A DICTIONARY

OF

MUSIC AND MUSICIANS

THE MACMILLAN COMPANY
NEW YORK · BOSTON · CHICAGO · DALLAS
ATLANTA · SAN FRANCISCO

MACMILLAN AND CO., Limited
LONDON · BOMBAY · CALCUTTA · MADRAS
MELBOURNE

THE MACMILLAN COMPANY
OF CANADA, Limited
TORONTO

GERMAN POSITIVE ORGAN, 1627
Victoria and Albert Museum, South Kensington

GROVE'S

DICTIONARY OF MUSIC AND MUSICIANS

THIRD EDITION

EDITED BY

H. C. COLLES, M.A. (Oxon.)

IN FIVE VOLUMES

VOL. III

NEW YORK

THE MACMILLAN COMPANY

1948

SET UP AND ELECTROTYPED BY J. S. CUSHING CO.
PRINTED IN THE UNITED STATES OF AMERICA
BY BERWICK & SMITH CO.

CONTRIBUTORS

v

W. B. CHASE, Esq., New York	W. B. C.
ALEXIS CHITTY, Esq.	A. C.
Mons. GUSTAVE CHOUQUET	G. C.
Mons. ERNEST CLOSSON, Professor at Brussels Conservatoire	E. C^N.
W. W. COBBETT, Esq.	W. W. C.
A. D. COLERIDGE, Esq.	A. D. C.
FREDERICK CORDER, Esq.	F. C.
GEORGE ARTHUR CRAWFORD, Major	G. A. C.
WALTER R. CREIGHTON, Esq.	W. R. C.
W. H. CUMMINGS, Esq., Mus.D., F.S.A.	W. H. C.
Sir WILLIAM GEORGE CUSINS	W. G. C.
WILLIAM H. DALY, Esq., Edinburgh	W. H. D.
H. G. DANIELS, Esq., Berlin	H. G. D.
EDWARD DANNREUTHER, Esq.	E. D.
PAUL DAVID, Esq.	P. D.
J. H. DAVIE, Esq.	J. H. D.
Sir H. WALFORD DAVIES, Mus.D., Gresham Professor of Music, etc.	H. W. D.
J. W. DAVISON, Esq.	J. W. D.
H. C. DEACON, Esq.	H. C. D.
EDWARD J. DENT, Esq., Professor of Music in Cambridge University	E. J. D.
L. M'C. L. DIX, Esq.	L. M'C. L. D
Miss JANET DODGE	J. D.
Herr ALFRED DÖRFFEL	A. D.
EDWARD H. DONKIN, Esq.	E. H. D.
GEORGE DYSON, Esq., Mus.D., Director of Music in Winchester College	G. D.
CLARENCE EDDY, Esq.	C. E.
F. G. EDWARDS, Esq.	F. G. E.
H. SUTHERLAND EDWARDS, Esq.	H. S. E.
Dr. ALFRED EINSTEIN, Editor of Riemann's *Lexikon,* 1922	A. E.
THOMAS ELLISTON, Esq.	T. E.
CARL ENGEL, Esq., Librarian of Music, Library of Congress, Washington	C. E^L.
EDWIN EVANS, Esq.	E. E.
The Rev. E. H. FELLOWES, Mus.D.	E. H. F.
GUSTAVE FERRARI, Esq.	G. F.
SHELLEY FISHER, Esq.	S. F.
Chevalier WM. HY. GRATTAN FLOOD, Hon. Mus.D., N.U.I., K.S.G.	W. H. G. F.
WALTER FORD, Esq.	W. F.
The Rt. Rev. WALTER H. FRERE, D.D., C.R., Lord Bishop of Truro	W. H. F.
ARTHUR M. FRIEDLANDER, Esq.	A. M. F.
Dr. MAX FRIEDLÄNDER	M. F.
H. FREDERICK FROST, Esq.	H. F. F.
JOHN T. FYFE, Esq.	J. T. F.
CHARLES ALAN FYFFE, Esq.	C. A. F.
The Rev. Canon F. W. GALPIN	F. W. G.
Signor GUIDO M. GATTI	G. M. G.
NICHOLAS COMYN GATTY, Esq., Mus.B.	N. C. G.
Dr. FRANZ GEHRING, Vienna.	F. G.
SCOTT GODDARD, Esq.	S. G.
M. VAN SOMEREN GODFERY, Major	M. V. S. G.
HARVEY GRACE, Esq.	H. G.
CHARLES L. GRAVES, Esq.	C. L. G.

J. C. Griffith, Esq. . . . . . . J. C. G.
Sir George Grove, C.B., D.C.L., Editor of the First Edition . . G.

Sir W. Henry Hadow, Mus.D., Vice-Chancellor of Sheffield University W. H. H^w
H. V. Hamilton, Esq. . . . . . . H. V. H.
Mrs. Robert Harrison . . . . . . B. H.
Herr Karl Hasse . . . . K. H^e.
L. W. Haward, Esq., Curator of the Manchester Art Gallery . L. W. H.
The Rev. T. Helmore . . . . . . T. H.
William Henderson, Esq. . . . . . W. H.
W. J. Henderson, Esq., New York . . . . . W. J. H.
George Herbert, Esq. . . . . . . G. H.
Arthur F. Hill, Esq. . . . . . . A. F. H.
Dr. Ferdinand Hiller . . . . . . F. H^R.
A. J. Hipkins, Esq., F.S.A. . . . . . A. J. H.
Miss Edith J. Hipkins . . . . . . E. J. H^s.
Claude Hobday, Esq. . . . . . . C. H.
Edward John Hopkins, Esq., Mus.D. . . . . E. J. H.
The Rev. Canon T. Percy Hudson (Canon Pemberton) . . T. P. H.
Francis Hueffer, Esq. . . . . . . F. H.
The Rev. Dom Anselm Hughes, O.S.B. . . . . A. H.
A. Hughes-Hughes, Esq. . . . . . . A. H.-H.
A. Eaglefield Hull, Esq., Mus.D. . . . . A. E. H.
John Hullah, Esq. . . . . . . J. H.
Duncan Hume, Esq. . . . . . . D. H.
W. Hume, Esq. . . . . W. H^e.
Hubert W. Hunt, Esq., Mus.D. . . . . . H. W. H.
Miss Kathleen D. Hurst . . . . . . K. D. H.
William H. Husk, Esq. . . . . . . W. H. H.

Ivor James, Esq. . . . . I. J.
F. H. Jenks, Esq. . . . . . . F. H. J.
Mons. Adolphe Jullien . . . . . . A. J.

H. J. Kalcsik, Esq. . . . . . . H. J. K.
A. Kalisch, Esq. . . . . A. K.
J. A. Kappey, Esq. . . . . . . J. A. K.
Cuthbert Kelly, Esq. . . . . . . C. K.
Frank Kidson, Esq. . . . . . . F. K.
Herman Klein, Esq. . . . . . . H. K.
The Rev. Dr. Alois Količek . . . . . A. K^K.
E. Krall, Esq. . . . . E. K.
H. E. Krehbiel, Esq. . . . . . . H. E. K.
Mons. Maurice Kufferath, Brussels . . . . M. K.

Herr Robert Lachmann . . . . . . R. L.
Morton Latham, Esq. . . . . . . M. L.
James Lecky, Esq. . . . . J. L.
Robin H. Legge, Esq. . . . . . . R. H. L.
J. Mewburn Levien, Esq. . . . . . . J. M. L.
Cecil Lewis, Esq. . . . . C. L.
H. J. Lincoln, Esq. . . . . . . H. J. L.
R. B. Litchfield, Esq. . . . . . . R. B. L.
R. E. Lonsdale, Esq. . . . . . . R. E. L.
Stanley Lucas, Esq. . . . . . . S. L.

R. F. M'Ewen, Esq.	R. F. M'E.
Sir G. A. Macfarren, Mus.D.	G. A. M.
The Rev. Charles Mackeson, F.R.S.	C. M.
Charles Maclean, Esq., Mus.D.	C. M^N.
H. S. Macran, Esq.	H. S. M.
Herr A. Maczewsky	A. M.
J. A. Fuller Maitland, Esq., F.S.A., Editor of the Second Edition	M.
Jeffery Mark, Esq.	J. M^K.
Mrs. Julian Marshall	F. A. M.
Julian Marshall, Esq.	J. M.
Russell Martineau, Esq.	R. M.
H. J. L. J. Massé, Esq.	H. J. L. M.
Signor Giannandrea Mazzucato	G. M.
The Rev. J. H. Mee	J. H. M.
Senhor Carlos de Mello	C. de M.
Herr Rudolf Mengelberg	R. M^G.
Miss Louisa Middleton	L. M. M.
The Rev. J. R. Milne	J. R. M.
R. O. Morris, Esq.	R. O. M.
D. L. Murray, Esq.	D. L. M.
V. E. Negus, Esq., F.R.C.S.	V. E. N.
Mrs. Rosa Newmarch	R. N.
E. M. Oakeley, Esq.	E. M. O.
Sir Herbert S. Oakeley, Mus.D.	H. S. O.
C. B. Oldman, Esq., British Museum	C. B. O.
The Rev. Sir F. A. Gore Ouseley, Bt., Mus.D.	F. A. G. O.
Sidney H. Pardon, Esq.	S. H. P.
Henry Parr, Esq.	H. P.
Sir Walter Parratt, Mus.D., M.V.O.	W. P^A.
Sir C. Hubert H. Parry, Bt., C.V.O., Mus.D.	C. H. H. P.
Mons. K. Paucitis, Riga	K. P.
Edward John Payne, Esq.	E. J. P.
The Rev. Hugh Pearson	H. P^N.
Edward H. Pember, Esq., K.C.	E. H. P.
The Rev. Canon T. P. Pemberton (formerly Hudson)	T. P. P.
Mlle. Marie Louise Pereyra	M. L. P.
Miss Phillimore	C. M. P.
F. Piggott, Esq.	F. P.
Mons. Marc Pincherle	M. P.
Herr C. Ferdinand Pohl	C. F. P.
William Pole, Esq., F.R.S., Mus.D.	W. P.
E. Polonaski, Esq.	E. P^I.
Victor de Pontigny, Esq.	v. de P.
Reginald Lane Poole, Esq.	R. L. P.
Mons. J. G. Prod'homme	J. G. P.
Ebenezer Prout, Esq., Mus.D.	E. P.
The Rev. W. Pulling	W. P^G.
Charles H. Purday, Esq.	C. H. P.
Miss Olga Racster	O. R.
Mons. Félix Raugel, Paris	F. R^L.

WILLIAM HENRY REED, Esq.	W. H. R.
LUIGI RICCI, Esq.	L. R.
EDWARD F. RIMBAULT, Esq., LL.D.	E. F. R.
Signor F. RIZZELLI	F. R^z.
W. S. ROCKSTRO, Esq.	W. S. R.
Dr. KURT ROGER, Vienna	K. R.
DESMOND LUMLEY RYAN, Esq.	D. L. R.
Mons. GUSTAVE SAMAZEUILH, Paris	G. S.
H. A. SCOTT, Esq.	H. A. S.
J. S. SHEDLOCK, Esq.	J. S. S.
A. J. SHELDON, Esq.	A. J. S.
CARL SIEWERS, Esq.	C. S^s.
The Hon. Mrs. SINCLAIR	G. A. S.
WARREN STOREY SMITH, Esq., Boston	W. S. S.
Miss BARBARA SMYTHE	B. S.
O. G. SONNECK, Esq., New York	O. G. S.
Dr. Ing. OTTOKAR SOUREK, Prague	O. S
T. L. SOUTHGATE, Esq.	T. L. S.
WALTER R. SPALDING, Esq., Professor of Music in Harvard University, Cambridge, Mass.	W. R. S.
Dr. PHILIPP SPITTA	P. S.
S. J. SPURLING, Esq.	S. J. S.
WILLIAM BARCLAY SQUIRE, Esq., M.V.O.	W. B. S.
Miss C. STAINER	C. S.
Sir JOHN STAINER, Mus.D.	J. S.
J. F. R. STAINER, Esq.	J. F. R. S.
W. W. STARMER, Esq.	W. W. S.
E. IRENAEUS PRIME STEVENSON, Esq.	E. I. P. S.
Sir ROBERT P. STEWART, Mus.D.	R. P. S.
T. L. STILLIE, Esq.	T. L. S^E.
WILLIAM H. STONE, Esq., M.D.	W. H. S.
E. VAN DER STRAETEN, Esq.	E. v. d. S.
A. H. FOX-STRANGWAYS, Esq.	A. H. F.-S.
R. A. STREATFEILD, Esq.	R. A. S.
The Rt. Rev. THOMAS B. STRONG, D.D., Lord Bishop of Oxford	T. B. S.
J. STUTTERFORD, Esq.	J. S^D.
Sir ARTHUR SEYMOUR SULLIVAN, Mus.D.	A. S. S.
FRANKLIN TAYLOR, Esq.	F. T.
CHARLES SANFORD TERRY, Esq., Litt.D. (Cantab.), Hon. Mus.D. (Edin.), Hon. LL.D. (Glasgow)	C. S. T.
Mons. ANDRÉ TESSIER, Paris	A. T.
ALEXANDER W. THAYER, Esq.	A. W. T.
Miss BERTHA THOMAS	B. T.
HERBERT THOMPSON, Esq., D.Litt., Leeds	H. T.
G. H. THRING, Esq., Incorporated Society of Authors, Playwrights and Composers	G. H. T.
H. JULIUS W. TILLYARD, Esq., Professor in Birmingham University	H. J. W. T
FRANCIS TOYE, Esq.	F. T^{YE}.
J. B. TREND, Esq.	J. B. T.
Mons. RICHARD VEŠELÝ, Prague	R. V.
Dr. BOLESLAV VOMAČKA	B. V.

Ernest Walker, Esq., Mus.D., Fellow of Balliol College, Oxford   .   E. W.
William Wallace, Esq.   .   .   .   .   .   .   W. W.
S. H. Walrond, Esq.   .   .   .   .   .   .   S. H. W.
Miss Sylvia Townsend Warner   .   .   .   .   .   S. T. W.
Edward Watson, Esq., National Institute for the Blind   .   .   E. W^N.
P. G. L. Webb, Esq.   .   .   .   .   .   .   P. G. L. W.
C. Welch, Esq.   .   .   .   .   C. W.
Frederick Westlake, Esq. .   .   .   .   .   .   F. W.
H. A. Whitehead, Esq.   .   .   .   .   .   .   H. A. W.
W. E. Whitehouse, Esq.   .   .   .   .   .   .   W. E. W.
C. F. Abdy Williams, Esq.   .   .   .   .   .   C. F. A. W.
R. Vaughan Williams, Esq., Mus.D.   .   .   .   .   R. V. W.
C. W. Wilson, Esq., Dublin   .   .   .   .   .   C. W. W.
Mrs. Edmond Wodehouse   .   .   .   .   .   .   A. H. W.
J. Muir Wood, Esq.   .   .   .   .   .   .   J. M. W.
H. E. Wooldridge, Esq.   .   .   .   .   .   .   H. E. W.
H. Saxe-Wyndham, Esq., Secretary of the Guildhall School of Music .   H. S.-W.

The Editor   .   •   •   •   •   •   •   C.

CONTRIBUTORS

LIST II. ARRANGED IN ALPHABETICAL ORDER OF THE INITIALS BY WHICH ARTICLES ARE SIGNED

The names of deceased writers are printed in italics

A. C.	ALEXIS CHITTY, Esq.
A. C. B.	ADRIAN C. BOULT, Esq., Mus.D.
A. D.	*Herr ALFRED DÖRFFEL.*
A. D. C.	*A. D. COLERIDGE, Esq.*
A. E.	Dr. ALFRED EINSTEIN.
A. E. H.	A. EAGLÉFIELD HULL, Esq., Mus.D.
A. F. H.	ARTHUR F. HILL, Esq.
A. H.	Rev. Dom ANSELM HUGHES, O.S.B.
A. H. F.-S.	A. H. FOX-STRANGWAYS, Esq.
A. H.-H.	A. HUGHES-HUGHES, Esq.
A. H. W.	*Mrs. EDMOND WODEHOUSE.*
A. J.	*Mons. ADOLPHE JULLIEN.*
A. J. H.	*A. J. HIPKINS, Esq., F.S.A.*
A. J. S.	A. J. SHELDON, Esq.
A. K.	A. KALISCH, Esq.
A. K^K.	Rev. Dr. ALOIS KOLIČEK.
A. M.	*Herr A. MACZEWSKY.*
A. M. F.	ARTHUR M. FRIEDLANDER, Esq.
A. S. S.	*Sir ARTHUR S. SULLIVAN, Mus.D.*
A. T.	Mons. ANDRÉ TESSIER.
A. W. T.	*ALEXANDER W. THAYER, Esq.*
B. H.	Mrs. ROBERT HARRISON.
B. S.	Miss BARBARA SMYTHE.
B. T.	Miss BERTHA THOMAS.
B. V.	Dr. BOLESLAV VOMAČKA.
C.	THE EDITOR.
C. A.	*CARL ARMBRUSTER, Esq.*
C. A. F.	*CHARLES ALAN FYFFE, Esq.*
C. B.	Mons. CHARLES BOUVET.
C. B. O.	C. B. OLDMAN, Esq.
C. E.	CLARENCE EDDY, Esq.
C. E^L.	CARL ENGEL, Esq.
C. F. A. W.	*C. F. ABDY WILLIAMS, Esq.*
C. F. P.	*Herr C. FERDINAND POHL.*

C. H.	.	.	.	.	. CLAUDE HOBDAY, Esq.
C. H. P.	.	.	.	.	. *CHARLES H. PURDAY, Esq.*
C. H. H. P.		.	.	.	. *Sir C. HUBERT H. PARRY, Mus.D., C.V.O.*
C. K.	.	.	.	.	. CUTHBERT KELLY, Esq.
C. L.	.	.	.	.	. CECIL LEWIS, Esq.
C. L. G.	.	.	.	.	. CHARLES L. GRAVES, Esq.
C. M.	.	.	.	.	. *Rev. CHARLES MACKESON, F.R.S.*
C. M^N.	.	.	.	.	. *CHARLES MACLEAN, Esq., Mus.D.*
C. de M.	.	.	.	.	. Senhor CARLOS DE MELLO.
C. M. P.	.	.	.	.	. Miss PHILLIMORE.
C. S.	.	.	.	.	. Miss C. STAINER.
C. S^s.	.	.	.	.	. CARL SIEWERS, Esq.
C. S. T.	.	.	.	.	. CHARLES SANFORD TERRY, Esq., Mus.D.
C. W.	.	.	.	.	. *C. WELCH, Esq.*
C. W. W.	.	.	.	.	. C. W. WILSON, Esq.

D. B.	.	.	.	.	. *DAVID BAPTIE, Esq.*
D. H.	.	.	.	.	. *DUNCAN HUME, Esq.*
D. J. B.	.	.	.	.	. D. J. BLAIKLEY, Esq.
D. L. M.	.	.	.	.	. D. L. MURRAY, Esq.
D. L. R.	.	.	.	.	. *DESMOND LUMLEY RYAN, Esq.*

E. B.	.	.	.	.	. ERIC BLOM, Esq.
E. B^L.	.	.	.	.	. Mons. E. BORREL.
E. C.	.	.	.	.	. *E. C. CHADFIELD, Esq.*
E. C^N.	.	.	.	.	. Mons. ERNEST CLOSSON.
E. D.	.	.	.	.	. *EDWARD DANNREUTHER, Esq.*
E. E.	.	.	.	.	. EDWIN EVANS, Esq.
E. F. R.	.	.	.	.	. *EDWARD F. RIMBAULT, Esq., LL.D.*
E. H.-A.	.	.	.	.	. E. HERON-ALLEN, Esq.
E. H. D.	.	.	.	.	. *EDWARD H. DONKIN, Esq.*
E. H. F.	.	.	.	.	. Rev. E. H. FELLOWES, Mus.D.
E. H. P.	.	.	.	.	. *EDWARD H. PEMBER, Esq., K.C.*
E. I. P. S.	.	.	.	.	. E. IRENAEUS PRIME STEVENSON, Esq.
E. J. D.	.	.	.	.	. EDWARD J. DENT, Esq.
E. J. H.	.	.	.	.	. *EDWARD JOHN HOPKINS, Esq., Mus.D.*
E. J. H^s.	.	.	.	.	. Miss EDITH J. HIPKINS.
E. J. P.	.	.	.	.	. *EDWARD JOHN PAYNE, Esq.*
E. K.	.	.	.	.	. E. KRALL, Esq.
E. M. O.	.	.	.	.	. E. M. OAKELEY, Esq.
E. O. B.	.	.	.	.	. Mrs. EDITH OLDHAM BEST (Miss Oldham).
E. P.	.	.	.	.	. *EBENEZER PROUT, Esq., Mus.D.*
E. P^L.	.	.	.	.	. E. POLONASKI, Esq.
E. v. d. S.	.	.	.	.	. E. VAN DER STRAETEN, Esq.
E. W.	.	.	.	.	. ERNEST WALKER, Esq., Mus.D.
E. W^N.	.	.	.	.	. EDWARD WATSON, Esq.

F. A. G. O.		.	.	.	. *Rev. Sir F. A. GORE OUSELEY, Bt., Mus.D.*
F. A. M.	.	.	.	.	. *Mrs. JULIAN MARSHALL.*
F. B.	.	.	.	.	. F. BONAVIA, Esq.
F. C.	.	.	.	.	. FREDERICK CORDER, Esq.
F. G.	.	.	.	.	. *Dr. FRANZ GEHRING.*
F. G. E.	.	.	.	.	. *F. G. EDWARDS, Esq.*
F. H.	.	.	.	.	. *FRANCIS HUEFFER, Esq.*
F. H^R.		.	.	.	. *Dr. FERDINAND HILLER.*

F. H. J.	.	*F. H. Jenks, Esq.*
F. J. A.	.	F. J. Arnold, Esq.
F. K.	.	*Frank Kidson, Esq.*
F. P.	.	F. Piggott, Esq.
F. R^z.	.	Signor F. Rizzelli.
F. R^l.	.	Mons. Félix Raugel.
F. T.	.	*Franklin Taylor, Esq.*
F. T^{ye}.	.	Francis Toye, Esq.
F. W.	.	*Frederick Westlake, Esq.*
F. W. G.	.	Rev. Canon F. W. Galpin.
G.	.	*Sir George Grove, C.B., D.C.L.*
G. A. C.	.	*Major George Arthur Crawford.*
G. A. M.	.	*Sir G. A. Macfarren, Mus.D.*
G. A. S.	.	The Hon. Mrs. Sinclair.
G. C.	.	*Mons. Gustave Chouquet.*
G. D.	.	George Dyson, Esq., Mus.D.
G. E. P. A.	.	G. E. P. Arkwright, Esq.
G. F.	.	Gustave Ferrari, Esq.
G. H.	.	*George Herbert, Esq.*
G. H. T.	.	G. H. Thring, Esq.
G. M.	.	*Signor Giannandrea Mazzucato.*
G. M. G.	.	Signor Guido M. Gatti.
G. S.	.	Mons. Gustave Samazeuilh.
G. S. K.-B.	.	*G. S. Kaye-Butterworth, Esq.*
H. A.	.	Herbert Antcliffe, Esq.
H. A. S.	.	H. A. Scott, Esq.
H. A. W.	.	H. A. Whitehead, Esq.
H. B.	.	Hugh Butler, Esq.
H. B^y.	.	Dr. Hermann Budy.
H. C. D.	.	*H. C. Deacon, Esq.*
H. E. A.	.	Lieut. H. E. Adkins.
H. E. K.	.	*H. E. Krehbiel, Esq.*
H. E. W.	.	*H. E. Wooldridge, Esq.*
H. F. B.	.	*Horatio Robt. Forbes Brown, Esq.*
H. F. F.	.	*H. Frederick Frost, Esq.*
H. G.	.	Harvey Grace, Esq.
H. G. D.	.	H. G. Daniels, Esq.
H. J. K.	.	H. J. Kalcsik, Esq.
H. J. L.	.	*H. J. Lincoln, Esq.*
H. J. L. M.	.	H. J. L. J. Massé, Esq.
H. J. W. T.	.	Professor H. Julius W. Tillyard.
H. K.	.	Hermann Klein, Esq.
H. P.	.	*Henry Parr, Esq.*
H. Pⁿ.	.	*Rev. Hugh Pearson.*
H. S. E.	.	*H. Sutherland Edwards, Esq.*
H. S. M.	.	H. S. Macran, Esq.
H. S. O.	.	*Sir Herbert S. Oakeley, Mus.D.*
H. S.-W.	.	H. Saxe-Wyndham, Esq.
H. T.	.	Herbert Thompson, Esq., D.Litt.
H. V. H.	.	H. V. Hamilton, Esq.
H. W. D.	.	Sir H. Walford Davies, Mus.D.
H. W. H.	.	Hubert W. Hunt, Esq., Mus.D.

I. J.	.	.	.	.	.	. IVOR JAMES, *Esq.*

J. A. K.	.	.	.	.	.	. *J. A. KAPPEY, Esq.*
J. B.	.	.	.	.	.	. Dr. JOSEF BARTOŠ.
J. B. T.	.	.	.	.	.	. J. B. TREND, Esq.
J. C. B.	.	.	.	.	.	. J. C. BRIDGE, Esq., Mus.D.
J. C. G.	.	.	.	.	.	. J. C. GRIFFITH, Esq.
J. D.	.	.	.	.	.	. Miss JANET DODGE.
J. F. R. S.	.	.	.	.	.	. J. F. R. STAINER, Esq.
J. G. P.	.	.	.	.	.	. Mons. J. G. PROD'HOMME.
J. H.	.	.	.	.	.	. *JOHN HULLAH, Esq.*
J. H. D.	.	.	.	.	.	. J. H. DAVIE, Esq.
J. H. M.	.	.	.	.	.	. *Rev. J. H. MEE.*
J. L.	.	.	.	.	.	. JAMES LECKY, Esq.
J. M.	.	.	.	.	.	. *JULIAN MARSHALL, Esq.*
J. Mᴷ.	.	.	.	.	.	. JEFFERY MARK, Esq.
J. M. L.	.	.	.	.	.	. JOHN MEWBURN LEVIEN, Esq.
J. M. W.	.	.	.	.	.	. *J. MUIR WOOD, Esq.*
J. R. M.	.	.	.	.	.	. Rev. J. R. MILNE.
J. R. S.-B.	.	.	.	.	.	. J. R. STERNDALE-BENNETT, Esq.
J. S.	.	.	.	.	.	. *Sir JOHN STAINER, Mus.D.*
J. Sᴰ.	.	.	.	.	.	. J. STUTTERFORD, Esq.
J. S. S.	.	.	.	.	.	. *J. S. SHEDLOCK, Esq.*
J. T. F.	.	.	.	.	.	. JOHN T. FYFE, Esq.
J. W. C.	.	.	.	.	.	. J. W. CAPSTICK, Esq.
J. W. D.	.	.	.	.	.	. *J. W. DAVISON, Esq.*

K. D. H.	.	.	.	.	.	. Miss KATHLEEN D. HURST.
K. Hᴿ.	.	.	.	.	.	. Herr KARL HASSE.
K. P.	.	.	.	.	.	. Mons. K. PAUCITIS.
K. R.	.	.	.	.	.	. Dr. KURT ROGER.

L. B.	.	.	.	.	.	. *LEONARD BORWICK, Esq.*
L. MᶜC. L. D.	.	.	.	.	.	. L. MᶜC. L. DIX, Esq.
L. M. M.	.	.	.	.	.	. Miss LOUISA MIDDLETON.
L. R.	.	.	.	.	.	. *LUIGI RICCI, Esq.*
L. W. H.	.	.	.	.	.	. L. W. HAWARD, Esq.

M.	.	.	.	.	.	. J. A. FULLER MAITLAND, Esq.
M. B.	.	.	.	.	.	. *The Hon. Mrs. M. BURRELL.*
M. C. C.	.	.	.	.	.	. Mrs. WALTER CARR.
M. D. C.	.	.	.	.	.	. M. D. CALVOCORESSI, Esq.
M. F.	.	.	.	.	.	. Dr. MAX FRIEDLÄNDER.
M. K.	.	.	.	.	.	. *Mons. MAURICE KUFFERATH.*
M. L.	.	.	.	.	.	. *MORTON LATHAM, Esq.*
M. L. P.	.	.	.	.	.	. Mlle. M. L. PEREYRA.
M. P.	.	.	.	.	.	. Mons. MARC PINCHERLE.
M. V. S. G.	.	.	.	.	.	. Major M. VAN SOMEREN GODFERY.

N. C. G.	.	.	.	.	.	. NICHOLAS C. GATTY, Esq.

O. G. S.	.	.	.	.	.	. O. G. SONNECK, Esq.
O. R.	.	.	.	.	.	. Miss OLGA RACSTER.
O. S.	.	.	.	.	.	. Dr. Ing. OTTOKAR ŠOUREK.

P. C. B.	.	.	.	. PERCY C. BUCK, Esq., Mus.D.
P. D.	.	.	.	. *PAUL DAVID, Esq.*
P. G. L. W.	.	.	.	. P. G. L. WEBB, Esq.
P. S.	.	.	.	. *Dr. PHILIPP SPITTA.*
R. A.	.	.	.	. RICHARD ALDRICH, Esq.
R. A. S.	.	.	.	. *R. A. STREATFEILD, Esq.*
R. B. L.	.	.	.	. *R. B. LITCHFIELD, Esq.*
R. E. L.	.	.	.	. R. E. LONSDALE, Esq.
R. F. M'E.	.	.	.	. *R. F. M'EWEN, Esq.*
R. H. L.	.	.	.	. ROBIN H. LEGGE, Esq.
R. H. M. B.	.	.	.	. *R. H. M. BOSANQUET, Esq.*
R. L.	.	.	.	. Herr ROBERT LACHMANN.
R. L. P.	.	.	.	. REGINALD LANE POOLE, Esq.
R. M.	.	.	.	. *RUSSELL MARTINEAU, Esq.*
R. M^G.	.	.	.	. Herr RUDOLF MENGELBERG.
R. N.	.	.	.	. Mrs. ROSA NEWMARCH.
R. O. M.	.	.	.	. R. O. MORRIS, Esq.
R. P. S.	.	.	.	. *Sir ROBERT P. STEWART, Mus.D.*
R. V.	.	.	.	. M. RICHARD VEŠELÝ.
R. V. W.	.	.	.	. R. VAUGHAN WILLIAMS, Esq., Mus.D.
S. F.	.	.	.	. SHELLEY FISHER, Esq.
S. G.	.	.	.	. SCOTT GODDARD, Esq.
S. H. P.	.	.	.	. *SIDNEY H. PARDON, Esq.*
S. H. W.	.	.	.	. S. H. WALROND, Esq.
S. J. S.	.	.	.	. S. J. SPURLING, Esq.
S. L.	.	.	.	. *STANLEY LUCAS, Esq.*
S. T. W.	.	.	.	. Miss SYLVIA TOWNSEND WARNER.
T. B. S.	.	.	.	. The Rt. Rev. THOMAS B. STRONG, D.D., Lord Bishop of Oxford.
T. E.	.	.	.	. THOMAS ELLISTON, Esq.
T. H.	.	.	.	. *Rev. THOMAS HELMORE.*
T. L. S.	.	.	.	. *T. L. SOUTHGATE, Esq.*
T. L. S^E.	.	.	.	. *T. L. STILLIE, Esq.*
T. P. H.	.	.	.	. *Rev. Canon T. PERCY HUDSON (Canon Pemberton).*
T. P. P.	.	.	.	. *Rev. Canon T. P. PEMBERTON (formerly Hudson).*
V. E. N.	.	.	.	. V. E. NEGUS, Esq., F.R.C.S.
V. de P.	.	.	.	. *VICTOR DE PONTIGNY, Esq.*
W. A. A.	.	.	.	. W. A. AIKIN, Esq., M.D.
W. B. C.	.	.	.	. W. B. CHASE, Esq.
W. B. S.	.	.	.	. *WILLIAM BARCLAY SQUIRE, Esq.*
W. C.	.	.	.	. *WILLIAM CHAPPELL, Esq., F.S.A.*
W. E. W.	.	.	.	. W. E. WHITEHOUSE, Esq.
W. F.	.	.	.	. WALTER FORD, Esq.
W. G. C.	.	.	.	. *Sir WILLIAM GEORGE CUSINS.*
W. H.	.	.	.	. *WILLIAM HENDERSON, Esq.*
W. H^E.	.	.	.	. W. HUME, Esq.
W. H. C.	.	.	.	. *W. H. CUMMINGS, Esq., Mus.D.*
W. H. D.	.	.	.	. WILLIAM H. DALY, Esq.
W. H. F.	.	.	.	. The Rt. Rev. W. H. FRERE, D.D., C.R., Lord Bishop of Truro.
W. H. G. F.	.	.	.	. W. H. GRATTAN FLOOD, Esq., Mus.D.

W. H. H.	.	.	.	. *WILLIAM H. HUSK, Esq.*
W. H. Hᵂ.	.	.	.	. Sir W. HENRY HADOW, Mus.D.
W. H. R.	.	.	.	. WILLIAM HENRY REED, Esq.
W. H. S.	.	.	.	. *WILLIAM H. STONE, Esq., M.D.*
W. J. H.	.	.	.	. W. J. HENDERSON, Esq.
W. P. .	.	.	.	. *WILLIAM POLE, Esq., F.R.S., Mus.D.*
W. Pᴬ.	.	.	.	. *Sir WALTER PARRATT, Mus.D., M.V.O.*
W. Pᴳ.	.	.	.	. *Rev. W. PULLING.*
W. R. C.	.	.	.	. WALTER R. CREIGHTON, Esq.
W. R. S.	.	.	.	. WALTER R. SPALDING, Esq.
W. S. R.	.	.	.	. *W. S. ROCKSTRO, Esq.*
W. S. S.	.	.	.	. WARREN STOREY SMITH, Esq.
W. W.	.	.	.	. WILLIAM WALLACE, Esq.
W. W. C.	.	.	.	. W. W. COBBETT, Esq.
W. W. S.	.	.	.	. W. W. STARMER, Esq.

LIST OF PLATES

VOLUME I

VOLUME II

VOLUME III

VOLUME IV

VOLUME V

ABBREVIATIONS

PERIODICALS AND WORKS OF REFERENCE, Etc.

Allgemeine Musikalische Zeitung	*A.M.Z.*
American Supplement of Grove's Dictionary	*Amer. Supp.*
Bach-Gesellschaft (complete critical edition of J. S. Bach's works)	*B.-G.*
Bach Jahrbuch	*B. J.-B.*
Baker's Biographical Dictionary	*Baker.*
British Musical Biography	*Brit. Mus. Biog.*
British Musical Society's Annual, 1920	*B.M.S. Ann.*, 1920.
Davey's *History of English Music*	*Hist. Eng. Mus.*
Denkmäler deutsche Tonkunst	*D.D.T.*
Denkmäler der deutsche Tonkunst in Österreich	*D.T.Ö.*
Dictionary of National Biography	*D.N.B.*
Eitner's *Quellen-Lexikon*	*Q.-L.*
Fétis's *Biographie universelle* (with Supplement)	*Fétis.*
Imperial Dictionary of Universal Biography	*Imp. Dict. Univ. Biog.*
Mendel's *Lexicon*	*Mendel.*
Monatshefte für Musikgeschichte, Leipzig	*M.f.M.*
Musical Antiquary	*Mus. Ant.*
Musical Association's Proceedings	*Mus. Ass. Proc.*
Musical Times	*Mus. T.*
Music and Letters	*M. and L.*
Oxford History of Music	*Oxf. Hist. Mus.*
Quarterly Musical Review	*Q. Mus. Rev.*
Revista de Filogia española, Madrid	*R.F.E.*
Revista musical Catalona, Barcelona	*R.M.C.*
Revista musical de Bilbao	*R.M.B.*
Revista musicale italiana, Turin	*R.M.I.*
Revue musicale, Paris	*R.M.*
Riemann's Musik Lexikon, 1922	*Riemann.*
Sammelbände der Internationalen Musikgesellschaft, Leipzig	*S.I.M.*, also *I.M.G.*
Studien zu Musikwissenschaft	*S.z M.W.*
Walker's *History of Music in England*	*Hist. Mus. Eng.*
Zeitschrift für Musikwissenschaft, Leipzig	*Z.M.W.*

ENGLISH LIBRARIES AND COLLECTIONS

Batten Organ Book at St. Michael's College, Tenbury	Tenb. O.B.
Bodleian Library, Oxford	Bodl. Lib.
British Museum	B.M.
Buckingham Palace Library (now in the British Museum)	Roy. Lib. B.M.
Caius College, Cambridge	Caius.
Christ Church, Oxford	Ch. Ch.
Commonplace Book of John Baldwin	Baldwin.
Durham Cathedral	Durh.
Ely Cathedral	Ely.
First Book of Selected Church Music, edited by John Barnard, 1641	Barnard.
Fitzwilliam Library, Cambridge	Fitzw.

ABBREVIATIONS

Harleian MSS., British Museum	Harl.
Lambeth Palace	Lambeth.
Organ Book at Christ Church	Ch. Ch. O.B.
Organ Book at Durham Cathedral	Durham O.B.
Oxford Music School Collection (now in the Bodleian Library)	Bodl. Mus. Sch.
Peterhouse, Cambridge	PH.
Royal Collection Appendix MSS., British Museum	Roy. MSS.
Royal College of Music	R.C.M.
Sadler Partbooks (now in the Bodleian Library)	Sadler.
St. George's Chapel, Windsor	St. G. Ch.
St. Michael's College, Tenbury	Tenb.
Wimborne Minster	Wimb.
Worcester Cathedral	Worc.
York Minster	Yk.

CHURCH MUSIC

Benedicite	(Bcte.)	Litany	(L.)
Benedictus	(B.)	Magnificat	(M.)
Creed	(C.)	Nunc Dimittis	(N.D.)
Gloria	(G.)	Sanctus	(S.)
Jubilate	(J.)	Te Deum	(T.D.)
Kyrie	(K.)	Venite	(V.)

INSTITUTIONS, Etc.

Bibliothèque National, Paris	Bibl. Nat. Paris.
Breitkopf & Härtel	B. &. H.
Guildhall School of Music, London	G.S.M.
Incorporated Society of Musicians	I.S.M.
International Musik Gesellschaft	Int. Mus. Ges.
Musical Antiquarian Society	Mus. Ant. Soc.
Musical Association	Mus. Ass.
Real Conservatorio di Musica, Naples	R.C.M. Naples.
Royal Academy of Music, London	R.A.M.
Royal College of Music, London	R.C.M.
Royal College of Organists, London	R.C.O

DICTIONARY

OF

MUSIC AND MUSICIANS

VOL. III

K—O

K

KADE, (1) OTTO (b. Dresden, May 6, 1819; d. Doberan, near Rostock, July 19, 1900), writer on music, showed a decided predilection for music while still a pupil at the Kreuzschule. He received lessons in harmony and counterpoint from Julius Otto and Moritz Hauptmann, and in pianoforte and organ-playing from J. G. Schneider. In 1846 he made a prolonged stay in Italy for the purpose of musical study, especially of the older vocal music. On his return he founded and conducted a Caecilien-Verein or mixed choir for the performance of older vocal works. In 1860 he received the first prize from the Maatschappij tot bevordering der Toonkunst in Amsterdam (Society for the Furtherance of Music) for his valuable monograph on 'Mattheus le Maistre,' a former Kapellmeister to the court of Saxony. In the same year he accepted the invitation from the Grand Duke of Mecklenburg-Schwerin, Friedrich Franz II., to be musical director of the Schloss-kapelle at Schwerin. The Schloss-chor, which was organised on similar principles to the Berlin Domchor, was brought by Kade to a high pitch of artistic refinement. During the same time he was entrusted with the musical editorship of the *Cantionale für die evangelisch-lutherischen Kirchen im Grossherzogtum Mecklenburg-Schwerin*, which appeared in parts from 1868–87. Along with this Cantional he also published a 'Choralbuch' for four voices, harmonised on the strict diatonic system of the 16th century. The first edition of this 'Choralbuch' appeared in 1869, a second in 1886. It appears to have been Kade who gave the first impulse to the foundation by Eitner of the Gesellschaft für Musikforschung, which led to the publication of the *Monatshefte für Musikgeschichte* from 1869. Kade edited for the Gesellschaft Johann Walther's *Wittenbergisch geistlich Gesanbuch* of 1524, and was joint-editor with Eitner and Erk of Ott's *Liederbuch* of 1544. In 1862 Kade had been commissioned by the firm of Leuckart, the publishers of Ambros's *Geschichte der Musik*, to edit a supplementary volume, containing specimens of the most celebrated masters of the 15th and 16th centuries. This volume only appeared in 1882, but represents the fruits of many years' research in the various libraries of Italy and Germany. In 1892 he published a volume entitled *Die älteren Passionskompositionen bis zum Jahre 1631* (Gütersloh, 1892), which gives an account of the various compositions of the Passion in the 16th century, and gives the actual notes of the Obrecht, Walther and Scandelli Passions. As part of his official work at Schwerin he published, in 1896, a Catalogue of the Grand-Ducal Musical Collection. Other works of Kade are *Der neu-aufgefundene Luther-Codex* (with facsimiles), 1871, and *Die deutsche weltliche Liedweise*, 1872. He retired from active service in 1893.

List of the pieces contained in Kade's supplementary volume to Ambros's *Geschichte der Musik*:

1. Okeghem. Sanctus and Benedictus from Missa ' Cujusvis toni.
2. ,, Chanson, ' Je n'ay deul,' a 4.
3. ,, ,, ' Lauter dantant,' a 3.
4. ,, ,, ' Se ne pas jeulx,' a 3.
5. ,, ,, ' Se vostre cœur,' a 3.
6. ,, Fuga 3 vocum in Epidiatessaron.
7. Obrecht. Ave Regina. a 4.
8. ,, Chanson, ' Forseulement,' a 4.
9. ,, ,, (without title), a 4.
10. ,, ,, ' La Tortorella,' a 4.
11. ,, ,, ' Se bien fait,' a 4.
12. ,, Salve Regina, a 3.
13. Josquin des Prés. Stabat Mater, a 5.
14. ,, ,, Missa, ' Pange Lingua,' a 4.
15. ,, ,, Chanson, ' J'ai bien cause,' a 6.
16. ,, ,, ,, ' Je say bien dire,' a 4.
17. ,, ,, ,, ' Adieu, mes amours,' a 4.
18. ,, ,, ,, ' Scaramella,' a 4.
19. Pierre de la Rue. Sanctus from Missa ' Tous les regrets,' a 4.
20. ,, ,, ' O salutaris hostia,' a 4.
21. A. Brumel. Missa festivalis, from Crucifixus to end, a 2, 3, 4.
22. ,, Regina Coeli, a 4.
23. A. Agricola. Chanson, ' Comme Femme,' a 3.
24. Gaspar Werbeke. Motet, ' Virgo Maria,' a 4.
25. Loyset Compère. Chanson, ' Nous sommes de l'ordre de St. Babouin,' a 4.
26. Ghiselin. Chanson, ' La Alfonsina,' a 3.
27. De Orto. Ave Maria, a 4.
28. ,, Agnus from Missa ' Mi-mi,' a 4.
29. Layolle. ' Salve Virgo singularis,' a 4.
30. ,, ' Media vita in morte sumus, a 4.
31. A. Fevin. Motet, ' Descendi in hortum meum,' a 4.
32. Eleazar Genet. Lamentations, a 3 and 4.
33. Nicolas Gombert. Ave Regina, a 4.
34-39. B. Ducis. 6 geistliche deutsche Lieder, a 4.
40. Heinrich Finck. Missa, ' De Beata Virgine,' a 3.
41. Thomas Stoltzer. Psalm 12. ' Hilf, Herr,' a 6.
42-44. Paul Hoffheymer. 3 deutsche weltliche Lieder, a 4.
45. Heinrich Isaac. Motet. ' Illumina oculos meos,' a 3.
46. ,, ,, ' Virgo Prudentissima,' a 6.
47. ,, ,, a 4.
48-49. ,, Introits and Alleluias, ' De Nativitate,' a 4.
50-53. ,, Chansons a 4 and 5 (without text).
54. M. Greiter. Lied, ' Ich stund an einem Morgen,' a 4.
55. David Köler. Geistliches Lied, ' O du edler brun der freuden,' a 4.
56. Arnold de Bruck. ' O du armer Judas,' a 6.
57. ,, ' O allmächtiger Gott,' a 5.
58. ,, ' Es geht gen diesen Sumer,' a 4.
59. L. Senfl. Motet, ' Ave rosa sine spinis,' a 5.
60. ,, Lied, ' Wol kumt der Mai,' a 4.
61. ,, ' Im Maien, im Maien,' a 4.
62. Johann Walther. Geistliches Lied ' Holdseliger meins Herzens Trost,' a 6.
63. Johann Walther. Geistliches Lied, ' Wach auf du deutsches Land,' a 4.
64. M. Le Maistre. Geistliches Lied, ' Hör, Menschenkind,' a 4.
65. ,, Weltliches Lied, ' Schem dich du tropf,' a 4.
66. Scandelli. Sanctus, Benedictus, Agnus from Missa, a 3-6.
67. ,, ' Nun komm der Heiden Heiland,' a 5.
68. ,, Trinklied, ' Der Wein, der schmeckt,' a 6.
69. ,, Canzonetta, ' Bonzorno Madonna,' a 4.
70. Rogier Michael. ' Ein feste Burg,' a 4.
71. Leonard Schröter. Te Deum (German text), a 8.
72. Thomas Walliser. ' Ein feste Burg,' a 5.
73-79. 7 Italian Frottole.
80. A. Willaert. Pater Noster and Ave Maria, a 4.
81. Hans Leo Hassler. ' Herzlich lieb hab' ich üich,' a 8.
82. Jacobus Gallus (Handl). ' Jerusalem laetare,' a 6.
83. Escobedo. Motet, ' Exurge quare obdormis,' a 4.
84. Morales. Motet, ' Sancte Antoni,' a 4.   J. R. M.

(2) REINHARD (b. Dresden, Sept. 25, 1859), son of the above, became professor of the Royal Gymnasium at Dresden and compiled the catalogue of the musical collection in the Royal Library (1890). He contributed the results of his researches to the publications of the Int. Mus. Ges. (*Riemann*).

KAFENDA, BEDŘICH (b. at Mošovce, 1883), Slovak composer and professor at the Slovak Music School, Bratislava, received his musical education at the Leipzig Conservatorium, and afterwards conducted light opera in Germany. He served in the army 1915–20, was taken prisoner, and joined the Czech legionaries. He entered upon his present appointment in

1920. His tendencies are classical and he has composed sonatas for violin and pianoforte, and violoncello and pianoforte ; a string quartet ; Slovak songs for solo and for chorus ; ' Ave Maria,' for soprano solo and organ ; and church music   R. N.

KAHN, ROBERT (*b.* Mannheim, July 21, 1865), studied with Lachner in his native town, with Kiel in Berlin and Rheinberger in Munich, and afterwards profited by the society of Brahms in Vienna and of Joachim in Berlin. In 1890 he undertook the direction of a choir of women's voices in Leipzig, a post which he held for three years, writing many compositions for female voices with and without orchestra. He became teacher of composition in the Hochschule of Berlin, and his chamber compositions are highly esteemed throughout Germany. A sonata for piano and violin in G minor, op. 5, was played in Mar. 1896 by Joachim at a Monday Popular Concert in London.

His principal compositions are :

String quartet in A minor, op. 60.
Quintet for PF. and strings in C minor.
Three quartets for PF. and strings, opp. 14, 30, 41.
Trios for PF. and strings, opp. 19, 33, 35.
Clarinet Trio, op. 45.
Three Sonatas, violin and PF., opp. 5, 26, 50.
Suite, violin and PF., op. 69.
Two violoncello sonatas, opp. 37, 56.
' Mahomet's Gesang,' choir and orch.
Many Songs, piano pieces, etc.
                                  M., with addns.

KAHRER, LAURA (*b.* Vienna, Jan. 14, 1853 ; *d.* Dresden, Aug. 2, 1925), a distinguished pianist.

On the nomination of the Empress Elisabeth she became a pupil of the Conservatorium at Vienna, under Dachs and Dessoff, from 1866–1869. After taking the first prize, she made a tour to the principal towns of Germany, ending at Weimar. There she studied under Liszt, and matured that beauty of touch, precision, fire, and intelligence which raised her to the first rank of pianists in Germany, and which induced Herr von Bülow—no lenient critic—to praise her playing of Beethoven's op. 106 in the highest terms. In 1874 she married Eduard RAPPOLDI (*q.v.*). She was the worthy colleague of her husband in the best concerts of Dresden.
                                             G.

KALCHER, JOHANN NEPOMUK (*b.* Feising, Bavaria, 1766 ; *d.* Munich, 1826), studied at Freising under the court organist Berger, and from 1790 under Grätz, at Munich, through whose recommendation he was appointed as court organist at the latter town in 1798. In purity and power his playing was considered unparalleled. Among his pupils was Carl Maria von Weber, then aged 13, who dedicated to him the second of his published works, 6 Variations for pianoforte (1800), in the dedication of which he expresses his sincere admiration of, and gratitude to, his revered master. Kalcher composed symphonies, masses, concertos, sonatas, songs, etc., of which most have remained in MS. (See *Q.-L.* and *Mendel.*)

KALINNIKOV, BASIL SERGEIVICH (*b.* Government of Orlov, Jan. 13, 1866 ; *d.* Yalta, Jan. 11, 1901 ; Dec. 29, 1900 O.S.), composer. He was the son of a police official, and was educated in the Orlovsky Seminary, where for a time he directed the choir. In 1884 he came to Moscow in great poverty, but succeeded in entering the Music School of the Philharmonic Society. He studied the bassoon and also composition under Ilyinsky and Blaramberg. Having completed a brilliant course at this school, Kalinnikov was appointed assistant conductor to the Italian Opera, Moscow, for the season 1893–94. Unhappily the privations he had undergone had told upon his health. Symptoms of consumption now began to show themselves, and he was ordered to relinquish his work and winter in the Crimea. The remaining years of his life were devoted entirely to composition. His first symphony is a spirited work, full of fresh and healthy inspiration, and very national in style. It met with great success in Russia, was heard in Vienna (1898), Berlin (1899), Paris (1900), and reached England in 1908, when it was heard both in London and at the Bristol festival. His principal works, published mostly by Jürgenson, include :

Cantata, ' St. John Chrysostom.'
Two symphonies (G minor and A major).
Two orchestral intermezzi.
Orchestral Suite.
Two symphonic sketches.
Incidental music to A. Tolstoi's play, ' Tsar Boris ' (1899).
String quartet.
' The Roussalka,' ballad for solo, ch., and orch.
Songs and pianoforte pieces.
                                             R. N.

KALKBRENNER, FRIEDRICH WILHELM MICHAEL (*b.* 1788 ; *d.* Enghien, near Paris, June 10, 1849), pianist and prolific composer for his instrument. He was born while his mother was on a journey between Cassel and Berlin. His father, Christian Kalkbrenner (1755–1806), of Hebrew extraction and a musician of considerable ability, began his son's training early.[1] In 1798 Friedrich entered the Conservatoire at Paris, and left it, after four years of assiduous study, with 1st prize for pianoforte-playing and harmony. In 1813 he played in public at Berlin and Vienna, heard Clementi, made Hummel's acquaintance, and was introduced by Haydn to Albrechtsberger, from whom he had lessons in counterpoint. From 1814–23 he resided in London, much sought after as a player and fashionable teacher. He was a champion of the system of LOGIER and the chiroplast. In 1824 he settled in Paris as a member of the pianoforte-making firm of Pleyel & Co. In Paris, too, his success as a performer and teacher was very great ; he was a shrewd man of business and managed to amass quite a fortune. Madame Camille Pleyel was his best pupil. When Chopin came to Paris

[1] Beethoven includes ' Kalkbrenner (Vater) ' with Sterkel and others of the ' old dead composers of the Empire ' in his denunciation of Gottfried Weber's mistakes in regard to Mozart's Requiem. ' Requiescat in pace,' says he (Letter, Feb. 6, 1826). He would hardly have been content with so mild a sneer if he had known that Kalkbrenner had ' arranged ' ' Don Giovanni ' (that is, had altered the music and interpolated fresh pieces for its appearance on the Paris stage, Sept. 17, 1805 (see Lajarte, *Bibl. mus. de l'Opéra,* ii. 3). (See LACHNITZ.)

in 1831, Kalkbrenner's reputation was at its height: his compositions, mostly written for the market and now forgotten, were upon the desks of all dilettanti, and his playing was upheld as a model. Chopin, who was then only 22 years of age, but had already written his two concertos, the études, op. 10, the first scherzo and ballade, etc., called on him and played his concerto in E minor, whereupon Kalkbrenner came forward with the astounding proposal that Chopin should bind himself to be his pupil for three years and thus under his guidance become a good artist! Chopin took no lessons, but attended certain class-meetings, and soothed Kalkbrenner by dedicating the concerto to him. In a letter dated Dec. 16, 1831, Chopin speaks in high terms of Kalkbrenner's technique, praises his charming, equable touch and quiet self-possession, and says that Herz was a zero compared with him. Still Chopin seems from the first to have been of Mendelssohn's opinion, who said to him soon after, ' You had nothing to learn from Kalkbrenner; you play better than he does.'

Professor Marx used to tell a story of how Kalkbrenner called on him in 1834 at Berlin, anxious to make a good impression, as the Professor was then editor of the new *Berliner Musikzeitung*, and an influential personage. The visitor in moving terms deplores the decay of the good old art of improvisation, saying that since Hummel had retired he was the only one who still cultivated it in the true classical spirit. He opens the piano and improvises for a quarter of an hour with fluent fancy and great neatness, interweaving all manner of themes, even a little fugue, much to the Professor's edification. Next day a parcel of music just printed at Paris arrives for review. The Professor, greatly interested, opens the topmost piece—' Effusio musica, par Fred. Kalkbrenner ': when lo and behold! he has yesterday's improvisation before him, fugue and all, note for note!

An instruction-book with études belonging to it[1] is the best thing Kalkbrenner left.[2] His attainments as a musician are shown in four pianoforte concertos, one for two pianos, a septet, sextet, and quintet, and various sonatas; all well written for the instrument, but dull and trite, spite of the glitter of what was called a ' brilliant ' style.[3]

Kalkbrenner died of cholera at Enghien, near Paris.   E. D.

KALLIWODA (KALÎVŌDA), (1) JOHANN WENZESLAUS (*b.* Prague, Mar. 21, 1800; *d.* Carlsruhe, Dec. 3, 1866), a violin-player and popular composer. From 1811–17 he was a pupil of the Conservatorium, under Dionys Weber and Pixis, and from 1817–23 a member

---

[1] ' *Méthode pour apprendre le pianoforte à l'aide du guide-mains contenant les principes de musique* ' . . . op. 108. Paris, 1830.
[2] He also wrote a *Traité d'harmonie du pianiste* (1849).
[3] See Mendelssohn's *Letters*, and the *Life of Moscheles*, passim; *Life and Letters of Sir Charles Hallé*, p. 212; and Niecks's *Chopin*, i. 232–40.

of the orchestra of that town. During a visit to Munich he was introduced to Prince Fürstenberg, who took a lively interest in his talent, and appointed him conductor of his private band at Donaueschingen, which post Kalliwoda retained, in spite of various offers from more important places, for the rest of his professional life, till he retired on a pension in 1853.

Kalliwoda, as a violinist, is regarded as one of the best representatives of the Prague school under F. W. Pixis. Without possessing very startling qualities of execution or style, his performances showed a well-finished technique, a sympathetic but not large tone, and were altogether more remarkable for elegance and a certain pleasantness than for vigour or depth of feeling. His compositions consist of :

Seven Symphonies—F minor (1826); E♭; D minor; C; B minor (op. 106); G minor; and F.
Overtures, Concertinos, and other Solo-pieces for the violin and oth'r orchestral instruments, especially the clarinet.
Quartets for stringed instruments.
Violin-Duets, Pianoforte-pieces, and a number of songs.

Many of his works enjoyed for some time, and chiefly in amateur circles, a considerable popularity; and the index of the Leipzig *A.M.Z.* shows a long list of performances. Their day is now over, but Schumann[4] speaks of Kalliwoda's fifth symphony with enthusiasm, and further testified his esteem by dedicating his Intermezzi (op. 4) ' al Sign. Kalliwoda.'

His son (2) WILHELM (*b.* Donaueschingen, July 19, 1827; *d.* Carlsruhe, Sept. 8, 1893) was for a short time a pupil of Mendelssohn at Leipzig in 1847, and at Hauptmann in 1848. He held various posts at Carlsruhe with credit to himself, and succeeded his father as conductor at Carlsruhe, but was compelled by ill-health to give up his work in 1875.   P. D.

KALNINS, A., see LATVIAN MUSIC.

KAMMERTON, see PITCH, subsection HISTORY.

KANDLER, FRANZ SALES (*b.* Kloster-Neuburg, Lower Austria, Aug. 23, 1792; *d.* Baden, near Vienna, Sept. 26, 1831), a musical historian, to whom we owe an admirable condensation of Baini's Palestrina. He belonged to the War Office, and went as interpreter with the army to Venice and Naples in 1817 and 1821. He died of cholera. His two works are *Cenni storico-critici alla vita ed opere del . . . G. Ad. Hasse* (Venice, 1820; 2nd ed., Naples, 1820), and that above mentioned, *Über das Leben und die Werke des . . . Palestrina*, etc. This was published after Kandler's death by Kiesewetter (Leipzig, B. & H., 1834). Another posthumous publication, collected from Kandler's contributions to musical periodicals, was *Cenni storico-critici sulle vicende e lo stato attuale della musica in Italia* (1836).

KAPELLMEISTER, see CHAPELLE.

KAPSBERGER, JOHANN HIERONYMUS (*d. circa* 1633), a prolific composer and skilled musician, flourished at Venice about 1604, and

---

[4] *Gesamm. Schriften*, iii. 278.

elsewhere in Italy. He attained great skill on instruments of the lute family, and among his publications were three books of ' Intabolatura di chitarrone ' (1604, 1616, 1626); four of ' Villanelle ' for voices, with chitarrone accompaniment (1610, 1619, 1619, 1623); besides motets, arias, a wedding chorus (1627), and an Apotheosis of Ignatius Loyola (1622). He is mentioned with great eulogium by Kircher (*Musurgia*). He seems to have died about 1633, as no work of his of later date is known. (For list see *Q.-L.*; also Ambros, *Gesch. d. Mus.* vol. iv. p. 126.)

KARAJAN, THEODOR GEORG, RITTER VON (*b.* Vienna, Jan. 22, 1810; *d.* Apr. 28, 1873), Dr. juris., philologist, and historian; clerk (1841) and custos (1854) in the court library, appointed vice-president (1851), and president (1859) of the Akademie der Wissenschaften; received the order of Leopold in 1870. His philological works are numerous and important; but his title to admission here is his pamphlet, *J. Haydn in London, 1791 und 1792* (Vienna, Gerold, 1861). In addition to matter from the well-known pamphlets of Dies and Griesinger, it contains a number of Haydn's letters, chiefly from London and Estoras, to his friend Maria Anna von Genzinger, the wife of Leopold Peter, Edler von Genzinger, an esteemed physician, with four from the lady herself. She played the piano well and even composed. Haydn wrote several sonatas for her, and whenever he was in Vienna spent much of his time at her house, where a pleasant musical society was generally to be found. Karajan also furnished his friend Otto Jahn with valuable material for his book on Mozart.   C. F. P.

KAREL, RUDOLF (*b.* Pilsen, now Plzen, Czechoslovakia, Nov. 1880), composer and teacher.

Karel attended the Gymnasium, first in Plzen and then in Prague, and later studied law in the Prague University. These studies, however, were not congenial to him, and finally, against his father's wish, he entered the Prague Conservatoire, where he became a pupil of J. Klička (organ) and Antonin Dvořák (composition). On completing his course, in 1904, he devoted himself exclusively to composition. For ten years he lived quietly in Prague, until the summer of 1914. He was then taking a holiday in Russia, where, on the outbreak of war, he was interned as an Austrian subject. After a few months, he was sent to teach in the State Music School at Taganrog, and two years later was appointed professor in the Conservatoire at Rostov-on-Don. When, in the autumn of 1917, the Bolshevist upheaval took place, Karel was forced to fly to Irkutsk, in Siberia. But even there he was pursued, and only rescued by the Czechoslovak Legionaries, whose ranks he joined. Finally he was appointed conductor of the Symphony Orchestra of the

Legion, in which capacity he eventually succeeded in getting home. He is now on the teaching staff of the Prague Conservatoire.

Karel is chiefly an instrumental composer; a typical ' absolute ' musician, even when he occasionally adopts a programme for his works (see below). In this respect he is a true pupil of Dvořák, in fact, his only successor among the Czech composers. Karel started with a thorough study of Bach, Mozart, Beethoven, Dvořák and Brahms, and afterwards found his own personal and modern idiom wherewith to fill the mould of classical instrumental forms. Thence his relationship to Bruckner, with whom he shares the tendency to breadth of structure, and also to Reger, and, in his later period, to Hindemith, and others. Like the Russians he usually employs in his works the old church tonalities. His instrumental music is epic rather than lyrical; it is not impressionistic; it lacks the softer qualities and is pervaded by a certain austerity. At the same time, much passion is often concealed within its broad themes. Karel's adagios are remarkable for their depth and are generally the strongest of his movements. In his scherzos, the humour is rather biting than careless, and Slavonic rhythms may be clearly heard. His themes are broad, his harmony rich; and the whole plan of modulation constructed upon the apparently simple relations of keys, combined at the same time with the allied church tonalities, a method which gives rise to new and interesting complications. His instrumentation avoids all affectations and is pithy, sane and real. In the ' Renaissance ' symphony (by which is meant the renaissance of classical music) he simplifies his orchestral resources so much, and strives for such a peculiarly transparent quality of tone, that he only uses a small orchestra (like Beethoven and Brahms he holds back the trombones for the last movement) in which, wherever possible, each instrument plays an independent part, and the tone of the full orchestra almost disappears. Hence the polyphonic tendency of Karel's work.

A special feature of Karel's art is his remarkable capacity for the use of the variation form. When he introduces a theme, he continues to elaborate it, so that his work actually consists of a continuous development. For this reason he likes to combine sonata-form or rondo-form with variation-form. It is characteristic of him that immediately after the composition of the Theme and Variations for piano, op. 13, he started to write a monothematic sonata (op. 14) in four movements on the same motive. Also his Capriccio for violin, op. 21, varies the same theme used in the preceding violin concerto, op. 20, which the composer calls a symphony for violin and orchestra. Besides these works, the symphonic epic, ' The Ideals,' the string quartet in E flat, and the pianoforte quartet in

A minor, are all monothematic ; on the other hand, Novák points out Karel's great power of thematic invention as shown in the 'Renaissance' symphony and the violin sonata.

Karel's programme music — 'The Ideals,' 'Demon' and 'The Awakening,' are not constructed on literary bases. They treat personal or universal problems, and merely originate from some definite idea, but their further structure is purely musical ; therefore it is impossible to attach to them any detailed programme. He has also a very marked feeling for dramatic art. In his youth he made a diligent study of Wagner and Smetana. His only opera, 'Ilseina srdce' (Ilsea's Heart), the libretto of which is taken from the modern artistic world of Bohemia, shows that the author possesses a powerful dramatic talent, with a special sense for stagecraft and scenic effect. Various external obstacles delayed the first production of this work for fifteen years after its composition. On this account, Karel has not up till now shown any wish to write a new work for the theatre. He has recently delighted his public with a song cycle of an epic character (op. 24).

ORCHESTRAL MUSIC

Orchestral Suite, op. 4 (arrangement for 4 hands, J. Otto, Prague); Comedy Overture (MS.), op. 5 ; Scherzo-Capriccio, op. 6 (score, parts and piano arrangement, 4 hands, Simrock) ; Fantasia for orchestra, op. 8 (MS.) ; 'The Ideals,' op. 11, symphonic epic (MS.) ; Renaissance Symphony, op. 15, in E flat minor (MS.) ; Four Slavonic Dances, op. 16 (score and arrangement 4 hands, Simrock) ; Symphony (concerto ?) for violin and orchestra, op. 20 (MS.) ; Capriccio for violin and orchestra, op. 21 (MS.) ; Symphonic poem 'Demon,' op. 23 (score and parts, Simrock) ; incidental music to K. P. Hamsun's drama 'The Game of Life,' op. 26 (also arranged as a Concert Suite, MS.) ; 'Awakening,' op. 27, a symphony for soli, chorus and orchestra (not quite finished).

CHAMBER MUSIC

String Quartet in D minor, op. 3 (MS.) ; Pianoforte Trio in G minor, op. 7 (MS.) ; String Quartet in E flat, op. 12 (Simrock) ; Pianoforte Quartet in A minor, op. 22 (only two movements out of seven preserved in MS.) ; Violin Sonata in D minor, op. 17 (Simrock).

PIANO

'An Eternal Legend,' op. 1, melodrama for piano (MS.) ; pieces for piano, op. 2 (J. Otto, Prague) ; Nocturne, op. 9 (Simrock) ; Thema con variazone, op. 13 (Simrock) ; Sonata in C minor, op. 14 (Simrock) ; Three Valses, op. 18 (Simrock) ; Burlesque, op. 19 (Simrock).

VOCAL AND CHORAL

'V. Zaři Helénského Slunce' (In the Glow of the Hellenic Sun) op. 24, four songs with Czech and German words (Hudební Matice, Prague) ; Regimental Marching Song, op. 25 (MS.).

OPERATIC

'Ilseina srdce' (Ilsea's Heart), op. 10, opera in 3 acts, first performance National Theatre, Prague, Nov. 11, 1924 ; pianoforte score published by Hudební Matice, Prague.

R. V.

KARGEL (KÄRGEL), SIXT, a 16th-century lutenist, in the service of the Prince-Bishop of Strassburg c. 1571 ; living at Zabern, Alsace, 1586. He published a number of important collective books of lute pieces, the first of which has apparently been lost, as the first known, dated 1571, is a reprint ; five books are enumerated in Q.-L.

E. v. d. s.

KARG-ELERT, SIGFRID (b. Oberndorf-on-Neckar, Nov. 21, 1879), composer. His real name was Karg, the 'Elert' having been added early in his career at the suggestion of his concert-agent. He studied at Leipzig Conservatoire under Reinecke, Jadassohn, Homeyer, etc., served for a time as professor at Magdeburg Conservatoire, and was appointed in 1919 to Leipzig Conservatoire, where he taught pianoforte, theory and composition. Though his earliest ambitions lay in the direction of composition, his chief distinction during his student days, and for some years after, was as a pianist of unusual brilliance. Some meetings with Grieg turned his ambitions once more towards composition, and the result has been a very large output in a great variety of forms —over 100 songs, sonatas for violin, pianoforte, etc., many sets of pieces for pianoforte, a symphony, string quartet, and much music for organ, etc.

There is also a valuable series of studies and pieces written specially for the 'Kunst-Harmonium,' an instrument, usually of two manuals, with considerable resources in tone-colour of the imitative-orchestral type. Karg-Elert toured as a recitalist on this instrument, and his works for it range from little pieces of delicate fancy to lengthy works, including a sonata and a highly original Passacaglia, the latter being subsequently re-written for organ, in which shape it ranks with the finest examples of the type. Probably this association with the 'Kunst-Harmonium' led Karg-Elert to take up the study of the organ, mainly with a view to composing for the instrument. (For a time he acted as accompanist and soloist at St. John's, Leipzig.) There can be little doubt that he found his true *métier* as an organ composer. Few modern organ works have been more widely and deservedly esteemed than his 'Sixty-six Choral Improvisations,' 'Twenty Choral Preludes and Postludes,' 'Ten Poetic Tone Pictures,' the Passacaglia in E flat minor, and, among lighter works, the 'Three Impressions,' and 'Three Pastels.' He shows great harmonic resource—a factor that appears to advantage in his frequent treatments of ground basses—and an easy mastery of contrapuntal devices. His strong feeling for colour no doubt led to his great interest in organ registration—indeed his enthusiasm and ingenuity in devising subtle schemes of organ tone-colour often lead to demands that few players or instruments can meet. A tendency to extravagance shows itself in other ways, *e.g.* over-chromaticism, the piling up of gigantic stacks of notes, with chords of three (and even four) notes for pedal, a too-frequent employment of *prestissimo* rushes up the keyboard, violent dynamic contrasts, etc. But his pronounced mannerisms are trifling blemishes on an organ output of nearly 200 pieces, some of large scale and many of rare beauty and originality. He is at his best in his numerous treatments of chorales. It is not too much to say that the present revival of interest in the Chorale Prelude in this country is largely due to the impression made on English organists by his 'Sixty-six Chorale Improvisations,' which appeared in 1909. They show a variety

of treatment, an intimacy of expression, and
a wealth of harmonic and contrapuntal resource
that make the collection the nearest approach,
and a worthy successor, to Bach's labours in
the same field.   There appears to be no method
of treatment used by Bach that Karg-Elert
does not also employ, plus some devices of
his own, *e.g.* an ingenious use of dance
measures as rhythmical bases.   But whatever
the chosen form may be, the music is intensely
alive and expressive.   He has also written
effectively for other instruments in combination with the organ ; and in certain of his
larger solo works has added, in the Coda, parts
for brass and drums.   Interest in England is
almost confined to the organ works, a list of
which is appended :

Op.
25b. Passacaglia in E flat minor.
34b. Improvisation.
36b. Interludium.
39b. Fantasia and Fugue in D.
46. Canzone.
65. Sixty-six Chorale-Improvisations.
72. Three Impressions.
73. Chaconne, Fugue-Trilogy and Chorale.
74. Sonatina in A minor.
75. (a) Funerale ;   (b) Improvisation on 'In dulci jubilo' ;   (c)
        Two Chorale Improvisations.
78. Twenty Preludes and Postludes (Chorale-Studier).
85. Three Symphonic Canzones.
86. Ten Characteristic Pieces.
87. Three Symphonic Chorales.
92. Three Pastels.
96. Seven Pastels from the Lake of Constance.
106. Cathedral Windows (Six Pieces on Gregorian Tunes).
        Homage to Handel (Fifty-four studies in Variation Form on a
            ground bass of Handel).

H. G.

KASHKIN, Nicholas Dmitrievich (*b.* Vo-
ronezh, Dec. 9, 1839 ; *d.* circa 1909), received
his first instruction in music from his father, a
bookseller, who was self-taught in the art.   As
early as 13, Kashkin found himself obliged to
give music lessons on his own account.   In 1860
he went to Moscow, where he studied the piano
under Dubuque.   N. Rubinstein observed his
talents, and offered him a post as teacher of
pianoforte and theory at the classes of the
Musical Society, which in 1866 developed into
the Conservatoire.   He retained this position
until 1896, and was one of the most popular
teachers in Moscow.   Kashkin, an able writer,
was musical critic of the *Russky Viedomosti* from
1877–78, and again from 1886–97.   He was also
on the staff of the *Moscow Viedomosti*.   He is
best known abroad by his *Reminiscences of
Tchaikovsky* (1896), with whom he was long
associated in intimate friendship.   R. N.

KASHPEROV, Vladimir Nikitich (*b.* Sim-
birsk, Russia, 1827 ; *d.* July 8, 1894), composer
and teacher of singing, first studied with Fotta
and Henselt in St. Petersburg, and in 1850
composed an opera, ' The Gipsies ' (' Tsiganer '),
some scenes from which were performed.   In
1856 he visited Berlin, where he worked under
the celebrated theorist Dehn.   From Germany
Kashperov went to Italy.   Here he made a
special study of vocal art.   His opera, ' Marie
Tudor ' (1859), was produced at Milan with
some success.   Other operas followed : ' Rienzi '
(Florence, 1863), ' Consuelo ' (Venice).   ' The

Storm ' (St. Petersburg, 1867), libretto by
Ostrovsky, was an attempt at national opera,
as was also ' Taras Boulba ' (Moscow, 1893).
From 1866–72 Kashperov was professor of
singing at the Moscow Conservatoire.   He did
great service to the musical life of the town by
organising gratuitous choral classes, which were
very much appreciated.   R. N.

KASTALSKY, Alexander Dmitrievich
(*b.* Moscow, Nov. 16/28, 1856), Russian composer and authority on the church music.   He
studied from 1878–82 at the Moscow Conservatoire under Tchaikovsky and Taneiev.   In
1887 he was appointed teacher of piano in the
Moscow Synodal School, of which he became
director in 1900.   After the revolution the
Synodal School became the People's Choral
Academy, abolished in 1923.   Kastalsky
led a new and progressive movement in
Russian church music, and wrote a number of
liturgical works.   His Requiem for the Fallen
Heroes of the Allied Army was given at Birmingham, Nov. 22, 1917, by the Festival
Choral Society under Sir Henry J. Wood.   It
is an ambitious attempt to unite East and West
in a solemn commemoration of the heroic dead.
Ecclesiastical themes from the Eastern Orthodox, Western Catholic and Anglican liturgies
are employed ; and even the Hymn to Indra
and the song of the Japanese soldiers are included.   Kastalsky had in view the lofty, but
impracticable, aim of a performance for which
each of the allied nations should furnish its own
choir.   Though coldly received, it is the work
of a highly-cultured church musician of broad-
minded ideals.   Kastalsky also composed an
opera, ' Clara Milich ' (based on Turgeniev's
tale) ; a Georgian Suite ; a symphony of the
tilling of the soil ; and wrote a book on the
harmonisation of the folk-songs by the people.
                                    R. N.

KASTNER, (1) Jean Georges (*b.* Strassburg,
Mar. 9, 1810 ; *d.* Paris, Dec. 19, 1867), was
destined to theology ; but music conquered,
and the successful performance of his opera,
' Die Königin der Sarmaten,' induced the town
council of Strasburg to grant him the means of
going to Paris in 1835, where he finished his
studies under Berton and Reicha, and resided till his death.   In 1837 he published his
Traité général d'instrumentation (2nd ed. 1844),
the first work of the kind published in France,
and the beginning of a long series of elementary
treatises.   Though fruitful as a dramatic composer—' Beatrice,' opera (German), 1839 ; ' La
Maschera,' opéra-comique, 1841 ; ' Le Dernier
Roi de Juda,' biblical opera given in concert
form at the Conservatoire, Dec. 1, 1844, under
Habeneck ; ' Les Nonnes de Robert-le-Diable,'
1845, and a number of vocal and instrumental
compositions large and small, including his
Livres-Partitions, half music, half treatises—he
cannot occupy a high rank amongst the masters

of the French school. On the other hand, his theoretical works and musical literature have acquired for him a solid reputation. Besides the numerous works enumerated below, Kastner was a voluminous contributor to the *Gazette musicale*, the *Ménestrel*, and the *Revue éirangère*, as well as to the German periodicals, *Iris, Allg. musikalische Zeitung, Neue Zeitschrift, Cecilia*, and many others. Every spare moment was directed to the preparation of a vast *Encyclopædia of Music*, which remained unfinished at his death. Kastner was made a free member of the Académie des Beaux-Arts in 1859, and was also decorated by a very large number of institutions outside of France.

For the details of his honourable and useful life we must refer to the exhaustive biography by Hermann Ludwig (Breitkopf & Härtel, 3 vols., 1886), with complete lists, indexes, etc., a monument raised to Kastner's memory by the devotion of his widow. His library was acquired by the Paris Conservatoire.

LIST OF WORKS

STRASSBURG, 1826–35. Five Operas ; three Symphonies ; five Overtures ; PF. Concerto ; Marches ; Choruses ; Waltzes ; ten Serenades for Wind Instruments.
PARIS. Operas : ' Beatrice ' (1839) ; ' La Maschera ' (1841) ; ' Le Dernier Roi de Juda ' (1844) ; ' Les Nonnes de Robert-le-Diable ' (1846). Hymns, Cantatas : ' La Résurrection ' (1835) ; ' Sardanapale ' (1852) ; Cantate alsacienne (1858). Scenes for Voices and PF., Songs, etc. : ' Les Derniers Moments d'un artiste,' ' Le Vétéran,' ' Le Nègre,' ' Glenallan,' ' Judas Iscariote,' etc., forty-one in all. Part-songs, chiefly for men's voices : ' Bibliothèque chorale,' 72 Nos. ; ' Heures d'amour,' 6 Nos. ; ' Les Chants de la vie,' 28 Nos. (1854) ; ' Les Chants de l'armée française,' 23 Nos. ; (1855) ' Les Orphéons,' etc. etc., twenty-six more in all. Piano : ' Valses et galops de Strasbourg,' three sets ; Waltzes, Polkas, Marches, etc., twenty-one more in all. Orchestra : two ' Ouvertures de Festival,' in E♭, and C ; ' Drame-symphonie ' two pieces for saxophone and PF. Treatises : 1. *Cours d'instr. considéré sous les rapports poétiques*, etc. 2. *Traité gén. d'instrumentation* (1837). 3. *Grammaire musicale* (1837). 4. *Théorie abrégée du contrepoint et du fugue* (1839). 5. *Méthode élémentaire d'harmonie*. 6. Suppléments to Nos. 1 and 2. The above were approved by the Institut, and Nos. 1, 2 and 6 adopted by the Conservatoire. 7. *Méthodes élément. de chant piano, violin, flûte, flageolet, cornet à p.'* (1837). 8. *De la composition*, etc., MS. (1841). 9. *Cours d'harmonie moderne*, MS. (1842). 10. *Méthodes élém. de violoncelle, hautbois, clarinette, cor. ophicléïde, trombone* (1844). 11. *Méthode . . . de saxophone* (1845). 12. *Méthode . . . de timbales* (1845). 13. *Manuel . . . de musique militaire* (1847). 14. *Traité de l'orthographie musicale*, MS. (1849). 15. *Les Danses des morts* (1852). 16. *La Harpe d'Éole et la musique cosmique* (1856). 17. *Les Chants de l'armée française avec un essai historique sur les chants militaires des Français* (1855). 18. *Les Voix de Paris* (1857). 19. *Les Sirènes* (1858). 20. *Parémiologie mus. de la langue française* (1866). Nos. 15, 16, 18, 19 and 20 contain large compositions orchestral and vocal.

Kastner's son, (2) GEORGES FREDERIC EUGEN (*b*. Strassburg, Aug. 10, 1852 ; *d*. Bonn, Apr. 6, 1882), devoted himself to physical science, especially to research on the law of vibrations. He was the inventor of the ' Pyrophone,' a small organ, the pipes of which were set in vibration by jets of lighted gas. He brought the subject before the Académie des Sciences, Mar. 17, 1873 ; and issued a book, *Le Pyrophone : Flammes chantantes*, which reached its 4th edition in 1876. (See also *Journal of Society of Arts*, Feb. 17, 1875). His memoir occupies the concluding chapters of his father's life by H. Ludwig (B. & H., 1886). G. ; rev. M. L. P.

KAUFFMANN, GEORG FRIEDRICH (*b*. Ostermondra, Merseburg, Feb. 14, 1679 ; *d*. Merseburg, Mar. 1735), pupil of Buttstedt of Erfurt and Alberti of Merseburg, whom he succeeded as court organist, afterwards becoming also Kapellmeister at the court. He composed an oratorio, 4 cantatas, and a considerable number of organ pieces. (See *Q.-L.*)

KAUFFMANN, PAUL, a 16th-17th century music publisher, who was manager of the business of ' Wittwe Katharina Gerlach ' at Nuremberg in 1590, which business he afterwards took over. Between 1597 and 1614 he published a number of collective volumes, an account whereof is given in *Q.-L.*

KAYSER, ISFRID, an 18th-century monk of the Praemonstratenses at Marchthal, where he was also Kapellmeister. He was a composer of masses, psalms, and other church music, as well as 3 suites (Parthiae), op. 4, for harpsichord, mostly published at Augsburg between 1743–54.   E. V. D. S.

KAYSER, MARGARETHE SUSANNA, of Hamburg, the first woman to sing as soloist in a Hamburg church choir, on Sept. 17, 1716, when Mattheson led her personally to the choir. She was also an excellent oratorio and operatic singer between 1716 and 1746, and between 1729 and 1733 undertook, with great success, the management of the opera, which she rescued from a critical condition. She appeared also at various times at Copenhagen opera. Her husband, JOHANN (*d*. 1729), was conductor of the band of the Hamburg council, and instituted oratorio performances with the assistance of his wife.   E. V. D. S.

KAYSER, PHILIPP CHRISTOPH (*b*. Frankfort-on-M., Mar. 10, 1755 ; *d*. Zürich, Dec. 24, 1823), pianist and composer. From 1775 he lived as music teacher at Zürich, whence Goethe called him to Rome in Nov. 1787 to discuss the composition of some of his Singspiele, as well as the music to *Egmont*. Goethe was a great friend and admirer of Kayser, and had often given him financial assistance when the loss of pupils, caused often through his eccentric behaviour which offended the parents, had reduced him to dire straits. There are many references to Kayser in Goethe's works and letters, while several essays and books have been written about their relations. Apart from Singspiele, motets, and cantatas, Kayser wrote songs and some harpsichord sonatas (*Q.-L.*).
    E. V. D. S.

KEARNS, WILLIAM HENRY (*b*. Dublin, 1794 ; *d*. Prince's Place, Kennington, Dec. 28, 1846), a prominent figure in London musical life in the middle part of the 19th century. He came to London in 1817, where he played the violin at Covent Garden Theatre. He wrote an operetta in that year, called ' Bachelors' Wives, or the British at Brussels.' He soon, however, became the musical adviser to Arnold and Hawes, and ' Der Freischütz,' ' Azor and Zemira,' ' Robert the Devil,' and many other foreign operas were brought out under his direction at Covent Garden. Kearns wrote the additional wind accompaniments to the ' Messiah ' and ' Israel in Egypt ' for the Festival at

Westminster Abbey in 1834, as well as for Handel's choruses at provincial festivals. In 1845 he assisted Gauntlett in editing the *Comprehensive Tune-book*. Henry Smart was among his pupils.   G.

KEEBLE, JOHN (*b.* Chichester, 1711; *d.* London, Dec. 24, 1786), was brought up as a chorister in Chichester Cathedral under Thomas Kelway. He afterwards became a pupil of Dr. Pepusch, and was in 1737 appointed successor to Thomas Roseingrave as organist of St. George's, Hanover Square, allowing Roseingrave one-half of the salary until his death in 1750. Keeble was also organist at Ranelagh Gardens. In 1784 he published *The Theory of Harmonics, or, an Illustration of the Grecian Harmonies*, a work which attracted attention. He published five books of organ pieces, and, jointly with Kirkman, ' 40 Interludes to be played between the verses of the Psalms.'
    W. H. H.

KEEL, FREDERICK (*b.* London, May 8, 1871), studied as a baritone singer at the R.A.M. and at Milan, and made his début in London at Queen's Hall (1898). Though successful as a singer and now teacher of singing at the R.A.M., it is as arranger of old songs that Keel is most widely known. He was honorary secretary of the FOLK-SONG SOCIETY (*q.v.*) (1911–19) and editor of that Society's journal. His editions of Elizabethan songs have done much to popularise many fine melodies.   C.

KEELEY, MRS. (MARY ANNE GOWARD) (*b.* Ipswich, Nov. 22, 1805; *d.* London, Mar. 12, 1899). Being endowed with a pure soprano voice of remarkable compass, she was apprenticed for seven years to the well-known teacher of music, Mrs. Smart (a sister-in-law of Sir George Smart and mother of Henry Smart), under whom she made her first appearance on the stage at Dublin in Nov. 1823. On July 2, 1825, she appeared in London at the Lyceum, then under the management of Arnold. The performance consisted of ' The Beggar's Opera ' (with Thorne, Miss Stephens and Miss Kelly), Shield's ' Rosina ' and ' The Spoiled Child,' in which last two pieces Miss Goward played. The event is thus chronicled in *The Times* (July 4) :

' Miss Goward, the débutante, appeared as Rosina in the opera of that title. She is young, of a slender figure, and with intelligent features. Her voice is pretty, and after she had overcome the first embarrassments of her entrance she went through the part very successfully. She sang the songs in a simple manner, which deserved the applause she received. It is dangerous to prophesy at first appearances, but we may, nevertheless, venture to say that this young lady promises to make a very fine actress. . . . Miss Goward played Little Pickle in the " Spoiled Child " very well indeed.'

In the same season she sang Annetta in ' Der Freischütz ' with Braham and Miss Paton. On Apr. 12, 1826, on the production of Weber's ' Oberon ' at Covent Garden, she undertook the

small but important part of the Mermaid, the music of which had been previously tried by Miss Love and Miss Hammersley, both of whom declined to sing it owing to the difficulty of hearing the delicate orchestral accompaniments at the back of the vast stage where the Mermaid had to appear. ' Little Goward shall sing it,' said Weber, and she overcame this obstacle, as J. R. Planché states (*Recollections and Reflections*, vol. i.) : ' She was even then artist enough to be entrusted with anything,' and her singing of the Mermaid's music earned for her the personal thanks of the composer. For the next few years Miss Goward continued to sing in English opera, but after her marriage with the well-known comedian, Robert Keeley (which took place on June 26, 1829), she devoted her talents entirely to comedy, in which she was one of the greatest artists of the English stage.
    W. B. S.

KEINSPECK (KÜNSPECK), MICHAEL (called ALEXANDRINUS), of Nuremberg, a 15th-century musician. He wrote *Lilium musice plane, Michaelis Keinspeck Musici Alexandrini* (Basle, 1496), one of the earliest books containing printed music, which was engraved on wood blocks. The book, which was used as a music text-book at the University of Basle, went through several editions. In the preface Keinspeck says that he studied music in foreign lands, and after weary and adventurous travels came to France and Lorraine, where the ' unconquerable kings ' had dedicated chapels, and drawn there many eminent men under whom he had perfected himself (*Q.-L.*).

KEIRNINE, a small wire-strung Irish harp (*PLATE XXXVIII*. No. 2; see HARP).

KEISER, REINHARD (*b.* Teuchern, near Weissenfels, Leipzig, 1673[1]; *d.* Hamburg, Sept. 12, 1739), an eminent German opera-composer.

He was grounded in music by his father, a sound church composer, and afterwards attended the Thomasschule of Leipzig, under Johann Schelle, at the same time coming frequently before the public at the many concerts renowned even then for their excellence. In 1692 he was at the court of Brunswick with Kusser (see COUSSER), where his opera ' Basileus ' was produced. A pastorale, ' Die wiedergesundenen Verliebten,' was also given there (1695), and revised as ' Ismene ' was later produced at Hamburg (1699) with extraordinary success. In 1694 he removed to Hamburg, presently succeeding Kusser as chief composer to the opera there, and retaining his preeminence, despite varying fortunes, through some forty years. ' Irene ' (1697) was the first of a series of 116 operas composed for the Hamburg theatre, each containing from 40 to 50 airs, besides operas in collaboration with others, and sacred music. Keiser was luxurious and self-indulgent, and led an adventurous life, but

[1] Bapt. Jan. 12, 1674.

without sacrificing his love of art or his taste for intellectual enjoyments. In 1700 he opened a series of winter-concerts, which formed a remarkable combination of intellectual and sensual gratification ; the most accomplished virtuosi, the finest and best-looking singers, a good orchestra, and carefully selected programmes, furnishing the former, and a banquet of choice viands and wines the latter. In 1703 he assumed the direction of the opera in conjunction with Drüsicke, but his partner absconded, and the whole burden fell upon the shoulders of Keiser. He proved equal to the emergency, for in one year (1709) he composed eight operas, married the daughter of a Hamburg patrician and musician to the municipality 'Oldenburg,' and, having completely reinstated his affairs, plunged into all his former extravagant indulgence. In 1716 he resumed his concerts, visited Copenhagen in 1717, and was at the court of Stuttgart from 1719–21 ; in 1722 he revisited Copenhagen to superintend the production of his opera 'Ulysses' and was appointed Kapellmeister to the King of Denmark ; in 1728 was made cantor and canon of Hamburg Cathedral, and again turned his attention to sacred music. He composed operas up to the year 1738. His wife and daughter are said to have been accomplished singers.

Keiser exercised an important though not a permanent influence on German opera. The perfection to which at first he raised the opera at Hamburg speedily degenerated into mere outward show and trivial if not vulgar farce ; but the sensation he produced at first is described by his contemporaries as extraordinary. Mattheson, who was not likely to exaggerate the successes of a rival, in his life-like picture of the musical condition of Hamburg, calls Keiser the first dramatic composer in the world, and says that no other music than that of 'dieser galante Komponist' was either sung or listened to.[1] His melodies were smooth and graceful, and fell upon the ear 'like charmed accents after the dull pedantries of the contrapuntists of the day.' That his melody was spontaneous his facility itself proves, and he was conspicuous in his endeavour to convey the sentiment of the character in the music. This was the secret of his success, and it was by this that he enabled German opera to hold its own against the declamation of the French, and the melody and fine singing of the Italians.

In sacred music he shines chiefly in oratorio, which he treated dramatically, but with an earnestness and dignity surprising in a man of his character. His sacred compositions include 'Der für die Sünde der Welt gemarterte und sterbende Jesus,' 1712 ; 'Der verurtheilte und gekreuzigte Jesus,' published 1715 (poem by

[1] See his *Musikalische Patriot* for list of operas given in Hamburg, and Mattheson's other books for criticism on his music. Keiser contributed some remarks to Mattheson's *Neu-eröffnetes Orchester*.

Brockes of Hamburg) ; a Passion according to St. Mark, and other historical oratorios, motets, cantatas and psalms. He published extracts from the two first-named works, viz. 'Auserlesene Soliloquia' (1714), and 'Selige Erlösungs-Gedanken' (1715) ; airs from various operas, cantatas for a single voice, and several vocal collections with various titles, such as 'Gemüthsergötzung' (1698) ; 'Divertimenti serenissimi' (1713) ; 'Musikalische Landlust' (1714) ; 'Kaiserliche Friedenspost' (1715), etc. Important modern reprints of Keiser's works are 'Octavia' (supplement to Händelgesellschaft edition (1902) and 'Krösus' and 'Inganno fedele,' *D.D.T.* xxxvii. and xxxviii. Portions of his operas and sacred works have been published by Lindner, in his *Erste stehende deutsche Oper*, ii. 3-15 ; Reissmann, in his *Allg. Geschichte der Musik*, iii. 54-73 and App. Nos. 7 and 8 ; and von Winterfeld in his *Evangelische Kirchengesang*, vol. iii. Examples are also to be found in the *Oxf. Hist. Mus.*, vol. iv., *The Age of Bach and Handel*. Adam Hiller included an unaccompanied motet—'Kindlich gross '—in his *Vierstimmige Motetten*, etc., vol. ii. ; and there is a fugue for four voices, 'Gott ist offenbaret,' in the *Auswahl vorzüglicher Musikwerke*. A full catalogue of his works is in the *Vierteljahrsschrift*, vol. vi. pp. 196-203, and a condensed list in *Q.-L.* A. M., rev.

(See OPERA and ORATORIO.)

BIBL.—CHRYSANDER, *Geschichte der Hamburger Oper (A.M.Z., 1878–79)* ; KLIEFELD, *Das Orchester der Hamburger Oper (J.M.G. Sammelb.* i. 213).

KÉLER BÉLA (ADALBERT VON KÉLER) (*b.* Bartfeld, Hungary, Feb. 13, 1820 ; *d.* Wiesbaden, Nov. 20, 1882). After attempting both the law and farming he settled himself to music, and in 1845 began regular study at Vienna under Schlesinger and Sechter, playing the fiddle in the band of the Theatre ' an der Wien ' at the same time. On May 7, 1854, he took the command of Gung'l's band in Berlin, and began his career as conductor, solo player and composer. After a few months in Berlin he returned to Vienna, and succeeded to Lanner's position at the head of that celebrated band in 1855. This again he left in 1856 for an infantry regiment. As bandmaster to the latter he was called to Wiesbaden in 1863, and in 1870 became Kapellmeister of the Kur orchestra there, a post which he resigned from ill-health in 1872. He celebrated his silver anniversary on May 7, 1879. His works, which reach op. 130, consist of overtures, dance music, and pieces for solo violin, all distinguished for showy, brilliant style and clever orchestration. Among the most popular are his 'Hoffnungssterne' waltz, 'Hurrah-Sturm' galop, and 'Friedrich-Karl' march. G.

KELLER, FORTUNATO, see CHELLERI.

KELLER, GODFREY (*d.* before 1707), a teacher of music who settled in London near the

end of the 17th century. In conjunction with Godfrey Finger he produced ' A set of Sonatas in five Parts for Flutes and Hautboys.' With this date John Cullen issued an engraved folio, *A Complete Method for Attaining to Play a Thorough-Bass upon either Organ, Harpsicord, or Theorbo Lute, by the late famous Godfrey Keller.* This, in its day, was a greatly esteemed work, and in 1731 it was reprinted in full, with corrections, as an appendix to Holder's *Treatise on Harmony.* F. K.

A set of six suites for 2 violins and flutes in unison, with violins *ad lib* and bass, MS. from the Granville Library, is now in private hands. E. v. d. s.

KELLER, KARL (*b.* Dessau, Oct. 16, 1784 ; *d.* Schaffhausen, July 19, 1855), a famous flute virtuoso, son of the court organist and chamber musician, Joh. Gotthilf Keller. He was engaged successively at the courts of Berlin (till 1806), Cassels (till 1814), Stuttgart (till 1816), Donaueschingen, where he was also Kapellmeister at the theatre, and his wife (Wilhelmine Meierhofer) operatic singer, 1817–49. In the latter year he retired to Schaffhausen on a pension. Keller composed chiefly for the flute (concertos, solos, etc.), and songs, some of which attained to great popularity (*Mendel*).

KELLEY, EDGAR STILLMAN (*b.* Sparta, Wisconsin, U.S.A., Apr. 14, 1857), an American composer and writer on musical subjects. He was a pupil, first, of F. W. Merriam, from 1870–1874 ; then of Clarence Eddy and N. Ledochowski in Chicago for two years. He went then to Stuttgart, where he studied for four years under Seifriz, Krüger, Speidel and Friedrich Finck. Kelley spent much of his time, upon his return to America, in California, acting as organist in San Francisco and Oakland, and as music critic, from 1893–95, for the *San Francisco Examiner.* While there he devoted some attention to study of the music of the Chinese, who dwell in large numbers on the Pacific coast. The influence of these observations is seen in his ' Aladdin ' suite, in which he has used Chinese motives. In 1890 he conducted a comic operetta company in the eastern States, and in 1892 he brought out a comic operetta of his own, entitled ' Puritania,' in Boston, where it had a success that was denied to it in other cities. In 1901–02 he was acting professor in Yale University. He taught pianoforte and composition in Berlin from 1902–10. Since 1910 he has been teacher of composition in the Cincinnati Conservatory and has held a fellowship from the Western College for Women at Oxford, Ohio, to enable him to devote himself to composition. Kelley's compositions, which are chiefly in manuscript, include, beside ' Puritania,' op. 11, and ' Aladdin,' op. 10, incidental music to *Macbeth* for orchestra and chorus, op. 7 ; incidental music to the play of *Ben Hur,* op. 17, for orchestra, solos, and chorus ; a pianoforte quintet ; an original theme with variations for string quartet, op. 1 ; a Wedding Ode for tenor solo, male chorus and orchestra, op. 4 ; ' Pilgrim's Progress,' a cantata ; ' Gulliver,' a symphony ; ' New England Symphony '; quintet for pianoforte and strings; quartet for strings ; and a number of songs and pieces for the pianoforte. He published, in 1913, *Chopin the Composer.* R. A.

KELLNER, DAVID (*b.* Leipzig, 1670 ; *d.* Stockholm, Apr. 6, 1748), organist and carillon-player at the time of his death. He was a captain in the service of the town of Hamburg, and an excellent musical theorist and lute-player. He went later into Swedish service, and was Kapellmeister at the German church at Stockholm (*c.* 1745). His *Treulicher Unterricht im General - Bass* (instructions in thoroughbass), Hamburg, 1732, appeared in many editions, the last being in 1797, and was translated into Swedish and Dutch. Thelemann wrote a preface to the second edition, and Dan. Solander of Upsala to the third, but Mattheson apparently wrote an adverse criticism. Kellner wrote also a book of lute pieces (1747). E. v. d. s.

KELLNER, (1) JOHANN PETER (*b.* Gräfenrode, Thuringia, Sept. 24, 1705 ; *d.* there, 1788), received his musical instruction chiefly from J. C. Schmidt, the organist of Zella St. Blasii, by whom he was early introduced to the works of Sebastian Bach. In 1725 he obtained the post of cantor at Frankenhain, but exchanged it in 1728 for a similar post at his birthplace, where, in spite of many tempting offers elsewhere, he remained till his death. It was his pride in later days to recall his personal acquaintance with Bach and Handel. For them and their works he always expressed the utmost veneration, and we owe the preservation of some of Bach's works to copies made by him. We are also told that once when Bach happened to come into the church where Kellner was playing, Kellner improvised in a masterly way a fugue on the theme b-a-c-h. From Kellner's manuscript of 1738 Spitta has printed Bach's *Vorschriften und Grundsätze zum vierstimmigen Spielen des General-Bass oder Accompagnement für seine Scholaren in der Musik.*[1] Kellner's own published works are :

1. ' Certamen musicum bestehend aus Präludien, Fugen, Allemanden,' etc., in six Suites (Arnstadt, 1739–49). Another edition in eight Suites (1749–56).
2. ' Manipulus Musices oder eine Hand voll kurzweiliger Zeitvertreib vors Clavier ' (Arnstadt, 1753–56), four pieces partly Suites, partly Sonatas.
3. Two Choralbearbeitungen for two Clav. and Pedal. Other organ works and church cantatas exist in MS.

Seiffert[2] expresses the opinion that Kellner's clavier works have been most undeservedly neglected by modern collectors and editors of the older music. He reckons the suites, more especially, as among the best of those produced after the form had been perfected by Muffat

[1] See Appendix xii. Spitta's *Bach,* Eng. trans. vol. iii. p. 315 ff.
[2] *Geschichte der Klaviermusik,* Bd. I. p. 361 ff.

and Bach. Naturally, various reminiscences of Bach and Handel occur in Kellner's works.

J. R. M.

His son, (2) JOHANN CHRISTOPH (b. Gräfenrode, Thuringia, Aug. 15, 1736; d. Cassels, 1803), pupil of his father and of Georg Benda, toured in Germany and Holland, and lived for some time at Amsterdam and the Hague. On his return he became organist at the court church at Cassels. He was an eminent theorist and composer of an operetta, a cantata, concertos, sonatas, organ pieces ; he wrote a book on thorough-bass (Mendel; Q.-L.).

KELLOGG, CLARA LOUISE (b. Sumterville, South Carolina, July 12, 1842 ; d. New Hartford, Connecticut, May 13, 1916), opera singer. She was of northern extraction. Her mother had considerable talent as a musician, and Clara was her only child. In 1856 they removed to New York, where she received the whole of her musical education. She made her first appearance there, at the Academy of Music (Opera), as Gilda in ' Rigoletto,' in 1861, and sang that season ten or twelve times. On Nov. 2, 1867, she made her début in London at Her Majesty's as Margherita, and sang also as Violetta, Linda, Martha and Zerlina (' Don Giovanni '), appearing in the last-named part on the night before the theatre was burnt down, Dec. 6. In 1868 she sang, with the company of Her Majesty's Theatre, at Drury Lane, and at various important concerts in the same season, and at the Handel Festival. From 1868–72 she was touring in the United States. On May 11, 1872, she reappeared in London at Drury Lane, Her Majesty's Opera, as Linda, and sang during that season also in ' Lucia,' and other parts. On her return to the United States she continued to sing in Italian opera till 1874, when she organised an English troupe, herself superintending the translation of the words, the mise en scène, the training of the singers, and the rehearsals of the chorus. Such was her devotion to the project, that in the winter of 1874–1875 she sang no fewer than 125 nights. She reappeared at the rebuilt Her Majesty's Theatre in 1879 as Aïda, and Philine in ' Mignon.' In 1881 she returned to America, singing principally in concerts. She married her manager, Carl Strakosch, in 1887, and soon afterwards retired. Her musical gifts were great. She is said to have been familiar with forty operas. She had great conscientiousness as an artist, ardent enthusiasm, and a voice of great compass and purity.

G. and A. C.

BIBL.—Memoirs of an American Prima Donna, New York, 1913.

KELLY, FREDERICK SEPTIMUS (b. Sydney, May 29, 1881 ; d. Beaucourt on the Ancre, France, Nov. 13, 1916), pianist and composer, was educated at Eton and Balliol College, Oxford (where he gained a musical scholarship, 1899), and later studied the piano under Knorr at Frankfort.

Kelly's musical influence among his contemporaries at Oxford was strong. He took his turn as president of the University Musical Club, and was active in promoting the Sunday evening concerts at Balliol. In connection with both, his fine taste and his admirable qualities as a pianist, particularly in concerted chamber music, made their mark. That he was also known as a first rate oarsman [1] naturally served to popularise the interests of his art among undergraduates. After his period of study abroad he was in London and acted as adviser to the CLASSICAL CONCERT SOCIETY (q.v.). His influence was exerted to direct that society's interests towards modern music and to combine it with the existing repertory of classical works, and he was largely responsible for the important place held by the society through several years. In 1911 he revisited Australia and gave some concerts at Sydney. He returned to London and gave an interesting series of chamber concerts in 1912. In 1914, on the outbreak of war, he joined the Royal Naval Division ; after distinguished service in Gallipoli he attained the rank of Lieutenant-Commander and was killed in action in France, Nov. 13, 1916. As a composer Kelly was chiefly known through some piano pieces which he had produced at his recitals, but a memorial concert of his compositions (Wigmore Hall, May 2, 1919) included an Elegy for small orchestra, written in Gallipoli (1915), in memory of his friend, Rupert Brooke, who had died there a few days before, a Serenade for flute solo and small orchestra (5 movements) and a number of songs. Other works are a sonata in G for violin and PF. played by Jelly D'Aranyi and Leonard Borwick at a concert of the Classical Concert Society ; ' Monographs ' and ' Allegro de Concert ' for PF. ; Theme, Variations and Fugue for two pianofortes.

C.

KELLY, MICHAEL (b. Dublin, Christmastide, 1762 ; d. Margate, Oct. 9, 1826), the son of Thomas Kelly, wine merchant and dancing-master, of Mary Street, Dublin, was a tenor singer, composer and author of much quoted Reminiscences.

When a lad in Dublin he took part in the ' Fantoccini' organised by Kane O'Hara at the theatre in Capel Street, and he was taught the piano by Morland (1770–72) and by Michael Arne (1777–1778)—his singing-masters being Passerini, Peretti and St. Giorgio. He finished his piano lessons with Dr. Cogan, and had a short course of instruction from Rauzzini. On May 1, 1779, he left Dublin for Naples. Before quitting Dublin, however, a fortuitous circumstance led to his appearance on the stage as the Count in Piccinni's ' Buona Figliuola,' and that again to his performing the hero in Michael Arne's ' Cymon,' and Lionel in ' Lionel and Clarissa.'

---

[1] He rowed in the Eton eight (1899), then in the Oxford eight and won the ' Diamond Sculls ' three times at Henley.

At Naples he placed himself under the tuition of Finaroli, head of the Conservatorio of La Madonna di Loreto. He subsequently studied under Aprile, with whom he visited Palermo, and then went successively to Leghorn, Florence, Bologna, Brescia, Verona, Gratz in Styria, and Venice, ultimately reaching Vienna, where he was engaged at the Court theatre. There he remained four years, enjoying the intimate friendship of Mozart, who on the production of his ' Nozze di Figaro ' (May 1, 1786) allotted to Kelly (whose name he spells ' Occhely ' in his MS. catalogue) the parts of Basilio and Don Curzio. Being anxious to visit England, Kelly obtained leave of absence from the Emperor, and in Feb. 1787 quitted Vienna in company with Stephen Storace, his mother and sister—Signora Storace—and Attwood. He appeared at Drury Lane on Apr. 20, as Lionel, in ' Lionel and Clarissa,' and continued there as first tenor until he quitted the stage. He also sang at the Concerts of Antient Music, the Handel performances in Westminster Abbey, and in the provinces.

In 1789 he made his first appearance as a composer by the production of the music to two pieces called ' False Appearances ' and ' Fashionable Friends,' and from that date till 1820 furnished the music for sixty-two dramatic pieces,[1] besides writing a considerable number of English, Italian and French single songs, etc. In 1793 he was engaged at the King's Theatre, of which he was for many years acting manager. On Jan. 1, 1802, he opened a music-shop in Pall Mall adjoining the Opera House, but this promising speculation failed owing to his inattention, and in 1811 he was made a bankrupt. He also engaged in the wine trade, and this circumstance, combined with the suspicion that some of Kelly's compositions were derived from foreign sources, led Sheridan to propose that he should inscribe over his shop, ' Michael Kelly, Composer of Wines and Importer of Music.' On Oct. 1, 1811, in Dublin, Kelly made his last appearance on the stage at his own benefit, when he sang ' The Bard of Erin,' composed by himself.

In 1826 he published his *Reminiscences* in 2 vols. 8vo. This entertaining work, which reached a second edition in the same year, was written by Theodore Hook from materials furnished by Kelly. Its personal notices of Mozart are both interesting and important, and have been done justice to by Otto Jahn (*Mozart*, ii. 242, etc.). Kelly died at Margate, and was buried in the churchyard of St. Paul's, Covent Garden. The following is a list of the pieces for which he composed the music :

' False Appearances ' and ' Fashionable Friends,' 1789 ; ' A Friend in Need,' ' The Last of the Family,' ' The Chimney Corner,' and ' The Castle Spectre,' 1797 ; ' Blue Beard,' ' The Outlaws,' ' The Captive of Spielberg ' (with Dussek), and ' Aurelio and Miranda,' 1798 ; ' Feudal Times ' and ' Pizarro,' 1799 ; ' Of age to-morrow,'

[1] For an account of the transactions by which ' Blue Beard ' was produced (Drury Lane, Jan. 16, 1798), see Kelly's *Reminiscences*, vol. ii. p. 144.

' De Montfort,' and ' The Indians,' 1800 ; ' Deaf and Dumb,' ' Adelmorn the Outlaw,' and ' The Gipsey Prince,' 1801 ; ' Urania,' ' Algonah,' and ' A House to be sold,' 1802 ; ' The Hero of the North,' ' The Marriage Promise,' and ' Love laughs at Locksmiths,' 1803 ; ' Cinderella,' ' The Counterfeit,' ' The Hunter of the Alps,' ' The Gay Deceivers,' ' The Bad Bargain,' and ' The Land we live in,' 1804 ; ' The Honey Moon,' ' A Prior Claim,' and ' Youth, Love and Folly,' 1805 ; ' We fly by night,' ' The Forty Thieves,' and ' Adrian and Orilla,' 1806 ; ' The Young Hussar,' ' Town and Country,' ' The Wood Demon ' (with M. P. King), ' The House of Morville,' ' Adelgitha,' and ' Time's a tell-tale,' 1807 ; ' The Jew of Mogadore,' ' The Africans,' and ' Venoni,' 1808 ; ' The Foundling of the Forest ' and ' The Jubilee, 1809 ; ' Gustavus Vasa ' and a Ballet, 1810 ; ' The Peasant Boy,' ' The Royal Oak,' and ' One o'clock,' 1811 ; ' The Absent Apothecary,' ' The Russians,' ' Polly,' ' The Illusion,' and ' Harlequin Harper, 1813 ; ' Remorse,' 1814 ; ' The Unknown Guest,' 1815 ; ' The Fall of Taranto,' 1817 ; ' The Bride of Abydos,' 1818 ; ' Abudah,' 1819 ; and ' The Lady and the Devil,' 1820.

Of his many songs, ' The Woodpecker ' is the only one that has survived until the present time.   w. h. h. ; addns. w. h. g. f. and *D.N.B.*

KELLY, Thomas Alexander Erskine, sixth Earl of (*b.* Sept. 1, 1732 ; *d.* Brussels, Oct. 9, 1781), an amateur composer of some degree of celebrity, and a violinist. He succeeded to the title in 1756, and died a bachelor. He studied music in Germany under Stamitz, and about the middle of the 18th century became famous for the composition of minuets, overtures and symphonies. His overture to ' The Maid of the Mill,' 1765, was long a popular piece. Robert Bremner of London and Edinburgh published his earlier compositions, and his copyright grant for them for nineteen years is dated 1761. Afterwards Lord Kelly's compositions were issued by William Napier. In 1836 Charles Kirkpatrick Sharpe edited a small quarto publication of his minuets and other pieces, with a biographical notice and list of compositions. It is likely that Lord Kelly formed one of that group of musicians among whom were James Oswald, Charles Burney and Captain (afterwards General) Reid, who formed the ' Society of the Temple of Apollo.' The compositions of this Society were for a time published anonymously by James Oswald of St. Martin's Lane.

f. k.

KELWAY, (1) Joseph (*d.* probably May 1782), a pupil of Geminiani, was organist of St. Michael's, Cornhill, about 1730, but resigned the post in 1736, on being appointed organist of St. Martin's-in-the-Fields *vice* Weldon deceased. Upon the arrival of Queen Charlotte in England in 1761, Kelway was appointed her instructor on the harpsichord. As a harpsichord-player he was remarkable for neatness of touch and rapidity of execution, and for his ability in performing Scarlatti's pieces. As an organist he excelled in extemporaneous performance, of which he was such a master as to attract the most eminent musicians in London (amongst them Handel) to the church in order to hear him. Burney (iv. 665) characterises his playing as full of a ' masterly wildness . . . bold, rapid, and fanciful.'[2] A fine portrait of Kelway seated at the harpsichord, probably by Battone, exists. Also a pastel from it.[3]

His elder brother, (2) Thomas (*d.* Chichester,

[2] See also Mrs. Delany's *Letters*, i. 579, ii. 61, and other books referred to in the *D.N.B.*
[3] The portrait belonged (1915) to Miss Musgrave, 63 Cadogan Gardens, London ; the pastel to Miss Leat of Yelverton, Devon.

May 21, 1749), was educated as a chorister in Chichester Cathedral, and became organist there in 1726. Seven services and nine anthems by him are contained in a MS. volume in the library of Chichester Cathedral. His Evening Service in B minor is printed in Rimbault's *Cathedral Music*, and two others in A minor and G minor are published by Novello. His epitaph may be read in West's *Cath. Org.*   w. h. h.

KELZ, Matthias, of Schongau, Upper Bavaria, was at Augsburg from 1658–69. He is the composer of ' Primitiae musicales ' and 'Epidigma harmoniae novae,' 2 books of sonatas and dance movements for one or two violins and viola da gamba.

KEMANTCHE (Arab. *Kemangeh*), a Persian bowed instrument with three strings, dating from unknown antiquity. The body is globular with flattened open ends, and made preferably of ' tut ' (mulberry) wood. One end is covered with skin upon which rests the bridge ; the tailpin is of metal, and lengthened for resting on the ground during performance. There are three strings, two of silk and one of metal, and the long bow is strung with black horse-hair (*PLATE LII.* No. 3). Amongst the Arabs the instrument takes a simpler and less ornamental form, the body being made out of a cocoa-nut or a hollow gourd, and there are generally but two strings of twisted horse-hair. The word means ' a little bow,' and the Arabic epithet *à gouz* (' ancient ') is usually added. It is undoubtedly one of the earliest of all bowed instruments, claiming identity with or descent from the somewhat mythical Ravan-astrom of India, from which the Urheen (Erh-hsien) of the Chinese is also supposed to have sprung. (See Violin Family.)   F. W. G.

KEMBLE, Adelaide (*b. circa* 1814 ; *d.* Aug. 4, 1879), younger daughter of Charles Kemble, the eminent actor, was educated for a concert singer. She appeared first in London at a concert of Ancient Music on May 13, 1835, and afterwards at the York Festival, but with little success. She then went to Paris for improvement, and from thence in 1837 to Germany, and early in 1839 to Italy, when she had lessons from Pasta on the Lake of Como. In that year she made her appearance at La Fenice, Venice, as Norma with decided success. In 1840 she sang at Trieste, Milan, Padua, Bologna and Mantua with increasing reputation. In 1841 she returned to England, and on Nov. 2 appeared in an English version of ' Norma ' with marked success. In 1842 she sang in English versions of ' Le Nozze di Figaro,' ' La Sonnambula,' ' Semiramide,' and ' Il Matrimonio Segreto.' In 1843 she was married to Edward John Sartoris, and retired from the profession. In 1867 she published her delightful *A Week in a French Country House*.

Bibl.—See her sister Fanny Kemble's *Records of a Girlhood*, and other reminiscences. Mrs. Sartoris's own recollections were embodied in *Past Hours*, 1880.

w. h. h. ; addns. from *D.N.B.*

KEMP, Joseph, Mus.D. (*b.* Exeter, 1778 ; *d.* London, May 22, 1824), was placed as a chorister in the cathedral under William Jackson, with whom he continued as a pupil after quitting the choir. In 1802 he removed to Bristol on being appointed organist of the cathedral. In 1807 he resigned his appointment and settled in London. In 1808 he took the degree of Mus.B. at Cambridge, his exercise being a War Anthem, ' A Sound of Battle is in the Land ' (composed 1803). In 1809 he was, by special dispensation, permitted to proceed Doctor of Music ; his exercise being an anthem entitled ' The Crucifixion.' On Oct. 25, 1809, ' The Jubilee,' an occasional piece by him, was produced at the Haymarket Theatre. In 1810 a melodrama called ' The Siege of Isca (Exeter); or, The Battles in the West,' written by Kemp, with music by himself and Domenico Corri, was produced at the theatre in Tottenham Street. In the same year he lectured on his *New System of Musical Education*, probably the first method propounded in England for teaching music to numbers simultaneously. In 1814 he returned to Exeter, resided there till 1818, then went to France, remained until 1821, and again returned to Exeter. Dr. Kemp published :

An anthem, ' I am Alpha and Omega.'
' Twelve Psalmodical Melodies,' 1818.
' Twelve Songs,' 1799.
' Twenty Double Chants.'
A set of pianoforte sonatas, published at Exeter.
' Musical Illustrations of the Beauties of Shakespeare.'
' Musical Illustrations of The Lady of the Lake.'
The Vocal Magazine.
The New System of Musical Education, Part I.
Numerous single glees, songs, duets and trios.   w. h. h.

KEMPIS, Nicolas à (*b.* Florence, mid-17th cent.), organist of St. Gudule, Brussels. He composed a book of 8-part masses and motets ; also Symphoniae 1, 2, 3 violinorum (Antwerp, 1644) ; Symphoniae 1, 2, 3, 4 et 5 instrum. . . . op. 2 (Antwerp, 1647). His violin sonatas of 1644 show considerable progress in the cantabile style. (See his sonata in A in Riemann's ' Alte Kammermusik,' Schott.)   E. v. d. s.

KENN, P., a famous German horn-player who went to Paris in 1782. He became 2nd horn at the Opéra in 1783 ; joined the Guarde Nationale in 1791 ; was teacher at the Conservatoire from 1795–1802, and retired from opera with a pension in 1808. He composed horn duets, trios, etc. Fétis declared him one of the finest of all low horn players.
          E. v. d. s.

KENNEDY, see Violin Family, subsection English Makers.

KENNEDY, (1) David (*b.* Perth, Apr. 15, 1825 ; *d.* Stratford, Ontario, Oct. 12, 1886), Scottish singer.

He received his first lessons in music from his father, an enthusiastic musician, and at the age of 18 assisted him as precentor of the North United Secession Church, Perth. At the age of 20 he succeeded his uncle as precentor of South Street Church in the same city. At an early age he was apprenticed to a house painter in

Perth. During this time, while working at a house ten or twelve miles distant, he resolved to hear Templeton, who was singing at the Perth Theatre. He started after leaving off work, running all the way, and clearing the distance in two hours. Having no money to pay for admission, he stood throughout the whole performance, in the pelting rain, with ear to keyhole, and then took to the road again to be ready for work at six in the morning. He afterwards worked as a journeyman in Edinburgh and London, but returned to Perth to start business on his own account. He had, however, the never-ceasing desire to become a public singer, and made frequent visits to Edinburgh to receive singing-lessons from Edmund Edmunds. Having secured an appointment as precentor in Nicolson Street United Presbyterian Church, Edinburgh, he struggled hard to support himself and family by occasional concert giving, teaching, etc., in Edinburgh and neighbourhood.

In January 1859 he received his first important engagement, for the Burns centenary at St. George's Hall, Liverpool. In the autumn he gave twelve concerts in Buccleuch Street Hall, Edinburgh. Every programme being different, he tested about 150 songs. Professor Aytoun and Robert and William Chambers were in the habit of attending; they became his personal friends, and gave him many friendly hints and great encouragement at the outset of his career. In 1860 he made short tours in Scotland, and 1861 went as far as the Orkneys. In the summer of 1862 he made his first appearance in London, at the Hanover Square Rooms. Four concerts were given, and the programmes contained selections from 'The Gentle Shepherd,' 'Noctes Ambrosianae,' etc., etc. The veteran John Templeton was present upon each occasion, and was one of the first to offer his warm congratulations. In December of the same year Kennedy gave a long series of concerts in the Egyptian Hall. After tours in the south of England and in Scotland he returned to London in 1864 to give a series of concerts in Store Street Hall, with fresh programmes, which included selections from 'Waverley,' and an entertainment called 'The Farmer's Ingle.' His eldest daughter, Helen, scarcely in her teens, had now become his accompanist. At one time or another his eleven sons and daughters all assisted in the entertainments. In the summer of 1866 he visited Canada and the United States, and sang in every city of importance North and South. For the next twenty years he toured at home and abroad, travelling through Australia, New Zealand, South Africa and India, and revisiting Canada several times. One of his first acts when at Quebec in 1867 was to visit the grave of John Wilson, the Scottish singer, who died there in 1849. He had photographs taken of the tombstone, and arranged

that the grave should be tended and cared for in perpetuity. Kennedy's last appearance in public was at a 'Burns Night,' in Sarnia, Oct. 4, 1886. The last concert given by the 'Kennedy Family' was at Stratford, Ontario, on the following evening. Kennedy being too ill to appear, his daughters carried out the programme, the Mayor of Stratford taking the chair. Kennedy probably hastened his end by resolving to revisit the grave of Wilson with the shadow of death almost upon him. He went out of his way to do so, and died in a few days. The body was embalmed and brought to his native land by his widow; a public funeral took place from his own house in Edinburgh to the Grange Cemetery. An interesting sketch, *David Kennedy, the Scottish Singer*, by his daughter MARJORY (Mrs. Kennedy Fraser; see below), was published in 1887. It contains also a condensation of three books, previously published, entitled *Kennedy's Colonial Tour*, *Kennedy in India*, and *Kennedy at the Cape*. One son and two daughters perished at the burning of the Théâtre des Italiens at Nice on Mar. 23, 1881. His eldest son was DAVID (b. Perth, 1849; d. Pietermaritzburg, Dec. 5, 1885). His youngest daughter, JESSIE, married Tobias MATTHAY (q.v.). Only a few years before his death Kennedy was at Milan receiving valuable hints from Lamperti; a true lover of his art, he ever felt the necessity for constant application and study. Among the Scottish singers who gave similar entertainments to those of Wilson and Kennedy, the Fraser family deserves mention. Its head was JOHN FRASER (b. Renfrewshire, c. 1794; d. Mar. 1879). He and his daughters attained considerable merit in their line.   w. h.; addns. f. k.

(2) MARJORY (Mrs. Kennedy Fraser) (b. Perth, Oct. 1, 1857), is the most distinguished of David Kennedy's children on account of her important work as collector and editor of Hebridean Folk-song. She, like the other members of the family, shared the travels and the musical activities of the father, whom she accompanied on the piano at the age of 12. He began her training as a singer, which was completed under Mathilde Marchesi in Milan and Paris. Her marriage to A. J. Fraser, a mathematician and schoolmaster of Glasgow, took place after her father's death, and, her husband dying not long after, she pursued her artistic career through many lecture-recitals on various aspects of song. Ducoudray's collection of Breton songs stimulated her interest in folk-song, and in 1905 she first visited the islands of the Outer Hebrides. Her own collections of Hebridean song, her extensive studies therein, and the numerous lecture-recitals by which she has brought these songs before the general public, have accomplished for the folk art of the Hebrides a popularity comparable to that achieved by Cecil Sharp for the folk-songs of

Somerset. Mrs. Kennedy Fraser visited New York in 1913, and has lectured in the United States. She made an appearance on the stage in the first production (1924) of Bantock's opera, 'The Seal Woman,' of which she was the librettist, and the music of which is largely founded on melodies of her collection. The following are her principal publications :

'Songs of the Hebrides,' 3 vols. (English and Gaelic text), 1909, 1917, 1921
'Hebridean Suite,' vcl. and PF.
'Scots Folk Tunes.'
Unison Songs for Schools.
Three handbooks, viz. :
   Laws of Interpretation and Hebridean Song.
   Lowland Scots Song.
   Pronunciation of Lowland Scots.

Her daughter, (3) PATUFFA KENNEDY-FRASER (*b.* Edinburgh, June 10, 1888), is well known for her singing to the harp of ' Songs of the Hebrides.' She has toured in America. She married J. C. F. Hood.   C.

KENNIS, GUILLAUME-GOMMAIRE (*b.* Lierre, Feb. 9, 1719 ; *d.* Louvain, May 10, 1789), maître de chapelle at Lierre Church, 1742–50 ; at St. Pierre, Louvain, 1750–89. He was an excellent violinist, and was presented with a Jac. Stainer violin by the Empress Maria-Theresa. (See Burney's *Diary*, p. 62.) He composed 6 sinfinie a quatro, trio sonatas, duets, and violin sonatas with basso continuo (*Q.-L.*).

KENT, JAMES (*b.* Winchester, Mar. 13, 1700; *d.* there, May[1] 6, 1776), son of a glazier, became a chorister of the cathedral there under Vaughan Richardson, from 1711–14, but was shortly afterwards removed to London and entered as a chorister of the Chapel Royal under Dr. Croft. There he attracted the attention of the sub-dean, Rev. John Dolben, through whose influence he obtained, in 1717, the post of organist of the parish Church of Finedon, Northamptonshire, the seat of the Dolbens. He resigned his office at Finedon in 1731, on obtaining the organistship of Trinity College, Cambridge, which he held till 1737, when on Jan. 13 he succeeded John Bishop as organist of the cathedral and college of Winchester. He married Elizabeth, daughter of John Freeman, a singer at the theatre in the time of Purcell, afterwards a member of the choirs of the Chapel Royal, St. Paul's, and Westminster, and who died Dec. 10, 1736. It was not until the decline of life that Kent could be induced to publish ; he then printed a volume containing twelve anthems. In 1774 he resigned his appointments in favour of Peter Fussell. After his death a volume containing a Morning and Evening Service and eight anthems by him was published under the editorship of Joseph Corfe. Kent assisted Dr. Boyce in the compilation of his ' Cathedral Music.' His anthems have been extravagantly extolled by some, and decried by others ; in both cases unjustly. They are smooth and even productions, generally pleas-

[1] Or in October, according to his monument in the cathedral.

ing, but rarely rising above mediocrity. His ' Hear my Prayer ' was at one time a great favourite, but it is a poor composition. He borrowed freely from Italian composers, without acknowledgment, as is shown by a volume full of his notes formerly in the possession of Sir F. A. G. Ouseley. (See BASSANI.)

    W. H. H. ; addns. West's *Cath. Org.*, etc.

KENT - BUGLE ; ROYAL KENT BUGLE ; REGENT'S BUGLE, see BUGLE.

KEOLANTHE, or THE UNEARTHLY BRIDE, opera in 2 acts ; words by Fitzball, music by Balfe. Produced Lyceum Theatre, Mar. 9, 1841.   G.

KEPER, JOHN, of Hart Hall, Oxford, who graduated as M.A. Feb. 11, 1569, produced in 1574 ' Select Psalms in four parts.'   W. H. H.

KERAULOPHON (from κεραύλης, a horn-blower, and φωνή, a voice). An 8-foot organ manual stop, of a reedy and pleasant quality of tone. It was invented by Messrs. Gray & Davison, and used by them for the first time in 1843 in the organ they made for St. Paul's Church, Wilton Place. An example was introduced by the French firm of Ducroquet into their organ at St. Eustache, Paris, erected in 1854.   E. J. H.

KERLE, JACOB VAN (*b.* Ypres, *c.* 1531 ; *d.* Prague, Jan. 7, 1591 [2]), a Flemish master who appears to have spent the earlier part of his musical career in Italy, whence the dedications of his earlier works from 1558 are dated. From 1562–75 he was in the service of the Cardinal-Archbishop of Augsburg—Otto von Truchsess—partly in Rome and partly in Augsburg. He is said to have accompanied the cardinal to the later sessions of the Council of Trent, 1562–63, and at any rate was commissioned by him to compose the music for a set of special prayers on behalf of the Council (see title below). He afterwards obtained a canonry at Cambrai, which he continued to hold while also in the service of the Emperor Rudolf at Vienna and Prague (1583 and 1585). His works are :

1. Hymni totius anni, etc., *a* 4. Rome, 1558, 23 n.
2. Magnificat octo tonum, *a* 4. Venice, 1561.
3. Sex missae, *a* 4 and 5. Venice, 1562. Dedicated to Duke Albert of Bavaria. It is in the title of this work Kerle is described as composer to the Cardinal of Augsburg.
4. Preces speciales pro salubri generalis concilii successu et conclusione, ponulique Christiani salute ac unione, etc., 10 Responsoria. *a* 4. Venice, 1562.
5. Cantiones sacrae, *a* 5 and 6. Nürnberg, 1571. 14 Motets and Te Deums.
6. Liber modulorum sacrorum, 5 et 6 voc., quibus addita est recens cantio, 8 voc., de sacro foedere contra Turcas (this last composition being a thanksgiving for the victory at Lepanto over the Turks). Munich, 1572.
7. Two other Books of Motets, *a* 4-6. 33 n. Munich, 1573.
8. Cantiones sacrae, *a* 5 and 6. Munich, 1575, 9 n.
9. 4 Missae, *a* 4, with Te Deum, *a* 5. Plantin, Antwerp, 1583 (this work a reprint).
10. Aliquot moduli, *a* 4-8, etc. Prag, 1585. Te Deum, Magnificat, Asperges and motets.

Ambros speaks very highly of Kerle's masses and motets. While still belonging to the older school of composition, they have a character of their own of grandeur and power. Proske's ' Musica Divina ' contains a vigorous motet by

[2] *Riemann.*

Kerle, 'Exurge quare obdormis Domine.'
Maldeghem in his 'Trésor' has reprinted three
masses, a Te Deum and a few motets.

BIBL.—OTTO URSPRUNG, *Jacobus de Kerle*, 1531/32—1591.
Sein Leben und seine Werke, pp. 113 (Munich, 1913). See note in
Z.M.W., Feb. 1920, p. 310.   J. R. M.

KERLL (KERL, CHERLL), JOHANN CASPAR [1]
(*b.* Adorf, Saxony, Apr. 9, 1627 [2]; *d.* there,
Feb. 13, 1693 [3]), celebrated organist.

Mattheson's *Ehrenpforte* contains details of
his life. He came early to Vienna, and learnt
the organ from Valentini, then organist, afterwards Kapellmeister to the court, on whose
recommendation Ferdinand III. sent him to
Rome to study under Carissimi. In all probability he also learnt from Frescobaldi, possibly
at the same time as his countryman Froberger.
Having returned to Germany he entered the
service of the Bavarian Elector on Feb. 22,
1656, and in that capacity was present at the
coronation of Leopold I. at Frankfort (July 22,
1658), where he is said to have been presented
by Schmelzer, vice-court-Kapellmeister, to the
Emperor, and invited to improvise on a given
theme in presence of the court. Some doubt is
thrown on this by the fact that Schmelzer did
not become vice-Kapellmeister till Jan. 1, 1671;
but he may well have been in attendance on the
Emperor at Frankfort, and at any rate Kerll's
reputation as an organist dates from the coronation. Kerll remained at Munich until 1674.
For the Italian singers there he composed a
'Missa nigra,' entirely written in black notes,
and a duet for two castrati, 'O bone Jesu,' the
only accompaniment of which is a ground bass
passing through all the keys. Besides other
church works, sonatas for two violins and a viola
da gamba, and a 'Modulatio organica super
Magnificat' (Munich, 1686), Mattheson mentions toccatas, canzonas, ricercars and batailles
of his composition for the organ. In 1674 he
threw up his post and went to Vienna, where
he gave lessons at what was then a high scale
of remuneration. He was appointed court
organist there in 1677, and seems to have retained the post until 1692, when it is supposed
that he returned to Munich.

His style is remarkable for the frequent
introduction of discord resolved in a new and
unexpected manner, in which respect he is deservedly considered a predecessor of Sebastian
Bach. He wrote the music of the operas
'Oronte,' 1657; 'Erinto,' 1661; of the serenata in honour of the birthday of the wife of
the Elector (Nov. 6, 1661), 'Le pretensioni del
Sole': and of 'I colori geniali' (1668). One
of his canzonas has been preserved to the world
in a singular but most efficient way—owing to
its insertion by Handel in 'Israel in Egypt'
to the words 'Egypt was glad when they de-

[1] Not von Kerl, as many dictionaries say.
[2] *Riemann.*
[3] His tomb, showing this date, was formerly in the Augustine
Church, but that is now the Custom-house, and the tomb is no
longer discoverable. The epitaph is given in *Q.-L.*

parted.' Hawkins gives the canzona in its
original form in his *History*, chap. 124. His
masses and motets are catalogued in *Q.-L.*, as
well as his other compositions in MS. A selection of his instrumental works is published in
D.D.T. (second series), ii. 2.

                                 F. G., with addns.

KES, WILLEM (*b.* Dordrecht, Holland, Feb.
16, 1856), violinist and conductor, studied with
many professors, at first under Tyssens, Noth-
durft and Ferdinand Böhm, and then, provided
with a stipend by the King of Holland, with
Ferdinand David at the Leipzig Conservatorium
(1871), with Wieniawski at the Brussels Conservatoire, and finally (1876) with Joachim at
Berlin. But his career has been rather that of
conductor than violinist. For several years he
divided his time between his native town and
Amsterdam, accepting in the latter city the
post of conductor of the Park Orchestra, and
Felix Meritis Society (1876), the Parkschouw-
burg Concerts (1883), and the Concertgebouw
Concerts (1890), directing also the Society Concerts at Dordrecht. In 1895 he undertook the
conductorship of the Scottish Orchestra in Glasgow, and in 1898 was appointed conductor of
the Moscow Philharmonic Society and director
of the Moscow Conservatoire. He returned to
Leipzig in 1904 for a few months; then removed to Dresden, and afterwards to Coblenz,
with musical activities in both towns. He has
written a symphony, a 'Ballade' for chorus, solo
voice and orchestra, besides smaller works.

                                            W. W. C.

KETTEN, HENRI (*b.* Baja, Hungary, Mar.
25, 1848; *d.* Paris, Apr. 1, 1883), attained a
rapid success as a pianist, being trained in Paris
by Marmontel and Halévy. His compositions
enjoyed a great vogue in their day, but are of
essentially trivial quality.   M.

KETTERER, EUGÈNE (*b.* Rouen, 1831;
d. Dec. 18, 1870), entered the Paris Conservatoire, obtaining a second prize for solfège in
1847, and a *premier accessit* in 1852, under Marmontel From that time until his death, which
took place during the siege of Paris, he appeared
constantly as a pianist, and wrote multitudes
of brilliant fantasias and drawing-room pieces,
which obtained ephemeral popularity.   M.

KETTLE-DRUM, see DRUM (1).

KEUCHENTHAL, JOHANNES, described as
'Pfarrherr auf dem St. Andreasberge,' published at Wittenberg in 1573 a comprehensive collection of liturgical music for the
use of the Lutheran Church (*Kirchengesang
lateinisch und deutsch*). It contains plain-song
melodies of the Introits, Sequences, Antiphons,
Responsoria, parts of the Mass and other offices
of the Church for all Sundays and Holydays,
besides some Deutsche Lieder, and a German
Passion-Music with the 'Turbae' set in falso-
bordone style for four voices. Otto Kade (*Die
ältere Passionscompositionen*, 1893) has proved

this Passion to be based on an older arrangement by Johann Walther. Tucher (*Schatz des evangelischen Kirchengesangs*, ii. p. 322) mentions that this Keuchenthal Passion continued to be used at Nuremberg down to 1806.

J. R. M.

KEY, an English word applied to music mainly in two senses, viz. (1) in relation to scales and (2a and 2b) as part of the mechanism of instruments, as follows :

(1) Equivalent to Fr. *tonalité* ; Ger. *Tonart* ; Ital. *tonalità*. In this sense the term is applicable to all European music written in accordance with either of the two modes, called major or minor, which were evolved by the process of harmony from the older melodic modes (see MODES, ECCLESIASTICAL). It is not coterminous with SCALE (*q.v.*), because the scale is merely the chart or outline of the key, and notes not contained in the scale are usable in the key (see ACCIDENTALS). Every note is possible as the key-note of two keys, based on the major and minor scales beginning from that note. The key is shown in notation by a group of sharps or flats placed after the clef on the stave and called the Key SIGNATURE (*q.v.*). For the historical development of key and its importance as a factor in composition, see the articles HARMONY and TONALITY.   C.

(2a) Equivalent to Fr *touche* ; Ger. *Taste* ; Ital. *tasto*. A key of a pianoforte or similar instrument is a lever, balanced see-saw fashion near its centre, upon a metal pin. It is usually of lime-tree, because that wood is little liable to warp. Besides the metal pin upon the balance rail of the key-frame, modern instruments have another metal pin for each key upon the front rail, to prevent too much lateral motion.[1] A key is long or short according to its employment. Those representing the notes of the natural scale are long, those of the intervening semitones (five to the octave) are short. Each long key is covered as far as it is visible with ivory or equivalent substance : and each short or raised key bears a block of ebony or other hard black wood. In old instruments the practice in this respect varied. (See KEY-BOARD.)   A. J. H.

(2b) Equivalent to Fr. *clef* ; Ger. *Klappe* ; Ital. *chiave*, the name given to the levers on wind instruments which serve the purpose of opening and closing certain sound-holes.

They are divided into open and closed keys, according to the function which they perform. In the former case they stand normally above their respective holes, and are closed by the pressure of the finger ; whereas in the latter they close the hole until lifted by muscular action. The closed keys are levers of the first, the open keys usually of the third mechanical

order. They serve the purpose of bringing distant orifices within the reach of the hand, and of covering apertures which are too large for the last phalanx of the finger. They are inferior to the finger in lacking the delicate sense of touch to which musical expression is in a great measure due. In the bassoon, therefore, the sound-holes are bored obliquely in the substance of the wood so as to diminish the divergence of the fingers. Keys are applied to instruments of the flute family, to reeds, such as the oboe and clarinet, and to instruments with cupped mouthpieces, such as the key bugle and the OPHICLEIDE (*q.v.*), the name of which is a compound of the Greek words for Snake and Key. (See articles on these instruments.) In the original SERPENT (*q.v.*) the holes themselves were closed by the pad of the finger, the tube being so curved as to bring them within reach.

The artistic arrangement of keys on all classes of wind instruments is a recent development. Flutes, oboes, bassoons and clarinets, up to the beginning of the 19th century or even later, were almost devoid of them. The bassoon, however, early possessed several in its bass joint for the production of the six lowest notes on its register, which far exceed the reach of the hand. In some earlier specimens, as stated in the article referred to, this mechanism was rudely preceded by plugs, requiring to be drawn out before performance, and not easily replaced with the necessary rapidity. (See BASSOON.)

The older flutes, clarinets and oboes only possess three or four keys at most, cut out of sheet metal, and closely resembling mustard-spoons. The intermediate tones, in this deficiency of keys, were produced by what are termed ' cross-fingerings,' which consist essentially in closing one or two lower holes with the fingers, while leaving one intermediate open. A rude approximation to a semitone was thus attained, but the note is usually of a dull and muffled character. BOEHM (*q.v.*), in the flute named after him, entirely discarded the use of these ' cross-fingered ' notes. (See FLUTE.)

Keys are now fashioned in a far more artistic and convenient form, a distinction in shape being made between those which are open and those normally closed ; so that the player may be assisted in performance by his instinctive sense of touch. (See BASSOON.) Besides the Bassoon, the Corno di Bassetto affords a good example of this contrivance, the scale being carried down through four semitones by interlocking keys, worked by the thumb of the right hand alone.   W. H. S.

KEYBOARD (Fr. *clavier* ; Ger. *Klaviatur* ; Ital. *tastatura*), a frame or, technically, a ' set ' of keys. The influence of the keyboard upon the development of modern music is as conspicuous as it has been important. To this day C major is ' natural ' on the keys, as it is in the

---

[1] The invention (1909) by Frederick Clutsam of the cradle key is an important modification of this mechanism. In ' Clutsam's Cradle Keyboard ' the key rests on a rocker and is so balanced that the metal weights usually employed can be dispensed with.

corresponding notation. Other scales are formed by substituting accidental sharps or flats for naturals, both in notation and on the keyed instruments, a fact which is evidence of the common origin and early growth together of the two. But the notation soon outgrew the keyboard. It has been remarked by Huxley that the ingenuity of human inventions has been paralleled by the tenacity with which original forms have been preserved. Although the number of keys within an octave of the keyboard are quite inadequate to render the written notation of the four-and-twenty major and minor modes, or even of the semitones allied to the one that it was first mainly contrived for, no attempts to augment the number of keys in the octave or to change their familiar disposition have yet succeeded. The permanence of the width of the octave again has been determined by the average span of the hand, and a Ruckers harpsichord of 1614 measures but a small fraction of an inch less in the eight keys than a concert-grand piano of the 20th century. We are without definite information as to the origin of the keyboard. A primitive keyboard is exhibited in the HYDRAULUS (q.v.). There is reason to believe that the little portable organ or regal may at first have had a keyboard derived from the T-shaped keys of the HURDY GURDY. The first keyboard would be diatonic, with fluctuating or simultaneous use of the B♭ and B♮ in the doubtful territory between the A and C of the natural scale. Praetorius, 1619, speaks of organs with such keyboards as being still in existence, i.e. with B♭ and B♮ only, making three semitones in the octave (really four : e—f, a—b♭, b♭—b♮, b♮—c). When the row of sharps was introduced, and whether at once or by degrees, we do not know. They are, doubtless, due to the frequent necessity for transposition, and we find them complete in trustworthy pictorial representations of the 15th century. There is a painting by Memling in the Hospital of St. John at Bruges, whence it has never been removed, dated 1479, wherein the keyboard of a regal is depicted exactly as we have it in the arrangement of the upper keys in twos and threes, though the upper keys are of the same light colour as the lower, and are placed farther back. Another painting of the Flemish school may be seen at Holyrood Palace, Edinburgh, wherein a positive organ has a perfect chromatic keyboard beginning at B♮. This picture has been proved by the late Mr. Laing, F.S.A., to date about 1484. The instrument is 'short octave,' there being two pipes for the deep G and A. The keys are white naturals and black sharps.

EARLY KEYBOARDS DESCRIBED.—The oldest keyed instruments we have seen with undoubtedly original keyboards are a spinet [1] in the museum of the Conservatoire at Paris, bear-

ing the inscription ' Francisci de Portalupis. Veronen. opus, MDXXIII,' the compass is four octaves and a half tone (from E to F) and the natural notes are black with the sharps white ; and a very interesting Roman Clavicembalo, acquired by the Victoria and Albert Museum in 1879. The date is 1521, and it was made by Geronimo of Bologna ; it has boxwood naturals, compass from E to d''', nearly four octaves. There was a spinet in the loan collection of the Bologna Exhibition (1888), made by Pasi of Modena, which was said to be dated 1490. (See also SPINET.) The Flemings, especially the Ruckers, oscillated between black and ivory naturals. The clavichords of Germany and the clavecins of France which we have seen have had black naturals, as, according to Dr. Burney, had those of Spain. Loosemore and the Haywards, in England, in the time of Charles II., used boxwood for naturals ; a clavichord of four and a half octaves existing near Hanover in 1875 had the same—a clue perhaps to its date. Keen and Slade, in the time of Queen Anne, used ebony. Dr. Burney writes that the Hitchcocks also had ivory naturals in their spinets, and two of Thomas Hitchcock's still existing have them. But one of John Hitchcock's, dated 1630, said to have belonged to the Princess Amelia, subsequently owned by Mr. W. Dale, has ebony naturals. All three have a strip of the colour of the naturals inserted in the sharps, and have five octaves compass—from G, to g''', sixty-one keys ! This wide compass for that time—undoubtedly authentic—may be compared with the widest Ruckers to be mentioned farther on.

COMPASS OF SPINETS AND HARPSICHORDS.— Under CLAVICHORD we have collected what information is trustworthy of the earliest compass of the keyboards of that instrument. The Italian spinets of the 16th century were nearly always of four octaves and a semitone, but divided into F and C instruments with the semitone E or B♮ as the lowest note. But this apparent E or B may from analogy with ' short octave ' organs—at that time frequently made —have been tuned C or G, the fourth below the next lowest note.[2] Another question arises whether the F or C thus obtained were not actually of the same absolute pitch (as near as pitch can be practically said to be absolute). We know from Arnold Schlick (Spiegel der Orgelmacher, 1511,[3] that F and C organs were made on one measurement or pitch for the lowest pipe, and this may have been carried on

---

[1] No. 215 of Chouquet's Catalogue (1875).

[2] Yet Praetorius distinctly describes the Halberstadt organ, built 1359, reconstructed 1494, as having the lowest note B♮—the scale proceeding by semitones upwards, and we know the sentiment for the leading note had not then been evolved. Mersenne gives a Psaltery this scale : G, C, D, E (not B, C be it observed). The writer's suggestion has been recently confirmed by the independent research of Professor A. Kraus, Junr., of Florence. He thus describes the lowest octaves of these Spinets. Apparent notes E, F♯, G♯, A, B♭, etc., or B, C♯, D♯, E, etc., real notes C, F, D, G, E, A, B♭, etc. G, C, A, D, etc., the B key frequently divided into F upper half, G for the lower. The primary disposition is, however, that of the semitone from the Greek tetrachord.

[3] Reprinted in M.f.M., Berlin, 1869, p. 103.

1. ENGLISH PIANO (Zumpe and Buntebart, 1770).
2. ITALIAN PIANO (by the inventor, B. Cristofori, 1726).

1. Galpin Collection.　　2. Heyer Museum, formerly Cologne, now Leipzig.

m spinets, which would account for the old tradition of their being tuned ' in the fifth or the octave,' meaning that difference in the pitch which would arise from such a system.

The Antwerp (Ruckers) harpsichords appear to have varied arbitrarily in the compass of their keyboards. We have observed E—c''' forty-five notes, C—c''' forty-nine, B,—d''' fifty-two, C—e''' fifty-three, C—f''' fifty-four, G,—d''' or A,—e''' fifty-six, G,—e''' or G,—f'' (without the lowest G♯) fifty-eight F,—f''' sixty-one, and in two of Hans Ruckers (the eldest) F,—g''' sixty-three notes. In some instances, however, these keyboards have been extended even, as has been proved, by the makers themselves.

COMPASS OF THE PIANOFORTE.—The English seem to have early preferred a wide compass, as with the Hitchcocks, already referred to. Kirkman and Shudi in the next century, however, in their large harpsichords never went higher than f''', although the latter, towards the end of his career, about 1770, increased his scale downwards to C. Here Kirkman did not follow him. Zumpe began making square pianos in London, about 1766, with the G,—f''' compass (omitting the lowest G♯)—nearly five octaves—but soon adopted the five octaves, F,—f''' in which John Broadwood, who reconstructed the square piano, followed him. The advances in compass of Messrs. Broadwood and Sons' pianofortes are as follows. In 1793, to five and a half octaves, F,—c''''. In 1796, six octaves, C,—c'''' : this was the compass of Beethoven's Broadwood Grand, 1817. In 1804, six octaves F,—f''''. In 1811, six and a half octaves, C,—f''''. In 1844 the treble g'''' was attained, and in 1852 the treble a''''. But before this the A,,—a'''' seven octave compass had been introduced by other makers, and soon after became general. The Broadwoods were late in adding these extreme notes : Pleyel's semigrand, used by Chopin in Paris, on his return from Majorca, had C,—g''''. Liszt played on a Erard C,—c'''' in Paris in 1824, and in London in 1825. Even c''''' appears in recent concert grands, and composers have written up to it ; also the deepest G,, which was, by the way, in Broadwoods' Exhibition grands of 1851. (See STAVELESS NOTATION.)

EXPERIMENTAL KEYBOARDS.—Innumerable attempts have been made during the last century to modify the keyboard either in order to approximate it to the system of just intonation or to gain some supposed facility in performance. None has yet (1926) gained any acceptance. The nature of these experiments is indicated by the following examples.

The invention of a ' symmetrical ' keyboard, by which a uniform fingering for all scales, and a more perfect tuning, might be attained, was attempted by R. M. Bosanquet, of St. John's College, Oxford, who had constructed an en-

harmonic harmonium with one. In *An Elementary Treatise on Musical Intervals and Temperament* (Macmillan, 1876), he described this instrument—with passing reference to other new keyboards independently invented by Poole and Colin Brown. In Bosanquet's harmonium the number of keys in an octave available for a system proceeding by perfect fifths was 53. But in the seven tiers of his keyboard he had 84, for the purpose of facilitating the playing of a ' round ' of keys.

In Germany an arrangement was proposed, almost identical with the ' sequential keyboard' invented and practically tried in England by William A. B. Lunn under the name of Arthur Wallbridge in 1843, in which six lower and six upper keys were grouped instead of the historical and customary seven and five in the octave. This gives all the major scales in two fingerings, according as a lower or upper key may be the keynote. The note C becomes a black key. In 1876–77 the partisans of the new German keyboard formed themselves into a society, ' Chroma - Verein des gleichstüfigen Tonsystems,' with the view of settling the still more difficult and vexed question of the reconstruction of musical notation. It published a journal, *Die Tonkunst* (Berlin, Stilke), edited by Albert Hahn, whose pamphlet, *Zur neuen Klaviatur* (Königsberg, 1875), with those of Vincent, *Die Neuklaviatur* (Malchin, 1875), and of Otto Quanz, *Zur Geschichte der neuen chromatischen Klaviatur* (Berlin, 1877), gives particulars of the system evolved. The inventor appears to have been K. B. Schumann (*d.* 1865), a physician at Rhinow in Brandenburg. Preuss of Berlin constructed the keyboard with C on a black key ; width of octave 14 centimetres [1] (5⅝ inches nearly), and with radiating keys by which a tenth became as easy to span as an octave is at present.

A later application of the principle (1887–88) is the invention of Paul von JANKÓ (*q.v.*). In this keyboard each note had three finger-keys, one lower than the other, attached to a key lever. Six parallel rows of whole tone intervals were thus produced. In the first row the octave was arranged c, d, e, f♯, g♯, a♯, c ; in the second row c♯, d♯, f, g, a, b, c♯. The third row repeated the first, the fourth the second, etc. The sharps were distinguished by black bands intended as a concession to those familiar with the old system. The keys were rounded on both sides and the whole keyboard slanted. The advantage claimed was a freer use of the fingers than is possible with the accepted keyboard. Von Jankó's invention was introduced to the English public by J. C. Ames at the Portman Rooms on June 20, 1888.

The fact that the fingering of the right hand upwards is frequently that of the left hand downwards led to the construction of a

[1] The width of six of the present keys.

'Piano à doubles claviers renversés,' shown in the Paris Exhibition of 1878 by Mangeot frères of that city. It was in fact two grand pianos, one placed upon the other, with keyboards reversed as the name indicates, the lower starting as usual with the lowest bass note at the left hand ; the higher having the highest treble note in the same position, so that an ascending scale played upon it proceeded from *right to left* ; the notes running the contrary way to what has always been the normal one. By this cumbersome contrivance an analogous fingering of similar passages in each hand was secured, while other advantages were claimed.　　　　　　　　　　　　　A. J. H.

KEY-BUGLE, an improvement of the original Bugle (*q.v.*). (See *PLATE LXXIV.* No. 9).

KEYED GUITAR. Towards the end of the 18th century a mechanical device was frequently attached to the English guitar or cither consisting of little buttons placed at the side of the instrument which, by a lever action, plucked the strings with small points or plectra, as in the spinet, or else struck the strings with small hammers, as in the pianoforte. For this latter purpose a detachable box furnished with 6 keys and 6 hammers (one for each set of strings) was affixed to the guitar just over the bridge, but notwithstanding the subsequent addition of so-called Trumpet, Harp, Hautboy and Cremona stops the keyed guitar failed to hold its own against the Spanish instrument (*PLATE XXXI.* No. 3 ; see Guitar).
　　　　　　　　　　　　　　　　　F. W. G.

KEYED HORN, see Bass Horn.

KEYNOTE, the note by which the key is named, and from which the scale starts, corresponding to the Final of the Ecclesiastical Modes : the Tonic. (See Key ; Tonic.)

KEYRLEBER, Johann Georg (*b.* Württemberg, 2nd half of 17th cent.), *Magister philosophiae et artium liberalium*, possessed a great facility for writing canons in any known species. For the birthday of the Emperor Joseph I., in 1691, he wrote an 'Aggratulatio musica-poetica' in a 'canon perpetuo' of 16 trebles and 16 violins of different melody, which could be increased to 256 vocal and 256 instrumental parts, *i.e.* 512 distinct parts. He also wrote circle and other trick canons in many parts (*Mendel*).

KHOVANTCHINA, opera in 5 acts ; text and music by Moussorgsky. Completed (finale to last act) and orchestrated by Rimsky-Korsakov. Produced St. Petersburg, 1885 ; Drury Lane, July 1, 1913 ; in English (Beecham), Covent Garden, Nov. 25, 1919.

KHUEN (Kuen), Johann (*b.* Mosbach (or Mosach), Bavaria ; *d.* Nov. 1675), beneficiary of St. Peter's, Munich ; a prolific composer of sacred songs, some of which have appeared in modern editions (*Q.-L.*).

KIALLMARK, (1) George (*b.* King's Lynn,

Feb. 1781 ; *d.* Islington, Mar. 1835), studied the violin under Barthélemon and Spagnoletti, and became leader in various orchestras. He wrote many songs which were popular in their day, and a great number of fantasias for the pianoforte. His son, (2) George Frederick (*b.* Islington, Nov. 7, 1804 ; *d.* Dec. 13, 1887), studied the piano under Moscheles, Logier and his father ; also at Paris under Kalkbrenner. He lived in London as a player and teacher (*Brit. Mus. Biog.*)

KIDSON, Frank (*b.* Leeds, Nov. 15, 1855 ; *d.* there, Nov. 8, 1926), was an antiquary who combined to a remarkable degree enthusiasm and accuracy, as his numerous publications show. He was among the earliest modern collectors of folk-songs, one of the founders of the Folk-Song Society and an editor of its journals. He contributed many articles on old English music and publishers to this Dictionary, in both the 2nd and the present editions, and his contributions always gave evidence of original, conscientious research. His speciality was the popular music, more particularly the songs, ballad operas, dances and publishers of the 18th century in this country, as to which he might be regarded as the leading authority. He was also a recognised authority on Leeds Pottery, on which he collaborated with his brother, J. R. Kidson, in writing a book, *Historical Notes of the Leeds Old Pottery* (1892), which is always quoted as the chief source of information on the subject. His local knowledge was shown in the valuable notes on music and musicians, painting, etching and pottery, which he contributed to the *Handbook* of the 'Old Leeds Exhibition' of July 1926. The honorary M.A. conferred on him by Leeds University in 1923 was a suitable recognition of his work.

His publications include :

Old English Country Dances (1890) ; *Traditional Tunes* (1891) ; *British Music Publishers, Printers and Engravers, from Queen Elizabeth's Reign to George the Fourth's* (1900) ; *English Folk-song* (1900) ; *The Beggar's Opera, its Predecessors and Successors* (1922).

He also edited, jointly with Alfred Moffat, several collections of old songs. (See also under Libraries.)
　　　　　　　　　　　　　　　　　H. T.

KIEL, Friedrich (*b.* Puderbach on the Lahn, Oct. 7, 1821 ; *d.* Berlin, Sept. 14, 1885), son of a schoolmaster, who taught him the pianoforte. At 14 he began the violin under Schulz, Konzertmeister to Prince Carl von Wittgenstein-Berleberg, and soon entered the band of the reigning Prince, who sent him first to Caspar Kummer at Coburg, and in 1843 to Dehn at Berlin. While there he received a salary from King Frederick William IV. His first compositions were for the pianoforte, 'Canons und Fugen' opp. 1 and 2 ; variations and fugue, op. 17 ; and several pieces for PF and violoncello, of which the 'Reisebilder' are specially interesting. In 1862 his Requiem (op. 20), a remarkable work, was performed by Stern's Choral Society — also by the University Musical Society of Cambridge, May 21, 1878. In 1865 he composed a ' Missa solennis,' and in 1871-72 an oratorio ' Christus.' A second Requiem (op. 80) was brought out a few years before his death. He was a member of the council of the Berlin Akademie der Künste from 1869, and was professor of composition in the Hochschule für Musik, in which capacity he was much esteemed. Kiel was a distinguished teacher of counterpoint and fugue, and as such forms one of the race of musicians of whom the late Moritz Hauptmann may be considered the chief. His compositions are of the sound classical school.   F. G.

KIENLEN, JOHANN CHRISTOPH (b. Ulm, 1784; d. Dessau, 1830), appeared as a prodigy, both of the voice and the piano, at the age of 7, and was sent by his Munich patrons to Paris, where he studied under Cherubini. On his return he became municipal music director of Ulm. In 1810 he produced his composition of Goethe's *Claudine von Villa Bella* at Leipzig with scant approbation. It met with a better reception at Stuttgart in 1811, and achieved distinct success at Berlin in 1818 after revision and a partial rewriting. About this time he received the title of 'Royal Bavarian Director of Music.' In 1811 he went to Vienna where he became the teacher of Schnyder von Wartensee. Between that time and 1823 he held various appointments and produced several operas. In the latter year he became singing-master at the Berlin opera. In 1828 a symphony was produced at Posen. He wrote an introduction and romance to E. T. A. Hoffmann's composition of Goethe's *Scherz, List und Rache*, many songs, and two pianoforte sonatas. He died in poverty.   E. V. D. S.

KIENZL, WILHELM (b. Waizenkirchen, Austria, Jan. 17, 1857), composer principally of operas, was the son of a lawyer. His father was elected in 1861 mayor of the town of Gratz, where Kienzl has lived nearly all his life. Kienzl studied composition under Dr. W. Mayer, who also had as pupils Weingartner and Busoni. Later he attended the Conservatorium at Prague, and concluded his studies in Munich under Rheinberger. Encouraged by the advice of Adolf Jensen and the sympathy of Liszt, he began to compose, simultaneously continuing his abstract studies, his work in this direction finding expression in a highly interesting and valuable work on musical declamation, which attracted the attention of Wagner, to whom Kienzl felt himself drawn by the similarity of their musical opinions. Kienzl stayed for some time at Bayreuth on terms of intimacy with the family, until his outspoken admiration of Schumann put an end to their amicable relations. Nevertheless, Kienzl remained, musically speaking, in the Wagnerian fold, and did not desert the tenets of Bayreuth.

His first opera, ' Urvasi,' which was produced at Dresden in Feb. 1886, attracted more attention by its melodic charm and the beauty of its orchestration than by the action of the drama, which was weak. His next opera, ' Heilmar der Narr,' was held in abeyance for some ten years owing to difficulties in the staging. In the meantime his third and best-known opera, ' Der Evangelimann,'[1] which had a conspicuous success all over Germany and Austria, rivalling that of Humperdinck's ' Hänsel und Gretel,' appeared in 1894. It was given at Covent Garden, July 3, 1897. In 1898 another opera, on the subject of Don Quixote, was produced in Berlin. In all these works Kienzl, like Humperdinck, retained the constructive features of the Wagnerian creed, but discarded the purely heroic drama, proving that the methods of Bayreuth are capable of being brought nearer to the people than their first propounder ever intended. His style, which is less intricate than that of Humperdinck, is full of musical interest, and is superior to most of the productions of his German contemporaries by the attractiveness of the material he uses. Later stage works of Kienzl are ' In Knecht Rupprechts Werkstatt ' (Gratz, 1907), ' Der Kuhreigen ' (Vienna, 1911), ' Das Testament ' (Vienna, 1916), and ' Hassan der Schwärmer ' (*Riemann*). ' Der Kuhreigen ' was given in English as ' The Dance of Death ' by the Moody-Manners Opera Company at Liverpool and London in 1914.

Besides his operas Kienzl has published over 100 songs, of which a representative selection exists, in the form of an album obtainable in the ' Universal Edition,' other interesting sets being op. 55, six songs, and op. 66, three songs. Further, some 150 piano pieces, amongst which the ' Dichterreise,' op. 46, and the ' Tanzbilder,' op. 41, the latter for piano duet, deserve mention. He has also contributed copiously to orchestral and chamber music, and has published a large number of smaller choral works. His most important production in musical literature, besides the book mentioned above, is an interesting monograph on Wagner, which appeared in 1903. In the same year a marble relief monument in his honour was unveiled in his native town.

     E. E., with addns.

KIESEWETTER, RAPHAEL GEORG, EDLER VON WIESENBRUNN (b. Holešov, Moravia, Aug. 29, 1773; d. Baden, near Vienna, Jan. 1, 1850), uncle to Ambros the historian of music, Imperial councillor from 1803, and learned author on musical subjects. He settled in Vienna in 1794. In 1816 he began to form a collection of scores of the old masters, and made his house a rendezvous for the first musicians of Vienna. There also, during Advent, Lent

---

[1] It was given in English (Moody Manners Co.) at Liverpool Apr. 1914.

and Holy Week, a first-rate amateur choir performed the principal works of the old Italian composers, and of Bach, Handel, etc. He was ennobled for his services as an official in the Kriegsrath, taking his title from his estate. Innumerable societies elected him a member in acknowledgment of his services as a musician. He left his musical MSS. and his correspondence with musical men of letters to Aloys Fuchs, and to the court library his invaluable collection of scores, with the condition that they should be kept together as the Kiesewetter collection. He was buried in the cemetery at Vienna, ' vor der Währinger Linie.'

That he was a most prolific writer the following list of his principal works will show :

1. *Die Verdienste der Niederländer um die Tonkunst* (received the gold prize-medal, Amsterdam, 1828). 2. *Geschichte der europäisch-abendländischen, das ist unserer heutigen Musik* (Breitkopf & Härtel, 1834; 2nd ed. 1846, translated into English by R. Müller, 1848). 3. *Über die Musik der Neugriechen*, with remarks on ancient Egyptian and ancient Greek music ; three treatises (*ibid.*, 1838). 4 *Guido von Arezzo*, life and works (*ibid.*, 1840). 5. *Schicksale und Beschaffenheit des weltlichen Gesanges*, from the early Middle Ages down to the discovery of the dramatic style and rise of opera (*ibid.*, 1841). 6. *Die Musik der Araber*, from original sources (*ibid.*, 1842). 7. *Über das Leben, und die Werke Palestrinas*, a condensation of Baini's work left unpublished by Kandler ; edited with preface and remarks (*ibid.*, 1834). 8. *Der neuen Aristoxener zerstreute Aufsätze* (*ibid.*, 1846). 9. *Über die Octave des Pythagoras*, supplement to the preceding (Vienna, 1848). 10. *Catalog über die Sammlung der Partituren alter Musik*, etc.[1] (Vienna, 1847), with preface and appendix *Gallerie der alten Contrapuntisten*, a selection from their works, chronologically arranged.

Also about fifty scattered articles in different periodicals, reviews, etc. A letter from him to R. L. de Pearsall, dated 1838, and expressed in very queer English, is printed in the *Mus. T.*, 1902, p. 93, from the original in the B.M.   C. F. P.

KILBURN, NICHOLAS (*b.* Bishop Auckland, Durham, Feb. 7, 1843 ; *d.* there, Dec. 4, 1923), a zealous and able amateur, who did a great work for the cultivation and appreciation of good music in the north of England. He graduated Mus.B. Cantab. in 1880, and received the hon. degree of Mus.D. from Durham University, 1914. His activity as a conductor was in connexion with three important northern societies : the Bishop Auckland Musical Society from 1875, the Middlesbrough Musical Union from its foundation in 1882, and the Sunderland Philharmonic Society from 1886. His independent position as an honorary conductor and adviser allowed him great freedom in arranging his programmes, which, while by no means neglecting the great classics of choral and orchestral music, introduced many works which were either new to the country or at least unfamiliar. His habit of attending the principal festivals, at home and abroad—he was a frequent visitor to Bayreuth—enabled him to keep in close touch with current music, and his influence on the music of the district in which he worked was healthful and enduring. He was an efficient organist, pianist and violoncellist, and composed several works for chorus and orchestra, of which the latest, a ' Choral In Memoriam, for Voices, Violins and Trumpet ' (Novello), composed ' in memory of our brave soldiers and sailors, 1914 and after,' may be cited.   H. T.

KIND, JOHANN FRIEDRICH (*b.* Leipzig, Mar. 4, 1768 ; *d.* Dresden, June 25, 1843), author of

the words of ' Der Freischütz ' ; was brought up to the law, but frequented the Thomasschule of his own accord. He began to practise literature as early as 1800, and after much success with novels and tales, settled in 1814 at Dresden, became a Hofrath, and definitely renounced the law for a literary life. Here Weber met him, at the house of von Nordstern. About Feb. 15, 1817, Kind read to him his *Vandyck's Landleben*, which so pleased the composer that he at once consulted him as to an opera-book. The choice of a source fell on Apel's *Gespensterbuch* (Ghost Stories). Weber had, several years before, been attached to the story of the Freischütz, and so entirely did his enthusiasm communicate itself to Kind, that by the evening of Feb. 23 he had completed the first act of the opera. This was the only important joint composition of the two, but Jähns's Catalogue contains eleven other pieces, the words of which were supplied by Kind. The chief of these is the ' Jubel Cantata,' another cantata called ' Natur und Liebe,' five songs, two part-songs, and a chorus. Some of these were taken from operas of Kind's—' Der Weinberg an der Elbe,' ' Der Abend am Waldbrunnen,' and ' Das Nachtlager in Granada.' The last of these was set to music by Conradin Kreutzer. Kind seems to have supplied Spanish materials for ' Preciosa,' and Weber had two librettos by him--' Alcindor,' 1819, and ' Der Cid,' 1821—under consideration, but ' Der Freischütz ' is the one which Weber adopted in full. Kind's ' Holzdieb ' (Woodthief) was composed by Marschner in 1824. He is described by Weber's son as a small person, with a great opinion of himself and a harsh voice. Two volumes of his works were published, Leipzig, 1821.   G.

KINDERMANN, AUGUST (*b.* Berlin, Feb. 6, 1817 ; *d.* Munich, Mar. 6, 1891), began his career at the opera as a chorus-singer, received instruction from Meyer, and played both bass and baritone parts at Leipzig in 1839–46, after which he was engaged at Munich, where he obtained a life engagement, and was always a great favourite, being a very versatile artist. He celebrated his twenty-fifth anniversary of his engagement there on June 15, 1871, as Figaro in ' Nozze,' the Cherubino being his elder daughter Marie, then engaged at Cassel. He sang Titurel at Bayreuth in 1882 ; and on Sept. 9, 1886, he celebrated the jubilee of his career, and the fortieth year of his engagement at Munich, playing the part of Stadinger in Lortzing's ' Waffenschmied.' For his daughter Hedwig, see REICHER-KINDERMANN.

KINDERMANN, JOHANN ERASMUS (*b.* Nuremberg, Mar. 29, 1616 ;[2] *d.* Apr. 14, 1655), Nuremberg organist. His chief work is entitled *Harmonia organica in tabulaturam Germanicam composita*, etc., first published in 1645,

---

[1] The scores left to the court library.

[2] *Riemann.*

and republished in 1665. It is remarkable, as being one of the earliest specimens of German copper-plate engraving, and is also of importance in the history of organ-playing and organ composition. As the title indicates, the music is given in the old German tablature notation.[1] The work opens with fourteen preludes mainly in the church tones, followed by fugal fantasias on Choral - tunes, and concludes with some Magnificat intonations and verses. The pedal is treated obbligato throughout. Ritter gives three examples from the work in modern notation. Kindermann's other works are partly sacred, partly secular compositions for voices with basso continuo and occasional viol and violin accompaniment. Selections from his works have been reprinted in *D.D.T.* (2nd series) xiii. and xxi. He also composed a large number of Choral-tunes, harmonised for three voices, to the Nuremberg preacher Dilherr's *Evangelische Schlussreimen* and *Göttliche Liebesflamme*, 1649–52. Some works for instruments only, partly viols, partly wind instruments, are also mentioned, but do not seem to exist complete. (See Eitner, *Q.-L.*)

BIBL.—PETER EPSTEIN, *Aus Frankfurter Ratsakten des 17. Jahrhunderts.* *Z.M.W.*, Apr. 1923, pp. 370-73.   J. R. M.

KINDERSLEY, ROBERT, a 16th-century English composer, who wrote 2 anthems in Leighton's ' Teares and Lamentacions ' (1614). One of these was also given in Myriell's ' Tristitiae remedium ' (1616) A sacred partsong mentioned in *Q.-L.* is not traceable from indications given, but apparently refers to an incomplete edition of one of the former.

KING, CHARLES, Mus.B. (*b.* Bury St. Edmunds, 1687 ; *d.* London, Mar. 17, 1748), became a chorister of St. Paul's under Dr. Blow and Jeremiah Clarke. He was next a supernumerary singer in the choir at the small annual stipend of £14. On July 12, 1707, he graduated as Mus.B. at Oxford. On the death of Clarke, whose sister he had married, he was appointed almoner and master of choristers of St. Paul's. In 1708 he became also organist of St. Benet Fink, Royal Exchange. On Oct. 31, 1730, he was admitted a vicar choral of St. Paul's. King composed several services and anthems, some of which are printed in Arnold's *Cathedral Music*, and others in Page's *Harmonia Sacra* ; and there are some in the Tudway Collection (Harl. MSS. 7341 and 7342). Although his compositions evince no originality they are vocal and long continued in frequent use in choirs, particularly his services in F and C. They have justified the joke of Dr. Greene, that King was a *serviceable* man. Six of them in all are published by Novello, besides five anthems. Hawkins intimates that his inferiority was the result rather of indolence than want of ability.   W. H. H.

KING, (1) MATTHEW PETER (*b.* London,

1773 ; *d.* there, Jan. 1823), studied composition under Charles Frederick Horn. His first productions were ' Three Sonatas for the Pianoforte,' ' Eight Songs and a Cantata,' and three other sets of Pianoforte Sonatas. In 1796 he published *Thorough-Bass made clear to every Capacity*, and in 1800 *A General Treatise on Music*, etc., a work of repute, with second edition, 1809. On June 1, 1816, his oratorio, ' The Intercession,' was produced at Covent Garden. One of the songs in it, ' Must I leave thee, Paradise ? ' (known as ' Eve's Lamentation ') became very popular, and long found a place in programmes of sacred music. King was also the composer of several glees (among them the popular ' Witches '), and of numerous pianoforte pieces. He composed several dramatic pieces, chiefly for the English Opera House, Lyceum, as follows :

' Matrimony,' 1804 ; ' The Invisible Girl,' 1806 ; ' False Alarms ' (with Braham) ; ' One o'clock, or The Wood Demon ' (with Kelly); and ' Ella Rosenberg,' 1807 ; ' Up all night,' 1809 ; ' Plots ' and ' Oh, this Love,' 1810 ; ' The Americans ' (with Braham), and ' Timour the Tartar,' 1811 ; and ' The Fisherman's Hut ' (with Davy), 1819.

His son, (2) C. M. KING, published in 1826 some songs which were favourably received.

     W. H. H.

KING, ROBERT, Mus.B., was one of the Royal band, appointed Feb. 6, 1679–80 *vice* John Bannister deceased. At Christmas 1689 a licence was granted to him to establish a concert.[2] He graduated at Cambridge in 1696. He was the composer of many songs published in ' Choice Ayres, Songs and Dialogues,' 1684 ; ' Comes Amoris,' 1687–93 ; ' The Banquet of Musick,' 1688-92 ; *The Gentleman's Journal*, 1692–94 ; and *Thesaurus musicus*, 1695–96. He composed the songs in Crowne's comedy, ' Sir Courtly Nice,' which were printed in *The Theater of Music*, Book ii. 1685. In 1690 he set Shadwell's Ode on St. Cecilia's Day, ' O Sacred Harmony.' In 1693 he set an Ode ' on the Rt. Hon. John Cecil, Earl of Exeter, his birthday, being the 21 of Sept.' beginning ' Once more 'tis born, the happy day,' the words by Peter Motteux. A collection of twenty-four songs by him, entitled ' Songs for One, Two, and Three voices, composed to a Through-Basse for yᵉ Organ or Harpsicord,' engraven on copper, was ' sold by John Crouch at the Three Lutes in Princes St., Drury Lane ' (1690). The date of his death has not been ascertained. He was living in 1711.

     W. H. H., with addns.

KING, WILLIAM (*b.* Winchester, 1624 ; *d.* Oxford, Nov. 17, 1680), son of George King (*d.* 1665), organist of Winchester Cathedral, was admitted a clerk of Magdalen College, Oxford, Oct. 18, 1648. He graduated B.A. June 5, 1649, and in 1652 was promoted to a chaplaincy at Magdalen College, which he held until Aug. 25, 1654, when he became probationer-fellow of All Souls' College. On Dec. 10, 1664, he was

---

[1] A detailed description of the contents is given in Ritter's *Geschichte des Orgelspiels*, pp. 146-7.

[2] Calendar of State Papers.

appointed successor to Pickhaver as organist of New College. He composed a service in B♭ and some anthems (a setting of the Litany remained in use in Lichfield Cathedral, and was republished by J. Bishop of Cheltenham and J. B. Lott), and in 1668 published at Oxford ' Poems of Mr. Cowley [The Mistress] and others, composed into Songs and Ayres, with a Thorough Basse to the Theorbo, Harpsicon, or Basse Violl.' He was buried in New College Cloister.

W. H. H.

KING CHARLES THE SECOND, a comic opera in 2 acts ; words adapted by Desmond Ryan from a comedy of Howard Payne ; music by G. A. Macfarren. Produced Princess's Theatre, Oct. 27, 1849. Payne's comedy had before been turned into a ballet-pantomime, ' Betty,' music by Ambroise Thomas, produced Opéra, Paris, July 10, 1846.   G.

KING COLE CHAMBER MUSIC CLUB, THE. This Club was founded Dec. 8, 1900, by Jan Mulder, a musical enthusiast of Dutch origin. Its object was to obtain performances of chamber music under more intimate and social conditions than in a concert hall. The season consists of 10 concerts and has been carried on continuously since the foundation, the meetings being held in a room lent by the proprietor of an hotel, who undertakes to serve dinner to the guests before the music begins. The venue was in the first instance at the Caledonian Hotel, Adelphi, and more recently at the Great Central, Marylebone.

Most of the leading instrumentalists of the period, 445 in number, have been engaged at these concerts, at which 380 works, including nearly all the masterpieces of chamber music, have been performed. Several modern works, and 66 by British composers, have up to 1925 appeared on the programmes, some for the first time. The aims and objects of the King Cole Club may be said to be unique.   W. W. C.

KING SAUL, see SAUL (2).

KING'S BAND OF MUSIC, THE. The custom of the kings of England to retain as part of their household a band of musicians, more or less numerous, is very ancient (see CHAPEL ROYAL). We learn that Edward IV. had 13 minstrels, ' whereof some be trompets, some with shalmes and smalle pypes.' Henry VIII.'s band in 1526 consisted of 15 trumpets, 3 lutes, 3 rebecks, 3 taborets, a harp, 2 viols, 10 sackbuts, a fife and 4 drumslades. In 1530 his band was composed of 16 trumpets, 4 lutes, 3 rebecks, 3 taborets, a harp, 2 viols, 9 sackbuts, 2 drumslades, 3 minstrels and a player on the virginals. Edward VI. in 1548 retained 8 minstrels, a player on the virginals, 2 lutes, a harper, a bagpiper, a drumslade, a rebeck, 7 viols, 4 sackbuts, a Welsh minstrel and a flute-player. Elizabeth's band in 1581 included trumpets, violins, flutes and sackbuts, besides musicians

whose instruments are not specified ; and six years later it consisted of 16 trumpets, lutes, harps, a bagpipe, 9 minstrels, 2 rebecks, 6 sackbuts, 8 viols and 3 players on the virginals. Charles I. in 1625 had in his pay 8 performers on the hautboys and sackbuts, 6 flutes, 6 recorders, 11 violins, 6 lutes, 4 viols, 1 harp and 15 ' musicians for the lute and voice,' exclusive of trumpeters, drummers and fifers, Nicholas Laniere being master of the band ; and in 1641 his band included 14 violins, 19 wind instruments and 25 ' musicians for the waytes,' besides a serjeant trumpeter and 18 trumpeters.

Charles II. in 1660 established, in imitation of Louis XIV., a band of 24 performers on violins, tenors and basses, popularly known as the ' four and twenty fiddlers.' This band not only played while the king was at meals, but was even introduced into the royal chapel, anthems being composed with symphonies and ritornels between the vocal movements expressly for them. After the death of Charles the band was kept up, but was somewhat changed in its composition ; it no longer consisted exclusively of stringed instruments, but some of its members performed on wind instruments. Besides its ordinary duties it was employed, together with the gentlemen and children of the Chapel Royal, in the performance of the odes annually composed for the King's birthday and New Year's day ; on the discontinuance of the production of such odes, its duties were reduced to attendance on royal weddings and baptisms, and other state occasions. The Band of Queen Victoria was reconstituted by Prince ALBERT (q.v.) on the lines of a modern orchestra. It was thus employed for State concerts, which, however, were discontinued by King Edward VII. The following is the succession of the ' Masters of the Musick ' responsible for the Band from the Restoration onwards :

Davis Mell and George Hudson, 1660 ; Thomas Baltzar, 1661 (?) ; John Banister, 1663 ; Louis Grabu, 1666 ; Thomas Purcell, 1672 (?) ; Dr. Nicholas Staggins, 1674 ; John Eccles, 1700 ; Dr. Maurice Greene, 1735 (?) ; Dr. William Boyce, 1755 ; John Stanley, 1779 ; Sir William Parsons, 1786 ; William Shield, 1817 ; Christian Kramer, 1829 ; François Cramer, 1834 ; George Frederick Anderson, 1848 ; Sir William George Cusins, 1870 ; Sir Walter Parratt, 1893-1924.

Robert Cambert is sometimes said to have held the office of Master of the Musick, but this is doubtful. Sir Edward ELGAR (q.v.) succeeded Sir Walter Parratt as Master, but the position is now advisory rather than executive.

W. H. H., with addns.

BIBL.—H. C. DE LA FONTAINE, The King's Musick.

KING'S CONCERTS, THE, see ANCIENT CONCERTS.

KING'S THEATRE, THE. In the early part of the 18th century, Sir John Vanbrugh, the architect and dramatist, proposed to the performers at Lincoln's Inn Fields Theatre to build them a new and splendid theatre in the Haymarket, and, his offer being accepted, he raised a subscription of £30,000 in sums of £100 each, in return for which every subscriber was to have a free admission for life. The undertaking was greatly promoted by the Kit-Cat Club, and the first stone of the building, which was wholly from the designs of Vanbrugh, was laid in 1704 with great solemnity by the beautiful Countess of Sunderland (daughter of the great Duke of Marlborough), known as 'The little Whig.' Congreve, the dramatist, was associated with Vanbrugh in the management, and the theatre was opened on Apr. 9, 1705, under the name of 'The Queen's Theatre,' which name was changed on the accession of George I. in 1714 to 'King's Theatre,' by which it continued to be called until the death of William IV. in 1837, after which it was styled HER MAJESTY'S THEATRE (*q.v.*), the reason for not resuming the name 'Queen's Theatre' being that the theatre in Tottenham Street at the time bore that appellation.

Vanbrugh's erection, although internally a splendid and imposing structure, was totally unfitted for its purpose, owing to the reverberations being so great as to make the spoken dialogue almost unintelligible. The defect necessitated extensive alterations. In the course of a few years the house became the established home of Italian opera. In it the greater part of Handel's operas and his early oratorios were first performed (see HANDEL). On the evening of June 17, 1789, the building was burned to the ground. It was rebuilt in 1790 from designs by Michael Novosielski, the lyre-shaped plan being then first adopted in England. When completed it was refused a licence for dramatic representations, but a magistrates' licence being obtained it was opened with a concert and ballet on Mar. 26, 1791. (See HAYDN.) A regular licence was, however, soon afterwards granted. The interior of the theatre was the largest in England; there were five tiers of boxes, exclusive of slips, and it was capable of containing nearly 3300 persons. It was admirably adapted for conveying sound. On the east side was a large and handsome concert-room, 95 feet long, 46 feet broad, and 35 feet high, on a level with the principal tier of boxes. About 1817 an important alteration was made in the exterior of the theatre by the erection of the colonnades on the north, south and east sides, and the formation of the western arcade. The northern colonnade was afterwards removed.[1] (See LAPORTE.) The theatre was again destroyed by fire on Friday night, Dec. 6, 1867.   W. H. H.

KINGSTON, MORGAN (*b.* Wednesbury, Staffs, Mar. 16, 1881), operatic tenor. Something of

romance attaches to the early life-story of this talented artist. He sang as a boy in the parish church choir, and when his voice broke he strengthened his chest by playing tenor horn in a brass band. He was then 14, and four years later he began work as a miner, hoping to become a mining engineer. He was still thus occupied at the age of 27 when his singing at a local bazaar drew attention to the exceptional beauty of his voice, and it was decided that he should enter the profession. After nearly three years' training under various teachers, he began his career as an oratorio and concert singer, quickly earning a reputation both in England and on the Continent by the singular purity and genuine tenor quality of his voice, the steadiness and ease of his *sostenuto*, and the dramatic ring of his high notes. These attributes pointed to his suitability for the operatic stage, and by 1913 he was ready for the American career which was to prove such a brilliant success for him. He made his début at the Century Theatre, New York, as Radamès in 'Aïda,' and, consequent upon the enthusiasm of his reception, his contract was extended with double fee from that night. He met with no less success in oratorio, and sang in his first season at no fewer than fifteen festivals, including Cincinnati. In 1916 he became a member of the Metropolitan Opera Company, and for seven or eight seasons held a high place in that world-famous troupe. Returning in 1924, he made his first appearance at Covent Garden as Canio in 'Pagliacci' on June 25, and met with emphatic success. He then remained in London for a long rest, the benefit of which was made apparent by the freshness and power of his singing at an Albert Hall concert in Jan. 1925, when he was heard to equal advantage in four languages.   H. K.

KIRBYE, GEORGE (*d.* Bury St. Edmunds, Oct. 1634), one of the best English writers of madrigals of the graver kind, may have been a native of Suffolk, where his life was chiefly spent.

The first mention of his name occurs in 1592, when he contributed to East's 'Whole Book of Psalms.' As he furnished more settings of tunes to this book than any other of the composers employed, excepting John Farmer, it is to be assumed that he had already made some reputation as a musician. In 1597 he published what he calls the 'first fruites of my poore knowledge in Musicke,' a set of twenty-four madrigals for 4, 5 and 6 voices, dedicated to two of the daughters of Sir Robert Jermyn of Rushbrooke, near Bury St. Edmunds, in whose house he seems to have lived as music-master, or domestic musician. On Feb. 16, 1597/8, George Kirbye married Anne Saxye, at Bradfield St. George, near Rushbrooke.

In 1601 appeared the 'Triumphes of Oriana,' for which Kirbye wrote a 6-part madrigal. In

---

[1] There is a good description of the pit, including the famous 'Fops' alley' in Lumley's *Reminiscences*, chap. vii.

some copies of the 'Triumphes' his composition appears to the words 'With angel's face and brightness,' elsewhere to the words 'Bright Phœbus greets most clearly,' the music being the same in both cases. It may be conjectured that Kirbye wrote his music to the words 'With angel's face,' to which it seems better suited, but that, as these words were also set by Daniel Norcome, the editor of the 'Triumphes' may have thought it advisable to supply new words to Kirbye's composition.

In 1626 Kirbye was living in Bury St. Edmunds. On June 11 of that year the burial of his wife is recorded in St. Mary's parish registers there, and in 1627–28 his name twice appears in the same registers, probably as one of the churchwardens. On Oct. 6, 1634, his burial is entered in St. Mary's registers. His will, dated Mar. 10, 1633, and proved at Bury, Oct. 7, 1634, shows that he owned property in Whiting Street, Bury St. Edmunds, which he left to his servant, Agnes Seaman, kinswoman to his late wife, together with all his goods, chattels and personal estate ; excepting small legacies to his brother, Walter Kirbye ; his sister, Alice Moore, widow ; and a few others. There is a note in a set of MS. part-books, copied by Thomas Hamond, of Cressners, Hawkdon, near Bury St. Edmunds, between the years 1631 and 1660 (Bodl. MS. Mus. f. 1-6), to the effect that the 'Italian songs to 5 and 6 voyces' contained in them were

'collected out of Master Geo. Kirbies blacke bookes wch were sould after ye decease of the said Geo. to the right woᵗʰʸ Sʳ Jo. Hollond in ye yeare 1634. And he paid as they said Kirbies maid, 40s.'

This note is of interest as showing that Kirbye possessed copies of motets, etc., by the best Italian composers of the day.

A large number of unpublished madrigals and motets by Kirbye exist in the Bodleian Library, and in the libraries of the R.C.M. and of St. Michael's College, Tenbury. Unfortunately they are all imperfect, excepting a 4-part madrigal, 'Farewell, false love,' in the R.C.M. Library. In the British Museum is an imperfect pavan for viols (Add. MSS. 30,826/8) and a 5-part hymn, 'O Jesu, look' (Add. MSS. 29,372/7). The complete sets of madrigals are published in Arkwright's OLD ENGLISH EDITION (q.v.), Nos. 3, 4, 5 and 21. Kirbye's 'First set of English Madrigalls' (1597) with his Oriana madrigal (including both sets of words) are republished in ENGL. MADR. SCH. vol. xxiv.   G. E. P. A.

KIRCHENMUSIK, AKADEMISCHES INSTITUT FÜR, see BERLIN.

KIRCHER, ATHANASIUS (b. Geisa, near Fulda, May 2, 1602 ; d. Rome, Nov. 28, 1680), early became a Jesuit, and taught mathematics and natural philosophy in the Jesuit College at Würzburg, where he was professor in 1630. About 1631 he was driven from Germany by the Thirty Years' War, and went in 1633 to the house of his Order at Avignon, and thence by way of Vienna (1635) to Rome, where he remained till his death. He acquired a mass of information in all departments of knowledge, and wrote books on every conceivable subject. His great work *Musurgia universalis sive ars magna consoni et dissoni*, two vols. (Rome, 1650), translated into German by Andreas Hirsch (Hall in Swabia, 1662), contains, among much rubbish, valuable matter on the nature of sound and the theory of composition, with interesting examples from the instrumental music of Frescobaldi, Froberger and other composers of the 17th century. The second volume, on the music of the Greeks, is far from trustworthy ; indeed Meibomius (*Musici antiqui*) accuses Kircher of having written it without consulting a single ancient Greek authority. His *Phonurgia* (Kempten, 1673), translated into German by Agathus Carione (apparently a *nom de plume*), with the title *Neue Hall- und Thonkunst* (Nördlingen, 1684), is an amplification of part of the *Musurgia*, and deals chiefly with acoustical instruments. In his *Magnes, sive de arte magnetica* (Rome, 1641) he gives all the songs and airs then in use to cure the bite of the tarantula. His *Oedipus aegyptiacus* (Rome, 1652–54) treats of the music contained in Egyptian hieroglyphics. (See J. E. Matthew's *Literature of Music*, p. 57.)   F. G.

KIRCHGESSNER, MARIANNA (b. Waghäusel, near Rastatt, Baden, 1770 ; d. Schaffhausen, Dec. 9, 1809), performer on the glass HARMONICA (q.v.). An illness in her fourth year left her blind for life, but this misfortune was compensated by a delicate organisation for music. She learned the harmonica from Schmittbauer of Carlsruhe, and made numerous successful concert tours. Mozart heard her in Vienna (1791), and composed a quintet for her (Köchel, 617). In London, about 1794, Fröschel made her a new instrument, which in future she always used. Here also she recovered a glimmering of sight under medical treatment. Much as they admired her playing, musicians regretted that she failed to bring out the true qualities of the harmonica, through a wrong method of execution. After living in retirement at Gohlis, near Leipzig, she undertook another concert tour, but fell ill and died at Schaffhausen.   C. F. P.

KIRCHHOFF, GOTTFRIED (b. Mühlbeck, near Bitterfeld, Sept. 15, 1685 ; d. Halle, Jan. 21, 1746), a pupil of Zachau, was Kapellmeister of the Duke of Holstein-Glücksburg in 1709 ; organist of the Benedictine Church, Quedlinburg, in 1711 ; and succeeded Zachau as organist of the Liebfrauenkirche, Halle, July 13, 1714. He was one of the foremost organ composers of the 18th century. (List of works in *Q.-L.*)

KIRCHNER, THEODOR (b. Neukirchen, near Chemnitz, Saxony, Dec. 10, 1823 ; d. Hamburg,

Sept. 19, 1903), one of the most gifted disciples of Schumann, a composer of 'genre pieces' for the pianoforte, had his musical training at Leipzig, under C. F. Becker, from 1838. Having completed his schooling at Leipzig and Dresden, he took the post of organist at Winterthur in Switzerland in 1843, which town in 1862 he left for Zürich, where he acted as conductor and teacher. In 1873 he became director of the Musikschule at Würzburg, but after two years he threw up that appointment and settled at Leipzig, until 1883, when he moved to Dresden as a teacher of ensemble in the Conservatorium. In 1890 he moved once more to Hamburg, where he died.

Kirchner's works extend to over 100 opus numbers. Except a string quartet, op. 20, a 'Gedenkblatt,' a 'Serenade' and 'Novelletten,' op. 59, for piano, violin and violoncello, some violin pieces, op. 63, and eight pieces for violoncello, op. 79, and a number of Lieder, they are all written for pianoforte solo or duet, are mostly of small dimensions, and put forth under suggestive titles such as Schumann was wont to give to his lesser pieces. The stamp of Schumann's original mind has marked Kirchner's work from the first ; yet though sheltered under Schumann's cloak, many minor points of style and diction are Kirchner's own, and decidedly clever. At best, his pieces are delicate and tender, frequently vigorous, now and then humorous and fantastic ; at worst, they droop under a taint of lachrymose sentimentality. They are always carefully finished and well shapen, never redundant, rarely commonplace. Among his early publications, 'Albumblätter,' op. 9, became popular as played by Madame Schumann ; and among his later, "Still und bewegt,' op.24, and particularly 'Nachtstücke,' op. 25, deserve attention.   E. D.

KIRKMAN. The name borne by a family of eminent harpsichord and subsequently pianoforte makers. (1) JACOB KIRCHMANN (afterwards KIRKMAN) (d. 1778), a German, came to England early in the 18th century, and worked for Tabel, a Flemish harpsichord maker, who had brought to London the traditions of the RUCKERS (q.v.) of Antwerp. Another apprentice of Tabel was SHUDI (q.v.) (properly Tschudi), who became Kirkman's rival, and founded the house of Broadwood. Tabel would have been quite forgotten but for these distinguished pupils, and for the droll anecdote, narrated by Dr. Burney, of Kirkman's rapid courtship of Tabel's widow, and securing with her the business and stock-in-trade. He proposed at breakfast-time, and married her (the Marriage Act being not then passed) before twelve o'clock the same day, just one month after Tabel's demise. Jacob Kirkman was organist of St. George's, Hanover Square ; he wrote several sets of pieces for organ and pianoforte, and published them himself at the sign of the King's Arms in Broad Street, Carnaby Market, now No. 19 Broad Street, Soho. Dr. Burney places the arrival of Jacob Kirkman in England in 1740, but he rented a house in Great Pulteney Street East from June 1739 to the end of 1749 (the ratebook of St. James's is missing for 1750). An interesting advertisement apropos of the date appeared in the Daily Gazetteer for May 8, 1739 :

'Whereas Mr. Hermann Tabel late of Swallow Street, the famous Harpsichord maker, dead, hath left several fine Harpsichords to be disposed of by Mr. Kirckman, his late Foreman ; this is to acquaint the Curious, that the said Harpsichords, which are the finest he ever made, are to be seen at the said Mr. Kirckmann's the corner of Pulteney Court in Cambridge Street, over against Silver Street, near Golden Square.'

Shudi was probably established by that time in Meard's Street, Dean Street, Soho, whence he removed in 1742 to the premises in Great Pulteney Street. There is no reason, however, to doubt the same generally excellent authority that Kirkman's death took place about 1778, and that he left nearly £200,000.

Burney, in Rees's Cyclopædia, gives Jacob Kirkman's harpsichords high praise, regarding them as more full in tone and durable than those of Shudi. These instruments retained certain features of the Antwerp model as late as 1768, preserving André Ruckers's keyboard of G,—f''' (nearly five octaves), with lowest G♯ wanting. This, as well as the retention of the rosette in the sound-board, may be seen in the Kirkman harpsichord of that year which belonged to the late C. K. Salaman, and in which we find King David playing upon the harp, between the letters I and K. Dr. Burney met with no harpsichords on the Continent that could at all compare with those made in England by Jacob Kirkman and his almost life-long competitor, Shudi.

Jacob Kirkman, having no children by his marriage, was succeeded by his nephew (2) ABRAHAM, whose son, (3) JOSEPH, followed him. The piano was introduced in Kirkman's workshops in the time of Abraham Kirkman, as there is record of a square piano inscribed Jacob and Abraham Kirchmann, which was dated 1775. A grand piano dated 1780 was also theirs, and the manufacture of both kinds of instrument went on side by side for some years, as there was a single harpsichord in the possession of the firm, dated 1778, and the double harpsichord, in the possession of Mr. J. A. Fuller Maitland, is dated 1798 ; it is inscribed 'Josephus Kirckman.' His son, (4) JOSEPH, died at the advanced age of 87 in 1877, his second son, (5) HENRY, to whom the business owed its extension, having died some years before. The warerooms were for many years in Soho Square. In 1896 the business was amalgamated with that of COLLARD (q.v.). The Kirkmans were the English agents for Signor Caldera's attachment known as the Melopiano.   A. J. H.

KIRMAIR, FRIEDRICH JOSEPH (d. Gotha,

1814,[1] an 18th century pianist-composer, teacher of the Prussian Crown Princess at Berlin in 1795; from 1803 Konzertmeister to the Duke of Gotha. He composed a Mass, trios, sonatas, variations for pianoforte, etc. (Q.-L.).

KIRNBERGER, JOHANN PHILIPP (b. Saalfeld, Thuringia, Apr.[2] 1721; d. Berlin, July 27, 1783), composer and writer on the theory of music, learnt the rudiments of music at home, the organ from Kellner of Gräfenrode, and the violin from Meil of Sondershausen. Gerber, court organist there, taught him to play Bach's fugues, and recommended him to Bach, whose pupil he was from 1739–41. Several years were passed at Leipzig, in Poland, and at Lemberg. On his return to Germany he resumed the study of the violin under Zickler of Dresden, and in 1751 entered the service of Frederick the Great at Berlin as violinist. In 1758 he became Kapellmeister to Princess Amalie, and remained with her until his death, in Berlin, after a long and painful illness. During these twenty-five years he formed such pupils as Schulz, Fasch and Zelter, and devoted his leisure to researches on the theory of music. Of his many books on the subject, *Die Kunst des reinen Satzes*, two vols. (Berlin, 1771–76), alone is of permanent value. He also wrote all the articles on music in Sulzer's *Theorie der schönen Künste*, and warmly criticises Marpurg's *Kritische Briefe*, in which various charges had been brought against him. (See Q.-L.) He prided himself on the discovery that all music could be reduced to two fundamental chords, the triad and the chord of the seventh, and invented a new interval bearing the relation of 4 : 7 to the keynote, and which he called I :—but neither of these ideas has stood the test of time. As a composer his most interesting works are his fugues, remarkable for their correctness. In 1773–74 he edited a large collection of vocal compositions by Graun, who was a kind friend to him, and ' Psalmen und Gesänge ' by Leo (Leonhard) Hassler. The autograph scores of several motets and cantatas, and a quantity of fugues, clavier-sonatas and similar works, are preserved in the State Library at Berlin and elsewhere. (See Q.-L.) Kirnberger was of a quarrelsome temper, and fond of laying down the law, which made him no favourite with his fellow-musicians.　　　　　　　　　　　F. G.

KISTLER, CYRILL (b. Grossaitingen, near Augsburg, Mar. 12, 1848; d. Kissingen, Jan. 2, 1907), composer of operas, displayed early taste for music, was a choir-boy at the age of 8, and could play the flute.

At first intended for the Church, he afterwards entered upon the career of a schoolmaster, and taught in various schools from 1867–75. In 1876 he entered the Munich Conservatorium, and studied regularly under

Wüllner, Rheinberger and Fr. Lachner. The last of these took him as a private pupil after his leaving the Conservatorium, and did all in his power to counteract the strong influence of Wagner which had even then declared itself. In 1883 he was appointed teacher of theory, etc., at Sondershausen, and in 1884 his most important work, an opera or music-drama, ' Kunihild,' was brought out at that place. It was not until its revival at Würzburg in 1893 that it was widely recognised as a piece of any great significance. It then excited a good deal of comment, stimulated by the polemical attitude adopted by the composer towards theatrical managers and others, and expressed in a series of *Musikalische Tagesfragen*, published between 1884 and 1894. The opera is constructed on purely Wagnerian principles, with numerous ' leading-motives.' Occasionally the composer declines into a style that is more akin to that of the usual German partsong, in choruses and such things, for, during his earlier life, he had written much music of a less ambitious aim. After 1885 he lived at Bad Kissingen, as principal of a private music-school, and as a publisher. In 1889 his comic opera, ' Eulenspiegel,' was brought out at Würzburg without much success, although in some ways it is more original than ' Kunihild.' ' Arm' Elslein ' was given at Schwerin in 1902, ' Röslein im Hag ' at Elberfeld in 1903, and ' Baldurs Tod ' at Düsseldorf in 1905. He left a 3-act opera, ' Die deutschen Kleinstädter ' (published), unperformed at the time of his death. Besides these dramatic works, Kistler published many pieces for orchestra, among them an interesting ' Trauerklänge,' choruses, songs, organ pieces, etc., method of harmony on Wagnerian principles (*Harmonielehre*, 1879 and 1903), a *Musikalische Elementarlehre*, a *Volksschullehrer* (1880), a *Tonkünstler-Lexikon*, which reached its third edition in 1887, and *Der einfache Kontrapunkt* (1904).　　　　M., addns.

BIBL.—*Riemann*; BAKER, *B. Dict. of Mus., Masters of German Music. Mus. T.*, Apr. 1893; H. RITTER, *Führer durch Kistlers Kunihild.*

KISTNER, a music-publishing firm of Leipzig. The business was founded in 1823 by PROBST, who was succeeded in 1831 by (1) KARL FRIEDRICH KISTNER (b. Leipzig, Mar. 3, 1797; d. Dec. 21, 1844), a man of some gifts for music and great business powers. The new name was not assumed till 1836. Kistner greatly improved the business, and secured important works of Mendelssohn, Schumann, Chopin, Moscheles, Sterndale Bennett, etc. He was succeeded by his son (2) JULIUS (d. May 13, 1868), who followed in his father's steps with equal success. He added the names of Hiller, Taubert and Rubinstein to the catalogue of the house, and will long be remembered by those who had to do with him for his kindness and liberality. He withdrew from the business in 1866 in favour of Karl Friedrich

Ludwig Gurckhaus (1821–84). The business was acquired by the brothers Linnemann in 1919.   G., addns.

KIT, a tiny violin, formerly carried by dancing-masters in their pockets. Hence the French and German names for it were 'pochette'

and 'Taschengeige,' though pochette is also applied to an instrument of long and narrow form resembling a sourdine. It was usually about 16 inches long over all : the woodcut shows its size relatively to that of the violin. Sometimes, however, the neck was longer and broader,[1] for convenience of fingering, which gave the Kit a disproportioned look (see also *PLATE LXXXVII.* No. 5).

The origin of the name may be connected with the beginning of some form of the word Cithara.[2] In Florio (1598 and 1611), Beaumont and Fletcher, Ben Jonson and Drayton, it seems evident that it is used without reference to size as a synonym for Crowd, Rebeck or Pandora. Cotgrave (1611) defines it as ' a small Gitterne.' Grew, in 1681, speaks of ' a dancing-master's Kit,' and as dancing-masters' Kits would naturally be smaller than other Kits, the name gradually adhered to them, as that of viol or violin did to the larger sizes. G.

KITCHINER, WILLIAM (*b.* London, 1775 ; *d.* there, Feb. 27, 1827), M.D. (Glasgow), an accomplished amateur musician, the son of a coal merchant, from whom he inherited an ample fortune, was educated at Eton. He composed an operetta entitled ' Love among the Roses, or, The Master Key,' and was author of *Observations on Vocal Music,* 1821, and editor of ' The Loyal and National Songs of England,' 1823 ; ' The Sea Songs of England,' 1823 ; ' The Sea Songs of Charles Dibdin,' 1824 ; and ' A Collection of the Vocal Music in

[1] Examples were Nos. 61*h* and 66 of the Special Exhibition of Ancient Musical Instruments, South Kensington Mus., 1872.
[2] Murray's *Dict.*

Shakspere's Plays.' He was also author of some eccentrically written but useful books, including *The Cook's Oracle* (1817), *The Art of Invigorating and Prolonging Life* (1822), *The Housekeeper's Ledger* (1825), *The Economy of the Eyes* (1824), *The Traveller's Oracle* (1827). (The titles of other books are given in the *D.N.B.*) In his fine musical library was the MS. collection of airs containing the supposed original of ' God save the King,' which, coming after Kitchiner's death into the possession of Richard Clark, was tampered with and has now totally disappeared.   W. H. H.; addns. F. K.

KITTEL, JOHANN CHRISTIAN (*b.* Erfurt, Feb. 18, 1732 ; *d.* there, May 18, 1809), one of the last pupils of J. S. Bach.

His first post was that of organist at Langensalza (1751), which he left in 1756 for that of the Predigerkirche at his native place. His pay was wretched, and had to be eked out by incessant and laborious teaching. Even when nearly 70 he was forced to make a tour to Göttingen, Hanover, Hamburg and Altona. In the latter place he stayed for some time, to the delight of the musicians there, and published a book of tunes for the Schleswig-Holstein Church (*Neues Choralbuch*, Altona, 1803). Thence he crept home to Erfurt, where he died in great poverty, but was saved from actual starvation by a small pension allowed him by Prince Primas of Dalberg. The fame of his playing was very great, but is hardly maintained by his works, which are not very important. The best are grand preludes for the organ in two books (Peters) ; six sonatas and a fantasia for the clavier (Breitkopf) ; and an organ school (*Der angehende praktische Organist,* in three books, 1801–08 ; Erfurt, Beyer ; third edition, 1831). His papers were inherited by his pupil, C. H. Rinck, one of many famous organists who perfected themselves under him. Fétis tells us—and we may accept the story as true, since he was intimate with Rinck—that Kittel had inherited a full-sized portrait of Bach, and that when satisfied with his pupils he drew the curtain, and allowed them a sight of the picture as the best reward he could afford them. It is a story quite in accordance with the devotion which Bach is known to have inspired in those who had to do with him.   G.

KITTEL, KASPAR, a 16th - century composer, was sent to Italy for study from 1624–28 by the Elector of Saxony. He studied also under Heinrich Schütz. In 1630 he was teacher of the theorbo at Dresden ; in 1632 inspector of instruments ; later court organist, which position he still held in 1669. A follower of the school of Caccini, he composed arias and cantatas 1, 2, 3, and 4 v. with basso continuo, op. 1 (1638), edited in score by Naue, Halle, 1824.   E. V. D. S.

KJERULF, HALFDAN (*b.* Christiania, Sept.

15, 1815 ; *d.* Grefsen, near Christiania, Aug. 11, 1868), became known as a composer in Norway and the surrounding countries during the time of Norway's struggle for freedom, and the consequent renascence of her intellectual and artistic spirit.[1]

In 1834 he was a graduate of the Christiania University, and he had as a matter of course devoted himself to the study of jurisprudence, for his father's high post under Government would have ensured for him a good start in official life. On the death of his father in 1840, a decided step was at last taken by Halfdan Kjerulf, and he began his professional career at the age of 25. He settled down as a teacher of music, and published some simple songs even before he had been introduced to the theory of music by some resident foreigner. In 1850 or thereabouts Kjerulf had begun to attract public attention; the Government awarded to him a grant by which he was enabled to study for a year at Leipzig under Richter. On his return to Christiania he did his best to establish classical subscription concerts in that city, but with no lasting success. In 1860 he was in active co-operation with Björnson, who wrote for him many poems; and it was during these years—1860–65—that Kjerulf did his best work, resigned to a contemplative and lonely existence, and content to exercise a quiet influence upon those who sought him out. Grieg, amongst others, was very glad of the older master's moral support. The portraits of Kjerulf represent him with a mild and pensive face, with traces of pain in the expression. He had indeed suffered for long from extreme delicacy in the chest, and death overtook him when he had withdrawn to a retreat at Grefsen, near Christiania. A wave of deep emotion and sympathy, the fervour of which would have astonished the composer himself, passed over the country he had loved and served so well.

The value of Kjerulf's stirring quartets and choruses for men's voices, as reflecting the national sentiment in the way most acceptable to his countrymen, has already been commented on. As absolute music they are of slight interest, but by their vigour and their straightforward simplicity they may be said to possess all the virtue which belongs to complete appropriateness to the subject. His few pianoforte pieces fully maintain the highly artistic standard to which Kjerulf was always faithful. Consideration of the purely musical side of Kjerulf's songs shows the perfect genuineness of their inspiration, and also the limits of that inspiration in intellectual depth and power. Among the Northern ballads and lyrics are to be found some really characteristic and quaintly

fascinating ditties. Such are Björnson's ' Synnöve's Song,' ' Ingrid's Song,' ' Young Venevil,' ' Evening Song ' and the Scotch ' Taylor's Song,' Munch's ' Night on the Fjord,' Theodor Kjerulf's ' Longing.' Several songs that spring from Kjerulf's sojourn at Leipzig recall the influence of Schumann, while his treatment of some English poems is almost startling. The polished verses of Moore are made the vehicle of outpourings in which the gentle Kjerulf is seen in his most impassioned mood—for instance, ' Love thee, dearest, love thee.' ' My heart and lute,' on the other hand, has inspired the composer with an intensity of dreamy melancholy. Unfortunately a certain amount of licence has been taken in the settings, and where the poem as a whole gains by the suggestiveness of the music, the lines and words now and then suffer from false accentuation. This is especially the case with some familiar verses by the late Lord Houghton. It would be impossible to enumerate all that is worthy of note in the collection of more than one hundred songs by Kjerulf ; but notice must be taken of the successful colouring of some Spanish subjects, and of the pleasing settings of Victor Hugo's Romances. Many of the songs are familiar to English amateurs through the compilation by T. Marzials, published by Messrs. Stanley Lucas, Weber & Co. Further testimony to the value of the Norwegian composer's work can be read in the *Musikalisches Wochenblatt* of Jan. 24, 1879, in an article from the pen of Edward Grieg.   L. M. M.

KLAFSKY, KATHARINA (*b.* Szt. Janos, Wieselburg, Hungary, Sept. 19, 1855 ; *d.* Sept. 22, 1896), famous Wagnerian singer, was the daughter of a poor shoemaker. In 1870 her mother died, and she left home for Oedenburg, where she had to beg her daily bread. Later she went to Vienna and entered service there as a nurserymaid. Her singing attracted the attention of her employers, who introduced her to Neuwirth, the organist of the Elizabeth Kirche, who gave her instruction. She was engaged in 1874 as a chorus-singer at the Komische Oper. There her voice attracted the attention of the conductor, the younger Hellmesberger, who induced Mme. Marchesi to teach her gratuitously. She was engaged in 1875 at Salzburg as a chorus-singer. In 1876 she married a merchant of Leipzig, and for a very brief space of time retired from the stage, but circumstances compelled her to accept an offer of Angelo Neumann to play small parts at the Leipzig theatre. From 1876–82 she gradually won recognition as Venus in ' Tannhäuser,' and especially, Jan. 2, 1882, as Brangäne, on the production of ' Tristan ' at Leipzig. In this last part she made a great success, after a fortnight's study only under the tuition of Paul Geisler, then chorus-master at Leipzig. In the same year she accompanied Neumann

[1] For a full account of Kjerulf as the representative of his country, and for extracts from his letters and details of his private life, the reader may be referred to the articles *Halfdan Kjerulf*, by Henrik Sundt, in the *Musical World* of Oct. 1, 8 and 15, 1887.

on his ' Nibelungen ' tour, still in an inferior capacity, and when the Trilogy was produced at Her Majesty's Theatre, London, Frau Klafsky's modest débuts were made, May 5 and 6, as Wellgunde (' Rheingold ') and Waltraute (' Walküre '). From 1883–86 she played all the principal parts, and in 1885 played the title part in a revival of Geisler's ' Ingeborg.' From 1886–95 she was the principal singer at Hamburg, and established her reputation as one of the greatest artists in Germany in an extraordinary number of parts. She also sang in opera and concerts at Stuttgart, the Rhenish Festival at Cologne, at St. Petersburg, etc. On July 2 she reappeared in England at Drury Lane in ' Fidelio,' and made an immediate success as Leonora, as Brünnhilde in the ' Trilogy,' and as Isolde and Elizabeth, singing both at Drury Lane and Covent Garden. In 1894 she made a welcome reappearance at Drury Lane, and sang for the first time here as Elsa, and Agatha in ' Der Freischütz.' Later in the year she sang at the Lamoureux Concerts, Paris. In the autumn she and her third husband, Otto Lohse, went to North America as principal singer and conductor of the Damrosch German Opera Company. In Aug. 1896 Frau Klafsky reappeared at Hamburg as Elizabeth, and on Sept. 11 appeared on the stage for the last time as Fidelio. Her life was written by Ludwig Ordemann (Fuendeling, Hameln and Leipzig, 1903), and has been of material assistance in the preparation of this notice.   A. C.

KLAPPENHORN. Horns of the bugle type, fitted with keys to close or open side-holes, preceded those with the cylinder or valve action. They all come under the Klappenhorn group in German nomenclature and comprised instruments in various pitches, from soprano to bass. The alto instrument in C or B flat, corresponding to the English ' Key ' or ' Kent-bugle,' (see *PLATE LXXIV.* No. 9) was (and still is when fitted with pistons) known more particularly as the Flügel horn. (See BASS-HORN, BUGLE, FLÜGEL HORN.)   D. J. B.

KLEBER, LEONHARD (*b.* Göppingen, Würtemberg, *c.* 1490; *d.* 1556), organist at Pforzheim, Baden, is known as the writer and compiler (from 1520–24) of a large MS. collection of organ and clavier music, in old tablature notation, now in the State Library, Berlin. A full account of the work will be found in Ritter's *Geschichte des Orgelspiels*, pp. 103-5, also in a monograph by H. Löwenfeld, Berlin, 1897. It has two parts, one for clavier alone in 3-part harmony, the second part requiring the use of the pedals. There are in all 116 pieces, some with the names of their composers, consisting of a certain number of preludes in various keys, described as being in *ut, re, mi, fa, sol* with and without B flat, *la* with and without B flat, and a large number of fantasias and organ arrange-

ments of sacred and secular songs. Ritter says :

'The whole collection shows the South German organ-playing in a very advantageous light; it extends and completes the work begun by Schlick, on whose principles it is based.'

Seventeen preludes and a fantasia are given in modern notation in the *M.f.M.*, 1888, and three other pieces by Ritter.   J. R. M.

KLEEBERG, CLOTILDE (*b.* Paris, June 27, 1866; *d.* Brussels, Feb. 7, 1909), was educated at the Conservatoire under Mme. Emile Réty and Mme. Massart, where she carried off the first piano prize at 12 years of age. Shortly afterwards she played Beethoven's C minor concerto with conspicuous success at one of Pasdeloup's concerts, and from that time onwards she made annual appearances at all the most important Parisian concerts. In 1883 she came to England, and appeared at a recital, at Mann's benefit at the Crystal Palace, and elsewhere. In the following year she appeared at the Philharmonic Society, and at all the first-rate London concerts. Richter, hearing her play in a private house, engaged her forthwith for the Philharmonic Concerts at Vienna, where she made a great success, as she did in Berlin in 1887, where Von Bülow greeted her with enthusiasm. She married the sculptor, Charles Samuel, and settled in Brussels. Her interpretative power was very remarkable, and her vigorous, artistic and unaffected playing was fully appreciated wherever she was heard. She was perhaps at her best in Bach and Schumann, and she made a speciality of the works of the old French clavecinistes.   M.

KLEIN, BERNHARD (*b.* Cologne, Mar. 6, 1793; *d.* Berlin, Sept. 9, 1832), a composer, whose father was a bass-player in Cologne. In 1812 he found means to get to Paris, where Cherubini's advice, the hearing of fine performers, and the study of the library of the Conservatoire, advanced him greatly. On his return to the Rhine he conducted the performances in Cologne Cathedral, and profited by an acquaintance with Thibaut and his fine library at Heidelberg. His first important works were a Mass (1816) and a Cantata on Schiller's ' Worte des Glaubens ' (1817). In 1819 he was sent officially to Berlin to make acquaintance with Zelter's system of teaching, and to apply it in Cologne Cathedral. He, however, found it more profitable to remain in Berlin, where he became connected with the Institut für Kirchenmusik, then recently established, and was made director of music and teacher of singing in the University. These occupations in no wise checked his productivity. He composed many sonatas and songs, an oratorio, ' Job ' (Leipzig, 1820), and two grand operas, ' Dido,' to Rellstab's text (1823), and ' Ariadne ' (1825). In 1823 he married and went to Rome, where he enjoyed intercourse with Baini, and copied from the ancient treasures of music there. On his return to Berlin he composed an oratorio, ' Jephthah,' for the Cologne Festival, 1828, and another, ' David,' for Halle, 1830.[1] He died suddenly in Berlin. Besides the compositions already mentioned, he left a Mass in D, a Paternoster for eight voices, a Magnificat and Responsoria for six voices, an opera, ' Irene,' and an oratorio, both nearly finished, eight books of psalms, hymns, and motets for men's voices, and other pieces both sacred and secular. His vocal music was much used by singing societies after his death. Hullah reprinted one of the 4-part psalms, ' Like as the hart,' in his collection called ' Vocal Scores.' It is sweet, dignified, religious music, very vocal in its phrases.   G.

KLEIN, HERMAN (b. Norwich, July 23, 1856), an able critic and teacher of singing, who was himself a pupil of Manuel Garcia. He edited Garcia's *Hints on Singing*, taught at the G.S.M. for 13 years, and has trained many professional singers privately.

Klein began work as a musical journalist in 1875 in London, was critic to *The Sunday Times* (1881–1901), and at the end of this period produced his book *Thirty Years of Musical Life in London* (1903), a valuable chronicle. He spent the years 1902–09 in America and wrote much for the *New York Herald*. Returning to England he resettled in London, resumed teaching work, and has been active in many musical and other societies, notably the Critic's Circle, of which he became chairman in 1924. He wrote *The Reign of Patti* (1920), the official life of the great singer, whom he had known personally and for whom he retained an unbounded admiration. *The Art of the Bel Canto* (1924), which followed, may be described as a study in Patti's method. A second book of chronicles, *Musicians and Mummers*, more an autobiography than its predecessor was, appeared in 1925. He was a contributor to the second edition of this Dictionary as well as to the present one.   c.

KLEINHEINZ, FRANZ XAVER (b. Mindelheim, Algäu, July 3, 1772 ; d. ? Budapest, c. 1832). After studying at Memmingen, he joined the Munich orchestra, went to Vienna c. 1803, where he studied under Albrechtsberger, and arranged Beethoven's pianoforte sonatas for string quartet. He was for a time Kapellmeister at Brünn, and in 1809 was in the service of Count Brunswick at Budapest. He composed a Mass, 2 operas, 1 cantata, settings of some of Schiller's poems, quintet for wind instruments, clarinet trio, pianoforte concerto, violin and pianoforte sonatas, etc. (Thayer's *Beethoven*; *Mendel*; *Q.-L.*).

KLEINKNECHT, a remarkable family of musicians. (1) A 17th-18th century Kleinknecht is represented with a piece in a lute-

book in the Augsburg town library (*Q.-L.*). (2) JOHANN, an early 18th century Konzertmeister and second organist at Ulm Cathedral. (3) JOHANN WOLFGANG, eldest son of Johann (2) (b. Ulm, Apr. 17, 1715 ; d. Anspach, Feb. 20, 1786), studied the violin under his father, with whom he toured as a prodigy c. 1723. He was chamber musician at Stuttgart in 1733, after filling similar positions at Eisenach and Bayreuth (1738), whence the court chapel was transferred to Anspach in 1769. He was one of the best violinists and orchestral leaders of his time. According to *Q.-L.* the Brussels Conservatoire possesses in MS. a violin concerto with orchestra. The authorship of the 3 sonatas for 2 violoncelli, given in the same place, is at least doubtful, as no Christian name is given on the title-page. (4) JAKOB FRIEDRICH, (b. Ulm, June 8, 1722 ; d. Anspach, Aug. 4, 1794) second son of Johann (2) In 1743 he was flautist, in 1747 violinist, in 1749 second Konzertmeister, then court-composer, and in 1761 Kapellmeister at the Bayreuth court. He composed sinfonia concertata, concerto 2 flutes and orchestra, 5 trios, 2 flutes and bass, sonatas for flute, for violin, for pianoforte, etc. (see *Q.-L.*). (5) JOHANN STEPHAN, third son of JOHANN (2) (b. Ulm, Sept. 17, 1731 ; d. Anspach, c. 1803), studied the flute under his father, followed his brothers to Bayreuth in 1750, where he completed his studies under Döbbert and Götzel and became a member of the court chapel. In 1766 he toured successfully in Germany, and followed the chapel to Anspach in 1769. His autobiography appeared in Cramer, i. 772, and again in J. J. Meusel's ' Miscellaneen,' Part 12, p. 334.   E. V. d. S.

KLEINMICHEL, RICHARD (b. Posen, Dec. 31, 1846; d. Charlottenburg, Aug. 18, 1901), pianist and composer, received his first instruction from his father (Friedrich H. H. Kleinmichel, 1827–94, a military and operatic conductor). In 1863–66 he completed his studies at the Leipzig Conservatorium, and settled at Hamburg, where he published many works of some importance, mostly for his own instrument. His second orchestral symphony was given at the Gewandhaus at Leipzig with success. In that town he held for some time the position of Kapellmeister at the Stadttheater, and subsequently held similar posts at Danzig and Magdeburg. His first opera, ' Manon,' was successfully produced at Hamburg in 1883, and his ' Pfeifer von Dusenbach ' at the same place in 1891. He has also made ' simplified ' arrangements of the pianoforte scores of Wagner's later works.   M.

KLEMM. This well-known Leipzig music publishing firm and circulating library was founded in 1821 by Carl August Klemm in the house known as the ' Hohe Lilie,' 14 in the Neumarkt. Klemm succeeded Wieck, the father of Madame Schumann, who had for some time carried on a musical lending library on the premises. In 1847 the house opened a branch at Chemnitz, and in 1856 at Dresden. Among the original publications of the house are to be found the names of J. S. Bach, Dotzauer, F. Abt, Dreyschock, Mendelssohn, Schumann (opp. 34, 35), Lachner, F. Schneider, Julius Rietz, Marschner, etc. etc.   G.

KLEMM (KLEMME), JOHANN (*b.* Oederan, near Zwickau, Saxony, before 1600 ; *d.* after 1651), was received as a boy into the choir of the Electoral Chapel at Dresden. He was afterwards sent, by the Elector Johann Georg I., for his further musical education, to Christian Erbach at Augsburg, with whom he remained from 1613–15. Returning to Dresden he became the pupil of Heinrich Schütz for composition, and was appointed court organist in 1625. He deserves honourable mention in musical history as having generously undertaken the publication of several of the works of Schütz, when Schütz was unable to bring them out at his own expense. The work by which he himself is known as a composer is an instrumental work entitled, ' Partitura seu Tabulatura Italica, exhibens 36 fugas, 2, 3 et 4 vocibus, ad duodecim consuetos tonos musicos compositas . . . non tantum organo sed aliis quoque instrumentis accommodatas,' Dresden, 1631. On this work see Seiffert-Fleischer, *Geschichte der Klaviermusik*, Bd. I. p. 101. (For other works see *Q.-L.*)   J. R. M.

KLENAU, PAUL VON (*b.* Copenhagen, Feb. 2, 1883), composer and conductor, studied the violin with Hilmer, and composition with Otto Malling at Copenhagen.

In 1902 he went to Berlin and entered the Hochschule, continuing the violin with Halir and composition with Max Bruch. Proceeding to Munich, he had lessons with Ludwig Thuille until joining the opera at Freiburg i. B. in 1907. The following year he was appointed to the opera at Stuttgart, and took the opportunity of working further with Max Schillings. In 1914 he returned for a time to Freiburg and thereupon settled again at Copenhagen in order to devote himself chiefly to composition. His gifts as conductor and his interest in modern music led to the foundation of the Copenhagen Philharmonic (Dansk filharmonisk Selskab), which he still directs. He is also director of the Wiener Konzerthausgesellschaft and of the Singakademie in Vienna. His work as a conductor is animated with a sincere enthusiasm, which easily communicates itself to the orchestra. In Denmark he has played the part of a pioneer, introducing the works of numerous contemporary composers of all countries. In Vienna and in Central Europe he is noted for his performances of Delius, and was chosen to conduct the festival concert given at Frankfort in 1924, on the occasion of the composer's sixtieth birthday. In 1925 he conducted, at

a Philharmonic concert in London, Delius's ' A Mass of Life,' which he had given some months previously in Vienna. He also directed the first Viennese performance of Milhaud's ' L'homme et son désir ' and of the revised version of Schönberg's ' Gurre-Lieder.'

As a composer his most important works are the opera ' Gudrun auf Island ' (a revised and more concise version of ' Kjartan und Gudrun ') and the series of symphonic poems or ' fantasies ' based upon Dante's Inferno. This cycle originated in a Dante symphony, which was performed at Dresden in 1913 and afterwards modified. It now comprises three sections, to which, however, more may be added. The ' Paolo and Francesca ' section, originally the slow movement of the symphony, was written as far back as 1904, and, though attractive musically, is less representative of the composer than the later sections. A ballet, ' Klein Idas Blumen ' (after Andersen), produced at Stuttgart in 1916, has been performed on several of the more important stages of Central Europe. It is graceful, unpretentious music, and contains a waltz which has become popular. Apart from a feeling for harmonic warmth, the most salient attributes of Klenau's music are its lyrical quality and its sensitiveness to ' mood.'

OPERAS

' Sulamith.' (Munich, 1908. Bruno Walter.)
' Kjartan und Gudrun.' (Mannheim, 1918. Furtwängler.) Revised version ' Gudrun auf Island.' 1924.

BALLET

' Klein Idas Blumen ' (after Andersen). (Stuttgart, 1916.)

ORCHESTRA

Three Symphonies.
Inferno ' fantasies ' :
    1. Descent to Hell.
    2. Paolo and Francesca.
    3. Ugolino.
' Bank Holiday—Souvenir of Hampstead Heath.'

VOICE AND ORCHESTRA

' Die Weise von Liebe und Tod des Cornet Christof Rilke ' (baritone solo, chor. and orch.).
' Ebbe Skammalsen,' ballad (baritone and orch.).
' Gespräche mit dem Tode ' (contralto and orch.).
' Hiob,' choral work in preparation (1925).
String Quartet in E minor. Several sets of piano pieces
                                   E. E.

KLENGEL, AUGUST ALEXANDER (*b.* Dresden Jan. 27, 1783 ; *d.* there, Nov. 22, 1852), son of a well-known portrait and landscape painter, first studied music with Milchmayer, inventor of a piano which could produce fifty different qualities of tone (see Cramer's *Magazin der Musik*, i. 10). In 1803 Clementi visited Dresden, and on his departure Klengel went with him as his pupil. The two separated on Clementi's marriage in Berlin, but, the young wife dying shortly after, they went together to Russia, where Klengel remained till 1811. He then spent two years studying in Paris, returned to Dresden in 1814, went to London in 1815, and in the following year was appointed court organist at Dresden, which remained his home till his death. During a visit to Paris in 1828 he formed a close friendship with Fétis, who with other musicians was much interested in his pianoforte canons. Of these he published only ' Les Avant-coureurs ' (Paul, Dresden,

1841).   After his death Hauptmann edited the
' Canons et fugues ' (Breitkopf & Härtel, 1854),
with a preface, in which he says :

> ' Klengel was brought up on Sebastian Bach, and
> knew his works thoroughly.   It must not be supposed,
> however, that he was a mere imitator of Bach's
> manner ; it is truer to say that he expressed his own
> thoughts in the way in which Bach would have done
> had he lived at the present day.'

He left several concertos, and many other
works.   His visit to London was commemorated
by the composition of a quintet for piano and
strings for the Philharmonic Society, which was
performed Feb. 26, 1816, he himself taking the
pianoforte.   There is a pleasant little sketch of
him in a letter of Mendelssohn to Eckert, Jan.
26, 1842.   F. G.

KLENGEL, (1) JULIUS (*b.* Leipzig, Sept. 24,
1859), violoncellist and composer.   He came
of a musical family, his father, a Professor of
Law, being the son of a professional musician,
and himself an excellent amateur player.
Moreover, his sister and brothers were all
skilled performers on either piano or strings, so
that the family circle was in a position to provide a full pianoforte quintet.   Julius showed
exceptional musical gifts at a very early age,
and when still quite a small boy was intimate,
through these family performances, with all the
best chamber-music, an experience to which he
constantly refers with gratitude both for its
educational value and its sheer musical delight.
He studied the violoncello with Émile Hegar,
and theory and composition with S. Jadassohn.
In 1874, at the age of 15, he became a member
of the famous Gewandhaus Orchestra, and in
1881 was appointed its principal violoncellist,
a post which he held until his resignation in
1924.   He was appointed, also in 1881, teacher
at the Leipzig Conservatorium, with the title of
' Royal Professor,' and he still carries on his
duties there.

Klengel began his career as soloist in 1875,
since when he has travelled repeatedly over the
greater part of Europe, including the British
Isles, both as soloist and with the Gewandhaus
Quartet, of which he is still a member.   On his
leaving the orchestra in 1924 after fifty years'
service, his ' Jubiläum ' was celebrated with
great enthusiasm.   At the first Gewandhaus
Concert of that season, on Oct. 9, with Furtwängler conducting, he played the violoncello
part in a fine double concerto for violin and
violoncello, which he had specially composed
for the occasion.   It is an interesting coincidence that his grandfather had also played, as
a first violin, for 50 years in the Gewandhaus
Orchestra, without missing a single concert.

As a performer Klengel ranks very high on
the musical as well as on the purely technical
side.   He makes his effects by subtlety of
accent and emphasis rather than by violent
contrasts or emotional climaxes.   He is a fine
and scholarly musician, with an admirable

taste and sense of style, and nowhere is this
more conspicuous than when he is taking part
in chamber-music or interpreting such music
as the Beethoven sonatas or the Bach solo-
suites.   On the technical side there is probably
no one who has surpassed him.   His least strong
point is in the matter of tone, which, though
clear and effective, is a little lacking in beauty
of quality.   He is an admirable teacher and has
trained many hundreds of pupils, of whom
Mme. Suggia, Paul Grümmer and Emanuel
Feuermann are probably the best known.   He
has composed a great deal of excellent music,
without perhaps any pronounced individuality
of idiom but showing a fine gift of melody and
finished workmanship.   He has also edited
many works of other composers—concertos,
sonatas, Bach suites, etc.—and has written a
large number of first-rate technical exercises.
Amongst his best compositions are the second
concerto for violoncello in D minor, the double
concerto for two violoncellos in E minor, the
' Caprice in the form of a Chaconne ' for violoncello alone, and the double concerto, already
referred to, for violin and violoncello.   Mention
should also be made of the beautiful ' Hymnus '
for 12 violoncellos, which was performed at
Nikisch's funeral service and has been repeated
many times since.

(2) PAUL (*b.* Leipzig, May 13, 1854), violinist,
pianist and composer, elder brother of the
above, was a pupil of the Leipzig Conservatorium from 1868–72 and afterwards graduated
at Leipzig University, and in 1876 took the
degree of Doctor of Philosophy with a dissertation on ' Æsthetic in Music.'   He conducted the ' Euterpe ' Concerts at Leipzig,
1881–86 ;   was second Hofkapellmeister in
Stuttgart, 1887–91 ;   conducted the ' Arion '
and ' Singakademie ' choral Societies at
Leipzig, 1892–98 ;   was conductor of the
' Deutsche Liederkranz ' in New York from
1898–1903, and then returned to Leipzig as
conductor of the ' Arion ' Society.   He is now
(1925) on the teaching staff of the Leipzig
Conservatorium.

He is a man of wide general culture and an
admirable example of the good all-round
musician.   As a violinist he possesses a sound
and competent technique, especially of the left
hand, but he is not the ' born violinist,' and it
is probably unfortunate that he did not concentrate in his youth on the piano, for which he
has very high natural qualifications, including
an exquisite touch, which makes him an ideal
accompanist.   He is a gifted composer, especially of songs and pieces in small form.   His
compositions, without any marked originality,
are beautifully finished in their workmanship,
and deserve to be better known than they are.
In particular, his two suites for violin would
make a pleasant addition to the repertory of any
violinist, for they are both attractive as music

and capitally written for showing off the possibilities of the instrument. He has done a great deal of ' arranging,' in which he shows exceptional skill and tact, occasionally amounting almost to genius. His arrangement of Brahms's clarinet quintet as a pianoforte and violin sonata is one of the best examples. It sounds at least as beautiful as the three genuine pianoforte and violin sonatas, and it won Brahms's enthusiastic approval, as well as Joachim's, who played it in public on more than one occasion with Professor Paul Klengel himself.
H. B.

KLENOVSKY, Nicholas Semenovich (b. Odessa, 1857), composer and conductor, was a pupil of the Moscow Conservatoire, under Hubert and Tchaikovsky. He was selected by N. Rubinstein to assist him in organising the first performance of Tchaikovsky's ' Eugene Oniegin ' (1879). Klenovsky was afterwards conductor of the University orchestra, and assistant conductor at the Imperial Opera, Moscow. Deeply interested in all that concerned racial music, he was associated with Melgounov (q.v.) in collecting and harmonising the Russian folk-songs. In 1893 he became director of the Music School at Tiflis, which gave him the opportunity of studying the music of the various Caucasian races. He was the first to organise ' Ethnographical Concerts ' in Russia. In 1902 he was appointed sub-director of the Imperial Chapel. He composed several successful ballets ; incidental music to plays, ' Messaline,' ' Antony and Cleopatra,' etc. ; cantatas and a ' Georgian Liturgy ' a cappella (1902). R. N.

KLIČKA, Josef (b. Klatovy, 1855), Czech composer, attended the Organ School as a pupil of Skuherský and began his musical life as an organist. From 1876–81 he acted as assistant conductor at the Czech theatre ; choirmaster of the choral society Hlahol from 1890–97 ; professor of organ in the master-school of the Prague Conservatoire since 1920. He has composed much music for choir and organ: the cantatas, 'The burial on the Kaňk'; 'The coming of the Czechs to the Říp-hill'; A Ballad of Czech music, ' Blaník '; some choral works of a humorous character—' The Goodman of the Mill,' ' The Gnat, ' The Thistle,' etc. ; masses, concert-fantasias for organ (his ' Fantasia on the Choral, St. Wenceslaus ' and ' Legend' are published in the 'Maîtres contemporains d'orgue,' Paris) ; an organ sonata in F sharp minor; some chamber music. R. N.

KLINDWORTH, Karl (b. Hanover, Sept. 25, 1830 ; d. Stolpe, July 27, 1916), was in early youth an accomplished performer on the violin. From his 17th to his 19th year he acted as conductor to a travelling opera troupe ; he then settled in Hanover and took to playing the piano and composing. In 1852 he went to Weimar to study pianoforte-playing under

Liszt, and had Hans von Bülow, W. Mason and Dionys Pruckner as his fellow-pupils.

In 1854 he came to London, where he remained fourteen years, appearing in public at intervals as a pianist and conductor of orchestral concerts, but in the main living the quiet life of a student and teacher. His first appearance in London was at one of Ella's ' Musical Winter Evenings ' on Mar. 30, 1854, and he played Henselt's concerto at the New Philharmonic concert on July 4, 1855. He organised two series of three chamber concerts in the spring of 1861 and 1862, and a series of three orchestral and vocal concerts in the summer of 1861, under the title of the ' Musical Art Union.' The most remarkable compositions brought forward at the latter were Rubinstein's ' Ocean ' symphony ; Gade's ' Erl King's Daughter '; Cherubini's Requiem, No. 1 ; Schumann's PF. concerto. They were well carried out, but were discontinued for want of capital. In 1868 Klindworth was appointed to the post of professor of the pianoforte at the Conservatorium of Moscow, and while there he brought out the works which have made his name famous, the pianoforte scores of Wagner's ' Der Ring des Nibelungen,' begun during Wagner's visit to England in 1855, and his critical edition of Chopin ; the latter beyond all praise for rare insight into the text and minute care bestowed on the presentation of it ; the former quite wonderful for the fidelity with which the transcript is contrived to reflect Wagner's complicated orchestration. In 1882 he returned to Germany, and was conductor of the Berlin Philharmonic Concerts, jointly with Joachim and Wüllner, and was also conductor of the Berlin Wagner Society. He established a school of music in Berlin, which existed until 1893, when he retired to Potsdam, and devoted himself to private teaching. He visited London once again to conduct a concert given by F. Dawson, on May 15, 1898.[1] His arrangement of Schubert's symphony in C major for two pianofortes, and the four-hand arrangement of Tchaikovsky's poème symphonique, ' Francesca da Rimini,' as also, amongst his original compositions, a very difficult and effective polonaise fantaisie for pianoforte, should be particularly mentioned. The manuscripts of a masterly rescoring of Chopin's concerto in F minor, and a condensation and orchestration of C. V. Alkan's concerto in G♯ minor (Études, op. 39), were well known to his friends. The new version of Chopin's concerto has been often played, and in the opinion of a large class of musicians the work is improved thereby, though others consider that the slighter accompaniment designed by the composer is really more effective. E. D., with addns.

KLINGENSTEIN, Bernhard. From 1575–1614 (the time of his death) he was priest and

Kapellmeister at Augsburg Cathedral. In 1580 he was still studying under J. de Cleve. He composed ' Rosetum Marianum ' (1604) ; ' Sacr. Symphoniarum,' Book i. (1607); single numbers are in various collective volumes (*Riemann*; *Q.-L.*).

KLÖFFLER (KLÖFLER), JOHANN FRIEDRICH (*d.* Castle Steinfurt, near Münster, 1792), a late 18th century flute virtuoso and instrumental composer. He was Kapellmeister of Count Bentheim-Steinfurt, Castle Steinfurt, near Münster, *c.* 1787. He composed a piece of programme music, ' The Battle,' which he produced in 1782 in Berlin and in 1783 in London. He wrote : *Zergliederung eines Instrumental Tonstückes von . . . 1787* (probably the analytical programme of the above) ; composed symphonies, flute-concertos, trios 2 flutes and basso continuo ; quartets 4 flutes, a nonet, sonatas, etc.   E. V. D. S.

KLOTZ, the name of a numerous family of violin-makers who lived at the little town of Mittenwald, in the Bavarian Alps, and founded a manufacture of stringed instruments which makes Mittenwald to this day only less famous than Markneukirchen in Saxony, and Mirécourt in the Vosges.

A variety of the pine, locally known as the ' Hasel-fichte ' (Bechstein calls it the ' harte oder späte Roth-tanne '), of delicate but strong and highly resonant fibre, flourishes in the Bavarian Alps. The abundance of this material, which the ingenious peasants of the neighbouring Ammerthal use for wood-carving, led to the rise of the Mittenwald violin manufacture. For about two centuries there was held in the town a famous fair, greatly frequented by Venetian and other traders. In 1679 this fair was removed to Botzen, and the Mittenwalders attribute the rise of the violin industry to the distress which thereupon ensued.

(1) EGIDIUS KLOTZ had already made violins at Mittenwald. Tradition says that he learned the craft from Stainer at Absam. He is more likely to have learned it from seeing Stainer's violins, which he imitated with success. His son, (2) MATTHIAS or MATTHEW (1653–1743), followed in the same path. He travelled, however, into Italy, sojourning both at Florence and Cremona. Tradition reports him to have returned to Mittenwald about 1683, and to have at once begun to instruct many of the impoverished Mittenwalders in the mystery of fiddle-making. The instruments found a ready sale. They were hawked about by the makers at the churches, castles and monasteries of South Germany ; and Mittenwald began to recover its prosperity. Most of the instruments of Matthias Klotz date from 1670–96. They are well built, on the model of Stainer, but poorly varnished.

His son (3) SEBASTIAN surpassed him as a maker. His instruments, though Stainer-like in appearance, are larger in size, of flatter model, and better designed : and his varnish is often of a good Italian quality. Another son of Matthias, (4) JOSEPH, still has a good reputation as a maker.

Until about the middle of the 18th century, a distinctive German style prevailed in violins, of which the above-mentioned makers are the best exponents. In several towns of Italy there were Germans working in their own style side by side with Italian makers. Tecchler worked thus in Rome, Mann in Naples, and the three Gofrillers (Gottfriedl) in Venice. It is certain, too, that there was a demand for German violins in Cremona itself. Two Germans, named Pfretschner and Fricker, who made violins of their own ugly pattern, gained a subsistence there in the golden days of Stradivarius : and the famous Veracini always used a German violin. But this competition could not long endure. The superiority of the Italian violin was established in the earlier half of the century : and wherever stringed instruments were made, imitation of the Italian models began. It penetrated to Mittenwald, as it did to London and Paris.

This stage of the art is represented by (5) GEORG KLOTZ, whose fiddles date from 1750–1770. They have lost their distinctive Tyrolese cut, without gaining the true Italian style, and are covered with a thin brittle spirit varnish, laid upon a coat of size, which keeps the varnish from penetrating the wood, and renders it opaque and perishable. Besides George, we hear of (6) MICHAEL, (7) CHARLES and (8) EGIDIUS, second of the name. Nine-tenths of the violins which pass in the world as ' Stainers ' were made by the Klotz family and their followers.

     E. J. P.

KLUGHARDT, AUGUST FRIEDRICH MARTIN (*b.* Cöthen, Nov. 30, 1847 ; *d.* Dessau, Aug. 3, 1902), was for twenty years a theatrical conductor before becoming court music-director, first at Weimar in 1869, then at Neustrelitz in 1873, and at Dessau in 1882. Under Liszt's influence he threw himself into the modern school of music, but stopped short of the extremes towards which many of Liszt's followers were led. Five overtures, five symphonies, two suites, concertos for oboe, violin and violoncello respectively, the oratorios ' Die Grablegung Christi,' ' Die Zerstörung Jerusalems ' (his best-known work), and ' Judith,' two psalms for soli and chorus, and much chamber music, represent his chief work apart from the stage, to which he contributed ' Miriam ' (Weimar, 1871), ' Iwein ' (1879), and ' Gudrun ' (1882), both produced at Neustrelitz), and ' Die Hochzeit des Mönchs ' (Dessau, 1886), given as ' Astorre ' at Prague in 1888. (*Riemann.*)

KNABE & COMPANY, an eminent firm of American pianoforte manufacturers with headquarters in Baltimore. Its founder, William

Knabe, was born in Kreutzburg, Saxe-Weimar, in 1797, and died in Baltimore in 1864. He began the business of making pianofortes in 1837, and some years later entered into partnership with Henry Gaehle. In 1854 he bought the latter's interests, and associated his son, Ernst (1837–94), with him, as also another son William (1841–89) a little later, and a son-in-law, Charles Keidel. In 1908 the firm was merged in the American Piano Co.   H. E. K.

KNAPP, WILLIAM (b. 1698 ; d. 1768), the author of a L.M. psalm tune called ' Wareham,' which was long a favourite in churches. He was parish clerk of Poole. He published a ' New Sett of Psalms and Anthems in four parts ' in 1738 (2nd edition, 1741, 3rd, 1747, all from engraved plates, 4th, 1750, 7th, 1762, 8th, 1770, the latter from type). In 1753 appeared ' The New Church Melody ' which was re-issued in 1756 and 1764, the last being the 5th edition. ' Wareham ' is in both—in the former called ' Blandford,' and in common time, in the latter in triple time. Another tune by him is given by the Rev. Henry Parr, *Church of England Psalmody.* (Information from Rev. H. Parr, the parish clerk of Poole, J. F. R. Stainer and F. Kidson.)   G.

KNAPTON, PHILIP (b. York, 1788 ; d. there, June 20, 1833), received his musical education at Cambridge from Dr. Hague. He then returned to York and followed his profession. He composed several overtures, pianoforte concertos and other orchestral works, besides arranging numerous pieces for the pianoforte and harp. He acted as one of the assistant conductors at the York Festivals of 1823, 1825 and 1828. His father, Samuel Knapton, was a music-publisher in Blake Street, and afterwards in Coney Street, York, at the end of the 18th century. Philip and others of the family, together with a York musician named White, kept on the business until about 1840, when it passed into the hands of a person named Banks.

                W. H. H. ; addns. F. K.

KNECHT, JUSTIN HEINRICH (b. Biberach, Suabia, Sept. 30, 1752 ; d. there, Dec. 1, 1817), received a good education, both musical and general (Boeckh was one of his masters), and filled for some time the post of professor of literature in his native town. He combined with this the office of music-director from the year 1771. By degrees he gravitated to music, and in 1807 became director of the opera and of the court concerts at Stuttgart ; but owing to successful intrigues against him, in a couple of years he resigned the post and returned to Biberach, where he died, with a great reputation as organist, composer and theoretician. In the last-named department he was an adherent of Vogler. The list of his productions as given in *Q.-L.* embraces many compositions, sacred and secular, vocal and instrumental, and eight theoretical and didactic works. Two of the

former have an historical interest, and that from an accidental cause. The first is ' Le Portrait Musical de la Nature,' a grand symphony [1] for two violins, viola and bass, two flutes, two oboes, bassoons, horns, trumpets and drums *ad lib.*, in which is expressed :

> (1) A beautiful country, the sun shining, gentle airs and murmuring brooks ; birds twitter, a waterfall tumbles from the mountain, the shepherd plays his pipe, the shepherdess sings, and the lambs gambol around.
> (2) Suddenly the sky darkens, an oppressive closeness pervades the air, black clouds gather, the wind rises, distant thunder is heard, and the storm approaches.
> (3) The tempest bursts in all its fury, the wind howls and the rain beats, the trees groan and the streams rush furiously.
> (4) The storm gradually goes off, the clouds disperse and the sky clears.
> (5) Nature raises its joyful voice to heaven in songs of gratitude to the Creator (a hymn with variations).

The second (if it be not an arrangement of a portion of the preceding) is another attempt of the same kind with a German title—' The Shepherds' pleasure interrupted by the storm, a musical picture for the organ.' These are precisely the subjects which Beethoven has treated, and Fétis would have us believe that Knecht actually anticipated not only the general scheme of the Pastoral Symphony but some of its figures and passages. But this is not the case. The writer purchased the score and parts of Knecht's work at Otto Jahn's sale, and is able to say that beyond the titles the resemblances between the two works are obviously casual, Knecht's being in addition commonplace, entirely wanting in that ' expression of emotions ' which Beethoven enforces, and endeavouring to depict the actual sights and sounds, which he deprecates.   G.

KNEISEL, FRANZ (b. Bucharest, Jan. 26, 1865 ; d. New York, Mar. 26, 1926), violinist, chiefly player and leader of chamber concerts.

His father, a native of Olmütz, Moravia, was the leader of a military band, and gave him his first musical instruction. He then studied at the Conservatorium in Bucharest, and had finished its courses and carried off the first prize for violin playing before he was 15 years old. In 1879 he entered the Vienna Conservatorium as a special pupil of Grün and Hellmesberger, devoting himself under the latter chiefly to chamber music. On the completion of his academical studies he took the first prize for violin playing in July 1882, and on Dec. 31 of the same year played Joachim's ' Hungarian ' concerto at a Philharmonic concert. He was at once appointed solo violinist at the Hofburg Theatre as successor of Jacob Dont. In 1884 he went to Berlin as Konzertmeister of the Bilse Orchestra, remaining in that position one year, when, in the autumn of 1885, he went to

---

[1] It is published at Spire by Bossler, with no year ; but the date may very well be 1784, since the list on the back contains the three early sonatas of Beethoven, which were published by Bossler in 1783. But the coincidence is curious. Beethoven must have been familiar with Bossler's advertisement page, on which his own first sonatas were announced, and which contains all the above particulars.

America, on the invitation of Wilhelm Gericke, conductor, to be principal and solo violinist of the Boston Symphony Orchestra. He performed the duties of that office uninterruptedly for eighteen years, resigning in May 1903 to devote himself thenceforward to solo work and the leadership of the KNEISEL QUARTET (q.v.).

As a lad Kneisel had conducted a Philharmonic Society of instrumentalists in Bucharest; in America similar duties of greater moment devolved upon him. In the absence of Arthur Nikisch he conducted the concerts of the Boston Symphony Orchestra at the World's Fair in Chicago in 1893, and also a concert tour through Western cities lasting three weeks, in the early summer of that year. In 1902 and 1903 he was associate conductor of the Worcester Festivals in Massachusetts. He visited England in 1904, playing at two of the Broadwood Concerts in March with his quartet, and in 1905 was appointed violin professor in the new Institute of Musical Art in New York. In 1917 Kneisel disbanded the quartet in order to devote himself entirely to his work as head of the violin department of the Institute. He was made Doctor of Music of Yale University in 1911 and of Princeton in 1915.   H. E. K.; addns. R. A.

KNEISEL QUARTET, a string quartet formed in 1885 by Franz KNEISEL (see above) for the cultivation of chamber music.

The original members were Franz Kneisel (1st violin), E. Fiedler (2nd violin), Louis Svecenski (viola) and Fritz Giese (violoncello). During the thirty-two years in which Kneisel led his quartet the following changes took effect :

Second violin : Otto Roth (1887), Karl Ondriček (1899), J. Theodorowicz (1902), Hans Letz (1914). Violoncello : Anton Hekking (1889), Alwin Schroeder (1891), Willem Willeke (1907). The quartet was disbanded in 1917, its last concert being given on Apr. 3 of that year. Its record was very fine and its services to music in America of the greatest.   R. A.

KNELLER HALL, see ROYAL MILITARY SCHOOL OF MUSIC.

KNIGHT, REV. JOSEPH PHILIP (b. Bradford-on-Avon Vicarage, July 26, 1812 ; d. Great Yarmouth, June 2, 1887), a popular song-writer.

At 16 he studied harmony and thorough-bass under Corfe, then organist of Bristol Cathedral. When about 20 Knight composed his first six songs, under the name of ' Philip Mortimer.' Among these were ' Old Times,' sung by Henry Phillips, and ' Go, forget me,' which was much sung both here and in Germany. After this he used his own name, and in company with Haynes Bayly produced a number of highly popular songs, among which the most famous were ' Of what is the old man thinking ? ' ' The Veteran,' ' The Grecian Daughter,' and ' She wore a wreath of roses.' He subsequently composed a song and a duet to words written for

him by Thomas Moore—' The parting,' and ' Let's take this world as some wide scene.' In 1839 Knight visited the United States. To this time are due, among other popular songs, his best song, ' Rocked in the cradle of the deep,' sung with immense success by Braham. On his return to England he produced ' Venice,' ' Say what shall my song be to-night,' and ' The Dream,' to words by the Hon. Mrs. Norton—all more or less the rage in their day. Some years afterwards Knight was ordained by the Bishop of Exeter to the charge of St. Agnes in the Scilly Isles.   G.

KNIGHT (KNIGHTE, KNYGHT), (1) THOMAS, organist and vicar choral of Salisbury Cathedral, 1535–40 or 45. He received an annuity out of the dissolved monastery of Spalding, 1545–47. It is as yet impossible to decide in most cases which of the compositions merely signed Knight (or Knyghte, etc.) belong to this or the following composer. The beautiful Magnificat arranged for Novello's Parish Choir Book, No. 898, by Royle Shore, is undoubtedly by Thomas, and probably also the Mass in the Peterhouse MS. (c. 1530–40), and Evening Canticles in John Day's ' Certaine Notes ' (1560–65), which contains also the above Magnificat. Of the Mass and two motets (B.M. Add. MSS. 17,802-05) or the motet in Sadler's partbooks (Bodl. Lib.) it is so far impossible to say whether they are by Thomas or by (2) ROBERT, who was a contemporary of the former, though he may have reached farther into the century, and author of the five-part motet, ' Propterea maestum ' at Peterhouse (W. H. Grattan Flood in Mus. T. vol. lxii. p. 331; Q.-L.).   E. V. D. S.

KNITTL, KAREL (b. Polná, 1853 ; d. Prague, 1907), a Czech teacher and conductor who entered the Organ School, Prague, in 1882 and was afterwards appointed professor of harmony at the Conservatoire (1890)   In 1901 he became the administrative director of this institution. Kn.ttl was active in the journalistic world of Prague, and his judgment was independent and decisive. He was an excellent conductor, and, as director of the choral society, Hlahol, he produced Berlioz's ' Requiem,' Liszt's ' Christus,' Dvořák's 'Stabat Mater ' and ' The Spectre's Bride ' and other works.   R. N.

KNÖFEL (KNEFELIUS) (b. Lauban, Silesia, latter half of 16th cent.), musician to the Duke of Liegnitz in 1571 ; in the service of the town of Breslau, 1575 ; from 1576–83 Kapellmeister of the Elector Palatine at Heidelberg ; in 1592 organist and choirmaster of St. Henry's at Prague. He composed between 1571 and 1592 five books of sacred and secular songs, apart from single numbers in collective volumes. (See Q.-L.)

KNORR, IWAN (b. Mewe, West Prussia, Jan. 3, 1853; d. Frankfort-on-M., Jan. 22, 1916), composer and teacher. When only 4 years of age, he was taken by his parents to Southern Russia, and soon began his musical training under his mother, a moderate pianist. In the various small Russian towns in which at this time the Knorr family lived, the lad had much to do for himself, all the while absorbing the influence of the Slavonic folk-music which he heard. His first efforts at composition were made when he was 7 years of age, but it was not until 1868, when the family settled in Leipzig, that he determined to adopt a musical career.

On entering the Conservatorium Iwan became a pupil for pianoforte of Ignaz Moscheles, for theory of Richter, and for composition of Carl Reinecke. After passing through the Conservatorium Knorr returned to Russia and became professor of music in the Imperial Institute for Noble Ladies. There he had ample time for composition, but, doubtful of his ability, he submitted some compositions to Brahms, at that time unknown to him, with a request for a judgment. The work submitted was the series of variations on an Ukrainish Volkslied (op. 7) for orchestra, on which Brahms expressed so highly favourable an opinion that a few years later (1883) Knorr was appointed, on Brahms's recommendation, principal teacher of composition at the Hoch Conservatorium in Frankfort - on - Main. There he numbered among his pupils many Englishmen: Cyril Scott, H. Balfour Gardiner, Norman O'Neill and Roger Quilter, for example. He believed firmly in training the mind of each pupil individually, and acted up to his belief; and he preferred the school of experience and the 'eternal laws' to the set 'rules' of composition. His text was that in harmony all is good that seems good to the thoroughly educated ear, whether it conform to the rules or not.

Knorr's published compositions include:

Op. 1, variations on a theme by Schumann for pianoforte trio; op. 3, pianoforte quartet; op. 6, the 'Ukrainische Liebeslieder' for vocal quartet and pianoforte, the poems by himself; op. 12, a symphonic Phantasie for orchestra; and a quantity of songs and pianoforte music for two and four hands.

In the mass of his manuscript music is 'Dunja'—a musical village-tale in two acts, which was successfully staged at Coblenz on Mar. 23, 1904, and a second opera, 'Durchs Fenster,' given at Carlsruhe in 1908. He wrote a biography of his friend Tchaikovsky (Riemann's *Berühmte Musiker*, 1900) and the following pedagogic works:

Aufgaben für den Unterricht in der Harmonielehre. (1903.)
Lehrbuch der Fugenkomposition. (1911.)
Fugen des wohltemperirten Klaviers in bildlicher Darstellung. (1912.)   R. H. L., with addns.

KNOTE, HEINRICH (b. Munich, 1870), operatic tenor. He learned singing from E. Kirschner in his native city, where he made his début at the Royal Opera in 1892. Deducting only a short stay at Hamburg, his career in Germany was exclusively restricted to Munich, Bayreuth and Berlin. From those centres his fame as a

'Heldentenor' was loudly trumpeted forth, and it must be admitted that he fully justified it on his first appearances in London (Covent Garden, 1901) and New York (Metropolitan Opera House, 1902–03), at both of which he sang frequently down to 1913. He was a typical interpreter of the heroes of Wagnerian music-drama; a particularly fine Siegfried, a noble Tristan, an impulsive Tannhäuser; his striking physique well matched by a clear, resonant, sympathetic voice and impressive declamation. In the summer of 1908 he sustained the rôle of Tristan (Miss Edyth Walker then making her first attempt as a soprano) in the 50th performance of 'Tristan und Isolde' at Covent Garden.

BIBL.—*Int. Who's Who in Music*; NORTHCOTT, *Covent Garden and Royal Opera.*   H. K.

KNOTT, JOHN (b. probably Sevenoaks, Kent; d. Edinburgh, 1837), a composer and compiler of church melodies. His father was a Baptist minister at Sevenoaks. John Knott became a chorister in Durham Cathedral, and in 1811 was precentor in the West Church, Aberdeen, and a teacher of singing. While there he issued an interesting little oblong volume, *Sacred Harmony, being a collection of Psalm and Hymn Tunes*, 1814, 2nd ed. 1815. In 1824 he was in Edinburgh, and issued a *Selection of Tunes in four parts, adapted to the Psalms and Paraphrases of the Church of Scotland.* While in Edinburgh he was music-master at Heriot's Hospital, and precentor at the New North Church.   F. K.

KNÜPFER, SEBASTIAN (b. Asch, Voigtland, Saxony, Sept. 7, 1633; d. 1676), received his education, musical and otherwise, at Regensburg. Coming to Leipzig to pursue his philological as well as musical studies, he succeeded, in 1657, Tobias Michael as Cantor of the Thomasschule and General Director of the Town Music. From the obituary notice contained in the so-called Leichenprogramm[1] or Funeral Invitation issued by the rector of Leipzig University we learn that, amongst his contemporaries, Knüpfer was as much esteemed for his philological as for his musical attainments. He is said to have edited Kircher's *Musurgia*, and the treatises of Guido, Boethius, Berno and others, although no traces of such works are now to be found. The only musical works published by him consist of a few Funeral Motets (Leichengesänge) for 4 to 8 voices; but the State Library at Berlin contains a collection of 22 of his church cantatas for 3 to 8 voices, with instrumental accompaniment, which Winterfeld characterises as a valuable possession, and as showing Knüpfer to have been a serious, solid, thoroughly trained musician. Four of these are reprinted in *D.D.T.* lviii. and lix.   J. R. M.

KNYVETT, (1) CHARLES (b. Feb. 22, 1752; d. London, Jan. 19, 1822), descended from an

1 Reprinted in *M.f.M.*, 1901, pp. 207-13.

ancient Norfolk family, was one of the principal alto singers at the Commemoration of Handel in 1784 ; he was also engaged at the Concert of Ancient Music. He was appointed a gentleman of the Chapel Royal, Nov. 6, 1786. In 1791 he, in conjunction with Samuel Harrison, established the VOCAL CONCERTS, which they carried on until 1794. On July 25, 1796, he was appointed an organist of the Chapel Royal, and a few years later resigned his former post.

His elder son, (2) CHARLES (b. London, 1773 ; d. Nov. 2, 1852), was placed for singing under William Parsons (afterwards Sir William Parsons), and for the organ and piano under Samuel Webbe. In 1801 he joined his younger brother William (3), Greatorex and Bartleman, in reviving the Vocal Concerts. In 1802 he was chosen organist of St. George's, Hanover Square. Besides this he taught the pianoforte and thorough-bass, wrote glees, etc., and published a ' Selection of Psalm Tunes,' 1823.

(3) WILLIAM, the younger son of Charles (1) (b. Apr. 21, 1779 ; d. Ryde, Nov. 17, 1856). In 1788 he sang in the treble chorus at the Concert of Ancient Music, and in 1795 appeared there as principal alto. In 1797 he was appointed gentleman of the Chapel Royal, and soon afterwards a lay-vicar of Westminster. In 1802 he succeeded Dr. Arnold as one of the composers of the Chapel Royal. For upwards of forty years he was principal alto at the best London concerts and all the provincial festivals, being greatly admired for the beauty of his voice and his finished style of singing, particularly in part music. Callcott's glee ' With sighs, sweet rose,' was composed expressly for him. In 1832 he became conductor of the Concert of Ancient Music, which office he resigned in 1840. He conducted the Birmingham Festivals from 1834–43, and the York Festival of 1835. He was the composer of several pleasing glees—one of which, ' When the fair rose,' gained a prize at the Harmonic Society in 1800 —and some songs, and wrote anthems for the coronations of George IV. and Queen Victoria.

(4) DEBORAH (b. Shaw, near Oldham, Lancs ; d. Feb. 10, 1876), second wife of William (3), and niece of Mrs. Travis, one of the Lancashire chorus singers engaged at the Concert of Ancient Music. In 1813 she was placed in the chorus of the Concert of Ancient Music, the directors of which, finding her possessed of superior abilities, soon withdrew her from that position, took her as an articled pupil and placed her under Greatorex. In 1815 she appeared at the concerts as a principal singer with success. In 1816 she sang at the Derby Festival, in 1818 at Worcester and in 1820 at Birmingham. From that time she was constantly in request, particularly as an oratorio singer, until 1843, when she retired. She married William (3) in 1826.   W. H. H.

KOBELIUS, JOHANN AUGUSTIN (b. Wählitz, near Halle ; d. Weissenfels, Aug. 17, 1731), studied under the Wählitz organists Brausen and Schieferdecker, and afterwards (for composition) under J. Ph. Krieger. After a period of travel, which took him as far as Venice, he became a chamber musician at Weissenfels. In 1712 he was organist at Sangershausen ; in 1713 Kapellmeister at Querfurt ; and in 1725 a government official and Kapellmeister at the court of Weissenfels. He composed 20 operas between 1716 and 1729 ; also church music, overtures, serenades, concertos, sonatas, etc.
                                      E. V. D. S.

KOCH, HEINRICH CHRISTOPH (b. Rudolstadt, Oct. 10, 1749 ; d. there, Mar. 12, 1816), the son of a member of the ducal orchestra there. In 1768 he was admitted into the band as a violinist, having received instruction from Göpfert of Weimar, and in 1777 obtained the title of ' Kammermusiker.' He composed various pieces of small importance for the court, but his fame rests upon his contributions to musical literature. His Versuch einer Anleitung zur Composition appeared in three parts between the years 1782 and 1793 ; and his Musikalisches Lexicon in 1802. This was republished in a condensed form in 1807 and 1828, but its complete revision dates from 1865, and is the work of Arrey von DOMMER (q.v.). He wrote several other works of less importance on harmony and other subjects connected with the art.   M.

KOCHETOV, NICHOLAS RAZOUMNIKOVICH (b. Oranienbaum, July 8, 1864), composer and musical critic. In 1889 he began to write for the Novoe Vremya, The Artist, The Moscow Viedemosti, etc. His compositions include : An opera, ' A Terrible Revenge,' on a subject from Gogol ; ' Arabian Suite ' for orchestra, op. 3 ; Symphony in E minor, op. 8 (1895) ; Valse Serenade for string orchestra ; numerous pianoforte pieces, including ' In the Heart of Nature,' op. 11, and ' Eastern Sketches,' opp. 12, 13 ; about twenty-four songs.   R. N.

KOCIÁN, JAROSLAV (b. Bohemia, Feb. 22, 1884), violinist, was from 1899–1901 pupil of Ševčik at the Prague Conservatoire. His successful concert tours in many countries spread the fame of his master's method and soon established his own reputation as a virtuoso of the first rank. His visits to England have been comparatively few but memorable. Important among them was the occasion of the Czechoslovak festival in London (1919), when he gave a performance of Dvořák's violin concerto with the orchestra of the Prague Philharmonic Society at the Queen's Hall. (See Mus. T., May 1915.)   C.

KOCZALSKI, RAOUL (b. Warsaw, Jan. 3, 1885), was taught by his father, and from the age of 7 was allowed to display his exceptional abilities as a pianist in public and on various tours. He appeared in London in May 1893, and a composition of his written about that time was marked op. 46 ; in 1896 he celebrated the 1000th appearance in public.   M.

He has since attained an eminent position as a pianist, and has specialised in the performance of Chopin. When he returned to London, after a long interval, in Nov. 1924, he gave a series of four recitals of Chopin's music. His compositions include two operas, ' Rymond' (Elberfeld, 1902) and ' Die Sühne ' (Mülhausen, 1909), a sonata in G and other works for the piano (*Riemann*).   C.

KODÁLY, ZOLTÁN (*b*. Kecskemét, Hungary, Dec. 16, 1882). composer, entered the Budapest Conservatoire in 1900 and studied under Hans Koessler. In his student days he was influenced at first by Brahms and afterwards by Debussy, but the immature works written under the sway of these two masters have remained unpublished. About 1905 he began the study of Hungarian folk-music, and became absorbed in the task of tracing the traditional tunes to their sources, which were greatly obscured by foreign and gipsy influences. Like Béla Bartók he began to collect the original melodies among the peasantry, in some cases by means of direct notation from their singing, in others with the aid of the gramophone. (The problems to be faced by the collector of Hungarian folk-music are set forth in the article, BARTÓK.) Kodály has collected between 3000 and 4000 traditional melodies, the majority of which are still in MS., although some are now published jointly with Bartók. He also wrote a book on *The Pentatonic Scale in Hungarian Folk-Music.*

In 1906 Kodály was appointed professor of composition at the Budapest Conservatoire. He was music critic to several prominent Hungarian papers for a number of years, and is still correspondent for some foreign musical periodicals.

Kodály's work reveals the influence of his country's folk-music no less unmistakably than that of Bartók, but it does so in a different way. Each composer filters the national idiom through his own personality. The fundamentals of folk-song provide merely the raw material, the vocabulary, as it were, which they fashion by the individuality of their creative gifts into works of art. Kodály's music is distinguished by an originality that appears startling at a first hearing, but on closer acquaintance reveals a certain leaning towards tradition. He does not abandon tonality and accepted forms, but creates a new music of astonishing vitality within their limits. His instrumental writing is extremely interesting, and there is a close interdependence between his creative impulse and the particular medium chosen for its expression. The piano pieces are predominantly harmonic and per-

cussive, the string quartets contrapuntal, and the pieces for solo string instruments (opp. 7 and 8) abound in appropriate technical problems and striking effects.

WORKS

Op.
1. 16 Songs. (1907–09.)
2. String Quartet No. 1. (1908.)
3. 10 Piano Pieces. (1909.)
4. Sonata for v'cl. and PF. (1909–10.)
5. 2 Songs with orch. (1912–13.)
6. 7 Songs. (1912–13.)
7. Duo for vln. and v'cl. (1914.)
8. Sonata for v'cl. solo. (1915.)
9. 6 Songs. (1914–15.)
10. String Quartet No. 2. (1916–17.)
11. 7 Piano Pieces. (1917–18.)
12. Serenade for 2 vlns. and vla. (1919–20.)
13. Psalm LV. for tenor solo, chorus and orch. (1923.)
Hungarian Folk-songs (2 vols.). (With Béla Bartók.)
           E. B.

KOEBERG, F. E. A. (*b*. The Hague, July 15, 1879), Dutch composer, received his musical education at the Conservatoire in his native town under W. F. G. Nicolai and Henri Viotta, and in Berlin at the Staatsakademie der Künste under Xaver Scharwenka. He played the violin and viola in various orchestras and also toured as a pianist, but on his return to Holland devoted himself to conducting, composition and teaching. He has been conductor of various amateur choruses and orchestras, the principal being the students' musical society, ' Sempre Crescendo,' at Leyden and the Orchestra ' Musica ' at The Hague. He is professor of composition in the Netherlands Academy for Music at The Hague. As a composer he has specialised in music demanding large forces, and many of his works have been written for open-air plays and pageants. From this it will be gathered that his style is broad and free from any fussiness or unnecessary detail, his melodies being thoroughly national and bearing an evident relation to those of such songs as the ' Wilhelmuslied,' ' Wier Neerlandsch bloed,' ' Piet Heijn,' etc. The broad simplicity of his melodies has caused a number of them to be adapted for the clock carillons in the great towers at Leyden and Middelburg. Nevertheless, as long ago as 1904, when the music of the modern French schools was utterly unknown in Holland, he wrote a setting of Bürger's ' Lenore' that was ' atonal' throughout.

His compositions include :

Open-air plays : ' Ydylle ' (Lucie Broedelet), ' Bloemensproke , (Lily Green), ' Plato ' (P. C. Boutens), ' Alianora ' (Boutens), ' Middelburg's Overgang in 1574 ' (Boutens), ' Koninginne Kantate ' (A. Heyting); an opera: ' Bloemenkind '; symphonic poems ' Zeelandia,' ' Zevenzot,' ' Zonneweg,' ' Zotskap,' ' Zelma,' ' Minone ' ' Kolma,' besides three symphonies, a large number of overtures and songs, and shorter works for chorus, violin, piano and string quartet.   H. A.

KÖCHEL, DR. LUDWIG, RITTER VON (*b*. Stein, near Krems on the Danube, Jan. 14, 1800 ; *d*. Vienna, June 3, 1877), learned musician and naturalist, tutor to the sons of the Archduke Karl (1828–42). From 1850–63 he lived at Salzburg, and from the latter year to his death at Vienna. His work as a botanist and mineralogist does not concern us : as a musician he has immortalised his name by his *Chronologisch-thematisches Verzeichniss* of all

W. A. Mozart's works, with an appendix of lost, doubtful and spurious compositions (Breitkopf & Härtel, Leipzig, 1862). As a precursor of that invaluable work, a small pamphlet should be named, *Über den Umfang der musikalischen Productivität W. A. Mozarts* (Salzburg, 1862). The complete edition of Mozart's works which Breitkopf & Härtel have published could scarcely have been made without his generous co-operation. In 1832 von Köchel was made an Imperial Councillor, and in 1842 he received the order of Leopold. Among his intimate friends was Otto Jahn, in whose work on Mozart he took an active interest.   See Jahn's *Mozart*, second edition, p. xxxi.   C. F. P.

KOECHLIN, CHARLES (*b*. Paris, Nov. 27, 1867), composer, belongs to an Alsatian family. He attended first the École Polytechnique, but soon changed the direction of his studies and entered the Conservatoire, where he learned harmony with Taudou, counterpoint with Gédalge and composition with Massenet, ultimately becoming a pupil of Fauré.

His first published compositions, settings of Rondels by Théodore de Banville and Charles d'Orléans, appeared in 1890, and one of them, 'Le Thé,' became almost immediately popular. Yet of the composer little was known, and his career has been not only uneventful, save for creative work, but isolated. At a time when the French composers of his generation were attracting world-wide attention to themselves, his growing list of compositions scarcely penetrated beyond a narrow circle. Few of them were published, and those in the larger forms were but rarely performed. Except as a song-writer, it is only since about 1921 that he has become more widely known. Now, not only the whole of his piano music and songs, but about half of his chamber music, and even a portion of his orchestral output is available in print, and it is gradually being discovered that Koechlin's contribution to the modern French movement has been far more important than was realised at the time. Though he never shared the delight of his contemporaries in *recherches harmoniques*, his writings as far back as the 'nineties abound in examples of harmonic independence. In other respects his style is remarkable for its unswerving sobriety and absence of all ingratiating concessions, amount-ing sometimes to dryness, but more often en-livened by melodic invention. He was an early exponent of the contrapuntal simplicity, the revival of which has been attributed to a more recent school; he has always had a fond-ness for extended melodic lines combined in the manner of the classic 'Invention,' and he has written many chorales. Apart from these features of his method his mode of thought is almost constantly lyrical, and in his later works characterised by a rhythmic freedom which frequently dispenses with time-signatures and

even bar-lines. It is impossible to do more than enumerate his principal works. Those for orchestra include many extended series, such as the 'Heures persanes,' which comprise sixteen pieces.

ORCHESTRAL

La Forêt' (opp. 25 and 29), 'En mer la nuit' (op. 27), 'Les Saisons' (opp. 30-47, 48-69), 'Études antiques' (op. 46), 'Nuit de Walpurgis classique' (op. 38), 'Rhapsodie sur des chansons françaises' (op. 62), 'Les Heures persanes' (op. 65).
Ballade piano and orchestra, op. 50.
Ballets : 1. La Forêt païenne, op. 45.
   2. La Divine Vesprée, op. 67.
Chorus and orchestra, L'Abbaye, op. 16.

CHAMBER MUSIC

3 String Quartets, opp. 51-57 and 72.
Quintet, piano and strings, op. 80.
Sonatas for piano with vln. (op. 64), vla. (op. 53), vcl. (op. 66), flute (op. 52), oboe (op. 58), clarinet (opp. 85 and 86), bassoon (op. 71), and horn (op. 70).
Sonata for two flutes (op. 75).

PIANO

Esquisses (op. 41), Sonatines (op. 59), 'Paysages et marines' (op. 63), Pastorales (op. 77), and two sets of 'Petites Pièces.'
A suite for two pianos (op. 6), and another for piano, four hands (op. 19).
Numerous songs and choral pieces.   E. E.

KÖHLER, the name of an eminent family of military wind-instrument makers. The founder of the family was (1) JOHN KÖHLER, a native of Volkenrode, a hamlet near Cassel. He came to England, acted as bandmaster to the Lancashire Volunteers, and in 1780 estab-lished himself as a musical instrument maker at 87 St. James's Street. Having no children, he sent for his nephew, (2) JOHN KÖHLER, from Germany, who succeeded to his business in 1801. The latter was appointed musical instru-ment-maker to the Duke of York, then Com-mander-in-Chief, and the Prince of Wales successively. He was succeeded by his only son, (3) JOHN AUGUSTUS (*d.* June 20, 1878), who removed the business to Henrietta Street. His inventions in brass instruments were many, and were successful in their day. He obtained prize medals at the Exhibitions of 1851 and 1862, and was favourably mentioned in the Report of the latter. His eldest son, (4) AUGUSTUS CHARLES, now deceased, succeeded to his business.   G.

KÖHLER, CHR. LOUIS HEINRICH (*b*. Bruns-wick, Sept. 5, 1820 ; *d.* Königsberg, Feb. 16, 1886), was educated at Brunswick and Vienna, being in the latter capital from 1839–43 as a pupil of Sechter for theory, and Bocklet for piano. He filled the post of conductor at Marienburg and Elbing, before settling down at Königsberg, which was his home from 1847 until his death. He wrote three operas, one of which, 'Maria Dolores,' was performed at Brunswick in 1844, and a ballet, 'Der Zauber-komponist,' at the same place in 1846. His chief work as a composer was in the direction of educational pianoforte music, such as studies of all kinds, arrangements of popular works, fantasias, etc. Two books of his studies, opp. 112 and 128, have more value than most of his works. He was a valued contributor to the *Neue Zeitschrift für Musik*, in 1867–78, and to the *Berliner Musik-Zeitung* in 1871–76.   M.

KÖLER, DAVID (b. Zwickau, Saxony, first half of 16th century; d. July 1565). His first appointment was at Altenburg, whence in 1563 he was called to be Kapellmeister at Güstrow in Mecklenburg. The town council of Zwickau afterwards called him back to his native town, giving him the post of cantor at St. Marien, the principal church.

His one published work consists of Ten Psalms with German words for four to six voices, composed throughout in several divisions ('Zehen Psalme Davids des Propheten mit vier, fünf und sechs Stimmen gesetzt durch David Köler von Zwickau,' Leipzig, 1554). The only known copy of this work is preserved in the public library at Zwickau. Otto Kade has the merit of first calling attention to this work, and rescuing its able composer from utter oblivion. Since then Dr. Georg Göhler of Leipzig has reprinted two of the Psalms, and conducted performances of them at Zwickau and elsewhere. In his preface to Psalm III. Dr. Göhler says :

'It may be considered as one of the most perfect pieces of contrapuntal art and genial interpretation of the text which we anywhere possess. . . . The realism of the musical drawing is as astonishing as the quite modern conception and presentation of the different parts of the text.'

In the Beilagen zu Ambros Kade printed from a MS. Köler's four-voice setting of the Geistliches Lied, ' O du edler Brunn der Freuden,' which is also an excellent piece of work. Among the few other works of Köler in MS. there is a Mass for seven voices on Josquin's Motet ' Benedicta es coelorum regina.'   J. R. M.

KÖMPEL, AUGUST (b. Brückenau, Aug. 15, 1831 ; d. Weimar, Apr. 7, 1891), a distinguished violinist, one of the best pupils of Spohr, whose quiet, elegiac style suited his talent precisely. His tone was not large, but very pure and sympathetic, his execution faultless. He was for a time member of the bands at Cassel and Hanover (the latter in 1852–61), and from 1863 was leader of that at Weimar. He retired on a pension in 1884.   P. D.

KÖNIG, JOHANN BALTHASAR (b. 1691 ; d. 1758), director of church music at Frankfort-am-Main, is best known as the editor of the most comprehensive Choral-book of the 18th century, Harmonischer Lieder - Schatz oder Allgemeines evangelisches Choral-buch, Frankfort, 1738. It contains 1940 tunes, including those to the French Calvinistic Psalms, but the older tunes and the French Psalm-tunes have all been deprived of their original variety of rhythm, and the more modern tunes from the Freylinghausen and other hymn-books have all been simplified by the retrenchment of slurs and appoggiaturas and other superfluous ornaments. All the tunes have thus been reduced to a uniform pattern with notes of equal length, and while this simplification has been of advantage in the case of the Freylinghausen tunes it has

rather spoilt the older melodies. The tunes are only provided with figured bass.   J. R. M.

KÖNIGIN VON SABA, DIE, opera in 4 acts ; words by J. Mosenthal, music by Carl Goldmark ; produced Vienna, Mar. 10, 1875 : in English, Carl Rosa Co., Theatre Royal, Manchester, Apr. 12, 1910. (See also REINE DE SABA, LA.)

KÖNIGSKINDER, dramatised fairy-tale in 3 acts, written by Ernst Rosmer, with music by Engelbert Humperdinck ; produced Munich, Jan. 23, 1897 ; in English, Court Theatre, Oct. 13, 1897. Originally the action was carried on in declamation through continuous music. Later Humperdinck transformed the work into opera, and it was so given for the first time, Metropolitan Opera House, New York, Dec. 28, 1910 ; Berlin, Jan. 14, 1911 ; Covent Garden, Nov. 27, 1911.

KÖNIGSPERGER, MARIAN (MARIANUS) (b. Roding, Bavaria, Dec. 4, 1708 ; d. Oct. 9, 1769), received his early education in the Benedictine Abbey of Prüfening near Ratisbon, where he afterwards took the vows, and spent the rest of his life as organist and director of the choir, and occupied in musical composition.

He enjoyed great reputation in his time as an organ player, and composer of works for the church. Lotter, the music publisher of Augsburg, acknowledged that he owed the foundation of his prosperity in business to his publication of Königsperger's works, and the profits which were obtained for the composer himself were all generously devoted by him to the benefit of the Abbey, providing it with a new organ, purchasing valuable books for the library, and furnishing the means for the publication of literary works by the other brethren. His works are enumerated in Q.-L., and even more fully by Ernst von Werra in Haberl's Kirchen-musikalisches Jahrbuch, 1897, pp. 32-34. Both E. v. Werra and Eitner say that Königsperger wrote for the theatre as well as for the church, but the works, as they enumerate them, are all for the church, and consist of—

(1) A large number of masses, offertoria, vespers, litanies, etc., all for voices with a considerable instrumental accompaniment— strings, horns, trumpets and drums.
(2) Sonatas or symphonies for strings and other instruments with organ, evidently for church use.
(3) Various sets of preludes and fugues or versetts in the church tones for organ.

Ritter (Geschichte des Orgelspiels, pp. 80, 161) considers the organ works to show good schooling, and to have more substance in them than similar works of his South German contemporaries. None appear to be reprinted in modern times.   J. R. M.

KOLB, KARLMANN (b. Köstlarn, Bavaria, 1703 ; d. Munich, 1765), received his first musical instruction as a choir-boy in the Benedictine Abbey of Aschbach. Taking the vows at this Abbey in 1723, he was ordained priest in 1729, and acted as organist. Later on, with the permission of his superiors, he entered the service of a noble family in Munich as resident-tutor, and died there.

His musical work, published at Augsburg in 1733, is entitled 'Certamen Aonium id est, Lusus vocum inter se innocue concertantum,' etc., and consists of preludes, short fugues or versetts, and cadences or concluding voluntaries, all intended for church use. Ritter (*Geschichte des Orgelspiels*) gives one of Kolb's preludes, and says of the work generally that it shows the composer to have been an original and capable musician, although it is also evident from extracts given in Seiffert (*Geschichte der Klaviermusik*) that many of the pieces are written in a somewhat unecclesiastical style, a style more suitable to the harpsichord or pianoforte than to the organ. There are some bold experiments in chromatic and enharmonic progressions. The whole work is characteristic of the lighter style of organ playing which, owing to Italian influence, was chiefly cultivated in Catholic South Germany and Austria. E. von Werra has reprinted three of Kolb's pieces in his ' Orgelbuch.' J. R. M.

KOLISEK, ALOIS (*b.* Protivanov, Moravia, 1868), one of six brothers who all entered the priesthood. He has travelled much, is an accomplished linguist, and an active propagandist of the folk-art of Moravia and Slovakia. He is professor of æsthetics in the theological faculty at Bratislava. Dr. Kolisek has contributed valuable information on the subject of Slovak music to this Dictionary.
R. N.

KOLLMANN, (1) AUGUST FRIEDRICH CHRISTOPH (*b.* Engelbostel, Hanover, *c.* 1756 ; *d.* London, Apr. 19, 1829),of a musical family, his father an organist and schoolmaster, his brother, George Christoph, an organist of great renown at Hamburg. Appointed organist at Lüne, near Lüneburg, about 1781, and in 1784 was selected to be chapel-keeper and schoolmaster at the German Chapel, St. James's, London. In 1792 George III. presented a chamber organ to the chapel, which was played by Kollmann under the title of ' clerk ' till his death on Easter Day, 1829.

He was a person of much energy, and in 1809, during a large fire in the palace, is said to have saved the chapel by standing in the doorway and preventing the firemen from entering to destroy it. His works are numerous : *Essay on Practical Harmony*, 1796 ; *Essay on Practical Musical Composition*, 1799 ;[1] *Practical Guide to Thorough Bass*, 1801 ; *Vindication of a Passage in Thorough Bass*, 1802 ; *New Theory of Musical Harmony*, 1806 ; *Second Practical Guide to Thorough Bass*, 1807 ; *Quarterly Musical Register*, 1812 (two numbers only) ; *Remarks on Logier*, 1824 (some of these went through two editions) ; *Analysed Symphony*

[1] One number of the *Wohltemperirtes Klavier* was printed in this essay.

(for piano, violin and bass), op. 3 ; First beginning on the PF., op. 5, 1796 ; ' Sinfonien,' *i.e.* trios for piano, violin and violoncello, op. 7 ; Concerto for PF. and Orchestra, op. 8 ; Melody of the 100th Psalm, with 100 harmonies, op. 9 ; Twelve analysed Fugues, for two performers on piano and organ, op. 10 ; Introduction to Modulation, op. 11 ; Rondo on the Chord of the Diminished Seventh. He is also said to have published an orchestral symphony, 'The Shipwreck, or the Loss of the East Indiaman Halsewell,' a piece of programme-music quite in the taste of the time ; songs, sonatas. He also proposed (1799) an edition of Bach's *Wohltemperirtes Klavier.*

His son, (2) GEORGE AUGUST (*b.* 1780 ; *d.* Mar. 19, 1845), was a good organ player, and on his father's death succeeded to his post as organist. On his death his sister, (3) JOHANNA SOPHIA (*d.* May 1849), succeeded him ; and on her death the post was bestowed on F. Weber.
G., with addns.

KONINK, SERVAAS VAN (*d.* Amsterdam, ? 1720), a 17th-18th century Dutch composer who composed music to Racine's *Athalia* (1697), an opera, church music, motets, songs, trios for various instruments, dance tunes, flute sonatas, etc. (*Mendel, Q.-L.*).

KONIUS, GEORGE EDWARDOVICH (*b.* Moscow, Sept. 30, 1862), studied at the Conservatoire of his native town under Taneiev and Arensky. From 1891–99 he held a professorship at this institution. In 1902 he transferred his services to the Music School of the Philharmonic Society. He was subsequently professor and director of the Saratov Conservatoire, and since the revolution (1916) professor at Moscow Conservatoire. His chief works are:

Orchestral suite, 'Child-life,' op. 1 ; Cantata in Memory of Alexander III., op. 8 ; Symphonic poem, 'From the World of Illusion,' op. 23 ; Symphonic poem, 'The Rustling Forest' (after Korolenko), op. 33 ; Ballet, 'Daita' (Moscow, 1896) ; about twenty pieces for pianoforte, opp. 3, 4, 6, 7, 13, 16, 17, 18, 24 ; over thirty songs, opp. 2, 5, 9, 12, 14, 20, 22.
R. N.

KONTSKI, DE, a family of virtuosi, of which (1) CHARLES, the eldest (*b.* Warsaw, Sept. 6, 1815 ; *d.* Paris, Aug. 27, 1867), appeared as a pianist in public at the age of 7, but, like the majority of prodigies, did not fulfil the promises of childhood. He made his first studies in Warsaw, and continued them at Paris, where he settled as teacher.

(2) ANTOINE (*b.* Cracow, Oct. 27, 1817 ; *d.* Nowogrod, Lithuania, Dec. 7, 1899) was a clever pianist, a pupil of Field at Moscow. He possessed great delicacy of touch and brilliance of execution, but was a superficial musician. He composed many ' pièces de salon,' of which the ' Réveil du lion ' (op. 115) became widely popular. He lived in Paris till 1851, then in Berlin till 1853, in St. Petersburg till 1867, when he settled in London, where an opera, ' Les Deux Distraits,' was given in 1872. He was in the United States in 1885, and later, and in 1896–1898 made a professional tour round the world, ending at Warsaw.

(3) STANISLAS (*b.* Oct. 8, 1820), pianist and pupil of Antoine, lived at St. Petersburg and in Paris.

(4) APOLLINAIRE (*b.* Warsaw, Oct. 23, 1825 ; *d.* there, June 29, 1879) was a violinist. His first master was his elder brother Charles (1). He showed the same precocity of talent as the rest of his family, performing in public concerts at an age of not much over 4 years. Later on he travelled a great deal, chiefly in Russia, but also in France and Germany, and made a certain sensation by his really exceptional technical proficiency, not unaccompanied by a certain amount of charlatanism. In 1837 he is said [1] to have attracted the attention of Paganini in Paris, and to have formed a friendship with the great virtuoso which resulted in his receiving some lessons [2] from him (an honour which he shared with Sivori) and ultimately becoming heir to his violins and violin compositions. This, however, requires confirmation. He made tours in France and Germany in 1847, and in 1853 was appointed solo-violinist to the Emperor of Russia, and in 1861 director of the Warsaw Conservatoire. He played a solo at one of the Russian concerts given in connection with the Exhibition at Paris in 1878. His compositions (fantasias and the like) are musically unimportant.

(5) EUGENIE, sister of the above, was a competent pianist, who performed with Stanislas and Apollinaire (*Riemann*).   P. D.

KONZERTMEISTER, see CONCERT-MASTER.

KORBAY, FRANCIS ALEXANDER (*b.* Budapest, May 8, 1846 ; *d.* London, Mar. 9, 1913), the son of parents distinguished as amateur musicians. He studied the piano under various masters, and composition, etc., under Moronyi and Robert Volkmann ; he was trained as a tenor singer under Gustave Roger, and sang in grand opera at the National Theatre in Budapest from 1865–68 ; the continued exertion was too much for his voice, and he took to the piano under the advice of his godfather, Franz Liszt. After touring in Europe as a pianist, he went to America in 1871, playing and teaching for two years. By this time his voice had recovered sufficiently to enable him to give song-recitals at which he accompanied himself, and to teach singing. He lectured and composed, besides singing and playing, during his residence in New York, and an orchestral piece, 'Nuptiale,' was often played in the United States. A Hungarian overture was performed in London (1912) ; a set of songs to Lenau's 'Schilflieder,' and other single songs, have been published and often sung, but his arrangements of Hungarian national songs to English versions of his own are the things by which his reputation was made in England. He lived in London from

1894, and was a professor of singing at the R.A.M., 1894–1903.   M.

KORESTCHENKO, ARSÈNE NICHOLAEVICH (*b.* Moscow, Dec. 18, 1870), composer and pianist. At the Conservatoire — which he quitted in 1891—Korestchenko carried off the first gold medal for proficiency in two branches : pianoforte (Taneiev) and theory (Arensky). He became professor of harmony at the Conservatoire, and took classes for counterpoint and musical form at the Synodal School, Moscow. He is a prolific composer, as will be seen from the following list of his works :

WORKS FOR THE STAGE

'Balthasar's Feast,' op. 7, opera in 1 act (Moscow Opera, 1892).
'The Angel of Death,' op. 10, opera in 2 acts, text from Lermontov.
Incidental music to 'The Trojans' of Euripides, op. 15.
Do. to 'Iphigenia in Aulis,' op. 18.
'The Ice Palace,' op. 38, opera, subject from Lajechnikov (Moscow Opera, 1900).
'The Magic Mirror,' op. 39, ballet.

ORCHESTRAL WORKS

Barcarolle, op. 6.	'Armenian Suite,' op. 20.
'A Tale,' op. 11.	'Scènes nocturnes' (second
'Scène poétique,' op. 12.	suite), op. 21.
Two Symphonic Sketches, op.	First Symphony (lyric), op. 23.
14.	'Musical Picture,' op. 27A.

VOCAL AND ORCHESTRAL

Cantata 'Don Juan,' op. 5.
'Armenian Songs,' opp. 8, 13.
'Prologue' for the twenty-fifth anniversary of the Moscow Conservatoire, op. 9.
'Georgian Songs,' op. 27c.

MISCELLANEOUS

Choruses, opp. 16, 29, 32, 37.
80 Songs, opp. 2, 26, 28, 31, 35, 36.
Pianoforte pieces, opp. 1, 3 (Concert Fantasia with orchestra), 19 22, 30, 33.
String quartet, op. 25.
Melody for violin and piano, op. 4.
Do. for violoncello and piano, op. 34.   R. N.

KORNAUTH, EGON (*b.* Olmuetz, Moravia, May 14, 1891), one of the most talented of the modern school of German composers. He studied in the Musikakademie in Vienna under Fuchs, Schreker and Schmidt, at the same time matriculating in Philosophy at the Viennese University. When taking this degree, he was writing his dissertation on the string quartets of Haydn which aroused general attention. A prolific writer, he pauses midway between the German romanticism and the modern school, and in many ways recalls the delicate intimacy of Schumann, the colour harmonie of Brahms, and the melodies of Reger.

WORKS.—Sonata, vln. and PF. C flat min., op. 3 ; sonatas, vln. E min. and D maj., opp. 9 and 13 ; rhapsody, vln. and orch., op. 15 ; sonata, clar. in E min., op. 5 ; PF. quintet, C min., op. 18 ; str. quartet, A min., op. 25 ; scherzo, fl. and PF., op. 11; little evening music, str., op. 11 ; str. quartet, G min., op. 26 ; five pieces for PF., op. 2 ; sonata, PF. in A flat, op. 4 ; piano-fantasy, E flat min. ; three PF. pieces, op. 23 ; songs, opp. 1, 12, 21, 22 ; songs with orch., opp. 7 and 24, sinfonietta, orch. in A min., op. 20 ; ballade, orch. and vcl., G min., op. 17 ; overture, E maj., op. 13 ; Symphony suite, op. 8, 'Gesang der späteren Lieder' for female chor. and orch., op. 16 ; music to 'Traumland' ' str. quintet, 2 vlns., 2 v'las. and v'cl., op. 30.   H. J. K.

KORNGOLD, (1) JULIUS (*b.* Brno, Dec. 24, 1860), studied law in Vienna (graduated Dr. Jur.) and music at the Conservatorium there. He succeeded Hanslick as critic of the *Neue Freie Presse* in Vienna, in which capacity he has wielded a considerable influence. His son, (2) ERICH WOLFGANG (*b.* Brno, May 29, 1897), early showed precocious talent as a composer. He was 11 years old when his

---

[1] Mendel.
[2] This is corrobora ed by Hanslick, *Aus dem Concert-saal*, p. 429.

pantomime, 'Der Schneemann,' was given at the Hofoper in Vienna. Two piano sonatas, an elaborate Lustspiel Ouvertüre for a large orchestra, and a Sinfonietta for orchestra and some chamber music followed in quick succession. His first opera was ' Der Ring des Polycrates '; two later operas, ' Violanta ' (Vienna and Munich, 1916) and ' Die tote Stadt ' (Hamburg, 1920), have been much acclaimed and frequently given. (*Riemann.*)   c.

KOTO, see JAPANESE MUSIC.

KOTTER, HANS (*b.* Strassburg, *c.* 1485 ; *d.* Berne, between 1541–43), organist at Freiburg from *c.* 1504. As a Protestant he was imprisoned, tortured and exiled in 1522. At the instance of the Strassburg council he obtained his freedom in 1531 (?) and went to Berne *c.* 1532; but, as the Reformation had banished all church organs, the only employment he could find was that of a schoolmaster. He remained at Berne except for a few fruitless journeys to obtain a more suitable position. The organ-book in tablature written by him for Bonifazius Amerbach in 1513, now in the University library, Basle, is one of the oldest monuments of the German school of organ-playing. He wrote also a second organ book without name of author, and a Salve Regina *a* 3 v. for organ (in the same library) (*Riemann, Q.-L.*).

KOTZWARA (KOCŽWARA), FRANZ (*b.* Prague ; *d.* London, Sept. 2, 1791), published six songs in London in 1785, was in Ireland in 1788, and was engaged in 1790 as tenor player in Gallini's orchestra at the King's Theatre. He returned to London in the latter year, and in 1791 he hanged himself in a house of ill-fame in Vine Street, St. Martin's. He had been one of the band at the Handel Commemoration in the preceding May. Kotzwara was the author of the ' Battle of Prague,' a piece for PF. with violin, violoncello and drum *ad libitum*, long a favourite in London. A copy of John Lee's edition of this piece exists, bearing the MS. date 1788, so that it must have been published before the date usually given, 1789. He also wrote sonatas, serenades, and other pieces.   G. ; addn. W. H. G. F.

KOVAŘOVIC, KAREL (*b.* Prague, Dec. 9, 1862 ; *d.* there, Dec. 9, 1920), for twenty years (1900–20) chief conductor of the National Opera (Národni Divadlo) in PRAGUE (*q.v.*), and the composer of two very popular operas founded on national subjects : ' Psohlavci ' (The Peasants' Charter) and ' Na starém Bĕlidle ' (At the Old Bleaching House).

On leaving the Prague Conservatoire, where he had made the clarinet and the harp his special studies, Kovařovic joined the orchestra of the National Opera as harpist until 1885. He then studied theory with Fibich. Being also an excellent pianist, he was engaged as accompanist by the violinist Fr. Ondříček, and toured with him from 1886–88. During the

next few years he was employed as conductor to several provincial societies, until in 1895 Prof. Hostinsky commissioned him to organise and direct an orchestra for the Ethnographical Exhibition in Prague. This brought his remarkable gifts as a conductor into prominence, and it was realised that he was the very man to be placed at the head of the National Opera. It was not without some opposition and delay that he was actually appointed conductor-in-chief, in 1900. His drastic methods raised the entire standard of performance, but naturally aroused some hostility in his professional surroundings. A stern disciplinarian with his personnel, he took also a very decided view as to the works suitable for production at the National Opera, and set his face against indiscriminate experimentalism. He was, however, an eclectic in his views, and his performances of Mozart were as carefully thought out and as exquisite in detail as were his famous revivals of Smetana's operas, which he popularised until they became a really vital part of the musical life of his people. Kovařovic put the National Opera in Prague on a level with the best continental opera houses, having regard to the size and resources of the city. As regards the appreciation and assimilation of very modern music he had his limitations, but made on the whole very few mistakes. His life and health were given ungrudgingly to the maintenance of first-rate opera, of which the Czechs were justly proud.

As a composer, Kovařovic appeared at first to be merely versatile and superficially gifted. As a young man he wrote several comic operas : ' Ženichove ' (The Bridegrooms) (1884), ' Cesta Oknem ' (The Way through the Window) (1886), and ' Noč Šimon a Judy ' (The Night of Simon and Jude) (1892), besides a picturesque ballet, influenced by Delibes, ' Haschish ' (1881), and ' Pohádka o nalezeném štěsti ' (A Tale of Luck Found) (1886). A sense for the stage and a certain musical wit assured some success for these works, and also for a burlesque operetta on ' Œdipus Rex,' and the incidental music which he furnished for Tyl's *Wood Nymph* and *The Excursions of Mr. Brouček.* But none suspected that his talent, hitherto somewhat unworthily employed, was maturing and aspiring in secret until, in 1898, it manifested itself in a serious opera, written in honour of .ne Jubilee of the Association of the Národni Divadlo. ' Psohlavci,' translated into German as ' Bauernrecht ' (The Peasants' Charter,) but meaning literally ' the Dog-heads,' is based on a tale by the popular historical novelist, Jirásek. The Chods, a small group of loyal peasants dwelling in the south-west of Bohemia, had proved such trusty guardians of the frontier that they were recompensed by various princes of Bohemia with unusual favours, amongst them the right to bear on their banners the symbol of a watch-dog's head. But in 1695 Austrian oppression touched its zenith, and the Chods were stripped of their privileges and treated with brutal injustice by their Governor, the implacable Laminger von Albenreuth, called ' Lomikar ' by the Slavonic peasants. The judicial murder of one of their leaders, Kozina, who remains to this day a traditional local hero, furnishes material for a touching and dramatic libretto. The homely and historical setting of the story may possibly limit its universal significance, while offering as compensation many picturesque suggestions—the local costumes, dances and scenery ; but the emotional scope is profound and untrammelled. There are stirring moments in ' Psohlavci ' : the mock trial scene in which the peasants' cherished charter is torn to shreds by the partial judge ; the tense mental agony of the prison scene, when Kozina refuses pardon at the price of his honour; the sudden death of the sinister Lomikar in the banquet hall— these are strong situations, and Kovařovic knew how to make them not merely effective, but poignant. Here he sloughs off the facile eclecticism of earlier years and produces music of real value.

While aiming to follow in some respects the operatic traditions of Smetana, Kovařovic could not, because of his delicate and distinguished musical personality, prevent his own work from taking a more modern and individual form. Between the master and the disciple lies the development of a whole generation. The immediate success of ' Psohlavci ' was sensational, and its popularity has lasted over a quarter of a century. Kovařovic followed this dramatic opera by a completely contrasting work. ' Na starém Bělidle ' (At the Old Bleaching House), the libretto founded on Mme. Němcova's novel of rural life, Babička (Grannie), is not so much an opera as a series of idyllic scenes from the life of an earlier generation, enveloped in a tender and delicate musical tissue, shot through with the colour of the folk music, a little reminiscent of Massenet, and touched with a wistful calm and mellow beauty which, emanating from the personality of Grannie, pervades the entire work. A few gay dances, the singing of the girls as they spin by the light of the log fire in Grannie's bleaching house, the brightness of the costumes, and the atmosphere of youth contrasted with that of serene old age, all combine to make a delicate little poem of ' Na starém Bělidle.'

Among Kovařovic's miscellaneous works are the symphonic poem ' The Rape of Persephone ' (1884), dramatic overture in C minor, incidental music to Šubert's play Raphael's Loves, and to Vojnovic's ' Equinox,' a violin sonata in F, a pianoforte concerto in F minor, string quartets in A minor, G major and E flat,

romance for clarinet, a few charming songs in the national style, including the popular ' Slovak Song,' to words by Destinnova, one or two melodramas and small choral works.

Kovařovic visited England in May 1919, when, with the orchestra of the Prague National Opera, he took part in the Czechoslovak Musical Festival in London. He was already in failing health, and a few months later underwent a severe operation which did little to alleviate his sufferings. He died at the age of 58, just at the time when the newly-won independence of Bohemia gave every hope that his devoted service to his country's art might become more widely appreciated.

R. N.

KOVEN, HENRY LOUIS REGINALD DE (b. Middletown, Connecticut, Apr. 3, 1859; d. Chicago, Jan. 16, 1920), an American composer, chiefly of comic operas and songs. He studied at St. John's College, Oxford, where he took his degree in 1879, and then devoted himself to music successively at Stuttgart, Frankfort, Florence, Vienna and Paris. He composed many light operas, beginning with ' The Begum ' in 1887. By far the most successful of them was ' Robin Hood,' first heard in 1890, and for many seasons thereafter in America, and given in London as ' Maid Marion.' His ' Rob Roy ' (1894), also gained considerable success. In 1902 De Koven formed the Philharmonic Orchestra in Washington, D.C., which he conducted for two seasons. In the season of 1916–17 his grand opera, ' The Canterbury Pilgrims,' was produced at the Metropolitan Opera House in New York ; a second grand opera, ' Rip Van Winkle,' was produced in Chicago and in New York by the Chicago Opera Company in 1920. De Koven was also a fertile writer of songs ; of 400 which he composed, some have gained a remarkable popularity. He had a gift for facile melody and, to a certain extent, for characterisation in comedy. But his powers did not extend to the successful creation of operas in the larger forms. His two ' grand operas,' comedies on a larger scale, show fundamental weaknesses ; and especially in the matter of ensemble writing and orchestral scoring.   R. A.

KOŽELUH (Ger. KOTZELUCH), (1) JOHANN ANTON (b. Welvarn, Dec. 13, 1738 ; d. Prague, Feb. 3, 1814), Bohemian musician, was choirmaster first at Rakonitz and then at Welvarn Desirous of further instruction he went to Prague and Vienna, where he was kindly received by Gluck and Gassmann, was appointed choirmaster of the Kreuzherrn church, Prague ; and on Mar.13, 1784, Kapellmeister to the cathedral, which post he retained till his death. He composed church-music, operas and oratorios, of which very little was published. Q.-L. gives a cantata for soprano, op. 7, as published by

Artaria of Vienna, and contains a list of MS. works. Of much greater importance is his cousin and pupil,

(2) LEOPOLD (b. Welwarn, 1754 [1] ; d. Vienna, May 7, 1818 [2]). In 1765 he went to Prague for his education, and there composed a ballet, performed at the national theatre in 1771, with so much success that it was followed in the course of the next six years by twenty-four ballets and three pantomimes. In 1778 he went to Vienna and became the pianoforte master of the Archduchess Elizabeth, and favourite teacher of the aristocracy. When Mozart resigned his post at Salzburg (1781) the Archbishop at once offered it with a rise of salary to Koželuh, who declined it on the ground that he was doing better in Vienna. To his friends, however, he held different language :

'The Archbishop's conduct towards Mozart deterred me more than anything, for if he could let such a man as that leave him, what treatment should I have been likely to meet with ? '

The respect here expressed was strangely at variance with his subsequent behaviour towards Mozart.[3] At the coronation of the Emperor Leopold II. at Prague (1791) even his own countrymen, the Bohemians, were disgusted with his behaviour to Mozart, who was in attendance as court composer. He nevertheless succeeded him in his office (1792), with a salary of 1500 gulden, and retained the post till his death. His numerous compositions include two grand operas, ' Judith ' and ' Debora und Sisara ' ; an oratorio, ' Moses in Aegypten ' ; many ballets, cantatas, about thirty symphonies, and much pianoforte music, at one time well known in England, but all now forgotten. (See list in Q.-L.) It should be added that he arranged some Scottish songs for Thomson of Edinburgh, in allusion to which, Beethoven, in a letter of Feb. 29, 1812 (Thayer, iii. 449), whether inspired with disgust at Koželuh's underselling him, or with a genuine contempt for his music, says, ' Moi je m'estime encore une fois plus supérieur en ce genre que Monsieur Kozeluch (miserabilis).' [4]   F. G.

KRAF, MICHAEL, a Frankonian, Kapellmeister and organist of the monastery of Weingarten, Würtemberg, between 1620–27. He was a prolific composer of masses, motets, other church music, and of songs. (List in Q.-L.)

KRAFFT, (1) FRANÇOIS (b. Ghent, 1728 ; d. there, Jan. 13, 1795), choir-boy at Ghent Cathedral, maître de chapelle, Brussels. He was at Ghent Cathedral from 1770 or 1771. He left some 60 compositions, mostly in private hands. (2) FRANÇOIS (b. Brussels, Oct. 3, 1733), music teacher at Brussels, 1760, composer to the Royal Chapel, 1770–83. According to Fétis he

was organist at Notre Dame au Sablon. Fétis quotes also FRANÇOIS-JOSEPH (b. Brussels, July 22, 1720). The history is so far greatly confused, and it is uncertain to which of the foregoing the sonatas in Haffner's ' Raccolta ' or the 12 minuets, 13 pièces en écho mentioned in Q.-L. have to be attributed. It appears certain, however, that the masses and sacred songs at the collegiate church of Anderlecht (dated 1783) are by François (2).

KRAFT, (1) ANTON (b. Rokitzan near Pilsen, Bohemia, Dec. 30, 1752 [5] ; d. Aug. 28, 1820), distinguished violoncellist, son of a brewer and amateur, who had his son early taught music, especially the violoncello. He studied law at Prague, where he had finishing lessons from Werner, and at Vienna, where Haydn secured him for the chapel of Prince Esterhazy, which he entered on Jan. 1, 1778. On the Prince's death in 1790 he became chamber-musician to Prince Grassalkowitsch, and in 1795 to Prince Lobkowitz, in whose service he died. On one of his concert-tours he was at Dresden in 1789, and with his son played before Duke Karl, and before the Elector the night after the court had been enchanted by Mozart. Both musicians were staying at the same hotel, so they arranged a quartet, the fourth part being taken by Teyber the organist.[6] Haydn valued Kraft for his power of expression, and for the purity of his intonation, and in all probability composed (1781) his violoncello concerto (André) for him. According to Schindler [7] the violoncello part in Beethoven's triple concerto was also intended for Kraft. As he showed a talent for composition, Haydn offered to instruct him, but Kraft taking up the new subject with such ardour as to neglect his instrument, Haydn would teach him no more, saying he already knew enough for his purpose. He published three sonatas with accompaniment, op. 1 (Amsterdam, Hummel) ; three sonatas, op. 2 (André) ; three grand duos concertantes for violin and violoncello, op. 3, and first concerto in C, op. 4 (Breitkopf & Härtel) ; grand duos for two violoncellos, opp. 5 and 6 (Vienna, Steiner) ; and divertissement for violoncello with double bass (Peters). Kraft also played the baritone in Prince Esterhazy's chamber music,[8] and composed several trios for two baritones and violoncello.

His son and pupil (2) NICOLAUS (b. Esterház, Dec. 14, 1778 ; d. May 18, 1853), early became proficient on the violoncello, accompanied his father on his concert-tours (see above), and settled with him in Vienna in 1790. He played a concerto of his father's at a concert of the Tonkünstler-Societät in 1792, and was one of

1 Riemann gives 1748.
2 The date, 1814, was given by Dlabač and Wurzbach, who have been followed by some later authorities.
3 See Jahn's Mozart, Engl. trans., ii. 347.
4 See Thayer, iii. 449 ; Krehbiel, ii. 219.

5 This is the date in the baptismal register ; 1751 and 1749 have been given.
6 Mozart also played with the Krafts his Trio in E (Köchel, 542) see Nohl's Mozart-Briefe, No. 251.
7 Vol. i. p. 147 ; see also Thayer's Beethoven, vol. ii. p. 299.
8 For an anecdote on this point see Josef Haydn, by C. F. Pohl vol. i. p. 252.

Prince Karl Lichnowsky's famous quartet party, who executed so many of Beethoven's works for the first time. The others were Schuppanzigh, Sina, and Franz Weiss, all young men.[1] In 1796 he became chamber-musician to Prince Lobkowitz, who sent him in 1801 to Berlin for further study with Louis Duport. There he gave concerts, as well as at Leipzig, Dresden, Prague and Vienna on his return journey. In 1809 he entered the orchestra of the court-opera, and the King of Würtemberg hearing him in 1814, at once engaged him for his chapel at Stuttgart. He undertook several more concert-tours (Hummel accompanied him in 1818), but an accident to his hand obliged him to give up playing. He retired on a pension in 1834. Among his pupils were Count Wilhorsky, Merk, Birnbach, Wranitzky's sons, and his own son (3) FRIEDRICH (b. Vienna, Feb. 12, 1807), who became violoncellist in the chapel at Stuttgart, 1824.

Among Nicolaus's excellent violoncello compositions may be specified—

Fantasia with quartet, op. 1 (André); concertos, opp. 3, 4 (B. & H.) and 5 (Peters); Scène pastorale with orchestra, dedicated to the King of Würtemberg, op. 9 (Peters); 8 divertissements progressifs with second violoncello, op. 14 (André); three easy duos for two violoncellos, op. 15, and three grand duos for ditto, op. 17 (André).   C. F. P.

KRAKOVIAK (CRACOVIAK, or CRACO-VIENNE), a Polish dance, belonging to the district of Cracow. ' There are usually,' says an eye-witness, ' a great many couples—as many as in an English country dance. They shout while dancing, and occasionally the smart man of the party sings an impromptu couplet suited for the occasion—on birthdays, weddings, etc. The men also strike their heels together while dancing, which produces a metallic sound, as the heels are covered with iron.' The songs, which also share the name, are innumerable and, as is natural, deeply tinged with melancholy. Under the name of Cracovienne the dance was brought into the theatre about the year 1840, and was made famous by Fanny Elssler's performance. The following is the tune to which she danced it ; but whether that is a real Krakoviak, or a mere imitation, the writer is unable to say :

It has been varied by Chopin (op. 14), Herz, Wallace, and others.   G.

[1] See Thayer's *Beethoven*, vol. ii. p. 278.

KRANZ, JOHANN FRIEDRICH (b. Weimar, 1754 ; d. Stuttgart, 1807), violinist and composer, pupil of Göpfert, Weimar (violin), and Jos. Haydn, Vienna. From 1778–81 he was a member of Weimar court orchestra ; was sent by the Duke to Italy for further studies ; returned in 1739, and was appointed second Konzertmeister in the court orchestra and music director of the opera. He composed several Singspiele, especially those by Goethe, who mentions him in *Tag und Jahreshefte*, 1791 (vol. 21, p. 12). In 1803 he became Zumsteeg's successor as Kapellmeister of the Stuttgart court theatre, which post he held till the time of his death.   E. V. D. S.

KRÁSNOHORSKÁ, ELIŠKA (b. Nov. 18, 1847), a distinguished Czech authoress who furnished librettos for many popular Bohemian operas in the second half of the 19th century. She showed musical talent in her girlhood, and studied singing and theory under Zvonař at the ' Žofin ' Academy, but literature finally claimed her whole attention. The chief operas for which she wrote the texts were : Bendl's ' Lejla ' (from Bulwer Lytton) (1868), ' Břetislava,' (1870), ' Dítě Tabora ' (The Child of Tabor) (1892), and ' Karel Škreta ' (1883) ; Fibich's ' Blanik ' (1881) ; while for Smetana she wrote the texts of ' Hubička ' (The Kiss) (1876), ' Tajemstvi ' (The Secret) (1878), and ' Čertova Stěna ' (The Devil's Wall) (1882). She also made a very happy translation into Czech of Bizet's ' Carmen.' Krásnohorská has been a frequent contributor to the leading musical and other journals, and her articles on ' Czech Poetry and Music Drama,' ' Czech Musical Declamation,' and her reminiscences of Smetana are useful to the student, especially her brochure *Bedřich Smetana*, published in 1885 in Em. Chávla's series of Musical Essays (*Rozpravy Hudebni*, Fr. Urbánek, Prague).   R. N.

KRAUS, JOSEPH MARTIN (b. Miltenberg, near Mainz ; d. Stockholm, Dec. 15, 1792), pupil of Abbé Vogler. He studied philosophy and law at Mainz, Erfurt and Göttingen ; and went with a Swedish co-student to Stockholm, where he became conductor at the theatre in 1778 and Kapellmeister in 1781. In 1782 he travelled at the expense of, and partly with, the King of Sweden through Germany, Italy, France and England, returning to Stockholm in 1787. In 1788 he succeeded Uttini as court Kapellmeister. He composed 4 operas, church music, secular songs, symphonies, overtures and string quartets ; he also wrote essays on music (anon.), poetry, and an autobiography. (List in *Q.-L.*)

KRAUS, FATHER LAMBERT (b. Pfreund, Palatinate ; d. Nov. 27, 1790), abbot of the monastery of Metten in Bavaria. He composed sacred and secular ' Singspiele ' (1762–70), 12 symphonies, 16 masses and other church music.

KRAUSE, CHRISTIAN GOTTFRIED (b. Winzig, Silesia, 1719 ; d. Berlin, July 21, 1770), son of

E

a town musician. He studied at the University of Frankfort-on-Oder, and became a barrister in 1753. He was a song composer, whom Riemann calls 'the soul of the Berlin Lieder-school,' and the author of important essays on music (A. Schering, *Studie über Krause*; see also *Riemann*).

KRAUSS, MARIE GABRIELLE (*b.* Vienna, Mar. 24, 1842; *d.* Paris, Jan. 5-6, 1906), received instruction at the Conservatorium in pianoforte playing and harmony, and in singing from Mme. Marchesi. She sang in Schumann's 'Paradise and Peri' at its publication in Vienna by the Gesellschaft der Musikfreunde, Mar. 1, 1858. She made her début at the opera there as Mathilde (' Tell ') in July 1859, and played also Anna (' Dame Blanche ') and Valentine. She became a favourite, and remained there for some years, until about 1867. She made her début at the Italiens, Paris, as Leonora (' Trovatore '), Apr. 6, 1867, and Lucrezia ; became very successful, and was engaged there every season until the war of 1870. She gained great applause by her performance of Donna Anna, Fidelio, Norma, Lucia, Semiramide, Gilda, etc., in a new opera of Mme. de Grandval's, ' Piccolino,' Nov. 25, 1869, and in Halévy's ' Guido et Ginevra ' (1870). She sang with great success at Naples in Petrella's ' Manfredo ' (1871), and ' Bianca Orsini ' (1874), also as Aida ; with less success at Milan as Elsa on the production there of ' Lohengrin,' and in Gomes's ' Fosca,' Feb. 16, 1873. She returned to the Italiens for a short time in the autumn of 1873, accepted the offer of an engagement for the Opéra, previous to which she played at St. Petersburg in 1874. She made her début at the Opéra, at the inauguration of the new house, as Rachel in ' La Juive ' (first two acts), Jan. 5, 1875, and in the same opera in its entirety, Jan. 8. With the exception of a short period, 1885–86, she remained a member of that company until the end of 1888. She played in operas produced there for the first time as the heroine (Mermet's ' Jeanne d'Arc '), Apr. 5, 1876 ; Pauline (Gounod's ' Polyeucte '), Oct. 7, 1878 ; Aida, Mar. 22, 1880 ; Hermosa (Gounod's ' Tribut de Zamora '), Apr. 1, 1881 ; Katharine of Aragon (Saint-Saëns's ' Henry VIII '), Mar. 5, 1883 ; the heroine on revival of Gounod's ' Sapho,' Apr. 2, 1884 ; Gilda (' Rigoletto '), Mar. 2, 1885 ; and Dolores (Paladilhe's ' Patrie '), Dec. 20, 1886.

' By degrees Gabrielle Krauss became as great an actress as she was a singer . . . and the French were right when they gave her the name of ' La Rachel chantante' (Marchesi).

After her retirement, she frequently sang at concerts, and for many years devoted herself to teaching.   A. C.

BIBL.—CHARNACÉ, *Les Étoiles du chant* (Paris, 1868–69); H. DE CURZON, *Croquis d'artistes* (Paris, 1893).

KREBS, (1) JOHANN LUDWIG (*b.* Buttel-

städt, Thuringia, Feb. 10, 1713 ; *d.* Altenburg, Jan.[1] 1780), distinguished organist. His father, JOHANN TOBIAS (*b.* Heichelheim, 1690 ; *d.* Buttelstädt, after 1728), himself an excellent organist, for seven years walked every week from Buttelstädt to Weimar, in order to take lessons from Walther, author of the Lexicon, who was organist there, and from Sebastian Bach, at that time Konzertmeister at Weimar. He was appointed organist at Buttelstädt about 1721. He so thoroughly grounded his son in music that when in 1726 the latter went to the Thomasschule in Leipzig he was already sufficiently advanced to be at once admitted by Bach into the number of his special pupils. He enjoyed Bach's instruction for nine years (to 1735), and rose to so high a place in his esteem that he was appointed to play the clavier at the weekly practices to which Bach gave the name of ' collegium musicum.' Punning upon his pupil's name and his own, the old cantor was accustomed to say that ' he was the best crab (Krebs) in all the brook (Bach).'

At the close of his philosophical studies at Leipzig he was appointed organist successively at Zwickau (1737), Zeitz (1744), and Altenburg, where he remained from 1756 till his death. He was equally esteemed on the clavier and the organ, and in the latter capacity especially deserves to be considered one of Bach's best pupils. His published compositions include ' Klavier-Uebungen ' (4 parts), containing Chorals with variations, fugues and suites ; sonatas for clavier, and for flute and clavier ; and trios for the flute. (See *Q.-L.*) Several of these have been reprinted in the collections of Körner and others. Among his unpublished works a Magnificat and two settings of the Sanctus with orchestral accompaniments are highly spoken of.

He left two sons, both sound musicians and composers, though not of the eminence of their father. The eldest, (2) EHRENFRIED CHRISTIAN TRAUGOTT, succeeded his father as court organist and Musik-director at Altenburg, and on his death was succeeded by his younger brother, (3) JOHANN GOTTFRIED, who wrote cantatas, songs, etc.   A. M.

KREBS, a musical family of the 19th century. (1) KARL AUGUST (*b.* Nuremberg, Jan. 16, 1804 ; *d.* May 16, 1880), the head, was the son of A. and Charlotte Miedcke, belonging to the company of the theatre at Nuremberg. The name of Krebs he obtained from the singer of that name at Stuttgart, who adopted him. His early studies were made under Schelble, and in 1825 under Seyfried at Vienna. In Mar. 1827 he settled in Hamburg as head of the theatre, and there passed twenty-three active and useful years, till called to Dresden in 1850 as Kapellmeister to the court, a post

[1] Buried Jan. 4.

which he filled with honour and advantage till 1871. From that date he conducted the orchestra in the Catholic chapel. His compositions are numerous and varied in kind— masses, operas (' Silva,' 1830, ' Agnes Bernauer,' 1835), a Te Deum, orchestral pieces, songs and pianoforte works, many of them much esteemed in Germany. In England, however, his name is known almost exclusively as the father of (2) MARIE KREBS (b. Dresden, Dec. 5, 1851; d. June 27, 1900), the pianist. On the side of both father and mother (ALOYSIA MICHALESI, an operatic singer of eminence, b. Aug. 29, 1826, married Krebs July 20, 1850) she inherited music, and like Mme. Schumann was happy in having a father who directed her studies with great judgment. Marie appeared in public at the early age of 11 (Meissen, 1862). Her tours embraced not only the whole of Germany and England, but Italy, France, Holland and America. She played at the Gewandhaus first, Nov. 30, 1865. To this country she came in the previous year, and made an engagement with Gye for four seasons, and her first appearances were at the Crystal Palace, Apr. 30, 1864; at the Philharmonic, Apr. 20, 1874; and at the Monday Popular Concerts, Jan. 13, 1875. She enjoyed many years of great popularity in England and on the continent, and retired from the profession on her marriage with Herr Brenning.

G., with addns.

KREHBIEL, HENRY EDWARD (b. Ann Arbor, Michigan, U.S.A., Mar. 10, 1854; d. Mar. 20, 1923), an eminent American critic and writer of music. He studied law in Cincinnati, but soon turned to journalism, devoting himself especially to music. He was music critic of *The Cincinnati Gazette* from 1874 to 1880, and then entered upon the same office for *The New York Tribune*, which post he held till his death. He occupied a position of outstanding authority and influence among American critics, was one of the ablest champions of musical progress, and at the same time a deep student of the classics. He did much to advance the understanding and love of Wagner's later music dramas in America, and was among the earliest to welcome and appraise discriminatingly the music of Brahms, Tchaikovsky, Dvořák and other modern composers. It was to some extent at any rate due to him that such work was made familiar in New York before it was widely known in many European capitals.

Krehbiel's activity was by no means confined to newspaper criticism. Amongst the list of his many books given below, the revised and completed edition of the English text of Thayer's *Life of Beethoven* is pre-eminent (see THAYER.) It was the work of his last years, and its publication was attained through the instrumentality of the Beethoven Association of New York.

(See BAUER, Harold.) Another line of original research in which his work is important was his study of the negro folk-songs, of which he made a large collection. His intimate and first-hand knowledge was ultimately embodied in *Afro-American Folk-songs* (1914). He was widely known as a lecturer; he accomplished a useful work for many years by means of the programme notes and analyses that he prepared for the principal New York concerts (see ANALYTICAL NOTES). He acted as editor for American matters to the second edition of this Dictionary and contributed to it many important articles. His principal books are as follows :

Notes on the Cultivation of Choral Music and the Oratorio Society of New York (1884) ; *Review of the New York Musical Season* (five volumes, 1885–90) ; *Studies in the Wagnerian Drama* (1891) ; *The Philharmonic Society of New York : a Memorial published on the occasion of the Fiftieth Anniversary of the Founding of the Philharmonic Society* (1892) ; *How to Listen to Music* (1897) ; *Music and Manners in the Classical Period* (1898) ; *Chapters of Opera*, a valuable history of opera in New York (1908, 2nd edition 1909) ; *A Book of Operas* (1909) ; *The Pianoforte and its Music* (1911) ; *Afro-American Folk-songs* (1914) ; *A Second Book of Operas* (1917) ; *More Chapters of Opera* (1919) ; Thayer's *Life of Beethoven* revised, completed and published for the first time in English (3 vols., 1921).

In 1900 he was on the jury for musical instruments at the Paris Exposition; and in 1901 received the cross of the Legion of Honour.

M. ; addns. R. A.

KREHL, STEPHAN (b. Leipzig, July 5, 1864; d. Apr. 7, 1924), composer and theorist, was a pupil at the Leipzig and Dresden Conservatoriums. In 1889 he was appointed teacher of piano and theory at the Carlsruhe Conservatorium. In 1902 he went in a similar capacity to the Conservatorium at Leipzig, attaining the title of ' Royal Professor ' in 1910, and in 1921 he succeeded Hans Sitt as director of that institution, a post which he occupied till his death. He was an admirable theorist, and possessed the invaluable gift of being able to express lucidly whatever he wished to say. In the main he followed Hugo Riemann's system of harmony and counterpoint, and wrote several handbooks for educational purposes, for the most part of an elementary kind: *Praktische Formenlehre* (1902) ; *Fuge* (1909) ; *Allgemeine Musiklehre* (1910) ; *Harmonielehre* (1911) ; *Kontrapunkt* (1912) ; and (more advanced) *Theorie der Tonkunst und Kompositionslehre*, 2 vols. (1921–24). His compositions, always well written and workmanlike, are in some instances attractive; notably his clarinet quintet, op. 19, and the ' Symphonic Prelude to Hannele,' op. 15. Amongst the better of his other compositions are a string quartet, op. 17, sonata for piano and violoncello, op. 20, a cantata called ' Tröstung,' op. 33, and a suite for string quartet written just before his death. H. B.

KREISLER, FRITZ (b. Vienna, Feb. 2, 1875), violinist, displayed musical gifts of an uncommon order in earliest infancy. These were recognised by his father, an eminent physician and enthusiastic musical amateur, who instructed and encouraged him to such purpose that at the age of 7 he appeared at a concert for children given in Vienna by Carlotta Patti, and entered the Vienna Conservatorium, where he studied under Hellmesberger and Auer. This was a special privilege, pupils being as a general rule ineligible for admission in that institution before the age of 14. He was in fact the youngest child who had studied there, and justified to the full the opinion formed of his exceptional talents by carrying off, in 1885, the gold medal for violin-playing at the age of 10. Passing on to Paris, where he studied at the Conservatoire under Massart (violin) and Delibes (theory), he there achieved at the age of 12 another remarkable success, gaining the gold medal (Premier Grand Prix de Rome) against forty competitors, all of whom had reached the age of 20. After a few years of further study he visited America (in 1889), and made a successful tour of the States with Moritz Rosenthal, the pianist, at the conclusion of which he returned to his native town and temporarily broke away from the musical life. He entered the Gymnasium at Vienna to take up a course of medicine, studied art in Paris and Rome, prepared for and passed a very stiff army examination, and duly became an officer in a regiment of Uhlans. In short, he gave to other sides of his nature, besides the musical, a chance of development. During his year of military service he laid the violin completely aside, and, as a result of the training received, became physically the more fitted for a profession which makes serious calls upon the vitality of those who practise it. Then came a transition period, during which he made a few public appearances, but with so little success that he was moved to make a preliminary retirement into the country, during which he worked uninterruptedly at his violin for eight weeks, and emerged triumphant, having completely regained his command over the instrument. He was then able once more to shine as a solo player, making a brilliant début at Berlin in Mar. 1899, in a programme which included concertos by Max Bruch and Vieuxtemps, and the ' Non più mesta ' variations of Paganini. In the same year he revisited the United States, where the public was quick to perceive the quality of greatness which is now universally attributed to him. Subsequently he paid frequent visits to America, and lived chiefly in New York from 1915–24. On the eve of war (July 31, 1914), he was recalled to the Austrian army from Ragaz in Switzerland, and returned wounded to America three months later. His appearances in all the continental musical centres have been very numerous. In London he made his début at a Richter Concert on May 12, 1901. On May 19, 1904, he was presented at a Philharmonic Concert with the gold medal of the society ; he played frequently in England up to the time of

the war, and reappeared after it at Queen's Hall on May 4, 1921. His style of playing is full of glow and high courage, above all intensely individual, his readings and even his methods of fingering being quite his own. His programmes include frequently works of major importance—notably he was the first to perform Elgar's violin concerto (at a Philharmonic Concert) in London, St. Petersburg, Moscow, Vienna, Berlin, Dresden, Munich and Amsterdam ; but the feature of his concerts lately has been his brilliant playing of his own works, a few of which are original (e.g. ' Caprice viennois,' ' Tambourin chinois,' 'Recitative and Scherzo' for violin alone, and ' Polichinelle Sérénade'). The bulk of them, however, are clever arrangements of pieces ancient and modern, and they are so much to the taste of the general public that Kreisler may be said to be the world's most popular violinist at the present time (1926).

He has written one string quartet (A minor). It contains no quartet writing of the conventional kind, but is charged with very deep and very personal feeling, and is so well laid out for the strings that it is sure of its effect.

                         w. w. c

KREISLERIANA, a set of 8 pieces for piano solo, dedicated to Chopin and forming op. 16 of Schumann's works. Kreisler is the Kapellmeister in Hoffmann's *Fantasiestücke in Callots Manier*, so much admired by Schumann. (See BÖHNER and HOFFMANN.) The pieces were written in 1838, after the Phantasiestücke (op. 12) and Novelletten (op. 21), and before the Arabeske (op. 18).[1] Schumann has added to the title ' Phantasien für das PF.' The Kreisleriana were published by Haslinger of Vienna shortly after Schumann's visit there (1838–39).   G.

KREISSLE VON HELLBORN, HEINRICH (b. Vienna, 1812 ; d. Apr. 6, 1869), Dr. juris, Imperial Finance Secretary at Vienna, and Member of the Direction of the Gesellschaft der Musikfreunde, finds a place here for his lives of Schubert, viz. *F. Schubert, eine biografische Skizze*, von Heinrich von Kreissle (small 8vo, Vienna, 1861), a preliminary sketch; and *Franz Schubert* (8vo, Vienna, Gerold, 1865), a complete and exhaustive biography, with a portrait. The latter has been translated in full by Arthur Duke Coleridge, *The Life of Franz Schubert . . . with an Appendix by George Grove* (giving a thematic catalogue of the nine symphonies, and mentioning other works in MS.), 2 vols., 8vo, London, Longmans, 1869 It has also been condensed by E. Wilberforce. 8vo, London, Allen, 1866.   C. F. P.

KRENEK, ERNST (b. Vienna, 1900), composer, of Czech family, studied composition with Franz Schreker in Vienna and Berlin, and is now domiciled in the latter city. His works, which have led to his recognition as one of the

[1] Wasielewsky, 181.

foremost composers of the younger generation in Germany, are remarkable for the austerity of his contrapuntal outlook. He appears to be swayed by strictly musical, not to say even technical, impulses, and rarely, if ever, allows his course to be deflected by emotional or temperamental considerations. He takes the ' linear ' view of polyphony which prevails in so much recent German music, and is in fact one of its most uncompromising adherents. As with others, this has committed him to atonality, but rather as a corollary to his methods than as an integral feature of them, for he does not wilfully avoid the assertion of tonality where it presents itself in the course of development. His strong feeling for rhythm is possibly a racial trait, but if so it stands alone, for he has nothing in common with the Czech national movement. His reputation was established by performances at various festivals, notably of a string quartet in 1921 and a symphony in 1923, followed in 1924 by the production of a comic opera in three acts, ' Der Sprung über den Schatten ' (op. 17).

The following is a list of his works :

1. (1) Double Fugue, and (2) 'Tanzstudie ' for PF.
2. Sonata for PF.
3 Sonata, vln. and PF.
4 Serenade for clar., vln., vla. and vcl.
5. Five Sonatinas for PF.
6. String Quartet I.
7. Symphony I.
8. String Quartet II.
9. Songs.
10. Concerto grosso I. For 6 solo instr. (vln., vla., vcl., flute, clar. and bassoon) and str. orch.
11. Symphonic Music I. For 9 solo instr. (flute, oboe, clar., bassoon, 2 vlns., vla., vcl. and double-bass).
12. Symphony II.
13 Toccata and Chaconne for PF.
14. ' Zwingburg.' Dramatic cantata.
15. Songs.
16. Symphony III.
17. ' Der Sprung über den Schatten.' Opera.
18. Piano Concerto in F sharp.
19. Songs.
20. String Quartet III.
21. Orpheus and Eurydike. Opera.
22. Three a cappella choruses.
23. Symphonic Music II. (Divertimento), for 9 solo instr.
24. String Quartet IV.
25. Concerto grosso II.
26. Two Suites for PF.
27. Concertino for flute, vln., cembalo and str. orch.
29. Violin Concerto.
35. ' The Seasons,' 4 short a cappella choruses (perf. Donaueschingen 1925).

Opp. 1 to 11 were composed whilst Krenek was studying with Schreker.   E. E.

KRESS, JAKOB (d. ? Darmstadt, c. 1736), a 17th-18th century violinist and composer, Konzertmeister in the court orchestra. He composed a symphony, overtures, violin and flute concertos, quartets, trios (1 for flute, viol d'amour, cembalo or lute; and 1 for flute viola da gamba and cembalo, MS. Rostock libr.), and sonatas for various instruments.   E. v. d. S.

KRESS (KRESSEN, CRESSE), JOHANN ALBRECHT (d. Stuttgart before 1701), vice-Kapellmeister of the court chapel at Stuttgart in 1674. He was a highly esteemed composer of sacred cantatas and songs and the author of a treatise on thorough-bass (Q.-L.).

KRETSCHMER, EDMUND (b. Ostritz, Saxony, Aug. 31, 1830 ; d. Dresden, Sept. 13, 1908), organist and dramatic composer. His father, the rector of the school in Ostritz, gave

him his early musical education. He studied composition under Julius Otto, and the organ under Johann Schneider at Dresden, where he became organist of the Catholic church in 1854, and to the court in 1863. He founded several ' Gesangvereine,' and in 1865 his composition, ' Die Geisterschlacht,' gained the prize at the first German ' Sängerfest,' in Dresden. Three years later he took another prize in Brussels for a Mass. His opera ' Die Folkunger,' in five acts, libretto by Mosenthal, was produced at Dresden, June 1875. It was well received and had a considerable run, but has since disappeared; nor has ' Heinrich der Loewe,' to his own libretto (produced at Leipzig, 1877), met with more permanent favour, though it was given on many German stages with success. The music is correct, and shows both taste and talent, but no invention or dramatic power. His vocal part-writing has little life ; and his duets, terzets, finales, etc., are too much like part-songs. Another opera, ' Der Flüchtling,' was produced at Ulm in 1881, and ' Schön Rohtraut ' in Dresden, Nov. 1887. Three later masses, ' Pilgerfahrt,' ' Sieg im Gesang,' for chorus and orchestra, and ' Musikalische Dorfgeschichten,' for orchestra, may also be mentioned.   F. G.

KRETZSCHMAR, AUGUST FERDINAND HERMANN (b. Olbernhau, Saxony, Jan. 19, 1848 ; d. Gross-Lichterfelde, May 10, 1924), distinguished as a writer on music and as Joachim's successor as head of the Hochschule at Berlin (1909-20), was educated at the Kreuzschule at Dresden, where he was taught music by J. Otto, and was sent later to the Leipzig Conservatorium, where he was a pupil of Richter, Reinecke, Paul and Papperitz.

He took the degree of Dr.Phil. with a thesis on musical notation before Guido, and became in the same year, 1871, a teacher in the Leipzig Conservatorium. He conducted several musical societies, and overworked himself to such an extent that he was forced to give up Leipzig altogether ; in 1876 he undertook the conductorship of the theatre in Metz ; in 1877 went to Rostock as music director at the University, and from 1880 as town music director. In 1887 he succeeded H. Langer as music director of the Leipzig University, and conductor of a male choir. He soon became a member of various important musical institutions, such as the Bach Gesellschaft, and was made conductor of the Riedel-Verein in 1888. In 1890 he organised the Academic Orchestral Concerts, which had a successful career, with especial regard to historical programmes, until 1895. In 1898 he retired from his conductorships, but retained his professorship, and continued to give lectures on musical history. His compositions include only some organ works and partsongs.

He contributed critical work to the *Musika-*

tisches Wochenblatt, and the *Grenzboten* ; published lectures on *Choral Music,* on *Peter Cornelius,* etc. One of his most useful undertakings is the *Führer durch den Konzertsaal,* the equivalent of our own analytical programmes, which began to be published in 1887, and have gone through many editions, being printed in separate portions in pamphlet form in 1898 and later. His collected essays (*Gesammelte Aufsätze*) appeared (1911), *Geschichte des neuen deutschen Liedes* (1912), *Geschichte der Oper* (1919), and *Einführung in die Musikgeschichte* (1920). He edited vols. viii. and ix. of *D.D.T.* He succeeded Joachim as director of the Berlin Hochschule in 1909.　　　　　　M.

KRETZSCHMER, FRANZ JOHANN KARL ANDREAS (called ANDREAS) (*b.* Stettin, Nov. 1, 1775 ; *d.* Anklam, Mar. 5, 1839), councillor of war at Berlin ; musical theorist and composer of pianoforte pieces, songs, etc. He published, in conjunction with von Zuccalmaglio and Dr. Massmann, an important collection of German folk-songs ; he also wrote an essay on musical theory (*Q.-L.*).

KREUBÉ, CHARLES FRÉDÉRIC (*b.* Luneville, Nov. 5, 1777 ; *d.* near St. Denis, 1846), studied the violin, became conductor at Metz theatre, studied in 1800 under Rod. Kreutzer in Paris, and joined the orchestra of the opéra-comique as violinist, becoming 2nd conductor in 1805, and 1st conductor in 1816. He was pensioned Nov. 1828, and retired to his country house at St. Denis. He was a member of the Royal Chapel from 1814–30. He composed 16 operas, quartets, trios, violin duets, etc. (*Fétis*).

KREUSSER, GEORG ANTON (*b.* Heidingsfeld, 1743 ; *d.* Frankfort-on-M.[1] before 1811), studied under his brother Adam, the horn player, at Amsterdam, where he remained for some years as violinist ; then went to Italy to study composition ; returned in 1775, and became Konzertmeister in the Elector's orchestra, Mainz, before 1779. He gave a concert of his own compositions at Frankfort-on-M., Nov. 12, 1779, and a passion music, ' The Death of Jesus,' by Ramler, in 1780. He became Kapellmeister at the Frankfort theatre. Apart from his passion music, he composed symphonies, chamber music and songs (*Fétis; Q.-L.*).

KREUTZER, CONRADIN (*b.* Messkirch, Baden, Nov. 22, 1780 ; *d.* Riga, Dec. 14, 1849), German composer, son of a miller ; chorister first in his native town, then at the Abbey of Zwiefalten, and afterwards at Scheussenried. In 1799 he went to Freiburg in Breisgau to study medicine, which he soon abandoned for music. The next five years he passed chiefly in Switzerland, as pianist, singer and composer (his first operetta, ' Die lächerliche Werbung,' was performed at Freiburg in 1800) ; and in 1804 he arrived in Vienna. There he took lessons from Albrechtsberger, and worked hard

at composition, especially operas. His first opera was ' Conradin von Schwaben ' (Stuttgart, 1812), and its success gained him the post of Kapellmeister to the King of Würtemberg ; thence in 1817 he went to Prince von Fürstenberg at Donaueschingen ; but in 1822 returned to Vienna and produced ' Libussa.' At the Kärthnerthor theatre he was Kapellmeister in 1825, 1829–32 and in 1837–40. From 1833–40 he was conductor at the Josephstadt theatre, where he produced his two best works, ' Das Nachtlager in Granada ' (1834) and a fairy opera, ' Der Verschwender.' In 1840 he was appointed Kapellmeister at Cologne, and in 1841 conducted the 23rd Festival of the Lower Rhine. Thence he went to Paris, and in 1846 back to Vienna. He accompanied his daughter, whom he had trained as a singer, to Riga, and there died.

Kreutzer composed about thirty operas ; incidental music to several plays and melodramas ; an oratorio, ' Die Sendung Mosis,' and other church works ; chamber and pianoforte music ; Lieder, and partsongs for men's voices in *Q.-L.* ; Fétis speaks of a one-act drama ' Cordelia ' as the most original of his works. In his partsongs Kreutzer displays a flow of melody and good construction ; they are still standard works with all the German Liedertafeln, and have taken the place of much weak sentimental rubbish. ' Der Tag des Herrn,' ' Die Kapelle,' ' Märznacht ' and others are models of that style of piece. Some of them are given in ' Orpheus.'　　　　　　A. M.

KREUTZER,[2] (1) RODOLPHE (*b.* Versailles, Nov. 16, 1766 ; *d.* Geneva, June 6, 1831), violinist and composer. He studied first under his father, a musician, and a pupil of Antoine, son of John Stamitz, but he owed more to natural gifts than to instruction. He began to compose before he had learnt harmony, and was so good a player at 16, when his father died, that through the intervention of Marie Antoinette he was appointed first violin in the Chapelle du Roi. Here he had opportunities of hearing Mestrino and Viotti, and his execution improved rapidly. The further appointment of solo-violinist at the Théâtre Italien gave him the opportunity of producing an opera. 'Jeanne d'Arc,' three acts (May 10, 1790), was successful, and paved the way for ' Paul et Virginie ' (Jan. 15, 1791), which was still more so.

The melodies were simple and fresh, and the musical world went into raptures over the new effects of local colour, poor as they seem to us. The music of ' Lodoïska,' three acts (Aug. 1, 1791), is not sufficiently interesting to counterbalance its tedious libretto, but the overture and the Tartars' March were for long favourites. During the Revolution Kreutzer was often suddenly called upon to compose *opéras de circon-*

---

[1] Fétis says Mainz.

[2] His name has been often transmuted into Kretsche by Frenchmen, and appeared in the London papers of 1844 as ' Greitzer.'

stance, a task he executed with great facility. In 1796 he produced ' Imogène, ou la Gageure indiscrète,' a three-act comedy founded on a story of Boccaccio little fitted for music. At the same time he was composing the concertos for the violin, on which his fame now rests. After the peace of Campo Formio (Oct. 17, 1797) he started on a concert-tour through Italy, Germany and the Netherlands ; the fire and individuality of his playing, especially in his own compositions, exciting everywhere the greatest enthusiasm.

In 1798 Kreutzer was in Vienna in the suite of Bernadotte,[1] and acquired that friendship with Beethoven which resulted later [2] in the dedication to him of the sonata (op. 47) which will now be always known by his name— though he is said [3] never to have played it— and he became ' first violin of the Academy of Arts and of the Imperial chamber-music '— titles which are attributed to him in the same dedication. He had been professor of the violin at the Conservatoire from its foundation in 1795, and on his return to Paris he and Baillot drew up the famous *Méthode de violon* for the use of the students. He frequently played at concerts, his ' Duos concertantes ' with Rode being a special attraction. On Rode's departure to Russia in 1801, Kreutzer succeeded him as first violin-solo at the Opéra, a post which again opened to him the career of a dramatic composer. 'Astyanax,' three acts (Apr. 12, 1801) ; 'Aristippe' (May 24, 1808), the success of which was mainly due to Lays; and 'La Mort d'Abel' (Mar. 23, 1810), in three acts, reduced to two on its revival in 1823, were the best of a series of operas now forgotten. He also composed many highly successful ballets, such as ' Paul et Virginie ' (June 24, 1806), revived in 1826 ; ' Le Carnaval de Venise' (Feb. 22, 1816), with Persuis ; and ' Clari ' (June 19, 1820), the principal part in which was sustained by Bigottini.

He was appointed first violin in the chapelle of the First Consul in 1802, violin-solo to the Emperor in 1806, maître de la chapelle to Louis XVIII. in 1815 and Chevalier of the Legion of Honour in 1824. He became vice-conductor of the Académie de Musique in 1816, and conductor in chief from 1817–24. A broken arm compelled him to give up playing, and he retired from the Conservatoire in the year 1825. His last years were embittered by the decline of his influence and the impossibility of gaining a hearing for his last opera, ' Mathilde.'

Besides his thirty-nine operas and ballets, all produced in Paris, he published :

Nineteen vln. concertos ; duos, and two symphonies concertantes, for two vlns. ; études and caprices for vln. solo ; sonatas for vln. and vcl. ; fifteen trios, and a symphonie concertante, for two vlns. and vcl. ; fifteen string quartets ; and several airs with variations. (See *Q.-L.*)   G. C.

1 *Thayer,* ii. 21.
2 See Beethoven's letter to Simrock, Oct. 4, 1804. *Krehbiel,* ii. 21.
3 See Berlioz, *Voyage,* i. 264, for this and for an amusing account of Kreutzer's difficulties over Beethoven's second symphony.

Rodolphe Kreutzer is the third, in order of development, of the four great representative masters of the classical violin-school of Paris ; the other three being VIOTTI, RODE and BAILLOT. His style, such as we know it from his concertos, is on the whole more brilliant than Rode's but less modern than Baillot's. Kreutzer did not require Beethoven's dedication to make his name immortal. His fame will always rest on his unsurpassed work of studies —' 40 Études ou caprices pour le violon '; a work which has an almost unique position in the literature of violin-studies. It has been recognised and adopted as the basis of all solid execution on the violin by the masters of all schools—French, German or any other nationality—and has been published in numberless editions. In point of difficulty it ranks just below Rode's twenty-four caprices, and is generally considered as leading up to this second standard work of studies.   P. D.

Kreutzer, on the testimony of Baillot (*Art du violon*, 1834, p. 183), and of A. L. Blondeau (*Hist. Mus.*, 1847, ii. p. 161), was probably one of the greatest improvisers of his time. There is a medallion of him by Peuvrier (1823). M. P.

Rodolphe's brother, (2) AUGUSTE (*b.* Versailles, Sept. 3, 1778 ; *d.* Paris, Aug. 31, 1832), was a member of the Chapelle de l'Empereur and of the Chapelle du Roi (1804–30) ; and succeeded his brother at the Conservatoire, Jan. 1, 1826, retaining the post till his death. His son, (3) LÉON (*b.* Paris, Sept. 23, 1817 ; *d.* Vichy, Oct. 6, 1868), was musical critic to *La Quotidienne* ; *feuilletoniste* to the *Union* ; and contributed a number of interesting articles to the *Revue contemporaine,* the *Revue et Gazette musicale* and other periodicals. G. C.

BIBL.—JOSEPH HARDY, *Rodolphe Kreutzer, sa jeunesse à Versailles* (Paris, 1910) ; PAUL FROMAGEOT, in *Les Compositeurs de musique versaillais* (Versailles, 1906).

KREUZ, EMIL (*b.* Elberfeld, May 25, 1867), violinist and composer. Began to play at the age of 3, but did not begin to study for the profession until his 10th year (under Japha of Cologne). In 1883 he gained an open scholarship at the R.C.M., where he studied for five years under Holmes (violin) and Stanford (composition). During the last two years he made a special study of the viola, making his début with that instrument on Dec. 11, 1888, in the ' Harold in Italy ' solo at a Henschel concert. He was soloist at Leeds Festival 1889, member of Gompertz Quartet 1888–1903, and of the Queen's Band 1900–3. He also played frequently at the Popular Concerts. In 1903 he joined the Hallé Orchestra in order to work under Richter. He left England before the war (1914). Amongst his compositions are a concerto for viola with orchestra, a trio for piano, violin and viola, op. 21, a prize quintet for horn and string quartet, op. 49, many songs and numerous pieces useful for teaching purposes.   W. W. C.

KŘIČKA, JAROSLAV (*b.* Kelč, Moravia, 1882), Czech composer, choirmaster and professor at the Prague Conservatoire.

Křička entered the Conservatoire as a student in 1902, working at composition under Stecker. He belongs, however, to the group of musicians directly influenced by Vít. Novák. Leaving the Prague Conservatoire in 1905 he spent a little time in Berlin before visiting Russia. Fascinated by the artistic life of that country, he settled down for several years as professor of composition at the Music School at Ekaterinoslav. Křička was a great admirer of Rimsky-Korsakov, and this Russian period left its traces upon his earlier works. He returned to Prague in 1909, and quickly made a reputation as a choirmaster, directing the famous choral society 'Hlahol' until 1920. In the meantime he discarded external influences in his creative work and formed a clear personal style which deepens as time goes on. Křička enjoyed a happy childhood in beautiful surroundings, and in the companionship of a younger brother, Peter, now a poet of distinction. From this unspoilt past he has kept a simple and delightful humour which enables him to sympathise with children, for whom, and about whom, he has written charmingly and—what is rarer—appropriately. Although much of his music is optimistic, he is by no means without a shadow. In his later choral works he touches chords of tragic memory and profound human sympathy. He has also a sincere religious sense, which is finely expressed in his cantata for chorus, soli and orchestra, 'Pokušení' (The Temptation in the Wilderness). Křička's best work is lyrical and choral. His earlier song cycles 'Severni noci' (Northern Nights), containing the remarkable song 'The Albatross,' 'O lásce a smtri' (Of Love and Death), and 'Pisně rozchodu' (Songs of Parting) would—if well translated—enrich the recital programmes of other lands. The later songs, including the 'Tři bajky' (Three Fables) and the 'Children's Songs' require more intimate interpretation. His overture to *The Blue Bird* of Maeterlinck is a happy inspiration. His short choral works are sung by all such Czech choirs as are equal to the demands they make upon the technical powers of the singers. Křička has only made one operatic essay: 'Hypolita,' based on a story from Maurice Hewlett's *Little Novels of Italy*, produced at the National Theatre, Prague, in 1917.

The following is a list of his chief compositions:

ORCHESTRAL: Symphony in D min., op. 3; 'Nostalgia.' for strings, op. 4; 'Vira' (Faith), symphonic poem, op. 6; Polonaise for Orchestra, op. 7a, and b, Elegy on the Death of Rimsky-Korsakov; Children's Suite for small orchestra; 'Venkovské Scherzo' (Idyllic Scherzo); 'Adventus'; Overture, 'Modry Pták' (*The Blue Bird*), 1912.
PIANOFORTE WORKS: Intimate Pieces; Lyrical Suite, op. 30; 'Rozmar' (Caprices), op. 11.
CHAMBER MUSIC: Preludium for two violins and piano, op. 9; string quartet in D, op. 10; sonata for vln. and piano.
CHORAL WORKS: Cantata, 'Pokušení' (The Temptation in the

Wilderness), for chorus, soli and orch., op. 34 (1921–22); 'Zrozen pramene' (The Fountain's Birth); 'Slovanska' (Slovakia), 'Koledy Vánoční' (Christmas Folk-songs), op. 22 (1917), for women's or children's voices; 'Zablesky' (Gleams), op. 26 (1917–1918). four choruses for mixed voices; 'Zornička' (Dawn-light) and other folk-songs and dances, op. 28 (1919–20), for male voice choir; 'Pozdrav' (Greeting), op. 31 A¹ (1920), for mixed voices; 'Ve vychodni zaři' (In the Eastern Light), op. 31 A² (1921), for mixed voices; 'Kruty Host' (The Grim Guest), op. 37 (1923), double chorus for male voices.
SONG CYCLES, ETC.: 'Severní noci' (Northern Nights), op. 14, 'O lásce a smrti' (Of Love and Death), op. 15; 'Pisně rozchodu' (Songs of Parting), op. 19; 'Tři ba'ky' (Three Legends), op. 21; 'Jaro pacholátko' (Spring, the Young Lad), op. 29, three recitatives for high voice and pianoforte; 'Památník ze staré školy' (The Old Schoolhouse), op 35, four songs for soprano.

R. N.

KRIEGER, ADAM (*b* Driesen in the Neumark, Prussia, Jan. 7, 1634; *d.* Dresden, June 30, 1666), was a pupil of Samuel Scheidt and Heinrich Schütz, and after being for a time organist at St. Nicholas, Leipzig, was appointed court-organist to the Elector of Saxony. He appears to have made an unsuccessful application for the post of cantor at St. Thomas's, Leipzig. He was poet as well as composer, and his compositions consist of so-called Arien on his own texts, songs for one, two, three and five voices with three or five-part instrumental Ritornelli between each verse. The Arias themselves have only basso continuo accompaniment, but are written in regular Lied form, while the Ritornelli have no thematic connexion with them. The original and complete edition of the Arien with their Ritornelli, published Dresden, 1676, has been republished in *D.D.T.* xix., with a valuable preface by Alfred Heuss. Specimens are given in the *M.f.M* xxix.

J. R. M.

BIBL.—KURT FISCHER, *Über eine Gelegenheitskomposition von Adam Krieger. A.M.,* July 1920.

KRIEGER, (1) JOHANN PHILIPP (*b.* Nüremberg, Feb. 26, 1649; *d.* Weissenfels, Feb. 6, 1725), travelled in Italy, and was for a while pupil of Johann Rosenmüller at Venice. Returning to Germany he was ennobled by the Emperor at Vienna, and after various wanderings entered the service of the Duke of Saxe-Weissenfels, first as chamber-musician and organist at Halle, in 1677, and afterwards as Kapellmeister at Weissenfels from 1712. For the Weissenfels court he wrote a quantity of Singspiele, the Arias of which for one, two and three voices were afterwards published with bass accompaniment only in two volumes published at Nüremberg, 1690, 1692. Specimens of them, with accompaniment written out, are given by Eitner in the *M.f.M.* xxix. Chrysander gives the titles of some operas of Krieger written for Brunswick-Wolfenbüttel in 1693, some of which were also performed in Hamburg in 1694. In 1693 Krieger published as his op. 2 an instrumental work consisting of twelve sonatas for violin and viola da gamba with cembalo accompaniment. The second and third of these sonatas are given in full by Eitner, *M.f.M.* xxix.-xxx. In 1704 there appeared also in Nüremberg 'Lustige Feld-Musik,' consisting of suites or 'Partien' (partitas) for four wind instruments (oboes and bassoons), or *ad libitum* for strings. Two of these 'Partien' are given in score by Eitner, who says of these compositions generally that they are so excellent in form and expression that one may unhesitatingly class them with similar works by Handel. Besides these published works by Krieger there exist a quantity of sacred compositions, arias for one, two, three and four voices, with various instrumental accompaniments, somewhat after the manner of Schütz, but of a lighter and more popular character. A selection is published in *D.D.T.* liii.-liv. Some of these are also given by Eitner, *M.f.M.* For a complete list see *Q.-L.*   J. R. M.

(2) JOHANN (*b.* Nüremberg, Jan. 1, 1652 ; *d.* Zittau, July 18, 1735), younger brother of Johann Philipp, was for a time the pupil of his brother, and in 1672 became court organist at Bayreuth, which post, however, he gave up in 1677. After a transient connexion with Weissenfels he finally settled at Zittau, where in 1681 he was appointed town music-director, and in 1701 organist also at the church of SS. Peter and Paul. Johann is of greater importance in the history of music than his brother Philipp. Mattheson praises him specially as a composer of double fugues, and puts him beside Handel. Handel himself confessed how much he owed to Krieger. Eitner comments on his excellent gift of melodic invention, and the cleverness of his thematic work. His works are—

(1) 'Neue musicalische Ergetzlichkeit,' 1684. Part 1. 'Geistliche Andachten,' thirty numbers. Part 2. Secular songs, thirty-four numbers. Part 3. Theatrical pieces performed in Zittau.
(2) 'Sechs musicalische Partien,' Nüremberg, 1697. Suites for Clavier alone (' Nach einer Ariensen Manier ausgesetzt ').
(3) 'Anmuthige Clavierübung,' consisting of preludes, fugues, a chaconne and a toccata for pedal, Nüremberg, 1699.

It was this last work which Handel specially valued and recommended as a model for organ and harpsichord composers. It was one of the few musical works which he brought with him to England, his copy of which he gave to his friend Bernard Granville, who has recorded for us Handel's appreciation of the work.[1] Eitner considers the pedal toccata of this work as approaching the grand style of Sebastian Bach.[2] Besides these published works Johann Krieger left in MS. various organ works (specimens given in Ritter, *Geschichte des Orgelspiels*, Nos. 80, 81, and in *D.D.T.* (2nd series), xviii.), and a large number of sacred compositions for various combinations of voices and instruments, a full list of which is given in *Q.-L.*
             J. R. M.

KRIEGK, J. J. (*b.* Bibra, Merseburg, June 25, 1750 ; *d.* Meiningen, 1813), violinist at the court of Meiningen *c.* 1762, leader of Flemish opera, Amsterdam, 1773. In 1774 he accompanied the Marquis de Taillefer to Paris, where J. L. Duport induced him to exchange the violin for the violoncello. After one year's study under that master he was for 4 years in

the service of Prince Laval-Montmorency and thence went to Meiningen as chamber musician at the court, where he became a Konzertmeister in 1798. He composed 3 concertos and 4 sonatas with bass which belong to the better productions of that time for the violoncello (E. van der Straeten, *History of the Violoncello*).

KŘÍŽKOVSKÝ, PAVEL (*b.* Holasovice, in Bohemian Silesia, Jan. 9, 1820; *d.* Brno, Moravia, 1885). His baptismal name in the secular world was Karel. He was the first Czech composer whose technical grasp of his art, combined with deep penetration into the spirit of the folk-songs, enabled him to weld the two elements in a satisfactory way. He was therefore the true precursor of Smetana in national music, as the more famous composer gladly acknowledged when he observed that it was not until he had heard Křížkovský's choruses that he began to realise the full significance of the Czech and Moravian folk melody.

Křížkovský came of a family of poor but talented rural musicians who had suffered too many deprivations to wish that the boy should follow in their steps. He was forbidden to touch any musical instrument or even to speak about music. But once having heard High Mass in the Church of St. Mary at Opava, he escaped from home every Sunday and tramped the long distance between his village and the town. At first he only ventured to stand listening at the door leading into the choir, but as week after week went by he became familiar to the choristers, and one kind singer asked permission to bring him in and let him sit among the sopranos. Of course he was not intended to sing, but when the leading boy went astray in his solo, Křížkovský took up the part and sang it correctly to the end, much to the astonishment of the choirmaster. After this he was admitted to the foundation of the choir school. Extreme poverty hindered his career after his voice broke, but he managed at last to take the degree of doctor of philosophy at Brno University. Here he entered the Augustinian community of St. Thomas in 1845, and on the completion of his novitiate became a professor in the Divinity school at the head of which was F. Sušil, an assiduous collector of the Moravian folk tunes, who inculcated in the young monk a genuine love of the national music.

Křížkovský began to arrange some of the folk-songs for four-part male voice choir, and showed an aptitude for the work which delighted Sušil. Brother Pavel was sent to Prague to study music for six months. The director of the music in the church of the community was Bohumir Rieger (1764–1855), who helped and encouraged Křížkovský during his earlier years of study, and eventually resigned his post in favour of his pupil. Křížkovský therefore had a sound training and some

---

[1] See Chrysander's *Händel*, Bd. iii p. 211.
[2] *M.f.M.* xxvii.

practical experience in composition before he took up his researches into the folk music. He entered deeply into its spirit and traditions, and the result was a series of stirring and beautiful male voice choruses. It is regrettable perhaps that he wrote always for a male choir, but natural enough considering his monastic life. His chorus ' Utonula ' (The Drowned Girl), 1860, was received with enthusiasm in Prague, and like most of Křížkovský's subsequent works now forms part of the repertory of every choral society in Czechoslovakia. Unfortunately he was too modest to realise the value of his compositions, and lent the manuscripts to choral societies in all directions, with the result that much of his music is lost. Of what remains, the most popular partsongs are : ' Divča ' (Lassie), tender, impassioned and charmingly harmonised ; ' Dar za lásku ' (The Love-gift) ; ' Prosba odvedenho ' (The Recruit's Prayer) ; ' Žaloba ' (The Plaint) ; ' Zatoč se ' (Turn around), for solo quartet and chorus, the words from a folk-song ; ' Zahrada Boži ' (God's Garden) ; ' Modlitba Sv. Cyrilla na sotnách ' (Prayer of St. Cyril on his Deathbed) ; ' The Shepherd and the Pilgrim ' ; and a humorous chorus in the polyphonic style, ' Vyprask ' (Threshing). In addition, Křížkovský composed the cantata ' Two Stars from the East,' in honour of the millenary anniversary of the first coming of these Slavonic evangelisers to Moravia ; a Funeral Song, with trombone accompaniment ; solo songs with piano accompaniment, a few original, and others arranged from folk-tunes.

Křížkovský was an excellent conductor and gave some memorable sacred concerts in Brno. Among his pupils in the choir school of St. Thomas were Jahn, afterwards conductor at the Vienna Opera, Vojáček, and the dramatic composer, Leoš JANÁČEK (*q.v.*). It is a pity that his finest choral compositions are not more widely known. He had strong dramatic instincts, but his cloistral life was unfavourable to his development on the secular side of his art. He died, after a paralytic stroke, in his old community of the Austin Friars at Brno. R. N.

KROLL, FRANZ (*b.* Bromberg, June 22, 1820 ; *d.* Berlin, May 28, 1877), began with medicine, but finally devoted himself to music under the guidance of Liszt, whom he accompanied on some of his tours. He settled in Berlin, and was for some years a successful teacher. He edited the *Wohltemperirtes Clavier* for the Bach Gesellschaft (14th year, 1864)—with a Preface containing a list of MSS. and Editions, and an Appendix of various readings, a highly creditable work as regards care and accuracy in collation, which Spitta has selected for honourable mention.[1] He also published editions of Bach's chromatic fantasia, Mozart's pianoforte fantasias and other important compositions.

[1] *J. S. Bach*, Eng. trans., ii. 166 note.

He was a thorough musician, and his style as a pianist was clear and eminently suggestive.
F. G.

KROMMER, FRANZ (*b.* Kamenitz, Moravia, Dec. 5, 1759 [2] ; *d.* Jan. 8, 1831), violinist and composer, learned music from an uncle, then choirmaster at Turas. From the ages of 17 to 25 he acted as organist, and composed much church music, still unpublished. He next entered the band of Count Styrum [3] at Simonthurm in Hungary as violinist, and in two years was promoted to the Kapellmeistership. Here he became acquainted with the works of Haydn and Mozart, and composed his pieces for wind instruments, which are of lasting importance, and perceptibly influenced modern military music. After several changes he at length became Kapellmeister to Prince Grassalkowitz, after whose death he lived comfortably in Vienna, enjoying a considerable reputation as a teacher and composer. The sinecure post of doorkeeper to the Emperor was conferred upon him, and in 1818 he succeeded Koželuk as court Kapellmeister and composer, in which capacity he accompanied the Emperor Francis to France and Italy. He died suddenly while composing a pastoral Mass.

As a composer he was remarkable for productiveness, and for a clear and agreeable style, most observable perhaps in his sixty-nine string-quartets and quintets, published at Vienna, Offenbach and Paris. This made him a great favourite in Vienna at the close of the century. Schubert, however, who as a boy of 11 had to play his Symphonies in the band of the ' Convict,' used to laugh at them, and preferred those of Koželuk. Krommer also composed a number of quartets and quintets for flutes, besides the pieces for wind instruments already mentioned. Two Masses in four parts with orchestra and organ are printed (André, Offenbach). F. G.

KRUMMHORN (CROMORNE). This obsolete crooked-horn was a wood-wind instrument of small cylindrical bore, played with a double reed, of the bassoon or bagpipe chanter type. The reed being enclosed with a cover, or cap, through which the air was directed, was not under the direct control of the lips, as in modern orchestral reed instruments. The lower end, or bell, was turned upwards in U form, hence the French name for the instrument, ' Tournebout.' The scale was obtained by means of seven finger-holes, supplemented in the case of some of the larger instruments by key-work to extend the compass downwards. The krummhorns were made in ' choirs ' or sets, from soprano to bass in compass, and were in very general use throughout Europe during the 14th, 15th and 16th centuries. Mersenne stated that the best were made in England. D. J. B.

[2] *Riemann* gives May 17, 1760.
[3] Fétis and Mendel call him Ayrum by mistake.

KRUMPHOLZ, (1) JOHANN BAPTIST (*b.* Zlo-nitz, near Prague, *c.* 1745 ; *d.* Feb. 19, 1790), celebrated harpist and composer ; son of a bandmaster in a French regiment, lived in Paris from his childhood, learning music from his father. The first public mention of him is in the ' Wiener Diarium ' for 1772 ; he had played at a concert in the Burg-theater, and advertised for pupils on the pedal-harp. From Aug. 1773 to Mar. 1776 he was a member of Prince Ester-hazy's chapel at Esterház, taking lessons from Haydn in composition, and already seeking after improvements in his instrument. He next started on a concert-tour, playing at Leipzig on an ' organisirte Harfe.' He then settled in Paris, where he was highly esteemed as a teacher and virtuoso. Nadermann built a harp from his specifications, to which attention was drawn by an article in the *Journal de Paris* (Feb. 8, 1786), and which Krumpholz described in a preface to his sonata, op. 14. His wife played some pieces on it before the Académie, Krumpholz accom-panying her on the violin, and on the ' piano-forte centrebasse ' or ' clavicorde à marteau,' another instrument made by Erard from his specifications. The Académie expressed ap-proval of the new harp in a letter to Krumpholz (Nov. 21, 1787). He drowned himself in the Seine from grief at the infidelity and ingratitude of his wife.

Gerber gives a list of his compositions. They comprise six grand concertos, thirty-two sona-tas with violin accompaniment, preludes, varia-tions, duets for two harps, a quartet for harp and strings, and symphonies for harp and small orchestra, published in Paris and London. (See *Q.-L.*)

His wife, *née* Meyer, from Metz,[1] eloped with a young man to London. She was even a finer player than her husband, making the instru-ment sound almost like an Æolian narp. In London she gave her first concert at Hanover Square Rooms, June 2, 1788,[2] and for many years appeared with great success at her own and Salomon's concerts, at the oratorios in Drury Lane, and at Haydn's benefit. She fre-quently played Dussek's duos concertantes for harp and pianoforte with the composer. She is mentioned in 1802, but after that appears to have retired into private life.

(2) WENZEL, brother of Johann (*b.* 1750 ; *d.* Vienna, May 2, 1817), became one of the first violins at the court-opera in Vienna in 1796. His name is immortalised by his intimacy with Beethoven, who was very fond of him, though he used to call him in joke ' mein Narr,' my fool. According to Ries[3] he gave Beethoven some instruction on the violin in Vienna. Krumpholz was one of the first to recognise Beethoven's genius, and he inspired others with his own enthusiasm. Czerny mentions this in his Auto-

[1] Or Liège, according to Gerber and Reichardt.
[2] Not 1790, as commonly stated.
[3] *Biographische Notizen*, p. 119.

biography,[4] and also that he introduced him to Beethoven, who offered of his own accord to give him lessons. Wenzel also played the man-doline, and Beethoven wrote a sonata in one movement (first published in this Dictionary, Edition I., see MANDOLINE) for PF. and mando-line for him.[5] Beethoven must have felt his death deeply, since he composed on the follow-ing day the ' Gesang der Mönche ' (from Schiller's ' Wilhelm Tell '), for three men's voices, ' in commemoration of the sudden and unexpected death of our Krumpholz.'[6] Only two of his compositions have been printed— an ' Abendunterhaltung ' for a single violin[7] (dances, variations, a short andante, etc.; Vienna and Pest, Kunst & Industrie-Comptoir); and ' Ein Viertelstunde für eine Violine,' dedi-cated to Schuppanzigh (Joh. Traeg). C. F. P.

KRUSE, JOHANN SECUNDUS (*b.* Melbourne, Australia, Mar. 22, 1859), violinist, of German parentage. He appeared in public when 9 years of age, playing at the first desk in the Phil-harmonic concerts of his native town. In 1875 he went to Berlin to study with Joachim in the Hochschule, in which institution he was later appointed professor. In 1882 he became prin-cipal violin and sub-conductor of the Berlin Philharmonic Society, and founded a string Quartet. In 1885 he visited Australia, but was called back by Joachim to relieve him of some of his work at the Hochschule, his activity as teacher continuing till 1891, when he relin-quished the appointment to go to Bremen as leader of the Philharmonic orchestra. In Oct. 1892 he joined the JOACHIM QUARTET (*q.v.*) as second violin though still resident in Bremen, where he also founded a Quartet of his own, travelling very constantly in Germany with the various organisations with which he was con-nected. In 1895 he revisited Australia for a short tour, and in 1897 left Germany and the Joachim Quartet to live in London, where he once more founded a Quartet, and gave a series of concerts at St. James's Hall. In Oct. 1902 he took over the Saturday Popular Concerts, of which only ten were announced, and the follow-ing year restored them to their original number of twenty, besides reviving the twenty Monday Popular Concerts. During the same season he gave a series of orchestral concerts (conductor, Felix Weingartner), in 1903 a Beethoven Festi-val of eight concerts, and in 1904 a second festival of seven concerts, so that the English public owes much to his enterprise and energy. In 1921 he was associated with Mathilde Verne and others in chamber concerts, and in 1926 he reappeared as leader of a new Quartet bearing his name. W. W. C.

KUBA, LUDVÍK (*b.* Poděbrady, 1863), a

[4] He calls Krumpholz ' an old man.' He was then about 50.
[5] *Autographische Skizze*, by Artaria.
[6] Compare Nottebohm's Thematic Catalogue, p. 161.
[7] Czerny took No. 1, a contredanse, as the theme of his XX con-cert variations for PF. and violin. This, his op. 1 (Steiner, 2nd edit.), is dedicated to Krumpholz—a fine trait of gratitude.

Czech painter who in his travels has been an assiduous collector of the Slavonic folk-songs. The results of his labour have recently been published by the Hudební Matice, Prague, under the general title *Slovanstvo ve svých zpěvech* (The Slavs in their Songs) ; the volumes which have so far appeared deal with Russian, Czech, Moravian, Slovak, Slovene Ruthenian, Serb, Croat and Montenegrin folk-songs. Before he became a painter Kuba studied music at the Organ School, Prague.

R. N.

KUBELIK, JAN (*b.* Michle, near Prague, July 5, 1880), violinist, was born of Czech parents. When the young Kubelik at the age of 5 years expressed a desire to learn the violin, he received from his father, a gardener by profession and a keen amateur of music, a thorough training which laid an excellent foundation for the virtuosity exhibited in later years. In an incredibly short space of time he was able to play the earlier studies of Kreutzer, and in 1888 made his first appearance in public at Prague, playing a concerto of Vieuxtemps and pieces by Wieniawski. In 1892 he entered the Conservatorium, and was favoured by the circumstance that Ottakar Sevčik returned in the same year from Russia. Taking the youth in hand at the most receptive age, the professor saw his laboriously thought-out theories of violin teaching carried to a triumphant issue by his pupil, who, after six years devoted to hard practice under the Sevčik method, played the Brahms concerto, with his own cadenzas, at a students' concert given in the German theatre, and on the occasion of his final appearance as a student in 1898, gave a brilliant performance of the D major concerto of Paganini, with Sauret's cadenza, and was recognised by examiners and critics as a virtuoso player of the first rank. He was no less successful on the occasion of his first appearance away from home in the autumn of 1898, before a critical audience at Vienna. He then went to Budapest, and later made a prolonged tour through Italy, receiving, when in Rome, the order of St. Gregory at the hands of Pope Leo XIII. In 1900 he visited many continental cities, including Paris, and on June 18 of the same year made his London début at a Richter concert, giving also, during the season, five concerts of his own at St. James's Hall.

The moment was ripe for the appearance of such an artist as Kubelik. When it was perceived that he was able to execute the most dangerous flights of the virtuoso school with consummate ease and precision, there was a scene of wild enthusiasm ; it was pronounced that the mantle of Paganini had fallen on his shoulders, and from that day to this he has secured crowded audiences whenever and wherever he has appeared.

His trip to America in 1902–03 produced remarkable financial results. He was less appreciated in Germany than elsewhere, but was the recipient of honours and decorations at several European courts. At Linz on the Danube he was once unable to appear through hostile demonstrations made by the anti-Czech population. In Hungary he married (Aug. 1903) the Countess Czaky Szell, daughter of an ex-President of the Senate at Debreczin, becoming at the same time a ' Polgar ' or naturalised Hungarian citizen. He visited Rome for the second time in 1905, and, in company with his wife, was received in audience by Pope Pius X. If his subsequent career has not quite equalled the brilliance of his first appearance, he yet holds an assured place as one of the foremost virtuosi of his age.

With regard to his technique, it may briefly be said that he possesses the complete equipment of the virtuoso player, but mention should be made of his exceptional facility in the playing of double harmonics. He has written three violin concertos, but has not achieved much success as a composer.

W. W. C.

KÜCKEN, FRIEDRICH WILHELM (*b.* Bleckede, Hanover, Nov. 16, 1810 ; *d.* Schwerin, Apr. 3, 1882), composer. His father, a country gentleman, was averse to the musical proclivities of his son, and the boy had to thank his brother-in-law, Lührss, music-director and organist of Schwerin, for being allowed to follow his bent, which he did under Lührss and Aron in Schwerin, and as flute, viola and violin player in the Duke's orchestra. His early compositions, ' Ach wie wär's möglich dann ' and others, became so popular that he was taken into the palace as teacher and player. But this did not satisfy him, and he made his way in 1832 to Berlin, where, while studying hard at counterpoint under Birnbach, he gradually composed the songs which rendered him famous. His opera, ' Die Flucht nach der Schweiz ' (the Flight to Switzerland), was produced at Berlin in 1839, and proved very successful throughout Germany. In 1841 he went to Vienna to study under Sechter. In 1843 he conducted the great festival of male singers at St. Gall and Appenzel. Thence he went to Paris, where he studied orchestration with Halévy, and writing for the voice with Bordogni. His stay in Paris lasted for three and a half years ; thence he went to Stuttgart, and brought out (Apr. 21, 1847) a new opera, ' Der Prätendent ' (the Pretender), with the greatest success, which followed it to Hamburg and elsewhere in Germany. In 1851 he received a call to Stuttgart as joint Kapellmeister with Lindpaintner, filling the place alone after Lindpaintner's death (Aug. 21, 1856) till 1861, when he resigned. In 1863 he joined Abt and Berlioz as judges of a competition in Strassburg, and had an extraordinary reception. He composed sonatas for pianoforte and violin, pianoforte and violoncello, etc., but his immense popularity sprang from his songs and duets,

some of which, such as ' Das Sternelein ' and
' O weine nicht,' were extraordinarily beloved
in their time. Almost exclusively, however,
by amateurs and the masses ; among musicians
they found no favour, and are already almost
forgotten. They were also very popular in
England (' Trab, trab,' ' The Maid of Judah,'
' The Swallows,' duet, etc., etc.), and Kücken
had an arrangement with Messrs. Wessel & Co.
for the exclusive publication of them.   G.

KÜFFNER, JOSEPH (b. Würzburg, Mar. 31,
1776 ; d. there, Sept. 8, 1856), studied law, then
took up the violin and was member of the
Würzburg court chapel from 1797. When
Würzburg fell to Bavaria in 1802, Küffner became a military bandmaster. He wrote an
operetta, symphonies, overtures, chamber
music, solo pieces, songs and pieces for military
band (Q.-L.).

KÜHMSTEDT, FRIEDRICH (b. Oldisleben,
Saxe-Weimar, Dec. 20, 1809 ; d. Eisenach,
Jan. 10, 1858), composer. When 19, he left
the University of Weimar and walked to Darmstadt (a distance of full 150 miles) to ask the
advice of C. H. Rinck. The visit resulted
in a course of three years' instruction in theoretical and practical music under that great
organist. At the end of that time he returned
to his family and began to write. His career,
however, was threatened by a paralysis of his
right hand, from which he never recovered,
and which but for his perseverance and energy
would have wrecked him. During several
years he remained almost without the means of
subsistence, till in 1836 he obtained the post
of music-director and professor of the Seminar
at Eisenach, with a pittance of £30 per annum.
This, however, was wealth to him ; he married,
and the day of his wedding his wife was
snatched from him by a sudden stroke as they
left the church. After a period of deep distress
music came, to his relief, and he began to
compose. As he grew older and published his
excellent treatises and his good music, he
became famed as a teacher, and before his
death was in easier circumstances. He died
in harness at Eisenach. His works extend to
op. 49. His oratorios (' Die Auferstehung,'
and ' Triumph des Göttlichen '), operas and
symphonies are forgotten, but his fame rests
on his organ works—his Art of preluding, op. 6
(Schotts) ; his Gradus ad Parnassum or introduction to the works of J. S. Bach, op. 4 (ibid.) ;
his Fantasia eroica, op. 29 (Erfurt, Körner) ;
and many preludes, fugues, and other pieces
for the organ, which are solid and effective
compositions. He also published a treatise on
harmony and modulation (Eisenach, Börnker,
1838).   G.

KÜHNAU, (1) JOHANN CHRISTOPH (b. Volk-
städt near Eisleben, Feb. 10, 1735 ; d. Oct. 13,
1805). Coming to Berlin as school teacher in
1763, he took further lessons in harmony and

musical composition from Kirnberger, and in
1788 was appointed cantor and director of the
music at the Dreifältigkeitskirche (Trinity
Church) in Berlin. He did much to stimulate
musical life in Berlin by conducting performances of the larger choral works. The only
published work by which he has any particular
claim to remembrance is his ' Vierstimmige
alte und neue Choralgesänge mit Provinzial-
Abweichungen,' the first part of which appeared
1786, and was followed by a second in 1790.
His son, (2) JOHANN FRIEDRICH WILHELM,
republished this Choralbuch in various editions
from 1817 onwards, and in a compressed form,
containing altogether 336 Chorals in four-part
harmony. Eight of the tunes are by Christoph
Kühnau himself. He also collected and
edited a book of Choral-Vorspiele by various
composers, including Emanuel Bach and Kirnberger.   J. R. M.

KÜHNEL, AUGUST (b. Delmenhorst, Aug. 3,
1645 ; d. Cassel, c. 1700), one of the greatest
German viola da gambists, whose claim upon
posterity rests on the sterling merit of his
sonatas.[1] He is said to have been a pupil in
composition of Agostino Steffani. He was a
member of the court chapel at Zeitz from 1661–
1681. In 1665 he visited France to acquaint
himself with the art of the French gambists.
On his return he played at various courts with
great success. He refused an engagement
offered by the Bavarian court as it was condi-
tional upon his conversion to Roman Catholicism. In Nov. 1685 he gave concerts in the
City and at York Buildings, London, when he
viol da gamba and the baritone, when he played
his own sonatas, which were published in 1698.
In 1686 he was Kapellmeister at the court of
Cassel, where he remained to the end of his
life.   E. v. d. S.

KÜHNEL, AUGUST (d. Leipzig, 1684), court
Kapellmeister at Zeitz about the same time as
the above, their biographies often appearing
confused. On Sept. 26, 1682, he was appointed
organist of St. Thomas, Leipzig.   E. v. d. S.

KÜHNEL, JOHANN MICHAEL (latter half of
17th cent.) virtuoso on the lute and bass viol, for
some time at the court of Berlin. He went to
Weimar in 1717 and afterwards entered the service of Marshal Flemming at Dresden. The
latter part of his life he spent at Hamburg. He
composed sonatas for 1 and 2 violas da gamba
(1730). (E. van der Straeten, History of the
Violoncello.)   E. v. d. S.

KÜRZINGER, (1) JGNAZ FRANZ XAVER,
court Kapellmeister c. 1750 at Mergentheim
(Würtemberg). He composed ' David et
Apollo ' . . ., and eight 6-part symphonies for
church or secular use, op. 1 (1758). His other
compositions remained unpublished. He wrote
also an instruction book for singing and for
violin playing (Augsburg, 1763).

[1] See Alfr. Einstein, *Zur deutschen Literatur für Viola da Gamba.*

(2) PAUL (b. Würzburg, c. 1760), son of the former, showed early talent for music, but was destined by his father for the study of the law. Overcoming all obstacles, however, he entered the Munich court chapel and in 1773 achieved success with an opera, ' The Countess ' (MS. now in Dresden Libr.). He intended to return to Würzburg, but finding no vacancy he went to Ratisbon, where he joined the chapel of the Prince of Turn and Taxis and wrote the music for the reception of the Emperor Joseph II., who was so pleased with his compositions that he engaged him for his court at Vienna, where he produced his operas, ' The Illumination ' in 1792, and ' Robert and Calliste ' in 1794. He wrote also some excellent church music, which was partly still in use during the latter part of last century ; and secular songs. Kürzinger was still living in Vienna in 1807 as music director of an educational institute (Fétis ; *Mendel*).   E. v. d. s.

KUFFERATH, (1) HUBERT FERDINAND (b. Mühleim on Ruhr, Rhenish Prussia, June 10, 1818 ; d. Brussels, June 23, 1896), was the youngest of eight brothers, all musicians, and grew up in musical surroundings. As a child of 7 he was accustomed to tune the church organs of the neighbourhood, and played both piano and violin in public at a very early age. His eldest brother, Johann, director of the music-school at Utrecht, undertook to teach him, and eventually sent him to Cologne to complete his studies in violin playing and composition. At the Niederrheinische Festival of 1839 at Düsseldorf, he played a violin solo so much to Mendelssohn's satisfaction that the master urged him to go to Leipzig, where, after studying the violin under David, Kufferath took up the pianoforte, studying composition under Mendelssohn and Hauptman. In the winter of 1840 he played his capriccio for piano and orchestra at a Gewandhaus concert, and the piece was noticed by Schumann in the *Neue Zeitschrift für Musik*. Kufferath was one of the band of brilliant students which included Bennett, Horsley, Verhulst, Eckert and Gade. On returning to Cologne in 1841 he became conductor of the Männergesangverein, and after spending some time as a travelling virtuoso, he settled in Brussels in 1844, where he was for some time conductor of the Choral Society, and, with Léonard and Servais, founded a regular series of chamber concerts, at which he played, alternately, pianoforte and viola. Schumann's concerted music was introduced to the Belgian public by this organisation, and Mme. Schumann occasionally took part in their concerts. The title of pianist to the King was conferred upon Kufferath by Leopold I. From 1872 until his death he held the post of professor of counterpoint and fugue at the Conservatoire ; he wrote an *École du Choral* which is in use in Belgium and France. Among his pupils may

be mentioned Charles de Bériot, Edouard Lassen, Franz Servais, Léon Jahin, Arthur de Greef and Edgar Tinel. Kufferath's works include a symphony, a piano concerto, a string quartet, a trio, many compositions for piano, books of songs, and an andante for violin and orchestra.

His son (2) MAURICE (b. Brussels, Jan. 8, 1852 ; d. there, Dec. 8, 1919) was a pupil of the two Servais for violoncello, took the degree of ' docteur en droit et en philologie ' at the university, where a thesis on the theatre of Molière was rewarded with a prize. In 1873 he joined the staff of the *Indépendance Belge* and remained there until 1900. He was especially responsible for the articles on foreign politics, etc. Later on he contributed frequently to the *Guide musical*, and eventually became its editor and chief proprietor. Under his control the paper became known for its championship of the best modern tendencies in music. For the exhibition at Brussels in 1880 he wrote a report on musical instruments, and subsequently was sent by the Belgian Government to report upon the conditions of German and Austrian theatres. Among his literary works, the most famous are his interesting monographs on Wagner's later works, *Les Maîtres Chanteurs, Lohengrin, Walkyrie, Siegfried, Tristan et Yseult*, and *Parsifal*. Most of them have gone through many editions. *Hector Berlioz et Schumann*, and *Henri Vieuxtemps* are the subjects of two more volumes, and Kufferath translated into French certain famous books of Wagner, Richter, etc., as well as Wagner's letters to Roeckel ; he wrote translations of the words of songs, etc., and of several operas, such as Mozart's ' Enlèvement au sérail,' etc. In 1900 he was appointed director of the Théâtre de la Monnaie with Guillaume Guidé. Under their direction the first complete performance of the Wagnerian trilogy in French took place, and the following operas were given for the first time : D'Indy's ' Étranger,' Ernest Chausson's ' Roi Arthus,' J. Albeniz's ' Pepita Jimenez,' and ' L'Ermitage fleuri,' Gilson's ' Captive,' and Blockx's ' Fiancée de la mer.' He was associated with Ysaÿe and Guillaume Guidé in founding the Ysaÿe concerts, was a member of the ' Comité de lecture des œuvres musicales,' a chevalier of the order of Leopold and of the Sauveur de Grèce, an officer of public instruction, and commander of the order of Alphonso XII.

BIBL.—L. SOLVAY, *Notice sur M. Kufferath*. Brussels, 1923.

The daughter of H. F. Kufferath, (3) ANTONIA (b. Brussels, Oct. 28, 1857), studied singing under Stockhausen and Mme. Viardot-Garcia. Her fine soprano voice and pre-eminently artistic singing were much admired at the Schumann Festival at Bonn in 1880, by which date she had made herself a name as an interpreter of Schumann and of Brahms's songs, etc., some of the latter of which were sung by her for the first time in public. She visited England in 1882, singing at the Popular Concerts, the Philharmonic, etc. On June 2, 1885, she married Edward Speyer, and retired from the regular exercise of her art.   M.

KUGELMANN, HANS (d. 1542), said to have been born at Augsburg, was in 1519 trumpeter at Innsbruck in the service of the Emperor Maximilian, and afterwards as first trumpet-major and then Kapellmeister at Königsberg in the service of Duke Albert of Brandenburg and Prussia. In 1540 he brought out a harmonised Gesangbuch for liturgical use in the Lutheran Church, one of the earliest of the kind after Johann Walther's book of 1524. Its title is :

'Concentus novi trium vocum ecclesiarum usui in Prussia praecipue accomodati . . . News Gesang mit dreyen Stimmen dem Kirchen und Schulen zu nutz . . . auch etliche Stück mit 8, 6, 5, 4 Stim. hinzugethan' . . . (Augsburg, 1540).

It contains thirty-nine pieces, eight of them with Latin texts, including a Missa and Magnificat, mostly for three voices, thirty of them being the composition of Kugelmann himself. Towards the end there are a few more elaborate pieces. A complete Psalm by Stoltzer for five voices, another by Hans Heugel for six voices, etc. Kugelmann's book is the first source for the Choral-tunes, ' Nun lob mein' Seel' den Herrn ' (of which there are three settings, a 3, a 5 and a 8), and ' Allein Gott in der Höh',' this latter, however, being based on a Plain-song Gloria in Excelsis. Winterfeld, in his *Evangelische Kirchenmusik*, gives three of Kugelmann's pieces.   J. R. M.

KUHE, (1) WILHELM (b. Prague, Dec. 10, 1823 ; d. Kensington, Oct. 8, 1912), was taught music by Tomaschek, with Schulhoff as a fellow-student. He made a concert tour with great success in 1844–45 at Linz, Salzburg, Innsbruck, Augsburg, Munich and Stuttgart. He visited London with Pischek in 1845, and played with success at the Musical Union in Mayseder's trio, op. 52, May 13. He then lived in England (London and Brighton) after 1847. Kuhe showed great enterprise by the annual festival held by him at Brighton from 1870–82, wherein he encouraged native talent by the new works composed at his instance and produced by him. He frequently appeared in London, where he gave an annual concert for many years from 1846. He was appointed a professor of the R.A.M. in 1886, a post he resigned in 1904. His numerous compositions include many drawing-room pieces, fantasias and studies, viz. ' Lieder ohne Worte,' op. 12 ; ' Le Carillon,' op. 13 ; ' Chanson d'amour ' ; ' Romance sans paroles,' op. 17 ; ' Le Feu Follet,' op. 38 ; ' Victoria Fantasia on National Anthem ' ; ' Fantasia on Austrian Anthem ' ; operatic fantasias, etc. In 1896 his *Musical Recollections* was published by Bentley & Sons.   A. C.

His son (2) ERNEST is well known in London

as a musical journalist, on the staff of the *Daily Telegraph.*

KUHLAU, FRIEDRICH (b. Uelzen, Hanover, Sept. 11, 1786 ; d. Copenhagen, Mar. 12, 1832), a musician of some distinction in his day. He was born of poor parents, and had the misfortune to lose an eye at an early age. The loss did not, however, quench his ardour for music. During a wandering life he contrived to learn the piano and the flute, and to acquire a solid foundation of harmony and composition. He was, about 1800, in Hamburg, and previously in Brunswick. Germany was at that time under French rule, and to avoid the conscription he escaped to Copenhagen, where he became the first flute in the king's band. He then settled in Denmark, acquired a house in Lyngbye, near Copenhagen, to which he fetched his parents, composed half-a-dozen operas, was made professor of music and court composer, and enjoyed a very great popularity. In the autumn of 1825 he was at Vienna, and Seyfried [1] has preserved a capital story of his expedition to Beethoven at Baden with a circle of choice friends, of the way in which the great composer dragged them at once into the open air, and of the jovial close of the day's proceedings. Kuhlau, inspired by champagne and the presence of Beethoven, extemporised a canon, to which Beethoven responded on the spot, but thought it wise to replace his first attempt next morning by another, which is one reiterated joke on the name of his guest (and, whether intentionally or not, on the name ' Bach ')—

Kuhl nicht   lau nicht lau Kuhl nicht

lau Kuhlau nicht lau   Kuhl nicht lau etc.

and was accompanied by the following note :

BADEN, *September* 3, 1825.

'I must confess that the champagne got too much into my head last night, and has once more shewn me that it rather confuses my wits than assists them ; for though it is usually easy enough for me to give an answer on the spot, I declare I do not in the least recollect what I wrote last night. Think sometimes of your most faithful   BEETHOVEN.'

In 1830 Kuhlau suffered two irreparable losses—the destruction of the greater part of his manuscripts by fire, and the death of his parents. This double calamity affected his health, and he died at Copenhagen, leaving a mass of compositions, of which a few for flute and a few for piano are still esteemed.   G.

KUHNAU, JOHANN (b. Geising, Bohemia, Apr. [2] 1660 ; d. June 25, 1722), a very remarkable musician, cantor of Leipzig, and one of the pillars of the German school of the clavier.

[1] *Beethovens Studien, Anhang*, p. 25. See also *Beethoven's Letters* (Nohl), No. 365.
[2] Baptized Apr. 6, 1660.

As a boy he had a lovely voice and a strong turn for music. He was put to the Kreuzschule at Dresden about 1669, where he became a ' Rathsdiscantist,' and obtained regular instruction in music. On the breaking of his voice he worked the harder, and in addition to his music learned Italian. The plague in 1680 drove him home, but Geising was no field for his talent, and he went to Zittau and worked in the school, till the excellence of a motet which he wrote for the Rathswahl, or election of the town council, procured him the post of cantor, with a salary on which he could study at leisure. He began by lecturing on French. His next move was to Leipzig, in 1682, whither his fame had preceded him, and in that city of music he cast anchor for the rest of his life. In 1684 he succeeded Kühnel as organist at St. Thomas's. In 1688 he founded a ' Collegium Musicum,' or set of concerts. At the same time he was studying law, and qualified himself for the rank of advocate. In 1700 he was made musical director of the University and of the two principal churches, and in 1701 cantor. After this no further rise was possible. He left translations from Hebrew, Greek, Latin, Italian and French, and wrote satirical poetry of no common order. Of his works on music the following are named : *Jura circa musicos ecclesiasticos* (Leipzig, 1688); *Der musickalische Quacksalber . . . in einer kurtzweiligen und angenehmen Historie . . . beschrieben* (Dresden, 1700); *Tractatus de tetrachordo*; *Introductio ad compositionem*; and *Disputatio de triade*—the last three in MS. He wrote motets on Chorals, and other sacred pieces ; but his clavier music is his glory, and he is the greatest figure among German composers for the clavier before Bach. He was the inventor of the sonata as a piece in several movements, not dance-tunes—the first of which, ' Eine Sonata aus dem B,' in three movements, is found in his ' Sieben Partien ' (Leipzig, 1695). He followed this with thirteen others—' Frische Clavier-Früchte, oder sieben Sonaten ' (Dresden and Leipzig, 1696) ; ' Biblische Historien nebst Auslegung in sechs Sonaten '—the last a curious offspring of the musician and the divine, and a very early instance of Programme music. J. S. Shedlock edited several of these quaint Bible sonatas for Novello & Co., and describes them fully in his *Pianoforte Sonata*. The whole set were published in the *D.D.T.*, vol. iv., edited by K. Päsler. In addition to these he published ' Clavierübung aus 14 Partien . . . bestehend ' (Leipzig, 1689)—a collection of Suites, that is, of dance-tunes. Becker has republished two of Kuhnau's pieces in his ' Ausgewählte Tonstücke ' ; and Pauer, who introduced several of them to the English public in his chronological performances in 1862 and 1863, printed a suite in his ' Alte Claviermusik ' (Senff), and a Sonata in his ' Alte Meister ' (Breitkopf).

BIBL.—*Sammelbände* of the Int. Mus. Ges., 1902, p. 473, list of literary and musical works in *Q.-L.*; A. Schering, *Ein Memoria Joh Kuhnaus, Z.M.W.*, Aug.-Sept. 1923, pp. 612-15 ; R. Rolland, *Musical Tour through the Land of the Past* (Eng. trans. B. Mall, 1922) contains an excellent account of the *Musikalische Quacksalber*.

G., with addns.

KULLAK, (1) THEODOR (*b.* Krotoschin, province of Posen, Sept. 12, 1818 ; *d.* Mar. 1, 1882), was famous chiefly as teacher of the piano. His father held the post of ' Landgerichts-sekretär ' at Krotoschin. He was first intended for the law, but preferred to devote himself to music. He was a pupil of Hauck from his eleventh year, having previously been under the tuition of Albert Agthe. In 1837 he went to Berlin to study medicine. In 1842 he became a pupil of Czerny, and in 1846 was made Hofpianist to the King of Prussia. He founded, in conjunction with Stern and Marx, a Conservatorium at Berlin in 1850 ; and in 1855, in consequence of some disagreement with his fellow-workers, he started a new institution under the name of ' Neue Akademie der Tonkunst ' in the same city, where he resided until his death. He devoted his attention principally to the ' drawing-room ' style of composition, and published many transcriptions and arrangements for the piano, which are very popular. Of his original works the following are the most remarkable :

Grand concerto in C minor for piano and orchestra (op. 55); Trio for piano and strings (op. 77) ; Duos for piano and violin ; Ballades, Boleros, etc., for piano solo ; ' Les Etincelles,' ' Les Danaïdes,' ' La Gazelle,' etc. ; also collections of small pieces, such as ' Deux Portefeuilles de musique, ' Kinderleben,' two sets of pieces (op. 81), ' Les Fleurs animées.' Among his later works may be mentioned ' Ondine ' (op. 112), ' Concert-étude ' (op. 121).

In 1877 he published a second edition of his ' Octave-school,' which is very valuable as an instruction book.

His brother, (2) ADOLF (*b.* Feb. 23, 1823 ; *d.* Berlin, Dec. 25, 1862), was a distinguished musical critic in Berlin, and wrote *Das Musikalisch-Schöne* (Leipzig, 1858), and *Aesthetik des Clavierspiels* (Berlin, 1861). M.

(3) FRANZ (*b.* Berlin, Apr. 12, 1844 ; *d.* there Dec. 9, 1913), son of Theodor, was educated in his father's Akademie, and produced some educational works as well as compositions. His opera ' Mes de Castro ' was given in Berlin in 1877.

(4) ERNST (*b.* Berlin, Jan. 22, 1855), son of Adolf, became a well-known teacher of the piano and of composition in Berlin (*Riemann*).

KUMMER, FRIEDRICH AUGUST (*b.* Meiningen, Aug. 5, 1797 ; *d.* Dresden, May 22, 1879), a great violoncellist. His father (an oboist) migrated to Dresden, where the lad learnt the violoncello under Dotzauer. It was his ambition to enter the King's band, but as there was then no vacancy for a violoncellist, he took up the oboe, and soon attained such proficiency as to obtain the desired appointment, in Nov. 1814. In 1817 he again took up his original instrument, and in time became known as the most accomplished virtuoso in Germany. With the exception of occasional musical tours principally in Germany and Italy, his career was confined to Dresden. In 1864 he celebrated the fiftieth anniversary of his appointment as a member of the Dresden orchestra, after which he retired on a pension, and was succeeded by F. Grützmacher. Kummer was a voluminous writer for his instrument. Of his works 163 have appeared in print, among which are Concertos, Fantasias, a good Violoncello School, etc. He also composed some 200 entr'actes for the Dresden Theatre. Among his many distinguished pupils, Goltermann of Stuttgart and Cossmann of Wiesbaden may be named.   T. P. P.

His grandson, (2) ALEXANDER CHARLES (b. Dresden, 1850), was trained under David at the Leipzig Conservatorium, and lived for many years in London in high esteem as a violinist.   A. C.

KUNC, JAN (b. Doubravice, Moravia, Mar. 27, 1883), composer, conductor, teacher and director of the State Conservatoire at Brno since June 1923.

He studied at the Organ School at Brno, under Leoš Janáček, passed his examinations in pianoforte and singing, and went on to the Conservatoire at Prague, where he worked first under Karel Stecker, and later under Vítězslav Novák for composition, and Kovařovic for conducting. He acted as musical critic for the leading Moravian paper, the *Lidové Noviny*, toured with his wife (a singer and also a pupil of the Prague Conservatoire) through Bohemia and Moravia (1918–19), was chorus-master and conductor at the Prague National Theatre (1919–20); appointed Secretary to the Brno Conservatoire, and, after it was taken over by the State in 1920, became successively Administrator and Director. Kunc is perhaps best known as a composer of choral works in the national spirit and as an interesting arranger of the folk-songs. But he has written in other styles, and his music is now beginning to be published in Czechoslovakia. His symphonic poem ' A Song of Youth,' op. 12, which won a prize offered by the Czech Academy, was produced at a concert of the Prague Philharmonic Society in 1920. Like many of his contemporaries, Kunc has found the urgent demands upon his services for the reorganisation of the educational life on a national basis a hindrance to creative activity. The following is a list of his principal works :

ORCHESTRA
Symphonic Poem for full orchestra, ' Píseň mládí ' (Song of Youth), second prize of the Czech Academy of Arts.

CHAMBER MUSIC
Trio, op. 3, in F minor, for vln. v'cl. and PF. (MS.) · String Quartet, op. 9, in G major, second prize of the Czech Academy (in the repertory of the Czech Quartet); A second String Quartet (still unfinished, 1925).

PIANOFORTE
Sonata in C minor, op. 1 (MS.) · Nálady (Moods), op. 13; Miniatures, op. 19 (children's pieces, Pazdírek, Brno).

CHORAL MUSIC
Male Voice Choruses, op. 4 (published separately by Fr. Urbánek, Prague, and by the Hudebni Matice of the Society of Arts); Seventy-Thousand,' for chorus and orchestra, op. 8 (MS.); A

Czech Mass, for soprano and organ, op. 7 (MS.); Male Voice Choruses, op. 11 (published separately by Hudebni Matice; in the repertory of the Prague and Moravian Choral Societies of Teachers); ' Stála Kačenka u Dunaja ' (There was a Duck by the Danube), ballad for alto voice and orchestra, op. 14 (Barvič & Novotný, Brno); ' Zahrada ' (The Garden), for women's voices, unaccompanied, op. 15 (Hudebni Matice, Prague); Choruses for mixed voices, op. 16 (Hudebni Matice); Festival Chorus for the Choral Society of Moravian Teachers, in honour of their Jubilee, op. 20 (O. Pazdírek Brno); Folk-songs arranged for chorus, op. 21 (O. Pazdírek, Brno). Many Solo Songs, at present chiefly in MS.   R. N.

KUNST DER FUGE, DIE, see ART OF FUGUE, THE.

KUNST-HARMONIUM, see KARG-ELERT.

KUNTZEN (KUNZEN). Three members of the family who bore this name, father, son and grandson, distinguished themselves as musicians of some consequence in their day. (1) JOHANN PAUL KUNTZEN (b. Leisnig in Saxony, Aug. 30, 1696; d. Mar. 20, 1757), whose father was a cloth manufacturer at Leisnig. While still attending the University of Leipzig in 1716, he was engaged at the Leipzig Opera, both as singer and instrumental performer. In 1718 he became Kapellmeister at Zerbst, and in 1719 at Wittenberg, where he established regular concerts. In 1723 he was invited to Hamburg as opera composer. In 1732 he was appointed organist to the Marien-Kirche at Lübeck, which post he held till his death. At Lübeck he also established regular concerts which may be considered as a continuation of the Advent Abendmusiken of Buxtehude. Mattheson speaks highly of his compositions (opera, oratorio, etc.), none of which, however, appear ever to have been printed.

(2) ADOLPH KARL (surname generally spelt KUNZEN), son of Johann Paul (b. Wittenberg, Sept. 22, 1720; d. 1781), early distinguished himself as a performer on the harpsichord and clavier generally, and made tours as a virtuoso, in the course of which he paid several visits to London. It was in London that his op. 1 appeared, 12 sonatas for the harpsichord, dedicated to the Prince of Wales. In 1749 he was appointed Konzertmeister to the Duke of Mecklenburg-Schwerin, and in 1757 succeeded his father as organist at the Marien-Kirche, Lübeck, where he continued till his death. In his official capacity at Lübeck, as also previously in Schwerin, he produced a large number of Passions, oratorios and church cantatas (see *Q.-L.*) The library at Schwerin contains a large number of instrumental works by him (concertos, symphonies) and birthday serenatas for members of the ducal family. Besides the few for the harpsichord already mentioned, the only other works published by him are three collections of songs with accompaniment of figured bass only, 1748–56 (' Lieder zum unschuldigen Zeitvertreib ').

(3) FRIEDRICH LUDWIG AEMILIUS (surname always spelt KUNZEN). son of Adolph Karl (b. Lübeck, Sept. 24, 1761; d. 1817), received his early musical instruction from his father, who in 1768 brought him to London, where,

F

along with his equally talented sister, he appeared as a juvenile prodigy, playing in a concerto for two claviers. In 1781 he attended the University at Kiel for the study of law. There he made the acquaintance of Professor K F. Cramer, a musical dilettante and writer, who encouraged him to devote himself to music. Giving up his legal studies in 1787, he obtained through Cramer's influence a minor post at the Copenhagen Opera, where in 1789 he produced his first Danish opera, ' Holger Danske ' (Oberon), which the same year was also published in a piano score edited by Cramer. Shortly afterwards he went to Berlin, where, in conjunction with Reichardt, he edited a musical journal. In 1792 he was musical director of the theatre at Frankfort, and in 1794 held a similar post at Prague. In 1795 he successfully produced his opera ' Das Fest der Winzer,' which also appeared in piano score. The same year he succeeded J. A. P. Schulz as director of the opera at Copenhagen, where he produced a large number of Danish operas. Most of these were published in piano score at Copenhagen. (For list see *Q.-L.*) J. R. M.

KUNTZSCH, JOHANN GOTTFRIED (*d.* 1854), one of those earnest, old-fashioned, somewhat pedantic musicians to whom Germany owes much ; who are born in the poorest ranks, raise themselves by unheard - of efforts and self-denial, and die without leaving any permanent mark except the pupils whom they help to form. The ' Baccalaureus Kuntzsch ' was teacher of the organ and clavier at the Lyceum of Zwickau when Schumann was a small boy, and it was by him that the great composer was grounded in pianoforte - playing. Kuntzsch celebrated his jubilee at Zwickau in July 1852, when Schumann wrote him a charming letter,[1] which his biographer assures us was but one of many. Schumann's studies for the pedal piano—six pieces in canon-form (op. 56), composed in 1845 and published in 1846—are dedicated to his old master, whose name is thus happily preserved from oblivion. Kuntzsch died at a great age.

G.

KUPSCH, KARL GUSTAV (*b.* Berlin, Feb. 24, 1807 ; *d.* Naumburg, July 30, 1846), demands a few lines as having been for a short time Schumann's instructor in the theory of music [2] —apparently in the latter part of 1830, after his accident to his finger. Kupsch was an average German Kapellmeister, and lived and worked in Berlin, Leipzig and Dresden as teacher, composer and conductor, till 1838, when he settled in Rotterdam as director of the Singing Academy, and one of the committee of the ' Eruditio musica ' Society. In 1845 he returned to Germany, became director of the theatre at Freiburg im Breisgau, and at Naumburg, where he died. G.

KURTH, ERNST (*b.* Vienna, June 1, 1886),

studied under Guido Adler, graduated D.Ph. 1908 with a thesis on *Der Stil der Opera Seria von Chr. W. Gluck bis zum Orfeo* (published in Adler's *Studien*) and, after holding a post at Wickersdorf in Thuringia, settled in 1912 as a teacher in Berne. ' He founded there his Collegium Musicum and received a professorship in 1920. He wrote in 1913 *Die Voraussetzungen der theoretischen Harmonik,* but his distinctive contribution to musical thought up to the present time is contained in two volumes, *Grundlagen des linearen Kontrapunkts* (1916) and *Romantische Harmonik* (1919). In the former he expounds his elaborate theory of ' linear counterpoint ' as the result of a detailed examination of Bach's melodic style. Similarly the latter is based on the study of Wagner's ' Tristan.' Together these works are held to be an important landmark in the evolution of a modern theory of music based on the German classics. C.

KURZ, SELMA, Austrian soprano, was famous as the chief lyric soprano at the court opera and the most popular singer in Vienna. Selma Kurz made her first appearance in London on June 7, 1904, at Covent Garden as Gilda in ' Rigoletto ' and enjoyed nothing less than a triumph. As a singer pure and simple she made perhaps an even stronger impression when she played Oscar, the page in ' Un ballo in maschera,' the perfection of her shake astonishing half the singing-masters in London and provoking comparison with the most celebrated sopranos of the past. In other circumstances Selma Kurz would very likely have become a permanent attraction at Covent Garden, but though she reappeared in 1905 and sang in ' Rigoletto ' with Caruso and Scotti, she was never a regular member of the company. Heard at Queen's Hall since the war, she sang as fluently as ever, with a quality of tone little impaired by time, but she was slightly uncertain in intonation. S. H. P.

KUSSER, see COUSSER.

KUSSEVITZKY, SERGEI ALEXANDROVITCH (*b.* Tver, June 30, 1874), is famous both as a virtuoso of the double bass and as orchestral conductor.

Educated at the Philharmonic Music School in Moscow he first entered the Imperial Orchestra, but cultivating the double bass as a solo instrument he soon began to give recitals. He proved not only his complete technical command, but also that the musical qualities of the instrument were capable of unlimited development in the hands of a master. Kussevitzky's fame spread through Europe and his virtuosity was first shown to England in 1907, when he gave double-bass recitals at the Bechstein (now Wigmore) Hall. In the following year he returned, giving further double-bass recitals and conducting the LONDON SYMPHONY ORCHESTRA (*q.v.*) for the first time in a programme of

[1] Wasielewsky gives it, p. 10.   [2] Wasielewsky, p. 97.

Beethoven's works. This began an association which has been fruitful in many conspicuously fine performances both of Beethoven and of Russian orchestral music in the interpretation of which Kussevitzky excels. Kussevitzky studied the methods of Nikisch in Berlin, but his genius as a conductor is of that intuitive kind which owes little to teaching. He formed an orchestra of his own in Russia with which he gave important symphony concerts in the great

appeared almost entirely in the 14th and 15th centuries from all except the Kyries. The troped or farced Kyries survived down to the Reformation. (See TROPE.) The Kyrie of the Missa pro Defunctis, exhibited in the subjoined example, is peculiarly interesting, not only from its own inherent beauty, but, as will be presently shown, from the use to which it was turned by Palestrina, in the 16th century.

Ky - ri - e   e   - le - i - son.   Christe e - - le - i - son.   Ky - ri - e   e   - le - i - son.

cities. He also founded a firm for the publication of Russian music. The revolution brought to an end his activities in Russia. Latterly he has conducted concerts in the capitals of Europe, and in 1924 was appointed to direct the Boston Symphony Orchestra. (See BOSTON.)

C.

KVAPIL, JAROSLAV (b. Fryštak, Moravia, Apr. 21, 1892), teacher and composer. He studied under Leoš Janáček at the Organ School, Brno, and immediately on completing his courses was appointed professor of organ and counterpoint. From 1911–13 he continued his education at the Leipzig Conservatorium, his teachers being Teichmüller (PF.), Max Reger (composition) and Hans Sitt (conducting). His diploma work consisted of Variations and a Fugue for Orchestra. Kvapil is at present professor of piano and composition at the State Conservatoire of Brno and conductor of the Brno Philharmonic Society. His works include :

2 Symphonies (A min., E maj.) ; a string quartet (G min.), a PF. trio, a PF. quintet ; 2 violin sonatas, a violoncello sonata, a PF. sonata ; many songs (some published by Hudební Matice, Prague) and piano pieces ; a cantata for baryton solo, chorus and orchestra, etc.

R. N.

KYRIE (Gr. Κύριε ἐλέησον ; *Kyrie eleison* ; ' Lord, have mercy ').

(1) That portion of the Ordinary of the Mass which immediately follows the Introit, and precedes the ' Gloria in excelsis.' It is, historically speaking, the end of the litany which preceded the Mass. Originally Kyries were sung *ad libitum*, but in the early mediæval period the number was reduced to nine — a threefold ' Kyrie eleison,' a threefold ' Christe eleison,' and a threefold ' Kyrie eleison ' repeated. The primitive music, as this history suggests, was very simple ; but with the change in form came a change of music, and from the 9th or 10th century onward ninefold Kyries were composed, as St. Dunstan composed the ' Kyrie Rex Splendens,' or else adapted from older melodies. The next step was that the elaborate melodies were farced, *i e.* provided with a set of words written so that a syllable went to each note ; and from the *incipit* of these words they took their name. Similar tropes were inserted into other pieces of the services, but they dis-

When, after the invention of figured music, these venerable melodies were selected as themes for the exercise of contrapuntal skill, the Kyrie naturally assumed a prominent position in the polyphonic Mass ; and at once took a definite form, the broad outlines of which passed, unaltered, through the vicissitudes of many changing schools. The construction of the words led, almost of necessity, to their separation into three distinct movements. Some of the earlier contrapuntists delighted in moulding these into canons, of excessive com plexity. The great masters of the 16th century preferred rather to treat them as short but well-developed real fugues, on three distinct subjects, the last of which was usually of a somewhat more animated character than the other two.

(2) The Response, ' Lord, have mercy upon us, and incline our hearts to keep this law ' ; sung, in the service of the Church of England, after the recitation of the Ten Commandments.

As the custom of reciting the Commandments during the Communion Service is of later date than the First Prayer Book of King Edward the Sixth, in Merbecke's ' Book of Common Praier Noted ' (1550), the old ninefold Kyrie is found in a simple form, borrowed from the Kyrie cited above. Dyce in his *Book of Common Prayer with Plain Tune* (1844) adapted this to the

Kyrie of the present[1] Prayer Book, and his adaptation is in frequent use. The Kyrie provided by Merbecke for a burial was taken with less alterations from the melody which was used in the lesser Litany as well as in the Mass, and is probably the primitive form of Kyrie.

[1] The proposals for revision of the Book of Common Prayer issued in 1927 contain permissive use of the original Kyrie.

The treatment of the English Kyrie by the early composers of the polyphonic school was extremely simple and dignified ; indeed, some of these responses, as set by Tallis (in the Dorian Mode), Byrd, Farrant, Gibbons and other old English writers, are perfect little gems of artistic beauty. (See Service.)

W. S. R. ; addns. W. H. F.

L

LA, the sixth note of the major scale in the nomenclature of France and Italy. See A; Hexachord; Solmisation.

LA BARRE, Michel de, see Barre.

LA BASSÉE, Adam de, see Bassée.

L'ABBÉ, see Abbé.

LABIAL PIPES, organ pipes possessing lips as distinguished from reeds.

LABITZKY, (1) Josef (b. Schönfeld, Eger, July 4, 1802 ; d. Carlsbad, Aug. 19, 1881), a well-known dance composer, was grounded in music by Veit of Petschau. In 1820 he became first violin in the band at Marienbad and in 1821 removed to a similar position at Carlsbad. He then formed an orchestra of his own, and made tours in South Germany. Feeling his deficiencies, he took a course of composition under Winter, in Munich, and in 1827 published his first dances there. In 1835 he settled at Carlsbad as director of the band, making journeys from Petersburg on the one hand, to London on the other, and becoming every day more famous. He lived at Carlsbad, and associated his son (2) August (b. Oct. 22, 1832 ; d. Aug. 28, 1903) with him as director from 1853. His second son, (3) Wilhelm, an excellent violinplayer, settled at Toronto, Canada, and his daughter was a favourite singer at Frankfort.

Labitzky's dances are full of rhythm and spirit. Among his waltzes, the ' Sirenen,' ' Grenzboten,' ' Aurora,' ' Carlsbader ' and ' Lichtensteiner ' are good. In galops he fairly rivalled Lanner and Strauss, though he had not the poetry of those two composers. F. G.

LABLACHE, Luigi (b. Naples, Dec. 6, 1794 ; d. Naples, Jan. 23, 1858), operatic singer. His mother was Irish, and his father, Nicolas Lablache, a merchant of Marseilles, had quitted that place in 1791 in consequence of the Revolution. But another Revolution in 1799 overwhelmed him with ruin in his new country, and he died of chagrin. His family was, however, protected by Joseph Buonaparte, and Luigi at the age of 12 was placed in the Conservatorio della Pietà de' Turchini, afterwards called San Sebastiano.

Gentilli taught him the elements of music, and Valesi instructed him in singing ; while, at the same time, he studied the violin and violoncello under other masters. His progress was not at first remarkable, for he was wanting in application and regularity ; but his aptitude was soon discovered by a singular incident. One day a contrabassist was wanted for the orchestra of S. Onofrio. Marcello-Perrino, who taught young Lablache the violoncello, said to him, ' You play the violoncello very well : you can easily learn the double bass ! ' The boy had a dislike for that instrument, in spite of which he got the gamut of the double bass written out for

him on a Tuesday, and on the following Friday executed his part with perfect accuracy. At this period his boy's voice was a beautiful contralto : his last use of it was to sing, as it was just breaking, the solos in the Requiem of Mozart on the death of Haydn in 1809. Before many months were passed, however, he became possessed of a magnificent bass, which gradually increased in volume until, at the age of 20, it was the finest of the kind which can be remembered, with a compass of two octaves, from E♭ to e'♭.

Continually dominated by the desire to appear on the stage, the young Lablache made his escape from the Conservatorio no less than five times, and was as often brought back in disgrace. He engaged himself to sing at Salerno at 15 ducats a month (40 sous a day), and received a month's salary in advance ; but, remaining two days longer at Naples, he spent the money. As he could not, however, appear decently without luggage, he filled a portmanteau with sand, and set out. Two days later he was found at Salerno by the vice-president of the Conservatorio, while the impresario seized the effects of the young truant in order to recoup himself the salary he had advanced, but found, to his horror, nothing in the portmanteau but what Lablache had put there ! [1] To these escapades was due, however, the institution of a little theatre within the Conservatorio ; and Lablache was satisfied for a time. A royal edict, meanwhile, forbade the impresario of any theatre, under severe penalties, to engage a student of the Conservatorio without special permission.

Having at length completed his musical education, Lablache was engaged at the San Carlino Theatre at Naples, as *buffo Napolitano*, in 1812, though then only 18. He made his début in ' La molinara ' of Fioravanti. A few months later he married Teresa Pinotti, the daughter of an actor engaged at the theatre and one of the best in Italy. His young wife persuaded Lablache, not without difficulty, to quit the San Carlino, a theatre in which two performances a day were given, to recommence serious study of singing, and to give up the patois in which he had hitherto sung and spoken. Accordingly, a year later, after a short engagement at Messina, he went as *primo basso cantante* to the Opera at Palermo. His first appearance was in the ' Ser Marc-Antonio ' of Pavesi, and his success was so great as to decide him to stay at Palermo for nearly five years. But the administration of La Scala at Milan engaged him in 1817, where he made his début as Dandini in ' Cenerentola ' with great success, due to his splendid acting and singing, and in spite

[1] Escudier.

69

of the provincial accent which still marred his pronunciation. Over the latter defect he soon triumphed, as he had over his want of application a few years before. It is said that at Naples he had enjoyed the great advantage of the society and counsels of Madame Méricofre, a banker's wife, known in Italy before her marriage as La COLTELLINI (q.v.). To such influence as this, and to that of his intelligent wife, Lablache perhaps owed some of the impulse which prompted him to continue to study when most singers cease to learn and content themselves with reaping the harvest ; but much must have been due to his own desire for improvement.

The opera ' Elisa e Claudio ' was now (1821) written for him by Mercadante ; his position was made, and his reputation spread throughout Europe. From Milan he went to Turin ; returned to Milan in 1822, then appeared at Venice, and in 1824 at Vienna, and always with the same success. At the last city he received from the enthusiastic inhabitants a gold medal bearing a most flattering inscription. After twelve years' absence he returned to Naples, with the title of singer in the chapel of Ferdinand I., and with an engagement at the San Carlo. Here he created a great sensation as Assur in ' Semiramide.' In 1829 we find him at Parma, singing in Bellini's ' Zaira.'

Although Ebers had endeavoured, as early as 1822, to secure him for London, on the strength of his reputation as ' perhaps even excelling Zucchini,' Lablache did not tread the English boards till the season of 1830, when he made his début on Mar. 30 in the ' Matrimonio segreto.' Here, as elsewhere, his success was assured from the moment when he sang his first note, almost from the first step he took upon the stage. It is indeed doubtful whether he was greater as a singer or as an actor. His head was noble, his figure very tall, and so atoning for his bulk, which became immense in later years : yet he never looked too tall on the stage. His strength was enormous. As Leporello, he sometimes carried off under his arm, apparently without effort, the troublesome Masetto, represented by Giubilei, a man of the full height and weight of ordinary men !

Like Garrick, and other great artists, Lablache shone as much in comic as in tragic parts. Nothing could exceed his Leporello ; of that character he was doubtless the greatest known exponent. But he had, at an earlier date, played Don Giovanni. As Geronimo, the Podestà in ' La gazza ladra,' again, in ' La prova d' un' opera seria,' as Dandini and the Barone di Montefiascone, he was equally unapproachable ; while his Henry VIII. in ' Anna Bolena,' his Doge in ' Marino Faliero,' and Oroveso in ' Norma,' were splendid examples of dignity and dramatic force. He appeared for the first time in Paris, Nov. 4, 1830, as Geronimo in the

' Matrimonio segreto,' and was there also recognised immediately as the first *basso cantante* of the day. He continued to sing in Paris and London for several years ; and it may be mentioned that his terms were in 1828, for four months, 40,000 frs. (£1600), with lodging and one benefit-night clear of all expenses, the opera and his part in it to be chosen by himself on that occasion, as also at his début. The modest sum named above, in no degree corresponding with the value of Lablache in an operatic company, was a few years later (1839) the price paid by Laporte to Robert, to whom Lablache was then engaged at Paris, for the mere cession of his services to the London Opera.

In 1833 Lablache sang again at Naples, renewing his triumphs in the ' Elisire d' amore,' and ' Don Pasquale.' He returned to Paris in 1834, after which he continued to appear annually there and in London, singing in our provincial festivals as well as at the Opera, for many years. In 1852 he sang at St. Petersburg with no less éclat than elsewhere. Whether in comic opera, in the chromatic music of Spohr, or in that of Palestrina, he seemed equally at home. Let it be never forgotten that he sang (Apr. 3, 1827) the bass solo part in Mozart's Requiem after the death of Beethoven, as he had, when a child, sung the contralto part at a memorial service for Haydn ; and let the former fact be a sufficient answer to those who say he had no notes lower than A or G. Be it recorded, at the same time, that he paid Barbaja 200 gulden for the operatic singers engaged on that occasion. He was also one of the thirty-two torch-bearers who surrounded the coffin of Beethoven at its interment. To him, again, Schubert dedicated his three Italian songs (op. 83), written to Metastasio's words and composed in 1827, showing thus his appreciation of the powers of the great Italian.

In 1856, however, his health began to fail, and he was obliged in the following spring to drink the waters of Kissingen, where he was met and treated with honour by Alexander II. of Russia. Lablache received the medal and order given by the Emperor with the prophetic words, ' These will do to ornament my coffin.' After this he returned for a few days in August to his house at Maisons-Lafitte, near Paris ; but left it on the 18th, to try the effect of his native climate at his villa at Posilipo. But the bright, brisk air was too keen for him, and he had to take refuge in Naples. The relief, however, served only to prolong his life a short while, and he died Jan. 23, 1858. His remains were brought to Paris, and buried at Maisons-Lafitte.

Lablache had many children ; one of his daughters married the great pianist, Thalberg. A *Méthode de chant*, written by Lablache, was published chez Mme. Vve Canaux, at Paris ; but it rather disappointed expectation.

He was Queen Victoria's singing - master (1836–37),[1] and the esteem and even affection which that intercourse engendered are expressed more than once in warm terms in Her Majesty's published Diaries and Letters.   J. M.

BIBL.—CASTIL-BLAZE, *Biographie de Lablache*; J. D'ORTIGUE, *Journal des Débats*, Feb. 24, 1858: *Lablache. Onori alla memoria di Luigi Lablache* (Naples, 1858).   M. L. P.

LA BORDE, J. B. DE, see BORDE.
LA CARAMBA, see CARAMBA.
LACH, ROBERT (*b.* Vienna, Jan. 29, 1874), studied at the Conservatoire, 1893–99, with Robert Fuchs, and musical history and research under Wallaschek and Guido Adler. He graduated D.Ph. Prague in 1902. His studies in folklore and melody bore fruit in the papers contributed to the *Sammelbände* of the Int. Mus. Ges. In 1911 he became director of the musical department of the Vienna State Library ; in 1915 a teacher of the University and in 1920 a professor. In addition to his important research work and his studies in the Wagnerian music drama, he has done much musical composition. He contributed to Adler's *Handbuch*, 1924, a chapter on *Musik der Natur- und orientalischen Kultur-Völker*.   C.

LACHNER, a prominent musical family of the 19th century. The father was an organist at Rain, on the Lech, in Bavaria, very poor and with a very large family, a man of worth and character. He was twice married. One of the first family, (1) THEODOR (*b.* 1798 ; *d.* Munich, May 22, 1877), was a sound musician, but unambitious, who ended his career as organist at Munich, and chorus-master at the court theatre. The second family were more remarkable. Of the daughters, (2) THEKLA was organist of St. George's Church, Augsburg, and (3) CHRISTIANE (*b.* 1805) held the same post in her native place.

Of the brothers, (4) FRANZ (*b.* Apr. 2, 1803 ; *d.* Munich, Jan. 20, 1890) was solidly educated in other things besides music, but music was his desire, and in 1822 he prevailed on his parents to let him go to Vienna. He put himself under Stadler and Sechter, and was constantly in Schubert's company, with whom he became very intimate. In 1826 he was made vice-Kapellmeister of the Kärnthnerthor Theatre, and the next year, on the retirement of Weigl, principal Kapellmeister. He retained this post till 1834, and it was a time of great productivity. In that year he went to Mannheim to conduct the opera there, and in 1836 advanced to the top of the ladder as Hof-Kapellmeister—in 1852 general music director—at Munich, and there remained till 1865, when he retired on a pension. In 1872 the University of Munich gave him the honorary degree of Doctor of Philosophy. Lachner's writings are of prodigious number and extent. Two oratorios, ' Moses ' and ' Die vier Menschenalter ' ; four operas (' Die Bürg-

schaft,' Pest, 1828 ; ' Alidia,' Munich, 1839 ; ' Catarina Cornaro,' Munich, 1841 ; and ' Benvenuto Cellini,' Munich, 1849) ; a Requiem ; three masses ; various cantatas, entr'actes, and other pieces ; many large compositions for male voices ; eight symphonies— among them those in D minor (No. 3), in C minor (op. 52)—which won the prize offered by the Gesellschaft der Musikfreunde—and in D (No. 6), which Schumann finds twice as good as the prize one—seven suites, overtures, and serenades for orchestra, the orchestration of Schubert's ' Song of Miriam ' ; five quartets ; concertos for harp and bassoon ; a nonet for wind instruments, trios, duos, pianoforte pieces of all dimensions ; and a large number of vocal pieces for solo and several voices. All that industry, knowledge, tact and musicianship can give is here—if there were but a little more of the sacred fire ! No one can deny to Lachner the praise of conscientiousness and artistic character ; he was deservedly esteemed by his countrymen almost as if he were an old classic, and held a similar position in the South to that of Hiller in the North.

The next brother, (5) IGNAZ (*b.* Sept. 11, 1807 ; *d.* Hanover, Feb. 24, 1895), was brought up to music, and at 12 years old was sent to the Gymnasium at Augsburg, where he is said to have had no less a person than Napoleon III. (then Count St. Leu) as a schoolfellow. In 1824 he joined his brother at Vienna, in 1825 was made vice-Kapellmeister of the Kärnthnerthor Theatre ; in 1831 a court music-director at Stuttgart, and in 1842 rejoined his brother in a similar position at Munich. In 1853 he took the conduct of the theatre at Hamburg, in 1858 was made court Kapellmeister at Stockholm ; and in 1861 settled down for good at Frankfort, where he filled many musical positions, and retired in 1875. He also produced a long list of works—three operas (' Der Geisterturm,' Stuttgart, 1837 ; ' Die Regenbrüder,' Stuttgart, 1839 ; and ' Loreley,' Munich, 1846) ; several ballets, melodramas, etc. etc. ; with masses, symphonies, quartets, pianoforte works, and many songs, one of which—' Überall Du '—was very popular in its day.

The third brother, (6) VINCENZ (*b.* July 19, 1811 ; *d.* Carlsruhe, Jan. 22, 1893), was also brought up at the Augsburg Gymnasium. He began by taking Ignaz's place as organist in Vienna in 1834, and rose, by the same course of goodness and indefatigable assiduity as his brothers, to be court Kapellmeister at Mannheim from 1836–73, when he retired on a pension. He was in London in 1842, conducting the German Company. After his retirement he settled at Carlsruhe, where he taught in the Conservatorium from 1884. His music to *Turandot*, his prize song ' In der Ferne,' and other pieces, are favourites with his countrymen.   G.

1 See *The Letters of Queen Victoria*, vol. 1., ed. by A. C. Benson and Viscount Esher, London, 1908.

LACHNITH, LUDWIG WENZEL (*b.* Prague, July 7, 1746; *d.* Oct. 3, 1820), migrated to the service of the Duke at Zweibrücken, and thence to Paris, where he made his début at the Concert Spirituel as a horn-player. He was a clever, handy creature, who wrote not only quantities of all kinds of instrumental music, but at least four operas, and several pasticcios and other pieces. His most notable achievements, however, were his adaptations of great operas, by way of making them pleasant to the public, such as ' Les Mystères d'Isis,' for which both libretto and music of the ' Zauberflöte ' were ' arranged ' into what Fétis calls ' a monstrous compilation ' [1] (Opéra, Aug. 23, 1801). No wonder that the piece was called ' Les Misères d'ici,' and that Lachnith was styled ' le dérangeur.' He was clever also at working up the music of several composers into one piece, and torturing it to the expression of different words and sentiments from those to which it had originally been set—as ' Le Laboureur chinois,' in which the music of ' several celebrated composers ' was ' arrangée par M. Lachnitch ' (Feb. 5, 1813). In these crimes he had an accomplice in the elder Kalkbrenner, who assisted him to concoct two ' Oratorios in action '—' Saul ' (Apr. 6, 1803), and ' The Taking of Jericho ' (Apr. 11, 1805). We were as bad in England several years later, and many fine operas of Rossini, Auber and quasi-Weber were first made known to Londoners by much the same expedients as those of Lachnith, in the hands of T. P. Cooke, Lacy and others.   G.

LACOMBE, LOUIS TROUILLON (*b.* Bourges, Nov. 26, 1818; *d.* St. Vaast-la-Hougue, Sept. 30, 1884), entered the Paris Conservatoire under Zimmerman at the age of 11, and at 13 carried off the first piano prize. In 1832 he undertook a concert-tour with his sister, and in 1834 settled in Vienna, where he had lessons from Czerny, and studied theory, etc., with Sechter and Seyfried. From 1839 he lived in Paris, and devoted himself mainly to composition, writing numerous pieces for piano solo, studies, etc., a quintet for piano, violin, oboe, violoncello and bassoon, and two trios, his best-known pieces of chamber music ; two dramatic symphonies— soli, choir and orchestra, ' Manfred ' (1847) and ' Arva ' (1850), as well as a melodrama with choruses, ' Sapho,' which received a prize in the Exhibition of 1878. The two operatic works performed in the composer's lifetime were ' L'Amour,' melodrama (Théâtre St. Marcel, Paris, 1859) and ' La Madone,' one act (Théâtre Lyrique, Jan. 16, 1861) ; the four-act ' Winkelried ' was given Feb. 17, 1892, at Geneva ; the two-act ' Le Tonnelier de Nuremberg ' in Hugo Riemann's adaptation, as ' Meister Martin und

[1] See the account by O. Jahn (*Mozart*, 2nd ed. ii. 537). The magic flute and all the comic music were omitted ; Papageno was turned into a shepherd sage ; while many pieces were left out, others were put in—as for instance ' Fin ch' an dal vino,' *arranged as a duet* ! The opera opened with Mozart's finale, and the disorder must have been complete. And yet it ran forty-nine nights !

seine Gesellen,' was given at Coblenz, Mar. 7, 1897, and the three-act ' Korrigane ' at Sondershausen in 1901. A monument was erected to his memory in 1887 in his native town. In 1896 his treatise *Philosophie et musique* appeared.   M.

LACOMBE, PAUL (*b.* Carcassonne, July 11, 1838), was taught harmony, counterpoint and fugue there by a former pupil of the Paris Conservatoire, an organist, François Teysserre. In 1866 he began to correspond with Bizet, and was his disciple until Bizet's death. Lacombe belonged to the group of composers whose desire was to reform French music after 1870. He has travelled in Europe, but resides in his native town. In 1901 he was elected ' corresponding member' of the Institut and was made chevalier of the Légion d'Honneur in 1902. He has produced more than 150 works—instrumental music, chiefly for piano, and songs. There are also some unpublished compositions. His first sonata for violin and PF. (1868) was played by Delaborde and Sarasate in 1869. A great many of his works have been performed at the Société Nationale de Musique, between 1872 and 1921. He also composed orchestral music : an ' Ouverture symphonique ' (Concerts Pasdeloup, 1876) ; 3 symphonies (the 3rd awarded the prize of the Société des Compositeurs de Musique, 1886) ; a suite for PF. and orch. In chamber music his important works are 3 sonatas (PF. and vln.), 1 sonata (PF. and v'cl.), 3 trios, 1 quartet. His latest works are : ' Marche dernière ' (orch.), ' Dialogue sentimental ' (flute, bassoon and PF., 1917), ' Petite suite,' ' Deux pièces ' (PF., 1922), ' Trois mélodies ' (1922), ' Berceuse ' (1924). Lacombe's music owes much to the romanticism of Mendelssohn, Chopin and Schumann.   M. L. P.

BIBL.—LÉON MOULIN, (1) *Le Romantisme musical allemand et l'âme française. Un classique français du piano : Paul Lacombe* (Montauban, 1915, 1917). (2) *Paul Lacombe et son œuvre* (Toulouse, *Éditions de Travail ;* Paris, 1924). HUGUES IMBERT, (1) *Profils d'artistes contemporains ;* (2) *Portraits et études.*

LA COSTE, see COSTE.

LACY, FREDERICK ST. JOHN (*b.* Blackrock, Co. Cork, Mar. 27, 1862) ; studied at the R.A.M., of which he became Associate (1888) and Fellow (1911) ; member of the Philharmonic Society (1918) ; taught in London from 1886 to 1900 ; appointed lecturer in music at Queen's College, Cork, in 1906, and has been professor of music at University College, Cork, since 1908. He became examiner for musical degrees at the N.U.I. in 1909, and examiner in theory to the Intermediate Board of Education in 1922 ; Vice-President of the Cork Orchestral Union, 1905–09 ; President of Cork Literary and Scientific Society, 1915–17. In addition to various songs, partsongs, song cycles and sacred music, Prof. Lacy has composed a fine Serenade for Orchestra (op. 21), and a book of Irish tunes for Irish regiments. He is also well known as a lecturer.   W. H. G. F.

LACY, JOHN (b. end of 18th cent. ; d. Devonshire, c. 1865), bass singer, was a pupil of Rauzzini at Bath. After singing in London he went to Italy, where he became complete master of the Italian language and style of singing. On his return he sang at concerts and the Lenten oratorios, but although he possessed an exceptionally fine voice and sang admirably in various styles, circumstances prevented him from taking any prominent position. In 1818 he accepted an engagement at Calcutta, and, accompanied by his wife, left England, returning about 1826. Had he remained here he would most probably have been appointed successor to Bartleman.

MRS. LACY, his wife, originally Miss Jackson (b. London, 1776 ; d. Ealing, May 19, 1858), appeared as a soprano singer at the Concert of Ancient Music, Apr. 25, 1798. In 1800 she became the wife of Francesco Bianchi, the composer, and in 1810 his widow. In 1812 she was married to Lacy, and sang as Mrs. Bianchi Lacy in 1812–15. She ' was the best representative of the great and simple style as delivered down by Mrs. Bates and Madame Mara, whilst her articulate delivery and pure pronunciation of Italian rendered her no less generally valuable in other departments of the art.'

w. h. h. ; addns. from S. S. Stratton.

LACY, MICHAEL ROPHINO (b. Bilbao, July 19, 1795 ; d. Pentonville, Sept. 20, 1867), son of an Irish merchant, learned music from an early age, and made rapid progress on the violin, appearing in public at 6 years old in a concerto by Jarnowick at a concert given at Bilbao by Andreossi. In 1802 he was at college at Bordeaux, and in 1803 was sent to Paris to finish his education, and attained to considerable skill as a linguist. Kreutzer was his principal instructor in music. About the end of 1804 he performed before Napoleon at the Tuileries. He was then known as ' Le petit Espagnol.' He played in the principal Dutch towns on his way to London, which he reached in Oct. 1805. He soon gave concerts at Hanover Square Rooms, under the sobriquet of ' The Young Spaniard,' his name not being announced until May 1807, when an engraved portrait of him by Cardon after Smart was published. He next performed at Catalani's first concert in Dublin, during a visit of Michael Kelly's opera company to Ireland, and was afterwards engaged for Corri's concerts at Edinburgh at 20 guineas per night. A few years later he quitted the musical for the theatrical profession, and performed the principal genteel comedy parts at the theatres of Dublin, Edinburgh, Glasgow, etc. In 1818 he was appointed leader of the Liverpool concerts vice Janiewicz, and at the end of 1820 returned to London and was engaged as leader of the ballet at the King's Theatre. Lacy adapted to the English stage both words and music of several popular operas ; and his adaptations

display great skill, although gross liberties were frequently taken with the original pieces, which can only be excused by the taste of the time. Among them are

' The Maid of Judah ' from *Ivanhoe*, the music from ' Semiramide,' 1829 ; ' Cinderella,' the music from Rossini's ' Cenerentola,' Armida,' ' Maometto Secondo,' and ' Guillaume Tell,' 1830 ; ' Fra Diavolo,' 1831 ; and ' Robert le Diable,' under the title of ' The Fiend Father,' 1832.

In 1833 he produced an oratorio entitled ' The Israelites in Egypt,' a pasticcio from Rossini's ' Mosè in Egitto,' and Handel's ' Israel in Egypt,' which was performed with scenery, dresses, and personation. In 1839 he brought forward a readaptation of Weber's ' Der Freischütz,' introducing the whole of the music for the first time. He rendered great assistance to Schœlcher in collecting the material for his *Life of Handel*.

w. h. h. ; addns. from *D.N.B.*, etc.

LADURNER, (1) IGNAZ ANTON (b. Aldein, Tirol, Aug. 1, 1766 ; d. Massy, Seine-et-Oise, Mar. 4, 1839), eldest son of Franz Xavier, educated at the monastery of Benediktbeuern. From 1782–84 he filled his father's post as organist. He made further studies at Munich and went with a countess of Heimhausen to Bar-le-Duc. He was succeeded in the latter appointment by his younger brother. In July 1788 he went to Paris as composer and teacher, became professor at the Conservatoire, and teacher of Auber and Boëly. He retired to his country seat near Massy in 1836. Ladurner composed 2 operas, sonatas for PF. and for violin, divertissements, variations, etc.

His younger brother, (2) JOSEPH ALOYS (b. Algund, Mar. 7, 1769 ; still living in 1835), was court chaplain, councillor of the consistory, etc., at Brixen. He was a talented composer of church music. (Works in *Q.-L.*)

e. v. d. s.

LADY HENRIETTE, OU LA SERVANTE DE GREENWICH, see MARTHA.

LÄNDLER, LÄNDERER, or LÄNDLERISCHE TANZ, a national dance popular in Austria, Bavaria, Bohemia and Styria. It probably derives its name from the Landel, a district in the valley of the Ens, where the dance is said to have had its origin ; but according to some authorities the word simply means ' country dance,' *i.e.* a waltz danced in a country fashion. In fact the Ländler is a homely waltz, and only differs from the waltz in being danced more slowly. It is in 3–4 or 3–8 time, and consists of two parts of eight bars, each part being repeated two or more times. Like most early dances, it occasionally has a vocal accompaniment. Both Mozart (Köchel, No. 606) and Beethoven (Nottebohm's *Cat.* pp. 150, 151) have written genuine Ländler, but the compositions under this name of Jensen, Raff, Reinecke and other modern musicians have little in common with the original dance. The following example is the first part of a Styrian

Ländler (Köhler, *Volkstänze* : Brunswick, 1854) :

The little waltz so well known as ' Le Désir,' usually attributed to Beethoven, though really composed by Schubert, is a Ländler. To know what grace and beauty can be infused into this simple form one must hear Schubert's ' Wiener Damen-Ländler ' or ' Belles Viennoises ' in their unsophisticated form, before they were treated by Liszt. W. B. S.

LA FAGE, J. A. L. DE, see FAGE.

L'AFFILARD, MICHEL, see AFFILARD.

LAFONT, CHARLES PHILIPPE (*b.* Paris, Dec. 1, 1781 ; *d.* Aug. 23, 1839), an eminent violinist.

Fétis relates that he got his first instruction on the violin from his mother, a sister of Berthaume, a well-known violinist of that period, whom he also accompanied on his travels through Germany, performing successfully, when only 11 years of age, at Hamburg, Oldenburg and other towns. On his return to Paris he continued his studies under Kreutzer ; and soon appeared at the Théâtre Feydeau, though not as a violinist, but as a singer of French ballads. After some time he again took up the violin, this time under the tuition of Rode. and soon proved himself a player of exceptional merit. Fétis credits him with a perfect intonation, a pure and mellow, though somewhat feeble tone, great powers of execution, and a remarkable charm of expression. From 1801–08 he travelled and played with great success in France, Belgium, Holland, Germany and Russia. In 1808 he was appointed Rode's successor as solo-violinist to the Emperor of Russia, a position in which he remained for six years. In 1815 he returned to Paris, and was appointed solo violinist to Louis XVIII. In 1816 he had a public contest with Paganini at Milan. (See PAGANINI for that artist's comment on the occasion.) In 1831 he made a long tour with Henri Herz, the pianist, which occupied him till 1839, when his career was suddenly ended by a carriage accident in the south of France, through which he lost his life.

Spohr, in his *Selbstbiographie*, praises his fine tone, perfect intonation, energy and gracefulness, but deplores the absence of deep feeling, and accuses him of mannerism in phrasing. He also relates that Lafont's repertory was confined to a very few pieces, and that he would practise a concerto for years before venturing on it in public—a method which, although leading to absolute mechanical perfection,

appears absurd from an artistic or even musical point of view. Lafont's compositions for the violin are of no musical value ; they comprise seven concertos, a number of fantasias, rondos, etc. He wrote a number of duos concertants in conjunction with Kalkbrenner, Herz, etc.; more than 200 ballads (romances), which for a time were very popular ; and two operas. P. D.

LA FRANCESINA, ELISABETH DUPARC, see FRANCESINA.

LAGARDE, N. DE (mid. 18th cent.), an excellent French singer and master of the children of the French Chapel Royal. He composed operettas, brunettes, aires, suites of songs with instruments, etc. (published 1742–1766). E. V. D. S.

LAGE (Ger.) = ' position,' used (1) of the positions in violin-playing (see FINGERING), and (2) of the positions of chords in harmony which in English are called INVERSIONS.

LAGKHNER, DANIEL (16th-17th cent.), of Marchpurg, Styria, organist to Count Losenstein at Losdorf *c.* 1607. He composed motets 4-8 v. and other church music ; also secular songs (published *c.* 1601–28) (*Q.-L.*).

LA GROTTE, NICOLAS DE, see GROTTE.

LAGUERRE, JEAN (*b. circa* 1700 ; *d.* London, 1748), commonly called Jack, was the son of Louis Laguerre, the artist who painted the greater part of Verrio's large picture in St. Bartholomew's Hospital, the ' Labours of Hercules ' in chiaroscuro at Hampton Court, the staircase at Wilton, etc., and is immortalised by Pope in the line

'Where sprawl the saints of Verrio and Laguerre.'

This painter came to England in 1683, and died in 1721, his son Jean having, as it is supposed, been born about 1700. The lad was instructed by his father for his own profession, and had already shown some ability ; but, having a talent for music, he took to the stage, where he met with fair success. He sang at concerts in 1723–25. It must be he whom we find, under the name of *Mr. Legar*,[1] playing the part of Metius in ' Camilla ' (revived), 1726, which had formerly (1706 and 1708) been sung by Ramondon, a low tenor. Again, he is advertised (*Daily Journal,* Mar. 13, 1731) as sustaining the added rôle of Corydon in ' Acis and Galatea,' ' for the benefit of M. Rochetti, at Lincoln's Inn, Theatre Royal, on Friday 26th,' his name being spelled as in the cast of ' Camilla.' In 1737 he sang in Capt. Breval's ' Rape of Helen ' the part of Mercury, when his name was correctly spelled in the cast. J. M.

LA GUERRE, MME. DE, see JACQUET, Elisabeth Claude.

LA HALE, ADAM DE, see HALE.

LAHEE, HENRY (*b.* Chelsea, Apr. 11, 1826 ; *d.* Apr. 29, 1912), studied under Sterndale Bennett, Goss and Cipriani Potter, held the

---

[1] 'Mr. Legar' sang with Leveridge and Mrs. Chambers on St. Cecilia's Day, 1723, at Lincoln's Inn Fields. W. H. G. F.

post of organist at Holy Trinity Church, Brompton, from 1847–74, and was well known also as a professor and composer. Lahee was the victor in various prize competitions for glees and madrigals : in 1869 with ' Hark, how the birds ' (Bristol) ; in 1878, with ' Hence, loathed Melancholy ' (Manchester) ; in 1879, with ' Away to the hunt ' (Glasgow) ; and in 1880 and 1884, with ' Love in my bosom ' and ' Ah ! woe is me ' (London Madrigal Society). Equally good work can be seen in his other choral songs, such as ' The Unfaithful Shepherdess,' ' Love me little, love me long,' and the popular ' Bells,' and in his anthems no less than in his various songs and instrumental pieces.

Good taste is shown by this composer in the choice of his words, and he has found Longfellow congenial with his musical style. The cantata ' The Building of the Ship ' was written in 1869 for John Curwen, who desired a work of moderate difficulty for the use of Tonic-Sol-faists. It was performed on a large scale in the Hanover Square Rooms, attained considerable popularity in the provinces, and made its way to Africa and America. The subject of another cantata, Tennyson's ' The Sleeping Beauty,' afforded Lahee scope for a greater variety of treatment, and contains some graceful writing for female voices. It has been heard on the Continent and in America.   L. M. M.

LA HÈLE, GEORGES DE, see HÈLE.

LAHOUSSAYE, PIERRE (b. Paris, Apr. 12, 1735 ; d. there, 1818), became a distinguished violinist much patronised by the nobility, and made a tour in Italy, where he was given a post by the Prince of Monaco. He spent the years 1770–75 in London, as director of the Italian opera,[1] and returned to Paris, where in 1779 he was given the direction of the Concert Spirituel, in 1781 that of the Comédie Italien, and in 1790 that of the Théâtre de Monsieur, afterwards the Théâtre Feydeau. He was also professor in the Conservatoire. He died in Paris in the latter part of 1818. (Q.-L.)

LAIDLAW, ROBENA ANNA,[2] (b. Bretton, Yorks, Apr. 30, 1819 ; d. London, May 29, 1901), pianist, a lady whom Schumann distinguished by dedicating to her his ' Fantasiestücke ' (op. 12), was educated at Edinburgh at the school of her aunt, and in music by Robert Müller, a pianoforte teacher there. Her family went to Königsberg in 1830, and there her vocation was decided, she improved in playing rapidly, and in three or four years appeared in public at Berlin with great applause. In 1834 she was in London studying under Herz, and played at Paganini's farewell concert. In 1836 she returned to Berlin, and played at a Gewandhaus concert in Leipzig on July 2, 1837. Soon

afterwards she received the dedication of the ' Fantasiestücke,' [3] and made the acquaintance of the composer. After a lengthened tour through Prussia, Russia and Austria, she returned in 1840 to London. She was appointed in that year pianist to the Queen of Hanover. In 1855 she married a Mr. Thomson, and retired.   G.

LAJARTE, THÉODORE ÉDOUARD DUFAURE DE (b. Bordeaux, July 10, 1826 ; d. Paris, June 20, 1890), French writer on music, was a pupil of Leborne at the Paris Conservatoire, and in early life wrote a good many small operettas (' Monsieur de Floridor,' 1 act, Opéra-Comique, Oct. 11, 1880 ; ' Les Deux Jumeaux de Bergame,' ballet, Opéra, Jan. 26, 1886), but was best known for his works on musical history. He published Bibliothèque musicale du Théâtre de l'Opéra (2 vols. 1876–79), a very important catalogue of the operas produced at the Opéra in Paris, with annotations based upon the archives of the institution ; Instruments Sax et fanfares civiles (1867) ; a Traité de composition musicale (in collaboration with Bisson, 1880) ; a collection of ' Airs à danser ' from Lully to Méhul, and a number of old operas and ballets in vocal score, in nine series, comprising in all forty compositions, under the title of Chefs-d'œuvre classiques de l'Opéra français (Paris) ; Curiosités de l'Opéra (1883).[4] He was sub-librarian of the Opéra from 1873 to 1890.   G. F. ; rev. M. L. P.

LAKMÉ, opéra-comique in 3 acts, words by Goudinet and Gille ; music by Delibes ; produced Paris, Apr. 14, 1883 ; London, Gaiety Theatre, June 6, 1885 ; New York, Academy of Music, Mar. 1, 1886.

LALANDE, DÉSIRÉ ALFRED (b. Paris, Dec. 5, 1866[5] ; d. London, Nov. 8, 1904), a distinguished oboe-player, being the son of a well-known bassoon-player. After studying for two and a half years at the Conservatoire he obtained his first important engagement under Lamoureux in that conductor's famous band. He came to England in 1886, joined the Hallé orchestra, and played in Manchester for five years. He next joined the Scottish Orchestra when conducted by Henschel, and subsequently became a member of the Queen's Hall orchestra, with which organisation he played till his death in London from pneumonia. It was during this latter part of his career that he may be said to have established his reputation completely as one of the most gifted instrumental players of his time, possessing, as he did, a beautiful tone, great powers of refined expression, and a perfect technique. He was also constantly in request for cor anglais solos.   N. C. G.

LALANDE, HENRIETTE - CLÉMENTINE MÉRIC- (b. Dunkerque, 1798 ; d. Chantilly,

1 Pohl's Mozart und Haydn in London, vol. ii. p. 370.
2 This is the original order of her names ; they were transposed to ' Anna Robena ' at the suggestion of Schumann, as being more euphonious. (See Dr. Annie Patterson's Life of Schumann.)
3 See the Zeitschrift of the Int. Mus. Ges. vol. iii. p. 188 ff
4 Lajarte directed this publication in collaboration with Weckerlin, Guilmant, Gevaert and others.   5 M. L. P.

near Paris, Sept. 7, 1867), operatic singer, daughter of Lamiraux-Lalande, the chief of a provincial operatic company.

She made her début with success in 1814 at Naples : Fétis heard her, and admired her as an actress of opéra-comique, at Douai in the following year. She continued to sing till 1822, with equal success, in the principal towns of France, and was then engaged at the *Gymnase Dramatique* at Paris, Ebers having made an unsuccessful attempt to engage her for London. Clever enough to perceive, however, after hearing the singers at the Italian Opera, how utterly she was without the knowledge of the proper manner of producing her voice, she took lessons of Garcia, and made her first appearance, Apr. 3, 1823, in ' Les Folies amoureuses,' a pasticcio arranged by Castil-Blaze. About this time she became the wife of Méric, a horn-player at the Opéra-Comique. Rejecting the offer of an engagement at the latter theatre, on Garcia's advice she went to Italy, and received additional teaching from Bonfichi and Banderali at Milan. After singing with increased éclat at Venice, Munich, Brescia, Cremona, Venice (again), and other Italian cities, she at length appeared in London during the season of 1830.

' She arrived in England too late, and her place, moreover, had been filled by women of greater genius. She was a good musician, and sang with taste ; but her voice, a soprano, ere she came had contracted a habit of trembling, in those days a novelty (would it had always remained so !), to which English ears were then averse. She gave little satisfaction.' [1]

Mme. Méric sang again in London in 1831. In Paris she pleased no better in these latter years, and at length retired, in 1833, as it is said, to Spain. A biography, with a portrait, of Mme. Méric-Lalande was published in the musical journal, *Teatro della Fenice*, Venice, 1826.

J. M.

LALANDE, MICHEL RICHARD DE (*b.* Paris, Dec. 15, 1657 ; *d.* Versailles, June 18, 1726), surintendant de la musique under Louis XIV. and XV., the best French writer of church music of his day. He spent forty-five years in the service of the court.

He was the fifteenth child of a tailor, and was at first a chorister of St. Germain l'Auxerrois, where he studied music under Chaperon, and learnt, almost entirely by himself, to play the violin, bass viol and harpsichord. When, on the breaking of his voice at the age of 15, he was obliged to leave the maîtrise, he bethought himself of turning his violin-playing to account, and applied for admission into Lully's orchestra. He was refused, and swore out of pique never to touch the violin again. He gave himself up to the organ, and made such progress that he was soon appointed organist of three different churches in Paris—St. Jean en Grève, Petit St. Antoine and the Jesuits of the Maison Professe, who confided to him the composition of sym-

phonies and choruses for several of the tragedies performed at their college. He soon afterwards applied for the post of organist to the king, but though Lully pronounced him to be the best of the competitors he was refused on account of his youth. He was recommended by the Maréchal de Noailles, to whose daughters he taught music, to Louis XIV., and the king chose him to superintend the musical education of the princesses, afterwards the Duchesse d'Orléans and Madame la Duchesse. Lalande was so successful in this capacity that the king appointed him master of his chamber music ; and in 1683, on the retirement of Henry du Mont and Robert from the superintendence of the chapelle, he obtained one of the appointments, for it was decided to appoint four officers to serve for three months by turns. Eventually the offices were united in the person of Lalande, who had now received several pensions and the cordon of the order of St. Michel. In 1684 the king had given him a wife, Anne Rebel, said to be the best singer of the court, had paid the expenses of the wedding, and given a dowry to the bride. In 1722, having lost his wife, and two gifted daughters, who died of smallpox in the same year as the Dauphin (1711), Lalande begged the king to allow him to remit three-quarters of his salary, thus returning to the original arrangement. He presented as his substitutes and assistants Campra, Bernier and Gervais. As a reward for his disinterested conduct the regent granted him a pension of 3000 livres. In the following year he married again—Mlle. de Cury, daughter of one of the Princesse de Conti's surgeons—and died three years later at the age of 68.

The cause of Lalande's superiority over his immediate rivals was that he knew how to adapt to French tastes the forms of concerted church music hitherto confined to the Italian school, and his compositions, besides possessing real imagination, show that, like the musicians of Lully's school, he gave special attention to declamation and to the proper agreement between words and music. He wrote no fewer than 42 motets for chorus and orchestra for the chapel at Versailles, which were published most luxuriously at the king's expense. They are contained in 20 books, and are usually found bound in 10 volumes. A copy in 7 volumes, containing in all 21 books (42 motets), is preserved (apparently the only copy known) in the Fitzwilliam Museum. [2] He did not contribute so much as is generally supposed to the ballet of ' Les Éléments,' by Destouches (Tuileries, Dec. 22, 1721 ; Académie de Musique, May 29, 1725), his portion being confined to a few pieces in the prologue. He wrote music for the heroic pastoral ' Mélicerte ' (1698), begun by Molière and altered by Guérin.

---

[1] Chorley.

[2] See the *Catal. of Music in the Fitz. Mus.* and Q.-L.

He composed various works for the court theatres : a cantata called 'La Concert d'Esculape,' 1683 ; the 'Ballet de la jeunesse ' (Versailles, 1686), 'Ballet de Flore, ou le Trianon,' 1689; 'Adonis' and 'Mirtil,' 1698 ; 'Ballet des fées,' 1699; 'L'Amour fléchi par la Constance' (Fontainebleau, 1697); 'L'Hymen champêtre,' 1700; 'Ballet de la paix,' 1713 ; 'Les Folies de Cardenio' (Tuileries, 1720); 'Ballet de l'inconnu,' Paris, 1720. He also composed 'Trois leçons de Ténèbres miserere' for solo voice ; 'Musique pour les soupers du Roy' (*Collection Philidor*). Fétis is of opinion that Lalande worked at several operas without allowing anything to be represented under his own name, and gives as his authority Titon du Tillet, to whom we owe the biographical details of Lalande ; but du Tillet does not mention it in his article on Lalande in the *Parnasse Française*. (See *The Age of Bach and Handel*, Oxf. Hist. Mus. pp. 290-98, etc.)

A. J.

BIBL.—MICHEL BRENET, in *Grande Encyl.* ; L. DE LA LAURENCIE, *France, XVIIe-XVIIIe siècles*, in *Encyl. de la Mus. et Dict. du Conservatoire* ; *Oxf. Hist. Mus.*, pp. 290–98, *The Age of Bach and Handel.*
Catalogue of Music in the Fitzwilliam Museum, Cambridge.
Reprints: Musique d'Église des XVIIe et XVIIIe siècles (Paris) ; *Panis angelicus* ; *Quando veniam.*

LA LAURENCIE, L. DE, see LAURENCIE.

LALLA ROOKH. Moore's poem has been the basis of a number of musical compositions.

1. An opera poem adapted by J. O'Sullivan, music by C. E. Horn, Dublin, June 4, 1818.

2. Spontini wrote introductory and incidental music for a set of tableaux vivants in Berlin, Jan. 27, 1821.

3. Opera, called 'Nurmahal,' to a libretto by Herklot in 2 acts, Berlin, May 27, 1822.

4. Opera in 2 acts ('Lalla Roukh '), words by Lucas and Carré, music by Félicien David, produced Opéra-Comique, May 12, 1862.

5. An opera in 2 acts by Anton Rubinstein (name afterwards changed to 'Feramors '), produced Dresden, March 1863.

6. Cantata, by Frederic Clay, produced Brighton Festival, 1877.

For operas, etc., on the subordinate poems of 'Lalla Rookh,' see PARADISE AND THE PERI; VEILED PROPHET.

LALLOUETTE, JEAN-FRANÇOIS (*b.* Paris, *c.* 1651 ; *d.* Versailles, Sept. 1, 1728 [1]), pupil of Lully (composition) and Guy Leclerc (violin). He is said to have orchestrated and written the recitatives for some of Lully's operas. He was violinist and afterwards conductor at the Opéra (1668–77), but was dismissed for having claimed collaboration in Lully's 'Isis.' He then became maître de chapelle of Rouen Cathedral, and in 1695 of Notre Dame, Versailles. He composed one or more masses, 2 books of motets, some Misereres, as well as interludes and ballets for the opera.   E. v. d. S.

[1] *Riemann* says : Paris, Aug. 31, 1728, as maître de chapelle of Notre Dame.

LALO, (1) VICTOR ANTOINE ÉDOUARD (*b.* Lille, Jan. 27, 1823 [2]; *d.* Paris, Apr. 22, 1892), a famous composer of Spanish origin, studied at the Lille Conservatoire under Muller for violin, and for violoncello under a German professor named Baumann, who had played at Vienna under Beethoven's conductorship.

When he came to Paris in 1839 he entered the Conservatoire, in Habeneck's violin class, and studied composition privately with the pianist Schuloff and the composer Crèvecoeur. He then played the viola in the Armingaud-Jacquard quartet from its foundation (1855). His first compositions date from about 1845, and he published in 1848 and 1849 songs bearing the mark of this epoch. He competed at the concours at the Théâtre Lyrique in 1867 with an opera, 'Fiesque' (1866), which took a third place ; it was subsequently printed and partly performed at the Concert National, 1873. The ballet music from this work, under the title of a Divertissement, was given with great success at the Concert Populaire, Dec. 8, 1872. Lalo next composed a violin concerto in F, played by Sarasate at the Concert National, Jan. 18, 1874 (and at the London Philharmonic Society in the following May), and a 'Symphonie espagnole,' for violin and orchestra, played by the same artist at the Concert Populaire, Feb. 7, 1875. It was produced in England at the Crystal Palace, Mar. 30, 1878.

After these two great successes, which gave Lalo a first-class position as a composer for the concert-room, he produced an 'Allegro symphonique,' [3] the overture to his opera 'Le Roi d'Ys,' a violoncello concerto, played by Fischer at the Concert Populaire, 1877, a scherzo [4] for orchestra (all performed in Paris), and a 'Fantaisie norvégienne' [5] for violin and orchestra, first given in Berlin. His 'Rhapsodie norvégienne' and his 'Concerto russe,' the latter played by Marsick at the Concert Populaire, were the last important works for the concert-room written before his ballet 'Namouna,' performed at the Opéra, Mar. 6, 1882. This work has something of a symphonic style, and is orchestrated in a manner far superior to that of many more popular ballets, but it was coldly received by the public. 'Namouna' was only given fifteen times, but when transferred to the concert-room in the form of an orchestral suite in five movements it achieved the success it deserved. An andantino, and two other movements from the same, arranged for violin and orchestra, were also received with favour at the Concerts Modernes, and a serenade, arranged for four stringed instruments, was also successful.

[2] Date verified by the register of birth.
[3] Composed from the allegro for PF. and v'cl., op. 16, 1875.
[4] The scherzo, taken from the trio in A min., op. 26, was orchestrated by Lalo and first performed at the Exhibition, 1869, and at the Concert Lamoureux, Nov. 12, 1906.
[5] Partly transformed into the 'Rhapsodie norvégienne,' for orch. alone; 1st perf. Concerts Colonne, Oct. 26, 1879.

After this reparation for his former failure, Lalo again set to work and orchestrated the whole of his ' Roi d'Ys,' of which the general plan had been sketched some five or six years before, and wrote a symphony in G minor, performed at the Concert Lamoureux, Feb. 13, 1887, which was much praised by musicians. The opera was produced at the Opéra-Comique, May 7, 1888, with well-deserved success. It was not heard in England till 1901, when it was produced at Covent Garden on July 17. Thus far we have only spoken of Lalo's orchestral compositions. An allegro for violoncello and piano, a sonata for the same,[1] a serenade and ' Chanson villageoise' for violoncello and piano, a sonata in three movements for violin, three trios, of which one is the trio in A minor for piano and strings (given at Hallé's recital, June 15, 1888), a string quartet in Eb, op. 45 (2nd version of op. 19), composed c. 1855, a ' Romance Sérénade' for violin and orchestra (1880), a piano concerto in C minor (1889), played by Diémer in that year, a charming ' Aubade-allegretto' (1872) for ten instruments, wind and string ; ' Néron,' pantomime in 3 acts (unpublished) (Hippodrome, Paris, Mar. 28, 1891) ; ' La Jacquerie,' an opera in 4 acts (only 1 act by Lalo ; finished by A. Coquard, and produced at Monte Carlo, Mar. 8, 1895 ; Paris, Opéra-Comique, Dec. 23, 1895) and more than 20 songs complete the list of works by one who gained a reputation both in Germany and France, though his dramatic work has received but tardy recognition. His talent was of an extremely individual kind, and was formed, not by the discipline of the Conservatoire, nor by the influence of professors, but by the direct study of such masters as Beethoven, Schubert and Schumann, for whom he had a special predilection. His chief characteristics were the expressive grace of certain ideas, the piquancy of some of his themes, and, above all, the richness and skill of his orchestration. Lalo was one of the most distinguished of French composers, and fully deserved the decoration of the Légion d'Honneur conferred upon him in July 1880.

A. J. ; addns. G. F. ; rev. M. L. P.

(2) PIERRE (b. Puteaux, Seine, Sept. 6, 1866), son of the above, a contributor to the *Journal des Débats*, first appeared as music critic in an article on V. d'Indy's ' Fervaal' (*Revue de Paris*, May 15, 1898). He succeeded J. Weber as musical critic of *Le Temps* in Oct. 1898. His own successor in that post is Henry Malherbe. Lalo has published a selection of his articles in *La Musique*, 1898–99 (Paris).

M. L. P.

BIBL.—OCTAVE SÉRÉ, *Musiciens français d'aujourd'hui* (Paris, *Mercure de France*, 1921 ; with bibl. and list of works) ; *Revue musicale*, 1923, No. 5 (articles by P. Dukas, A. Jullien, Pierre Lalo) ; GEORGES SERVIÈRES, *Lalo* (Paris, 1925 ; bibl. and list of works).

[1] First performed at the Société Nationale de Musique by Sarasate and Georges Bizet.

LA LUCCHESINA, MARIA ANTONIA MAR-CHESINI, see LUCCHESINA.

LA MARA, see LIPSIUS, MARIE.

LA MARRE, J. M. H. DE, see MARRE.

LAMB, BENJAMIN, organist of Eton College in the first quarter of the 18th century, and also verger of St. George's Chapel, Windsor, was the composer of some church music. An evening ' Cantate' service and four anthems by him are in the Tudway collection (Harl. MSS. 7341-42). He was also a composer of songs.
W. H. H.

LAMBARDI, CAMILLO (16th-17th cent.), maestro di cappella of the Church of the Annunciation, Naples ; wrote church music for Holy Week for 2 choruses (1592), 2 books of madrigals, etc.

LAMBARDI, FRANCESCO (early 17th cent.), maestro (1607) and organist from 1614 of the Royal Chapel, Naples ; composer of a villanelle and canzonette.

LAMBARDI, GIROLAMO (16th-17th cent.), Venetian composer of a large quantity of church music ; some call him a pupil of Palestrina, others of Zarlino (Q.-L.).

LAMBE, WALTER (2nd half of 15th cent.), English composer of church music. An early 16th-century MS. in the Eton College Library, which, as an index shows, once contained 97 compositions, but now only contains 43 complete pieces, includes the following motets (Hymns to the Virgin) by Lambe :

' Ascendit Christi,' a 4 ; ' Nesciens Mater Virgo virum,' a 5 ; ' Salve Regina,' a 5 ; ' Stella coeli,' a 4 ; ' Magnificat et exultavit,' a 5.

Besides these, the MS. still contains imperfect copies of two others by him : ' O Regina celestis gloriae' and ' O Maria, plena gratia.' A complete copy of this latter motet is at Lambeth. For a detailed description of it see H. O. Anderton, *Early English Music*. ' An Inventarye of the Pryke Songys longynge to the Kyngys College in Cambryge (1529),' printed in *The Ecclesiologist* for Apr. 1863, refers to ' 6 bokys of parchmente conteynynge Wa[l]ter Lambes Exultavit.' This is presumably the same composition as that in the list above. The presence of a 3-part Sanctus by Lambe in a 15th-century MS. at the Roman Catholic College of St. Edmund's, Old Hall, Ware, Herts, shows either that there were two composers of this name, or that Lambe is of an earlier generation than any of the composers, except Dunstable, whose music is in the Eton MS. If there is only one Lambe, he is either a contemporary of Dunstable, Power and Bedyngham, or one of a small group of composers who link these names with the Fayrfax school. W. Barclay Squire [1] refers to a man of this name in a list of the clerks of St. George's, Windsor, from 1468-79.
J. MK.

LAMBERT, GEORGE JACKSON (b. Beverley, Yorks, Nov. 16, 1794 ; d. Jan. 24, 1880), son of

[1] See *Sammelb*. Int. Mus. Gas.. Band ii.

George Lambert, organist of Beverley Minster, studied under his father until he was 16, then in London under Samuel Thomas Lyon, and finally became a pupil of Dr. Crotch. In 1818 he succeeded his father at Beverley. His compositions include overtures, instrumental chamber music, organ fugues, pianoforte pieces, etc. In 1874 ill-health and deafness compelled him to relinquish his post and retire from active life.

The two Lamberts successively held the office of organist of Beverley Minster for the long period of ninety-six years, the father for forty and the son for fifty-six years, and but for the latter's deafness would have held it for a century, a circumstance probably unparalleled.

W. H. H.

LAMBERT, Lucien (b. Paris, Jan. 1861), French pianist and composer, began his musical studies with his father, and had a successful career as a pianoforte virtuoso in America and on the Continent. On returning to Paris he worked with Massenet and Théodore Dubois, and produced ' Prométhée enchaîné,' a scène - lyrique which gained the Rossini prize of the Institut (Conservatoire, Apr. 19, 1885); ' Sire Olaf,' incidental music for a play by A. Alexandre, given at Lille in 1887 and in Paris 1889 ; ' Brocéliande,' a 4-act opera, Rouen, Feb. 25, 1893, the overture to which became widely popular ; ' Le Spahi,' in 4 acts, Opéra-Comique, Paris, Oct. 18, 1897 ; ' La Flamenca,' in 4 acts, at the Théâtre de la Gaieté, Paris, Oct. 30, 1903; ' La Roussalka,' ballet, Opéra, Paris, Dec. 8, 1911 ; two more operas, ' Penticosa ' and ' La Sorcière,' have not yet been given. In the concert - room Lambert is represented by an 'Andante et Fantaisie tzigane,' for piano and orchestra ; ' Tanger le soir,' a Moorish rhapsody for orchestra ; and other things, most of which were heard for the first time at the Société Nationale de Musique. He has also published songs, piano pieces, etc.   G. F. ; rev. M. L. P.

LAMBERT, Michel (b. Vivonne, Poitou, c. 1610 ; d. Paris, 1696), famous singer and lutenist ; master of the royal chamber music, and of the children of the Chapel Royal (from 1663). He composed several books of airs which attained great popularity. He was the father-in-law of Lully.

LAMBERTINI, Giovanni Tommaso (b. Bologna, 16th-17th cent.), priest, and composer of a book of madrigals (1560), 7 penitential psalms (1569), viollote, etc., in collective volumes. From 1556–1628 he was a singer, and from 1545 treasurer at San Petronio, Bologna.   E. v. d. S.

LAMBERTINI, Luiz Joaquim (b. Bologna, Mar. 17, 1790 ; d. Lisbon, Nov. 13, 1864), founder of a great firm of Portuguese piano manufacturers.

He was related to the celebrated Cardinal Lambertini, Archbishop of Bologna, who be-

came Pope Benedict XIV. ; and is said to have been a fellow-student of Rossini, and an excellent pianist. In 1836 he left Italy for Portugal, and by 1838 had established his business in Lisbon, where it still exists.

A descendant of Luiz Joaquim, Michel Angelo Lambertini is known as a historian and writer on Portuguese music.   J. B. T.

LAMBETH, Henry Albert (b. Hardway, near Gosport, Jan. 16, 1822 ; d. Glasgow, June 27, 1895), studied for some time under Thomas Adams, went to Glasgow about 1853 as city organist, on the recommendation of Henry Smart, and in 1859 was appointed conductor of the Glasgow Choral Union. This post he held till 1880. In 1874 he formed a choir of from 20 to 30 selected voices, and in the department of Scotch music their concerts met with great success under the name of the Glasgow Select Choir. Lambeth left this society in 1878. Lambeth harmonised several of the best Scottish melodies in a most effective manner. He composed several songs and pianoforte pieces, also settings of Psalms 86 and 137, both of which were performed by the Glasgow Choral Union. He was organist and choirmaster successively at St. Mary's Episcopal Church, and at Park Church. He edited the Scottish Book of Praise with D. Baptie in 1876.   W. H^E.

LAMENT. In Scottish and Irish folk-music are melodies named ' Laments ' or ' Lamentations.' In Scottish music these were mainly confined to the Highlands, and were generally purely bagpipe tunes, consisting of an air, sometimes set vocally, with a number of more or less irregular variations or additional passages. Each of the clans or important families had its particular ' lament,' as well as its ' gathering,' and the former was played on occasions of death or calamity. Many of the laments are of wild and pathetic beauty : ' McGregor a ruaro ' and ' Mackrimmon's lament ' are among those which have become more widely familiar. The latter, Sir Walter Scott says,

' is but too well known from its being the strain with which the emigrants from the West Highlands and Isles usually take leave of their native shore.'

The burden of the original Gaelic words is ' we return no more.' Of the same class is ' Lochaber no more,' which is a true ' Lament ' to the Highlander. The melody in one of its earlier forms is entitled ' Limerick's Lamentation ' or ' Irish Lamentation,' and there seems to be but little doubt that the song has been written to an air then generally recognised as a ' Lamentation.' For examples of the Gaelic laments the reader is referred to Patrick McDonald's Highland Vocal Airs, 1783 ; Albyn's Anthology, 1816–18 ; and other collections of Highland airs.

Bunting supplies several current in Ireland, and in the Aria di camera, c. 1727, are some of the earliest in print, viz. ' Limerick's,'

'Irish,' 'Scotch,' 'Lord Galloway's' and 'MacDonagh's' Lamentations.   F. K.

LAMENTATIONS (Lat. *Lamentationes Hieremiae*). On the Thursday, Friday and Saturday in Holy Week the three First Lessons appointed in the Roman Breviary for the Office of Matins (commonly called *Tenebrae*) are taken from the Lamentations of Jeremiah ; and the extraordinary beauty of the music to which they are sung, in the Sistine Chapel and other large churches, contributes not a little to the impressive character of the service. (See TENEBRAE.)

It is impossible to trace to its origin the plain-song melody to which the Lamentations were anciently adapted. The most celebrated version—though not, perhaps, the purest—is that printed by Guidetti, in his 'Directorium chori,' in 1582. The best modern editions are those of Solesmes, *e.g.* the *Officium ultimi tridui majoris hebdomadis* ; in which the Lessons are given, at full length, in Gregorian notation, although the music is really no more than a simple chant in Mode vi., repeated, almost *notatim*, not only to each separate verse of the Sacred Text, but even to the prefatory 'Incipit Lamentatio Jeremiae Prophetae,' and the names of the Hebrew letters with which the several paragraphs are introduced.

In-ci-pit Lamentatio Jere - mi-æ pro-phe - tæ.   A - leph.

Early in the 16th century, the use of the plain-song Lamentations was discontinued, in the Pontifical Chapel, to make room for a polyphonic setting, by Elziario GENET (*q.v.*)—more commonly known by his Italian cognomen, Carpentrasso—who was attached to the papal court in 1508–18. These compositions remained in constant use till the year 1587, when Pope Sixtus V. ordained that the First Lamentation for each day should be adapted to some kind of polyphonic music better fitted to express the mournful character of the words than that of Carpentrasso ; and, that the Second and Third Lessons should be sung, by a single soprano, to the old plain-song melody as revised by Guidetti. The disuse of Carpentrasso's time-honoured harmonies gave great offence to the choir : but, the Pope's command being absolute, Palestrina composed some music to the First Lamentation for Good Friday, in a manner so impressive, that all opposition was at once silenced ; and the Pope himself, on leaving the Chapel, said that he hoped in the following year to hear the other two First Lessons sung in exactly the same style. Palestrina produced, in Jan. 1588, a volume containing a complete set of the nine Lamentations—three for each of the three days—which were printed the same year by Gardan, under the title of *Lamentationum liber primus*. The work was prefaced by a formal dedication to the Supreme Pontiff, who, though he still adhered to his resolution of having the Second and Third Lessons sung always in plain-song, expressed great pleasure in accepting it : and in 1589 it was reprinted at Venice, in 8vo by Girolamo Scoto.

More complex in construction than the great composer's 'Improperia,' though infinitely less so than his masses and motets, these Lamentations are written throughout in the devout and impressive style which produces so profound an effect in the first-named work, and always with marked attention to the mournful spirit of the words They do not, like the plain-song rendering, embrace the entire text ; but, after a certain number of verses, pause on the final chord of a prolonged cadence, and then pass on to the strophe, 'Jerusalem, Jerusalem' with which each of the nine Lessons concludes. In the single Lesson for Good Friday —which, though not included in the original printed copy, is undoubtedly the most beautiful of all —the opening verses are sung by two soprani, an alto and a tenor ; a bass being added, in the concluding strophe, with wonderful effect. A similar arrangement is followed in the third Lamentation for the same day : but the others are for four voices only, and most of them with a tenor in the lowest place ; while in all, without exception, the introductory sentences, 'Incipit Lamentatio,' or, 'De Lamentatione,' as well as the names of the Hebrew initial letters, are set to harmonies of infinite richness and beauty.

Since the death of Palestrina, the manner of singing the Lamentations in the Pontifical Chapel has undergone no very serious change. In accordance with the injunction of Pope Sixtus V., the Second and Third Lessons for each day have always been sung in plain-song : generally by a single soprano, but sometimes by two, the perfection of whose unisonous performance has constantly caused it to be mistaken for that of a single voice. Until the year 1640, the First Lesson for each day was sung from Palestrina's printed volume. In that year, the single unpublished Lesson for Good Friday, composed in 1587, was restored to its place, and the use of the published one discontinued ; while a new composition, by Gregorio Allegri, was substituted for Palestrina's Lesson for Holy Saturday.

Benedict XIII. inaugurated a radical change, by decreeing that the First Lessons should no longer be sung in this shortened form, but, with the entire text set to music. To meet his desire, three Lamentations, by modern writers, were submitted for approval, but unanimously rejected by the College, who commissioned Giovanni Biordi to add to the compositions of Palestrina and Allegri whatever was necessary to complete the text. His work was unhesitatingly accepted, and retained in use till the year

1731, when Pope Clement XII. restored the Lamentations to their original shortened form. In this form they were suffered to remain, till 1815, when the indefatigable Baini restored Palestrina's printed Lamentation for the first day, retaining the MS. of 1587 for the second, and Allegri's really beautiful composition for the third ; while the last-named composer's inferior work (of 1651) was suffered to fall into disuse.

Besides the printed volume already mentioned, Palestrina composed two other entire sets of Lamentations, which, though written in his best and purest style, remained, for two centuries and a half, unpublished. One of them was prepared, as early as the year 1560, for the use of the Lateran Basilica, where the original MS. is still preserved. The other reaches us only through the medium of a MS. in the Altaemps Otthoboni collection, now in the Vatican library. In the year 1842 Alfieri printed the three sets entire, in the fourth volume of his *Raccolta di musica sacra*, together with the single Lamentation for Good Friday, to which he appended Biordi's additional verses, without, however, pointing out the place where Palestrina's work ends, and Biordi's begins. The three single Lamentations, sung in the Pontifical Chapel, are given, with Biordi's now useless additions, in a volume of the same editor's *Excerpta*, published in 1840 ; and, without Biordi's verses, in Choron's 'Collection des pièces de musique religieuse.' Both these editions are now out of print, and difficult to obtain ; but a fine reprint of the nine pieces contained in the original 'Lamentationum liber primus' will be found in Proske's 'Musica divina,' vol. iv. Capes, in his Selection from the works of Palestrina (Novello), has given the first Lamentation in Coena Domini, and the first in Sabb. Sancto, from the 1st book (1588), and has introduced between them the single Lesson for Good Friday (1587) already mentioned. The Lamentations of Palestrina are contained in vol. xxv. of Haberl's Collected Edition. In 1919 CASIMIRI (*q.v.*) published ' Il Codice 59,' containing the corrected MS. of Palestrina's Lamentations in the composer's autograph.

Though the Lamentations of Carpentrasso, Palestrina and Allegri are the only ones that have ever been actually used in the Pontifical Chapel, many others have been produced by composers of no small reputation. Those of Okeghem date from 1474. As early as the year 1506, Ottaviano dei Petrucci published, at Venice, two volumes containing settings by Johannes Tinctoris, Ycaert, De Orto, Francesco (d' Ana) da Venezia, Johannes de Quadris, Agricola, Bartolomeo Tromboncino and Gaspar and Erasmus Lapicida. All these works were given to the world before that of Carpentrasso, which, with many more of his compositions, was first printed at Avignon, by Johannes Channay, in 1532. But the richest collection extant is that entitled 'Piissimae ac sacratissimae Lamentationes Jeremiae prophetae,' printed in Paris, by A. le Roy and Robert Ballard, in 1557, and containing, besides Carpentrasso's *capo d' opera*, some extremely fine examples by De la Rue, Fevin, Arcadelt, Festa and Claudin le Jeune.   w. s. r., rev.

Lamentations by English composers of the 16th century are now known to be more numerous than was formerly supposed. See TALLIS, BYRD and Robert WHYTE.

LAMOND, FREDERICK A. (*b.* Glasgow, Jan. 28, 1868), famous pianist, was at first a pupil of his brother, David Lamond, and in 1880 obtained the post of organist at Laurieston parish church. He studied the violin with H. C. Cooper, and in 1882 went to Frankfort to the Raff Conservatorium, where Heermann was his master for the violin, Max Schwarz for the piano, and Urspruch for composition. Here he laid the foundation of his wide musical culture, and his pianoforte studies were completed under Von Bülow and Liszt. His first important appearance as a mature pianist took place at Berlin, Nov. 17, 1885, when he made a great success, and appeared at Vienna soon afterwards. His first piano recital in Great Britain took place in Glasgow, Mar. 8, 1886, and soon afterwards he gave a set of recitals at Princes Hall, London. For the fourth of these, on Apr. 15, St. James's Hall was taken, and Liszt's presence set the seal on the young player's reputation. The recitals showed the depth of Lamond's interpretations of Beethoven, a master in whom he takes especial delight. During the next few years he played much in Germany, but appeared occasionally in London. On Apr. 5, 1890, he played Saint-Saëns's C minor concerto at the Crystal Palace, when his own symphony in A was given (it was first played at the Glasgow Choral Union, Dec. 23, 1889, and revived at Queen's Hall in 1912).

His first appearance at the Philharmonic Society took place on May 14, 1891, when he played Brahms's second concerto with great skill. The same society performed his overture, ' Aus dem schottischen Hochlande,' on Mar. 7, 1895. In 1896 Lamond played in Russia, and in 1897 gave a series of recitals in London, at one of which a couple of piano pieces of his own were played. From 1904, when he married the actress, Irene Triesch, he lived in Berlin, but he made an annual appearance in England up to 1914. His performances here were renewed in 1919. In 1917 he accepted a professorship in the Conservatoire at the Hague (*Riemann*). Among his other compositions may be mentioned a trio for piano and strings, and a sonata, op. 2, for piano and violoncello. (*Brit. Mus. Biog.*)   M., with addns.

LAMOTTE (LAMOTA), FRANZ (*b.* Vienna,[1] c. 1751 ; *d.* Netherlands, 1781). At the age of 12

[1] Or in the Netherlands.

he played a violin concerto before the Emperor, who sent him to Italy for further studies, and on his return placed him in his private chapel. In 1769 he competed successfully with Jarnovick in Paris, and in 1776 appeared in London. Reichard praises his staccato in single and double notes, and his unfailing technique. He composed concertos, solos and sonatas for his instrument. He died while on a visit to the Netherlands.　　　　　　　　　　E. v. d. s.

LAMOUREUX, CHARLES (b. Bordeaux, Sept. 21, 1834; d. Paris, Dec. 21, 1899), a famous orchestral conductor, began his violin studies under Beaudoin, and was then sent to the Paris Conservatoire, where he was in Girard's class.

He obtained in 1852 a second *accessit* for the violin, the second prize in the following year, and the first in 1854. He also studied harmony under Tolbecque, and attended the counterpoint course of Leborne at the Conservatoire, where he finished his theoretical studies under the famous organist Alexis Chauvet. He was solo violinist in the Gymnase orchestra (1850), and afterwards joined that of the Opéra, where he played for many years. He was admitted a member of the Société des Concerts du Conservatoire, and, like all the members of these orchestras, gave private lessons. But these insignificant posts were not sufficient for the activity of Lamoureux, who dreamt of great undertakings in the musical art of France. Together with Colonne, Adam and A. Pilet he founded in 1860 a society for chamber music of a severe character, in which he showed a taste for new works by producing compositions hitherto unnoticed. He had also the honour of first performing in France Brahms's sextets. He was not content with this, for having travelled in Germany and England he was anxious to organise performances on a large scale, such as he had heard under Hiller and Costa, of the masterpieces of Handel, Bach and Mendelssohn.

After several preliminary trials at the Salle Pleyel, where he performed among other things the 'Streit zwischen Phöbus und Pan' of Bach, he succeeded by his own energy and resources in founding the Société de l'Harmonie Sacrée on the model of the Sacred Harmonic Society of London. The first festival was given at the Cirque des Champs-Élysées, Dec. 19, 1873. The success of an admirable performance of 'Messiah' was such that amateurs came in crowds to the following performances. Lamoureux then produced Bach's 'St. Matthew Passion,' Mar. 31, 1874, and 'Judas Maccabæus,' Nov. 19, 1874. Not content with confining himself to well-known masterpieces, he produced Massenet's 'Eve,' then unpublished, Mar. 18, 1875. These great performances showed that Lamoureux was a conductor of great merit, who succeeded in obtaining from his orchestra

a matchless precision of attack and regard to expression. When Carvalho became director of the Opéra-Comique in 1876 he offered Lamoureux the post of conductor, but in less than a year the latter resigned, owing to some difficulties arising out of the rehearsal of Chaumet's 'Bathyle' in May 1877. In December of the same year Lamoureux was appointed conductor of the Opéra (1877–79; 1891) by Vaucorbeil, and gave up the sub-conductorship of the Concerts du Conservatoire, which he had held since 1872. In 1878 he was decorated with the Légion d'Honneur, and in the following year he resigned his post at the Opéra on account of a dispute with Vaucorbeil as to the tempo of one of the movements in 'Don Juan.'

From that time he determined to be self-dependent, and, after having carefully prepared the undertaking, he founded on Oct. 23, 1881, the Nouveaux Concerts, called the Concerts Lamoureux, which were held for some years in the theatre of the Château d'Eau, and afterwards at the Eden Théâtre (1885) and the Cirque des Champs-Élysées (1887), where their success constantly increased. In the year of their foundation he appeared as a conductor in London, giving two concerts in St. James's Hall, on Mar. 15 and 22, 1881. Not only did Lamoureux develop as a conductor a precision and firmness, a care for the perfection of the smallest details, without excluding passion and warmth of expression ; he also gave a welcome to the works of contemporary musicians such as Reyer, Saint-Saëns, Lalo, d'Indy, Chabrier, Franck, Dukas, etc., and succeeded in placing himself at the head of the Wagnerian movement in France. He gave excellent performances of selections from Wagner's operas to a public that had been too long deprived of these compositions. The first Act of 'Lohengrin,' Acts I. and II. of 'Tristan' and Act I. of 'Die Walküre' were given in their entirety. Encouraged by the warmth of the applause and the moral support of his audience, Lamoureux decided to give a performance in a Paris theatre of 'Lohengrin,' then unknown in France. After a whole year of preparation a perfect performance was given at the Eden Théâtre (May 3, 1887), which was not repeated. Lamoureux lived, however, to see the ultimate triumph of Wagner in Paris.

In Apr. and Nov. 1896, in Mar. and Nov. 1897, and in the spring of 1898 he gave concerts with his orchestra in the Queen's Hall, London ; and in May 1899 he and his band were the chief attraction of a 'London Musical Festival' in the Queen's Hall. He was succeeded as conductor by his son-in-law, Camille CHEVILLARD (q.v.).　　　　　　　　A. J.

BIBL.—H. IMBERT, *Portraits et études*; A. JULLIEN, *Ch. Lamoureux* (*R.M.I.*, 1900) ; G. DORET, *Musique et musiciens* (Lausanne, 1915).

LAMPE, (1) JOHN FREDERICK (b. Saxony, 1703 ; d. Edinburgh, July 25, 1751), came to

England about 1725, and was engaged as a bassoon-player at the Opera.

He is heard of previously as playing in ' De colloquio Croesi et Solonis ' at St. Catherine's School, Brunswick, Aug. 19, 1717.[1] In 1732 he composed the music for Carey's ' Amelia,' produced Mar. 13. In 1737 he published *A Plain and Compendious Method of teaching Thorough-Bass*, etc., and also furnished the music for Carey's burlesque opera ' The Dragon of Wantley,' which met with remarkable success. It is an admirable example of the true burlesque, and is said to have been an especial favourite of Handel's. In 1738 he composed music for the sequel, ' Margery ; or, A Worse Plague than the Dragon.' In 1740 he published *The Art of Musick*, and in 1741 composed music for the masque of ' The Sham Conjuror.' In 1745 he composed ' Pyramus and Thisbe, a mock opera, the words taken from Shakespeare.' A composition to celebrate the repression of the Stuart rebellion of 1745 was performed in the Savoy Chapel, Oct. 9, 1746, and published. Lampe was the composer of many single songs, several of which appeared in collections, as ' Wit musically embellish'd, a Collection of Forty-two new English Ballads ' ; ' The Ladies' Amusement ' and ' Lyra Britannica.' Many songs by him were included in ' The Vocal Musical Mark,' ' The Musical Miscellany,' etc. Lampe married Isabella, daughter of Charles Young, and sister of Mrs. Arne ; she was a favourite singer, both on the stage and in the concert-room. In 1748 he went to Dublin, and in 1750 to Edinburgh, where he died, leaving behind him the reputation of an accomplished musician and excellent man. He was buried on July 28, 1751, in the Canongate Churchyard. Charles Wesley, whose hymns he set to music in ' Hymns on the Great Festivals,' etc. (1746), often mentions him with great affection, and wrote a hymn on his death —' 'Tis done ! the Sovereign Will's obeyed ! '

(2) CHARLES JOHN FREDERICK, his son, succeeded his grandfather, Charles YOUNG (*q.v.*), as organist of Allhallows, Barking, in 1758, and held the appointment until 1769. In 1763 (May) he was also organist at Covent Garden, and married Miss Smith, a singer at Marylebone Gardens, May 7.[2] A catch by him is in a ' Second Collection of Catches ' (Welcker, 1766).   W. H. H.

LAMPERTI, FRANCESCO (*b.* Savona, Mar. 11, 1813 ; *d.* Como, May 1, 1892), teacher of singing.

His father was an advocate, and his mother a prima donna of considerable repute. As a child he showed great talent for music, and was placed under Pietro Rizzi of Lodi. In 1820 he entered the Conservatorio at Milan, and there studied the pianoforte and harmony under Sommaruga d' Appiano and Pietro Ray. Devoting himself afterwards to the teaching of singing, he became

1 Cf. J. C. Brewer (*Schema*).   W. B. S.
2 *Lloyd's Evening Post*.   W. B. S.

associated with Masini in the direction of the Teatro Filodrammatico at Lodi. Selecting many of the members of his company from the natives of the surrounding country, he educated and brought out at his theatre many famous singers.

Attracted by their success pupils flocked to him from Bergamo, Milan and other parts of Europe, and he there trained many of the most distinguished operatic vocalists, amongst whom may be named Jeanne Sophie Löwe, Cruvelli, Grua, Brambilla, Hayes, Artôt, Tiberini, La Grange. Appointed in 1850 by the Austrian government professor of singing to the Conservatorio at Milan, he brought out amongst others Angelica Moro, Paganini, Galli, Risarelli, Angeleri, Peralta ; and as private pupils, Albani, Sembrich, Stoltz, Waldmann, Aldighieri, Campanini, Vialletti, Derevis, Mariani, Palermi, Everardi and Shakespeare. After twenty-five years' service he retired from the Conservatorio upon a pension in 1875, and henceforward devoted himself entirely to private pupils.

A friend of Rubini and Pasta, and associated with the great singers of the past, Lamperti followed the method of the old Italian school of singing, instituted by Farinelli and taught by Crescentini, Velluti, Marchesi and Romani. Basing his teaching upon the study of respiration, the taking and retention of the breath by means of the abdominal muscles alone, and the just emission of the voice, he thoroughly grounded his pupils in the production of pure tone. His memory and his intuition were alike remarkable, and enabled him to adapt to each of his pupils such readings of the music and cadenzas as are warranted by the traditions of the greatest singers and are best adapted to their powers.

He was Commendatore and Cavaliere of the order of the Crown of Italy, and a member of many academies and foreign orders. He wrote several series of vocal studies and a treatise on the art of singing (Ricordi & Co.), which has been translated into English by one of his pupils.   J. C. G.

LAMPUGNANI, GIOVANNI BATTISTA (*b.* Milan, *c.* 1706), came to London in the autumn of 1743 as conductor and composer to the opera in the place of Galuppi. In November of that year his ' Roxana ' was given, on Jan. 3, 1744, his ' Alfonso,' on Apr. 28 his ' Alceste,' and in 1755 his ' Siroe.' Burney, in the fourth volume of his *History*, refers to these successive operas, and to various pasticcios to which he contributed, in terms which imply that his music was considered of very light, flimsy quality. He was a clever craftsman in the concoction of the pasticcios that were in fashion at the time, and his recitative was unusually expressive. In many of his pasticcios Hasse collaborated ; and after his return to Italy, where he lived at Milan and held the post of maestro al cembalo in the theatre from 1779–89, he seems to have written two more operas, 'Semiramide,' given at Milan in 1762 (the score printed by Walsh), and 'L' Amore contadino,' given at Lodi in 1766 (score in the Fitzwilliam Museum, Cambridge). His name is not found after 1789. (*Q.-L.*, etc.)   **M.**

LANCERS' QUADRILLE, THE, a square dance, for eight or sixteen couples. It is said to have been the invention of a Dublin dancing-master, John Duval; but Joseph HART claimed to have invented it in 1819, according to the title-page of his original edition, published in 1820:

'Les Lancier·, a second set of Quadrilles for the Piano Forte, with entirely new figures, as danced by the Nobility and Gentry at Tenby in the summer of 1819. Composed and most respectfully dedicated to Lady and the Misses Beechy by Jo·eph Hart. London, for the Author, Whitaker & Co., 75 St. Paul's Churchyard.'

The dance consisted of five figures—La Rose, La Lodoiska, La Dorset, Les Lanciers, and L'Étoile, danced to Airs by Spagnoletti, by Kreutzer, from the 'Beggar's Opera' ('If the heart of a man'), by Janiewicz, and by Storace ('Pretty Maiden,' from the 'Haunted Tower') respectively. In Duval's version [1] the names of the figures and music are substantially the same, though in the figures themselves there is considerable difference. Hart's figures, with a slight difference or two, are still danced, L'Étoile being now called Les Visites, and Les Lanciers danced last.   **W. B. S.**

LAND, JAN PIETER NICOLAAS (*b.* Delft, 1834; *d.* Arnhem, Apr. 30, 1897), Oriental scholar and musician. Although of Scandinavian descent, he was a thorough Dutchman [2]; brought up at Leevwarden in Friesland, educated at the well-known Moravian school at Neuwied, on the Rhine, and subsequently at the University of Leyden, where he devoted himself to Semitic philology and took his degree of Doctor of Theology. He next spent two years in England working among the Syriac manuscripts at the British Museum. On returning to Holland, he was made professor of classical and Oriental languages at the Academy (now the Municipal University) of Amsterdam; whence, in the 'seventies, he was speedily promoted to the chair of Logic and Metaphysics at Leyden.

This latter post he held over twenty years, filling in due course the office of Rector of the University, and lecturing on Syriac when required, until 1895, when a paralytic seizure compelled his retirement to Arnhem—where he occupied himself with learned tasks until his death.

He was devoted to music, especially of the 17th century, and fond of transcribing, from the original Tablature, lute music for his friends. The following works concern music:

Noord Nederlands muziekgeschiedenis. (1874–81.)
De Koorboeken van de S'Pieterskerk te Leyden. (1880.)

---

[1] Danced at the Countess of Farnham's ball in Dublin, Apr. 9, 1817.   **W. H. G. F.**
[2] His grandfather had been taken prisoner at Camperdown by the English.

Over de toonladders der arabische muziek. (1880.)
Huygens. *Correspondance et œuvres musicales.* (1882.) (See HUYGENS.) In this work Jonckbloet collaborated.
De Pathodia van Constantijn Huygens.
Recherches sur l'histoire de la gamme arabe. (1884.)
Essai de notation musicale chez les Arabes et les Persans. (1885.)
Het Tijdschrift der Vereeniging voor Noord Nederlands muziek-geschiedenis. (1885.)
Quirinus van Blankenburg en zijne Fuga Obligata. (1882.)
Joan Albert Ban en de theorie der Toonkunst. (1882.)
Het Luitboek van Thysius. (Containing, among others, both English and French songs.)
Tonschriftversuche und Melodieproben aus dem muhammedanischen Mittelalter. (1886.) (A continuation of the lute-book of Thysius, with songs and dance music.)
Het volmaeckte Klaewvier of Joan Albert Ban.
De Gamélan te Jogjākartā, with examples of Javanese music.
Werken van Sweelinck te Oxford.   **E. J. Hˢ.**

LANDI, CAMILLA (*b.* Geneva, 1866), the daughter of Milanese parents, both of them singers, became one of the most distinguished concert singers of her day.

On Dec. 8, 1884, she made her début at a concert given by Servais at the Sala ·di Filar-monica, Florence, and she made a very favourable impression in songs of Tosti and Marchetti From 1886–92 she lived in Paris, and made *ı*· great success at the Lamoureux Concerts, and at Rouen, Bordeaux, etc. On Oct. 1, 1888, she played for one night at the Opéra, Paris, as Amneris in 'Aïda'; and on June 5, 1890, at the Odéon as Ursula on the production in Paris of Berlioz's 'Béatrice et Bénédict' by the Société des Grandes Auditions. On that and subsequent evenings the success of the performance was her singing with Mlle. Levasseur (Hero) of the well-known Duo Nocturne, 'Vous soupirez, Madame.' On Nov. 10, 1892, she made her début in this country, under Hallé at Manchester, and became an immediate favourite there at subsequent concerts under him in that city and elsewhere. On Feb. 22, 1893, under Hallé, she made her début at an orchestral concert at St. James's Hall, when she sang 'La Captive' of Berlioz. On Mar. 25, at the Crystal Palace, she confirmed the favourable impression she had made, and later in the autumn she sang at the Bristol Festival. For the next few years she lived in London, where her mother had established herself as a teacher, and became a great favourite at the above concerts, the Philharmonic, Ballad Concerts, and elsewhere. In 1897 and 1898, announced as from London, Mlle. Landi sang in Germany and Austria-Hungary, with the greatest success, her singing of Handel's 'Ombra mai fu' from 'Serse' being particularly appreciated. Her German engagements were principally at Berlin, her mother having settled for the time at Leipzig, where she had made her German début. In 1899 she sang in Holland, Belgium, Russia and Poland, and in 1900 again in Germany, etc. She reappeared in London, giving vocal recitals 1904–07 at the Bechstein (now Wigmore) Hall. She has lived subsequently in Geneva. Mlle. Landi's voice had a large compass, from the low *d* to *a″*, and a quality of infinite charm.   **A. C.**

LANDI, STEFFANO (*b.* Rome, *c.* 1590; *d.* there, *c.* 1655), maestro di cappella at Padua

c. 1619; alto singer in the Papal Chapel *c.* 1629.
He was one of the foremost composers of his
time, and was responsible, with others, for the
appearance of the cantata, and first representative of Roman opera. He composed 2 operas,
masses, madrigals, 6 books of arias for a solo
voice, 4-part psalms, etc.   E. v. d. s.

LANDINO,[1] FRANCESCO (FRANCISCUS
CAECUS, etc.[2]) (*b.* Florence, *c.* 1325; *d.* there,
Sept. 2, 1397), son of a painter. He lost the
sight of both eyes as a child through smallpox,
and devoted himself to music, playing lute,
guitar, flute and a clavier instrument—' Serena
serenorum '—of his own invention and construction. But he shone particularly as an
organist (S. Lorenzo, Florence) and composer.
In the latter capacity he is one of the chief
representatives of the *ars nova* of the 14th
century (see MADRIGAL). Of his compositions,
a large number are still in existence, viz.
madrigals, ballads, canzonas and secular songs.
(See *Riemann* and *Q.-L.*)   E. v. d. s.

LANDOLFI, CARLO FERDINANDO (LAN-
DULPHUS), a reputable violin-maker of Milan,
where he lived in the Street of St. Margaret,
1750-60. The Landolfi violoncellos are especially striking in quality and appearance, and are
in greater demand than the violins. E. J. P.

LANDOWSKA, WANDA (*b.* Warsaw, July 5,
1881), distinguished pianist and harpsichordist,
has devoted her career to the interpretation of
keyboard music written before the era of
romanticism. Her tours in Europe and
America have done much to recreate an understanding of the classical style of playing on
keyboard instruments. She has combated the
theory that the *Wohltemperirtes Clavier* was
written for the clavichord and given practical
evidence that J. S. Bach's technique is laid out
for the double harpsichord (see *Neue Zeitschrift
für Musik*, Jahrg 78, No. 10). Her books *Bach
et ses interprètes* (1906) and *La Musique
ancienne* (1908) show that her æsthetic principles are based on thorough scholarship. C.

LANDSBERG, LUDWIG (*d.* Rome, May 6,
1858), a German musician, native of Breslau,
who went to Rome and remained there for
twenty-four years, teaching the piano and
amassing a wonderful collection of music, both
printed and MS. On his death his library was
taken, part to Berlin and part to Breslau, and
a catalogue of the ancient portion was printed
(Berlin, 1859, imprimé chez Ernest Kuhn)—
whether the whole or a part, does not appear.
It contains compositions by more than 150
musicians of the old Italian and Flemish
schools, down to Casali. Fétis, however, who
had received a MS. catalogue of the collection
from Landsberg during his life, insists upon the
fact that many of the most important works
have disappeared.   G.

[1] Wooldridge, *Oxf. Hist. Mus.* ii. p. 47, etc., gives the name as
Landini; so also Ludwig, Adler's *Handbuch*, p. 240.
[2] Riemann.

LANFRANCO, GIOVANNI MARIA (*b.* Terenzio,
Parma, end of 15th or beginning of 16th cent.),
was, according to Fétis, maestro di cappella, and
canon at Brescia Cathedral. He wrote ' Scin-
tille di Musica ' (published 1533), important for
its information about contemporary musical
instruments.   E. v. d. s.

LANG, BENJAMIN JOHNSON (*b.* Salem, Mass.,
U.S.A., Dec. 28, 1837; *d.* Boston, Mass., Apr.
3, 1909), an American pianist, conductor, organist and teacher. His father was a well-
known teacher of the pianoforte in Salem, and
he began his studies under him, continuing
them under Francis G. Hill of Boston. By the
time he was 15 years old he held a post as
organist of a Boston church. In 1855 he went
to Europe to study composition in Berlin and
elsewhere in Germany, and pianoforte with
Alfred Jaell; he also had some intercourse
with Liszt. On his return to Boston he made
his first public appearance as a pianist in 1858.
His first appearance as a conductor was made
in Boston in May 1862, when he gave the first
performance in that city of Mendelssohn's
' Walpurgisnacht.' The next year he shared
with Carl Zerrahn the direction of the music at
the jubilee concert in honour of President Lincoln's Emancipation Proclamation, and from
that time forth he figured more and more extensively in Boston as a leader. He was appointed conductor of the Apollo Club, a men's
singing society, at its formation in 1871, and
remained as such until 1901. He was also conductor of the Cæcilia, a mixed chorus, since its
establishment in 1874, and was conductor of
the Handel and Haydn Society for two seasons,
1895-97. He gave several complete performances of ' Parsifal ' in concert form.

In the early sixties Lang became prominent as a concert pianist in Boston, playing
frequently at the concerts of the Harvard
Musical Association, at chamber concerts of
his own, and with the Mendelssohn Quintette
Club. His labours as a composer were less
important than as an interpreter; yet he left
an oratorio, ' David,' symphonies, overtures,
chamber music, pieces for the pianoforte,
church music and many songs, mostly in manuscript. In 1903 Yale University conferred on
him the degree of Master of Arts. (See
BOSTON.)   R. A.

LANG, a family of German musicians originally from Mannheim, but settling at Munich,
and mentioned here for the sake of (1) JOSE-
PHINE LANG (the second of that name)
(*b.* Munich, Mar. 14, 1815; *d.* Tübingen, Dec.
2, 1880), a young lady of very remarkable
musical gifts and personality, who attracted
the notice of Mendelssohn when he passed
through Munich in 1830 and 1831. There is
an enthusiastic account of ' die kleine Lang ' in
his letter of Oct. 6, 1831; in writing to Bärmann (July 7 and Sept. 27, 1834), he inquires

for her, and in a letter, seven years later (Dec. 15, 1841), to Professor C. R. Köstlin of Tübingen, to whom she was married in 1842, he shows how deeply her image had impressed itself on his susceptible heart. She published several books of songs (up to op. 38), which from the reviews in the *A.M.Z.*, appear to be full of imagination, and well worthy of the warm praise bestowed on them by Mendelssohn in the letters just mentioned. Hiller tells the story of her life at length in his *Tonleben* (ii. 116), and selects her songs, opp. 12 and 14, as the best. Connected with the same family at an earlier date was (2) REGINA (*b*. Würzburg, 1786), a singer whose name was originally Hitzelberg, educated at Munich by Winter, Cannabich and Vogel, and appointed chamber singer at the Bavarian court. When Napoleon I. was at Munich in 1806 she sang before him in Winter's 'Interrupted Sacrifice' and Mozart's 'Don Giovanni,' and so pleased him that he is said to have urged her to come to Paris.[1] She, however, remained in Munich, and married Theobald Lang, a violinist in the court band. In 1812 or 1813 she was at Vienna, and Beethoven wrote in her album a song 'An die Geliebte,' to Stoll's words, 'O dass ich dir vom stillen Auge,' which was published about 1840 in a collection called 'Das singende Deutschland.' It is his second version of the song—the former one being dated by himself Dec. 1811, and having been published in 1814. See Nottebohm's *Thematic Catalogue*, p. 183.   G.

LANGDON, RICHARD, Mus.B. (*d*. Exeter, Sept. 8, 1803), grandson of the Rev.Tobias Langdon, priest-vicar of Exeter Cathedral, graduated as Mus.Bac. at Oxford in 1761. In 1753 he received the appointments of organist and sub-chanter of Exeter Cathedral, but resigned them in 1777, when he became organist of Ely Cathedral. This post he held only for a few months, being appointed to Bristol Cathedral in 1778. He quitted Bristol in 1782 to become organist of Armagh Cathedral, a post he resigned in 1794. In 1774 he published 'Divine Harmony, a Collection, in score, of Psalms and Anthems.' His published compositions include 'Twelve Glees,' 1770, two books of songs, and some canzonets. Two glees and a catch by him are contained in Warren's 'Vocal Harmony.'   W. H. H.

LANGE (LANGIUS), HIERONYMUS GREGOR (*b*. Havelberg, Brandenburg ; *d*. Breslau, May 1, 1587), obtained in 1574 the post of school-cantor at Frankfort-on-the-Oder, but becoming paralysed in his hands and feet he removed to Breslau in 1583, where he was received into a charitable institution, and in spite of his infirmity continued to devote himself to musical composition till his death. There are 2 books of 'Cantiones sacrae,' published 1580 and 1584 respectively, containing 35 Latin motets

for 4, 5, 6, 8 and 10 voices ; and 2 books of Deutsche Lieder, 1584, 1586, containing forty German secular songs for 3 voices. Besides these, there are only a few occasional compositions published separately, chiefly 'Epithalamia' or wedding-songs in the form of motets. The Deutsche Lieder for 3 voices were frequently reprinted, and in 1615 Christoph Demantius rearranged them for 5 voices. Although highly thought of in their time, Eitner says, these songs are less attractive than those of Regnard, being somewhat stiff and wanting in melody. The rearrangement by Demantius is of greater merit. But Lange's Latin motets stand upon a higher level. In 1899 Reinhold Starke edited for the Gesellschaft für Musikforschung a selection of 24 of these motets (*Publikation*, Jahrgang 29), among which are several very interesting numbers. 'Vae misero mihi,' with its second part, 'O vos omnes qui transitis,' is very remarkable, on account of its unusual chromatic modulations. A motet, 'Media vita,' composed on the occasion of the death of the General Superintendent, Musculus, one of Lange's chief Frankfort patrons, the editor considers as being quite in the mood of Sebastian Bach. These motets must have enjoyed considerable favour, as some of them were also transcribed for the lute. Besides the published works Starke enumerates a considerable number of works which have remained in MS., among which are 2 masses and 30 other Latin motets, and 20 German songs for 4 and 5 voices, partly sacred. See his monograph on Lange contributed to the *M.f.M.*, 1899, pp. 101-23.   J. R. M.

LANGE, DE, a Dutch family of musicians and organists ; the father, (1) SAMUEL (*b*. June 9, 1811 ; *d*. Rotterdam, May 15, 1884), was organist of the church of St. Lawrence there, and an eminent teacher, as well as a composer of pieces for the organ. He was the teacher of his elder son, (2) SAMUEL (*b*. Rotterdam, Feb. 22, 1840 ; *d*. Stuttgart, July 7, 1911), who further studied with Verhulst, and in Vienna with A. Winterberger. After travelling as a virtuoso in Galicia in 1858-59, he settled at Lemberg for four years, and in 1863 was appointed organist at Rotterdam, and given a teaching appointment in the music school of the Maatschappij tot bevordering van Toonkunst, making occasional concert tours in Switzerland, Germany, France, etc. From 1874-76 he taught at the music school at Basle, and in 1877 was called to Cologne to teach in the Conservatorium. While there he directed the Kölner Männergesangverein and the choir of the Gürzenich concerts. In 1885 he went to the Hague as rector of the Oratorio society, and remained there until 1893, when he went to Stuttgart as substitute for Immanuel Faisst, on whose death in 1894 he became professor of the organ and counterpoint in the Conservatorium. In 1900 he was appointed director of the Conservatorium. His works include eight organ sonatas, a piano concerto, three quartets, a trio, a quintet, four sonatas for violin and two for violoncello, a concertstück for violoncello, and many partsongs for male voices, besides three symphonies, and an oratorio, ' Moses,' performed while he was at the Hague.

His brother, (3) DANIEL (b. Rotterdam, July 11, 1841 ; d. Caiifornia, Jan. 31, 1918), was a pupil of Ganz and Servais for the violoncello, and of Verhulst for composition. He taught at the music school at Lemberg in 1860–63, and then went to Paris to perfect his pianoforte and organ playing. While there he was organist of the Protestant church at Montrouge, and remained there until the outbreak of the war, when he went back to Holland, taking up his abode at Amsterdam, as teacher in the music school, which afterwards became the Conservatorium. He was made secretary of the Maatschappij tot bevordering van Toonkunst. He conducted several choral societies with great distinction, and formed a party of eminent solo singers with which he performed old Netherlandish music. They gave concerts in the Albert Hall, London, during the Music and Inventions Exhibition of 1885, and created a great sensation by the exquisite finish of their performances. De Lange became director of the Amsterdam Conservatorium (1895–1913). His works include two symphonies, cantatas, an opera, ' De val van Kuilenburg ' ; an overture ' Willem van Holland ' ; music to ' Hernani ' ; a Mass, a Requiem ; a setting of Ps. xxii., for soli, choir and piano ; a violoncello concerto, etc. (Riemann.)   M.

L A N G E - M Ü L L E R , PETER ERASMUS (b. Frederiksberg, Denmark, Dec. 1, 1850 ; d. Feb. 25, 1926), composer, educated at the Royal Conservatorium in Copenhagen. He wrote incidental music to several Danish plays and several operas produced at Copenhagen and Stockholm, as well as symphonic music. His 200 songs and choral pieces are regarded as the work most characteristic of him and his country, which claims him as a representative Danish composer.   C.

LANGHANS, FRIEDRICH WILHELM (b. Hamburg, Sept. 21, 1832 ; d. Berlin, June 9, 1892), author, composer and violinist. His early general education was received at the Johanneum in Berlin, and in 1849 he entered the Leipzig Conservatorium, where his violinteacher was David and his composition-master Richter. On leaving Leipzig Langhans went to Paris to study the violin further under Alard. For five seasons, 1852–56, he played first violin in the Gewandhaus orchestra in Leipzig ; from 1857–60 was Konzertmeister at Düsseldorf ; and then settled temporarily, as teacher and violinist, in Hamburg, Paris and Heidelberg. From 1874–81 he was professor of the history

of music at Kullak's Neue Akademie der Tonkunst, when he joined Scharwenka's newly founded Conservatorium, and ultimately acted as its director. In 1871 the University of Heidelberg conferred the degree of Doctor upon Langhans, who was an honorary member of the Liceo Filarmonico of Florence and of the St. Cecilia at Rome. He visited England in 1881, and subsequently, after hearing some open-air music in Glasgow, the Worcester Festival, and ' Patience ' in London, wrote articles on music in England for the Musikalisches Centralblatt. Langhans's compositions, which include a string quartet that gained a prize offered by a Florentine gentleman in 1864, a violin sonata, and a symphony, are quite unimportant ; but his literary work has been more prized. It includes Das musikalische Urtheil (1872) ; Die Musikgeschichte in 12 Vorträgen (1878) ; a Geschichte der Musik des 17., 18. und 19. Jahrhunderts in continuation of Ambros, and a history of the Berlin Hochschule. In 1858 he married the pianist Luise Japha, a pupil of Robert and Clara Schumann.

                           R. H. L.

LANGLÉ-LANGLOIS, HONORÉ FRANÇOIS MARIE (b. Monaco, c. 1741 ; d. Paris, Sept. 20, 1807), studied at the Conservatorio de la Pietà at Naples. He was maestro di cappella at Genoa c. 1764 ; in 1768 he went to Paris as teacher of singing and composer, and became also the singing-master of Queen Marie Antoinette. In 1784 he became teacher at the École Royale de chant, which was merged into the Conservatoire in 1791, where he was professor of harmony and librarian. On the reconstruction of that institution he only retained the latter position, but retired in 1802 to his country house near Paris. He composed several operas, cantatas, etc., and wrote a number of important theoretical works (Riemann ; Fétis ; Q.-L.).   E. V. D. S.

LANGSAM, i.e. slow, the German equivalent for Adagio.

LANGSHAW, (1) JOHN (d. 1798), was employed about 1761, under the direction of John Christopher Smith, in setting music upon the barrels of an organ, of much larger size than had been theretofore used for barrels, then being constructed for the Earl of Bute, which he did ' in so masterly a manner that the effect was equal to that produced by the most finished player.' In 1772 he became organist of the parish church of Lancaster.

His son, (2) JOHN (b. London, 1763), became in 1779 a pupil of Charles Wesley, and in 1798 succeeded his father as organist at Lancaster. He composed many hymns, chants, organ voluntaries, pianoforte concertos, songs and duets, and made numerous arrangements for the pianoforte.   W. H. H.

LANIERE (LANIER, LANEIR, LANYER, LANEER, LANNEARE, LANEARE), the name of a family [1] of musicians at the English court in the 17th century. The head of the family, or rather of the English branch of the family, was (1) JOHN LANIER (d. 1579),[2] described as a native of Rouen, who had property in Crutched Friars. A player of the sackbut, named (2) JOHN LANYER, from 1565–1605, was probably identical with the John Lannyer who, on Oct. 12, 1585, married, at Holy Trinity, Minories, the daughter of Mark Antony Galliardello, another court musician. He had property at East Greenwich, and the registers of Greenwich mention several of the family. This John Lanier was the father of (3) NICHOLAS (see below), the most distinguished of the family, who must not be confused with two other bearers of the same name. One (4) NICHOLAS (d. 1612), owned property at East Greenwich, and seems to have been another son of John of Rouen ; he was musician to Queen Elizabeth in 1581, and died leaving six sons and four daughters. The sons were all court musicians, and one of them, Jerome, had two sons, Jeremy and William, who were musicians in 1634–35. Another (5) NICHOLAS LANIER (d. 1646) pub-lished some etchings from drawings by Parmigiano, and in 1638 a set after Giulio Romano ; he is presumed to be identical with the Nicholas Lanier who was buried in St. Martin's-in-the-Fields, Nov. 4, 1646, aged 78.[3]

Coming now to the most eminent of the family, (3) NICHOLAS LANIERE (as he was generally called) (b. 1588 ; bapt. Sept. 10 ; d. Feb. 1666). It is probable that he, rather than either of his namesakes, was the musician for the flutes in 1604 ; he was attached to the household of Henry, Prince of Wales, and it is assumed that he is the 'Laniere' alluded to by Herrick in a poem to Henry Lawes. In 1613 he joined Coprario (see COOPER, John) and others in the composition of Campian's masque for the marriage of Robert Carr, Earl of Somerset, and Lady Frances Howard, performed at Whitehall, St. Stephen's night, 1614. The first song, ' Bring away the sacred tree,' is reprinted in Stafford Smith's ' Musica antiqua.' He composed the music for Ben Jonson's masque ' Lovers made Men ' at Lord Haye's house, Feb. 22, 1617, and is described as introducing the ' stylo recitativo ' apparently for the first time in England. He sang in the piece and painted the scenery. He also wrote the music for the same poet's masque ' The Vision of Delight ' in 1617. His skill in the art of painting was turned to account in 1625, when he was sent to Italy by Charles I. to buy pictures for the royal collection.[4] He remained in Italy about three years, and stayed at Mantua with Daniel Nys,

the agent through whom the King acquired Mantegna's ' Triumph of Caesar ' now at Hampton Court. Correggio's ' Mercury instructing Cupid ' in the National Gallery, was another of the pictures bought through Laniere (see D.N.B. for other details unconnected with music). The patent of his appointment as Master of the King's Musick at a salary of £200 a year is dated July 11, 1626. In 1630 he set Herrick's poem on the birth of Prince Charles. He was appointed keeper of the king's miniatures, and in 1636 the King granted to Laniere and others a charter, incorporating them as ' The Marshal, Wardens, and Cominalty of the Arte and Science of Musicke in Westminster,' and appointed Laniere the first Marshal. At the outbreak of the civil war, Laniere lost his appointments, and seems to have spent much of his time abroad. There are passes among the State Papers, for him to journey with pictures and musical instruments between Flanders and England. In Jonckbloet and Land's *Musique et musiciens au XVII⁰ siècle*, p. xxi., is a letter from Lanier (as he spells it), dated Mar. 1, 1645, and in 1646 he begs Huygens to get him a passport to go to Holland. In 1655 the Earl of Newcastle gave a ball at the Hague at which a song set to music by Laniere was sung. At the Restoration he was reinstated in his posts as master of the king's music and marshal of the corporation of music. He composed New Year's Songs in 1663 and 1665, and died in Feb. 1666. The entry in the Greenwich registers is dated Feb. 24, 1665–66, ' Mr. Nicholas Laniere buried away ' (i.e. elsewhere). Songs and other pieces by him are contained in ' Select Musicall Ayres and Dialogues,' 1653 and 1659 ; ' The Musical Companion,' 1667 ; ' The Treasury of Musick,' 1669 ; and ' Choice Ayres and Songs,' book iv., 1685. Several songs and dialogues by him are in the B.M. Add. MSS. 11,608, 29,396 ; Eg. MS. 2013. A cantata, ' Hero and Leander,' is in B.M. Add. MSS. 14,399, 33,236. Other music is in MS. in the Bodl. Mus. Sch. and Christ Church. Vandyck painted Laniere's portrait for Charles I., and at the dispersal of the royal collection it was bought by Laniere himself. Another portrait is in the Bodl. Mus. Sch., both painted and presented by Laniere.[5]

BIBL.—*D.N.B., Q.-L.*, Nagel's *Annalen*, etc. ; information from Sir A. S. Scott-Gatty, Garter King of Arms.   M.

LANNER, (1) JOSEPH FRANZ KARL (b. Oberdöbling, near Vienna, Apr. 11/12, 1801 ; d. Apr. 14, 1843), famous as composer of dance music contemporary with Johann Strauss, was the son of a glove-maker ; he early showed a talent for music, taught himself the violin, and by means of theoretical books learned to compose.

Next came the desire to conduct an orchestra ; and in the meantime he got together a quartet party, in which the viola was taken by Strauss,

---

[1] For details of the less eminent members, their relationship to each other, and dates of their appointments, etc., the reader must be referred to Willibald Nagel's *Annalen der englischen Hofmusik*, and *Geschichte der Musik in England*. The register of St. Olave, Hart Street, London, also supplies some subsidiary dates of family history.

[2] *D.N.B.*   [3] Nichol's *Progresses*, ii. 710.

[4] Bertolotti's *Musici alla corte dei Gonzaga in Mantova*.

[5] Reproduced *Mus. Ant.*, 1913, pp. 144-8.

his subsequent rival. They played potpourris from favourite operas, marches, etc., arranged by Lanner. He next composed waltzes and Ländler, first for a small, then for a full orchestra, and performed them in public. His popularity increased rapidly, and important places of amusement eagerly competed for his services. He also appeared in most of the provincial capitals, but declined all invitations abroad. He conducted the dance music in the large and small Redoutensaal, and also that at the court balls, alternately with Strauss. As a mark of distinction he was appointed Kapellmeister of the second Bürger regiment. When thus at the height of prosperity he died, and was buried in the churchyard of Döbling, near Vienna. A memorial tablet was placed on the house in which he was born, May 15, 1879.[1]

Lanner may be considered the founder of Viennese dance music. His galops, quadrilles, polkas and marches, but especially his waltzes and Ländler, bear traces of the frank, genial disposition which made him so beloved. All his works, from op. 1 (' Neue Wiener Ländler ') to his swan-song (' Die Schönbrunner '), are penetrated with the warm national life of Vienna. The titles often contain allusions to contemporaneous events and customs, and thus have an historical interest. His printed works amount to 208, and he left others unpublished. The following numbers are dedicated to crowned heads, and distinguished persons—opp. 74, 81, 85, 91, 101, 110-12, 115-116, 120, 128, 131-32, 138 (' Victoria-Walzer ' dedicated to Queen Victoria), 143, 146, 155, 161-62. The ' Troubadour-Walzer,' op. 197, are dedicated to Donizetti, and the ' Norwegische Arabesken,' op. 145, to Ole Bull. Diabelli published opp. 1-15 ; Haslinger 16-32 and 170-208 ; Mechetti 33-169.

Of Lanner's three children, (2) AUGUST (b. Vienna, 1834 ; d. Sept. 27, 1855), a young man of great promise, followed his father's profession. (3) KATHARINA (b. Vienna, 1831), was a well-known dancer, who made her début at the court opera in Vienna in 1845, and appeared at all the important theatres in Europe. In 1858 she formed a children's ballet in Hamburg, which gave forty-six performances in Paris with great success. At a later date she was engaged also at the Italian Opera in England, and under her admirable management a high standard of dancing was maintained at the Empire Theatre in London.   C. F. P.

BIBL.—FRITZ LANGE, Josef Lanner und Johann Strauss. Ihre Zeit, ihr Leben und ihre Werke. Nach authentischen Quellen und nach den neuesten Forschungen dargestellt. 2nd edn. (Leipzig, 1919.)

LANTINS (LANTIUS, LATINIS), the name of two Netherlandish composers of the 15th century. (1) ARNOLDUS DE, appointed as singer in the Papal Chapel, Nov. 1431.

(2) HUGO DE (c. 1400). A considerable number

[1] Owing to a curious error in the entry of his baptism, his name was for long overlooked in the register.

of his church compositions, sacred and secular songs in MS. are preserved in the libraries of Bologna, Oxford (Bod. Lib.), and Cod. Trient, Vienna. Some of these have been republished in Stainer's Dufay and ' Hausmusik,' etc., by Riemann, who considers them almost equal to Binchois.   E. v. d. s.

LANZETTI, DOMENICO (18th-19th cent.), a violoncellist of whom the Berlin Library possesses 10 violoncello concertos and 2 sonatas with instruments and basso continuo, all in MS.

LANZETTI, SALVATORE (b. Naples, c. 1710; d. Turin, c. 1780), famous violoncellist who studied at Naples, came to London c. 1739, and is mentioned by Burney as one of those who brought the violoncello into favour in England, where he still was in 1754, after a visit to Germany, where he gave concerts at Frankfort-on-M. on May 29 and 31, 1751. From London he went to Turin as member of the royal chapel. He composed a number of sonatas for one and two violoncellos with bass, and a Tutor for his instrument. Several of his sonatas have been republished by Piatti and by Schröder (Q.-L.).

LAPARRA, RAOUL (b. Bordeaux, May 13, 1876), operatic composer, who attained international recognition with his opera ' La Habañera.'

His first work of the kind was ' Peau d'Ane ' (1899) ; ' La Habañera,' produced (1908) at the Opéra-Comique, was brought to Covent Garden two years later, when its skilful use of Spanish dance rhythms and other evidences of local colour in the orchestration produced a favourable impression. It has since been given with success in America. Another opera, ' La Jota,' was produced at the Opéra-Comique in 1911. A suite, ' Un Dimanche basque,' for piano and orchestra, was heard at Queen's Hall (1923), the composer playing the piano part.
       C.

LAPICIDA, ERASMUS, nearly contemporary with Josquin des Prés, is mentioned by Ornithoparcus as one of the approved composers of his time, and is also referred to as an authority in musical theory in certain correspondence between Spataro and Giovanni del Lago. Petrucci printed some Lamentations by him with the plain-song melody in the tenor, also three motets. In Forster's Liederbuch, 1539, seven German songs bear his name, which Ambros thought to be adaptations of other compositions of Lapicida to German words ; but Eitner claims to have proved them to be original settings of the German texts since the cantus firmus is in each case the original melody to the text. None of Lapicida's compositions have been reprinted in modern times.
       J. R. M.

LAPIS SANTO (early 18th cent.), Italian composer, singer and mandolinist, member of the Philharmonic Academy, Bologna. Two operas of his were performed at Venice in 1729 and 1730. About the middle of the century he was music master at The Hague, and *c.* 1758 in London. He wrote a third opera, which was in Breitkopf's library in 1754, and several works of sonatas for various instruments. (See *Q.-L.*)

LAPORTE, L'ABBÉ JOSEPH DE (*b.* Belfort, *c.* 1713 ; *d.* Paris, Dec. 19, 1779), entered the Jesuit Order, where he finished his studies. He settled in Paris and devoted himself chiefly to literature, including an *Almanach des spectacles,* a *Dictionnaire dramatique* (*c.* 1776), and *Anecdotes dramatiques,* which give much interesting information about the stage and musical life in Paris (*Riemann*).

LAPORTE (DELAPORTE), PIERRE FRANÇOIS (*b.* 1799 ; *d.* near Paris, Sept. 24 or 27, 1841), a French comedian,[1] came to London as a member and joint manager of a company which, in Jan. 1824, began performing French plays at the theatre in Tottenham Street. On Nov. 18, 1826, he appeared on the English stage, as a member of the Drury Lane company, as Sosia in Dryden's 'Amphitryon,' and afterwards played a variety of parts, mostly original, and amongst them Wormwood in 'The Lottery Ticket.' He next joined the Haymarket company, in which he first appeared June 15, 1827. In 1828 he became manager of the King's Theatre, and continued such until 1831. In 1832 he was lessee of Covent Garden Theatre, and actor as well as manager, but was compelled to retire, with heavy loss, before the end of the season. In 1833 he resumed the management of the King's Theatre, and retained it until his death, which occurred in his father's house at Soisy-sous-Etiolles, near Paris. A notable feature of his last season (1841) was the 'Tamburini Row,' a disturbance of the performance occasioned by the admirers of Tamburini, who resented his non-engagement for that season, and by their tumultuous proceedings for two or three evenings forced the manager to yield to their wishes. Another curious feature of this year was the reappearance of Laporte in his original capacity as an actor, with Rachel, on three nights of her first London season. Laporte first introduced to the English public, amongst other operas, Rossini's 'Comte Ory' and 'Assedio di Corinto'; Bellini's 'Pirata,' 'Sonnambula,' 'Norma' and 'Puritani'; Donizetti's 'Anna Bolena,' and Costa's 'Malek Adel'; and amongst singers, Sontag, Méric-Lalande, Persiani, Assandri, Albertazzi, Pisaroni, Donzelli, David, jun., Ivanoff, Mario ; and, above all, the famous quartet who so long held supremacy on the opera stage, Grisi, Rubini, Tamburini and Lablache. Though his dilatory and unbusinesslike habits ruined his management, Laporte was not without good qualities. Amongst others, his tact and coolness were

[1] He was son of the actor Laporte (*b.* Mar. 1775; *d.* Oct. 17, 1841),

great, and many of his *bons mots* were current at the time. When Cerrito returned the ticket of a box on the upper tier with the remark that she was much too young to be exalted to the skies before her time, Laporte—having already given a box on the same tier to Taglioni—replied that he ' had done his best, but that perhaps he had been wrong in placing her on the same level with Mlle. Taglioni.'

W. H. H. ; rev. M. L. P.

LA POUPLINIÈRE, ALEXANDRE, J. J. LE RICHE DE, see POUPLINIÈRE.

LAPPI (LAPPUS), PIETRO (*b.* Florence, latter part of 16th cent.). From 1600 until after 1628 he was maestro di cappella at the church ' delle Grazie,' Brescia. He was a prolific composer of masses and other church music ; also instrumental music (*Q.-L.* ; *Riemann*).

LARA, ISIDORE DE (*b.* London, Aug. 9, 1858), opera composer. At the age of 15 he entered the Milan Conservatorio, obtaining the gold medal for composition, which he studied with Mazzucato. He also studied singing under Lamperti. He then went to Paris and continued to work at composition under Lalo. On his return to England De Lara was at first known as a singer and song-writer, but his attention was turned to the stage when, on the suggestion of Victor Maurel, he transformed his cantata ' The Light of Asia ' into an opera and secured its production at Covent Garden in 1892. The following year his ' Amy Robsart ' was given at the same theatre and two years later in French at Monte Carlo. He lived for a time at Monte Carlo, producing ' Moïna ' in 1897, and ' Messaline ' in 1899, the last-named being heard at Covent Garden in 1901. ' Soléa ' was produced, in German, at the Cologne Opera House in 1907 ; ' Sanga ' at the Opéra-Comique, Paris, in 1908, and ' Naïl ' at the Théâtre de la Gaieté, Paris, in 1911, and Covent Garden during the summer season of 1919. ' Les Trois Masques ' was first given at Marseilles in French in 1912, and later in English at Glasgow, ' The Three Musketeers ' at Cannes in 1921, and by the Carl Rosa Company at Newcastle, May 2, 1924, and subsequently in London.

During the war (1914–18) De Lara gave in London many orchestral and chamber concerts of British music, at which numerous works were heard for the first time. He has worked hard to promote the establishment of a permanent opera in London, and believes it can only be done with a theatre specially designed to hold a large number of low-priced seats. As a composer De Lara works on the French model as represented by Massenet, and has a sure instinct for comic and orchestral effect. He is a Chevalier of the Legion of Honour and a Commander of the Crown of Italy. N. C. G.

LARCHET, JOHN F., Mus.D., (*b.* Dublin, 1885), studied at the R.I.A.M., graduated

Mus.B. (1915) and Mus.D. (1917) of Dublin University. He was for some years organist of the Jesuit Church, Dublin, and conductor of the Abbey Theatre orchestra, and, in 1920, was appointed professor of music at the National University, in succession to Dr. Kitson. He has composed many song cycles, tone poems and songs, and arranged some Irish folk-tunes in an unconventional way, and is regarded as a promising Irish composer.

W. H. G. F.

LARGE (Lat. *maxima*), the note of greatest time-value in the early system of Measured Music. It could be triple or duple (*i.e.* equalling three or two Longs), according to the mood.

	Large rest Perfect	Large rest Imperfect
1. or		

(The black form is the earlier. In some very early examples the tail is omitted, but this is rare.)

With the increasing articulation of polyphonic music the Large became a somewhat fossilised form, and was seldom called for except in the plain-song canti fermi when a note was prolonged through several measures as a pedal-point.

The final note of a composition was usually written as a Large; here the Large was used without mensural significance, indicating an indefinite prolongation of tone, as does the *fermata* or pause mark. In such cases the Large often appears in this form:

2.

The breaking-up of the note into two is merely a convention of ornament, it has no vocal import. (See NOTATION.)

S. T. W.

LARGHETTO, partaking of the broad style of Largo, but about the same pace with Andante.

LARGO, *i.e.* broad, an Italian term meaning a slow, broad, dignified style.

The term *Largamente* has come into use to denote breadth of style without change of *tempo*. Largo implies a slow pace, but the very varying metronome marks applied to it show conclusively that style and not pace is its principal intention.

G.

In the B.M. Add. MSS. 31,424, fol. 46, 53*b* are two gigues marked Largo, the others in the same set being marked vivace or allegro.

M.

LARIGOT, from an old French word, *l'arigot*, for a small flute or flageolet, now obsolete, hence among organ stops the old name for a rank of small open metal pipes, the longest of which is only 1⅓ ft. speaking-length. Its pitch is a fifth above that of the fifteenth. It is first met with, in English organs, by HARRIS (*q.v.*), who passed many years in France, and who

placed one in his instrument in St. Sepulchre's, Snow Hill, erected in 1670.

E. J. H.

LAROCHE, HERMAN AUGUSTOVICH (*b.* St. Petersburg, May 25, 1845; *d.* there, Oct. 18, 1904), musical critic. He received his musical education at the Conservatoire, where he was a contemporary of Tchaikovsky (1862–66). In 1867 he was appointed to a professorship at the Moscow Conservatoire. He returned to St. Petersburg in 1871, where most of his life was spent. Laroche was a voluminous contributor to many of the leading Russian newspapers and periodicals, and was regarded as the chief representative of conservative principles in music. His writing was distinguished for its excellency of style, erudition, and flashes of original thought; but his work as a whole lacks system, and shows more personal bias than reasoned conviction. Laroche translated Hanslick's *Vom Musikalisch-Schönen* into Russian. He was one of the first to appreciate the genius of Tchaikovsky, and devoted many articles to his personality and his works.

R. N.

LAROCHE, JAMES (JEMMY LAROCH, or LAROCHE) (*b. circa* 1680–82), was a popular singer in London, though probably French by origin or birth, at the end of the 17th and beginning of the 18th centuries. He played, as a boy, the part of Cupid in Motteux's 'Loves of Mars and Venus,' set to music by Eccles and Finger, in which the part of Venus was played by Mrs. Bracegirdle, in 1696. His portrait appears on a very rare print, called

'The Raree Show, Sung by Jemmy Laroch in the Musical Interlude for the Peace, with the Tune set to Musick for the Violin. Ingraved Printed Culred and Sold by Sutton Nicholls next door to the Jack etc. London.'

It was afterwards published by Samuel Lyne. There are thirty-three verses, beginning 'O Raree Show, O Brave Show' below the engraving, which represents Laroche with the show on a stool, exhibiting it to a group of children; and at foot is the music. The Peace of Utrecht was signed in Apr. 1713, and this interlude was played in celebration of it, at the Theatre in Little Lincoln's Inn Fields, the music being written by John Eccles. The portrait of Laroche was also engraved by Laroon in his *Cries of London.*

J. M.

LA RUE, P. DE, see RUE.

LARUETTE, JEAN LOUIS (*b.* Toulouse, Mar. 27, 1731; *d.* there, Jan. 1792), singer and actor at the Opéra-Comique and Comédie Italienne, Paris, and composer of 10 operas and operettas.

LASERNA, BLAS (*d.* Madrid, after 1801), Spanish musician. In 1779 he was appointed official composer to several of the Madrid theatres; and in 1790 he succeeded ESTEVE (*q.v.*). His comic opera, 'La Gitanilla por amor.' (Teatro de la Cruz, 1791) was a notable success; he composed an immense number of 'Tonadillas' (see MISSON, Luis), of which the Bibl. Nacional, Madrid, contains 13 vols., the Bibl. Municipal many more in unbound MSS. He also wrote incidental music for several of the great Spanish plays of the 17th century, by Calderón, Lope de Vega, Moreto and others. In 1801 he was conducting at the Cruz and Principe theatres at Madrid.   J. B. T.

LASSALLE, JEAN (b. Lyons, Dec. 17, 1847 ; d. Paris, Sept. 7, 1909), singer, the son of a silk-merchant at Lyons, was intended for the same business, and studied industrial design at the Beaux-Arts, Lyons, and later in Paris.

He abandoned the idea of a mercantile career, and for a time studied painting in Paris. He studied singing for a time at the Conservatoire, but making little progress he left the school and studied privately under Novelli (Lavessière). He made his début at Liège as St. Bris in the 'Huguenots' (Nov. 19, 1868). He sang next at Lille, Toulouse, the Hague and Brussels, where on Sept. 5, 1871, he made his début, with great success, as De Nevers, and was heard during the season as Ashton in 'Lucia,' Nelusko, Telramund, etc. On June 7, 1872, he made a successful début at the Paris Opéra as Tell. With the exception of visits, on leave of absence, to London, Russia, Madrid, Milan, Vienna, Prague, Warsaw, the United States, etc., Lassalle remained at the Opéra for twenty-three years, and became principal baritone there (1872–92) on the retirement of Faure. His parts included Don Juan, played by him in 1887 at the centenary performance, and Rigoletto on production of Verdi's opera there. He created the parts of Scindia (Massenet's 'Roi de Lahore '), Apr. 27, 1877 ; Sévère (Gounod's ' Polyeucte '), Oct. 7, 1878 ; Ben Saïd (ib. ' Tribut de Zamora '), Apr. 1, 1881 ; Lanciotto Malatesta (Thomas's ' Françoise de Rimini '), Apr. 14, 1882 ; Henri VIII. (Saint-Saëns), Mar. 5, 1883 ; Gunther (Reyer's ' Sigurd '), June 12, 1885 ; De Rysoor (Paladilhe's ' Patrie '), Dec. 20, 1886 ; Benvenuto Cellini ('Ascanio '), Mar. 21, 1890 ; the High Priest (' Samson and Dalila '), Nov. 23, 1892 ; these last two both by Saint-Saëns. On May 5, 1876, on leave of absence, he played at the Théâtre Lyrique (May 5, 1876) as the Count de Lusace in Joncières's ' Dimitri.' On Dec. 11, 1890, he played Escamillo in 'Carmen' at the Opéra-Comique with Mesdames Galli-Marié and Melba, and J. de Reszke, in aid of the Bizet memorial.

On June 14, 1879, he made his début at Covent Garden Theatre, under Gye, as Nelusko, and played there for three seasons with great success ; Scindia in Massenet's opera abovementioned, and June 21, 1881, the Demon in Rubinstein's opera of that name, on the production of these works in England. From 1888–93 he played at the same theatre under Harris, with unvarying success, a great variety of parts, notably July 13, 1889, Hans Sachs on production of ' Meistersinger ' in Italian, and in some operas new at that theatre, the most important

being Claude Frollo (Goring Thomas's 'Esmeralda '), July 12, 1890. In 1896 and 1897 he played in Germany. After 1901, Lassalle devoted himself to teaching in Paris, and in Nov. 1903 was appointed a professor at the Conservatoire. Excellent alike, both as a singer and an actor, the possessor of a beautiful voice, an indefatigable worker, Lassalle was one of the finest artists of his time.
                         A. C. ; rev. M. L. P.

LASSEN, EDUARD (b. Copenhagen, Apr. 13, 1830 ; d. Weimar, Jan. 15, 1904), though a native of Copenhagen, was virtually a Belgian musician, since he was taken to Brussels when only 2, entered the Conservatoire there at 12, in 1844 took the first prize as PF. player, in 1847 the same for harmony, and soon afterwards the second prize for composition. His successes, which were many, were crowned by the Grand Prix de Rome in 1851, after which he started on a lengthened tour through Germany and Italy. Disappointed in his hopes of getting a five-act opera performed at Brussels, he betook himself to Weimar, where in 1857 it was produced, as ' Landgraf Ludwig's Brautfahrt,' under the care of Liszt, with great success. In the following year he was appointed court music-director, and on the retirement of Liszt in 1861, succeeded him as conductor of the opera. A second opera, ' Frauenlob,' was given in 1861, and a third, ' Le Captif,' was brought out in Brussels in 1868. At Weimar Lassen had the satisfaction to produce ' Tristan und Isolde ' in 1874, at a time when no other theatre but Munich had dared to do so. He there published a Symphony in D, a ' Beethoven ' overture and a Festival ditto, music to Sophocles' ' Oedipus,' to Hebbel's ' Nibelungen,' Goethe's ' Faust,' Parts 1 and 2, to Devrient's version of Calderon's ' Circe,' and to Goethe's ' Pandora ' (1886). His works include a second symphony in C, op. 78, cantata, a Fest-Cantate, a Te Deum, a set of ' Biblische Bilder,' for voices and orchestra, a large number of songs and other pieces. In 1881 he was decorated with the order of Leopold. His ' Faust ' music long kept the stage all over Germany.   G.

LASSERRE, JULES BERNARD (b. Tarbes, July 29, 1838 ; d. there, Feb. 19, 1906), eminent violoncellist, entered the Paris Conservatoire in 1852, where he gained the second prize in 1853 and the first prize in 1855. When the popular concerts of Pasdeloup were first started, he was appointed solo violoncellist ; he also played with great success in the principal towns of France. During 1859 he was solo violoncellist at the court of Madrid, and travelled through Spain. In 1869 he took up his residence in England, and played principal violoncello under Sir Michael Costa and at the Musical Union. Lasserre wrote various compositions both for his own instrument and for the violin:

Études, Fantasies, Romances, Tarantelles, Transcriptions, a violoncello Method, etc.

T. P. P.

LASSUS, ORLANDE DE (b. Mons, Belgium, 1530 or 1532; d. Munich, June 14, 1594), is probably the original name of the great Netherland musician of the 16th century who more frequently subscribed himself as ORLANDO LASSO or ORLANDUS LASSUS, sometimes with the preposition di or de between the two names. In one exceptional case his name is latinised as LASSUSIUS.

EARLY LIFE.—There is no proper authority for the assertion that his original name was Roland de Lattre. He was born at Mons in Belgium, but the most recent investigation still leaves it uncertain whether in 1530 or 1532. Dr. Adolf Sandberger,[1] after reviewing all the available evidence, confesses himself unable absolutely to decide between the two dates, but is personally inclined to give the preference to 1530. The earlier date of 1520, which was adopted by H. Delmotte,[2] must be unhesitatingly rejected. Delmotte relied too exclusively on one writer, François Vinchant, who in his *Annals of Hainault*, written not long before 1635, stated that the composer was born ' in the year in which Charles V. was crowned Emperor at Aix-la-Chapelle.' Sandberger is able to show that Vinchant did not make this statement on any first-hand information, but merely copied it along with other mistaken dates from an earlier writer in 1615, who is as little to be relied on as a first-hand authority. As will appear below, the early date of birth is quite irreconcilable with the other known facts of Orlando's life, and with the evidence of the inscriptions on his various portraits. It seemed to be supported for a time by Baini's statement in his life of Palestrina that Orlando was choirmaster at St. John Lateran in Rome in 1541, and by the further statement that his First Book of Motets was published in 1545. But no trace of such a book has ever been found, and Baini's statement is proved to be erroneous by the discovery of the precise date of Orlando's presence at Rome as 1553.[3]

It is also Vinchant who has given currency to the story that Orlando's father was found guilty of being a coiner of false money, and that on this account the composer changed his name from Roland de Lattre to Orland de Lassus. This story has been proved to be false by the discovery that the name of the criminal was not de Lattre, but Jehan de Lassus, so that the reason alleged for change of name becomes meaningless. Nor is there any evidence to connect this Jehan with the family of the composer. As Ch. van den Borren assures us, the name de Lassus was

quite a common name in Hainault, being simply a contraction of de là-dessus, and has nothing to do with de Lattre (= de l'âtre), and Roland is simply a variant of Orlande, but the latter was more commonly used in the 16th century.[4] On the ground of local tradition, Sandberger allows that some credence may be given to Vinchant's further statement with regard to the situation of the house in which the composer was born, as also of his having been one of the boy-choristers of the Church of St. Nicolas in Mons. But for a fuller and more trustworthy account of Orlando's early life we must refer to that given by Samuel Quickelberg, a physician to the court of Munich personally acquainted with Orlando, in a biographical dictionary, H. Pantaleon's *Prosopographiae heroum atque illustrium vivorum*, etc., published at Basle in 1565. Quickelberg begins his account with the definite statement that Orlando was born at Mons in 1530. This date is also attested by the inscriptions on various portraits of the composer up to the year 1580, but has against it the inscription on the last portrait of all, an engraving dedicated to Orlando himself by Johann Sadeler, the artist attached to the court of Munich. This inscription reads, 'Aetat. suae LXI. Anno Dñi 1593.' A copy of this engraving appears on the title-page of Orlando's last publication signed by him shortly before his death in 1594, and his epitaph also describes him as aged 62 at the time of his death. Dr. Sandberger would account for these discrepancies of date between the earlier and later portraits on the supposition that Orlando in the last years of his life had come to believe in the later date of birth. But there are also, as Sandberger points out, certain discrepancies in Quickelberg's enumeration of years which would leave the way open to the acceptance of the 1532 date.

Quickelberg relates that from his ninth year Orlando made great progress in his knowledge of music, and the beauty of his voice attracted so much attention that he was thrice abducted, but that on the third occasion his parents permitted him to be taken into the service of Ferdinand Gonzaga, Viceroy of Sicily, who was then commander of the emperor's forces at St. Dizier. This brings us to the year 1544, as it is otherwise known that the siege of St. Dizier took place in July and August of that year. Orlando accompanied Gonzaga first to Sicily, then for a longer period to Milan. After six years, Quickelberg says, Orlando's voice broke, and at the age of 18, Constantin Castriotto took him to Naples, where he lived for three years with the Marquis of Terza. Here Quickelberg's narrative is somewhat inconsistent, or he is loose in his reckoning of years. For if Orlando was six years with

[1] *Beiträge zur Geschichte der bayerischen Hofkapelle unter Orlando di Lasso.* (Leipzig, 1894.)
[2] *Notice biographique*, etc. (1836.)
[3] Casimiri, *Orlando de Lasso, maestro de cappella al Laterano nel 1553.*
[4] Van den Borren, *Orlande de Lassus* (Paris, 1920), p. 2.

Gonzaga before his voice broke at the age of 18, then Orlando can only have been born in 1532. Quickelberg goes on to relate that from Naples Orlando came to Rome, where he was the guest of the Archbishop of Florence for six months, and was then appointed choirmaster to the celebrated Church of St. John Lateran. This latter statement was previously open to doubt, as apart from Baini's reference to it with the mistaken date of 1541, there was no further evidence, but all doubt may now be considered as set at rest by the discovery of some documents which indirectly appear to show that Orlando did actually occupy this post from at least Apr. 1553 to Dec. 1554.[1] According to Quickelberg he was two years altogether in Rome, and was then recalled to Flanders on hearing of the illness of his parents, but arriving too late and finding them dead he accepted the invitation to accompany Cesare Brancaccio, a Neapolitan nobleman and musical amateur, on a visit first to England and then to France, and afterwards settled for two years in Antwerp, where he enjoyed the society of men of rank and culture, rousing their interest in his music, and gaining their esteem and affection. Some doubt has been entertained about this alleged visit to England, as Quickelberg's own reckoning of years hardly leaves room for it, or it must have been of very short duration. Brancaccio indeed is known to have been in England before July 1554, and if Orlando was with him he must have left Rome early in 1554. We know from Orlando himself that he was settled in Antwerp some time before May 1555, and in the preface to his first publication at Antwerp in 1555 he makes no mention of any visit to England, but speaks of having come straight from Rome to Antwerp, and in the dedication of his Cantiones of 1562 he mentions only Italy, France and Flanders as countries known to him. Apart from this last point, and making allowance for discrepancies of dates, we may accept Quickelberg's account of the successive phases of Orlando's youthful career as true in the main, whether 1530 or 1532 be taken as the year of birth.

By his 22nd or 23rd year he had already obtained a very extensive and varied experience of life in the society of distinguished patrons, and besides his musical talents he must have had remarkably engaging social qualities to have secured the favour of so many in high positions. It also says much for his strength of character in his youthful years that in spite of the dissipations of court life he found time for the serious study of musical composition. Who were his actual masters we have no means of knowing, but both at Milan and Naples, the two places where he made the longest stay of his adolescent years, there were musicians of distinction from whom

he may have learned to pay less attention to the scholastic formalities of canon and cantus firmus than was customary at Rome, and rather to concentrate his efforts on the art of expression by a freer system of counterpoint and chordal harmony.

ANTWERP PUBLICATIONS.—With his settlement in Antwerp at the end of 1554 or the beginning of 1555, there is no longer any uncertainty with regard to the details of Orlando's career. He emerges to the light of day as the fully-equipped musician with an already strongly marked individuality of style. His two first publications appeared in 1555, one indeed printed at Venice, which may have been left or sent there shortly before his arrival in Antwerp. This was his First Book of Italian Madrigals a 5, containing 22, not reckoning second parts separately, mostly on verses by Petrarch. The madrigal was then the highest and most refined form of secular music, and its cultivation exercised a beneficial influence on the composition of the Latin motet and Mass by calling for greater attention to the proper expression of words and sentiments. It was in 1555 that Palestrina also published his First Book of Madrigals, and it is interesting to notice from the first the difference of style of the two great masters, in that while Palestrina endeavours to express the general sentiment of the words by smooth flowing melodic phrases, Orlando aims at emphasising the significance of particular words by abrupt turns of melody and harmony, and also by unusual chromatic modulations. Orlando's other publication of 1555 is even more interesting, as showing from the first the remarkably versatile and cosmopolitan character of his musical activity. It is a miscellaneous collection of Italian madrigals and villanellas, French chansons and Latin motets, all a 4. This was published by Tylman Susato of Antwerp in two editions, one with an Italian title and dedication by Orlando, the other with a longer French title and without dedication, and then again in the same year there was another edition printed by Waelrant and Laet, rivals of Susato in the Antwerp publishing trade, all which seems to show that Orlando's works were already being much sought after. His dedication is addressed to a Signor Stefano, an Antwerp musical dilettante, who expected from the composer music easily understood and generally pleasing. The book may be said to satisfy these requirements. The 7 madrigals, one of which is a sestina, are written in a more spontaneous and less artificial style than those of the First Book a 5. These are followed by 6 villanellas, the fruits no doubt of his earlier stay at Naples, which differ from the madrigals in being of a humorous character and written in a lighter and more popular style with the simplest homophonic

---

[1] Casimiri, *op. cit.*

XLI

PALESTRINA

Portrait by an unknown artist in the Vatican

ORLANDO DI LASSO

From a painting at the Erziehungsinstitut, Munich

harmony and repetition in several verses. The villanella was originally a simple popular song current in the territory of Naples, which was often sung with an improvised three-part harmony consisting of a free use of consecutive fifths and thirds. When first adopted as an art-form about 1545, it continued to be written in this rustic style of harmony with the tune at the top, and such compositions were styled 'Canzoni villanesche alla Napolitana,' and afterwards 'Napolitane' simply. There is one example by Orlando of this rustic style of three-part harmony with consecutive fifths in a composition entitled Moresca contained in a collection 'Il terzo libro delle villotte alla Napolitana de diversi con due moresche,' which first appeared in 1560. But by his use of four-part harmony in the book of 1555 he gave greater refinement to this class of work, though it also appears that in some of these pieces his tenor part is simply adopted from an earlier composer of such trifles. The 6 French chansons [1] which come next are of a sentimental cast, exquisite miniatures in the madrigal style with perhaps some influence from the villanella, though this latter influence is more apparent afterwards in the chansons of a comic or satirical character. Then come 4 Latin motets, which are remarkable as showing from the first Orlando's marked predilection in church music for the composition of texts of a deeply penitential or meditative prayerful character, in which generally speaking he was more successful than in the composition of texts of a joyous festival character. As Ch. van den Borren says, the sentiment of penitence is expressed with a singular intensity in the two motets on texts from the Office of the Dead, 'Peccantem me quotidie' and 'Domine quando veneris.' The appearance of such works so early in his career seems to show that in spite of the dissipations of the brilliant court life to which he had been accustomed, and with the keen appreciation of the humorous aspects of life which find expression in so much of his secular work, there was still a vein of deep religion in his nature which found sincere expression in his church music. With all his keen interest in the ordinary social life of the world, he was not too much a man of the world to ignore the higher interests and aspects of human life. At the end of this miscellaneous work of 1555 there are two secular pieces with Latin words, one 'Alma Nemes,' by Orlando, the other 'Calami sonum ferentes,' by Cyprian de Rore, which are remarkable as being very bold experiments for the time in chromatic writing, showing the desire to illustrate particular words and phrases by unusual chromatic progressions and harmonies, as for instance in 'Alma Nemes,'

[1] The first of the chansons, 'Las voulez-vous qu'une personne chante,' is published with English words in L. Benson's Oriana Series.

specially on the words 'Simul dulce novumque melos.' Orlando seems to have been influenced in this direction by Cyprian, whose acquaintance he may have made in Italy, and therefore included in his own publication an example by Cyprian, as if to justify his own attempt. This indeed is implied by the words in the title of the French edition, 'à la nouvelle composition d'aucuns d'Italie.' In the Magnum Opus of 1604 'Alma Nemes' was provided with sacred words beginning 'Alme Deus,' retaining wherever possible the original words, and in this edition we might even see a punning reference to Cyprian in the chromatic treatment of the words 'rore tegens.'

In 1556 Orlando published another important work at Antwerp, his First Book of Motets, 12 a 5 and 6 a 6. This book is dedicated to Antoine Perrenot, Bishop of Arras, afterwards more generally known as the statesman Cardinal Granvelle, who had just recently in 1555, become chief minister to Philip II. of Spain for the government of the Netherlands. In the dedication Orlando expresses his gratitude for benefits already received, describing Perrenot as being at that time his only patron and benefactor, and calls his special attention to the first motet of the book, 'Delitiae Phoebi,' on verses written in his praise, in which the composer also makes a strong appeal for his further patronage by the words 'Musarum famulum ne despice, sustine Lassum,' duly emphasised in their musical setting. Evidently Orlando was just then anxious to obtain some permanent church position in the Netherlands through the patronage of this powerful statesman bishop. Another motet, a 5, 'Te spectant, Reginalde, poli,' is addressed to Cardinal Pole, with a flattering pun upon his name. Orlando may have come in contact with Pole through Bishop Perrenot on some occasion of Pole's passage through Antwerp. The verses were also probably written by Orlando himself, and suggest that his political and religious sympathies were all on the Roman side in the great controversies of the day. Two motets a 6, 'Heroum Soboles' and 'Si qua tibi obtulerint,' are addressed to the Emperor Charles V., indirectly soliciting his patronage by lauding his merits as a musical connoisseur and a generous patron of musicians. 'Heroum Soboles' is written in a very jubilant style with mostly homophonic harmony. 'Si qua tibi obtulerint' is mistakenly described in the Breitkopf & Härtel edition of Orlando's Magnum Opus [2] as addressed to Bishop Perrenot, but the last line plainly shows that the reference is to the Emperor, 'maxima (merces) laudari principis ore boni,' and in the original edition it is an immediate sequel to the 'Heroum Soboles.' It is also noticeable for its combination of texts, the second alto having only the words, 'aequabit

[2] See below, under POSTHUMOUS PUBLICATIONS.

laudes nulla camena tuas,' with its musical phrase as cantus firmus throughout. Of the church motets in this publication the penitential pieces are again remarkable for a peculiar intensity of expression. 'Gustate et videte,' a 5, has a story attached to it which will be referred to later on. 'Fremuit spiritu Jesus', a 6, the story of the resurrection of Lazarus, is written in a very dramatic style, the second soprano having only in long sustained notes the words, 'Lazare veni foras,' which the other voices take up after the word 'exclamavit,' and repeat with greater emphasis. Orlando does not often use the strict canon form, but we may just note his impressive setting of 'Creator omnium Deus,' with its canon in subdiapente post unum tempus between second soprano and second tenor. This piece concludes with the words, 'Da pacem in diebus nostris,' and the two pieces which follow are two quite different, but both considered to be fine, settings of the whole of this antiphon, 'Da pacem,' the second piece using the plainsong melody in the tenor. The circumstances of the time may have induced Orlando to conclude his work with these three earnest prayers for peace.

RESIDENCE AT MUNICH.—It was probably through his patron, the Bishop of Arras, who had relations with the Bavarian court, that Orlando was recommended to the notice of Albert V., Duke of Bavaria, who was just then anxious to increase and reorganise the musical resources of his chapel at Munich by recruiting new members from the Netherlands. Quickelberg dates Orlando's engagement in 1557, but Sandberger is able to show that Orlando must have been already at Munich before the end of 1556. A MS. mass by him in Munich already bears the date 1556, and his first quarter's salary is paid from some time in December. Ludwig Daser still remained Kapellmeister, and Orlando was at first engaged simply as one of the singers or chamber musicians, but occupied an exceptional position, having a higher salary than the others, and even than Daser himself, apart from what Daser received for the maintenance and instruction of the choir-boys. From December 1557 he received 200 florins per annum. In 1558 he married Regina Weckinger, daughter of a lady of the Munich court. A very expressive motet a 5, 'Sponsa, quid agis, mea lux,' first published in the Magnum Opus of 1604, is thought to have been written and composed by Orlando to celebrate the occasion of his own marriage. In the 'Secondo libro delle Muse, a 4,' published at Rome by A. Barré in 1558, appeared a madrigal by Orlando, 'Deh or foss' io,' which Ch. van den Borren considers a real pearl of madrigal composition, and which it is interesting to compare with Palestrina's setting of the same words as the first number of his First Book of Madrigals

a 4, 1555. We may specially notice the simple way in which Orlando endeavours to illustrate the single word 'addormentato.' In 1559 appeared his Second Book of Madrigals a 5, containing 10 numbers, beginning with a sestina, but also including 3 contributions by other composers. But most of these pieces had previously appeared in 'Secondo Libro delle Muse a 5,' published at Rome in 1557, with a dedicatory preface by a Roman admirer of Orlando's works, which he describes as 'full of sweetness and art.' He was unwilling that these 'fruits of a most rare genius,' which he had already obtained from the composer himself in Rome, should be withheld from the public. The madrigals of the second book of 1559 might thus appear to be earlier than those which Orlando had selected for his first book of 1555, and they are less chromatic with more use of homophonic harmony after the manner of the Villanellas. In 1560 two different editions of what is described as the First Book of Madrigals a 4, appeared, one at Rome, the other at Venice, containing the seven madrigals of the miscellaneous collection of 1555, with two new ones different in each case. Publishers seem to have had a free hand in these matters. These parallel publications were afterwards combined in 1569 as together constituting Orlando's First Book of Madrigals a 4, containing 11 numbers which was then frequently reprinted. 1560 was also the year of publication of a large number of chansons in the collections of Le Roy and Ballard in Paris, and of Peter Phalèse in Louvain. Among them may be specially mentioned 'Mon cœur se recommende à vous,' a 5[1]; 'Le Rossignol' and 'Susanne un jour,' both a 5, which reappear in Yonge's Musica Transalpina of 1588, where also are independent settings of the same texts by Alfonso Ferrabosco. In Ferrabosco's setting of 'Susanne un jour,' we may just notice a slight resemblance in the soprano part to some of Orlando's phrases. As Ferrabosco is known to have been intimate with Byrd, it may have been he who called Byrd's attention to Orlando's settings, and incited him to provide his independent settings of the English words, 'Susanna fair,' a 5, in his 'Psalms and Sonnets' of 1588, and in 1589, 'Susanna fair' and 'The Nightingale,' a 3.[2] But what is also worth mentioning and apparently has not been noticed before, is that Giles Farnaby in his setting of 'Susanna fair,'[3] a 4 in his book of 1598, has simply taken over Orlando's soprano part into his own soprano as a cantus firmus in longer notes for his independent counterpoint in shorter notes in the other voices. Included with the chansons of 1560 there is an interesting setting a 6 of the first ten lines of dialogue from Virgil's First Eclogue, 'Tityre tu

[1] Edited by L. Benson, with English words in Arion, vol. i.
[2] See Eng. Madr. Sch. vol. xiv. 29, and vol. xv. 8 and 9.
[3] See ibid. vol. xx. 12.

patulae,' almost entirely with homophonic harmony and with a fairly close observance of Latin quantities. In 1561 Orlando's only publications are three madrigals of an elegiac character contributed to the 'Terzo Libro delle Muse a 5,' published by Gardano at Venice, one of which, ' Oh d' amarissime onde,' is reprinted in Hawkins's *History*. It is also perhaps of some interest to note that in this collection Orlando appears in company with Palestrina, who contributes 8 numbers, one of which, very popular, ' Io son ferito,' Orlando afterwards takes as the title and basis of one of his masses. In the 'Terzo Libro delle Muse a 4,' published by Anton Barré at Rome in 1562, are three more madrigals by Orlando, simpler and more homophonic, but graceful and expressive.

In June 1562 a more important work saw the light. Orlando published at Nuremburg his ' Sacrae cantiones 5 vocum,' dedicated to Duke Albert, containing 25 numbers. This work shows the master in the full possession of all the resources of his art for the devout expression of the various phases of personal religious feeling from penitential sorrow and prayerful meditation to joyous praise and thanksgiving. Without specifying particular masterpieces, we may just note as characteristic of his style his fondness for the picturesque illustration of prominent words and phrases, as in ' Videntes stellam Magi ' and ' Jerusalem plantabis ' ; in ' O Domine salvum fac,' on the words ' non moriar, sed vivam,' and in the very expressive ' Quam benignus ' the words ' in silentio.' The strangest instance is perhaps on the word ' laborem ' in ' Deus qui sedes.' ' Clare sanctorum,' an old sequence of the 9th century for the Feasts of Apostles, may be referred to as showing how Orlando got over the difficulty of setting a list of names, by using the old melody of Notker Balbulus as a cantus firmus in one or other of the voices. Proske esteemed this work very highly, describing it as ' eine höchst werthvolle Komposition.'

From 1563, if not somewhat earlier, Orlando became full Kapellmeister at Munich, Ludwig Daser retiring on a handsome pension. The circumstances of Daser's retirement are somewhat obscure. He was not so much older than Orlando, and was a composer of talent. It has been thought that through prolonged ill-health he may have been no longer equal to the duties of his position, specially in view of the increase of the staff of musicians, but religion also may have had something to do with the matter. Daser would appear to have had Lutheran sympathies, and though in 1556 and before the final sessions of the Council of Trent, Albert V., like Ferdinand of Austria, had been obliged to make concessions to Protestant feeling by allowing the communion of the cup to the laity in the mass, and by a relaxation of strict rules

of fasting, from 1563 onwards these privileges were being gradually withdrawn, under the influence of the Jesuit mission in Bavaria, until in 1569 they were absolutely revoked, and the old form of religion was definitely reestablished. Daser continued to live in Munich for some years afterwards, until he accepted another post at the Lutheran court of Würtemberg, but his pension was not withdrawn, and in 1578 he published at Munich a setting of the Passion a 4, which he dedicated to Duke Albert in gratitude, as he says, for the singular clemency of the Duke towards him and for many exceptional kindnesses.[1] All this speaks well for the Duke as for Daser, and a pension was still allowed by the Bavarian court to Daser's widow as late as 1601.

THE PENITENTIAL PSALMS.—To Orlando and his compositions special honour was now shown by Duke Albert. At his instance Orlando had undertaken the composition of the Seven Penitential Psalms, and the task was evidently very congenial to the mind of the composer. The Duke admired these works so highly that he had them beautifully transcribed on parchment and adorned with miniatures by his court painter, Hans Mülich, and then handsomely bound in two folio volumes in red morocco with silver clasps. The carrying out of the Duke's wishes occupied several years, from 1563–70. In the first volume, completed in 1565, is a portrait[2] of the composer without any indication of age, but with this inscription round the outside of the oval, ' In corde prudentis requiescit sapientia et indoctos quosque erudiet. Prov. xiii.' In the second volume, which was not completed till 1570, is another portrait full-length with the inscription, ' Imago excellentissimi musici Orlandi de Lassus suae aetatis 40 anno.' With these volumes are associated two others, smaller, one containing Quickelberg's commendatory notice of Orlando's music, and an explanation of the first set of miniatures ; the other has a continuation of this explanation written by some one else after Quickelberg's death in 1567.

Quickelberg describes Orlando's music as being of the style known as ' musica reservata,' which he explains as that which aims at the dramatic expression of the words. These four volumes are some of the chief treasures of the State Library at Munich. Ambros observes that ' if any music ever merited a splendid outward adornment as a symbol of its intrinsic value, it is that of these Psalms. Besides their masterly construction they have a quite peculiar colouring of spiritual nobility, and a magical fragrance of beauty hovers over them.' So, too, Van den Borren writes :

[1] Pro singulari Celsitudinis tuae in me clementia multisque eximiis beneficiis.
[2] This portrait, with others, is reproduced in Sandberger's *Beiträge*, Bd. 1.

'The celebrity of this work is justified by its exceptional merit. It is marvellous that, having to treat a subject relatively monotonous, Orlando has remained throughout equal to his task. Without any failure of inspiration he makes to pass before us all the states of soul which the Psalmist describes, ranging from the profoundest grief to the brightest hope. . . . All this he has depicted in a musical language ideally concise, in which the madrigalesque element intervenes largely, but with the utmost discretion and with a most exquisite sense of proportion.'

These Psalms are written mainly *a* 5, but always with several verses interspersed as duos, trios, and quartets, and the last verse 'Sicut erat' always more elaborately set *a* 6. The duos and trios are specially masterly in construction. The 'De profundis' has in one or other of the voices the 6th Psalm tone as cantus firmus, which in two of the verses is treated in canon form. To the Psalms of Penitence [1] there is appended the two Laudate Psalms 148 and 150, treated as one Psalm in four divisions.

VARIOUS PUBLICATIONS.—The only publication of Orlando in 1563 was the Third Book of Madrigals *a* 5, not, however, issued by Orlando himself, but consisting of 13 older and newer pieces collected and edited by the publisher Antonio Barré in Rome. In 1564 appeared two books of chansons, one published by Jacob Susato at Antwerp containing 27 numbers *a* 4, short pieces mostly of a humorous or satirical character, the other published by Phalèse at Louvain, with similar pieces *a* 4 and 5, including three with Latin words. Some numbers *a* 4 are common to both publications.[2] It is interesting to notice in so many of Orlando's publications the strange mixture of sacred and secular work. So in Susato's publication we find ' Du fond de ma pensée,' Marot's translation of Psalm 130, with the Huguenot Psalm tune in the tenor. In Phalèse there appears for the first time the mediæval drinking-song, 'Fertur in conviviis,' set *a* 4 in a striking fashion, which in the Magnum Opus of 1604 has the words slightly altered to express quite opposite sentiments. It had been previously adapted in 1576 to new words, 'Tristis ut Eurydicen,' as an elegy on the death of the older master Clemens non Papa. This transformation may have been suggested by the use which Orlando makes of the plain-song 'Requiem' at the conclusion. Whether Orlando had anything to do with these alterations of text must remain uncertain. In Phalèse we have again the curious mixture of the sacred with the outrageously secular. With ' Fertur in conviviis ' there are two motets *a* 5, ' Pater peccavi,' and ' Quid prodest stulto,' the latter noticeable for its peculiar cantus firmus in the tenor with the words ' Vanitas

[1] A modern edition of the Seven Penitential Psalms was issued by S. W. Dehn in 1838.
[2] From th.m have been edited separately in modern form such pieces as ' Bon jour, mon coeur ' with English words in L. Benson's Oriana Series, the amusing ' Quand mon mari ' by Barclay Squire, and ' Qui dort ici ' by H. Expert.

vanitatum, omnia est vanitas.' To the great collection in 5 volumes entitled ' Thesaurus musicus,' published at Nuremberg in 1564 by Montanus and Neuber and dedicated by them to Duke Albert of Bavaria, Orlando contributes a considerable number of new motets. In the first volume *a* 8 we find the splendid piece ' Confitebor tibi ' written in the Venetian style for two responsive choirs, immediately followed by the satirical parody of a church hymn ' Jam lucis orto sidere,' in the form of a drinking - song ; very cleverly written for two choirs in homophonic harmony, but rather out of place in this collection, into which one might think it had only gained admission in virtue of its title. The second volume *a* 7 has two very fine motets by Orlando, ' Estote misericordes ' and ' Decantabat Israel.' The third volume *a* 6 has 5 new motets among them ' Timor et tremor,' remarkable for its depth of expression by the appropriate use of chromatic semitones. The fourth volume *a* 5 has four new motets, including ' Confisus Domino,' with its interestingly varied cantus firmus with the words ' Confide et ama.' In the fifth volume *a* 4 is a fine complete setting of Psalm 64, ' Te Decet,' in short sections verse by verse with purely syllabic declamation. One might wish to have had more psalms set in this simple style. In 1565 Orlando published, with a dedication to Duke Albert, ' Sacrae lectiones novem ex propheta Job ' *a* 4, the lessons from the Vigil Office of the Dead. This is one of the more important works of the master, but no modern complete edition of it is yet available for study. It furnishes one of many indications from his works generally how, with all his capacity for the humorous enjoyment of ordinary life in the world, and apart from the urgency of any special occasion, his mind, like that of Sebastian Bach and Johannes Brahms, was apt to brood deeply over the mystery of death. A second book of ' Sacrae cantiones ' *a* 5 and 6 was published at Venice in 1565, consisting of motets which had come into the hands of Guelio Bonagiunta of St. Mark's, Venice, an industrious collector of good compositions, who had received Orlando's permission to publish them. This was followed in 1566 by a third book published by Gardano, containing the motets of 1556 with some additions, and a fourth book containing new motets *a* 6 and 8, but these editions were superseded by more comprehensive collections afterwards which we shall have occasion to mention later on. To Bonagiunta's collection of madrigals by various composers, entitled ' Il Desiderio,' Orlando contributed a sestina, which is interesting for some strange experiments in chromatic harmony with a view to greater expressiveness.

THE MUNICH CHAPEL.—In 1567 Orlando

travelled to Venice to engage new singers and instrumentalists for the Bavarian court. Here, anticipating a little, we may mention that among those engaged about this time whose names appear on the pay-rolls of the Munich court from 1568 onwards, were some distinguished musicians who were also composers of merit, as Antonio Morari, who became leader of the instrumentalists (capo della musica instrumentale), Gioseffo Guami and Ivo de Vento, who were appointed organists, Francesco Guami, Simone Gatti and Fileno Cornazzano, trumpet or trombone players; Anton Gosswin, a pupil of Orlando, who was one of the alto singers, and had charge of some of the choir-boys, and Massimo Trojano, an alto singer and comedian, who has left us some interesting accounts of the Munich court and its affairs. With them may be mentioned Johann von Lockenburg, a musician of older date in the ducal service, one of whose MS. masses, 'Orsus à coup' a 4, has been mistakenly attributed to Orlando. At its maximum, the musical staff of the Bavarian court, employed in church and chamber service, consisted of about 90 members—60 vocalists (including the boys) and 30 instrumentalists. The instrumental music of the time was elementary. It consisted mainly in doubling the voice parts with the voices, or in playing the voice-parts without the voices. The motet collections of the time, like the Thesaurus Musicus of 1564, describe their contents as ' ad omnis generis instrumenta musica accomodatas.' (Q.-L.) In compositions a 8 for two choirs, instruments would frequently take the place of one of the two choirs. In chamber music there was also the frequent practice of one part being sung by a single voice while the lute alone or lute and viols played the other voice parts. But already in 1547 and 1559 Jacques Buus and Adrian Willaert had published pieces entitled Ricercari or Fantasie, meant to be played by instruments alone, although written very much in the vocal style. A step further was taken by the Spanish musician Diego Ortiz, engaged as choir-master to the Vice-regal Chapel at Naples, whom it is possible Orlando may there have met, and who published at Rome in 1553, just when Orlando was also there, a treatise [1] showing in much detail how madrigals might be converted into instrumental pieces by one or other instrument playing one of the vocal parts in a style of florid variation, while the other parts were played simply as originally written. We may add that an instrumental ' Symphonie a 6,' alleged to be written by Orlando, is given in Wasielewski's Geschichte der Instrumental Musik im 16ten Jahrhundert (Berlin, 1878), which, however, is written in a purely vocal style.

Returning from this digression, we may follow Orlando on his journey from Venice to Ferrara to present in person his Fourth Book of Madrigals a 5, just recently printed at Venice, to Alfonso II., Duke of Ferrara. Orlando had previously come into contact with Duke Alfonso, on occasion of a visit paid by the Duke to Munich to his relative Duke Albert. Alfonso had then expressed himself greatly pleased with a sestina of Orlando's sung in his presence, and had handsomely rewarded the composer. In his dedication Orlando tactfully recalls this incident, and expresses the hope that his Book of Madrigals would be equally pleasing to the Duke. But on this occasion he was coldly received and would have been dismissed without reward, had not the Florentine ambassador at Ferrara intervened on Orlando's behalf to avoid diplomatic difficulties, and save the credit of the Duke. The book itself, containing 12 numbers including two lengthy pieces, sestinas, deserved a better reception, as it shows a great advance on the composer's previous work of the kind, a greater refinement of workmanship and expression, with a more restrained use of chromatic modulation. Another publication of 1567 is a Book of Magnificats on the eight tones, printed at Nuremburg, with 24 numbers, 8 a 4, 8 a 5, 8 a 6, the alternate verses only being composed, the others being sung in unison to the proper tone in each case. The 8 numbers a 4,[2] are very simple and concise, mostly with homophonic harmony, the others a 5 and 6 are more elaborate, some verses being set as duos or trios, etc. A third publication of the year, printed at Munich, is even more important as testimony to the versatility of Orlando's genius, his first book of compositions to German words. Its full title is ' Neue teutsche Liedlein mit fünff Stimmen welche ganz lieblich zu singen und auf allerley Instrumenten zu gebrauchen.' It was dedicated to Duke William, the eldest son of Duke Albert, and has 15 numbers, including three religious pieces, two being settings of Lutheran hymns, ' Vater Unser ' and ' Ich ruf zu dir, Herr Jesu Christ,' with their proper tunes used as a free cantus firmus; the other, 'Wie lang, O Gott, in meiner Noth,' is throughout Orlando's own composition. The other numbers are German songs of a popular humorous character. With Duke William, Orlando stood on a more confidential footing than with his father, on terms, indeed, of an intimate personal friendship, as a large number of letters which have been preserved, shows. Through the intervention of Duke William he was enabled to obtain a grant from the ducal treasury of 1000 florins, for the purchase of a convenient house near the court. His salary in 1567 was raised to

---

[1] Tratado de glosas sobre clausulas y otros generos de puntos en la musica de violones (Roma, 1553). This work has been reprinted Berlin, 1913.

[2] They may be found in Proske's Musica divina tom. iii. pp. 253-81.

280 florins. In 1568 took place the marriage of Duke William to Renata or Renée, daughter of Duke Francis of Lorraine. Massimo Trojano in his books entitled *Discorsi* and *Dialogi*, published 1568 and 1569, has left a detailed account of the musical and dramatic festivities on this occasion, in which Orlando took a prominent part, not only as director of the music, but to the great delight of the illustrious guests, as a comic actor in an improvised Italian commedia dell' arte. A Te Deum *a* 6 and some masses were specially composed by him for the occasion, also two motets, ' Quid trepidas ' *a* 6, and ' Gratia sola Dei ' *a* 5-6. The Te Deum is composed very elaborately, only, however, the even verses and the Sanctus, the other odd verses being sung antiphonally in unison plain-song. Some verses are set as duos, trios, quatuors, sung no doubt by select solo-voices. The motet ' Gratia sola Dei ' is a setting of 14 hexameter lines, the first letters of which form the acrostic ' Guilhelmus-Renea.' Massimo [1] Trojano tells us that this was sung at table, and during the singing of the second part *a* 4 by four select voices, all present were so spellbound by the singing as to stop in the middle of their feasting to listen intently to the sweet harmonies, and at the end of the third part *a* 6, Orlando was greatly applauded.

MOTETS AND CHANSONS.—In 1568 two comprehensive collections of Orlando's motets were published at Nuremberg, in which these works were included, one ' Selectissimae cantiones ' *a* 6 to 10, including, with considerable additions, all that had previously appeared *a* 6 to 8 in the Venetian publications of 1565, 1566, making altogether 38 numbers *a* 6, 3 *a* 7, 4 *a* 8, 1 *a* 10; the other, similarly including what had appeared, *a* 5 and 4, making 39 numbers *a* 5, and 11 *a* 4. These new collections would seem to have been intended to oust the Italian editions from the German market. There may have been a certain amount of jealousy between German and Italian publishers. Among the motets *a* 6 we may notice the effective epic-dramatic settings of the liturgical Gospels for Christmas and Epiphany-tide : ' In principio erat verbum,' ' Cum natus esset Jesus,' ' Nuptiae factae sunt,' also some splendid settings of Church hymns, ' Jesu nostra redemptio,' ' Vexilla regis,' etc., without any reference to their plain-song tunes, but with beautiful duos and trios for solo voices interspersed. Among shorter pieces *a* 6, the best known is the quiet but very expressive ' In Monte Oliveti.' A beautiful Passion piece is also ' Huc me sidereo,' with a fine trio in the middle. Nor can we altogether pass by those pieces in which Orlando gives us his solemn meditations on the mystery of death, such as ' O mors, quam amara ' (Eccles. xli.

vv. 1-3),[2] the same verses which Brahms has set in his ' Ernste Gesänge,' in connection with which we may notice the strange coincidence that in the Magnum Opus of 1604 this motet is immediately followed by a splendid setting of the Pauline verses in praise of charity (1 Cor. xiii.) just as in Brahms. Other motets of the same kind are 'Audi Tellus,' 'Anni nostri,' and specially ' Libera me Domine,' with its cantus firmus of five descending notes of the diatonic scale to the words ' Respice finem.' There are also some fine compositions of complete psalms, ' Beatus vir qui non abiit,' ' Lauda Jerusalem,' with verses set as trios and quartets. It is exceptional that the Psalm Jubilate should be set with a cantus firmus, ' Si Deus nobiscum, quis contra nos.' There is one striking motet set ' chromatico more,' ' Concupiscendo concupiscat.' The last piece *a* 10, ' Quo properas, facunde nepos Atlantis,' as also ' Edite Cesareo ' *a* 8, are brilliantly composed panegyrics of Duke Albert. In the companion publication *a* 5 we may just notice some secular pieces, which by slight changes of the words were afterwards, much to their advantage, transformed into sacred motets, ' Ave color vini clari,' changed to ' Ave decus coeli clari,' and ' Quis mihi . . . dulcissima Phylli,' a disappointed lover's farewell to life transformed into the prayer of a penitent sinner, ' Quid tibi . . . dulcissime Jesu.' Even in the edition of 1567 itself two pieces with somewhat objectionable secular words in earlier books of chansons, ' Alma Venus ' (1560) and ' Veux-tu ton mal ' (1564), were provided with new sacred words, 'Christe Patris Verbum' and ' Alleluia vox laeta.' In all these cases the music seems even more appropriate to the sacred than to the original secular words. The comic spelling piece on the words ' Super flumina Babylonis,' though it serves to show Orlando's love of fun and persiflage, might well have been dispensed with. His fondness for combination of appropriate texts is once more exhibited in ' Tu Domine benignus es,' with its cantus firmus, ' clamantem ad te, exaudi me Domine.'

In 1569 appeared another book of motets, ' Cantiones aliquot,' 13 numbers *a* 5, 1 *a* 6, published at Munich and dedicated to the Custos of Augsburg Cathedral, in which the most interesting numbers are three [3] Christmas pieces, ' Quem vidistis pastores,' ' Resonet in laudibus ' (which makes use of the old German tune to these words), and ' Sidus ex claro,' also the concluding number of the book, ' Quemadmodum desiderat cervus,' [4] *a* 6, with its canon ad septimam. One madrigal *a* 7 appeared in a Venetian collection of this year.

---

[1] In more modern times Proske speaks of these works in the highest terms of praise.

[2] Strangely enough, the modern editor of the Magnum Opus (Haberl) has overlooked the scriptural origin of these words, ascribing them to a contemporary. It may also be noted that the last word of the motet, ' sapientiam,' should be corrected into ' patientiam,' as in the Vulgate.
[3] The first two of these have been edited with English words by Sir F. Bridge.
[4] Also edited with English words by Bridge.

It is a sonnet of Petrarch, ' Che fai, alma,' a dialogue of the poet with his own soul, which is also treated dialogue-wise in the music by the alternation of the three higher voices with the four lower, all uniting on the last line of the poem. In this year, too, Massimo Trojano brought out at Venice a collection of madrigals *a* 5 by all the composer-musicians of the Bavarian court, including Orlando and himself, but unfortunately this book has not been preserved complete, the tenor part being missing. Trojano intended to have followed this up with a second book, but, although in his *Dialogi* he had been so loud in his praises of the pleasant and peaceful life at Munich of all the musicians of the court, it was he himself who was the first to break up this beautiful harmony, by being concerned with another in the following year, 1570, in a murderous attack on one of his fellow-musicians, which obliged him to flee the country, and we hear no more of him.

In January 1570 Orlando published at Munich and dedicated as a new-year gift to the Abbot of Weingarten in Würtemberg another book of ' Cantiones sacrae,' containing 10 numbers *a* 6 (not reckoning separate parts) and 3 dialogues *a* 8. The abbot had expressed the wish to have some original compositions of Orlando. One of Orlando's pupils, Jacob Reiner, had come from the abbey school of Weingarten, and was afterwards choirmaster there. In this book there are three complete psalms in several divisions with verses *a* 3 and 4, of all of which Proske in his Annotations speaks in terms of highest praise, and we may just note the greater liveliness of manner in the setting of the psalm ' Cum invocarem,' which shows the extraordinary variety in Orlando's style of composition. Van den Borren considers the Easter motet ' Ego sum qui sum ' the pearl of this set. Of greater importance for Orlando's growing reputation in France was the publication in Paris in this year by Le Roy and Ballard of a book of ' Mellanges cont. plusieurs chansons tant en vers latin qu'en ryme françoyse a 4, 5, 6, 8, 10 parties.' This publication was ushered into the world with a portrait of the composer, 'Aet. suae 39,' accompanied with a series of lengthy laudatory verses by Gohory and Jodelle, concluding with a sonnet by Jodelle to a female singer of the day, which shows that Orlando's works were often sung by a single voice, while instruments played the other vocal parts. The Latin pieces in this book are all secular, and taken from earlier publications, with the exception of two which appear for the first time, ' Deus qui bonum vinum,' *a* 4, a somewhat profane piece, which in the Magnum Opus of 1604 was transformed into a sacred penitential piece by a clever slight alteration of words [1]; and ' Dulces

exuviae,' Dido's lament in Virgil's *Æneid*, Book iv., set *a* 5 and 6, in a severely homophonic style of solemn grandeur, more epically descriptive than properly dramatic, as Van den Borren observes. Of the chansons along with some of earlier date, 13 appear for the first time, among them the nonsense verses ' un jour vis un foulon,' which, as afterwards provided with English words beginning ' Monsieur Mingo,' J. F. R. Stainer has shown to be the song partly quoted as sung by Silence in Shakespeare's *Henry IV*. pt. 2, act v. sc. 3, and in the usual editions with the unintelligible word ' Samingo,' which he rightly suggests should be read ' Sir Mingo.' [2] The other songs *a* 4 are also of a humorous cast; a few *a* 5 written more on the madrigal style are of a sentimental character, one ' Vive sera,' on verses by Orlando himself in praise of friendship, in which he introduces his name Lassus. In 1570 Phalèse of Louvain published a collective work comprising four books of chansons by Orlando, Cyprian Rore and Philip de Monte, which, so far as Orlando is concerned, mostly includes work which had appeared elsewhere, but also a set of six new madrigals *a* 4 and one *a* 5, two of which, ' Vien' dolc' Imeneo ' and ' Quando fia mia,' were written to celebrate the marriage in 1565 of Alessandro Farnese, son of Margaret of Parma, with Maria of Portugal.

A further honour was done to Orlando at this time on Dec. 7, 1570, at the Diet of Spires. Emperor Maximilian conferred on him and his posterity a patent of nobility with the grant of a coat of arms,[3] on the shield of which, in recognition of his musical genius, the musical signs of the Diesis, the Bécarre and Bémol, were displayed with other heraldic emblems. This honour might also be regarded as a return compliment for Orlando's greeting to Maximilian in an excellent motet, ' Pacis amans ' *a* 6, on the occasion of his first coronation at Frankfort in 1562 as King of Bohemia and King of the Romans.

VISIT TO THE FRENCH COURT.—Encouraged by the success of his works in Paris, Orlando in 1571 was induced to pay a visit there, provided with recommendations to the French court from the Bavarian Dukes, and his travelling expenses paid from the Bavarian treasury. He was entertained in the house of Adrian Le Roy, his Parisian publisher, and was well received and rewarded by King Charles IX., who had himself some knowledge and skill in music. He had not come empty-handed. In anticipation of his visit he had ready for presentation to the King a new book of chansons *a* 5, with a flattering dedication in verses of his own. The first two pieces in this book are on

---

[1] Original text, ' Deus qui bonum vinum creasti et ex eodem multa capita dolere fecisti, da nobis quaesumus intellectum ut

saltem possimus invenire lectum,' altered *to* ' Deus qui non vis mortem peccantis sed ut de suis velit integre dolere peccatis, da nobis, quaesumus, ut amissum possimus favorem invenire tuum.'
[2] See *Mus. T.*, Feb. 1902, pp. 100-101.
[3] A representation of Orlando's arms is given as a frontispiece to Sandberger's *Beiträge*, iii.

poems by Ronsard, the first originally addressed to King Henry II. of France, but by
Orlando transferred to Charles IX.; the other,
a longer poem in praise of the Queen-mother,
Catherine de Medicis, set in a more brilliant
and varied style, as if indeed it were more important to secure her favour than that of the
weak Charles. No. 10, ' Paisible demain,' is a
fine short setting of a eulogy on Paris as the
city of peace and justice, the Paris which was
to witness in the following year the massacre
of St. Bartholomew, which, however, Orlando
could not foresee, or might even with other
partisans of Rome have approved. The other
pieces are as usual partly humorous, partly
moralising or sentimental, but what is particularly noticeable about them musically is
the adoption into the chanson of the higher
refinements of the madrigal style. There
are 16 numbers a 5 and 2 a 8 in dialogue
form, one of the latter, ' Hola Caron,' of
a semi-dramatic character between a disappointed lover wishful for death and Charon,
the ferryman of Hades, who refuses him a
passage in his boat. The other dialogue, ' O
doux parler,' on verses by Ronsard, consists
more of an interchange of beautiful phrases
between two choirs. Orlando's visit was taken
by Le Roy as a good opportunity for the publication and dedication to King Charles of two
books of motets, consisting of works which had
already appeared elsewhere, but Orlando himself had also ready for publication by Le Roy
a new book of motets a 5, which from Paris he
dedicated to Duke William at Munich. Accompanying the dedication are some French
verses of his own addressed to the Duke and
Duchess, testifying his devotion, at the same
time showing that in spite of the attractions of
the French court he had then no idea of leaving
the Bavarian service. In this book of motets
Van den Borren notes the increased refinement
of style by a greater utilisation of all the expressive methods of the madrigal. One very
striking piece for its wonderful depth of expression is ' Pater Abraham,' a musical transcription of part of the dialogue from the
Gospel parable of Dives and Lazarus. ' Emendemus in melius ' is remarkable for the peculiar
distribution of the words to the different voices,
and here as in similar pieces we may also note
how carefully he underlines the word ' miserere '
wherever it occurs. Of another kind is the fine
Christmas motet with a very melodious cantus
firmus on an ascending and descending hexachord to the words ' Quis audivit talia, dic
mirabilia.' In the last piece, ' Nuntium vobis
fero,' the musical rhythm is adapted to the
poetical metre as in an earlier piece of the same
kind, ' Sidus ex claro.'

FURTHER PUBLICATIONS FROM MUNICH.—On
his return to Munich, Orlando soon had ready
for publication in 1572 by Adam Berg, a second

book of ' Teutsche Liedlein,' 15 numbers a 5,
which he dedicated to Duke Ferdinand, Count
Palatine of the Rhine, the second son of Duke
Albert. In this book there are 5 settings of
Lutheran hymns with their proper tunes as
cantus firmus in the tenor, among them ' Es
sind doch selig alle die,' with Matthäus Greiter's
Strassburg tune, better known afterwards as
adapted to the later hymn, ' O mensch bewein
dein Sünde gross.' Another piece, ' Der
Meye,' is the spiritual version of a popular
song, also with its tune in the tenor. The other
pieces are free settings of humorous and sentimental Volkslieder, in this respect differing
from the French chansons, the verses of which
are usually by witty court poets like Marot, De
Magny and others.

From 1572–79 we have a series of intimate confidential letters [1] of Orlando addressed
to Duke William in a curious medley of languages,
French, Italian, bad Latin, with occasional
German, showing Orlando's exuberant love of
fun and merriment of all sorts, with an occasional tendency to melancholy, especially when
temporarily in disfavour with Duke Albert.
The year 1573 is distinguished by two important publications. One is a composite work
dedicated to four members of the Fugger family
of Augsburg, then greatly esteemed as munificent patrons of music, containing 28 numbers,
6 Latin motets, 6 Italian madrigals, 6 French
chansons, 6 Teutsche Lieder, all a 4, but with
a dialogue a 8 to each set of 6. The other publication of 1573 is the first volume of a series
entitled ' Patrocinium musices,' undertaken on
the responsibility of Duke William, for which
Adam Berg, the music-printer of Munich, had
provided specially large and entirely new type.
A portrait of Duke William appears as a frontispiece to the first volume, and the music is not
in separate partbooks as usual, but the separate parts are together on opposite pages. In
the dedication Orlando enlarges on the nature
and mission of music in its connexion with
religion, and eulogises the princely house of
Bavaria for the energy and constancy with
which in troublous times it had upheld the
interests both of church music and Catholic
piety. The first volume has 21 motets, 7 a 4,
7 a 5, and 7 a 6, works all remarkably interesting
from the great variety both of technique and
expression displayed in them. Here in passing
we might just notice, as indeed we might have
done before, the great range of Orlando in the
choice of texts for musical setting. He does
not confine himself, as most musicians of the
time did, to the liturgical texts of the Breviary
and Missal, but ranges freely over the books of
Scripture to find texts which make some sort of
personal appeal to him as the expression of his
own sentiments. He thus often chooses texts

---

[1] The whole correspondence is given at length in Sandberger's
Beiträge, iii.

of a sententious moralising nature which might
seem quite intractable to musical setting,
which, however, by his great mastery as a
sculptor of musical motives he is able to endow
with appropriately picturesque or otherwise
solemnly expressive musical phrases. In the
course of this year 1573 he received a commission from the court of France to compose
some music in connexion with a mythological
ballet and other festivities got up by Catherine
de Medicis to celebrate the election of her
younger son Henry as King of Poland. For
this purpose he composed the introductory
piece, consisting of a Latin dialogue sung between one character representing the kingdom
of France, and other two the allegorical figures
of Peace and Prosperity. Brantome speaks of
Orlando's music as the most melodious that
one had ever heard. Sandberger and Van den
Borren suppose this music to have been lost,
but a comparison of the text as given by Sandberger,[1] with the text of the Latin dialogue *a* 8
in the publication of 1573 dedicated to the
brothers Fugger, shows that the music has not
been lost, but is preserved in the latter piece,
only that the text which was originally intended for the glorification of the French court
has been ingeniously transformed into a glorification of Duke Albert and the Bavarian
house. The very first line indicates the resemblance and yet a significant difference between the two texts. 'Unde recens reditus
Pax Prosperitasque sorores' is altered to 'Unde
revertimini pax religioque sorores.' The piece
would be sung originally by three solo voices
in dialogue, with instruments playing the other
parts.

A letter of Adrian Le Roy informs us that
Charles IX. was so delighted with various
pieces of Orlando performed before him, that he
offered to engage him as chamber musician
with an annual salary of 1200 livres, beginning
Jan. 1, 1574, even paying at once half of this
sum for the previous half year. This proposal
may have been a very tempting one to Orlando,
and one account says that he had already set
out with his family on the journey to Paris, and
had come as far as Frankfort, when he was
met with tidings of the French king's death on
May 20, 1574, and at once returned to Munich.
This account, however, is difficult to reconcile
with what we learn from his letters, that he had
gone to Italy in Feb. 1574 to engage new
musicians for Munich, and was back again in
Munich for some time in May. Sandberger
concludes that already in January or February
Orlando had definitely decided to remain in
Munich. His good relations with Le Roy and
the French court continued unimpaired.
Henry III. allowed him a pension and a special
privilege for the publication of his works.

[1] Bd. xii. of the Breitkopf & Härtel edition of Orlando's works,
pp. xvii-xviii.

THE 'PATROCINIUM MUSICES.' — In 1574
appeared the second and third volumes of the
'Patrocinium musices.' The second volume
contains five of his masses *a* 5, bearing the
titles, 'Ite rime dolenti,' 'Scarco di doglia,'
'Sidus ex claro,' 'Credidi propter,' and
'Le Berger et la bergère.' This volume
was dedicated to Pope Gregory XIII., and
Orlando travelled to Rome to present it in
person to the Pope, the expenses of his journey
and stay in Rome being met by Duke Albert.
He was well received at Rome, and solemnly
invested as Knight of the Golden Spur in the
Papal Chapel. The first two masses in this
volume would seem to take their themes from
two madrigals of Cyprian de Rore. 'Sidus ex
claro,' based on his own motet, is the only one
of the five which has yet appeared in a modern
edition. The rhythmical themes of the motet
might not seem suited to the words of the mass.
These are not indeed the first published masses
of Orlando. Already in 1566 Gardano of
Venice had published in a collection one, 'In te
Domine speravi' *a* 6, and Phalèse of Louvain
in 1570 had similarly published 3 *a* 5. The
third volume of the 'Patrocinium,' dedicated
to the Bishop of Augsburg, contains Orlando's
settings of the Vidi Aquam and Asperges with
the offices for Christmas, Easter, Pentecost
and Corpus Christi. By the 'offices' are
meant the introits and other variable parts of
the mass, based on the plain-song. These are
not reckoned amongst his best compositions,
the plain-song in this case being somewhat of a
drag on the inspiration of the composer. The
fourth volume of the 'Patrocinium' appeared
in 1575, and contains an interesting setting of
the 'Passion according to St. Matthew,' the 9
lessons from the Book of Job *a* 4, which had
already appeared in 1565, and the 3 lessons of
Christmas Matins *a* 4. In the 'Passion' the
parts of an Evangelist and of Christ are understood to be recited in plain-song, while the
other utterances are set *a* 3 to 5. There are 3
other settings of the 'Passion' from the other
Gospels, *a* 5 and 4 by Orlando still preserved
in MS. in the Munich Archives, for an account
of which see Kade 'Die ältere Passionskom-
position' (Gütersloh, 1893), pp. 134-40. In
1575 Cosimo Bottegari, a Florentine lutenist,
very much in favour with Duke Albert, published a second Book of Madrigals *a* 5, in continuation of Trojano's book of 1569, with contributions by the various Bavarian musicians,
including two by Orlando, one *a* 10 or for two
choirs each, *a* 5 and 4 by Orlando still preserved
song. Bottegari, however, shortly afterwards
used his great influence with Duke Albert to
injure Orlando in the Duke's opinion, and it
was with some difficulty that a reconciliation
was brought about through the mediation of
Duke William.

The year 1576 was an important one for

publication. There was first, the fifth volume of the ' Patrocinium,' containing five Magnificats —2 a 4, 1 a 5, and 2 a 8. In the 1 a 5 Orlando departs from the usual way of setting according to the church tone, and takes his themes from a madrigal of Cyprian de Rore. In the 2 a 8, all the verses are set by means of answering chorus a 4. A third book of ' Teutsche Lieder,' 11 nos. a 5, was dedicated to Duke Ernst, third son of Duke Albert. It opens with a fine setting of ' Susannen frumm,' the German version of ' Susanne un jour,' with what seems to be its proper popular tune in the tenor. Some numbers are moralising pieces, others drastically humorous. Under the title of ' Meslanges d'Orlande de Lassus,' Le Roy republished nearly all his previous chansons, with the exception of the book dedicated to Charles IX. in 1571. It contains 93 chansons, with 26 Latin secular pieces and 6 Italian madrigals, only a very few of which were really new. About the same time two other editions of the chansons appeared with the texts altered in a religious sense, to make several of them less offensive to Christian ears, and also to satisfy the growing taste for psalm-singing in the Huguenot circles of France. One was published at La Rochelle, the headquarters of French Protestantism, another more complete, and more thoroughgoing in its alterations was entitled ' Thresor de musique,' etc., and appears to have been published at Lyons. 1577 brings a small work of interest, a set of 24 cantiones a 2, twelve being vocal duets, and the other twelve for instruments, or it may be also for vocal practice. In later editions these latter are described as ' Fantasiae ' or ' Ricercari.' The first twelve show Orlando's wonderful skill in the picturesque setting of meditative texts. This work was dedicated to Duke William alone, but was followed by a book of motets a 3, introduced with an exquisite musical dedication to all three brothers, Dukes William, Ferdinand and Ernest. There are 18 numbers, mostly on verses of the Psalms, and written in the older imitative style with many beautiful melismatic passages. To these there are appended in the Magnum Opus six other numbers, including two very expressive settings of ' Adoramus te Christe ' which have been described as ' marvels of angelic grace.' In this year, too, Le Roy brought out at Paris a splendid edition of 18 masses by Orlando, including with several additions all those previously published. Of these the finest is one entitled ' Puisque j'ay perdu ' a 4, written in a very noble style.

Generally speaking, his masses, with some exceptions, are not on the same high level as his motets. Some are very short, and especially in the Gloria and Credo, written in a rapid homophonic syllabic style, which leaves no room for much expression. But not all have yet been published in modern form, to enable a proper judgment, and besides those published in the old editions, there are a considerable number in MS. in the Munich Archives. ' Puisque j'ay perdu,' with others have been edited by Proske in his ' Musica Divina.' No new publications of Orlando appeared in 1578. In 1579 Leonard Lechner, who had been a choir-boy under Orlando in the Bavarian chapel, brought out at Nuremberg new enlarged editions of the two sets of Selectissimae Cantiones of 1568, in a few cases altering the original words. The additional pieces are not for the most part really new, but only taken over from other publications. ' Si bene perpendi,' the drinking-song ascribed to Walter Mapes, might, along with other pleasantries, have better found their place among the chansons than among serious motets.

WORKS IN MANY STYLES.—On Oct. 24, 1579, Duke Albert died. He had done a last act of kindness to Orlando in the previous April by guaranteeing his yearly salary of 400 florins for life. From 1575 Orlando had been receiving this amount as salary, with 150 florins extra described in the Munich accounts as ' Gnadengeld.' This addition to his regular salary was also continued by Duke William. Early in 1580 he was offered, but declined, the post of Kapellmeister to the court of Dresden, then vacant by the death of Antonio Scandelli. But with the death of Duke Albert the more splendid days of the Bavarian chapel came to an end. The finances of the court were in an embarrassed condition, and Duke William was obliged to reduce the number of his musicians from 44 to 17, although in the course of the years following it was gradually raised again to a maximum of 38 in 1591. These circumstances may have induced Orlando to entertain some scruples of conscience about receiving the interest of his capital invested in the State Funds. But the Duke magnanimously reimbursed to him as a personal gift what he offered to renounce. Early in 1581 there appeared at Nuremberg a book of five masses a 4-5 by Orlando which, however, was not published by himself but by Leonard Lechner, and consists of early work of the master. Of these Commer has reprinted one on the tune ' La, la, maître Pierre,' but not, as Commer says, on the tune set by Clemens non Papa, which is quite different.[1] This is one of Orlando's shorter masses, but we may notice that while in these masses he seems to treat the Kyrie, Gloria and Credo, somewhat perfunctorily, he bestows much greater care on the setting of the Sanctus, Benedictus and Agnus, which are often very beautiful. On another of these masses, ' Entre vous filles de

[1] See the chanson of Clemens non Papa in Arion, vol. iii., ed. L. Benson.

quinze ans,' which is really based on a chanson of Clemens,[1] Peter Wagner comments at some length in his *Geschichte der Messe*, pp. 359-368. Much earlier work of quite a different complexion, Orlando himself in this year reproduced in his ' Libro de villanelle, moresche et altre canzoni a 4, 5, 6 et 8 voci,' published at Paris by Le Roy and Ballard. In the Italian dedication of this work to Duke William, he acknowledges that it would have been more suitable if he had published these works in his earlier years when he composed them, but that in publishing them now in his graver years he had rather acceded to the wishes of friends than followed his own judgment. There are 23 numbers, written in the rhythmical homophonic villanella style, all of a comic character, some drastically representing scenes of low life in Naples and Venice, and probably sung dramatically in character with accompanying instruments and the voices imitating them. They serve to show the comic dramatic verve embedded in Orlando's musical nature, and at the same time the beginning of that peculiar style of Italian music which was afterwards to be developed into the opera buffa. From the account of Massimo Trojano it would appear that the morescas a 6 were performed both vocally and instrumentally on the occasion of Duke William's marriage in 1568. Of all these pieces the best known in modern times is the comic serenade ' Matona mia cara ' a 4. The last number in the book, ' O la, o che bon eccho '[2] a 8, is thought to be of later origin than the others ; it is an ' echo ' piece in the Venetian style, one choir a 4 echoing another.

With 1582 we come back to more serious work. With the accession of Duke William, indeed, a more serious religious spirit had begun to pervade the court of Munich. Through the influence of his Jesuit advisers Duke William became more attentive to religious duties, earning for himself afterwards the surname of William the Pious. Lassus followed suit with his master, and also entered into relations with the Jesuit seminary at Munich, where there still exists a portrait of him in oil supposed to have been painted by his son-in-law Hans von Ach, representing him as he was in 1580 (see *PLATE XLI.*). Yet, too, Orlando had shown himself somewhat recalcitrant to the enforced introduction of the Roman rite into the Bavarian chapel in place of the old Germanic usages, as a good deal of laxity had previously been tolerated in Munich, but conformity with Rome had become the watchword of the counter-Reformation movement under the auspices of the Jesuit order. In

1582 Orlando published three important books of church music. One dedicated to the Bishop of Wurzburg contains a new setting of the Nine Lessons from the Book of Job, along with 11 new motets a 4. The new set of lessons are composed quite differently from the earlier set of 1565. The text is simply declaimed syllable by syllable in homophonic harmony, the melody being chiefly in the upper part, but with abrupt chromatic changes. This set is equally beautiful with the first set, some would say, even more beautiful, because simpler. It is only to be regretted that it has not yet appeared in any modern edition. Among the 11 new motets are some very fine numbers which we must pass over, only mentioning that at the end of the book, and without connexion with its other contents, there is a short tuneful setting of the curious words :

' Quid facies, facies Veneris cum veneris ante
  Ne sedeas sed eas, ne pereas per eas.'

It is as if after more serious work Orlando liked to unbend himself and vent his humorous delight in verbal witticisms. The next important publication of this year is ' Sacrae cantiones 5 voc.' dedicated to the Senators of Nuremberg, 21 numbers, almost all of the highest value. Among them are the two which gained first prize at the Puy de Musique of Evreux in 1575 and 1583, ' Domine qui cognoscis,' a deeply penitential piece, and ' Cantantibus organis ' for St. Cecilia's Day, also ' Justorum animae,' which has always been greatly admired, and which it is interesting to compare with Byrd's setting of the same words, and ' Christus resurgens,' a very brilliant Easter motet. At the end of the book Orlando indulges in a musical witticism on the verse of the old hymn for St. John Baptist's day, ' Ut queant laxis ' (see SOLMISATION). He makes the tenor alone sing the hexachordal syllables to their proper note without any regard to the sense, while it joins with the other voices only on the last line ' Sancte Joannes.'

The third publication of 1582 is ' Motetta sex vocum,' dedicated to Jacob Fugger, Baron of Kirchberg, and described as only recently composed, ' singulari authoris industria.' There are 20 numbers, among them fine settings of the Marian Antiphons and the ' Ave Verum,' and other distinguished pieces are, ' O altitudo divitiarum ' and ' Benedictio et claritas.' It may be said generally that in the decade 1580 to 1590, Orlando's genius had reached its full maturity in his masterly freedom and boldness of technique combined with a rare subtlety and depth of expression. All these works are described as equally available for instruments as for voices.

In 1583 appeared a new book of ' Teutsche Lieder ' a 4, dedicated, strangely enough, to Maximilian, the ten-year-old son of Duke William. There are 11 numbers, but as some of

[1] See this chanson very suitably adapted by Cornelius Freundt of Zwickau to a Christmas Carol ' Ein Kindlein ist uns heut geboren' C. Freundt, *Weihnachtsliederbuch*, ed. G. Göhler, 1897).
[2] It has been edited with English words in L. Benson's Oriana Series.

them are lengthy pieces broken up into several divisions, they are often reckoned as making up 33 separate pieces. They are written in simple four-part counterpoint, but are beautiful and expressive in Orlando's most refined style. Five are of a definitely religious character, among them the old Easter hymn of the 12th century, ' Christ ist erstanden,' with its proper melody in the bass, and ' Aus meiner Sünden tiefe ' in four divisions, a metrical paraphrase of the Psalm De profundis. But perhaps the more generally interesting may be two short amusing secular pieces, ' Ich weiss mir ein Meidlein hübsch '[1] and ' Baur was trägst im Sacke.' There was also a reprint about the same time of the three earlier sets of ' Teutsche Lieder ' a 5 in one complete edition. Mention may here be made of a collection entitled ' Harmoniae miscellae '[2] a 5 and 6, edited by Leonard Lechner and published at Nuremberg in 1583, containing three excellent motets of Orlando, never published by himself. The collection is otherwise interesting as including works mostly by Orlando's pupils and associates in the Bavarian chapel.

LAST DECADE OF COMPOSITION.—The year 1584 is distinguished by the first appearance in print of the Seven Penitential Psalms, originally composed for Duke Albert, but now in their printed form dedicated to Pfalzgraf Philip, Bishop of Ratisbon. The only other publication of 1584 is the ' Continuation de Mellange ' (Paris, Le Roy and Ballard). This contains 19 chansons a 3 to 6, along with four new Italian madrigals a 5 to 10. Some of the chansons appear to be older work written in the villanella style of homophonic harmony, others are composed on popular tunes, as especially the last a 6, ' Dessus le marché d'Arras.' There are two sacred pieces a 5, ' Père qui habitez dans les cieux,' and ' A toi je crie, ô Jesu Christ,' which are French translations of the Lutheran hymns, ' Vater unser ' and ' Ich ruf zu dir.' Sandberger considers them as in their expressive character among the finest examples of Orlando's fully mature style, but has strangely omitted to observe that these French settings are practically identical with the settings to the German words of the first set of ' Teutsche Lieder,' 1567. Of the four Italian madrigals in this book the last, ' Passan vostri trionfi ' a 10 on a text from Petrarch, is specially noticeable as a magnificent example of contrapuntal art, written partly in alternating choirs, but with powerful outbursts of ten-part harmony, somewhat resembling in this respect the effect of a modern orchestra, as Sandberger observes. Two other madrigals a 7 and 10, in the Dialogue and Echo form appeared in a miscellaneous collection.

On the Feast of Corpus Christi in 1584 pre-

parations were made for the customary procession with the Sacrament through the streets of Munich, but a severe thunderstorm with heavy downpour of rain intervened, and it seemed that the procession would have to be confined to the interior of St. Peter's Church. But no sooner had the Sacrament been borne to the porch of the church, and the choir under Orlando's direction had begun to sing his motet, ' Gustate et videte,' ' O taste and see how gracious the Lord is,' than there was a sudden lull in the storm. The rain ceased, the sun shone out brilliantly, and the procession was able to continue as usual. This was regarded as a special instance of Divine favour accorded on account of Orlando's music, and on future occasions of outdoor church procession this motet continued to be sung as if a sure talisman for the securing of fair weather.

The year 1585 was a great one for new and important publications by Orlando. The increasingly religious and moralising bent of his mind is manifested in his Fifth Book of Madrigals a 5, which though not so named, are in reality 'Madrigali spirituali.' Of the 12 numbers, 7 are on texts from the ' Rime spirituali ' of Gabriel Fiamma, Bishop of Chioggia, the others are from verses of Petrarch which specially dwell on the transitoriness of earthly things, and the need of penitence for the errors of youth. But the music is on a higher level than in any of the preceding books. The intense seriousness of the poetry is even more powerfully reflected in the music. All chromaticism foreign to the diatonic system is carefully avoided, except for very occasional use on words to which, as Van den Borren observes, some idea of blame attaches. He seems to pass censure on his own excessive indulgence in chromaticism in his earlier days as a musical fault. In the last number of the book, ' Come la cera al fuoco ' a 6, a mystic symbolism may be thought to be implied in his use of a canon all ' unisono ' as expressing the idea of wax melting in the fire, the wax of earthliness melting in the fire of Divine love. This book of madrigals was dedicated to Count Mario Bevilaqua of Verona, a distinguished musical amateur of the time and a munificent patron of musicians. He maintained in his palace at Verona a regular concert called a ' ridotto,' and the best musicians of the day, as Luca Marenzio, Philip de Monte, Orazio Vecchi and others dedicated their compositions to him. Orlando was about to make a journey to Italy at this time, and it is probable that he passed by Verona to present his book personally to Bevilaqua. Of this journey we shall speak presently, but first have to mention the other publications of the year. On the 1st of March 1585 he dedicates to the Abbot of Benedictbenern a book of Lamentations with 11 new motets a 5. Of the Lamentations it is sufficient to say that for expressiveness they are

[1] Edited with English words in Arion, vol. i.
[2] S. W. Dehn of Berlin published a large number of these works in a modern edition of 1837.

worthy to rank with the Lessons from the Book of Job and the Penitential Psalms. The Hebrew letters are composed in beautiful arabesques, and Orlando sets three of the verses of each Lesson, but treats the 'Jerusalem, convertere,' more concisely than Palestrina. The motets which follow show the direction of Orlando's mind at this time. The long piece, 'Dixi in cordo meo' (Eccl. ii. 1-11) is set in a very rhythmical fashion, largely homophonic, as if to express the vanity of earthly delights suggested by the text. In the next piece there is the same dwelling on the ideas, 'Quid valet hic mundus,' 'Pulvis et umbra sumus,' but by way of contrast we have in 'Quocumque loco fuero,' a beautiful setting of three stanzas of the hymn, 'Jesu dulcis memoria,' from which Orlando seems to derive comfort for himself. A book of motets, 17 nos. *a* 6 and 8, is dedicated to Count Eytel Fritz of Hohenzollern, at whose court at Hechingen his son Ferdinand was now engaged as Kapellmeister. It may seem a little strange that in this book should be included a brilliant congratulatory ode to Duke Ernest, Duke William's brother, on his appointment in 1583 to the Archbishopric of Cologne. Another book of motets, 31 numbers *a* 4, with a Stabat Mater *a* 8, was dedicated to Alexander Fugger, Provost of Freysing Cathedral. This book has a character of its own, as not being so miscellaneous in its contents as so many of the other books. It is considered to contain the very best of Orlando's sacred pieces *a* 4, and consists almost entirely of short offertory texts from the Missal, mostly of a prayerful or meditative character. The Stabat Mater alone is thought to come short of the high level of the other pieces.

In the autumn of this year Orlando set out on his journey to Italy, its first object being to make a pilgrimage to the Holy House of Loretto. He afterwards proceeded to Ferrara, where he was better received by Duke Alfonso d'Este than on the occasion of his first visit eighteen years before. Before we leave this busy year 1585, we cannot altogether pass over without mention two fine settings by Orlando of some lines of Tasso, 'Ardo si ma non t' amo,' contributed to a collection entitled 'Sdegnosi ardori,' which consists of nothing else but settings of the same lines by about 30 other composers, many of them in the Bavarian service, but also including Philip de Monte, Costanzo Porta and others. The lines are meant to express the disdain of a disappointed and deceived lover, and Orlando has set them in a very dramatic fashion.

The numerous publications from 1580, which we have had occasion to mention, bear testimony to the wonderful industry of the composer during this period. 1586 brings the first warning of declining strength. It is a blank so far as publications are concerned,

and the opening of 1587 brings with it the gift from Duke William of a country house at Geising on the Ammer, probably as a place of occasional retirement. Then he came back to work, and in gratitude, no doubt, for better health, on April 15 dedicated a new book of Italian madrigals to the court physician, Dr. Thomas Mermann, a man of great culture, and a lover of music, who became one of his best friends. This book has 23 numbers, 7 *a* 4, 7 *a* 5 and 9 *a* 6, and is regarded as the crown of Orlando's achievements in madrigal writing. The pieces are almost entirely of a religious character, nine taken from the 'Rime spirituali' of Gabriel Fiamma, one an Italian verse translation of Psalm vi., others from various sources known and unknown. The mood of love complaint characteristic of the ordinary madrigal is here spiritualised into that of penitential lament and heavenly aspiration, and the music gains thereby in artistic elevation and expressive power. In August a new volume of the 'Patrocinium musices' appears, containing 13 magnificats *a* 4 to 6. Here Orlando manifests an opposite tendency to that of his later madrigal writing. Into the madrigal he had infused greater seriousness and solemnity, but in the Magnificat he shows his desire to impart to his spiritual work something of the lightness and grace of his earlier secular work. This may have been by way of relief to his heavily oppressed mind. So he borrows the themes on which these magnificats are composed largely from secular songs, his own or those of other composers, in a few cases from motets. We have magnificats, like Masses, named from such secular songs as 'Si par souhait,' 'Dessus le marché,' 'Susanne un jour,' etc., and the result of the alliance does not appear to be any more unsatisfactory in the one case than in the other. Two masses *a* 6 based on his own motets, 'Locutus sum' and 'Beatus qui intelligat,' were also published separately this year by Le Roy and Ballard.

In consequence of his failing health Orlando's mind began to be much occupied with concern for the future of his wife and family, and on Nov. 6, 1587, he obtained the assurance of an annuity of 100 florins for his wife in case she should survive him. A month later Duke William grants him at his own request a dispensation from further service in the chapel, but with a reduction of 200 florins from his salary, and on the other hand offers his son Ferdinand a salary of 200 florins to take part of his father's duties, and also appoints his second son Rudolf as organist with a salary of 200 florins, and the further obligation of giving musical instruction to the younger members of the choir. The composer does not seem to have been satisfied with this arrangement, and remained at his post with his full salary, but probably with some alleviation of his duties and help from his son Rudolf. Ferdinand does not appear to have left the service of Count Eytel Fritz of Hohenzollern or to have entered again the Bavarian service until 1589 or 1590.

In 1588 Orlando brought out, in conjunction with his son Rudolf, a book of 'Teutsche geistliche Psalmen' *a* 3. The book contains 50 numbers, the texts and melodie taken from Caspar Ulenberg's metrical version of the Psalter of 1582, the best that had then been produced on the Catholic side. Orlando composed the 25 psalms with the odd numbers up to the fiftieth, Rudolf, the alternate 25 with the even numbers. The book was dedicated to Abbot Gallus of Ottobeuern, and seems to show that in German Catholic circles and even in monastic houses some interest was taken in German Psalm-singing. Orlando's settings are very beautiful and interesting ; he treats Ulenberg's tunes with great freedom, and not as a cantus firmus in any one part. We have no means of judging the merit of Rudolf's settings, as only Orlando's are reproduced in modern editions.

In 1589 a new volume of the 'Patrocinium musices' appears, the last to which Orlando contributes, containing 6 masses *a* 5, with the titles ' Dites maîtresse,' ' Amar donne,' ' Qual donna attende,' ' In die tribulationis,' ' Io son ferito,' ' Pro defunctis.' Their composition, however, is of older date, as they are found in MSS. of 1578–80. ' Io son ferito ' takes its themes from a then well-known madrigal of Palestrina, and is thought to have something of the grace of the Palestrina style. ' Qual donna attende ' and ' In die tribulationis ' would seem to take their themes from a madrigal and motet of Cyprian de Rore. We know that Cyprian's works were highly esteemed at Munich, and that Orlando was personally acquainted with him in earlier days, and influenced by him in certain directions. Proske has edited these two masses in the second series of his 'Musica divina,' and considers that for pure Church expression and style they take a very high place among the works of the master. The ' Pro defunctis ' is composed with the plain-song intonations sung *unisono* at the beginning of each movement, and with the cantus firmus mostly in the tenor, but sometimes also in the bass, and used with considerable freedom, as when in the third Kyrie it appears first in minims, then in breves and afterwards in semibreves. The Tractus 'Absolve' is set, but not the Dies Irae, as this was not then even generally 'used. In this mass, with the fetters of cantus firmus, the genius of the master is not thought to burn so brightly as in other works.

In 1590 Orlando dedicated to the Bishop of Bamberg his ' Neue teutsche und etliche frantzösiche Gesäng ' *a* 6. The dedication is dated on the Feast of St. Henry, July 15, this date being appropriately chosen as recalling both to Orlando himself and the Bishop the fact that it was Henry II., Duke of Bavaria and Holy Roman Emperor, who at the beginning of the 11th century founded and endowed the Bishopric of Bamberg, and who was afterwards with Cunigunde his wife canonised for his fervent piety and benefactions to the Church. The book contains 12 numbers, 9 German and 3 French. The French pieces, however, are merely corrected editions of some which had appeared in 1584. With one exception the German pieces are all of a religious character, showing the increasing preoccupation of Orlando's mind with religious subjects. ' Ich ruf zu dir ' is yet another version of the ' De profundis,' with the tune from Ulenberg's Psalm as cantus firmus unchanged in all 5 divisions. ' Aus hartem Weh ' is a German Catholic Advent hymn with its tune in the tenor, resembling the Lutheran ' Erbarm dich mein.' Other pieces are free compositions in which Orlando seems to assume the rôle of a Christian preacher exhorting mankind to penitence, patience and humility. To these he adds one amusing secular piece from Hans Sachs, ' Der Körbelmacher,' describing a dispute between a basket-maker and his wife.

On Nov. 6 of this year Orlando's third son, Ernest, was admitted as a singer of the chapel with a salary of 60 florins. Meantime the master's mental faculties become more and more disturbed ; it seems as if the fresh effort to work had completely prostrated him. His wife Regina, on one occasion returning from Geising, finds him gloomy and morose, failing to recognise her and unwilling to speak to any one. At her request the Princess Maximiliana at once sends Dr. Mermann, and there is a temporary recovery, but the mind is still at fault. A spirit of melancholy settled on him. ' Cheerful and happy no longer,' says Regina, ' he has become gloomy and speaks only of death.' In an access of melancholy he wrote to the Duke complaining that he had never carried out his father Albert's intentions towards him, and it needed all that Regina and the Princess Maximiliana could do to soften the effect of this act. In 1592 his material position was improved by the Duke increasing his salary to 800 florins. Ferdinand and Rudolf were also benefited by increase of salary. In 1593, under the sympathetic care of Dr. Mermann, there came about a great improvement in his state of health, so that he was able to return to work and fulfil his duties as choirmaster on the Festival of Corpus Christi. He also resumes the labours of composition, and on Michaelmas Day (Sept. 29) dedicates to Johann Otto, Bishop of Augsburg, his book of ' Cantiones sacrae ' *a* 6. In the very interesting and touching dedication he alludes to this work as being probably his swan-song (' cygneum forte melos'), and expresses the hope that as the light of the setting sun is more pleasing to the eye, so these graver songs of his closing days may perhaps delight the mind and ear better than the gayer and more festive songs of his youth. The book contains 30 numbers *a* 6 and 2 *a* 12, which show no diminution of the composer's technical skill or power of expression. It includes pieces of the highest quality, some of his best work in a great variety of form, and which show his increased earnestness of religious feeling. We may notice that 'Prolongati sunt dies mei' is a pathetic farewell Nunc Dimittis, which the composer, with a presentment of his approaching end, addresses to Duke William. It is matter for surprise that the modern editor of the Magnum Opus has overlooked the extremely personal nature of the references in this motet, and has mistakenly represented the text as only the usual combination of Scripture texts. Orlando has himself compiled the text out of a tissue of Scripture phrases, only to apply them to himself and his relation to Duke William. Very touching is the reference he makes to the account he must give of his stewardship. 'Heu quis armorum' is a powerful setting in homophonic harmony of a Sapphic poem describing the struggle between good and evil in the world. Another part of the same poem is in the posthumous Magnum Opus. With other similar pieces in the Magnum Opus it seems to show how much Orlando's mind was exercised in the last years of his life with the thought of the Divine Judgment. They serve also to point to that kinship of his mind generally with Dante and Michael Angelo, which has often been dwelt upon. One of the last pieces in the book is a touching setting of the verse from the Dies Irae 'Recordare Jesu pie.' But even in this very serious book Orlando must find some outlet for his vein of jovial or saturnine humour in his clever setting of a drinking song in leonine verses, 'Ad primum morsum,' which Van den Borren considers to bear the impress of his genius.

In 1593 Orlando was able to accompany Duke William to the Diet of Ratisbon, where he came into contact with Philip de Monte and other musicians of note. The earlier part of 1594 must have been occupied with the preparation for publication of his last work, 'Lagrime di San Pietro,' which, on May 24, he dedicated to Pope Clement VIII. This work consists of 20 spiritual madrigals on verses by the Italian religious poet, Tansillo, and one Latin motet *a* 7, 'Vide quae pro te patior.' Haberl describes it as a 'truly magnificent work,' and intended to have published it in a modern edition, but this unfortunately has never appeared, and we only know the beautiful Latin piece by its inclusion in the Magnum Opus. Before his last work appeared in print, Orlando died on June 14, 1594. By his last will, besides bequeathing alms to the poor and to a Munich hospital, he provided that two low masses and a sung Requiem should be celebrated for him annually on St. John Baptist's Day in the Church of Geising. He was buried in the cemetery of the Franciscans at Munich. When the Franciscan property was secularised, the monument which had been erected over his grave was removed, and remained for some time in the possession of a private family, but has now been set up in the gardens of the National Museum at Munich. It is of reddish marble, 3½ ft. high and 7 ft. wide, with a carving of the burial of Christ in the upper part, and below this, his arms, on one side of which are ten kneeling male figures, Orlando himself, his sons and grandsons, and on the other side eight kneeling female figures, Regina with her daughters and granddaughters. The epitaph consists of twelve lines of elegiac verse, of which we may quote the first two and last two lines :

> 'Orlando cineres eheu ! modo dulce loquentes
> Nunc mutos eheu ! flebilis urna premit

> Nunc quia complevit totum concentibus orbem,
> Victor cum superis certat apud superos.'

The epitaph states that he died at the age of 62, and with this agrees the inscription on the portrait prefixed to the 'Lagrime,' but, as was mentioned before, the inscriptions on the various portraits are not in agreement with each other, so that the question of his exact age must be left doubtful. Regina survived her husband to June 5, 1600. Of the marriage there were four sons, Ferdinand, Rudolf, Johann and Ernst, and two daughters, Anna and Regina, the latter married to the court artist, Hans von Ach. Of the sons, Johann appears to have died early ; we hear no more of Ernst after 1594. Ferdinand had returned to the Bavarian chapel in 1590, and succeeded Fossa as Kapellmeister in 1602, dying in 1609. Rudolf also remained in the Bavarian service as composer and organist till his death in 1625. Both, besides being composers themselves, were active in the further publication of their father's works.

POSTHUMOUS PUBLICATIONS.—In 1596 Georgius Victorinus, choirmaster of the Jesuit Church in Munich, edited a collection entitled 'Thesaurus litaniarum,' in which appear 12 litanies *a* 4—9 by Orlando, 3 of which *a* 4, 5, very simple works, appear again in Proske, 'Musica divina.' In 1597 Ferdinand published 11 motets *a* 5 of his father interspersed with 12 of his own. One of them, 'Memento peccati tui,' may be noticed as a characteristic penitential piece by Orlando with its strange emphasis at the end on the words 'ne desperes.' In 1600 Rudolf published his father's 'Prophetiae Sibyllinae chromatico more,' 12 numbers *a* 4. The first mention of this work occurs in a letter of the French publisher, Le Roy, to Orlando in 1574, telling him of the performance of some numbers from it before Charles IX., to the King's great delight and astonishment. It has not yet been published in any modern edition. We know that Orlando in his later years was rather opposed to the chromaticism in which he indulged earlier. In 1602 Ferdinand published 5 Magnificats of Orlando with some of his own.

In 1604 both brothers joined together to issue a more important work entitled, ' Magnum Opus musicum O. de Lasso,' preserving in six volumes of a moderate size, most clearly and beautifully printed, no less than 516 sacred and secular motets, including all those previously published, with nearly 100 previously unpublished. The work was dedicated to Duke Maximilian, and from the dedication it would appear to have been undertaken partly at the instigation of Dr. Thomas Mermann, the friend and physician of Orlando's later years. There are 24 numbers *a* 2 (including the 12 Ricercari of 1577), 24 *a* 3, 100 *a* 4, 167 *a* 5, 159 *a* 6, 11 *a* 7, 24 *a* 8, 2 *a* 9, 3 *a* 10 and 2 *a* 12. The modern edition of Breitkopf & Härtel has remained incomplete, lacking the last 24 numbers, owing to the death of its editor, Dr. Haberl, in 1910.

After his brother's death, Rudolf issued ' 6 Missae posthumae ' in 1610, 4 *a* 6, ' Amor Colei,' 'Certa fortiter,' 'Deus in adjutorium,' ' Ecce nunc benedicite,' and 2 *a* 8, 'Bell' Amfitritt ' and ' Vinum bonum.' These have all appeared in a modern reprint by Commer. Under the title 'Jubilus B.V.M.' Rudolf issued in 1619 a complete collection of Orlando's magnificats, 100 numbers *a* 4-10, by far the greater number of which were previously unpublished. Of these about 30 have appeared in modern editions.

Reckoning up, then, the number of Orlando's separate compositions published up to 1620, but without including their various divisions as separate numbers, we find that even then the total amounts to 1183, made up as follows: the 516 numbers of the Magnum Opus, 41 masses, 100 magnificats, 57 other church pieces, 230 madrigals including the ' Lagrime ' and ' Sibyllinae,' 146 chansons, and 93 Deutsche Lieder. Of these, 20 madrigals and 11 chansons have not been perfectly preserved. Besides these there exist in MSS. in the Munich Archives, 10 or more masses, a book of Lamentations *a* 4, 3 Passions, 32 Latin hymns, 10 settings of Nunc Dimittis, and some other works, which bring up the number of separate compositions to the amazing total of over 1250.

In 1625 a certain Caspar Vincentius, organist at Würzburg, brought out there a new edition of the Magnum Opus, but with a figured bass part, which, as Haberl says, disfigures and misrepresents the original. The modern edition of Orlando's works published by Breitkopf & Härtel, which was intended to be complete, but has been broken off for the present, contains in 10 volumes 492 nos. of the Magnum Opus edited by Dr. Haberl, and in 10 other volumes 173 madrigals, 135 chansons and 93 Deutsche Lieder, edited with valuable introductions by Dr. Adolf Sandberger of Munich.[1]

DESCENDANTS.—It would seem from the Munich accounts that Ferdinand and Rudolf continued to use only Orlando's adopted name, De Lasso, in place of the original De Lassus. From the list of his works in *Q.-L.*, Rudolf would appear to have been a fairly prolific composer, and in later years to have also adopted the new style of composition with Bassus ad Organum. Two of his motets are given by Proske in 'Musica divina,' tom. II., one showing something of an inclination to the new monodic style of Italy. A son of Ferdinand, also called Ferdinand, was sent by Duke Maximilian to study music at Rome under Crivelli, and afterwards became Kapellmeister at Munich, but later on, at the instance of the Duke himself, gave up his musical calling to accept some office in the civil service. Descendants of Orlando would appear to have been still living in 1895.

LASSUS AND PALESTRINA

Lassus and Palestrina, both dying in 1594, have long been recognised as twin summits in musical history, representing the highest achievements of the 16th century in the department of pure vocal and choral music. This was the only really artistic music of the time. The music of both was often indeed performed by instruments as well as sung by voices, but the instruments only played the vocal parts, and the style is vocal and not instrumental. Lassus, however, was more familiar with the use of instruments, and often imitates them in his vocal writing, as in his villanellas, and even occasionally in his masses, and in his motets when in the words there was any suggestion of instruments. The choral art of the 16th century is often designated as the *a cappella* style in music, and regarded as betokening the original ecclesiastical domination of music. But the designation *a cappella* is somewhat of a misnomer, when we find the same style in secular as in sacred music, and when we also find on further examination that the so-called *a cappella* style in such masters as Palestrina and Lassus is really secular in origin, and only the successful adaptation of the style of the secular Italian madrigal to sacred purposes. The Renaissance in music is often supposed to have only begun with the rise of monody and instrumental music leading to the opera. But there is the spirit of the Renais-

---

[1] We are informed by Dr. Sandberger that further volumes of Orlando's works are to be published under his editorship.

sance already in the music of both Palestrina and Lassus, perhaps more manifest in the latter than the former. Both start from the same ground of the secular madrigal, but their paths and their aims diverge, and while Palestrina is distinguished for the exquisite grace and beauty of his music with its smooth flow of melody and the crystalline clearness of its harmony, Lassus excels in greater variety and depth of expression, with a greater command of all means of expression, though his style thus became more abrupt and less melodious. Both are equally great in their special excellences, and there is no need to exalt one to depreciate the other, though it may be admitted that Palestrina is more open to immediate appreciation than Lassus. Schweitzer has familiarised us with the distinction between those musicians who are mainly tone-poets, and those who are specially tone-painters, and we may apply this distinction to the present case by saying that Palestrina is more the lyrical tone-poet who aims at expressing the general sentiment underlying the words, while Lassus is more the epic-dramatic tone-painter who endeavours to depict in tones the words themselves in all the significance they have to him personally. While Palestrina for general grace and beauty of style has been compared to Raphael and Mozart, Lassus in his depth of thought has been considered to belong to the lineage of Michael Angelo and Sebastian Bach.

BIBLIOGRAPHY

Eugen Schmitz: *Orlando di Lasso.* (Leipzig, 1915.)
Charles Van den Borren : *Orlande di Lassus,* pp. 254. (Paris, 1920.)
Adolf Sandberger : *Ausgewählte Aufsätze,* a large number of which deal with Orlando di Lasso (Munich, 1921); *Beiträge zur Geschichte der bayr. Hofkapelle,* Bd. I. and III. (Leipzig, 1894).
Raffaello Casimiri : *Orlando di Lasso, Maestro di Capella al Laterano nel 1553,* pp. 13 (Rome, 1920). See notice in *Z.M.W.,* Oct. 1920, pp. 51, 52.
J. R. M.

LAST JUDGMENT, THE, the English version, by Prof. Taylor, of Spohr's ' Die letzten Dinge,' an oratorio in 2 parts ; text by Rochlitz, music by Spohr. Composed in the autumn of 1825, and produced in the Lutheran church, Cassel, on Good Friday, Mar. 25, 1826 (see Spohr's *Selbstbiographie,* ii. 171) ; Norwich Festival, Sept. 24, 1830 ; Sacred Harmonic Society, July 11, 1838, Spohr conducting. This oratorio must not be confounded with ' Das jüngste Gericht,' produced Erfurt Festival, Aug. 15, 1812 (*Selbstbiographie,* i. 169). G.

LATES, (1) John James (*d.* in or near Oxford, 1777), an English violinist and composer of the early 18th century. He studied under the best Italian masters of that day, and became leader of the concerts at Oxford. His patron, the Duke of Marlborough, gave him a professional position at Blenheim. His published works include violin solos, duets and trios.

Charles (2) (*d. circa* 1810), his son, studied church music under Philip Hayes of Oxford, in

which city both father and son resided, and had some degree of fame as a performer on the organ and the pianoforte. He published some sonatas for the pianoforte and other works. F. K.

LATILLA, Gaetano (*b.* Bari, *c.* 1713 ; *d.* Naples, 1789), was a choir-boy in the cathedral at Bari, and was later educated at the Conservatorio di San Onofrio in Naples, where he was a pupil of Domenico Gizzi. In 1732 his first opera, ' Li mariti a forza ' had a great success, and was followed by many others, among which the most popular was ' Orazio,' brought out in Rome, 1738. On the last day of that year he was appointed vice-maestro di cappella at Santa Maria Maggiore. Incapacitated by illness, he returned to Naples in 1741, and in 1756 he went to Venice as choir director at the Conservatorio della Pietà, and in 1762 was made second conductor at St. Mark's. In 1772 he once more returned to Naples, where his ' Antigono ' was performed at the San Carlo in 1775 ; he died there, having written some thirty-six operas, much church music (preserved at the Conservatorio della Pietà and elsewhere), six string quartets published in London, and many arias and duets. Seven operas and two intermezzi are all that are now known to exist of his dramatic compositions (see *Q.-L.*). M.

LATROBE, (1) Rev. Christian Ignatius (*b.* Fulneck, Leeds, Feb. 12, 1757 ; *d.* Fairfield, near Manchester, May 6, 1836), eldest son of Rev. Benjamin Latrobe, superintendent of the congregations of the United (Moravian) Brethren in England. In 1771 he went to college of the United Brethren at Niesky, Upper Lusatia, returned to England in 1784, took orders in the same church, became in 1787 secretary to the Society for the Furtherance of the Gospel, and in 1795 was appointed secretary to the Unity of the Brethren in England.

Although Latrobe never followed music as a profession he cultivated it assiduously from an early age. His earlier compositions were chiefly instrumental ; three of his sonatas, having met with the approval of Haydn,[1] were published and dedicated to him. His other published compositions include Lord Roscommon's translation of the Dies Irae, 1799 ; ' The Dawn of Glory,' 1803 ; Anthem for the Jubilee of George III., 1809 ; Anthems, by various composers, 1811 ; Original Anthems, 1823 : ' Te Deum, performed in York Cathedral ' : ' Miserere, Ps. 51 ' ; and ' Six Airs on serious subjects, words by Cowper and Hannah More.' He edited the first English edition of the Moravian Hymn Tunes. But his most important publication was his *Selection* [2] *of Sacred Music from the works of the most eminent composers of*

---

[1] A Letter of Latrobe to Vincent Novello (1828) gives a full account of his friendship with Haydn. It, together with a study of Latrobe's life and work by E. Holmes, was published in *Mus. T.,* Sept. 1851.
[2] The full contents of the *Selection,* arranged alphabetically, was published in earlier editions of this Dictionary.

Germany and Italy, six vols. 1806–25, through the medium of which many fine compositions, including much of Graun, Hasse, Haydn and Mozart, were first introduced to the notice of the British public.

(2) Rev. JOHN ANTES LATROBE, M.A., his son (*b.* London, 1799 ; *d.* Gloucester, Nov. 19, 1878), was composer of several anthems. He was educated at St. Edmund Hall, Oxford, was B.D. in 1826 and M.A. in 1829, took holy orders in the Church of England, and was incumbent of St. Thomas's, Kendal, from 1840–1865, and honorary canon of Carlisle Cathedral from 1858. He was author of *The Music of the Church considered in its various branches, Congregational and Choral*, London, 1831, and *Instructions of Chenaniah*, a book of directions for accompanying chants and psalm tunes (1832).   w. H. H.

LATVIAN MUSIC. The history of Latvian music consists of two epochs : (1) popular music as a naïve and direct expression of the people's common emotion, and (2) artistic music, as a conscious and elaborated expression of the individual's action of the mind or soul.

(1) POPULAR MUSIC.—The popular songs existed long before the establishment of Christianity by Germans, who invaded and conquered Latvia in the 12th century (about 1158). We find the texts of popular songs celebrating pagan idols. But the greatest part of the popular songs collected until now have their origin in the age of Catholicism, *i.e.* from the 13th-16th century. After the introduction of Lutheranism (1530) the German barons tightened their hold, and Protestant pastors tried by all means to abolish the Latvian popular songs. Forcibly introducing not only German hymn tunes for singing in church, but also German secular songs (translated into Latvian) for singing in the schools and in the home, they nearly succeeded in banishing all Latvian characteristics.

The first full account of Latvian songs and singing, dating from 1632 (*Syntagma de origine Livonarum di Fridericus Menius*), shows that the popular songs written down about the end of the 16th century are like those of the 17th. A great many songs perished, because they were handed down from mouth to mouth ; some which survived were put on paper only in the 19th century. The most zealous and conscientious collector of the popular songs, Andrejs Jurjans (1856–1922), only began to gather them about the year 1890. The musical material now gathered surpasses 2000 numbers, consisting of songs, dance tunes and fragments of instrumental music. The tunes of the prehistoric epoch moved in the limits of a fourth and were performed more in a declamatory than in a singing manner. The tunes of the next epoch were more melodious, and moved in the limits of an octave. These tunes were sung in solo as well as in chorus, in unison or in octaves. Besides common measures we find an abundance of measures of five, seven and other mixed times.

The principal musical intruments of the ancient Latvians were (1) the Kokles, a species of harp with broad and long sounding-board, furnished with five to seven strings ; (2) Aza Rags, a goat's or bull's horn with a mouth-piece like that of our modern brass wind instruments, and with three or five holes for fingering ; (3) Bungas, primitive drums ; and (4) various wooden trumpets and fifes made in a simple manner. Particularly beloved was the Kokles as an instrument for accompaniment to singing.

(2) ARTISTIC MUSIC.—This branch of Latvian music could arise and unfold itself only after the emancipation of the serfs in Livonia and Courland (1819) ; the Latvian's affection for music showed itself in the four-part vocal music, and displayed itself particularly about the end of the last century, when choral societies existed not only in towns, but also in the country. In the beginning the choral societies sang separately, then the neighbouring societies jointly, and finally from all Latvia together ; in 1873 the first general singing festival in Riga had 1000 singers ; in 1880, the 2nd, 1627 ; in 1888, the 3rd, 2618 ; in 1895, the 4th, 4000 ; and in 1910, the 5th festival had 6000 singers (from about 250 singing societies). That was a considerable success for an agricultural nation of only two million, oppressed during seven centuries. In the war (1914–18) Latvians suffered greatly from German and Russian armies ; but now Latvia is independent and can develop her musical as well as other faculties without hindrance.

The first-fruits of artistic music were popular tunes harmonised for four-part singing. The first harmoniser of Latvian songs, Janis Cimze (1814–81), altered the characteristic qualities of popular tunes by putting them into the modern major and minor keys. More national are the songs harmonised by E. Vigners (*b.* 1850), A. Jurjans and E. Melngailis (*b.* 1871). The first original compositions were written by K. Baumanis (1835–1905), author of the national hymn, 'God Bless our Latvia' ; but the most important composers are J. Vitols and A. Kalnins. For foreigners the most interesting are the works of Kalnins (*b.* 1879), as having true national colouring. The compositions of J. Vitols (*b.* 1863) are refined, but not specially characteristic of the country. J. Vitols excels in nearly all branches of music ; his orchestral works are brilliant ; *e.g.* his overture ' Spriditis,' his suite of popular songs, etc. In piano music Vitols until now was the only composer whose works require virtuosity from the performer. A. Kalnins has written for the piano and organ, but much more for voice and for orchestra, and the first more important national opera 'Banuta.' His orchestral works have true national content and expression; for instance, 'Pie Staburaga,' 'The Song of the Native Country,' etc. Among A. Jurjans's works are interesting popular dances for orchestra: 'Ackups,' 'Jandalins,' and 'Beggar's Dance.' Among the younger composers the most remarkable is Janis Medins (b. 1890), author of two operas and many other works. The other Latvian composers, who have written mostly vocal music, are N. Alunans, E. Darzins, D. Milits, L. Betins (pianist), J. Straume, P. Jurjans, J. Jurjans, A. Ore, H. Ore, J. Zalits, A. Abels, P. Suberts, B. Valle, J. Reinholds, J. Graubins, M. Gubene, J. Kade, O. Kaulins, J. Ozols, O. Sepskis, K. Zigmunds, J. Sprogis, etc.

The most important stimulants to the development of Latvian music are now the Latvian National Opera (director, T. Reiters), the Latvian Conservatory (Riga), and several Popular Conservatoires in the other towns. The Latvian Opera Company was founded in 1912 by P. Jurjans as a private enterprise; its further development was checked by the war. Only after the proclamation of independent Latvia (1918) could the opera renew its activity as the Latvian National Opera, with a government subsidy. As the highest music school there is now the Latvian (State) Conservatoire,

toire, and first violin at the Musical Society, with great liberty of action. But Russia did not agree with him, and the state of his health compelled him in 1874 to take the baths at Carlsbad.

Laub was certainly one of the greatest violinvirtuosi of his time. He had a fine and very powerful tone and a brilliant technique, and played with much feeling and passion. His repertory was very large, comprising all the important classical works and a great many modern compositions. His frequent performances of Joachim's Hungarian concerto deserve special mention. He had also much success as a quartet player, but his style, especially in latter years, was not unjustly reproached with mannerism and a tendency to exaggeration.   P. D.

LAUD, a kind of citterne, see BANDURRIA.

LAUDA SION, the name of a Sequence, sung at Mass on the Feast of Corpus Christi. (See SEQUENTIA.)

The text of the *Lauda Sion*, written about the year 1264 by S. Thomas Aquinas, has always been regarded as a masterpiece of mediæval scholarship. The plain-song to which the sequence is adopted belongs originally to the Sequence 'Laudes Crucis attolamus'; it is written in Modes VII. and VIII. combined. The following is the opening:

founded in 1919 under the direction of Prof. J. Vitols, formerly a professor at St. Petersburg Conservatoire for over thirty years.   K. P.

LAUB, FERDINAND (b. Prague, Jan. 19, 1832; d. Gries, near Botzen, Tyrol, Mar. 17, 1875), one of the most remarkable violinplayers of his day. His father was a musician at Prague.

At 6 he mastered Variations by De Bériot, and at 9 performed regularly in public. He was a pupil of the Prague Conservatoire under Mildner, and at 11 years old he attracted the notice of Berlioz and Ernst, and shortly after was taken up by the Grand Duke Stephen, and by him sent to Vienna in 1847. After this he visited Paris, and, in 1851, London, where he played at the Musical Union, and in 1853 succeeded Joachim at Weimar. Two years later we find him at Berlin as Kammervirtuos and leader of the court band, teacher in the Stern Conservatorium, and leader of quartetconcerts of his own. At length, after considerable wandering, he settled at Moscow in 1866 as head professor of the violin in the Conserva-

The Sequence has been many times subjected to polyphonic treatment of a very high order. Palestrina has left us two settings of it for eight voices, arranged in a double choir, and a shorter one for four. The first, and best known, was printed, in 1575, by Alex. Gardanus, in the Third Book of Motets for five, six and eight voices, and is one of the earliest examples of that peculiar combination of two choirs, consisting of unequally balanced voices, which Palestrina has made so justly famous—the voices selected being, in this case, cantus I. and II., altus and bassus, in the first choir, and altus, tenor I. and II. and bassus, in the second.

A reprint of this beautiful composition will be found in vol. iii. of the complete edition of Palestrina's works published by Breitkopf & Härtel. The other eight-part setting, in triple measure throughout, formerly known only through the medium of a MS. in the Library of the Collegio Romano at Rome, has been published in vol. vii. of the same series.

      w. s. r., rev.

LAUDI SPIRITUALI, a name given to certain collections of devotional music, compiled for the use of the ' Laudisti '—a Religious Confraternity, instituted, at Florence, in the year 1310, and afterwards held in great estimation by S. Charles Borromeo, and S. Philip Neri.

The poetry of the ' Laudi '—some ancient specimens of which are attributed, by Crescentini, to S. Francis of Assisi (d. 1226), was originally written entirely in Italian, and bears no trace of classical derivation. The music to which it is adapted—inclining rather to the character of the sacred canzonet, than to that of the regular hymn—was, at first, unisonous, and extremely simple ; though, after a time, the ' Laudisti ' cultivated part-singing with extraordinary success.[1]

A highly interesting MS. volume, once belonging to a company of ' Laudisti ' enrolled in the year 1336 at the Chiesa d' Ogni Santi at Florence, is now preserved in the Magliabecchi Library : and, from this, Burney (Hist. ii. 328) quotes a very beautiful example—' Alta Trinità beata.' The earliest printed collection is dated 1485. This, however, would seem to have been either unknown to, or unrecognised by, the disciples of S. Philip Neri ; for, in 1565, Giovanni Animuccia, who acted as his maestro di cappella, published a volume entitled ' Il primo libro delle Laudi,' followed by a ' Secondo libro,' of more advanced character, in 1570. These sacred songs, which formed the germ of the performances afterwards called oratorio, became so popular among the youths who flocked to S. Philip for instruction, that, in 1588— seventeen years after the death of the saintly Animuccia—P. Soto thought it desirable to edit a third volume, containing unacknowledged works, for three and four voices, by some of the greatest composers of the age. In 1589 the same zealous editor published an amended reprint of the three volumes, consolidated into one ; succeeded, in 1591, by a fourth volume, dedicated to the Duchessa d'Aquasparta. Serafino Razzi published a large collection, in 1563, and many others followed—for, at this period, almost every large town, and even many an important parish, had its own company of ' Laudisti,' who sang the poetry of Lorenzo de' Medici, Poliziano, Pulci, Bembo, Ludovico Martelli, Giambellari, Filicaia and other celebrated writers, with undiminished interest, though, as time progressed, the character of the music sensibly deteriorated.

In the year 1770, Burney heard the company of Laudisti attached to the Church of S. Maria Maddalena de' Pazzi, in Florence, sing, with excellent effect, in some street processions, as well as in some of the churches, from a book then just published for their use.   w. s. r.

LAUDS (Lat. Laudes), the name given to that division of the Canonical Hours which immediately follows Matins.

The Office of Lauds opens, according to the Ritual of the Western Church, with the series of Versicles and Responses beginning ' Deus in adjutorium meum intende,' followed by select Psalms with Antiphons. These are succeeded by the ' Capitulum ' (or ' Little Chapter ') ; the Hymn for the Day, with its proper Versicle and Response ; and the ' Benedictus.' The Service then concludes with the Collect for the Day and the Commemorations (as at Vespers).

The plain-song music proper to it will be found in the Antiphonal. (See MATINS ; ANTIPHON.)   w. s. r. ; rev. by w. h. f.

LAUFENBERG (LOUFENBERG), HEINRICH VON (d. Mar. 31, 1460),[2] mediæval ecclesiastic and poet, was, in 1434, dean at Zofingen, between Basle and Lucerne, later at Freiburg-im-Breisgau, and in 1445 entered the Johanniterkloster at Strassburg. He deserves mention as being one of the first to adapt German sacred words to old secular tunes, so as to save the beautiful tunes while rejecting the objectionable words with which they were at first associated, a practice which was afterwards so much in vogue at the time of the Reformation. His poems may be found in Wackernagel, Das deutsche Kirchenlied, Bd. II. Nos. 701-798. Ambros[3] quotes his German paraphrase of the Salve Regina, words and music, but mistakenly attributes the melody to Laufenberg, though he afterwards so far corrects himself as to describe it as ' eine volksthümliche Umbildung der kirchlichen Melodie.' R. von Liliencron[4] has shown that the melody is nothing else but that of the plain-song Salve Regina, the text of which Laufenberg has so paraphrased in German verses that every note of the plain-song melisma is sung to a separate syllable. The whole piece is an interesting example of the practice by which the originally textless melismata on the final syllable of the Gradual Alleluias were developed into the Proses and Hymns called Sequences. For the use of his choir at Leipzig, Carl Riedel edited several 'Altdeutsche geistliche Lieder' by Laufenberg, arranged for four voices, and published by E. W. Fritzsch.   J. R. M.

LAUKO, DESIDERIUS (b. Sarvaš, in the district of Béckeš, Nov. 8, 1872), Slovak composer, LL.D. and financial secretary at Bratislava. His father, a Slovak schoolmaster, early awakened the sense of music in his son. After passing through the secondary school and the gymnasium at Sarvaš, he proceeded to study law at the University of Budapest. His musical education was carried on at the Academy in the Hungarian capital, under Professor Szendy. His early musical training was

---

[1] For a study of the technique and example of the style see Adler's Handbuch der Musikgeschichte (Ludwig), p. 176 et seq.

[2] Riemann.   [3] Geschichte der Musik, ii. pp. 256-9.   [4] Monatschrift für Gottesdienst und kirchliche Kunst. 1896, p. 265.

Magyar rather than Slavonic; later on, however, his enthusiasm for Slovak scenery and folk-music awakened a desire to treat some of the popular tunes in art forms—rhapsodies, humoresques, berceuses, etc. His best work of the kind is the arrangement of the Slovak dances (7 books, still in MS.).   A. K. and R. N.

LAURENCE, FREDERICK (b. London, May 25, 1884), composer, at first followed a commercial career, but studied music privately under Josef Holbrooke. Afterwards he travelled in Germany, France and Austria, gaining musical experience in various ways. On his return to England he became librarian to one or two of the most important orchestral organisations in London, doing much useful work in the way of arranging and scoring. He was also for a time a partner in a London firm of music librarians and publishers. In 1924 he transferred some of his activities to other fields. Between 1910–12 he composed an opera, 'The Pariah,' which he afterwards destroyed, a fate shared by several early and immature works. An orchestral Legend, 'The Spirit's Wayfaring,' was produced by Sir Henry J. Wood at the Queen's Hall Promenade Concerts on Oct. 2, 1918, and another work for orchestra, 'The Dance of the Witch Girl,' on Oct. 12, 1920. A lighter piece for string orchestra, 'Tristis,' has a certain vogue. In 1922 and 1923 Laurence visited Vienna, where he conducted some of his works.

The music of Frederick Laurence is daring as regards harmony, exceedingly complex in texture, and richly scored. In spite of its non-conformity with established usages, it does not reveal indiscriminate sympathy with all the new tendencies. It is absolute music in so far as it seeks to express only such conceptions as lie outside the scope of any other art. Most frequently it deals with occult matters and aims at arousing a mystical emotion rather than at making its appeal to the senses or the intellect.

Other works by Laurence are:

'A Miracle,' 'Enchantment,' 'Fire Earth,' 'Milandor,' Night,' 'The Dream Harlequin,' 'The Passionate Quest,' all for orchestra; Sextet for strings; Trio for vln., vcl. and PF.; Sonata for vln. and PF.; various pieces for PF.   E. B.

LAURENCIE, LIONEL DE LA (b. Nantes, July 24, 1861). While following the study of law and of science, he early initiated himself into musical technique with Leon Reynier for violin, Alph. Weingartner and Bourgault-Ducoudray (at the Paris Conservatoire, 1891–92) for harmony. At the end of 1898 he devoted himself entirely to the study of music, gave some very popular courses at the École des Hautes-Études Sociales, on such subjects as: 'Quelques maîtres de l'ancienne école de violon' (1906), 'Les Origines de l'Opéra-Comique' (1907), 'Le Ballet de cour avant Lully' (1910), 'Les Pastorales en musique au XVIIIème siècle' (1911), 'Les Formes instrumentales'

(1913). He has also given numerous lectures both in France and abroad.

De La Laurencie has contributed a number of articles to the Mercure musical (1905–06), the review S.I.M., the Revue musicale, to the quarterly publications of the I.M.G., to the R.M.I.; he has also written books, of which the best known are Le Goût musical en France (1905), the Académie de musique et le concert de Nantes (1906), Quelques documents sur Jean Philippe Rameau et sa famille (1907), Rameau (1908), the École française de violon de Lully à Viotti (3 vols., Paris, 1922–24). A work on the lutenists is in preparation (1926).

He has been president at different times of the Société Française de Musicologie, of which he was one of the founders, and has succeeded Lavignac as editor of the Encyclopédie de la Musique et Dictionnaire du Conservatoire, published by Delagrave.   M. P.

LAURENTI, (1) BARTOLOMEO GIROLAMO (b. Bologna, c. 1644; d. there, Jan. 18, 1726), violinist-composer, violinist at S. Petronio and member of the Academia Filarmonica, Bologna. He composed 'Sonate da camera a vn°. e vcl°.' op. 3; 'Sei concerti a . . . vn°., vcl°. ed org.'; 1 sonata violin and basso continuo in collective volumes published by Buffagnotti, 1700.

(2) GIROLAMO NICOLO (b. Bologna; d. there, Dec. 26, 1752), son of Bartolomeo, pupil of Torelli and Vitali; violinist at San Petronio. He composed 6 concertos for 3 violins, viola, violoncello and organ. By 'Laurenti' without Christian name, are 6 concertos and 1 solo piece. (See Q.-L.)

LAURENTIUS VON SCHNÜFFIS (real name JOHANN MARTIN) (b. Schniffis, Vorarlberg, Aug. 24, 1633; d. Constance, Jan. 7, 1702). As an itinerant scholar he earned his subsistence by singing and rhyming until he received an engagement at the Innsbruck court theatre in 1660. In 1665 he entered a religious order, and sometime after was made a poet laureate by the Emperor Leopold I. He is one of the few monodic song-writers of the 17th century, but of the nine books of his songs (list in Q.-L.) the melodies are at least partly by Father Romanus Vötter.   E. V. D. S.

LAURO, DOMENICO (b. Padua, c. 1540), went to Mantua c. 1598 and became maestro di cappella at the cathedral. He composed masses, madrigals, etc. (Q.-L.).

LAUTENCLAVICYMBEL, 'lute-harpsichord,' invented by J. S. Bach in 1740, strung with gut strings for the two 'unison' stops, and with an octave stop of wire. Its tone, when checked by a damper of cloth, was so like a lute as to deceive a lute-player by profession. (See HARPSICHORD, and Adlung's Mus. Mech. ii. 139; Spitta's J. S. Bach, Engl. transl. ii. 47.)

LAUTERBACH, JOHANN CHRISTOPH (b. Culmbach, Bavaria, July 24, 1832; d. Dresden, Apr. 1918), distinguished violinist.

His education he received at the school and
gymnasium of Würzburg, where he also learnt
music from Bratsch and Fröhlich. In 1850 he
entered the Conservatoire at Brussels as pupil
of De Bériot and Fétis ; in 1851 received the
gold medal, and during Léonard's absence took
his place as professor of the violin. In 1853 he
became Konzertmeister and professor of the
violin at the Conservatorium of Munich ; in
1861, on the death of Lipinski, was appointed
second Konzertmeister of the royal band at
Dresden, and in 1873 succeeded to the first
place. From 1861–77 he also held the post of
principal teacher of the violin in the Conservatorium of Dresden, with great and increasing
renown. He travelled much, and always with
success. He spent the seasons of 1864 and
1865 in England, appearing at the Philharmonic on May 2 of the former and May 15 of
the latter year, and playing also at the Musical
Union. In Paris he played at the last concert
at the Tuileries before the war ; and received
from the Emperor Napoleon a gold snuff-box
set with diamonds. He was decorated with
many orders, both of North and South Germany. In the summer of 1876 he met with a
serious mountain accident in Switzerland, by
which several of his companions were killed and
he himself severely injured. He, however,
completely recovered.   Lauterbach's style
united the best peculiarities of the Belgian
school, great polish and elegance, with the
breadth of the German.   P. D.

LAVENU, (1) LEWIS, an important London
music-publisher, who was in business in 1796
at 23 Duke Street, St. James's. About 1800 he
had removed to 29 New Bond Street, and in
1803 he entered into partnership with Mitchell.
In 1809 Mitchell dropped out of the firm, and
L. Lavenu was sole proprietor.

(2) ELIZABETH, probably a relative, was in
business on her own account about 1820 at
24 Edwards Street, Manchester Square, but
she appears shortly before 1822 to have succeeded to the business at 28 Bond Street, where
in 1838 Louis Henry Lavenu was in partnership with Nicholas Mori the violinist.

The Lavenu family issued great quantities of
sheet music, vocal and instrumental, almost
always printed on coarse, blue-tinged paper.
                                          F. K.

(3) LOUIS HENRY (b. London, 1818 ; d. Sydney, Australia, Aug. 1, 1859), son of a flautist
and music-seller. He was a pupil of the
R.A.M., where he studied composition under
Bochsa and Potter. Before leaving the Academy he was engaged as a violoncellist at the
Opera and the Westminster Abbey Festival of
1834. He was also in business as a music-seller
in partnership with his stepfather, Nicholas
Mori, the eminent violinist, after whose death
in 1839 he continued the business alone for a
few years. During this time he published a few

songs and short pianoforte pieces composed by
himself. His opera, ' Loretta, a Tale of Seville,'
words by Bunn, was produced at Drury Lane,
Nov. 9, 1846, with success. Dissatisfied with
his position, Lavenu emigrated to Australia,
and obtained the post of director of the music
at the Sydney Theatre.   w. H. H.

LAVIGNAC, ALEXANDRE JEAN ALBERT
(b. Paris, Jan. 22, 1846 ; d. there, May 28,
1916), was a pupil of the Conservatoire, carrying off the first prize for solfège in 1857, the
first prize for piano in 1861, the first for harmony and accompaniment in 1863, the first for
counterpoint and fugue in 1864 and the second
for organ in 1865. He was appointed assistant
professor of solfège in 1871 ; professor in 1875 ;
and professor of harmony in 1891. In 1915 he
became honorary professor. His Cours complet
théorique et pratique de dictée musicale (1881),
suggested to most French conservatoires and
schools the practical value of musical dictation.
                              G. F. ; rev. M. L. P.

In 1902 Lavignac formed the scheme for the
great publication, Encyclopédie de la musique et
Dictionnaire du Conservatoire, which started
publication on May 30, 1913 (see HISTORIES OF
MUSIC), and which he edited until his death.
Its present editor is L. de La LAURENCIE (q.v.).

BIBL.—Bulletin de la Société Française de Musicologie, 1917, i.
                                          M. L. P.

LIST OF WORKS

Cinquante leçons d'harmonie.
8 vols. of Solféges.
L'Éducation musicale. (1902.)
Notions scolaires de musique. (1905, 1906, 2 vols.)
Théorie complète des principes fondamentaux de la musique moderne.
    (1909.)
Cours d'harmonie pratique. (1909.)
Solfège des solfèges (33 vols.), (Danhauser - Lemoine), additions by
    Lavignac.
L'École de la pédale. (1889.)
La Musique et les musiciens ; Le Voyage artistique à Bayreuth
    (Paris, 1895, 1897), the 2nd transl. into English by Esther
    Singleton as The Music Drama of Richard Wagner (London,
    1898.)
Les Gaietés du Conservatoire. (1899.)

LAVIGNE, ANTOINE JOSEPH (b. Besançon,
May [1] 23, 1816 ; d. Manchester, Aug. 1, 1886),
oboe-player, received his early musical education from his father, a musician in an infantry
regiment. On Jan. 24, 1830, he was admitted
a pupil of the Conservatoire at Paris, where he
studied the oboe under Vogt, but was obliged
to leave on May 3, 1835, on account of his
father's regiment being ordered from Paris. He
resumed his position on Oct. 17, 1836, and
obtained the first prize in 1837. He was for
several years principal oboe at the Théâtre
Italien at Paris. In 1841 he came to England,
and appeared as oboe soloist at the Promenade
Concerts at Drury Lane, and was for many
years a member of Hallé's orchestra at Manchester. He fell into great poverty and distress, and was admitted into the infirmary of
St. Saviour's, Southwark, in 1885, and removed
thence to the Royal Infirmary, Manchester,
where he died.

Lavigne addressed himself with great earnest-

[1] Date given by M. L. P.

ness to applying to the oboe the system of keys which Boehm (or Gordon) had contrived for the flute, and devoted several years to perfecting the instrument. This admirable player had great execution and feeling; but what was most remarkable was his power and length of breath, which, by some secret known to himself, enabled him to give the longest phrases without breaking them.   w. h. h. ; addns. w. h. c.

LAVOIX, HENRI MARIE FRANÇOIS (b. Paris, Apr. 26, 1846 ; d. there, Dec. 27, 1897) (known as Lavoix fils, to distinguish him from his father, the conservateur of the collection of coins in the Bibliothèque Nationale), eminent writer on music, was educated at the university of the Sorbonne, where he took the degree of bachelier, while studying harmony and counterpoint with H. Cohen. His writings on musical history are as follows : *Les Traducteurs de Shakespeare en musique*(1869); *La Musique dans l'imagerie du moyen âge* (1875) ; *La Musique dans la Nature* (1877) ; *Histoire de l'instrumentation* (1878, crowned by the Institut) ; *Le Chant, ses principes et son histoire* (with Th. Lemaire) ; *La Musique du siècle de Saint-Louis* ; *Histoire de la musique* ; *Histoire de la musique française* ; and many articles in magazines, etc. He was appointed librarian of the Bibliothèque Nationale in 1865.   G. F. ; rev. M. L. P.

LAWES. The name of an English family of musicians in the 17th century, of whom

(1) THOMAS was the founder. The identification of Thomas Lawes of Dinder,[1] near Wells, Somerset, with the vicar - choral of Salisbury of the same name has not been ascertained with certainty. The latter died Nov. 7, 1640, and was buried in the north transept of Salisbury Cathedral. He is presumed to have been twice married and the father of three sons, two of whom, William (4) and Henry (2), are of historical importance.

In the registers of Dinton in Wiltshire there are two entries which establish Thomas of Dinder as the father of Henry ; the marriage (1593–94) on Feb. 3 of ' Thomas Lawes of Dynder in the countie of Somerset and Lucris Shepharde, the daughter of Junne Shepharde of Dinton,' and (1595–96), ' In this yeare ye fift day of January Thomas Lawes had a sonne christened named Henry.' [2]

(2) HENRY (b. Dinton, Wilts, c. Dec. 1595 ; d. Oct. 21, 1662), received his musical education from John COOPER (Coprario). On Jan. 1, 1625–26, he was sworn in as epistler of the Chapel Royal, and on Nov. 3 following, one of the gentlemen, and afterwards became clerk of the cheque. In 1633 he furnished music for Thomas Carew's masque, ' Coelum Britannicum,' performed at court, Feb. 18, 1633–34. In this masque the Earl of Bridgewater's two

sons took part, and this circumstance very probably led to his being employed as music-teacher in the family, and so to the production of Milton's masque, ' Comus,' [3] written at his request and produced at Ludlow Castle on Michaelmas night, Lawes performing the part of the Attendant Spirit. Both Hawkins and Burney have printed ' Sweet Echo,' one of the songs in ' Comus.' The whole of the songs are in the B.M. Add. MSS. 11,518, and the music was published entire by the Mermaid Society in 1904. In 1637 appeared

' A Paraphrase vpon the Psalmes of David. By G[eorge] S[andys]. Set to new Tunes for private Devotion. And a thorow Base, for Voice or Instrument. By Henry Lawes ' ;

and in 1648

' Choice Psalmes put into Musick for Three Voices. . . . Composed by Henry and William Lawes, Brothers and Servants to His Majestie. With divers Elegies set in Musick by several friends, upon the death of William Lawes. And at the end of the Thorough Base [4] are added nine [5] Canons of Three and Four Voices made by William Lawes.'

A copper-plate portrait of Charles I., believed to be the last published in his lifetime, accompanies each part, and amongst the commendatory verses prefixed to the work is the sonnet, addressed by Milton to Henry Lawes in Feb. 1645–46,[6] beginning ' Harry, whose tuneful and well-measured song.' Lawes composed the Christmas songs in Herrick's ' Hesperides,' and the songs in the plays and poems of William Cartwright.

Comedies, and tragi-Comedies, with other poems by Mr. William Cartwright. . . . The Ayres and Songs set by Mr. Henry Lawes . . . London, 1651.

It contains no music, however. In 1652 some of his songs appeared in Playford's ' Select Musical Ayres,' and in 1653 Lawes published ' Ayres and Dialogues for One, Two and Three Voyces,' with his portrait [7] finely engraved by Faithorne on the title. This was received with such favour as to induce him to issue two other books with the same title in 1655 and 1658. In 1656 he was engaged with Capt. Henry Cooke, Dr. Charles Colman and George Hudson in providing the music for Davenant's ' First Day's Entertainment of Musick at Rutland House.' On the Restoration in 1660, Lawes was reinstated in his court appointments. He composed the anthem ' Zadok the Priest,' for the coronation of Charles II. He died Oct. 21, 1662, and was buried (Oct. 25) in the cloisters of Westminster Abbey. Many of his songs are to be found in ' Select Musical Ayres and Dialogues,' 1652, 1653 and 1659, and ' The Treasury of Musick,' 1669.

Henry Lawes was highly esteemed by his contemporaries, both as a composer and performer. Milton praises him in both capacities, and Herrick in an epigram places him on a level with some of the most renowned singers

---

[1] The Rev. M. Y. McClean, rector of Dinder, kindly made search of his parish registers for the present edition of this Dictionary, but without result.
[2] This agrees with the evidence of the portrait in the Bishop's palace at Salisbury inscribed ' H Lawes aetat 26, 1622.' See *D.N.B*
[3] See Peck's *New Memoirs*, etc., p. 12
[4] The work is in separate parts.   [5] Really ten.
[6] As to the difficulties connected with this date, and the original title, see *Notes and Queries*, 2nd ser. vi. 337, 395, 492.
[7] Reproduced in former editions of this Dictionary.

and players of his time ; but later writers have formed a lower estimate of his abilities as a composer. Burney declares his productions to be ' languid and insipid, and equally devoid of learning and genius ' ; and Hawkins speaks of his music as deficient in melody and ' neither recitative nor air, but in so precise a medium between both that a name is wanting for it.' But both appear to judge from a false point of view. It was not Lawes's object to produce melody in the popular sense of the word, but to set ' words with just note and accent,' to make the prosody of his text his principal care ; and it was doubtless that quality which induced all the best poetical writers of his day, from Milton and Waller downwards, to desire that their verses should be set by him. To effect his object he employed a kind of ' aria parlante,' a style of composition which, if expressively sung, would cause as much gratification to the cultivated hearer as the most ear-catching melody would to the untrained listener. His work of this kind is historically important apart from its intrinsic merits, since it marks a stage in the setting of the English language to music in a way which reached its consummation in Purcell (see under PURCELL, CHARACTERISTICS OF PURCELL'S ART ; also SONG, section ENGLAND). Lawes was careful in the choice of words, and the words of his songs would form a very pleasing volume of lyric poetry. Hawkins says that notwithstanding Lawes ' was a servant of the church, he contributed nothing to the increase of its stores ' ; but, besides the coronation anthem before mentioned, there are (or were) in an old choir book of the Chapel Royal fragments of eight or ten anthems by him, and the words of several of his anthems are given in Clifford's ' Divine Services and Anthems,' 1664. In 1901 Dr. Cooper Smith, Rector of Basingstoke, owned a MS. volume (formerly belonging to Gostling, R. Smith and Dr. Hayes), dated in the binding 1634, containing many compositions by H. Lawes. These include ' Dispairs Banquet, sung in The Pasions written by Mr. Wm. Strood, presented by ye scollers of Ch. Ch. before both their Majestys, 1636,' ' Come from the Dungeon, sung in . . . ye Royal Slave—written by Mr. Wm. Cartwright presented by the scollers of Ch. Ch. in Oxford before their Majestys 1636,' ' The five songs in Comus . . . presented . . . Oct. 1634,' etc., and ' Cupid to ye Knights Templars in a Maske at ye Middle Temple.' A portrait of Henry Lawes is in the Music School, Oxford (reproduced on *PLATE XLII.*). Another painted in 1622, is in the bishop's palace at Salisbury.[1]

[1] This is said in a note to the Cooper Smith MS. mentioned above to have been picked up at a stall in Salisbury by Elderton, a chapter clerk, and left by Bishop Barrington in 1791 as an heirloom to the palace with a portrait of Bishop Jewel, ' the Musical Bishop.'
W. B. S.

(3) JOHN, a brother of Henry, was a lay-vicar of Westminster Abbey. He died in Jan. 1654–55, and was buried in the Abbey cloisters.

(4) WILLIAM [2] (d. Chester, 1645), elder half-brother of Henry, received musical instruction from Coprario at the expense of the Earl of Hertford. He became a member of the choir of Chichester Cathedral, which he quitted in 1602, on being appointed a gentleman of the Chapel Royal. He was sworn in Jan. 1, 1602–1603. On May 5, 1611, he resigned his place in favour of Ezekiel Waad, a lay-vicar of Westminster Abbey, but on Oct. 1, following, was readmitted ' without paie.' He was also one of the musicians in ordinary to Charles I. In 1633 he joined Simon Ives in the composition of the music for Shirley's ' Triumph of Peace.' In 1635 he wrote the music for Davenant's masque, ' The triumph of the Prince d'Amour,' preserved in the Bodleian (Music Sch. MSS. B, 2, 3, and D, 229). An anthem by him is printed in Boyce's ' Cathedral Music ' ; songs and other vocal compositions in ' Select Musicall Ayres and Dialogues,' 1653 and 1659 ; ' Catch that catch can,' 1652 ; ' The Treasury of Musick,' 1669 ; and ' Choice Psalms,' 1648 ; and some of his instrumental music in ' Courtly Masquing Ayres,' 1662. His portrait is in the Music School, Oxford. ' The Royal Consort ' for viols, consisting of sixty-six short pieces, and some ' Airs ' for violin and bass are in the B.M. Add. MSS. 10,445, 31,431-2 ; the latter MS. contains also a canon, ' 'Tis joy to hear,' and fifty-five vocal compositions. B.M. Add. MSS. 29,410-4, and 17,798 contain more of his pieces, and in the Christ Church Library are his ' Great Consorte ' (I. 5, 1-6) and other works (I. 4, 79-82, 91-3, K. 3, 32, and H. I. 12 and 18). Canons and MS. songs are contained in B.M. Eg. MS. 2013, Add. MSS. 29,396-7, 30,273, 31,423, 31,433, 31,462. His best-known work is the partsong ' Gather ye rosebuds while ye may.' On the breaking out of the Civil War he joined the Royalist army, and was made a commissary by Lord Gerrard, to exempt him from danger, but his active spirit disdaining that security, he was killed by a stray shot during the siege of Chester, 1645.

w. H. H. ; with addns. c., incorporating information from W. B. S., etc.

LAWROWSKA, ELIZABETH ANDREJEWNA LAWROWSKAJA, known as Mme. Lawrowska (b. Kaschin, Twer, Russia, Oct. 12, 1845), mezzo-soprano singer. She was taught singing by Fenzi at the Elizabeth Institute, and by Mme. Nissen-Saloman at the Conservatoire of St. Petersburg.

In 1867 she made her début as Orpheus at three performances of Gluck's opera, given by

[2] An entry in the register of Dinton of 1594 of the marriage of William Lawes does not apparently relate to the musician, since the description reads ' William Lawes, son of Henry Lawes of Styple Langforde,' etc

XLII

HENRY LAWES

From a painting in the Music School Collection, Oxford

JOHN PLAYFORD

After a print by Logan

the students of the Conservatoire under Rubinstein, at the Palace of the Grand Duchess Helena, thanks to whose kindness she was enabled to study abroad. From 1868–72 she was engaged at the Russian Opera-Theatre Marie, and on July 31, 1871, she married the Prince Zereteiev at Odessa. In 1868 she was announced to sing at the Italian Opera, Covent Garden, but did not appear. She left the opera for a time and sang in concerts all over Europe, having received further instruction from Mme. Viardot-Garcia. She visited this country in 1873, and made her first appearance, Feb. 24, at the Monday Popular Concerts, and Mar. 1 at the Crystal Palace. During her stay she made a great impression by her grand mezzo-soprano voice and fine declamatory powers of singing in operatic airs of Handel and Glinka, and in the Lieder of Schubert, Schumann, etc. In 1881 she reappeared in England in concerts, but for a very short period. In 1878 she returned to the St. Petersburg Opera. The principal Russian operas in which she performed were ' La Vie pour le Czar ' and ' Russlan and Ludmila ' of Glinka, ' Russalka ' of Dargomijsky, and ' Wrazyïa Silow ' of Serov.   A. C.

LAY, a Provençal word, originally probably Celtic, meaning at first a sound or noise, and then a song, especially the tune, as the quotations from Spenser, Milton and Dryden in Johnson's Dictionary prove. Beyond this general sense the term has no application to music. The German ' Lied ' is another form of the word.
                                          G.

LAYOLLE, FRANCISCUS DE, or FRANCESCO DELL' AIOLLE, a French composer of the earlier part of the 13th century, who settled as organist at Florence about 1540, and was Benvenuto Cellini's teacher in music. He edited, for the Lyons music-printer Jacques Moderne or Modernus, a book of ten masses (' Liber decem Missarum,' 1532–40), among which are three masses and three motets by himself. His Mass ' Adieu, mes amours,' Ambros describes as a remarkable work. His other works are canzoni *a* 5 and *a* 4, published by Modernus, 1540 and later, and other madrigals and motets in various collections. From a rare work entitled *Contrapunctus seu figurata musica super plano cantu,* etc., Lyons, 1528, Kade in his *Beilagen zu Ambros* has reprinted two motets by Layolle, ' Salve Virgo singularis ' and ' Media vita,' both *a* 4, which, as the title of the work indicates, are contrapuntal studies on a plain-song tenor. From this connexion of Layolle with works printed in Lyons, it would seem as if Lyons had been his birthplace, and it appears that Aleman Layolle, his son, was for a while organist at Lyons, but afterwards returned to Florence, and was music-teacher to a daughter of Benvenuto Cellini.   J. R. M.

LAYS, FRANÇOIS (b. La Barthe de Nesthes, Old Gascony, Feb. 14, 1758 ; d. Ingrande, near Angers, Mar. 30, 1831), a famous French singer, whose real name was LAY or LAÏ. He learned music in the monastery of Guaraison, but before he was 20 his fame as a singer had spread, and in Apr. 1779 he found himself at Paris to be tried for the Opéra. His name first appears in Lajarte's catalogue of first representations, as Pétrarque, in a ' pastoral héroïque ' by Candeille, called ' Laure et Pétrarque,' July 2, 1780, and is spelt Laïs. His next mention is in the ' Iphigénie en Tauride ' of Piccinni, Jan. 23, 1781, where he has the rôle of a coryphée.[1] After that he appears frequently in company with Mlle. Saint-Huberti, a famous soprano of that day. He was also attached to the concerts of Marie Antoinette, and to the Concert Spirituel. He was a poor actor, unless in parts specially written for him ; but the splendour of his voice made up for everything, and he preserved it so well as to remain in the company of the Opéra till Oct. 1823.

Lays was a violent politician on the popular side, which did not please his colleagues, and some quarrels arose in consequence, but with no further result than to cause him to write a pamphlet, and to force him, after the 9th Thermidor, to appear in parts distasteful to him, and to sing before the Bourbons after the Restoration. He was professor of singing at the Conservatoire from 1795–99, when he retired from the post ; and from 1819–26 held the same office in the ' École royale de chant et de déclamation.' He had been principal singer in the chapel of Napoleon from 1801 till the fall of the Emperor, but was cashiered by Louis XVIII. After leaving the École he retired to Ingrande, where he died. We have said that he was not a good actor, but Fétis pronounces him not even a good singer, saying that his taste was poor and that he had several bad tricks ; but he had warmth and animation, and the beauty of his voice so far atoned for all that for a long time no opera could be successful in which he had not a part.   G.

LAY-VICAR or LAY-CLERK, a singer in English Cathedral Choirs. (See VICARS-CHORAL.)

LAZARI, FRATE ALBERTO, a carmelite monk, maestro di cappella and organist at the parochial college of Massa Lombarda in 1635 ; academician at Cesena, 1637 ; afterwards at Perugia. He composed 2 books of church music (*Q.-L.*).

LAZARINI, FRA SCIPIONE (17th cent.), Augustinian monk and composer at Ancona. His earliest known composition is a 3-part song in a collective volume, 1646, followed by 2 books of motets, opp. 1 and 2 (1674), and a book of psalms (1675). In MS. in the Bologna Library are 3 masses and 4 motets, 4-8 v.
                                          E. v. d. S.

[1] The rôle of the ' Seigneur bienfaisant ' is said by Fétis to have been written for him, but his name does not appear in the company at the first performance of that piece.

LAZARO, VALVASENSI (b. Valvasone, Udine, late 16th cent.), organist at Murano, 1622; maestro di cappella and organist at Tolmezo, Friuli, 1626; organist at Valvasone, 1630. He composed church music, 2-5 v., a book of sacred songs, and two books of secular monodic songs between 1620–34 (Q.-L.).

LAZARUS, HENRY (b. London, Jan. 1, 1815; d. London, Mar. 6, 1895), clarinettist, began the study of the clarinet when a boy under Blizard, bandmaster of the Royal Military Asylum, Chelsea, and continued it under Charles Godfrey, sen., bandmaster of the Coldstream Guards. After fulfilling engagements in various theatrical and other orchestras he was, in 1838, appointed as second to Willman at the Sacred Harmonic Society. On the death of Willman in 1840 Lazarus succeeded him as principal clarinet at the Opera and all the principal concerts, festivals, etc., in London and the provinces, a position he retained for many years with great and ever-increasing reputation. He was a professor of his instrument at the R.A.M. from 1854, and at Kneller Hall from 1858. He gave a farewell concert in St. James's Hall, May 31, 1892.   W. H. H.

LAZZARI, SYLVIO (b. Botzen, Tyrol, Jan. 1, 1860), a composer who after studying law at Innsbruck and Munich, entered the Paris Conservatoire in 1883–84, but his chief studies were carried on under César Franck. The following works have been publicly performed : The pantomime, 'Lulu,' brought out in 1887; the musical drama, ' Armor,' at the Landestheater in Prague in 1898, and ' L'Ensorcelé,' in Paris in 1903; 'La Lépreuse' (Ger. 'Die Angeschlossene,' translated by Emma Klagenfeld and Sylvio Lazzari), performed Paris, Opéra-Comique, Feb. 7, 1912; 'Melaenis' (Paris, 1915); 'Le Sauteriot,' performed Paris, Opéra-Comique Apr. 8, 1920. For orchestra he has written a 'Rhapsodie espagnole,' 'Ophélie,' a symphonic poem; 'Impressions d'Adriatique'; 'Effet de nuit ' (1904), 'Marche de fête,' a fantasia for violin and orchestra, and a Concertstück for piano and orchestra. His chamber compositions include a sonata for piano and violin (1894), a trio, a string quartet (1911), an octet for wind instruments, Concertstück for violin and orchestra, ' Trois pièces pour piano ' (1912), Barcarolle for violoncello and piano (1914), ' Suite d'orchestre,' F major, symphony in E flat major, 'Rhapsodie ' for violin and piano (1922), 'Romanzetta ' for PF. (1923), second ' Rhapsodie hongroise ' for PF. (1924), songs to poems by Verlaine, Bataille, Rollinat, Maeterlinck, Tristan Klingsor, etc.

G. F. ; addns. M. L. P.

BIBL.—GUSTAVE DORET, Musique et musiciens (Lausaune, 1915); AD. BOSCHOT, Chez les musiciens (Paris, 1924).

LAZZARINI, GUSTAVO (b. Padua, or Verona,[1] c. 1765), a tenor singer, whose début was made

[1] Biographers differ as to the place of his birth.

at Lucca in 1789, in Zingarelli's ' Ifigenia in Aulide,' with great éclat.

In the two following years he appeared in London, singing both in serious and comic operas, such as Bertoni's ' Quinto Fabio ' and the ' Locanda ' of Paisiello, in the former with Pacchierotti, but taking the principal rôle in the latter. Lord Mount-Edgcumbe thought him 'a very pleasing singer with a sweet tenor voice.' During the Carnival of 1794 he sang at Milan, with Grassini and Marchesi, in Zingarelli's 'Artaserse' and the 'Demofoönte' of Portogallo, and bore the comparison inevitably made between him and those great singers. He sang there again in 1795, and once more in 1798, appearing on the latter occasion in Cimarosa's ' Orazzi ' and Zingarelli's 'Meleagro,' with Riccardi and Crescentini. In 1801 he was one of the Opera Buffa troupe at Paris, where he was again heard to advantage by Lord Mount-Edgcumbe (1802), singing in company with La Strinasacchi and Georgi Belloc. But his voice had now lost much of its freshness, though the great style remained. Lazzarini published two volumes of Italian airs, and a Pastoral, both at Paris (Carli). His portrait was engraved there by Nitôt Dufrêne, an operatic singer.   J. M.

LEACH, JAMES (b. Wardle, near Rochdale, Lancashire, 1762; d. near Manchester, Feb. 8, 1798), was at first a handloom weaver. From 1789 he was a tenor singer and teacher in Rochdale, and at Salford a few years later. He published a ' New Sett of Hymn and Psalm Tunes, etc.' (Preston, London, 1789); and a ' Second Sett ' of the same, probably about 1794. His tunes are found in several of the American collections, as the Easy Instructor (Albany, New York, 1798), and the Bridgewater Collection (Boston, 1802). The David Companion or Methodist Standard (Baltimore, 1810) contains forty-eight of his pieces.[2] In the Rev. H. Parr's ' Church of England Psalmody ' will be found Mount Pleasant, Oldham and Smyrna, by him, which used to be favourites in certain congregations. His ' Psalmody ' was brought out in 1886, with a biographical sketch by Thomas Newbigging. Leach died from a stage-coach accident, near Manchester, and is buried at Rochdale.   G.

LEADER. (1) The chief of the first violins is in England called the leader of the orchestra, the Konzertmeister of the Germans, and chef d'attaque of the French. He is close to the conductor's left hand. The position is a most important one, as the animation and ' attack ' of the band depend in great measure on the leader. The great precision and force of the Gewandhaus orchestra, for instance, is said to have been mainly due to David being for so long at the head of them. It is the leader's duty to play any passages for solo violin that may occur in works other than violin concertos ; and in

[2] See a letter signed G. A. C. in Mus. T., Apr. 1878, p. 226.

orchestras that are not organised institutions the leader often makes the engagement with the individual members.

(2) In America the conductor (Fr. *chef d'or-chestre*, Ger. *Dirigent*) is generally spoken of as the 'Leader.'   c.

LEADING NOTE (Fr. *note sensible*, Ger. *Leitton*) is the seventh note of the scale, and 'leads' to the principal note, the tonic, by a semitone. In three principal Ecclesiastical modes, those on D, G and A, the note below the tonic (and also above) was at the distance of a tone. The advent of harmony gradually changed that by insisting on a major chord on the dominant. The arrival of the leading note, being due to harmonic considerations, was strongly protested against (for instance, in John XXII.'s Bull of 1322) by a Church which felt strongly the melodic associations of the modes. It has established itself in the classical period so firmly as a harmonic element that recent experiments with folk-song and the tonal scale have done little, if anything, to shake it.

But, even so, it is not unaffected by melody, for, as the French name for it reminds us, its intonation is variable. The experiments of Cornu and Mercadier (see Helmholtz, *Sensations of Tone*, 1st edn. pp. 787-91) showed that in ordinary playing on strings the major third as such was sharpened, in melody not in harmony, by a comma, but the major third on the dominant, *i.e.* the leading-note, by $1\frac{1}{3}$ commas—obviously because of the attraction of the tonic.   A. H. F. S.

LEAGUE OF COMPOSERS, see under NEW YORK.

LE BÈGUE, NICOLAS ANTOINE, see BÈGUE.

LEBERT, SIGMUND (real name LEVY) (*b.* Ludwigsburg, Würtemberg, Dec. 12, 1822; *d.* Stuttgart, Dec. 8, 1884), the virtual founder of the Stuttgart Conservatorium, received his musical education from Tomaschek and D. Weber at Prague. He settled in Munich as a pianoforte teacher for some years before 1856, where, with Faisst, Stark and others, he started the music school. He was a very accomplished and successful teacher.   G.

The *Grosse Pianoforte Schule*, which he edited with Stark, was published by the house of Cotta, and afterwards revised by Max Pauer (1904); the famous edition of Beethoven's pianoforte sonatas, issued by the same firm, was begun by these editors and continued by Hans von Bülow.   M.

LEBHAFT, *i.e.* 'lively,' the German equivalent for *Vivace*.

LEBORNE, AIMÉ AMBROISE SIMON (*b.* Brussels, Dec. 29, 1797; *d.* Paris, Apr. 1 or 2, 1866), obtained the Grand Prix de Rome in 1820, as composition pupil of Cherubini, and successively taught 'solfège' counterpoint, fugue and composition at the Paris Conserva-

toire, the latter branch 1836–66, replacing Reicha. He became librarian at the Opéra and of the Imperial Chapel under Napoleon III. He composed 'Les Deux Figaro' performed at the Odéon (1827), wrote treatises of harmony and counterpoint and gave out a new edition of Catel's harmony treatise.   M. L. P.

LE BORNE, FERNAND, see BORNE.

LEBRUN, JEAN (*b.* Lyons, Apr. 6, 1759; *d.* Paris *c.* 1809), famous horn-player; studied in Paris under Punto. He possessed great technical ability, and produced the highest notes with perfect ease. From 1786–92 he was at the Paris Opéra when the Revolution drove him to London, whence he went to Berlin as member of the royal chapel. In 1802 he toured on the Rhine and in the Netherlands, and returned to Paris in 1806, where he failed to find an appointment and died in poverty. He is credited with the invention of the mute for the horn. Some horn concertos of his remained in MS. (*Mendel*; *Q.-L.*).

LEBRUN, (1) LUDWIG AUGUST (*b.* Mannheim, *c.* 1746; *d.* Berlin, Dec. 15, 1790), one of the greatest of oboe virtuosi of the 18th century. In 1764 he became a member of the Mannheim court orchestra, and followed it, on its transference to Munich in 1778. With his wife, the famous singer (see below), he toured all over Europe and met with triumphant success, especially in London and Paris. He composed 7 oboe concertos; 12 trios for oboe, violin and bass; a flute concerto and duets for flutes. (*Mendel*; *Riemann*; *Q.-L.*)

(2) FRANCESCA (*b.* Mannheim, 1756; *d.* Berlin, May 14, 1791), famous soprano singer, married Ludwig Lebrun.

She was the daughter of DANZI (*q.v.*), the violoncellist, made her first appearance (1771) when scarcely 16 years old, and charmed the court; in the next year she was engaged at the Mannheim Opera. Fétis says that in 1775 she became the wife of Lebrun, the oboist, whom she accompanied to Italy, singing first at Milan (1778) in Salieri's 'Europa riconosciuta.' The Milanese were delighted with her clear and beautiful voice and easy vocalisation, in spite of the intrigues of La Balducci, the *prima donna* of La Scala, who endeavoured to set them against her young rival. This account must, however, be corrected; for, whereas Fétis says that she only came to England in 1781, there is no doubt that she was here five years earlier, then unmarried, arriving with Roncaglia, with whom she sang in Sacchini's 'Creso.' It is clear that she did not marry Lebrun until after 1777. She reappeared in London as Mme. Lebrun in 1779, being again the *prima donna* for serious opera, and continued with Pacchierotti to sing in London for two or three seasons.

She sang in 1785 at Munich, after which she returned to Italy, achieving the same brilliant success at Venice and Naples as elsewhere. In

1788 and 1789 she appeared at Munich in Mozart's 'Idomeneo,' Prati's 'Armida,' and the 'Castor and Pollux' of Vogler. She started for Berlin in Dec. 1790 to fulfil an engagement, but on her arrival lost her husband, and herself died May 14, 1791. Mme. Lebrun, besides being a great singer, was an accomplished pianist, and published at Offenbach (1783) some sonatas with violin accompaniment, and some trios for piano, violin and violoncello.

Of her two daughters, the elder (3) SOPHIE, better known as Mme. Dulcken [1] (b. London, June 20, 1781), became celebrated as a pianist. She made successful concert-tours through France, Italy and Germany. On Apr. 18, 1799, she married Dulcken, a famous maker of pianos at Munich. She composed, but never published, some sonatas and other pieces for the piano.

(4) ROSINE, her younger sister (b. Munich, Apr. 13, 1785), was at first taught by Streicher for the piano, but afterwards studied singing under her uncle, Danzi, the Kapellmeister. She made a successful début ; but, having married Stenzsch, an actor of the Court Theatre, Nov. 30, 1801, gave up the opera to play in comedy, in which she displayed a fair amount of talent.

J. M.

LEBRUNO, LOUIS SEBASTIAN (b. Paris, Dec. 10, 1764 ; d. there, June 27, 1829), a tenor at the Paris Opéra and Opéra-Comique ; maître de chapelle of Napoleon's private music ; and composer of operas and a Te Deum (Fétis ; Q.-L.).

LECHNER, LEONHARD (b. before 1550 in the Etschthal, Austrian Tyrol ; d. Würtemberg, 1604), composer of the school of Lassus. From his birthplace comes the designation Athesinus, which he usually appended to his name. He was brought up as a chorister in the Bavarian court chapel at Munich under Orlando Lassus, of whose works he always remained an ardent admirer. In 1570 he held some post as schoolmaster in Nuremberg, and while still there began to be known as a diligent composer of motets and German songs in the madrigal or villanella style, also as editor of various collections of music. Thus in 1579 he introduced some degree of order into the chaos of the frequent republications of earlier works of Lassus, by bringing out, evidently in concert with the composer himself, a revised and enlarged edition of his two books of motets of 1568, one a 4 and 5, the other a 6-10, incorporating more of Lassus' earlier work of the same kind. In 1581 he brought out a book of five previously unpublished masses by Lassus ; and in 1583 a collection entitled Harmoniae miscellae, containing motets a 5 and 6, mostly by composers connected at one time or another with the Bavarian chapel. Dehn in his Sammlung aelterer Musik, published a selection from

this latter work, including a good motet by Lechner himself, 'Ne intres in judicium.' In 1584, probably on the recommendation of Lassus, he was appointed Kapellmeister at Hechingen to Count Eitel Friedrich of Hohenzollern, but suddenly gave up his post in 1585, without any ostensible reason. Religion may have been the determining motive, as we know that he was succeeded at Hechingen by Ferdinand Lassus, the son of Orlando ; and it was also in 1585 that Orlando dedicated to Count Eitel Friedrich a book of motets, and meanwhile Lechner, after an unsuccessful application for the post of Kapellmeister at Dresden to the then Lutheran court of Saxony, in 1587 became Kapellmeister at Stuttgart to the court of Würtemberg, where he remained till his death. It would almost appear as if he continued to cherish a hankering after the Saxon court, and endeavoured to keep up some relation with it, since his last work was the composition of a wedding-motet ('Laudate Dominum,' for fifteen voices) for the marriage of the Elector Johann Georg I. of Saxony. Besides his editorial work already referred to, Lechner's own works may be summarised as follows :

1. Two books of Motetta- or Sacrae cantiones a 4-6, containing eighty-six numbers, 1575, 1581.
2. Liber Missarum 6 et 5 voc. 1584, containing three masses and ten introits.
3. Magnificat sec. octo tonos, 1578, eight numbers.
4. Septem Psalmi Poenitentiales, etc., 6 v., 1587.
5. Various collections of Teutsche Lieder, geistliche und weltliche a 3, 4 and 5, 1575-89.

F. Commer, in his volume of 'Geistliche und weltliche Lieder,' republished four good specimens of Lechner's work : two geistliche Lieder, 'Christ ist erstanden,' a 4, and 'Herr Jesu Christ dir lebe ich,' a 5 ; two weltliche, 'Wol komt der Mey,' a 4, and 'Will uns das Meidlein nimmer han,' a 5. Also in the Publikation der Gesellschaft für Musikforschung, Bd. xix., 1895, Eitner has republished Lechner's lieder, 1579, containing his rearrangement, a 5, of twentyone Lieder a 3, from Regnart's Tricinia, and three Italian madrigals of Lechner's own. See also D.D.T. (2nd series), vol. v. 1.   J. R. M.

LECLAIR, (1) JEAN-MARIE (b. Lyons, May 10, 1697 ; d. Oct. 22, 1764), l'aîné (so called to distinguish him from his brother Antoine-Remi), an eminent violin-player, and composer for his instrument.

It has been stated that he began his public life as a dancer at the Rouen Theatre ; but this is doubtful.[2] In 1722 he went to Turin as ballet-master, where he composed some interludes for the 'Semiramide' of Orlandini, and where SOMIS (q.v.) was so much pleased with some ballet music of his that he induced him to take up the violin, which up to this time he had cultivated as a secondary pursuit only, and to place himself under his tuition. His first stay in Turin, near Somis, was only until 1723, but he returned in 1726. Leclair appears to have

---

[1] Not to be confounded with the later artist of that name.

[2] See the article by L. de La Laurencie, in the Sammlungen of the Int. Mus. Ges. vi. 250.

continued his studies for a considerable time before going to Paris in 1728. From 1728–36 he won a brilliant success in Paris at the Concert Spirituel and at the court. During this period he studied composition under Chéron. In 1734 he became a member of the royal band, but owing to a dispute with Guignon as to the leadership of the second violins, gave up his post again, and about 1735 retired from the Opéra. His name ceases to appear in the programmes of the Concert Spirituel about 1736. For the rest of his life he appears to have been exclusively occupied with the composition and publication of his works, and with teaching. He was already an old man when he made a journey to Holland at the invitation of the Princess of Orange, for the purpose of hearing and meeting Locatelli, of whose powers as a violinist he, led by the extraordinary and novel difficulties presented in the caprices of that artist, had probably formed a great idea. On his return he visited the court of Don Philip of Spain at Chambéry, in 1743–44. His opera, ' Scylla et Glaucus,' was performed in 1746, and in 1748 the Duc de Gramont appointed Leclair first violin in his private orchestra at Puteaux. Here he wrote various ballets and divertissements. Soon after his return from Holland, he was assassinated, late at night, close to the door of his own house. Neither motive nor author of the crime has ever been discovered.

Owing to the merit of his compositions for the violin, Leclair occupies a prominent place among the great classical masters of that instrument. As to his powers as a performer we have but the indirect evidence of the difficulties presented in his compositions. These are very considerable; and, barring Locatelli's eccentricities, greater than any that we find in the works of his predecessors or contemporaries. He very freely employs—in fact not seldom writes whole movements in—double-stops ; and altogether, even according to the modern standard of technique, his music is exacting both for the left hand and the bow. In one instance he directs a note to be stopped with the left thumb. As a composer, judging him after his best works, Leclair must be accorded the first place among French writers for the violin. It has been justly remarked that a great deal of what he wrote is antiquated ; but much remains that is truly charming. He is no mere imitator of the Italians, but there is a distinct individuality in many of his movements ; and also a definite national French element. On the whole, grace-fulness and vivacity are more prominent than depth of feeling ; his frequent employment of double-stops, already mentioned, giving much richness and brilliancy of sound.

The two sonatas of his, edited by Ferd. David (' Hohe Schule des Violinspiels '), are good examples of his higher powers, especially the pathetic one, surnamed ' Le Tombeau.' On

the other hand, a Saraband and Tambourin, often played with great success by Joachim and others, are good specimens of his lively style. This is a list of his works, as appended to his op. 12 :

Op.
1. Sonatas for vln. alone with a bass. (1st book.) (1723.)
2. Sonatas. (2nd book.) (c. 1728.) Another set is called ' opus 1' and published by Walsh.
3. Sonatas for two vlns. without bass. (1730.) (c. 1732.)
4. Sonatas en trio for two vlns. and basso continuo. (c. 1730.)
5. Sonatas for vln. alone (3rd book.) (1734.)
6. ' Première Récréation de musique . . . pour deux violons et B.C.' (1737.)
7. Six concertos. (c. 1737.)
8. ' Deuxième Récréation de musique . . . pour deux flûtes ou deux violons et B.C.' (c. 1737.)
9. Sonatas. (4th book.) (1738.)
10. Six concertos (2nd book). (c. 1743 or 1744.)
11. Scylla et Glaucus (musical tragedy). (1746.)
12. Sonatas for two vlns. without bass. (c. 1747.) (2nd book.)
13. Ouvertures et sonates en trio, two vlns. and basso continuo. (1753.)
14. Trio for two vlns. and bass. (1766.) Posthumous.
15. Sonatas for vln. and bass. (1767.) Posthumous.

MODERN REPRINTS.—Sonatas for vln. alone and bass, fragmentary reprints by Alard, F. David, Deldevez, d'Indy, Jensen, Kreisler, Moffat, etc. ; the entire two first books, by Debroux and Guilmant (Demets-Eschig) ; Concertos, by Herwegh (Peters) and Borrel (Senart) ; Sonatas for two vlns. without bass, Book I., by Pincherle (Senart) ; Sonate à trois, ré maj., by Bouvet (Demets-Eschig).

BIBL.—LA LAURENCIE, L'École française de violon, i. (Paris, 1922; pp. 268-340) ; LÉON VALAS, Une Famille de violonistes lyonnais, les Leclair, Bulletin of the Société de Musicologie, July 1921 ; LIONEL DE LA LAURENCIE, L'École française de violon de Lully à Viotti, 1922–23, vol. i. pp. 269-340, deal with the elder Leclair (pp. 340-349 deal with the younger).

There is a portrait of him, by Alexis Loir, engraved by François (Lyons, 1741).

As a rule his works were engraved by his wife, whose name was Louise Roussel, and whom he married in 1730.

P. D. ; addns. and rev. M. P.

His brother, (2) ANTOINE REMI, called le Cadet (b. Lyons), was a violinist and composed a book of sonatas for the violin published about 1760 (Fétis).

LE COCQ, JEHAN, see GALLUS, Joannes.

LECOCQ, ALEXANDRE CHARLES (b. Paris, June 3, 1832 ; d. there, Oct. 24, 1918), composer of opéra-bouffe, entered the Conservatoire in 1849 and in 1850 obtained the first prize for harmony and accompaniment. He took the second prize for fugue in Halévy's class in 1852. He left the Conservatoire towards the close of 1854.

Lecocq found the usual difficulty in obtaining access to the stage, and would probably have had to wait a long time but for a competition for an operetta opened by Offenbach in 1856. He was bracketed with Bizet, and ' Le Docteur Miracle ' was produced at the Bouffes Parisiens, Apr. 8, 1857. The operetta was evidently the work of a clever musician, who understood how to write for the voice. Notwithstanding this good beginning the small theatres still closed their doors to him, and Lecocq was driven to teaching for a livelihood. He then tried a different line, publishing, in conjunction with Besozzi, a collection of sacred songs for women's voices called ' La Chapelle au couvent ' (1865) —less incongruous when we remember that he was a good organist ; but the stage was irresistible, and after the failure of ' Huis clos ' (1859), a little one-act piece ' Le Baiser à la porte ' (1864) was followed by ' Liline et

Valentin' (1864), 'Les Ondines au champagne' (1866),[1] ' Le Mysotis ' (1866), ' Le Cabaret de Ramponneau ' (1867) and ' Fleur de thé,' three acts (1868).[2]

This last piece was a brilliant success. Lecocq at last found himself established with the public and produced in rapid succession :

' L'Amour et son carquois,' two acts (1868) ; ' Gandolfo ' and ' Le Rajah de Mysore,'[3] both in one act (1869) ; ' Le Beau Dunois,' one act (1870)[4] ; ' Le Barbier de Trouville ' and ' Le Testament de M. de Crac,' both in one act (1871) ; ' Sauvons la caisse ' (1871), one act, and ' Les Cent Vierges '[5] three acts (Brussels, 1872) ; ' La Fille de Mme Angot,' three acts (Brussels, Dec. 4, 1872),[6] which ran for 500 nights consecutively ; ' Les Prés St. Gervais '[7] and ' Girofle-Girofla,'[8] both in three acts (Brussels, Mar. 21, 1874) ; ' Les Jumeaux de Bergame,' (1868), one act, and ' Le Pompon,' three acts (1875) ; ' La Petite Mariée,' three acts (1875)[9] ; ' Kosiki ' (1876) and ' La Marjolaine '[10] (1877), both in three acts ; ' Le Petit Duc '[11] and ' Camargo,' both in three acts (1878) ; ' La Jolie Persane,' 1879 ; ' La Petite Mademoiselle,' three acts (1879)[12] ; ' Le Grand Casimir,' 1879[13] ; Janot, ' Le Jour et la nuit,'[14] 1881 ; ' Le Cœur et la main,' 1882 ; ' La Princesse des Canaries,'[15] 1883 ; ' L'Oiseau bleu ' (1884).

An attempt at a higher class of music, ' Plutus,' produced at the Opéra - Comique, Paris, Mar. 31, 1886, failed and was withdrawn after eight representations ; the earlier style was returned to in

' Les Grenadiers de Mont-Cornette (Paris, 1887) ; ' Ali-Baba ' (Brussels, 1887) ; ' La Volière ' (Paris, 1888) ; ' L'Égyptienne ' (Paris, 1890) ; ' Nos Bons Chasseurs ' (ib. 1894) ; ' Ninette ' (ib. 1896) ; ' Ruse d'Amour ' (1898) ; ' Barbe-Bleue ' (1898) ; ' Le Cygne ' (Opéra-Comique, 1899) ; ' La Belle au bois dormant ' (1900) ; ' Rose Mousse ' (1904), ' La Salutiste ' (1905) ; ' Le Chevrier ' (not performed) ; ' Yetta ' (1908) ; ' La Trahison de Pan ' (1911) ; also 4 works in MS. not performed—' Renza,' ' Ma Cousine,' ' Don Japhet d'Arménie,' ' Les Picaros.' To this long list must be added 4 vols. of pieces for PF., 5 vols. of songs with PF. accompaniment, orchestral music and compositions for various instruments, a sonata for PF. and vln., 2 choruses. He arranged Rameau's ' Castor et Pollux ' as a vocal score.

Lecocq realised that what the public really liked was light, gay, sparkling melodies. His style, not a very elevated one, made small demand on the poetry or the intellect of the composer ; but it required tact, ease, freedom and, above all, animation. These qualities are conspicuous in Lecocq's operettas, which have become universally popular owing to the life, *brio* and easy gaiety which pervade them.

G. C. ; addns. A. C. and G. F. ; rev. M. L. P.

BIBL.—LOUIS SCHNEIDER, *Les Maîtres de l'opérette française—Hervé et Charles Lecocq* (Paris, 1924, with list of works) ; *Revue musicale* (1924, Feb.-Aug. ; 1925, June-Oct.), *Lettres inédites de Lecocq à Saint-Saëns.*

LE COUPPEY, FÉLIX, see COUPPEY.

LEDGER LINES, see LEGER LINES.

LEDUC (LE DUC), (1) SIMON L'AÎNÉ (b. Paris, c. 1748 ; d. there, Jan. 1777), violinist, pupil of Gaviniès. He appeared as soloist in violin concertos at the Concert Spirituel up to 1763, and afterwards, on various occasions, almost up to the time of his death.

As a composer, he published at the end of 1768 2 books of sonatas, 2 books of duos for

1 Folly Theatre, London, Sept. 1877.
2 Lyceum Theatre, 1871, and (in English) at the Criterion, 1875.
3 Park Theatre, London, 1875.
4 Lyceum Theatre, 1871.
5 In London at St. James's Theatre (French), June 21, 1873.
6 In London at St. James's Theatre (French), May 17, 1873 ; at Royal Philharmonic Theatre (English, Byron), Oct. 4, 1873 ; in another version at the Gaiety, Nov. 10, 1873 ; Paris, Feb. 21, 1873.
7 In London at Criterion Theatre (English, Reece), Nov. 28, 1874.
8 In London at Opéra-Comique (French), June 6, 1874 ; at Royal Philharmonic Theatre (English), Oct. 3, 1874.
9 Opéra-Comique, London, 1876.
10 Royalty Theatre, London, 1877.
11 Philharmonic Theatre, London, 1878.
12 Alhambra, London, 1879.
13 Gaiety Theatre, London, 1879.
14 Strand Theatre, London, as ' Manola,' 1882.
15 Liverpool, as ' Pepita,' 1886, and Toole's Theatre, London, 1888.

2 violins without bass, 6 trios for 2 violins and bass, 3 violin concertos, worthy of his master Gaviniès.

His work as a publisher is no less important. At the end of 1767 he published not only his own works, but the German and Italian compositions of J. C. Bach, Haydn, Nardini and others. About 1775 he acquired the publishing business of De Roullède de La Chevardière.

(2) PIERRE (b. Paris, c. 1755 ; d. Holland, 1816[16]), brother of the above, made a remarkable début as violinist at the Concert Spirituel in 1770. He followed his elder brother as publisher, succeeding in 1775 to the publisher Venier, rue Saint Thomas du Louvre, and, after the death of Simon, carrying on his brother's business until 1804. His son, (3) AUGUSTE, of whom little is known, succeeded him, and published *Les Principes de composition des écoles d'Italie*, by A. Choron. It is from him that (4) ALPHONSE (b. Nantes, Mar. 9, 1804), whose relationship with him is not known, acquired the business in 1841. The firm is now directed by his son (5) ALPHONSE (b. 1878), honorary president of the Chambre Syndicale des Éditeurs de Musique.

BIBL.—LA LAURENCIE, *L'École française de violon*, ii., 1923, pp. 380-94.

M. P.

LEE, GEORGE ALEXANDER (b. 1802 ; d. Oct. 8, 1851), theatrical manager and composer, was son of Harry Lee, a pugilist and landlord of the Anti-Gallican tavern, Shire Lane, Temple Bar. When a boy he entered the service of Lord Barrymore as ' tiger,' being the first of the class of servants known by that name ; but on the discovery that he had a fine voice and a natural taste for music, he was withdrawn from that position and placed under a master for instruction. In 1822 he appeared as a tenor singer at the Dublin theatre, where he acted as conductor 1823–26, and in 1826 in London at the Haymarket Theatre, where he became conductor in 1827, and soon afterwards began business as a music-seller in the Quadrant.

In 1829, with Melrose, the tenor singer, and John Kemble Chapman, he entered upon the management of the Tottenham Street Theatre, and gave performances of popular English operas. Lee seceded in 1830, on account of the heavy penalties incurred through the infringement of the right of the ' patent theatres,' and became lessee of Drury Lane Theatre. He was soon afterwards joined by Captain Polhill, but at the end of the season he withdrew, leaving Polhill sole manager. In 1831 he undertook the management of the Lenten oratorios at both Drury Lane and Covent Garden. In 1832 he was composer and music director at the Strand Theatre, and in 1845 the same at the Olympic. He had a music shop at 59 Frith Street, Soho,

16 According to Fétis.

in 1835–36. Lee composed the music for several dramatic pieces, amongst which were—

'The Sublime and Beautiful' and 'The Invincibles,' 1828 ; 'The Nymph of the Grotto' and 'The Witness,' 1829 ; 'The Devil's Brother' (principally from Auber's 'Fra Diavolo') and 'The Legion of Honour,' 1831 ; 'Waverley' (with G. Stansbury), 1832; 'Love in a Cottage,' 'Good Husbands make Good Wives,' 'Sold for a Song,' 'The Fairy Lake' and 'Auld Robin Gray,'

the last composed about 1838 but not performed until 1858. He was also composer of many songs and ballads, highly popular in their day ('Away, away to the mountain's brow,' 'Come where the aspens quiver,' 'The Macgregors' Gathering,' etc.), and author of a 'Vocal Tutor.' As other publishers brought out his works, it would appear that the business referred to above was either of short duration or very unimportant. He must not be confounded with Leoni Lee of Albemarle Street, who had a large publishing business. In Feb. 1837 he was part proprietor of the Abbey Street Theatre in Dublin, and in 1849 he was conducting at Vauxhall. Lee married Mrs. Waylett, the popular singer and actress, whose death (Apr. 26, 1851) so seriously affected him that he died the following October.

w. h. h. ; addns. w. h. g. f. and f. k.

LEE, SAMUEL (d. Feb. 21, 1776), a distinguished Irish violinist and musical director, who flourished during the second half of the 18th century. Handel often visited his house in 1742, and employed him as copyist. In 1751 he was appointed conductor of the 'City Music,' or Corporation Band, and in 1753 his salary was increased from £40 to £60 a year (*Calendar of Ancient Records of Dublin*). In the autumn of 1750 he opened a music-shop at the Little Green, off Bolton Street, and printed much music, including 'Lee's Masque, a collection of popular songs,' four in each number, 'price a British sixpence each' (1753–1756). In July 1751 he was one of the syndicate (the others being Signor Marella, Joseph de Boeck, Daniel Sullivan and Stephen Storace) which took a lease of Crow Street Music Hall, for six years, at an annual rent of £113 : 15s. He led the band at Marlborough Green from 1752–1756, and in 1758 was appointed musical director of Crow Street Theatre. In 1768 he removed his music-shop to No. 2 Dame Street, and published a miscellaneous lot of music. Three years later he opened a coffee-house in Essex Street, which was largely patronised by theatrical folk. See O'Keefe's *Recollections*, i. 320.   w. h. g. f.

LEEDS. Music in Leeds is best described under the two headings of MUSICAL FESTIVAL and CONCERTS.

MUSICAL FESTIVAL.—The first of these important meetings took place on Sept. 7-10, 1858, and formed part of the ceremony connected with the opening of the Town Hall by Queen Victoria. Sterndale Bennett was the conductor, and his 'May Queen' was the chief

novelty of the festival. In spite of the great success (£2000 was given out of the profits to the Leeds medical charities) there were difficulties in the way of establishing the festival as a triennial event ; and the second did not take place until 1874, Oct. 14-17, when Costa conducted. At the third festival, Sept. 19-22, 1877, Costa was again the conductor, and Macfarren's 'Joseph' was the most important new work. From 1880 (Oct. 13-16) until 1898 inclusive, Sullivan was the conductor. In 1880 Sullivan's 'Martyr of Antioch' and J. F. Barnett's 'Building of the Ship' were commissioned. Oct. 10-13, 1883, was the date of the fourth meeting, at which Macfarren's 'David,' Alfred Cellier's 'Gray's Elegy,' Barnby's 'Psalm xcvii.' were commissioned, and Raff's 'End of the World' was performed for the first time in England. In 1886 (Oct. 13-16) Sullivan's 'Golden Legend,' Stanford's 'Revenge,' Mackenzie's 'Story of Sayid' and Dvořák's 'Saint Ludmila' were commissioned, and a memorable performance took place of Bach's B minor Mass. In 1889 (Oct. 9-12) the profits of the festival rose to the high figure of £3142 ; the new works were Parry's 'St. Cecilia's Day,' Stanford's 'Voyage of Maeldune,' Corder's 'Sword of Argantyr,' and Creser's 'Sacrifice of Freia.' In 1892 (Oct. 5-8) Alan Gray's 'Arethusa' and a symphony by Frederick Cliffe were the novelties. Instead of the choir being drawn only from Leeds, the influence was extended this year (and until 1898) by obtaining singers from different centres in the West Riding of Yorkshire, who were trained in their separate towns, and met occasionally at Leeds for general rehearsals. This plan was dropped in 1901, but was resumed in and since 1910. In 1895 (Oct. 2-5) Parry's 'Invocation of Music,' Somervell's 'Forsaken Merman,' and orchestral pieces by Massenet and Edward German were the new works. In 1898 (Oct. 5-8) Stanford's Te Deum, Elgar's 'Caractacus,' Cowen's setting of Collins's 'Ode on the Passions,' Otto Goldschmidt's 'Music,' Alan Gray's 'Song of Redemption,' and a symphonic poem by Humperdinck were the novelties, and the *diapason normal* was employed for the first time. For the festival of 1901 (Oct. 9-12) Stanford was appointed conductor and the programme was commemorative of the music of the 19th century. Among actual novelties were Coleridge Taylor's 'Blind Girl of Castel-Cuillé,' and a Memorial Cantata by Glazounov ; a most interesting performance of Beethoven's Mass in D took place, in which Joachim took part, as well as playing a concerto of Mozart. In 1904 (Oct. 5-8) Stanford again conducted, and the new works were Mackenzie's 'Witch's Daughter,' Walford Davies's 'Everyman,' Stanford's 'Songs of the Sea,' Charles Wood's 'Ballad of Dundee,' Joseph Holbrooke's 'Queen Mab' and Stanford's violin concerto (played by Kreisler)

At the festival of 1907 six new works by native composers were given : Stanford's Stabat Mater, Somervell's 'Intimations of Immortality,' Vaughan Williams's 'Toward the Unknown Region,' Bantock's 'Sea Wanderers,' Rutland Boughton's choral variations on Two Folk-Songs, and Brewer's 'Pastorals.' Glazounov's 8th Symphony had its first performance in England. In 1910, from which time onwards the chorus had sectional rehearsals in Leeds and Huddersfield, only two novelties were introduced, Vaughan Williams's 'Sea Symphony' and Stanford's 'Songs of the Fleet.' After this festival Stanford resigned the conductorship, and for the festival of 1913 (Oct. 1-4), Nikisch, Elgar, and H. P. Allen shared the duties. The novelties were Elgar's 'Falstaff,' Harty's 'Mystic Trumpeter,' Butterworth's 'Shropshire Lad,' and Basil Harwood's 'On a May Morning.' Preparations were being made for a festival in 1916, but the war intervened, and it was not till 1922 (Oct. 4-7) that the festivals were resumed, Albert Coates and H. P. Allen being the conductors. The only new work was Holst's 'Ode to Death,' but a programme of Hubert Parry's compositions, and another of shorter works by Bach, were interesting features of the event. For the festival of 1925 (Oct. 7-10) the same conductors were engaged, and the programme included a choral symphony by Holst (on poems of Keats), a work for orchestra and chorus by Albert Coates, 'The Eagle,' and compositions by two American musicians, J. D. Taylor and Howard Hanson.

BIBL.—A *History of the Leeds Festivals* (1858–89), by JOSEPH BENNETT and F. R. SPARK (Hon. Secretary of the Festival from 1877–1907) (1892).

M., with addns. H. T.

CONCERTS.— The oldest existing Leeds Concert organisation is the LEEDS PHILHARMONIC SOCIETY, founded in 1871, and active ever since. Its first conductor was James Broughton, who was succeeded in 1884 by his brother Alfred, both of whom were also chorus-masters of the Leeds Festivals. Adolf Beyschlag was conductor for two seasons, 1895–97, and then Stanford conducted the society for eleven years, 1897–98 to 1908–09. For some years the society had no official conductor, one being engaged for each concert, but in 1916 the old method was resumed, and Dr. Fricker was conductor for the season 1916–17. On his leaving for Canada, Dr. E. C. Bairstow was appointed, and has occupied the position till now (1927). In 1896 the Leeds Subscription Concerts were run jointly with those of the Philharmonic, but this arrangement came to an end in 1909.

Among the more important events in the career of the Philharmonic may be mentioned the first performance at Leeds of Brahms's 'German Requiem' (1878), and of Elgar's

'Dream of Gerontius'; visits to London in 1889 (Choral Symphony under Henschel), 1891, 1897 (Choral Symphony under Mottl), and many subsequent occasions, to sing important works, such as Beethoven's Mass in D (under Richter), etc. For many years the Philharmonic supplied choral contingents for the festivals of Worcester, Hereford, Chester, Norwich, Hanley, Hovingham, Scarborough, etc. In 1906 the society paid the first visit to Paris by an English society's chorus, singing under Stanford's direction the Sanctus from Bach's B minor Mass, Beethoven's Choral Symphony, etc., and repeated the visit in 1912, when the Requiem of Berlioz was given. Besides the conductors already mentioned, the choir has sung under Sir Henry Wood, Weingartner, Nikisch, Verbrugghen and others. One of Stanford's last public appearances was at a concert of his music on Nov. 23, 1923, when his Stabat Mater was given under Dr. Bairstow's direction, and he was the guest at a dinner given by the members of the society.

The LEEDS CHORAL UNION began operations on Mar. 26, 1896, with the first and only performance of Gounod's 'Redemption' ever given at Leeds. Alfred Benton, organist of the Leeds Parish Church, was the society's first conductor, and was succeeded in 1905 by Henry Coward, who still retains the post. During this period the society has introduced to Leeds many choral works, among them 'Samson and Delilah' (Saint-Saëns), 'Swan and Skylark' (Goring Thomas), 'Hero and Leander' (Mancinelli), 'Rinaldo' (Brahms), Te Deum (Dvořák), 'King Saul' (Parry), 'Byron' (Holbrooke), Choral Ballads (Coleridge Taylor), 'John Gilpin' and 'The Veil' (Cowen), 'Atalanta in Calydon' (Bantock), and Psalm (Florent Schmitt). It has also paid special attention to Elgar's works, and has given most of his choral compositions, in many cases for the first time at Leeds. The Choral Union has had an advantage of no little moment in these days in being subsidised by an enthusiastic amateur, H. C. Embleton, through whose munificence the choir has been taken far afield, several times to London, twice to Canterbury, to Germany in 1912, and to Paris in 1912 and 1924. On the second visit to Paris the choir was accompanied by the London Symphony Orchestra for a series of concerts, and the whole of the proceeds were given to French charities, without any deduction for expenses, all of which were borne by Mr. Embleton.

Another Leeds society of high aims is the Leeds NEW CHORAL SOCIETY, founded by H. M. Turton, a Leeds organist. Under his conductorship it has done good work, which since his departure for Canada has been carried on by Dr. C. H. Moody of Ripon; and now by H. Bardgett. An effort to make Bach's Christmas Oratorio a recognised alternative to

Messiah ' at Christmastide is one of its most interesting enterprises.

Perhaps the most influential agency for bringing the best music before the people of Leeds has been the orchestral concerts given on Saturday evenings. These had their origin in the Municipal Concerts, initiated in the autumn of 1903 by Dr. Fricker, then organist of the Town Hall, who adopted an orchestra which had been organised by some local professional musicians. It consisted at first of fifty professionals, a number afterwards increased to about sixty. It had no direct subsidy from public money, but as Dr. Fricker as conductor received no further remuneration than his stipend as organist, and the concerts took the place of the customary Saturday organ recitals, there was no additional expense for hall, lighting, etc., and the small charges made for admission nearly sufficed to maintain the concerts. They were carried on for some years under these conditions, until the economists on the Council discovered that they involved an expenditure of something over £200 a year, and it was decided that this was more than Leeds could afford to expend on an institution whose object was merely artistic, so they were reorganised by a committee under the title of the Leeds Saturday Orchestral Concerts. For a good many years these prospered artistically and financially, but in the season 1925–26 they, in common with nearly all Leeds concert enterprises, suffered from a lack of support which made their future less assured than it had seemed. Since Dr. Fricker left Leeds for Toronto, the conductorship has been in various hands — Hamilton Harty, Eugene Goossens, Aylmer Buesst and Julius Harrison. The programmes have consisted chiefly of favourite classics, and unfamiliar works have been exceptional, but a high standard has always been maintained.

From the orchestra engaged at these concerts was organised the Leeds Symphony Orchestra, which was made into a limited company in 1908, and consists of 35 shareholders, all playing members. The orchestra is augmented according to requirements, and averages about 55 artists. For the season 1926–27 it took the entire responsibility for the Saturday concerts.

Mention should also be made of the LEEDS BOHEMIAN CONCERTS, the 28th season of which took place during 1926–27. A string quartet of West Riding artists, supplemented occasionally by a pianist or other instrumentalist, takes part in a series of four concerts, at which it is customary to sandwich a contemporary work between two classics.   H. T.

LEEVES, REV. WILLIAM (b. Kensington, June 11, 1748; d. Wrington, May 28, 1828), entered the first regiment of Foot-Guards in 1769, and was promoted lieutenant 1772. After taking holy orders he was appointed in 1779 rector of Wrington, Somerset, the birthplace of John Locke, the philosopher, and the home of Hannah More. He was a good violoncellist, and composed much sacred music, but will be remembered only as the author of the air of ' Auld Robin Gray ' (words by Lady Anne Barnard, born Lindsay of Balcarres, written in 1772, autograph in the B.M. Add. MSS. 29,387), published by Exsham of Dublin, 1781, and by Corri and Sutherland in 1783, but not publicly acknowledged by the composer until 1812, when in the dedication of ' Six Sacred Airs ' he admitted the authorship of ' Auld Robin Gray.'

W. H. H. ; addns. from D.N.B.,
W. H. G. F., etc.

LEFÉBURE-WÉLY, LOUIS JAMES ALFRED (b. Paris, Nov. 13, 1817; d. there, Jan. 1, 1870), son of Antoine Lefébvre, organist and composer, who took the name of Lefébure-Wély and died 1831.

He learned his notes before the alphabet, and as soon as he could speak showed a marvellous aptitude for music. At 8 he was his father's deputy at the organ, accompanying the plain-song and playing short pieces. Though only 15 when his father died, he was appointed his successor at St. Roch through the influence of Queen Marie Amélie. Feeling the need of solid study, he entered the Conservatoire in 1832, and obtained the second prizes for pianoforte and organ in 1834, and the first for both in the following year. He then took lessons in counterpoint from Halévy, and in composition from Berton, but, not satisfied with these professors, studied privately with Adolphe Adam, and with Séjan, the organist, who initiated him in the art of improvising and in the management of the stops. He told the author of this article that he owed much to both these men, widely different as they were, and he often sought their advice after he had left the Conservatoire in order to marry. To support his young family he took to teaching, and composed a quantity of pianoforte pieces, some of which were popular at the time.

But it is as an organist that he will be remembered. His improvisations were marvellous, and from the piquancy of his harmonies, the unexpectedness of his combinations, the fertility of his imagination, and the charm which pervaded all he did, he might justly be called the Auber of the organ. The great popularity in France of the free-reed instruments of Debain and Mustel is largely owing to him ; indeed, the effects he produced on the instruments of the harmonium class were really astonishing. Endowed with immense powers of work, Lefébure-Wély attempted all branches of composition—chamber music ; symphonies for full orchestra ; masses ; an opéra-comique

in three acts, ' Les Recruteurs ' (Dec. 13, 1861),
etc. Among his best works are his ' Cantiques,'
a remarkable ' O Salutaris,' his ' Offertoires,'
many of his fantasias for harmonium and his
organ - pieces. He received the Legion of
Honour in 1850, being at the time organist of
the Madeleine, where he was from 1847–58.
After this he had for some time no regular post,
but in 1863 accepted the organ of St. Sulpice,
so long held with success by his friend and
master Séjan. Here he remained, till his death
from consumption.　　　　　　　　　　　　　　G. C.

LEFEBVRE, CHARLES ÉDOUARD (b. Paris,
June 19, 1843 ; d. Paris, Sept. 8, 1917),
was a pupil of the Conservatoire, and gained
the first Prix de Rome with his cantata, ' Le
Jugement de Dieu.' He was a composer of
sincere and delicate accomplishment in many
forms.

His church music includes a setting of Psalm
xxiii. and some motets. His ' Judith,' of which
portions had been given at concerts of the Conservatoire, was brought out as a whole at the
Pasdeloup Concerts in 1879, being later heard
in many other French towns, as well as in
Belgium and Germany. An ' Ouverture dramatique ' was played at the Colonne Concerts ;
and ' Dalila,' orchestral scenes, and a symphony
in D are important works for orchestra. For
the stage Lefebvre wrote, ' Lucrèce,' three-act
opera, not performed ; ' Le Trésor ' a one-act
opéra-comique (Angers, 1883) ; ' Zaïre,' four-
act opera (Lille, 1887) ; ' Djelma,' three-act
opera (Paris, Opéra, May 25, 1894) ; ' Singo-
alla,' three-act opera, unperformed. ' Eloa,' a
poème lyrique ; ' Melka,' a ' legend ' given at
the Lamoureux Concerts ; ' Sainte Cécile,' for
soli, chorus and orchestra (Concerts de l'Opéra,
1896) ; ' La Messe du fantôme,' for voice and
orchestra (Colonne Concerts) ; a Serenade, an
Overture, ' Toggenburg ' (Colonne Concerts,
1904) ; sonatas, trios, quartets, suites, etc., for
various instruments, a suite for wind instruments, etc. In 1884 he obtained the Prix
Chartier for his concerted compositions, and in
1895 he succeeded Benjamin Godard as professor of the instrumental ensemble class in the
Conservatoire.　　　　　G. F. ; rev. M. L. P.

LEFÈVRE, JEAN XAVIER (b. Lausanne, Mar.
6, 1763 ; d. Paris, Nov. 9, 1829), celebrated
clarinettist, pupil of Michel Yost, for many
years member of the Opéra orchestra. From
1795–1825 he was professor of the clarinet at
the Conservatoire ; from 1807 member of the
Imperial (afterwards Royal) Chapel. He composed concertos, sonatas, trios, duets, etc., for
his instrument, to which he added a sixth key.
He also wrote the official clarinet Tutor for the
Conservatoire which appeared in 1802 ; also
in a German edition ; and was translated into
Italian (Riemann ; Q.-L.).

LEFFLER, (1) JAMES HENRY (d. 1819), was
bassoon player and organist of St. Katherine's

Hospital by the Tower, the German Lutheran
church in the Savoy and Streatham Chapel.
He died suddenly in the street in 1819. His
son, (2) ADAM (b. London, 1808 ; d. there, Mar.
28, 1857), was soon after his father's death admitted a chorister of Westminster Abbey. On
attaining manhood he was endowed with a bass
voice of exceptionally fine quality and extensive compass, from E below the stave to g'
above it—and a natural gift for singing. He
first attracted notice in Oct. 1829 at a Festival
at Exeter, when the casual absence of another
performer gave him the opportunity of appearing as a principal singer. He acquitted himself so satisfactorily that he was immediately
appointed a deputy at Westminster Abbey, and
shortly afterwards took and maintained a good
position on the English operatic stage and in
the concert-room.　　　　　　　　　　　W. H. H.

LE FROID, see MEREAUX.

LEGATO (Ital., sometimes written ligato ;
Fr. lié ; Ger. gebunden) = ' connected,' and is
the term used to mean the passage from note to
note without any perceptible hiatus between
the ending of one and the beginning of the next.

A legato style of singing or playing is presumed in the notation of music unless indications to the contrary (see STACCATO) are given.
There are, however, physical limits to the possibility of maintaining the legato in singing and
in playing wind instruments supplied by the
lungs of the player, due to the necessity for
taking breath, though in both these cases the
ability to take breath with as little interruption
as possible of the tone is a first essential of
technique. Similarly in the case of the bowed
strings the change of direction of the bow implies a partial interruption of the legato ; hence
the necessity for the SLUR (q.v.) to indicate
where the legato may be broken induced its use
as an indication of the legato itself.

On keyboard instruments the legato can be
maintained indefinitely, and slurs therefore are
only required for the sake of PHRASING (q.v.).

Occasionally the word legato is written at the
beginning of a movement or passage as a
special warning. The use of the superlative,
Legatissimo, has no real meaning. It merely
indicates the extreme desire of the composer
for the maintenance of the legato style.　　C.

LÉGENDE DE ST. CHRISTOPHE, LA,
lyric drama, in 3 acts and 8 tableaux ; words
and music by V. d'Indy. First performance,
Opéra, June 6, 1920.

LEGER (LEDGER) LINES (Fr. lignes pos
tiches, supplémentaires ; Ger. Hilfslinien, Neben-
linien ; Ital. ligne d' ajuto) are the short lines
drawn above and below the staff for those notes
which exceed its limits.

The origin of the term is not known. It is
proposed to derive it from the French léger,
light, or from the Latin legere, to read, or as if
it were equivalent to layer—additional lines

laid on above or below ; but none of these is quite satisfactory. The term came into use in the year 1700. (See C. J. Evans, *Mus. T.*, June 1879, and the *Oxf. Dict.* s.v. The analogous use of the word ledger, as ' a horizontal timber in a scaffolding, lying parallel to the face of the building,' is interesting.)   G.

LEGGE, ROBIN HUMPHREY (*b*. Bishop's Castle, Shropshire, June 28, 1862), has been musical editor of the *Daily Telegraph* since 1908.

Legge was educated at Trinity Hall, Cambridge, when he read law, and then studied music at Leipzig, Frankfort-on-Main and elsewhere on the Continent. He joined the staff of *The Times* in 1891 and acted as assistant musical critic to FULLER MAITLAND (*q.v.*) for fifteen years. In 1906 he became musical critic to the *Daily Telegraph*, succeeding to full responsibility for its musical policy two years later when Joseph BENNETT (*q.v.*) retired. He has chosen to exert his influence rather as editor than as critic, and his choice has been salutary. A man of wide interests and generous enthusiasms, Legge was exactly fitted to sweep away the repressive style of dogmatic criticism to which Bennett had clung, and through the ' Music Page ' of the *Daily Telegraph* he has stimulated the general reader's interest in music and musicians to an uncommon extent. His active pen has been exercised in many directions outside daily journalism. He was a contributor to the second edition of this Dictionary and also to the *D.N.B.*   C.

LEGGIERO (Ital. also *leggieramente*) = ' lightly.' The word is usually applied to a rapid passage, and in pianoforte playing indicates an absence of pressure, the keys being struck with only sufficient force to produce the sound.

Leggiero passages are usually, though not invariably, *piano*, and they may be either legato or staccato ; if the former the fingers must move very freely and strike the keys with enough percussion to ensure distinctness, but with the slightest possible amount of force. Examples of legato passages are *leggieramente* are found in the twenty-fifth variation of Beethoven's op. 120, and in the finale of Mendelssohn's concerto in G minor (which also contains the unusual combination of *forte* with *leggiero*) ; and of staccato single notes and chords in the finale of Mendelssohn's concerto in D minor.

On stringed instruments leggiero passages are as a rule played by diminishing the pressure of the bow upon the strings, but the word generally refers rather to the character of the movement than to any particular manner of bowing. The scherzo of Beethoven's quartet in E♭, op. 74, is marked *leggieramente*, although it begins *forte*, and the same indication is given for the second variation of the andante in the Kreutzer sonata. which is *piano* throughout.   F. T.

LEGRANT, (1) GUILHEME, an early 15th-century composer, whose real name was probably Guillaume, while Legrant (le grand) was merely a qualificative. Some songs of his from the Bodleian Library have been republished by Stainer ; others are preserved in the libraries of Bologna, Trient (now Vienna) and Lochheim.

(2) JOHANNES, early 15th-century composer. Songs by him are in the Cod. Trient (Vienna) and the Bodleian Library.   E. V. D. S.

LEGRENZI, GIOVANNI (*b*. Clusone near Bergamo, *c*. 1625 ; *d*. July 26, 1690), composer and conductor, learned music, and received his first appointment, that of organist to the church of St. Maria Maggiore, at Clusone. He next became maestro di cappella of the church of the Spirito Santo at Ferrara, where he still was in 1664. When Krieger, Kapellmeister to the Duke of Weissenfels, visited Venice in 1672, he found Legrenzi settled there as director of the Conservatorio dei Mendicanti. In 1681 he became vice-maestro, and in 1685 maestro di cappella of St. Mark's, and exercised both functions till his death. He entirely reorganised the orchestra of St. Mark's, augmenting it to 34 performers, thus disposed—8 violins, 11 violette, 2 viole da braccia, 2 viole da gamba, 1 violone, 4 theorbos, 2 cornetts, 1 bassoon, and 3 trombones. He composed industriously, and left specimens of his skill in most departments of music—church sonatas (1654, 1655, 1663 and 1677), motets (1655, 1660, 1670, 1692), masses, psalms (1657, 1667), instrumental music of various kinds, and 17 operas, of which the most remarkable are ' Achille in Sciro,' his first (1664) ; ' La divisione del mondo ' (1675) ; ' I due Cesari ' (1683), mentioned in the Paris *Mercure galant* (Mar. 1683) ; and ' Pertinace ' (1684), his last. The number in *Q.-L.* is 14. They were nearly all produced in Venice. Like Scarlatti, and other composers of his time, he did not attempt to banish the comic element from his serious operas. One of his orchestral compositions is in seven real parts, and all are important. His best pupils were Lotti and Gasparini.

Legrenzi's name has been handed down to posterity by Bach and Handel, both of whom have treated subjects from his works, the former in an organ fugue in C minor on a ' Thema Legrenzianum elaboratum cum subjecto pedaliter ' [1] (*B.-G.* xxxviii. p. 94) ; and the latter in the phrase ' To thy dark servant light and life afford,' in the chorus ' O first-created beam ' from ' Samson ' ; this is taken from a motet of Legrenzi's—' Intret in conspectu,' [2] of which a copy in Handel's handwriting is to be found among the MSS. of the Royal Library now at the British Museum.

                                        F. G., with addns.

[1] This is the fugue about the autograph of which Mendelssohn writes, June 18, 1839.
[2] Chrysander, *Händel*, i. 179.

LEGROS, Joseph (*b.* Monampteuil, Laon, Sept. 7, 1730; *d.* Rochelle, Dec. 20, 1793), made his début as operatic tenor at the Paris Opéra on Mar. 1, 1764. When Gluck came to Paris to produce his operas he chose Legros as singer for the principal male parts; but he retired from the stage on account of increasing stoutness. In 1777 he became managing director of the Concert Spirituel until its dissolution in 1791, when he retired to Rochelle. He was a good musician, who, together with Désormery the elder, rearranged and wrote some new music for the opera 'Hylas et Sylvie,' performed in 1775.   E. v. d. S.

LEHMANN, Elizabetta Nina Mary Frederika, known as Liza Lehmann (*b.* London, July 11, 1862; *d.* Pinner, Sept. 19, 1918), composer and singer, was daughter of Rudolf Lehmann, the painter, by his wife Amelia, daughter of Robert Chambers of Edinburgh, author and publisher.

She was first taught singing by her mother, a highly cultivated amateur, and well known in the musical world, both as a composer and arranger of old classical songs under the initials 'A. L.' Later she studied singing with Randegger, and composition with Raunkilde at Rome, Freudenberg at Wiesbaden, and Hamish MacCunn. On Nov. 23, 1885, she made her début at the Monday Popular Concerts with great success, and was a favourite at these concerts during the nine years she remained in the vocal profession. She appeared at all the chief concerts in the kingdom, receiving especial encouragement from Frau Clara Schumann [1] and Joachim. On July 14, 1894, she gave a farewell concert at St. James's Hall, previous to retiring from the vocal profession on her marriage to Herbert Bedford (*q.v.*) in October of the same year. Her voice—a light soprano, with an extensive compass from A to *b'*, and of a carrying nature—was perfectly produced.

On her retirement, Liza Lehmann devoted herself to composition with conspicuous success. In 1896 her song-cycle, 'In a Persian Garden,' the words taken from FitzGerald's translation of the Rubáiyát of Omar Khayyám, was introduced in private at a concert in the house of Mrs. E. L. Goetz, by Mesdames Albani and Hilda Wilson, Ben Davies and Bispham. It was afterwards produced publicly at the Monday Popular Concerts and elsewhere, being received with remarkable enthusiasm, both in America and England.

By this and other song-cycles, 'In Memoriam' (from Tennyson), 'The Daisy-Chain,' 'More Daisies,' 'Songs of Love and Spring,' etc., Liza Lehmann may be said to have established a vogue for song-cycles in England. She was the first woman to be commissioned to

undertake the composition of a Musical Comedy, 'Sergeant Brue' (book by Owen Hall), produced at the Strand Theatre, June 14, 1904, transferred to the Prince of Wales's Theatre, and later retransferred to the Strand. Her larger productions for the theatre were 'The Vicar of Wakefield,' a romantic light opera (1906), and a stage setting of 'Everyman,' produced by Beecham, Feb. 1916. She also wrote incidental music for plays, ballads for voice and orchestra, and many songs and pianoforte pieces, several of which gained considerable popularity.   A. C.

LEHMANN, (1) Lilli (*b.* Würzburg, May 15, 1848), was taught singing by her mother, Marie Lehmann, formerly a harp-player and prima donna at Cassel under Spohr, and the original heroine of some of the operas of that master.

The daughter made her début at Prague as the First Boy ('Zauberflöte'), and was engaged successively at Dantzig in 1868 and at Leipzig in 1870. She made her début at Berlin as Vielka (Meyerbeer's 'Feldlager in Schlesien'), Aug. 19, 1870, with such success that she was engaged there as a light soprano, remaining there till 1885. In 1876 she played Woglinde and Helmwige, and sang the 'Bird' music in Wagner's trilogy at Bayreuth. In that year she was appointed Imperial chamber singer. She made a successful début at Her Majesty's as Violetta, June 3, as Philine ('Mignon'), June 15, 1880, and sang there for two seasons. She appeared at Covent Garden in German with great success as Isolde, July 2, 1884. In passing through England to America, she gave a concert with Franz Rummel at the Steinway Hall, Oct. 22, 1885. From 1885–90 she sang in German opera in America, but returned to Her Majesty's in June 1887, singing three times in Italian as Fidelio, to the Florestan of her husband, Herr Kalisch. In 1890 she returned to Germany, singing both in operas and concerts. In 1899 she reappeared at Covent Garden as Fidelio, Sieglinde, Norma, Isolde, Ortrud and Donna Anna, and won warm appreciation. She also sang in Paris at the Lamoureux Concerts, and appeared at the Nouveau Théâtre as Donna Anna in 1903.   A. C.

It should be mentioned that this gifted artist took part, as one of the Rhine maidens, in the first performance in England of 'Der Ring des Nibelungen,' at Her Majesty's Theatre in 1882. The development of her voice from a light to a dramatic soprano followed closely on the growth of her power as a tragic artist. An accomplished musician and actress as well as a magnificent singer, all styles came alike to her. Apart from her striking Wagnerian assumptions, she will be best remembered for her Fidelio, the finest seen in this country since the death of Tietjens. After an active stage career of nearly thirty-

---

[1] On Mar. 15, 1888, at the Philharmonic, Mme. Schumann accompanied her in Schumann's 'Nussbaum' and 'Frühlingsnacht.'

five years, she settled down as a teacher in the Berlin suburb of Grunewald, and there, in Oct. 1900, completed her celebrated book on singing, *Meine Gesangskunst*, which was ably translated into English by Richard Aldrich, and published three years later in New York. Under the title of *How to Sing*, it met with great success, and it remains an enduring record of sound scientific methods, intelligent observation and practical experience, marred only by some superfluity of physiological illustration and detail.   H. K.

A younger sister (2), MARIE (*b.* 1851), also a soprano, sang at Bayreuth as Wellgunde and Ortlinde in the ' Trilogy ' in 1876, and was for many years a valued member of the company at Vienna, and an excellent concert singer.
                                                 A. C.

L E I B L, KARL (*b.* Bavaria, *c.* 1784 ; *d.* Cologne, Oct. 4, 1870). In his youth he was teacher of music at the Munich court, afterwards becoming organist and Kapellmeister of Cologne Cathedral and conductor of the famous Cologne male choir, which he brought to a high state of excellence.   E. V. D. S.

LEICHTENTRITT, HUGO (*b.* Posen, Jan. 1, 1874), eminent writer on music and editor, has pursued a career singularly free from official appointments of a professional kind.

Leichtentritt spent his youth in America and studied at Harvard under J. K. PAINE (*q.v.*) ; he continued his musical studies at the Hochschule in Berlin, and graduated D.Ph. in 1901 with a dissertation on the opera of Reinhard Keiser. He then joined the staff of the Klindworth Schwarenka Conservatorium. He brought out several books of an educational kind, and began biographical work with *Chopin* (Riemann's *Berühmte Meister*, 1905). A collection of Beethoven's Letters (1912), *Erwin Lendvai* (1912), *Busoni* (1916), *Analyse der chopinschen Klavierwerke* (1920) show the versatility of his interests, and his *Händel* (1924) is one of the chief modern authorities on its subject (see HANDEL). His *Geschichte der Motette* (1908), the several volumes he has edited for the *D.D.T.* (see DENKMÄLER) and many other editions of old music (for list see *Riemann*) show the substantial nature of his scholarship. He has also found time for a considerable amount of composition.   C.

LEIDER, FRIDA (*b.* Berlin, Apr. 18, 1892), operatic soprano, pupil of Leo Leissner. This excellent artist made her mark in Germany, both on the stage and in the concert-room, during the years that followed the close of the war. She made her début at Halle ; her first important successes being at Hamburg and at the Berlin Staats-Oper. Under the auspices of Bruno Walter, chief conductor of the German season given at Covent Garden in 1924, she made her début here on May 8 in ' Tristan and Isolde ' ; appearing a few nights later as

Brünnhilde in the second cycle of the ' Ring.' Her success in both characters was emphatic and her talent evoked the most favourable criticism. She may be reckoned among the few German sopranos of recent years who have understood the art of investing Wagnerian declamation with sympathetic charm as well as strong dramatic feeling. In addition, she is an actress of unusual gifts—a Brünnhilde and an Isolde of the true heroic stamp—and in these parts of the modern school, more particularly, she has, become a reigning favourite at the Berlin Staats-Oper, where she has been engaged for some years. She sang again in London in 1925 and 1926. She has also sung at Vienna and other leading continental theatres.
                                                 H. K.

LEIGHTON, SIR WILLIAM, Knight (*d.* before 1617 [1]), one of the band of Gentlemen Pensioners of Elizabeth and James I., published in 1614

' The Teares or Lamentacions of a Sorrowfvll Soule ; Composed with Musicall Ayres and Songs both for Voyces and Divers Instruments. Set foorth by Sir William Leighton, Knight, one of his Majesties honourable Band of Gentlemen Pensioners. And all Psalmes that consist of so many feete as the fiftiethe Psalme, will go to the four partes for Consort.' London, 1614, Wm. Stansby.

The work consists of 54 metrical psalms and hymns, 17 of which are for 4 voices, with accompaniments in tablature for the lute, bandora and cittern ; and 13 for 4 voices and 24 for 5 voices without accompaniment. The first 8 (of the 17) pieces are of Leighton's own composition, and the rest were contributed by the following composers :

John Bull, William Byrd, John Coprario, John Dowland, Alfonso Ferrabosco, Thomas Ford, Orlando Gibbons, Nathaniel Giles, Edmond Hooper, Robert Johnson, Robert Jones, Robert Kindersley, Thomas Lupo, John Milton, Martin Peerson, Francis Pilkington, Timolphus Thopul (a pseudonym),[2] John Ward, Thomas Weelkes and John Wilbye.

From the dedication to Prince Charles we learn that the collection was compiled while Leighton was—unjustly, as he alleges—incarcerated for debt. He had in the preceding year published the poetry alone in a duodecimo volume. Some verses by him were prefixed to Alison's ' Psalms ' (1599), and he wrote a poem in praise of James I., called *Vertue Triumphant* (1603) (*D.N.B.*). A wordless round printed on the title-page was resolved by E. T. Warren Horne and set to the words ' Resolutio of the Rota,' etc. This is now in B.M. Add. MSS. 31,418/70b. A fragment of a 4-part piece called ' Surdus Melopaeus ' or ' The deafe composer of tunes ' is also in B.M. Add. MSS. 4388/84. The words of an anthem by him are given in Clifford's ' collection ' (1663). W. H. H. ; addns. J. MK.

LEIPZIG. Leipzig, in Saxony, has for some centuries been one of the foremost musical towns in the world, and owes its high position to several causes, chief of which are : (1) the THOMASSCHULE, with its famous choir and

1 He was evidently dead in 1617, as his name does not occur in the list of wages due to the Gentlemen Pensioners at the beginning of that year. (B.M. Add. MSS. 34,122 B.)   A. H.-H.
2 Th. *Lupo.* spelt backwards.   E. H. F.

its long list of distinguished cantors, amongst whom John Sebastian Bach, who reigned from 1723–50, stands out pre-eminent ; (2) the GEWANDHAUS CONCERTS, with a glorious history of nearly 200 years ; (3) the CONSERVATORIUM, founded in 1843 through the instrumentality of Mendelssohn, who was its first chief ; (4) the presence of several great music publishing houses, with BREITKOPF & HÄRTEL (*q.v.*) at the head of the list.

(1) The THOMASSCHULE, or School of St. Thomas, is a public school of ancient foundation consisting of several hundred boys from the ages of 10 to 19, of whom about 60 are musical ' scholars ' and receive a free education. These scholars, or ' alumni ' as they are called, in addition to their ordinary schoolwork, are given a thorough musical education under the direction of the cantor and form the choir. They furnish the music at both the Thomaskirche and the Nikolaikirche ; and at one or other of these churches on Sunday mornings, either immediately before or in the course of the service, they perform with the assistance of a portion of the Gewandhaus Orchestra a cantata, nearly always one of Bach's. On Saturdays at 1.30 in the Thomaskirche it has long been the practice for the choir to sing unaccompanied motets, which are preceded by some big organ-work— generally by Bach, but also by other of the great organ-writers ancient and modern. The motets embrace music of all periods, from the earliest Netherland and Italian writers down to contemporary composers. For example, Vaughan Williams's unaccompanied Mass in G minor was given in this way more than once in the winter of 1923 with great effect. It has in recent years become the custom to have a ' Hauptprobe ' on Friday evenings at 6, with the addition of a short service of about ten minutes inserted between the organ-playing and the motets, and the Friday Hauptprobe has tended to outdo in importance the actual Saturday performance, owing no doubt to the more convenient hour at which it takes place. The large church is always crowded with listeners of all classes and ages, some 3000 people in all, many of them standing in the aisles. It is impossible to exaggerate the influence of these evenings on the musical education of the Leipzig inhabitants, numbers of whom never miss a performance for years together. The choir is remarkable for the precision of its singing and the accuracy of its intonation : nothing is too hard for the singers. The quality of the tenors and basses naturally lacks richness and mellowness owing to the youth of the singers, but the general effect, helped by the superb acoustic qualities of the church, is extremely impressive. There are many distinguished names [1] in the

[1] For a full list see *Riemann.*

long succession of cantors. Johann Urban, appointed in 1439, was the first holder of the office, and Sethus Calvisius (1594–1615), Johann Hermann Schein (1615–30) and Johann Kuhnau (1701–22) are some of the most famous of Bach's predecessors. The present cantor is Karl STRAUBE (*q.v.*), appointed in 1918, formerly organist at the Thomaskirche. In this latter office he was succeeded by his brilliant young pupil, Günther Ramin, whose powers and virtuosity are scarcely inferior to his master's. The organ in the Thomaskirche is a specially fine one, and the magnificent organ-playing of these two men has for many years been one of the leading features of Leipzig musical life.

(2) The GEWANDHAUS CONCERTS are so called from their having been held in the hall of the Gewandhaus, the ancient market-hall of the Saxon linen-merchants of Leipzig. They date from the time when Bach was cantor of the Thomasschule, and the original title was ' das grosse Concert.' The first performance was held in a private house in 1743 ; the conductor was Doles, afterwards cantor of the Thomasschule (1756–89), and the orchestra consisted of 16 performers. They were interrupted by the Seven Years' War, but resumed on its termination in 1763, under the direction of J. A. Hiller, who conducted them at his own risk, and gave them the title of ' Liebhaberconcerte.' The orchestra was increased to 30, and regular performances were held down to Easter 1778. After a pause of three years the concerts were resumed, and located in the Gewandhaus, to which a hall for balls and concerts had lately been added. The credit for this change is due to Bürgermeister Karl Wilhelm Müller, who has a right to be considered as the founder of the institution in its present form. He and eleven of his friends constituted themselves a board of directors, appointed J. A. Hiller as conductor, and opened a subscription list for 24 concerts. The first concert in the new rooms took place on Sept. 29, 1781 ; the first regular subscription concert on Nov. 25. In process of time the old Gewandhaus became too small and inconvenient for modern conditions, and in 1884 a magnificent new building was opened, containing a large hall for the orchestral concerts and a smaller one for chamber music, both of which possess admirable acoustic properties. At the present day some 20 orchestral concerts, generally with a vocal or instrumental soloist, take place weekly on Thursdays between the middle of October and Easter ; and there are usually two or three choral concerts, in which the Gewandhauschor, an excellent voluntary choir, take part. The regular conductor of the concerts (since 1922) is Wilhelm FURTWÄNGLER (*q.v.*), while Karl Straube, conductor of the Gewandhauschor, directs the choral concerts.

The orchestra is a magnificent one, the strings being especially brilliant. Mendelssohn was the conductor from 1835–43, and was succeeded by Ferdinand Hiller (1843–44). Since then Niels Gade (1844–48), Julius Rietz (1848–60), Karl Reinecke (1860–95) and Arthur Nikisch (1895–1922) have been successively in charge. The most brilliant periods in the past have undoubtedly been those under Mendelssohn and Nikisch; but Furtwängler has already shown that there is little likelihood of any falling away from his predecessor's high standard. For some time past it has been the custom to have a public 'Hauptprobe' of the concerts on the Thursday morning (in the case of big choral works on the previous evening). This Hauptprobe is to all intents and purposes a duplicate of the actual concert, for all the necessary rehearsing has been finished beforehand. In addition to the orchestral concerts, there have been (since 1809) 8 chamber-music evenings in the course of the winter, in which the leading part is borne by the Gewandhaus Quartet, consisting (1925) of Edgar Wollgandt, Karl Wolschke, Carl Herrmann and Julius Klengel. For the centenary celebrations of the concerts in 1881, a history of the institution was written by A. Dörffel.

BIBL.—E. KRESHKE'S *Die 150jährige Geschichte der Leipziger Gewandhauskonzerte, 1743–1893.* (1893.)

(3) CONSERVATORIUM. The foundation of the Conservatorium was entirely due to Felix Mendelssohn. It was opened on Apr. 3, 1843, with a brilliant staff of teachers. Mendelssohn himself was the first head, and gave lessons in piano-playing and composition, in both of which subjects he had the co-operation of Robert Schumann. The chief violin-teacher was Ferdinand David, leader of the Gewandhaus Orchestra and one of Joachim's masters. The business and financial management was placed, then as now, in the hands of a committee of leading Leipzig citizens, while the purely musical side was administered by the chief members of the teaching staff. If the Conservatorium cannot boast to-day of quite the same renown as it possessed in those early radiant days, when it was first and alone in the field, that is explained by the subsequent springing up of similar institutions all over Germany. But it has succeeded in maintaining a very high standard of efficiency, particularly perhaps on the theoretical side and in composition, and need not fear comparison with its competitors. At the present day there are between five and six hundred students of many nationalities. The head of the institution is Professor Max PAUER (*q.v.*), who succeeded Stephan Krehl in 1924, and prominent amongst the many excellent teachers are Karl Straube and Günther Ramin (organ), Robert Teichmüller and, of course, Pauer himself (piano), Julius Klengel (v'cl.), Walther Davisson

(violin), Hermann Grabner and Sigfrid Karg-Elert (composition) and Frau Hedmondt (singing). The students' orchestra gives, in the Conservatorium Hall, from 8 to 10 concerts every year, and there are about twice as many student chamber-concerts, all of them open to the public. Professor Pauer has also instituted a series of 'Hausmusik' evenings, when he, either alone or assisted by other members of the staff, plays to the students.

(4) OPERA has seldom taken a very prominent position in the musical life of Leipzig. It has had one or two brief periods of brilliance; but Leipzig has always been handicapped by lack of funds and by the possession of too small a theatre. Until it possesses a larger stage it will be impossible for it to compete with such places as Berlin, Dresden or Munich, at all events in the performance of such works as the 'Meistersinger,' 'Götterdämmerung,' etc. But under its present able chief, Gustav Brecher, it has recently made great strides, and very good performances are to be heard, especially of the less exacting works. The body of singers is thoroughly competent, and the orchestra, being the Gewandhaus Orchestra, could scarcely be better.

(5) Amongst other musical institutions should be mentioned the RIEDEL-VEREIN, a choral society founded in 1854 and named after its first conductor, Carl Riedel. It gives a series of excellent concerts every year, and, in particular, has done a great work in popularising by annual performance Bach's B minor Mass. The LEIPZIG SYMPHONY ORCHESTRA, though not in the same class as the Gewandhaus Orchestra, gives capital concerts, and, after going through bad times during the inflation period, is now (1926) well on the upward grade. Finally, a striking feature of musical life in Leipzig—as indeed in many other German towns—is the very large number of admirable male choral societies—many of them composed entirely of working-men. In nearly every case the standard of performance is extraordinarily high, both in quality of tone and on the purely musical side.   H. B.

LEITE, ANTONIO DA SILVA (*b.* Oporto, May 23, 1759; *d.* there, Jan. 10, 1833), Portuguese composer. His master is said to have been Girolamo Sertori, an Italian resident in Oporto, many sacred works by whom are now in the Lisbon Public Library. Leite's own church music (Bibl. Nac., Lisbon) shows a technical mastery of his material; his two operas, performed in 1807 (Theatro de S. João, Lisbon), have not been preserved. His printed works include a 'Tantum ergo,' 4 v. with orchestra, printed in London (1815), an instruction book, 'Rezumo de todas as regras, e preceitos da cantoria' (Oporto, 1787). Of more interest are his works for guitar 'Estudo de guitarra' (Oporto, 1796) and '6 Sonatas de guitarra'

(Oporto, 1792); some of these have accompaniments for a violin and 2 horns.　　　J. B. T.

LEIT - MOTIV (LEIT - MOTIF) (Ger. plur. *Leitmotive*) =leading or guiding theme; a term invented by Hans von Wolzogen [1] to mean a short figure of melody or progression of harmony (frequently the two in combination) of marked character, used to illustrate situations, personages, objects and ideas essential in a story or drama to which music forms a counterpart.

' Leit-motive ' are appropriate alike to descriptive instrumental music called PROGRAMME MUSIC (*q.v.*) and the opera. Though the principle of using them as recurrent features to present to the hearers associations of ideas may be traced back to much earlier times, it was Richard Wagner who gave the term a general currency by his reliance on the ' Leit-motiv ' as a primary means of characterisation in all his mature music-dramas.[2] He pushed the method to its extreme limits in ' Der Ring des Nibelungen,' which is constructed on the most elaborate network of ' leading themes.' In his later works, ' Tristan,' ' Meistersinger ' and ' Parsifal ' Wagner showed that the ' Leit-motiv ' principle was no obsession with him, as it became with his immediate followers in dramatic composition. In these works Wagner uses the ' Leit-motiv ' more sparingly than in the ' Ring '; in fact it may be said that the simpler the stage situation the less he relied on these guides, and the more he indulged in a lyrical development of his material. The 'Ring,' indeed, contains powerful development of certain ' Motive.' A comparison of the Walhalla theme at the beginning of ' Rheingold,' Scene II. (where it emerges from the ' Ring ' theme), with the same at the end of ' Götterdämmerung ' gives an outstanding instance of the force of development. It also contains conspicuous transformations, not quite the same thing as development, *e.g.* that of Siegfried's horn into the majestic form it assumes in ' Götterdämmerung ' (see the ' Trauermarsch '). Nevertheless there are many ' Motive ' in the ' Ring,' notably those associated with inanimate objects, *e.g.* the sword and the anvil, which remain the musical labels of those objects, and are never completely merged into the psychological progress of the drama. The same is not the case with the later dramas, and ' Tristan ' particularly holds its musical pre-eminence on account of what may be called the symphonic development of its leading themes.

As regards earlier history it may be noted that J. S. Bach illustrates the principle of leading themes in his allusive use of Chorals throughout the church cantatas and kindred works. The introduction of ' Meine Seel' erhebt ' by the solo oboe in the ' Suscipit

[1] *Riemann.*
[2] See G. E. H. Abraham, *The Leit-Motif since Wagner.* M. and L. vol. vi. No. 2.

Israel' of the Magnificat in D is a typical case in point. The romantic movement of the early 19th century favoured the exploitation of all kinds of literary allusiveness and quotation in music. Berlioz's *idée fixe* in the ' Symphonie fantastique,' Mendelssohn's references to his own leading themes in ' Elijah ' and Schumann's quotations of the ' Grossvatertanz ' in the ' Carnaval ' and the ' Marseillaise ' in the ' Faschingsschwank ' show the principle gaining hold in different kinds of music not connected with the stage. Naturally, however, the stage most often suggested the sort of relevance of idea which led composers to something approaching the ' Leit-motiv,' and pre-Wagnerian opera affords numerous instances, from the theme of mourning which links the opening chorus of Gluck's ' Orfeo ' with the song ' Ché faro ' to the magic theme in Weber's ' Der Freischütz,' the most immediate predecessor of Wagner.

Wagner's exhaustive use of the ' Leit-motiv ' and perhaps still more the blind copying of his methods by his followers has produced a certain reaction amongst 20th-century composers against this means of expression. Debussy's ' Pelléas et Mélisande ' (1902) marks the turn of the tide. For while the analyst may find themes more or less associated with the several personages of drama, they are no longer ' leading themes ' in the true sense of the word, since it is not by them that the hearer's attention is focussed and directed.　　　　c.

LE JEUNE, C., see JEUNE.

LEJEUNE, GABRIELLE GILIBERT (*b.* Liège, Belgium), operatic soprano. After her vocal studies at the Liège Conservatoire she graduated to the Monnaie at Brussels, making a promising début there in 1892 as Aïda. This led to her engagement at the Opéra-Comique, Paris, where she gained valuable experience and sang in a variety of rôles. She first appeared at Covent Garden on May 15, 1895, as Bertha in ' Le Prophète,' a performance notable for the fact that in it Tamagno sang Jean de Leyden for the first time in England, and that it was the 150th representation of Meyerbeer's opera at this house. Thenceforward until 1909 she sang here regularly, singing among others the part of Suzuki on the production of 'Madama Butterfly ' in 1905, with a cast that included Destinn, Caruso and Scotti. She also created the part of Joan in d'Erlanger's opera ' Tess,' on July 14, 1909. Her voice was of very musical quality and excellently trained, but not powerful enough to stand the strain of high parts. She was married to the baritone, Charles Gilbert, and accompanied him to New York, where they both took part in Oscar Hammerstein's opening season at the Manhattan Opera House, 1906–07.

BIBL.—NORTHCOTT, *Covent Garden and the Royal Opera.*
　　　　　　　　　　　　　　　　　　　H. K.

LEKEU, GUILLAUME (*b.* Heusy, province of Liège, Jan. 20, 1870; *d.* Angers, Jan. 21, 1894), composer, whose works made considerable mark considering the shortness of his life. He died of typhoid.

Lekeu studied with César Franck (1888) and Vincent d'Indy in Paris. He obtained (1891) the second Prix de Rome in Belgium, with his scène lyrique 'Andromède,' which was followed by various symphonic compositions, works for voice and different instruments, many of which were unfortunately left incomplete at his early death. His works include a sonata in G for piano and violin, dedicated to Ysaÿe, much played by him and subsequently by others; a trio for piano and strings, in which passages of very high rank alternate with weak and confused portions; a string quartet, finished by d'Indy; and a 'fantaisie sur deux airs populaires angevins,' frequently played in Belgium and France, and given in London by Wood (1903). Ysaÿe often conducted Lekeu's Étude symphonique on 'Hamlet,' an intimately poetical work, and an adagio for quartet and orchestra, of finely elegiac character. Most of Lekeu's compositions are published by Baudoux of Paris and Muraille of Liège.

LIST OF WORKS

2 Symphonie études. (1889–90.)
Introduction and Adagio for brass instr. (1891.)
Sonata PF. (1891.)
'Chant lyrique,' choir and orch. (1891.)
'Trois Poèmes' (songs). (1892.)
Sonata in G, vln. and PF. (1892.)
'Fantaisie sur deux airs populaires angevins.' (1892.)
'L'Ombre plus dense.' (1893.)
Sonata, PF. and v'cl. (finished by d'Indy).
String Quartet (finished by d'Indy).

BIBL.—A. PISSIER, *Guillaume Lekeu* (1906); O. SÉRÉ, *Musiciens français d'aujourd'hui* (1922); *Le Courrier musical*; *La Terre wallonne*, 1924, seven letters; M. LORRAIN, *Guillaume Lekeu, sa correspondance, sa vie, son œuvre* (Liège, 1923).
M. K.

LE MAISTRE, M., see MAISTRE.

LEMARE, EDWIN HENRY (*b.* Ventnor, Isle of Wight, Sept. 9, 1865), was elected to the Goss scholarship at the R.A.M. in 1878, and became an associate on the completion of his studies. He was subsequently elected to a fellowship of the same institution, and in 1884 was made a fellow of the R.C.O. His successive appointments as organist are as follows: St. John the Evangelist's, Brownswood Park; St. Andrew's Church, and the Public Hall, Cardiff; the Parish Church, Sheffield (1886); Holy Trinity, Sloane Street; and St. Margaret's, Westminster. During his tenure of these last two posts, he became famous as a solo-player and a giver of recitals of more than the usual interest.
M.

He made a prominent feature of transcriptions of modern orchestral music, and his work in this field had a good deal of influence on the subsequent development of the art of registration, and even of organ building. In 1900 Lemare made a recital tour of Canada and the United States, and from 1902–15 he held the post of organist at the Carnegie Institute, Pittsburgh, Pa. He was recitalist at the Panama-Pacific Exposition, San Francisco, 1915, municipal organist at San Francisco, 1917–21; and since 1921 he has held a similar post at Portland, Maine. Lemare is one of the most brilliant players of to-day, an unusually gifted improvisor, and a prolific and successful composer, chiefly of organ music. His works for the instrument number about a hundred, among the best being two symphonies, a 'Toccata di concerto' and a 'Fantaisie fugue.' The bulk of the remainder is in popular style, and shows a pleasant vein of fancy and a dexterous management of effect.
H. G.

LEMLIN (LAMMLEIN), LORENZ, a German composer of the earlier part of the 16th century, came from Eichstätt in Bavaria, and in 1513 attended the University of Heidelberg. He was afterwards singer and Kapellmeister to the Elector Palatine at Heidelberg. Georg Forster mentions him with respect as his worthy preceptor in music, and inserts fifteen of his master's Lieder in his collections of 1539 and 1549. Eitner [1] speaks very slightingly of these Lieder, while on the other hand Ambros [2] judges them very favourably. The only one accessible in a modern reprint is a humorous 'cuckoo' song for six voices, which Ambros describes as quite a charming piece *im Volkston*, 'Der Gutz-gauch auf dem Zaune sass.' This was first republished by C. F. Becker in his book, *Die Hausmusik in Deutschland*, Leipzig, 1840, and is also contained in Eitner's republication of Forster's *Liederbuch* of 1540. The only other known works of Lemlin are a few Latin motets in collections from which Ambros singles out for special mention 'a very beautiful' 'In manus tuas.'
J. R. M.

LEMMENS, (1) NICHOLAS JACQUES (*b.* Zoerle-Parwys, Westerloo, Belgium, Jan 3, 1823; *d.* Castle Linterport, near Malines, Jan. 30, 1881), a distinguished organist, whose performances on the Mustel organ (see MUSTEL) were specially remarkable.

His father was provost and organist at Zoerle-Parwys. His career was attached to the organ from the first. At 11 years of age he was put under Van der Broeck, organist at Dieste. In 1839 he entered the Conservatoire at Brussels, but soon left it owing to the illness of his father, and was absent for a couple of years. In the interval he succeeded his former master at Dieste, but fortunately gave this up and returned to the Conservatoire at the end of 1841. There he became the pupil of Fétis and was noted for the ardour and devotion with which he worked. He took the second prize for composition in 1844 and the first in 1845, as well as the first for organ-playing. In 1846 he went, at the government expense, to Breslau, and remained there a year, studying the organ under A. Hesse, who sent him back at the end

[1] *Monatshefte.* xxvi., 1894, p. 89.
[2] *Geschichte der Musik.* iii. pp. 403-4.

of that time, with a testimonial to the effect that ' he played Bach as well as he himself did.' In 1849 he became professor of his instrument at the Conservatoire, and Fétis, as the head of the establishment, bears strong testimony to the vast improvement which followed this appointment, and the new spirit which it infused through the country.

Though distinguished as a pianist, it is with the organ that his name will remain connected. In 1857 Lemmens married Miss Sherrington, and from that time lived much in England. His great work is his *École d'orgue*, which was adopted by the Conservatoires at Paris, Brussels, Madrid, etc. He also published Sonatas, Offertoires, etc., for the organ, and was engaged for twenty years on a Method for accompanying Gregorian Chants, which was edited by J. Duclos after the author's death, and published at Ghent in 1886. Four volumes of *œuvres inédites* were published by Breitkopf & Härtel. On Jan 1, 1879, he opened a college at Malines, under the patronage of the Belgian clergy, for training Catholic organists and choirmasters, which was soon largely attended.

(2) Madame LEMMENS, *née* Sherrington (*b*. Preston, Oct. 4, 1834 ; *d*. Brussels, May 9, 1906), came of a family who had lived for several generations in Preston : her mother was a musician. In 1838 they migrated to Rotterdam, and there Miss Sherrington studied under Verhulst. In 1852 she entered the Brussels Conservatoire, and took first prizes for singing and declamation. On Apr. 7, 1856, she made her first appearance in London, and soon rose to the position of leading English soprano, both in sacred and secular music, a position which she maintained for many years. In 1860 she appeared on the English, and in 1866 on the Italian, operatic stage, and her operas included ' Robin Hood,' ' Amber Witch,' ' Helvellyn,' ' L'Africaine,' ' Norma,' ' Huguenots,' ' Roberto,' ' Don Giovanni,' ' Domino noir,' ' Fra Diavolo,' ' Marta,' etc.   G.

LEMOINE, a well-known Paris firm of music-publishers. It was founded in 1793 by (1) ANTOINE MARCEL LEMOINE (*b*. Paris, Nov. 3, 1763 ; *d*. there, Apr. 1817), who was a performer on the guitar, and played the viola in the orchestra of the Théâtre de Monsieur. His son, (2) HENRI (*b*. Paris, Oct. 21, 1786 ; *d*. there May 18, 1854), was a pupil of the Conservatoire in 1798–1809, and was one of the most successful piano-teachers of Paris ; he took over the business on his father's death, and raised it to a high position. His educational compositions include a *Petite méthode élémentaire* for piano ; a *Traité d'harmonie pratique* ; a *Solfège des solfèges*, in ten small volumes ; *Tablettes du pianiste*, etc. (3) ACHILLE PHILIBERT, the son of Henri (*b*. Paris, 1813 ; *d*. Sèvres, Aug. 13, 1895), was a partner from 1850, and two years afterwards undertook the sole direction of the

firm. In 1858 he added to it an establishment for engraving and music-printing, which gave a great impulse to the business ; this was carried still further by the acquisition of the ' fonds Schonenberger.' In 1885 Lemoine founded a branch establishment at Brussels, in association with his sons, (4) HENRY (*d*. 1895) and (5) LÉON, who carried it on. Among the numerous publications of the house may be mentioned the *Répertoire classique du chant français*, and the *Répertoire de l'ancien chant classique*, both edited by Gevaert. The firm is now carried on under the title Henri Lemoine & Cie, a nephew of the former, Henry, being the present director (1926).

G. F. ; rev. M. L. P.

LEMOYNE, JEAN BAPTISTE (*b*. Eymet, Perigord, Apr. 3, 1751 ; *d*. Paris, Dec. 30, 1796). After several engagements as conductor in provincial theatres he went to Berlin in 1770 and studied under Graun, Kirnberger and I. A. P. Schulz ; but emotionalism and theatrical effect were more in accordance with his nature than purity of style. After a short engagement as second Kapellmeister at the court theatre, Berlin, he went to Warsaw, and thence to Paris, where he produced an opera, ' Electra ' (1782), imitating the style of Gluck, of whom he declared himself to be a pupil. When Gluck indignantly repudiated that statement, Lemoyne revenged himself by writing (in 1786) another opera, ' Phèdre,' in the style of Piccinni. This met with great success, owing largely to the fine libretto by Hoffmann, and the beautiful singing and acting of Mme. Saint-Huberty, Lemoyne's pupil. After a visit to Italy he returned to Paris in 1788, where in the following year he achieved with ' Nephté ' the (in Paris) unprecedented success of being called before the curtain. Fétis enumerates 16 operas by this composer.   E. v. d. S.

LENDVAI, ERWIN (*b*. Budapest, June 4, 1882), studied music under Koessler in Budapest, and was the winner of a State prize to Milan, where he received a further musical training from Puccini. In 1913 he was appointed teacher of theory at the Jaques-Dalcroze School of Dancing in Hellerau, and in 1919 professor of composition at the Klindworth-Scharwenka Conservatorium in Berlin. His music is of a fine, delicate texture and expresses happily the poetic soul of the composer.

WORKS.—Three string trios, opp. 11, 14, 16 ; string quartet in E min., op. 8 ; symphony in D maj., op. 10 ; scherzo, ' Masken,' for orch., op. 7 ; Archaic Dances, for small orch., op. 30 ; quintet for wind and brass, op. 23 ; pieces for PF., opp. 6, 9, 12, 13, 15 ; songs, opp. 2, 6 ; ' Nippon,' for women's choir, op. 5 ; ' Jungbrunnen,' for voice and orch., op. 20 ; ' Stimmen der Seele,' for 8-voiced choir, op. 25 ; four male choruses, op. 29 ; Minnelieder, op. 21 ; cycle for male choir and baritone, op. 26 ; military march for orch., op. 22 ; four pieces for v'cl. and PF., op. 3 ; three pieces for organ, op. 4 ; opera, ' Elga ' (first perf. in Mannheim, Dec. 6 1916).

K. D. H.

LENEPVEU, CHARLES FERDINAND (*b*. Rouen, Oct. 4, 1840 ; *d*. Paris, Aug. 16, 1910), composer. After finishing his classical studies at his native place he came to Paris by his father's

desire to study law, and at the same time he
learnt solfège from Savard, a professor at the
Conservatoire. His first essay as a composer
was a cantata composed for the centenary of
the Société d'Agriculture et de Commerce of
Caen, which was crowned and performed July
29, 1862. After this success he resolved to
follow the musical profession, and through the
intervention of Savard he entered the Conservatoire and joined Ambroise Thomas's class. He
carried off the Prix de Rome in 1865 as the first
competitor, and his cantata, 'Renaud dans les
jardins d'Armide,' was performed at the opening of the restored Salle du Conservatoire, Jan.
3, 1866. When he was at Rome he took part in
the competition instituted by the Minister of
Fine Arts in 1867, and his score of 'Le Florentin,' written on a poem by St. Georges, was
accepted from among sixty-two compositions,
without hesitation on the part of the judges, or
murmurs on the part of the rival competitors.
The prize work was to have been given at the
Opéra-Comique, but political events and the
war delayed the fulfilment of the promise, and
Lenepveu, instead of composing for the Concerts Populaires, which were always ready to
receive new works, made the mistake of holding
aloof, resting on his laurels, while his companions, Massenet, Dubois, Guiraud, Bizet, etc.,
all of whom were waiting for admittance into
the theatres, devoted themselves to symphonic
music, and thereby acquired skill in orchestration, as well as the recognition of the public.
Lenepveu, who on his return from Rome had
resumed his contrapuntal studies with the
organist CHAUVET (q.v.), while waiting for the
production of 'Le Florentin,' brought forward
nothing except a funeral march for Henri Ré-
gnault, played under Pasdeloup, Jan. 21, 1872.
In the preceding year he had produced a Requiem at Bordeaux for the benefit of the widows
and orphans of those killed in the war, May 20,
1871 ; fragments of these works given at the
Concerts du Conservatoire, Mar. 29, 1872, and
at the Concerts Populaires, Apr. 11, 1873,
showed an unfortunate tendency in the composer to obtain as much noise as possible.

At length, after long delays and repeated
applications, 'Le Florentin' was given at the
Opéra-Comique, Feb. 26, 1874, and was wholly
unsuccessful. After this Lenepveu was never
able to get any work represented in France.
Having completed a grand opera, 'Velléda' (on
the subject of Chateaubriand's 'Martyrs '), he
determined to produce it in London, where it
was performed in Italian, with Mme. Patti in
the principal part (Covent Garden, July 4,
1882). Lenepveu produced a 'drame lyrique,'
'Jeanne d'Arc,' performed in the Cathedral at
Rouen (June 1, 1886); a 'Hymne funèbre et
triomphal,' at Rouen, 1889; an 'Ode triom-
phale à Jeanne d'Arc' at the same place, 1892;
and a Requiem, 1893. From Nov. 1880 he took

a harmony class for women at the Conservatoire
in the place of Guiraud. In this capacity
Lenepveu was decorated with the Légion
d'Honneur on Aug. 4, 1887. He was professor
of composition in the Conservatoire from 1894,
and was elected a member of the Institute in
1896.　　　　　　　A. J. ; addns. by G. F.

LENER QUARTET. The four artists
composing this quartet are wholly the product
of the Musical Academy of Budapest, Jeno
Lener, the leader (b. 1894), Joseph Smilovits,
the second violin (b. 1894), and Sandor Roth,
the viola (b. 1895), being pupils of Jeno Hubay,
who, as far as chamber music is concerned,
owed much to the influence of his master and
intimate friend Joachim. Imre Hartman, the
violoncellist (b. 1895), was a pupil of the
equally famous David Popper.

All won many distinctions and were members
in 1918 of the Opera orchestra in Budapest when, at the outbreak of revolution in
Hungary, Lener gathered around him his three
friends, and the four together retired to a
remote Hungarian village, dedicating their
best energies to the study of chamber music.

After two years of work they made an
appearance in Vienna before an international
gathering of musicians, amongst them Maurice
Ravel, who personally invited them to Paris,
where the concerts they gave proved a revelation to the exacting public of that city. Since
then they have played with success in all the
musical centres of Europe.

Their fourth visit to London in 1925 was
signalised by an historical series of quartet
performances, from Stamitz to Debussy, given
in Wigmore Hall, and by a unique recital in
the Albert Hall, in which a platform was
erected in the centre of the hall.

The playing of the Lener Quartet is characterised by fine tone quality, homogeneity of
style and technical brilliancy. Gramophone
records of their playing are in great demand.
　　　　　　　　　　　　　　W. W. C.

LENTO = 'slow,' implies a pace and style
similar to a slow Andante.

LENTON, JOHN (b. 1656), appointed musician for the violin to Charles II., Aug. 2, 1693,
one of the band of music of William and Mary
and of Queen Anne, from 1692–1718, published
in 1694 'The Gentleman's Diversion, or the
Violin explained,' with some airs composed by
himself and others at the end. A second
edition, with an appendix, and the airs omitted,
appeared in 1702, under the title of 'The Useful Instructor on the Violin.' It is remarkable
that in neither edition is there any mention of
'shifting,' and the scale given reaches but to
c'''. In 1692, in conjunction with Thomas
Tollet, he published 'A Consort of Musick in
three parts.' Lenton composed the overtures
and act tunes to the following plays : 'Venice
Preserved,' 1682 ; 'The Ambitious Step-

mother,' 1700; 'Tamburlain,' 1702; 'The Fair Penitent,' 1703; 'Liberty asserted,' 'Abra Muley,' 1704; and 'The Royal Captive.' Songs by him are in several of the collections of the period, and other vocal pieces in 'The Pleasant Musical Companion' (1685). He contributed to D'Urfey's 'Third Collection of New Songs,' to 'Apollo's Banquet,' and revised the tunes for the earlier editions of his 'Pills to purge Melancholy.' The second vol. of Playford's *Dancing Master*, 1713, is 'carefully corrected by J. Lenton, one of Her Majesties Servants.' The date of his death has not been ascertained, but it was probably soon after 1718, when his name disappears from the royal band.   w. h. h. ; addns. from *D.N.B.*, etc.

LENTZ, HEINRICH GERHARD (*b.* Cologne, *c.* 1764; *d.* Warsaw, Aug. 21, 1839), a pianoforte virtuoso and composer who played at the Concert Spirituel, Paris, in 1785, and at Salomon's concerts in London, 1792. He went to Hamburg in 1795, and was engaged in the same year by Prince Louis Ferdinand of Prussia; but supplanted by Dussek in 1802, he went via Halle to Warsaw, where he became teacher at the Conservatoire in 1826 and retired on the dissolution of that institute in 1831. He composed 3 symphonies, concertos, solos and sonatas, with and without flute or violin, 9 pianoforte trios, and songs.   E. V. D. S.

LENZ, WILHELM VON (*b.* 1808 ; *d.* St. Petersburg, Jan. 31, 1883), Russian councillor at St. Petersburg, and author of *Beethoven et ses trois styles* (2 vols., St. Petersburg, 1852), in which the idea, originally suggested by Fétis, that Beethoven's works may be divided into three separate epochs, has been carried out to its utmost limits. This was followed by *Beethoven : eine Kunststudie*, in 6 vols.—i.-iii., Cassel, 1855–56 ; iv.-vi., Hamburg, 1860. This is an entirely different work from the foregoing, and though often extravagant in expression, has a certain value from the enthusiasm of the writer and the unwearied manner in which he has collected facts of all kinds about Beethoven's works. He also published *Die grossen Pianofortevirtuosen unserer Zeit* (Berlin, 1872), a collection of articles on Liszt, Chopin, Tausig, Henselt, and many other great artists, from personal knowledge, well translated in the *Monthly Musical Record* for 1878. *Aus dem Tagebuche eines Livländers* appeared in Vienna, without date.
                                                    F. G.

LEO, LEONARDO (*b.* S. Vito degli Sclavi, Aug. 5, 1694 ; *d.* Naples, Oct. 31, 1744), more correctly Lionardo Oronzo Salvatore de Leo, was born of humble parents at S. Vito degli Sclavi, now called S. Vito dei Normanni, not far from Brindisi. He was the youngest of the three sons of Leonardo de Leo and Saveria Martino, and was named Leonardo after his father, who died before his birth, Oronzo after an ancestor whose name has been perpetuated in the family

up to the present day, and Salvatore because he came into the world poor like our Saviour. According to the family traditions recorded by Cavaliere Giacomo Leo, a descendant of his brother Giuseppe, he was educated at S. Vito by the Dominicans, who discovered his musical talent and persuaded his mother and his uncles Don Stanislao de Leo, cantor of the church of S. Vito, and Doctor Teodomiro de Leo to send him to pursue his musical studies at Naples. He was admitted to the Conservatorio della Pietà dei Turchini in 1703, being then 9 years old, and remained there until he came of age in 1715. He must not be confused with a relative of his, Leonardo Leo (not de Leo), son of Corrado Leo, who was in easy circumstances, and was living at Naples ' in domibus Conservatori,' *i.e.* in a house belonging to the Conservatorio della Pietà dei Turchini at this time. This Leonardo married in 1713 ; his namesake would not have been allowed to do so while still a pupil of the Conservatorio, and indeed he remained single all his life.

At Naples Leonardo studied first under Provenzale, and later under Nicola Fago il Tarentino. It has been stated that he was also a pupil of Pitoni at Rome, and of Alessandro Scarlatti at Naples ; but although his work was certainly much influenced by both these masters, he cannot have received direct tuition from either of them. He could not have gone to Rome for lessons while a poor student at a Neapolitan Conservatorio, and A. Scarlatti on his return to Naples towards the close of the year 1708 was teaching, not at the Pietà dei Turchini, but at the Poveri di Gesù Cristo.

Leo made his first appearance as a composer with a sacred drama on the subject of Santa Chiara, entitled 'L' Infedeltà abbattuta,' performed by the students of the Conservatorio during the carnival of 1712, and repeated on Feb. 14 of that year at the royal palace, by command of the Viceroy. Florimo names as his first composition another sacred drama, 'Il trionfo della castità di S. Alessio,' produced, according to him, on Jan. 4, 1713, at the Conservatorio, but no trace of either score or libretto is to be found, and it is not mentioned in the newspapers of the time. His first secular opera was 'Pisistrato' (Teatro di S. Bartolomeo, May 13, 1714), which was much admired. In the following year the young composer was made second master at the Pietà dei Turchini, and (according to Florimo) organist of the cathedral ; in 1716 he appears to have been appointed supernumerary organist of the royal chapel, and on June 23, 1717, organist, with a stipend of 12.75 lire a month. This promotion was probably connected with the departure for Rome of A. Scarlatti, which took place in the autumn, after which he received no stipend, but continued to hold the title of Primo Maestro della Real Cappella. Leo also became maestro di cappella at the church of S. Maria della Solitaria, which belonged to a convent of Spanish nuns. In 1718 he produced ' Sofonisba,' hitherto supposed to have been his first opera, and in any case the first which definitely established his reputation as a composer for the stage. The scores of most of his operas of this time have disappeared, and only the more important ones need be mentioned here. In 1722 he composed recitatives and comic scenes for Gasparini's ' Bajazette,' first produced under the name of ' Tamerlano ' at Venice in 1710. The comic scenes were written by Bernardo Sabdumene, who afterwards became famous as a writer of comic libretti in Neapolitan dialect. This seems to have been the beginning of Leo's brilliant career as a composer of comic opera. ' La mpeca scoperta ' (' L' imbroglio scoperto ') was produced in 1723 at the Teatro dei Fiorentini, a theatre already celebrated for the comedies of A. Scarlatti and Leonardo Vinci, and was the first of a long series of successes in this line.

In 1725 Alessandro Scarlatti died, and a number of promotions took place on the staff of the royal chapel, Leo now becoming first organist. It was probably at this date that he became master at the Conservatorio di S. Onofrio. His fame now extended outside Naples. ' Timocrate ' had been given in Venice in 1723, and in 1726 his ' Trionfo di Camilla ' was produced at Rome. The charming pastorale ' In van la gelosia,' which occurs in this opera, enables us to fix the date of the Neapolitan comic opera ' La semmeglianza di chi l' ha fatta,' in which the same air is sung as a show-piece by one of the minor characters. In 1732 he produced his two celebrated oratorios ' La morte di Abele ' and ' Sant' Elena al Calvario.' ' Demofoönte,' perhaps the most successful of all his operas, appeared in 1735 ; in this opera occur the well-known duet ' La destra ti chiedo ' and the pathetic air ' Misero pargoletto,' considered by Piccinni as a model of dramatic expression. In 1737 he was at Bologna for the production of ' Siface,' which was given twenty-seven times at the Teatro Malvezzi, and for which the composer received 1595 lire. ' Farnace ' (1737) was the last opera given at the old Teatro di S. Bartolomeo before its final conversion into a church, the newly built San Carlo having taken its place as court theatre. Leo's L' Olimpiade ' (1737) was the second opera performed there. In 1738 he composed ' Le nozze di Amore e di Psiche,' a ' festa teatrale ' in honour of the marriage of Charles III. with Maria Amalia Walburga of Saxony, and was so much taken up with this work that he was unable to finish the opera ' Demetrio,' on which he was engaged, in spite of being imprisoned in his house and guarded by soldiers to ensure his working. He wrote the first act and part of the second, which was finished by De Majo.

Lorenzo Fago, and Logroscino, the third being written by Riccardo Broschi, brother of Farinelli. The whole opera was, however, eventually finished by Leo himself, and produced at Rome in 1742.

Two important compositions belong to the year 1739 : the celebrated Miserere and the comic opera ' Amor vuol sofferenze.' The Miserere was composed in March, for the use of the royal chapel, and afterwards presented to King Charles Emmanuel of Savoy ; Florimo tells a story of Leo's refusing to allow it to be copied after this, until his pupils contrived to do so secretly and perform it before him. The comic opera ' Amor vuol sofferenze ' is that described with so great delight by the Président Des Brosses to de Neuilly :

' Nous avons eu quatre opéras à la fois sur quatre théâtres différents [i.e. S. Carlo, Fiorentini, Nuovo, and della Pace]. Après les avoir essayés successivement j'en quittai bientôt trois pour ne pas manquer une seule représentation de la Fresquatana, comédie en jargon dont la musique est de Leo . . . Quelle invention ! Quelle harmonie ! Quelle excellente plaisanterie musicale ! '

The heroine of the opera, Eugenia, disguises herself as a maidservant from Frascati : hence the title La finta Frascatana, under which the opera was revived at Bologna in 1742, and by which it was no doubt conveniently known at the time of its first production. It was also known as ' Il cioè,' from the absurd character Fazio, a muddle-headed person who is always explaining and contradicting himself with the word ' cioè '—' that is to say.' In Nov. 1740 Leo went to Turin for the production of ' Achille in Sciro,' and to Milan for that of ' Scipione nelle Spagne,' being absent from Naples for four months. On Jan. 1, 1741, he succeeded Nicola Fago as first master at the Pietà dei Turchini, and, with the exception of a short visit to Rome in November of that year, he seems to have remained in Naples until his death. On Saturday morning, Oct. 31, 1744, he was found dead, having succumbed to apoplexy while seated at his harpsichord : the romantic statement of Florimo that he was engaged at the moment on the composition of ' La finta Frascatana ' is obviously untrue. The records of his death are conflicting, owing to a confusion with his namesake mentioned above ; for the various documents the reader may be referred to Cav. G. Leo's biography. He was buried at the church of Montesanto, the last resting-place of A. Scarlatti and many other musicians of his school.

In person, Leo was of middle height and handsome features ; in manner he was dignified and urbane. He was a man of serious character, working hard at night when his other occupations left him little opportunity for composition in the daytime, and so careful in the preparation of music for performance that he would begin on Ash Wednesday rehearsing the Miserere to be sung in Holy Week. As a teacher he was severe, but greatly beloved of his pupils, the most distinguished of whom were Piccinni and Jommelli.

As a composer, his fame rests chiefly on his sacred music and his comic operas. He was the first of the Neapolitan school to obtain a complete mastery over modern harmonic counterpoint. In the fugal movements of his psalms and masses he is entirely free from modal influences, and is careful to secure a strong rhythmic contrast between his subjects and counter-subjects, a means of effect but vaguely attempted by A. Scarlatti. Leo is in this respect an important factor in the development of modern scholastic counterpoint. In other respects he presents little that is new. His melody is flowing and dignified, but rarely passionate ; his harmony clear and logical, with no attempt at romantic expression. Of his ecclesiastical style the Dixit Dominus in C, published by Novello, is a very typical specimen ; another Dixit Dominus, for ten voices and orchestra, in D, exhibits similar qualities. Of his masses that in D major for five voices and orchestra is the best ; the well-known Miserere and the series of Introits, etc., for Lent, composed in 1744, show a successful adaptation of old methods to modern needs of expression, combining poetic feeling with a studiously restrained style. His sacred music for solo voices is less severe in manner ; we may mention the beautiful Lamentations for Holy Week, a graceful and florid Salve Regina, and a fine motet, ' Inter tot vana insana blandimenta,' for soprano solo and double quartet of strings.

As a composer of serious opera Leo is not especially interesting, and the scarcity of his scores makes it difficult to trace his development. His comic operas, however, are full of life and humour. ' Amor vuol sofferenze ' fully merits the praise bestowed on it by Des Brosses, and no more amusing ' plaisanterie musicale ' could be found than Fazio's great air, ' Io non so dove mi sto,' in which the mock-ecclesiastical accompaniment admirably illustrates the grotesque pomposity of the character. ' La semmeglianza ' shows a keen sense of musical parody ; and all the comic operas are full of sparkling and vivacious music, generally including one or two ensemble movements which are spirited, though never developed to a strong climax, either dramatic or musical. Mention must also be made of his instrumental music, which includes a concerto for four violins and six admirable violoncello concertos composed in 1737 and 1738, for the Duke of Maddaloni.

The best collection of Leo's operas is at Montecassino ; the British Museum and Fitzwilliam Museum afford the best materials for the study of his sacred music. A complete catalogue of his works, with the libraries where

they are to be found, is printed in Cav. G. Leo's biography. The writer's special thanks are due to Cav. Leo for help in the preparation of this article.

I. OPERAS AND OTHER DRAMATIC WORKS

Pisistrato (Naples, 1714). Score, Montecassino.
*Il gran giorno d' Arcadia (Naples, 1714). Serenata.
Diana amante (Naples, 1717). Serenata. Libretto, Brussels Conservatoire.
Sesostri, Re d' Egitto (with Gasparini). Libretto, Brussels Conservatoire (Naples, 1717).
Le nozze in Danza, favoletta pastorale (Naples, 1718).
Sofonisba (Naples, 1718). Libretto, Naples R.C.M.
*Serenata for Sir George Byng, British Ambassador (Naples, 1719).
Lucio Papiro (Naples, 1720). (?) (Revived at Venice, 1737 ; fragments, Brussels Conserv.)
Caio Gracco (Naples, 1720). Libretto, Naples R.C.M.
Arianna e Teseo (Naples, 1721). Libretto, Bologna, Liceo Musicale.
Bajazette Imperador de' Turchi, tragicomedia (Naples, 1722), a modification by Leo of an opera by Gasparini called Tamerlano. Libretto, Naples R.C.M., Bologna.
Artaserse ?
*La mpeca scoperta (L' imbroglio scoperto) (Naples, 1723).
Timocrate (Venice, 1723). Libretto, Bologna, Venice (Bibl. Marc.).
*L' Ammore fedele (Naples, 1724).
*Lo pazzo apposto (Il Finto Pazzo) (Naples, 1724).
Le fiente Zingare (Naples, 1724). Libretto, Naples (Bibl. Naz.).
Turno Aricino (Naples, 1724). By Leo and Vinci. Libretto, Brussels Conservatoire.
Zenobia in Palmira (Naples, 1725). Score and libretto, Naples R.C.M.
Il trionfo di Camilla (Rome, 1726). Score, Montecassino, Vienna, Dresden ; libretto, Bologna ; fragments, Münster.
La Semmeglianza di chi l' ha fatta (Naples, 1726). Score, Montecassino ; libretto, Naples R.C.M. ; fragments, Naples R.C.M.
Dalli sdegni d' Amore ovvero L' Orismene (Naples, 1726). Score, Montecassino ; libretto, Naples R.C.M.
Il Cid (Rome, 1727). Libretto, Brussels Conservatoire, Bologna ; fragments, Münster ?
Argene (Venice, 1728). Libretto, Bologna, Venice. Reproduced at Naples in 1731 ; the autograph score of this version is at Montecassino.
La pastorella Commattuta (Naples, 1728). Libretto, Bologna. The composer's name appears under the anagram ' Onorio Ladel.'
Catone in Utica (Venice, 1729). Score, Brussels Conservatoire ; libretto, Brussels Conservatoire, Bologna, Venice.
La schiava per Amore (Naples, 1729). Libretto, Naples (Bibl. Naz.). The composer's name appears as ' Onorio Ladel.'
Rosmene (Naples, 1730). Libretto, Naples R.C.M.
Evergete (Rome, 1731). Score, Montecassino.
La Vecchia Trammera (Naples, 1732). By Orefice, airs added by Leo. Libretto, Naples (Bibl. Naz.).
Li mariti a forza (Naples, 1732) ?
La festa di Bacco (Leo and Vinci) (Naples, 1732). Libretto, Brussels Conservatoire.
Rosilla (Leo and Orefice) (Naples, 1733). Libretto, Naples (Bibl. Naz.).
Amor dà senno (Naples, 1733). Libretto, Rome (Bibl. Angelica).
Il castello d' Atlante (Naples, 1734). Libretto, Brussels Conservatoire.
La clemenza di Tito (Venice, 1735). Libretto, Bologna, Venice ; fragments, Naples R.C.M.
*Demetrio (Torre Maggiore, 1725).
Demofoönte (Naples, 1735). Score, Brit. Mus., Naples R.C.M., Montecassino.
Emira (Naples, 1735). Score, Naples R.C.M., Montecassino ; libretto, Bologna, Naples R.C.M.
Onore vince Amore (Naples, 1736) ?
Farnace (Naples, 1736). Score, Vienna. Paris Conservatoire ; libretto, Naples R.C.M.
Siface (Bologna, 1737). Score, Montecassino ; libretto, Bologna ; fragments, Brussels Conservatoire.
Ciro riconosciuto (Naples, 1737). Score, Montecassino, Naples R.C.M., Paris Conservatoire ; fragments, representing a later revival, at Montecassino.
L' amico traditore (Naples, 1737). Libretto, Naples R.C.M.
La simpatia del sangue (Naples, 1737). Libretto, Naples R.C.M. autograph overture, Paris Conservatoire.
L' Olimpiade (Naples, 1737). Score, Montecassino, Berlin, Venice, Paris Conservatoire ; libretto, Bologna ; fragments at Montecassino representing a later revival.
Il conte (Naples, 1738).
Le nozze di Amore e di P iche (Naples, 1738). Festa Teatrale. Score, Berlin, Naples R.C.M., Paris Conservatoire.
Demetrio (Naples, 1738). A different opera from that produced in 1735. Leo was unable to finish it and was assisted by G. de Majo, Lorenzo Fago, Nicola Logroscino and Riccardo Broschi. Leo completed the opera later (score at Paris Conservatoire), and it was given at Rome in 1742 (libretto at Brussels).
Choruses for Cammarota's tragedy Sofronia (1738).
Temistocle (Florence, 1739). Fragments, Brussels Conservatoire. Probably additions to an opera by G. B. Ristori.
*Intermezzo and *Festa teatrale for the Spanish Court (Madrid, 1739), for the marriage of the Infante Fhilip.
Amor vuol sofferenze (also called Il cioè, or La finta Frascatana) (Naples, 1739). Score, Montecassino, Paris Conservatoire ; libretto and fragments, Naples R.C.M.
Achille in Sciro (Turin, 1739). Fragments, Montecassino, Naples.
Alidoro (Naples, 1740). Score, Montecassino ; libretto, Naples.
Scipione nelle Spagne (Milan, 1740). Libretto, Bologna.
Viriati (Pistoja, 1740). Libretto, Bologna.
L' Alessandro (Naples, 1741) ?
L' impresario delle Isole Canarine (Venic , 1742). Intermezzo ; libretto, Brussels Conservatoire.
L' Andromaca (Naples, 1742). Score and libretto, Naples.

---

* Neither score nor libretto survive, but the work is mentioned in contemporary journals or other records.

*Airs added to Hasse's Issipile (Naples, 1742).
L' Ambizione delusa (Naples, 1742). Score, Paris Conservatoire (partly autograph, a revised version). Libretto, Naples.
*Serenata del felice parto della Regina di Napoli (1743, not performed). Bv Leo, Mannia and Logroscino.
Decebalo (?) festa teatrale. Score at Paris Conservatoire. A modern German manuscript apparently copied from an autograph. Apparently composed for the birth of the Archduchess Maria Elizabeth, daughter of the Empress Maria Theresa, born 1743.
fl fantastico od Il nuovo Don Chisciotte (Naples, 1743).
La Fedeltà odiata (Naples, 1744) ?
*Vologeso (Turin, 1744).
La contesa dell' Amore colla Virtù (1744, for the marriage of the Dauphin of France with the Infanta of Spain). Autograph score, Paris Conservatoire.

OPERAS OF UNCERTAIN DATE

Il Medo. Score, Brussels.
Lo matremonio annascuso. Score, Montecassino.
Nitocri, Regina d' Egitto. Score, Montecassino.
I viaggiatori. Libretto (Paris, 1754), Brussels and Bologna.
Le nozze di Iole ed Ercole. Score at Münster.
Andromeda. Score at Vienna. A pasticcio with some airs of Leo, 1750.

II. ORATORIOS

*S. Chiara o l' Infedeltà abbattuta (Naples, 1712).
Il trionfo della castità di S. Alessio (Naples, 1713) ?
*Dalla morte alla vita (S. Maria Maddalena). (Atrani near Amalfi, 1722.)
Oratorio per la B. V. del Rosario (Naples, 1730). Score at Münster.
La morte di Abele (Naples, 1732). Score, Naples R.C.M., Montecassino, Bologna, Brussels Conservatoire, Munich, Dresden, Berlin, Paris Conservatoire, Vienna. Libretto, Bologna.
S. Elena al Calvario (Naples, 1732). Score, B.M., Naples R.C.M., Cambridge Fitzwilliam, Berlin, Dresden, Montecassino, Münster, Paris Conservatoire.
S. Francesco di Paola nel deserto (Lecce, 1738).
S. Genoviefa. Score, Naples R.C.M. (by Leo ?).
Fragments of an oratorio (autograph) in which the characters are Abdia and Eliseo. Paris Conservatoire.

III. MASSES

? S.A.T.B. and orch. in A (K. and G.). Paris Conservatoire.
S.S.A.T.B. and orch. in B flat (K. and G.). Paris Conservatoire (autograph) Berlin, copied by Winterfeld from parts in the Mathiasstift at Breslau, 1817.
? S.S.A.T.B. and str. in D. Paris Conservatoire. Doubtful.
S.S.A.T.B. and orch. in D (K. and G.). Naples R.C.M., Dresden, Berlin, Paris Conservatoire.
S.S.A.T.B. and orch. in F (K. and G.). B.M., Berlin. Fitzwilliam has a fragmentary copy of the voice part only.
S.S.A.T.B. and orch. in G (K. and G.). Two versions of this Mass exist.

A	B
For S. Vincenzo Ferrero, ᴢ733.	Berlin.
Berlin.	B.M.
Cambridge.	Münster.
Dresden.	Munich.
London R.C.M.	
Paris Conservatoire.	

Gloria S.S.A.T.B. and orch. in G (1734). Berlin.
Credo S.A.T.B. and str. in A. Berlin, Munich, Paris Conservatoire.
Credo, Sanctus and Agnus, S.S.A.T.B., S.S.A.T.B. and str. Naples R.C.M.
Credo, Sanctus Benedictus and Agnus, S.S.A.T.B. and org. in C. Naples R.C.M.
Credo, S.A.T.B. str. and org. in C. Berlin, Münster, B.M.

IV. MOTETS, PSALMS, ETC.

A solis ortu, S.S.T. and org. (autograph). Naples R.C.M.
? Ave Regina Caelorum, T.T.B.B. Berlin.
Cessate eia cessate, S. and str. B.M.
Chr'stus factus est, S.S. and org. Fitzwilliam.
Christus factus est, S. and org. B.M., Vienna, Naples.
Christus factus est, S. solo, S.A.T.B. and str. Naples.
? Credidi propter quod, S.A.T.B. Berlin, Münster.
Dixit Dominus, S.A.T.B. and orch. in A. Palermo R.C.M., Berlin, Fitzwilliam, Paris Conservatoire.
Dixit Dominus, S.A.T.B., S.A.T.B. and orch in C (1742 ?). Fitzwilliam; autograph (date cut off by binder). (Edited by Stanford, Novello.) Naples R.C.M. (1742), Dresden, Berlin, Münster, Vienna Gesellschaft der Musikfreunde, London R.C.M., B.M., Paris Conservatoire.
? Dixit Dominus, S.S.A.T.B. and orch. in D. Paris Conservatoire.
Dixit Dominus, S.A.T.B., S.A.T.B. and orch. in D. Münster.
Dixit Dominus, S.S.A.T.B., S.A.T.B. and orch. in D. Fitzwilliam (1730), Naples R.C.M. (1741), Berlin, Paris Conservatoire.
? Dixit Dominus, S.A.T.B. and orch. in F. R.C.M.
Dixit Dominus, S.S.A.T.B. and orch. in G. Münster.
Dixit Dominus, S.A.T.B. and orch. in G. Naples (org. part only).
Heu nos miseros, S.S.A.T.B., S.A.T.B. B.M., Berlin, Cambridge, Darmstadt, Dresden, Munich, Naples, Paris Conservatoire. (The Dresden MS. is inscribed ' Fatto a richiesta de' Pittoni,' which might be an error for ' di ' or ' del Pitoni,' but Cav. G. Leo reads de' Pittoni, i.e. for the Congregazione dei Pittori in Naples.
Inter tot vana insana blandimenta, S. and double quartet of str. Naples R.C.M.
Laudate Dominum omnes gentes, S.A.T.B. and str. Dresden.
Laudate Pueri Dominum, S.S.S.S. soli, S.A.T.B., S.A.T.B. coro and org. Naples R.C.M.
? Laudate Pueri, S.S.A. and orch. Dresden.
Lezioni della settimana santa, S.A. and org. Munich, Berlin, Münster, B.M., Paris Conservatoire.
Magnificat, S.S.A.T.B., str. and org. in C min. Berlin, Paris Conservatoire.
Magnificat, S.S.A.T.B., str. and org. in G min. Berlin, Munich, Milan, Naples.

---

* Neither score nor libretto survive, but the work is mentioned in contemporary journals or other records.

Miserere, S.A.T.B., S.A.T.B. and org. in C min. (1739). Naples R.C.M. (autograph) Fitzwilliam, Munich, Berlin, Vienna, B.M., Paris Conservatoire, R.C.M.
Miserere, S.A.T.B. and orch. in C min. Munich, Milan.
Introits, Graduals, Offertories, and Communions for the Sundays of Lent. Composed for the Royal Chapel, Naples, 1744 :
Ash Wednesday. Introit : Misereris omnium Domine. S.A.T.B and org. B.M.
First Sunday in Lent. Introit : Invocabit me et ego exaudiam eum Gradual : Angelis suis Deus mandavit de te. Offertory. Scapulis suis obumbrabit tibi Dominus, S.A.T.B. and org. B.M. Aut. Berlin, Münster.
Second Sunday in Lent. Introit : Reminiscere miserationum tuarum. Gradual : Tribulationes cordis mei dilatatae sunt. S.A.T.B. and org. Communion : Intellige clamorem meum, S. solo, S.A.T.B. and org. B.M. Aut.
Fourth Sunday in Lent. Introit : Laetare Jerusalem. Gradual : Laetatus sum in his ; S.A.T.B. and org. B.M. Aut., Berlin, Münster. Offertory : Laudate Dominum quia benignus est, S.S. soli, S.A.T.B. and org. B.M. Aut.
Passion Sunday. Introit : Judica me Deus, S.A.T.B. and org. Gradual : Eripe me Domine, S.A.T.B. and org. Aut. B.M., Berlin, Münster, Paris Conservatoire. Communion : Hoc corpus quod pro nobis traditur, S.S. soli, S.A.T.B. and org. B.M. Aut., Münster.
Pange lingua (for the Cons. di S. Onofrio, 1744). S.A.T.B. and str, Naples R.C.M., Dresden.
Praebe Virgo benignas aures, S. and org. Berlin, Münster.
Quae Virtus infinita, S.A.T. and str. Berlin.
Responsorij di S. Antonio di Padova (Si quaeris miracula). S.A.T.B. and str. Naples R.C.M.
Responsorij for Holy Week. S.A.T.B. and org. (In monte Oliveti). Naples R.C.M., Berlin, Münster, Munich, B.M.
Salve Regina, S. and str. in C min. R.C.M.
Salve Regina, S. and str. in F. Berlin, Münster.
Te Deum, S.A.T.B. and orch. in D. Berlin, Paris Conservatoire, R.C.M. Chorus, S.A.T.B. and orch., with two sets of words, (a) Cum Sancto Spiritu, and (b) Alleluia. The Cum Sancto Spiritu, written above the notes, appears to be autograph. Naples R.C.M.

V. STUDIES IN COUNTERPOINT, ETC.

Fugues for two voices. Naples R.C.M.
Various. Berlin, Naples, Montecassino, Bologna, Milan.

VI. INSTRUMENTAL MUSIC

Concerto for four vln. and bass in D. Berlin, Dresden.
Six Concerti (one called a Sinfonia Concertata) for v'cl., with two vlns. and bass. Composed for the Duke of Maddaloni, aut., 1737 and 1738. Naples R.C.M., Milan.
Toccatas for Cembalo. Milan, Montecassino, Naples ; one in G min., published in a modernised form under the name of ' Arietta ' has become very popular.
Aria con variazioni per cembalo. Montecassino.

BIBLIOGRAPHY

(Used as authorities for the above)
Fétis, Florimo, Cav. G. Leo, Leonardo Leo, musicista del secolo xviii e le sue opere musicali, Naples, 1905 ; I Signori Leo, i Di Leo ricchi e poveri nei secoli xvii e xviii, etc., Naples, 1901 ; Leonardo Leo ed il suo omonimo, Naples, 1901 ; S. Vito dei Normanni, Naples, 1904.

In addition to the above works there are numerous cantatas for a single voice, arias from operas, etc., in various libraries.   E. J. D.

LEO DI MODENA, an early 17th-century Jewish composer of Mantua, wrote an essay on choral singing in the Synagogue, in Rossi's Schirha-Schirim (Venice, 1623).

LÉONARD, HUBERT (b. Bellaire, Belgium, Apr. 7, 1819 ; d. Paris, May 6, 1890), famous violinist, entered the Paris Conservatoire in 1836, and studied under Habeneck. He established his reputation as a brilliant player by a tour through Germany in 1844, and was the first to play Mendelssohn's Violin Concerto in Berlin, under the immediate direction of the composer. In 1847 he succeeded de Bériot as first professor of the violin at the Brussels Conservatoire. In 1867 he resigned on account of ill-health and went to live in Paris, where he died. He was an eminently successful teacher, and counted among his pupils many of the best modern Belgian, German and French violinists. Léonard was a brilliant virtuoso, excelling especially in arpeggios and staccatos.

Madame Léonard (née Antonia Sitcher de Mendi, a niece of Manuel Garcia) gained much distinction in concert singing, and was for many years a successful teacher of singing in Paris.

LEONARDA, ISABELLA (*b.* Novara, *c.* 1641), abbess of the convent of St. Ursula, Novara ; composer of masses, motets (the last book, op. 20, Bologna, 1700) and other church music. (List in *Q.-L.*)

LEONARDO, GIOVANNI, DELL' ARPA (late 16th cent.), Neapolitan composer of villanelle and canzone in collective volumes (*Q.-L.*).

LEONCAVALLO, RUGGIERO (*b.* Naples, Mar. 8, 1858 ; *d.* Montecatini, near Florence, Aug. 9, 1919), composer of ' Pagliacci ' and other less famous operas, was the son of a magistrate. His musical studies began with the pianoforte, which he learnt, first, from a musician named Siri, and afterwards from Simonetti, a teacher of some repute at Naples, the author of an *Enciclopedia del pianista.* In due course Leoncavallo was admitted to the Neapolitan Conservatoire, where he became the pupil of Beniamino Cesi for the piano, of Michele Ruta for harmony, and of Lauro Rossi for composition.

At the age of 18 he left the Conservatoire with the diploma of ' maestro,' and set to work upon an opera. His subject was the tragic story of Chatterton, the libretto being an adaptation of Alfred de Vigny's drama. At Bologna, whither he had gone to attend the lectures of the famous poet and littérateur Carducci, he completed the opera and arranged for its production, but at the last moment the impresario decamped, leaving the unfortunate composer almost penniless. In despair Leoncavallo was compelled to undertake any work that would keep him from starvation. He gave lessons in singing and in piano-playing, and played accompaniments at café-concerts. In the latter capacity he travelled far, visiting England, France, Holland and Germany, and going even as far as Cairo. After many years' wandering he returned to Italy, and presented himself to the house of Ricordi, with the scenario of a vast trilogy dealing with the history of the Renaissance in Italy, for which he had already completed the libretto of the first section, ' I Medici.' The latter was accepted, and in a year Leoncavallo had finished the music.

For three years he waited vainly in the hope of seeing his opera produced, and then betook himself in despair to the rival house of Sonzogno. Here he was well received, and for this firm he wrote his 2-act opera ' Pagliacci,' which was produced at the Teatro dal Verme, Milan, on May 21, 1892, with very great success. Leoncavallo's name soon became famous throughout Italy, and on Nov. 10, 1893, his ' Medici,' the first section of his Renaissance trilogy, ' Crepusculum,' was produced at the Teatro dal Verme. The work, which deals with the Pazzi conspiracy and the murder of Giuliano de' Medici, was a failure ; and the composer, discouraged by its unfavourable reception, never completed, or at any rate never published, the remaining

sections of the trilogy, ' Savonarola ' and ' Cesare Borgia.' Leoncavallo's early opera, 'Chatterton,' which was finally given at the Teatro Nazionale, Rome, on Mar. 10, 1896, was no more successful than ' I Medici,' but ' La Bohème ' (Teatro della Fenice, Venice, May 6, 1897), an adaptation of Henri Murger's novel, was far more favourably received, although handicapped by inevitable comparisons with Puccini's opera on the same subject, which had been produced with overwhelming success a few months earlier, and was actually being played to crowded audiences at another theatre in Venice at the same time.

Leoncavallo's next opera, ' Zaza,' an adaptation of the play by Berton and Simon, was produced at the Teatro Lirico, Milan, on Nov. 10, 1900, with fair success, and has subsequently been performed in Germany, Holland and Paris. ' Der Roland ' was written in response to a commission of the German Emperor, Wilhelm II., who heard ' I Medici ' in Berlin in 1894, and believed that in the Italian poet and musician he had found a bard worthy of celebrating the glory of the house of Hohenzollern, as in ' I Medici ' he had celebrated that of the great Florentine family. ' Der Roland ' is founded upon Willibald Alexis's romance, ' Der Roland von Berlin,' which deals with the subjugation of Berlin by the Elector Frederick II. Of this work an Italian translation was made for Leoncavallo's benefit by the Emperor's orders, from which he constructed his own libretto. This, after the music was finished, was translated back into German by Georg Droescher, and the opera was produced at the Royal Opera House in Berlin, on Dec. 13, 1904. In spite of the patronage of the Emperor, and the favour of the Court, ' Der Roland ' attained no permanent success. It was, in fact, in his most ambitious works, such as this and ' I Medici,' that Leoncavallo showed to least advantage. In operas of the type of ' Zara ' and ' Pagliacci,' his strong feeling for theatrical effect served him well, but his musical inspiration was singularly deficient, and his more pretentious works were hardly more than strings of ill-digested reminiscences.

In 1910 two new operas by him were produced in Rome within four days of each other, ' Maia ' in 3 acts, libretto by Paul de Choudens, at the Costanzi Theatre, Jan. 15, 1910 ; and ' Malbruk,' a comic opera in 3 acts, libretto by Signor Nessi, at the Teatro Nazionale, on Jan. 19.

Later works, several of them no more than operettas of slight quality, were ' I Zingari ' (London, 1912). ' La reginalla delle rose ' (Rome, 1912), ' Are you there ? ' (London, 1913), 'La Candidata' (Rome, 1915), 'Goffredo Mameli ' (Genoa, 1916), ' Prestami tua moglie ' (Montecatini, 1916), ' Edipo Re ' (Chicago, 1920).

As a librettist Leoncavallo showed uncommon dramatic ability. Not only did he write the libretti for his own operas, but, like Boïto, he occasionally placed his talent at the service of his friends, as in the case, for instance, of 'Mario Wetter,' an opera by the Portuguese composer, Augusto Machado. Apart from his operatic works, Leoncavallo was the composer of a symphonic poem, 'Serafita,' founded upon Balzac's novel, and of a ballet entitled 'La Vita d' una Marionetta.'

R. A. S., with addns.

LEONETTI, GIOVANNI BATTISTA, of Crema, organist of S. Agostino of that town in 1617. He composed a book of masses, 8 v., and a book of madrigals, 5 v.; also 4 madrigals *a* 6 in Orazio Scaletta's 'Affettuosi affetti' (1604).

LEONI (*d.* Kingston, 1797 [1]), a vocalist of repute during the latter part of the 18th century. His real name was Myer Lyons, and he was uncle to John Braham. After being a chorister at the Great Synagogue in Aldgate, London, he made an appearance in opera at Covent Garden in the part of Arbaces, in 'Artaxerxes,' by Dr. Arne, in 1775. He sang in other Covent Garden operas, including Shield's 'Flitch of Bacon,' in 1778.

He joined Giordani in the management of an English opera-house in Dublin, and was also engaged by Palmer for the Royalty Theatre. After remaining some time in England and Ireland, he was appointed 'bazzan' at the Jewish Synagogue at Kingston, Jamaica, being the first to hold that office in the English colonies.

His voice is said to have been of fine quality, surpassing even that of his talented nephew, John Braham. He composed small pieces for the theatre, and for use in the Jewish ritual. The hymn-tune 'Leoni' was named after him from the circumstance that he supplied Thomas Oliver, the hymn-writer, with it, the tune being sung as a 'Yigdal' in the Synagogue. It was first published in a collection in 1781.   F. K.

LEONI, GIOVANNI ANTONIO (17th cent.), Italian violinist, composed Sonate di violino a voce sola di . . . lib. 1, op. 3, Rome, 1652. These 31 sonatas are among the earliest written for the violin. A motet by Leoni appears in a collective volume of 1625.

LEONI, LEONE, maestro di cappella at the Duomo of Vicenza from at least 1588, belongs to the Venetian school of composers, whose chief merit does not so much consist in the polyphonic interweaving of the separate voices in skilful and elaborate counterpoint, as in the variety and brilliance of colouring by expressive harmony and the contrasts of double choirs.

His publications are five Books of Madrigals *a* 5, containing twenty or twenty-one each,

<hr>

[1] The *Jewish Encyclopædia* gives about 1800, but Oxberry, probably more trustworthy in this matter, furnishes the former date.

Venice, 1588–1602; 'Penitenza,' a book of Spiritual Madrigals *a* 5, 21 *n*, 1596; 'Sacri fiori,' four Books of Motets for one to four voices with organ accompaniment, 1606–22; 'Sacrae cantiones,' lib. I. *a* 8, with double organ score 20 *n*, 1608; 'Psalmodia,' with two Magnificats *a* 8, 1613; 'Aurea corona,' concerti *a* 10 for four voices and six instruments, etc., 25 *n.*, 1615. It will thus be seen that Leoni also followed in the wake of Giovanni Gabrieli in the combining of voices and instruments, using the instruments *obbligato*. The works of Leoni which would seem to have been most valued by his contemporaries are his motets for double choir *a* 8, fifteen of which appear in the *Promptuarium* of Schadaeus, 1611, and four in the *Florilegium* of Bodenschatz, 1621. Of these Ambros singles out two for special mention. A Passion motet, 'O Domine Jesu Christe adoro te,' he describes as of an almost heavenly beauty, and of 'Petre amas me' he says that hardly any one has given a more beautiful and touching expression to the rapturous utterance of divine love. In Torchi's *L' arte musicale in Italia*, vol. ii., there are two madrigals of Leoni from the volume of 1602, both interesting, one a nightingale echo song, the two upper voices meant to represent one nightingale echoing the other in canon.   J. R. M.

LEONINUS, MAGISTER LEO, a 12th-century organist and maître de chapelle at 'Beatae Mariae Virginis' (afterwards rebuilt as Notre Dame), Paris, one of the first to mark the different time values of notes. He is said to have surpassed his successor, Perotinus, in the art of organ-playing (*Q.-L.*).

LEONORA OVERTURES. The four overtures to Beethoven's 'Fidelio' are known as the 'Leonora' Nos. 1, 2 and 3 in C major, and 'Fidelio' in E major. The order and the occasion of their composition is as follows: 'Leonora' No. 2 for production of the opera, Nov. 20, 1805; 'Leonora' No. 3 for the revival, Mar. 1806; 'Leonora' No. 1 for a performance at Prague, May 1807, which never materialised; and 'Fidelio' for final revision of the opera, May 26, 1814. (See FIDELIO.)

LÉONORE, OU L'AMOUR CONJUGAL, the original title of Beethoven's opera FIDELIO (*q.v.*). The book, written by Bouilly, had been set by Gaveaux (Opéra-Comique, Paris, Feb. 19, 1798); an Italian version was set by Paër (Dresden, Oct. 3, 1804).

LÉPINE, a family of French organ-builders.

(1) JEAN FRANÇOIS (*d.* Toulouse, Oct. 21, 1762), established at the beginning of the 18th century the reputation of the firm. His principal instruments are the great organ of the Cordeliers at Toulouse (1727) and that of the Cathedral at Lodève (1752). He was nearly 80 years of age at his death.

(2) JEAN FRANÇOIS (*b.* Toulouse, July 18,

1732; *d.* Pézenas, July 30, 1817), son of the preceding, pupil and friend of Dom Bédos, and the most celebrated of the family. He established his factory at Pézenas. His principal instruments are : the organ at Pézenas (1757); the reconstruction of the organ in the church at Saint-Just de Narbonne (1770–71); the organ of the Cathedral at Saint-Pierre at Montpellier (1776–80), 48 stops and 3471 pipes.

(3) ADRIEN (*b.* Toulouse, July 15, 1735), brother of (2), established himself at Paris about 1758 and there became the brother-in-law of François Henri Clicquot. In 1767 he restored the great organ of Nantes Cathedral, in 1777 constructed that of the Church of La Chapelle near St. Denis, and in 1778 restored that of the Church of St. Médard in Paris. In 1772 he submitted to the Académie des Sciences (*T.I.* p. 109) a system of *forte piano organisé*, of his own invention. A second keyboard combined the speech of an eight-foot bass, a treble flute, a bassoon and oboe stop.   F. R^L.

L'ÉPINE, FRANCESCA MARGHERITA DE, see ÉPINE.

LEPORIN, JOHANN CHRISTOPH, German organist. Dates of birth and death unknown. Was organist of the Domkirche [1] at Halle from 1697–1702. Leporin was removed from his post by Frederick of Prussia owing to his dissolute manner of living, and was succeeded by the 17-year old G. F. Handel. Handel was a Lutheran, but was appointed to this post, a fitting member of the Reformed Church not being obtainable. It is most important to realise that it was Leporin who was the author of the scandals with which many Handel biographers (starting with Mainwaring, who was followed by Schoelcher) have burdened Friedrich Wilhelm Zachau, Handel's master. Zachau's name has been finally cleared (after a general mention of the falseness of the accusations by Mattheson in his *G. F. Händels Lebensbeschreibung*) by Chrysander (i. p. 61).   S. G.

LEROUX, XAVIER HENRY NAPOLEON (*b.* Velletri, Italy, Oct. 11, 1863; *d.* Paris, Feb. 2, 1919), was a pupil of Massenet at the Paris Conservatoire, where he gained in 1881 a second *accessit* for piano and a first prize for harmony; in 1882 a second prize for counterpoint and an honourable mention for the Prix de Rome; in 1884 a first prize for counterpoint and the second Prix de Rome; and finally, in 1885, the Prix de Rome itself with his cantata 'Endymion.' Leroux's dramatic works are 'Cléopâtre,' incidental music to a five-act drama by Sardou and Moreau (Porte Saint-Martin, Oct. 23, 1890); 'Évangeline,' lyric drama in four acts (Brussels, Dec. 1895); incidental music for 'Les Perses,' adapted from Aeschylus (Odéon, Nov. 5, 1896); music for 'La Montagne enchantée' (in collaboration with A. Messager, Porte Saint-Martin,

[1] Mattheson has U.L. Frauenkirche. This is an error. Leporin was a member of the Reformed Church, and this body worshipped at the Domkirche.

Apr. 12, 1897); 'Astarté,' four-act opera (Paris Opéra, Feb. 15, 1901); 'La Reine Fiammette' (after Catulle Mendès), in four acts (Opéra-Comique, Dec. 23, 1903); 'William Ratcliffe' (Opéra-Comique, Jan. 22, 1906); 'Théodora' (Monte Carlo, Mar. 19, 1907); 'Le Chemineau' (Opéra-Comique, Nov. 6, 1907); 'Xantho chez les courtisanes' (1910); 'Le Carillonneur' (1913); 'La Fille de Figaro' (Paris, Apollo, Mar. 11, 1914); 'Les Cadeaux de Noël' (1916); '1814,' lyric drama (Monte Carlo, Apr. 6, 1918); 'Nausithoé' (Nice, Apr. 9, 1920); 'La Plus Forte' (Opéra-Comique, Jan. 11, 1924). Apart from the stage, Leroux's works include an overture 'Harald,' given at the Lamoureux Concerts; 'Vénus et Adonis,' lyric scene (Concerts de l'Opéra, 1897); and many songs. He also wrote church music, a Mass with orchestra, motets, etc., and filled the post of professor of harmony at the Paris Conservatoire from 1896 till his death. He edited *Musica* and founded the music-school known as the Conservatoire Musica.   G. F. ; addns. M. L. P.

LE ROY, ADRIEN, see ROY, A. Le.

LE ROY, BARTHOLOMEO, see ROY, B. Le.

LE SAGE DE RICHÉE, P. F., see SAGE DE RICHÉE.

LESCHETIZKY, THEODOR (*b.* Lancut, Austrian Poland, June 22, 1830; *d.* Dresden, Nov. 14, 1915), a distinguished pianist, whose fame, however, rested more on his teaching than on personal performance. He attracted notice in Vienna by his pianoforte-playing in 1845. He was at St. Petersburg (1852–78) as a professor at the Conservatorium, then settled in Vienna, where he developed his own school of piano-playing, and was responsible for the training of a large number of distinguished pianists, including Paderewski. While at St. Petersburg he married Mlle. Friedeburg, a concert singer. His three subsequent marriages were with pupils, namely, Annette Essipoff (*q.v.*) (1880–92), Donimirska Benislavska (1894–1908), Marie Gabriele Rozborska (1908). The last-named made her appearance in London as Mme. Leschetizky in the year of her marriage.

Leschetizky's compositions chiefly consist of morceaux de salon for the piano, but an opera, 'Die erste Falte,' was given with success at Prague in 1867, at Wiesbaden in 1881, and elsewhere. He made his début in England at the Musical Union concerts in 1864, playing in the Schumann Quintet, and solos of his own composition, and later frequently appeared at the same concerts. An account of his method was published as *Die Grundlage des Methode Leschetizky* by Malwine Brée in 1902. The following books shed further light on the principles of his teaching and the qualities of his personality :

MARIE UNSCHULD VON MELASFELD : *Die Hand des Pianisten.* (1901.)

ANGELA POTOCKA : *Th. Leschetizky.* (Translated into English from

the French by Geneviève Seymour Lincoln. (New York, 1903.)
ANNETTE HULLAH: *Th. Leschetizky. Living Masters of Music.* (London, 1906.)
ETHEL NEWCOMB: *Leschetizky as I knew him.* (New York and London, 1921.) M. ; addns. C.

LESLIE, (1) HENRY DAVID (*b.* London, June 18, 1822 ; *d.* Llansaintfraid, near Oswestry, Feb. 4, 1896), important in the history of choral music in England for the choir which he directed and brought to a high pitch of excellence, began his musical education under Charles Lucas in 1838.

For several years he played the violoncello at the Sacred Harmonic Society and elsewhere. In 1847, on the formation of the Amateur Musical Society, he was appointed its honorary secretary, and continued so until 1855, when he became its conductor, which post he retained until the dissolution of the Society in 1861. The choir which bore his name was actually formed by Joseph Heming in 1853, and conducted at first by Frank Moir ; Leslie undertook the leadership in 1855, and the first concert took place in 1856. At first the number of voices was limited to about sixty, but afterwards it was increased to 240, so that a large work could replace the madrigals, for the sake of which the choir was originally founded. In 1878 it gained the first prize in the International Competition of choirs at Paris. In 1863 Leslie was appointed conductor of the Herefordshire Philharmonic Society, an amateur body at Hereford. In 1874 he became the director and conductor of the Guild of Amateur Musicians. In 1880 his choir was broken up ; it was subsequently reorganised under Randegger, and in 1885–1887 Leslie resumed its management. Leslie's compositions were numerous, and included practically every form. They are not now considered important. W. H. H. ; rev. C.

His son (2) WILLIAM HENRY PERRY (*b.* 1860 ; *d.* Llansaintfraid, May 23, 1926) united something of his father's musical gifts and enthusiasm with a successful business career. He was a member of Lloyd's (Godwin & Leslie) and was the first chairman of Lloyd's Brokers Association. He furthered various societies for amateur music in connexion with Lloyd's. As a director of John Broadwood & Son he promoted the interesting concerts given by that firm in London. He was a member of the Council of the R.C.M. and Master of the Musicians' Company (1924). His most individual work for music, however, was accomplished in the singing festivals and competitions which he organised in the neighbourhood of his country estate in Wales. C.

LESSEL, FRANZ (*b.* Pulawy on the Vistula, Poland, *c.* 1780 ; *d.* Aug. 1838), one of Haydn's three favourite pupils, his father, a pupil of Adam Hiller and Dittersdorf, being Musikdirector at the neighbouring castle of Prince Czartoryski.

In 1797 he came to Vienna to study medicine, but the love of music proved a great distraction. Haydn eventually took him as a pupil, a service he repaid by tending him till his death with the care and devotion of a son. In 1810 he returned to Poland, and lived with the Czartoryski family, occupied entirely with music. After the Revolution of 1830 had driven his patrons into exile, Lessel led a life of great vicissitude, but being a man of varied cultivation always managed to maintain himself, though often reduced to great straits. In 1837 he was superseded in his post as principal of the gymnasium at Petrikau on the borders of Silesia, and feeling a presentiment of approaching death, he composed his Requiem, and shortly after expired of the disease commonly called a broken heart. He left songs, chamber music and symphonies ; also church music, specially indicating gifts of no common order. Among his effects were some autographs of Haydn presented by himself. Some of his works were published by Artaria, Weigl and Breitkopf & Härtel, among them being three sonatas for PF. (op. 2), dedicated to Haydn ; fantasia for PF. (op. 8), dedicated to Clementi ; another fantasia (op. 13), dedicated to Cecily Beidale ; a piano concerto, etc. (See *Q.-L.*) Lessel's life was a romantic one. He was believed to be the love-child of a lady of rank. Mystery also enveloped the birth of his first love, Cecily Beidale, and he discovered that she was his sister only just in time to prevent his marrying her. One of his Masses—' Zum Cäcilientag '—was composed in all the fervour of this first passion. C. F. P.

LESSON (LEÇON), a name in common use from the beginning of the 17th century to the close of the 18th, to denote pieces for the harpsichord and other keyed instruments. It was generally applied to the separate pieces which in their collected form made up a Suite.

The origin of the name seems to be that these pieces served an educational purpose, illustrating different styles of playing, and being often arranged in order of difficulty. This is borne out by the fact that Domenico Scarlatti's ' Forty-two Lessons for the Harpsichord, edited by Mr. Roseingrave,' are in the original edition called ' Esercizi—xxx. Sonatas per gravicembalo,' though they have little of the educational element in them.[1] Rameau's Lessons for the Harpsichord, opp. 2 and 3, are not arranged in order of difficulty, but are connected by the relation of their keys. In the case of Handel's 3 Leçons, the first consists of a Prelude and air with variations in B♭, the second of a Minuet in G minor and the third of a Chaconne in G major ; so they may be presumed to be intended for consecutive performance. The

[1] See also Sir John Hawkins's *History of Music*, chap. 148, where he uses the word ' lessons ' for ' suites of lessons.'

' Suites de pièces pour le clavecin,' in two Books, were called ' Lessons ' in the first edition, but in the later editions this name was discarded for that which they now bear. Instances of the use of the word to indicate a composition in three movements are to be found in the works of many 18th-century composers.[1]

Although in general the name was applied to pieces for the harpsichord alone,[2] yet it was sometimes used for concerted chamber music, as in the ' Firste Booke of consort lessons,' collected by Thomas MORLEY (q.v.) (London, 1611), and in Mathias Vento's ' Lessons for the Harpsichord with accompaniment of Flute and Violin.' (Cf. ÉTUDE.)   M.

L'ESTOCART, PASCHAL DE, see ESTOCART.

LESTOCQ, opera in 4 acts ; words by Scribe, music by Auber. Produced Opéra-Comique, May 24, 1834 ; in English, Covent Garden, Feb. 21, 1835.   G.

LESUEUR, JEAN FRANÇOIS (b. Drucat-Plessiel, near Abbéville, Feb. 15, 1760[3]; d. Paris, Oct. 6, 1837), grandnephew of the celebrated painter Eustache Lesueur. He became a chorister at Abbéville at the age of 7. At 14 he went to the college at Amiens, but two years later, in 1779, broke off his studies to become, first, maître de musique at the cathedral of Séez, and then sous-maître at the church of the Innocents in Paris. Here he obtained some instruction in harmony from the Abbé Roze, but it was not any systematic course of study, so much as his thorough knowledge of plainsong and deep study, that made him the profound and original musician he afterwards became.

His imagination was too active, and his desire of distinction too keen, to allow him to remain long in a subordinate position ; he therefore accepted in 1781 the appointment of maître de musique at the cathedral of Dijon, whence after two years he removed to Le Mans and then to Tours. In 1784 he came to Paris to superintend the performance of some of his motets at the Concert Spirituel, and was reappointed to the church of the Holy Innocents as headmaster of the choristers, in place of the Abbé Roze. He now mixed with the foremost musicians of the French school, and with Sacchini, who gave him good advice on the art of composition and urged him to write for the stage. In 1786 he competed for the musical directorship of Notre Dame, which he obtained, and immediately entered upon his duties. He was allowed by the chapter to engage a full orchestra, and thus was able to give magnificent performances of motets and Messes solennelles. His idea was to excite the imagination and produce devotional feeling by means of dramatic

effects and a picturesque and imitative style, and he even went so far as to precede one of his masses by a regular overture, exactly as if it had been an opera. Crowds were attracted by this novel kind of sacred music, and his masses were nicknamed the ' Beggar's Opera ' (' L'Opéra des gueux ').

This success soon aroused opposition, and a violent anonymous attack was made upon him, under pretext of a reply to his pamphlet Essai de musique sacrée, ou musique motivée et méthodique pour la fête de Noël (1787). Lesueur's rejoinder was another pamphlet, Exposé d'une musique, une imitative et particulière à chaque solennité (Paris, Hérissant, 1787), in which he gives a detailed sketch of an appropriate musical service for Christmas, and states expressly that his aim was to make sacred music ' dramatic and descriptive.' Meantime the chapter, finding that his projects had involved them in heavy expense, curtailed the orchestra, while at the same time strong pressure was put upon him by the Archbishop to take Orders. He willingly assumed the title of Abbé, but declined the priesthood, especially as he was composing an opera, ' Télémaque,' which he was anxious to produce. Finding his reduced orchestra inadequate for his masses he resigned, upon which an infamous libel was issued, accusing him, the most upright of men, of having been dismissed for fraud. Completely worn out, he retired in the autumn of 1788 to the country house of a friend, and here he passed nearly four years of repose and happiness. On the death of his friend in 1792 he returned to Paris, invigorated and refreshed in mind, and composed a series of three-act operas—' La Caverne ' (Feb. 15, 1793), ' Paul et Virginie ' (Jan. 13, 1794) and ' Télémaque ' (May 11, 1796), all produced at the Théâtre Feydeau. The brilliant success of ' La Caverne ' procured his appointment as professor in the École de la Garde Nationale (Nov. 21, 1793), and he was also nominated one of the inspectors of instruction at the Conservatoire from its foundation in 1795. In this capacity he took part with Méhul, Gossec, Catel and Langlé in drawing up the Principes élémentaires de musique and the Solfèges du Conservatoire.

He was then looking forward to the production of two operas which had been accepted by the Académie ; and when these were set aside in favour of Catel's ' Semiramis ' his indignation knew no bounds and he vehemently attacked not only his colleague but the director of the Conservatoire, Catel's avowed patron. His pamphlet, Projet d'un plan général de l'instruction musicale en France (Paris, an IX. (1801) anonymous), raised a storm and Lesueur received his dismissal from the Conservatoire on Sept. 23, 1802. Having a family to support, the loss of his salary crippled him severely, and he was only saved from utter indigence by his

---

[1] One such lesson by Nares is quoted in the Oxf. Hist. Mus. vol. iv. ; The Age of Bach and Handel, pp. 329-38.
[2] Lessons for the lute were published as early as 1577. W. H. G. F.
[3] See Q.-L. for the evidence of this date

appointment in Mar. 1804 as maître de chapelle to the First Consul, on the recommendation of Paisiello, who retired on account of his health. As the occupant of the post most coveted by musicians in France, Lesueur had no difficulty in securing the representation of ' Ossian, ou les Bardes ' (five acts, July 10, 1804). The piece inaugurated the new title of the theatre as ' Académie Impériale.' Its success was extraordinary, and the Emperor, an ardent admirer of Celtic poems, rewarded the composer with the Legion of Honour, and presented him with a gold snuff-box inscribed ' L'Empéreur des Français à l'auteur des Bardes,' intended also as an acknowledgment for a Te Deum and a Mass performed at Notre Dame on the occasion of his coronation (Dec. 2, 1804). During the next five years Lesueur undertook no work of greater importance than a share in Persuis's intermède ' L'Inauguration du Temple de la Victoire ' (Jan. 2, 1807), and in the same composer's three-act opera ' Le Triomphe de Trajan ' (Oct. 23, 1807), containing the well-known ' Marche solennelle '; but on Mar. 21, 1809, he produced ' La Mort d'Adam et son apothéose ' in three acts—the original cause of his quarrel with the management of the Académie and the Conservatoire. The scenery and decorations of the new opera excited the greatest admiration ; when complimented on his work, Degotti the scene-painter replied quite seriously, ' Yes, it certainly is the most beautiful paradise you ever saw in your life, or ever will see.'

In 1813 Lesueur became a member of the Institut (Académie des Beaux-Arts) ; and after the Restoration became, in spite of his long veneration for Napoleon, surintendant and composer of the chapel of Louis XVIII. On Jan. 1, 1818, he was appointed professor of composition at the Conservatoire, a post which he retained till his death. His lectures were largely attended and very interesting from the brilliant remarks with which he interspersed them. Of his pupils no less than twelve gained the Prix de Rome—namely, Bourgeois, Ermel, Paris, Guiraud, Hector Berlioz, Eugène Prévost, Ambroise Thomas (whom he called his ' note sensible,' or leading note, on account of his extreme nervousness), Elwart, Ernest Boulanger, Besozzi, Xavier Boisselot (who married one of his three daughters) and, lastly, Gounod. Lesueur also wrote *Notice sur la Mélopée, la Rhythmopée et les grands caractères de la musique ancienne*, published with Gail's French translation of Anacreon (Paris, 1793). Ancient Greek music was a favourite subject with him, and he would with perfect seriousness expound how one mode tended to licence and another to virtue ; unfortunately, however, some wag in the class would occasionally mislead his ear by inverting the order of succession in the chords and thus betray him into taking the licentious for the virtuous mode, and *vice versa*.[1]

Lesueur died at a patriarchal age and in universal respect ; even Berlioz [2] loved and honoured him to the last. He left three operas which had never been performed, ' Tyrtée,' three acts, composed in 1794 ; ' Artaxerse,' three acts, accepted by the Opéra in 1801 ; and ' Alexandre à Babylone,' of which the score has been engraved and considerable portions performed at the Conservatoire concerts. Of his numerous oratorios, masses, motets, etc., the following have been published :

' L'Oratorio ou Messe de Noël.'
Three Messes solennelles.
Mass with ' Domine Salvum.'
Three ' Oratorios pour le couronnement des princes souverains.'
Te Deum (3 settings).
' Domine Salvum ' (2).
Two ' Oratorios de la Passion.'
Stabat Mater.
The oratorios ' Debora,' ' Rachel,' ' Ruth et Noémi,' ' Ruth et Booz.'
Cantata for the marriage of the Emperor Napoleon.
Motet for the baptism of the King of Rome.
Prière for the Emperor on airs of Languedoc.
' O Salutaris.'
Psalms and Motets, including a ' Super flumina Babylonis.'

The five operas previously mentioned and all this sacred music furnish ample materials for forming an estimate of Lesueur's talent. His most marked characteristic is a grand simplicity. No musician ever contrived to extract more from common chords or to impart greater solemnity to his choruses and ensembles ; but in his boldest flights and most original effects of colour the ear is struck by antiquated passages which stamp the composer as belonging to a past school. ' His biblical characters are set before us with traits and colours so natural as to make one forget the poverty of the conception, the antique Italian phrases, the childish simplicity of the orchestration.' [3] By another critic he was said to have taken the theatre into the church and the church into the theatre. Thus, looking at the matter from a purely musical point of view, it is impossible to consider Lesueur the equal of his contemporaries Méhul and Cherubini ; though the novelties he introduced derive a special interest from the fact that he was the master of Hector Berlioz.   G. C.

BIBLIOGRAPHY

RAOUL-ROCHETTE : *Notice historique sur la vie et les ouvrages de M. Lesueur.* (Paris, 1837).
STEPHEN DE LA MADELAINE : *Biographie de Jean-François Le Sueur.* (Paris, 1841).
BERLIOZ : *Les Musiciens et la musique.*
OCTAVE FOUGUE : *Les Révolutionnaires de la musique.* (Paris, 1883.)
G. SERVIÈRES : *Épisodes d'histoire musicale* (Paris, Fischbacher, 1914) ; *Les Oratorios de J. F. Le Sueur, La Chapelle royale sous la Restauration.*   M. L. P.

LETZTEN DINGE, DIE, see LAST JUDGMENT, THE.

LEUTGEB (LEITGEB), JOSEF (*d.* Feb. 27, 1811 [4]), a horn-player to whom Mozart was much attached. They became acquainted in Salzburg, where Leutgeb was one of the band, and on Mozart's arrival in Vienna he found him

---

1 This is said to have been a favourite amusement with Gounod as a boy.   3 *Ibid.* chap. vi.
2 Berlioz, *Mémoires*, chaps. vi. and xx.
4 See Jahn's *Mozart*, 2nd ed. ii. 26.

settled there, in the Altlerchenfeld, No. 32, keeping a cheesemonger's shop and playing the horn. Mozart wrote four Concertos for him (Köchel, 412, 417, 447, 495), a Quintet (407), which he calls ' das Leitgebische,' and probably a Rondo (371). This shows that he must have been a good player. There must also have been something attractive about him, for with no one does Mozart appear to have played so many tricks. When Leutgeb called to ask how his pieces were getting on Mozart would cover the floor with loose leaves of scores and parts of symphonies and concertos, which Leutgeb must pick up and arrange in exact order, while the composer was writing at his desk as fast as his pen could travel. On one occasion he was made to crouch down behind the stove till Mozart had finished. The margins of the Concertos are covered with droll remarks— ' W. A. Mozart has taken pity on Leutgeb, ass, ox and fool, at Vienna, March 27, 1783, etc.' The horn part is full of jokes—' Go it, Signor Asino '—' take a little breath '—' wretched pig ' —' thank God here's the end '—and much more of the like. One of the pieces is written in coloured inks, black, red, green and blue, alternately. Such were Mozart's boyish romping ways ! Leutgeb throve on his cheese and his horn, and died richer than his great friend. G.

LEVA, ENRICO DE (b. Naples, Jan. 19, 1867), famous for his very numerous songs, chiefly Neapolitan ' canzonette.' In early youth he studied the pianoforte under Pannain and Rossomandi, receiving lessons in composition from Puzone and D'Arienzo, professors at the R. Conservatorio Musicale of Naples. Ricordi, after the extraordinary success of his Neapolitan canzonetta, ' Non mi guardà,' entered into a contract with the young composer to write for them five songs each year. De Leva's celebrity was still further increased in 1890 by royal favour, when Queen Margherita commissioned him to write a vocal piece for an open-air festivity at the Royal Palace of Capodimonte. This work, a serenata entitled ' A Capomonte,' was directed by the composer, whose songs enjoyed, thenceforward, the advantage of being interpreted by the foremost singers of the day. Of the hundreds of songs written by Enrico de Leva, it must suffice to mention only a few of the most successful, such as ' 'E spingole frangese,' ' Triste aprile,' ' Voi siete l' alba,' ' Ultima serenata,' ' Voce fra i campi,' ' Ammore piccerillo,' ' Ho sognato ' and ' Lacrime amare.' Some of his best have been written for popular local festivals. In these, the composer has skilfully preserved the spirit of the old Neapolitan folk-song, adapting it to the requirements of modern harmony with admirable spontaneity. Among de Leva's larger works may be mentioned his ' Sirenetta,' a setting of some verses from D'Annunzio's *Gioconda,* and an opera in four acts, ' La Camargo,'

produced in Turin in 1898 at the Teatro Regio and in Naples at San Carlo.

De Leva is widely known as a teacher of singing in its higher branches, and as a successful advocate of improved methods in the cultivation of choral singing in elementary schools throughout Italy. In 1907 he succeeded D'Arienzo as director of the Istituto dei SS. Giuseppe e Lucia in Naples (*Riemann*).

                           H. A. W.

LEVASSEUR, JEAN HENRI, called 'le jeune' (b. Paris, c. 1765 ; d. there 1823), violoncellist, pupil of Cupis and Duport. He joined the Opéra orchestra in 1789, was professor at the Paris Conservatoire, and a member of the imperial (afterwards royal) private music. He was a collaborator in the official violoncello Tutor for the Conservatoire, and composed sonatas and duets for his instrument (E. van der Straeten, *History of the Violoncello*).

LEVASSEUR, MARIE CLAUDE JOSÈPHE (called ROSALIE) (b. Valenciennes, Oct. 8, 1749 ; d. Neuwied-on-the-Rhine, May 6, 1826), was a French singer, the natural daughter of Jean-Baptiste Levasseur and Marie-Catharine Tournay. She went young to Paris, where her parents married (Feb. 2, 1761) ; she first appeared in a fragment of ' L'Europe galante ' (1766), and until about 1770 she only took secondary parts, that of l'Amour, among others. Her real gifts, her beautiful voice, her recognised talents as a singer and an actress, would not have served her without the protection of the Austrian ambassador, Count Mercy-Argenteau, who became her lover about this time. In 1775, after the comedy by Palissot, ' Les Philosophes,' of which the heroine was called Rosalie, she retook her own name of Levasseur, which made her say to Sophie Arnould : ' Cette Rosalie, au lieu de changer de nom, elle aurait bien fait de changer de visage,' making allusion to her ugliness, which, it seems, was not without charm.

At the production of ' Iphigénie en Aulide ' (Gluck, 1774), by Sophie Arnould, Rosalie Levasseur played a small part, and in that of ' Orphée,' in the same year, she took the part of l'Amour. But at the revivals of these works (1776) she took the principal rôles. In 1775 she created the part of ' Alceste,' then ' Armide,' 1777, and ' Iphigénie en Tauride ' (1779). Gluck chose her as his interpreter (he stayed with her at two revivals). She sang further : ' Ernelinde ' (Philidor, revived 1777); created ' Roland ' (Piccinni, 1777), Amadis (Christian Bach, 1779), ' Persée ' (Philidor, 1780), ' Électre ' (Lemoynhe, 1782) and ' Renaud ' (Sacchini, 1783). She had only a short career as a singer entrusted with principal parts, between the retirement of Sophie Arnould and the début of Saint-Huberti, who succeeded her in ' Roland ' and in ' Armide.' Rosalie Levasseur had obtained special terms of 9000 livres ; her patent of pension (Jan. 14, 1788), was for 2000. She left France at the Revolution, consorting with the ' Émigrés,' and returned about 1801. She married ; again left France, and died at Neuwied, aged 77.

Bibl.—Campardon, *L'Académie Royale de Musique au XVIIIe siècle*, 1884 ; Welvert, *Mercy - Argenteau a - t - il épousé R.L. ?* (*Archives historiq. de Charavay*, 1st series, 1899) ; J.-G. Prod'homme, *Rosalie Levasseur: Ambassadress of Opera* (*Musical Quarterly*, Apr. 1916) ; cf. *Revue Pleyel* (1925).   J. G. P.

LEVASSEUR, Nicholas Prosper (*b.* Bresles, Oise, Mar. 9, 1791 ; *d.* Paris, Dec. 6,[1] 1871), bass singer, entered the Paris Conservatoire in 1807, and became a member of Garat's singing class, Feb. 5, 1811. He made his débuts at the Opéra as Osman Pacha (Grétry's ' La Caravane '), Oct. 14, 1813, and as Œdipus (Sacchini's ' Œdipe à Colonos '), Oct. 15, and was engaged there. According to Fétis he was successful only as the Pacha ; the repertory was either too high for his voice, or unfavourable to the Italian method which he had acquired. He made his début at the King's Theatre, London, in Simon Mayr's ' Adelasia ed Alderano,' Jan. 10, 1815, and played there two seasons with success in ' La Clemenza di Tito,' in ' Gli Orazi,' as Pluto (Winter's ' Ratto di Proserpina ') at Mme. Vestris's début, July 20, 1815 ; in Paër's ' Griselda,' Farinelli's ' Rite d' Efeso,' Ferrari's ' Heroine di Raab ' and Portogallo's ' Regina di Lidia.' He reappeared there with some success in 1829, and again in French as Bertram on production of ' Robert,' June 11, 1832. He reappeared at the Opéra about 1816, and remained there as an under-study, but obtained much reputation in concerts with his friend Ponchard. He made his début at the Italiens as Figaro, Oct. 5, 1819, and remained there until about 1827, where he sang in new operas of Rossini, in Meyerbeer's ' Crociato,' and Vaccaj's ' Romeo.' He sang at Milan on the production of Meyerbeer's ' Margherita d'Anjou,' Nov. 14, 1820. He reappeared at the Opéra as Moses on the production of Rossini's opera there, Mar. 26, 1827, a part which he had previously played at the Italiens, Oct. 20, 1822 ; returned there permanently the next year, and remained until his retirement, Oct. 29, 1853. He created the part of Zacharie in the ' Prophète ' at the request of Meyerbeer, who admired his talent as much as his noble character. He was appointed head of a lyric class at the Conservatoire, June 1, 1841, and on his retirement in 1869 was made a Chevalier of the Legion of Honour. He became blind a short time before his death.   A. C.

LEVERIDGE, Richard (*b.* London, *c* 1670 ; *d.* Mar. 22, 1758), a singer noted for his deep and powerful bass voice. His name appears as one of the singers in Dr. Blow's Te Deum and Jubilate for St. Cecilia's day 1695, and he took part in Motteux's ' Island Princess ' in 1699, composing some of the music himself. In 1702

' Macbeth ' was given at Drury Lane, ' with music by Leveridge.' This is now in the Fitzwilliam Museum at Cambridge. Leveridge usually took the part of Hecate. He appeared in various operas, etc., of Purcell. He sang in the Anglo-Italian operas, ' Arsinoë,' ' Camilla,' ' Rosamond ' and ' Thomyris,' at Drury Lane Theatre in 1705–07. In 1708 he was engaged at the Queen's Theatre and sang in ' The Temple of Love,' etc., and in Handel's ' Faithful Shepherd ' (' Il pastor fido ') on its production in 1712. He subsequently transferred his services to Rich, and sang in the masques and pantomimes at Lincoln's Inn Fields and Covent Garden for nearly thirty years. His voice remained unimpaired so long, that in 1730, when sixty years old, he offered, for a wager of 100 guineas, to sing a bass song with any man in England. About 1726 he opened a coffeehouse in Tavistock Street, Covent Garden. He sang in the first performance of Arne's ' Rosamond,' Mar. 7, 1733, and appeared in pantomimes, etc., until 1751, taking his last benefit in that year. He wrote ' Brittaine's Happiness,' an interlude performed at both the theatres, in 1704, and ' Pyramus and Thisbe,' a comic masque, in 1716, compiled by him from ' A Midsummer Night's Dream.' In 1727 he published his songs, with the music, in two small 8vo vols. The best known are ' All in the Downs ' and ' The Roast Beef of Old England.' Some of his songs are said to be adaptations from Irish traditional tunes. Many others were published singly. In his old age he was maintained by an annual subscription among his friends, promoted by a city physician. There is a good mezzotint of him by Pether, from a painting by Frye.

w. h. h. ; addns. *D.N.B.* etc.

LEVEY, (1) Richard Michael (real name O'Shaughnessy) (*b.* Dublin, Oct. 25, 1811 ; *d.* June 28, 1899), was apprenticed to James Barton in 1821, with whom he continued till 1826, when he entered the Theatre Royal orchestra. Balfe, Wallace and Levey were intimate friends. Levey's earliest recollection was seeing Horn's opera, ' Lalla Rookh,' in Dublin, and he had pleasant memories of G. A. Lee and G. F. Stansbury as conductors of the ' old ' Royal, of which he himself became leader in 1834. His accounts of the ' stars ' between 1827 and 1847 make capital reading (a summary of them is given in his *Annals of the Theatre Royal*), and he often told the present writer stories of the two Keans, Alfred Bunn, Tyrone Power, Macready, Cooke, Miss Smithson (who married Berlioz), Taglioni, Paganini, Ole Bull, Bochsa, Lablache and Grisi.

In all, from 1836–80 (the ' Royal ' was burned on Feb. 9, 1880), Levey composed fifty overtures, and he arranged the music for forty-four pantomimes. His first pantomime was ' O'Donoghue of the Lakes,' the book of which was written by Alfred Howard ('Paddy Kelly'). In 1839 he toured with Balfe's opera company in Ireland, and in 1840 he conducted the first performances in Dublin of ' The Maid of Artois ' (with Balfe himself in the cast) and ' The Siege of Rochelle.' Levey often alluded with pardonable pride to Sir Robert Stewart and Sir Charles Villiers Stanford as his pupils. The latter's first appearance in public as a composer, at the age of 8, was as the writer of incidental music for the pantomime of ' Puss in Boots,' duly performed at the Theatre Royal during the Christmas of 1860, under Levey's baton.

In 1850 Levey was one of the founders of the Royal Irish Academy of Music—the other three being John Stanford, Joseph Robinson and Sir Francis Brady, K.C.—and the infant institution was removed to more suitable premises, at 36 Westland Row, in 1870. In 1852-55 he was leader of the ' Dublin Quartet Concert Society ' ; in 1859-62 he formed and led the ' Classical Quartet Union.' In spite of the short duration of these enterprises, he helped to start the ' Monthly Popular Concerts ' in 1868, when the quartet was led by Joachim, and the concerts lasted till 1871. He had a ' jubilee benefit,' Apr. 20, 1876, and was presented with 250 guineas. Sir Robert Stewart conducted a new comic opera, ' The Rose and the Ring,' for Levey's benefit, on Mar. 23, 1878. Levey lived to see the opening of the ' new ' Theatre Royal on Dec. 13, 1897, and repeated his favourite joke that ' he still struggled to beat Time.' Among his published pieces are two volumes of old Irish airs. He married three times.

His eldest son, (2) RICHARD MICHAEL (b.1833; d. 1904), became a famous violinist, and played at Musard's concerts in Paris in 1851-58. He then engaged in London in an entertainment called ' Paganini's Ghost,' in which he was got up to represent that player, and performed his most difficult feats of virtuosity. In 1865-85 he gave concerts, etc., under the name of ' Paganini Redivivus,' and after 1888 he appeared at the music-halls.   W. H. G. F.

Another son, (3) WILLIAM CHARLES (b. Dublin, Apr. 25, 1837 ; d. London, Aug. 18, 1894), studied at Paris under Auber, Thalberg, and Prudent, and was elected a member of the Société des Auteurs et Compositeurs. He was conductor at Drury Lane from 1868-74, and held the same post at Covent Garden, Adelphi, Princess's, Avenue and Grecian Theatres, etc. His compositions include two operettas, ' Fanchette,' Covent Garden, Jan. 2, 1864 ; ' Punchinello,' Her Majesty's, Dec. 28, 1864 ; ' The Girls of the Period,' musical burletta, libretto by Burnand, Mar. 1869 ; incidental music to ' Antony and Cleopatra,' 1873 ; music to the dramas ' King o' Scots,' ' Amy Robsart,' ' Lady of the Lake,' ' Rebecca ' and ' Esmeralda,' and to several pantomimes ; ' Robin Hood,' can-

tata for boys' voices ; Saraband for piano on a theme by Henry VIII. ; several drawing-room pieces and many songs, one of which, ' Esmeralda,' originally sung by Miss Furtado at the Adelphi in the drama of that name, and in the concert-room by Mme. Bodda-Pyne, obtained considerable popularity.   A. C.

The youngest son, (4) JOHN, author and comedian, died at Seaforth, Liverpool, Sept. 17, 1891.   W. H. G. F.

LEVI, HERMANN (b. Giessen, Nov. 7, 1839 ; d. Munich, May 13, 1900), studied with Vincenz Lachner from 1852-55, and for three years from that time at the Leipzig Conservatorium. His first engagement as a conductor was at Saarbrücken in 1859 ; in 1861 he became director of the German Opera at Rotterdam ; in 1864 Hofkapellmeister at Carlsruhe ; and finally, in 1872, was appointed to the Court Theatre of Munich, a post which he filled with great distinction until 1896. He attained to a prominent place among Wagnerian conductors, and to him fell the honour of directing the first performance of ' Parsifal ' at Bayreuth, on July 28, 1882. In 1895 he came to England, but only conducted one concert, on Apr. 25, in the Queen's Hall. His mental disease showed itself soon afterwards, and, though in 1898 he rearranged the libretto of ' Così fan tutte,' he was never able to resume active work.   M.

BIBL.— E. POSSART, Erinnerungen an H. Levi, 1900. See also Brahms's Letters (Briefwechsel, vol. 7).

LEVY, ALEXANDRE (b. S. Paulo, Brazil, Nov. 10, 1864 ; d. there, Jan. 17, 1892), Brazilian pianist and composer. His works include a ' Suite brasileira ' (orch.), and ' Variações para piano sobre um thema brasileiro ' (PF.). He aimed at the creation of national Brazilian music based on popular melodies.   J. B. T.

LEWIS, THOMAS C., originally an architect, started business as an organ-builder in London about the year 1861. He built the organs of the Anglican and Roman Catholic Cathedrals at Newcastle-on-Tyne, Ripon Cathedral, and in London those of St. Peter's, Eaton Square ; Holy Trinity, Paddington, and the People's Palace. But his largest work is the organ of St. Andrew's Hall, Glasgow.   V. de P.

LEY, HENRY GEORGE (b. Chagford, Dec. 30, 1887), one of the most brilliant of English organists, was educated at St. George's, Windsor (1896), Uppingham, and the R.C.M. (under Parratt). Ley won the organ scholarship at Keble College, Oxford, and while still an undergraduate was appointed organist of Christ Church Cathedral (1909) in succession to HARWOOD (q.v.). His remarkable skill and taste as a performer were quickly recognised, but like most English organists of the first rank he devoted himself to his cathedral work and refused the temptation to gain notoriety by touring as a recitalist. He was appointed

Choragus of the University and joined the staff of the R.C.M. as teacher of the organ. The last of these appointments he still (1926) holds, but his Oxford appointments were resigned this year in favour of that of Director of the Music at Eton College. (See *Mus. T.*, Dec. 1922, p. 837.)   c.

L'HÉRITIER, Jean, see Héritier.

L'HOMME ARMÉ (Lome Armé; Lomme Armé). (1) The name of an old French chanson, the melody of which was adopted by some of the great masters of the 15th and 16th centuries, as the canto fermo of a certain kind of Mass— called the ' Missa L'Homme armé '—which they embellished with the most learned and elaborate devices their ingenuity could suggest.

The origin of the song has given rise to much speculation. P. Martini calls it a ' canzone provenzale.' Burney (who, however, did not know the words) is inclined to believe it identical with the famous ' Cantilena Rolandi,' anciently sung by an armed champion at the head of the French army when it advanced to battle. Baini confesses his inability to decide the question ; but points out that the only relic of this poetry which remains to us—a fragment preserved in the ' Proportionale Musices ' of Tinctor—makes no mention of Roland, and is not written in the Provençal dialect.[1]

> ' Lome, lome, lome armé.
> Et Robinet tu m'as
> La mort donnée,
> Quand tu t'en vas.'

The melody—an interesting example of the use of the seventh mode—usually appears either in perfect time or the greater prolation. Slight differences are observed in the canti fermi of the various masses founded upon it ; but they so far correspond, that the reading adopted by Palestrina may be safely accepted as the normal form. We therefore subjoin its several clauses, reduced to modern notation, and transposed into the treble clef.

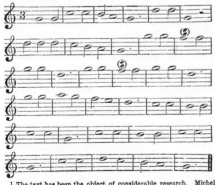

[1] The text has been the object of considerable research. Michel Brenet (*La Chanson de L'Homme armé, Journal musical*, Nov. 1898 ; also *Palestrina*) discovered one line of it only. A whole verse was more lately found by Dr. Dragan Plamenac at the Biblioteca Nazionale, Naples, in the MS., Cod. VI., E. 40, which contains 6 anonymous masses built on the theme. (See the *Proceedings* of the Congrès Historique et Archéologique Bruges, Aug. 1925.)   M. L. P.

Upon this unpretending theme, or on fragments of it, masses were written by Guglielmo du Fay, Antonio Busnoys, Regis, François Caron, Joannes Tinctor, Philippon di Bruges, La Fage (or Faugues), De Orto, Vacqueras, Monsieur mon Compère, at least three anonymous composers who flourished between the years 1484 and 1513, Antonio Brumel, Josquin des Prés, Pierre de la Rue (Petrus Platensis), Pipelare,Mathurin Forestyn,Cristofano Morales, Palestrina, and even Carissimi.

(2) The title is also attached to another melody, quite distinct from the foregoing—a French dance tune, said to date from the 15th century, and printed, with sacred words, by Jan Fruytiers, in his *Ecclesiasticus*, published, at Antwerp, 1565. The tune, as there given, is as follows :

w. s. r., abridged.

L'HOSTE, Spirito, see Hoste.

LHOTSKY, see Ševčik-Lhotsky String Quartet.

LIADOV, Anatol Constantinovich (*b.* St. Petersburg, May 11 (Apr. 29, O.S.), 1855 ; *d.* Novgorod, Aug. 28, 1914), composer. His father and grandfather had been professional musicians.

He received his first musical instruction from his father, after which he went through a course —including composition under Rimsky-Korsakov—at the Conservatoire, St. Petersburg. He left with a brilliant record in 1877, returning the following year as assistant teacher in the elementary classes for theory, and later holding a professorship at this institution, taking special classes for harmony and composition. He also held a similar post in the Imperial Court Chapel. Together with Balakirev and Liapounov, he was charged by the Imperial Geographical Society to make researches into the folk-songs of various districts. As a composer Liadov wrote his best work for the pianoforte. His compositions for this instrument are delicate and graceful in form. The influence of Chopin is clearly evident in them ; at the same time their distinctively Russian colouring, and gay—frequently humorous—character, saves them from the reproach of servile imitation. Much of Liadov's piano music has been orchestrated and used for ballets in the repertory of the Diaghilev troupe. The following is a list of Liadov's chief compositions :

PIANOFORTE MUSIC

Op. 2, 'Birioulki'; op. 3, Six Pieces; op. 4, Arabesques; op. 5, Studies; opp. 6, 7 and 8, Intermezzi; opp. 9 and 10, Preludes and Mazurkas; op. 11, *idem*; op. 12, Studies; op. 13, Four Preludes; op. 15, Two Mazurkas; opp. 17, 20, 21, 'From Days of Old,' ballades; op. 23, 'On the Sward'; op. 24, Two Pieces; op. 25, Idyll; opp. 26 and 27, Marionettes; opp. 30, 31, 32, Musical Snuff-box; op. 34, Three Canons; op. 35, Variations on a theme by Glinka; op. 36, Three Preludes; op. 37, Studies; op. 38, Mazurkas; op. 39, Four Preludes; op. 40, Studies and Preludes; op. 44, Barcarolles; op. 46, Preludes; op. 48, Studies and Canzonetta; op. 51, Variations on a Polish Song; op. 52, Morceaux de ballet.

VOCAL MUSIC, SOLO WITH PF. ACCOMPANIMENT

Op. 1, Four Songs; opp. 14, 18, 22, Albums of Six Songs for Children to national words; op. 45, Ten National Songs for Female Voice; op. 48, Russian National Songs, 120 National Songs, in three volumes.

CHORAL

Op. 28, Last scene from Schiller's 'Bride of Messina,' for mixed chorus and orchestra; op. 47, 'Slava,' for women's voices, two harps and two pianofortes—eight hands; op. 50, Songs for Female Chorus and PF. accompaniment; Female Chorus (in honour of Valdimir Stassov, 1894).

WORKS FOR ORCHESTRA

Op. 16, First Scherzo; op. 19, Scena: The Inn-Mazurka; op. 49, Polonaise in memory of Poushkin.

Besides the above, Liadov collaborated in 'The Paraphrases' (see BORODIN), the string quartet 'B-la-f' (see BELAIEV), in the 'Fanfare' for the jubilee of Rimsky-Korsakov, etc.

R. N.

LIAPOUNOV, SERGIUS MIKHAILOVICH (*b*. Yaroslav, Nov. 30, 1859; *d*. Paris, Nov. 11,[1] 1924), composer. He attended the classes of the Imperial Musical Society at Nijny Novgorod, and afterwards joined the Moscow Conservatoire, which he quitted in 1863. He was appointed by the Geographical Society to collect folk-songs in the governments of Vologda, Viatka and Kostroma (1893). From 1894–1902 Liapounov was assistant director of the court chapel. His chief compositions are :

ORCHESTRA: Ballade (1883); Solemn Overture (1896); Symphony in B minor, op. 12 (1887); Polonaise, op. 16; symphonic poem 'Hashish'; Second Symphony in B flat (completed but unpublished at date of death).
PIANOFORTE: Two Concertos (opp. 4, 38), preludes, valses, mazurkas, studies (12 Études d'exécution transcendante), etc.
VOCAL: 35 national songs with PF. accompaniment.

R. N.

LIBERATI, ANTIMO, of Foligno, a pupil of Gregorio Allegri and Orazio Benevoli, became in 1661 a singer in the Papal Chapel. He was also for some time choirmaster and organist to two other churches in Rome. He is chiefly known as the author of an Open Letter addressed to a musical friend (*Lettera scritta . . . in risposta ad una del Sig. Ovidio Persapegi . . .*), printed and published at Rome in 1685, which has been relied on by Baini and others as the main authority for various statements with regard to the early life and works of PALESTRINA (*q.v.*). Besides this Letter, Liberati wrote another work, *Epitome della musica*, which only exists in MS., also two letters in defence of a passage in one of Corelli's sonatas. Baini mentions madrigals, arias and oratorios of Liberati in Roman Archives.   J. R. M.

LIBERT, HENRI (*b*. Paris, Dec. 15, 1869), composer, organist and piano virtuoso, regular organist of the great organ of the Basilica of St. Denis, and professor of the organ at the

American Conservatoire at Fontainebleau. At the Paris Conservatoire he was a pupil of Marmontel, Diémer, César Franck, Widor and Massenet, and won the first organ prize in 1894. He has written numerous organ pieces in a large style : 'Variations symphoniques' (Lemoine), 'Chorals,' 'Préludes et fugues,' some piano pieces, songs, motets, and some remarkable didactic works, suggesting a new basis for the formation and perfecting of the technique of pianists and organists.   F. R[L].

LIBERTI, HENRI (HENDRIK) (*b*. Groeningen, *c*. 1600), organist of Antwerp Cathedral, 1630–1661. He composed a book of Cantiones sacrae (1621), a book of 'Paduanes et galiardes' (1632); also songs in collective volumes (*Q. L.*).

LIBERTI, VINCENZO, of Spoleto, composed 2 books of madrigals *a* 5 v. (Bologna, 1608 and 1609).

LIBON, FELIPE (*b*. Cadiz, Aug. 17, 1775; *d*. Paris, Feb. 5, 1838), Spanish violinist. He was a pupil of Viotti in London, studied composition with Cimador, and afterwards held court appointments at Lisbon (1796) and Paris (1800). His compositions include 6 violin concertos, string trios, duets, etc.   J. B. T.

LIBRARIES AND COLLECTIONS OF MUSIC. I. EUROPE.—This article is arranged alphabetically ; first by countries and then by towns within those countries. The territorial adjustments brought about by the Treaty of Versailles have naturally necessitated a regrouping of many of the headings. Strassburg, for instance, is now treated as a French town, and the independent town of Danzig has been entered separately as a 'country.'[2] An alphabetical arrangement of the individual libraries was not found feasible, as many of them have no distinctive or generally recognised title. Private libraries are entered under the place where they are situated, and after the list of public libraries in that place. It should be pointed out that the main purpose of this article is to give particulars of libraries where the student is likely to find material that is not generally accessible, and for this reason no mention has been made of many excellent municipal libraries which make a special feature of their music collections, since such libraries are forced as a rule to confine their attention to the standard literature of the art. The absence of any detailed reference to them must therefore not be attributed to a failure to recognise the importance of the part they are playing in the musical life of the community. In preparing the present notes as to the musical contents of the libraries of Europe, considerable use has been made of Dr. Emil Vogel's paper, 'Musikbibliotheken nach ihrem wesentlichsten Bestande,' which appeared in the *Jahrbuch der Musikbibliothek Peters* for

[2] Variable details such as the names of librarians were revised in 1926.

1904. A. Aber's *Handbuch der Musikliteratur* (1922) and the tenth edition of Dr. Riemann's *Musik-Lexikon* have also been consulted, and much kind help has been given by various owners of private collections and by many friends and librarians. Information has also been derived from Dr. W. H. Frere's *Bibliotheca musico-liturgica* (1901); W. H. J. Neale's *Descriptive Catalogue of MSS. and Liturgical Books at the Music Loan Exhibition* (London, 1885); Riaño's *Critical and Bibliographical Notes on early Spanish Music* (1887); the Catalogues and Guides to the Music Loan Exhibition (London, 1885); Victorian Era Exhibition (London, 1897); International Loan Exhibition (Crystal Palace, 1900); Company of Musicians' Loan Exhibition (London, 1904); and especially from the Catalogues of the Vienna Music Exhibition of 1892. To these works, as well as to E. Vogel's *Bibliothek der gedruckten weltlichen Vocalmusik Italiens aus den Jahren 1500–1700* (Berlin, 1892), to Eitner's *Quellen-Lexikon*, and the pages of the *Monatshefte für Musikgeschichte*, the reader may be referred to supply the inevitable deficiencies and shortcomings of the following lists. Information concerning regulations for admission to the various libraries mentioned, and their hours of opening and other administrative details, will be found in such periodical publications as *Minerva* and the *Index generalis*.

Austria

EISENSTADT. The Library of Prince Esterhazy's castle contains much MS. music of the 18th and 19th centuries, amongst which are autograph symphonies and quartets by Haydn; a series of masses (from *c.* 1770 to *c.* 1830), including works by Haydn, Vogler, etc., and many German and Italian operas.

GÖTTWEIG. The Library of the Benedictine Abbey contains two MS. collections of songs by Mastersingers of the 16th century, and a MS. collection of organ music by Claudio Merulo. Librarian : P. Hartmann Srohsacker.

GRAZ. The University Library possesses some printed theoretical works. Librarian : Dr. J. Fellin.

INNSBRUCK. The University Library contains some rare early printed books on music, some treatises in a MS. of 1460, and a MS. with two-part compositions of the 14th century. Librarian : H. Pogatscher.

KLAGENFURT. The Library of the Historical Society (' Geschichtsverein ') possesses *inter alia* two valuable MS. lute-books of the 16th century. Director : Prof. Dr. H. P. Meier.

KLOSTER NEUBURG. The Monastery of Austin Canons contains liturgical MSS. of the 13th and 15th centuries, and some printed music of the 16th century. See *Catalogus codicum manu scriptorum qui in Bibliotheca Canonicorum Regularium S. Augustini Claustroneoburgi*

asservantur (Vienna, 1922, etc.). Librarian : Prof. Dr. V. O. Ludwig.

KREMSMÜNSTER. The Benedictine Monastery contains a legendarium of the 11th century, with music in neumes; printed theoretical works of the 16th-19th centuries; about 1000 masses, 300 symphonies, and several operas (mostly of the 18th century). See Huemer : *Die Pflege der Musik im Stifte Kremsmünster* (Wels, 1877). Librarian : P. B. Lehner.

MELK. Besides a few printed musical works, the Library of the Benedictine Monastery contains liturgical MSS. of the 13th and 14th centuries, and a collection of MS. masses of the 16th century by Orlando di Lasso, A. Scandelli, etc. Librarian : Dr. W. Schier.

REIN. The Library of the Cistercian Monastery contains some printed music of the early 17th century. Librarian : O. Patteder.

SALZBURG. *a.* The Benedictine Abbey of St. Peter contains church music of the late 18th and early 19th centuries, including compositions by Michael Haydn. Librarian : P. B. Huemer, O.S.B.

b. The Chapter Library, attached to the Cathedral, possesses some MS. music of the early 16th century by Victoria, Palestrina, etc., and some compositions by Michael Haydn. Librarian : J. Strasser, O.S.B.

c. Mozart Museum (Getreidegasse No. 9). Catalogue by J. Horner (1st edition, 1882), continued by J. E. Engl (2nd and 3rd editions). Fourth edition, published by the Mozarteum, 1906. Later editions have appeared in summary form only. The most important Mozart MSS. have, however, now been transferred to the Mozarteum.

d. Mozarteum. The Mozarteum, opened in 1914, possesses a valuable collection of Mozart MSS., books about Mozart and printed editions of his works.

e. Museum Carolino-Augusteum. The Library contains the score of O. Benevoli's mass in fifty-three parts (1628), published in Jahrg. x. of the *D.T.Ö.* Director : J. Leisching.

ST. FLORIAN, near ENNS. The Monastery of Austin Canons possesses a Library of over 100,000 volumes, including 802 incunables and 882 MSS. On the latter see Albin Czerny, *Die Handschriften der Stiftsbibliothek St. Florian.* (Linz, 1871.) Librarian : Prof. F. Asenstorfer.

ST. PAUL, LAVANT THAL, CARINTHIA. The Library of the Benedictine Monastery contains a valuable MS. collection of French Troubadour songs of the 13th century, besides treatises by Hucbald and J. de Muris. Librarian : Prof. P. T. Raichl.

VIENNA. *a.* The Nationalbibliothek (formerly Hofbibliothek) received in 1826 and 1829 all the music not connected with church music in the archives of the court chapel. In course of time it has acquired much scarce music (printed by Petrucci, etc.), and is also rich in autographs of different musicians, including a number of letters and MSS. by Beethoven ; of special interest to English musicians is a volume of Bull's organ music in tablature. The manuscripts have been catalogued by Dr. Joseph Mantuani. His work appeared in two volumes (in 1897–99) as parts ix. and x. of the *Tabulae codicum manuscriptorum . . . in bibliotheca Palatina Vindobonensi asservatorum*. The Ambros and Kiesewetter collections, which form part of the library, are not included in this catalogue, but are to form a supplementary volume. A list of recent acquisitions to the Library, by R. Haas, was printed in the *Z.M.W.* for Sept. 1924. Director : Prof. Dr. J. Bick.

b. Gesellschaft der Musikfreunde (see VIENNA).

c. The University Library possesses printed theoretical works of the 16th and 17th centuries, and lute-books by Judenkunig, Ochsenkhun, Caroso and Deuss. Director : G. A. Crüwell.

d. The Library of the Landesarchiv contains some musical works printed at Vienna about 1600. Librarian : Dr. K. Lechner.

e. The Ministry for Education. Here are deposited the six precious volumes of MSS. formerly in the Chapter Library at Trent, from which volumes of selections have been printed by Dr. Guido Adler and Dr. Oscar Koller in the *D.T.Ö.* Director : Dr. V. Kreuzinger.

f. St. Peter's Church. See C. Roulland : *Katalog des Musik-Archives der St. Peterskirche in Wien* (Augsburg and Vienna, 1908).

g. The Benedictine Abbey of our Lady of the Scots (Schottenkloster) possesses some valuable early liturgical MSS. and a small collection of MS. and printed works of the 16th century. See A. Hübl : *Catalogus codicum manuscriptorum qui in bibliotheca Monasterii B.M.V. ad Scotos Vindobonae servantur* (1899), and the same author's *Die Inkunabeln der Bibliothek des Stiftes Schotten in Wien* (1901).

h. Monastery of the Minorites. The Library contains some MS. and printed organ music of the 17th and 18th centuries, including three works by Frescobaldi and G. B. Fasolo's *Annali* (Venice, 1645), and also some vocal music of the 17th century.

i. The Haydn - House (Mariahilferstrasse, 102) contains a small collection of printed and MS. documents relating to Joseph and Michael Haydn.

j. The Arnold Schönberg-Bibliothek, founded in 1924 in celebration of the composer's fiftieth birthday, confines its collections to the music of the last thirty years. Over 1000 volumes have already been acquired to form the nucleus of the library.

Belgium

The musical libraries of the Netherlands have been very fully described by J. G. Prod'homme

in an article in Jahrg. 1913/14 of the *Sammelbände der Internationalen Musik-Gesellschaft*, which has been freely used in the compilation of the following notices.

BRUSSELS. *a.* Royal Library. In 1872 the Belgian Government was induced by F. A. Gevaert, Director of the Brussels Conservatoire, to purchase the library of Fétis for 152,000 francs. This collection, which comprises 7525 works, together with the collection of C. J. E. van Hulthem, forms the bulk of the musical library. The contents are very valuable, comprising about 4500 theoretical works, about 500 liturgies, over 100 Italian operas, about 170 French operas, and many rarities. The Van Hulthem collection is catalogued in vol. ii. of C. A. Voisin's *Bibliotheca Hulthemiana* (Ghent, 1836–37) ; the Fétis Library in the *Catalogue de la bibliothèque de F. J. Fétis* (by L. J. Aloin) (Brussels, 1870). See also J. van den Ghen : *Catalogue des manuscrits de la Bibliothèque Royale de Belgique. Tome I. Écriture sainte et liturgie* (Brussels, 1901). Conservateur-en-chef : L. Paris.

b. Conservatoire Royal de Musique. This valuable library, which now numbers some 31,000 items, was in 1904 greatly enriched by the acquisition of the collection of Professor Wagener, of Marburg, which is especially rich in works printed in England in the 18th century. Four volumes of an excellent catalogue by Wotquenne, covering about half the total collection of the library, have been issued (vol. 1, 1898 ; vol. 2, 1902 ; vol. 3, 1908 ; vol. 4, 1912), with an elaborate supplement : *Libretti d'opéras et d'oratorios italiens du XVIIᵉ siècle* (1901). A catalogue of the remaining portion of the library exists in manuscript. Librarian : C. van den Borren.

GHENT. The Town and University Library contains liturgical MSS. of the 10th - 12th centuries, a copy of Monteverdi's 'Lamento d' Arianna ' (Venice, 1623), early theoretical works, and printed music from the presses of Phalèse and Gardano. The library of the Grand-Théâtre, including operas and ballets in score and a large number of librettos, is also housed here. See C. A. Voisin : *Bibliotheca Gandavensis* (Ghent, 1839) ; J. de Saint Genois: *Catalogue méthodique . . . des manuscrits de la bibliothèque de la ville et de l'université de Gand* (Ghent, 1849–52), the *Monatshefte für Musikgeschichte* for 1873, p. 62, and P. Bergmans : *Une collection de livrets d'opéras italiens* (1669–1710) *à la bibliothèque de l'université de Gand* (*Sammelbände*, I.M.G., 1910/11). Head Librarian : P. Bergmans.

LIÈGE. *a.* Conservatoire Royal de Musique. The library contains two extensive special collections, a Grétry library, forming part of the ' Musée Grétry,' and the library formed by the singer Léonard Terry, which includes some 2000 musical works. See *Catalogue de la bibliothèque du Conservatoire Royal de Musique de Liège* (1862).

b. Société Libre d'Émulation. See *Catalogue de la bibliothèque musicale de la Société Libre d'Émulation de Liège* (1861).

OUDENAERDE. The church of St. Walpurga possesses a collection of church music of the 18th century. See *Liste générale de la musique appartenant à l'église parochiale de Ste. Walpurga à Audenarde (s.a.).*

TOURNAI. The Chapter Library contains a three-part mass of the 13th century, which was published by Coussemaker in the *Bulletin de la Société Historique de Tournai*, and reprinted separately in 1861.

Czecho-Slovakia

BARTFELD. The Church of St. Aegidius contains a small collection of printed vocal music of the late 16th and early 17th centuries.

OLMÜTZ. The Studienbibliothek (Studijni knihovna v Olomouci) contains a copy of Schmid's *Tabulaturbuch* (1607), some printed music of the early 17th century, and MS. graduals of the 13th and 14th centuries. Keeper : B. Vybiral.

PRAGUE. *a.* The Chapter Library possesses copies of masses by Luyton (Prague, 1609, etc.), and a collection of sacred music of the late 16th and early 17th centuries. See the catalogues by the librarian, Dr. A. Podlaha (Prague, 1904, 10).

b. The Library of the Count von Nostitz-Rieneck contains copies of the *Frottole intabulate da sonare per organi, libro primo* (Rome, 1517), the *Canzoni frottole e capitoli* (Rome, 1531), and other printed works of the 16th and 17th centuries.

c. The Library of the Premonstratensian Monastery of Strakow contains a small collection of music, chiefly works of the late 16th and early 17th centuries. Librarian : C. Straka.

d. The Church of St. Thomas contains a copy of Uberti's Contrasto Musico (Rome, 1630).

e. The University Library contains MS. treatises of the 11th and 15th centuries ; old Bohemian songs of the 14th and 15th centuries ; two Easter mystery plays of the 15th and 16th centuries ; printed theoretical works of the 16th and 17th centuries, and lute-books by Caroso, Negri, and Schmid (1607). Librarian : J. Borecký.

RAUDNITZ. The Library of the princely family of Lobkowicz contains some rare MS. and printed music chiefly of the 17th and 18th centuries. Of special interest are a number of 17th-century MSS. of lute, guitar and mandoline music in tablature. See P. Nettl : *Musicalia der Fürstlich Lobkowitzschen Bibliothek in Raudnitz (Mitt. des Vereines für Geschichte der Deutschen in Böhmen*, Jahrg. 58, Heft 1, 1919).

SAAZ. The Capuchin Monastery possesses some sacred and secular music by Orlando de Lasso, Scandelli, Joachim à Burck, etc.

TEPL. The Premonstratensian Abbey contains a number of liturgical MSS., the earliest of which is a Penitential of the 8th or 9th century, with music in neumes. A catalogue of the manuscripts (by M. Nentwich) and a short description of some of the more important (by W. Vacek) are to be found in the volume *Zum 700jährigen Todestage des s. Hroznata* (Marienbad, 1917). Librarians : M. Nentwich. J. W. Vacek.

Danzig

a. The Town Library contains a valuable collection, principally of works of the second half of the 16th century. See O. Günther : *Katalog der Handschriften der Danziger Stadtbibliothek. Teil 4. Die musikalischen Handschriften* (Danzig, 1911). There is also a MS. catalogue of the collection, by S. W. Dehn, in the Royal Library at Berlin. Librarian : Dr. H. Bauer.

b. The Allerheiligen-Bibliothek, in the Marienkirche, contains a small collection of sacred music, mostly printed works of the 17th century.

Denmark

COPENHAGEN. *a.* The Royal Library contains a collection of MS. organ music (in tablature) by German composers of the 17th century, Italian printed music of the late 16th and early 17th centuries, and some rare printed works from Copenhagen and Antwerp presses. Principal Librarian : C. S. Petersen.

b. The Musikhistorisk Museum possesses a number of theoretical works relating to musical instruments and a few liturgical works, both printed and MS., exhibited to illustrate the development of notation. See A. Hammerich : *Musikhistorisk Museum. Beskrivende illustreret Katalog* (Copenhagen, 1909 ; German trans., *ibid.*, 1911).

Finland

HELSINGFORS. The University Library possesses a collection of fragmentary MSS., rescued from old bindings, containing a large number of fragments of missals, of which a catalogue (by T. Haapanen) was issued in 1922 (*Universitetsbiblioteks Skrifter*, vol. 4). See also *Die Neumenfragmente der Universität Helsingfors* (1924), by the same author. Director : Dr. G. C. A. Schauman.

France

AIX (PROVENCE). The Bibliothèque Méjanes contains a 14th-century MS. of French Troubadour songs, and an early 17th-century collection of nearly 100 chansons with lute accompaniment. See catalogue by the Abbé J. H. Albanes, in *Catalogue général des manuscrits des bibliothèques publiques de France*, tome xvi.

(1894), and the supplements in tome xl. (1902) and tome xlv. (1915). Conservateur : E. Aude.

AMIENS. The Bibliothèque Communale contains a few early printed treatises, a number of French psalters of the 17th century, operas and song-books of the 18th century, and seventeen volumes of sacred music and five volumes of operas by Lesueur. For the printed music see *Catalogue méthodique de la bibliothèque communale de la ville d'Amiens : Sciences et Arts* (1859). Among the MSS. there are many interesting liturgies, etc., and a collection of sequences (with music), which belonged in 1572 to a monk named Guglielmus Lovel (described in the *Ecclesiologist* for October 1859). For the MSS. generally, see the catalogue by E. Coyecque in *Catalogue général des manuscrits des bibliothèques publiques de France*, tome xix. (1893), and the supplement in tome xl. (1902). Librarian : H. Michel.

AVIGNON. The Bibliothèque de la Ville contains many fine early MS. missals and liturgical works ; motets by Mondonville, Blanchard, etc., and some miscellaneous 18th - century music. See catalogue by J. Quicherat, in tomes xxvii.-xxix. of *Cat. gén. des MSS. des bibl. pub. de France* (1894–1901), and the supplements in tome xl. (1902) and tome xliv. (1911). Librarian : J. Girard.

BESANÇON. The Bibliothèque de la Ville possesses a Boethius de Musica of the 9th century on vellum. See tomes xxxii., xxxiii. and xlv. of *Cat. gén. des MSS. des bibl. publ. de France* (1897–1915). Librarian : G. Gazier.

BORDEAUX. Bibliothèque de la Ville. See J. Delas : *Catalogue des livres composant la bibliothèque de la ville de Bourdeaux, musique* (Bordeaux, 1856), and tomes xxiii. and xl. of *Cat. gén. des MSS. des bibl. publ. de France* (1894, 1902). Librarian : J. de Maupassant.

CAEN. Bibliothèque Municipale. See Carlez : *Liste des œuvres musicales et des œuvres relatives à la musique* (Caen, s.a.), and the catalogues in tomes xiv. (1890) and xli. (1903) of the *Cat. gén. des MSS. des bibl. publ. de France*. Librarian : M. Guillaume.

CAMBRAI. The Public Library contains a precious collection of MS. church music by early Flemish and Burgundian musicians, besides songs for two, three, and four parts, dating from the 14th century. The collection was described in Coussemaker's *Notice sur les collections musicales de la bibliothèque de Cambrai et des autres villes du Département du Nord* (1843). See also A. J. Le Glav : *Catalogue . . . des manuscrits de la bibliothèque de Cambrai* (Cambrai, 1831). Much of the library's stock was destroyed or damaged in the war (1914–18). Librarian : G. Leboyer.

CARPENTRAS. The Bibliothèque municipale possesses a MS. of Kepler's *Principium musice* ; some 18th- and 19th-century music ; autographs of Schumann, Brahms, Gounod, etc.

The library contains the collections of Peiresc, J. B. Laurens and others. See *Cat. gén. des MSS. des bibl. publ. de France*, tomes xxxiv.-xxxvi. (1899–1903). Librarian : R. Caillet.

DOUAI. The Bibliothèque Municipale possesses a 12th-century MS. with two-part music, a hymnarium of the 12th century, and some printed theoretical works of the 16th century. See Coussemaker's work (quoted under Cambrai) and the catalogue of the MSS. by the Abbé C. Debraisnes in *Cat. gén. des MSS. des bibl. publ. de France*, tome vi. (1878). Librarian : L. Noël.

DUNQUERQUE. The Bibliothèque de la Ville possesses some music printed by Phalèse (16th century). See Coussemaker's work (quoted under Cambrai). Librarian : L. Baron.

FOIX. In the Bibliothèque de la Ville there are nine antiphoners and other liturgical works (formerly belonging to the Cathedral of Mirepoix), written between 1497 and 1535. See *Cat. gén. des MSS. des bibl. publ. de France*, tome xxxi. (1898). Librarian : J. Eychenne.

GRENOBLE. The Bibliothèque de la Ville is rich in valuable liturgies. See the catalogue by P. Fournier, E. Maignien and A. Prudhomme, in tome vii. of *Cat. gén. des MSS. des bibl. publ. de France* (1889) and the *Catalogue des incunables*, by E. Maignien (1899). Librarians : L. Royer, N. de Bonfils.

LE HAVRE. In 1894 the Bibliothèque Musicale Publique contained about 4000 works, mostly dating from the latter part of the 18th century.

LILLE. Bibliothèque municipale. See *Catalogue des ouvrages sur la musique et des compositions musicales de la bibliothèque de la ville de Lille* (Lille, 1879). The collection is rich in operas. See also Coussemaker's work (quoted under Cambrai). The contents of this library were seriously damaged by fire in Apr. 1916, and although the greater number of the books were saved, many were irreparably injured by water. The collection is at present housed in the University. Librarian : P. Vanrycke.

MARSEILLES. a. The Bibliothèque de la Ville possesses some valuable liturgical MSS. of the 12th century. See the catalogue by the Abbé J. H. Albanès, in *Cat. gén. des MSS. des bibl. publ. de France*, tome xv. (1892), and the supplement in tome xlii. (1904). Librarian : J. Billioud.

b. Sainte Madeleine. The library contains a collection of liturgical MSS. from the 12th century downwards.

MONTPELLIER. The Bibliothèque de la Faculté de Médecine possesses a precious antiphoner (noted in neumes and letters) of the 9th century, published in the *Paléographie musicale*, and a 14th-century collection of French chansons for two and more voices. See Coussemaker : *L'Art harmonique*, etc. (Paris, 1865), and *Cat. gén. des MSS. des bibl. publ. de France*, tome i. (1849), and supplement, tome xlii. (1904).

ORLEANS. The Bibliothèque de la Ville contains a valuable MS. collection of mystery plays of the 12th century. See *Cat. gén. des MSS. des bibl. publ. de France*, tome xii. (1889), and supplement, tome xlii. (1904). Librarian : A. Bouvier.

PARIS. *a.* Bibliothèque de l'Arsénal. The library of the Arsenal contains very interesting MSS., such as the ' Mazarinades '—songs sung under the Fronde—with their airs ; collections of airs by Michael Lambert, and other little-known compositions of the 17th and 18th centuries, etc. See H. Martin : *Catalogue des manuscrits de la Bibliothèque de l'Arsénal* (9 vols., Paris, 1885–94, issued as tomes iv.-xii. of *Cat. gén. des MSS. des bibl. publ. de France*, Paris). There is a good index of the music in tome vii. p. 457. See also the supplementary lists in tome xliii. (1904) and tome xlv. (1915) of the same catalogue. Administrateur : M. Battifol.

b. The Bibliothèque Historique de la Ville de Paris (Musée Carnavalet) is valuable for its MS. and printed works on the theatres of Paris and the instrument-makers of the city. Keeper : G. Cain.

c. Bibliothèque Musicale du Théâtre de l'Opéra. See T. de Lajarte : *Catalogue historique*, etc. (2 vols., Paris, 1878). Administrateur : Ch. Bouvet.

d. Bibliothèque Nationale. The Bibliothèque Nationale is very rich in French music, both printed and engraved. It is also more complete than any other in Paris in respect of musical literature, periodicals, almanacs, dictionaries and similar works of reference. It is rich in valuable MSS. of Dom Caffiaux, Parfait, Baini, Adrien de La Fage and other distinguished writers, but the great value of the collection consists in its early MSS., in which it occupies the first position for the study of the origins of music in Europe. The library contains MSS. with musical notation from the 9th century downwards, and is especially rich in Troubadour songs of the 13th century, and French and Italian compositions of the 14th century, while later times are well represented in operas, oratorios, etc. See J. Écorcheville : *Catalogue du fonds de musique ancienne de la Bibliothèque Nationale* (8 vols., Paris, 1910–14). A new catalogue is in preparation. The MSS. are also catalogued in the various printed catalogues of J. Taschereau, H. Omont, L. V. Delisle, etc., and the books on music are included in the catalogue of the printed books now in course of publication. Administrateur : P. Roland-Marcel.

e. Bibliothèque Ste-Geneviève. This library contains a large number of rare works on music, a fine collection of chansons and dramatic works, with the music, and many curious MSS., including a valuable MS. of the 11th century. See E. Poirée and G. Lamouroux : *Les Éléments d'une grande bibliothèque-Catalogue abrégé de la Bibliothèque Ste-Geneviève* (Paris, 1897 – 1910). Administrateur : M. Boinet.

f. Conservatoire des Arts et Métiers. The library contains few musical works, but is rich in materials for the history of the music trade, such as patents, trade registers, etc. Librarian : E. M. Lévy.

g. Conservatoire National de Musique et de Déclamation. Some account of the library has already been given (see CONSERVATOIRE). To the rare works there mentioned may be added the autograph score of Mozart's ' Don Juan ' (presented by Mme. Viardot Garcia), a copy of the *Harmonice musices odhecaton* (printed by Petrucci in 1504), and the *Liber primus missarum* of Carpentras (Avignon, 1532). Of especial interest to English musicians are a large folio MS. containing compositions by Coprario, Lawes, Locke, Gibbons, Jenkins, Ferabosco and Ward ; and an account-book of the Academy of Vocal Music (from Jan. 7, 1725 to 1726), formerly belonging to Owen Flintoft. The library secured many fine and rare works at the dispersal of the Borghese collection in 1892. See J. B. Weckerlin : *Bibliothèque du Conservatoire National de Musique. Catalogue . . . de la Réserve* (Paris, 1885). Librarian : H. Expert.

ROUEN. The Bibliothèque Municipale contains a superb illuminated missal, liturgical MSS. of the 9th-11th centuries, and collections of operas and church music. See F. I. Licquet : *Catalogue de la Bibliothèque de la Ville de Rouen* (1830), and the catalogue by H. Omont, in tomes i. and ii. of *Cat. gén. des MSS. des bibl. publ. de France. Départements* (1886–88), and the supplement in tome xliii. (1904). Director : H. Labrosse.

STRASSBURG. *a.* Bibliothèque Universitaire et Régionale. This library possesses a small collection of early printed musical works, the rarest of which are the *Harmonie* of Tritonius (Augsburg, 1507) and the *Novus partus sive concertationes musicae* of Besardus (Augsburg, 1617). Director : Dr. E. Wickersheimer.

b. Library of the Priester-Seminar. A list of the music, by J. Victori, was published in No. 10 of the *Kirchliche Rundschau* for 1901, and reprinted as a ' Beilage ' to the *Monatshefte f. M.* for 1902.

c. The Cathedral Library contains over 100 MSS. of church compositions by F. X. Richter, who was maître de chapelle at the cathedral from 1769–80. See the catalogue by F. X. Mathias in the *Riemann Festschrift* (Leipzig, 1909).

TOURS. The Bibliothèque de la Ville possesses a Sacramentarium of the 9th-10th centuries with neumes ; mystery plays of the

12th century; liturgies of the 15th-18th centuries; motets of the 17th century; organ music (including autographs by N. Le Bègue, 1676); a MS. of J. de Muris (15th century), and much else of interest. See A. J. Dorange: *Catalogue . . . des manuscrits de la bibliothèque de Tours* (1875); *Cat. gén. des MSS. des bibl. publ. de France. Départements*, tome xxxvii. (1900); and *Sammelbände* of the I.M.G. for 1905 (p. 356, etc.). Librarian : F. Galabert.

TROYES. The Bibliothèque de la Ville possesses a copy of Praetorius's *Syntagma* ; lutebooks ; publications of Phalèse (Louvain, 1573, etc.) ; organ and viol music of the 18th century, etc. See E. Socard : *Catalogue de la bibliothèque de la ville de Troyes* (1875, etc.), tome xiv. pp. 281-300. Librarian : L. Morel-Payen.

VALENCIENNES. The Bibliothèque Municipale possesses some early MS. treatises, including 9th-century MSS. of Hucbald, Isidore of Seville, etc. See *Cat. gén. des MSS. des bibl. publ. de France*, tome xxv. (1894), and also Coussemaker's work (quoted under Cambrai).

VERSAILLES. Bibliothèque de la Ville. This library is rich in sacred music, dramatic works and books on music, and also contains several interesting MSS. of the 17th and 18th centuries, including the Philidor collection. See *Manuscrits musicaux de la bibliothèque de Versailles* (1884) and *Cat. gén. des MSS. des bibl. publ. de France*, tome ix. (1888), and the supplement in tome xliii. (1904). Librarian : C. Hirschauer.

Germany

ANSBACH. The Regierungsbibliothek contains a small collection of vocal printed music of the 16th century and MS. scores of Cavalli's ' Pompeo ' and Ziani's ' Annibale in Capua.' Librarian : Georg Freiherr von Kress.

ARNSTADT. The Church Library possesses six folio volumes of vocal music of the 16th century.

AUGSBURG. The Stadtbibliothek, the Archives and the Historical Society possess valuable collections of early printed and MS. music, chiefly collected from the suppressed monasteries of the city. See H. M. Schletterer : *Katalog der in der Kreis- und Stadtbibliothek, dem städtischen Archiv und der Bibliothek des historischen Vereins zu Augsburg befindlichen Musikwerke.* (Leipzig, 1878. *Monatshefte für Musikgeschichte*, Bde. 11 and 12. Beilagen.) Librarian : Dr. R. Schmidbauer.

AUGUSTUSBURG, SAXONY. The Parish Church contains some music of the 16th and 17th centuries.

AURICH, EAST FRIESLAND. The Staats-Archiv contains a 17th-century MS. collection of songs. (See *Monatshefte* for 1874 and 1894.) Archivist : Dr. A. Eggers.

BAMBERG. The Public Library contains some liturgical MSS. with neumes of the 11th-13th centuries, and printed music of the late 17th century. See F. Leitschuh and H. Fischer : *Katalog der Handschriften der Kgl. Bibliothek zu Bamberg.* 3 vols. (Bamberg, Leipzig, 1887 – 1912.) Librarian : Dr. M. Müller.

BERLIN. *a.* The Preussische Staatsbibliothek, founded in 1661, possesses one of the finest musical collections in the world, thanks mainly to the liberality of a long series of donors and to the efforts of its librarians, in particular of S. W. Dehn and his successor F. Espagne. The library acquired its first important accession in 1824 when J. F. Naue's extensive collection of liturgical music was added. Its real nucleus, however, was the magnificent Pölchau collection, rich in Bach autographs and copies, and in practical and theoretical works of the 16th and 17th centuries, which was purchased in 1841. Since then the most important acquisitions have been the following : in 1843 Schindler's Beethoven MSS., including a MS. of the Ninth Symphony, an autograph transcript of ' Leonore,' the quartet op. 59, No. 2, and sketches, letters and 136 ' conversation-books ' ; in 1851 Count von Voss-Buch's collection of music from 1680 to 1750, including several Bach MSS. ; in 1854 the Bach autographs from the Singakademie ; in 1855 Karl von Winterfeld's collection of 103 volumes of old church music in score ; in 1859 J. Fischof's collection which included many Beethoven MSS., and Prof. L. Landsberg's collection of early printed music and treatises and MSS. by later composers, especially Schubert ; in 1869 Otto Jahn's Mozart library ; in 1873 the whole of the Mozart MSS. still in the possession of André's heirs, some 531 compositions in all ; in 1874 the score of Mozart's ' Ascanio in Alba,' the first of a series of gifts from Professor R. Wagener which subsequently included autographs of the ' Wohltemperirtes Clavier ' and the French Suites of Bach ; in 1877 the Mendelssohn MSS. ; in 1878 the Cherubini MSS. ; in 1881 Jähn's Weber library; in 1890 the Schumann MSS. ; in 1901 the library of the music-publisher Artaria, particularly rich in Beethoven MSS. ; in 1904 F. Hauser's Bach library, with the autographs of nineteen cantatas and Nos. 2-6 of the English Suites ; in 1908 Ernst von Mendelssohn-Bartholdy's collection which included autograph scores by Beethoven (4th, 5th and 7th symphonies, the Septet and the B♭ Trio), by Mozart (' Die Entführung ') and by Haydn (several symphonies). In 1915 Meyerbeer's whole musical library, including autographs of most of his works, was deposited on loan. No catalogue of the music has yet been published. For further particulars see the articles by W. Altmann in the *Zeitschrift für Musikwissenschaft* for 1919–20, 1920–21, 1923 and 1926. Director : Dr. H. Krüss ; Director of the Music Section : Dr. W. Altmann.

b. Staatliche Hochschule für Musik. This institution possesses the musical libraries of Professor Spitta, Bach's biographer, and also contains some rare printed music of the 17th and 18th centuries, and a number of printed scores of French 18th-century operas.

c. The Library of the Joachimsthal Gymnasium received in 1787 the music collected by Princess Amalia of Prussia, and in 1858 190 vols. of musical works from the library of Dr. Spiker (see Meierotti's *Nachricht*, etc., Berlin, 1788). Amongst the music are autographs and many ancient copies of the works of J. S. Bach. See R. Eitner: *Katalog der Musikalien-Sammlung des Joachimsthalschen Gymnasium* (*Monatshefte*, Beilage, 1884), and also *Thematischer Katalog der von Thulemeier'schen Musikalien-Sammlung in der Bibliothek des Joachimsthal'schen Gymnasium* (by R. Jacobs) (*Monatshefte*, Beilage, 1898–99).

d. The Library of the Grey Friars (zum Grauen Kloster) contains an important collection of works of the 16th and 17th centuries, in parts, carefully arranged so as to present a view of ancient vocal music. See H. Bellermann: *Verzeichniss des grösstentheils von S. Streit dem grauen Kloster geschenkten Musikalien* (in the Programme of the Gymnasium for 1856).

e. The Kgl. Hausbibliothek. See G. Thouret: *Katalog der Musiksammlung auf der Königlichen Hausbibliothek im Schlosse zu Berlin* (Berlin, 1895).

f. The Akademie für Deutsche Schul- und Kirchenmusik, formerly the Kgl. Institut für Kirchenmusik. The library contains a collection of 18th-century MSS.

BONN. *a*. The University Library contains about 600 vols. of music, chiefly of the 19th century. Amongst the few early works is a copy of the 1517 edition of the *Micrologus* of Ornithoparcus. Director: E. von Rath.

b. The Beethoven-Haus contains a collection of Beethoven MSS. and of old and modern editions of his works. Since 1920 it has published some of the MSS. in critical editions.

BRANDENBURG. The Church of St. Catherine contains an important collection of partbooks and of vocal music of the 16th, 17th and 18th centuries. See J. F. Täglichsbeck: *Die musikalischen Schätze der St. Katharinen-Kirche zu Brandenburg a/H* (in the Programme of the Brandenburg Gymnasium, Easter, 1857).

BREMEN. About seventy-four musical works belonging to the Stadtbibliothek are in the care of the Bremen Tonkünstler-Verein.

BRESLAU. *a-c*. See E. Bohn: *Bibliographie der Musik-Druckwerke bis 1700, welche in der* (*a*) *Stadtbibliothek*, (*b*) *der Bibliothek des academischen Instituts für Kirchenmusik, und* (*c*) *der Kgl. u. Universitäts-Bibliothek zu Breslau aufbewahrt sind* (Berlin, 1883). Also E. Bohn: *Die musikalischen Handschriften des 16. und 17.*

Jahrhunderts in der Stadtbibliothek zu Breslau (Breslau, 1890), and E. Kirsch: *Die Bibliothek des Musikalischen Instituts bei der Universität Breslau* (Berlin, 1922). The Brieg collection (see *infra*) is now in the University Library of Breslau. Directors: (*a*) M. Hippe, (*b*) O. Günther, (*c*) R. Oehler.

d. The Cathedral Library contains about 1000 musical works, of which sixty are in manuscript. The collection chiefly consists of church music of the 18th and 19th centuries. Director: A. Nowack.

e. The Domstifts-Bibliothek contains a small collection of MSS.

f. The Church of St. Elisabeth contains about 4200 musical works, chiefly church music of the 18th and 19th centuries.

BRIEG. The musical collection formerly in the Kgl. Gymnasium is now preserved in the University Library at Breslau. See F. Kuhn: *Beschreibendes Verzeichniss der alten Musikalien . . . des Königlichen Gymnasiums*, etc. (Leipzig, 1897. *Monatshefte*, Beilage.)

CASSEL. *a*. The Landesbibliothek contains about 340 musical works, printed and MS. Amongst the former are copies of Morley and Weelkes's madrigals. Most of the works date between 1560 and 1620. See C. Israel: *Übersichtlicher Katalog der Musikalien der ständischen Landesbibliothek zu Cassel* (Cassel, 1881). Director: W. Hopf.

b. The Hoftheater possesses the autograph scores of Spohr's 'Jessonda' and of Marschner's 'Templer und Jüdin' and 'Hans Heiling.'

CELLE. The Kirchen- und Ministerialbibliothek contains some printed music of the 16th century (1539–64), mostly by Italian composers.

CHARLOTTENBURG. Kaiserin-Augusta-Gymnasium. See F. Schultz: *Der ältere Notenschatz des Kaiserin-Augusta-Gymnasiums* (Charlottenburg, 1900).

COLOGNE. *a*. The Universitäts- und Stadtbibliothek possesses a MS. treatise (*Musica enchiriadis*) of the 12th century, and a few printed partbooks from Venetian and Antwerp presses of the 16th century. Director: Prof. K. Löffler.

b. Conservatorium der Musik. See F. Bölsche: *Bücher-Katalog des Conservatoriums der Musik in Cöln* (Cologne, 1909).

c. The Jesuitenbibliothek has a small collection of printed 16th-century music, including copies of the *Lilium musice plane* of 1506, and Wollick's *Enchiridion* (Paris, 1512).

d. Musikhistorisches Museum von Wilhelm Heyer. This museum, opened in 1913, in addition to a fine collection of musical instruments,[1] possesses about 20,000 musical autographs, many rare books on music, and a large number of portraits. Three volumes of an excellent

---

[1] Transferred to Leipzig in 1926. See COLLECTIONS OF MUSICAL INSTRUMENTS. The MSS. have since been sold by auction.

illustrated catalogue by the Curator, Dr. G. Kinsky, have been published (1910–16).

CRAYN, near LIEGNITZ. The library contains some printed music of the 17th century.

DARMSTADT. The Landesbibliothek, formerly Grossherzog. Hofbibliothek. See P. A. F. Walther: *Die Musikalien der Grossherzoglichen Hofbibliothek in Darmstadt* (Darmstadt, 1874), and supplementary notices, by F. W. E. Roth, in the *Monatshefte* for 1888. Director: Dr. L. Voltz.

DESSAU. The Hoftheater possesses a large musical library which includes church music and instrumental compositions as well as dramatic works. See the chapters on the library in A. Seidl's *Ascania* (Regensburg, 1913).

DONAUESCHINGEN. The Library of Prince Fürstenberg contains thirteen MS. antiphoners (14th-18th century) and a fragment of a MS. treatise on music of the 15th century. See C. A. Barack: *Die Handschriften der fürstlich-Fürstenbergischen Hofbibliothek zu Donaueschingen* (Tübingen, 1865). Director: E. Johne.

DRESDEN. *a.* Sächsische Landesbibliothek, formerly Kgl. Öffentliche Bibliothek. See Eitner and Kade: *Katalog der Musik-Sammlung der Kgl. öffentlichen Bibliothek zu Dresden* (*im Japanischen Palais*). (Leipzig, 1890. *Monatshefte*, Beilage, 1890.) See also *M.f.M.* for 1904, No. 1. The musical MSS. are also catalogued in Bd. 4 of the *Katalog der Handschriften der Sächsischen Landesbibliothek* (Dresden, 1923). They include parts of Bach's B minor Mass and the score of Weber's 'Euryanthe.' At the beginning of the present century the library absorbed a number of smaller musical collections, including that of the Landesschule at Grimma (see below). The Royal Private Music Collection, which is rich in 18th-century MS. and printed works, and includes an extensive collection of libretti, is also now housed in the Landesbibliothek. Director: Dr. M. Bollert.

b. The State Archives contain some MSS. and printed music of the early 17th century. See *Monatshefte* for 1888. Director: Dr. W. Lippert.

c. The Archives of the court church contain about 2000 pieces of church music, mostly of the late 18th and 19th centuries, including some autographs.

d. The Tonkünstlerverein Library (founded in 1854) possesses over 2500 works, chiefly instrumental music of the 18th and 19th centuries, also symphonies by J. J. Fux.

e. The Dreikönigskirche possesses a few rare printed works, including the descant and tenor parts of Walther's Wittenberg hymn-book (1524).

EICHSTATT, BAVARIA. The Staatsbibliothek contains liturgies, works printed by Attaignant (1529–31), and music of the 17th and 18th centuries. See *Monatshefte* for 1870.

ELBING. *a.* The Marienkirche Library contains seventy-six works of the 16th century and eighty-five of the 17th; thirteen Polish cantionales (1571–1792), and many MS. church compositions of the 18th and 19th centuries. See T. Carstenn: *Katalog der St. Marienbibliothek zu Elbing* (Kirchenmusikalischer Jahrbuch for 1896), and G. Döring: *Die musikalischen Erscheinungen in Elbing* (Elbing, 1868).

b. The Town Library possesses a few rare books, including a copy of the *Syntagma* of Praetorius. See L. Neubaur: *Katalog der Stadtbibliothek zu Elbing* (Elbing, 1893), and the list appended to T. Carstenn's catalogue of the Marienkirche Library. Librarian: T. Lockemann.

ERFURT. *a.* The Town Library has many mediæval treatises on music, liturgical MSS. and printed books, chiefly derived from suppressed convents. See W. Schum: *Beschreibendes Verzeichniss der Amplonianischen Handschriften-Sammlung* (Berlin, 1887), R. Hernried: *Erfurter Notenschätze* (*Neue Musikzeitung*, Feb. 1925), and the general catalogue of the library, publication of which was begun in 1903. Librarian: Dr. W. Suchier.

b. The Library of the Michaeliskirche. See Noack, E.: *Die Bibliothek der Michaeliskirche zu Erfurt* (*Archiv für M.-W.*, April 1925).

ERLANGEN. The Institute for Church Music, which forms part of the University, has a library of its own. Director: Prof. Schmidt.

FRANKFORT-ON-M. *a.* The Town Library contains a large collection of printed music (of the period 1537–1697) and of musical MSS. (of the period 1623–1790), chiefly from the archives of the Churches of St. Paul, St. Catherine and St. Peter, part of which was formerly included in the library of the Town Gymnasium. See C. Israel: *Die musikalischen Schätze der Gymnasial-Bibliothek und der Peterskirche in Frankfurt a. M.* (in the Programme of the Town Gymnasium for Easter, 1872), the articles by C. Valentin: *Musikbibliographisches aus Frankfurt a. M.* in the *Monatshefte f. M.* for 1901 and 1902, and C. Süss: *Die Manuskripte protestantischer Kirchenmusik zu Frankfurt a. M.* in the *Liliencron-Festschrift* (Leipzig, 1910). Acting Director: Prof. Dr. H. Traut.

b. Paul Hirsch possesses an extensive musical library which is especially rich in early theoretical works. In recent years Herr Hirsch has begun the publication of some of his rarer treasures in facsimile editions. He has also issued a catalogue of his Mozart collection (Frankfort, 1906).

c. Nicholas Manskopf owns a particularly rich musical collection, comprising some 10,000 objects. The autographs include works of F. Tunder, D. Buxtehude, G. P. Telemann, Weber.

Spohr, Cornelius, Schumann and Wagner; there is also a valuable collection of documents relating to Handel and his family, besides relics of Beethoven and an extensive collection of portraits.

FREIBERG, SAXONY. Libraries of the Gymnasium Albertinum and the Altertumsverein. See O. Kade : *Die älteren Musikalien der Stadt Freiberg* (*M.f.M.*, Beilage, 1888).

GELENAU, SAXONY. The Pfarrkirche contains some vocal music by German composers of the second half of the 17th century.

GÖTTINGEN. The University Library contains 145 musical works, mostly of the 15th and 16th centuries, many of which are of great rarity. The Library is now entitled to a copy of every work published in the Province of Hanover. See A. Quantz : *Die Musikwerke der Kgl. Universitäts-Bibliothek in Göttingen* (*M.f.M.*, Beilage, 1883). Director : Dr. R. Fick.

GOTHA. The Landesbibliothek contains a small but interesting collection, comprising several rare early theoretical works of the 16th century, and about seventy hymnals of the 16th and 17th centuries. Principal Librarian : Prof. Dr. A. Krüger.

GRIMMA, SAXONY. The Landesschule formerly possessed about 131 works of the 16th and 17th centuries which have now been incorporated in the music collections of the Dresden Public Library. See N. M. Petersen : *Verzeichniss der in der Bibliothek der Königl. Landesschule zu Grimma vorhandenen Musikalien aus dem 16. und 17. Jahrhundert.* (Grimma, 1862, reprinted from the Programme of the Landesschule for 1861).

GÜSTROW, MECKLENBURG-SCHWERIN. The Domschule Library contains a small but valuable collection of rare early printed musical works, chiefly of the 16th century. They are described in the school Programme for 1865.

HALLE. *a.* The Marienkirche has a small collection of vocal music of the 17th century, and a few earlier works. See *M.f.M.* for 1894. Librarian : Dr. B. Weissenborn.

b. The Waisenhausbibliothek contains an important collection of hymnals, theoretical works of the 17th and 18th centuries, and practical music of the 18th century.

HAMBURG. The Staatsbibliothek contains theoretical works of the 16th and 17th centuries ; Italian music of the same period ; a valuable collection of libretti of operas performed at Hamburg, and eighty volumes of Handel's works—copies, partly in the handwriting of J. C. Smith, and formerly in the possession of Kerslake, of Bristol, and of Victor Schoelcher. There is an excellent MS. catalogue by A. von Dommer. Director : Dr. G. Wahl.

HANOVER. *a.* The Public Library contains some valuable early theoretical works, a few madrigals of the 16th and 17th centuries, and seven vols. of programmes of Hanover theatres from 1785–96. Director : Dr. K. Kunze.

b. The Kestner Museum contains a collection of folk-songs, and also a collection of libretti (from 1686). Director : Dr. C. Küthmann.

HEILBRONN. Gymnasialbibliothek. See E. Mayser : 'Alter Musikschatz,' No. 2 of *Mitteilungen aus der Bibliothek des Heilbronner Gymnasiums.* (Heilbronn, 1893.)

HELMSTEDT. *a.* The Gymnasialbibliothek contains some theoretical and practical works, mostly by German musicians of the 16th and 17th centuries.

b. The church of St. Stephen possesses some German 17th-century music, chiefly by M. Praetorius, J. H. Schein and A. Hammerschmidt.

JENA. The University Library contains many musical treasures, the chief of which is the 'Jenaer Handschrift' of 14th- and 15th-century songs (published in facsimile with an introduction by C. C. Müller : Jena, 1896 ; and in a critical edition by G. Holz, C. Saran and E. Bernouilli : Leipzig, 1901). The Library also contains liturgical MSS., the printed collections of Lieder of Ott (1544) and Forster (1539–56), etc. See *Nachricht von alten Musikalien auf der Jenaischen Universitäts-Bibliothek* (in *Allg. Mus. Zeitung* for 1828). Chief Librarian : B. Willkomm.

KAMENZ, SAXONY. Rathsbibliothek. A Catalogue was printed in the *Serapeum* (Leipzig) for 1853.

KARLSRUHE. The Badische Landesbibliothek contains some mediæval treatises and a good collection of 16th- and 17th-century hymnals. See H. Ehrensberger : *Bibliotheca liturgica manuscripta. Nach Handschriften der grossherzoglich. Badischen Hof- und Landesbibliothek,* etc. (Karlsruhe, 1889). Director : Dr. T. Längin.

KÖNIGSBERG, PRUSSIA. The Staats- und Universitätsbibliothek contains the collection made by Director F. A. Gotthold (died 1858), which is of importance for hymnology, and is rich in vocal music of the 17th century and works by minor composers of the 18th century. The library also possesses a number of MS. and printed volumes from the library of the Archduke Albert (1490–1568), and has in recent years been enriched by a number of accessions from various sources. It now numbers more than 50,000 volumes. See Jos. Müller : *Die musikalischen Schätze der Königlichen und Universitäts-Bibliothek zu Königsberg i. Pr.,* etc. (Bonn, 1870), and an article, with the same title, by J. Müller-Blattau in the *Zeit. für Musikwissenschaft,* Jan./Feb. 1924. Director : Dr. C. Wenael.

LEIPZIG. *a.* The Town Library possesses a valuable 10th-century MS. treatise by Regius of Prüm, and also a collection of theoretical works and instrumental music of the 17th century, collected by C. F. BECKER (*q.v.*), the well-known writer. Principal Librarian : Dr. E. Kroker.

b. The University Library possesses a small collection of theoretical works and a number of libretti (from 1662 to about 1836), mostly of performances at Dresden and Hanover. Director : Prof. O. Glauning.

c. The Musikbibliothek Peters. This valuable institution, founded by the firm of C. F. PETERS (*q.v.*), was opened on Jan. 2, 1894, in which year a catalogue (by the first librarian, Dr. Emil Vogel) was published. Accessions have been noted in the interesting *Jahrbücher* issued from the Library. The collection is particularly complete in modern practical and theoretical works, musical journals, etc., and is kept up to date by the liberality of the founders. There are also many musical autographs, a number of works of antiquarian interest, and some valuable portraits and prints. A catalogue of the important collection of Bach manuscripts, part of the collection of autographs bequeathed by Ernst Rudorff in 1916, was printed in the *Jahrbuch* for 1919. Librarian : Dr. Rudolf Schwartz.

LIEGNITZ. The Bibliotheca Rudolfina of the Ritter-Akademie contains an extremely valuable collection of 16th- and 17th-century music. See Dr. E. Pfudel : *Mittheilungen über die Bibliotheca Rudolfina der Kgl. Ritter-Akademie zu Liegnitz* (printed in the three Easter Programmes of the Ritter-Akademie for 1876–78) ; and the same author's *Die Musik-Handschriften der Kgl. Ritter-Akademie zu Liegnitz* (*M.f.M.*, Beilage, 1886).

LÜBECK. The Stadtbibliothek contains valuable early German and Italian printed music. See C. Stiehl : *Katalog der Musiksammlung auf der Stadtbibliothek zu Lübeck* (Lüb., 1893), and also *M.f.M.* for 1884. Librarian : Dr. W. Pieth.

LÜNEBURG. The Town Library contains a miscellaneous collection of music, chiefly dating from the 17th to the 19th centuries. There is some important organ music, and also a copy of Book I. of the *Parangon des chansons*, printed by J. Moderne. See *M.f.M.*, 1873. Librarian : Dr. W. Reinecke.

MAIHINGEN, near NÖRDLINGEN. The Library of Prince Oettingen-Wallerstein contains much MS. music : 390 symphonies, 214 cantatas and oratorios, 114 masses, and 111 works for stringed instruments—chiefly by composers of the late 18th century. There are also 120 works on theory. Among the rarer printed books are copies of Genet's *Liber primus missarum* (Avignon, 1532) ; Morales's *Missarum libri duo* (J. Moderne, Lyons, 1546) and *Magnificat* (same printer and place, 1550) ; and the works in tablature of Paix

(1583) and Schmid (1607). Librarian : Dr. F. Zoepfl.

MAINZ. The Town Library contains some theoretical works of the 16th-18th centuries, and some partbooks of the 15th and 16th centuries. See *M.f.M.* for 1889. Principal Librarian : Dr. A. Ruppel.

MANNHEIM. The Court Theatre Archives. See F. Walter : *Archiv und Bibliothek des Grosherzöglichen Hof- und Nationaltheaters in Mannheim, 1779–1839* (2 vols., Leipzig, 1899).

MEININGEN. Herzogliche Öffentliche Bibliothek. This library contains an important collection of operas, oratorios and cantatas by 18th-century composers in score, formerly in the library of the Hofkapelle. See C. Mühlfeld : *Die Meininger Musikbibliothek* (*Neue Zeit. f. Mus.*, 1912, No. 16). Librarian : T. Linschmann.

MÜNSTER, WESTPHALIA. The Library of the Abbate Santini (of Rome) was bought about 1856 by the See of Münster for a Collegium Gregorianum, which has never been founded. It consists chiefly of MSS. and printed music of the 16th to the 18th centuries, and is at present lodged in very inadequate quarters in the Episcopal Museum of Christian Antiquities. See J. Killing : *Kirchenmusikalische Schätze der Bibliothek des Abbate F. Santini* (Düsseldorf, 1910), Stassoff : *L'Abbé Santini et sa collection musicale* (Florence, 1854), and *Catalogo della musica existente presso F. Santini in Roma* (Rome, 1820).

MUNICH. *a.* Staatsbibliothek. The musical collections of this library rank with those of the National Library at Vienna and the State Library at Berlin as the most important on the Continent. Here is preserved Duke Albert's famous copy of the Penitential Psalms of LASSUS (*q.v.*). The printed books are rich in works from the early presses of Italy and Germany. See J. J. Maier : *Die musikalischen Handschriften der Kgl. Hof- und Staatsbibliothek in München, I. Theil. Die Handschriften bis zum Ende des 17ten Jahrhunderts* (Munich, 1879). Director : Dr. H. Schnorr von Carolsfeld.

b. The Frauen-Kirche contains some printed 17th-century music and a collection of MS. choir-books, dating from *c.* 1600, containing masses, etc., by Orlando and Rudolfo di Lasso, J. Reiner, G. Croce, J. C. Kerl, Praetorius, etc.

c. The University Library has some printed music of the early 16th century and a MS. collection of compositions by Obrecht, Josquin, Senfl, etc., in the autograph of Glareanus, written at Basel in 1527. Director : Dr. A. Hilsenbeck.

NEISSE, PRUSSIAN SILESIA. The Kreuzheiliges Stift has a few printed works of the 16th century and also some MS. liturgical works.

NUREMBERG. *a.* The Germanic Museum contains some important liturgies, including missals and antiphoners of the 12th and 13th centuries, and rare hymnals of the 16th century. There are also examples of the chief Nuremberg printing-presses, and valuable lute-books in tablature. The autograph score of Wagner's 'Meistersinger' is now in the Museum's possession. Director: Dr. E. H. Zimmermann.

b. The Stadtbibliothek possesses some musical works printed at Nuremberg in the 17th century, theoretical works, and a collection of theatre programmes between 1779 and 1788. Librarian : Dr. F. Bock.

PIRNA. The collection of musical works formerly in the Stadtkirche is now at Dresden. It consists of eight 16th-century MSS. and sixty-three printed musical works of the 16th and 17th centuries. See O. Kade : *Die Musikalien der Stadtkirche in Pirna* (in the *Serapeum*, Leipzig, 1857).

QUEDLINBURG. See T. Eckardius : *Codices manuscripti Quedlinburgenses* (Quedlinburg, 1723).

REGENSBURG. *a.* The Kreisbibliothek. See C. T. Gmeiner : *Kurze Beschreibung der Handschriften in der Stadtbibliothek Regensburg* (Ingoldstadt, 1791). Librarian : J. Schmatz.

b. The Episcopal Library comprises the very extensive and valuable collections of Proske (about 20,000 vols.), Mettenleiter and F. X. Witt. The musical MSS. (from the 13th to the 17th century) number about 1000, and there are about 2000 printed books from the 15th to the 17th century, with many of later date. See K. Weinmann : *Die Proskesche Musikbibliothek in Regensburg* (*Kirchenmus. Jahrbuch*, 1911).

c. Library of Prince Thurn and Taxis. This library contains about 53,000 volumes and 300 MSS. The printed music dates chiefly from the late 16th and early 17th centuries ; among the MSS. are four volumes in organ tablature, and compositions by G. Aichinger (about 1610). Librarian : Dr. R. Freytag.

ROSTOCK. The University Library contains a small collection of musical works printed at Lyons and Venice in the 16th century ; also operas, oratorios, etc., of the 17th and 18th centuries. Principal Librarian : Dr. W. Golther.

SCHWARZENBERG, SAXONY. The Church Library contains some German vocal music of the 17th century.

SCHWERIN. The Regierungsbibliothek. See O. Kade : *Die Musikalien-Sammlung des Grossherzoglich Mecklenburg - Schweriner Fürstenhauses aus den letzten zwei Jahrhunderten* (2 vols., Schwerin, 1893) ; and (same author) *Der musikalische Nachlass weiland Ihrer Königlichen Hoheit der verwittweten Frau Erbgrossherzogin Augustavon Mecklenburg-Schwerin*, etc. (Schwerin, 1899). Director : Dr. P. Crain.

SONDERSHAUSEN. The Schlosskirche Library contains much MS. music, chiefly sacred cantatas of the first half of the 18th century.

SORAU, BRANDENBURG. Hauptkirche Library. See G. Tischer and K. Burchard: *Musikalienkatalog der Hauptkirche zu Sorau N. L.* (*M.f.M.*, 1902, Beilage).

STUTTGART. Landesbibliothek. See A. Halm : *Katalog über die Musik - Codices des 16. und 17. Jahrhunderts auf der K. Landes-Bibliothek in Stuttgart* (*M.f.M.*, Beilage, 1902). There is also an important collection of over 500 MS. scores of operas and other dramatic works of the 18th century. Director : Dr. E. Rath.

THORN, PRUSSIA. Gymnasialbibliothek. See the Schulprogramm for 1871.

TORGAU, SAXONY. The Library of the Cantorei (founded in 1864) contains church music of the 18th and 19th centuries.

ULM. The Stadtbibliothek has about 142 volumes of printed music, chiefly vocal works dating from the end of the 16th and early 17th century. Librarian : Prof. Dr. Greiner.

WEIMAR. *a.* The Landesbibliothek contains the music collected by the Duchess Amalia during her visit with Goethe to Italy, including interesting operas of the Neapolitan school. Also the score of Haydn's opera ' La vera costanza,' the autograph of the finale of Act II. of Gluck's ' Orfeo,' and a valuable 14th-century MS. of Meistersingers' compositions. Directer : Prof. Dr. W. Deetjen.

b. The Liszt Museum contains a collection of Liszt's autographs.

WERNIGERODE. In 1923 the Library of Count Stolberg contained 128,757 volumes. The hymnological collection comprises over 5000 volumes. The chief treasure of the Library is the Locheimer Liederbuch (15th-cent. MS.), on which see Chrysander's *Jahrbücher* (Bd. II., Leipzig, 1867) and the *M.f.M.* for 1872. See also E. W. Förstemann : *Die Gräflich Stolbergsche Bibliothek zu Wernigerode* (Nordhausen, 1866). Librarian : Dr. W. Herse.

WIESBADEN. The Nassauische Landesbibliothek. See *M.f.M.* for 1888. Director : Prof. E. Liesegang.

WOLFENBÜTTEL. The Landesbibliothek (formerly Herzogliche Bibliothek). See E. Vogel : *Die Handschriften nebst den älteren Druckwerken der Musik-Abtheilung der Herzoglichen Bibliothek zu Wolfenbüttel* (Abth. 8 of *Die Handschriften der Herzoglichen Bibliothek zu Wolfenbüttel*, 1890). Librarian : Dr. H. Schneider.

WÜRZBURG. *a.* The University Library contains liturgical MSS. of the 12th-14th centuries, besides theoretical works (from 1497), and some early operas of the 17th century. Principal Librarian : Dr. F. Segner.

b. The Music School contains MSS. and printed music of the 18th and 19th centuries.

c. The Episcopal Seminary possesses a small collection of printed sacred music of the late 17th and early 18th centuries.

ZITTAU. The Stadtbibliothek has seven missals, dating from 1435, decorated with illuminations of great beauty ; ten volumes of MS. sacred music of the 17th century ; some editions of Moravian hymnals, and many printed works of A. Hammerschmidt. Librarian : Dr. T. Gärtner.

ZWICKAU. a. The Ratsschulbibliothek, now incorporated in the Stadtbibliothek, is rich in early printed music, particularly in psalters and collections of hymns. There are also a few MSS. In 1904 the Library contained 20,000 vols. and 260 MSS. See R. Vollhardt : Bibliographie der Musik-Werke in der Ratsschul-bibliothek. (Leipzig, 1896. M.f.M. Beilage, 1893–96.) Librarian : Dr. Kleinebreil.

b. The Robert Schumann Museum, opened in 1910, contains a collection of autograph and printed music by Schumann and a library of Schumann literature. Director : M. Kreisig.

Great Britain and Ireland

ABERDEEN. The University Library contains about 2500 musical works, mostly acquired by the copyright privileges possessed by the University in the early part of the 19th century. In 1910 the Library acquired the extensive collection of psalm-books brought together by William Lawrence Taylor. A catalogue of this collection was issued in 1921. Librarian : W. D. Simpson.

ASHSTEAD, SURREY. J. F. R. Stainer is the present possessor of the valuable musical library formed by his father, the late Prof. Sir John Stainer. The collection is especially rich in printed song and books. See the Catalogue of English Song-Books forming a portion of the Library of Sir John Stainer, with appendices of Foreign Song-Books, Collections of Carols, Books on Bells, etc. (printed for private circulation, London, 1891).

BOURNEMOUTH. The Public Library contains the collection of orchestral scores and other music formed by Mr. John B. M. Camm, and presented by him to the Borough in 1912. The collection is housed in a large room specially designed as a music library. Consisting originally of about 4000 volumes, it now numbers nearly 5000, and is continually being added to. Librarian : C. Riddle.

BRISTOL. The Baptist College contains the Lea Wilson collection of Bibles, included in which are 258 editions of the Psalms, many of the earlier of which are of great rarity. See Lea Wilson : Bibles, Testaments, Psalms, and other Books of the Holy Scripture in English, in the collection of Lea Wilson, Esq. (London, privately printed, 1845).

CAMBRIDGE. a. Caius College. The Library contains a large MS. volume, dating from the early 16th century, containing masses and motets for five and six voices, by Fayrfax, Ludford, Cornysh, Turgis, Prentes and Pasche. The

volume seems to have belonged to Edward Higgyns, Canon of Lincoln and Prebendary of Carleton cum Thirleby, Sept. 3 ; 27 Hen. VIII. (See Valor ecclesiasticus, temp. Hen. VIII., 1821, p. 19.) Librarian : G. A. S. Schneider.

b. Corpus Christi College. The library contains the unique MS. of Walter de Odington's De speculatione musices and a 10th-century MS. containing two treatises by Hucbald and the Enchiridion of Odo of Cluny. See the catalogue of the MSS. in the library by Dr. M. R. James (1912). Librarian : Sir G. G. G. Butler.

c. Fitzwilliam Museum. See J. A. Fuller Maitland and A. H. Mann : Catalogue of the Music in the Fitzwilliam Museum, Cambridge (London, 1893). Not included in this catalogue is the Musical Library of the late Richard Pendlebury, fellow of St. John's College, comprising about 2000 modern works, presented to the Museum between 1880 and 1902, and a selection from the Musical Library of the late G. F. Cobb, Bursar of Trinity College, presented by his widow. In recent years the Museum has been enriched by a number of important accessions. Thanks to the generosity of various donors, it now possesses autograph MSS. of Bach (the cantata ' Mache dich, mein Geist, bereit '), Beethoven (musical sketches and a letter), Brahms (the songs op. 63, Nos. 7 and 9, and the vocal duet op. 75, No. 1), Chopin (a letter), Haydn (a song), Mozart (the PF. duet, K. 497), Purcell (a volume consisting chiefly of transcripts of works by other composers), Scarlatti (a nameless opera, dated 1710), Schubert (four songs), Schumann (a letter), Wagner and Weber (letters), S. Wesley (' O sing unto the Lord '), and the 67 volumes of J. C. Smith's MS. copies of Handel's works. There have also been large additions of modern music and books on music. Director : S. C. Cockerell.

d. Magdalene College. The Pepysian Library contains a few early works on music by Butler, Holder, Morelli, Victorini, Wallis and Alstedius; valuable MS. collections of vocal music of the time of Edward IV., Henry VII. and Henry VIII. (comprising compositions by J. Gwinneth, R. Davis, W. Corbronde, G. Banaster, J. Tuder, Sir William Hawte, Nesbet, Fowler and Garnesey) ; English, French, Scotch and Latin psalters ; compositions by Blome, de Bacilly, Kircher, Mersenne, Morley, Salmon, Dering, Merbecke, Coprario, Lawes, King, Purcell and Finger ; ballads, songs and other compositions adjusted to the compass of Mr. Pepys's voice, and solos, duets and trios for stringed and wind instruments. A MS. of special importance is the Remède d'Amour of G. de Marchant, containing musical settings of several lyrics. A catalogue by W. Barclay Squire is in the press. Librarian : O. F. Morshead.

e. St. Peter's College (Peterhouse). In the College Library is a valuable collection of MS.

anthems, services, masses, motets, etc., both Latin and English, in separate partbooks. The anthems and services are by composers of the early 17th century, and were probably collected when Dr. Cosin was Master of Peterhouse (1634–1660). They are in various handwritings, and contain some autograph compositions by Cambridge organists of the period. The masses and motets (in four partbooks) date from the early part of the 16th century, and contain many rare and valuable compositions of the time of Henry VII. and Henry VIII., including four masses by Fayrfax, a Stabat Mater by Hunt, three masses by Ludford and eleven compositions by Taverner. The collection contains works by upwards of eighty different musicians, as well as many anonymous compositions. There is a catalogue by the Rev. Dr. Jebb, which was printed in vol. xx. of the *Ecclesiologist* (1859). See also an account of the collection (by R. C. Hope) in the *Antiquarian Magazine and Bibliographer* (vol. iii., 1883). Librarian: E. C. Francis.

f. Trinity College. The Library contains a small collection of musical works and treatises, including copies of Wilson's *Psalterium Carolinum* (1657) and *Cheerful Ayres* (1660) ; Locke's *Present Practice of Music Vindicated* (1673) ; Carr's *Vinculum societatis* (1687) ; four volumes of Zarlino's works (1589), and early editions of the works of Byrd, Watson, Morley, Playford, Simpson, Bannister, Wilson, Gamble, Lawes, Mace, etc. Among the MSS., which have been catalogued by Dr. M. R. James in his *Catalogue of the Western MSS. in the Library of Trinity College, Cambridge* (1901–04), the most valuable is a 15th-century roll of English carols, which has been published by J. A. Fuller Maitland and W. S. Rockstro (London, 1891). Other MSS. of interest are the volume of ' Ayres to be sunge to ye Lute and Base vyole,' by G. Handford (1609), the medius of some anthems by G. Loosemore (1664), and two 15th-century Greek MSS. which contain some music. Of modern MSS. the Library possesses the autograph scores of Hubert Parry's ' Blest Pair of Sirens ' and his ' Ode at a Solemn Musick,' and the autograph of C. V. Stanford's treatise *Musical Composition.* Librarian: H. M. Adams.

g. The University Library, besides a considerable collection of printed music, which is continually being augmented in virtue of the privileges enjoyed by the Library under the Copyright Act, contains a few musical MSS., consisting principally of collections of well-known airs, dance-tunes and lessons for the lute, bass viol and recorder, arranged and composed by Bachelor, Dowland, Holborne, Byrd, Tallis, R. and J. Johnson, Alison, Cutting, Pilkington, Reade, Nicolson, Robinson and other composers of the early part of the 17th century. They are written in tablature, and date principally from 1600–40. Besides these there is

the tenor part of a 16th-century collection of masses and motets by Fayrfax, Prowett, Davy, Austen, Taverner, Lovell, Pasche and Ashwell. The bass part of this collection is in the library of St. John's College, Cambridge. Amongst the masses in this volume may be mentioned a ' Missa regalis ' and a mass, ' God save King Harry.' There is also preserved here a 15th-century mass in two parts, unfortunately wanting one page, and the superius and tenor parts of an anonymous mass of the time of Queen Mary. A collection of lute music (in tablature) by R. Taylor, R. Johnson, J. Daniel and T. Greaves is also of interest. MS. installation odes by Boyce and Walmisley are also in the library, and a collection of exercises for the University musical degrees is being gradually accumulated. Librarian: A. F. Scholfield.

CANTERBURY. The Cathedral Library contains a number of volumes of music and works on music, including an incomplete copy of the contra-tenor cantoris of Barnard's Church Music (1641). Librarian: Canon A. J. Mason.

CHATSWORTH, DERBYSHIRE. The Library of the Duke of Devonshire, though not very rich in music, contains a few works of interest. The chief rarities are a volume of altus parts of works printed by Petrucci, comprising the masses of P. de la Rue (Venice, 1503), A. Agricola (Venice, 1504), A. de Fevin (Fossombrone, 1515), J. Mouton's Book I. (Fossombrone, 1515), and Josquin's Book I. (Fossombrone, 1516); there are also a few theoretical works; copies of ' The Maske of Flowers ' (1613) and Coprario's ' Funeral Teares ' (1606) ; Campian and Coprario's ' Songs of Mourning ' (1613), and a number of single partbooks of English and Italian madrigals, among which are a bassus part of E. Bonnizoni's *Primo libro delle canzoni a quattro voci* (Venice, 1569), and a canto part of the *Lieti amanti* of 1586. Librarian: F. W. Thompson.

CARDIFF. F. J. Arnold possesses an extensive collection of chamber music of the 17th and 18th centuries; with a number of contemporary treatises on the art of accompanying from a THOROUGH-BASS (*q.v.*).

CHESTER. The Cathedral Library contains a good collection of modern church music.

DUBLIN. *a.* Royal Irish Academy of Music. This Society possesses a good library of scores and orchestral parts of the works of the great composers. It also includes the Library of the long defunct ' Antient Concerts.' Secretary : C. E. Grahame-Harvey.

b. The Library of Christ Church Cathedral contains valuable MS. copies of anthems and services by Purcell, Child, Battishill and others, which are said to differ greatly from those printed in England during the last seventy years.

c. Trinity College. Besides a miscellaneous collection of modern music received under the

Copyright Act, the Library contains a few liturgical MSS. and some 16th-18th century music, among which is Thomas Dallis's Lute Book (1583). See T. K. Abbott, *Catalogue of the MSS. in the Library of Trinity College, Dublin* (Dublin, 1900). Librarian : Dr. J. G. Smyly.

d. Archbishop Marsh's Library. This library contains a good deal of printed and MS. music, chiefly of the late 16th and 17th centuries. The partbooks include a complete set of Adson's ' Courtly Masquing Ayres ' (1621) ; the C.T.B. and quintus of *Prima stella de madrigali* . . . *di O. Lasso, di G. Nascho, di Zanetto, di Palestrina*, etc. (Venice, 1570) ; nine partbooks of ' Gratulationes Marianae ' (Antwerp, Phalèse, 1636) ; twelve partbooks of the Masses of G. Messaus (Antwerp, 1633) ; eight partbooks of the ' Primitiae Marianae ' of J. Willems (Antwerp, 1639) ; five partbooks of Viadana's First Book of Masses (Antwerp, 1625) ; and many other partbooks, chiefly by English and Italian composers. The MSS. consist largely of instrumental fantasias, lute pieces, etc., by B. Rogers, R. Dering, S. Ives, T. Giles, G. Jeffreys, J. Coprario, T. Lupo, W. Cranford, Tomkins, R. Mico, Jenkins, Brewer, J. Ward, Lawes, A. Ferabosco, O. and R. Gibbons, C. Coleman, R. Nicolson and other English and Italian composers of the 17th century. Librarian : Rev. N. J. D. White.

e. The National Library. The most important musical works in this library are contained in the collection (upwards of 23,500 volumes) formed by Dr. Jasper Joly, and presented by him to the Library. The musical portion of this collection consists principally of 18th-century works, comprising Irish and Scottish song-books with a number of collections of country dances, some of great rarity. In all there are 683 volumes, 175 of Irish music, 176 of Scottish, 84 of English, 17 of Welsh, and 231 of a miscellaneous character. This latter class includes rare works by Campian, Playford, Durfey, etc., early ballad operas, and sheet-songs of the 18th century. In addition to the Joly Collection there are three others—the Banks, Omeath and Hamilton gifts—comprising about 120 large volumes. Librarian : Dr. R. T. Best.

DUNDEE. The Free Library contains a valuable collection of works relating to Scottish music, formed by A. J. Wighton (1802–66), and bequeathed by him to the Library. The number of volumes is 421. The collection contains many very rare books, besides most of the musical works printed in Scotland down to the early 19th century, as well as several scarce English and Irish musical books. Various letters addressed to Wighton by French, German and British composers and music publishers are also preserved in the collection. In the Music section of the Reference Library there is a comprehensive series of volumes illustrating the folk-songs of all the nations of Europe. A Lending Library of music has recently been formed. Chief Librarian : A. H. Millar.

DURHAM. The Cathedral Library contains a few books of glees and catches of the early 18th century, and an interesting collection of old MS. partbooks, containing anthems and services formerly used in the cathedral. These MSS. were carefully collated and indexed by the late organist, Professor Armes. They consist of four sets of books, all unfortunately imperfect. The old set contains about forty full and fifty verse anthems by Tallis, White, Parsons, Hooper, Morley, Weelkes, Byrd, Batten, Giles, Tomkins, East, Gibbons, etc. The second set is rich in anthems and services for men's voices only. The third consists of eight out of ten magnificent folio volumes containing Preces and Psalms for special days by Byrd, Gibbons, William and Edward Smith ; and services by Shepherd, Parsons, Batten and others. The fourth set consists of organ parts of practically all the anthems and services used in the cathedral from Tallis to Purcell. Other works of note are : D. Petersen's ' Speelstukken ' (Amsterdam, 1683), the 8th edition of ' Apollo's Banquet ' (1701), John Eccles's ' Theater Musick ' (2 books, published by Walsh ; i. undated, ii. ab. 1699, with a frontispiece showing a scene at the Theatre Royal ; iii. 1700), many works by J. Schenck, published at Amsterdam, and the ' Collection of New Ayres for 2 Bass Viols ' by Wm. Gorton, organist of Greenwich (Young, London, 1701). Honorary Librarian : J. Meade Falkner.

EDINBURGH. *a.* The University Music Library has been formed by bequests and donations from the Reid Fund, from General Reid, Professor John Thomson, and M. T. Bucher and others. It was largely added to by the late professor of music (F. Niecks) and his predecessors (Donaldson and Sir H. S. Oakeley). It is well supplied with modern full scores and standard editions, besides works on theory, and also contains some valuable old printed music, such as the *Musica getutscht* (1511) of Virdung ; Praetorius's *Syntagma* ; Morley's *Introduction* (1597) ; Heyden's *Ars canendi* (1537) ; Cerone's *Melopeo* (1613) ; the five volumes of Lasso's *Patrocinium musices* (1573–79), etc. Among the MSS. are a collection of oratorios by Hasse, and a Kyrie and Gloria in forty-eight real parts by G. Balabene. There is also a fine collection of musical instruments and acoustical apparatus. The Library is in charge of the professor of music, D. F. Tovey.

b. The Advocates' Library, which forms the main part of the newly established National Library of Scotland, receives, under the Copyright Act, copies of all music published in Great Britain. The Library contains some works of special interest to the students of Scottish music, but its chief musical treasures are the Skene MS. (see DAUNEY and SCOTTISH NATIONAL MUSIC), and the important MS. known as the Scone 'Antiphonarium,' or more accurately as the Carver MS. The latter dates from the first half of the 16th century and contains 12 masses, 6 settings of the Magnificat and about 30 motets composed by Robert CARVER (q.v.), Canon of Scone, some of the compositions being in as many as nineteen parts. Keeper : W. K. Dickson.

c. Library of the Society of Writers to the Signet. The Catalogue, with two Supplements, appeared in three parts, 1871–91. The last volume contains a subject-index, in which music occupies a column and a half, chiefly consisting of theoretical and historical works, with a small collection of Scottish airs, etc. Principal Librarian : J. Minto.

d. The Public Library, in addition to a good general collection of music and books on music, contains the collection formed by the late Robert A. Marr. This consists of 481 volumes, comprising chiefly 18th - century music and musical literature, and a few MSS. The latter include three Antiphoners, a Gradual, the autograph score of Sir M. Costa's 'Eli,' and an autograph MS. of a mass by Luigi Rossi. Chief Librarian : E. A. Savage.

e. A very interesting collection of works illustrating the national music of Scotland was formed, during many years of collecting, by John GLEN (q.v.). The collection contains, with the exception of a very few of the rarest works, everything relating to Scottish music that has been printed down to the early 19th century, besides a few MSS. and some collections of English Country Dances and rare English and Irish books. For a detailed list of a great portion of the Library, see J. Glen's *Early Scottish Melodies* (1900). The collection is now the property of Lady Dorothea Ruggles-Brise, who intends to present it to the newly formed National Library of Scotland.

ELY. The Cathedral Library contains a valuable collection of MSS., principally of English church music, thanks chiefly to the pious care and industry of James Hawkins, its organist from 1682–1739. It consists of 36 volumes—21 of anthems, services and chants in score, 11 of voice parts, and 4 of organ parts. The number of compositions is over 580, and includes some of large dimensions, as Handel's Utrecht Te Deum and Jubilate for voices and orchestra, and a composition inspired by the same occasion by Croft. See W. E. Dickson : *A Catalogue of Ancient Choral Services and Anthems, preserved among the Manuscript scores and Partbooks in the Cathedral Church of Ely* (Cambridge, 1861).

ETON. The College Library possesses a very fine and valuable MS. of English sacred music of the 16th century. See W. B. Squire : *On an Early Sixteenth Century Manuscript of English Music in the Library of Eton College* (*Archæologia*, vol. lvi., London, 1898).

GLASGOW. a. The Euing Library. This Library, containing over 5000 volumes, was collected by the late W. Euing, of Glasgow. In 1866 he founded a musical lectureship in Anderson's University, Glasgow, now merged in the Royal Technical College, which is affiliated to the University. He bequeathed the whole of his musical library to the University for the use of the lecturer and students. It is a large and valuable collection, particularly rich in treatises and histories of music. The anonymous catalogue, which was prepared and printed in accordance with Euing's will, is unfortunately altogether inadequate, and displays the grossest ignorance. Now that the Library is better housed and more accessible, it is hoped that a new catalogue will be printed. Amongst the ancient music in this collection the following works may be mentioned : early editions of Byrd's 'Psalms,' etc. ; the *Corale Constantini* (1550 – 57); Faber's *Melodiae Prudentianae* (1533) ; 3 volumes of Frescobaldi's works; Nicolas de la Grotte's 'Chansons' (1575) ; 47 volumes of Praetorius's works (1607–18) ; 9 volumes of G. de Wert's works (1583–89) ; and a valuable and extensive collection of English psalters and hymn-books, including the 'Gesangbuch' of the Picard Brethren (1538), referred to in Burney's *History*, iii. 31. See *Catalogue of the Musical Library of the late Wm. Euing* (Glasgow, 1878) and the select list by A. Hubens, published in *R.M.I.*, 1916. Librarian: W. R. Cunningham.

b. The Stillie Musical Library in Glasgow University was collected and bequeathed to the University by Thomas L. Stillie, a well-known musical critic, who died at Glasgow in 1883. It contains 760 volumes, including many full scores and modern operatic works.

c. The Mitchell (Public) Library contains the collection of music and musical literature, some 1700 items in all, formed by the late Robert Turnbull, for many years music critic of the *Glasgow Herald*. City Librarian : S. A. Pitt.

GLOUCESTER. The Cathedral Library possesses several old choir-books containing unpublished anthems by Rogers, Tye, Wise, Blackwell, Turner, Pickhaver, Henstridge, Davies, Jefferies, Portman, Parsons, etc., unfortunately wanting several of the parts ; a complete full service (in F), and two anthems in MS. by Fortunato Santini ; a full MS. score of Boyce's anthem 'Blessed is he that considereth ' ; a few leaves of illuminated MS. music, and some printed and MS. church music of the 17th century.

GREAT WARLEY, ESSEX. Miss Willmott has an interesting musical Library containing many rare MSS. and printed works. Among the former are two sets of partbooks of Italian church music of the early 17th century—one formerly in the Altempi Library—containing many compositions by Palestrina and his school; finely bound volumes of French 18th-century chansons ; cantatas by Scarlatti ; an autograph of J. S. Bach and a collection of autographs—chiefly of the 19th century. The printed books comprise several complete sets and odd partbooks of English madrigalists of the late 16th and early 17th centuries. Miss Willmott also owns many interesting musical instruments, among which are three clavichords, two harpsichords, two spinets, etc.

HEREFORD. The Cathedral Library contains a few old organ books and other volumes for the use of the choir, and a copy of Kircher's *Musurgia* (1650).

LEEDS. *a.* Central Public Free Library. A fairly extensive collection of scores was bought some years ago, and in recent years the Committee has greatly extended the musical portion of the Library. A large quantity of theoretical and historical books has been acquired, considerable purchases being made at the sale of the Taphouse collection (July 1905), and the Library is now one of the most useful in Yorkshire for musical students. A printed catalogue of the music was issued in 1902, but since then much has been added to the collection. Librarian : T. W. Hand.

b. The late Frank Kidson[1] possessed a fairly large library formed to show the development of British vocal and dance music. Besides a mass of 17th- and 18th-century English publications, it was especially representative in Scottish, Welsh and Irish early collections ; also in country-dance books and ballad operas. There was also a considerable number of song-books (words only) and of 18th-century tune-books of sacred music.

LICHFIELD. There are 189 volumes of printed and MS. music belonging to the Cathedral. The MSS. include a volume of Croft's anthems and Te Deum (in D) with orchestral accompaniments ; two volumes of Blow's anthems ; two volumes of anthems by Purcell, Blow, etc.; and a large collection of partbooks. The chief treasure of the printed works is seven parts (three counter-tenors, two tenors and two basses) of Barnard's Church Music (1641).

LIVERPOOL. The Public Library contains a good general selection of musical works, including a number of 18th-century song-books. The music is incorporated in the general catalogue. Chief Librarian : G. T. Shaw.

LONDON. *a.* British Museum. The musical portion of the library of the British Museum belongs partly to the department of Printed Books, and partly to that of MSS. The foundation of both collections consists in the musical

works in the old Royal Library, which was presented by George II., and to this were added a number of treatises presented in 1778 by Sir John Hawkins ; the musical library of Dr. Burney, which was bequeathed by its owner to the Museum, and transferred to Bloomsbury on his death in 1814, and the collection of Dragonetti, consisting of 182 volumes of scores of classical operas which became the property of the Museum by bequest on his death in 1846. In 1863 a notable purchase was made of duplicates from the Berlin Library, consisting mainly of old German and Italian madrigals, and church music, valued at about £1000. The collection was increased in 1886 by the acquisition from M. Kockx, of Antwerp, of a large number of works printed by the Phalèses at Louvain and Antwerp. Many of these volumes were exhibited at the Brussels Exhibition of 1880, and described in section D of the catalogue. At the dispersal of the Borghese Library in 1892, the British Museum, the Paris Conservatoire and the Academy of St. Cecilia at Rome were the three principal purchasers ; a list of the works acquired for the Museum will be found in the *Jahrbuch* of the Musikbibliothek Peters for 1896. At the second sale of the Heredia collection in 1892, the British Museum acquired several very rare Spanish treatises and musical works. Besides these important accessions, old music has been steadily bought by the Trustees since the middle of the 19th century, and many valuable works have been received by presentation or bequest, so that from an antiquarian point of view the collection is now fully worthy the national position of the institution. The *Catalogue of Printed Music published between 1487 and 1800 now in the British Museum*, by W. Barclay Squire (2 vols., 1912), covers the greater part of the older music, but does not include purely liturgical works, which are to be found in the general catalogue of the library. Since its compilation, moreover, approximately 1000 additional titles have been prepared for inclusion in a supplementary volume. Particulars of some of the most important recent accessions may be found in an article in *Mus. T.*, Oct. 1924. The great bulk of the collection, however, consists of music deposited at the museum in accordance with the provisions of the Copyright Act. The disposal of this enormous body of printed matter has been greatly facilitated by the recent adoption of a system by which the great mass of unimportant music which the Museum receives and is bound to preserve is not catalogued, bound and placed in the ordinary way, but is simply arranged in alphabetically ordered bundles, grouped according to the period of issue. Any work of this character that is required can thus be readily found, and the cost of the system is only a fraction of what the ordinary methods

---

[1] On Kidson's death (1926) a proposal was made to acquire this collection for the University of Leeds.

of treatment would entail. Until 1884 the catalogue of the printed music remained in manuscript. In 1858 it filled twenty-two volumes; at present it occupies 314 volumes, partly manuscript and partly printed. Since 1884 all the accessions have been printed and issued in separate volumes, the titles in which are afterwards incorporated in the old MS. catalogue. The printed volumes of accessions of modern music issued up to date are as follows: 1884 (452 pp.), 1886 (154 pp.), 1888 (712 pp.), 1889 (197 pp.), 1891 (948 pp.), 1894 (610 pp.), 1895 (292 pp.), 1896 (287 pp.), 1897 (539 pp.), 1898 (372 pp.), 1900 (572 pp.), 1902 (585 pp.), 1903 (537 pp.), 1904 (545 pp.), 1906 (518 pp.), 1908 (580 pp.), 1909 (616 pp.), 1910 (539 pp.), 1912 (547 pp.), 1913 (578 pp.), 1914 (391 pp.), 1915 (161 pp.), 1916 (473 pp.), 1921, 1922 (745 pp.), 1924 (433 pp.), 1925 (2 pts., 233 pp. and 169 pp.), 1926 (2 pts., 229 pp. and 172 pp.). Before the outbreak of the war a start was made with the revision of the larger headings of the catalogue, with a view to the preparation of special and comprehensive lists of the works of individual composers, but the work has been delayed. Besides modern works acquired by copyright, a considerable amount of foreign music is bought every year, special attention being paid to the acquisition of full scores and other works beyond the means of the ordinary musical student. Considerable additions of Russian music and of miniature scores of the works of modern composers have recently been made. The most valuable musical accessions are mentioned in the yearly British Museum Returns to Parliament.

The collection of musical MSS., including ancient service-books and treatises, but excluding Oriental MSS., amounts to about 3000 volumes. The following are among the most noteworthy items: A large volume of autograph music by Purcell; a volume known as Thomas Mulliner's book, containing airs and chants for the virginals, by Tallis and others, and including the earliest known copy of Richard Edwards's madrigal ' In going to my naked bed'; services and anthems of the Church of England down to Queen Anne's reign, collected by Dr. Tudway, 1715–20, in six volumes, containing works by Aldrich, Blow, Gibbons, Humfrey, Purcell, Tudway, etc.; an autograph of Part 2 of Bach's ' Wohltemperirtes Clavier'; two or three volumes of autograph pieces by Handel, some leaves of which supply the place of leaves wanting in the autograph of ' Admetus' in the Royal Music Library; also the thirty-seven volumes of transcripts of Handel's music, mainly in the hand of J. C. Smith, formerly in the possession of Mr. Bernard Granville of Calwich Abbey; the original MSS. of ten string quartets by Mozart, including the sets dedicated respectively

to Haydn and to the King of Prussia; several volumes of rough drafts by Beethoven, in which the first ideas of themes of some of his great works were jotted down; eleven volumes of autograph musical extracts, chiefly vocal, made by Dr. Burney for his *History of Music*; twenty-eight volumes of MS. motets, masses, madrigals, duets, etc., by Italian and English composers, copied by Henry Needler from the libraries at Oxford, and bequeathed in 1782; John Barnard's first book of Selected Church Music, a manuscript copy scored by John BISHOP of Cheltenham, from the various part books; many interesting collections of Italian and early English (16th and 17th centuries) songs, having both words and music; autograph compositions by Haydn, Mozart, Schubert, Schumann, Mendelssohn, Weber, Wagner, Liszt, Gounod, etc.; collections for a dictionary of music, etc., by Dr. J. W. Callcott; musical compositions and works on music by R. L. Pearsall; thirty-nine operas or musical dramas by Sir Henry R. Bishop, in autograph score; forty volumes of scores of Balfe's operas, presented by his widow; and a large collection of Dibdin's songs and operas. There is also a good deal of lute music in tablature. Among the more important manuscripts acquired by purchase from time to time are numerous operas in contemporary transcripts— many, if not most, probably unpublished in score—especially by Rossini, Meyerbeer, Donizetti, Paisiello, Hasse, Winter, Ricci and Mercadante; and church music, chiefly Italian, in 18th-century copies, comprising compositions by Palestrina, the Scarlattis, Durante, Leo, Bai, Clari, Perez, Pergolesi and others. See the *Catalogue of Manuscript Music in the British Museum*, by A. Hughes-Hughes, 3 vols., 1906–1909. For the Royal Music Library and the collections of the Royal Philharmonic Society deposited at the British Museum see below. Director: Sir Frederick G. Kenyon, K.C.B.

b. Victoria and Albert Museum. The Science and Art Libraries contain useful collections of works on music and musical instruments, besides some printed editions of German operas of small value, and the autograph MSS. of Mendelssohn's ' Hear my prayer' and Bishop's ' Legends of the Rhine.' The musical works formerly belonging to John Ella were transferred to the Royal College of Music some years ago. The Museum contains a fine collection of old instruments, many of which are of remarkable beauty. Director: Eric Maclagan.

c. Royal Academy of Music. The Library of this institution, of which there is a MS. Catalogue by Henry Davey, contains many interesting and valuable works, amongst which may be mentioned a collection of English glees (in sixteen volumes) by Atterbury, Callcott, Danby, etc., and MS. operas by Leonardo Leo

Gasparini, Bononcini, Porpora and others, which were presented to the R.A.M., together with the whole of his valuable musical library, by R. J. Stevens. From the same source came the MS. full score of Purcell's ' Fairy Queen,' partly in the composer's autograph—the only known complete copy of the work (printed by the PURCELL SOCIETY, 1904) ; copies of the treatises of Morley and Bevin, three copies of Mace's *Musick's Monument*, copies of Tallis and Byrd's ' Cantiones ' (1575), Yonge's ' Musica Transalpina ' (1588), Byrd's ' Songs of Sundrie Natures' (1589), Hilton's ' Ayres' (1627) and Lawes's Psalms (1648). The modern MSS. in the Library include the autograph score of Sullivan's ' Mikado.' There is also a collection of the works of Sebastian Bach, being the library of the defunct Bach Society ; a large number of Liszt's works (presented by Miss Constance Bache), and a collection of modern orchestral scores (presented by the publishers, Messrs. Novello). In 1903, the Angelina Goetz Library was founded in memory of Mrs. Goetz by her children ; this consists of a valuable collection of full scores, and includes many modern operatic works, etc., rarely found in either public or private libraries. Principal : Dr. J. B. McEwen.

d. Royal College of Music. In addition to an extensive working library, the Royal College possesses the most extensive purely musical library in the United Kingdom. The basis of this collection is the fine library of the old Sacred Harmonic Society, which was acquired for the R.C.M. in 1883 for the sum of £3000, £2000 being contributed by Sir Augustus Adderley and the rest by fifteen subscribers. The Sacred Harmonic collection is catalogued in W. H. Husk's *Catalogue of the Library of the Sacred Harmonic Society. A new Edition, revised and augmented* (London, 1872), with a Supplement published in 1882. With the exception of No. 1826 in this catalogue (the manuscript score of Mendelssohn's ' Elijah,' which, according to the original terms of its gift to the society, was returned to Mrs. Bartholomew), the whole library, together with the original bookcases, is arranged in a large room specially fitted up for the purpose, extending the whole length of the college buildings. But this collection has been so largely increased by other donations and bequests that it now constitutes less than one-half of the R.C.M. Library. Among the most important accessions the following may be mentioned : the library of the Concerts of Ancient Musick, formerly preserved at Buckingham Palace and presented by Queen Victoria, comprising a very large collection of MS. scores and parts, chiefly of 18th and early 19th century music, and including many volumes of autographs of Bishop, interesting autographs of Croft, an opera by Keiser, and early copies of Handel ; the large

musical library of Sir George Grove, including autographs by Beethoven, Mendelssohn and Schubert (unfinished symphony in E), and especially rich in musical literature ; the collections of Mr. J. W. Windsor (of Bath) and his family, among which are an autograph string quartet (in C) by Haydn and some fine prints of musicians ; several hundred bound volumes of music collected by Mr. S. W. Waley ; several hundred volumes of duplicates from the Musical Library of the British Museum ; a large collection of chamber music formerly belonging to Franz Ries ; over 300 volumes of printed and MS. music (formerly belonging to John Ella, and including 20 MS. volumes of operas by D. Perez) transferred from the Victoria and Albert Museum ; the full scores of ' The Golden Legend ' and ' The Yeomen of the Guard ' (bequeathed by Sir Arthur Sullivan) ; autographs of H. H. Pierson, A. W. Bach, C. Neate, Benedict (symphony in F), Pearsall and Monk ; the full score (MS.) of ' Love in a Village ' ; MSS. of Mozart, Michael Haydn, Purcell, Durante, Hammerschmidt, Anfossi, Paisiello, Saratelli and many others ; a collection of autographs and other MSS. of A. Goring Thomas ; over 100 volumes from the library of the late E. Dannreuther ; many autographs of S. Wesley, C. Wesley and S. S. Wesley (bequeathed by the last-named's last surviving son) ; and much printed music and musical literature of all kinds. This immense accumulation of music has naturally resulted in there being a good many duplicates. A sale of a portion of these took place a few years ago, and the proceeds have been devoted to binding, the acquisition of new works, etc. A catalogue of the printed music was published in 1909 ; the MSS. (over 4000 in number) have been catalogued, as well as the greater part of the large collection of general literature : both these catalogues are at present in manuscript. On the death of Sir Hubert Parry, as a practical memorial to him, a small fund was raised, by which the central bay of the Library was fitted up as a Reading Room for the use of the students. To this ' Parry Room ' many contributions of books were given, while volumes from the old collection were moved there for purposes of general reference. A set of the Bach Society's volumes was given by Dr. Emily Daymond, and a special case was set aside for Parry's own compositions and many of his autographs—the latter lent by his executors. Current periodicals are available here, and new books are added from time to time. Though not a public library, access is generally granted on application (during term time) to the director. Besides the MSS. and printed books the library contains many interesting instruments, presented or bequeathed by the late Duke of Saxe-Coburg, Sourindro Mohun Tagore, Mrs. Day, Dr. Turpin, Mr. Hipkins and others. There is also a small collection of paintings, drawings and prints; the former include portraits of Bononcini (by Hogarth) (see *PLATE X.*), Corelli (by Howard), Attwood (see *PLATE II.*), Weber (by Cawse) (see *PLATE LXXI.*), Joachim (by Bendemann), Salomon (by Dance), Hullah (by Bower), M. A. Paton (by T. Sully), E. Paton (by E. T. Crawford), Dibdin, and several portraits of S. S. Wesley (see *PLATE XCII.*). There are also busts of Mendelssohn, Thalberg (see *PLATE LXXXI.*), Mario, Grisi and other musicians. The Donaldson Collection of Old Instruments is preserved in a separate museum (see COLLECTIONS OF MUSICAL INSTRUMENTS). Director: Prof. Sir Hugh P. Allen.

e. Trinity College of Music. The Bridge Memorial Library, opened in 1924 in honour of the late Sir Frederick Bridge, consists at present of some 3000 volumes. There are some old copies, in score, of works by Piccinni, Sacchini, Grétry, Cimarosa, Monsigny, etc.; a fine copy of the second edition of 'Orpheus Britannicus,' and two short pieces for pianoforte in the autograph of W. Sterndale Bennett. Secretary: C. N. H. Rodwell.

f. Gresham College. The College possesses a small collection of printed and MS. music (see the *Catalogue of Books and Music in the Library of Gresham College*, London, 1872), mostly of the 18th and early 19th centuries, including the MS. and printed glees formerly belonging to the Concentores Society (1798–1805). The rarest works are 8 masses by Henri Fremart (Paris, 1642–45); MSS. by S. Bolio, G. B. Borghi, C. Burney, T. Carapella, G. B. Casali, Cordicelli, Durante; 'fancies' by Locke, Jenkins and W. Young; masses, etc., by G. Fideli, Galuppi, Paisiello, Pergolesi, and a score of Jommelli's 'Don Trastullo.'

g. The Madrigal Society. This Society possesses a valuable collection of more than 300 madrigals, anthems, etc., comprising works by more than 100 composers, principally of the English and Italian schools. The greater part of the collection consists of MS. copies of the 18th century, but there are some early printed partbooks and some MSS. of the 17th century, including some interesting instrumental fancies by English composers of the time of James I. and Charles I. The Library is at present deposited at the Royal College of Music.

h. The Royal Philharmonic Society. This Library, which dates from the formation of the Society in 1813, has now been deposited on loan at the British Museum. It contains all the parts of the principal works of the classical composers necessary for an orchestra, and many full scores and MSS. of unique interest. Amongst the autographs may be mentioned two of Haydn's grand Symphonies; Beethoven's dedication to the Society of his Ninth Symphony; a MS. symphony by Cherubini; Mendelssohn's Symphony in C ('No. XIII.' known as 'No. I.'), dedicated to the Society; also 'Melusina,' the 'Trumpet Overture,' and the original setting of the scena 'Infelice,' with violin obbligato—all three with notes or alterations by himself; also original scores by Cipriani Potter, Ries, Clementi, Spohr and other composers.

i. Westminster Abbey. The Chapter Library contains a collection of music (chiefly in MS.) by Italian and English composers of the 17th and 18th centuries, and a number of madrigals, both English and Italian, of the late 16th and 17th centuries. See W. B. Squire: *Musik-Katalog der Bibliothek der Westminster-Abtei in London* (*M.f.M.*, Beilage, 1903). Librarian: Rev. L. H. Nixon.

j. Lambeth Palace. The Archiepiscopal Library contains many fine Psalters, Missals and Breviaries, both printed and MS.; a good collection of early editions of psalms and hymnbooks; MS. treatises collected by W. Chelle; a MS. volume of English, French and Italian songs with lute accompaniment (written in tablature), containing compositions by Charles and Edward Coleman, Alphonso Marsh, Matthew Locke and John Gulgrum, and an explanation of the tablature; a MS. volume of harpsichord music (dances and airs) by R. Ayleward and others; a copy of Tye's 'Acts of the Apostles'; and a MS. volume containing the bass part of services and anthems by Tallis, Parsons, Byrd, Tomkins, Gibbons, Munday, Portman, Strogers, Morley, and many anonymous compositions. See W. H. Frere: *Bibliotheca musico-liturgica*, vol. i. (fasc. 1, 1901). Librarian: A. B. Robinson.

k. The Royal Music Library, which is the private property of His Majesty, since 1911 has been deposited on permanent loan in a special room at the British Museum. It consists principally of the collection formerly at Buckingham Palace, to which has been added a large amount of music from Windsor Castle. In the main the library was formed by George III., but it was largely increased by George IV., whose music (formerly at Carlton House) is here; important additions of printed music were also made by Queen Victoria and the Prince Consort. The library is chiefly renowned for its priceless Handel manuscripts (see HANDEL, subsection BIBLIOGRAPHY). But besides these the collection is remarkable for its many fine bindings and rare manuscripts and printed works. Amongst the chief treasures are a splendid volume of autograph MSS. by Purcell; a valuable volume of English 16th-century music written by John Baldwin of Windsor, the Virginal Books of B. Cosyn and W. Forster; a curious volume of puzzle canons by Dr. John Bull; a collection of puzzle canons, in from two to twenty parts, by Elway Bevin, in the composer's own handwriting; a fine copy of the second edition of Monteverdi's 'Orfeo'; a MS. volume of 'Aires and Phantasies' by

Coprario, which formerly belonged to Charles I.; an original copy of Mendelssohn's 'Oedipus in Colonos,' sent by the composer to the Prince Consort for the production of the work at Buckingham Palace; curious masques by Schmied; a copy of 'Parthenia'; a valuable and extensive collection of Steffani's music, including a set of his operas, bound for the use of the opera at Hanover; many full scores of operas by Lully, Mozart, Christian Bach, Graun, etc.; autograph symphonies by A. Scarlatti; musical compositions by King George IV.; and a very fine collection of madrigals, most of which were formerly in the possession of Sir John Hawkins. Catalogues of the whole collection by Barclay Squire, late Hon. Curator, are in preparation and will eventually be printed. That of the Printed Music and Musical Literature is finished (in manuscript). A catalogue of the Handel MSS. is in the press.

l. Richard Northcott possesses a collection of some 2000 books relating to the Opera and to operatic singers and composers. The two most interesting items are Vice-Chamberlain Coke's papers (see *Proceedings of the Musical Association,* Jan. 1914), and the volume, with Della Bella illustrations, of the festivities arranged for the marriage at Florence in 1637 of the Grand Duke of Tuscany and the Princess Vittoria of Urbino. Mr. Northcott has also a fine collection of unpublished autograph letters of composers, *e.g.* of Balfe, Berlioz, Bishop, Bizet, Brahms, M. Costa, Donizetti, Flotow, Gounod, Massenet, Mendelssohn, Meyerbeer, Offenbach, Puccini, Rossini, Saint-Saëns, Sullivan, Verdi and Wagner; and a collection of programmes, portraits of artists, and libretti relating to opera performances in London, particularly at Covent Garden, of which theatre he is the archivist. These papers form the basis of the recently established Royal Opera Museum.

MANCHESTER. *a.* Public Library. In 1899 Dr. Henry Watson of Salford transferred the ownership of his Musical Library to the Manchester Free Libraries Committee, with the stipulation that the collection should remain in his custody and under his control during his lifetime, access to the books being granted to students on application to the chief librarian. Dr. Watson died in 1911, and the library is now housed in Portland Street. The library consisted originally of some 16,700 volumes, but now numbers about 40,000. It is extremely valuable for general purposes of reference, and also contains many rare works, among which may be mentioned a MS. Antiphoner of the 14th century, sets of English madrigals by Byrd, Farmer, East, Lichfield, Ward, Pilkington, Tomkins, etc., and many printed treatises of the 16th and 17th centuries. See the *Manchester Public Free Libraries Quarterly*

Record for 1899. A series of 'music lists' has been issued as a guide to the collection, and a brief catalogue of the rarer books and MSS. was printed in connexion with an exhibition held at the Town Hall, Manchester, in 1905. Librarian: J. F. Russell.

b. Chetham Library. Here is preserved a collection of nearly 4000 proclamations, broadsides, ballads and poems, accumulated by and presented to the Library by the late J. O. Halliwell-Philipps. Amongst these will be found the music of many old popular songs ranging through the 16th, 17th and 18th centuries; songs, catches, odes, etc., by Purcell, Eccles, Leveridge, Courteville, Croft, Carey, Weldon and Pepusch, and a large collection of single sheet songs with music, published between 1680 and 1740. Many of the songs in this collection were introduced into operas for special occasions, and are therefore not to be found in the printed editions. There is a privately printed catalogue of this collection prepared by Halliwell-Philipps. Librarian: C. T. E. Phillips.

c. John Rylands Library. This library possesses a certain number of items of musical interest. There are several liturgical MSS. which serve to illustrate the development of notation from the 9th to the 15th century, the most important of which are: the 'Trier Psalter' (9th cent.); 'Cantica ecclesiastica pro dominicis et festis, cum notis musicis' (10th cent.); the 'Sarum Missal' (first half of the 13th cent.); and the 'Colonna Missal' (1517). The collection of early printed books also includes many of the famous Missals, and items such as Merbecke's 'Booke of Common Praier noted and described' (1550), Sternhold and Hopkins's Psalter (1562) and theoretical works by Gaforius. In the collection of Chinese drawings and paintings there is an interesting volume containing about forty coloured drawings of musical instruments, two of which show the arrangement of an orchestra of 32 instruments. Librarian: H. Guppy.

NEWBURY, BERKS. G. E. P. Arkwright has a collection of musical works containing a few manuscripts and many rare books. Among the former are a 12th-century gradual (with neumes) in vellum, and a set of motets for three voices by Steffani. The printed books include Victoria's Masses (Rome, 1583, folio); several partbooks of Italian sacred music of the 17th century; Bevin's *Briefe Introduction* (1631), and other theoretical works; Coprario's 'Funeral Teares' (1606) and 'Songs of Mourning' (1613); Danyel's 'Songs for the Lute' (1606); Gibbons's 'Madrigals' (1612); 'The Lamentations of Jeremie with apt Notes' (London, J. Wolfe, 1587); Pilkington's 'First Book of Songes' (1605); Ward's 'Madrigals' (1613); and Weelkes's 'Ayres or Phantasticke Spirites' (1608) and 'Balletts and Madrigals' (1608).

Oscott, St. Mary's College. The Library contains a collection of masses, sequences, offertories, psalms, hymns, responses, etc., in seven volumes, by Palestrina; masses by Alfieri, and unpublished MSS. by Guglielmi, Alfieri, Morales, Zingarelli, Marotti, Festa, Rovalli, Casciolini, Bolloffi, Fioravanti and Borroni.

Oxford. *a*. Bodleian Library. In 1759 and 1769 music began to be received by the Bodleian Library from Stationers' Hall. It was allowed to accumulate until, in the 19th century, it was arranged and bound up in some 400 vols. The cataloguing began in 1882, and since then all accessions, with the exception of certain of the less important works received under the Copyright Act, have been catalogued. Some 3000 or 4000 musical works are received yearly under the Copyright Laws; classified hand-lists of all the music are available for reference. In 1801 a large collection of both MS. and printed music was bequeathed by the Rev. O. Wright. It consists of 209 bound volumes, and includes compositions by Ariosti, Blow, Boyce, Caldara, Clarke, Croft, East, Ford, O. and C. Gibbons, Greene, Lotti, Morley, Purcell, Rogers, Scarlatti, Taylor, etc., besides numerous works by W. and P. Hayes. Much of this collection is autograph. Among musical MSS. acquired from other sources are five partbooks, dated 1585, of motets by Byrd, Tye, Taverner, Fayrfax, Tallis and others. A large number of MSS. also contain mediæval music, mostly liturgical. Among these are a *Winchester Troper* (date 979 or 980), a *Winchester Proser* (date after 984), and an 11th-century *Winchester Sequentiary* (MS. Bodl. 775); the (10th- and) 11th-century *Leofric Missal*; the 11th-century *Heidenheim Troper and Sequentiary*, and *Novalesa Troper and Proser*; MS. Ashmole, 1285, containing (f. 235v.) a Norman-French song, apparently written in England about 1185; MS. Rawlinson G. 22, containing (f. lv.) an English song of about 1225; MS. Selden B. 26, containing a collection of secular and sacred songs written about 1450; and MS. Canonici misc. 213, a collection of 15th-century Belgian, French and Italian songs by Dufay, Binchois, Hugh and Arnold de Lantins, and others; 18 French and Italian songs; 61 sonatas (*a* 4) by Corelli, Matteis, Ruggieri, Purcell, etc. In the Bodleian is also now deposited the library of the Music School, containing about 880 volumes of manuscripts, among which are six partbooks containing 18 masses by Taverner, Burton, Merbecke, Fayrfax, Rasar, Aston, Ashwell, Norman, Shepperde, Tye and Alwood; three Edwardine cathedral partbooks, perhaps in John Taverner's autograph; a collection of In Nomines, in four and five parts, by Byrd, Ferrabosco, Bull, Taverner, Tye, Tallis, etc.; motets by Felice Sances, etc.; motets with instrumental accompaniments by Rosenmüller, Schelling and

Knüpfer; sonatas, symphonies, etc., by Corelli and others; 235 pieces from Lully's operas; Henri de Gallot's 'Pièces de guitarre' (1680-84); two fine folio volumes containing fantasias, music to masques, etc., by William and Henry Lawes; fantasias in six parts by J. Jenkins, Cooper, Lupo, T. Tomkins, Byrd, etc.; John Jenkins's 'Fancyes and Ayres,' and fantasias for two trebles, two basses and organ; pavans, galliards, corantos, dated 1654, by Coleman, Lawes, John Taylor, etc.; about 179 instrumental pieces *a* 4 by Benj. Rogers; Sylvanus Taylor's Ayres for two trebles and a bass; vocal and instrumental parts of Dryden's 'Secular Masque'; 9 instrumental pieces by C. Gibbons; songs by Purcell, Blow, W. Child, etc.; the 'Oxford Act Music' (or commemoration music) by Blow, Goodson, etc.; Chris. Simpson's 'Months and Seasons' for two basses and a treble (1668), and his 'little Consort'; complete set of Occasional Odes by Boyce for the King's birthday and New Year (1755-79), etc. A good MS. catalogue of the Music School collection was compiled in 1854. Exercises submitted for Oxford musical degrees, from about 1710 onwards, are also deposited in the Bodleian Library. These and the other musical MSS. in the Library (including those of the Music School) are included in the printed *Summary Catalogue of the Western MSS. in the Bodleian Library*, vols. iv. and v. See also Stainer's *Dufay and his Contemporaries* (1898), Stainer and Nicholson's *Early Bodleian Music* (1901, 1913), and Frere's *Bibliotheca musico-liturgica* (vol. i. fasc. 1), in which are also noticed some early musical treatises in the libraries of Balliol and St. John's Colleges. Librarian: Dr. A. E. Cowley.

b. Oxford University Music Students' Library. In addition to the music in the Bodleian Library there is at Oxford a collection of music designed particularly for use as a working and lending library by persons reading music at the University. This collection of about 4000 vols. consists of the so-called Music Students' Library, the Mee bequest, and the library of the late Captain F. B. Ellis, of Christ Church. The library, which contains most standard works and is rich in modern full scores, is open in the mornings during term. It is housed temporarily in the Clarendon Buildings. Librarian: Dr. T. Wood.

c. Christ Church. The Library of this college contains a very large and valuable collection of early English and foreign music, chiefly bequeathed to the college by Dean Aldrich and Mr. Goodson, but since then increased by many additions. The printed works comprise compositions by more than 180 different composers, while the MSS. contain 1075 anonymous pieces, and 2417 pieces by known composers, of whom 182 are English, 80 Italian, and 14 composers of other nations. This estimate does not include the many separate movements of operas, services, etc., and the Fancies for instruments, which if enumerated would amount to nearly 5000. Amongst the MSS. here are 30 anthems by Dr. Aldrich; 23 anthems, 7 motets, 4 services and a masque (' Venus and Adonis ') by Dr. Blow; 29 anthems, 43 motets, 19 madrigals, etc., and a very curious piece of programme music ('Mr. Bird's Battle') by W. Byrd; 18 motets by R. Dering; 20 anthems and 21 madrigals and canzonets by T. Ford; 24 anthems by Orlando Gibbons; 21 anthems by John Goldwin; 33 motets by M. Jeffrey; 21 canzonets by J. Jenkins; 17 motets by W. Mundy; 15 dramatic works by Henry Purcell; 39 motets by J. Shepperde; 17 motets by John Taverner; 10 madrigals by J. Warde; 25 motets by R. Whyte; 47 motets and 45 cantatas by Carissimi; 15 cantatas by Cesti; 67 motets by Gratiani; 27 cantatas by Micheli; 30 motets by Palestrina; 112 cantatas by Luigi Rossi; 12 cantatas, a serenata, 2 dramas, and an opera by A. Scarlatti; and the following anonymous compositions: 239 motets, 162 cantatas, etc., to English words, and 408 cantatas, etc., to Italian words. In 1918 the Library acquired the set of 10 volumes of Barnard's Church Music formerly in the possession of the Cathedral Library at Hereford. See the catalogues of the MSS., by G. E. P. Arkwright (vol. i., 1915; vol. ii., 1923—a third volume is in preparation), and of the printed music prior to 1801, by A. Hiff (1919).

d. St. John's College. The Library of this college possesses two MS. bass partbooks, date between 1625–32. Both books bear the autograph of William Juxon and contain important works not found elsewhere, notably Tallis's five-part service. The conjecture that they were written by Tomkins and East is founded on an error.

RIPON. In the Minster Library is preserved an interesting volume of theological tracts by Gerson and others, on blank leaves of which are written two 16th-century ballads for three voices. The first is entitled 'A ballet of yᵉ deth of yᵉ Cardinall' (*i.e.* Wolsey), and the second, 'A lytyll ballet mayde of yᵉ yong dukes gᵃce' (*i.e.* Henry Fitzroy, Duke of Richmond and Somerset, a natural son of Henry VIII., who died in 1536). The words of these ballads are printed in the *Yorkshire Archæological and Topographical Journal*, ii. 396. The library also contains some rare liturgical printed books, particularly a *York Manuale* (W. de Worde) of 1509, and a *York Missal* (Rouen) of 1517.

ROCHESTER. The Music Library of the Cathedral consists of 478 volumes, 84 of which are in MS., and contain anthems and services (some of which are unpublished) by the following composers: Hopkins, Henstridge, Loch, Wootton, Hine, Turner, Elvey, Child, Dupuis, Lambert, Fussell, Mason, Walmisley, Russell Rogers, Marsh and Pratt.

SEVENOAKS. Newman Flower possesses a Handel Library which includes some transcripts of Handel's works made by John Christopher Smith (from the Aylesford Collection), and a number of early printed editions, the most important of which is an issue of the 'Songs in Messiah,' apparently earlier than any previously recorded. The collection also includes some transcripts of works by other 18th-century composers. See the *Catalogue of a Handel Collection formed by Newman Flower* (Sevenoaks, 1921).

SHENLEY, HERTS. Edward Speyer has a valuable collection of musical autographs, many of which are of great interest and rarity. The following are the chief musicians represented: Albrechtsberger, Auber, C. P. E. Bach, J. S. Bach (cantata, 'Wo Gott der Herr'); Beethoven (several letters, sketches, and proof-sheets); Bellini, Berlioz, Boccherini, Boieldieu, Brahms (vocal quartets, op. 112, Nos. 1 and 2, and many letters); Bülow, Burney, Cherubini, Chopin, Clementi, Dalayrac, Donizetti, Elgar, Farinelli, Gluck (score of aria from 'Issipile'); Grétry, Handel, Josef and Michael Haydn, Joachim, Liszt, Martini, Méhul, Mendelssohn, Meyerbeer, Monteverdi, Mozart and his family, Neefe, Paër, Paganini, Philidor, Piccinni, Rousseau, Sacchini, Salieri, Schubert, Schumann, Schütz, Spohr, Spontini, R. Strauss, Thalberg, A. Thomas, Verdi, Wagner and Weber.

SHERBORNE. The school Library contains a few rare musical printed works, including complete sets of both parts of the 'Selectissimae Cantiones' (Nuremberg, 1587) and 'Lectiones Hiob' (Nuremberg, 1588) of Lasso; the 'Balletti' of Gastoldi (Antwerp, 1601); 'Paradiso musicale' (Antwerp, 1596); and the five-part madrigals of Marenzio (Antwerp, 1593).

STAMFORD. The Library of the Marquess of Exeter at Burghley House, near Stamford, contains a small collection of MS. music, chiefly operas, church music and cantatas by 18th-century composers, amongst whom may be mentioned Astorga, P. Auletta, Clari, Durante, Giaji, Hasse, Pazzaglia, Pergolesi and Vinci.

STONYHURST. This college possesses the original MS. of de Vico's responses for Holy Week, MS. music by Cartoni, and a few litanies, motets, sequences, etc., by Palestrina.

TENBURY. St. Michael's College possesses the Library of the late Rev. Sir F. A. Gore Ouseley, containing nearly 4000 volumes, and is by far the most important private music library in the United Kingdom. The printed books include a large number of very scarce treatises, and among other great rarities are the four works of Gafori and Case's *The praise of Musicke* (1586); there is also a good collection of partbooks of English and Italian madrigals. But the chief importance of this library rests upon the manuscripts. The most valuable of these are the numerous sets of partbooks dating about the year 1600 and containing the text of sacred and secular music of the polyphonic school. The works both of continental and English composers are to be found in these books, and they supply the only known text of certain pieces by Taverner, Whyte, Byrd and other Tudor musicians. Perhaps the most notable manuscript in this library belonging to this period is the famous organ-book in the hand of Adrian BATTEN (q.v.) containing a vast store of early English church music. (See *Tudor Church Music*, vol. ii. xxvi.) The school of Purcell is richly represented in this library by contemporary MSS., and some of the works of Purcell and Blow have survived nowhere else. In this collection are autographs of Blow, Purcell, Croft and Jeremiah Clarke. The later periods of English music are also well represented, and include autographs of Boyce, Burney, Charles Wesley, Crotch, S. Arnold and many more modern composers.

Perhaps the most famous MS. in this library is Handel's ' conductor's ' score of ' Messiah ' used by the composer at the first performance in Dublin in 1742. Certain numbers and some pencil notes are in Handel's autograph. This MS. is one of the four recognised sources of the text of the oratorio. It is fully described by Chrysander in vol. xxiv. of the German Handel Society Edition, and all the autograph portions may be seen in Chrysander's facsimile reproduction of ' Messiah.'

One further feature of this library is the remarkably large collection of printed and MS. scores of operatic works ranging from the 17th to the 19th century. Among these are a very fine set of scores in the hand of Philidor *aîné*, which together with vocal and instrumental partbooks (numbering over 200 vols.) once formed part of the Royal Music Library of the French kings. The scores are in especially good condition and the covers are stamped with the coat of arms of the Bourbons. These scores include operas, ballets and motets by Lully, Campra, Colasse and others of the same school. Also in Philidor's hand is a fine set of service books from the French Chapel Royal.

The library has recently been entirely rearranged and catalogued by the present librarian, Rev. Dr. E. H. Fellowes.

WARE, HERTS. St. Edmund's College, Old Hall. The Library contains a valuable English manuscript of the 15th century, containing sacred music by English composers of the period, including two numbers ascribed to King Henry VI. For a full account and thematic catalogue, see *Sammelbände* of the Int. Mus. Ges. ii. (1900–01), pp. 342-92, 719-22. Librarian : Rev. J. O'Brien.

WELLS. The Cathedral Library contains some fragmentary parts of a vocal composition or compositions by Fayrfax.

WIGAN. The Free Public Library contains a good collection of works on music, mostly English publications of the 19th century, as well as a few pianoforte scores of operas, etc. See Folkard (H. T.): *Music and Musicians. A list of Books and Pamphlets relating to the History, Biography, Theory, and Practice of Music, preserved in the . . . Wigan Free Public Library* (Wigan, 1903). Librarian : A. G. Hawkes.

WIMBORNE MINSTER. Among the books preserved in the famous ' chain-library ' in the Minster are five 17th-century partbooks, an alto, two tenors and two basses. They provide texts of no inconsiderable value as regards Byrd's short service and other English church music.

WINDSOR. a. The Royal Library at Windsor Castle. Most of the music from this library has now been removed to form part of the Royal Music Library (see above under London) now housed at the British Museum. The most important item that remains is the autograph score of Mozart's cantata ' Die Schuldigkeit des ersten Gebotes.'

b. St. George's Chapel. The Chapter Library contains a few 17th-century MS. partbooks ; some of these are in the hand of William Child and include several of his services, besides anthems by Tallis and other Tudor composers. Here also are two of the partbooks (and one duplicate) of Tomkins's *Musica Deo sacra* (1668).

WORCESTER. The Cathedral Library possesses a fine Sarum Missal, a Benedictine Antiphoner of the 13th century, now in process of facsimile reproduction in *Paléographie musicale*, the primus contratenor, bassus, decani, secundus contratenor and tenor cantoris of Barnard's Church Music, a valuable tenor partbook containing Byrd's Great Service, and, above all, a quantity of fly-leaves of harmonised music, mostly dating from about 1275 to about 1325, which have been recovered from old bindings. Parts of the same collection exist at the Bodleian, at the British Museum, and at Magdalen College, Oxford, and the whole provides the most considerable body of material for the history of English composition during this period that is at present available, containing as it does about thirty complete and eighty incomplete items. See *Cathedral Quarterly*, Dec. 1916 ; *Proceedings of the Musical Association* for 1924, *Music and Letters*, Apr. 1925, and the article MOTET. Librarian : Canon J. E. H. Blake.

YORK. The Minster Library contains 258 musical works, both printed and MS., besides a large quantity of anthems and services. Amongst the MSS. the following works may be mentioned : a collection of duets, glees, etc., by Aldrich, Wise, Blow, etc. ; an installation ode by Hague ; Te Deums by Haydn, Neukomm, Schicht, and Weber ; ' The Nativity,' an oratorio by Homilius; a mass by Naumann; ' The Intercession,' an oratorio by King ; a set of three-part Fancies by Jenkins ; a very important set of eight choir-books (formerly belonging to W. Gostling), containing the voice parts complete of a large number of anthems and services of the 17th century. There is also a considerable collection of printed musical works of the 17th century.

Holland

For further particulars of Dutch libraries, see the article by J. G. Prod'homme referred to under the heading *Belgium*, above.

AMSTERDAM. *a.* Vereenigung voor Noord-Nederlands Muziekgeschiedenis. (Maatschappij tot bevordering der Toonkunst.) See *Catalogus van de bibliotheken der Maatschappij tot bevordering der Toonkunst en der Vereenigung von Noord-Nederlands Muziekgeschiedenis* (Amsterdam, 1884). Lists also appeared in the Society's two first *Bouwsteenen*, afterwards continued as the *Tijdschrift* of the Society.

b. The late J. W. Enschedé possessed an extensive musical Library particularly rich in books on church music, with special reference to the history of the organ.

THE HAGUE. *a.* The Royal Library (Koninklijke Bibliotheek) contains about 1100 volumes of musical interest, which have been catalogued in the *Catalogue van schoone kunsten en kunstnijverheid* ('s Gravenhage, 1905). Director: P. C. Molhuysen.

b. D. F. Scheurleer possesses a very fine and extensive musical Library, of which he has published an admirable catalogue, containing facsimiles of title-pages, etc. See *Catalogus der Muziekbibliotheek van D. F. Scheurleer* (Deel i. and ii., 's Gravenhage, 1893, Verfolg, 1903 ; 2de Verfolg, 1910), and *Muziekhistorisch Museum van Dr. D. F. Scheurleer. Catalogus van de muziekwerken en de boeken over muziek* (3 vols., 's Gravenhage, 1923–25).

LEYDEN. *a.* The St. Pieterskerk possesses six choir-books containing compositions of the 16th century. They are described at length in the third of the *Bouwsteenen* of the Vereenigung voor Noord-Nederlands Muziekgeschiedenis, p. 37, etc.

b. The University Library contains liturgical manuscripts of the 10th, 11th and 15th centuries ; a collection of Souterliedekens and some chamber music of the 18th century. See the third of the *Bouwsteenen*, p. 111, etc. Director : Dr. F. C. Wieder.

c. The Bibliotheek Thysius contains a volume of 17th-century lute music that is of the very greatest importance, partly on account of its size—there are over 1000 pages of music—

partly on account of the variety of styles and of composers represented. The MS. has been described at length by G. P. Land in the *Tijdschrift* of the Vereenigung voor Noord-Nederlands Muziekgeschiedenis, Deel 1-3, 1885–91.

UTRECHT. The University Library possesses valuable liturgical manuscripts of the 12th-15th centuries, among which a 14th-century collection of sequences is especially noteworthy. See *Catalogus codicum manuscriptorum bibliothecae Universitatis Rheno-Trajectinae* (2 vols., Utrecht, 1887, 1909). Librarian : Dr. A. Hulshof.

Italy

In 1909 the Associazione dei Musicologi Italiani began the issue of a Bulletin, which consists of a valuable series of catalogues of the musical libraries of Italy (referred to below as *Boll. Ass. Mus. It.*). The following cities have at present been dealt with, either in whole or in part : Assisi, Bologna, Ferrara, Florence, Milan, Modena, Naples, Parma, Rome, Venice, Vicenza. See also *Le Biblioteche governative italiane nel* MDCCCXCVIII (Rome, 1900).

AREZZO. The Biblioteca Comunale contains some liturgical manuscripts of the 11th, 12th and 15th centuries.

ASSISI. Biblioteca Comunale. See the catalogue by the librarian, F. Pennacchi (*Boll. Ass. Mus. It.*, 1921).

BERGAMO. The Biblioteca Civica possesses some works printed by Petrucci ; madrigals of the 16th and 17th centuries ; manuscript vocal and instrumental music of the 18th century, and eleven volumes of youthful autograph compositions by Donizetti. Most of the music preserved here formerly belonged to J. S. Mayr. Librarian : A. Mazzi.

BOLOGNA. *a.* Liceo Musicale. This magnificent Library was founded in 1798 and opened in 1805. It contains the collections of Padre Martini, S. Mattei and G. Gaspari, and is one of the finest and most valuable musical libraries in existence. The musical instruments formerly here are now in the Museo Civico. See the elaborate published Catalogue, vol. i. (1890) and vol. ii. (1892), by G. Gaspari and F. Parisini ; vol. iii. (1893), by G. Gaspari and L. Torchi ; vol. iv. (1905), by R. Cadolini ; and F. Vatielli's *La Biblioteca del Liceo Musicale di Bologna* (Bologna, 1917). Librarian : F. Vatielli.

b. R. Biblioteca Universitaria. The music here is only manuscript, but it includes a missal of the 11th century, a valuable collection of sacred vocal music of the 15th century (see *Vierteljahrsschrift für Musikwissenschaft* for 1885), two operas by Scarlatti, and some sacred music of the early 17th century. Director : C. Frati.

c. R. Accademia Filarmonica. This Library

contains a small collection of printed and MS. music, chiefly of the 17th and 18th centuries, including the various compositions submitted for the Academy's Diploma. See the catalogue by A. Bonora (*Boll. Ass. Mus. It.*, 1910–13). There is also a collection of MSS., chiefly autograph letters, presented by Dr. M. Masseangeli, of which a catalogue was issued in 1881. Librarian : A. Bonora.

d. San Petronio. The church archives contain some vocal sacred music (both printed and manuscript) of the 16th century. See Dr. L. Frati : *Notizie storiche sugli scrittori e miniatori dei libri corali della chiesa di S. Petronio,* etc. (in the *Rivista delle Biblioteche,* Ann. vi. p. 169, etc.), and the catalogue by A. Bonora (*Boll. Ass. Mus. It.*, 1913).

e. Raimondo Ambrosini possesses a Library of works relating to Bologna, which includes a small collection of musical works of the 17th and 18th centuries, for the most part printed at Bologna. See the catalogue in the *Boll. Ass. Mus. It.*, 1913.

CESENA. Biblioteca Malatestiana (now Comunale). This celebrated Library possesses some old manuscript treatises. See J. M. Muccioli, *Catalogus codicum manuscriptorum Malatestinae Caesenatis bibliothecae,* etc. (Cesena, 1780–84), and Zazzeri, *Sui codici e libri a stampa della biblioteca Malatestiana di Cesena* (Cesena, 1887). Director : M. T. Dazzi.

CESTONA. The Biblioteca Comunale possesses some liturgical manuscripts, including an Antiphoner of the 12th century.

CIVIDALE. The Biblioteca Capitolare possesses some liturgical manuscripts (in neumes) of the 11th century, and some valuable mystery plays of the 14th century. See Coussemaker : *Les Drames liturgiques* (Rennes, 1860). Director : Prof. Dr. R. della Torre.

CORTONA. See G. Mancini : *I manoscritti della libreria del Comune e dell' Academia Etrusca di Cortona* (1884). Director : W. Mancini.

CRESPANO. For the contents of the Canal Library see *Bibliotheca musicale del Prof. P. Canal in Crespano Veneto* (Bassano, 1885).

FABRIANO. The Biblioteca Comunale contains a small collection of Italian madrigals, etc., printed between 1565 and 1611. They are not included in Vogel's bibliography. See the catalogue by Dr. E. Filippini in Ann. v. of the *Rivista delle biblioteche,* p. 168, etc.

FERRARA. Biblioteca Comunale. The music here chiefly consists of printed vocal works by Italian composers of the 16th, 17th and early 18th centuries. See the catalogue in the *Boll. Ass. Mus. It.*, 1917. Librarian : Prof. G. Agnelli.

FLORENCE. *a.* Biblioteca Nazionale Centrale (since 1861 combined with the Magliabechiana and Palatina). The musical collections here are very important. The manuscripts include theoretical works of the 12th and 15th centuries, Laudi of the 14th century, and sacred and secular music from the 15th to the 18th centuries. The printed music is also very important, and includes early operas of the 17th century, and many works printed by Marescotti. Among the autographs, Vincenzo Galilei is especially well represented. See F. Fossi : *Catalogus codicum saeculo XV. impressorum qui in publica bibliotheca Magliabechiana Florentiae adservantur,* etc. (Florence, 1793–95) ; F. Palermo : *I manoscritti Palatini di Firenze ordinati ed espositi* (Florence, 1853–68) ; A. Bartoli : *I manoscritti italiani della Biblioteca Nazionale di Firenze . . . Sezione prima. Codici Magliabechiani* (Florence, tomo 1, 1879 ; tomo 2, 1881 ; tomo 3, 1883 ; tomo 4, 1885) ; *I codici Panciatichiani. I manoscritti della Biblioteca Nazionale . . . Sezione Palatina* (Rome, 1887, vol. vii. of the *Indici e cataloghi* published by the Minister of Public Instruction) ; *Illustrazioni di alcuni cimeli concernanti l' arte musicale in Firenze* (Florence, 1892) ; *Monatshefte f. Musikgeschichte* for 1872. Director : A. Bruschi.

b. Biblioteca Mediceo - Laurenziana. The liturgical manuscripts here are important, and include an Antiphoner of the 11th century. A precious collection of 13th-century music is described (with extensive excerpts) in vol. i. of the *Oxford History of Music.* The library also contains a portion of the Ashburnham manuscripts, among which are liturgies from the 10th to the 15th century, Greek hymnologia of the 12th and 14th centuries, treatises of the 14th and 15th centuries, etc. See C. Paoli, *I codici Ashburnhamiani della R. Biblioteca Mediceo-Laurenziana,* vol. i. (Rome, 1887–97 ; vol. viii. of the *Indici e cataloghi* published by the Minister of Public Instruction) ; and *Illustrazioni di alcuni cimeli concernanti l' arte musicale in Firenze* (Florence, 1892).

c. Bibliotheca Riccardiana. This Library possesses some treatises and printed and manuscript music of the 16th and 17th centuries, including a German organ-book (in tablature) of the early 17th century. See *Catalogus codicum manuscriptorum qui in bibliotheca Riccardiana Florentiae adservantur* (Leghorn, 1756), and R. Morpurgo : *I manoscritti della R. Biblioteca Riccardiana,* vol. i. (Rome, 1893–1900, vol. xv. of the *Indici e cataloghi* of the Minister of Public Instruction).

d. R. Istituto Musicale. This Library possesses the collections of the late A. Basevi, containing valuable theoretical and practical works of the 15th-17th centuries. The Tuscan Court Library, rich in 18th- and early 19th-century operas, is also preserved here. See Burbure : *Étude sur un manuscrit du 16ᵉ siècle* (Brussels, 1882) and *Illustrazioni di alcuni cimeli concernanti l' arte musicale in Firenze* (Florence, 1892), and R. Gandolfi : *Biblioteca del R. Istituto Musicale di Firenze*

(Florence, 1901). A catalogue was published in the *Boll. Ass. Mus. It.* in 1910–11. Librarian: A. Bonaventura.

e. Biblioteca Marucelliana. Here are a few musical works printed in the early 16th century (described in Vogel's Bibliography, vol. ii.). Librarian : Dr. G. Tamburini.

GENOA. The R. Biblioteca Universitaria possesses a few printed works and some MS. lute-books, the most important of which is described by A. Neri in vol. vii. of the *Giornale storico della letteratura italiana*. Librarian : P. Nurra.

LEGHORN. The Biblioteca Comunale Labronica possesses a collection of libretti printed between 1706 and 1782.

LORETO. See G. Tebaldini : *L' archivio musicale della Capella lauretana. Catalogo storico-critico* (Loreto, 1922).

LUCCA. *a*. The Biblioteca dei Canonici contains liturgical MSS. (in neumes) of the 11th and 14th centuries, and choir-books of the 15th century.

b. The Biblioteca Comunale contains a few printed music-books of the 16th century and a MS. lute-book of the same period. For the latter see the *Giornale storico della letteratura italiana*, vol. viii. p. 312. Librarian: E. Boselli.

MILAN. *a*. The Biblioteca Ambrosiana contains liturgical MSS. of the 10th-13th centuries ; printed works (mostly sacred) by Italian composers of the late 16th and early 17th centuries, and autographs of Gaforius, C. de Rore, Zarlino, etc. See the catalogue, not yet completed, by G. Cesari (*Boll. Ass. Mus. It.*, 1910–11). Prefect : Dr. G. Galbiati.

b. The Biblioteca del R. Conservatorio contains a very large musical library, to which additions are being constantly made by the deposit of copyright copies. The library is strong in printed vocal sacred music of the 16th century, and also possesses autographs of Durante, Leo, Paisiello, Zingarelli, Donizetti, Bellini, Generali and Rossini. In 1889 the collection of G. A. Noseda was deposited here : it contains 700 autographs, 300 masses, 200 orchestral scores of operas, etc. See E. de' Guarinoni : *Indice generale dell' Archivio Musicale Noseda . . . con . . . alcuni cenni intorno . . . alla biblioteca del R. Conservatorio di Musica di Milano* (Milan, 1897). Librarian : G. Cesari.

c. Biblioteca Nazionale Braidense. This Library contains valuable liturgical MSS. of the 12th-16th centuries, and also some printed theoretical works and lute-books in tablature. See F. Carta : *Codici corali e libri a stampa miniati della Biblioteca Nazionale di Milano, Catalogo descrittivo* (Rome, 1891, vol. xiii. of the *Indici e cataloghi* issued by the Minister of Public Instruction). Chief Librarian : Count T. Gnoli.

d. The Archivio del Duomo contains a valu-

able collection of sacred music, comprising MSS. of the 15th-18th centuries, and a few rare printed works of the 16th and 17th centuries. See *Elenco dei maestri di musica le cui composizioni si conservano nell' archivio musicale della cappella del duomo di Milano* (Appendix iii. *a* to vol. ii. of *Annali della fabbrica del duomo di Milano*, 1877–85).

MODENA. Biblioteca Estense. The musical collections here, both MS. and printed, are important. The former contain valuable compositions of the 15th century, in which Dunstable and his English and foreign contemporaries and immediate successors are unusually well represented. There is a very rich collection of MSS. by Stradella and many 18th-century oratorios, operas, etc. For the printed works, which are almost entirely Italian and French, dating from the 16th to the 18th centuries, see V. Finzi : *Bibliografia delle stampe musicali della R. Biblioteca Estense (Rivista delle biblioteche*, ann. iii., iv. and v., containing careful descriptions of 321 works, with a good index). The Stradella collection is described by A. Catelani : *Delle opere di A. Stradella esistenti nell' archivio musicale della R. Biblioteca Palatina di Modena. Elenco con prefazione e note* (Modena, 1866). A catalogue of the whole library, by P. Lodi, has now been published (*Boll. Ass. Mus. It.*, 1916–24). Director: D. Fava.

MONTE CASSINO. Besides liturgical MSS. and treatises of the 11th-16th centuries, the Abbey Library contains a large collection of Neapolitan music in MS. (bequeathed by Maestro Rignano), including operas by A. Scarlatti, Leo, Vinci, etc., and the autograph of Pergolesi's ' Stabat Mater.' A Martyrology of the 14th century (formerly in the Cistercian monastery of SS. Vincent and Anastasius at Rome) is bound up with a valuable collection of 15th- and early 16th-century compositions for one to four voices, containing works by Bernardus, Cornago, Dufay, Okeghem, Oriola, Gaforius, Loyset Compère, Damianus, etc. The words are Latin, French, Italian and Spanish. Director: D. G. Piccinino.

MONZA. The Biblioteca Capitolare contains some valuable liturgical MSS. of the 10th-14th centuries.

NAPLES. *a*. The Biblioteca Nazionale possesses some liturgical MSS. of the 12th and 13th centuries, and a little printed vocal music of the 16th and 17th centuries. Superintendent : Dr. G. Burgada.

b. The library of some 40,000 volumes illustrative of theatrical and operatic history collected by Count Lucchesi Palli was made over by him to the town of Naples some years ago, and is now administered as an independent section of the Biblioteca Nazionale. Librarian : S. di Giacomo.

c. Real Conservatorio di Musica (Conservatorio S. Pietro a Majella). The Library is important for its collection of MS. Italian music (especially of the Neapolitan school) of the 18th and early 19th centuries. The printed works date from 1550–1728, and include some rare sets of madrigals printed at Naples. There is also a good collection of libretti. Some account of the contents of the library will be found in F. Florimo's *La scuola musicale di Napoli e i duoi Conservatorii* (3 vols., Naples, 1882). See also *Indici di tutti i libri e spartiti di musica che si conservano nell' archivio del Real Conservatorio della Pietà de' Turchini* (Naples, 1801). Director : F. Cilèa.

d. The Oratory of St. Philip Neri possesses an important collection of church music, chiefly of the 16th and 17th centuries. See the catalogue by S. di Giacomo (*Boll. Ass. Mus. It.*, 1918).

NOVARA. The archives of the Cathedral contain some sacred vocal music, mostly of the latter part of the 17th century.

PADUA. *a.* Biblioteca Nazionale. This Library, which is incorporated in the Museo Civico, contains a few printed musical works of the 16th and 17th centuries. Librarian : O. Ronchi.

b. The Biblioteca Universitaria contains MS. French and Italian songs (for one and two voices) of the 15th century ; MS. music in organ tablature by Hasler, Erbach, Sweelinck, etc., and a little printed vocal music of the 16th and 17th centuries. Librarian : F. Ageno.

c. The Library of the Episcopal Seminary possesses a small collection of theories and other music of the 16th and 17th centuries. Librarian : T. Lancerotto.

d. S. Antonio. The archives of the Cappella Antoniana contain some rare printed music and several autographs of Tartini. See G. Tebaldini: *L' archivio musicale della Cappella Antoniana in Padova. Illustrazione storico-critica* (Padua, 1895).

PARMA. R. Istituto Musicale. The musical works formerly in the Biblioteca Palatina of Lucca are preserved here and form what is known as the R. Biblioteca Palatina di Parma (Sezione Musicale). Some of the earlier printed works are described by Prof. G. Maruffi in the *Rivista delle biblioteche* (anno iv. p. 7), and the whole collection has now been catalogued in the *Boll. Ass. Mus. It.*, 1909–12. This catalogue also includes works from other libraries in Parma. Director : G. Gasperini.

PERUGIA. The Biblioteca Capitolare contains some liturgical MSS., including an Antiphoner of the 11th century.

PESARO. Biblioteca Oliveriana. A 16th-century MS. (songs and lute music) in this Library is described by A. Saviotti in vol. xiv. (1889) of the *Giornale storico della litteratura italiana.* Director : Prof. L. Castaldini.

PISA. The University Library contains a few theoretical works and a copy of Bucchianti's ' Arie, scherzi e madrigali ' (Venice, 1627). Director : U. Ortensi.

ROME. *a.* Vatican Library. The music in this library chiefly consists of liturgical and theoretical works. The former—both printed and MS.—are especially valuable, and there are many MS. treatises from the 10th to the 15th century. A collection of French Troubadour songs (13th and 14th centuries) and a manuscript (in the Urbino collection) containing vocal compositions of the 15th century (Dunstable, Binchois, Ciconia, etc.) may also be mentioned, but the contents of the library are still but imperfectly known. A complete catalogue of the MSS. under the title *Bibliotheca Apostolica Vaticana codicibus manuscriptis recensita* began to appear in 1885 and is still in progress. See also H. Ehrensberger : *Libri liturgici bibliothecae Apostolicae Vaticanae manuscripti* (Freiburg, Breisgau, 1897) ; H. Stevenson : *Inventario dei libri stampati Palatino-Vaticani* (Rome, vol. i. 1886–89 ; vol. ii. 1886–91) ; and G. B. de Rossi : *La biblioteca della Sede Apostolica ed i cataloghi dei suoi manoscritti* (Rome, 1884). Prefect : G. Mercati.

b. Barberini Library. This collection is now transferred to the Vatican. It contains some liturgical MSS. of the 12th to the 15th centuries, and valuable printed musical works of the early 17th century.

c. Archives of the Sistine Choir. For the valuable MSS. preserved here, see F. X. Haberl : *Bibliographischer und thematischer Musikkatalog des päpstlichen Kapellarchivs im Vatikan* (Leipzig, 1888. Beilage to the *M.f.M.*).

d. Archives of St. Peter's. The music here includes an Antiphoner of the 14th century, and some important collections of vocal compositions of the latter part of the 15th and beginning of the 16th centuries. See *Vierteljahrsschrift für Musikwissenschaft* for 1885 and 1887, and J. Wolf : *Die Musikbibliothek der Cappella Giulia in Rom* (*Kirchenmusikalisches Jahrbuch*, 1908).

e. Lateran Choir. The Archives contain MS. and printed sacred music of the 16th and 17th centuries.

f. Santa Maria Maggiore. This church possesses some graduals of the 16th century.

g. Biblioteca Casanatense (S. Maria sopra Minerva). The musical collections of Baini are preserved here. The library contains liturgies of the 11th–14th centuries ; MS. treatises by Ugolino of Orvieto, etc. ; a volume of three-part compositions by Okeghem and his contemporaries, and MS. works by Scarlatti and Hasse. The collection is rich in printed works —practical and theoretical—of the 16th and 17th centuries. Librarian : L. de Gregorio.

h. Accademia di S. Cecilia. This library is especially rich in printed music and libretti, and receives constant accessions by the copyright laws. Among the rarer books are the 'Liber quindecim missarum,' printed by Andreas de Montona (Rome, 1516), and the only complete copy known of Cavaliere's 'Rappresentazione di anima e di corpo' (Rome, 1600). Valuable purchases were made at the dispersal of the Borghese Library in 1892. There is also a collection of musical autographs. See the catalogue by O. Andolfi (*Boll. Ass. Mus. It.*, 1912–13). See also the *Catalogo delle opere di musica . . . che dall' anno 1836 all' anno 1846 sono state depositate nell' archivio della Congregazione ed Accademia di Santa Cecilia di Roma (s.l. et a.)* and the *Elenco delle opere musizali donate alla biblioteca della Regia Accademia di S. Cecilia da S. M. la Regina* (Rome, 1896). Librarian : Cav. F. Mantica.

i. Biblioteca Nazionale Centrale Vittorio Emanuele. Besides some liturgical MSS. of the 15th-17th centuries this library contains a few musical MSS. of the 16th-19th centuries, among which are a valuable copy of Vittoria's Psalms for four voices (with autograph corrections and additions by the composer), and some compositions by A. Scarlatti. Director : G. Bonazzi.

j. Biblioteca Chigiana. This Library possesses a valuable 15th-century MS. collection containing twelve masses by Okeghem, masses and motets by P. de la Rue, Josquin des Prés, and other contemporary composers. Librarian : Prof. G. Baronci.

SIENA. Biblioteca Comunale. This Library contains a small collection of musical works, both printed and manuscript. Among the former are a few 16th- and 17th-century madrigals, among the latter a 15th-century MS. containing treatises by J. de Muris, Marchettus of Padua, etc., and collection of songs by French minstrels of the 13th century. The music is catalogued under the heading 'Belle arti' in vol. vii. of L. Ilari's *Indice per materie della biblioteca comunale di Siena* (Siena, 1844–1848); the French songs are described by L. Passy in tome 5 (série 4) of the *Bibliothèque de l'École des Chartes* (Paris, 1859), and in *Mus. T.*, Nov. 1886. Librarian : F. Jacometti.

TREVISO. The Chapter Library of the Cathedral contains some manuscript vocal sacred music of the 16th and 17th centuries, but the greatest treasure is a complete copy of the rare 'Harmonice musices odhecaton,' printed by Petrucci in 1501. Librarian : A. Marchesan.

TURIN. *a.* Biblioteca Nazionale. The fire of January 1904, which destroyed so many priceless treasures in this library, fortunately spared the musical collections. These include a considerable number of printed madrigals of the 16th century, and a valuable series of ballets performed at the Court of Savoy between the years 1645 and 1660. A selection of music from this library was exhibited at the National Exhibition of Turin in 1898; the catalogue, after appearing in the *Rivista delle biblioteche* (anno ix.), was issued separately as *Esposizione Nazionale di Torino*, 1898. *Manoscritti e libri a stampa musicali espositi della Biblioteca Nazionale di Torino* (Florence, 1898). See also L. A. Villanis : *Alcuni codici manoscritti di musica del secolo XVI, posseduti dalla Biblioteca Nazionale di Torino (Atti del Congresso internazionale di scienze storiche*, vol. 8, Rome, 1905). Chief Librarian : L. Torri.

b. Biblioteca Civica. See *Biblioteca Civica di Torino : cataloghi, sezione teatrale* (Turin, 1913). Director : Prof. Dr. H. Mussa.

c. Cathedral (S. Giovanni Battista). The Library possesses some sacred vocal music (both printed and manuscript) of the 16th-18th centuries.

d. The Museo Civico possesses some liturgical MSS. of the 17th and 18th centuries. Director : L. Rovere.

URBINO. Biblioteca Universitaria. The only musical work appears to be an imperfect copy of Cavaliere's 'Rappresentazione di anima e di corpo' (Rome, 1600). Librarian : Count L. Nardini.

VENICE. *a.* The Library of St. Mark's (now transferred to the Zecca) contains much interesting music. Amongst the theoretical books are copies of the works of Galilei, Aron, Artusi, L. Folianus, Zacconi, Zarlino, J. Froschius, Gafori, Ornithoparcus, Burtius (*Opusculum*, 1487) and many others. The collection of practical music is rich in partbooks of madrigals, chiefly in Venetian editions. The following is a list of composers whose works are contained in this section of the Library : Agostini, Anerio, Antegnati, Arcadelt, Asola, Baccusi, Balbi, Berchem, Bertani, Bianco, Caccini, Cambio Perissone, Corvus, Croce, Donato, Doni, Dorati, La Faya, Ferretti, Fiesco, Freddi, A. Gabrieli, Giovanelli, Gero, Gombert, della Gostena, Sigismondo d' India, Ingegneri, Orlando Lasso, G. de Macque, Manara, Marenzio, A. Marien, Masotti, Mazzone, Merulo, F. di Monte, Monteverdi, Nasco, Peri, Petrino, Phinot, G. da Ponte, Pordenone, Porta, Portinaro, Primavera, Renaldi, Romano, de Rore, Rossi, Rosso, Rubini, Ruffo, Sabino, Spontini, Stabile, Stivori, Striggio, Tarditi, Tigrini, G. da Udine, Vecchi, Verdelot, dalla Viola, G. de Wert, Zacchino, Zappasorgo, Zuccarini, G. A. Bontempi, Crescentini, Crivelli, Frescobaldi, Grossi, Hartmann-Stunz, T. Merula, Miniscalchi, Moretti, Morlacchi and Rinuccini. The MSS. include works by Marcello (two Intermezzi and a Serenata, autograph, a treatise (1707), two cantatas, an aria and two operas) ; S. Albero ; D. Scarlatti (a Serenata *a* 4, and thirteen vols. of Sonatas, 1752–57) ; Perez (eight operas, 1752–55) ; Cafara ; T. Traetta ; L. Vinci ;

Sarti; Graun; Perotti; Haydn; Mysliweczek ('Demofoonte,' played at Venice in 1769); Bonno; Galuppi; Guglielmi ('Il re pastore,' 1767); Naumann; Leardini; C. Grossi; Venier (Procurator of St. Mark's, 1732–45); Stradella; Mattheis; Brusa; Giaji (Theatre Airs, 1738); G. Porta; Porpora (Theatre Airs, 1727); D. Terradellas; Hasse (five operas (1730–58) and two oratorios); A. Scarlatti (opera, 'L' Eurillo'); and the following twenty-seven operas by Cavalli: 'Gli Amori d' Apollo e di Dafne,' 'Alcibiade,' 'L' Artemisia,' 'La Calisto,' 'Il Ciro,' 'La Didone,' 'La Doriclea,' 'L' Egista Elena,' 'L' Eliogabalo,' 'Ercole amante,' 'L' Erismena' (two settings), 'L' Eritrea,' 'Il Giasone,' 'L' Hipermestra,' 'Muzio Scevola,' 'Le nozze di Teti e Peleo,' 'L' Orimonte,' 'L' Orione,' 'L' Oristeo,' 'L' Ormindo,' 'Pompeo Magno,' 'La Rosinda,' 'Scipione Africano,' 'La Statira,' 'La virtù degli strali d' Amore,' 'Xerse.'

There are also many detached cantatas and songs. For the Contarini collection, which is extremely rich in operas (some autograph) of the early Venetian school, see T. Wiel: *I codici musicali Contariniani del secolo XVII nella R. Biblioteca di San Marco* (Venice, 1888). Librarian: L. Ferrari.

b. The Museo Correr has a considerable collection of music, chiefly MS. compositions of the later Venetian schools. There are many autographs of B. Furlanetto, and church music, operas, intermezzos, etc., by Morlacchi, Bernasconi, Perotti, Salari, Pergolesi, Jommelli, Mayer, Lotti, Burzolla, Bertoni and many others. In 1881 the collection of Count Leopardo Martinengo, consisting chiefly of detached vocal and instrumental pieces, was added to the collection. See the catalogues in the *Boll. Ass. Mus. It.*, 1913–14.

c. Biblioteca Querini - Stampaglia. This library contains some manuscript vocal music of the late 17th century. See the catalogue by G. Concina in the *Boll. Ass. Mus. It.*, 1914. Librarian: A. Segarizzi.

VERONA. *a.* The Biblioteca Capitolare possesses some liturgical MSS., including a troper of the 11th century and a missal of the 13th century, and some MS. vocal music of the 16th and 17th centuries, including a volume containing nineteen masses by Orlando di Lasso. See G. B. C. Guiliari: *La Capitolare Biblioteca di Verona*. Parte Prima. Lib. I. e II. (Verona, 1888). Librarian: Prof. G. Zamboni.

b. Biblioteca Comunale. This library contains a little printed and manuscript music, mostly of the 16th-19th centuries, including autographs of G. B. Beretta, G. Ceffis, F. Morlacchi and others. See G. Biadego: *Storia della Biblioteca Comunale di Verona con documenti e tavole statistiche* (Verona, 1892), and the same author's *Catalogo descrittivo dei*

manoscritti della Bibl. Com. di Verona (Verona, 1892). Librarian: V. Fainelli.

c. Teatro Filarmonico. The collection of printed music of the 16th and 17th centuries preserved here is said to be of importance.

VICENZA. Biblioteca Comunale Bertoliana. This library possesses a small number of printed works (theoretical and practical) of the 16th and 17th centuries. See the catalogue by S. Rumor (*Boll. Ass. Mus. It.*, 1923). Librarians: Mons. D. Bortolan and Abb. S. Rumor.

Luxemburg

The Bibliothèque Nationale contains a small collection of early printed musical works, including copies of Wollick's *Opus aureum* (Cologne, 1505), and Twyvel (or Tzwyvel) de Montegaudio's *Introductorium musice pratice* (Cologne, 1513). See A. Namur: *Catalogue . . . des éditions incunables de la Bibliothèque de l'Athénée* (Brussels, 1865). Librarian: W. Colling.

Poland

CRACOW. See A. Chybinsky: *Die Musikbestände der Krakauer Bibliotheken von 1500–1650* (*Sammelbände* I.M.G., 1911/12).

a. The Musikverein possesses autograph and other MS. compositions by Polish musicians.

b. The University Library possesses over 4000 works of musical interest. For the MSS. see W. Wislocki: *Catalogus codicum manuscriptorum Bibliothecae Universitatis Jagellonicae Cracoviensis* (1877–81). The early printed works are described in the same author's *Incunabula typographica Bibliothecae Universitatis Jagellonicae Cracoviensis* (1900), issued as vol. iii. of *Munera saecularia Universitatis Cracoviensis*. Director: F. Papée.

c. The Chapter Library, in addition to music by Polish composers, possesses a small number of rare works of the 16th and 17th centuries.

Portugal

The great musical library of John IV. (1604–56) was destroyed in the Lisbon earthquake of 1755. The catalogue, however, was saved and has been printed and indexed by Vasconcellos. Besides a large number of religious works, printed and MS., by the best masters, the library contained madrigals by Lasso, Marenzio, Monteverdi, Morley, Willaert, and the Amfiparnasso of Orazio Vecchi; copies of early Italian operas: 'Euridice' (Peri or Caccini), Cavalieri's 'Rappresentazione dell' anima e del corpo,' and Monteverdi's 'Orfeo.'

EVORA. *a.* Cathedral. Magalhães, Masses (1631).

b. Bibl. Publica. Duarte Lobo, Natalitiae Noctis, 8 v., and another battered printed work by the same composer. Mendez, church music (MS.), and numerous MSS. of later masses.

LISBON. *a.* Bibl. da Ajuda. (Lib. of the Ajuda palace.) Some thirty MS. scores of operas by Jommelli, granted a pension by King Joseph (1750–77) on condition of sending copies of all his works ; Portuguese operas by Antonio d'Almeida ; and nine Italian operas by Marcos Portugal. Lima, operas and oratorios. Printed : Correia de Araujo, Libro de Tientos (1626).

b. Cathedral. A quantity of Portuguese church music including MSS. of John IV. Adjuva nos, 4 v.

c. Bibl. Nacional. MSS., Leite, church music ; Marcos Portugal, opera 'Semiramide' (1801) ; Rebello, Psalms, etc. (1657), part-books (incomplete), Correia de Araujo, Libro de Tientos (1626).

MAFRA. Bibl. Publ. Church music for male voices (unaccomp.), by Marcos Portugal.

Spain

AVILA. Cathedral. As in most Spanish cathedrals, much music disappeared during the invasion of 1808 and subsequent disturbances. MS. masses of Juan del Vado, showing transition from polyphonic style to figured bass ; Ave Virgo (6 v.) on themes from Guerrero's motet, has organ part and a note that the voice parts were doubled by strings. Late MS. of Morales, Off. Defunctorum, and Aguilera, Magnif. Printed T. and B. partbooks of Guerrero, Motets (1597).

R. Monasterio de Santa Ana. MS. part-books (16th cent., incomplete) of early works of Guerrero and Ribera. Printed : Guerrero, Motets, 1597 (completing those in Cathedral) ; Lassus, Sacrae Cantiones (1578), Victoria, Motets (1572).

BARCELONA. *a.* Bibl. Musical de la Diputació. MSS. : Spanish madrigals, Flecha and Vila (one by Morales) ; music to Calderon's 'Jardin de Falerina.' Printed : Motetti de la Corona [1526] and other early sets ; Flecha, Ensaladas, bass (1581) ; Guerrero, Canciones y villanescas, Sup. 2 (1589) ; Morales, Masses (1544) ; magnificats (1583) ; Peri, 'Euridice' (1600) ; Raval, motets, 5 v. (1593) ; Ruimonte, madrigals, quintus (1614) ; Vasquez, Agenda defunctorum (1556) ; Victoria, Masses, etc., 8-12 v. (1600), incomplete ; Vila, Madrigals, alto (1561). Tablature : L. Milan (1535), Fuenllana (1554), Amat (1639 ?), Sanz (1674). Catalogue, 2 vols. By Felipe Pedrell (Barcelona, 1908–09). Librarian : Sr. D. A. Rubio y Lluch. Director of the Music Section : Mossen H. Anglés.

b. Orfeó Català. 15th-century MS. of Peñalosa and others ; Morales, Masses, Magnificats and Lamentations. Librarian : Sr. D. Francisco Pujol.

c. University Library. Printed works in tablature : Enriquez de Valderrabano (1547) ; Santa María (1565) ; Cabezón (1578).

CORDOBA. Cathedral. Printed : Guerrero, Masses, Lib. II. (1582) ; Victoria, Motets (1585) ; and a quantity of Spanish polyphonic music in MS. choir-books.

ESCURIAL. *a.* Biblioteca. MSS. : Cantigas of Alfonso X. (13th cent.), music and miniatures ; two 15th-century MSS., of which V. iij. 24 contains an English work (3 v.), 'Princesse of youth and flore of godlihede,' and discantus of unidentified piece by Dunstable, 'Durer ne puis.' Printed : Lassus, Moduli (1588), Sacrarum cantionum (1587), 9 Quiritationes divi Job (1587), Lamentations (1586), Thesaurus Litaniarum (1596). Spanish lute tablature : Fuenllana (1554), Mudarra (1546), Pisador (1552), Santa Maria (1565). Librarian : Excmo. Sr. Dr. Don Guillermo Antolín. Introduction advisable.

b. Archivo de Musica. Early MS. choir-books of Morales ; also Cevallos, Comes, Guerrero, A. Lobo, Rogier. 17th-century MS. Folías, etc., with variations for organ, and other early Spanish organ works. 18th-century MSS. (parts) music for plays by Calderon. Soler, quartets, str. and organ. Musical Director ; R. P. Isidoro Cortázar.

LEON. Cathedral. Mozarabic MSS., including 10th-century Antiphonary of King Wamba. Catalogue by Z. García Villada (Madrid, 1919).

MADRID. *a.* Bibl. Medinaceli. MSS. : Unpublished collection of Madrigals with Spanish words (*c.* 1580) by R. Cevallos, D. Garzon, Guerrero (Francisco and Pedro), Navarro and others, including motets by Morales and Cipriano di Rore ; a similar collection of early 17th century ; a set of parts of unidentified Italian comic opera (early 18th cent.) in style of Leo or Vinci. Printed : Harmonice musices odhecaton A, May 25, 1504 (Venice, Petrucci) ; and the following rare Spanish works : Guerrero, Canciones y villanescas (1589) ; sup. only (complete at Valencia, Patriarca) ; id., Motets (1555 and 1589) ; Ruiz de Ribayaz, Luz y Norte musical, guitar tablature (1677) ; Sancta María, Arte de tañer fantasía (1565) ; Vasquez, Villancicos, 3-4 v. (1551) ; id., Recopilacion, 4-5 v. (1560). Librarian : Sr. Don Antonio Paz y Melia. (Since this is the private library of the Duke of Medinaceli, an introduction is essential.) Catalogue in preparation.

b. Bibl. Municipal. 18th-century tonadillas and incidental music to Spanish plays (Calderón, Lope de Vega, Tirso de Molina) ; from the Teatro de la Cruz and T. Principe. Sbarbi Collection : 18th-century church music, Aranaz, Doyagüe and Soler. Catalogue : Madrid (1902).

c. Bibl. Nacional. The music is in the 'Sección de Bellas Artes' ; but tablatures are under 'Raros.' These include Cabezon, Daza, Enriquez, Fuenllana, Milan, Mudarra, Narvaez, Pisador, Venegas ; also Bermudo and Ortiz.

MSS.: M. 2431, masses by Morales and Clemens non Papa; M. 2433, Gombert, Magnif.; M. 1370, 1, 2. Romances, 3 v. (early 17th cent.); Pizarro, Tonos humanos, 3-4 v. (17th cent.); a modern copy of the Sablonara MS. (17th cent.) at Munich: 17th-century Spanish operas by Duron; A. Scarlatti, Cantatas (M. 2245-6), oratorio S. Casimiro, Ballo delle Ninfe (1706), from library of the Dukes of Osuna; Marcello, Ioaz, azione sacra; Spanish theatre music (18th cent.): Tonadillas, by Laserna; Soler, str. quartets with organ; Spanish Seguidillas and Portuguese Modinhas. ' Papeles Sueltos ' (unbound MSS.) include secular works of early 17th century, for 3-4 v. or solo and continuo; M. 811, guitar tablature (1705), M. 816 and 2478, harp tablature. Arabic Musical MSS. include al-Fárábi's Elements of the Art of Music. The Mozarabic (Visigothic) MSS. are described by Riaño, ' Early Spanish Music ' (1887). These and a second MS. of Alfonso X., Cantigas, are in the ' Sección de MSS.' Printed works include: Gesualdo, Responsoria, 6 v. (1611); Lassus, Mellange (1570–1584), Chansons nouvelles, 5 v. (1576), 1 and 2 Lib. Modulorum (1571–72), Moduli, 5 v. (1571), Patrocinium musices (1574). Madrigals: tenor of Notte Negri, Lib. 2, 4 v. (1567); Dolci affetti, 5 v. (1590); Spoglia amorosa, 5 v. (1590). Motets: Lib. 5 Eccles. cantionum, 5 v., quint. (1553); Peu d'argent, Lib. 1 and 2, Sacr. Cant., 5 v. (1555); Willaert, Musica nova (1559). A collection of 17th- and 18th-century books on the dance. Librarian: Excmo. Sr. Don Francisco Rodríguez Marín. Keeper of the Music; Sr. Don Francisco Suarez Bravo. Catalogue not accessible.

d. Bibl. Real (Library of the Royal Palace). 15th-century MS. ' Cancionero del Palacio,' published 1890 by Barbieri. The existence of MSS. of Domenico Scarlatti is denied, but the greater part of the music is inaccessible. Librarian: Excmo. Sr. Conde de las Navas. Diplomatic introduction desirable.

e. R. Conservatorio de Música y Declamación. Infantas, Sacrarum varii styli cantionum (1568, missing part in Bibl. Nac.). Director: Excmo. Sr. Don Antonio Fernández Bordas.

MALAGA. Cathedral. MSS.: Morales, Tu es Petrus, 5 v.; Guerrero, psalms, hymns and motets. Printed: Aguilera, Magnif. (1618).

MONTSERRAT. Monastery. 14th - century MS. ' Llibre Vermell ' (Red Book), Pilgrims' songs, showing beginnings of polyphony; Caças (caça = caccia = ' catch '), 2-3 v.; Dance of Death, said to be the earliest known (v. P. Suñol, Analecta Montserratensia, and Z.M.W., 1922, iv. 136-60). Printed works include Morales, Missarum Lib. i. (1544).

SANTIAGO. a. Cathedral. Codex Calixti II. (1120–40), including Pilgrims' Songs, 1, 2 and 3 v.

b. University Library. Liber Ferdinandi Regis (1055), Mozarabic MS.

SEVILLE. a. Cathedral (' Bibl. del Coro '). MSS.: Morales, motets; Guerrero, Passionarium (1580), masses, motets; Verdelot, Willaert, Josquin des Prés. A. Lobo, Credo, with organ; Lamentations. Printed: Aguilera, Magnif. (1618); Duarte Lobo, Masses (1621). An ' Inventario ' of 1721 shows how many MSS. of Guerrero, Josquin, Morales and Victoria have since disappeared. Musical Director: Sr. Don Eduardo Torres.

b. Chapter Library (' Bibl. Columbina,' founded by Ferdinand Columbus). MS.: ' Cantinelas vulgares,' early secular Spanish songs (end of 15th cent.), and another 15th-century MS. Printed: Rare works printed by Petrucci; Frottole, Lib. xi. (1514), the only example known; Harmonice musices odhecaton A. (1502, Jan. 14) (catalogued under Castellanus); Bossinensis, Tenori e contrabassi intabulati (1509); Damonis, Laude Lib. ii. (1507); Motetti, B., Lib. i. (1503), Lib. iii. (n.d.); Pisano, Le canzone del Petrarcha (1520); counter-tenor of Neuf basses dances, printed by Attaignant (1530). All these were bought by Ferdinand Columbus (son of the discoverer of America). They bear the name of the place, the price paid, and the rate of exchange on the day. The library also contains a complete set of Guerrero, motets (1597). Librarian: Sr. Dr. Don José Moreno Maldonado. The catalogue of printed books includes the printed music. 5 vols. published, as far as T.

TOLEDO. a. Cathedral. The Mozarabic MSS. are described by Riaño, ' Early Spanish Music.' Polyphonic MSS. include a splendid collection of Morales in 16th-century illuminated choirbooks. Also Escobedo, F. and P. Guerrero, A. Lobo, Navarro, Victoria, and many works by Josquin des Prés. Printed: Guerrero, Masses (1582); Rogier, Masses (1598); Victoria, Motets (1585). Librarian: Sr. Dr. Don Eduardo Estella.

b. Bibl. Provincial. MSS.: Reglas de canto plano e de contrapunto (1410); Peñalosa, 10 motets (6 published by Eslava). Printed: Narvaez, tablature (1538).

VALENCIA. a. Cathedral. MSS. of Guerrero, hymns and requiem; Ginés Pérez and Victoria.

b. Colegio del Patriarca. MS.: partbooks of Guerrero, Lassus, G. Pérez, Ribera, Robledo and Navarro. Choir-books containing Clemens non Papa, Comes, A. Lobo, Morales, Navarro, B. Ribera, Vecchi and Victoria. Printed: Guerrero, Masses (1582); Canciones y villanescas (1589), complete; A. Lobo, Masses (1602); Victoria, Motets (1572 and 1585). Catalogue: v. Ripollés, Bol. de la Soc. Castellonense de Cultura, vi. (1925); and H. Anglés, Joan Pujol (Barcelona, 1926).

Sweden

On the music libraries of Sweden, see T. Norlind : *Vor 1700 gedruckte Musikalien in den schwedischen Bibliotheken* (*Sammelbände der I.M.G.*, 1907/08), where particulars will be found of some smaller collections not mentioned here.

FINSPONG. The Library contains Swedish liturgies of the 16th-18th centuries ; a few theories ; some partbooks of Italian madrigals ; and some French 17th-century chansons (both printed and manuscript). See B. Lundstedt : *Catalogue de la Bibliothèque de Finspong* (Stockholm, 1883). In 1904 the whole collection passed into the possession of the town of Norrköping.

STOCKHOLM. *a.* Kongl. Musikaliska Akademien. The Library contains 10,000 volumes of musical works, mostly modern, but including a few of the 16th and 17th centuries. See B. Lundstedt : *Notice sur les bibliothèques publiques de Suède* (Paris, 1895), reprinted from the *Revue Internationale des Archives, des Bibliothèques et des Musées*. A catalogue of the collection began to appear in 1905 with a list of scores and pianoforte arrangements of operas. In 1910 the first part of the list of books on music followed.

b. The Royal Theatre library is rich in music of the 18th century.

UPSALA. Kongl. Universitets - Biblioteket. The printed music includes many French and Italian works of the 16th and 17th centuries. The manuscripts chiefly date from the 17th and 18th centuries, and include over 100 autographs of D. Buxtehude. See the *M.f.M.*, 1889 ; the *Catalogus librorum impressorum Bibliothecae Regiae Academiae Upsalensis* (Upsala, 1814), and R. Mitjana : *Catalogue critique et descriptif des imprimés de musique des XVIe et XVIIe siècle conservés à la Bibliothèque de l' Université Royale d'Upsala*. Tom. 1. *Musique religieuse* (Upsala, 1911). Librarian : Dr. J. M. Hulth.

WESTERÅS. The Gymnasium Library contains some printed music of the 16th and 17th centuries. Librarian : S. Landtmanson.

Switzerland

BASEL. The University Library contains a few early printed works, but is chiefly notable for an important collection of MS. parts of symphonies and chamber music by some of the lesser - known 18th - century composers. See J. Richter : *Katalog der Musik-Sammlung auf der Universitäts-Bibliothek in Basel* (Leipzig, 1892, Beilage of the *M.f.M.*), the *Catalog der Schweizerischen Musikbibliothek* [established in 1902]. Pt. 1. *Musikgeschichtliche und theoretische Werke* (Basel, 1906), and E. Refardt's *Katalog der Musikabteilung der Öffentlichen Bibliothek der Universität Basel und der in ihr erhaltenen Schweizerischen Musikbibliothek*, of which the first volume dealing with the

musical compositions was published in 1925. Principal Librarian : Prof. Dr. G. Binz.

BERN. The Stadtbibliothek possesses some early liturgical MSS. and treatises, many containing music in neumes. See H. Hagen : *Catalogus codicum Bernensium* (*Bibliotheca Bongarsiana*) (Bern, 1875). Principal Librarian : Dr. T. Steck.

EINSIEDELN. The Library of the Benedictine Monastery contains important MS. treatises of the 10th - 15th centuries. See G. Meier : *Catalogus codicum manuscriptorum qui in Bibliotheca Monasterii Einsidlensis O. S. B. servantur* (tom. i., Einsiedeln, 1899). See also A. Schubiger : *Die Sängerschule St. Gallens vom 8. bis 12. Jahrhundert* (Einsiedeln, 1858), and (same author) *Die Pflege des Kirchengesanges und der Kirchenmusik in der deutschen katholischen Schweiz* (Einsiedeln, 1873). The library also contains the valuable and extensive collection of musical treatises brought together by R. L. Pearsall and presented to the Monastery by his heirs. Principal Librarian : Dr. P. I. Staub.

FRAUENFELD. The Kantonsbibliothek contains some 16th- and 17th-century printed musical works. Librarian : W. Gonzenbach.

GENEVA. The Bibliothèque publique et universitaire possesses some missals of the 10th, 14th and 15th centuries, and a small general collection of printed theoretical and practical works, including a few early treatises and some French 18th-century operas. See J. Senebier : *Catalogue raisonné des manuscrits conservés dans la Bibliothèque de la Ville et République de Genève* (Geneva, 1779), and *Catalogue de la Bibliothèque Publique de Genève*, pp. 1631-5 (vol. iii. 1879), 2661-2 (vol. v. 1885) and 3523-3530 (vol. viii. 1899). Director : F. Gardy.

ST. GALL. Stiftsbibliothek. The early MS. liturgies (with music in neumes) are most important. There are also a few early printed theories, among them the *Melopoiae* of Tritonius (Augsburg, 1507), and two MS. volumes containing 204 sacred compositions by Manfredus Barbarinus Lupas of Correggio, written in 1562 by H. Keller of Rapperswyl, with illuminations by C. Härteli. Some of the liturgical MSS. are described in Weale's *Catalogue of MSS. and Printed Books at the Music Loan Exhibition, London, 1885* (London, 1886). See also G. Scherrer : *Verzeichniss der Handschriften der Stiftsbibliothek von St. Gallen* (Halle, 1875) ; and the same author's *Verzeichniss der Incunabeln der Stiftsbibliothek von St. Gallen* (St. Gall, 1880). Librarian : Dr. A. Fäh.

SCHAFFHAUSEN. The Town Library contains a small collection of works on musical history, theory, etc., including a few early treatises. See *Fach-Katalog der Schaffhauser Stadtbibliothek* (2 vols., Schaffhausen, 1903–05). Librarian : Dr. K. Henking.

ZURICH. The Zentralbibliothek, formed in

1916 by the amalgamation of the Cantons-bibliothek, the Stadtbibliothek and a few smaller libraries, possesses some liturgical MSS. of the 11th and 14th centuries and some valuable 16th-century organ music and treatises on the organ. (On the latter see *Monatshefte für Musikgeschichte* for 1891.) Principal Librarian: Dr. H. Escher.

Yugoslavia

LAIBACH (LJUBLJANA). *a.* Prince Auersperg possesses a copy of F. Boccella's very rare *Primavera di vaghi fiori musicali* (Ancona, 1653).

b. The Lycealbibliothek contains a MS. gradual of the 14th century, and a small collection of printed music of the 16th and 17th centuries.

c. The Studienbibliothek contains some printed music of the early 17th century. Keeper : Dr. J. Šlebinger.

w. b. s.; rev. with addns. by c. b. o. Information on certain English libraries from e. h. f.; Spanish and Portuguese by j. b. t.

II. UNITED STATES OF AMERICA

The number and importance of music collections in the United States is constantly growing. They are no longer found exclusively in the main centres of population or at the chief institutions of learning. In response to a wide demand, music departments have been established in libraries all over the country.[1] In most cases, the purpose of these departments is to fill the wants of the general reader. They furnish information and diversion. The contents are primarily modern ; the accessions consist in current publications. In not a few instances, books and music are supplemented by piano-rolls and phonograph records. These are circulating libraries as distinguished from reference libraries. There are exceptions, however, which combine the two types. Notably the public libraries of New York and Boston continue to collect older works or rarities, and supply the needs of the student and scholar as well. The increasing space conceded to music in academic education is responsible for the large and excellent music libraries attached to many of the universities and colleges. A number of conservatories and schools of music maintain collections which exceed the scope of pedagogy. Certain historical and musical societies collect music and books on musical subjects for the use of their members. Musical autographs and similar treasures which the market may offer go frequently into the hands of private collectors. The most comprehensive and richest collection, of course, is the one in the country's national library, known as the Library of Congress, in Washington.

[1] See U.S. Department of the Interior, Bureau of Education, Bulletin, 1921, No. 33, *Music Departments of Libraries*, by a committee of the Music Teachers' National Association (Washington: Government Printing Office, 1922).

LIBRARY OF CONGRESS. The music division was created in 1897. In 1902 the Librarian of Congress, Dr. Herbert Putnam, appointed O. G. Sonneck chief of the division. With extraordinary skill and energy Sonneck organised and built up a music collection which not only stands first in America, but need no longer fear comparison with similar and much older collections in Europe. Except for the wealth of old manuscripts and autographs of the masters, which can be consulted only in some of the great European libraries, the Library of Congress offers to student and investigator more than ample material for reference and research. In certain fields (opera scores and libretti) the collection has attained a position unequalled anywhere. A provision of the U.S. copyright law demands the deposit, in the Library of Congress, of all works registered. This accounts, in part, for the rapid growth of the collection, especially in current publications. For the study of contemporary music its full significance will not be understood until fifty or a hundred years hence, when the historian of that day, bent on an examination of the musical trends of our own time, will find it for his purposes the most complete in the world.

The music collection in 1924 contained close upon 1,000,000 entries. It increases at a rate of over 15,000 a year. Not all the copyright deposits are placed on the shelves of the division. A great number of them is left in the custody of the Register of Copyrights or distributed among other Government libraries. The purchases average 3000 a year. Since 1903, the notable accessions of each fiscal year are mentioned in the annual report of the librarian. They form an impressive array. Suffice it to single out a few of the most conspicuous, such as the collection of books on music printed before 1800 (over one-third of all that were published before that date) ; orchestral scores of dramatic and symphonic works (over 10,000) ; opera libretti, including the Schatz collection (*c.* 25,000) ; early Americana (rare hymn-books and patriotic pieces) ; music of the Civil War and of the Great War ; over 2600 autographs by *c.* 650 composers (of whom 375 are American, represented by over 1400 works, most of which are gifts) ; a considerable number of autograph letters. The musical holographs include several unpublished symphonies of Clementi [2] ; interesting pieces by Wagner (a setting of the omitted passage in the 3rd act of ' Die Götterdämmerung ' in his hand, the Parsifal music he arranged for his birthday, 1880, sketches for ' The Flying Dutchman ' and the ' Ring ') ; the entire musical manuscripts of J. Peter Ritter (1763–1846) ; Mrs. F. S. Coolidge's gift of all the composers' holograph scores of chamber music which have won the ' Berkshire Prize ' ; and important specimens

[2] See Georges de St. Foix in *R.M.I.* vol. xxxi. No. 1, 1924.

in the handwriting of the older masters. Among 34 letters of Wagner are 14 to Bertha Goldwag, and a number of unpublished ones. An object of particular pride is the holograph music book cf Francis Hopkinson, the first native American composer (1731–91), and one of the signers of the Declaration of Independence. The Library possesses unpublished manuscript works of Haydn, Tartini, C. Ph. Em. Bach, Boccherini, and many later composers. One of its special features is the large number (over 600) of transcripts of rare orchestral scores of old operas or unique collections (such as Philidor's compilation of ballets) which are in the permanent keeping of European institutions and are not likely to come into the market. At the sale of the Cummings, Weckerlin, Martorell, Prieger and other collections, the library made large acquisitions. Among several en bloc purchases were those of the Albert Schatz collection of libretti and part of the music library of the house of Braganza.

The material is classified according to a plan devised by Sonneck. It was adopted in Dec. 1902 and revised in Apr. 1917. The classification is published. It serves as a model in many other libraries. The music and books are shelved according to their class, not according to composers, year of publication, or date of accession. The card catalogue is divided into three groups corresponding with the scheme of classification : Music (M), Literature of Music (ML), Theory of Music (MT). The last includes all works of instruction and instructive editions, school readers, etc. The catalogue of music is subdivided in a composer-, a class- or subject-, and a title-index. For the literature of music and instructive works, the dictionary form of catalogue is used. There are separate card catalogues of Americana prior to 1820, American prints between 1820 and 1860, libretti (according to author, composer and title), and an extensive index to American and European periodicals. There is no printed catalogue for the entire collection. But certain sections, as well as special composers, have been dealt with in catalogues prepared in the division and published by the library :

Classification : Class M, Music ; Class ML, Literature of Music ; Class MT, Music Instruction. Adopted 1902. 1917 (revised).
Dramatic music, catalogue of full scores, comp. by O. G. Sonneck, 1908.
Catalogue of early books on music (before 1800), by Julia Gregory, 1913.
Catalogue of first editions of Stephen C. Foster (1826–64), by Walter R. Whittlesey and O. G. Sonneck, 1915.
Catalogue of first editions of Edward MacDowell (1861–1908), by O. G. Sonneck, 1917.
Catalogue of opera libretti. Printed before 1800, prepared by O. G. Sonneck, 1914. 2 vols.
Catalogue of orchestral music, pt. 1, scores, comp. under the direction of O. G. Sonneck, 1912.
Report on ' The Star - spangled Banner,' ' Hail, Columbia,' ' America,' ' Yankee Doodle,' comp. by O. G. Sonneck, 1909.
Revised and enlarged edition of the chapter on the ' Report on " The Star-spangled Banner "' (issued in 1909), by O. G. Sonneck.

Detailed descriptions of the collection and of its workings are contained in several articles [1]

[1] Amer. Library Journal, 1915, vol. 40, No. 8, pp. 587–9 ; in the 1908 Proceedings of the Music Teachers' National Association, pp. 260-87.

by Sonneck. For an account of the current accessions, especially in rare and valuable items, consult the Annual Report of the librarian of Congress. The present chief of the music division (since Jan. 1922) is Carl Engel.

BALTIMORE. The Peabody Conservatory Library embraces about 2700 volumes of books and music. It is particularly strong in orchestral scores and text-books on harmony. Several small private collections have been absorbed.

BOSTON. a. The Public Library of Boston contains over 31,500 bound volumes ; 15,500 of these belong to the ' Allen A. Brown Collection ' and are for reference only. The balance forms part of the circulating library. The average yearly growth is about 600 volumes. Until 1894 music was not a feature of special significance, though efforts had been made to improve this state of things at various times. In 1858, Bates, the benefactor of the institution, gave the de Kondelka collection to the library. This was purchased in Europe through the agency of A. W. Thayer, who added 100 volumes of his own to the original 400 : among these were publications of the 15th-18th centuries. Some time later, 48 MS. scores were selected and copied by S. W. Dehn at Bates's request ; but in 1883, when William F. Apthorp reported on the musical contents of the library, it was deficient in classical and modern orchestral scores. This deficiency was speedily and richly made good by the late Allen A. Brown, who gave 6382 vols. of music in 1894, thus raising the collection to a very high place among musical libraries. The donor continued his generosity until his death in 1916, adding about 300 vols. a year. Symphonies by Haydn to the number of 87, operatic scores of the 18th and 19th centuries (including 20 by Simon Mayr), are contained in this collection. Among European rarities are Caccini's ' Euridice,' 1600, and a good collection of 16th-century theoretical works. Of American rarities there are Hopkinson's Seven Songs, 1788 ; two copies of the Bay Psalm Book, 1640 ; Flagg's Collection of Psalms (Boston), 1764 ; and Billing's Music in Miniature (Boston), 1779. The collection has been enriched by many gifts from the private library of Philip HALE. A printed catalogue of the Allen A. Brown Collection was published by the trustees of the library in 1916. From time to time brief reading lists have been issued, notably Landmarks in Music, Boston, 1630–1924, compiled by R. G. Appel, the present curator of the collection.

b. The New England Conservatory of Music, founded in 1867, maintains a library of over 5000 vols. for the special use of its faculty and students. It contains among its treasured possessions the autograph sketches of Claude Debussy for his opera ' Pelléas et Mélisande,' and several autograph scores by its present director (since 1897), George W. Chadwick.

c. The library of the Harvard Musical Association (not connected with the University) numbers about 10,000 volumes of music and books. It is well supplied with the scores of the classic repertory and with chamber music. It has an excellent assortment of Russian and other modern music.

d. The private collection of Francis Driscoll specialises in early Americana and first editions of Stephen C. Foster.

BUFFALO. The Grosvenor Library music collection began to extend when the music room was provided in the addition built in 1921–22. The collection at present comprises approximately 1900 books, and 27,000 pieces of sheet music. It is strongest in songs, 1810–1920. The charter prohibits the removal of books from the library. During the past few years the library has secured the Delaney collection of popular songs (about 13,000 pieces); the W. W. Nolen collection of sheet music (about 8000) ; the F. C. M. Lautz collection of symphony scores (on deposit) ; the Louis C. Elson music library (about 9000 volumes and pieces) ; the Buffalo Philharmonic library (on deposit) ; the Ossian Lang collection of songs (about 1000) ; the Frank Dumont collection of songs (about 2000). The yearly growth is irregular. The great advance has come since 1922. The average number of readers is about 1200 annually, but the music room, which has two grand pianos, has an attendance of about 4000, including musicales, rehearsals, meetings, visitors, as well as readers.

CHICAGO. a. The music section of the Chicago Public Library was organised in 1915, the first selections being made, at the invitation of the library, by a group of Chicago music critics, Felix Borowski, Glenn Dillard Gunn and Karleton Hackett. The collection is chiefly of a popular nature and for purposes of circulation. A catalogue of its contents was published in 1923. At present the number of bound volumes is about 7000, and that of pieces of sheet music 15,000. It has an average of 5500 readers a year.

b. The Newberry Library is a free library of reference, which was established in 1887 and is maintained by the moiety of the estate of Walter Loomis Newberry, who died in 1868. Its musical collection contained, in December 1923, 13,756 volumes of music and books on music. The most important features are (1) the collection of scores of the classical composers, such as Bach, Beethoven, Berlioz, Chopin, Gluck, Grétry, Handel, Haydn, Lanner, Lasso, Liszt, Löwe, Mendelssohn, Mozart, Palestrina, Purcell, Rameau, Schein, Schubert, Schumann, Schütz, Sweelinck and Victoria ; (2) full scores of many of the rarer early operas ; (3) files of the older musical periodicals ; and (4) an ex-

tensive collection of American church hymnology. The collections which have been merged in it include that of Count Pio Resse, of Florence, purchased in 1889, containing many rare Italian works and a copy of the original edition of Peri's ' Euridice ' (1600), together with the libretto by Rinuccini ; the collection of the Beethoven Society of Chicago, added in 1890 ; the private library of Julius Fuchs in 1891, and that of Otto Lob in 1892. Hubert H. Main's collection of hymn-books and sacred music, numbering 3000 volumes, was acquired in 1891. The library of Theodore Thomas (566 vols.), given by his widow, which is kept intact, contains many orchestral scores annotated by Thomas, and three original manuscripts written by him. By his will, the set of programmes of concerts conducted by him 1855–1904, to the number of 10,000, was bequeathed to the library. In 1911 the library acquired the collection of Mme. T. Le Carpentier-Morphy of New Orleans, and in 1920 that of the late George P. Upton, presented by his widow. Additional noteworthy rarities of the Newberry collection are : a MS. volume of compositions for the lute by Vincenzo Capirola, with illuminated borders, early 16th century ; a 16th-century MS. vesper book of the Russian church ; the Graduale Dominicale, Mexico, 1576, the first choir-book printed in North America, of which only four copies are known ; ' Musica Transalpina,' by Nicholas Yonge, London, 1588 ; the holograph MS. of Richard Wagner's ' Festmarsch ' (1876) (in the Theodore Thomas collection) ; holograph MS. of Edward A. MacDowell's ' First Concerto ' (1882), presented by his widow ; and a considerable number of liturgical MSS. of the 13th to the 18th centuries, used in European or Mexican monasteries.[1]

CLEVELAND. The music division of the Cleveland Public Library includes about 600 volumes for reference use. In the circulating collection there are approximately 1950 books about music, 3300 bound volumes of scores, and 2300 pieces of sheet music. The music division houses also 332 volumes of orchestral music which are the property of the city of Cleveland, making the total number of volumes in this division nearly 8500. In addition there are about 1500 volumes of music and musical literature in the John G. White collection of Folk-lore and Orientalia, the most extensive library in these subjects in the United States. This collection is the gift to the Cleveland Public Library of a Cleveland attorney, for a long period President of the Library Board of Trustees. It now comprises over 50,000 volumes, with additions at the rate of 3000 to 4000 annually. Through this collection the library has unusually fine resources in ballads,

[1] George P. Upton published an article on the musical department of this library in the *Nation*, New York, 1889, vol. xlviii. pp. 361-2 and an article on the same subject, by W. N. C. Carlton, is printed in *Proceedings of the Music Teacher·National Association*, 1909.

folk-songs and dances, mediæval and Oriental music. Many volumes have been transferred to the music division, but the greater number are kept with the other John G. White books. The rarer portion of the great folk-song library gathered by the Joliet family of Dijon was purchased by White in 1923. A number of original manuscripts by Jean-Baptiste Weckerlin, the well-known collector of folk-songs, are of unusual interest.

DETROIT. The music department of the Detroit Public Library has been organised and largely developed since the library moved into its new building, and a special room was devoted to this department in 1921. The greater part of the collection is available for outside use, but a reference collection is being developed which includes such works as the complete Bach in the Bach Gesellschaft edition, the Handel Gesellschaft edition, the complete Palestrina, the Denkmäler Deutscher Tonkunst and Denkmäler der Tonkunst in Österreich, and the full orchestra scores of 8 of Wagner's operas. The complete collection includes books on music and the literature of music ; a large number of miniature scores, full orchestral scores with parts, and scores of chamber music with parts ; also the vocal and piano scores of operas, with the full orchestral scores of a few others, and many libretti. It also includes a collection of 3752 anthems and choral works which are loaned to choirs in sufficient numbers for their use. Besides normal increase the Library has added to its collection by the acquisition of the library of the late Theodore Spiering. The violin section has been increased by the acquisition of the music library of the late Maud Powell. The library also owns many phonograph records, which are loaned to schools and colleges for the use of classes in the music courses.

MINNEAPOLIS. The music collection of the Minneapolis Public Library now includes over 2500 books about music, 3300 bound music scores, and some 7000 pieces of sheet music. The library has acquired several small private collections as gifts, and in 1919 purchased the collection of Gustav Schoettle, which comprised several thousand pieces. The average yearly growth is about 700 items. During the year 1923 the music department circulated 20,000 pieces and served approximately 7000 readers.

NEW YORK. a. The Public Library of the city of New York has over 30,000 catalogued volumes devoted to music, besides several thousand uncatalogued pieces of sheet music

It consists of what were originally three distinct foundations—the Astor, Lenox and Tilden, established respectively in 1849, 1870 and 1887, and consolidated in 1892. The first had a fair collection of music, with the publications of the Plain-song and Mediæval Music Society of London, and of the Continental antiquarian societies, as special features. The nucleus of the truly remarkable Lenox Library is the musical collection made by Joseph W. Drexel of Philadelphia, and given to the library by will. Drexel began the formation of his library in 1858 by purchasing and combining the collections of H. F. Albrecht, a musician who came to America with the Germania Orchestra in 1848, and Dr. R. La Roche. Many purchases were made at the sale of Dr. E. F. Rimbault's library in London in 1877. A moderately trustworthy catalogue made in 1869 contains 12 vols. of 16th-century musical publications, 48 of the 17th, and 483 of the 18th. The unique copy of ' Parthenia inviolata ' is in this library. There are also several theoretical works of the 15th century, and some autograph scores of classical composers. Among the MSS. are two of great beauty and value, one a magnificent gradual on vellum, on which the writer, who calls himself Brother Leonard of Aix-la-Chapelle (Leonardo di Aquisgrano), laboured, according to his own statement, for seven years. It was finished in 1494, and is supposed to have been commissioned by one of the princes who assisted at the coronation of Maximilian as King of the Romans. The other MS. is a gorgeous Antiphoner of 1695, formerly belonging to Charles X. of France. A valuable historical collection of sacred and secular compositions of the 16th century is contained in a MS. vol. entitled ' ffrancis Sambrook his book,' which was in the Rimbault collection. Dr. Rimbault states that Sambrooke died in 1660, aged 70, and was buried in Salisbury Cathedral. A note in the MS., attributed to Dr. Alcock, says that the music was ' wrote out of the Vatican (or Pópe's Library) at Rome.'

The Astor and Lenox collections were united and transferred to the new building of the library at Fifth Avenue and 42nd Street in 1911. Since then the following collections have been absorbed by the music division : 1914, Julian Edwards (over 800 vocal and orchestral scores of operas, cantatas, overtures, suites, etc.) ; 1918, Doane collection presented by Mrs. George W. Doane (777 volumes of scores, books about music, sacred and secular American song-books, etc.) ; 1921, 1923, 1924, parts of the collections belonging to James G. Huneker, Henry E. Krehbiel and Arthur Mees ; 1922, musical manuscripts of Horace Wadham Nicholl. The number of readers in the music division during the year 1923 exceeded 23,717. This part of the library is for reference only.

The circulation department of the New York Public Library has its headquarters in the 58th Street branch. It supplies 47 branches of the Public Library system of New York City. Its musical collection contained in 1924 about 25,000 volumes. Since 1920 the department has specialised in the acquisition of contemporary music, chiefly orchestral scores. The strongest section is that of 19th- and 20th-century opera scores. Among recent additions is the collection of the late Charles T. Griffes (mainly scores of modern American composers), purchased and presented by the American Music Guild (1922). The growth of the collection since 1920 has been over 1000 items annually. Statistics of readers are taken only at the 58th Street branch, where the circulation averages 1500 a month.

b. Interesting musical items (old manuscripts and liturgical chants) are in the library of the Hispanic Society of America.

c. The private library of John Pierpont Morgan contains a number of rare musical publications and manuscripts.

NORTHAMPTON, MASS. The Forbes Library has about 1500 books on music, about 6000 bound volumes of music, and over 12,000 unbound pieces of music. Four phonographs with an adequate number of records are kept for use in schools.

PHILADELPHIA, PENN. The library of the Historical Society of Pennsylvania has valuable manuscripts and publications of the Colonial period.

PORTLAND, OREGON. The Library Association of Portland maintains a music collection which in 1924 contained more than 5000 volumes. Its aim is to serve the general reader. In 1923 a total of 19,525 music books circulated among about 6500 readers. A committee of three prominent musicians of Portland supervises the selection and recommends the purchase of new acquisitions.

SALEM, MASS. The Essex Institute has 1000 volumes of or upon music, and 4000 pamphlets, chiefly early American.

SPRINGFIELD, MASS. The City Library Association, in the Grace Rumrill Department of Music, maintains a collection of about 4000 volumes and a large number of phonograph records.

WASHINGTON, D.C. a. The Public Library of the District of Columbia maintains a music collection for purposes of circulation. Its accessions are in part derived through transfers of copyright deposits from the Library of Congress.

b. Frank J. Metcalf, compiler of a valuable bibliography on ' American Psalmody ' (1917), has gathered a private collection of some 1600 hymn- and tune-books. The earliest item in the collection is ' The American Harmony,' published by Daniel Bayley at Newburyport, Mass., in 1771. Other books of particular rarity or interest are : Gospel Hymn Book, by Abraham Maxim, printed in Maine, 1813 ; Psalms, Hymns and Anthems for the Catholic Church, printed in Washington, D.C., in 1830 ; Manual of the Broad Church, by William D.

Haley, pastor of the Unitarian Church in Washington, D.C., 1859, containing a collection of 70 hymns ; Hymns for the Unitarian Church in Washington, D.C., 1821 ; Hymns and Spiritual Songs, by D. Millard and J. Badger, printed at Union Mills, New York, 1831.

WORCESTER, MASS. The American Antiquarian Society has a collection of about 3000 volumes, including about 1600 volumes of early American psalmody.

UNIVERSITIES AND COLLEGES.[1] a. Harvard is not only the oldest American university (1636), but it was the first to establish a chair for music, in 1862, to which the American composer and organist John Knowles PAINE was appointed. The Harvard University Library has a special musical collection of 14,500 volumes and pamphlets, and includes the collected works of the most prominent composers, full scores of a number of important operas, and a fairly well rounded-out collection of treatises and musical biography and criticism. In addition to the main collection, the library has in its folklore stack an unusually complete set of folk-music (all countries) and ballads and songs (especially English and American). The library has also (not included in its special music collection) a fair collection of hymnology which is supplemented by that contained in the departmental Theological Library. A special file of 25,000 sheet-music songs is worth noting. These are arranged alphabetically by titles, and are in major part American. A similar file of instrumental sheet music has been arranged by composer. A series of 224 manuscript volumes contains the words of over 1500 Italian operas, sacred dramas and cantatas, which are uncatalogued. The musical manuscripts include autographs of Bellini, Haydn (part of the opera ' Armida '), J. J. Rousseau, Gabriel Fauré, J. K. Paine and other American composers. The average yearly growth of the collection is between 300 and 400 volumes. In addition to the main collection of Harvard in the Widener Library, there is a reference library in the Music Building comprising some 2000 volumes.

b. Yale University Library. The music section in the General University Library contains about 6000 volumes. These are divided between the literature of music, with a very good collection of historical and theoretical works, and vocal and church music. Instrumental music has been transferred to the library of the School of Music. The library is particularly strong in song collections. The rate of growth is about 100 volumes a year. The library of the School of Music is intended as a working collection for the benefit of students in the Music School, specialising in works to which reference is made in the very complete courses in musical history which are

[1] Cf. the article DEGREES IN MUSIC: AMERICAN UNIVERSITIES.

part of the curriculum, as well as in any music which students may wish to perform or which they may have an opportunity of hearing. The most complete sections are orchestral scores, chamber music, compositions for the pianoforte, and works of modern French composers in all forms. The collection of Horatio Parker's compositions, published works and manuscripts, has found a fitting place in the University, whose first dean of the music department he was.

The Lowell Mason collection of church music is at present kept at the School of Music. It contains about 6000 volumes of works published before 1870. It consists principally of treatises in English and German and in collections of hymns. It has a very complete list of song- and hymn-books published in the United States. Its most notable rarity is a copy of the first edition of Bach's first published work, the 'Klavier Übung, Leipzig, In Verlegung des Autoris, 1726.' No additions are made to the Lowell Mason Library.

A catalogue of both the University and the Lowell Mason collections was made by J. Sumner Smith.

c. University of Illinois, Urbana, Ill. The music collection of the University library contains about 6500 compositions, about 2000 books on musical subjects, 250 bound volumes of musical periodicals, and about 400 pamphlets, catalogues, etc.

d. Oberlin College, Oberlin, Ohio. The music collections of Oberlin College are two: first, a circulating library of music which is maintained by the Conservatory of Music. This collection includes about 25,000 pieces of sheet music for voice, piano, organ, string, wind and other instruments; second, the Oberlin College Library takes care of the literature of music, including the history of music, and musical theory, biographies and periodicals. In addition it has a good working collection of operas, oratorios, songs and music of historical interest. The two collections comprise a total of about 10,000 volumes. It is a general collection rather carefully selected, particularly strong for purposes of the historical worker. Additions average 750 a year.

e. University of Rochester, Rochester, N.Y. The library is attached to, and housed in, the Eastman School of Music. It was established in 1904 (and is supported) by Hiram W. Sib'ey of Rochester. The collection is strong in chamber music and in literature on French music and the French theatre. A complete set of French musical and dramatic almanacs from 1750 to date, with unique copies of those for the years 1735-6-7, is especially notable. The collection, though comparatively young, has absorbed the libraries of Arthur Pougin (literature of French music and theatre), H. P. Kreiner (history of Russian music, operas and

folk-songs), O. G. Sonneck (miscellaneous music and literature, including periodicals), Dr. M. J. Fleming (literature concerning violin, pamphlets, clippings, manuscript dictionary of violin and bow makers A-F), H. E. Krehbiel (material on folk-song and folklore from his collection), and chamber music, orchestral music, operas and manuscripts from Arthur Hartmann's library. The average yearly growth averages 1600 volumes. Among signal rarities is the autograph manuscript score of Sir Henry R. Bishop's opera 'Clari, or The Maid of Milan,' containing the song 'Home, sweet Home,' and the autograph of an early work by C. Saint-Saëns, for violin and piano, entitled 'Caprice brillant.' The Brown collection, which through Mrs. C. K. Rogers became the repository of all the works by her father John BARNETT (q.v.), contains many interesting autographs. The librarian is Miss Barbara Duncan (1924).

f. Hartford, Connecticut. The Theological Seminary has about 1000 volumes on music.

g. Bowdoin College, Brunswick, Maine. The Bowdoin College Library specialises in collecting musical settings of Longfellow's poems. It has collected about 1000 of these compositions.

Other universities which maintain considerable music collections as part of their libraries are Columbia (New York), Kansas (Lawrence) and North-western (Evanston, Ill.).

LIBRARIES FOR THE BLIND. a. The New York Institute for the Education of the Blind (New York City) has about 800 pieces of music. The Institute also publishes music for the blind.

b. The Perkins Institution and Massachusetts School for the Blind (Watertown, Mass.) contains in its special library about 250 books on music and over 5000 separate compositions. These are chiefly solos for the piano and songs, with a few choruses for mixed voices. The yearly additions average 200. The average number of readers is 2000 a year.

c. The Iowa College for the Blind (Vinton, Ia.) has about 1000 pieces of music and books on musical subjects.   C. E^L.

LIBRETTO, diminutive of the Italian libro, and meaning 'little book,' is the term generally used to denote the text of an opera or oratorio, but more especially the former. Libretti have undergone many changes in style and character corresponding to changes in musical development; indeed the librettist has frequently played nearly as important a part in such developments as the composer.

An opera libretto is to all intents and purposes a stage play cast in a certain mould, conditioned by musical requirements, and it may be noted that it was really the development of the aria and the formal musical number which marked the first differentiation. Thus the early Florentine experimenters in the opera form would employ their musica parlante in their setting of the text of a play, so that the librettist as such did not come into his own until it was found necessary for the composer to break the monotony of his recitative with moments of purely lyrical expression. Thus arose the aria for which the poem had to be provided, and the difficulty with which the librettist was confronted, owing to the claims of the singers, in maintaining a proper balance between musical and dramatic interest, a balance which Gluck and Calzabigi sought to restore after the type represented by Metastasio's libretti had become prevalent. In later operatic developments the fanciful and fantastic elements of the ' romantic ' school offered special opportunities to the imagination of the librettist, while the more recent Italian school again has offered scope for the invention of plots with swiftly moving dramatic action. Meanwhile Wagner had solved all difficulties for himself by writing his own texts, as did Charpentier and Borodin, and in two important cases Debussy (' Pelléas et Melisande) ' and Strauss (' Salome ') have reverted to the setting of actual plays practically in their entirety.

History has shown that the indispensable requirements for a successful opera libretto cannot be absolutely defined. Sometimes it appears that the musical expression is sufficient to outweigh dramatic and literary deficiences of the text, and we may predicate that real human interest in the central situations comes first in importance ; next, it must afford scope to the composer for musical illustration and expression of those moments. In fact the sway of music is such that it can easily compensate for the absence of literary or poetic style ; there are innumerable instances where it has been successfully left to the singer to simulate the delivery of true elevation of thought or passion, only suggested by the text in the crudest form. This, however, is ultimately a matter which concerns the composer alone, for we measure his inspiration by the result. Another example of the power of the music lies in the modern rejection of Wagner's doctrine that the period of an opera must necessarily be put back into legendary times. Many theoretic ideals are shattered by the colder logic of practice, for, in opera, music can idealise almost everything it couches, and its truthfulness of expression or the reverse is not to be measured by comparison with actualities.

Many famous librettists will be found under their own names in this Dictionary ; attention may be called to : RINUCCINI, the Florentine poet, whose texts were set by Peri, Caccini, Monteverdi and Gagliano ; FERRARI, poet and composer ; ZENO, 1668–1750, court poet in Vienna and Venice, supplied texts for, amongst others, Caldara ; METASTASIO, whose work enjoyed enormous popularity, being set by all the leading opera composers of his time—Hasse,

Porpora, Piccinni, Paisiello, Gluck, Mozart, Caldara, etc., many texts, indeed, being set over and over again. Arne's ' Artaxerxes ' was a translation of Metastasio's text.

In the foundation of French opera Perrin was associated with Cambert and Lully. The ' Armide ' of Quinault, who wrote for Lully, was later set by Gluck. Other French librettists to be mentioned are Sedaine (1719–97), librettist to Philidor, Monsigny and Grétry, and Favart (1710–92) (his ' Bastien et Bastienne ' was set in a German version by Mozart).

Calzabigi (1714–95) was Gluck's collaborator in ' Orfeo,' ' Alceste ' and ' Paride ed Elene.'

DA PONTE wrote ' Nozze di Figaro,' ' Don Giovanni ' and ' Così fan tutte,' and SCHIKANEDER ' Die Zauberflöte.'

Weisse, 1726–1804, collaborated with Hiller in the foundation of the German Singspiel, and Kind wrote ' Der Freischütz ' for Weber. Bouilly was the author of ' Les Deux Journées ' and the original version of ' Fidelio.'

The text of Cherubini's ' Anacreon ' was by Mendouze, and that of Spontini's ' La Vestale ' was by Jouy (V. J. Étienne).

In Italian opera of the 19th century the chief librettists were : ROMANI, associated with Bellini and Donizetti ; Carmmarano, wrote ' Lucia ' and ' Il Trovatore ' ; Piave, ' Rigoletto,' ' Traviata ' ; Ghislanzoni, ' Aïda,' and BOITO, ' La Gioconda,' ' Falstaff,' ' Otello ' and his own ' Nerone.'

In French opera of the same period SCRIBE wrote for Boieldieu ' Dame Blanche ' ; Auber, ' Fra Diavolo ' ; Verdi, ' Vêpres siciliennes ' ; and Meyerbeer, ' L'Africaine ' and ' Robert le Diable.' He was associated with Deschamps in ' Les Huguenots ' and ' Le Prophète.' (See also SAINT - GEORGES.) Barbier and Carré wrote ' Faust ' and ' Mignon ' ; Meilhac was associated with Halévy in ' Carmen ' and with Gille in ' Manon ' ; Massenet was also supplied with texts by Gallet and H. Cain.

The librettos of Puccini's most famous operas, ' La Bohème,' ' Tosca ' and ' Madame Butterfly,' are by L. Illica and G. Giacosa.

H. von Hofmannsthal wrote for Strauss ' Elektra,' ' Salome,' ' Der Rosenkavalier,' etc.

Among English librettists there should be mentioned Nahum Tate, the author of ' Dido and Aeneas ' (Purcell), Bickerstaffe and Gay of the ballad opera period.

J. R. PLANCHÉ wrote ' Oberon ' for Weber. Alfred BUNN wrote ' The Bohemian Girl,' J. Oxenford ' Lily of Killarney,' Fitzball ' Maritana ' and H. F. CHORLEY ' The Amber Witch,' etc.

In a later period Mackenzie's ' Colomba ' and ' Troubadour ' had texts by F. HUEFFER. Julian Sturgis wrote ' Ivanhoe ' (Sullivan), ' Nadeshda ' (Goring Thomas) and ' Much Ado about Nothing ' (Stanford).

In light opera the outstanding names have

been W. S. Gilbert, Basil Hood and Sydney
Grundy, the first of whom, through his masterly
collaboration with SULLIVAN (*q.v.*), created a
unique type.

It remains to add a few words about translations of libretti into English. This is a difficult
matter for the translator, who has often failed
in trying to satisfy all the claims of poetic diction, correct accentuation, correspondence between the salient notes and words in a phrase,
rhyme and literalness. It is obvious that
something has to be sacrificed, and it is a safe
rule to sacrifice rhyme and literalness first. A
carefully written paraphrase can be made to
fit the case, and occasionally it is legitimate to
make a slight alteration in the music itself, at
any rate as regards note values in the vocal
part. It is a matter for satisfaction that the
standard of translation into English has improved in recent years, for inferior work is
unquestionably hampering to the English temperament, and hinders truth of expression in
performance, besides annoying the hearer, and
even tending to discourage the appreciation of
opera as an art-form. The best work has been
done in the translation of the Wagner operas ;
there are now several good versions of the
' Ring,' notably that by Ernest NEWMAN. It
is, however, one thing to possess a good translation and quite another to get it into general use,
owing to the unsettled conditions under which
the performance of opera in English is conducted in this country.   N. C. G.

LICHARD, MILAN (*b.* Uherska Skalice, Feb.
24, 1853), one of the earlier group of Slovak composers and a great authority on the folk-songs ;
now living in Bratislava. He was educated
in Skalice, Veľka Revúce and Šoprona, and
became a railway official under the Magyar
regime. His interest in music, which was at
first of a general nature, was his chief consolation under hardships and political disabilities.
Later on he specialised in the folk-music which
gave colour to his compositions, of which the
best known are : ' Škovránok ' (The Lark), for
mixed choir and soprano solo ; ' Sláva Ti
najvyšší ' (Praise to Thee, All-Highest), text by
the poet Vajansky ; ' Zmlknite žialne Kvíl'by '
(Hush your Laments), a funeral ode ; a Book of
Slovak Songs (composed in prison) ; the ' Songs
of Jonaš ' (16) ; a choral ode for the funeral of
Mudroň, words by Leštinsky ; a Rhapsody in
F ; six ' Garlands of Popular Song,' transcribed
in their appropriate modes, and the chorus
' Orel ' (The Eagle), composed for the first
celebration of Slovak independence (1919) but
never performed.

Lichard has done great service in the cause of
the Slovak folk-songs by insisting upon their
modal character and special rhythmic characteristics. In his versions he respects the archaic
nature of the songs and ruthlessly eliminates
the injurious influence of the gipsy music, with
its so-called ' Magyar scale,' and the spasmodic
nature of its rhythm.

An interesting article on Slovak songs by
Milan Lichard appeared in a pamphlet entitled
Slovak Peasant Art and Melodies (reprinted
from Prof. Seton-Watson's *Racial Problems in
Hungary*, Constable & Co., 1911).

                              A. K. ; transl. R. N.

LICHFILD, HENRY, madrigal composer,
fl. 1613. He published

' The First Set of Madrigals of 5 Parts ; apt for both Viols and
Voyces. Newly composed by Henry Lichfild London : Printed
for M. L., I. B. and T. S. tne Assignes of W Barley 1613.' (See
Engl. Madr. Sch. vol. xvii.)

The volume was dedicated to Lady Cheyney,
or Cheney, of Toddington House, near Luton.
Lord Cheney died many years earlier, in 1587.
The widow survived till 1614. Lichfild may
have been resident musician at Toddington,
but it is more likely that he was household
steward and that, like Henry WARD (*q.v.*), he
was an amateur musician. Lady Cheney
bequeathed a legacy of £20 to Lichfild.
Lichfild is one of the smaller figures among
the English madrigalists, yet some of his works
are pleasant to sing. Perhaps the best of the
set is ' I always loved to call my lady Rose.'

                                          E. H. F.

LICHNOWSKY, (1) CARL (*b.* 1758 ; *d.* Apr.
15, 1814), Fürst (Prince), by Russian patent
issued Jan. 30, 1773, was descended from an old
Polish family whose estates were so situated
that, after the partition of Poland, it owed
allegiance to all three of the plunderers. The
principal seat of Prince Carl was Schloss Grätz,
near Troppau in Silesia ; but Vienna was his
usual place of residence. He claims a place in
this work as the pupil and friend of Mozart and
the Mæcenas of Beethoven.

Readers of Burney's *Present State of Music*
will remember his eulogies of the Countess
Thun-Klösterle, so celebrated for her beauty,
intellect and culture, whose disregard for mere
form gave her the reputation of eccentricity,
but whose house and family had charms that
attracted even the Emperor Joseph and his
brothers thither on the footing of friendly
visitors. Of her taste in music it is sufficient to
say that she was a profound admirer of the
compositions of both the young Mozart and the
young Beethoven, at a time when such appreciation was by no means universal. Her
daughters—Georg Forster's ' Three Graces '—
were worthy of their mother. Elizabeth
married Rasoumowsky ; Christine (*b.* July 26,
1765) married Nov. 21, 1788, Lichnowsky ; and
the third the English Lord Guilford. Schönfeld, a Viennese, writes in 1796 of Lady ' Gil-
fort ' as a guitar-player of very high rank and a
singer of uncommon excellence, and of Princess
Lichnowsky as ' a *strong* musician who plays
the pianoforte with feeling and expression.'

Lichnowsky, without pretending to rival the
great magnates Esterhazy, Lobkowitz and

their peers in maintaining a complete ' chapel ' of vocal and instrumental music, had within five years after his marriage his regular Friday quartet of youthful virtuosi, Schuppanzigh, Sina, Weiss and Kraft, all of whom became famous, and also gave musical entertainments on a scale requiring a full orchestra.

His relations to the Prussian court compelled him occasionally to appear there ; and he thus found opportunity to give Mozart—only two years his senior—a practical and substantial proof of his affection, by inviting him, in those days of tedious and expensive travelling, to join him on one of these occasions free of expense. This was the journey in the spring of 1789, during which the King of Prussia offered Mozart the then noblest musical position in Germany ; a kind word from the Emperor, after his return, led him to reject it, without securing an equivalent. There seems to be no doubt that Lichnowsky, deeply moved by the distressing condition of his teacher and friend, had taken him to Berlin in the hope of improving his circumstances, and that the King's offer was partly due to his influence. Two and a half years later Mozart was dead, leaving a void in the Lichnowsky-Thun circle which there was no one to fill. Another two years and young Beethoven had come from Bonn.

The relations between him and the Lichnowskys are sufficiently indicated in the article BEETHOVEN ; but a current error must be corrected, namely, that the breach caused by the quarrel at Gratz in 1806 was final. Lichnowsky lived in a large house over the Schotten gate— both house and gate disappeared long since— and in the storey below him dwelt Beethoven's friends, the Erdödys. The Schotten and Mölker bastions were contiguous, and the Pasqualati house, on the latter, was in the same row with that of Lichnowsky, though a few doors away from it. This then was the reason why Beethoven was content to live in rooms in the fourth storey, looking to the cold north, and without a direct ray of the sun. He remained there from 1804–07, and then removed into rooms provided him by the Countess Erdödy.

An outbreak with the Countess led him to remove to the other side of the city, where he passed the years 1809 and 1810. Meantime, so complete a reconciliation had taken place between him and both Lichnowsky and the Countess Erdödy, that in 1811 he went again to Gratz, and on his return once more took his old lodging in the Pasqualati house, where he remained until the death of Lichnowsky.[1] It

1 Reichardt, under date Nov. 30, 1808, writes : ' Beethoven lodges with a Hungarian Countess Erdödy, who occupies the front part of the huge house, but he has broken completely with Prince Lichnowsky, who lives in the upper part of the house, and with whom he for some years resided.' During the ten years 1804–14, then, Beethoven moved from the Pasqualati house once only, but then for three years ; at the end of that period he departed finally. When, therefore, Ries (writing avowedly from hearsay) states ' he removed from it several times, and Pasqualati said " The lodging shall not be let, Beethoven will come again," ' he was evidently misinformed, at least in part ; but his error has been adopted and made the most of in all biographies and biographical sketches of

was during these last years that Schindler records the frequent visits of the Prince to the composer.

(2) EDWARD MARIA (b. Sept. 19, 1789 ; d. Munich, Jan. 1, 1845), son and successor of Prince Carl, distinguished himself as an agriculturist, but more as a man of letters. He stands high in Austrian literature as a national antiquary, especially for his great *History of the House of Hapsburg*.

(3) COUNT MORITZ, a younger brother of Prince Carl, was one of that small circle of most intimate friends of Beethoven faithful to the last. He was probably that Count Lichnowsky who published (1798) the seven Variations for PF. on ' Nel cor più.' After the death of his first wife he became deeply attached to the opera singer Mlle. Stummer ; but not until after the death of Prince Carl, when their daughter had already passed the stage of infancy, were they able to marry. It is in relation to this attachment that Beethoven is said to have written the Sonata in E minor, op. 90.

A. W. T.

LICHTENSTEIN, KARL AUGUST BARON VON (b. Lahm, Franconia, Sept. 8, 1767 ; d. Berlin, Sept. 16, 1845), studied music under Forkel at Göttingen. He served in the English army, returning to Germany, 1793, as gentleman of the bedchamber at the court of Hanover, where he produced his opera ' Knall und Fall,' of which he had written both words and music. In 1798 he became Intendant of the court theatre at Dessau, which, under his management, became a model theatre for all Germany. In about 1800 he was for some time co-director with Baron von Braun of the Vienna court theatre. After a period of directorship of the Bamberg theatre, he took over in 1823 the stage management of the playhouse, and in 1825 that of the Opera at Berlin. He composed a number of operas and operettas (Singspiele). (See list in *Q.-L.*)

LICHTENTHAL, PETER (b. Pressburg, May 10, 1780 ; d. Milan, Aug. 18, 1853), Doctor of Medicine, composer and writer on music. He studied medicine in Vienna, where he wrote several books on music and musical subjects, and settled at Milan, producing there in 1826 his important *Dizionario e biografia della musica*, which was followed by several other theoretical, æsthetical and biographical works. He composed 3 operas, 4 ballets, chamber music, pianoforte pieces, church music, songs, etc. (See *Q.-L.*)

LICKL, (1) JOHANN GEORG (b. Kornneuburg, Austria, Apr. 11, 1769 ; d. Fünfkirchen, May 12, 1843), church Kapellmeister from 1806 till his death. He composed operettas (Singspiele)

Beethoven since 1838. The new lodging in 1814 was in the lower storey of the Bartenstein house, on the same bastion. He retained it but one year ; for, on the departure of the Erdödys from Vienna in 1815, there was no inducement to remain, and Beethoven moved away from the Mölker Bastei, never to return.

O

for Schikaneder's theatre ; also masses, motets and chamber music.

His son, (2) KARL GEORG (b. Vienna, Oct. 28, 1801), was a virtuoso on the physharmonica, for which he composed a number of works, as also church music.

Another son, (3) AEGIDIUS FERDINAND KARL (b. Vienna, Sept. 1, 1803), was a guitar virtuoso, who also wrote Singspiele and an oratorio.

E. v. d. s.

LIDARTI, CRISTIANO GIUSEPPE, a popular 18th-century violoncellist and composer, lived, according to Burney, at Pisa, his birthplace, in 1770 ; and for some time in Vienna. Judging from the number of compositions published in London, as well as a fine portrait of his, apparently the work of an English painter, now in the possession of Messrs. W. E. Hill & Sons, he must have been in London between 1768 and 1780. Although represented therein as a violoncellist, he wrote apparently no solo work for that instrument, his compositions consisting of violin and flute sonatas, duets, trios, quartets, a sonata for viola pomposa, a musical drama, an aria with orchestra, and some catches and glees (E. van der Straeten, *History of the Violoncello*).

LIDL (LIDEL), ANDREAS (b. Vienna, c. 1740 ; d. ? London before 1789). He was one of the greatest baryton virtuosi, who increased the number of wire strings at the back of the instrument to 27. After visiting all the big continental cities, he made his début in London in 1778 with great success, and appears to have remained there till his death. He wrote a considerable number of quintets, quartets, trios, duets and a song. His baryton compositions remained in MS. The ' Anton ' Lidel which appears in many biographical works is the same as Andreas, the former name arising from an error.   E. v. d. s.

LIE, SIGURD (b. May 23, 1871 ; d. Sept. 29,[1] 1904), an eminent Norwegian musician, was a pupil of the Leipzig Conservatorium in 1891–94. He was soon afterwards appointed conductor of the Harmonien choral society in Bergen, and was the conductor of the Central Theatre. He underwent a second course of musical study in Berlin, and on returning to Christiania was appointed conductor of one of the best choral societies ; he was a good violinist, and among his compositions are a symphony in A minor, a ' marche symphonique,' an ' Orientalisk Suite ' for orchestra, a quintet for piano and strings, duets, cantatas, songs and choral works, many of which show such high qualities that if he had lived he would have taken a very high place among Scandinavian writers.   M.

LIEBE, CHRISTIAN (b. Freiberg, Nov. 5, 1654 ; d. Zschoppau, Saxony, Sept. 3, 1708), went to Leipzig in 1676 ; was organist at Frauenstein, 1684, afterwards rector ; became

rector at Zschoppau in 1690. He composed masses, motets and other church music, 4-8 v., mostly with instrumental accompaniments.

E. v. d. s.

LIEBESVERBOT, DAS, opera in 2 acts, text [2] (founded on ' Measure for Measure ') and music by Wagner. Produced Magdeburg, Mar. 29, 1836.

LIEBLICH GEDACT (*i.e. gedeckt*), literally ' sweet-toned covered or closed ' pipe. This class of organ stop is a variety of the old quite-stopped Diapason or Gedact. It was invented by the elder Schulze, of Paulinzelle, near Erfurt, and was first brought under notice in England in his organ in the Great Exhibition of 1851. It is made either of 16-foot tone (Lieblich Bourdon), 8-foot (Lieblich Gedact) or 4-foot (Lieblich Flöte). The pipes are made five or six sizes narrower than the Gedact, but are more copiously winded, and the mouths cut up higher. The tone, therefore, is nearly or quite as strong as that of the Gedact, though not so full, yet brighter and sweeter. When the three stops, 16, 8 and 4 feet, are grouped together on the same manual their effect is very beautiful. The late Edmund Schulze combined them in this manner in the choir organ at the Temple Church in 1860, also in his fine organ at Doncaster (1862). Lewis adopted the same plan at Ripon Cathedral, and it was followed by Willis at Salisbury Cathedral.   E. J. H.

LIED, see SONG, subsection GERMANY.

LIEDERKREIS, LIEDERCYCLUS or LIEDER-REIHE (Ger.), a circle or series of songs relating to the same object and forming one piece of music. The first instance of the thing and the first use of the word appears to be in Beethoven's op. 98, ' An die ferne Geliebte. Ein Liederkreis von Al. Jeitteles.' [3] It was followed by Schubert's ' Die schöne Müllerin, ein Cyclus von Liedern,' twenty songs, composed 1823, and published Mar. 1824. Schubert's two other series, the ' Winterreise ' and the ' Schwanen-Gesang,' [4] have not the special title. Schumann has left several Liederkreise—by Heine (op. 24); by Eichendorff (op. 39) ; ' Dichterliebe, Liedercyklus ' (op. 48) ; ' Liederreihe ' von J. Kerner (op. 35) ; ' Frauenliebe und Leben ' (op. 42). Of all these Beethoven's most faithfully answers to the name. The songs change their tempo, but there is no break, and the *motiv* of the first reappears in the last, and closes the circle.

G.

The English equivalent, ' song cycle,' is now in common use, and often applied to any set of songs by one composer meant to be sung in series, not necessarily the work of one poet. Song cycles are now so frequent as to

1 *Riemann.*

2 See *Quarterly Magazine*, Int. Mus. Ges., Jan. 1912.
3 Of the poet of these charming verses little information can be gleaned. He was born at Brünn, June 20, 1794, so that when he wrote the Liederkreis he was barely 21. Like many amateurs of music he practised medicine, and he died at his native place, Apr. 16, 1858.   G.
4 A publisher's title.

make any enumeration of their composers impossible.   C.

LIEDERSPIEL (Ger.), a play with songs introduced into it, such songs being either well-known and favourite airs—Lieder—or, if original, cast in that form. It is the German equivalent of the French Vaudeville, and of the English BALLAD OPERA (*q.v.*).

The thing and the name are both due to J. F. Reichardt, whose ' Lieb' und Treue ' was the first Liederspiel. It was an attempt to bring back the musical stage of Germany from artifice to natural sentiment. Reichardt's interesting account of his experiment and the reasons which led to it, will be found in the *A.M.Z.*, 1801 (709 - 17). After Reichardt, Himmel, Lortzing, Eberwein and a number of other second-class writers composed Liederspiel which were very popular, and they still are to be heard. Mendelssohn often speaks of his ' Heimkehr ' (Son and Stranger) as a Liederspiel, but that can only be by an extension of the phrase beyond its original meaning.

G., rev.

LIEDERTAFEL (Ger.), originally a society of men who met together on fixed evenings for the practice of vocal music in four parts, drinking forming part of the entertainment. These clubs arose during the political depression caused by Napoleon's rule in Germany ; and the first, consisting of twenty-four members only, was founded by Zelter in Berlin, Dec. 28, 1808. Others soon followed at Frankfort and Leipzig, gradually relaxing the rules as to numbers. Bernhard Klein founded the Jüngere Berliner Liedertafel, which aimed at a higher standard of art. These societies gave an immense impetus to men's part-singing throughout Germany. Since the establishment of the Männergesangvereine proper (male singing societies), the word Liedertafel has come to mean a social gathering of the ' Verein,' *i.e.* a gathering of invited ladies and gentlemen at which the members perform pieces previously learned. They are in fact informal concerts, where the guests move about, eat, drink and talk as they please, provided they keep silence during the singing. The Liedertafeln of the large male singing societies of Vienna, Munich and Cologne are pleasant and refined entertainments, not without a musical significance of their own.   F. G.

LIED-FORM. The term Lied-form has unfortunately been used by different writers with different significations; and the vagueness which results, conjoined with the fact that the term is not happily chosen, renders it doubtful whether it had not better be entirely abandoned.

Some people use it merely to define any slight piece which consists mainly of a simple melody simply accompanied, in which sense it would be perfectly adapted to many of Mendelssohn's ' Lieder ohne Worte,' and innumerable other pieces of that class of small compositions for the pianoforte by various authors, as well as to songs. On the other hand, some writers have endeavoured to indicate by the term a form of construction, in the same sense as they would speak of the forms of the movements of sonatas. For the diffusion of this view Bernhard Marx appears to be responsible, and his definition will be best given in his own terms :

' Under this name of Lied-form we group all such pieces of music as have one single main idea, which is presented either in one developed section, or as a period (with first and second phrase), or even as a period divided into first and second similar parts, or into first, second and third parts (in which case the last is generally a repetition of the first). It is possible in Lied-form to have even two such complete forms aggregated into one piece ; but then they occur without close connexion or interweaving with one another, perhaps with the two parts twice or three times repeated ; in which case the second group will be called a Trio, and the third the second Trio, and be treated as a second independent piece. For the sake of contrast, such Trios will often be in another key, or in other key relationship, such as minor corresponding to major, and major to minor, of the same key, etc., return being afterwards made to the first portion and the original key to make the piece complete. In this Lied-form are cast most of the Lieder which are intended to be sung, dances, marches, many études, introductions, etc.' [1]

Marx further gives formulas, or types, of the harmonic distribution of this kind of composition,[2] and discusses the details of the structure at length.[3]

To this classification there appear to be two main objections. The first is the choice of the distinctive name ' Lied ' for a form which comprises dances, marches and other alien forms of music. Were there nothing else to say against it, it would certainly jar against our sense of fitness to have to speak of the funeral march in the Eroica Symphony, or the Scherzo of the Ninth Symphony, or even of far less conspicuously alien examples, such as the waltz in the ' Freischütz,' or a minuet of Haydn or Mozart, as in ' Lied-form.'

The other objection to the classification is its vagueness when formulated in such an empirical way ; but in order to understand fully both this objection and the former it will be necessary to go somewhat deeper into the matter.

In every artistic whole there must be balance and proportion. In musical works this is chiefly obtained by the grouping of harmonies. An artistic whole may be obtained in one key by throwing stress first upon one harmonic centre, passing from that to one which represents an opposite phase, and then passing back to the original again. The harmonies of the Tonic and the Dominant represent the most complete opposition of phase in the diatonic series of any key ; the most perfect simple balance is therefore to be found in their alternation. For example, the first fifteen bars of the Trio in the Scherzo of Beethoven's Symphony in A form

---

[1] *Allgemeine Musiklehre*, sec. 4, div. 5.
[2] *Lehre von der musikalischen Komposition*, sec. 3, div. 4.
[3] *Ibid.* vol. ii. bk. 3.

a complete artistic whole of themselves. There are six bars of tonic harmony and one of dominant forming the first group, and then six of dominant harmony followed by one of tonic harmony forming the second group. The balance is perfect, and the form the simplest in all music ; and it might reasonably be called the 'simple primary form.' It is to be found in the most diverse quarters, such as single chants of the Anglican Church, sailors' hornpipes, German popular waltzes and Ländler, and the trivial snatches of tunes in a French opéra-bouffe. The manner of obtaining the balance is, however, not necessarily restricted to the above order, for it is quite equally common to find each of the two groups containing a balance in themselves of tonic and dominant harmony. In that case the balance is obtained thus—$\overline{C\ G}\ \overline{C}\ \ \overline{C\ G}\ C$, instead of $\overline{C\ G}\ \overline{G\ C}$ as in the former instance ; but the principle which underlies them is the same, and justifies their being classed together. The subsidiary harmonies which are associated with these main groups are independent, but are most effective when they converge so as to direct attention to them. When greater extension is required, the balance is found between key and key, each key being severally distinguished by an alternation of harmonic roots so as to be severally complete when they are to be a prominent part of the form. Subsidiary transitions occur much as the subsidiary harmonies in the preceding class, and must be regarded in the same light. The identity of principle in these two classes is obvious, since in both alike it consists of taking a definite point to start from and marking it clearly, then passing to another point which will afford the needed contrast, and returning to the original to conclude. But as in the latter class the process is complicated by the changes of key, it may best be distinguished from the former as 'complex primary form.'

It is not necessary to enter into details on the subject of the extent, treatment and distribution of the keys; neither is it possible, since the principle when put upon this broad basis admits of very great variety, as indeed it is desirable that it should. But to guard against misapprehension, it may be as well to point out a few of the broadest facts.

In the first place, the several sections which serve to mark the elements of form need not be distinct and independent pieces, though they most frequently are so in the older opera and oratorio songs, and in the minuets and trios, or marches and trios, of instrumental music. In many examples, especially such as are on a small scale, there is no marked break in the continuity of the whole, the division at most amounting to nothing more than a cadence or half-close and a double bar, and often to not even so much as that. With regard to the dis-

tribution of ideas, it may be said that the several sections are often characterised by totally independent subjects, especially when the piece is on a large scale; but there are many examples, especially in the form of themes for variations, when, notwithstanding a certain freedom of modulation, the predominance of one main idea is unbroken.

Professor Marx has called attention to the fact that this form is sometimes amplified by repetition ; that is to say, when the return to the original key has been made to follow the contrasting section or Trio, a fresh departure is made, and another contrasting section or Trio is given, after which follows the final return to the original key and idea. Examples of this occur in the symphonies of Beethoven and Schumann, as well as in less important works ; and it is well to take note of the fact that in this case the form under consideration shows its close relationship to the rondo form ; for that form in the hands of early instrumental composers such as Rameau and Couperin was little else than the frequent repetition of a main idea in a principal key, interspersed with contrasting episodes, which in the present case answer to the trios.

The occurrence of codas with this form is very common, but for the discussion of that point reference must be made to the article under that head and to the article Form.

Finally, it will be well to return shortly to the consideration of the distinctive name of 'Lied' which has been given to this form. In the choice of it its author was probably guided by a well-grounded opinion of the superior antiquity of song to other kinds of music, which led him to infer that the instrumental forms which he put under the same category were imitated from the 'Lieder.' But this is not by any means inevitable. It will have been seen from the above discussion that in this form the simplest means of arriving at artistic balance and proportion are made use of ; and these would have been chosen by the instinct of the earliest composers of instrumental music without any necessary knowledge that vocal music was cast in the same mould. And there is more than this. In songs and other vocal music the hearer is so far guided by the sense of the words that a total impression of completeness may be obtained even with very vague structure in the music ; whereas in instrumental music, unless the form is clear and appreciably defined, it is impossible for the most intelligent hearer to realise the work as a whole. So that, in point of fact, vocal music can do without a great deal of that which is vital to instrumental music : and therefore the Lied is just the member of the group which it is least satisfactory to take as the type : but as this form has been classified under that head, it has been necessary so to review it fully, in order that a just estimation may be formed of its nature, and the reason for taking exception to the title. The form itself is a very important one, but inasmuch as it admits of great latitude in treatment, it appears that the only satisfactory means of classifying it, or making it explicable, is by putting it on as broad a basis as possible, and giving it a distinctive title which shall have reference to its intrinsic constitution, and not to one of the many kinds of music which may, but need not necessarily, come within its scope.

C. H. H. P.

LIED OHNE WORTE, *i.e.* Song without words (Fr. *romance sans paroles*), Mendelssohn's title for the pianoforte pieces which are more closely associated with his name than any other of his compositions. (See MENDELSSOHN, p. 426.)

LIE-NISSEN, ERIKA (*b.* Kangsviger, Jan. 17, 1845; *d.* Christiania, Oct. 27, 1903), a distinguished Norwegian pianist, was brought up in a family where many eminent musicians were guests. On the death of her father, a lawyer, the family went to live at Christiania, where Erika Lie became the pupil of Kjerulf; in 1860 she went to Berlin to study the piano with Kullak, and her progress was so rapid that she was appointed a teacher in his conservatorium. In 1866 she went to Paris and had some lessons from Tellefsen, and in 1870 she went to Copenhagen as professor of the piano at the Conservatorium there. She undertook many concert tours all over Europe, making a great success in the works of Chopin and the romantic school. In 1874 she married Dr. Oscar Nissen of Christiania; in 1894 she received a yearly grant from the Norwegian Storthing. She died at Christiania and was buried at the Vor Frelsers Church. Edvard Grieg conducted the musical part of the service (*Musical News*, obituary notice, Nov. 28, 1903).

M.

LIFE FOR THE TSAR, A, opera in 4 acts and an epilogue; text by Baron Rosen; music by Glinka. Produced St. Petersburg, Nov. 27, 1836; Covent Garden (in Italian as ' La Vita per lo Czar '), July 12, 1887.

LIGATURE, (1) (Fr. *liaison*; Ital. *legatura*; Lat. *ligatura*), a passage of two or more notes sung to a single syllable. (See NOTATION.)

(2) (In reed instruments.) The flexible metal band, regulated by two adjusting screws, which is used to secure the reed to the mouthpiece in instruments such as the clarinet and the saxophone. In former days the reed was held in position merely by a binding of waxed thread.   D. J. B.

LIGHT, EDWARD, a musician who claimed the invention of the harp-lute and a kindred instrument named the Apollo-lyre. The HARP-LUTE (*q.v.*), known also as the dital harp, was popular at the junction of the 18th and 19th centuries, and the Apollo-lyre less so. The

latter took the form of the ancient instrument, but it had a centre finger-board and a sound chamber. In 1794 Light was living at Kensington, and about this period he was making the above two instruments for sale. He soon removed to 8 Foley Place, Cavendish Square, and was ' lyrist to the Princess of Wales.' In 1818 [1] he took out a patent in connexion with the harp-lute which shortly after this date was made by Wheatstone & Co. Light was a teacher of the guitar, and arranged some music for it. He published a number of works, being arrangements and instructions for the harp-lute, Apollo-lyre, and for the guitar.   F. K.

LIGHT OF THE WORLD, THE, an oratorio in 2 parts; words compiled from the Scriptures; music by Sullivan. Produced Birmingham Festival, Aug. 27, 1873.

LILIENCRON, ROCHUS FREIHERR VON (*b.* Plön, Holstein, Dec. 8, 1820; *d.* Coblenz, Mar. 5, 1912). After going through a course of theology and law at Kiel and Berlin, and graduating both as Doctor of Theology and Philosophy, he devoted himself chiefly to Germanistic studies, including Old Norse languages and literature, on which he contributed various essays to periodicals. From 1848-50 he was in the diplomatic service of the Schleswig-Holstein Government during the war with Denmark. In 1850 he became professor of Old Norse languages and literature at Kiel, and in 1852 of ' Germanistik' at Jena. From 1855-68 he was Geheimer Kabinetsrat (Privy Cabinet Councillor) to the Duke of Meiningen. In 1855 he published ' Lieder und Sprüche aus der letzten Zeit des Minnesangs,' containing twenty melodies with texts from the celebrated Jena Minnesänger codex, written about 1320. Dr. Wilhelm Stade of Jena provided the melodies with a modern setting in four-part harmony. Liliencron afterwards settled at Munich as editor of the *Allgemeine deutsche Biographie*. It was also during his stay at Munich that he published *Die historischen Volkslieder der Deutschen vom 13.–16. Jahrh.* in five volumes (1865–69), the last volume containing valuable notes on the old tunes, besides eighteen polyphonic settings of some of them by H. Isaac, Senfl, H. Finck, Mahu and others. For Kürschner's *Deutsche National-Literatur*, Bd. 13 (1884), he published *Deutsches Leben im Volkslied um 1530*, which contains 147 Volkslieder of the 16th-century texts and melodies.

From 1876 Liliencron chiefly resided at Schleswig as Prälat des St. Johannisstiftes. Later he occupied himself much with the question of church music. Besides contributing various essays on the subject to *Siona* and other church and musical periodicals, he published in 1893 *Liturgisch-musikalische Geschichte der evangel.-Lutherischen Gottesdienste von 1523 bis 1700*, which is a valuable sketch of the

[1] W. H. G. F. gives 1816.

history of Lutheran church music from the liturgical point of view up to the rise of the form of church cantata as perfected by Sebastian Bach. It is based on a thorough liturgical as well as musical knowledge, and is in effect a plea for the closer welding of music with the liturgy by a return to the older forms of liturgical music. Practical proposals to the same effect were embodied in *Chorordnung für die Sonn- und Festtage des evangel. Kirchenjahres* (Gütersloh, 1900). The task of providing a musical setting for the liturgical texts contained in this work in accordance with the author's principles, he entrusted to a Berlin musician, H. van Eyken. Another historico-musical work by Liliencron of some importance is *Die Horazischen Metren in deutschen Komponisten des 16ten Jahrhunderts*, which includes nineteen Odes of Horace as set in simple note-for-note counterpoint, and in accordance with metrical principles by Tritonius, Senfl and Hofhaimer. An edition of these settings in modern score was published by Breitkopf & Härtel. Among the recent works of Liliencron may be mentioned a novel, *Wie man im Amwald Musik macht* (1903), written to further the cause of reform in church music. Mention may also be made of an earlier writing on the Danish composer C. E. F. Weyse, and Danish music generally (1878). From 1900 he was appointed president and leading director of the Royal Prussian Commission for the editing and publication of the *D.D.T.*   J. R. M.

LILLIBURLERO, a 17th-century party tune, and used to-day by Irish Orangemen to a song called 'Protestant Boys.' It has been attributed to Henry Purcell, but whether Purcell composed the melody or only fitted the bass is a question not finally settled.[1]

The tune first appears as a 'Quick Step' in the 2nd edition of *The Delightful Companion, or Choice New Lessons for the Recorder or Flute*, 1686, as follows :

The words are a doggerel set of satirical verses upon the appointment of General Talbot to the Lieutenancy of Ireland in 1687. They begin :

'Ho ! broder Teague, dost hear de decree,
     Lilliburlero, bullen a la,
Dat we shall have a new deputie,
     Lilliburlero, bullen a la,
     Liero, lero, lilliburlero lero, lero, bullen a la.

---

[1] See Purcell Society's edition, vol. vi. p. 31.

'Ho ! by Shaint Tyburn it is de Talbote,
     Lilliburlero, etc.,
And he will cut all de English troate,
     Lilliburlero, etc., etc.'

The whole words will be found in Percy's *Reliques of Ancient English Poetry*. The words or the tune quickly caught on, and Bishop Burnet in his *History of His Own Time* mentions the effect that the 'foolish ballad, treating the Papists and chiefly the Irish in a ridiculous manner,' had upon the political events of that day. 'The whole army and at last the people, both in the city and country, were singing it, and perhaps never had so slight a thing so great an effect.' There were numerous songs set to the air, all having a strong Protestant bearing.

Whether the tune which we now know as 'Lilliburlero' is the original one for the song is rather doubtful, for in the Bodleian Library is an early broadside, with music, headed 'A New Song,' the words being the same as above quoted. The broadside formerly belonged to Antony à Wood.

The music is as follows :

It will be noticed that the tune is 'Cold and Raw' or 'Stingo.'

Henry Purcell's name was first associated with the tune in the second part of *Musick's Hand Maid, containing the newest Lessons, Grounds, Sarabands, Minuets and Jiggs set forth for the Virginal and Spinet*, 1689. It is set down there as 'A New Irish Tune,' and on the same line 'H. Purcell,' either as composer or merely responsible for the bass. There are no words given. Purcell used the air as a ground bass to the fifth piece in 'The Gordian Knot unty'd ' in 1691.

An attempt has been made to fathom the mystery of the words 'Lilliburlero,' etc., but nothing that can be relied upon has been elicited. The chances are they are merely nonsense words.   F. K.

LILT (verb and noun), to sing, pipe or play cheerfully, or, according to one authority, even sadly ; also, a gay tune. The term, which is of Scottish origin, but is used in Ireland and occurs in Chaucer, would seem to be derived from the bagpipe, one variety of which is described in the 'Houlate' (an ancient allegorical Scottish poem dating 1450) as the 'Lilt-pype.' Whenever, in the absence of a musical instrument to play for dancing, the Irish peasant girls sing lively airs to the customary syllables la-la-la, it is called 'lilting.' The classical occurrence of the word is in the Scottish song 'The Flowers of the Forest,' a lament for the disastrous field of Flodden, where it is contrasted with a mournful tone :

'I've heard them liltin' at the ewe milkin',
    Lasses a-liltin' before dawn of day ;
Now there's a moanin' on ilka green loanin',
    The Flowers of the Forest are a' wede away.'

The Skene MS., ascribed (though not conclusively [1]) to the reign of James VI. of Scotland, contains six lilts : ' Ladie Rothemayeis ' (the air to the ballad of the Burning of Castle Frindraught), 'Lady Laudians' (Lothian's), 'Ladie Cassilles' (the air of the ballad of Johnny Faa), Leslies, Aderneis and Gilcreich's Lilts. We quote ' Ladie Cassilles ' :

W. Dauney, editor of the Skene MS., supposes the Liltpipe to have been a shepherd's pipe, not a bagpipe, and the Lilts to have sprung from the pastoral districts of the Lowlands.

R. P. S.

LILY OF KILLARNEY, opera in 3 acts, founded on Boucicault's ' Colleen Bawn ' ; words by John Oxenford ; music by Benedict. Produced Covent Garden (Pyne & Harrison), Feb. 8, 1862.   G.

LIMA, JERONYMO FRANCISCO DE (b. Lisbon, Sept. 30, 1743 ; d. there, Feb. 19, 1822), Portuguese operatic composer. He came from a musical family ; his younger brother, Bras Francisco de Lima (d. 1813) was the composer of several oratorios (Bibl. da Ajuda, Lisbon). Jeronymo was early recognised as a composer, as his early election to the Brotherhood of St. Cecilia (1767) shows. He visited Italy, and afterwards (1798) succeeded Carvalho as conductor of the Royal Opera. His works (Bibl. da Ajuda) include six operas to Italian libretti performed between 1772–85, occasional cantatas and church music.   J. B. T.

LIMPUS, RICHARD (b. Isleworth, Sept. 10, 1824 ; d. Mar. 15, 1875), organist, was a pupil of the R.A.M., and organist successively of Brentford ; of St. Andrew's, Undershaft ; and St. Michael's, Cornhill. He composed a good deal of minor music, but his claim to remembrance is as one of the founders of the College of Organists, which, owing to his zeal and devotion, was established in 1864. He

was secretary to the College till his death. (See ROYAL COLLEGE OF ORGANISTS.)   G.

LINCKE,[2] JOSEPH (b. Trachenberg, Prussian Silesia, June 8, 1783 ; d. Mar. 26, 1837), eminent violoncellist and composer, learnt the violin from his father, a violinist in the chapel of Prince Hatzfeld, and the violoncello from Oswald. A mismanaged sprain of the right ankle left him lame for life.[3] At 10 he lost his parents, and was obliged to support himself by copying music, until in 1800 he procured a place as violinist in the Dominican convent at Breslau. There he studied the organ and harmony under Hanisch, and also pursued the violoncello under Lose, after whose departure he became first violoncellist at the theatre, of which C. M. von Weber was then Kapellmeister. In 1808 he went to Vienna, and was engaged by Prince Rasoumowsky [4] for his private quartet party, at the suggestion of Schuppanzigh. In that house, where Beethoven was supreme, he had the opportunity of playing the great composer's works under his own supervision.[5] Beethoven was much attached to Lincke, and continually calls him 'Zunftmeister Violoncello,' or some other droll name, in his letters. The State Library at Berlin [6] contains a comic canon in Beethoven's writing on the names Brauchle and Lincke :

The two sonatas for PF. and violoncello (op. 102) were composed by Beethoven while he and Lincke were together at the Erdödys in 1815.[7]

Lincke played in Schuppanzigh's public quartets, and Schuppanzigh in turn assisted Lincke at his farewell concert, when the programme consisted entirely of Beethoven's music, and the great composer himself was present. His playing appears to have been remarkable for its humour, and he is said to have been peculiarly happy in expressing Beethoven's characteristic style, whence no doubt the master's fondness for him.[8] He then went to Grätz, and from thence to Pancovecz, near Agram, the residence of Countess Erdödy, as her chamber virtuoso, where he remained a year and a half. In 1818 he was engaged by Freiherr von Braun as first violoncellist in the theatre ' an der Wien,' and in 1831 played with Merk, the distinguished violoncellist, in the orchestra of the Court Opera.

---

[1] See W. Chappell's criticisms, Popular Music, p. 614.

[2] He always wrote his name thus, though it is usually spelled Linke.
[3] It is perhaps in allusion to this that Bernard writes, ' Lincke has only one fault—that he is crooked ' (krumm).
[4] Weiss played the viola, and the Prince the second violin.
[5] Compare Thayer's Beethoven, iii. 49.
[6] See Nohl's Beethoven's Briefe, 1867, p. 92, note.
[7] See Thayer, iii. 343.
[8] See the Neue Zeitschrift für Musik, 1837, No. 32.

His compositions consist of concertos, variations, capriccios, etc., his first three works only (variations) having been published.   c. f. p.

LINCOLN, (1) HENRY CEPHAS (b. 1789; d. 1864), an organ-builder in London. He built the organ in the Pavilion, Brighton, which is now in Buckingham Palace.   v. de p.

His son, (2) HENRY JOHN (b. London, Oct. 15, 1814; d. Hampstead, Aug. 16, 1901), began as organist of Christ Church, Woburn Square, and from 1846 was employed upon the *Daily News*, succeeding G. Hogarth as its critic in 1866, and retaining the post till 1886. He lectured frequently on musical subjects, in London, Edinburgh, Glasgow, Manchester, Liverpool, etc. In a lecture on Mendelssohn, at the Western Literary Institution, on Dec. 23, 1845, that master's violin concerto was played for the first time in England by Kreutzer, with Lincoln at the pianoforte. (*Brit. Mus. Biog.*)

LINCOLN'S INN FIELDS THEATRE stood nearly in the centre of the south side of Lincoln's Inn Fields, the principal entrance being in Portugal Street. It was erected by Christopher Rich, and opened (after his death) in 1714 by his son, John Rich, with Farquhar's comedy 'The Recruiting Officer.' Here Rich first introduced his pantomimes, a curious mixture of masque and harlequinade in which he himself, under the name of Lun, performed the part of Harlequin. Galliard was his composer and Pepusch his music director. (See GALLIARD; PEPUSCH.) Here THE BEGGAR'S OPERA (*q.v.*) was first produced in 1727. Rich removing in 1732 to the new theatre in Covent Garden, the house in Lincoln's Inn Fields was let for a variety of purposes. Here in 1734 Italian operas were given, in opposition to Handel's at the King's Theatre, with Porpora as composer and Senesino as principal singer; and here, when Handel was compelled to quit the King's Theatre, he, in his turn, gave Italian operas, and also, occasionally, oratorio performances. His 'Dryden's Ode on St. Cecilia's Day' was first performed here in 1739, and in 1740 his 'L' Allegro, Il Pensieroso, ed Il Moderato,' his serenata 'Parnasso in Festa,' and his operetta 'Hymen.' Plays were occasionally performed here until 1756, when the building was converted into a barrack. It was afterwards occupied as Spode & Copeland's Salopian China Warehouse, until it was taken down in 1848 for the enlargement of the College of Surgeons.

This theatre must not be confounded with two others which previously stood near the same spot, viz. the Duke's Theatre, erected by Sir William Davenant in 1662, and occupied until 1671, when the company removed to Dorset Garden Theatre, and the Theatre in Little Lincoln's Inn Fields, built upon the same site and opened in 1695 with Congreve's 'Love for Love,' and occupied until the company

removed to the Queen's Theatre in 1705, when it was abandoned. (See KING'S THEATRE.)
          w. h. h.

LIND, JENNY (b. Stockholm, Oct. 6, 1820; d. Wynd's Point, Malvern, Nov. 2, 1887), famous soprano.

When she was 9 years old, Count Puke, director of the Court Theatre, admitted her to the school of singing which is attached to that establishment, and she received there her first lessons from the singing-master and court secretary Croelius, and subsequently from a master named Berg. After appearing in children's parts from 1830 onwards, she made her début at the Opera in her native city, Mar. 7, 1838, as Agatha in Weber's 'Freischütz,' and played afterwards the principal rôle in 'Euryanthe,' Alice in 'Robert le Diable,' and finally 'La Vestale,' all with brilliant success. In 1840 she was made a member of the Royal Swedish Academy of Music, and was appointed court singer. She upheld the Royal Theatre until July 1841, when she went to Paris in hope of improving her style of singing. There Manuel Garcia, after expressing the opinion that her voice had been worn out by faulty method and overwork, ultimately gave her lessons, during a period of eleven months. Meyerbeer, who happened to be at Paris at the time, heard her, was delighted, and foretold a brilliant future for the young singer. He arranged a private 'audition' for her at the Opéra, and recommended her for the Opera at Berlin. She returned to Stockholm for two years, and in 1844 went to Dresden to study German. In September she returned to Stockholm and took part in the fêtes at the crowning of King Oscar, but went to Berlin in October, and obtained an engagement at the Opera through the influence of Meyerbeer, who had written for her the principal rôle in his 'Feldlager in Schlesien,' afterwards remodelled as 'L'Étoile du nord.'

She appeared first, Dec. 15, as Norma, and was welcomed with enthusiasm; and afterwards played, with equal success, her part in Meyerbeer's new opera. She also appeared as Euryanthe and in 'La Sonnambula.' In the following spring she sang at Hanover and Hamburg. After this tour she returned again to Stockholm and once more enjoyed a triumphant success. She sang before Queen Victoria and Prince Albert at Stolzenfels in the following August, and appeared at Frankfort, Darmstadt and Copenhagen; she was again in Berlin in the winter, appearing in the parts of Donna Anna, Agatha, the Vestalin, and Valentine in 'Les Huguenots.' At the Gewandhaus, Leipzig, she made her first appearance Dec. 4, 1845. Engaged soon after for Vienna, she appeared there Apr. 22, 1846, and at Whitsuntide of the same year sang in the Niederrheinische Fest at Aix-la-Chapelle, appearing at Hanover

XLIII

MALIBRAN

From a pencil drawing by A. E. Chalon, R.A., bequeathed by the late W. Barclay Squire to the R.C.M.

JENNY LIND

From an engraving by W. Holl after a Daguerreotype

and Hamburg in the summer. After engagements at Darmstadt, Munich, Stuttgart and various cities of South Germany in the autumn, she returned to Vienna and added 'La figlia del reggimento' to her list of characters.

Difficulties had arisen between the two London managers, Bunn and Lumley, as to the validity of a contract which Jenny Lind had been induced to sign with the former, and it was not until May 4, 1847, that she appeared at Her Majesty's Theatre in 'Robert.' Moscheles had already met her in Berlin, and wrote thus (Jan. 10, 1845) of her performances in 'The Camp of Silesia':

'Jenny Lind has fairly enchanted me; she is unique in her way, and her song with two concertante flutes is perhaps the most incredible feat in the way of bravura singing that can possibly be heard. . . . How lucky I was to find her at home! What a glorious singer she is, and so unpretentious withal!'

This character, though true to life, was, however, shamefully belied by the management of the London Theatre, both before and after her arrival. It is curious now to look back upon the artifices employed, the stories of broken contracts (this not without some foundation), of long diplomatic *pourparlers*, special messengers, persuasion, hesitation and vacillations, kept up during many months,—all in order to excite the interest of the operatic public. Not a stone was left unturned, not a trait of the young singer's character, public or private, unexploited, by which sympathy, admiration, or even curiosity, might be aroused.[1]

The interest and excitement of the public at her first appearance was, therefore, extraordinary. Yet her great singing in the part of Alice disappointed none but a very few, and those were silenced by a tumultuous majority of idolaters. She certainly sang the music splendidly, and acted the part irreproachably.

'From that first moment till the end of that season, nothing else was thought about, nothing else talked about, but the new Alice—the new Sonnambula—the new Maria in Donizetti's charming comic opera, —his best. Pages could be filled by describing the excesses of the public. Since the days when the world fought for hours at the pit-door to see the seventh farewell of Siddons, nothing had been seen in the least approaching the scenes at the entrance of the theatre when Mlle. Lind sang. Prices rose to a fabulous height. In short, the town, sacred and profane, went mad about "the Swedish nightingale." '[2]

Her voice, which then at its very best showed some signs of early wear, was a soprano of bright, thrilling and remarkably sympathetic quality, from *b* to *g'''*. The upper part of her register was rich and brilliant, and superior both in strength and purity to the lower. These two portions she managed, however, to unite in the most skilful way, moderating the power of her upper notes so as not to outshine the lower. She had also a wonderfully developed 'length of breath,' which enabled her to perform long and difficult passages with ease, and to fine down her tones to the softest pianis-

simo while still maintaining the quality unvaried. Her execution was very great, her shake true and brilliant, her taste in ornament altogether original, and she usually invented her own *cadenze*. In a song from 'Beatrice di Tenda' she had a chromatic cadenza ascending to E in alt, and descending to the note whence it had arisen, which could scarcely be equalled for difficulty and perfection of execution. The following, sung by her at the end of 'Ah! non giunge,' was given to the present writer by an ear-witness:

In this comparatively simple cadenza the highest notes, though rapidly struck, were not given in the manner of a shake, but were positively *martelées*, and produced an extraordinary effect. Another cadenza,[3] which, according to Moscheles, 'electrified' them at the Gewandhaus, occurred three times in one of Chopin's mazurkas:

Moscheles wrote (1847):

'What shall I say of Jenny Lind? I can find no words adequate to give you any real idea of the impression she has made. . . . This is no short-lived fit of public enthusiasm. I wanted to know her off the stage as well as on; but, as she lives some distance from me, I asked her in a letter to fix upon an hour for me to call. Simple and unceremonious as she is, she came the next day herself, bringing her answer verbally. So much modesty and so much greatness united are seldom if ever to be met with; and, although her intimate friend Mendelssohn had given me an insight into the noble qualities of her character, I was surprised to find them so apparent.'

Meanwhile Mlle. Lind maintained the mark which she had made in 'Robert' by her impersonation of the Sonnambula, a most effective character — Lucia, Adina in 'L'Elisir,' 'La figlia del reggimento,' and perhaps, altogether her best part, Giulia in Spontini's 'Vestale.' She also created the part of Amalia in Verdi's 'I masnadieri' (July 22), and sang that of Susanna in 'Figaro.' In 1848 she returned to Her Majesty's Theatre, and added to these 'Lucia di Lammermoor' and 'L'Elisir d'amore.' In 1849 she announced her intention not to appear again on the stage, but so far modified this resolution as to sing at Her Majesty's Theatre in Mozart's 'Flauto magico' arranged as a concert, without acting (Apr. 12); the experiment was so unsuccessful that instead of similar concert performances previously announced, she gave six more operatic perform-

---

[1] See Lumley's *Reminiscences*, 1847.   [2] Chorley.

[3] Further cadenzas in the *Musical Union Record*, 1849, and in *Jenny Lind, the Artist* (see BIBL.).

ances, appearing as Amina, Lucia, Maria and Alice. Her last appearance ' on any stage ' took place in ' Roberto,' May 10, 1849. Henceforward she betook herself to the more congenial platform of the concert-room.

' The wild, queer northern tunes brought here by her, her careful expression of some of Mozart's great airs, her mastery over such a piece of execution as the Bird song in Haydn's " Creation," and lastly, the grandeur of inspiration with which the " Sanctus " of angels in Mendelssohn's " Elijah " was led by her (the culminating point in that oratorio). These are the triumphs which will stamp her name in the Golden Book of singers.' [1]

On the other hand, the wondrous effect with which she sang a simple ballad, in the simplest possible manner, can never be forgotten by those who ever heard it. After another season in London, and a visit to Ireland in 1848, Mlle. Lind was engaged by Barnum,[2] the American speculator, to make a tour of the United States. She arrived there in 1850 and remained for nearly two years, during part of the time unfettered by an engagement with any impresario, but accompanied by Mr., afterwards Sir, Julius Benedict. The Americans, with their genius for appreciation and hospitality, welcomed her everywhere with frantic enthusiasm, and she made £20,000 in this progress. Here it was, in Boston, on Feb. 5, 1852, that she married Otto GOLDSCHMIDT (q.v.).

Returned to Europe, Mme. Goldschmidt now travelled through Holland, and again visited Germany. Dresden was her home from 1852–1855. In 1856 she came once more to England, and for some years appeared frequently in oratorios and concerts. Her actual last appearance was at a concert for a charity at Malvern, July 23, 1883. In that year she accepted an appointment as teacher of singing at the R.C.M., which she held till 1886.

It must be recorded that the whole of her American earnings was devoted to founding and endowing art scholarships and other charities in her native Sweden ; while in England, the country of her adoption, among other charities she gave a whole hospital to Liverpool and a wing of another to London. In the winter of 1848–49 she raised a sum of £10,500 for charities. The scholarship founded in memory of her friend Felix Mendelssohn also benefited largely by her help and countenance. (See MENDELSSOHN SCHOLARSHIP.)

Madame Lind-Goldschmidt was respected and admired by all who knew her, the mother of a family, mixing in society, but in no degree losing her vivid interest in music. The Bach Choir, conducted by Goldschmidt, which gave the English public the first opportunity of hearing in its entirety the B minor Mass of that composer, profited in no small degree by the careful training bestowed on the female portion

of the chorus by this great singer, and the enthusiasm inspired by her presence among them. On Apr. 20, 1894, H.R.H. Princess Christian unveiled a medallion of Jenny Lind in Westminster Abbey. (See Billroth's *Studies in Music*, p. 252.)   J. M., with addns.

BIBLIOGRAPHY

SCOTT HOLLAND and W. S. ROCKSTRO, *Jenny Lind, the Artist*, 2 vols. (London, 1891) ; Ditto, abridged edition (London, 1893).
SVEN DORPH, *Jenny Lind's triumftåg genom nya världen och öriga leonadsöden*, 2nd ed. (Upsala, 1918). *Jenny Lindiane till hundraårsminnet* (Upsala, 1919).
TOBIAS NORLIND, *Jenny Lind. En minnesbok till hundraårsdagen* (Stockholm, 1919).
SIGRID ELMBLAD, *Jenny Lind. En lifsstudie. Svenska Kinnor 1* (Upsala, 1920).
Jenny Lind, 1820–1920. Studier utgivna av Svenska Sanfundet för Musikförskning, pp. 149 (Stockholm, 1920). Contains a Jenny Lind bibliography, pp. 139-49.

LINDA DI CHAMOUNI, opera in 3 acts ; words by Rossi, music by Donizetti. Produced Kärnthnerthor Theatre, Vienna, May 19, 1842 ; in Paris, Nov. 17, 1842 ; in London, Her Majesty's, June 1843 ; New York, Palmo's Opera House, Jan. 4, 1847.   G.

LINDBLAD, ADOLF FREDRICK (b. near Stockholm, Feb. 1, 1801 ; d. there, Aug. 23, 1878). This Swedish composer passed several years of his early life in Berlin, and studied music there under Zelter. In 1827 he returned to Stockholm and there resided, giving singing lessons and composing until his death.

Lindblad composed little instrumental music; a symphony in C,[3] which was given under Mendelssohn's[4] direction at one of the Gewandhaus Concerts at Leipzig in Nov. 1839, and a duo for pianoforte and violin (op. 9) are considered the best, but they aim so little at effect and are so full of the peculiar personality of their author that they can never be popular. His vocal compositions made him famous. He was eminently a national composer. He published a large collection of songs for voice and piano to Swedish words, which are full of melody, grace and originality. Written for the most part in the minor mode, they are tinged with the melancholy which is characteristic of Swedish music. In such short songs as 'The Song of the Dalecarlian Maiden,' 'Lament,' 'The Wood by the Aaren Lake,' etc., of which their extreme simplicity is of the very essence of their charm, his success has been most conspicuous. In longer and more elaborate songs, where the simplicity at which he aimed in his accompaniment has limited the variety of harmony and figures. the effect is often marred by repetition and consequent monotony. Yet even in this class of work there are many beautiful exceptions, and 'A Day in Spring,' 'A Summer's Day ' and ' Autumn Evening ' are specially worthy of mention.

Jenny Lind, who was Lindblad's pupil, introduced his songs into Germany, and their rapidly acquired popularity earned for the author the

---

[1] Chorley.
[2] For an American account of this tour see *P. T. Barnum*, by M. R. Werner (1923).

[3] Analysed in *A.M.Z.*, Oct. 23, 1839.
[4] There is a pleasant reference to Lindblad in a letter of Mendelssohn, Dec. 28, 1833.

title of 'the Schubert of the North.' His only opera, ' Frondärarne,' was performed at Stockholm, 1835, and revived for the opening of the new opera-house there in 1898. Several of his vocal duets, trios and quartets have a considerable reputation in Sweden.   A. H. W.

LINDBLAD, OTTO JONAS (b. Karlstorp, Småland, Mar. 31, 1809 ; d. N. Mellby, Skåne, Jan. 24, 1864), was a composer, particularly of choral music and quartets for men.

He was sent to Växsjö to be educated as a clergyman. Here he was also instructed in music by Svensson, whom Lindblad himself mentions as an excellent organ-player 'à l'abbé Vogler.' In 1829 he matriculated at Lund, and about this time fell ill with smallpox. During his long convalescence he drifted, owing to his musical bent, further and further away from his academic studies. Together with two friends, Lindblad organised a trio, arranged for vocal as well as instrumental music, in which he took part as second tenor and also performed on the violin ; it was by studying music and practising it that he developed his own talent in composition, in which he only had a few lessons from Krebs during a visit to Copenhagen. He was taught the violin by K. M. Lundholm, in whose home he lived for three years. Of great significance to Lindblad's musical education became the Henserska Theatre Company, which in 1836 visited the south of Sweden, producing operas by Weber, Mozart, Rossini, Boieldieu, etc. Lindblad took part in the orchestra and joined the company on their tour as orchestral leader. In 1841 he visited Hamburg, where he was invited as guest of honour to the musical festival. Whilst Haeffner and Geijer founded the Swedish Student Song in Upsala, it was not long before Otto Lindblad organised the same in Lund, and it is due to him that it was raised to one of the foremost in the north.

He composed 124 songs, of which 66 were quartets ; 5 choruses, with solos ; 14 trios ; 3 duets ; and 36 solo songs.   G. A. S.

LINDEMANN, MAGISTER JOHANN (b. Gotha, c. 1550), cantor at Gotha from c. 1571 or 1572, resigning 1631. He wrote sacred songs, words and music, and published a collection of New Year and Christmas songs by various masters (1598). Only the second of three volumes has been rediscovered so far ; it contains 2 songs by Pevernage (Q.-L.).

LINDLEY, (1) ROBERT (b. Rotherham, Mar. 4, 1776 ; d. London, June 13, 1855), showed so early a predilection for music that when he was about 5 years of age his father, an amateur performer, began teaching him the violin, and at 9 years of age, the violoncello also. He continued to practise the latter until he was 16, when Cervetto, hearing him play, encouraged him and undertook his

gratuitous instruction. He quitted Yorkshire and obtained an engagement at the Brighton theatre. In 1794 he succeeded Sperati as principal violoncello at the Opera and all the principal concerts, and retained undisputed possession of that position until his retirement in 1851. His intimacy with DRAGONETTI (q.v.) lasted for half a century. He was appointed professor of his instrument in the R.A.M. on its foundation in 1822.[1] Lindley's tone was remarkable for its purity, richness, mellowness and volume, and in this respect he has probably never been equalled. His technique, for that date, was remarkable, and his accompaniment of recitative was perfection. He composed several concertos and other works for his instrument, but his composition was by no means equal to his execution. His daughter married John Barnett the composer.

His son, (2) WILLIAM (b. 1802 ; d. Manchester, Aug. 12, 1869), was also a violoncellist. He was a pupil of his father, first appeared in public in 1817, and soon took a position in all the best orchestras. He gave great promise of future excellence, but was unable to achieve any prominence owing to extreme nervousness.   W. H. H.

LINDNER, FRIEDRICH (b. Liegnitz, Silesia, c. 1540 ; d. Nuremberg, Sept. 15, 1597), was first a boy chorister in the Electoral Chapel at Dresden, received his further education at the famous school at Pforta, and afterwards studied at Leipzig University. After serving for a while as Hof-musikus to the Margrave of Brandenburg at Ansbach, he received in 1574 the appointment of cantor to the important St. Aegidien Kirche at Nuremberg, where he died. Although Lindner published none of his own compositions, he is known to have sent to the Duke of Würtemberg in 1567 a Cantional-buch for which he received the then considerable honorarium of 30 thaler, and again in 1570 and 1572 he also sent two musical settings of the Passion for which he received 6 and 10 thalers respectively (Eitner, Monatshefte, xxxi. pp. 18, 19). But he is chiefly known as the meritorious editor of various collections of music, sacred and secular, published by the Nuremberg firm of Gerlach, which are important as testifying to the kind of music which continued to be cultivated and favoured in the Lutheran churches and schools of Nuremberg and elsewhere. They are as follows :

1. Sacrae cantiones, 1585, 41 n. a 5-9 ; motets by Italian composers, chiefly of the Venetian school, but including some by Palestrina.
2. Continuatio Cantionum sacrarum, 1588, 56 n. a 4-12.
3. Corollarium Cantionum sacrarum, 1590, 70 n. a 4-12.
4. Missae quinque, a 5.
5. Magnificat octo tonorum, 1591 ; three sets by Guerrero, Ruffo and Varotto, a 4 and 5.
6. Bicinia sacra, 80 n.
7. Gemma musicalis ; three books, 1588, 1589, 1590, containing altogether 190 Italian madrigals by the most representative composers of the genre, such as Marenzio, the Gabrielis, Striggio and many others.   J. R. M.

LINDPAINTNER, PETER JOSEPH VON (*b.* Coblenz, Dec. 9, 1791 ; *d.* Nonnenhorn, Aug. 21, 1856), studied the violin, piano and counterpoint at Augsburg, and subsequently appears to have received some instruction at Munich from Winter. In 1812 he accepted the post of Musik-director at the Isarthor Theatre in Munich, and whilst so engaged completed his musical studies under Jos. Grätz, an excellent contrapuntist. In 1819 he was appointed Kapellmeister to the Royal Band at Stuttgart, and held that post until his death, which took place during a summer holiday at Nonnenhorn, on the Lake of Constance. He was buried at Wasserburg. He died full of honours, a member of almost every musical institution of the Continent, and the recipient of gifts from many crowned heads—amongst others a medal from Queen Victoria, in 1848, for the dedication of his oratorio of ' Abraham.'

By quiet and persistent labour he raised his band to the level of the best in Germany, and acquired a very high reputation. ' Lindpaintner,' says Mendelssohn, describing a visit to Stuttgart in 1831,

' is in my belief the best conductor in Germany ; it is as if he played the whole orchestra with his baton alone ; and he is very industrious.'

Of the many professional engagements offered him in other towns and foreign countries, he accepted but one, and that, in 1853, three years before his death, was to conduct the New Philharmonic Concerts in London, at which his cantata ' The Widow of Nain,' his overtures to ' Faust ' and ' The Vampyre,' and others of his compositions were given with success, including the song of ' The Standard-bearer,' at that time very popular, sung by Pischek. He conducted some of the New Philharmonic Concerts in 1854. He wrote 28 operas, 3 ballets, 5 melodramas and oratorios, several cantatas, 6 masses, a Stabat Mater, and above 50 songs with pianoforte accompaniment. To these were added symphonies, overtures, concertos, fantasias, trios and quartets for different instruments. He rescored ' Judas Maccabaeus.' Some of his symphonies, his operas ' Der Vampyr ' and ' Lichtenstein,' his ballet ' Joko,' the overture to which was often heard at concerts, his music to Goethe's ' Faust ' and Schiller's ' Song of the Bell,' have been pronounced to be among the best of his works. And two of his songs, ' The Standard-bearer ' and ' Roland,' created at the time a veritable furore.

Though wanting in depth and originality Lindpaintner's compositions pleased by their clearness and brilliancy, melody and well-developed form ; and the hand of a clever and practised musician is everywhere visible in them. A. H. W.

LINIKE (LINECKE), JOHANN GEORG, was appointed violinist in the court orchestra, Berlin, 1711 ; left in 1713 at the dissolution of the orchestra ; was Konzertmeister at the court of Weissenfels in 1718 ; went thence to England, and became leader at the Hamburg theatre in 1725, where he wrote the recitatives to some of Handel's operas. His own compositions, overtures, suites, concertos, trios, duos and sonatas for various instruments, remained in MS. (See *Q.-L.*)

LINKE, see LINCKE.

LINLEY, FRANCIS (*b.* Doncaster, 1771 ; *d.* there, Sept. 13, 1800 [1]), blind from his birth, studied music under Dr. Miller and became an able organist. He was chosen organist of St. James's Chapel, Pentonville, and soon afterwards married a blind lady of considerable fortune. He purchased the business of Bland, the music-seller in Holborn, in 1796, but his affairs becoming embarrassed, his wife parted from him and he went to America in the same year, where his playing and compositions were much admired. He returned to England in 1799. His works consist of songs, pianoforte and organ pieces, flute solos and duets, and an *Organ Tutor*. His greatest amusement was to explore churchyards and read the inscriptions on the tombstones by the sense of touch.

W. H. H. ; addns. and corr., F. K.

LINLEY, GEORGE (*b.* Leeds, 1798 ; *d.* Kensington, Sept. 10, 1865), composer. His birthplace [2] was a house in Briggate, where his father, James Linley, carried on business as a tinplate worker. As a young man he amused himself with much satirical literature, directed against the magnates of the town. He removed to London, and besides doing much literary work of sundry kinds, wrote the words or the music (frequently both) of some of the most popular drawing-room lyrics of the day : ' Ever of thee,' ' I cannot mind my wheel, mother,' ' Thou art gone from my gaze,' being among these productions.

His operas include ' Francesca Doria,' 1849 ; ' La Poupée de Nuremberg,' acted at Covent Garden in 1861 ; ' The Toymaker,' produced Nov. 10, in the same year at the same theatre, and ' Law versus Love,' 1862. He edited and arranged several collections of songs as : ' Scottish Melodies,' ' Songs of the Camp,' ' Original Hymn Tunes,' etc. Two books of Nursery Rhymes were among his latest musical works. His *Musical Cynics of London*, 1862, was an attack on the metropolitan music critics, H. F. Chorley being severely treated. The *Modern Hudibras* was published in 1864. He is said to have been a skilled violoncellist, and to have played at the Italian Opera. He was buried at Kensal Green. F. K.

LINLEY, (1) THOMAS (*b.* Badminton, Jan. 17, 1733 [3] ; *d.* Covent Garden, Nov. 19, 1795),

1 Wilson's *Biography of the Blind*.
2 The statement made in Batty's *History of Rothwell*, 1877, p. 230, that he was born at Glass Houses, near Rothwell, is undoubtedly erroneous. 3 See *The Linleys of Bath*.

began the study of music under Thomas Chilcot, organist of Bath Abbey church, and completed his education under Paradies. He established himself as a singing-master at Bath, and for many years carried on the concerts there with great success. On the retirement of John Christopher Smith in 1774 Linley joined Stanley in the management of the oratorios at Drury Lane, and on the death of Stanley in 1786 continued them in partnership with Arnold. In 1775, in conjunction with his eldest son, Thomas (5), he composed and compiled the music for 'The Duenna,' by his son-in-law, Sheridan, which had the then unparalleled run of seventy-five nights in its first season. In 1776 he purchased part of Garrick's share in Drury Lane, removed to London and undertook the management of the music of the theatre, for which he composed several pieces of merit. He became a member of the Royal Society of Musicians in 1777. Linley died at his house in Southampton Street, Covent Garden, and was buried in Wells Cathedral. His dramatic pieces were :

The Royal Merchant, 1768.
The Duenna, 1775.
Selima and Azor (chiefly from Grétry, but containing the charming original melody, No flower that blows), 1776.
The Camp, 1778.
The Carnival of Venice, The Gentle Shepherd and Robinson Crusoe, 1781.
The Triumph of Mirth, 1782.
The Spanish Maid, 1783.
The Spanish Rivals, 1784.
Tom Jones, 1785.
The Strangers at Home, Richard Cœur de Lion (from Gretry), 1786, and Love in the East, 1788.
The song in The School for Scandal, 1777, and accompaniments to the songs in The Beggar's Opera.

He also set such portions of Sheridan's Monody on the Death of Garrick, 1779, as were intended to be sung. 'Six Elegies' for three voices, composed at Bath (much commended by Burney), and 'Twelve Ballads' were published in his lifetime. The posthumous works of himself and his son Thomas, which appeared a few years after his death, in two vols., consist of songs, cantatas, madrigals and elegies, including the lovely five-part madrigal by him, 'Let me, careless,' one of the most graceful productions of its kind. As an English composer Linley takes high rank.

BIBL.—PARKE, *Musical Memoirs* ; BUSBY, *Concert-Room Anecdotes.*

(2) ELIZABETH ANN, his eldest daughter, 'The Maid of Bath' (*b.* Bath, Sept. 7, 1754 ; *d.* Bristol, June 28, 1792), received her musical education from her father, and appeared at an early age with great success at the Bath concerts as a soprano singer. In 1770 she sang at the oratorios in London and at Worcester Festival, and rose high in public favour. In 1771 she sang at Hereford Festival, and in 1772 at Gloucester. On Apr. 13, 1773, she became, in romantic circumstances, the wife of Richard Brinsley Sheridan, and, after fulfilling engagements at Worcester Festival and at Oxford, contracted before her marriage, she retired at the zenith of her popularity. Her voice was of

extensive compass, and she sang with equal excellence in both the sustained and florid styles. She was painted by Sir Joshua Reynolds as St. Cecilia, and sat for the Virgin in his 'Nativity.' She died of consumption at Hotwells, Bristol. (See the *D.N.B.*, *s.v.* ' Sheridan, Elizabeth Ann,' from which corrections have been taken.)

(3) MARY (*b.* Bath; *d.* Clifton, July 27, 1787), his second daughter and pupil, also a favourite singer, sang with her sister at the oratorios, festivals, etc., and for a few years afterwards, until her marriage in 1780 with Richard Tickell, commissioner of stamps.

(4) MARIA (*d.* Bath, Sept. 15, 1784), third daughter of Thomas (1), was also a concert and oratorio singer. She died at an early age. Shortly before her death she raised herself in bed, and with momentary animation sang part of Handel's air 'I know that my Redeemer liveth,' and then, exhausted with the effort, sank down and soon afterwards expired.

(5) THOMAS (*b.* Bath, May 1756 ; *d.* Lincolnshire, Aug. 7, 1778), eldest son of Thomas (1), displayed at an early age extraordinary skill on the violin, and at 8 years old performed a concerto in public. After studying with his father he was placed under Boyce. He then went to Florence and took lessons on the violin from Nardini, and whilst there became acquainted with Mozart, then about his own age, and a warm attachment sprang up between them; when they parted they were each bathed in tears, and Mozart often afterwards spoke of Linley with the greatest affection. On returning to England he became leader and soloplayer at his father's concerts at Bath, and subsequently at the oratorios, etc., at Drury Lane. In 1773 he composed an anthem with orchestra ('Let God arise') for the Worcester Festival. In 1775 he assisted his father in 'The Duenna' by writing the overture, three or four airs, a duet and a trio. He subsequently composed a chorus and two songs for introduction into 'The Tempest.' In 1776 he produced 'An Ode on the Witches and Fairies of Shakspere.' He also composed a short oratorio, 'The Song of Moses,' performed at Drury Lane, and added accompaniments for wind instruments to the music in 'Macbeth.' He was unfortunately drowned, through the upsetting of a boat, whilst on a visit at the Duke of Ancaster's, Grimsthorpe, Lincolnshire. The greater part of his miscellaneous compositions are contained in the two vols. of posthumous works above mentioned.

Another son, (6) OZIAS THURSTON (*b.* 1765 ; *d.* Dulwich College, Mar. 6, 1831), was also instructed in music by the father. He entered the Church and obtained a living, which he resigned on being appointed, May 5, 1816, a junior fellow and organist of Dulwich College.

(7) WILLIAM (*b. circa* 1771 : *d.* London, May

6, 1835), youngest son of Thomas (1), was educated at St. Paul's and Harrow, and learned music from his father and Abel. Fox procured for him a writership at Madras. He came back to England in 1796, joined his brother-in-law, Sheridan, in the management of Drury Lane Theatre, and between that year and 1880 brought out three pieces, ' Harlequin Captive,' ' The Honeymoon ' and ' The Pavilion ' (afterwards called ' The Ring '). They were unsuccessful, and in 1800 the author resumed his official duties at Madras. He was subsequently paymaster at Nellore, and in 1805 was sub-treasurer to the presidency, Fort St. George. In 1806 he returned from India with a competence, and devoted his attention to literature and music, composed many glees (' At that dread hour ' won the Glee Club prize in 1821), published a set of songs, two sets of canzonets, and many detached pieces, edited *Shakspere's Dramatic Songs*, two vols. fol. 1815–16, and wrote two novels and several pieces of poetry.

w. h. h. ; addns. *D.N.B.*

LINTERN, J. and W., music publishers in Bath at the end of the 18th century. Their place of business was in the Abbey Churchyard. One of the partners had been a blacksmith, and is said to have first given the title ' The Harmonious Blacksmith ' to Handel's well-known composition on a copy which he published. ' The Harmonious Blacksmith ' had been a nickname bestowed on Lintern himself.

F. K.

LIPINSKI, KARL JOSEPH (*b*. Radzyn, Poland, Oct. 30,[1] 1790 ; *d*. Orlow, near Lemberg, Dec. 16, 1861), eminent violinist, was son of a land-agent and amateur violinist, who taught him the elements of fingering.

He became in 1810 first Konzertmeister, and then Kapellmeister, of the theatre at Lemberg. Not being able to play the piano, he used to lead the rehearsals with his violin, and thus acquired that skill in part-playing which was one of his great characteristics as a virtuoso. In 1814 he resigned his post and gave himself up to private study. In 1817 he went to Italy, chiefly in the hope of hearing Paganini. They met in Milan, and Paganini took a great fancy to him, played with him daily, and even performed in public with him at two concerts (Apr. 17 and 30, 1818), a circumstance which greatly increased Lipinski's reputation. Towards the close of the year Lipinski returned to Germany, but soon went back to Italy, attracted by the fame of an aged pupil of Tartini, Dr. Mazzurana. Dissatisfied with Lipinski's rendering of one of Tartini's sonatas, but unable on account of his great age (90) to correct him by playing it himself, Mazzurana gave him a poem, which he had written to explain the master's intentions. With this aid Lipinski mastered the sonata, and in consequence endeavoured for the future to embody some poetical idea in his playing—the secret of his own success, and of that of many others who imitated him in this respect. In 1829 Paganini and Lipinski met again in Warsaw, but unfortunately a rivalry was excited between them which destroyed the old friendship. In 1835 and 1836, in the course of a lengthened musical tour, he visited Leipzig, and there made the acquaintance of Schumann, which resulted in the dedication to him of the ' Carneval ' (op. 9), which had been composed in 1834. In 1836 he visited England and played his military concerto at the Philharmonic Concert of Apr. 25. In 1839 Lipinski became Konzertmeister at Dresden, where he entirely reorganised the Royal Chapel, thus doing very much the same service to Dresden that Hellmesberger subsequently did to Vienna. He retired with a pension in 1861, and died of sudden paralysis of the lungs at Orlow, his country house near Lemberg.

His compositions (now forgotten) are numerous, and his concertos, fantasias and variations are valuable contributions to violin music. One of the best known was the ' Military Concerto,' which for years was much played. In conjunction with Zalewski, the Polish poet, he edited an interesting collection of Galician ' Volkslieder ' with pianoforte accompaniments.

F. G.

LIPKOWSKA, LYDIA (*b*. Russia), operatic soprano. Her musical studies were carried on in St. Petersburg during the three or four years preceding 1910, when she made her début there at the Maryinsky Theatre. She was engaged in the following year for the summer season at Covent Garden, and made her first appearance on July 11 in Wolf-Ferrari's ' Segreto di Susanna.' To a voice of singular purity and sweetness, not lacking power in the head register, mounting easily to the E flat in *alt*, and admirably trained, she added the charm of an engaging stage presence and a refined, intelligent style. Her success as Susanna she followed up with others as Mimi, Gilda and Violetta, sustaining the last-named rôle on May 22, 1912, when ' La Traviata ' was given at Covent Garden for the 150th time. In these same years she also sang with marked acceptance at New York, Boston and Chicago, extending her repertory by singing Tatiana (in Tchaikovsky's ' Eugen Onégin '), Manon Lescaut and Juliette.

BIBL.—*Int. Who's Who in Music* ; NORTHCOTT, *Covent Garden and the Royal Opera.*

H. K.

LIPOWSKY, FELIX JOSEPH (*b*. Wiesensteig, Jan. 25, 1764 ; *d*. Munich, Mar. 21, 1844), a high official and councillor in the Bavarian Government, who, on the dissolution of the religious orders under Napoleon, saved the documents and collected them in the State Library, of which he became the head. In 1811 he produced his *Baierisches Musik-Lexikon.*

---

[1] Or, according to a family tradition, Nov. 4.

He composed a Mass, 4 v. (1789), and a number of pianoforte solos and sonatas with and without other instruments, which remained in MS.

E. V. D. S.

LIPPARINO, GUGLIELMO, of Bologna, a 16th-17th century Augustinian monk ; maestro di cappella at Como Cathedral from 1619 ; returned afterwards to Bologna, and composed, between 1609 and c. 1639, 8- and 9-part masses with a Te Deum, madrigals, 5 v. (1614), motets (1635), psalms, 8 v. (1637),. sacri concerti, canzonets, canzoni, etc. (Q.-L.).

LIPPIUS, JOHANN, Ph.D. (b. Strassburg, June 25, 1585 ; d. on journey to Speyer, Sept. 24, 1612), Doctor of Philosophy, theologian and musician ; pupil of Calvisius. He wrote a number of theoretical works on music which were held in high repute, and was one of the pioneers who changed the view-point from polyphony to harmony.   E. V. D. S.

LIPSIUS, MARIE (known under the pseudonym 'LA MARA') (b. Leipzig, Dec. 30, 1837 ; d. there, Mar. 2, 1927), a member of a literary family, devoted her life to the literature of music. Her works consist of the following : Musikalische Studienköpfe (five volumes, 1868–82, of which the first series went through nine editions) ; Musikalische Gedanken-Polyphonie (1873), a collection of musicians' sayings about their art ; Beethoven (2nd ed. 1873) ; Das Bühnenfestspiel in Bayreuth (1877) ; a translation of Liszt's Chopin (1880) ; Musikerbriefe aus fünf Jahrhunderten (1886) ; Klassisches und Romantisches aus der Tonwelt (1892) ; and many other books of value. She edited several collections of letters, such as Liszt's correspondence from 1828–86 (translated into English by Constance Bache, and issued with some additional letters, in 1894) ; three volumes of letters to Liszt from various contemporaries (1893–1904) ; the correspondence between Liszt and Von Bülow (1898) ; and Berlioz's letters to the Princess Karolyne zu Sayn-Wittgenstein (1903). Further volumes of Liszt records include Liszt und die Frauen (1911) and Briefe F. Liszts an seine Mutter (1918). (See LISZT BIBL.) In her book Beethoven und die Brunsviks (1920) she held that the 'unsterbliche Gebiebte' was Josephine, Therese's younger sister. She held the title of Royal Professor till her 80th birthday (1917), and in that year published her autobiography, Durch Musik und Leben im Dienste des Ideals (2 vols.). (Riemann.) M.

LIRA. A name given in mediæval times to the smaller bowed instruments such as the rebec and also to the hurdy-gurdy, but from the 15th century onward more especially to bowed instruments furnished with additional strings, some of them placed at the side of the fingerboard, like the free-vibrating 'bourdons' of the large theorbo lutes and chitarroni. According to Praetorius (1618) the principal forms were

two, viz. the Lira da braccio with 7 strings, two off the fingerboard (see PLATE LXXXVIII. No. 5, and VIOL FAMILY), and the Lira da gamba (Lirone perfetto or Arciviola de lira) with 12, 14 or 16 strings, two of them generally at the side (PLATE LXXXVIII. No. 4). Sixteenth-century specimens of both these forms are preserved in the Museum of the Conservatoire de Musique at Brussels and in the Heyer Musikhistorisches Museum, formerly Cologne, now Leipzig.

For the Lira da braccio, a favourite instrument of Ferdinand IV., King of Naples, Haydn wrote seven nocturnes and five concertos. The tuning was that of the violin for the first three strings, the 4th string (G) was doubled by another an octave higher, while the two strings off the fingerboard were tuned to C (Tenor C) and its upper octave.

The Lira da gamba or Lirone was a much more elaborate instrument, its strings being tuned in a succession of consecutive fifths with two 'bourdons' in octaves : this unique arrangement, together with the almost flat bridge and the long bow, facilitated the execution of chords as an accompaniment to the voice (see art. CRWTH). Hence according to Ceruti (1776) it was called in Italy the Accordo. The English lyra viol of the 17th century was an attempt to reproduce by various tunings the full-chord effect of the Lira upon the Viola da gamba. (See LYRA VIOL ; VIOLIN FAMILY.)

F. W. G.

LISCHEN ET FRITZCHEN, operetta in 1 act ; words by Paul Dubois, music by Offenbach. Produced at Ems ; and reproduced Bouffes-Parisiens, Paris, Jan. 5, 1864 ; in London (French), St. James's, June 2, 1868.

G.

LISLEY, JOHN, contributed a six-part madrigal—'Faire Citharea presents hir doves'—to 'The Triumphes of Oriana,' 1601 (see Eng. Madr. Sch. vol. xxxii.), but no other composition by him has survived, nor is anything known of his biography.   W. H. H.

LISTENIUS, MAGISTER NIKOLAUS (b. Brandenburg, c. 1500), wrote a small compendium of music, 'Rudimenta musica,' etc., published at Wittemberg, 1533, which until 1583 appeared in numerous editions, legitimate and pirated.

LISZT, FRANZ (FERENCZ) (b. Raiding, Hungary, Oct. 22, 1811 ; d. Bayreuth, July 31, 1886), as pianist and composer one of the outstanding figures of 19th-century music, was the son of Adam Liszt, a steward in the service of Prince Esterhazy, and a musical amateur of sufficient attainment to instruct his son in the rudiments of pianoforte-playing.

At the age of 9 young Liszt made his first appearance in public at Ödenburg with such success that several Hungarian noblemen guaranteed him sufficient means to continue his studies for six years. For that purpose he went to Vienna, where he made his first public appearance Dec. 1, 1822. His genius was acknowledged with an enthusiasm in which the whole musical republic from Beethoven downward joined unanimously. He took lessons from Czerny on the pianoforte and from Salieri and Randhartinger in composition. The latter introduced the lad to his friend Franz Schubert. His first appearance in print was probably in a variation (the 24th) on the waltz of Diabelli which prompted Beethoven's famous set. (See VATERLÄNDISCHE KÜNSTLERVEREIN.) In 1823 he proceeded to Paris, where it was hoped that his rapidly growing reputation would gain him admission to the Conservatoire in spite of his foreign origin. But Cherubini refused to make an exception in his favour, and he continued his studies under Reicha and Paër. In 1824 he paid his first visit to England, appearing in the Argyll Rooms, London, on June 21, and on June 29 at Drury Lane, having, in the words of the original playbill, ' consented to display his inimitable powers on the New Grand Piano Forte, invented by Sébastien Erard.' In the following season he came to London again and played at the Duke of Devonshire's, May 13, 1825, and elsewhere, and in June he played twice in Manchester. Shortly afterwards he made his first serious attempt at composition, and an operetta in one act, called ' Don Sancho,' was produced at the Académie Royale, Paris, Oct. 17, 1825.[1] Artistic tours to Switzerland and England occupy the period till 1827, when Liszt lost his father, and was thrown on his own resources to provide for himself and his mother. During his stay in Paris, where he settled for some years, he became acquainted with the leaders of French literature, Victor Hugo, Lamartine and George Sand, the influence of whose works may be discovered in his compositions. More important still was his intercourse with Chopin. For a time also he was attracted by the tenets of the St. Simonians, but in after years he denied that he had ever joined that body. In 1834 he became acquainted with the Countess d'Agoult, better known by her literary name of Daniel Stern, with whom he formed an intimacy which lasted till 1844, and by whom he had three children, a son, one daughter who became the wife of Émile Ollivier the French statesman, and another, Cosima, married first to Von Bülow, and later to Wagner.

The public concerts which Liszt gave during the latter part of his stay in Paris placed his claim to the first rank amongst pianists on a firm basis, and at last he was induced, much against his will, to adopt the career of a virtuoso proper. The dazzling career of Paganini, to which his own was to be in some sort a parallel, no doubt attracted him forcibly, as did also the compositions of that artist ; the transcriptions

for piano of his famous studies were first published in 1839. The interval from 1839–47 Liszt spent in travelling almost incessantly from one country to another ; in England he played at the Philharmonic Concerts of May 21, 1827, May 11, 1840, June 8, 1840, June 14, 1841. His reception [2] seems to have been less warm than was expected, and Liszt, with his usual generosity, at once undertook to bear the loss that might have fallen on his agent. Of this generosity numerous instances might be cited. The charitable purposes to which Liszt's genius was made subservient are legion. The disaster caused at Pest by the inundation of the Danube (1837) was considerably alleviated by the princely sum—the result of several concerts—which he contributed. When two years later a sum had been collected for a statue to be erected to him at Pest, he insisted upon the money being given to a struggling young sculptor, whom he, moreover, assisted from his private means. The poor of Raiding also had cause to remember the visit paid by Liszt to his native village about the same time. It is well known that Beethoven's monument at Bonn, erected in 1845, owed its existence, or at least its speedy completion, to Liszt's liberality. When the subscriptions for the purpose began to fail, Liszt offered to pay the balance required from his own pocket, provided only that the choice of the sculptor should be left to him.

From about 1842 dates Liszt's more intimate connexion with Weimar, where in 1849 he settled for the space of twelve years. This stay was to be fruitful in more than one sense. The Princess Karolyne zu Sayn-Wittgenstein united her life with his in 1847, and their house at Weimar, the ' Altenburg,' was for many years a centre of artistic influence, always exerted on behalf of the most modern tendencies in music. The princess undoubtedly collaborated with Liszt in the composition of various literary efforts that made a considerable stir at the time ; such were the very untrustworthy Life of Chopin, and certain pamphlets on the early works of Wagner.[3] When he closed his career as a virtuoso and accepted a permanent engagement as conductor of the Court Theatre at Weimar, he did so with the distinct purpose of becoming the advocate of the rising musical generation, by the performance of such works as were written regardless of immediate success, and therefore had little chance of seeing the light of the stage. At short intervals eleven operas of living composers were either performed for the first time or revived on the Weimar stage. Amongst these may be counted such works as ' Lohengrin,' ' Tannhäuser ' and ' The Flying Dutchman ' of Wagner, ' Benvenuto Cellini ' by Berlioz, Schumann's ' Genoveva,' and music to Byron's ' Manfred.'

---

[1] See the *Harmonicon*, vol. iii. p. 224.

[2] Some amusing English criticisms may be read in Ramann's *Life*, vol. ii. pp. 82, 83, 109, etc.

[3] See W. Ashton Ellis's *Life of Wagner*, vol. iv.

Schubert's ' Alfonso und Estrella ' was also rescued from oblivion by Liszt's exertions. For a time it seemed as if this small provincial city were once more to be the artistic centre of Germany, as it had been in the days of Goethe, Schiller and Herder. From all sides musicians and amateurs flocked to Weimar, to witness the astonishing feats to which a small but excellent community of singers and instrumentalists were inspired by the genius of their leader. It was, indeed, at these Weimar gatherings that the musicians who formed the so-called School of the Future, till then unknown to each other and divided locally and mentally, came first to a clear understanding of their powers and aspirations.

But in a still higher sense the soil of Weimar, with its great traditions, was to prove a field of rich harvest. When, as early as 1842, Liszt undertook the direction of a certain number of concerts every year at Weimar, his friend Duverger wrote : ' Cette place, qui oblige Liszt à séjourner trois mois de l'année à Weimar, doit marquer peut-être pour lui la transition de sa carrière de virtuose à celle de compositeur.' This presage was verified by a number of compositions which have done much to elucidate some of the most important questions in Art. (See the symphonic poems in the list of works below.)

The last concert given by Franz Liszt for his own benefit was that at Elisabethgrad towards the end of 1847,[1] since when his artistic activity was exclusively devoted to the benefit of others. No more striking evidence of the nobility of Liszt's purpose and of the gracious manner in which he fulfilled it could be wished for than that contained in the published correspondence between Liszt and Wagner.[2] The two volumes cover the Weimar period, but by no means represent the extent of the friendship between these two great men, which was only interrupted by death.

Liszt made Weimar, during the twelve years of his residence, the centre of musical life in Germany. ' I had dreamed for Weimar a new Art period,' he wrote in 1860, ' similar to that of Karl August, in which Wagner and I would have been the leaders as formerly Goethe and Schiller, but unfavourable circumstances brought these dreams to nothing.' Though he did not accomplish all he wished for Weimar, the little city still ranks high among German art centres, and in some degree the work of advancement so firmly established between the years 1844 and 1861 was carried on in subsequent years.

The aspect of Liszt's everyday life at Weimar has become known through the accounts of some of the host of aspiring pianists and music lovers who gathered around him there. Liszt's

teaching had already borne fruit in the achievements of his most distinguished pupils—Von Bülow, Tausig and others—and no wonder that the music-room which the generous artist had thrown open to all comers was thronged by a number of gifted young people in search of inspiration—no other word so well describes the ideal character of the instruction they were privileged to receive.

Liszt held his classes in the afternoon, during which several of the pupils would play in the presence of the rest—some dozen or more, perhaps—all being expected to attend the séance. At times he would seat himself at the piano and play, but this supreme pleasure could never be counted upon. A lively description of this professorial life has been given by an American lady who visited Weimar in 1873.[3] In 1859 Liszt left his official position at the Weimar Opera owing to the captious opposition made to the production of Cornelius's ' Barber of Bagdad.' There then ensued a period with Rome as his headquarters which Liszt called his *vie trifurquée*, divided between Budapest, Weimar and Rome. The Hungarian Government, in order to ensure Liszt's presence in Budapest during part of the year, invented for him (1870) the post of president o an institution which at the moment did not exist, but which soon afterwards rose as the Academy of Music. Impressive scenes occurred when the Magyars publicly fêted their compatriot,[4] and hero-worship was at its height on such occasions as the jubilee of the master's career in 1873, when ' Christus ' was performed at the Hungarian capital. The ' Legend of St. Elizabeth ' had already been given there in 1865.

In Rome again Liszt found himself the centre of an artistic circle of which von Keudell and Sgambati were the moving spirits. The significance, however, of his residence there lies rather in the view he took of it as his *années de recueillement*, which ultimately led to his binding himself as closely as he could to the Church of Rome. He who in his youth, with the thirst for knowledge upon him, had enjoyed the writings of freethinkers and atheists (without being convinced by them), was now content with his breviary and book of hours ; the impetuous artist who had felt the fascination of St. Simonianism [5] before he had thoroughly understood its *raison d'être*, who had been carried away by the currents of the Revolution and had even in 1841 joined the Freemasons,[6] became in 1856 or 1858 a tertiary of St. Francis of Assisi. In 1879 he was permitted to receive the tonsure and the four minor orders (doorkeeper, reader, exorcist and acolyth), and an

[3] *Music Study in Germany*, Amy Fay. See also F. Hueffer in the *Fortnightly Review*, Sept. 1886.
[4] Janka Wohl's *François Liszt*.
[5] ' I neither officially nor unofficially belonged to the St. Simonians.' See Ramann, vol. i. Heine is inaccurate on this and some other points.
[6] At Frankfort-on-Main, during the period of his sojourn at Nonnenwerth with the Countess d'Agoult.

[1] Ramann's *F. Liszt als Künstler und Mensch*, vol. ii. Breitkopf & Härtel.
[2] *Briefwechsel zwischen Wagner und Liszt*. Breitkopf & Härtel.

honorary canonry. The Abbé Liszt, who as a boy had wished to enter the priesthood but was dissuaded therefrom by his parents and his confessor, now rejoiced in the public avowal of his creed as conveyed by his priestly garb, although he was indeed no priest, could neither say Mass nor hear a confession, and was at liberty to discard his cassock, and even to marry if he chose, without causing scandal. Thus, in the struggle with the world which the youth of 16 had so much dreaded, his religious fervour was destined to carry the day. Extracts from Liszt's private papers throwing further light on his inmost thoughts have been published,[1] but can be only referred to in this place.

In the last year of his life he received special honours in the two capitals where his earliest successes had been won. On Mar. 25, 1886, his ' Graner Messe,' first performed at the consecration of Gran cathedral, Aug. 31, 1856, was given at St. Eustache, Paris, while his former triumphs in England were destined to be eclipsed by the enthusiasm of the reception which awaited him upon his return. In 1824 George IV. had given the sign to the aristocracy of homage to the child prodigy ; and his visits in the following year and in 1827 were successful enough. In 1840–41 [2] the Queen's favour was accorded to him, and he shared with Thalberg a reputation as a skilful pianist in fashionable circles. But it was not until 1886 that the vast popularity which had hitherto been withheld from him, owing to the conditions of musical life in our country, was meted out to him in full measure.

Liszt paused awhile in Paris on his way to England and received much attention, his musical friends and followers gathering to meet him at the concerts of Colonne, Lamoureux and Pasdeloup. At length on Apr. 3 the Abbé Liszt reached our shores, and on the same evening three or four hundred people met at Mr. Littleton's house at Sydenham to do him honour, and a programme consisting entirely of his compositions was gone through by Walter Bache and others. Liszt, however, chose to play Chopin's nocturne in A♭. On the following day Liszt played part of his E♭ concerto before a few friends. On the Monday he attended the rehearsal of his oratorio ' St. Elizabeth ' in St. James's Hall, and in the evening he astonished his host and a circle of friends by an improvisation on some of the themes. Apr. 6 was the date of the concert, which was conducted by MACKENZIE (q.v.), and when the composer walked into the hall he received such ovations as had probably never been offered to an artist in England before. Even before he entered, his arrival was announced by the shouts of the crowd outside,

who hailed him as if he were a king returning to his kingdom. During the afternoon Liszt had been entertained at the R.A.M., where the Liszt Scholarship, raised by the zeal of Walter Bache, was presented by him to the master. A short programme was performed, Shakespeare and Mackenzie conducting, and then Liszt rose and moved to the piano and played, to the delight of all present. A visit to Windsor, where he played to Queen Victoria a reminiscence of the Rose Miracle scene from ' St. Elizabeth,' filled up most of the following day (Apr. 8), on the evening of which Walter Bache's reception at the Grosvenor Gallery took place. (See BACHE.) The events which followed in the course of the visit included a performance of ' St. Elizabeth ' at the Crystal Palace on the 17th. On the 22nd, a week later than he intended, Liszt left England, pleased with his reception, and promising to repeat his visit. No wonder that his death was felt by English people as the loss of a personal friend. The last music he wrote was a bar or two of Mackenzie's ' Troubadour,' upon which he had intended to write a fantasia.

Paris gave him a performance of ' St. Elizabeth ' at the Trocadéro. Leaving Paris in May, Liszt visited in turn Antwerp, Jena and Sondershausen. He attended the summer festival here while suffering from weakness and cold. ' On m'a mis les bottes pour le grand voyage,' he said, excusing himself to a friend for remaining seated. His last appearance upon a concert platform was on July 19, when, accompanied by M. and Mme. Munkácsy, he attended a concert of the Musical Society of Luxemburg. At the end of the concert he was prevailed upon to seat himself at the piano. He played a fantasia and a ' Soirée de Vienne.' In the pages of Janka Wohl's *François Liszt* there is an account of a scene during Liszt's stay at the Munkácsys' house, according to the writer a record of the last time the greatest master of the pianoforte touched his instrument. A flying visit had been paid to Bayreuth on the marriage of Daniela von Bülow—Liszt's granddaughter—with von Thode on July 4. Liszt returned again for the performance of ' Parsifal ' on the 23rd. He was suffering from a bronchial attack, but the cough for a day or two became less troublesome, and he ventured to attend another play, an exceptionally fine performance of ' Tristan,' during which the face of Liszt shone full of life and happiness, though his weakness was so great that he had been almost carried between the carriage and Mme. Wagner's box. This memorable performance of ' Tristan,' in which the singers (Sucher, Vogl, etc.) and players surpassed themselves, lingered in Liszt's mind until his death. When he returned home he was prostrate, and those surrounding him feared the worst. The patient was confined to his bed and kept perfectly quiet. The case

[1] *Allgemeine Musik-Zeitung*, May 13, 1887.
[2] His project of conducting German opera in London in 1842 came to nothing,

was from the first hopeless, the immediate cause of death being general weakness rather than the severe cold and inflammation of the lungs which supervened on July 31, 1886. His death that night was absolutely painless.

Since the funeral in the Bayreuth cemetery on Aug. 3, Liszt's ashes have not been disturbed, although Weimar and Budapest each asserted a claim to the body of the illustrious dead. Cardinal Haynauld and the Princess Wittgenstein (heiress and executrix under his will) gave way before the wishes of Liszt's sole surviving daughter Cosima Wagner, supported as they were by public opinion and the known views of Liszt himself, who had not looked with favour on the removal of the remains of Beethoven and Schubert, and had expressed a hope that it might not also be his fate to *herumfahren*. These towns, as well as others, have therefore raised monuments to the genius who was associated with them. The memory of Liszt has been honoured in a practical way in many places. Liszt societies existed during the master's lifetime, and since his death they have been multiplied. Immediately after the funeral a meeting of the leading musicians was held at Bayreuth, at which Richter made a speech and urged that all the living forces of the artistic world should unite to preserve the memory of the master by perfect renderings of his own and other modern works. The Grand Duke of Weimar, Liszt's friend and protector, sent the intendant of the theatre to Bayreuth to confer with Richter upon the best means of perpetuating Liszt's intentions. He proposed a Liszt foundation after the manner of the Mozarteum at Salzburg. A Liszt museum was to be established in the house where he lived at Weimar, and scholarships were to be offered to promising young musicians, and on similar lines scholarships have been instituted elsewhere. The outcome of this project was the Fondation-Liszt.

The first competition for the Liszt R.A.M. scholarship took place in Apr. 1887.[1] The scholarship is open for competition by male and female candidates, natives of any country, between 14 and 20 years of age, and may be awarded to the one who may be judged to evince the greatest merit in pianoforte-playing or in composition. All candidates have to pass an examination in general education before entering the musical contest. The holder is entitled to three years' free instruction in the R.A.M., and after that to a sum for continental study.

Among portraits of the master, the bust executed by Boehm, and exhibited at the Grosvenor Gallery in 1886, has great interest for English people, as Liszt sat for it during his visit to Sydenham in the same year. The head of Liszt upon his death-bed has been successfully represented in a plaster cast by Weissbrod &

[1] Walter Bache raised upwards of £1100 for the purpose.

Schnappauf of Bayreuth. On pp. 149 and 219 of Janka Wohl's volume, and in the second volume of L. Ramann's Life, a detailed account and list of portraits and paintings may be found.   F. H.

QUALITIES OF THE ARTIST.—As an interpretative artist and a creator of music, Liszt stands before us as a man in whom sympathy was a far stronger thing than imagination. He had a marvellous intuition for what was good in the work of a multitude of men whose paths ultimately diverged as far as the poles asunder. It must be remembered that the narrowness of artistic views, of which the Liszt school has often been accused—not altogether without warrant—was not due to the master, whose affections were large enough to hold a world of composers, and to enter with surprising fullness into the ideals of each. In Schumann, Brahms, Joachim, he found, at one time or another, points with which he could sympathise, however great was the distance which eventually separated the composers of his special devotion from the classical school of their time. The fortune which he had made during his early career as the most astonishing virtuoso of any time upon the pianoforte, was in later life held as it were in trust for the use of his poorer brethren in the art, and his correspondence—more particularly the collection of the letters addressed to him by his contemporaries—shows how unscrupulously his generosity was in many cases abused. Still, his influence was far from being wasted, for without his help it is quite certain that the fame of Wagner would have been greatly delayed, while the catalogue of operas produced during his artistic reign at Weimar shows how catholic his tastes were. His brave defence of Cornelius, as a consequence of which he gave up the most useful duties of his life, was the kind of action that appeals to the imagination and no doubt helped to advance the cause of contemporary music, both for good and evil. For of course with such open-handed liberality there was little room for discrimination, and a great many of the disciples of the Liszt school were very poor musicians, just as many of his pianoforte pupils were entirely unworthy of his name.

His sympathy for all sorts of music was again manifested in his interpretation of the music of widely different schools on the pianoforte. He lived before the time when musical archæology was in vogue, and it was owing to his ecclesiastical tastes rather than to any antiquarian instinct that he was moved to practical admiration of Palestrina. His playing of the older music (before Beethoven) was never the most remarkable side of his art, and it must have been the difficulty of combining the pedal and manual parts of Bach's organ works which drew him to arrange them for the piano. But with all music of his day he was in fullest sympathy, up to the time when he gave up the regular career of a virtuoso. In regard to pianoforte technique his work was of the utmost importance; the full discussion of this point must be left to another place (see PIANO-FORTE-PLAYING). It must suffice here to say that, even to those who only heard him in the last year of his life, his playing was a thing never to be forgotten, or approached by later artists. The peculiar quiet brilliance of his rapid passages, the noble proportion kept between the parts, and the meaning and effect which he put into the music, were the most striking points, for it is quite a mistake to suppose that the habit of thumping, which so many of his pupils and followers thought fit to adopt, came from himself.

His pianoforte transcriptions and arrangements cover an immense field of music, good, bad and indifferent. Yet very few of the productions suggest that they were done 'to order,' or that the task was at all uncongenial to the arranger. Among the most famous of these, and as a matter of fact among the very best, are the arrangements of Schubert's songs, in many of which he contrives to throw a new light on Schubert's ideas, and, in the opinion of a good many people, to enhance their beauty. Naturally there are cases where his additions cannot meet with unqualified approval from every one; but his sympathy with this master was so complete that he very seldom erred in taste in treating his music. Even operatic fantasias, which for the most part are the dreariest of imaginable compilations, became, in Liszt's hands, things of some beauty and musical interest, besides reproducing the theatrical situation with success. One of the many paradoxes of Liszt's nature was his warm admiration for the kind of themes that we associate with Bellini and Donizetti, combined with a rather uncouth type of melodic invention, in the case of his own creations, which assorts remarkably ill with the Italian sentimentality. In his own original work as a composer it is remarkable that he nearly always required a poetic idea to illustrate in his compositions. (In this connexion it is of course possible that the process was similar to that employed by Schumann, i.e. the music may have been composed first, and the fancy title found for it afterwards; but, taking all the compositions into consideration, it would seem more likely that, in the great majority of instances, the music was deliberately written up to an impression produced by some other art, or by some natural scene.) It is not exactly that the imagination was defective, but it required to be kindled from without. Liszt's efforts at abstract music are very few and, for the most part, very unsatisfactory. This is no doubt explained by the circumstance that so much of his early life had been given to the attainment of his wonderful pianoforte technique that he could not undergo the drudgery of learning how to develop musical themes and how to make them self-dependent and inherently interesting. Their actual fabric as well as their invention often leaves much to be desired, more especially in such things as the pianoforte ballades or the sonata in B minor. Liszt's themes, in fact, are most rarely such as to produce the feeling in the hearer that a new revelation was made in them. Where he was supreme was in his handling of the orchestra, and it must for ever be a problem how he learnt the art of scoring. The 'Hungarian Rhapsodies,' in the transference between the piano and the orchestra of the special effects of the national bands, must have been the means by which he became the master of the orchestra that we know him to have been. The 'Symphonic Poems' mark the point of greatest divergence from the classical ideals, and the discussion they aroused was the chief cause of the defection of Joachim and others from the Liszt camp. Even Wagner hesitated for a time before accepting some of the perversities which occur in them, just as in earlier days some of Liszt's extravagances in his pianoforte works had repelled Chopin. The symphonic poems and the 'Faust' and 'Dante' symphonies are the works in which the theories of 'programme music' were pushed to the furthest point reached in that peculiar department of art until the advent of Strauss. The fact that this latter composer has out-Liszted Liszt must not blind us to the boldness of Liszt's work at the time it was written. (See ABSOLUTE MUSIC; PROGRAMME MUSIC.) From the purely musical point of view the 'Faust' symphony is far superior to the 'Dante,' and the conception of the work seems more spontaneous than that of the other, or of most of the symphonic poems. Of the finale Dannreuther (see below) says:

'This movement exhibits the outlines of symphonic structure . . . but the details for the most part have reference to the exigencies of the poetical idea, and such exigencies are permitted to overrule considerations of musical consistency and beauty.'

In this class of his compositions Liszt laid great stress upon an innovation which has been generally associated with his name, although it had been practically used from time to time long before his days. The system of 'Transformation of Themes,' as he called it, is beyond question an easier thing to handle than the logical development which the older masters preferred. This may or may not have been the reason why Liszt adopted it so readily. It is easy to see that it lends itself well to the illustrative music of which he and his followers were so fond; for a theme appearing in a new guise, altered in tempo and rhythm—so long as it is easy to recognise in its changed shape—stands well as the counterpart of one character in different circumstances. (See LEIT-MOTIV.)

The larger compositions of Liszt intended for ecclesiastical use have been analysed very minutely, and with great insight and acumen, by Dannreuther in the *Oxford History of Music, Romantic Period*, vol. vi. He points out that in the 'Graner Festmesse,' and in the two oratorios which Liszt completed, there is a copious use of Wagner's method of employing representative themes, the various movements of the Mass being connected by these means. He says :

'Liszt came to interpret the Catholic ritual in a histrionic spirit, and tried to make his music reproduce the words not only as *ancilla theologica et ecclesiastica*, but also as *ancilla dramaturgica*. The influence of Wagner's operatic method . . . is abundantly evident ; but the result of this influence is more curious than convincing' (p. 200).

In speaking of the 'Hungarian Coronation Mass' (1866–67) Dannreuther says :

'Liszt aimed at characteristic national colour, and tried to attain it by persistently putting forward some of the melodic formulae common to music of the Hungarian type. . . . The style of the entire mass is as incongruous as a gipsy musician in a church vestment' (*ib.* pp. 204, 209).

The same author sums up the other pieces by Liszt that belong to sacred music in these words :

'The majority of them can hardly be accounted good music in the full sense of the word. Taken simply as music, and without regard to any symbolism or casual association with the Ritual, they convey an undefinable sense of effort and weakness' (*ib.* p. 220).

The 'concert oratorio' called 'The Legend of St. Elizabeth' is a living illustration of the dual personality of Liszt ; it is fervently religious in character, and yet is far more of an opera than a real oratorio. It had a far greater success on the stage (at Munich, Weimar, Hanover, Leipzig and elsewhere) than on the concert platform. The scene of the miracle of the roses is by far the finest point of the work, and, as Dannreuther says, 'one of the best things Liszt ever produced.' For an analysis of 'Christus' the reader must be referred to the volume already quoted.

It remains to speak of two branches of art in which Liszt was at his very best. The purely lyrical pianoforte pieces, such as the 'Consolations,' many of the 'Années de pèlerinage,' the beautiful 'Bénédiction de Dieu dans la solitude,' and several of the other 'Harmonies poétiques et religieuses,' have an amount of inspiration which is rarely found in the more ambitious works of the composer ; and in his songs he reaches a level of invention that is untouched for the most part elsewhere. All, or almost all, the songs are highly original, effectively written for the voice, and interesting in the accompaniment ; some are a little forced in sentiment, but in all the natural accentuation of the words is followed with singular fidelity, and a few are among the most expressive lyrics of the world. 'Kennst du das Land' is held by many good judges to be the best of the many excellent settings of the words ;

'Der König von Thule' is another of finest quality ; 'Es muss ein Wunderbares sein' has an emotional directness, and 'Comment, disaient-ils' a whimsical grace, that are obvious to every hearer ; 'Die Lorelei' and 'Du bist wie eine Blume' are perfect counterparts of Heine's words, and if Liszt had been nothing more than a song-writer, he would have been hailed as a composer of rare gift.   M.

A branch of Liszt's work that has only recently received due attention in this country is his organ music. His correspondence shows that he was always interested in the organ, and no doubt his compositions and arrangements for it would have been more numerous had the instrument of his day been more tractable in touch and less imperfect in regard to facilities for registration. Owing to these drawbacks he seems to have worked generally with the pedal-piano in view (A. W. Gottschalg's 'Repertorium,' a bulky three-volume collection of transcriptions issued under Liszt's general editorship, and containing his arrangements of some Bach cantata choruses and Chopin's preludes in E minor and E major, was described as being 'für Orgel, Harmonium, oder Pedal-Flügel'), and the bulk of his organ music appeared also in pianoforte versions. As a result, the manual passage work is often suggestive of the pianoforte, and much of it —especially certain bravura passages—must have been difficult to negotiate on old organs. Despite some inevitable lack of consistency in the matter of style, and a tendency to development of a somewhat diffuse character, the outstanding examples of Liszt's organ music are worthy of ranking with the pick of his pianoforte and orchestral music. The best-known appears to be the Fantasia and Fugue on B. A. C. H., a work so much in the style of a dashing improvisation (which was probably its origin) that one readily accepts some lapses into superficiality. Less known, but perhaps finer, is the 'Evocation in the Sistine Chapel,' a picturesque tone-poem based on Mozart's 'Ave Verum' and a phrase from the well-known Miserere of Allegri. With an easily made 'cut,' and a little adaptation in passages that are more effective on the pedal-pianoforte than on the organ, this makes a vivid recital piece. The variations on 'Weinen, Klagen' contain much that is striking, especially in the use of enharmonic changes, but the work is too long. Liszt here, in over three hundred bars, says no more—perhaps less—than does Bach in his brief treatment of the same ground bass in the *Crucifixus* of the B minor Mass. The finest of Liszt's organ works, and one of the greatest of his essays in any field, is the Fantasia and Fugue on the Choral 'Ad nos, ad salutarem undam' from Meyerbeer's 'Le Prophète.' It is on an immense scale, containing nearly eight hundred bars, and taking over half an hour in performance. (The Fugue alone is a good deal longer than Bach's G minor Fantasia and Fugue.) The Fantasia is now generally played in a much shortened form. In spite of a few passages in which the counterpoint is of the over-facile 'padding' type, the Fugue is a truly splendid example of free use of the form. It is an epitome of Liszt's method, all the thematic material being derived from the Choral. (An interesting point in connexion with the Fugue is its obvious influence on the famous 'Sonata on the 94th Psalm' of Liszt's pupil, Julian REUBKE (q.v.). Before the 'Ad nos' Fugue became generally known it was customary to ascribe much of the Reubke harmonic and thematic treatment to Wagner.) That these works have been neglected until recent times is no doubt due to the fact that they call for an organ of ample and easily managed resource. Now that such instruments are plentiful, and organ technique has developed a good deal along pianoforte lines, justice is likely to be done to this small but striking side of Liszt's output.   H. G.

The following catalogue of Liszt's works is as complete as it has been possible to make it, while the collected and revised edition of his works undertaken by the Liszt-Stiftung is still in progress. This is compiled with the help of the various published lists, and based on the *Thematisches Verzeichniss* published by Breitkopf & Härtel (as No. 14,373) shortly before the master's death. The earlier edition of the catalogue, published in 1855, contained mention of early editions and some compositions which Liszt afterwards disowned.

I. ORCHESTRAL WORKS

1. ORIGINAL

1. Symphonie zu Dante's Divina Commedia, orch. and female chorus: ded. to Wagner. 1. Inferno; 2. Purgatorio; 3. Magnificat. Score and parts. B. & H. Arr. for 2 PFs.
2. Eine Faust-Symphonie in drei Charakterbildern (nach Goethe), orch. and male chorus: ded. to Berlioz. 1. Faust; 2. Gretchen (also for PF. 2 hands); 3. Mephistopheles. Score and parts; also for 2 PFs. Schuberth.
3. Zwei Episoden aus Lenau's Faust. 1. Der nächtliche Zug. 2. Der Tanz in der Dorfschenke (Mephisto-Walzer). Score and parts; also for PF. 2 and 4 hands. Schuberth.
4. Symphonische Dichtungen. 1. 'Héroïde funèbre,' begun in 1830, but not completed until 1849, published in 1857; was at one time intended to form the first movement of a 'Symphonie Révolutionnaire,' an intention never carried out. 2. Tasso ('Lamento e Trionfo'), conceived in 1840 as a pianoforte work; orchestrated in 1848; produced as introduction to Goethe's 'Tasso' at the Goethe Festival at Weimar, Aug. 28, 1849; revised in 1854 and published in 1856. 3. 'Les Préludes,' after Lamartine's 'Méditations poétiques,' conceived at Marseilles in 1845; completed at Weimar in 1850. 4. 'Hungaria,' sketch dated 1846; published as a 'Hun-

garian March' for pianoforte; orchestrated in 1853; revised in 1856; published in 1857. 5. 'Bergsymphonie' ('Ce qu'on entend sur la montagne'), sketch dated 1847; development and orchestration, 1849; first performance, 1853, at Weimar; revised in 1854 and again in 1856; published, 1857. 6. 'Mazeppa' dates from about the same period as No. 5, but was originally destined for a pianoforte étude (see below, No. 29, 4), enlarged and orchestrated in 1858; published for pianoforte in 1857. 7. 'Prometheus' in original form dates from 1850, but a complete revision of the choruses, etc., for concert purposes with text by Richard Pohl, followed in 1859. 8. 'Festklänge' dates from 1853; on the fiftieth anniversary of the first performance of Schiller's 'Huldigung der Künste,' it served in the theatre and as a mark of respect for the jubilee of the entry into power of the Grossfürstin Marie Paulowna, Nov. 9, 1854. An edition was published in June 1856, but in 1860 this was revised, added to, and republished in its new form as at present known. 9. 'Orpheus,' conceived in January 1854, during the rehearsals of Gluck's 'Orfeo' at Weimar, and first performed in the middle of February of that year. 10. 'Hunnenschlacht,' conceived

in 1856 after Liszt saw Kaulbach's painting which bears the same title; apparently completed between January and March 1857. 11. 'Die Ideale' (after Schiller's poem), written for the unveiling of the Goethe-Schiller monument at Weimar, September 1857. 12. 'Hamlet,' composed in 1859, apparently was not publicly performed until undertaken by the Allgem. D. Musikv. at Sondershausen in 1886. 13. 'Von der Wiege bis zum Grabe,' founded upon a sketch by Michael Zichy, consists of three parts : (1) Die Wiege ; (2) Der Kampf ums Dasein ; (3) Am Grabe, der Wiege des zukünftigen Lebens.
5. Fest-Vorspiel, for Schiller and Goethe Festival, Weimar, 1857. Score, Hallberger.
6. Fest-Marsch, for Goethe's birthday. Score and parts, also for PF. 2 and 4 hands. Schuberth.
7. Huldigungs-Marsch, for accession of Duke Carl of Saxe-Weimar, 1853. Score ; and for PF. 2 hands. B. & H.
8. 'Vom Fels zum Meer' : Patriotic March. Score and parts; also for PF. 2 hands. Schlesinger.
9. Künstler Fest-Zug ; for Schiller Festival, 1859. Score ; and for PF. 2 and 4 hands. Kahnt.
10. 'Gaudeamus igitur': Humoreske for orch., soli and chorus for the centenary of the Academische Concerten at Jena, 1870. Score and parts ; also for PF. 2 and 4 hands. Schuberth.
11. Music to Halm's play, 'A Hundred Years Ago' (Prague, 1859), not published.

2. ARRANGEMENTS

12. Schubert's Marches. 1. Op. 40, No. 3 ; 2. Trauer-; 3. Reiter-; 4. Ungarischer-Marsch. Score and parts. Fürstner.
13. Schubert's Songs for voice and small orch. 1. Die junge Nonne ; 2. Gretchen am Spinnrade ; 3. Lied der Mignon ; 4. Erlkönig. Score and parts. Forberg.
14. 'Die Allmacht,' by Schubert, for tenor, men's chorus and orchestra. Score and parts ; and vocal score. Schuberth.
15. H. v. Bülow's Mazurka-Fantasie (op. 13). Score and parts. Leuckart.
16. Festmarsch on themes by E. H. zu S. Score ; also for PF. 2 and 4 hands. Schuberth.

---

17. Ungarische Rhapsodien, arr. by Liszt and F. Doppler ; 1. in F ; 2. in D ; 3. in D ; 4. in D minor and G major ; 5. in E ; 6. Pester Carneval. Score and parts ; and for PF. 4 hands. Schuberth. (See below, No. 49.)
18. Ungarischer Marsch, for Coronation at Buda - Pest, 1867. Score ; also for PF. 2 and 4 hands. Schuberth.
19. Rákoczy-Marsch ; symphonisch bearbeitet. Score and parts ; also for PF. 2, 4 and 8 hands. Schuberth.
20. Ungarischer Sturm-Marsch. New arr. 1876. Score and parts; also for PF. 2 and 4 hands. Schlesinger.
21. 'Szózat' and 'Hymnus' by Béni and Erkel. Score and parts ; also for PF. Rózsavölgyi, Pest.

II. FOR PIANOFORTE AND ORCHESTRA

1. ORIGINAL

22. Concerto No. 1, in E flat. Score and parts ; also for 2 PFs. Schlesinger.
23. Concerto No. 2, in A. Score and parts ; also for 2 PFs. Schott.
24. 'Todten-Tanz.' Paraphrase on 'Dies Irae.' Score ; also for 1 and 2 PFs. Siegel.

2. ARRANGEMENTS, PF. PRINCIPALE

25. Fantasia on themes from

Beethoven's 'Ruins of Athens.' Score ; also for PF. 2 and 4 hands, and 2 PFs. Siegel.
26. Fantasie über ungarische Volksmelodien. Score and parts. Heinze.
27. Schubert's Fantasia in C (op. 15), symphonisch bearbeitet. Score and parts ; also for 2 PFs. Schreiber.
28. Weber's Polonaise (op. 72). Score and parts. Schlesinger.

III. FOR PIANOFORTE SOLO

1. ORIGINAL

29. Études d'exécution transcendante. 1. Preludio ; 2, 3. Paysage ; 4. Mazeppa ; 5. Feux Follets ; 6. Vision ; 7. Eroica ; 8. Wilde Jagd ; 9. Ricordanza ; 10, 11. Harmonies du soir ; 12. Chasse-neige. B. & H.
30. Trois Grandes Études de concert. 1. Capriccio ; 2. Capriccio ; 3. Allegro affettuoso. Kistner.
31. Ab-Irato. Étude de perfection. Schlesinger.
32. Zwei Concertetuden, for Lebert and Stark's Klavierschule. 1. Waldesrauschen ; 2. Gnomenreigen. Trautwein.
33. Ave Maria, for ditto. Trautwein.
34. Harmonies poétiques et religieuses. 1. Invocation ; 2. Ave Maria ; 3. Bénédiction de Dieu dans la solitude ; 4. Pensée des morts ; 5. Pater Noster ; 6. Hymne de l'enfant à son réveil ; 7. Funérailles ; 8. Miserere d'après Palestrina ; 9. Andante lagrimoso; 10. Cantique d'amour. Kahnt.
35. Années de pèlerinage Première année, Suisse. 1. Chapelle de Guillaume Tell ; 2. Au lac de Wallenstadt ; 3. Pastorale ; 4. Au bord d'une source ; 5. Orage ; 6. Vallée d'Obermann ; 7. Eglogue ; 8. Le Mal du pays ; 9. Les Cloches de Genève (Nocturne). Seconde année, Italie. 1. Sposalizio ; 2. Il Pensoroso ; 3. Canzonetta di Salvator Rosa ; 4-6. Tre sonetti del Petrarca ; 7. Après une lecture de Dante. Venezia e Napoli. 1. Gondoliera ; 2.

Canzone ; 3. Tarantelle. Schott, 3me. année (see below).
36. Apparitions, 3 Nos. Schlesinger, Paris.
37. Two Ballades. Kistner.
38. Grand Concert-Solo: also for PFs. (Concerto pathétique). B. & H.
39. Consolations, 6 Nos. B. & H.
40. Berceuse. Heinze.
41. Weinen, Klagen, Sorgen, Zagen : Präludium nach J. S. Bach. Schlesinger.
42. Variations on theme from Bach's B minor Mass ; also for organ. Schlesinger.
43. Fantasie und Fuge, theme B.A.C.H. Siegel. Also for organ. Schuberth.
44. Scherzo und Marsch. Litolff.
45. Sonata in B minor. Dedicated to Schumann. B. & H.
46. 2 Polonaises. Senff.
47. Mazurka brillante. Senff.
48. Rhapsodie espagnole, Folies d'Espagne and Jota aragonese. Siegel.
49. Trois Caprice-Valses. 1. Valse de bravoure ; 2. V. mélancolique ; 3. V. de Concert. Schlesinger.
50. Feuilles d'album. Schott.
51. Deux feuilles d'album. Kahnt.
52. Grand Galop cromatique. Also for 4 hands. Hofmeister.
53. Valse impromptu. Schuberth.
54. 'Mosonyi's Grab-Geleit,' Táborszky & Parsch, Pest.
55. Élégie. Also for PF., violoncello, harp and harmonium. Kahnt.
56. 2nd Élégie. Also for PF., vln. and violoncello. Kahnt.

57. Légendes. 1. St. François d'Assise ; 2. St. François de Paul. Rózsavölgyi.

58. L'Hymne du Pape ; also for 4 hands. Bote & Bock.

59. Weihnachtsbaum (Fürstner) (12 pieces), and Via Crucis.

60. Impromptu—Thèmes de Rossini et Spontini, in E. 'Op. 3.' Schirmer.

61. Capriccio al'a Turca sur des motifs des Ruines d'Athènes de Beethoven. Mechetti.

62. Liebesträume—3 Notturnos, transcribed from his own songs. Kistner.

63. L'Idée fixe—Andante amoroso d'après une mélodie de Berlioz. Mechetti.

64. Impromptu, in F sharp. B. & H.

65. Variation on a Waltz by Diabelli. No. 24 in Vaterländischer Künstlerverein. Diabelli (1823).

66. 'The Pianoforte'—Frstes Jahrgang ; Parts I.-XII.—34 pieces by modern composers. Out of print.

2. ARRANGEMENTS

67. Grandes Études de Paganini, 6 Nos. (No 3, La Campanella). B. & H.

68. Sechs (organ) Präludien und Fugen von J. S. Bach, 2 parts. Peters.

69. Bach's Orgelfantasie und Fuge in G minor : for Lebert & Stark's Klavierschule. Trautwein.

70. Divertissement à la hongroise d'après F. Schubert, 3 parts ; also easier ed. Schreiber.

71. Märsche von F. Schubert. 1. Trauer-Marsch ; 2, 3. Reiter-Marsch. Schreiber.

72. Soirées de Vienne. Valsescaprices d'après Schubert. 9 Nos. Schreiber.

73. Bunte Reihe von Ferd. David. 24 Nos. Kistner.

74. Élégie d'après Sorriano. Troupenas.

75. Russischer Galopp von Bulhakow. Schlesinger.

76. Zigeuner-Polka de Conradi. Schlesinger.

77. La Romanesca. Schlesinger.

78. Leier und Schwert (Weber). Schlesinger.

79. Élégie, Themes by Prince Louis of Prussia. Schlesinger.

80. Gaudeamus igitur, paraphrase of No. 10.

81. God Save the Queen. Concert-Paraphrase. Schuberth.

82. Hussiten-Lied. Hofmeister.

83. La Marseillaise. Schuberth.

3. PARAPHRASES, TRANSCRIPTIONS, ETC., FROM OPERAS

84. La Fiancée (Auber) ; Masaniello ; La Juive ; Sonnambula ; Norma ; Puritani (3) ; Benvenuto Cellini ; Don Sébastien ; Lucia di Lammermoor (2) ; Lucrezia Borgia (2) ; Faust (Gounod) ; Reine de Saba ; Roméo et Juliette ; Robert le Diable ; Les Huguenots ; Le Prophète (3) ; L'Africaine (2) ; Szep Jlonka (Mosonyi) ; Don Giovanni ; König Alfred (Raff) (2) ; I Lombardi ; Trovatore ; Ernani ; Rigoletto ; Don Carlos ; Rienzi ; Der fliegende Holländer (2) ; Tannhäuser (3) ; Lohengrin (4) ; Tristan und Isolde ; Meistersinger ; Ring des Nibelungen.

85. Fantaisie de bravoure sur la Clochette de Paganini. Schreiber

86. Trois morceaux de salon. 1. Fantaisie romantique sur deux mélodies suisses ; 2. Romance fantastique sur un thème espagnol ; 3. Divertissement sur une cavatine de Pacini, also for 4 hands. Schlesinger.

87. Paraphrase de la Marche de Donizetti (Abdul Medjid Khan); also easier ed. Schlesinger.

88. ' Jagdchor und Steyrer,' from ' Tony ' (Duke Ernest of Saxe-Coburg-Gotha). Kistner.

89. Tscherkessen - Marsch from Glinka's ' Russlan und Ludmilla.' Also for 4 hands. Schuberth.

90. 'Hochzeit-Marsch und Elfenreigen ' from Mendelssohn's Midsummer Night's Dream. B. & H.

91. Fest-Marsch for Schiller centenary (Meyerbeer). Schlesinger.

92. Fantaisies (2) sur des motifs des Soirées musicales de Rossini. Schott.

93. Trois morceaux suisses. 1. Ranz de vaches ; 2. Un Soir dans la montagne ; 3. Ranz de chèvres. Kahnt.

4. RHAPSODIES, ETC.

94. Rhapsodies hongroises. 1. in E ; 2. in C sharp (also for 4 hands, and easier ed.) ; 3. in B flat ; 4. in F flat ; 5. in E minor ; 6. in D flat ; 7. in D minor ; 8. Capriccio F sharp minor ; 9. in E flat, ' Carneval de Pesth ' ; 10. Preludio ; 11. in A minor ; 12. in C sharp minor (also for PF. and violin by Liszt and Joachim) ; 13. in A minor ; 14. in F minor ; 15. Rákoczy March. Senff and Schlesinger. (See below.)

95. Marche de Rákoczy. Edition populaire. Kistner.

96. Do. Symphonisch. Schuberth.

97. Heroischer-Marsch im ungarischen Styl. Schlesinger.

98. Ungarischer Geschwindmarsch. Schindler. Pressburg.

99. Einleitung und Ungarischer Marsch von Graf E. Széchényi. Rózsavölgyi.

5. PARTITIONS DE PIANO

100. Beethoven's Septet. Schuberth.

101. Nine Symphonies. B. & H.

102. Hummel's Septet. Schuberth.

103. Berlioz's ' Symphonie fantastique.' Leuckart. Marche des pèlerins, from ' Harold in Italy.' Rieter - Biedermann. ' Danse des sylphes,' from ' La Damnation de Faust.' *Ibid.* Overtures to ' Les Francs-Juges.' Schott. ' Le Roi Lear.'

104. Rossini's Overture to Guillaume Tell.

105. Weber's Jubelouvertüre and Overtures to Der Freischütz and Oberon. Schlesinger.

106. Wagner's Overture to Tannhäuser. Meser.

6. TRANSCRIPTIONS OF VOCAL PIECES

107. Rossini's ' Cujus animam ' ' La Charité.' Schott.

108. Beethoven's Lieder, 6 ; Geistliche Lieder, 6 ; Adelaide ; Liederkreis. B. & H.

109. Von Bülow's ' Tanto gentile.' Schlesinger.

110. Chopin's ' Six Chants polonais,' op. 71. Schlesinger.

111. Lieder. Dessauer, 3 ; Franz, 13 ; Lassen, 2 ; Mendelssohn, 9 ; Schubert, 57 ; Schumann, R. and Clara, 14 ; Weber, Schlummerlied, and ' Einsam bin ich.'

112. Meyerbeer's ' Le Moine.' Schlesinger.

113. Wielhorsky's ' Autrefois.' Fürstner.

114. Alleluja et Ave Maria d'Arcadelt ; No. 2 also for organ. Peters.

115. A la Chapelle Sixtine. Miserere d'Allegri et Ave Verum de Mozart ; also for 4 hands and for organ. Peters.

116. Zwei Transcriptionen, 'Confutatis et Lacrymosa ' aus Mozart's Requiem. Siegel.

117. Soirées italiennes, sur des motifs de Mercadante. 6 Nos. Schott.

118. Nuits d'été à Pausilippe, sur des motifs de l'Album de Donizetti, 3 Nos. Schott.

119. Canzone napolitaine. Schott.

120. Faribolo Pastour, and Chanson du Béarn. Schott.

121. Glanes de Woronince. 3 Nos. Kistner.

122. Deux Mélodies russes. Arabesques. Cranz.

123. Transcriptions of his own songs ; Loreley, Kahnt; 6 Songs, Schlesinger ; Die Zelle in Nonnenwerth ; Hofmeister ; Liebesträume. Kistner.

124. Ungarische Volkslieder, 5 Nos. Táborszky & Parsch.

125. Soirées musicales de Rossini, 12 Nos. ; also for 4 hands and for 2 PFs. Schott.

IV. ARRANGEMENTS FOR 2 PIANOFORTES

126. Variations de Concert on March in I Puritani (Hexaméron). Schuberth.

127. Beethoven's Ninth Symphony. Schott.

V. PIANOFORTE AND VIOLIN

128. Epithalam ; also for PF. 2 hands. Táborszky & Parsch.

129. Grand duo concertant sur ' Le Marin.' Schott.

VI. FOR ORGAN OR HARMONIUM

130. Andante religioso. Schuberth.

131. Einleitung, Fuge und Magnificat, from Symphony 'Zu Dante's Divina Commedia.' Schuberth.

132. Ora pro nobis. Litanei. Körner.

133. Fantasie und Fuge on the Choral in 'Le Prophète.' B. & H.

134. Orlando di Lasso's Regina coeli. Schuberth.

135. Bach's Einleitung und Fuge, from motet ' Ich hatte viel Bekümmerniss.' Schuberth, Comp. No. 40.

136. Chopin's Praeludien, op. 28, Nos. 4 and 9. Schuberth.

137. Kirchliche Fest-Ouvertüre on ' Ein' feste Burg.' Hofmeister.

138. ' Der gnade Heil ' (Tannhäuser). Meser.

VII. VOCAL

1. MASSES, PSALMS AND OTHER SACRED MUSIC

139. Missa solennis (Graner) Fest-messe in D. Score and parts ; also vocal score, and for PF. 4 hands. Schuberth.

140. Ungarische Krönungs-Messe in E flat. Score and parts, and vocal score ; Offertorium and Benedictus, for PF. 2 and 4 hands, PF. and violin, organ, organ and violin. Schuberth.

141. Mass in C minor, with organ. B. & H.

142. Missa Choralis in A minor, with organ. Kahnt.

143. Requiem, men's voices and organ. Kahnt.

144. NeunKirchen-Chor-Gesänge, with organ. 1. Pater Noster ; 2. Ave Maria (also for PF.) ; 3. O Salutaris ; 4. Tantum ergo ; 5. Ave Verum ; 6. Mihi autem ; 7. Ave Maris Stella, also for PF. ; 8. OSalutaris ; 9. Libera me. Kahnt.

145. Die Seligkeiten. Kahnt. (See ' Christus.')

146. Pater noster, for mixed chorus and organ. Kahnt.

147. Pater Noster et Ave Maria, *a 4* and organ. B. & H.

148. Psalms 13th, 18th (E.V. 19th), 23rd and 137th. Kahnt.

149. Christus ist geboren ; chorus and organ. Arr. for PF. Bote & Bock.

150. An den heiligen Franziskus, men's voices, organ, trumpets and drums. Táborszky & Parsch

151. Hymne de l'enfant à son réveil, female chorus, organ and harp. Táborszky & Parsch.

2. ORATORIOS

152. Christus. Score, vocal score and parts. Schuberth. 'Pastorale,' No. 4, and ' Marsch der heiligen drei Könige ' No. 5, for instruments only ; also for PF. 2 and 4 hands. ' Tu es Petrus,' No. 8, for organ and for PF. 2 and 4 hands as ' Hymne du Pape.'

153. Die Legende von der heiligen Elisabeth. Score, vocal score and parts. Kahnt. ' Einleitung,' for organ ; ' Marsch der Kreuzritter ' and 'Interludium,' for PF. 2 and 4 hands ; ' Der Sturm,' for PF. 4 hands.

3. CANTATAS AND OTHER CHORAL MUSIC

154. Zur Säcular-Feier Beethovens, for chorus, soli and orch. Score, vocal score and parts. Kahnt.

155. Choruses (8) to Herder's 'Ent fesselte Prometheus.' Score, vocal score and parts. Kahnt. Pastorale (Schnitterchor) for PF. 2 and 4 hands. Kahnt.

156. Fest-Album for Goethe centenary (1849). Fest-Marsch ; 1. Licht ! mehr Licht ; 2. Weimar's Todten ; 3. Über allen Gipfeln ist Ruh' ; 4. Chor der Engel. Vocal score and parts. Schuberth.

157. Wartburg - Lieder Einleitung and 6 Lieder. Vocal score. Kahnt.

158. Die Glocken des Strassburgen Münsters. Baritone solo, chorus and orch. Score, vocal

score and parts. Schuberth. ' Excelsior ' (Prelude) for organ, and PF. 2 and 4 hands.

159. Die heilige Cäcilia. Mezzo-soprano, chorus and orch., or PF., harp and harmonium. Score, vocal score and parts. Kahnt.

4. FOR MEN'S VOICES

160 1. Vereinslied ; 2. Ständchen ; 3. Wir sind nicht Mumien ; 4-6. Geharnischte Lieder (also for PF.) ; 7. Soldatenlied ; 8. Die alten Sagen ; 9. Saatengrün ; 10. Der Gang um Mitternacht ; 11. Festlied ; 12. Gottes ist der Orient. Kahnt.

161. Das düstre Meer. Unter allen Wipfeln. Eck.

162. Vierstimmige Männergesänge. 1. Rheinweinlied ; 2. Studentenlied ; 3. Reiterlied ; 4. Ditto Schott.

163. An die Künstler. With orch. Kahnt.

164. Fest-Chor (Herder-Memorial, 1850). Weber.

165. Festgesang. Kthhn.

166. Das Lied der Begeisterung. Táborszky & Parsch.

167. Was ist des Deutschen Vaterland ? Schlesinger.

168. Weimar's Volkslied. Also for organ and PF. 2 and 4 hands. Kühn.

5. FOR SINGLE VOICE AND PF

169. Gesammelte Lieder. Kahnt' 1. Mignon's Lied (also with orch. accomp. and for PF.) ; 2. 3. Der du vom Himmel bist und leidvoll) ; 5. Wer nie sein Brod ; 6. Über allen Gipfeln ist Ruh' ; 7. Der Fischerknabe (also with orch.) ; 8. Der Hirt (also with orch.) ; 9. Der Alpenjäger (also with orch.) ; 10. Die Loreley (also with orch. and for PF.) ; 11. Am Rhein (also for PF.) ; 12. Vergiftet sind meine Lieder ; 14. Anfangs wollt' ich ; 15. Morgens steh' ich auf ; 16. Ein Fichtenbaum (2) ; 17. Comment disaient - ils ? 18. Oh ! quand je dors ; 19. S'il est un charmant gazon ; 20. Enfant si j'étais roi ; 21. Es rauschen die Winde ; 22. Wo weilt er ? 23. Nimm einen Strahl ; 24. Schwebe, blaues Auge ; 25. Die Vätergruft ; 26. Angiolin dal biondo crin (also for PF.) ; 27. Kling leise ; 28. Es muss ein Wunderbares sein ; 29. Mutter Gottes Sträusslein (1); 30. Ditto (2) ; 31. Lasst mich ruhen ; 32. Wie singt die Lerche ; 33. In Liebeslust ; 34. Ich möchte hingehn ; 35. Nonnenwerth (also for PF.); 36. Jugendglück ; 37. Wieder möcht' ich dir begegnen ; 38. Blume und Duft ; 39. Ich liebe dich; 40. Die stille Wasserrose ; 41. Wer nie sein Brod ; 42. Ich scheide ; 43. Die drei Zigeuner (also with orch.); 44. Lebe wohl ; 45. Was Liebe sei ; 46. Die todte Nachtigall ; 47. Bist du ; 48. Gebet ; 49 Einst ; 50. An Editam ; 51. Und sprich ; 52. Die Fischers, tochter ; 53. Sei still ; 54. Der

Glückliche; 55. Ihr Glocken von Marling. Kahnt.
170. Il m'aimait tant (also for PF.). Schott.
171. Drei Lieder. 1. Hohe Liebe; 2. Gestorben war Ich; 3. O lieb'; also for PF. as 'Liebesträume.' Kistner (see No. 123).

VIII. PIANOFORTE ACCOMPANIMENT TO DECLAIMED POEMS

176. Bürger's Leonore, Kahnt; Lenau's Der traurige Mönch, Kahnt; Jokai's Des todten Dichters Liebe, Táborszky & | Parsch; Strachwitz's Helge's Treue, Schuberth; Tolstoy's Der blinde Sänger, Bessel, Petersburg, also for PF.

IX. REVISED EDITIONS OF CLASSICAL WORKS

177. Beethoven. I. & II. Sonatas complete. III. Variations for PF. solo. IV. Various PF. compositions for 2 and 4 hands. V. Duets for PF. and violin. VI. Duets for PF. and violoncello, or horn. VII. Trios for PF., violin and violoncello. X. Masses, vocal score. XIV. String quartets. XV. Trios for strings, wind and strings, and wind only. Holle.

178. Field. 18 Nocturnes, annotated. Schuberth.
179. Hummel's Septet; also as quinte for PF. and strings. Schuberth.
180. Schubert's PF. Sonatas and Solos (selected); 2 vols. Cotta.
181. Weber's PF. Sonatas and Solos; 2 vols. Cotta.
182. Viole's Gartenlaube; 100 Études in 10 parts. Kahnt.

X. LITERARY WORKS

183. De la Fondation-Goethe à Weimar. Brockhaus, 1851.
184. Lohengrin et Tannhäuser de Richard Wagner. Brockhaus, 1851.
185. R. Wagner's Lohengrin und Tannhäuser; with musical illustrations. Eyssen.
186. Fréd. Chopin. B. & H. 1852.
187. Die Zigeuner und ihre Musik in Ungarn. In German and Hungarian; the former revised by Cornelius. Heckenast, Pressburg, 1861.
188. Über Field's Nocturnes; French and German. Schuberth, 1859.

189. Robert Franz. Leuckart. 1872.
190. Contributions to *Gazette musicale de Paris*, and in the *Neue Zeitschrift für Musik*. Kahnt.
191. Schumann's Musikalische Haus- und Lebensregeln; translated into French. Schuberth, 1860.
    A complete edition of the writings in a German version by L. Ramann is prepared by that writer. 6 vols. out of 7 published (1894). General Index by J. Kapp (1910).

                F. H.

The task of collecting Liszt's posthumous works has not been an easy one, the composer having distributed his MSS. amongst his friends and pupils.

Published by Táborszky & Parsch, Budapest:

'Ungarisches Königslied,' for male voices or mixed chorus with orchestral accompaniment; the same in PF. score, and in arrangements for baritone solo, and for 4 hands and 2 hands on the PF.
'Ungarn's Gott,' for baritone solo and *ad lib.* chorus of male voices. Also for PF. 2 hands; also for PF. left hand; also for organ or harmonium; also for cymbal.
Csárdás for PF. 2 hands.
Csárdás macabre or obstiné. Do.
Dem Andenken Petöfi's for PF. 2 and 4 hands.
16th Hungarian Rhapsody (Munkácsy), 2 hands; also 4 hands.
17th do. (Aus dem Figaro Album). 18th do. (Für das Album der Budapester Ausstellung). 19th do. (nach C. Ábrányi's 'Csárdás nobles ').

Published by Kahnt's Nachfolger

'Christus,' PF. arrangements, 2 and 4 hands.
Antiphon for St. Cecilia's Day, contralto solo and 5-part mixed choir, and orchestral accompaniment. Also PF. or vocal score.
'Le Crucifix,' for contralto solo, with harmonium or PF. accompaniment.
Missa pro Organo.
Sacred Choruses. No. X., Anima Christi; No. XI., Tu es Petrus; No. XII., Dominus conservet eum.
'Salve Regina ' (Gregorian), for harmonium or organ.
Songs ; 'Verlassen,' 'Ich verlor die Kraft.'
Duet ; 'O Meer im Abendstrahl.'
'Sonnenhymnus.' Baritone solo, male voice chorus, organ and orchestra. Also vocal score.
'Stanislaus,' oratorio, unfinished. Full score. Vocal score.
Single numbers published.
'Salve Polonia,' Interludium. Full score. Also arrangement for PF.
'De Profundis,' Ps. cxxix., bass or alto solo, with PF. or organ.
Responses for soli and choir and organ, called 'Septem Sacramenta,' 1877-78.
Collected Songs.

By various Publishers :

'Von der Wiege bis zum Grabe,' symphonic poem, after a drawing by Michael Zichy.
Varianten und Zusätze to 'Festklänge.'
'Le Triomphe funèbre de Tas e,' epilogue to 'Tasso.'
Two new Mephisto-Walzer, orch. and PF. 2 or 4 hands (Fürstner).
'Crux,' Hymne des marins, chorus and accompaniment *ad lib.*
Pax vobiscum,' motet, 4 male voices.
'Natus est Christus,' 4 male voices.
'Qui Mariam absolvisti,' baritone so'o and chorus.
'O heilige Nacht,' tenor solo and 3-part female chorus (Fürstner).
'Nun danket alle Gott,' chorus, organ, trumpets, trombones and drums.
Antiphon for St. Cecilia's Day, contralto solo and 5-part female chorus.
'Gruss,' for male choir, published 1887.

172. Tre sonetti di Petrarca. Haslinger.
173. Die Macht der Musik. Kistner.
174. Jeanne d'Arc au bûcher. Mezzo-soprano and orch., or PF. Schott.
175. Ave Maris Stella. Kahnt.

Original, for Pianoforte :

Années de pèlerinage. Troisième année: No. 1. Angelus (also for string quartet). No. 2. Aux Cyprès de la Villa d'Este. No. 3. Do. No. 4. Les Jeux d'eaux à la Villa d'Este. No. 5. ' Sunt lacrymae rerum ' en mode hongrois. No. 6. Marche funèbre. No. 7. ' Sursum corda' (also for solo voices, Schott), 'Abschied,' russisches Volkslied). ' Die Trauer-Gondel ' (Fritzsch). 3 Valses oubliées ; Valse élégiaque (Bote & Bock) ; Étude in C ; Andante maestoso (Rosvölgy). Grosses Concert-Fantasia über spanische Weisen (Licht). En Rûr, nocturne. Twelve books of Technical Studies, with more to follow (Schuberth).

Transcriptions :

Processional March from 'Parsifal ' (Schott). Other Wagner transcriptions (Schott, and B. & H.). Berlioz's ' Harold ' Symphony (Leuckart). Verdi's ' Aïda ' and ' Requiem,' Lassen's ' Hagen und Kriemhilde,' ' Faust ' and Intermezzo from ' Über allen Zaubern Liebe ' (Bote & Bock). Liebesscene and Fortuna's Kugel from Goldschmidt's ' Die sieben Todsünden.' Rubinstein's ' Gelb rollt ' and ' Der Asra ' (Kistner). Schumann's ' Provençalisches Minnelied ' (Fürstner). Forty-two Lieder by Beethoven, Franz, Schumann and Mendelssohn (B. & H.). Paraphrase of themes from Handel's ' Almira.' Paraphrase of themes from modern Russian works. Wilhorsky's ' Romance.' Arrangements of Fest-Cantata for 4 hands ; nocturne, 4 hands. Schubert's Marches, 4 hands. Beethoven's Concertos, 2 PFs.
The works still unpublished include a Requiem on the death of the Emperor Maximilian of Mexico ; ' Hosannah ! ' for organ and trombone ; ' Rosario ' for organ or harmonium, 3 pieces, 1879 ; ' Quasi Cedrus ' tenor solo, female chorus and harmonium ; ' Mariengarten,' vocal trio with organ ; ' Verlassen,' song ; ' Romance oubliée, 27, 1880; ' Am Grabe R. Wagners,' string quartet, 1883 ; ' UngarischeBildnisse ' (3), for PF., 1884 ; from Mephisto-Walzer for piano, and Mephisto Polka ; ' Pax vobiscum,' male voice quartet with organ, 1886 ; a 20th Hungarian Rhapsody.
Liszt had completed, or is said to have partly written : New symphonic poem for organ, on lines by Herder, ' The Organ ' ; ' Lo sposalizio ' (organ) ; score of Zarembski's duets ; ' Die Macht der Musik,' song ; Fantasia for orch. and PF. on Schubert's ' Der Wanderer ' ; ' Die Nebensonnen ' and ' Aufenthalt ' (Schubert) for PF. ; ' Weihelied ' to Leo XIII. ; ' Der ewige Jude,' for PF. with declaimed poem (Schubart).
The discovery of a concerto entitled ' Malédiction,' and of a choral work, ' The Creation,' has been reported.[1]

BIBLIOGRAPHY

LETTERS

Briefwechsel z. Wagner und Liszt (2 vols., 3rd ed. 1910, E. Kloss).
Liszt's Briefe (9 vols., 1893-1904). Edited with the following volumes by La Mara. (See Lipsius.)
Briefe hervorragender Zeitgenossen an F. Liszt (3 vols., 1895-1904).
Briefwechsel z. F. Liszt und H. von Bülow (1898).
Briefwechsel z. F. Liszt und dem Grossherzog K. A. von Sachsen (1908).
Briefe an seine Mutter (1918).
Liszt's Briefe an K. Gille (1903). Ed. by A. Stern.
Ungedruckte Originalbriefe (1902). Ed. by R. von Seydlitz.
F. Liszt's Briefe an Baron A. Augusz (1911).
Römische Briefe (1864-69). Ed. R. von Schlözer (1913).

BIOGRAPHIES, ETC.

1. During Liszt's life :
L. Rellstab : *F. Liszt* (1842).
R. Pohl : *F. Liszt* (1883).
A. Habets : *Borodin et Liszt* (1885). English version by R. Newmarch.
L. Ramann : *F. Liszt als Künstler und Mensch* (1880). English translation, E. Cowdrey (2 vols., 1882).

2. Since Liszt's death :
O. Lüning : *F. Liszt* (1896, A. M. G. Neujahrstück).
A. Göllerich : *F. Liszt* (Berlin, 1908).
J. Kapp : *Liszt und Wagner* (1909) ; *F. Liszt* (1909, 7th ed. 1918).
B. Schrader : *F. Liszt* (Leipzig, 1914).
E. Reuss : *F. Liszt, ein Lebensbild* (1898) ; *F. Liszt's Lieder* (1907).
A. Taddei : *La Divina Commedia . . di F. Liszt* (1903).
La Mara (see Lipsius) : *Bilder und Briefe aus dem Leben der Fürstin K. Sayn-Wittgenstein* (1906).
Cosima Wagner : *F. Liszt* (Munich, 1911).
J. C. Huneker : *F. Liszt* (New York, 1911).
J. Chantavoine : *F. Liszt* (Paris, 1910, *Maîtres de la Musique*).
M. Calvocoressi : *Liszt* (Paris, 1906, *Musiciens Célèbres*).
A. Hervey : *F. Liszt* (London).
P. Raabe : *Grossherzog Karl Alexander und Liszt* (Leipzig, 1918).
J. G. Prod'homme : *Franz Liszt* (Paris, Fabre, 1910).
A. Salles : *Le Centenaire de Liszt—Liszt à Lyon* (Paris, Fromont, 1911).
P. L. Robert : *Études sur Boïeldieu, Chopin et Liszt* (Rouen, Lainé, 1913).
L. Bourguès et Al. Dénéréaz : *La Musique et vie intérieure* (Paris, Alcan, 1921).

PERIODICALS

S.I.M., 1907 A. de Bertha, *Franz Liszt*. *S.I.M.* 1911 (No. 11) : Vincent d'Indy, *Franz Liszt en 1873*. K. d'Isoz *Lettres de Liszt —Lettres de Berlioz à Liszt conservées au Musée de Weimar*. A. Sommsich : *Liszt Ferencz élete* (*La Vie de F. Liszt*), Budapest, 1925.

            L. M. M., with addns.

---

[1] All posthumous MSS. were handed over to the Allg. Deutsche Musikverein by the Princess Hohenlohe, the daughter of Liszt's faithful friend and testatrix the Princess Wittgenstein who died in 1887.

LITANIAE LAURETANAE (Litany of Loreto), a solemn Litany, sung in honour of the Blessed Virgin Mary.

It is no longer possible to ascertain when, where or by whom this Litany was originally written ; but, if we may trust the very generally received tradition that it was first chanted at Loreto, and carried thence, by pilgrims, to all parts of the world, it cannot be of earlier date than the closing years of the 13th century. In other places than Loreto (where it is sung every evening) it is most frequently sung either in solemn Processions or during the Exposition of the Blessed Sacrament at Benediction ; but its use—especially on the Continent—is by no means restricted to those particular occasions. In Rome, for instance, it is constantly sung, at almost every popular service, to a simple plain - song melody familiar to all Italians, and printed in the Ratisbon edition of the *Directorium Chori*. This is probably the oldest music to which the words were ever adapted. Its date, like theirs, is uncertain : but it is at least old enough to have attracted the attention of the great polyphonic composers of the 16th century, some of whom have treated it in their best and most devout style.[1]

Palestrina was especially devoted to the Litany, and, in 1593, published a volume containing, in two books, ten different settings of exquisite beauty, composed for the use of the Confraternity of the Holy Rosary. One of the most beautiful divisions of the work is reprinted in the fourth volume of Proske's *Musica divina*, and all are published in the complete edition of Breitkopf & Härtel.

Another volume of Litanies, by various authors, was published at Munich in 1596 by Georgius Victorinus, under the title of *Thesaurus litaniarum*. We here find among other interesting works a charming Litany, by Orlando di Lasso, founded entirely upon the plain-song canto fermo, and so simple in construction that the most modest choir need feel no hesitation in attempting it. This Litany is also reprinted entire in the fourth volume of *Musica divina*, together with some others from the same rare work, which fortunately is not the only collection that has been preserved to us from the 16th century. Under the title of *Litaniae Catholicae ad Christum, Beatam Virginem, et Sanctos*, a highly interesting work was printed by Wolfgang Eder at Ingolstadt in 1589. Another, called *Sacrae litaniae variae*, was published at Antwerp in 1595. A precious volume, believed to be unique, wanting the title and first nine pages—and therefore without date—is preserved in the library bequeathed by Dr. Proske to the cathedral of Ratisbon. And many other printed collections

[1] The most ancient printed copy is that of Dilingen (1558). Costanzo Porta set it 1575. The Litany of Loreto was officially approved by Pope Sixtus V. (1587).   W. H. G. F.

are still extant, containing quite a little treasury of Art.

At Notre-Dame the Litany is annually sung, in grand procession, on the afternoon of the Feast of the Assumption, to a form of the First Tone, which, set with the melody in the tenor, produces an indescribably solemn effect.   W. S. R.

LITANY, see RESPONSE ; TALLIS.

LITERES, ANTONIO (*d.* Madrid, after 1752), Spanish operatic composer. The earliest dated work in the National Library, Madrid, is ' Jupiter y Danae ' (1700), a piece in three acts and ballet, scored for violins and bass. ' Azis y Galatea ' is dated 1709, while the libretto of a lost oratorio, ' S. Vicente,' belongs to 1720. In a collection of ' Psalmos de Visperae,' etc., printed at Madrid, 1731 (Bibl. Provincial, Toledo), Literes is described as *musico violon* (musician, bass-viol) in the Chapel Royal. After the disastrous fire at the Royal Palace, Madrid (1734), in which most of the music was lost, Literes and NEBRA (*q.v.*) were ordered to arrange the MSS. which had survived and write what music was necessary for services in the Chapel Royal. Literes was possibly second organist at the time, and he certainly held that appointment in 1752. He was praised by the moralist Padre Feijoo for the loftiness and sweetness of his style : an example of his music is given by Mitjana.[2] Besides the opera mentioned above, the Nat. Library at Madrid possesses MS. scores of ' Los Elementos ' and ' Dido y Eneas,' both described as *opera armonica al estilo Ytaliano*, and ' Coronis,' a ZARZUELA (*q.v.*) in 2 acts (the last two are unsigned). There exists a quantity of church music by him (Chapel Royal, Madrid). Two hymns were printed by Eslava.

               J. B. T.

LITOLFF, HENRY CHARLES (*b.* London, Feb. 6, 1818 ; *d.* Bois le Combes, near Paris, Aug. 6, 1891). His father, a French Alsatian soldier taken prisoner by the English in the Peninsular War, had settled in London as a violinist after the declaration of peace, and had married an Englishwoman. In the beginning of the year 1831 Henry Litolff was brought by his father to Moscheles, who on hearing the boy play the piano, was so much struck by his unusual talent that he offered to take him gratis as a pupil ; and under his generous care Litolff studied for several years. He made his first appearance (or one of his first) at Covent Garden Theatre, July 24, 1832, as ' a pupil of Moscheles, 12 years of age.' In his 17th year a marriage of which the parents disapproved obliged him to leave England and settle for a time in France. For several years after this event Litolff led a wandering life, and during this period he visited Paris, Brussels, Leipzig, Prague, Dresden, Berlin and Amsterdam, giving in these towns a series of very successful

[2] *Encl. de la musique: Espagne*, pp. 2111-13.

concerts. In 1851 he went to Brunswick, and undertook there the business of the music publisher Meyer, marrying, as his second wife, the widow of the owner. In 1860 he transferred this business to his adopted son Theodor Litolff, and he, in 1861, started the well-known 'Collection Litolff,' as a cheap and accurate edition of classical music, which was among the earliest of the many series of similar size and aim now existing. It opened with the sonatas of Beethoven, Mozart and Haydn (vols. i.-iv.). Henry Litolff himself went to Paris. His third wife was a Comtesse de Larochefoucauld. His opera 'Les Templiers' was produced at Brussels in Jan. 1886.

About 115 of his works, including several operas, a violin concerto, a short oratorio, 'Ruth et Boaz' (1869) and much chamber music, have been published. Among the best of them may be reckoned some of his pianoforte pieces, such as the well-known 'Spinnlied,' a few of his overtures and his symphony concertos, especially Nos. 3, 4 and 5 ; the latter are remarkable for their wealth of original ideas in harmony, melody and rhythm, and for their beautiful instrumentation (see Berlioz's *Les Musiciens*, p. 303).   A. H. W.

LITUUS. The *lituus* was used by the cavalry, and answered to the 'cavalry trumpet' of modern armies. It was cylindrical in bore with an expanding bell-mouth, and was turned back upon itself only at the bell-end, so that its general form was that of a crooked staff, or the letter J. (See *PLATE LXVIII.* No. 2.) The pitch of one discovered in 1827 at Cervetri, and now preserved in the palace of the Vatican at Rome, is *g*, an octave higher than the Buccina, and a major third higher than the modern cavalry trumpet of the British Army, which is in E flat. That the distinction between the Roman *tuba* and *lituus* is real needs for proof no more scholarship than is contained in Horace's 'First Ode to Maecenas':

> 'Multos castra iuvant, et lituo tubae
> Permixtus sonitus.'

On this passage Torcellini comments, 'Sunt qui lituum a tuba distinguunt, ex eo quod ille equitum sit, haec vero peditum.' The distinction is good to-day. The *tuba* was the 'Infantry Bugle'; the *lituus* the 'Cavalry Trumpet.' The derivation of *lituus* may indeed be originally Greek ; certainly it is proximately from the hooked augur's staff of the Oscans, which had been Mercury's wand, and has become the bishop's crozier. Both *tuba* and *lituus* figure on Trajan's column, in the triumphal procession. Vegetius defines the former : 'Tuba—quae directa est, appellatur.' This straight form reappears even in more recent times, as in a fine picture by Baltazarini; by comparing it with the average height of the players, it may be estimated at about seven feet long. The *lituus* is figured by Bartolini from a marble Roman tombstone with the inscription :

> 'M. Julius Victor
> ex collegio
> Liticinum Cornicinum,'

which is perhaps the first mention of a society of professional musicians.   D. J. B.

LITVINNE, FELIA (LITVINOV) (*b.* Russia, 1861), operatic soprano. Her vocal training took place in Paris under Mme. Barth-Banderoli and Victor Maurel. Her sister was the wife of Edouard de Reszke, and she married Dr. Emmanuel Depoux. After a promising début at the Théâtre des Italiens, Paris (1885), she joined Mapleson's American company and appeared at the Academy of Music, New York, in the following winter as Leonora in 'Il Trovatore,' Arditi being the conductor. On her return she sang with success at St. Petersburg and Moscow ; also at the Lamoureux Concerts in Paris during a lengthy period of study entirely devoted, by the advice of the De Reszkes, to the mastery of the leading Wagnerian rôles. In some of these— notably Isolde and Brünnhilde—she created a good impression in France, her fine voice and excellent declamation earning warm praise. She sang meanwhile under Cortot at the Château d'Eau in 1902, and afterwards at the Opéra-Comique and the Gaieté. Later on she appeared with Jean de Reszke in 'Tristan' and 'Siegfried' at the Metropolitan Opera House, New York, and in 1899 made a successful début with him at Covent Garden as Isolde, besides taking part in subsequent seasons as Donna Anna, Brünnhilde, Aïda, La Gioconda, etc. She last sang in London in the winter season of 1910.   H. K.

LIVERATI, GIOVANNI (*b.* Bologna, *c.* 1772), pupil of Mattei and Gibelli, singer and composer. In 1792 he was tenor singer at Barcelona theatre. After a position in Madrid he became Kapellmeister to the King of Prussia ; left Potsdam in 1800 for Prague ; went to Trieste in 1804 and thence to Vienna, where he settled as singing-master, and produced successfully some operas. In 1814 he went to London as composer for the opera, but returned to Italy, 1817. He composed operas, chamber duets, arias, etc.   E. V. D. S.

LIVERPOOL. The most important musical organisation in Liverpool is the PHILHARMONIC SOCIETY, founded Jan. 10, 1840. Occasional concerts at first were given in the Collegiate Hall, Shaw Street. In 1849, however, the Philharmonic Hall was opened, which is said to be acoustically one of the most perfect in England. At first a permanent conductor was appointed to conduct orchestral or choral concerts every year, and this position has been held in turn by Sir Julius Benedict (1867), Max Bruch (1880), Sir Charles Hallé (1883) and Sir Frederic Cowen (1896). This policy was abandoned in 1910 in favour of guest conductors. The Liverpool Philharmonic Society possesses a choir of 250 voices under a permanent chorus-master (Dr. A. W. Pollitt).

Chamber music is represented mainly by the RODEWALD CONCERTS SOCIETY, which was founded in 1911 and named after a wealthy patron of music, the late A. E. Rodewald. The Society has a membership of 200 and provides six chamber concerts every season.

Liverpool claims to itself the most flourishing branch of the BRITISH MUSIC SOCIETY (q.v.), which, founded in 1919, possesses its own club-room and library and has been the means of introducing to Liverpool celebrated singers and quartets. Its activities extend to many fields, for the Society has a Choral Circle, a con-temporary Music Circle, and affiliated to it is the LIVERPOOL AMATEUR ORCHESTRAL SOCIETY of 80 performers. The first provincial Con-gress of the British Music Society was held in Liverpool in 1924.

Choral music is cultivated by the LIVERPOOL CHURCH CHOIR ASSOCIATION, which was founded in 1899. It became the means of bringing together all the church choirs of the city for the purpose of an annual festival. Before the war 14 such festivals were given in the St. George's Hall. After a period of suspension during the war the Association was revived in 1921, and the first Festival Service in the new Liverpool Cathedral was given in 1924. H. A. Brans-combe has been hon. conductor of the Associa-tion since its inception.

The best known of the many choral societies is the LIVERPOOL WELSH CHORAL UNION, founded in 1901, with a chorus of 250 voices. Its first conductor was Harry Evans, after whose death in 1914 T. Hopkin Evans was appointed. In 1923 the choir visited London on the invitation of Lord Howard de Walden, to sing Holbrooke's Dramatic Choral Symphony.

Two organisations undertake to educate young people in musical appreciation :

(1) THE ART STUDIES ASSOCIATION, founded in 1908 by elementary school teachers. It secured a grant from the Education Committee in 1923, which enables it to give 52 recitals every season attended by some 14,000 school children.

(2) THE RUSHWORTH AND DREAPER OR-CHESTRAL CONCERTS FOR YOUNG FOLK, which started in 1922, represented a first attempt in England to provide a systematic course of appreciation in orchestral music for children. Eight concerts are given every year. At the invitation of the Annual Conference of the British Association a demonstration concert was given in 1923 before the delegates in the St. George's Hall, and a similar demonstration was given the following year for the delegates of the British Music Society's Congress.

LIVERPOOL UNIVERSITY.—The Alsop Lecture-ship in Music was founded in 1925 and Gustav Holst gave the inaugural lecture.

ORGAN MUSIC.—The great organ in the St. George's Hall is a particularly fine example of its maker, Willis. Weekly recitals are given by the city organist, H. F. Ellingford, who succeeded Dr. A. L. Peace, who held the appointment after the death of the renowned W. T. Best. The new cathedral has provided Liverpool with a still more magnificent speci-men of the organ-builder's art, the gift of Mrs. James Barrow, and the creation of Henry Willis, junior. The instrument was opened on Oct. 18, 1926, by Henry GOSS-CUSTARD (q.v.), the cathedral organist.

LIVERPOOL MUSICAL FESTIVALS.—These did not take place with regularity. The first was held in 1784, the next in 1790, and the next in 1799. They were then suspended till 1823, 1830 and 1836 (Oct. 4-7, Sir G. Smart, con-ductor), when Mendelssohn's ' St. Paul ' was performed for the second time, and for the first time in England. Up to this date the concerts had been held in churches, but the next fes-tival took place at the Philharmonic Hall in 1874 (Sept. 29–Oct. 1)—conductor Sir Julius Benedict. The St. George's Hall, containing rooms available for music, was opened in September 1854.   F. B.

LLOYD, CHARLES HARFORD (b. Thornbury, Glos., Oct. 16, 1849 ; d. Slough, Oct. 16, 1919), a distinguished organist whose compositions take a minor but distinct place in the English revival of the Victorian era.

The son of Edmund Lloyd, a solicitor, he was educated at Thornbury Grammar School and Rossall School. From the latter he went to Magdalen Hall (now Hertford College), Oxford, in Oct. 1868 as the holder of an open classical scholarship. He graduated Mus.B. 1871, B.A. 1872, M.A. 1875, taking a second class in the Final Theological School, but it was not till 1892 that he proceeded to the degree of Mus.D. While an undergraduate he was instrumental in establishing the Oxford University Musical Club, and was elected its first president (see OXFORD). Lloyd was appointed organist of Gloucester Cathedral in June 1876 as successor to S. S. Wesley, and the appointment was backed by the personal recommendation of Wesley, who had been greatly impressed by Lloyd's powers of improvisation. In this capa-city he conducted the festivals of the Three Choirs in 1877 and 1880. In Sept. 1882 he succeeded Corfe as organist of Christ Church Cathedral, Oxford, and in the same year became conductor of the Oxford Choral Society in succession to Walter Parratt. From 1887–92 he taught organ and composition at the R.C.M. In 1892 he succeeded Barnby as precentor and musical instructor of Eton College. On his re-tirement from that post he became (1914) organist of the Chapel Royal, St. James's. In

1902 he was placed on the Council of the R.C.M.; he was at various times examiner in music to the universities of Oxford, Cambridge and London, and was president of the R.C.O. A memorial window to Lloyd has been placed in Gloucester Cathedral, and a scholarship for a chorister to continue his musical training after leaving the choir has been founded there.

As a composer Lloyd was more than the writer of ephemeral works for festival performances. He has left something of permanent value in two directions, Anglican church music and short works for unaccompanied choirs in the madrigal and partsong styles. While these show the influence of Wesley and Parry, and he may be described as a lesser light in the school of which they were the masters, an individual touch appears here and there. There is a poetic subtlety in his 'To morning' (8 voices), dedicated to the Leeds Philharmonic, which is spontaneous, not derived, and the lyrical handling of the voices in 'Mark when she smiles' (Spenser) makes it an example of the English partsong at its best.

LIST OF PUBLISHED WORKS

Cantatas.—' Hero and Leander,' for soli, chorus and orchestra (Worcester Festival, 1884) ; ' Song of Balder,' for soprano solo and chorus (Hereford Festival, 1885) ; 'Andromeda,' for soli, chorus and orchestra (Gloucester Festival, 1886) ; ' The Longbeards' Saga,' male chorus and PF. acct., 1887. ' A Song of Judgment ' (Hereford, 1891) ; ' Sir Ogie and Lady Elsie ' (Hereford, 1894) ; ' A Hymn of Thanksgiving ' (Hereford, 1897) ; motet, ' The Souls of the Righteous ' (Gloucester, 1901).

Choruses and incidental music to ' Alcestis ' (see GREEK PLAYS, MUSIC TO), for male chorus, flutes, clarinets and harp, 1887. ' The Gleaner's Harvest ' for female chorus.

Services in E♭ (full Cathedral), Evening Service in D and A, in F and G (Parochial). Magnificat and Nunc Dimittis in F, soli, chorus and orchestra (Gloucester Festival, 1880).

Anthems.—' Art thou weary ? ' eight voices unaccompanied. ' Blessed is he,' with full orchestral accompaniment (Gloucester Festival, 1883). ' Fear not, O land,' ' Give the Lord the honour,' etc.

Duo concertante for clarinet and piano.

Organ.—Sonata in D minor ; concerto in F minor (MS. written for Gloucester Festival, 1895), and other pieces.

Madrigal, five parts, ' When at Corinna's eyes.' Various partsongs, including ' To morning ' (Blake, eight parts), ' Allen-a-Dale,' with orchestral accompaniment, ' Twelve by the clock ' (female voices), etc. Also several songs.

M. ; addns. C.

LLOYD, EDWARD (b. Westminster, Mar. 7, 1845 ; d. Worthing, Mar 31, 1927), was the most famous English tenor of his generation.

The son of Richard Lloyd (b. Mar. 12, 1813 ; d. June 28, 1853), chorister, afterwards assistant lay-vicar of Westminster Abbey, and assistant vicar-choral of St. Paul's, and Louisa (née HOPKINS, q.v.), he received his early musical education in the choir of Westminster Abbey under James Turle. His was a curious instance of a voice which never ' broke,' but deepened gradually from treble to tenor. In 1866 he obtained the appointment of tenor singer in the chapels of Trinity and King's College, Cambridge, which he resigned in 1867 in order to join the choir of St. Andrew's, Wells Street, under Barnby ; he retained this post on being appointed a gentleman of the Chapel Royal in 1869, a place which he held about two years. Subsequently he devoted himself entirely to concert singing. He made his first great success at Gloucester Festival in 1871 in Bach's St. Matthew Passion music, and in 1874 won universal admiration by his singing of ' Love in her eyes sits playing ' at the Handel Fest.val at the Crystal Palace. In a very short time Lloyd reached a position of great importance, both as an oratorio and concert singer. He was associated with the production of many important works in the concert-room. The list includes :

The Martyr of Antioch (Sullivan).
The Redemption (Gounod).
Mors et Vita (Gounod).
The Rose of Sharon (Mackenzie).
The Golden Legend (Sullivan).
Saint Ludmilla (Dvořák).
Judith (Parry).
The Voyage of Maeldune (Stanford).
Eden (Stanford).
The Swan and the Skylark (Goring Thomas).
King Saul (Parry).
Caractacus (Elgar).
The Dream of Gerontius (Elgar).

The title-part in this was the last part of importance studied by Lloyd before his retirement from the profession, while still at the top of his powers, in 1900, when he had a series of farewell concerts, and then went to live in Sussex. He emerged from his retirement to sing a solo in the anthem at King George's coronation (1911), and again to sing at a Mansion House concert for the benefit of Belgian refugees (Feb. 3, 1915).

Lloyd's exceptional value as a festival tenor was perhaps not fully realised until his retirement, for no one of his successors had a voice equal to his in range and beauty, or so comprehensive a talent. In looking back on Lloyd's career of about thirty years as a leading tenor, something more than passing mention should be made of his unvarying success in singing Wagner's music in the concert-room. He made the ' Preislied ' a familiar melody to thousands of people who had never heard 'Die Meistersinger.' At different times he was heard in the third acts of ' Lohengrin ' and ' Tannhäuser,' in the great duet in the first act of ' Die Walküre,' and in the Forging Songs of ' Siegfried.'

W. H. H. ; addns. S. H. P., etc.

LOBE, JOHANN CHRISTIAN (b. Weimar, May 30, 1797 ; d. Leipzig, July 27, 1881), musician and writer of some eminence on music, owed his musical instruction to the Grand Duchess Maria Paulowna. The flute was his instrument, and after performing a solo at the Gewandhaus, Leipzig, in 1811, he settled at his native place as second flute in the Duke's band. He wrote five operas (' Wittekind,' ' Die Flibustier,' ' Die Fürstin von Granada,' ' Der rote Domino,' ' König und Pachter,' all performed at Weimar), besides overtures and two symphonies for the orchestra, PF. quartets, and other compositions. But it is as a littérateur that he is most interesting to us. He resigned his place at Weimar in 1842, and in 1846 undertook the editing of the *Allgemeine Musik Zeitung* of Leipzig, which post he retained until the termination of that periodical in 1848. In 1853 he began a publication called *Fliegende Blätter für Musik*, of which about twenty numbers were published; he then edited the musical department of the Leipzig *Illustrirte Zeitung*, and made endless contributions to other periodicals. His principal books, some of which appeared first in the periodicals, are :

Musikalische Briefe . . . von einer Wohlbekannten two vols., Leipzig, 1852.
Aus dem Leben eines Musiker (*ib.* 1859).
Catechism of Composition, and another of music (both translated into English).
Consonanzen und Dissonanzen (*ib.* 1869).
Lehrbuch der musikalischen Composition (4 vols., *ib.* 1850 to 1867).

G.

LOBGESANG, EINE SYMPHONIE CANTATE. Mendelssohn's cantata (op. 52), known in England as the 'Hymn of Praise,' was produced at St. Thomas's Church, Leipzig, June 25, 1840; at Birmingham (Mendelssohn conducting), Sept. 23, 1840. Revised and produced at Leipzig, Nov. 27, 1840; Gloucester Festival, Sept. 10, 1841; London, Sacred Harmonic Society, Mar. 10, 1843.

LOBKOWITZ[1] (LOBKOWICZ), a noble and distinguished Czech family, founded early in the 15th century, by Mikuloš Chudý z Ujezda (Nicholas Chuzy von Ujezd), and deriving its name from a place in Bohemia. The chief country seat of the family is at Roudnice (Raudnitz) on the Elbe, near Terezin (Theresienstadt), and its town residences are the Lobkowicz Palace at Prague and the palace on the Lobkowitz-Platz, Vienna. The family has been closely and honourably connected with music.

(1) PHILIP HYACINTH (beginning of 18th cent.), had musical relations with Sylvius Leopold Weiss, the last famous lutenist.

(2) FERDINAND PHILIP (*b.* Prague, Apr. 17, 1724; *d.* Vienna, Jan. 11, 1784). By the death of his father and two elder brothers he became the head of the house before he was fifteen. Gluck, whose father was in his service, was much aided in his early success by the assistance of the Prince. The two were present together at the coronation of Francis I. (Sept. 28, 1745); after which they went to London in company with the Duke of Newcastle, who had represented the English Court at the coronation. There[2] Lobkowicz is said to have lived in a house of the Duke's for two years, and it was during this time that Gluck produced his operas at the King's Theatre, and appeared in public in the strange character of a performer on the musical glasses. (See GLUCK; HARMONICA.) A story is told by Burney of his having composed a symphony bar by bar alternately with Emanuel Bach. The feat was an absurd one, but at least shows that he had considerable practical knowledge of music. He was succeeded by his son.

(3) JOSE FRAN (JOSEPH FRANCIS) MAXIMILIAN (*b.* Dec. 7, 1772; *d.* Dec. 16, 1816). This is the prince whose name *is* familiar in

connexion with Beethoven. He seems, notwithstanding the temptations of his immense early wealth, to have been an exemplary character, with no vices, and with no fault but an inconsiderate generosity rising to prodigality, which ultimately proved his ruin. He married Princess Marie Caroline Schwarzenberg, Aug. 2, 1792. His taste for music was an absorbing passion. He played both violin and violoncello, and had a splendid bass voice, which he cultivated thoroughly and with success. He maintained a complete establishment of orchestra, solo and chorus singers, with Anton Wranitzky (Antonín Vranický) and Cartellieri at their head, for the performances of masses, oratorios, operas, symphonies, etc. When Beethoven arrived at Vienna in Nov. 1792, Lobkowicz was twenty, and the two young men soon became extremely intimate. True, beyond the frequent mention of his name in Ries's *Recollections*, there is not much definite proof of this[3]; but it is conclusively shown by the works dedicated to him by Beethoven; for we must remember that the dedication of a work by this most independent of composers was, in nineteen cases out of twenty, a proof of esteem and affection. Excepting those inscribed with the name of the Archduke Rudolph they form the longest and most splendid list of all his dedications. Chief[4] among them are :

Six quartets, op. 18 (1801-5)[5]; Sinfonia Eroica, op. 55 (1806); triple concerto, op. 56 (1807); 5th and 6th symphonies (1809), (shared by Lobkowicz with Rasoumowsky); quartet in E♭, op. 74 (1810); 'Liederkreis,' 'An die ferne Geliebte,' op. 98 (1816).

We must not suppose that the course of such a friendship as this betokens was always smooth; the anecdote told on p. 264 of Vol. I. of this work, shows that Prince Lobkowicz, like all the intimates of Beethoven, and other men of genius, had occasionally a good deal to put up with. No doubt the Prince was a kind and generous friend to the composer. It was he who advised him to apply for the position of composer to the opera, and promoted two profitable concerts for him in his own palace and with his own band in 1807. Two years later he joined Kinsky and the Archduke in subscribing to Beethoven's annuity, contributing 700 florins (paper) per annum. On Jan. 1, 1807, an association of noblemen, with Lobkowicz at its head, took charge of the court theatres, and during 1810, 1811 and 1812 the Prince had the sole direction of the opera. He was one of the promoters and founders of the Gesellschaft der Musikfreunde in Vienna, and sang the bass solos at the second performance of 'Alexander's Feast,' Dec. 3, 1812. He was also one of the leading spirits of the noblemen of Bohemia who, in 1810, founded the 'Jednota ku zvelebení hudebního umění v

---

[1] The German form of the name is here retained since it is in that form that it has become famous in musical history, through Prince Josef Franz's association with Beethoven.
[2] Cf. Burney, *Hist.* iv. 452.

[3] Beethoven nicknames him 'Prince Fitzli Putzli'—but then he nicknames every one.
[4] See catalogue of Beethoven's works, Vol. I.
[5] These are dates of publication.

Cechách ' (Association for the Promotion of the Art of Music in Bohemia) at Prague, which in 1811 started the famous Prague Conservatorium of Music. He had Haydn's ' Creation ' translated by Jan Kruchina into Czech, and had it performed in this language for the first time at his castle of Roudnice, on Oct. 27, 1805, conducted by Anton Cartellieri, and himself taking the bass part. Both there and at his other country seat of Jezeří (Eisenberg), at which latter place the theatre still exists, operas and plays were performed, witnessed amongst others by Goethe, and at which occasionally artists from Vienna took part. In addition to his great expenditure on music, he, like Kinsky, raised, equipped and maintained a body of riflemen during the campaign of 1809. At length came the depreciation in the Austrian currency, the bankruptcy of the Government and the Finance-patent of 1811. Lobkowicz was unable to change his habits or reduce his expenditure, and in 1813 his affairs were put into the hands of trustees, and he left Vienna for Prague and Roudnice. By the Finance-patent Beethoven's 700 florins were reduced to 280 flor. 26 kr. in Einlösungsscheine —all that the trustees had power to pay. Beethoven was clamorous, and his letters are full of complaints against the Prince—most unjust as it turned out, for early in 1815, through the Prince's own exertions, the original amount was restored with arrears. Beethoven acknowledged this by the dedication of the Liederkreis. On Jan. 24, 1816, the Princess Lobkowicz died, and in less than a year was followed by her husband.[1]

A. W. T. ; addns. from information supplied by Vladimir Blarek.

(4) His eldest son, FERDINAND (b. Apr. 13, 1797 ; d. Dec. 18, 1868), was also a supporter of music. He had his own orchestra and a brass band and cultivated singing himself.

(5) His son, MAURICE (MORIZ) (b. Feb. 1, 1831 ; d. Feb. 4, 1903), was, in his turn, a music lover, played the piano, and enriched the musical archive of the family with valuable collections.

(6) FERDINAND, a cousin of the former (b. Dolní Beřkovice, 1850), the last marshal of the Diet of the Kingdom of Bohemia, was from 1885 until 1909 president of the above-mentioned ' Jednota ku zvelebení hudebního umění v Čechách ' and rendered great services in the development of the Prague Conservatorium.

(7) Prince Maurice's grandson, FERDINAND JOSEPH (b. Bílina, Dec. 27, 1885), in addition to his studies in law (Doctor juris), devoted himself to music and became a brilliant pianist. He studied under Jindřich Káan of Albest (Prague), Stavenhagen and Pembaur (Munich).

[1] For fuller details of the Lobkowicz family the reader is referred to a paper by Thayer in the *Musical World* of May 17, 24, 31, 1879.

He performed as a soloist both in Prague and in Vienna, and in chamber music, together with the famous BOHEMIAN QUARTET (q.v.). As a patron of art he became an enthusiastic supporter of the rhythmic-pedagogical method of Jaques-Dalcroze. He frequently visited the latter's school at Hellerau near Dresden, which he ran from 1910–14, and helped to propagate Dalcroze schools in his own country. He founded (1912) societies in Prague and in Vienna for the promotion of the Dalcroze method by means of lectures and classes. He followed in the musical traditions of his ancestors and caused a thorough research and reorganisation of the musical archive at Roudnice to be made.   R. V.

LOBO, ALFONSO (b. Borja, about 1555 ; d.? Seville, after 1610), Spanish church musician (also claimed by the Portuguese, though this is probably owing to confusion with Duarte Lobo). He held an appointment in Lisbon. His name appears in the records of Toledo Cathedral as having been elected maestro de capilla in 1593 ; he is described as having been assistant to the maestro at Seville. In 1602 he published a book of masses :

Liber primus missarum Alfonsi Lobo de Borja Sanctae Ecclesiae Toletanae Hisp. Primatis Portionarii Musicesque Praefecti . . . Madrid, 1602. (Córdoba ; Valencia, Patriarca.)

This was seen through the press by VICTORIA (q.v.). In 1604 Lobo was succeeded at Toledo by Alonso de Texeda ; he returned to Seville, and was in charge of the choir-school until 1610. The following works are known in MS. :

Lectio prima de Ieremia propheta . . . In officio Tenebrarum. Sabbati Sancti. Ildephonso Lupo, auctore (Seville).
Credo Romano ad organo grande. (Escurial; Seville.)
Passions. (Toledo, MS. 21.)
Responso para el dia de defunctos, 5 v. (Toledo, MS. 24.)
Vivo Ego dicit Dominus, a 5. (Escurial.)   J. B. T.

LOBO, DUARTE (' Eduardus Lupus,' or ' Lopez ' (b. 1540 ; d. 1643), Portuguese church composer. He studied at Evora under Manuel MENDES (q.v.), and then became choir-master there, perhaps in succession to his teacher, who died in 1605, or more likely under him. He moved to Lisbon, and held an appointment at the Royal Hospital, being transferred to the Cathedral before 1594. Many of his works were printed by Plantin, at Antwerp, and letters are preserved from the composer to the printer. He lived to the age of 103. His style has been compared with that of BENEVOLI, but without justice. Lobo never employed so many voices or so many different groups as Benevoli ; his style has more in common with the later manner of Victoria (in the ed. of 1600) but is without Victoria's imagination.

PRINTED WORKS

Opuscula : Natalitiae noctis responsoria, 4 v. et 8. Missa . . . 8 v, B.M.V Antiphonae, 8 v. . . . Salve, choris 3, et 11 v. Antwerp, Plantin, 1602. (Seville ; Valladolid Evora, Bibl. Publ.)
Officium defunctorum. Lisbon, Craesbeck, 1603.
Cantica B.M.V. vulgo Magnificat, 4 v. Antwerp, Plantin, 1605. (Munich ; Vienna, Staatsbibl.)
Liber processionum et stationum Ecclesiae Olyssiponensis. Lisbon, Craesbeck, 1607.

Liber missarum, 4, 5, 6 et 8 v. Antwerp, Plantin, 1621. (MS. copy in score, Brit. Mus.)
Liber II. missarum, 4, 5 et 6 v. Antwerp, Plantin, 1634.

MSS.

B.M. Score of Lib. missarum, 1621, Motets in score ; Vidi aquam, Audivi vocem, Pater peccavi, 6 v. ; Asperges, 4 v. ; Missa pro defunctis, 2 choirs, 8 v.
R.C.M. Mass, 8 v. Missa pro defunctis. Motet, Audivi vocem, 6 v. Asperges, 4 v.
Fitzwilliam Coll. : Audivi vocem, 6 v.
Granada Cathedral : Asperges, 4 v.
Toledo Cathedral : Pater peccavi, 4 v. ; Audivi vocem, 6 v. (MS. 23.)

J. B. T.

LOCATELLI, PIETRO (*b.* Bergamo, 1693 ; *d.* Amsterdam, Apr. 1, 1764 [1]), a celebrated violinist, was still very young when he became a pupil of Corelli at Rome. Very little is known of his life, but he appears to have travelled a good deal, and finally to have settled at Amsterdam, where he established regular public concerts.

There can be no doubt that Locatelli was a great and original virtuoso. As a composer we must distinguish between a number of caprices and études—which he evidently wrote merely for practice, to suit his exceptional powers of execution, and which have no musical value— and the sonatas and concertos, which contain very graceful and pathetic movements, and certainly prove him to have been an excellent musician. In these serious works he shows himself as a worthy disciple of his great master. All the more striking is the contrast when we look at his caprices and études. Here his sole aim appears to have been to endeavour to enlarge the powers of execution on the violin at any price, and no doubt in this respect he has succeeded only too well ; for, not content with legitimately developing the natural resources of the instrument, he oversteps all reasonable limits, and aims at effects which, being adverse to the very nature of the violin, are neither beautiful nor musical, but ludicrous and absurd. A striking example of this tendency of his is to be found in a caprice entitled, ' Le Labyrinthe,' where the following arpeggiando passages occur :

and

This savours strongly of charlatanism, and it is astonishing to find a direct pupil of Corelli one of the first to introduce such senseless feats of execution into the art of violin-playing. Wasielewsky not unjustly speaks of him as the great-grandfather of our modern ' Finger-heroes ' (Fingerhelden).

[1] Date communicated by Arthur F. Hill.

Locatelli published ten different works :

Op.	Op.
1. Twelve concerti grossi. Amsterdam, 1721.	6. Six sonatas for violin solo. 1737.
2. Sonatas for flute. Amsterdam, 1732.	7. Six concerti a quattro. 1741.
3. L' arte del violino, containing 12 concerti grossi and 24 caprices. 1733.	8. Trios. 2 violins and bass. 1741.
4. Six ' Introduzioni teatrali ' and six concertos. 1735.	9. L' arte di nuova modulazione. Caprices énigmatiques.
5. Six sonatas en trio. 1737.	10. Contrasto armonico : concertos a quattro.

Modern editions of some of his sonatas and caprices have been issued by Witting, Alard and David.

BIBL.—*Un celebre violinista bergomasco precursore di Nicolo Paganini, 1695–1764. Lettere e documenti inediti* (Estratte del Bolletino della Civica Biblioteca di Bergamo, Jan.-Dec. 1920), pp. 16. Anon., Bergamo, 1921.

P. D.

LOCATELLO, GIOVANNI BATTISTA, a 16th-century composer of the Roman school, who composed a book of madrigals, 2-7 v. (1628), songs and canzonets in collective volumes, 1585–91 (*Q.-L.*).

LOCKE, MATTHEW (*b.* Exeter, *c.* 1630 ; *d.* Aug. 1677), was a chorister of the cathedral there in 1638–41 under Edward Gibbons, and afterwards, it has been generally supposed, studied under William Wake.[2] He is important in musical history as the most eminent of the predecessors of Henry Purcell in the composition of English stage music (see under PURCELL, CHARACTERISTICS OF PURCELL'S ART).

Locke and Christopher Gibbons composed the music for Shirley's masque ' Cupid and Death,' ' represented at the Military Ground in Leicester Fields ' before the Portuguese Ambassador, Mar. 26, 1653. In 1656 he published his ' Little Consort of Three Parts ' for viols or violins, composed, as he tells us, at the request of William Wake, for his scholars. He composed part of the music for Davenant's ' Siege of Rhodes ' in 1656, and sang in it himself. He composed the music, ' for ye king's sagbutts and cornets,' performed during the progress of Charles II. from the Tower through the city to Whitehall on Apr. 22, 1661, the day before his coronation, for which he received the appointment of Composer in Ordinary to the King. The Register of St. Mary Woolchurch contains the following entry :

Marrd. Mch. 21. 1663–4
Mr. Mathew Locke of Westminster gent.
& Mrs. Alice Smith of Annables, co.
Herford Spinster.

It cannot be definitely stated that this was the musician. There was another Matthew Locke, and in Aubery's *Lives* (ii. 254) it is stated that one or other of them married ' Mr. Garnon's daughter, of Herefordshire.'

He composed several anthems for the Chapel Royal, and on Apr. 1, 1666, produced there a Kyrie and Credo, in which he departed from the ordinary usage by composing different music to each response. This occasioned some opposition on the part of the choir, in conse-

[2] Davy, *History of English Music*, denies that Locke's reference to Wake as ' an intimate friend and great master in music ' implies that Wake had been Locke's own teacher.

quence of which he published his composition, with an angry preface, on a folio sheet, under the title of

'Modern Church Music ; Pre-Accused, Censur'd, and Obstructed in its Performance before His Majesty, April 1, 1666, Vindicated by the Author, Matt. Lock, Composer in Ordinary to His Majesty.'

(Of this publication, now excessively rare, there is a copy in the R.C.M. Another is in the Fitzwilliam Museum, Cambridge.) To this period may probably be assigned the production of 13 anthems for 3 and 4 voices, all contained in the same autograph MS., which Roger North describes as ' Psalmes to musick in parts for the use of some vertuoso ladyes in the city.' Soon afterwards, having, according to A. Wood's MS. notes (Bodl. Lib.), become a convert to Rome, he was appointed organist to the queen. He had in 1664 composed ' the instrumental, vocal and recitative music ' for Sir Robert Stapylton's tragi-comedy, ' The Stepmother.' In 1672 Davenant's alteration of ' Macbeth,' with the songs and choruses from Middleton's ' Witch ' introduced, was produced at the theatre in Dorset Garden ; and Downes, the prompter, in his *Roscius Anglicanus,* 1708, expressly states that the vocal music was composed by Locke. The music then performed remained unpublished until about the middle of the 18th century, when it appeared under the editorial care of Dr. Boyce, with Locke's name as composer, and as his it was long undisputedly accepted. But Downes's proved inaccuracy in some other things at length occasioned doubts of the correctness of his statement as to the authorship of the ' Macbeth ' music, and eventually Locke's right to it was denied and its composition claimed by some for Purcell, by others for Eccles, and by others again for Leveridge. No positive proof, however, has been adduced in support of any one of these claims, and until such is forthcoming it would be premature to set aside the long-standing traditional attribution of the music to Locke. (See MACBETH MUSIC.) In 1673 Locke composed the music (with the exception of the act tunes, by Draghi) for Shadwell's ' Psyche,' which he published in 1675, under the title of ' The English Opera,' together with his instrumental music to Shadwell's version (1673–74) of the TEMPEST (*q.v.*). The work is prefaced by some observations, written with his usual asperity, but is valuable as an exposition of his views of the proper form for opera. The varied songs and dances of ' Psyche ' show Locke combining the lessons learnt from the example of the French stage with the traditions of the English masque as he had helped to develop them in ' Cupid and Death.' Locke's personal enterprise is nowhere more strongly shown than in a ' Curtain tune' of ' The Tempest,' [1] which in its directly de-

scriptive features may be regarded as one of the earliest of the many storm fantasies of programme music.

In 1672 an extraordinary controversy was begun between Locke and Thomas Salmon, who had published *An Essay to the Advancement of Musick by casting away the Perplexity of different Cliffs and writing all sorts of musick in one universal character.* Locke attacked the work in *Observations upon a late book entitled An Essay, etc.,* written in a most acrimonious and abusive tone, to which Salmon replied in *A Vindication* of his essay, and Locke in 1673 retorted in *The Present Practice of Music vindicated, &c.* To which is added *Duellum Musicum, by John Phillips* [Milton's nephew]. *Together with a Letter from John Playford to Mr. T. Salmon in confutation of his Essay,* which closed the dispute [2] (see PLAYFORD). In 1673 Locke published a small treatise entitled

'Melothesia, or Certain General Rules for playing upon a Continued Bass, with a Choice Collection of Lessons for the Harpsichord or Organ of all sorts,'

said to be the first of the kind published in England. [3]

His compositions were numerous and various. His anthem, ' Lord, let me know mine end,' was printed by Boyce, and several other anthems exist in MS. in the Tudway collection, the Fitzwilliam Museum, at Westminster Abbey, Ely and elsewhere. Some anthems and Latin hymns are in ' Cantica sacra, 2nd set,' 1674 ; some hymns in ' Harmonia sacra,' 1688 and 1714 ; songs in ' The Treasury of Musick,' 1669 ; ' Choice Ayres, Songs and Dialogues,' 1676–84 ; and ' The Theater of Music,' 1687 ; and eight three-part vocal compositions by him (including ' Ne'er trouble thyself at the times or their turning,' reprinted in some modern collections) in ' The Musical Companion,' 1667. Instrumental compositions by him are printed in ' Courtly Masquing Ayres,' 1662 ; ' Musick's Delight on the Cithern,' 1666 ; ' Apollo's Banquet,' 1669 ; ' Musick's Handmaid,' 1678 (reprinted in J. S. Smith's ' Musica antiqua ') ; and Greeting's ' Pleasant Companion,' 1680. In several of these is ' A Dance in the Play of Macbeth,' evidently written for an earlier version than that above mentioned. [4] A song by him is in D'Urfey's ' Fool turned Critic ' (see D'Urfey's Songs, 1683). The R.C.M. possesses the autograph MS. of a ' Consort of ffoure Parts ' for viols, containing six suites, each consisting of a fantazia, courante, ayre and saraband, which Roger North (1728) tells us was ' the last of the kind that hath been made.' Autographs are in the library of King's College, Cambridge, the

[1] Parts of it are quoted by Parry, *Oxf. Hist. Mus.* vol. iii. p. 289.

[2] For a description of Salmon's proposal for a revised notation see Burney, *General History of Music,* vol. iii. p. 473.
[3] William Penny's *Art of Composition, or, Directions to play a Thorow Bass* is mentioned in Clavel's *Catalogue of Books printed in England since the Dreadful Fire,* 1670, and in a catalogue of Henry Playford's, but no copy has been found.
[4] Pepys, who from Nov. 5, 1664, to Dec. 21, 1668, saw ' Macbeth performed seven times, mentions (Apr. 19, 1667) the ' variety of dancing and musick ' in it.

R.C.M. and the B.M. Add. MSS. 17,801, 31,437, 17,799. Locke is said to have been buried in the Savoy, but the fact cannot be verified, the existing registers extending no farther back than 1680. Purcell composed an elegy on his death, printed in ' Choice Ayres,' etc., Book II., 1689. A portrait of him is in the Music School, Oxford.

         w. h. h. ; addns. *D.N.B.*, etc. ; rev. c.

LOCKENBURG (Giovanni Lochenburgo), Johann von (*d. circa* 1591–92), chamber-valet to the Duke of Bavaria *c.* 1568, and an excellent composer. He was organist at the Bavarian court *c.* 1558–91, and was mentioned in 1574 as a member of the ducal chapel. He composed masses, madrigals and sacred songs. (See *Q.-L.*)

LOCKEY, Charles (*b.* Thatcham, near Newbury, Mar. 23, 1820 ; *d.* Hastings, Dec. 3, 1901), son of Angel Lockey of Oxford, was admitted a chorister of Magdalen College, Apr. 1, 1828, remaining so until 1836, when he went to Bath to study under Edward Harris. In 1842 he became a pupil of Sir George Smart and lay-clerk of St. George's Chapel, Windsor. In 1843 he was appointed vicar-choral of St. Paul's Cathedral. In 1846 he was engaged (as the youngest of four tenors) for the Birmingham Festival, and allotted the air ' Then shall the righteous,' in the first performance of ' Elijah.' On hearing him rehearse the song, Mendelssohn immediately requested him also to sing ' If with all your hearts,' which had before been assigned to another singer. ' A young English tenor,' says the composer,[1] ' sang the last air so very beautifully that I was obliged to collect myself to prevent my being overcome, and to enable me to beat time steadily.' In Apr. 1848 Lockey was appointed a gentleman of the Chapel Royal. He married, May 24, 1853, Miss Martha Williams, contralto singer, who died at Hastings, Aug. 28, 1897. In 1859 an affection of the throat deprived him of voice and compelled his retirement.   w. h. h.

LOCO (Lat.), ' in (the usual) place,' a term used to re-establish the actual pitch of notes, after their transposition an octave higher or lower, as is explained under ALL' OTTAVA. m.

LOCRIAN MODE (Lat. *Modus Locrinus* ; *Modus Hyperaeolius*), see MODES, ECCLESIASTICAL.

LODER (1), John David (*b.* Bath, 1788 [2] ; *d.* London, Feb. 13, 1846), father of Edward James, the song-writer (see below), was a skilled violinist, and his *General and Comprehensive Instruction-Book for the Violin*, 1814 ; his *Modern Art of Bowing*, 1842 ; and *Violin School*, had considerable reputation. He was a music publisher at 46 Milsom Street, Bath, and about 1820 issued an edition of Handel's songs, as well as many other more or less important publications. From 1826–45 he was

orchestral leader at the Three Choirs Festivals. In 1840 he became a professor of the R.A.M., and in 1845 succeeded Cramer as leader of the Ancient Concerts. Another of the same family, A. Loder, was about the same period established as a music-seller at 4 Orange Grove, Bath.   f. k.

(2) John Fawcett (*b.* 1812 ; *d.* Apr. 16, 1853), son of the above, an excellent violinist and able orchestral leader, for many years resided at Bath and managed the concerts there. When Bath ceased to be a place of fashionable resort Loder removed to London, and on the death of his father succeeded him as leader at most of the best concerts and festivals.

        w. h. h. ; addns. *D.N.B.*, etc.

(3) Edward James (*b.* Bath, 1813 ; *d.* Apr. 5, 1865), son of John David (1), was in 1826 sent to Frankfort to study music under Ferdinand Ries. He returned to England in 1828, and went back to Germany with the view of qualifying himself for the medical profession, but soon changed his mind and again placed himself under Ries. When he again came back to England he was commissioned by Arnold to compose the music for ' Nourjahad,' an old drama of his to which he had added songs, etc., to convert it into an opera, for the opening of the new English Opera House, then building. The opera was produced in July 1834, and, notwithstanding very general admiration of the music, proved unattractive owing to the poverty of the libretto. In 1835 Loder set Oxenford's ' Dice of Death.' He next entered into an engagement with Dalmaine & Co., the music publishers, to furnish them with a new composition every week, in part performance of which he produced his ' Twelve Sacred Songs,' dedicated to Sterndale Bennett. As it became necessary that some of the pieces produced under this arrangement should be heard in public, an opera entitled ' Francis I.' was written to incorporate them and produced at Drury Lane in 1838. As might have been expected, so heterogeneous a compound met with little success, although one song, ' The old house at home,' obtained a widespread popularity. ' The Foresters, or twenty-five years since,' and ' The Deer-stalkers ' were brought out in 1845, and ' The Night Dancers,' his finest work, was produced at the Princess's Theatre in 1846, revived there in 1850, and again at Covent Garden in 1860. ' Puck,' a ballad opera, additions to ' The Sultan,' and ' The Young Guard,' were brought out at the Princess's in 1848. His cantata ' The Island of Calypso ' was written for the National Concerts at Her Majesty's Theatre in 1850, but, owing to their cessation, remained unperformed until given at the New Philharmonic Concerts in 1852. ' Raymond and Agnes,' an opera, was produced at Manchester, Aug. 14, 1855.

Besides these works Loder wrote some string

---

[1] Letter of Aug. 26, 1846.
[2] One account gives the date 1798

quartets and numerous songs, of which 'The Diver,' 'The brave old oak,' and 'Invocation to the deep' are well known. After his retirement a set of twelve songs, six sacred and six secular, was brought out by subscription. Among these, together with several remarkably fine lyrics, there is a setting of an English version of 'Wohin' (immortalised by Schubert) called 'The Brooklet' which is among the most beautiful and effective songs in existence, quite worthy to stand beside Schubert's setting of the original words. His compositions are distinguished by the melodiousness of the parts and their skilful instrumentation. He was for several years conductor at the Princess's Theatre, and afterwards at Manchester, but although musically well qualified for the office his want of regular, business-like habits militated greatly against his success. About 1856 he was attacked by cerebral disease, which long afflicted him, and prevented his resuming his old avocations. Albums of collected songs were issued by Messrs. Novello and Joseph Williams many years after his death.

w. h. h. ; addns. from *D.N.B.*, etc.

(4) KATE FANNY (*b*. Bath, Aug. 1825 ; *d*. Headley, Surrey, Aug. 30, 1904), only daughter of George Loder, and first cousin to E. J. Loder. Educated at the R.A.M., she gained a King's scholarship (1839), she became a distinguished pianist. She quitted the R.A.M. in 1844, in which year she played the adagio and rondo from Mendelssohn's G minor concerto in presence and to the satisfaction of the composer at Mrs. Anderson's concert at Her Majesty's Theatre. She was then appointed professor of harmony at the R.A.M. She first appeared at the Philharmonic Society, Mar. 15, 1847, when she played Weber's concerto in E♭, and in 1848 (May 29) her performance there of Mendelssohn's G minor concerto received the unprecedented distinction of an encore. In 1851 she was married to Mr. (afterwards Sir) Henry Thompson, the eminent surgeon. On Mar. 6, 1854, at the Philharmonic Concert, she made her last public appearance. Among her compositions was an opera, 'L'elisir d' amore.'

About 1871 she gradually became paralysed, but up to the end of her life Lady Thompson was a good friend to young artists of all kinds, and was a powerful influence on the art of her time, even after she had ceased to play. It was at her house, on July 7, 1871, that Brahms's Requiem was first performed in England, three years after it was written ; she and Cipriani Potter played the accompaniments as a pianoforte duet.   w. h. h. ; addns. m.

LODOÏSKA, comedy in 3 acts. (1) Words by Fillette-Loreaux, music by Cherubini. Produced at the Théâtre Feydeau, July 18, 1791. (2) Words by Dejaure (same story), music by R. Kreutzer. Produced at the Italiens, Aug. 1, 1791.   G.

LODOLETTA, opera in 3 acts ; text by Gioacchino Forzano, after Ouida's *Two Little Wooden Shoes* ; music by Mascagni. Produced Rome, Apr. 30, 1917 ; New York, Metropolitan Opera House, Jan. 12, 1918.

LOEFFLER, CHARLES MARTIN TORNOV (*b*. Mulhouse, Alsace, Jan. 30, 1861), Alsatian-American composer and violinist. The son of a specialist in agriculture and chemistry, as a boy Loeffler was taken to Smjela in Russia, and later to Debreczin in Hungary, the former sojourn in particular exercising an important influence on the formation of his musical tastes and tendencies. In 1875, after two years spent in Switzerland, Loeffler set out to become a professional violinist, studying with Rappoldi and Joachim in Berlin and with Massart in Paris, while his teachers in harmony and composition were Kiel and Bargiel in the former and Guiraud in the latter city. After a season under Pasdeloup in Paris, two years in the private orchestra of Baron Paul von Derwies at Nice and Lugano and a second season with Pasdeloup, Loeffler went, in 1881, to New York City. There he played under Leopold Damrosch and Theodore Thomas. A year later he became a member of the Boston Symphony Orchestra, and from 1885–1903 shared the first violin desk with Franz Kneisel. In this latter year he resigned, simultaneously with Kneisel, that he might devote himself more completely to composition, his orchestral and chamber pieces having already won him conspicuous recognition, and since then he has appeared as violinist only semi-publicly. In May 1887, Loeffler became an American citizen and since 1910 he has made his permanent residence in Medfield, Mass.

As composer Loeffler defies precise classification. The strong feeling for line as well as for colour in his music renders somewhat inaccurate the grouping of him with the French impressionists. A bold and individual harmonist, his dissonances are the outcome of a free polyphony rather than the arbitrary use of discord for its own sake. Loeffler has cultivated the macabre, the mystical and the idyllic. Modal influences derived both from the music of the Russian liturgy and from plain chant play an important part in his style. Although his music has never been influenced by the country of his adoption, it has variously reflected the idioms of Russia, Ireland and Spain. In an era of virtuoso orchestration his instrumention has commanded especial admiration. A fastidious workman and much given to self-criticism, Loeffler has subjected many of his compositions to repeated and often sweeping revision. Of his orchestral pieces those most widely known are 'La Mort de Tintagiles,' after Maeterlinck, and 'A Pagan Poem,' after Virgil. His Russian-inspired 'Memories of My Childhood,' awarded the prize of $1000 offered in connexion with the

1923 Chicago (Ill.) North Shore Festival, came quickly into popular favour.

The list of his more important compositions includes :

Symphony in one movement. 'Hora Mystica,' with men's chorus.
'Vilanelle du diable,' after Rollinat, symphonic poem.
'La Mort de Tintagiles,' after Maeterlinck, symphonic poem.
'Pagan Poem,' after Virgil, for orchestra with PF. obbligato.
'Poem,' for orchestra.
'Memories of My Childhood,' symphonic poem.
'Les Veillées de l'Ukraine,' suite for vln. and orchestra.
Divertimento in A min., for vln. and orchestra.
'Five Irish Fantasies,' for voice and orchestra.
'Psalm CXXXVII.,' for women's chor., with small instrumental accompaniment.
'For One Who Fell in Battle,' 8-part chor. for mixed voices a cappella.
Octet for two vlns., vla., v'cl., two clars., harp and double bass.
'Music for Four Stringed Instruments,' three movements for str. quartet.
Two Rhapsodies, for oboe, vla. and PF.
'Canticle of the Sun,' for voice and chamber orchestra.
Also a one-act opera as yet (1926) unperformed, numerous orchestral, concerted and chamber pieces and several songs, the latter mostly with obbligati. W. S. S.

LÖHLEIN, GEORG SIMON (b. Neustadt a. d. Heide, Coburg, 1727 ; d. Danzig, Dec. 17, 1781). Caught on a journey to Copenhagen, in 1743, by a Prussian pressgang he was, on account of his tall stature, placed in the famous Potsdam Guards. After being wounded at the battle of Collin he went to Jena in 1760, studied music and became Musikdirektor. In 1763 he went to Leipzig as violinist and pianoforte soloist in the concert orchestra and instituted a kind of conservatoire. In 1779 he accepted an appointment as Konzertmeister at Danzig. His importance lay in his exceptional gifts as music pedagogue. His pianoforte Tutor (Part I., 1765; Part II., 1788) appeared in many editions, the latest revised and edited by Reichard (1797), A. E. Müller (1804), and Czerny (18—?); his violin Tutor (1774) appeared in at least 7 editions, the latter revised and edited by Reichard and A. E. Müller. His compositions, concertos, quartets, trios, duets, sonatas, etc., are of lesser importance. E. v. d. s.

LŒILLET, a family of distinguished Flemish musicians, whose biographies in some instances have become inextricably confused.

(1) JEAN BAPTISTE of Ghent (b. 2nd half of 17th cent.), a flute-player, oboist and composer, who attained great proficiency at an early age. He went to Paris in 1702, where he published 4 sonatas for flute alone and a set of sonatas for 2 flutes, and flute trios. In 1705 he became a member of the orchestra at the Haymarket Theatre, London. Walsh of London published several sets of sonatas by him c. 1710–15, and Roger of Amsterdam published in 1725 his 6 sonatas for flute, oboe or violin, op. 5. On the title-page he calls himself chamber musician of the Elector of Bavaria, and concert-master of the Duke Ferdinand.

(2) JOHN, 'of London' (as he calls himself on the title-pages of his compositions) (d. 1728), was a flute, oboe and harpsichord player and composer, and either a brother or cousin of the former. In 1710 he started weekly concerts at his house in Hart Street, Covent Garden,

where some of Corelli's works were first performed in London.[1] He left at his death a fortune of £16,000. He wrote several books of sonatas for flute, oboe or violin, some flute trios and a book of harpsichord sonatas, published c. 1725–26.

(3) JACQUES (d. Paris c. 1746), oboist at the court of Munich. In Aug. 1727 he appeared before the French King at Paris, when he played on the oboe, various kinds of flutes, the bassoon and the violin, and sang a motet with accompaniment of a violin and 2 flutes, after which the King appointed him as chamber oboist. Several other Lœillets were members of the Royal Chapel and the cathedral of St. Gudule, Brussels. E. v. d. s.

LOESCHHORN, ALBERT (b. Berlin, June 27, 1819 ; d. there, June 4, 1905), a pupil of Ludwig Berger. He studied subsequently at the Royal Institute for Church Music in Berlin, where from 1851 he was teacher of the pianoforte. The title of Royal Professor was conferred upon him in 1858. For many years he carried on concerts of chamber music at Berlin with eminent success. He served the advancement of classical music by his conscientious and thorough discipline as a teacher ; many of his pupils have distinguished themselves. He became most widely known through his numerous studies for the pianoforte, although he published a long list of other worthy compositions, such as quartets and sonatas. C. E.

LÖWE, FERDINAND (b. Vienna, Feb. 19, 1865), was a pupil of Bruckner at the Vienna Conservatorium and in his work as a conductor has since been specially identified with the furtherance of his master's work (see VIENNA). In 1883 he became a piano teacher at the Vienna Conservatorium, and in 1897 conductor of the Kaim orchestra at Munich. His subsequent career as a conductor has been pursued chiefly in these two cities, and has included such important posts as the ' Singakademie ' and ' Gesellschaftskonzerte ' in the former and the ' Konzertverein ' in the latter. He has also directed concerts in Budapest and Berlin. c.

LOEWE, JOHANN CARL GOTTFRIED (b. Loebejuen, near Halle, Nov. 30, 1796 ; d. Kiel, Apr. 20, 1869), famous as the creator of the German ballad as an art-form (voice and piano), was twelfth and youngest child of a cantor and schoolmaster.

Near his home were collieries employing 300 miners, and this underground world, so near in his boyish fancy to the world of spirits, took powerful hold on his imagination, to reappear later when he was composing ' Der Bergmann ' (The Miner). His father taught him music early, and his singing having attracted attention, he was offered in 1807 a place in the choir of Cöthen. There he remained two years and went thence to the Gymnasium of the Franke

1 See E. van der Straeten, *The Romance of the Fiddle.*

Institution at Halle. Türk, the head of this, was director of the town choral society, and at the twelve annual concerts produced much good music, although he had some curious notions.[1] Niemeyer, chancellor of the Gymnasium, was proud of the choir, and made them sing to distinguished visitors, among others to Mme. de Staël, who made Loewe a present, and to King Jerome, who at Türk's instigation gave him an annuity of 300 thalers.

This enabled him to devote himself entirely to music. He had already become a pianist by studying Bach's *Wohltemperirtcs Clavier*, and he now took daily lessons from Türk, and worked hard at Kirnberger, Marpurg and Forkel. He also learned French and Italian. Two of his songs cf this date, ' Clothar ' and ' Die Einsetzungsworte des Abendmahls ' (op. 2)[2] have survived. Meantime the war of 1812–13 broke out, and Loewe has left a graphic account of its horrors in his *Selbstbiographie* (see Bibl.). Türk died in 1814, and the flight of King Jerome (Oct. 26, 1813) deprived Loewe of his income, but by the aid of Niemeyer he entered the University of Halle as a theological student under Michaelis. Naue, Türk's successor, founded a Singakademie like that of Zelter at Berlin. Loewe joined this, and thus became acquainted with his future wife, Julie von Jacob, a very gifted person, whom he married Sept. 7, 1821.

In 1818 he composed his first ballads, 'Edward,' and the 'Erl-König,' followed in 1824 (after his wife's death) by ' Der Wirthin Töchterlein,' which, by Marx's assistance, were printed. In 1819 and 1820 he paid visits to Dresden, Weimar and Jena, making the acquaintance of Weber, Hummel and Goethe. In 1820 he was invited to Stettin, and having passed with credit through various tests, such as a musical exercise submitted to Zelter, and a trial sermon, was duly installed professor at the Gymnasium and Seminary, and cantor. In 1821 he became Musikdirector to the municipality, and organist of St. Jacobus. He made a considerable mark both as a conductor and professor[3] in Stettin and throughout Pomerania. In 1837 he was elected member of the Akademie of Berlin. He was a favourite with both Frederick William III. and IV., the latter being especially fond of his ballads. He travelled much, and was present at the Musical Festivals of Düsseldorf (1837) and Mayence (the Gutenberg Commemoration), visiting Hamburg, Lübeck and Bremen on the way. In 1844 he went to Vienna, and in 1847 to London. The Duchess of Coburg had specially recommended him to the Prince Consort and Queen Adelaide;

he sang and played at court, the Prince turning over his music ; and here he heard Jenny Lind for the first time ; but he left not the least trace of his presence behind him. In 1851 he went to Sweden and Norway, and in 1857 to France. In 1864 he had a singular illness—a trance of six weeks' duration, and in 1866 the authorities of Stettin asked him to resign. After this mortification—somewhat atoned for by the King's opportune bestowal of a higher grade of the Order of the Red Eagle than he had before enjoyed—he left Stettin for Kiel, where he quietly expired after another trance. His heart was buried near his organ in St. Jacobus at Stettin.

Carl Loewe was an industrious composer. He wrote five operas, of which one only was performed—' Die drei Wünsche ' (Theatre Royal, Berlin, 1834). Mantius was the tenor ; Spontini took unusual pains ; the opera was a great success, and the Crown Prince presented the composer with a gold medal. The list of his oratorios includes :

' Die Festzeiten ' ; ' Die Zerstörung Jerusalems ' (1829) ; ' Die sieben Schläfer '[4] (1833) ; ' Die eherne Schlange ' (1834) ; ' Die Apostel von Philippi ' (1835, for voices only) ; ' Gutenberg ' (1836) ; ' Palestrina ' (1841) ; ' Huss ' (1842) ; ' Hiob,' ' Der Meister von Avis,' ' Das Sühnopfer des neuen Bundes,' ' Das hohe Lied Salomonis,' and ' Polus Atella ' (all between 1848 and 1860) ; ' Die Heilung des Blindgebornen ' (1861) ; ' Johannes der Täufer ' (1862); and ' Die Auferweckung des Lazarus ' (1863).

The last has an organ accompaniment, but the two that precede it, like ' Die Apostel von Philippi,' were for voices only, without accompaniment, a species of composition of which he was specially fond. His second wife and pupil, Auguste Lange of Königsberg, sang in his oratorios with himself.

He published 145 works with opus numbers, symphonies, concertos, duets and other pieces for PF., but above all, ballads, in which he specially excelled, and in which he may be considered as the successor of Zumsteeg. His complete songs were ultimately published in a series of eight volumes (B. & H., Schesinger, etc.). His poetic feeling and power of musical expression gave him a high rank among composers. He was the author of a *Gesanglehre* (Stettin, 1826 ; 3rd ed., 1834), and of *Musikalischer Gottesdienst, Anweisung zum Kirchengesang und Orgelspiel* (1851, four editions). The University of Greifswald conferred on him a Doctor's degree.   F. G.

BIBLIOGRAPHY

Selbstbiographie, ed. by Bitter. (Berlin, 1870.)
A. B. BACH : *The Art-Ballad ; Loewe and Schubert.* (London, 1890.)
H. BULTHAUPT : *K. Loewe ; Deutschlands Balladenkomponist.* (Reimann's *Berühmte Meister*, 1898.)
KARL ANTON : *Karl Loewes Bedeutung für unsere Zeit und deren Ziele.* Z.M.W., May 1919, pp. 483-499 ; *Aus Karl Loewes noch unveröffentlichter Lehre des Balladengesangs*, etc. Z.M.W. Jan. 1920, pp. 235-9.
LEOPOLD HERSCHBERG : *Carl Loewes Instrumentalwerke. Ein Monographie*, etc. (Hildburghausen, 1919.)

LOEWE, (1) JOHANNA SOPHIE (*b.* Oldenburg, Mar. 24, 1816 ; *d.* Pest, Nov. 29, 1866), dramatic singer, granddaughter of Friedrich August Leopold Loewe (who died 1816 as

---

[1] Loewe tells that he always omitted the introduction to the finale of Beethoven's first symphony as ' ludicrous,' and for fear of making the audience laugh.
[2] He afterwards printed three ballads by Herder and Goethe as op. 1.
[3] Some experiments in acoustics, conducted with his colleague Grassmann, produced results of real value.

director of the Lübeck theatre) and daughter of Ferdinand Loewe, an actor. She accompanied her father to Mannheim, Frankfort and Vienna, where he was engaged at the Burg Theatre, through the influence of his sister, Julie Loewe, a celebrated actress. Here Sophie studied singing under Ciccimara and other good masters. Her début as a concert singer was so successful that she was at once engaged for the court opera, and first appeared on the stage in 1832 in a German version of Donizetti's ' Otto mese in due ore.' Towards the close of 1836 she went to Berlin, where she created a furore as Isabella in ' Robert le Diable,' and was at once engaged at a high salary, appearing as Amina in the ' Sonnambula ' on Apr. 28, 1837. In 1838 she was appointed chamber singer to the King, but soon resigned, and travelled to London, Paris and Italy. In London she appeared at Covent Garden, May 13, 1841, in Bellini's ' Straniera,' but her success was only temporary.[1] She never returned to England. She failed to obtain an engagement in Paris, and in 1845 sang again in Berlin, but coming just after Jenny Lind, was only moderately received. In 1848 she married Prince Lichtenstein and retired. Her special characteristic was the singular harmony between her bodily and mental gifts. In conversation she was witty and intellectual, and as a singer had a great diversity of rôles, playing both Elvira and Donna Anna, Jessonda and Madeleine (' Postillon '), Lucrezia and Adine (' Elisir '). An admirable portrait of her was painted by Krüger, and engraved by Sachse of Berlin.

Her niece and namesake, (2) SOPHIE LOEWE (b. 1848; d. 1926), a soprano, daughter of the régisseur of the Court Theatre at Stuttgart, and pupil of Stockhausen, made her first appearance in London in 1871, and sang at the concerts for several seasons with success, till her marriage with W. von Glehn in 1877.   F. G.

LOEWENSTERN, MATTHAEUS APELLES VON (b. Neustadt, Upper Silesia, Apr. 20, 1594; d. Bernstadt, Apr. 16, 1648), Silesian poet and composer. Was the son of a saddler of the name of Loewe, and is said to have studied at the University of Frankfort on the Oder, but devoted himself chiefly to music. He was for a while schoolmaster and cantor at Neustadt and Leobschütz. The troubles of the Thirty Years' War obliged him to seek a home elsewhere.

He settled at Bernstadt near Breslau, where he was appointed Secretary and Privy Councillor to the Duke of Oels-Bernstadt, and was also director of the church music. About the same time he was raised to noble rank by the Emperor Ferdinand II., and took the name of Loewenstern. His chief published work is a book of thirty Geistliche Lieder, for two to four

[1] See Chorley, Modern German Music, i. pp. 210-13.

voices, entitled ' Frühlings-Mayen ' (the words also by him). The first dated edition is 1644. Some of these hymns and tunes were received into the various Choralbücher up to modern times, of which the best known are ' Christe du Beistand deiner Kreuz gemeinde,' and ' Mein Augen schliess ich jetzt.' He also composed the choruses to Martin Opitz's tragedy ' Judith,' for three voices with basso continuo, which were published at Rostock, 1646. There remain in MS. a number of Latin and German motets for four to eight voices, and sacred concertos in the style of Viadana with instrumental accompaniment.   J. R. M.

LOGIER, JOHANN BERNARD (b. Kaisersläutern, Palatinate, Feb. 9, 1777; d. July 27, 1846) a descendant of a family of French refugees, attained great notoriety by his invention of the ' chiroplast,' a mechanism for training the hands for piano - playing, and a system of piano teaching based on its use.

His father and grandfather were organists at Kaisersläutern. He received his early musical education from his father. After the death of his parents, and when about 10 years old, he came to England and studied the flute and pianoforte. He then joined the band of a regiment commanded by the Marquis of Abercorn, of which Willman, father of the celebrated clarinet-player, was master, and with which he went to Ireland. In 1796 he married Willman's daughter, and engaged in composing for and instructing military bands and teaching the pianoforte. At the close of the war, his regiment being disbanded, he became organist at Westport, Ireland, holding the post till 1807, when he was appointed bandmaster of the Kilkenny Militia. He settled in Dublin in 1809, as did also his brother-in-law Willman, the clarinettist. He opened a music shop at 27 Lower Sackville Street in July 1811, and was musical director of the Royal Hibernian Theatre, Peter Street, for twelve months.

Whilst there he invented the ' chiroplast,' the merits of which were widely debated. His method[2] included the plan of making several pupils, to the number of twelve or more, play at the same time on as many pianofortes. To this end he wrote a number of studies which were published in his *First Companion to the Royal Chiroplast*, and other works in which several studies of varying degrees of difficulty were capable of being played simultaneously. He gave his first musical lecture on Nov. 23, 1814. In 1821 the Prussian

[2] A full description of the chiroplast and of the controversy provoked by the method was given by Franklin Taylor in the earlier editions of this Dictionary under the head GYMNASTICS. He there quotes the following :
Favourable letter from Spohr, *A.M.Z.*, 1820.
Hostile criticisms in *Quarterly Mus. Mag.*, i. 111 :
   General Observations, R. Burdie. (Edinburgh, 1817.)
   Strictures on Mr. Logier's System, H. de Monti. (Glasgow.)
   Exposition of the New System, etc., by a committee of London professors, 1818.
Logier's replies in pamphlets. *An Authentic Account*, etc., 1818.
   A Refutation of the Fallacies and Misrepresentations, etc.

government sent Franz Stoepel to London to inquire into the merits of the system, and the result was that Logier was invited to Berlin to superintend the promulgation of it in Prussia. He remained in Berlin three years, being allowed an annual vacation of three months to visit England. In 1826, having acquired a competency by the sale of his chiroplast and elementary works, his very numerous classes, and the fees received for permission to use his invention and teach on his system—it was asserted that he had received 100 fees of 100 guineas each for that purpose—he retired and settled in Dublin. He reopened a music shop at 46 Upper Sackville Street ; in 1843 we find him at 28 Westmoreland Street, and two years later at 45 St. Stephen's Green. His *Thorough-bass* was the first musical text-book used by Wagner in 1828. He composed some sonatas and other pieces, besides making numerous arrangements for the pianoforte. He also composed an ode on the beginning of the fiftieth year of the reign of George III., Oct. 25, 1809, performed in Dublin. Besides the publications connected with his chiroplast, he was author of *A Complete Introduction to the Keyed Bugle.*   W. H. H. ; addns. from F. T., W. H. G. F., etc.

LOGROSCINO (LO GROSCINO), NICOLA (*b.* Naples, *c.* 1700 ; *d.* there, *c.* 1763), became a pupil of Durante at the Conservatorio di Loreto. He is first heard of in 1738, when he collaborated with LEO (*q.v.*) and others in the production of ' Demetrio ' ; in the autumn of the same year he produced a comic opera, ' L' inganno per inganno,' at the Teatro dei Fiorentini. This was followed by a long series of comic operas, which were so successful that Logroscino was called by the Neapolitans ' Il Dio dell' Opera buffa.' It was probably in 1747 that he went to Palermo to teach counterpoint at the Conservatorio dei Figliuoli Dispersi, the study of music being first introduced there in that year. (It should be remembered that the Italian Conservatori were originally not schools of music, but simply orphanages.) He is last heard of as a composer in 1760, and is supposed to have died in 1763 at Naples ; this, however, is doubtful, since the Conservatorio at Palermo possesses a receipt for his stipend signed by him in August of that year.

It has been stated that Logroscino would never compose except for words in Neapolitan dialect, and that he was the inventor of the concerted finale in several movements. Both statements are untrue, as far as can be gathered from his few remaining works. He wrote a certain amount of quite uninteresting church music and at least one serious opera, ' Giunio Bruto ' (score at Münster). His finales show no structural advance on those of Leo, but are distinctly superior to them in humorous treat-

ment of voices and instruments. For genuine comic feeling Logroscino stands in the front rank of operatic composers.

LIST OF EXTANT WORKS

SACRED MUSIC

Stabat Mater in E flat for S.A. and strings. ' In Palermo, 1760, autograph, Naples R. Conservatorio di Musica.
A second Stabat Mater in G minor, mentioned by Florimo, has disappeared.
Psalms for S.A.T.B., two violins and cont., Palermo R.C.M.

OPERAS

Giunio Bruto. (Score at Münster, Bibl. Santini.)
Il Governatore. (Score at Münster, Bibl. Santini.)
L' inganno per inganno, Naples, 1738 (libretto, Naples R.C.M.).
L' inganno felice, Naples, 1739 (libretto, Naples R.C.M.).
La Ciommetella corrervata, Naples, 1744 (libretto, Naples R.C.M.).
Revived as Il Cicisbeo, Naples, 1751 (libretto, Naples R.C.M.).
Il Leandro, Naples, 1744 (libretto, Naples R.C.M.). (Finale to Act I. Pare che sento mpietto at Cambridge, Fitzwilliam Museum ; libretto, Naples R.C.M.).
Le Zite, Naples, 1745 (libretto, Naples R.C.M.).
Don Paduano, Naples, 1745 (libretto, Naples R.C.M.).
Le Griselda, Naples, 1752 (libretto, Naples R.C.M.).
Le Finte Magie, Naples, 1756 (libretto, Naples R.C.M.).

OPERAS partly composed by Logroscino

Le Chiajese Cantarine, Naples, n.d. (libretto, Naples R.C.M.).
L' innamorato balordo, Naples, n.d. (libretto, Naples R.C.M.).
La Rosmonda, Naples, 1755 (libretto, Naples R.C.M.).
La furba buriata, Naples, 1760 (libretto, Naples R.C.M.).
A single act from an anonymous Neapolitan comic opera in Brit. Mus. Add. MSS. 14,235 is probably by Logroscino, but does not correspond with any of the above-mentioned libretti.

The names of a few more are mentioned by Florimo. A few airs and concerted pieces from not yet identified operas are to be found in the British Museum, Naples R.C.M., Milan Conservatorio and Montecassino.   E. J. D.

LOHENGRIN, a romantic drama in 3 acts ; words and music by Wagner. Produced at Weimar, under Liszt, Aug. 28, 1850 ; New York, Stadt Theatre, Apr. 3, 1871 ; in London, in Italian, Covent Garden, May 8, 1875 ; in English, Carl Rosa Co., Her Majesty's Theatre, Feb. 7, 1880 ; in German, Drury Lane, May 1882 ; Paris, Eden-Théâtre, in French, under Charles Lamoureux ; May 3, 1887 ; Opéra, Sept. 16, 1891.

LOHET, SIMON, was appointed organist to the court of Würtemberg at Stuttgart, in 1571, and his name is mentioned up to 1611.

Woltz in his Organ *Tabulatur-Buch* of 1617, inserts twenty-four pieces by Lohet, with some commendatory words *in memoriam.*[1] Twenty of these pieces are called fugues, though they are not developed fugues in the modern sense, the subjects being very short, and the answer coming in before the subject itself is completed. These fugues are followed by a canzona, and two 'Choral-bearbeitungen,' one on the plainsong melody of the ' Media vita in morte sumus,' with the melody in the bass throughout. Ritter has high words of praise for Lohet's pieces, and gives four specimens (Nos. 68-71 in his book), two fugues, the canzona and the ' Media vita ' pieces. The first of these fugues has the familiar theme of the E major fugue in the second part of the *Wohl-temperirtes Klavier.* Of the ' Media vita ' piece Ritter says it alone would suffice to justify for Lohet a high place among the best

[1] See Ritter, *Geschichte des Orgelspiels*, 1884, p. 109.

masters of organ music. 'In feeling so deep, in expression true and touching, it is a perfect piece from the old time, and therefore for all times.'[1]   J. R. M.

LOISEAU DE PERSUIS, Louis Luc, see Persuis.

LOLLI, Antonio (b. Bergamo, 1728–33; d. Sicily, 1802), a celebrated violinist.

It is generally assumed that he was almost entirely self-taught. We know for certain that he was at Stuttgart in 1762 with Nardini. There he was attached to the court of the Duke of Würtemberg, till 1773, when he went to St. Petersburg, where he is said to have enjoyed the special favour of the Empress Catherine II. He remained in her service till 1778. In 1779 he came to Paris, and played with great success at the Concert Spirituel. After this he went to Spain, and in 1785 we find him in London, where, however, according to Burney, he appeared but seldom in public. He continued to travel, and we read of his appearance now at Palermo, now at Copenhagen; then again at Paris, Vienna or Naples.

According to all contemporaneous testimony Lolli was an extraordinary performer, but an indifferent musician. Schubart, the well-known German poet and musician, who had many opportunities of hearing both him and Nardini, speaks with unmeasured praise of Lolli's feats of execution, the wonderful ease and absolute certainty with which he played the most difficult double stops, octaves, tenths, double-shakes in thirds and sixths, harmonics, etc. As to his having been a bad musician, or rather no musician at all, the testimonies are equally unanimous. The Abbé Bertini plainly states that Lolli could not keep time, could not read even easy music, and was unable to play an adagio properly. On one occasion, when asked to play an adagio, he said: 'I am a native of Bergamo; we are all born fools at Bergamo,—how should I play a serious piece?' When in England, he almost broke down in a quartet of Haydn which the Prince of Wales had asked him to play. If, with all these drawbacks as a musician, he nevertheless created, wherever he played, an immense sensation, we are all the more compelled to believe that his powers of execution were of the most exceptional kind.

He is described as a handsome man, but a great dandy and charlatan, very extravagant, and a gambler. The Emperor Joseph II., himself a very fair musician, habitually called him 'muddle-headed Lolli' (der Faselhans). Burney[2] writes that

'owing to the eccentricity of his style of composition and execution, he was regarded as a madman by most of the audience. In his freaks nothing can be imagined so wild, difficult, grotesque and even ridiculous as his compositions and performance.'

[1] See Ritter, *Geschichte des Orgelspiels*, 1884, p. 110.
[2] *Hist.* iv. 680.

True, Burney adds,

'I am convinced that in his lucid intervals he was in a serious style a very great, expressive and admirable performer,'

but it appears doubtful whether Burney ever heard him in a 'lucid interval.'

His compositions (concertos and sonatas for the violin), poor and insipid as they are, yet are said to have been his own productions in a limited sense only. We are assured that he wrote a violin part only, and that this was corrected, furnished with accompaniments, and brought into shape, by another hand. The list is in *Q.-L.*, where some other references to his career are given.

Bibl. — Andreas Moser, *Arcangelo Corelli und Antonio Lolli. Zwei künstlerische Ehrenettungen.* Z.M.W., Apr. 1921, pp. 415-25.
                                             P. D.

LOMAKIN, Gabriel Joachimovich (b. Apr. 6 (Mar. 25, O.S.), 1812; d. Gatchina, May 21, 1885). As a boy he sang in the celebrated choir of Count Sheremetiev, of which he became choirmaster in 1830. He also taught singing in the court chapel (1848–59) and the Theatrical School. His services were greatly in demand, and he held singing-classes in the most important educational establishments in St. Petersburg. In 1862 he joined Balakirev in founding the Free School of Music, in which he directed the choral classes until 1870. In 1874 he was compelled, on account of failing health, to retire from active life. Lomakin arranged a great number of the old church tunes, national airs, etc. He exercised a considerable influence upon the musical life of his day.   R. N.

LOMBARDI, I, alla prima crociata, opera in 4 acts; libretto by Solera, music by Verdi. Produced La Scala, Milan, Feb. 11, 1843; London, Her Majesty's, Mar. 3, 1846; Paris, Théâtre Italien, Jan. 10, 1863. A French adaptation, under the title 'Jerusalem,' words by Royer and Walez, was produced at the Opéra, Nov. 26, 1847.   G.

LOMBARDINI, Maddalena, see Sirmen.

LONATI (Lunati), Carlo Ambrogio, called 'il gobbo' (the hunchback), a 17th-18th century violinist and composer of Milan, who had a great reputation in both capacities. He was the first teacher of Geminiani, and composed an opera (Venice, 1684), an oratorio, cantata, arias, etc., and violin sonatas, all of which remained in MS. (*Q.-L.*).

LONDON ACADEMY OF MUSIC, THE. Dr. Henry Wylde started a music-school under this name in 1861, and in 1867 St. George's Hall, Langham Place, was opened to accommodate it. At his death in 1890 the school passed into the hands of Herr Pollitzer, Messrs. Raimo and Denza, and in 1904 was amalgamated with three other teaching institutions: The London Music School (formerly called the London Organ School), founded in 1865 by the Rev. Scotson Clark, and after his death directed by Dr. T. H. YORKE TROTTER; the FOREST GATE COLLEGE OF MUSIC, founded in 1885 by W. Harding Bonner (who became chairman of the Board of Directors); and the METROPOLITAN COLLEGE OF MUSIC, founded in 1889 by the Finsbury Choral Association at Finsbury Park, with C. J. Dale at its head. In 1905 the HAMPSTEAD CONSERVATOIRE, founded in 1885 by G. F. Geaussent, and subsequently directed by Cecil Sharp, was added to the number of amalgamated schools. The present premises of the combined institutions, under the direction and style of 'The United Music Schools, Limited,' are at 22 Princes Street, Cavendish Square.   M.

LONDON CHORAL SOCIETY. This society, which gave its first concert in Oct. 1903 at the Queen's Hall, was founded by its present (1926) conductor, Arthur FAGGE (*q.v.*). Since its first season, when Elgar's ' Dream of Gerontius ' was performed publicly for the first time in London, the society's policy of performing the new and unfamiliar rather than relying on the usual repertory has done much towards maintaining interest in choral singing in central London. Among works given which were new to London, mention may be made of ' Omar Khayyám ' (Bantock), ' Everyman ' (Walford Davies) and ' Pied Piper ' (Parry). On account of the war no concerts were given from the autumn of 1916 till the spring of 1919.

LONDON MUSICAL SOCIETY, THE (1878–87). This society was formed in 1878 by Heathcote Long and other prominent amateurs for 'the practice and performance of the works of composers which are not generally known to the musical public ' (Rule 2). Barnby was appointed musical director, and Long and Alfred Littleton honorary secretaries. An efficient choir was formed, and the first concert was given on June 27, 1879, in St. James's Hall, although, strictly speaking, the occasion was a private one. Goetz's Psalm cxxxvii. was introduced to London at that concert, the solos being sung, as on many subsequent occasions, by competent amateurs. From 1884 until the last season of the society's existence, Heathcote Long was alone in the honorary secretaryship. After the season of 1886, Barnby was succeeded as conductor by Mackenzie, who conducted the final concert on May 24, 1887. In the course of that year the society was disbanded, and a sum of £100 was handed over from its funds to the R.C.M. During the nine years of its existence the institution performed the following works for the first time in England :

CHORAL WORKS

Beethoven   Cantata on the death of the Emperor Joseph the Second.
Brahms. Vier Gesänge, op. 17.
Dvořák. ' Stabat Mater.'
Goetz. Psalm cxxxvii. and ' Noenia.'
Gounod. Troisième Messe (selections).
Grieg. ' Klosterthor.'
Hiller. ' O weep for those.'

Hofmann, Heinrich. ' Cinderella.'
Jensen. ' Feast of Adonis.'
Rheinberger. ' Christoforus.'
Silas, E. Magnificat.
Schumann. ' The King's Son,' ' The Minstrel's Curse,' and 'Spanische Liebeslieder.'

ORCHESTRAL WORKS

Bach. Toccata in F, arranged.
David, Ferd. Violin Concerto in E minor (Miss Shinner).
Dvořák. Legenden.
Schubert. Overture, ' Des Teufels Lustschloss.'   M.

LONDON SACRED HARMONIC SOCIETY, THE (1848–56), was formed on Mar. 6, 1848, after the dismissal of Surman from the post of conductor to the Sacred Harmonic Society. The Rev. George Roberts was president, Surman conductor, and the affairs of the society were managed by a committee. Six concerts were given in Exeter Hall during the year 1848, resulting in a loss of £394. The society lingered on for some years, and gave its last concert on Dec. 22, 1856 (' Messiah ').
                                                          G.

LONDON SCHOOL OF DALCROZE EU-RHYTHMICS, see JAQUES-DALCROZE.

LONDON STRING QUARTET, THE, founded in 1908, stands in the forefront of quartet parties of British nationality. Its composition has varied from time to time, the original leader being Albert Sammons, who relinquished the post in favour of James Levey in July 1917. The original 2nd violin was Thomas Petre, and he is still one of the party ; but during the war his post was taken successively by H. Wynn Reeves and Edwin Virgo. The viola, H. Waldo Warner, conspicuous by his dual talent as composer and executant, and the violoncellist, C. Warwick Evans, an artist of wide experience in ensemble playing, have performed continuously from the beginning.

After 2 years of rehearsing, a concert was given on Jan. 26, 1910, the first of a series the avowed object of which was to revive the glories of the old St. James's Hall popular concerts, but with this addition—to seek to bring not only the old masters but modern and living composers' chamber music before the public. After 117 of these concerts had been given, the party started (in Sept. 1920) for a 3 months' tour in the United States, and received a welcome so unmistakably cordial that it was repeated in the years following, the tour in 1925 being the fifth. Their absence (1922–23) spread over a year and a half. They have also visited many European countries and played on several further occasions in London, with programmes which included practically the whole of the classical repertory, and so many new works that space will not allow of their enumeration.

A cycle of the Beethoven quartets, including the ' Grosses Fuge,' has been played (up to Jan. 1925) 14 times, and British composers have from the first received liberal attention.
                                                        W. W. C.

LONDON SYMPHONY CONCERTS, see HENSCHEL, (1) Sir George.

LONDON SYMPHONY ORCHESTRA. This organisation, which gave its first concert on June 9, 1904, was formed by a large number of players belonging to the Queen's Hall Orchestra. Their action was due principally to the vexed question as to the right to send deputies. As the Queen's Hall Orchestra was quickly re-formed, London and the musical public generally gained greatly by the establishment of two permanent orchestras of first-rate quality. The London Symphony Orchestra is run as a 'commonwealth,' the players sharing the risks and controlling the direction. It began operations with a series of symphony concerts conducted by Richter, and these have been continued regularly, although not necessarily under one conductor, the policy of the orchestra being to avail itself of any opportunity that may arise of engaging the best talent for the whole or part of the season. The programmes have maintained the usual orchestral repertory, while a number of new works by British composers have found a place. Eminent soloists have been engaged, and from time to time leading choral societies, to take part in the performance of the larger choral works. Richter was the principal conductor down to 1911, his last appearance being on Apr. 10 of that year. In 1907 a special concert was given to celebrate his thirty years' work in England. The list of conductors includes the names of Nikisch, Safonov, Arbos, Mlynarski, Kussevitsky, Elgar, Steinbach, Mengelberg, Beecham, Walter Damrosch, Furtwängler, Coates, Sokolov and Goossens. In 1912 the orchestra toured America with Nikisch. In 1924 it appeared in Paris with the Leeds Choir. It has been regularly engaged to take part in some of the leading provincial festivals, such as the Three Choirs and Leeds.

LONDON TRIO. This organisation was formed in 1901 by Amina Goodwin (pianoforte), A. Simonetti being the violinist and W. E. Whitehouse the violoncellist. In 1912 L. Pécskai was appointed violinist, being replaced in 1917, while serving in the British Army, by A. Sammons; and in 1925 Lebell succeeded Whitehouse. Subscription concerts, at which the leading pianoforte trios are performed, were initiated in 1905, and until 1912 were given at the Aeolian Hall. Since then they have taken place at the Wigmore Hall, and amount in 1925 to over 300. The Trio has also toured in France and Italy.

LONG (Lat. *longa, notula caudata*), the note intermediate in value between the Large and the Breve in the early system of Measured Music. It could be triple or duple (*i.e.* equalling three or two Breves), according to the mood.

	Long rest Perfect	Long rest Imperfect
or		

(The black form is the earlier.) In early printed music the Long usually supplants the Large in its function of indicating an indefinite pause on the last note of a composition, *i.e.* used as a *fermata*, and both in printed music and MSS. it was a conventional form for the last note of a section. Merbecke in his *Booke of Common Praier Noted* (1550) uses it thus at the end of a verse, and calls it a 'close.' The *Duplex Longa* of the Franconian Treatises is another name for the Large (*q.v.*). It does not mean double Long as opposed to triple Long, but a Long of double the usual length. (See NOTATION.)   s. t. w.

LONG, SAMUEL (latter 18th cent.), organist and composer of glees and catches, including the 3-part prize glee, 'Where'er you tread' (1764, for the Catch Club), psalms in Riley's collection, four lessons and two voluntaries for the harpsichord or organ (1770), and a song for the Mall (1761).

LONGHURST, (1) JOHN ALEXANDER (*b.* London, 1809; *d.* 1855), studied under John Watson, musical director at Covent Garden, and on Apr. 22, 1820, came out at Covent Garden as the Page in Bishop's 'Henri Quatre,' and gained great popularity by his singing in the duet 'My pretty page' with Miss Stephens. During that and the next four years Bishop composed original parts for him in 'Montrose,' 'The Two Gentlemen of Verona,' 'Maid Marian,' 'Clari,' 'The Beacon of Liberty,' and 'As You Like It,' besides giving him the boys' parts in 'The Miller and his Men,' 'The Slave,' etc., which he had formerly written for Gladstanes and Barnett. Early in 1826 he was allotted the part of Puck in Weber's 'Oberon,' then in preparation; but shortly afterwards, whilst in the middle of a popular ballad, 'The Robin's Petition,' his voice suddenly broke, and he was compelled to relinquish singing. Weber mentions the event in a letter to his wife, Mar. 9, 1826: 'The young fellow who was to have sung Puck has lost his voice, but I have a charming girl,[1] who is very clever and sings capitally.' After a short time he became known as a teacher of singing and the pianoforte and an excellent accompanist.

His younger brother, (2) WILLIAM HENRY, Mus.D. (*b.* Lambeth, Oct. 6, 1819; *d.* Canterbury, June 17, 1904), was admitted a chorister of Canterbury Cathedral, Jan. 6, 1828, under Highmore Skeats, sen., having afterwards Stephen Elvey and Thomas Evance Jones as his masters. In 1836 he was appointed lay-clerk and assistant organist of the cathedral. In 1865 he was one of the earliest Fellows of the College of Organists. On Jan. 26, 1873, he was chosen to succeed Jones as organist and master of the choristers. He retired in 1898, after a period of seventy years' service in the cathedral. His doctor's degree was conferred on him by the

[1] Miss Harriet Cawse, afterwards Mrs. John Fiddes.

Archbishop of Canterbury (Tait), Jan. 6, 1875. His compositions consist of anthems, services, songs, etc., and a MS. oratorio, 'David and Absalom.'   w. h. h., with addns.

LONGMAN & BRODERIP, a well-known firm of London music publishers during the latter half of the 18th century. The business was founded in or before 1767, when James Longman with others, as 'J. Longman & Co.,' were established at the Harp & Crown, 26 Cheapside. The sign of the Harp & Crown was that also of another Cheapside music publisher, John JOHNSON (q.v.), but Longman's was nearer St. Paul's, and on the opposite side of the road, i.e. the south side, between Friday Street and Mitre Court.

In the latter part of 1771 the house became known as Longman & Lukey, and this title remained until 1777 or 1778, when, Francis Broderip entering, it was styled Longman, Lukey & Broderip. In 1779 Lukey's name is absent, and the firm remained as Longman & Broderip until 1798. Before 1785 an additional address was at 13 Haymarket. In or near the year 1798 the firm became bankrupt, and John Longman, who had succeeded the original James, held for a couple of years a partnership with Muzio CLEMENTI (q.v.) at the old address, 26 Cheapside; while the other partner, Broderip, entered with Wilkinson at 13 Haymarket (see BRODERIP & WILKINSON). Fresh information which has come to hand makes it very doubtful whether he was Robert Broderip as has been suggested; it is certain that Francis was the original partner.

John Longman in 1802 had left Clementi and set up for himself at 131 Cheapside, where about 1830 the name stands as G. Longman.

The first James Longman and Longman & Lukey issued much music now of an interesting antiquarian character, while Longman & Broderip's publications embrace a wide range of musical productions. They were also makers, in great quantity, of spinets and harpsichords, pianofortes and the smaller class of musical instruments. Their catalogues chronicle an immense variety of these, and some curious items are mentioned as 'Glove horns,' 'Sticcado pastorales,' 'pipes and tabors' (1781–82); also 'upright harpsichords with a curious new invented swell,' 'pianofortes in commodes, sideboards and dressing-tables for convenience of small rooms (1786); and in the 1789 catalogue is — 'Portable Clavecins . . . agreeable for travelling with, as they may be conveyed and even performed on in a coach.'   f. k.

LONGO, ALLESANDRO (b. Amantea, Italy, Dec. 30, 1864), was a pupil of Beniamino Cesi and P. Serrao; at an early age he was made professor for pianoforte at the Naples Conservatory of Music. The founder of the 'Circolo Scarlatti,' and the 'Società del Quartetto' in Bologna he also edits Arte pianistica, a monthly

review on musical matters, though chiefly devoted to pianoforte music. His compositions are of the strong classical style, and many of them are excellent imitations of the style of old Italian masters with a certain influence of German classicism and romanticism clearly visible. His works comprise many works for PF., a quintet and several suites. He also edited and published the complete works of Domenico Scarlatti for harpsichord (in 11 vols.) and many editions of old Italian PF. music.

                                          k. d. h.

LOOSEMORE, (1) HENRY, Mus.B. (d. Cambridge, 1670), was a chorister in one of the Cambridge colleges, afterwards lay-clerk there, and organist of King's College 1627 until his death.[1] He graduated at Cambridge in 1640. There is a composition by Loosemore for '3 vialls to the organs' (B.M. Add. MSS. 34,800). His church music includes a service in D minor, 4, 5 and 6 v. (Harl. MS. 7337), two Latin litanies (in D minor and G minor) printed in Jebb's Choral Responses and Litanies (PH.) and anthems at Durham, PH. and B.M.

His son, (2) GEORGE, Mus.D. (d. ?1682), was a chorister of King's College, Cambridge, under his father, and in 1660 became organist of Trinity College, retaining the post till 1682. He took his Doctor's degree at Cambridge in 1665. Anthems by him include 'Glory be to God on High' (Harl. 7339) described as 'a hymn composed by Mr. George Loosemore, organist of Trinity College, Cambridge, at the Restauration,' and others in B.M. Add. MSS. 34,203.

(3) JOHN (d. 1681), son or possibly brother of Henry (1), built the organ of Exeter Cathedral in 1665. Parts of his work still remain in that organ.

                    w. h. h. ; addns. J. Mᴷ. and
                                    West's Cath. Org.

LOPEZ DE VELASCO, SEBASTIAN (b. Segovia, end of 16th cent.; d. ? Madrid, after 1628), Spanish church composer. In 1628 he was maestro de capilla to the Infante Juana, in the convent (Descalzas Reales) founded by her in Madrid, a post occupied from 1586–1603 by Victoria.

His printed works are entitled :

<small>Libro de Missas, Motetes, Salmos, Magnificas y otras cosas tocante al culto divino. 8 partbooks. Madrid, 1628. (Bibl. Nac., Madrid ; Barcelona, Bibl. de la Diputació; Valencia, Patriarca.)</small>
                                          J. B. T.

LORELEY, DIE, an opera, words by Geibel,[2] upon the composition of which Mendelssohn was engaged at the time of his death. The completed and published portions are a finale to the first act (performed at Leipzig and at the Birmingham Festival, Sept. 8, 1852, English adaptation by Bartholomew) an Ave Maria and a Vintagers' Chorus. This subject has been

<hr />

<small>[1] Hawkins's statement that Henry Loosemore became organist of Exeter Cathedral after the Restoration is probably due to s confusion with John LOOSEMORE (q.v.).
[2] Dem Andenken Felix Mendelssohn - Bartholdys (Hanover, Rümpler, 1861).</small>

treated by several other composers such as
Lachner (text by Molitor), Munich, 1846 ; Max
Bruch, Cologne, 1864 ; Catalani (3 acts, text
by Carlo d'Ormeville and A. Zanardini), Turin,
1880 (under another title), revised and reproduced, Feb. 16, 1890, Covent Garden, July
12, 1907 ; Adolph Mohr, 1884 ; Johann Bartholdy, 1887 ; Hans Sommer (3 acts, text by
Gustav Gurski) Hoftheater, Brunswick, 1891.

LORENZ, FRANZ (b. Stein, Lower Austria,
Apr. 4, 1805 ; d. Wien-Neustadt, Apr. 8, 1883),
physician and writer, took his doctor's degree
in 1831. Like many other physicians, he did
much for music, and his publications are of
special interest and value : *In Sachen Mozarts*
(Vienna, 1851), much praised by Köchel in his
Mozart-Catalogue (Preface, p. xvii.) ; *Haydn,
Mozart and Beethovens Kirchenmusik*, etc. ;
W. A. Mozart als Clavier-Componist (Breslau,
1866) ; various accurate and interesting contributions on Mozart, Beethoven and Haydn,
to the *Deutsche Musik-Zeitung*,[1] 1861, 1862; the
Wiener Zeitung,[2] Aug. 3, 1850, Aug. 16, 1863.[3]
It is to Dr. Lorenz that we owe Krenn's important account of Beethoven's last autumn,
and the other anecdotes and traits there given.

C. F. P.

LORENZANI, PAOLO (b. Rome, 1640 ;
d. there, Oct. 28, 1713), pupil of the maestro
di cappella of the Vatican, Orazio BENE-
VOLI (q.v.), famous contrapuntist. Lorenzani early showed himself in possession of
original talent and a solid style. He made a
career as maestro di cappella outside his native
town (possibly at Turin), but Benevoli having
died in 1672, Lorenzani returned to Rome to
scheme for his office.

His fellow-pupil Bernabei was preferred to
him, but he gained at all events the post
of 'maestro di cappella di Gesu e seminario
romano.' He held this important musical
post at the Jesuit College for several years,
until 1675 apparently, when he accepted
from a Sicilian delegation who had come to
Rome to engage a maestro, the equally important post at the cathedral of Messina. It was
just at the moment when the citizens of that
town revolted against the Spaniards, a revolt
which gave to Louis XIV., already engaged in
wars against the whole of Europe, an opportunity of helping the despatch of an expedi-
tionary force.

Marshal de Vivonne, who became viceroy
of Sicily, appreciated Lorenzani, and when
the time of evacuation came after the *pourparlers* of peace, 1678, he engaged him to go
and seek his fortune in France. Lorenzani
took passage on a vessel of the French fleet
at the same time as those inhabitants of

Messina who were prominently involved in
the revolution, and who dared not expose
themselves to the vengeance of the returning
Spaniards.

Thanks to the influence of Vivonne and of his
sisters, Mmes. de Montespan and de Thianges,
Lorenzani succeeded at the court of Louis XIV.
He arrived in Aug. 1678, was presented, had
one of his motets performed with success,
and ten months later (May 1679), thanks
to the personal intervention of the king, he
was able to buy from Jean-Baptiste Boësset
one of the two posts of ' maître de musique '
to the Queen. The following month he went
on a mission to Italy, officially with the object
of engaging five castrati for the music of the
chapel, but also without doubt to arrange his
personal affairs. He returned in December,
and in the following years a number of his
compositions were performed before the king
or court, and all were well received : pastorales,
serenades, Italian airs, motets, dance airs,
instrumental pieces. The *Mercure*, jealously
hostile to Lully and his monopoly of the opera,
saw in Lorenzani a champion of Italian music,
a rival to the Surintendant, and never lost
an opportunity of praising him. Lully, on
the other hand, who had made great efforts
to create a purely French music and who
until then had succeeded in destroying all
recollection of the Italian influence which had
been so strong at the time of Mazarin, did not
view with any satisfaction the arrival of this
Roman musician. Their quarrel, however,
owing to diplomatic intervention, never came
to open hostility. But the death of the Queen
(July 1683) gave a fatal blow to the fortunes of
Lorenzani in depriving him of his place at
court. On June 20, 1685, he accepted as a
waiting post the employment of ' maître de
chapelle ' to the convent of the Théatins—an
Italian order, a branch of which had been
established in Paris by Mazarin. His motets
were the best known of his works ; they were
esteemed by amateurs with those of Du Mont,
Lalouette and of Lully himself. They made
the success of the famous Wednesdays at the
Théatins ' Saluts en musique,' to which both
court and townspeople went eagerly for almost
ten years.

However, in spite of the death of Lully
(Mar. 1687), Lorenzani did not readily find
access to the king. The French musicians
jealously barred the way. Nevertheless, he
found means to present an opera with French
words (1688), ' Orontée,' which the Prince de
Condé had ordered for the festivities at
Chantilly in the summer of that year. In spite
of good mounting and playing by the Académie
de Musique, this opera, on which the composer had founded such great hopes, had no
success. His failure was due far more to the
absurd libretto in the Italian style which

<hr>

[1] *Mozart's Requiem* (1861, Nos. 33, 48) ; *Mozart's Klavier-
Sonaten* (do. 41, 42) ; *Mozart's Masses* (1862, Nos. 34, 35) ; *Beethoven at Gneizendorf* (do. 10) ; *Haydn and his princely patrons*
(do. 45, 47, 48).
[2] *Mozart's death.*   [3] *Haydn and Beethoven.*

Michel Le Clerc had taken from 'l'Orontea,' by Cicognini and Cesti, than to the music, of which the score unhappily has never been recovered. A few years later Lorenzani embarked again on another scheme which was to cost him very dear. He began to publish his motets (1693) in sumptuous editions (Ballard). In his dedication to the King he let it appear that he hoped to be employed afresh by him. This work sold badly, and Brossard says that the very cause which should have favoured it was of disservice. The motets of Lorenzani were too famous; too many copies of them had been already distributed for the 'maîtres de chapelle' to rush to acquire them in this expensive edition.

Then Lorenzani dreamed of returning to his own country. The post of maestro di cappella at St. Peter's, for which he had schemed years before, was vacant by the death of Francesco Beretta; it was offered to him; he accepted and was nominated July 19, 1694, in the centenary year of the death of his illustrious predecessor Palestrina. After Lorenzani had left France, Ballard published a collection of Italian airs which had a great success. At Rome Lorenzani, director of the Cappella Giulia and Guardiano dei Maestri of the congregation St. Cecilia, had a brilliant career of close on twenty years. He died at the age of 73 and was buried, like Benevoli, at San Spirito in Sassia.

The works of Lorenzani which the circumstances of his life attach at one time to the history of Italian music and at another to that of French music, are valuable. They exist in sufficient numbers in France and probably also in Rome, although in the latter place they have not been counted. His vocal compositions in Italian words, cantatas, detached airs, serenades, and even a little opera, 'Nicandro e Fileno,' presented at Fontainebleau, 1681, denote a musician of the Roman school and a follower of Carissimi. But his melody, already more luscious and with a subtly refined symmetry, his finished harmony, his little developed recitatives recall that he belonged to an epoch of transition, and allow him to be considered as one of the most interesting representatives of the 'bel canto' links between Carissimi and Bononcini. His music to French words is more curious, because it shows that he knew (in order to succeed in France) how to adapt his style to that of Lully as far as he wished; his airs, in the style of Ballard's collections, are in no way distinguished from those of other contemporary composers of works in the same manner. Nevertheless, the motets of his Parisian period take their place in the literature of the French classical motet, alternating soli, chorus and symphonic ritornelles. They hold an important place, and are

worthy of the favour in which they were held by the public.

WORKS

'Motets à I, II, III, IV et V parties. Avec symphonies et basse continue. Par Monsieur Lorenzani, maistre de musique de la feuë Reyne.' (Paris, Ballard, 1693.) Contains 25 motets. Other motets are found in the following collections : 'Scelta di motetti sacri . . . a 2 e 3 voci.' (Rome, 1675.) 'Sacri concerti a 2 e 3 voci . . .' (Bologna, 1675.) 'Airs italiens de Monsieur Lorenzani, maistre de la musique de la feuë Reyne.' (Paris, 1695.) Contains 6 Italian airs.
'Airs italiens composez par les plus célèbres autheurs . . . recueillis par les sieurs Fossard et Philidor l'aisné.' (Paris, 1695.)
Mercure Galant, May 1680, an air ' Printemps, ne reviens plus,' by ' M. Laurencin ' (probably Lorenzani).
'Airs sérieux et à boire.' (Paris, 1696.) An ' Air sérieux,' ' Quand mon destin, belle Silvie.'
Théâtre italien de Gherardi. (Paris, 1700.) The air of ' L'Empereur dans la lune,' 1684, ' Tornami in petto, speranza cara.'
MSS. of airs and cantatas are preserved in the Bibliothèque Nationale, Paris. (Brossard Collection.)
Outside the Brossard Collection : Treble parts of the overture and of the dance airs of the opera ' Orontée ' (with a false attribution to Carissimi). The only known fragment of this part.
Fétis points to Rome (after Baini) for some MS. psalms for 4 choirs, and also a volume of Magnificats a 9 voices which would have been printed there in 1690. Q.-L., on the other hand, indicates MS. works in the Library of Modena. The mention which is there made to an oratorio, ' Dimma ' in the Bibliothèque Mazarine, rests on a mistake. It should be the ' Santa Dimna,' sung at Rome in 1687, and of which the libretto is by Gio. Andrea Lorenzani.

MODERN REPRINT.—' Scène du sommeil de Filli,' from the opera ' Nicandro e Fileno,' edited by Hy. Prunières (Revue musicale, Aug. 1922, p. 117).

BIBLIOGRAPHY

Mercure Galant, vols. between 1678 and 1694 ; Gazette de France, 1687 ; Le Cerf de la Viéville de Fresneuse, Comparaison de la musique italienne et de la musique françoise, vols. iii. and iv.
SÉNECÉ : Lettre de Clément Marot . . . touchant ce qui s'est passé à l'arrivée de Jean-Baptiste de Lulli aux Champs-Élysées. (Cologne, 1688.)
LA BRUYÈRE : Caractères.
BAINI : Memorie storico-critiche della vita e delle opere di G. P. da Palestrina. (Rome, 1828.)
BRENET, MICHEL : Les Concerts en France sous l'ancien régime. (Paris, 1900.)
PRUNIÈRES, HENRY : L'Opéra italien en France avant Lulli. (Paris, 1913.) Un opéra de Paolo Lorenzani (Actes du Congrès d'histoire de l'art de Paris, 1921). (Paris, 1924.) Paolo Lorenzani à la cour de France. (Revue musicale, Aug. 1922.)
TESSIER, ANDRÉ : L'Orontée de Lorenzani et l'Orontea du Padre Cesti. (Communication à la Société française de Musicologie, 1925.)
BOYER, FERDINAND : La Princesse des Ursins et la musique italienne. (Revue musicale, Apr. 1924.)
MANUSCRIPT SOURCES.—Arch. Nat. : États de la Maison de la Reine ; Registres de délibérations capitulaires du couvent des Théatins. Bibl. Nat. : Abbé de Dangeau. Dict. des Bienfaits du Roi, art. Boisset.
A. T.

LORTZING, GUSTAV ALBERT (b. Berlin, Oct. 23, 1801 ; d. Jan. 21, 1851), opera composer, son of an actor.

He studied for a time under Rungenhagen, but the wandering life entailed by his father's profession made steady instruction an impossibility, and at 9 he was thrown upon his own resources, played the pianoforte, violin and violoncello, studied the works of Albrechtsberger and others, and soon began to compose. At the same time he habitually sang and acted on the stage. In 1822 he went with his parents to Cologne, where he married in 1823, and produced his first operetta, 'Ali Pascha von Janina,' in 1824. The company to which he belonged served the theatres of Detmold, Münster and Osnabrück, in addition to that of Cologne, and at all these his opera was repeated. In 1828 an oratorio, ' Die Himmelfahrt Christi,' was performed. In 1833 he was engaged as first tenor at the Stadttheater at Leipzig, and here he passed a happy and successful ten years. In 1837 he wrote and composed two comic operas, ' Die beiden Schützen ' and ' Czaar und Zimmermann.' Both were successful, and the latter was at once performed all over Germany. His next few works, however, fell flat, and it was not till 1842 that his 'Wildschütz,' arranged from Kotzebue's comedy, again aroused the public.

He then gave up acting, and in 1844 was appointed Kapellmeister of the theatre, a post for which he was unfitted, both by his easy disposition and his defective education, and which he resigned in the following year. He next produced 'Undine' (1845) with success at Hamburg and Leipzig, and 'Der Waffenschmied' (1846) at Vienna, where he was for a short time Kapellmeister at the theatre ' an der Wien.' In 1849 the success of his 'Rolandsknappen' at Leipzig again procured him the offer of the Kapellmeistership, but to his disappointment the negotiations fell through, and Rietz was appointed. His life was now a hard one ; he travelled from place to place with his numerous family, earning a precarious existence now as an actor, now by conducting his own operas ; enduring at the same time the mortification of having his later operas rejected by all the more important theatres. In 1850 he obtained the conductorship at the Friedrich-Wilhelmstadt Theatre in Berlin, where he had only farces and vaudevilles to direct; but he was completely worn out, and died on Jan. 21, 1851.

The public discovered its neglect too late, honoured his remains with a solemn funeral procession, and raised a subscription which placed his family above want. He left an opera, 'Regina' (first performed at Berlin, 1899), several overtures, a second oratorio, 'Petrus,' incidental music for various plays, Lieder and partsongs, all unpublished. His operas are still stock pieces at the comic theatres in Germany, and 'Undine' is frequently performed, although romantic subjects were not his forte. 'Czaar und Zimmermann' was produced as 'Peter the Shipwright' at the Gaiety Theatre, London, on Apr. 15, 1871 ; his 'Beiden Schützen' by the London Academy of Music in St. George's Hall, Mar. 31, 1898 ; and the 'Wildschütz' by the Saxe-Coburg Opera Company at Drury Lane, July 3, 1895.

As a composer Lortzing aimed at expressing natural and healthy sentiments by means of graceful and pleasing music, and his keen sense of humour enabled him to give an interest to commonplace situations. He was never able to free himself entirely from a slight amateurishness in the technical part of his work, but his compositions, though not belonging to the highest branch of art, are good of their kind, and in spite of an occasional tendency to farcical exaggeration, are sound and artistic music.

                         A. M.

BIBLIOGRAPHY

Ph. Düringer : *A. Lortzing, sein Leben in seinen Werken.* (1851.)
G. R. Kruse : *Lortzings Briefe.* (1902.)
R. Bürner : *Lortzing in Detmold.* (1900.)
Eugen Müller : *Albert Lörtzing. Ein Lebensbild des berühmten Musikers unter besonderer Berücksichtigung seiner Wirkens und Schaffens in Münster.* (Münster i. W., 1921.)

LOSSIUS, Lucas (*b.* Vacha, Hesse-Cassel, 1508 ; *d.* 1582), was rector or corrector of the school at Lüneburg from 1533 to his death.

He is author of a theoretical work, *Erotemata musicae practicae* . . ., Nuremberg, 1563, which passed through many editions ; also the compiler of a comprehensive collection of liturgical music for the use of the Lutheran Church, entitled *Psalmodia hoc est Cantica sacra veteris ecclesiae selecta* . . ., Nuremberg, 1553. This latter work is introduced with a preface by Philip Melanchthon, and is divided into four parts ; the first part containing the Latin texts and plain-song melodies of the antiphons, responsoria, hymns and sequences for all Sundays and chief holydays, also the Passion according to St. Matthew and the Lamentations ; the second part makes a similar provision for all the minor holydays of the year ; the third part contains the plain-song melodies for the mass and for funerals ; the fourth contains the psalms and canticles with their antiphons and intonations according to the eight tones. Only a few German hymns appear in the collection. A second revised and enlarged edition of this work was published by George Rhaw at Wittenberg in 1561, and two others in 1569 and 1579. The musical editor of Schöberlein's *Schatz des liturgischen Gesangs*, F. Riegel, claims that the psalm-tones, with all their differences, have been preserved in greater purity in Lossius than in the form in which they have been current in the Roman Church, based on Guidetti's *Directorium chori* ; Lossius in 1553 being in closer contact with the older Catholic tradition than Guidetti in 1589.

                         J. R. M.

LOTTI, Antonio (*b.* ? Venice,[1] *c.* 1667 ; *d.* there, Jan. 5, 1740), eminent composer, son of Matteo Lotti, a Venetian, Kapellmeister to the then Catholic court of Hanover.[2] His early years were passed in Venice, and before he was 16 he produced an opera, 'Il Giustino,' to words by a nobleman, Nicolo Beregani. His master was Legrenzi, then maestro di cappella to the Doge. Lotti entered the Doge's chapel as a boy ; in 1687 joined the Confraternità musicale di Santa Cecilia ; was appointed, May 30, 1689, 'cantore di contra alto,' with a salary of 100 ducats ; and Aug. 6, 1690, became deputy organist, with an addition of 30 ducats. On May 31, 1692, the Procuratori of St. Mark's unanimously elected him organist in place of Pollarolo, appointed vicemaestro di cappella. As second organist he composed a book of masses, for which he received 100 ducats, July 22, 1698. On Aug. 17, 1704, he succeeded Spada as first organist, and retained the post forty years, receiving

[1] He styles himself 'Veneto' on the title-page of his book of madrigals (1705), and his brother Francesco was lawyer to the Procuratori, a post tenable only by a native.
[2] Through the kindness of Dr. Kestner of Hanover I am able to say that no documents as to music or musicians at the court of Hanover in the 17th century are now to be found there. The Register of the Catholic church at Hanover contains, under Nov. 5, 1672, an entry of the baptism of Hieronymus Dominicus, son of Matthias de Lottis and Marina de Papirinis, and under Nov. 9, 1673, of that of a daughter of Matteo de Lotti. The Register was begun in May 1671, so that it does not go far enough back for our purpose.   F. G.

permission in 1732 to employ as substitute his pupil Saratelli, who eventually succeeded him.

In 1733 the maestro di cappella, Antonio Biffi, died, and an eager competition for the vacant post ensued. Lotti's chief rivals were Pollarolo and Porpora, and at the first election, Mar. 8, 1733 (the dates throughout are from State documents), he obtained six votes out of twelve. A majority being necessary, the matter remained in suspense, and meantime Lotti was authorised to call himself maestro di cappella. Porpora retired before the second election (Apr. 2, 1736), but his place was taken by a scarcely less formidable competitor, Giovanni Porta. Lotti, however, received nine votes and thus obtained the post, with its salary of 400 ducats and an official residence. In the interim he composed his celebrated Miserere, which superseded that of his master Legrenzi, and has been performed in St. Mark's on Maundy Thursday ever since. This was followed by a number of masses, hymns and psalms, with organ accompaniment only, although his predecessors had employed the orchestra. He also composed seventeen operas,[1] produced with success between the years 1693 and 1717 at the theatres of S. Angelo, S. Cassiano, S. Giovanni Crisostomo and SS. Giovanni e Paolo. Some of these having attracted the attention of the Crown Prince of Saxony during his stay in Venice (1712), he engaged Lotti to visit Dresden with a company of singers, including Boschi and Personelli, both members of the chapel, and his own wife, a Bolognese singer named Santa Stella. The joint salary of husband and wife was fixed at 2100 'doppii' (about £1600). The party set out on Sept. 5, 1717, having obtained special leave of absence from the Procuratori of St. Mark's—' per farvi un opera.'

In Dresden Lotti composed ' Giove in Argo ' (1717), ' Ascanio, ovvero gl' odi delusi del sangue ' (1718), and ' Teofane ' with Pallavicini (1719) ; intermezzi, and various other pieces, including church works, among which may be specified the eight-part ' Crucifixus ' occurring in a Credo for five voices and instruments. The Procuratori gave him one extension of leave, but in 1719 he was compelled to return or vacate his post ; and accordingly left Dresden in October in a travelling-carriage which he ever after retained as a memorial of his visit, and finally bequeathed to his wife. After his return to Venice he composed entirely for the church and chamber. Lotti died of dropsy, and was buried in the church of S. Geminiano, where his widow (who died 1759 and was buried with him) erected a monument to his memory. It was destroyed with the church in 1815.

Besides the compositions already mentioned he wrote for Vienna an opera, ' Constantino,'

overture by Fux (1716), and two oratorios, ' Il voto crudele ' (1712) and ' L' umiltà coronata ' (1714) ; for Venice, the oratorios ' Gioa Rè di Giuda,' ' Giuditta ' (printed by Poletti), and the celebrated madrigal ' Spirito di Dio '[2] for the Doge's espousal of the Adriatic, performed on the Bucentoro in 1736—a very effective composition. His book of madrigals (1705), dedicated to the Emperor Joseph I., contains the one in five parts, ' In una siepe ombrosa,' which Bononcini claimed in London as his own composition, and which led to his disgrace (see BONONCINI). Another is given as a model by Padre Martini in his Esemplare di contrappunto. Nevertheless they were severely handled at the time in a Lettera famigliare d' un accademico filarmonico, circulated in MS. anonymously, but attributed on Fontana's authority to Marcello, who had been a pupil of Lotti.[3] Many of his compositions[4] are still in the King of Saxony's musical library, and Breitkopf & Härtel once possessed several of his MSS., as did also Dr. Burney.

Lotti's rank among musicians is a high one, from the fact that though the last representative of the old severe school, he used modern harmonies with freedom and grace. The expression and variety of his music struck even his contemporaries, especially Hasse, when he was at Venice in 1727. Burney,[5] who heard his church music sung in Venice in 1770, credits him with ' grace and pathos,' and characterises his choral music as both solemn and touching, and so capable of expression, though written in the old contrapuntal style, as to have affected him even to tears. Of his cantatas he says that they contain recitatives full of feeling.[6] As a specimen of his writing for a single voice we may cite the favourite song ' Pur dicesti.' He was so afraid of overloading the voices that he never used orchestral accompaniments in church music. There are wind instruments as well as the four strings in his Dresden operas, but not in those produced in Venice.

Besides Saratelli and Marcello, Alberti, Bassani, Gasparini and Galuppi were among his pupils. A motet of Lotti's, ' Blessed be thou,' and a madrigal, ' All hail, Britannia,' both for four voices, are given in Hullah's Part Music (1st ed.), and a fine Credo in C, also for four voices, in his Vocal Scores and Part Music (2nd ed.). Proske has a Mass of his (a 4) in Musica divina, vol. i., and Rochlitz a Crucifixus, a 6, and another a 8, and a Qui tollis, a 4, in his Sammlung. There is also a Kyrie in the Auswahl vorz. Musikwerke (Trautwein). Four masses and a Requiem are in Lück's Sammlung, and various other pieces in the collections of Schlesinger, Moskowa, etc.   F. G.

[1] Fétis gives a list.

[2] A MS. of this is in the R.C.M.
[3] See Chrysander's Händel, ii. 294 and 303.
[4] Q.-L. enumerates twelve operas as still extant, and gives the names of fifteen more, and a list of masses, church music of different kinds, and arias and madrigals.
[5] Present State, France and Italy, p. 145.   [6] Hist. iv. 534.

LOTTINI, Antonio, the principal Italian basso in London in 1737 and 1738. He sustained that part in Handel's ' Faramondo ' in 1737, in his ' Serse,' and in the ' Conquista del Vello d' oro ' in 1738.   J. M.

LOUISE, musical romance in 4 acts; text and music by Gustave Charpentier. Produced Opéra-Comique, Paris, Feb. 2, 1900; Covent Garden, June 18, 1909; in English (Quinlan Opera Co.), Palace Theatre, Manchester, Oct. 17, 1912.

LOUIS FERDINAND, Prince—accurately Friedrich Christian Ludwig—(b. Nov. 18, 1772; d. Saalfeld, Oct. 13, 1806), was the son of Prince August Ferdinand of Prussia, and therefore nephew of Frederick the Great and of Prince Henry (the patron of J. P. Salomon and cousin of Frederick William II.), the violoncello-player, for whom Beethoven wrote his op. 5. His sister Louise married Prince Radziwill, who composed the Faust music, and to whom Beethoven dedicated the overture, op. 115.

Louis Ferdinand thus belonged to a musical as well as a royal family. That he very early entered the army was a matter of course, for no other career was open to a Prussian prince; but that, amid all the distractions of a military life no small part of which (1792–1806) was spent in hard service, he should have become a sound practical musician and composer, proves his energy and perseverance no less than his talent; but music was his passion, and in garrison or camp he had musicians with him and kept up his practice. He preferred English pianofortes, of which he is said to have purchased no fewer than thirteen.

We find no account of his masters and early studies, nor any but vague notices of his rapid progress, until 1793. He was then with his regiment at Frankfort, and is reported to have aided a poor musician not only with his purse, but by a very fine performance of a sonata in a concert. Three years later, in 1796, Beethoven, then in Berlin, formed that opinion of his playing which he afterwards expressed to Ries,[1] that, though the playing of Himmel—then among the most renowned of pianists—was elegant and pleasing, it was not to be compared with that of the Prince. Ries also records Beethoven's compliment to him—that he did not play at all like a king or a prince, but like a thorough, solid pianist. In 1804 the Prince made a journey to Italy. In Bohemia he visited Prince Lobkowitz at his seat, Raudnitz. We see no sufficient reason to doubt the truth of an anecdote the scene of which lay then and there. Lobkowitz had purchased from Beethoven the recently composed Heroic Symphony, and had had it performed in his palace at Vienna. He consulted with Wranitzky, his Kapellmeister, as to a programme for the entertainment of his guest. Wranitzky proposed the new symphony.

1 Biog. Not. p. 110.

Louis Ferdinand listened with the utmost interest, and at the close of the performance requested a repetition, which was of course granted. After supper, having to depart early the next morning, he besought the favour of a third performance, which was also granted.

It was under the fresh impression of this music that Louis Ferdinand renewed his acquaintance with Beethoven. We have no particulars of the meeting. Ries[2] only relates that an old Countess,[3] at the supper after a musical entertainment, excluded Beethoven from the table set for the Prince and the nobility, at which the composer left the house in a rage. Some days later Louis Ferdinand gave a dinner, and the Countess and Beethoven being among the guests, had their places next the Prince on either hand, a mark of distinction of which the composer always spoke with pleasure. A pleasant token of their intercourse survives in the dedication to the Prince of the PF. concerto in C minor, which was first played in July 1804, and published in November.

In the autumn of the next year (1805), the Prince being at Magdeburg on occasion of the military manœuvres, Spohr was invited to join them. ' I led,' says Spohr,[4]

' a strange, wild, stirring life, which for a short time thoroughly suited my youthful tastes. Dussek and I were often dragged from our beds at six in the morning and called in dressing-gown and slippers to the Prince's reception-room, where he, often in shirt and drawers (owing to the extreme heat), was already at the pianoforte. The study and rehearsal of the music selected for the evening often continued so long, that the hall was filled with officers in stars and orders, with which the costume of the musicians contrasted strangely enough. The Prince, however, never left off until everything had been studied to his satisfaction.'

Louis Ferdinand was killed at the battle of Saalfeld.

His compositions, like his playing, were distinguished for boldness, splendour and deep feeling; several of those which are in print were composed before the intercourse with Dussek had ripened his taste, and made him more fully master of his ideas. These he would gladly have suppressed. The pianoforte quartet in F minor is considered to be his best work.

Ledebur's list of the published compositions (made 1861) is as follows:

Op.	C—.
1. Quintet for PF. and strings, C minor.	10. Trio for PF., violin and violoncello, Eb. (The same number is affixed in the Q.-L. to the octet op. 12.)
2. Trio for PF., violin and violoncello, Ab.	
3. Trio for PF., violin and violoncello, Bb.	11. Larghetto, variations, PF., with violin, viola and violoncello obbligati.
4. Andante, and variations, for PF., viola and violoncello, Bb.	12. Octet for PF., clarinet, 2 horns, 2 violins, 2 violoncellos.
5. Quartet for PF., violin, viola and violoncello, Eb.	13. Rondo for PF.
6. Quartet for PF., violin, viola and violoncello, F minor.	Also a 2nd Quintet for PF. and strings.
7. Fugue, 4 parts, for PF. solo.	A fourth Trio, without opus number.
8. Notturno for PF., flute, violin, violoncello obbligati and 2 horns ad lib., F.	A Rondo for PF. and orch.
9. Rondo for PF., 2 violins, flute, 2 clarinets, 2 horns, viola and violoncello, B.	March for trumpet, 2 oboes and basso.
	A. W. T.

2 Biog. Not., p. 11.
3 Not the Countess Thun, as has been stated—she died long before.
4 Selbstbiographie.

LOULIÉ, ETIENNE, protégé of Mlle. de Guise, and music-master, in the second half of the 17th century, was a pupil of Gehenault and of Ouvrard ; entered the Sainte-Chapelle,[1] Paris, in 1663–64, and left it in 1673. He is known as the author of *Éléments ou principes de musique dans un nouvel ordre . . . . avec l'estampe et l'usage du chronomètre* (Paris, 1696; National Lib.), at the close of which is an engraving and description of his ' Chronomètre.' Loulié was the first to attempt to indicate the exact tempo of a piece of music by means of an instrument beating the time. The one he invented took the minute as the unit, and went up to seventy-two degrees of rapidity ; but being six feet in height was too cumbrous for general use. Nevertheless to Loulié belongs the merit of the idea which more than a century later was carried into practice by MAELZEL.   G. C.; addns. M. L. P.

LOURE (Fr.), a term of uncertain derivation, signified originally a kind of bagpipe common in many parts of France, but especially in Normandy.

From its primary signification the word ' loure ' came to mean a dance, in slower time than the gigue, generally in 6–4 time. As this was danced to the nasal tones of the ' loure,' the term ' louré ' was gradually applied to any passage meant to be played in the style of the old bagpipe airs. Thus ' lourer ' is to play legato with a slight emphasis on the first note of each group. The ' louré ' style is chiefly met with in pastoral, rustic and mountaineer music. A ' loure ' occurs as the sixth movement of the fifth of the French Suites of Bach, in G.   G. C.

LOUYS, MAÎTRE JAN, a 16th-century Flemish singer and composer, member of the Imperial Chapels of Maximilian I. and Ferdinand; organist of the Royal Chapel of the Netherlands in 1576. He composed 3 books of psalms (published Antwerp, 1555) ; motets, etc., in various collective volumes (*Q.-L.*).

LOVE IN A VILLAGE, the earliest and the most famous work of the second period of English BALLAD OPERA (*q.v.*). The libretto was by Isaac Bickerstaffe, and the music was probably arranged and selected by Dr. Arne.

LOVELL, THOMAS, a 15th-16th century English composer, who, in 1501, at the wedding festivities of Prince Arthur with Catherine of Aragon, had ' the orderinge and guydinge ' of the trumpeters and minstrels, and who is probably identical with the sub-dean of Wells, who died in 1524. Only 2 MS. songs of his are known so far in the University Library and in St. John's College, Cambridge (*Q.-L.*).

LOVER, SAMUEL (*b.* Dublin, Feb. 24, 1797 ; *d.* St. Heliers, Jersey, July 6, 1868), dramatist and composer, was the eldest son of a stock-

broker, and displayed talent in many directions at an early age.

After an unsuccessful attempt to follow his father's business he devoted himself to miniature-painting, and was elected a member of the Royal Hibernian Academy in 1828, becoming its secretary two years afterwards. Ten years before this he had sung a song of his own composition at the banquet given to Moore in Dublin. He also achieved success as a writer of prose and verse, before the publication of his *Legends and Stories of Ireland* in 1831. On Feb. 9, 1832, his opera, ' Graine Uaile, or The Island Queen,' was given in Dublin. In 1832 he gained much fame by the exhibition of a miniature he had painted of Paganini. In 1835 he settled as a miniature-painter in London, and attained a good deal of social and artistic success. He was associated with Dickens in the foundation of *Bentley's Miscellany*. His first novel, *Rory O'More* (the title taken from his own song of the same name, dated 1826), came out in 1836, and he dramatised it in the same year for the Adelphi Theatre, where it ran for more than a hundred nights. Other dramatic pieces were : ' The White Horse of the Peppards,' 1838 : ' The Happy Man,' 1839; ' The Olympic Picnic' ' The Beau Ideal' and ' The Greek Boy,' 1840 ; ' Il Paddy Whack in Italia ' (a burlesque Italian opera, English Opera House, Lyceum, 1841). His last play was ' M'Carthy More,' 1861. Meanwhile he was writing novels, etc., and the best known of his works, ' Handy Andy,' came out in 1842. In 1844 the regular practice of his art had to be abandoned, owing to failing eyesight, and on Mar. 13, 1844, he started a musical entertainment, called ' Irish Evenings,' in the Princess Concert Rooms. The success of his experiment was so great that he repeated the entertainment in the chief towns of England, Scotland and Ireland, going to America in 1846. In 1848 he returned to London, and appeared in a new entertainment called ' Paddy's Portfolio.' He wrote two libretti for Balfe, married for the second time in 1852 (his first marriage was to Miss Berrill, 1827), and brought out some books of poems which were not successful.

From 1864 he wrote no more, and in the latter years of his life went back to live in Dublin. He died in Jersey, but was buried at Kensal Green, London. Among his most popular songs were ' The Angel's Whisper,' ' Molly Bawn ' and ' The Low-backed Car.' Some of these were adapted to old Irish tunes. (*D.N.B.* ; W. H. G. F.)   M.

LOVE'S TRIUMPH, an opera in 3 acts ; words by J. R. Planché, after ' Le Portrait vivant,' music by W. Vincent Wallace. Produced Royal English Opera, Covent Garden (Pyne and Harrison), Nov. 3, 1862.   G.

In addition to the above the title has been

---

[1] See Brenet's *Les Musiciens de la Sainte Chapelle du Palais*, 1910.

used for other earlier musical productions :
(1) 'Love's Triumph thro' Callipos,' printed
in 1640. This was a masque written by Ben
Jonson, and acted in the court of Charles I. in
1630. The name of the composer of the music
has not survived ; the decorations for its
staging were by Inigo Jones. (2) 'Love's
Triumph or the Royal Union' was a tragedy
acted in 1678. (3) An opera, 'Love's Triumph,'
produced at the Haymarket Theatre in 1708,
and printed in folio by Walsh and Hare about
that year. Richard Leveridge and Mrs. Tofts
were the principal English singers, while the
other parts were taken by Italians. The words
were adapted from the Italian of Cardinal
Ottoboni by Peter Anthony Motteux, and
the music was by C. F. Cesarini [1] and F.
Gasparini.   F. K.

LOWE, EDWARD (b. Salisbury, c. 1610 ;
d. Oxford, July 11, 1682), was a chorister in the
cathedral there under John Holmes, the
organist. About 1630 he succeeded Dr. William
Stonard as organist of Christ Church Cathedral,
Oxford. He married Alice, daughter of Sir
John Peyton of Doddington, in the diocese of
Ely, who died Mar. 17, 1648–49.[2] In 1660 he
was appointed one of the organists of the Chapel
Royal. In 1661 he published at Oxford *A
Short Direction for the performance of Cathedrall
Service, published for the information of such
as are ignorant of it and shall be called upon to
officiate in Cathedral or Collegiate Churches
where it hath formerly been in use*, containing
the notation of the Preces, Responses, Litany,
etc., for ordinary days, and, under the title of
Extraordinary Responses upon Festivalls, a
version of Tallis's Responses and Litany, and
also 'Veni Creator,' harmonised for four voices.
In 1662, on the resignation of Dr. Wilson, he
was appointed Professor of Music at Oxford,
having been deputy for some time before. In
1664 he published *A Review* of his *Short
Direction*, adapted to the then newly revised
Liturgy, and including also several chants and
John Parsons' Burial Service. This edition
was reprinted by Dr. Rimbault in 1843, and by
Dr. Jebb in his *Choral Responses* in 1857. Lowe
composed several anthems, some of which are
in the Tudway collection and at Ely Cathedral.
He is buried in the Divinity Chapel on the north
side of the cathedral at Oxford.   W. H. H.

LOWE, THOMAS (d. Mar. 1, 1783), favourite
tenor singer, made his first appearance on any
stage at Drury Lane, Sept. 11, 1740, as Sir John
Loverule in 'The Devil to pay ' ; on Oct. 17 he
performed Macheath, and on Dec. 20 had the
distinction of being the original singer of Arne's
beautiful songs, 'Under the greenwood tree '
and 'Blow, blow, thou winter wind ' in 'As
You Like It.' In 1743 he appeared in Dublin
in 'The Provoked Wife,' singing O'Carolan's

1 Fétis gives the name as Cesarini, but both Hawkins and Burney
speak of him as Carlo Cesarini Giovanni, surnamed Del Violone.
2 Wood's *Life*, i. 151.

song, 'Bumpers, Squire Jones.' He was the
original singer of the following parts in Handel's
oratorios : Priest of Dagon and Israelitish Man
in 'Samson,' 1742 ; First Elder in 'Susanna,'
1743 ; Joshua, 1746 ; Zadok in 'Solomon,'
1749 ; and Septimus in 'Theodora,' 1750. In
1745 and several subsequent years he sang at
Vauxhall Gardens, and in 1763 became lessee
and manager of Marylebone Gardens, and continued so until 1768, when an unsuccessful
season compelled him in Feb. 1769 to assign
his interest in the place to trustees for the
benefit of his creditors. His powers beginning
to fail, he was compelled to accept engagements
at Finch's Grotto Garden, Southwark, and
similar places. In 1772 he was engaged at
Sadler's Wells. Lowe is said to have possessed
a finer voice than Beard, but to have been
inferior as musician and singer.

     W. H. H. ; addns. *D.N.B.* and W. H. G. F.

LUARD-SELBY, BERTRAM, see SELBY.

LUCAS, CHARLES (1) (b. Salisbury, July 28,
1808 ; d. Mar. 30, 1869), was a chorister in the
cathedral under Arthur Thomas Corfe from
1815–23, when he became a pupil of the R.A.M.
and studied the violoncello under Lindley, and
harmony and composition under Lord and
Dr. Crotch. He remained there for seven
years. In 1830 he became a member of Queen
Adelaide's private band, and composer and
arranger of music for it, and soon afterwards
music preceptor to Prince George (afterwards
Duke) of Cambridge and the Princess of Saxe-
Weimar. In 1832 he succeeded Cipriani
Potter as conductor at the R.A.M. He also
became a member of the opera and other
orchestras as a violoncellist. In 1839 he was
appointed organist of Hanover Chapel, Regent
Street. He was for some time conductor of the
Choral Harmonists' Society, and in 1840–43 he
occasionally conducted at the Ancient Concerts.
On the retirement of Lindley he succeeded him
as principal violoncello at the opera, the provincial festivals, etc. From 1856 to June 30,
1865, he was a member of the music-publishing
firm of Addison, Hollier & Lucas. In 1859 he
was appointed successor to Potter as Principal
of the R.A.M., which office he held until
July 1866, when ill-health compelled him to
relinquish it. His compositions include 'The
Regicide,' opera, three symphonies, string
quartets, anthems, songs, etc. He edited
'Esther' for the Handel Society.

His son, (2) STANLEY (b. 1834 ; d. Hampstead, July 24, 1903), was Secretary to Leslie's
Choir from its formation to Oct. 1855 ; Secretary
to the Royal Society of Musicians from 1861 ;
and to the Philharmonic Society from 1866 ;
and as a publisher did good work in London
for many years.   W. H. H.

LUCAS, CLARENCE (b. Niagara, Canada,
Oct. 19, 1866), composer and conductor, of
mixed Dutch and Irish extraction. He re-

ceived his early musical education in Montreal, where he played trombone in a military band, and second violin in the local Philharmonic Society, besides acting as organist at different churches. At the age of 20 he went to Paris, and studied under Georges Marty before entering the harmony class of Théodore Dubois at the Conservatoire. In 1889 he returned to Canada and became professor of harmony and counterpoint at the College of Music, Toronto, and conductor of the Philharmonic Society at Hamilton, Ontario. In 1893 Lucas took up his residence in London, acting as critic and correspondent for several papers. He was appointed conductor of the Westminster Orchestral Society in Dec. 1902, but resigned in the summer of 1904. Between 1880 and 1897 he wrote seven operas. He also composed four oratorios and cantatas, one of which, ' The Birth of Christ,' was performed in the Chicago Auditorium, Feb. 17, 1902. His overtures to ' Othello,' ' As You Like It,' and ' Macbeth ' have been heard at Queen's Hall under Sir Henry Wood. He has written nearly forty pieces for piano, while a list of sixty-four songs comprises many varieties of styles. Lucas is now living in America.   H. K.

LUCCA, PAULINE (b. Vienna, Apr. 25, 1841; d. there, Feb. 28, 1908), one of the most brilliant operatic artists of a brilliant epoch, born of Italian parents. When a child she sang in the choir of the Karlskirche, in 1856. One Sunday the principal singer was missing, and the young chorister, put forward to supply her place in the solo of a Mass by Mozart, revealed a beauty of voice and charm of style that startled all present. She studied under Uschmann and Lewy, and, her parents being in straitened circumstances, entered the chorus of the Opera at Vienna, which she quitted in 1859 to come out at Olmütz. On Sept. 4, 1859, she made her début at Olmütz as Elvira in ' Ernani,' and there became a favourite at once. In Mar. 1860 she appeared at Prague as Valentine in ' The Huguenots,' and as Norma. At Meyerbeer's instigation Mlle. Lucca was engaged for Berlin, where she first appeared in Apr. 1861, and soon roused an enthusiasm rarely equalled by any former singer. She studied the rôle of Selika (' Africaine ') and others under Meyerbeer's personal supervision. At Berlin she was engaged as court singer for life; and on July 18, 1863, made her first appearance in England, at Covent Garden, in the part of Valentine, creating an extraordinary impression, further enhanced by her performance of Margherita, in ' Faust,' during her second visit in the following year. On July 22, 1865, the ' Africaine ' was produced at Covent Garden, and Mlle. Lucca's impersonation of Selika was of the highest rank. She reappeared in London every season (excepting 1869) up to 1872; and in 1882–84 she sang again at Covent Garden, in the parts of

Selika, Cherubino, Carmen, etc. She sang throughout Germany with triumphant success, and at St. Petersburg, where she was received with the wildest enthusiasm. Her voice, a full soprano, with a compass of 2½ octaves extending easily to C in alt, and sympathetic throughout, seemed capable of taking every grade of expression ; and to her rare lyrical endowments she united one still rarer—a genius for representation. In London, besides the parts specified above, she was heard mostly in Zerlina (' Fra Diavolo '), Leonora (' Favorita ') and Cherubino ; but Berlin knew better the extent of a repertory said to include over fifty-six rôles. Auber was so delighted with her singing of his music that he presented her with the pen with which ' Fra Diavolo ' was written, in token of his admiration. In 1872 she severed her connexion with Berlin, and went to America, where she remained two years, on an operatic tour through the States. She returned to Europe in 1874, and sang at all the chief cities of Germany, except Berlin. At Vienna she remained one of the chief attractions of each season. Besides starring engagements in Germany, she reappeared in Brussels, 1876 ; St. Petersburg and Moscow, 1877 ; and Madrid, 1878. In 1869 she married Baron van Rahden, but was separated from him in 1872. While in America she married Herr von Wallhofen, who died in 1899. She was honorary member of the court opera in Vienna.

                                    B. T.

LUCCA. In 1640 an Academy, that of the ' Accesi,' was founded at Lucca entirely for dramatic musical representation.   C. M. P.

LUCCHESI, ANDREA (b. Motta, Venice, May 28, 1741), opera composer, came to Bonn, 1771, appointed Kapellmeister there in 1774, and was still there in 1784, when the young Beethoven was playing in the orchestra. Lucchesi was a good organist, conductor, composer of 8 operas, symphonies, cantatas, church music, violin sonatas, etc. (Q.-L.; Riemann).

LUCCHESINA, MARIA ANTONIA MARCHESINI, an Italian mezzo-soprano, who sang in London, 1737–39. In the former year she played Rosimonda in Handel's ' Faramondo ' ; in the following year, besides other parts, that of Arsamene, a male character, in ' Serse ' ; and she sang the music of David in ' Saul ' on its first production, Jan. 16, 1739.   J. M.

LUCIA, FERNANDO DE (b. Naples, 1860 ; d. there, Feb. 21, 1925), tenor singer, studied at the Conservatoire of St. Peter at Naples and made his first appearance at the San Carlo in ' Faust ' in 1883.

Having gained his reputation at Lisbon and elsewhere he came to London in 1887, being engaged by the late Sir Augustus Harris for that manager's experimental season of opera at Drury Lane. At first, however, de Lucia made no impression on London audiences. He was altogether overshadowed at Drury Lane by the brilliant success of Jean de Reszke, and, moreover, the parts in which he appeared—one of them Don Ottavio in ' Don Giovanni '—were scarcely suited to his voice and style. His real opportunity in London came in 1893, when, again under Sir Augustus Harris's management, he appeared as Canio in the first production in England of Leoncavallo's ' Pagliacci.' He remained associated with Covent Garden for some time, singing in ' Faust,' ' Cavalleria rusticana,' Boito's ' Mefistofele ' and also in the first performance in England of Mascagni's ' L' amico Fritz.' Ceasing to be a member of the Covent Garden company, de Lucia sang much in America and had not been in London for some years when he reappeared at the new Waldorf Theatre in May 1905, singing in ' Pagliacci,' ' L' amico Fritz ' and other operas with undiminished power. De Lucia's full tones did not fall very pleasantly on English ears, but he had a beautiful *mezza voce*. He was an admirable actor, especially in parts like Canio, that demand vigour and passion. He was a professor of singing at the Royal Conservatoire of Naples.   s. h. p., with addns.

LUCIA DI LAMMERMOOR, opera in 3 acts ; libretto by Cammarano, music by Donizetti. Produced San Carlo, Naples, Sept. 26, 1835 ; Paris, in 4 acts (words by A. Royer and Waez). Théâtre de la Renaissance, Aug. 10, 1839, and Académie-royale, Feb. 20, 1846 ; London, Her Majesty's, Apr. 5, 1838 ; in English, Princess's Theatre, Jan. 19, 1843 ; New York, Park Theatre (in English), Nov. 17, 1845.   G.

LUCIO, FRANCESCO, a 17th-century Venetian composer, singing-master at the Conservatorio dei Incurabili there from 1650. His operas were held in high esteem, and he composed also 2 books of motets, a book of arias, sacred songs in various collective volumes between 1649 and 1658 (Q.-L.).

LUCIO SILLA, a *dramma per musica*, in 3 acts ; libretto by G. da Gamera, music by Mozart. Produced Milan, Dec. 26, 1772.
G.

LUCREZIA BORGIA, opera in 3 acts ; libretto adapted by Romani from Victor Hugo ; music by Donizetti. Produced La Scala, Milan, spring, 1834 ; Théâtre Italien, Paris, Oct, 27, 1840. Victor Hugo then stopped the performance, and the words were rewritten under the title of ' La rinnegata.' In England it was produced (in two acts) Her Majesty's Theatre, June 6, 1839 ; in English, Princess's Theatre, Dec. 30, 1843 ; New York, Astor Place Opera House, in 1847.   G.

LUDFORD, NICHOLAS, an English church composer of the late 15th and early 16th centuries, an important contemporary of Fayrfax. It has been supposed that he was a member of the Chapel Royal, but Grattan Flood[1] traces the

biography of a Nicholas Ludford who was born about 1480, married in 1535, and died about 1542, without giving any information which definitely identifies him with the composer. Ludford is mentioned at the end of Morley's *Plaine and Easie Introduction* as one of the ' practicioners ' in music whose work he had consulted. There is a collection of 6 masses (B.M., Roy. App. 45-48), one for each day of the week, bearing the composer's name—Nicholas Ludford. The collection dates from before 1536 (the date of the death of Katharine of Aragon—whose arms, together with those of Henry VIII., are on the binding), and is peculiar in that each Mass begins with a Kyrie and contains a long Sequence inserted between the Gloria and the Credo. They are all for 3 voices (treble, tenor and contra-tenor) and are ' lighter in texture than Fayrfax's work . . . [but] rather more advanced in character, the parts of ten entering in one after another with points of imitation, showing a transition to a late style.'[2] Part of the first Mass of this interesting series is contained in two greatly mutilated pages (B.M. Add. MSS. 30,520) ; it is there called ' Le Roy,' as the Mass is founded on a melody of that name (Tye also used it as a basis for a Kyrie).

MASSES

Six Masses for solo and 3-part chorus. Roy. MSS. 45-48.
' Le Roy.' B.M. Add. MSS. 30,520/2. 2nd tenor and bass solo parts of R. Treble and 1st tenor of Agnus Dei.
Benedicta, *a* 6. Lambeth ; Caius.
Christi Virgo, *a* 5. Caius, PH.
Inclina Domine, *a* 5. PH.
Lapidaverunt Stephanum, *a* 5. Lambeth ; Caius.
Regnum mundi, *a* 5. PH. (tenor part wanting).
Sine Nomine. PH. (tenor part wanting).
Videte miraculum, *a* 6. Caius.

MOTETS

Ave cuius Conceptio, *a* 5. PH. (tenor part wanting).
Ave Maria ancilla, *a* 5. PH.   do.
Domine Jesu Christi, *a* 5. PH.   do.
Salve Regina Mater misericordie. PH. Harl. MSS. 1709/49*b*, medius part only.
Salve Regina pudica Mater. Harl. MSS.1709/9, medius part only.
J. M^K.

LUDWIG, FRIEDRICH (*b*. Potsdam, May 8, 1872), became teacher of musical science in the University of Strassburg in 1905, and has made a special study of the music of the 13th and 14th centuries. His contributions to the *Sammelbände* of the Int. Mus. Ges. and the Riemann *Festschrift*, 1909 (*Die liturgischen Organa des Leoninus Perotinus*), as well as his chapter on the non-liturgical and secular vocal music of the Middle Ages in Adler's *Handbuch*, record these researches. He has held a professorship at Göttingen since 1911.
c.

LUDWIG, JOSEPH (*b*. Bonn, Apr. 6, 1844), violinist and composer. He began the study of music at the age of 11, and was sent, four years later, to the Cologne Conservatorium, where he studied for four and a half years under Grünwald (violin), and Ferd. Hiller

[2] H. B. Collins, *Latin Church Music by Early English Composers Proceedings of the Musical Association*, 1916–17.

(composition). Later he went to Hanover and was taken in hand by Joachim, with whom he remained two years. Then came the inevitable military examinations, and a period during which music was put aside, after which he accepted engagements to play solos in various German towns.

He came in 1870 to London, where he received, shortly after his arrival, an appointment at the R.A.M. in succession to Leopold Jansa. He identified himself with English musical life, took out naturalisation papers, and won a respected position as a performer of chamber music, both in public and private. He gave numerous quartet concerts in London and provinces, his colleagues being usually G. Collins (2nd violin), A. Gibson or A. Hobday (viola) and W. E. Whitehouse (violoncello).

w. w. c.

LUDWIG, WILLIAM (real name LEDWIDGE), (b. Dublin, July, 1847; d. London, Dec. 25, 1923), operatic baritone. He was educated at the National Schools, Marlborough Street, Dublin, where he received musical instruction from John W. Glover, grandfather of James M. Glover, the conductor. Developing a fine baritone voice, he sang for several years in chorus at the Old Gaiety Theatre in the Strand, under the management of John Hollingshead, and also took small parts in the operatic productions there, in some of which Santley appeared towards the end of his stage career. What first brought him prominently into public notice was his remarkable performance of Vanderdecken in ' The Flying Dutchman.' The part fell to him when in 1877 he succeeded Santley as chief baritone in the Carl Rosa Company, and for many years he played it with unvarying success. The sombre tone of his voice was exactly suited to the music, and he acted with an imaginative force that even the most famous of German artists can scarcely have excelled. In opera in English there have been few achievements so striking. Ludwig's success both in London and the provinces in the Wagner operas was by no means limited to ' The Flying Dutchman.' He was excellent as Wolfram and Frederic of Telramund, and late in his career, in performances otherwise imperfect, he did excellent work for the Carl Rosa Company, as Wotan in the ' Walküre,' and (in 1896) Sachs in the ' Meistersinger.' It was a pity that the chance of playing Sachs did not come to him while his voice was still in its prime. His conception of the great part was admirable in its blend of dignity, tenderness and kindly humour. Ludwig's voice was always marred by a pronounced tremolo, but he sang with such fervour and sincerity that the defect was readily forgiven. He played Claude Fiollo in the production of Goring Thomas's ' Esmeralda ' at Drury Lane, in 1883, and on the following night the small part of

Barracini in the first performance of Sir Alexander Mackenzie's ' Colomba.' As a concert singer he was never given in London or at the Festivals the opportunities he deserved, but he sang ' Elijah ' for Willing's Choir at St. James's Hall in the 'eighties, with Joseph Maas as the tenor.   s. h. p. ; addns. h. k.

LÜBECK (1), JOHANN HEINRICH (b. Alphen, Holland, Feb. 11, 1799; d. The Hague, Feb. 7, 1865), conductor and violinist, held the post of Kapellmeister and head of the Conservatoire at The Hague until his death. His eldest son, (2) ERNST (b. Aug. 24, 1829; d. Sept. 17, 1876), a very distinguished pianist, first appeared in public at 12 years of age, when he played Beethoven's Eb concerto. He made a tour to the United States, Mexico and Peru, which lasted from 1849–54. On his return he was made court pianist at The Hague. In 1855 he moved to Paris, where he principally resided until driven from the city by the disturbances of the Commune, which gave a shock to his brain, from which it never recovered, and he became at length hopelessly insane. He wrote only for piano. Among his compositions are the following : Berceuse in Ab, op. 13 ; Tarentelle ; Polonaise, op. 14 ; ' Trilby the Sprite, Rêverie caractéristique.' The two former were chosen by him for performance at the Philharmonic Concert, May 7, 1860, when he also played Mendelssohn's concerto in G minor. In the same year he first appeared at the Musical Union. His playing was distinguished for brilliancy and technical dexterity. Berlioz says of him :

' Son talent est tout à fait extraordinaire, non seulement par un mécanisme prodigieux, mais par un style musical excellent et irréprochable. C'est la verve unie à la raison, la force unie à la souplesse ; c'est brillant, pénétrant, et élastique comme une lame d'épée.'

His brother, (3) LOUIS (b. The Hague, 1838 ; d. Berlin, Mar. 8, 1904), was for some years teacher of the violoncello at the Leipzig Conservatorium, until about 1872, when he moved to Frankfort. He was a member of the court orchestra at Berlin from 1880.   M.

LÜBECK, (1) VINCENT (b. Padingbüttel, Hanover, 1654 ; d. Hamburg, Feb. 9, 1740), an organist of the North German school, famous alike as performer and teacher.

His first appointment, gained when he was 20 years years old, was at Stade, where he remained about 30 years. In 1702 he was appointed to the church of St. Nicholas, Hamburg, where he remained till his death. His compositions include three cantatas, seven large works for organ and Choral-preludes. They have been published (1921) in a collected edition by Gottlieb Harms.

Of Lübeck's two sons, the elder, (2) PETER PAUL, was his father's successor at Slade, the younger, (3) VINCENT, was (1724–35) organist of St. George's Church, Hamburg, and his father's assistant and successor at St. Nicholas (*Riemann*).

BIBL.—His complete works, edited by Gottlieb Harms, published at Klecken in 1921. See review *Z.M.* June/July 1923, pp. 574, 575; Paul F. H. RUBARDT, *Vincent Lübeck, sein Leben und seine Werke, selbst Nachrichten über seine Familie und Beiträgen zur Geschichte der Kirchenmusik in Stade und Hamburg im 17. u. 18. Jahrhundert.* Leipzig Dissertation, 1921.

LUGG (LUGGE), JOHN (early 17th cent.), English composer and organist. His Service in D (see below) is described in the MS. as being ' composed in King James ye 1^{sts} time.' He is apparently identical with John Lugg who was a vicar-choral at Exeter in 1634,[1] and who, for some time also, was ' organist in St. Peters in Exeter.' This last description is given in MSS. at Ch. Ch., which, among other compositions by ' John Lugge,' includes some (probably) autograph copies of organ scores of motets and 3 organ voluntaries (MS. 49) by him, as well as a ' Jigg for Harpsichord ' (MS. 431). Some canons by a John Lugg are included in the 2nd edition of Hilton's ' Catch that catch can ' (1658), as well as an anthem, ' It is a good thing to give thanks,' in Thomas Myriell's collection, ' Tristitiae remedium ' (1616).

SERVICES (see also ROBERT LUGG below)

Whole Service in D.   Harl. 7340/46-53*b*.   Score.
Service, including T.D.; J.; K.; C.; M. and N.D   Ch. Ch. 437.
   Organ score.
Short Service, *a* 4, including T.D.; B.; K.; C.; M. and N.D. Ch. Ch 6, organ score with words.

ANTHEMS

Behold, how good and joyful.   Verse anthem, *a* 5.   PH.; Harl. 7339/149.   Score, with organ part.   Harl. 4142/2*b*.   Words only.
I am the resurrection.   Harl. 4142/11, words only.   Ch. Ch. 437.
   Organ score.
It is a good thing to give thanks.   B.M. Add. MSS. 29,372-7.
Keepe, we beseech thee.   Harl. 4142/12.   Words only.
Let my complaint.   PH.; Harl. 4142/14*b*.   Words only.   Ch. Ch. 437.   Organ score.
Not every one that saith.   Harl. 4142/16.   Words only.
Stir up, we beseech thee.   Harl. 4142/25*b*.   Words only.

J. M^K.

LUGG, ROBERT, English church composer and organist, contemporaneous with, and probably a relation of, John LUGG (*q.v.*). He graduated Mus.B. at Oxford, 1638, and later became organist of St. John's College there. According to the *Oxonienses alumni*, he ' changed his religion for that of Rome, and went beyond the seas.' A Service in G and 3 anthems are in a MS. organ-book which once belonged to St. John's College.[2] With regard to a Service at Ely (*Q.-L.*) and a Short Service by ' Lugg ' (B.M. Add. MSS. 17,792-6), there is no means of ascertaining whether they are the work of John or Robert.   J. M^K.

LUIGINI, ALEXANDRE CLÉMENT LÉON JOSEPH (*b.* Lyons, Mar. 9, 1850; *d.* Paris, July 29, 1906), famous conductor, was a violin pupil of the Paris Conservatoire, gaining a third *accessit* in 1867, a first *accessit* in 1868 and a second prize in 1869. In the latter year he was appointed leader of the orchestra in the Grand Théâtre at Lyons, becoming conductor there in 1877. He held this post till 1897, when he became conductor at the Opéra-

Comique in Paris, at first with Danbé, and afterwards (May 4, 1904) as principal conductor. While at Lyons he was professor in the Conservatoire there, and founded the ' Concerts Bellecour ' (Lyons) and the concerts of the École de Musique, now the ' Concerts du Conservatoire.' He wrote numerous ballets, and also composed symphonic music : ' Ballet égyptien,' ' Ballet russe,' ' Marche de l'émir,' ' Carnaval turc,' ' Marche solennelle,' etc. ; chamber music ; a cantata, ' Gloria victis,' performed at Lyons, 1887 ; and lastly, ' Faublas,' an opéra-comique in 3 acts, Th. Cluny, Oct. 25, 1881.   G. F.

LUINIG (LUINEAG), a choral song used to accompany labour, sung (or formerly sung) principally by women in the remote Highlands and Islands of Scotland. Patrick M'Donald, 1783, says that they were of a plaintive character, and were then most common on the north-west coast of Scotland and in the Hebrides. He mentions that Luinigs were ' sung by the women not only at their diversions but also during almost every kind of work where more than one person is employed, as milking cows, fulling cloth, grinding of grain,' etc. When the same airs were sung as a relaxation the time was marked by the motions of a napkin held by all the performers. One person led, but at a certain passage he stopped, and the rest took up and completed the air. As they were sung to practically extempory words by the leader with a general chorus, they resembled the sailors' ' shanty ' of modern times. A ' Luineag ' is given in *Albyn's Anthology*, 1818, vol. ii.   F. K.

LUISA MILLER, opera in 4 acts ; text (from Schiller's ' Cabale und Liebe ') by Cammarano, music by Verdi. Produced Naples, Dec. 8, 1849 ; in French, Opéra, Paris, Feb. 2, 1853 ; in English, Sadler's Wells, June 3, 1858 ; in Italian, Her Majesty's, June 8, 1858 ; New York, Academy of Music, Oct. 20, 1886.   G.

LULLUS, RAYMUNDUS, Doctor illuminatus (*b.* Palma, Majorca, 1236 ; stoned to death in Africa, 1315), a famous philosopher and occultist, devotes 3 chapters of his *Ars generalis* to music.   E. V. D. S.

LULLY (LULLI), (1) JEAN - BAPTISTE (*b.* at or near Florence, Nov. 29, 1639 [3]; *d.* Paris, Mar. 22, 1687). The correct orthography of this name may be settled by the fact that all extant authentic documents signed by him end with the *y*. It is probable that he dropped the Italian *i* and substituted the *y* when he became a naturalised Frenchman. Lully, who was greatly in favour with Louis XIV.—whose band of ' Petits-Violons ' he led—was a graceful composer of the minuets and dances then in vogue, and was the first composer of legitimate French opera. The

[1] Davey, *Hist. Eng. Mus.*   [2] West's *Cath. Org.* p. 125.   [3] See *Ménestrel* for Mar. 13, 1909.

whole history of his earliest childhood is veiled in obscurity. In spite of the statement in his *lettres de naturalisation* granted to him by Louis XIV., in Dec. 1661, wherein he is declared to be the son of Lorenzo de' Lulli, a ' Florentine Gentleman,' and Caterina del Serta, it is most probable that Lully's origin was humble, and that France only learned that about this brilliant genius which he himself chose to reveal. An old shoemaker monk gave the gifted but mischievous child some elementary instruction, and taught him the guitar and the rudiments of music. Lully was in the midst of these studies when the Chevalier de Guise, returning from Malta, chanced to come across him, and, to please his niece Mlle. de Montpensier (who wanted a ' joli petit Italien ' to teach her his language), brought this child, then about 10 or 12 years of age, with him to France. It is doubtful whether ' La Grande Mademoiselle ' thought Lully *joli*, for we are told he entered her service as a scullion in the kitchen, and employed his leisure in learning the songs of the day and playing them upon his second-rate violin. The Comte de Nocent, chancing to hear him one day, was so struck with his talent that he mentioned it to Mlle. de Montpensier, with the result that he was promoted from the kitchen to the princess's band, where he soon outdistanced the other violinists. Thus, when quite young, fortune smiled upon the little Lully and further favours were probably in store for him at the Palais d'Orléans, when his mischievous habit of writing sarcastic verses and setting them to characteristic music brought him all at once into disgrace with the princess. Mademoiselle having discovered that he had composed the air of a satirical song, full of gaiety and ' go,' at her expense, promptly dismissed him from her service. However, that which seemed a loss was really a gain to Lully, for the young King Louis—then a youth of fifteen or so—had previously taken a fancy to Baptiste, as he was then called, and astutely perceiving his superior gifts made him a member of his band of ' Twenty-four violins ' (*Les vingt-quatre violons du Roi*). Here his wonderful powers on the violin, ' an instrument which he played with a perfection none had heretofore attained,' [1] so impressed Louis XIV. that His Majesty was pleased to establish a band entirely for his favourite to train. He named these players *Les Petits-Violons*, and under Lully's instruction they soon surpassed the famous ' Twenty-four violins ' both in power and celebrity. His new post enabled him to perfect himself as a solo-player, and gave him valuable practice as a conductor and composer for the orchestra. With his band of Petits-Violons as a means, he completely revolutionised the dull methods of composition formerly employed. Instead of

[1] Charles Perrault, *Hommes illustres.*

treating his subjects as airs with an accompaniment (as was generally the custom) he studied the capacity of each instrument, and arranged his harmony and counterpoint in such a manner that each one was allotted a ' part ' of individual interest, thus greatly adding to the novelty and balance of the whole composition. Baptiste had common sense as well as ambition, and soon perceived that without deeper study he could not make full use of his talents. To remedy his defective education he took lessons on the harpsichord, and in composition, of Nicholas Mertu, a professor of singing ; of François Roberdet, who combined the functions of valet de chambre to the queen-mother with those of organist at the Église des Petits-Pères, and of Gigault, the greatest man of the three, who filled the post of organist at several churches, and was also a composer of talent. Lully's brilliant intellect and natural gifts were not slow in profiting by the superior knowledge of these masters, and in the meantime he lost no opportunity of ingratiating himself with men of rank. A born courtier, full of the resource and aplomb necessary to face an intriguing court, he knew, above all, how to please and amuse the king, and how to profit by this precious favour at the beginning of a reign full of youth, passion and art. In the midst of his dissipated life he continued tenaciously composing, and found time to write innumerable songs (amongst them ' Au Clair de la lune '), dances, violin solos and even church music, and gained such a reputation that no court fête was complete without Baptiste's music. He was soon chosen to compose the music for the court ballets, in which Louis XIV. himself danced side by side with Lully ; and after the success of ' Alcidiane ' (1658, words by Benserade) was commissioned to write the divertissements for ' Serse,' an Italian opera by Cavalli, performed at the Louvre (Nov. 22, 1660) in honour of the king's recent marriage with Marie Thérèse of Austria (June 9 previous), and a year and a half later the ballets for ' Ercole amante,' another opera by Cavalli, performed at the opening of the magnificent ' Salle de Spectacles ' at the Tuileries (Feb. 7, 1662). The royal favour was not slow in manifesting its pleasure in these performances in a palpable form. On May 16, 1661, Lully received the ' Brevet de la charge de Composition de la Musique de la Chambre du Roi ' ; on July 3, 1662, a new brevet, ' La charge de Maître de Musique de la Famille royale.' These two united were fixed at a value of 30,000 livres, and the *bénéfice* of them was extended after Lully's death to his daughter for her life. In 1664 Lully married the daughter of Michel Lambert, ' maître de musique de la cour '— a man greatly esteemed for his talents, his singing and his amiable character — who

XLIV

RAMEAU

From a print by A. St. Aubin after J. J. Caffieri

LULLY

From a painting by P. Mignard in the Musée Condé, Chantilly

brought with her a dot of 20,000 livres. In the same year he became very friendly with Molière, and collaborated with him in the composition of numberless ballets until 1671. It was by studying the works of the Venetian composer Cavalli, and observing his method, that Lully laid the foundation of his own individual style. In composing the divertissements of ' Le Mariage forcé,' ' Pourceaugnac,' ' La Princesse d'Élide ' and ' Le Bourgeois Gentilhomme ' he made good use of the feeling for rhythm which he had imbibed from Cavalli, and also endeavoured to make his music express the life and variety of Molière's situations and characters. The exquisitely comic scene of the polygamy in ' M. de Pourceaugnac ' (which Lully himself impersonated to such perfection that he often employed it as a means to gain the king's pardon when His Majesty was displeased) is, in itself, sufficient evidence of the point to which he had attained, and of the glorious future which awaited him.

From 1658–71—the year in which Molière produced his tragedy ' Psyché '—Lully composed no less than thirty ballets, all unpublished.[1] These slight compositions, in which he personally took part with considerable success as dancer and comic actor, confirmed him still further in the favour of Louis XIV. But neither the lucrative posts granted him by the king nor his constantly increasing reputation were sufficient to appease his insatiable ambition. With all his genius he possessed neither honour nor morals, and would resort to any base expedient to rid himself of a troublesome rival. His envy had been roused by the privilege conceded to the Abbé Perrin (June 28, 1669) of creating an Académie de Musique, and was still further excited by the success of Cambert's operas, ' Pomone ' and ' Les Peines et les plaisirs de l'amour ' (1671). With the astuteness of a courtier Lully took advantage of the squabbles of the numerous *associés directeurs* of the opera, and with the aid of Mme. de Montespan procured the transference of Perrin's patent to himself (Mar. 1672). Once master of a theatre, the man whom honest Boileau branded as a *cœur bas*, a *coquin ténébreux* and a *bouffon odieux* proved his right to a place in the first rank among artists, though as a man he could claim neither sympathy nor respect. In the poet Quinault he was fortunate enough to discover a *collaborateur* of extraordinary merit, and a docile, modest character, admirably adapted to agree with that of the excitable, domineering court musician. In conjunction with him, Lully composed the first legitimate French opera, ' Les Fêtes de l'Amour et de Bacchus,' which was produced with great éclat

[1] Philidor's precious MS. collection in the library of the Paris Conservatoire de Musique contains the music of several of these divertissements. Some, notably that of ' Le Bourgeois Gentilhomme,' have been revived on the Parisian stage.

at the new theatre on Nov. 15, 1672. The partnership so auspiciously inaugurated continued for a space of fourteen years, within which time Lully composed no less than twenty operas, paying Quinault a retaining fee of 4000 livres to supply him annually with an operatic libretto.

The following is a list of the works produced :

1. Les Fêtes de l'Amour et de Bacchus (pasticcio). 3 acts. Nov. 15, 1672.
2. Cadmus et Hermione. 5 acts. Apr. 1673.
3. Alceste. 5 acts. Jan. 19, 1674.
4. Thésée. 5 acts. Jan. 11, 1675.
5. Le Carnaval. Masquerade (pasticcio). Oct. 17, 1675.
6. Atys. 5 acts. Jan. 10, 1676.
7. Isis. 5 acts. Jan. 5, 1677.
8. Psyché. 5 acts. Apr. 19, 1678.
9. Bellérophon. 5 acts. Jan. 31, 1679.
10. Proserpine. 5 acts. Feb. 3, 1680.
11. Le Triomphe de l'Amour. Ballet. Apr. 19, 1681.
12. Persée. 5 acts. Apr. 17, 1682.
13. Phaéton. 5 acts. Jan. 6, 1683.
14. Amadis de Gaule. 5 acts. Jan. 18, 1684.
15. Roland, 5 acts. Jan. 18, 1685.
16. Idylle sur la paix. Divertissement. 1685.
17. L'Eglogue de Versailles. Divertissement. 1685.
18. Le Temple de la Paix. Ballet. Sept. 12, 1685.
19. Armide et Renaud. 5 acts. Feb. 15, 1686.
20. Acis et Galatée. 3 acts. Sept. 6, 1686.

An act of Colasse's ' Achille et Polyxène ' (1687) is by Lully.

The variety of subjects in this list is surprising, but Lully was perfectly at home with all, passing easily from lively and humorous divertissements to scenes of heroism and pathos, from picturesque and dramatic music to downright comedy, and treating all styles with equal power. He revolutionised the ' ballets de la cour,' replacing the slow and stately airs by lively allegros, as rapid as the pirouettes of the danseuses whom he introduced on the stage, to the great delight of the spectators. For the ' recitativo secco ' of the Italians he substituted accompanied recitative, and in this very important part of French opera scrupulously confirmed to the rules of prosody and left models of correct and striking declamation. On the other hand, he made no attempt to vary the form of his airs, but slavishly cut them all after the fashion set by Cavalli in his operas, and by Rossi and Carissimi in their cantatas. But although the ' chanson à couplets,' the ' air-complainte ' (or ' arioso ' as we call it) and the ' air déclamé '—afterwards brought to such perfection by Gluck—unduly predominate in his works, that monotony of form is redeemed by a neatness of execution and a sweetness of expression worthy of all praise. He thoroughly understood the stage—witness the skill with which he introduces his choruses ; had a true sense of proportion, and a strong feeling for the picturesque. The facts that his works are not forgotten, but are still republished, in spite of the progress of the lyric drama during the last 200 years, is sufficient proof of his genius. Not but that he has serious faults. His instrumentation, though often laboured, is poor, and his harmony not always correct : a great sameness of treatment disfigures his operas, and the same rhythm and the same counterpoint serve to illustrate the rage of Roland and the rocking of Charon's boat. In criticising works of art of a bygone age we should put them back in their original frames ; and according to this rule we have no right to demand from the composer of 'Thésée,' 'Atys,' 'Isis,' 'Phaéton' and 'Armide' outbursts of passion or agitation which would have disturbed the solemn majesty of his royal master, and have outraged both stage propriety and the strict rules of court etiquette. The chief business of the king's surintendant de la musique undoubtedly was to please his master, who detested brilliant passages and lively melodies ; and making due allowance for these circumstances we affirm that Lully's operas exhibit the grace and charm of Italian melody and a constant adherence to that good taste which is the ruling spirit of French declamation.

Lully was also successful in sacred music. Ballard published his motets for double choir in 1684, and a certain number of his sacred pieces, copied by Philidor, exist in the libraries of Versailles and of the Conservatoire. (See *Q.-L.*) Mme. de Sévigné's admiration of his *Miserere* and ' Libera ' (letter, May 6, 1672) is familiar to all. Equally well known is the manner of his death. While conducting a Te Deum (Jan. 8, 1687) in honour of the king's recovery from a severe illness, he accidentally struck his foot with the baton ; an abscess followed ; the quack in whose hands he placed himself proved incompetent, and he died in his own house in the Rue de la Ville-l'Évêque.

During the whole of his fifteen years' directorship of the Opéra, Lully guarded his privileges with the uttermost care and jealousy. The national archives chronicle the numerous commands issued in favour of Lully by Louis XIV. : Aug. 12, 1672, Order forbidding any theatre other than Lully's to employ more than six violins or twelve musicians in all ; forbidding Lully's actors and dancers to play at any other theatres but his own, unless expressly given leave by Lully. Apr. 1673, Forbidding any of the other theatres to employ more than ' two voices and six violins ' in any of their representations. In 1684 a Royal Command that no Opera should be played in the kingdom unless by the permission of the ' Sieur Lully ' ; for infringement of this rule a penalty of 500 livres was demanded.

Mounting still higher in the king's favour, Lully was granted in 1681 his *Lettres de naturalisation* and his *Lettres de noblesse*, and, through sheer impudence, was made one of the *Secrétaires du Roi*, a privilege previously only accorded to the *noblesse* of the land.

As both surintendant de la musique and secretary to Louis XIV., Lully was in high favour at court, and used his opportunities to amass a large fortune. At his death he left four houses, all in the best quarters of Paris, besides securities and appointments valued at 342,000 livres (about £14,000). His wife, Madeleine, daughter of Lambert the singer (or of Michel Cambert, according to *Q.-L.*), whom he married

July 24, 1662, and by whom he had three sons and three daughters, shared his economical tastes. For once laying aside their parsimonious habits, his family erected to his memory a splendid monument surmounted by his bust, which still exists in the left-hand chapel of the church of the ' Petits-Pères,' near the Place des Victoires. Cotton [1] was the sculptor, and the Latin epitaph was composed by Santeul :

Perfida mors, inimica, audax, temeraria et excors,
Crudelisque, e caeca probris te absolvimus istis,
Non de te querimur tua sint munia magna.
Sed quando per te populi regisque voluptas,
Non ante auditis rapuit qui cantibus orbem
LULLIUS eripitur, querimur modo surda fuisti.

Lulli musicien, a pamphlet to which both Fétis and the author of this article are indebted, was chiefly compiled by Le Prévost d'Exmes from various articles written by Sénecé, de Fresneuse and Titon du Tillet. There are many portraits of Lully, of which the best known are those engraved by Edelinck, Thomas, St. Aubin (from the bust by Colignon) and Desrochers. The full-length engraving by Bonnard, which forms the frontispiece to the score of ' Psyché,' published by Fourcault, is now extremely scarce.

Lully's eldest son, (2) LOUIS (*b*. Paris, Aug. 4, 1664 ; *d. circa* 1715), composed with his brother Jean-Louis 'Zéphire et Flore,' five acts (1688), revived in 1715 ; by himself, ' Orphée ' (1690), a failure ; and with Marais, ' Alcide,' five acts, successfully produced in 1693, and revived in ' La Mort d'Hercule,' in 1705, as ' La Mort d'Alcide ' in 1716, and again under its original title in 1744. He also composed with Colasse a four-act ballet, ' Les Saisons,' the memory of which has been preserved by one of J. B. Rousseau's satires. The second son, (3) JEAN-BAPTISTE DE LULLY (*b*. Paris, Aug. 6, 1665 ; *d*. June 9, 1761 [2]), was appointed surintendant de la musique in 1695, and wrote a cantata, ' Le Triomphe de la raison,' performed at Fontainebleau in 1696.

(4) JEAN-LOUIS (*b*. Sept. 23, 1667 ; *d*. Dec. 28, 1688), third son of the great composer, was a musician of considerable promise. His father's court appointments devolved on him, and on his death his brother became ' Surintendant ' and ' Compositeur de la Chambre du roi,' to which posts he owed the slender reputation he succeeded in acquiring.

BIBL.—F. LE PRÉVOST D'EXMES, *Lulli musicien* (Paris, 1779); C. MAROT, *J. B. Lully* (Lyons, 1825); A. POUGIN, *J. B. Lully* (Paris, 1883); E. RADET, *Lully homme d'affaires, propriétaire et musicien* (Paris, 1891); M. DE MONTROND, *Les Musiciens les plus célèbres* (Lille, 1853, p. 41). Article in *The People's Magazine* (London, Nov. 1, 1869), with a print of De la Charlerie's picture of Lully in Mlle. de Montpensier's kitchen. *Fétis*, vol. v.

G. C. ; addns. E. H.-A.

A complete chronology of Lully's works (instrumental, motets, ballets, *comédie ballets*, *mascarades*, pastorals, dramatic works) will be found in the following : HENRY PRUNIÈRES, *Lully* (Paris), and LA LAURENCIE, *Lully* (Paris, 1911, pp. 235–42). Other biographical details in : H. PRUNIÈRES, *Recherches sur les années de jeunesse de Lully* (*R.M.I.* xvii. 3, 1910); PRUNIÈRES and LA LAURENCIE, *La Jeunnesse de Lully* (*S.I.M.*, 1909); ROMAIE ROLLAND, *Musiciens d'autrefois* (Paris, 1908).

M. P.

---

[1] Not Gosson, as Fétis has called him.   [2] Fétis.

LUMBYE, (1) HANS CHRISTIAN (b. Copen-hagen, May 2, 1810 ; d. Mar. 20, 1874), Danish composer of marches and dance music. Like Strauss and Lanner he had an orchestra, which, when not travelling professionally, was engaged from 1848 at the Tivoli near Copenhagen. His many marches and dances " Krolls Ballklänge,' ' Eine Sommernacht in Danemark,' ' Der Traum des Savoyarden,' etc.), were long popular. On his retirement in 1865 he was created a Kriegsrath. His son, (2) KARL (b. Copenhagen, July 9, 1841 ; d. there, Aug. 10, 1911), succeeded his father in his office of conductor, and composed dance music. His second son, (3) GEORG (b. Copenhagen, Aug. 26, 1843), was the composer of an opera, ' Die Hexenflöte ' (1869), and other musical pieces for the stage.   F. G. ; addns.

LUMLEY, BENJAMIN (b. 1811 ; d. Mar. 17, 1875) (the son of a Jewish merchant named Levy), was bred to the law, and in Nov. 1832 admitted a solicitor. Being concerned for Laporte he became mixed up with the affairs of the opera in London, and on Laporte's death in 1841 was induced to become its manager at HER MAJESTY'S THEATRE (q.v.).

Pursuing a policy initiated by his predecessor, he gave prominence to the ballet to the neglect of the opera, and in a few years had so alienated his performers that at the end of the season of 1846 nearly the whole of his principal singers, band and chorus, seceded and joined the newly formed establishment at Covent Garden. The popularity of Jenny Lind sustained him during the next three seasons ; and after her retirement from the stage in 1849, the return of Sontag to public life enabled him to maintain his position for a time, but afterwards the fortune of the house waned, until, at the end of the season of 1852, the manager was compelled to close the theatre until 1856, when the burning of Covent Garden induced him again to try his fortune. Meantime in 1850–51 he had been also manager of the Paris Théâtre des Italiens.

He struggled on at Her Majesty's for three seasons, but at the end of 1858 was forced to submit. Four benefit performances were given for him in 1863. He produced during his period of management the following operas for the first time in England :

Donizetti's 'Figlia del reggimento,' 'Don Pasquale,' 'Linda di Chamouni' and 'Favorita'; Verdi's 'Ernani,' 'Attila,' 'Nabucco,' 'Traviata,' 'Trovatore' and 'Masnadieri'; Costa's 'Don Carlos,' and Halévy's ' Tempesta,'

and introduced, among others, the following singers :

Jenny Lind, Tadolini, Frezzolini, Cruvelli, Parodi, Castellan, Johanna Wagner, Piccolomini, Tietjens, Gardoni, Calzolari, Fraschini, Giuglini, Fornasari, Ronconi and Belletti.

After his retirement he returned to his original profession. In 1863 appeared (2nd edition)

an account of his trouble with Lord Dudley, as The Earl of Dudley, Mr. Lumley and Her Majesty's Theatre. In 1864 he published an account of his managerial career, under the title of Reminiscences of the Opera (Hurst & Blackett. 1864).   w. H. H. ; addns. D.N.B.

LUNN, CHARLES (b. Birmingham, Jan. 5, 1838 ; d. London, Feb. 28, 1906), tenor singer, teacher, writer and controversialist, studied singing in Italy under Cattaneo, whom he esteemed highly, and other masters. He started professional life as a singer of considerable promise : in 1867 he settled in his native town as a teacher of singing, removing in 1895 to London. Lunn's chief publication, Philosophy of Voice, which ran through nine editions, was a scientific and historical exposition of the old Italian school of singing, associated principally with the names of Porpora and Manuel Garcia. It contained an original and interesting description of the action of the false cords and their influence in the production of true tone ; and the development and preservation of the voice, allowing the singer to make full and unhampered use of his elocutionary powers and artistic gifts. Though a noted predilection for the clash of intellectual armour militated against his success in the world at large, Lunn was much esteemed in certain circles for his entertaining and informative conversation and his fearless and untiring championship of what he felt to be the truth.   J. M. L.

LUNN, LOUISA KIRKBY (b. Manchester, Nov. 8, 1873), mezzo-soprano, was first taught singing there by J. H. Greenwood, organist of All Saints' Church ; later, 1893–96, by Visetti at the R.C.M., where in 1894 she gained a scholarship.

On Dec. 6, 1893, as a student, Miss Lunn made her débuts in opera at Drury Lane as Margaret in Schumann's ' Genoveva,' and at the Prince of Wales's Theatre on Dec. 13, 1894, as the Marquise de Montcontour in Delibes's ' Le Roi l'a dit,' on the production of these operas in England by the R.C.M. Her success, both as singer and actress, was such that Sir Augustus Harris engaged her for five years to sing in opera, but the contract became void by his death in 1896. In the meantime, on Mar. 2 of the last-named year, she played with great success as Norah on the production of Stanford's ' Shamus O'Brien ' at the Opéra-Comique Theatre, since demolished, and later in the summer played small parts at Covent Garden. From 1897–99 she was the principal mezzo or contralto of the Carl Rosa Company, both in London and in the provinces. Her parts included Ortrud, Brangäne, Magdalena, Carmen, both Frederick and the heroine in ' Mignon,' Julia in a stage version of Sullivan's ' Martyr of Antioch ' (Oct. 23, 1897), Eila on the production of MacCunn's ' Diarmid ' at Covent Garden, etc. In June 1899 she married

W. J. K. Pearson of London. For a time she
sang in concerts only at the Queen's Hall and
elsewhere, under the direction of Robert Newman, with whom she had signed a contract.
On May 14, 1901, she reappeared at Covent
Garden with the Grand Opera Syndicate as
the Sandman in Humperdinck's 'Hänsel und
Gretel.' In 1904 she made a great advance
there in public favour, notably as Amneris and
Fricka ; June 20, Pallas in Saint-Saëns's
'Hélène,' and July 6, Hesotoade in 'Salome,'
a new version of Massenet's 'Hérodiade,' on
the production of these two last operas in
England. She continued singing each year at
Covent Garden up to and including 1914, and
has made occasional appearances there since
the war.

Mme. Kirkby Lunn, with her fine mezzo-
soprano of over two octaves in compass from
g to b'' flat, is equally successful in the concert-
room in oratorio, Lieder, and ballads, singing
with equal facility in four languages. On
Nov. 12, 1902, she sang at the Queen's Hall on
the production of Prout's version of the
'Messiah' by the Royal Society of Musicians,
having previously sung the same year at the
Festivals of Sheffield and Norwich. Later in
this year she went to the United States and
played in opera at New York as Brangäne,
Ortrud, Erda in 'Siegfried,' Amneris, etc. She
also sang six times with the Symphony
Orchestra at Boston and elsewhere, twice at
Chicago with the Pittsburg Orchestra, and
twice with the Chicago Orchestra under
Theodore Thomas. In 1904 she took part in
the 'Elgar Festival' at Covent Garden, and,
late in the summer, she sang at the Kursaal,
Ostend, under Léon Rinskoff. In the autumn
she went again to America, and on Oct. 17 sang
as Kundry at Boston in the first English performance of 'Parsifal' by the Savage Company,
under the conductorship of Rothwell, with
great success.   A. C.

LUPACCHINO, BERNARDINO, DAL VASTO
(mid. 16th cent.), a composer famous for his 2-
part solfeggi written in collaboration with J. M.
Tasso (1559), which appeared in numerous editions down to the 18th century. He also composed 2 books of madrigals a 4 v. (1543 and
1546), and a book of madrigals a 5 v. (1547)
(Q.-L.).

LUPO, the name of a family of musicians, 7
members whereof appear in the State Calendars
as musicians at the English court. (1) AMBROSO
DA MILAN ($d.$ 1594) appears first in the list of
royal musicians as 'Viall' (viol-player) in
1540 ; AMBROSIUS (de Millane) and Mark Anthony (Bassano ?) are the only musicians mentioned as having received the Queen's customary New Year's gift in 1578–79, and in 1587
Ambrose's New Year gift to the Queen consisted
of '2 glasses of sweet water' (bottles of scent ?).
We find (2) JOSEPH and (3) PETER first men-

tioned in 1570 as 'vyolons' (the word was then
used for viols). In 1593–94 we find among 'the
violins' (still used for viols) (4) JOSEPH, (5)
PIETRO and (6) THOMAS (the latter was Joseph's
son), and in 1602 'Peter and Thomas his son'
and 'Joseph and Thomas his son' appear in
the same capacity ; Peter's son Thomas was
appointed violinist, Nov. 17, 1599. One of the
two cousins, Thomas, the son of Joseph, was
not only a violist, but also lute-player, singer
and a composer of distinction. He died about
April or beginning of May 1628, and his various
appointments were filled by different musicians,
his son (7) THEOPHIL becoming his successor as
violinist on Dec. 1 of that year. He appears
still among Charles I.'s musicians in 1640.[1]
(8) HORATIO, whose relationship to the foregoing does not appear from the lists, was
appointed in 1612 as violinist for lifetime, but
his name does not occur in the lists of the king's
musicians later than 1625.   E. V. D. S.

LUPOT, a family of famous French violin-
makers. The family came from the village
of Mirécourt in the Vosges mountains, which
has been for three centuries or more the
seat of a violin manufacture. (1) JEAN LUPOT,
the great-grandfather of Nicolas, was a violin-
maker here. His son (2) LAURENT ($b.$ 1696)
established himself in the trade at Lunéville
(1751–56) and Orléans (1756–62). (3) FRAN-
ÇOIS, son of Laurent, first worked with his
father at Lunéville, and in 1758 migrated to
Stuttgart, where he remained for twelve years
as fiddle-maker in ordinary to the Grand Duke
of Würtemberg. In 1770 he returned and
settled at Orleans. He was the father of two
sons, (4) NICOLAS, the 'French Stradivarius'
($b.$ Stuttgart, 1758 ; $d.$ 1824), and (5) FRANÇOIS
($b.$ Orleans, 1774 ; $d.$ 1837), in his time a reputable bow-maker. Nicolas began his career
early. We have good instruments made by
him at Orleans (Rue d'Illiers) before he had
completed his twentieth year.

In 1794 Nicolas Lupot removed to Paris and
set up a shop in the Rue de Grammont (1798–
1803). He afterwards removed to the Rue
Croix des Petits Champs, where he made those
famous copies of the great Italian makers on
which his reputation rests. Lupot wisely
dropped all pretensions to originality, and became the first of copyists. His favourite
pattern was the Stradivarius : his few copies of
Guarnerius violins are less successful. Many
instruments are signed with his autograph.
He made several quintets of two violins, two
tenors and bass, to which he sought to give a
perfect unity of tone and appearance. Nicolas
Lupot ranked in his time as the first of his trade

1 Eitner (Q.-L.) suggests that Trimolphus Thopull, contributor
to Leighton's 'Teares' is a pseudonym of Theophil Lupo.
The 'Ayre' in Elizabeth Rogers's Virginal book is attributed by
Hughes-Hughes (Brit. Mus. Cat.) to Thomas, son of Peter.
Lupo (Thomas ?), one 5-part fancye (2 parts missing). Add. MSS.
29,366-8 ; one 3-part fancye, Add. MSS. 37,402-6.
(W. Nagel, Annalen d. Engl. Hofmusik ; D.N.B.; Q.-L.)

in Europe. Spohr, who long played on one of his violins, recommends him as a maker. His weakest point is his varnish. He employed several kinds : the usual one is a thick and not very transparent oil varnish, which is sometimes badly dried, and presents a rough and lumpy appearance. His business descended to his son-in-law, Charles Francis Gand, who was his pupil at the end of 1806 and had left him in 1812 to succeed the *luthier* Koliker. C. F. Gand took the title of 'Luthier du Conservatoire.' At his death, May 10, 1845, his eldest son, Charles Adolphe, took over the firm, at first alone, then (1855) with his brother Eugène, under the name Gand Frères.

Charles Adolphe Gand died in 1866. Eugène then took as his partners Ernest and Gustave Bernardel, sons of Sébastien Philippe Bernardel, an old workman of Nicolas Lupot. The name Gand et Bernardel Frères became in 1884 Gand et Bernardel, by the retirement of Ernest. In 1892 Eugène died. In 1901 Gustave handed over his house to Albert Caressa (*b.* Dec. 25, 1866), who had entered the firm May 20, 1891, and Henri Français, his partner from 1880. From 1920 Albert Caressa remained sole director of this firm.   M. P.

François Lupot (5), the bow-maker, and brother of Nicolas, invented the 'coulisse,' or metal groove attached to the 'nut,' and carefully fitted to the stick, on which it works. He left as his successor Dominique PECCATE, who ranks as the best bow-maker after Tourte.   E. J. P.

LUPRANO (LURANO), PHILIPPO DE, a 15th-16th century Italian composer, wrote 31 Frottole in collective volumes by Petrucci and others, published between 1504 and 1517.

LUPUS, JOHANNES DE, see HELLINCK, J. LUPUS.

LUR (LUUR, *i.e.* Great Horn). A prehistoric instrument of bronze whereof many specimens in a remarkable state of preservation have been discovered from time to time in the peat bogs of Denmark and Sweden, nineteen of them being in the National Museum at Copenhagen.

Its peculiar shape resembles somewhat that of a contorted S, the bell of the instrument— here represented by a flat ornamental disc attached to the larger end of the tube—projecting above the head of the performer. (*PLATE LXVIII.*)

The natural sound of this horn is rough and blatant, and small pendant plates of metal are attached to the smaller end of the tube apparently for the purpose of increasing by their rattling the terrifying effect of the blast, as noted by Polybius and Diodorus Seculus in connexion with the Celtic and Gallic warriors before the Christian era.

Under the lip and embouchure of a modern player the longer horns easily produce the eleven natural harmonics above the prime or funda-

mental note, and also certain chromatic sounds descending below the prime. Some writers have therefore supposed that the intervals of the modern scale were known to those horn-blowers of 2500 years or more ago ; but it is more probable that as the player's cheeks were in those days puffed out in blowing (whence the need of the *capistrum* or cheek bandage used by Greeks and Romans), only one or two of the lower harmonics were obtained, the octave and possibly the twelfth.   F. W. G.

LURLINE, legendary opera in 3 acts ; words by E. Fitzball ; music by W. Vincent Wallace. Produced Covent Garden, Feb. 23, 1860.   G.

LUSCINIUS, OTTOMAR (Nachtgall) (*b.* Strassburg, 1487 [1] ; *d.* near Freiberg-im-Breisgau, 1537), a pupil of Hofhaimer, was organist at Strassburg in 1515, and afterwards canon of St. Stephen's. Owing to the reformation troubles he was obliged to leave Strassburg in 1523, and led a somewhat wandering life, dying at the Carthusian house near Freiberg-im-Breisgau. He was the author of *Musicae institutiones*, 1515, also of *Musurgia*, 1536, the latter work mainly a translation into Latin of Virdung's *Musica getutscht*. His name appears as the composer of a three-part organ piece in Kleber's organ *Tabulatur-Buch*, with the date 1516.   J. R. M.

LUSINGANDO (LUSINGHIERO), literally 'flattering' or 'coaxing,' whence its musical meaning comes to be 'in a soft, tender manner,' resembling *Amoroso* in character, with perhaps a hint of coquetry in it, except that the latter is generally used at the beginning of movements, and the former as applying only to a short passage.   M.

LUSITANO, VICENTE (*b.* Olivença, 1st quarter of 16th cent. ; *d.* after 1553), Portuguese composer and theorist. In his own country he was known as Vicente de Olivença ; but in Rome, where he established himself about 1550, he was called Lusitano (the Portuguese). His name came prominently forward in musical circles in 1551, through an academic dispute with Nicola Vicentino, in which the Spaniard Escobedo and the Netherlander Danckerts were appointed as judges. Baini (ii. 342-7) has related the affair in a footnote which occupies six pages, though in this as in other matters the authority of Baini should not be accepted without question. The verdict was given in favour of the Portuguese, who, to make sure of his position, published an 'Introdutione facilissima et nouissima de canto fermo . . .' (Rome, 1553, with two later editions at Venice.)

He also composed a book of motets, 'Epigrammata, quae vulgo motetta dicuntur, cum 5, 6 et 8 v.,' Rome, 1551 (Munich).   J. B. T.

LUSSAN, ZÉLIE DE (*b.* Brooklyn, U.S.A., Dec. 21, 1863), married, 1907, Angelo Fronani,

---

[1] Between 1478 and 1480, according to Vogeleis.

pianist, who died 1918. Her parents, who settled in New York in the '50's, were both French, the mother, a singer, claiming descent from Mme. de Sévigné. In spite of the girl's promising talent, they refused to let her follow a professional career until persuaded by Mme. Christine Nilsson, who heard her privately. Trained by her mother, she first appeared in opera with the Boston Ideals in 1886 as Arline in ' The Bohemian Girl' and won immediate success. In 1888 she came to London and was engaged by Augustus Harris for his first Covent Garden season, appearing in a single performance of ' Carmen ' on July 7, directly after Minnie Hauk and Nordica. Comparisons, however, did not prevent her gaining marked favour in a part which she subsequently made her own and sang over 500 times in the United Kingdom and America. Nature and art had combined to make her an ideal exponent of Bizet's heroine ; it was alike vocally and histrionically picturesque, forcible and attractive, yet free from exaggeration. With a range of 2½ octaves, her voice had the rich timbre of a mezzo-soprano, whilst mounting easily to a bright, ringing tone in the head register ; and thus, thanks to rare technical facility, she was able to do justice to a wide range of parts, including Zerlina, Mignon, Juliette, Desdemona (these two created by her in English), Nedda and Musetta. She appeared more or less regularly at Covent Garden, chiefly as Carmen, between 1890 and 1910. During the same period she was a leading member of the Carl Rosa Company, with which her versatile labours will perhaps be best remembered. In 1894-95 she sang at the Metropolitan Opera House, New York, taking among other parts that of Anne in Verdi's 'Falstaff' on its production in America. In the following year she toured successfully in France, Spain and Portugal, and in 1900 again sang in New York with H. W. Savage's English Opera Company. She retired from the stage on her marriage and made her permanent home in London. H. K.

LUSTIG, JAKOB WILHELM (b. Hamburg, Sept. 21, 1706 ; d. Gröningen, 1796), organist of Gröningen from 1728. He wrote a number of theoretical works of merit, and also translations into Dutch of Burney's Diary, Quantz's Flute Tutor and other well-known works. He composed 12 sonatas for pianoforte. E. V. D. S.

LUSTIGE WEIBER VON WINDSOR, DIE, see MERRY WIVES OF WINDSOR, THE.

LUTE (Fr. luth ; Ger. Laute ; Ital. liuto or leuto ; Dutch luit ; Spanish laud ; Port. alaude), a large and beautiful stringed instrument with a long neck and fretted finger-board ; at one time much in use, but now obsolete. (See PLATE XLV.). In mediæval Latin the lute is called testudo, and the guitar cithara, both inaccurate identifications of ancient Greek

instruments of very different construction. (See LYRE.) The lute is of Oriental origin, and its Arabic name is al'ud—from which its European names are derived by the omission of the initial vowel of the definite article al.[1] The Portuguese alaude alone retains it. The lute became known throughout the West in the time of the Crusades. We class the Russian kobsa as a lute ; while the balalaïka of the same country is of the guitar kind. As in the viola da gamba and violoncello, the formal difference between a lute and a guitar is to be found in the back, which in the lute is pear-shaped and in the guitar is flat. The lute is without ribs, which are essential to the framing of the GUITAR (q.v.).

The invention of stringed instruments with finger-boards, or the neck serving as a finger-board, precedes the earliest historical monuments. The long-necked Egyptian guitar was certainly depicted in the fourth dynasty ; and wall-painting of the time of Moses, preserved in the British Museum, shows that it then had frets. We observe a similar instrument in Assyrian monuments. Strangely enough the Greeks had it not. The Arabs derived the lute from Persia, and with the instrument a finesse in the division of the octave into smaller parts than our semitones, rendered possible by the use of frets, and still an Asiatic peculiarity ; the best authorities assuring us that the modern Arabian ud and tambura are thus adjusted. Kiesewetter,[2] however, gives the Persian-Arab scale as a division of seventeen in the octave ; twelve of the intervals being the Pythagorean limma (not quite our equal semitone) and five of the dimension of the comma, an interval, though small, quite recognisable by a trained ear. (See COMMA.) Carl Engel [3] states that the Arabs became acquainted with the Persian lute before their conquest of the country, and names an Arab musician who, sent to the Persian king to learn singing and performance on the lute, brought it to Mekka in the 6th century of our era. The strings of the Arab lute are of twisted silk—an Asiatic, especially Chinese, material for strings. The same, bound round the neck, has served for the FRETS (q.v.). The modern Egyptian lute, named oud [4] or e'oud. of which there is a specimen at South Kensington, and an excellent woodcut in Lane's Modern Egyptians, chap. v., has seven pairs of gut strings, and is, moreover, played with a plectrum of eagle's or vulture's quill.

The Western lute was a mediæval and a Renaissance instrument. It flourished during the creative period of Gothic architecture and later, its star beginning to pale as the violin quartet arose. There were publications for the

<hr/>

[1] In the same way el-arz, the cedar, became in English larch.
[2] Musique des Arabes, Leipzig, 1842, pp. 22, 33.
[3] Musical Instruments, 1874, p. 60.
[4] Observe the elision of the consonant.

1. MANDORE or LUTINA (18th cent.).   2. PANDURINA (M. A. Bergonzi, 1756).
3. LUTE (Sixtus Rauwolf, 1593).   4. THEORBO (Mathye Hofman [*sic*] the elder, 1619).
5. ARCHLUTE or CHITARRONE (Italian, 17th cent.).   6. GUITAR (R. Champion, *c.* 1725).

lute as late as 1740—six sonatas by Falkenhagen, Nuremberg; and, 1760, Gellert's Odes by Beyer. The latest use of the instrument in the orchestra seems to have been in Handel's 'Deidamia,' 1741. The great J. S. Bach himself wrote three sets of pieces[1] for the lute, besides introducing the instrument in the 'St. John Passion.'

To proceed to the description of the instrument; the pear-shaped or vaulted body of the lute is built up of staves of pine or cedar. The belly is of pine, and has one or more sound-bars for support and to assist the resonance. It is graduated in thickness towards the edges and is pierced with from one to three sound-holes in decorative knots or 'rose' patterns. Great pains were evidently taken in choosing and making this very essential part of the instrument. Attached to the body is a neck of moderate length covered by a finger-board divided by frets of brass or catgut into a measured scale. The strings were entirely of catgut until towards the end of the 17th century, when silver-spun bass strings were introduced. There would appear by comparison of old lutes to have been much diversity in the stringing and tuning, and there is a broad division in the large lutes between those notes, generally in pairs of unisons, which lie over the finger-board and frets, and the diapason notes that are not stopped, and serve only to determine the key or modulation. When off the finger-board these deeper strings were attached to pegs elevated by a second and higher neck. These extended instruments became afterwards known as theorboes, and in time virtually banished the older single-necked lutes. Mersenne's engraving of lute and theorbo (*tuorba*, *téorbe*) gives nine frets besides the nut, to the lute twenty-one strings, and to the theorbo twenty-three strings (eight to the upper neck). (See CHITARRONE; THEORBO; ARCHLUTE, the bass theorbo.) The fingers of the right hand, without a plectrum, touched the strings *pizzicato* in melody or chords. The tender charm and colouring of the lute-player's tone can, in these days of exaggerated sonorousness, be scarcely imagined. The frets of the finger-board followed a division by half-tones, and in the old lutes were eight to each pair of strings. Later, as will be presently shown, they were carried farther in the higher strings. Mace[2] said nine was the best number, but there was a limitation to this stopping nearer the bridge, by the proportions of the strings in length, thickness and weight being unduly disturbed to the detriment of the tone. According to Baron[3] and an older authority, Praetorius, the lute had originally four open notes (*a*); in course of time two G's were added (*b*). Mel-

chior Neusiedler of Augsburg, who was living A.D. 1574, added low F, making thirteen strings

in all, the highest, or Chanterelle, being a single string. Baron calls compass (*b*) Gamaut, and the deeper bass strings he calls Brummer or Bombarte, the finer ones Bombärtlein. Brummer was usually applied, and the appellations in German, Italian and English were as follows :

g'. Quintsaite.—Canto.—Treble.
d'. Kleinsangsaite.—Sottana.—Small Mean.
a. Grossangsaite.—Mezzana.—Great Mean.
f. Kleinbrummer.—Tenore.—Counter Tenor.
c. Mittelbrummer.—Bordone.—Tenor.
G. Grossbrummer.—Basso.—Bass.

At page 122 of his work Baron gives the compass of an 'eleven course' lute, thus :

the two highest (the melody strings) being single, the remainder pairs. His division of the finger-board has ten frets for the F ; eleven for the G ; and twelve for each of the highest six. There is thus a compass of 3½ octaves from C below the bass stave to the *f''*. We gather further from him that this tuning would represent 'cammer,' or theatre pitch ; for the 'chor,' or church pitch, the chanterelle would be tuned to the treble G, to the greater peril of the strings.[5] This would be the 'Discant lute' of Praetorius ; see below. Praetorius[6] has G for the chanterelle. There were at last thirteen pairs of strings in large lutes, descending at the tuner's pleasure to the deep A or G. Mace (p. 41) explains a large compass of strings as bringing the stopping 'to a natural form and aptitude for the hand.' There were other tunings besides the above D minor. Mace gives a new French tuning in E minor, and a 'flat' tuning which he preferred ; referring to that we quote from Baron (*b*) as the old lute, theorbo or viol way : but he wisely remarks (p. 191):

'That tuning upon any instrument which allows the artist most scope, freedom and variety, with most ease and familiarity, to express his conceptions most fully and completely, without limitation or restraint throughout all the keys, must needs be accounted the best.'

It must have been very troublesome to keep a lute in order. Mace, in his often-quoted work, recommends that a lute should be kept in a bed which is in constant use, and goes on to say that once in a year or two, if you have

1 Carl F. Becker described them in *Die Hausmusik in Deutschland*, Leipzig, 1840.
2 *Musick's Monument*, London, 1676, p. 50.
3 *Untersuchung der Instruments der Lauten*, Nuremberg, 1727.

4 According to the *Encyclopédie*, about the middle of the 18th century the accordance was—

C, D, E, F, G.	A, d, g, b, e', a'.
Open.	Fingered.

5 Mahillon's *Catalogue*, 1880, p. 247.
6 *Organographia*. Wolfenbüttel, 1619, p. 49.

not very good luck, you will be constrained to have the belly taken off as it will have sunk from the stretch of the strings, ' which is a great strength.' Mattheson said a lutenist of eighty years old had certainly spent sixty in tuning his instrument, and that the cost in Paris of keeping a horse or a lute was about the same. Baron replied that the horse would soon be like one of Pharaoh's lean kine.

In Italian lutes of early date the tuning pegs were disposed diagonally across the head in two rows, the projections for tuning being at the back. They were afterwards inserted at the side of the head as in a violin, the head being bent back at an obtuse or even a right angle to the neck. Ultimately metal screws replaced the pegs, but only when large single strings were put on instead of double strings. The lute is now esteemed solely for the great beauty of its form and design. Inlays of various hard woods, tortoiseshell, ivory and mother-of-pearl, and sometimes painting on the sound-board, have been employed to decorate them. Through their decorative value many lutes have been preserved ; and many were trans-formed into Vielles or Hurdy-gurdies. Lutes and viols having been made by the same artists, the word *luthier* in French still desig-nates a maker of violins.

The lute-player had not our musical notation ; systems special to the instrument, and known as TABLATURE (*q.v.*), being long in vogue. The lute and organ are the two instruments for which the oldest instrumental compositions we possess were written.[1] Many instruction-books were written for the lute, with examples in tablature ; the oldest known to exist in this country is the *Lauttenbuch* of Wolf Heckel (Strassburg, 1562), preserved at the R.C.M. The next in order of date are *The Science of Luting*, licensed to John Allden in 1565 ; *A Brief and easy instruction to learne the tableture, to conduct and dispose the hand into the Lute* [by Adrien Le Roy]. Englished by J. Alford, Londoner, 1568 ; an English translation by F. K. (London, 1574), of the famous Tutor of Adrien Le Roy, which had appeared in Paris in 1551 ; Thomas Dallis's MS. Lute-Book (1583), in the library of Trinity College, Dublin ; and William Ballet's MS. Lute-Books (1594) in the same library. There is another in the British Museum by Thomas Robinson, written in the form of a dialogue (London, 1603). We must not omit the treatise by Thomas Mace (London, 1676), to which we have so frequently referred, and the lute-books of Thysius.

Praetorius, in his *Organographia*, was careful to describe the then (1619) familiar lute. He gives (p. 51) a graduated family of lutes with their quints or chanterelles, which show how

[1] Mahillon's *Catalogue*, 1880, p. 246.

much variety in size and scale was permitted. They are—(1) Klein Octav (*a*) ; (2) Klein Discant (*b*) ; (3) Discant (*c*) ; (4) Recht Chorist oder Alt (*d*) ; (5) Tenor (*e*) ; (6) Bass (*f*) ; (7) Gross Octav Bass (*g*).

Thus it will be seen that the lute generally known and described here, the ' French ' lute of Mace, is the Alto lute. Vincentio Galilei, the father of the astronomer, was the author of a dialogue on the lute (Venice, 1583) and a book on lute tablature (1620). Other noteworthy continental publications were by Judenkünig, Vienna, 1523 ; Gerle, Nuremberg, 1545 ; Hans Neusiedler, Nuremberg, 1556 ; Melchior Neu-siedler, 1574 ; Ochsenkhuns, Heidelberg (1558) ; Kargel, Strassburg, 1586 ; Besardus, Cologne, 1603 ; Campion, Paris, 1710 ; and Baron, Nuremberg (already quoted from), 1727.

Much valuable information collected about lute-makers and the literature of the lute is communicated by Carl Engel [2] in his admirable catalogue of the Victoria and Albert Museum referred to. The finest lutes were made in Italy ; and Bologna, Venice, Padua and Rome were especially famous for them. There would appear to have been a fusion of German and Italian skill in northern Italy, when the Bolo-gnese lutes were reputed to excel all others. Evelyn in his *Diary* (May 21, 1645) remarks their high price, and that they were chiefly made by Germans. One of the earliest of these was Lucas (or Laux, as he inscribed his name on his instruments) Maler, who was living in Bologna about 1500–20. There is one of his make at South Kensington, but the head is modernised to correspond with that of the modern guitar. There is a perfect specimen in the University Museum, Philadelphia, U S.A.[3] According to Thomas Mace, ' pittifull old, batter'd, crack'd things ' of Laux Maler would fetch a hundred pounds each. He (p. 48) quotes the king (Charles I.) as having bought one for £100 through the famous lutenist Gaultier ; but the correspondence of Huygens [4] relates that the lute belonged to Jehan Ballard, who would not part with it. After his death Charles I. bought it of the relations for £100, and gave it to Gaultier. The discant lute dated 1593, shown in *PLATE XLV*. No. 3, is typical of the instrument used in England in the 16th and early 17th centuries. The head is turned sharply backward, not merely for portability but to secure a firm pressure of the 13 strings on

[2] A lute, once Engel's, now at the R.C.M., is a rare specimen. It bears the inscription ' 1600. In Padova Vvendelio Venere.' It was bought by Hipkins when Engel died.   E. J. H[S].
[3] This rare example of an early lute has the head turned back at a sharp angle ; a single ' rose ' is cut in the belly ; there are 5 pairs of strings (the highest tuned to treble G) and 9 flat ribs in the body, which is of the dark black-reddish colour so much praised by Mace. The label within is not dated.   F. W. G.
[4] *Musique et musiciens*, etc., ed. Jonckbloet and Land, 1882.

the upper nut.   Both lutes and theorboes are now being made again on the Continent.

BIBLIOGRAPHY

Mace's *Musick's Monument* gives full details of the lute and the method of playing practised in England in the 17th century; but the following recent treatises may be consulted :
F. W. GALPIN : *Old English Instruments* (1911).
H. SOMMER : *Die Laute in ihrer musikgeschichtlichen kultur- und kunsthistorischen Bedeutung.   Eine Bildmonographie* (Berlin, 1920).
A. TOSCANELLI : *Il liuto, con un cenno su le intavolature* (Milan, 1922).
J. PULVER : *The Lute in England* (*Mus. Opinion*, Apr.-Aug. 1923).
A. J. H. ;   rev. F. W. G.

LUTE-HARPSICHORD, see LAUTENCLAVI-CYMBAL.

LUTENIST, a lute player. In the 16th and 17th centuries lutenists, or, as they were sometimes called, ' lewters ' or ' luters,' invariably formed part of the musical retinue of kings and princes, and one at least was commonly attached to the households of nobles and landed gentry.   As late as Aug. 8, 1715, a lutenist's place was created in the Chapel Royal of St. James's, and John Shore was appointed to it, who held it until his death in 1752, when it was given to John Immyns, who filled it until his death in 1764.   The office afterwards became a sinecure, and was eventually annexed to the Mastership of the Children as a means of increasing the stipend.   It continued until the death of William Hawes in 1846, when it was abolished.   W. H. H.

LUTHER, MARTIN (*b.* Eisleben, St. Martin's Eve, Nov. 10, 1483 ; *d.* there, Feb. 18, 1546). For the main facts of the life of the great Reformer the reader must consult some other work. as our space compels us to confine ourselves to his relation to music, and especially to the hymns and services of the Church.   It was after his departure from the Wartburg, Mar. 22, 1522, that he began to occupy himself with projects for the reform of the services of the Church, among which his alterations in the musical parts of the Mass led to important results.   There is ample evidence that German hymns were sung during the service before Luther's alterations ; but, if not the actual founder, there is no doubt that he was the establisher of congregational singing.   In his first ' Formula Missae ' (1523), Luther objects to the singing of long graduals, and recommends that the choice of certain hymns should be left to the priest.   The Reformer had long cherished the idea of a German Mass, and during the latter part of the year 1524 he was occupied with arranging that service.   In order to help him in the musical part of his work he summoned to Wittenberg two able musicians, Conrad Rupff, Kapellmeister to the Elector of Saxony, and Johann Walther, cantor at the court of Frederick the Wise at Torgau. To the latter we are indebted for much information about Luther as a musician.

He says that at this time he stayed with Luther at Wittenberg for three weeks, and that the Reformer himself set to music several

Gospels and Epistles and the words of Consecration, inventing the tunes on his flute, while Walther noted them down.   Luther used also to discuss the eight church tones ; giving the Epistle to the 8th tone, and the Gospel to the 6th.   ' For,' said he, ' Christ is a gentle Lord, and His words are lovely ; therefore let us take the 6th tone for the Gospel ; and since St. Paul is a grave apostle, we will set the Epistle to the 8th tone.'   The result of these labours was the publication of the ' Order of the German Mass,' which contained the following alterations.   Instead of the introit there was ordered to be sung a hymn or German psalm (' Ich will den Herrn loben,' or ' Meine Seele soll sich rühmen ').   Then followed the Kyrie Eleison, sung three times (instead of nine). After the Collect and Epistle a German hymn (' Nun bitten wir den heil'gen Geist,' or another) was sung, and after the Gospel, instead of the Latin Creed, the German (' Wir glauben all ').   The sermon then followed, and after this a paraphrase of the Lord's Prayer, and the Exhortation to Communicants.   After the Consecration was sung ' Jesaia dem Propheten,' Huss's hymn ' Jesus Christus, unser Heiland,' or ' Christe, du Lamm Gottes.'

This form of service was first used on Christmas Day, 1524, in the parish church of Wittenberg, but it was not published until the following year.   It is evident that while introducing a more popular element into the music of the Mass, Luther did not despise the singing of a trained choir.   In the ' Vermahnung zum Gebet wider den Türken ' (1541) he says :

' I rejoice to let the 79th Psalm, " O God, the heathen are come," be sung as usual, one choir after another. Accordingly, let one sweet-voiced boy step before the desk in his choir and sing alone the antiphon or sentence " Domine, ne secundum," and after him let another boy sing the other sentence, " Domine, ne memineris " ; and then let the whole choir sing on their knees, " Adjuva nos, Deus," just as it was in the Popish Fasts, for it sounds and looks very devotional.'

At the same time that he was engaged in arranging the German Mass, Luther was turning his attention to writing and adapting hymns to be sung during the service.   In 1524 he wrote to his friend, George Spalatin :

' I wish, after the example of the Prophets and ancient Fathers of the Church, to make German psalms for the people, that is to say, sacred hymns, so that the word of God may dwell among the people by means of song also.'

In the same year (1524) the first Protestant hymn-book appeared :

' Etlich christliche Lyeder Lobgesang und Psalm dem reinen Wort Gottes gemess auss der h. gschrifft durch mancherlay Hochgelerter gemacht, in der Kirchen zu singen, wie es den zum tail bereyt zu Wittenburg in yebung ist.   Witenburg, 1524.'

It is not certain whether Luther actually arranged this book ; it contains only eight hymns (four of which are by him), and five tunes.   During the same year several other collections appeared, and their number increased rapidly.   (See CHORAL.)   Scattered through these different collections there is great difficulty in deciding what hymns are really Luther's, and what are merely adaptations. The immediate popularity which these early Protestant hymns attained was immense ; they were taught in the schools, and carried through the country by wandering scholars, until his enemies declared that Luther had destroyed more souls by his hymns than by his writings and speeches.

On June 11, 1525, Luther was married to Catherine von Bora, formerly a nun at Nimptsch in Saxony. This marriage proved a most happy connexion, and the letters of his friends abound with descriptions of the domestic felicity to which it gave rise. We are told that after supper he used to sing motets and hymns with his children and friends, his favourite composers being Senfl and Josquin des Prés, the works of the latter of whom he particularly admired. Luther possessed a fine deep voice, and played both the flute and lute, the latter so well as to attract the attention of passers-by as he journeyed to Worms. It has been said that he wrote motets himself, but there is no proof of this, and it is probably a mistake arising from the existence, in the Munich Library, of a collection of motets with a preface by the Reformer. In 1538 Luther wrote a short treatise in praise of music ; a poem by him on the same subject (entitled ' Frau Musika ') also exists, and may be found in the *Leipziger A.M.Z.* for 1811. The latter years of Luther's life were principally spent at Wittenberg, but he died at Eisleben. He was buried in the Schloss-Kirche at Wittenberg ; his greatest hymn, ' Ein' feste Burg,' being sung over his grave.

The following is a list [1] of hymns, the words of which were written or arranged by Luther, together with their dates, so far as it is been possible to ascertain them :

I. Translations and Arrangements of Latin Hymns.

1. ' Jesus Christus unser Heiland,' 1524. From John Huss's hymn ' Jesus Christus nostra salus.'

2. ' Verleih uns Frieden gnädiglich,' 1529. From ' Da pacem Domine,' an antiphon of the 6th or 7th century.

3. ' Christum wir sollen loben,' 1524. From a Christmas hymn by Coelius Sedulius (5th cent.), ' A solis ortus.'

4. ' Der du bist drei,' 1543. From ' O Lux beata,' an Epiphany hymn of the 5th century.

5. ' Herr Gott, dich loben wir,' 1529. From the ' Te Deum.'

6. ' Komm, Gott, Schöpfer,' 1524. From the ' Veni Creator.'

7. ' Komm, heiliger Geist,' 1524. From the ' Veni sancte Spiritus ' attributed to King Robert of France, 997.

8. ' Nun komm der Heiden Heiland,' 1524. From a Christmas hymn by St. Ambrose, ' Veni Redemptor.'

9. ' Was fürcht'st du Feind,' Dec. 12, 1541. From ' Hostis Herodes impie,' an Epiphany hymn by Coelius Sedulius.

10. ' Wir glauben all' an einen Gott,' 1524. From the creed ' Patrem credimus.'

II. Amplifications of early German translations of Latin Hymns.

11. ' Gelobet seyst du,' 1524. Six verses added to a 15-century translation of the Christmas Sequence of Gregory the Great, ' Grates nunc omnes.'

12. ' Mitten wir im Leben sind,' 1524. Two verses added to a 15th-century funeral hymn on Notker's Antiphon ' Media vita in morte sumus.'

III. Corrections or Arrangements of early German Hymns.

13. ' Christ lag in Todesbanden,' 1524. From the 12th-century hymn ' Christ ist uferstanden.'

14. ' Gott der Vater wohn uns bei,' 1524. From a 15th-century Litany.

15. ' Gott sei gelobet und gebenedeiet,' 1524. From a sacramental hymn of the 16th century.

16. ' Nun bitten wir den heiligen Geist,' 1524. From a 13th-century Whitsuntide hymn.

IV. Hymns based upon Latin Psalms.

17. ' Ach Gott vom Himmel,' 1523. Ps. xii. ' Salvum me fac.'

18*a*. ' Aus tiefer Noth,' 1523. First version, containing four verses. Ps. cxxx. ' De profundis.'

18*b*. Do., 1524. Second version, containing five verses.

19. ' Ein' feste Burg,' 1529. Ps. xlvi. ' Deus noster refugium.'

20. ' Es spricht der Unweisen,' 1524. Ps. xiv. ' Dixit insipiens.'

21. ' Es wollt uns Gott,' 1524. Ps. lxvii. ' Deus misereatur.'

22. ' Wär' Gott nicht mit uns,' 1524. Ps. cxxiv. ' Nisi qui Dominus.'

23. ' Wohl dem, der in Gottesfürchte,' 1524. Ps. cxxviii. ' Beati omnes.'

V. Hymns based upon passages of the Bible.

24. ' Christ unser Herr,' 1541. The Baptism of Christ.

25. ' Diess sind die heiligen zehn Gebot,' 1524. The Decalogue.

26. ' Jesaia, dem Propheten,' 1526. The Vision of Isaiah.

27. ' Mensch, willst du leben,' 1524. Abbreviated version of the Decalogue.

28. ' Mit Fried und Freud,' 1524. The ' Nunc Dimittis.'

29. ' Sie ist mir lieb,' 1535. The Christian Church (Rev. xii.).

30. ' Vater unser,' 1539. The Lord's Prayer.

31. ' Vom Himmel hoch,' 1535. The Nativity (a children's hymn).

VI. Original Hymns.

32. ' Ein neues Lied,' 1523. A hymn to the memory of two Lutheran martyrs, H. Voes and J. Esch, who were burnt at Brussels, July 1, 1523.

33. ' Erhalt uns, Herr,'1541. A children's hymn against the two arch-enemies of Christ, the Pope and the Turk.

34. ' Jesus Christus, unser Heiland,' 1524. An Easter hymn.

35. ' Nun freut euch,' 1523. A hymn of thanksgiving.

36. ' Vom Himmel kam,' 1543. A Christmas hymn.

The following are the hymn tunes which have been ascribed to Luther, though none with any degree of certainty :

1. ' Jesaia dem Propheten das geschah.' Appeared in the place of the Sanctus in Luther's ' Eine Weiss, Christlich Mess zu halten,' 1526.

2. ' Ein' feste Burg ist unser Gott.' First appeared in ' Geistliche Lieder, auffs new gebessert zu Wittenberg. Dr. Mart. Luther. 1529.' This book was printed by Joseph Klug.

The following arrangements of this hymn appeared during Luther's life :

(*a*) For 3 voices, with the melody in the tenor, in ' News Gesang, mit dreyen stimmen den Kirchen und Schulen zu nutz, neulich in Preussen durch Joannem Kugelmann gesetzt ' (Augsburg, 1540). Hans Kugelmann was Kapellmeister to Duke Albert of Brandenburg.

(*b*) For 4 voices, with the melody in the bass, in G. Rhaw's ' Newe deutsche geistliche Gesenge cxxiii.' (Wittenberg, 1544).

(*c*) For 5 voices, with the melody in the tenor, by Stephen Mahu, in G. Rhaw's Hymn-book.

(*d*) For 4 voices, with the melody in the bass, by M. Agricola, in G. Rhaw's Hymn-book.

(*e*) For 4 voices, with the melody in the bass, by L. Hellinck, in G. Rhaw's Hymn-book.

3. ' Aus tiefer Noth ruf' ich zu dir.' First appeared in the ' Geistliche Gesangbüchlein. Tenor.' (Wittenberg, 1524.)

4. ' Ein neues Lied wir heben an.' First appeared in ' Enchi-

ridion, Oder eyn Handtbüchlein eynem yetzlichen Christen fast nutzlich bey sich zu haben zur stetter vbung vnnd trachtung Geystlicher gesenge vnd Psalmen, Rechtschaffen vnd kunstlich vertheutscht. 1524.' Printed at Erfurt.

5. ' Es spricht der Unweisen Mund wohl.' Appeared in the ' Gesangbüchleyn,' 1524.

6. ' Mensch, willst du leben seliglich.' From the ' Gesangbüchleyn,' 1524.

7. ' Mit Fried und Freud ich fahr dahin.' From the Gesangbüchleyn,' 1524.

8. ' Vom Himmel hoch, da komm ich her.' Appeared in Lotther's Magdeburg Gesangbuch, 1540.

9. ' Jesus Christus unser Heiland.' From the ' Enchiridion,' 1524.

10. ' Nun freut euch, liebe Christen g'mein.' From the so-called ' Achtliederbuch,' 1524. In Adam Dyson's Hymn-book (Breslau, 1525) it is set to the tune of ' Es ist das Heil,' which was probably composed by Speratus.

11. ' Nun freut euch, liebe Christen g'mein.' From Klug's ' Geistliche Lieder ' (Wittenberg, 1529).

12. ' Vater unser im Himmelreich.' In Köphyl's Strassburg Gesangbuch (1537) and in Lotther's Magdeburg Hymn-book (1540).

13. ' Wohl dem, der in Gottesfürchte steht.' In the ' Geistliche Gesangbüchleyn,' 1524.

         W. B. S.

LUTHIER, a general title which has denoted the makers of lutes and viols as well as of the other more modern bowed instruments, of which the violin is chief.   E. H. ⸏.

LUTZ, WILHELM MEYER (*b.* Männerstadt, Kissingen, 1822 [2] ; *d.* London, Jan. 31, 1903). His father was organist and teacher of harmony to the Schoolmasters' Institute at Männerstadt. He showed a gift for the piano at a very early age, and when twelve played in public with the orchestra. His father removing to Würzburg, he entered the Gymnasium and University there, and at the same time studied music under Eisenhofer and Keller. From 1848 Lutz was settled in England, first

[2] The dates 1829 and 1830 are given by various authorities, but the above is probably correct.

as organist to St. Chad's, Birmingham, and St. Ann's, Leeds, and then organist and choirmaster to St. George's R.C. Cathedral, London, for which he composed several masses and much other music.

Meyer Lutz also had a long and wide experience of the stage as *chef d'orchestre*, first at the Surrey Theatre (1851–55), and from 1869 at the Gaiety Theatre; and also had the management of the operatic tours of Grisi and Mario, Pyne and Harrison, and other eminent artists. Many of his operas and operettas were favourably known in England, amongst them ' Faust and Marguerite' (Surrey Theatre, 1855), ' Blonde and Brunette' (1862), ' Zaïda' (1868), ' Miller of Milburg' (1872), ' Legend of the Lys' (1873), a cantata entitled ' Herne the Hunter,' etc. etc. More generally popular than these are the many compositions for the Gaiety Theatre in its most fashionable days. The well-known tune of the ' Pas de Quatre' was by him. A string quartet, which he wrote for Sainton's chamber concerts, was very well spoken of, and he left much music, orchestral and chamber, in MS.   G.

LUYTON (LUYTHON), CARL (*b.* Antwerp, *c.* middle of 16th cent.; *d.* Prague, 1620), important both as a vocal and instrumental composer.

The earliest known date in his life is 1576, in which year he dedicated a Mass to the Emperor Maximilian II., and in the same year was appointed Kammer-musikus or organist to the Emperor. On Maximilian's death at the end of 1576, Luyton was reappointed organist at Prague to the new Emperor Rudolf II., and also for a time held other offices about the court. On Rudolf's death in 1612, Luyton seems to have remained in Prague up to his own death in 1620, although even then the arrears of pay due to him for his service under Rudolf had never been made up. (See *Q.-L.*)

His chief vocal works are : one book of Italian madrigals *a* 5, 1582, 21 n.; Sacrae cantiones *a* 6, Prague, 1603, 29 n.; Lamentationes *a* 6, Prague, 1604; Lib. I. Missarum, Prague, 1609, 9 masses *a* 3-7. Of these F. Commer republished the Lamentations in vol. 20 of his *Musica sacra*, and 3 masses *a* 3-4, in vols. 18 and 19. See Eitner for a characterisation of these masses. Ritter describes two of Luyton's motets appearing in the Promptuarium of Schadaeus as masterly in treatment and full in harmony. Generally speaking, Luyton is remarkable as a pioneer in the use of chromatic modulation without any sacrifice of harmonic euphony or pleasing melody.

Of his instrumental works only two are preserved, one entitled a Fuga suavissima, which appeared in Woltz's *Tabulatur-Buch* of 1617, and fully deserves its name. It is reproduced in Ritter's *Geschichte des Orgelspiels*, Ex. 29, and is remarkable for its union of attractive melody

with a freedom of modulation into different keys after the modern fashion. The other work is an organ Ricercare in a MS. of 1624, concerning which and the Fuga suavissima see Ritter, pp. 51, 52. In connexion with these experiments in chromatic modulation, it is interesting to be told by Michael Praetorius that he had seen, in the possession of Luyton at Prague, a clavicymbal of Vienna manufacture, in which different keys were provided for two distinct semitones between each whole tone, so as to have pure major thirds, and to allow the transpositions of the church modes on any key; also two keys were inserted between the semitones *e-f* and *b-c*, for enharmonic modulation; there were thus, as Praetorius says, seventy-seven keys in the four octaves from C to *c′′′* (*Syntagma*, vol. ii. c. xl.).   J. R. M.

BIBL.—L. DE BURBURE, *Ch. Luyton. Sammelb.* Int. Mus. Ges. ix. 4 (1908); A. A. SMIJERS, *K. Luyton als Motettenkomponist* (Vienna Dissertation, 1907).

LUZZASCHI, LUZZASCO, of Ferrara (*d.* 1607) was a pupil of Ciprian de Rore at Ferrara, before Ciprian left that city in 1558, and was afterwards first organist at the court chapel of the Duke of Ferrara, Alfonso II. He is also designated as maestro di cappella. Van der Straeten [1] communicates the text of a document, relating to a composition of Rore, subscribed by Luzzaschi in 1606. Frescobaldi was his most illustrious pupil. His compositions consist of seven books of madrigals *a* 5, published from 1575 to 1604, but not all perfectly preserved (two books altogether missing); another book of madrigals for one, two and three soprani, 1601; and a Liber I. Sacrarum Cantionum *a* 5, 1598, containing fourteen motets. A few other madrigals appeared in collections. In Diruta's *Il Transilvano* there is an organ Toccata in the fourth tone, reprinted in Ritter, *Geschichte des Orgelspiels*, also two Ricercari in the first and second tones.

J. R. M.

LUZZO, FRANCESCO (mid. 17th cent.), an Italian composer, four of whose operas were produced at Venice between 1651 and 1658.

LVOV (LWOFF), (1) FEODORE PETROVICH, succeeded Bortniansky as Director of the Imperial Court Chapel in 1825. He was an authority upon church music and folk-songs.

(2) ALEXIS FEODOROVICH (*b.* Reval, June 6 (May 25, O.S.), 1799 or 1798; *d.* near Kovno, Dec. 16, 1870), son of the above. Before entering the army he received some musical education at home. He rose rapidly in the military service, and was appointed Adjutant to the Emperor Nicholas I. In 1836 Alexis Lvov succeeded his father as director of the Imperial Court Chapel. An excellent violinist, he was well known in Russia and Germany as a good quartet player. The permanent string quartet which he organised in St. Petersburg was celebrated for its perfection of ensemble.

[1] *Musique aux Pays-Bas*, vol. vi. p. 134.

Lvov composed a violin concerto, a fantasia ('Le Duel'—for violin and violoncello), and twenty-four caprices. His operas 'Bianca e Gualtiero' (Dresden and St. Petersburg, 1845), 'Undine' (1846), and 'Starosta Boris' (1854) had very little success. He also wrote a considerable quantity of church music, but the work by which his memory lives is the Russian National Hymn, 'God save the Tsar' (words by Joukovsky) composed in 1833. Previously to this the English or Prussian national anthems had been used on State occasions. The tune is devoid of those national characteristics which endear the 'Slavsia' from Glinka's opera 'A Life for the Tsar' to the hearts of musical Russians. Lvov, who suffered from deafness, retired from active service in 1867, and died on his estate near Kovno.   R. N.

LYCEUM THEATRE. The original theatre bearing this name occupied the site of a building erected in 1765 (on ground formerly belonging to Exeter House) for the exhibitions of the 'Society of Artists' (subsequently 'Royal Academy of Arts'), but afterwards used for a great variety of entertainments. It was constructed about 1798 under the direction of Dr. Arnold, who contemplated performing in it operas and other musical pieces, but being unable to obtain a licence was compelled to abandon his intention, and the house was occupied, occasionally only, for pictorial exhibitions, table entertainments, etc., until 1809, when Samuel James Arnold, the Doctor's son, succeeded in getting a licence for English operatic performances during four months in each year, June 3 to Oct. 3.

Drury Lane Theatre having been burnt down, Feb. 24, 1809, the company performed at the Lyceum from Apr. 11 following during the rebuilding of their own house. Arnold opened the theatre June 26, under the title of 'The English Opera House,' for the performance of operas, melodramas and musical farces. In 1815, having obtained a ninety-nine years' lease of the ground, he employed Samuel Beazley to rebuild the theatre on the same site, behind the houses on the north side of the Strand, a narrow avenue from which formed the approach to the box entrance, the pit and gallery doors being in Exeter Court to the westward. On Apr. 2, 1818, the elder Charles Mathews gave here his 'Mail Coach Adventures,' the first of that remarkable series of entertainments known as his 'At Home.' The most noticeable operatic event in the history of the house was the production on the English stage of Weber's 'Der Freischütz,' July 23, 1824. The house being burnt down, Feb. 16, 1830, another theatre (also designed by Beazley) was erected. It did not occupy the exact site of its predecessor, advantage having been taken of the opportunity to form the continuation of Wellington Street on the north

side of the Strand, by building the stage of the new house at the west instead of the east end. During the rebuilding the company performed at the Adelphi and Olympic Theatres.

The new house opened July 14, 1834, the first new opera performed in it being Loder's 'Nourjahad,' and Barnett's 'Mountain Sylph,' produced later in the year, achieving a great success. Early in 1839 'Promenade Concerts à la Musard' (the first of the kind given in England) took place here under the conductorship of Signor Negri. In 1841 the management passed into the hands of Balfe, who produced his opera 'Keolanthe,' but his career was brief.

The house then ceased to be an English opera-house and became, under its old name of 'Lyceum,' a theatre for the performance of the general drama, Keeley, Madame Vestris, Madame Celeste, Falconer, and others by turns holding the reins of management. In four seasons, 1837, 1838, 1841 and 1871 under Bottesini, Italian opera buffa was given here in the winter, and the house was frequently occupied by French comedians. During the rebuilding of Covent Garden Theatre after the fire in 1856 the performances of the Royal Italian Opera were given at the Lyceum, and in the same year the Pyne and Harrison English Opera Company performed there. It was occupied for the performance of operas in English by the Carl Rosa Company in 1876 and 1877, and as a special enterprise, Verdi's 'Otello' was given there in July 1889. The history of the long and successful management of the late Sir Henry Irving does not belong to a musical dictionary; in 1904 the building, very much modified in design, was turned into a music hall, but the Carl Rosa Opera Company once more occupied it for a season of opera in English in 1919.   W. H. H., addns.

LYDIAN MODE (Lat. *Modus Lydius*; *Modus V*; *Tonus V.*), see MODES, ECCLESIASTICAL.

LYRA, a form of Chimes. See GLOCKENSPIEL.

LYRA, see LIRA.

LYRA BARBERINA, see DONI, Giov. Battista.

LYRA VIOL (sometimes 'Lero Viol' or 'Viol Lyra way'), a term used in the 17th century to indicate a method of playing the ordinary viola da gamba from a letter TABLATURE (*q.v.*) instead of from note.

This was in use in 1650 to the end of the 17th century, and it was considered a simpler and easier way of reading for the instrument than from the ordinary notation. John Playford, who printed several editions of a work on the subject, speaks of it as 'but a late invention in imitation of the old English lute or bandora'; and that the first authors he

'had met with in setting lessons this way to the Viol, was Mr. Daniel Farrant, Mr. Alphonso Ferabosco, and Mr. John Coperario, who composed lessons not only to play alone, but for two or three viols in consort.' [1]

Playford also, in his *Introduction to the Skill of Musick*, mentions that the viol used to play 'Lyra-way' is 'somewhat less in size, with strings proportionable, than the other two sizes of viols.' The principle of the lyra viol is the simple adaptation of the lute tablature to the fretted six-stringed viol, the music being written on a six-line stave, each line corresponding to a string on the instrument. Burney [2] says that 'the lyra viol was a viol da gamba with more strings, but differently tuned from the common six string base. Its notation, like that of the lute, was written in entablature.' It is possible that in odd cases the viol played lyra-way had more than six strings, but contemporary writers always treat it as being a six-stringed instrument (see *PLATE LXXXVII.* No. 8). The stopping is indicated by letters placed either on or above the lines, thus: *a*, open string; *b*, first fret; *c, d, e, f, g, h*, succeeding half note stoppings. The viol finger-board only having seven frets, other letters, *i, k, l, m*, etc., are to be stopped, ' according to the judicious ear of the performer,' above the last fret. The time duration in viol tablature is shown by the crotchets, quavers, etc., being placed above the stave. The reading of the tablature is of course simplicity itself, provided that the tuning is known; but as this tuning seems to have been somewhat elastic, each viol-player apparently having one of his own, the translation of viol tablature from manuscript is sometimes puzzling; in a printed source, however, the tuning is generally given, which renders the task easier. For ease of fingering in certain pieces, tunings named 'harp-way sharp,' and 'harp-way flat,' besides some others, were in use (see TABLATURE and VIOL). The principal English work on the lyra viol was, as above indicated, by John Playford who, in his *Musicall Banquet*, 1651 (Bodl. Lib.), published some ' new lessons for the Lira Viol,' afterwards developing this into *Musick's Recreation on the Lyra Viol*, which in some editions is named *Musick's Recreation on the Viol Lyra-way*. The work consists of ' lessons ' and instructions besides a number of popular melodies all in viol tablature. Copies are dated 1651 (in *Musicall Banquet*), 1652–53, 1661, 1669 and 1682 with other issues, whose existence is mainly proved by old advertisements.

F. K.

LYRE (λύρα), an ancient musical instrument, in use among the Greeks, and undoubtedly derived by them from Asia. It consisted of a hollow body or sound-chest, from which were raised two arms, sometimes also hollow, which were curved both outward and forward. These arms were connected near the top by a crossbar or yoke. Another crossbar was on the sound-chest, and formed a bridge to convey

[1] *Musick's Recreation.*   [2] *Hist.* iii. 409.

the vibrations of the strings to it. The strings —at different times, four, seven, or ten in number—were made of gut, and were stretched between the yoke and the bridge, or carried on to a tail-piece below the bridge. The lyre differs from the harp in having fewer strings, and from the lute or guitar in having no finger-board. It was played by being struck with the plectrum, which was held in the right hand, but the fingers of the left hand were also used to touch the strings. The larger lyres (*Cithara*) were supported by a ribbon slung across the player's shoulders, or held as shown in the illustration, but the treble lyre (or *Chelys*) was held by the left arm or between the knees. The illustration is taken from a drawing upon an amphora (B.C. 440–330) in the British Museum, first vase-room, Case 53, No. 744. The portion engraved represents Apollo holding a Cithara or large lyre as rarely shown in detail in Greek art. With his left hand he at once supports the instrument and stops the strings. The plectrum would be held in the right hand and be guided by the thumb, the fingers closing over it.

The modern Greek ' lyra ' is a kind of rebec, a bowed instrument with three strings, having no connexion with the ancient lyre or cithara (see REBEC).   A. J. H.; revised F. W. G.

LYRE-GUITAR, a guitar, called in England the Apollo lyre, modelled on the lines of the ancient lyre, the six strings, however, being placed over a fretted finger-board. It appeared in France towards the end of the 18th century when the classical style was in vogue (*PLATE XXIII.* No. 6). The 'Harpo-Lyre,' invented by Salomon of Besançon in 1829, has a guitar body from which rise three fretted necks united at the top, the left-hand neck having 7 chromatic bass strings, the middle neck 6 strings for accompaniment, as in the ordinary guitar, and the other neck 8 diatonic strings for melodic passages.   F. W. G.

LYRIC; LYRICAL. The term Lyric is obviously derived from the lyre, which served as an accompaniment or support to the voice in singing the smaller forms of poetry among the ancient Greeks. The poems thus accompanied were distinguished by the name of Odes, and all Odes were in those times essentially made to be sung. Among the Romans this style of poetry was not much cultivated, and the poems which fall under the same category, such as those of Horace and Catullus, were not expressly intended to be sung ; but, inasmuch as they were cast after the same manner as the Greek poems which had been made to be sung, they also were called Odes or Lyrics.

On the same principle, the name has been retained for a special class of poems in modern times which have some intrinsic relationship in form to the Odes of the ancients ; though, on the one hand, the term Ode has considerably changed its signification, and become more restricted in its application ; and, on the other, the term Lyric is not generally associated either in the minds of the poets or their public with music of any sort. It is true that a great proportion are not only admirably fitted to be sung, but actually are set to most exquisite music ; but this fact has little or no influence upon the classification. Thus the able and intelligent editor of the beautiful collection of modern lyrics called *The Golden Treasury* explains in his preface that he has held the term ' Lyrical ' ' to imply that each poem shall turn upon a single thought, feeling, or situation,' and though he afterwards uses the term ' Song ' as practically synonymous, he does not seem to imply that it should necessarily be sung. In another part of his preface he suggests an opinion which is no doubt very commonly held, that the lyrical and dramatic are distinct branches of poetry ; and Mendelssohn has used the word in this sense even in relation to music in a letter where he speaks of his ' Lobgesang ' as follows : ' The composition is not a little oratorio, its plan being not dramatic but lyrical.'

But it is in respect of this sense of the term that its use in modern times is so singularly contradictory. It is true that the class of poems which modern critics have agreed to distinguish as Lyrics are quite different in spirit from the dramatic kind—Robert Browning's ' Dramatic Lyrics ' notwithstanding— but the principle of classification has really been erroneous all along, as though a man were called a sailor because he chose to wear a sailor's hat. Consequently the apparent anomaly of calling dramatic works lyrical when they are associated with music is not the fault of musicians, but of the long-continued habit of mankind of classifying things according to outward resemblance, instead of regarding the true basis of the terms of classification.

The term Lyric, then, originally implied music, and the Lyre stood as the type of accompaniment, of whatever kind ; and it is strictly in conformity with this derivation to give the name ' Lyrical ' to dramatic works which are associated with music ; and we have a forcible and substantial reminder of this use of the term in the name of the celebrated ' Théâtre Lyrique ' in Paris.

It has been necessary to enter into some detail on this subject in order to explain the confusion which exists in the use of the word. It must be confessed that nothing can now be gained by trying to go back to its original meaning ; for the modern sense, as expressed by the editor of *The Golden Treasury*, has a prescriptive title of such great antiquity as would suffice to bar the most unquestionable prior claim. It would be well to bear in mind, however, that the term can have two significations, and that in relation to poetry pure and simple it does not necessarily imply music, in our language at least ; and that in relation to the stage it should imply nothing else.

                                        C. H. H. P.

LYRICHORD, see Sostinente Pianoforte.

LYSBERG, Charles Samuel, originally named Bovy, and better known under the pseudonym ' Bovy-Lysberg ' (b. Lysberg, Canton Bern, Mar. 1, 1821 ; d. Geneva, Feb. 25, 1873), was an admirable pianist and composer of *morceaux de salon.*

He was the son of Antoine Bovy, a wellknown stamp-engraver, who after giving his son a good musical education sent him, at the age of 15, to Paris, where he became a pupil of Chopin and studied composition under Belaire. Subsequently he returned to his native country, and was appointed a professor of the Conservatoire at Geneva. He was chiefly successful as a writer of brilliant pieces for the pianoforte, and it was in this capacity that he borrowed the name of his birthplace as a pen-name. He published over 130 compositions in various styles, including barcaroles, nocturnes, caprices, waltzes, concert-études and operatic paraphrases ; also a romantic sonata entitled ' L'Absence,' and an opera, ' La Fille du carillonneur,' which was produced with tolerable success at Geneva, but never attained the dignity of a stage performance elsewhere.   H. K.

LYTTICH, Johann (d. Eisleben, c. 1612), a 15th-16th century composer of Plauen, cantor of St. Nicolas, and teacher at the college at the time of his death. He composed several books of songs and instrumental pieces ; also occasional songs, separate and in collective volumes. (See *Q.-L.*)

XLVI

MUSICAL INSTRUMENTS — SPAIN, c. 1270

(Library of the Escorial. Cantigas de S. Maria)

1 and 2. Viol (*Vihuela de arco*).   3. Lute (*Laúd*).   4. Rebab (*Rabé morisco*).   5. Rebec (*Rabé*).   6. Lutina (*Mandurria*).

M

MAAS, Joseph (b. Dartford, Jan. 30, 1847; d. London, Jan. 16, 1886), began his career as a chorister at Rochester [1] Cathedral, and was taught singing by J. L. Hopkins, the organist, and later by Mme. Bodda-Pyne. He was for some time a clerk in Chatham dockyard, but went to Milan in 1869, and studied under San Giovanni. He made his début at one of Leslie's concerts, Feb. 26, 1871, and sang 'Annabell Lee' in the place of Sims Reeves, with great success. He played the hero in 'Babil and Bijou' at Covent Garden, Aug. 29, 1872; he then went to America, and played in Miss Kellogg's English Opera Company. He reappeared in England at the Adelphi under Carl Rosa, as Gontran on the production of Brüll's 'Golden Cross,' Mar. 2, 1878, and was engaged by Rosa for three years as his principal tenor both at Her Majesty's and in the provinces. His principal parts were Rienzi on its production at Her Majesty's, Jan. 27, 1879; Raoul, Feb. 12, 1879; Wilhelm Meister on the production in English of 'Mignon,' Jan. 12, 1880; Radamès on the production in English of 'Aïda,' Feb. 19, 1880; also Faust, Thaddeus, Don César, etc. He played at Her Majesty's in Italian in 1880, at Covent Garden (as Lohengrin) in 1883, and under Rosa at Drury Lane in 1883–85, his new parts being Edgar of Ravenswood, Apr. 19, 1884, and the Chevalier des Grieux on production in London of Massenet's 'Manon,' May 7, 1885.

He was very popular on the stage, on account of his very fine voice, which was said to resemble Giuglini's in character, rather than for his dramatic gift, since he was a very indifferent actor. He was equally popular in the concert-room, where he appeared first at the Sacred Harmonic, in the 'Messiah,' Apr. 4, 1879, and at the Philharmonic, May 21, 1879. He sang at all the principal concerts, and at the various Handel and provincial festivals. He sang also in Paris at Pasdeloup's concerts, Apr. 6, 1884, and at Brussels at the Bach and Handel Festival of 1885. His last important engagement was at the Birmingham Festival of 1885, where he sang in Dvořák's 'Spectre's Bride,' Aug. 27, and Stanford's 'Three Holy Children,' Aug. 28, on the production of those works. At the Norwich Festival of the previous year he had introduced 'Apollo's Invocation,' a scena written for him by Massenet. He died from a complication of disorders, brought on from a cold taken while fishing. He was buried in West Hampstead Cemetery. Maas's greatest triumphs were gained in the concert-room rather than on the stage. For several years he has stood in the very first rank of tenor singers, not only by reason of his magnificent voice, but of his

[1] There is a memorial to Maas in Rochester Cathedral placed there by his widow.

thoroughly finished and artistic style. . . . By his amiable personal character the deceased artist won the esteem and affection of all who had the privilege of his friendship.' [2]

A 'Maas Memorial Prize' was established at the R.A.M.　　　　　　　　　　　　　　　A. C.

MAATSCHAPPIJ TOT BEVORDERING DER TOONKUNST (Society for the Furtherance of Tonal Art) is the largest musical society in Holland. Founded in 1829, it to-day includes 40 branches in different places, with altogether about 8000 members. The chief centre is Amsterdam. The objects of the Society include: the improvement of musical teaching; the education of capable instrument-makers; the performance of choral and orchestral works; the systematic encouragement of young talent; the support and pensioning of old musicians; the collection and circulation of a comprehensive music library. The chief activity of the branches is choral singing. Amongst numerous choirs that of the Toonkunst in AMSTERDAM (q.v.), conducted by W. Mengelberg, has received world-wide recognition. The annual Palm Sunday performance of the Matthew Passion in the Concertgebouw, Amsterdam, has been famous since 1899. The Society also controls altogether seventeen schools of music in the large and smaller towns of Holland.　　　　　　　　　　　　　　　R. M^{g.}

MABELLINI, Teodulo (b. Pistoia, Apr. 2, 1817; d. Florence, Mar. 10, 1897), was a pupil of the Istituto Reale Musicale in Florence, and when he was only 19 years of age, his opera, 'Matilda di Toledo,' was given at Florence (1836), with the result that the Grand Duke Leopold II. gave the composer funds to study under Mercadante at Novara. His second opera, 'Rolla,' was given at Turin in 1840 with great success. Mabellini settled in Florence in 1843, becoming conductor of the Società Filarmonica, and eventually court maestro di cappella and conductor at the Pergola (from 1848); from 1859–87 he was professor in his old school, until his death.

His other operas were: 'Ginevra degli Almieri' (Turin, 1841), 'Il Conte di Savagna' (Florence, 1843), 'I Veneziani a Constantinopoli' (Rome, 1844), 'Maria di Francia' (Florence, 1846), 'Il Venturiero' (with L. Giordani, Leghorn, 1851), 'Baldassare' (Florence, 1852), 'Fiammetta' (Florence, 1857). Two oratorios, 'Eudossia e Paolo' and 'L'Ultimo Giorno di Gerusalemme,' the cantatas, 'La Caccia,' 'Il Ritorno,' 'Elegiaca,' 'Rafaele Sanzio,' 'Lo Spirito di Dante,' are among his more important works, as well as a great quantity of church music (Riemann).

BIBL.—A. SIMONATTI, Teodulo Mabellini. Pistoia, 1923.

MACBETH. (1) Music for Davenant's version

[2] Athenæum, Jan. 23, 1886.

of ' Macbeth ' (produced Dorset Gardens, 1672) was, according to Downes,[1] composed by Matthew Locke. The authorship of the score published with Locke's name under the editorship of Boyce (1750) is still disputed. (See LOCKE.) ECCLES and LEVERIDGE (q.v.) composed music for ' Macbeth,' 1696 and 1702 respectively.

(2) Tragedy in 3 acts ; words by Rouget de Lisle and Hix, music by Chelard. Produced Opéra, Paris, June 29, 1827 ; in London, King's Theatre, July 4, 1832.

(3) Opera in 4 acts ; libretto by Piave, music by Verdi. Produced Pergola, Florence, Mar. 17, 1847 ; Paris, with alterations, Théâtre Lyrique, Apr. 21, 1865.

(4) An overture for orchestra in B minor, by Spohr (op. 75).

(5) The first act of an opera, ' Macbeth,' was published by von Collin in 1809 ; and sketches by Beethoven for the overture (D minor, 6–8) and first chorus therein, are given by Nottebohm in *Mus. Wochenblatt*, 1879, No. 10.

(6) A tone-poem for orchestra by Strauss, (op. 23).

MACBETH, ALLAN (b. Greenock, Mar. 13, 1856 ; d. Glasgow, Aug. 25, 1910), received his musical education chiefly in Germany, studying at the Leipzig Conservatorium under F. Richter, Jadassohn and Reinecke in 1875–76. In 1880 he was appointed conductor to the Glasgow Choral Union, but resigned the post in 1887. He was organist of various churches in Edinburgh and Glasgow, being appointed to St. George's-in-the-Fields Established Church in 1884. He was appointed principal of the music school connected with the Glasgow Athenæum in 1890. Macbeth, in spite of much occupation of his time in teaching (pianoforte and singing), wrote a number of pleasing pianoforte pieces, besides two or three orchestral movements played at the Choral Union Concerts, and since transcribed for piano. As a song-writer he was specially successful ; he ably arranged for voices several Scots melodies, and wrote some original partsongs. His cantata, ' The Land of Glory,' won a prize given by the Glasgow Society of Musicians, and was performed in 1890. He left other cantatas, short orchestral pieces and chamber music, as well as incidental music to a play, ' Bruce (Lord of the Isles),' and an operetta in MS., 'The Duke's Doctor.'   w. H^E.

MacCARTHY, MAUD (b. Clonmel, Ireland, July 4, 1884), violinist, singer and lecturer. She gave evidence of great talent at an early age, but was not sent to a musical college, her parents preferring to place her under the direction of Señor Arbós. She made her début in London at the age of 9, and in the ensuing years, after an interval of further study, made many public appearances under August Manns, Richter, Wood, Nikisch, etc. During a tour

in the U.S.A. she played with the leading American orchestras, her repertory including the principal violin concertos. At the age of 23 she was compelled to give up solo-playing owing to neuritis, and went to India with Mrs. Annie Besant, where she studied Indian music. On her return she gave a series of Indian vocal lecture-recitals before the Musical Association, the Oxford Folk-Song Society, etc. She was an early exponent of unaccompanied song and of the performance upon Indian instruments of minute subdivisions of the scale (microtones). She married John Foulds, the composer, in 1915, and led the orchestra during the performance of his ' World Requiem ' on Armistice Night, 1923.   w. w. c.

McCORMACK, JOHN (b. Athlone, June 14, 1884), tenor singer, won the Gold Medal for singing at the National Irish Festival (Feis Ceoil), Dublin, joined the choir of the Dublin R.C. Cathedral in the following year, and in 1904, with that choir, sang at the St. Louis Exhibition. In 1905 he went to Milan and received instruction in singing from Sabbatini.

On Feb. 17, 1907, he sang at a Sunday League concert in London, and on Mar. 1, 1907, appeared at a London Ballad Concert, when he sang with such success that Messrs. Boosey engaged him for the remaining concerts of the season.   On Oct. 15 he made a successful début on the stage at Covent Gorden as Turiddu in ' Cavalleria,' and confirmed his success the same season as Don Ottavio and as the Duke in ' Rigoletto.' He established his reputation as an oratorio singer when on Nov. 7 he undertook the tenor music in ' Elijah ' at the Royal Choral Society's concert, and subsequently he fulfilled several engagements at the English festivals. In the spring of 1909 he sang at the San Carlo, Naples, and in the autumn (Nov. 10) made a successful début at the Manhattan Opera House, New York, as Edgardo in ' La Traviata.' He has pursued his career principally in America, becoming a citizen of the United States in 1917. He sang with the Boston Opera Company (1910–11) and with the Chicago Opera Company (1912–13), but later devoted himself more especially to concert work, in which his success has been gained not only through the natural qualities of a remarkable voice, but through his interpretative power. Trained in the Italian style, he has added German Lieder to his repertory. He paid a visit to England after a prolonged absence, and gave a highly successful recital at Queen's Hall on June 10, 1924.   A. C. ; addns. C.

MacCUNN, HAMISH (b. Greenock, Mar. 22, 1868 ; d. London, Aug. 2, 1916), son of James MacCunn, shipowner of Greenock, showed an early aptitude for music, and on the opening of the R.C.M. in 1883, won a scholarship for composition. He was a pupil there of Sir Hubert Parry, and resigned his scholarship in

1886. An overture (see list) was given at the Crystal Palace in Oct. 1885, and a cantata, 'The Moss Rose,' was sung at the R.C.M. in December of that year, but it was not until 1887 that his name became widely known, from the success of his overture, ' Land of the Mountain and Flood,' produced at the same place. It was at once evident that the young composer had a strongly individual note of his own, and in quick succession other orchestral works were brought forward, for the most part at the Crystal Palace, where his first cantata, ' Lord Ullin's Daughter,' was given on Feb. 8, 1888. In that year he was commissioned to write a cantata for the Glasgow Choral Union; this was ' The Lay of the Last Minstrel,' given at Glasgow, Dec. 18, 1888, and at the Crystal Palace, Feb. 16, 1889. ' Bonny Kilmeny ' had been given at one of Paterson's concerts in Edinburgh a few days before. In 1888 he gave a series of orchestral concerts in the studio of John Pettie, R.A., whose daughter he married in 1889. In 1894 his opera, ' Jeanie Deans,' was produced by the Royal Carl Rosa Company in Edinburgh, and performed in London by the same company, after much success throughout the provinces, on Jan. 22, 1896. He was for some years connected with this company as conductor. He directed the production in English of many of the later works of Wagner, including ' Tristan ' and ' Siegfried,' as well as the stock repertory. After the death of Sullivan, during the last seasons of the Savoy Theatre as a home of English light opera, he conducted the run of ' Merrie England ' and ' A Princess of Kensington.' His compositions show a strongly national colouring, and certain sides of Scottish music, particularly those which deal with the more intimate and tender emotions, had scarcely been brought into the world of artistic or ' composed ' music until his time.

List of works :

OPERAS, etc.

' Jeanie Deans ' (libretto by Joseph Bennett), in 4 acts, Lyceum Theatre, Edinburgh, Nov. 15, 1894.
' Diarmid.' Grand opera in 4 acts, libretto by the Duke of Argyll (then Marquis of Lorne), Covent Garden Theatre, Oct. 23, 1897.
' Breast of Light.' Grand opera unfinished (libretto by the Duke of Argyll). MS.
' The Masque of War and Peace ' (libretto by Louis N. Parker), given at a single special performance for the benefit of the Household Troops, Her Majesty's Theatre, Feb. 13, 1900.
' The Golden Girl.' Musical comedy, written by Captain Basil Hood ; produced at the Prince of Wales's Theatre, Birmingham, Aug. 5, 1905 (not yet performed in London).
' Prue.' Light opera in 3 acts. MS. (libretto by C. Taylor).
' Pageant of Darkness and Light.' Stage pageant in 6 episodes (John Oxenham).

CANTATAS, BALLADS, etc. (for Choir and Orchestra)

' Lord Ullin's Daughter,' Crystal Palace, Feb. 18, 1888.
' The Lay of the Last Minstrel,' with soli, Glasgow Choral Union, Dec. 18, 1888 ; Crystal Palace, Feb. 16, 1889.
' Bonny Kilmeny,' with soli, Paterson's Concerts, Edinburgh, Dec. 15, 1888, and at the Crystal Palace, Mar. 8, 1889.
' The Cameronian's Dream,' with baritone solo, Paterson's Concerts, Edinburgh, Jan. 27 1890 ; Crystal Palace, Dec. 6, 1890.
' Queen Hynde of Caledon,' with soli, Glasgow Choral Union, Jan. 28, 1892 ; Crystal Palace, Mar. 5, 1892.
' The Death of Parcy Reed,' for male chorus and orchestra, performed London, 1925.
' The Wreck of the Hesperus,' produced with pictorial illustrations at the Coliseum Theatre, Aug. 28, 1905.
' Kinmont Willie.'
' Lambkin.'
' The Jolly Goshawk.'
' Livingstone, the Pilgrim ' (libretto by Sylvester Horne).

ORCHESTRAL OVERTURES, etc.

' Cior Mhor,' Crystal Palace, Oct. 27, 1885.
' The Land of the Mountain and Flood,' Crystal Palace, Nov. 5, 1887.
' The Ship o' the Fiend,' Henschel Concerts, Feb. 21, 1888 ; Crystal Palace, Apr. 21, 1888.
' The Dowie Dens o Yarrow,' Crystal Palace, Oct. 13, 1888.
' Highland Memories,' three descriptive pieces, Crystal Palace, Mar. 13, 1897, and at the Philharmonic on May 20 of the same year.
Psalm VIII., for chorus and organ, was performed at the Glasgow Exhibition of 1901.
Nine partsongs, six original pieces, ' Scotch Dances ' for piano solo, three pieces for violoncello and piano, extra numbers for various musical comedies, and about eighty songs. are also among MacCunn's published works.   M., with addns.

M'DONALD, MALCOLM, a Scottish composer of Strathspeys of some note during the latter part of the 18th century. Little is known of his personal history save that he was associated with the Gow family, and that he lived (and probably died) at Inver, the birthplace of Niel Gow. A footnote in The Beauties of Niel Gow states that he played the violoncello in Gow's band at Edinburgh. His published collections of Strathspey reels number four. The first in oblong folio was published in 1788 ; 2nd in folio, circa 1789 ; 3rd folio, circa 1792 ; a 4th folio, circa 1797.   F. K.

M'DONALD, (1) PETER (b. Durness Manse, Sutherland, Apr. 22, 1729 ; d. Sept. 25, 1824), a Scottish minister and son of one. He was educated at St. Andrews, and ordained minister of Kilmore in Argyllshire, Oct. 12, 1756. He remained in this position for sixty-nine years. He was one of a musical family, and was a skilled performer on the violin. He is deserving of remembrance for his valuable work (the first attempt at such a gathering), a ' Collection of Highland Vocal Airs,' issued in Edinburgh in 1783. In his preface he mentions that a number of the melodies were noted down by his brother (2) JOSEPH (b. Feb. 26, 1739 ; d. 1762), also a clever musician, who left Scotland for India in 1760. Joseph was the author of a Treatise on the Theory of the Scots Highland Bagpipe, which forms part of a work, a Collection of Bagpipe Music, published in Edinburgh in 1808.   F. K.

MacDOWELL, EDWARD ALEXANDER (b. New York City, Dec. 18, 1861 ; d. there, Jan. 24, 1908), American composer and pianist, was descended from a Quaker family of Scotch-Irish extraction that emigrated to America about the middle of the 18th century.

As a boy he studied the pianoforte with Juan Buitrago, a South American, and Pablo Desvernine, a Cuban, and for a brief space with Teresa Carreño, a native of Venezuela. The nationality of these early teachers is recorded to enable the curious to study or speculate on the influences which, with the varied training received in Europe, may have helped to shape the artistic character of MacDowell, who, though entitled to rank with contemporary composers of the highest class irrespective of country, is yet specially significant as a representative of the best that America has produced in music.

His European studies were varied. In 1876 he became a pupil of Savard in composition, and Marmontel in pianoforte at the Paris Conservatoire. For three years he remained under French influences, then exchanged them for German, going first to Stuttgart to Lebert ; but wearying of that teacher's pedagogic methods in less than a month, he went to Wiesbaden, where he studied with Louis Ehlert during the summer months of 1882. In the autumn he joined the pianoforte class of Karl Heymann at the Conservatorium, and the class in composition under Joachim Raff, director of the institution. The admiration which he felt for Raff's music, and the attachment which sprang up between master and pupil were among the strongest influences which shaped his creative career, and speak out of much of his music, especially the first suite for orchestra, op. 42. On Heymann's departure from the Conservatorium MacDowell was a candidate for the position vacated by him, but failed of appointment, ostensibly because of his youthfulness, probably because of his adherence to the romantic ideals exemplified in Heymann's playing. Thereupon he went to Darmstadt as chief teacher at the Conservatorium there. The duties were onerous, and the compensation inadequate. MacDowell had made up his mind to stay in Germany as a country more congenial to his artistic nature than his native land. He returned to Frankfort as a private teacher. In 1882, at the instance of Raff, he went to Weimar to visit Liszt. He played his first concerto for that master with D'Albert at the second pianoforte, and was invited to take part in the approaching meeting of the Allgemeiner Deutscher Musikverein at Zurich. There he played his first pianoforte suite. Raff died shortly after, and MacDowell set up a home in Wiesbaden, where he devoted himself to composition for four years, that is, till 1887. Then he went to America, settled in Boston, where he made his first appearance as a pianist with the Kneisel Quartet, Nov. 19, 1888, taught and gave concerts, producing his two pianoforte concertos with the Boston Symphony Orchestra in Boston, and the Theodore Thomas Orchestra in New York. The second concerto was played by the composer at the Philharmonic Concert, London, on May 14, 1903. In 1896 he was called to Columbia University in New York to fill the chair of music [1]—a new foundation. He remained professor at the institution until Jan. 1904, when he resigned the post because of a disagreement with the faculty touching the proper footing of music and the fine arts in the curriculum. For two years he was conductor of the Mendelssohn Glee Club, one of the oldest and best male choruses in the United States. Princeton University and the University of Pennsylvania conferred on him the degree of Mus.Doc. MacDowell's career ended in the

[1] His lectures at Columbia University were edited by W. J. Baltzell and published, 1911, as *Critical and Historical Essays.*

spring of 1905, when overwork and insomnia, the consequence of morbid worry over disagreeable experiences, brought on what eminent medical specialists pronounced to be a hopeless case of cerebral collapse.

When MacDowell went to Boston he gave a healthy impulse to American composition, chiefly through the performances of his works which had been stimulated by his return to his native land, but also by the attitude which he assumed as to the proper treatment of the American composer by the American public and press. He expressed himself as opposed to their segregation for the purpose either of laudation or condemnation. Naturally this came somewhat easier to him than to some of his fellows. He had grown artistically into man's estate in Germany, and had won quite as much recognition there as he found waiting for him in America when he returned thither. It deserves to be said that he found his position upheld by the majority of American musicians worthy of association with him. As a composer MacDowell was a romanticist. He believed in poetical suggestion and programmatic titles ; but he was not a musical cartoonist. He aimed at depicting the moods of things, and the moods awakened by things rather than the things themselves. He was fond of subjects and titles which, like those of his master Raff, smack of the woods ;—not the greenwood of the English ballads, but the haunted forests of Germany, in which nymphs and dryads hold their revels and kobolds frolic.

The supernaturalism which is an ineradicable element of German romanticism breathes through his first suite for orchestra. In his second suite, entitled 'Indian,' he makes use of aboriginal American idioms, forming his principal themes out of variants of Indian melodies — a harvest - song, war - song and women's dance of the Iroquois, and a love-song of the Iowas. A similar device is practised in the fifth of his 'Woodland Sketches for pianoforte, op. 51,' which has a melody of the Brotherton Indians as its theme. MacDowell was contemporaneous with Dvořák in thus calling attention to the existence of native American folk-song elements capable of use in a characteristic body of artistic music, though, unlike the composer of the symphony 'From the New World,' he never permitted himself to be influenced by the melodic idioms of the negro slave. His 'Indian' suite, op. 48, first played by the Boston Symphony Orchestra in New York, Jan. 23, 1896, was fully sketched before Dvořák's symphony appeared, though it was not performed till three years afterwards, the composer wishing to become better acquainted with what to him, as well as the world, was a new kind of music. As for the rest : great concentration, refined and highly emotionalised harmonisation, exalted poetical feeling and a spirit of breezy freshness are the characteristics chiefly to be found in MacDowell's compositions for the pianoforte. His published works are as follows :

WORKS WITH OPUS NUMBERS

Early works (opp. 1-8) published under the name of 'Edgar Thorn' as follows :

Op.
1. 'Amourette.' PF.
2. 'In Lilting Rhythm.' PF.
3. Two partsongs for male choir: 'Love and Time,' 'The Rose and the Gardener.'
4. 'Forgotten Fairy-tales.' Four pieces for PF.
5. 'The Witch.' Male voice choir.
6. 'War Song.' Ditto.
7. Six Pieces. PF.
8. Waltz. PF.
9. Two Old Songs.
10. First Modern Suite. PF.
11 & 12. Album of Five Songs.
13. Prelude and Fugue. PF.
14. Second Modern Suite. PF.
15. First Concerto in A minor. PF. and orch.
16. Serenata. PF.
17. Two Fantastic Pieces for concert use. PF.
18. Barcarolle in F and Humoreske in A. PF.
19. Wald-Idyllen. PF.
20. Three Poems. PF. 4 hands.
21. Moon Pictures, after Hans Andersen. PF., 4 hands.
22. 'Hamlet and Ophelia.' Two Poems for orch.
23. Second Concerto in D minor. PF. and orch.
24. Four Compositions. PF.
25. 'Lancelot and Elaine.' Symphonic poem for orch.
26. 'From an Old Garden.' Six songs.
27. Three Songs. Male chorus.
28. Six Idyls after Goethe. PF.
29. 'Lamia.' Third Symphonic Poem for orch.
30. 'The Saracens ' and ' Lovely Alda '; two Fragments from the 'Song of Roland.' Orch.
31. Six Poems after Heine. PF.
32. Four Little Poems. PF.
33. Three Songs.
34. Two Songs.
35. Romance for Violoncello with orchestral accompaniment.
36. Étude de Concert. PF.
37. 'Les Orientales.' Three pieces for PF.
38. 'Marionettes.' Six little pieces for PF. (with Prologue and Epilogue in revised edition).
39. Twelve Studies. PF.
40. Six Love Songs.
41. Two Songs. Male chorus.
42. Suite No. 1. Orch.
43. Two Northern Songs. Mixed chorus.
44. Barcarolle. Song for mixed chorus.
45. Sonata Tragica (No. 1). PF.
46. Twelve Virtuoso Studies. PF.
47. Eight Songs.
48. Second (' Indian ') Suite. Orch.
49. (Some Dances published in a Boston collection.)
50. Second Sonata, 'Eroica.' PF.
51. 'Woodland Sketches.' PF.
52. Three Choruses. Male voices.
53. Two Choruses. Male voices.
54. Two Choruses. Male voices.
55. 'Sea Pieces.' PF.
56. Four Songs.
57. Third Sonata, 'Norse.' PF.
58. Three Songs.
59. Fourth Sonata, 'Keltic.' PF.
60. Three Songs.
61. 'Fireside Tales.' PF.
62. 'New England Idyls.' PF.

WORKS WITHOUT OPUS NUMBERS

Two Songs from the Thirteenth Century. Male Chorus.
Six Little Pieces after Sketches by J. S. Bach. PF.
Technical Exercises for the Pianoforte (Two Books).
Columbia College Songs.
Many Transcriptions of old harpsichord music.

H. E. K. ; addns. *Amer. Supp.*

BIBLIOGRAPHY

LAURENCE GILMAN : *Ed. MacDowell.* New York and London, 1906 ; *Ed. MacDowell, a Study.* Enlarged from above, 1909.
E. F. PAGE : *Ed. MacDowell, his Works and Ideals.* 1910.
T. P. CURRIER : *MacDowell as I knew him.* (*Musical Quarterly*, Jan. 1915.)
O. G. SONNECK : *Catalogue of First Editions of Edward MacDowell* (Library of Congress Pub.) Washington, 1917.
J. F. PORTE : *Edward MacDowell.* 1922.

MacDOWELL MEMORIAL ASSOCIATION, THE.

On the death of Edward MacDowell his widow transferred to this Association the property at Peterboro', New Hampshire, which had been his summer home, in order that it might be maintained as a

' centre of interest to artists working in varied fields, who, being there brought into contact, may learn to appreciate fully the fundamental unity of the separate arts.'

This idea, which originated with MacDowell himself, has been carried out in the summer colony at which artists foregather for work and intercourse. Since 1910 an annual festival, chiefly musical, has been held there.

(*Amer. Supp.*)

MACE, JOHN, an English church composer, possibly the father of Thomas MACE (*q.v.*). He presumably lived some time at the end of the 16th century or early in the 17th, as the bassus cantoris part of an anthem by him, ' Let Thy merciful ears,' is included in Barnard's MS. collection (R.C.M. 1051).   J. Mᴷ.

MACE, THOMAS (*b.* Cambridge *c.* 1619), was one of the clerks of Trinity College, Cambridge, and author of a remarkable book published (in small folio, 272 pp., besides 18 pp. of prefatory matter) in 1676, entitled :

' Musick's Monument : or A Remembrancer of the best Practical Musick, both Divine and Civil, that has ever been known to have been in the world,'

the first part of which treats of the then condition of parochial psalmody and cathedral music and the means of improving their performance ; the second of the lute, including directions for choosing, tuning, repairing, performing on and composing for the instrument, with a full explanation of the tablature and numerous lessons ; and the third of the viol and of music generally, with other curious matter.

The book is written in a quaint, familiar style, intermingled with a profusion of strangely compounded terms, and produces a striking impression of the author's love of his art and his devout and amiable disposition. It was published by subscription at 12s. per copy in sheets. A lengthy epitome of it is given in Hawkins's *History*, pp. 727-33, Novello's edition. A few scanty biographical particulars are culled from it, viz. that Mace married in or shortly after 1636 ; that before the marriage his wife resided in Yorkshire, he in Cambridge ; that in 1644 he was in York during the siege of the city by the Parliamentary army ; that in consequence of having broken both arms he was compelled to make a shake upon the lute in an irregular manner ; that he invented a ' table organ ' (described in his book, with an engraving) to accompany a ' consort of viols '; that in consequence of partial deafness, rendering the soft tones of the lute inaudible to him, he in 1672 invented a lute of fifty strings, which he termed the Dyphone, or Double Lute ; that he had a family, and that his youngest son, John, learned in 1672 to play well upon the lute almost solely by the perusal of the MS. of his book (see IMMYNS, John) ; that the writing of the work was not begun until after Christmas 1671, and it was licensed for publication May 5, 1675 ; and lastly that owing to his increased deafness, which we may presume prevented him pursuing his profession, he was in somewhat straitened circumstances. Hawkins asserts that Mace was born in 1613, evidently arriving at that conclusion from the inscription beneath the portrait (engraved by Faithorne after Cooke) prefixed to his book, 'Ætat. suæ. 63.' The date of his death is not known, but 1709 is conjectured. See an important advertisement in the Bagford Collection (Harl. MS. 5936 (384)). Mace was further responsible for another quaint work, *Profit, conveniency and pleasure to the whole Nation, being a short rational discourse lately presented to His Majesty concerning the Highways of England*, etc. 1675. A copy is in the British Museum. An anthem, ' I heard a voice ' (MS. at PH.) is the only record of Mace as composer.

W. H. H.; addns., F. K. and J. Mᴷ.

BIBL.—HENRY WATSON, *Th. Mace. The Man, the Book and the Instruments*, Mus. Ass. Proc., 1908–9, pp. 87-107.

MACEDONIO DI MUTI, GIOVANNI VINCENZO, Neapolitan knight (*cavaliere*), living at Naples during the early 17th century, composed 2 books o madrigals, 1603 and 1606 (*Fétis*; Q.-L.).

McEWEN, JOHN BLACKWOOD (*b.* Hawick, Apr. 13, 1868), composer, teacher and Principal of the R.A.M. (1924), was educated at Glasgow, where from 1871 his father was minister of Sydney Place Church. He entered the university there, took his M.A. degree in 1888 and studied music while he held the choirmastership of St. James's Free Church and subsequently of Lanark Parish Church.

He came to London in 1891 and entered the R.A.M. as a student two years later. There Prout, Corder and Matthay were his teachers. His studentship was, however, comparatively short, for in 1895 he returned to Scotland and settled at Greenock as choirmaster of South Parish Church and teacher of pianoforte and composition at the Athenæum School of Music at Glasgow. In 1898 he was invited to join the teaching staff of the R.A.M. as professor of harmony and composition, and henceforward his life as a teacher became bound up with that of the R.A.M. He exerted an ever increasing influence not only on the pupils who passed through his hands, but on the policy of the institution in the direction of a sane liberalism of outlook. On the retirement of Sir Alexander Mackenzie in 1924, the appointment of McEwen to succeed him in the principalship was widely approved as an assurance of continuity and progress in the work of the R.A.M. While his personal career has been uneventful it has been one of incessant activity, particularly in undertakings for the advancement of British music. He was one of the founders of the SOCIETY OF BRITISH COMPOSERS (*q.v.*) in 1905 and later of the ANGLO-FRENCH MUSIC PUBLISHING COMPANY (*q.v.*), which was begun with similar educational aims. He was for a time musical adviser to the Æolian Company, but these latter interests he resigned on assuming the

principalship of the R.A.M. In 1926 he received the degree of Mus.D. *honoris causa* from the University of Oxford.

Apart from his executive work, McEwen has steadily pursued his way as a creative artist in composition, though few modern composers have been so little concerned as he about the problem of bringing their work before the public. He has never composed for the festivals, though a short prelude for orchestra was played at the Gloucester festival of 1925, and scarcely one of the long list of his works (see *B.M.S. Ann.*, 1920) bears any trace of having been composed for an occasion. Incidental music for three scenes of the Empire Pageant held at the Crystal Palace in 1910 is almost the only work so marked ; a concerto for viola seems to be a recognition of the demand of Lionel Tertis for such music for his instrument. Otherwise the major events of McEwen's output are symphonic works for orchestra and string quartets, the qualities of which he has left performers to discover when publication allowed them opportunity. His work first became generally known through ' Grey Galloway,' one of three Border ballads for orchestra, which has been widely played. Of his several symphonies that in C sharp minor known as ' Solway ' (produced Bournemouth 1922) has alone received repeated performance owing to its publication by the Carnegie Trust. The suggestions of a programme in the one case and of some delicate landscape painting in the other are incidental rather than essential. McEwen's characteristics, found most decisively in the string quartets, notably those in E minor, C minor, A minor and the one called ' Biscay ' (which may almost be said to be popular), are a seriousness of musical purpose which is never dull because the composer always remains free from the conventions of style, and an aptness of expression which, while perfectly direct, leaves the hearer feeling that the composer could say more if he would. A concert of his chamber-music given as part of the R.A.M. centenary celebrations (1922) gave a rare opportunity of hearing a number of his works together. Their total impression was described as music ' for those who are ready to forego excitement and take measured delight in fine quality.' [1]   C.

MACFARREN, (1) SIR GEORGE ALEXANDER, Mus.D. (*b.* London, Mar. 2, 1813; *d.* Oct. 31, 1887), composer and teacher, was son of George Macfarren, dramatist. In early life he displayed partiality for music, but did not begin regular study until 1827, when he became a pupil of Charles Lucas.

In 1829 he entered the R.A.M., and made composition his principal study, learning also the pianoforte and trombone : and in 1834 he was appointed one of its professors. On Oct. 27,

[1] *Mus. T.*, Aug. 1922.

1834, he produced at the Society of British Musicians his first important work, a symphony in F minor, and in 1836 his fine overture ' Chevy Chase.' In Aug. 1838 his ' Devil's Opera,' produced at the English Opera House, Lyceum, at once drew public attention to him. In 1840 he produced at Drury Lane an ' Emblematical Tribute on the Queen's Marriage,' and also edited, for the Musical Antiquarian Society, Purcell's opera, ' Dido and Æneas.' In 1843 he became secretary of the Handel Society, for which he edited ' Belshazzar,' ' Judas Maccabaeus ' and ' Jephthah.' In Jan. 1845 he directed the successful production of Mendelssohn's ' Antigone ' at Covent Garden Theatre. In 1846 his opera ' Don Quixote ' was successfully produced at Drury Lane, and in 1849 his opera ' Charles II.' was given at the Princess's. His serenata, ' The Sleeper Awakened,' was brought out at the National Concerts at Her Majesty's Theatre in 1851, and in the same year he composed his cantata ' Lenora.' His cantata ' May Day ' (long a favourite with choral societies) was written for the Bradford Festival, 1856, and his cantata ' Christmas ' was composed in 1859. He then resumed the composition of opera, and brought out ' Robin Hood ' at Her Majesty's Theatre in 1860, with great success. This was followed by ' Freya's Gift,' masque, and ' Jessy Lea,' opera, 1863 ; ' She stoops to conquer,' 'The Soldier's Legacy ' and ' Helvellyn,' operas, 1864. Several more operas remained in MS., and Macfarren also wrote music for a number of farces and melodramas.

Macfarren's eyesight had at a comparatively early age become impaired ; the malady increased year by year, until it terminated in total blindness. But this calamity did not diminish his exertions ; and with extraordinary energy he continued to perform his duties as a professor at the R.A.M. and to compose, dictating his compositions to an amanuensis. On Oct. 23, 1873, his oratorio ' St. John the Baptist ' was produced at the Bristol Festival with marked success. On Mar. 16, 1875, he was elected Professor of Music at Cambridge on the death of Sterndale Bennett, and greatly distinguished himself by the manner in which he performed the duties of the office. In April following he accumulated the degrees of Bachelor and Doctor of Music. In 1876 he was appointed Principal of the R.A.M. ' The Resurrection,' oratorio, was produced at the Birmingham Festival in 1876 ; ' Joseph,' oratorio, at the Leeds Festival in 1877 ; ' The Lady of the Lake,' a cantata, at Glasgow, on Nov. 15, 1877 ; the music to ' Ajax ' was performed with the play at Cambridge in 1882 ; the oratorio ' King David ' was produced at the Leeds Festival of 1883, and in that year Macfarren was knighted. Besides the beforementioned works his compositions are very

numerous ; they include a cathedral service, anthems, chants and psalm tunes, and ' Introits for the Holy Days and Seasons of the English Church,' 1866 ; ' Songs in a Cornfield,' 1868 ; ' Shakespeare Songs for 4 voices,' 1860–64 ; Songs from Lane's ' Arabian Nights,' and Kingsley's and Tennyson's poems ; very many songs (among which the beautiful ' Pack, clouds, away,' with clarinet obbligato, is perhaps the best known), duets, etc. ; overtures to ' The Merchant of Venice,' ' Romeo and Juliet,' ' Hamlet,' ' Chevy Chase ' (already mentioned) and ' Don Carlos ' ; symphonies, string quartets and a quintet ; a concerto for violin and orchestra ; and sonatas for pianoforte alone and in combination with other instruments. He harmonised the airs in Chappell's *Popular Music of the Olden Time*, and arranged ' Moore's Irish Melodies,' 1859, and Scotch Songs. He was eminent as a writer on music having produced *Rudiments of Harmony*, 1860, and *Six Lectures on Harmony*, 1867 ; analyses of oratorios, etc., for the Sacred Harmonic Society, 1853–57, and of orchestral works for the programme-books of the Philharmonic Society, 1869–71 ; also many articles in *The Musical World* and lives of musicians for the *Imperial Dictionary of Universal Biography*. He lectured at the Royal and London Institutions. His *Addresses and Lectures* were published in 1888. His last published work was an Andante and Rondo in E for violin and organ, contained in the *Organist's Quarterly Journal* for Oct. 1887. A cantata for female voices, ' Around the Hearth,' was published posthumously. He was buried in the Hampstead Cemetery; his life, by H. C. Banister, appeared in 1891.   w. h. h.

(2) NATALIA MACFARREN, *née* ANDRAE (*b.* Lübeck, 1828 ; *d.* Bakewell, Derbyshire, Apr. 9, 1916, appeared as contralto singer at the Princess's Theatre, London, Oct. 1849, in Macfarren's ' Charles II.' ; having previously appeared in the United States with Catherine Hayes in ' Linda,' with great success.

She was married at 17, to George Macfarren at Marylebone Church ; her life was spent in teaching and in translating operas and German Lieder. She was endowed with a fine intellect, her power of musical interpretation was extraordinary, and she was an excellent linguist.

                                    E. J. H[8].

(3) WALTER CECIL (*b.* Aug. 28, 1826 ; *d.* Sept. 2, 1905), brother of Sir George, was chorister of Westminster Abbey under James Turle from 1836–41, and pupil of the R.A.M. from 1842–46, studied the pianoforte under W. H. Holmes, and composition under his brother and Cipriani Potter. He was a professor of the pianoforte at the R.A.M. from 1846–1903, and conductor of its concerts from 1873–80. He was elected a director of the Philharmonic Society in 1868, and its treasurer in 1876. He

composed two Church Services and a number of chants and hymn-tunes ; a symphony in B flat, produced at Brighton, 1880 ; overtures, ' A Winter's Tale ' (1844) ; ' Taming of the Shrew ' (1845) ; ' Beppo ' (1847) ; ' Pastoral ' (1878) ; ' Hero and Leander ' (Brighton Festival, 1879) ; ' Henry V.' (Norwich Festival, 1881) ; ' Othello ' (Queen's Hall, 1896) ; a pianoforte concerto ; sonatas for pianoforte alone and in combination with other instruments ; songs both sacred and secular ; many madrigals and partsongs ; and numerous pieces of all kinds for pianoforte. He edited Mozart's pianoforte works, Beethoven's sonatas and the extensive series of pianoforte pieces known as ' Popular Classics.' He was buried at St. Pancras Cemetery, East Finchley, on Sept. 7. A biographical article appeared in the *Mus. T.* for Jan. 1898, and a volume of Reminiscences was published in 1905.

w. h. h., with addns.

M'GIBBON, WILLIAM (*b.* end of 17th cent. ; *d.* Edinburgh, Oct. 3, 1756), a musician residing in Edinburgh in the earlier half of the 18th century. Little is known of his biography save what is related of him and of other Scottish musicians by William Tytler of Woodhouselee, who contributed to the *Transactions of the Society of Antiquaries of Scotland*, vol. i., 1792, some personal remembrances of them.

He was the son of Matthew M'Gibbon, who was a hautboy-player in Edinburgh. William was early sent to London, and studied the violin under William Corbett. On his return to Edinburgh he was appointed leader of the orchestra in the Gentlemen's Concerts, and held the post for a long period. He was considered an excellent performer. In 1740 M'Gibbon published ' Six Sonatos [*sic*] or Solos for a German Flute or Violin. Edin. : R. Cooper for the author, 1740,' ob. folio. A copy of this now very rare publication was sold at the Taphouse Sale, July 1905. Another of his compositions is ' Six Sonatas for two German Flutes, compos'd by Mr. Wm. M'Gibbon of Edinburgh.' Lond. : J. Simpson, royal 8vo. His most important work, however, was a valuable collection of Scots Tunes, in three oblong folio volumes, of great value in the study of Scots music. These were issued in Edinburgh, and originally published in 1742, 1746 and 1755, though there are several later reprints. He died in Edinburgh and was buried in Greyfriars' Churchyard, having bequeathed the whole of his effects to the Royal Infirmary. He is mentioned in a verse by Robert Ferguson, the poet, and a portrait of him occurs in the title-page of *Flores Musicae* (Edin. : J. Clark, 1773), which is reproduced in Glen's *Early Scottish Melodies*, 1900. F. K.

M'GLASHAN, ALEXANDER (*d.* May 1797), an Edinburgh musician and performer on the violoncello and violin during the latter half of

the 18th century. From his stately appearance and dress he was nicknamed ' King M'Glashan.' He was in the habit of giving fashionable concerts at St. Cecilia's Hall, near the Cowgate, and issued three important books of Scottish national airs, of great value in tracing the history of these melodies, viz. : ' A Collection of Strathspey Reels ' (1780), ' A Collection of Scots Measures ' (1781) and ' A Collection of Reels ' (1786), all in oblong folio, and published by Stewart of Edinburgh. He was buried in Greyfriars' Churchyard. F. K.

M'GUCKIN, BARTON (*b.* Dublin, July 28, 1852 ; *d.* Stoke Poges, Apr. 17, 1913), tenor singer, began his career as a chorister at Armagh Cathedral. He received instruction from R. Turle, then organist there, in singing, organ, violin and pianoforte. He became first tenor at St. Patrick's Cathedral, Dublin, in 1871, and was for a time a pupil of Joseph Robinson. He sang at one of the Philharmonic Concerts in Dublin in 1874, and in the following year made his début at the Crystal Palace Concerts, July 5, 1875, after which he went to Milan and studied under Trevulsi. He reappeared with success at the same concerts, Oct. 28, 1876, where he first appeared as an oratorio singer in the ' Lobgesang,' Nov. 3, 1877. He made his début on the stage as Thaddeus under Carl Rosa at Birmingham, Sept. 10, 1880 ; at Dublin as Wilhelm Meister, May 9, 1881 ; in the same part at Her Majesty's, Jan. 20, 1882, and as Moro on the production in England of ' The Painter of Antwerp,' an English version of Balfe's Italian opera ' Pittore e duca,' Jan. 28, 1882. He remained in Rosa's company both in London and the provinces until the summer of 1887, and became a great favourite both as a singer and actor. His most important parts were Lohengrin, Faust and Don José ; in new operas he created at Drury lane the parts of Phœbus (' Esmeralda '), Mar. 26, 1883 ; Orso (' Colomba '), Apr. 9, 1883 ; Waldemar (' Nadeshda '), Apr. 16, 1885 ; Guillem de Cabestanh (' Troubadour '), June 8, 1886 ; Oscar (' Nordisa '), May 4, 1887 ; at Edinburgh, Renzo on the production in English of Ponchielli's ' Promessi sposi,' and at Liverpool, Des Grieux (' Manon '), Jan. 17, 1885. He sang in opera in America in 1887–88, and rejoined the Carl Rosa Company from 1889–96, adding to his repertory the part of Eleazar in ' La Juive,' and that of Thorgrim in Cowen's opera of that name, Apr. 22, 1890. A. C.

MACHAUT, GUILLAUME DE (*b.* Diocese of Reims, *c.* 1300 ; *d.* there, 1377), was the first practical exponent of the *Ars nova* of Philippe de VITRY (*q.v.*). He took holy orders at an early age, and about 1323 became secretary to John of Luxembourg, King of Bohemia, and accompanied that monarch on his expeditions to Poland, Lithuania and Italy. After the King's death at Crécy in 1346, Machaut entered the service of his daughter, the Duchess of Normandy, and on her death in 1349 he found a new patron in Charles, King of Navarre. The Dauphin of France (afterwards King Charles V.) and his brother Jean, Duke of Berry, were among his later patrons. Machaut had been made a canon of Reims Cathedral in 1333, and the later part of his life was passed chiefly in that city. (For a full account of his life see V. Chichmaref, *Poésies lyriques de Guillaume de Machaut*, vol. i. Introduction, published by H. Champion, Paris; or E. Hoepffner, *Œuvres de Guillaume de Machault*, vol. i. Introduction, published by the 'Société des anciens textes français,' Paris.)

Machaut is an important figure in the history of French music and poetry. His musical compositions include a Mass for four voices, 23 motets and a wordless 'double hoquet,' and musical settings of 45 *ballades*, 22 *rondeaux*, 32 *chansons baladées* and 18 *lais*. In addition to the latter there are musical settings of 7 lyrical poems — 1 *lai*, 1 *chanson royal*, 1 *complainte*, 1 *rondel*, 1 *chanson baladée* and 2 *ballades*—interpolated into a narrative poem, 'Le Remède de Fortune.'

Musically, the most important of his compositions is the Mass, which is traditionally said to have been composed for the coronation of Charles V. in 1364 at Reims, though we have no proof that this was the case. With the exception of the anonymous 3-part 'Messe de Tournai' it is the oldest extant polyphonic setting of the Mass (described in the *Oxf. Hist. Mus.* vol. ii.; in P. Wagner: *Geschichte der Messe*, vol. i.; and in 'Earliest Polyphonic Masses' (in *Blackfriars*, vol ii., June 1921) by Barbara Smythe).

The motets, which include 6 with Latin words of a sacred character, 15 with secular French words in the upper parts and 2 which are bi-lingual (*i.e.* with Latin words in *motetus* and French words in *triplum*; see MOTET), are written for three voices, with the exception of 1 French and 3 Latin examples, which are in four parts. The fourth part, both in these and in the Mass, is a second tenor (contra-tenor). Three of the French motets are written over French tenors, but the majority have liturgical Latin tenors, according to the more usual custom of the time.

The *lais* (long lyrical poems written in twelve pairs of stanzas, each pair having a different metrical form and a different melody from the rest, except the last pair, which repeats metre and melody of the first) are all set to one musical part only, as are also the majority of the *chansons baladées*. The latter are the simplest and musically the most attractive of all Machaut's songs. The majority of the Ballades and all the Rondeaux have a polyphonic setting. The second part is a tenor, the third,

when there is one, a contra-tenor. Words are given only to the topmost part, and it is generally supposed that the tenor and contra-tenor were intended to be played on instruments. Four Ballades and two Rondeaux have a fourth part, a triplum, written above the voice part, but this, too, is wordless, and probably instrumental. Machaut was an innovator in supplying a written accompaniment to his songs. Polyphonic Rondeaux had been written in the previous century, but these were really vocal trios, and the majority of the lyrics of trouvères and troubadours have a purely melodic setting. He was, on the other hand, the last of the French poets to compose the music for his songs.

His music is written according to the rules laid down by Philippe de Vitry in the *Ars nova*, with regard both to harmony and to rhythm. He makes much use of binary rhythm —hitherto unknown in French music—and he is the first French composer to use the minim (♦).

The musical works of Guillaume de Machaut are preserved wholly or in great part in six MSS., five of which are in the Bibliothèque Nationale, Paris—Nos. 22,545-6, 1584, 1585, 1586 and 9221 of the *fonds français*—and one in the private collection of the Marquis de Vogüé. Nos. 1585 and 1586 are of the 15th century, the others are of the 14th, and Nos. 22,545-6 and 1584, which are the most authoritative, were probably compiled under the poet's own direction. For a full description of the musical contents of all the Paris MSS., and a list of other MSS. containing a few of Machaut's songs, see J. Wolf, *Geschichte der Mensural-Notation*, vol. i. part iii. The account of the MSS. is followed by an account of Machaut's musical notation.

A good account of Machaut's music is given by F. Ludwig in Adler, *Handbuch der Musik-Geschichte*. See also the same writer's article on *Die mehrstimmige Musik des 14ten Jahrhunderts* in *Sammelbände der Int. Musikgesellschaft*, vol. iv.

No complete edition of Machaut's music has yet been published. Specimens of it — in modern notation unless otherwise indicated— have been published as follows :

J Wolf, *Geschichte der Mensural-Notation*, vol. ii. (original notation) and vol. iii. (modern notation).
Kyrie and Credo (omitting last section, from Confiteor to Amen).
3 3-part French motets.
1 4-part Latin motet.
3 Ballades, two in 3 and one in 2 parts.
4 Rondeaux, one in 4, two in 3 and one in 2 parts.
1 Chanson baladée in 2 parts.
F. Ludwig, in appendix to E. Hoepffner, *Œuvres de G. de Machault* : All the songs from the 'Remède de Fortune.'
P. Aubry, *Les plus anciens monuments de la musique française* : 1 chanson baladée in 1 part (facsimile and transcription).
P. Aubry, *Recherches sur les 'Ténors' français dans les motets du XIIIe siècle* : 1 3-part French motet.
B. Smythe, *Earliest Polyphonic Masses* (*Blackfriars*, vol. ii.) : Gloria and Sanctus (omitting Benedictus).
H. E. Wooldridge, *Oxford History of Music*, vol. ii. : Agnus Dei (part).
One of the Rondeaux given by Wolf is reproduced in Combarieu's *Histoire de la musique*, vol. i.
Adler, *Handbuch der Musik-Geschichte* (p. 232), quotes a ballade *a* 4, with two parts instrumental.   B. S.

MACHÊTE, a small 4-stringed guitar used by the Portuguese and found also in Madeira and the Azores. (See GUITAR.) 　　F. W. G.

MACICOTATICUM or MACHICOTAGE, a species of ornamentation applied to PLAIN-SONG (q.v.) melodies by means of extraneous notes inserted between those of the true Canto fermo, after the manner of *fioritura*. To the once prevalent custom of *machicotage* in France are to be attributed many of the corruptions observable in Gallican Office Books before the modern revisions. The *Processionale Parisiense* (Paris, 1787) directs that the melodies shall be *machicotée* by the clergy, and continued by the choir ' *sine macicotatico* '; and in former times the ecclesiastics entrusted with the duty of so singing them were called *maceconici* or *machicots*. 　　　　　　　　　　　W. S. R.

MACINTYRE, MARGARET, soprano, possessed a voice of exceptional beauty, but she had a tendency to force the tone and her career as a leading singer was rather short. She made her début in 1888 on the second night of Augustus Harris's first season at Covent Garden, playing Micaela to the Carmen of Madame Nordica. Her success was emphatic, and during the season she sang Inez in ' L'Africaine,' Mathilde in ' Gulielmo Tell ' to the Tell of Lassalle, and Marguérite in Boïto's ' Mefistofele.' In the following year she sang, among other parts, Marguérite in Faust. Soon in request as a concert singer, she made her first festival appearance at Leeds in 1889. She was the first Rebecca in Sullivan's ' Ivanhoe ' at D'Oyly Carte's English Opera House, on Jan. 31, 1891, alternating the part with Miss Thudichum. At Covent Garden in 1892 she sang Senta in the ' Flying Dutchman ' to Lassalle's Vanderdecken. She was at the Leeds Festivals in 1892 and 1895, and at the Birmingham Festival in 1891. While her voice was still at its best she sang at St. Petersburg and Moscow, an interesting feature of her visit to Russia being her appearance as Elizabeth in ' Tannhäuser ' with Battistini as Wolfram. 　　　　　　　　　　　S. H. P.

MACKAY, ANGUS (d. near Dumfries, Mar. 21, 1859), a famous Highland piper, who collected and published some interesting pipe melodies taken down from traditional sources. The book is now rare, and its title runs : ' A Collection of Ancient Piobaireachd or Highland pipe music,' folio, 1838. Another of his works is ' The Piper's Assistant.' He was piper to Queen Victoria, and was accidentally drowned in the Nith, near Dumfries. 　　　　F. K.

MACKENZIE, SIR ALEXANDER CAMPBELL (b. Edinburgh, Aug. 22, 1847), both as composer and as teacher (he was Principal of the R.A.M. for 36 years) is accounted one of the leaders of the British musical renaissance.

He was the fourth musician of his family in direct descent. His great-grandfather belonged

to the Forfarshire Militia Band ; his grandfather, John Mackenzie (1797–1852), was a violinist in Aberdeen and Edinburgh ; and his father, Alexander Mackenzie (1819–57), was also a violinist, pupil of Sainton and Lipinski ; he edited the ' National Dance Music of Scotland,' and was leader of the band at the Theatre Royal in Edinburgh.

A. C. Mackenzie was educated at Hunter's School in Edinburgh, and, when only 10 years old, was sent to study music at Schwarzburg-Sondershausen in Germany on the recommendation of a member of Gung'l's band named Bartel. Here he was a pupil of K. W. Uhlrich for the violin, and for theory, of Eduard Stein, the conductor of the Sondershausen Ducal orchestra. The boy played second violin in the orchestra, and took part in many performances of the most advanced music, Liszt, Berlioz and the then existing works of Wagner being his daily bread. In 1862 he returned to Edinburgh, and soon afterwards came to London, intending to take lessons from Sainton ; but on the latter's advice Mackenzie entered for the King's Scholarship at the R.A.M., and won it in December of the same year, remaining at the Academy till 1865. Besides Sainton, who taught him the violin, his masters were Charles Lucas for harmony and counterpoint, and F. B. Jewson for piano. While at the Academy Mackenzie played in various theatre orchestras, and thereby acquired experience of orchestral work at first hand. On the conclusion of his course at the Academy, Mackenzie returned to Edinburgh, where he quickly became known as an excellent violinist ; he also gave chamber concerts, at which Schumann's pianoforte quartet and quintet were given for the first time in Scotland. He was appointed conductor of the Scottish Vocal Music Association in 1873, and meanwhile fulfilled many teaching engagements, and officiated as precentor in St. George's Church. He found time to compose some chamber music, a PF. trio and string quartet (unpublished), besides a pianoforte quartet in E flat, published by Kahnt of Leipzig as op. 11.

Hans von Bülow had seen the proof-sheets at the German publishers', and had made inquiries about the composer. When he came to Glasgow and Edinburgh in 1877–78, he made Mackenzie's personal acquaintance, and accepted his overture ' Cervantes ' (performed at Sondershausen in 1877) for performance at Glasgow, where it was given on Dec. 17, 1879. As Mackenzie added to his other labours by playing in the orchestra of the Birmingham Festivals of 1864, 1867, 1870 and 1873, it is not surprising that his health was affected by the strain of his work. He wisely went abroad, and settled in Florence in order to devote himself to composition. For about ten years, in fact until his appointment to the principal ship of the R.A.M., Florence was his residence for at least part of the year; but as time went on his importance in regard to music in London steadily increased, and at last he was obliged to live altogether in England. From the beginning of his residence in Florence dates the first of his more important choral works, the cantata ' The Bride,' performed at the Worcester Festival of 1881. Each year after this saw some work of large calibre, and many festival and other commissions followed rapidly. In 1885–86 Mackenzie was appointed conductor of Novello's Oratorio Concerts, and introduced many important works to London audiences. It was primarily in order to hear his ' Saint Elizabeth ' under Mackenzie's direction that Liszt paid his final visit to England in 1886, and Mackenzie renewed his old friendship with the composer. By this time his second Scottish Rhapsody called ' Burns,' the opera ' Colomba,' and ' The Rose of Sharon,' an oratorio composed for the Norwich Festival of 1884, had raised Mackenzie to a high position among English composers, and on the death of Sir George Macfarren he was appointed to succeed him as Principal of the R.A.M. He undertook the duties of the post on Feb. 22, 1888. Mackenzie's long tenure of office at the R.A.M. (1888–1924) was begun when the institution was feeling the pressure of criticism and the competition of younger teaching schools (see ROYAL ACADEMY OF MUSIC). He brought his musicianship to bear on its internal problems, and showed such statesmanship in guiding its fortunes that not only was the artistic reputation of the Academy completely vindicated, but its material resources were increased and stabilised. Mackenzie taught composition, conducted the students' orchestra and lectured for many years in addition to all the administrative work which he personally controlled. The Academy's move into its new building (1911) and the celebration of its centenary (1922) witnessed the triumph of Mackenzie's organisation; the subsequent careers of the innumerable students who passed through his hands are still more decisive evidence of his power as a teacher and leader.

As a concert conductor Mackenzie's work outside the R.A.M. was important. He conducted the Royal Choral Society occasionally during the lifetime of Sir Joseph Barnby, on whose death he directed the concerts for the remainder of the season. In 1892 he was appointed conductor of the Philharmonic Society, and during his tenure of the post, which he resigned in 1899, introduced Tchaikovsky's Pathetic symphony to London, as well as Borodin's symphony in B minor. In 1903 he undertook a tour in Canada, in the course of which he conducted concerts of British music in all the most important towns of the Dominion.

The tour (organised by Charles A. E. Harriss) lasted six weeks, and extended from Halifax, N.S., to Victoria, B.C. Eleven new choral bodies were raised for this scheme; other existing ones were augmented, and thus, besides introducing many contemporary British works for the first 'ime in Canada, a movement in the direction of choral singing was begun which was the foundation of the present widespread cultivation of the art, furthered by the competition festivals. Mackenzie was General President of the International Musical Society (Int. Mus. Ges.) 1908–1912, a period which included congresses at Vienna (1909) and London (1911). As a lecturer Mackenzie has done important work in frequent courses delivered before the Royal Institution. One lecture, given there in 1919, on ' Hubert Parry, his work and place as a British composer,' was of peculiar value as the estimate of a close friend and contemporary.

Mackenzie received the Mus.D. degree from St. Andrews in 1886; Cambridge in 1888; Edinburgh in 1890; that of D.C.L. from Glasgow, 1901, and the M'Gill University in 1903; that of LL.D. from Leeds in 1904, and Mus.D. from Oxford in 1922. He received the gold medal for art and science from the Grand Duke of Hesse in 1884, and the Saxe-Coburg and Gotha Order for Arts and Science in 1893. He is a corresponding member of the Istituto Reale Musicale of Florence, a member of the Royal Swedish Academy and honorary member of the Accademia di S. Cecilia in Rome. In 1895 he was knighted; he was created Knight Commander of the Victorian Order (1922); and received the gold medal of the Royal Philharmonic Society (1923).

M. ; with addns. C.

QUALITIES OF COMPOSITION.—Mackenzie's high importance to his generation rests primarily on the fact that he is essentially both a Briton and a cosmopolitan. His early upbringing in Scotland was removed from those influences of the church and the organ loft which set their stamp both for good and ill on so many of his English contemporaries. As a violinist he lived in the freer atmosphere of the orchestra and the theatre, and his long periods of life on the Continent, besides giving him a command of the German and Italian languages equal to his command of English, enabled him to mix with the keenest musical minds of his time, to breathe their air and live their life, without for one moment being deflected from his own course, or belying his character as a sturdy long-sighted North Briton. These qualities are reflected in his music.

His appointment to the R.A.M. suggests a natural division of his compositions into two periods at about opus 40. Before that time

(1888) composition was the first business of his career ; after that it had to take second place, to be accomplished in time snatched from other duties, and be undertaken either for a special occasion or for relaxation.

Equality of output is scarcely to be expected, and for the most part Mackenzie's reputation has rested on his earlier works. Among these none served to establish his position more firmly than the oratorio 'The Rose of Sharon,' when it was produced at the Norwich Festival in 1884. Its romantic style, the warmth and fervour of its orchestral colouring and its freedom from the conventions of current English oratorio, marked its composer as a man of individual outlook and originality of ideas. Fortunately the libretto, though devised in a quasi-operatic manner, was put together by Joseph Bennett from the words of Holy Scrip-ture, so that the work is saved from the worst literary banalities of Bennett's own texts. Mackenzie, however, has suffered seriously from his librettists, both in his larger choral works and in his operas. At a time when English composers, led by Stanford and Parry, were rediscovering the musical possibilities of great English literature and poetry, Mackenzie accepted too readily the hackwork of Bennett and Hueffer for cantatas and operas respectively. They stultified much fine and imaginative work on his part. Mackenzie's apparent indifference to the qualities of a libretto seems, however, to be the defect of one of his strongest qualities. Without the literary sensitiveness of Stanford or the philosophic mind of Parry, he took his stand on purely musical values, and wrote with a freedom and frankness which showed genuine creative impulse.

It is significant that the list of his instrumental works contains neither symphony nor sonata ; but suites and overtures, generally with descriptive titles, rhapsodies, ballads, preludes and entr'actes are numerous, and testify to his refusal of any classical pose. The three Scottish rhapsodies, the piano concerto, the Pibroch suite for violin and 'The Cottar's Saturday Night' (one of his most effective choral works) have sufficient reference to Scottish folk-song and other suggestions of local colour to give him a place among musical nationalists ; but his idiom is really cosmopolitan, and he does not generally handle Scottish themes with special native sensitiveness. Max Bruch's Scottish fantasia, for example, might be placed beside his Scottish concerto. His nationality finds expression in more general characteristics less easily defined, in a steadfast persistence in the pursuit of an aim, in an imagination which is not afraid of the commonplace, and, by no means least, in a buoyant sense of humour. A volume of reminiscences by Mackenzie is (1927) in the press.

WORKS WITH OPUS NUMBERS

Op.
1-7. Songs and PF. pieces.
8. Seven Partsongs.
9. Rustic Scenes for PF.
10. Larghetto and Allegretto for vcl.
11. Quartet for PF. and strings in E flat (Classical Chamber Concerts, Edinburgh).
12. Songs.
13. Five pieces for PF.
14. Drei Lieder. (Heine.)
15. Trois Morceaux pour piano.
16. Three Songs.
17. Three Songs. (Christina Rossetti.)
18. Three Songs.
19. Three Anthems.
20. Six Pieces for PF.
21. Rhapsodie Écossaise, for orch. No. 1 (Glasgow, under Manns, Jan. 1880).
22. Three Vocal Trios.
23. 'In the Scottish Highlands,' for PF.
24. 'Burns,' second Scottish Rhapsody (Glasgow, under Manns, 1881).
25. Cantata, 'The Bride' (Worcester Festival, 1881).
26. Cantata, 'Jason' (Bristol Festival, 1882).
27. Three Organ Pieces.
28. Opera 'Colomba.' Drury Lane, Carl Rosa, Apr. 9, 1883 ; revised 1912 (R.C.M., His Majesty's).
29. Orchestral Ballad, 'La Belle Dame sans merci' (Philharmonic, 1883).
30. Oratorio, 'The Rose of Sharon' (J. Bennett). (Norwich Festival, 1884 ; revised 1910 (Alexandra Palace).
31. Five Songs.
32. Concerto for vln. (Birmingham Festival, 1885, Sarasate).
33. Opera, 'The Troubadour' (F. Hueffer, Drury Lane, Carl Rosa, June 8, 1886).
34. Cantata, 'The Story of Sayid' (J. Bennett ; Leeds Festival, 1886).
35. Three Songs by Shakespeare.
36. Jubilee Ode (Crystal Palace, 1887).
37. Six Pieces for vln. (including 'Benedictus '), (Monday Popular Concerts, Lady Hallé, 1888).
38. Ode, 'The New Covenant' (R. Buchanan, Glasgow Exhibition, 1888).
39. 'The Cottar's Saturday Night' (Burns), for chorus and orch.
40. Overture, 'Twelfth Night' (Richter Concerts, 1888).
41. Cantata, 'The Dream of Jubal' (J. Bennett, Liverpool Philharmonic, 1889).
42. Suite for vln., 'Pibroch' (Leeds Festival, played by Sarasate, 1889).
43. Prelude, Entr'actes and Songs for 'Marmion' (Glasgow, 1889 ; songs only published).
44. Spring Songs.
45. Music to 'Ravenswood' (Lyceum Theatre, 1890).
46. 'Veni Creator,' for chorus, solo quartet, and orch. (Birmingham Festival, 1891).
47. (a) Highland Ballad for vln. and orch. (Westminster Orchestral Society, 1893). (b) Barcarolle and Villanelle for vln.
48. Two Choral Odes for Buchanan's 'Bride of Love' (1893).
49. Oratorio, 'Bethlehem' (J. Bennett, Royal Choral Society, 1894).
50. Three Sonnets of Shakespeare.
51. 'Phœbe,' comic opera by B. C. Stephenson (not performed).
52. Overture, 'Britannia' (R.A.M. Commemoration Concert, May 17, 1894).
53. 'From the North,' nine pieces for vln. and PF. (three of them were scored and played at the Philharmonic, 1895).
54. Three Songs.
55. Scottish Concerto for PF. and orch. (Philharmonic, played by Paderewski, 1897).
56. Comic Opera, 'His Majesty' (F. C. Burnand and R. C. Lehmann (Savoy Theatre, Feb. 20, 1897).
57. Overture, Entr'actes, and Incidental Music to 'The Little Minister' (Haymarket Theatre, Nov. 6, 1897).
58. Three Preludes and Vocal Music to 'Manfred' (written for the Lyceum Theatre, but not performed). (Nos. 2 and 3, 'Pastoral' and 'Flight of Spirits,' performed at the London Musical Festival, 1899. No. 1, 'Astarte,' performed at Arthur Newstead's Concert, Dec. 12, 1904.)
59. Five Recitations with PF. accompaniment.
60. Six Rustic Songs.
61. Preludes, Entr'actes and Incidental Music to 'Coriolanus' (Lyceum Theatre, Apr. 15, 1901).
62. Opera, 'The Cricket on the Hearth,' in three acts (Julian Sturgis) ; the overture played at the Philharmonic, July 2, 1902 ; opera produced R.A.M. 1914.
63. Coronation March (Westminster Abbey, 1902).
64. Suite for orch., 'London Day by Day' (Norwich Festival, 1902).
65. 'The Knights of the Road,' operetta (H. A. Lytton, Palace Theatre, Feb. 27, 1905).
66. Cantata, 'The Witch's Daughter' (Whittier, Leeds Festival, Oct. 1904).
67. Canadian Rhapsody for orch. (Philharmonic, 1905).
68. Suite for vln. and orch. (London Symphony Orchestra, Feb. 18, 1897. Mischa Elman).
69. Cantata, 'The Sun-God's Return' (J. Bennett, Cardiff Festival, 1910 ; Singakademie, Vienna, 1911).
70. Fantasia for PF.
71. Four Partsongs.
72. 'La Savannah,' air de ballet for orch.
73. Three Trios for female voices.
74. 'Tam o' Shanter,' Scottish Rhapsody No. 3 (Int. Musical Congress, London, 1911).
75. 'An English Joy-peal,' for orch. (Coronation, Westminster Abbey, 1911).
76. Invocation for orch. (Philharmonic, 1912).
77. 'Perfection,' partsong.
78. 'The Walker of the Snow,' song for baritone.
79. Four Songs (Tennyson).
80. Four Dance Measures, for vln.
81. 'An English Air with Variations,' for PF.
82. Ancient Scots Tunes, for strings.
83. 'Odds and Ends,' 2 books for PF.

op.
84. 'Jottings,' 6 pieces for PF.
85. Three School Songs.
86. Six Easy Impromptus, for vln.
87. 'The Eve of St. John,' opera in 1 act (Eleanor Farjeon). (B.N.O.C. Liverpool, 1924.)
88. Four pieces for PF.
89. 'Distant Chimes,' vln. solo.
90. Overture, 'Youth, Sport, and Loyalty,' for orch. (R.A.M. Centenary, 1922).

WITHOUT OPUS NUMBERS
(With places and dates of first performance.)

Trio, PF. and strings, in D (Classical Chamber Concerts, Edinburgh, 1874). MS
String Quartet in G (Do. 1875). MS.
Overture to a Comedy (played under Julius Tausch at Düsseldorf, 1876). MS.
Overture,' Cervantes ' (played under Max Erdmannsdörfer, Sondershausen, 1877, and under Bülow, Glasgow, 1879). MS.
Scherzo for orchestra (Glasgow, 1878). MS.
Oratorio, ' The Temptation ' (in 3 parts), words by Milton. MS.
Postlude, 'In Memoriam,' organ and strings (Temple Church Memorial Service, 1919).
' Firm in her native strength,' choir and orch. (published).
' With wisdom, goodness, grace.' Partsong (published).
' To singers.' Partsong (published).
' Indian Reverie.' Song (Punch, Jan. 7, 1903).
The Willow Song (Othello) and many other songs.　　　　C.

MACKINTOSH, (1) JOHN (b. London, 1767 ; d. there, Mar. 23, 1844), an eminent performer on the bassoon, who from 1821–35 held the first place in all the principal London and provincial orchestras. He produced a full, rich and powerful, but somewhat coarse tone. His son (2) ALPHONSO was a violinist.

W. H. H.

MACKINTOSH, (1) ROBERT (d. London, Feb. 1807), a Scottish musician and famous composer of Strathspey reels, etc., nicknamed ' Red Rob.' He was from the Highlands (probably from the Vale of Athole), and was established as a musician in Skinner's Close, Edinburgh, in 1773. At various addresses in the northern capital he advertised himself as teacher of the violin, and he organised concerts ; ultimately conducting the orchestra at the Theatre Royal. He removed to London in 1803. He was a clever violinist, and his Scottish dance music is of considerable merit. He published four books of compositions and arrangements as under : ' Airs, Minuets, Gavottes and Reels ' (1783) ; ' Sixty-eight new Reels ' (1792) ; a second book (1793) ; ' A Third Book of Sixty-eight new Reels ' (1796) ; and ' A Fourth Book of new Strathspey Reels,' c. 1804–05 ; all, except the last, which was published in London, being issued in Edinburgh, in folio. It is said that Mackintosh gave the first professorial lessons on the violin to Nathaniel Gow, on the latter's first coming to Edinburgh.

(2) ABRAHAM, his son (b. Edinburgh, June 15, 1769), followed his father's profession. He published ' Thirty new Strathspey Reels,' Edinburgh, folio (1792), and some other works. He removed about the beginning of the 19th century to Newcastle-on-Tyne, where he was established in 1807 as a musician and a teacher of dancing. For many interesting details of the Mackintosh family, see the late John Glen's work, ' The Glen Collection of Scottish Dance Music,' book i., 1891.

MACKLEAN, CHARLES, a violinist and composer who, living in Edinburgh in 1737, pub-

lished in that year ' Twelve Solos or Sonatas for a Violin and Violoncello,' op. prima. R. Cooper, for the author, 1737. It is doubtful whether he is the same Charles M'Lean mentioned on the title-page of ' A Collection of Favourite Scots Tunes . . . by the late Mr. Chs. M'Lean and other eminent Masters,' ob. folio, c. 1772. This last-named collection is of some antiquarian interest.　　　　F. K.

MACLEAN, (1) CHARLES DONALD (b. Cambridge, Mar. 27, 1843 ; d. S. Kensington, London, June 23, 1916), educated at Shrewsbury and Exeter College, Oxford (he was both classical scholar and organist of the latter), studied music under Ferdinand Hiller at Cologne, and had an early career as a composer and organist in London. From 1871–75 he was musical director to Eton College. He then spent 22 years in India as a Civil servant, and subsequently his most important work for music was done in connexion with the International Musikgesellschaft. He became English editor of that society's publications in 1899 and general secretary of the whole society in 1908. He edited the Report volume of the society's Congress held in London 1911, and continued as secretary until the disruption of the society caused by the war (1914–18). (See INTERNATIONAL MUSICAL SOCIETY). His literary interests and his linguistic powers fitted him for such work as this. His compositions are numerous but not important.

His son (2) ALICK (ALEXANDER MORVAREN) (b. Eton, July 20, 1872), was educated at Eton and intended for the army. He began operatic composition with ' Crichton ' (3-act comic opera) and the first version of ' Quentin Durward ' (1892–93), and has had considerable success both as composer and conductor. In 1895 he won the Moody-Manners prize for a one-act opera by a British subject with ' Petruccio ' ; he became musical director to Sir Charles Wyndham (1899), to the Spa Company at Scarborough (1911), and conducted at Chappell's Ballad Concerts (Queen's Hall, London), 1915–23. His principal operatic productions have been—

' Petruccio.' June 1895, at Covent Garden.
Die Liebesgeige. Easter 1906, at Mayence.
' Maitre Seiler.' Aug. 1909, by Moody-Manners, London.
' Quentin Durward.' Jan. 1920, by Carl Rosa at Newcastle.

For lists of works by both father and son see B.M.S. Ann., 1920.　　　　C.

M'LEOD, PETER (b. West Calder, Midlothian, May 8, 1797 ; d. Bonnington, near Edinburgh, Feb. 10, 1859),[1] published several collections of original airs to the words of Scottish poets, as ' Original National Melodies of Scotland ' (1838), ' Original Scottish Melodies,' ' New National Songs, the melodies never before published,' etc., and was the composer of many now favourite Scots songs, ' Oh ! why left I my hame ? ' being among the most

[1] According to Brit. Mus. Biog.

famous of these. His collection of ' Original
Scottish Melodies ' was published with a view
to the completion of the Burns Monument in
Edinburgh, and the profits of it enabled this
to be effected.   F. K.

M'MURDIE, JOSEPH, Mus.B. (b. parish of St.
Bride, London, 1792 ; d. Merton, Surrey, Dec.
23, 1878), graduated at Oxford in 1814. He
was a pupil of Crotch, and composed many
glees (principally for the Concentores Sodales)
and songs, and made numerous arrangements
for the pianoforte. He was for some time a
director of the Philharmonic Society.

                                   W. H. H.

McNAUGHT, (1) WILLIAM GRAY (b. London, Mar. 30, 1849 ; d. there Oct. 13, 1918),
furthered the spread of popular music in
England by many activities, but specially as
a judge of the COMPETITION FESTIVALS (q.v.),
and as editor of the Musical Times (1909–18) [1]
in succession to F. G. EDWARDS (q.v.).

McNaught had been engaged in a business
career before he entered the R.A.M. as a student
(1872–76). During his studentship he was
active as a choir conductor, notably at the
Bow and Bromley Institute, with which he
was closely associated for sixteen years. In
such work he naturally became convinced of
the practical value of the tonic sol-fa notation,
and in his subsequent work as a teacher,
lecturer, and journalist he laid stress on its
uses. For some years he was in charge of
music at the Homerton Training College, and
he then became assistant inspector in music
under the Board of Education. In 1892 the
School Music Review was founded by Novello
under his editorship, a publication through
which a large number of folk-songs, national
songs, and new compositions were made
available for school use. As a judge at the
Competition Festivals McNaught's wide experience and kindly good sense carried great
weight and exerted a far-reaching influence on
the quality of the performances achieved
therein. His son

(2) WILLIAM (b. Sept. 1, 1883), educated at
University College School and at Worcester
College, Oxford, became assistant editor of the
Musical Times under his father. He still (1927)
holds that post, and until recently was on the
musical staff of the Morning Post.   C.

MAÇON, LE, opéra-comique in 3 acts; words
by Scribe and Delavigne, music by Auber.
Produced Opéra-Comique, May 3, 1825 ; in
England, St. James's Theatre, Mar. 13, 1850.

                                        G.

MACPHERSON, CHARLES (b. Edinburgh,
May 10, 1870; d. London, May 28, 1927),
organist of St. Paul's Cathedral, spent a great
part of his life in the service of the cathedral.

His father was Burgh Architect to the city
of Edinburgh. At nine years old Charles

Macpherson entered the choir of St. Paul's
Cathedral and remained there till 1887, when
he was appointed choirmaster under Dr. Pearce
at St. Clement's, Eastcheap. Sir George
Martin gave him organ lessons. He entered
the R.A.M. in 1890, and won the Charles Lucas
prize in 1892, becoming A.R.A.M. in 1896.
After holding the post of private organist to
the late Sir Robert Menzies, at Weem, Perthshire, and Mme. de Falbe, Luton Hoo, Bed-
fordshire, in succession, he was appointed in
1895 sub-organist of St. Paul's, a post of much
responsibility as regards the choir as well as
organ playing, and this position he filled until
the death of Sir George MARTIN (q.v.) in 1916,
when he succeeded to the organistship. He
conducted the London Church Choirs Association from 1914 till his death, served as President of the R.C.O., and was a professor of
the R.A.M. The degree of Mus.D. was conferred on him (honoris causâ) by Durham
University in 1919. His compositions include
a setting of Psalm cxxxvii. for choir and
orchestra ; nine anthems and other church
music ; three Gaelic melodies, accompanied on
strings and harp ; an overture, ' Cridhe an
Ghaidhil,' played at the Crystal Palace in 1895;
a Highland suite for orchestra ; another suite,
' Hallowe'en ' ; a quartet for piano and strings
in E flat ; and two movements of a sextet for
wind instruments. His glee, ' There sits a
bird,' gained the prize given in 1893 by the
Bristol Orpheus Glee Society.   M. ; addns. C.

MACPHERSON, STEWART (b. Liverpool,
Mar. 29, 1865), teacher and writer on music,
was educated at the City of London School,
won the ' Sterndale Bennett ' open scholarship
at the R.A.M., entering that institution in 1880.
He was a pupil of Sir G. A. Macfarren for composition, and of Walter Macfarren for the pianoforte. He gained the Balfe scholarship in 1882,
the Charles Lucas medal for composition in
1884, and the Potter exhibition in 1885. At
the conclusion of his studentship in 1887 he
was appointed professor of harmony and composition and an Associate of the institution,
becoming a Fellow in 1892. He was appointed
organist of Immanuel Church, Streatham Common, in 1885, and in the same year became conductor of the Westminster Orchestral Society,
a post which he held until 1902. He also
conducted the Streatham Choral Society from
1886–1904. In 1898 he was appointed examiner to the Associated Board of the R.A.M.
and R.C.M., and in that capacity visited
Canada, Australia, New Zealand and Ceylon
in 1900. In 1903 he succeeded Corder as
professor of composition at the Royal Normal
College for the Blind, and was appointed a
member of the Board of Musical Studies in the
University of London. He has lectured at the
R.A.M., the Normal College and elsewhere,
and has specialised in the teaching of ' Musical

Appreciation' and kindred matters. His educational works (see list) have had a wide influence. He has edited a complete edition of Beethoven's PF. sonatas.

His compositions include a symphony in C, 1888; two overtures, and short pieces for orchestra, mostly written for the Westminster Orchestral Society. More important than these is a remarkably beautiful Mass in D for solo, choir and orchestra, produced at St. James's Hall, May 1898. Many songs, pianoforte pieces and services have been published; and 'Concerto alla fantasia,' for violin and orchestra, was played at the Queen's Hall Promenade Concert in 1904. His theoretical works are:

Practical Harmony (trans. German) with Appendix, 350 exercises, etc.
Evolution of Musical Design.
Practical Counterpoint.
Rudiments of Music.
Form in Music.
Music and its Appreciation.
Aural Culture based upon Musical Appreciation, with Ernest Read. 3 parts.
Studies in Phrasing and Form.
Musical Education of the Child.
Melody and Harmony.
The Appreciation Class.
                 M., with addns.

MACQUE, JEAN DE, a Flemish musician, pupil of Philip de Monte, who settled in Italy, living from 1576–82 in Rome, and from 1586 in Naples. Only in 1610 is he definitely named as being choirmaster to the Royal Chapel in Naples. His publications extend from 1576–1613, and consist almost entirely of madrigals, of which there were two Books *a* 6, six *a* 5, two *a* 4, one *a* 4, five, six, and two Books entitled 'Madrigaletti e Napolitane,' *a* 6. Some of these are now lost, and several have parts missing. A considerable number of his madrigals and a few motets were received into the various collections of the time. Two were adapted to English words in Yonge's 'Musica Transalpina' of 1588, and Morley's 'Italian Madrigals' of 1598.   J. R. M.

MADAMA BUTTERFLY, opera in 2 acts, text by Luigi Illica and G. Giocosa, founded on David Belasco's dramatisation of a story by John Luther Long; music by Puccini. Produced Scala, Milan, in 1904, in a revised form; Brescia, May 28, 1904, the second act divided into two distinct parts; and Covent Garden, July 10, 1905; Washington, D.C., Oct. 1906; in English, Lyric Theatre (Moody-Manners Co.), Aug. 16, 1907.

MADAME SANS GÊNE, opera in 4 acts, text by Renato Simoni, after the play by Sardou and Moreau, music by Giordano. Produced New York, Metropolitan Opera House, Jan. 25, 1915.

MADIN (*recte* MADDEN), HENRI (*b.* Verdun, 1698; *d.* Versailles, 1748), came of Irish parents (from Eyrecourt, Co. Galway), and developed a taste for music at an early age. His uncle, Rev. Dr. Ambrose Madden, of Loughrea, was advanced to the bishopric of Kilmacduagh (Ireland) on the nomination of the Pretender, James III., in 1705. In 1730 we find Henri Madden a cleric, and maître de musique in the Cathedral of Tours, a position which he vacated in 1737 for the more important one of deputy maître de chapelle to the King. He published a treatise on counterpoint in 1742, and was nominated maître de chapelle to the King, in succession to Campra (see CAMPRA, André). In June 1742 he is described as 'Canon of the Chapel Royal of St. Quentin and Master of the Music to the King.' Not only was he a good theorist, but he was also a successful choir-trainer, and composed many popular motets.   W. H. G. F.

MADRIGAL (Ital. *madrigale*), a form of secular composition for two or more voices, practised originally in North Italy in the 14th century and revived in the 16th and early 17th centuries, during which period it assumed the style by which it is chiefly known and became popular over the greater part of Europe.

The etymology of the word has puzzled philologists for several centuries. It was applied originally to a particular form of short poem of pastoral character, and since such poems were often called *mandriali* in the 14th century, it was supposed that the word was derived from *mandria* (Latin *mandra* and Greek μάνδρα), a herd. The form *madriale* also appears, and gave rise to the theory that the madrigal was originally a hymn to the Virgin Mary. It has recently been shown by Prof. Leonardo Biadene of the University of Pisa that the word comes from a mediæval Latin word *matricale* meaning a rustic song in the mother tongue. Italian writers on literature in the early 14th century also make use of the words *mandriale* and *marigale* as synonymous, the latter word being more in common usage. The forms *madrigale*, *marigale* and *madriale* are all easily and naturally derived from *matricale* under the influence of various North Italian dialects; Biadene regards *mandriale* as a word invented by the literary men of the 14th century resulting from a fusion of *madriale* and *mandria*.

The madrigal as a musical composition makes its first appearance about 1340. Its origin may be traced to the CONDUCTUS (*q.v.*) of the French composers in the 13th century, but the great Florentine school of the 14th century has an individual style of its own. The most important composers of this school were Giovanni da Cascia, Jacopo da Bologna and Francesco Landini (*d.* 1397). Landini is described by contemporary writers as being not only a composer of very moving love-songs, but also as a marvellous performer on the *organetto* (portative organ). Specimens of his madrigals are quoted by Wooldridge (*Oxford History of Music*) and Ludwig (in Adler's *Handbuch der Musikgeschichte*). The madrigal of this period consists generally of two or three stanzas of three lines each, repeated to the same music and followed by a pair of lines in a different rhythm. The subjects are chiefly amorous, but often satirical or political as well. The music is generally for two voices. Another form common at this period is the *caccia* (chase), originally used for poems dealing with the chase; the music is for two voices in canon, with a free instrumental bass. It has been suggested by German writers that the English Catch is derived from the *Caccia*. Both madrigal and *caccia* often illustrate the words with a strong sense of musical wit. The madrigals often begin with long florid passages, and it has been suggested by Riemann and others that these were played by instruments.

The period of Landini shows secular music considerably in advance of music for the church, but in the 15th century the church seems to have taken the lead. The secular music of the early Netherland school is of comparatively little importance in the history of technical developments. From the beginning of the 16th century onwards the leadership passes to the Italians again. The madrigal and various other secular forms return to prominence, and by the end of the century the madrigal, especially in Italy, represents the most daring advance in the technique of musical composition. The transition is well summarised by Alfred Einstein (Adler's *Handbuch der Musikgeschichte*) as the passage of the principal melody from the tenor to the uppermost part. In the early years of the 15th century the favourite secular form was the chanson of the French and Netherlandish composers (see SONG, subsection FRANCE). It was in most cases a traditional popular tune, sung by the tenor and accompanied by the other voices in more or less elaborate counterpoint. During the course of the century composers gradually learned to give organic unity to their work by making the subsidiary voices sing free imitations on motives taken from the main tune. It has been well pointed out that the principle of perpetual free and fragmentary imitation was a very important step in musical technique, because it was the first step towards thematic unity and thematic development, neither of which were possible so long as the ideal of absolutely strict canon prevailed. This aspect of technique is best studied in the church music of the period which offered larger forms than the chanson in which to develop the principle. The chanson, which eventually imposed its definitely French style of expression on the Netherlanders as well, found its most artistic exponent in Josquin des Prés (*d.* 1521), who has been regarded by the general consensus of musical historians as the first composer whose music appeals unmistakably to our modern sense of the art. From Josquin onwards secular music maintains its own independent life as free composition, not merely the harmonisation of traditional tunes.

The name *madrigale*, after having been apparently forgotten (as a musical form) for over a hundred years, was revived again in 1533, when a collection of 'Madrigali noui de diuersi excellentissimi musici' was published by Valerio Dorico at Rome. Out of twenty compositions sixteen have Italian words, the rest French; the composers of the Italian pieces are given as Carlo (3), Constantio F[esta] (2), Sebastiano F[esta] (1), Maistre Jan (1), Jacobo de Tho-[scana?] (1), Verdelot (7), and Anon. (1). The poetical form of the Madrigal has been variously defined, according as the authorities followed the examples of the 14th or the 16th centuries. Bembo, the greatest literary authority of the later madrigal period, to whom also the actual musical composition of madrigals owed some of its instigation, says that the madrigal is bound by no rule as to the number of its lines or the arrangement of its rhymes. It was a short poem rarely exceeding twelve lines; its rhymes could be arranged as the poet pleased, provided that the last two lines, which generally formed some sort of pointed *coda*, should rhyme together; and its lines were free as to length, the metre being iambic, usually of seven or eleven syllables, more rarely of five.

The literary aspect of the madrigal is of great importance. It has been discussed at some length by G. Cesari (*R.M.I.* xix.). There existed in Italy during the first years of the 16th century a type of song called FROTTOLA (*q.v.*), popular mainly in North Italy (Verona, Mantua, Padua, Venice, Bologna). The poems were frivolous, but obviously written by educated people for educated audiences; they are clever and amusing adaptations of the folk-song style. Some are intended for four unaccompanied voices, others for one voice with the lute or other instruments. Two things should be noted about them—their music is definitely melodious, with the melody at the top, and their poems are generally in stanzas with a refrain and in trochaic lines of eight syllables. The composers of the frottole are all Italians. The madrigal was a reaction against the frivolity and vulgarity of the frottola. In its early stages it was mainly the work of Netherlandish composers; but it could not have come into existence but for the incentive of Italian poets. Bembo was the leader of the movement towards an essentially aristocratic poetry that deliberately avoided all contact with that of the common people. The last collection of frottole was printed in 1531; Bembo's famous 'Canzoniere' appeared in 1530, and the first collection of madrigals set to music in 1533. The disciples of Bembo took Petrarch as their model, and Petrarch himself was one of the poets most often set to music by the madrigalists; but, as Symonds pointed out, the conditions of social life in Petrarch's own day were very different from those of the Renaissance, and the imitation of Petrarch in the 16th century merely led to preciosity and affectation. Yet this movement, disastrous as it was in some ways to poetry, had a certain very valuable influence on music. In the first place, it made the madrigal the musical expression of the highly cultivated life of the small Italian courts; a definitely aristocratic type of music was created. The Netherlandish composers brought to it the accomplished contrapuntal technique of the motet; but that technique soon had to learn to adjust its paces to the swift and supple rhythms of the new Italian poetry. A typical example of the early madrigal is the well-known poem of Monsignor Guidiccioni set to equally well-known music[1] by Arcadelt:

> Il bianco e dolce cigno
>   Cantando more, ed io
>   Piangendo giungo al fin del viver mio.
> Strana e diversa sorte,
>   Ch' ei more sconsolato,
>   Et io moro beato.
> Morte, che nel morire,
>   M' empie di gioia tutto e di desire ;
>   Se nel morir altro dolor non sento,
>   Di mille mort' il di sarei contento.

The ingenious irregularity of its lines and rhymes compel the composer to invent musical forms that will correspond with them. As the ten lines are a complete poem there is no need for a simple tune to which a succession of stanzas are to be sung. The poem is short enough to admit of *melismata* and of contrapuntal elaboration, but, in conformity with the artificial spirit of the words, the counterpoint must be suggested rather than worked out. Music for a cultivated and elegant society must not become boring. Every line of the poem contains at least one word that is full of emotional suggestion—*dolce, cantando, piangendo, strana, sconsolato,* etc. The word *morire* bears the erotic double sense familiar in the madrigal poets of our own country. The epigrammatic point made by the final rhymed couplet gives the composer the opportunity of 'driving a point' of imitation, in order to end his work with an effective coda. In most madrigals, early or late, this coda, so carefully provided by the poet, is made still more pointed in the music by a repetition.

Most of these early madrigals are largely homophonic, but the parts (at this period four is the usual number) are all melodious and agreeable to sing, whether they move contrapuntally or not. They are intended to be sung by four unaccompanied voices; but it is clear that the uppermost part has the chief melody, and there can be little doubt that in many cases the three lower parts were played by instruments. There are definite records of madrigals being sung to instrumental accompaniment,

---

1 Published as No. 22 of 'Ausgewählte Madrigale' (select Madrigals), ed. by W. Barclay Squire. (B. & H.)

---

voices and instruments sometimes uniting in all parts, sometimes a voice singing the top part only. But the fact that the collection of 1533 was the first issue of separate partbooks with the words printed in full for each part shows that musicians had begun to require a more careful adjustment of words to notes in all voices; the previous practice had been to print all four parts in the same book, not in score but on facing pages, and to print words for the soprano alone in full.

The madrigal composers of this early period are almost exclusively Netherlanders occupying positions at the various small Italian courts. The chief representatives are Arcadelt, Verdelot, Willaert and Gero. The only Italians of distinction are Costanzo Festa and Alfonso della Viola. The madrigal, however, soon became an important feature of the courtly life. At the marriage of Cosmo de' Medici and Eleonora of Toledo at Florence in 1539 a whole series of madrigals was performed, some as entr'actes to a comedy, others as accompaniments to the entrance and exit of the ducal couple. The list of madrigals, singers and instruments gives in itself quite a vivid picture of the scene.

Ingredere, à 8, sung over the archway of the great door of the Porta al Prato with 24 voices on one side and on the other 4 trombones and 4 *cornetti* on the entrance of the most illustrious Duchess.
Sacro et santo himeneo, à 9.
Vattene almo riposo, à 4, sung by Aurora and played by a harpsichord and little organs with various stops at the beginning of the comedy.
Guardane almo pastore, à 6, sung at the end of the 1st act by 6 shepherds and then repeated by them and played as well by 6 other shepherds with *storte* (? krummhorn).
Chi me l' a tolt' oime, à 6, sung at the end of the 2nd act by 3 sirens and 3 sea-monsters, played by 3 flutes and 3 sea-nymphs with 3 lutes all together.
O begli anni dell' oro, à 4, played at the end of the 3rd act by Silenus with a violone, playing all the parts and singing the soprano.
Hor chi mai cantera, à 4, sung at the end of the 4th act by 8 huntress nymphs.
Vientene almo riposo, à 5, sung at the end of the 5th act, at nightfall, and played by 4 trombones.
Bacco, Bacco evoè, à 4, sung and danced by 4 bacchanals and 4 satyrs with various instruments all at once which at nightfall was the end of the comedy.

There were innumerable madrigals composed for social events such as weddings, as their words plainly show. Palestrina and others often allude to the lasciviousness of the madrigals; Corteccia, the composer of the wedding madrigals just mentioned, apologised for this in the dedication to Cosmo de' Medici of these and others which he published in 1544, being then a priest. He excuses himself partly on the ground that they were composed in his youth but mainly because they had been printed incorrectly by unauthorised persons and ascribed to other composers. Peter Wagner (*Das Madrigal und Palestrina,* in *Vierteljahrsschrift für Musikwissenschaft,* viii. 423) quotes the words of a very curious specimen which must be left in the decent obscurity of a learned periodical.

The chief composers of the second period of madrigal writing are Willaert and his pupil Cipriano de Rore, who was also a Fleming; Orlando Lasso, Palestrina and Andrea Gabrieli also belong to this group, though Palestrina's contributions to madrigal literature are of comparatively small importance. The output of minor Italian composers, almost all of considerable merit, was enormous. The typical madrigal of this period is for five voices, which not only enriched the harmony but allowed of frequent division of the singers into opposing groups, the middle voice often having to do duty in both. Six-part madrigals are also common. Counterpoint becomes the adroit servant of emotional expression; phrases are much broken up by rests which emphasise the rhetoric of the words and illustrate the sighs and groans of unsatisfied desire; both words and music acquire a marvellously skilful technique of delicate voluptuousness. But love is by no means the only subject of the madrigals; the whole life of the later Renaissance is mirrored in them. Jacques du Pont, organist of S. Luigi dei Francesi at Rome, shows us the street seller of roast chestnuts; Giovanni Croce of Chioggia teaches us to play the game of the Goose, still popular with Italian children to-day; Striggio describes the chattering of the women washing clothes in the river—their gossip of love-affairs, their grumbles at their mistresses, their ghost stories, their quarrels and the folk-songs which another group suddenly start to sing by way of putting an end to abusive language—and from Striggio it is only a short step to the 'Amfiparnaso' of Vecchi and the rather puerile buffooneries of Banchieri.

The third and most interesting period of the Italian madrigal is represented by Luca Marenzio, Monteverdi and Gesualdo Prince of Venosa. Their madrigals have been very severely criticised by earlier writers on musical history, such as Burney, Rockstro, Wooldridge and even Parry[1]; but it may be noted that Martini, the teacher of Mozart, speaks of them with the highest praise. The free use of chromatic alteration brings about the complete break-down of the modal tonality; modulations are introduced which even to-day sound bewildering. In the earlier years of the madrigal it is fairly clear that madrigals were written more for the pleasure of the singers than for that of an audience; the delight of singing them arises from the fact that every part is contrapuntally interesting as well as admirably vocal. In the third period the personality of the composer dominates; the separate voices have to sink their individuality in the organic whole. The madrigal is not the choral expression of a corporate body such as may perhaps be found in the church music of the period; the voices are the skilled and sensitive servants of the composer, like the instruments in a late quartet of Beethoven. The madrigal becomes in fact a conscious and accomplished work of art.

The madrigal broke down in the early years of the 17th century because it was becoming

[1] But see The Significance of Monteverdi, by C. H. H. Parry Proc. Mus. Ass., 1915-16.

steadily more and more literary. The madrigals of Monteverdi and Gesualdo, notwithstanding their daring harmonies and their consummate musical technique, seem to be inspired more by a passionate devotion to poetry than by a purely musical creative faculty. Some of the English composers described their madrigals as 'apt for voices or viols.' One could have Arcadelt's madrigals played by strings alone with no great loss to their beauty; but to treat those of Monteverdi and Gesualdo in this way would be unthinkable. Without their poems they would be meaningless; and perhaps the reason why some writers failed to appreciate the beauty of them was that they looked at them from too exclusively musical a point of view.

Galilei and Peri, the creators of the *stilo recitativo* which eventually became the foundation of the musical drama, had pushed the literary ideal of music still farther. We can see from the description of Corteccia's wedding madrigals how the ideal of solo song accompanied by intruments had interested musicians almost a hundred years before; but it was the madrigal of Cipriano de Rore, Marenzio and Monteverdi himself which prepared the expressive technique of the early operas. Monteverdi took over the madrigal style in the choruses of his operas; but it must not be overlooked that the style of his recitatives is derived no less from that of the madrigals. The madrigal did not altogether die out in the 17th century, in spite of the new orientation of music. Madrigals were composed even by such men as Stradella, Alessandro Scarlatti and Lotti, though it must be admitted that their numbers are very few. In the 16th century Luzzasco Luzzaschi had composed elaborately florid madrigals with accompaniment of the harpsichord for three ladies who sang at the court of Ferrara, and it is probably from these that the name passed to contrapuntal duets for two voices with figured bass which were written in large quantities by Alessandro Scarlatti, Steffani, Handel, Perez and others in the late 17th and early 18th centuries.

Alongside of the madrigals there existed in the 16th century a number of smaller secular vocal forms. The frottole have already been described. The 'Giustiniana' belongs to the same date and to much the same category. It derives its name not (as Morley and Prætorius supposed) from that of a notorious courtesan of Bergamo but from Leonardo Giustiniani, the Venetian statesman and humanist (*b.* 1385), who in his youth was a prolific poet and composer of songs in the popular Venetian manner. They were greatly admired in his own day and won the praise even of Bembo. The later songs called by Giustiniani's name were of less value. Giustiniani in later life wrote 'laudi spirituali,' and it has been conjectured that some of his own melodies have been preserved in various collections of laudi. The 'villanella' (Venetian *villota*) is of the same type, and closely allied with it are the 'canti carnascialeschi,' four-part settings of poems in several stanzas. Their words show that they were to be sung by people dressed up in various characters, who in the carnival procession present themselves to the ladies with language that is generally more or less obscene. An amusing example is the 'Canto delle Lancresine' (*i.e.* le *Inglesine*, or *Dames Anglaises*, English nuns whose complaints of the discomforts of foreign travel oddly resemble those of the English spinster in Italy to-day). The 'canti carnascialeschi' generally have the melody in the tenor. The villanelle are more usually in three parts, and one of their characteristics is the frequent use of three or more consecutive triads. This practice was pursued not from ignorance but from a deliberate intention to offend the 'good taste' which cultivated the madrigal, as the words show pretty clearly. The villanelle were not written for the lower classes, but for the same classes as the madrigals were, and among their most spirited composers we find Orlando Lasso and Luca Marenzio. Fifths of exactly the same kind are numerous among the 'laudi spirituali,' as these were popular tunes, supplied, for words, with edifying parodies of the far from edifying originals.

More important is the 'balletto,' belonging chiefly to the second half of the 16th century; its principal exponent is Giovanni Gastoldi. The balletto, which, as its name implies, was a song for dancing, is mainly homophonic, and has a quasi-instrumental refrain to the syllables *fa la la*. Gastoldi's balletti enjoyed a great popularity outside Italy, and had a considerable influence on the English school of madrigal composers.

BIBLIOGRAPHY

A. W. AMBROS, *Geschichte der Musik*, vol. iv. New edition. revised by H. Leichtentritt. Leipzig, 1909.
G. CESARI: *Le Origini del madrigale cinquecentesco. R.I.M.* xix. 1, 1912.
E. J. DENT: *Notes on the 'Amfiparnaso' of Orazio Vecchi. S.I.M.G.* xii. 330, 1911.
EINSTEIN, A. : *Augenmusik im Madrigal. Z.I.M.G.* xiv. 8, 1921.
Die Parodie in der Villanella. Z.M.W. ii. 212, 1920.
Eine Caccia im Cinquecento (von Luca Marenzio). Liliencron-Festschrift, 1910 ; *Claudio Merulo's Ausgabe der Madrigale des Verdelot. S.I.M.G.* viii. 220, 516 ; *Die mehrstimmige weltliche Musik von 1450–1600*, in G. Adler's *Handbuch für Musikgeschichte*. Frankfurt a/M., 1924.
P. HESELTINE : *Carlo Gesualdo* (with C. Gray), 1926.
A. HEUSS : *Claudio Monteverdi als Charakteristiker in seinen Madrigalen.* Liliencron-Festschrift, 1910.
J. HOL : *Horatio Vecchi als weltlicher Komponist.* Basel, 1917.
K. HUBER : *Ivo de Vento.* München, 1917.
F. KEINER : *Die Madrigale des Gesualdo di Venosa.* Leipzig, 1914.
O. KINKELDEY : *Luzzasco Luzzaschi's Solo-Madrigale mit Klavier-Begleitung. S.I.M.G.* ix. 538.
TH. KROYER : *Die Anfänge der Chromatik im italienischen Madrigal des 16. Jahrhunderts.* Beiheft der *I.M.G.* 1902.
Dialog und Echo in der alten Chormusik. Peters-Jahrbuch, 1909.
H. LEICHTENTRITT : *Claudio Monteverdi als Madrigalkomponist. S.I.M.G.* xi. 255, 1910.
A. SANDBERGER : *Vorreden zu der Gesamtausgabe Orlando di Lasso*, reprinted in *Ausgewählte Aufsätze zur Musikgeschichte.* München, 1921.
Roland Lassus's Beziehungen zur italienischen Literatur. S.I.M.G. v. 402. 1904 ; reprinted *ib.*
A. SCHERING : *Das kolorierte Orgelmadrigal des Trecento. S.I.M.G.* xiii. 172.
R. SCHWARTZ : *Die Frottole im 15. Jahrhundert. V.M.W.* ii. 427, 1886.
H. SPRINGER : *Zu Leonardo Giustiniani und den Giustinianen. S.I.M.G.* xi. 25, 1909.
E. SCHMITZ : *Zur Geschichte des italienischen Continuo-Madrigals im 17. Jahrhundert. S.I.M.G.* xi. 509, 1910.
L. TORRI : *Vincenzo Ruffo madrigalista. R.I.M.* iii. 635 ; iv. 233.
Giovanni Croce Chiozzotto. R.I.M. xvi. 550.
F. VATIELLI : *Canzonieri musicali del 1500. R.I.M.*, 1921.
E. VOGEL : *Bibliothek der gedruckten weltlichen Vokalmusik Italiens aus den Jahren 1500–1700.* Berlin, 1892.
P. WAGNER : *Das Madrigal und Palestrina. V.M.W.* viii. 423, 1892.

FRANCE

In the 16th century it is difficult to draw a clear distinction between the French and Netherlandish composers. A number of Josquin's pupils were connected with the French court in the days of Francis I. and Henri II.; several of them are mentioned by Rabelais and other contemporary men of letters. A collection of chansons by various composers, of whom Claude de Sermisy and Jannequin are the best known, was published by Attaingnant in Paris in 1529. This was followed by a number of other collections, in which a definitely French style soon makes its appearance. The general technique is more or less that which we have seen in the works of Josquin and Arcadelt, but the characteristic rhythms of French poetry make themselves clearly felt. The French temperament reveals itself here as in the 17th century; instead of the outspoken passion of the Italians, which was often uncongenial to French taste, we find a more delicate sentimentality and a lighter handling of the frivolous aspects of love. Clement Marot was a favourite poet for musical setting. Jannequin appears to have been the creator of the descriptive style with his 'Bataile de Marignan' and 'Les Cris des oiseaux,' which even to-day sound extraordinarily vivid. Descriptive madrigals of this type were also composed by Nicholas Gombert and Guillaume Costeley. The style was not confined to France; street cries and cuckoo songs are to be found in Germany and England as well; but Jannequin is the most elaborate of the descriptive composers.

The French never pursued the Italian ideals of madrigal-writing as exhibited in Marenzio and Monteverdi. In the second half of the 16th century the French composers came under the literary influences of Ronsard and the Pléiade. Ronsard, in spite of his deafness, was devoted to music; one of his first biographers tells us that he held the view 'que sans la Musique la Poësie était presque sans grâce.' Jannequin, Goudimel, Certon and eventually Orlando Lasso set his poems to music. The *vers mesurés* (quantitative verses) of Jean Antoine de Baïf were set by Claude le Jeune, whose collection entitled 'Printemps' is dedicated to King James I. of England, and also by Jacques Mauduit, who lived on into the 17th century and contributed to the new ideals of dramatic music. These settings of Ronsard and Baïf are almost entirely homophonic, though composed for four voices. Goudimel makes more use of counterpoint, but the general impression of the musical settings of Ronsard and his friends is frigid and formal.

The French chanson of the 16th century has a further historical importance in view of its connection with the Huguenot Psalter, for Goudimel's settings of the metrical versions of the Psalms made by Marot and Beza are clearly derived from the style of secular songs.

BIBLIOGRAPHY

R. BRANCOUR: *Les Maitres musiciens de la Renaissance Française. S.I.M.G.* viii. 115.
M. BRENET: *Musique et musiciens de la vieille France,* 1911.
O. CHILESOTTI: *Les Maitres musiciens de la Renaissance Française. R.M.I.* vii. 482 and 730.
J. COMBARIEU: *Histoire de la musique,* vol. 1, 1913.
H. KLING: *Les Compositeurs de la musique du psautier Huguenot. R.M.I.* vi 496.
L. LALOY: *La Chanson française au XVIe siècle. Revue musicale,* 1901.
J. TIERSOT: *Ronsard et la musique de son temps. S.I.M.G.* iv. 70.

GERMANY

The 'Lochamer Liederbuch' (1460) and other manuscript collections of the same date contain secular polyphonic music by Dufay, Busnois and other Netherlanders, but also an important quantity of similar songs by German composers, who exhibit considerable skill in counterpoint. Most of these songs are folk-songs sung by a tenor and accompanied by instruments. The first German composer of distinction who composed original four-part songs for voices was Heinrich Finck (1445-1527); a collection was printed at Nürnberg in 1536. Like most of the leading German composers of his day he was attached to the court of the Emperor Maximilian, which resided chiefly at Innsbruck, Augsburg, Constance and Vienna. To this group belong Paul Hofhaimer (1459–1537), Heinrich Isaac (1450?–1517), known as Arrigo tedesco, but of Flemish origin, and Ludwig Senfl (1490–1550?), a Swiss. Isaac spent a considerable time at the court of Lorenzo il Magnifico at Florence, and composed French and Italian songs as well as German. His work shows the influence of the 'Canti carnascialeschi' and the frottole. Otto Kade says of these three that Hofhaimer is eminently a harmonist, Isaac a melodist and Senfl a contrapuntist. The German 'Carmina,' as they were generally called, show the influence of German folk-song and German poetry in their style, which is much heavier than that of the Italians—one might almost call it pedestrian. Another characteristic form of German vocal music was the 'Quodlibet,' in which each voice entered with a different folk-tune; these show considerable contrapuntal ingenuity, but the original melodies are of necessity much distorted. Towards the middle of the 16th century the German courts employed a large number of Netherlanders and Italians, to the detriment of the native German composers, who could seldom hope for anything better than municipal appointments. The foreigners seem, however, to have done their best to adapt themselves to German life. Matthäus Le Maistre, a Fleming, and his successor Antonio Scandello from Bergamo, both Kapellmeister at the court of Dresden, even became Protestants and composed Lutheran church music. Both of them wrote secular songs for four or five voices to German words, mostly of a convivial type, in the manner of the villanelle. With these may be associated Orlando Lasso during his residence at Munich; he, too, although a Catholic, set words of Luther himself and wrote characteristically German drinking songs. Regnart, another Netherlander, published three sets of 'kurtzweiligen teutschen Liedern' for three voices in the style of the Neapolitan villanelle, with their typical chains of consecutive fifths. In 1579, the year of Regnart's last collection, Leonhard Lechner, a German, rearranged Regnart's songs for five voices in correct counterpoint. Lechner, who came from Tyrol, was the teacher of Hans Leo Hassler (1564–1612), who is the chief German madrigalist. Hassler spent some fifteen months at Venice, and was the first notable German musician to be educated in Italy. Many of his madrigals are set to Italian words; but the 'Neue teutsche Gesang' of 1596 and the 'Lustgarten' of 1601 have German words written by Hassler himself. Hassler was influenced mainly by the two Gabrielis, from whom he derived his partiality for double chorus in 8 parts, and by Gastoldi; his German madrigals are full of life and feeling, but are mainly homophonic and squarely rhythmical. Like most of the Germans he avoids chromaticism. Johann Staden (1581–1634) is another composer of humorous and popular songs, but his chief work belongs to the style of the 17th century.

As in France, the secular vocal music of Germany is closely related to the Protestant musical movement. Another German product which must be mentioned here was the musical setting of classical Latin poems, chiefly the Odes of Horace. Horace was set to music in Latin by various composers outside Germany; 'Integer vitae' is to be found among the Italian frottole, and Goudimel also set some of the Odes. The earliest German settings are those of Petrus Tritonius of Ingolstadt (1507); there are others by Hofhaimer and Senfl, as well as by many lesser composers. They were written for use in schools, and it was only in Germany that this musical aid to classical education was systematically practised.

BIBLIOGRAPHY

A. EINSTEIN: *Die mehrstimmige weltliche Musik von 1450–1600* in Adler's *Handbuch der Musikgeschichte.*
H. J. MOSER: *Geschichte der deutschen Musik,* Band 1, 1920.

ENGLAND

The records of early English secular music are scanty. 'SUMER IS IOUMEN IN' (13th century) is far in advance of any Continental work of its period, but it is an isolated specimen; nevertheless it may be presumed that in England at any rate other compositions of the same kind were produced in some quantity. Up to the death of Dunstable England took the lead in musical technique; after that the leadership passed to the Netherlanders, and English music is of less importance. A few secular songs for voices by Fayrfax and Cornysshe have been preserved, and the madrigalian period may be said to begin with the collection of secular songs published by Wynkyn de Worde in 1530. Edwards's 'In going to my naked bed,' which is not later than 1564, corresponds in its style to the early madrigals of Arcadelt. There are a few others by Tallis and Tye belonging to this period. The next collection to be printed in England was Thomas Whythorne's 'Songes of three, fower and five voyces' (1571). To judge from the examples quoted by Dr. Fellowes these songs, attractive as they are, are a long way behind the contemporary Italian music in their technique. Dr. Fellowes brings forward evidence to prove that Italian madrigals by Willaert, Verdelot, Lasso, Arcadelt and others, as well as contemporary French chansons, were sung in England as early as 1564. In 1588 Nicholas Yonge published his first volume of 'MUSICA TRANSALPINA,' a collection of Italian madrigals with words translated into English. This seems to have been the stimulus which produced the copious output of madrigals and kindred works by English composers from 1588–1627. But it is evident from Yonge's preface that 'Musica Transalpina' was published later in the year than Byrd's 'Psalmes, Sonets and Songs of Sadnes and Pietie,' also printed in 1588. In the 'Epistle to the Reader' Byrd says,

'If thou delight in Musicke of great compasse, heere are divers songs, which being originally made for Instruments to expresse the harmonie, and one voyce to pronounce the dittie, are now framed in all parts for voyces to sing the same. If thou desire songs of small compasse & fit for the reach of most voyces heere are most in number of that sort.'

On the opposite page is a list of 'these songs which are of the highest compasse.' The collection includes ten Psalms in metrical translations by an unknown author, sixteen 'sonnets and pastorals' of which only two are poems in sonnet-form, and nine 'songs of sadness and piety,' the last two being funeral songs for Sir Philip Sidney. All are for five voices, and it is fairly clear that all of them were originally solo songs with accompaniment for four viols. A large number have one voice marked as 'the first singing part,' which is generally the uppermost voice, sometimes the second and occasionally the third. Even where this direction is not given, the uppermost part can be clearly recognised as 'the first singing part.' It is

distinguished from the accompanying parts by various characteristics. It does not enter until after the other voices, which often have a complete series of imitations on the theme; its successive entries are separated by rests while the other voices continue; its words are as a rule set in a strictly syllabic way, and they are never repeated, whereas in the other parts two or three notes may be given to one syllable, and sentences may be broken up and fragments repeated, in order to fill up the musical phrase, since the accompanying voices have many more notes to sing than the 'first singing part.' There are exceptions to these rules, but they are rare.

In view of what has already been said about the treatment of the madrigal in Italy, this collection of Byrd's seems to point to a very highly developed system of accompanied solo singing in England. These Psalms and songs of Byrd are akin to the frottole in that they are poems in square and simple metres with several stanzas sung to the same music; but their contrapuntal elaboration ranks them with the most accomplished of the Netherlandish madrigals. The Psalms, too, are a good deal more elaborate than Goudimel's, which may possibly have served as a model for them. Byrd's songs are akin further to the songs by various composers written for the plays of the Elizabethan choristers, and they exhibit the same rhythmical ingenuities. This appears to be peculiar to the English composers. Byrd's elaborate cross rhythms and alternations of 3/2 and 6/4 bars are hardly to be paralleled in the Italians, who were either more directly passionate or more directly jovial, and wasted no time on ingenious learning. But with Byrd this ingenious learning is far remote from pedantry, for Byrd's chief characteristic is his exuberance of melody; these English songs are conspicuously more tuneful, both in the 'first singing part' and in the others, than any of the chansons or carmina of Continental composers.

In Byrd's next Set (1589) he approximates more to the true madrigal style of Marenzio in some cases. In others we can still trace his habit of building up on a plain and regular tune, even when this is elaborated near the end with imitations and repetitions. Byrd's music, in spite of its wonderful constructive skill and its unfailing beauty of melody, is not expressive in the Italian manner; its inspiration is purely musical and hardly ever literary.

The next publication was Morley's 'Canzonets to three voyces' (1593). Morley is the most popular, the most attractive and perhaps the most characteristically English of all the English madrigalists. He was strongly influenced by Gastoldi and made the Ballet or *Fa la* as much an English as an Italian form of composition. Morley delighted in cheerful subjects, and his madrigals present many vivid and fascinating pictures of English country life. It is interesting to note that Morley's set of ballets was published by East in two separate editions, both in 1595, one with English words and the other with Italian words which in most cases, if not all, are the original poems of which the English is a translation. Another edition with German words was published at Nürnberg in 1609.

Thomas Weelkes and John Wilbye, unlike Byrd and Morley, were both quite young men in their early twenties when they produced their first Sets of Madrigals, and both of them showed remarkable originality and daring. They adopted the extreme chromatic style of the Italians and rivalled Marenzio and Monteverdi in their power of passionate expression. Like the Italians, they conceived of the body of singers as the instrument of the composer's own thought and feeling; their madrigals are works of art intended for listeners, whereas in the earlier writers it often seems as though they were composed mainly for the pleasure of the singers. Weelkes was not only a master of painful emotion, but also a very picturesque and dramatic writer of descriptive music; in his 'Ayres or Phantasticke Spirites' of 1608 he shows himself a witty satirist and his ballets are fully equal to those of Morley.

Of the later madrigalists the most important are Orlando Gibbons, John Ward and Thomas Tomkins. Gibbons confined himself to madrigals of a serious type such as the well-known 'What is our life?' Ward, who seems to have been an amateur, had no great power of expression, but showed sound musicianship and constructive ability, which gives his madrigals a singular dignity. Tomkins, a pupil of Byrd, invented a happy combination of madrigal and ballet, in which he gave evidence of notable rhythmic originality.

Mention must also be made of Thomas Ravenscroft, whose three collections, 'Pammelia' (1609), 'Deuteromelia' (1609), 'Melismata' (1611), and 'A Brief Discourse of the True (but neglected) Use of Charact'ring the Degrees, by their Perfection, Imperfection and Diminution in Measurable Musicke, against the Common Practise and Custome of these Times' (1614), are of great value for the history of popular English music. They contain a number of tavern songs, rounds, catches, etc., many of which, such as 'Three Blind Mice,' are still familiar to all Englishmen however unskilled in music. In England, as in France, there seems to have been no equivalent of the villanelle in the Neapolitan style, though these were well known to Morley.

England was the only country in which the Italian madrigal became completely naturalised; no other country outside Italy produced madrigals either in such quantity or in so high a standard of quality. Continental writers have sometimes suggested that the English schoo' was no more than a mere imitation of that of Italy; but even in those composers, such as Morley, Weelkes and Wilbye, who came most obviously under Italian influence, a definitely English character is always apparent. The English language imposed its own rhythms on them, and English surroundings affected their style, partly by providing them with singers and audiences whose home was the English country-house instead of the Italian palace, and partly by offering them the sights and sounds of English rural life as appropriate subjects for illustration.

BIBLIOGRAPHY

E. H. Fellowes : *English Madrigal Composers.* Oxford, 1921.
   English Madrigal Verse. Oxford.
E. Walker : *History of Music in England.*
Ch. van den Borren : *The Aesthetic Value of the English Madrigal.*
   Proc. Mus. Ass., 1925–26.

SPAIN

The records of early Spanish music are scanty compared with those of the other countries described above; but the 'caccia' was practised in Catalonia (Spanish *caça*), though chiefly to sacred words. Spain, during the 15th century, kept up a close musical connexion with the Netherlands; Spanish musicians went there to study, and it has recently been proved that Netherlandish and also English musicians went to Spain. Petrucci's 'Harmonice musices odhecaton' (1502) contains four Spanish tunes set in four parts, which seem to be more instrumental than vocal in character. J. B. Trend [1] suggests that the editor of the book, Petrus Castellanus, was a Spaniard. In the earlier part of the 16th century Spain produced a large number of 'villancicos,' which are the Spanish equivalent of the Italian frottole, the chief composer of them being Juan del Enzina (1469–1534). Juan Vasquez (1560) and Diego Garzón are also attractive writers of villancicos. A manuscript collection in the Medinaceli library contains a large number of villancicos and madrigals by Spanish composers, along with sacred works of Gombert, Cipriano de Rore and others. Of the Spaniards, the brothers Pedro and Francisco Guerrero, and Rodrigo Cevallos are the most interesting among the early composers, but they seem to have been more at home in sacred music than in secular. Many of the madrigals and villancicos were afterwards adapted to sacred words in the manner of the Italian laudi spirituali. But the Spaniards were by no means without humour; there is in this collection an anonymous madrigal, rather in the style of Orazio Vecchi, describing a friar who mixes gallantry with religion and is ignominiously ridiculed by his two girl penitents. Comic madrigals were written by Matheo Flecha (1481–1553), whose nephew, also called Matheo Flecha, published a set of Italian madrigals at Venice in 1568. But there seems to

[1] *The Music of Spanish History.*

have been no great interest in madrigals in Spain, as compared with Italy and England; the only collections printed in Spain were those of Vasquez ('Villancicos y canciones,' Seville, 1551, and 1560), Brudieu ('Madrigales,' Barcelona, 1585) and Pedro Vila ('Madrigales,' Barcelona, 1561). In 1585 Joan Brudieu, a Frenchman by birth, but maestro de capilla at Urgell in the Pyrenees, composed a series of madrigals in Catalan for the reception at Barcelona of Charles Emmanuel, Duke of Savoy, who was on his way to Saragossa to marry Doña Catarina de Austria. (Cf. Corteccia's madrigals with instruments described above.)   Victoria wrote no madrigals, and of Morales only two are known. Of the later period the most finished and elaborate madrigals are those of Pedro Ruimonte (Parnaso Españo de Madrigales, Antwerp, 1614), which are worthy to stand by those of Marenzio.

BIBLIOGRAPHY

J. B. TREND: *The Music of Spanish History to 1600.* Oxford, 1925.
Spanish Madrigals, Proc. Mus. Ass., 1925–26.
R. MITJANA: *Estudios sobre algunos músicos españoles del siglo xvi.* Madrid, 1918.

E. J. D.

MADRIGAL SOCIETY. Founded in 1741 by John IMMYNS (*q.v.*), this Society enjoys the distinction of being the oldest musical association in London.

Its first meetings were held at the Twelve Bells in Bride Lane, whence it removed to the Anchor and Crown, Whitefriars, as proved by the earliest minute-book in the Society's library, dated 1744. In 1745 the Society removed to the Founders' Arms, Lothbury, where rules were adopted limiting the number of members to sixteen, with an admission fee of 8s. and a subscription of 3s. per quarter. Having returned for a time to the Twelve Bells, its original home, the Society afterwards migrated to the Queen's Arms, Newgate Street, in 1748, when the rules were revised. One rule enacted 'That all musical performances shall cease at half an hour after ten o'clock, unless some of the members shall be cheerfully incited to sing catches, in which case they shall be indulged half an hour, and no longer.' Numerous fines were imposed for such offences as the retention of books from the Society's library; and any member eating his supper, or a part thereof, during practice time was to forfeit sixpence, to be applied to buying ruled paper. The performance on each night was to be divided into two 'acts,' with an interval of half an hour, and in each act four madrigals were to be sung.

Between 1750 and 1757 additional rules were adopted, by one of which each member, to whose turn it came to serve as President, was bound to present a score and parts of a madrigal ready for performance, or 'to forfeit a penny extraordinary to the plate' every night until he did so. By another rule any gentleman who

had been educated in, or at the time belonged to, any cathedral or choir was to be admitted to visit the Society at his pleasure; and a similar privilege was accorded to any of 'the gentlemen of the Academy of Ancient Music.' Membership was confined to persons belonging to cathedral choirs, or those 'vouched for by two or more members of the Society as being capable of singing their part in concert both in time and in tune'; and others proposed for election were required, by way of probation, to sing between the acts their proper parts in an ancient madrigal for three or four voices, or some two-part song to be sung with double voices.

The Society at this time (1749–50) met every Wednesday evening, and consisted of twenty-one members, who subscribed 4s. 6d. a quarter. According to Sir John Hawkins (who was himself a member),

'most of them were mechanics, some weavers from Spitalfields, others of various trades and occupations, who were well versed in the practice of Psalmody and who, with a little pains and the help of the ordinary solmisation, which many of them were very expert in, became soon able to sing almost at sight a part in an English or even an Italian madrigal.'

At times they took country excursions, and the minutes record that on Whit-Monday, 1751, 'the party proceeded up the river, breakfasting at Wandsor [Wandsworth], dining at Richmond, besides stopping to whet their whistles at Mortlack [Mortlake].' In 1768 the subscription was raised to 8s. a quarter, the number of members being about thirty, and it was agreed to hold an entertainment for their friends once at least every year. In 1769 the Society removed to the Feathers Tavern, Cheapside; in 1775 to the King's Arms, Cornhill; in 1778 they were at the Half Moon, Cheapside, and the London Tavern; in Apr. 1792, at the King's Head in the Poultry; in May 1792, at the Globe, Fleet Street; and in 1795 removed to the Crown and Anchor, when the charge for supper, 'on account of the advance in wine,' was raised to 2s. 6d. for members, 4s. for visitors, and 3s. for professors. Festival dinners were held in 1798, 1802, 1803 and 1809, and were continued at intervals, and in 1876 ladies dined at the festival for the first time. In 1814 the subscription was raised to £3, and in 1816 the charge for supper, including a pint of wine, was fixed at 6s. On Sept. 27, 1821, the supper meeting, after being held for eighty years, gave place to a monthly dinner, held, successively, at the Freemasons' Tavern, Willis's Rooms, and the Holborn Restaurant during the season, which then lasted from Oct. to July, but now numbers six meetings, beginning in Nov. Since 1919 the meetings have been held at Carpenter's Hall.

In 1811 was offered for the first time a prize of a silver cup, value ten guineas,

'for the best madrigal in not less than four nor more than six parts, the upper part or parts to be for one or two treble voices. The character of the composition to be after the manner of the madrigals by Bennet, Wilbye, Morley, Weelkes, Ward, Marenzio, and others, and each part to contain a certain melody either in figure or imitation ; therefore, a melody harmonised will be inadmissible.'

The prize was given to W. Beale's ' Awake, sweet muse.' The earlier members of the Society included :

Immyns, Dr. John Worgan, Sir John Hawkins, Rev. C. Torriano, Jonathan Battishill, E. T. Warren, Dr. Arne and his son Michael, Luffman Atterbury, Theodore Aylward, Joah Bates, Dr. B. Cooke, James Bartleman, J. P. Street, librarian of the Society, R. J. S. Stevens. W Horsley, Spofforth, Robert Cooke, W. Beale, Dr. Callcott, W. Hawes, W. Linley, G. E. Williams, Sir J. L. Rogers, T. Greatorex, J. T. Cooper, Jonathan Nield, Rev. W. J. Hall, P. J. Salomons, Vincent Novello, Thomas Oliphant, J. W. Hobbs, J. Calkin, G. Cooper, James Turle.

Up to 1820 the members presided in rotation, but in that year it was resolved to appoint Sir J. L. Rogers as permanent president. The office has since been filled by various well-known music-lovers and professional musicians, including,

Lord Saltoun, Lord Alverstone, Lord Howard de Walden, Sir E. E. Cooper, Otto Goldschmidt, Sullivan, Sir G. Martin, and Sir F. Bridge.

The conductors or musical directors permanently appointed since W. Hawes, 1809–46, have been : James Turle, 1846–49 ; James King, 1849–54 ; Cipriani Potter, 1855–70 ; Otto Goldschmidt, 1871–77 ; Sir John Stainer, 1878–87 ; Sir J. F. Bridge, 1887–1924 ; and Stanley Roper to the present time. Under the present rules the Society consists of forty members, elected by ballot, the subscription (including dinner fees) being five guineas. From 1881 two prizes, T. Molineux's of £10 and the Society's of £5 were awarded annually until 1889, and triennially from 1891. The office of hon. secretary, held from July 1871 by J. Edward Street, afterwards by his son, Oscar W. Street, is now filled by Stanley Edgar.   c. m., with addns.

MAELZEL, JOHANN NEPOMUK (b. Ratisbon, Aug. 15, 1772 ; d. July 21, 1838), son of an organ-builder, was an inventor, whose fame is preserved by the METRONOME (q.v.) called by his name.

In 1792 he settled in Vienna, and devoted himself to teaching music, and to constructing an automaton instrument of flutes, trumpets, drums, cymbals, triangle, and strings struck by hammers, which played music by Haydn, Mozart and Crescentini, and was sold for 3000 florins. His next machine was the Panharmonicon; like the former, but with clarinets, violins and violoncellos added. It was worked by weights acting on cylinders, and was exhibited in Vienna in 1804. Maelzel then bought Kempelen's Chessplayer ; and took it with the Panharmonicon to Paris. The Chessplayer he afterwards sold to Eugène Beauharnais. He next constructed a Trumpeter, which played the Austrian and French cavalry

marches and signals, with marches and allegros by Weigl, Dussek and Pleyel. In 1808 he was appointed court mechanician, and about that time made some ear trumpets, one of which Beethoven used for years. In 1812 he opened the ' Art Cabinet,' among the attractions of which were the Trumpeter and a new and enlarged Panharmonicon ; and soon afterwards made public a musical chronometer, an improvement of a machine by Stöckel, for which he obtained certificates from Beethoven and other leading musicians.

Maelzel and Beethoven were at this time on very friendly terms. They had arranged to visit London together, and Maelzel had meantime aided the great master in his impecuniosity by urging on him a loan of 50 ducats in gold. In order to add to the attractions of the Panharmonicon, which they proposed to take with them, Maelzel conceived and sketched in detail the design [1] of a piece to commemorate the battle of Vittoria (June 21, 1813), which Beethoven composed for the instrument. While it was being arranged on the barrel, Maelzel further induced him to score it for the orchestra, with the view to obtain funds for the journey ; and it was accordingly scored, and performed at a concert on Dec. 8, 1813, the programme of which consisted of the Symphony No. 7, the marches of Dussek and Pleyel, by the automaton, and the Battle-piece. The concert was repeated on the 12th, and the two yielded a net profit of over 4000 florins. At this point Beethoven took offence at Maelzel's having announced the Battle-piece as his property, broke completely with him, rejected the Trumpeter and his marches, and held a third concert (Jan. 2, 1814) for his own sole benefit. After several weeks of endeavour to arrange matters, Maelzel departed to Munich with his Panharmonicon, including the Battle-piece, and also with a full orchestral score of the same, which he had obtained without Beethoven's concurrence and caused to be performed at Munich. Beethoven on this entered an action against him in the Vienna courts, and it is his memorandum of the grounds of the action, as prepared for his advocate, which is usually entitled his ' deposition.' [2] He further addressed a statement [3] to the musicians of London, entreating them not to countenance or support Maelzel.

The action came to nothing, and Maelzel does not appear to have gone to London. He stopped at Amsterdam, and there got from Winkel, a Dutch mechanic, the idea of employing a new form of pendulum as a METRONOME (q.v.). He soon perfected the instrument, obtained a patent for it, and in 1816 we find him in Paris established as a manufacturer of this metronome, under the style of ' Mälzl et Cie.' A wish

---

[1] Moscheles, note to his *Schindler*, i. 154.
[2] Schindler. Thayer, iii. 465.   [3] Thayer, iii. 467

to repurchase Kempelen's Chessplayer and to push his Metronome took him back to Munich and Vienna in 1817. Beethoven's good word was of more consequence than any one else's, and knowing Maelzel's cleverness, Beethoven's amenability to a good companion, and the fact that the performance on which the lawsuit was grounded having taken place out of Austria, the action could not lie, it need not surprise us to find that the suit was given up, and the costs divided equally. After this Maelzel travelled much, and even reached the United States, where he passed the rest of his life, except a voyage or two to the West Indies, exhibiting the Chessplayer, the Conflagration of Moscow and his other curious inventions.[1] He was found dead in his berth on board the American brig *Otis*. Maelzel was evidently a sharp, shrewd, clever man of business, with a strong propensity to use the ideas of others for his own benefit.

His Metronome was entirely different from the Stöckel-Mälzel 'Chronometer,' and it was upon the latter and not upon the Metronome that Beethoven wrote the catch which is connected with the Allegretto of his Symphony No. 8.   A. W. T.

MÄNNERGESANGVEREIN (Ger.), an association of men formed for the cultivation of singing in parts—tenors and basses. They sprang from the Liedertafeln ; famous examples are those founded by Dr. A. Schmid in Vienna (1845), and by Franz Weber in Cologne. They now flourish and are an important part of the popular musical life in all German-speaking countries. (See LIEDERTAFEL.)   F. G.

MÄNNERGESANGVEREIN ARION, see NEW YORK.

MÄSSIG = suitable. Applied to *tempo* it is the German equivalent of Moderato, used much by Schumann, as in the sixth of the fugues on the name Bach. ' Im mässigen Tempo ' occurs in the fourth figure of his op. 72, ' Sehr mässig ' in the Lager-scene, No. 3 of op. 76. His 'Mässig durchaus energisch,' in the second movement of the Fantasia in C, op. 17, is translated ' Moderato con energia.'   M.

MAESTOSO = ' with majesty,' or in a dignified way. It is used either alone, as a direction of time, in which case it indicates a pace rather slower than andante, or, combined with other indications of tempo, as a guide to the expression. Beethoven uses it frequently in both these ways.   M.

MAESTRO = master. Maestro di cappella is the exact Italian equivalent to the German term Kapellmeister, or conductor.

Maestro dei putti (master of the boys) is an office which was founded in 1538 (not, as is generally supposed, in the Papacy of Julius II., which was much earlier), and which was first

held by Arcadelt. Its duties are to teach singing to the boys of St. Peter's, in Rome, and more or less to superintend the choir arrangements. It thus represents our ' Choirmaster.' (See ARCADELT.)

Maestro al cembalo was an officer at the Opera, next in importance to the conductor, and occasionally taking his place. His duties consisted of superintending the rehearsals of the music, and accompanying at them. This post was held by Handel at Hamburg, when he was quite young (see HANDEL), and afterwards by Mattheson.   M.

MAGADA, or MAGAS (Greek), the semicircular wooden bridge fixed at one or both ends of the monochord. The name was also applied to the movable bridge inserted below the string of the monochord to mark the harmonic intervals (Boethius, iv. 18), and generally to the bridge in stringed instruments (Philostratus, 778). (See MONOCHORD.)   J. F. R. S.

MAGADIS, an ancient Greek instrument, our knowledge of which is almost wholly derived from a passage in the fourteenth book of Athenaeus, in which the scattered references to it in Greek literature are brought together. Athenaeus died in A.D. 194. The instrument had then long been obsolete, and the doubts which existed as to its exact form and structure are no nearer solution at the present day. From the conflicting statements of the authorities quoted, some of whom identify it with the pectis, others with the sambuca and others again with the psaltery, it would seem that the magadis was an instrument of the dulcimer type, provided with a bridge (magas) or bridges so placed that octaves could be played on adjoining strings. It was introduced from the East through the Lydians, and was in use in Greece as early as the 6th century B.C., when Anacreon speaks of playing on a magadis of twenty strings. According to Aristoxenus it was played without a plectrum. The characteristic of the instrument was the production of sounds in octaves, and consequently we find the name also applied to a species of double flute, also said to be of Lydian origin, on which octaves could be played, and a verb magadizein signifying to play in octaves on any instrument (Pseudo-Aristotle, 18).   J. F. R. S.

MAGALHÃES, FILIPPE DE (b. Azeitão, Lisbon, end of 16th cent.), Portuguese composer. After working with Manuel MENDES at Evora, he became choirmaster at the Misericordia at Lisbon, and in 1614 master of the Chapel Royal, Lisbon, under the Spanish King Philip III. His printed works include ' Missarum Liber,' Lisbon, Craesbeck, 1631 (Evora Cathedral) ; ' Cantica B.V.,' Lisbon, Craesbeck, 1636. 'Cantus ecclesiasticus,' Lisbon, 1641, 1642 ; Antwerp, 1691 (B.M.).   J. B. T.

MAGE, PIERRE DU, organist at the Collégiale de Saint-Quentin, 1703–13, was a pupil of

Marchand in Paris. In 1733 he took part in the installation of the great organ at Notre Dame, Paris. His fine 'Livre d'orgue,' which appeared in 1708 and was republished by Guilmant and Pirro, was known by J. S. Bach and his pupils.   F. R^L.

MAGGIELLO (Magiello), Dominico, of Valeggio, near Verona (second half of 16th cent.), composed 2 books of madrigals *a* 5 v. (Venice 1567 and 1568).

MAGGINI, Gio. Paolo (*b.* Brescia, 1581; *d.* there, *c.* 1628), a celebrated Italian violin-maker. According to information culled from the Brescian State Archives, Maggini's family came originally from Botticino, a village in the neighbouring hills of Brescia. His grandfather, Bartolommeo de Maggini, lived and died at Botticino, but after his death his son Zovan or Giovanni, migrated with his wife Giulia, to Brescia, where Paolo, their second son, was born. The Brescian Income Tax papers for 1568 state that Gio. Paolo's elder brother was a shoemaker, but no mention is made of his father following any profession or trade. In all probability he was a retired farmer with private means.

Nothing is known of Gio. Paolo's childhood, or what caused him to adopt the profession of violin-making, but a legal document, signed by him in 1602, proves two things clearly : first, that his signature is that of a person of scanty education, and, secondly, that at the age of 21 he was working in Brescia as an apprentice under Gasparo da Salò. On Jan. 20, 1615, he married Maddalena Anna, daughter of Messer Faust Forrestio, and after his marriage he and his wife settled in a house in the Contrada del Palazzo Vecchio del Podesta. In this home, with the assistance of his apprentice, Jacopo de Lanfranchini, Maggini built up a very successful business in the manufacture of citharas, violoncellos, violas and violins. In 1626 he prospered still more, and acquired a second house and shop in the Contrada delle Bombasaire, whither he removed with his wife and family. He also purchased property in the hills and plains surrounding Brescia, and a residential farm-house and land, which abutted upon the grandfather's old home near the village of Botticino. The date of his death is conjectural. After 1626 the Brescian Income Tax papers cease to mention his name, and in 1632 he was undoubtedly dead, as, in a schedule presented in that year by his son Carlo, he uses the formula ' Filius quondam Johannis Pauli.' Although documentary evidence proves that Maggini's wife died on Nov. 24, 1651, and was buried in the church of St. Agatha, all research for the certificate of her husband's death and burial has been in vain. It is possible that as the town of Brescia was ravaged by an excessively severe plague in 1632, Maggini was one of its victims, and being taken to one of the ' pest-houses ' which were organised for the sick, at the public expense,

died away from home, without any note of his death or burial being made.

As a maker, Maggini's name is associated with many progressive innovations in the construction of the violin, and especially in the method of cutting the wood. In his earliest work these alterations are not discernible, as he was still under the influence of Gasparo da Salò, whose inaccuracy of modelling, rough workmanship, and dark brown varnish he at first copied. But when he once cast aside the methods of his veteran master, and of the old school of viol-makers, Maggini created an era in the history of violin-making, which has deservedly immortalised his name. He was among the first makers who discarded the then customary method of cutting the soft pine-wood used for the bellies of violins in what is termed ' slab fashion,' *i.e.* parallel with the upward growth of the tree, and instead, adopted the practice of using the wood the straight way of the grain, brought about by cutting it wedge-ways out of the tree from the bark inwards to the core. He was almost, if not quite the earliest maker to use corner blocks and linings such as are now employed, and he modulated his thicknesses with far more intention and accuracy than any of his predecessors. Maggini's purfling is beautifully executed. His instruments are mostly ornamentally or double purfled, but there are some violins of his bearing the single line. Three of these, and one viola are known to exist. Many of his violins bear a purfled or painted conventional design upon the back, but as his violin model advanced in originality, so he gradually discarded the customary ornamentations so dear to the viol-makers, probably having discovered that this practice only served to muffle the tone of his instruments. His violins are large in size, and are made of the best materials. The model is quite original, and bears no resemblance to the Amati pattern ; the varnish of his best instruments is orange-yellow, the ff holes are clearly cut, the lower circles, in contradistinction to those of Stradivarius, being always smaller than the upper ones, a feature peculiar to Maggini. The scroll is well cut, but shorter than that of other makers, and for this reason appears to be wider than it really is. The labels are placed close to the centre of his instruments : they are in black Roman type, and, like those of his master da Salò, are undated.

Maggini was not a prolific maker, the result of his life's work, as represented by extant instruments, numbering about fifty violins and under two dozen tenors and violoncellos. For this reason authentic specimens of his work are scarce. Some of his finest fiddles have been in the hands of Ole Bull, Léonard, Vieuxtemps and de Bériot ; the last-named possessed two fine examples, one of which he picked up in an old curiosity shop in Paris for 15 francs. An excellent summary of Maggini's contributions to the development of violins, violas and violon-cellos is given in Lady Huggins's *Gio. Paolo Maggini*, published by the firm of Hill & Sons. No authentic pupils of Maggini have come to light. None of his seven children followed their father's profession; his only surviving son, Carlo Francesco, became a silk merchant, but the Maggini influence can be clearly traced both in the Guarnerius and the 'Long Strad' models. In modern times few makers have been more copied, both honestly and dishonestly. Fine copies were made by Bernard Simon Fendt and Remy (two French makers who settled in London); by Darches, and N. F. Vuillaume in Belgium; by Gand (père), Bernadel, Chanot and Vuillaume in Paris, and at Mirecourt, where it is one of the favourite models.

BIBL.—*Gio Paolo Maggini, his Life and Work*, compiled and edited from material collected and contributed by WILLIAM EBS-WORTH HILL and his sons, WILLIAM, ARTHUR and ALFRED HILL, by MARGARET L. HUGGINS (London, 1892). *The Violin and its Famous Makers and Imitators*, by GEORGE HART (London, 1875). *History of the Violin*, by WILLIAM SANDYS and SIMON ANDREW FORSTER (London, 1864). *Old Violins and their Makers*, JAMES M. FLEMING (London, 1883). *La Lutherie et les luthiers*, A. VIDAL (Paris, 1889). *Le Violon*, A. ROYER (Paris, 1886). *Maggini (Jean Paul), Biog. univ. des musiciens*, F. J. FÉTIS. *Luthomonographie historique et raisonnée*, LE PRINCE N. YOUSOUPOFF (Paris, 1856). *I liutai antichi e moderni*, G. DE PICOLELLIS (Florence, 1885). *I miei violini*, M. VILLA (Savignano, 1888). *Di Giovanni Paolo Maggini celebre liutaio bresciano*, D. ANGELO BERENZI (Brescia, 1890). *La patria di Giovanni Paolo Maggini*, D. ANGELO BERENZI (Cremona, 1891). *Die Violine und ihre Meister*, VON J. V. WASIELEWSKI (Leipzig, 1883).
E. H.-A.

MAGGIORE (Ital.) = 'major.' It is used as a supplementary guide in passages of music where a change is made from the minor to the major mode, generally to the tonic, not the relative major, lest a careless reader should disregard the correction of the minor signature.
M.

MAGIC FLUTE, see ZAUBERFLÖTE.

MAGNARD, LUCIEN DENIS GABRIEL AL-BÉRIC (*b*. Paris, June 9, 1865; killed at Baron, Oise, Sept. 3, 1914), French composer, was the son of Francis Magnard, who was editor of *Le Figaro* from 1879–94.

He studied the piano in his youth, and in 1886 matriculated at the Paris Conservatoire, where his first masters were Dubois (harmony) and Massenet (composition). He left this institution in 1888 and became a pupil of Vincent d'Indy. He was at that period strongly under the influence of Wagner's music. In 1889–90 he wrote his first symphony, and in 1891 completed his first dramatic score, 'Yolande.' This first symphony was performed in 1893 at Angers (no other performance was ever given), and 'Yolande' in 1893 at Brussels. The 'Chant funèbre,' written under the influence of his father's death, was completed in 1895, at a time when he was already planning his lyric drama 'Guercœur,' which was finished in 1901. In 1902 Ysaÿe and Pugno gave the first performance of his violin sonata. At that time Magnard, who was saturnine and distrustful by nature, had already developed a tendency to receive advances with suspicion, and an intense dislike for anything resembling self-advertisement. He became his own publisher, and thereby sacrificed all the aids to diffusion which a competent business organisation may provide. The public, on the other hand, did not prove responsive to his music (except at Nancy, where his friend and colleague, Guy Ropartz, made all his chief works known). The few, often inadequate, performances of his works that took place in Paris (*e.g.* string quartet, 1904; third symphony, 1906; concert performance of one act of 'Guercœur,' 1910; 'Bérénice' at the Opéra-Comique, 1911) did not create a profound impression except among a very small circle. But if his admirers were few, they were enthusiastic; and they never ceased to support his music staunchly. This was the one bright spot in the tragedy of his artistic career. At the outset of the war, when the Germans reached Baron, where he lived, he fired on them from his window; he was killed, and his house burned down. The fire destroyed the only existing copies of his 'Yolande,' of his songs op. 3, of the score two acts of 'Guercœur,' and of a newly completed set of twelve songs.

Magnard's music is austere in character. He did not believe in the possibility of poetic expression in music. Deeply interested in musical architecture, he devoted his utmost attention to form, and aimed at achieving new forms without infringing traditional principles. For colour and ornamentation he cared very little. His harmonic schemes and his scoring are plain and unadorned. Gaston Carraud [1] defines the main idiosyncrasies of his music thus :

' His tendency was to intensify the dramatic element in his instrumental music, and to introduce into dramatic music the logic and restraint of pure symphonic music. He expected from the co-operation of symphony and drama that symphony should govern the flow of dramatic matter, endow that matter with an order, a logic, a rhythm similar to its own. For him, symphony and drama are two parallel things, which, in the course of their evolution, may be brought closer to one another, but never intermingle. Symphonic music will acquire a greater wealth of dramatic significance without ceasing to be self-supporting; and the texture of dramatic music will be improved by the operation of principles which are those of pure music.

' His later works illustrate his progress in that twofold respect: the lyric drama " Bérénice " is an instance of pure, severe classicism; whereas in the violoncello sonata and the fourth symphony the dramatic character is more intense than ever.

' From the interpenetration of drama and music, Magnard expected the long-desired form which would satisfy both senses and mind, æsthetic conceptions and spontaneous emotions. His works are so many steps towards that gradual concourse of two modes of expressing the same inner activity.'

Magnard's works remain untried and practically unknown outside France. Even in France there has been no adjustment so far between the high praise of his admirers and the unqualified detractions of a limited number of writers. But what may be confidently asserted is that his music is worthy of earnest attention. It may never become popular, but it has power

1 *La Vie, l'œuvre et la mort d'Albéric Magnard.* (Paris, 1921.)

and depth, and is remarkable for its impassioned earnestness, stern resolution, gravity, and concentration.   M. D. C.

MAGNIFICAT. The 'Song of the Blessed Virgin Mary' has been used as the Vesper canticle of the Western Church from time immemorial; and the evening office has always been so constructed as to lead up to it as its chief point of interest.

In plain-song services it is sung to the same tones as the psalms, but to a different form, with more elaborate intonations and mediations (see PSALMODY).

After the invention of descant a custom arose of singing Magnificat in alternate verses of plain-song and FAUX BOURDON (*q.v.*). Sometimes the Faux Bourdon was simply a harmonised psalm-tune, with the melody in the tenor, as in the following example of a very beautiful 'Use' which has long been traditional in French cathedrals.

Magnificat, Primi Toni.

Sometimes the plain-song was contrasted with an original Faux Bourdon, written in the required mode, but not, like the former example, on the actual melody of the psalm-tune. Dr. Burney, during his visit to Rome, met with an exceedingly interesting MS. collection of Faux Bourdons of this description, by some of the greatest masters of the 16th century. From his autograph transcription of this volume—now preserved under the name of *Studij di Palestrina*, in the British Museum—we extract the following beautiful example by Giovanni Maria Nanini.[1]

[1] It will be seen that Nanini has ended his chant with the harmony of the dominant, instead of that proper to the final of

Ton. IV.

But the development of the idea did not rest here. It is scarcely possible to name any great church composer who has not illustrated the text of the canticle with original music over and over again.   W. S. R.

For the English treatment of Magnificat see SERVICE.

MAGPIE MADRIGAL SOCIETY, THE. In 1885 and 1886 Alfred Scott Gatty collected a small choir to sing choruses and glees at the concerts given by Helen Countess of Radnor for charitable purposes. These practices proved so popular that in November 1886 a society was founded under the name of 'The Magpie Minstrels,' its object being, to quote the Society's minutes—'to give Concerts for charitable purposes, the nature of which shall be left to the discretion and selection of the Committee.'

Lionel Benson was the conductor, and the numbers which in the first instance were limited to 80, rose by rapid degrees to nearly 200. In 1889 H.R.H. Princess Louise, Duchess of Argyll, became President of the Society. In 1889 the first Invitation Concert was given, and later one Charity Concert and one Invitation Concert were given annually. Over £4500 has been handed over to various Charitable Institutions. At first 'The Magpies' were associated at their concerts with 'The Wandering Minstrels' Amateur Orchestral Society,' also conducted by Lionel Benson. The name of the society was altered from 'The Magpie Minstrels' to 'The Magpie Madrigal Society' in 1896. In order to encourage good vocal part writing 'a cappella' the society, from time to time, gave prizes for competition among the students of the R.C.M. and R.A.M., the prize works being performed at the Invitation Concerts. Many of the best known madrigals have been included in the programmes, but a special feature was the performance of many fine works

the mode. A similar peculiarity is observable in many other Faux Bourdons adapted by the old masters to alternate verses of Canticles and Psalms. The reason of this is self-evident. One or other of the subsidiary cadences of the mode is employed, in order that its true final cadence may be reserved for the conclusion of the antiphon which is to follow. The Sistine *Miserere* may be cited as the exception which proves the rule. It ends with the proper final cadence, because, in the office of *Tenebrae*, it is always sung without an antiphon (see ANTIPHON).

of all schools of the 16th and 17th centuries. Most of them were unearthed and edited by the conductor. Nearly all the unaccompanied choral works of Brahms were performed by the society at one time or another ; and some of the unaccompanied choral works of Peter Cornelius were introduced to the English public for the first time.

Many compositions were specially written for the society by Parry (who was elected President of the Society in 1906), Stanford, C. H. Lloyd, Alan Gray, Henschel, R. Vaughan-Williams, Eaton Faning, Maude V. White, Arthur Somervell and J. Blumenthal. The society came to an end in 1911. See *The Magpie Madrigal Society*, 1886–1911 (Chiswick Press, 1911), a privately printed souvenir giving a complete list of concert programmes and other information.   S. H. W.

MAGYAR [1] (Hungarian) MUSIC. ' The so-called Hungarian style of music,' says the writer of two excellent articles on this subject in the *Monthly Musical Record* for Feb. and Mar. 1877,

' as it has come to be recognised, cannot by any means be regarded as indigenous, but may most properly be briefly defined as the product of a commixture of several races. More than one-fourth of the population of Hungary proper (*i.e.* Transleithan Hungary, as it has come to be called since its union with the Austrian empire in 1869) consists of Magyars, the descendants of the ancient Scythians of the Tartar-Mongolian stock, who, after wandering from the Ural mountains to the Caspian Sea, and thence to Kiev, established themselves in Hungary in the 9th century. The remainder of the population is made up of Slavs, Germans, Wallachians, Jews and Gipsies. Of this mixed population, the Magyars, as the dominant lords of the soil, and the Gipsies, as the privileged musicians of the country, are in the main to be regarded as the joint originators of the national style.'

The union of these two latter races resulted in the combination of their musical characteristics. That of the Magyar music is the peculiarity of its rhythms, and that of the Gipsy music is the presence of turns, embellishments, and ' gracenotes ' added to and built upon the melody, and eventually becoming a most important feature in it.[2]

This latter peculiarity, together with the scale which is characteristic of the music of Hungary in common with many other nations of Eastern Europe—a scale with two superfluous seconds, or the harmonic minor with a sharp fourth—

seem to indicate an Asiatic origin. (The ordinary European scales are also in use.) These two chief characteristics will be examined in order.

(1) The rhythms, of Magyar origin.—The great distinctive feature of the bar-rhythms is *syncopation*, generally consisting of the accentuation of the second quaver in the bar of 2–4

1 For the true Hungarian folk-song see the article SONG.
2 See an essay by Carl Engel on *The Music of the Gipsies, Mus. T.,* 1880, pp. 219, 274, 332, 389.

time (the rhythm known as *alla zoppa*, ' in a limping way '), but sometimes extending over larger spaces, as in No. 2 of the ' Ungarische Tänze ' of Brahms, bars 1–2, 5–6, etc., where the syncopation extends over two bars. Even where the melody is without syncopation, the accompaniment almost always has it. The phrase-rhythms are not confined to strains of 4 and 8 bars, but phrases of 3, 5, 6, 7, and 8 bars are not unfrequently to be met with. As examples of 3- and 6-bar rhythms may be cited the third and first of Brahms's ' Ungarische Tänze,' and of 7-bar rhythm, the first part of the following melody :

3–4 time, and consequently 6–8, is almost unknown in genuine Magyar music, although some modern Hungarian composers have introduced it in slow movements. The following very fine ' Hallgató ' is referred to triple time by the best authorities ; it is a ' Lassú ' or slow movement, but is not intended for the dance—

In the ' Lassú ' the actual value of the notes depends far more upon the accentuation of the words sung, than is the case in the quicker movements. A very beautiful rhythm of seven in a bar (written, for greater clearness, as a bar of 3-4 followed by a bar of common time) occurs in the ' Hungarian Song ' on which Brahms has written variations, op. 21, No. 2.

(2) The turns and embellishments added to the melody, of Gipsy, and hence Oriental, origin.—This peculiarity has been observed by travellers in India, who say that in the performance of the natives any embellishments and ' fioriture ' are permitted to be introduced at the will of the performer, provided only that the time of the melody remains intact. The following is a list of the most characteristic turns and ' gracenotes ' used in this music :

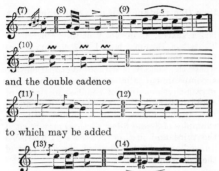

and the double cadence

to which may be added

But the importance of ' Hungarian ' music lies not so much in its intrinsic beauty or interest, as in the use made of it by the classical masters, and the influence which it exercises on their works. The first composer of note who embodies its peculiarities is Haydn. The most obvious instance of course is the well-known ' Rondo all' Ongarese,' or ' Gipsy Rondo,' in the Trio No. 1 in G major ; but there are many passages in his works which show that the years during which he held the post of conductor of Prince Esterhazy's private (and almost entirely Hungarian) band, were not without their effect. Instances of this may be found in many of the ' Salomon symphonies ' (the symphony in B♭, No. 9), etc. (see further, *A Croatian Composer*, by W. H. Hadow, 1897). The composer who has made the greatest use of ' Hungarian ' characteristics is Schubert. Constantly throughout his works we come upon a peculiarity which at once tells us of its nationality. The C major symphony (No. 9) for instance, the A minor string quartet, and the fantasia in C major, op. 15, are full of ' Hungarian' feeling and character, while almost all the peculiarities of the style are present in the splendid ' Divertissement à la hongroise ' (op. 54).

It is enough to cite the names of Liszt, Brahms and Joachim, to bring to the mind of every reader the use made by each of them of ' Hungarian' forms and themes. We may think it only natural that the first and the last of these should, being natives of Hungary, have a natural love for their national music, as we see in the 'Legend of St. Elizabeth,' the symphonic poem ' Hungaria,' the fourteen ' Rhapsodies hongroises,' by Liszt, and the noble Hungarian violin concerto of Joachim. In the case of Brahms, however, there is no national prejudice to which the partiality for the Hungarian element might be ascribed, and yet here we meet with many Magyar characteristics, not only in the ' Ungarische Tänze,' which are nothing more than transcriptions for the piano of the wild performance of the Hungarian bands (according to the best authorities on this subject), but also in the sextets for strings, the G

minor quartet for pianoforte and strings, the pianoforte variations, etc.

The following are some of the most important Magyar forms of composition :

DANCES.—The Csárdás (the name derived from Csárda, an inn on the Puszta (plain), where this dance was first performed). It was introduced into Hungary from Bohemia by Csermák, and was very quickly adopted as a national dance. Every Csárdás consists of two movements,—a ' Lassú,' or slow movement, andante maestoso and a ' Friss,' or ' quickstep,' allegro vivace. These two alternate at the will of the dancers, a sign being given to the musicians when a change is wished.

The ' Kör-táncz,' or Society-Dance, of which a part consists of a *Toborzó*, or Recruiting dance. A great number of these were arranged or composed by Lavotta.

The ' Kanász-táncz,' or Swineherd's Dance, is danced by the lower classes only.

OPERAS.—Among national Magyar operas— *i.e.* operas of which the libretti are founded on national historic events, and the music is characterised by Magyar rhythms, etc.—may be mentioned ' Hunyady László,' ' Báthori Maria,' ' Bánk Bán,' and ' Brankovics,' by Franz Erkel, and the comic opera ' Ilka,' by Doppler. Besides these two composers, the names of Mocsonyi, Császár, Fáy and Bartha, may be given as examples of operatic writers.

SONGS.—Many collections of Népdal, or popular songs, have been published. The best collection is that of Gyula Káldy, containing songs of the first part of the 19th century ; the seven volumes of Bartalus, and the collection made in the middle of the 18th century by Adám Horváth, are of value. Panna Czinka's collection of gipsy melodies may also be mentioned. One tune, ' Repülj Fecském,' has been made widely known by Remenyi's adaptation of it for the violin.

The famous national tune, the ' Rákoczy March,' was, in its original form, a lament for the hero Rákoczy, played on the tárogató—an instrument resembling a cor anglais—about the end of the 18th century. It was arranged as a march early in the 19th century by Scholl, the conductor of a military band at Nagyvárad, and was heard in this form by Berlioz, who introduced it into his ' Damnation de Faust,' with the result that it made a furore all over Europe.

Many of the best of the national songs of Hungary have become widely popular in England since the publication of F. Korbay's admirable arrangement of them with English words.

That the Magyars know how to value their own national music may be shown by the establishment at Budapest of a National Conservatorium, and of the Royal Academy of Music, of which Liszt was the first Director ; there are two national theatres, one for opera and the other for drama, besides the ' Népszinház,' or People's Theatre. The interest in folk-song has borne excellent fruit in Hungary, where phonographic records have been made of many thousands of traditional tunes, and preserved in the National Museum at Budapest.

The chief musical periodical of Hungary is the *Zenevilág*, edited and carried on by Pongrác Kacsoh. (Information from Arthur Diósy, Béla Bartók, etc.)   M.

MAHILLON, a Belgian family rendered famous by (1) CHARLES MAHILLON (*b.* 1813; *d.* 1887), who founded in Brussels (1836) the firm of wind instrument-makers called by his name. Three of his sons entered the business.

Of them, (2) VICTOR (*b.* Brussels, Mar. 10, 1841 ; *d.* St. Jean, Cap-Ferrat, June 17, 1924) is of outstanding importance as a writer on acoustics and musical instruments, and the honorary and zealous custodian of the museum of the Brussels Conservatoire.

After studying music under some of the best professors there, he applied himself to the practical study of wind-instrument manufacture, and was taken into his father's business in 1865. He started a musical journal, *L'Écho musical*, in 1869, and continued it until 1886, when his time became too much occupied to attend to its direction. In 1876 he became the honorary curator of the museum of the Conservatoire, which, begun with Fétis's collection of 78 instruments, was, through his special knowledge and untiring energy, increased (1888) to upwards of 1500 ! An important contribution to it, of Indian instruments, has been a division of the fine collection of the Rajah Sir Sourindro Mohun Tagore between the Brussels Conservatoire and the R.C.M., London. Victor Mahillon published two very important works, besides three synoptical tables of harmony, voices and instruments. The first is *Les Éléments d'acoustique musicale et instrumentale*, an octavo volume published in 1874, which gained for him at Paris in 1878 the distinction of a silver medal. The other is the catalogue of the Conservatoire, which appeared in volumes annually from 1877, and is of the highest interest. As well as these noteworthy works he contributed to the ninth edition of the *Encyclopædia Britannica* several historical and technical articles of great value upon wind instruments, both wood and brass. As soon as Mahillon could introduce a workshop into the Conservatoire he did so, and he had reproductions made of many rare instruments which, through their antiquity or the neglect of former owners, had become too much deteriorated for purposes of study. Among these reproductions the Roman LITUUS and BUCCINA in the Music Loan Collection at Kensington, in 1885, will be remembered as prominent objects of interest in the fine selec-

tion contributed under Mahillon's auspices by the Brussels Conservatoire. He has reproduced from authentic sources the complete families of wind instruments that were in use in the 16th and 17th centuries.

Victor Mahillon's services to the Inventions Exhibition of 1885, in the above-named contribution of instruments to the Loan Collection, and the historical concerts under his direction performed by professors and students of the Brussels Conservatoire, at which several rare instruments were actually played upon in contemporary compositions, were so highly appreciated by the Executive Council of that Exhibition that a gold medal was awarded to him.   A. J. H.

BIBL.—*Bulletin de la Société Union Musicologique*, 1924, ii. E. CLOSSON, *Victor Mahillon.*

MAHLER, GUSTAV (*b.* Kalischt, July 7, 1860 ; *d.* Vienna, May 18, 1911), symphonic composer and conductor. As a composer he took the symphonic form and, with a seldom restrained impetuosity, enlarged and inflated it until it had lost all the features of balance and form which are generally taken to be its characteristics, and became something which though still structurally sound and self-sufficient yet differed in feeling and idea from the classical model. As a conductor and as a producer of opera he always worked at high tension and with a meticulous attention to detail which did much to raise the standard of performance both on the concert platform and the operatic stage.

Mahler was born at Kalischt in Czecho-Slovakia (at that time Bohemia), of Jewish parents, the second of a family of twelve. From 1869–75 he went to the grammar-school at Iglau, the neighbouring large town. From there he was sent to Vienna, where he studied in the Conservatoire until 1878, in which year he met Anton Bruckner, an occurrence which made a great impression on the younger man. Hugo Wolf had entered the Conservatoire in the same year as Mahler, but was not able for long to submit to its discipline. Mahler, however, prospered under such teachers as Julius Epstein for piano, Robert Fuchs for harmony (Hellmesberger is said to have excused him from counterpoint owing to his exceptional gifts of composition, a freedom which Mahler later regretted), and Theodor Krenn for composition. By 1877 he had started on a course of history, philosophy and the history of music at the University of Vienna, but in 1879 he gave up the course. In 1880 he left Vienna and took up the post of Kapellmeister during the summer season at Hall in Austria. This year saw the completion of his first mature composition, ' Das klagende Lied.'

From then onwards Mahler worked unremittingly as opera conductor in different towns in Austria and Germany, gradually making his way from post to post until he reached the summit of the profession. In 1881 he was Kapellmeister at Laibach, and in 1882 at Olmütz. In 1883 he was back again in Vienna, this time with a small appointment, chorus-master of the Italian opera at the Carltheater, and it was in this year that he made a pilgrimage to Bayreuth and was deeply moved on hearing 'Parsifal.' In 1883 he finished the 'Lieder eines fahrenden Gesellen' and took up a fresh post, the most important and extended hitherto, that of Kapellmeister at Cassel. He stayed at this work for two years and conducted operas of all styles. His letters from this time show him dissatisfied with his situation. He was already beginning to find a second-rate position irksome.

In 1885 he went to fill a post at Prague similar to that which he had previously held at Olmütz. Anton Seidl was first Kapellmeister in Prague, but soon went on tour to America, leaving Mahler virtually in charge. At last things began to fall out for him as he had wished. His performance of Beethoven's 9th Symphony awakened enthusiasm, and to a great extent he was able to have his own way with productions of Mozart and Wagner. In 1886 he went, again as second Kapellmeister, to Leipzig, remaining in the post for two years and increasing his knowledge of opera scores and his capabilities as producer whenever the chance offered. Here his chief was Arthur Nikisch.

In 1888 he was given his first appointment as director, this time at Budapest, where he found affairs in a chaotic state with the new Intendant, von Beniczky, struggling to keep the balance between the old school of opera-goers who preferred Rossini and Meyerbeer and the new Magyar element which clamoured for national opera. Mahler signed a contract for ten years and started with the utterance 'I will work with enthusiasm.' But within two years he gave up the post and left Budapest disillusioned. While there he had managed to produce 'Don Giovanni' with such vitality that Brahms ejaculated 'famos' and 'grossartig' and called the young conductor a 'devil of a fellow.' In 1889 'Rheingold' and 'Die Walküre' were produced in Hungarian.

From 1891–97 he filled the post of first Kapellmeister in the municipal theatre at Hamburg. It was a step backward from his former directorship, but for all that these years in Hamburg were the most enjoyable of his life as a conductor of opera, and he was able to find real quiet, to give himself up to composition and to the comparatively unhindered production of opera. In 1892 he visited London and conducted performances of German opera, with a contingent from Hamburg, in Augustus Harris's season at Drury Lane. It was during these years that his second and third symphonies were finished. In 1895 he became a Roman Catholic.

In 1897 he was given the appointment of Kapellmeister at the Hofoper (now Staatsoper) in VIENNA (q.v.). The post came to him largely through the strong recommendation of Brahms. Shortly before this Mahler had visited Brahms at Ischl, where he lay dying, and it is possible that the elder man remembered the performance of 'Don Giovanni,' which had so stirred him at Budapest. It was not long after Mahler's return to Vienna that his duties were enlarged, and he was given the title of Artistic Director and placed at the real head of affairs. This had a liberating influence on his work, and enabled him to bring about the reforms which he at once started upon. During the ten years that he spent in this post he got through a mass of production of opera, wiped out the debt that had been crippling the Hofoper, and gathered about him not only a cultured and enthusiastic audience but a strong artistic following. There was nothing that he did not look into. Every detail of production as well as of stage deportment and musical phrasing he considered to be within his province and worthy of his close attention. And all this immense zeal was expended for the sake of the work. For himself he cared nothing, except in so far as he was a chosen instrument for the doctrines of faultless opera-production. But he lacked a sense of tactful management, and as fast as he made friends who were uplifted by his energy and by the largeness of his vision, he made enemies who could not brook the methods he employed of riding rough-shod over the feelings of all who had the misfortune to get in his way. And so the time came when affairs reached such a pass that it was borne in upon him that the only hope of the Hofoper pulling together was for him to depart and leave for his successor the possible continuation of his work. This he did.

The rest of his life was spent in a strenuous effort to amass, as swiftly as possible, a fortune large enough to ensure for himself a period of rest, and for his wife, Alma Maria Schindler, whom he had married in 1902, and his children a competency against the future. With this in view he journeyed to America as soon as his duties in Vienna were at an end in 1907. In the previous year he had visited that country, and now returned there to obtain a great success as conductor of the Philharmonic Society of New York. (See NEW YORK.) In 1908 he came again to America to fill this post. In this year also he conducted some memorable opera performances of Beethoven, Wagner and Mozart at the Metropolitan Opera House in New York, and gave there the first American performances of 'The Bartered Bride' and of 'Pique Dame.' In 1910 he was once more in America. But this time he returned to Europe broken in health, and after a few concerts of his own works in Munich, Paris and Amsterdam (the last named, both then and since, the centre of the Mahler cult and the home of the most complete performances of his works under the guidance of his friend Willem Mengelberg), he returned to Austria and died in his 51st year.

SYMPHONIC COMPOSITIONS. — The symphonies of Mahler trace descent from Beethoven through Bruckner. From Brahms he got little, from Wagner much. It is worthy of note that this man, who had been so identified with the opera and had acquired such a sound technique in its production, should never, but for such early discarded attempts as ' Die Argonauten ' and ' Der Herzog von Schwabe,' have made one of his own. It is probable that the looseness of structure and emotionalism which marks his works and increases with each fresh composition up to and including the 8th symphony may be put down to the influences which came to him from his very close connexion with the operatic stage, and a reason for the excellence of his two last completed works, the ' Lied von der Erde ' and the 9th symphony, may well be found in the fact that by the time he wrote them he had given up for good his activities in opera.

Mahler gradually developed from an artist mainly interested in the manifestations of nature (the 1st, 2nd, 3rd and 4th symphonies), through a period when vaster problems attracted him ; the soul of man, its relation to the world of nature which had held him in earlier years, its battle with circumstance (the 5th, 6th and 7th symphonies). In the last two works he had reached a period of resignation (' Das Lied von der Erde ' and the 9th symphony). In each section one work may be discussed as a type.

The 2nd symphony is a good example of all Mahler's work, being lengthy, scored nearly always heavily for a large orchestra, restless and stormy in places, monumentally exalted in others. Van Wessem likens the first movement to a sequence of frescoes before which we quickly pass. The second movement is a light dance, a rather cultured *Ländler*, with a contrasted middle section. The third shows Mahler's habit of using up old material in his symphonies, the song ' Des Antonius von Padua Fischpredigt ' (' Des Knaben Wunderhorn ') being incorporated. The fourth is remarkable for the use of a contralto voice which sings some lines from the Wunderhorn, a beautiful calm preparation for the brilliant last movement which ends with orchestra and large chorus united on the word ' Auferstehen.'

The 5th symphony may be taken as typical of Mahler's second period. The change in the composer's mental outlook which had taken place since the earlier works can here be seen in its full effect. This symphony is disjointed in form and unsettled in matter. The orchestra used is not so large as that of the 2nd symphony, but the demands made on it are greater. The work is in three large parts. The first is subdivided into two movements, the first of which is the exposition, the second the working-out and restatement of the various subjects. The second part is a scherzo and the third a rondo of huge proportions, preceded by a short adagietto which points the way to the slow movement of the 9th symphony.

This 9th symphony, for orchestra alone, is characteristic of the comparative spiritual calm which Mahler reached in his later years. The orchestra used is, as ever, a large one, but the manner of its use is more personal, the individualities of each instrument receive more careful attention than hitherto. There are some moments of really delicate scoring. The thought, too, is clearer, and directed with more certainty. The slow movement which ends the work, written with great breadth and a fine command of the strings, reaches a plane which is surely the highest that Mahler ever attained to.

In a different category from the rest of his work, the ' Lied von der Erde ' and the 8th symphony stand apart. The 8th symphony is set for a very large orchestra, two-part chorus, eight solo voices and boys' chorus. The work is in two parts. The words of the first part are those of the Latin hymn of Hrabanus Maurus, ' Veni, Creator Spiritus.' Those of the second are taken from the end of the second part of Goethe's ' Faust.' Between the two sets of words a certain affinity exists in the longing of the soul for the ' Creator Spiritus' and in Faust's yearning towards the ' Höchste Herrscherin der Welt,' and this linking of the two sections at certain well-chosen moments is strengthened by the use of themes in the second part which had previously served in the first part. Technically there is nothing new to note in the work. Apart from a tendency to use the chorus at places in an orchestral manner, the choral writing does not add anything to the technical invention of Mahler's contemporaries.

The ' Lied von der Erde ' dates from the next year to that of the 8th symphony. Six poems from the *Chinesische Flöte* of Hans Bethge are set for voice (3 for tenor, 3 for alto or baritone) and full orchestra with as nice a sensibility of the underlying philosophy of the lines as ever Mahler showed. The change from the blustering of the 8th symphony to the fine perceptions of this set of songs is noteworthy. The scoring has often an almost Latin delicacy. Mahler's position as a composer will rest more certainly on these songs and on the 9th symphony than on all the remainder of his work, even including the 8th symphony.

PUBLISHED WORKS

1880. 'Das klagende Lied.'
1882. Songs. 'Lieder und Gesange aus der Jugendzeit.'
1883. Songs with orchestra. 'Lieder eines fahrenden Gesellen.'
1887 Weber's unfinished opera, 'Die drei Pintos,' edited and completed.
1888. 1st Symphony (D major).
     First set of 'Knaben Wunderhorn' songs.
1894. 2nd Symphony (C minor).
1895. 3rd Symphony (G major).
1900. 4th Symphony (G major).
1902. Songs.
     'Ich atmet' einen linden Duft' (Ruckert).
     'Liebst du um Schönheit' (Ruckert).
     'Blicke mir nicht in die Lieder' (Ruckert).
     'Ich bin der Welt abhanden gekommen' (Ruckert).
     'Um Mitternacht' (Ruckert).
   'Kindertotenlieder,' 5 songs to words by Ruckert.
   5th Symphony (C minor).
1904. 6th Symphony (A minor).
1905. 7th Symphony.
1907. 8th Symphony (E major).
1908. 'Das Lied von der Erde.'
1909. 9th Symphony.

UNPUBLISHED WORKS

Two early operas :
   'Die Argonauten.'
   'Der Herzog von Schwabe.'
10th Symphony (1910, unfinished).   S. G.

BIBLIOGRAPHY

RICHARD SPECHT : Gustav Mahler (1905 ; enlarged, with 90 illustrations, 1913).
PAUL STEFAN : G. Mahler. Eine Studie über Personlichkeit und Werk.
G. ADLER : Gustav Mahler (Vienna, 1916 ; enlarged edition, 1920).
PAUL BEKKER : G. Mahlers Sinfonien (Berlin, 1921).
ALFRED ROLLER : Die Bildnisse von G. Mahler (1922).
FRITZ EGON PAMER : Die Lieder G. Mahlers (1923).
VON WESSEM : Gustav Mahler (Arnhem, 1920).
R. MENGELBERG : Gustav Mahler (Leipzig, 1923).

MAHOON (MOHOON), JOSEPH, a London harpsichord and spinet maker near the middle of the 18th century. His name is present on the harpsichord figured in Hogarth's Rake's Progress, Plate II. 1735. In Rider's Court Register for 1759 he is entered as 'Joseph Mohoon, harpsichord maker to the king.'   F. K.

MAHU, STEPHAN, a German composer, who flourished in the earlier part of the 16th century, is said to have been a singer in the chapel of the Archduke Ferdinand at Vienna, though this is only a conjecture from the fact of some of his compositions being received into Joanelli's Thesaurus of 1568. His works appeared only in collections. Ambros and others speak highly of a set of Lamentations a 4-6, which appeared in Joanelli, and have since been republished by Commer. Mahu's other works consist chiefly of a few contrapuntal settings a 4 and 5 of German songs, sacred and secular, in Ott, Rhau and Foster's collections. Eitner and Ambros judged his secular songs very favourably. The former [1] describes a setting of 'Ach hilf mich Leid und sehnlich Klag,' a 5, as excellent both in technique and expression. He also gives in shortened notes a characteristic setting of an old Tanzlied in triple time, 'Es ging ein wolbezogner Knecht.' Ott's Liederbuch of 1544, reprinted in 1872, contains four songs by Mahu, three sacred and one secular. From the text of one of the sacred songs, 'Lobt Gott ihr Christen all,' being a fierce diatribe against Roman abuses, as well as from the fact of Mahu having contributed a setting a 5 of Luther's 'Ein feste Burg' to Rhau's Geistliche Gesänge, 1544,

[1] See M. f. M. xxvi. 57.

we may conclude that Mahu was more Lutheran in his sympathies than Roman.   J. R. M.

MAICHELBECK, FRANZ ANTON (b. Reichenau, near Constance, 1702 ; d. June 14, 1750), was sent by some generous patrons to Rome to complete his musical training. He is afterwards described as being professor of the Italian language and praesentiarius of the minster at Freiburg-im-Breisgau. By praesentiarius would appear to be meant a prebendary or beneficed priest on the staff of a collegiate or cathedral church. Fétis took it to mean a 'beadle,' and mistakenly described Maichelbeck as 'bédeau de la cathédrale de Freyberg' ; and unfortunately Eitner, in Q.-L., has adopted Fétis's mistake, though it was corrected, and the word itself sufficiently explained, in an article by E. von Werra in Haberl's Kirchenmusikalisches Jahrbuch, 1897, pp. 28-30. The whole staff of a collegiate church was denominated praesentia.

Maichelbeck's works are of some importance in the history of clavier-music. He cultivated the lighter Italian homophonic style, which influenced the earlier development of the clavier sonata. His opus 1 is entitled

'Die auf dem Clavier spielende und das Gehör vergnügende Cäcilia, das ist viii Sonaten, so nach der jetzigen welschen Art, Regel- und Gehör-mässig ausgearbeitet' . . . Augsburg, 1736.

These eight sonatas are partly suites, having dance movements intermingled with adagios, allegros, capriccios and toccatas. The whole work shows the study of Italian models.[2] The only other known published work of Maichelbeck is his opus 2 entitled 'Die auf dem Clavier lehrende Cäcilia . . . Augsburg, 1737.' The first two parts of this work are theoretical, but the third part consists of preludes, fugues and versetts on the eight church tones, which, however, are treated not in any proper organ style, but in the lighter and more florid clavier style.   J. R. M.

MAID OF ARTOIS, THE, opera in 3 acts ; words by Bunn, music by Balfe. Produced Drury Lane, May 27, 1836.   G.

MAID OF HONOUR, THE, comic opera in 3 acts ; words by Fitzball, music by Balfe. Produced Drury Lane, Dec. 20, 1847.   G.

MAID OF ORLEANS, see JOAN OF ARC.

MAILLARD, JEAN, a French composer of the earlier part of the 16th century, is said to have been a pupil of Josquin des Prés.

Several masses by him were published separately by Le Roy and Ballard of Paris from 1557-1559, one of which, entitled 'Je suis déshéritée,' has a peculiar history, and is of interest because of its connexion with the work of Palestrina. It was republished by the same French firm, and almost about the same time, as being the work of another French composer, Nicholas de Marle, and there might thus have been considerable doubt as to its authorship, but it was also copied, probably at some earlier date, into

[2] For some illustrative quotations see Seiffert, Geschichte der Claviermusik, Bd. i. pp. 332-4.

the choir-books of the Sistine Chapel at Rome, and there ascribed to Maylard. It thus became known to Palestrina, who adopted the themes of Maillard's Mass for a Mass of his own, which was afterwards published as No. 3 'sine nomine,' of the sixth book of his masses 1592.[1] 'Je suis désheritée' was in fact a popular French song, on which many musicians, including Lassus and Gombert, but especially French writers, composed masses, and this may account for the confusion between Marle and Maillard, as Marle may also have composed a Mass on it which was confused with that of Maillard. The song itself, as set for four voices by Pierre Cadéac, may be seen in Eitner's Selection of Chansons, 1899, No. 11 ; and a comparison of this with Palestrina's Mass will show that the tune, as given by Cadéac partly in the tenor, but even more completely in the descant, reappears in all the leading themes of Palestrina's work, and is given complete to start with, in the three divisions of the Kyrie. Palestrina's Mass should thus, equally with that of Maillard, be denominated ' Je suis désheritée,' though Palestrina himself left it without a name, out of deference, no doubt, to the later ecclesiastical scruples against the use of secular names and tunes for works intended for the Church. But there is nothing really secular about the tune, and it is just worth notice that the opening strain of both song and Mass is identical with the opening strain of the oldest known German choral tune, ' Christ ist erstanden.'

Other works by Maillard besides the three Masses, a 4-5, and a Patrem for eight voices, are Magnificats, motets and chansons which appeared in the various collections of the time. Ambros describes his motets as characterised by a noble and expressive melodious elegance, and reckons him generally as one of the better masters of the French School. A chanson by Maillard, which has all this characteristic of melodious elegance, may be seen in Eitner's Selection of Chansons, No. 39.   J. R. M.

MAILLART, LOUIS (called AIMÉ), (b. Paris, Mar. 24, 1817 ; d. Moulins, department of Alliers, May 26, 1871), was a pupil of the Conservatoire, where he studied composition with Halévy and Leborne, and the violin with Guérin. He won the Grand Prix de Rome in 1841, with his ' Lionel Foscari,' and the first of his six operas, ' Gastibelza ' (3 acts), was successfully produced in 1847. His ' Moulin des tilleuls ' was given at the Opéra-Comique in 1849, and ' La Croix de Marie ' in 1852, but the work which most kept his name before the public was ' Les Dragons de Villars,' produced at the Opéra-Comique in Paris in 1856. His later comic operas, ' Les Pêcheurs de Catane ' (1860), and ' Lara ' (1864), were less successful. Maillart also wrote some cantatas, such

as ' La Voie sacrée ' (1859), ' Le 15 août' (1860), etc.   G. F.

MAINZER, JOSEPH, LL.D. (b. Trêves, 1801[2]; d. Manchester, Nov. 10, 1851). His father was a butcher at Trêves. He was educated in the Maîtrise of Trêves Cathedral, learnt to play several instruments, and developed considerable musical gifts, then spent some time in the coal-mines near Saarbruck, with the view of being an engineer, and at length embraced the ecclesiastical profession, was ordained priest in 1826, and afterwards became Abbé. His first practical introduction to music was as singing-master to the seminary at Trêves, for which he published a Singschule or Method (Trêves, 1831). His political tendencies obliged him to leave Germany, and we find him in 1833 at Brussels writing an opera (' Triomphe de la Pologne ') and editing the musical portion of L'Artiste. His next destination, at the end of 1834, was Paris, where he opened workmen's classes for music and singing, joined the staff of the Gazette musicale and wrote the musical feuilletons for the National. Between 1835 and 1841 he published several educational works on music, chiefly for very young beginners, as well as other works, and an opera, ' La Jacquerie,' which was damned on Oct. 10, 1839. He came to England in June 1841, competed for the musical professorship at Edinburgh in 1844, lived in Edinburgh in 1842-47, and finally established himself at Manchester. In February of that year Hullah had started his classes on Wilhem's system, and Mainzer attempted to follow suit in the north, and with considerable success. His Singing for the Million[3] (1842) was at that time well known, and went through many editions. He overworked himself in this cause, and died, much esteemed and regretted. He was buried at Rusholme Road Cemetery, Manchester. A periodical started by him in July 1842, and entitled Mainzer's Musical Times, was the predecessor and basis of the present Musical Times. See the Musical Herald for June 1895, and an extended notice in Chambers's Journal, Feb. 14, 1852.   G.

MAISTRE, MATTHÄUS LE (d. circa 1577), a Flemish musician of the 16th century, supposed to have come originally from Liège, succeeded Johann Walther in 1554 as Kapellmeister to the Saxon court at Dresden. He retired on a pension in 1568. Otto Kade, in his otherwise excellent monograph on this composer (published 1862), made the mistake of identifying him with Matthias Hermann, surnamed Werrecorensis (see WERRECORE), choirmaster at Milan, and so represented Le Maistre as having come from Milan to Dresden ; but the Milan choirmaster has since been proved to be a

---

[1] See Haberl's Preface to vol. xv. of Palestrina's Works, complete edition of Breitkopf & Härtel, also his Catalogue of the Music of the Sistine Chapel, p. 28.

[2] This date is established by the epitaph at Manchester. *Riemann* gives May 7, 1807, as the date of birth.
[3] Fétis amusingly infers from this title that Mainzer expected to number a million pupils.

different person altogether from Le Maistre the Dresden Kapellmeister. Le Maistre's publications are (1) 'Catechesis' (Nuremberg, 1563); this work consists mainly of a few simple, note-for-note settings of the chief parts of the Lutheran Catechism in Latin, the Paternoster for four voices on the plain-song melody, the Creed, and other pieces, for three voices. (2) 'Geistliche und weltliche Gesänge' *a* 4 and 5 (Wittenberg, 1566), seventy sacred songs and twenty-two secular. (3) 'Liber I. sacrarum cantionum' (Dresden, 1570), fifteen Latin Motets *a* 5. (4) 'Deutsche und lateinische geistliche Gesänge' (Dresden, 1577), twenty-four numbers *a* 3. Two motets by Le Maistre were received into the great collection *Thesaurus musicus* (Nuremberg, 1564), one of which *Estote Prudentes* for four voices, has been reprinted by Commer in his *Collectio*, etc., tom. viii. Also a mass *a* 5 was published in 1568. Other masses and officia have remained in MS. Kade's Monograph contains ten of Le Maistre's 'Geistliche Gesänge,' and five 'Weltliche Gesänge,' two of which are Quodlibets, that is, pieces with various texts and melodies combined. Two other pieces are contained in the *Beilagen zu Ambros Geschichte*.   J. R. M.

MAITLAND, see FULLER MAITLAND.

MAÎTRE DE CHAPELLE, LE. Opéracomique in 2 acts, by Ferdinando Paër. Produced Théâtre Feydeau, Paris, Mar. 29, 1821. It was afterwards reduced to one act; in English, Prince of Wales's Theatre, Feb. 16, 1897.

MAÎTRE DE CHAPELLE, see CHAPELLE.

MAÎTRISE, a term formerly applied in France both to the quarters assigned in cathedrals and collegiate churches to the choristers and their master, and to the institution itself, which originally included a complete education, lay and ecclesiastical. These schools turned out many great men, several rising to be bishops and popes; among the latter Pope Urban IV., a cobbler's son, whose early years were passed in the 'Psallette' at Troyes. Some centuries later, when the Maîtrises had undergone great changes, they were still the only establishments in which even secular musicians could obtain their training. From the Maîtrises the Church obtained choristers, organists and maîtres de chapelle, and the world its favourite composers. Here also, although instrumental music was neglected, and dramatic music positively forbidden, the regimental bands found their bassoon-players, and the lyric theatres their 'clavecinistes-accompagnateurs,' violoncellists and singers.

The Maîtrises were real schools of music, the pupils being maintained at the cost of the chapters. Indeed they much resembled the Conservatorios of Italy, both in their mode of administration, and in the course of instruction given. They were not, however, all organised

alike, but varied with local circumstances. Thus in some the boys, the master, and the priests lived in common, in others separately; in some the maintenance of the children was in the hands of the master, in others there was a regular purveyor. But in all, the main end was the study of music. Before the Revolution there were in France 400 Maîtrises and choirs, with as many maîtres de chapelle, maintained either by the chapters of cathedrals and collegiate churches, the curés or the monasteries. Each Maîtrise contained, on an average, from 25 to 30 persons, and the musicians thus diffused throughout the country numbered in all about 10,000, of whom 4000 were pupils or choristers. There was naturally much rivalry among the different establishments, which was of great benefit to music. (Cf. SONG-SCHOOL.)

The Maîtrises, though suppressed in 1791, were afterwards reconstituted, on a different footing. The CONSERVATOIRE DE MUSIQUE (*q.v.*) is now the great nursery of French musicians, but many a church has still its Maîtrise, where the choristers—boys and men —are trained by a maître de chapelle in everything necessary to ensure a good execution of plain-song and sacred music. We have already spoken of Choron's school of music (see CHORON), still in existence as the 'École Niedermeyer.' Niedermeyer and D'Ortigue also founded a periodical called *La Maîtrise*, specially devoted to sacred music. It survived only four years. Besides Gantez's work (*Entretien des musiciens*, Auxerres, 1643, sm. 12mo., very scarce), another book, also published in 1643 by Jean de Bordenave, a Canon of Béarn, *L'Estat des églises collégiales et cathédrales*, contains much information, though impaired by its want of method and arrangement. G. C.

MAJO, GIAN FRANCESCO DI (*b.* Naples, *c.* 1740; *d.* Rome, Jan. 18, 1771), was the son of Giuseppe de Majo (1698–1772), who was maestro di cappella to the King of the Two Sicilies in the early part of the 18th century, and wrote various church and chamber compositions.

The son was a pupil of Padre Martini, and first appeared as an opera composer in 1759, with 'Riccimero' at Naples; this was followed at short intervals by many others, written either by himself alone or in collaboration. 'Cajo Fabricio' was given at Naples in 1760, and the same year saw the production of 'Astrea placata'; in 1761 'L' Almeria' was given at Leghorn; in 1762 'Artaserse'; 'Ipermestra' in 1763; and in 1764 'Alcide negli Orti Esperidi' in Vienna; 'Adriano in Siria' was given in Rome about 1766; 'Ifigenia in Tauride' is of uncertain date; and his last, 'Eumene,' of which he only finished one act, was completed by Insanguine, and produced at Naples in 1771. Among the operas that have music by di Majo in them are 'Agamemnon,'

'Cleofide,' 'Demofoönte,' and 'Ezio.' Two arias by him are quoted in Marx's *Gluck und die Oper*. Cantatas and church music are mentioned in *Q.-L.*   **M.**

MAJOR. (1) When intervals have two forms which are alike consonant or alike dissonant, these are distinguished as major and minor, the former being always a semitone greater than the latter. Thus thirds and sixths have two forms, which are both consonant, and are respectively called major and minor. Seconds, sevenths and ninths have each two forms, which are dissonant, and are similarly distinguished as major and minor.

(2) The major forms of triads are such as contain a major third from the root note, and these are both more harmonious and better defined than the minor triads ; for, in the first place, the major third agrees with the fourth harmonic of the fundamental tone, and, in the second, the combinational tones of the chord for the most part only double notes already existing in the chord ; whereas in the minor triads the minor third does not correspond with any of the really perceptible harmonics of the root note, and the triad cannot in any position be free from false combinational tones. It is mainly for these reasons that the major chord is so often found at the conclusion of a piece of music in a minor mode in the works of the earlier masters, from Josquin des Prés up to Mozart. (See HARMONY; TIERCE DE PICARDIE.)

(3) The most important and best defined scale of modern music is called ' major,' because it has a major third from the tonic in the ascending series ; whence in former times it was common to distinguish the scale or mode by the terms ' greater ' or ' lesser ' third, as, ' in the key of G with the greater third,' where one would now say ' G major.' This major scale is the natural diatonic series of modern music, represented by the series starting from C. It is fundamentally the most perfect for harmonic purposes, as it presents the greatest number of concords, and the larger proportion of these in their most harmonious form ; and it also provides most perfectly and simply the means of making the tonal relationship intelligible, since, as Helmholtz points out, ' the tones [of the scale] are constituents of the compound tone of the tonic, or the fifth above or the fifth below it. By which means all the relations of tones are reduced to the simplest and closest relationship existing in any musical system—that of the fifth.' This scale corresponds to the Greek Lydian and the Ecclesiastical Ionian Mode.

(4) The term ' major ' is also used in a theoretical sense of tones, to distinguish the interval of a tone which has the ratio 9:8 from that which has the ratio 10:9, which is called a minor tone. For example, in the key of C, C—D is a major tone and D—E a minor tone, and the difference between them is a comma.   **C. H. H. P.**

MAJORANO, GAETANO, see CAFFARELLI.

MALAGUEÑAS, see FANDANGO ; SONG, sub-section SPAIN (4).

MALÁT, JAN (*b.* Staré Bydžov, Bohemia, June 16, 1843 ; *d.* Prague, Dec. 2, 1915), collector of folk-songs, composer and pedagogue.

From 1913 Malát was director of the Communal School for girls at Smíchov, a suburb of Prague. He was an enthusiastic collector of the folk-songs of Bohemia, Moravia and Slovakia, and the results of his life-work are published as ' Český národni poklad ' (A Treasury of Czech National Songs) in a series of popular albums (Fr. Urbánek, Prague). A second collection, ' Zlatá pokladnice ' (The Golden Treasury), is less of a household possession. He also harmonised a number of individual songs and transcribed a few in various instrumental arrangements. His original works include Czech Dances (Furiant, Round and ' Obkročák ') for orchestra, and several good partsongs and choruses. His accompaniments to the folk-songs are full and pleasing, but his treatment of the national material is popular rather than scientific.   **R. N.**

MALBECQUE (MALEBEKE), GUILLAUME DE MEDIATORIS, probably so-called from Malbecque in Flanders, a Papal singer, 1431–38 (except May to Aug. 1433). Five songs of his in a collective Codex of the Bodl. Lib. have been republished by Stainer.   **E. v. d. s.**

MALBROOK, a French nursery song of the 18th or 17th centuries. Its connexion with our own Duke of Marlborough as the hero of the words is doubtful.

Upon the birth of one of Marie Antoinette's children, about 1781, a provincial girl named, or nicknamed, Madame Pointrine, sang it to the child as a lullaby. The Queen was immensely taken with the song, and presently all the court were singing it. The tune, as current in England towards the end of the 18th century, is as follows, as printed in Aird's ' Selections of Scotch, English, Irish and Foreign Airs,' vol. iii. [1788].

The French words are a series of couplets beginning :

> Malbrook s'en va-t-en guerre ;
> Mironton, mironton, Mirontaine,
> Malbrook s'en va-t-en guerre
> Ne sait quand reviendra.

The lengthy song goes on to say 'He will return at Easter' or perhaps at 'Trinity.' Malbrook does not return, and the lady mounts her castle and then beholds his page, who tells her that his lord is dead, etc.

The pretty and somewhat melancholy tune took Europe by storm, and numberless songs were set to it. The first English use of the tune the present writer can trace is a song on the defeat of the French and Spanish combined forces in the siege of Gibraltar on Sept. 13, 1782.

The first verse, out of many, runs :

> D'Artois returns from Spain,
> Oh, what a rare campaign (bis).
> We thought that with a look
> He would the place have took ;
> But the thunders of his wrath
> Was not a cracker worth. Etc.

This was published by Preston of London on a half-sheet music page.

About 1790, among other songs, the air was adapted to a lyric, 'The Maid of Primrose Hill.'

There have been many foolish statements made regarding the air. The favourite came from Chateaubriand, who, having heard (or fancied he had heard) the tune sung among the Arabs, assumed it to have been carried to the East by the Crusaders and sung by them before the walls of Jerusalem.

The air is now known in England solely by the convivial song, 'We won't go home till morning,' with the second verse 'For he's a jolly good fellow.'   F. K.

MALCHAIR, JOHN BAPTIST (b. Cologne, 1731 ; d. Oxford, Dec. 12, 1812). The son of a watchmaker, he early came to England and taught music. He had a talent for water-colour painting, and taught drawing in ladies' schools. He settled at Bristol and Hereford, and by his amiable qualities won many friends. He removed to Oxford, where he married. In 1760 he was appointed leader of the Oxford Music Room Band. He painted many interesting views round about Oxford, and made excursions into North Wales. Many of his drawings are in private hands at Oxford.

When William Crotch came as a young organist to Christ Church, Oxford, the two became great friends. Malchair took great pains in helping Crotch to gather materials for his 'Specimens of Various Styles of Music,' which formed the basis of a series of lectures which Crotch gave. (See CROTCH.)

Malchair entered into the musical life of Oxford and was greatly esteemed, though he does not appear to have published any compositions. He was a violinist of considerable ability. In the Bodleian Library there are some notes made by Crotch on his friend's musical life in Oxford. The Folk-Song Society possesses a manuscript book of airs noted by Malchair.   F. K.

MALCOLM, ALEXANDER (b. Edinburgh, 1687), was author of A Treatise of Musick, Speculative, Practical and Historical, 8vo, Edinburgh, 1721 ; second edition, 8vo, London, 1730 ; a well-executed work. An ill-made abridgment by an 'eminent musician' appeared in London, 1776. In 1721 one Mitchell published 'An Od > on the Power of Musick,' dedicated to Malcolm, the greater part of which is prefixed to the two editions of the Treatise.   W. H. H.

His work is the first important treatise on the theory of music issued in Scotland. Prior to it are the few leaves of general instructions in the Aberdeen Cantus (1662, 1666, 1682), and a thin folio volume entitled An Introduction to the Knowledge and Practice of Musick, by A. B., 1717. The copy, probably unique, was sold at the Taphouse sale in 1905, and had bound up with it a contemporary manuscript essay on The Institutions of Musick wherein are sett forth the practicall principles of Musicall Composition. Another manuscript treatise is of the 16th century, and written in the Scottish dialect. It is mentioned by Hawkins and belonged to him ; it is now in the British Museum.

Malcolm's work is in octavo, and the first edition contains 608 pp. with engraved musical examples ; it was issued at 'Edinburgh, printed for the author, 1721.'

Hawkins and later writers speak in the highest terms of its merits. The book was dedicated to the 'directors of the Royal Academy of musick' (i.e. the Italian Opera in London, see HANDEL), who are named individually. It is advertised as just issued, in the Edinburgh Evening Courant of Nov. 6, 1721, and from this advertisement we learn that the author then lived 'in the Cowgate, opposite Burnet's Close.'   F. K.

MALDÉGHEM, ROBERT JULLIEN VAN (b. Deuterghem, Flanders, 1810 ; d. Ixelles, near Brussels, Nov. 13, 1893), organist and composer, is chiefly memorable as the editor of TRÉSOR MUSICAL (q.v.), a collection in 29 volumes of vocal works, sacred and secular, by Flemish composers of the 16th century.

MALDERE, PIERRE VAN, the younger (b. Brussels, May 13, 1724 ; d. there, Nov. 2, 1768), younger brother of Jean Baptiste, a 2nd violinist at the Brussels Opera. Pierre was engaged as 1st violinist in the private music of the Duke of Lorraine who took him to Paris, where his first opera was performed in 1762. He acquired European fame as symphony and chamber music composer and retained his popularity until the arrival of Haydn (Q.-L. ; Riemann).

MALEINGREAU, PAUL DE (b. Trélon et

Thiérache, Nov. 23, 1887), organist and composer. His father was Belgian and his mother
French. Three years later the family removed
to Namur. After some parental opposition
he was allowed to enter the Brussels Conservatoire in 1905, and studied composition
with Edgar Tinel. He devoted himself for
some time to liturgical studies, and was on the
point of accepting a remote organistship when
he was recalled to the Conservatoire to superintend the harmony classes. During the period
of the German occupation he gave many
recitals on private organs, and after the war
continued his work of popularising the best
organ music and reviving forgotten masterpieces. In 1921–22 he gave, in a series of organ
recitals at Brussels, the whole of Bach's works
for that instrument. His compositions are
mostly for organ, and, next to Bach, the
influence most readily discerned in them is
that of César Franck, especially in their
spiritual fervour. Though somewhat aloof
from the contending currents of contemporary
music, he displays some degree of modern
freedom in harmony and in form, combined
with personal inventiveness. In addition to
his compositions he has written some theoretical works.

PIANO

Op. 7. Prelude, Choral and Fugue.
Op. 9. Suite : Toccata-Overture, Allemande, Courante, Sarabande,
        Gigue.
Op. 12. Sonatine.
Op. 17. Les Angelus de printemps (suite pittoresque).
        Sonata for v'cl. and PF.

ORGAN

Op. 10. Opus sacrum (in Nativitate Domini), 7 pieces.
Op. 14. Suite : Prelude, Choral, Pastorale, Toccata.
Op. 18. No. 1, Offrande musicale in C major.
Op. 18. No. 2, Offrande musicale in G major.
Op. 18. No. 3, Toccata.
Op. 19. Symphonie de Noël.
Op. 20. Symphonie de la Passion.
Op. 22. Opus sacrum, (11. In feriis Quadragesima.)
Op. 25. Préludes à l'introit (7 pieces).
        Triptyque pour la Noël.
        20 liturgical pieces.   E. E.

MALEK ADEL, opera in 3 acts ; words by
Count Pepoli, music by Costa. Produced
Théâtre Italien, Paris, Jan. 14, 1837, and in
London, Her Majesty's, May 18, 1837.   G.

MALHERBE, CHARLES THÉODORE (b. Paris,
Apr. 21, 1853 ; d. Cormeil, Eure, Oct. 6, 1911).
On the completion of his literary and legal
studies (having reached the grade of ' licencié ')
he took up music and studied various branches
of composition with Danhauser, Wormser and
Massenet. From 1881 he contributed to
various musical publications : Revue d'art
dramatique ; Le Ménestrel ; Guide musicale ;
Le Monde artiste ; La Revue internationale de
musique, and in 1896 was appointed ' archiviste-
adjoint ' to the Paris Opéra (1895), and in 1898
succeeded Nuitter as archiviste. His private
collection of musical autographs became one of
the richest in the world, after those of the public
libraries of Berlin, Vienna, London and Paris.
He bequeathed them to the library of the Paris
Conservatoire.
The following may be mentioned among

Malherbe's works on music : Notices of ' Esclarmonde ' (1889) and ' Ascanio ' (1890) ; the
Catalogue bibliographique des œuvres de Donizetti (1897). In collaboration with M. A.
Soubies : L'Œuvre dramatique de R. Wagner
(1886) ; Précis de l'histoire de l'Opéra-Comique
(1887 ; pseudonym, B. de Lomague) ; Mélanges
sur Richard Wagner (1892) ; Histoire de la
seconde Salle Favart (two vols., 1892 and 1893,
crowned by the Institut); P. Tchaikovsky (1901);
Le Galliamathias musicum de Mozart (Riemann's
Festschrift, 1909) ; and a biography of Auber
(Musiciens célèbres, 1911). Malherbe edited
with Saint-Saëns the collected edition of
Rameau's works. He composed several opéras-
comiques (' L'Ordonnance,' etc., not published), incidental music for ' Les Yeux clos '
(Odéon, 1896), orchestral and chamber music,
as well as numerous transcriptions.
                                        G. F., with addns.

MALIBRAN, MARIA FELICITA (b. Paris,
Mar. 24, 1808 ; d. Manchester, Sept. 23, 1836),
one of the most distinguished singers of her
time, was the daughter of Manuel GARCIA (q.v.).
When 3 years old she was taken to Italy,
and at the age of 5 played a child's part in
Paër's ' Agnese,' at the ' Fiorentini,' Naples.
So precocious was she that, after a few nights
of this opera, she actually began to sing the
part of ' Agnese ' in the duet of the second
Act, a piece of audacity which was applauded
by the public. Two years later she studied
solfeggi with Panseron, at Naples ; and Hérold
gave her her first instruction on the piano.
In 1816 Garcia took her to Paris with the rest
of his family, and thence to London in the
autumn of 1817. Already speaking fluently
Spanish, Italian and French, Maria picked up
a tolerable knowledge of English in the two and
a half years she spent in London. Not long
after, she learned German with the same
facility.
    At the early age of 15 she was made by her
father to learn singing under his own direction.
Two years had barely elapsed when (1824)
Garcia allowed her to appear for the first time
before a musical club which he had just established. There she produced a great sensation,
and her future success was confidently pre-
dicted. Two months later, Garcia returned to
London, where he was engaged as principal
tenor ; and here he set on foot a singing-class,
in which the education of Maria was continued,
if not completed. Fétis says that it was in
consequence of a sudden indisposition of Mme.
Pasta that the first public appearance of Maria
was unexpectedly made ; but this account is
not the same as that given by Ebers or by
Lord Mount-Edgcumbe. The latter relates
that, shortly after the repair of the King's
Theatre,

' the great favourite Pasta arrived for a limited
number of nights. About the same time . . . it

became necessary to engage a young singer, the daughter of the tenor Garcia who had sung here for several seasons. She was as yet a mere girl, and had never appeared on any public stage; but from the first moment of her appearance she showed evident talents for it both as singer and actress. Her extreme youth, her prettiness, her pleasing voice, and sprightly easy action, as Rosina in "Il barbiere di Siviglia," in which part she made her début, gained her general favour; but she was too highly extolled, and injudiciously put forward as a *prima donna*, when she was only a very promising débutante, who in time, by study and practice, would in all probability, under the tuition of her father, a good musician, but (to my ears at least) a most disagreeable singer, rise to eminence in her profession.'

Ebers says, 'her voice was a contralto, and managed with great taste.'

Her début took place June 7, 1825. She was immediately afterwards engaged for the remainder of the season (about six weeks) at £500.[1] On July 23 she sang Felicia in the first performance of Meyerbeer's 'Crociato.' At the end of the season, Garcia went, with his daughter, to the provincial festivals, and then embarked for New York. In this new sphere Maria rapidly improved, and acquired confidence, experience, and the habit of the stage. She appeared in 'Otello,' 'Romeo,' 'Don Giovanni,' 'Tancredi,' 'Cenerentola,' and in two operas written for her by her father, 'L' amante astuto,' and 'La figlia dell' aria.' She had scarcely made her début when the enthusiasm of the public knew no bounds; and, in the midst of her popularity, Garcia gave her in marriage to Malibran, an elderly and seemingly wealthy French merchant, in spite of her repugnance to the union. This marriage, celebrated Mar. 25, 1826, was as unhappy as it was ill-assorted; a year had hardly elapsed before the young wife found herself, on Malibran's bankruptcy, free to leave him, and she at once seized the opportunity. In Sept. 1827 she had returned to France. Preceded by a bright reputation, she began by reaping a harvest of applause in private concerts, followed in Jan. 1828 by a great and genuine success, at Galli's benefit, in 'Semiramide.' Her genius for dramatic singing was at once recognised, though her style was marred by a questionable taste in her choice of ornament. This she had, in Paris, the best opportunity of correcting. Engaged for the season at the Italian opera, she made her début, Apr. 8. The public, at first doubting, soon welcomed her as a really great singer.

In the season of 1829 Malibran made her reappearance in London, where she shared the applause of the public with Sontag, and the same result followed her singing with that artist at Paris in the autumn. She was principal soprano at the Gloucester Festival of 1829, and was engaged again at the Italian Opera in Paris in Jan. 1830.

Sontag, marrying and retiring from the stage early in 1830, left Malibran mistress of the

[1] Many details of Malibran's fees will be found in earlier editions of this Dictionary.

field, and henceforth she had no rival, but continued to sing each season in London and Paris with ever-increased éclat. In 1830 an attachment sprang up between her and Charles de Bériot the violinist; and this ended only with her life. They built in 1831 a handsome villa at Ixelles, a suburb of Brussels, to which they returned after every operatic campaign. In the summer of 1832 a sudden inspiration took this impulsive artist to Italy in the company of Lablache, who happened to pass through Brussels; and an Italian tour was improvised, which was a sort of triumphal progress. Milan, Rome, Naples and Bologna were visited with equal success.

Malibran retired to Brussels in Dec. 1832, and her son, Charles Wilfrid, was born Feb. 12, 1833. In the following spring she came to London, and sang at Drury Lane, in English Opera.

Having played here in English versions of 'Sonnambula' and 'Fidelio,' Malibran returned to Naples, where she remained until May 1834, proceeding then to Bologna, and thence to Milan. She soon came back, however, to London for a flying visit; and was singing at Sinigaglia in July. On the 11th of the next month she went to Lucca, where her horses were taken from her carriage, which was drawn to her hotel by enthusiastic admirers after her last appearance. She next went to Milan, and thence to Naples where she sang at the Fondo in 'Otello,' and at the San Carlo, Dec. 4, 1834, in Rossi's 'Amelia.' Persiani's 'Ines de Castro' was produced at the San Carlo for her in the same winter. From Naples she went, in the same triumphant manner, to Venice, her arrival being announced by fanfares of trumpets. There she was besieged with fresh enthusiasm, which followed her in her return to Paris and London. She returned in August to Lucca.

At this juncture her marriage was annulled by the courts at Paris, and on Mar. 26, 1836, she married de Bériot, with whom she returned immediately to Brussels.

In the following April, once more in London, Mme. Malibran de Bériot had a fall from her horse and received serious injuries to her head, from which she never entirely recovered. She returned to Brussels, from whence she went to Aix-la-Chapelle, and gave two concerts there with de Bériot. In September she had come to England again, for the Manchester Festival —at which her short, brilliant life came to an end. She sang through three days of the festival, but on Wednesday, Sept. 14, her last notes in public were heard, in the duet, with Mme. Caradori Allan, 'Vanne se alberghi in petto,' from 'Andronico.' She died, after nine days of nervous fever, at the Moseley Arms Hotel, Market Street. She was buried on Oct. 1, in the south aisle of the collegiate church,

Manchester. Her remains were, soon afterwards, removed to Brussels, where they were reinterred in the cemetery of Laeken, where a mausoleum was erected by de Bériot, containing a bust of the great singer by the celebrated sculptor Geefs.

Malibran's charm seems to have consisted chiefly in the peculiarity of timbre and unusual extent of her voice, in her excitable temperament which prompted her to improvise passages of strange audacity upon the stage, and on her strong musical feeling which kept those improvisations nearly, but not quite, always within the bounds of good taste. That her voice was not faultless, either in quality or uniformity, seems certain. It was a contralto, having much of the soprano register superadded, and with an interval of dead notes intervening, to conceal which she used great ingenuity, with almost perfect success.

Many portraits of Malibran have appeared, none very good. A large one, after Hayter, representing her with a harp, as ' Desdemona,' is usually accounted the best; but it is only indifferent. Another, by R. J. Lane, A.R.A., showing her made up as ' Fidalma,' and then, afterwards, in a stage-box, in her usual dress, is much better.

Several biographies have appeared of this extraordinary person ; that which was written by the Comtesse Merlin is little better than a romance. Malibran composed and published many nocturnes, songs and chansonnettes ; some of the unpublished pieces were collected and published by Troupenas at Paris under the name of ' Dernières Pensées musicales de Marie-Félicité Garcia de Bériot,' in 4to.　J. M.

BIBL.—E. HERON-ALLEN, *Contributions towards an accurate biography of de Bériot and Malibran* (*De fidic. opuscula*, op vi.), by which the above article has been revised ; A. POUGIN, *Marie Malibran, the Story of a Great Singer* (London, 1911); E. LEGOUVÉ, *Maria Malibran* (*Études et souvenirs de théâtre*) (Paris, no date); LOUIS HÉRITTE DE LA TOUR, *Une Famille de grands musiciens: mémoires de Louise Héritte Viardot* (Paris, Stock, 1923).

MALIPIERO, G. FRANCESCO (*b.* Venice, Mar. 18, 1882), studied at first at the Liceo Musicale of Bologna, then in Germany with Max Bruch. In 1921 he was appointed professor of composition at the Royal Conservatoire of Parma, which position he still holds.

Malipiero belongs to the most advanced group of Italian composers of the present day. He has been described as ' a classic imbued with the restless spirit of romanticism.' The definition is hardly adequate. There is little in his music to connect its author either with classics or romantics. On the other hand, the desire to break new ground, the characteristic restlessness of the present time, is evident everywhere —in the string quartet which won the prize at the Coolidge competition of 1920, as in the works he has written for the theatre. These are all marked by strong individuality as by wealth and originality of invention. Malipiero repudiates thematic development as he repudi-

ates anything which savours of tradition—the orchestra of Beethoven, the form of Italian opera. For him perfect fusion of drama and music is found only in ' Pelléas et Mélisande.' But the Debussy opera is far from giving Malipiero the solution of the old problem of the relation between voice and orchestra in an ideal form of art. He wants music to respect not only the claims of the word, but even more the claims of mimic action. These reforms are embodied in the four operas—' Pantea,' ' Sette canzoni,' ' Le Baruffe Chiozzotte,' ' Orfeo '—written in less than two years (1917-1919). Of these the most interesting is the ' Sette canzoni,' a succession of episodes each of which centres round a *canzone*, while the rest is mimic action. ' Pantea ' is mimic action pure and simple, the protagonist being the dancer whose motions are not meant to suggest beauty but ' moods of the soul.' The ' Baruffe Chiozzotte ' is lively comedy based on Goldoni's masterpiece of that name. ' Orfeo ' is pure satire. The staging of these works for the theatre is not less revolutionary than the music, which obeys no traditional law of harmony but only the composer's fancy. ' Sette canzoni ' can be staged with the help of Gordon Craig's screens. But ' Orfeo ' demands not only a stage on the stage, but a stage on which three additional platforms are utilised. If Malipiero's outspoken criticism of existing institutions has been resented, his reforms and daring have won him some stout defenders and admirers, notably Henry Prunières and G. M. Gatti.

Besides the compositions already mentioned Malipiero has written :

FOR THE THEATRE

' Ellen e Fuldano,' in 3 acts ; text by S. Benco.
' Sogno d' un tramonto d' autunno,' on D'Annunzio's poem.
' Canossa,' in 1 act, text by S. Benco.
' Le Mascherata delle principesse.'
' San Francesco d' Assisi,' a mystery.

SYMPHONIC WORKS

' A Symphony of Heroes.' (1905.)
' A Symphony of the Sea.' (1906.)
' Symphonies of Silence and Death.' (1908.)
' Impressioni del vero.' (Part i. 1911 ; Part ii. 1914.)
' Pause del silenzio.' (1917.)
' Ditirambo tragico.' (1917.)
' Armenie.' (1917.)
' Per una favola cavalleresca.' (Rome, 1921.)
' Oriente immaginario.'
  Songs and pianoforte pieces ; a solo for baritone, chorus and orchestra, ' Canto notturno di un pastore errante nell' Asia,' a sonata for v'cl. and pianoforte.

His literary contributions include, besides articles published in the *Rivista musicale italiana*, a short monograph on *The Orchestra* (Zanichelli, Bologna) and the texts of the four works for the theatre, ' Pantea,' ' Sette canzoni,' ' Baruffe Chiozzotte,' ' Orfeo.' He is also director of the library of the Instituto Editoriale of Milan.　F. B.

MALLINGER, MATHILDE (*b.* Agram, Croatia, Feb. 17, 1847 ; *d.* Berlin, Apr. 19, 1920), a distinguished dramatic singer, was first taught singing there by her father, a professor of music, and Professor Lichtenegger later by Gordigiani and Vogl at the Prague Conservatorium from 1863–66, and finally by Richard Lewy at Vienna.

On the recommendation of Franz Lachner she was engaged at Munich, where she made her début as Norma, Oct. 4, 1866. She was the original Eva in the 'Meistersinger,' June 21, 1868. She made her débuts at Berlin as Elsa, Apr. 6, and Norma, Apr. 9, 1869. She was an excellent actress and a great favourite, married the Baron Schimmelpfennig von der Oye at Berlin, and remained there during her whole musical career until 1882. On leave of absence she played with success at Vienna, Munich, etc., and in Italian opera at St. Petersburg and Moscow, but with indifferent success. About 1871 a certain section of the Berlin public tried to establish her claim as leading singer as against Pauline Lucca, the then reigning favourite. Endless quarrels ensued on their account, which culminated in a performance of the 'Nozze,' Jan. 27, 1872, where they were both playing. On Lucca's entry as Cherubino she was hissed—in consequence of which she broke her contract in the following autumn and left for America. In 1890 Mme. Mallinger became professor of singing in the Conservatorium of Prague, and in 1895 returned to Berlin to teach in the Eichelberg Conservatorium.

A. C.

MALLORIE (MALORIE, MALLERY MALORY), an English church composer of the 16th century. There is a 5-part Miserere by him in Ch. Ch. partbooks (984-8), and also the tenor part of an anthem, 'O consider mine adversitie' by 'Malorie' (B.M. Add. MSS. 22,597/67). Another late 16th century MS. (B.M. Add. MSS. 31,390) contains fancies, In Nomines and arrangements of anthems, motets, etc., for viols by 16th century (chiefly English) composers, and includes a 5-part In Nomine by 'Malory,' an arrangement of a 5-part anthem by him, 'Prayse the Lord, O my sowll,' as well as a 'Sol re sol my sol' for 6 viols. These various compositions (all in MSS. of the same period) are apparently the work of the same man.   J. Mᴷ.

MALTEN (properly MÜLLER), THÈRESE (b. Insterburg, Eastern Prussia, June 21, 1855), was taught singing by Gustav Engel of Berlin. She made her début as Pamina and Agatha at Dresden in 1873, where she remained for thirty years as principal soprano, retiring at last on a pension. Her parts included Armida, Iphigenia, Fidelio, Jessonda, Genoveva, Leonora ('Trovatore'), Margaret; the heroines of Wagner; the Queen of Sheba in Goldmark's opera of that name; the Princess Marie in Kretschmer's 'Folkunger' on its production in 1874; Fulvia on the production of Hofmann's 'Arminius' in 1877, etc. On leave of absence she played in London, Berlin, Vienna.

In Aug. 1882 she appeared at Bayreuth as Kundry, at the instance of Wagner, who had a very high opinion of her ability, again in 1884, and at Munich, where she played the same part in private before King Ludwig, from whom she received the gold medal of Arts and Science.

She made a great impression on her début at Drury Lane under Richter as Fidelio, May 24, 1882, and during the season as Elsa, May 27; Elizabeth, June 3, and Eva, June 7. She re-appeared in England at the Albert Hall on the production of 'Parsifal,' Nov. 10 and 15, 1884; at a Richter Concert in 1886; and at the Bristol Festival of 1896.

She possessed a voice of extraordinary compass, with deep and powerful notes in the lower register, and was an admirable actress, being especially successful in Wagner's operas.

A. C.

MALVEZZI, CRISTOFANO (b. Lucca, July 27, 1547; d. Florence, Dec. 25, 1597),[1] was in 1571 a canon at the church of San Lorenzo in Florence, and on the death of Francesco Corteccia succeeded him as maestro di cappella to the Grand Duke of Tuscany.

He is chiefly known as the editor of a collection of dramatic intermezzi which were performed on the occasion of the marriage of the Grand Duke Ferdinand with Christina of Lorraine in 1589. The work was published in fourteen partbooks for voices and instruments under the title,

'Intermedii et concerti, fatti per la commedia rappresentata in Firenze nelle nozze del . . . Ferdinando Medici e Madama Christiana di Lorena' . . . Venice, 1591.

It is remarkable as a foreshadowing of the attempts made, a few years later, towards the creation of a proper dramatic music by means of vocal monody with instrumental accompaniment. It is only a foreshadowing, however, as the pieces are all written in a simple madrigal style for 3, 4, 5, 6, 8 voices with dialoghi for 6 to 15 voices. The instruments employed are chiefly lutes and viols of different kinds with trombones and organ. Only in the larger pieces are all the instruments employed with the voices. Besides the editor himself the composers represented are Luca Marenzio, Jacopo Peri, Emilio de' Cavalieri and Giovanni Bardi, the three latter becoming afterwards the creators of the later Monodic style. The piece composed by Luca Marenzio is entitled 'Il combattimento d' Apolline col serpente.' From this a madrigal chorus for four voices, 'O valoroso Dio,' is reprinted by Kiesewetter in his *Schicksale und Beschaffenheit des weltlichen Gesanges*, 1841, who also gives three other pieces by Peri, Cavalieri and Archilei, which, though written in the simplest four-part counterpoint, were sung by one voice with one or two instruments playing the other parts.

Other works by Malvezzi are a book of Madrigals a 5, Venice, 1583, and one a 6, Venice, 1584, also a book of Ricercari a 4, 1577. A

[1] *Riemann.*

canzona by him transcribed from Schmid's organ - tablature book, 1607, is given in Ritter's *Geschichte des Orgelspiels*, No. 9.

J. R. M.

MANARA, FRANCESCO, ducal musician at the court of Ferrara, and (according to Fétis) singer at S. Antonio, Padua, between c. 1548–1591. He composed 4 books of madrigals a 4 v., 1 book of madrigals a 6 v., psalms, vespers, etc. (*Q.-L.*).

MANCHESTER. Before the war (1914–18) Manchester was undoubtedly the most important centre of music in the English provinces. To some extent this pre-eminence was due to the generous support given to the two most important institutions—the Hallé Concerts and the Royal Manchester College of Music, both founded by Sir Charles Hallé. The war, however, was a severe test for Manchester, for, having ever extended a liberal invitation to foreign, and mostly German, musicians, it was consequently dependent on their co-operation for its most important concerts. The genuine love of music of the Lancashire man and the enterprise of Sir T. Beecham, however, won through the difficult period, and its orchestral concerts are now as prosperous an undertaking as they have ever been.

The HALLÉ SOCIETY was formed to finance and control the concerts founded by Sir Charles Hallé after the Manchester Exhibition in 1857. Under his guidance the concerts soon became famous in the North of England. The Manchester orchestra and its conductor extended their activities to other Lancashire and Yorkshire towns. After the death of Hallé (1895) the orchestra was conducted for a time by visiting conductors, but the plan did not work satisfactorily and a temporary solution was found with the appointment of Frederic Cowen. In the meantime, however, Hans Richter had retired from the position he had long held with great distinction in Vienna, and learning this, the Manchester committee approached him with an offer which was finally accepted. Richter became the conductor of the Hallé Concerts in 1899 and held the appointment until 1911, when he resigned.

In many ways these were the most prosperous years for music in Manchester. While the fame of its conductor gave new lustre to the orchestra, Arthur Johnstone—whose high promise was cut short by untimely death—was doing much to stimulate interest in musical matters throughout the North of England with his brilliant contributions in the columns of the *Manchester Guardian*. Those were the years of Elgar's swift rise to fame, and the composer found in Richter not only a very gifted exponent but a friend. Between the two there sprang up a friendship of far-reaching importance. If Richter did much to make Elgar's

music appreciated in the North, Elgar on his part made no secret of his preference for Richter and his orchestra. The Manchester orchestra and its conductor were engaged for the Elgar Festival at Covent Garden. Richter, who had first conducted 'The Dream of Gerontius' at Birmingham (1900), was again engaged with his Manchester orchestra for the festivals of 1903 and 1906, when 'The Apostles' and 'The Kingdom' were first produced. The first symphony of Elgar was produced for the first time in Manchester and dedicated by the composer to Richter, 'true artist and true friend.' In the meantime the excellent tuition imparted at the Royal Manchester College of Music began to bear fruit, and the orchestra found employment for many a capable player trained at the local college.

As for the programmes performed during the Richter regime certain lacunæ can be found, but they are far less important than one would have reason to expect in the case of an institution guided by one man, whose sympathies, however catholic, must needs have some limitation. As an interpreter of the classics Richter, of course, was supreme. His concert performances of acts from Wagner's operas were equally celebrated. Of French composers he liked Berlioz best and this name appeared frequently in Richter's programmes. Franck he did not appreciate. But he devoted great care to the preparation of a performance of Debussy's 'L'Après-midi d'un Faune,' and the remark he made that 'there was something in his music which was not apparent in the score' defines aptly impressionistic art. Richard Strauss's compositions were frequently performed and with considerable success.

After Richter's retirement the conductorship of the orchestra for a while passed through various hands. Visiting conductors were responsible for the concerts given in the season 1911–12. In 1912 Michael BALLIN (*q.v.*) was appointed and continued as conductor till the outbreak of war in 1914. Amongst the most notable musicians associated some time or other with the orchestra should be remembered L. Strauss, Willy Hess, Adolph Brodsky, C. Risegari, C. Rawdon Briggs and Arthur Catterall (leaders); Simon Speelman (leader of the violas), Vieuxtemp and Carl Fuchs (leaders of the violoncelli). The post of chorus-master to the Hallé Society was long held by R. Wilson, who retired in 1924. After the war Hamilton Harty was appointed conductor, and under his leadership the high traditions of the orchestra have been worthily upheld.

The Hallé Concerts are a development of a much older society—the GENTLEMEN'S CONCERTS. These trace their origin as far back as 1745, when the concerts appear to have been a meeting-place of Jacobites.[1] In recent times

---

[1] See *Monthly Review* for Dec. 1905, *Underground Jacobitism*.

the Hallé and the Gentlemen's Concerts shared the conductor. Mayas, Schira, Julius Benedict and George Smart preceded Hallé and Richter. Before Richter's retirement, however, it was sought to give the older society individual character with the appointment of Sir Henry J. Wood. But the Gentlemen's Concerts which had been concerned in the Musical Festivals held in 1828 and 1836 had no longer a *raison d'être* after the establishment of the Hallé Concerts, and with the war their activities came to an end.

At the beginning of the century two new organisations were started — the LADIES' CONCERTS and the FRENCH CONCERTS — the latter given with the avowed purpose to popularise French music. Saint-Saëns was once the guest of the French Concert Society, whose concerts were held in the hall of the Midland Hotel. Neither society lived long. The war also inevitably brought to an end the excellent series of chamber concerts which used to be given under the direction of Carl Fuchs at the Schiller Anstalt.

As regards opera Manchester is entirely dependent on visiting companies. When Richter first held the conductorship of the Hallé orchestra he made various suggestions with a view to establish opera in the North on a sound basis. But his advice was rejected, as were also rejected various proposals made later by Beecham, who played a prominent part in the music of Manchester from 1914–19.

The ROYAL MANCHESTER COLLEGE OF MUSIC was founded by Hallé in 1893. On his death the then leader of the Hallé orchestra, Adolph Brodsky, was appointed to succeed him, and the college has prospered under his able direction. Amongst the artists who taught there have been Fillunger, Marie Brema, Egon Petri, Willy Hess, Carl Fuchs and Arthur Catterall sometime student under Brodsky. Most teachers of theory in the College hold also lectureships in the Manchester University, and students can prepare for the degrees of Bachelor and Doctor of Music.

Chamber music is mainly represented by the BRODSKY QUARTET CONCERTS established in 1896, of which there are six every year—all well attended and much appreciated. The balance of the receipts is devoted to the assistance of the students at the Royal Manchester College of Music.

Of the other Concert Societies the most notable is the MANCHESTER PHILHARMONIC SOCIETY, founded in 1880 by G. Brand Lane. Its speciality is choral music, but thanks to the co-operation of Sir Henry J. Wood very successful orchestral performances have also been secured.

The Manchester Vocal Society was formed in 1867, largely on the initiative of J. St. J. B. Joule. In 1885 Dr. Henry Watson was ap-

pointed as conductor, an appointment held now by Dr. Keighley.

Manchester possesses two specially fine organs—one by Cavaillé-Coll, in the Town Hall, and one by Henry Willis, at the Whitworth Hall of the Manchester University. Dr. J. Kendrick Pyne, the city organist, gives occasional recitals on the latter, and regular Saturday evening recitals on the former. For the Henry Watson Music Library, see LIBRARIES.　　　　　　　　　F. B.

MANCHICOURT, PIERRE DE (b. Béthune, Artois), French-Flemish composer of the earlier part of the 16th century. In 1539 he is described as Phonascus or choirmaster of Tournai Cathedral, and some time before 1556 received a canonry at Arras. He is said to have lived afterwards at Antwerp. His compositions, fairly numerous, chiefly motets and chansons with a few masses, mostly appeared in the miscellaneous collections of the time. Some volumes, however, contain works exclusively or almost exclusively by Manchicourt; a book of motets, nineteen in all, a 4-6, was published by Attaingnant in 1539, another book of motets containing 14 a 5-6, was published by Phalèse at Louvain in 1554. This latter volume was dedicated by Manchicourt to Antoine Perrenot, Bishop of Arras, known afterwards as Cardinal Granvelle, and probably it was to him that the composer owed his canonry at Arras. In 1545 Tylman Susato of Antwerp published a book of twenty-nine chansons by Manchicourt. One of these chansons, ' Sortez mes pleurs,' has been reprinted in Commer's *Collectio*, tom. xii. Eitner, in *Q.-L.* (which, with *Fétis*, contains full list of titles), speaks in the highest terms of a motet, ' Vidi Speciosam,' a 8, taken from the *Thesaurus* of Montanus and Neuber, 1564; but none of Manchicourt's motets have yet been reprinted in modern score.　　　　J. R. M.

MANCINELLI, LUIGI (b. Orvieto, Feb. 5, 1848; d. Rome, Feb. 2, 1921), conductor and composer. At the age of 12 he went to Florence to be a pupil of Sbolci. The boy showed great aptitude for the violoncello, and his progress was very rapid.

Mancinelli's professional career began in Florence, where he was for a time one of the first violoncello-players in the orchestra of La Pergola. He was engaged in the same capacity at the Apollo in Rome in 1874, when this theatre, by unexpected circumstances, was left without a conductor. The impresario Jacovacci, thought of trying the ability of his first violoncellist, of whom he had heard favourable reports; and so Mancinelli was suddenly raised from the ranks to appear as a conductor. ' Aïda ' was the first opera conducted by him. In the following year Mancinelli was engaged to be the musical director at Jesi during the fêtes of Spontini's centenary. On this occasion he revived Spontini's ' La Vestale,' and he was re-engaged for the direction of the orchestra of the Apollo. In 1876 Mancinelli had his first success as a composer with his intermezzi to 'Messalina,' a drama by Pietro Cossa. The following year he wrote intermezzi to the 'Cleopatra' of the same author.

Mancinelli left Rome in 1881 for Bologna, where he was engaged to be the Principal of the Liceo Musicale, and at the same time the conductor of the Teatro Comunale, and the maestro di cappella of San Petronio, the old basilica of the famous university town. During his stay there he composed two masses and many other sacred pieces, introduced several improvements in the Liceo, organised a symphony and quartet society, and was the first to acquaint the Bolognese with vocal and instrumental music by foreign composers. In 1884 he gave the first performance of his opera, 'Isora di Provenza,' which was well received.

After five years he left Bologna, attracted, perhaps, to other countries by the prospect of pecuniary improvement in his position. During the season of 1886 he visited London, and gave a concert, in which he conducted classical works and some of his own compositions. The success of this concert brought him an invitation to write an oratorio for the next Norwich Festival, and the engagement to conduct the Italian Opera during the Jubilee season at Drury Lane. His powers as a conductor received full recognition; and his oratorio 'Isaias,' performed at Norwich in Oct. 1887, was unanimously praised. He was re-engaged by Harris as conductor for the season of 1888 at Covent Garden, and revisited London annually many times. His opera, 'Ero e Leandro,' first performed in concert form at the Norwich Festival of 1896, was presented on the stage at Madrid, Nov. 30, 1897, and at Covent Garden on July 11, 1898. From 1888–95 Mancinelli held the place of musical director and conductor at the Theatre Royal of Madrid. He was conductor of the operatic enterprises carried on by Harris at the Metropolitan Opera, New York. His cantata, 'Saint Agnes,' was given at the Norwich Festival of 1905. His opera, 'Paolo e Francesca,' was produced at Bologna, Nov. 11, 1907.

F. R^Z.

BIBL.—G. OREFICE, *L. Mancinelli.* (Rome, 1921.)

MANCINI, FRANCESCO (b. Naples, 1679; d. there, 1739), an Italian composer, important in English musical history for his opera 'Hydaspes' or 'L' Idaspe fedele,' produced at the Haymarket (or Queen's) Theatre in London, May 23, 1710.

Mancini was a pupil at the Conservatorio di San Loreto at Naples and afterwards a teacher there and its principal master (1728). He composed at least 20 operas for performance at Naples, some oratorios, and other works, and his reputation in Italy was very high.

'Hydaspes' or 'L' Idaspe fedele' followed the anonymous 'ALMAHIDE' (q.v.) which was performed in the January of the same year. 'Almahide' and 'Hydaspes' were of the series of Italian operas given before Handel's advent in England, and were the first to be wholly given in that language. 'Camilla,' 1706, and some others were, according to Colley Cibber (*Life,* 1740 ed. p. 262), sung at their representation by the singers in their native tongues, Italian or English as the case might be. 'Hydaspes' was brought on to the stage by Nicolini, and the libretto was dedicated to the then Lord Chamberlain, the Marquis of Kent; it was staged with much finery in decoration. The principal singers in it were Nicolini, Valentini, Signora Margarita de l'Epine, afterwards the wife of Dr. Pepusch, and some other Italians. One of the features of the piece was a combat between Nicolini and a sham lion; this incident is amusingly treated in No. 13 of the *Spectator.* 'Hydaspes' was performed twenty-one times, and was well received. The songs were published in a folio volume by Walsh and Hare, contemporary with the production of the opera. At the Lincoln's Inn Fields Theatre in 1719 was performed a parody of it by a Mrs. Aubert, entitled 'Harlequin Hydaspes, or the Greshamite.'   F. K.

MANCINI, GIAMBATTISTA (b. Ascoli 1716; d. Vienna, Jan. 4, 1800), was a celebrated teacher of singing, a pupil of Bernacchi and Padre Martini. He settled in Vienna about 1760 as singing-teacher to the royal princesses. He produced a book on the art of coloratura singing called *Pensieri e riflessioni pratiche sopra il canto figurato* (1774), which was twice translated into French. (*Riemann.*) His estimate of Farinelli's art is quoted in the article FARINELLI (q.v.).   C.

MANCINUS, THOMAS (b. Schwerin, Mecklenburg 1550; d. Wolfenbüttel, c. 1620 [1]), was cantor at the Dom-Schule (Cathedral School) at Schwerin from 1572–78; in 1584 became a member of the chapel of the Duke of Brunswick at Wolfenbüttel, and in 1587 was appointed Kapellmeister. He was afterwards employed as librarian to the Duke. He is the author of two simple settings of the Passion according to St. Matthew and St. John, first published in 1620, and since reprinted in Schöberlein's *Schatz des liturgischen Gesanges.* With the exception of a book of German secular songs a 4 and 5, his other works are mostly occasional compositions for weddings and funerals, in the form of motets and madrigals, with Latin or German texts. See *Q.-L.*   J. R. M.

MANDOLINE (Ital. *mandolino*) is a small and very beautifully formed stringed instrument of the lute kind, with deeper convexity of back than the lute. It is, as its name implies, less in size than the MANDÓLA or MANDÓRA, a

[1] Kade gives the date 1612.

much scarcer instrument.[1] Mandóla, or man-dórla, signifies 'almond,' and it has been supposed that the shape of the instrument has given it the name. But this cannot be accepted, since the almost universal use of the syllable 'man' unchanged, or changed by phonetic variation to 'ban,' 'pan,' 'tan,' etc., for the first syllable of names of lute instruments from East to West, removes it to a wider etymological field.

There are two varieties of mandoline, the Neapolitan (see *PLATE XXIII.* No. 2) and the Milanese; the former having four pairs of strings, the latter usually five. The Milanese 'mandurina' is tuned

There is one at South Kensington with six pairs, tuned

The Milanese variety, however, is rare in comparison with the Neapolitan, the tuning of which is like that of the violin, in fifths. The lowest pair of strings is of gut, spun over with silver or copper, like a guitar first string; the next of steel also spun over; the second and first pairs are of steel only. Mahillon,[2] says that the lowest pair is of gut, the third pair of steel, the second pair of copper, and the first pair of gut. Berlioz recommends that the G strings should be of gut spun with wire, the D strings of brass, the A of steel and the E of thin gut. The mandoline is played with a plectrum of tortoiseshell, whalebone, horn or ostrich-quill, more or less flexible, which is held in the right hand, the left being employed to stop the strings, for which purpose there are seventeen frets across the finger-board. The scale of the instrument is three octaves and one note, from the G below the treble stave to the octave of A above it. The serenade in Mozart's 'Don Giovanni,' 'Deh vieni,' was written to be accompanied by the mandoline, and Grétry wrote a charming accompaniment for it in the serenade in 'L'Amant jaloux.' There is a song with mandoline accompaniment in Michael Arne's 'Almena' (1764).[3]

The mandoline is not, however, the correct instrument for Don Juan, who would have played a bandurria, a kind of half-guitar and

truly national Spanish instrument, sometimes incorrectly called a mandoline. The back of the bandurria is flat; it has only in common with the mandoline that it is played with a plectrum of tortoiseshell, called in Spanish 'pua,' and that it is the practice to insert a plate of the same substance in the table below the sound-hole to prevent the plectrum scratching. The bandurria has now twelve strings tuned in pairs, though in the 17th century it had only half that number; the higher three notes of catgut, the lower of silk overspun with metal. It is tuned much more deeply than the mandoline. The compass is in all three octaves.

In Spain the bandurria is not entirely a popular instrument. A trio of two bandurrias and a guitar is an admirable combination for the performance of serious music in the open air; pieces by Falla, Albéniz, Granados, Debussy and even Domenico Scarlatti have been arranged for it, with very happy results.

Beethoven's friend Krumpholz was a virtuoso on the mandoline, and this probably explains the fact of Beethoven's having written a piece for the instrument (Thayer, ii. 49). The autograph is to be found in the volume of MS. sketches and fragments preserved in the B.M., Add. MSS., 29,801. Though entitled 'Sonatina per il mandolina (*sic*). Composta da L. v. Beethoven,' it is only in one movement, and was probably printed for the first time in the first edition of this Dictionary. Together with an adagio in E flat for mandoline and harpsichord, it is contained in the supplementary volume (serie xxv.) of Beethoven's works in Breitkopf & Härtel's complete edition.

A. J. H.; rev. with addns. J. B. T.

MANDORE (LUTINA, TESTUDO MINOR). A small stringed instrument of the lute class having a rounded back, 4 strings or sets of strings, a short neck, and played with a plectrum. (See *PLATES XLV., XLVI.*) The name is probably a corruption of the oriental word Pandoura (see PANDORE and TAMBURA). It was very popular with the Jongleurs of the 12th and 13th centuries, and appears in illustrations of English workmanship towards the close of the 14th century, but it does not seem to have been much esteemed in this country as the citole and gittern. Among the sculptures and carvings which adorn our ancient churches it is frequently portrayed in the hands of angelic minstrels and placed across the breast. A 16th century collection of pieces for the mandore, preserved in the Advocate's Library, Edinburgh, shows us that it at that time had 5 pairs or sets of double strings and that either the fingers or a plectrum were used in playing it. The mandorichen or pandurina, described by Praetorius, was still smaller and could be

1 For a discussion of the two different instruments confused under these names, see Curt. Sachs, *Real-lexikon der Musikinstrumente*, Berlin, 1913, pp. 251-2.
2 Catalogue of the Musical Instruments in the Brussels Conservatoire, p. 245.
3 The mandoline was first heard in England at a concert given for the benefit of Sodi (at Hickford's Rooms, London, on Mar. 25, 1713), who was announced to play 'a Concerto on the Mandoline, being an Instrument admired in Rome, but never Publick here.' Handel introduced the mandoline in 'Alexander Balus,' produced on Mar. 9, 1748. In 1750 Sodi played solos on the mandoline at Paris, and on Mar. 17, 1766, Leoné performed on this instrument at Hickford's Rooms, London.   W. H. G. F.

conveniently carried under the performer's cloak: it survives in the MANDOLINE (q.v.).

F. W. G.

MANDYCZEWSKI, EUSEBIUS (b. Czernowitz, Aug. 18, 1857), is famous as an editor and as keeper of the archives of the Gesellschaft der Musikfreunde in VIENNA (q.v.).

The son of a Greek Orthodox priest, Mandyczewski studied with Nottebohm in Vienna and there laid the foundation of his profound scholarship in the masters of the Viennese school. His publications are by no means commensurate with his learning, but we owe to him the complete edition of Schubert's works, and that of Haydn's works still (1927) in progress. In 1897 began his connexion with the Conservatorium at Vienna, where he has taught the history of music and of instruments, counterpoint and composition. (See Riemann.) c.

MANÉN, JUAN (b. Barcelona, Mar. 14, 1883), Spanish violinist and composer ; author of the operas ' Neron y Acte ' (performed Leipzig, Dresden, Cologne, Wiesbaden), ' Camino del Sol ' ; a symphony ; violin concerto ; caprices (vln. and orch.) and other works and transcriptions for violin. He has edited the complete works of Paganini, and is a violinist of outstanding ability and perfection of style.

J. B. T.

MANENTI, GIOVANNI PIERO, of Bologna; musician to the Grand-Duke of Tuscany in 1574 ; still living in 1586. He composed 3 books of madrigals, 4-6 v., 1 book of songs (li pratolini) a 5 v., and single numbers in collective volumes (Q.-L.).

MANGOLD, a numerous 18th-century family of excellent musicians, the most prominent being (1) AUGUST DANIEL (b. Darmstadt, July 25, 1775; d. there, 1842). About the beginning of the 19th century he was solo violoncellist at the Frankfort Theatre, toured for some time with his nephew, the violinist Wilhelm, and in 1814 became solo violoncellist of the Grand-Ducal orchestra at Darmstadt with the title Konzertmeister. He wrote solos, etc., for his instrument. (2) WILHELM (b. Darmstadt, Nov. 19, 1796; d. there, May 23, 1875), nephew of August Daniel, studied under Rinck and Abbé Vogler, and through the recommendation of Spontini and Méhul he was permitted to study at the Paris Conservatoire under Méhul and Cherubini, 1815-18. He was an excellent violinist, and after the tour with his uncle in Holland he became court-Konzertmeister at Darmstadt in 1819 and court-Kapellmeister in 1825. He composed several operas, overtures, chamber music, etc. (3) KARL LUDWIG AMAND (b. Darmstadt, Oct. 8, 1813 ; d. Oberstdorf (Allgäu), Aug. 5, 1889), brother of Wilhelm, from whom and from his father he received his first musical education. He studied at the Paris Conservatoire, 1836-39; became court Musikdirektor in 1848, and after

being pensioned he conducted the Mozart Society, 1869-73. He composed oratorios, operas, cantatas, orchestral works, etc., but his chief claim to fame rests on his excellent songs for male chorus which still retain their popularity (Q.-L. ; Mendel ; Riemann).

MANICORDE, see CLAVICHORD.

MANIER (Ger.), lit. ' manner ' ; derived, like our word ' manner,' through the French manière ' a manner,' and manier, ' to handle,' from the Latin manus, ' a hand.' It has two entirely distinct meanings, one dealing with the æsthetics of music, the other with its technicalities. In the first of these connections the word signifies ' mannerism,' or the faulty adherence to some peculiarity in style, bringing such peculiarity into undue prominence. It is the abuse of individuality, without which quality no great thing can be accomplished in any art.

The second meaning of the word is the same as the French agrément, ornaments introduced into, and built upon, the melody, whether indicated by small notes, or marks, or added at the will of the performer. (See ORNAMENT, where the subject is fully treated.) J. M.

MANN, ARTHUR HENRY, Mus.D. (b. Norwich, May 16, 1850), was a chorister in the cathedral under Dr. Buck. He was a Fellow of the College of Organists in 1871, and took the Mus. B. degree at Oxford in 1874 and that of Mus.D. in 1882. He held the post of organist at St. Peter's, Wolverhampton, from 1870 ; at Tettenhall Parish Church from 1871 ; and was appointed to Beverley Minster in 1875. In the following year he was elected organist and director of the choir at King's College, Cambridge. Here his work as a choir-trainer has borne good fruit. His more ambitious compositions include an oratorio, ' Ecce Homo,' 1882 ; and a Te Deum, 1887, besides services, anthems, etc. He has written numerous hymn tunes, which have become widely known, and has edited several successful hymn-books, as well as bringing out an edition of Tallis's famous ' Forty-part Song ' (1888). He is an earnest student of the work of Handel, and made a minute study of the sketches, etc., in the Fitzwilliam Museum, contributing an important section on them to the Catalogue of Music, published in 1893. In 1894 the discovery of the original wind parts of the ' Messiah ' in the Foundling Hospital—in which he was partly concerned—was followed by a performance of the oratorio with a reconstructed score, in King's College Chapel. He was appointed choirmaster of the Norwich Festival in 1902. (Brit. Mus. Biog.) M.

MANNERS, CHARLES (real name SOUTHCOTE MANSERGH) (b. London, Dec. 27, 1857), was the son of Colonel Mansergh, R.H.A. and J.P. for Cork and Tipperary. He was taught singing at the Royal Irish Academy of Music in Dublin and the R.A.M. in London, at the latter for a short time by Shakespeare, and later in Italy. In 1881 he began his career as a chorus-singer, and joined Carte's travelling company. On Nov. 25, 1882, he made a successful début as Private Willis on the production of 'Iolanthe' at the Savoy Theatre. He next sang in the provinces with the Carl Rosa Company, and appeared in 1890 at Covent Garden as Bertram in 'Roberto.' On Oct. 17, 1892, he sang the part of Prince Gremin on the production in England of Tchaikovsky's 'Eugene Oniegin' under Lago at the Olympic Theatre, and later as the King in 'Lohengrin.' In 1893 he sang in America. From 1894–96 he was engaged by Harris both for English and Italian opera, also by Hedmondt in the autumn of 1895, notably as the King in 'Maritana,' Mephistopheles, etc. His voice was a *basso cantante* of remarkably fine quality. In 1896–97 he undertook a successful English opera tour in South Africa. On his return he established the Moody-Manners Opera Company, and made extensive tours in the provinces, with three separate companies, the principal company being 115 in number, with a repertory of thirty operas. In 1902 and 1903 he gave two seasons at Covent Garden, and in 1904 a longer one at Drury Lane. In the latter year and in 1906, with characteristic generosity, he gave an operatic festival, without personal profit, at Sheffield, in aid of funds for the foundation of a university in that town. By giving prizes for the best operas produced by British composers, and by giving opportunities to provincial amateurs of seeing great operas, the Moody-Manners Company exerted a good influence on contemporary music.

His wife, *née* FANNY MOODY (*b.* Redruth, Cornwall, Nov. 23, 1866), was taught singing by Mme. Sainton-Dolby at her private Academy. On Apr. 25, 1885, she sang the principal soprano music in her mistress's last composition, 'Florimel,' a cantata for female voices, at a Memorial Concert at Prince's Hall, under Sainton. In Feb. 1887 she made her début as Arline in the 'Bohemian Girl' at Liverpool with the Carl Rosa Company, and on Apr. 30 appeared very successfully as Micaëla at Drury Lane. After singing in the provinces with that company for three years she reappeared at Drury Lane in 1890 as Mignon, Margaret, etc. She was married to Charles Manners on July 5, 1890, and in October sang in Italian as Margaret and Alice. In 1892 she was the original English Tatiana in Tchaikovsky's opera above mentioned. She accompanied her husband on all his tours, and sang in his London seasons, in addition to parts mentioned, Elizabeth, Elsa, Brünnhilde in 'Siegfried,' Juliet; Sept. 26, 1902, the heroine on the production of Pizzi's 'Rosalba' at Covent Garden; Sept. 22, 1903, Militza on the production at Covent Garden of M'Alpin's 'Crescent and the Cross,'

founded on Coppée's 'Pour la Couronne,' which won the £250 prize offered by the artists; on June 17, 1904, she sang the part of Senta in the revival of 'The Flying Dutchman,' at Drury Lane, etc. The possessor of a pleasant light soprano voice, an actress and singer of great charm, Madame Fanny Moody excelled in the poetic and pathetic parts formerly associated with Christine Nilsson.   A. C.

MANNS, SIR AUGUST (*b.* Stolzenburg, near Stettin, Mar. 12, 1825; *d.* Norwood, Mar. 1, 1907), a German bandmaster, who settled in England, created the CRYSTAL PALACE SATURDAY CONCERTS (*q.v.*) and as their conductor exerted a powerful influence on English music.

Born of poor parents his first teacher was the village musician at the village of Torgelow, from whom he learnt the violin, clarinet and flute. His next instruction was received from Urban, the town musician of Elbing, near which his parents had removed, and to whom he was apprenticed. Here he had regular practice in an orchestra, especially that of the Dantzig opera company during its annual visits to Elbing; and this led to his entering one of the regimental bands of Dantzig as first clarinet, while he played among the first violins at the theatre. He now began to arrange and compose for the band, and generally to take a prominent part in the music of the place. In 1848 the regiment was transferred to Posen, and here Manns was noticed by Wieprecht, and through his assistance transferred himself from the military band to Gung'l's orchestra in Berlin, and was at length advanced to the post of conductor and solo-violin player at Kroll's Garden—the Crystal Palace of Berlin. Here, under Gyer, he worked hard at harmony and composition, and produced much dance music and other pieces which were very popular. After the destruction of Kroll's establishment by fire in 1851, Manns was chosen by von Roon (subsequently war minister), then in command of a crack infantry regiment at Königsberg, to be his bandmaster. Colonel von Roon gave his bandmaster every opportunity of display. At his instance Beethoven's symphonies were arranged for the band, and in other ways the music of the regiment was made very prominent. It was soon afterwards moved from Königsberg to Cologne, and there enjoyed a still greater reputation. Manns, however, longed for a wider field, and he fortunately accepted, in the spring of 1854, an engagement as sub-conductor in the band of the Crystal Palace, then a wind band only, under Herr Schallehn. This position he gave up in October, and after following his profession at Leamington and Edinburgh (in Wood's opera band) he became conductor of the summer concerts at Amsterdam in 1855, and finally, in the autumn of that year, was engaged as conductor of the Crystal Palace band, a post upon which he entered on Oct. 14,

1855. Manns's duties as conductor, both of the daily music and of the Saturday concerts, as well as of the numerous fêtes and extra performances, where music had to be arranged, for large combined masses of wind and string, were naturally very arduous. In 1859 he conducted the Promenade Concerts at Drury Lane, and the winter series at Glasgow in 1879 and following years. In 1883 he replaced Sir Michael Costa as conductor of the Handel Festival, and conducted the subsequent festivals until 1900. He conducted the Sheffield Festivals of 1896 and 1899. He continued to conduct the Saturday Concerts at the Crystal Palace until 1901. He was knighted in 1903.

It was said that—

' the German conductor makes the orchestra express all the modifications of feeling that an imaginative soloist would give voice to on a single instrument.' [1]

To this power of wielding his band Manns accustomed his audience during the years of his conductorship. It is not too much to say that his persistent performance of the works of Schumann—to name but one composer out of several — in the early part of his career at Sydenham, made the London public acquainted with them years before they would otherwise have become so.   G., rev.

BIBL.—H. S. WYNDHAM, *August Manns and the Saturday Concerts.* (London, 1909.)

MANON LESCAUT. The Abbé Prévost's famous romance has attracted many opera-composers.

(1) Ballet in 3 acts, by Halévy. Produced Opéra, Paris, May 3, 1830.

(2) Opéra-comique, in 3 acts, by Auber, libretto by Scribe. Produced Opéra-Comique, Paris, Feb. 23, 1856.

(3) Manon. Opera in 3 acts, libretto by Meilhac & Gille, music by Massenet. Produced Opéra-Comique, Paris, Jan. 19, 1884; in English, Carl Rosa Co., Liverpool, Jan. 17, 1885; New York, Academy of Music, Dec. 23, 1885; in French, Covent Garden, May 19, 1891. Massenet also wrote the supposed sequel ' Le Portrait de Manon,' in one act, text by Georges Boyer, produced Opéra-Comique, May 8, 1894.

(4) Manon Lescaut. Opera in 4 acts, libretto anonymous, music by Puccini. Produced Turin, Feb. 1, 1893; Covent Garden, May 14, 1894; Philadelphia, Grand Opera House (in English), Aug. 29, 1894; Shaftesbury Theatre (Beecham Co.), Feb. 15, 1916.

MANRIQUE DE LARA, MANUEL (b. Cartagena, Oct. 24, 1863), Spanish composer. By profession a soldier, now holding the rank of Brigadier-General, he has devoted his leisure to the serious study of music. A pupil of CHAPÍ (*q.v.*), he composed music to ' La Orestiada '; a symphony; string quartet; and a comic opera in 3 acts, ' El ciudadano Simón.' A symphonic fragment from an unfinished opera, ' El Cid,' has

[1] *The Times,* Apr. 28, 1857.

been performed under Fernández Arbós at Madrid. Gen. Manrique de Lara has also done valuable research in Spanish musical folk-lore, having collected a large number of melodies to traditional Spanish ballads, sung by exiled Jewish communities in the Near East.
                                        J. B. T.

MANRU, opera in 3 acts; text by A. Nossig, music by Paderewski. Produced Court Theatre, Dresden, May 29, 1901; New York, Metropolitan Opera House, Feb. 14, 1902.

MANSFELDT, EDGAR, see PIERSON, H. H.

MANTIUS, EDUARD (b. Schwerin, Jan. 18, 1806; d. Ilmenau, Thuringia, July 4, 1874), a tenor singer of great reputation in Northern Germany. He studied law, first in 1825, at the university of Rostock, and afterwards at Leipzig. It was at the latter place that his fine voice attracted general attention and that he began to study singing under Pohlenz. After having sung with great success at a festival at Halle, conducted by Spontini, he went to Berlin, and by his interpretation of the tenor parts in Handel's oratorios (Samson, Judas, etc.), soon became the declared favourite of the Berlin public. How much his talent was appreciated in the house of the Mendelssohn family may be gathered from many passages in the published letters and other books relating to Mendelssohn. It was Mantius who sang the principal tenor part in the Liederspiel, ' Die Heimkehr aus der Fremde ' (' Son and Stranger '), at the celebration of the silver wedding of the elder Mendelssohns (Devrient, p. 89). In 1830 he made his first appearance on the stage at Berlin as Tamino in the ' Zauberflöte.' In 1857 he gave his farewell performance as Florestan in ' Fidelio.' During twenty-seven years he had appeared in no less than 152 characters. After quitting the stage he devoted himself with much success to teaching. Mantius not only had an exceptionally fine voice, which he knew how to use in a truly artistic and musical manner, but was also a remarkably good actor. His representations of the tenor parts in Mozart's and Gluck's operas were justly regarded as models of their kind.   P. D.

MANTOVANO, ALBERTO, see RIPA, Alberto da.

MANUAL (from *manus,* ' a hand '), a clavier, or set of keys, to be played by the hands. The term is used chiefly in reference to the organ, where the keyboards for the hands and the keyboard for the feet have, for convenience, to be distinguished by some brief and suggestive name. Clavier (from *clavis,* a key) simply means a keyboard, without reference to the members of the body with which it is to be played.   E. J. H.

MANUALITER, a direction of fairly frequent occurrence in the organ works of Bach and his contemporaries, indicating that the passage or piece so inscribed is to be played upon the manuals alone, the direction 'pedaliter' being used at the entry of the pedal.

MANUSCRIPT SOCIETY, see New York.

MANX MUSIC. The isolated position of the Isle of Man might be expected to produce a distinct type of national music. So little attention has hitherto been devoted to collecting the traditional melodies of the island that we are really left much in the dark as to the chief characteristics of the music that may be said to have had its origin there. In most of the tunes noted down from peasant singers in the Isle of Man the present writer finds much of Celtic character, a character common to certain classes of Gaelic music.

It must be admitted that in music claimed as Manx we find imperfect recollections of English and Irish folk-tunes, as well as of some well-known published airs. For instance, in one collection there is a shortened version of the well-known air 'Push about the Jorum,' and again the 17th-century tune, 'The Buff Coat hath no fellow' (see Chappell's 'Popular Music of the Olden Time'). There is also among Manx folk-song versions of the airs, generally accepted as Irish, 'Charley Reilly' (see Bunting, 1840), and 'Green Bushes,' while we also find 'Seventeen come Sunday,' and 'Colin and Phoebe.' This is sufficient to indicate that outside influence has had its effect at an early time on the music born of the people. The passing of fishermen to and from the Irish and Scottish coasts easily accounts for this diffusion of popular melody.

There can be no doubt that a great store of beautiful melody lies hid, or at any rate at one time existed among the farmers and the fishermen of the remoter districts, and it is to be hoped that following the lead of such bodies as the 'Folk-Song Society,' a combined effort will be made to rescue what is left of it.

Apparently the first notice of Manx national song is the mention made by Robert Burns in a letter to George Thomson, dated Nov. 1794. Speaking of the air now known as 'Ye Banks and Braes o' bonny Doon,' Burns, after mentioning that an Irish gentleman had told him that it was known among the old women of Ireland, continued, that 'a Countess informed me that the first person who introduced the air into this country was a baronet's lady of her acquaintance, who took down the notes from an itinerant piper in the Isle of Man.'

Probably what is now recognised as the national tune of the Isle of Man is 'Mylecharane.' The melody of this is strikingly original, with a peculiar plaintiveness in it. Several versions of it have been published, together with the long ballad associated with the air of which there are several translations. Copies of the air are to be found in 'English

County Songs,' edited by Miss L. E. Broadwood and J. A. Fuller Maitland, 1893, and 'Manx National Songs' arranged by W. H. Gill (1896). Another song, and a very beautiful one, that has all the elements of original Manx feeling in it, is 'Ny Kirree fo-sniaghtey' ('The Sheep under the Snow'). Copies of this are to be found in 'English County Songs,' 'Manx National Songs' (Gill), and Moffat and Kidson's 'Minstrelsy of England,' the version in this last case being taken from 'Mona's Melodies,' edited by C. St. George, and published in London in 1820. This work is the first attempt to put into print Manx melodies. The book is extremely scarce. It contains but thirteen tunes, and it is doubtful how much, or how little these airs have been 'edited.' The tunes have verses thereto bearing no relation to the Manx originals. The next issue of Manx music was in July 1896, 'Manx National Songs, with English words, selected from the MS. collection of The Deemster Gill, Dr. J. Clague, and W. H. Gill. (Boosey.) This contains fifty-one melodies, many of great excellence.   F. K.

MANZUOLI, Giovanni (b. Florence, c. 1725). Having acquired a reputation in Italy, he repaired, in 1753, to Madrid, where he was engaged at a high salary by Farinelli. In 1764 and 1765 he came to London, and, by his performance, 'the serious opera acquired a degree of favour to which it had seldom mounted since its first establishment in this country.'[1] His voice was the most powerful soprano that had been heard on our stage since the time of Farinelli, and his style was full of taste and dignity. The applause he earned was hearty and unequivocal; 'it was a universal thunder.' Other singers had more art and feeling; none possessed a sweeter or fuller organ. As to execution, he had none; but he was a good actor, though unwieldy in figure, and ill-made. Nor was he young; but the sensation he excited seems to have been irresistible. All the composers struggled to have the honour of writing for him; even Dr. Arne composed his unsuccessful 'Olimpiade' for the popular singer. Manzuoli, however, left England at the end of the season, and did not return. In the same year he was at Vienna, and he shortly afterwards retired to his native place, with the title of 'Singer to the Court of the Grand Duke of Tuscany.'

In a letter of Mozart's,[2] his first after starting on his Italian tour, Jan. 7, 1770, he says of a singer whom he heard, 'canta un poco Manzuolisch ed a una bellissima voce forte ed è già vecchio,' etc. Burney heard him again, in September of that year, taking part in a service in a convent near Florence, and was delighted, though the voice seemed less powerful, even in

[1] Burney.
[2] Was in the collection of the writer and sold at his death.

a small church, than when he was in England. His name occurs once more, in one of the elder Mozart's letters, written in the following August, ' Manzuoli often visits us ' ; and he is included among ' the singers, not only celebrated in their profession, but good-hearted and sensible people.' He took part in the ' Serenata ' composed by the young Mozart in honour of the nuptials of the Archduke Ferdinand, at Milan, Oct. 17, 1771, and was encored in one of his songs. Mozart writes again, Nov. 24, 1771 :

' Herr Manzuoli, the *musico*, who has always been considered and esteemed as the best of his class, has in his old age given a proof of his folly and arrogance. He was engaged at the Opera for the sum of 500 gigliati [ducats], but as no mention was made of the *Serenata* in the contract, he demanded 500 ducats more for singing in it, making 1000. The court only sent him 700 and a gold box (and enough too, I think), but he returned the 700 ducats and the box, and went away without anything. I don't know what the result of this history will be,—a bad one, I fear !'

A good portrait of Manzuoli was engraved by G. B. Betti, after a design by L. Betti. Among his pupils was the celebrated Coltellini.

J. M.

MAOMETTO SECONDO, opera by Rossini. Produced San Carlo, Naples, during the Carnaval of 1820 ; adapted and extended as LE SIÈGE DE CORINTHE.   G.

MAPLESON, JAMES HENRY (*b.* 46 Leicester Square, London, May 4, 1830; *d.* London, Nov. 14, 1901), a well-known impresario. He became a student at the R.A.M. (1844), appeared in public as a singer, and for some time played among the violas in the orchestra. In Feb. 1854 he sang in op'ra at Verona, under the name of Enrico Mariani. Later he was assistant to E. T. Smith at Her Majesty's Theatre, and when Smith announced, in 1861, his intention of abandoning Italian Opera, Mapleson took the Lyceum, and began his career as a manager. He opened there on June 5, 1861 ; and on the 15th produced Verdi's ' Ballo in maschera ' for the first time in England. His first season at Her Majesty's was 1862, when Trebelli made her début in England ; the burning of Her Majesty's drove him to Drury Lane in 1868. He joined Gye in 1869 ; the coalition lasted two seasons, and in 1871 he returned to Drury Lane. On Apr. 28, 1877, he reopened Her Majesty's Theatre, and had a few seasons there with varying success. ' Colonel ' Mapleson, as he was called, was in the habit of taking his company to the United States in the intervals of the London season. *The Mapleson Memoirs*, an amusing volume of reminiscences, appeared in 1888.

G., with addns.

MARA, LA, see LIPSIUS, Marie.

MARA, GERTRUDE ELISABETH (*b.* Cassel, Feb. 23, 1749 ; *d.* Revel, Jan. 20, 1833), one of the greatest singers of the 18th century. Her mother died soon after the birth of this child, and her father, a poor musician, named Schme-

ling, is said to have adopted the plan of securing his little daughter in an arm-chair, while he attended to his affairs. From this cause, it appears, she fell into a rickety state, from which it was long ere she recovered, if indeed she ever recovered entirely. Schmeling contrived to increase his income by mending musical instruments, and the little Gertrude one day got hold of a violin, and began to draw musical sounds from it, being then only 4 years old. For this she was punished by her father ; but the temptation was too strong to be resisted, and she seized every opportunity of practising on such instruments as she could find, whenever Schmeling's back was turned. He found her, however, before long, to his astonishment, playing on a violin, on which she had mastered a scale. Struck with her genius, he gave her a few lessons, and found her so apt a pupil that, not long afterwards, he was able to play duets with her before a few amateurs. But even now, in her fifth year, the poor child could not stand without support, and her father was obliged to carry her to the place where she was to play. By favour of an amateur, Schmeling and his child were enabled to visit the fair at Frankfort, where the little girl's performance excited great wonder. A subscription was set on foot, a better education was given to her, and when she had reached the age of 9 her health had improved, and she was able to proceed to Vienna with her father, and there give some concerts. The English ambassador advised Schmeling to take the child to England, advice on which the poor musician, furnished with letters of introduction by the ambassador, gladly acted. He soon obtained the patronage of many noble and influential persons, including the Queen, for his wonderful child. The little girl, petted and admired by all the great ladies, was, however, persuaded by them to give up the violin, which they thought an unfeminine instrument, and was encouraged to sing. Her voice was already resonant and clear, but she had, of course, had no instruction. Schmeling, by the help of her protectresses, placed the young Gertrude under the tuition of the *musico* Paradies. She made rapid progress, but it soon became necessary to remove her from the power of her profligate instructor.

Returning to Cassel, Schmeling found it impossible to get an engagement for his daughter, as he had hoped, at the court ; for the King would not hear of any but Italian singers. Hiller now received her into his music school, at Leipzig, where she remained for five years. In 1771 she came out from this academy, with a voice remarkable for its extent and beauty, a great knowledge of music, and a brilliant style of singing. She was the first great singer that Germany had produced. Her education had been formed on the music of Hasse, Graun, Benda, Jommelli, Pergolesi, Porpora and

Sacchini; but Hasse, with his vocal passages and facile style, was her favourite master. Her voice extended from the g' to e'''. She made her début in an opera of Hasse's at Dresden, and was successful. With difficulty, the King, Frederick II.,was persuaded to hear her; and, though strongly prejudiced against her on account of her nationality, he was immediately converted by her singing an air of Graun's at sight, and finally engaged her for life to sing at court, with a salary of fr. 11,250. Here she profited by the hints of Concialini and Porporino, and perfected her singing of slow and legato airs.

It was at this juncture that, in spite of all advice, and although the King twice refused his consent, she married the violoncellist, Mara. She soon discovered her folly, and regretted it when too late. This part of her life was extremely unhappy; she was made miserable on the one hand by the excesses of a debauched and dissipated husband, and on the other by the tyranny of a king who allowed her no liberty or indulgence. On one occasion she was actually brought from her bed, by his orders, transmitted through an officer and guard of soldiers, and forced to sing at the Opera, though complaining, truly or untruly, of indisposition. She at length succeeded in escaping to Dresden, where she was detained by the Prussian ambassador. Frederick, however, who had lost some front teeth, and could no longer play the flute, cared now but little for music, and gave her a tardy permission to annul her engagement. Mme. Mara, free at last, arrived in 1780 at Vienna, where Storace was playing in *opera buffa*, for which the Emperor had a great liking. This was not Mara's line, and she was coldly received. Provided, however, with a letter to Marie-Antoinette from the Empress, she passed through Germany, Holland and Belgium, singing at various places on her way. At Munich Mozart heard her, but was not favourably impressed. He wrote, Nov. 13, 1780:

'Mara has not the good fortune to please me. She does too little to be compared to a Bastardella (yet this is her peculiar style), and too much to touch the heart like a Weber [Aloysia], or any judicious singer.'

He tells a story of her and her husband a few days later (letter of Nov. 24), which shows both of them in a very unpleasant light, as behaving with foolish effrontery and pretension. She was again at Vienna in Mar. 1781, and Mozart mentions her as giving a concert there. She reached Paris in 1782. Here she found the celebrated Todi, and a rivalry immediately sprang up between these two singers, which divided society into factions, as when Handel and Bononcini, or Gluck and Piccinni, were opposed to each other by amateurs incapable of admiring both. Many anecdotes are told of the Mara and Todi dispute, among which one has become famous. At a concert where both singers appeared, an amateur asked his neighbour, 'Quelle était la meilleure': to which the other replied, 'C'est Mara.' 'C'est bien Todi' (bientôt dit) was the punning answer.

Two years later, in the spring of 1784, Mara made her first appearance in London, where her greatest successes awaited her. She was engaged to sing six nights at the Pantheon. Owing to the general election, she sang to small audiences, and her merits were not recognised until she sang at Westminster Abbey, in the Handel Commemoration, when she was heard with delight by nearly 3000 people. She sang in the repeated Commemoration in 1785, and in 1786 made her first appearance on the London stage in a serious pasticcio, 'Didone abbandonata,' the success of which was due entirely to her singing. In Mar. 1787 Handel's opera of 'Giulio Cesare' was revived for a benefit, and Mara played in it the part of Cleopatra, which Cuzzoni had sung in 1724. It was so successful that it was constantly repeated during the season. Mara again took a leading part in the Festival in Westminster Abbey in 1787, and she remained connected with the opera in London till 1791, after which, though she sang occasionally on the stage, and even in English ballad operas, she was more frequently heard in concerts and oratorios. For these she was better suited, as her figure was not good enough for the theatre, nor was she a good actress. It is, indeed, not impossible that her stage-presence was still to some extent spoiled by the disease which crippled her as a child; and there is a caricature in which she is shown, singing at a 'Wapping Concert' *seated* (Feb. 28, 1786), with the following apology below:

'MADAM MARY . . . begs her Polite Audience will excuse her sitting during the Performance, as she contracted in her infancy a Disorder called Le Genoue Inflexible, or (Stiff Knee) which prevents her standing, even in the most Sacred Pieces of Music—her Enemies call it Pride, but it must appear only malice, when she could not rise before their Majesties; or at the Sacred Name of Jehovah.'

There is, again, a letter of Mara's extant,[1] in which she apologises for not being able even to sit on a platform throughout a concert, a thing she had never been able to do, owing to the heat and fatigue, which she could not bear. Her health was, in fact, never strong. She had, however, the advantage of knowing our language, which she had learnt in childhood, during her first visit to England; and she is said to have gained large sums here by her oratorio-singing.

In 1788 she was singing in the Carnival at Turin, and the following year at Venice. She returned to London in 1790, and went to Venice again in 1791. Coming once more to London in the next season, she remained here for ten years. After this time, she found her voice losing strength, and she quitted England in

[1] Was in the collection of the writer and sold at his death.

1802, after enjoying a splendid benefit of over £1000 at her farewell concert. She sang without effect at Paris, where she had the misfortune to come after Grassini ; and then, after passing through Germany, Mara retired to Moscow, where she bought a house.

Her worthless husband, and her numerous lovers — among whom the last was a flute player named Florio—had helped her to spend the immense sums which she had earned, until she found herself without means, and compelled to support herself by teaching. By following this occupation, she acquired a small competence, which was again lost to her (1812) in the fire of Moscow, which destroyed the merchant's house in which she had placed it. Forced to begin once more to seek a means of subsistence, when almost 64 years old, Mara travelled in Livonia, where she was kindly received, and settled in Revel. She now supported herself again for about four years by teaching, and then formed the strange desire to revisit London, the scene of her former glory. Here she arrived in 1819 (according to Fétis), though Lord Mount-Edgcumbe puts her visit before the burning of Moscow. In any case, the poor old woman, announced in a mysterious manner by Messrs. Knyvett as 'a most celebrated singer whom they were not at liberty to name,' appeared at the King's Theatre, when it was discovered that not a shred of her voice remained — and never appeared again. She returned to Livonia, and died at the advanced age of 84, soon after receiving from Goethe a poem for her birthday, ' Sangreich war dein Ehrenweg ' (Weimar, 1831).

A life of Mara, by G. C. Grosheim, was published at Cassel in 1823, and a more interesting one by Rochlitz in his *Für Freunde der Tonkunst*, vol. i. The best portrait of her was engraved (oval) by J. Collyer, after P. Jean, 1794.   J. M.

MARAIS, (1) MARIN (b. Paris, Mar. 31, 1656 ; d. there, Aug. 15, 1728), an important musician of the time of Lully.

At an early age he entered the choir of the Sainte-Chapelle, where he was a pupil of Chaperon. He learnt the bass viol from Hottemann (or Hautmann) and his pupil Sainte-Colombe. After studying six months with the latter his master dismissed him, saying that he could teach him nothing further. In 1685 he entered the Royal Band as a soloist ; he was also a member of the orchestra of the Académie Royale de Musique, where he studied composition under Lully, sharing with Colasse the direction of the orchestra. In 1686 he published his first book of ' Pièces à son 2 violes,' dedicated to Lully ; he was then living in the Rue du Jour, near St. Eustache. In the same year he produced at court, before the Dauphiness, an ' Idylle dramatique.' In Apr. 1693 he brought out at the Académie de Musique a

setting of A. Houdart de la Motte's ' Alcide,' in which he collaborated with Louis de Lully. The work was revived in 1705, 1716 and 1744. With the same collaborator he wrote a ' Panto-mime des pages,' part of the score of which is preserved at Berlin. His other writings for the stage were ' Ariane et Bacchus ' (words by Saint-Jean), produced in 1696 ; ' Alcyone ' (words by Houdart de la Motte), 1706 ; and ' Sémélé ' (words by the same poet), 1709. The most successful of his operas was ' Alcyone,' in which was a representation of a storm, long much admired.

In 1692 he published a set of ' Pièces en trio pour les flûtes, violon et dessus de viole.' A second book of ' Pièces de viole ' appeared in 1701 ; a third in 1711 (when he was living in the Rue de la Harpe) ; a fourth in 1717 and a fifth in 1725. Reprints of some of these exist. In 1723 he published a set of ' Sinfonies ' for violin, viol and harpsichord, entitled ' La Gamme.' About 1725 Marais retired to his house in the Rue de Lourcine, where he occupied himself with horticulture. He still, however, gave lessons two or three times a week at a room in the Rue du Battoir. On his death in 1728, he was buried in the Church of St. Hippolyte in the Quartier Saint-Marcel. The parish was suppressed in 1791, and shortly afterwards the church was destroyed. No trace of it now remains, but the name is preserved in the Rue Saint-Hippolyte.

Marais left in MS. a Te Deum (written and performed on the convalescence of the Dauphiness) and some concertos for violin and bass viol, written for the elector of Bavaria. At an early age Marais married Catherine Damicourt, who survived him. By her he had nineteen children, four of whom (three sons and a daughter) were also violists. On one occasion he presented his three musician sons to Louis XIV., before whom the children and their father gave a concert, while a fourth boy turned over the leaves of the music. One of his daughters married a musician named Bernier. Marais improved the bass viol by adding a seventh string, and by increasing the sonority of the three lower strings by covering or twisting them. There is a painting [1] of ' M. Marais, musicien,' in the museum at Blois, and there also exists a mezzotint of Marin Marais, painted and engraved by A. Bouys and published in 1704. In this he is represented seated, full length, with his bass viol across his knees. The seven strings and the covering of the lower strings of the instrument have evidently been emphasised by the artist. Of his musician sons, the name of (2) JEAN LOUIS MARAIS occurs in the imprint of the fourth and fifth books of ' Pièces de violes,' together with that of (3) ROLAND MARAIS, the only one who

[1] A fine portrait of Marais also appears in the group of Lully and his musicians (attributed to Hyacinthe Rigaud) in the National Gallery, London.   B. v. d. s.

attained any distinction. He published (in 1711) a *Nouvelle Méthode de musique*, and in 1725 became a solo violist in the Royal Band, probably succeeding to his father's post. Quantz heard him in 1726, and praises him as a great performer. He published (in 1735 and 1738) two books of 'Pièces de violes.'   w. b. s.

MARAZZOLI (Marazzuoli), Marco, of Parma (*d*. Rome, Jan. 24, 1662), singer in the Papal Chapel, Rome, *c*. 1637, and a harp virtuoso. He assisted at the concerts of Queen Christina of Sweden, for whom he wrote in 1658 the music drama ' La vita humana,' and composed the two first comic operas, ' Chi soffre speri' (Rome, 1639) and ' Dal male il bene' (Rome, 1654), both the texts having been written by the Marquis Ruspigliosi, afterwards Pope Clemens IX. He composed two more operas, oratorios, cantatas and songs which remained in MS. (*Riemann*; *Q.-L.*).

MARBECK, see Merbecke.

MARCATO (Ital.), ' in a marked, decisive manner.' The principal use of this direction is to draw the attention to the melody or subject when it is in such a position that it might be overlooked, as for instance, ' Il basso ben marcato,' in Chopin's Krakowiak, op. 11 ; or when there are two subjects both of which are to be brought prominently forward, as in the Ninth Symphony of Beethoven (last movement),where the two subjects come together in 6-4 time, the words being ' Freude, schöner Götterfunken,' and ' Seid umschlungen,' etc. ; and in the Études symphoniques of Schumann, No. 2, ' Marcato il canto' and ' Marcato il tema.' Beethoven also uses ' Queste note ben marcato' (*sic*) in the string quartet, op. 18, No. 6, slow movement, and ' Melodia marcata,' in the Trio, op. 9, No. 2.

' Marcatissimo' is used by Chopin, Étude, op. 25, No. 11, at the end, by Schumann in the last movement of the Sonata in F♯ minor, op. 11, and in No. 8 of the Études symphoniques.   M.

MARCELLO, (1) BENEDETTO (*b*. Venice, July 31 or Aug. 1, 1686 ; *d*. Brescia, July 24, 1739), eminent composer, was son of Agostino Marcello and Paola Capello.

He was highly educated, and had great natural gifts for music, and was a pupil of Lotti and Gasparini. The violin was his first instrument, but he soon gave his whole attention to singing and composition. His father, objecting to the time thus occupied, sent him from home to study law, but on his death Benedetto returned to Venice, and contrived to combine the practice of music with his professional avocations. He held important government posts, was a member of the Council of Forty in 1711, and afterwards Provveditore of Pola (1730). Here he remained eight years, when his health having been ruined by the climate he became Camerlengo at Brescia, and

there died. His monument in the church of S. Giuseppe states his age to have been 52 years, 11 months, and 23 days.[1] He was elected Cavaliere of the Filarmonici of Bologna in 1812, and was also a member of the Pastori Arcadi of Rome. In his youth he was wild, but sobered down in middle life.

His great work, in eight volumes, folio, ' Estro poetico-armonico, Parafrasi sopra i primi 50 Psalmi, Poesia di Girolamo Giustiniani,' appeared in two parts of twenty-five Psalms each (Venice, 1724 – 27). They are composed for one, two, three, and four voices, with figured basses, and occasionally with two violins and violoncello obbligati ; and for expression far surpass any other work of the kind. Burney, in his notice of Marcello (*Hist.* iv. 543), considers that they have been overpraised, and that even in the composer's day his airs and themes were neither new nor original. In spite, however, of this judgment it is not too much to say that, as a whole, they constitute one of the finest productions of musical literature. An English edition, edited by Avison and Garth, was published in London in 1757 in 8 vols. ; a second in Italian soon after (Venice) ; and a third by Valle (1803-08).

Marcello also composed instrumental concertos (1701), and ' Canzoni madrigaleschi' (Bologna, 1717) ; besides ' Calista in Orsa,' pastoral (libretto printed in 1725, music unpub.) ; ' La Fede riconosciuta,' opera (Vicenza, 1702) ; ' Arianna,' cantata ; and ' Giuditta,' oratorio, all to his own words. As a poet he was above the average, and furnished the libretto for Ruggieri's ' Arato in Sparta' (Venice, 1709). In 1720 he published a satirical pamphlet, *Il teatro alla moda*, reprinted in 1727, 1733, 1738 (Venice), and 1741 (Florence). A German translation with notes by Alfred Einstein was published in 1917. The Library of St. Mark in Venice contains a MS. *Teoria musicale* ; the State Library of Dresden ancient copies of two cantatas, ' Timotheus,' to his own Italian translation of Dryden's poem, and ' Cassandra' ; the Court Library of Vienna many autographs and other works, including the cantatas ' La morte d' Adone,' ' Clori e Daliso,' and ' La stravaganza' ; and the Royal Library of Brussels ' Il trionfo della musica nel celebrarsi la morte di Maria Vergine,' an oratorio for six voices and chorus. This score was once in the possession of Fétis, who speaks highly of its expression, pathos, and effective instrumentation. Rossini has borrowed one of the most prominent themes in his overture to the ' Siege of Corinth' note for note from Marcello's 21st Psalm. For Marcello's *Lettera famigliare*, see Lotti. A catalogue of his works is in *M.f.M.* vol. 23 (1891), pp. 187-97 supplemented in *Q.-L.*   F. G., addns.

---

[1] Both Eitner and Riemann overlook this definite statement, and give the date of birth, like that of death, as July 24.

(2) ALESSANDRO (b. Venice, c. 1684; d. there, c. 1750), musician, philosopher and mathematician; elder brother of Benedetto. He composed under the name of Eterico Stinfalico, as member of the Academy of the Arcadians; held weekly meetings at his house, where chiefly his own compositions were performed. His published works are: solo cantatas, sonatas for violin and basso continuo, 6 concertos for 2 flutes or violins, 6 concertos for oboe or flute with violin principale and orchestra (Gerber; Fétis; Q.-L.).   E. v. d. s.

MARCH (Fr. marche; Ger. Marsch; Ital. marcia), a form originally associated with military movements, and afterwards imported into the music of the stage, the orchestra, the chamber and the oratorio. In ancient times the sound of instruments was used as a means of stimulating the action of large numbers of people, whether in processes of labour requiring consentaneous effort, or as a means of exciting ardour in armies advancing to battle by the tones of the 'shrill trump, the spirit-stirring drum, the ear-piercing fife'—equally familiar being Milton's reference to the effect of the sound 'of trumpets loud and clarions,' and the influence on a mighty host of 'Sonorous metal blowing martial sounds.' (Cf. MILITARY SOUNDS AND SIGNALS.) Like most forms, however, in instrumental music, the development of the march followed that of vocal music. We find marches in the early operas, in the stage works of Lully, and later in those of Handel and Rameau. In harpsichord music, too, it appears at a comparatively early date, the 'Suites des pièces' of the French composer Couperin offering examples.

Of the military march as now understood, as a strictly rhythmical and harmonised composition, written for a band of wind instruments, and intended not only to stimulate courage but also to ensure the orderly advance of troops, it does not appear that any examples are extant earlier than about the middle of the 17th century, and these seem to have originated during the Thirty Years' War, and are to be traced to the form of the Volkslied; war-songs, in which patriotic and military ardour was expressed lyrically, having long preceded the exclusive use of instruments for that purpose. A good specimen of the old German military march is that which Meyerbeer introduced in his 'Ein Feldlager in Schlesien,' and afterwards, with other portions of that work, in his 'L'Étoile du nord,' in the camp scene of which the fine old 'Dessauer March' stands prominently out from the elaborations with which the composer has surrounded it.

In England the military march would seem to be of considerable age. Sir John Hawkins, however, in his History of Music, says: 'It seems that the old English march of the foot was formerly in high estimation, as well

abroad as with us; its characteristic is dignity and gravity, in which respect it differs greatly from the French, which, as it is given by Mersennus, is brisk and alert.' On this subject Sir John quotes a bon mot of Sir Roger Williams, a soldier of Queen Elizabeth's time, in answer to the French Marshal Biron's remark that 'the English march being beaten by the drum was slow, heavy and sluggish'; the reply being, 'That may be true, but, slow as it is, it has traversed your master's country from one end to the other.' Hawkins (writing in 1776) speaks of 'the many late alterations in the discipline and exercise of our troops, and the introduction of fifes and other instruments into our martial music'; and, in reference to an earlier condition thereof, quotes, from Walpole's Catalogue of Royal and Noble Authors, a warrant of Charles I. to the following effect:

'Whereas the ancient custome of nations hath ever bene to use one certaine and constant forme of March in the warres, whereby to be distinguished one from another. And the March of this our nation, so famous in all the honourable atchievements and glorious warres of this our kingdom in forraigne parts (being by the approbation of strangers themselves confest and acknowledged the best of all marches) was through the negligence and carelessness of drummers, and by long discontinuance so altered and changed from the ancient gravity and majestie thereof, as it was in danger utterly to have been lost and forgotten. It pleased our late deare brother prince Henry to revive and rectifie the same by ordayning an establishment of one certaine measure, which was beaten in his presence at Greenwich, anno 1610. In confirmation whereof wee are graciously pleased, at the instance and humble sute of our right trusty and right well-beloved cousin and counsellor Edward Viscount Wimbledon, to set down and ordaine this present establishment hereunder expressed. Willing and ccmmanding all drummers within our kingdome of England and principalitie of Wales exactly and precisely to observe the same, as well in this our kingdome, as abroad in the service of any forraigne prince or state, without any addition or alteration whatsoever. To the end that so ancient, famous, and commendable a custome may be preserved as a patterne and precedent to all posteritie,' etc. etc.

This document also contains the following notation [1]:

Voluntary before the March.

Pou tou pou tou pou R   pou tou pou pou tou pou R poung

The March.

Pou tou pou tou poung

Pou tou pou R poung

R   pou tou R poung

R R pou R poung

R R pou tou R pou tou pou R tou pou R poung

R R R R poung

R R R pou R R pou tou pou R tou pou R poung potang.

[1] The notes are lozenge-shaped in the original.

subscribed 'Arundell and Surrey. This is a true copy of the original, signed by his Majestie. Ed. Norgate, Windsor.'

The primary (indeed absolute) importance of the drum in the early form of the March is very evident. Rousseau, in his *Dictionnaire de musique*, in his article on that subject, thus defines it : ' Marche : Air militaire qui se joue par des instrumens de guerre, et marque le mètre et la cadence des tambours, laquelle est proprement la Marche.' The same author, writing towards the close of the 18th century, speaks of the superiority of the German military music, and says that the French troops had few military instruments for the infantry excepting fifes and drums ; and very few marches, most of which were ' très malfaites.' Rousseau gives— as follows—the first part of the March of the Musketeers of the King of France, as illustrating ' L'accord de l'air et de la Marche.'

Hautbois. tr.

Tambours.

In its earlier instrumental form the German march had two reprises, each of eight, twelve or even sixteen bars, and its melodic origin would seem to have been influenced by the national dance called the ' Allemande,' in 2–4 time.

The modern march is now usually in common time—four crotchets in a bar—consisting of reprises of four, eight or even sixteen bars, and it usually begins with a crotchet before the opening phrase, with a subsidiary movement entitled a ' Trio ' (generally in the dominant or sub-dominant key), which occupies a similar place to that of the trio associated with the MINUET or SCHERZO (*q.v.*) of a symphony ; that is, following the march, which is repeated after it. With the ordinary (Parade) March, about 75 steps go to the minute; with the Quick March (Ger. *Geschwind Marsch* ; Fr. *Pas redoublé*), about 108 ; while the Storming March (Ger. *Sturm Marsch* ; Fr. *Pas de charge*) implies about 120 steps per minute, these being measured by rapid beats of the drum.

Military Marches, intended to stimulate enthusiasm, are generally written in a bright major key, trumpets, drums and other instruments of percussion being prominently used ; and Funeral Marches in a solemn minor one— a remarkable exception to the latter rule being offered by the Dead March in ' Saul,' the key of which is C major. ' The stormy music of the drum ' is still an important element, as it exercises a commanding influence on rhythmical precision, as already indicated. Formerly, as above indicated, that instrument was the all-essential feature in the march, instead of being, as afterwards, subsidiary in a musical sense.

Marches written for the stage and concert-room originally followed the simple structure of the military march, and conformed to their steady rhythmical design and avoidance of elaboration of figure. They are thus equally suitable for performance by a marching band, which, for purely physical reasons, the more developed type is not.

Chopin's Sonata in B flat minor has a Funeral March for slow movement which presents the feature of beginning on the strong beat. So also does Mendelssohn's ' Wedding March ' and the March in ' Tannhäuser,' these further using the preliminary flourish of trumpets (see FANFARE) such as is found in some of the older marches. Beethoven's Sonata in A flat, op. 26, also has a Funeral March for slow movement, while in the ' Eroica ' symphony there is an example of the march form treated symphonically. The freedom of structure in the ' Trauermarsch ' in ' Die Götterdämmerung ' is no less remarkable than is its preservation of the Funeral March spirit. Mention may also be made of the second movement of Elgar's Symphony in E flat, a symphonic Funeral March ; of his ' Imperial ' and Coronation Marches, or the set of military marches 'Pomp and Circumstance.'

There is also, as already said, a description of march in half time—2–4 (two crotchets in a bar), called with us the quick march—see Schubert's opp. 40 and 51 ; while in his op. 121 there are examples of marches in 6–8 tempo, one sometimes, but not often, employed in the march style; another such specimen worth referring to being the ' Rogues' March,' associated for more than a century (probably much longer) with army desertion. This is also in the style of the quick march, the tune being identical with that of a song once popular, entitled ' The tight little Island '—it having, indeed, been similarly employed in other instances. The following is the first part of this march, whose name is better known than its melody :

Quick March.

Besides the march forms already referred to, there is the torch-dance (see FACKELTANZ), which, however, is only associated with pageants and festivities. These and military marches being intended for use in the open air, are of course written entirely for wind instruments and those of percussion; and in the performance of these pieces many regimental bands, British and foreign, have arrived at a high degree of excellence. (See WIND BAND and WIND INSTRUMENTS.)

H. J. L.; addns. N. C. G.

MARCHAND, (1) JEAN-BAPTISTE (b. Paris, c. 1670), son of Jean Marchand (b. 1656; d. Versailles, July 19, 1691), ordinaire of the king's music. Marchand entered the Chapel Royal in 1691 as player on the small lute and dessus de violon.'[1] After the death of his brother Nöel he obtained (June 1, 1710) the emoluments attached to his brother's post as lute-player 'de la chambre,' which he had held since 1705. According to Michel Brenet he was still living in 1754; on Dec. 1 Louis Joseph Franceur obtained his position as 'joueur de luth de la chambre du roi.' These posts as lutenist, or theorbist, were at that time sinecures. Musicians on whom they were conferred more often played the guitar.

(2) JEAN-NOËL (b. 1666; d. Paris, May 31, 1710), (? elder) brother of the preceding, lutenist 'de la chambre,' received on Aug. 2, 1674, the position of his father as 'ordinaire de la musique de la chambre.' He succeeded Chabanceau de la Barre in 1705.

BIBL.—*Documents des Archives nationales* (*Maison du roi*); MICHEL BRENET, *R.M.I.*, 1898–99; L. DE LA LAURENCIE, *L'Ecole française du violon.*
J. G. P.

MARCHAND, LOUIS (b. Lyons, Feb. 2, 1669[2]; d. Paris, Feb. 17, 1732), a French organist of great reputation whose encounter with J. S. Bach has remained famous. He was the son of Jean Marchand, 'maître de musique et joueur d'instruments.' He went to Paris at an early age, became renowned there for his organ-playing, and ultimately became court organist at Versailles. A confusion between him and Jean Louis Marchand of Auxerre (b. 1679) has led to much uncertainty as to the tenure of various posts as organist (see Q.-L.). Louis Marchand became organist of the church of the Jesuits, Rue St. Jacques, at St. Benoît (1699), at St. Honoré (1703), at the Royal Chapel (1708–14) and at the convent of the Cordeliers. By his recklessness and dissipated habits he got into trouble and was exiled in 1717. The story goes that the King, taking pity on Marchand's unfortunate wife, caused half his salary to be withheld from him and devoted to her sustenance. Soon after this arrangement, Marchand coolly got up and went away in the middle of a Mass which he was playing, and when remonstrated with by the King, replied, 'Sire, if my wife gets half my salary, she may play half the service.' On

[1] Fétis.
[2] Spitta, in his *Life of Bach*, gives the date 1671, as an inference from an old engraving. But see Fétis (s.v.) who quotes an article in the *Magasin encyclopédique* 1812 tom. iv. p. 341, where this point is thoroughly investigated, and a register of Marchand's birth given. He was baptized in the church of St. Nizier, Lyons.

account of this he was exiled, on which he went to Dresden, and there managed to get again into royal favour. The King of Poland offered him the place of court organist, and thereby enraged Volumier, his Kapellmeister, who was also at Dresden, and who, in order to crush his rival, secretly invited Bach to come over from Weimar. At a royal concert, Bach being incognito among the audience, Marchand played a French air with brilliant variations of his own, and with much applause, after which Volumier invited Bach to take his seat at the harpsichord. Bach repeated all Marchand's showy variations, and improvised twelve new ones of great beauty and difficulty. He then, having written a theme in pencil, handed it to Marchand, challenging him to an organ competition on the given subject. Marchand accepted the challenge, but when the day came it was found that he had precipitately fled from Dresden, and, the order of his banishment having been withdrawn, had returned to Paris, where his talents met with more appreciation. He now set up as a teacher of music, and soon became the fashion, charging the then unheard-of sum of a louis d'or a lesson. In spite of this, however, his expensive habits brought him at last to extreme poverty, and he died in great misery. His organ works (wholly posthumous) reprinted in Guilmant's 'Archives des maîtres de l'orgue,' comprise a 'Grand Dialogue,' 'Livre d'orgue,' 'Pièces choisies pour l'orgue,' 'Pièces d'orgue' (from MSS. at the Library of Versailles). For harpsichord: 'Pièces de clavecin,' 2 books (Paris, 1702–03) and an opera, 'Pyrame et Thisbé,' never performed.[3]

His ideas, says Fétis, are trivial, and his harmonies poor and incorrect. There is a curious criticism of him by Rameau, quoted by La Borde, *Essai sur la musique* (vol. iii.), in which he says that 'no one could compare to Marchand in his manner of handling a fugue'; but, as Fétis shows, this may be explained by the fact that Rameau had never heard any great German or Italian organist.

It is a well-known fact that J. S. Bach used some of his themes, namely, a fugue theme in one of his Brandenburger Concertos. Among his numerous pupils were Pierre du Mage and Louis-Claude Daquin. L. Marchand represents, with A. Raison, the French organ tradition of the 17th century; although to some extent an innovator, he yielded to the musical taste of his epoch; but his music bears certain characteristics which are well his own.

BIBL.—*Encyclopédie de la Musique et Dictionnaire du Conservatoire*, Part I., L. DE LA LAURENCIE, *France, XVIIe-XVIIIe siècles*: Part II., articles by GUILMANT and PIRRO; A. GUILMANT, *Archives des maîtres de l'orgue*, with biographical studies by A. PIRRO; *Tribune de Saint Gervais*, 1900: Louis Marchand, by A. PIRRO.
M.; rev. M. L. P.

MARCHAND, MARGUERITE, see DANZI, Franz.

MARCHESI, LUIGI (LODOVICO), sometimes

[3] Fétis.

called MARCHESINI (*b.* Milan, 1755 ; *d.* there, Dec. 18, 1829), one of the latest of the famous male soprani of the 18th century.

His father, who played the horn in the orchestra at Modena, was his first teacher ; but his wonderful aptitude for music and his beautiful voice soon attracted the attention of some amateurs, who persuaded the elder Marchesi to have the boy prepared for the career of a sopranist. This was done at Bergamo, and young Marchesi was placed under the *evirato* Caironi, and Albujo, the tenor, for singing ; while his musical education was completed by the maestro di cappella, Fioroni, at Milan.

Marchesi made his début on the stage at Rome in 1774, in a female character, the usual introduction of a young and promising singer with a soprano voice and beautiful person. Towards the close of 1775 the Elector of Bavaria engaged Marchesi for his chapel, but his sudden death, two years after, put an end to this engagement, and the young singer went to Milan, where he performed the part of ' second man,' with Pacchierotti as first, and to Venice, where he played second to Millico. He was advanced in that same year to first honours at Treviso. In the next and following years he sang as ' first man ' at Munich, Padua and Florence, where he created a furore by his exquisite singing of ' Mia speranza, io pur vorrei,' a rondo in Sarti's ' Achille in Sciro.' In 1778 he had worked his way to the great theatre of San Carlo, and continued there during two seasons. He was now looked upon as the first singer in Italy, and was fought for by rival *impresarj.* Once more in Milan (1780), he sang in Mysliweczek's ' Armida,' in which he introduced the famous rondo of Sarti, which all Italy had been humming and whistling since he sang it at Florence, and also an air by Bianchi, almost as successful, ' Se piangi e peni.' His portrait was engraved at Pisa, and the impressions were quickly bought up. He now sang in turn at Turin, Rome, Lucca, Vienna and Berlin, always with renewed éclat ; and he went in 1785 to St. Petersburg with Sarti and Mme. Todi. The rigorous climate of Russia, however, filled him with alarm for his voice, and he fled rapidly back to Vienna, where he sang in Sarti's ' Giulio Sabino.'

We next find him (1788) in London, singing in the same opera by Sarti, having just completed an engagement at Turin. His style of singing now seemed to Burney ' not only elegant and refined to an uncommon degree, but often grand and full of dignity, particularly in the recitatives and occasional low notes.' From this time till 1790 he continued to delight the English, appearing meanwhile at short intervals in the various capitals and chief cities of Europe. In 1794 he sang at Milan in the ' Demofoönte ' of Portogallo, and was described in the cast as ' all' attual servizio di

S. M. il Re di Sardegna.' This memorable occasion was that of the début of Mme. Grassini. He continued to sing at Milan down to the spring of 1806, when he left the stage. He composed some songs, published in London (Clementi), at Vienna (Cappi) and at Bonn (Simrock). An air written by him, ' In seno quest' alma,' was also printed.

A beautiful portrait of Marchesi was engraved (June 1790) by L. Schiavonetti, after R. Cosway ; and a curious caricature (now rare) was published under the name of ' A Bravura at the Hanover Square Concert,' by J. N[ixon], 1789, in which he is represented as a conceited coxcomb, bedizened with jewels, singing to the King, Prince of Wales and courtiers.   J. M.

MARCHESI, (1) SALVATORE, CAVALIERE DE CASTRONE, MARCHESE DELLA RAJATA (*b.* Palermo, Jan. 15, 1822 ; *d.* Paris, Feb. 20, 1908), husband of Mme. M. Marchesi, a baritone singer and teacher. His family belonged to the nobility, and his father was four years Governor-General of Sicily. In 1838 he entered the Neapolitan Guard, but, for political reasons, resigned his commission in 1840. Whilst studying law and philosophy at Palermo, he took lessons in singing and composition from Raimondi ; and he continued his musical studies at Milan under Lamperti and Fontana. Having participated in the revolutionary movement of 1848, he was forced to seek shelter in America, where he made his début, as an operatic singer, in ' Ernani.' He returned to Europe to take instruction from Garcia, and settled in London, where, for several seasons, he was favourably known as a concert singer. He married Mlle. Graumann in 1852, and with her made numerous concert tours in England, Germany and Belgium, appearing also in opera with success, both in England and on the Continent. He held posts as teacher of singing at the Conservatoires of Vienna and Cologne, and was appointed chamber singer to the court of Saxe-Weimar, 1862. From the King of Italy he received the orders of the Knights of St. Maurice and St. Lazarus. Marchesi was known also as the composer of several German and Italian songs, and as the Italian translator of many French and German libretti —' Medea,' ' La Vestale,' ' Iphigenia,' ' Tannhäuser,' ' Lohengrin,' etc. He wrote various books and some exercises.   B. T.

(2) MATHILDE DE CASTRONE, *née* GRAUMANN (*b.* Frankfort - on - the - Main, Mar. 26, 1826 ; *d.* London, Nov. 17, 1913), mezzo-soprano and famous teacher of singing, was the daughter of a wealthy merchant. She was very highly educated, but in 1843, her father having lost his fortune, she adopted the musical profession.

She studied singing at Vienna with Nicolai, but in 1845 went to Paris to learn from Garcia. Here she took lessons in declamation from Samson, Rachel's master, and had the advan-

tage of hearing all the first singers of the age—
Persiani, Grisi, Alboni, Duprez, Tamburini,
Lablache. Her own aptitude for teaching was
already so remarkable that Garcia, whilst prevented by the effects of an accident from giving
his lessons, handed over his whole clientèle
for the time to his young pupil. In 1849 Mlle.
Graumann removed to London, where she
obtained a high standing as a concert singer.
She sang successfully in Germany, Belgium,
Holland, Switzerland, France and the United
Kingdom, married Salvatore Marchesi in
1852, and in 1854 accepted the post of professor of singing at the Vienna Conservatoire,
the vocal department of which was then in its
infancy. But she soon won high distinction
for it and herself. Among her pupils at this
period were Mlles. Ilma di Murska, Fricci and
Kraus. She resigned her appointment in 1861,
and removed with her husband to Paris, where
pupils came to her from far and wide. At this
time appeared her ' École de chant.' Rossini,
in acknowledging the dedication of a volume of
' Vocalizzi,' extols her method as an exposition
of the true art of the Italian school of singing,
inclusive of the dramatic element ; and specially valuable when, he complains, the tendency
is to treat the vocal art as though it were a
question of the capture of barricades ! In 1865
she accepted a professorship at the Cologne
Conservatoire, but resigned it in 1868 to return
to Vienna to resume her post as teacher of
singing at the Conservatoire, which she held for
ten years. Among her famous scholars there
were Mlles. d'Angeri and Smeroschi, Mmes.
Schuch-Proska and Etelka Gerster. She resigned her appointment at the Conservatoire
in 1878, but continued for some time to reside
and teach in Vienna, where her services to art
met with full recognition. From the Emperor
of Austria she received the Cross of Merit of the
first class, and she held decorations and medals
from the King of Saxony, the Grand Duke of
Saxe-Weimar, the Emperor of Germany and
the King of Italy. She was a member of the
St. Cecilia Society in Rome and of the Academy
of Florence. In 1881 she returned to Paris,
where she prepared many of the greatest
singers of the younger generation for a public
career, notably Melba. She published a
Method of Singing, and twenty-four books of
exercises.   B. T.

Her reminiscences appeared in 1897. She
died at the house of her daughter, (3) BLANCHE
(b. Paris, Apr. 4, 1863), to whom the book is
dedicated. The latter was at first trained as
a violinist, but from 1881 devoted herself to
singing, and, until her marriage with Baron A.
Caccamisi, assisted her mother in teaching. In
1895 she appeared at Berlin and Brussels, and
on June 19, 1896, gave a vocal recital in the
small Queen's Hall, London. Subsequently
she lived in England and enjoyed great suc-

cess as a concert singer and as the teacher
of many pupils. She made an operatic début
at Prague in 1900 as Brünnhilde in ' Die
Walküre,' and occasionally appeared on the
English stage with the Moody-Manners Company.   A. C.

MARCHESINI, see LUCCHESINA ; MAR-
CHESI, Luigi.

MARCHETTI, FILIPPO (b. Bolognola, province of Macerata, Feb. 26, 1831 ; d. Jan. 18,
1901 [1]), successful composer of operas. At the
age of 12 he began to study with a master
named Bindi, and in his 15th year determined
to make music his profession.

In 1850 his parents sent him to Naples,
where he was admitted as a paying student at
the Real Collegio di San Pietro a Majella. His
principal instructor there was Carlo Conti, with
whom he studied counterpoint and composition. In 1854 Marchetti left Naples and returned home, where he devoted himself to the
composition of an opera, ' Gentile da Verano,'
the libretto of which was written by his brother
Raffaele. This work was produced at the
Teatro Nazionale, Turin, in Feb. 1856, with so
much success that the impresario of the theatre
hastened to secure the performing rights of
a second opera, ' La Demente,' upon which
Marchetti was then engaged. ' La Demente '
was produced at the Teatro Carignano, Turin,
on Nov. 27, 1856, and in the following year it
was revived at Rome and at Jesi. It was well
received at both places, but Marchetti found
it impossible to persuade any impresario to
produce his next opera, ' Il Paria,' which in
fact has never been performed or published.
Marchetti fell back upon the composition of
ballads and romances, of which he wrote many
at this period of his career, though even these
he found much difficulty in recommending to
the good graces of publishers. In the year
1862 he was recommended by his brother to
move his quarters from Rome to Milan, which
was the real centre of musical life in Italy. In
Milan Marchetti made the acquaintance of a
young poet named Marcelliano Marcello, who
persuaded him to undertake the composition
of a new version of ' Romeo and Juliet,' the
libretto of which he had himself arranged from
Shakespeare's tragedy. Marchetti hesitated
to attack a subject which had already been
treated by Bellini and many other composers,
and his diffidence would probably have been
augmented had he known that Gounod was at
the same time hard at work upon an opera
founded upon the same subject. Marcello,
however, succeeded in overcoming Marchetti's
scruples, and the new ' Romeo e Giulietta ' was
produced at Trieste on Oct. 24, 1865. Its
success at first was only moderate, but when
it was revived two years later at the Teatro
Carcano at Milan it was very favourably

<hr>

[1] Birth certificate published *Gazzetta musicale*, Feb. 6, 1902.

received, in spite of the formidable rivalry of Gounod's 'Roméo et Juliette,' which was being given at La Scala at the same time. With 'Ruy Blas,' his next work, which was produced at La Scala, Milan, on Apr. 3, 1869, Marchetti reached the zenith of his achievement. 'Ruy Blas,' written to a libretto taken by D'Ormeville from Victor Hugo's drama, speedily became popular in Italy, and in process of time carried the composer's fame across the Alps. It was performed in London with no little success at Her Majesty's Theatre, under the management of Mapleson, on Nov. 24, 1877, Mlle. Salla appearing as the Queen, Mlle. de Belocca as Casilda, Mme. Lablache as Donna de la Cueva, Signor Fancelli as Ruy Blas, and Signor Galassi as Don Sallustio. After 'Ruy Blas' Marchetti never succeeded in winning the popular suffrages. His two remaining works, 'Gustavo Wasa' (La Scala, Milan, Feb. 7, 1875) and 'Don Giovanni d' Austria' (Teatro Regio, Turin, Mar. 11, 1880), made little impression. After 1880 Marchetti wrote no more for the stage, but devoted his energies entirely to teaching. In 1881 he was appointed President of the Reale Accademia di Santa Cecilia in Rome, and in 1885 he undertook the onerous duties of director of the Liceo Musicale in the same city, a post which he held until his death. Marchetti's fame as a composer was short-lived. Changes in musical taste soon made 'Ruy Blas' seem old-fashioned, and in his later works the composer showed no power of adapting his style to the requirements of modern audiences. He may be described as a typical Italian composer of the second rank. In his music the influence of Verdi is not unnaturally supreme, but unfortunately it is the Verdi of earlier days, not the composer of 'Aïda' and the Manzoni Requiem, who served as Marchetti's model. Marchetti's capacity for sheer musical invention was limited; but in 'Ruy Blas,' his most careful and most meritorious work, the musicianship is often admirable, the orchestration effective without vulgarity, while the composer displays a commendable feeling for characterisation, notably exemplified in the music allotted to the three female characters.   R. A. S.

MARCHETTUS of Padua, a musical theorist ot the early part of the 14th century. Of his life nothing is known except that he was in the service of Rainier, Prince of Monaco, and that some of his works were written at Cesena and Verona. He was the author of two treatises, the *Lucidarium in arte musicae planae* and the *Pomerium artis musicae mensurabilis*, both of which are printed in the third volume of Gerbert's *Scriptores*. The dedications of these two books point to their having been completed later than 1309, though the Milan manuscript of the *Lucidarium* is said to be dated 1274 and the Vatican manuscript of the *Pomerium*, 1283.

The *Lucidarium* is remarkable for the chromaticism employed and for the division of the whole tone either into three-fifths and two-fifths (diatonic and enharmonic semitones) or into four-fifths and one-fifth (chromatic semitone and diesis). The *Pomerium* is of great interest as marking the transition from the Franconian system of notation, in which the shortest musical note admitted was the semibreve, equal to one-third of a breve, to the 'ars nova' of Philip de Vitry and his successors, in which the minim and semiminim were differentiated and brought into the scheme of perfection and imperfection. Marchettus meets the growing need for notes of smaller value by reckoning any number of semibreves from two to twelve to the breve, and distinguishes their values by the addition or omission of tails above or below.[1] He also points out the differences between Italian and French notation. An epitome of the *Pomerium* entitled *Brevis compilatio Magistri Marchetti musici de Padua in arte musice mensurate primis rudibus et modernis* is printed in the third volume of Coussemaker's *Scriptores* from a 14th-century manuscript at St. Dié, which also contains the *Lucidarium*, the *Ars mensurabilis musice* of Franco, and other musical treatises. Fétis's manuscript containing the *Lucidarium*, the *Pomerium* and the *Brevis compilatio* is now in the Royal Library at Brussels. Other manuscripts are at Florence, at Pisa, and in the monastery of Einsiedeln.

Marchettus deserves credit for his attempt to amplify the means of musical expression, but his system of notation was too complex to become of practical utility, and was soon displaced by the bolder and simpler methods of the 'ars nova.' He suffered the penalty of failure, and met with much abuse at the hands of some of his successors. In 1410 Prosdocimus de Beldemandis wrote an *Opusculum contra theoricam partem sive speculativam Lucidarii Marcheti Patavini*, of which there is a manuscript copy at Bologna. In it he asserts that Marchettus was altogether ignorant of theory, and scoffs at his presumption in posing as a scientific musician. Joannes Carthusiensis wrote that Marchettus deserved a schoolboy's whipping; and in the *Musices opusculum* of Nicolaus Burtius (Bologna, 1487) the worst that the author can say of his opponent, Ramis de Pareia, is that he 'imitated the crass stupidity and fatuity of Marchettus.'   J. F. R. S.

MARCHISIO, The Sisters, (1) BARBARA (b. Turin, Dec. 12, 1834; d. Mira, Apr. 19, 1919); (2) CARLOTTA (b. Turin, Dec. 6, 1836; d. there, June 28, 1872). Both were taught singing at Turin by Luigi Fabbrica, and both made their débuts as Adalgisa, the elder (who afterwards became a contralto) at Vienna in 1856, the younger at Madrid. They played at Turin in 1857–58, and made great success there

[1] See Wolf, *Geschichte der Mensural-Notation*, 1904, p. 30.

as Arsace and Semiramide; also on a tour through Italy, and at the Paris Opéra on the production of ' Semiramis,' July 9, 1860. They first appeared in England with great success at Land's concerts, St. James's Hall, Jan. 2 and 4, 1862, in duets of Rossini and Gabussi, and made a concert tour through the provinces with Willert Beale. They also made a success in ' Semiramide ' at Her Majesty's, May 1, 1860, on account of their excellent duet singing, though separately their voices were coarse and harsh, their appearance insignificant, and they were indifferent actresses. Carlotta played the same season Isabella in ' Robert,' June 14, and Donna Anna, July 9. They sang also at the Crystal Palace, twice at the New Philharmonic, at the Monday Popular, etc. They sang together for some time abroad. Carlotta married a Viennese singer, Eugen Kuhn (1835–75), who sang with her in concerts, and at Her Majesty's in 1862 under the name of Coselli, and who afterwards became a pianoforte manufacturer at Venice.   A. C.

MARCOUX, VANNI (b. Turin, June 12, 1879), operatic baritone of French parentage. He first learned singing whilst studying for the law, but, after being admitted to the bar, relinquished the latter and went to Paris to complete his vocal training under Boyer. He had a naturally fine organ, with a dramatic quality and ringing timbre, as well as the histrionic temperament fitting him for a stage career. After a successful début at Bayonne in 1899 as Frère Laurent, he made his mark at Nice the same winter as Marcel in the first performance there of Puccini's ' La Bohème.' Then for four or five years he gained experience in France and also at the Brussels Monnaie. In 1905 he was engaged for Covent Garden, and among other parts sang Basilio in ' Il Barbiere ' and created that of Vim-sci in Leoni's ' L' oracolo.' Later on (1908–1914) he appeared in England in many of the leading baritone rôles, his best being Mephistopheles, Scarpia and Marcello. During the same period he was singing with unfailing success at the Paris Opéra, where he created (Jan. 1909) the rôle of Colonna in Février's ' MonnaVanna '; but perhaps his chief triumph in France was the creation, at Monte Carlo in Feb. 1910, of Don Quichotte in Massenet's opera of that name, which during the next six years he sang no fewer than 150 times at the Paris Opéra alone. His American career began, in 1912, at the Boston Opera House, with what was considered a singularly fine impersonation of Golaud in ' Pelléas et Mélisande.' Subsequently he joined the Chicago Opera Company and remained with it for several years.

BIBL.—Int. Who's Who in Music.   H. K.

MARÉCHAL, CHARLES HENRI (b. Paris, Jan. 22, 1842 ; d. there, May 10, 1924), opera composer, worked at first at solfège with A. Chevé and E. Batiste, studied the piano with Chollet,

and harmony with B. Laurent; finally, at the Conservatoire, studied the organ with Benoist, counterpoint with Chauvet, and composition with Victor Massé. In 1870 he obtained the Grand Prix de Rome with the cantata ' Le Jugement de Dieu.' He was chorus-master at the Théâtre Lyrique in 1867, and was appointed in 1896 inspector of musical education. His first important composition was a sacred piece, ' La Nativité,' in 1875, but he afterwards devoted himself to the theatre, for which he wrote the following : ' Les Amours de Catherine ' (one act, Opéra-Comique, 1876) ; ' La Caverne des Trabans ' (three acts, gained the Prix Monbinne in 1876, produced Opéra-Comique, 1881) ; ' L'Étoile ' (one act, 1881) ; ' Déidamie ' (two acts, Opéra, 1893) ; ' Calendal ' (four acts, Rouen, 1894) ; ' Ping-Sin ' (1895) ; ' Daphnis et Chloé ' (three acts, Théâtre Lyrique, 1899) ; incidental music for ' L'Ami Fritz ' (Comédie Française, 1876), ' Les Rantzau,' ' Smilis,' ' Crime et châtiment,' etc. For the concert-room he wrote ' Les Vivants et les morts,' for vocal quartet with orchestra (1886) ; ' Le Miracle de Naim,' sacred drama (1887) ; ' Esquisses vénitiennes ' (1894), and ' Antar ' (1897), both for orchestra. He also published many choral and instrumental compositions. He published Souvenirs d'un musicien, Paris, 1907 ; Lettres et souvenirs, 1920.   G. F.

MARÉCHAL, MAURICE (b. Dijon, Oct. 3, 1892), violoncellist, took the first prize at the Paris Conservatoire in 1911. After a remarkable début his career was interrupted by the war, but in 1919 he again took up his musical work.

He was soloist at the Concerts Lamoureux in 1919, at the Société des Concerts du Conservatoire in 1920, and at the Philharmonic in 1923. He became a member of the Board of examiners at the Paris Conservatoire in June 1921.

Maurice Maréchal has made a success throughout Europe and in the United States. He has played a number of compositions for the first time, such as the duo of Ravel (S.I.M., Apr. 1922) and the trio of Guy Ropartz (Nationale, 1921).   M. P.

MARENZIO, LUCA (b. before 1560 ; d. Aug. 22, 1599). The oldest account we can find of this great Italian composer is given by O. Rossi,[1] in 1620. It tells us of Marenzio's birth at Coccaglia, a small town on the road between Brescia and Bergamo, of the pastoral beauty of his early surroundings, and the effect they may have had in forming the taste of the future madrigal composer, of the patronage accorded him by great princes, of his valuable post at the court of Poland, worth 1000 scudi a year, of the delicate health which made his return to a more genial climate necessary, of the kind treatment

---

[1] Elogi historici di Bresciani illustri di Ottavio Rossi. (Brescia, Fontana, 1620.)

he received from Cardinal Cintio Aldobrandino at Rome, of his early death in that city, and burial at S. Lorenzo in Lucina. The same author gives an account of Giovanni Contini, organist [1] of the cathedral at Brescia, and later in the service of the Duke of Mantua, under whose direction Marenzio completed his studies, having for his fellow-pupil Lelio Bertani,[1] who afterwards served the Duke of Ferrara for 1500 scudi a year, and was even asked to become the Emperor's maestro di cappella.

Donato Calvi, writing in 1664,[2] anxious to claim Marenzio as a native of Bergamo, traces his descent from the noble family of Marenzi, and finds in their pedigree a Luca Marenzo. He adds further details to Rossi's account, how the King of Poland knighted the composer on his departure, how warmly he was welcomed by the court of Rome on his return, how Cardinal C. Aldobrandino behaved like a servant rather than a patron to him. We are also there told that he died Aug. 22, 1599, being then a singer in the Papal Chapel (though on this point compare later statements), and that there was a grand musical service at his funeral.

In the next account Brescia again puts in a claim, and Leonardo Cozzando [3] asserts that Marenzio was born at Coccaglia, that his parents were poor, and that the whole expense of his living and education was defrayed by Andrea Masetto, the village priest. To Cozzando we are also indebted for a special article on Marenzio's great merits as a singer, and after reading of him under the head of Brescian composers, we find him further mentioned under 'Cantori.'[4]

A fourth account, quite independent of these, and one of the earliest of all, is that given by Henry Peacham, published in 1622.[5] Of the composers of his time, Byrd is his favourite, Victoria and Lassus coming next. Then of Marenzio he says :

'For delicious Aire and sweete Invention in Madrigals, *Luca Marenzio* excelleth all other whosoever, having published more Sets than any Authour else whosoever : and to say truth, hath not an ill Song, though sometime an oversight (which might be the Printer's fault) of two *eights* or *fifts* escape him ; as betweene the *Tenor* and *Base* in the last close, of, *I must depart all haplesse* : ending according to the nature of the Dittie most artificially, with a Minim rest. His first, second, and third parts of *Thyrsis, Veggo dolce mio ben che fæ hoggi mio Sole Cantava,* or *sweete singing Amaryllis,*[6] are Songs, the Muses themselves might not have beene ashamed to have had composed. Of stature and complexion, hee was a little and blacke man : he was Organist in the Popes Chappell at *Rome* a good while, afterward hee went into *Poland,* being in displeasure with the Pope for

[1] For list of works see *Q.-L.*
[2] *Scena litteraria de gli scrittori bergamaschi.* Donato Calvi. (Bergamo, 1664.)
[3] *Libreria Bresciana.* Leonardo Cozzando. (Brescia, Rizzardi, 1685.)
[4] *Vago e curioso ristretto, etc., dell' Historia Bresciana.* Leonardo Cozzando. (Brescia, Rizzardi, 1694.)
[5] *The Compleat Gentleman,* by Henry Peacham, M[r.] of Arts. (London, 1622.)
[6] The proper titles of these, which are given in the above confused manner in Peacham's book, are—' Tirsi morir volea (a 5) ' ; ' Veggo dolce mio bene (a 4)' ; ' Che fa hogg' il mio sole (a 5) ' ; and ' Cantava la piu vaga (a 5),' the English words ' Sweete Singing Amaryllis ' being adapted to the music of the last.

overmuch familiaritie with a kinswoman of his (whom the Queene of *Poland,* sent for by *Luca Marenzio* afterward, she being one of the rarest women in *Europe,* for her voyce and the Lute :) but returning, he found the affection of the Pope so estranged from him, that hereupon hee tooke a conceipt and died.'

The above accounts agree in all important points, and even the descent from a noble Bergamese family is not inconsistent with the parents' poverty and their residence at Coccaglia. Marenzio certainly died at a comparatively early age, in 1599, and we may therefore place his birth about 1560, though not later, for he began to publish in 1581. On Apr. 10 in that year he was in Venice, dedicating his first book of madrigals (a 5) to Alfonso d' Este, Duke of Ferrara. He was in Rome, Dec. 1, 1582,[7] on Apr. 24,[8] and Dec. 15, 1584,[9] was maestro de cappella to the Cardinal d' Este in the same year, [10] and was still in the same city on July 15, 1585.[11]

We do not think he went to Poland just yet, but we have no more publications for some years. Marenzio probably received his appointment soon after the accession of Sigismund III. (1587), and is said to have kept it for two years, either from 1588–90, or from 1591–93.

He was back in Rome in 1595, writing to Dowland, July 13,[12] and to Don Diego de Campo, Oct. 20,[13] and in the same year is said to have been appointed to the Papal Chapel.[14] It was now that he lived on such familiar terms with Cardinal Aldobrandino, the Pope's nephew, and taking into this account Peacham's tale may have some truth in it, and Marenzio may have fallen in love with a lady belonging to his patron's family. If, however, he died of a broken heart, as is suggested, it must have been caused simply by the Pope's refusal to allow a marriage.

Marenzio's principal works are : 9 books of madrigals (a 5), 6 books (a 6), each book containing from 13 to 20 nos., and 1 book (a 4) containing 21 nos. ; 5 books of ' Villanelle e arie alla Napolitana,' containing 113 nos. (a 3) and 1 (a 4) ; 2 books of four-part motets, many of which have been printed in modern notation by Proske [15] ; 1 Mass (a 8), two books of motets (4 v.), 1588, 1592; a book of motets (12 v.), 1614; a book of ' Sacri concenti,' 1616 ; a complete series of motets for all church festivals. (See list in *Q.-L.*) Haberl has republished the motets of Marenzio. The first five books of madrigals a 5 were printed ' in uno corpo ridotto,' in 1593, and a similar edition of those

[7] See dedication to the Philharmonic Academicians of Verona of 3rd Book of Madrigals (a 5). (Venice, Gardane, 1582.)
[8] See ' Madrigali spirituali a 5 di L. M.' (Rome, Gardano, 1584.)
[9] Dedication of ' Il quinto lib. de madrigali a 5.' (Vinegia Scotto, 1585.)
[10] Title-page of ' Primo lib. de madr. a 6.' (Venice, Gardano, 1584.)
[11] Dedication of ' Madr. a 4 di L. M.' Lib. primo. (Venetia, Gardano, 1592.)
[12] ' First booke of Songs or Ayres of 4 parts by John Dowland.' (Short, Bred St. Hill, 1597.) Reprinted by Fellowes, *Eng. Sch. of Lutenist Songwriters,* vol. i.
[13] ' Di L. M. il 7mo lib. dt madr. a 5.' (Venetia, Gardano, 1595.)
[14] We cannot find any old authority for the date of appointment, and Eitner (*Q.-L.*) doubts it.
[15] ' Musica divina,' etc. Carl Proske, vol. ii. (Ratisbon, 1853.)

a 6 in 1594. These books, containing 78 and 76 pieces respectively, are both in the British Museum. (See MADRIGAL.)

Marenzio's works were introduced into England in 1588, in the collection entitled ' MUSICA TRANSALPINA ' (*q.v.*) (1588) and two years afterwards a similar book was printed, to which he contributed 23 out of 28 numbers.[1] His reputation here was soon established, for in 1595 John Dowland, the lutenist, ' not being able to dissemble the great content he had found in the proffered amity of the most famous Luca Marenzio,' thought the mere advertisement of their correspondence would add to the chance of his own works being well received. Burney does not hesitate to say that the madrigal style was brought to the highest degree of perfection by Marenzio's superior genius, and that the publication of the ' Musica transalpina ' gave birth to that passion for madrigals which became so prevalent among us when our own composers so happily contributed to gratify it.[2] Thus it came to pass that Luca Marenzio became bound up in our own musical history, and few foreign musicians of the 16th century have been kept so constantly before the English public. The Madrigal Society became a home for his works more than 150 years ago, and they have been sung continually by much younger societies. ' To guard faithfully and lovingly the beautiful things, and to reverence the great masters, of olden times, is quite a part of the English character, and one of its most beautiful traits.'[3]　　　J. R. S.-B.

MARESCHALL, SAMUEL (*b.* Tournay, May 1554 ; *d.* after 1640), was town and university organist at Basle from 1577 to his death some time after 1640. In 1606 he published at Basle a Choralbuch for four voices, containing Lobwasser's German versified translation of the Psalter with the original French tunes as in Goudimel, the melody, however, in the soprano; also some additional German hymns and tunes. Some of his settings are given in Winterfeld and Schöberlein. In MS. there exist a large number of his organ arrangements of some of these French psalm tunes, and other French and German songs. See *Q.-L.*　　　J. R. M.

MARGHERITA, see ÉPINE, F. M. de L'.

MARIA ANTONIA WALPURGA (or WALPURGIS) (*b.* Munich, July 18, 1724 ; *d.* Dresden, Apr. 23, 1780), Electress of Saxony, daughter of the Elector of Bavaria, afterwards the Emperor Charles VII., learnt music from Giovanni Ferrandini, Porpora, and finally Hasse. She was a member of the Arcadian Academy in Rome, and the initials of her academical name, ' Ernelinda Talia Pastorella Arcada ' were used by her to sign her compositions. The most important of these were

two operas, ' Il trionfo della fedeltà,' performed at Potsdam in 1753 before Frederick the Great, and furnished with additional numbers by him, Hasse, Graun and Benda ; and ' Talestri Regina dell' Amazone,' performed in 1763. Both were published by Breitkopf & Härtel, the former in 1756 being one of the first printed with their newly invented types, and the latter appearing in 1765. (*Q.-L.*) See also *M.f.M.* vol. xi. p. 167.　　　M.

MARIA DI ROHAN, opera in 3 acts ; music by Donizetti. Produced Vienna, June 5, 1843 ; Théâtre Italien, Paris, Nov. 20, 1843 ; Covent Garden, May 8, 1847.　　　G.

MARIANI, ANGELO (*b.* Ravenna, Oct. 11, 1822 ; *d.* Genoa, Oct. 13, 1873), a famous Italian conductor ; began to study the violin when quite young, under Pietro Casolini ; later on he had instruction in harmony and composition from a monk named Levrini, of Rimini, who was a celebrated contrapuntist. He was at the Liceo Filarmonico at Bologna, where he had instruction from Rossini. It was in 1844, at Messina, that he assumed the baton—which after all was only the bow of his violin, for at that time the conductor of an Italian orchestra was named *Primo Violino direttore dell' orchestra.*

After several engagements in different theatres in Italy, Mariani was appointed, in 1847, conductor of the Court Theatre at Copenhagen. While there he wrote a Requiem Mass for the funeral of Christian VIII. At the beginning of 1848 he left Denmark and went to Italy to fight in the ranks of the volunteers for the freedom of his country. At the end of the war he was called to Constantinople, where his ability won him the admiration of the Sultan, who made him many valuable presents ; and Mariani, as a mark of gratitude, composed a hymn which he dedicated to him. In Constantinople also he wrote two grand cantatas, ' La fidanzata del guerriero ' and ' Gli esuli,' both works reflecting the aspirations and attempts of the Italian movement. He returned to Italy in 1852, landing at Genoa, where he was at once invited to be the conductor of the Carlo Felice. In a short time he reorganised that orchestra so as to make it the first in Italy. His fame soon filled the country and spread abroad ; he had offers of engagements from London, St. Petersburg and Paris, but he would never accept them ; he had fixed his headquarters in Genoa, and only absented himself for short periods at a time, to conduct at Bologna, at Venice, and other important Italian towns. Mariani exercised an extraordinary personal fascination on all those who were under his direction. For him, no matter the name of the composer, the music he conducted at the moment was always the most beautiful, and he threw himself into it with all his soul. Great masters as well as young

[1] ' First part of Italian Madrigals Englished,' etc. Published by Thomas Watson (1590).
[2] *Gen. Hist. of Music*, vol. iii. pp. 201, 119.
[3] Ambros, *Geschichte der Musik*, iii. 460.

composers were happy to receive his advice, and he gave it in the interest of art and for the improvement of the work. At rehearsal nothing escaped him in the orchestra or on the stage.

In 1864 Mariani was the director of the grand fêtes celebrated at Pesaro in honour of Rossini, and was himself greeted enthusiastically by the public, which was in great part composed of the most eminent musicians of the world. On Nov. 1, 1871, he introduced 'Lohengrin' at the Comunale of Bologna, and, thanks to his efforts, the opera was such a success that it was performed through the season several times a week—and he had only nine orchestral rehearsals for it! On this occasion Richard Wagner sent him a large photograph of himself, under which he wrote 'Evviva Mariani.'

The day of Mariani's funeral was a day of mourning for the whole of Genoa. His body was transported to Ravenna at the request of the latter city. The Genoese municipality ordered a bust of him to be placed in the vestibule of the Carlo Felice; all the letters written to him by the leading composers and literary men of the day to be preserved in the town library; the portrait sent by Wagner hung in one of the rooms of the Palazzo Civico; and his last baton placed by the side of Paganini's violin in the civic museum.

Besides the works already named, and other orchestral pieces, he published several collections of songs, all of which are charmingly melodious: 'Rimembranze del Bosforo,' 'Il Trovatore nella Liguria,' 'Liete e tristi rimembranze,' 'Otto pezzi vocali,' 'Nuovo album vocale.'

BIBL.—T. MANTOVANI, *Angelo Mariani*. (Rome, 1921.)

F. R^z.

MARIMBA, a curious instrument (said to possess great musical capabilities) in use in the southern parts of Mexico. In type it is of the wooden harmonica species, but is much larger, of more extended range, and has a sound-box to each note. Its compass is five octaves extending upwards from A. A large table-like frame, five or six feet in length, on legs supports a graduated series of strips of hard and well-seasoned wood. Below each of these is fixed an oblong cedar box equally graduated in size. The box, which serves as a resonator, is entirely closed except at the top, but has a small hole covered with thin bladder at the lower end. The wooden note being struck with a drumstick has its vibrations increased by the resonator with the addition of a peculiar buzzing sound. The instrument, which also bears another name, 'Zapotecano,' is to be played by four performers, each armed with a pair of drumsticks varying in size and weight, the heads generally of soft crude indiarubber. A description, with illustrations from photo-

graphs, is to be seen in the *Mus. T.* for May 1901 (cf. XYLOPHONE).

The marimba is also known in Africa, its original home, where it is formed in a similar but rather more primitive fashion, gourds taking the place of the wooden sound-boxes. (*PLATE XXIV.* No. 7).   F. K.

MARIMBA GONGS, an instrument which takes its name from the foregoing but is akin to the GLOCKENSPIEL in effect. It consists of a series of bell-metal plates fitted with resonators which produce a fairy-like tone.

N. C. G.

MARIN, JOSÉ (*b.* Madrid, 1619; *d.* there, Mar. 17, 1699), Spanish composer. In 1644 he was engaged as tenor in the choir of the Convent of the Incarnation at Madrid. Twelve years later, however, he is mentioned by a contemporary diarist as being one of three notorious highwaymen, imprisoned for robbery with violence. Marin and one of the others are described as belonging to the clergy; and Marin is further identified by the description *musico de la Encarnación*. He is called the best musician in Madrid, but one who had already committed a murder and had fled to Rome and there been ordained priest. He was put to the torture, deprived of his orders, and sentenced to banishment for ten years. Meanwhile he was strictly confined in chains; but he managed to escape, and lived to be a celebrated musician, known in Italy as well as Spain. He died in old age, full of honour; his death was announced in the official gazette. His songs, with continuo, or with accompaniment definitely written for the guitar, have something approaching the quality of Purcell. Examples are given by Pedrell in his 'Teatro lírico,' iv. (1897); his MSS. are preserved in the Bibl. Nac., Madrid, and other songs by him are found in a MS. in the Bibl. Marciana, Venice (Cod. 470, Gir. Contarini).   J. B. T.

MARIN, MARIE-MARTIN MARCEL DE, Viscount, of Venetian descent (*b.* St. Jean de Luz, Bayonne, Sept. 8, 1769; still living in 1861), excellent harpist, violinist and composer; Fétis characterises his harp compositions as truly classical. On his second voyage to Italy in 1783 he was elected member of the Arcadians at Rome. At the outbreak of the French Revolution he came to London, where he met with great success, and some of his harp sonatas, etc., were published by Clementi in 1799–1800. He settled afterwards at Toulouse. Fétis gives a list of his compositions for harp and for violin, sonatas and chamber music, as well as an account of his varied adventures (See also *Q.-L.*)

MARIN DE LA GUERRE, ELISABETH, *see* JACQUET DE LA GUERRE.

MARINI, BIAGIO (*b.* Brescia; *d.* ? Padua, *c.* 1660), was employed as a violinist in Venice in 1617, was director of the music at Sant'

Eufemia in Brescia in 1620; in 1622 entered the service of Ferdinand Gonzaga at Parma, and in 1626 was maestro della musica to the Duke of Bavaria. He was at Düsseldorf about 1640, and in 1653 was maestro to the Accademia della Morte at Ferrara, and in the following year to Santa Maria della Scala at Milan. He is said by Fétis to have died at Padua, where he was a member of the Academy of the Occulti; the date of his death is given in Cozzando's *Libreria Bresciana* as 1660. He is important as one of the earliest of those Italian violinists who published concerted instrumental music. The following is a list of the most important :

Op.
1. Affetti musicali. . . . symfonie, canzone, sonate, balletti, arie, brandi, gagliarde e corenti, a 1, 2, 3 (for violins, cornets and other sorts of instruments). Venice, 1617.
2. Madrigale et symfonie, a 1, 2, 3, 4, 5. Venice, 1618.
3. Arie, madrigali et corenti, a 1, 2, 3. Venice, 1620. (These two books contain vocal as well as instrumental pieces.)
5. Scherzi e canzonette a 1 e 2 voci. Parma, 1622.
6. Le Lagrime d' Erminia in stile recitativo. Parma, 1623.
7. Canto per le musiche di camera concerti, a 4-6 voci, ed instromenti. Venice, 1634.
8. Sonate, symphonie, canzoni pass' emezzi, baletti, corenti, gagliarde, e ritornelli a 1-6 voci, per ogni sorte d' instrumenti . . . con altre curiose e moderne inventioni. Venice, 1626.
9. Madrigaletti, a 1-4 voci. Venice, 1635. (The only known copies of this and of 7 are in the Christ Church Library, Oxford.)
13. Compositioni varie per musica di camera, a 2-5 voci. Venice, 1641.
15. Corona melodica ex diversis sacrae musices floribus concinnata, 2-6 voc. ac instrumentis. Antwerp, 1644.
16. Concerto terzo delle musiche da camera a 3-6 e più voci. Milan, 1649.
18. Salmi per tutti le solennità dell' anno . . . ad 1-3 voci. Venice, 1653.
20. Vespri per tutte le festività dell' anno, a 4 voci. Venice, 1654.
21. Lacrime di Davide sparse nel Miserere concertato in diversi modi a 2-4 e più voci. Venice, 1655.
22. Per ogni sorte d' istromento musicale diversi generi di sonate da chiesa e da camera, a 2-4. Venice, 1655.

(*Q.-L.*, etc.)   M.

MARINO, CARLO AMBROSIO, violinist at S. Maria Maggiore, Bergamo, 1687; composed solo cantatas and a large number of sonatas for two violins and bass with and without other instruments; also solo sonatas for violin, and a book of 'Balletti, correnti, gighe,' etc., for 2 vlns. and v'cl. or spinet (*Q.-L.*).

MARINO FALIERO, opera in 2 acts; music by Donizetti. Produced Paris, Théâtre Italien, 1835; London, King's Theatre, May 14, 1835.

G.

MARIO (GIOVANNI MATTEO), CAVALIERE DI CANDIA (*b.* Cagliari, Oct. 17, 1810 [1]; *d.* Rome, Dec. 11, 1883), the greatest operatic tenor of his generation, was of an old and noble family. His father had been a general in the Piedmontese army; and he himself, after ten years in the Turin Military Academy, was an officer in the Piedmontese Guard, when he first came to Paris in 1836, and immediately became a great favourite in society. Never was youth more richly gifted for the operatic stage; beauty of voice, face and figure, with the most winning grace of Italian manner, were all his. But he was then only an amateur, and as yet all unfitted for public singing, which his friends constantly suggested to him, even if he could reconcile his pride with the taking of such a step. Tempted as he was by the offers made to him by

Duponchel, the director of the Opéra—which are said to have reached the sum of frs. 1500 a month, a large sum for a beginning—and pressed by the embarrassments created by expensive tastes, he still hesitated to sign his father's name to such a contract; but was finally persuaded to do so at the house of the Comtesse de Merlin, where he was dining one evening with Prince Belgiojoso and other well-known amateurs; and he compromised the matter with his family pride by signing only the Christian name, under which he became afterwards so famous—Mario.

He is said to have spent some time in study, directed by the advice of Michelet, Ponchard and the great singing-master, Bordogni; but it cannot have been very long nor the study very deep, for there is no doubt that he was a very incomplete singer when he made his first appearance. This was on Nov. 30, 1838, in the rôle of 'Robert le Diable.' Notwithstanding his lack of preparation and want of habit of the stage, his success was assured from the first moment when his delicious voice and graceful figure were first presented to the French public. Mario remained at the Opéra during that year, but in 1840 he passed to the Italian Opera, for which his native tongue and manner better fitted him.

In the meantime, he had made his first appearance in London, where he continued to sing through many years of a long and brilliant career. His début here was in 'Lucrezia Borgia,' June 6, 1839: but, as a critic [2] of the time observed,

'the vocal command which he afterwards gained was unthought of; his acting did not then get beyond that of a southern man with a strong feeling for the stage. But physical beauty and geniality, such as have been bestowed on few, a certain artistic taste, a certain distinction—not exclusively belonging to gentle birth, but sometimes associated with it—made it clear, from Signor Mario's first hour of stage-life, that a course of no common order of fascination was begun.'

Mario sang, after this, in each season at Paris and in London, improving steadily both in acting and singing, though it fell to his lot to 'create' but few new characters—scarcely another beside that of the 'walking lover' in 'Don Pasquale,' a part which consisted of little more than the singing of the serenade 'Com' è gentil.' In other parts he only followed his predecessors, though with a grace and charm which were peculiar to him, and which may possibly remain for ever unequalled.

'It was not till the season of 1846 that he took the place of which no wear and tear of time had been able to deprive him.' [3]

He had then played Almaviva, Gennaro, Raoul, and had shown himself undoubtedly the most perfect stage-lover ever seen, whatever may have been his other qualities or defects. His singing in the duet of the fourth Act of the 'Ugonotti' raised him again above this; and

[1] Baptismal register, Cathedral of S. Cecilia, Cagliari, Oct. 18, 1810. See also *The Romance of a Great Singer: a Memoir of Mario*, by C. M. Pearse and F. Hird. (London, 1910.)

[2] Chorley.   [3] *Ibid.*

in 'La favorita' he achieved, perhaps, his highest point of attainment as a dramatic singer.

Like Garcia and Nourrit, Mario attempted 'Don Giovanni,' and with similarly small success. The violence done to Mozart's music partly accounts for the failure of tenors to appropriate this great character; Mario was unfitted for it by nature. The reckless profligate found no counterpart in the easy grace of his love-making; he was too amiable in the eyes of the public to realise for them the idea of the 'Dissoluto punito.'

As a singer of 'romances' Mario has never been surpassed. The native elegance of his demeanour contributed not a little to his vocal success in the drawing-room; for refinements of accent and pronunciation create effects there which would be inappreciable in the larger space of a theatre. Mario was not often heard in oratorio, but he sang 'Then shall the righteous,' in 'Elijah,' at the Birmingham Festival of 1849, and 'If with all your hearts,' in the same oratorio, at Hereford, in 1855. For the stage he was born, and to the stage he remained faithful during his artistic life. To the brilliance of his success in opera he brought one great helping quality, the eye for colour and all the important details of costume. His figure on the stage looked as if it had stepped out of the canvas of Titian, Veronese or Tintoretto. Never was an actor more harmoniously and beautifully dressed for the characters he impersonated — no mean advantage, and no slight indication of the complete artistic temperament.

For five-and-twenty years Mario remained before the public of Paris, London and St. Petersburg, constantly associated with Mme. Grisi. In the earlier years (1843–46) of that brilliant quarter of a century, he took the place of Rubini in the famous quartet, with Tamburini and Lablache; this, however, did not last long; and he soon remained alone with the sole remaining star of the original constellation, Mme. Grisi. To this gifted prima donna Mario was united, after the dissolution of her former marriage; and by her he had three daughters. He left the stage in 1867, and retired to Paris (his farewell appearance took place at Covent Garden in 1871, in 'La favorita '), and then to Rome, where he died. About 1880 it became known that he was in reduced circumstances, and his friends got up a concert in London for his benefit.   J. M.

MARIONETTE-THEATRE, a small stage on which puppets, moved by wires and strings, act operas, plays and ballets, the songs or dialogue being sung or spoken behind the scenes. The repertories included both serious and comic pieces, but mock-heroic and satiric dramas were the most effective. Puppet-plays,[1] in England and Italy called 'fantoccini,' once popular with

all classes, go back as far as the 15th century.[i] From that period to the end of the 17th century Punch was so popular as to inspire Addison with a Latin poem, 'Machinae gesticulantes.' In 1713 a certain Powell erected a Punch theatre under the arcade of Covent Garden, where pieces founded on nursery rhymes, such as the 'Babes in the Wood,' 'Robin Hood' and 'Mother Goose,' were performed; later on they even reached Shakespeare and opera. About the same period marionette-theatres were erected in the open spaces at Vienna, and these have reappeared from time to time ever since.[3] Prince Esterhazy, at his summer residence, Esterház, had a fantastically decorated grotto for his puppet-plays, with a staff of skilled machinists, scene-painters, playwrights, and above all a composer, his Kapellmeister Haydn, whose love of humour found ample scope in these performances. His opera 'Philemon und Baucis' so delighted the Empress Maria Teresa, that by her desire Prince Esterhazy had the whole apparatus sent to Vienna for the amusement of the court. In London, fantoccini were playing between the years 1770 and 1780 at Hickford's large Rooms in Panton Street, Haymarket, Marylebone Gardens and in Piccadilly. In Nov. 1791 Haydn was present at one of these performances[4] in the elegant little theatre called Variétés Amusantes, belonging to Lord Barrymore, in Savile Row. He was much interested, and wrote in his diary, 'The puppets were well-managed, the singers bad, but the orchestra tolerably good.' The playbill may be quoted as a specimen.

FANTOCCINI

Dancing and music.

Overture, Haydn.	Spanish Fandango.
A comedy in one act, 'Arlequin valet.'	Concertante, Pleyel.
Overture, Piccini [sic.].	A comedy in one act, 'Les Petits Riens,'
The favourite opera (5th time)	the music by Sacchini and Paisiello.
'La buona figliuola,' the music by Piccini, Giordani and Sarti.	To conclude with a Pas de deux à-la-mode de Vestris and Hillisberg.

Leader of the band: Mr. Mountain.

First hautboy: Sgr. Patria.

To begin at 8; the doors open at 7 o'clock.

The theatre is well aired and illuminated with wax.

Refreshments to be had at the Rooms of the theatre. Boxes, 5/. Pit, 3/.

A critic in The Gazetteer says:

'So well did the motion of the puppets agree with the voice and tone of the prompters, that, after the eye had been accustomed to them for a few minutes, it was difficult to remember that they were puppets.'
                                        C. F. P.

The vogue of the marionette-theatre lasted through the 19th century in Italy (where it was generally managed by English performers), but the performances of regular plays became rarer than exhibitions of single dancing dolls. At the

---

[1] See Strutt's *Sports and Pastimes of the People of England*, London, 1830.

[2] The experiment of employing puppets for operatic representation was tried in Venice in the 17th century. (See OPERA, p. 694.)
[3] In 1877 Raupach's *Müller und sein Kind*, and the *Ring des Nibelungen* were performed there and elsewhere by puppets.
[4] See Pohl's *Mozart und Haydn in London*, p. 162.

XLVII

Photo, W. & D. Downey, Ltd.

MARIO

GRISI

From a mezzotint engraved by George Zobel

'Théâtre Guignol' the same kind of entertainment maintained its popularity for many years in the Champs Elysées, Paris.

With the 20th century a new era, one of more conscious artistry, began in the life of the marionette-theatre. In Rome the Teatro dei Piccoli, directed by Vittorio Podrecca, particularly attracted musicians by the production of a repertory of complete operas acted by the puppets and sung by singers behind the stage. The 'Teatro dei Piccoli' visited London (New Scala) in Apr. 1923, giving, amongst other things, 'The Sleeping Beauty,' an opera written for them by RESPIGHI (*q.v.*). Falla's 'El Retablo' ('The puppet show of Master Pedro ') is among the most delightful of modern experiments in the technique of the marionette-theatre. (See FALLA.)   C.

MARIOTTE, ANTOINE (*b.* Avignon, Dec. 22, 1875), composer, started life as a naval officer. He retired in 1897, and became, on the foundation of the Schola Cantorum in Paris, the pupil of Vincent d'Indy. He was conductor first of the orchestra at St. Étienne, then at Lyons, being appointed director of the Orleans Conservatoire in 1920. He has written for the theatre in a way which shows dramatic temperament expressed in a rich style, with characteristic harmonies and daring effects.

WORKS.—PF. sonata; 'Sonatines d'automne'; 'Impressions urbaines'; 20 songs for voice and PF.; operas: 'Salomé' (Lyons, 1908; Paris, Opéra, 1919); 'Le Vieux Roi' (Lyons, 1913); 'Esther' (Paris, Opéra, 1925); unpublished: 'Gargantua'; 'Nele Dooryn' (Enoch).   F. R^L.

MARITANA, opera in 3 acts, founded on Don César de Bazan; words by Fitzball, music by W. V. Wallace. Produced Drury Lane, Nov. 15, 1845.   G.

MARKULL, FRIEDRICH WILHELM (*b.* Reichenbach, near Elbing, Prussia, Feb. 17, 1816; *d.* Danzig, Apr. 30, 1887), studied composition and organ-playing under Friedrich Schneider at Dessau; became in 1836 principal organist at the Marienkirche at Danzig, and conductor of the 'Gesangverein' there. Markull enjoyed a high reputation as a pianist, and gave excellent concerts of chamber music, besides acting as critic for the *Danziger Zeitung*. His compositions include three operas, 'Maja und Alpino,' or 'Die bezauberte Rose' (1843); 'Der König von Zion' (1848); 'Das Walpurgisfest' (1855); two oratorios, 'Johannes der Täufer' and 'Das Gedächtniss der Entschlafenen,' produced by Spohr at Cassel in 1856, the 86th Psalm, several symphonies, numerous works for organ, voice and piano, a 'Choralbuch' (1845), and arrangements.   H. S. O., with addns.

MARMONTEL, (1) ANTOINE FRANÇOIS (*b.* Clermont-Ferrand, Puy de Dôme, July 16, 1816 [1]; *d.* Paris, Jan. 16, 1898), pianoforte pupil of Zimmermann at the Paris Conservatoire, where he obtained the first prize in 1832. Succeeding his master in 1848, he taught piano

until 1887, and enjoyed a high reputation as a teacher. Amongst his pupils were Guiraud, Paladilhe, A. and E. Duvernoy, Bizet, Dubois, etc. His piano compositions are of an instructive character. He wrote also: *L'Art classique et moderne du piano* (1876), *Les Pianistes célèbres* (1878), *Symphonistes et virtuoses* (1881), *Histoire du piano et de ses origines, influence de sa facture sur le style des compositeurs et virtuoses* (1885), etc.

(2) ANTONIN EMILE LOUIS CORBAZ (*b.* Paris, Apr. 24, 1850; *d.* there, July 23, 1907), son of the preceding, also a well-known pianist and teacher, obtained the first piano prize in 1867 at the Conservatoire, where he became teacher of a women's class from 1901 till his death. He won a 'mention honorable' at the Rome Concourse, and acted as second chorus-master at the Opéra, 1878–89.   M. L. P.

MARMONTEL, JEAN FRANÇOIS (*b.* Bort, Limousin, July 11, 1723; *d.* Abloville,[2] Eure, Dec. 31, 1799), librettist and defender of Piccinni. He wrote: *Essai sur les révolutions de la musique en France* (1777).   M. L. P.

MARPURG, FRIEDRICH WILHELM (*b.* Marpurgshof, near Seehausen, Brandenburg, Nov. 21, 1718 [3]; *d.* Berlin, May 22, 1795), eminent writer on music. Little is known of his musical education, as Gerber gives no details, although Marpurg furnished him with the history of his life. Spazier [4] says that in 1746 he was secretary to General Rothenburg (or Bodenberg) in Paris, and there associated with Voltaire, Maupertuis, D'Alembert and Rameau. He lived later in Berlin and Hamburg, and from 1763 until his death was director of the government lottery in Berlin. Eberhard remarks that his acquaintance with good society would account for his refined manners and his tact in criticism. The absence in his works of personality and of fine writing, then so common with musical authors, is the more striking as he had great command of language and thoroughly enjoyed discussion. His active pen was exercised in almost all branches of music—composition, theory, criticism and history.

Of his theoretical works the most celebrated are—the *Handbuch bey dem Generalbasse und der Composition*, founded on Rameau's system (3 parts, 1755–62, Berlin); *Der critische Musicus an der Spree* (Berlin, 1750), containing, on p. 129, a lucid explanation of the old Church Modes; the *Anleitung zur Singe-composition* (Berlin, 1758), and the *Anleitung zur Musik* (Berlin, 1763), both still popular: the *Kunst das Clavier zu spielen* (1750); the *Versuch über die musikalische Temperatur* (Breslau, 1776), a controversial pamphlet intended to prove that Kirnberger's so-called fundamental bass was merely an interpolated bass; and the *Abhandlung*

---

[1] Constant Pierre.

[2] Not Abbéville, as given by Fétis and others.
[3] The date of birth was discovered in the registers of Seehof in Wendemark by Dr. W. Thamhayn (see *Q.-L.*).
[4] *Leipzig. musik. Zeitung*, ii. 553.

von der Fuge, 62 plates (Berlin, 1753–54 ; 2nd
edition, 1806 ; French, Berlin, 1756), a masterly
summary of the whole science of counterpoint
at that period, with the solitary defect that it is
illustrated by a few short examples, instead of
being treated in connexion with composition.
This Marpurg intended to remedy by publishing
a collection of fugues by well-known authors,
with analyses, but he only issued the first part
(Berlin, 1758).

Of his critical works the most important is
the *Historisch-kritische Beyträge,* 5 vols. (Berlin,
1754–78). Among the historical may be specified a MS. *Entwurf einer Geschichte der Orgel,* of
which Gerber gives the table of contents ; and
the *Kritische Einleitung in die Geschichte der
. . . Musik* (Berlin, 1759). A *jeu d'esprit,
Legende einiger Musikheiligen von Simeon
Metaphrastes dem Jüngeren* (Cologne, 1786),
appeared under a pseudonym.

Of compositions he published, besides collections of contemporary music, ' 6 Sonaten für
das Cembalo ' (Nuremberg, 1756) ; ' Fughe e
capricci ' (Berlin, 1777) ; and ' Versuch in
figurirten Chorälen,' vols. 1 and 2 ; ' Musikalisches Archiv,' an elucidation of the *Historisch-
kritische Beyträge,* was announced, but did not
appear. (Other works and editions are given
in *Q.-L.*)　　　　　　　　　　　　　　F. G.

BIBL.—HERMANN VON HASE, *Beiträge zur Breitkopfschen Geschäfts-
geschichte,* Z.M.W., May 1920, pp. 459-63, F. W. *Marpurg* ; JEFFREY
PALVER, *Friedrich Wilhelm Marpurg,* Mus. T., June 1912, pp. 375-7.

MARRE, LA (LAMARE), JACQUES MICHEL
HUREL DE (*b.* Paris, May 1, 1772 ; *d.* Caen,
Mar. 27, 1823), a famous violoncello virtuoso,
who was called by Clementi ' the Rode of the
violoncello.' He toured all over Europe with
immense success, and visited Russia, but retired from public life in 1815. Four concertos
and an *air varié* published under his name are
the work of his friend, the famous AUBER (E.
van der Straeten, *History of the Violoncello*).

MARRIAGE OF FIGARO, see NOZZE DI
FIGARO.

MARSCHALL, SAML., see MARESCHALL.

MARSCHNER, HEINRICH AUGUST (*b.* Zittau,
Saxony, Aug. 16, 1795 ; *d.* Hanover, Dec. 14,
1861), celebrated German opera composer,
began to compose sonatas, Lieder, dances, and
even orchestral music, with no further help
than a few hints from various musicians with
whom his beautiful soprano voice and his
pianoforte-playing brought him into contact.

As he grew up he obtained more systematic
instruction from Schicht of Leipzig, whither he
went in 1813 to study law. Here also he made
the acquaintance of Rochlitz, who induced him
to adopt music as a profession. In 1816 he
travelled with Count Thaddäus von Amadée, a
Hungarian, to Pressburg and Vienna, where he
made the acquaintance of Koželuh and of
Beethoven, who is said to have advised him to
compose sonatas, symphonies, etc., for practice.

In Pressburg he composed ' Der Kyffhäuser-
berg,' ' Saidor,' ' Heinrich IV. und Aubigné.'
Weber produced the last at Dresden, July 19,
1820, and Marschner was in consequence appointed in 1823 joint-Kapellmeister with Weber
and Morlacchi of the German and Italian Opera
there. He was appointed musikdirector in
1824, but resigned on Weber's death in 1826,
and after travelling for some time, settled in
1827 at Leipzig as Kapellmeister of the theatre.
Here he produced ' Der Vampyr ' (Mar. 28,
1828), his first romantic opera, to a libretto by
his brother-in-law Wohlbrück, the success of
which was enormous in spite of its repulsive
subject. In London it was produced, Aug. 25,
1829, in English, at the Lyceum, and ran for
sixty nights, and Marschner had accepted an
invitation to compose an English opera, when
Covent Garden Theatre was burnt down. His
success here doubtless led to his dedicating his
opera ' Des Falkners Braut ' to King William
IV., in return for which he received a gracious
letter and a golden box in 1833. His attention
having been turned to English literature, his
next opera, ' Der Templer und die Jüdin ' (produced at Leipzig, Dec. 1829), was composed to
a libretto constructed by himself and Wohlbrück from ' Ivanhoe.' The freshness and
melody of the music ensured its success at the
time, but the libretto, disjointed and overloaded
with purely epic passages which merely served
to hinder the action, killed the music. In 1831
Marschner was appointed court Kapellmeister
at Hanover.

He produced ' Hans Heiling ' at Berlin [1]
(May 24, 1833) to a libretto by Eduard
Devrient, which had been urged upon Mendelssohn in 1827.[2] This opera is Marschner's
masterpiece. Its success was instantaneous and
universal, and it retains to this day an honourable place at all the principal theatres of
Germany. In 1836 it was performed under his
own direction at Copenhagen with marked
success, and he was offered the post of Generalmusikdirector in Denmark, an honour which
the warmth of his reception on his return to
Hanover induced him to decline. After ' Hans
Heiling '—owing chiefly to differences with the
management of the theatre—Marschner composed little for the stage, and that little has
not survived. He was pensioned, with the title
of Generalmusikdirector, in 1859. A monument
was erected to his memory at Hanover in 1877.
Besides the operas already mentioned he composed ' Schön Ell ' (incidental music) (1822) ;
' Der Holzdieb ' (Dresden, 1825) ; ' Lucretia '
(Danzig, 1826) ; ' Des Falkner's Braut ' (Leipzig, 1832 ; Berlin, 1838) ; ' Der Bäbu ' (Hanover, 1837) ; ' Das Schloss am Aetna ' (Berlin,
1838) ; ' Adolf von Nassau ' (Hanover, 1843) ;
' Austin ' (1851). He also composed incidental

---

[1] See *Allg. deutsche Biographie.* Also *The Harmonicon,* 183?.
[2] Devrient's *Recollections,* p. 40.

music for von Kleist's play ' Die Hermanns-schlacht,' and published over 180 works of all kinds and descriptions, but principally Lieder for one and more voices, and choruses for men's voices, many of which are excellent. An over-ture, embodying ' God save the King,' is men-tioned as being performed in London at a concert on the occasion of the baptism of the Prince of Wales (King Edward VII.), Jan. 25, 1842.

As a dramatic composer of the romantic school, Marschner ranks next to Weber and Spohr, but it is with the former that his name is most intimately connected, though he was never a pupil of Weber. The strong similarity between their dispositions and gifts, the harmo-nious way in which they worked together, and the cordial affection they felt for each other, are interesting facts in the history of music. Marschner's favourite subjects were ghosts and demons, whose uncanny revels he delineated with extraordinary power, but this gloomy side of his character was relieved by a real love of nature and outdoor life, especially in its lighter and more humorous characteristics. He worked with extreme rapidity, which is the more re-markable as his scores abound in enharmonic modulations, and his orchestration is unusually brilliant and elaborate. Such facility argues an inexhaustible store of melody, and a perfect mastery of the technical part of composition.

A. M.

Bibl.—Georg Fischer, *Marschner-Erinnerungen*. (Hanover, 1918.)

MARSEILLAISE, LA. The words and music of this popular French hymn are the composi-tion of Claude Joseph Rouget de Lisle, a captain of engineers, who was quartered at Strassburg when the volunteers of the Bas Rhin received orders to join Luckner's army. Diet-rich, the Mayor of Strassburg, having, in the course of a discussion on the war, regretted that the young soldiers had no patriotic song to sing as they marched out, Rouget de Lisle, who was of the party, returned to his lodgings,[1] and in a fit of enthusiasm composed, during the night of Apr. 24, 1792, the words and music of the song which has immortalised his name. With his violin he picked out the first strains of this inspiriting and truly martial melody ; but being only an amateur, he unfortunately added a symphony which jars strangely with the vigorous character of the hymn itself. The following copy of the original edition, printed by Dannbach of Strassburg under the title ' Chant de guerre pour l'armée du Rhin, dédié au Maréchal Lukner ' (*sic*), will be interesting from its containing the symphony, which has been since suppressed, and from an obvious typographical error, the crotchet marked * being evidently intended for a quaver.

The ' Chant de guerre ' was sung in Diet-rich's house on Apr. 25, copied and arranged

[1] In the Maison Böckel, No. 12, Grande Rue.

for a military band on the following day, and performed by the band on the Garde Nationale at a review on Sunday the 29th. On June 25 a singer named Mireur sang it at a civic banquet

at Marseilles with so much effect that it was immediately printed, and distributed to the volunteers of the battalion just starting for Paris. They entered Paris on July 30, singing their new hymn ; and with it on their lips they marched to the attack on the Tuileries on Aug. 10, 1792. From that day the ' Chant de guerre pour l'armée du Rhin ' was called ' Chanson ' or ' Chant des Marseillais,' and, finally, ' La Marseillaise.' The people, shouting it in the streets, probably altered a note or two ; the musicians, Edelmann, Grétry, and most of all, Gossec, in their accompaniments for pianoforte and orchestra, greatly enriched the harmonies, and soon the ' Marseillaise,' in the form we have it now (which need hardly be quoted),[2]

[2] See *Mus. T*. Sept. 1915, p. 551, where four versions are quoted by Tom S. Wotton, viz.: (1) The melody as given in the official military band arrangement approved by the French Minister of War ; (2) Berlioz's arrangement (see article by E. Newman, *Mus. T*., Aug. 1915, p. 461) ; (3) Gossec's version ; (4) The first edition as quoted above.

was known from one end of France to the other.

The original edition contained only six couplets ; the seventh was added when it was dramatised for the Fête of the Fédération, in order to complete the characters—an old man, a soldier, a wife, and a child—among whom the verses were distributed. Rouget de Lisle had been cashiered for expressing disapproval of the events of Aug. 10, and was then in prison, from which he was only released after the fall of Robespierre, on the ninth Thermidor (July 28), 1794. The following fine stanza for the child was accordingly supplied by Dubois, editor of the *Journal de Littérature* :

> Nous entrerons dans la carrière,
> Quand nos aînés n'y seront plus ;
> Nous y trouverons leur poussière
> Et la trace de leurs vertus.
> Bien moins jaloux de leur survivre
> Que de partager leur cercueil,
> Nous aurons le sublime orgueil
> De les venger ou de les suivre.

Dubois also proposed to alter the concluding lines of the sixth stanza—

> Que tes ennemis expirants
> Voient ton triomphe et notre gloire

to

> Dans tes ennemis expirants
> Vois ton triomphe et notre gloire.

That Rouget de Lisle was the author of the words of the ' Marseillaise ' has never been doubted—indeed Louis Philippe conferred a pension upon him ; but it has been denied over and over again that he composed the music. Strange to say, Castil-Blaze,[1] who should have recognised the vigour and dash so characteristic of the French, declared it to have been taken from a German hymn.

In F. K. Meyer's *Versailler Briefe* (Berlin, 1872) there is an article upon the origin of the 'Marseillaise,' in which it is stated that the tune is the same as that to which the Volkslied ' Stand ich auf hohen Bergen ' is sung in Upper Bavaria. The author of the article heard it sung in 1842 by an old woman of seventy, who informed him that it was a very old tune, and that she had learnt it from her mother and grandmother. The tune was also said to exist in the Credo of a MS. Mass composed by Holtzmann in 1776, which is preserved in the parish church of Meersburg.[2] Subsequently inquiry (Aug. 1879) on the spot from the curate of Meersburg has proved that there is no truth in this story.

Fétis, in 1863, asserted that the music was the work of a composer named Navoigille, and reinforces his statement in the second edition of his *Biographie universelle.* Georges Kastner[3] and several other writers, including the author of this article[4] have clearly disproved these allegations ; and the point was finally settled

by a pamphlet, *La Vérité sur la paternité de la Marseillaise* (Paris, 1865), written by A. Rouget de Lisle, nephew of the composer, which contains precise information and documentary evidence, establishing Rouget de Lisle's claim beyond a doubt. The controversy is examined at length by Loquin in *Les Mélodies populaires de la France,* Paris, 1879. The ' Marseillaise ' has been often made use of by composers. Of these, two may be cited—Salieri, in the opening chorus of his opera ' Palmira ' (1795), and Grison, in the introduction to the oratorio ' Esther ' (still in MS.), both evidently intentional. Schumann slyly alludes to it in the ' Faschingsschwank aus Wien,' uses it in his song of the Two Grenadiers with magnificent effect, and also introduces it in his Overture to ' Hermann and Dorothea.'

A picture by Pils, representing Rouget de Lisle singing the ' Marseillaise,' is well known from the engraving.   G. C.

BIBLIOGRAPHY

JULIEN TIERSOT : (1) *Histoire de la chanson populaire en France* (Paris, 1889, pp. 281–86) ; (2) *Histoire de 'La Marseillaise,' Nombreuses gravures documentaires, facsimilés, autographes, œuvres musicales de Roger de Lisle.* (Paris, 1915.)
RENÉ BRANCOUR : *La Marseillaise et le Chant du départ.* (Paris, 1916.)
LOUIS FIAUX : *La Marseillaise. Son histoire dans l'histoire des Français depuis 1792.* (Paris, 1918.)
VLADIMIR HELFERT : *Contributo alla storia della ' Marseillaise.'* (*R.M.I.,* 1922.)
CONSTANT PIERRE : (1) *La Marseillaise, comparaison des différentes versions, variantes, etc.* (Paris, 1887) ; (2) *Les Hymnes et chansons de la Révolution* (Paris, 1901).

MARSH, (1) ALPHONSO (*bapt.* St. Margaret's, Westminster, Jan. 28, 1627 ; *d.* Apr. 9, 1681), son of Robert Marsh, one of the musicians in ordinary to Charles I., was appointed a gentleman of the Chapel Royal in 1660. Songs composed by him appear in ' The Treasury of Musick ' (1669), ' Choice Ayres and Dialogues ' (1676), and other publications of the time. His son (2) ALPHONSO (*d.* Apr. 5, 1692) was admitted a gentleman of the Chapel Royal, Apr. 25, 1676. Songs by him are contained in ' The Theater of Music ' (1685–87), ' The Banquet of Musick ' (1688–92), and other publications. He was buried, Apr. 9, in the west cloister of Westminster Abbey.

W. H. H.

MARSH, JOHN (*b.* Dorking, 1752 ; *d.* 1828), a distinguished amateur composer and performer, was articled to a solicitor at Romsey in 1768, resided at Salisbury (1776–81), Canterbury (1781–86), and Chichester (1787–1828), in each of which places he led the band at the subscription concerts and occasionally officiated for the cathedral and church organists. He composed two services, many anthems, chants and psalm tunes, glees, songs, symphonies, overtures, quartets, etc., and organ and pianoforte music, besides treatises on harmony, thorough-bass, etc. A fully detailed account of his career is given in the *Dictionary of Musicians,* 1824.   W. H. H.

MARSHALL, WILLIAM (*b.* Fochabers, Banffshire, Dec. 27, 1748 ; *d.* Dandaleith, May 29,

---

[1] See *Molière musicien,* vol. ii. pp. 452–4.
[2] See the *Gartenlaube* for 1861, p. 256.
[3] *Revue et Gazette musicale,* Paris, 1848.
[4] See Chouquet's *L'Art musical,* Sept. 8, 1864–Mar. 9, 1865.

1833), a Scottish musician. As a boy he entered the service of the Duke of Gordon, rising, during a thirty years' residence in the family, to the posts of butler, house-steward and factor. He taught himself the violin, and became the best amateur performer of his day. His compositions, which are Strathspeys and a similar class of Scottish violin music, have been held in much favour, the best known being ' The Marquis of Huntley's ' and ' Miss Admiral Gordon's ' Strathspeys, the latter being the air to which Burns wrote ' Of a' the airts the wind can blaw.' He married in 1773, and had a family, dying in his 85th year. A number of his compositions appear in the Gow publications, but Stewart of Edinburgh issued a couple of small collections of his Strathspeys in 1781. A third and much fuller collection was published in 1822 and a later one, after his death, in 1847. An excellent portrait of Marshall is extant, engraved by Turner ; it is reproduced in *The Glen Collection of Scottish Dance Music*, book ii., 1895, where there is also much interesting information concerning him.   F. K.

MARSHALL, (1) WILLIAM, Mus.D. (*b.* Oxford, 1806 ; *d.* Handsworth, Aug. 17, 1875), son of William Marshall of Oxford, music-seller, was a chorister of the Chapel Royal under John Stafford Smith and William Hawes. He was appointed organist of Christ Church Cathedral and St. John's College, Oxford, in 1825, and was also organist of All Saints' Church from 1839. He graduated as Mus.B. Dec. 7, 1826, and Mus.D. Jan. 14, 1840. He resigned his Oxford appointments in 1846, and afterwards became organist of St. Mary's Church, Kidderminster. He was author of *The Art of Reading Church Music* (1842), the composer of some church music and songs, and editor (jointly with Alfred Bennett) of a collection of chants, 1829, and also editor of a book of words of anthems, 1840, fourth edition, 1862.

His younger brother, (2) CHARLES WARD (*b.* 1808 ; *d.* Islington, Feb. 22, 1874), appeared about 1835, under the assumed name of Manvers, on the London stage as a tenor singer, with success. In 1842 he quitted the theatre for concert and oratorio singing, in which he met with greater success. After 1847 he withdrew from public life.   W. H. H.

MARSICK, MARTIN PIERRE JOSEPH (*b.* Jupille, near Liège, Mar. 9, 1848 ; *d.* Oct. 1924), violinist. At the age of 8 he entered the Liège Conservatoire, studying under Desiré Heynberg, and gaining, two years later, the first prize in the preparatory class. In 1864 he secured the gold medal of the institution for ' exceptional merit.' In the following year and until 1867 he was pupil of Léonard (violin) and Kufferath (composition), and in 1868–69 of Massart at the Paris Conservatoire, the expense of his musical training being defrayed by a

music-loving lady of distinction. In 1870–71 he was the recipient of a stipend from the Belgian Government, and was enabled to proceed to Berlin to study under Joachim. Thus exceptionally equipped, he made a successful début, in 1873, at the ' Concerts populaires ' in Paris, travelled a good deal in various European countries, founded a Quartet at Paris in 1877 with Rémy, Von Waefelghem and Delsart, and 1892–1900 was violin professor at the Conservatoire in succession to Massart. In 1895–1896 he toured in the United States, and occasionally visited England, but without achieving in either country a great popular success. His compositions include three concertos and a number of smaller pieces for the violin.   W. W. C.

MARSOLO, PIETRO MARIA, Doct. Jur., of Messina, maestro di cappella at Ferrara Cathedral, 1612 ; composed 3 books of motets and 5 books of madrigals, one apparently lost (*Q.-L.*).

MARSON, GEORGE (*d.* Canterbury, Feb. 1631/2), organist and composer. About the year 1598 he became master of the choristers and organist of Canterbury Cathedral and held office till his death. The Cathedral registers record his burial on Feb. 5, 1631/2, and state that he was formerly one of the minor canons. He was married at Canterbury in 1599. According to Wood he took the B.Mus. degree at Cambridge in 1601, and Wood also states that Marson was a relative of Nathaniel GILES (*q.v.*). He contributed an excellent 5-part madrigal to ' The Triumphes of Oriana '—' The nymphs and shepherds danced lavoltas.' Some church music of Marson is in MS. at the R.C.M. and includes a service, preces and psalms and a few anthems.   E. H. F.

MARTEAU, HENRI (*b.* Rheims, Mar. 31, 1874), professor of the violin at the Geneva Conservatoire. His father was an amateur violinist and president of the Philharmonic Society of Rheims ; his mother, an accomplished pianist, a pupil of Madame Schumann. Sivori first discovered Henri Marteau's talent, and presented him with a violin, at the same time persuading his parents to allow him to study it as a profession. His first master was Bunzl, a pupil of Molique, his second, Léonard. In 1884, when only 10 years of age, he appeared under Richter at the Vienna Philharmonic Society, and elsewhere in Germany and Switzerland ; in the year following he was chosen by Gounod to play the violin obbligato of a piece composed for the Joan of Arc Centenary celebration at Rheims. In July 1888 he appeared at a Richter concert in London. In 1892 he gained the first prize at the Paris Conservatoire, and Massenet wrote a concerto expressly for him. He toured in America with success in 1893 and 1898, and in Russia in 1897–99. Having studied composition with Théodore Dubois, he brought out a cantata,

' La voix de Jeanne d'Arc,' for soprano, chorus and orchestra, in 1896. Marteau's compositions include a quantity of chamber music, 2 violin concertos, a violoncello concerto and an opera, ' Meister Schwalbe ' (Plauen, 1921). In 1900 he became teacher at the Geneva Conservatorium and succeeded Joachim (1908–15) as violin teacher in the Berlin Hochschule. In 1921 he became teacher at the Prague Conservatoire.

BIBL.—*Baker* ; HENRY C. LAHEE, *Famous Violinists of To-day and Yesterday*, Boston, U.S.A., 1899 ; additions from *Riemann*.

E. H.-A.

MARTELÉ, and MARTELLATO (Ital.), from *marteler* and *martellare*, to ' hammer ' ; said of notes struck or sung with especial force, and left before the expiration of the time due to them. Notes dashed, dotted or emphasised by $>$ or $fz.$ are Martelées or Martellate in execution. The term Martellement is sometimes employed for acciaccatura.   J. H.

In violin, violoncello and viola music this sign is used to indicate a detached hammered style of bowing. The effect is usually produced by a series of short quick *up* and down strokes at the point of the bow, without allowing the bow to leave the strings. The stick is held firmly, and the thumb pressed in the direction of the index finger, as each note is played. The arm should remain quite loose, and care should be taken to give a stronger pressure to the up bow than the down bow, or else the Martelé will become uneven.

BIBL.—C. SCHROEDER, *Catechism of Violin Playing* (Leipzig, 1889 ; London, 1895) ; CARL COURVOISIER, *Technique of Violin Playing* (Cologne, 1878 ; London, 1880) ; H. W. and G. GRESSWELL, *How to Play the Fiddle* (London, 1886).   O. R.

MARTHA, opera in 3 acts, music by Flotow. Produced—Vienna, Nov. 25, 1847. London, Drury Lane (in German), June 5, 1849 ; Covent Garden (in Italian), July 1, 1858 ; Drury Lane (in English), Oct. 11, 1858. New York, Niblo's Garden (in English), Nov. 1, 1852. Paris, Salle Ventadour (in Italian), Feb. 11, 1858 ; Théâtre Lyrique, Dec. 16, 1865.

The opera is an extension of 'Lady Henriette, ou La Servante de Greenwich,' ballet-pantomime in 3 acts, by St. Georges, with music by Flotow, Burgmüller and Deldevez, produced, Opéra, Paris, Feb. 21, 1844. The necessary alterations in the book were made by St. Georges, and the German translation by Friedrich.   G. ; rev. M. L. P.

MARTIN, CLAUDE, of Couches, near Autun, lived in Paris c. 1540–55. A Magnificat *a* 4 v., published by Attaingnant 1540, and 9 chansons *a* 4 in collective volumes by Claude du Chemin, are the only compositions of his still left ; he also wrote two theoretical works (titles, etc., in *Q.-L.*).

MARTIN, SIR GEORGE CLEMENT (*b.* Lambourne, Berks, Sept. 11, 1844 ; *d.* London, Feb. 23, 1916), received instruction in organ-playing from J. Pearson and Sir John (then Dr.) Stainer, also in composition from the latter

during the time he was organist there at the parish church. He was appointed private organist to the Duke of Buccleuch, at Dalkeith, in 1871 ; master of the choristers, St. Paul's Cathedral, in 1874, deputy organist at the same on the death of George Cooper in 1876, and organist on the resignation of Stainer in 1888. He received the degrees of Mus.B., Oxon., in 1868, Fellow of the College of Organists in 1875, and Mus.D. (degree conferred by the Archbishop of Canterbury) in 1883, and was appointed the same year teacher of the organ at the R.C.M., which post he later resigned ; He was made Mus.D. of Oxford in 1912. His compositions include Morning Communion Service in C for voices and orchestra ; Communion Service in A, Magnificat and Nunc Dimittis in A, for the same ; the same in B♭ for voices, organ and military band ; the same in G for voices and orchestra ; 7 anthems ; also a variety of compositions for parochial use ; songs, partsongs, etc. His most important work is the Te Deum sung on the steps of St. Paul's at the Diamond Jubilee of Queen Victoria, 1897, shortly after which event he was knighted. (See *Mus. T.*, July 1897.) Martin died in London and was buried in the crypt of St. Paul's Cathedral. A memorial tablet with portrait in relief was placed near the grave by public subscription. (See *Mus. T.*, Dec. 1917.)

A. C.

MARTIN, GEORGE WILLIAM (*b.* Mar. 8, 1828; *d.* Bolingbroke House Hospital, Wandsworth, Apr. 16, 1881), received his early musical education in the choir of St. Paul's Cathedral under William Hawes. He was professor of music at the Normal College for Army Schoolmasters ; music-master at St. John's Training College, Battersea (1845–53), and organist of Christ Church, Battersea, in 1849. He composed many glees, madrigals and partsongs, for some of which he was awarded prizes, and edited and published cheap arrangements of the popular oratorios and other works of Handel, Haydn and others. For some years he directed performances given under the name of the National Choral Society, which was begun in 1860. He had an aptitude for training choirs of school children, and conducted many public performances by them. He edited the *Journal of Part Music* in 1861–62, and did much to make good music popular. He died in great poverty at Bolingbroke House Hospital.   W. H. H.

MARTIN, JONATHAN (*b.* 1715 ; *d.* April 4, 1737), was a chorister of the Chapel Royal under Dr. Croft. On quitting the choir he was placed under Thomas Roseingrave for instruction on the organ, and soon attained such proficiency as to be able to act as deputy for his master at St. George's, Hanover Square, and for Weldon at the Chapel Royal. On June 21, 1736, he was admitted organist of the Chapel Royal on the death of Weldon, and promised ' to compose anthems or services for the use of His Majesty's Chapel, whenever required by the Subdean for the time being.' Probably he was never called upon to fulfil his promise, as his only known composition is a song in Rowe's tragedy, 'Tamerlane,' 'To thee, O gentle sleep.' He died of consumption, and was buried (Apr. 9) in the west cloister of Westminster Abbey.

W. H. H.

MARTINENGO, GABRIELE, composed 2 books of madrigals a 4 v. (Venice, Scotto, 1544 and 1548), 1 book of madrigals a 5 v. (Venice, Gardano, 1580); also madrigals and motets in collective volumes (1548–77).

MARTINES (MARTINEZ), MARIANNE (b. Vienna, May 4, 1744; d. Dec. 13, 1812), composer, was daughter of the master of the ceremonies to the Pope's Nuncio.

Metastasio, a great friend of her father, lived for nearly half a century with the family, and undertook her education. Haydn, then young, poor, and unknown, occupied a wretched garret in the same house, and taught her the harpsichord, while Porpora gave her lessons in singing and composition, her general cultivation being under Metastasio's own care. Of these advantages she made good use. Burney, who knew her in 1772,[1] speaks of her in the highest terms, specially praising her singing; and she also won the admiration of both Hasse and Gerbert. After the death of the parents, and of Metastasio, who left them well off, she and her sister gave evening parties, which were frequented by all the principal artists. On one of these occasions Kelly[2] heard Marianne play a 4-hand sonata of Mozart with the composer. Latterly Marianne devoted herself to teaching talented pupils. In 1773 she was made a member of the Musical Academy of Bologna. In 1782, the Tonkünstler Societät performed her oratorio 'Isacco,' to Metastasio's words. She also composed another oratorio 'Santa Elena al Calvario,' a Mass, and other sacred music; a Psalm, to Metastasio's Italian translation, for four and eight voices; solo-motets, arias and cantatas, concertos, overtures and symphonies, and harpsichord sonatas, two of which were reprinted by E. Pauer ('Alte Meister'). The Gesellschaft der Musikfreunde possesses the autographs of many of these works. Marianne died a few days after the death of her younger sister Antonie.

C. F. P.

MARTINI, GIOVANNI BATTISTA (or GIAMBATTISTA, commonly called 'Padre Martini') (b. Bologna, Apr. 24, 1706; d. Oct. 3[3] or Aug. 4,[4] 1784), one of the most important scientific musicians of the 18th century; was first taught music by his father, Antonio Maria, member of

a musical society called 'I Fratelli.' Having become an expert violinist, he learned to sing and play the harpsichord from Padre Predieri, and counterpoint from Antonio Riccieri, a castrato of Vicenza, and composer of merit. At the same time he studied philosophy and theology with the monks of San Filippo Neri.

Having passed his noviciate at the Franciscan convent at Lago, he was ordained on Sept. 11, 1722, and returning to Bologna in 1725 became maestro di cappella of the church of San Francesco. Giacomo Perti held a similar post at San Petronio, and from him Martini received valuable advice on composing church music, at the same time laying a scientific foundation for the whole theory of music by a conscientious study of mathematics with Zanotti, a well-known physician and mathematician. He thus gradually acquired an extraordinary and comprehensive mass of knowledge, with an amount of literary information far in advance of his contemporaries. His library was unusually complete for the time,[5] partly because scientific men of all countries took a pleasure in sending him books. Burney, whose own library was very extensive, expressed his astonishment at that of Martini, which he estimates to contain 17,000 vols.[6] After his death a portion found its way to the court library at Vienna; the rest remained at Bologna in the Liceo Filarmonico.

His reputation as a teacher was European, and scholars flocked to him from all parts, among the most celebrated being Paolucci, Ruttini, Sarti, Ottani and Stanislao Mattei, afterwards joint founder of the Liceo Filarmonico. These he educated in the traditions of the old Roman school, the main characteristic of which was the melodious movement of the separate parts. Martini was also frequently called upon to recommend a new maestro di cappella or to act as umpire in disputed questions. He was himself occasionally involved in musical controversy; the best-known instance being his dispute with Redi about the solution of a puzzle-canon by Giovanni Animuccia, which he solved by employing two keys in the third part. This, though approved by Pitoni, was declared by Redi to be unjustifiable. To prove this point Martini, therefore, wrote a treatise maintaining that puzzle-canons had not infrequently been solved in that manner, and quoting examples. Another important controversy was that held with EXIMENEO (q.v.). In spite of these differences of opinion his contemporaries describe him as a man of great mildness, modesty and good nature, always ready to answer questions and give explanations. It is difficult to think without emotion of the warm welcome which he, the most learned and one of the oldest musicians of his country,

---

[1] See Present State of Music in Germany, i. 311-13, 352, 354, 362.
[2] Kelly's mistakes of detail are innumerable. He gives the name Martini,' and imagining Marianne to be the sister of her father— 'a very old man' and 'nearly his own age'—speaks of her as 'in the vale of years,' though still 'possessing the gaiety and vivacity of a girl.' She was barely forty.
[3] According to Moreschi, Gandolfi and Della Valle.
[4] According to Fantuzzi.

[5] He had ten copies of Guido d' Arezzo's Micrologus.
[6] Present State of Music in France and Italy, p. 195.

bestowed on Mozart when he visited Bologna in 1770 as a boy of 14. His courtesy and affability brought the Bolognese monk into friendly relations with many exalted personages, Frederick the Great and Frederick William II. of Prussia, Princess Maria Antonie of Saxony and Pope Clement XIV. among the number.

He suffered much towards the close of his life from asthma, a disease of the bladder and a painful wound in the leg; but his cheerfulness never deserted him, and he worked at the fourth volume of his *Storia della musica* up to his death. His favourite pupil Mattei stayed with him to the last. Zanotti's Requiem was sung at his funeral, and on Dec. 2, the Accademia Filarmonica held a grand function, at which a funeral Mass, the joint composition of thirteen maestri di cappella, was performed, and an 'Elogio' pronounced by Lionardo Volpi. All Italy mourned for him, and a medallion to his memory was struck by Tadolini. He was a member of two Accademie, the 'Filarmonici' of Bologna, and the 'Arcadici' of Rome, his assumed name in the latter being Aristoxenus Amphion.

Martini's two great works are the *Storia della musica* (3 vols. Bologna, 1757, 1770, 1781), and the *Esemplare ossia saggio . . . di contrappunto* (2 vols., Bologna, 1774, 1775). The first is a most learned work; each chapter begins and ends with a puzzle-canon, the whole of which were solved and published by Cherubini. The three volumes all treat of ancient music; the music of the Middle Ages down to the 11th century was to have been the subject of the fourth volume, which he did not live to finish. A report having sprung up that the completed MS. was in the Minorite convent at Bologna, Fétis obtained access to the library through Rossini, but found only materials, of which no use has yet been made. The *Saggio* is a most important collection of examples from the best masters of the ancient Italian and Spanish schools, and a model of its kind. Besides a number of small treatises and controversial writings (for list see *Fétis*) Martini left masses and other church music in the style of the time. The following were printed: 'Litaniae,' op. 1 (1734); 'XII Sonate d' intavolatura,' op. 2 (Amsterdam, Le Cène, 1741), excellent and full of originality; 'VI Sonate per organo e cembalo' (Bologna, 1747). 'Duetti da camera' (Bologna, 1763). The Liceo of Bologna possesses the MSS. of a Mass, a Requiem, etc., three oratorios, 'San Pietro' (two separate compositions), 'Il sagrifizio d' Abramo,' and 'L' assunzione di Salomone al trono d' Israello'; a farsetta 'La Dirindina'; and three intermezzi, 'L' impresario delle Canarie,' 'Don Chisciotto,' and 'Il maestro di musica.' A Requiem (103 sheets), and other church compositions are in Vienna. Pauer, in his 'Alte Klaviermusik,' gives a gavotte and ballet of Martini's. Farrenc

has published twelve sonatas in the 'Trésor musical,' and other works are given by Lück, Körner, Ricordi, etc. (See *Q.-L.*)   F. G.

BIBLIOGRAPHY

Pietro Della Valle: *Memorie storiche del padre G. Martini.* 1785.
L. Busi: *Il padre G. B. Martini.* 1891.
F. Parisini: *Della vita e delle opere del Padre Martini.* 1887; also a volume of letters. 1888.
G. Gandolfi: *Elogio di G. B. Martini.* 1913.

MARTINI IL TEDESCO ('the German'), the name by which the musicians of his time knew JOHANN PAUL AEGIDIUS SCHWARTZENDORF (*b.* Freistadt, Upper Palatinate, Sept. 1, 1741; *d.* Paris, Feb. 10, 1816), who was organist of the Jesuit seminary at Neustadt, on the Danube, when he was 10 years old. From 1758 he studied at Freiburg, and played the organ at the Franciscan convent there. When he returned to his native place, he found a stepmother installed at home, and set forth to seek his fortune in France, notwithstanding his complete ignorance of the language. At Nancy he was befriended, when in a penniless condition, by the organ-builder Dupont, on whose advice he adopted the name by which he is known.

From 1761–64 he was in the household of King Stanislaus, who was then living at Nancy. After his patron's death Martini went to Paris, and immediately obtained a certain amount of fame by successfully competing for a prize offered for the best march for the Swiss Guard. At this time he wrote much military music, as well as symphonies and other instrumental works. In 1771 his first opera, 'L'amoureux de quinze ans,' was performed with very great success, and after holding various appointments as musical director to noblemen, he was appointed conductor at the Théâtre Feydeau, when that establishment was opened under the name of Théâtre de Monsieur for the performance of light French and Italian operas. Having lost all his emoluments by the decree of Aug. 10, 1792, he went to live at Lyons, where he published his *Mélopée moderne*, a treatise on singing. In 1794 he returned to Paris for the production of his opera 'Sapho,' and in 1798 was made inspector of the Conservatoire; then professor of composition. From this post he was ejected in 1802, by the agency, as he suspected, of Méhul and Catel. At the restoration of 1814 he received the appointment of superintendent of the court music, and wrote a Requiem for Louis XVI., which was performed at St. Denis, Jan. 21, 1816. Besides the operas mentioned above he wrote 'Le Rendez-vous nocturne' (1773); 'Henri IV' (1774); 'Le Droit du seigneur' (1783); 'L'Amant sylphe' (1795); 'Annette et Lubin' (1789); 'Camille ou le souterrain' (1796); and 'Ziméo' (1800). In the department of church music he wrote several masses, psalms, Requiems, etc. (See *Q.-L.*) A cantata written for the marriage of Napoleon with Marie Louise exists, besides much chamber music, but Martini's best-known composition is probably the charming song, ' Plaisir d'amour.' M.

BIBL.—POUGIN, *Martini.* 1864.

MARTIN PEU D'ARGENT (DARGENT, PEUDARGANT), Kapellmeister to the Duke of Jülich, Cleve and Berg, 1561; master of Joan. Orydrius. He composed motets and chansons, and made a collection of motets *a* 4, 5, 6 v., together with Orydrius and Buysius, all published at Düsseldorf, 1555–61.

          E. v. d. s.

MARTIN Y SOLAR, VICENTE (*b.* Valencia,[1] *c.* 1754 ; *d.* May 1810), was a choir-boy in the cathedral of his native town, and afterwards organist at Alicante. On the advice of an Italian singer, named Giuglietti, he went to Florence, where he was commissioned to write an opera for the next Carnival. His ' Ifigenia in Aulide ' was accordingly brought out in 1781. Soon after this ·he produced a new opera, ' Astartea,' in Lucca, as well as a ballet, ' La Regina di Golconda.' In 1783 ' La donna festeggiata ' and ' L' accorta cameriera ' were brought out at Turin, and in the following year ' Ipermestra ' at Rome. In 1785 he went to Vienna, where he became acquainted with Da Ponte, who wrote for him the libretto of ' Il burbero di buon cuore,' produced Jan. 4, 1786. Here as elsewhere he speedily became the fashion, his operas ' La capricciosa corretta,' ' L' arbore di Diana ' and ' Una cosa rara ' following one another in quick succession. This last work, produced Nov. 11, 1786, for a time threw ' Figaro ' (produced six months before) into the shade. (See MOZART.) In the autumn of the following year ' Don Giovanni ' appeared, and Martin unwittingly obtained immortality at the hands of his rival, since a theme from ' Una cosa rara ' makes its appearance in the second finale of Mozart's masterpiece.[2] (See also Köchel's Catalogue, pp. 582, 583.) In 1788 Martin was appointed director of the Italian Opera at St. Petersburg, where he brought out ' Gli sposi in contrasto,' and a cantata, ' Il sogno.' In 1801 the fashion for Italian opera passed away for a time, and French opera took its place. Martin, thus deprived of his post, employed the rest of his life in teaching. A Mass, and a ' Domine salvum fac,' and another opera, ' L'Île de l'amour,' are mentioned in *Q.-L.*, and the latter is stated to have been produced in Florence about 1784. M.

MARTORETTA, GIANDOMENICO LA (2nd half of 16th cent.), of Calabria, composer of 3 books of madrigals and a book of motets between 1548 and 1566 ; single numbers in collective volumes. (See *Q.-L.*)

---

[1] Whence he was known in Italy as ' Lo Spagnuolo.'
[2] The article in Mendel's *Lexikon* contains several mistakes, such as the statement that ' Don Giovanni ' was brought out before ' Una cosa rara ' (in which case it would have been difficult for Mozart to have used one of the themes from the latter opera in the former !), and the inclusion, among works by him, of the book of canons with pianoforte accompaniment, published by Birchall in London, and ¢dited by Cianchettini. These are by Padre Martini.

MARTUCCI, (1) GIUSEPPE (*b.* Capua, Jan. 6, 1856 ; *d.* Naples, June 1, 1909), pianist, orchestral conductor and composer.

He was taught the elements of music by his father, a military bandmaster, and made, as a child, some stir in Naples by his clever performances on the piano. At the age of 11 he was admitted to the R. Conservatorio in that city. Here he devoted five years to the study of the pianoforte under Beniamino Cesi, whose training was supplemented by lessons in theory and composition with Carlo Costa, Paolo Serrao and Lauro Rossi. He left the Conservatorio in 1872 ; but after two years passed in teaching and playing in public he returned to it as professor, gaining the post by competition. Having appeared with remarkable success at concerts in Rome and Milan, Martucci undertook, in 1875, a tour through France, Germany and England. In London, where he played at Arditi's Concert, St. George's Hall, June 14, the character of his reception warranted a stay of four months ; he also played in Dublin. On the occasion of a second visit to Paris in 1878 he·was heard by Rubinstein, who not only expressed the highest opinion of his executive talent, but honoured Martucci as a composer by directing a performance of his Concerto in B♭ minor with Cesi at the piano. The work was also played in after years by Eugen d'Albert at the Berlin Philharmonic.

Martucci's progress at home was marked by his association with the Quartetto Napoletano whose performances he directed during eight years, and still further by his appointment as conductor of the orchestral concerts instituted by the Prince d' Ardore, a choice fully justified by his enterprise in introducing classical and modern masterpieces before unheard in Naples. He also took his orchestra from Naples to Turin, where he gave a series of performances during the exhibition of 1884. Nominated director of the Liceo Musicale at Bologna in 1886, Martucci continued his concerts in other towns. His programmes, broadly eclectic, sometimes included the works of Hubert Parry, Stanford and other English composers. During his residence in Bologna he made his only appearance as orchestral conductor in a theatre to direct the first performance in Italy of Richard Wagner's ' Tristan und Isolde ' (1888). After an absence of sixteen years he was once more recalled to the scene of his early labours, having been named director of the R. Conservatorio in Naples, Mar. 5, 1902. He was a member of the Accademia Reale of Naples, Commendatore della Corona d' Italia and Cavaliere dei S.S. Maurizio e Lazzaro. Martucci occupied a place in the front rank of pianoforte virtuosi. As an author his style was formed on the best classical models. His works are remarkable for their finish, and often display considerable originality. In writing for the pianoforte his intimate knowledge of its resources produced effects of a quite exceptional kind.

His very numerous compositions include :

Symphony No. 1 in D minor (op. 75) played at the R.C.M., Mar. 18, 1898.   A detailed analysis is in *R.M.I.*, iii. 125.
Symphony No. 2 in F major (op. 81).
Concerto in B flat minor for piano and orchestra (op. 66).
Four piccoli pezzi for orchestra.
Poemetto lirico, 'La canzone dei ricordi,' for voice and orchestra.
Quintet for piano, two violins, viola and violoncello (op. 45).
Trio No. 1 in C for piano, violin and violoncello (op. 59).
Trio No. 2 in E flat for piano, violin and violoncello (op. 62) (played at one of Hallé's Concerts, St. James's Hall, May 17, 1889).
Sonata for violoncello and piano (op. 52).
Three pieces for violoncello and piano (op. 69).
Due Romanze for violoncello (op. 72).
Three pieces for violin and piano (op. 67).
Momento musicale e Minuetto for two violins, viola, and violoncello.
'Pagine sparse,' melodies for voice and piano (op. 68).
'Due sogni,' for voice and piano (op. 68 bis).
Six volumes of compositions for pianofortes.
Variations for two pianofortes.
Fantasia for two pianofortes (op. 32).
Two pieces for pianoforte : 'Capriccio ' and 'Toccata ' (op. 77).
Three pieces for piano solo : 'Novelletta,' 'Notturno,' and ' Scherzo ' (op. 76).
Two pieces for piano : 'Serenata ' and 'Gavotta ' (op. 73).
'Trèfle à quatre feuilles ' (op. 74).
Three little pieces for pianoforte solo : 'Serenata,' 'Minuetto,' 'Capriccio ' (op. 78).
Three little pieces for pianoforte solo : 'Preludio,' 'Canzonetta,' 'Saltarello ' (op. 79).
Due Capricci for pianoforte (op. 80).
Unpublished compositions :
Oratorio, 'Samuel.'
Concerto for piano and orchestra in D minor.
Sonata for organ.
Numerous pianoforte transcriptions of classical works, and Raccolta of sixteen pieces for piano by classical authors transcribed for violoncello and pianoforte.

H. A. W.

(2) PAOLO (*b.* Naples, Oct. 8, 1883), son and pupil of the above, is an excellent pianist, who settled for a time in England, then in America ; he taught at the Cincinnati Conservatory (1911) and in New York (1913).

MARTY, EUGÈNE GEORGES (*b.* Paris, May 16, 1860 ; *d.* there, Oct. 11, 1908), was a pupil of the Conservatoire, where he obtained the first prize in solfège in 1875, the first in harmony in 1878, and the Grand Prix de Rome in 1882 with his cantata, ' Edith.' In 1892 he was appointed chorus-master at the Théâtre Eden, and in the same year was made director of the vocal ensemble classes at the Conservatoire, a post he resigned in 1904 ; he was chorus-master at the Opéra in 1893, and conducted the Opéra-Comique in 1900. From June 12, 1901, till 1908, he was conductor of the Concerts du Conservatoire. From 1906 he conducted classical concerts at the Casino of Vichy. Marty wrote much, and was greatly influenced by his master, Massenet. We may mention : 'Ballade d'hiver ' (1885); 'Balthazar' overture (1887) ; a suite, 'Les Saisons' (1888) ; a symphonic poem, 'Merlin enchanté,' all for orchestra ; 'Lysic,' a one-act pantomime (1888) ; 'Le Duc de Ferrare,' 3-act opera, Théâtre Lyrique (1899) ; 'Daria,' 2-act opera (Opéra, Jan. 27, 1905) ; songs, and pianoforte pieces, etc.

G. F.

MARTYRS, LES, see POLYEUCTE.

MARX, ADOLPH BERNHARD (*b.* Halle, May 15, 1795 ; *d.* Berlin, May 17, 1866), learned musician and author, son of a physician, learned harmony from Türk, studied law, and held a legal post at Naumburg. His love of music led him to Berlin, where he soon gave up the law, and in 1824 he founded, with Schlesinger the

publisher, the *Berliner Allgemeine Musikalische Zeitung.* This periodical, which only existed seven years, did important service in creating a juster appreciation of Beethoven's works in North Germany, a service to which Beethoven characteristically refers in a letter [1] to Schlesinger, Sept. 25, 1825. His book on the same subject, however, *Beethovens Leben und Schaffen* (Berlin, 1859 ; 2nd ed., 1865 ; 5th, 1901), is a fantastic critique, too full of mere conjecture and misty æstheticism. In 1827 he received his doctor's diploma from the University of Marburg, and was made ' Docent,' or tutor, in the history and theory of music, at the University of Berlin. He became professor in 1830, and in 1832 Musikdirector of the university choir. In 1850 he founded with Kullak and Stern the ' Berliner Musikschule,' afterwards the ' Berliner Conservatorium,' and now the ' Sternsche Conservatorium,' but withdrew in 1856 (Kullak having resigned in 1855), and henceforth devoted himself to his private pupils and to his work at the University.

His numerous works are of unequal merit, the most important being the *Lehre von der musikalischen Composition,* four vols. (Breitkopf & Härtel, 1837, 1838, 1847). His *Gluck und die Oper* (Berlin, two vols., 1863) contains many ingenious observations, but is of no historical value. The others are *Über Malerei in der Tonkunst* (1828), *Über die Geltung Händelschen Sologesänge,* etc. (1829), *Allgemeine Musiklehre* (1839), *Die alte Musiklehre* (1842), *Die Musik des 19. Jahrhundert,* etc. (1855), *Anleitung zum Vortrag Beethovenschen Klavierwerke* (1863), *Erinnerungen* (1865), and a posthumous work, *Das Ideale und die Gegenwart* (1867). Besides what he did for Beethoven's music, Marx deserves credit for bringing to light many little-known works of Bach and Handel. His compositions are not remarkable ; neither his oratorios ' Johannes der Täufer,' ' Moses ' and ' Nahid und Omar,' nor his instrumental music, obtaining more than a ' succès d'estime.' His opera, ' Jery und Bätely,' was performed at Berlin in 1827, and a *melodram,* ' Die Rache wartet,' in 1829. Nevertheless some particulars given in his *Erinnerungen* (Berlin, 1865) as to his manner of composing are well worth reading, as indeed is the whole book for its interesting picture of the state of music in Berlin between 1830 and 1860. With Mendelssohn he was at one time extremely intimate, and no doubt was in many respects useful to him ; but his influence diminished as Mendelssohn grew older and more independent.

F. G.

MARX, JOSEPH (*b.* Graz, Austria, May 18, 1882), composer, studied history of arts and music, taking a Ph.D. degree with a dissertation on ' The Functions of Intervals in Harmony and Melody for the Comprehension of Time-complexes.' In 1922 he was appointed director of the Academy of Music in Vienna succeeding Ferdinand Loewe.

At the age of 18 he wrote his first songs, which immediately attracted keen interest for the delicate and exquisite charm therein expressed. Starting in the popular manner of Robert Franz he was for some time strongly influenced by Hugo Wolf till he found his own style, which shows clearly marked local colour, bold part-writing, abundant feeling and richly coloured orchestral sound. A pure romanticist, he belongs to the transition-period between Brahms, Wolf and Schoenberg, with all of whom he has certain affinities in clear architectural structure and freshness of thought. In his later years he has produced chamber music and orchestral works.

WORKS

ORCHESTRAL.—Romantic Concerto for PF. and orch., 1919; Autumn Symphony, 1922.
CHAMBER MUSIC.—PF. Quartet (Ballade, Rhapsody and Scherzo), 1911; Trio Phantasy for vln. v'cl. and PF., 1910; Sonata for vln. and PF., 1914; Sonata for v'cl. and PF., 1915.
CHORAL.—Chorus to Pan in Autumn, 1911; Evening Song, 1910; Morning Song, 1910; Hymn for the New Year, and about 120 songs, all published by U. E. Vienna.)   H. J. K.

MARXSEN, EDUARD (b. Nienstädten, near Altona, July 23, 1806; d. Altona, Nov. 18, 1887). His father was organist at Altona. He was intended for the Church, but devoted himself to music, which he studied at home and with Clasing of Hamburg. He then assisted his father till the death of the latter in 1830, when he went to Vienna, and took lessons in counterpoint from Seyfried, and the pianoforte from Bocklet. He also composed industriously, and on his return to Hamburg gave a concert (Oct. 15, 1834) at which he played eighteen pieces of his own composition. He subsequently lived at Hamburg in great request as a teacher. Brahms was his most illustrious pupil. Of his sixty or seventy compositions, one for full orchestra, called ‘Beethoven's Schatten,’ was performed in 1844 and 1845 at concerts in Hamburg.   F. G.

MARYLEBONE GARDENS. This once celebrated place of entertainment was situated at the back of and appurtenant to a tavern called ‘The Rose of Normandy’ (or briefly ‘The Rose’), which stood on the east side of High Street, Marylebone, and was erected about the middle of the 17th century. The earliest notice of it is in Memoirs by Samuel Sainthill, 1659, printed in The Gentleman's Magazine, vol. 83, p. 524, where the garden is thus described :

‘The outside a square brick wall, set with fruit trees, gravel walks, 204 paces long, seven broad ; the circular walk 485 paces, six broad, the centre square, a Bowling Green, 112 paces one way, 88 another ; all except the first double set with quickset hedges, full grown and kept in excellent order, and indented like town walls.’

It is next mentioned by Pepys, May 7, 1668 :

‘Then we abroad to Marrowbone and there walked in the garden, the first time I ever was there, and a pretty place it is.’

Long's bowling green at the Rose at Maryle-

bone, half a mile distant from London, is mentioned in the London Gazette, Jan. 11, 1691/92. Count de Tallard, the French ambassador, gave a splendid entertainment before leaving England to the Marquis of Normanby (afterwards Duke of Buckingham) and other persons of note ‘at the great Bowling Green at Marylebone,’ in June 1699. About that time the house became noted as a gaming-house much frequented by persons of rank ; Sheffield, Duke of Buckingham, was a constant attendant, and, as Quin told Pennant, gave, every spring, a dinner to the chief frequenters of the place, at which his parting toast was ‘May as many of us as remain unchanged next spring meet here again.’ It was he who was alluded to in Lady Mary Wortley Montagu's oft-quoted line, ‘Some dukes at Marybone bowl time away.’ Gay, in his ‘Beggar's Opera,’ 1727, makes Marylebone one of Macheath's haunts, and mentions the ‘deep play’ there. Prior to 1737 admission to the gardens was gratuitous, but in that year Daniel Gough, the proprietor, charged 1s. each for admission, giving in return a ticket which was taken back in payment for refreshments to that amount.

In 1738 Gough erected an orchestra and engaged a band of music ‘from the opera and both theatres,’ which performed from 6 to 10 o'clock, during which time they played eighteen pieces. In August ‘two Grand or Double Bassoons, made by Mr. Stanesby, junior, the greatness of whose sound surpass that of any other bass instrument whatsoever ; never performed with before,’ were introduced. In 1740 an organ was erected by Bridge. In 1746 robberies had become so frequent and the robbers so daring that the proprietor was compelled to have a guard of soldiers to protect the visitors from and to town. In 1747 Miss Falkner appeared as principal singer (a post she retained for some years), and the admission to the concert was raised to 2s. In 1748 an addition was made to the number of lamps, and Defesch was engaged as first violin, and about the same time fireworks were introduced. In 1751 John Trusler became proprietor ; ‘Master [Michael] Arne’ appeared as a singer, balls and masquerades were occasionally given, the doors were opened at 7, the fireworks were discharged at 11, and ‘a guard was appointed to be in the house and gardens, and to oblige all persons misbehaving to quit the place.’ In 1752 the price of admission was reduced to 6d., although the expense was said to be £8 per night more than the preceding year. In 1753 the bowling green was added to the garden, and the fireworks were on a larger scale than before.

In 1758 the first burletta performed in the gardens was given ; it was an adaptation, by Trusler junior and the elder Storace, of Pergolesi's ‘La Serva Padrona,’ and for years was a great favourite. The gardens were opened in the morning for breakfasting, and Miss Trusler made cakes which long enjoyed a great vogue. In 1762 the gardens were opened in the morning gratis, and an organ performance given from 5 to 8 o'clock. In 1763 the place passed into the hands of Thomas (familiarly called Tommy) Lowe, the popular tenor singer, the admission was raised to 1s. and Miss Catley was among the singers engaged. In the next year the opening of the gardens on Sunday evenings for tea-drinking was prohibited ; and in October a morning performance, under the name of a re-hearsal, was given, when a collection was made in aid of the sufferers by destructive fires at Montreal, Canada, and Honiton, Devonshire. Lowe's management continued until 1768, when he retired, having met with heavy losses. In 1769 ARNOLD (q.v.) became proprietor, and engaged Mrs. Pinto (formerly Miss Brent), Master Brown and others as vocalists, Pinto as leader, Hook as organist and music director, and Arne to compose an ode. In 1770 Bar-thélemon became leader, and Mrs. Barthélemon, Bannister and Reinhold were among the singers. A burletta by Barthélemon, called ' The Noble Pedlar,' was very successful. In 1771 Miss Harper (afterwards Mrs. John Bannister) ap-peared, Miss Catley reappeared, and several new burlettas were produced. In 1772 Torrè, an eminent Italian pyrotechnist, was engaged, and the fireworks became a more prominent feature in the entertainments, to the great alarm of the neighbouring inhabitants, who applied to the magistrates to prohibit their exhibition, fearing danger to their houses from them. Torrè, however, continued to exhibit during that and the next two seasons. But the gardens were losing their popularity ; in 1775 there appear to have been no entertain-ments of the usual kind, but occasional per-formances of Baddeley's entertainment, ' The Modern Magic Lantern,' deliveries of George Saville Carey's ' Lecture upon Mimicry,' or ex-hibitions of fireworks by a Signor Caillot. In 1776 entertainments of a similar description were given, amongst which was a representa-tion of the Boulevards of Paris. The gardens closed on Sept. 23, and were not afterwards regularly opened. In or about 1778 the site was let to builders, and is now occupied by Beaumont Street, Devonshire Street, and part of Devonshire Place. The tavern, with a piece of ground at the back, used as a skittle alley, continued to exist in nearly its pristine state until 1855, when it was taken down, and rebuilt on its own site and that of an adjoining house, and on the ground behind it was erected the Marylebone Music Hall. A list of names of artists who appeared at Marylebone Gardens is given, with dates, in J. T. Smith's *Book for a Rainy Day.*   W. H. H.

MASANIELLO, the name in England of Auber's opera, LA MUETTE DE PORTICI ; in 5

acts ; words by Scribe and Delavigne. Pro-duced at the Paris Opéra, Feb. 29, 1828; Drury Lane, in English (3 acts), May 4, 1829 ; in Italian, Covent Garden (3 acts), Mar. 15, 1849 ; Her Majesty's, Apr. 10, 1851, as ' La muta di Portici.'

An earlier opera on the same subject was based on a contemporary account of the re-bellion at Naples under Tommaso Annello ; D'Urfey was the author, and Samuel Ackeroyde (or Akeroyde) the principal composer. It was printed in 1700, with the title, ' The famous history of the rise and fall of Massaniello, in two parts.' The songs remained in favour through the early part of the 18th century.

MASCAGNI, PIETRO (b. Leghorn, Dec. 7, 1863), an eminent composer of opera.

His father, who was a baker, intended his son to be a lawyer, and discouraged his attempts to learn the rudiments of music. The budding composer, compelled to prosecute his musical studies by stealth, entered himself surrepti-tiously as a pupil at the Istituto Luigi Cherubini, where his principal instructor was Alfredo Soffredini. In due course Mascagni's father found out how his son was spending his leisure time, and the musical career of the future com-poser of ' Cavalleria rusticana ' would there-upon have come to an untimely close had it not been for the intervention of an amiable uncle, who came forward and offered to adopt the young musician. Transferred to his uncle's house, Mascagni devoted himself in earnest to music, and the first fruits of his labours appeared in the shape of a symphony in C minor for small orchestra, and a 'Kyrie' written to celebrate the birthday of Cherubini, both of which were per-formed at the Istituto in 1879. These were fol-lowed after two years by ' In Filanda,' a cantata for solo voices and orchestra, which was favour-ably mentioned in a prize competition instituted by the International Exhibition of Music at Milan. These successes reconciled Mascagni's father to the idea of making his son a musician ; and at the death of his uncle in 1881 the boy returned to his father's house, when he was allowed to pursue his musical studies in peace. His next composition was a setting of a trans-lation of Schiller's ' Ode to Joy,' which was per-formed at the Teatro degli Avvalorati with so much success that Count Florestano de Lar-derel, a wealthy amateur, offered on the spot to pay for the composer's education at the Milan Conservatoire. Mascagni's career at Milan was not a success. In spite of the sympathy and en-couragement of his teachers, among whom were Amilcare Ponchielli and Michele Saladino, he found the course of regular study insupportable. For some time he chafed silently against the trivial round of counterpoint and fugue, and eventually took French leave of his professors, joined a travelling operatic company in the capacity of conductor, and turned his back upon

Milan to seek his fortune elsewhere. For many years he led a life of obscurity and privation, travelling through the length and breadth of Italy with one company after another. He had no spare time for composition, but doubtless gained much valuable experience in practical orchestration. After many wanderings Mascagni married and settled at Cerignola near Foggia, where he managed to make a meagre livelihood by giving pianoforte lessons and managing the municipal school of music.

From this obscurity he was suddenly rescued by the success of his one-act opera, ' Cavalleria rusticana,' which won the first prize in a competition instituted in 1889 by the publisher Sonzogno, and was produced at the Costanzi Theatre in Rome, May 18, 1890. The libretto was founded by Signori Menasci and Targioni-Tozzetti upon a well-known story of Sicilian village life by Giovanni Verga. The opera was received at its first performance with tumultuous applause, and the next day Mascagni awoke to find himself famous. ' Cavalleria ' at once made the tour of Italy, and speedily crossed the Alps. It was produced in Berlin in the summer of 1890, and in London, at the Shaftesbury Theatre, under the management of Signor Lago in Oct. 1891. It was first performed in Paris at the Opéra-Comique, Jan. 19, 1892. Everywhere its success was unquestionable. The public, tired, perhaps, of imitations of Wagner, welcomed the crisp action and direct emotional appeal of the little work. It became the fashion, and was responsible for a mushroom crop of one-act melodramas.

Since the days of ' Cavalleria ' Mascagni's fame has steadily declined. His next work, ' L' amico Fritz ' (Teatro Costanzi, Rome, Oct. 31, 1891), an adaptation of Erckmann-Chatrian's well-known novel, made by Daspuro under the anagram of P. Suardon, had more refinement than ' Cavalleria,' and was more carefully written, but the composer scarcely attempted to fit his grandiose manner to the exigencies of an idyll. ' I Rantzau ' (Teatro della Pergola, Florence, Nov. 10, 1892), another adaptation from Erckmann-Chatrian, by Menasci and Targioni-Tozzetti, was even less successful than ' L' amico Fritz.' ' Guglielmo Ratcliff ' (La Scala, Milan, Feb. 1895) was a work of the composer's student days, subsequently revised and rewritten. Mascagni had conceived the extraordinary notion of setting to music a literal translation of Heine's gloomy tragedy, which was alone sufficient to doom the work to failure, and his music did little to relieve the tedium of the libretto. No less decisive was the failure of ' Silvano ' (La Scala, Milan, Mar. 1895), a half-hearted bid for popularity in the composer's most hackneyed manner. Meanwhile (1895) Mascagni had been appointed director of the Conservatoire at Pesaro, where his next opera, ' Zanetto,' was

produced, Mar. 2, 1896. ' Zanetto ' is slight in structure, being scored only for strings and harp, but has considerably more refinement of thought and expression than is customary in Mascagni's work. ' Iris ' (Teatro Costanzi, Rome, Nov. 22, 1898), on a Japanese subject, is handicapped by a singularly unpleasant libretto, but nevertheless has won more favour than any of the composer's works since ' Cavalleria.' It shows much skill in the handling of the orchestra, but its lack of original invention is conspicuous. Mascagni's idea of producing his next work, ' Le maschere ' (Jan. 17, 1901), simultaneously in seven different cities, was a piece of audacious impertinence; but no amount of advertisement could galvanise ' Le maschere ' into a success. At Milan, Venice, Verona, Naples and Turin it was soundly hissed, while at Genoa the audience would not even allow the performance to be finished. Only at Rome was it received with any degree of favour. ' Amica ' (Monte Carlo, Mar. 1905), though produced in more modest fashion, shared the fate of its predecessor.

Mascagni wrote a cantata for the Leopardi centenary, which was performed at Recanati in 1898, and incidental music for Hall Caine's play, *The Eternal City*, which was produced at His Majesty's Theatre, London, in October 1902. Later operas of Mascagni are: ' Isabeau ' (libretto by Iilica), first performed at Buenos Ayres, 1911; ' Parisina ' (on a text by D' Annunzio), given at Milan, 1913; ' Lodoletta ' (text by G. Forzano), produced at Rome, 1917, and ' Il Piccolo Marat ' (text by G. Forzano and Giovanni Targioni-Tozzetti), given at Rome, 1921. The composer has also written an operetta in 3 acts, entitled ' Si,' on a book supplied by C. Lombardo and A. Franci, which was first produced at Rome in 1919. A Requiem in memory of King Humbert was performed in the Pantheon at Rome in 1900. There exists also a ' Rapsodia satanica,' a symphonic poem written for a film.

Mascagni has won some fame as a conductor, chiefly owing to repeated tours with specially chosen orchestras through the cities of Europe and America. A protracted tour in the United States in 1903 cost him his place at Pesaro.

Mascagni's reputation rests almost entirely upon ' Cavalleria rusticana.' It owes much to its direct if somewhat brutal libretto, but the music undeniably shows a natural instinct for theatrical effect, and it boasts plenty of catchy, commonplace tunes. The speedy exhaustion of a shallow vein of musical invention, together with the carelessness engendered by a dangerously sudden success, is in great part responsible for the complete collapse of what at one time seemed a talent of bright promise.

R. A. S. ; rev. F. B.

MASCHERA, FLORENTIO, succeeded Merulo, Aug. 1, 1557, as organist of Brescia Cathedral;

composed a book of instrumental Canzone *a* 4 v. (Brescia, 1584; republ. Venice, 1588 and 1593). Whether he was still alive at the latter date (1593) is uncertain. Some of his pieces for organ (also for lute) appeared in collective volumes (*Q.-L.*).

MASCHERONI, EDOARDO (*b.* Milan, Sept. 4, 1857), composer, and eminent conductor of Italian opera.

As a boy he showed no special aptitude for music, and was sent to the Liceo Beccaria, where he distinguished himself particularly in mathematics. As he grew up he developed a marked taste for the study of literature, and joined the little band of enthusiasts, among whom were De Marchi, Pozza, G. Mazzucato and Borghi, who founded the journal, *La vita nuova*, to which he contributed numerous articles on literary subjects. But with manhood came the consciousness that music was to be his career, and he placed himself under Boucheron, a composer and teacher well known in Milan at the time, with whom he worked assiduously for several years. In his younger days Mascheroni composed much music of various kinds, but as time went on he became persuaded that his real vocation lay in conducting. He made his first serious essay in this branch of his art in 1883, when he was engaged as conductor at the Teatro Goldoni at Leghorn. From Leghorn Mascheroni moved to Rome, where he had been appointed conductor of the Teatro Apollo. Here he remained seven years, gaining each year in experience and reputation, so that at last he might fairly claim to be considered the leading Italian conductor of his day, a claim which was tacitly recognised in 1893 by his being chosen to produce and conduct Verdi's 'Falstaff' at La Scala.

Mascheroni, although best known as conductor, has also won laurels as a composer. During his Roman period he wrote a good deal of chamber music, which was performed with much applause, and an Album for pianoforte of his won a prize in a *Concorso* at Palermo. But his masterpiece at that time was the Requiem for solo voices, chorus and orchestra, which he wrote in memory of the death of Victor Emmanuel. So profound an impression did this work create, that the composer was commissioned by the royal family to write another Requiem for voices only, for exclusive performance in the Royal Chapel, where it was at once performed. In spite of his success in conducting other men's music, Mascheroni did not himself tempt fortune on the stage until his 'Lorenza' was produced successfully at the Teatro Costanzi, Rome, on Apr. 13, 1901. Another opera, 'La Perugina,' libretto by Illica, was performed and favourably received at the S. Carlo Theatre, Naples, in 1909.   R. A. S. ; addns. F. B.

MASINI, ANGELO (*b.* Forlì, 1845), is the only Italian tenor of that generation who won a very high position without having appeared on the operatic stage in England. He came to this country in 1875 as a member of the famous quartet, which, under the composer's own direction, sang at the Albert Hall in Verdi's Requiem Mass, the other singers being Mme. Stoltz, Mme. Waldmann and Signor Medini. At that time Masini was the first of the younger tenors of Italy, and in 1876 he sang the part of Rhadamès when, with Verdi himself conducting, 'Aïda' was produced for the first time in Paris. This performance added greatly to his reputation, and in 1879 Mapleson engaged him to sing at Her Majesty's Theatre. A stupid contretemps, however, for which Masini was himself solely responsible, prevented his appearance. The story is fully set forth in the *Mapleson Memoirs*. This blunder proved a bar to his future career in England, as Mapleson had an injunction against him for breach of contract—compromised at last by the payment of £200. In Madrid, Buenos Ayres and elsewhere, however, Masini sang with the utmost success, and gained both fame and fortune. He was for many seasons the leading tenor at the Italian Opera at St. Petersburg, resigning his position at last for the reason that he could no longer withstand the severe climate. At St. Petersburg, late in his career, he sang Lohengrin to the Elsa of Sigrid Arnoldson. That Masini at his best was a tenor of exceptional gifts cannot be doubted. Distinguished singers, who appeared with him at St. Petersburg, have spoken of him in enthusiastic terms. It was stated at the time that before the production of 'Falstaff' in Milan, Verdi offered to write a romance for Masini if he would undertake the part of Fenton. However, nothing came of the proposal. Possibly Masini thought that, even with a song thrown in, it was a poor compliment to offer him a small part, and no set-off against the distinction Verdi had conferred on his great rival, Tamagno, by selecting him for Otello.   S. H. P.

MASNADIERI, I—*i.e.* The Brigands—opera in 4 acts : libretto by Maffei, from Schiller's 'Die Räuber,' music by Verdi. Produced Her Majesty's Theatre, London, July 22, 1847, Verdi conducting. An experiment had been made by Mercadante eleven years before on a libretto adapted from the same play, under the title of 'I briganti,' produced at the Italiens, Paris, Mar. 22, 1836.   G.

MASNELLI (MASENELLI), PAOLO (*b.* Verona), court organist at Mantua, Feb. 6, 1585–Mar. 24, 1592; afterwards organist at Verona Cathedral (*c.* 1596). He composed 1 book of madrigals *a* 4 v. (1582) ; 2 books of madrigals *a* 5 v. (1586, 1596) (*Q.-L.*).

MASON, DANIEL GREGORY (*b.* Brookline, Mass., Nov. 20, 1873), American composer, author, lecturer and associate professor of music at Columbia University (New York). He graduated from Harvard in 1895; his teachers in music were Johns, Nevin, Paine, Whiting, Chadwick and Goetschius, and later d'Indy. Although associated with Columbia since 1910, his activities as lecturer have extended to numerous other institutions, and for the Board of Education he has given some hundreds of popular lectures. His books are many; particularly notable are:

From Grieg to Brahms (1902).
Beethoven and his Forerunners (1904).
The Romantic Composers (1906).
Contemporary Composers (1918).
The Appreciation of Music (1907) with T. W. Surette.
He was editor-in-chief of *The Art of Music*, 14 vols. (1914–17).

His compositions include:

Symphony, C minor, op. 11.
Prelude and Fugue, piano and orchestra, op. 20.
'Russians,' baritone and orchestra, op. 18.
Quartet, piano and strings, op. 7.
Three Pieces for Flute, Harp and String Quartet, op. 13.
Pastorale, violin, clarinet and piano, op. 8.
String Quartet on Negro Themes, op. 19.
Intermezzo, string quartet, op. 17.
Sonata, violin and piano, op. 5.
Sonata, clarinet and piano, op. 14.
Many piano pieces and songs.

         W. S. S.

MASON, GEORGE (*fl.* 1618), with John Earsden composed and published:

'The Ayres that were sung and played, at Brougham Castle in Westmerland, in the King's Entertainment; given by the Right Honourable the Earle of Cumberland, and his Right Noble Sonne the Lord Clifford.'

The authorship of the words is attributed to Thomas CAMPIAN (*q.v.*) in Percival Vivian's edition of Campian's works. E. H. F.

MASON, JOHN, Mus.B. (*d.* 1543 [1]), was admitted clerk of Magdalen College, Oxford, in 1508, graduated Feb. 12, 1509, and was in the same year appointed instructor of the choristers and chaplain of Magdalen College. Wood says he was in much esteem in his profession. He was collated prebendary of Pratum Minus, July 21, and of Putston Minor, July 22, 1525, and treasurer of Hereford Cathedral, May 23, 1545. He is mentioned by Morley in his *Introduction* as one of those whose works he had consulted. Four motets (tenor wanting) are at PH.

         W. H. H.

MASON, (1) LOWELL, Mus.D. (*b.* Medfield, Massachusetts, Jan. 24, 1792; *d.* Orange, New Jersey, Aug. 11, 1872), was self-taught, and in his own words 'spent twenty years of his life in doing nothing save playing on all manner of musical instruments that came within his reach.' At 20 he went to Savannah in Georgia, as clerk in a bank, and there continued to practise, lead and teach. In the course of these labours he formed, with the help of F. L. Abel, a collection of psalm tunes based on Gardiner's 'Sacred Melodies'—itself adapted to tunes extracted from the works of Haydn, Mozart and Beethoven. (See GARDINER.) This collection was published by the Handel and Haydn Society of Boston in 1822 under the title of 'The Handel and Haydn Society's collection of Church Music,' Mason's name being almost entirely suppressed. The book sold well; it initiated a purer and healthier taste for music

 [1] See C. F. Abdy Williams, *Degrees in Music*, p. 65.

in New England, and it led to Mason's removal to Boston and to his taking 'a general charge of music in the churches there,' in 1827. He then became president of the society; but as his object was not so much the cultivation of high-class music as the introduction of music as an essential element of education in the common schools, he soon left it and established (with G. J. Webb) the Boston Academy of Music in 1832. He founded classes on the system of Pestalozzi, and at length in 1838 obtained power to teach in all the schools of Boston. He also published a large number of manuals and collections which have sold enormously and produced him a handsome fortune. He visited Europe first in 1837 with the view of examining the methods of teaching in Germany, and embodied the results in a volume entitled *Musical Letters from Abroad* (New York, 1853). He was for long closely connected with the Public Board of Education of Massachusetts. His degree of Doctor in Music, the first of the kind conferred by an American College, was granted by the New York University in 1835. The last years of his life were spent at Orange in New Jersey, the residence of two of his sons. He formed a very fine library, which he collected far and wide, regardless of expense. The list of his popular collections of secular and sacred music is given in *Baker*.

Of his sons, (2) WILLIAM (*b.* Boston, Jan. 24, 1829; *d.* New York, July 14, 1908) received a liberal education in music, and after a successful début at Boston in 1846, and a period of study at Leipzig in 1849, under Moscheles, Hauptmann and Richter, and at Weimar, under Liszt, was long recognised as a leading pianist in New York. He founded chamber-music concerts with Theodore Thomas and others in 1854, and received the degree of Mus.D. from Yale University in 1872. Special interest attaches to his *Memories of a Musical Life* (New York, 1901), which contains a valuable account of the Weimar circle in 1853.

         A. W. T.

MASON, MATHIAS, groom of the chamber to James I., is mentioned in Dowland's 'Varietie of Lute Lessons' (1610) as having invented three frets for the lute.

MASON, REV. WILLIAM (*b.* Kingston-upon-Hull, Feb. 12, 1724; *d.* Aston, Apr. 5, 1797), son of a clergyman, graduated at Cambridge, B.A. 1745, M.A. 1749; took orders 1754, became rector of Aston, Yorkshire, in that year, and afterwards prebendary (1756), canon residentiary and precentor (1763) of York Minster. He was appointed chaplain to Lord Holderness in 1754 and to the King in 1757. In 1782 he published a book of words of anthems, to which he prefixed a *Critical and Historical Essay on Cathedral Music* (another edition, 1794). He also wrote essays *On Instrumental Church Music, On Parochial Psalmody,* and *On the Causes of the Present imperfect Alliance between Music and Poetry.* (See also PIANO-FORTE, subsection THE SQUARE PIANO). He composed some church music, the best known of which is the short anthem ' Lord of all power and might.' He was author of several poems, and of two tragedies, ' Elfrida ' and ' Caractacus ' (see ARNE, Thomas Augustine), and was the friend and biographer of the poet Gray. He also invented an instrument called the ' Celestinette.'   W. H. H., addns.

BIBL.—JOHN W. DRAPER, *William Mason,* New York 1924.

MASQUE (MASKE, MASK). A dramatic entertainment—usually upon an allegorical or mythological subject, and combining poetry, vocal and instrumental music, scenery, dancing, elaborate machinery and splendid costumes and decorations — which was performed at court or at noblemen's houses on festive occasions, the performers being usually persons of rank. Masques were frequently exhibited at the courts of James I. and Charles I., and vast sums were lavished upon their production. The Masque of the Inner Temple and Gray's Inn, presented in Feb. 1612/13, on the marriage of the Princess Elizabeth to the Elector Palatine of the Rhine, cost £1086 : 8 : 11.[1] The principal author of those masques was Ben Jonson, whose genius was peculiarly fitted to a style of composition which afforded him ample opportunity of displaying his erudition. Beaumont, Chapman, Samuel Daniel, Campian, Shirley, Heywood and Carew also employed their talents upon masques, as did a greater than they, Milton, whose ' Comus ' was represented at Ludlow Castle in 1634. Inigo Jones devised the machinery and designed the costumes and scenes for the court masques [2]; Laniere and others painted the scenery ; and FERRABOSCO, CAMPIAN, H. and W. LAWES, IVE (Ives), LANIERE, LOCKE, C. GIBBONS and others composed the music. (See OPERA, subsection ENGLISH MASQUES.) Two of Ben Jonson's masques—' The Masque of Queens,' 1610, and ' The Twelfth Night's Revels,' 1606—were printed from his autograph MSS. in the British Museum by the Shakespeare Society at the end of Cunningham's *Life of Inigo Jones.* The evolution of the masque in its dramatic and literary form is traced in Herford and Simpson's *Ben Jonson (Masques and Entertainments,* vol. ii.).

After the Restoration what were called masques were occasionally given at court, but they appear to have been rather masked or fancy-dress balls than dramatic entertainments. An exception was Crowne's masque, ' Calisto ; or, the Chaste Nymph,' performed at court by the princesses and courtiers, Dec. 15 and 22, 1675. In the 18th century masques were not

[1] In regarding these figures the difference in the value of money then and now must be borne in mind.
[2] Many of his sketches for this purpose are in the possession of the Duke of Devonshire. Several are reproduced in Herford and Simpson, *Ben Jonson.*

unfrequently to be seen on the public stage. The ' pantomimes ' produced by Rich (for most of which Galliard composed the music) were really masques with harlequinade scenes interspersed. More recently masques have been performed on occasion of royal weddings ; thus ' Peleus and Thetis,' a masque, formed the second act of the opera ' Windsor Castle,' by William Pearce, music by J. P. Salomon, performed at Covent Garden on the marriage of the Prince of Wales, 1795, and ' Freya's Gift,' masque by John Oxenford, music by G. A. Macfarren, was produced at the same house on the marriage of Edward VII., 1863. Soon after the death of Sir Walter Scott in 1832, ' The Vision of the Bard,' masque by James Sheridan Knowles, was produced at Covent Garden. In 1887, in honour of Queen Victoria's Jubilee, ' The Masque of Flowers ' was revived at Gray's Inn, and was again performed in 1897 for the Diamond Jubilee. ' Comus ' (with the music of Lawes) has received repeated performances in all sorts of conditions. Revivals of the earlier 17th-century masques are becoming more frequent in the 20th century. A masque by Campian was given at the G.S.M. under the title of ' The Golden Tree,' by the Worshipful Company of Musicians, June 29, 1905. (See *Mus. T.,* 1900, p. 248.) Another masque of Campian was given at Hatfield Palace, May 30, 1924, and a limited edition privately printed by the Cayme Press, Chelsea.

                                        W. H. H., with addns.

BIBLIOGRAPHY

R. BROTANEK : *Die englische Maskenspiele.* (1902.)
PAUL REYHER : *Les Masques anglais ; Étude sur les ballets et la vie de cour en Angleterre, 1512-1640.* (1909.)
C. H. HERFORD and R. SIMPSON : *Ben Jonson,* vol. ii. (1925.)
W. J. LAURENCE : *Notes on a Collection of Masque Music, M. and L.* iii. 49.
JEFFREY MARK : *The Jonsonian Masque, M. and L.* iii. 358.

MASS (*missa*) is employed as a musical term for a setting of the unvarying portion of the text of the Liturgy, called the Ordinary, and consisting normally and mainly of *Kyrie, Gloria in excelsis, Credo, Sanctus* and *Agnus Dei.* For the varying portions little music besides the original Gregorian chant has ever been provided : their turn and opportunity for performance came too rarely. The main exception to this general statement is the Requiem. Because of the frequent repetition of this form of Mass, it has been worth while to provide fresh settings of the variables — the Introit Gradual, etc.—as well as of the invariable elements which make up the Ordinary of the Mass. See REQUIEM ; GREGORIAN MUSIC.

THE LITURGICAL FORM

Many different plain-song settings of the component parts of the Ordinary were made in the period between the 9th and the 12th centuries ; but they remained isolated compositions, unconnected in idea and even in tonality. Among them the *Credo* was the most stable element, for it kept to its one original setting.

But of the rest, any setting of *Kyrie, Gloria, Sanctus* or *Agnus* might be associated with it ; and these individually were freely chosen from the stock available without reference to one another, and combined at will. In time a certain allotment of the repertory took place. But the pieces were still viewed individually and allocated severally to particular occasions—Easter, Greater Saints' Days, etc.—rather than associated with one another. Such allotment as there was took place rather at haphazard and without any uniform practice. Thus the ' Mass,' as an art-form—a cantata in four or five movements—did not yet exist.

It was only at the end of the Middle Ages that anything like the *Missa de Angelis*, a plain-song Mass continuous in theme and tonality, came into existence. The way to it had been made, not by monody but by polyphony. When part-singing arose, under the name of *Organum* or *Diaphonia*, it began to make its way into the church music, though long faced by considerable opposition. The earliest *Organa* were probably improvisations, analogous to those which find favour with Bantu tribes, or to those which are still to be heard in Russian churches. As such, they could be applied as easily to the variable items as to the invariables ; and indeed the latter as belonging to special days and great feasts seem at first to have had the preference. The examples given in the Theorists show this ; and the earliest large collection of two-part *Organa* that we have—those in the *Winchester Troper* (Henry Bradshaw Society) bear this out. But as the writer of *Organa* became more scientific, he fastened upon those curious interpolations called the tropes as giving him his best field. For in the tropes only a single syllable was set to each note ; and this arrangement facilitated the task of writing and singing in two parts. So while the main text was sung in unison, the intercalated tropes gave occasion for *organum*. Among all the tropes those of the Ordinary, recurring as they did in frequent use, supplied the best opportunities. The farsed *Kyries*, and the tropes of *Gloria, Sanctus* and *Agnus* are the best xamples of the earliest harmony in two parts.

While this remained the position so far as the Mass-music was concerned through the 12th and 13th centuries, the art of harmony was being considerably developed meanwhile, in another connexion, namely, by the MOTET (*q.v.*). The motet in origin was a trope or prose that broke away from the host of which it had been a parasite, and set up for itself an independent existence. Consisting thus of a *canto fermo*, drawn out of some liturgical text, with one or more added parts, it acquired a freedom, which any composition that remained embedded in its liturgical position could not secure. The development was then made with considerable rapidity. New *canti fermi* could soon be taken at will, and modified freely as to rhythm and time values. This freedom facilitated also the combining of a known melody with a *canto fermo*, or the superposing of new parts. And with this freedom came the clearer conception of measurable, as distinct from plain, chant, and the development of the *Ars nova discantus*.

In course of time the contrapuntal skill, learned in connexion with the motet, became available for the Mass. Not merely the intercalated trope but the whole liturgical melody then could be made mensurable and taken as *canto fermo* : and there thus emerged a setting in two or three parts of a whole *Sanctus* or *Agnus*. The earliest known setting in parts of the whole ordinary comes from the first half of the 14th century. The *canto fermo* for each portion is drawn from the plain-song repertory. The result is a ' Mass ' in the special sense of the term : but as yet there is still no unity in it. The combination of *Kyrie, Gloria, Credo, Sanctus* and *Agnus* is still fortuitous ; and the Mass is a group of five distinct compositions in different modes, not a single uniform composition in five connected movements. In the *Gloria* and *Credo* the liturgical intonation, as sung by the celebrant, is preserved; and the choir begins the words ' Et in terra ' and ' Patrem omnipotentem ' respectively.

A further stage of development yet remained which should bring the whole into a unity linked by common thematic material and a uniform tonality. This change was brought about only gradually in the course of the 15th century ; and it was to a large extent bound up with the gradual emancipation of composers from the traditional habit of using the plainchant as *canto fermo* throughout. When this was gone the component parts drew together. In this emancipation probably the motet led the way and the Mass followed. The *Credo* was the latest portion of the ordinary to be brought into line, partly because it was that which most pertinaciously preserved its old plain-song melody, and partly also, perhaps, because, like the *Gloria in excelsis*, it was not always needed, not being used on ordinary week-days, or in Advent and Lent. But eventually and by degrees all fell into line, and the homogeneous Mass in 5 movements arose, more or less closely knit. While this emancipation was coming, the door was also opening for another great advance. The thematic material could be polyphonically employed, imitation and other devices of counterpoint could come increasingly into use, and there arose new rhythmical independence among the parts, Thus the composer had worked himself free to write his four or five parts unhampered, and free to choose as his theme and starting-point either a plain-song phrase in the old manner or some secular melody like 'L'Homme armé' or 'The Western Wind,' or else an original phrase or motto : free also to handle his themes and develop them at will.

These are the principal stages to be noted in tracing the development of the 'Mass' as a musical form. Incidentally there are many curious details to be observed. It is not possible to do more than mention two here. (1) In regard to the handling of the tenor—it long continued to be the lowest voice; and this arrangement remained the rule even after the experiment had been made of placing it in the highest voice, or in the middle one of the parts. It was only in the 16th century that it became commonly identified with the 'tenor voice.' (2) In regard to the handling of the liturgical text—in the earlier stages this was sung in due order and respectfully treated. The alternation of unisonous plain-song with occasional passages set in harmony did not alter this ; though it had the result that the choir-books exhibited only some portions of the text, to the exclusion of the rest, which was sung to the plain-chant. But the growing elaboration of the harmonised music brought in some disrespect for the text. A notable example is afforded by the *Sanctus*. The settings became so long that they were not concluded by the time when the celebrant reached the Consecration. So, to overcome this difficulty, the text was cut into two portions. It was clumsily divided. The logical point of subdivision would have been before the first 'Hosanna,' for that begins a new section, which is both historically an addition to the primitive *Sanctus* and also logically distinct from it ; but an unintelligent division into two equal halves was made at 'Benedictus qui venit.' This gave the composer the opportunity of dividing his work into two movements of more or less equal length, one occupying the available time up to the Consecration, and the other the available time after it. But the sense suffered ; and this unfortunate mishandling has its evil effects even until now. Musically it is convenient, but ritually it is indefensible. Other results of disrespect to the words may be found in the course of the history—clauses of the *Credo* are sung simultaneously by different voices, or omitted altogether, because the composer had spent too much time over the rest. And, more generally speaking, a habit of making meaningless repetitions of the words grew out of the exigencies of imitation and counterpoint ; and again the sense suffered.

But in spite of these flaws, the development of the Mass as an art-form was a great achievement. It was completed by the early part of the 16th century. Since, then, though music has gone through many phases, and most of them have made some contribution to the great series of masses extending down to the present day, the form itself has remained stable.   w. h. f.

INDIVIDUAL DEVELOPMENTS

Only the briefest summary can be attempted here of the principal influences which have modified composers' treatment of the Mass from the time when the individual artist assumed complete freedom of action.

(1) The development of what is known as the polyphonic style can be most consistently traced in the several generations of composers proceeding from the Netherlands, of which the names of DUFAY, OKEGHEM, OBRECHT, JOSQUIN DES PRÉS and Orlandus LASSUS are representative. Various national groups owed their technical methods to the Netherlanders ; Robert FAYRFAX, followed by the early Tudor composers, TAVERNER and TYE in England, by ISAAC in Germany, SERMISY (Claudin), DE FEVIN and MOUTON in France, are representative names. The Italian school of the 16th century, of which PALESTRINA is the head and forefront, drew to itself composers both from the Netherlands and Spain (see GUERRERO, MORALES, VICTORIA), and formed the culmination of the style (see under POLYPHONY : Principles of the 16th century). William BYRD, whose three masses are masterpieces, is the last landmark of the contrapuntal Mass in England, after religious and political considerations had banished the Latin Office from the English Church. (See SERVICE.)

Up to this point church music with the Mass as its central feature had guided secular music (cf. MADRIGAL). From the beginning of the 17th century onward the growth of instruments and the rise of the opera becoming the most potent factors in the development of the art as a whole, reversed this position. Henceforward developments in the music of the Mass (as of all other Latin church music) consisted in the adoption of the devices of secular music.[1]

(2) The method adopted by VIADANA (q.v.) in his 'Cento concerti ecclesiastici' introduced new principles of construction into church music (see THOROUGH-BASS). His Mass for 1-3 voices with *basso continuo* for organ (1605) marks the starting-point of the new style in which BANCHIERI, MERULA and other Italians followed him. In the first half of the century the conflict between the polyphonic and monodic styles, the ecclesiastical and the secular, is traceable in composers of the Roman school. The victory of the latter, however, soon becomes decisive. The growth of instrumental accompaniment keeps pace with the operatic orchestra ; the musical form accommodates itself to the aria, the dramatic chorus and

---

[1] The *Motu Proprio* of Pope Pius X. (1903), in claiming polyphonic music together with that of the Gregorian chant as proper to the sacred offices, is historically accurate.

ensemble of solo-singers. The masses of Alessandro SCARLATTI exhibit fully all the qualities of his style in opera and cantata.[1]

(3) Broadly speaking, the same is true of the Neapolitan school which followed Scarlatti in the 18th century, of which VINCI, LEO, DURANTE and PERGOLESI are representative. They are a ' school ' in virtue of their operatic productions, and they wrote masses in the style cultivated by the theatre.[2]

(4) Bach's Mass in B minor stands alone as a supreme musical setting of the Mass in the middle of the 18th century. It must be remembered, however, that it was not conceived primarily as a setting of the Mass as a whole, but was begun with a view to performance of those parts of the text sung in Lutheran churches. The whole might be more fitly considered to be a series of church cantatas. The splitting up of *Gloria* and *Credo* into distinct movements (soli and chorus), according to the individual taste of the composer, had already become prevalent in the more elaborate settings intended for liturgical use, and was the natural outcome of the adoption of the aria form into the Mass.

(5) Later in the century the Viennese school as represented by the two brothers HAYDN, and by MOZART, dominated the situation and lasted into the 19th century in the works of BEETHOVEN, SCHUBERT, HUMMEL and others. The style, in so far as it is anything besides purely individualistic, is governed by the conditions of patronage in which composers worked. The resources of the private chapels and the wishes of patrons determined the form of the works produced, in many cases entirely unfitting them for transference to the conditions of public worship.

(6) The rise of the public concert in the 19th century completes the list of secular influences operating on the composition of the Mass. Beethoven's ' Missa solennis ' in D, despite its ecclesiastical origin, stands beside its companion work, the ' Choral Symphony,' as music for public performance on the scale of the festival choir and symphonic orchestra. The most conspicuous Masses and Requiems of the century are essentially works of the concert-room. To this category belong those of SPOHR, BERLIOZ, SCHUMANN, LISZT, VERDI, DVOŘÁK, BRUCKNER, notwithstanding the fact that some of them were undertaken for special occasions of the Church. In all, despite their different styles, the text is regarded as a libretto for dramatic and emotional treatment in music intended to be heard as a self-sufficient work of art.

(7) Meantime, the tradition of strict church writing was not entirely destroyed. From CARISSIMI, the last composer to write a Mass

on the old tune, ' L'Homme armé,' it survived through the 18th century in Italy, notably by means of the teaching of Padre MARTINI, to find more than a reflection of its original manner in the contrapuntal masses of CHERUBINI. An ever-decreasing stream of what came to be known as *a cappella* works (in distinction from the operatic and instrumental masses) trickled through the ages, and the tradition was maintained more vigorously in the Catholic churches of Southern Germany than anywhere else in Europe. It has been enriched through that revival of scholarship in the latter half of the 19th century which has included research into the principles of the ancient plain-song, carried on by the monks of SOLESMES (*q.v.*), the re-study of the MODES (*q.v.*), the publication of the complete works of Palestrina (see HABERL), and of much other music of the same period. In England it has had the special stimulus of what almost amounts to a rediscovery of ɛ national school of composition of the 16th century, ranging from TAVERNER to BYRD.[3] The realisation of these achievements of the past has brought several significant works from modern composers of which the Mass by R. VAUGHAN WILLIAMS is an outstanding example.

C.

BIBLIOGRAPHY

P. WAGNER : *Geschichte der Messe.* 1. Teil : Bis 1600. (Leipzig, 1913.) Teil 2 not yet published.
A. SCHNERICH : *Messe und Requiem seit Haydn und Mozart*, pp. 178. (Vienna, 1909.)
GUIDO ADLER : *Zur Geschichte der Wiener Messenkomposition in der zweiten Hälfte des 17. Jahrhunderts. S.z.M.W.* Heft 4, 1916.
JOHANN RÖCK : *Handschriftliche Missalien in Steiermark*, pp. 200, pl. 10. (Graz and Vienna, 1916.) See notice in *Z.M.W.*, Oct. 1920, p. 56.

MASSAINO (MASSAINI), TIBURTIO (*b.* Cremona), Augustinian monk, maestro di cappella at Salo 1587, Prague 1590, Salzburg 1591, Cremona 1594, Piacenza 1598 and Lodi 1600. He composed masses, psalms, motets, madrigals, also canzonas, including one each for 8 trombones, for 4 violins and 4 lutes, and one for 16 trombones. (For list see *Q.-L.* ; *Riemann*.)

MASSART, JOSEPH LAMBERT (*b.* Liège, July 19, 1811 ; *d.* Paris, Feb. 13, 1892), a famous violin teacher, professor at the Paris Conservatoire. Massart received his first instruction in violin-playing from an amateur named Delavau, who was so impressed with the talent displayed by his pupil, that he persuaded the municipal authorities of Liège to grant him a scholarship which would enable him to study in Paris. On his arrival in the city Massart sought admission as a student to the Conservatoire, but was refused by the then director, Cherubini, on account of his being a foreigner. Notwithstanding this first rebuff, Massart's gifts were soon recognised by Rudolph Kreutzer, who

---

[1] See Dent, *Alessandro Scarlatti.*
[2] The masses of this school are amply quoted from by Alfred Orel in Adler's *Handbuch der Musikgeschichte*, p. 471, *et seq.*

[3] The coincidence of the consecration of the Roman Catholic Cathedral at Westminster with the issue of the *Motu Proprio* on church music of Pope Pius X., and the fact that the new Cathedral, under the musical direction of R. R. TERRY (*q.r.*), set itself to illustrate the principles in the revival of polyphony, having special regard to the old English music, gave composers and other English musicians practical experience of the style beyond anything which pure scholarship could afford.

willingly undertook the task of developing the young artist's talents. Although Massart became a fine executant under Kreutzer's tuition, yet, on account of his excessive shyness, he never attained much fame as a public player. An instance of his modesty, when his performance with Liszt of the Kreutzer Sonata was shouted down by an audience anxious to hear Liszt's Fantasia on 'Robert le Diable,' is related by Sir Charles Hallé in his Autobiography. In 1843 the Paris Conservatoire appointed him professor of the violin, and in this position his energy and thoroughness gained for him a world-wide renown. Among his many famous pupils were : Henri Wieniawski, Lotto, Pablo de Sarasate, Martin Marsick and Teresina Tua. Massart was an excellent quartet-player, and together with his wife, Louise Aglae Marson—who succeeded Farrenc as professor of piano at the Paris Conservatoire—gave many delightful chamber-music concerts.

BIBL.—HENRY C. LAHEE, *Famous Violinists of To-day and Yesterday* (Boston, 1899) ; *Fétis* ; *Baker*.

E. H.-A.

MASSÉ, FÉLIX MARIE (known as VICTOR) (*b.* Lorient, Mar. 7. 1822 ; *d.* Paris, July 5, 1884), entered the Conservatoire at 12, obtained the first prizes for piano, harmony and fugue, and in 1844, after some years' study with Halévy, the Grand Prix de Rome for composition. His cantata 'Le Rénégat' was given three times at the Opéra (Feb. 1845), a rare event. During his stay in Rome he composed a 'Messe solennelle,' performed at the church of St. Louis des Français (May 1, 1846), a careful and clever work, though wanting in religious sentiment—never Massé's strong point. The unpublished score is in the library of the Conservatoire. After his two years in Rome he travelled through Italy and Germany, and returned to Paris, where he was much appreciated in society. Publishers readily accepted his 'Mélodies' and 'Romances,' and he gained access to the stage with little delay. 'La Chambre gothique' (Opéra-Comique, 1849), and 'La Chanteuse voilée,' one-act (Opéra-Comique, Nov. 26, 1850), were followed by 'Galathée,' two acts (Apr. 14, 1852), and 'Les Noces de Jeannette' (Feb. 4, 1853), a charming lyric comedy in 1 act. These early successes justified the hope that in Massé the French stage had found a composer as fruitful and melodious, if not as original, as Auber ; but his later efforts were less fortunate. 'La Reine Topaze' (Dec. 27, 1856) indeed succeeded completely, but 'La Fiancée du Diable' (June 3, 1854), 'Miss Fauvette' (Feb. 13, 1855), 'Les Saisons' (Dec. 22, 1855), 'Les Chaises à porteurs' (Apr. 28, 1858), 'La Fée Carabosse' (Mar. 7, 1859), 'Mariette la Promise' (1862), 'La Mule de Pedro' (Mar. 6, 1863), 'Fior d' Aliza' (Feb. 5, 1866), and 'Le Fils du brigadier' (Feb. 25, 1867), though fairly received, soon disappeared. Some, however, contain good music, especially

'Les Saisons' and 'Fior d' Aliza.' In 1860 he became chorus-master to the Opéra and in 1866 succeeded Leborne as professor of composition at the Conservatoire—gratifying appointments, as showing the esteem of his brother artists, although the work they entailed left him little time for composition. On June 20, 1872, he was elected to the Institut as successor to Auber.

After a long period of silence Massé produced 'Paul et Virginie,' three acts (Nov. 15, 1876 : given in Italian at Covent Garden, June 1, 1878). In spite of its success and its evident ambition, this opera seems less original and less homogeneous in style than 'Galathée' or 'Les Noces de Jeannette,' and its best parts, as in all his operas, are the short pieces and the simple romances.

To complete the list of his operas we may mention 'La favorita e la schiava' (Venice, 1855), and 'Le Cousin Marivaux' (Baden, 1857) ; also two drawing-room operettas, 'Le Prix de famille' and 'Une Loi somptuaire' (published in 1879). He published three sets of twenty songs each, selected from his numerous romances. Many of these are charming little pieces. In 1877 he was made an officer of the Legion of Honour. G. C.

A painful illness compelled him to resign his post at the Opéra in 1876, and rendered him totally incapable of active work. During seven years of suffering his only consolation lay in composition, and in this way his opera 'Une Nuit de Cléopâtre,' intended for the Opéra, was written. After his death, a representation of the work took place at the Opéra-Comique ir the composer's honour (Apr. 25, 1885), though the reception of 'Paul et Virginie' did not hold out much hope of success for a work evidently written in the same style and aiming too high. A. J.

BIBL.—LEO DELIBES, *Notice sur Victor Massé* ; DELABORDE, *Notice sur la vie et les ouvrages de Victor Massé* (Paris, 1885, 1888).

MASSENET, JULES ÉMILE FRÉDÉRIC (*b.* Montaud, near St. Étienne, May 12, 1842 ; *d.* Paris, Aug. 13, 1912) was one of the most famous composers of French opera of his day.

When Massenet was 6 years old his father, an ironmaster and the inventor of a steel-hammer, was obliged for reasons of ill-health to leave his foundry and remove to Paris. Here his mother, who was his father's second wife and bore three other musical children besides the composer, helped to support the family by turning her musical talents to account and giving lessons on the pianoforte. From her he first learnt to play, and at the age of 11 he was sufficiently advanced in music to be able to pass successfully into the Conservatoire, where he became a pupil of Adolphe Laurent at the pianoforte, and of Savard in solfège. When the family, again for reasons of health, left Paris for Chambéry, he went too, but returned for good after some months' absence, and in 1860 entered Reber's harmony class and shortly after took up composition with Ambroise Thomas. Whilst still at the Conservatoire he earned a small pittance first by playing triangle at the Gymnase, and then by acting as drummer three nights a week at the Théâtre Lyrique, and with the knowledge of instrumentation which he thus acquired he scored for orchestra a Mass for military band by Adam. After having won successively the first prize for pianoforte, and the second and first prizes for fugue, he gained the 'Prix de Rome' in 1863 with a cantata, 'David Rizzio.' At the Villa Medici, where he had as fellow-students Carolus Duran the painter and Chaplain the engraver, he met Liszt, and at his request gave lessons to the daughter of Mme. Sainte-Marie who, before his three years in Rome were up, became his wife. On his return to Paris with the MS. of an opera, 'Esméralda,' which was never performed or printed, he was again driven to do hack-work, but owing to the influence of Ambroise Thomas had his first opera, 'La Grand'tante,' produced at the Opéra-Comique (1867), and Pasdeloup played his first orchestral suite at one of his popular concerts the same year. Soon after this he made the acquaintance of Hartmann the publisher, who accepted his two song-cycles 'Poème d'avril' and 'Poème du souvenir.' After the Franco-Prussian War his second orchestral suite, 'Scènes hongroises,' was played by Pasdeloup; and then by the production of his opéra-comique 'Don César de Bazan' in three acts and four tableaux (1872) he found himself in the front rank of the younger composers of the day. An opera, 'Méduse,' completed two years before this, remains unpublished, and another one, 'La Coupe du roi de Thulé,' was never performed, for though it gained a *proxime accessit* in a competition organised by the Ministère des Beaux-Arts, Massenet recognised the justice of the jury's opinion that it was unsuited to the stage, and remodelled the best numbers, transferring some of them to his next opera, 'Le Roi de Lahore' (1877), and others to the incidental music which he wrote for Leconte de Lisle's drama *Les Erynnies* (1873). This incidental music did not make much impression, but it contained an air which, issued separately as an 'Élégie' with accompaniment for violoncello and pianoforte, became one of the most famous of all his songs.

Between the production of 'Don César de Bazan' and that of 'Le Roi de Lahore' came two small operas produced in the Cercle de l'Union Artistique—'L'Adorable Bel-Boul,' which was suppressed by the composer, and 'Bérengère et Anatole'—together with a large harvest of miscellaneous works in the shape of two more orchestral suites, 'Scènes drama-tiques' and 'Scènes pittoresques,' an 'Ouverture de Concert,' an overture to *Phèdre*, a 'Sarabande espagnole' for orchestra, some choruses for four equal voices, various works for pianoforte, and a number of songs and duets. The most important, however, of his compositions at this period (1872–77), was the oratorio, or 'Sacred Drama' as it was called, 'Marie Magdeleine,' which was produced by Colonne in 1873 with Mme. Pauline Viardot-Garcia in the part of the Magdalen, and which at once brought him fame. In 1906 this work was rearranged as an opera and given at the Opéra-Comique, with Mme. Aïno Ackté and M. Salignac in the parts of the Magdalen and Christ. Owing to the success of the music in its original form as an oratorio, Massenet composed two more works on much the same model, 'Ève' (1875), which was almost as great a success as 'Marie Magdeleine' and 'La Vierge' (1880), which was a failure. Soon after the production of 'Le Roi de Lahore' he wrote a cantata, 'Narcisse,' for voice and orchestra, and eventually three more orchestral suites, 'Scènes napolitaines,' 'Scènes alsaciennes,' and 'Scènes de féerie,' all of which were produced at the Concerts du Châtelet. These, with a short work, 'Biblis,' for voice and orchestra, another oratorio, 'La Terre promise' (1900), a pianoforte concerto (1903) and various songs, practically constitute, with the works already mentioned, the whole of Massenet's miscellaneous output. Everything else was written for the theatre.

In 1881 'Hérodiade' was produced at Brussels, where it enjoyed success for a season, and after being partly rewritten was given three years later in Paris at the Opéra Italien, where it was sung in Italian with Victor Maurel, Fidès-Devriès, Tremelli and the two De Reszkes in the cast. It did not meet with favour at the time, though when revived in 1903 at the Théâtre de la Gaîté, with Emma Calvé as Salome, it soon grew into public favour, and has since then been popular in America, where Lina Cavalieri has played Salome, and has even penetrated into England, having been given under the title of 'Salome,' with the scene transferred to Ethiopia and certain details altered to suit the requirements of British taste, at Covent Garden in 1904. 'Manon,' which came out at the Opéra-Comique in 1884, is usually considered to be Massenet's operatic masterpiece. In it he used leading themes in the manner of Wagner and tried the experiment of having the dialogue not sung in the usual *recitativo secco* but spoken over a slightly orchestrated accompaniment. The work has been played in the leading opera-houses in most countries, and the number of famous singers who have been heard in the rôles of Manon and Des Grieux is legion.

His other works for the stage are as follows :

'Le Cid' (Opéra, 1885).
'Esclarmonde,' lyric drama in 4 acts (Opéra-Comique, May 15, 1889).
'Le Mage,' opera in 5 acts (Opéra, Mar. 16, 1891).
'Werther,' opera in 3 acts (Vienna, Feb. 16, 1892).
'Le Carillon,' 1-act ballet (Vienna, Feb. 21, 1892).
'Thaïs,' lyric comedy in 3 acts (Opéra, 1894).
'Le Portrait de Manon,' opéra-comique in 1 act (Opéra-Comique, May 8, 1894).
'La Navarraise,' lyric drama in 2 acts (London, Covent Garden, June 20, 1894, Brussels later in the same year, and Paris 1895).
'Sapho,' lyric play in 5 acts (Opéra-Comique, Nov. 27, 1897).
'Cendrillon,' fairy tale in 4 acts (Opéra-Comique, May 1899).
Grisélidis,' in 3 acts and a prologue (Opéra-Comique, Nov. 20, 1901).
Le Jongleur de Notre-Dame,' 'miracle' in 3 acts (Monte Carlo, Feb. 18, 1902 ; Covent Garden, June 14, 1906).
Chérubin,' 'comédie chantée,' in 3 acts (Opéra-Comique, Feb. 14, 1905).
'Ariane,' opera in 5 acts (Opéra, Oct. 31, 1906).
'Thérèse,' musical drama in 2 acts (Monte Carlo, 1907).
'Bacchus,' opera in 4 acts (Opéra, May 1, 1909).
'Don Quichotte,' heroic comedy in 5 acts (Monte Carlo, Feb. 19, 1910).
'Roma,' tragic opera in 5 acts (Monte Carlo, 1912).
'Panurge,' lyric comedy in 4 acts (Paris, 1913).
'Cléopâtre' (Monte Carlo, 1914).
'Amadis,' legendary opera in 4 acts (Monte Carlo, 1924).

Besides these operas Massenet wrote a one-act ballet, ' Cendrillon ' (Vienna, 1892), and a divertissement-ballet in two acts, ' La Cigale,' as well as incidental music to Sardou's plays *Théodora* and *Le Crocodile* (Th. Porte St. Martin, 1884, 1886) and to *Phèdre* (Th. Sarah Bernhardt, 1901). He also orchestrated and completed the opera ' Kassya,' which Delibes had left unfinished at the time of his death.

In 1878 he was appointed professor of advanced composition at the Conservatoire, where Alfred Bruneau, Gustave Leroux, Gabriel Pierné and Gustave Charpentier were amongst his pupils, and held the post until his death. The same year he was elected a member of the Académie des Beaux-Arts in place of Bazin, whom he had succeeded at the Conservatoire, and to the exclusion, by five votes, of Saint - Saëns. He was only 36 at the time, and was the youngest member ever elected to the Académie des Beaux-Arts. In 1876 he was decorated with the Légion d'Honneur and became Grand-Officier in 1899.

During his lifetime, and for a period of some forty years, Massenet, thanks to his undoubted gifts for melody of a suave, voluptuous character—gifts which are as much in evidence in his operas and larger choral and orchestral works as in his songs for single voice and pianoforte—ingratiated himself with that large section of the public which, whether in Paris or elsewhere, regards music as an agreeable after - dinner entertainment. At the same time he was a sufficiently astute musician not merely to reflect the taste of his day (which he gratified by his regular and effortless supply of what M. Vincent d'Indy called a ' discreet and semi-religious eroticism ') but even to some extent to mould it. By grafting the idiom of Gounod on to the method of Wagner with a sensibility to the requirements of singers and an understanding of effective but conventional characterisation that belonged essentially to the theatre, he succeeded in appealing to 'the

average sensual man ' [1] without alienating those who expected opera to be something more than a series of pleasant tunes. His own tunes, whilst invariably singable, were usually short-winded and, in the operas at least, had a way of reverting, after a series of mild attempts at getting under way, to a restatement of the initial subject ; the orchestration, often piquant, was unambitious and varied little from scene to scene. In fact with all his skill as a composer Massenet was strictly confined by a temperament of narrow range, so that to have heard ' Manon ' is to have heard the whole of him. His personal charm and the continued vogue during the last quarter of the 19th century of the kind of musical delicacies he enjoyed purveying, account for his popularity during his lifetime. There have since been signs of reaction. But however far this reaction may go it would be absurd to deny that within its marked limitations, of which he himself was obviously aware, ' Manon,' so eminently typical both of the composer and of the public for which he wrote, is in its own way a masterpiece.

BIBL. — Séré, *Musiciens français d'aujourd'hui*, 2nd ed., 1921, with bibliography and list of works; Brancour, *Massenet* (Paris, 1922).

L. W. H.

MASSOL, Jean Étienne Auguste (*b.* Lodève, Hérault, 1802 ; *d.* Paris, Oct. 31, 1887), was taught singing at the Paris Conservatoire in 1823–25, and gained a first prize there. He made his début at the Opéra as Licinius (' Vestale '), Nov. 17, 1825, and remained there until Oct. 8, 1845. He first played second tenor parts in several new operas and the baritone parts of Tell and Jolicœur (' Philtre '), etc. He played for a time in Brussels, London (Drury Lane, 1846), etc., and returned as principal baritone to the Opéra in 1850, where he remained until his farewell benefit, Jan. 14, 1858. The Emperor was present on that occasion, immediately after the attempt made on his life by Orsini on his arrival at the theatre. His best new parts were Reuben (Auber's ' Enfant prodigue '), Dec. 6, 1850, and Ahasuerus (Halévy's ' Juif errant '), Apr. 23, 1852. He was a good singer, admirably suited for heroic drama, having the proper figure and height, and a splendid voice.   A. C.

MASSON, Elizabeth (*b.* 1806 ; *d.* Jan. 9, 1865), was taught singing by Mrs. Henry Smart, sen., and in Italy by Mme. Pasta. She made her first appearance in public at Ella's second subscription concert, in the Argyll Rooms, Mar. 11, 1831, and sang afterwards at the Ancient Concerts, Mar. 16, 1831, and at the Philharmonic, Mar. 11, 1833 ; she sang frequently at those Societies' concerts during a public career of about twelve years, and revived there forgotten airs of Handel, Purcell, Pergolesi, Gluck, Mozart, etc. She was in great

1 ' The average sensual man ' is a standardised French phrase.

request at private concerts, since she possessed, apart from her musical attainments, great talents and accomplishments, and was an excellent linguist. She sang occasionally in oratorio, viz. at the festival in Westminster Abbey, 1834, and at the Sacred Harmonic Society, where she took the parts of Solomon, Nov. 22, 1839, and Storge on the revival of 'Jephtha,' Apr. 7, 1841. She afterwards devoted herself to teaching and composition. She wrote many songs to the words of Scott, Byron, Adelaide Proctor, etc., and edited a series of 'Original Jacobite Songs' (Lonsdale, 1839), and 'Songs for the Classical Vocalist' (Leader & Cock, first series of twelve songs, 1845 ; a second series, 1860), which enjoyed a well-deserved popularity. She founded the Royal Society of Female Musicians in 1839 (see ROYAL SOCIETY OF MUSICIANS), and was its hon. treasurer until her death.   A. C.

MASTER, THE, see SCHAUSPIELDIREKTOR.

MATASSINS (MATACINS ; MATACHINS)—also called *Bouffons*—a dance of men in armour, popular in France during the 16th and 17th centuries. It was probably derived from the ancient Pyrrhic dance, although the name has been traced to an Arabic root. Jehan Tabourot in his *Orchésographie* (Langres, 1588) gives a long and interesting account of this dance, with six illustrations of the different positions of the dancers,

' qui sont vestus de petits corcelets, auec fimbries és espaules, et soubs la ceinture, une pente de taffetats soubz icelles, le morion de papier doré, les bras nuds, les sonnettes aux iambes, l'espée au poing droit, le bouclier au poing gaulche.'

The Matassins were four in number, generally all men, but sometimes two men and two women. They danced several distinct figures, between which they performed mimic fights with one another. Molière has introduced Matassins into his comédie-ballet of ' M. de Pourceaugnac,' and the dance is said to have been common at Bordeaux, Marseilles and Strassburg as late as 1735. The following, according to Tabourot, is the air which usually accompanied the dance.

Air des Bouffons.

W. B. S.

MATELOTTE, a Dutch sailors' dance somewhat similar to the English hornpipe. The dancers wore wooden shoes, and their arms were interlaced behind their backs. The music of the Matelotte consists of two parts in 2-4 time, and is remarkable for its short decided rhythm. There is a sabot dance in Lortzing's ' Czaar und Zimmermann,' but it is not a true Matelotte,

being written in waltz time. Schubert, *Die Tanzmusik* (Leipzig, 1867) gives an example of the time.   W. B. S.

MATERNA, AMALIE (Frau FRIEDRICH) (*b.* St. Georgen, Styria, July 10, 1845; *d.* Jan. 18, 1918), a distinguished prima donna in German opera.

Her father was a schoolmaster at St. Georgen. Her first stage appearance was made at the Thalia-Theater, Gratz, about 1864. She married soon afterwards Karl Friedrich, a popular German actor, and together with him was engaged at the suburban Karlstheater, Vienna, where she sang for some time in operetta. But her qualifications for the higher lyrical walks could not long remain undiscovered, and in 1869 she made her début at the Imperial Opera House as Selika in the ' Africaine,' with signal success, at once winning for herself a high position among opera-singers of the German school. With a soprano voice of unusual volume, compass and sustaining power, a fine stage presence, and much musical and dramatic intelligence, Materna left nothing to be desired in the great Wagner parts. At the Wagner Festival at Bayreuth, 1876, she first earned a world-wide reputation by her magnificent impersonation of Brünnhilde in the Nibelungen Trilogy. She sang in England with great success at the Wagner concerts at the Albert Hall in 1877. She was the first exponent of the part of Kundry in 'Parsifal,' on July 28, 1882, at Bayreuth, and she retired on Apr. 23, 1897.   B. T.

MATHIEU, EMILE LOUIS VICTOR (*b.* Lille, Oct. 16, 1844), composer and teacher, was the son of musical parents, his father having been eminent as a singer and as director of the theatre at Antwerp, while his mother was a professor of singing in the Académie des Beaux-Arts at Louvain. Emile Mathieu began his studies very early at the Brussels Conservatoire, and in 1869 obtained the second Prix de Rome with his cantata, ' La Mort du Tasse,' which was performed four years afterwards in Brussels. In 1881 he was appointed director of the Académie de Musique at Louvain, and moved from there to Ghent, where he succeeded Adolphe Samuel as director of the Conservatoire Royal (1896–1924). His compositions include a Te Deum for soli, chorus and orchestra; six Ballads from Goethe for voice and piano; three descriptive poems, ' Le Hoyoux,' ' Freyir ' and ' Le Sorbier,' for soli, chorus and orchestra. For the stage he has composed a series of dramatic works, of which, for the most part, he has written the words himself : ' Richilde,' in four acts (the leading part created by Mme. Rose Caron at the Théâtre de la Monnaie in 1888) ; ' L'Enfance de Roland ' (1889) ; and three opéras-comiques, dating from his earlier years— ' Georges Dandin ' (after Molière), given at Brussels in 1879 ; ' L'Exchange ' (Liège, 1863) ;

and ' Le Bernoise ' (Brussels, 1885) to a poem by M. Lucien Solvay.   M. K.

MATHILDE DI SHABRAN, opera buffa in 3 acts; music by Rossini. Produced Apollo Theatre, Rome, in the Carnival of 1821; Théâtre Italien, Paris, 1857; in London, King's Theatre, July 3, 1823.   G.

MATILDA OF HUNGARY, opera in 3 acts; libretto by Bunn, music by W. Vincent Wallace. Produced Drury Lane, Feb. 22, 1847.

MATINS (Lat. *matutinae*; *officium matutinum*), the first division of the Canonical Hours. It contains the great Responds of the Gregorian Repertory, and a large portion also of the Antiphons of that collection. (See GREGORIAN MUSIC.)   W. H. F.

MATRIMONIO SEGRETO, IL, opera buffa in 2 acts; libretto by Bertatti, adapted from Colman's *Clandestine Marriage*, music by Cimarosa. Produced Vienna in 1792; London, 1794[1]; Paris, May 10, 1801; in English, Covent Garden, Nov. 1, 1842, and with new translation by W. Grist, Crystal Palace, Dec. 13, 1877.   G.

MATTEI, FILIPPO (commonly known as 'Pipo'), a violoncellist in London, and performer at the operas given by the Royal Academy of Music in the theatres in the Haymarket in the early 18th century. His claim to remembrance is based on Handel's MS. conducting score of the opera ' Muzio Scaevola,' in which ' Pipo ' is mentioned as the composer of the first act, which has often been ascribed to Attilio ARIOSTI (*q.v.*), the second and third being by Bononcini and Handel respectively. See Chrysander's *G. F. Handel*, vol. ii. p. 56, where the opera ' Arsace, overo Amore e Maestà ' is attributed to him. See also *Mus. Ant.* i. 255.   M.

MATTEI, STANISLAO, ABBATE (*b.* Bologna, Feb. 10, 1750; *d.* May 12, 1825), pupil of Martini and master of Rossini. Though of humble parentage (his father was a locksmith) he was sent to the Latin school. Having been present accidentally at a service in the Minorite convent, he was so enchanted with the music that he became a constant attendant, and thus attracted the notice of Padre Martini, by whose advice he entered upon his noviciate. Master and pupil became tenderly attached, and as soon as Mattei had been ordained he became the Padre's confessor, and remained with him till his death. He acted as Martini's deputy from 1770, and succeeded him as maestro di cappella. From 1776 his compositions were produced in the service. On the suppression of the monasteries in 1798 he went to live with his aged mother, and began an active career as a teacher. From this time he was known as the Abbate Mattei. Later he became maestro di cappella of San Petronio, and professor of counterpoint at the Liceo from its foundation in 1804. Among his pupils were Rossini,

[1] According to W. B. S.; Grove gave Jan. 25, 1803.

Morlacchi, Donizetti, Perotti, Robuschi, Palmerini, Bertolotti, Tadolini, Tesei and Pilotti, who succeeded him at San Petronio. He lived in complete retirement, accessible only to his pupils. He was president of the Filarmonici in 1790 and 1794, and was a member of the Subalpine Académie and of the Institut de France (Jan. 24, 1824). He had a thorough practical acquaintance with the old traditions, as may be seen by his *Prattica d' accompagnamento sopra bassi numerati*, 3 vols. (Bologna, 1788, 1829, 1830), which consists mainly of well-chosen examples, with a few rules. The libraries of San Giorgio and the Minorite convent in Bologna contain most of his compositions, including eight masses, much church music, and the scores of an intermezzo, ' La bottega del libraio,' and of a Passion performed in 1792.

BIBL.—FILIPPO CANUTI, *Vita di Stanislao Mattei* (Bologna, 1829, with portrait).   F. G.

MATTEIS, (1) NICOLA, an eminent Italian violinist, came to England about 1672. The earliest notice of him is found in Evelyn's *Diary* under date of Nov. 19, 1674 :

' I heard that stupendous violin, Signor Nicholao (with other rare musicians), whom I never heard mortal man exceed on that instrument. He had a stroke so sweet, and made it speak like the voice of a man, and, when he pleased, like a concert of several instruments. He did wonders upon a note, and was an excellent composer. Here was also that rare lutanist, Dr. Wallgrave, but nothing approached the violin in Nicholao's hand. He played such ravishing things as astonished us all.'

Roger North also [2] speaks very highly of his abilities. ·When he first came to England he exhibited many singularities of conduct which he afterwards abandoned. He published here, without date (about 1688) :

(1) ' Arie, preludij, alemande, sarabande, etc., per il violino. Libro primo.'
(2) ' Altre Arie, etc., più difficile e studiose per il violino. Libro secondo.'
(3) ' Ayres for the Violin, to wit, Preludes, Fuges, Alemands, Sarabands, Courants, Gigues, Fancies, Divisions, and likewise other Passages, Introductions, and Fugues for Single and Double stops with divisions somewhat more artificial for the Emproving of the Hand upon the Basse-Viol or Harpsichord. The Third and Fourth Books.'

This last has the date 1685 concealed in the ornamentations of the title-page ; other books of the series are dated 1687. The books are in oblong octavo, engraved on copper-plates by T. Greenhill. A set was sold at the Taphouse sale in 1905. He was likewise author of

' The False Consonances of Musick, or, Instructions for playing a true Base upon the Guittarre, with Choice Examples and clear Directions to enable any man in a short time to play all Musicall Ayres. A great help likewise to those that would play exactly upon the Harpsichord, Lute, or Base-Viol, shewing the delicacy of all Accords, and how to apply them in their proper places. In four parts,'

—which even in North's time had become scarce, and is now excessively rare. In 1696 Matteis composed an Ode on St. Cecilia's Day for the then annual celebration in London, and was also one of the stewards of a Cecilian celebration at Oxford. Another and lesser known work by the same composer is

' A Collection of New Songs set by Mons. Nicola Matteis, made purposely for the use of his Scholars : Fairly engraven on Copper plates,'

two books, 1696, folio, Walsh and Hare. A

[2] *Memoirs of Musick*. See note on p. 122 of Rimbault's edition.

copy of this was sold at Dr. Rimbault's sale. With 'Symphonies for two flutes by a person of quality, fairly engraved on copper plates,' these songs by Matteis are advertised by Walsh and Hare in the *London Gazette* for May 11, 1696. A song by him is included in a collection of 'Twelve New Songs,' published in 1699. According to North,

'he fell into such credit and imployment that he took a great hous, and after the manner of his country lived luxuriously, which brought diseases upon him of which he dyed.'

He is said to have been the inventor of the half-shift, but it is claimed also for others.

His son, (2) NICHOLAS, was taught the violin by his father, and became an excellent player. He went to Germany and resided for some time at Vienna, being a member of the court orchestra there from 1700, but in 1737 returned to England and settled at Shrewsbury as a teacher of languages as well as of the violin, where Burney learned French and the violin of him. He died there about 1749. (See Burney's *History*, iii. p. 515, etc.)

w. h. h. ; addns. f. k.

MATTHAY, TOBIAS (*b.* London, Feb. 19, 1858), a successful teacher of the pianoforte whose many publications on technique and psychology in association, embodying the sum of his thinking, have become known as the 'Matthay System.'

Matthay's parents came from North Germany; his father was a naturalised British subject. Matthay entered the R.A.M. in 1871, where he won the Sterndale Bennett scholarship. He became a sub-professor in 1876, and full professor in 1880, and maintained his connexion with the R.A.M. until 1925, when he left it to continue his work in his own school founded in 1900. *The Act of Touch* (1903), in which he made a close analysis of the pianist's touch, was the first important enunciation of his views. *The First Principles of Pianoforte Playing*, *Relaxation Studies*, *Method in Teaching* and *Musical Interpretation*, all deal with various aspects of the application of the problem with which *The Act of Touch* grapples. He has composed a considerable amount of pianoforte music, but it is of slight importance in comparison with his educational work. In 1893 he married JESSIE, youngest daughter of David KENNEDY (*q.v.*). Mrs. Tobias Matthay is well known as a reciter.　　　　　c.

MATTHESON, JOHANN (*b.* Hamburg, Sept. 28, 1681; *d.* there, Apr. 17, 1764), German musician and writer, son of a clerk of excise.

As a child he showed striking symptoms of versatility, which his parents carefully cultivated. Besides the ordinary education he studied music, and at 9 years could play the harpsichord and organ, sing and compose. His ability and versatility were truly extraordinary. A good classical scholar and a proficient in modern languages, a student of law and political science, a fine player both on harpsichord and organ, and thoroughly skilled in theory, an elegant dancer, a master of fence, and a cultivated man of the world. The first step in his changeful career was his appearance in 1696 as a singer (of female parts) in the Hamburg opera, then in its most flourishing condition. In 1699 he produced his first opera, 'Die Pleyaden'; in another, 'Cleopatra' (1704), he took the part of Antony, and after singing his part on the stage, was in the habit of sitting down at the harpsichord to conduct the orchestra. To this period belongs his acquaintance, and the famous duel, with Handel, who came to Hamburg in 1703, Mattheson tells us that he recognised Handel's genius immediately, that they became at once attached and that their friendship continued, with occasional breaks caused by Mattheson's vanity, during the whole time of Handel's stay in Hamburg (1709) (see HANDEL). He claims to have done Handel an important service by introducing him to the musical world of Hamburg, at that time very celebrated; but he acknowledges that he picked up from him many a 'contrapuntal device.' In 1703 he went with Handel to Lübeck in order to see whether the post of organist, which he had been offered by the town in succession to Buxtehude, were to his liking. The offer was not accepted by Mattheson, he feeling unable to comply with one clause in the agreement, which stipulated that the new organist should marry Buxtehude's daughter. In 1704 he was invited to Holland as organist at Haarlem, but refused. Handel's 'Nero' (1705) was the last opera in which Mattheson appeared; he then retired from the stage, and declined more than one organist's post which was offered to him. He became tutor to the son of the English envoy, Sir Cyrill Wych, and in 1706 was made secretary of legation. His post was one of labour and responsibility, but he still continued to teach, conduct, compose and write on musical subjects. In 1712, on the death of Wych, Mattheson filled the post of English Resident in Lower Saxony until Wych's son, Mattheson's old pupil, was appointed, Mattheson continuing in the post of secretary. In 1715 he was appointed cantor and canon of the cathedral; and took an active part in the development of the church cantata, so soon after carried to its highest pitch by J. S. Bach (see CANTATA). This was the result of an attempt, made more particularly by the Hamburg composers, to vary the monotony of congregational singing by the introduction of airs, duets, choruses, etc., and was considered by the orthodox an impious and sacrilegious innovation. Mattheson supported this 'adapted dramatic' style, as it was called, both as a composer and as a pamphleteer; and even ventured on a further innovation, by introducing female singers into church.

In 1719 he received from the Duke of Holstein the title of court Kapellmeister. In 1728 he was attacked with deafness, which obliged him to resign his post at the cathedral. Thenceforward he occupied himself chiefly with writing. He is said to have resolved to publish a work for every year of his life, and this aim he more than accomplished, for when he died at 83 his printed literary works amounted to eighty-eight, besides a still larger number of completed MSS.

He composed twenty-four oratorios and cantatas ; eight operas ; sonatas for flute and violin ; suites for clavier ; arias ; *pièces de circonstance* for weddings, funerals, etc. (See *Q.-L.* for list.) His vocal music is overburdened with declamatory passages—a fault easily explained by his own experience on the stage, but one which is often detrimental and must have been very incongruous in church music.

His books are of far greater value than his compositions. In these, notwithstanding a peculiar self-satisfied loquacity, he shows himself a ready and skilful champion for earnestness and dignity in art, for progress, and for solidity of attainment in the practical part of music. In both branches, theoretical and practical, he attacked and demolished much that was antiquated, furnishing at the same time a great deal that was new and instructive, and bequeathing to posterity a mine of historical material. He also found time for much other literary work, especially translations (chiefly from English works on politics and jurisprudence), and even translated a small treatise on tobacco. This extraordinary versatility and his untiring industry go far to redeem the vanity which animated his character and actions and continually shows itself in his writings. His autobiography in the *Ehrenpforte* contains an amusingly egotistical description of his manifold labours. His more important books are standard sources of information on the state of music at that period, especially in Hamburg. These are *Das neu eröffnete Orchester* (1713), followed by *Das beschützte* and *Das forschende Orchester* (1717 and 1721) ; *Critica musica* (1722–25) ; *Der musikalische Patriot* (1728) ; and the *Grundlage einer Ehrenpforte* (1740),[1] a collection of biographies of contemporary musicians. The last two are the most important. His theoretical works are the *Exemplarische Organisten Probe* (1719), republished in 1731 as the *Grosse Generalbassschule* ; the *Kleine Generalbassschule* (1735) ; the *Kern melodischer Wissenschaft* (1737) ; and finally the *Vollkommene Capellmeister* (1739), perhaps his most valuable work. As a controversial writer he was wanting in temper ; his ' Ephorus Göttingensis ' 1727), directed against Professor Joachim

<hr>

1 Modern edition by Max Schneider (Berlin, 1910).

Meyer of Göttingen on the church cantata question, is the only work of that class we need specify. The complete list of his writings is given in *Q.-L.*   A. M. ; rev. S. G.

MATTHIAS, HERMANN, see WERRECORE.

MATZENAUER, MARGARET (*b.* Temesvár, Hungary, June 1, 1881), operatic mezzo-soprano, was educated at Hanover and studied singing under various teachers at Berlin. She made her début in 1901, as Fatima in ' Oberon,' at the Stadttheater, Strassburg, and remained there until 1904. She was next engaged for the Hoftheater at Munich, where she sang for seven years and by degrees established her reputation as an artist of rare ability. Possessing a voice of exceptional range, richness and power (admirably trained by Fritz Emerich in the school of Manuel Garcia), and endowed with unusual dramatic intelligence and versatility, she acquired a repertory which practically covered the whole field of modern opera. She excelled alike in soprano and mezzo-soprano rôles, proving herself equally at home, for example, as Aïda and Amneris, Azucena and Leonora, Amelia and Ulrica, Donna Anna and Donna Elvira, Ortrud and Venus, Brünnhilde and Erda, Norma and Mignon, Carmen and Santuzza, Selika and La Gioconda. No part came amiss to her, since her choice was always tempered by discretion, her command of character and *tessitura* correctly judged. She sang frequently as ' guest ' at Bayreuth and Munich, but her European career practically closed from the season (1911–12) when she first appeared at the Metropolitan Opera House, won the undivided suffrages of the American public, and settled down permanently in New York. She sang at Covent Garden during the summer that the war began, making her début here as Kundry and appearing also as Ortrud ; but has not since been heard in this country. She was the recipient of many German decorations, including the Saxe-Coburg medal for ' Kunst und Wissenschaft.'   H. K.

MAUCOTEL (1) ADOLPHE (*b.* Mirecourt, Lorraine, 1820 ; *d.* 1858), French violin-maker. He worked under J. B. Vuillaume in Paris from 1839–44, and then opened a workshop of his own in the Galérie Vivienne. Later he removed to the Rue Croix-des-Petits-Champs, and lastly settled in the Rue Princesse. His instruments are greatly esteemed for their tone, their durability and their excellent workmanship. H. copied the Stradivarius model very successfully, and but for his untimely end should have ranked among the foremost French makers. He committed suicide at the age of 38, by cutting his throat whilst in a state of feverish delirium. The Paris Conservatoire owns a violoncello by this maker, which is considered to be the finest instrument he ever produced. His brother (2) CHARLES (*b.* Mirecourt, 1807 ;

d. 1860), was also an excellent violin-maker and a pupil of Bloise Mast, of Mirecourt. He went to Paris in 1834 and studied under Gand, after which, in 1850, he established himself in London.

BIBL.—WILLIBALD FREIHERRN VON LUTGENDORFF, *Die Geigen-und Lautenmacher* (Frankfort-on-M., 1904); H. R. HAWEIS, *Old Violins* (London, 1898).   E. H.-A.

(3) ERNEST (*b.* 1867), great-nephew of Charles and Adolphe, is also a luthier of some renown. In 1892 he entered the house of H. C. Silvestre, great-nephew of the no less celebrated Pierre and Hippolyte Silvestre, with whom he entered into partnership on Apr. 1, 1900. Left sole partner, Ernest Maucotel applied to Paul Deschamp (*b.* Mar. 7, 1887), a talented violinist and an expert on violin-making, who became his partner in 1922. Their house, in the Rue de Rome, contains, in addition to instruments of their own make, a wonderful collection of old instruments.   M. P.

MAUDUIT, JACQUES (*b.* Paris, Sept. 16, 1557; *d.* Aug. 21, 1627), French lute-player and composer. He succeeded his father as 'greffier des requêtes,' registrar in the courts of justice at Paris, but his talent and reputation as a musician acquired for him in France the title of Père de la Musique. In 1581 he obtained the first prize at the musical competition, which took place yearly at Evreux in Normandy, for the best motets and chansons. A Requiem *a* 5 by Mauduit, written for the funeral of the poet Ronsard, was published by the Père Mersenne in the seventh book of his *Harmonie universelle*, 1636. Ambros speaks slightingly of this work, describing it as a simple Fauxbourdon without any particular merit. In 1570 the poet Antoine Baïf received permission from Charles IX. to found the Académie Française de Musique et de Poésie, the original object of which was to bring about a closer union between music and poetry by making musical rhythm entirely subordinate to the metrical rhythm of prosody. Mauduit would appear to have associated himself with the efforts which Baïf made in this direction, and to have taken part in the concerts which were held in Baïf's house. Henry Expert, in his collection entitled *Les Maîtres-musiciens de la Renaissance Française*, has republished the 'Chansonnettes mesurées de Jan-Antoine de Baïf mises en musique à quatre parties par Jacques Mauduit,' Paris, 1586, in which Mauduit has endeavoured to carry out the classical theories of Baïf. They are slight compositions, but graceful enough. After Baïf's death in 1590, the concerts continued to be carried on by Mauduit, but as Brenet [1] says, 'The equilibrium jealously maintained by Baïf, between poetry and music, was broken to the advantage of the latter,' and more freedom was gained for the independent development of

music by the greater prominence given to instrumental music. For the story of his saving Claude Le Jeune's manuscripts from the flames, see JEUNE, Le.   J. R. M.

MAUGARS, ANDRÉ,[2] viol-player of the early 17th century, was a politician-musician of the French court. He is described by THOINAN (*q.v.*) as
'Célèbre Joueur de Viole, Musicien du Cardinal de Richelieu, Conseiller, Secrétaire, Interprète du Roi en langue Anglaise, Traducteur de F. Bacon, Prieur de Saint-Pierre Eynac.'

About 1620 he spent four years in England playing the viol at the court of James I., and the first-fruit of his sojourn was a translation of Bacon's *Advancement of Learning*, which was published in Paris in 1624 (P. Billaine), under the title *Le Progrez et avancement aux sciences divines et humaines*, dedicated to de Lomenie. Soon after this he became a creature of Cardinal Richelieu, useful to that prelate in the capacity of Secretary-Interpreter, in which capacity he served likewise in the court of Louis XIII., and became a favourite butt of the courtier-wit Bois-Robert, whom he distinguished by a hatred which, though impotent, has passed into history. His political satires, etc., and the story of his various quarrels, may be read in the authorities referred to below. All that we know of his death is the record of Tallemant to the effect that he 'returned to France and died a few years later. On his death-bed he sent to ask forgiveness of his old enemy Bois-Robert.' To this period belongs his pamphlet, reprinted by Thoinan, *Response faite à un curieux sur le sentiment de la musique d'Italie, escrite à Rome le premier Octobre 1639.*

As a violist he was classed by Mersenne [3] with Hottman, and his eulogy is similarly expressed by Jean Rousseau in his *Traité de la viole*. His compositions, which must have been significant, appear wholly lost to posterity, but he himself lauds their excellence with no uncertain voice.

BIBL.—P. SAINT-GLAS, *Divers Traitez d'histoire de morale et d'éloquence* (Paris, 1672); L'ABBÉ BORDELON, *Les Malades de belle humeur ou lettres divertissantes*, etc. (Paris, 1697), reprinted in vol. viii. of *Diversitez curieuses* (Paris, 1700); TALLEMANT DES RÉAUX, *Les Historiettes pour servir à l'histoire du XVIIe siècle*.   E. H.-A.

MAUREL, VICTOR (*b.* Marseilles, June 17, 1848; *d.* New York, Oct. 22, 1923), operatic baritone, received instruction at the Paris Conservatoire in singing from Vauthrot, and in opera from Duvernoy, and gained the first prizes in both subjects, co-equal with Gailhard, in 1867. He made his début at the Opéra as De Nevers ('Huguenots') and Conte di Luna ('Trouvère') in 1868. He was next in Italy, where he played the Cacique on the production of Gomes's 'Guarany' at Milan, Mar. 19, 1870. He made his début at the Royal Italian Opera, London, as Renato, Apr. 21, 1873, made a great success, and was engaged there every year until 1879 inclusive. His

---

[1] See Michel Brenet, *Les Concerts en France sous l'ancien régime*, 1900, p. 37.

[2] Fétis has Aude, but his notice in *Biog. des Mus.* is unreliable.
[3] *De instr. harm.* lib. 1. prop. 30.

parts comprised Don Giovanni, Tell, Almaviva, Hoël, Peter the Great, Valentine, Hamlet, the Cacique; in operas new to England, Telramund, May 8, 1875; Wolfram, May 6, 1876; the Flying Dutchman, June 16, 1877; and Domingo in Massé's ' Paul et Virginie,' June 1, 1878. He reappeared at the French Opéra as Hamlet, Nov. 28, 1879, and also played Amonasro on the production in Paris of ' Aïda,' Mar. 22, 1880. After a tour in Spain, he undertook, in 1883, the management with Corti of the Italian Opera at the Théâtre des Nations (afterwards the Théâtre Sarah - Bernhardt), with disastrous financial results, in spite of a company including Mesdames Marimon, Adler-Dévriès, Nevada and Tremelli, Gayarré, the brothers De Reszke and himself, and the successful production of Massenet's ' Hérodiade,' Feb. 1, 1884. He played at the Opéra-Comique (Peter), Oct. 6, 1885, Falstaff in Thomas's ' Songe d'une nuit d'été,' and Zampa, Jan. 19, 1886, with great success. He played again at Covent Garden in 1886, and at Drury Lane for the first time in 1887 in favourite parts. Between these engagements he created, with the greatest success, Iago in Verdi's ' Otello,' Milan, Feb. 5, 1887, and showed himself the best acting baritone on the Italian stage since Faure. He introduced this fine impersonation to the English public at the Lyceum Theatre on July 5, 1889, and on Feb. 9, 1893, created the part of Falstaff in Verdi's last opera at Milan. Both these parts were sung by him for the first time in Paris in 1894, the latter first in London on June 10, 1895. In 1896 he returned to the Opéra-Comique, where he created the part of Mathias in Erlanger's ' Juif polonais,' Apr. 11, 1900. For a short time after that he appeared as an actor at non-musical theatres, but returned to the operatic stage and reappeared in London in the part of Rigoletto on Nov. 15, 1904. In 1909 he settled as a teacher in New York. His Dix ans de carrière (1897) was translated into German by Mme. Lilli Lehmann. Other publications are Le Chant renové par la science (1892), Un Problème d'art (1893) and A propos de la mise-en-scène de Don Juan (1896). A. C.

MAURER, Ludwig Wilhelm (b. Potsdam, Feb. 8, 1789; d. St. Petersburg, Oct. 25, 1878), distinguished violinist, pupil of Haak, Konzert-meister to Frederick the Great.

At 13 he appeared with great success at a concert given in Berlin by Mara, and was in consequence admitted to the royal chapel as a probationer. After the battle of Jena (1806) the chapel was dismissed, and Maurer travelled, first to Königsberg and Riga, where he made the acquaintance of Rode and Baillot, and then to Mittau and St. Petersburg, his playing being everywhere appreciated. At Moscow he again met Baillot, through whose good offices he became Kapellmeister to the Chancellor Wsowologsky, who had a private orchestra. Here he

remained till 1817, when he made another successful tour, being particularly well received in Berlin and Paris. In 1832 he returned to Wsowologsky and stayed till 1845, when after another tour he settled finally in Dresden. His compositions include a ' Symphonie concertante' for four violins and orchestra, first played in Paris by himself, Spohr, Müller and Wich in 1838; and three Russian airs with variations (op. 14). Of his operas ' Alonzo' (c. 1830), ' Aloise' (1838), ' Der entdeckte Diebstahl ' and ' Der neue Paris,' the overtures only were printed. He also published several concertos—one of which was at one time very often played at the Philharmonic Concerts in London—and two collections of quartets (opp. 17 and 26). His two sons, Wsevolod, a violinist, and Alexis, a violoncellist, were good musicians who settled in Russia.   F. G.

MAXWELL, Francis Kelly (sometimes called John), D.D. (d. 1782), chaplain of the Asylum, Edinburgh, published anonymously An Essay upon Tune, being an attempt to free the scale of music and the tune of instruments from imperfection (Edinburgh, 1781; London, 1794)—an able work.   w. h. h.

MAY, (1) Edward Collett (b. Greenwich, Oct. 29, 1806; d. Jan. 2, 1887), son of a ship-builder at Greenwich. His first teacher was his brother Henry, an amateur musician and composer of considerable ability. When about 15 years of age, Thomas Adams, then organist of St. Paul's, Deptford, and an intimate friend of the May family, struck by the promise and intelligence of Edward, offered to take him as a pupil. Subsequently he became a pupil of Cipriani Potter for the pianoforte, and of Crivelli for singing. In 1837 he was appointed organist of Greenwich Hospital, an office he held till the abolition of the institution in 1869. From 1841 to his death he devoted himself enthusiastically and exclusively to the musical teaching of the masses. At one institution alone, the National Society's Central School, more than a thousand teachers and many more children were instructed by him. At Exeter Hall, the Apollonicon Rooms, and subsequently St. Martin's Hall, several thousand adults passed through his classes; while for many years he was the sole musical instructor at the Training Schools, Battersea, St. Mark's, White-lands, Home and Colonial, and Hockerill; institutions from which upwards of 250 teachers were annually sent forth to elementary schools. After many years' connexion with the Institution, May was appointed in 1880 professor of vocal music in Queen's College, London.   J. H.

His daughter, (2) Florence, became known in London as a pianoforte-player of considerable cultivation and power, and a successful teacher. She had the great advantage of being a pupil of Brahms, and distinguished herself as an interpreter of his music, playing many of his pianoforte works for the first time in England. She wrote *The Life of Johannes Brahms*, 2 vols., 1905.

MAYER, CHARLES (*b.* Königsberg, Mar. 21, 1799; *d.* Dresden, July 2, 1862), pianist. His father, a clarinet-player, went soon after the boy's birth to St. Petersburg, and four years after to Moscow, where he settled with his family.

Charles first learned from his mother, a good pianoforte teacher, and later became a pupil of Field. After the burning of Moscow in 1812 the family fled to St. Petersburg, where the mother became pianoforte teacher, and where the lessons with Field were resumed. The pupil played so exactly like his master that connoisseurs were unable to tell which was at the piano if a screen was interposed. In 1814 Mayer accompanied his father to Paris, where he was well received. He first played his concert-variations on 'God save the King' in Amsterdam. In 1819 he returned to St. Petersburg, where he worked hard and successfully at teaching, and formed as many as 800 pupils. In 1845 he travelled to Stockholm, Copenhagen, Hamburg, Leipzig and Vienna, but this was his last tour. In 1850 he settled in Dresden, where he taught, gave concerts, and composed up to his death. His pieces reach the astonishing number of 900. A mazurka by him in F♯ major was for some time considered to be by Chopin, and as such was included in the first issue of Klindworth's edition. It has been removed from later issues.

F. G.

MAYNARD, JOHN, a lutenist, published in 1611

'The XII Wonders of the World, Set and composed for the Violl de Gambo, the Lute and the Voyce to sing the Verse, all three jointly and none severall; also Lessons for the Lute and Base Violl to play alone; with some Lessons to play Lyra-waye alone, or if you will to fill up the parts with another Violl set Lute-way.'

The work contains twelve songs severally describing the characters of a Courtier, Divine, Soldier, Lawyer, Physician, Merchant, Country Gentleman, Bachelor, Married Man, Wife, Widow and Maid; and twelve pavans and galliards for the lute. A curious canon, 'Eight parts in one upon the Plaine Song,' is on the title-page. The composer described himself as 'Lutenist at the most famous Schoole of St. Julian's in Hartfordshire,' and dedicated his work 'To his ever-honoured Lady and Mistris the Lady Joane Thynne, of Cause Castle in Shropshire.' Some organ pieces by one Maynard (presumably the same) are contained in a MS. in the library of the Sacred Harmonic Society (R.C.M.).

W. H. H.

MAYR, JOHANN SIMON (SIMONE MAYER) (*b.* Mendorf, Bavaria, June 14, 1763; *d.* Dec. 2, 1845), esteemed opera composer in the beginning of the 19th century. He early showed talent for music, which he first learned from his father, the village schoolmaster and organist.

When about 10 he entered the Jesuit seminary at Ingolstadt, but did not neglect his music either then or when, after the banishment of the Jesuits, he studied law in Ingolstadt. Having made the acquaintance of a nobleman, Thomas de Bessus of the Grisons, he lived in the house as music master, and was afterwards sent by his patron to Bergamo to study with Lenzi, maestro di cappella there. Mayr found, however, that his master knew little more than himself, and was on the point of returning to Germany when Count Presenti, a canon of Bergamo, provided him with the means of going to F. Bertoni in Venice. Here again his expectations were deceived, but he picked up some practical hints and a few rules from Bertoni, and hard work and the study of good books did the rest. He had already published some songs in Ratisbon; and in Bergamo and Venice he composed masses and vespers. After the success of his oratorio 'Jacob a Labano fugiens,' composed in 1791 for the Conservatorio dei Mendicanti and performed before a distinguished audience, he was commissioned to compose three more oratorios for Venice ('David,' 'Tobiae matrimonium' and 'Sisara'). For Forlì he wrote 'Jephte' and a Passion. Thrown on his own resources by the sudden death of his patron, he was urged by Piccinni to try the stage, and his first opera, 'Saffo, ossia i riti d' Apollo Leucadio,' was so well received at the Fenice in Venice (1794) that he was immediately overwhelmed with commissions, and between that date and 1814 composed no less than seventy-seven operas. Indeed it was not till Rossini's success that his fame declined. Many of his melodies were sung about the streets, such as the pretty cavatina 'O quanto l' anima' from 'Lauso e Lidia.' In 1802 he became maestro di cappella of Santa Maria Maggiore in Bergamo, and was so much attached to his work there that he declined not only invitations to London, Paris, Lisbon and Dresden, but also the post of censor to the Conservatorio of Milan, his appointment to which had been signed by the Viceroy of Italy in 1807. As professor of composition in the Musical Institute of Bergamo—founded in 1805, reorganised in 1811—he exercised great and good influence; Donizetti was one of his pupils there. He was the founder of two institutions for decayed musicians and their widows, the Scuola Caritatevole di Musica and the Pio Istituto di Bergamo. From 1816 onwards he wrote only church music, such as masses, psalms, motets, etc. (See *Q.-L.*) He had been blind for some years before his death. The city of Bergamo erected a monument to him in 1852, and in 1875 his remains and those of Donizetti were removed with much ceremony to the church of Santa Maria Maggiore. The most celebrated of his operas are 'Lodoïska' (1800), 'Ginevra di Scozia' (1801),

'Medea' (1813) and 'Rosa bianca e Rosa rossa' (1814). *Q.-L.* mentions 28 operas as still extant. He is said to have been the first to introduce the crescendo of the orchestra to which Rossini owes so much of his fame. He wrote a small book on Haydn (1809), a biography of Capuzzi the violinist, and poems on his death in 1818; also *La dottrina degli elementi musicali*, still in MS. in Bergamo.

BIBLIOGRAPHY
C. SCHMIDL : *Cenni biografici su G. S. Mayr.* 1901.
C. SCOTTI : *G. S. Mayr.* 1903.
H. KRETSCHMAR : *Die musikgeschichtliche Bedeutung S. Mayrs.* 1904.
L. SCHIEDERMAIR : *Simon Mayr,* 2 vols. 1907–10.
Zeitschr. of the *Int. Mus. Ges.* vii. 224.
Kirchenmusikalisches Jahrbuch, 1894.
Le Guide musical, Mar. 11, 1906.
             F. G.

MAYR, RICHARD (*b.* Salzburg, Oct. 18, 1877), operatic baritone or basso-cantante. After preliminary study at the local Gymnasium in Salzburg, where his father was a wealthy brewer, he decided to take up medicine, and for that purpose worked some time at the University of Vienna. During that period, however, his fine natural voice gradually attracted so much attention that he decided to abandon the career of a physician for that of a singer. Accordingly he entered the Conservatoire, and, from the age of 21 until he was nearly 25, studied hard to master an extensive repertory of operatic rôles. Declining any tentative appearance at the smaller theatres, he imitated the unique example of the Dutch singer, Anton van Rooy, by obtaining his initial engagement at Bayreuth, where he sang for the first time on any stage in Sept. 1902, as Hagen in ' Götterdämmerung.' His resonant voice and splendid declamation won for him an unequivocal success : but his supreme gifts as an actor were yet to be made manifest in their full maturity. The opportunity for development was immediately afforded through his engagement by Gustav Mahler for the Hofoper at Vienna. Making his début as Don Gomez in ' Ernani,' he sang there for several years in succession, and, whilst laying in a rich store of experience, displayed amazing versatility in a round of leading parts of various schools, serious and comic alike, that extended from the Wotan of the ' Ring ' to the Baron Ochs in ' Der Rosenkavalier.' The latter, a superb creation in every detail, was the character in which he made his first appearance at Covent Garden when Strauss's opera was revived on May 23, 1924. This success was enhanced in the following year, when he sang with no less ability in other strongly-contrasted rôles.

BIBL.—NORTHCOTT, *Covent Garden and the Royal Opera.*
             H. K.

MAYSEDER, JOSEPH (*b.* Vienna, Oct. 26, 1789 ; *d.* Nov. 21, 1863), violinist and composer, son of a poor painter. Beginning at 8, he learnt the violin from Suche and Wranitzky. Schuppanzigh took a great interest in the lad, and entrusted him with the second violin in

his quartet. In 1800 he gave his first concert in the Augarten with brilliant success. In 1816 he entered the court chapel, in 1820 became solo-violin at the court theatre, and in 1835 was appointed chamber-violinist to the Emperor. The municipality awarded him the large gold Salvator Medal in 1811, and presented him with the freedom of the city in 1817. In 1815 he gave, with Hummel (afterwards replaced by Moscheles) and Giuliani, the so-called ' Dukaten Konzerte.' He also gave concerts with Merk the violoncellist, but after 1837 he never appeared in public. He never played abroad ; even on his visit to Paris in 1820, he would only play before a select circle of artists, including Kreutzer, Baudiot, Cherubini, Habeneck, Lafont and Viotti. In 1862 the Emperor bestowed on him the order of Franz - Joseph. With the exception of a Mass he composed only chamber music. He published sixty-three works, including concertos, polonaises, variations, five quintets and eight quartets for strings, études and duets for violin, four trios, sonatas, etc., for PF., trio for violin, harp and horn, etc.   C. F. P.

MAZAS, JACQUES-FÉRÉOL (*b.* Beziers, Sept. 23, 1782 ; *d.* there, 1849), French violinist and composer. He entered the Paris Conservatoire in 1802, and after having studied for three years under Baillot, obtained the first prize for violin-playing. He had great success at Paris, especially with his performance of a violin-concerto, written for him by Auber, at the Conservatoire. He travelled through a very large part of Europe, and returned in 1829 to Paris, without, however, gaining his former success. In 1837 he left Paris again, and accepted the directorship of a music-school at Cambrai, remaining there till 1841.

Mazas wrote a large number of brilliant violin pieces, quartets, trios and duets for stringed instruments, an instruction-book for the violin and one for the viola. Fétis mentions also two operas (one, ' Le Kiosque,' performed in Paris in 1842), two violin-concertos and an overture.   P. D.

MAZEPPA. (1) Opera in 3 acts, libretto from Poushkin's *Poltava,* by Bourenin and others, music by Tchaikovsky. Produced at Moscow and St. Petersburg, almost simultaneously, in 1883 ; at the Alexandra Theatre, Liverpool, in 1888, by a Russian Company.

(2) Symphonic poem by Liszt. Originally designed as a pianoforte étude, it was revised and scored for orchestra in 1858.

MAZURKA (MAZOURKA, MASUREK, MASURE), a national Polish dance, deriving its name from the ancient Palatinate of Masovia. The Mazurka was known as early as the 16th century ; it originated in national songs [1]

[1] This feature it has retained. Chopin, in a letter of Aug. 26, 1829, says, ' The thought fortunately struck Maciejowski to write four stanzas for a Mazurka, and I set them to music ' (Karasowski, i. 89).

accompanied with dancing. It was introduced into Germany by Augustus III., Elector
of Saxony and King of Poland (1733–63), and
after becoming fashionable in Paris, reached
England towards 1845. The Mazurka was
naturalised in Russia after the subjugation of
Poland, but the Russian dance differs from the
Polish in being performed by an indefinite
number, while the latter is usually danced by
four or eight couples. The Mazurka is remarkable for the variety and liberty allowed in its
figures, and for the peculiar steps necessary to
its performance. Indeed, the whole dance
partakes of the character of an improvisation,
even the invention of new steps and figures
being allowable. The music (in 3-4 or 3-8
time) consists usually of two or four parts of
eight bars, each part being repeated. In the
earliest Mazurkas the bass was invariably on
one note, usually the tonic. There is generally
a strong accent on the third beat of the bar.
The tune should also end on the second beat of
the bar, but in old Mazurkas there is often no
definite conclusion, and the repeats are made
ad libitum. (See BEAT (3)). The *Tempo* is
much slower than that of the ordinary waltz.
Chopin treated the dance in a new and characteristic manner. He extended its original
forms, eliminated all vulgarity, introduced all
sorts of Polish airs, and thus retained little
more than the intensely national character of
the original simple dance tune.[1] No less
than fourteen sets of his Mazurkas have been
published, containing fifty-two in all (opp.
6, 7, 17, 24, 30, 33, 41, 50, 56, 59, 63, 67, 68,
and one without opus number). Weber gives
the title ' Masurik ' to the fourth of his six
pieces for the PF. à quatre mains (op. 10).

The following example is a simple Mazurka
popular in the neighbourhood of Warsaw. The
first part of the melody has a vocal accompaniment :

W. B. S.

MAZZAFERRATA, GIOVANNI BATTISTA
(*b.* Como, 2nd half of 17th cent.), maestro di cappella at the Accademia della Morte at Ferrara.
He composed : Salmi concertati, 3-4 v. (1676) ;
cantatas (1680) ; madrigals, 2-3 v. (1668),
canzonets and cantatas (1680) ; solo chamber
cantatas (1677) ; 12 sonatas for 2 violins with

a ' bassetto viola ' *ad lib.* (1674 ; republ. 1678).
One of these was republished by Wasielewski.
An Oratorio by him was performed at Siena,
1684 (*Q.-L.* ; *Riemann*).

MAZZINGHI, a family of musicians of
Corsican extraction settled in England.

(1) THOMAS (*d.* May 20, 1775) was violinist
at Marylebone Gardens. ' Six solos for the
violin,' published in London about 1763 (see
Q.-L.), may be ascribed with reasonable probability to him. He was buried in St. Pancras.[2]
His son,

(2) JOSEPH (*b.* London, Dec. 25, 1765 ;
d. 1839[3]), was a pupil of John Christian Bach,
under whom he made such progress that, on
the death of his father, in 1775, he was, although
but 10 years of age, appointed organist of the
Portuguese Chapel. He then studied under
Bertolini, Sacchini and Anfossi. In 1784 he
became musical director and composer at the
King's Theatre, and produced the operas of
' Il tesoro ' and ' La Belle Arsène,' besides
many songs, duets, etc., for introduction into
other operas, and the music for several ballets.
The score of Paisiello's opera ' La Locanda '
having been consumed in the fire of the Opera
House in June 1789, Mazzinghi rescored the
work so faithfully as to admit of its continued
performance. For the English theatre he set
the following pieces :

' A Day in Turkey,' 1791.
' The Magician no Conjuror,' 1792.
' Ramah Droog,' 1798.
' The Turnpike Gate,' 1799.
' Paul and Virginia,' 1800.
' The Blind Girl,' 1801.
' Chains of the Heart,' 1802 (the last five in collaboration with
    Reeve).
' The Wife of two Husbands,' 1803.
' The Exile,' 1808.
' The Free Knights,' 1810.

The last piece contained the duet, ' When a
little farm we keep,' which for nearly half a
century was highly popular and constantly
introduced into other pieces.

Mazzinghi was music-master to the Princess
of Wales, afterwards Queen Caroline, and had
an extensive practice as a teacher of the pianoforte, for which instrument he composed nearly
seventy sonatas and arranged a multitude of
pieces, besides writing an ' Introduction ' to it.
His glees, trios, harmonised airs, songs and
other vocal pieces were legion. His pastoral
glee, ' The Wreath ' (' Tell me, shepherds '), was
long in favour. He likewise composed a Mass
for three voices, and six hymns.   W. H. H.

(3) THOMAS (TOMMASO) (*d.* Downside, near
Bath, Jan. 15, 1844), violinist, was ennobled in
Italy in 1834.[4] His title of Count has been
supposed to belong to Joseph, and the ' Six
solos for the violin ' named above have been
attributed [5] to him despite the obvious incom-
patibility of dates. He may have been another
son of THOMAS (1).   C.

MAZZOCCHI (1), DOMENICO (*b.* Veja, near

---

[1] See Karasowski's *Life of Chopin*, chap. vii. ; and also the somewhat rhapsodical but still interesting remarks of Liszt in his *Chopin*.

[2] Cansick's *St. Pancras Inscriptions.*
[3] C. F. Pohl, *Mozart und Haydn in London*, vol. ii. p. 370.
[4] *Ibid.*   [5] *Riemann.*

Civita Castellana, *c.* end of 16th cent.), was a pupil of Nanini, and published an opera, ' La catena d' Adone,' in 1626, a book of 5-part madrigals, a set of ' Dialoghi e sonetti ' in 1638, and a volume of ' Musiche sacre ' in 1640.

In the dedication of this last he states that he has been for twenty years in the service of the family of Aldobrandini Borghese. He seems to have been the first to use the sign $\prec\succ$ for a crescendo and diminuendo, or a ' swell.'

His brother (2) VIRGILIO (*d.* Oct. 1646) was from 1628–29 maestro di cappella at St. John Lateran in Rome, and in the latter year was appointed to a similar place in St. Peter's. He held this post until his death. In 1640 he published, as op. 1, ' Sacrae flores ' for two, three and four voices, and in 1648 a set of psalms for double chorus was issued (*Q.-L.*).

MAZZONE, MARC' ANTONIO, of Miglionico, Naples, composed 1 book of madrigals *a* 5 v., 1 book of madrigals *a* 4 v. (both Venice, 1569) ; 1 book of Magnificats to serve for choirs of limited compass (*ib.* 1593) (*Q.-L.*).

MAZZONI, ANTONIO (*b.* Bologna, *c.* 1718), pupil of Predieri. After filling appointments as maestro di cappella in various towns, he entered the Accademia Filarmonica of Bologna in 1743 ; visited Spain and Portugal where he produced several of his operas, and returned in 1752, writing operas for Parma, Naples, Venice and Bologna, where he became Prince of the Accademia Filarmonica in 1757. He then visited St. Petersburg, Sweden and Denmark, returning to Bologna in 1761 as maestro di cappella of S. Giovanni in Monte. In 1767 he was deputy maestro di cappella at the Cathedral of St. Peter, and 1773 again Prince of the Accademia Filarmonica. Apart from a number of operas, he composed an oratorio and a considerable amount of church as well as secular music. Burney and Dittersdorf speak very highly of his ability. His Solfeggi for middle voice have been re-edited by Jul. Stern (*Q.-L.*; *Fétis*).

MAZZUCATO, GIAN ANDREA (*b.* Milan ; *d.* London, Aug. 1900), writer and critic. On the death of his father (Alberto Mazzucato) he was appointed professor of musical aesthetics at the Milan Conservatoire (1878). He contributed also various critical articles to the *Corriere della sera*, then in its infancy. About 1880 he left Milan for London, where he earned a living by giving lessons in Italian, translating, and occasional articles on musical subjects, including biographical and critical notes for the first edition of this Dictionary.   F. B.

MEAN (Old Eng. *meane, mene*; Lat. *medius*). (1) An old name for a middle voice-part, whether alto or tenor.

(2) A name given to the second instrument in a Consort of Viols, such as Orlando Gibbons's ' Fantasies in three parts, for Viols.'

(3) The name of the second and third strings of the viol—the former being called the Small and the latter the Great Meane.

(4) The title of an ingenious Fugue for the Organ composed by William Blitheman, and printed by Hawkins in the Appendix to vol. v. of his *History*.   W. S. R.

MEANTONE, see TEMPERAMENT.

MEARES, RICHARD, father and son with the same Christian name. The father was a skilled maker of viols, lutes, and other instruments, and as his labels inform us, lived ' Without Bishop-gate, near to Sr. Paul Pinder's, London.' The earliest of these labels of which the present writer has knowledge is dated 1669 ; others 1677, etc. Hawkins, who gives an account of father and son (misspelling the name ' Mears '), says that his shop was opposite the Catherine Wheel Inn, without Bishopgate, and that he was advertising in 1688, ' lutes, and viols fretted according to Mr. Salmon's proposal.'

Richard Meares the son is mentioned by Hawkins as a ' whimsical man,' bred up to his father's business, who, ' seeing the slovenly manner in which music was published by Walsh & Hare, and being desirous to participate in so gainful a trade, became their rival.'

A card in the Bagford collection (*B.M.*) indicates that the younger Meares was first established in Leadenhall Street at the sign of the Golden Viol, but that he is then removed from thence to the north side of St. Paul's Churchyard at the Golden Viol and Hautboy, where he sells all sorts of musical instruments, books and songs ' as also ye best sort of cutlery ware.'

Meares's first publication is stated to be Mattheson's ' Pièces de clavecin,' which is dated from St. Paul's Churchyard, 1714. After this he became the publisher selected by Handel, during his periodical squabbles with Walsh, to issue his works, partly in conjunction with J. C. Smith. ' Radamisto ' is ' printed and sold by R. Meares and C. Smith not to be sold anywhere else in England.' ' Suites de pièces ' and the additional airs in ' Floridant ' are others by Handel having Meares's imprint. He published also Corelli's ' Sonatas ' and ' Concertos,' Ariosto's ' Coriolanus,' and Dr. Croft's ' Musicus apparatus academicus.' One of his late issues is *Introduction to Psalmody*, J. Church, 1723, 8vo. According to Hawkins he was not very successful, and in due course removed to Birchin Lane, and finally to London-house Yard, where he died about 1743. He must not be confused with a typographical music-printer named H. Meere, who printed one or two works for Walsh in 1716 and 1718.   F. K.

MEARS & STAINBANK. This bell-foundry was established in 1570 and removed from Essex Street, Whitechapel, to its present site in Whitechapel Road in 1738.

The history of the firm begins with Robert Mot, 1570, who was succeeded by the following founders : Carter (2), Bartlet (3), Phelps (2), Lester, Pack and Chapman.

In 1784 the ownership passed to William Mears, and remained in that family until 1865, since which time the business has been carried on under the name of Mears & Stainbank. At different times the foundries of Abraham Rudhall (Gloucester), John Briant (Hertford), Osborn and Dobson (Downham), and Robert Wells (Aldbourne), have been absorbed by the Mears foundry. Amongst the best-known peals cast at this foundry may be mentioned :

12 bells :

Bow Church, Cheapside .	tenor 53 cwts.
Norwich : St. Peter Mancroft	„ 43 „
York Minster	„ 54 „

10 bells :

Coventry : St. Michael's .	tenor 31 cwts.
Stepney : St. Dunstan's .	„ 31 „
Stockport : St. George's .	„ 30 „

W. W. S.

MEASURE (1) originally denoted any dance remarkable for its well-defined rhythm, but in time the name was applied to a solemn and stately dance, of the nature of a Pavan or a Minuet. The dignified character of the dance is proved by the use of the expression ' to tread a measure ' ; a phrase of frequent occurrence in the works of the Elizabethan dramatists. In the reigns of Elizabeth and James I., Measures were danced at court, and at the public entertainments periodically given by the Societies of Law and Equity. On these occasions the great legal and state dignitaries took part in them, but the custom seems rapidly to have died out under Charles I. It is somewhat remarkable that no trace can be found of any special music to which Measures were danced ; this circumstance seems to prove that there was no definite form of dance tune for them, but that any stately and rhythmical air was used for the purpose.

(2) Equivalent to BAR (q.v.).   W. B. S.

MECHANICAL APPLIANCES CONNECTED WITH MUSIC. The earliest instance of mechanical music-making seems to be the CARILLON, described under its own heading, which could be played either by the hand or by mechanism. Several other appliances are discussed below in chronological order.

(1) BARREL ORGAN, a musical instrument, of all others the most easy of manipulation, as it requires nothing beyond the regular rotary motion of a handle to keep it playing. In some examples even this power is applied mechanically, either by means of clock-work, or by weights. These instruments are of the most various capacities, from the simple street organ —the ' barrel organ ' of ordinary parlance—to large and complicated machines representing the full orchestra. But the principle of action is the same in all. A wooden cylinder, or barrel, placed horizontally, and armed on its outside circumference with brass staples or

pins, slowly revolves, in the direction from back to front ; and in doing so the pins raise certain trigger-shaped keys, which correspond with simple mechanism communicating with valves that on being opened allow wind to enter the required pipes. In this way either melody or harmony is produced. The wind is provided by bellows which are worked by the same motion that turns the barrel. The most simple kind of instrument of this nature is the small ' bird organ,' used, as its name implies, for teaching bullfinches to pipe—which plays the simplest music in melody only.

It is not positively known when barrel organs were first made, but they are supposed to date from about the beginning of the 18th century. An organ-builder of the name of Wright, the great-grandfather of ROBSON, made a barrel organ for Fulham Church, which alone would carry the date a long way back. FLIGHT of Exeter Change was also a celebrated maker of barrel organs in his day. The finest and most elaborate specimen of a ' Finger and Barrel ' organ that was ever made was the APOLLONICON (q.v.). The firms of Flight and Robson, and of BRYCESON, made perhaps the greatest number of barrel organs, a kind of instrument in much demand many years ago, for churches and chapels. These were set with psalm and hymn tunes, chants, and occasionally with voluntaries.

A church barrel organ had rarely a chromatic compass of notes, but usually only a greater or less approximation thereto. Thus it would generally have either 8, 14, 17, 21, 27, 28 or 31 keys. In the case of one having 14 keys, two diatonic scales, of short range, would be presented, namely G and D, into which all the tunes ' marked ' upon the barrel would be transposed, and a few pipes at somewhat large intervals apart would be supplied by way of bass, such as D and G. In organs with more keys, the G♯ would be inserted, allowing the scale of A to be used. In organs having a further increased number of keys the D♯ would be introduced, permitting the scale of E to be employed ; and so on. Strange to say, scales with flats were never planned unless specially ordered ; nor was there much provision for tunes in the minor mode in organs with comparatively but few ' keys.'

Organs having the complete compass and with all the chromatic semitones have been made to play overtures, movements of symphonies, selections from operas, sets of waltzes, and other music. The place occupied in the making of these instruments by John Robson was taken by Imhof and Mukle of London, who during the 19th century supplied a large number of these mechanical organs called ' Orchestrion ' to private houses in the country at prices ranging from £100 to £1500. One of the completest of these instruments contains

8 ordinary stops, ranging through a complete chromatic scale of $5\frac{1}{3}$ octaves, and 6 solo stops ; with a swell of 3 stops in addition to drums, triangle, cymbals and castanets. Three machines work the whole of this elaborate apparatus. The barrels can be changed very rapidly, and as each barrel takes $11\frac{1}{2}$ minutes to complete its revolution whole movements of symphonies and overtures can be performed. Instruments of this character have been occasionally furnished with a manual, and are then known as ' Barrel and Finger Organs.'

The ordinary street organ was first made by a builder named Hicks at the beginning of the 19th century. It flourished in the streets of London and other English towns during that century, but has now almost disappeared. The smallest kind having 24 keys, sounded the following notes :

Larger sizes had a fuller compass. There were 2 stops, an open (rarely of metal) and a closed (wood). The barrel was set to play 9 or 10 tunes. The instruments weighed from 40 to 56 lbs., and cost from £18 upwards.

The annexed illustration shows a cross section of an ordinary barrel organ.

Barrel organs have been made with three and four barrels in a circular revolving iron frame. The first of the kind, containing four barrels, was made by BISHOP, sen., for Northallerton Church, Yorkshire, about the year 1820. Many years later Messrs. Gray and Davison made grinder organs with three barrels in one frame.

E. J. H.

(2) PIANO MÉCANIQUE, an invention of Debain of Paris (d. 1877), for the mechanical performance of musical compositions upon a pianoforte without disturbing its keyboard, or its capability for manual performance. To manage this the pinned barrel employed in the street pianos and barrel-organs had to give place to a novel and ingenious apparatus invented and adapted to his ' Piano mécanique ' by Debain, about the year 1850. To an ordinary upright piano he supplied a second set of hammers working the reverse way to the ordinary ones, that is, from above. These hammers were set in motion by iron levers, the further ends of which were tempered hard, and projected as ' beaks ' through a comb of four or five inches long, into which space five octaves of the keyboard were compressed. The comb crossed transversely a smooth iron plate fixed along the top of the instrument. 'Planchettes,' or small boards upon which the piece to be played was pinned (as on a barrel), were connected with a handle, made to travel along this plate, the pins doing the work of the fingers upon the levers. The dynamic shades of piano

and forte, accent, etc., were produced by varying the height of the pins. Perhaps the greatest merit of Debain's invention was that his upper system of hammers had the same 'striking-place' (i.e. measured division of the string for the impact of the hammers) that the keyboard hammers have. This was achieved by moving the latter forward when the mechanical apparatus came into play. The great defect of the contrivance was the want of damping during performance. When applied by Debain and Co. to the organ or harmonium it was styled ' Antiphonal.'

(3) The ' Handle-pianos,' popularly known as PIANO-ORGANS, merely because being stringed instruments they succeeded the street organs as the chief means of musical mendicancy in

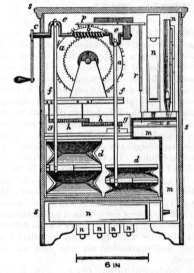

6 IN

a is the barrel, ' set ' round its circumference with ' pins,' at the various intervals, and of the various lengths, necessary for the music, and turned by the worm *b* on the shaft *c* ; *d d* are the bellows worked by the cranks *e e* on the shaft and the connecting rods *f f*, and delivering the wind into an air chamber *g*, which runs to the farther end of the case, and is kept at an uniform pressure by the spiral springs *h h*. The air vessel again delivers the wind into the wind-chest *m*, which communicates with the pipes *n n*. Each pipe has its valve *o*, which is kept closed by a spring until the corresponding pin on the barrel raises the trigger *p*, and, forcing down the connecting wire *r*, opens the valve and admits wind to the pipe. *s s* is the case. Space being very valuable in these instruments, the pipes are packed together very closely, and are often bent in shape to fit the demands of the case. In the diagram one is shown lying beneath the floor of the bellows.

England, come principally from Italy. These instruments are strongly made, to stand hard work and weather ; the felt hammers have leather coating, and there are three, and in the treble often four, strings to each note. The action is of the simplest kind, the pin of the barrel pressing down a crank, which gives the blow ; a spring causing the immediate return of the hammer. There are no dampers excepting in a few instances in the lowest bass notes, and no attempt to regulate the pinning of the barrel to produce louder or softer notes.

(4) MUSICAL SNUFF-BOX, etc.—Musical boxes were invented about the beginning of the 19th century, probably in Switzerland, the chief seat of their production. The motive power is a pinned cylinder resembling the barrel of a mechanical organ, and made to shift on the same principle ; the working power is a spring; the mechanism and rotation are closely allied to those of a watch or clock ; and the teeth of the comb which produce the notes are measured to scale.

The original musical boxes are small and not unlike a snuff-box in appearance. They are now made of all sizes.

About 1830 a very favourite composition with amateurs of the pianoforte was the ' Snuff-box Waltz,' the composer of which preserved his anonymity under the initials M. S. Such a passage as the following illustrates the kind of imitation that was possible :

Bells, drums, castanettes, free reeds worked by bellows, and more recently a ' zither,' produced by a sheet of thin paper resting on the teeth of the comb, have been introduced, and have not raised the musical value of the instrument, any more than similar introductions early in the 19th century raised the value of the pianoforte. As pointed out by Moonen in his Report on the Melbourne Exhibition, the real improvements have been in the mechanical portion, by the accurate ' pointing ' or adjustment on the cylinder of as many as 36 airs ; the obtaining a constant movement for an hour and a half without requiring to wind up the spring during that time ; the possibility of shifting the barrel in such a manner that an air ' noted ' may be played without the necessity of going through all the others in rotation, and the important one of the interchange of barrels made to fit any box.   A. J. H.

(5) PLAYER-PIANO (PIANOLA, etc.).—Of late years a refined form of mechanical piano has come into extraordinary vogue for domestic use. A patent was taken out in the United States as early as 1860 for a keyboard pianoplayer, and the first pneumatic keyboard instrument was made in France in 1863. The main principles of the action are much the same in all these attachments. A roll of cardboard

pierced with openings corresponding to the duration and pitch of the notes in the composition to be repeated passes over a cylinder furnished with small apertures, through which a puff of air is drawn or pushed as often as the passage is left free by the occurrence of one of the openings in the cardboard roll. This puff of air sets in motion a series of hammers which act as substitutes for the human fingers ; the movement of the roll, and the force with which the notes are struck, are regulated by pedals like those of the harmonium, with the assistance of certain handles by which the speed and force of the apparatus can be rapidly changed. It is not necessary to discuss the relative merits of the innumerable and variously named inventions which are now before the public ; the greater number of them are of American origin, though practically all piano manufacturers build player-pianos, that is, instruments capable of being played either through the mechanism or by the hands of the pianist. All of them claim that by means of the mechanism the performer can put an individual interpretation into music for which his manual technique would be quite insufficient, and that one person's manner of manipulating the instruments will be altogether different from another's.

An immense collection of music of all grades is now published in the form of rolls, and the technique of performance through the player-piano has been fully explored. A few composers have been induced to write specially for the instrument. The following books afford useful information :

CONSTRUCTION.—WILLIAM BRAID WHITE, *The Player-piano up to date* (1914) ; HARRISON LOUIS VAN ATTA, *The Piano and Piano-player* (1914).
TECHNIQUE AND AESTHETICS.—SYDNEY GREW, *The Art of the Player-piano* (1922) ; E. NEWMAN, *The Piano-player and its Music.*

An important modification of the player-piano mechanism is the reproducing action which requires no individual control at all. By means of it the previous performance of a pianist is recorded and reproduced with more or less faithfulness as to tone values, time, phrasing, etc. The principal patents which mark successive stages of accuracy in this mechanism are the ' Welte - Mignon,' the ' Duo-Art ' and the ' Ampico.'

The principle of the player-piano has been successfully applied to the organ in the form of the Æolian and Orchestrelle. See ÆOLIAN COMPANY for details of the manufacture in England of these several instruments, and more especially the ' Duo-Art ' player-piano.

      M. ; addns. C.

(6) GRAMOPHONE (PHONOGRAPH) is the instrument by far the most widely used at the present day for the mechanical reproduction of music. Its principle rests on the formation of an actual record of the vibrations set up by voice or instrument and their subsequent re-creation. A stylus attached to the

sensitive diaphragm, which receives the vibrations, makes indentations on a revolving disc or cylinder of wax or other impressionable material. From this a copy is produced in metal by a process of electrolysis and is used as a matrix from which further copies in a hard composite material can be multiplied.

The name gramophone (in America phonograph) is commonly given to the machine through which these records reproduce the sound. It reverses the recording process. The needle, following the groove of the record placed on a rotating plate, is the agent by which the indentations once more set up vibrations. These conducted through the tone arm into contact with a mica diaphragm and sound box are converted into sound waves. A horn or other apparatus supplies the necessary amplification.[1]

The invention is attributable to Thomas A. Edison who patented his Phonograph, Nov. 1877. The record was made on a cylinder, and one instrument served both to record and to reproduce. Edison's first object was the transmission of speech, but music soon entered into his experiments. The adoption of the disc form of record and its almost unlimited multiplication from a matrix, which made possible the popular vogue of the gramophone, was due to Émile Berliner of Washington, D.C. (1887). By about the year 1900, the immense commercial possibilities of the gramophone becoming apparent, the ingenuity of American inventors was concentrated on the improvement of its processes. The majority of inventions of the first quarter of the 20th century have been directed to secure greater accuracy in the transmission of musical qualities. There is still much to be done in this direction, particularly with regard to the recording of orchestral values, but what has been effected in this comparatively short period has been sufficient to make gramophone reproduction acceptable to musicians, who not only commend its educational value to others but profess pleasure in it themselves. Recording has become a very lucrative occupation for executive artists of all kinds, and by means of the gramophone every type of music from the highest to the lowest has been disseminated[2] all over the world.   C.

MÉDECIN MALGRÉ LUI, LE, opera by Gounod, the text adapted from Molière by Barbier and Carré ; produced Théâtre Lyrique, Jan. 15, 1858 ; in English, as ' The Mock Doctor,' Covent Garden, Feb. 27, 1865. G.

Henry Fielding made a ballad opera, ' The Mock Doctor, or the Dumb Lady cured,' acted at Drury Lane in 1732, and often revived afterwards. It was published with the airs of the songs by J. Watts in 1732.   F. K.

MÉDÉE, opera in 3 acts ; words by Hoff-

[1] For fuller description of the principle and action of the gramophone see E. W. Scripture, *Elements of Experimental Phonetics.*
[2] See ' *His Master's Voice* ' *Record Catalogue,* 1922. Additions are made almost daily to the large catalogues of this and other companies.

mann, music by Cherubini. Produced Théâtre Feydeau, Mar. 13, 1797 ; in London, Her Majesty's Theatre, in Italian, with recitatives by Arditi, June 6, 1865.   G.

MEDER, JOHANN VALENTIN (*bapt.* Wasungen on the Werra, May 3, 1649 ; *d.* Riga, July 1719), studied theology at Leipzig and Jena, then turned to music. After various engagements as singer, and wanderings which brought him as far as Copenhagen, he became in 1674 cantor at Reval College, and in 1687 at St. Mary's, Danzig, where his attempt to introduce opera (with two of his own works, ' Nero ' and ' Coelia ') met with the opposition of the town council. He left there and became Kapellmeister at Königsberg Cathedral, but exchanged that post for a similar position at Riga Cathedral. He was greatly esteemed as a composer by Buxtehude, Mattheson, etc., his works including operas, an oratorio, motets and other church music, as well as trios for 2 violins, and bass for the organ, and a MS. trio for 2 treble viols with bass and harpsichord (J. Bolte, *Vierteljahrsschrift für Musikwissenschaft,* 1891 and 1892 ; *Q.-L.*).

MEDESIMO TEMPO, ' in the same time,' is occasionally used in the same way as L' ISTESSO TEMPO (*q.v.*).   M.

MEDIAL CADENCE, see CADENCE (I.), section (2).

MEDIANT (from the Lat. *medius,* 'middle').

(1) For the use of this term in the Modal system see MODES, ECCLESIASTICAL.

(2) In modern music the term is always applied to the third of the scale, by reason of its intermediate position, between the tonic and the dominant. The office of this note is extremely important, inasmuch as it determines whether the tonality of the scale is major or minor.   W. S. R.

MEDIATION (Lat. *mediatio*), the inflexion which occurs half-way through a psalm-tone before the point of division marked in the words by a colon. (See INFLEXION ; GREGORIAN TONES.)

MEDTNER, NICOLAI RASLOVITCH (*b.* Moscow, Dec. 24, 1879), Russian composer of German descent, entered the Moscow Conservatoire in 1891, studying the piano under Safonov. In 1900 he won the Gold Medal awarded by that institution and the Rubinstein Prize. In 1901–02 he toured Europe as a pianist, and on his return became professor of his instrument at the Conservatoire. In 1903 he retired in order to devote himself exclusively to composition, a branch of his art for which, although he had cultivated it comparatively little during his student days, he had an astonishing aptitude. He had no difficulty in bringing his work before the public. His first piano sonata was published by Belaiev, and P. Jurgenson issued all his other works for some time, until he attracted the attention of the Russian Music Publishing Society. After the Revolution he taught music at a school in the outskirts of Moscow, and in 1922 he set out on another European tour.

Medtner's music is firmly rooted in tradition. He does not break new ground, but devotes himself to extending the fields cultivated by the classics. Although not averse to the use of new idiomatic resources, he regards them as acquisitions destined to enrich the old system, not to destroy it. Even his curious experiments in rhythm must be considered as old devices used in a new and interesting way rather than as actual innovations.

Both on account of his neo-classicism and his predilection for cross-rhythms, Medtner has often been described as the ' Russian Brahms ' ; but, apart from the fact that this designation is in itself contradictory, the resemblances that have occasioned it are only superficial ones. The two composers have a certain earnestness of purpose and self-sufficing gravity in common, but such a similarity of outlook may be found in artists whose creative faculties manifest themselves in totally dissimilar ways. Medtner is undoubtedly a modern descendant of the Beethoven-Brahms line of classical development, but he is not therefore more like Brahms than the latter is like Beethoven.

Medtner is a firm believer in absolute music. His output is almost exclusively restricted to chamber music, the piano works being the most significant and characteristic as well as the most numerous. The stage and the orchestra have apparently no attraction for a composer who aims at creating works of an intimate and purely musical nature. Even in his songs, where a literary element necessarily obtrudes itself, the music remains abstract as far as possible.

The form in which Medtner expresses himself most completely is that of the sonata. He does not adhere very closely to the classical model, which he bends to his creative fancy with considerable freedom, but its fundamental principles serve him as the ideal mould for all his larger works. Perhaps the sonata form is occasionally apt to be his master rather than his servant. The op. 11, for instance, may be suspected to have originally been planned as a sonata in three movements, and it would seem that, as the work progressed, each movement shaped itself inevitably into the first-movement form, and that the work thus became a ' Sonata-Triad ' of three separate and fully developed movements. Much the same appears to have happened in the case of op. 25, No. 1, and of op. 27, which may have been intended as a ' Fairy Tale ' and a ' Ballade ' respectively, but grew imperceptibly into sonatas.

In spite of the organic structure of Medtner's music, it is by no means coldly formal. It is clear that each work sprang from a poetical conception, even when this is left to the hearer's imagination. In some cases it is indicated by a verbal motto, in others implied by a title such as ' Dithyramb ' or ' Fairy Tale.' The latter has become especially typical of the romantic aspects of Medtner's work.

The difference between the early and the later works is not vast, for, in spite of some classical influences, the composer's personality is apparent from the beginning. His style of pianistic writing is invariably ideally suited to the instrument. Comparatively conventional in its first stages, it has constantly enriched itself by new devices, and its intricate and endlessly varied texture is the more interesting for being at times almost invincibly difficult. Here and there the problems are made unnecessarily hard to solve by Medtner's curious manner of making his rhythmic complexities apparent to the reader's eye ; phrasing and accent are frequently not only indicated by the conventional signs, but reinforced by a method of linking together the groups of notes which is logical in theory but confusing in practice.

The most extensive work for the piano is the concerto, op. 33. In technical ingenuity it is inferior to none of the earlier piano music, but the composer's excessive preoccupation with contrapuntal problems, which are overcome with consummate mastery, involves the sacrifice of much of the fanciful imagination and soaring poetry that characterises his best work.

For violin and piano Medtner has written a sonata and three ' Nocturnes,' which not only represent him at his best as regards invention, but are admirably laid out for the two instruments, both individually and in combination.

In the songs the vocal line is somewhat lacking in lyrical breadth and adaptability to the varying character of the poetry. The great variety Medtner achieves in his vocal work is too much due to his interesting but unduly prominent accompaniments. An advantage, on the other hand, is the treatment of each poem from a purely musical point of view. Each song is confined to a definite range of colours that expresses the feeling of the poem without resorting to the description of details, which are made sufficiently salient by the words alone and need no strengthening by duplication.

A curious and interesting vocal work on a larger scale is the 'Sonata-Vocalise,' op. 41, for voice and piano, which, save for a ' motto ' culled from Goethe, is sung without words.

The following is a list of Medtner's works (PF. solo unless otherwise stated) :

Op. 1, 8 Mood Pictures. Op. 2, 3 Improvisations. Op. 3, 3 Songs. Op. 4, 4 Pieces (Etude, Caprice, Moment musical, Prelude). Op. 5, Sonata, F minor. Op. 6, 9 Songs (Goethe). Op. 7, 3 Arabesques. Op. 8, 2 Fairy Tales. Op. 9, 3 Fairy Tales. Op. 10, 3 Dithyrambs

Op. 11, Sonata-Triad (A flat major, D minor, C major). Op. 12 3 Songs (Heine). Op. 13, 2 Songs. Op. 14, 2 Fairy Tales. Op. 15, 12 Songs (Goethe). Op. 16, 3 Nocturnes, Vn. & PF. Op. 17, 3 Novels. Op. 18, 6 Songs (Goethe). Op. 19, 3 Songs (Nietzsche), Op. 19a, 2 Songs (Nietzsche). Op. 20, 2 Fairy Tales. Op. 21, Sonata, B minor, Vn. & PF. Op. 22, Sonata, G minor. Op. 23. 4 Lyric Fragments. Op. 24, 8 Songs. Op. 25, No. 1, Fairy-Tale Sonata, C minor ; No. 2, Sonata, E minor. Op. 26, 4 Fairy Tales. Op. 27 Sonata-Ballade, F sharp minor. Op. 28, 7 Songs. Op. 29, 7 Songs (Pushkin). Op. 30, Sonata, A minor. Op. 31, 3 Pieces (Improvisation, Marche funèbre, Fairy Tale). Op. 32, 6 Songs (Pushkin). Op. 33, Concerto, C minor, PF. & Orch. Op. 34, 4 Fairy Tales. Op. 35, 4 Fairy Tales. Op. 36, Songs (Pushkin). Op. 37, 5 Songs. Op. 38, Forgotten Melodies, vol. i. Op. 39, Forgotten Melodies, vol. ii. Op. 40, Forgotten Melodies, vol. iii. Op. 41, Sonata-Vocalise, Voice & PF. Op. 42, No. 1, Russian Fairy Tale. Op. 44, Sonata No. 2, G major, vln. and PF 2 Cadenzas to Beethoven's PF. Concerto No. 4.　　　　　E. B.

MEERESSTILLE UND GLÜCKLICHE FAHRT, *i.e.* Calm Sea and Prosperous Voyage, a poem by Goethe, which has been set to music by—

(1) Beethoven, for chorus and orchestra. Composed in 1815, first performed at the Great Redoutensaal in Vienna on Christmas Day of that year, and published Feb. 28, 1823, by Steiner. It is dedicated ' to the immortal Goethe.' The reverse of the title-page contains three lines from Voss's translation of the *Odyssey* (viii. 479), thus rendered by Lang and Butcher :

' For from all men on earth minstrels get their meed of honour and worship ; inasmuch as the muse teacheth them the paths of song, and loveth the tribe of minstrels.'

A letter from Beethoven to the publisher, dated June 12, and apparently belonging to the year 1824, calls it a cantata, and asks for the loan of the score, that he ' might write a kind of overture to it.' This intention does not appear to have been carried out.

(2) Mendelssohn, for orchestra only. Written in the summer of 1828, first performed at Berlin, Dec. 1, 1832, remodelled and ' made thirty times as good as before,' and published as op. 27 and No. 3 of his Concert Overtures in 1834. We learn from a passage in his sister's diary [1] that Mendelssohn wished to avoid the form of an introduction and overture, and to throw his work into two companion pictures.　　　　G.

MEERTS, LAMBERT JOSEPH (*b.* Brussels, Jan. 6, 1800 ; *d.* there, May 12, 1863), distinguished violinist and composer for his instrument, a pupil of Lafont, Habeneck and Baillot. At the age of 16 he became a member of the theatre orchestra in Antwerp. After completing his studies in Paris he returned to Brussels and established himself as a teacher and performer. In 1835 he was appointed professor of the violin at the Brussels Conservatoire. He wrote several instructive works for the violin, including a series of duets for two violins, each study being founded on a particular rhythm extracted from one of Beethoven's symphonies.

BIBL.—A. MASON CLARKE, *Fiddlers Ancient and Modern*, London, 1896.　　　　　　　　　　　　　　　E. H.-A.

MEFISTOFELE, opera in a prologue and 5 acts ; words (after Goethe) and music by Boïto. Produced Milan, Mar. 5, 1868 ; remodelled, prologue and 4 acts, Bologna, Oct. 4,

[1] Hensel's *Die Familie Mendelssohn*, i. 194.

1875 ; Her Majesty's, July 6, 1880 ; New York, Academy of Music, Nov. 24, 1880 ; in English (Carl Rosa Co.), 1912. See also FAUST.

MEGLI (MELIO, MELLI), DOMENICO (16th-17th cent.), of Reggio, Doct.Jur., lived at Padua. He composed several books of madrigals, canzoni, arias, etc., between 1602 – 09, some in 2 editions ; 1 song in Robt. Dowland's ' A Musicall Banquet,' 1610 (*Q.-L.*).

MEHLIG, ANNA (*b.* Stuttgart, July 11, 1846), a distinguished pianist, received her musical education at the Conservatorium of her native town, and afterwards spent a year at Weimar studying under Liszt. In 1866 she made her first appearance in England, playing Hummel's Concerto in B Minor at the Philharmonic on Apr. 30. She revisited England each year till 1869 inclusive, playing regularly at the Philharmonic and Crystal Palace and other concerts. She then took a long tour in America, where she met with great success. In 1875 she reappeared in England, playing Chopin's E minor Concerto at the Crystal Palace on Oct. 9. She married Herr Falk of Antwerp.　　　　　　　　　　　　G.

MÉHUL, ÉTIENNE HENRI (ÉTIENNE-NICOLAS) (*b.* Givet in the Ardennes, June 22, 1763 ; *d.* Paris, Oct. 18, 1817), son of a cook, who was too poor to give him much education. Even in childhood he showed a passion for music, and a remarkable perseverance in overcoming obstacles, and at 10 was appointed organist to the convent of the Récollets at Givet. Having learned all that his master, a poor blind organist, could teach him, he was thrown on his own resources, until the arrival, at the neighbouring convent of La Val Dieu, of a new organist, Wilhelm Hauser, whose playing had attracted the attention of the Abbot Lissoir, when visiting the Abbey of Scheussenried in Swabia. The monks of La Val Dieu, wishing to make music a special feature in their services, had a good organ, and the playing of Hauser, who was a sound and good musician, caused quite an excitement in that secluded corner of the Ardennes. La Val Dieu was several leagues from Givet, but Méhul often walked over to hear Hauser ; and at length, with the consent of his father, was admitted into the convent, and became the most diligent, as he was the most gifted, of the eight pupils under Hauser's training. At 14 he became deputy-organist ; and a distinguished amateur who heard him play was so struck by his evident power of imagination, that he determined to take him to Paris, and in 1778 Méhul bade farewell to the flowers he loved to cultivate, and the instructor who had put him in the way to become a great musician. On his arrival in Paris he at once went to Edelmann for instruction in pianoforte-playing and composition. To earn his bread he gave lessons, and composed two sonatas (1781) which bear no traces of a master mind ; but this was not the line in which he was destined to distinction. In 1779 he was present at the first performance of ' Iphigénie en Tauride,' and the effect produced on one with his cultivated intellect, his love of the beautiful, and passionate though reserved nature, was immense. He expressed his admiration to Gluck himself, who received the young enthusiast graciously, gave him valuable advice, and undertook his instruction in the philosophical and poetical parts of music. Encouraged by the success of a cantata with orchestra composed to one of Rousseau's sacred odes, and produced at the Concert Spirituel in Mar. 1782, he might have gone on writing church music, had not Gluck shown him his true vocation, and directed his attention to the stage. Solely for practice, he composed, one after another, three operas, ' Psyché et l'Amour,' a pastoral by Voisenon previously set by Saint Amans ; ' Anacréon,' the third act of a ballet by Bernard and Rameau, produced in 1757 as ' Les Surprises de l'Amour'; and ' Lausus et Lydie,' three acts, to a libretto adapted by Valadier from Marmontel. These unpublished scores are lost, no trace of them being discoverable in any of the public libraries of Paris.

Méhul now felt himself in a position to appear before the public, and Valadier having furnished him with the libretto of ' Cora et Alonzo,' four acts, also taken from Marmontel, the score was soon ready, and accepted by the Opéra, but there the matter ended. Tired of waiting, he resolved to try his fortune at another theatre, and having made the acquaintance of Hoffmann he obtained from him the libretto of ' Euphrosine et Coradin, ou le Tyran corrigé,' three acts (Sept. 4, 1790). In this opéra-comique the public recognised at once a force, a sincerity of accent, a dramatic truth, and a gift of accurately expressing the meaning of the words, which were throughout the main characteristics of Méhul's mature genius. Its success was instantaneous ; and the duet ' Gardez-vous de la jalousie,' the close of which contains a modulation as unexpected as it is effective, speedily became a favourite throughout France. Henceforth Méhul had ample opportunities of satisfying his productive instinct, and he brought out successively :

' Cora ' (1791) ; ' Stratonice ' (May 3, 1792) ; ' Le jeune Sage et le vieux Fou ' (1793) ; and the third act of ' Le Jugement de Paris ' (the other acts by Haydn and Pleyel) ; ' Horatius Coclès ' and ' Mélidore et Phrosine ' (1794) ; ' La Caverne ' (1795), not so successful as Lesueur's on the same subject ; ' Doria ' (1795) ; ' Le Jeune Henri ' (1797) ; ' Adrien ' (June 4) and ' Ariodant ' (Oct. 11, 1799) ; ' Épicure,' with Cherubini (Mar. 14), and ' Bion ' (Dec. 27, 1800) ; ' L' Irato, ou l'Emporté ' (Feb. 17, 1801) ; ' Une Folie ' (Apr. 4), ' Le Trésor supposé,' ' Joanna ' and ' L'Heureux malgré lui ' (1802) ; ' Héléna ' and ' Le Baiser et la quittance,' with Kreutzer, Boieldieu, and Nicolo (1803) ; ' Les Deux Aveugles de Tolède ' (Jan. 28), ' Uthal ' (May 17), and ' Gabrielle d'Estrées ' (June 25, 1806) ; ' Joseph ' (Feb. 17, 1807).

Astonishing as it may seem, these twenty-four operas were not the only works Méhul produced within seventeen years. He composed and published in addition many patriotic songs and cantatas, among others the ' Chant national du 14 juillet,' the ' Chant du départ,' the ' Chant

du retour,' the ' Chanson de Roland,' and choruses to ' Timoléon ' (1794), a tragedy by Joseph Chénier ; two ballets, ' La Dansomanie' (1800) and ' Daphnis et Pandrose ' ; several operettas, and other ' morceaux de circonstance,' such as ' Le Pont de Lodi,' etc., all unpublished except the ' Chant lyrique ' for the inauguration of the statue voted to Napoleon by the Institut. A Mass, written for the coronation of Napoleon, but not performed then, was published in Paris in 1879.

The epoch at which he composed ' Uthal ' and ' Joseph ' was the culminating point of Méhul's career. He was already a member of the Institut (1795) and a chevalier of the Legion of Honour (1802), and had been inspector of instruction at the Conservatoire from its foundation. His pupils looked up to him and he was a favourite in the best society, but such homage did not blind him to the fact that in science his colleagues Cherubini and Catel were his superiors, owing to his want of early systematic training. This accounts for his laborious efforts to change his style and excel in more than one department of music. His symphonies, though performed at the Conservatoire, cannot rank with those of Haydn and Mozart ; indeed none of his other orchestral works rise to the level of his overtures Of his ballets ' Le Retour d'Ulysse ' (1807), and ' Persée et Andromède ' (1810) in which he introduced many pieces from ' Ariodant,' were well received, but ' Les Amazones, ou la fondation de Thèbes ' (1811) disappeared after nine performances. An opéra-comique in one act, ' Le Prince Troubadour ' (1813), was not more successful, and in 1814 he collaborated with Paër, Berton and Kreutzer in ' L'Oriflamme ' ; his last work, ' La Journée aux aventures,' three acts (Nov. 16, 1816), kept the boards for some time. Its success was partly due to its being known at the time that Méhul was dying of consumption. Two months after its production he was sent to Provence, but the change came too late ; he returned to Paris, and died there. Besides six unpublished operas composed between 1787 and 1797, he left the unfinished score of ' Valentine de Milan,' a three-act opéra-comique, completed by his nephew and pupil DAUSSOIGNE-MÉHUL (q.v.) (b. Givet, June 10, 1790 ; d. Liège, Mar. 10, 1875), and produced Nov. 28, 1822.

The most conspicuous quality of Méhul's work as a whole is its absolute passion. This is exemplified most strikingly in ' Stratonice ' and ' Ariodant.' Not less obvious are the traces of the various influences under which he passed. Between ' Ariodant ' and ' Joseph ' must be placed all those repeated attempts to vary his style and convince his detractors that he could compose light and graceful airs as well as grand, pathetic and sustained melodies, which cannot be considered as anything but failures, although the ignorant amateurs of the day pronounced

'L' Irato' to be true Italian music. 'Joseph,' which dates from the midst of the Revolution, before the Empire, belongs to a different epoch, and to a different class of ideas. Méhul's noble character, his refined sentiment, and religious tendencies, the traces of his early education, his acquaintance with the church modes and plain-song, and his power of writing excellent church music, are all apparent in this powerful work, the simplicity, grandeur and dramatic truth of which will always command the admiration of impartial musicians.

Méhul was not so fortunate as Grétry in finding a poet whose creative faculties harmonised thoroughly with his own; and he was fascinated by any subject—antique, chivalrous, Ossianic, Spanish, patriarchal or biblical—so long as it afforded him opportunities for local colouring, the importance of which he often exaggerated. His overtures to 'Le Jeune Henri,' 'Horatius Coclès,' 'Timoléon,' and 'Les Deux Aveugles de Tolède' are, however, incomparably superior to anything of the kind which preceded them; and most striking are such passages as the introduction to 'Ariodant,' where three violoncellos and a trombone hold a kind of dialogue, and that in 'Mélidore et Phrosine,' where four horns, which have a complete part throughout the score, accompany the voice of a dying man with a kind of smothered rattle. In 'Uthal' the violins are entirely absent, their places being taken by the violas, in order to produce a soft and misty effect. Grétry was shocked at this innovation, and so wearied by its monotony that he cried, on leaving the theatre after the first performance, 'Six francs for a chanterelle (E-string)!'

Though Méhul's new and ingenious combinations were not always successful, and though his melodies were often wanting in that life and dash which rouse an audience, it must be acknowledged that his work bears the stamp of a very individual mind and character, and the impress of that mighty race of 1789, with whom to will was to do, but amongst whose many gifts that of grace was too often wanting. Had he but possessed this fascinating quality, Méhul might have been the Mozart of France. As it is, we cannot withhold our admiration from the man who carried on Gluck's work with even more than Gluck's musical skill, regenerated opéra-comique, and placed himself at the head of the composers of his own time and nation.

A portrait[1] of Méhul exists in a remarkable print by Quenedey, 1808. Quatremère de Quincy pronounced his eulogium at the Institut in Oct. 1818, and Vieillard, one of his intimate friends, published an interesting *Notice* of him (Paris, 1859). The library of the Conservatoire contains many of his auto-

[1] A woodcut therefrom was given in former editions of this Dictionary

graphs, several being fragments of unpublished operas. The writer of this article discovered among them 'La Naissance d'Oscar Leclerc,' not elsewhere mentioned, an opéra-comique 'La Taupe,' and an 'Ouverture burlesque' for piano, violin and reeds, interesting merely as musical curiosities. A statue of Méhul was unveiled at Givet, Oct. 2, 1892.

BIBL.—*Fétis* and Supplement *Q.-L.*; *Encyclopédie de la Musique et Dictionnaire du Conservatoire*: RADIGUER, *France, XVIIIe-XIXe siècles*; A. POUGIN, *Méhul, sa vie, son génie* (Paris, 1889); M. THIERY, *Notice sur Méhul* (Paris, 1892); R. BRANCOUR, *Méhul* (Paris, Laurens, 1913); *Revue musicale*, Nov. 1925; G. DE SAINT FOIX, *Les Premiers Pianistes parisiens*: *Méhul*. Reprints: Op. 2, Sonata III., for pianoforte and violin *ad libitum*, edited by Mme. M. Gallet (Paris, 1917, École de gravure féminine) out of print; Symphonie II. (piano score, revision by P. Vidal, Paris, Sénart). Breitkopf and Härtel, op. 1, Piano Sonatas; 2 Symphonies.
G. C.

MEIBOM (Latin, MEIBOMIUS), MARCUS (*b.* Toenningen, Schleswig-Holstein, early 17th century; *d.* Utrecht, 1711), learned historian of music.

His great work, *Antiquae musicae auctores septem graece et latine* (Amsterdam, Elzevir), was published in 1652, which suggests that the date of his birth can hardly have been as late as 1626 as commonly stated. The work was dedicated to Queen Christina of Sweden, at whose court he resided for some time. On one occasion, however, while singing at the Queen's request his version of an ancient Greek melody, the whole court burst out laughing, and Meibom, imagining that the Queen's physician Bourdelot was the instigator of this unseemly mirth, gave him a box on the ear, and was in consequence dismissed. He took refuge with Frederick III. of Denmark, who gave him a professorship at Upsala, but he soon returned to Holland. Having endeavoured in vain to find a capitalist who would carry into execution his plan of restoring the ancient triremes, he came to England in 1674 with the view of making arrangements for a new edition of the Old Testament. This project also failed, and he returned to Holland. The book already mentioned is one of the most valuable sources of information on ancient music, and may be considered a precursor of Gerber and Coussemaker. Its usefulness is much enhanced in the modern reprints, notably that by Karl von Jan (1895). For his numerous works on music and geometry the reader is referred to *Fétis*.
F. G.

MEILAND, JACOB (*b.* Senftenberg in Saxony, *c.* 1542; *d.* 1577), was brought up as a chorister in the Saxon Court Chapel at Dresden. After attending the University of Leipzig, and spending some time in travelling, he was appointed Kapellmeister to the Margrave of Anspach, till the dissolution of this chapel in 1574. The rest of his life, to his early death, Meiland spent chiefly as an invalid at Frankfort-on-the-Main, though busy to the last in bringing out his fairly numerous publications. He was highly thought of in his time as a composer of Latin and German motets, and considered even the equal of Orlando Lassus. His harmonies are often rugged, after the manner of Orlando. In the composition of German secular songs he was one of the first to introduce into Germany the Italian Villanella style, paying more attention to the rhythmical declamation of the words than to the artifices of counterpoint. His works are:

1. Cantiones sacrae, 1564, 17 Nos. *a* 5 and 6
2. Neue auserlesene teutsche Liedlein, 1569, 15 Nos. *a* 4 and 5.
3. Selectae cantiones, 1572, 17 Nos. *a* 5 and 6.
4. Sacrae aliquot cantiones latinae et germanicae, 1575, 33 Nos. *a* 4 and 5.
5. Neue auserlesene teutsche Gesäng, 1575, 18 Nos. 4 and 5.
6. Cantiones novae, etc., 1576, 19 Nos. *a* 5.
7. Cygneae cantiones latinae et germanicae, 1590, 22 Nos. *a* 4 and 5.

Other works, including three settings of the Passion, are preserved in MS. Three Latin motets were republished in Commer's *Musica sacra*, and two German sacred songs *a* 4 are contained in Schöberlein.   J. R. M.

MEINARDUS, LUDWIG SIEGFRIED (*b.* Hooksiel, Oldenburg, Sept. 17, 1827 ; *d.* Bielefeld, July 12, 1896), composer, teacher and writer on music, was at first educated at the Gymnasium at Jever, where his father held an official post. He was intended to study theology, but was at length allowed to devote himself to the art, his parents imposing the curious condition that he was to become a public performer on some instrument. To this end he took up the violoncello, learning what he could from the Stadtmusikus of the place, who was a violinist. After making himself ill with excessive practice, he returned to school, and it was not till he had finished his studies there that he finally determined, on the advice of Schumann, who had seen some of his compositions, to embrace the profession of a composer. At Christmas, in 1846, he entered the Leipzig Conservatorium, but after half a year, finding that private instruction from Riccius would be more to his advantage, he accordingly remained with him for two years. In 1850 he went to Berlin in order to study with A. B. Marx, but for some reason or other he fell under the suspicions of the police, and was not allowed to remain. He betook himself to Liszt at Weimar, where he stayed some months, after which he went to Erfurt as conductor of a small theatrical company, and subsequently in a similar capacity to Nordhausen. At last he was provided with better credentials, and succeeded in remaining in Berlin. In 1853, having finished his education with Marx, he was appointed conductor of the Singakademie at Glogau, where he remained until, in obedience to a call from Julius Rietz, he went to the Dresden Conservatorium as a teacher in 1865. In 1874 he settled in Hamburg, where he was for many years continuously active as a composer and as critic of the *Hamburger Korrespondent*. In 1887 he moved to Bielefeld, to take up a post as organist, and died there. His most prominent compositions are the oratorios ' Simon Petrus,' ' Gideon,' ' König Salomo,' ' Luther in Worms,' ' Odrun ' ; two operas, ' Bahnesa ' (three acts, finished

1881) and ' Doktor Sassafras ' (neither of them performed) ; four ballads for chorus, ' Rolands Schwanenlied,' ' Frau Hitt,' ' Die Nonne,' ' Jung Baldurs Sieg ' ; two symphonies, and many chamber compositions. A memoir of Mattheson, an autobiographical sketch, and collected criticisms are his most important contributions to literature.   M.

MEISTERSCHULE, see BERLIN.

MEISTERSINGER (Ger. = Master-singers), the name given to the guilds of poet-musicians which flourished in the 14th-16th centuries in various towns of Germany. The founder of the first guild is supposed to have been Heinrich von Meissen, called Frauenlob, who instituted a company at Mainz in 1311. As to the original signification of the name authorities are divided, but it seems fairly certain that as in other crafts the grades of apprentice, journeyman and master were differentiated, so the members of these guilds passed successively through the stages of Schüler, Schulfreund, Sänger, Dichter and Meister. For a list of famous mastersingers, the chief of whom was Hans Sachs, see SONG, subsection GERMANY. The guild was a kind of counterpart, in what would now be called the middle classes of German society, to the MINNESINGER, who were exclusively of noble birth.   M.

BIBLIOGRAPHY

ADAM PUSCHMANN : *Gründlicher Bericht des deutschen Meistergesangs zusamt der Tablatur.* (1571, reprinted by Niemeyer.)
WAGENSEIL : *Buch von der Meistersinger holdseliger Kunst.* (1697.)
GRIMM : *Über den altdeutschen Meistergesang.* (1811.)
SCHNORR VON CAROLSFELD : *Zur Geschichte des deutschen Meistergesangs.* (1872.)
RUNGE : *Über die Notation des Meistersangs.* (1907.)
K. DRESCHER : *Nürnberger Meistersinger. Protokolle von 1575 bis 1689.* 2 vols. (1898.)
G. MÜNZER : *Über die Notation der Meistersinger.*
Das Singebuch des Adam Puschmann (numerous melodies). (1907.)
A. KÜHN : *Rhythmik und Melodik Michel Behaims.* (1907.)

MEISTERSINGER VON NÜRNBERG, DIE, opera in 3 acts ; words and music by Wagner, completed in Oct. 1867, and produced at Munich, June 21, 1868 (the overture was first performed at Leipzig, Nov. 1, 1862) ; in England, under Richter, Drury Lane, May 30, 1882 ; New York, Metropolitan Opera House, Jan. 4, 1886 ; Covent Garden, in Italian (G. Mazzucato), July 13, 1889 ; in English, Carl Rosa Co., Manchester, Apr. 16, 1896 ; Paris, Opéra, Nov. 10, 1897.   G.

MEL, RINALDO DEL, ' Gentilhuomo fiammengo,' and distinguished composer of the 16th century. The date of his birth is not known, but his nationality is assured, not only by the above title, which appears on more than one of his works, but by his own words, ' la natione nostra fiammengo.' In the ' Sacrae cantiones ' of 1589, he implies that Schlettstadt in Lorraine was his birthplace. He is not to be confused with Gaudio Mell, a name which Adami,[1] Liberati[2] and Martini[3] give to GOUDIMEL (*q.v.*).

[1] *Osservazioni per ben regolare Capella pontif.* (Rome, 1711). (B.M. C. 20 c.)
[2] *Lettera in risposta ad una del Sig. Pers.* (B.M. 556 c. 8.)
[3] *Giudicio di Apollo* bound up with third volume of Martini's *Storia della musica.* (B.M. 557 ∞.)

Having served Sebastian, King of Portugal, and his successor, Cardinal don Henriquez, as maestro de capilla, he arrived in Rome in 1580. This change in his career may be accounted for by the annexation of Portugal to Spain in that year. If Philip II. was unwilling to keep up a useless retinue in Lisbon, he would certainly make no exception in favour of ' Flemish gentle-men,' who indeed were never to his liking. At Rome, Mel entered the service of Cardinal Paleotto, and Baini[1] declared that he also studied under Palestrina. His publications began in 1581, with a first book of motets, a 4-8, and between that year and 1595 he published five books of motets and fifteen books of mad-rigals, besides contributing to various collections which carried his name from Rome to Venice, Nuremberg, Antwerp and Munich. (See Q.-L.)

Up to 1590 he probably lived chiefly in Rome, though we find him at Liège in 1587,[2] where some of his family were in the service of Ernest, Duke of Bavaria, in whose employ we find the composer in the following year. In 1591 he was again in the service of Cardinal Gabriel Paleotto, archbishop of Bologna, who had him-self some knowledge of music.[3] When the diocese of Sabina was placed under Paleotto's charge in 1591 he founded a college, improved the cathedral at Magliano and made many changes in the internal government. The appointment of a new maestro di cappella agrees well enough with these facts, and it is in the year 1591 that we hear of Mel's appointment to the cathedral and the new college. He dates from Calvi, a little town near Magliano, Mar. 20, 1593, and from Magliano[4] itself, 1595. From this time his publications cease, and we have no further record of him. He is said to have been already well advanced in life when he left Portugal, and by this time was probably an old man. So we may assume that the end of life was near, and that he did not long survive Palestrina.

Proske prints a Litany in the ' Musica divina,' Ann. II. vol. iii. (Ratisbon, 1869), and Commer's 'Musica sacra' contains seven motets and a litany; the Motet Society published an anthem, ' O praise the Lord,' adapted by Aldrich from a work of Mel, in vol. iii. p. 128.

J. R. S.-B.

BIBL.—G. VAN DOORSLAER, René del Mel, compositeur du XVIe siècle (I. 1554–I. 1598). (With a very full bibliography.) Annales de l'Académie Royale d'Archéologie de Belgique. 6th ser. tom. 9, ev. 4, pp. 221-88.

MELANI, a 17th-century sexton of Pistoja, eight of whose sons became eminent musicians. (1) JACOPO (b. Pistoja, July 6, 1623) was, with Mazzocchi and others, one of the pioneers of comic opera in Rome, and was famous for his arias on a basso ostinato. Of his operas which appeared between 1657–73 only three, and a

[1] Memorie di Palestrina
[2] Madrigali a 6 (Antwerp, 1588). See also Fétis, Biographie, under Melle, Renaut de.
[3] See Fantuzzi, Notizie delli scrittori bolognesi (Bologna, 1788).
[4] See dedication of ' Liber 5us motectorum ' (Venice, 1595).

few libretti, are still in existence. (2) ALESS-ANDRO (d. Rome, 1703), maestro di cappella successively of St. Petronio, Bologna (1660), S. Maria Maggiore, Rome (from 1667), S. Luigi de Francesi, Rome (from 1672), composer of operas, oratorios, cantatas, motets and other church music, arias, etc. (3) ANTONIO, in the service of Archduke Ferdinand Karl of Austria (1659), composed Scherzi Musicali, etc., for 2 violins and viola (Innspruck, 1659). (4) BARTOLOMEO (b. Pistoja, Mar. 6, 1634), 1657–58 singer in the Munich court chapel, when he was arrested for political intrigues. (5)_DOMENICO (d. before Nov. 12, 1693), castrato at the Dresden court from 1654, returned to Italy in 1680 as agent of the Elector. (6) NICOLA, also castrato at the Dresden court from 1654. (7) ATTO (b. Pistoja, Mar. 31, 1626; d. 1714), castrato, sang in the title rôle of Rossi's Orfeo at Paris in 1647. (8) FRANCESCO MARIA, Servite monk under the name of Filippo (b. Pistoja, Nov. 3, 1628), also a castrato, who sang Amastris in Cavalli's ' Serse ' at Paris in 1660. (For further particulars see Riemann; also Q.-L.)

MELBA, DAME NELLIE (b. Burnley on the ' Yarra Braes,' near Melbourne, May 19, 1861), is the professional name and title of Helen Porter Armstrong (née Mitchell), celebrated operatic soprano.

Her father, David Mitchell, a Scottish con-tractor, had settled in Australia. He was proud of his child's precocious musical talent, and allowed her to sing at a concert in the Richmond (Melbourne) Town Hall when only 6 years old. He objected, however, to her adopting music as a profession. It was only after her marriage in 1882 to Captain Charles Armstrong that the young soprano finally determined to follow a musical career ; nor did she come to Europe until the spring of 1886, when, after a solitary appearance at Prince's Hall, London (June 1), she went to Paris to study under Madame Marchesi.

Her period of tutelage was rapid and brilliant, for after twelve months' work her teacher pro-nounced her ready for the stage, and on Oct. 12, 1887, she made her début as Gilda at the Théâtre de la Monnaie, Brussels, under the name of ' Melba,' obviously derived from that of her native city, Melbourne. She achieved instantaneous success, and was soon afterwards engaged by Harris for his first season of Italian Opera at Covent Garden in 1888, where she appeared as Lucia on May 24.

From the outset the London public was rapturous in its warmth. Calmer critics readily perceived what was still lacking to the equip-ment of a really great and finished artist ; but none could gainsay the uncommon character of her endowments—the extraordinary beauty of her silvery tone, its bright, ' girlish ' quality and remarkable evenness throughout a compass of two and a half octaves (b flat to f'''), and above all the excellence of a method that plainly owed as much to nature as it did to art. In her brilliant execution of the most difficult *fioriture* nothing impressed more than the wonderful flexibility of the organ, unless it was the unfailing ease and perfect sense of restraint with which the singer accomplished her *tours de force.* This rare faculty for using her tone within rather than beyond its true limit of resonant power has remained one of the most striking and beneficial features of Melba's method. Once, in America, she was so ill-advised as to essay the part of Brünnhilde in ' Siegfried.' But it was for a single night only. Fortunately she perceived that disaster must ensue, and took care never to repeat her error.

In the spring of 1889 Mme. Melba made her début at the Paris Opéra, and sang Ophélie with great success to the Hamlet of Lassalle. She also prepared the rôles of Marguerite and Juliette under the personal instruction of Gounod, and later in the year undertook both at Covent Garden, where ' Roméo et Juliette ' was then performed in French for the first time. In conjunction with Jean and Edouard de Reszke she shared a memorable triumph in these operas, while her vocal and dramatic resources alike manifested a marked advance. Thenceforward she took part regularly in every Covent Garden season without missing a single summer. In 1890 Mme. Melba added to her repertory the parts of Elsa (' Lohengrin ') and Esmeralda (in the French revival of Goring Thomas's charming opera) ; subsequently Violetta in ' La Traviata,' Micaela in ' Carmen,' Rosina in ' Il Barbiere,' and the Queen in ' Les Huguenots.' In 1894 she created here the rôle of Nedda in ' Pagliacci,' and ten years later that of Hélène in the opera so named, written for her by Camille Saint-Saëns.

In 1891 she accompanied the De Reszkes to St. Petersburg, by special invitation of the Czar, and was welcomed there with extraordinary warmth. In 1892 she sang at La Scala, Milan, and followed up her triumphs there with a brilliant tour through Italy. Next year she fulfilled the first of many successful engagements in the United States, making her début with the De Reszkes at Chicago during the ' World's Fair.' In 1894 she sang for the first time at the Handel Festival (Selection Day). In 1902, after an absence of sixteen years, she revisited Australia, making her reappearance in Melbourne on Sept. 27, and subsequently gave concerts at Sydney, Brisbane, Adelaide and many other towns. During the next twenty years she continued to travel much, to work constantly, and to add to her honours in different parts of the world ; dividing her home-life pretty equally between England and Australia. She has also received numerous decorations, among the more prominent being that

of a Dame Commander of the Order of the British Empire.

Among her more notable tours were those in Canada and the United States in 1903. It was while travelling there that she studied the rôle of Hélène in Saint-Saëns's opera, already mentioned, which she first created at Monte Carlo in Jan. 1904, and also at Covent Garden on June 20 of the same year. During that season she organised a very successful concert at the Queen's Hall in aid of Queen Charlotte's Hospital ; and, *inter alia*, sang for King Edward and Queen Alexandra at Buckingham Palace for the entertainment of the Archduke Franz Ferdinand of Austria, whose assassination at Serajevo in July 1914 was the signal for the outbreak of the Great War. On this occasion the Queen pinned on her breast the Order of Science, Art and Music. Whilst in New York the following winter she was compelled by a long and dangerous illness to cancel most of her tour, but sang once in ' La Bohème ' at the Metropolitan Opera House. She appeared regularly at Covent Garden, and in 1905 her English engagements included the Bristol Musical Festival.

In January 1907 the appearances of Dame Melba at the Manhattan Opera House, New York, rescued from financial disaster Oscar Hammerstein's initial enterprise in the domain of grand opera. She then sang the parts of Lucia, Gilda, Mimi and Violetta with, if possible, greater success than ever before in America, and the houses were extraordinary. Later in the year she revisited Australia, chiefly for a holiday, but in May 1908 was back in London taking part at a gala performance at Covent Garden in honour of President Fallières. And so the record went on for year after year, until 1926, when her final farewells of the public were announced—in opera at Covent Garden in the summer, and in the concert room at the Royal Albert Hall in the autumn.

H. K.

BIBL.—AGNES MURPHY, *Nellie Melba.* (1909.)

MELCHISSÉDEC, PIERRE LÉON (*b.* Clermont - Ferrand, Puy - de - Dôme, May 7, 1843 ; *d.* Paris, Mar. 23, 1925), baritone singer. Educated at the Paris Conservatoire, he won the 2nd prize for opera and opéra-comique in 1865, and made his début the same year at the Opéra-Comique in ' Le Toréador ' and ' Le Châlet ' of Adolphe Adam. He created the principal parts in ' Le Premier Jour de bonheur ' (Auber, 1868), Ourrias in ' Mireille ' (Gounod, 1874), and ' L'Amour africain ' (Paladilhe, 1875). He went on to the Théâtre-Lyrique, first appearing there in 1876 in V. Joncière's ' Dimitri ' ; and there created the chief parts in ' Paul et Virginie ' (V. Massé) and ' Le Timbre d'argent ' (Saint-Saëns, 1877), etc.

Melchissédec joined the Opéra, Nov. 17, 1879, in ' Les Huguenots,' and remained there until 1892. Among his most important rôles may be mentioned those in 'Le Tribut de Zamora' (Gounod, 1881), 'Françoise de Rimini' (Ambroise Thomas, 1882), 'Le Cid' (Massenet, 1885), 'Roméo et Juliette' (Gounod, 1888), etc.

Melchissédec was professor of vocal declamation at the Conservatoire, 1894–1923; among his pupils may be mentioned Gresse, Gilly, Friant, Mmes. Chenal, Courso, A. Daumas, etc. He was an excellent singer, but was generally regarded as an inferior actor. He possessed a fine baritone, well-modulated, and was a capable vocalist. He published two works of instruction : *Pour chanter* ; *ce qu'il faut savoir* ; *ma méthode* (1913) ; and *Le Chant, la déclamation lyrique* (1924).

BIBL.—*Comoedia* (Apr. 25, 1913, Mar. 25, 1925).

J. G. P.

MELGOUNOV, JULIUS NICHOLAEVICH (*b.* Vetlouga, Govt. of Kostroma, Aug. 30 (Sept. 12), 1846 ; *d.* Moscow, Mar. 19/31, 1893), pianist and musical writer. In his school days he took pianoforte lessons with Dreyschock, and at 18 made his début in St. Petersburg as a pianist. He studied theory with Laroche, and was for a short time a student of the Moscow Conservatoire. About 1875 Melgounov became acquainted with Rudolph WESTPHAL (*q.v.*), then professor in the Katkov Lycée at Moscow. Melgounov was attracted to Westphal's theories, and co-operated with him in bringing out ten of Bach's fugues in a special edition, with a preface entitled : 'The rhythmic execution of Bach's Fugues.' When, shortly afterwards, Westphal gave a series of sixty concerts in Germany in order to propagate his views upon musical rhythm, Melgounov accompanied him as pianist. He also toured in Russia with the violinist Laub and the violoncellist Carl Davidov. Melgounov's most important work was the elaboration of a more accurate method of noting down the folksongs. The results of his researches in popular music are published under the following title :

'Russian Songs, written down directly from the singing of the people, transcribed for pianoforte with text ; Part I. with the co-operation of Klenovsky, Moscow, 1879 ; Part II. with the co-operation of Blaramberg, St. Petersburg, 1885.'

His leading ideas were : that the folk-songs are based upon two diatonic scales, the major and natural minor, and that the intervals of the latter are exactly the same as those of the major reversed $\begin{cases} e & d & c & b & a & g & fe \\ 1T. & 1T. & \frac{1}{2}T. & 1T. & 1T. & 1T. & \frac{1}{2}T \end{cases}$; that they are sung 'polyphonically,' not, as was once erroneously supposed, in unison ; that their harmony is formed by working out the principal melody in independent contrapuntal parts (*podgoloski*), and unison is only found at the close of the songs, or in their rhythmic sections ; that the rhythm is inseparably connected with the text and conforms to the rhythmic principles of the Greeks. Melgounov

finds no chromatic or enharmonic changes in the folk-songs, and the perfect fifth is of rare occurrence. By writing down all the secondary parts, Melgounov revealed the entire structure of the songs. As these *podgoloski* are generally free improvisations, and to write them all down from ear at once is practically impossible, it often happens in Melgounov's songs that all his secondary parts do not harmonise with the principal melody. Subsequently Mme. Eugénie Liniev carried Melgounov's work much farther, and by the help of the phonograph obtained some very accurate records of the peasant partsongs, just as they are sung by the people. Besides the above publication, Melgounov left the following treatises on this subject : *On Russian National Music* (*Russ. Ethnographical Review*, v. vi.), *A Correct Method of Writing Down the Folk-songs, The Rhythm of the Slavonic Folk-songs*, etc.

R. N.

MELISMA (Gr. μέλισμα, a 'song'). (1) In plain-song the term is used for a group of notes set to a single syllable ; hence the more elaborate plain-song style is often called melismatic.

W. H. F.

(2) Any kind of air or melody, as opposed to recitative or other music of a purely declamatory character. It is frequently used in the sense of *fioritura* or even *cadenza*.

MELL, DAVIS, familiarly called Davie Mell (*b.* Wilton, near Salisbury, Nov. 15, 1604), an eminent violinist and clockmaker, resident in London about the middle of the 17th century, was one of the signatories of the Cromwellian petition for the establishment of a national college of music,[1] and is honourably mentioned by Aubrey and Anthony Wood. In the year 1657 he visited Oxford, where, as we learn from Wood's *Diary* :

'Peter Pett, Will. Bull, Ken. Digby, and others of Allsoules, as also A. W. did give him a very handsome entertainment in the Taverne cal'd " The Salutation" in S. Marie's Parish. . . . The Company did look upon Mr. Mell to have a prodigious hand on the Violin, & they thought that no person, as all in London did, could go beyond him. But, when Tho. Baltzar, an Outlander, came to Oxon. in the next yeare, they had other thoughts of Mr. Mell, who, tho he play'd farr sweeter than Baltzar, yet Baltzar's hand was more quick, & could run it insensibly to the end of the Finger-board.'

He succeeded Laniere as Master of the King's Band at the Restoration, and was followed, at the close of 1661, by Thomas BALTZAR (*q.v.*). Pieces by him are in Christopher Simpson's 'Division Violin,' 1684.

Aubrey[2] tells a curious story of a child of Mell's, who was cured of a crooked back by the touch of a dead hand.

W. S. R.

MELLON, ALFRED (*b.* London, Apr. 17, 1821; *d.* Mar. 27, 1867), lived first at Birmingham, became a violinist in the opera and other orchestras, and afterwards leader of the ballet at the Royal Italian Opera, Covent Garden. He

1 Davey, *Hist. of English Music* (1922), p. 272.
2 *Miscellanies*, under the article 'Miranda.'

was next director of the music at the Haymarket and Adelphi theatres, and subsequently conductor of the Pyne and Harrison English Opera Company, which in 1859 produced his opera, ' Victorine,' at Covent Garden ; he was conductor of the Musical Society, and of the Promenade Concerts which for several seasons were given under his name at Covent Garden, begun in the Floral Hall, in Aug. 1860. In Sept. 1865 he was chosen conductor of the Liverpool Philharmonic Society. He married Miss Woolgar (*d.* Sept. 8, 1909), a well-known actress. He is buried in Brompton Cemetery.

W. H. H.

MELNGAILIS, E., see LATVIAN MUSIC.

MELODISTS' CLUB, THE (1825-1856), a society founded in 1825 by admirers of Charles Dibdin, ' for the promotion of ballad composition and melody.' In 1827 and 1828 a library was formed, and prizes offered for songs ; and the prize songs were afterwards published in a volume. In 1833 two prizes of ten guineas were offered for songs in the style of Arne, Shield or Dibdin, and gained by Blewitt and Hobbs. In 1837 prizes of five guineas for words and ten guineas for music of a song were gained by Wilson and Hobbs for the song ' Send round the wine.' The object of the Club was well described by Sir H. Bishop in presenting some music to the Library in 1840 :

' It is from my perfect conviction that good and appropriate melody is the chief attribute of excellence in music of every style, from the simple ballad to the most elaborate composition, that I hail the establishment of the Melodists' Club, from its patronage of native genius, and its encouragement of melody, as essentially calculated to aid the cause of the musical art in this country.'

The entrance-fee was five guineas, and the subscription eight guineas. Its professional members included Sir George Smart, Braham, Balfe, T. Cooke, Hawes, Sterndale Bennett and other eminent English musicians. Among the artists who took part in the music in its earlier day were J. B. Cramer, Moscheles, Hummel, Field, Benedict, Lipinski. T. Cooke was musical director, and John Parry hon. secretary.

C. M.

MELODRAMA (Fr. *mélodrame* ; Ger. *Melodram*), a kind of dramatic composition in which the actor recites his part while the orchestra plays a more or less elaborate commentary on the situation of the moment, as in the classic instance of the grave-digging scene in ' Fidelio,' the dream in ' Egmont,' the incantation scene in ' Der Freischütz ' and scenes in Mendelssohn's ' Midsummer Night's Dream.' For earlier examples see DUODRAMA.

The same principle has been adopted for concert-room performance in the shape of recitations to music, for which the term declamation has often been used, and of which examples are Schubert's ' Abschied von der Erde,' Schumann's ' Schön Hedwig ' (Hebbel), op. 106 ; ' Vom Haideknabe ' (Hebbel), and Shelley's

' Fugitives,' op. 122. Hiller's ' Vom Pagen und der Königstochter ' (Geibel) is a slighter specimen. In these ' ballads for declamation ' the accompaniment is always for pianoforte, and as a kind of impromptu adjunct to recitations the same instrument came into use some years ago in connexion with the recitals of Clifford Harrison. A long series of ' Recitation Music,' *i.e.* compositions for piano intended to accompany the declamation of various well-known poems, was written by Stanley Hawley, and a shorter series by Sir A. C. Mackenzie came out about the same time. A more important work was the musical accompaniment to Tennyson's *Enoch Arden* by Richard Strauss (1902).

The melodrama has been much cultivated in Czecho-Slovakia, *e.g.* see FIBICH; JANÁČEK, etc.   M.; revd. N. C. G.

MELODY is the general term vaguely used to denote successions of single notes which are musically effective. It is sometimes used as if synonymous with TUNE or AIR (*q.v.*), but in point of fact many several portions of either tunes or airs may be accurately characterised as ' melody ' which could not reasonably be made to carry the name of the whole of which they form only a part.

Tunes and airs are for the most part constructively and definitely complete, and by following certain laws in the distribution of the phrases and the balance of the groups of rhythms, convey a total impression to the hearer (see FORM) ; but melody has a more indefinite signification, and need not be a distinct artistic whole according to the accepted laws of art, though it is obvious that to be artistic it must conform to such laws as lie within its range. For example, the term ' melody ' is often with justice applied to the inner parts of fine contrapuntal writing, and examples will occur to every one in numerous choruses, symphonic movements and other instrumental works, where it is so perfectly woven into the substance of the work that it cannot be singled out as a complete tune or air, though it nevertheless stands out from the rest by reason of its greater beauty.

The elements of effect in melody are extremely various and complicated. In the present case it will only be possible to indicate in the slightest manner some of the outlines. In the matter of rhythm there are two things which play a part—the rhythmic qualities of language, and dance rhythms. For example, a language which presents marked contrasts of emphasis in syllables which lie close together will infallibly produce corresponding rhythms in the national music ; and though these may often be considerably smoothed out by civilisation and contact with other peoples, no small quantity pass into and are absorbed in the mass of general music, as characteristic Hungarian rhythms have done through the intervention of Haydn,

Schubert, Brahms and other distinguished composers. (See MAGYAR MUSIC.)

DANCE-RHYTHMS (*q.v.*) play an equally important part, and those rhythms and motions of sound which represent or are the musical counterpart of the more dignified gestures and motions of the body which accompany certain states of feeling, which, with the ancients and some mediæval peoples, formed a beautiful element in dancing (cf. BALLET-DANCING).

In the distribution of the intervals which separate the successive sounds, harmony and harmonic devices appear to have very powerful influence. Even in the times before harmony was a recognised power in music we are often surprised to meet with devices which appear to show a perception of the elements of tonal relationship, which may indicate that a sense of harmony was developing for a great length of time in the human mind before it was definitely recognised by musicians. However, in tunes of barbaric people who have no notion of harmony whatever, passages of melody also occur which to a modern eye look exceedingly like arpeggios or analyses of familiar harmonies; and as it is next to impossible for those who are saturated with the simpler harmonic successions to realise the feelings of people who knew of nothing beyond homophonic or single-toned music, we must conclude that the authors of these tunes had a feeling for the relations of notes to one another, pure and simple, which produced intervals similar to those which we derive from familiar harmonic combinations. Thus we are driven to express their melody in terms of harmony, and to analyse it on that basis; and we are, moreover, often unavoidably deceived in this, for transcribers of national and ancient tunes, being so habituated to harmonic music and to the scales which have been adopted for the purposes of harmony, give garbled versions of the originals without being fully aware of it, or possibly thinking that the tunes were wrong and that they were setting them right. And in some cases the tunes are unmercifully twisted into forms of melody to which an harmonic accompaniment may be adjusted, and thereby their value and interest both to the philosopher and to every musician who hears with understanding ears is considerably impaired. (See IRISH MUSIC.)

Modern melody is almost invariably either actually derived from, or representative of harmony, and is dependent for a great deal of its effect thereupon. In the first place it is immediately representative in one of two ways: either as the upper outline of a series of different chords, and therefore representing changing harmonies; or else by being constructed of different notes taken from the same chord, and therefore representing different phases of permanent harmony. Examples of either of these forms being kept up for any length of time are not very common; of the first the largest number will be found among hymn tunes and other forms of simple note-against-note harmony;—the first phrase of ' Batti batti ' approaches it very nearly, and the second subject of the first movement in Beethoven's Waldstein sonata, or the first four bars of ' Selig sind die Todten ' in Spohr's ' Die letzten Dinge ' are an exact illustration. Of the second form the first subject of Weber's sonata in A♭ is a remarkable example:

since in this no notes foreign to the chord of A♭ are interposed till the penultimate of all. The first subject of the Eroica symphony in like manner represents the chord of E♭, and its perfectly unadorned simplicity adds force to the unexpected C♯, when it appears, and to its yet more unexpected resolution; the first subject of Brahms's violin concerto is a yet further example to the point:

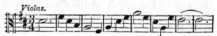

The simplest variation of these forms is arrived at by the interposition of passing notes between notes which are part of the essential chord or chords, as in the following from ' Cet asile aimable,' in Gluck's ' Orphée ':

The notes with asterisks may be all regarded as passing notes between the notes which represent the harmonies.

This often produces successions of notes which are next to each other in the scale; in other words, progression by single degrees, of which we have magnificent examples in some of the versions of the great subject of the latter part of Beethoven's ninth symphony, in the second subject of the first movement of his violin concerto, and in the last chorus of Bach's ' Matthew Passion.' When these passing notes fall on the strong beats of the bar they lead to a new element of melodic effect, both by deferring the essential note of the chord and by lessening the obviousness of its appearance, and by affording one of the many means, with suspensions, appoggiaturas and the like, of obtaining the slurred group of two notes which is alike characteristic of Bach, Gluck, Mozart and other great inventors of melody, as in the following example from Mozart's quartet in D major :

The use of chromatic preparatory passing notes pushes the harmonic substratum still further out of sight, and gives more zest and interest to the melodic outline ; as an example may be taken the following from the second Act of ' Tristan und Isolde ' :

Along with these elements of variety there are devices of turns and such embellishments, such as in the beginning of the celebrated tune in ' Der Freischütz,' which Agatha sings in the second scene of the second act :

Süss ent - - zückt ent - - ge - - gen ihm.

Sequences also, and imitations and anticipations, and all the most elaborate devices of resolution, come into play, such as interpolation of notes between the discordant note and its resolution. Further, there are endless refinements of grouping of phrases, and repetition of rhythms and groups of intervals in condensed forms and in different parts of the scale, which introduce an intellectual element even into the department of pure melody.

Lastly, it may be pointed out that the order and character of the successions of harmony which any special form of melody represents has a great deal to do with its importance. Commonplace tunes represent commonplace and trite successions of harmony in a commonplace way, while melody of a higher order usually represents successions which are in themselves more significant and more freely distributed. The giants of art have produced tunes the melody of which may represent the simplest harmonic successions, but they do it in their own way, and the result is proportionate to their powers and judgment. Unfortunately, the material of the simpler order of melody tends to be exhausted, and a large proportion of new melody has to be constructed on a more complicated basis. To take simple forms is often only to make use of what the great masters rejected ; and indeed the old forms by which tunes are constructively defined are growing so hackneyed that their introduction in many cases is a matter for great tact and consideration. More subtle means of defining the outlines of these forms are possible, as well as more subtle construction in the periods themselves. The result in both cases will be to give melody an appearance of greater expansion and continuity, which it may perfectly have without being either diffuse or chaotic, except to those who have not sufficient musical gift or cultivation to realise it. In instrumental music there is more need for distinctness in the outline of the subjects than in the music of the drama ; but even in that case it may be suggested that a thing may stand out by reason of its own proper individuality quite as well and more artistically than if it is only to be distinguished from its surroundings by having a heavy blank line round it. Melody will always be one of the most important factors in the musical art, but it has gone through different phases, and will go through more. Some insight into its direction may be gained by examination of existing examples, and comparison of average characters at different periods of the history of music, but every fresh great composer who comes is sure to be ahead of our calculations, and if he rings true will tell us things that are not dreamed of in our philosophy.   C. H. H. P.

MELOPHONE, a free-reed instrument in the shape of the guitar or sometimes the violoncello, with a rudimentary keyboard for the left hand on the neck. The bellows, concealed within the body of the instrument, are worked by the right hand. It was invented by Leclerc, a Parisian clockmaker, and introduced by Halévy into one of his operas. (See HARMONIUM.)   F. W. G.

MELOPHONIC SOCIETY, THE, established 1837, ' for the practice of the most classical specimens of choral and other music,' by band and choir, under the management of J. H. Griesbach, H. Westrop, J. Surman and H. J. Banister. The first performance, on Nov. 23, 1837, at Wornum's Music Hall, Store Street, was the ' Creation,' followed during the season by Beethoven's Mass in C, Romberg's Ode 'The Transient and the Eternal,' 'Judas Maccabæus,' and 'St. Paul.'   C. M.

MELOPIANO, see SOSTINENTE PIANOFORTE.

MELSA, DANIEL (b. Warsaw, Aug. 1892), violinist, entered the Conservatoire of Lodz, Poland, at the age of 7, when he already showed some proficiency as a violinist. His studies continued till 1905, when they were interrupted by the revolution and its attendant tragedies (among the victims were his father and sister), but they were resumed in Berlin in 1906 under Carl Flesch. In 1912 he gave his first recital in the Beethoven Saal, playing 3 concertos with orchestra. The following year he appeared in Paris under Nikisch and came to London for the season 1913–14 to give 6 recitals. He was chosen by Clara Butt as soloist during her Empire tour, and has since then played in every town of importance in the United Kingdom, his appearances including 3 recitals given in London with his wife, Joan Carr. His elegance of style ingratiates him with the public, whilst his remarkably sure technique commends his playing to musicians.   W. W. C.

MEMMO (MEMO), FRATE DIONISIO, a 15th-16th-century Italian musician, pupil of Giovanni di Maria, appointed Sept. 22, 1507, first organist of St. Mark's, Venice. He came to London 1516, where he was made a vicar choral, and stood in high esteem at the court of Henry VIII. (W. Nagel, Gesch. d. Mus. am engl. Hofe).

MENDEL, HERMANN (b. Halle, Aug. 6, 1834; d. Berlin, Oct. 26, 1876), editor of the famous dictionary of music (see DICTIONARIES OF MUSIC), studied music in Leipzig and Berlin.

From 1862–68 he carried on a music business in the latter city, and at the same time wrote in various musical periodicals and took an active part in music generally. His lives of Meyerbeer (1868) and Otto Nicolai have been published separately. In 1870 Mendel started the work already mentioned—Musikalisches Conversations-Lexikon—with the help of a large and distinguished staff of writers. The Lexicon was completed after his death, in 11 vols. under the editorship of Dr. August Reissmann, who brought out the twelfth, supplementary, volume in 1883.   G.

MENDELSSOHN, JAKOB LUDWIG FELIX MENDELSSOHN-BARTHOLDY (b. Hamburg, Feb. 3, 1809; d. Leipzig, Nov. 4, 1847), was the composer whose versatile abilities dominated the musical taste of Germany during his life and of England for a generation or more after his death.

The article by Sir George Grove printed below was written for the first edition of this Dictionary published in 1880. It is retained as a masterly presentation of the view of Mendelssohn accepted when his reputation stood highest.

The text follows as far as possible that of the first edition. The additions contributed by F. G. Edwards to the second edition, as well as many details formerly scattered through the Dictionary under other headings, are incorporated in footnotes[1]; a few cuts have been made, and subheadings have been added to facilitate reference.   C.

JAKOB LUDWIG FELIX MENDELSSOHN-BARTHOLDY was born in a house in the thoroughfare now called the Grosse Michaelisstrasse.[2]

The family was already well known from Moses Mendelssohn, the grandfather of Felix, 'The Modern Plato,' whose Phädon, a dialogue upon the immortality of the soul, based on the Phaedo of Plato, was translated, long before the birth of his illustrious grandson, into almost every European (and at least one Asiatic) language.[3] Moses (b. Dessau, Sept. 6, 1729; d. Berlin, Jan. 4, 1786), was the son of Mendel, a poor Jewish schoolmaster of Dessau, on the Elbe. The name Mendelssohn, i.e. 'son of Mendel,' is the ordinary Jewish, oriental way of forming a name. Moses migrated at 14 years old to Berlin, settled there in 1762, married Fromet, daughter of Abraham Gugenheim, of Hamburg, had many children, of whom six attained maturity, three sons and three daughters, published his Phädon at Berlin in 1767,

[1] The following abbreviations are used for the references in this article:
F.M.=Die Familie Mendelssohn, 1729–1847, von S. Hensel. Berlin, 1879, English trans. London, 1882. The references are to the first German edition in 3 vols. The second and revised German edition (from which the English trans. was made) is in 2 vols., and was published in 1880.
L.=Letters contained in the two published volumes. In order to facilitate reference to both the German and English versions, the dates of the letters are given in preference to the pagination. For full titles of these volumes of correspondence see p. 176a.
Dev.=My Recollections of Felix Mendelssohn-Bartholdy, and his Letters to Me. By Eduard Devrient. London, 1869.
H.=Mendelssohn, Letters and Recollections. By Dr. Ferdinand Hiller. English trans. by M. E. von Glehn. London, 1874.
G. & M.=Goethe and Mendelssohn (1821–1832). English trans. by M. E. von Glehn, second edition. London, 1874.
B.=Sketch of the Life and Works of the late Felix Mendelssohn-Bartholdy. By Jules Benedict. London 1853.
Mos.=Life of Moscheles . . . By his wife (2 vols.), London, 1873. This originally appeared with German text—Aus Moscheles Leben, etc., Leipzig, 1872; but the references are to the English version.
C.=Henry Fothergill Chorley, Autobiography, etc., by Henry G. Hewlett. London, 1873.
P.=Reminiscences of Felix Mendelssohn-Bartholdy. By Elise Polko. English trans. by Lady Wallace. London, 1869.
Sch.=Reminiscences of Mendelssohn. By J. Schubring, Musical World, May 12 and 19, 1866. Trans. from Daheim (Leipzig) 1866, No. 26. N.B. the references are to the English version.
C.E.H.=Reminiscences of Mendelssohn. By Charles Edward Horsley. The Choir, Jan. 11 and 25, Feb. 8 and 15, 1873.
Dorn=Recollections of Felix Mendelssohn and his Friends. By Dr. Dorn, Temple Bar, Feb 1872.
A.M.Z.=Allgemeine musikalische Zeitung. (Leipzig.)
N.M.Z.=Neue musikalische Zeitung. (Leipzig.) Robert Schumann's paper.
Hogarth=The Philharmonic Society of London. . . . By George Hogarth. London, 1862.
Lampadius=Life of Felix Mendelssohn-Bartholdy. From the German of W. A. Lampadius. London, 1876. For the German title of the original edition see p. 176a.
[2] Ferdinand David, destined to become so great a friend of Mendelssohn's, was born in the same house the year after. The house is at the corner of the Brunnenstrasse, and is now, through the affectionate care of Mr. and Madame Otto Goldschmidt, decorated with a memorial tablet over the front door. The house was numbered 14 when Grove wrote, and later numbered 54.
[3] Dutch (Hague, 1769); French, 2 versions (Paris, 1772; Berlin, 1772); Italian, 2 do. (Chur, 1773; Parma, 1800); Danish (Copenhagen, 1779); Hebrew (Berlin, 1786); English (London, 1789); also Russian, Polish and Hungarian. It is a curious evidence of the slowness with which music penetrated into literary circles in England that the excellent article on Moses Mendelssohn in the Penny Cyclopedia, though published in 1839, makes no mention of Felix, who had then been five times in this country. The 'Phädon' attracted the notice of no less a person than Mirabeau.—Sur M Mendelssohn, etc. London, 1787.

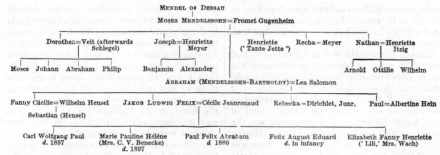

MENDEL OF DESSAU
|
MOSES MENDELSSOHN = Fromet Gugenheim

Dorothea = Veit (afterwards   Joseph = Henriette   Henriette   Recha = Meyer   Nathan = Henriette
Schlegel)   Meyer   (' Tante Jette ')   Itzig

Moses Johann Abraham Philip   Benjamin Alexander   Arnold Ottilie Wilhelm

ABRAHAM (MENDELSSOHN-BARTHOLDY) = Lea Salomon

Fanny Cäcilie = Wilhelm Hensel   JAKOB LUDWIG FELIX = Cécile Jeanrenaud   Rebecka = Dirichlet, Junr.   Paul = Albertine Hein
Sebastian (Hensel)

Carl Wolfgang Paul   Marie Pauline Hélène   Paul Felix Abraham   Felix August Eduard   Elizabeth Fanny Henriette
d. 1897   (Mrs. C. V. Benecke)   d 1880   d. in infancy   (' Lili,' Mrs. Wach)
d. 1897

and died there. He was a small, humpbacked man, with a keen, eager face, bright eyes, and a humorous mouth. The first peculiarity is traceable in his grandchild Fanny, and the bright eyes were one of Felix's most noticeable characteristics. After the death of Moses his widow left Berlin with Joseph, the eldest son, and returned to her native city.

Abraham, the second son (*b*. Dec. 11, 1776), went to Paris, and in 1803 was cashier in Fould's bank there. In 1804 he resigned this post and went into partnership with his elder brother Joseph ; married, Dec. 26, 1804, Lea Salomon (*b*. Mar. 26, 1777), of a Jewish family in Berlin, and settled in Hamburg, carrying on his business at the house above mentioned, and having also a house out of town called ' Marten's Mühle.' He remained in Hamburg till 1811, and there were born to him Fanny Cäcilie (Nov. 14, 1805), Jakob Ludwig Felix (Feb. 3, 1809), and Rebecka (Apr. 11, 1811). During the French occupation of Hamburg, life became intolerable, and shortly after Rebecka's birth the whole family escaped in disguise to Berlin, where they started the eminent banking-house, and lived in a large house on the Neue Promenade, in the N.E. quarter of the town, a broad open street or place between the Spree and the Haacksche Markt, with houses on one side only, the other side lying open to a canal with trees, a sufficiently retired spot as late as 1820 for Felix and his friends to play in front of it.[1] There, eleven days after the battle of Leipzig, Abraham's second son and youngest child, Paul, was born (Oct. 30, 1813). The daughters of Moses Mendelssohn, Dorothea and Henriette, became Roman Catholics. Dorothea married Friedrich von Schlegel, and Henriette was governess to Fanny, the only daughter of General Sebastiani, afterwards (1847) so unfortunate as the Duchesse de Praslin. The sons remained Jews; but at length Abraham saw that the change was inevitable, and decided[2] to have his children baptized and brought up as Protestant Christians. This decision was taken on the advice and example of his wife's brother Salomon Bartholdy, to whom also is due the adoption of the name

Bartholdy, ' after the former proprietor of the garden belonging to the family.' He himself had taken it, and he urged it on his brother-in-law as a means of distinction from the rest of the family. Salomon was a man of mark. He resided in Rome for some time as Prussian Consul-General; had his villa on Monte Pincio (Casa Bartholdy) decorated with frescoes,[3] by Veit, Schadow, Cornelius, Overbeck and Schnorr, collected objects of art, and died there in 1827, leaving his fortune to his sister Lea. He was cast off by his mother for his conversion, and was only reconciled long after, at the entreaty of Fanny.[4] At a later date Abraham and Lea were received into the Christian Church at Frankfort, and Lea took the additional names of Felicia Paulina, from her sons.

. Abraham Mendelssohn was accustomed to describe his position in life by saying ' formerly[5] I was the son of my father, now I am the father of my son.'[6] But though not so prominent as either, he was a man of strong character, wise judgment and very remarkable ability. These qualities are strikingly obvious in the success of his method for the education of his children, and in the few of his letters[7] which are published; and they are testified to in a very remarkable manner by his son in many passages of his letters, and in the thorough deference which he always pays to the judgment of his father, not only on matters relating to the conduct of life, but on points of art. Though not, like Leopold Mozart, a technical musician, and apparently having no acquaintance with the art, he had yet an insight into it which many musicians might envy. ' I am often,' says his son, ' quite unable to understand how it is possible to have so accurate a judgment about music without being a technical musician, and if I could only say what I feel in the same clear and intelligent manner that you always do, I would certainly

---

[1] *Dev.* p. 2.   [2] *F.M.* i. 83.

[3] *L.* Rome, Feb. 1, 1831 ; Fanny's letter in *F.M.* ii. 127.
[4] *F.M.* i. 83.
[5] ' Früher war ich der Sohn meines Vaters, jetzt bin ich der Vater meines Sohnes ' (*F.M.* i. 77). Said Talleyrand : ' Non, monsieur, l'on disait, il y a douze ans, que M. de Saint-Aulaire étoit beau-père de M. de Cazes ; l'on dit maintenant que M. de Cazes est gendre de M. de Saint-Aulaire.'—G. O. Trevelyan's *Life and Letters of Lord Macaulay* (1876), i. 232.
[6] Elsewhere he describes himself as a mere dash, a *Gedankenstrich* (—) between father and son. (*F.M.* i. 367.)
[7] *L.* Nov. 23, 1834, and March 10, 1835 ; *F.M.* i. 84, 87, 91; 347-86.

never make another confused speech as long as
I live.' [1] Or again, this time after his death,
' not only my father, but . . . my teacher both
in art and in life.' [2]

Though apparently cold in his manners, and
somewhat stern in his tone, and towards the
end perhaps unduly irritable, Abraham Mendelssohn was greatly beloved by his wife and
children. Felix, in particular, is described as
' enthusiastically, almost fanatically, fond of
him,' [3] and the letters show how close was the
confidence which existed between them. Hardly
less remarkable was the mother. She was
one of those rare persons whose influence seems
to be almost in proportion to the absence of
any attempt to exert it. Hiller when a boy
saw her once, and the impression made upon
him by the power of her quiet kindness and
gentleness remained fresh in his mind after
more than half a century.[4] When her house
was thronged with the intellect and wit of
Berlin, she was the centre of the circle and the
leader of the conversation.[5] Her letters, of
which large numbers exist in manuscript, are
full of cleverness and character. Her practical
sense of the value of money comes out in her
letters to Ferdinand David.[6] The education of
her children was her great object in life. She
was strict—we may now think over strict [7];
but no one who looks at the result in the
character of her children can say that her method
was not a wise one. They loved her dearly to
the end, and the last letters which Felix wrote
to her are full of an overflowing tenderness and
a natural confidential intimacy which nothing
can surpass. Calm and reserved like her husband,
she was full of feeling, and had on occasion
bursts of passion. Felix's intention to leave
Berlin affected her to a ' terrible ' degree—a
degree which surprised him. He confesses that
his yielding to the wishes of the King, after
having made up his mind to retire, was due
solely to her. ' You think that in my official
position I *could* do nothing else. It was not
that. It was my mother.' [8]

How far she was herself a pianoforte player we
are not told, but the remark which she made
after Fanny's birth, ' that the child had got
Bach-fugue fingers,' shows that she knew a good
deal about the matter. We learn also that
she herself for some time taught the two eldest
children music, beginning with lessons five
minutes long, and gradually increasing the time
until they went through a regular course of
instruction.[9] For many years Felix and Fanny
never practised or played without the mother
sitting by them, knitting in hand.

EARLY LIFE.—Felix was scarcely 3 when

his family escaped to Berlin. The first definite
event of which we hear after this is a visit to Paris
by Joseph and Abraham in 1816, for the liquida-
tion of the indemnity to be paid by France to
Prussia on account of the war. Abraham took
his family with him, and Felix and Fanny,
then 7 and 11 respectively, were taught the
piano by Madame Bigot, a remarkable musician,
and apparently an excellent teacher. She was
the daughter of a Madame Kiéné, and in 1816
was 30 years old. Miniatures of the four
children were taken during this visit, which
are still in existence.[10] Soon after their return
from Paris to the grandmother's house at the
Neue Promenade, where the family still lived,
the children's education seems to have begun
systematically. Heyse [11] was their tutor for
general subjects, Ludwig Berger for the piano,
Zelter for thorough-bass and composition, Henning for the violin and Rösel for landscape.
Felix learned Greek with Rebecka, two years
his junior, and advanced as far as Aeschylus.[12]

On Oct. 28, 1818, he made his first appearance
in public at a concert given by a certain Herr
Gugel, in which he played the pianoforte part
of a trio for pianoforte and two horns by Woelfl,
and was much applauded.[13] The children were
kept very closely to their lessons, and Felix is
remembered in after-life to have said how much
they enjoyed their Sundays, because then they
were not forced to get up at 5 o'clock to work.
Early in his eleventh year, on Apr. 11, 1819,
he entered the singing-class of the Singakademie
as an alto, for the Friday practisings. There and
elsewhere 'he took his place,' says Devrient,[14]
' amongst the grown-up people in his child's
dress, a tight-fitting jacket, cut very low at
the neck, over which the wide trousers were
buttoned, into the slanting pockets of these
the little fellow liked to thrust his hands, rocking his curly head [he had long brown curls]
from side to side, and shifting restlessly from
one foot to the other.'

With 1820, that is to say with his twelfth
year, Felix seems to have begun systematically
to compose ; at least with that year begins the
invaluable series of forty-four volumes, in which
Mendelssohn's methodical habits have preserved
a collection of autographs or copies of a great
part of his works, published and unpublished,
down to the time of his death, the majority
carefully inscribed with both date and place—
which are now deposited in the State Library
at Berlin.

To the year 1820 are attributable between
fifty and sixty movements, including amongst
them a trio for pf. and strings (three movements);
a sonata in F for pf. and violin (three do.) ;
two movements in D minor for the same ; two
full sonatas for pf. solo ; the beginning of a

1 *L.* Mar. 23, 1835.   2 *L.* to Pastor Bauer, Dec. 9, 1835.
3 *F.M.* i. 424. Compare p. 349.
4 *Hiller*, p. 3.   5 *Dev.* p. 38.
6 See *Ferdinand David und die Familie Mendelssohn-Bartholdy*,
von Julius Eckhardt (1888), pp. 42 and 45.
7 Devrient gives an instance or two of it ; see pp. 8 and 57, note.
8 *L.* to Klingemann, Jan. 3, 1843 ; and to his mother, Nov. 4
1834.   9 *B.* p. 6.

10 Photographs of the miniatures of Fanny and Felix were reproduced in the *Musical Times* of Nov. 1897, p. 731.
11 Father of Paul Heyse the novelist.
12 *Sch.* p. 301a.   13 *A.M.Z.*, 1818, p. 791.   14 *Dev.* p. 2.

third in G minor, finished the next year, and
published in 1868 (as op. 105) ; six pieces for
pf. solo ; three pieces for the same instrument,
four hands ; four pieces for organ ; three songs;
two partsongs for men's voices; a cantata, ' In
rührend feierlichen Tönen ' ; and a Lustspiel,
or little comedy, for voices and pf. in three
scenes, beginning ' Ich. J. Mendelssohn.' The
earliest date is that to the cantata—Jan. 13,
1820. The extraordinary neatness and finish,
which characterise Mendelssohn's MSS. to the
end, are observable in the earliest of these childish
productions, and the mysterious letters L.v.g.G.,
or H. d. m., so familiar to those who know his
latest scores, are usually at the head of each.

Among the pieces for 1821 are five sinfonies
for string quartet, each in three movements ;
nine fugues for ditto ; the completion of the
G minor pf. sonata (op. 105) ; motets for four
voices ; a couple of songs ; a couple of études
for pf. solo ; two one-act operas, ' Soldatenliebschaft ' and ' Die beiden Pädagogen '[1]; and half
a third opera, ' Die wandernden Comödianten.'
1821 was the year of his acquaintance with
Weber, then in Berlin for the production of 'Der
Freischütz,' and of an enthusiasm on the part of
the boy for that romantic composer which he
never lost.[2] This, too, was the year of his first
visit to Goethe. Zelter took his pupil to Weimar
in November, and they passed sixteen days
under the old poet's roof.[3]

In 1822 Felix made a second appearance in
public of a more serious nature than before, viz.
on March 31, at a concert of Aloys Schmitt's,
in which he played with Schmitt a duet of
Dussek's for two pianos. In the summer the
whole family made a tour in Switzerland.
Starting on July 6, they went by Cassel (for
Spohr), Frankfort, Darmstadt, Schaffhausen,
Amsteg, Interlaken, Vevey and Chamounix ; a
large and merry party of ten, besides servants.
The tour was taken at great leisure, and on the
return two important halts were made—first at
Frankfort, to make the acquaintance of Schelble,
the conductor of the famous Cäcilien-Verein,
whom Felix astonished by extemporising on
Bach's motets ; and at Weimar, for a second
visit to Goethe.[4]

At Secheron, near Geneva, two songs were
written (Sept. 18, 1822) ; and the pianoforte
quartet in C minor, afterwards published as op.
1, was begun to be put on paper (the autograph
being marked ' Begun at Secheron, Sept. 20,
1822 '), and was finished after the return home.
Besides this, the records of these two years
(1822 and 1823) contain six more symphonies,
Nos. 7, 8, 9, 10, 11, 12 ; six detached pieces for
strings ; five concertos for solo instruments
with quartet accompaniment, viz. one for violin
solo, one for pf. solo, one for pf. and violin, and

two for two pfs.; two quartets for pf. and strings,
viz. in C minor (op. 1) and in F minor (op. 2) ;
sonata for pf. and violin (op. 4) and for pf. and
viola (MS.) ; a fantasia and three other pieces
for the organ ; a fugue and fantasia for pf. ; a
Kyrie for two choirs ; a psalm, three songs, a
piece for contralto solo and strings, in three
movements, to Italian text; two songs for men's
voices, and the completion of the fourth opera,
'Die beiden Neffen,' or 'Der Onkel aus Boston,'
which was a full-grown piece in three acts. The
symphonies show a similar advance. They are
in four movements instead of three as before,
and the length of the movements increases.
No. 8, in D, written between Nov. 6 and Nov. 27
(1822), after the return from Switzerland, has
an *Adagio e grave* before the opening *Allegro*.
The slow movement is for three violas and bass,
and the finale has a prominent part for the
violoncello. This symphony must have pleased
the composer or some of his audience in whose
judgment he believed, since within a month he
began to re-score it for full orchestra. He wrote
a new trio for the minuet, and in this form it
became symphony No. 9. The three last of the
six are for quintet, and the scherzos of Nos. 10
and 12 are founded on Swiss tunes, in No. 12
with the addition of triangles, cymbals and
drums. The independent violoncello part is
conspicuous throughout. This advance in his
music is in keeping with the change going on in
Felix himself.   He was now nearly 14, was
growing fast,[5] his features and his expression
were altering and maturing, his hair was cut
short,[6] and he was put into jackets and trousers.
His extemporising—which he had begun to
practise early in 1821 [7]—was already remarkable,[8] and there was a dash of audacity in it
hardly characteristic of the mature man. Thus
Goethe wished to hear a certain fugue of Bach's,
and as Felix could not remember it all he developed it himself at great length, which he
would hardly have done later.[9] After his
return home, on Dec. 5, 1822, he appeared at a
concert given by Madame Anna Milder, when he
played a pianoforte concerto of his own, probably that in A minor with quintet accompaniment.[10]

The same incessant and varied production of
previous years marks those of 1822 and 1823.
It must not be suppoted that the symphonies
operas, quartets, concertos and other work
mentioned were written as exercises only. It
had been the custom in the Mendelssohn house
for some time past to have musical parties on
alternate Sunday mornings, with a small orchestra, in the large dining-room of the house,
and the programmes included one or more of
Felix's compositions. As a rule the pianoforte
part was taken by himself or Fanny, or both,
while Rebecka sang, and Paul played the violon-

---

[1] Words by Dr. Caspar (*Dev.* p. 5).   [2] *H.* p. 32.
[3] See details in *G. & M.* See also Rellstab, *Aus meinem Leben*,
ii. 135 ; and Lobe's *Recollections of Mendelssohn*, in *Once a Week*,
May 11, 1867.   [4] *G. & M.* p. 33.

[5] Zelter, in *G. & M.* p. 35.   [6] *F.M.* i. 130 ; *Dev.* p. 10.
[7] *F.M.* i. 100.   [8] *Dev.* p. 11.
[9] *F.M.* i. 129.   [10] *A.M.Z.* 1822, p. 273 ; 1823, p. 55.

cello. But Felix always conducted, even when so small as to have to stand on a stool to be seen ; thus he enjoyed the benefit not only of hearing his compositions played (a benefit for which less fortunate composers—Schubert, for example—have sighed in vain) but of the practice in conducting and in playing before an audience.[1] The size of the room was not sufficient for a large audience, but on these occasions it was always full, and few musicians of note passed through Berlin without being present.[2] In performing the operettas and operas, no attempt was made to act them. The characters were distributed as far as the music went, but the dialogue was read out from the piano, and the chorus sat round the dining-table. Zelter, in strong contrast to his usual habit of impartial neglect of his pupils, was not only regularly there, but would criticise the piece at the close of the performance, and if he often praised would sometimes blame. The comments of his hearers, however, were received by Felix with perfect simplicity. Devrient has well described how entirely the music itself was his aim,[3] and how completely subordinated were self-consciousness and vanity to the desire of learning, testing and progressing in his art. These Sunday performances, however, were only one feature of the artistic and intellectual life of the house. Music went on every evening more or less, theatricals, impromptu or studied, were often got up, and there was a constant flux and reflux of young, clever, distinguished people, who made the suppers delightfully gay and noisy, and among whom Felix was the favourite.

The full rehearsal of his fourth opera, ' Die beiden Neffen,' on his fifteenth birthday, Feb. 3, 1824, was an event in the boy's life. At supper, after the conclusion of the work, Zelter, adopting freemason phraseology, raised him from the grade of ' apprentice,' and pronounced him an ' assistant,' ' in the name of Mozart, and of Haydn, and of old Bach.'[4] A great incentive to his progress had been given shortly before this in the score of Bach's Passion, copied by Zelter's express permission from the MS. transcript in the Singakademie, and given him by his grandmother at Christmas, 1823. The copy was made by Eduard Rietz,[5] who had succeeded Henning as his violin teacher, and to whom he was deeply attached. His confirmation took place about this date, under Wilmsen, a well-known clergyman of Berlin.

In the compositions of 1824 there is a great advance. The symphony in C minor (op. 11)—which we now know as ' No. 1,' but which on the autograph in the library of the Philharmonic

Society is marked ' No. XIII.'—was composed between March 3 and 31. The sestet for pt. and strings (op. 110), the pianoforte quartet in B minor[6] (op. 3), a fantasia for four hands (pf.), and a motet in five numbers are all amongst the works of this year. An important event in the summer of 1824 was a visit of the father, Felix, and Rebecka, to Dobberan, a bathing-place on the shores of the Baltic near Rostock. For the wind-band at the bath-establishment at Dobberan Felix wrote an overture which he afterwards scored for a full military band and published as op. 24. But the chief result of the visit was that he there for the first time saw the sea, and received those impressions and images which afterwards found their tangible shape in the Meeresstille overture.

Among the great artists who came into contact with Felix at this time was Moscheles, then on his way from Vienna to Paris and London. He was already famous as a player, and Frau Mendelssohn calls him ' the prince of pianists.' He remained in Berlin for six weeks in Nov. and Dec. 1824, and was almost daily at the Mendelssohns' ; and after a time, at the urgent request of the parents, and with great hesitation on his own part, gave Felix regular lessons on the pianoforte every other day. Moscheles was then 30. It is pleasant to read of his unfeigned love and admiration for Felix and his home—

' a family such as I have never known before ; Felix a mature artist, and yet but fifteen ; Fanny extraordinarily gifted, playing Bach's fugues by heart and with astonishing correctness—in fact, a thorough musician. The parents gave me the impression of people of the highest cultivation. They are very far from being over-proud of their children ; indeed, they are in anxiety about Felix's future, whether his gifts are lasting, and will lead to a solid, permanent future, or whether he may not suddenly collapse, like so many other gifted children.'

' He has no need of lessons ; if he wishes to take a hint from me as to anything new to him, he can easily do so.'

Such remarks as these do honour to all concerned, and it is delightful to find Mendelssohn, years afterwards, in the full glory of his great fame, referring to these very lessons as having fanned the sacred fire within him and urged him on to enthusiasm.[7]

Moscheles has preserved two of the Sunday morning programmes :

' Nov. 28. Morning music at the Mendelssohns' :— Felix's C minor quartet ; his D major symphony ; Concerto by Bach (Fanny) ; Duet for two pianos in D minor, Arnold.'

' Dec. 12. Sunday music at Mendelssohns' :— Felix's F minor quartet. I played my Duet in G for two pianos. Little Schilling played Hummel's Trio in G.'

Moscheles was followed by Spohr, who came to superintend the first performance at Berlin of his opera ' Jessonda ' (Feb. 14, 1825). He was often at the house, and on very intimate terms, though he does not mention the fact in his Autobiography.[8]

---

[1] It seems that he accompanied the quartet symphonies on the piano. Dorn, in his *Recollections*, expressly says so, and the slow movement of the Symphony No. 10 contains a note in Mendelssohn's own writing, ' Das Klavier mit dem Basse,' which seems to prove it. The practice, therefore, did not end with the 18th century, as has been supposed (Prof. E. Prout, *On the Growth of the Modern Orchestra, Proceedings of the Musical Association*, 1878–79, p. 37).
[2] *F.M.* i. 137.   [3] *Dev.* p. 4.   [4] *F.M.* p. 140 ; *Dorn*, p. 399.
[5] Or Ritz, as Mendelssohn always spells it. He seems to have been on the whole Felix's most intimate early friend.

[6] Last movement dated Jan. 18, 1825.
[7] *Mos.* i. 99 ; ii. 161.   [8] *F.M.* i. 144.

One or two accounts by competent judges of Felix's style of playing at this time have been preserved. Hiller was with him in Frankfort in the spring of 1825, and speaks both of his extemporising and of his playing the music of others.[1] With the latter he delighted both Hiller and André (who relished neither his face, his ideas, nor his manners) by playing the *Allegretto* of Beethoven's Seventh Symphony in such a ' powerful orchestral style ' as fairly to stop André's mouth. With the former he carried Hiller away by extemporising on Handel's choruses in ' Judas,' as he had done Schelble, in the same room three years before, on subjects from Bach's motets. This time his playing was quite in the vein of his subject ; ' the figures which he used were thoroughly Handelian, and the power and clearness of his passages in thirds, sixths and octaves were really grand, and yet it all belonged to the subject-matter, thoroughly true, genuine, living music, with no trace of display.' Dorn is more explicit as to his accompanying—the duet in ' Fidelio.' ' He astonished me in the passage, " Du wieder nun in meinen Armen ! " by the way in which he represented the violoncello and the bass parts on the piano, playing them two octaves apart. I asked him why he chose that striking way of rendering the passage, and he explained it all to me in the kindest manner. How many times since,' says Dorn, ' has that duet been sung in Berlin to the pianoforte, but how rarely has it been accompanied in such a manner ! '[2] He rarely played from book, either at this or any other time of his life. Even works like Beethoven's Ninth Symphony, and the sonata in B flat (op. 106), he knew by heart.[3] One of the grounds of Spontini's enmity to him is said to have been a performance of the Ninth Symphony by Felix, without book, before Spontini himself had ever heard it, and it is known on the best authority that he played the symphony through by heart only a few months before his death. Here we may say that he had a passion for Beethoven's latest works, his acquaintance with which dated from their publication, Beethoven's last years (1820–27) exactly corresponding with his own growth to maturity. It was almost the only subject on which he disagreed with his father.[4] On the other hand, the devotion of such very conservative artists as David, Rietz and Sterndale Bennett to those works is most probably due to Mendelssohn's influence. Marx[5] challenges his reading of Beethoven ; but this is to fly in the face of the judgment of all other critics.

In 1825 the elder Mendelssohn made a journey to Paris, for the purpose of fetching his sister Henriette back to Germany, and took Felix with him. They arrived on Mar. 22.

One of the first things he mentions is the astonishment of his relatives at finding him no longer a child.[6] He plunged at once into musical society. Hummel, Onslow, Boucher, Herz, Halévy, Kalkbrenner, Moscheles (on his way back from Hamburg to London, with his bride), Pixis, Rode, Baillot, Kreutzer, Rossini, Paer, Meyerbeer, Plantade and many more, were there, and all glad to make acquaintance with the wonderful boy. At Madame Kiéné's— Madame Bigot's mother—he played his new pianoforte quartet (in B minor) with Baillot and others, and with the greatest success.

The French musicians, however, made but a bad impression on him. Partly, no doubt, this is exaggerated in his letters, as in his criticism on Auber's ' Léocadie '[7] ; but the ignorance of German music — even Onslow,[8] for example, had never heard a note of ' Fidelio '—and the insults to some of its masterpieces (such as the transformation of ' Der Freischütz ' into ' Robin des bois,'[9] and the comparison of a passage in Bach's A minor organ prelude to a favourite duet of Monsigny), and the general devotion to effect and outside glitter—these were just the things to enrage the lad at that enthusiastic age. With Cherubini their intercourse was very satisfactory. The old Florentine was more than civil to Felix, and his expressions of satisfaction (so very rare in his mouth) must have given the father the encouragement which he was so slow to take in the great future of his boy.[10] Felix describes him in a few words as ' an extinct volcano, now and then blazing up, but all covered with ashes and stones.' He wrote a Kyrie ' *a 5 voci* and *grandissimo* orchestra' at the instance of Cherubini,[11] which he describes as ' bigger than anything he had yet done.'[12] The Kyrie seems to have been lost. Through all this the letters home are as many as ever, full of music, descriptions and jokes— often very bad ones. Here, for instance, is a good professional query: 'Ask Ritz if he knows what *Fes moll* is.'

On May 19, 1825, the father and son left Paris with Henriette (' Tante Jette '), who had retired from her post at General Sebastiani's with an ample pension, and thenceforward resided at Berlin. On the road home they paid a short visit (the third) to Goethe, at Weimar. Felix played the B minor pianoforte quartet (op. 3), and delighted the poet by dedicating it to him.[13] It is a marvellous work for a boy of 16, and an enormous advance on either of its two predecessors ; but probably no one—not even the composer—suspected that

[1] *Hiller*, pp. 5 6.   [2] *Dorn*, p. 398.

[3] Marx, *Erinnerungen*, ii. 117 ; confirmed to me by the Duke of Meiningen, Taubert, Schleinitz, Klengel, J. W. Davison, and others.   [4] *L.* Nov. 22, 1830.   [5] *Erinn.* ii. 135.

[6] *F.M.* i. 146.   [7] *G. & M.* p 43.

[8] *F.M.* i. 149, and MS. letter.   [9] *G. & M.* p. 48.

[10] Marx (*Erinn.* ii. 113, 114) says that the father's hesitation as to his son's future was so great, that, even to a late date, he constantly urged him to go into business. He believed that his son had no genius for music, and that it was all the happier for him that he had not.

[11] *Briefwechsel zwischen Goethe und Zelter in den Jahren 1796 bis 1832* (Berlin, 1834) ; iv. 35 ; *G. & M.* p. 49.

[12] ' An Dickigkeit alles übertrifft.'

[13] For the details see *G. & M.* p. 50.

the scherzo (in F sharp minor, 3-8) was to be the first of a ' family of scherzi which, if he had produced nothing else, would stamp him as an inventor in the most emphatic signification of the word.' It must be admitted that Goethe made him a very poor return for his charming music. Anything more stiff and ungraceful than the verses which he wrote for him, and which are given in *Goethe and Mendelssohn*, it would be difficult to find, unless it be another stanza, also addressed to Felix, and printed in vol. i. p. 477 of the poet's works (Stuttgart, 1860):

Wenn das Talent verständig wal-tet,	If Talent reigns with Wisdom great,
Wirksame Tugend nie veraltet.	Virtue is never out of date.
Wer Menschen gründlich konnt' erfreun	He who can give us pleasure true
Der darf sich vor der Zeit nicht scheun;	Need never fear what time can do;
Und möchtet ihr ihm Beifall geben.	And will you Talent your approval give?
So gebt ihn uns, die wir ihn frisch beleben.	Then give it us who make her newly live.

They were at home before the end of May. The fiery Capriccio in F sharp minor for pf. (afterwards published as op. 5), so full of the spirit of Bach, is dated July 23 of this year, and the score of 'Camacho's Wedding'—an opera in two acts by Klingemann, founded on an episode in ' Don Quixote '—is dated Aug. 10. The Capriccio was a great favourite with him, and he called it *une absurdité*.

The Mendelssohn-Bartholdy family was beginning to outgrow the accommodation afforded by the grandmother's roof, and at the end of the summer of 1825 they removed from No. 7 Neue Promenade to a large house and grounds which had formerly belonged to the noble family of Reck, namely to No. 3 of the Leipziger Strasse, the address so familiar to all readers of Felix's subsequent letters. If we were writing the life of an ancient prophet or poet, we should take the name of the ' Leipzig Road ' as a prediction of his ultimate establishment in that town ; but no token of such an event was visible at the time. The new residence lay in a part of Berlin which was then very remote, close to the Potsdam Gate, on the edge of the old Thiergarten, or deer park, of Frederick the Great, so far from all the accustomed haunts of their friends that at first the laments were loud. The house was of a dignified, old-fashioned kind, with spacious and lofty rooms ; behind it a large court with offices, and behind that again a beautiful stretch of ground, half park, half garden, with noble trees, lilacs and other flowering shrubs, turf, alleys, walks, banks, summer-houses and seats—the whole running far back, covering about ten acres, and being virtually in the country. Its advantages for music were great. The house itself contained a room precisely fitted for large music parties or private theatricals ; and at the back of the court, and dividing it from the garden, there was a separate building called the ' Gartenhaus,' the middle of which formed a hall capable of

containing several hundred persons, with glass doors opening right on to the lawns and alleys —in short, a perfect place for the Sunday music.[1] Though not without its drawbacks in winter —reminding one of Hensel's almost pathetic description of the normal condition of too many an English house—it was an ideal summer home, and ' 3, Leipziger Strasse ' is in Mendelssohn's mouth a personality, to which he always turned with longing, and which he loved as much as he hated the rest of Berlin. It was identified with the Mendelssohn-Bartholdys till his death, after which it was sold to the State ; and the Herrenhaus, or House of Lords of the German government, now stands on the site of the former court and Gartenhaus.

FIRST WORKS OF MATURITY.—Devrient takes the completion of ' Camacho ' and the leaving the grandmother's house as the last acts of Felix's musical minority ; and he is hardly wrong, for the next composition was a wonderful leap into maturity.[2] It was no other than the octet for strings (afterwards published as op. 20), which he finished towards the end of Oct. 1825, and dedicated to Eduard Ritz as a birthday gift. It is the first of his works which can be said to have fully maintained its ground on its own merits, and is a truly astonishing composition for a boy half-way through his seventeenth year. There is a radiance, a freedom and an individuality in the style which are far ahead of the 13th symphony, or any other of the previous instrumental works, and it is steeped throughout in that inexpressible captivating charm which is so remarkable in all Mendelssohn's best compositions. The scherzo especially (G minor, 2-4) is a movement of extraordinary lightness and grace, and the Finale, besides being a masterly piece of counterpoint (it is a fugue), contains in the introduction of the subject of the scherzo a very early instance of ' transformation of themes.' Felix had confided to Fanny[3] that his motto for the scherzo was the following stanza in the Intermezzo of ' Faust ':

Orchester.—(pianissimo)

Wolkenzug und Nebelflor	Floating cloud and trailing mist
Erhellen sich von oben;	Bright'ning o'er us hover;
Luft im Laub, und Wind im Rohr	Airs stir the brake, the rushes shake—
Und Alles ist zerstoben.	And all their pomp is over.

and never was a motto more perfectly carried out in execution. The whole of the last part, so light and airy—and the end, in particular, where the fiddles run softly up to the high G, accompanied only with staccato chords—is a perfect illustration of ' Alles ist zerstoben.' He afterwards instrumented it for full orchestra, but it is hard to say if it is improved by the process.[4] The so-called Trumpet Overture, in C (op. 101), was almost certainly composed this autumn, and was first heard at a concert given by Maurer, in Berlin, on Nov. 2, at which Felix played the pianoforte part of Beethoven's

1 *F.M.* i. 142.   2 *Dev.* p. 20.   3 *F.M.* i. 154.
4 MS. in the possession of the Philharmonic Society (London).

Choral Fantasia.[1] This overture was a special favourite of Abraham Mendelssohn's, who said that he should like to hear it while he died. It long remained in MS. in the hands of the Philharmonic Society, and was not published until many years after the death of the composer. 1826 opens with the string quintet in A (op. 18),[2] which, if not perhaps so great as the octet, is certainly on the same side of the line, and the scherzo of which, in fugue form, is a worthy companion to its predecessors. The pianoforte sonata in E (op. 6) is of this year (Mar. 22, 1826). So is an interesting-looking Andante and Allegro (June 27), written for the wind band of a Beergarden which he used to pass on his way to bathe ; the MS. is safe in the hands of Dr. Paul Mendelssohn-Bartholdy's widow at Berlin.

But all these were surpassed by the overture to ' A Midsummer Night's Dream,' which was composed during the peculiarly fine summer of 1826, under the charming conditions of life in the new garden,[3] and the score of which is signed ' Berlin, August 6, 1826.' [4] It appears to have been the immediate result of a closer acquaintance with Shakespeare, through the medium of Schlegel and Tieck's version, which he and his sisters read this year for the first time. Marx claims to have been much consulted during its progress, and even to have suggested essential modifications.[5] Fanny also no doubt was in this, as in other instances, her brother's confidante, but the result must have exceeded even the fondest wishes of those who knew him best. It is asserted by one who has the best right to judge, and is not prone to exaggeration,[6] ' that no one piece of music contains so many points of harmony and orchestration that had never been written before as does this, and they have none of them the air of experiment, but seem all to have been written with certainty of their success.' In this wonderful overture, as in the octet and quintet, the airy fairy lightness, and the peculiar youthful grace, are not less remarkable than the strength of construction and solidity of workmanship which underlie and support them. Not the least singular thing about it is the exact manner in which it is found to fit into the music for the whole play when that music was composed seventeen years later. The *motives* of the overture all turn out to have their native places in the drama.[7] After many a performance as a duet on the piano, the overture was played by

an orchestra in the Mendelssohns' garden-house, to a crowded audience, and its first production in public seems to have been at Stettin, in Feb. 1827, whither Felix went in very severe weather to conduct it.[8] With the composition of this work he may be said to have taken his final musical degree, and his lessons with Zelter were discontinued.

' Camacho ' had been submitted to Spontini as General Music-Director in the preceding year by Felix himself. Spontini was then, by an odd freak of fortune, living in a house which had for some time been occupied by the Mendelssohns in the early part of their residence in Berlin, viz. 28 Markgrafen Strasse, opposite the Catholic church. Taking the young composer by the arm, Spontini led him to the window, and pointing to the dome across the street, said, ' Mon ami, il vous faut des idées grandes comme cette coupole.' [9] This from a man of 52, in the highest position, to a boy of 17, could hardly have been meant for anything but kindly, though pompous, advice. But it was not so taken. The Mendelssohns and Spontini were not only of radically different natures, but they belonged to opposite parties in music, and there was considerable friction in their intercourse. At length, early in 1827, after various obstructions on Spontini's part, ' Camacho ' was given out for rehearsal and study, and on Apr. 29 was produced. The house — not the Opera-house, but the smaller theatre—was crowded with friends, and the applause vehement ; at the end the composer was loudly called for, but he had left the theatre, and Devrient had to appear in his stead. Owing to the illness of Blum, the tenor, the second performance was postponed, and the piece was never again brought forward. Partly from the many curious obstructions which arose in the course of the rehearsals, and the personal criticisms which followed it, partly perhaps from a just feeling that the libretto was poor and his music somewhat exaggerated, but mainly no doubt from the fact that during two such progressive years as had passed since he wrote the piece he had outgrown his work,[10] Felix seems to have so far lost interest in it as not to press for another performance. The music was published complete in pianoforte score by Laue, of Berlin, in 1828.[11]

A nature so keenly sensitive as his could hardly be expected to pass with impunity through such worries as attended the production of the opera. He was so sincere and honest

1 *A.M.Z.*, 1825, p. 825. The autograph was once in possession of Mr. Schleinitz. From him it went into the omnivorous maw of Julius Rietz : it is now in the State Library at Berlin. The MS. in our Philharmonic library is a copy with corrections made by Mendelssohn.
2 Zelter's letter to Goethe of June 6, 1826. This MS., too, seems to have disappeared.
3 The first letter that I have found dated from the Leipziger Strasse, ' am 7. Juli 1826, im Garten,' says, ' to-day or to-morrow I shall begin to dream the Midsummer night's dream.'
4 The score was published with those of the ' Hebrides ' and ' Meeresstille ' as ' 3 Concert Overtures ' by B. & H., Mar. or Apr. 1835.
5 For example, the introduction of the Bergomask dance (*Dev.* p. 35). Marx, *Erinn.* ii. 231-3.
6 G. A. Macfarren, Philharmonic programme-book, Apr. 30, 1877.
7 August Reissmann's *Felix Mendelssohn-Bartholdy*, 1867, p. 62.

8 *F.M.* i. 156. Felix's MS. letter from Stettin, Feb. 17, 1827, is the first in which his father is addressed as ' Herr Stadtrath.'
9 ' My friend, your ideas must be grand—grand as that dome.' Marx, *Erinn.* i. 247.
10 ' For God's sake, do not let my old sin of Camacho's Wedding be stirred up again ! ' (Letter to Wm. Bartholomew, July 17, 1843. *Polko*, 217.) In the same manner in 1835 he protests to Mrs. Voigt against the performance of his C minor Symphony—at least without the explanation that it was written by a boy of barely fifteen. (*Acht Briefe, von Felix Mendelssohn-Bartholdy*, Leipzig, 1871, p. 20.)
11 In the original Grove here drew attention to the use of ' Leitmotiv ' in the part of Don Quixote and claimed the term as Mendelssohn's own invention.

that the sneers of the press irritated him unduly.
A year before (in 1826) he had vented his feelings in some lines which will be new to most readers :

Schreibt der Komponiste ernst, Schäfert er uns ein ; Schreibt der Komponiste froh, Ist er zu gemein ;	If the artist gravely writes, To sleep it will beguile. If the artist gaily writes, It is a vulgar style.
Schreibt der Komponiste lang, Ist es zum Erbarmen ; Schreibt ein Komponiste kurz, Kann man nicht erwarmen.	If the artist writes at length, How sad his hearers' lot ! If the artist briefly writes, No man will care one jot.
Schreibt ein Komponiste klar, Ist's ein armer Tropf ; Schreibt ein Komponiste tief, Rappelt's ihm im Kopf.	If an artist simply writes, A fool he's said to be. If an artist deeply writes, He's mad ; 'tis plain to see.
Schreib' er also wie er will, Keinem steht es an, Darum schreib' ein Komponist Wie er will und kann.[1]	In whatsoever way he writes He can't please every man ; Therefore let an artist write How he likes and can.

But on the present occasion the annoyance was too deep to be thrown off by a joke. It did in fact for a time seriously affect his health and spirits, and probably laid the foundation for that dislike of the officialism and pretension, the artists and institutions, the very soil and situation of Berlin, which so curiously pervades his letters whenever he touches on that city.[2] His depression was increased by the death of an old friend, named Hanstein, who was carried off this spring, and beside whose deathbed Felix composed the well-known fugue in E minor for pianoforte (op. 35, No. 1). The chorale in the major, which forms the climax of the fugue, is intended, as we are told on good authority, to express his friend's release.[3] But Felix was too young and healthy, and his nature too eager, to allow him to remain in despondency. A sonata in B flat for pf. (afterwards published as op. 106) is dated May 31, 1827 ; and on Whitsunday, June 3, we find him at Sakrow, near Potsdam, the property of his friend Magnus, composing the charming Lied, ' Ist es wahr ? ' which within a few months he employed to advantage in his string quartet in A minor (op. 13). Meantime—on May 2, 1826—he had entered the University of Berlin, where his tutor Heyse was now a professor. For his matriculation essay he sent in a translation in verse of the *Andria* of Terence, which primarily served as a birthday present to his mother (Mar. 15).[4] This translation was published in a volume, with a preface and essay, and a version of the ninth Satire of Horace, by Heyse.[5] Mendelssohn's translation has been examined by an eminent English scholar, who reports that as a version it is precise and faithful, exceedingly literal, and corresponding closely with the original both in rhythm and metre, while its language, as far as an Englishman may judge of German, is quite worthy of repre-

senting the limpid Latin of Terence. Professor Munro also points out that as this was the first attempt in Germany to render Terence in his own metres, it may be presumed to have set the example to the scholars who have since that date, as a rule, translated Plautus and Terence and other kindred Greek and Latin classics in the original metres. It was by no means his first attempt at verse ; for a long mock-heroic of the year 1820 has been preserved, called the *Paphleïs*, in three cantos, occupied with the adventures of his brother Paul (Paphlos), full of slang and humour, and in hexameters.

Whether Felix went through the regular university course or not, does not appear, but no doubt the proceeding was a systematic one, and he certainly attended several classes, amongst them those of Hegel,[6] and took especial pleasure in the lectures of the great Carl Ritter on geography. Of his notes of these, two folio volumes, closely written in a hand like copper-plate and dated 1827 and 1828, still exist. Italian he was probably familiar with before he went to Italy ; and in later years he knew it so thoroughly as to be able to translate into German verse the very crabbed sonnets of Dante, Boccaccio, Cecco Angiolieri and Cino, for his uncle Joseph in 1840.[7] Landscape drawing, in which he was ultimately to excel so greatly, he had already worked at for several years. For mathematics he had neither taste nor capacity, and Schubring pathetically describes the impossibility of making him comprehend how the pole-star could be a guide in travelling.

The change into the new house was a great event in the family life. Felix began gymnastics, and became a very great proficient in them. He also learned to ride, and to swim, and with him learning a thing meant practising it to the utmost, and getting all the enjoyment and advantage that could be extracted from it. He was a great dancer, now and for many years after. Billiards he played brilliantly. Skating was the one outdoor exercise which he did not succeed in—he could not stand the cold. The garden was a vast attraction to their friends, and *Boccia* (a kind of bowls) was the favourite game under the old chestnut trees which overshadowed the central alley. The large rooms also gave a great impetus to the music and to the mixed society which now flocked to the house more than ever. We hear of Rahel and Varnhagen, Bettina, Heine, Holtei, Lindblad, Steffens, Gans, Marx, Kugler, Droysen ; of Humboldt, W. Müller,[8] Hegel (for whom alone a card-table was provided) and other intellectual and artistic persons, famous, or to be famous afterwards. Young people, too, there were in troops ; the life was free, and it must have been a delightful, wholesome and thoroughly enjoy-

---

[1] Written for his mother's birthday, Mar. 15, 1826. See *Über Land und Meer*, 1873, No. 36, p. 702.
[2] See the two letters to Verkenius, Aug. 14 and 23, 1841 ; also one to Hiller, Mar. 25, 1843 (*H.* p. 207), and far more strongly in many an unpublished letter.
[3] *Sch.* p. 318a.   [4] *Ibid.* p. 302a.
[5] ' Das Mädchen von Andros, eine Komödie des Terentius, in den Versmassen des Originals übersetzt von F****. Mit Einleitung und Anmerkungen herausgegeben von K. W. L. Heyse. Angehängt ist die 9te Satire des Horatius, übersetzt von dem Herausgeber. Berlin, 1826. Bei Ferdinand Dümmler.' The preface is dated ' Berlin, im Juli, 1826.'

[6] One course of these was on Music. Zelter, in *G. & M.* p. 54.
[7] They are given in their place in the later editions of the German version of the Letters.
[8] Father of Max Müller, and author of Schubert's ' Schöne Müllerin.'

able time. Among the features of the garden life was a newspaper, which in summer was called *Garten-zeitung* ('The Garden Times'), in winter *Thee- und Schneezeitung* ('Tea and Snow Times'). It appears to have been edited by Felix and Marx, but all comers were free to contribute, for which purpose pens, ink and paper lay in one of the summer-houses. Nor was it confined to the younger part of the society, but grave personages, like Humboldt and Zelter even, did not disdain to add their morsel of fun or satire. In all this brilliant interchange of art, science and literature, Felix, even at this early date, was the prominent figure. It was now as it was all through his life. When he entered the room every one was anxious to speak to him. Women of double his age made love to him, and men, years afterwards, recollected the evenings they had spent with him, and treasured every word that fell from his lips.[1] One who knew him well at this time, but afterwards broke with him, speaks of the separation as 'a draught of wormwood, the bitter taste of which remained for years.'[2]

The latter half of August and the whole of September (1827) were passed in a tour with Magnus and Heydemann[3] through the Harz mountains to Baden-Baden (where his amusing adventures must be read in his letters in *F.M.*), and thence by Heidelberg, where he made the acquaintance of THIBAUT[4] (*q.v.*) and his old Italian music, to Frankfort. At Frankfort he saw Schelble and Hiller, and delighted them with his new A minor string quartet (op. 13)— not then fully written down; and also with the 'Midsummer Night's Dream' overture, which although a year old was still new to the world.

The annoyance about 'Camacho' had vanished with the tour, and Felix could now treat the story as a joke, and take off the principal persons concerned. The A minor quartet (op. 13) was completed directly after his return home, and is dated 'Berlin, Oct. 26, 1827.' Of further compositions this year we know only of the beautiful fugue in E flat for strings (on his favourite old ecclesiastical subject), which after his death was published as the last movement of op. 81. It is dated 'Berlin, Nov. 1, 1827.' Also a 'Tu es Petrus' for choir and orchestra, written for Fanny's birthday (Nov. 14), and published as op. 111. A very comic 'Kinder-symphonie' for the Christmas home party, scored for the same orchestra as Haydn's, and a motet for four voices and small orchestra on the chorale 'Christe du Lamm Gottes,' are named by Fanny in a letter.[5] Soon after this their circle sustained a loss in the departure of Klingemann, one of the cleverest and most

genial of the set, to London as Secretary to the Hanoverian Legation.

THE REVIVAL OF BACH.—During the winter of 1827, Felix—incited thereto by a complaint of Schubring's, that Bach always seemed to him like an arithmetical exercise—formed a select choir of sixteen voices, who met at his house on Saturday evenings, and at once began to practise the Matthew Passion.[6] This was the seed which blossomed in the public performance of that great work a year later, and that again in the formation of the BACH GESELLSCHAFT (*q.v.*). Long and complicated as the Passion is, he must have known it by heart even at that early date ; for among other anecdotes proving as much, Schubring, who may be implicitly believed, relates that one evening after accompanying one of the choruses at the piano without book, he said, 'at the twenty-third bar the sopranos have C and not C sharp'!

Mar. 1828 was occupied by the composition of a long lyric poem (*lyrische Dichtung*), to words by Levezow, for the Tercentenary Festival of Albert Dürer, at the Singakademie at Berlin, on Apr. 18.[7] It was undertaken at the request of the Akademie der bildenden Künste und dem Künstlervereine, and is written for solo voices, chorus and orchestra, and contains fifteen numbers. The 'Trumpet Overture' preceded it in performance. Felix was not in love with his task, but as the work grew into shape and the rehearsals progressed, he became reconciled to it ; the performance was good, and Fanny's sisterly verdict is that 'she never remembers to have spent a pleasanter hour.'[8] The work remains in MS. at the Singakademie and the Royal Library at Berlin, and has probably the faults of almost all such compositions. Even Beethoven failed when he had to write to order. Fate, however, had a second task of the same kind in store for Felix, with some curious variations. This time the cantata was for a meeting (or, as we should now call it, a 'congress') of physicians and investigators of natural science, to whom a festival was given by A. von Humboldt as president. Rellstab wrote the words, and Felix was invited to compose the music. It contains seven numbers for solo and chorus. Owing to a whim of Humboldt's the chorus was confined to men's voices, and the orchestra to clarinets, horns, trumpets, violoncellos and basses. The thing came off in September ; but no ladies—not even Fanny —were admitted, no report is given in the musical paper, and as there is no mention of it in the MS. Catalogue the autograph has probably vanished. Chopin was present at the sitting of the congress, and saw Mendelssohn with Spontini and Zelter ; but his modesty kept him from introducing himself, and their acquaintance was put off to a later date.[9]

---

[1] For instances of this see Dorn.
[2] Marx, *Erinn.* ii. 138.
[3] Louis Heydemann was a very eccentric person. He possessed many MSS. of Mendelssohn's—amongst others the pianoforte sonata in E (op. 7) and the violoncello variations (op. 17). These—ten 'n number, dating from 1824–29—are now (1906) all in the possession of Dr. Paul Mendelssohn-Bartholdy's widow at Berlin.
[4] *F.M.* i. 164–6. [5] *Ibid.* i. 180, 181.

[6] *Sch.* p. 318a. [7] *A.M.Z.*, 1828, p. 364. [8] *F.M.* i. 169.
[9] Karasowski's *Life of Chopin*, chap. iv.

Felix had, however, during the summer been occupied in a more congenial task than such *pièces d'occasion* as these, viz. in the composition of the overture to Goethe's ' Calm sea and prosperous voyage,' on which we find him employed in June (1828). Fanny gives us the interesting information that he especially avoided the form of an overture with introduction, and wished his work to stand as two companion pictures.[1] She mentions also his having written pianoforte pieces at this time, including some ' Lieder ohne Worte ' (a title not destined to come before the world for some years) and a great Antiphona and Responsorium for four choirs, ' Hora est,' etc., which still remains in MS.

For Christmas he wrote a second Kindersymphonie, which delighted every one so much that it had to be repeated on the spot.[2] He also re-scored Handel's ' Acis and Galatea,' and the ' Dettingen Te Deum,' at Zelter's desire, for the use of the Singakademie.[3] They have since been published, but are not satisfactory specimens of such work (see ADDITIONAL ACCOMPANIMENTS). He also wrote the Variations in D for pf. and violoncello (op. 17), dated ' Jan. 30, 1829,' and dedicated to his brother Paul, who was more than a fair violoncello-player. The ' Calm sea and prosperous voyage ' was finished, or finished as nearly as any score of Mendelssohn's can be said to have been finished, before it was publicly performed and had received those innumerable corrections and alterations and afterthoughts which he always gave his works, and which in some instances caused the delay of their appearance for years—which in fact prevented the appearance of the Italian Symphony till his removal made any further revision impossible. We have already seen that the basis of the work was furnished by the visit to Dobberan. A MS. letter from that place to Fanny (July 27, 1824) gives her an account of the sea in the two conditions in which it is depicted in the overture.[4]

Felix's little choir had steadily continued their practice of the Passion, and the better they knew the mighty work the more urgent became their desire for a public performance by the Singakademie (300 to 400 voices) under Felix's own care. Apart from the difficulties of the music, with its double choruses and double orchestra, two main obstacles appeared to lie in the way—the opposition of ZELTER (*q.v.*) as head of the Akademie, and the apathy of the public. Felix, for one, ' utterly disbelieved ' in the possibility of overcoming either,[5] and with him were his parents and Marx, whose influence in the house was great. Against him, in this opinion, were Devrient, Schubring, Bauer and one or two other enthusiasts. At length Devrient and

Felix determined to go and board Zelter in his den. They encountered a few rough words, but their enthusiasm gained the day. Zelter yielded, and allowed Felix to conduct the rehearsals of the Singakademie.[6] The principal solo singers of the opera at once gave in their adhesion ; the rehearsals began ; Felix's tact, skill and intimate knowledge of the music carried everything before them, and the public flocked to the rehearsals.

On Wednesday, Mar. 11, 1829, the first performance of the Passion since the death of Bach took place ; every ticket was taken, and a thousand people were turned away from the doors. Thus in Felix's own words (for once and once only alluding to his descent) ' it was an actor and a Jew who restored this great Christian work to the people.' [7] There was a second performance under Felix on Bach's birthday, Mar. 21. It is probable that these successes did not add to Felix's popularity with the musicians of Berlin. Whether it was his age, his manner, his birth, the position held by his family, or whatever else, certain it is that he was at this time in some way under a cloud. He had so far quarrelled with the Royal Orchestra that they refused to be conducted by him, and concerts at which his works were given were badly attended.[8]

Paganini made his first appearance in Berlin this month (March), gave four concerts, and bewitched the Berliners as he did every one else.[9] He very soon found his way to the Leipziger Strasse.[10] It would be interesting to know if he heard the Passion, and if, like Rossini, some years later, he professed himself a convert to Bach.

Whistling's *Handbuch* shows that by the end of this year (1829) Felix had published his three pf. quartets ; the sonata for pf. and vln. ; the Capriccio for pf. (op. 5) ; the sonata for pf. solo ; the ' Wedding of Camacho ' ; and the first two books of songs. The dedications of these throw an interesting light on some things. The pf. quartets are inscribed respectively to Prince A. Radzivil (a friend of the family, who was present at the first performance of ' Die beiden Pädagogen ' at the Neue Promenade), Zelter and Goethe ; the violin sonata (op. 4) to Eduard Ritz, Felix's favourite violin-player ; and the seven 'Characteristic Pieces,' pf. (op. 7), to Ludwig Berger, his pianoforte-teacher. The rest have no dedications.

FIRST VISIT TO ENGLAND.—The engagement of Fanny Mendelssohn to William Hensel the painter, of Berlin, took place on Jan. 22, 1829, in the middle of the excitement about the Passion ; and on Apr. 10 Felix started for England. He was now 20. His age, the termination of his liability to military service,[11] the friction

1 *F.M.* i. 194.   2 *Ibid.* p. 199.
3 *Ibid.*, compared with *Devrient*, p. 161.
4 · 'Sometimes it lies as smooth as a mirror, without waves, breakers, or noise . . . sometimes it is so wild and furious that I dare not go in.'   5 *Dev.* p. 46.

6 They began about the end of Jan. 1829. *F.M.* i. 204.
7 *Dev.* p. 57.
8 See his letter to Leopold Ganz, in *G. & M.* p. 186.
9 *A.M.Z.*, 1829, p. 256.
10 Marx, *Erinn.* ii. 75.   11 *F.M.* i. 188.

just alluded to between himself and the musical world of Berlin—all things invited him to travel, and Zelter [1] was not wrong in saying that it was good for him to leave home for a time. Hitherto also he had worked without fee or reward. He was now to prove that he could make his living by music.[2] But more than this was involved. His visit to England was the first section of a long journey,[3] planned by the care and sagacity of his father, and destined to occupy the next three years of his life. In this journey he was ' closely to examine the various countries, and to fix on one in which to live and work ; to make his name and abilities known, so that where he settled he should not be received as a stranger ; and lastly to employ his good fortune in life, and the liberality of his father, in preparing the ground for future efforts.' [4] The journey was thus to be to him what the artistic tour of other musicians had been to them ; but with the important difference, resulting from his fortunate position in life, that the establishment of his musical reputation was not the exclusive object, but that his journey was to give him a knowledge of the world, and form his character and manners. Music had not been adopted as a profession for Felix without much hesitation, and resistance on the part of some of his relations, and his father was wisely resolved that in so doing nothing should be sacrificed in the general culture and elevation of his son. The reason alleged to have been given by a young Scotch student for going to Oxford, ' To improve myself, and to make friends,' was Mendelssohn's motto, not only during his grand tour but throughout his career.

It was their first serious parting. His father and Rebecka accompanied him to Hamburg. The boat (the *Attwood*) left on the Saturday evening before Easter Sunday, Apr. 18, and it was not till noon on Tuesday, the 21st, that he reached the Custom House, London. The passage was a very bad one, the engines broke down, and Mendelssohn lay insensible for the whole of Sunday and Monday. He was welcomed on landing by Klingemann and Moscheles, and lodged at the house then numbered 103 Great Portland Street, where his landlord was Heinke, a German ironmonger.[5]

It was the middle of the musical season, and on the night of his arrival Malibran made her first reappearance at the opera, as Desdemona.[6] Other singers in London at that time were Sontag, Pisaroni, Mme. Stockhausen and Don-

zelli ; also Velluti, the castrato, a strange survival of the ancient world, whom it is difficult to think of in connexion with Felix Mendelssohn - Bartholdy. De Bériot and Madame Dulcken were among the players. Fétis, too, was in London with the object of delivering his lectures (of which only one was given) on ' La musique à la portée de tout le monde,' in French, to English audiences. Felix was much with Mr. and Mrs. Moscheles, and there met Neukomm, with whom, in everything but his music, he sympathised warmly.

His first appearance before an English audience was at the Philharmonic Concert, then held in the ARGYLL ROOMS (*q.v.*), on Monday evening, May 25, when he conducted his symphony in C minor. Old John Cramer ' led him to the piano, as if he were a young lady.' [7] The applause was immense, and the scherzo (scored by him from his octet for this occasion, in place of the original minuet and trio) was obstinately encored against his wish.[8] How deeply he felt the warmth of his reception may be seen from his letter to the Society.[9] He published the symphony with a dedication to the Philharmonic,[10] and they on their part elected him an honorary member of the Society on Nov. 29, 1829. It was thus an English body which gave him his first recognition as a composer.[11] The simple applause of London had wiped out the sneers and misunderstandings of Berlin. This he never forgot : it recurs throughout his correspondence, and animates his account of his latest visits to us. Near the close of his life he spoke of it as ' having lifted a stone from his heart.' [12] The English had much to learn, and he could laugh heartily at them ; but at least they loved him and his music, and were quite in earnest in their appreciation.[13] Five days afterwards, on the 30th, at 2 P.M., he appeared again in the Argyll Rooms at what is vaguely called in *The Times* of June 1 ' The fourth grand concert.' He played the Concertstück of Weber —as the same journal informs us—' with no music before him.' A charming letter,[14] equal to any in the whole collection for its gaiety and bright humour, describes his coming to the rooms early to try the piano—a new Clementi —and his losing himself in extemporising till he was recalled by finding that the audience were taking their seats. Two other concerts must be mentioned : one by Drouet, the flute-player, on Midsummer Night, at which, most appropriately, the overture to the ' Midsummer Night's Dream' was given, for the first time in England, and he himself played the E flat concerto of Beethoven. After the concert the score

[1] Zelter's *Correspondence with Goethe*, letter 641, Mar. 9, 1829.
[2] *L.* to Schleinitz, Apr. 16, 1835.
[3] ' My great journey ' he calls it, *G. & M.* pp. 100, 187.
[4] *L.* Feb. 21, 1832.
[5] The corner of Ridinghouse Street, since 1858 numbered 79. The house was rebuilt in 1904 ; a photograph of it, taken before the rebuilding, will be found in *Musical Haunts in London*, by F. G. Edwards (1895), p. 42. See also *Mus. T.*, Dec. 1899, p. 528, and Sept. 1904, p. 581.
[6] His account of her, with other letters describing this period, will be found in *F.M.* i. 214-94, in *Dev.*, and in *Letters of Felix Mendelssohn to Ignaz and Charlotte Moscheles* (1888).

[7] *F.M.* i. 226.　　　　[8] *Ibid.*
[9] *Hogarth*, p. 51. The letter is in French.
[10] The autograph of the Symphony—in the green cloth boards so familiar to those who know his MS. scores—is now in the Society's Library.
[11] See the statement to this effect in *A.M.Z.* for 1836, p. 337.
[12] Letter to Mme. Jenny Lind-Goldschmidt.
[13] See *F.M.* i. 232, and *Dev.* pp. 81, 82.
[14] *F.M.* i. 227, dated June 7, 1829.

of the overture was left in the hackney coach by Attwood, and lost.[1] The other concert on July 13 was for the benefit of the sufferers from the floods in Silesia.[2] At this the overture was repeated, and Felix and Moscheles played (for the first and only time in England) a concerto by the former for two pianofortes and orchestra, in E.[3] All this was a brilliant beginning, as far as compositions went; it placed him in the best possible position before the musical society of London, but it did not do much to solve the question of livelihood, since the only commission which we hear of his receiving, and which delighted him hugely, he was compelled for obvious reasons to decline, viz. a festival hymn for Ceylon for the anniversary of the emancipation of the natives ! — an idea so comical that he says it had kept him laughing inwardly for two days.[4] A MS. letter of this time (dated June 7) is signed ' Composer to the Island of Ceylon.'

But he found time for other things besides music ; for the House of Commons, and picture galleries, and balls at Devonshire House and Lansdowne House, and so many other parties, that the good people at home took fright and thought he was giving up music for society, and would become a drawing-room ornament.[5] The charm of his manner and his entire simplicity took people captive, and he laid a good foundation this year for the time to come.

An amusing little picture of himself and his friends Rosen and Mühlenfeld, coming home late from a state dinner given by the Prussian Ambassador, buying three German sausages, and then finding a quiet street in which to devour them, with a three-part song and peals of laughter between the mouthfuls, shows how gaily life went on outside the concert-room.[6]

At length the musical season was over. Felix and Klingemann left London about July 21, and stopping at York (23rd) and Durham (24th),[7] were in Edinburgh by the 28th.[8] On the 29th they were present at the annual competition of Highland Pipers in the Theatre Royal.[9] On the 30th, before leaving ' the grey metropolis of the north,' they went over Holyrood Palace, saw the traditional scene of the murder of Rizzio, and the chapel with the altar at which Mary was crowned standing ' open to the sky, and surrounded with grass and ivy, and everything ruined and decayed ' : ' and I think,' he continues, ' that I found there the beginning of

my Scotch Symphony.' The passage which he then wrote down was the first sixteen bars of the Introduction, which recurs at the end of the first movement, and thus forms, as it were, the motto of the work.[10]

From Edinburgh they went to Abbotsford, and thence by Stirling, Perth and Dunkeld, to Blair-Atholl ; then on foot by Fort-William to Tobermory, sketching and writing enormous letters at every step. On the way they visited Fingal's Cave, and Felix, writing ' auf einer Hebride '—' on one of the Hebrides '—Aug. 7, gives twenty bars of music, ' to show how extraordinarily the place affected me.' These twenty bars,[11] an actual inspiration, are virtually identical with the opening of the wonderful overture which bears the name of ' Hebrides ' or ' Fingal's Cave.' Then came Glasgow, and then Liverpool. At Liverpool they went over a new American liner called the Napoleon, and Felix, finding a Broadwood piano in the saloon, sat down to it and played for himself and his friend the first movement of Fanny's ' Easter-Sonata ' —whatever that may have been. Home was always in his thoughts. Then to Holyhead for Ireland, but the weather was dreadful. He says : ' Yesterday was a good day, for I was only wet through three times.' So he turned back to Liverpool, there said good-bye to Klingemann, and went on by Chester to the house of John Taylor,[12] a mining engineer, at Coed-du near Holywell. Here he remained for some days, seeing a very pleasant side of English country life, and making an indelible impression on his hosts ; and here he composed the three pianoforte pieces which form op. 16, the first of which in key, tempo and melody closely resembles the introduction to the Scotch Symphony.[13]

His head was at this time full of music—the E flat violin quartet (op. 12)[14]; an organ piece for Fanny's wedding[15]; the Reformation Symphony, the Scotch Symphony, the ' Hebrides ' overture, as well as vocal music, ' of which he will say nothing.' Other subjects, however, occupied even more of his letters than music. Such were a private plan for a journey to Italy in company with his parents and Rebecka, for which he enters into a little conspiracy with his sister ; and a scheme for the celebration of his parents' silver wedding (Dec. 26, 1829), by the perform-

[1] The discovery in 1906 at the R.A.M. of a German copyist's score from which Mendelssohn had undoubtedly conducted the London performance of 1830, and possibly also this one of 1829, seems to disprove the story originally told here of Mendelssohn rewriting the score from memory.   C.

[2] This was suggested by Mendelssohn's uncle Nathan, who lived in Silesia, to his brother Abraham, and by him communicated to Felix (*F.M.* i. 236).

[3] See Felix's letters describing this, July 10, 16, and 17 (*F.M.* i. 233-40) ; also *Mos.* i. 227. The autograph of the Concerto is dated Oct. 17, 1823.

[4] *F.M.* i. 230.   [5] *Dev.* p. 78.

[6] *F.M.* i. 235.

[7] Their journey can be traced by Felix's sketches.

[8] *F.M.* i. 240.

[9] *Ibid.* ; *Hogarth*, p. 77. I owe the date to the kindness of John Glen of Edinburgh.

[10] *F.M.* i. 244.

[11] Ten of the present score, as he afterwards diminished the notation by one-half. A facsimile is given in *F.M.* i. 257.

[12] A letter from Miss Anne Taylor, afterwards Mrs. Worsley, was quoted at length here in former editions. It gives a charming picture of Mendelssohn's personality and of his relations with his hosts. It mentions the piano piece, ' " The Rivulet," which he wrote at that time for my sister Susan.' Cf. *Dev.* p. 175.

[13] Both Allegros are in 6-8, and the Andante is repeated at the end of each. The piece is dated ' Coed-du, Sept. 4,' [1829].

[14] *F.M.* pp. 276, 279, 280. The autograph of the Quartet, in the possession of Mr. Rudorf, is dated ' London, Sept. 14, 1829.' Though published as No. 1, it is thus really his second string quartet. See above, p. 118. The quartet was dedicated to ' B[etty] P[istor] ' ; but after her engagement to Rudorf, Mendelssohn requested David to alter the initials (' durch einen kleinen Federschwanz ') to ' B. R.' (see Eckardt's *Ferdinand David*, p. 35). In the same letter he calls it ' Quartet aus S.'

[15] Fanny herself wrote the piece which was actually played at the wedding, Oct. 3, 1829 (*F.M.* i. 296). Felix's piece, however, was finished and written out (*L.* to Fanny, July 25, 1844).

ance of three operettas (Liederspiel), his own 'Soldatenliebschaft,' a second to be written by Hensel and composed by Fanny, and the third an 'Idyll' by Klingemann and himself, which when once it entered his head rapidly took shape, and by the end of October appears to have been virtually complete.[1]

By Sept. 10 he was again in London, this time at 35 Bury Street, St. James's, Klingemann's lodgings[2]; on the 14th he finished and signed the E flat quartet, and on the 17th was thrown from a gig and hurt his knee, which forced him to keep his bed for nearly two months, and thus to miss not only a tour through Holland and Belgium with his father, but Fanny's wedding. Confinement to bed, however, does not prevent his writing home with the greatest regularity. On Sept. 22 he ends his letter with the first phrase of the 'Hebrides' overture— 'aber zum Wiedersehn,

F.'

On Oct. 23 he informs them that he is beginning again to compose—and so on. He was nursed by Klingemann, and well cared for by Sir Lewis and Lady Moller, by Attwood and Hawes (the musicians), the Goschens and others. His first drive was on Nov. 6, when he found London 'indescribably beautiful.' A week later he went to Norwood to the Attwoods,[3] then back to town for 'the fourteen happiest days he had ever known,' and on Nov. 29 was at Hôtel Quillacq, Calais, on his road home.

He reached Berlin to find the Hensels and the Devrients inhabiting rooms in the garden-house. His lameness still obliged him to walk with a stick; but this did not impede the mounting of his piece for the silver wedding,[4] which came off with the greatest success on Dec. 26, and displayed an amount of dramatic ability which excited the desire of his friends that he should again write for the stage.[5] The Liederspiel, however, was not enough to occupy him, and during this winter he composed a symphony for the tercentenary festival of the Augsburg Confession, which was in preparation for June 25, 1830.[6] This work, in the key of D, is that which we shall often again refer to as the 'Reformation Symphony.'[7] He also wrote the fine Fantasia in F sharp minor (op. 28) for pf., which he called his 'Scotch Sonata'[8]—a piece too little

played. A chair of music was founded in the Berlin University this winter expressly with a view to its being filled by Mendelssohn. But on the offer being made he declined it, and at his instance Marx was appointed in his stead.[9] There can be no doubt that he was right. Nothing probably could have entirely kept down Mendelssohn's ardour for composition; but it is certain that to have exchanged the career of a composer for that of a university teacher would have added a serious burden to the many occupations which already beset him, besides forcing him to exchange a pursuit which he loved and succeeded in, for one for which he had no turn—for teaching was not his *forte*.[10]

The winter was over, his leg was well, and he was on the point of resuming his 'great journey' in its southern portion, when, at the end of Mar. 1830, both Rebecka and he were taken ill with measles. This involved a delay of a month, and it was not till May 13 that he was able to start.[11] His father accompanied him as far as Dessau, the original seat of the family, where he remained for a few days with his friend Schubring.

CONTINENTAL TRAVELS.—He travelled through Leipzig, Weissenfels and Naumburg, and reached Weimar on the 20th. There he remained a fortnight in the enjoyment of the closest intercourse with Goethe and his family, playing and leading what he calls a mad life— *Heidenleben*.[12] There his portrait was taken, which, though like, 'made him look very sulky,' and a copy of the score of the Reformation Symphony was made and sent to Fanny. On June 3 he took leave of Goethe for the last time,[13] and went by Nuremberg to Munich, which he reached on June 6.[14] At Munich he made a long halt, remaining till the end of the month; made the acquaintance of Josephine Lang, Delphine Schauroth and other interesting persons, and was fêted to an extraordinary extent[15]—'several parties every evening and more pianoforte playing than I ever recollect' —all which must be read in the letter of Marx, and in his own delightful pages.[16] On June 14, he sends Fanny a little Song without Words (Lied) in A, and on the 26th, 'on the birth of her son,' a much longer one in B flat minor, which he afterwards altered, and published as op. 30, No. 2.[17] Both here and at Vienna he is disgusted at the ignorance on the part of the best players— Mozart, Haydn and Beethoven utterly ignored, Hummel, Field and Kalkbrenner accepted as classics. He himself played the best music, and with the best effect, and his visit must

[1] *F.M.* i. 302-4; *Dev.* p. 86.　　[2] *F.M.* i. 301.
[3] Op. 16, No. 2, is dated 'Norwood, Surrey, Nov. 18.' There is a MS. letter from the same address, Nov. 15. The house was on Beulah Hill. (A photograph of it is given in *Musical Haunts in London*, p. 5.)
[4] 'Heimkehr aus der Fremde' (The Return from Abroad). It was translated by Chorley as 'Son and Stranger,' and produced at the Haymarket Theatre, July 7, 1851.
[5] *Dev.* p. 94.
[6] The first mention of the symphony appears to be in a letter of his own from North Wales, Sept. 2, 1829. The tercentenary was intended to be celebrated throughout Germany, but the political troubles of 1830 prevented any festive demonstrations.
[7] For some curious details regarding this, see *Dev.* p. 96. Schubring (302*b*) tells the same story of the Trumpet Overture.
[8] The MS., formerly in Mr. Schleinitz's possession, is entitled 'Sonate écossaise,' and dated 'Berlin, Jan. 29, 1833'; but he played it at Goethe's, May 24, 1830 (*L*, May 25, 1830).

[9] *Dev.* p. 98.
[10] See a remark in Hauptmann's *Letters to Hauser* (i. 157) in reference to a similar attempt in 1835.
[11] *F.M.* i. 313 (inaccurately August, but corrected in the second edition, from which the English translation was made).
[12] *L.* May 25, 1830. See also letters in *G. & M.*
[13] *G. & M.* p. 70.　　[14] *L.* June 6, 1830.
[15] *L.* to Zelter, Oct. 16, 1830.　　[16] *F.M.* i. 313-27.
[17] In this, as in several other cases, he has altered the notation from quavers to semiquavers.

have marked an epoch in the taste of both places.[1]

From Munich he went through the Salzkammergut, by Salzburg, Ischl and the Traunsee, to Linz, and thence to Vienna, Aug. 13. Here he passed more than a month of the gayest life [2] with Hauser the singer,[3] Merk the violoncellist, the Pereiras, the Eskeles and others, but not so gay as to interfere with serious composition— witness a cantata or anthem on ' O Haupt voll Blut und Wunden ' (MS.),[4] and an ' Ave Maria ' for tenor solo and 8-part chorus (op. 23, No. 2), both of this date. On Sept. 28 we find him at Pressburg, witnessing the coronation of the Crown Prince Ferdinand as King of Hungary[5]; then at Lilienfeld ; and by Gratz, Udine, etc., he reached Venice on Oct. 9.

His stay in Italy, and his journey through Switzerland back to Munich, are so fully depicted in the volume of his Letters from Italy and Switzerland, that it is only necessary to allude to the chief points. He went from Venice by Bologna to Florence, reaching it on Oct. 22, and remaining there for a week. He arrived in Rome on Nov. 1—the same day as Goethe had done, as he is careful to remark—and he lived there till Apr. 10, 1831, at No. 5 Piazza di Spagna. The latter half of April and the whole of May were devoted to Naples (Sti. Combi, Sta. Lucia, No. 13, on the 3rd floor) and the Bay —Sorrento, Ischia, Amalfi, etc. Here he met Benedict, and renewed the acquaintance which they had begun as boys in Berlin in 1821, when Benedict was Weber's pupil.[6] By June 5 he was back in Rome, and after a fortnight's interval set out on his homeward journey by Florence (June 24), Genoa, Milan (July 7-15), Lago Maggiore and the Islands, the Simplon, Martigny and the Col de Balme, to Chamounix and Geneva. Thence on foot across the mountains to Interlaken ; and thence by Grindelwald and the Furka to Lucerne, Aug. 27 and 28. At Interlaken, besides sketching, and writing both letters and songs, he composed the only waltzes of which—strange as it seems in one so madly fond of dancing—any trace survives.[7] At Lucerne he wrote his last letter to Goethe,[8] and no doubt mentioned his being engaged in the composition of the 'Walpurgisnacht,' which must have brought out from the poet the explanation of the aim of his poem which is printed at the beginning of Mendelssohn's music, with the date Sept. 9, 1831. Then, still on foot, he went by Wallenstadt and St. Gall to Augsburg, and returned to Munich early in September.

Into both the nature and the art of this extended and varied tract he entered with enthusiasm. The engravings with which his father's house was richly furnished, and Hensel's

copies of the Italian masters, had prepared him for many of the great pictures ; but to see them on the spot was to give them new life, and it is delightful to read his rapturous comments on the Titians of Venice and Rome, the gems in the Tribune of Florence, Guido's ' Aurora,' and other masterpieces. His remarks are instructive and to the point ; no vague generalities or raptures, but real criticism into the effect or meaning or treatment of the work ; and yet rather from the point of view of an intelligent amateur than with any assumption of technical knowledge, and always with sympathy and kindness.[9] Nor is his eye for nature less keen, or his enthusiasm less abundant. His descriptions of the scenery of Switzerland during the extraordinarily stormy season of his journey there are worthy of the greatest painters or letter-writers. Some of his expressions rise to grandeur.

' It was a day,' he says, describing his walk over the Wengern Alp,

' as if made on purpose. The sky was flecked with white clouds floating far above the highest snow-peaks, no mists below on any of the mountains, and all their summits glittering brightly in the morning air, every undulation and the face of every hill clear and distinct. . . . I remembered the mountains before only as huge peaks. It was their height that formerly took such possession of me. Now it was their boundless extent that I particularly felt, their huge broad masses, the close connection of all these enormous fortresses, which seemed to be crowding together and stretching out their hands to each other. Then, too, recollect that every glacier, every snowy plateau, every rocky summit was dazzling with light and glory, and that the more distant summits of the further ranges seemed to stretch over and peer in upon us. I do believe that such are the thoughts of God Himself. Those who do not know Him may here find Him and the nature which He has created, brought strongly before their eyes.' [10]

Other expressions are very happy :

" The mountains are acknowledged to be the finest after rain, and to-day looked as fresh as if they had just burst the shell.' [11]

Again, in approaching Naples :

' To me the finest object in nature is and always will be the sea. I love it almost more than the sky. I always feel happy when I see before me the wide expanse of waters.'

In Rome he devoted all the time that he could spare from work to the methodical examination of the place and the people. But his music stood first, and surely no one before or since was ever so self-denying on a first visit to the Eternal City. Not even for the sirocco would he give up work in the prescribed hours.[12] His plan was to compose or practise till noon, and then spend the whole of the rest of the daylight in the open air. He enters into everything with enthusiasm—it is ' a delightful existence.' Rome in all its vast dimensions lies before him like an interesting problem, and he goes deliberately to work, daily selecting some different object—the ruins of the ancient city,

1 L. to Zelter, June 22 (not included in the English trans.), and Oct. 16, 1830.   2 Dev. p. 105.
3 Afterwards director of the Munich Conservatorium and Spohr's correspondent.
4 Dev. p. 105.   5 L. to Paul, Sept. 27, 1830.
6 B. p. 7.   7 L. Aug. 11, 1831.   8 G. & M. p. 80.

9 L. Oct. 25, 1830 ; June 25, 1831 ; Sept. 14, 1839.
10 L. Aug. 14, 1831.   11 L. Aug. 24.
12 Berlioz, Voyage musical, i. 76.

the Borghese Gallery, the Capitol, St. Peter's, or the Vatican.

'Each day is thus made memorable, and, as I take my time, each object becomes indelibly impressed upon me. . . . When I have fairly imprinted an object on my mind, and each day a fresh one, twilight has usually arrived, and the day is over.'

Into society he enters with keen zest, giving and receiving pleasure wherever he goes, and 'amusing himself thoroughly and divinely.' 'My looking-glass is stuck full of visiting-cards, and I spend every evening with a fresh acquaintance.' [1] His visits to Horace Vernet and Thorwaldsen, Santini's visits to him ; the ball at Torlonia's, where he first saw the young English beauty, and that at the Palazzo Albani, where he danced with her ; the mad frolics of the Carnival, the monks in the street (on whom he 'will one day write a special treatise '), the peasants in the rain, the very air and sunshine —all delight him in the most simple, healthy and natural manner.

'Oh! if I could but send you in this letter one quarter of an hour of all this pleasure, or tell you how life actually flies in Rome, every minute bringing its own memorable delights.' [2]

On the other hand, he has no mercy on anything like affectation or conceit. He lashes the German painters for their hats, their beards, their dogs, their discontent, and their incompetence, just as he does one or two German musicians for their empty pretension. The few words which he devotes to Berlioz (who although always his good friend is antagonistic to him on every point) and his companion Montfort, are strongly tinged with the same feeling.[3] On the other hand, nothing can be more genuinely and good-naturedly comic than his account of the attempt to sing Marcello's psalms by a company of dilettanti assisted by a Papal singer.[4]

This sound and healthy habit of mind it is, perhaps, which excludes the sentimental—we might almost say the devotional—feeling which is so markedly absent from his letters. Strange that an artist who so enjoyed the remains of ancient Italy should have had no love of antiquity as such. At sight of Nisida he recalls the fact that it was the refuge of Brutus, and that Cicero visited him there.

'The sea lay between the islands, and the rocks, covered with vegetation, bent over it then just as they do now. These are the antiquities that interest me, and are much more suggestive than crumbling mason-work.' . . .
'The outlines of the Alban hills remain unchanged. There they can scribble no names and compose no inscriptions . . . and to these I cling.'

In reference to music the same spirit shows itself still more strongly in his indignation at the ancient Gregorian music to the Passion in the Holy Week services.

'It does irritate me to hear such sacred and touching words sung to such insignificant dull music. They say it is *canto fermo*, Gregorian, etc. No matter. If at that period there was neither the feeling nor the capacity to write in a different style, at all events we have now the power to do so ' ;

and he goes on to suggest two alternative plans for altering and reforming the service.

He was very fortunate in the time of his visit to Rome. Pope Pius VIII. died while he was there, and he came in for all the ceremonies of Gregory XVI.'s installation, in addition to the services of Holy Week, etc. These latter he has described in the fullest manner, not only as to their picturesque and general effect, but down to the smallest details of the music, in regard to which he rivalled Mozart's famous feat. They form the subject of two long letters to Zelter, dated Dec. 1, 1830,[5] and June 16, 1831 ; and as all the particulars had to be caught while he listened, they testify in the strongest manner to the sharpness of his ear and the retentiveness of his memory. Indeed it is impossible not to feel that in such letters as these he is on his own ground, and that, intense as was his enjoyment of nature, painting, society and life, he belonged really to none of these things—was 'neither a politician nor a dancer, nor an actor, nor a *bel esprit*, but a musician.' [6] And so it proved in fact. For with all these distractions his Italian journey was fruitful in work. The 'Walpurgisnacht,' [7] the result of his last visit to Weimar, was finished, in its first form, at Milan (the MS. is dated 'Mailand, July 15, 1831 '); the 'Hebrides,' also in its first form, is signed 'Rome, Dec. 16, 1830.' [8] The Italian and Scotch Symphonies were begun and far advanced before he left Italy. Several smaller works belong to this period—the Psalm 'Non Nobis' (Nov. 15, 1830) ; the three church pieces which form op. 23 ; a Christmas Cantata, still in MS. (Jan. 28, 1831) ; the hymn 'Verleih' uns Frieden ' (Feb. 10) ; the three motets for the nuns of the Trinità de' Monti at Rome ; and although few of these minor pieces can be really said to live, yet they embody much labour and devotion, and were admirable stepping-stones to the great vocal works of his later life. In fact, then, as always, he was what Berlioz calls him, 'un producteur infatigable,' [9] and thus obtained that facility which few composers have possessed in greater degree than Mozart and himself. He sought the society of musicians. Besides Berlioz, Montfort and Benedict, we find frequent mention of Baini, Donizetti, Coccia and Madame Fodor. At Milan his encounter with Madame Ertmann, the intimate friend of Beethoven, was a happy

---

1 *L.* from Rome, Nov. 2, 1830, to Apr. 4, 1831.
2 *L.* Feb. 8, 1831.
3 *L.* Mar. 29, 1831. It is curious to compare Berlioz's account (*Voyage mus.* i. 73) of Mendelssohn with the above.
4 *L.* Mar. 1, 1831.

5 This was added to the *Reisebriefe* in a subsequent edition, and is not included in the English translation.
6 *L.* to Fanny, Dec. 28, 1831.
7 The vocal portion was begun in April. Feb. 13, 1832, is the date of the completion of the overture—' Saxon Overture ' as he calls it—in the ' Walpurgisnacht.'
8 The date of the revised version is ' London, June 20, 1832.'
9 *Voyage musical*, i. 76.

accident, and turned to the happiest account. There, too, he met the son of Mozart, and delighted him with his father's overtures to ' Don Juan ' and the ' Magic Flute,' played in his own ' splendid orchestral style ' on the piano. Not the least pleasant portions of his letters from Switzerland are those describing his organ-playing at the little remote Swiss churches at Engelberg, Wallenstadt, Sargans and Lindau —from which we would gladly quote if space allowed.

The great event of his second visit to Munich was the production (and no doubt the composition) of his G minor concerto, ' a thing rapidly thrown off,' [1] which he played on Oct. 17, 1831, at a concert which also comprised his symphony in C minor, his overture to the ' Midsummer Night's Dream,' and an extempore performance. Before leaving he received a commission to compose an opera for the Munich Theatre.[2] From Munich he travelled by Stuttgart (Nov. 7) and Heidelberg to Frankfort, and thence to Düsseldorf (Nov. 27), to consult Immermann as to the libretto for the Munich opera, and arrange with him for one founded on ' The Tempest.' [3] The artistic life of Düsseldorf pleased him extremely, and no doubt this visit laid the foundation for his future connexion with that town.

He arrived in Paris about the middle of December, and found, of his German friends, Hiller and Franck settled there. He renewed his acquaintance with the Parisian musicians who had known him as a boy in 1825, especially with Baillot ; and made many new friends, Habeneck, Franchomme, Cuvillon and others. Chopin, Meyerbeer, Herz, Liszt, Kalkbrenner, Ole Bull, were all there, and Mendelssohn seems to have been very much with them. He went a great deal into society and played frequently, was constantly at the theatre, and as constantly at the Louvre, enjoyed life thoroughly, saw everything, according to his wont, including the political scenes which were then more than ever interesting in Paris ; knew everybody ; and in fact, as he expresses it, ' cast himself thoroughly into the vortex.' [4] His overture ' Midsummer Night's Dream ' was performed at the Société des Concerts (Conservatoire) on Feb. 19, 1832, and he himself played the concerto in G of Beethoven at the concert of Mar. 18. His Reformation Symphony was rehearsed, but the orchestra thought it too learned, and it never reached performance.[5] His octet was played in church at a mass commemorative of Beethoven, and several times in private ; so was his quintet (with a new Adagio [6]) and his quartets, both for strings and for piano. The pupils of the Conservatoire, he writes, are

working their fingers off to play ' Ist es wahr ? ' : [7] His playing was applauded as much as heart could wish, and his reception in all circles was of the very best.

On the other hand, there were drawbacks. Eduard Ritz, his great friend, died (Jan. 23) while he was there ; the news reached him on his birthday. Goethe, too, died (Mar. 22). The rejection of his Reformation Symphony, the centre of so many hopes,[8] was a disappointment which must have thrown a deep shadow over everything ; and no doubt after so much gaiety there was a reaction, and his old dislike to the French character—traces of which are not wanting in a letter to Immermann dated Jan. 11, 1832—returned. In addition to this his health had not latterly been good, and in March he had an attack of cholera.[9] Though he alludes to it in joke, he probably felt the truth of a remark in the Figaro that ' Paris is the tomb of all reputations.' [10] Brilliantly and cordially as he was received, he left no lasting mark there ; his name does not reappear in the programmes of the Conservatoire for eleven years, and it was not till the establishment of the Concerts Populaires in 1861 that his music became at all familiar to the Parisians.[11] He himself never again set foot in Paris.

LONDON AND BERLIN.—On Apr. 23, 1832, he was once more in his beloved London, and at his old quarters, in Great Portland Street. ' That smoky nest,' he exclaims, amid the sunshine of the Naples summer, ' is fated to be now and ever my favourite residence ; my heart swells when I think of it.' [12] And here he was back in it again ! It was warm, the lilacs were in bloom, his old friends were as cordial as if they had never parted, he was warmly welcomed everywhere, and felt his health return in full measure. His letters of this date are full of a genuine heartfelt satisfaction. He plunged at once into musical life. The ' Hebrides ' overture was played from MS. parts by the Philharmonic on May 14, and he performed his G minor concerto, on an Erard piano, at the concerts of May 28 and June 18. He gave a MS. score of his overture to the Society, and they presented him with a piece of plate. During his stay in London he wrote his Capriccio Brillant in B minor (op. 22), and played it at a concert of Mori's on May 25.[13] On Sunday, June 10, he played the organ at St. Paul's Cathedral.[14] He also published a four-hand arrangement [15] of the ' Midsummer Night's

---

[1] L. to his father, Dec. 28, 1833.
[2] L. to his father, Dec. 19, 1831.
[3] L. Dec. 19, 1831 ; Jan. 11, 1832.
L. Dec. 28, 1831 ; Jan. 11, 1832.   [5] H. p. 21.
[6] Written in memory of Eduard Ritz, and replacing a Minuet in F sharp minor, with Trio in double Canon.

[7] The Lied embodied in the A minor Quartet. See above, p. 382.
[8] H. p. 22.
[9] H. p. 33.   Letter to Bärmann, Paris, Apr. 16, 1832, in Letters of Distinguished Musicians, p. 406.
[10] Fétis is inaccurate in citing this as Mendelssohn's own expression.   See L. Mar. 31, 1832.
[11] This want of sympathy, combined with an astonishing amount of ignorance, is amusingly displayed in the following description from the catalogue of a well-known French autograph collector : ' Mendelssohn - Bartholdy (Felix) remarquable intelligence, mais cœur égoïste et froid ; qui n'ayant pu gravir d'un pas sur les sommets de l'art, s'est réfugié dans la musique de chambre.' Can ignorance and confidence go further ?
[12] L. to his sisters, May 28, 1831.
[13] Mos. i. 271.   [14] Ibid. p. 272.   [15] Ibid.

Dream' overture with Cramer, and the first book of the 'Songs without Words' with Novello,[1] and played at many concerts. A more important thing still was the revision of the 'Hebrides' overture,[2] to which he appears to have put the final touches on June 20 (five weeks after its performance at the Philharmonic), that being the date on the autograph score in possession of the family of Sterndale Bennett, which agrees in all essentials with the printed copy.

On May 15 Zelter died, and he received the news of the loss of his old friend and teacher at Attwood's house at Norwood. The vision of a possible offer of Zelter's post at the Singakademie crossed his mind, and is discussed with his father; but it was not destined to be fulfilled. Among the friends whom he made during this visit, never to lose till death, were the Horsleys, a family living in the country at Kensington. William Horsley was one of our most eminent glee-writers; his daughters were unusually musical; one of the sons, John Calcott Horsley, became R.A., and another, Charles Edward Horsley, was for many years a bright ornament to English music. The circle was not altogether unlike his Berlin home, and in his own words[3] he seldom spent a day without meeting one or other of the family.

In July 1832 he returned to Berlin, to find the charm of the summer life in the garden as great as before. His darling sister Rebecka[4] had been married to Professor Dirichlet in May. Another change was that the Devrients had migrated to another place, and Hensel's studios now occupied all the spare space in the garden-house. Immermann's promised libretto was waiting for him on his return, but from the terms in which he asks for Devrient's opinion on it, it is evident that it disappointed him, and we hear no more of the subject.[5] 'St. Paul' was beginning to occupy his mind (of which more anon), and he had not long been back when the election of the conductor for the Singakademie in Zelter's place came on the tapis. The details may be read elsewhere[6]; it is enough to say here that chiefly through the extra zeal and want of tact of his friend Devrient, though with the best intentions, Mendelssohn, for no fault of his own, was

dragged before the public as an opponent of Rungenhagen; and at length, on Jan. 22, 1833, was defeated by 60 votes out of 236. The defeat was aggravated by a sad want of judgment on the part of the family, who not only were annoyed, but showed their annoyance by withdrawing from the Singakademie, and thus making an open hostility. Felix himself said little, but he felt it deeply. He[7] describes it as a time of uncertainty, anxiety and suspense, which was as bad as a serious illness; and no doubt it widened the breach in his liking for Berlin, which had been begun by the rejection of 'Camacho.' He doubtless found some consolation in a grand piano which was forwarded to him in August by Pierre Erard of London.

His musical activity was at all events not impaired. Besides occupying himself with the Sunday music at home, Felix, during this winter, gave three public concerts at the room of the Singakademie in Nov. and Dec. 1832 and Jan. 1833,[8] at which he brought forward his 'Walpurgisnacht,' his Reformation Symphony, his overtures to the 'Midsummer Night's Dream,' 'Meéresstille' and 'Hebrides,'[1] his G minor concerto and his Capriccio in B minor for pf.; besides playing Beethoven's pf. sonatas (opp. 27 and 53) and his G major concerto, also a concerto of Bach in D minor—all, be it remembered, novelties at that time even to many experienced musicians. In addition to this he was working seriously at the Italian Symphony. The Philharmonic Society of London had passed a resolution on Nov. 5, 1832, asking him to compose 'a symphony, an overture and a vocal piece,' and offering him a hundred guineas for the exclusive right of performance during two years.[9] Of these the Italian Symphony was to be one, and the MS. score of the work accordingly bears the date 'Berlin, Mar. 13, 1833.' On Apr. 27 he wrote to the Society offering them the symphony with 'two new overtures, finished since last year' (doubtless the 'Fingal's Cave' and the Trumpet overtures), the extra one being intended 'as a sign of my gratitude for the pleasure and honour they have again conferred upon me.' Graceful and apparently spontaneous as it is, the symphony had not been an easy task. Mendelssohn was not exempt from the lot of most artists who attempt a great poem or a great composition; on the contrary, the bitterest moments he 'ever endured or could have imagined' were those which he experienced during the autumn when the work was in progress, and up to the last he had his doubts and misgivings as to the result. Now, however, when it was finished, he found that it pleased him and showed progress[10]—a very

---

[1] Under the title of 'Original Melodies for the Pianoforte' (Novello). It was during this visit also that he played to Vincent Novello Bach's little E minor prelude and fugue for the organ, a circumstance which led to its being published in England (by Novello) before it appeared in any other country, including Germany. (See *Mus. T.*, Nov. 1896, p. 724.)

[2] The first score, dated 'Rome, Dec. 16, 1830,' and entitled 'Die einsame Insel,' was formerly in possession of Felix Moscheles. The differences between this and the above-mentioned autograph are very great, chiefly in the working out. In an English letter, written from Attwood's house at Norwood, to Sir George Smart, and dated 'June 6, 1832,' he offers to the Philharmonic Society 'the score of my Overture to the "Isles of Fingal," as a sign of my deep and heartfelt gratitude for the indulgence and kindness they have shown to me during my second visit in this country' (B.M. Add. MSS. 33,965, fol. 251). The MS. does not, however, appear to be in the Society's library.

[3] *G. & M.* p. 97.

[4] A little book containing water-colour sketches and songs which Mendelssohn began for his sister, Rebecka Dirichlet, and dated Christmas 1832, was formerly in the possession of Sir Charles Santley, who left it to Miss Marie Pezze (Mrs. Duncan Montgomerie).　　　　c.

[5] *Dev.* p. 142.

[6] See especially *Dev.* pp. 145-56.

[7] *L.* to Pastor Bauer, Mar. 4, 1833.

[8] *A.M.Z.*, 1833, pp. 22, 58, 125. The dates are not given of all the concerts, but the second took place on Dec. 1, 1832.

[9] See the Resolution and his answer in *Hogarth*, pp. 59, 60.

[10] *L.* to Pastor Bauer, Apr. 6, 1833.

modest expression for a work so full of original thought, masterly expression, consummate execution and sunny beauty as the Italian Symphony, and, moreover, such a prodigious advance on his last work of the same kind ! [1]

On Feb. 8, 1833, a son was born to the Moscheleses, and one of the first letters written was to Mendelssohn, asking him to be godfather to the child. He sent a capital letter in reply, with an elaborate sketch,[2] and later on he transmitted a cradle song—published as op. 47, No. 6—for his godchild, Felix Moscheles. Early in April he left Berlin for Düsseldorf, to arrange for conducting the Lower Rhine Festival which took place May 26-28. As soon as the details had been completed, he went on to London for the christening of his godchild, and also to conduct the Philharmonic Concert of May 13, when his Italian Symphony was performed for the first time, and he himself played Mozart's D minor piano concerto. This was his third visit. He was there by Apr. 26—again at his old lodgings in Great Portland Street—and on May 1 he played at Moscheles's annual concert a brilliant set of four-hand variations on the Gipsy March in ' Preciosa,' which the two had composed together.[3]

On or after May 16 he left London and returned to Düsseldorf, in ample time for the rehearsal of the Festival, which began on Whitsunday, May 26, and was an immense success. ' Israel in Egypt ' [4] was the *pièce de résistance*, and among the other works were Beethoven's Pastoral Symphony and overture to ' Leonora,' and Felix's own Trumpet overture. Abraham Mendelssohn had come from Berlin for the Festival, and an excellent account of it will be found in his letters,[5] admirable letters, full of point and wisdom, and showing better than anything else could the deep affection and perfect understanding which existed between father and son. The brilliant success of the Festival and the personal fascination of Mendelssohn led to an offer from the authorities of Düsseldorf that he should undertake the charge of the entire musical arrangements of the town, embracing the direction of the church music and of two associations, for three years, from Oct. 1, 1833, at a yearly salary of 600 thalers (£90).[6] He had been much attracted by the active artistic life of the place when he visited Immermann at the close of his Italian journey, and there appears to have been no hesitation in his acceptance of the offer. This important agreement concluded, Felix returned to London for the fourth time, taking his father with him. They arrived about June 5, and went into the

old lodgings in Great Portland Street. It is the father's first visit, and his letters are full of little hits at the fog, the absence of the sun, the Sundays and other English peculiarities, and at his son's enthusiasm for it all. As far as the elder Mendelssohn was concerned, the first month was perfectly successful, but in the course of July he was laid up with an accident to his shin, which confined him to his room for three weeks, and although it gave him an excellent idea of English hospitality, it naturally threw a damp over the latter part of the visit. His blindness, too, seems to have begun to show itself.[7]

His son, however, experienced no such drawbacks. To his father he was everything. ' I cannot express,' says the grateful old man,

' what he has been to me, what a treasure of love, patience, endurance, thoughtfulness and tender care he has lavished on me ; and much as I owe him indirectly for a thousand kindnesses and attentions from others, I owe him far more for what he has done for me himself.' [8]

Only a few letters by Felix of this date have been printed,[9] but enough information can be picked up to show that he fully enjoyed himself. His Trumpet overture was played at the Philharmonic on June 10, 1833. He played the organ at St. Paul's (June 23), Klingemann and other friends at the bellows, and the church empty—introduction and fugue, extempore ; Attwood's Coronation Anthem, four hands, with Attwood; and three pieces of Bach.[10] He also evidently played a great deal in society, and his father's account of a mad evening with Malibran will stand as a type of many such.[11] The Moscheleses, Attwoods,[12] Horsleys and Alexanders are among the most prominent English names in the diaries and letters.[13] Besides Malibran, Schröder-Devrient, Herz and Hummel were among the foreign artists in London. On Aug. 4 the two left for Berlin,[14] Abraham having announced that he was bringing home ' a young painter named Alphonse Lovie,' who, of course, was no other than Felix himself.[15] They reached Berlin in due course, and by Sept. 27, 1833, Felix was at his new post.

WORK AT DÜSSELDORF.—Düsseldorf was the beginning of a new period in his career—of settled life away from the influences of home, which had hitherto formed so important an element in his existence. At Berlin both success and non-success were largely biassed by personal considerations ; here he was to start afresh, and to be entirely dependent on himself. He began his new career with vigour. He first attacked the church music, and as ' not one tolerable mass ' was to be found, scoured the country as far as Elberfeld, Cologne and Bonn,

---

[1] *I.e.* the early Symphony in C minor.
[2] A facsimile will be found in *Mos.* i. 284.
[3] *Mos.* i. 290. The duet was published by Cramer.
[4] It had been performed by the Singakademie of Berlin, Dec. 8, 1831, but probably with re-instrumentation. It was now done as Handel wrote it.
[5] *F.M.* i. 347-64.
[6] I cannot discover his exact status or title at Düsseldorf. In his own sketch of his life (see below) he styles himself Music-director of the Association for the Promotion of Music in Düsseldorf.

[7] *F.M.* i. 397.   [8] *Ibid.* p. 384.
[9] See *Letters of F. M. to I. & C. Moscheles*, pp. 70-74, and the amusing facsimiles of sketches therein.
[10] *F.M.* p. 372.   [11] *Ibid.* p. 377.
[12] See his letters to Attwood, *Mus. T.*, Dec. 1900, pp. 792 and 800.
[13] *Mos.* i. 298 ; Abraham M. in *F.M.* i. 368, 380, 382, etc.
[14] *Mos.* i. 299.   [15] *F.M.* i. 386.

and returned with a carriage-load of Palestrina, Lasso and Lotti. 'Israel in Egypt,' the 'Messiah,' 'Alexander's Feast' and 'Egmont' are among the music which we hear of at the concerts. .At the theatre, after a temporary disturbance, owing to a rise in prices, and a little over-eagerness, he was well received and successful ; and at first all was *couleur de rose*— 'a more agreeable position I cannot wish for.'[1] But he soon found that the theatre did not suit him ; he had too little sympathy with theatrical life, and the responsibility was too irksome. He therefore, after a few months' trial, in Mar. 1834,[2] relinquished his salary as far as the theatre was concerned, and held himself free, as a sort of Honorary Intendant.[3] His influence, however, made itself felt. 'Don Juan,' 'Figaro,' Cherubini's 'Deux Journées,' were amongst the operas given in the first four months ; and in the church we hear of masses by Beethoven and Cherubini, motets of Palestrina and cantatas of Bach, the Dettingen Te Deum, 'and on the whole as much good music as could be expected during my first winter.'[4] He lived on the ground floor of Schadow's house,[5] and was very much in the artistic circle, and always ready to make an excursion, to have a swim, to eat, to ride (for he kept a horse[6]), to dance or to sleep ; was working hard at water-colour drawing, under Schirmer's tuition, and was the life and soul of every company he entered.[7] May 18 - 20 was the Lower Rhine Festival at Aix-la-Chapelle, conducted by Ferdinand Ries ; there he met Hiller,[8] and also Chopin, whose acquaintance he had already made in Paris,[9] and who returned with him to Düsseldorf. During the spring of 1834 he was made a member of the Berlin Academy of the Fine Arts.[10]

Meantime, through all these labours and distractions, of pleasure or business alike, he was composing busily and well. The overture to 'Melusina'[11] was finished Nov. 14, 1833, and tried ; the Rondo Brillant for piano and orchestra in E flat (op. 29) on Jan. 29, 1834 ; 'Infelice,' for soprano and orchestra, for the Philharmonic Society (in its first shape),[12] is dated Apr. 3, and the fine Capriccio for piano-

forte in A minor (op. 33, No. 1), Apr. 9, 1834. He had also rewritten and greatly improved the 'Meeresstile' overture[13] for its publication by Breitkopf with the 'Midsummer Night's Dream' and 'Hebrides' overtures. A symphony which he mentions as on the road appears to have been superseded by a still more important work. In one of his letters from Paris (Dec. 19, 1831), complaining of the low morale of the opera librettos, he says that if that style is indispensable he 'will forsake opera and *write oratorios*.' The words had hardly left his pen when he was invited by the Cäcilien-Verein of Frankfort to compose an oratorio on St. Paul.[14] The general plan of the work, and such details as the exclusive use of the Bible and Choral-book, and the introduction of chorales, are stated by him at the very outset. On his return to Berlin he and Marx made a compact by which each was to write an oratorio-book for the other ; Mendelssohn was to write 'Moses' for Marx, and Marx 'St. Paul' for Mendelssohn.[15] Mendelssohn executed his task at once, and the full libretto, entitled 'Moses, an Oratorio, composed by A. B. M..' and signed 'F. M. B., 21 Aug. 1832,' is now in the possession of the family.[16] Marx, on the other hand, not only rejected Mendelssohn's book for 'Moses,' but threw up that of 'St. Paul' on the ground that chorales were an anachronism. In fact, this singular man's function in life seems to have been to differ with everybody. For the text of 'St. Paul,' Mendelssohn was indebted to his own selection, and to the aid of his friends Fürst and Schubring.[17] Like Handel, he knew his Bible well ; in his oratorios he followed it implicitly, and the three books of 'St. Paul,' 'Elijah' and the 'Lobgesang' are a proof (if any proof were needed after the 'Messiah' and 'Israel in Egypt') that, in his own words, 'the Bible is always the best of all.'[18] He began upon the music in Mar. 1834, not anticipating that it would occupy him long ;[19] but it dragged on, and was not completed till the beginning of 1836.

Though only Honorary Intendant at the Düsseldorf theatre, he busied himself with the approaching winter season, and before leaving for his holiday corresponded much with Devrient as to the engagement of singers.[20] Sept. 1834 he spent in Berlin,[21] and was back at Düsseldorf for the first concert on Oct. 23,[22] calling on his way at Cassel, and making the acquaintance of Hauptmann,[23] with whom he was destined in later life to be closely connected. The new theatre opened on Nov. 1.

1 *L.* to l. Fürst, July 20, 1834.
2 *L.* to his father, Mar. 28, 1834.
3 *L.* to Schubring, Aug. 6.
4 *L.* to his father, Mar. 28.　　5 *H.* p. 38.
6 The acquisition of this horse gives a good idea of his dutiful attitude towards his father. *L.* to his father, Mar. 28, 1834.
7 *Dev.* p. 174.　　8 *L.* to his mother, May 23, 1834 ; *H.* p. 36.
9 Karasowki's *Life of Chopin*, chap. xiv.
10 *L.* to his father, Dec. 28, 1833, and to Fanny, Apr. 7, 1834. On this occasion he sent in the following 'Memorandum of my biography and art-education.' 'I was born Feb. 3, 1809, at Hamburg ; in my 8th year began to learn music, and was taught thorough-bass and composition by Professor Zelter, and the Pianoforte, first by my mother and then by Mr. Ludwig Berger. In the year 1829 I left Berlin, travelled through England and Scotland, South Germany, Italy, Switzerland and France ; visited England twice more in the spring of 1832 and 1833, was there made Honorary Member of the Philharmonic Society, and since October 1833 have been Music-director of the Association for the Promotion of Music in Düsseldorf.' This is preserved in the archives of the Academy, and I am indebted for it to the kindness of Dr. Joachim.
11 First public performance at Düsseldorf in July of the following year.
12 The vocal piece of his contract with the Society. It was first sung by Mme. Caradori at the Philharmonic Concert of May 19, 1834, with violin obbligato by Henry Blagrove.

13 *L.* to Schubring, Aug. 6, 1834.
14 *L.* to Devrient, pp. 137, 138.　　15 *Marx*, ii. 139, etc.
16 It shows how fully Mendelssohn realised the connexion of the Old and New Testaments that his concluding chorus, after the giving of the Law, is 'This is the love of God, that we keep His commandments.'—1 John v. 3.
17 See *Sch.* ; and *Letters*, vol. fi.
18 *L.* to Schubring, July 15, 1834.
19 *Ibid.*, Sept. 6, 1833, etc.　　20 *Dev.* pp. 177-83.
21 *Ibid.* pp. 183, 184.　　22 *N.M. Zeitung.*
23 Hauptmann's letters to Hauser, i. 139.

He and Immermann quarrelled as to pre-cedence, or as to the distribution of the duties. The selection of singers and musicians, the bargaining with them, and all the countless worries which beset a manager, and which, by a new agreement, he had to undertake, proved a most uncongenial and, moreover, a most waste-ful task ; so uncongenial that at last, the day after the opening of the theatre, he suddenly ' made a *salto mortale* ' and threw up all connexion [1] with it, not without considerable irritability and inconsistency.[2] After this he continued to do his other duties, and to con-duct occasional operas, Julius Rietz being his assistant.

REMOVAL TO LEIPZIG.—With the opening of 1835 he received an invitation from Leipzig through Schleinitz, which resulted in his taking the post of Conductor of the Gewandhaus Con-certs there. His answers [3] to the invitation show not only how very careful he was not to infringe on the rights of others, but also how clearly and practically he looked at all the bearings of a question before he made up his mind upon it.

Before the change, however, several things happened. He conducted the Lower Rhine Festival of 1835 at Cologne (June 7-9) (see NIEDERRHEINISCHE MUSIKFESTE). The principal works were Handel's ' Solomon '—for which he had written an organ part in Italy ; Beethoven's symphony No. 8, and overture op. 124, a ' religious march ' and hymn of Cherubini's, and the Morning Hymn of his favourite J. F. Reichardt. The Festival was made more than ordinarily delightful to him by a present of Arnold's edition of Handel in thirty-two vols. from the committee. His father, mother and sisters were all there. The parents then went back with him to Düsseldorf; there his mother had a severe attack of illness, which prevented his taking them home to Berlin till the latter part of July.[4] At Cassel the father too fell ill, and Felix's energies were fully taxed on the road.[5] He remained with them at Berlin till the end of August, and then left for Leipzig to make the necessary prepara-tions for beginning the subscription concerts in the Gewandhaus on Oct. 4.

His house at Leipzig was in Reichel's garden, off the Promenade. Chopin visited him during the interval, and Felix had the pleasure of introducing him to Clara Wieck, then a girl of 16. His first introduction to Schumann is said to have taken place at Wieck's house on Oct. 3, the day before the Gewandhaus Concert, at which Clara played Beethoven's B flat trio.[6] Later came his old Berlin friend Ferdinand

David from Russia to lead the orchestra,[7] and Moscheles from London for a lengthened visit. Mendelssohn's new engagement began with the best auspices. The relief from the worries and responsibilities of Düsseldorf was immense,[8] and years afterwards he refers to it as ' when I first came to Leipzig and thought I was in Paradise.' [9] He was warmly welcomed on taking his seat, and the first concert led off with his ' Meeresstille ' overture.

Rebecka passed through Leipzig on Oct. 14 (1835) on her way from Belgium, and Felix and Moscheles accompanied her to Berlin for a visit of two days, returning to Leipzig for the next concert. Short as the visit was, it was more than usually gay. The house was full every evening, and by playing alternately, by playing four hands, and by the comical extempore tricks of which the two friends were so fond, and which they carried on to such perfection, the parents, especially the father, now quite blind, were greatly mystified and amused.[10] And well that it was so, for it was Felix's last oppor-tunity of gratifying the father he so tenderly loved and so deeply reverenced. At half-past 10 A.M. on Nov. 19, 1835, Abraham Mendels-sohn was dead. He died the death of the just, passing away, as his father had done, without warning, but also without pain. He turned over in his bed, saying that he would sleep a little; and in half an hour he was gone. Hensel started at once for Leipzig, and by Sunday morning, the 22nd, Felix was in the arms of his mother. How deeply he felt under this peculiarly heavy blow the reader must gather from his own letters. It fell on him with special force, because he was not only away from the family circle, but had no home of his own, as Fanny and Rebecka had, to mitigate the loss. He went back to Leipzig stunned, but determined to do his duty with all his might, finish ' St. Paul,' and thus most per-fectly fulfil his father's wishes. He had com-pleted the revision of his ' Melusina ' overture on Nov. 17, only three days before the fatal news reached him, and there was nothing to hinder him from finishing the oratorio. He had played in Bach's concerto in D minor for three pianofortes with Clara Wieck and Rakemann at the Gewandhaus Concert on Nov. 9, 1835.

The business of the day, however, had to go on. One of the chief events in this series of concerts was a performance of the Ninth Sym-phony of Beethoven, Feb. 11, 1836.[11] Another was Mendelssohn's performance of Mozart's D minor concerto ' as written ' (for it seems to have been always hitherto played after some adaptation),[12] on Jan. 29, with cadenzas which electrified his audience. Leipzig was particu-

1 *L.* to his mother, Nov. 4 ; to Rebecka, Nov. 23, 1834.
2 This is brought out in his father's letter, printed on p. 57 of *Letters from 1833-47.* See also Felix's letter to his mother of Nov. 4, 1834.
3 *L.* to Schleinitz, Jan. 26 and Apr. 16, 1835.
4 *L.* to Mrs. Voigt, Düsseldorf, July 17, 1835.
5 *L.* to F. W. von Schadow, Berlin, Aug. 9, 1835, in *Polko*, p. 19
6 Moscheles' *Life*, i. 301.

7 He joined definitely Feb. 25, 1836, after Matthai's death (*A.M.Z.*, 1836, p. 133).
8 *L.* to Hildebrandt, Leipzig, Oct. 31, 1835 in *Polko*, p. 191 ; also *Hiller*, p. 47.
9 *L.* to Fanny, June 18, 1839.   10 *F.M.* i. 422.
11 *A.M.Z.*, 1836, p. 273.   12 *Ibid.* p. 105.

'arly congenial to Mendelssohn. He was the idol of the town, had an orchestra full of enthusiasm and devotion, a first-rate coadjutor in David, who took much of the mechanical work of the orchestra off his shoulders ; and, moreover, he was relieved of all business arrangements, which were transacted by the committee, especially by Herr Schleinitz. Another point in which he could not but contrast his present position favourably with that at Düsseldorf was the absence of all rivalry or jealousy. The labour of the season, however, was severe, and he confesses that the first two months had taken more out of him than two years' composing would do.[1] The University of Leipzig showed its appreciation of his presence by conferring on him the degree of Doctor of Philosophy in March.[2]

Meantime Schelble's illness had cancelled the arrangement for producing ' St. Paul ' at Frankfort, and it had been secured for the Lower Rhine Festival at Düsseldorf (May 22-24, 1836). The programmes included, besides the new oratorio, the two overtures to 'Leonore,' both in C, ' No. 1 ' (then unknown) and ' No. 3 ' : one of Handel's Chandos anthems, the ' Davidde penitente ' of Mozart, and the Ninth Symphony. ' St. Paul ' was executed with the greatest enthusiasm, and produced a deep sensation. It was performed on the 22nd, not in the present large music-hall (Kaisersaal), but in the long low room which lies outside of that and below it, known as the Rittersaal, a too confined space for the purpose. For the details of the performance, including an escapade of one of the false witnesses, in which the coolness and skill of Fanny alone prevented a break-down, we must refer the reader to the contemporary accounts of Klingemann, Hiller and Polko.[3] To English readers the interest of the occasion is increased by the fact that Sterndale Bennett, then 20 years old, and fresh from the R.A.M., was present.

Schelble's illness induced Mendelssohn to take the direction of the famous Cäcilien-Verein at Frankfort. Leipzig had no claims on him after the concerts were over, and he was thus able to spend six weeks at Frankfort practising the choir in Bach's ' Gottes Zeit,' Handel's ' Samson,' and other works, and improved and inspired them greatly. He resided in Schelble's house at the corner of the ' Schöne Aussicht,' with a view up and down the Main. Hiller was then living in Frankfort ; Lindblad was there for a time ; and Rossini remained for a few days on his passage through, in constant intercourse with Felix.[4]

Mendelssohn's visit to Frankfort was, however, fraught with deeper results than these. It was indeed quite providential, since here he

met his future wife, Cécile Charlotte Sophie Jeanrenaud, a young lady of great beauty, nearly ten years younger than himself, the second daughter of a clergyman of the French Reformed Church, who had died many years before, leaving his wife (a Souchay by family) and children amongst the aristocracy of the town. The house was close to the Fahrthor, on the quay of the Main.[5] Madame Jeanrenaud was still young and good-looking, and it was a joke in the family that she herself was at first supposed to be the object of Mendelssohn's frequent visits. But though so reserved, he was not the less furiously in love, and those who were in the secret have told us how entirely absorbed he was by his passion, though without any sentimentality. He had already had many a passing attachment. Indeed, being at once so warm-hearted and so peculiarly attractive to women—and also, it should be said, so much sought by them—it is a strong tribute to his self-control that he was never before seriously or permanently involved. On no former occasion, however, is there a trace of any feeling that was not due entirely, or mainly, to some quality or accomplishment of the lady, and not to her actual personality. In the present case there could be no doubt either of the seriousness of his love or of the fact that it centred in Mlle. Jeanrenaud herself, and not in any of her tastes or pursuits. And yet, in order to test the reality of his feelings, he left Frankfort, at the very height of his passion, for a month's bathing at Scheveningen near the Hague.[6] His friend F. W. Schadow, the painter, accompanied him, and the restless state of his mind may be gathered from his letters to Hiller.[7] His love stood the test of absence triumphantly. Very shortly after his return, on Sept. 9, the betrothal took place, at Kronberg, near Frankfort[8] ; three weeks of bliss followed, and on Oct. 2 he was in his seat in the Gewandhaus, at the first concert of the season. Five days later (Oct. 7), in the distant city of Liverpool, ' St. Paul ' was performed for the first time in England,[9] under the direction of Sir George Smart. The season at Leipzig was a good one ; Sterndale Bennett, who had come over at Mendelssohn's invitation, made his first public appearance in his own pianoforte concerto in C minor, and the series closed with the Choral Symphony.

His engagement soon became known far and wide, and it is characteristic of Germany, and of Mendelssohn's intimate relation to all concerned in the Gewandhaus, that at one of the

1 L. to Hiller, Dec. 10, 1837.
2 A.M.Z., Mar. 30, 1836, p. 216.
3 See *Musical World*, June 17, 1836, and *B*. pp. 27, 28 ; *H*. p. 51 ; and *Polko*, p. 43 ; also *Mus. T*., Mar. 1891, p. 137.
4 *H*. p. 55 *et seq*.

5 A pencil-drawing of the Main and the Fahrthor, with the 'Schöne Aussicht ' in the distance, taken from the Jeanrenauds' windows, has the following inscription : ' Vendu à Mendelssohn au prix de l'exécution d'un nombre indéterminé de Fugues de J. S. Bach, et de la Copie d'un Rondo du même Maître. LAURENS à Montpellier.'
6 *H*. ch. iv. p. 51 *et seq*. ; *F.M*. ii. 30 ; *Dev*. p. 196.
7 *H*. pp. 62-72.
8 *L*. to his mother in *F.M*. ii. 27 ; *Polko*, p. 63.
9 The music had been revised since the Düsseldorf production and 14 numbers rejected. The English version was by William Ball, and the score was published in England, Nov. 1836.

concerts, the Finale to 'Fidelio,' 'Wer ein holdes Weib errungen,' should have been put into the programme by the directors with special reference to him, and that he should have been forced into extemporising on that suggestive theme, amid the shouts and enthusiasm of his audience. The rehearsals for the concerts, the concerts themselves, his pupils, friends passing through, visits to his fiancée, an increasing correspondence, kept him more than busy. Sterndale Bennett was living in Leipzig, and the two friends were much together. In addition to the subscription series and to the regular chamber concerts, there were performances of 'Israel in Egypt,' with a new organ part by him, on Nov. 7, and 'St. Paul,' on Mar. 16, 1837. The compositions of this winter are few, and all of one kind, namely, preludes and fugues for pianoforte.[1] The wedding took place on Mar. 28, 1837, at the Walloon French Reformed Church, Frankfort. For the wedding tour they went to Freiburg and into the Palatinate, and by the 15th of May had returned to Frankfort.[2] A journal which they kept together during the honeymoon is full of sketches and droll things of all kinds. In July they were at Bingen, Horchleim, Coblenz and Düsseldorf for some weeks. At Bingen, while swimming across to Assmannshausen, he had an attack of cramp which nearly cost him his life, and from which he was only saved by the boatman. The musical results of these few months were very important, and include the 42nd Psalm, the string quartet in E minor (op. 44, No. 2), an Andante and Allegro for pianoforte in E, published posthumously as a Capriccio (op. 118), the second pianoforte concerto, in D minor, and the three preludes[3] for the organ (op. 37). He was also in earnest correspondence with Schubring[4] as to a second oratorio, on the subject of St. Peter.

'ST. PAUL,' ORGAN MUSIC, etc.—It must have been hard to tear himself away so soon from his lovely young wife—and indeed he grumbles about it lustily[5]—but he had been engaged to conduct 'St. Paul,' and to play the organ and his new pianoforte concerto, at the Birmingham Festival. Accordingly on Aug. 24 he left Düsseldorf for Rotterdam, crossed to Margate in the *Attwood*, the same boat which had taken him over in 1829, and on the 27th is in London, on his fifth visit, at Klingemann's house, as cross as a man can well be.[6] But this did not prevent his setting to work with Klingemann at the plan of an oratorio on Elijah[7] over which they had two mornings'

consultation.[8] Before leaving London for Birmingham, he played the organ at St. Paul's—on Sunday afternoon, Sept. 10—and at Christ Church, Newgate Street, on Tuesday morning, the 12th. It was on the former of these two occasions that the vergers, finding that the congregation would not leave the Cathedral, withdrew the organ-blower, and let the wind out of the organ during Bach's prelude and fugue in A minor[9]—'near the end of the fugue,[10] before the subject comes in on the pedals.'[11] At Christ Church he was evidently in a good vein. He played 'six extempore fantasias,' one on a fugue subject given by old Wesley at the moment, and the Bach fugue just mentioned and Bach's toccata. Samuel Wesley—our own ancient hero, though 71 years old—was present and played. It was literally his Nunc Dimittis : he died on Oct. 11, 1837, a month from that date. Mendelssohn's organ-playing[12] on these occasions was eagerly watched. He was the greatest of the few great German organ-players who had visited this country, and the English organists, some of them no mean proficients, learned more than one lesson from him. 'It was not,' wrote Dr. Gauntlett,

'that he played Bach for the first time here,—several of us had done that. But he taught us how to play the *slow* fugue, for Adams and others had played them too fast. His words were, "Your organists think that Bach did not write a slow fugue for the organ." Also he brought out a number of pedalfugues which were not known here. We had played a few, but he was the first to play the D major, the G minor, the E major, the C minor, the short E minor,' etc.[13]

Even in those that were known he threw out points unsuspected before, as in the A minor fugue, where he took the episode on the Swell,

---

[1] Published as op. 35. See the Catalogue at the end of this article.
[2] *Dev.* p. 200.
[3] The fugues appear to have been composed later.
[4] *L.* to Schubring, July 14, 1837.
[5] *F.M.* ii. 51.
[6] *H.* p. 99.
[7] The earliest known reference to the oratorio of 'Elijah' is in a letter to Klingemann, dated 'The Hague, Aug. 12, 1836.' He says : 'If you would only give all the care and thought you bestow now upon St. Paul to an Elijah, or a St. Peter, or even an Og of Bashan !' See *The History of Mendelssohn's 'Elijah,'* by F. G. Edwards, p. 3 *& seq.*

[8] His private journal. He mentioned it to John C. Horsley, R.A., during this visit.
[9] For a very interesting account of these two performances by Dr. Gauntlett, see *Musical World,* Sept. 15, 1837, p. 8.
[10] His private journal.
[11] See a letter from Dr. Gauntlett to Sir George Grove in *Mus. T.,* Feb. 1902, p. 96.
[12] Mendelssohn's biographers have usually ignored his organ compositions, yet his 'Six Sonatas' and 'Three Preludes and Fugues' for the instrument have proved to be among the most vital of his works. Even the organ music of Bach himself is hardly more sure of its place in the repertory alike of student, church organist and recitalist. The Sonatas owe their origin to the enterprise of Messrs. Coventry & Hollier, a London firm of music publishers, who, noting the interest roused by Mendelssohn's organ-playing during his visits to England, commissioned him to write some organ music, suggesting the English title 'voluntary' as being specially suitable. Mendelssohn, however, preferred to call them 'sonatas,' although they contain scarcely a movement in sonata form as the term is generally understood (See SONATA, where their form is analysed.) Moreover, it is clear that he wrote them as independent movements, and with no view to their subsequent grouping. Writing to Coventry from Frankfort in 1844, he says : 'I hope soon to send you the promised organ pieces. Nine are ready, but I want to have twelve before I make a parcel of them.' The Sonatas were published in the following year, one hundred and ninety subscribers coming forward, and the composer receiving £60 for the English copyright. They made their way slowly, owing to the scarcity of good organs and players in England at the time. However, the Sonatas roused the enthusiasm of the few players able to do them justice. Dr. Chipp (apparently the first to perform them in public) played the half-dozen at a single recital, and from memory ! Mendelssohn himself only once did this, and found the physical effort too great. Writing to his sister Fanny, he says : 'I will play the organ sonatas to you at Ober-Liederbach ; that is to say, by three at a time, for all six are too fatiguing, as I found the other day when trying them.' For a full analysis of the Sonatas and many interesting details concerning their origin, the reader is referred to Dr. C. W. Pearce's *On Mendelssohn's Organ Sonatas* (Schirmer). The 'Three Preludes and Fugues' were written about seven years before the Sonatas, and, though less immediately attractive, are sterling organ music.   H. G.
[13] He had learned these since his Swiss journey. See *L.* Sept. 3, 1831.

returning to the Great Organ when the pedal re-enters, but transferring the E in the treble to the Great Organ a bar before the entry of the other parts, with very fine effect.[1] One thing which particularly struck our organists was the contrast between his massive effects and the lightness of his touch in rapid passages. The touch of the Christ Church organ was both deep and heavy, yet he threw off arpeggios as if he were at a piano. His command of the pedal clavier was also a subject of much remark.[2]

On the evening of the Tuesday, Sept. 12, he attended a performance of his oratorio 'St. Paul' by the Sacred Harmonic Society at Exeter Hall. He had conducted three rehearsals, but could not conduct the performance itself, owing to the prohibition of the Birmingham committee. It was the first time he had heard 'St. Paul' as a mere listener, and his private journal says that he found it 'very interesting.' His opinion of English amateurs may be gathered from his letter to the Society, with which his journal fully agrees.

'I can hardly express the gratification I felt in hearing my work performed in so beautiful a manner, indeed, I shall never wish to hear some parts of it better executed than they were on that night. The power of the choruses—this large body of good and musical voices—and the style in which they sang the whole of my music, gave me the highest and most heartful treat; while I thought on the immense improvement which such a number of *real amateurs* must necessarily produce in the country which may boast of it.'

On the Wednesday he went to Birmingham, and remained there, rehearsing and arranging, till the Festival began, Tuesday, Sept. 19. At the evening concert of that day he extemporised on the organ, taking the subjects of his fugue from 'Your harps and cymbals sound' ('Solomon'), and the first movement of Mozart's symphony in D, both of which had been performed earlier in the day; he also conducted his 'Midsummer Night's Dream' overture. On Wednesday he conducted 'St. Paul,' on Thursday evening played his new pianoforte concerto in D minor, and on Friday morning, the 22nd, Bach's prelude and fugue ('St. Anne's') on the organ.[3] The applause throughout was prodigious; but it did not turn his head, or prevent indignant reflections on the treatment to which Neukomm had been subjected, reflections which do him honour. Moreover, the applause was not empty. Mori and Novello were keen competitors for the D minor pianoforte concerto, and it became the prize of the latter, at what we should now consider a very moderate figure, before its composer left Birmingham. He travelled up by coach, reaching London at midnight, and was intercepted at the coach-office by the committee of the Sacred Harmonic

Society, who presented him with a large silver snuff-box, adorned with an inscription.[4]

He then went straight through, arrived in Frankfort on the 27th, and was at Leipzig at 2 P.M. of the day of the first concert, Sunday, Oct. 1.[5] His house was in Lurgenstein's Garden, off the Promenade, the first house on the left, on the second floor.[6]

LEIPZIG CONCERTS, ETC.—The next few years were given chiefly to Leipzig. He devoted all his heart and soul to the Gewandhaus Concerts, and was well repaid by the increasing excellence of the performance and the enthusiasm of the audiences. The principal feature of the series 1837–38 was the appearance of Clara Novello for the first time in Germany—a fruit of his English experiences. She sang first at the concert of Nov. 2, 1837, and remained till the middle of January, creating an extraordinary excitement. But the programmes had other features to recommend them. In Feb. and Mar. 1838 there were four historical concerts (1. Bach, Handel, Gluck, Viotti; 2. Haydn, Cimarosa, Naumann, Righini; 3. Mozart, Salieri, Méhul, Romberg; 4. Vogler, Beethoven, Weber), which excited great interest. Mendelssohn and David played the solo pieces, and it is easy to imagine what a treat they must have been. In the programmes of other concerts we find Beethoven's 'Glorreiche Augenblick,' and Mendelssohn's own 42nd Psalm. His Serenade and Allegro giojoso (op. 43)—like his 'Ruy Blas' overture, a veritable impromptu—was produced on Apr. 2,[7] and his string quartet in E flat (op. 44, No. 3) on the following day.

His domestic life during the spring of 1838 was not without anxiety. On Feb. 7 his first son was born, afterwards named Carl Wolfgang Paul, and his wife had a very dangerous illness.[8] This year he conducted the Lower Festival at Cologne (June 3-6). He had induced the committee to include a cantata of Bach,[9] then an entire novelty, in the programme, which also contained a selection from Handel's 'Joshua.' A silver cup (Pokal) was presented to him at the close of the Festival.[10]

The summer was spent at Berlin, in the lovely garden of the Leipziger Strasse, and was his wife's first introduction to her husband's family.[11] To Felix it was a time of great enjoyment and much productiveness. Even in the early part of the year he had not allowed the work of the concerts to keep him from composition. The string quartet in E flat just mentioned, the violoncello sonata in B flat (op. 45),

---

[1] Dr. E. J. Hopkins's recollection.
[2] H. C. Lincoln's recollection.
[3] For these details see *Musical World*, Sept. 22 and 29, 1837, pp. 34-40. He had resolved on the Prelude and Fugue two months before. See *L.* to his mother, July 13, 1837.

[4] *L.* to his mother, Oct. 4, 1837.
[5] On Oct. 12, 1837, he writes to thank the Gesellschaft der Musikfreunde of Vienna for its diploma of membership. The letter is in the Society's archives.　　　[6] *H.* p. 149.
[7] Conceived and composed in two days for Mme. Botgorscheck's concert. See *L.* Apr. 2, 1838.　　　[8] *H.* p. 115.
[9] The Bach novelty appears to have been a garbled version of the Himmelfahrts cantata, 'Gott fähret auf mit Jauchzen,' though Mendelssohn probably found it in that state. The double chorus—to which he refers in a letter to J. A. Novello, printed in *G. & M.*, p. 182, as being alone worth the journey from London to Cologne to hear—was 'Nun ist das Heil, und die Kraft.' This information is obtained from a word-book of the festival. See *Mus. T.*, June 1906, p. 387.　　　[10] *A.M.Z.*, 1838, p. 439.　　　[11] *F.M.* i. 57, 63.

the 95th Psalm, and the Serenade and Allegro giojoso are all dated during the hard work of the first four months of 1838. The actual result of the summer was another string quartet (in D ; op. 44, No. 1), dated July 24, 1838,[1] and the Andante Cantabile and Presto Agitato in B (Berlin, June 22, 1838). The intended result is a symphony in B flat which occupied him much, which he mentions more than once as complete in his head, but of which no trace on paper has yet been found.[2] He alludes to it in a letter to the Philharmonic Society (Jan. 19, 1839)—answering their request for a symphony —as ' begun last year,' though it is doubtful if his occupations will allow him to finish it in time for the 1839 season. So near were we to the possession of an additional companion to the Italian and Scotch symphonies! The violin concerto was also begun in this holiday,[3] and he speaks of a Psalm [4] (probably the noble one for eight voices, ' When Israel out of Egypt came '), a sonata for pianoforte and violin (in F, dated ' Berlin, June 13, 1838,' still in MS.), and other things. He was now, too, in the midst of the tiresome correspondence with J. R. Planché,[5] on the subject of the opera which that gentleman had agreed to write, but which, like Mendelssohn's other negotiations on the subject of operas, came to nothing ; and there is the usual large number of long and carefully written letters. He returned to Leipzig in September, but was again attacked with measles,[6] on the eve of a performance of ' St. Paul,' on Sept. 15. The attack was sufficient to prevent his conducting the first of the Gewandhaus Concerts (Sept. 30), at which David was his substitute. On Oct. 7 he was again at his post.[7] The star of this series was Mrs. Alfred Shaw, whose singing had pleased him very much when last in England. Its one remarkable novelty was Schubert's great symphony in C,[8] which had been brought from Vienna by Schumann, and was first played in MS. on March 21, 1839, at the last concert of the series. During the autumn of 1839 he received from Erard the grand piano which became so well known to his friends and pupils, and the prospect of which he celebrates in a remarkable letter now in the possession of that firm.

' Elijah ' is now fairly under way. After discussing with his friends Bauer and Schubring the subject of St. Peter,[9] in terms which show how completely the requirements of an oratorio book were within his grasp, and another subject not very clearly indicated, but apparently approaching that which he afterwards began to treat as ' Christus' [10]—he was led to the contemplation of that most picturesque and startling of the prophets of the Old Testament, who, strange to say, does not appear to have been previously treated by any known composer. Hiller [11] tells us that the subject was suggested by the passage [12] (1 Kings xix. 11), ' Behold, the Lord passed by.' We may accept the fact more certainly than the date (1840) at which Hiller places it. Such a thing could not but fix itself in the memory, though the date might easily be confused. We have already seen that he was at work on the subject in the summer of 1837, and his correspondence [13] shows that much consultation had already taken place upon it, and that considerable progress had been made in the construction of the book of the oratorio. Mendelssohn had drawn up a number of passages and scenes in order, and had given them to Schubring for consideration. His ideas are dramatic enough for the stage ! [14] The music does not seem to be yet touched.

During the spring of 1839 he finished the 114th Psalm, and wrote the overture to ' Ruy Blas.' This, though one of the most brilliantly effective of his works, was, with a chorus for female voices, literally conceived and executed à l'improviste between a Tuesday evening and a Friday morning—a great part of both Wednesday and Thursday being otherwise occupied—and in the teeth of an absolute aversion to the play.[15] The performance took place at the theatre on Mar. 11. A letter to Hiller, written a month [16] after this (Leipzig, Apr. 15), gives a pleasant picture of his care for his friends. A great part of it is occupied with the arrangements for doing Hiller's oratorio in the next series of Gewandhaus Concerts, and with his pleasure at the appearance of a favourable article on him in Schumann's paper, Neue Zeitschrift für Musik, from which he passes to lament over the news of the suicide of Nourrit, who had been one of his circle in Paris in 1831.

In May (1839) he is at Düsseldorf, conducting the Lower Rhine Musical Festival (May 19-21) —the ' Messiah,' Beethoven's Mass in C, his own 42nd Psalm, the Eroica Symphony, etc. From there he went to Frankfort, to the wedding of his wife's sister Julie to Mr. Schunck of Leipzig, and there he wrote the D minor trio[17]; then to Horchheim, and then back to Frankfort On Aug. 21 [18] they were at home again in Leipzig, and were visited by the Hensels, who remained with them till Sept. 4, and then departed for Italy. Felix followed them with a

1 Autograph in possession of the Sterndale Bennetts.
2 L. to F. David, July 30, 1838; to Fanny, June 18, 1839 : H. p. 126.   3 L. to F. David, July 30, 1838.   4 H. p. 126.
5 For the whole of this, see J. R. Planché's Recollections and Reflections, 1872, vol. i. p. 279 et seq. Mr. Planché's caustic deductions may well be pardoned him even by those who most clearly see their want of force.   6 A.M.Z., 1838, p. 642.   7 Ibid. p. 696.
8 He was very anxious that the Philharmonic Society (London) should perform Schubert's symphony; and, indeed, he sent the parts to London, but without any practical result. See his letters to the secretary of the Society, W. Watts, in the concert programme-book of Feb. 5, 1880.   9 L. to Schubring, July 14, 1837.

10 L. to Pastor Bauer, Jan. 12, 1835.   11 H. p. 171.
12 He liked a central point for his work. In ' St. Peter ' it would have been the Gift of Tongues ; see L. to Schubring, July 14, 1837.
13 Published in Hist. of Mendelssohn's Elijah, chap. i.
14 ' Elijah ' has been put on the stage as an opera by the Moody Manners Opera Company in 1912.
15 L. to his mother, Mar. 18, 1839. In fact it was only written at all because the proceeds of the concert were to go to the Widows' Fund of the orchestra. He insisted on calling it ' The Overture to the Dramatic Fund '   16 H. p. 133.
17 The autograph is dated—1st Movement, Frankfort, June 6; Finale, Frankfort, July 18, 1839.   18 F.M. ii. 85.

long letter [1] of hints and instructions for their guidance on the journey, not the least characteristic part of which is the closing injunction to be sure to eat a salad of broccoli and ham at Naples, and to write to tell him if it was not good.

The summer of 1839 had been an unusually fine one ; the visit to Frankfort and the Rhine had been perfectly successful ; he had enjoyed it with that peculiar capacity for enjoyment which he possessed, and he felt ' thoroughly refreshed.' [2] He went a great deal into society, but found none so charming as that of his wife. A delightful picture of part of his life at Frankfort is given in a letter to Klingemann of Aug. 1, and still more so in one to his mother on July 3, 1839. Nor was it only delightful. It urged him to the composition of partsongs for the open air, a kind of piece which he made his own, and wrote to absolute perfection. The impulse lasted till the end of the winter, and many of his best partsongs—including ' Love and Wine,' ' The Hunter's Farewell,' ' The Lark '—date from this time.[3] In addition to these the summer produced the D minor pianoforte trio already mentioned, the completion of the 114th Psalm, and three fugues for the organ, one of which was worked into the organ sonata No. 2.[4]

On Oct. 2 his second child, Marie, was born. Then came the christening, with a visit from his mother and Paul, and then Hiller arrived. He had very recently lost his mother, and nothing would satisfy Mendelssohn but that his friend should come and pay him a long visit,[5] partly to dissipate his thoughts, and partly to superintend the rehearsals of his oratorio of ' Jeremiah the Prophet,' which had been bespoken for the next series of Gewandhaus Concerts.[6] Hiller arrived early in December, and we recommend his description of Mendelssohn's home life to any one who wishes to know how simply and happily a great and busy man can live. Leipzig was proud of him, his wife was very popular, and this was perhaps the happiest period of his life. His love of amusement was as great as ever, and his friends long recollected his childish delight in the Cirque Lajarre and Paul Cousin the clown.

The concert season of 1839–40 was a brilliant one. For novelties there were symphonies by Lindblad, Kalliwoda, Kittl, Schneider and Vogler. Schubert's symphony in C was played no less than three times,[7] and one concert [8] (Jan. 9, 1840) was rendered memorable by a performance of Beethoven's four overtures to Leonora (' Fidelio '). Mendelssohn's own 114th Psalm was first performed ' sehr glorios ' [9] on New Year's Day, and the new trio in D minor on Feb. 10. The quartet Concerts were also unusually brilliant. At one of them Mendelssohn's octet was given, he and Kalliwoda playing the two violas ; at another he accompanied [10] David in Bach's ' Chaconne,' then quite unknown. Hiller's oratorio was produced on Apr. 2 with great success. Ernst and, above all, Liszt were among the virtuosi of this season ; and for the latter of these two great players Mendelssohn arranged a soirée at the Gewandhaus, which he thus epitomises: ' 350 people, orchestra, chorus, punch, pastry, Meeresstille, Psalm, Bach's triple concerto, choruses from St. Paul, Fantasia on Lucia, the Erl King, the devil and his grandmother ' [11]; and which had the effect of somewhat allaying the annoyance which had been caused by the extra prices charged at Liszt's concerts.

How, in the middle of all this exciting and fatiguing work (of which we have given but a poor idea), he found time for composition, and for his large correspondence, it is impossible to tell, but he neglected nothing. On the contrary, it is precisely during this winter that he translates for his uncle Joseph, his father's elder brother—a man not only of remarkable business power but with considerable literary ability—a number of difficult early Italian poems into German verse. They consist of three sonnets by Boccaccio, one by Dante, one by Cino, one by Cecco Angiolieri, an epigram of Dante's and another of Gianni Alfani's. They are printed in the later editions of the letters (German version only), and are accompanied by a letter to his uncle Joseph, dated Feb. 20, 1840, describing half-humorously, half-pathetically, the difficulty which the obscurities of the originals had given him amid all his professional labours. With irrepressible energy he embraced the first moment of an approach to leisure, after what he describes as a ' really overpowering turmoil,' [12] to write a long and carefully studied official communication to the Kreis-Director or Home Minister of Saxony, urging that a legacy recently left by a certain Herr Blümner should be applied to the formation of a solid music academy at Leipzig.[13] This was business ; but, in addition, during all these months there are long letters to Hiller, Chorley, his mother, Fanny, Paul and Fürst (and remember that only a small part of those which he wrote has been brought within our reach) ; and yet he managed to compose both the ' Lobgesang ' and the ' Festgesang ' for the Festival in commemoration of the invention of Printing, which was held in Leipzig on June 25, the former of which is as characteristic and important a work

1 *L.* to Fanny, Sept. 14, 1839.
2 *L.* to Klingemann, Aug. 1, 1839.
3 For a full and graphic account of a musical Festival which Mendelssohn conducted at Brunswick, Sept. 6-8 of this year, see Chorley's *Modern German Music*, vol. i. p. 1 *et seq.* ; and *A.M.Z.*, 1839, p. 791.
4 The fugue in F minor, No. 3 of the set, which was published by Stanley Lucas & Co., London, in 1885.
5 *H.* p. 147.   6 *Ibid.* p. 134.
7 Dec. 12, 1839, and Mar. 19. The second performance was interfered with by a fire in the town.
8 *L.* to Fanny, Jan. 4, 1840.
9 *L.* to Fanny, Jan. 4, 1840.
10 Probably extempore ; the published version is dated some years later.   11 *L.* to his mother, Mar. 30, 1840.
12 *Ibid.*   13 *L.* Apr. 8, 1840.

as any in the whole series of his compositions. The music for both these was written at the express request of the Town Council, acting through a committee whose chairman was Dr. Raymond Härtel, and the first communication with Mendelssohn on the subject was made about the end of the previous July. We know from Mendelssohn himself [1] that the title ' Symphonie Cantata ' is due to Klingemann, but the words are probably Mendelssohn's own selection, no trace of any communication with Schubring, Bauer or Fürst being preserved in the published letters or recollections, and the draft of the words having vanished.

The Festival extended over two days, Wednesday and Thursday, June 24 and 25, 1840. On Tuesday evening there was a ' Vorfeier ' in the shape of an opera by Lortzing, ' Hans Sachs,' composed for the occasion. At 8 A.M. on Wednesday was a service in the church with a cantata by Richter (of Zittau), followed by the unveiling of the printing-press and statue of Gutenberg, and by a performance in the open market-place of Mendelssohn's ' Festgesang ' [2] for two choirs and brass instruments, he conducting the one chorus and David the other. On Thursday afternoon a concert was held in St. Thomas's Church, consisting of Weber's Jubilee Overture, Handel's Dettingen Te Deum, and Mendelssohn's ' Lobgesang.'

Hardly was this over when he went to Schwerin with his wife, to conduct ' St. Paul ' and other large works, at a Festival there (July 8-10). On the way back they stopped in Berlin for ' three very pleasant days.' [3] Another matter into which at this time he threw all his devotion was the erection of a monument to Sebastian Bach in front of his old habitat at the ' Thomas School.' The scheme was his own, and he urged it with characteristic heartiness.[4] But dear as the name and fame of Bach were to him, he would not consent to move till he had obtained (from the Town Council) an increase to the pay of the orchestra of the Gewandhaus Concerts. For this latter object he obtained 500 thalers,[5] and on Aug. 6 gave an organ performance *solissimo* in St. Thomas's Church, by which he realised 300 thalers.[6] Even this he would not do without doing his very best, and he describes to his mother how he had practised so hard for a week before ' that he could hardly stand on his feet, and the mere walking down the street was like playing a pedal passage.' [7] After such a six months, no wonder that his health was not good, and that his ' physician wanted to send him to some Brunnen instead

of a Musical Festival.' [8] To a Festival, however, he went.

' LOBGESANG ' AT THE BIRMINGHAM FESTIVAL. —The ' Lobgesang ' had not escaped the attention of the energetic Mr. Moore, who managed the music in Birmingham, and some time before its first performance he had written to Mendelssohn with the view of securing it for the autumn meeting. On July 21, Mendelssohn writes in answer, agreeing to come, and making his stipulations as to the other works to be performed.[9] It was his sixth visit to England.

There was a preliminary rehearsal of the work in London under Moscheles's care. Mendelssohn arrived on Sept. 18,[10] visited all his London friends, including the Alexanders, Horsleys, Moscheles, and Klingemann (with whom he stayed, at 4 Hobart Place, Pimlico), went down to Birmingham with Moscheles on Sunday the 20th and stayed with Mr. Moore. On Tuesday he played a fugue on the organ ; on Wednesday, the 23rd, conducted the ' Lobgesang,' [11] and after it was over, and the public had left the hall, played for three-quarters of an hour on the organ.[12] The same day he played his G minor concerto at the evening concert in the theatre. On Thursday, after a selection from Handel's ' Jephthah,' he again extemporised on the organ, this time in public. The selection had closed with a chorus, the subjects of which he took for his improvisation,[13] combining 'Theme sublime ' with ' Ever faithful ' in a masterly manner.

On his return to town he played on the organ at St. Peter's, Cornhill, on Sept. 30, Bach's noble prelude and fugue in E minor, his own in C minor (op. 37, No. 1) and F minor,[14] and other pieces, concluding with Bach's Passacaglia. Of this last he wrote a few bars as a memento, which still ornament the vestry of the church.[15] He had intended to give a charity concert during his stay in London,[16] after the Festival, but it was too late in the season for this, and he travelled from London with Chorley [17] and Moscheles in the mail-coach to Dover ; then an eight hours' passage to Ostend, and by Liège and Aix-la-Chapelle to Leipzig. It was Moscheles's first introduction to Cécile.

The concerts had already begun, on Oct. 4, but he took his place at the second. The 'Lobgesang ' played a great part in the musical life of Leipzig this winter. It was performed at the special command of the King of Saxony at an extra concert in October.[18] Then Mendelssohn set to work to make the alterations and additions which the previous performances had

1 *L.* to Klingemann, Nov. 18, 1840.
2 The words of this were by Prof. Prölss of Freiberg (*N.M.Z.*, 1840, ii. 7). The ' statue ' which is mentioned in the accounts was probably something merely temporary. The second number of the ' Festgesang,' adapted by Dr. W. H. Cummings to the words ' Hark, the herald angels sing,' is a very favourite hymn-tune in England. In a letter to his English publisher, Mr. E. Buxton (Ewer & Co.), Mendelssohn says that the tune ' will *never* do to sacred words.' See *Mus. T.*, Dec. 1897, p. 810.   3 *C.* i. 320.
4 *N.M.Z.*, 1843, i. 144.   5 *L.* to Paul, Feb. 7, 1840.
6 See *Mus. T.*, Jan. 1903, p. 21.
7 *L.* to his mother, Aug. 10, 1840.

8 Letter in *C.* i. 314 ; *Polko*, p. 231.   9 *Polko*, p. 231.
10 *Mos.* ii. 67, where the date is wrongly given as the 8th.
11 The English adaptation was made with his concurrence by J. A. Novello.   12 *Mos.* ii. 70.
13 From the recollections of Mr. Turle and Mr. Bowley.
14 On the authority of Miss Elizabeth Mounsey, then organist of the church.
15 See *Mus. T.*, Nov. 1905, p. 718, for details of this and hi subsequent visit to the church in 1842.
16 See his letter of July 21, 1840, in *C.* i. 319.
17 *Mos.* ii. 71.   18 *L.* to his mother, Oct. 27. 1840.

suggested to him, including the scene of the watchman, preparatory to a benefit perform- ance on Dec. 3 ; and lastly it was performed at the ninth Gewandhaus Concert, on Dec. 16, when both it and the Kreutzer Sonata were commanded by the King and the Crown Prince of Saxony. The alterations were so serious and so universal as to compel the sacrifice of the whole of the plates engraved for the perform- ance at Birmingham. Now, however, they were final, and the work was published by Breitkopf & Härtel early in the following year. Before leaving this we may say that the scene of the watchman was suggested to him during a sleepless night, in which the words ' Will the night soon pass ? ' incessantly recurred to his mind. Next morning he told Schleinitz that he had got a new idea for the ' Lobgesang.'

THE INTERVENTION OF BERLIN.—From 1841 began the worries and troubles which, when added to the prodigious amount of his legiti- mate work, gradually robbed him of the serene happiness and satisfaction which he had for long enjoyed, and in the end, there can be little doubt, contributed to his premature death. Frederick William IV., to whom, as Crown Prince, Mendelssohn dedicated his three con- cert overtures in 1834, had succeeded to the throne of Prussia on June 7, 1840 ; and being a man of much taste and cultivation, one of his first desires was to found an Academy of Arts in his capital, to be divided into the four classes of Painting, Sculpture, Architecture and Music, each class to have its director, who should in turn be superintendent of the whole Academy. In music it was proposed to connect the class with the existing establishments for musical education, and with others to be formed in the future, all under the control of the director, who was also to carry out a certain number of concerts every year, at which large vocal and instrumental works were to be performed by the royal orchestra and the Opera company.

Such was the scheme which was communi- cated to Mendelssohn by Herr von Massow, on Dec. 11, 1840, with an offer of the post of director of the musical class, at a salary of 3000 thalers (£450). Though much gratified by the offer, Mendelssohn declined to accept it without detailed information as to the duties involved. That information, however, could only be afforded by the Government Depart- ments of Science, Instruction and Medicine, within whose regulation the Academy lay, and on account of the necessary changes and adjust- ments would obviously require much considera- tion. Many letters on the subject passed between Mendelssohn, his brother Paul, Herr von Massow, Herr Eichhorn the Minister, Klingemann, the President Verkenius, from which it is not difficult to see that his hesitation arose from his distrust of Berlin and of the official world which predominated there, and

with whom he would in his directorship be thrown into contact at every turn. He con- trasts, somewhat captiously perhaps, his free- dom at Leipzig with the trammels at Berlin ; the devoted, excellent, vigorous orchestra of the one with the careless, perfunctory execution of the other. His radical, *roturier* spirit revolted against the officialism and etiquette of a great and formal court, and he denounces in distinct terms

' the mongrel doings of the capital—vast projects and poor performances ; the keen criticism and the slovenly playing ; the liberal ideas and the shoals of subservient courtiers ; the Museum and Academy, and the sand.'

However, the commands of a king are not easily set aside, and the result was that by the end of May 1841 he was living in Berlin, in the old home of his family—to his great delight.

His life at Leipzig during the winter of 1840– 1841 had been unusually laborious. The interest of the concerts was fully maintained ; four very interesting programmes, occupied entirely by Bach, Handel, Haydn, Mozart and Beethoven, and involving a world of consideration and minute trouble, were given. He himself played frequently ; several very important new works by contemporaries—including symphonies by Spohr, Maurer and Kalliwoda, and the Choral Symphony, then nearly as good as new—were produced, after extra careful rehearsals [1] ; and the season wound up with Bach's Passion. In a letter to Chorley [2] of March 15, 1841, he says his spring campaign

' was more troublesome and vexatious than ever . . . nineteen concerts since then [Jan. 1], and seven more to come in the next three weeks, not to speak of rehearsals, of which we always had *at least* three in a week.'

The amount of general business and corre- spondence, due to the constant rise in his fame and position, was also alarmingly on the in- crease. In a letter to his mother, Jan. 25, 1841, he tells of thirty-five letters written in two days, and of other severe demands on his time, temper and judgment. And when we remember what his letters often are—the large quarto sheet of ' Bath paper,' covered at least on three sides, often over the flaps of the fourth, the close straight lines, the regular, extra- ordinarily neat writing, the air of accuracy and precision that pervades the whole down to the careful signature and the tiny seal—we shall not wonder that with all this, added to the Berlin worries, he composed little or nothing. ' I have neither read nor written in the course of this music-mad winter,' says he,[3] and accord- ingly, with one exception, we find no composi- tion with a date earlier than the latter part of Apr. 1841. The exception was a pianoforte duet in A, which he wrote expressly to play with his friend Madame Schumann, at her concert

1 It was at this performance of the Choral Symphony that Schumann for the first time heard the D in the bass trombone which gives so much life to the beginning of the trio. See his words in *N.M.Z.*, 1841, i. 89. 2 *C.* i. 334. 3 *Ibid.*

on Mar. 31. It is dated Leipzig, Mar. 23, 1841, and was published after his death as op. 92. As the pressure lessens, however, and the summer advances, he breaks out with some songs, with and without words, and then with the ' 17 Variations sérieuses ' (June 4), going on, as his way was, in the same rut, with the variations in E flat (June 25) and in B flat.[1] It was known before he left Leipzig that it was his intention to accept the Berlin post for a year only, and therefore it seemed natural that the ' Auf Wiedersehen ' in his Volkslied, ' Es ist bestimmt,' should be rapturously cheered when sung [2] by Schröder-Devrient to his own accompaniment, and that when serenaded at his departure with the same song he should himself join heartily in its closing words.[3] He took his farewell, as we have said, with a performance of Bach's Passion, in St. Thomas's Church, on Palm Sunday, Apr. 4, and the appointment of Kapellmeister to the King of Saxony followed him to Berlin.[4]

For some time after his arrival there matters did not look promising. But he had bound himself for a year. Many conferences were held, at which little was done but to irritate him. He handed in his plan for the Musical Academy,[5] received the title of Kapellmeister [6] to the King of Prussia, the life in the lovely garden at the Leipziger Strasse reasserted its old power over him, and his hope and spirits gradually returned. He was back in Leipzig for a few weeks in July, as we find from his letters, and from an organ prelude in C minor, a perfectly strict composition of thirty-eight bars, written ' this morning ' (July 9), on purpose for the album of Henry E. Dibdin of Edinburgh.[7] He then began work in Berlin. The King's desire was to revive some of the ancient Greek tragedies. He communicated his idea to Tieck, the poet, one of the new directors ; the choice fell on the *Antigone* of Sophocles, in Donner's new translation ; and by Sept. 9 [8] Mendelssohn was in consultation with Tieck on the subject. He was greatly interested with the plan, and with the novel task of setting a Greek drama, and worked at it with the greatest enthusiasm. By the 28th of the same month he had made up his mind on the questions of unison, melodrama, etc. The first full stage rehearsal took place on Oct. 22, and the performance itself at the Neue Palais at Potsdam on Oct. 28, with a repetition on Nov. 6. Meantime he had taken a house of his own opposite the family residence. A temporary arrangement had been made for the Gewandhaus Concerts of this winter to be con-

ducted by David, and they began for the season on that footing. Mendelssohn, however, ran over for a short time, after the second performance of ' Antigone,' and conducted two of the series, and the concert for the benefit of the orchestra, returning to Berlin for Christmas.

On Jan. 10, 1842, he began a series of concerts by command of the King, with a performance of ' St. Paul ' in the concert-room of the theatre ; but, if we may believe Devrient, there was no cordial understanding between him and the band ; the Berlin audiences were cold, and he was uncomfortable. ' A prophet hath no honour in his own country.' It must, however, have been satisfactory to see the hold which his ' Antigone ' was taking both in Leipzig and Berlin,[9] in each of which it was played over and over again to crowded houses. During the winter he completed the Scotch Symphony, which is dated Jan. 20, 1842. His sister's Sunday concerts were extraordinarily brilliant this season, on account not only of the music performed, but of the very distinguished persons who frequented them ; Cornelius, Thorwaldsen, Ernst (a constant visitor), Pasta, Madame Ungher-Sabatier, Liszt, Böckh, Lepsius, Mrs. Austin, are specimens of the various kinds of people who were attracted, partly no doubt by the music and the pleasant *réunion*, partly by the fact that Mendelssohn was there.

He made his escape to his beloved Leipzig for the production of the Scotch Symphony on Mar. 3,[10] but though it was repeated a week later, he appears to have returned to Berlin. For the sixth time he directed the Lower Rhine Festival at Düsseldorf (May 15-17) ; and passing on to London, for his seventh visit, with his wife, conducted his Scotch Symphony at the Philharmonic, amid extraordinary applause and enthusiasm, on June 13, and played his D minor concerto there on the 27th,[11] and conducted the ' Hebrides ' overture, which was encored. The Philharmonic season wound up with a fish dinner at Greenwich, given him by the directors.

On June 12 he revisited St. Peter's, Cornhill. It was Sunday, and as he arrived the congregation were singing a hymn to Haydn's well-known tune. This he took for the subject of his voluntary, and varied and treated it for some time extempore in the happiest and most scientific manner. On the 16th he paid a third visit to Christ Church, Newgate Street, and it was possibly on that occasion that he played an extempore fantasia on ' Israel in Egypt ' which positively electrified those who heard it. He also again treated Haydn's hymn, but this time as a fantasia and fugue, entirely distinct from his performance of four days previous.[12] On

1 *L.* to Klingemann, July 15, 1841, and MS. Cat.
2 Schumann in *N.M.Z.*, 1841, i. 118.
3 *Dev.* p. 218.   4 *A.M.Z.*, July 14, 1841, p. 550.
5 ' Memorandum '; dated Berlin, May 1841, p. 238 of *Letters, 1833-47*.   6 *A.M.Z.*, Oct. 20, 1841, p. 856.
7 See Catalogue at end of this article. Dibdin had asked him to compose a psalm-tune. ' I do not know what " a long measure psalm-tune " means,' Mendelssohn writes in English, ' and there is nobody in this place [Leipzig] at present to whom I could apply for an explanation. Excuse me, therefore, if you receive something else than what you wished.'   8 *Dev.* p. 223.

9 First performance in Leipzig, Mar. 5 ; in Berlin, Apr. 13, 1842.
10 *N.M.Z.*, 1842, i. 108.
11 For an amusing and anagrammatic criticism of this concert, by J. W. Davison, see the *Musical Examiner* of June 17, 1843, reprinted in *Mus. T.*, May 1906, p. 322.
12 On the authority of Miss Elizabeth Mounsey, Dr. E. J. Hopkins and the *Athenæum*, June 18, 1842.

the 17th, at a concert of the Sacred Harmonic Society at Exeter Hall, mostly consisting of English anthems, he played the organ twice ; first, Bach's so-called ' St. Anne's ' fugue, with the great prelude in E flat, and, secondly, an extempore introduction and variations on the ' Harmonious Blacksmith,' ending with a fugue on the same theme.[1] After this he and his wife paid a visit to their cousins in Manchester, with the intention of going on to Dublin, but were deterred by the prospect of the crossing. During the London portion of this visit they resided with his wife's relations, the Beneckes, on Denmark Hill, Camberwell.[2] He was very much in society, where he always enjoyed himself extremely, and where his wife was much admired ; and amongst other incidents described in his letters to his mother [3] are two visits to Buckingham Palace, the first in the evening of June 20, and the second on the afternoon of July 9, which show how thoroughly Queen Victoria and the Prince Consort appreciated him. On the latter occasion he obtained Her Majesty's permission to dedicate the Scotch Symphony to her.[4]

They left London on July 12, and by the middle of the month were safe at Frankfort, in the midst of their relatives, ' well and happy,' and looking back on the past month as a ' delightful journey.' [5] August was devoted to a tour in Switzerland, he and Paul, with their wives. Montreux, Interlaken, the Oberland, the Furka, Meiringen, the Grimsel are all mentioned. He walked, composed, and ' sketched furiously ' ; visited the old scenes, found the old landladies and old guides, always glad to see him ; his health was perfect, his mood gay, and all was bright and happy, save when the spectre of a possible prolonged residence in Berlin intruded its unwelcome form.[6] On Sept. 3 they were at Zürich,[7] on the 5th, 6th and 7th at the Rigi and Lucerne.[8] While at Zürich he visited the Blind Institution, spent two hours in examining the compositions of the pupils, praised and encouraged them, and finished by extemporising on the piano at great length.[9] On his return he stayed for a gay fortnight at Frankfort. Hiller, Charles Hallé and their wives were there, and there was much music made, and a great open-air fête at the Sandhof, with partsongs, *tableaux vivants*, etc., etc.[10] A very characteristic and beautiful letter to Simrock, the music publisher, urging him to accept some of Hiller's compositions (an appeal promptly responded to by that excellent

personage), dates from this time.[11] So well was the secret kept that Hiller never knew of it till the publication of the letter in 1863.

During the summer the King of Prussia had conferred on Mendelssohn, in company with Liszt, Meyerbeer and Rossini, the great honour of the ' Ordre pour le Mérite,' [12] and the Order itself reached him at Frankfort. He set no store by such distinctions, nor perhaps was its Berlin origin likely to increase the value of this particular one. Shortly after it arrived he was taking a walk with a party of friends across the bridge at Offenbach. One of them (Mr. Speyer) stayed behind to pay the toll for the rest. ' Is not that,' said the toll-keeper, ' the Mr. Mendelssohn whose music we sing at our society ? ' ' It is.' ' Then, if you please, I should like to pay the toll for him myself.' On rejoining the party, Mr. Speyer told Mendelssohn what had happened. He was enormously pleased. ' Hm,' said he, ' I like that better than the Order.' [13]

He took Leipzig on his way to Berlin, and conducted the opening concert of the Gewandhaus series on Oct. 2 (1842), amid the greatest enthusiasm of his old friends. A week later and he was in Berlin, and if anything could show how uncongenial the place and the prospect were, it is to be found in his letter to Hiller, and even in the Italian *jeu d'esprit* to Hiller's wife.[14] It is as if his very teeth were set on edge by everything he sees and hears there. Nor were matters more promising when he came to close quarters. A proposition was made to him by the minister immediately after his arrival that he should act as superintendent of the music of the Protestant Church of Prussia, a post at once vague and vast, and unsuited to him. At the same time it was now evident that the plans for the organisation of the Academy had failed, and that there was no present hope of any building being erected for the music school. Under these circumstances, anxious more on his mother's account than on his own not to leave Berlin in disgrace, in fact ready to do anything which should keep him in connexion with the place where she was,[15] he asked and obtained a long private interview with the King, in which His Majesty expressed his intention of forming a choir of about thirty first-rate singers, with a small picked orchestra, to be available for church music on Sundays and festivals, and to form the nucleus of a large body for the execution of grand musical works. Of this, when formed, he desired Mendelssohn to take the command, and to write the music for it ; meantime he was to be at liberty to live where he chose, and—his own stipulation—to receive half the salary previously granted. The King evidently had the

---

[1] *Atlas* newspaper, June 18 ; and *Musical World*, June 23, 1842.
[2] Here he composed Nos. 30 and 43 of the Songs without Words, also the Kinderstücke, op. 72, known in England (*Mus. T.*, Aug. 1892, p. 466, and Dec. 1901, p. 807) as Christmas pieces.
[3] *L.* to his mother, June 21, 1842 ; and specially the letter to his mother of July 19, 1842, printed in *G. & M.* p. 141.
[4] *G. & M.* p. 148.   [5] *Ibid.* p. 141.
[6] *L.* to his mother, Aug. 18, 1842.   [7] *Ibid.*, Sept. 3, 1842.
[8] Diary of Mr. Ella. The above dates preclude the possibility of his having attended the Mozart Festival at Salzburg on Sept. 4 and 5. There is no trace of his having been invited, and the full report in the *A.M.Z.* (1842, pp. 780, 806), while giving the names of several musicians present, does not allude to him.
[9] *A.M.Z.*, 1842, p. 907.   [10] *H.* p. 187.

[11] *L.* to Simrock, Sept. 21, 1842 ; *H.* p. 189.
[12] *A.M.Z.*, 1842, p. 534.
[13] Told to the writer by Mr. Edward Speyer, son of Mr. Speyer
[14] Oct. 8 ; *H.* p. 194.
[15] *L.* to Klingemann, Nov. 23, 1842.

matter very closely at heart. He was, says Mendelssohn, quite flushed with pleasure, could hardly contain himself, and kept repeating 'You can scarcely think *now* of going away.' When kings ask in this style it is not for subjects to refuse them. Moreover, Mendelssohn was as much attracted by the King as he was repelled by the official etiquette of his ministers, and it is not surprising that he acceded to the request. The interview was followed up by a letter from His Majesty dated Nov. 22,[1] containing an order constituting the Domchor or Cathedral Choir, conferring on Mendelssohn the title of General Music-Director, with a salary of 1500 thalers, and giving him the superintendence and direction of the church and sacred music as his special province. This involved his giving up acting as Kapellmeister to the King of Saxony, and for that purpose he had an interview with that monarch at Dresden, in which he obtained the King's consent to the application of the Blümner legacy to his darling scheme of a Conservatorium at Leipzig.[2]

RETURN TO LEIPZIG.—Thus then ' this long, tedious, Berlin business ' was at length apparently brought to an end, and Mendelssohn was back in his beloved Leipzig, and with a definite sphere of duty before him in Berlin, for he had learnt in the meantime that he was at once to supply the King with music to Racine's *Athalie*, the *Midsummer Night's Dream*, *The Tempest* and *Œdipus Coloneus*.[3] This, with the proofs of the Scotch Symphony and ' Antigone ' to correct, with the ' Walpurgisnacht ' to complete for performance, the new Conservatorium to organise, the concerts, regular and irregular, to rehearse and conduct, and a vast and increasing correspondence to be kept up, was enough for even his deft and untiring pair of hands. He is cheerful enough under it, and although he complains in one letter that composition is impossible, yet in the next letter ' Athalie,' ' Œdipus,' the ' Midsummer Night's Dream,' the ' Walpurgisnacht ' and the new violoncello sonata (in D) are beginning again to fill his brain, and he finds time to be pleasant over old Madame Schröder, and to urge the claims of his old Meiringen guide to a place in Murray's *Handbook*.[4] In the midst of all this whirl he lost his mother, who died in the same rapid and peaceful manner that his father had done. She was taken ill on the Sunday evening—her husband's birthday—and died before noon on Monday, Dec. 12—so quickly that her son's letter of the 11th could not have reached her.[5] The loss affected him less violently than that of his father had done, perhaps because he was now older and too hard worked, and also because of the home-life and ties by which he was surrounded. But it caused him keen suffer-

ing, from which he did not soon recover. It brings into strong relief his love of the family bond, and his fear lest the disappearance of the point of union should at all separate the brothers and sisters ; and he proposes, a touching offer for one whose pen was already so incessantly occupied, that he should write to one of the three every week, and the communication be thus maintained with certainty.[6]

The house now became his, but the hesitation with which he accepts his brother's proposal to that effect, lest it should not be acceptable to his sisters or their husbands, is eminently characteristic of his delicate and unselfish generosity.[7] He admits that his mother's death has been a severe trial, and then he drops an expression which shows how heavily the turmoil of so busy a life was beginning to press upon him.—' In fact, everything that I do and carry on is a burden to me, unless it be mere passive existence.' This may have been the mere complaint of the moment, but it is unlike the former buoyant Mendelssohn. He was suffering, too, from what appears to have been a serious cough. But work came to his relief ; he had some scoring and copying to do which, though of the nature of

> The sad mechanic exercise,
> Like dull narcotics, numbing pain,

yet had its own charm—' the pleasant intercourse with the old familiar oboes and violas and the rest, who live so much longer than we do, and are such faithful friends,'[8] and thus kept him from dwelling on his sorrow. And there was always so much in the concerts to interest and absorb him. He still clung, though as fastidiously as ever, to the hope of getting an opera-book. A long letter in French to M. Charles Duveyrier, dated Jan. 4, 1843,[9] discusses the merits of the story of Jeanne d'Arc for the purpose, and decides that Schiller's play has preoccupied the ground. At this time he rewrote 'Infelice,' the second published version of which is dated ' Leipzig, Jan. 15, 1843.'

At the concert of Feb. 2, 1843, the ' Walpurgisnacht ' was produced in a very different condition from that in which it had been performed at Berlin just ten years before, in Jan. 1833. He had rewritten the score ' from A to Z,' amongst other alterations had added two fresh airs, and had at length brought it into the condition in which it is now so well known. On Jan. 12 a symphony in C minor, by Niels Gade, of Copenhagen, was rehearsed. It interested Mendelssohn extremely, and gave him an opportunity to write a letter[10] full of sympathy and encouragement to the distant and unknown composer, one of those letters which were native to him, but which are too seldom written, and for more of which the world would be all

1 *L.* to Paul, Dec. 5, 1842.
2 *L.* to Klingemann, Nov. 23.   3 *Ibid.*, Nov. 23.
4 *L.* Nov. 28 and 23 ; compare with letter of Sept. 3.
5 *L.* to his mother, Dec. 11.

6 *L.* to Paul, Dec. 22, 1842.   7 *Ibid.*
8 *L.* to Klingemann, Jan. 13, 1843.
9 I am indebted for this to Mr. J. Rosenthal.
10 *L.* to Klingemann, Jan. 13, 1843.

the better. The work was produced on Mar. 2, amid extraordinary applause.

Berlioz visited Leipzig at this time, and gave a concert of his compositions. Mendelssohn and he had not met since they were both at Rome, and Berlioz was foolish enough to suppose that some raillery of his might be lurking in Mendelssohn's memory, and prevent his being cordially welcomed. But he was soon undeceived. Mendelssohn wrote at once offering him the room and the orchestra of the Gewandhaus, on the most favourable terms, and asking him to allow one of his works to be played at the approaching concert (Feb. 22) for the benefit of the orchestra.[1] An account of the whole, with copious souvenirs of their Roman acquaintance (not wholly uncoloured), will be found in Berlioz's *Voyage musical*, in the letter to Heller.[2] It is enough here to say that the two composer-conductors exchanged batons, and that if Berlioz did not convert Leipzig, it was not for want of an amiable reception by Mendelssohn and David. (See BATON.)

On Mar. 9 an interesting extra concert was given under Mendelssohn's direction, to commemorate the first subscription concert given in 1743.[3] The first part of the programme contained compositions by former cántors, or directors of the concerts—Doles, Bach, J. A. Hiller and Schicht, and by David, Hauptmann and Mendelssohn (114th Psalm). The second part consisted of the Choral Symphony.

FOUNDATION OF THE CONSERVATORIUM.— Under the modest title of the Music School, the prospectus of the Conservatorium was issued on Jan. 16, 1843, with the names of Mendelssohn, Hauptmann, David, Schumann, Pohlenz and C. F. Becker as the teachers ; the first trial was held on Mar. 27, and on Apr. 3 it was opened in the buildings of the Gewandhaus.[4] Thus one of Mendelssohn's most cherished wishes was at last accomplished. A letter on the subject to Moscheles, dated Apr. 30, is worth notice as showing how practical his ideas were on business matters, and how sound his judgment. On Sunday, Apr. 23, he had the satisfaction of conducting the concert at the unveiling of the monument to Sebastian Bach, which he had originated, and for which he had worked so earnestly.[5] The programme consisted entirely of Bach's music, in which Mendelssohn himself played a concerto. Then the monument was unveiled, and the proceedings ended with Bach's eight-part motet ' Singet dem Herrn.' Such good services were appropriately acknowledged by the Town Council with the honorary freedom of the city (Ehrenbürgerrecht).[6]

In the spring of 1843 he made the acquaintance of Joseph Joachim, who came to Leipzig from Vienna as a boy of 12, attracted by the fame of the new music school, and there began a friendship which grew day by day, and only ended with Mendelssohn's death.

On May 1 his fourth child, Felix, was born. On account no doubt partly of his wife's health, partly also of his own—for it is mentioned that he was seriously unwell at the dedication of the Bach monument—but chiefly perhaps for the sake of the Conservatorium, he took no journey this year, and, excepting a visit to Dresden to conduct ' St. Paul,' remained in Leipzig for the whole summer. How much his holiday was interfered with by the tedious, everlasting affair of Berlin—orders and counter-orders, and counter-counter-orders—may be seen from his letters,[7] though it is not necessary to do more than allude to them.

For the unveiling of the statue of Friedrich August I. of Saxony at Dresden on June 7, 1843, he and Wagner each contributed a composition. Wagner, then Kapellmeister at Dresden, confirms the opinion, which he says was formed, that ' his simple, heartfelt composition had entirely eclipsed the complex artificialities of Mendelssohn ' ! Wagner's piece, for male voices only, was published at Berlin in 1906 : Mendelssohn's (still in MS.) is for two choirs of men's voices (tenor and bass) with accompaniment of brass instruments. ' Its complex artificialities ' (as Wagner was pleased to call them) consist in the singing of the Saxon national anthem (our ' God save the King ') by the second choir as a counter theme to, and concurrently with, the singing of Mendelssohn's original music by the first choir.[8]

WORKS FOR BERLIN.—By the middle of July he had completed the ' Midsummer Night's Dream ' music,[9] had written the choruses to ' Athalie,' and made more than a start with the music to ' Oedipus,' and some progress with a new symphony [10] ; had at the last moment, under a pressing order from court, arranged the chorale ' Herr Gott, dich loben wir ' (Te Deum) for the celebration of the 1000th anniversary of the empire, ' the longest chorale and the most tedious job he had ever had,' and had also, a still harder task, answered a long official letter on the matter of his post, which appeared to contradict all that had gone before, and cost him (in his own words) ' four thoroughly nasty, wasted, disagreeable days.'

He therefore went to Berlin early in August (1843), and on the 6th conducted the music of the anniversary ; returned to Leipzig in time to join his friend Madame Schumann in her husband's Andante and Variations for two

[1] Jan. 25. Letter now in Brit. Museum Add. MSS. 33,965. In printing it Berlioz has shortened it by one-half, and sadly garbled it by correcting Mendelssohn's French.

[2] And in Berlioz's *Mémoires*.

[3] *N.M.Z.*, 1843, i. 95.

[4] *Ibid.* i. 102. Hauptmann, letter to Spohr, Feb. 6, 1843, says: ' Our music-school is to begin in April, but not on the 1st; Mendelssohn thought that unlucky.'

[5] See *Lampadius*, p. 111 ; *N.M.Z.*, 1843, i. 144.

[6] *A.M.Z.*, 1843, p. 334.

[7] *L.* July 21, 26 ; Aug. 26 ; Sept. 16, 1843.

[8] For further details see *Mus. T.*, June 1906, p. 385 ; *Life of Richard Wagner*, by William Ashton Ellis, vol. ii. p. 26 ; and *Athenœum*, Apr. 14, 1906, p. 459. This paragraph is an addition to the text contributed to the second edition of the Dictionary by F. G. Edwards.

[9] *L.* July 21, 1843.   [10] *F.M.* iii. 20—' marschirt langsam.'

pianofortes at Madame Viardot's concert on Aug. 19,[1] and on Aug. 25 was pursued thither by orders for a performance of ' Antigone,' and the production of the ' Midsummer Night's Dream ' and ' Athalie ' in the latter half of September.   At that time none of the scores of these works had received his final touches ; ' Athalie ' indeed was not yet scored at all, nor was a note of the overture written.   Then the performances are postponed, and then immediately resumed, at the former dates; and in the end ' Antigone ' was given on Sept. 19, in the Neue Palais at Potsdam,[2] and the ' Midsummer Night's Dream ' at the same place—after eleven rehearsals [3]—on Oct. 18, and on the 19th, 20th and 21st,[4] at the King's Theatre in Berlin.   The music met with enthusiastic applause each time ; but the play was for long a subject of wonder to the Berliners.   Some disputed whether Tieck or Shakespeare were the author ; others believed that Shakespeare had translated it from German into English.   Some, in that refined atmosphere, were shocked by the scenes with the clowns, and annoyed that the King should have patronised so low a piece ; and a very distinguished personage [5] expressed to Mendelssohn himself his regret that such lovely music should have been wasted on so poor a play—a little scene which he was very fond of mimicking.[6] ' Antigone' procured him the honour of membership of the Philologen-Versammlung of Cassel.[7]

Mendelssohn's position at Berlin had now apparently become so permanent that it was necessary to make proper provision for filling his place at the Leipzig concerts, and accordingly Ferdinand Hiller was engaged to conduct them during his absence.[8] The first of the series was on Oct. 1.   Hiller conducted, and Felix supported his friend by playing his own G minor concerto.   Two days afterwards, on Oct. 3, he writes a long communication to the Town Council of Leipzig, praying for an increase in the salaries of the town orchestra for their services at the theatre.   On Oct. 30 he joined Mme. Schumann and Hiller in the triple concerto of Bach ; on Nov. 18 there was a special farewell concert at which he played his new violoncello sonata (op. 58), and which closed with his octet, he and Gade playing the two viola parts ; and by Nov. 25 he had left Leipzig ' with wife and children, and chairs and tables, and piano and everything,' [9] and was in Berlin, settled in the old family house, now his own.   On Nov. 30 he conducted the first of the weekly subscription concerts, which he

and Taubert directed alternately and at which he often played.   With all his aversion to the Berlin musicians he was obliged to acknowledge that, in some respects at least, the orchestra was good.   ' What pleases me most,' he says to his old friend and confidant David,

' are the basses, because they are what I am not so much accustomed to.   The eight violoncellos and four good double-basses give me sometimes great satisfaction with their big tone.' [10]

Then came performances of the ' Midsummer Night's Dream ' music, of ' Israel in Egypt,' entertainments and dinners—which amused him notwithstanding all his dislike to aristocrats—and Fanny's Sunday performances.   Once immersed in life and music, and freed from official correspondence and worries, he was quite himself.   ' He is,' says his sister,

' indescribably dear, in the best of tempers, and quite splendid, as you know he can be in his best times.   Every day he astonishes me, because such quiet intercourse as we are having is a novelty to me now, and he is so versatile, and so original and interesting on every subject, that one can never cease to wonder at it.' [11]

His favourite resort during his later Berlin life was the house of Professor Wichmann the sculptor, in the Hasenjäger (now Feilner) Strasse.   Wichmann's wife was a peculiarly pleasant artistic person, and their circle included Magnus the painter, Taubert, Werder, Count Redern and other distinguished people, many of them old friends of Mendelssohn's. There, in 1844, he first met Jenny Lind.   The freedom of the life in this truly artistic set, the many excursions and other pleasures, delighted and soothed him greatly.

Christmas was kept royally at his house ; he was lavish with presents, of which he gives Rebecka (then in Italy) a list.[12] A very characteristic Christmas gift to a distant friend was the testimonial, dated Berlin, Dec. 17, 1843,[13] which he sent to Sterndale Bennett for use in his contest for the professorship of music at Edinburgh University.   His exertions for his friend did not stop at this testimonial, but led him to write several long letters pressing his claims in the strongest terms, the drafts of which will be found in the ' green books ' at Leipzig.   The Edinburgh professorship, however, was not bestowed on Bennett.

The compositions of the winter were chiefly for the Cathedral, and include the fine setting of the 98th Psalm (op. 91) for eight-part choir and orchestra, for New Year's Day, 1844 ; the 2nd Psalm, for Christmas, with chorales and ' Sprüche,' and pieces ' before the Alleluja ' ; also the 100th Psalm, the 43rd ditto, and the 22nd, for Good Friday, for eight voices, each with its ' Spruch ' or anthem—and seven psalm-tunes or chorales with trombones.   At these great functions the church was so full[14] that not

1 *N.M.Z.*, 1843, ii. 68 ; and *Lampadius.* Joachim, then 12 years old, made his first appearance in Leipzig at this concert.
2 *Dev.* p. 245.
3 *H.* p. 213.   The band was small—only six first and six second fiddles ; but ' the very pick of the orchestra ' (Joachim).
4 On the 18th Mendelssohn was called for, but did not appear : *F.M.* iii. 51.
5 *F.M.* iii. 73.   These court-people were only repeating what the Italian villagers had said to him in 1831. See *L.* July 24, 1831.
6 Mr. Sartoris's recollection.
7 *A.M.Z.*, 1843, p. 804.   8 *H.* p. 210 ; *N.M.Z.*, 1843, ii. 135.
9 To G. A. Macfarren, *G. & M.* p. 160.

10 *L.* to David, Dec. 19, 1843, printed in Eckardt's *Ferdinand David*, p. 192.   11 *F.M.* iii. 89.   12 *Ibid.* iii. 91.
13 The letter was first printed in this article.   It will be found in the *Life of Sterndale Bennett* (1907), by his son, p. 153.
14 *F.M.* iii. 99.

even Fanny Hensel could get a place. The lovely
solo and chorus, ' Hear my prayer,' for soprano
solo, chorus and organ,[1] belongs to this time.
It is dated Jan. 25, 1844, and was written for
William Bartholomew, the careful and laborious
translator of his works into English, and sent
to him in a letter dated Jan. 31.[2] Also the duets
' Maiglöckchen,' ' Volkslied ' and ' Herbstlied '
(op. 63, Nos. 6, 5 and 4), and many songs, with
and without words. The concerts finished with
a magnificent performance of Beethoven's
Ninth Symphony on Mar. 27, and on Palm
Sunday (Mar. 31) ' Israel in Egypt ' was sung
in St. Peter's Church. The rehearsals for these
two difficult works, new to Berlin, had been
extremely troublesome and fatiguing.

THE PHILHARMONIC SOCIETY OF LONDON.—
At the end of February he received a letter
from the Philharmonic Society of London, offering him an engagement as conductor of the last
six concerts of the season. He looked forward
with delight to an artistic position ' of such tremendous distinction,' [3] and one which promised
him the opportunity of doing a service to a
Society to which he felt personally indebted [4] ;
and on Mar. 4 he writes ' with a feeling of true
gratitude ' accepting for five concerts.[5] Meantime the old annoyances and heartburnings at
Berlin had returned. Felix had been requested
by the King to compose music to the *Eumenides* of Æschylus, and had replied that the difficulties were immense, and perhaps insuperable,
but that he would try ; and in conversation
with Tieck he had arranged that as the work
could only be given in the large new opera-
house, which would not be opened till Dec. 15,
it would be time enough for him to write his
music and decide after his return from England
whether it was worthy of performance. Notwithstanding this, he received, as a parting gift,
on Apr. 28, a long, solemn, almost scolding,
letter from Bunsen,[6] based on the assumption
that he had refused to undertake the task, and
expressing the great disappointment and annoyance of the King. No wonder that Mendelssohn's reply, though dignified, was more than
warm. It appeared to him that some person
or persons about the court disbelieved in the
possibility of his writing the music, and had
pressed their own views on the King as his, and
he was naturally and justifiably angry. A dispute with the subscribers to the Symphony
Concerts, where he had made an innovation on
ancient custom by introducing solos, did not
tend to increase his affection for Berlin.[7]

His presence was necessary on Easter Day
(Apr. 7) in the Cathedral, but by the end of the

month he had left Berlin with his family. On
May 4 they were all at Frankfort, and by the
10th or 11th he himself was settled in London at Klingemann's house, 4 Hobart Place.[8]
This was his eighth visit. He conducted
the Philharmonic Concert of May 13, and
each of the others to the end of the series,
introducing, besides works already known, his
' Midsummer Night's Dream ' music and the
' Walpurgisnacht,' as well as Beethoven's overture to Leonora, No. 1, the Ruins of Athens,
Bach's suite in D, Schubert's overture to
Fierrabras, and playing Beethoven's concerto
in G (June 24), then almost a novelty to an
English audience. He had brought with him
Schubert's symphony in C, Gade's in C minor,
and his own overture to ' Ruy Blas.' But the
reception of the first two at the trial by the
band was so cold, not to say insulting, as to
incense him beyond measure.[9] With a mag-
nanimity in which he stands alone among
composers, he declined to produce his own
overture, and it was not publicly played in
England till after his death.[10]

With the directors of the Philharmonic his
intercourse was most harmonious. 'He attended
their meetings, gave them his advice and assistance in their arrangements, and showed the
warmest interest in the success of the concerts
and the welfare of the Society.' [11] By the band
he was received with 'rapture and enthusiasm.' [12]
And if during the earlier concerts one or two
of the players acted in exception to this, the
occurrence only gave Mendelssohn the opportunity of showing how completely free he was
from rancour or personal feeling.[13] No wonder
that the band liked him. The band always likes
a conductor who knows what he is about. His
beat, though very quiet, was certain, and his
face was always full of feeling, and as expressive
as his baton. No one perhaps ever possessed
so completely as he the nameless magic art of
inspiring the band with his own feeling ; and
this power was only equalled by his tact and
good nature. He always touched his hat on
entering the orchestra for rehearsal. He was
sometimes hasty, but he always made up for it
afterwards. He would run up and down to a
distant desk over and over again till he had
made the meaning of a difficult passage clear to
a player. If this good nature failed, or he had
to deal with obstinacy, as a last resource he
would try irony—sometimes very severe. Such
pains and tact as this are never thrown away.

The band played as if under a new influence.
The season was most successful in a pecuniary
sense ; Hanover Square Rooms had never been

<hr />

[1] *Polko*, p. 220. It was originally written with an organ accompaniment, but Mendelssohn afterwards scored it at the instance of
Joseph Robinson, of Dublin. For an account of the dedication of
' Hear my prayer ' to Taubert, see *Felix Mendelssohn und Wilhelm
Taubert* in *Deutsche Revue*, Jan. 1893, p. 57.
[2] This letter and the autograph score of the music are now at the
Victoria and Albert Museum, South Kensington.
[3] *F.M.* iii. 92.   [4] *L.* to Paul, July 19, 1844.   [5] *Hogarth*, p. 82.
[6] *L.* (from Bunsen) Apr. 28, 1844.   [7] *Lampadius*, p. 116.

[8] Eaton Square, opposite St. Peter's Church, on the south side.
[9] Few things are more curious than the terms in which Schubert's
splendid works were criticised at this date in London, compared
with the enthusiasm which they now excite.
[10] At Mrs. Anderson's Concert, Hanover Square Rooms, May 25,
1849. The MS., which differs in a few passages from the published
score, is now in the Royal collection of music at the British Museum.
[11] *Hogarth*, p. 83.   [12] *Mos.* ii. 118.
[13] *L.* to Moscheles, June 26, 1846.

so crammed; as much as 120 guineas were taken on single nights in excess of the usual receipts ; and whereas in 1842 the loss had been £300, in 1844, with the interest on capital, etc., nearly £400 were added to the reserve fund.[1] Among the events which combined to render this series of concerts historical were the first appearances at the Society's concerts of Ernst (Apr. 15), Joachim (May 27) [2] and Piatti (June 24). His playing of the Beethoven G major concerto on June 24 was memorable, not only for the magnificence of the performance, but for some circumstances attending the rehearsal on the previous Saturday. He had not seen the music of the concerto for two or three years, and ' did not think it respectful to the Philharmonic Society to play it without first looking through it '—those were his words. He accordingly called at Sterndale Bennett's on the Friday night to obtain a copy, but not succeeding, got one from Miss Horsley after the rehearsal on the Saturday. At the rehearsal itself, owing to some difficulty in the band coming in at the end of his cadenza in the first movement, he played it three times over, each time quite extempore, and each time new, and at the performance on the Monday it was again different.[3]

In addition to the Philharmonic, Mendelssohn took part in many other public concerts—conducted ' St. Paul ' for the Sacred Harmonic Society on June 28 and July 5, extemporised at the British Musicians, played his own D minor trio, and his duet variations (op. 83a), and took part twice in Bach's triple concerto — once (June 1) with Moscheles and Thalberg, when he electrified the room with his sudden improvisation in the cadenza,[4] and again (July 5) with Moscheles and Döhler. He also finished a scena for bass voice and orchestra, to words from Ossian—' On Lena's gloomy heath,' which he undertook at the request of Henry Phillips in 1842, and which was sung by that gentleman at the Philharmonic, Mar. 15, 1847. On June 12 he and Dickens met for the first time. On June 18 he is at Manchester, writing to Mr. Hawes, M.P., to secure a ticket for the House of Commons.[5] Piatti he met for the first time during this visit, at Moscheles's house, and played with him his new duo in D. No one had a quicker eye for a great artist, and he at once became attached to that noble player. One of his latest words on leaving England for the last time was, ' I must write a concerto for Piatti.' In fact, he had already composed the first movement.

The enthusiasm for him in London was greater than ever, and all the more welcome

after the irritations of Berlin. He was more widely known at each visit, and every acquaintance became a friend. He never enjoyed himself more than when in the midst of society, music, fun and excitement. ' We have the best news from Felix,' says Fanny during this visit,[6]

' and when I tell you that he has ordered a large *Baum-Kuchen* [a peculiar Berlin cake, looking like a piece of the trunk of a tree] to be sent to London for him, you will know that that is the best possible sign.'

' A mad. most extraordinarily mad time,' says he ; ' I never had so severe a time before—never in bed till half-past one ; for three weeks together not a single hour to myself in any one day.' [7]

' My visit was glorious. I was never received anywhere with such universal kindness, and have made more music in these two months than I do elsewhere in two years.' [8]

But even by all this he was not to be kept from work. He laboured at his edition of ' Israel in Egypt ' for the Handel Society ; and on official pressure from Berlin—which turned out to be mere vexation, as the work was not performed for more than a year—actually, in the midst of all the turmoil, wrote (in London) the overture to ' Athalie,' the autograph of which is dated June 13, 1844. Very trying ! and very imprudent, as we now see ! but also very difficult to avoid. And his power of recovery after fatigue was as great as his power of enjoyment, so great as often no doubt to tempt him to try himself. Three things were in his favour—his splendid constitution ; an extraordinary power of sleep, which he possessed in common with many other great men, and of being lazy when there was nothing to do ; and most of all that, though excitable to any amount, he was never dissipated. The only stimulants he indulged in were those of music, society and boundless good spirits.

HOLIDAYS.—On July 10 he left London, and on the 13th was in the arms of his wife and children at Soden, near Frankfort. During his absence they had been seriously ill, but his wife had kept the news from him, and when he returned he found them all well, brown and hearty. For the life of happy idleness which he passed there in the next two months—

' eating and sleeping, *without* dress coat, *without* piano, *without* visiting-cards, *without* carriage and horses ; but *with* donkeys, *with* wild flowers, *with* music-paper and sketch-book, *with* Cécile and the children ' [9]—

interrupted only by the Festival which he conducted at Zweibrücken on July 31 and Aug. 1, the reader must be referred to his own charming letters.[10] ' Idleness ' does not mean ceasing to compose, so much as composing only when he had a mind to it. And that was often : he had no piano, but he completed the violin concerto on Sept. 16, after a long and minute correspondence with David, and many of the movements of the six organ sonatas appear in the

[1] *Musical World*, Aug. 1, 1844.

[2] The bearer of a letter of introduction from Mendelssohn to Klingemann, for which see *Polko*, p. 157.

[3] I owe this to the recollection of Mr. Kellow Pye and Mr. J. W. Davison.

[4] See an account of this (somewhat exaggerated) by C. E. Horsley in the *Choir*, Feb. 8, 1873, p. 81.

⁵ [Letter in Brit. Museum, Add. MSS. 33,965.]

[6] *F.M.* iii. 168.　　　　[7] *Ibid.* p. 176.

[8] *L.* to Paul, July 19, 1844.　　[9] *F.M.* iii. 177.

[10] *L.* (from Soden) July 17, 19, 25, Aug. 15, 1844.

MS. Catalogue, with dates ranging from July 22 to Sept. 10.[1] Doubtless, too, he was working at the book of 'Christus,' a new oratorio, the first draft of which he had received from Bunsen on Easter Monday of this year. At this time also he edited a collection of organ pieces by Bach commissioned by the firm of Coventry & Hollier,[2] by whom they were published in London in the spring of 1845.

The pleasure in his simple home life which crops out now and then in these Frankfort letters is very genuine and delightful. Now, Marie is learning the scale of C, and he has actually forgotten how to play it, and has taught her to pass her thumb under the wrong finger! Now, Paul tumbles about so as to crack their skulls as well as his own. Another time he is dragged off from his letter to see a great tower which the children have built, and on which they have ranged all their slices of bread and jam—' a good idea for an architect.' At ten Carl comes to him for reading and sums, and at five for spelling and geography—and so on. 'And,' to sum up, 'the best part of every pleasure is gone if Cécile is not there.'[3] His wife is always somewhere in the picture.[4]

RETURN TO WORK.—But the time arrived for resuming his duties at Berlin, and, leaving his family behind him at Frankfort, he arrived there on Sept. 30, alone, and took up his quarters with the Hensels. We are told that before leaving in the spring he had firmly resolved not to return for a permanence; and the extraordinary warmth and brilliance of his subsequent reception in England, both in public and in social circles, and the delights of freedom in Frankfort, when compared with the constraint and petty annoyances of Berlin —the difficulty of steering through those troubled official waters, the constant collisions with the Singakademie, with the managers of the theatre, the clergy, the King and the Ministers; the want of independence, the coldness of the press, the way in which his best efforts appeared to be misunderstood and misrepresented, and above all the consciousness that he was at the head of a public musical institution of which he did not approve [5]—all these things combined to bring about the crisis. His dislike to the place, and the way in which it haunts him beforehand, is really quite plaintive in its persistence—'If I could only go on living for half a year as I have lived the last fortnight (Soden, Aug. 15), what might I not get through? But the constant arrangement and direction of the concerts, and the exertion of it all, is no pleasure to me, and comes to nothing after all.'[6] So he once more communicated with the King, praying to be

freed from all definite duties, and from all such commissions as would oblige him to reside in Berlin.[7] To this the King good-naturedly assented; his salary was fixed at 1000 thalers, and he was free to live where he liked. It is easy to understand what a blow this was to his sister,[8] but it was evidently the only possible arrangement for the comfort of the chief person concerned. 'The first step out of Berlin' was to him 'the first step towards happiness.'[9] He remained till the end of November, at the special wish of the King, to conduct a few concerts and a performance of 'St. Paul' (Nov. 25), and the time was taken advantage of by Lvov to commission Hensel to paint a portrait of him, which has been engraved by Caspar, but can hardly be called a favourable likeness. On the 30th he left Berlin amid regret and good wishes, but the coldness of the ordinary musical circles towards him was but too evident.[10]

Very early in December he was in Frankfort, where he found his youngest boy Felix dangerously ill; the child recovered, but only after being in great danger for many weeks. It was probably a relief in the very midst of his trouble to write a long letter to G. A. Macfarren (Dec. 8, 1844),[11] giving him minute directions as to the performance of 'Antigone' at Covent Garden. His own health began to give him anxiety, and his resolution was to remain in Frankfort for the whole year and to have a thorough rest.[12] He had always good spirits at command, looked well, and would rarely confess to any uneasiness. But when hard pressed by those with whom he was really intimate, he confessed that his head had for some months past been in constant pain and confusion.

'I myself am what you know me to be; but what you do not know is that I have for some time felt the necessity for complete rest—*not* travelling, *not* conducting, *not* performing—so keenly that I am compelled to yield to it, and hope to be able to order my life accordingly for the whole year. It is therefore my wish to stay here quietly through winter, spring, and summer, *sans* journeys, *sans* festivals, *sans* everything.'[13]

This resolve he was able to carry out for some months of 1845,[14] even to resisting a visit to Leipzig when his violin concerto was first played by David on Mar. 13; and his letters to his sisters show how thoroughly he enjoyed the rest.

'Antigone' was brought out at Covent Garden on Jan. 2, 1845, under the management of M. Laurent, the orchestra conducted by G. A. Macfarren. Musically its success was not at first great, owing to the inadequate way in which the chorus was put on the stage. Writing

1 See *Mendelssohn's Organ Sonatas* by F. G. Edwards, in *Proceedings of the Musical Association*, 1894-95, p. 1.
2 See the letters in *Polko*, p. 245, etc.   3 *F.M.* iii. 151.
4 A tablet has been placed upon the house at Soden in which he lived in 1844. See *Mus. T.*, Aug. 1899, p. 528.
5 *F.M.* iii. 205.   6 *L.* to Fanny, Aug. 15, 1844.

7 *L.* Sept. 30, in *F.M.* iii. 191.   8 *F.M.* iii. 192.
9 *Dev.* p. 252. His own words.
10 Recollection of Piatti, who was there at the time.
11 *G. & M.* p. 165.
12 At the end of 1844, or the beginning of 1845, he was much gratified at receiving an invitation to conduct a musical festival at New York in 1845; his letter declining the invitation and other information leading to the proposal is given by H. E. Krehbiel in the *New York Daily Tribune* of Oct. 29, 1905.
13 *F.M.* iii. 204.   14 *Ibid.* p. 219 *et seq.*

to his sister at Rome on March 25,[1] Mendelssohn says :

'See if you cannot find *Punch* for Jan. 18. It contains an account of "Antigone" at Covent Garden, with illustrations, especially a view of the chorus which has made me laugh for three days. The chorus-master, with his plaid trousers shewing underneath, is a masterpiece, and so is the whole thing, and most amusing. I hear wonderful things of the performance, particularly of the chorus. Only fancy, that during the Bacchus chorus there is a regular ballet with all the ballet-girls !'

A woodcut which made Mendelssohn laugh for three days has *ipso facto* become classical, and needs no apology for its reproduction.

given him considerable trouble, owing apparently to the wish of the council of the Handel Society to print Mendelssohn's marks of expression as if they were Handel's, and also to the incorrect way in which the engraving was executed. These letters are worth looking at,[6] as evidence how strictly accurate and conscientious he was in these matters, and also how gratuitously his precious time was often taken up.

Gade had conducted the Gewandhaus Concerts for 1844–45; but having got rid of the necessity of residing in Berlin, and having

The play improved after a short time, and the fact that it ran for forty-five nights (Jan. 2–Feb. 1, Feb. 8-21), and that the management applied to him for his 'Œdipus,'[2] proves that it was appreciated. His letters show how much work he was doing at this time. By April 20 the six organ sonatas (op. 65) were in the hands of the copyist, the C minor trio was finished—'a trifle nasty (*eklig*) to play, but not really difficult—seek and ye shall find '[3]; and the splendid string quintet in B flat (dated July 8). The sixth book of Songs without Words was shortly to be published, and dedicated to Klingemann's fiancée; a symphony was well in hand (oh that we had got it !); nor had the desire to write an opera by any means left him, 'if only the right material could be found.'[4]

He had not forgotten his promise to consider the possibility of setting the choruses of the *Eumenides* of Æschylus with effect, and a correspondence had taken place between him and the Geheim-cabinetsrath Müller, in which, in reply to something very like an offensive innuendo, Mendelssohn stated that in spite of strenuous efforts he had utterly failed to see any way of carrying out the commission to his own satisfaction.[5] The 'Œdipus Coloneus,' the 'Œdipus Rex' and the 'Athalie' were, however, finished, and at His Majesty's disposal. The editing of 'Israel in Egypt' had

enjoyed the long rest which he had proposed, it was natural that Mendelssohn should return to his beloved Leipzig. But in addition to this he had received an intimation from Von Falkenstein as early as June 5, 1845, that the King of Saxony wished him to return to his former position. He accordingly once more took up his residence at Leipzig early in September (this time at No. 3 Königsstrasse, on the first floor [7]), and his reappearance in the conductor's place at the opening concert in the Gewandhaus on Oct. 5 was the signal for the old applause, and for hearty recognition from the audience and the press. The season was rendered peculiarly brilliant by the presence of Madame Schumann, and of Jenny Lind, who made her first appearance in Leipzig at the subscription concert of Dec. 4. Miss Dolby also made her first appearance Oct. 23, sang frequently, and became a great favourite. Among the more important orchestral works of the season 1845–46 were Schumann's symphony in B flat, and Mendelssohn's violin concerto (David), brought forward together on Oct. 23, 1845.

After the first concert he left for Berlin to produce his 'Œdipus Coloneus,' which was first performed at Potsdam on Nov. 1, and his 'Athalie' at Charlottenburg, both being repeated at Berlin. He returned to Leipzig on

---

[1] *F.M.* iii. 221.   [2] *Ibid.*   [3] *Ibid.* p. 227.
[4] *Ibid.* p. 221 ; *Dev.* pp. 258, 259, 262.   [5] *L.* Mar. 12, 1845.
[6] There are seven of them, and they are given in the Appendix to *G. & M.* p. 169.
[7] The house has since been renumbered, and is now 21. A bronze tablet on the front states that he died there.

Dec 3, bringing Jenny Lind [1] with him, and remained there till the close of the season, taking an active part in all that went on, including her farewell concert on Apr. 12, 1846—the last occasion of his playing in public in Leipzig.

At the end of 1845 a formal offer was made to Moscheles, at that time the fashionable pianoforte-teacher in London, to settle in Leipzig as professor of the pianoforte in the Conservatorium. He took time to consider so important an offer, and on Jan. 25, 1846, with a sacrifice of income and position which does his artistic feeling the highest honour, decided in its favour. Mendelssohn's connexion with the school was no sinecure. He had at this time two classes—pianoforte and composition.[2] The former numbered about half-a-dozen pupils, and had two lessons a week of two hours each. The lessons were given collectively, and among the works studied during the term were Hummel's 'Septuor'; three of Beethoven's sonatas; preludes and fugues of Bach; Weber's Concertstück and sonata in C; Chopin's studies. The composition class had one lesson a week of the same length. The pupils wrote compositions,of all kinds,which he looked over and heard and criticised in their presence. He would sometimes play a whole movement on the same subjects, to show how they might have been better developed. Occasionally he would make them modulate from one key to another at the piano, or extemporise on given themes, and then would himself treat the same themes. He was often extremely irritable : ' Toller Kerl, so spielen die Katzen ! ' or (in English, to an English pupil) ' Very ungentlemanlike modulations ! ' etc. But he was always perfectly natural. A favourite exercise of his was to write a theme on the blackboard, and then make each pupil add a counterpoint ; the task of course increasing in difficulty with each addition. On one occasion the last of the pupils found it impossible to add a single note, and after long consideration shook his head and gave in. ' You can't tell where to place the next note ? ' said Mendelssohn. ' No.' ' I am glad of that,' was the reply, ' for neither can I.' But in addition to the work of his classes, a great deal of miscellaneous work fell upon him as virtual head of the School. Minute lists of the attendance and conduct of the pupils, drawn up by him, still remain to attest the thorough way in which he did his duty, and we have Moscheles's express testimony [3] that during the overwhelming work of this summer he never neglected his pupils.[4] But it was another ounce added to his load. The fixed labour, the stated hours, when combined with his composition, his correspondence, his hospitality, and all his other pursuits, were too much, and to his intimate

friends he complained bitterly of the strain, and expressed his earnest wish to give up all work and worry, and devote himself entirely to his Art—in his own words, to shut himself into his room and write music till he was tired, and then walk out in the fresh air.[5]

PRODUCTION OF 'ELIJAH.'—Meantime ' Elijah' [6] was fast becoming a realised fact: by May 23, 1846,[7] the first part was quite finished, and six or eight numbers of the second part written, and a large portion despatched to London to be translated by Bartholomew.[8] ' I am jumping about my room for joy,' he writes to a very dear friend [9] on the completion of part I. ' If it only turns out half as good as I fancy it is, how pleased I shall be ! ' And yet, much as the oratorio engrossed him, he was corresponding with Mme. Birch-Pfeiffer about an opera, and writes to the same friend as if the long-desired libretto were virtually within his grasp. At this date he interrupted his work for three weeks to conduct a succession of performances on the Rhine—at Aix-la-Chapelle (the Lower Rhine Festival, May 31–June 2) for the seventh and last time [10] ; at Düsseldorf, a soirée ; at Liège, on Corpus Christi Day, June 11, his hymn 'Lauda Sion,' composed expressly for that occasion, and dated Feb. 10, 1846 ; and at Cologne the first festival of the German-Flemish association, for which he had composed a Festgesang on Schiller's poem ' An die Künstler ' (op. 68). His reception throughout this tour was rapturous, and delighted him. The three weeks were one continued scene of excitement. Every moment not taken up in rehearsing or performing made some demand on his strength. He was in the highest spirits all the time, but the strain must have been great, and was sure to be felt sooner or later. It will all be found in a delightful letter to Fanny of June 27, 1846.[11]

On June 26 he is again at Leipzig, writing to Moscheles to protest against the exclusion from the band at Birmingham of some players who had been impertinent to him at the Philharmonic in 1844.[12] The summer was unusually hot, and his friends well remember how exhausted he often became over his close work. But he kept his time. The remainder of the oratorio was in Bartholomew's hands by the latter part of July[13]; the instrumental parts were copied in Leipzig, and rehearsed by Mendelssohn there on Aug. 5.

---

1 Rockstro's information.
2 This information I owe to Mr. Otto Goldschmidt and Mr. W. S. Rockstro, who belonged to both of his classes.   G.   3 Mos. ii. 162.
4 The English pupils for 1844 and 1845 embraced the names of Ellis, Wells, Hasker, Ascher and Rockstro.

5 L. to Jenny Lind.
6 On June 11, 1845, the Committee of the Birmingham Musical Festival invited him to conduct all the performances, and to ' provide a new oratorio, or other music for the occasion.' He declined to conduct the Festival, and added in an English letter : ' Since some time I have begun an oratorio, and hope I shall be able to bring it out for the first time at your Festival.' This proved to be ' Elijah.'   (Hist. of ' Elijah.' p. 31 et seq.)
7 L. to Schubring, May 23, 1846.
8 L. to Moore ; Polko, p. 241.   9 Jenny Lind.
10 On this occasion he discovered the two redundant bars in the Trio of Beethoven's C minor Symphony, which had remained uncorrected, notwithstanding Beethoven's protest to the publishers in 1810. See Musical World, May 26, 1860, p. 328 ; also Sir George Grove's Beethoven and his Nine Symphonies (Novello, 1896), p. 174.
11 F.M. iii. 239-43. See also Chorley's Modern German Music, ii. 320-50.
12 L. to Moscheles, June 26, 1846.
13 (The long and minute correspondence (entirely in English) with Bartholomew, together with an important letter in facsimile, will be found in the Hist. of ' Elijah,' chapters iii. and v.)

One of the last things he did before leaving was to give his consent to the publication of some of Fanny's compositions, which, owing to his 'tremendous reverence for print,' he had always opposed,[1] and now only agreed to reluctantly.[2]

He arrived in London, for the ninth time, on the evening of Aug. 17 or 18, had a trial rehearsal with piano at Moscheles's house, two band rehearsals at Hanover Square Rooms, went to Birmingham on Sunday the 23rd, had full rehearsals on Monday morning and Tuesday evening, and the oratorio was performed on the morning of Wednesday, Aug. 26. The Town Hall was densely crowded, and it was observed that the sun burst forth and lit up the scene as Mendelssohn took his place,[3] amid a deafening roar of applause from band, chorus and audience. Staudigl was the Elijah, and Charles Lockey sang the air ' Then shall the righteous ' in a manner which called forth Mendelssohn's warmest praise.[4] ' No work of mine,' says he in the long letter which he wrote his brother the same evening—

' no work of mine ever went so admirably at the first performance, or was received with such enthusiasm both by musicians and the public, as this.' ' I never in my life heard a better performance—no, nor so good, and almost doubt if I can ever hear one like it again.' [5]

No less than four choruses and four airs were encored.[6] The applause at the conclusion of both first and second parts was enormous—almost grotesquely so ; and an old member [7] of the band well remembered the eagerness with which Mendelssohn shook hands with all who could get near him in the artists' room, thanking them warmly for the performance. He returned to London with Mr. and Mrs. Moscheles, ' on purpose for a fish dinner at Lovegrove's,' spent four days at Ramsgate with the Beneckes ' to eat crabs,' [8] and on Sept. 6 recrossed the Channel with Staudigl. His visit this time had been one of intense hard work, as any one who knows what it is to achieve the first performance of a great work for solos, chorus and orchestra will readily understand. And the strain was unremitting, for, owing partly to Moscheles's illness, he had no relaxation, or next to none. In consequence he was so tired as to be compelled to rest three times between Ostend and Leipzig.[9] It is a sad contrast to the buoyancy of the similar journey ten years before.[10]

But notwithstanding the success of the oratorio the reader will hardly believe that he himself was satisfied with his work. Quite the contrary. His letter to Klingemann of Dec. 6 shows the eagerness with which he went about his corrections.[11] The oratorio was then en-

graved, and published by Simrock of Berlin, and Ewer & Co., London, in June 1847.

Meantime Mendelssohn had been again reminded of his duties at Berlin by an urgent command from the King to set the German Liturgy to music. This (still in MS.), and an anthem or motet (published as op. 79, No. 5), both for double choir, are respectively dated Oct. 28 and Oct. 5, 1846. A song for the Germans in Lyons [12]—dear to him as the birthplace of his wife—and a Psalm-tune for the French Reformed Church in Frankfort, are dated the 8th and 9th of the same month. On Oct. 21 the Moscheleses arrive at Leipzig, and Moscheles begins his duties as professor of pianoforte-playing and composition. Gade again conducted the Gewandhaus Concerts for this season. A trace of Mendelssohn's interest in them remains in a pianoforte accompaniment to the E major violin prelude of Bach,[13] which he evidently wrote for David's performance at the concert of Nov. 12, 1846. The MS. is dated the day before, and is amongst David's papers.[14] During October and November he was very much occupied with the illness of his faithful servant Johann Krebs, to whom he was deeply attached—' mein braver guter Diener,' as he calls him—and whose death, on Nov. 23, distressed him much. It was another link in the chain of losses which was ultimately to drag him down. Fortunately he had again, as at the time of his mother's death, some mechanical work to which he could turn. This time it was the comparison of the original autograph parts of Bach's B minor mass with his (Mendelssohn's) score of the same work.[15] As time went on, however, he was able to apply himself to more independent tasks, and by Dec. 6 was again hard at work on the alterations of ' Elijah.' [16] Since the middle of October he had been in communication with Lumley,[17] then lessee of Her Majesty's Theatre, London, as to an opera to be founded by Scribe on The Tempest, already tried by Immermann ; and a long correspondence between himself, Scribe and Lumley appears to have taken place, no doubt exhaustive on his part. It came to nothing, from his dissatisfaction with the libretto,[18] but it was accompanied by extreme and long-continued annoyance, owing to his belief that the opera was announced in London as if he were under a contract to complete it, and that for the season of 1847.[19] He was at this moment more or less committed to the subject of ' Loreley,'

---

1 L. to his mother, June 2, 1837.   2 F.M. iii. 234.   3 B. p. 51.
4 L. to Paul, dated 'Birmingham, Aug. 26, 1846,' the day of the performance.   5 Ibid.
6 Mrs. Moscheles says 11 pieces : Mos. ii. 157.
7 Mr. J. T. Willy.   8 F.M. iii. 244.   9 Ibid. iii. 244.
10 L. to his mother, Oct. 4, 1837.
11 For a detailed examination by Mr. Joseph Bennett of the alterations in the oratorio, see Mus. T. from Oct. 1882 to Apr. 1883 inclusive. Also Hist. of ' Elijah.' A MS. copy of the original full score, in a copyist's hand, is in the possession of Messrs. Novello.

12 Op. 76, No. 3.
13 Dörffel's Thematisches Verzeichniss der Instrumentalwerke von J. S. Bach, No. 634. The Prelude is well known in London through Joachim's playing of it.
14 ' An F. David zur und aus der Erinnerung niedergeschrieben F. M. B. Leipzig d. 11te Nov. 1846.' This (which with many other things in this article I owe to my friend Mr. Paul David) looks as if the accompaniment had been originally extemporised.
15 L. to Klingemann, Dec. 6, 1846.
16 Ibid.
17 Lumley's Reminiscences, p. 166.
18 Ibid. p. 168.
19 Long letters to influential London friends are in existence, full of bitter complaints—most justly founded, if his information was correct.

on which he had communicated with Geibel the poet as early as the preceding April.[1] Geibel, a friend of Mendelssohn's and a warm admirer of his wife's, was at work on the book and completed it at the beginning of 1847.

Mendelssohn occasionally conducted the later Gewandhaus concerts of this season, and some of the programmes were of special interest, such as two historical concerts on Feb. 18 and 25, 1847. One of these gave him the opportunity to write a charming letter to the daughter of Reichardt,[2] a composer for whom he always had a special fondness, and whose Morning Hymn (from Milton) had been performed at the Festival at Cologne in 1835 at his instance.

This was not on the whole a satisfactory autumn. After the extra hard work of the spring and summer, especially the tremendous struggle against time in finishing ' Elijah,' he ought to have had a long and complete rest, like that which so revived him in 1844 ; whereas the autumn was spent at Leipzig, a less congenial spot than Frankfort, and, as we have shown, in the midst of grave anxiety and perpetual business, involving a correspondence which those only can appreciate who have seen its extent, and the length of the letters, and the care and neatness with which the whole is registered and arranged by his own hands. Knowing what ultimately happened, it is obvious that this want of rest, coming after so much stress, must have told seriously upon him. He himself appears to have felt the necessity of lessening his labours, for we are told that he had plans for giving up all stated and uncongenial duty, and doing only what he felt disposed to do ; for building a house in Frankfort,[3] so as to pass the summer there, and the winter in Berlin with his sisters, and thus in some measure revive the old family life to which he so strongly urges his brother-in-law in a remarkable letter of this time.[4] Nothing, however, could stop the current of his musical power. He was at work on ' Christus,' the new oratorio.[5] As Kapellmeister to the King of Saxony he had to arrange and conduct the court concerts at Dresden ; and he took a large part in the management of the Gewandhaus concerts this season, though suffering much from his head, and being all the time under the care of his doctor.[6] How minutely, too, he did his duty at this time as chief of the Conservatorium is shown by a MS. memorandum, dated Jan. 10, 1847, containing a long list of students, with full notes of their faults, and of the recommendations to be made to their professors.

His enjoyment of life is still very keen, and his birthday was celebrated with an immense amount of fun. His wife, and her sister, Mrs. Schunck—a special favourite of Mendelssohn's —gave a comic scene in the Frankfort dialect ;

and Joachim (as Paganini), Moscheles (as a cook) and Mrs. Moscheles acted an impromptu charade on the word ' Gewandhaus.' Happily no presentiment disturbed them ; and the master of the house was as uproarious as if he had fifty birthdays before him. On Good Friday (Apr. 2) he conducted ' St. Paul ' at Leipzig, and shortly afterwards—for the tenth, and alas ! the last time—was once more in England, where he had an engagement with the Sacred Harmonic Society to conduct three (subsequently increased to four) performances of ' Elijah ' in its revised form.[7]

One of those kindnesses which endeared him so peculiarly to his friends belongs to this time. Madame Frege had a son dangerously ill, and was unable to hear the performance of ' St. Paul.' ' Na nun,' said he, ' don't distress yourself ; when he gets out of danger I'll come with Cécile and play to you all night.' And he went, began with Beethoven's ' Moonlight' sonata, and played on for three hours, ending with his own ' Variations sérieuses.' A day or two afterwards, he left, travelled to London with Joachim,[8] and reached the Klingemanns' house on Monday evening, Apr. 12. The performances of ' Elijah '[9] took place at Exeter Hall on the 16th, 23rd, 28th, with a fourth on the 30th. The Queen and Prince Albert were present on the 23rd, and it was on that occasion that the Prince wrote the note in his programme book, addressing Mendelssohn as a second Elijah, faithful to the worship of true Art though encompassed by the idolators of Baal, which has often been printed.[10] In the interval Mendelssohn paid a visit to Manchester for a performance of ' Elijah '[11] on the 20th, and another to Birmingham, where he rehearsed and conducted the oratorio at the Town Hall on the 27th.[12] He conducted his ' Midsummer Night's Dream ' music and Scotch Symphony at the Philharmonic on Apr. 26, and played Beethoven's G major concerto with even more than his usual brilliancy and delicacy. He probably never played that beautiful concerto—' my old *cheval de bataille*,' as he called it years before—more splendidly than he did on this occasion. To a friend [13] who told him so after the performance he replied : ' I was desirous to play well, for there were two ladies present whom I particularly wished to please, and they were the Queen and Jenny Lind.' A little trait remembered by more than one who heard the performance, is that during the cadenza to the first movement —a long and elaborate one, and, as before (see

[7] The engagement for one performance had been tendered as early as Sept. 14 ; see Mendelssohn's reply of Oct. 7, 1846, to the letter of the secretary to the Society (Thomas Brewer) of that date, in *Polko*, p. 227. The other two were proposed Jan. 26, and arranged for between that date and Mar. 10, 1847 ; see the letter of that date to Bartholomew, *Polko*, p. 229. The fourth was an afterthought.
[8] *Musical World*, Apr. 17, 1847.
[9] The first in the revised form.
[10] *L.* to Paul. Sir Theodore Martin's *Life of the Prince Consort* i. 489.
[11] Letter to Moore, dated ' Manchester, Apr. 21, 1847,' in *Polko* p. 244. The performance was by the Hargreaves Choral Society.
[12] For the benefit of Mr. Stimpson, the organist.
[13] William Bartholomew.

[1] *Dev.* p. 276.
[2] *L.* Feb. 1847, p. 388, *English* ed.
[3] *Dev.* p. 291.
[4] *L.* to Dirichlet, Jan. 4, 1847.
[5] *Dev.* p. 290.
[6] *Lampadius*, p. 131.

p. 408), entirely extempore, Costa, who conducted, raised his baton, thinking that it was coming to an end, on which Mendelssohn looked up, and held up one of his hands, as much as to say, ' Not yet.'

On May 1 he lunched at the Prussian embassy and played, and also played for more than two hours at Buckingham Palace in the presence of the Queen and Prince Albert only. On the 4th, at the Beethoven Quartet Society, he played Beethoven's thirty-two variations, without book, his own C minor trio, and a Song without Words ; and the same evening was at the opera at Jenny Lind's début. On the evening of the 5th at the Antient Concert he played on the organ a prelude and fugue on the name of Bach. The morning of the 6th he spent at Lord Ellesmere's picture-gallery, and in the afternoon played to his friends the Bunsens and a distinguished company, including Mr. and Mrs. Gladstone, at the Prussian embassy. He left the room in great emotion, and without the power of saying farewell.[1] The same day he wrote a Song without Words in the album of Lady Caroline Cavendish, and another in that of the Hon. Miss Cavendish, since published as op. 102, No. 2, and op. 85, No. 5, respectively. On the 8th he took leave of the Queen and Prince Albert at Buckingham Palace, and left London the same evening, much exhausted, with the Klingemanns. He had indeed, to use his own words, ' stayed too long here already.' [2]

It was observed at this time by one [3] who evidently knew him well, that though in the evening and when excited by playing, he looked as he had done on former visits, yet that by daylight his face showed sad traces of wear and a look of premature old age. He crossed on Sunday, the 9th, to Calais, drove to Ostend, and on the 11th was at Cologne.[4] At Herbesthal, through the extra zeal of a police official, who mistook him for a Dr. Mendelssohn of whom the police were in search, he was stopped on his road, seriously annoyed, and compelled to write a long statement which must have cost him as much time and labour as to compose an overture.

BREAKDOWN IN HEALTH.—He had been only a day or two in Frankfort when he received the news of the sudden death of his sister Fanny at Berlin on May 14. It was broken to him too abruptly, and acting on his enfeebled frame completely overcame him. With a shriek he fell to the ground, and remained insensible for some time. It was the third blow of the kind that he had received, a blow perhaps harder to bear than either of the others, inasmuch as Fanny was his sister, more of his own age, and he himself was older, more worn, and less able in the then weak state of his nerves to sustain the shock. In his own words, ' a great chapter

was ended, and neither title nor beginning of the next were written.' [5]

Early in June, as soon as he had sufficiently recovered to move, the whole family (with Frl. Jung as governess, and Dr. Klengel as tutor) went to Baden-Baden, where they were joined by Paul and Hensel ; thence by Schaffhausen to Lucerne, Thun and Interlaken, in and about which they made some stay. To Felix the relief was long in coming. On July 7, though well, and often even cheerful, he was still unable to do any musical work, write a proper letter, or recover a consistent frame of mind. He worked at his drawing with more than usual assiduity at this time. Thirteen large water-colour pictures illustrate the journey, beginning with two views of the Falls of Schaffhausen (June 27 and 29), and ending with one of Interlaken (Sept. 4). Many of them are very highly finished, and all are works which no artist need hesitate to sign. They are on a larger scale than any of his previous sketches, and there is a certainty about the drawing, and a solidity in the perspective, which show how well he understood what he was about. The same love of form that shines so conspicuously in his great symphonies is there, and the details are put in, like the oboe and clarinet phrases in his scores, as if he loved every stroke. They are really beautiful works. In addition to these finished drawings, he sketched a good deal in Indian ink.[6]

In the middle of the month Paul and Hensel returned home, but Felix and his family remained till September.[7] Meantime the world was going on, regardless of private troubles ; friends visited him, and plans for music began to crowd round him. Among the former were Professor Graves [8] and his wife, Mr. Grote the historian—old friends, the last of whom had taken a long journey on purpose to see him [9]— and Chorley the musical critic. He had received a request from the Philharmonic Society for a symphony for 1848 ; an application to write a piece for the opening of the Philharmonic Hall, Liverpool [10] ; had a new cantata in view for Frankfort, and something for the inauguration of Cologne Cathedral. ' Elijah ' was to be given under his baton both at Berlin (Nov. 3) and Vienna—at the latter with Jenny Lind—and the long-cherished opera exercised its old charm over him. But his nerves were still too weak to bear any noise, and he suffered much from headache and weariness ; his piano was ' not for playing, but for trying a chord,' ' it was the very worst he had ever touched in his life,' [11] and he shrank from the organ at Fribourg when proposed to him.[12] The organ in the village church of Ringgenberg, on the lake of Brienz, was his only resource, and it was

---

[1] *Life of Bunsen*, ii. 129, 130.   [2] *B.* p. 56.
[3] *Fraser's Magazine*, Dec. 1847, p. 732.   [4] Mrs. Klingemann.

[5] *L.* to Rebecka, July 7, 1847.   [6] *L.* to Paul, Aug. 3, 1847.
[7] Chorley's *Modern German Music*, ii. 384.
[8] Afterwards Bishop of Limerick (see GRAVES).
[9] *Personal Life of G. Grote*, p. 176.
[10] *L.* to Chorley, July 19, 1847, in *C.* ii. 67 ; (see also *Musical World*, Jan. 8, 1848, p. 27).   [11] *Personal Life of G. Grote*, p. 177.
[12] *Mod. Germ. Music*, ii. 394.

there that for the last time in his life he touched the organ keys. He put aside the music for Liverpool, ' for the present,' and declined the request of the Philharmonic,[1] on the ground that a work for the Society ought not to bear the least trace of the hurry and bustle in which he would have to live for the rest of the year. At the same time he was much agitated at the state of home politics, which were very threatening, and looked with apprehension on the future of Germany. For himself he returned strongly to the plans already alluded to at the end of 1846, of giving up playing and concert-giving, and other exciting and exacting business, and taking life more easily, and more entirely as he liked.[2]

LAST WORKS.—At length the power of application came, and he began to write music. We shall not be far wrong in taking the intensely mournful and agitated string quartet in F minor (op. 80) as the first distinct utterance of his distress. This over, he arrived by degrees at a happier and more even mental condition, though with paroxysms of intense grief and distress. The contrast between the gaiety and spirit of his former letters and the sombre, apathetic tone of those which are preserved from this time, is most remarkable, and impossible to be overlooked. It is as if the man were ' broken,'[3] and accepted his lot without an idea of resistance. He continually recurred to the idea of retirement from all active life but composition.

Of the music which is due to this time we find, besides the quartet just mentioned, an andante and scherzo in E major and A minor, which form the first movements of op. 81 ; the fragments of ' Loreley '[4] and of ' Christus '[5]; a Te Deum,[6] Jubilate, Magnificat and Nunc dimittis for four voices (op. 69), which he began before going to London, and finished in Baden-Baden on June 12, and a few songs, such as ' Ich wandre fort ' (op. 71, No. 5).

With the close of the summer the party returned homewards, and on Sept. 17 were again in Leipzig.[7] He found there a new Broadwood grand piano which had been forwarded by the firm during his absence in Switzerland, and is said to have played upon it for several hours. Those who knew him best found him ' unaltered in mind, and when at the piano or talking about

music still all life and fire.'[8] During these days he played to Dr. Schleinitz a new string quartet, complete except the slow movement, which was to be a set of variations—but not yet put on paper. He took leave of Mr. Buxton (Ewer & Co.) one of his English publishers, with the words ' You shall have plenty of music from me ; I will give you no cause to complain.'[9] But such moments of vivacity would be followed by great depression, in which he could not bear to speak or to be spoken to even by old friends. He was much changed in look, and he who before was never at rest, and whose hands were always in motion, now often sat dull and listless, without moving a finger. ' He had aged, looked pale and weary, walked less quickly than before, and was more intensely affected by every passing thing than he used to be.' Also he complained of the oppressive air of the town.[10] And yet, not even those most near him appear to have realised the radical and alarming change for the worse which had taken place in his strength.

ILLNESS AND DEATH.—The Gewandhaus concerts began on Oct. 3, but he took no part in them, and left the conducting to his old colleague Rietz. A friend recollects his saying how happy he was—' as cheerful as a set of organ-passages '—that he had not to make out the programmes. He dreaded all public music, and complained much, though blaming himself as not deserving the happiness he had in his ' dear Cécile ' and in the recovery of his boy Felix. He had been to Berlin for a week, very shortly after his return, and the sight of his sister's rooms, exactly as she left them, had agitated him extremely,[11] ' and almost neutralised the benefits of his Swiss retirement.'[12] He had definitely given up the performance of ' Elijah ' at Berlin, but was bent on undertaking that at Vienna on Nov. 14,[13] where he was to hear his friend Jenny Lind in the music which he had written for her voice. On the morning of Oct. 9, he called on the Moscheleses and walked with them to the Rosenthal. He was at first much depressed, but it went off, and he became for the moment almost gay. After this he went to Madame Frege's house, and here his depression returned, and worse than before. His object was to consult her as to the selection and order of the songs in op. 71,[14] which he was about to publish—one of the minute matters in which he was so fastidious

---

[1] Letter to Philharmonic Society, Interlaken, Aug. 27, 1847 ' (printed in the programme-book of the concert given Feb. 5, 1880).
[2] *Mod. German Music.* ii. 392 ; *Dev.* p. 272.
[3] This expression was used to the writer by Dr. Klengel, the tutor of his boys, who was constantly with him during the last two or three years of his life, and knew him intimately. Dr. Klengel died in Nov. 1879.
[4] The completed and published portions of ' Loreley ' are the finale to Act 1, an Ave Maria, sop. and chorus (sc. 3), and a vintagers' chorus (sc. 4). Portions of scenes 2 and 7 were left more or less advanced towards completion. The finale has been frequently staged in Germany.
[5] ' Christus ' had been projected to form the third of a trilogy with ' St. Paul ' and ' Elijah.' During this last visit to Switzerland, 8 numbers of recitative and chorus were sufficiently completed to be published as op. 97 (No. 26 posth. works). The fragments were first heard at the Birmingham Festival, Sept. 8, 1852.
[6] Mendelssohn appears to have composed the Te Deum fifteen years earlier, though he may have rewritten it in 1847. See his letter (in English) of Aug. 22, 1832, in Brit. Mus. Add. MSS. 11,730, fol. 129 ; printed in *Mus. T.*, Oct. 1903, p. 652.   [7] *Mos.* ii. 177.

[8] *Mos.* ii. p. 177.
[9] For extracts from his long and pleasant correspondence with Mr. Buxton (Ewer & Co.), see *Mus. T.* of Jan. and Mar. 1905, pp. 20, 167. A memorial window, jointly to commemorate Mendelssohn and Buxton, his English publisher, has been placed in the chancel of Cranford Church, Middlesex.
[10] *Lampadius*, pp. 134, 151.
[11] Mme. Frege ; *Mos.* ii. 181.   [12] *B.* p. 57.
[13] The last letter stuck into the last (the 29th) of his green volumes is from Fischhoff of Vienna on this subject, and is dated Oct. 29. It must have been received too late to have been read by him.
[14] Of the seven songs which he brought, the ' Altdeutsches Frühlingslied,' though put on paper on Oct. 7, was composed in the summer. The ' Nachtlied ' was composed and written for Schleinitz's birthday, Oct. 1, and is therefore virtually Mendelssohn's last composition. ' An odd birthday present,' said he to Mme. Frege, ' but I like it much, for I feel so dreary.'

and difficult to satisfy. She sang them to him several times, they settled the order, and then he said he must hear them once more, and after that they would study ' Elijah ' ; she left the room for lights, and on her return found him on the sofa shivering, his hands cold and stiff, his head in violent pain. He then went home, and the attack continued ; leeches were applied, and by the 15th he had recovered so far as to listen with interest to the details of the reception of Hiller's new opera at Dresden, and actually to make plans for his Vienna journey.

On the 25th he writes to his brother in the old affectionate vein. He is taking tonics, but Paul's face would do him more good than the bitterest medicine. He was not, however, destined to speak to him again. On the 28th he was so much better as to take a walk with his wife, but it was too much, and shortly afterwards he had a second attack, and on Nov. 3 another, which last deprived him of consciousness. He lingered through the next day, fortunately without pain, and expired at 9.24 P.M. on Thursday, Nov. 4, 1847, in the presence of his wife, his brother, Schleinitz, David and Moscheles.

During the illness, the public feeling was intense. Bulletins were issued, and the house was besieged by inquirers. After his death it was as if every one in the town had received a blow and sustained a personal loss. ' It is lovely weather here,' writes a young English student [1] to the *York Courant*, ' but an awful stillness prevails ; we feel as if the king were dead. Clusters of people are seen speaking together in the streets.' The streets were placarded at the corners with official announcements of his death, as if he had been a great officer of state.

On the Friday and Saturday the public were allowed to see the dead body. On Sunday the 7th it was taken to the Pauliner Church at Leipzig. A band preceded the hearse, playing the Song without Words in E minor (Book 5, No. 3), instrumented by Moscheles ; and after this came a student [2] of the Conservatorium with a cushion, on which lay a silver crown formerly presented to Mendelssohn by his pupils, and his Order ' pour le mérite.' The pall was borne by Moscheles, David, Hauptmann and Gade ; the professors and pupils of the Conservatorium, the members of the Gewandhaus orchestra, the chief functionaries of the Corporation and the University, and several guilds and societies accompanied the coffin, and Paul Mendelssohn was chief mourner. In the church the chorale ' To thee, O Lord,' and the chorus ' Happy and blest,' from ' St. Paul,' were sung, a sermon or oration was delivered by Herr Howard, the pastor of the Reformed Congregation, and the service closed with the concluding chorus of Bach's St. Matthew Passion. At 10 P.M. the coffin was conveyed to the Leipzig station and transported by rail to Berlin. On the road, during the night, it was met at Cöthen by the choir of the place, under Thile their director, and at Dessau by Friedrich Schneider, who wiped away the recollection of early antagonisms by a farewell partsong, composed for the occasion, and sung by his choir at the station. The coffin arrived at Berlin at 7 A.M., and, after more funeral ceremonies, was deposited in the enclosed burial-place of the family in the Alte Dreifaltigkeits Kirchhof, close outside the Hallethor. His tombstone is a cross. He rests between his boy Felix and his sister Fanny. His father and mother are a short distance behind.

The fifth Gewandhaus concert, which, it was piously observed, would naturally have ended at the very moment of his death, was postponed till Nov. 11, when, excepting the Eroica Symphony, which formed the second part of the programme, it was entirely made up of the compositions of the departed master. Among them were the Nachtlied of Eichendorf (op. 71, No. 6), sung by Madame Frege.

In London the feeling, though naturally not so deep or so universal as in his native place, was yet both deep and wide. His visits had of late been so frequent, and the last one was so recent, and there was such a vivid personality about him, such force and fire, and such a general tone of health and spirits, that no wonder we were startled by the news of his death. The tone of the press was more that of regret for a dear relation than of eulogy for a public character. Each writer spoke as if he intimately knew and loved the departed. This is especially conspicuous in the long notices of *The Times* and *Athenæum*, which are full not only of keen appreciation, but of deep personal sorrow. From his private friends I shall only permit myself two quotations. Mrs. Grote, writing nearly thirty years afterwards, names four friends whose deaths had occasioned her the most poignant sorrow of her life ; and among these are Felix Mendelssohn, Alexis de Tocqueville and John Stuart Mill. Mrs. Austin, the aunt of his early friends the Taylors, and herself one of his most intimate allies, in a tribute to his memory as beautiful as it is short, says :

' His is one of the rare characters which cannot be known too intimately. Of him there is nothing to tell that is not honourable to his memory, consoling to his friends, profitable to all men. . . . If I admired him as an artist, I was no less struck by his childlike simplicity and sportiveness, his deference to age, his readiness to bend his genius to give pleasure to the humble and ignorant ; the vivacity and fervour of his admiration for everything good and great, his cultivated intellect, refined tastes, and noble sentiments.' [3]

---

[1] Mr. Thomas Simpson Camidge (see CAMIDGE (4)).
[2] Mr. de Sentis.

[3] *Fraser's Magazine*, Apr. 1848, p. 426.

Nor was the public regret out of proportion to that of his intimate friends. We are not perhaps prone to be very demonstrative over artists, especially over musicians ; but this was a man who had wound himself into our feelings as no other musician had done since Handel. What Handel's songs, the ' Harmonious Blacksmith,' and other harpsichord pieces, had done for the English public in 1740, that Mendelssohn's Songs without Words, and partsongs, had done in 1840, and they had already made his name a beloved household word in many a family circle both in town and country. He had been for long looked upon as half an Englishman. He spoke English well, he wrote letters and familiar notes in our tongue freely ; he showed himself in the provinces ; his first important work was founded on Shakespeare, his last was brought out in England, at so peculiarly English a town as Birmingham ; and his Scotch Symphony and 'Hebrides' overture showed how deeply the scenery of Britain had influenced him. And, perhaps more than this, there were in the singular purity of his life, in his known devotion to his wife and family, and his general high and unselfish character, the things most essential to procure him both the esteem and affection of the English people.

The Sacred Harmonic Society, the only Society in London having concerts at that period of the year, performed ' Elijah ' on Nov. 17, preceded by the Dead March in ' Saul,' and with the band and chorus all dressed in black. At Manchester and Birmingham similar honours were paid to the departed composer. In Germany commemorative concerts (*Todtenfeier*) were given at Berlin, Vienna, Frankfort, Hamburg and many other places. His bust was set up in the Theatre at Berlin, and his profile in the Gewandhaus at Leipzig. The first concert of the Conservatoire at Paris, on Jan. 9, 1848, was entitled 'À la mémoire de F. Mendelssohn-Bartholdy,' and comprised the Scotch Symphony and 'Hebrides' overture, the violin concerto, and airs from ' St. Paul.' Among the very numerous letters of condolence addressed to his widow we will only mention those from Queen Victoria, the King of Prussia and the King of Saxony.

POSTHUMOUS PUBLICATIONS. — Two works were in the printers' hands at the time of Mendelssohn's death—the Six Songs (op. 71) and the Six Kinderstücke (op. 72), known in England as ' Christmas pieces.' These were quickly published. Then there was a pause, and at length, as he had left no will, Madame Mendelssohn confided to a kind of committee, composed of her husband's most intimate musical friends, the task of deciding which pieces out of the immense mass of MS. music should be published, and of supervising the publication. These gentlemen were Dr. Schleinitz, the acting member of the council of the Conservatorium, David, Moscheles and Hauptmann, all resident in Leipzig, with Paul Mendelssohn in Berlin, and Julius Rietz in Dresden. The instrumental works then (1847) in MS. embraced the Trumpet overture (1825) and Reformation Symphony (1830), the Italian Symphony (1833), the overture to ' Ruy Blas ' (1839), two sets of pianoforte variations (1841), the quintet in B flat (1845), the quartet in F minor (1847), and fragments of another quartet in E, Songs without Words, and other pianoforte pieces. The vocal works comprised the Liederspiel ' Heimkehr aus der Fremde ' (1829), the concert-aria ' Infelice ' (1843), the music to 'Athalie' and to ' Œdipus Coloneus' (both 1845), ' Lauda Sion ' (1846), fragments of the opera ' Loreley,' and of the oratorio ' Christus,' on which he had been at work not long before his death, Psalms and Sprüche for voices with and without accompaniment, songs and partsongs.

The work of publication began with ' Lauda Sion,' which appeared as op. 73, in Feb. 1848. This was followed by ' Athalie,' and by other works, down to the four partsongs which form op. 100, and No. 29 of the posthumous works, which came out in Jan. 1852. Here a pause took place.

In the meantime, borne down by her great loss, and also by the death of her third boy, Felix, in 1851, Madame Mendelssohn herself died on Sept. 25, 1853. The manuscripts then came into the hands of Dr. Carl Mendelssohn, the eldest son, and after some years publication recommenced with the Trumpet overture, which appeared in 1867, and continued at intervals down to the ' Responsorium et Hymnus ' (op. 121), and other works without opus numbers.

Many of the pieces referred to in the above enumeration are included in the series of MS. volumes already mentioned. Forty-four of these volumes were deposited in the Imperial Library at Berlin, in pursuance of an arrangement dated Dec. 23, 1877, by which, in exchange for the possession of them, the German government agreed with the Mendelssohn-Bartholdy family to found two perpetual scholarships of 1500 marks (£75) per annum each, tenable for four years, for the education of students of music elected by competition from the music schools of Germany. The Trustees of the Fund are three—the Director of the High School of Music at Berlin, a second nominated by the government, and a third by the family. The first election took place on Oct. 1, 1879, and the successful candidates were Engelbert Humperdinck of Siegburg, and Josef Kotek of Podolia. In addition, Ernst Seyffardt of Crefeld, and Johann Secundus Kruse of Melbourne, Australia, received allowances of 750 marks each out of the arrears of the Fund

Long before the foundation of the Berlin Scholarships, however, practical steps in the same direction had been taken in England. In Nov. 1847 a resolution was passed by the Sacred Harmonic Society of London for the erection of a public memorial in honour of Mendelssohn. £50 was subscribed thereto by Queen Victoria and Prince Albert and like sums by the Sacred Harmonic and Philharmonic Societies. Other subscriptions were raised amounting in the whole to over £600. In Apr. 1859, after many negotiations, a model of a statue by Mr. C. Bacon was approved by the subscribers; it was cast in bronze in the following November and on May 4, 1860, was set up on the Terrace of the Crystal Palace at Sydenham.

A more appropriate memorial was the Mendelssohn Scholarship originated by Madame Jenny Lind - Goldschmidt in the year 1850, which will be found described under its own heading. (See MENDELSSOHN SCHOLARSHIP.)

PERSONALIA AND PORTRAITS.—In person Mendelssohn was short,[1] not so much as 5 ft. 7 ins. high, and slight of build ; in figure lithe, and very light and mercurial. His look was dark and very Jewish ; the face unusually mobile, and ever varying in expression, full of brightness and animation, and with a most unmistakable look of genius. After a breakfast with him at B. Hawes's, Thackeray told Richard Doyle (who told the writer), ' His face is the most beautiful face I ever saw, like what I imagine our Saviour's to have been.' Sir Frederick Pollock [2] ' was much struck by his fine face and figure, and the excellence of his conversation.' His complexion was fresh, and showed a good deal of colour. His hair was black, thick and abundant, but very fine, with a natural wave in it, and was kept back from his forehead, which was high and much developed. By the end of his life, however, it showed a good deal of grey, and he began to be bald. His mouth was unusually delicate and expressive, and had generally a pleasant smile at the corners. His whiskers were very dark, and his closely shaven chin and upper lip were blue from the strength of his beard. His teeth were beautifully white and regular ; but the most striking part of his face were the large dark-brown eyes. When at rest he often lowered the eyelids as if he were slightly short-sighted—which indeed he was ; but when animated they gave an extraordinary brightness and fire to his face and ' were as expressive a pair of eyes as were ever set in a human being's head.' They could also sparkle with rage like a tiger's.[3] When he was playing extempore, or was otherwise much excited, they would dilate and become nearly twice their ordinary size, the brown pupil changing to a vivid black. His laugh was hearty and frequent;

and when especially amused he would quite double up with laughter and shake his hand from the wrist to emphasise his merriment. He would nod his head violently when thoroughly agreeing, so that the hair came down over his face. In fact his body was almost as expressive as his face. His hands were small, with taper fingers.[4] On the keys they behaved almost like ' living and intelligent creatures, full of life and sympathy.' [5] His action at the piano was as free from affectation as everything else that he did, and very interesting. At times, especially at the organ, he leant very much over the keys, as if watching for the strains which came out of his finger tips. He sometimes swayed from side to side, but usually his whole performance was quiet and absorbed.[6]

He refused more than once, from motives of modesty, to have his likeness taken.[7] But a great number of portraits were painted and drawn at different times of his life. The best of these, in the opinion of those most capable of judging, is that painted by his friend Professor Edward Magnus at Berlin in the year 1844, and although deficient in that lively speaking expression which all admit to have been so characteristic of him, it may be accepted as a good representation.[8] It is very superior to the various replicas and copies in existence, which are distinguished by a hopeless meek solemnity of look, absolutely impossible in the original, and which, therefore, convey an entirely wrong idea of the face.

Other portraits worth notice are (1) a pencil sketch taken in 1820, in possession of Mr. C. V. Benecke, lithographed in Goethe and Mendelssohn. (2) A half-length taken by Begas in 1821, in the possession of the Paul Mendelssohn-Bartholdy family at Berlin. This is very poorly engraved, both as to resemblance and execution, in Goethe and Mendelssohn. The original is probably much idealised, but it is a striking picture. (3) A three-quarter-length, in a cloak, painted by Hildebrand, and engraved as the frontispiece to ' Elijah ' ; in possession of Herr Killmann of Bonn. (4) A whole length, sitting, and looking to the side, taken by Hensel in 1844, in the possession of the Paul Mendelssohn-Bartholdy family. This, though clever as a picture, can hardly convey the man. The hand is perhaps the most remarkable thing in it, and must be a portrait. (5) A profile taken after death by Hensel, in possession of Mr. C. V. Benecke. This, which is said by many to be the best representation of him, is fairly engraved as the frontispiece to Lady Wallace's translation of the letters.

---

[1] He was shorter than Sterndale Bennett, who was 5 ft. 7.
[2] Reminiscences, i. 215.   [3] Moscheles's Life, i. 324.

[4] A plaster cast of his hand can be bought.
[5] The late Dr. Charles Graves, Bishop of Limerick.
[6] I owe the above description of Mendelssohn's looks chiefly to Mr. John C. Horsley, R.A. Few knew him better, or are more qualified to describe him.
[7] L. Dec. 20, 1831 ; Apr. 18, May 18, 1835.
[8] This portrait was presented by Magnus himself to Madame Jenny Lind-Goldschmidt, who bequeathed it to Mendelssohn's elder daughter, the late Mrs. C. V. Benecke.

XLVIII

Photo, Augustus Littleton

LISZT

Photographische Gesellschaft, Berlin

MENDELSSOHN

From a painting by Horace Vernet

A portrait of him in crayons was taken at Weimar for Goethe,[1] which he describes as ' very like, but rather sulky ' ; another was painted at Rome by Horace Vernet,[2] (see *PLATE XLVIII.*) and another by a painter named Schramm.[3] The sketch by his brother-in-law, taken in 1840, and given as frontispiece to vol. ii. of the *Familie Mendelssohn* must surely be too young-looking for that date. Miniatures of the four children were taken in Paris in 1816, and passed into the possession of Herr Ernst von Mendelssohn - Bartholdy, Berlin, nephew of the composer.

The bust by Rietschel (engraved as frontispiece to Devrient) and the profiles by Knauer and Kietz are all said to be good. There is a bust by Peter Hollins (1800–86), a Birmingham artist, now in the City of Birmingham Museum and Art Gallery.[4]

CHARACTER AND FRIENDSHIPS.—Not less remarkable than his face was his way and manner. It is described by those who knew him as peculiarly winning and engaging ; to those whom he loved, coaxing. The slight lisp or drawl which remained with him to the end made the endearing words and pet expressions, which he was fond of applying to his own immediate circle, all the more affectionate. But outside this immediate circle also he was very fascinating, and it is probable that, devotedly as he was loved at home, few men had fewer enemies abroad. The strong admiration expressed towards him by men of such very different natures as Schumann[5] and Berlioz,[6] both of whom knew him well, shows what a depth of solid goodness there was in his attractiveness. ' His gentleness and softness,' says one of his English friends, ' had none of the bad side so often found with those qualities ; nothing effeminate or morbid. There was a great deal of manliness packed into his little body,' as all readers of the early part of this sketch must be aware. Indeed he had a great capacity for being angry. Anything like meanness or deceit, or unworthy conduct of any kind, roused his wrath at once. ' He had a way,' says a very old friend, ' of suddenly firing up on such occasions, and turning on his heel, in a style which was quite unmistakable,' and astonishing to those who only knew his smoother side. Towards thoughtlessness, negligence or obstinate stupidity he was very intolerant, and under such provocation

said things the sting of which must have remained for long after, and which he himself deeply regretted.[7] But these were rare instances, and as a rule his personal fascination secured him friends and kept them firm to him. And to those to whom he was really attached— outside his own family, of which we are not speaking—there could hardly be a better friend. The published letters to General von Webern, to Verkenius, Klingemann, Schubring, Hiller, Moscheles, are charged with an amount of real affection rarely met with, which yet never leads him to sink his own individual opinion on any point which he thought material, as may be seen in many cases. Talent and perseverance he was always ready to encourage, and the cases of Taubert, Eckert, Gade, Joachim, Rietz, Naumann, Sterndale Bennett, Hiller, and the anonymous student whose cause he pleads so earnestly to the King,[8] show how eager he always was to promote the best interests of those whom he believed to be worthy. His warm reception of Berlioz, Liszt and Thalberg has been already mentioned, but must be again referred to as an instance of the absence of jealousy or rivalry in his nature, and of his simple wish to give everybody fair play.

The relations of Mendelssohn and Schumann were thoroughly good on both sides. There is a remarkable absence of Schumann's name in Mendelssohn's published letters[9] ; but this may have arisen from considerations which influenced the editors, and would possibly be reversed if the letters had been fully given, and if others which remain in MS. were printed. The two men were always good friends. They differed much on some matters of music. Mendelssohn had his strong settled principles, which nothing could induce him to give up. He thought that everything should be made as clear as a composer could make it, and that rough or awkward passages were blemishes, which should be modified and made to sound well. On the other hand, Schumann was equally fixed in the necessity of retaining what he had written down as representing his intention. But such differences of opinion never affected their intercourse ; they were always friendly, and even affectionate, and loved to be together. More than one person living[10] remembers the strong interest which Mendelssohn took in ' Paradise and the Peri '[11] on its first appearance, and how anxious he was that his friends should hear it. Of Schumann's string quartets he records that they ' pleased him extremely ' ; and it is surely allowable to infer

---

[1] *L.* Weimar, May 25, 1830.
[2] *L.* Jan. 17 and Mar. 15, 1831. See Rebecka's letter in Eckardt's *Ferdinand David*, p. 39. Vernet's portrait, painted in return for an extempore fantasia on ' Don Juan,' was reproduced as a supplement to the *Mus. T.*, Mar. 1905. Another portrait, drawn by Edward Novello (a son of Vincent Novello), was reproduced as a supplement to the *Mus. T.*, Nov. 1897.
[3] Possibly taken in 1840 ; since in Ernst Mendelssohn-Bartholdy's possession is the autograph of three songs inscribed ' Dem Maler Schramm zu freundlichem Andenken und mit bestem Dank. F. M. B. Leipzig, d. 4 Nov. 1840.' It was reproduced as frontispiece to F. G. Edwards's *History of ' Elijah '* (1896).
[4] Addition by F. G. E.
[5] *Life of Robert Schumann*, by von Wasielewski. Eng. trans. p. 221 ; see also several references in *The Life of Robert Schumann*, told in his *Letters*, translated by May Herbert, 2 vols., London, 1890.
[6] Letter from Berlioz to Hiller, Rome, Sept. 17, 1831. Berlioz's *Correspondance inédite* (Paris, 1879), p. 88 ; *Voyage musical*, Letter 4 in vol. i. 71 et seq.

[7] He complained bitterly to the late Dr. Charles Graves, Bishop of Limerick, in 1847 of his short temper at rehearsals or with his pupils.
[8] *L.* Berlin, p. 325 of *Letters from 1833-47*, English ed.
[9] See the fuller discussion of this question under SCHUMANN, subsection RELATIONS WITH MENDELSSOHN.
[10] *I.e.* in 1879, the date of writing.
[11] See Mendelssohn's letter to Buxton (Ewer & Co.), suggesting the publication in England of ' Paradise and the Peri,' quoted in the letter from Sir George Grove in the *Times* of Sept. 11, 1894 ; also printed in the *Mus. T.*, Nov. 1905, p. 716.

that it was the expression of his pleasure that made Schumann dedicate them to him. He had a particular love for some of Schumann's songs, and as this feeling was not shared by all the members of his family he would sometimes ask for the 'forbidden fruit,' as a kind of synonym for something peculiarly pleasant. The fact that he placed Schumann among his colleagues at the starting of the Leipzig Conservatorium of itself shows how much he valued him.

On the other hand, Schumann is never warmer or more in earnest than when he is praising Mendelssohn's compositions, as may be seen by many an article in his *Gesammelte Schriften*. He dedicated his string quartets to him, as we have said. He defended him with ardour when attacked; during his last sad years Mendelssohn's name was constantly in his mouth as that of his best friend, and his last clearly expressed wish was that his youngest boy should be called after him. A proof of his affectionate feeling is to be found in the No. 28 of his 'Album für die Jugend' (op. 68), which is inscribed 'Erinnerung (Nov. 4, 1847),' and therefore expresses his feelings at the death of his friend. It is not necessary to discover that definite direct meaning in this touching little piece which Mendelssohn found in all music, in order to recognise sadness tempered by a deep sense of grace and sweetness; the result showing how beautiful was the image which Mendelssohn left in the mind of one so completely able to appreciate him as Schumann.

Nowhere is Mendelssohn's naturalness and naïveté more evident than in his constant reference to his own foibles. The hearty way in which he enjoys idleness, and boasts of it,[1] the constant references to eating and drinking, are delightful in a man who got through so much work, who was singularly temperate, and whose only weakness for the products of the kitchen was for rice milk and cherry pie. In this, as in everything else, he was perfectly simple and natural. 'I do not in the least concern myself as to what people wish or praise or pay for : but solely as to what I myself consider good.'[2] No doubt he was very fortunate in being able to disregard 'what people paid for,' but that he did so is a part of his character.

His fun and drollery were more the result of his high spirits than of any real turn for wit. Unlike Beethoven, he rarely indulges in plays on words, and his best efforts in that direction are the elaborately illustrated programmes and *jeux d'esprit* which are preserved in the albums of some of his friends, and in which caricatures, verses, puns and jokes are mixed up in a very droll fashion. There is much humour in some of his scherzos, but especially in the funeral march for Pyramus and Thisbe in the 'Mid-

summer Night's Dream' pieces, one of the most comical things in all music. It is much to be regretted that he has left no other specimen of his remarkable power in this direction. Probably he indulged in a good deal of such fun which has not been preserved, since both he and his sister refer to that march as a specimen of a style in which he often extemporised.[3] In mimicry he was great, not only in music but in taking off speech and manner. The most humorous passage that I have met with in his letters is still in MS. :

'Dass jenseits auch Musik gemacht werden könne, das glauben Sie ja, und haben mirs oft gesagt. Dann wird's wohl kein schlechtes Instrument geben, wie bei Geyer, und keine dumme Flöte pustet da, und keine Posaune schleppt nach, und nirgends fehlt es, und wankt es, und eilt es, das glaube ich wohl.'[4]

PURSUITS—SKETCHES AND CORRESPONDENCE.—No musician—unless perhaps it were Leonardo da Vinci, and he was only a musician in a limited sense—certainly no great composer, ever had so many pursuits as Mendelssohn. Mozart drew, and wrote capital letters, Berlioz and Weber also both wrote good letters, Beethoven was a great walker and intense lover of nature, Cherubini was a botanist and a passionate card-player, but none of them approach Mendelssohn in the number and variety of his occupations. Both billiards and chess he played with ardour to the end of his life, and in both he excelled. When a lad he was devoted to gymnastics ; later on he rode much, swam more, and danced whenever he had the opportunity. Cards and skating were almost the only diversions he did not care for. But then these were diversions. There were two pursuits which almost deserve to rank as work —drawing and letter-writing. Drawing with him was more like a professional avocation than an amusement. The quantity of his sketches and drawings preserved is very large. They begin with the Swiss journey in 1822, on which he took twenty-seven large ones, all very carefully finished, and all dated, sometimes two in one day. The Scotch and Italian tours are both fully illustrated ; and so they go on year by year till his last journey into Switzerland in 1847, of which, as already said, fourteen large highly finished water-colour drawings remain, besides slighter sketches.[5] At first they are rude and childish, though with each successive set the improvement is perceptible. But even with the earliest ones there is no mistaking that the drawing was a serious business. The subjects are not what are called 'bits,' but are usually large comprehensive views, and it is impossible to doubt that the child threw his whole

---

[1] *L.* July 14, 1836, and in many others.
[2] *L.* to his mother, Oct. 4, 1837.

[3] *F.M.* iii. 51, 54. A 'Bärentanz' is described in *Mus. T.*, Aug. 1892.
[4] 'That there may be music in the next world I know you believe, for you have often told me so ; but there will certainly be no bad pianos there like Geyer's, no stupid puffing flutes, no dragging trombones, no stopping, or wavering, or hurrying—of that I am quite sure.' MS. letter.
[5] Coloured facsimiles of two of his water-colour sketches formed supplements to the *Mus. T.*, Dec. 1897, which also contains one of his humorous pen-and-ink sketches, as does the issue of Nov. 1900, p. 723.

mind into it, did his very best, and shirked nothing. He already felt the force of the motto which fronted his conductor's chair in the Gewandhaus—' Res severa est verum gaudium.' Every little cottage or gate is put in with as much care as the main features. Every tree has its character. Everything stands well on its legs, and the whole has that architectonic style which is so characteristic of his music.

Next to his drawing should be placed his correspondence, and this is even more remarkable. During the last years of his life there can have been but few eminent men in Europe who wrote more letters than he did. Many even who take no interest in music are familiar with the nature of his letters—the happy mixture of seriousness, fun and affection, the life-like descriptions, the happy hits, the naïveté which no baldness of translation can extinguish, the wise counsels, the practical views, the delight in the successes of his friends, the self-abnegation, the bursts of wrath at anything mean or nasty. We all remember, too, the length to which they run. Taking the printed volumes, and comparing the letters with those of Scott or Arnold, they are on the average very considerably longer than either. But the published letters bear only a small proportion to those still in MS.[1] In fact the abundance of material for the biographer of Mendelssohn is quite bewildering. That, however, is not the point. The remarkable fact is that so many letters of such length and such intrinsic excellence should have been written by a man who was all the time engaged in an engrossing occupation, producing great quantities of music, conducting, arranging and otherwise occupied in a profession which more than any demands the surrender of the entire man. For these letters are no hurried productions, but are distinguished, like the drawings, for the neatness and finish which pervade them. An autograph letter of Mendelssohn's is a work of art ; the lines are all straight and close, the letters perfectly and elegantly formed, with a peculiar luxuriance of tails, and an illegible word can hardly be found. Down to the folding and the sealing everything is perfect. It seems impossible that this can have been done quickly. It must have absorbed an enormous deal of time.

While speaking of his correspondence, we may mention the neatness and order with which he registered and kept everything. The forty-four volumes of MS. music, in which he did for himself what Mozart's father so carefully did for his son, have been mentioned. But it is not generally known that he preserved all letters that he received, and stuck them with his own hands into books. Twenty-seven large

thick green volumes exist,[2] containing apparently all the letters and memorandums, business and private, which he received from Oct. 29, 1821, to Oct. 29, 1847, together with the drafts of his oratorio books, and of the long official communications which, during his latter life, cost him so many unprofitable hours. He seems to have found time for everything. Hiller tells us how, during a very busy season, he revised and copied out the libretto of his oratorio for him.[3] One of his dearest Leipzig friends has a complete copy of the full score of ' Antigone,' including the whole of the words of the melodrama, written for her with his own hand ; a perfect piece of caligraphy, without spot or erasure ! and the family archives contain a long minute list of the contents of all the cupboards in the house, filling several pages of foolscap, in his usual neat writing, and made about the year 1842. We read of Charles Dickens that ' no matter was considered too trivial to claim his care and attention. He would take as much pains about the hanging of a picture, the choosing of furniture, the superintending of any little improvement in the house, as he would about the more serious business of his life ; thus carrying out to the very letter his favourite motto that, What is worth doing at all is worth doing well.'[4] No words could better describe the side of Mendelssohn's character to which we are alluding, nor could any motto more emphatically express the principle on which he acted throughout life in all his work.

His taste and efficiency in such minor matters are well shown in the albums which he made for his wife, beautiful specimens of arrangement, the most charming things in which are the drawings and pieces of music from his own hands. His private account-books and diaries are kept with the same quaint neatness. If he had a word to alter in a letter, it was done with a grace which turned the blemish into a beauty. The same care came out in everything—in making out the programmes for the Gewandhaus concerts, where he would arrange and rearrange the pieces to suit some inner idea of symmetry or order ; or in settling his sets of songs for publication as to the succession of keys, connexion, or contrast of words, etc. In fact he had a passion for neatness, and a repugnance to anything clumsy. Possibly this may have been one reason why he appears so rarely to have sketched his music. He made it in his head, and had settled the minutest points there before he put it on paper, thus avoiding the litter and disorder of a sketch. Connected with this neatness is a certain quaintness in his proceedings which perhaps strikes an Englishman more forcibly than it would a German. He used

[1] In the hands of his family, of Mr. Robi von Mendelssohn (Berlin), Felix Moscheles, Professor Paul Schubring (Berlin), Paul David, Otto Goldschmidt, Miss Preusser, Euler of Düsseldorf, the Sterndale Bennetts, and others.

[2] In the hands of Mrs. Wach (Lili Mendelssohn-Bartholdy). Two others seem to be missing.   [3] H. p. 167.
[4] Preface to the Letters of Charles Dickens, 1879.

the old-fashioned C clef for the treble voices in his scores to the last ; the long flourish with which he ornaments the double bar at the end of a piece never varied. A score of Haydn's Military Symphony which he wrote for his wife bears the words ' Possessor Cécile.' In writing to Mrs. Moscheles of her little girls, whose singing had pleased him, he begs to be remembered to the ' drei kleine Diskantisten.' A note to David, sent by a child, is inscribed ' Kinderpost,' and so on. Certain French words occur over and over again, and are evidently favourites. Such are *plaisir* and *trouble*, *à propos*, *en gros*, and others. The word *hübsch*, answering to our ' nice,' was a special favourite,[1] and *nett* was one of his highest commendations.

But to return for a moment to his engrossing pursuits. Add to those just mentioned the many concerts, to be arranged, rehearsed, conducted ; the frequent negotiations attending on Berlin ; the long official protocols ; the hospitality and genial intercourse, where he was equally excellent as host or as guest ; the claims of his family ; the long holidays, real holidays, spent in travelling, and not, like Beethoven's, devoted to composition—and we may almost be pardoned for wondering how he can have found time to write any music at all. But on the contrary, with him all this business does not appear to have militated against composition in the slightest degree. It often drove him almost to distraction ; it probably shortened his life ; but it never seems to have prevented his doing whatever music came before him, either spontaneously or at the call of his two posts at Berlin and Dresden. He composed ' Antigone ' in a fortnight, he resisted writing the music to ' Ruy Blas,' he grumbled over the long chorale for the thousandth anniversary of the German Empire, and over the overture to ' Athalie ' in the midst of his London pleasures ; but still he did them, and in the cases of ' Antigone ' and the two overtures it is difficult to see how he could have done them better. He was never driven into a corner.

The power by which he got through all this labour, so much of it self-imposed, was the power of order and concentration, the practical business habit of doing one thing at a time, and doing it well. This, no doubt, was the talent which his father recognised in him so strongly as to make him doubt whether business was not his real vocation. It was this which made him sympathise with Schiller in his power of ' supplying ' great tragedies as they were wanted.[2] In one way his will was weak, for he always found it hard to say ' No ' ; but having accepted the task it became a duty, and towards duty his will was the iron will of a man of business. Such a gift is vouchsafed to very few artists. Handel possessed it in some degree ; but with that one exception Mendelssohn seems to stand alone.

Of this method of composing, little or nothing is known. He appears to have made few sketches, and to have arranged his music in his head at first, much as Mozart did. Probably this arose from his early training under Zelter, for the volumes for 1821, 1822, 1823 of the MS. series now in the Royal Library at Berlin appear to contain his first drafts and rarely show any corrections, and what there are are not so much sketches as erasures and substitutions. Devrient and Schubring tell of their having seen him composing a score bar by bar from top to bottom ; but this was probably only an experiment or *tour de force*.

Alterations in a work after it was completed are quite another thing, and in these he was lavish. He complains of his not discovering the necessity for them till *post festum*.[3] We have seen instances of this in the ' Walpurgisnacht,' ' St. Paul,' ' Lobgesang,' ' Elijah ' and some of the concert-overtures. Another instance is the Italian Symphony, which he retained in MS. for fourteen years, till his death, with the intention of altering and improving the finale. Another, equally to the point, is the D minor trio, of which there are two editions in actual circulation, containing several important and extensive differences.[4] This is carrying fastidiousness even further than Beethoven, whose alterations were endless, but ceased with publication. The autographs of many of Mendelssohn's pieces are dated years before they were printed, and in most, if not all, cases they received material alterations before being issued.

MENDELSSOHN AS PIANIST.—Of his pianoforte-playing in his earlier days we have already spoken. Of the various recollections with which I have been favoured, I cannot do better than give entire those of Madame Schumann and Ferdinand Hiller. In reading them it should be remembered that Mendelssohn was fond of speaking of himself as a player *en gros*, who did not claim (however great his right) to be a virtuoso, and that there are instances of his having refused to play before great virtuosi.

1. ' My recollections of Mendelssohn's playing,' says Madame Schumann,

' are among the most delightful things in my artistic life. It was to me a shining ideal, full of genius and life, united with technical perfection. He would sometimes take the *tempi* very quick, but never to the prejudice of the music. It never occurred to me to compare him with virtuosi. Of mere effects of performance he knew nothing—he was always the great musician, and in hearing him one forgot the player and only revelled in the full enjoyment of the music. He could carry one with him in the most incredible manner, and his playing was always stamped with beauty and nobility. In his early days he had acquired perfection of technique ; but latterly, as he often told me, he hardly ever practised and yet he surpassed every one. I have heard him in

---

[1] *Mos.* ii. p. 165.   [2] *L.* Engelberg. Aug. 23, 1831.

[3] *L.* to Klingemann, Dec. 6, 1846.
[4] The parts of the ' Hebrides ' overture are not in exact accordance with the score of ' Fingals Höhle.' The pianoforte arrangement of the ' Midsummer Night's Dream ' overture published in London is given in notes of half the value of those in the score, published after it in Leipzig : but the difference here is only apparent.

Bach, and Beethoven, and in his own compositions, and shall never forget the impression he made upon me.'

2. ' Mendelssohn's playing,' says Ferdinand Hiller,

' was to him what flying is to a bird. No one wonders why a lark flies, it is inconceivable without that power. In the same way Mendelssohn played the piano because it was his nature. He possessed great skill, certainty, power and rapidity of execution, a lovely full tone—all in fact that a virtuoso could desire ; but these qualities were forgotten while he was playing, and one almost overlooked even those more spiritual gifts which we call fire, invention, soul, apprehension, etc. When he sat down to the instrument music streamed from him with all the fulness of his inborn genius,—he was a centaur, and his horse was the piano. What he played, how he played it, and that he was the player—all were equally riveting, and it was impossible to separate the execution, the music and the executant. This was absolutely the case in his improvisations, so poetical, artistic and finished ; and almost as much so in his execution of the music of Bach, Mozart, Beethoven or himself. Into those three masters he had grown, and they had become his spiritual property. The music of other composers he knew, but could not produce it as he did theirs. I do not think, for instance, that his execution of Chopin was at all to be compared to his execution of the masters just mentioned ; he did not care particularly for it, though when alone he played everything good with interest. In playing at sight his skill and rapidity of comprehension were astonishing, and that not with pianoforte music only, but with the most complicated compositions. He never practised, though he once told me that in his Leipzig time he had played a shake (I think with the second and third fingers) several minutes every day for some months, till he was perfect in it.'

' His staccato,' says Dr. Joachim,

' was the most extraordinary thing possible for life and crispness. In the Frühlingslied (Songs without Words, No. 30), for instance, it was quite electric, and though I have heard that song played by many of the greatest players, I never experienced the same effect. His playing was extraordinarily full of fire, which could hardly be controlled, and yet was controlled, and combined with the greatest delicacy.'

' Though lightness of touch and a delicious liquid pearliness of tone,' says another of his pupils,[1]

' were prominent characteristics, yet his power in fortes was immense. In the passage in his G minor Concerto where the whole orchestra makes a crescendo, the climax of which is a 6-4 chord on D (pianoforte alone), it seemed as if the band had quite enough to do to work up to the chord he played.'

As an instance of the fullness of his tone, the same gentleman mentioned the five bars of piano which begin Beethoven's G major concerto, and which, though he played them perfectly softly, filled the whole room.

' His mechanism,' says another of his Leipzig pupils,[2]

' was extremely subtle, and developed with the lightest of wrist (never from the arm) ; he therefore never strained the instrument or hammered. His chord-playing was beautiful, and based on a special theory of his own. His use of the pedal was very sparing, clearly defined and therefore effective ; his phrasing beautifully clear. The performances in which I derived the most lasting impressions from him were the Thirty-two Variations and last sonata (op. 111) of Beethoven, in which latter the variations of the final movement came out more clearly in their structure and beauty than I have ever heard them before or since.'

[1] W. S. Rockstro.   [2] Otto Goldschmidt.

Of his playing of the Thirty-two Variations, Macfarren remarks that

' to each one, or each pair, where they go in pairs, he gave a character different from all the others. In playing at sight from a MS. score he characterised every incident by the peculiar tone by which he represented the instrument for which it was written.'[3]

In describing his playing of the Ninth Symphony, Schleinitz testified to the same singular power of representing the different instruments. A still stronger testimony is that of Berlioz, who, speaking of the colour of the ' Hebrides ' overture, says that Mendelssohn ' succeeded in giving him an accurate idea of it, such is his extraordinary power of rendering the most complicated scores on the piano.'[4]

His adherence to his author's meaning, and to the indications given in the music, was absolute. Strict time was one of his hobbies. He alludes to it, with an eye to the sins of Hiller and Chopin, in a letter of May 23, 1834, and somewhere else speaks of ' nice strict tempo' as something peculiarly pleasant. After introducing some ritardandos in conducting the introduction to Beethoven's second symphony, he excused himself by saying that ' one could not always be good,'[5] and that he had felt the inclination too strongly to resist it. In playing, however, he never himself interpolated a ritardando, or suffered it in any one else.[6] It especially enraged him when done at the end of a song or other piece. ' Es steht nicht da ! ' he would say ; ' if it were intended it would be written in—they think it expression, but it is sheer affectation.'[7] But though in playing he never varied the tempo when once taken, he did not always take a movement at the same pace, but changed it as his mood was at the time. We have seen in the case of Bach's A minor Fugue (p. 396) that he could on occasion introduce an individual reading ; and his treatment of the arpeggios in the Chromatic Fantasia shows that, there at least, he allowed himself great latitude.[8] Still, in intimating this it should be remembered how thoroughly he knew these great masters, and how perfect his sympathy with them was. In conducting, as we have just seen, he was more elastic, though even there his variations would now be condemned as moderate by some conductors. Before he conducted at the Philharmonic it had been the tradition in the coda of the overture to ' Egmont ' to return to a piano after the crescendo ; but this he would not suffer, and maintained the fortissimo to the end—a practice now always followed.

He very rarely played from book, and his prodigious memory was also often shown in his sudden recollection of out-of-the-way pieces. Hiller has given two instances of this.[9] His power of retaining things casually heard was

[3] See Dorn, p. 398.
[4] Voyage musical, Letter 4 (vol. i. 71, et seq.).   [5] Kellow Pye.
[6] Hans von Bülow.   [7] Mrs. Moscheles and W. S. Rockstro.
[8] L. to Fanny, Nov. 14, 1840.   [9] H. pp. 28, 29.

also shown in his extempore playing, when he would recollect the themes of compositions which he heard then and there for the first time, and would combine them in the happiest manner. An instance of this is mentioned by his father,[1] in which, after Malibran had sung five songs of different nations, he was dragged to the piano, and improvised upon them all. He himself describes another occasion, a ' field day ' at Baillot's, when he took three themes from the Bach sonatas and worked them up to the delight and astonishment of an audience worth delighting.[2] At the matinée of the Society of British Musicians in 1844, he took his themes from two compositions by C. E. Horsley and G. A. Macfarren which he had just heard, probably for the first time—and other instances could be given.

His extemporising was, however, marked by other traits than that of memory. ' It was,' says Macfarren, ' as fluent and as well planned as a written work,' and the themes, whether borrowed or invented, were not merely brought together but contrapuntally worked. Instances of this at Birmingham and elsewhere have been mentioned. His tact in these things was prodigious. At the concert given by Jenny Lind and himself on Dec. 5, 1845, he played two Songs without Words—No. 31 in E flat, and No. 30 in A major, and he modulated from the key of one to that of the other by means of a regularly constructed intermezzo, in which the semiquavers of the first song merged into the arpeggios of the second with the most consummate art and with magical effect.[3] But great as were his public displays, it would seem that, as with Mozart, it was in the small circle of intimate friends that his improvisation was most splendid and happy. Those only who had the good fortune to find themselves (as rarely happened) alone with him at one of his Sunday afternoons are perhaps aware of what he could really do in this direction,[4] and he ' never improvised better ' or pleased himself more than when tête à tête with Queen Victoria and Prince Albert. A singular fact is mentioned by Hiller,[5] which is confirmed by another friend of his : that in playing his own music he did it with a certain reticence, as if not desiring that the work would derive any advantage from his execution. The explanation is very much in consonance with his modesty, but whether correct or not, there is no reason to doubt the fact.

His immense early practice in counterpoint under Zelter—like Mozart's under his father—had given him so complete a command over all the resources of counterpoint, and such a habit of looking at themes contrapuntally, that the combinations just spoken of came more or less

naturally to him. In some of his youthful compositions he brings his science into prominence, as in the fugue in A (op. 7, No. 5) ; the finale of the E flat string quartet (1823) ; the original minuet and trio of the string quintet in A (op. 18), a double canon of great ingenuity ; the chorus in ' St. Paul,' ' But our God,' constructed on the chorale ' Wir glauben all '' ; but with his maturity he mostly drops such displays and ' Elijah,' as is well known, ' contains no fugues.' In extemporising, however, it was at his fingers' ends to the last.

He was also fond of throwing off ingenious canons,[6] of which the following, written on

Etude for one violin, or Canon for two violins.

the moment for Joachim, on March 11, 1844, is a good example. A somewhat similar canon, written in the album of John Parry in 1846, is printed in the *Musical World* for August 19, 1848. Another for two violas—' Viola 1, Sir G. Smart ; Viola 2, F. M. B.'—is given in Sir Frederick Bridge's *Primer of Double Counterpoint and Canon.*[6]

Of his organ-playing we have already spoken. It should be added that he settled upon his combinations of stops before starting, and steadily adhered to the plan on which he set out[7] ; if he started in three parts he continued in three, and the same with four or five. He took extraordinary delight in the organ ; some describe him as even more at home there than on the pianoforte, though this must be taken with caution. But it is certain that he loved the organ, and was always greatly excited when playing it.

He was fond of playing the viola, and on more than one occasion took the first viola part of his own octet in public. The violin he learned when young, but neglected it in later life. He however played occasionally, and it was amusing to see him bending over the desk and struggling with his part just as if he were a boy. His practical knowledge of the instrument is evident from his violin music, in which there are few difficulties which an ordinarily good player cannot surmount. But this is characteristic of the care and thoughtfulness of the man. As a rule in his scores he gives each instrument the passages which suit it. He appears to have felt somewhat of the same natural dislike to brass instruments that Mozart did. At any rate in his early scores he uses them with great

1 *F.M.* i. 377.　　2 *L.* to Rebecka, Paris, Dec. 20, 1831.
3 Recollections of Joachim and Rockstro.
4 Dr. Klengel and Sterndale Bennett once had this good fortune, and it was a thing never to be forgotten.　　5 *H.* p. 18.

6 Yet another canon, written in the album of Miss Eliza Wesley (daughter of Samuel Wesley), will be found in the *Mus. T.*, Feb. and Apr. 1896, pp. 89 and 233.
7 *Musical World*, Feb. 16, 1838, p. 102.

moderation,[1] and somewhere makes the just remark that the trombone is ' too sacred an instrument ' to be used freely.

COMPOSITIONS

The few of Mendelssohn's very early works which he published himself, or which have been issued since his death, show in certain points the traces of his predecessors—of Bach, Mozart, Beethoven and Weber. But this is only saying what can be said of the early works of all composers, including Beethoven himself. Mendelssohn is not more but less amenable to this law of nature than most of his compeers. The traces of Bach are the most permanent, and they linger on in the vocal works even as late as ' St. Paul.' Indeed Bach may be tracked still later in the solid construction and architectonic arrangement of the choruses, even of the ' Lobgesang,' the grand Psalms, the 'Walpurgisnacht' and 'Elijah,' works in all respects emphatically Mendelssohn's own, not less than in the religious feeling, the union of noble sentiment with tender expression, and the utter absence of commonness or vulgarity which pervade all his music alike.

SYMPHONIC WORKS.—In the instrumental works, however, the year 1826 broke the spell of all external influence, and the octet, the quintet in A, and, above all, the ' Midsummer Night's Dream ' overture, launched him upon the world at 17 as a thoroughly original composer. The concert-overtures, the two great symphonies, the two PF. concertos and the violin concerto fully maintain this originality, and in thought, style, phrase and clearness of expression, no less than in their symmetrical structure and exquisite orchestration, are eminently independent and individual works. The advance between the symphony in C minor (1824)—which we call ' No. I.,' though it is really ' No. XIII.'—and the Italian Symphony (Rome, 1831) is immense. The former is laid out quite on the Mozart plan, and the working throughout recalls the old world. But the latter has no model. The melodies and the treatment are Mendelssohn's alone, and while in gaiety and freshness it is quite unrivalled, it is not too much to say that the slow movement is as great a novelty as that of Beethoven's piano concerto in G. The Scotch Symphony is as original as the Italian, and on a much larger and grander scale. The opening andante, the scherzo, and the finale are especially splendid and individual. The concert-overtures are in all essential respects as original as if Beethoven had not preceded them by writing ' Coriolan '—as true a representative of his genius as the ' Hebrides ' is of Mendelssohn's. That to the ' Midsummer

Night's Dream,' which brought the fairies into the orchestra and fixed them there, and which will always remain a monument of the fresh feeling of youth ; the ' Hebrides ' with its intensely sombre and melancholy sentiment, and the ' Melusina ' with its passionate pathos, have no predecessors in sentiment, treatment or orchestration. ' Ruy Blas ' is as brilliant and as full of fire as the others are of sentiment, and does not fall a step behind them for individuality.

In these works there is little attempt at any modification of the established forms. Innovation was not Mendelssohn's habit of mind, and he rarely attempts it. The Scotch Symphony is directed to be played through without pause, and it has an extra movement in the form of a long coda, which appears to be a novelty in pieces of this class. There are unimportant variations in the form of the concertos, chiefly in the direction of compression. But with Mendelssohn, no more than with Schubert, do these things force themselves on the attention. He has so much to say, and says it well, the music is so good and so agreeable, that it never occurs to the hearer to inquire if he has altered the external proportions of his discourse.

His scherzos are still more peculiarly his own offspring, and really have no prototypes. That in a movement bearing the same name as one of Beethoven's most individual creations, and occupying the same place in the piece, he should have been able to strike out so entirely different a path as he did, is a wonderful tribute to his originality. Not less remarkable is the variety of the many scherzos he has left. They are written for orchestra and chamber, concerted and solo alike, in double and triple time indifferently ; they have no fixed rhythm, and notwithstanding a strong family likeness—the impress of the gay and delicate mind of their composer—are all independent of each other. In his orchestral works Mendelssohn's scoring is remarkable not more for its grace and beautiful effect than for its clearness and practical efficiency. It gives the conductor no difficulty. What the composer wishes to express comes out naturally, and, as already remarked, each instrument has with rare exceptions the passages best suited to it.

Mendelssohn's love of 'Programme' is obvious throughout the foregoing works. The exquisite imitation of Goethe's picture in the scherzo of the octet is the earliest instance of it ; the overture founded on his ' Calm sea and prosperous voyage' is another; and as we advance each overture and each symphony has its title. He once said, in conversation with Friedrich Schneider on the subject, that since Beethoven had taken the step he did in the Pastoral Symphony, every one was at liberty to follow.[2]

---

[1] Neither of his three concert-overtures, nor the Italian and Scotch Symphonies, have trombones. As to ' St. Paul,' see his letter to J. C. Horsley, R.A., Aug. 23, 1834, in *G. & M.* p. 115.

[2] Schubring, p. 347b, note.

But the way in which he resented Schumann's attempt [1] to discover ' red coral, sea monsters, magic castles and ocean caves' in his 'Melusina' overture shows that his view of Programme was a broad one, that he did not intend to depict scenes or events, but held fast by Beethoven's canon, that such music should be ' more expression of emotion than painting'—*mehr Ausdruck der Empfindung als Malerei.* Thus he quotes the first few bars of the 'Hebrides' overture (see p. 387) not as his recollection of the sound of the winds and the waves, but ' to show how extraordinarily Fingal's cave had affected him ' *wi—e seltsam mir auf den Hebriden zu Muthe geworden ist.* True, in the 'Midsummer's Night's Dream' overture we are said to hear the bray of Bottom in the low G of the ophicleide ; and in the three North Wales pieces for pianoforte (op. 16) we are told of even more minute touches of imitation ; but these, if not imaginary, are at best but *jeux d'esprit.*

Connected with this tendency to Programme is a curious point, namely, his belief in the absolute and obvious ' meaning' of music. ' Notes,' says he, ' have as definite a meaning as words, perhaps even a more definite one,' [2] and he devotes a whole letter to reiterating that music is not too indefinite to be put into words, but too definite ; that words are susceptible of a variety of meanings, while music has only one.[3] This is not the place to discuss so strange a doctrine, which, though true to him, is certainly not true to the majority of men, and which obviously rests on the precise force of the word ' to mean ' (*heissen*) ; but it is necessary to call attention to it *en passant.*[4]

CHAMBER MUSIC.—His great works in chamber music are on a par with those for the orchestra. The octet, the quintets and the six quartets are thoroughly individual and interesting, nothing far-fetched, no striving after effect, no emptiness, no padding, but plenty of matter given in a manner at once fresh and varied. Every bar is his own, and every bar is well said. The accusation which is sometimes brought against them, that they are more fitted for the orchestra than the chamber, is probably to some extent well founded. Indeed Mendelssohn virtually anticipates this charge in his preface to the parts of the octet, which he desires may be played in a symphonic style ; and in that noble piece, as well as in parts of the quintet in B flat and of the quartets in D and F minor, many players have felt that the composer has placed his work in too small

a frame, that the proper balance cannot always be maintained between the leading violin and the other instruments, and that to produce all the effect of the composer's ideas they should be heard in an orchestra of strings rather than in a quartet of solo instruments. On the other hand, the pianoforte quartet in B minor and the two pianoforte trios in D minor and C minor have been criticised, probably with some justice, as not sufficiently concertante, that is as giving too prominent a part to the piano. Such criticism may detract from the pieces in a technical respect, but it leaves the ideas and sentiments of the music, the nobility of the style and the clearness of the structure, untouched.

His additions to the technique of the pianoforte are not important. Hiller tells a story which shows that Mendelssohn cared little for the rich passages of the modern school ; his own were quite sufficient for him.[5] But this is consistent with what we have just said. It was the music of which he thought, and as long as that expressed his feelings it satisfied him, and he was indifferent to the special form into which it was thrown. Of his pianoforte works the most remarkable is the set of seventeen ' Variations sérieuses ' ; but the Fantasia in F sharp minor (op. 28), the three great Capriccios (op. 33), the Preludes and Fugues and several of the smaller pieces, are splendid works too well known to need further mention. The Songs without Words stand by themselves, and are especially interesting to Englishmen on account of their very great popularity in this country. Mendelssohn's orchestral and chamber works have been greatly played and much enjoyed here, but it is to his oratorios, songs, Songs without Words and partsongs that he owes his firm hold on the mass of the English people. It was some time before the Songs without Words reached the public ; but when once they became known, the taste for them quickly spread, and probably no pieces ever were so much and so permanently beloved in the country. The piece, like the name (*Lieder ohne Worte*), is virtually his own invention. Not a few of Beethoven's movements—such as the adagio of the 'Sonate pathétique' or the minuet of op. 10, No. 3—might be classed as songs without words, and so might Field's nocturnes ; but the former of these are portions of larger works, not easily separable, and the latter were little known ; and neither of them possess that grace and finish, that intimate charm, and above all that *domestic* character, which have ensured the success of Mendelssohn's Songs without Words in many an English family. They soon became identified with his name as it grew more and more familiar in England ; some of them were composed here, others had names or stories

---

1 *L.* to Fanny, Jan. 30, 1836. The reference is to an article in the *N.M.Z.* When asked what he meant by this overture he once replied, ' Hm. une mésalliance.'
2 *L.* to Frau von Pereira, Genoa, July 1831.
3 *L.* to Souchay, Oct. 15, 1842, and compare that written to Frau von Pereira, Genoa, July 1831.
4 Mrs. Austin (*Fraser's Mag.*, Apr. 1848, p. 426) relates that he said to her on one occasion, ' I am going to play something of Beethoven's, but you must tell them what it is about. What is the use of music, if people do not know what it means ? ' She might surely have replied, ' What, then, is the use of the imagination ? '

5 *H.* pp. 154, 155.

attached to their origin[1] : there was a piquancy about the very title—and all helped their popularity. His own feeling towards them was by no means so indulgent. It is perhaps impossible for a composer to be quite impartial towards pieces which make him so very popular, but he distinctly says, after the issue of Book 3, 'that he does not mean to write any more at that time, and that if such *animalculae* are multiplied too much, no one will care for them,' etc.[2] It is difficult to believe that so stern a critic of his own productions should not have felt the weakness of some of them, and the strong mannerism which, with a few remarkable exceptions, pervades the whole collection. We should not forget, too, that he is not answerable for the last two books, which were published after his death, without the great alterations which he habitually made before publication. One drawback to the excessive popularity of the Songs without Words is, not that they exist—for we might as well quarrel with Goethe for the 'Wandrers Nachtlied' or the 'Haidenröslein'—nor yet the number of imitations they produced, but that in the minds of thousands these graceful trifles, many of which were thrown off at a single sitting, are indiscriminately accepted as the most characteristic representatives of the genius of the composer of the violin concerto and the 'Hebrides' overture.

VOCAL MUSIC.—His songs may be said to have introduced the German *Lied* to England, and to have led the way for the deeper strains of Schumann, Schubert and Brahms in English houses and concert - rooms. No doubt the songs of those composers do touch lower depths of the heart than Mendelssohn's do ; but the clearness and directness of his music, the spontaneity of his melody, and a certain pure charm pervading the whole, have given a place with the great public to some of his songs, such as 'Auf Flügeln des Gesanges,' which they will probably retain for a long time to come. Others, such as the Nachtlied, the Volkslied ('Es ist bestimmt') and the Schilflied, are deeply pathetic ; others, as the 'Lieblingsplätzchen,' are at the same time extremely original ; others, as 'O Jugend,' the 'Jagdlied' and 'An die Entfernte,' the soul of gaiety. He was very fastidious in his choice of words, and often marks his sense of the climax by varying the last stanza in accompaniment or otherwise, a practice which he was perhaps the first to adopt. One of his last commissions to his friend Professor Graves, before leaving Interlaken in 1847, was to select words from the English poets for him to set to music. His partsongs gave the majority of English

amateurs a sudden and delightful introduction to a class of music which had long existed for Germans, but which till about 1840 was little known here. Many can still[3] recollect the utterly new and strange feeling which was then awakened in their minds by the new spirit, the delicacy, the pure style, the delicious harmonies, of these enchanting little compositions ! Ever since Handel's time, oratorios have been the favourite public music here. Mendelssohn's works of this class, 'St. Paul,' 'Elijah,' the 'Lobgesang,' soon became well known. They did not come as strangers, but as the younger brothers of the 'Messiah' and 'Judas Maccabæus,' and we liked them at once. Nor only liked them ; we were proud of them, as having been produced or very early performed in England ; they appealed to our national love for the Bible, and there is no doubt that to them is largely owing the position next to Handel which Mendelssohn occupies in England. 'Elijah' at once took its place, and it is now on a level with the 'Messiah' in public favour. Apart from the intrinsic qualities of the music of his large vocal works, the melody, clearness, spirit and symmetry which they exhibit, in common with his instrumental compositions, there is one thing which remarkably distinguishes them, and in which they are far in advance of their predecessors—a simple and direct attempt to set the subject forth as it was, to think first of the story and next of the music which depicted it. It is the same thing that we formerly attempted to bring out in Beethoven's case, 'the thoughts and emotions are the first things, and the forms of expression second and subordinate' (Vol. I. p. 306). We may call this 'dramatic,' inasmuch as the books of oratorios are more or less dramas ; and Mendelssohn's letters to Schubring in reference to 'Elijah,' his demand for more 'questions and answers, replies and rejoinders, sudden interruptions,' etc., show how thin was the line which in his opinion divided the platform from the stage, and how keenly he wished the personages of his oratorios to be alive and acting, 'not mere musical images, but inhabitants of a definite active world.'[4] But yet it was not so much dramatic in any conscious sense as a desire to set things forth as they were. Hauptmann[5] has stated this well with regard to the three noble Psalms, 'Judge me, O God,' 'Why rage fiercely the heathen ?' and 'My God, why hast Thou forsaken me ?' He says that it is not so much any musical or technical ability that places them so far above other similar compositions of our time, as the fact that Mendelssohn has

'just put the Psalm itself before him : not Bach, or Handel, or Palestrina, or any other style or composer, but the words of the Psalmist ; and the result is not

[1] Such as the well-known one in A (No. 30), which, though in Germany known as Frühlingslied was in England for a long time called 'Camberwell Green,' from the fact of its having been composed during his visit to the Beneckes, who resided at Denmark Hill, near Camberwell Green. The Duet (No. 18) represents a conversation between the composer and his fiancée.
[2] *L.* to Simrock, Mar. 4, 1839.

[3] *i.e.* in 1879, the date of writing.
[4] *L.* to Schubring, Nov. 2, Dec. 6, 1838.
[5] Hauptmann's letter to Hauser, Jan. 18, 1850.

anything that can be classed as new or old, but the Psalm itself in thoroughly fine musical effect ; the music not pretending to be scientific, or anything on its own account, but just throwing life and feeling into the dry words.'

Any one who knows these psalms will recognise the truth of this description. It is almost more true in reference to the 114th Psalm, ' When Israel out of Egypt came.' The Jewish blood of Mendelssohn must surely for once have beat fiercely over this picture of the great triumph of his forefathers, and it is only the plain truth to say that in directness and force his music is a perfect match for the splendid words of the unknown Psalmist. It is true of his oratorios also, but they have other great qualities as well. ' St. Paul ' with all its great beauties is an early work, the book of which, or rather perhaps the nature of the subject, does not wholly lend itself to forcible treatment, and it is an open question whether it can fully vie with either the ' Lobgesang ' or ' Athalie,' or still more ' Elijah.' These splendid compositions have that air of distinction which stamps a great work in every art, and which a great master alone can confer. As instances of this, take the scene of the Watchman and the concluding chorus in the ' Lobgesang '—' Ye nations ' ; or in ' Elijah ' the two double quartets ; the arioso, ' Woe unto them,' which might be the wail of a pitying archangel ; the choruses, ' Thanks be to God,' ' Be not afraid,' ' He watching over Israel,' ' Behold ! God the Lord passed by ' ; the great piece of declamation for soprano which opens the second part ; the unaccompanied trio ' Lift thine eyes,' the tenor air 'Then shall the righteous.' These are not only fine as music, but are animated by that lofty and truly dramatic character which makes one forget the vehicle, and live only in the noble sentiment of the scene as it passes.

' Lauda Sion,' though owing to circumstances less known, has the same great qualities, and is a worthy setting of the truly inspired hymn in which St. Thomas Aquinas was enabled to rise so high above the metaphysical subtleties of his day. This piece of Roman Catholic music— Mendelssohn's only important one—shows what he might have done had he written a Mass, as he once threatened to do.[1] It would have been written ' with a constant recollection of its sacred purpose ' ; and remembering how solemn a thing religion was to him, and how much he was affected by fine words, we may well regret that he did not accomplish the suggestion.

' Antigone ' and ' Œdipus,' owing to the remoteness of the dramas, both in subject and treatment, necessarily address themselves to a limited audience, though to that audience they will always be profoundly interesting, not only for the lofty character of the music, but for the able and thoroughly natural manner in which Mendelssohn carried out a task full of diffi-

culties and of temptations to absurdity, by simply ' creating music for the choruses in the good and scientific style of the present day, to express and animate their meaning.' [2]

The ' Midsummer Night's Dream ' music is a perfect illustration of Shakespeare's romantic play, and will be loved as long as beauty, sentiment, humour and exquisite workmanship are honoured in the world.

How far Mendelssohn would have succeeded with an opera, had he met with a libretto entirely to his mind—which that of ' Loreley ' was not—it is difficult to say. Fastidious he certainly was, though hardly more so than Beethoven (see Vol. I. p. 297), and probably for much the same reasons. Times had changed since the lively intrigues and thinly veiled immoralities of Da Ponte were sufficient to animate the pen of the divine Mozart ; and the secret of the fastidiousness of Beethoven and Mendelssohn was that they wanted librettists of their own lofty level in genius and morality, a want in which they were many generations too early. Opera will not take its proper place in the world till subjects shall be found of modern times with which every one can sympathise, treated by the poet, before they come into the hands of the composer, in a thoroughly pure, lofty and inspiriting manner.

' Camacho ' is too juvenile a composition, on too poor a libretto, to enable any inference to be drawn from it as to Mendelssohn's competence for the stage. But, judging from the dramatic power present in his other works, from the stage-instinct displayed in the ' Midsummer Night's Dream ' music, and still more from the very successful treatment of the finale to the first act of ' Loreley '—the only part of the book which he is said really to have cared for— we may anticipate that his opera, when he had found the book he liked, would have been a very fine work. At any rate we may be certain that of all its critics he would have been the most severe, and that he would not have suffered it to be put on the stage till he was quite satisfied with his treatment.

We must now close this long and yet imperfect attempt to set Mendelssohn forth as he was. Few instances can be found in history of a man so amply gifted with every good quality of mind and heart ; so carefully brought up amongst good influences ; endowed with every circumstance that would make him happy ; and so thoroughly fulfilling his mission. Never perhaps could any man be found in whose life there were so few things to conceal and to regret.

Is there any drawback to this ? or, in other words, does his music suffer at all from what he calls his ' habitual cheerfulness ' ? It seems as if there was a drawback, and that arising more

---

[1] L. to Pastor Bauer, Jan. 12, 1835.

[2] L. to Müller, Mar. 12, 1845.

or less directly from those very points which we have named as his best characteristics—his happy healthy heart, his single mind, his un-failing good spirits, his simple trust in God, his unaffected directness of purpose. It is not that he had not genius. The great works enumer-ated prove that he had it in large measure. No man could have called up the new emotions of the ' Midsummer Night's Dream ' overture, the wonderful pictures of the Hebrides, or the pathetic distress of the lovely Melusina, without genius of the highest order. But his genius had not been subjected to those fiery trials which seem necessary to ensure its abiding possession of the depths of the human heart. ' My music,' says Schubert, ' is the product of my genius and my misery ; and that which I have written in my greatest distress is that which the world seems to like best.' Now Mendelssohn was never more than temporarily unhappy. He did not know distress as he knew happiness. Perhaps there was even something in the con-stitution of his mind which forbade his harbour-ing it, or being permanently affected by it. He was so practical that as a matter of duty he

would have thrown it off. In this as in most other things he was always under control. At any rate he was never tried by poverty, or dis-appointment, or ill-health, or a morbid temper, or neglect, or the perfidy of friends, or any of the other great ills which crowded so thickly around Beethoven, Schubert or Schumann. Who can wish that he had been ? that that bright, pure, aspiring spirit should have been dulled by distress or torn with agony ? It might have lent a deeper undertone to his songs, or have enabled his adagios to draw tears where now they only give a saddened pleasure. But let us take the man as we have him. Surely there is enough of conflict and violence in life and in art. When we want to be made un-happy we can turn to others It is well in these agitated modern days to be able to point to one perfectly balanced nature, in whose life, whose letters and whose music alike all is at once manly and refined, clever and pure, brilliant and solid. For the enjoyment of such shining heights of goodness we may well forgo for once the depths of misery and sorrow.   G.

List of Mendelssohn's Published Works taken from the Thematic Catalogue published by Messrs. Breitkopf & Härtel in 1882, with additions and corrections from other sources. The dates of composition are also given, when discoverable, together with the names of the persons to whom the works were dedicated, and the *original* English and German publishers, so far as they can be traced.

Op.	Title.	Da.e of Composition.	Dedicated to	English Publisher.	German Publisher.
1	Quartet in C minor, No. 1, pf. and strings.	*Begun,* Secheron. Sept. 20, 1822—*ended,* Berlin, Oct. 18, 1822.	Anton, Count Radzi-will.	..	Schlesinger, Berlin.
2	Do. in F minor, No. 2.	Nov.19 and 30; Dec. 3, 1823.	Prof. Zelter.	..	Do.
3	Do. in B minor, No. 3.	Oct. 7, 1824 ; Jan. 3, 1825—*at end,* Jan. 18, 1825.	Goethe.	..	Laue, Berlin.
4	Sonata, in F minor, pf. and vln.	Berlin, July 23, 1825.	Eduard Ritz (or Rietz).	..	Do.
5	Capriccio, in F sharp minor, pf.	Berlin, July 23, 1825.	..	Clementi.	Schlesinger.
6	Sonata, in E, pf.	Berlin, Mar. 22, 1826.	..	Ewer & Co.	Laue, Berlin.
7	Seven characteristic pieces, pf.	..	Ludwig Berger.	Wessel & Co.	Do.
8	12 Songs (No. 12 duet). *N.B.—*Nos. 2, 3 and 12 are by Fanny Mendelssohn-Bartholdy.	..	..	Ewer.	Schlesinger.
9	12 Songs (Part I., The Youth ; Part II., The Maiden). *N.B.—*Nos. 7, 10 and 12 are by Fanny Mendelssohn-Bartholdy.	No. 3, Berlin, Apr. 3, 1829 (?).	..	Do.	Do.
10	' The Wedding of Camacho,' comic opera in 2 acts.	*At the end,* Berlin, Aug. 10, 1825.	..	Wessel (overture).	Laue.
11	Symphony in C minor, No. 1, ' Sinfonia xiii.,in C,' orch.	Mar. 3, 9, 31, 1824.	The Philharmonic So-ciety, London.	Cramer (pf. arrt. 4 hands).	Schlesinger.
12	Quartet in E flat, No. 1, strings.	London, Sept. 14, 1829.	..	..	Hofmeister.
13	Do. in A, No. 2.	Berlin, Oct. 26, 1827.	..	..	Breitkopf & Härtel.
14	Rondo capriccio in E, pf.	..	..	Cramer.	Mechetti, Vienna.
15	Fantasie in E, pf. On the Irish air, ' The Last Rose of Sum-mer.'	..	..	Do.	Do.
16	3 Fantasies (or Caprices) in A minor, E minor, and E major, pf.	No. 1, Coed-du, North Wales, Sept. 4, 1829. ' Rosen und Nelken in Menge ' ; No. 2, Norwood, Surrey, Nov. 13, 1829 ; No. 3, Coed-du, Sept. 5, 1829.	Miss (Anne) Taylor (of Coed-du). Miss Honoria Taylor. Miss Susan Taylor.	Do.	Do.
17	Variations concertantes in D, pf. and violoncello.	Berlin, Jan. 30, 1829.	Paul M.-B. (brother of Felix).	Do.	Do.
18	Quintet in A, strings.	*Andante,* ' Nachruf,' Paris, Sept. 23, 1821.	..	..	Simrock.
19	6 Songs, voice and pf.	..	..	Ewer.	Breitkopf & Härtel.
19	6 Songs without words, Book I., Original English title : ' Melo-dies for the pianoforte.'	No. 6, ' Auf einer Gondel,' Venice, Oct. 16, 1830.	..	Novello.	Simrock.
20	Octet in E flat, strings.	..	E. Ritz (or Rietz).	..	Breitkopf & Härtel.
21	'A Midsummer Night's Dream,' Concert overture, in E, No. 1, orch.	Berlin, Aug. 6, 1826.	Crown Prince of Prus-sia.	Cramer (pf. arrangements).	Do.
22	Capriccio brillant in B minor, pf. and orch.	..	..	Mori & Lavenu.	Do.

Op.	Title.	Date of Composition.	Dedicated to	English Publisher.	German Publisher.
23	3 Pieces of Church music, solo, chorus and organ : No. 1, Aus tiefer Noth (' In deep distress '). No. 2, Ave Maria (8 voices). No. 3, Mitten wir (8 voices).	..	..	Ewer & Co.	Simrock.
24	Overture in C, Wind band, ' für Harmoniemusik.'	..	..	Cramer (pf. arrt.) (4 hands, and called ' Military duet ').	Do.
25	Concerto in G minor, pf. and orch., No. 1.	..	Fräulein D. von Schauroth.	Mori & Lavenu.	Breitkopf & Härtel.
26	' The Hebrides,' or ' Fingal's Cave,' Concert overture in B minor, No. 2, orch.	First form, Rome, Dec. 16, 1830 ; revised form, London, June 20, 1832.	Crown Prince of Prussia.	Do. (pf. 4 hands).	Do.
27	' Calm sea and prosperous voyage,' Concert overture in D, No. 3, orch.	..	..	Do. (pf. 4 hands).	Do.
28	Fantasie in F sharp minor, ' Sonate écossaise,' pf.	Berlin, Jan. 29, 1833.	Ignaz Moscheles.	Do.	Simrock.
29	Rondo (or Capriccio) brillant in E flat, pf. and orch.	Düsseldorf, Jan. 29, 1834.	Do.	Do.	Breitkopf & Härt
30	6 Songs without words, pf., Book II., English titles : ' Six Melodies' and ' Six Romances.'	No. 4, Jan. 30, 1833 (?). No. 5, Dec. 12, 1833.	Fräulein Elisa von Woringen.	Do.	Simrock.
31	Psalm 115, solo, chorus and orch., ' Not unto us, O Lord.'	Nov. 15, 1830.	..	Novello.	Do.
32	' To the story of the lovely Melusina,' Concert overture in F, No. 4, orch.	Düsseldorf, Nov. 14, 1833.	Crown Prince of Prussia.	Cramer (pf. solo).	Breitkopf & Härtel,
33	3 Caprices in A minor, E, B flat minor, pf.	No. 1, Apr. 9, 1834 ; No. 3, London, July 25, 1833.	Carl Klingemann.	Mori & Lavenu.	Do.
34	6 Songs, voice and pf.	No. 1, Düsseldorf, May 11, 1834; No. 5, Dec. 28, 1834.	Fräulein Julie Jeanrenaud.	Ewer.	Do.
35	6 Preludes and Fugues, pf.	No. 2, Prel., Leipzig, Dec. 6-8, 1836 ; No. 3, Fugue, Berlin, Sept. 21, 1832 ; No. 4, Fugue, Düsseldorf, Jan. 6, 1835 ; No. 5, Prel., Leipzig, Nov. 19, 1836, Fugue, Düsseldorf, Dec. 3, 1834 ; No. 6, Prel., Leipzig, Jan. 3, 1837, Fugue, Nov. 27, 1836.	..	Mori & Lavenu.	Do.
36	' St. Paul,' oratorio.	Part I., Leipzig, Apr. 8, 1836 ; Part II., Leipzig, Apr. 18, 1836.	..	Novello.	Simrock.
37	3 Preludes and Fugues, organ.	No. 1, Prel., Spires, Apr. 2, 1837 ; No. 2, Prel., Spires, Apr. 4, 1837, Fugue, Leipzig, Dec. 1, 1837 ; No. 3, Prel., Spires, Apr. 6, 1837.	Thomas Attwood, ' mit Verehrung und Dankbarkeit.'	Do.	Breitkopf & Härtel
38	6 Songs without words, pf., Book III.	No. 5, Spires, Apr. 6, 1837 ; No. 6, ' Duet,' Frankfort, June 27, 1836.	Fräulein Rosa von Woringen.	Do.	Simrock.
39	3 Motets, female voices and organ (or pf.), ' Für die Stimmen der Nonnen auf Sta-Trinità de' Monti.'	Rome, Dec. 31, 1830. Another version of ' Surrexit Pastor,' headed ' No. 2,' in the MS., is dated ' Coblentz, Aug. 14, 1837.'	..	Do.	Do.
40	Concerto in D minor, pf. and orch., No. 2.	Horchheim, Aug. 5, 1837.	..	Do.	Breitkopf & Härtel.
41	6 Partsongs, S.A.T.B., ' for singing in the open air,' 1st set. The earliest appearance of Mendelssohn's Four-part songs in England was in No. 55 of Ewer & Co.'s Orpheus collection, which began in 1836.	No. 4, Düsseldorf, Jan. 22, 1834.	..	Do.	Breitkopf & Härtel.
42	Psalm 42, soli, chorus and orch., ' As the hart pants.'	..	..	Do.	Do.
43	Serenade and Allegro giojoso in B minor, pf. and orch.	Apr. 11, 1838.	..	Do.	Simrock.
44	3 Quartets in D, E minor, E flat, strings, Nos. 3, 4 and 5.	No. 3, Berlin, July 24, 1838 ; No. 4, June 18, 1837 ; No. 5, Feb. 6, 1838.	The Prince of Sweden.	..	Breitkopf & Härtel.
45	Sonata in B flat, pf. and violoncello.	Leipzig, Oct. 13, 1838.	..	Novello.	F. Kistner, Leipzig.
46	Psalm 95, tenor solo, chorus and orch., ' O come let us worship.'	Final chorus (in F flat), Leipzig, Apr. 11, 1893.	..	Do.	Do.
47	6 Songs, voice and pf.	No. 3, Leipzig, Apr. 17, 1839 ; No. 4, Apr. 18, 1839 ; No. 5, London, May 1832.	Frau Constanze Schleinitz.	Wessel.	Breitkopf & Härtel.
48	6 Partsongs, S.A.T.B., 2nd set.	No. 1, July 5, 1839 ; No. 3, Leipzig, Dec. 28, 1839 ; No. 4, June 15, 1839 ; No. 5, Nov. 18, 1839 ; No. 6, Leipzig, Dec. 26, 1839.	Dr. Martin and Dr. Spiess.	..	Do.
49	Trio in D minor, pf., violin and violoncello.	Allegro, Frankfort, June 6, 1839 ; Finale, Frankfort, July 18, 1839, and Leipzig, Sept. 23, 1839.	..	Ewer & Co.	Breitkopf & Härtel.
50	6 Partsongs, male voices.	No. 2, ' Der Jäger Abschied,' with wind accompaniments, Leipzig, Jan. 6, 1840 ; No. 5, Dec. 7, 1839 ; No. 6, Jan. 6, 1840.	Die Liedertafel, Leipzig.	Do.	Kistner.
51	Psalm 114, 8-part chorus and orch., ' When Israel out of Egypt came.'	Horchheim, Aug. 9, 1839.	J. W. Schirmer (the painter).	Novello.	Breitkopf & Härtel.
52	Lobgesang (Hymn of Praise), Symphony-cantata.	Leipzig, Nov. 27, 1840 (revised form).	Frederic Augustus, Duke of Saxony.	Do.	Do.
53	6 Songs without words, pf., Book IV.	No. 5 Apr. 30, 1841 ; No. 6, May 1, 1841.	Miss Sophy Horsley.	Ewer.	Simrock.

Op.	Title.	Date of Composition.	Dedicated to	English Publisher.	German Publisher.
54	17 Variations sérieuses in D minor, pf.	June 4, 1841.	..	Ewer.	Mechetti, Vienna.
55	Antigone of Sophocles; music to, male voices and orch.	Berlin, Oct. 10, 1841.	Frederick William IV., King of Prussia.	Do.	Kistner.
56	Symphony in A minor, ' The Scotch,' No. 3, orch.	Berlin, Jan. 20, 1842.	Queen Victoria.	Do.	Breitkopf & Härtel.
57	6 Songs, voice and pf.	No. 2, Apr. 20, 1839 (cf. op. 88, No. 3); No. 5, 'Rendez-vous,' Berlin, Oct. 17, 1842; No. 6, 'Frische Fahrt,' Apr. 29, 1841.	Miss Dolby.	Wessel.	Do.
58	Sonata in D, pf. and violoncello, No. 2.	..	Count Mathias Wielhorsky.	Ewer.	Kistner.
59	6 Partsongs, S.A.T.B., 3rd set.	No. 1, Leipzig, Nov. 23, 1837; No. 2, Jan. 17, 1843; No. 3, Leipzig, Mar. 4, 1843; No. 4, Leipzig, June 19, 1843; No. 5, Mar. 4, 1843; No. 6, 'Vorüber,' Mar. 5, 1843.	Frau Henriette Benecke.	Do.	Breitkopf & Härtel.
60	First Walpurgis night, Music to Goethe's Ballad, chorus and orch.	1st version, Milan, July 15, 1831, and Paris, Feb. 13, 1832.	..	Do.	Kistner.
61	'A Midsummer Night's Dream,' Music to, solo, chorus and orch. (exclusive of overture, for which see op. 21).	..	Heinrich Conrad Schleinitz.	Do.	Breitkopf & Härtel.
62	6 Songs without words, pf., Book V.	No. 1, Jan. 6 and 12, 1844; No. 2, July 29, 1843; No. 6, Denmark Hill, June 1, 1842.	Frau Clara Schumann.	Do.	Simrock.
63	6 Duets, voices and pf.	No. 1, Frankfort, Dec. 1836; No. 4, originally for pf. duet; No. 5, Berlin, Oct. 17,1842; No. 6, Jan. 23, 1844.	..	..	Kistner.
64	Concerto in E, vln. and orch.	Sept. 16, 1844.	..	Ewer.	Breitkopf & Härtel.
65	6 Sonatas, organ. [For the history of these organ sonatas, see Mus. T., 1901, p. 794, and 1906, p. 95.]	Son. 1: No. 1, Frankfort, Dec. 28, 1844; No. 2, Dec. 19, 1844; No. 4, Aug. 18, 1844. Son. 2: No. 1, Frankfort, Dec. 21, 1844; No. 3 (Fugue), July 14, 1839, and Dec. 19, 1844. Son. 3: No. 1, Aug. 9, 1844; No. 2, Aug. 17, 1844. Son. 4: Nos. 1 and 2, Frankfort, Jan. 2, 1845. Son 5: Nos. 2 and 3, Sept. 9, 1844. Son. 6: No. 1, Frankfort, Jan. 26, 1845; No. 4 (Fugue), Frankfort, Jan. 27, 1845.	Dr. F. Schlemmer.	Coventry & Hollier.	Do.
66	Trio in C minor, pf., vln. and violoncello.	1845.	Louis Spohr.	Ewer.	Breitkopf & Härtel.
67	6 Songs without words, pf., Book VI.	No. 1, June 29, 1843; No. 2, Frankfort, May 3, 1845; No. 5, Jan. 5 and 12, 1844.	Fräulein Sophie Rosen.	Do.	Simrock.
68	'An die Künstler' (' To the sons of art '). Schiller's poem, Festgesang. Male voices and brass instruments. Composed for the opening of the first German-Flemish vocal festival at Cologne, June 1846.	..	..	Do.	Do.
69	3 English Church pieces, solo voices and chorus—(1) Nunc dimittis; (2) Jubilate; (3) Magnificat.	No. 1, Baden-Baden, June 12, 1847; No. 2, Leipzig, Apr. 5, 1847; No. 3, Baden-Baden, June 12, 1847.		Do.	Breitkopf & Härtel.
70	'Elijah,' oratorio.	At the end, Leipzig, Aug. 11, 1846.	..	Do.	Simrock.
71	6 Songs, voice and pf.	No. 1, Leipzig, Dec. 22, 1845; No. 2, Frankfort, Apr. 3, 1845; No. 3, Leipzig, Sept. 22, 1847; No. 4, Berlin, Nov. 3, 1842; No. 5, Interlaken, July 27, 1847; No. 6, Oct. 1, 1847.	..	Do.	Breitkopf & Härtel.
72	6 Kinderstücke, pf. Known in England as ' Christmas pieces,' and composed at Denmark Hill, London.	No. 1, June 24, 1842; No. 3, June 21, 1842.	No. 1, Lilli Benecke; No. 3, Edward Benecke.	Do.	Do.

FROM OP. 73 TO OP. 121 ARE POSTHUMOUS WORKS

Op.	Title.	Date of Composition.	Dedicated to	English Publisher.	German Publisher.
73	Lauda Sion, cantata, chorus and orch. For St. Martin's church, Liège.	Feb. 10, 1846.	..	Ewer.	Schott.
74	'Athalie,' Music to Racine's, soli, chorus and orch.	Choruses, Leipzig, July 4, 1843; Overture, London, June 13, 1844, and Berlin, Nov. 12, 1845.	..	Do.	Breitkopf & Härtel.
75	4 Partsongs, male voices.	No. 1, Feb. 8, 1844; No. 2, Nov. 14, 1839.	..	Do.	Kistner.
76	4 Partsongs, male voices.	No. 2, Feb. 9, 1844; No. 3, Leipzig, Oct. 8, 1846.	..	Do.	Do.
77	3 duets, voices and pf. No. 3 is from ' Ruy Blas.'	No. 1, Leipzig, Dec. 3, 1836; No. 2, Leipzig, Jan. 18, 1847; No. 3, Leipzig, Feb. 14, 1839.	..	Do.	Do.; No. 3, Cranz, Hamburg.

Op.	Title.	Date of Composition.	Dedicated to	English Publisher.	German Publisher.
78	3 Psalms—the 2nd, 43rd and 22nd, solo and chorus. For the Domchor, Berlin.	No. 2, Berlin, Jan. 17, 1844.	..	Ewer.	Breitkopf & Härtel.
79	6 Anthems, 8-part chorus. For the Domchor, Berlin.	No. 2, Berlin, Dec. 25, 1843; No. 4, Feb. 14, 1844; No. 5, Oct. 5, 1846; No. 6, Feb. 18, 1844.	..	Do.	Do.
80	Quartet in F minor, strings.	Interlaken, Sept. 1847.	..	..	Do.
81	Andante in E, Scherzo in A minor. Capriccio in E minor, Fugue in E flat, strings.	..	..	..	Do.
82	Variations in E flat, pf.	Leipzig, July 25, 1841.	..	Ewer.	Do.
83	Variations in B flat, pf.	..	..	Do.	Do.
83a	Variations arranged for 4 hands.	..	..	Do.	Do.
84	3 Songs for a low voice and pf.	No. 1, Düsseldorf, Dec. 5, 1831; No. 2, Feb. 26, 1839; No. 3, May 25, 1834.	..	Do.	Do.
85	6 Songs without words, pf., Book VII.	No. 2, Düsseldorf, June 9, 1834; No. 4, Frankfort, May 3 and 6, 1845; No. 5, Frankfort, May 7, 1845; No. 6, May 1, 1841.	..	Do.	Simrock.
86	6 Songs, voice and pf.	No. 3, Unterseen, Aug. 10, 1831; No. 6, Oct. 7, 1847.	..	Do.	Breitkopf & Härtel.
87	Quintet in B flat, strings.	Soden, July 8, 1845.	..	..	Do.
88	6 Partsongs, S.A.T.B. (4th set).	No. 1, Aug. 8, 1844; No. 2, Leipzig, June 20, 1843; No. 3, Apr. 20, 1839; No. 4, Leipzig, June 19, 1843; No. 6, Leipzig, Mar. 10, 1840.	..	Ewer.	Do.
89	Heimkehr aus der Fremde ('Son and Stranger'), Singspiel in 1 act.	..	..	Do.	Do.
90	The 'Italian Symphony,' Symphony in A, orch.	Berlin, Mar. 13, 1833.	..	Do.	Do.
91	Psalm 98, 'Sing to the Lord,' 8-part chorus and orch. For the Festival Service in Berlin Cathedral on New Year's Day, 1844.	Dec. 27, 1843.	..	Do.	Kistner.
92	Allegro brillant in A, pf., 4 hands.	Leipzig, Mar. 23, 1841.	..	Do.	Breitkopf & Härtel.
93	Œdipus in Colonos by Sophocles, Music to, male voices and orch.	Frankfort, Feb. 25, 1845.	..	Do.	Do.
94	'Infelice!' Concert-air in B flat, soprano solo and orch.	1st version, with vln. obbl., Apr. 3, 1834; 2nd version, Leipzig, Jan. 15, 1843.	..	Do.	Do.
95	'Ruy Blas,' Overture, orch.	Leipzig, Mar. 8, 1839.	..	..	Kistner.
96	Hymn, alto solo, chorus and orch. Composed for Mr. [Dr.] C. Broadley.	Leipzig, Dec. 14, 1840; Jan. 5, 1843 (final chorus). Autograph in British Museum (Add. MS. 31,801).	..	Ewer.	Simrock.
97	Christus, unfinished oratorio. Recitatives and choruses.	..	..	Do.	Breitkopf & Härtel.
98	(1) Loreley, unfinished opera, solo, chorus and orch. Finale to 1st act.	..	..	Do.	Do.
98	(2) Loreley, Ave Maria, solo and chorus of female voices.	..	..	Novello.	J. Rieter-Biedermann
98	(3) Loreley, Vintage chorus, male voices and orch.	..	..	Do.	Do.
99	6 Songs, voice and pf.	No. 1, Berlin, Aug. 9, 1841; No. 4, June 6, 1841; No. 5, Leipzig, Dec. 22, 1845.	..	Ewer.	Breitkopf & Härtel.
100	4 Partsongs, S.A.T.B.	No. 1, Aug. 8, 1844; No. 2, June 20, 1843; No. 4, Frankfort, June 14, 1839.	..	Do.	Do.
101	Overture in C ('Trumpet overture'), orch.	..	..	Novello.	Do.
102	6 Songs without words, pf., Book VIII.	No. 1, London, June 1, 1842; No. 2, Frankfort, May 11, 1845, Pfingsten; Nos. 3 and 5 (Kinderstück), Dec. 12, 1845.	..	Do.	Simrock.
103	Trauer-Marsch in A minor, orch. For funeral of Norbert Burgmüller.	..	..	Do.	J. Rieter-Biedermann
104	3 Preludes and 3 Studies, pf. (2 parts).	Bk. 1, No. 1, Leipzig, Dec. 8, 1836; No. 2, Oct. 12, 1836; No. 3, Nov. 27, 1836. Bk. 2, No. 1, June 9, 1836; No. 2, Düsseldorf, Apr. 21, 1834.	..	Do.	Bartholf Senff.
105	Sonata in G minor, pf.	Begun, June 16, 1820. Presto, Aug. 18, 1821.	..	Do.	J. Rieter-Biedermann
106	Sonata in B flat, pf.	Berlin, May 31, 1827.	..	Do.	Do.
107	'The Reformation Symphony' in D, No. 5, orch.	..	..	Do.	Simrock.
108	March in D, orch. For the Fête given to the painter Cornelius at Dresden in Apr. 1841.	..	..	Do.	J. Rieter-Biedermann
109	Song without words in D, violoncello and pf.	..	Mlle. Lisa Cristiani.	Do.	Bartholf Senff.
110	Sextet in D, pf., vln., 2 violas, violoncello and bass.	Apr. and May 1824.	..	Do.	Kistner.
111	Tu es Petrus, 5-part chorus and orch.	Nov. 1827.	..	Do.	Simrock.
112	2 Sacred songs, voice and pf. (No. 2, composed originally for 'St. Paul')	..	..	Do.	Do.

Op.	Title.	Date of Composition.	Dedicated to	English Publisher.	German Publisher.
113 & 114	2 Concerted pieces, clarinet and basset-horn, with pf. accompt., in F major and D minor.	No. 1, Berlin, Jan. 19, 1833.	Heinrich Bärmann, Senr., and Carl Bärmann, Junr.	Novello.	J. André (Offenbach).
115	2 Sacred choruses, male voices.			Do.	J. Rieter-Biedermann.
116	Funeral song, mixed voices.	Soden, July 8, 1845.		Do.	Do.
117	Album-Blatt, song without words in E minor, pf.			Do.	Kistner.
118	Capriccio in E, pf.	Bingen, July 11, 1837.		Do.	Do.
119	Perpetuum mobile in C, pf.			Do.	Do.
120	4 Partsongs, male voices.	No. 2, Leipzig, Feb. 20, 1847.		Do.	Do.
121	Responsorium et Hymnus, male voices, with accompt. of violoncello and bass (organ).				F. E. C. Leuckart (Leipzig).

WORKS WITHOUT OPUS NUMBERS

Op.	Title.	Date of Composition.	Dedicated to	English Publisher.	German Publisher.
	Étude in F minor, pf. For the 'Méthode des méthodes.'	Leipzig, Mar. 13, 1836.			Schlesinger.
	Scherzo in B minor, pf.				Do.
	Scherzo and Capriccio in F sharp minor, pf. For the Pianist's Album.			Cramer.	Simrock.
	2 Romances of Lord Byron's, voice and pf.: 'There be none of beauty's daughters,' and 'Sun of the sleepless.'	No. 2, Düsseldorf, Dec. 31, 1834.			Breitkopf & Härtel.
	'Verleih' uns Frieden'; 'Grant us Thy peace,' Prayer, chorus and orch.	Rome, Feb. 10, 1831.	President Verkenius.	Novello.	Do.
	Andante cantabile and Presto agitato in B, pf. For the Album of 1839.	Berlin, June 22, 1838.		Mori & Lavenu.	Do.
	The Garland, voice and pf., poem by Thomas Moore.	London, May 24, 1829.		Ewer.	Spehr, Brunswick.
	Ersatz für Unbestand, partsong, male voices, poem by Rückert. For Tauchnitz's Musen-almanach.	Nov. 22, 1839.			Kistner.
	Festgesang, male chorus and orch. Composed for the Gutenberg Festival at Leipzig, held in 1840, in celebration of the invention of printing. [No. 2 is associated in England with the words of Charles Wesley's Christmas hymn, 'Hark! the herald angels sing,' to which it was adapted by Dr. W. H. Cummings.]			Ewer.	Breitkopf & Härtel.
	Gondellied in A, pf. 'Auf einer Gondel'	Leipzig, Feb. 5, 1837.		Ewer.	F. W. Arnold (Elberfeld).
	3 Volkslieder, 2 voices and pf.			Do.	Schlesinger.
	'Lord, have mercy upon us' (Kyrie). 'For evening service.' Voices only. 'For Mr. Attwood.' In the 'Album für Gesang.' First published in England in Ewer's Orpheus, Book XII.	Berlin, Mar. 24, 1833.		Do.	Schuberth.
	Prelude and fugue in E minor, pf. For the Album Notre temps.	Prelude, Leipzig, July 13, 1841; Fugue, June 16, 1827.			Schott.
	3 Sacred choruses, forming part of op. 96.	Leipzig, Jan. 5, 1843.			Simrock.
	'Hear my prayer.' hymn, soprano solo, chorus and organ; afterwards orchestrated, the full score is only published in England, not in Germany.	Jan. 25, 1844.	Wilhelm Taubert.	Ewer. Orchestral Score, Novello.	E. Bote & G. Bock.
	Warnung vor dem Rhein, poem by C. Simrock, voice and pf.				Simrock.
	2 Songs, voice and pf.	No. 1, Berlin, Aug. 17, 1835.			F. W. Arnold.
	2 Songs, voice and pf.	No. 1, Apr. 20, 1841.			C. A. Klemm (Leipzig).
	2 Clavier tücke, in B flat and G minor, pf.			Mori & Lavenu.	B. Senff (Leipzig).
	Seemann's Scheidelied, poem by Hoffmann v. Fallersleben, voice and pf.			Printed in 'Apollo's Gift, or The Musical Souvenir,' for 1831, p. 36 (Chappell).	Schlesinger.
	Nachtgesang, 4 male voices.	Berlin, Jan. 15, 1842.			C. F. Kahnt (Leipzig).
	Die Stiftungsfeier, 4 male voices. 'Für die Stiftungsfeier der Gesellschaft der Freunde in Berlin, Jan. 1842.'				Do.
	Des Mädchens Klage, Romance, voice and pf.				Schuberth & Co. (Leipzig).
	Kyrie Eleison, mixed voices, double chorus (Deutsche Liturgie).	Oct. 28, 1846.			E. Bote & G. Bock.
	Ehre sei Gott in der Höhe; Heilig: Psalm 100. Three sacred pieces, Nos. 1 and 2, double choir; No. 3, 4 voices, from 'Musica sacra,' Band 7, Nos. 17 and 18, Band 8, No. 10.				Do.
	Te Deum in A (English Church Service).			Novello.	(Not published in Germany.)
	'The Evening Bell,' for harp and pf. The 'bell' was that of Attwood's gate. See Musical Haunts in London, p. 5.	Norwood, Nov. 1829.		Chappell.	(Not published in Germany.)
	Fugue in F minor, organ.	Frankfort, July 18, 1839.		Stanley Lucas & Co. (1885).	(Not published in Germany.)
	Two pieces, organ. (1) Andante with variations in D. (2) Allegro in B flat.	July 23, 1844. Dec. 31, 1844.		Novello (1898).	(Not published in Germany.)
	Duo concertant, variations upon the March in Weber's Preciosa, pf., 4 hands jointly composed by Mendelssohn and Ignaz Moscheles.		Mme. la Baronne O. de Goethe.	Cramer.	Kistner.

NOT INCLUDED IN THE THEMATIC CATALOGUE

Title.	Date of Composition.	Dedicated to	English Publisher.	German Publisher.
Hymn-tune, Psalm xxxi., 'Defend me, Lord, from shame.' Composed for the 'National Psalmist' (1839), edited by Charles Danvers Hackett.	Feb. 27, 1839.	..	..	..
Praeludium in C minor for the organ. Composed for Mr. Henry E. Dibdin	Leipzig, July 9, 1841.	..	Paterson & Co. (Edinburgh).	(Not published in Germany.)
Additional (final) chorus to Psalm 95 (op. 46).	Leipzig, Apr. 11, 1839.	..	Novello.	(Not published in Germany.)
String quartet in E flat. Autograph in British Museum (Add. MS. 30,900).	Mar. 5-30, 1823.	..	..	Erler (Berlin).

COMPOSITIONS EDITED, ETC., BY MENDELSSOHN

Handel's 'Dettingen Te Deum,' with additional accompaniments. Score and parts. (Kistner.)

Handel's 'Acis and Galatea,' with additional accompaniments. (Novello.)

Handel's 'Israel in Egypt,' edited for the London Handel Society; Mendelssohn wrote a special organ part, and the edition was published by Cramer & Co. in June 1846. For the interesting correspondence with G. A. Macfarren on the subject of this edition, see *Goethe and Mendelssohn*, 2nd edition, 1874, p. 169 *et seq.*

J. S. Bach's Chaconne for violin, with pf. accompt. (Ewer.)

J. S. Bach's 'Organ compositions on Corales (Psalm tunes),' Organ Preludes, etc., 2 books. (Coventry & Hollier, 1845.)

J. S. Bach's 'Eleven variations on the Corale Sey gegrusset Jesu gütig' (All hail, good Jesus), edited from the original manuscript. (Coventry & Hollier.)

The collection of autograph MSS. of Mendelssohn contained in the green volumes, already mentioned, now preserved in the State Library, Berlin, comprise the following unpublished compositions :

11 Symphonies for strings.
1 Symphony for full orchestra.
Many Fugues for strings.
Concertos for pf.; vln.; pf. and vln. with quartet accompaniment.
2 Concertos for 2 pianos and orch.
Trio for pf., vln. and viola.
2 Sonatas for pf. and vln. (one dated 1838).
1 Sonata for pf. and viola.
1   do.   for pf. and clarinet.
2 Sonatas for pf. solo.
Many Studies, Fantasias (one for four hands), Fugues, etc., for pf. solo.
Many Fugues for organ.
5 Operas and music to Calderon's 'Steadfast Prince.'
1 secular and 3 sacred Cantatas.
Many Songs and vocal pieces.
Organ part to Handel's 'Solomon.'

A fragment of a symphony in C found among the loose papers of Mendelssohn was printed in former editions of this Dictionary by permission of the composer's daughter, the late Mrs. C. Victor Benecke.

BIBLIOGRAPHY

I. Letters

(1) Two volumes have been published by authority. The first, edited by his brother Paul, is entitled *Reisebriefe . . . aus den Jahren 1830 bis 1832* (Leipzig, 1861); the second, edited by his brother and his eldest son, *Briefe aus den Jahren 1833 bis 1847* (Leipzig, 1863), with an Appendix purporting to be a list of all Mendelssohn's compositions, compiled by Julius Rietz, which is, however, both vagu: and incomplete.

These were translated (not adequately) by Lady Wallace and published with the titles, *Letters from Italy and Switzerland*, etc., and *Letters from 1833 to 1847* (Longmans, 1862 and 1863). At a later date some important letters were added to the German edition of vol. ii., amongst others one containing Mendelssohn's translations of Dante, Boccaccio, etc., and Indexes were appended; but no change has been made in the contents of the English translation. There is reason to believe that the letters of vol. i. were in many ways altered by the editor.

(2) Eight letters published for the benefit of the Deutschen Invaliden-Stiftung—*Acht Briefe und ein Facsimile* (Leipzig, 1871). English translation in *Macmillan's Magazine*, June 1871.

The name of the lady to whom they were written is suppressed, but it is understood that she was Mrs. Voigt, a musical amateur of Leipzig. The last of the eight contains a facsimile of a sketch by Mendelssohn.

(3) *Musiker Briefe*, by C. F. Ludwig Nohl (Leipzig, 1867), contains thirty letters dating from 1826 to Aug. 26, 1847. They are included by Lady Wallace in her translation of the entire work entitled *Letters of Distinguished Musicians* (London: Longmans, 1867).

(4) Other letters are contained in Devrient's *Recollections*; Hiller's *Mendelssohn*; *Goethe und Mendelssohn*; Polko's *Reminiscences*; Hensel's *Die Familie Mendelssohn*; Moscheles's *Life*; Chorley's *Life*; Eckardt's *Ferdinand David*; F. Moscheles's *Briefe*; and F. G. Edwards's *History of 'Elijah*,' etc.

II. Biographical Works

(1) Lampadius (Wilhelm Adolf). *Felix Mendelssohn-Bartholdy. Ein Denkmal für seine Freunde* (Leipzig, 1848), translated into English by William Leonhard Gage, with supplementary sketches by Benedict, Chorley, Ludwig Rellstab, Bayard Taylor, R. S. Willis and J. S. Dwight (New York, 1866; London, 1876).

(2) Benedict (Julius). *A Sketch of the Life and Works of the late Felix Mendelssohn-Bartholdy* (London: John Murray, 1850; 2nd ed., with additions, 1853).

(3) Devrient (Eduard). *Meine Erinnerungen an F. M.-B. . . .* (Leipzig, 1869). English translation by Lady Macfarren (London: Bentley, 1869).

Contains thirty-two letters and portions of letters.

(4) Mendelssohn-Bartholdy (Carl). *Goethe und Felix Mendelssohn-Bartholdy* (Leipzig, 1871). By the composer's eldest son; an account of the three visits paid to Goethe, from journals, letters, etc., with a poor engraving from Begas's portrait. English translation by Miss M. E. von Glehn—*Goethe and Mendelssohn*, 'with additions and with letters of later date' (London: Macmillan, 1872; 2nd ed. 'with additional letters,' thirty-seven in all (1874).

(5) Hiller (Ferdinand). *Mendelssohn. Letters and Recollections*, etc., first published in *Macmillan's Magazine* (from Jan. to May 1874), the English translation by Miss M. E. von Glehn. Also in a volume (London: Macmillan, 1874); and in German (Cologne, 1874). Contains twenty-six etters not before printed.

(6) Polko (Elise). *Erinnerungen an F. M.-B.* (Leipzig, 1868). Contains twelve letter . English translation by Lady Wallace—*Reminiscence of Felix Mendelssohn-Bartholdy*, etc. (London: Longmans, 1869), with Appendix of thirty-three additional letters and fragments of letters addressed to English correspondents.

(7) Hensel (Sebastian). *Die Familie Mendelssohn (1729–1847) . . . with eight portraits* (3 vols., Berlin, 1879). Engli h translation, *The Mendelssohn Family* (from the second revised German edition, 2 vols., London: Sampson Low & Co., 1880), by Carl Klingemann and an American collaborator, with a notice by Sir George Grove, London, 1881.

By the son of Fanny Hensel—the Sebastian of the Letters. Compiled from journals and family papers, and containing seventy-three letters or portions of letters hitherto unpublished.

(8) Hogarth (George). *The Philharmonic Society of London* (London, 1862). Contains notices of Mendelssohn's connexion with the Philharmonic, with three letters in the body of the work and seven others in the appendix.

(9) Moscheles (Charlotte). *Aus Moscheles Leben . . . von seiner Frau* (2 vols., Leipzig, 1872 and 1873). English translation by A. D. Coleridge (2 vols., London: Hurst & Blackett, 1873). Contains many valuable notices, and some letters.

(10) Schubring (Julius). *Erinnerungen an F. M.-B.* In the magazine *Daheim* (Leipzig) for 1866, No. 26. English translation in *Musical World*, May 12 and 19, 1866.

One of the most detailed, valuable and interesting of all the notices.

(11) Horsley (Charles Edward). *Reminiscences of Mendelssohn.* First published in *Dwight's Journal of Music* (Boston, U.S.A.) and reprinted in *The Choir* (London) for Jan. 11, 25; Feb. 8, 15, 1873.

Full of information, now and then a trifle exaggerated.

(12) Dorn (Heinrich L. G.). *Recollections of F. M. and his Friends.* An article in *Temple Bar*, Feb. 1872; probably translated from a German original.

(13) Chorley (Henry Fothergill). 1. *Modern German Music* (2 vols., London: Smith, Elder & Co., 1854).

(14) Chorley (Henry Fothergill). Brief notice prefixed to the third edition (1864) of *Mendelssohn's Letters from Italy and Switzerland*, translated by Lady Wallace.

(15) Hewlett (Henry G.). *Henry Fothergill Chorley, Autobiography, Memoir and Letters* (2 vols., London: Bentley, 1873). Contains some information, and six letters.

(16) Marx (Adolph Bernhard). *Erinnerungen aus meinem Leben* (2 vols. Berlin, 1865).

Contains many recollections of the Mendelssohn house from 1824–1832, and personal anecdotes of Felix, with whom Marx was at one time extremely intimate.

(17) Rellstab (Heinrich F. L.). *Aus meinem Leben* (2 vols., Berlin, 1861).

Contains (vol. ii. chap. 11) an account of Mendelssohn's playing at Goethe's house at Weimar in 1821.

(18) Lobe (Johann Christian) has reported some conversations with Mendelssohn in his *Fliegende Blätter für Musik* (Leipzig, 1853). He has also described the evening at Goethe's mentioned just above in the *Gartenlaube* for 1867, No. 1.

(19) Eckardt (Julius). *Ferdinand David und die Familie Mendelssohn-Bartholdy* (Leipzig 1888).

Contains thirty letters of Mendelssohn's.

(20) Moscheles (Felix). *Briefe von Felix Mendelssohn an Ignaz und Charlotte Moscheles* (Leipzig, 1888). English translation, *Letters of Felix Mendelssohn* (London: Trübner & Co., 1888). Contains many fresh letters.
(21) Edwards (F. G.). *The History of Mendelssohn's 'Elijah'*: with an introduction by Sir George Grove (London: Novello, 1896). Contains the Mücke portrait of Mendelssohn, and portraits of William Bartholomew, Staudigl and others; also several unpublished letters, including one in facsimile.
(22) Stratton (Stephen S.). *Mendelssohn*; in Dent's 'The Master Musicians' series (London: J. M. Dent & Co., 1901), with illustrations and portraits.
(23) Edwards (F. G.). *Musical Haunts in London* (London: Curwen, 1895). Contains a facsimile of a sketch of St. Paul's Cathedral and its surroundings, by Mendelssohn, and photographs of two houses at which he stayed in London, pp. 5 and 42.
(24) Wolff (Ernst). *Felix Mendelssohn-Bartholdy* (Berlin, 'Harmonie, Verlagsgesellschaft für Literatur und Kunst,' 1905).
(25) Dahms (Walter). *Mendelssohn* (Berlin and Leipzig, 1919).
(26) Kahl (Willi). *Zu Mendelssohns Liedern ohne Worte* (Z.M.W. May 1921).
(27) Schünemann (Georg). *Mendelssohn's Jugendopern* (Z.M.W. June–July 1923).

MENDELSSOHN CHOIR, TORONTO, see VOGT, Augustus Stephen.

MENDELSSOHN GLEE CLUB, see NEW YORK.

MENDELSSOHN SCHOLARSHIP. This is the most valuable musical prize in the United Kingdom. It originated in a movement among the friends of Mendelssohn at Leipzig, who, shortly after his death, resolved to found scholarships in his memory, to be competed for and held in that Conservatorium in the foundation of which, not long before, he had greatly assisted. They appealed for help in this undertaking to English admirers of the departed composer, and were met with ready sympathy and co-operation. A committee was formed in London, with Sir G. Smart as chairman, Carl Klingemann, Mendelssohn's intimate friend, as secretary, and E. Buxton (Ewer & Co.), treasurer.

The first effort towards raising money was made in the shape of a performance of ' Elijah ' on a large scale, to which Mlle. Jenny Lind gave her willing and inestimable services. This took place Dec. 15, 1848, under the direction of Julius Benedict, at Exeter Hall, the Sacred Harmonic Society and John Hullah's Upper Schools contributing to the efficiency of the choral force. A large profit was derived from the performance ; and this, with a few donations, was invested in the purchase of £1050 Bank 3 per cent annuities—the nucleus of the present Scholarship Fund.

The original plan of amalgamating the London and Leipzig projects fell through, and the money was allowed to accumulate till 1856, when the first scholar was elected—Arthur S. Sullivan.   J. M.

The funds of the trust were increased in later years by subscriptions and donations, now enabling a grant of £100 a year to be made to the successful candidate. At first the candidates, natives of Great Britain and Ireland, of either sex, were required to be between the ages of 14 and 20. In 1871 the limit was between 14 and 24 : in 1885, 16 and 21 : in 1890, 16 and 22 : and in 1923 below the age of 30.

The original qualification was a decided talent for music in composition, or instrumental

or vocal performance. In 1890 it was changed to composition only. The scholars are elected for one year, subject to renewal, but no scholarship is held for more than four years. The education is in this country or abroad.

The original Committee consisted of the following : Sir George Smart, C. Klingemann (secretary), E. Buxton (treasurer), Sir Julius Benedict, Sir W. Sterndale Bennett, J. W. Davison, John Hullah, C. E. Horsley and H. F. Chorley.

At the present time (1926) the committee includes among its members, Sir Hugh Allen, Sir A. C. Mackenzie, Sir Landon Ronald, Sir H. Walford Davies, J. B. M'Ewen, P. V. M. Benecke (treasurer) and J. F. R. Stainer (secretary).

The scholars have been :

A. S. Sullivan	.	.	1856–60
C. S. Heap	.	.	1865–67
W. Shakespeare	.	.	1871–75
F. Corder	.	.	1875–78
Maude V. White	.	.	1879–81
E. D'Albert	.	.	1881–82
Marie Wurm	.	.	1884–87
S. P. Waddington	.	.	1891–93
H. C. Wilson	.	.	1895–98
P. H. Miles	.	.	1899–1902
G. Dyson	.	.	1904–07
E. W. Gritton	.	.	1909–12
J. A. Taffs	.	.	1912–15
P. Lévi	.	.	1916–19
A. L. Sandford	.	.	1921–23
P. P. Turnbull	.	.	1923–26.

In addition short scholarships at the R.A.M. were granted to Mary Crawford, 1872, E. Faning, 1873, and G. J. Bennett, 1884.

MENDÈS, MANUEL (*b.* Evora, early 16th cent. ; *d.* there, Dec. 16, 1605), Portuguese church musician, master of Duarte Lobo, Filippe de Magalhães and other distinguished composers. He was for a time choirmaster at Portalegre, and then occupied that post in his native town of Evora. His pupil, Duarte Lobo, endeavoured to get some of his master's work printed ; in 1610 he wrote to the manager of Plantin's printing-house at Antwerp on the subject, but without success. A Mass (4 v.) by him is to be found in a 17th-century MS. choir-book at Evora (Bibl. Publ.) ; the catalogue of the library of John IV. mentions four motets and a theoretical treatise.   J. B. T.

MENESSON, ÉMILE (*b.* Mirecourt), a violin-maker, trained at Mirecourt, but working at Rheims from about 1870, whose instruments were considered worthy of a special ' rapport ' in the *Travaux de l'Académie Nationale de Reims* (1875–76, No. 1, p. 44), by L. S. Fanart, which was afterwards printed separately as a pamphlet. The peculiarity which he introduced as an improvement was the covering of the outer periphery of his violins with a single coat of tender varnish, the central portions only, of the back and table, being covered with hard varnish. By this means Menesson claimed that the elasticity of the sound-box was increased.   E. H.-A.

MENGELBERG, RUDOLF (b. Crefeld - on - Rhine, Feb. 1, 1892), composer and musical writer. He studied (first in Jura) in Geneva, Munich, Leipzig and Bonn; he graduated under Hugo Riemann in Leipzig with an essay on G. A. Ristori.

Since 1915 he has lived in Amsterdam, being engaged in the artistic direction of the Concertgebouw. He organised the Mahler Festival in Amsterdam, 1920. His chief compositions are songs, orchestral and chamber works.

Op. 1, 2. Songs Op. 6. 'Lieder des Abschieds.' (Universal Edition.)
Op. 8.   'Idyllen.' (Leuckart, Leipzig.)
Op. 7.   Violin Sonata. (Fischer u. Jagenberg, Cologne.)
Op. 9.   Symphonische Elegie for orchestra. (Rahter, Hamburg and
          Leipzig.)
Composed 1922, performed in Amsterdam, New York, Hamburg,
          etc.
Numerous Songs, including 'Verlaine - Lieder' and songs with
          orchestra (in MS.).
'Requiem' for baritone and orchestra.
'Trauermusik' for violin and orchestra.

LITERARY WORKS

Gustav Mahler, a little biography. (Breitkopf und Härtel, 1923.)
Mahler-Feestboek. (Amsterdam, 1920.)
Editor of: Das Mahlerfest in Amsterdam. (May 1920.) Vorträge
und Berichte. (Universal Edition.)

MENGELBERG, WILLEM (b. Utrecht, Mar. 28, 1871), conductor. He comes of a Rhenish family and is the son of Friedrich Wilhelm Mengelberg, church architect. He studied at the Cologne Conservatoire and became an excellent pianist under Isidor Seiss, studying composition and conducting, at the same time, with Franz Wüllner. At the age of 21 he was appointed music director in Lucerne, and in 1895 he was invited to Amsterdam, as conductor of the 'Concertgebouw.' Since 1898 Mengelberg has also conducted the choir of the Maatschappij tot Bevordering der Toonkunst. From 1907–20 he was also director of the Museumgesellschaft, and (from 1908) of the Caecilienverein in Frankfort-on-Main. From 1911–14 he conducted regularly concerts of the London Symphony Orchestra and of the Royal Philharmonic Society, and also visited Italy, Russia and other countries as a guest conductor. Since 1921 Mengelberg has conducted each season in New York : first the National Symphony Orchestra, which, on his initiative, in 1922 was united with the Philharmonic Orchestra, and which is now one of the finest orchestras in the United States.

Mengelberg also makes many tours in other countries with his famous and magnificent Amsterdam orchestra ; in 1898, at Grieg's invitation, to the first Northern Music Festival in Bergen (Norway) ; in 1903 to the Strauss Festival in London ; in 1912 to the Church Music Festival at Frankfort-on-Main ; in 1914 and 1924, in conjunction with the Toonkunst Choir, to Paris (Bach's Matthew Passion and Beethoven's Ninth Symphony) ; in 1922 to Berlin and Hamburg for a three-days' 'Netherland-Hamburg' music festival.

Mengelberg's importance as a conductor lies especially in the refinement and individuality of his orchestral and choral technique, and his power of revealing the utmost expression in the music. His interest in contemporary music is worthy of note, especially for that of Gustav Mahler. He celebrated his 25 years' anniversary as conductor of the Concertgebouw, 1920, with a Mahler Festival ; the first big international festival to take place after the war. This was followed in 1922 by a French Music Festival, and in 1924 by a Strauss Festival under his direction.

Mengelberg has composed, in his younger years, a Mass for mixed choir, solo voices and orchestra ; also songs, 'Rembrandt Variations' (in connexion with the Rembrandt celebrations in 1906), and a 'Praeludium' upon the Dutch national hymn, for full orchestra.   R. M[G].

MENGOZZI, BERNARDO (b. Florence, 1758 ; d. Mar. 1800), distinguished both as a singer and a composer. Studied music at Florence and at Venice from Pasquale Potenza, cantor of St. Mark's.

In Lent of 1785, Lord Mount Edgcumbe found him singing in oratorio at Naples, with Signora Benini, whom he soon afterwards married. After singing together at several Italian theatres, the two came to London in 1786, but our climate was very ill-suited to Mengozzi, whose voice, a good tenor, but wanting in power, suffered much and permanently from its rigour. He played, however, the principal part in 'Il Tutor Burlato' of Paisiello, and showed himself 'a good musician, with a good style of singing.'[1] In March, Handel's 'Giulio Cesare' was revived, with additions from others of his works ; and in this pasticcio (1787) Mengozzi took part.

From London Mengozzi went to Paris (about 1787), where he was heard to advantage in the concerts given by Marie Antoinette, and among the Italian company of the Théâtre de Monsieur, with Mandini and Viganoni. He remained at Paris after the Revolution, and supported himself by giving lessons and writing operettas for the Feydeau and Montansier Theatres. When the Conservatoire was established, he was named 'Professeur de Chant.' Mengozzi had, during many years, compiled the materials for a Méthode de chant for the Conservatoire ; but he died before he had completed it. The work was edited by Langlé. Fétis gives a list of his 14 operas.   J. M.

MENO MOSSO, lit. 'with less motion'; hence, rather slower. A direction, which, like Più lento, generally occurs in the middle of a movement, the latter term properly being used where the whole movement is already a slow one, and the former in a quick movement.   M.

MENOU, TUTTOVALE (TUTUALLE), 16th-century musician. Fétis says he was a Frenchman who lived in Italy, mostly at Correggio ; he was the teacher of Claudio Merulo and composed 1 book of madrigali d' amore a 4 v.

[1] Burney.

(Ferrara, 1548) which appeared in several editions, 4 canzone in P. Bozzi's 'Giardinetto,' 1588 (*Q.-L.*).

MENSURAL MUSIC, see MUSICA MENSURATA ; NOTATION.

MENTER, (1) JOSEPH (*b.* Deutenkofen, Bavaria, Jan. 19, 1808 ; *d.* Munich, Apr. 18, 1856), celebrated violinist. His first instrument was the violin, but before long he transferred his attention to the violoncello, which he studied under P. Moralt at Munich. In 1829 he took an engagement in the orchestra of the Prince of Hohenzollern-Heckingen, but in 1833 became a member of the Royal Opera band at Munich. With the exception of various artistic tours in Germany, Austria, Holland, Belgium and England, he remained at Munich till his death.   T. P. P.

His daughter, (2) SOPHIE (*b.* Munich, July 29, 1848 ; *d.* Feb. 23, 1918) was a distinguished pianoforte-player, and after a childhood of great precocity entered the Munich Conservatorium under Professor Leonhard. At 13 she left that establishment for private tuition under Niest ; in her 15th year took her first artistic tour ; in 1867 appeared at the Gewandhaus, Leipzig, and studied with Tausig ; in 1869 became a pupil of Liszt, and in 1872 married the violoncellist, David POPPER (*q.v.*), from whom she was divorced in 1886. In 1883–87 she was professor at St. Petersburg. She first appeared in England in 1881.   G.

MENUETTO, MENUETT, see MINUET.

MEO, ASCANIO, in 1608 maestro di cappella of S. Jacomo delli Spagnoli, Naples, composed 5 books of madrigals, only the 3rd and 5th books of which are still known to exist (*Q.-L.*).

MERBECKE (MERBECK, MARBECK, MARBECKE), JOHN (*d.* Windsor, *c.* 1585), a church musician and composer of more than ordinary importance, since he produced *The Booke of Common Praier noted* (1550), being the first setting to music of the English Liturgy as authorised by the Act of Uniformity of 1549.

Merbecke is first heard of as a lay-clerk and organist (1541) of St. George's Chapel, Windsor. In the dedication to King Edward VI. of his *Concordance* (published 1550), he describes himself as

'altogether brought up in your highnes College at Wyndsore, in the study of Musike and plaiyng on Organs, wherin I consumed vainly the greatest part of my life.'

In 1543 Merbecke was arrested, his papers, including notes on the Bible and his half-completed *Concordance*, were seized, and he was tried for heresy and condemned [1] July 26, 1544. He was, however, saved from the death penalty by the personal interposition of Gardiner, Bishop of Winchester, and Sir Humphrey

Foster, one of the Commissioners. He was not only pardoned but left in the possession of his office at Windsor. In 1549 he supplicated for the degree of Mus.B.[2] at Oxford. It was in that year that

'The Booke of the Common Prayer and Administracion of the Sacramentes, and other Rites and Ceremonies of the Churche, after the use of the Churche of England,'

known as the First Prayer Book of Edward VI., was brought into general use as from Whitsunday (June 9) ; it may safely be assumed, therefore, that Merbecke's few surviving Latin compositions belong to an earlier date. The 'Injunctions' (4 Ed. VI., Oct. 26, 1550) refer to Merbecke and one George Thexton as receiving fees for playing on the organ, and these emoluments are secured to them

'during their lyves, if they continue in that Colledge, in as large and ample a maner as if organ plaing had still continued in the Church.' [3]

The implied intention to abolish organ-playing never took effect.

Merbecke's unique contribution to English liturgical music, *The Booke of Common Praier Noted*, was published in this year, but the First Prayer Book survived in use only till the second Act of Uniformity substituted its successor, the Second Prayer Book, on All Saints Day, Nov. 1, 1552. Had Merbecke followed this up with a noted version of the second book the course of English Church musical history might have been materially altered. (See CHANT and CHANTING.) The second Prayer Book introduced considerable modifications in the liturgical text which necessarily threw much of Merbecke's setting out of use. Moreover, it compromised on the musical question as on much else. Its rubrics provided for the use of singing,[4] but did not command or expect it as the first had done. Opposition to the sung Office was strengthening ; Merbecke may have sympathised with the opposition ; the dedication of his *Concordance*, quoted from above, suggests that he had come to regard church music as a 'vanity.' The immense industry of that work shows him absorbed in Biblical studies. Nevertheless he apparently remained in his office of organist at Windsor, was undisturbed by the Marian reaction, and in the reign of Queen Elizabeth published the following books and pamphlets, which leave no doubt of his personal attitude in the theological controversy as one of uncompromising Protestantism :

The Lyves of Holy Sainctes, Prophets, Patriarches, etc. 1574.
The Holie History of King David . . . drawne into English meetre for the Youth to Reade. 1579.
A Ripping up of the Pope's Fardel.[5] 1581.
A Booke of Notes and Commonplaces. 1581.
Examples drawn out of Holy Scriptures. 1582.
A Dialogue between Youth and Age. 1584.

---

[2] Wood, *Fasti Oxon.*   [3] See West, *Cath. Org.*
[4] Notably in the Gloria in Excelsis of the Communion Service, now for the first time transferred to its position near the end of the Office.
[5] Entered in the register of Stationer's Company anonymously. Terry says he has been unable to discover a copy.

---

[1] Fox, *Acts and Monuments* (1562), relates the whole story and more than the story, since he declares Merbecke to have suffered 'martyrdom.' This Fox had to correct in the edition of 1576.

With Merbecke as Biblical student and anti-papist controversialist we are not here concerned, beyond noting that his active participation in the questions of the day so far increased as to banish artistic creativeness. We are therefore left to consider two aspects of Merbecke as artist, (1) the composer of Latin church music, (2) the pioneer in English church music. Of these the latter is of by far the greater historical importance.

LATIN COMPOSITIONS.—The known compositions of this type include the following :

> Mass. 'Per arma justiciae' (5 v.). (Bod. Mus. Sch.)
> Motet. 'Domine Jhesu Christe' (5 v.). (Bod. Mus. Sch.)
> Motet. 'Ave Dei Patris Filia.' (PH. Tenor missing.)

Sir R. Terry, who scored the Mass for use at Westminster Cathedral, has given a full analysis of it.[1] The melody, much used as a *canto fermo* by English composers of the period, is that of an Antiphon, and, comparing Merbecke's work with that of Taverner, Terry has drawn attention to its high qualities and also proved its remarkable beauties in performance. With the Latin works must also be mentioned the exquisite English carol 'A Virgine and Mother,'[2] of which, however, no original has been found. Nevertheless the small bulk of Merbecke's surviving polyphonic compositions leaves him in the position of a minor composer of the school in which Taverner and Tye are the acknowledged masters.

THE BOOKE OF COMMON PRAIER NOTED.—The pioneer character of Merbecke's service to the first liturgy in the English language increases his historical importance immeasurably. His object was to provide a 'playne tune'[3] for priest and clerks (in unison) for the daily Offices of the church[4] which should be in keeping with the traditions of plain-song and also be conformable to the accentual qualities of the English language. His method shows extraordinary insight into the necessities of the case and subtle artistry in dealing with it. The *Booke* contains full directions for the singing in this manner (if necessary without organ accompaniment) of Mattins, Evensong, 'Quicunque vult,' Communion, the Burial of the Dead and 'Communion when there is a Burial.'

He used traditional melodies freely, more particularly the psalm tones, simplifying where necessary in conformity with Cranmer's view that there should be 'for every syllable a note,'[5] and writing original music on similar lines. Thus in the Communion, Gloria and Creed are

---

[1] *Proceedings* of the Musical Association, 45th session, 1918–19.
[2] Quoted by Hawkins, *Hist.* p. 451 (Novello ed.). Its general acceptance as Merbecke's work rests solely on Hawkins's statement.
[3] A rubric of Mattins in both Prayer Books of Edward VI., but omitted from Elizabeth's book, reads : 'And (to thende the people may the better heare) in such places where they do syng, there shall the lessons be songe in a playne tune and lykewise the Epistle and Gospell.'
[4] Terry points out that in doing so he followed 'a practice common enough on the Continent, as exhibited in the well-known "Missa Regia" and the Masses of Dumont and others' (*Proc. Mus. Ass.*, 1918–19).
[5] Cranmer's letter to Henry VIII., quoted by Burney, *Hist.* vol. ii. p. 577.

original save for the traditional intonation of the former, while Kyrie, Sanctus, Benedictus and Agnus Dei are traceable to several Sarum sources.[6]

But the essential value of Merbecke's treatment, whether of traditional music or of his own, lies in his study of the rhythmic qualities of the English language as opposed to Latin. The short preface to the *Booke* sufficiently defines this and is as follows :

IN THIS BOOKE

is conteyned so much of the Order of Common prayer as is to be song in Churches ; wherein are used only these iiii sortes of notes,

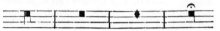

The first note is a strene note, and is a breve. The second a square note, and a semy breve. The iii a pycke, and is a mynymme. And when there is a prycke by the square note, that prycke is half as muche as the note that goeth before it. The iiii is a close, and is only vsed at ye end of a verse.

It must be remembered that in 16th-century NOTATION (*q.v.*) the relative values of breves, semibreves and minims were not fixed in the proportion of 1 : 2 as they are to-day. Time signatures required for the purposes of polyphony and not employed here determined the proportion as 1 : 2 or 1 : 3. Study of the music shows that Merbecke regards the square note (or semibreve) as the normal note and that he uses it continuously for recitations and wherever he considers it unnecessary to give any strict rhythmic value to the phrase beyond that which the words themselves secure. His setting of Venite to Tone VIII. first ending without intonation shows the method.

O come, let us sing un-to the Lorde, let

our sal-va-cion.

The 'strene'[7] note or breve is merely a prolonged note for the purpose of stressing an important word. Again, where he feels the necessity to express groups of syllables he avails himself of the 'pycke'[8] or minim either with or without the 'prycke' (or dot) to lengthen the square note. These devices are amply illustrated in the opening to the Creed.[9]

---

[6] The sources have been analysed by Terry, *cit ob.*
[7] Burney defines this as 'strained or stretched.'
[8] Stainer and Barrett, *Dict. of Musical Terms*, and Terry, *Proc. Mus. Ass.*, misquote this as 'prycke,' thus confusing the pycke (pike-head, referring to the shape) with the prycke or dot.
[9] The quotations are from the copy of the original edition in the British Museum. The type of the first note of the Creed has slipped a little. In copies from other impressions it seems to have slipped more. Hence some modern reprints give C as the first note of the intonation. The B.M. copy clearly gives two notes on the lowest line, but printed a little unevenly.

I Be-lieve in one God. The Fa-ther al-might-ie

ma-ker of heaven and earth, and of all thyngs

vi - si - ble and in - vi - si - ble.

Here the words ' One God ' receive the accents of prolonged notes, the ' close ' naturally marking the end of the priest's intonation ; the values of ' Father ' are rendered precisely by the dotted note and minim, and the minims to ' visible and invisible ' deal successfully with the troublesome problem of the short English finals. To singers accustomed to sing ' visibilium omnium et invisibilium ' this would demand careful safeguarding. This examination then shows that Merbecke's ' playne ' tune is neither ' plain-song ' in the technical sense (notes of undefined value) nor mensural music (notes of strict value) but a typically English compromise between the two, designed to guide the singer in his new problem of singing an accentual language in place of a quantitative one.

These principles have been either misunderstood or frequently ignored by modern editors with fatal results both to the character of the melody and to the reading of the liturgical text.[1] The errors have been in two directions. One is represented by Stainer's [2] harmonised version where the whole is forced into a time of four beats in a bar ; the other [3] by attempts to smooth out the rhythmic figures into the even notes of plain-song. Merbecke in the preface to his *Concordance* disclaimed learning, but his treatment of the English language here shows him to have been an instinctive master of its problems. He created an art of free rhythm to deal with them, an art in which, unfortunately, he had no followers, since it was crushed out alike by the enemies and the friends of church music. The enemies refused altogether the ideal of a common song in the Church's Offices ; the friends concentrated on the preservation and extension of harmonised music and the creation of the choral SERVICE (*q.v.*). It was not until the revival of the 19th century that Merbecke's importance received recognition by others than historians.[4] In 1844 *The Booke of Common Praier Noted* was reprinted in

---

[1] It must be remembered, however, that all modern editions are adaptations to the text of the present Book of Common Prayer, based on the second Book of Edward VI., which differs materially from the wording set by Merbecke.
[2] *The Cathedral Prayer Book*, where above the harmonised version is given a blacknote notation, which must not be mistaken for that of Merbecke, as a comparison with the example above will show.
[3] See the *English Gradual*, edited by Francis Burgess.
[4] Both Hawkins and Burney devoted considerable attention to him ; the one following Fox discussing the circumstances of his life, the other laying stress on the achievements of *The Booke of Common Praier Noted*.

facsimile by Whittingham for Pickering, Rimbault issued an edition in the following year and Jebb included it in ' Choral Responses and Litanies ' (vol. ii.) in 1857. Since then prints of various parts, and more particularly of the Communion Office, have issued from the press with increasing frequency and his melody has been widely accepted as the groundwork of the sung Eucharist in the English church.   c.

MERCADANTE, GIUSEPPE SAVERIO RAFFAELLE (*b.* Altamura near Bari, 1795 [5]; *d.* Naples, Dec. 17, 1870), entered at 12 the Collegio di San Sebastiano at Naples, of which Zingarelli was chief, and where he learnt the flute and violin, and became leader in the orchestra. He was suddenly dismissed, and to gain a living attempted composing for the stage. His first work, a cantata for the Teatro del Fondo (1818) was followed by another, 'L' Apoteosi d' Ercole,' produced at San Carlo (1819) with extraordinary success. In the next year he produced his first opera buffa, 'Violenza e costanza,' and after this came several ' opere serie,' of which ' Elisa e Claudio ' (Milan, 1821) was the most successful.

From this period Mercadante steadily maintained his reputation, and the verdict of Italy in his favour was endorsed by Vienna in 1824. He passed the years 1827 and 1828 in Madrid, 1829 in Cadiz, and in 1831 returned to Naples. In 1833 he became Generali's successor as maestro di cappella at the cathedral of Novara. In 1836 he composed and superintended the production of ' I briganti ' in Paris. His next fine opera was ' Il giuramento ' (Milan, 1837). In the opera buffa ' I due illustri rivali,' 1838, he changed his style, marking the accents strongly with the brass instruments. In 1839 he became musical director of the cathedral at Lanciano, and in 1840 director of the Conservatorio of Naples. He was a member of the Institut de France. Though he lost an eye at Novara, he continued to compose by dictation ; but became totally blind in 1862. Besides his operas, which number nearly 60, he wrote 20 masses, many psalms and motets, secular cantatas, instrumental pieces and songs.

BIBL.—G. BUSTICO, *Saverio Mercadante a Novara. R.M.I.*, 1921, pp. 361-96.   F. G.

MERCATOR, MICHAEL (*b.* 1491 ; *d.* 1544), was a Venetian maker of virginals, who made instruments for Henry VIII. and Cardinal Wolsey, 1529-32. He was included in the list of the musical establishment of Henry VIII. in 1526. There is a medallion portrait of him in the British Museum.   E. J. H[s].

MERCKER (MERKHER), MATHIAS (MATTHAEUS), of Amsterdam, a 16th-17th-century composer and skilful performer on the organ, trombone, cornetto, flute and viols. From before 1599 till after 1622 he was organist at St. Nikolas, Strassburg. He composed 1 book of

[5] Bapt. Sept. 17.

pavanes, galliards, etc., in 5 parts (1609), and
'Odae spirituales' (1619); also a MS. (copied in
1599) of 'Christ Gottes und Mariae Sohn,' 5 v.
(*Q.-L.*).

MERCY (MERCI), LOUIS (*b.* early 18th
cent.), an Englishman of French extraction,
was an eminent performer on the flûte-à-bec, or
English flute, for which he composed several
sets of solos. But he lived at a time when his
favourite instrument was gradually becoming
superseded by the traverse, or German flute,
and in the hope of averting the change, about
1735 he allied himself with Stanesby the
instrument-maker, in an endeavour to promote
the use of the modified form of the flûte-à-bec
manufactured by the latter, and published
12 solos, six of which were said to be adapted
to the traverse flute, violin or Stanesby's new
English flute, with a preface strongly insisting
on the merits of Stanesby's invention. Mercy's
solos, two sets for the flute and bassoon (or
violoncello) respectively, are in the British
Museum.   W. H. H.

MEREAUX, (1) NICOLAS JEAN LE FROID DE,
(*b.* Paris, 1745; *d.* there, 1797), was organist
of the Church of St. Sauveur [1] (1767) and at
the Petits Augustins and royal chapel. His
oratorios 'Samson' and 'Esther' were given
at the Concert Spirituel in 1774 and 1775
respectively. These, and an Ode on the birth
of the Dauphin, performed at the same concerts
in Dec. 1781, are his only works of importance
besides his operas, of which the following list
is given in the supplement to *Fétis* :

'La Ressource comique,' 1772; 'Le Retour de tendresse,' 1774;
Le Duel comique' (partly arranged from Paisiello), 1776;
'Laurette,' 1777; 'Alexandre aux Indes,' 1783; 'Œdipe et
Jocaste,' 1791; 'Fabius,' 1793; 'Les Thermopyles' and 'Scipion
à Carthage.'

(2) JEAN NICOLAS (*b.* Paris, June 22, 1767;
d. there, Feb. 1838), pupil of his father, organist
and pianist, composed sonatas, fantasias, etc.
His son

(3) JEAN AMÉDÉE (*b.* Paris 1803; *d.* Rouen,
Apr. 25, 1874), became a remarkable pianist and
a most successful teacher. He studied under
Reicha from the age of 10, and appeared with
great success in Paris and London before 1835,
when he settled in Rouen as a teacher. Of his
original compositions his studies are the most
important, but his fame rests chiefly upon his
excellent collection published in 1867 under
the title of 'Les Clavecinistes de 1637 à 1790.'
He was also in great repute as a musical
journalist.   M. ; addns. M. L. P.

MERIC, MADAME DE, an accomplished
singer, who appeared in London in 1832, and
was very successful in an unsuccessful season.
She was a clever actress, with a good voice and
considerable versatility of talent, rendering her
very useful, as she sang in serious or comic
operas, first parts or second, and in any
language. While in this country, she per-

1 Not St. Jacques du Haut-Pas as stated by *Fétis.*

formed in Italian, German, French and English,
and could have done so equally well in Spanish,
had it been required.

She appeared in 'Der Freischütz' on its first
production here with the original German
words, when German opera, for a time at least,
drove Italian from the London boards. Madame
de Meric played also Donna Elvira to the
Donna Anna of Schröder-Devrient, who rather
eclipsed her; but in Chelard's 'Macbeth' she
distinguished herself.   J. M.

MÉRIC-LALANDE, see LALANDE, Hen-
riette-Clementine-Méric.

MERIGHI, ANTONIA, a fine operatic contralto profondo, was first engaged for the
London stage by Handel, as announced in the
Daily Courant of July 2, 1729. The first part
she undertook was that of Matilda in 'Lotario'
(Handel), Dec. 2, 1729, in which she created a
favourable impression; but her songs, when
printed in the published opera, were transposed
into much higher keys. This opera was
followed by a revival of 'Tolomeo,' in which she
sang soprano music transposed for her, and next
by 'Partenope,' in which Merighi appeared as
Rosmira with equal success in 1730 and 1731.
In the latter year she sang the part of Armida
in the revival of 'Rinaldo.'

After the close of that season, however, her
name was not found again in the bills until
1736. The *Daily Post* of Nov. 18 in that year
informs us that

'Signora *Merighi*, Signora *Chimenti*, and the
Francesina, had the honour to sing before her
Majesty, the duke, and princesses, at Kensington, on
Monday night last, and met with a most gracious
reception.'

In Jan. 1738, Merighi appeared in the new
opera, 'Faramondo,' just finished by Handel
after his return from Aix-la-Chapelle, and again
in 'La conquista del Vello d' Oro' (Pescetti).
In April of the same season she took the part
of Amastre in 'Serse'—the last she sang in
England.   J. M.

MERK, JOSEPH (*b.* Vienna, Jan. 18,
1795; *d.* there, June 16, 1852), a distinguished
Austrian violoncellist. His first musical studies
were directed to singing, the guitar, and especially to the violin, which last instrument he
was obliged to abandon (according to Fétis)
in consequence of an accident to his arm. He
then took to the violoncello, and under the
tuition of an excellent master, named Schind-
löcker, speedily acquired great facility on the
instrument. After a few years of desultory
engagements he settled at Vienna as principal
violoncellist at the Opera (1818), professor at
the newly founded Conservatorium (1823), and
Kammervirtuos to the Emperor (1834). He
was much associated with Mayseder, and was
often called the Mayseder of the violoncello.
His compositions for his instrument are
numerous.   T. P. P.

MERKEL, GUSTAV (*b.* Oberoderwitz, Saxony,

Nov. 12, 1827; d. Dresden, Oct. 30, 1885), organist and composer of organ music, studied music under Julius Otto, and Johann Schneider of Dresden, and also received some instruction from Reissiger and Schumann; was appointed organist of the Waisenkirche, Dresden, in 1858, of the Kreuzkirche in 1860, and court organist in 1864.

From 1867–73 he was director of the Dresden Singakademie, and from 1861 was a professor at the Conservatorium there. Merkel's printed compositions reach the number of 180. Of these a large proportion is for his instrument, for which he composed preludes, fugues, fantasias, variations, sonatas, etc., and pieces for violin (or violoncello) and organ. He also published many solos and duets for pianoforte, motets (op. 106), and songs with pianoforte accompaniment. Many of his fugues are 'alla cappella,' and in five parts, and all are well constructed.   H. S. O.

His organ works include 9 organ sonatas, an 'Organ School,' 30 studies for pedal technique, 3 fantasias and many Choral preludes. (*Riemann*.)

MERKLIN, SCHÜTZE & CIE, see DAUBLAINE & CALLINET.

MERLIN, opera in 3 acts; libretto by Siegfried Lippiner, music by Goldmark. Produced Hof Oper, Vienna, Nov. 19, 1886.

MERLIN, JOSEPH, an ingenious instrument maker in London in the latter part of the 18th century. He had a place in Oxford St. described as ' Merlin's Cave.'

A piano of his, No. 91, 1782, gives him precedence of Broadwood in making grands, and perhaps even of Kirkman, but not Stodart.

His only patent is for a combined harpsichord and piano with a pedal for the 2 unisons and octave, replacing the stops (1774): No. 1081.

A single keyboard Kirkman harpsichord, 1758, came to light in 1924 with an adapted pianoforte movement by Merlin (1779).

' He may have been one of Burney's harpsichord-makers who followed Backer's lead in making grand pianos, before Kirkman and Shudi took them up.

' Broadwood has a square piano by him with an organ beneath.

' The square piano in the portrait by Gainsborough of his son-in-law Fischer, the oboe-player, is by Merlin.' [1]   E. J. H⁸.

MERLO, ALESSANDRO (b. Rome, c. 1530), singer and violist (also called Alessandro Romano and Alessandro della Viola), pupil of Willaert and Rore. In c. 1575 he came into prominence through his phenomenal basstenor voice with a compass of three octaves. In 1594 he was singer in the Papal Chapel. His compositions are: two books of Canzoni alla napolitana, 5 v. (1572, 1575); two books of madrigals, 5 v. (1565, 1577); a book of

[1] Notes by A. J. Hipkins.

villanelle (1579); one book of madrigals, 4 v. (' Le vergini,' 1554, 1562, 1585, 1587); one book of motets (1579); one piece in 'Delle Muse libri III.' (1555–61). (*Riemann*.)

MERMET, AUGUSTE (b. 1810; d. Paris, July 4, 1889), composer, was a pupil of Lesueur and Halévy. His operas include ' La Bannière du roi ' (Versailles, 1835), ' Le Roi David ' (Paris, Opéra, 1846), ' Roland à Roncevaux ' (Opéra, 1864), and ' Jeanne d'Arc ' (1876). The last named is memorable as the first new production in the present Opera House of Paris (see ACADÉMIE DE MUSIQUE, Vol. I. p. 11).

MERRICOCKE, T. (MERRICOCK, MARCOCK), an English church music composer of the 16th or early 17th century, who is among the composers of the 40 In Nomines included in partbooks (Bodl. Mus. Sch.). The name is an unusual one, and he is probably the ' Merricock,' the altus part of whose Te Deum and Evening Service is in an early 17th-century MS. (B.M. Add. MSS. 29,289/80b), and whose 3-part motet, ' Gloria laus et honor ' is in the Commonplace Book of John BALDWIN (*q.v.*) (written between 1581 and 1606).   J. Mᴷ.

MERRIE ENGLAND, comic opera in 2 acts; libretto by Basil Hood, music by Edward German. Produced Savoy Theatre, London, Apr. 2, 1902.

MERRY WIVES OF WINDSOR, THE (Die lustigen Weiber von Windsor), opera in 3 acts; words from Shakespeare, by Mosenthal; music by Nicolai. Produced Berlin, Mar. 9, 1849; Her Majesty's (in Italian), as ' Falstaff,' May 3, 1864; in Paris Théâtre Lyrique as ' Les Joyeuses Commères de Windsor,' May 25, 1866; in English, Carl Rosa Co., Adelphi, Feb. 11, 1878. For the operas by Balfe and Verdi, founded on the same play, see FALSTAFF.

MERSENNUS, MARIN (LE PÈRE MERSENNE) (b. Oizé, Maine, Sept. 8, 1588; d. Paris, Sept. 1, 1648), was the writer of valuable treatises on music.

Educated at Le Mans and La Flèche, Mersenne became a Minorite, entering upon his noviciate July 17, 1611, and receiving full orders (after a course of theology and Hebrew in Paris) from Monsignor de Gondi in 1613. For a time he taught philosophy at Nevers, but soon returned to Paris, where, with other kindred spirits such as Descartes, Pascal (père), Roberval and Peiresc, he studied deeply both mathematics and music. He corresponded with Doni, Huygens and other learned men in Italy, England and Holland; and visited Italy three times (1640, 1641 and 1645). His most important work is his *Harmonie universelle* (1636), which had been preceded by a smaller work, *Traité de l'harmonie universelle* (1627), of which he published an epitome in Latin. *Harmonie universelle*, two folio volumes, with numerous illustrations, includes full descriptions of contemporary instruments. These are more important even than

Cerone's great work as sources of information on music in the 17th century, especially French music and musicians. His other musical treatises are *Questions harmoniques* (1634), *Les Préludes de l'harmonie universelle* (1634), *Harmonicorum libri XII.* (1635) (enlarged edition 1648, with the names of three publishers, Baudry, Cramoisy and Robert Ballard), *De la nature des sons* (1635). The full titles of these and of Mersennus's miscellaneous writings, are given in *Q.-L.*   F. G.

MERULA, TARQUINIO, a composer of the early 17th century, the facts of whose life are gathered from the title-pages of his compositions. His birthplace is never definitely given in these, but it is supposed to have been Cremona. He was maestro di cappella at Santa Maria of Bergamo in 1623, court and church organist at Warsaw in 1624, and in 1628 was organist at Sant' Agata and maestro of the cathedral at Cremona. In 1639 he resumed the office at Bergamo, and in 1640 was maestro and organist of the cathedral there. He belonged to the Bolognese academy of the ' Filomusi,' and in 1652 was once more maestro and organist of the cathedral at Cremona. At one time, before 1680, he held a court appointment at Florence. His works are interesting as early specimens of the use of voices and instruments in combination. They are :

Canzoni a 4 per stromenti, lib. 1. Venice, 1615.
Madrigali et altre musiche concertate a 1-5. Venice, 1623.
Madrigaletti a 3, lib. 1, op. 4. Venice, 1624.
Madrigali a 4-8 voci, lib. 1, op. 5. Venice, 1624.
Motetti e sonate concertati, a 2-5 voci, lib. 1, op. 6. Venice, 1624.
Satiro, e Corsica, dialogo. Venice, 1626.
Concerti spirituali, etc., a 2-5 voci, lib. 2. Venice, 1628.
Canzoni, overe Sonate concertate per chiesa, lib. 2, op. 12. Venice, 1637.
Curtio precipitato et altri capricij, etc., lib. 2, op. 13. Venice, 1638.
Canzoni da suonare a tre, op. 9. Venice, 1639.
Concerto decimo quinto . . . Messi, salmi, . . . concertati, a 2-12. Venice, 1639.
Pegaso, salmi, motetti, etc., a 2-5, lib. 3, op. 11. Venice, 1640.
Arpa Davidica . . . salmi et messa . . . op. 16. Venice, 1640.
Canzoni da suonare a 2-3, lib. 4, op. 17. Venice, 1651.
Salmi et messa concertati a 3-4, lib. 2, op. 18. Venice, 1652.

For other works in MS., see *Q.-L.* The Fitzwilliam Museum at Cambridge and the R.C.M. contain a comic madrigal for three voices, ' Nominativo, hic, haec, hoc.'   M.

MERULO, (1) CLAUDIO, or CLAUDIO DA CORREGGIO (*b.* Correggio, 1533 [1]; *d.* Parma, May 4, 1604), organist and distinguished teacher. At the age of 24, after competition with nine other candidates, he took his place at the second organ of St. Mark's, Venice. He had been appointed organist at Brescia in the previous year (Sept. 17, 1556). It is delightful to be carried back [2] to a May evening more than 300 years ago, to find Zarlino waiting on the Piazza of St. Mark till Vespers are over, that he may present ' M. Claudio Merulo soavissimo organista of the detto tempio ' to Francesco Viola,[3] who was visiting Venice,

[1] Entered in baptismal register of S. Quirino on Apr. 8 as son of Antonio and Giovanni Merlotti, which was the true form of his name.
[2] *Dimostrationi harmoniche* (Zarlino, Venice, 1571). See Introduction.
[3] Maestro di cappella to the Duke of Ferrara, and an old pupil of Willaert.

and then to follow them all to the house of old Adrian Willaert, kept at home by the gout, yet holding a grand reception, and ready to discuss with them the subjects of Zarlino's famous book. Merulo's salary was increased from time to time,[4] and he became first organist of St. Mark's in 1566. He set up as a publisher in 1566,[5] and twelve years later (between 1578–81) as a composer of motets and madrigals. Gardane printed in 1578 two books of Sacrae cantiones (*a* 5) and in 1579 and 1580 respectively two books of madrigals (*a* 4 and *a* 3). The first and second books of motets (*a* 6) were not printed till 1583 and 1593 respectively. The third book of motets was not published till 1605, after the composer's death. A first book of four masses appeared in 1573 and ' Sacrorum concentuum 8-16, lib. 1 ' in 1594. Two masses (*a* 8 and *a* 12) and litanies (*a* 8), were published some years after his death.

After twenty-seven years' service Claudio left Venice, went first to Mantua, and thence to Parma, in 1584, as organist of the Steccata, or ducal chapel. Here he lived sixteen years, was knighted by the Duke, and died at the age of 71. The following letter was written at the time by one of his pupils to Sig. Ferrante Carli.[6]

' According to your wish I send you some particulars of Sig. Claudio's death. On Sunday the 25th of April, S. Mark's Day, after playing the organ at Vespers in the Steccata, he enjoyed an evening walk before going home. In the night he was aroused by a pain in his right side, succeeded by great fever and violent sickness. The fever continued from day to day, giving him no rest even for a few minutes. The doctors, Sig. Cernidore and Cerati, his son-in-law, after using many remedies with little or no success, determined at last to give him a medicine with strong ingredients—rhubarb, etc. This was on Sunday, May 2nd. When the poor old man had taken the draught he cried out, " Alas ! how cruelly these doctors have treated me " ; for they had given him to understand it was merely a syrup. The effect was so severe that he died just as the clock struck 12 on the 4th of May. The Duke arranged the funeral, and had him crowned with laurel and ivy, these marks of respect giving great consolation to all. He was dressed as a Capuchin monk, music books were placed on his coffin, at each corner of which one of his scholars, clothed in black, held a lighted candle. They were D. Chris. Bora, M. Ant. Bertanelli, M. And. Salati, the fourth scarcely venturing to add his name, for he had only been under the good old man's care for a month, thanks first to his own gentleness and kindness, and next to that of our Sig. Christophero, who introduced me and entered me at S. Claudio's great school. . . . The Monday following, May 10th, the service took place in the Cathedral, when he was buried next to Cipriano [Rore], near the altar of S. Agatha. . . . We sang the Mass with double choir, one placed near the organ, the other on the opposite side. . . .

' Your affectionate servant,
' ALESSANDRO VOLPIUS.

' PARMA, *May* 14, 1604.'

Claudio's organ toccatas and ricercari,[7] given to the world late in life, many published

[4] Catelani, *Memorie della vita* . . . *di C. Merulo* (Milan, Ricordi).
[5] Editing madrigals by Verdelot, and, as a partner with Betanio. a set of the same by Porta. Betanio only joined him for a short time, perhaps owing to an unexpected pressure of work at St. Mark's by the resignation of the other organist and delay in appointing another. Claudio published one set of madrigals (*a* 5) of his own.
[6] G. Tiraboschi, *Biblioteca Modenese*, tom. vi. pt. i. (Modena, 1786).
[7] ' Canzoni d' intavolatura,' etc. lib. 1, 1592 ; lib. 2, 1606 ; lib. 3, 1611. ' Ricercari d' intavolatura,' lib. 1, 1567 ; lib. 2, 1607 ; lib. 3, 1608. ' Messe d' intavolatura d' organo,' lib. iv. 1568. ' Toccate d' intavolatura,' etc. lib. 1, 1598 ; lib. 2, 1604.

posthumously, cannot bring back to us the wonderful power of his playing, which could fascinate the most orthodox musicians, and attract students from all parts of Italy, Germany and the North of Europe. They compare favourably with other works of the period. As historical examples they are also valuable. Six vocal pieces are in Torchi's *L'arte musicale in Italia*, vol. i., and four toccatas in vol. iii. See full list of extant works in *Q.-L.*

J. R. S.-B.

(2) GIACINTO, nephew of Claudio, succeeded the latter as court organist at Parma. One book of madrigals *a* 4 with one instrumental Canzona (Venice, 1623) by him is known to exist.

E. V. D. S.

MERULO, GIOVANNI ANTONIO, appointed singer in the Papal Chapel Sept. 12, 1551; was elected maestro di cappella in 1587 for one year by the college of singers by the order of Pope Sixtus V., being the first musician to hold this position, which before that time had been held by a prelate of the Papal court, chosen by the Pope (Haberl, *Jahrbuch*, 1891, p. 84).

MÉSANGEAU (MÉZENGEAU), RENÉ (*b.* Paris, ? end of 16th cent.; *d.* there, *c.* 1639), lutenist, 'ordinaire' to the king's music. Some pieces by him are in the Bibliothèque Nationale de Paris, the library of Copenhagen (under the name of Meschanson), in a MS. of Rostock's, etc. 'Gautier le vieux' composed the 'Tombeau' de Mézangeau in 1653 or later.

BIBL.—L. DE LA LAURENCIE, *Revue de musicologie* (Nov. 1923).

J. G. P.

MESSA DI VOCE, the art of swelling out and diminishing the tone on a long-held note in singing. See SINGING.

MESSAGER, ANDRÉ CHARLES PROSPER (*b.* Montluçon, France, Dec. 30, 1853), composer of French opéra-comique and English light opera, studied music for some time at the École Niedermeyer in Paris, and subsequently worked at harmony and composition under Camille Saint-Saëns. In 1876 he won the gold medal of the Société des Compositeurs for a symphony in four movements, which was performed the same year at the Châtelet concerts under the direction of Édouard Colonne. He also carried off the second Premier Prix at the Concours de la Ville de Paris with a cantata for chorus and orchestra entitled 'Prométhée enchaîné.'

Messager's first effort as a writer for the stage was in connexion with an unfinished comic opera by Firmin Bernicat, 'François les Bas-bleus,' which he completed, on the composer's death, for production at the Folies-Dramatiques on Nov. 8, 1883. Two years later, at the same theatre, was brought out his 3-act operetta, 'La Fauvette du Temple,' which was favourably received. His first real success, however, was 'La Béarnaise,' a 3-act operetta given at the Bouffes-Parisiens in Dec. 1885, and in the following Oct. mounted at the Prince of Wales's Theatre, London, where, with Miss Florence St. John and Miss Marie Tempest in the principal parts, it achieved a lengthy run. To tunefulness was added a refinement and musicianship quite unusual in works of this class. It was followed in successive years by 'Les Deux Pigeons,' a 3-act ballet (Opéra, and Covent Garden, June 21, 1906), 'Le Bourgeois de Calais,' a 3-act operetta (Folies-Dramatiques) 'Isoline,' a fairy spectacle (Renaissance), 'Le Mari de la reine,' a 3-act operetta (Bouffes-Parisiens), and 'La Basoche,' a comic opera in 3 acts, produced at the Opéra-Comique on May 30, 1890.

The opera last named marked a turning-point in Messager's career. It was recognised as aiming at a higher standard; and, despite a certain lack of originality (which the Parisian critics have invariably pointed out in their countryman's music), was warmly welcomed as a pleasant contrast to the serious and often heavy works that had too long monopolised the active repertory of the Opéra-Comique. An English version of 'La Basoche,' written by Sir Augustus Harris and Eugène Oudin, was mounted in London by D'Oyly Carte at the Royal English Opera (now the Palace Theatre of Varieties), Shaftesbury Avenue, on Nov. 3, 1891, with Miss Esther Palliser, Ben Davies, and David Bispham (then a débutant) in the principal parts. (See CARTE; SULLIVAN.) It met with considerable success, and established its composer's reputation in the British metropolis as a musician of ability, imagination and resource.

His next important work was a comédie-lyrique on a Japanese subject, 'Madame Chrysanthème,' founded upon Pierre Loti's novel of the same name, and performed at the Théâtre-Lyrique (Renaissance) for its inauguration on Jan. 30, 1893. This ambitious score was greatly admired for its 'tasteful and elegant orchestration, the limpid clearness of its ensemble, and the rare delicacy of its harmonies.' At the same time, it left to be desired, 'even at the cost of less perfection of form, a higher degree of solidity, a little more individuality; in a word, greater freshness, novelty, and individuality of melodic inspiration.' In the same year the same industrious pen gave forth a 4-act ballet entitled 'Scaramouche,' and a 3-act operetta, 'Miss Dollar,' both produced at the Nouveau Théâtre. On July 3, 1894, his 3-act comic opera 'Mirette,' specially written for the Savoy Theatre, London, was brought out there with fair success. Next came 'Le Chevalier d'Harmental' (Opéra-Comique, 1895), 'Le Chevalier aux fleurs,' ballet (Théâtre Marigny, 1896), 'Les Petites Michus' (Bouffes-Parisiens, 1897), 'Véronique' (Bouffes-Parisiens, 1898), 'Une Aventure de la Guimart,' ballet (Opéra-Comique, 1900), and 'Les Dragons de l'impératrice' (Variétés, 1905). Of these 'Véronique' and ' Les Petites Michus ' were both transferred to the London stage with remarkable success, while the former was also given in America during the winter of 1905.

Messager was for several years one of the conductors of the Paris Opéra-Comique. He was appointed joint ' directeur de la Musique ' with Albert Carré, and ' Directeur Général ' in 1898. He filled the post of ' Artistic Director' at the Royal Opera, Covent Garden (1901–06). He then became associated with M. Bronssau as director of the Paris Opéra, and occupied that position until his resignation in 1913. During his connexion with Covent Garden many novelties were produced, some of which he himself conducted. These included Bunning's ' La Princesse Osra ' (1902), Saint-Saëns's poème-lyrique, ' Hélène ' (1904), Leoni's ' L' Oracolo ' (1905), and Gluck's ' Armide ' (1906). He was succeeded here as musical director in 1907 by Percy Pitt. Further operas were ' Fortunio ' at the Opéra-Comique (1907) and ' Béatrice ' (Monte Carlo, 1914). ' Monsieur Beaucaire,' an English light opera, was produced for a run at Prince's Theatre, London, Apr. 19, 1919. He has also written minor compositions for various instruments, piano duets for four hands, and several songs.   H. K.

MESSCHAERT, JOHANNES (b. Hoorn, Holland, Aug. 22, 1857 ; d. Zürich, Sept. 10, 1922), baritone singer. He began his career as a violinist, but changed to singing and became a pupil of Stockhausen. He lived and worked also as a teacher, chiefly in Holland and Germany, but he appeared also in London and other music centres. The Messchaert - Röntgen Lieder evenings (with Julius Röntgen as pianist) were well known. Messchaert was one of the most notable concert singers of his time ; as a baritone of wide range he was equally remarkable as an oratorio and ' Lieder ' singer. His interpretation of the part of Christus in Bach's Matthew Passion was unequalled. He sang the bass solos in Elgar's ' Gerontius ' at Dusseldorf (1902).

Franziska Martienssen wrote in German upon his methods, *Johannes Messchaert, contribution to the understanding of the true art of singing.*   R. Mᴳ.

MESSIAH, oratorio by Handel ; libretto from Holy Scripture by Charles Jennens. Composition begun Aug. 22, 1741 ; first part completed Aug. 28 ; second part, Sept. 6 ; third part, Sept. 12 ; instrumentation, etc., filled in, Sept. 14 ; in all twenty-four days only. First performed (during Handel's sojourn in Ireland) in the Music Hall, Fishamble Street, Dublin, for the benefit of the Society for relieving Prisoners, the Charitable Infirmary, and Mercer's Hospital, Apr. 13, 1742. First performed in England at Covent Garden Theatre, Mar. 23, 1743. After the original performance Handel revised and rewrote much of

the work, which was published in 1767. The ADDITIONAL ACCOMPANIMENTS of Mozart and others are discussed under that heading.

MESSIDOR, lyric drama in 4 acts ; text by Emile Zola, music by Bruneau. Produced Opéra, Paris, Feb. 19, 1897.

MESTO, ' sadly ' ; a term used twice by Beethoven, in the pianoforte sonata, op. 10, No. 3, and in the slow movement of the string quartet, op. 59, No. 1. The slow movement of the first of these is called *Largo e mesto,* and of the second *Adagio molto e mesto.*   M.

MESTRINO, NICCOLO (b. Milan, 1748 ; d. Paris, Sept. 1790), violinist and composer. Having begun life as a street player, he entered the service of Prince Esterhazy, and later that of Count Erdödy in Hungary. Undergoing imprisonment for some foolish prank, he occupied the period of his confinement by perfecting his technique. He went to Paris in 1786, and performed with marked success at the Concert Spirituel. Becoming an established teacher in Paris, he was appointed leader of the Italian Opera orchestra in 1789. Compositions : twelve concertos for violin and orchestra ; duos for two violins ; sonatas for violin and bass ; and studies for the violin alone. (A. M. Clarke's *Biog. Dict. of Fiddlers,* London, 1896.)

     E. H.-A.

METALLO, D. GRAMMATIO (b. Bisaccia, Naples, 1541 ; still living in Venice in 1615 [1]). Metallo appears to have been living at his birthplace in 1577. In 1602 he was at Cairo, after a journey to the Holy Land where he finished his book of Ricercari *a* 2 v. (note on title-page), published 1603 at Venice, where he was maestro di cappella at S. Marcuola, still holding that position in 1610. He composed masses, motets, madrigals and other church music, ' Vilanelle alla Napolitana,' and one Moresca (1592), Canzoni alla francese for instruments, book 4 (1594), and the above-mentioned Ricercari *a* 2 v. ' to play and sing,' which appeared in many editions until 1685 (list of works in *Q.-L.*). The dedication mentioned by Eitner as signed in Alexandria, 15/9/1601, the writer has been unable to trace.   E. V. D. S.

METAMORPHOSIS is the modification of a musical figure or idea, made with the view of putting it in a new light, or adapting it to changed conditions.

In the later stages of the development of abstract music, composers have concentrated a great deal of energy on devising new ways of enhancing the intellectual interest of their works—as by making the continuity of the component sections more close, and giving a new aspect to the relationship of various movements, or distinct portions of single movements ; and most of these are based upon some varia-

---

[1] According to Romano Micheli (*Musica vaga,* etc.), who gives his age at that time as 74.

tion or modification of a well-defined melodic or rhythmic figure. Such devices can be found occasionally in the early stages of modern instrumental music, as in J. S. Bach; and an example from Mozart, in which he welds together a minuet and trio, is quoted in the article FORM. Beethoven was the first to make any very conspicuous use of them, and they are frequently met with in the 'development' portion of the movements of his sonatas and symphonies. A most notable instance is the dovetailing of the 'working-out' to the 'recapitulation' in the first movement of his sonata, op. 90, in E minor. An ornamental passage put over a part of a subject with a phrase quoted in the working-out ends as at (a) Ex. 1, which has at first sight no ostensible connexion with the principal subject. But in order to make the continuity of the movement as close as possible, and also of course to introduce a feature of interest, Beethoven makes this figure pass through five modifications, and then come out as the first phrase of the subject in recapitulation. The changes are as follows, (a) being the end of the ornamental passage, (b) (c) (d) and (e) its successive modifications, and (f) the beginning of the recapitulation of this principal subject. The device is enhanced in this case by the echoes of imitation, and by the dying away of the old figure in a constant diminuendo, and its bursting out with renewed vigour as the impulsive first subject.

Ex. 1.

(a)

(b)   (c)

(d)   (e)

(f)

The device is to be met with also in other situations, as in the first movement of the C minor symphony, where the figure (a) at

Ex. 2.

(a)   (b)

the outset becomes (b) in the contrasting key.

Berlioz makes ingenious and characteristic use of the device in his 'Symphonie fantastique,' in his treatment of what he calls the 'idée fixe.' Liszt also makes it a conspicuous feature in his experiments in programme music. Wagner makes more elaborate use of it than any one else in his great music dramas, and constantly transforms the character of his LEITMOTIVE (q.v.) in conformity with the varying nature of the situations.   C. H. H. P.

METASTASIO, PIETRO ANTONIO DOMENICO BONAVENTURA (b. Rome, Jan. 3, 1698; d. Vienna, Apr. 12, 1782), a celebrated Italian poet and most famous of all operatic librettists, was the son of Trapassi, of Assisi, a papal soldier. As a child he showed an astonishing power of improvisation, which so struck Gravina, that, with his parents' consent, he took him into his family, had him educated, and changed his name.[1] He was studying the classics, and engaged in translating the Iliad into Italian verse, when his benefactor died suddenly—a loss he felt deeply, although he was eventually consoled by the attachment of Maria Bulgarini the singer. In the meantime his fame had reached Vienna, and, at the instigation of Apostolo Zeno, the late court poet, the Emperor Charles VI. offered him that post. He arrived in Vienna in 1730, and remained there till his death, living with his friend Martines in the 'Michaeler Haus.' Henceforth he furnished the principal attraction at the private festivals of the court, composing verses to be recited or sung by the young Archduchess, set to music in the latter case by the court composers, Reutter, Predieri, Caldara or Bonno. Metastasio was also musical; he played the harpsichord, sang (' come un serafino,' as he used to say) and composed.[2] He may be considered as the originator of a real improvement in the musical drama, though long since superseded. His popularity as a dramatic poet was great; the charm, grace, melody and sweetness of his verse induced the composers to overlook the absence of contrast and strong passion; and in consequence some of his libretti have been set as many as thirty or forty times.[3] His poems include twenty-nine dramas, eight oratorios, thirty-nine pièces de circonstance, nearly fifty cantatas and scenas; elegies, idylls, sonnets, canzonas, sestines, terzines, etc., published in nearly fifty different editions.[4] His portrait has often been engraved; that by Mansfield and Heath after Steiner is the best. Burney describes his appearance in 1772 in enthusiastic

1 'Metastasio,' trapassamento, or transition, is a play on Trapassi.
2 Cappi of Vienna published his 'XXXVI Canzoni as sole tre voci.'
3 See *R.M.I.* vol. xi. p. 228.
4 Vol. i. of *Opere del Signor Abbate Pietro Metastasio*, seventeen small vols. 12mo (Nice, 1785), contains a life by Cristini. A selection of his poems was published in Paris (1804) with the title *Pensieri di Metastasio.*

terms.[1] There are also busts and medallions of him. He was buried in a vault in the Michaelerkirche, and in 1855 an amateur named Galvagni placed a marble monument to his memory (by Luccardi) in the church of the Minorites, bearing the following lines by the Abbé Guido Ferrari :

' Dat patriam Assisium, nomen Roma, Austria famam,
    Plausum orbis, tumulum haec urna Metastasio.'

Chronological List of Metastasio's secular dramas, with the chief composers and dates of production.

Didone abbandonata. Sarri,1724 ; Scarlatti, about 1724 ; Porpora, 1742 ; Hasse, 1743 ; Jommelli, 1745 ; Bonno, 1752 ; Piccinni, 1767 . Koželuh, 1795 ; Paisiello, 1797 ; Paër, 1810 ; Mercadante, 1823 ; Reissiger, 1823.
Siface. Porpora, 1726 ; Leo, 1737.
Siroe. Vinci, 1726 ; Handel, 1728 ; Hasse, 1733 ; Piccinni, 1759.
Catone in Utica. Vinci, 1727 ; Leo and Hasse. 1732 ; Graun, 1744, Jommelli 1749 ; Piccinni, 1770.
Ezio. Auletta, 1728 ; Porpora, 1729 ; Handel, 1731 ; Jommelli, 1749 ; Hasse, 1755; Graun, 1755; Gluck, 1763; Mercadante, 1826.
Semiramide. Vinci, 1729 ; Porpora, 1729 ; Hasse, 1747 ; Gluck, 1748 ; Meyerbeer, 1819.
Alessandro nell' Indie. Leo, 1727; Vinci 1730 ; Handel (as 'Poro'), 1731 ; Hasse (as Cleofide '), 1731 ; Gluck, 1745 ; Piccinni, 1758 and 1774.
Artaserse.[2] Vinci, 1730 ; Hasse, 1740 ; Leo, 1740; Gluck, 1741 ; Galuppi, 1749 ; G. Scarlatti, 1763 : forty settings in all.
Demetrio. Caldara, 1731 ; Hasse, 1732 ; Gluck (as 'Cleonice '), 1742.
Adriano in Siria. Caldara, 1731; Hasse,1752; twenty-six settings in all.
Issipile. Porpora, 1723 ; F. Conti, 1732.
Olimpiade.[3] Caldara, 1733; Pergolesi, 1735 ; Leo,1740 ; Wagenseil, 1749 ; Hasse, 1756 ; Gassmann, 1764 ; Jommelli, 1765 ; Piccinni, 1761 and 1771.
Demofoonte. Caldara, 1733 ; Leo, 1741; Gluck, 1742; Hasse,1748 ; Piccinni, 1762 ; Paisiello, 1773.

La clemenza di Tito. Caldara, 1734 ; Leo, 1735 ; Hasse, 1737 ; Wagenseil, 1746 ; Gluck, 1751 ; G. Scarlatti, 1760 ; Mozart, 1791.
Achille in Sciro. Caldara, 1736 ; Jommelli, 1745 ; Hasse, 1759.
Ciro riconosciuto. Scarlatti, 1712 ; Leo, 1727 ; Caldara. 1736 ; Jommelli, 1744 ; Hasse, 1751.
Temistocle. Porpora,1742; Pacini. 1823.
Zenobia. Predieri, 1740 ; Hasse, 1763.
Antigono. Hasse, 1743 ; Gluck, 1754.
Ipermestra. Hasse, 1744 and 1751; Gluck, 1742 ; Jommelli, 1752.
Attilio Regolo. Hasse, 1750 ; Jommelli 1752.
Il rè pastore. Bonno, 1751 ; Sarti, 1753; Hasse, 1755; Gluck, 1756; Mozart, 1775.
L' eroe cinese. Bonno, 1752 ; Hasse, 1753 ; Gluck, 1754 ; Sacchini, 1771 ; Cimarosa, 1783.
L' isola disabitata. Bonno, 1754 ; G. Scarlatti, 1757 ; Jommelli, 1762 ; Haydn, 1779 ; Spontini, 1798.
Nitteti. Jommelli, 1759 ; Hasse, 1759 ; Sarti, 1765 ; Sacchini, 1774.
Alcide al Bivio. Hasse, 1760 ; Paisiello, 1779.
Il trionfo di Clelia. Gluck, 1760 ; Hasse, 1762.
Tetide. Gluck, 1760.
Egeria. Hasse, 1764.
Romolo ed Ersilia. Hasse, 1765.
Il Parnasso confuso. Gluck, 1765.
Il trionfo d' Amore. Gassmann, 1765.
Partenope. Hasse, 1767.
Il Ruggiero, ovvero L' eroica gratitudine. Hasse, 1771.

Sacred dramas or oratorios, performed in the Imperial Chapel, Vienna, in Passion week.

La Passione, etc. Caldara, 1730.
Sant' Elena. Caldara, 1731.
La Morte d' Abel. Caldara, 1732.
Giuseppe riconosciuto. Porsile, 1733.
La Betulia liberata. Reutter, 1734.
Gioas, Re di Giuda. Reutter, 1735.
Isacco. Predieri, 1740.

One drama, ' Per la Fest. di S. Natale,' composed by G. Costanza, was performed at Rome, 1727, in a theatre with scenery and action.

BIBLIOGRAPHY   C. F. P.
C. BURNEY : Life and Letters of Metastasio. 3 vols. 1796.
J. A. HILLER : Über Metastasio und seine Werke. 1786.
CAV. MATTEI : Memorie per servire alla vita di Metastasio e di Jomelli. 1785.
M. ZITO : Studio su Pietro Metastasio. 1904.
LUIGI RUSSO : Metastasio. 1921.
Also in R.M.I.—
    M. CALLEGARI : Il melodramma e P. Metastasio. 1919-20.
    A. DELLA CORTE : Appurti sull' estetica musicale di P. Metastasio. 1921.

METHFESSEL, ALBERT GOTTLIEB (b. Stadt Ilm, Thuringia, Oct. 6, 1785 ; d. Mar. 23, 1869), became Kammermusikus at Rudolstadt, 1810, and was Hof Kapellmeister in Brunswick in 1832–42. He published a large number of

[1] ' For that time of life [he was about 74] he is the handsomest man I ever beheld. There are painted on his countenance all the genius, goodness, propriety, benevolence, and rectitude which constantly characterise his writings. I could not keep my eyes off his face, it was so pleasing and worthy of contemplation.'—Present State of Music in Germany, i. 295.
[2] Set by Arne in a translation of his own, 1762.
[3] Written to celebrate the birthday of Elizabeth, wife of Charles VI.

songs of a popular type, and partsongs for male voices ; some of his productions, as for instance 'Kriegers Abschied,' 'Rheinweinlied ' and ' Deutscher Ehrenpreis,' were popular. He wrote an opera, ' Der Prinz von Basra,' and an oratorio, ' Das befreite Jerusalem.'   M.

METNER, see MEDTNER.

METRE. In a succession of notes, equal in length and intensity

the ear soon picks out one of them as longer or stronger than the others, and contrasts it with its neighbour to left or right

We have then two cases : (a) thesis precedes arsis, or ; and (b) arsis precedes thesis, or . Since we use the bar-line to express accent we write (a) as above, but (b) as or .

ARSIS AND THESIS.—The Greeks called the weak beat arsis and the strong thesis. This is clear from Baccheios's catechism (Meibom, p. 24) :

Q. What shall we say arsis is ?
A. The time during which the foot is raised when we are going to take a step.
Q. And what is thesis ?
A. The time when it is on the ground. We need not go into such a detail as the moment between arsis and thesis, for by its brevity it escapes both eye (in the dance) and ear (in song).

Unfortunately the Romans, perhaps because they thought much of recited poetry and little of dancing, inverted the meanings, and used arsis for the (strong) rise and thesis for the (weak) fall of the voice. The Greek meaning is chosen here because the words are Greek (and are used then in their original sense), and because that sense agrees with the motion of the conductor's stick.

Here are a few of these Greek feet arranged on either side of a bar-line according to the times into which they fall :

Common Time.

(a) spondee (' solemn ')
    dactyl (' finger joints ').
    proceleusmatic (' inciting ')
(b) amphibrach (' long between shorts ')
    anapæst (' reversed ' dactyl)
    orthios (' stirring ')

2/4 *Time.*

(a)
(b) } pyrrhic (a dance measure)

3/4 *Time.*

(a) trochee (' tripping ')
(b) tribrach (' three shorts ')
    iamb (associated with lampoons)

It is to be noticed that *thesis* means rather the accented part of the foot than the accented note merely, and that if we apply what they said of the foot to our bar we get such articulation as

(Quavers) *th. ar. th. ar.   th. ar. th. ar. th.*   etc
(Crotchets) *th.   ar.   th.   ar.   th.*   etc.
(Minims) *thesis   arsis   thesis*   etc.

They were saying, in fact, a practical thing, that the accent (thesis) controls every section, small or great, of the phrase.

THE COMPOUND FOOT, THE PERIOD.—Out of these simple feet they went on to make compound. (See also PERIOD.) One of these, to take an instance, was

iamb. | pyrrh. | iamb. | troch.
ᴗ – | ᴗ ᴗ | ᴗ – | – ᴗ

We do not know how they put this into their music, but we can almost hear an Elizabethan writing it; this, from Wilbye's 'Draw on, sweet night,' is, in fact, not very far off :

A ˙ rise   from pain-ful   me - lan-cho - ly.

This, by the way, is a good example of metrical articulation, one of the main conditions of sound melody. Other examples are 'Il mio tesoro' ('Don Giovanni'), Schubert's 'Über allen Gipfeln,' the theme of the slow movement of Brahms's A minor Quartet, Purcell's 'I attempt from love's sickness,' the opening theme of Beethoven's violoncello Sonata in A, and most of the themes in Bach's maturer work.

FOOT AND BAR.—The example just given shows clearly the difference between foot and bar. For instance | ♩♩ |, | ♩♪ | and | ♫ | are all equally trochees but they make different kinds of bar, as, conversely, a bar of any one time makes different kinds of foot. In the example, the first iamb is of the (*b*) form, the second of the (*a*), and the pyrrhic has half the value it should have to correspond with the others. A foot, therefore, is a uniform combination of time-units independent of 'time,' and a bar a uniform division of time regardless of the particular time-units it contains. We think musical phrases in feet and afterwards arrange them in bars. It does not disturb us in a *stretto* that these phrases begin on different bar-accents, since the foot is uniform.

METRICAL FIGURE.—A small, easily recognisable nucleus (see FIGURE) of similar time-units (Mozart's violas at the beginning of the G minor Symphony), or dissimilar (the 'cyclical dactyl' for the flute which begins the *Vivace*

in Beethoven's seventh), is called a metrical figure. It ranges from the ALBERTI BASS (*q.v.*) to the protean forms of Wagner's motives, and is especially useful in establishing by its recurrence, by way of *basso ostinato* or inverted pedal or otherwise, the unity of a piece.

CHOICE OF TIME-UNIT.—Rousseau in his Dictionary (1781) remarks, under 'Mesure,' that if the many different time-units in use (eight, after the lapse of the *Maxime* and *Longue*) were adopted to mark differences of time they are too many, and if of tempo, too few. Commenting on this, Westphal, *Theorie der musikalischen Rhythmik*, p. 83, points out as a curious case that ♪ ♫ ♫ are usual in Adagios and ♩ ♩ ♪ in Allegros, and quotes an explanation offered in 1794 by Sulzer. This was that musicians, having come to regard ♩ ♩ as heavy notes and ♪ ♫ as light, now, when they see a piece of which ♫ is the shortest note, play it in a heavy manner, and if ♩ is the longest in a light manner. As he observes, this does not account for the waltz, which, with ♩ for time-unit, is of a decidedly light character. He does not account for this himself, but he reminds us that Bach's minuets in | ♫♫♫ | became in Haydn's hands | ♩♩♩ | at a quicker pace; and adds, what has not proved true, that no one would be likely to depart from writing scherzos in Beethoven's | ♩♩♩ |.

It is possible also that as slow movements are apt to be variational and to indulge in groups composed of every sort of fraction of the original time-unit, the fact that the tails could be joined (whereas with ♩ and ♩ they cannot) proved a substantial argument for the smaller time values in such movements. If it is not altogether true that quaver and semiquaver suggest lightness, yet minim and semibreve do, to us now, look heavy, and so the true character of the madrigal, for instance, is expressed better in the former.   A. H. F. S.

METRONOME (Fr. *métronome*. Ger. *Metronom*, and *Taktmesser*. From the Gr. μέτρον, 'a measure,' and νόμος, 'a law '), an instrument, constructed for the purpose of enabling composers to indicate the exact pace at which they wish their works to be performed.

EARLY EXPERIMENTS.—Étienne Loulié in a work entitled *Élémens ou principes de musique, mis dans un nouvel ordre* (Paris, 1696; Amsterdam, 1698) describes an instrument, called a *chronomètre*, formed of a bullet suspended to a cord, and provided with means for lengthening or shortening the latter at pleasure, in such a manner as to indicate seventy-two different degrees of velocity. This was a good beginning. Nevertheless, the machine does not seem to have become generally known; for in many curious treatises of later date we find vague glimmerings of similar ideas put forth in apparent ignorance of Loulié's discovery. Joseph Sauveur—the inventor of the word 'Acoustics,' and the author of a series of valuable papers on music contributed to the *Mémoires de l'Académie* between the years 1700 and 1711—is said to have proposed a *Chronomètre* of his own. In 1732 an article on a species of Musical Timekeeper was contributed to the *Mémoires des Sciences* by Enbrayg. Gabory recommended the use of the pendulum in his *Manuel utile et curieux sur la mesure du tems* (Paris, 1771). John Harrison's *Description concerning such a machine as will afford a nice and true mensuration of time ; as also an account of the Scale of Music* (London, 1775) serves to show that the connexion between music and chronometry was not unnoticed in England. Davaux wrote an article on the subject for the *Journal Encyclopédique* in 1784. Not long afterwards, Pelletier made use of the pendulum in a way sufficiently ingenious to call forth a treatise on his invention from Abel Burja of Berlin in 1790. In the same year Breitkopf & Härtel printed, at Leipzig, *Zwölf geistliche prosaische Gesänge, mit Beschreibung eines Taktmessers*, by J. G. Weiske. And enough was done, both in France and in Germany, to show that even before the close of the 18th century the matter had attracted no small amount of serious attention.

In 1813 Gottfried Weber advocated the use of a pendulum, formed of a small bullet attached to the end of a string, upon which the necessary divisions were marked by knots ; the whole being so contrived that it could be carried in the pocket—a far more simple and convenient arrangement than that of Loulié.[1] New plans were proposed by G. E. Stöckel, Zmeskall and other musicians of reputation, and Beethoven is known to have discussed them with interest. The subject excited an equal amount of attention in England, where many attempts were made to produce a perfect instrument. (See WRIGHT, Thomas.) Dr. Crotch, discarding Loulié's cord, used in place of it a stiff pendulum, formed of a long thin strip of boxwood, graduated in inches and hung upon a suitable frame. Another musical time-keeper invented by Henry Smart is described in the *Quarterly Musical Review* (vol. iii., London, 1821).

All these inventions failed, however, more or less completely, through the inconvenience caused by the length of the pendulum necessary to produce beats of even moderate slowness. In order to perform sixty oscillations in a minute a pendulum must, in our latitude, be 39·2 inches long. One long enough to execute forty would

[1] A pocket Metronome was registered by Greaves in 1850, and another, 'scala Mälzl, system Decher,' was patented by Aibl, of Munich. A still further development of this simple kind of metronome, the principle of which is identical with an ordinary tape-measure, but with a spring to fasten the measure at any length, is that now sold by J. Curwen & Sons.

be difficult to manage. This difficulty was eventually removed through the ingenuity of a celebrated mechanist named WINKEL, an inhabitant of Amsterdam, who first entertained the idea of constructing a metronome upon a system before untried, involving the use of a certain kind of double pendulum, the motions of which are governed by mathematical laws of extreme complexity though, practically considered, the principle is simple.

If a rod be suspended from its centre, and equally weighted at both ends, its centres of motion and gravity will coincide, and its position, when at rest, will be perfectly horizontal. But if the weight at one end be diminished, or moved a little nearer to the central pivot than the other, the centre of gravity will be displaced, and the unaltered end will gradually descend, until the rod hangs perpendicularly ; the rapidity with which the change of position takes place depending upon the amount of diminution to which the upper weight is subjected, or its nearness to the pivot. In either case, the upper weight will exercise so strong a retarding influence on the lower one, that by carefully adjusting the proportion between weights and distances, it will be found possible to make a double pendulum, of the kind we have described, oscillate as slowly as an ordinary one five or six times its length.

WINKEL AND MAELZEL.—The possibility of constructing a metronome upon this principle is said to have first suggested itself to Winkel about the year 1812 ; but it is difficult, in the face of conflicting statements, to arrive at a just conclusion as to the circumstances in which his invention was first given to the world. It is indeed known to have been warmly commended by the Dutch Academy of Sciences in a report dated Aug. 14, 1815 ; and, judging from this, we may surmise that it had by that time assumed a complete, if not a perfect form. We have, however, no definite proof of its then condition. It may have been finished, or it may not ; but, finished or unfinished, it is certain that Winkel derived very little benefit from his discovery. Johann Nepomuk MAELZEL (*q.v.*) had long meditated an improvement upon Stöckel's machine for beating time, and succeeded about this time in producing a species of so-called 'Chronometer,' which fairly satisfied Salieri, Weigl and even Beethoven himself. Fortified by the approval of these high authorities, he determined to bring out his invention in London. Meanwhile, he exhibited it, in company with other mechanical curiosities, in a travelling museum, which he carried about with him from city to city, through some of the principal countries of Europe. Among other places, he visited Amsterdam, where he saw Winkel's instrument. Struck with the superiority of the double pendulum to the principle adopted in his own time-keeper, he at once offered to purchase the invention. Winkel declined to cede his rights; but Maelzel, having now learned all he wanted to know, proceeded to Paris, patented the double pendulum in his own name, and in 1816 set up the first metronome manufactory on record. Winkel afterwards obtained possession of one of the Paris instruments; established its identity with his own; and (as Wurzbach states) took advantage of Maelzel's return to Holland to submit his case to the 'Niederländische Akademie' for decision. A Commission was appointed to investigate its merits; and as it was proved that the graduated scale was the only part of the instrument really originated by Maelzel, a formal judgment was recorded in Winkel's favour—too late, however, to do him full justice, for to this day his share in the work is, by common consent, suppressed, and Maelzel is universally regarded as the inventor of the instrument which bears his name.[1]

THE METRONOME DESCRIBED.—The first metronomes made at the new manufactory differed so little in any point of vital consequence from those now in daily use, that a description of the one will include all that need be said concerning the other. The most important part of the business is a flat steel rod, about seven and a half inches long, and an eighth of an inch in breadth, pierced, at a distance of about five and a half inches from its upper end, by a hole, through which is passed the pivot upon which it is made to oscillate. This rod—answering to the double pendulum already described—is suspended, by means of the pivot, in front of a wooden case, and kept in a perpendicular position by a stout leaden bullet, fixed to its shorter end, which, thus weighted, sinks, of course, when at rest, to the lowest place. On its upper and longer end is placed a smaller weight, of brass, made to slide up and down at will, and so proportioned to the lower weight, that, by changing its position, the pendulum may be made to execute any number of oscillations, between 40 and 208 in a minute. As a guide to the position of the upper weight, the rod is backed by a graduated scale—really the invention of Maelzel—affixed to the wooden case; and by means of this the instrument may be so adjusted as to beat, silently, for a few minutes, at any required pace. To render it still more effective—capable of beating for a longer time, and with a distinctly audible sound —it is provided with a strong spiral spring, adapted to an escapement exactly similar to that of an ordinary loud-ticking clock.[2] In

this form it is complete enough to answer its intended purpose perfectly; nevertheless, an attempt is sometimes made to increase its efficiency still farther, by the addition of a little bell, which can be made to strike at every second, third, fourth or sixth oscillation of the pendulum, and thus to indicate the various accents, as well as the simple beats of the bar. The scale does not include all the units between 40 and 208—which, indeed, would be a mere useless encumbrance—but proceeds from 40 to 60 by twos, from 60 to 72 by threes, from 72 to 120 by fours, from 120 to 144 by sixes, and from 144 to 208 by eights. In order to indicate the exact *Tempo* in which he wishes his piece to be performed, the composer uses a formula, beginning with the letters M. M. followed by a musical note, connected by the sign = with a number. The letters signify Maelzel's Metronome. The note implies that the beats of the pendulum are to be understood as representing minims, crotchets or quavers, as the case may be. The number indicates the place on the graduated scale to the level of which the top of the upper weight must be raised or lowered. Thus ' M. M. $\downarrow$ = 60 ' would show that the metronome was to be so arranged as to beat minims at the rate of 60 in a minute; ' M. M. $\downarrow$ = 100 ' that it was to beat crotchets at the rate of a hundred in a minute. Some metronomes are marked with the words *Andante, Allegretto, Allegro*, etc., in addition to the numbers. This is a useless contrivance; for it is evident that if $\downarrow$ = 100 be held to indicate *Moderato*, $\downarrow$ = 100 will stand for *Allegro* and $\downarrow$ = 100 for *Largo*. The word *Moderato*, therefore, without the minim, crotchet or quaver to qualify it, means nothing at all.   W. S. R.

For the purpose of silently indicating the time, the tape-measure already mentioned in the footnote, p. 448, and the ingenious and compact apparatus called 'Pinfold's Patent Metronome,' are of great use. The latter has the weight moving on a graduated scale, and a swinging weight below a small tripod.   M.

METZLER. The founder of this well-known business was (1) VALENTINE METZLER, a native of Bingen on the Rhine, who opened a shop in Wardour Street for the sale of flutes and other instruments about the year 1790. He married an Englishwoman, and his only child was (2) GEORGE RICHARD METZLER (1797–1867). The name Metzler first appears in the London directories in 1812, and the style Metzler & Son was adopted in 1819; V. Metzler probably died in 1840, as the name after 1841 is G. Metzler & Co. The firm is said to have entered upon music-publishing in 1816, and removed in 1842 to

---

[1] We are indebted, for most of these particulars, to A. W. Thayer, whose careful researches have placed him in possession of much valuable information on this subject. Bernsdorf tells a different story, to the effect that Maelzel, unable to overcome some difficulty connected with his improvement of Stöckel's time-keeper, took Winkel into consultation; that Winkel solved the problem for him; and that he then proceeded to Paris and there patented Winkel's invention in his own name.

[2] In the first time-keeper made by Maelzel, in his attempt to improve upon Stöckel's Chronometer, the sound was produced by a lever. (*Hebel*), striking upon a little anvil (*Amboss*). This explains

a curious expression contained in a letter written by Beethoven to Zmeskall—'*Erste Schwungmann der Welt, und dies ohne Hebel*' ('first swingman of the world, and that without a lever'). For a description of the instrument—known as the 'Stöckel-Maelzel Chronometer'—see the *A. M. Z.* for Dec. 1, 1813.

37 Great Marlborough Street. The only surviving child of George Richard was (3) GEORGE
THOMAS METZLER (1835–79). He gained a
practical knowledge of the pianoforte in Germany, and had a distinct literary bias, which
he followed as far as opportunity permitted.
He became known as a writer of words for
songs, Mrs. George March (Virginia Gabriel),
Mme. Sainton-Dolby, Henry Smart and J. L.
Hatton having set his graceful lyrics to music.
In 1867, Frank Chappell, who had acquired his
knowledge of business in the Bond Street firm
of that name, joined G. T. Metzler in partnership, and from his suggestion the important
agency of Messrs. Mason & Hamlin, which
practically introduced the American organ into
this country, became a speciality of the Metzler
business. This firm was early in the field with
the precursors of the harmonium; their ' improved Seraphines ' are advertised in the *Musical World* in 1838. Frank Chappell died in
1886, and from that date the business was
carried on by the trustees of his estate until
1893, when it became a limited company.

About 1810–12 a certain ' Mr. Metzler,' of
9 Newman Street, issued a small oblong book
of airs for the flageolet, called ' The Magic
Flageolet.' This came out in numbers, many
being issued by James Power, and others by
Metzler himself, whose name was affixed to
many of the pieces.   A. J. H.; addns. F. K.

MEYER, GREGOR, was organist of the Cathedral Church at Solothurn in Switzerland in the
earlier part of the 16th century. Our whole
knowledge of him is derived from Glarean, who
in his *Dodecachordon*, 1547, frequently mentions
him in terms of the highest respect for his musical abilities, and obtained from him for the
purposes of his work various compositions as
examples of the proper use of the ecclesiastical
modes in polyphonic music, inattention to
which Glarean is disposed to censure in the
works of Josquin and others. So, for instance,
he communicates of Meyer eleven somewhat
elaborate settings *a* 4 and 3 of the Kyrie and
Christe Eleison as illustrations of the proper
use in conjunction of the Æolian and Hypoæolian modes, also a motet, ' Confitebor
Domino,' as an example of the Lydian and
Hypo-Lydian united, and two settings of the
antiphon ' Qui mihi ministrat,' etc., one as
an example of what Glarean describes as
the genuine form of the Lydian mode without
B flat, and the other in the more commonly
used form of the Lydian with the flat. J. R. M.

MEYER, SIGTENHORST, see SIGTENHORST
MEYER.

MEYERBEER, GIACOMO (properly JAKOB
LIEBMANN BEER) (*b.* Berlin, Sept. 5, 1791;
d. Paris, May 2, 1864), famous dramatic composer, of Jewish parentage. His father, Herz
Beer, a native of Frankfort, was a wealthy
banker in Berlin; his mother (*née* Amalie
Wulf) was a woman of rare mental and intellectual gifts, and high cultivation. He was
their eldest son, and a legacy from a rich relation named Meyer caused his name to take the
form in which it was known. He seems to
have been the sole member of his family remarkable for musical gifts; but two of his brothers
achieved distinction in other lines—Wilhelm as
an astronomer, and Michael (who died young)
as a poet.

His genius showed itself early. His first
instructor was Lauska, an eminent pianoforte-
player, and pupil of Clementi; and old
Clementi himself, although he had long given
up teaching, was so much struck, during a visit
to Berlin, with the promise displayed in the
boy's performance as to consent to give him
lessons. As early as 7 years old he played
in public the D minor concerto of Mozart, and
two years later was reckoned one of the best
pianists in Berlin. It was as a pianist that he
was expected to win his laurels, but as he had
also, from an early age, shown much talent for
composition, he was placed under Zelter for
instruction in theory, and subsequently (for
Zelter's rigid severity was insupportable to the
young prodigy) under Bernard Anselm Weber,
director of the Berlin Opera, and a pupil of the
then celebrated Abbé VOGLER (*q.v.*). In 1810
Meyerbeer became an inmate of Vogler's house.
He had for companions Gänsbacher and Carl
Maria von Weber, who had studied with Vogler
some years before, and was now attracted to
Darmstadt by his presence there, and between
whom and Meyerbeer, eight years his junior,
there sprang up a warm and lasting friendship.
Each morning after early Mass, when the young
men took it in turns to preside at the organ, they
assembled for a lesson in counterpoint from
the Abbé. Organ fugues were improvised in
the Cathedral, on subjects contributed by all in
turn. In this way Meyerbeer's education was
carried on for two years. His great powers of
execution on the pianoforte enabled him to
play at sight the most intricate orchestral
scores, with a full command of every part. His
4-part ' Geistliche Oden von Klopstock ' were
published at this time, and an oratorio of his,
entitled ' Gott und die Natur,' was performed
in presence of the Grand Duke, who appointed
him composer to the court. His first opera,
'Jephthas Gelübde,' was also written during this
Vogler period and produced at Munich in 1813.
Biblical in subject, dry and scholastic in treatment, it resembled an oratorio rather than an
opera, and although connoisseurs thought it
promising, it failed to please the public. A
comic opera, 'Alimelek,' or ' Die beiden Kalifen,'
met with a better fate at Stuttgart in 1813. It
was bespoken and put in rehearsal by the
manager of the Kärnthnerthor theatre in
Vienna.

To Vienna, in consequence, Meyerbeer now

XLIX

MEYERBEER

ROSSINI

From a drawing by Louis Dupré in the possession of A. F. Hill

repaired, with the intention of making his appearance there as a pianist. But on the very evening of his arrival he chanced to hear Hummel, and was so much impressed by the grace, finish and exquisite *legato*-playing of this artist that he became dissatisfied with all he had hitherto aimed at or accomplished, and went into a kind of voluntary retirement for several months, during which time he subjected his technique to a complete reform, besides writing a quantity of pianoforte music, which, however, was never published. He made a great sensation on his first appearance, and Moscheles, who heard him at this time, was wont to say that, had he chosen a pianist's career, few virtuosi could have rivalled him. But to be a composer was the only goal worthy of his ambition, although at this moment it seemed to recede as he pursued it. 'Die beiden Kalifen,' performed in Vienna in 1814, had been an utter failure. Salieri, however, assured him that he wanted nothing in order to succeed but freedom from scholastic trammels, and, above all, knowledge of the human voice and how to write for it, a knowledge, Salieri added, only to be acquired in Italy.

Accordingly, in 1815, Meyerbeer went to Venice. It was Carnival time. Rossini's 'Tancredi' was then at the height of its popularity, and all Venice resounded with 'Di tanti palpiti.' To Meyerbeer this was a revelation, and he surrendered spell-bound to the genial charm. Hope awoke, emulation was rekindled. He had no style of his own to abandon, but he abandoned Vogler's without regret, and set to work to write Italian operas. His success was easy and complete. 'Romilda e Costanza' (produced at Padua in 1818, Pisaroni in the leading part), 'Semiramide riconosciuta' (Turin, 1819), 'Eduardo e Cristina' and 'Emma di Resburgo' (Venice, 1820) were all received with enthusiasm by the Italian people, and this at a time when it was difficult for any one but Rossini to obtain a hearing. The last-named opera was played in Germany under the title of 'Emma von Leicester,' and not unsuccessfully. 'Margherita d'Anjou,' the best of these operas, was written for La Scala at Milan and given there in 1820. 'L' esule di Granata' (1822) made but little impression. 'Almansor' was begun at Rome, but not completed. In 1823, while engaged in writing the 'Crociato,' the composer went to Berlin, where he tried, but failed, to get a performance of a 3-act German opera— 'Das Brandenburger Thor.' This was a time of transition in his life. He was wearying of the Italian manner, and he could not be insensible to the murmurs of dissatisfaction which everywhere in Germany made themselves heard at the degradation of his talent by his change of style. Foremost among the malcontents was C. M. von Weber, who had looked on his friend as the hope of that German opera in which were centred his own ardent aspirations, and who in 1815 at Prague, and subsequently at Dresden, had mounted 'Die beiden Kalifen' with extraordinary care and labour, hoping perhaps to induce him to return to his old path. 'My heart bleeds,' he wrote, 'to see a German composer of creative power stoop to become an imitator in order to win favour with the crowd.' In spite of all this the friendship of the two men remained unshaken. On his way back to Italy Meyerbeer spent a day with Weber, who wrote of it :

'Last Friday I had the happiness of having Meyerbeer with me. It was a red-letter day—a reminiscence of dear old Mannheim. . . . We did not separate till late at night. He is going to bring out his "Crociato" at Trieste, and in less than a year is to come back to Berlin, where perhaps he will write a German opera. Please God he may! I made many appeals to his conscience.'

Weber did not live to see his wish fulfilled, but the desire which he expressed before his death, that an opera he left unfinished should be completed by Meyerbeer, showed that his faith in him was retained to the last.

The 'Crociato' was produced at Venice in 1824, and created a furore, the composer being called for and crowned on the stage. In this opera, written in Germany, old associations seem to have asserted themselves. More ambitious in scope than its predecessors, it shows an attempt, timid indeed, at dramatic combination which constitutes it a kind of link between his 'wild oats' (as in after years he designated these Italian works) and his later operas.[1]

In 1826 he was invited to witness its first performance in Paris, and this proved to be the turning-point of his career. He eventually took up his residence in Paris, and lived most of his subsequent life there. From 1824–31 no opera appeared from his pen. A sojourn in Berlin, during which his father died, his marriage and the loss of two children, were among the causes which kept him from public life. But in these years he undertook that profound study of French character, French history and French art which resulted in the final brilliant metamorphosis of his dramatic and musical style, and in the great works by which his name is remembered.

Paris was the headquarters of the unsettled, restless, tentative spirit which at that epoch pervaded Europe. The prevailing spirit of eclecticism found its perfect musical counterpart in the works of Meyerbeer. The assimilative power that, guided by tenacity of purpose, enabled him to identify himself with any style he chose, found in this intellectual ferment, as yet unrepresented in music, a wellnigh inexhaustible field, while these influences in return proved the key to unlock all that was original

[1] It is significant that, with the exception of the 'Crociato,' not one of these early works, so enthusiastically received, held the stage after their composer had left Italy.

and forcible in his nature. And he found a fresh stimulus in the works of French operatic composers.

'He did not shrink, as a man, from the unremitting, insatiable industry he had shown as a boy, and he buried himself in the literature of French opera, from the days of Lulli onwards. . . . It was interesting to see in his library hundreds of opera-scores great and small, many of which were hardly known by name even to the most initiated. . . . In his later works we see that to the flowing melody of the Italians and the solid harmony of the Germans he united the pathetic declamation and the varied, *piquant* rhythm of the French.' [1]

Last, but not least, in his librettist, Eugène Scribe, he found a worthy and invaluable collaborator.

Many vicissitudes preceded the first performance, in 1831, of ' Robert le Diable,' the opera in which the new Meyerbeer first revealed himself, and of which the unparalleled success extended in a very few years over the whole civilised world. It made the fortune of the Paris Opéra. Scenic effect, striking contrast, novel and brilliant instrumentation, vigorous declamatory recitative, melody which pleased none the less for the strong admixture of Italian-opera conventionalities, yet here and there (as in the beautiful scena ' Robert ! toi que j'aime ') attaining a dramatic force unlooked for and till then unknown, a story part heroic, part legendary, part allegorical—with this strange picturesque medley all were pleased, for in it each found something to suit his taste.

The popularity of the opera was so great that the ' Huguenots,' produced in 1836, suffered at first by contrast. The public, looking for a repetition, with a difference, of ' Robert,' was disappointed at finding the new opera quite unlike its predecessor, but was soon forced to acknowledge the incontrovertible truth, that it was immeasurably the superior of the two. It is, as treated by Meyerbeer, the most vivid chapter of French history that ever was written. The splendours and the terrors of the 16th century—its chivalry and fanaticism, its ferocity and romance, the brilliance of courts and the ' chameleon colours of artificial society,' the sombre fervour of Protestantism—are all here depicted and endued with life and reality, while the whole is conceived and carried out on a scale of magnificence hitherto unknown in opera.

In 1838 the book of the ' Africaine' was given to Meyerbeer by Scribe. He became deeply interested in it, and the composition and re-composition, casting and recasting of his work, occupied him at intervals to the end of his life. His excessive anxiety about his operas extended to the libretti, with which he was never satisfied, but would have modified to suit his successive fancies over and over again, until the final form retained little likeness to the original. This was especially the case with the ' Africaine,' subsequently called ' Vasco de Gama ' (who,

1 Mendel.

although the hero, was an afterthought !), and many were his altercations with Scribe, who got tired of the endless changes demanded by the composer, and withdrew his book altogether ; but was finally pacified by Meyerbeer's taking another libretto of his, ' Le Prophète,' which so forcibly excited the composer's imagination that he at once set to work on it and finished it within a year (1843).

A good deal of his time was now passed in BERLIN (*q.v.*),[2] where the King had appointed him Generalmusikdirector in 1842. Here he wrote several occasional pieces, cantatas, marches and dance music, besides the 3-act German opera, ' Ein Feldlager in Schlesien.' The success of this work was magically increased, a few weeks after its first performance, Dec. 7, 1844, by the appearance in the part of the heroine of Jenny Lind.

He at this time discharged some of the debt he owed his dead friend, C. M. von Weber, by producing ' Euryanthe ' at Berlin. His duties at the opera were heavy, and he had neither the personal presence nor the requisite nerve and decision to make a good conductor. From 1845 he only conducted—possibly not to their advantage—his own operas, and those in which Jenny Lind sang.

The year 1846 was marked by the production of the overture and incidental music to his brother Michael's drama of ' Struensee.' This very striking work is its composer's only one in that style, and shows him in some of his best aspects. The overture is his most successful achievement in sustained instrumental composition. A visit to Vienna (where Jenny Lind achieved a brilliant success in the part of Vielka in the ' Feldlager in Schlesien ') and a subsequent sojourn in London occurred in 1847. In the autumn he was back in Berlin, where, on the occasion of the King's birthday, he produced, after long and careful preparation, ' Rienzi,' the earliest opera of his future rival and bitter enemy, Richard Wagner. The two composers had seen something of one another in Paris. Wagner was then in necessitous circumstances, and Meyerbeer exerted himself to get employment for him, and to make him known to influential people in the musical world. Subsequently Wagner, while still in France, composed the ' Fliegende Holländer,' to his own libretto. The score, rejected by the theatres of Leipzig and Munich, was sent by its composer to Meyerbeer, who brought about its acceptance at Berlin. Without claiming any extraordinary merit for these good offices of one brother artist to another, we may, however, say that Meyerbeer's conduct was ill-requited by Wagner.

' Le Prophète,' produced at Paris in 1849, after long and careful preparation, materially

2 On the conditions of his life at Berlin, see the *Sammelbände* of the Int. Mus. Ges. iv. 519.

added to its composer's fame. Thirteen years had elapsed since the production of its predecessor. Once again the public, looking for something like the ' Huguenots,' was disappointed. Once again it was forced, after a time, to do justice to Meyerbeer's power of transferring himself, as it were, according to the dramatic requirements of his theme. But there are fewer elements of popularity in the ' Prophète ' than in the ' Huguenots.'

Meyerbeer's health was beginning to fail, and after this time he spent a part of every autumn at Spa, where he found a temporary refuge from his toils and cares. Probably no great composer ever suffered such a degree of nervous anxiety about his own works as he did. During their composition, and for long after their first completion, he altered and retouched continually, never satisfied and never sure of himself. During the correcting of the parts, the casting of the characters, the ' coaching ' of the actors, he never knew, nor allowed any one concerned to know, a moment's peace of mind. Then came endless rehearsals, when he would give the orchestra passages scored in two ways, written in different coloured inks, and try their alternate effect; then the final performance, the ordeal of public opinion and of possible adverse criticism, to which he was so painfully susceptible that, as Heine says of him, he fulfilled the true Christian ideal, for he could not rest while there remained one unconverted soul, ' and when that lost sheep was brought back to the fold he rejoiced more over him than over all the rest of the flock that had never gone astray.'

Faithful to change, he now challenged his adopted countrymen on their own especial ground by the production in 1854 of ' L'Étoile du nord.' To this book he had intended to adapt the music of the ' Feldlager in Schlesien,' but his own ideas transforming themselves gradually while he worked on them, there remained at last only six numbers of the earlier work. ' L'Étoile ' achieved considerable popularity, although it aroused much animosity among French musicians, jealous of this invasion of their own domain, which they also thought unsuited to the melodramatic style of Meyerbeer. The same may be said of ' Le Pardon de Ploermel ' (Dinorah), founded on a Breton idyll, and produced at the Opéra-Comique in 1859. Meyerbeer's special powers found no scope in this comparatively circumscribed field. The development of his genius since 1824 was too great not to be apparent in any style of composition, but these French operas, although containing much that is charming, were, like his Italian ' wild oats,' the result of an effort of will—the will to be whomsoever he chose.

After 1859 he wrote, at Berlin, two cantatas, and a grand march for the Schiller Centenary Festival, and began a musical drama—never finished—called ' Göthe's Jugendzeit,' introducing several of Goethe's lyrical poems, set to music. His life was overshadowed by the death of many friends and contemporaries, among them his old coadjutor, Scribe, to whom he owed so much.

In 1862 he represented German music at the opening of the London International Exhibition by his ' Overture in the form of a March.' (He had before visited England in 1832.) The next winter he was again in Berlin, still working at the ' Africaine,' to which the public looked forward with impatience and curiosity. For years the difficulty of getting a satisfactory cast had stood in the way of the production of this opera. His excessive anxiety and fastidiousness resulted in its being never performed at all during his lifetime. In Oct. 1863 he returned, for the last time, to Paris. The opera was now finished, and in rehearsal. Still he corrected, polished, touched and retouched : it occupied his thoughts night and day. But he had delayed too long. On Apr. 23 he was attacked by illness, and on May 2, 1864, he died.

The ' Africaine ' was performed after his death at the Opéra in Paris, Apr. 28, 1865. When it appeared in London (in Italian) on the 22nd July following, the creation by Pauline Lucca of the part of Selika was long remembered by those who saw it. The work itself had suffered somewhat from the incessant change of intention of its composer, having occupied him from 1838–43. Laid aside at that time for many years, and the book then undergoing a complete alteration, a second story being engrafted on to the first, the composition, when resumed, was carried on intermittently to the end of his life. The chorus of bishops, and Nelusko's two airs, for instance, were written in 1858 ; the first duet between Vasco and Selika in 1857 ; while the second great duet took its final form as late as the end of 1862. The excessive length of the opera on its first production (when the performance occupied more than six hours) necessitated considerable curtailments detrimental to coherence of plot. But in spite of all this, the music has a special charm, a kind of exotic fragrance of its own, which will always make it to some minds the most sympathetic of Meyerbeer's works. It is, in fact, the most purely musical of them all.

Subjoined is a list of his principal works :

OPERAS AND DRAMATIC PIECES

1. Jephthas Gelübde (performed 1811) ; 2. Les Amours de Tevelinde (in German, monodrama for soprano, chorus and clarinet obbligato, in which the instrumentalist figured as a dramatic personage) ; 3. Alimelek, or The Two Caliphs (German. Wirth und Gast), 1813 ; 4. Romilda e Costanza, 1818 ; 5. Semiramide riconosciuta, 1819 ; 6. Emma di Resburgo, 1819 ; 7. Margherita d' Anjou, 1820 ; 8. L' esu'e di Granata, 1822 ; 9. Das Brandenburger Thor, 1823 ; 10.

Il crociato in Egitto, 1824 ; 11. Robert le Diable, 1831 ; 12. Les Huguenots, 1836 ; 13. Ein Feldlager in Schlesien, 1840 ; 14. Struensee (overture and entr'-actes), 1846 ; 15. Le Prophète, 1849 ; 16. L'Étoile du nord, 1854; 17. Le Pardon de Ploermel (Ital. Dinorah), 1859 ; 18. L'Africaine, 1864.

An Oratorio—Gott und die Natur (performed 1811).

Choruses to the Eumenides of Aeschylus.

CANTATAS AND VOCAL MUSIC

Seven sacred cantatas of Klopstock, for four voices, unaccompanied.
An Gott. Hymn, by Gubitz. For four voices.
Le Génie de la musique à la tombe de Beethoven. For solos and chorus.
Cantata, for four voices. Written for the inauguration of Gutenberg's statue at Mainz.
Cantata, 'Maria und ihr Genius.' Composed for the silver wedding of Prince and Princess Charles of Prussia. For solos and chorus.
Serenade, 'Braut geleite aus der Heimath.' Composed for the wedding of Princess Louise of Prussia. For eight voices, unaccompanied.
La festa nella corte di Ferrara. Grand Cantata, with tableaux.

March of the Bavarian Archers. Cantata for four voices and male chorus, with accompaniment of brass instruments.
Ode to Rauch, the sculptor. Solos, chorus and orchestra.
Festal Hymn. Composed for the silver wedding of the King of Prussia. Four voices and chorus.
Freundschaft. Quartet for men's voices.
The 91st Psalm, for eight voices. Composed for the choir of Berlin Cathedral. Published, in score, by Brandus at Paris.
Pater Noster, for four voices, with organ accompaniment.
Twelve Psalms, for double chorus, unaccompanied. (MS.)
Stabat Mater. (MS.)
Miserere. (MS.)
Te Deum. (MS.)

SONGS

A large number of songs with PF. accompaniment, among which the best known are perhaps 'Le Moine' (for bass) and 'Das Fischermädchen.' The whole of them were published, together with 'Le Génie de la musique à la tombe de Beethoven,' in one volume, entitled 'Quarante Mélodies à une et plusieurs voix,' by Brandus at Paris.

'Neben Dir,' song for tenor voice, with violoncello obbligato.
'Des Jägers Lied,' for bass voice, with horns obbligati.
'Dichters Wahlspruch,' canon for three voices.
'A Venezia,' barcarole.
'Des Schäfers Lied,' for tenor voice with clarinet obbligato.
And many others of less importance.

INSTRUMENTAL MUSIC

First Dance, with torches (Fackeltanz), for brass orchestra.
Composed for the King of Bavaria's wedding, 1846.
Second ditto, for the wedding of Princess Charlotte of Prussia, 1850.
Third ditto, for the wedding of Princess Anne of Prussia, 1853.

Grand March, for the Schiller Centenary Festival, 1859.
Overture, in the form of a march, for the opening of the International Exhibition in London, 1862.
Coronation March, 1863.
A quantity of PF. music, written in youth, all unpublished.

F. A. M.

BIBLIOGRAPHY

There are Lives and general studies of Meyerbeer's work by—
A. DE LASSALLE. (1864, with catalogue of works.)
A. POUGIN. (1864.)
H, BLAZE DE BURY. (1865.)
H. MENDEL. (1868.)
J. WEBER. (1898.)
L. DAURIAC (Les Maitres de la musique). (1913.)
HERMANN ABERT. (1918.)
JULIUS KAPP. (1920.)

Special studies include—
G. R. KRUSE: Meyerbeers Jugendopern. (Z.M.W., Apr. 1919.)
W. ALTMANN: Meyerbeer im Dienste des preussischen Königshauses. (Z.M.W., Nov. 1919.)
J. KAPP: Wagner-Meyerbeer, ein Stück Operngeschichte, etc. (Die Musik, Oct. 1923.)

MS. diaries of Meyerbeer (1812–64) are now in the Preussische Bibliothek.

MEYER-HELMUND, ERIK (b. St. Petersburg, Apr. 25, 1861), after learning the rudiments of music from his father, went to Berlin to study composition with Kiel and singing with Stockhausen. He had a successful career as a concert singer, but his fame, at all events in England, chiefly rests upon his many graceful songs, all of which are of a kind to appeal at once to a large number of hearers, and many of which are written to his own words. The operas 'Margitta' (Magdeburg, 1889), 'Der Liebeskampf' (Dresden, 1892) were very successful; his ballet, 'Rübezahl,' or 'Der Berggeist,' was given at Leipzig with great success; and a 1-act burlesque opera, 'Trischka,' was given at Riga in 1894. It was followed by 'Lucullus' (Riga, 1905), 'Münchener Bilderbogen' (Munich, 1910), another opera, 'Heines Traumbilder,' and a light opera, 'Taglioni' (both Berlin, 1912). (Riemann ; Baker.)   M.

MEZARI, MADALENA (called CASULANA) (b. Vincenza, 2nd half of 16th cent.), a composer who apparently lived afterwards at Venice. She was a madrigal composer of distinction to whom A. Gardano dedicated a book of madrigals by Filippo de Monte. She composed 1 book of madrigals a 4 v. (1568 ; 2nd edition, 1583), 1 book of madrigals (1570), and a third book of madrigals a 5 v. (1583). Various numbers are in collective volumes (Q.-L.).

MÉZENGEAU, see MÉSANGEAU.

MEZZO, MEZZA (Ital.), 'half' or 'medium'; is used of voices as a qualification both as regards tone and range. Hence 'mezza voce' means singing at half-power, a quiet, unforced utterance. (Cf. MEZZO-SOPRANO.)

MEZZOGORRI, GIOVANNI NICOLO, an early 17th-century Italian church composer, vicar and maestro di cappella of Comacchio Cathedral, 1612. He composed a large amount of sacri concerti, masses, madrigals, motets, etc., published between 1611 and 1623 (list in Q.-L.).

MEZZO-SOPRANO, the name given to the woman's voice which combines some of the rich quality of the true CONTRALTO (q.v.) with the bright ring of the true SOPRANO (q.v.), and with a compass generally of about two octaves up to b' flat. The tessitura lies in a most effective register, between those of the contralto and the soprano, and the voice in consequence is greatly used for music of a dramatic character.

MI, the third note of the major scale in the nomenclature of France and Italy. See E ; HEXACHORD ; SOLMISATION.

MIASKOVSKY, NICOLAI YAKOVLEVITCH (b. Novogeorgievsk, Russia, now Poland, Apr. 8/20, 1881), composer, son of a general of engineers in the Russian army, was educated for a military career, but studied music with Glière in Moscow and afterwards entered the St. Petersburg Conservatoire as a pupil of Rimsky-Korsakov and Liadov. At the outbreak of war in 1914 he joined the army, which he did not leave until 1920. The following year he became professor of composition at the Moscow Conservatoire.

In his own country Miaskovsky is regarded as the musician destined to carry forward the evolution of Russian symphonic music. His works are for the most part planned on a large scale and show a predilection for vast formal conceptions and elaborate thematic development. The first orchestral work of importance was a symphoniette, begun in 1907, finished in 1910, and revised in 1922. The first symphony followed in 1908, and was also rewritten in 1922. The symphonic poems 'Nevermore '(after Poe) and 'Alastor' (after Shelley) belong to the years 1909–11 and 1912–14 respectively. The second symphony was finished in 1911, the third in 1914, the fourth in 1917, the fifth in 1918. Nos. 6 and 7 appeared in 1922 and No. 8 was completed in 1925.

Only one or two of the symphonies being published, Miaskovsky's work has not yet been adequately performed outside Russia. A few isolated works have been heard in London, New York, Berlin and elsewhere. Sir Henry J. Wood performed 'Alastor' at a Queen's Hall Promenade Concert in Oct. 1923. It made no profound impression, but was probably not a representative work. The sixth symphony was given in London by the same conductor on Mar. 5, 1927.

Victor Belaiev sees in Miaskovsky's music some superficial influences, such as that of Glazounov as regards symphonic structure and that of Scriabin in respect of harmonic idiom, while he attributes the composer's care to relate his music as much to human experience as to artistic principles to a certain affinity with Moussorgsky; but he maintains that such derivations confine themselves to generalities and that Miaskovsky's work reveals above all a strongly original creative personality.

Miaskovsky has also written three sonatas for piano, several smaller pieces for that instrument, a number of songs, and a sonata for violoncello and piano.   E. B.

MICHAEL, (1) ROGIER (b. Bergen, Dutch Brabant; d. circa 1619), was the son of a certain Simon Michael, who is described as Mechanicus and Musicus to the Emperor Ferdinand I.

He is first mentioned as being before 1574 in the service of the Markgraf of Ansbach as tenor singer. In 1575 he became tenor singer at the Electoral Chapel at Dresden, and in 1587 became Kapellmeister to the Elector. For some years before his death, owing to Michael's age and growing infirmities, the Elector was obliged to send for Michael Praetorius, and afterwards Heinrich Schütz, to take his place on all important occasions. Heinrich Schütz definitely succeeded Michael in 1619. The second part of the Dresden Gesangbuch of 1593 contains fifty - two Choralbearbeitungen by Michael, which Otto Kade describes as simple four-part settings, nota contra notam, with the Choral melody in the descant; but, judging from the specimen Kade himself gives in his Beilagen zu Ambros, a setting of 'Ein' feste Burg,' we cannot call them simple harmonic settings in the modern sense, as they have also something of the freedom of the motet style. Another work, not preserved complete, is a book of Introits for Sundays and Festivals, set as motets for five voices, 1603. A few other occasional works, printed and MS., are enumerated in Q.-L.

(2) TOBIAS (b. Dresden, 1592; d. 1657), son of Rogier, was first a soprano singer at the court chapel in Dresden, and receiving his further education at Schulpforta and Wittenberg, became in 1619 Kapellmeister at Sondershausen. In 1631 he succeeded Johann Hermann Schein as cantor and Musikdirector of the Thomaskirche at Leipzig. His chief work

is 'Musikalischer Seelenlust,' of which the 'Erster Theil,' 1634–35, contains thirty sacred pieces, a 5, in the madrigal style, and the 'Ander Theil,' 1637, fifty pieces, a 1-6, in the concerto style for voices and instruments. Other occasional and MS. works are enumerated in Q.-L.   J. R. M.

MICHEL ANGELO CANCINEO, a 16th-17th-century composer of Viterbo, a Carmelite monk and maestro di cappella at Viterbo Cathedral. He appears in some works [1] under Cancineo, but generally signed himself only Michel Angelo. He composed 2 books of motets a 5 v. (only 2nd book, of 1608, still known), and a book of madrigals a 4, 5, 6 and 8 v. (Venice, 1590); also some songs in collective volumes (Q.-L.).

MICHELI, DOMENICO, lived at Bologna 1564 and Ravenna 1581. He composed 1 book of masses a 5 v., and 5 books of madrigals a 5 and 6 v., with some 'Dialoghi' of 8 and 10 parts (Q.-L.).

MICHELI, ROMANO (b. Rome, c. 1575), studied music in Rome under Francesco Soriano, and acquired fame among his contemporaries as a learned contrapuntist. Doni [2] describes him as a 'peritissimo contrapuntista, ed allievo in questa professione del Soriani.' Printz [3] also praises Micheli's work 'in dem stylo canonico.' Micheli made a tour of all the more important towns in Italy — Milan, Ferrara, Bologna, Venice, Florence and Naples; he met many celebrated musicians, with whom there was much friendly rivalry in the pastime of composing music on given themes. In the preface to Musica vaga, 1615, he gives an account of his travels; he was warmly received in Venice, and adds :

'non solo darmi occasione di comporre diverse opere ecclesiastiche a mio beneplacito, ma anche alcuni motetti con oblighi, e canoni diversi, datomi da ciascheduno il soggetto, come in essi motetti e canoni è annotato.'

In 1616 he was maestro di cappella at the church of Concordia, Modena. He became a priest; in 1610 he was already a 'clerico,' and in 1621 was placed for a time at Aquileia. He returned to Rome in 1625 as maestro di cappella at S. Luigi de' Francesi. One of Banchieri's Lettere armoniche,[4] Bologna, 1628, p. 50, is addressed to 'Sig. D. Romano Micheli, Roma.' In 1659 he was still alive at the age of 84.

Micheli took part in an amusing squabble as to the relative merits of German and Italian composers, between the Italian organist Marco Scacchi and Paul Syfert, organist at Danzig. The latter asserted that Italian compositions were of a trivial character, and that their authors should go to Danzig and study genuine music. Micheli promptly sent copies of his musical works to both Syfert and Forster of

1 Fétis; Vogel.   2 Annotazioni, Rome, 1640. p. 395.
3 Sing- und Klingkunst, 1690, ch. xii.   4 Parisini, i. 4.

Danzig, with a request that they would test Italian work before they condemned it. The effect was immediate, a polite reply was received in Feb. 1647, and the matter then dropped. Scacchi himself was not so ready to acknowledge Micheli's pre-eminence. The work, ' Canoni musicali composti sopra le vocali di più parole da Romano Micheli romano, del qual modo di comporre egli è inventore,' Rome, 1645, roused him to publish a protest (Warsaw, Mar. 16, 1647) against the assumption that Micheli was the originator of this type of canon, which could be traced to a much earlier date. Micheli replied by the publication of a collection of canons, full of the most ingenious devices, entitled ' La potestà pontificia diretta dalla santissima Trinità.' The manuscript inscribed ' Canoni musicali di Romano Micheli romano ' was preserved in the library of S. Agostino.[1]

LIST OF WORKS

Psalmi ad officium vesperarum musicis notis expressi, et ternis vocibus decantan‑li. Una cum parte organica. Romano Michaele clerico romano auctore. Liber primus. Romae. J. B. Roblectum, 1610. 4to.

Musica vaga et artificiosa continente motetti con oblighi, e canoni diversi, etc. Di D.R.M. rom. Venetia. Giacomo Vincenti, 1615. Folio. Is in the British Museum ; the music, writes Burney (*Hist. of Music*, iii. 319), shows nothing but ' toil and pedantry.'

Salmi per i vesperi a tre voci in concerto da cantarsi in diversi modi . . . con il basso continuo per l' organo. Libro secondo. Opera terza. Venetia. Magni, 1615. 4to.

Compieta a sei voci con tre tenori concertata all' uso moderno con il basso continuo per l' organo di D.R.M. rom. maestro di cappella nella cattedrale di Concordia. Venetia. 1616. Fétis gives an edition of 1618.

Lettera di R.M. . . . sig. eccellentiss. musici della cappella di N.S. ed altri musici romani miei Patroni osservandissimi. Venetia. G. Vincenti, 1618. Contains a canon in twelve parts.

Madrigali a sei voci in canone, con la resolutione delle parti, nel quale per mezzo de gli accidenti l' armonia ch'un' tuono e di poi ascende il tuono già disceso, potendosi anco cantare per i suoi riversi, come il musici periti sanno ; studio curioso non più veduto. Con un avviso a tutti li Sig. musici di Roma. Dato in luce da R.M. rom. Beneficiato nella metropoli d' Aquileia. Roma. Soldi, 1621. Contains the madrigal ' O voi che sospirate,' which was afterwards printed by Angelo Berardi both in his *Miscellanea musicale*, Bologna, 1689, p. 60, and in his *Arcani musicali*, 1690, p. 14 ; he describes it as written ' con nobilissimo artificio.'

Certezza d' artificii musicali, non più fatti, contenuti nelli dieci oblighi della messa a dieci voci ; con la risposta all' opposizione, fatta dal Sig. A. Antonelli, musico in Roma, sopra la quantità di essi obblighi. Dato in luce da R.M. rom. Beneficiato nella metropoli di Aquileia. Venetia. Bonfadino, 1621. 4to.

Copia di lettera con manoscritta mandata dal Sig. A. Antonelli musico in Roma a me R.M., ecc., con la risposta fattagli nelle presente stampe, etc. Venetia. Bonfadino, 1621. 4to.

Vivit Deus. Canones super plurium verborum vocalibus : quod artificium componendi, neque in Italia, nec alibi hactenus visum est nonnullaque curioso artificio ad musices peritissimos pertinentia. Auctore R.M. rom. Opus sextum. Romae. L. Grignani, 1649. Folio.

Avviso inviato da me R.M. insieme col foglio reale del canone musicale Fons Signatus, alli famosi e peritissimi sig. musici d' Italia e di tutti gl' altri Regni, etc. Roma. Grignani, 1650. 4to. This work gives approximately the date of Micheli's birth as it was written ' nella sua riguardevole età di anni 75 ' (Parisini, i. 89).

Canone musicale a quattro voci, ad honore della concettione della B.V.M., composto sopra le vocali di nuovo, e curioso artificio. etc. Opera et inventione pellegrina di R.M. rom. Roma, L. Grignani, 1650.

Baini also mentions the following three works :
Li salmi a quattro voci. Venetia, 1638.
Le messe a quattro voci. Roma, 1650.
Li responsori a cinque voci. Roma, 1658.

Kircher, *Musurgia universalis*, Rome, 1650, i. pp. 583-4, prints a canon in thirty-six parts, distributed among nine choirs, composed by Micheli, ' one of those who had revived the forgotten art of writing canons.'

MSS. In the Dresden Library, MS. 375b, an aria scored for voice and instruments. (Eitner.)

In the British Museum Add. MSS. 11,588, ff. 148, 149, ' Canon di Romano Micheli,' 1615 ; and ' Canone del Metallo, dal Romano Micheli ' ; both from Micheli's *Musica vaga et artificiosa*, 1615.

C. S.

MI CONTRA FA, see TRITONE.

MICROLOGUS (from the Gr. adj. μικρο-λόγος, ' having regard to small things '—from μικρός, ' little,' and λόγος, ' a word '; Lat. *sermo brevis*, an ' epitome,' or ' compendium '), a name

given by two celebrated authors to works containing an epitome of all that was known of music at the time they were written.

(1) The Micrologus of GUIDO D' AREZZO (*q.v.*) is believed to have been compiled about the year 1025. Valuable MS. copies of this curious work are preserved in the Vatican Library, as well as in the Bibliothèque Nationale at Paris, the British Museum and in other European collections. The treatise was printed in 1784 by Gerbert, Prince Abbot of S. Blasien, in his great work entitled *Scriptores ecclesiastici de musica* ; and in 1876 Hermesdorff published a copy of the original text at Treves, side by side with a German translation. Considerable variations occur in the ancient MSS. An admirable edition of Guido's *Micrologus* was prepared by Dom Ambrogio Amelli, O.S.B., Prior of Monte Cassino, and published in 1904.

(2) A less celebrated but scarcely less valuable treatise entitled *Musice active micrologus* was printed at Leipzig in 1517, by Andreas ORNITHOPARCUS (*q.v.*) (or Ornitoparchus).

The following are the various editions through which it passed :

1. Leipzig, Jan. 1517. The colophon runs as follows :

Excussum est hoc opus Lipsiae in aedibus Valentini — Schuman. Mēse Januario, Anni virginei partus De | cimiseptimi supra sesquimillesimū Leone de | cimo pont. max. ac Maximiliano | gloriosissimo Impatore orbi terrax | praesidentibus. |

This is the first edition, and only one copy is known to exist, viz. in the Bibliothèque Nationale at Paris, the whole of sheet A of which is wanting. It was described by Fétis, who, however, confuses it with the second edition.

2. Leipzig, Nov. 1517. Described in Panzer (ix. 496). The colophon is :

Excussum est hoc opus, ab ipso authore denuo casti-gatum, | recognitumq : Lipsie in edibus Ualentini Schumanni, calco- | graphi solertissimi : Mense Nouēbr : Anni virginei partus de- | cimi septimi supra sesquimillesimū. Leone decimo Pont. Max. | ac Maximiliano inuictissimo impatore orbi terrax psidētibus. |

This edition, though the colophon clearly proves the contrary, is generally described as the first. Copies of it are in the British Museum ; Kgl. Bibliothek, Berlin; Hofbibliothek, Darmstadt; Library of St. Mark's, Venice ; University of Bonn; and one was in the 'Rosenthal Antiquariat,' Munich, May 1888.

3. Leipzig, 1519. The colophon runs :

Excussum est hoc opus : denuo castigatum recogni-tum⊣ : | Lipsie in edibus Ualentini Schumanni : calco-graphi solertissi | mi : Mense Aprili ; Anni virginei partus vndeuigesimi supra | sesquimillesimum. |

There are copies of this at Berlin (State Library), Munich (State Library), Königsberg (see *M.f.M.*, 1870, p. 47), Göttingen (University Library) and Brussels (see *Catalogue de la Bibliothèque de F. J. Fétis*, p. 621). A copy is said (*M.f.M.* viii. p. 22) to be in the Rathsschulbibliothek of Zwickau. Fétis says there is an edition of 1521 at the Bibliothèque Nationale in Paris, though on inquiry the only copy found there was that of Jan. 1517. The colophon he quotes is that of the 1519 edition, but he seems to have imagined that 'undevigesimi' meant twenty-one, instead of nineteen. His statement has been copied by Mendel.

4. Cologne, 1533. The title-page runs :

Andræ Ornitoparchi Meyningensis, De arte cantandi micrologus, libris quatuor digestus, omnibus musicæ studiosis non tam utilis quam necessarius, diligenter recognitus. Coloniæ, apud Joannem Gymnicum, anno 1533.

A copy of this edition is in the Bibliothèque du Conservatoire Nationale de Musique, Paris (see Weckerlin's *Catalogue*, p. 209).

5. Cologne, 1535. An edition without colophon, similar to the preceding. A copy is in the State Library at Munich.

6. Gerber (*Lexicon*, ed. 1813, iii. p. 618) quotes Schacht's *Bibl. Music.* (1687) to the effect that there exists an edition in oblong 8vo, printed by Johannes Gymnicus at Cologne in 1540, but no copy of this is known to exist.

This work, written in the quaint Latin peculiar to the 16th century, contains the substance of a series of lectures delivered by the author at the Universities of Heidelberg, Mainz and Tübingen; and is divided into four separate books.

In 1609 John Dowland printed a correct though deliciously quaint English translation in London (quoted from in the article COUNTERPOINT); and it is through the medium of this that the work is best known in this country. Hawkins, indeed, though he mentions the Latin original, gives all his quotations from Dowland's version.   w. s. r. ; w. b. s.

MIDAS, a famous work of the second period of English BALLAD OPERA (*q.v.*). It is a classical extravaganza, and a parody of Italian opera. Its first appearance on the English boards was at Covent Garden in 1764.[1]

The music was selected from popular melodies, and the piece held the stage for many years. It was revised and acted at Drury Lane, Oct. 25, 1802, when Michael Kelly took the part of 'Apollo,' previously filled by Vernon, and by Mattocks. Another revival took place at Covent Garden in 1814, Sinclair taking 'Apollo.' The pretty song, 'Pray Goody please to moderate the rancour of your Tongue,' appears in the opera, the air of which has been variously ascribed to Rousseau, Oswald and Burney. The music of the opera was first published by Walsh; the revised edition of 1802 by Birchall.   F. K.

MIDDLE C. The note, c', indicated by the C clef, or by the first ledger line below the treble stave, and the first above the bass stave. (See STAVELESS NOTATION.)

MIDLAND INSTITUTE SCHOOL OF MUSIC, see BIRMINGHAM.

[1] It was played privately at Lurgan in 1760, and was brought out at the Crow Street Theatre, Dublin, Jan. 22, 1762.   W. H. G. F.

MIDSUMMER NIGHT'S DREAM MUSIC, by Mendelssohn, consists of two parts. (1) The overture was written between July 7 and Aug. 6, 1826, and was first performed in public at Stettin in Feb. 1827, and in London, Argyll Rooms, June 24, 1829, Mendelssohn conducting. (2) The music for the play was composed in 1843 in obedience to the desire of the King of Prussia, and was produced on the stage at the New Palace at Potsdam, on Oct. 14 of that year; first performance at the Philharmonic was under the composer's direction, May 27, 1844.   G.

MIGNON, opéra-comique in 3 acts, words by Carré and Barbier, founded on 'Wilhelm Meister'; music by Ambroise Thomas. Produced Opéra-Comique, Paris, Nov. 17, 1866; Drury Lane, July 5, 1870; New York, Academy of Music, Nov. 22, 1871; in English, Carl Rosa Co., Her Majesty's Theatre, 1880.   M.

MIKADO, THE, comic opera in 2 acts; words by W. S. Gilbert, music by Sullivan. Produced Savoy Theatre, Mar. 14, 1885.   M.

MILAN. A school of music was founded at Milan in 1483 by Lodovico Sforza, Duke of Milan. Some writers affirm that this was the first public school of music in Italy, but that of Bologna, founded in 1482 by Pope Nicholas V., preceded it by one year. Franchino Gafurio of Lodi was the first public professor of music in Milan. Costanza Porta, the pupil of Willaert, Zarlino, Caimo, Gastoldi, Biffi and others were also eminent composers in the old Lombard school of music, but Claudio Monteverdi (*b.* Cremona, 1570) was the first to found a new epoch in this school and to make it one of the richest and most powerful in Italy. The result of his studies appears in some valuable innovations in the old rules of counterpoint, which, although they excited much cavil and discussion at the time, were soon adopted not only by dilettanti but by professors.

Besides making these important discoveries, he is considered to be one of the inventors of recitative in the musical drama. Orazio Vecchi (*b.* about 1550) was another writer of operatic music of the Lombard school. His opera of 'L' Amfiparnaso' was one of the earliest operatic representations. These and many other writers of dramatic music were formed in the Lombard school, which was also illustrated by composers for the Church, such as Viadana, Noscimbeni, Simpliciano Olivo, Giuseppe Vignati, Antonio Rosetti, Gio. Andrea Fioroni, etc. etc.

In the first part of the 18th century the famous school of singing of Giuseppe Ferdinando Brivio flourished at Milan, but there does not seem to have been any special 'Accademia' or Conservatorio for public musical instruction till the year 1807, when, by a decree of Napoleon Buonaparte, the present Royal Conservatorio of Milan was established.

By order of the viceroy, Eugène Beauharnais,

the building annexed to the church of Santa Maria della Passione, formerly a convent, was set apart for the new musical institute. It was opened on Sept. 8, 1808, and formally inaugurated by the Marquis de Brème, Minister of the Interior ; and it was to be modelled on the pattern of the old Conservatorios of Naples.

The first president of the Conservatorio was Bonifazio Asioli, chosen by the celebrated Gian Simone Mayr, who traced out the rules for the new institution ; and the first professors of the various branches of musical instruction were Federigi, Secchi, Ray, Piantanida, Negri, Rolla, Sturioni, Andredi, Adami, Belloli, Buccinelli. In 1814, on account of the large increase of pupils, two extra professors were nominated. During the years 1848 and 1849, when the Austrians were in Milan, the Conservatorio was also occupied by their troops, but the musical instruction of the pupils was carried on in the private houses of the professors. In 1850 the Conservatorio was reopened under the presidency of Lauro Rossi on a larger scale, with a considerable change in its form of government, and fresh provision was made for instruction in the organ, the harp, the history and philosophy of music. In 1858 a school of instruction in singing for the performers at the royal theatres was likewise added.

An Academical Council was instituted in 1864 to determine what prizes should be distributed to the pupils, and every year those who distinguish themselves most at the yearly examinations receive a monthly pension arising out of the endowment of the institution. In this same year the ' Società del Quartetto ' was formed, of which many of the most notable musicians of the present day are honorary members. Every year this society causes six or eight concerts of classical music to be performed, and offers a prize for the best musical composition on a given subject. The ' Scuole popolari ' for the lower classes of the people, at the cost of the State, are also offshoots of the great Milanese Conservatorio.

The programme of musical instruction in the Royal Conservatorio, as translated from the report of Jan. 1873 of the president, Lodovico Melzi, comprehends two kinds of instruction in music, artistic and literary, and these may again be subdivided into a preliminary and a superior course of instruction in either of these two branches.

The Conservatorio professes to give a complete musical and a fair literary education. The musical instruction is directed by twenty-nine professors, assisted by about thirty teachers selected from the best pupils of both sexes. For the literary branch there are seven professors. There are other professors for deportment, pantomime, ballet and drill.

Each pupil previous to admission must pass through a preliminary examination. This ex-

amination when passed only gives the pupil a right to enter the Conservatorio probationally for a year, and not till he has passed the second examination at the end of the probationary year is he admitted as a pupil.   C. M. P.

LA SCALA.—The proprietors of the Ducal Theatre of Milan, which was burnt in 1776, obtained, by a decree of July 15, 1776, from the Empress Maria Theresa of Austria, leave to build a new opera-house on the site of the church of S. Maria della Scala. The celebrated architect Piermarini of Foligno made the designs, and it was inaugurated Aug. 3, 1778. The building was not only the grandest theatre then existing in Europe, but the most artistically beautiful and complete. Levati and Reina painted the ceiling, the boxes and the great hall or ridotto ; and the curtain, representing Parnassus, was the work of Riccardi. The cost of the whole amounted to one million lire (£40,000), an enormous sum for that time. Until 1857 the principal entrance of La Scala was from a by-street, but since that date it opens on to a large and beautiful piazza.

The interior of the house is in the horseshoe form, with five tiers of boxes and a gallery above them, all in white, relieved by gilded ornaments. The lowest three tiers have each thirty-six boxes, and a royal box above the entrance to the stalls. The fourth and fifth tiers have each thirty-nine boxes, and there are four on each side of the proscenium, making a total of 194 boxes, besides the large royal box and the gallery, each box having a private room at its back for the convenience of its occupants.

The length of the whole building is 330 ft., and its width 122 ft. The height from the floor to the ceiling is 65 ft. The stage, with the proscenium, is 145 ft. long and 54 wide between the columns of the proscenium, but is 98 ft. wide farther behind. The ridotto, a large hall for promenading between the acts, is 82 ft. long and 30 ft. wide. The total capacity of the house is 3600. This immense institution permanently employs 922 persons on its staff, distributed in the following way : Artist-singers, 20 ; orchestra, 100 ; band, 28 ; choristers, 110 ; ' supers,' 120 ; ballet, 140 ; dressmakers and tailors, 150 ; doctors, 6 ; servants, 36, etc.

The gentlemen who provided the funds for the building of La Scala enjoy the use of its boxes at a nominal rental whenever the theatre is open, each box having its owner. In all other respects the theatre has been the property of the town of Milan since 1872. The theatre is controlled by a Commission elected by the Common Council of Milan and the owners of its boxes.

Annexed to the theatre is a celebrated dancing school, with sixty pupils, where the most famous ballet-dancers have been trained, and a singing school for about fifty choristers. Two charitable institutions—*I Filarmonici*, founded by Marchesi in 1783, and the *Teatrale*, by Modrone in 1829—are also dependent for their income upon the greatest theatre of Italy. The theatre was restored in 1878, and again later, reopening in 1922 after important alterations had been carried out.

Its archives have been most carefully preserved and an interesting museum is now housed in the theatre. As the most important opera-house in Italy, La Scala has seen the first production of most of Verdi's operas, including ' Otello ' and ' Falstaff '; of Boito's ' Mefistofele ' and ' Nerone '; of Puccini's ' Madame Butterfly ' and ' Turandot.' (See TOSCANINI.)   L. R. ; rev., with addns., F. B.

BIBLIOGRAPHY

LUIGI ROMANI : *Teatro alla Scala, 1778–1862.* (Milan, 1862.)
CAMBIASI : *Reali teatri di Milano.* (1881.)
HENRI DE CURZON : *La Scala de Milan.* (*Le Guide musical,* 1906.)
GUIDO MARANGONI AND CARLO VANBIANCHI : *La Scala. Studie e ricerche. Note storiche e statistiche.* 1906–1920. (Bergamo, 1922.)

MILAN, LUIS (*b.* ? Valencia, about 1500 ; *d.* there, after 1561), Spanish lutenist. He was the third son of Don Luis del Milan (*d.* before 1516) and Violante Eixarch. His first book, ' Libro de Motes ' (a book of parlour games), was published in 1535 ; ' El Maestro ' (lute tablature) in 1536 ; ' El Cortesano ' (a manual of polite conversation and descriptions of life and music at the court of Germaine de Foix at Valencia) in 1561. ' El Maestro ' is dedicated to Prince John, afterwards John III. of Portugal (1521–57), from whom the author received a pension of 7000 *cruzados*. His visit to Portugal (if he ever visited it) must have taken place after 1538, or he would certainly have mentioned the fact in the dedication. He describes Portugal as being ' a sea of music,' so much was the art appreciated and understood there. He may have been in Italy ; though the fact that he set six Italian sonnets to music proves no more than the Portuguese villancicos also included in ' El Maestro.' He was certainly familiar with contemporary Italian music and systems of lute tablature, and it has been conjectured that ' El Maestro ' was printed from type brought from Venice. The printer describes himself as a Roman (Francisco Diaz *Romano*), but the book was printed in Valencia. No lute music is known to have been printed in Rome as early as this; the only Italian lutebooks in existence at the time were three printed by Petrucci at Venice.

The instrument for which Luis Milan wrote was not, strictly speaking, a lute at all, but the VIHUELA (*q.v.*). His tablature is in principle Italian, the frets being designated by numbers (not by letters, as in England and France) ; but the top line of his ' stave ' is the top string and not, as usually the case, the bottom one (see TABLATURE). In vocal music, the voice part is distinguished by the figures being printed in red. The book consists of Spanish and Portuguese villancicos, Spanish ballads and Italian sonnets. The purely instrumental pieces include *fantasías* and pavanes. Luis Milan has a real instrumental style, and shows considerable variety in his methods of accompaniment : simple chords, passages in imitation of the voice part, and, above all, rapid brilliant passages, especially at the end of a verse. His settings are real solo songs, not mere transcriptions of polyphonic music. Copies of his ' Libro de musica de vihuela de mano, intitulado El Maestro ' (1536) are in the Brit. Mus. ; Bibl. Nat., Paris ; Bibl. Nac. and Bibl. Real, Madrid ; Bibl. de la Diputació, Barcelona. (See Morphy, *Les Luthistes espagnoles* (Leipzig, 1902); *Luis Milan* (Oxford, 1925).)   J. B. T.

MILANOLLO, (1) DOMENICA MARIA TERESA (*b.* Savigliano, near Turin, Aug. 28, 1827 ; *d.* Paris, Oct. 25, 1904), the elder and better known of the two sisters. (2) Her sister MARIA (*b.* Savigliano, July 19, 1832 ; *d.* Paris, Oct. 21, 1848), whose career was suddenly cut short at the age of 16. They were two exceptionally gifted youthful violinists.

Their father, according to Fétis, was a poor carpenter, and his little daughters were two out of thirteen children. Teresa's talent was so precocious that her father migrated to Turin, when the little girl— scarcely 6—received instruction from Gebbaro and Mora, two violinists attached to the Cappella Carlo Alberto. After a year of struggle and trial in Turin, Milanollo père resolved to tempt fortune by taking Teresa to Paris. Armed with an introduction to Lafont, they finally arrived in Paris in 1837. Lafont at once recognised Teresa's gifts, made her one of his pupils, allowed her to play five times at the Opéra-Comique concerts, and took her on tour with him through Holland and Belgium. After a severe illness in Amsterdam, which prevented her from finishing the tour, she reappeared at The Hague, and played to the Prince of Orange, who presented her with a handsome diamond ornament. From Holland she went to England ; played in Covent Garden Theatre at five concerts ; received some tuition from the Anglo-Italian violinist, Mori, and then toured in the provinces and Wales, playing at forty concerts in less than a month. Previously to this, Teresa had started giving her sister Maria violin lessons. Maria's gifts were also of a high order, though her style was quite different. Teresa's playing was full of warmth and feeling, while Maria's was brilliant and sparkling, characteristics which caused them to be nicknamed Mademoiselle Adagio and Mademoiselle Staccato. After Maria's début in Boulogne at the age of 6, the two sisters were inseparable, and travelled together everywhere, playing in France, Holland and Belgium. In 1839 they returned to Paris. A year later, the sisters appeared again in public at Rennes, Nantes and Bordeaux, where they gave twelve concerts with great success. In Paris they played before King Louis Philippe at Neuilly, and at Habeneck's special request made a most successful appearance at the Paris Conservatoire. Making the acquaintance of De Bériot at Boulogne, Teresa received some lessons from him, and then travelled with her sister in Belgium and Germany, played before the King of Prussia, gave twelve concerts at Frankfort, and in 1843 arrived in Vienna, where they created a furore at twenty-five concerts. In the same year they returned to their native country, and on June 9, 1845, appeared in London at the Philharmonic Concert. In 1848, Maria, who had been ailing for some months, suddenly died of rapid consumption, and was buried in the Cemetery of Père Lachaise. Teresa was so overcome with grief at the loss of her companion that she retired from public life for some time, remaining mostly on an estate which her father had bought near Malezeville, in Lorraine. Gradually she resumed her concert appearances, which she continued with remarkable success in Germany and Italy, until 1857, when she married, on Apr. 16, an eminent French military engineer, Monsieur Charles Joseph Théodore Parmentier (b. Barr, Lower Rhine, Mar. 14, 1821). After her marriage she abandoned the concert platform. During the lifetime of Maria the sisters were greatly interested in the poor of Lyons, and as soon as Teresa had roused herself from the grief which her sister's death caused her, she exerted herself in establishing her Concerts des Pauvres, which she carried out in a systematic manner in almost every town in France. Teresa's compositions include:

Ave Maria, chorus for male voices; Fantaisie-élégiaque for violin; two romances; transcriptions and variations for violin and pianoforte.

BIBLIOGRAPHY

Fétis: *Biographie des musiciens.*
A. C. Lahee: *Famous Violinists of To-day and Yesterday.*
A. M. Clarke: *Fiddlers Ancient and Modern; Les Sœurs Milanollo, études biographiques, artistiques et morales.* (Lyons, 1847.)
Theresa Milanollo et Maria Milanollo, par C.M. (Nantes, n.d.)

E. H.-A.

MILANUZ (Milanuzzi), Fra Carlo, Augustinian monk and B.D. of Santa Natoglia, near Camerino, Venice; organist (1619) of the Augustinians at Perugia, maestro di cappella (1622) at S. Eufemia, Verona; organist (1623–1630) of S. Stefano, Venice; maestro di cappella of Camerino Cathedral, 1636, and maestro di cappella and organist at S. Mauro at Noventa di Piave, Lombardy, 1643. He was a prolific composer of masses, psalms, litanies and other church music, and wrote 8 books of secular songs (ariose) between 1619 and 1635 (Q.-L.).

MILDENBURG, Anna von (b. Vienna, Nov. 29, 1872), operatic soprano, married Hermann Bahr, 1909. She studied for some time with Mme. Rosa Papier, and did her final preparatory work for the stage under Pollini of the Hamburg Stadttheater, where she made her first appearance in 1895. Voice and physique alike indicated her fitness for the

heroic characters of Wagnerian opera, and in these she earned invariable success. She became a favourite in Hamburg, and in 1906 was engaged for the German performances at Covent Garden, making her début as Isolde on June 6. In 1908 she became a member of the Imperial Opera in Vienna and took up her residence permanently in her native city, where her talent was deservedly appreciated. Her next appearance at Covent Garden was in 1910 as Klytemnestra, in Beecham's production of Strauss's 'Elektra,' wherein she several times created a highly satisfactory impression during both the spring and winter seasons. She sang the same rôle here in the revival of 1913. She was joint-author with her husband of *Bayreuth und das Wagner-Theater* (1912; Eng. trans. by T. W. Shakespeare).

Bibl.—*Int. Who's Who in Music;* Northcott, *Covent Garden and the Royal Opera.*

H. K.

MILDER-HAUPTMANN, Pauline Anna (b. Constantinople, Dec. 13, 1785; d. Berlin, May 29, 1838), a celebrated German singer and tragic actress, the daughter of Milder, a courier in the Austrian service. Her fine voice and handsome person attracted the notice of Schikaneder, who urged her to enter the profession, offering to be responsible for her musical education and to superintend her début on the stage. The offer was accepted, and she became the pupil of an Italian singing-master named Tomascelli, and subsequently of Salieri. She made her first public appearance on Apr. 9, 1803, as Juno, in Süssmayer's opera 'Der Spiegel von Arkadien.' That the part of 'Fidelio' should have been written for her is sufficient testimony to the capabilities of the organ which caused Haydn to say to her, 'Dear child, you have a voice like a house!'

Her fame spread rapidly, and in 1808 she made a brilliantly successful professional tour, obtaining, on her return to Vienna, a fresh engagement at court as *prima donna assoluta.* In 1810 Anna Milder married a rich jeweller named Hauptmann. Her greatest series of triumphs was achieved at Berlin, where she appeared in Gluck's 'Iphigenia in Tauris' in 1812. After singing with equal éclat in other great German towns, she contracted, in 1816, a permanent engagement with the royal theatre of Berlin. Her great parts were those of the classical heroines of Gluck—Iphigenia, Alcestis, Armida—for which she was pre-eminently fitted, both by her imposing presence and by her magnificent soprano voice, full, rich and flawless, which both in amount and quality seems to have left nothing to desire. At times, especially in her later years, she attempted some lighter parts, such as Mozart's Donna Elvira, and Susanna, but her lack of execution prevented her from succeeding in these as she did in Weigl's opera 'Die Schweizerfamilie' (made celebrated by her impersonation of Emmeline), or in the broad declamatory style of Gluck. Although ' Fidelio ' became one of her principal rôles, her performance in this opera was never, either vocally or dramatically, irreproachable. Thayer [1] relates a conversation with her, in 1836, when she told him what ' hard fights ' she used to have with the master about some passages in the adagio of the great scena in E major, described by her as ' ugly,' ' unvocal ' and ' inimical (*widerstrebend*) to her organ.'

In 1829 she left Berlin owing to misunderstandings and differences with Spontini. She then visited Russia, Sweden and Denmark, but her voice was failing fast. Her last public appearance was at Vienna in 1836, two years before her death.   F. A. M.

MILES, PHILIP NAPIER (*b.* Shirehampton, Gloucestershire, Jan. 21, 1865), is a composer who has combined to a quite remarkable extent the single-minded enthusiasm of the amateur with the practical workmanship of the professional musician.

The heir to a large landed property in the west of England (King's Weston), Napier Miles studied music seriously both at Dresden and at home under Parry and Dannreuther. He has since constantly devoted himself to the encouragement of music in Bristol and its neighbourhood. He formed and has conducted the Shirehampton Choral Society on his own estate, and brought its performances to a high degree of proficiency, performing a wide repertory of music which has ranged from the Elizabethan madrigals to the works of such modern composers as Vaughan Williams and Holst. He has been president of the BRISTOL MADRIGAL SOCIETY (*q.v.*), and he furthered in many ways the Glastonbury Festival scheme (see BOUGHTON). He organised the performances of opera at Clifton in 1924 at which de Falla's puppet opera, ' El Retablo de Maese Pedro,' received its first English performance. Other works of great interest, including some of his own, were there heard. A similar season was undertaken in Bristol in 1926. The University of Bristol gave to Napier Miles the honorary degree of LL.D. in 1925.

The greater part of Napier Miles's own composition has been for the stage. ' Westward Ho ! '—an opera in three acts, the book by E. F. Benson after Charles Kingsley's novel —was heard in London (Lyceum Theatre) in 1913, and portions of another grand opera, ' Queen Rosamond,' have been given at Shirehampton. But later works of less ambitious scope show surer handling, and among them the one-act opera, ' Markheim ' (after R. L. Stevenson's story), is a subtle piece of musical characterisation. It has been given both at Clifton at Bristol and in London, and it received an award from the Carnegie Trust. The vocal score was published in 1926. ' Music Comes,' a

choral dance (poem by John Freeman—Boosey & Co.), was written for Glastonbury, produced there, and subsequently given by the Glastonbury Players in London (Old Vic.). Its skilful treatment of combined rhythms and the delicate scoring for tenor voice, women's choir and small orchestra, are typical of the composer's refined talent. Similar in imaginative quality, though without the stage, is his setting of Keats's ' Ode to Autumn ' (baritone voice, oboe, clarinet and string quartet), heard in London in 1926. He has written many other songs (some published by Acott of Oxford, others still unpublished) which deserve attention.   C.

MILHAUD, DARIUS (*b.* Aix-en-Provence, Sept. 4, 1892), composer, studied at the Paris Conservatoire, where he successively gained prizes for violin, counterpoint and fugue. The outbreak of the European war interrupted his studies before he was able to compete for the Prix de Rome. From 1917–19 he was attached to the French Legation in Brazil. Milhaud was a member of the group of young French composers who became known as the ' Six.'

The productivity of Darius Milhaud so far has been extraordinary, and his contributions to almost every species of music are numerous. In 1911 appeared a sonata for violin and piano, which still reveals the influence of the post-Franck school ; like the first string quartet, it is a distinctly romantic work. But it soon became clear that the composer began to lean more and more towards sombre and violent expressions. He has proved by his incidental music to Greek tragedies that he is capable of lifting dark and sinister themes to a high level. His most daring experiment in this direction is his curious ' orchestration of stage noises ' in the music to the ' Choëphori ' of Aeschylus, where he employs a number of percussion instruments in combination with such things as whistling winds, human groans and cries of despair. On the other hand, Milhaud is equally well versed in the comic side of his art ; in the pantomime ' Le Bœuf sur le toit ' (produced in London as ' The Nothing-doing Bar '), for instance, he has exploited with brilliant effect the humorous possibilities of the Brazilian tango, and in the ballet ' Le Train bleu ' (produced in Paris in June 1924) he makes an amusingly parodistic use of the conventions of musical comedy. But his humour, too, is of a somewhat crude type, and in works such as his setting of a florist's catalogue for voice and chamber orchestra it verges disastrously on mere eccentric trifling. We must turn to his chamber music and to some of the song-cycles in order to discover that delicate tints and lyrical emotions are by no means outside his wide range of expression.

The following are Milhaud's principal works up to 1924 :

Five String Quartets ; 2 Sonatas for violin and piano ; several Suites and a Sonata for piano ; a considerable number of sets of

[1] Thayer, ii. 290 ; Krehbiel, ii. 64.

Songs, including 'Soirées de Pétrograde' and 'Poèmes juifs'; 'Catalogue des fleurs' for voice and chamber orchestra; Sonatina for flute and piano; Sonata for flute, oboe, clarinet and piano; Symphony for vocal quartet, oboe and clarinet; Études and a Poem for piano and orchestra; several orchestral Suites; incidental music for the 'Choëphori' and 'Agamemnon' of Aeschylus; the pantomime 'Le Bœuf sur le toit'; a satiric drama, 'Protée'; the Ballets, 'La Création du monde,' 'Le Train bleu' and 'Salade'; and a work for the stage described as a 'musical novel,' based on 'La Brebis égarée' by Francis Jammes.

E. B.

MILITARY BAND, see WIND BAND.

MILITARY DRUM, another term for the side drum. (See DRUM, 3.)   V. de P.

MILITARY SOUNDS AND SIGNALS. The use of musical instruments in war by the ancients—a use which is found in all countries and at all times—appears to have been more as an incentive to the courage of the troops than as a means of conveying orders and commands.

It is in the 13th century of our era that we first find undoubted evidence of the sounding [1] of trumpets in a field of battle as a signal for attack. At the battle of Bouvines (1215) the French charge was signalled in this manner, and numerous other instances are to be found in the chronicles of the period. For the next 200 years at least the instrument used for signalling seems to have been the trumpet alone. The question of the introduction of the drum into Europe is one involving too much discussion to be entered upon here, but it may be mentioned as a fact that the first clear evidence of its use is the passage in Froissart (Bk. I. pt. i. chap. 322) describing how, in the year 1347, Edward III. and his company entered into Calais 'à grand foison de menestrandies, de trompes, de tambours, de nacaires, de chalemies et de muses '— no mean military band to attend the king of 'unmusical' England !

It is in Italy that the drum seems first to have been used for signalling purposes. Macchiavelli, in several passages in his *Art of War* (written for Lorenzo de' Medici in 1521), clearly states that the drum commands all things in a battle, proclaiming the commands of the officer to his troops. He also recommends the use of trumpets and flutes, the latter being apparently an idea of his own borrowed from the Greeks; he would give the signals to the trumpets, followed by the drums, and advises that the cavalry should have instruments of a different sound from those used by the infantry. This use by the Italians of both trumpets and drums is confirmed by a passage in Zarlino [2]:

'Osservasi ancora tal costume alli tempi nostri; perciocche di due esserciti l' uno non assalirebbe l' inimico, se non invitato dal suono delle Trombe e de' Tamburi, overo da alcun' altra sorte de' musicali istrumenti.'

It was in all probability from Italy that the earliest musical signals came : spread over Europe by mercenaries, they were modified and

[1] In connexion with this word we have an instance of Tennyson's extreme accuracy in the choice of terms. Where the bugle is used as a means of awakening the echoes he says—
    '*Blow*, bugle, *blow*, set the wild echoes flying ':
but where it is to be used as a signal he employs the strictly correct term—
    'Leave me here, and when you want me, *sound* upon the bugle-horn.'
[2] *Istituzioni armoniche*, Venice, 1558, pt. i. cap. 2.

altered by the different troops which adopted them, but the two signalling instruments were everywhere the same (with perhaps the exception of Germany, where the fife seems to have been introduced), and the names given to the different sounds long retained evidence of their Italian origin.

The first military signals which have been handed down to us in notation are to be found in Jannequin's remarkable composition, 'La Bataille,' which describes the battle of Marignan (1515), and was published at Antwerp in 1545, with a fifth part added by Verdelot. A comparison of this composition with the same composer's similar partsongs, 'La Guerre,' 'La Prinse et reduction de Boulogne,' [3] or Francesco di Milano's 'La battaglia,' would be most interesting, and would probably disclose points of identity between the French and Italian military signals. The second part of Jannequin's 'Bataille' (of which the first ten bars are given here in modern notation) evidently contains two trumpet calls, 'Le Bouteselle' and 'A l'Étendart.'

[3] Fifth book of Nicolas du Chemin's Chansons, 1551; Eitner Bibl. d. Sammelwerke, 1551, i.

In the same year in which Jannequin's ' Bataille ' was published, we find in England one of the earliest of those 'Rules and Articles of War' of which the succession has been continued down to the present day. These ' Rules and Ordynaunces for the Warre ' were published for the French campaign of 1544. Amongst them are the following references to trumpet signals :

' After the watche shal be set, unto the tyme it be discharged in the mornynge, no maner of man make any shouting or blowing of hornes or whisteling or great noyse, but if it be trumpettes by a special commaundement.' ' Euery horseman at the fyrst blaste of the trumpette shall sadle or cause to be sadled his horse, at the seconde to brydell, at the thirde to leape on his horse backe, to wait on the kyng, or his lorde or capitayne.'

There is here no mention of drums, but it must be remembered that by this time the distinction of trumpet sounds being cavalry signals and drum-beats confined to the infantry was probably as generally adopted in England as it was abroad. In a virginal piece of William Byrd preserved at Christ Church, Oxford, and called ' Mr. Birds Battel,' which was probably written about the end of the 16th century, we find different sections, entitled ' The Souldiers Summons,' ' The March of the footemen,' ' The March of the horsemen,' ' The Trumpetts,' ' The Irish March ' and ' The Bagpipe and the Drum.' The

first and fifth of these contain evident imitations of trumpet sounds which are probably English military signals of the period, the combination of bagpipes and drums being a military march. Jehan Tabourot, in his valuable *Orchésographie* (1588) (see ARBEAU), says that the musical instruments used in war were ' les buccines et trompettes, litues et clerons, cors et cornets, tibies, fifres, arigots, tambours, et aultres semblables ' (fol. 6*b*), and adds that

' Ce bruict de tous les dicts instruments, sert de signes et aduertissements aux soldats, pour desloger, marcher, se retirer : et à la rencontre de l'ennemy leur donne cœur, hardiesse, et courage d'assaillir, et se defendre virilement et vigourousement.'

Tabourot's work also mentions that it was the custom among certain German troops for the cavalry to use kettledrums. The illustrations to the 1566 edition of L. Fronsperger's *Kriegsbuch* give more than one example of this. Similarly in Rabelais we find a description of the Andouille folk attacking Pantagruel and his company to the sound of ' joyous fifes and tabours, trumpets and clarions.' But though from these passages it would seem as if signals were given by other instruments than the drum and trumpet, there can be no doubt that if this was the case they were soon discontinued. ' It is to the voice of the Drum the Souldier should wholly attend, and not to the aire of the whistle,' says Francis Markham in 1622 ; and Sir James Turner, in his *Pallas Armata* (1683), has the following :

' In some places a Piper is allowed to each Company ; the *Germans* have him, and I look upon their Pipe as a Warlike Instrument. The Bag-pipe is good enough Musick for them who love it ; but sure it is not so good as the *Almain* Whistle. With us any Captain may keep a Piper in his Company, and maintain him too, for no pay is allowed him, perhaps just as much as he deserveth.'

In the numerous military manuals and works published during the 17th century we find many allusions to and descriptions of the different signals in use. It would be unnecessary to quote these *in extenso*, but Francis Markham's *Five Decades of Epistles of Warre* (London, 1622) demands some notice as being the first work which gives the names and descriptions of the different signals. In Decade I., Epistle 5, ' Of Drummes and Phiphes,' he describes the drum signals as follows :

' First, in the morning the discharge or breaking up of the *Watch*, then a preparation or Summons to make them repaire to their colours ; then a beating away before they begin to march ; after that a *March* according to the nature and custom of the country (for diuers countries have diuers Marches), then a *Charge*, then a *Retrait*, then a *Troupe*, and lastly a *Battalion* or a *Battery*, besides other sounds which depending on the phantasttikenes of forain nations are not so useful.'

He also states that a work upon the art of drumming had been written by one Hindar ; unfortunately of this no copy apparently exists. Markham is no less explicit with regard to Trumpet Sounds than he is with Drum Signals :

' In Horse-Troupes . . . the *Trumpet* is the same which the *Drum* and *Phiph* is, onely differing in the tearmes and sounds of the Instrument: for the first point of warre is *Butte sella*, clap on your saddles; *Mounte Cauallo*, mount on horseback; *Tucquet*, march; *Carga, carga*, an Alarme to charge; *A la Standardo*, a retrait, or retire to your colours; *Auquet*,[1] to the Watch, or a discharge for the watch, besides diuers other points, as Proclamations, Cals, Summons, all which are most necessary for euery Souldier both to know and obey' (Dec. III. Ep. 1).

It is noticeable in this list that the names of the trumpet sounds evidently point to an Italian origin, while those of the drum signals are as clearly English. To the list of signals given by Markham we may add here the following, mentioned only in different English works, but in which, unfortunately, no musical notes are given: Reliefe, Parado, Tapto (*Count Mansfields Directions of Warre*, translated by W. G., 1624); March, Alarm, Troop, Chamadoes and answers thereunto, Reveills, Proclamations (Du Praissac's *Art of Warre*, Englished by J. Cruso, 1639); Call, Preparative, Battle, Retreat (W. Barriffe's *Military Discipline: or the Young Artillery Man*, second edition, 1639, and Elton's *Compleat Body of the Art Military*, 1650); Take Arms, Come to Colours, Draw out into the Field, Challenge, General, Parley (*English Military Discipline*, 1680); Gathering (Turner's *Pallas Armata*, 1683).

To return to those signals the notes of which have come down to us, the earliest collection extant is to be found in the second book of Mersenne's *De instrumentis harmonicis*, Prop. xix. (1635), where the following cavalry signals are given—L'entrée; Two Boute-selles; A cheval; A l'estendart; Le simple cavalquet; Le double cavalquet; La charge; La chamade; La retraite; Le Guet. Of these signals (copies of which will be found in a MS. of the 17th century in the British Museum, Harl. 6461) we give here the first Boute-selle:

The next collection known is that of Girolamo Fantini, Trumpeter to Ferdinand II., Duke of Tuscany, whose work is entitled

Modo per imparare a sonare di tromba tanto di guerra quanto musicalmente in organo, con tromba sordina, col cimbalo e ogn' altro istrumento; aggiuntovi molte sonate, come balletti, brandi, capricci, serabande, correnti, passaggi e sonate con la tromba e organo insieme (Frankfort, 1636).

This rare work, to which M. Georges Kastner first drew attention in his *Manuel de musique militaire*, contains specimens of the following trumpet calls—Prima Chiamata di Guerra; Sparata di Butta Sella; L' Accavallo; La marciata; Seconda Chiamata che si và sonata avant la Battaglia; Battaglia; Allo Stendardo; Ughetto; Ritirata di Capriccio; Butte la Tenda; Tutti a Tavola. Some of these are very elaborate. The Boute-selle, for instance, consists of an introduction of four

bars in common time, followed by a movement in 6-4 time, twenty-nine bars long, which is partly repeated. We give here one of the shorter signals, ' Allo Stendardo ':

(Three times.)

With regard to the German signals of this period, and indeed with regard to the whole history of military music in Germany, we are reluctantly compelled to treat the subject very cursorily, owing to the almost total want of material. It has been seen that the use of the kettledrum for the cavalry came from Germany, and frequent allusions are made in French works of the 18th century to the superiority of German military music. But owing perhaps to the more general musical intelligence of the soldiers, the different signals seem to have been handed down orally to a greater extent than they were with other nations. It is said that their signals were better in point of form than those of other nations, and that they were often derived from popular Volkslieder, etc. Their musical superiority they retain to the present day. An interesting point with regard to the German signals is the habit the soldiers had of inventing doggerel verses to them. Some of these rhymes are said to be very ancient, going back so far as the 16th century. The verses were not confined to the signals of their own armies, but were sometimes adapted to those of their traditional enemies, the French. Freiherr von Soltau gives several of these in his work on German Volkslieder (Leipzig, 1845). The following are some of the most striking:

Wahre di bure
Di garde di kumbt. (1500.)

Hüt dich Bawr ich kom
Mach dich bald davon. (16th cent.)

Zu Bett zu Bett
Die Trommel geht
Und das ihn morgen früh aufsteht,
Und nicht so lang im Bette lêht.
(Prussian Zapfenstreich, or Tattoo.)

Die Franzosen haben das Geld gestohlen,
Die Preussen wollen es wieder holen!
Geduld, geduld, geduld!
(Prussian Zapfenstreich.)

Kartoffelsupp, Kartoffelsupp,
Und dann und wann ein Schöpfenkop',
Mehl, mehl, mehl. (Horn Signal.)[2]

[2] In England similar nonsense rhymes are invented for some of the calls. Their chief authors and perpetuators are the boy buglers. The following Officers' Mess Call is an example:

Oh, offi - cer's wives have puddings and pies, but
sol - diers' wives have skil - ly.

---

[1] *Auquet*, i.e. *Au guet*—to the watch.

Another probable reason of the scarcity of old collections of signals in Germany is that the trumpeters and drummers formed a very close and strict guild. The origin of their privileges was of great antiquity, but their real strength dates from the Imperial decrees confirming their ancient privileges, issued in 1528, 1623 and 1630, and confirmed by Ferdinand III., Charles VI., Francis I. and Joseph II. Sir James Turner (*Pallas Armata*, Lond. 1623) [1] has some account of this guild, from which were recruited the court, town and army trumpeters. Their privileges were most strictly observed, and no one could become a master-trumpeter except by being apprenticed to a member of the guild. [2]

Returning to France, we find from the time of Louis XIV. downwards a considerable number of orders of the Government regulating the different trumpet and drum signals. Many of these have been printed by M. Kastner in the Appendix to his *Manuel*, to which work we must refer the reader for a more detailed account of the various changes which they underwent. In 1705 the elder Philidor (André) inserted in his immense autograph collection (see PHILIDOR), part of which is now preserved in the library of the Paris Conservatoire, many of the 'batteries et sonneries' composed by himself and Lully for the French army. The part which Lully and Philidor took in these compositions seems to have been in adapting short airs for fifes and hautbois to the fundamental drum-beats. (See the numerous examples printed in Kastner's *Manuel*.)

From this time the number and diversity of the French signals increased enormously. Besides Philidor's collection, a great number will be found in Lecocq Madeleine's *Service ordinaire et journalier de la cavalerie en abrégé* (1720) and Marguery's *Instructions pour les Tambours*, for the most part full of corruptions, and too often incorrectly noted. Under the Consulate and Empire the military signals received a number of additions from David Buhl, who prepared different sets of ordonnances for trumpets, drums and fifes, which were adopted by the successive French Governments during the first half of the 19th century, and still form the principal body of signals of the French army.

The French signals are much too numerous for quotation in these pages. They are superior to the English in the three essentials of rhythm, melody and simplicity, but in all three respects are inferior to the German. Perhaps the best

French signal is 'La Retraite,' played as arranged for three trumpets:

Returning to the English signals, after the Rebellion and during the great continental wars of the 18th century the English army underwent many changes, and was much influenced by the association of foreign allies. The fife had fallen into disuse, but was re-introduced by the Duke of Cumberland in 1747. Fifes were first used by the Royal Artillery, who were instructed in playing them by a Hanoverian named Ulrich. They were afterwards adopted by the Guards and the 19th, and soon came into general use. Grose

Of recent years several collections of Trumpet and Bugle Sounds with adapted words have been published ; that by A. C. Atherley (1902) is especially complete.
[1] See also *Ceremoniel u. Privilegia d. Trompeter u. Paucker* (Dresden, no date. Quoted in Weckerlin's *Musiciana*, p. 110).
[2] Further information on this subject will be found in Mendel, *sub voce* 'Trompeter,' and in the work quoted in that article, *Versuch einer Anleitung zur heroisch-musikalischen Trompeter- und Pauken-Kunst* (Halle, 1795).

(*Military Antiquities*) alleges that the trumpet was first adopted in 1759 by the Dragoons instead of the hautbois ; but this is evidently an error, as by an order of George II., dated July 25, 1743, ' all Horse and Dragoon Grand Guards are to sound trumpets, and beat drums, at marching from the Parade and Relieving.' On the formation of light infantry regiments, drums were at first used by them, in common with the rest of the army, but about 1792 they adopted the bugle for signalling purposes. ' Bugle Horns ' are first mentioned in the *Rules and Regulations for the Formations, Field-Exercise and Movements of His Majesty's Forces,* issued June 1, 1792.[1] In Dec. 1798 the first authorised collection [2] of trumpet-bugle Sounds was issued, and by regulations dated Nov. 1804 these Sounds were adopted by every regiment and corps of cavalry in the service. The bugle was afterwards (and still is) used by the Royal Artillery, and about the time of the Crimean campaign was used by the cavalry in the field, although the trumpet is still used in camp and quarters. The use of the drum for signalling is almost extinct in our army, except for parade purposes to convey orders, but combined with the fife (now called the flute) it is used for marching purposes.[3] Like many other musical matters connected with the British army, the state of the different bugle and trumpet sounds calls for considerable reform. The instruments used are trumpets in E♭ and bugles in B♭, and though the former are said to be specially used by the Horse Artillery and Cavalry, and the latter by the Royal Artillery and Infantry, there seems to be no settled custom in the service, but—as in the similar case of the different regimental marches—one branch of the service adopts the instrument of another branch whenever it is found convenient. The two collections of Sounds formerly published for the respective use of the Mounted Services and Garrison Artillery and the Infantry have been superseded, since Dec. 1902, by *The Trumpet and Bugle Sounds for the Army,* which was compiled under the direction of the Commandant, Royal Military School of Music, and is issued by authority. In this all calls have been assimilated, so that they can be sounded either by trumpet or by bugle. The work contains Regimental Calls, War and Peace Calls, for all arms, and Instructions for Trumpeters and Buglers. The sounds are formed by different combinations of the open notes of the bugle and trumpet. Their scales are as follows:

---

[1] Grose, *Military Antiquities* (first ed.), says that in the year 1761 there were some troops of Light Dragoons who used horns like post-bags.
[2] In James Gilbert's *Bugle Horn Calls of Riflemen,* etc. (London, 1804), the author states that he was ' in the year 1795 the First that Arranged and Published the compleat Duty of the Trumpet and Bugle Horn for the Light Horse Regiments and Associations throughout Great Britain.'
[3] Compare the table of early marching rhythms given under MARCH.

Bugle.

Trumpet.

The B♭ of the trumpet is, however, never used. Many of the English signals are intrinsically good, while many are quite the reverse; and they are noted down without much regard to the manner in which they should be played. A comparison with the sounds used by the German army (especially the infantry signals) shows how superior in this respect the latter are, the rests, pauses, marks of expression and tempi being all carefully printed, and the drum-and-fife marches being often full of excellent effect and spirit, while in the English manuals attention to these details is more the exception than the rule.

In conclusion we must refer the reader who would further investigate this subject to Kastner's *Manuel général de Musique Militaire* (Paris, 1848), where are to be found a large number of the signals and sounds in use in the different European armies in the author's time, as well as much information on the subject of military music in general—a subject which has been hitherto strangely neglected in both Germany and England. Some little information will also be found in Mendel's *Lexikon* (arts. ' Militair - Musik ' and ' Trompeter '). The present writer is much indebted to the kindness of Col. Thompson and Col. Barrington Foote, former Commandants of the Military School of Music, Kneller Hall ; Sir Lionel Cust ; Lieut. A. J. Stretton ; Mr. J. A. Browne, bandmaster of the South Metropolitan Schools ; and H. Potter & Co., who have furnished information for this article. The last-named firm publish a *Drum, Flute and Bugle Duty Tutor.*   W. B. S.

MILLER, EDWARD, Mus.D. (*b.* Norwich, 1731 ; *d.* Doncaster, Sept. 12, 1807), studied music under Dr. Burney, and was elected organist of Doncaster, July 25, 1756, upon the recommendation of Nares. He graduated as Mus.D. at Cambridge in 1786. His compositions comprise elegies, songs, harpsichord sonatas, flute solos, psalm tunes, etc., and he was the author of ' The Elements of Thorough-bass and Composition,' 1787, and a *History of Doncaster,* 1804. In his ' Psalms of David for the use of Parish Churches ' occurs the famous hymn-tune ' Rockingham.' See *Mus. T.,* 1901, p. 736.

W. H. H.

MILLERAN, an undated MS. of lute music, entitled : *Livre de lut de M. Milleran, interprète du Roy . . . Recueil des plus belles pièces de lut des meilleurs maîtres sur les 14 modes de la musique, savoir sept en bémol et sept en bécarre,* belonging to the Conservatoire Library, Paris. It must have been compiled at the end of the 17th century ; though Weckerlin assigns it the date of 1725. Its author, René Milleran, was a grammarian, teacher of the English and German languages in Paris, an amateur lutenist and a pupil of Mouton. This valuable MS. contains : pieces by Mouton (24), Dupré d'Angleterre, Gautier, Gautier le vieux (in all 17), Gallot de Paris, le vieux Gallot d'Angers, Emond (Hémon) de Launay, le père Bocquet and some anonymous ; also a list of the principal lute-masters of the time.

BIBL.—WECKERLIN, *Catalogue de la Réserve de la Bibliothèque du Conservatoire* ; MICHEL BRENET, *Notes sur l'histoire du luth en France* (*Rivista musicale italiana*, 1899).   M. L. P.

MILLET, LUIS (*b.* Apr. 18, 1867), Spanish (Catalan) conductor and composer, founder of the Barcelona Choral Society, *Orfeó Català*, in 1891. His works consist mainly of choral arrangements of Catalan folk-songs, though he has also written for orchestra.   J. B. T.

MILLEVILLE, (1) G. ALESSANDRO (*b.* 1521, either Paris [1] or Ferrara ; *d.* Ferrara, Sept. 7, 1589). His father was Jean de Milleville.[2] From 1544–73 he was at the court of Modena as teacher of the Princess of Este. He was appointed singer in the Papal Chapel, Rome, Oct. 30, 1552 ; was organist at the court of Ferrara in 1575, and was still there in 1584. He composed 2 books of sacred songs and 3 books of madrigals.[3]   (2) BARNABA (*b.* Ferrara), maestro di cappella of Chioggia Cathedral, 1619–20. In 1628 he was at Siena, according to Adr. Banchieri,[4] who calls him P. D. Barnaba Milleville. He composed masses, madrigals, motets and other church music.   (3) FRANCESCO (*b.* Ferrara), a son of Alessandro, late 16th century, according to Fétis at first engaged at the Polish court, then at the court of Rudolph II. He went to Rome in 1614, became maestro di cappella at Volterra Cathedral; afterwards at Chioggia (?). In 1622 he was maestro di cappella and organist at S. Giorgio, Ferrara ; in 1627 organist at S. Benedetto, Siena. He composed between 1617–1639 masses, 3-8 v., psalms, litanies, concerti spirituali, sacre gemine, concerti *a* 1-4 v. with basso continuo, the last a Fantasia alla Francese for instruments (1617) ; also 7 books of motets, 2-6 v. (*Riemann ; Q.-L.*).

MILLICO, GIUSEPPE (*b.* Terlizzi, Modena, 1739), a good composer and better singer. Gluck, who heard him in Italy, thought him one of the greatest soprani of his day, and, when Millico visited Vienna in 1772, and was attached to the court theatre, Gluck showed his estimation of him by choosing him as singing-master for his own niece. In the spring of that year Millico had already come to London, where, however, he found the public but little disposed in his favour. By the end of the season, however, he had reversed the first unfavourable impression. He had then appeared in ' Artaserse ' and ' Sofonisba,' and he took part in ' Il Cid ' and ' Tamerlano ' in the following year. In 1774 he appeared here in ' Perseo,' after which he went to Berlin. In 1780 he was in Italy again, attached to the Neapolitan court. Fétis gives a list of his compositions, including three operas, three cantatas, a collection of canzonets, published in London (1777), and other pieces. The canzonets are apparently a small oblong quarto publication of Italian songs, ' Six Songs with an accompanyment (*sic*) for the Great or Small harp, fortepiano, or harpsichord . . . dedicated to the Hon. Mrs. Hobard by Giuseppe Millico,' issued originally by Welcker and republished by Birchall at a much later date.   J. M. ; addns. F. K.

MILLÖCKER, KARL (*b.* Vienna, May 29, 1842 ; *d.* Baden, near Vienna, Dec. 31, 1899), a most prolific composer of operettas, was educated in the Conservatorium der Musikfreunde there. After being Kapellmeister at Graz in 1864, and at the short-lived Harmonie-theater in Vienna two years later, Millöcker was, in 1869, appointed conductor of and composer to the Theater-an-der-Wien, for which he accomplished all of his most brilliant work. The list of his compositions is very long. It includes, besides a number of musical farces and the collection of pianoforte pieces, which were issued as the *Musikalische Presse* in monthly parts, the operettas ' Der todte Gast ' and ' Die beiden Binder,' written for Graz ; ' Diana,' produced at the Harmonie-theater ; ' Fraueninsel,' brought out at Buda-Pest ; ' Ein Abenteuer in Wien,' ' Das verwunschene Schloss,' with dialect songs, ' Gräfin Dubarry,' ' Der Bettelstudent ' (1882), which enjoyed an enormous vogue in Germany and Austria especially, and was produced at the Alhambra Theatre, Apr. 12, 1884 ; ' Der Feldprediger,' ' Der Vice-admiral,' ' Die sieben Schwaben,' ' Der arme Jonathan,' ' Das Sonntagskind,' ' Gasparone,' and a host of other operettas. Millöcker's music was piquant and cheerful, and aimed at popularity, which it very easily attained.   R. H. L.

MILLS, ROBT. WATKIN-, see WATKIN-MILLS.

MILLS, SEBASTIAN BACH (*b.* Mar. 1, 1838 ; *d.* Dec. 21, 1898), a pianist, English by birth, but a resident of the United States for the last thirty years of his life. His first teachers were his father and Cipriani Potter ; later he studied at the Conservatorium in Leipzig, under Moscheles, Plaidy, Rietz and Hauptmann, and then came within the circle of young men who were so strongly influenced by Liszt. Mills's first professional engagement was as organist of the Roman Catholic cathedral at Sheffield, which he took in 1855. He did not drop out of sight, however, as a public pianist, and in 1858 he appeared as solo performer at the Gewandhaus in Leipzig. In 1859 he went

[1] Fétis.   [2] *Riemann.*   [4] *Lettere armoniche*, p. 116.   [3] *Q.-L.*

to New York, making his first appearance
there at a concert of the Philharmonic Society
on Mar. 26, in Schumann's A minor concerto.
In 1859, 1867 and 1878 he made brilliant and
successful concert tours in Germany. His appearances in the United States were frequent,
and he was an especial favourite in New York,
where he played every season in the Philharmonic Society's concerts from 1859 down to
1877, his last performance being on Nov. 24 of
the latter year.   R. A.

MILOYEVICH, MILOYE (b. Belgrade, Oct. 15,
1884), Serbian composer, studied in Belgrade
and Munich. He is now settled as assistant
lecturer in musical æsthetics at the University
of Belgrade. His works include :

Antique Legend, for solo v., chor. and orch. ; Symphonic Poem,
Smrt Majke Jugovica (Death of the Mother of Jugovich) ; National
Melodies of Serbia ; Serbian Dance for vln. and PF. ; Legende for
violoncello and piano ; partsongs and piano pieces.   R. N.

MILTON, JOHN (b. circa 1563 ; d. in the
Barbican, London, Mar. 1646/47), composer,
father of the poet, was the son of Richard
Milton, a well-to-do yeoman of Stanton St.
John, near Oxford.

Aubrey says that he was brought up at
Christ Church, Oxford ; the fact that his name
is not found in the University registers does
not make this impossible, for they were care-
lessly kept at that time. Perhaps it was at
Oxford that he received a gold medal and chain
from a Polish prince, in reward for an In
Nomine of forty parts, as related by his grandson Phillips on the authority of the poet ; this
prince, it has been conjectured, may have been
Albertus Alasco, vaiode or palatine of Siradia
in Poland, who visited Oxford in 1583, and
was entertained by the University with
'learned recreations.' Milton was 'cast out by
his father, a bigoted Roman Catholick, for ab-
juring the Popish tenets,' and accordingly
went to London to seek his fortune. In 1595
he was apprenticed to James Colbron, a member
of the Scriveners' Company, and on Feb. 27,
1599 (1600), was himself admitted to the freedom of the Company. He married Sarah
Jeffrey about the same date, and settled in
Bread Street. Of his children (five of whom
were baptized at Allhallows, Bread Street)
three survived : John, the poet ; Christopher,
the judge ; and a daughter, Ann, who married
Edward Phillips and was the mother of Edward
and John Phillips, the authors.

About the year 1632, Milton, who had
acquired a considerable fortune, retired to
Horton in Buckinghamshire. In 1634 he was
elected to the Mastership of the Scriveners'
Company, but avoided serving the office.[1] On
Apr. 3, 1637, Milton's wife died at Horton, and
soon afterwards his son Christopher came with
his family to live with him, until at some date
between Jan. 1639/40 and Aug. 1641 he moved

[1] For particulars as to his business career, and a lawsuit brought
against him and his partner which was decided in their favour, see
Masson's Life of Milton, vol. i.

with them to Reading. Here he remained till
the taking of Reading by Lord Essex's forces
in 1643, when he went to live in London with
his son the poet, at first in Aldersgate Street,
and later in a house in the Barbican, where
he died. He was buried in the chancel of
St. Giles', Cripplegate, on Mar. 15, 1646/47.

Milton's musical abilities are alluded to in
his son's poem ' Ad Patrem.' His compositions display sound musicianship, but are of
no remarkable interest. The following were
printed in his lifetime. In ' The Triumphes of
Oriana,' 1601, ' Fair Oriana in the morn,' a
6. In Leighton's ' Teares or Lamentacions,'
1614, ' Thou God of might,' a 4 (printed by
Burney) ; ' O Lord behold,' a 5 ; ' O had I
wings,' a 5 (printed by Hawkins) ; and ' If that
a sinner's sighs,' a 5. For Ravenscroft's
Psalter, 1621, he set two Psalm-tunes, one of
them twice over. Of his other compositions,
' When David heard ' and ' I am the Resurrection ' (both a 5) have been printed in No. xxii.
Old English Edition, from B.M. Add. MSS.
29,372-7, which also contain ' O woe is me,'
a 5, ' Precamur sancte Domine,' ' How doth
the Holy City,' and ' She weepeth continually '
(all a 6). At Christ Church, Oxford, are ' If ye
love me,' a 4, and five Fancies in five and six
parts.   G. E. P. A.

MINACCIANDO, ' threateningly ' ; a term
used once by Beethoven, in a letter to Schott,
dated Jan. 28, 1826 (Nohl, Neue Briefe Beethovens, p. 282), in which, after some playful
abuse, the following postscript occurs :

Posaun
16 füssig

                                   M.

MINGOTTI, REGINA (b. Naples, 1728 ;
d. Neuberg on Danube, 1807), a very celebrated
singer, born of German parents, whose family
name was VALENTINI. Her father, an officer
in the Austrian service, being ordered to
Graz in Silesia in the same year, took his
daughter with him. Here he died, leaving her
to the care of an uncle, who placed her in the
Ursuline Convent, where she received her first
instruction in music. At the age of 14, however, she lost her uncle by death, and the
pension which ensured her an asylum with the
nuns ceased with his life. Compelled to return
to her family, she spent some time very unhappily.

In order to escape from this miserable life,
though still a mere child, she married Mingotti,
an old Venetian musician, impresario of the
Dresden opera. Perceiving all the advantage
that might be derived from the great gifts of
his young wife, Mingotti placed her at once

under the tuition of Porpora, where she made rapid progress in her art. From a slender salary, she soon rose to receiving more considerable pay, while her growing popularity aroused the jealousy of a powerful and established rival, the celebrated Faustina, who actually vacated the field and left Dresden for Italy. Soon afterwards the younger singer went also to Italy, and obtained a lucrative engagement at Naples. There she appeared with great éclat (1748) in Galuppi's 'L' Olimpiade,' astonishing the Italians no less by the purity of her pronunciation than by the beauty of her voice and style. Engagements were immediately offered her for many of the great Italian operas, but she refused all in order to return to Dresden, where she was already engaged. Here she played again in 'L' Olimpiade' with enormous success. Faustina and her husband, Hasse the composer, were also now again in Dresden; and Burney tells an anecdote which, if true, shows that their jealous feelings towards Mingotti had not ceased.[1] From Dresden she went to Spain (1751), where she sang with Gizziello in the operas directed by Farinelli, who was so strict a disciplinarian that he would not allow her to sing anywhere but at the Opera, nor even to practise in a room that looked on the street!

After spending two years in Spain, Mingotti went to Paris, and thence to London for the first time. Her arrival here retrieved the fortunes of the opera in England, which were in a languishing condition. In Nov. 1755 Jommelli's 'Andromaca' was performed, but 'a damp was thrown on its success by the indisposition of Mingotti.' She told Burney,[2] indeed, in 1772, 'that she was frequently hissed by the English for having a toothache, a cold, or a fever, to which the good people of England will readily allow every human being to be liable except an actor or a singer.' She seems to have been a very accomplished singer and actress; her only fault, if she had one, being a little want of feminine grace and softness.

Her contentions with Vaneschi, the manager, occasioned many private quarrels and feuds.

At the close of the season of 1763, Signora Mattei left England, and Giardini and Mingotti again resumed the reins of opera government, and Mingotti sang in 'Cleonice,' 'Siroe,' 'Enea e Lavinia' and 'Leucippe e Zenocrita.' She afterwards sang with considerable success in the principal cities of Italy, but she always regarded Dresden as her home, during the life of the Elector Augustus. In 1772 she was settled at Munich, living comfortably, well received at court, and esteemed by all such as were able to appreciate her understanding and conversation. In 1787 Mingotti retired to Neuburg on the Danube, where she died. Her portrait in

[1] See HASSE; and Burney, *Present State (Germany)*, i. 157.
[2] From whose account most of these details are derived.

crayons, by Mengs, is in the Dresden Gallery. It represents her, when young, with a piece of music in her hand; and, if faithful, it makes her more nearly beautiful than it was easy for those who knew her later in life to believe her ever to have been. 'She is painted in youth, plumpness, and with a very expressive countenance.' The dog in Hogarth's 'Lady's Last Stake' is said to be a portrait of Mingotti's dog.   J. M.

MINIM (Fr. *blanche*; Ger. *halbe Note*, whence the American term *Half-note*; Ital. *minima*). The half of a semibreve and equal to two crotchets. It is written ♩, and its rest is ▬, a block-stroke placed above a line of the stave: *i.e.* the inversion of the semibreve rest.

MINNESINGER, or MINNESÄNGER, were the German counterpart of the troubadours, but of somewhat later date. They flourished in the 12th and 13th centuries, and were succeeded by the MEISTERSINGER (*q.v.*). The Minnesinger were almost exclusively of noble or gentle birth, and to modern musicians, the names of Walther von der Vogelweide, Wolfram von Eschenbach and Tannhäuser are the most familiar, from the dramas of Wagner. The work of F. H. von der Hagen, *Minnesänger* (1838–56), is the best authority on the subject. The name implies that love was the principal subject dealt with in the songs of these knightly minstrels. (See MEISTERSINGER; SONG, subsection GERMANY.)

BIBLIOGRAPHY

FRIEDRICH VOGT: *Des Minnesangs Frühling. Mit Bezeichnung der Abweichungen von Lachmann und Haupt und unter Beifügung ihrer Anmerkungen neu bearbeitet.* Ed. 3. (Leipzig, 1920.)
KONRAD BURDACH: *Über den Ursprung des mittelalterlichen Minnesangs, Liebesromans und Frauendienstes.* (Berlin, 1918.)
GÜNTHER HASE: *Der Minneleich Meister Alexanders und seine Stellung in der mittelalterlichen Musik.* Pp. 96. Halle a. S., 1921. (Sächsisches Forschungsinstitut für neuere Philologie in Leipzig.) Alt-germanische Abt. Heft. 1.
ALFRED ROTTAUSCHER: *Das Taghorn. Dichtungen und Melodien des bayrisch-österreichischen Minnesangs.* 3 Bde. (Bd. 1 consists of introduction.) (Vienna, 1922.)   M.

MINOJA, AMBROGIO (*b.* Ospitaletto, near Lodi, Oct. 2, 1752; *d.* Milan, Aug. 3, 1825), pupil of S. Anselmi, Lodi and Sala at Naples. From 1781–1801 he was maestro al cembalo (conductor) at La Scala Theatre, Milan, where he produced his first opera in 1787. In 1795 he was maestro al cembalo at Parma Theatre, afterwards maestro di cappella at La Scala Theatre and director of Milan Conservatoire. He composed masses and other church music, coronation music for Napoleon and music for members of his court, etc.; orchestral and chamber music and a book of Solfeggi which are still largely used. He also wrote *Letters on Singing* (addressed to B. Asioli), which were translated into German. The MS. of his *Autobiography* is in the Wm. Heyer Museum, Leipzig (*Q.-L.*; *Riemann*).

MINOR. When intervals have two forms which are alike consonant or alike dissonant, these are distinguished as major and minor. The minor form is always a semitone less than the major.

The consonances which have minor forms are thirds and sixths; the dissonances are seconds, sevenths and ninths; of these the minor thirds and sixths are the roughest of consonances, and the minor second is the roughest and the minor seventh the smoothest of dissonances.

Minor scales are so called because their chief characteristic is their third being minor. Minor tones are less than major by a comma. (See MAJOR; HELMHOLTZ; SCALE.)   C. H. H. P.

MINOR CANONS, priests in cathedrals and collegiate churches whose duty it is to superintend the performance of daily service. They are not of the Chapter, but rank after the canons and prebendaries. They were formerly called vicars choral, and were originally appointed as deputies of the canons for church purposes, their number being regulated by the number of the capitular members. Laymen were frequently appointed as vicars choral, but it is necessary that minor canons should be in Holy Orders. According to the statutes, they should also be skilled in church music. (Hook's *Church Dictionary*.)   W. B. S.

MINORE (Ital. *minor*) is used as a warning sign in music which changes suddenly into the tonic (or sometimes the relative) minor of the original key, and in which the change of signature might escape the observation of the performer. It is most commonly found, like its counterpart, MAGGIORE (*q.v.*), in variations. M.

MINSTREL (Fr. *ménétrier*). The name so vaguely used in modern romantic language as the equivalent of musician, had originally a far more definite signification. Its most probable derivation is from *minister*, and at first the minstrels seem to have been employed by the troubadours as their attendants, possibly in order to accompany them on some stringed instrument. Through all the development of music, the idea of an instrumental performer has clung to the name minstrel, who appears to have corresponded in the north of France to the jongleur of the south, and to have performed the same functions. The name minstrel has undergone no such debasing change of meaning as has been the fate of jongleur in its modern form of juggler. (See SONG; TROUBADOUR.)   M.

MINUET (Fr. *menuet*; Ger. *Menuett*; Ital. *menuetto*), a dance of French origin. The name is derived from the French *menu* (small), and refers to the short steps of the dance. According to some authorities it came originally from the province of Poitou, while others say that the first was composed by Lully.

In its earliest form the minuet consisted of two eight-bar phrases, in 3–4 time, each of which was repeated; sometimes beginning on the third, but more frequently upon the first, beat of the bar, and of a very moderate degree of movement. As a complement to the short movement, a second minuet was soon added,

similar in form to the first, but contrasted in feeling. This was mostly written in 3-part harmony, whence it received its name trio, a name retained down to the present time, long after the restriction as to the number of parts has been abandoned. A further enlargement in the form of the minuet consisted in the extension of the number of bars, especially in the second half of the dance, which frequently contained sixteen, or even more, bars, instead of the original eight. It is in this form that it is mostly found in the Suite.

SUITES.—In the works of the composers of the 18th century, especially Handel and Bach, the minuet is by no means an indispensable part of the suite. As compared with some other movements, such as the allemande, courante or sarabande, it may be said to be of somewhat infrequent occurrence. Its usual position in the suite is among the miscellaneous dances, which are to be found between the sarabande and the gigue, though we exceptionally meet with it in the third suite of Handel's second set as a final movement, and with three variations. In Handel, moreover, it is very rare to find the second minuet (or trio) following the first. On the other hand, this composer frequently gives considerable development to each section of the movement, as in the eighth suite of the second set, where the minuet (written, by the way, as is frequently the case with Handel, in 3–8 instead of 3–4 time) contains thirty-four bars in the first part, and seventy-one in the second. This piece has little of the character of the ordinary minuet excepting the rhythm. Handel also frequently finishes the overtures of his operas and oratorios with a minuet; one of the best-known instances will be found in the overture to 'Samson.'

The minuets of Bach are remarkable for their variety of form and character. In the partita in B♭ (No. 1) the first minuet contains sixteen bars in the first section and twenty-two in the second; while the second minuet is quite in the old form, consisting of two parts of eight bars each. The minuet of the fourth partita (in D) has no trio, and its sections contain, the first eight, and the second twenty bars. In a suite for clavier in E♭ (B.-G. xxxvi. p. 12) we find an early example of a frequent modern practice. The first minuet is in E♭ major, and the second in the tonic minor. It may be remarked in passing that Bach never uses the term 'trio' for the second minuet, unless it is actually written in three parts. In the fourth of the six sonatas for flute and clavier we meet with another departure from the custom of the day which ordained that all movements of a suite must be in the same key. We here see the first minuet in C major, and the second in A minor—a precedent often followed in more modern works. Another example of the same relation of keys will be found in the fourth of the so-called 'English Suites'—the only one which contains a minuet. Here the first minuet is in F and the second in D minor. Of the six French suites four have minuets, two of which are worth noticing. In the second minuet of the first suite the latter half is not repeated —a very rare thing; and in the third suite we meet with a genuine trio in three parts throughout, and at the end the indication 'Menuet da capo.' Though it was always understood that the first minuet was to be repeated after the second, it is very rare at this date to find the direction expressly given. One more interesting innovation of Bach's remains to be mentioned. In his great concerto in F for solo violin, two horns, three oboes, bassoon and strings, will be found a minuet with three trios, after each of which the minuet is repeated. (B.-G. xix. p. 27.) We shall presently see that Mozart, half a century later, did the same thing.

THE SYMPHONIC MINUET.—The historic importance of the minuet arises from the fact that, unlike the other ancient dances, it did not become obsolete, but continued to hold a place in the symphony (the descendant of the old suite), and in other large instrumental works written in the same form. The first composer to introduce the minuet into the symphony appears to have been Haydn; for in the works of this class which preceded his (those of C. P. E. Bach, Sammartini and others) we find only three movements. And even with Haydn (as also in many of the earlier works of Mozart) we find the minuet at first by no means of invariable occurrence. On the other hand, we sometimes see in the same work two minuets, each with a trio, one before and one after the slow movement. Examples will be met with in Haydn's first twelve quartets (opp. 1 and 2) and also in some of Mozart's serenatas, divertimenti, etc. (Köchel's Catalogue, Nos. 63, 99, 204, 247 and others).

While in general retaining the old form of the minuet, Haydn greatly changed its spirit. The original dance was stately in character, and somewhat slow. With Haydn its prevailing tone was light-hearted humour, sometimes even developing into downright fun. The time became quicker. While in the earlier works the most frequent indications are *Allegretto*, or *Allegro ma non troppo*, we find in the later quartets more than once a *Presto* (opp. 76 and 77). These minuets thus become an anticipation of the Beethoven scherzo. Curiously enough, in one set of quartets, and in only one (op. 33), Haydn designates this movement 'Scherzando,' in Nos. 1 and 2, and 'Scherzo' in Nos. 3 to 6. As the tempo here is not more rapid than in the other minuets, it is evident that the term only refers to the character of the music, and is not used in the modern sense. As we learn from Pohl's *Haydn* (p. 332) that the composer care-

fully preserved the chronological order of the quartets in numbering them, we are in a position to trace the gradual development of the minuet through the entire series. We find one of Haydn's innovations in some of the later works, in putting the trio into a key more remote from that of the minuet, instead of into one of those more nearly related (quartet in F, op. 72, No. 2—minuet in F, trio in D♭; quartet in C, op. 74, No. 1—minuet in C, trio in A major). This relation of the tonics was a favourite one with Beethoven. In only one of Haydn's quartets (op. 9, No. 4) do we find a trio in three parts, though the name is always given to the second minuet. A curious departure from the ordinary form is to be seen in the quartet in E♭, op. 2, No. 3. Here the trio of the second minuet has three variations, one of which is played, instead of the original trio, after each repetition of the minuet.

It is no uncommon thing in the works of Haydn to meet with another variety of the minuet. The finales of his smaller works are often written in a 'Tempo di minuetto.' Here the regular subdivisions of minuet and trio, sometimes also the double bars and repeats, are abandoned. In the piano sonatas and trios many examples will be met with. An instance of a similar movement by Mozart is furnished in the finale of his sonata in F for piano and violin. Haydn's predilection for the minuet is further shown by the fact that in several of his sonatas in three movements the minuet and trio replace the slow movement, which is altogether wanting.

With Mozart the form of the minuet is identical with that of Haydn; it is the spirit that is different. Suavity, tenderness and grace, rather than overflowing animal spirits, are now the prevailing characteristics. It is in Mozart's concerted instrumental works (serenatas, etc.) that his minuets must be chiefly studied; they are singularly rare in his pianoforte compositions. Of seventeen solo sonatas, only two (those in E♭ and A major) contain minuets; while out of forty-two sonatas for piano and violin, minuets are only found in four as intermediate movements, though in the earlier works a 'Tempo di minuetto' often forms the finale. In many of the earlier symphonies also we find only three movements, and even in several of the later and finer symphonies (*e.g.* Köchel, Nos. 297, 338, 444, 504) the minuet is wanting. On the other hand, in the serenades and divertimenti, especial prominence is given to this movement. Frequently two minuets are to be found, and in some cases (Köchel, Nos. 100, 203, 250) three are to be met with. The variety of character and colouring in these minuets is the more striking as the form is approximately the same in all. In the divertimento in D (Köchel, 131), for strings, flute, oboe, bassoon and four horns, there are two

minuets, the first of which has three trios and
the second two. The first minuet in D major
is given to strings alone ; the first trio (also in
D major) is a quartet for the four horns ; the
second (in G) is a trio for flute, oboe and bassoon ; while the third (in D minor) is for the
seven wind instruments in combination. After
the last repetition of the minuet, a coda for all
the instruments concludes the movement. The
three trios are as strongly contrasted in musical
character as in orchestral colour. Many similar
instances might easily be given from the works
of Mozart.

To Beethoven we owe the transformation of
the minuet into the SCHERZO (q.v.). Still Beethoven does not entirely abandon the older
minuet. Out of sixty-three examples of the
minuet or scherzo (not counting those in common time) to be found in his works, seventeen
are entitled ' Minuet,' or ' Tempo di minuetto.'
Besides this, in two works (the piano and violin
sonata in G, op. 30, No. 3, and the piano solo
sonata in E♭, op. 31, No. 3) the tempo di
minuetto takes the place of the slow movement ; in the sonata, op. 49, No. 2, it serves as
finale (as with Haydn and Mozart) ; and in the
sonata, op. 54, the first movement is a tempo
di minuetto. In these minuets we sometimes
find a grace akin to that of Mozart (sonata, op.
10, No. 3 ; septet), sometimes, as it were, a
reflection of the humour of Haydn (sonata, op.
22) ; but more often the purest individuality of
Beethoven himself. In some cases a movement is entitled ' Minuet ' though its character
is decidedly that of the scherzo (e.g. in the first
symphony). The only one of the nine symphonies in which a minuet of the old style is to
be seen is No. 8.

The transformation of the minuet into the
scherzo, just adverted to, has had an important
influence on modern composers. In the large
majority of works produced since the time of
Beethoven, the scherzo has replaced its predecessor.   E. P.

THE DANCE IN ENGLAND.—Minuets began to
appear in English musical publications in the
latter part of the 17th century ; one is in
Salter's *Genteel Companion for the Recorder*,
1683, and in the first half of the 18th century
they were a feature in English dancing. The
period of their greatest popularity here was
from about 1730–70, owing, no doubt, to their
court patronage. Annually, on the King's
birthday, a special minuet was composed for
the occasion, and this with the other French
dances was published in a small oblong volume
issued yearly by such publishers as Walsh and
Wright. Later, other music-sellers brought
out similar yearly collections. The earliest of
these issues of minuets with which the present
writer is acquainted is for 1716, and the latest,
Thompson's, for 1791. After that date the
decline of the minuet as a dance caused such

yearly sets to be abandoned. Though so
greatly in favour, much of this minuet music
was decidedly uninteresting, and as an example
of the type common at the middle of the 18th
century the following is appended ; it is notable
as having been used at the Coronation ball of
George the Third in 1761—

The Coronation Minuet.

From *Thompson's Minuets for* 1762.

Other minuets of greater musical quality
were Martini's ; that from 'Ariadne,' Foot's,
etc. ; these were in great favour for flute and
fiddle pieces.   F. K.

MIOLAN, MARIE CAROLINE FÉLIX, see
CARVALHO.

MIREILLE, opera in 5 acts ; words by Carré
(from Mirèio, a Provençal poem by Mistral) ;
music by Gounod. Produced Théâtre Lyrique,
Mar. 19, 1864 ; reduced to 3 acts, Dec. 15,
1864, same theatre. In London, in Italian,
5 acts, as 'Mirella,' Her Majesty's Theatre,
July 5, 1864.   G.

MISERERE, Psalm li. in the Hebrew and
English reckoning, or 50th in the Latin,
Miserere mei Deus, has special musical importance from its position at the end of the Office
of TENEBRAE (q.v.).

There is reason to believe that the idea of
adapting the Miserere to music of a more solemn
character than that generally used for the
Psalms, and thus making it the culminating
point of interest in the service of Tenebrae,
originated with Pope Leo X., whose Master of
Ceremonies, Paride Grassi, tells us that it was
first sung to a Fauxbourdon in 1514. No trace
of the music used on that occasion can now be
discovered. The oldest example we possess
was composed in 1517 by Costanzo Festa, who
distributed the words of the Psalm between
two falsi-bordoni, one for four voices and the
other for five, relieved by alternate verses of
plain-song—a mode of treatment which has
survived to the present day. Festa's Miserere
is the first of a collection of twelve, contained
in two celebrated MS. volumes preserved
among the archives of the Pontifical Chapel.
The other contributors to the series were Luigi
Dentice, Francesco Guerrero, Palestrina, Teofilo
Gargano, Francesco Anerio, Felice Anerio, an
anonymous composer of very inferior ability,
Giovanni Maria Nanini,[1] Sante Naldini, Ruggiero Giovanelli, and lastly Gregorio ALLEGRI

---

[1] Nanini's work is little more than an adaptation of Palestrina's
with an additional verse for nine voices.

(q.v.)—whose work is the only one of the twelve now remaining in use in the Papal Chapel. Later works by Tommaso Bai (produced 1714) and Giuseppe Baini (1821) have shared in the fame of Allegri's Miserere as performed by the SISTINE CHOIR (q.v.). w. s. r., rev.

MISSA; MISSA DE ANGELIS, see MASS.

MISSON, LUIS (b. ? Barcelona; d. Madrid, Feb. 13, 1766), Spanish composer, inventor of the 'Tonadilla.' In 1748 he was admitted to the royal orchestra as a player on the flute and hautboy, and he soon gained a reputation for virtuosity, especially on the flute. He became conductor in 1756. The first tonadilla dates from 1757. It is a duet between the landlady of an inn and an itinerant Bohemian, and was so successful that it was followed by many others, for various numbers of voices and written by various composers. Misson takes as his subject some simple scene of popular life (usually in Madrid) and draws out of it all the music of which the scene is capable. His writing is strongly national, and inspired by popular songs (e.g. Seguidillas); his works are genre-pictures, the musical counterpart of the paintings and tapestries of Goya.

The Bibl. del Ayuntamiento, Madrid, contains four MS. scores of Misson, including ' Lo que puede verse . . .' (for 5 v.), which may be translated ' Things seen in the street on a public holiday.' Misson also composed 3 comic operas (ZARZUELAS (lost)), and 6 sonatas for flute and bass (Library of the Duke of Alba, Madrid). J. B. T.

MITJANA Y GORDON, RAFAEL (b. Malaga, Dec. 6, 1869; d. Stockholm, Aug. 15, 1921), Spanish diplomat and musical historian. He studied music with Pedrell and Saint-Saëns; but his importance lies less with his operatic works (e.g. ' La Buena Guarda ') than with his historical research. A far better writer than Pedrell, hardly less learned, and more accurate, he was able to give a clearer account of the course of Spanish musical history, while his diplomatic appointments enabled him to discover in foreign libraries new information of great importance. He was particularly fortunate in his discoveries in Sweden, where he found and described an unknown Cancionero (song-book) dating from the mid-16th century : 'Villancicos de diversos autores' (2-5 v.), printed at Venice by H. Scotus, 1556 (Univ. Lib., Upsala). He also discovered two early and unknown secular cantatas by MORALES (q.v.), and published a catalogue of printed music at Upsala. He was responsible for the Spanish vol. of the Encl. du Conservatoire (Paris, Delagrave); but owing to unforeseen causes his MS., dated 1914, was only printed in 1919. Many printers' errors remained uncorrected, especially in the musical illustrations, while the indispensable index and table of contents were omitted. The final results of his researches

will be found in the following, published subsequently :

Estudios sobre algunos músicos españoles del siglo XVI. Madrid, 1918. (Including Morales and Victoria.)
Don Fernando de las Infantas. Madrid, 1918.
Francisco Guerrero. Madrid, 1922.

He also wrote valuable articles on secular music in Spain in the 16th and 17th centuries for the Revista de Filología Española, and a short life of Morales. This, however, has not yet been published. J. B. T.

MIXED CADENCE, see CADENCE (II.), section (3).

MIXED MODES. Writers on plain-song apply this term to tonalities which embrace the entire compass of an Authentic Mode in combination with that of its plagal derivative (see MODES, ECCLESIASTICAL). w. s. r.

MIXED VOICES, the English term for a combination of female and male voices, as opposed to EQUAL VOICES (q.v.), which denotes male or female voices alone. G.

MIXOLYDIAN MODE (Lat. modus mixolydius ; modus angelicus), the seventh of the Ecclesiastical Modes, see MODES, ECCLESIASTICAL.

MIXTURE, an organ stop ordinarily furnished with from two to five comparatively small pipes to each key. It is compounded of the higher-sounding and therefore shorter members of the ' foundation ' and ' mutation ' classes of stops, combined or ' mixed,' and arranged to draw together, as in practice they are seldom required to be used separately. The Mixture represents or corroborates the higher consonant harmonic sounds suggested by nature, and in the bass produces tones to the third or fourth octave above the unison or chief foundation tone. As the musical scale ascends the higher harmonics become weak and inaudible to the ear ; hence in a Mixture stop it is customary to discontinue the higher ranks as they ascend, one or more at a time, and insert in lieu a rank of lower tone than was previously in the stop, but appearing as a separate stop. This alteration is called a ' break.' A Full Mixture is generally of three ranks, consisting of the following intervals in relation to the unison : 15, 19, 22, or c'', g'', c''', when c is struck. (See MUTATION and J. J. Wedgwood's Dictionary of Organ Stops.) E. J. H.

MIZLER (MITSLER) VON KOLOF, LORENZ CHRISTOPH (b. Heidenheim, Würtemberg, July 25, 1711 ; d. Warsaw, Mar. 1778), was educated at the Gymnasium of Anspach and the University of Leipzig. He was one of Bach's scholars. In 1734 he became a magistrate, and was generally a cultivated and prominent person. His claim to perpetuity is his connexion with the ' Association for Musical Science,' which he founded at Leipzig in 1738 and kept together. Amongst its members were Handel, Bach and Graun. Bach composed a 6-part canon and the canonic variations on ' Vom Himmel hoch ' as his diploma pieces.   Mizler edited a periodical, the *Neu-eröffnete Musik-Bibliothek* (1739–54), wrote a treatise on Thorough-bass, *Die Anfangsgründe des General basses*, in which he seems to have pushed the connexion of music and mathematics to absurdity.   (See Spitta, *Bach*, Engl. trans. iii. 22-25.)   He translated Fux's *Gradus* into German (1742).   (See *Q.-L.* for other works.)   G.

MLYNARSKI, EMIL (*b.* Kibarty, Poland, July 18, 1870), orchestral conductor, studied as a violinist under Auer in St. Petersburg and became second conductor and director of symphony concerts at Warsaw (1893), and succeeded to the senior conductorship both of the Opera and of the Warsaw Philharmonic Society (1901–05).   In 1907 he conducted orchestral concerts with the LONDON SYMPHONY ORCHESTRA (*q.v.*), and in 1910 he took charge of the SCOTTISH ORCHESTRA (*q.v.*), with which he did much important work.   Later (1919–22) he returned to Poland and resumed the director-ship of the Opera and of the Conservatoire at Warsaw.

Among his more important compositions are a concerto in D minor for violin and orchestra and a symphony in F, ' Polonia.'   c.

MOCK DOCTOR, THE, see MÉDECIN MALGRÉ LUI, Le.

MOCQUEREAU, DOM ANDRÉ (*b.* Tessoualle, near Chollet, Maine-et-Loire, June 6, 1849), a French Benedictine, entered the Solesmes monastery in 1875, after solid musical study. He founded the *Paléographie musicale*, a monumental publication intended to spread the knowledge of the liturgical chants of the Catholic Church in all their forms and in all epochs.   In order to complete the melodic restoration, Dom Mocquereau published before the prefaces to the volumes of the *Paléographie* a number of theoretical and practical works on the traditional rules for the performance of the Gregorian chant: *L'Art grégorien ; Petit traité de psalmodie ; Méthode de chant grégorien* (1899) ;   *Le Nombre musical grégorien ou Rythmique grégorienne* (1908).   F. R^L.

MODERATO, ' in moderate time,' or ' mod-erately.'   This direction is used either singly as a mark of time, or as qualifying some other mark of time, as Allegro moderato, or Andante moderato, when it has the result of lessening the force of the simple direction.   Thus Allegro moderato will be slightly slower than Allegro alone, and Andante moderato slightly faster than Andante.   M.

MODERNE, JACQUES, also GRAND JACQUES (on account of his stoutness) or ' PINGUENTO,' probably from his birthplace (?) in Istria ; early 16th-century musician ; maître de chapelle at Notre Dame du Confort at Lyons, where he established a music-printing business and pub-lished between 1532–67 several books of masses, motets, chansons, including motets and chan-

sons of his own composition which appear to be lost (*Q.-L.* ; *Riemann*).

MODES, ECCLESIASTICAL.   All mediæval art-music is based upon a system of eight modes. This system is the result of a long, intricate and controverted history ; and it will be best explained by an historical method of treatment

HISTORY—THE GREEK SYSTEM.—The first question that arises is with regard to the anti-quity of the modes.   It has been taken for granted that when ancient Greek writers such as Plato and Aristotle speak of certain *Har-moniai* (ἁρμονίαι) distinguished by Greek tribal names as Dorian, Lydian, Phrygian, etc., they are referring to modes such as were in use in the later Middle Ages under those names.   In the article GREEK MUSIC reasons have been given to prove that this is a false assumption, and to show that the groups of notes described as Dorian, Phrygian, etc., by the Greek writers of classical times were distinguished from one another by pitch and grouping, and not, properly speaking, by tonality.

Now the mediæval modal system is one which depends on differences of tonality, and is comparatively indifferent to pitch.   The history of the mediæval modes is therefore, to a con-siderable extent, the history of the evolution of tonality.   Tonality may be defined as the musi-cal character belonging to a mode or a melody by reason of the mutual relation of the notes employed.   It is determined chiefly by three things, (1) the range and sequence of the notes, and their relation to the two fixed points of (2) the Dominant, and (3) the Final.

The early Greek *Harmoniai* or groupings of notes and tetrachords were experimental in character.   One of them proved to be more valuable than all the rest, viz. the Octave-system (see MONOCHORD).   It came, in theory at any rate, to supersede all the others, though, they being no doubt associated with particular instruments, continued to be in practical use long after theory had advanced beyond them. This Octave-system represented only one form of tonality.   Variety was provided not by differ-ences of tonality but by differences of *genus* (γένος), the enharmonic, the chromatic and the diatonic *genera*.   (See GREEK MUSIC.)   In the diatonic genus (which alone need be taken into account for the present purpose) the tonality may be roughly described as that of the modern minor scale or mode, for the series of notes pre-sented tones and semitones in the following order ascending

T S T T S T T | T S T T, etc.

equivalent to the white notes of the pianoforte from A upwards.

A reader unaccustomed to the modes and the idea of tonality will realise what this implies by contrasting the T S T T S T T series of intervals of the modern minor scale or mode, with the familiar T T S T T T S series of the modern major scale or mode. This Greek diatonic system, standing as it did alone, afforded no sufficient opportunity for any idea of differences in tonality. Yet even so the Greeks began to see that the character of a melody depended upon its reference to a given note of the series. The fixed note in their series of notes was the Mese ($\mu\epsilon\sigma\eta$), the central note, which served as the hinge or meeting-point for the two conjunct tetrachords of the Octave-system (E–e), or in later days for the two octaves of the Perfect System (A–a). (See MONOCHORD.) Thus Aristotle called attention (*Probl.* xix. 20) to the way in which the character of a melody depended upon the relation of its notes to the constantly recurring Mese. Here are the first signs of the sense of tonality, and of a Mese or Dominant ; but they are only rudimentary as yet.

The *Harmoniai* and their designations fell into the background as the advance was made first towards the Octave-system and then the Perfect System ; thereupon that sense of pitch to which the early Greeks attached so much significance, was satisfied in a new way, viz. by transposing the Octave-system to different pitches. When thus set at a special pitch it was called $\tau\acute{o}\nu os$; and it was natural to give to these various $\tau\acute{o}\nu oi$ the same designation which had previously been employed to denote pitch, viz. Dorian, Lydian, etc.

Thus when the old (Dorian, Phrygian, Lydian, etc.) *Harmoniai* or groups went out of vogue, there came up in their place the (Dorian, Phrygian, Lydian, etc.) *Tonoi*, each formed by transposing the Octave-system to the Dorian, the Phrygian, the Lydian, etc., pitch. At this point there appeared upon the scene Aristoxenus of Tarentum, a pupil of Aristotle (*fl. c.* 310), the author of many developments in musical theory. He noted the indefiniteness of the old use of the designations Dorian, Phrygian, etc., and gave them a definite pitch. He made out a scheme of thirteen *Tonoi*, placing one on each semitone of the octave, and he attached to each some one of the old designations. The enumeration is found in two forms in the writings of Cleoneides, a disciple of Aristoxenus ; his own account is not extant. In the one form thirteen designations are used, in the other only eight, five of them being utilised for a pair of *Tonoi*.

			Mese.	
1 (highest).	Hypermixolydian		e	Hypermixolydian or Hyperphrygian.
2.	}	Mixolydian	d♯	Mixolydian or Hyperionian.
3.	}		d	Hyperdorian.
4.	}	Lydian	c♯	Lydian.
5.	}		c	Æolian.
6.	}	Phrygian	b	Phrygian.
7.	}		a♯	Ionian.
8.	.	Dorian	a	Dorian.
9.	}	Hypolydian	G♯	Hypolydian.
10.	}		G	Hypoæolian.
11.	}	Hypophrygian	F♯	Hypophrygian.
12.	}		F	Hypoionian.
13 (lowest).	Hypodorian		E	Hypodorian.

At a later date the Aristoxeneans raised the number to fifteen by adding a Hyperlydian and a Hyperæolian : the *Tonoi* thus fell into three groups of five each, the upper group distinguished by the prefix Hyper and the lower by the prefix Hypo.

This system of *Tonoi* or keys remained the chief feature of Greek musical theory for the next 500 years. It provided only for one tonality or mode, viz. that represented by the Octave-system, or later by the Perfect System of two octaves ; but it provided for it at every possible pitch. (See Vol. II. pp. 444-7.) Meanwhile advances were being made towards a fuller sense of tonality and towards the modal system.

Aristoxenus himself was active in this direction. He showed that as there are in the diatonic genus three different species of tetrachord possible, viz. those represented by the formulas T T S, T S T and S T T, so there are seven possible species of octave. In the writings of his followers (his own treatise unfortunately breaks off at this point) these are thus described :

1.	S T T S T T ^{m} T	{ Hypate Hypaton to Paramese	(B—b) Mixolydian.
2.	T T S T T ^{m} T S	{ Parhypate Hypaton to Trite Diezeugmenon	(C—c) Lydian.
3.	T S T T ^{m} T S T	{ Lichanos Hypaton to Paranete Diezeugmenon	(D—d) Phrygian.
4.	S T T ^{m} T S T T	{ Hypate Meson to Nete Diezeugmenon	(E—e) Dorian.
5.	T T ^{m} T S T T S	{ Parhypate Meson to Trite Hyperbolæon	(F—f) Hypolydian.
6.	T ^{m} T S T T S T	{ Lichanos Meson to Paranete Hyperbolæon	(G—g) Hypophrygian.
7.	^{m} T S T T S T T	{ Mese to Nete Hyperbolæon	(a—a') Hypodorian.

These seven octaves were distinguished from one another in range and sequence of intervals ; so far they exhibited the first element of tonality. But they were not distinguished from one another by difference of Mese or Dominant, and there is as yet no idea of a Final. The note Mese (=a) acted as Dominant throughout, and this accounts for the designations. Mixolydian, signifying high pitch, is given to No. 1 because it has its Mese at the highest point, Lydian at the next highest, and so on. The position is marked above by ^{m}. Thus the designations Mixolydian, Lydian, etc., here appear in inverse order as compared with their use for the *Tonoi* or keys. The contradiction is more apparent than real. In each case it is the Mese that determines the sense of pitch. In the *Tonoi*, being transpositions of the scale, the Mese varies actually in pitch just as all the other notes of the *Tonos* vary in pitch ; and the highest *Tonos* in range is the highest also in pitch. In the Seven Species of Octave, however, being mere sections of a fixed scale, the Mese is at a fixed pitch, and only varies relatively to the other notes of the octave. Consequently the octave which is the lowest in range gives the effect of the highest pitch, since its melodies group round the Mese, which is at the top of the Octave ; conversely, the octave which has the highest range gives the effect of low pitch, because of the prevalence of its lowest note. In other words, the designations are given to the *Tonoi* in regard to the actual pitch of the Mese, but to the Seven Species of Octave in regard to the relative pitch of the Mese (see Vol. II. p. 443).

This doctrine of the Seven Species of Octave remained without further development among the disciples of Aristoxenus until the advent of Ptolemy in the middle of the 2nd century A.D. Differences of pitch were now felt to be of less importance, and distinctions of species were more highly appreciated; the consequence was that interest was transferred from the *Tonoi* or keys, which merely gave the same scale at different pitches, to the Seven Octaves, which represented different species. Ptolemy reduced the *Tonoi* to seven in number, equating them to the Seven Species of Octave, and using transposition as a way of setting all the species at a uniform pitch, but with varying signatures. When this was done it was natural to ascribe to each species a Mese of its own, which should be a real Mese or middle note of the octave, exercising the same function with regard to it that the original Mese exercised with regard to the original (Dorian) octave of the Perfect System. This necessitated the double nomenclature described in Vol. II. p. 447. According to the new method (κατὰ θέσιν) each species of octave could have a Mese as its central note, a Nete as its highest note, and so on. As each octave thus acquired its own Mese, which was not as formerly in a varying position but always the central note, the inverted series of denominations formerly given to the octaves became inappropriate, and the series of names was attached to the Seven Species of Octave in the same order in which it was attached to the *Tonoi* and not in the inverse order.

Thus Ptolemy's Seven Octaves, which we may now begin to call modes because they are distinguished by their tonality and valued accordingly, may be set down in tabular form thus : First as seven modes varying in pitch, but each formed of a section of the Perfect System or white notes of the pianoforte.

		Mese.		
1 (highest).	Mixolydian	(a—a') d	= Paranete Diezeugmenon.	
2.	Lydian	(G—g) c	= Trite Diezeugmenon.	
3.	Phrygian	(F—f) b	= Paramese.	
4.	Dorian	(E—e) a	= Mese.	
5.	Hypolydian	(D—d) G	= Lichanos Meson.	
6.	Hypophrygian	(C—c) F	= Parhypate Meson.	
7.	Hypodorian	(B—b) E	= Hypate Meson.	

(κατὰ θέσιν ... κατὰ δύναμιν)

Secondly, reduced by the system of *Tonoi* to uniform pitch but varying in signature :

| Mixolydian. | Lydian. | Phrygian. | Dorian. | Hypolydian. | Hypophrygian. | Hypodorian. |

The successors of Ptolemy, as it appears from the late Byzantine writer Bryennius, came to regard each of these modes as a pair of conjunct tetrachords meeting in Mese ; they then added

below a Proslambanomenos or disjunct note to make up the octave, thus repeating again the process which had taken place years before in the extension downwards of the two lower conjunct tetrachords of the Perfect System (see MONOCHORD) ; and the old names of the notes in the octave were reapplied to each mode in slightly altered form, thus : Proslambanomenos, Hypate, Parhypate, Lichanos, Mese, Parhypate, Lichanos, Nete.

The main results of these changes were as follows : (1) The Seven Species of Octave of the theorists became seven practical working modes,[1] distinguished from one another essentially by their different sequence of intervals, and only incidentally by difference of pitch. (2) The Mese became the regular Dominant of the mode : and (3) the modes ranged a note lower than they had previously done owing to the addition of the Proslambanomenos. Thus the Dorian mode is found to have its seat as ever in the octave from E upwards, with *a* as its Mese or Dominant : but it now descends to D. Similarly the Phrygian has *b* for its dominant and E for its lowest note : while the Lydian has *c* and F, the Mixolydian *d* and G.

So far it has been possible to trace the evolution of the modal system in the writings of the theorists. Two out of three chief features of tonality have emerged, viz. (1) the range and succession of the intervals in each mode, and (2) the idea of the Dominant. Hitherto, however, there is no sign of any idea of the importance of the Final, which is the third chief ingredient of tonality. The conception of the Dominant is traceable back as far as Aristotle, but the significance of the closing note of a melody had not as yet been scientifically recognised, at any rate by the theorists. At this point in the evolution the series of writers on the theory of music, who have hitherto been our guides, to all intents and purposes comes to an end. No Greek writers are forthcoming after the 4th century A.D. until Bryennius in the 14th ; the Latin writers do little to fill the gap, at any rate until the 9th. Boethius, Cassiodorus and Martianus Capella in the 5th and 6th centuries are of little value, as they merely repeat, after the manner of an encyclopædist, such information as they derived from the Greek writers. Happily at this date, when the theorists fail, there becomes available for the Western history a large collection of actual musical compositions in which the further evolution of the modal system may be traced.

THE ROMAN SCHOOL.—The developments in the West between the 6th and the 9th centuries

---

[1] Later followers of Ptolemy added a Hypermixolydian **Mode** thus making eight.

are bound up with the great music school (*Schola Cantorum*) of Rome. They go forward in silence ; for it is only when the Roman chant reaches the Frankish Empire that the silence is broken by fresh writings of theorists, called forth here, as in the case of the Liturgy, by the new ways recently imported from Rome. The early Roman Church was pre-eminently Greek in character and personnel, therefore its church music was not different in this respect from the Roman secular music which clung closely to the Greek traditions. From the 6th century onward the music school of the Roman Church grew in importance and organisation ; and, even when Greek ceased to be the liturgical language of the Roman Church, there is no reason to think that any break came in the continuity of the Greek tradition so far as the music was concerned. The bulk of the so-called GREGORIAN MUSIC (*q.v.*) was composed in these surroundings, and whatever importations there were at this period from outside were from Greek sources. It is therefore to be expected that the theory that lies behind the Gregorian music should prove to be in line with the Greek traditions. For a full discussion of the character of this music the reader is referred to the article PLAIN-SONG ; but one or two points must be taken into account here.

The bulk of the music falls into two classes, and is either responsorial or antiphonal in its style. Now the responsorial music, which is the older class of the two, is characterised by a Dominant note, which serves as the note on which the greater part of the text is recited ; but it sets no great store on the Final. It therefore corresponds with the state of development already reached and expounded. The antiphonal style was of later introduction, coming from the East in the 4th century. Here the Final is of greater moment, for the antiphon consists of a melody which has no reciting note, and in which, therefore, tonality is largely determined by the close. It is safe, therefore, to suppose that with the progress of the antiphonal style there went along a growth in the conception and importance of the Final. Meanwhile a transformation from simple to elaborate music was taking place, as musical proficiency grew within the Roman School. The responsorial class of music was more affected by it than the antiphonal. The elaborate embroideries which decorated the chant of the Graduals and other Responds tended to obscure the primitive reciting note ; the Final, however, was only brought into greater prominence by the process of elaboration. Consequently, as the music grew more ornate, tonality came to depend more upon the newly conceived Final and less upon the older conception of the Dominant. This change is one which may safely be said to have come about during this intervening period from the 5th to the 8th centuries in which the theorists are silent.

A more difficult change to account for is that by which the so-called ' plagal ' modes came into existence in their mediæval form. The germ of them is clearly discernible in the prefix ' Hypo,' which characterised the lowest three of the Seven Modes. But in Ptolemy's time these were not accounted of a different class from the rest ; they had the same general character (*mutatis mutandis*) ; and the prefix merely denoted that they were each in pitch a fourth below the mode with the corresponding designation. The mediæval plagal modes took from these their names and ranges, but they had not their independent position and other characteristics. Each plagal mode depended upon the corresponding authentic mode ; it had the same Final, and was so closely related to it that, when the modes came to be denoted by numbers, it was at first thought more natural to put the two under one number, only distinguishing them from one another by the term ' Authentic' and 'Plagal.' Thus the Greeks reckoned them as four pairs ; but the Latins, as they emancipated themselves from Greek influence, came to denote them by the numbers from one to eight.

			Range.	Domi-nant.	Final.
1st.	First Mode	Authentic (Dorian)	D—*d*	*a*	D
2nd.		Plagal (Hypodorian)	A—*a*	F	D
3rd.	Second Mode	Authentic (Phrygian)	E—*e*	*b*	E
4th.		Plagal (Hypophrygian)	B—*b*	*a*	E
5th.	Third Mode	Authentic (Lydian)	F—*f*	*c*	F
6th.		Plagal (Hypolydian)	C—*c*	*a*	F
7th.	Fourth Mode	Authentic (Mixolydian)	G—*g*	*d*	G
8th.		Plagal (Hypomixolydian)	D—*d*	*c*	G

This arrangement of eight modes in four pairs must be subsequent to the evolution of the idea of the Final ; for it is the Final that is made the main link between each pair of modes. It also seems to be subsequent to the decay of the Dominant in importance ; for while the Dominants of the authentic modes keep to the old line as being the Mese of the mode, those of the plagal modes are determined only with reference to the corresponding authentic Dominant, being normally a third lower.

It is further to be observed that a new mode has been added to the seven, viz. the Hypomixolydian (quite unlike the previous one of that name), which occupies the same octave as the Dorian, but in the new condition of things is entirely unlike it in any other respect.

There is also conceived to be a structural difference between authentic and plagal. The extra note that was added to the two conjunct tetrachords in the form of a Proslambanomenos (see above) came to be regarded, when the old Greek tetrachordal system faded, as forming with the lower tetrachord of the two a pentachord or fifth ; consequently, each authentic mode was looked upon as a pentachord with a tetrachord above it. This pentachord it shared with its plagal brother ; and thus a plagal mode was conversely viewed as a tetrachord with a pentachord above it. In the former case the Dominant (or ' Media ' as the Latins called it,

$=\mu\acute{\epsilon}\sigma\eta$) was the hinge or meeting-point of the two, and in the latter case the Final.

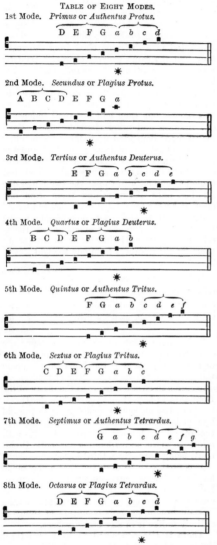

TABLE OF EIGHT MODES.
1st Mode. *Primus* or *Authentus Protus.*

2nd Mode. *Secundus* or *Plagius Protus.*

3rd Mode. *Tertius* or *Authentus Deuterus.*

4th Mode. *Quartus* or *Plagius Deuterus.*

5th Mode. *Quintus* or *Authentus Tritus.*

6th Mode. *Sextus* or *Plagius Tritus.*

7th Mode. *Septimus* or *Authentus Tetrardus.*

8th Mode. *Octavus* or *Plagius Tetrardus.*

This brief analysis tends to show that, though the exact genesis of the dual system of authentic and plagal modes cannot be traced, it proceeded along very natural lines, and arrived at a very convenient and symmetrical result. The development still went on under the Greek ægis, as the terminology would alone be sufficient to prove. Its date is a matter of more difficulty. The earliest literary mention of the system of eight modes, or Octoechos as the latest Greeks called it, is found in a table given in some editions of Boethius ; but as there is

no mention of it in the text it must be taken to be a later addition. The next mention is to be found in a passage of Alcuin of the end of the 8th century, where the system is spoken of as a matter of common knowledge. Among Greek writers (so far as they have been explored) an even greater conspiracy of silence prevails.[1] So literary evidence is entirely wanting. The history of the Schola Cantorum suggests the 6th or 7th century as a suitable date for such a settlement ; and this view of the case is amply borne out by an examination of the Gregorian music itself.

The older class, the responsorial music, demands in its highly elaborated form an eight-mode system. The Responds of the Hours, though they use various reciting notes for the Respond, employ normally for the ' Verse ' one of eight set formulas corresponding to the modes. Similarly in the antiphonal music there are the eight Gregorian tones corresponding also to the modes. (See PSALMODY.) These two facts alone are enough to prove that the music, as we now have it, presupposes the eight-mode system. Now there are many lines of evidence that converge to show that the main bulk and nucleus of this music is to be dated as belonging to the 6th century. A persistent tradition ascribes the final regulation of it to St. Gregory (590–604). The festivals and other occasions for which the music was written are as a rule earlier than his date ; and the festivals of later origin differ markedly from the pre-Gregorian festivals in having borrowed music instead of original music provided for them ; this is especially the case in regard to the Mass. Further, the text of the Latin Bible employed is an ancient one that was for most purposes superseded in the 5th and 6th centuries. These and other considerations all point in the same direction. From them it may be concluded, though with some considerable hesitation owing to the difference of views among students of the question, that the eight-mode system lay behind the great plain-song compositions that form the musical *corpus* of the Western Church ; and must, therefore, have arisen at least as early as the 6th century.

FRANKISH THEORISTS ; NINTH CENTURY.— When literary evidence as to the modes again becomes available in the Carlovingian era, the system is regarded as an old-established tradition. Greek theory still holds the field, and Aurelian, the first of a new group of writers that gives any full discussion or statement of the modes, quotes Greek teachers as his authorities. In fact the theory was already so ancient that some of it was no longer intelligible to the Greek teachers, and the actual

---

[1] If it were possible to discover what was the Octoechos of the Greek Church, say in the days of St. John of Damascus, we should probably have the clue to the formulation of the system of the Ecclesiastical Modes ; but the Greek Church has lost the system, and only preserves a conventional distinction, not a modal one, in its Octoechos. Failing the East, we turn back to the West.

practice of liturgical singers had in some respects moved away from it. One of the difficulties, therefore, that confronted the Franks, as new disciples of the *Cantilena Romana,* was that of reconciling the practice and the theory; indeed, we owe the treatises written in the 9th century, by such writers as Aurelian, Regino and Odo, to the fact that such discrepancies existed, and that the Franks desired to reconcile them.

It will be well to sum up what was clear and fixed at this important epoch before going on to discuss what was doubtful or what was changing in practice.

(1) The Greek Perfect System was the basis of all. This gave the following possibilities.

Γ A B C D E F G a b♮ bb c d e f g a'

The range was ample for vocal purposes; it was even extended on occasions one further note downwards (φ), and several notes upwards; while the use of the ♭ gave an opportunity not only for transposition but also for obtaining some variety by the use of an accidental. Moreover, by combining transposition and the use of the ♭ some further chromatic effects could be obtained, and were in fact employed.

(2) This range was subdivided into tetrachords, and this arrangement accorded with the position of the eight modes, for the lowest tetrachord comprised the four lowest limits of the plagal modes: the next comprised the four Finals, and was always so described; the third in fact comprised the four Dominants (Mese) of the authentic modes, but it was not so described.

(3) The doctrine of the Final was very clearly held, though the doctrine of the Dominant had almost entirely dropped out of sight.

(4) The distinction between authentic and plagal was clearly drawn in theory, though it was being found a difficult task to draw the line in practice. No tradition survived as to the origin of the distinction. (The fable that St. Ambrose made the authentic modes and St. Gregory the plagal is of much later date.) It is only supposed that the plagal were devised to include the melodies of lower range, and no significance is attached to the difference of dominant between the authentic and plagal.

Yet even with all these four points clear, there remained much for the new musicians to do in the way of exposition and development of the modal system. They had before them (1) a great collection of masterpieces which had been in use two hundred years and more, (2) an eight-mode system of Greek origin and unknown antiquity, which even their Greek teachers could not fully explain, and (3) works of theorists (such as we have already had in review) extending only down to the 5th or 6th century and exhibiting the theory at an inchoate stage of development.

The works of Boethius and the rest of the theorists were, so far as the modes went, far more a source of mystification than of enlightenment. Valiant and clumsy attempts were made by the writers of the 9th and 10th centuries to reconcile the earlier with the later, the past theory and the actual practice (*e.g.* in the nomenclature of the modes); but they only resulted in much confusion both at the time and since. When, however, this element is eliminated from their writings, there remains a real development and a true exposition of the modal system to be found even in the earliest of the Frankish writers; and when once Guido d' Arezzo had had the courage to say that ' the book of Boethius is of no use to singers, but only to philosophers,' emancipation had come, and the road of progress lay open to future generations.

The chief features of the modal system which we have already brought to light, *e.g.* the combination of pentachord and tetrachord in the authentic, and its inversion in the plagal, were duly expounded by these writers. They have also the credit of having resisted an attempt to make twelve modes instead of eight; they rightly pointed out that twelve were quite unnecessary, granted the power to transpose and the use of the *b♭*. They laboured to expound and maintain the real tonal independence of the modes; and this in itself was no easy task in the days before Guido when the singers had in the neums no absolute guide as to the intervals and notes which they were to sing.

The chief innovation for which this period was responsible was the change of the Dominant of the third mode from the dubious note *b* to *c*; it took place in the 10th or 11th century, and, though the improvement was universally accepted in theory and the innovation was adopted in the most prominent position possible, *i.e.* in the case of the reciting note of the third tone, which thenceforward was *c* not *b*, the change was never carried out thoroughly, and plenty of traces of the old use of *b* as Dominant have survived.

The main difficulties that the writers of this period had to face lay in two very practical directions, and were caused by a change in practice. Both the antiphons and the responds had ceased to be used in the old way, and much trouble was caused to the singers in consequence. In many of the responds the custom had arisen of repeating, after the verse or verses, only the latter part of the respond itself instead of the whole. It thus became necessary to lay down rules for the establishing of a proper musical relation between the end of the verse and the opening notes of the repeat. A similar process of shortening had caused the antiphon to be repeated no longer after each verse of the psalm, but only once or twice in the course of the psalmody. Now the endings of the tones had always been carefully adapted so as to fit on to the opening phrases of the antiphons; but when the repetition of the antiphon decayed, this close intimacy was no longer so necessary. This change of custom affected also the view taken of the tonality of the antiphon. As originally used, its opening phrase was all-important; and it was assigned to this or that mode (and associated therefore with this or that tone) according to the character of its opening. When, however, it came to be used rarely, or only once at the end of the psalm, the end of the antiphon and its Final became far more important than its opening; consequently, according to the newer plan, its tonality was determined no longer by its *incipit* but by its last note.

The difficulty with the Responds was soon settled once for all, by making, where necessary, some slight but permanent accommodation in the music; but the other difficulty was a more or less permanent one; the mediæval tonals continued to offer varying solutions of it, and out of it there grew such further developments of modal theory as the settlement of the Absolute Initials (see INITIALS, ABSOLUTE), *i.e.* the notes in each mode on which a melody may begin.

The development that produced the sequences (see SEQUENCE) entailed a further modification in the modal theory that went far to break down again the distinction between authentic and plagal. In many cases the sequence-melodies were written, as it were, in two registers; their compass, therefore, exceeded the normal limits assigned to any one mode by the theorists of the 10th to 12th centuries (who in this respect were much more strict than the original writers of the music had been); it then became usual to regard them as being both in the authentic and in the corresponding plagal mode.

LATER INFLUENCES.—This was the last modification of any great moment that plain-song brought to the theory of the modes. Such other modifications as came to it between the 12th and the 16th centuries were due principally to two other causes, (1) the invasion of popular music or the spirit of folk-song, and (2) the growth of harmonised and measured music.

The tonality that was congenial to folk-song especially in France was one that had always been uncongenial to the classical plain-song, viz. the scale which resulted from the uniform use of the $b\flat$ with the fifth and sixth modes, and is identical with the modern major scale or mode. This pair of modes had always been the least used of all the four; without the flat, there was too much tritone in it, even for

mediæval ears that were not so sensitive in that respect as modern ones; with the flat, the mode did not much differ from the fourth pair except in having a semitone below the final, *i.e.* in possessing a leading note, which from the point of view of unharmonised music was rather a disadvantage than an advantage. The major scale, however, is the joy of folk-song; and, as such, it tended to invade the art-music and even to claim a place cheek by jowl with the severe ecclesiastical plain-song.

This tendency was still further emphasised by the growing art of harmony. When at last the perfect close was invented it became the centre of the harmonic art, and the leading note became a necessity. The F mode with $b\flat$ and the C mode without it, became favourites; other modes had to submit to chromatic alteration in the interests of harmony. For a surprisingly long time the feeling for the old tonality was so strong that this alteration had to be disguised (see MUSICA FICTA), yet it was clear that eventually it would have to yield before the steady pressure of the advancing art of harmony. The period of the rise of harmony is thus the period of the decay of the old tonality, and of the modal system. The ancient modes gradually disappeared until only the major and minor modes remain. A good deal of richness in melodic beauty was sacrificed in the process, and modern melody, even with all its chromatic freedom, has not such a wide range of variety as the old modal system afforded. No one will doubt that the gains in harmony more than compensated for the losses in melody; but it must be emphasised that all was not clear gain.

The modal system as handled and transformed by the pioneers of modern harmony is a matter of far less interest, for all was in a continual state of transition; and though at certain points a halt seems to be called and a permanent interest stirred by the genius of Dunstable, or of the great Flemings, or Palestrina and his contemporaries, yet from the point of view of harmony the old modal system cannot be regarded as anything else but a slavery, from which it was desirable that the polyphonic school should work its escape as soon as possible.

In the closing stages of the decay an attempt was made to revive the proposal to reckon twelve (or even fourteen) modes. (See DODECA-CHORDON.) There was much more to be said for this from the point of view of polyphony in the 16th century than there had been in the 9th from the point of view of plain-song; but the modes were then a vanishing quantity, and the enumeration is only misleading if it is applied to the classical plain-song of earlier days. The Renaissance sent the musicians back afresh to the old writers on musical theory, but the attempts of Gafori and his followers to combine the old and new were as little successful in the 16th century as they had been in the 9th ; they added nothing but some fresh elements of confusion to the theory of the modes.

The following tables of the fourteen modes as given by Glareanus may be compared with the table given above to represent the eight modes of the mediæval plain-song :

mediæval music, Gevaert has also put forward a view of the evolution of the mediæval modes out of the ancient in his *Mélopée antique,* Ghent, 1895—a book of great value even to those who cannot accept his theories. Another view, also based on Westphal, is given by Gaisser in his *Système musical de l'Église Grecque* (Rome, 1901). The account given above differs entirely from these as regards the mediæval period, and follows Monro and Macran as regards the earlier history. See GREEK MUSIC.

W. H. F.

THE MODES IN POLYPHONIC MUSIC. — Besides its Final and Dominant, every

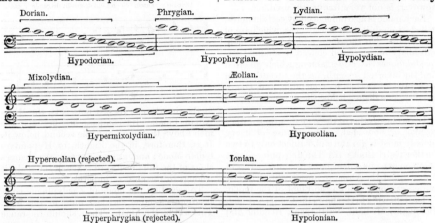

Dorian.   Phrygian.   Lydian.

Hypodorian.   Hypophrygian.   Hypolydian.

Mixolydian.   Æolian.

Hypermixolydian.   Hypoæolian.

Hyperæolian (rejected).   Ionian.

Hyperphrygian (rejected).   Hypoionian.

The following are the eight representative melodies (or Neums) devised in the later Middle Ages in order to show off the special characteristics of each mode :

mode is distinguished by two other highly characteristic notes—its Mediant and Participant.

The Mediant — so called from its position

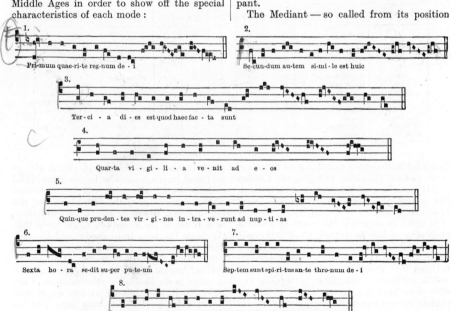

1.
Pri-mum quae-ri-te reg-num de - i

2.
Se-cun-dum au-tem si-mi - le est huic

3.
Ter - ci - a di - es est quod haec fac - ta sunt

4.
Quar-ta vi - gi - li - a ve - nit ad e - os

5.
Quin-que pru-den - tes vir - gi - nes in - tra - ve - runt ad nup - ti - as

6.
Sexta ho - ra se-dit super pu-te-um

7.
Sep-tem sunt spi-ri-tus an-te thro-num de - i

8.
Oc-to sunt be - a - ti - tu-di-nes

BIBL.—The ancient authorities are enumerated in the article headed SCRIPTORES. Among modern writers the following may be named. Greek Music—Westphal, *Harmonik und Melopoie der Griechen,* 1863, and Gevaert, *Histoire de la musique d'antiquité,* Ghent, 1875 and 1881 These writers and their followers are opposed by Monro, *The Modes of Ancient Greek Music,* Oxford, 1894, and Macran, *Harmonics of Aristoxenus,* Oxford, 1902. As regards

between the Final and Dominant—is always the third of the scale in the authentic modes, unless that note should happen to be B, in which case C is substituted for it. In the plagal modes its position is less uniform. The Participant is an auxiliary note, generally in the immediate neighbourhood of the Mediant in authentic modes, and, in the plagal forms, coincident with the Dominant of the corresponding authentic scale. Some modes have a second Participant ; and one has a second Mediant, which, however, is not very frequently used.

Each mode is also influenced by certain notes, called its modulations or cadences, which are of two kinds. To these are added two or more subsidiary notes, called conceded modulations (*modulationes concessae*), among which we often find the inverted seventh, *i.e.* the seventh taken an octave lower than its true pitch, and, consequently, one degree below the natural compass of the scale.

Upon one or other of these modulations, either regular or conceded, every phrase of every melody must begin and end, subject only to two further restrictions : (i.) The first phrase must begin on one of a somewhat less ample series of notes, called the Absolute Initials ; (ii.) The last phrase can only end on the Final of the mode.

The following table shows the Compass, Final, Dominant, Mediant, Participant, Regular and

that the mode has been transposed ; and the true Final will then lie a fourth below the written one. For example, the plain - song melody ' Angelus autem Domini ' has no B flat

Ange-lus   autem   do - mi - ni descendit de cae-lo   et

ac - ce - dens re - vol-vit la - pi - dem   et se - de-bat

su-per   e - um, al - le - lu - ya, al - le - lu - ya.

at the signature. Its last note is G, the Mixolydian Final. Its compass lies between the fifth above that note and the second below it. It is, therefore, in the Eighth, or Hypomixolydian Mode ; and, as its range falls two degrees short of the full downward range of the scale, it belongs to the class of imperfect melodies.

To ascertain the mode of a polyphonic composition, examine the last note in the bass. This will be the Final. Then, should the range

Modulations.

					Regular.			Conceded.	
Numbers.	Names of the Modes.	Range.	Fin.	Dom.	Med.	Part.	Mod. Con.	Absolute Initials.
I.	Dorian.	D—D	D	A	F	G	C[1]. E	C[1]. D. F. G. A.
II.[2]	Hypodorian.	A—A	D	F	E	A. A[3]	C. G	A. C. D. E[4]. F
III.	Phrygian.	E—E	E	C	G	A. B	D[1]. F	E. F. G[4]. C
IV.[2]	Hypophrygian.	B—B	E	A	G	C. F	D. B[2]	C. D. E. F. G[4]. A[4]
V.	Lydian.	F—F	F	C	A	G	B. D. E	F. A. C
VI.[2]	Hypolydian.	C—C	F	A	D	C[6]	B[1]. G. B (♭)	C. D[4]. F
VII.	Mixolydian.	G—G	G	D	C	A	B. E	G. A[4] B. C. D
VIII.[2]	Hypomixolydian.	D—D	G	C	F. A	D	B. D[3]	C[1]. D. F. G. A. C
IX.	Æolian.	A—A	A	E	C	D	G[1]. B	G[1]. A. C. D. E
X.[2]	Hypoæolian.	E—E	A	C	B	E. E[3]	G. D	E. G. A. B[4]. C
{ XI.	Locrian.	B—B	B	G	D	F	A[1]. C	B. C[4]. D. G }
{ XII.[2]	Hypolocrian.	F—F	B	E	C	C	A. F[3]	G. A. B. C. D[4]. E[4] }
XIII. (or XI.)	Ionian.	C—C	C	G	E	D	F. A. B	C. D[5]. E. G
XIV. (or XII.)[2]	Hypoionian.	G—G	C	E	A	G[6]	F[1]. D. F	C. D[5]. G. A

Conceded Modulations, and Absolute Initials of every mode in the series, including the Locrian and Hypolocrian, which, in spite of their manifest imperfection, have sometimes been used in secular music.

In order to ascertain the mode in which a plain-song melody is written, observe the last note, which will, of course, show the required Final. Should the compass of the melody lie between that Final and its octave, the mode will be authentic. Should it lie between the fifth above and the fourth below, it will be plagal. Should it extend throughout the entire range, from the fourth below the Final to the octave above it, it will be mixed. Should there be a B flat at the signature, it will indicate

of the *canto fermo*—which will almost always be found in the tenor—lie between the Final and its octave, the mode will be authentic. Should it lie between the fifth above and the fourth below, it will be plagal. Should there be a B flat at the signature, it will show that the mode has been transposed ; and the true Final will then lie a fourth below the last bass note. Thus, Palestrina's motet, ' Dies sanctificatus,' has no B flat at the signature. The last note in the bass is G. The compass of the *canto fermo*, as exhibited in the tenor, lies, almost entirely, between that note and its octave. The motet, therefore, is in the seventh, or Mixolydian Mode. The same composer's Missa, ' Aeterna Christi munera,' has a B flat at the signature, and is, therefore, transposed. The last note in the bass is F, the fourth below which is C—the Ionian Final.

1 The Inverted 7th.   2 Plagal Modes.
3 The 5th above the Final.
4 Rarely used in an Absolute Initial.
5 Used as an Absolute Initial chiefly in polyphonic music.
6 The lowest note of the Mode.

The compass of the *canto fermo*, in the tenor, lies between the transposed Final and its octave. Consequently, the Mass is in the Thirteenth or Ionian Mode, transposed.

According to strict law, it is as necessary for the *canto fermo* to end on the Final of the mode as the bass ; but, when the last cadence is a very elaborate one, it frequently contents itself with just touching that note, and then glancing off to others, after the manner of what we should now call a *coda*. (See POLYPHONY.)

In order to accommodate the range of 'unequal' voices, it constantly happens that the treble and tenor are made to sing in an authentic mode, while the alto and bass sing in a plagal one, and *vice versa*. In these cases the true character of the mode is always decided by the compass of the *canto fermo*.   W. S. R.

MODULATION is the process of passing out of one key into another.

In classical harmonic music, especially in its instrumental branches, it is essential that the harmonies should be grouped according to their keys ; that is, that they should be connected together for periods of appreciable length by a common relation to a definite tonic or keynote. If harmonies belonging essentially to one key are irregularly mixed up with harmonies which are equally characteristic of another, an impression of obscurity arises ; but when a chord which evidently belongs to a foreign key follows naturally upon a series which was consistently characteristic of another, and is itself followed consistently by harmonies belonging to a key to which it can be referred, modulation has taken place, and a new tonic has supplanted the former one as the centre of a new circle of harmonies.

THREE TYPES.—The various forms of process by which a new key is gained are generally distributed into three classes—Diatonic, Chromatic and Enharmonic. The first two are occasionally applied to the ends of modulation as well as to the means. That is to say, Diatonic would be defined as modulation to relative keys, and Chromatic to others than relative. This appears to strain unnecessarily the meaning of the terms, since Diatonic and Chromatic apply properly to the contents of established keys, and not to the relations of different shifting ones, except by implication.

Moreover, if a classification is to be consistent, the principles upon which it is founded must be uniformly applied. Hence if a class is distinguished as Enharmonic in relation to the means (as it must be), other classes cannot safely be classed as Diatonic and Chromatic in relation to ends, without liability to confusion. And lastly, the term Modulation itself clearly implies the process and not the result. Therefore in this place the classification will be taken to apply to the means and not to the end—to the process by which the modulation is accomplished and not the keys which are thereby arrived at.

(1) The Diatonic forms, then, are such as are effected by means of notes or chords which are exclusively diatonic in the keys concerned. Thus in the following example (Bach, *Wohlt. Clav.* Bk. 2, No. 12) :

the chord at * indicates that F has ceased to be the tonic, as it is not referable to the group of harmonies characteristic of that key. However, it is not possible to tell from that chord alone to what key it is to be referred, as it is equally a diatonic harmony in either B♭, E♭ or A♭ ; but as the chords which follow all belong consistently to A♭, that note is obviously the tonic of the new key, and as the series is Diatonic throughout it belongs to the Diatonic class of modulations.

(2) The Chromatic is a most ill-defined class of modulations ; and it is hardly to be hoped that people will ever be sufficiently careful in small matters to use the term with anything approaching to clear and strict uniformity of meaning. Some use it to denote any modulation in the course of which there appear to be a number of accidentals—which is perhaps natural but obviously superficial. Others again apply the term to modulations from one main point to another through several subordinate transitions which touch remote keys. The objection to this definition is that each step in the subordinate transitions is a modulation in itself, and as the classification is to refer to the means, it is not consistent to apply the term to the end in this case, even though subordinate. There are further objections based upon the strict meaning of the word Chromatic itself, which must be omitted for lack of space. This reduces the limits of chromatic modulation to such as is effected through notes or chords which are chromatic in relation to the keys in question. Genuine examples of this kind are not so common as might be supposed ; the following example (Beethoven, op. 31, No. 3), where passage is made from E♭ to C, is consistent enough for illustration :

(3) The Enharmonic, which tends to be more and more conspicuous in modern music, is such as turns mainly upon the translation of intervals which, according to the fixed distribution of notes by equal temperament, are identical, into terms which represent different harmonic relations. Thus the minor seventh, G–F, appears to be the same interval as the augmented sixth G–E♯; but the former belongs to the key of C, and the latter either to B or F♯, according to the context. Again, the chord which is known as the diminished seventh is frequently quoted as affording such great opportunities for modulation, and this it does chiefly enharmonically; for the notes of which it is composed being at equal distances from each other can severally be taken as third, fifth, seventh, or ninth of the root of the chord, and the chord can be approached as if belonging to any one of these roots, and quitted as if derived from any other.

Enharmonic treatment really implies a difference between the intervals represented, and this is actually perceived by the mind in many cases. In some especially marked instances it is probable that most people with a tolerable musical gift will feel the difference with no more help than a mere indication of the relations of the intervals. Thus in the succeeding example the true major sixth represented by the A♭–F in (a) would have the ratio 5 : 3 (= 125 : 75), whereas the diminished seventh represented by G♯–F♮ in (b) would have the ratio 128 : 75; the former is a consonance and the latter, theoretically, a rough dissonance, and though they are both represented by the same notes in our system, the impression produced by them is to a certain extent proportionate to their theoretical rather than to their actual constitution.

Hence it appears to follow that in enharmonic modulation we attempt to get at least some of the effects of intervals smaller than semitones; but the indiscriminate and ill-considered use of the device will certainly tend to deaden the

musical sense, which helps us to distinguish the true relations of harmonies through their external apparent uniformity.

SALIENT DEVICES.—A considerable portion of the actual processes of modulation is effected by means of notes which are used as pivots. A note or notes which are common to a chord in the original key and to a chord in the key to which the modulation is made, are taken advantage of to strengthen the connexion of the harmonies while the modulation proceeds; as in the following modulation from G♯ major to B major in Schubert's Fantasie-Sonata, op. 78.

This device is found particularly in transitory modulation, and affords peculiar opportunities for subtle transitions. Examples also occur where the pivot notes are treated enharmonically, as in the following example from the chorus 'Sein Odem ist schwach' in Graun's 'Tod Jesu':

These pivot-notes are, however, by no means indispensable. Modulations are really governed by the same laws which apply to any succession of harmonies whatsoever, and the possibilities of modulatory device are in the end chiefly dependent upon intelligible order in the progression of the parts. It is obvious that a large proportion of chords which can succeed each other naturally—that is, without any of the parts having melodic intervals which it is next to impossible to follow—will have a note or notes in common; and such notes are as useful to connect two chords in the same key as they are to keep together a series which constitute a modulation. But it has never been held indispensable that successive chords should be so connected, though in earlier stages of harmonic music it may have been found helpful; and in the same way, while there were any doubts as to the means and order of modulation, pivot-notes may have been useful as leading strings, but when a broader and freer conception of the nature of the modern system has been arrived at, it will be found that though pivot-notes may be valuable for particular purposes, the range of modulatory device is not limited to such successions as can contain them, but only to such as do not contain inconceivable progression of parts. As an instance, we may take the progression from the dominant seventh of any key to the tonic chord of the key which is represented by the flat submediant of the original key : as from the chord of the seventh on G to the common chord of A♭ ; of which we have an excellent example near the beginning of the Leonora overture, No. 3. Another remarkable instance to the point occurs in the trio of the third movement of a quartet of Mozart's in B♭, as follows :

Key D♭.   Key C Minor.

Other examples of modulation without pivot-notes may be noticed at the beginning of Beethoven's Egmont overture, and of his sonata in E minor, op. 90 (bars 2 and 3), and of Wagner's ' Götterdämmerung ' (bars 9 and 10).

An impression appears to have been prevalent with some theorists that modulation ought to proceed through a chord which was common to both the keys between which the modulation takes place. The principle is logical and easy of application, and it is true that a great number of modulations are explicable on that basis ; but inasmuch as there are a great number of examples which are not, even with much latitude of explanation, it will be best not to enter into a discussion of so complicated a point in this place. It will be enough to point out that the two principles of pivot-notes and of ambiguous pivot-chords between them cover so much ground that it is not easy to find progressions in which either one or the other does not occur— and even though in a very great majority of instances one or the other may really form the bond of connexion in modulatory passages, the frequency of their occurrence is not a proof of their being indispensable. The following passage from the first act of ' Die Meistersinger ' is an example of a modulation in which they are both absent :

The real point of difficulty in modulation is not the manner in which the harmonies belong-

ing to different keys can be made to succeed one another, but the establishment of the new key, especially in cases where it is to be permanent. This is effected in various ways. Frequently some undoubted form of the dominant harmony of the new key is made use of to confirm the impression of the tonality, and modulation is often made through some phase of that chord to make its direction clear, since no progression has such definite tonal force as that from dominant to tonic. Mozart again, when he felt it necessary to define the new key very clearly, as representing a definite essential feature in the form of a movement, often goes at first beyond his point, and appears to take it from the rear. For instance, if his first section is in C, and he wishes to cast the second section and produce what is called his second subject in the dominant key G, instead of going straight to G and staying there, he passes rapidly by it to its dominant key D, and having settled well down on the tonic harmony of that key, uses it at last as a dominant point of vantage from which to take G in form. The first movement of the quartet in C, from bar 22 to 34 of the allegro, will serve as an illustration. Another mode is that of using a series of transitory modulations between one permanent key and another. This serves chiefly to obliterate the sense of the old key, and to make the mind open to the impression of the new one directly its permanency becomes apparent. The plan of resting on the dominant harmony for a long while before passing definitely to the subjects or figures which are meant to characterise the new key is an obvious means of enforcing it ; of which the return to the first subject in the first movement of Beethoven's Waldstein sonata is a strong example. In fact insistence on any characteristic harmony or on any definite group of harmonies which clearly represent a key is a sure means of indicating the object of a modulation, even between keys which are remote from one another.

In transitory modulations it is less imperative to mark the new key strongly, since subordinate keys are rightly kept in the background, and though they may be used so as to produce a powerful effect, yet if they are too much insisted upon, the balance between the more essential and the unessential keys may be upset. But even in transitory modulations, in instrumental music especially, it is decidedly important that each group which represents a key, however short, should be distinct in itself. In recitative, obscurity of tonality is not so objectionable, as appears both in Bach and Handel ; and the modern form of melodious recitative, which often takes the form of sustained melody of an emotional cast, is similarly often associated with subtle and closely woven modulations, especially when allied with words. Of recitative forms which show analogous freedom of modulation in purely instrumental works, there are examples both by Bach and Beethoven, as in an adagio in a toccata in D minor and the Fantasia Cromatica by the former, and in the introduction to the last movement of the A♭ pianoforte sonata (op. 110) of the latter.

When transitory modulations succeed one another somewhat rapidly they may well be difficult to follow if they are not systematised into some sort of appreciable order. This is frequently effected by making them progress by regular steps. In Mozart and Haydn especially we meet with the simplest forms of succession, which generally amount to some such order as the roots of the chord falling fifths or rising fourths, or rising fourths and falling thirds successively. The following example from Mozart's C major quartet is clearly to the point :

etc.

Bach affords some remarkably forcible examples, as in the chorus 'Mit Blitzen und Donner' in the Matthew Passion, and in the last movement of the fantasia for organ in G (B.-G. xxxviii. p. 81), in which the bass progresses slowly by semitones downwards from C♯ to D. A passage quoted by Marx at the end of the second volume of his *Kompositionslehre* from the 'Christe Eleison' in Bach's A major [1] Mass is very fine and characteristic ; the succession of transitions is founded on a bass which progresses as follows :

etc.

In music of a later date a common form is that in which the succession of key-notes is by rising or falling semitones, as in the following passage from the first movement of the Eroica Symphony :

etc.

Of this form there are numerous examples in Chopin, as in the latter part of the ballade in A♭, and in the prelude in the same key (No. 17). Beethoven makes use of successions of thirds in the same way ; of which the most remarkable example is the largo which precedes the fugue in the pianoforte sonata in B♭, op. 106. In this there are fully eighteen successive steps of thirds downwards, most of them minor.[2] This instance also points to a feature which is important to note. The successions are not perfectly symmetrical, but are purposely distributed with a certain amount of irregularity so as to relieve them from the obviousness which is often ruinous to the effect of earlier examples. The divisions represented by each step are severally variable in length, but the sum total is a complete impression based upon an appreciable system ; and this result is far more artistic than the examples where the form is so obvious that it might almost have been measured out with a pair of compasses.[3]

This point leads to the consideration of another striking device of Beethoven's, namely, the use of a caesura in modulation, which serves a similar purpose to the irregular distribution of successive modulations. A most striking example is that in the prestissimo of the pianoforte sonata in E major, op. 109, in bars 104 and 105, where he leaps from the major chord of the supertonic to the minor of the tonic, evidently cutting short the ordinary process of supertonic, dominant and tonic ; and the effect of this sudden irruption of the original key and subject before the ordinary and expected progressions are concluded is most remarkable. In the slow movement of Schumann's sonata in G minor there is a passage which has a similar happy effect, where the leap is made from the dominant seventh of the key of D♭ to the tonic chord of C to resume the first subject, as follows :

etc.

AN HISTORICAL SURVEY.—In the study of
the art of music it is important to have a clear
idea of the manner in which the function and
resources of modulation have been gradually
realised. It will be best, therefore, at the risk
of going occasionally over the same ground
twice, to give a short consecutive review of the
aspect it presents along the stream of constant
production.

To a modern ear of any musical capacity
modulation appears a very simple and easy
matter, but when harmonic music was only
beginning to be felt, the force even of a single
key was but doubtfully realised, and the
relation of different keys to one another was
almost out of the range of human conception.
Musicians of those days no doubt had some
glimmering sense of a field being open before
them, but they did not know what the problems
were which they had to solve. It is true that
even some time before the beginning of the
17th century they must have had a tolerably
good idea of the distribution of notes which we
call a key, but they probably did not regard it
as an important matter, and looked rather to
the laws and devices of counterpoint, after the
old polyphonic manner, as the chief means by
which music was to go on as it had done before.
Hence in those great polyphonic times of
Palestrina and Lasso, and even later in some
quarters, there was no such thing as modulation
in our sense of the word. They were gradually
absorbing into their material certain accidentals
which the greater masters found out how to use
with effect ; and these being incorporated with
the intervals which the old church modes
afforded them, gave rise to successions and
passages in which they appear to us to wander
with uncertain steps from one nearly related
key to another ; whereas in reality they were
only using the actual notes which appeared to
them to be available for artistic purposes,
without considering whether their combinations
were related to a common tonic in the sense
which we recognise, or not. Nevertheless, this
process of introducing accidentals irregularly

was the ultimate means through which the art
of modulation was developed. For the musical
sense of these composers, being very acute,
would lead them to consider the relations of the
new chords which contained notes thus modified,
and to surround them with larger and larger
groups of chords which in our sense would be
considered to be tonally related ; and the very
smoothness and softness of the combinations to
which they were accustomed would ensure a
gradual approach to consistent tonality, though
the direction into which their accidentals turned
them was rather uncertain and irregular, and
not so much governed by any feeling of the
effects of modulation as by the constitution of
the ecclesiastical scales. Examples of this are
given in the article HARMONY ; and reference
may also be made to a pavin and a fantasia by
our great master, Orlando Gibbons, in ' Parthenia,' republished in the ' Trésor des pianistes,'
in Pauer's ' Old English Music,' and (fantasia
alone) in Dannreuther's *Ornamentation*. In
these there are remarkably fine and strong
effects produced by means of accidentals ; but
the transitions are to modern ideas singularly
irregular. Gibbons appears to slip from one
tonality to another more than six times in as
many bars, and to slide back into his original
key as if he had never been away. In some of
his vocal works he presents broader expanses of
distinct tonality, but of the power of the effect
of modulation on an extended scale he can have
had but the very slightest possible idea. About
his time and a little later in Italy, among such
musicians as Carissimi and Cesti, the outlines
of the modern art were growing stronger.
They appreciated the sense of pure harmonic
combinations, though they lost much of the
force and dignity of the polyphonic school ;
and they began to use simple modulations, and
to define them much as a modern would do,
but with the simplest devices possible. Throughout the 17th century the system of keys was
being gradually matured, but their range was
extraordinarily limited, and the interchange of
keys was still occasionally irregular. Corelli,
in the latter part of it, clearly felt the relative
importance of different notes in a key and the
harmonies which they represent, and balanced
many instrumental movements on principles
analogous to our own, though simpler ; and the
same may be said of Couperin, who was his
junior by a few years ; but it is apparent that
they moved among accidentals with caution,
and regarded what we call extreme keys as
dangerous and almost inexplorable territory.[1]
In the works of the many sterling and solid
composers of the early part of the 18th century,
the most noticeable feature is the extraordinary
expanse of the main keys. Music had arrived
at the opposite extreme from its state of a

1 The limitations of keyboard instruments tuned on a system of
unequal TEMPERAMENT (*q.v.*) accounted to some extent for this.

hundred years before ; and composers, having realised the effect of pure tonality, were content to remain in one key for periods which to us, with our different ways of expressing ourselves, would be almost impossible. This is in fact the average period of least modulation. Handel is a fairer representative of the time than Bach, for reasons which will be touched upon presently, and his style is much more in conformity with most of his contemporaries who are best known in the musical art. We may take him, therefore, as a type ; and in his works it will be noticed that the extent and number of modulations is extremely limited. In a large proportion of his finest choruses he passes into his dominant key near the beginning—partly to express the balance of keys and partly driven thereto by fugal habits ; and then returns to his original key, from which in many cases he hardly stirs again. Thus the whole modulatory range of the Hallelujah Chorus is not more than frequent transitions from the tonic key to the key of its dominant and back, and one excursion as far as the relative minor in the middle of the chorus, —and that is all. There are choruses with a larger range, and choruses with even less, but the Hallelujah is a fair example to take, and if it is carefully compared with any average example of the 19th century such as Mendelssohn's ' The night is departing,' in the ' Hymn of Praise,' or ' O great is the depth,' in ' St. Paul,' or the first chorus in Brahms's Requiem, a very strong impression of the progressive tendency of modern music in the matter of modulation will be obtained. In choruses and movements in the minor mode, modulations are on an average more frequent and various, but still infinitely less free than in modern examples. Even in such a fine example as ' The people shall hear,' in 'Israel,' the apparent latitude of modulation is deceptive, for many of the changes of key in the early part are mere repetitions ; since the tonalities range up and down between E minor, B and F♯ only, each key returning irregularly. In the latter part it is true the modulations are finely conceived, and represent a degree of appreciation in the matter of relations of various keys, such as Handel does not often manifest.

Allusion has been made above to the practice of going out to a foreign key and returning to the original again in a short space of time. This happens to be a very valuable gauge to test the degrees of appreciation of a composer in the matter of modulation. In modern music keys are felt so strongly as an element of form, that when any one has been brought prominently forward, succeeding modulations for some time after must, except in a few special cases, take another direction. The tonic key, for instance, must inevitably come forward clearly in the early part of a movement, and when its importance has been made sufficiently clear by insist-

ence, and modulations have begun in other directions, if it were to be quickly resumed and insisted on afresh, the impression would be that there was unnecessary tautology ; and this must appear obvious on the merest external grounds of logic. The old masters, however, must, on this point, be judged to have had but little sense of the actual force of different keys as a matter of form ; for in a large proportion of examples they were content to waver up and down between nearly related keys, and constantly to resume one and another without order or design. In the ' Te gloriosus ' in Graun's Te Deum, for instance, he goes out to a nearly related key, and returns to his tonic key no less than five several times, and in the matter of modulation does practically nothing else. Even Bach occasionally presents similar examples, and Mozart's distribution of the modulations in ' Splendente te Deus ' (in which he probably followed the standing classical models of vocal music) are on a similar plan, for he digresses and returns again to his principal key at least twelve times in the course of the work.

Bach was in some respects like his contemporaries, and in some so far in advance of them that he cannot fairly be taken as a representative of the average standard of the day. In fact, his more wonderful modulatory devices must have fallen upon utterly deaf ears, not only in his time but for generations after ; and, unlike most great men, he appears to have made less impression upon the productive musicians who immediately succeeded him than upon those of a hundred years and more later. In many cases he cast movements in the forms prevalent in his time, and occasionally used vain repetitions of keys like his contemporaries ; but when he chose his own lines he produced movements which are perfectly in consonance with modern views. As examples of this the ' Et resurrexit ' in the B minor Mass and the last chorus of the Matthew Passion may be taken. In these there is no tautology in the distribution of the modulation, though the extraordinary expanse over which a single key is made to spread, still marks their relationship with other contemporary works. In some of his instrumental works he gives himself more rein, as in fantasias, and preludes, and toccatas, for organ or clavier. In these he not only makes use of the most complicated and elaborate devices in the actual passage from one key to another, but also of closely interwoven transitions in a thoroughly modern fashion. Some of the most wonderful examples are in the fantasia in G minor for organ (B.-G. xv. p. 177), and others have been already alluded to.

It is probable that his views on the subject of the relation of keys had considerable influence on the evolution of the specially modern type of instrumental music ; as it was chiefly his sons and pupils who worked out and traced in clear

and definite outlines the system of key-distribu-
tion upon which Haydn and Mozart developed
their representative examples of such works.

In the works of these two great composers we
find at once the simplest and surest distribution
of keys. They are in fact the expositors of the
elementary principles which had been arrived at
through the speculations and experiments of
more than a century and a half of musicians.
The vital principle of their art-work is clear and
simple tonality ; each successive key which is
important in the structure of the work is marked
by forms both of melody and harmony, which,
by the use of the most obvious indicators, state
as clearly as possible the tonic to which the
particular group of harmonies is to be referred.
This is their summary, so to speak, of existing
knowledge. But what is most important to
this question is that the art did not stop at this
point, but composers having arrived at that
degree of realisation of the simpler relations of
keys, went on at once to build something new
upon the foundation.

Both Haydn and Mozart—as if perceiving
that directly the means of clearly indicating a
key were realised, the ease with which it could
be grasped would be proportionately increased
—began to distribute their modulations more
freely and liberally. For certain purposes they
both made use of transitions so rapid that the
modulations appear to overlap, so that before
one key is definitely indicated an ingenious
modification of the chord which should have
confirmed it leads on to another. The occasions for the use of this device are principally
either to obtain a strong contrast to long
periods during which single keys have been or
are to be maintained ; or, where according to
the system of form it so happens that a key
which has already been employed has soon to
be resumed—as, for instance, in the recapitulation of the subjects—to lead the mind so
thoroughly away that the sense of the more
permanent key is almost obliterated. Occasionally, when the working-out section is very
short, the rapid transitions alluded to are also
met with in that position, as in the slow movement of Mozart's E♭ quartet. The example
quoted above from the last movement of his
quartet in C will serve as an example on this
point as well as on that for which it was
quoted.

A yet more important point in relation to the
present question is the use of short breaths of
subordinate modulation in the midst of the
broader expanses of the principal keys. This
is very characteristic of Mozart, and serves
happily to indicate the direction in which art
was moving at the time. Thus, in the very
beginning of his quartet in G (Köchel, 387), he
glides out of his principal key into the key of
the supertonic, A, and back again in the first
four bars. A similar digression, from F to D

and back again, may be observed near the beginning of the slow movement of the Jupiter
Symphony. But it requires to be carefully
noted that the sense of the principal keys is not
impaired by these digressions. They are not to
be confounded either with the irregular wandering of the composers who immediately succeeded the polyphonic school, nor with the frequent going out and back again of the composers
of the early part of the 18th century. This
device is really an artificial enlargement of the
capacity of a key, and the transitions are
generally used to enforce certain notes which
are representative and important roots in the
original key. A striking example occurs in the
first movement of Mozart's symphony in G
minor (1st section), where after the key of B♭
has been strongly and clearly pointed out in
the first statement of the second subject, he
makes a modulatory digression as follows :

etc.

This is in fact a very bold way of enforcing
the subdominant note ; for though the modulation appears to be to the key of the minor
seventh from the tonic, the impression of that
key is ingeniously reduced to a minimum, at
the same time that the slight flavour that remains of it forms an important element in the
effect of the transition.

The force with which Beethoven employed
the device above illustrated from Mozart is
shown in the wonderful transition from E♭ to
G minor at the beginning of the Eroica (bars
7-10), and the transition from F to D♭ at the
beginning of the Sonata Appassionata. These
are, as in most of Mozart's examples, only
single steps ; in many cases Beethoven makes
use of several in succession. Thus in the beginning of the E minor pianoforte sonata, op. 90,
the first section should be theoretically in E
minor, but in this case a quick modulation to G
begins in the third bar, in the seventh a modulation to B minor follows, and in the ninth, G
is taken up again, and through it passage is
made back to E minor, the original key, again.
Thus the main centre of the principal key
is supplemented by subordinate centres ; the

different notes of the key being used as points of vantage from which a glance can be taken into foreign tonalities, to which they happen also to belong, without losing the sense of the principal key which lies in the background.

These transitions often occur in the early part of movements before the principal key has been much insisted on, as if to enhance its effect by postponement. Thus we find remarkable examples in Beethoven's Introductions, as for instance in the Leonora overture, No. 3, and in the Introduction to the quartet in C, op. 59, No. 3.

In composers of note since Beethoven, we find a determination to take full advantage of the effect of such transitions. Brahms, for instance, makes constant use of them in his instrumental works from the earliest to the latest. The first two pages of the G minor quartet for pianoforte and strings, show at once how various are the subordinate centres of which he makes use. In the pianoforte quartet in C minor, op. 60—he presents a short version of his principal subject in the principal key, and then passes to B♭ minor, D♭ major, E♭ minor, A♭, G♭ minor and B♭ major in rapid succession before he resumes his original key, in order to propound his first subject more fully. Schumann was equally free in his use of subordinate modulations. In the fine intermezzo of the 'Faschingsschwank,' which has the signature of E♭ minor, the first chord is in that key, but the second leads to D♭ major, and a few chords farther on we are in B♭ minor, from which an abrupt return is made to E♭ minor only to digress afresh. Such are the elaborate transitions which are developed by an extension of the device of single transitions used so frequently by Mozart; and it may be noted that a closely connected series of transitory modulations occupies in music of the 19th century an analogous position to that occupied by a connected series of harmonies, based on quickly shifting root-notes, in the music of a century or a century and a half earlier. Similarly, in the closely connected steps of modulation, like those used by Haydn and Mozart between one strongly marked expanse of key and another, later composers have packed their successions of keys so closely that it is often a matter of some difficulty to disentangle them with certainty. For instance, the passage in the slow movement of Beethoven's B♭ sonata, op. 106, just before the resumption of the principal key and the first subject (in variation), is as follows:

In this, besides the number of the transitions (exceeding the number of bars in the example), the steps by which they proceed are noticeable with reference to what was touched upon above in that respect. Many similar examples occur in Schumann's works. For instance, in the last movement of his sonata in G minor, where he wishes to pass from B♭ to G major, to resume his subject, he goes all the way round by B♭ minor, G♭ major, E♭ major, D♭ minor, F♯, B, A, D, C minor, B♭, A♭, and thence at last to G; there is a similar example in the middle of the first movement of his pianoforte quartet in E♭; examples are also common in Chopin's works, as for instance bars 29 to 32 of the prelude in E♭, No. 19, in which the transitions overlap in such a way as to recall the devices of Haydn and Mozart, though the material and mode of expression are so markedly distinct.

From this short survey it will appear that the direction of modern music in respect of modulation has been constant and uniform. The modern scales had first to be developed out of the chaos of ecclesiastical modes, and then they had to be systematised into keys, a process equivalent to discovering the principle of modulation. This clearly took a long time to achieve, since composers moved cautiously over new ground, as if afraid to go far from their starting-point, lest they should not be able to find a way back. Still, the invention of the principle of passing from one key to another led to the discovery of the relations which exist between one key and another; in other words of the different degrees of musical effect produced by their juxtaposition. The bearings of the more simple of these relations were first established, and then those of the more remote and subtle ones, till the way through every note of the scale to its allied keys was found.

In the meanwhile groups of chords belonging to foreign keys were subtly interwoven in the broader expanses of permanent keys, and the principle was recognised that different individual notes of a key can be taken to represent subordinate circles of chords in other keys of which they form important integers, without destroying the sense of the principal tonality.[1] Then as the chords belonging to the various groups called keys are better and better known, it becomes easier to recognise them with less and less indication of their relations, so that groups of chords representing any given tonality can be constantly rendered shorter, until at length successions of transitory modulations make their appearance, in which the group of chords representing a tonality is reduced to two, and these sometimes not representing it by any means obviously.

It may appear from this that we are gravitating back to the chaotic condition which harmony represented in the days before the invention of tonality. But this is not the case. We have gone through all the experiences of the key-system, and by means of it innumerable combinations of notes have been made intelligible which could not otherwise have been so. The key-system is therefore the ultimate test of harmonic combinations, and the ultimate basis of their classification, however closely chords representing different tonalities may be brought together. There will probably always be groups of some extent which are referable to one given centre or tonic, and effects of modulation between permanent keys; but concerning the rapidity with which transitions may succeed one another, and the possibilities of overlapping tonalities, it is not safe to speculate; for theory and analysis are always more safe and helpful to guide us to the understanding of what a great artist shows us when it is done, than to tell him beforehand what he may or may not do.

C. H. H. P.

The processes of modulation thus broadly indicated by Sir Hubert Parry leave little to add, though they have been illustrated in widely different ways by composers since his article was written. Max Reger's *Beiträge zur Modulationslehre* (12th edition, 1919) goes some way towards codifying later German practices. The article HARMONY, together with George Dyson's *The New Music* (1924), may be consulted for further analysis. Modulation is necessarily modified by new views as to the scope of TONALITY (*q.v.*). The adoption of pure CHRO-

[1] Illustrations of this process might be drawn from any composer of the later 19th century, but the chromatic style of César Franck exemplifies it with peculiar clearness.   C.

MATICISM (*q.v.*) or the acceptance of the doctrine of ' atonality ' would necessarily banish modulation.   C.

MODULATIONS, REGULAR AND CONCEDED (Lat. *modulationes* [*vel clausulae*] *regulares et concessae*). See MODES, ECCLESIASTICAL, subsection THE MODES IN POLYPHONIC MUSIC.

MODULATOR, see TONIC SOL-FA.

MÖLLER, JOHANN (late 16th to mid-17th cent.), town and court organist at Darmstadt; composed German motets, 5-8 v. (1611), a 6-part ' Vater unser '; 2 books of pavans, galliards, etc., for 5 instruments (1610 and 1612), etc. (See *Q.-L.*)

MOERAN, ERNEST JOHN (*b.* Osterley, near London, Dec. 31, 1894), composer, is of Irish extraction but has lived much in Norfolk, where he has been an assiduous collector of folk-songs. He was educated at Uppingham but was practically self-taught in music until he entered the R.C.M. in 1913. Eighteen months later he joined the army and served through the war, being demobilised in 1919. Since then he has had some guidance from John Ireland, whose influence can be traced in a few works of that period. Robustness is the outstanding quality of his idiom. Several of his early works have remained unpublished and are now discarded. These include a few orchestral scores, three string quartets, three violin sonatas, a violoncello sonata and a trio. His published works comprise :

Orchestral.—Two Rhapsodies (Halle, Norwich Festival, Promenades, etc.). Symphonic impression, ' In the Mountain Country.'
Chamber Music.—String Quartet. Sonata (vln. and PF.). Trio (PF., vln. and v'cl.).
Piano.—Variations, legends, fancies, toccata, etc.
Songs.—Cycle, ' Ludlow Town " (from ' A Shropshire Lad '), and numerous others. ' Six Folk-songs from Norfolk,' and other folk-song settings, including two for baritone and male voice quartet. A few partsongs.

E. E.

MÖSER, KARL (*b.* Berlin, Jan. 24, 1774; *d.* there, Jan. 27, 1851), violinist, pupil of Böttcher and Karl Haak. After a short activity as member of the Royal Chapel, Berlin, he went to Hamburg, where his personal intercourse with Rode and Viotti encouraged him to renewed studies. After extended journeys he returned to his former position at Berlin in 1811, where he formed a quartet party with Kelz as violoncellist. Soon after he widened the scope of his public concerts by the introduction of symphonies and overtures, which gradually developed into the symphony concerts of the Royal Chapel for the benefit of the orphan fund. On Nov. 27, 1826, he conducted the first performance of Beethoven's 9th Symphony. In 1842 he celebrated his jubilee, received the title of ' royal Kapellmeister,' and was pensioned, but continued to preside over the instrumental class. Among the foremost of his pupils are Karl Müller and his son August (*b.* 1825; died on a concert tour in America, 1859). His compositions are unimportant (Wasielewski, *Die Violine*; *Q.-L.*).

MOFFAT, ALFRED (*b.* Edinburgh, Dec. 4,

1866), composer and editor of old music. Studied composition for five years at Berlin, under Professor Ludwig Bussler, and remained in Berlin for another five years working for most of the large music-publishing firms.

He settled in London about the end of the 'nineties, turned his attention to the forgotten British violin composers of the 18th century and earlier, and had a hard fight to get any one to believe there had been a school of English violin composers. In fact it was only after Simrock had published so many of the old English sonatas, arranged by Moffat, that he induced Novello to embark on his 'Old English Violin Music' series, mostly of forgotten works. He has arranged much of Purcell's works and others of the old English school of vocal and instrumental music. His *Meisterschule der alten Zeit* (Simrock) embraces 36 classical violin sonatas, 18 violoncello sonatas, and 22 trio sonatas. It contains many old English works by Purcell, Richard Jones, Robert Valentine, John Collett, Charles Avison and Henry Eccles. His *Kammersonaten* (Schott) contains 30 violin sonatas, brought to light for the first time. His French 18th-century music (Schott) contains 18 numbers, and his English 18th-century music (Schott) contains 24 numbers.

His arrangements of British music are comprised in 'The Minstrelsy of England,' 'The Minstrelsy of Scotland,' of 'Wales,' of 'The Highlands,' and a valuable book, 'The Minstrelsy of Ireland,' all enriched with historical notes. There are many others of his arrangements of the English and Scottish vocal and instrumental music published in book form. Moffat regards his *Meisterschule* as one of his most important works. It began with 24 numbers, and has been very popular all over Europe.

In 1925 he was engaged upon a series of books of 'Melodious Scotland.' One of his notable books is 'Songs and Dances of all Nations,' in conjunction with the late J. D. Brown. He has a fine and unique library of early violin music, 17th-18th centuries, including many rare works. His daughter, Alice Moffat, is a talented actress.   F. K.

MOLINARA, LA (Ger. *Die schöne Müllerin*), opera by Paisiello, produced at Naples in 1788 ; in London at the King's Theatre, Mar. 22, 1803. Its name is preserved by a duet, 'Nel cor più non mi sento,' which has served as the theme of many variations, amongst others of six by Beethoven.   G.

The song, 'Hope told a flattering tale,' adapted to Paisiello's 'Nel cor più non mi sento,' became, near the close of the 18th century, one of the most favourite English sentimental songs; it was introduced by Mara in a revival of Arne's 'Artaxerxes,' and was republished in all imaginable forms.   F. K.

MOLINARO, SIMONE (*b.* Genoa), was nephew and pupil of Giovanni Battista dalla Gostena, whom he succeeded in 1599 in his office of maestro di cappella at the Cathedral of Genoa. In 1613 he edited in score, in one folio volume, the six books of chromatic madrigals of GESUALDO (*q.v.*), Prince of Venosa, which, as Ambros says, shows that these strange works had begun to be a subject of study for musicians. Of Molinaro's own publications, consisting of motets, sacred concertos with organ score, including some Masses and Magnificats, a book of madrigals and canzonets, hardly any are preserved complete, partbooks being missing in nearly every case. A certain number of his motets for five voices have been preserved complete in the collections of Hasler ('Sacrae symphoniae,' 1598) and Schadaeus ('Promptuarium,' 1611), from which Commer in modern times has reprinted ten. These are mostly quite simple and melodious on a harmonic basis, without anything of imitative counterpoint to speak of. But Molinaro is also known as a lutenist, and from his 'Intavolatura di liuto,' 1599, containing Saltarelli, Passamezze and Gagliarde, and including twenty-five fantasias by his master Gostena, Oscar Chilesotti has reprinted fourteen little pieces in modern notation in his 'Lautenspieler des XVI. Jahrhunderts' (Breitkopf & Härtel, 1891). In these pieces, as Eitner says, Molinaro despises all counterpoint, and shows himself as a pure melodist and harmonist, but both in so simple and pretty a way that they all have something uncommonly attractive (see *M.f.M.* xxiv. p. 29).   J. R. M.

MOLIQUE, WILHELM BERNHARD (*b.* Nuremberg, Oct. 7, 1802; *d.* Cannstadt, near Stuttgart, May 10, 1869), celebrated violinist and composer.

His father, a member of the town band, at first taught him several instruments, but Molique soon made the violin his special study. Spohr,[1] relates that while staying at Nuremberg, in 1815, he gave some lessons to the boy, who already possessed remarkable proficiency on the instrument. Molique afterwards went to Munich, and studied for two years under Rovelli. After having lived for some time at Vienna, as member of the orchestra of the Theater-an-der-Wien, he returned in 1820 to Munich, and succeeded his master Rovelli as leader of the band. From Munich he made several tours through Germany, and soon established his reputation as an eminent virtuoso and a solid musician. In 1826 he accepted the post of leader of the Royal Band at Stuttgart, and remained there till 1849. In that year he came to England, where he spent the remaining part of his professional life. The sterling qualities of Molique as a player, and his sound musicianship, soon procured him an honourable position in the musical world of London. His first appearance at the Philharmonic was on

1 *Selbstbiographie*, i. 228.

May 14, 1840, when he played his own A minor concerto. With the general public he was equally successful as a soloist, quartet-player and teacher, while the serious character and the fine workmanship of his compositions raised him high in the estimation of connoisseurs and musicians.

As an executant he showed a rare perfection of left-hand technique, but his bowing appears to have been somewhat wanting in breadth and freedom. His style of playing was usually very quiet, perhaps deficient in animation. As a composer the influence of Spohr is evident, not only in the character of most of his subjects, but also in his manner of treating and working them out, yet some of his works—especially the first two movements of his third concerto in D minor, and of the fifth in A minor—are fine compositions. His other compositions, though evincing the same technical mastery, are very inferior in interest to these concertos—they bear hardly any traces of inspiration and had no great or lasting success.

Molique gave a farewell concert at St. James's Hall, May 3, 1866, and five days afterwards retired to Cannstadt, near Stuttgart, where he died. His principal published works are :

6 Violin Concertos ; 8 Quartets for stringed instruments ; 2 Pianoforte Trios ; a Symphony ; 2 Masses ; an Oratorio, ' Abraham ' (performed at the Norwich Festival in 1860) ; Duos for two violins, and for flute and violin.

BIBL.—FRITZ SCHRÖDER, *Bernhard Molique und seine Instrumentalkompositionen. Mit einem Verzeichnis aller nachweisbaren Werke Moliques und einem thematischen Katalog des wichtigsten Instrumentalkompositionen.* (Stuttgart, 1923.)   P. D.'

MOLL and DUR are the German terms for minor and major respectively.

MOLLE, HENRY (early part of 17th cent.), English composer of church music, went to King's College, Cambridge, and was Public Orator to that University while Cosin was Master of Peterhouse (1635–40). His English Litany was ' made for Cosin.' One of the madrigals in Thomas Tomkins' ' Songs ' of 1622 is dedicated to Molle. In the Tudway Collection (B.M. Harl. MSS. 7337-7342) are 2 Evening Services by Molle ; the first in D, written in 1636, and the second in F, dated 1639, and ' . . . commonly called Molle's 2nd Service.' In PH. are the following compositions by him :

Latin T.D. and L., English L., M. and N.D., Second M. and N.D. a 4, and an anthem, ' Great and Marvellous.'

The words also of another anthem by him are given in Clifford's ' Collection ' (1663).   J. M^K.

MOLLENHAUER, EDWARD R., a violin-maker established in New York in the latter half of the 19th century, who introduced an '·improvement ' in violin construction which was patented in this country (1881, No. 621).

' The invention consists in placing a board between the sounding-board and the back of the instrument, and parallel to these two boards, so as to divide the interior into two compartments. This intermediate board is provided with sound-holes and a bass bar.'

This contrivance was considered of sufficient importance by Count Luigi Francesco Valdrighi to form the subject of No. 9 of his *Musurgiana* under the title *Strumenti ad arco rinforzati* (Modena, 1881).   E. H.-A.

MOLLER, JOACHIM, see BURCK, Joachim à.

MOLTER, JOHANN MELCHIOR (d. Durlach, Jan. 12, 1765), from 1722–33 Kapellmeister at the court of the Markgrave of Baden at Durlach, whence he went to Italy, at the latter's expense, for further studies. In 1733 he went to Eisenach as church-music director but returned to Durlach in 1743, where he occupied his former position till his death. He was a prolific composer of instrumental music. Most of his compositions, including 169 symphonies, 95 concertos and concertini, and 66 sonatas, for various instruments, 14 overtures, 14 cantatas, etc., are preserved in MS. in the State Library at Karlsruhe, and the MS. score of a Passion Music in the Sondershausen Library (*Riemann* ; *Q.-L.*).

MONASTERIO, JESUS DE (b. Potes, province of Santander, Spain, Apr. 18, 1836 ; d. there, Sept. 28, 1903 [1]), eminent violinist, showed strong inclination for music at a very early age, and enjoyed royal patronage from the age of 7 years. He was taught by the best masters at Madrid, and for a time followed the career of a prodigy ; but the death of his father compelled him to return to his home, and through the influence of a wealthy amateur he was sent to Brussels to study with De Bériot. Here he remained at the Conservatoire from 1849–52, when he returned home and played in Madrid with great success ; in 1861 he appeared in Belgium, Holland and Germany as a finished performer. His success in these countries and in France was remarkable ; at Weimar he was offered the post of court Kapellmeister, but he preferred to return to his native country, and in a short time he was appointed violin professor at the Conservatoire of Madrid. His quartet-playing was of remarkable excellence, and he introduced the works of the classical masters to the musical amateurs of Spain. He wrote many successful works for his instrument, as well as two ecclesiastical compositions without accompaniment.   M.

MONDAY POPULAR CONCERTS, see POPULAR CONCERTS.

MONDONVILLE, (1) JEAN JOSEPH CASSANEA DE (b. Narbonne, Dec. 24, 1711 ; d. Belleville, near Paris, Oct. 8, 1772), son of well-born but poor parents.[2] His taste for music showed itself early, and he acquired considerable powers of execution as a violinist. He was in Paris in 1733, and from there went to Lille, where he was well received, and still more so at the Concert Spirituel in 1737. He returned to Paris in 1734 and achieved success as a violinist

1 Obituary in the *Zeitschrift* of the Int. Mus. Ges., 1903, p. 224.
2 The only information about his youth is in the *Nécrologe des hommes célèbres de France.* (1773.)

and composer of popular chamber music and organ pieces (for Balbâtre).

We lose sight of him from this time until 1738, when he began to compose motets. These religious compositions appeared in the programmes of the Concert Spirituel from then until 1770. Mondonville attempted the stage, but his first opera, ' Isbe ' (Académie, Apr. 10, 1742), failed. In 1744 he succeeded Gervais as Surintendant de la Chapelle du Roi, and under court patronage he produced at the Académie ' Le Carnaval du Parnasse ' (Sept. 23, 1749), an opéra-ballet in three acts, containing some graceful music. When the contest between the partisans of Italian and French music, known as the Guerre des Bouffons, arose in 1752 in consequence of the success of ' La serva padrona,' Mondonville, a protégé of Mme. de Pompadour, was chosen champion of the national school ; and his opera ' Titon et l'Aurore ' (Jan. 9, 1753) owed its success largely to this circumstance. ' Daphnis et Alcimadura' (Dec. 29, 1754), a pastoral in the Langue d'Oc, in which he introduced many Provençal airs, completed his popularity ; and of this he made use to procure his appointment as director of the Concert Spirituel. That post he occupied for seven years (1755–62) showing great ability both as an administrator and conductor, and producing at the concerts with much success three short oratorios, ' Les Israëlites au Mont Oreb,' ' Les Fureurs de Saül' and ' Les Titans.' ' Les Fêtes de Paphos ' (May 9, 1758), originally written for Mme. de Pompadour's private theatre, was the only opera performed at the Académie during the same period. His last operas, ' Thésée ' (1767) and ' Psyché ' (1769, a mere adaptation of the third act of ' Les Fêtes de Paphos '), were unsuccessful. Twelve motets, a book of trios, sonatas for violin and harpsichord, etc., are mentioned in *Q.-L.*, and a very amusing *jeu d'esprit* was published in 1760. It is a musical setting in cantata form of the ' Privilège du Roi ' which appears in all publications of the period ; it has parts for strings, oboes and horns.

The following are his chief instrumental works, arranged chronologically, of which the ' Pièces de clavecin en sonates,' the first of the kind, and the ' Sons harmoniques,' which, for the violin were equally original, are the most important :

1. Sonatas for vln. with basso continuo. (1733.)
2. Trio Sonatas for two vlns. or flutes with basso continuo.
3. Sonatas for PF. with vln. accomp. (c. 1734.)
4. ' Les Sons harmoniques,' sonatas for vln. solo with basso continuo (c. 1738.)
5. PF. pieces with voice or vln. (c. 1748.)

There is a good portrait of Mondonville in pastel by La Tour, formerly in the possession of Ambroise Thomas, now in the Musée de St. Quentin ; and another by C. N. Cochin, engraved by Saint-Aubin.

(2) JEAN (*b.* Narbonne, Apr. 15, 1716) (called le Jeune or le Cadet), his younger brother, was

' Ordinaire de la musique du roi,' and composed a collection of sonatas (1767). He is lost sight of after 1769.   G. C. ; addns. M. P.

BIBL.—L. DE LA LAURENCIE, *L'École française de violon de Lully à Viotti*, i. 1922–23, pp. 376-436.

MONFERRINA, a kind of country dance, originating in Piedmont. The tunes used in Italy and Malta became fashionable in England in the early years of the 19th century, and were employed for country dances. In this country the name stood as ' Monfrina,' ' Monfreda ' or ' Manfredina.' The favourite tune with the title ' Italian Monfrina ' was—

Copies will be found in Wheatstone's *Country Dances for* 1810, *Companion to the Ball-Room, circa* 1816, and other collections of country dances.   F. K.

MONGINI (*d.* 1874), a tenor singer, who first sang in London at Her Majesty's Theatre in 1859, and again about 1862. The best part of his London career, however, dated from 1866, when the premature death of Giuglini had left Mapleson without a leading tenor possessed of any great attraction for the public. Mongini could not fill Giuglini's place, but he had a voice of extraordinary power and range, and in certain parts—Arnold in ' William Tell,' Manrico in ' Trovatore,' and John of Leyden in ' The Prophet ' among the rest—he met with marked success. When Gye and Mapleson joined forces at Covent Garden in 1869, Mongini was one of the leading tenors in the company, and he afterwards sang under Mapleson's management down to 1873. He was a typical *tenore di forza*.   S. H. P.

MONIUSZKO, STANISLAUS (*b.* dept. of Minsk, Lithuania, May 5, 1820 ; *d.* Warsaw, June 4, 1872), received his first musical education from the organist Aug. Freyer and went to Berlin in 1837, where he was a pupil of Rungenhagen for two years. He settled down at Wilna as a teacher and organist of the church of St. John, and in 1846 his first opera, ' Halka,' was given at Warsaw. In 1858 he became Kapellmeister at the opera in Warsaw, and afterwards professor at the Conservatorium. Among his operas [1] and dramatic pieces the most noteworthy are ' Die Gräfin ' and ' Der Paria,' the latter produced in 1869. He wrote five masses, church music, cantatas and choral music, an overture ' Bajka,' music to ' Hamlet ' and ' The

<hr/>

[1] *Riemann* enumerates fourteen, with three ballets.

Merry Wives of Windsor,' and many songs and pianoforte pieces, besides an instruction book in harmony in Polish. One of his best songs, ' Le Cosaque,' enjoyed great popularity for many years. Twenty years after his death a branch of the Warsaw Musical Society was founded with the special object of publishing his MS. works and founding a museum in his honour.   M.

BIBL.—BRONISLAWA WOJCIKOWNA, *Szkice Muzukologiczne.* (Warsaw, 1923). (Discusses Moniuszko's settings of ballads by Mickiewicz.)

MONK, EDWIN GEORGE, Mus.D. (*b.* Frome, Somerset, Dec. 13, 1819 ; *d.* Radley, near Oxford, Jan. 3, 1900), was initiated in music by his father, an amateur. He studied pianoforte-playing at Bath under Henry Field, and organ-playing under George Field. He then went to London and learned choral singing in Hullah's classes, and solo singing from Henry Phillips. Later he studied harmony with G. A. Macfarren. After holding several appointments as organist in his native county he went to Ireland in 1844, and became organist and music-master of the newly formed College of St. Columba ; at Stackallan, near Navan, County Meath, afterwards transferred to Rathfarnham, County Dublin ; he remained there till 1846, when he was succeeded by J. B. Calkin. In 1847 he settled in Oxford, and was concerned in the formation of ' The University Motett and Madrigal Society.' In 1848 he obtained the appointments of lay-precentor, organist and music-master at the new College of St. Peter, Radley, and graduated Mus.B. at Oxford. In 1856 he proceeded Mus.D., his exercise being a selection from Gray's ode, ' The Bard,' which he published in the same year in vocal score. In 1859 he was appointed successor to Dr. Camidge as organist and choirmaster of York Cathedral. He resigned in 1883, and was succeeded by Dr. J. Naylor. He published a service, several anthems, a Veni Creator Spiritus, and other pieces, and various secular compositions, and edited *The Anglican Chant Book* and *The Anglican Choral Service Book*, also, with the Rev. R. Corbet Singleton, *The Anglican Hymn Book*; and, with Sir F. A. G. Ouseley, *The Psalter and Canticles pointed for chanting* (two series), and *Anglican Psalter Chants*. He was the compiler of the libretti of Macfarren's oratorios, ' St. John the Baptist,' ' The Resurrection ' and ' Joseph.' He was a student of astronomy, and became F.R.A.S. in 1871.   W. H. H. ; addns. W. H. G. F.

MONK, WILLIAM HENRY (*b.* London, Mar. 16, 1823 ; *d.* there, Mar. 1, 1889), is remembered for his widespread influence on English hymnody through the part which he took in editing the music of HYMNS ANCIENT AND MODERN (*q.v.*).

He studied under Thomas Adams, J. A. Hamilton and G. A. Griesbach. After filling the office of organist at Eaton Chapel, Pimlico ;

St. George's Chapel, Albemarle Street ; and Portman Chapel, St. Marylebone, he was appointed in 1847 director of the choir in King's College, London, and in 1849 organist. In 1874, upon the resignation of Hullah, he became professor of vocal music in the college. He was early associated with Hullah in his work of popular musical education. In 1851 he became professor of music at the School for the Indigent Blind. In 1852 he was appointed organist of St. Matthias, Stoke Newington, where a voluntary choir, under his direction, for many years sustained a daily choral service. He delivered lectures on music at the London Institution (1850–79); the Philosophical Institution, Edinburgh ; and the Royal Institution, Manchester. He was appointed a professor in the National Training School for Music, 1876, and in Bedford College, London, 1878. He was musical editor of *The Parish Choir* after the fortieth number, and one of the musical editors of *Hymns Ancient and Modern*. He edited many other works of a similar character, including some for the Church of Scotland, and made various contributions to many of the modern hymnals.   W. H. H.

MONN, GEORG MATTHIAS (*b.* Austria, 1717 ; *d.* Vienna, Oct. 3, 1750), organist of the Karlskirche, composer of symphonies, trio sonatas, quartets, etc., which are in a style of transition from the old to the modern school of instrumental composition. K. Horwitz, C. Riedel and G. Adler held that to him and not to Stamitz belonged the credit of having inaugurated the modern style, but this claim must fail on closer examination, as Riemann has justly pointed out. Some compositions attributed to him (also in *Q.-L.*) are by a younger composer, G(iovanni) M(atteo) Monn or Mann (*Riemann* ; *Q.-L.*).

MONOCHORD (from the Greek Μονόχορδον and the Latin ' Monochordon '), a single vibrating string, which, being subdivided in simple mathematical ratios, gives the main notes of the scale which underlie all musical theory. This scientific basis of music has been known from very early times. It is especially connected with the name of Pythagoras, the great Greek of the 6th century B.C. He very possibly obtained his knowledge of it from the Egyptian priests, and he certainly handed on to a Greek school of his own a developed musical or rather acoustical theory, on which all subsequent theory has been based. The earliest full statement of it is in the treatise of Euclid (*c.* 300 B.C.), called ' Sectio Canonis,' the precursor of a large number of such treatises extending into the Latin Middle Ages.

The first interval to be established is the octave, which is sounded by $\frac{1}{2}$ the vibrating string ; the fifth will similarly be given by $\frac{2}{3}$ of the string and the fourth by $\frac{3}{4}$ of it. A tone is the difference between the fourth and the fifth, that is to say, it is represented by the fraction $\frac{9}{8}$. Thus the whole skeleton of the scales is arrived at. The Greeks subdivided the fourth in three different ways : (1) into a tone, a tone and a semitone : or else (2) into a semi-tone, a semitone and a sesquitone : or else (3) into a quarter-tone, a quarter-tone and a ditone, these three methods give the three *genera* of scale called respectively diatonic, chromatic and enharmonic.[1] (See GREEK MUSIC.)

The first of the three is the one that has been perpetuated in modern Western music, and therefore is the only one that need be taken into account here. The immediate result of it was an Octave-System made up thus :

T	Nete (νήτη or νεάτη,	lit. ' lowest '), our highest note.
T	Paranete (παρανήτη,	*i.e.* ' next to Nete ').
S	Trite (τρίτη,	*i.e.* ' third string ').
	Paramese (παραμέση,	*i.e.* ' next to Mese ').

T	Mese (μέση,	*i.e.* ' middle string ').
T	Lichanos (λιχανός,	*i.e.* ' forefinger string ').
S	Parhypate (παρυπάτη,	*i.e.* ' next to Hypate ').
	Hypate (ὑπάτη	*i.e.* ' highest '), our lowest note.

The terminology is taken from the Cithara or Lyre. The interval from Nete to Hypate is that of an octave ; from Paramese to Hypate is a fifth or pentachord ; from Nete to Paramese or from Mese to Hypate is a fourth or tetrachord. These four notes are ' stable,' *i.e.* of fixed position, whether the scale be diatonic, enharmonic, or chromatic ; but the inner notes of the tetrachord vary according to the character of the scale. On the left-hand side the intervals of the diatonic scale are indicated by the initials T and S ; and it will be noticed that the two tetrachords are exactly alike in the arrangement of their intervals, each being represented by the formula STT ascending. This octave, therefore, consists of two similar tetrachords separated from one another by a tone, and therefore called in technical language ' disjunct.'

As the range of musical instruments and of musical ideals became more extended this conception of the scale was widened. In the extant writings of Aristoxenus (4th cent. B.C.) there is little trace of any more extended scale than this of one octave ; but at least by the time of Euclid (c. 300 B.C.) the standard scale was regarded as consisting of two octaves. A tetrachord was added both above and below the twin tetrachords of the original octave, and then, in order to complete the range of two octaves an additional note was added below. The result was the Double Octave-System, consisting of the following series of notes, and known thence-

[1] There are further subtleties of subdivision which may here be left unnoticed.

forward as the ' Perfect System ' (σύστημα τέλειον) :

T	Nete Hyperbolaion (νήτη ὑπερβολαίων)	
T	Paranete Hyperbolaion (παρανήτη ὑπερβολαίων)	Tetrachord Hyperbolaion.
S	Trite Hyperbolaion (τρίτη ὑπερβολαίων)	
T	Nete Diezeugmenon (νήτη διεζευγμένων)	
T	Paranete Diezeugmenon (παρανήτη διεζευγμένων)	Tetrachord Diezeugmenon.
S	Trite Diezeugmenon (τρίτη διεζευγμένων)	
T	Paramese (παραμέση)	
T	Mese (μέση)	
T	Lichanos Meson (λιχανὸς μέσων)	
S	Parhypate Meson (παρυπάτη μέσων)	Tetrachord Meson.
	Hypate Meson (ὑπάτη μέσων)	
T	Lichanos Hypaton (λιχανὸς ὑπατῶν)	
S	Parhypate Hypaton (παρυπάτη ὑπατῶν)	Tetrachord Hypaton.
	Hypate Hypaton (ὑπάτη ὑπατῶν)	
	Proslambanomenos (προσλαμβανόμενος	

It is evident at once that this nomenclature is only the extension of the preceding. There are only three new terms : the tetrachord added above is called Hyperbolaion (ὑπερβολαίων) additional ; the upper tetrachord of the two original ones is called Diezeugmenon (διεζευγμένων) disjunct ; the note added to complete the two octaves is called Proslambanomenos (προσλαμβανόμενος) additional. This enlargement of the scale grew up during the course of the 4th century B.C. Its earliest extant exposition is in the treatise of Euclid already mentioned, but probably its growth was gradual. It will be observed that each of the two new tetrachords is more closely attached to its neighbour than were the two original tetrachords ; each pair is in technical language not disjunct but ' conjunct ' (συνημμένων), because the two meet and share one note in common.

This conjunction of tetrachords was not a new thing, for there had long been in existence, side by side with the octave, a Heptachord consisting of two conjunct tetrachords which met in the note Mese. The full Greek system therefore was not complete without a tetrachord conjunct having Mese as its base. This formed an alternative to the intervals and notes of the Tetrachord Diezeugmenon ; and thus a tetrachord called Synemmenon (συνημμένων) found a place alongside and parallel to it. The middle of the scale therefore offered two alternatives :

T	Paranete Diezeugmenon.	Nete Synemmenon.
T	Trite Diezeugmenon.	T Paranete Synemmenon
S	Paramese.	T Trite Synemmenon.
T	Mese.	S Mese.

Thus, by a combination of these two—known as the Greater Perfect System and the Lesser

Perfect System—there was reached the full development in the Perfect Unmodulating System σύστημα τέλειον ἀμετάβολον, which consisted of a pair of octaves corresponding, so far as notes went, with the modern minor scale without accidentals, but with the possibility that the note above the middle note of the series could be flattened by a semitone.

This series had no particular pitch of its own ; in other words these Greek names correspond with the modern terms tonic, supertonic, mediant, etc., not with the names that denote a definite pitch. They were therefore applicable to any pitch. The early notions of pitch among the Greeks were denoted by tribal names—Dorian, Locrian, Lydian, etc., which in themselves were necessarily somewhat indeterminate. (See Modes.) Such methods, though for the moment they might satisfy the theorists, were necessarily insufficient as a working notation for practical musicians. An alphabetical system of notation was therefore devised by them for their use in early days. This policy was begun by the instrumentalists who assigned fifteen letters of a Greek archaic alphabet to the fifteen degrees of the Perfect System. These applied in the first instance to the diatonic form, but by modifications in form and in position the same set of symbols was made to serve also for the chromatic and enharmonic forms. The highest note of the series was called *alpha* ; *beta* stood for the fourth below and *gamma* for its octave, *delta* for the sixth below and *epsilon* for its octave, and thus the series went on, each pair of letters signifying two notes an octave apart. (See Greek Music.) The antiquity of the system is shown not merely by the employment of the digamma, but also by the archaic form of other letters and by the use of a second form of *lambda*, the second of which is said to be peculiar to the alphabet of Argos. The strange method of arrangement is probably to be explained as due to the technique of the instruments (see the Table, p. 498).

This system was sufficient not only to provide a short notation for each note of the Perfect System, but also (with the help of some modifications to express the chromatic semitones) to provide for the old Octave Scale to be pitched at each of the thirteen pitches which the teaching of Aristoxenus showed to be required, corresponding with the thirteen semitones of the diatonic octave. (See Modes.) When the neo-Aristoxenean teaching demanded fifteen pitches instead of thirteen, the series was insufficient, and had to borrow from elsewhere, as will be seen shortly.

Meanwhile the singers had devised their own method of notation, a simpler one and more modern. They reckoned up all the notes that they would use whether in the diatonic, the chromatic, or the enharmonic form, gave *alpha* to the highest note, and the succeeding letters to the succeeding notes. No digamma or other archaic form was used ; all the notes of the alphabet down to *phi* were required for the higher octave, owing to the number of the true chromatic, enharmonic, and diatonic subdivisions of the octave. The lower octave then followed suit, beginning with the *chi, psi* and *omega* that were left over and then starting a fresh alphabet with slightly modified letter-symbols, which in turn had reached to *phi* by the time that the lowest note was reached. This notation, like the other, was sufficient to represent the octave at the thirteen Aristoxenean pitches. To provide for the set of fifteen the vocalists extended their notation upwards, and adopted notes above their original *alpha*, denoting them by the letters of the alphabet from *tau* to *omega*.

It seems to have been at this point in the evolution that the two systems of notation— that of the vocalists and that of the instrumentalists—were for the first time confronted with one another. At once a discrepancy was seen to exist between them in point of pitch ; for the *alpha* of the instrumentalist was a minor third above the *alpha* of the vocalist. As, however, the vocalist had adopted the notes just mentioned above his original *alpha*, he had something to equate with the instrumentalist's *alpha*, and thus the two were easily brought into line, so far as the upper end of the scale was concerned. At the lower end the discrepancy was more marked, because the instrumentalist had not yet extended his notation so as to meet the requirements of the neo-Aristoxenean fifteen pitches. He was able, however, to do this very simply by adding to the lower end of his scale the lower notes of the vocalist's scale that overlapped his. Thus the two methods of notation were made to conform to one another. No further devices were required, except that when it was desired to note the Double-octave of the Perfect System, and not merely the old Single-octave, at the different pitches, the additional notes that this change entailed were added above, and the notation of the lower octave was repeated (with a distinguishing dash) alike in both the systems of notation.

Thenceforward the two systems prevailed side by side ; each note was represented by two signs, and it is in this form that the Greek notation is known to us. The full description of it is only found in writers of the Christian era such as Gaudentius and Alypius ; but it is clear that it is of great antiquity, and some such history as that which has been reconstructed here must lie behind it.

The Perfect System and its notation are of importance because they pass from Greek music through Greco-Latin music into the music of the Middle Ages, and their effect still remains in modern music. The further history as regards the theory of music is traced in the article MODES, but the question of pitch must be dealt with here. Though the Perfect System could be set at any pitch, it was natural to look upon some one particular pitch as the normal one, and upon others as transpositions. The Lydian pitch was adopted for that purpose, and consequently the symbol ⊢, which represented Proslambanomenos at the Lydian pitch, is constantly found as the normal equivalent of Proslambanomenos, the Γ (*gamma*) a note higher as the equivalent of Hypate Hypaton, and so on, the notation being the instrumental one. The reason for this convention is not clear; certainly it was settled without reference to the origin of either of the systems of notation, for each of these presupposes a different pitch as the normal one, as its use of the letter *alpha* shows. If the ancient and modern notations are to be compared it is evident that the normal pitch at which the Perfect System can most naturally be set is from *a'* to A, for its intervals are those of our minor scale, or else from *dd* to D when the *b♭* is used instead of *b♮*. To bring the old Greek instrumental notation into line with modern notation it is therefore natural to take the modern *aa* as the equivalent of the highest note of the old instrumental system (which was its starting-point, and was in fact called *alpha*). The starting-point of the old vocal system will then have F♯ as its modern equivalent; while the Lydian pitch, which was adopted as the normal pitch of the Perfect System, will be represented by the range from *dd* to D. And the whole range covered by the Perfect System in all its possible pitches will be from *gg* (the top note of the Hyperlydian pitch) to FF, the bottom note of the Hypodorian pitch. Within these extreme limits lies the whole of ancient and mediæval music.

The Perfect System, with its double Greek notation, appears in the early Latin writers such as the celebrated Roman philosopher Boethius (470–524), and through him it reappears in the Latin writers on music in the 9th century. The Lydian pitch still continued to be for Boethius and his followers the normal pitch; and thus the description of the Perfect System in Hucbald's treatise *De harmonica institutione* (c. 900) is accompanied by the ancient signs derived from the primitive Greek alphabet, but in a yet more degraded form, and with letters drawn from the vocalist's system of alphabetical notation substituted where the instrumentalist's symbol was too uncouth to be easily reproduced (see below).

This fusion of the two Greek alphabetical methods of noting the Perfect System, called Dasian Notation, did not last long. Later writers are content to describe the Greek scale without the Greek notation, and with a new Western alphabetical system in its stead. The two tables following will make all clear.

TABLE OF GREEK NOTATION FOR EVERY SEMITONE

(Compare the Tables, Vol. II. pp. 444-447.)

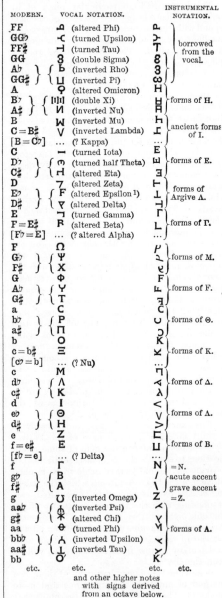

MODERN.	VOCAL NOTATION.	INSTRUMENTAL NOTATION.
FF	⅏ (altered Phi)	borrowed from the vocal.
GG♭	(turned Upsilon)	
FF♯	(turned Tau)	
GG	(double Sigma)	
A♭	(inverted Rho)	
GG♯	(inverted Pi)	
A	(altered Omicron)	forms of H.
B♭	(double Xi)	
A♯	(inverted Nu)	
B	(inverted Mu)	ancient forms of I.
C = B♯	(inverted Lambda)	
[B = C♭]	(? Kappa)	forms of E.
C	(turned Iota)	
D♭	(turned half Theta)	
C♯	(altered Eta)	
D	(altered Zeta)	forms of Argive Λ.
E♭	(altered Epsilon[1])	
D♯	(altered Delta)	
E	(turned Gamma)	forms of Γ.
F = E♯	(altered Beta)	
[F♭ = E]	(? altered Alpha)	
F	Ω	forms of M.
G♭	Ψ	
F♯	Χ	
G	Φ	forms of F.
A♭	Υ	
G♯	Τ	
a	Σ	forms of Θ.
b♭	Ρ	
a♯	Π	
b	Ο	forms of K.
c = b♯	Ξ	
[c♭ = b]	(? Nu)	forms of Δ.
c	Μ	
d♭	Λ	forms of Λ.
c♯	Κ	
d	Ι	
e♭	Θ	forms of B.
d♯	Η	
e	Ζ	
f = e♯	Ε	=N.
[f♭ = e]	(? Delta)	acute accent
f	Γ	grave accent
g♭	Β	=z.
f♯	Α	
g	Ʊ (inverted Omega)	forms of Λ.
aa♭	(inverted Psi)	
g♯	(altered Chi)	
aa	(turned Phi)	
bb♭	(inverted Upsilon)	
aa♯	(inverted Tau)	
bb	Ο'	
etc.	etc.	etc. etc.

and other higher notes with signs derived from an octave below.

[1] Not really Digamma though called so.

TABLE OF GRECO-LATIN NOTATION

The Dasian Notation of Hucbald derived from the Greek runs thus :

(Iota.)	[V]	Nete hyperbolaion.
	Π	Paranete hyperbolaion.
	[Y]	Trite hyperbolaion.
(Form of Alpha.)	N	Nete diezeugmenon.

[Ω]	Paranete diezeugmenon.	Ω	Nete synemmenon.
[E]	Trite diezeugmenon.	[E]	Paranete synemmenon.
⊐	Paramese.	[Θ]	Trite synemmenon.
[I]	Mese.	[I]	Mese.
[M]	Lichanos meson.		
[P]	Parhypate meson.		
C	Hypate meson.		
(Digamma.) F	Lichanos hypaton.		
[B]	Parhypate hypaton.		
(Gamma.) Γ	Hypate hypaton.		
(Dasian.) Ⅼ	Proslambanomenos.		

The lower notes are, as was then usual, placed below and the upper ones above ; and this table reads in the inverse order to the preceding one. Proslambanomenos here is the equivalent of D there.

The signs which are bracketed are those taken from the Vocal Notation. Compare the Lydian Table (given in Vol. II. p. 445) from which Hucbald took his signs. For the other Dasia Notation of Pseudo-Hucbald, see NOTATION.

W. H. F.

MONOCORDO (Ital.), MONOCORDE (Fr.), an indication which instructs a player of a stringed instrument to execute a given passage or whole piece on one string. This excellent effect originated with PAGANINI (q.v.). Having played his ' Love Scene,' which he had written for the G and E strings, before the court at Lucca with great success, he was asked if he could not execute something on one string only. The idea immediately caught his fancy, and he set to work and composed his sonata ' Napoleon ' for the G string. This he performed before the court on the Emperor Napoleon's birthday, in the presence of the Princess of Piombo, Napoleon's favourite sister, and other royalties, and the success of this composition led to many others of a similar character.　　　　　O. R.

MONODY (from the Gr. μόνος, ' single,' and ᾡδή, ' song '), a term applied to music written in what is sometimes called the homophonic style ; that is to say, music in which the melody is confined to a single part, instead of being equally distributed between all the voices employed, as in the polyphonic schools.

The rise of the homophonic school was extraordinarily rapid. It sprang suddenly into notice ; and, without having previously passed through any of the usual stages of gradual development, at once began to exercise an irresistible influence upon the progress of art.

Giov. Battista Doni tells us that at the celebrated *réunions* which took place in Florence about the close of the 16th century, at the house of Sig. Giov. Bardi de' Conti di Vernio, ' Vincenzo Galilei was the first who composed songs for a single voice ' ; and that Giulio Caccini (detto Romano), ' in imitation of Galilei, but in a more beautiful and pleasing style, set many canzonets and sonnets written by excellent poets,' and sang them ' to a single instrument, which was generally the theorbo, or large lute, played by Bardilla.' [1] (See CACCINI, Giulio.) The success of these early efforts was so encouraging that the inventors of the opera and the oratorio were content to write the whole of their recitatives, and even the rudimentary arias with which they were interspersed, with no richer accompaniment than that of an exceedingly simple - figured bass, in which we soon find indications of the unprepared discords first introduced by Monteverdi. (See THOROUGH - BASS.) No doubt unisonous vocal music with little or no accompaniment had been heard in the canzonetta, villanella, and other forms of national melody, ages and ages before the birth of Galilei ; and that the recognition of what we now call the ' Leading Note ' as an essential element of melody was no new thing, may be gathered from the words of Zarlino, who, writing in 1558, says—

' even Nature herself has provided for these things ; for not only those skilled in music, but also the *Contadini*, who sing without any art at all, proceed by the interval of the semitone '

—*i.e.* in forming their closes. Nevertheless, whatever may have been the popular practice, it is certain that the polyphonic style alone had hitherto been taught in the schools. We must understand therefore that those who met at the house of Bardi, though undoubtedly the first to introduce this simple music to real lovers of art, were not its actual inventors. The latent germs of the monodic style must have been present wherever national melody existed.

The example on the next page from Caccini's ' Nuove musiche ' (Venice, 1602) will show the kind of effect contemplated by the Count of Vernio's enthusiastic disciples. We need scarcely say that the figure 14, under the last D, in the last bar but one, indicates a dominant seventh ; but before this canzonetta was published, Monteverdi had already printed his Fifth Book of Madrigals ; he would not, therefore, be robbed of any portion of the credit universally accorded to him, even if it could be proved—which it cannot—that the discord in this instance was not intended to appear as a passing-note. The seventh on the E, in the third bar, is of course a suspension. (See MONTEVERDI ; FORM ; HARMONY ; OPERA ; ORATORIO.)

1 Giov. Batt. Doni. *Op. Omn.* Florence, 1763, vol. ii.

Di - te - li vo - i   se di me vi - ca - le

ch'il mio gran ma - le   vien da gl'occhi suo - i

Di - te - li che ri - mi - ri Di - te - li che ri-mi-ri Mentre ch'io

moro al-me - - no mie - i   mar - ti - - ri.

BIBLIOGRAPHY

WILHELM KRABBE: *Die Lieder Georg Nieges von Allendorf. Zur Geschichte der Monodie im 16. Jahrhundert. A.M.Z.,* Jan. 1922, pp. 48-84.
HANS VOLKMANN: *Johann Nauwachs Leben. Z.M.W.,* June-July 1922, pp. 553-62.
ARNOLD SCHMITZ-BONN: *Monodien der Kölner Jesuiten aus der ersten Hälfte des 17. Jahrhundert. Z.M.W.,* Feb. 1922, pp. 266-85.
PAUL NETTL: *Über ein handschriftliches Sammelwerk von Gesängen italienischer Frühmonodie. Z.M.W.,* Nov. 1919, pp. 83-93.

W. S. R., rev.

MONOTONE (from μόνος, 'single,' and τόνος, a 'note,' or 'tone'), Prayers, Psalms, Lessons and other portions of the Divine Office, when declaimed on a single note, are said to be monotoned, or recited in monotone. (Cf. INFLEXION.)

The use of monotonic recitation is of extreme antiquity, and was probably suggested, in the first instance, as an expedient for throwing the voice to greater distances than it could be made to reach by ordinary means.   W. S. R.

MONPOU, FRANÇOIS LOUIS HIPPOLYTE (b. Paris, Jan. 12, 1804; d. Orleans, Aug. 10, 1841), at 5 became a chorister at St. Germain l'Auxerrois, and at 9 was transferred to Notre Dame. In 1817 he entered as a pupil in the school founded by Choron, which he left in 1819 to be the organist at the Cathedral at Tours. For this post he proved unfit, and soon returned to Choron, who was extremely fond of him, and made him, although a bad reader and a poor pianist, his 'accompagnateur' (or assistant) at his Institution de Musique Religieuse. Here he had the opportunity of studying the works of ancient and modern composers of all schools, while taking lessons in harmony at the same time from Porta, Chelard and Fétis; but notwithstanding all these advantages he showed little real aptitude for music, and seemed destined to remain in obscurity. He was organist successively at St. Nicholas des Champs, St. Thomas d'Aquin, and the Sorbonne, and sacred music appeared to be his special vocation until 1828, when he published a pretty nocturne for three voices to Béranger's song, 'Si j'étais petit oiseau.' He was now taken up by the poets of the romantic school, and became their musical interpreter, publishing in rapid succession romances and ballads to words chiefly by Alfred de Musset and Victor Hugo.

Monpou found himself after the close of Choron's school without regular employment, and being a married man found it necessary to have some certain means of support. The stage seemed to offer the best chance of fortune, and though entirely unpractised in instrumentation, he unhesitatingly came forward as a composer of operas. Within a few years he produced 'Les Deux Reines' (Aug. 6, 1835); 'Le Luthier de Vienne' (June 30, 1836); 'Piquillo,' 3 acts (Oct. 31, 1837); 'Un Conte d'autrefois' (Feb. 20, 1838); 'Perugina' (Dec. 20, 1838); 'Le Planteur,' 2 acts (Mar. 1, 1839); 'La Chaste Suzanne,' 4 acts (Dec. 27, 1839); and 'La Reine Jeanne,' 3 acts (Oct. 12, 1840). His progress was undeniable, but he never became a really good musician. He overworked himself, and the effort to produce with greater rapidity than his powers would justify resulted in his premature death. He left unfinished 'Lambert Simnel' (Sept. 16, 1843), completed by Adolphe Adam, and a short opéra-comique, 'L'Orfèvre,' which has never been performed.   G. C.

MONRO (MONROE), GEORGE, an 18th-century organist, who held an appointment at St. Peter's in Cornhill, and who played the harpsichord in the orchestra of Goodman-fields theatre from 1729 to his death a few years later (1731 ?). His principal fame was gained, however, by a great number of vocal compositions which were in great favour during the early part of the 18th century. After appearing on single music sheets many were transferred to *The Merry Musician,* vols. ii. and iii., c. 1728-29; to Watt's *Musical Miscellany,* 1731; to Walsh's *British Musical Miscellany,* 1733-34, and similar collections. He composed the music for Fielding's *Temple Beau,* acted in 1729.   F. K.

MONRO, HENRY (b. Lincoln, 1774), was a chorister in the cathedral there, and afterwards a pupil of John James Ashley, Dussek, Dittenhofer and Domenico Corri. In 1796 he was appointed organist of St. Andrew's, Newcastle-upon-Tyne. He composed a sonata for pianoforte and violin, and a few pianoforte pieces and songs.   W. H. H.

MONSIGNY, PIERRE ALEXANDRE (b. Fauquemberque, near St Omer, Oct. 17, 1729; d. Jan. 14, 1817), composer, whom Choron used to call the French Sacchini, showed a taste for music in childhood, and studied the violin with success, though not intended for the profession of music.

His father died just as he had completed his classical education, and wishing to help his family, Monsigny went to Paris in 1749 and obtained a clerkship in the Bureaux des Comptes du Clergé. Having good patrons, for his family was a noble one, and being well educated, refined in manners and a skilful violinist, he was soon attached to the household of the Duke of Orleans as maître d'hôtel, with a salary which placed him above want and enabled him to provide for his younger brothers. He then resumed his musical studies, and Pergolesi's 'Serva padrona' having inspired him with a vehement desire to compose a comic opera, he took lessons from Gianotti, who played the double-bass at the Opéra and taught harmony on Rameau's system. He was a good teacher, and his pupil made so much progress that it is said Gianotti would not have been averse to putting his own name on the score of 'Les Aveux indiscrets,' which Monsigny submitted to him after only five months' tuition, and which at once established his fame when produced at the Théâtre de la Foire (Feb. 7, 1759).

Encouraged by this first success he composed for the same theatre 'Le Maître en droit' (Feb. 13, 1760) and 'Le Cadi dupé' (Feb. 4, 1761), which contains an animated and truly comic duet. His next opera, 'On ne s'avise jamais de tout' (Sept. 14, 1761), was the first in which he had the advantage of a libretto by Sedaine, and the last performed at the Théâtre de la Foire before it was closed at the request of the artists of the Comédie Italienne, in fear of the new composer's increasing reputation. After the fusion of the two companies Monsigny composed successively 'Le Roi et le fermier,' three acts (Nov. 22, 1762); 'Rose et Colas,' one act (Mar. 8, 1764); 'Aline, Reine de Golconde, three acts (Apr. 15, 1766); 'L'Île sonnante,' three acts (Jan. 4, 1768); 'Le Déserteur,' three acts (Mar. 6, 1769); 'Le Faucon,' one act (Mar. 19, 1772); 'La Belle Arsène,' three acts (Aug. 14, 1773); 'Le Rendezvous bien employé,' one act (Feb. 10, 1774); and 'Félix ou l'enfant trouvé,' three acts (Nov. 24, 1777). After the immense success of this last work he never composed again. Two other operas, 'Pazanius de Monègne' and 'Philémon et Baucis,' written about 1770, remained unperformed. He had acquired a considerable fortune as steward to the Duke of Orleans and inspector-general of canals, but the Revolution deprived him of his employment and of nearly all his resources. However in 1798 the sociétaires of the Opéra-Comique came to his assistance, and, in recognition of his services to the theatre, allowed him an annuity of 2400 francs (nearly £100). On the death of Piccinni, two years later, he was appointed inspector of instruction at the Conservatoire de Musique, but he resigned in 1802, being aware that he could not adequately perform the duties of the

office from his own insufficient training. In 1813 he succeeded Grétry at the Institut; but it was not till 1816 that he received the Legion of Honour. His last years were soothed by constant testimonies of sympathy and respect.

As an artist Monsigny's greatest gift was melody. His desultory training accounts for the poverty of his instrumentation, and for the absence of that ease, plasticity and rapidity of treatment which are the most charming attributes of genius. He was not prolific; and, either from fatigue or from a dread of an encounter with Grétry, he ceased to compose immediately after his greatest triumph; his exquisite sensibility and his instinct for dramatic truth have, however, secured him a place among original and creative musicians. G. C.

BIBL.—A POUGIN, *Monsigny et son temps* (1908); *Encyclopédie de la musique et Dictionnaire du Conservatoire*, L. DE LA LAURENCIE, *France XVIIe-XVIIIe siècles*; QUATRENIÈRE DE QUINCY, *Notice historique sur la vie et les ouvrages de Monsigny* (Paris, 1818); HEDOUIN, *Éloge de Monsigny* (Paris, 1821); F. DE MÉNIL, *Les Grands Musiciens du nord: Monsigny* (Paris, 1893).

MONT, HENRY DU, see DUMONT.

MONTAGNANA, ANTONIO, a celebrated basso, who appeared in England in the autumn of 1731. He made his début on the London boards in 'Poro' (revived); and in Jan. 1732 he created the bass rôle in 'Ezio,' Handel having written specially for him the famous song 'Nasce al bosco,' which was clearly intended to exhibit the peculiar powers of the singer. This opera was followed by 'Sosarme,' in which Montagnana had again an air, 'Fra l' ombre e l' orrori,' in which the depth, power and mellow quality of his voice, and his rare accuracy of intonation in hitting distant and difficult intervals, were displayed to full advantage. In the same year he sang in Handel's 'Acis,' a revival of 'Alessandro,' 'Flavio,' 'Coriolano,' and in 'Esther.' In 1733 Montagnana took part in 'Deborah,' 'Tolomeo,' 'Ottone,' 'Orlando,' and 'Athaliah' (at Oxford). In 'Orlando' he had another very difficult song composed expressly for him, 'Sorge infausta,' which has remained a trial of compass and execution since his day for the most accomplished bassi.

In the following year, however, Montagnana seceded, with Senesino and Cuzzoni, to the Theatre in Lincoln's Inn Fields, under the direction of Porpora; and here he appeared in 'Onorio' by that master, and other pieces. In 1735 and 1736 he was still with Porpora, singing in his 'Polifemo,' and the 'Adriano' of Veracini. In Jan. 1738 he returned to his allegiance to Handel, singing in 'Faramondo,' then first produced, 'La Conquista del Vello d' Oro' and 'Serse.' J. M.

MONTAGNANA, DOMENICO (1700–40), a great violin-maker whose name is not as renowned as others of his class, owing to the misleading labels bearing the names of 'Guarnerius,' 'Bergonzi,' etc., which have been dishonestly inserted in his instruments from time to time to enhance their market value. He was an apprentice of Antonius Stradivarius, and ranks with Carlo Bergonzi as one of the master's best pupils. He first established a workshop of his own in Cremona, but later he settled in Venice, where his superior knowledge of qualities, materials, thicknesses and varnish—gained in the workshops of Cremona—brought him into prominence. His instruments show the influence of Stradivarius's teaching, but bear little resemblance to the Stradivarius form. The outline is less graceful, the upper and lower curves flatter. The sound-holes somewhat resemble the ' Guarnerius ' type, and the scroll is much larger and bolder than that of Stradivari. The extreme richness and velvety softness of his varnish rivals that of his master, and has excited the admiration of connoisseurs throughout Europe. Montagnana made violas and magnificent violoncellos besides violins, but not being a prolific maker, his instruments are scarce and valuable. It is as a violoncello-maker that the best tribute has been paid to him by Charles Reade, who called him ' the mighty Venetian ' in his letters to the *Pall Mall Gazette* in 1872.

BIBLIOGRAPHY
HART : *The Violin.* (London, 1875.)
P. VIDAL : *Les Instruments à archet.* (Paris, 1876.)
CHARLES READE : *A Lost Art Revived,* reproduced from the *Pall Mall Gazette* by George Muntz. (Gloucester, 1873.)
Les Luthiers italiens, au XVIIe et XVIIIe siècles. (Jules Gallay, Paris, 1869.)
                          E. H.-A.

MONTANARI, FRANCESCO (*b.* Padua, latter part of 17th cent.; *d.* 1730), a distinguished violinist. He was a pupil of Corelli, and established himself in Rome, where he became a member of the orchestra of St. Peter's in 1700, and, according to Dr. Burney, died in 1730 of a broken heart when Bini came to Rome and proved himself to be the finest performer of the period. He composed twelve sonatas for violin which are published by a Boulogne firm.

BIBL.—A. M. CLARKE, *Fiddlers Ancient and Modern* ; *Fétis.*
                          E. H.-A.

MONTE, PHILIPPE DE (FILIPPO DE ; sometimes PHILIPPE DE MONS) (*b.* Mons,[1] *c.* 1521 or 1522[2] ; *d.* July 4, 1603). As to his history, we gain little by consulting old authorities, as Boissart,[3] Bullart,[4] Freher,[5] Sweertius,[6] etc., and are told as much by the title-pages of Philippe's own publications. Bullart, however, gives a portrait of the composer, after Sadeler, which is well worth seeing, and much superior to the smaller copies of it in Boissart and Hawkins. Elisabeth Weston's poem,[7] often

referred to in biographies of Philippe, gives no information at all.

De Monte published his first book of masses at Antwerp in 1557,[8] just at the end of Lassus's residence in that city, and we may safely credit the common tradition of a friendship existing between the two composers. It was probably on Orlando's recommendation that Philippe was called to Vienna, May 1, 1568, to become Maximilian's Kapellmeister. Rudolph II., the next emperor, moved his court to Prague, and thither Philippe followed him. Thus we find him dating from Vienna, April 15, 1569,[9] and from Prague, Sept. 20, 1580,[10] and Oct. 10, 1587.[11]

Fétis gives interesting details of de Monte's appointment as treasurer and canon of the cathedral at Cambria, a benefice which he apparently held without residence. He resigned these appointments early in 1603, and died on July 4 of the same year.[12]

De Monte published over thirty books of madrigals—nineteen books *a* 5, eight *a* 6 and four *a* 4.[13] Eight books of these in the British Museum contain 163 numbers, so we may assume that 630 madrigals were printed, not to speak of many others contributed to collections. His sacred publications include two books of masses and seven of motets. (See *Q.-L.* for list.) Of reprints, Hawkins contributes a madrigal *a* 4, Dehn and Commer a motet each, and Van Maldeghem some numbers in his ' Trésor musical.' The Mass ' Benedicta es ' (*a* 6) has been edited (1920) by A. Smijers. The most comprehensive, however, is the study *La Vie et les œuvres de Ph. de Monte* (Brussels, 1921), by G. van Doorslaer, with list of the composer's works, bibliography and reprints. See also *Quatorze lettres inédites du compositeur Ph. de Monte* (Brussels, 1921), by Paul Bergmans.
           J. R. S.-B., with addns.

MONTÉCLAIR, MICHEL PINOLET DE (*b.* Chaumont in Bassigny, *c.* 1666; *d.* St. Denis, Sept. 1737), was a chorister in the cathedral of Langres, and subsequently sang in various other churches. He entered the service of the Prince de Vaudémont, as music-master, and went with him to Italy. In 1700 he went to live in Paris, and became a double-bass player in the Opéra orchestra in 1707, remaining there until 1737, when he retired with a pension. He was a distinguished teacher of the violin, and a composer of some importance, both for the stage and the chamber. His ' Festes de l'Été,' an *opéra-ballet,* was produced on June 12, 1716,

1 According to Dlabacz at Mechlin. *Allgem. histor. Künstler-Lex. für Böhmen.* 4to. (Prague, 1815.) Dlabacz founds his statement on a list of the Imperial Chapel dated 1582. For a full discussion of the subject see Fétis's *Biographie,* under ' Philippe de Mons.'
2 Sadeler's portrait, the single authority for this date, gives Philippe's age as 72 in 1594.
3 Boissardus, *Icones viror. illustr.* pars 3, p. 32 (1593).
4 Bullart, *Académie des Sciences,* etc., vol. ii. bk. 4, p. 299 (Brusselles, 1682).
5 Freheri, *Theatrum vir. clarorum* (Nuremberg, 1688).
6 Sweertius, *Athenae Belgicae,* p. 645 (Antwerp, 1628).
7 From the *Parthenicon,* by E. J. Weston, ' ex familia Westoniorum Angla ' (Prague, Aug. 16, 1610). The poem in Philippe's honour consists of forty-six Latin lines.

8 *Missarum a* 5, 6, 8, lib. i. (Antwerp, 1557). This on the authority of Fétis.
9 See Alto copy of second book of six-part Madrigals (Venice, 1569), in B.M.
10 Ninth book of Madrigals (*a* 5) (Venice, 1580), in B.M.
11 Sacr. cantionum lib. ii. (Venice, 1587), in B.M.
12 For this date, and that of the Vienna appointment, see Eitner, *Verzeichnis neuer Ausgaben* (Berlin, Trautwein, 1871), and the *Q.-L.*
13 Fétis speaks of the nineteenth book. The B.M. has the fourteenth. Fétis mentions no four-part Madrigals ; but the Catalogue of the Bibliothèque Fétis contains ' Di Fi. di M. il 4°. lib. di Mad. à 4.'

and his *tragédie lyrique* ' Jephté,' in five acts and a prologue, on Feb. 28, 1732. In the prologue of this latter is a curious scene in which various mythological divinities are driven from the opera-house by Truth and the Virtues, and their places taken by the scriptural personages. Montéclair wrote a *Nouvelle Méthode pour apprendre la musique* (Paris, 1709) ; a *Méthode facile pour apprendre à jouer du violon* (1711 or 1712) ; *Principes de musique*, divided into 4 parts (1736) which Fétis has taken for a second edition of the *Méthode*. A number of examples from ' Jephté ' were there given. It contains a valuable explanation of the more usual ornaments, and hints on the proper accentuation of words in music. (See *The Oxf. Hist. Mus.*, vol. iv. : *The Age of Bach and Handel*, p. 301.)

M. ; rev. M. P.

MONTELLA, GIOVANNI DOMENICO (*d.* Naples, *c.* 1601/02), lutenist in the Royal Chapel, Naples, 1594. According to Florimo [1] he was also harp-player and organist. He composed 8 books of madrigals, 5 v., 2 books of madrigals, 4 v., 1 book of motets, 5 v., 4 books of villanelle, 4 v., psalms and other church music (list in *Q.-L.*).

MONTEMEZZI, ITALO (*b.* Vigasio, province of Verona, May 31, 1875), began early the study of the piano without, however, showing any marked predilection for music. It was only after being sent to Milan to complete his technical studies that he decided to abandon engineering for musical composition. Lacking sound elementary training, he did not find it easy to gain admission to the Conservatorio of Milan, and he succeeded only after two fruitless attempts. Once admitted, however, his progress was very rapid under the guidance of M. Saladino (counterpoint) and Ferroni (composition). He obtained his final diploma in 1900. But there were apparently still some lacunæ in his education, and he has confessed that his knowledge of orchestration was gained not from text-books but from the gallery of La Scala Theatre. After leaving the Conservatorio he lived and worked for some years in retirement. His first opera, ' Giovanni Gallurese,' was given in 1905 at Turin, where it made so favourable an impression that Montemezzi came at once to be looked upon as one of the most promising composers of the younger generation. A second opera, ' Hellera,' was less successful, but the third, 'L' Amore dei tre re,' founded on the tragedy of Sem Benelli, then very popular in Italy, was received at La Scala with considerable sympathy and performed in most Italian theatres and also in England, Germany and America. A fourth opera on D'Annunzio's ' La Nave ' has met with favour in Italy.

Montemezzi himself has given us a definition of his artistic aims in an article published in America. Music without melody, he there declares, is inconceivable. Neither scholasticism nor realism appeal to him. His main aim is to create the musical atmosphere in which the characters of the drama must live and express themselves by means of melody. Certainly his chief asset at present appears to be his obvious sincerity and a certain modesty of style, which is never over-elaborate though often finished and neat.

Montemezzi has been engaged for some time in setting to music Edmond Rostand's ' La Princesse lointaine.' He has also composed a ' Song of Songs,' performed in Milan in 1900.

F. B.

MONTESARDO, see TABLATURE.

MONTEVERDI (MONTEVERDE), CLAUDIO (*b.* Cremona, May, 1567; *d.* Venice, Nov. 29, 1643), was the pupil of INGEGNERI (*q.v.*) of whom Rolland,[2] says that he was ' the principal theoretician of the theatre in the second half of the 16th century.' From Ingegneri Monteverdi would seem to have obtained a thorough grounding in the contrapuntal method for his later works bear testimony to the efficacy of this teaching. His ability to write in a severely classical style did not leave him even when he appeared most positively to be forsaking the older methods for a yet more advanced incursion among the newer. In 1583 he published his first works, the four-part ' Madrigali spirituali,' and in 1584 the Canzonette à tre voci.

MANTUA.—In 1589–90 he was accredited to the Mantuan court as violinist. In 1595 he travelled to Hungary in the suite of the Duke Vincenzo I., who was aiding the Emperor Rudolph in his war against the Turkish Sultan. Again in 1599 Monteverdi was included in the suite which accompanied Vincenzo I. to Flanders [3] where, at Spa, the Duke stayed during a month for reasons of health. Pallavicino, maestro di cappella to the House of Gonzaga at Mantua, died in Nov. 1601 and Monteverdi at once applied for the post and eventually obtained it. From the fact that the Duke created him a citizen of Mantua by a decree dated Apr. 10, 1602, it would seem that it was in this year that his appointment as maestro di cappella was finally ratified. Mantua had already become an artistic centre of some renown. The members of the House of Gonzaga, Dukes of Mantua, were inclined towards music, though in differing ways, Guglielmo, father of Vincenzo I., as an amateur composer and as a patron who was indefatigable in attracting the best contemporary talent to his court, Vincenzo I. as one who used all he could procure in the way of musicians and music that would gratify his desire for lavish display. Lacking the

---

[1] *La scuola mus. di Napoli.*

[2] *Musiciens d'autrefois*, p. 45.
[3] See Henry Pruniéres for possible French influence on Monteverdi at this time. Art. *Sackbut*, Nov. 1922.

intellectual brilliance that had characterised the court of the Estensi at Ferrara as GESUALDO (*q.v.*), Prince of Venosa, found it in 1594, Mantua in 1602 was awakening to a realisation of the potentialities of art as a means to enjoyment and was attentive at least to its seductive properties. Vincenzo I., curious mixture of the Maecenas and the miser, appears to have treated his artists, Monteverdi among them, to alternating manifestations of this two-sided character.

THE FIRST FIVE BOOKS OF MADRIGALS.—In 1587 the first book of five-part madrigals appeared. The second was published in 1590, the third in 1592, the fourth in 1603 and the fifth in 1605. The unwontedness of the harmonic progression in these early madrigals did not go unchallenged. (It must be noted, in this connection, that Gesualdo had, by the time of his death in 1614, reached harmonic spheres as distant as any to be found in Monteverdi's first five books or indeed in all the range of his compositions.) Giovanni Maria Artusi, a canon of S. Salvatore in Bologna, launched a bitter attack on the methods of the new school (*L' Artusi ovvero delle imperfettioni della moderna musica*, part 1, 1600; part 2, 1603) in which he cited the illegal progressions to be found in certain of Monteverdi's madrigals (books 4 and 5). The answer to this was contained in the *Dichiaratione* written by Monteverdi's brother Giulio Cesare as preface to the 1607 'Scherzi musicali.' It is generally considered that Monteverdi's journey to Flanders in 1599 should be held to account for a change of style which took place between the first three books and those that follow, though it is not clear what really was the exact nature of the causes which brought about that change. It seems hardly feasible that a visit to Flanders should have made more impression than did the acquaintance with that Flemish music which was already to be heard in Italy.

ORFEO.—In 1607 'Orfeo' was produced at Mantua, first at the Accademia degli Invaghiti (Feb. 24) and later (Mar. 1) before the court, these being the first of many contemporary performances. The libretto is by Alessandro Striggio, secretary to the Duke and son of the madrigalist of the same name (see STRIGGIO (2)). The work seems to have attracted the attention of Mantua as being an authentic example of the Florentine *stile rappresentativo*. Time has shown how greatly Monteverdi in 'Orfeo' surpassed the achievements of 1600. The work sums up the endeavours of past years. It is more truly the climax of what had gone before, the consummation of traditional technique, than the starting-point of new methods (Adler). 'Orfeo' has been looked on in the past as the first noticeable step in the direction of the orchestral methods of the 17th century. In reality it shows the last

stages of the older methods of Peri and the Florentine operatic composers (Goldschmidt). Monteverdi did not return again to the instrumental style of 'Orfeo.' Already in 'Arianna' (1608) the orchestra, placed behind the scenes as in 'Orfeo,' although possibly still as bewilderingly rich in instruments (Adler), was almost certainly overshadowed in interest by the greater one of the stage action. If we may judge 'Arianna' by all that now remains of the opera, the 'Lamento' (famous throughout Italy from its first appearance as a solo song, later scored by Monteverdi as a five-part madrigal and included in the 6th book of 1614, and, again, fitted with sacred words as the five-part 'Pianta della Madonna,' 1640), the histrionic style is more certain in the portrayal of emotion than that of 'Orfeo,' and has greater importance here than details of orchestral method. Again it is not in 'Orfeo' that experiments in orchestration were carried out, but in later and smaller works such as 'Tancredi e Clorinda.' And from the point of view of orchestral organisation 'Orfeo,' and possibly 'Arianna,' are seen as the final examples of the old methods of Peri, soon to give place to the 'Ballo delle ingrate' (1608), wherein the string orchestra shows signs of a more distinct existence (Goldschmidt). Monteverdi, finding the new movement, initiated in Florence, already in being, showed in 'Orfeo' what, as regards orchestral technique, could be obtained from the contemporary orchestra, and as regards dramatic technique what great advances could be made on the achievements of 1600. In the former connection he could go no farther and was forced to reorganise on narrower lines. In the latter, he was to go onward and reach the more intense dramatic style of 'L' incoronazione di Poppea.' In 1608 Monteverdi also wrote the prologue, now lost, to 'L' idropica,' a comedy by Guarini and the 'Ballo delle ingrate,' later printed in the 'Madrigali guerrieri' (1638).

VENICE.—In 1610 Monteverdi went on a short visit to Rome. Vincenzo I. of Mantua died in 1612 and Monteverdi was relieved of his duties by the new duke. In September of that year he went to Milan, after a short stay in his native Cremona. In Aug. 1613 he was appointed maestro di cappella at St. Mark's in Venice by the Procuratori. His success seems to have been immediate and he definitely settled himself at Venice. His powers were ample and his financial position assured. In such surroundings he was able to apply himself to solving those problems of musical evolution which had been postulated in Florence by the Bardi fraternity and to which he himself had contributed in his Mantuan period. Placed in absolute control of a body of singers and players, he could gauge to a nicety the material at his disposal as well as impose his will on those who showed themselves to be at variance with his innovating genius.

In 1614 the sixth book of madrigals appeared, and already what Prunières aptly calls 'the disintegration of the madrigal' set in. This book contains declamatory pieces for 2 or for 3 voices in a style far removed from the accepted utterances of Marenzio or di Lasso. The dramatic urgency of the 'Lasciatemi morire' is more sustainedly intense than even Gesualdo, and certainly more definitely descriptive of the actual emotion portrayed than anything the older school had produced. The seventh book (1619) consists in 2, 3 and 4-part madrigals and even solos, all with accompaniment either orchestral or a basso continuo. And in the eighth book ('alcuni opusculi in genre rappresentativo'), the 'Madrigali guerrieri e amorosi' (1638), the pieces are clearly conceived as for a theatre, the 'Ballo delle ingrate' and the 'Combattimento di Tancredi e Clorinda' being included in this set. That Monteverdi should term such pieces 'Madrigali' is evidence of the position to which the madrigal had attained in Italy by the end of the third decade of the 17th century. Since Artusi's attack on the modern school in 1600 swift changes had come over music. It was now no longer details of harmonic behaviour that exercised the minds of the leading composers, but questions of the deeper meaning that was guessed at as lying behind and beyond that kind of disquisition. Monteverdi was armed with an unerring knowledge of contrapuntal methods, and where he destroyed he did so wittingly. In his church music he shows himself the equal of the contemporary ecclesiastical composers, conforming to their conventions as to the contrapuntal treatment of voices and the formal disposition of material. At the same time the charge brought against him in contemporary chronicles that his church music was, by reason of its style, often better fitted to the theatre, is comprehensible. He had the ability for keeping two seemingly antipathetic styles equally in order. And with the 'Messe' of 1610, the 'Selva morale e spirituale' of 1640 and the 'Messa à quatro voci e salmi' of 1650, this twofold activity can be apprehended, so austere and polyphonic a work as the 'In illo tempore' for six voices appearing in the same book (1610) as the brilliant polyphonic 'Sonata sopra Sancta Maria' for eight instruments (five wind and three strings) and solo voice.

OPERAS OF THE VENETIAN PERIOD.—In 1615 Monteverdi wrote the opera-ballet 'Tirsi e Clori,' commissioned by Ferdinand Gonzaga for performance at Mantua (printed in the 7th book of madrigals, 1619). In 1617 he co-operated with Muzio Effrem, Salomo Rossi and Alessandro Guivizzani in the religious drama 'Maddalena.' In the same year an opera, 'Amori di Diana e d' Endimione,' was performed

in Parma. In 1618 the opera 'Andromeda' (unfinished) is placed. Of greatest importance up to this time, however, is the setting of 'Il combattimento di Tancredi e Clorinda' (str. 52–68, omitting str. 63, from canto 12 of Tasso's *Gerusalemme liberàta*), performed in 1624 at the Palace of Girolamo Mocenigo. Dramatic in intention, this work is cast in the form of a secular cantata. The advance in power of characterisation on 'Orfeo' is remarkable, the command both of the ways and the means of emotional delineation, most noticeable. In this work the first effective use of string *tremolo* and of *pizzicato* for strings is made. But apart from such interesting considerations the artistic merits of the 'Combattimento' are of a sufficiently high order to warrant its being held in remembrance. What Monteverdi called the 'stile concitato,' that which was fashioned in order to express the agitated and warring elements of human relationships, was here manifested. Each subtlety of spirit and action in the protagonists is reflected from the music.

In 1627 the operas 'Armide' and 'La finta pazza Licori' (both lost) were composed. In 1633 Monteverdi was admitted to the priesthood. Other operas which came after this, and might possibly help to show the expansion of his genius, are most unfortunately no longer to be found. In 1637 the Teatro San Cassiano was opened as a public opera-house, and two years later Monteverdi wrote 'Adone' (also among the lost works) for performance there. Not until the 'Ritorno d' Ulisse in patria' (1642) is it possible to regain touch with Monteverdi's development as a composer of operas. The libretto of this opera is by Badoaro.

'L' INCORONAZIONE DI POPPEA.' — In the 'Ritorno d' Ulisse' Monteverdi faced the great task of setting an extended historical subject in the realistic manner. He was not wholly successful. The value of the work is only relative. The involved libretto weakens the interest of the tale. The story might well have been retold in such a way as to make an exceedingly moving operatic spectacle. Even as it stands the scene of the recognition of Ulysses by Penelope gave Monteverdi an opportunity for one of his finest achievements.

In 1642 'L' incoronazione di Poppea,' an opera on a libretto by Busenello, was produced in Venice at the Teatro San Cassiano, and in this work Monteverdi gave final proof of his genius for truthful characterisation and his talent as a technician in the craft of music and of dramatic presentation. No longer is there any chance that the attention may be deflected to orchestral effects as in the 'Combattimento.' (Only voice parts and continuo are to be found in the sole existing copy of 'L' incoronazione.'[1]) However the orchestra may have been organised

[1] See Hugo Goldschmidt's practically complete edition of the opera in vol. ii. of his 'Studien.'

and written for, the intensity of the dramatisation is such as to take possession of the audience from the moment when the first act opens to Ottone's restless ' E pur si torno ' until at the end Poppea and Nero sing the triumphal ' Pur ti miro, pur ti godo.' The *ritornelli* are few, fewer still the *sinfonie*. Nothing interrupts the unfolding of the bitter and extremely unmoral plot by the singers. Scenes such as that of the death of Seneca and the lullaby sung to Poppea by her nurse in Act 2, or the love scenes between Poppea and Nero in Acts 1 and 3, are more deeply felt and more delicately treated than anything that Monteverdi had previously written. The characters are finely differentiated and keep their individuality to the end. As ' Orfeo,' Monteverdi's first significant work, sums up the achievement of the early attempts at operatic representation, ' L' incoronazione di Poppea,' his last dramatic composition, securely founds that operatic style [1] which was to take possession of Italy, reaching thence out into the whole of Europe and attaining unimagined heights in the stage works of G. F. Handel.

MONTEVERDI'S POSITION IN HISTORY.—As an orchestrator Monteverdi's innovations in the ' Combattimento di Tancredi e Clorinda ' are not to be minimised. But as an organiser of the orchestra his importance is still greater. Already in ' Orfeo ' he exercised discrimination in the choice of instruments he used (as can be seen when the early orchestras of Marenzio and others are compared with that of ' Orfeo ' [2]), and he abandoned such antiquated instruments as were no longer effective in the orchestral ensemble. By the time of the composition of the ' Combattimento' Monteverdi had effected still further changes in the organisation of the orchestra, which had the result of freeing composers from the cumbersome machinery set in motion by the first exponents of the ' Nuove musiche.' This limitation of orchestral resources had the effect of refining the technique of orchestration at the same time as it simplified the organisation of the orchestra and made it a more malleable medium for the expression of subtleties of thought through music. The instrumentation of ' Orfeo ' was rich in the same way as that of the accompanied madrigal of the preceding century. That of ' L' incoronazione ' was bare, as though it were left purposely void in order not to impede the unfolding of the principles of operatic form.

Monteverdi stands midway between Palestrina and Handel. He was gifted with an intellect that could understand and practice the art of a Gabrieli as well as that of a Gesualdo. At no one time during all his career does this

---

[1] See Goldschmidt, *op. cit.* vol. ii., for a discussion of Monteverdi's first use of the *da capo* aria with change of key in the middle section, also first use of *leitmotiv* and special treatment of basso ostinato in 'L' incoronazione.'
[2] See Goldschmidt, *op. cit.* vol. i.

dual nature forsake him. And in ' L' incoronazione di Poppea ' he used his knowledge of the tried methods of harmonic and contrapuntal procedure and of formal construction in alliance with those revolutionary ideas which informed the art of his time and which he, having done more than any other composer to advance, eventually guided into the paths of a saner evolution.

LIST OF WORKS

Note.—In the case of Operas, Ballets and Intermezzi, date of performance is given. In all other cases, that of publication. Lost works in *italics*.

1583. 4-pt. Madrigali spirituali.
1584. Canzonette a tre voci.
1587. 1st book 5-pt. madrigals.
1590. 2nd   „   „
1592. 3rd   „   „
1603. 4th   „   „
1605. 5th   „   „
1607. Scherzi musicali a tre voci.
    Some of the madrigals are printed in the ' Raccolta nazionale ' (Ricordi, Milan), books 76, 77, 78, 79, 224, 225. Three 5-pt. madrigals have been edited by M. Vincent d'Indy (Rondaney, Paris, 1914). Three motets for solo voice have been published by Senart, Paris (1913).
    ' Orfeo.' Libretto by Alessandro Striggio. Published Venice, 1609. Reprinted Venice, 1615. Eitner, ' Die Oper ' I.; Vincent d'Indy prepared a shortened version for performance in 1904. This has since been published. A definitive edition by Signor Malipiero appeared in 1923 (Chester).
1608. ' Arianna.' Libretto by Rinuccini. The ' Lamento,' published Mantua, 1623.
    ' Ballo delle ingrate.' Libretto by Rinuccini. Published in the ' Madrigali guerrieri,' 1638.
    L' idropica. Prologue. Libretto by Chiabrera.
1610. Messe.
1614. 6th book 5-pt. madrigals.
1615. ' Tirsi e Clori,' ballet with voices. Published 1619, 7th book 5-pt. madrigals.
1617. ' Maddalena.' Opera, libretto by Rossi, composed in conjunction with others.
    ' Gli amori di Diana e d' Endimione.' Libretto by the Duchess of Parma.
1618. *' Andromeda.' Libretto by Marigliani.*
1619. 7th book 5-pt. madrigals.
    ' Lamento di Apollo.' Libretto by Striggio.
1624. ' Combattimento di Tancredi e Clorinda.' Poem by Tasso (' Gerusalemme liberata '). Published in the ' Madrigali guerrieri,' 1638.
1627. *' Armide.'* Poem by Tasso (' Gerusalemme liberata ').
    ' La finta pazza Licori.' Libretto by Giulio Strozzi.
    ' Melissa e Bradamante.' Poem by Tasso. Intermezzo.
    ' Aminta.' Poem by Tasso. *Intermezzo.*
    ' Didone.' Libretto by Pii. Intermezzo.
    ' Gli Argonauti.' Libretto by Pii. Intermezzo.
    ' Mercurio e Marte.' Libretto by Claudio Achillini. Intermezzo.
1628. *' I cinque fratelli.'* Five sonnets by Strozzi.
1630. *' Proserpina rapita.'* Libretto by Strozzi.
1632. Scherzi musicali a 1 e 2 voci.
1634. Seconda Pratica.
1638. 8th book 5-pt. madrigals. The ' Madrigali guerrieri e amorosi.'
1639. *' Adone.'* Libretto by Vendramin.
1640. Selva morale e spirituale.
1641. ' Il ritorno d' Ulisse in patria.' Libretto by Giacomo Badoaro. *D.T.Ö.* xxix. (i.)
    ' Nozze d' Enea con Lavinia.' Libretto by Badoaro.
1642. ' L' incoronazione di Poppea.' Libretto by Busenello. Shortened performing edition prepared by M. d'Indy, 1905. Complete edition (some omissions) by Hugo Goldschmidt, ' Studien,' vol. 2.
    ' La vittoria d' Amore.' Ballet with voices. Libretto by Morandi.
1650. Messe a 4 voci e salmi. (Posthumous.)
1650. Madrigali e canzonette a due e tre voci. (Posthumous.)

BIBLIOGRAPHY

DAVARI : *Notizie biografiche.* (Mantua, 1885.)
GOLDSCHMIDT : *Studien zur Geschichte der italienischen Oper im 17. Jahrhundert.* (Leipzig, 1904.)
SCHNEIDER : *Claudio Monteverdi.* (Paris, 1921.)
ADLER : *Handbuch der Musikgeschichte.* (Frankfort, 1924.)
PRUNIÈRES : *Monteverdi.* (Paris, 1925.)
Articles in *Revue musicale* (Nov. 1922, June 1922, Aug. 1923) and in *Sackbut* (Nov. 1922, Apr. 1923, Sept 1923).

                                    S. G.

MONTGOMERY, HUGH (*b.* Nov. 29, 1739; *d.* Dec. 14 or 15, 1819), afterwards 12th Earl of Eglintoun, joined the army and became a colonel. On succeeding to the title and estates in Ayrshire he devoted himself to musical studies and became a fair amateur composer. He became a prominent figure in Edinburgh musical society, and patronised the Gow family.

Some of his compositions appear in the Gow publications, and in 1796 Nathaniel Gow issued a thin folio volume (24 pp.) entirely of his Strathspeys. It was issued anonymously, its title being *New Strathspey Reels . . . composed by a gentleman, and given with permission to be published by Nathaniel Gow.* 'Ayrshire Lasses,' his best-known Strathspey, is included in this work. Niel Gow dedicated his *Fourth Collection of Strathspey Reels,* 1800, to him. A volume of his vocal airs and marches, apparently from his hitherto unpublished MSS., was issued in Glasgow about 1835–40 with pianoforte arrangements by John Turnbull. Mrs. John Hunter had in most instances supplied the words. F. K.

MONTICELLI, ANGELO MARIA (*b.* Milan, *c.* 1710 ; *d.* Dresden, 1764), soprano singer. He first appeared in opera at Rome in 1730, and, having a beautiful face and figure, began in that city, where no women were then allowed upon the stage, by representing female characters. His voice was clear and sweet, and singularly free from defects. 'He was,' says Burney, ' a chaste performer, and . . . a good actor.' In 1731 and 1732 he appeared at Venice with Carestini, Bernacchi and Faustina. He came to London in the autumn of 1741, and made his début here in the pasticcio ' Alessandro in Persia.' In the beginning of 1742, after other attempts, another opera was brought out by Pergolesi, called ' Maraspe, o L' Olimpiade,' the first air of which, ' Tremende, oscuri, atroci,' in Monticelli's part, was sung for ten years after the end of the run of this opera; and 'the whole scene, in which " Se cerca se dice " occurs, was rendered so interesting by the manner in which it was acted as well as sung by Monticelli that the union of poetry and music, expression and gesture, have seldom had a more powerful effect on an English audience.'[1]

He continued to perform in London through 1743 ; and in 1744 he sang, in ' Alfonso,' songs of more bravura execution than he had previously attempted. During 1745 and 1746 Monticelli still belonged to our Opera ; and in the latter year he sang in Gluck's ' Caduta de' Giganti,' and described one of his songs as an ' aria Tedesca ' from the richness of the accompaniment. The ' Antigono ' of Galuppi (produced May 13) was the last opera in which Monticelli appeared on our stage. He sang at Naples with Regina Mingotti in the same year, and afterwards at Vienna. In 1756 Hasse engaged him for the Dresden theatre.

A capital mezzotint portrait of Monticelli was scraped by Faber after Casali. J. M.

MONTIGNY-RÉMAURY, FANNY MARCELLINE CAROLINE (*b.* Pamiers, Ariége, Jan. 22, 1843; *d.* there, June 29, 1913). Her elder sister and godmother, Elvire Rémaury (Mme.

Ambroise Thomas), an excellent pianist, first taught her music, but anxious to secure her every advantage, entered her in 1854 at the Conservatoire, in the pianoforte class of Professeur Le Couppey. In 1858 she gained the first prize for piano ; in 1859 a medal for solfège ; and in 1862 the first prize for harmony. Shortly after this Mme. C. Rémaury played Mendelssohn's concerto in G minor at one of the concerts of the Conservatoire, and her animated and vigorous interpretation of this favourite work at once placed her in the first rank of French pianists. In 1866 she married Léon Montigny, a political writer on the staff of the *Temps,* but was left a widow in 1871. She was for long the head of the pianoforte virtuosi of France, and her visits to England and tours on the Continent extended her reputation over Europe. G. C.

MONZANI, THEOBALD, a celebrated Italian flute-maker and player. As early as 1790 he was established as a flute-maker and seller at 1 Duke Street, Grosvenor Square ; and before 1800, after sundry changes of address, had settled down at 2 Pall Mall, in partnership with one Cungdor, Cundon or Cinador, for the name is variously spelled in contemporary references. In 1804 they removed to 3 Old Bond Street, and in 1808 Monzani was in partnership with Hill. Monzani & Hill were, in 1814, at 100 Cheapside ; in 1814, at 24 Dover Street ; and finally, 1820, at 28 Regent Street, close to Regent Circus. They issued a great deal of sheet music, much of it being Italian vocal pieces, while their reputation as flute-makers was at the highest. The elder Monzani acquired some fame as an orchestral flautist, and wrote several instruction-books, etc., but his son excelled the father in taste and execution, and in 1826 is referred to, in W. N. James's *A Word or Two on the Flute,* as ' the most promising performer in England.' F. K.

MOOD (Lat. *modus*; Ital. *modo*; Old Eng. *mode* or *moode*), a term employed in mediæval music to indicate the relative duration of the Large and the Long, the Long and the Breve. (See NOTATION, under subsection TIME SIGNATURES.)

MOODY, FANNY, see MANNERS.

MOONLIGHT SONATA, an absurd title which for years has been attached both in Germany and England to the ' Sonata quasi una fantasia' in C♯ minor, the second of the two which form together Beethoven's op. 27. It is dedicated to the ' Damigella Contessa Giulietta Guicciardi.' The title is said to have been derived from an expression of Rellstab, the critic, comparing the first movement to a boat wandering by moonlight on the Lake of Lucerne.[2] In Vienna it is sometimes known as the Laubensonate,[3] from a tradition that

[1] Burney. The air is given at length in *The Oxf. Hist. Mus.* vol. iv., *The Age of Bach and Handel,* p. 221.

[2] Lenz, *Beethoven et ses trois styles,* i. 225.
[3] Ib., *Beethoven, eine Kunststudie,* Pt. 2, 79.

the first movement was composed in the leafy alley (Laubengang) of a garden.

MOÓR, EMANUEL (b. Hungary, 1862), composer and inventor of the Duplex Coupler Grand Pianoforte, studied in Budapest and Vienna and then toured in Europe and America as conductor and pianist. Several operas by him have been produced in Germany, namely, 'Die Pompadour' and 'Andreas Moser' (both Cologne, 1902), and 'Hochzeitsglocken' (Cassel, 1908). Of seven symphonies three (op. 45 in D minor, op. 65 in E minor, op. 67 in C) have been published. Of his four violin concertos, that in G (op. 62) was introduced by Ysaÿe who played it at Queen's Hall first in 1907 and again later. At about the same period some of his chamber works were heard in programmes of the CLASSICAL CONCERT SOCIETY. Moór gave a concert of his own pianoforte works in London in 1910.

Moór has been much occupied with instrumental problems and has written a pamphlet on the reconstruction of the orchestra. Of his inventions, that which has come nearest to practical realisation is the Duplex-Coupler piano, the rights in which were bought by the Aeolian Company (see PIANOFORTE).　　c.

MOOR, KAREL (b. Bělohrad, 1873), Czech composer, operatic conductor and writer. His works include : two operas, 'Viy' (1901), based on Gogol's tale of witchcraft, and 'Hjördis' (1899), from Ibsen's tragedy ; the symphonic poems 'Polonia' (reminiscences of Mickiewicz) ; 'Requiem' (the life of Smetana) ; 'The Sea' ; Polish dances ; songs ; quartet, etc. Moor has also written a novel of musical life, Karel Martens (1904–05). R. N.

MOORE, THOMAS (b. 12 Aungier Street, Dublin, May 28, 1779 ; d. Feb. 28, 1852), poet and musician, was the son of John Moore and Anastasia, his wife.

In his fragmentary 'Memoirs' Moore speaks of himself as a 'Show Child,' and tells of his infantile recitations and his taking part in private theatrical performances. One cannot but recall how in his manhood days he was wont to delight the company by his exquisite rendering of his own songs.

After some private schooling he entered Trinity College, Dublin, in 1793, and remained until 1798. At this time he became associated with Robert Emmet and other members of a revolutionary party. He escaped the fate which befell some of the others, and in 1799 he came to London to enter the Middle Temple. All this while he had written much ephemeral work and translated the Odes of Anacreon, which formed a small volume. It is not necessary here to refer in any detail to his literary work, which during his life was very varied and popular. His musical education was mostly what he picked up from the music-master of his sister and his own independent study.

He came to England, but in 1803 was appointed to a Government post in Bermuda. Not liking his position he left the affair in the hands of a deputy who involved him in a deficit of something like £3000. The debt was paid by Lord Lansdowne, who was afterwards repaid by Moore. He went to America and Canada. In the latter-named country he wrote the 'Canadian Boat Song,' one of the most popular of his early pieces.

About 1802–03 he was fully engaged in writing songs which were published, with the music (much of it being his own composition), by James Carpenter of Old Bond Street.

Of single songs he was prolific, some published by Carpenter and at a later period by Power. 'The Woodpecker,' with the music by Michael Kelly, is even now heard ; 'O Lady Fair,' a glee for 5 voices, had its fame ; 'A Song of the Olden Time' had its vogue, and many another. When the 'Irish Melodies' came forth they eclipsed all Moore's previous efforts. William Power, music-seller of Dublin, projected an edition of Irish airs with English words by different poets. The musical arrangements were to be done by Dr. John Stevenson. In Feb. 1807 Power wrote to Thomas Moore telling him of his project and soliciting his aid. Moore replied enthusiastically, and promised all the help he could give.

It is quite evident that Power's scheme was suggested by Geo. Thomson's Collection of Scottish Songs, then publishing, to which work Robert Burns was the chief contributor. The scheme was launched and the 'Selection of Irish Melodies, with Symphonies and Accompaniments by Sir John Stevenson, Mus. Doc., and characteristic words by Thomas Moore, Esq.,' began publication in numbers, Thomas Moore being the sole poet employed. The 'Melodies' reached ten numbers and a supplement extending to 1834.

The first number was issued at the latter end of 1807 or beginning of 1808, and consisted of 51 pages. It contained about twelve songs, some of which were arranged for two or more voices. The numbers were published at 15 shillings each. The work was issued in green paper boards, decorated with a rude woodcut depicting a lady (supposed to be 'Erin') reclining against a harp. It is said that this woodcut had adorned a Dublin ballad sheet. It was replaced by a far more beautiful design after Stotherd in 1821. In their get-up the numbers were evidently a distinct copy of Geo. Thomson's Scottish collection.

The dates of the publications of the numbers are as follows : 1807–08, 1810–11, 1813, 1815–1818, 1821, 1824–34. The six early numbers contain all the most popular of Moore's songs. The popularity of these from the date of their publication was simply enormous, and the numbers were republished again and again.

For the airs Moore robbed without scruple the collections of Irish airs made by Edward Bunting and published in 1796 and 1807, much to Bunting's chagrin. It is said that Moore made serious alterations in the airs, but an examination of Bunting's and Holden's works, which he also used, will show that these alterations, when present, were of the slightest. Sir Charles Stanford published in 1895 'The Irish Melodies of Thomas Moore ; the original airs restored.' Stanford's restorations are not always justified, as pointed out in Moffat's *Minstrelsy of Ireland.*

One thing has not been before noticed ; that Moore was bold enough to take for serious songs tunes which were familiar with comic or semi-comic songs, as 'Paddy Whack' for 'While History's Muse,' and 'The Pretty Girl of Darby, O' for 'Eveleen's Bower.'

After the publication of the seventh number William Power brought an action against his brother James, who then had an extensive trade in London, to prevent him publishing the eighth number, 1821, contending that he had the sole copyright. James, however, won the case.

The ninth and tenth numbers were harmonised by Bishop, who afterwards did most of the musical arrangements for Moore. At James Power's death, in Aug. 1836, his widow retained the copyright of the Irish melodies, which afterwards passed into the hands of Addison and Hollier, who reissued them in the same style of paper boards as the original. When the 'Melodies' became free from copyright, numerous musicians edited them and wrote new arrangements of the airs, as Sir John Stevenson's were old - fashioned and by no means satisfactory for modern singing.

In 1816 Moore published the first number of 'Sacred Songs, the words by Thomas Moore, Esq., the music composed and selected by Sir John Stevenson and Mr. Moore,' folio. After that came a 'Selection of Popular National Airs,' in six numbers, beginning in 1818, and continuing to 1828. The first number was arranged by Sir John Stevenson, and contained the charming song 'Oft in the Stilly Night.' The remaining numbers were harmonised by Henry Bishop. A volume of 'Evenings in Greece' followed.

In 1811 Moore wrote an unsuccessful opera called 'M.P., or the Blue Stocking,' produced at the English Opera House in Sept. 1811, the music composed by Charles Edward HORN (*q.v.*). In 1811 Moore married an actress, Miss Bessie Dykes. He died from softening of the brain.

Moore's songs were, during the first fifty or sixty years after their publication, in immense favour, and they were sung among all classes of people. They entered into the literature of the country, and to go no further they are greatly quoted and referred to in Dickens's novels.

His voice was delightful, and charmed everybody with its sweetness. He was fond of singing his songs at the society functions which he attended, and his small stature was hidden by the cluster of admirers who surrounded him. His relations with his publisher, James Power, were extraordinary. Although he drew immense sums for his works he was continually overdrawing his account with Power, and looked upon him for the performance of many extraordinary tasks. Power said, 'I am his banker, his bill acceptor and fish agent, letter carrier, hotel keeper and publisher, and now he wants me to be his shoe-black.'

In the latter part of his life, by the exertions of Lord John Russell, he was granted a Government pension.   F. K.

MOORE, THOMAS, a 17th-century London printer, who was the first to introduce the 'new tied' note in musical typography, where the tails of the quavers and semiquavers are united instead of being printed separately, as was the case before Moore printed. 'The new tied' note is used in the second book of *Comes Amoris*, 1688, the first book, 1687, having the old lozenge-shaped notes.

Moore was afterwards associated with J. Heptinstall, another London printer. In 1700 William Pearson made great improvements in the 'new tied note,' and Fougt, at a much later date, effected still greater improvements.
                                              F. K.

MOOREHEAD, (1) JOHN (*b.* Ireland, middle of 18th cent. ; *d.* near Deal, Mar. 1804) received his first musical instruction in Ireland. He came to England when young, and was for several years engaged in the orchestras of various country theatres. He was one of the violins at the Worcester Festival of 1794, and in 1796 was principal viola at Sadler's Wells Theatre. In 1798 he was engaged in the orchestra at Covent Garden, and soon after was employed to compose for that theatre. During his engagement he composed music for ' The Philosopher's Stone,' 1795 ; ' Birds of a Feather,' 1796 ; ' The Volcano ' and ' Speed the Plough,' ' Harlequin's Tour ' and ' The Dominion of Fancy ' (both with Attwood), 1800 ; ' Il Bondocani ' (with Attwood) and ' Perouse ' (with Davy), 1801 ; ' Harlequin's Habeas,' ' The Cabinet ' (with Braham, Davy, etc.) and ' Family Quarrels ' (with Braham and Reeve), 1802. In that year he became insane, and having transgressed the laws, was confined successively in Tothill Fields Prison and Northampton House, Clerkenwell. On his liberation he entered the navy as a common sailor, and was quickly promoted to be bandmaster. A short time afterwards he hanged himself in a fit of insanity near Deal. The ' F. Moorehead ' who is described as the composer of ' The Naval Pillar,' 1799 (see *Q.-L.*) is probably a printer's error for John Moorehead. His brother, (2) ALEXANDER, was also a violinist of merit, and led the band at Sadler's Wells ; he also became insane and died in an asylum in Liverpool.[1]   W. H. H. ; addns. F. K.

MOOSER, ALOYS (*b.* Fribourg, 1770 ; *d.* there, Dec. 19, 1829), a famous Swiss organbuilder, whose greatest instruments are those at Fribourg and in the New Temple at Berne. Mooser also made pianos.   G.

MORALES, CRISTOBAL (*b.* Seville, *c.* 1500 ; *d.* ? Marchena, between Sept. 4 and Oct. 7, 1553). Morales always described himself as *Hispalensis*, a native of Sevil e. His father is believed to have been a certain Cristobal de Morales who was in Seville in 1503, a singer in the service of the Duke of Medina Sidonia. As the son was already maestro de capilla in 1526, he cannot have been born much later than 1500. He was a pupil of Fernandez de Castilleja, maestro de capilla at Seville Cathedral, 1514–74. He was evidently brought up on Flemish traditions, and MS. choir books of Josquin des Prés, apparently dating from this time, are still preserved in the choir library. They also include motets by Gombert, who probably visited Seville in 1526 as maestro de capilla to the Emperor Charles V. at the time of his marriage to Isabella of Portugal, and it was in two collections of motets by Gombert that Morales's earliest works were printed, in 1541. His first appointment was maestro de capilla at Avila (Aug. 8, 1526), with a salary of 100 ducats, a post which he held until Oct. 12, 1530.[2] The three masses he is said to have left there have disappeared. He is next heard of in Rome, being admitted as cantor in the Cappella Pontificia under Pope Paul III. (Sept. 1, 1535). He was already a priest, and is described as *Clericus Hispalensis*.[3] Calasanz, Escribano and other Spaniards were already members of the choir, and Morales was soon joined by Escobedo (Aug. 23, 1536) and Ordoñez (Apr. 29, 1539). His earliest known work is a secular cantata (6 v.) written for the Peace Conference at Nice (1538) between the Emperor Charles V., Francis I. of France and Pope Paul III., while in the following year he composed a similar cantata for the elevation of Ippolito d' Este to the dignity of cardinal. Both of these works are constructed on the principle of one voice (quintus or ' vagans ') repeating the same succession of notes at regular intervals, to words which are different from those sung by the other voices—a device much used by Josquin des Prés, Gombert and other 16th-century composers down to the time of Lassus. (Cf. Lassus's 6-part, ' Fremuit spiritus Jesu,' in which the sextus sings nothing but *Lazare, veni foras*). In the same year

(1539) a madrigal by Morales (' Ditimi o si o no ') was printed in Arcadelt's 4th book. Two others were published later. To Morales's Roman period also belong some, if not all, his magnificats (1542 and 1545), his 3 vols. of motets (1543 and 1546) and his 2 vols. of masses (1544).

Morales had visited Spain in 1540 (Apr. 4 : *obtinuit licentiam eundi ad patriam*). In 1545 he was granted 10 months' leave (May 1 : *abiit ad partes de licentia per menses decem*)— leave from which he never returned. In the autumn of that year he was appointed maestro de capilla at Toledo. There, however, he remained for less than two years (Aug. 30, 1545–Spring, 1547). He had been granted, in addition to the usual stipend, an allowance towards the maintenance of the *seises*, the boys of the choir-school. Yet early in the next year (Mar. 26, 1546) the chapter lent 20 ducats to the ' Venerable Cristobal de Morales,' owing to the famine and the high prices resulting from it ; while on Oct. 3 they made him a further advance, on account of illness : ' 28 ducats produced by the sale of the 25 dead elm-trees in the garden of Alaytique.' By July 1547 Morales seems to have left Toledo. A new ' Rector of the College ' (the choir-school ?) was appointed, and on Aug. 9 the post of maestro de capilla was announced to be vacant.[4]

The whereabouts of Morales between 1547 and 1550 are uncertain ; but in that year (Oct. 22) he describes himself (in a letter printed in the 2nd ed. of Bermudo's *Declaracion de instrumentos*) as maestro de capilla to the Duke of Arcos at Marchena, near Seville. In Nov. 1551 we find him elected maestro at Malaga ; but he is next heard of at Toledo (Mar. 29, 1552). He returned to Malaga, however, and his name appears frequently in the *Actas Capitulares* of the cathedral. His value was not appreciated ; he fell out with the canons and was more than once fined for petty offences.[5] On July 13, 1552, he asked for leave to go home (to Marchena ?) ; but in 1553 he was once again at Malaga, where, in June, he applied once more for leave of absence. He was trying for a second time for the post of maestro at Toledo, which he had resigned in 1547. It had been decided at a meeting of the Toledo Cathedral chapter (Aug. 11, 1553) that Morales would be welcome back again, but that he must perform his *oposición* (examination) as laid down by the regulations. Morales entered his name (by proxy) on Sept. 4 ; but he was never heard of again, and on Oct. 7 the chapter at Malaga disposed of ' the house left vacant through the death of Morales.' The election of a maestro de capilla took place at Toledo on Dec. 4, the successful candidate being Bartholomé de Quevedo.

1 See T. Dibdin's *Reminiscences*, 1827, vol. i. pp. 314-33.
2 Mitjana ; see also *Z.M.W.*, 1920, ii. 551.
3 Celani, *Rev. Mus. Ital.*, 1907, xiv. 98.
4 Rubio Piqueras, *Musicos Toledanos.* Toledo, 1922.
5 Mitjana, *Estudios.* Madrid, 1918.

Morales was famous among his contemporaries. As early as 1541 he is described as the 'most excellent' Morales; there were personal qualities in his style which could be recognised—the spacing of the voices, the recourse to purely homophonic writing when the words gave point to the music, and the realisation of the expressive possibilities of the 3rd and 4th modes. These have been favourites in Spain from that day to this. A constant feature of southern Spanish folk-music (and of the works of Granados and Albéniz) is the recurrence of the 4th mode 'Phrygian' cadence, with its drop of a semitone to the final; and this helps to explain Pedrell's enthusiasm for the essentially Spanish qualities which he felt in Morales. Two or three characteristic cadences are probably enough to give the Spanish effect, just as 'Purcellian' cadences and false relations give an English effect to the 'Euge Bone' mass of Morales's contemporary, Tye. The fact that Morales sometimes broke the rules by allowing 'hidden 5ths' and even the tritone, and that like the Tudor composers he had a certain affection for the 'quinta falsa,' did not blind his contemporaries to his complete mastery of the technique of composition. Strict counterpoint with him was not a restraint, but a means of expression; Padre Martini and others have justly admired his skill in fugue and his imaginative use of structural principles. He does not make lucky shots like Taverner; but if he is less surprising than his English contemporaries, he always seems to know what he is doing. Clearness of thought and expression were evidently a passion with him, and his one recorded saying confirms this attitude. Discussing the organ with Juan BERMUDO (q.v.); he remarked: 'If what some of these organists do could be brought out clearly, we should find grand mistakes.' (*Si lo que hazen algunos tañedores de órgano se sacasse en limpio, grandes faltas hallaríamos.*) The object of music, he held, was 'to give nobility and austerity to the soul'; yet it is precisely the nobility and austerity of his music which has tended to banish him from the Church service, in favour of Victoria. The formal perfection and austerity of Morales are also found in the later composer, in an intenser form; but the modern reputation of Victoria, unlike that of Morales, depends upon a few of his more expressive responses and motets, which have been sentimentalised by transposing them into flat keys and accompanying them on the organ. Morales, on the other hand, is remarkable for his lyrical sense, and for his feeling for the expressive possibilities of a good tune. His favourite principle of construction, as mentioned above, was that of an independent voice singing words which were different from those the other voices were singing. This can be seen in all stages of development. In the

5-part motet 'Tu es Petrus' the quintus has nothing to sing except the short phrase of six notes with which the motet begins. The same is the case with the beautiful 'Veni, Domine,' 6 v., though the phrase repeated is longer. In 'Andreas Christi famulus,' 5 v., the Superius 2 enters at regular intervals on G and D, singing a well-known tune from the Litania Sanctorum: 'Sancte Andrea, ora pro nobis,' which was used by Gombert in his 5-part motet 'Veni, dilecta mea.' In the celebrated 'Emendemus in melius' (printed by Eslava and Pedrell), the 1st tenor repeats a long melody to the words: *Memento, homo, quia pulvis es et in pulverem reverteris*; while in 'Quanti mercenarii,' 6 v., the independent voice sings the whole of the Lord's Prayer, to the accompaniment of the other voices—having, in fact, become 'the first singing part' as it is found in BYRD's 'Psalms, Sonnets and Songs' (1588). Morales also applied this principle to the Mass. In 'Ave Maria,' 'Tu es vas electionis' and 'De Beata Virgine,' one voice sings the theme and its corresponding words, while the other voices proceed with the Kyrie, Gloria or Credo. (Cf. Palestrina's Mass, 'Ecce Sacerdos magnus,' in which the same device is used.) Morales's 5-part Mass, 'Tristezas me matan' (MS., Sistine Chapel) is even more curious; for the independent voice sings not only the tune of the folk-song but also the Spanish words, while the other voices continue in Latin.

Three portraits of Morales are described by Mitjana. (1) A woodcut in the frontispiece to the 'Missarum liber secundus' (Rome, 1544) in which the composer, dressed as a cantor in the Pontifical choir, offers his work to Paul III. and receives his blessing. (2) An engraving published by Adami da Bolsena, 'Osservazioni per ben regolare il coro della Cappella Pontificia' (Rome, 1711), and reproduced by Hawkins. (3) A drawing in the National Library, Madrid, made for Barbieri from an original said to exist in the Sistine chapel.

Morales published two books of masses, two of magnificats and two of motets. The Lamentations were printed after his death, while the motets appeared mainly in collections of works by various composers (*v.* Eitner, *Bibliographie d. Musik-Sammelwerke des 16. und 17. Jahrhunderts*, 1877). Pedrell's edition (*Hisp. Schol. musica sacra*, i.) reprints the Officium Defunctorum, 4 v., 2 Magnificats, and the motets previously published by Eslava. A madrigal and two motets are only known in the lute transcriptions of FUENLLANA (*q.v.*), while 24 more have been found in choir-books in Spanish cathedrals, particularly Toledo, Seville and the Escurial. A provisional list is given in *Music and Letters*, 1925, vi. 28-31.

PRINTED WORKS

MASSES

Missarum Lib. I. Rome, 1544. Folio. (Rome: St. Peter's Lateran; Modena; Ferrara; Berlin, State Lib.; Munich

Barcelona, Diputació ; Montserrat ; Tortosa.) Reprinted Lyons, 1545. (Munich ; Königsberg ; Bonn ; Rostock ; Vienna, State Lib. ; Falset (Tarragona). Contents :
  4 v. : Aspice Domine, De Beata Virgine (printed P. Wagner, *Gesch. d. Messe*, i. 457 ff.), Vulnerasti cor meum. 5 v. : Ave Maris Stella, L'homme armé, Queramus cum pastoribus (Ed. Ch. Bordes). 6 v. : Mille Regrets, Si bona suscepimus.
  The 4-part masses were printed separately in partbooks. Venice, L. Scotus, 15˙1 (B.M.) and 1563 ; A. Gardanus, 1544 and 1580.
  Missarum Lib. II. Rome, 1544. Folio. (Sistine Chapel ; Bologna ; Munich.) Reprinted Lyons, 1551-55 (Rome : St. Peter's, Lateran ; Vienna ; Königsberg ; Bonn.) Contents :
  4 v. : Ave Maria, Benedicta es Cœlorum Regina, Gaude Barbara, L'homme armé, Tu es vas electionis. 5 v. : De Beata Virgine, Pro Defunctis (ed. Pedrell), Quem dicunt homines.
  Quinque Missarum harmonia cum 5 v. Moralis Hispani . . . Venice, 1565, H. Scotus. 5 partbooks (B.M.) L'homme armé and Queramus cum pastoribus, from Lib. I., and De Beata Virgine, from. Lib. II.

MAGNIFICATS

Magnificat Moralis Hispani aliorumque authorum. Lib. I. Venice, 1542. H. Scotus. Partbooks. 5 Magn. by Morales. (Bologna ; Jena.)
  Magnificat Moralis Ispani cum 4 v. Lib. I Venice, 1545, Gardane. Partbooks. 8 Magn (Berlin ; Bologna ; Munich.) Later edns. 1559, 1563 and 1568 (all in B.M.), 1583 (Barcelona), 1614.
  Magnificat omnitonum cum 4 v. Venice, 1562. Gardane. Folio. 16 Magn. 8 with the odd verses and 8 with the even. (B.M. ; Rome : Sistine Chapel, Lateran ; Bologna ; Brussels ; Berlin.)

LAMENTATIONS

Lamentationi di Morales, 4, 5, et 6 v. Venice, 1564. Gardano. Partbooks ; (Munich ; Bologna ; Upsala.)

MOTETS

Gomberti . . . musica 4 v. . . . additis nonnullis excellentissimi Morales Motectis (4 by Morales). Venice, 1541. Scotus. Part-books.
  N. Gomberti Pentaphthongos harmonia. (3 by Morales.) Venice, 1541. Scotus. Partbooks.
  Morales et reliquorum Musica vocum 4. Venice, 1543. H. Scotus. (Berlin ; Munich ; Bologna.) 25 motets.
  Morales et multorum eximiæ artis virorum musica cum voc. 4. Venice, 1546. Gardanus. (Berlin ; Munich ; Königsberg ; Bologna ; Vienna, Staatsbibl.) 9 Motets.
  Many others in collections of motets by various composers (16th cent.).

MADRIGALS

Ditimi o si o no, 4 v. (in Arcadelt, Lib. IV.) ; Quando lieto sperai, 5 voc. (in ' Nuova spoglia amorosa ') ; Caronte, 5 v. (in ' Fronimo,' lute arr.). De Antequera sale el moro, 4 v. (in Fuenllana).

EARLY MSS. (IN SPAIN)

Avila.—Officium Defunctorum 4 v.
  Barcelona.—(Diputació.) Masses : Tu es vas electionis, 4 v., Benedicta es cœlorum regina, 4 v. (incompl. score). Madrigal : Si no os hubiera mirado, 3 v. (Boscán).
  (Orfeó Catalá.) Masses : Benedicta es cœlorum regina, 4 v., Mille Regrets, 6 v. ; Magnificats ; Lamentations, 4 v. (incomplete) ; Per tuam crucem 4 v.
  Escurial.—Masses : Benedicta es cœlorum regina, 4 v., Mille Regrets, 6 v. Lamentations, 6th tone (part), 6 v. Off. Defunctorum (part). Motets : Andreas Christi famulus, 5 v., Emendemus, 5 v., O crux ave, 5 v., O vos omnes, 4 v., Verbum iniquum, 5 v., Vigilate, 4 v.
  Madrid.—(Bibl. Medinaceli.) Lamentations, 4 v. (part) ; 2 Magnificats ; Motets : Accepit Jesus panes, 4 v., Dixit Dominus, t v., Inter natos mulierum, 4 v., Inter vestibulum, 4 v., Salve, 4 v. (Bibl. Nacional.) Masses : L'homme armé, 5 v., Si bona suscepimus, 6 v.
  Malaga.—Tu es Petrus, 5 v.
  Seville.—Ave Maria, 5 v., Ecce virgo, 4 v., Noctis recolitur, Per tuam crucem, 4 v., Quod Eva tristis, Regina coeli, 5 v., Salve, 5 v., Sancta et immaculata, 4 v., Tu es Petrus, 5 v.
  Toledo.—Masses : Aspice Domine, 4 v., Ave Maris Stella, 5 v., Benedicta es, 4 v., De beata Virgine, 4 v. and 5 v., Gaude Barbara, 4 v. L'homme armé, 4 v., Mille Regrets, 6 v., Pro Defunctis, 5 v., Si bona suscepimus, 6 v., Tu es vas electionis, 4 v., Vulnerasti cor meum, 4 v. Lamentations, 5 v. Motets, etc. : Agnus redimitoris, 4 v., Andreas Christi famulus, 5 v., Asperges, 5 v., Circumdederunt me, 5 v., Clamabat autem mulier, 5 v., Gloriosus confessor, 5 v., Hi sunt olivæ duæ, 4 v., In die tribulationis, 3 v., Inter natos mulierum, 4 v., Israel es tu, rex Davidis, 4 v., Lamentabatur Jacob, 5 v., O Sacrum convivium, 5 v., Per tuam crucem, 4 v., Regina coeli, 4 v., Salva nos stella maris, 4 v., Salve, 5 v., Sancta et immaculata, 4 v., Tu es Petrus, 5 v., Verbum iniquum, 5 v., Vidi aquam, 4 v.

　　　　　　　　　　　　　　　　　　　　　　　　J. B. T.

MORALES, OLALLO JUAN MAGNUS (*b.* Almeria, Oct. 13, 1874), Spanish composer, educated in Sweden, his mother being Swedish. In Berlin he worked with Teresa Carreño, and later with Pfitzner (conducting). After holding appointments at Lausanne (1904) and Gothenburg (1905-9), he moved to Stockholm, where he became professor at the Conservatoire. His compositions include a symphony in G minor ; concert - overture, ' Försommer ' (1910), and other orchestral pieces ; Berceuse for flute and strings ; string quartet He has also done important critical and historical work.　J. B. T.

MORALES, PEDRO GARCÍA (*b.* Huelva, 1879), Spanish composer. Studied at Seville and then R.C.M., London. Being himself a poet, whose verse is praised by the best judges of Spanish literature, his activities as a composer are chiefly concerned with the modern Spanish song. His instrumental works include ' Esquisse andalouse ' (vln. and orch.) and ' Bagatelle ' (vln. and PF.). His energy during the war, in organising concerts of Spanish music in aid of war victims, made modern Spanish music (especially the works of Falla, Granados and Turina) well known in England.　J. B. T.

MORALT, five brothers, four of whom were celebrated in Munich for their rendering of Haydn's quartets.

(1) JOSEPH (*b.* 1775 ; *d.* 1828) entered the court band in 1797, and became Konzertmeister in 1800, which post he held till his death.

(2) JOHANN BAPTIST (*b.* Jan. 10, 1777 ; *d.* Oct. 7, 1825) was violinist in the Mannheim court band, and entered the Munich band in 1792. He was the second violin in the quartet, and also composed two symphonies for orchestra, and ' Leçons méthodiques ' for the violin, two string quartets, besides a MS. Mass, etc.

(3) PHILIPP (*b.* 1780 ; *d.* Mar. 18, 1847), the violoncello of the quartet, was in the band from 1795 to his death. He had a twin brother, (4) JACQUES, who played in the orchestra, but not in the celebrated quartet.

(5) GEORG (*b.* 1781 ; *d.* 1818), tenor-player.

A Moralt, probably one of the same family, was well known in England in the early part of the 19th century. He was first viola player at the Philharmonic till 1842, when his name disappears, possibly on account of his death, and is succeeded by that of Hill. He took a prominent part in the provincial festivals and music generally.　M.

MORATA, GINÉS DE (16th cent.), Spanish madrigalist, of whom nothing is known beyond 12 pieces for 3 and 4 v. in the Bibl. Medinaceli, Madrid. (MS. 13230.)　J. B. T.

MORDENT (Fr. *pincé* ; Ger. *Mordent*, also *Beisser* ; Ital. *mordente*), one of the most important of the *agréments* or graces of instrumental music. It consists of the rapid alternation of a written note with the note immediately below it.

Mordents are of two kinds, the simple or short mordent, indicated by the sign 𝄿, and consisting of three notes, the lower or auxiliary note occurring but once, and the double or long mordent, the sign for which is 𝄿, in which the auxiliary note appears twice or oftener. Both kinds begin and end with the principal note, and are played with great rapidity, and, like all graces, occupy a part of the value of the written note, and are never introduced before it.

The appropriateness of the term Mordent (from *mordere*, ' to bite ') is found in the sudden

1. *Single Mordent.*   *Double Mordent.*

Written.

Played.

ness with which the principal note is, as it were, attacked by the dissonant note and immediately released. Walther says its effect is ' like cracking a nut with the teeth,' and the same idea is expressed by the old German term *Beisser* and the French *pincé*.

The mordent may be applied to any note of a chord, as well as to a single note. When this is the case its rendering is as follows :

2.   BACH, Sarabande from ' Suite française No. 4.'

3.   BACH, Overture from ' Partita No. 4.'

Sometimes an accidental is added to the sign of the mordent, thus ♮, or ♯ ; the effect of this is to raise the lower or auxiliary note a semitone. This raising takes place in accordance with the rule that a lower auxiliary note should be only a semitone distant from its principal note, and the alteration must[1] be made by the player even when there is no indication of it in the sign (Ex. 4), except in certain understood cases. The exceptions are as follows—when the note bearing the mordent is either preceded or followed by a note a whole tone lower (Exs. 5 and 6), and, generally, when the mordent is applied to either the third or seventh degree of the scale (Ex. 7). In these cases the auxiliary note is played a whole tone distant from its principal.

4.   BACH, Organ Fugue in E minor.

[1] It should be mentioned that the passage referred to in Ex. 4 is, to the opinion of many excellent authorities, to be played without the accidental, *i.e* with A♮ not A♯ as the auxiliary note. See Spitta, *J. S. Bach.* Eng. trans., i. 403, note 89.

5.   Air from ' Suite française No. 2.'

6.   ' Well-tempered Clavier,' No. 1, vol. 2.

7.   Sarabande from ' Suite française No. 5.'

The long mordent (*pincé double*) usually consists of five notes, though if applied to a note of great length it may, according to Emanuel Bach, contain more ; it must, however, never fill up the entire value of the note, as the trill does, but must leave time for a sustained principal note at the end (Ex. 8). Its sign is ⅏, not to be confounded with ⅏, or ⅏, the signs for a trill with or without a turn.

8.   BACH, Sarabande from ' Partita No. 1.'

Besides the above, Emanuel Bach gave the name of mordent to two other graces, now nearly or quite obsolete. One, called the abbreviated mordent (*pincé étouffé*), was rendered by striking the auxiliary note together with its principal, and instantly releasing it (Ex. 9). This grace, which is identical with the ACCIACCATURA (*q.v.*), was said by Marpurg to be of great service in playing full chords on the organ, but its employment is condemned by the best modern organists. The other kind, called the slow mordent, had no distinctive sign, but was introduced in vocal music at the discretion of the singer, usually at the close of the phrase or before a pause (Ex. 10).

9.   *Abbreviated Mordent.*   10.   *Slow Mordent.*

(Cf. PRALLTRILLER.)   F. T.

MORE (MOORE), WILLIAM (*d.* 1565), an English composer who is described (B.M. Add. MSS. 30,480-4) as 'harpour to Edw. VI.' This is a MS. of Elizabeth's time and includes a motet by More, 'Levavi oculose' (*sic*), arranged for 4 viols. His name occurs, however, as early as 1525 among the list of payments to the King's musicians in the Household Book of Henry VIII. (B.M. Egerton MSS. 2604). Apparently also he held similar office in the royal household under Elizabeth, for in the 'Declaration of the accounts by Sir John Masone, knight' for 1560 (Public Record Office) he is described as a harper and is granted '12ᵈ a day to be paid quarterly during life, paid for 2 years & three quarters ended Michaelmas 2 (Eliz.).' A further entry under his name occurs in 1562, and in 1565 there is a record of the last payment made on his account. 'William Moore, Harper, due for half a year ending at the Annunciation, at which time he died.' [1] He is probably identical with the 'Morum' mentioned in John Case's *Apologia musices* (1588) along with Taverner, Blitheman and Tallis, as below :

'Angli non ita pridem Tavernerum, Blithmanum, Tallesium, Morum, aliosque insignos musicos magnis premiis affecerunt.' [2]

Besides the motet referred to above (score in B.M. Add. MSS. 31,226/103), there is a single part of another 5-part one, 'Ad Dominum contribularer' (Harl. 7578/104*b*).   J. Mᴷ.

MOREAU, JEAN-BAPTISTE (*b.* Angers, 1656 ; *d.* Paris, Aug. 24, 1733), church musician and composer. He early showed a musical disposition, and was educated as a choir boy in the cathedral of Angers. Whilst still quite a lad he composed motets which were notable. He continued his career as a church musician in the provinces, and became successively 'maître de musique' at Langres Cathedral (a post which he quitted after his marriage, celebrated in that town), then at Dijon, where he remained about a year. He then went to Paris, without introductions and without a post. The exact date of his arrival is not known, but he was there in 1686. At that time, when in all the Parisian churches thanksgiving services were held for the recovery of the king, a Te Deum, sung on Jan. 24, 1687, in the church of St. Côme, at the expense of the Company of Master Surgeons, is announced as being the composition of Moreau.

A little later he succeeded in obtaining the protection of the Dauphine, and through her mediation entered the court. He went to Versailles and succeeded in slipping into the apartments of the princess. He had the audacity to address her direct and to propose to sing to her an air of his own composition. The Dauphine, who was very musical, was amused by the unconventionality of the unknown countryman, but granted his request,

and being pleased with his song she spoke of Moreau forthwith to the king. The king bade him come two days later to the apartments of Mme. de Maintenon, where he wished to hear him in his turn. The king liked him and ordered from him the music of several little operas, which were given in the years 1687 and 1688. This gave Moreau the right, without being, properly speaking, in charge of the court music, to take the title 'maître de musique du roi.' The first of these divertissements to be sung, called 'Les Bergers de Marly,' composed on a libretto by Banzy, was given at Marly, in the summer of 1687, two months after Moreau's audition at Mme. de Maintenon's; it was much applauded.

In 1688 Racine received the command for *Esther*, a play intended to serve for a literary exercise and for the amusement of the young ladies of St. Cyr; Moreau was chosen by the king and Mme. de Maintenon to write the musical interludes to the tragedy, which was composed of recitatives and choruses in the classic manner. The famous representations of *Esther* at St. Cyr, Jan. and Feb. 1689, established the reputation of Moreau, whom Racine esteemed highly, and to whom the king gave several distinctions, together with a pension of 600 livres, continued until his death. After this Moreau became, concurrently with the organist Nivers and later with Clérambault, the official musician to St. Cyr. For this institution he composed in the following year the music for a great number of tragedies and divertissements which were not otherwise played in public, Mme. de Maintenon having asserted that representations of *Esther* had introduced a spirit of disorder and worldliness into her religious house. The most celebrated of these compositions are the interludes to *Athalie* (Racine, 1691); to *Jephté* (1692) and *Judith* (1695), by the Abbé Boyer; those to *Jonathas* (1700), *Absalon* (1702) and *Débora* (1706), by Duché; the music to an '*Idylle sur la naissance de Notre Seigneur*'; and lastly the music to the three 'Cantiques spirituels' which Racine wrote for St. Cyr in 1689.

He adapted, in 1697, his interludes to *Esther* into a kind of oratorio called 'Concert spirituel, où le peuple juif est délivré par Esther.' The alterations in the text and the necessary additions are by Banzy. The work was performed in Paris, under the direction of the author, but it has not been preserved in this form.

The works of Moreau, of which the library of the 'Dames de St. Louis' has numerous copies, remained during the whole of the 18th century, together with those of Nivers and Clérambault, with the 'Stances chrétiennes' of Oudot and the prologues of the operas of Lully, the foundation of the musical repertory at St. Cyr.

---

[1] See *Mus. Ant.*, Oct. 1910.   [2] Davey, *Hist. Eng. Mus.*

Appreciated as a composer, assured of the favour of the king and of Mme. de Maintenon, Moreau would have made a fine fortune if he had led a regular life, and if he had not had such a great intimacy with the bacchic poet Laînez, whose libertine ways were disapproved in high quarters. Moreau employed a great deal of his time in setting to music the songs of Laînez, which were widely distributed in manuscript copies and which had great success. In 1694 he accepted the charge of 'Intendant de la musique des États de Languedoc,' but as he preferred Parisian to provincial life, he spent little time in this employment, and sold the reversion to a musician called Mallet. His chief resource outside his royal salary came from his teaching. He was renowned for his method of singing, and amongst his pupils, both for singing and composition, were to be counted some of the best musicians of the 18th century: Montéclair, Clérambault, Jean-François d'Andrieu; the celebrated singers Marie-Claude Moreau, his daughter (who died before he did, after her marriage to the viol master Deniau), and Louise Couperin, cousin-german to François Couperin.

During the last years of his life Moreau was employed by the curé of St. Sulpice Languet to teach singing to the daughters of the Jesuit community, a convent instituted by this priest. They performed the famous choruses of *Esther* and *Athalie*.

Moreau died Aug. 24, 1733, and was buried in his parish church, St. Josse. He left a widow and a daughter.

Besides the tragedies of St. Cyr and the chansons by Laînez he composed a certain number of works, both sacred and secular, left in MS. and now lost. Amongst these, his contemporaries praised a motet 'In exitu Israel de Egypto,' with choruses in counterpoint on a plain chant of the psalm; a Requiem Mass; a divertissement written to words by Laînez to be given at the 'Ermitage de Franchard' during a sojourn of the king at Fontainebleau; and, finally, an essay on teaching, *L'Art mélodique*, a subject which Moreau, whose special characteristics were justness of accent and formal grace of melody, should have treated in an interesting way.

For posterity, he remains as the musician of Racine. His recitatives and his songs which, like those of other Lullist-composers, are smooth and clear in declamation; his choruses simple in style but informed with elegance and nobility; above all the personal character of his music, so expressive and touching, spontaneous, Christian, with something fresh and virginal, accord to perfection with the style and spirit of the poet. These religious and literary divertissements, for the use of an institution for girls, which Racine, in spite of his humility, accounted his *chefs-*

d'œuvre, found at the first moment the music which fitted them. It would be vain to try and remake them.

WORKS

PUBLISHED.—'Chœurs de la tragédie d'Esther, avec la musique composée par J. B. Moreau, maistre de musique du roy.' (Paris, 1689.) A second edition was published with the title: 'Intermèdes en musique de la tragédie d'Esther propres pour les dames religieuses, et toutes autres personnes. Par Monsieur Moreau, maistre de musique et pensionnaire de Sa Majesté' (Paris, 1696); 'La Musique d'Athalie par J. B. Moreau, maistre de musique du roy. Composée par ordre de Sa Majesté, gravée par H. de Baussen. . . .' (Paris, without date.)
'Cantiques chantez devant le Roy, et composez par Monsieur Moreau, maistre de musique et pensionnaire de Sa Majesté. Propres pour les dames religieuses, et toutes autres personnes.' (Paris, 1695.)

MANUSCRIPTS.—'Intermèdes de la tragédie de Jephté.' (Library of Versailles; from St. Cyr.) 'Intermèdes de la tragédie de Jonathas,' with Moreau's autograph, dated 1725 (from St. Cyr). The Versailles Library has many other copies of 'Jonathas,' and of 'Athalie'; one with Moreau's autograph and a copy of the 'Cantiques spirituels': all from St. Cyr. The library of the Paris Conservatoire also possesses, from the same source, many MSS. of these works, as well as of 'Esther.'
'Idille sur la naissance de Notre Seigneur,' Versailles Library (from St. Cyr), and the Bibliothèque Nationale.
'Le Feu de Joye du Sr. Moreau pour Mgr. le Duc de Bretagne,' Versailles Library.
The MS. of the Bibl. Nat. contains some copies of 'Athalie,' 'Esther,' and the 'Cantiques spirituels.'
Rigaudon de M. Moreau, Bibl. Nat.
'Zaïre cantatille,' Darmstadt Library (see Q-L).

MODERN REPRINTS.—'*Musique des chœurs d'Esther et d'Athalie et des cantiques spirituels.*' Works of J. Racine; ed. by Paul Mesnard. (*Supplément musical,* Paris, 1873, exact reproduction of original editions.) 'Esther' (ed. by Ch. Bordes), Paris, Schola, without date (not a precise reproduction). 'Athalie' (ed. by Ch. Bordes and Léon Saint-Réquier), Paris, Schola, without date.

BIBLIOGRAPHY

TITON DU TILLET: 'Le Parnasse françois.' (*Supplément* of 1743.)
Mercure Galant, vols. between 1687 and 1702.
LAVALLÉE, TH.: *Histoire de la maison royale de St. Cyr.* (Paris, 1856.)
TAPHANEL, ACHILLE: *Le Théâtre de St. Cyr.* (Paris, 1876.)
HALLAYS, ANDRÉ: '*Racine, poète lyrique*' (*Tribune de St. Gervais.* May and June 1899; and excerpts, Paris, Schola, 1899.)
BORDES, CHARLES: *Les Chœurs d'Esther et d'Athalie par Jean-Baptiste Moreau.* (Preface to the reprint of 'Esther' and 'Athalie' by Bordes.)
TIERSOT, JULIEN: '*Les Chœurs d'Esther de Moreau.*' (*Revue musicale,* Jan. 1903.)

A. T.

MORELLI, GIOVANNI, a basso with a voice of much power, compass, sweetness and flexibility. He first appeared in London in Paisiello's 'Schiavi per Amore,' with Storace and Sestini, and Morigi, who had long been the first *buffo caricato,* but now became second to Morelli. The latter was a very good actor, but, having been 'running-footman' to Lord Cowper at Florence, he was probably not much of a musician. He continued for many years in great favour, and sang at the Opera from time to time till he had scarcely a note left; but he was always received kindly as an old and deserving favourite.

He sang the bass part in the 'Serva padrona,' with Banti, so successfully that the performance was repeated by Royal command; and he was singing with Catalani and Miss Stephens (her first appearance) at the Pantheon, when that house was rebuilt. He sang in the Commemoration of Handel in 1787, with Mara and Rubinelli.   J. M.

MORENDO, 'dying,' is used to indicate the gradual 'decrescendo' at the end of a cadence. Its meaning is well given by Shakespeare in the words, 'That strain again! it had a *dying fall.*' It is used by Beethoven in the trio, op. 1, No. 3, at the end of the fourth variation in the slow movement, and in the quartet, op. 74, also at the end of the slow movement. As a rule it is only used for the end of the movement or in a cadence, but in the quartet, op. 18, No. 7, slow movement, and in the ninth symphony, slow movement, it is not confined to the end, but occurs in imperfect cadences, to give the effect of a full close. It thus differs from *smorzando*, as the latter can be used at any time in the movement. 							M.

MORERA, ENRIC (*b.* Barcelona, May 22, 1865), Spanish composer. His youth was spent in Argentina (Buenos Ayres and Córdoba); his musical studies were prosecuted at Barcelona and Brussels, and the influence of the Belgian school is noticeable in his work. His compositions include operas ('Emporium,' 'Bruniselda,' 'Don Joan de Serrafonga,' 'La Nit de St. Joan,' 'La Font de l'Albera,' 'La Fada') and incidental music to a number of Catalan plays, *e.g. l'Alegria que passa*, by Rusiñol. His chief interest, however, is in choral works and arrangements of Catalan folk-songs, and this preference has tended to prevent his music from becoming widely known in Spain and consequently in other countries.

BIBL.—I. IGLESIAS, *Enric Morera: Estudi biográfici* (Barcelona, 1921). 							J. B. T.

MORGAN, JOHN (*b.* Newburgh, Anglesey, *c.* 1711; living in 1771), was the last of the Welsh bards who played their national instrument, the crwth (Edw. Jones, *Welsh Bards*). A 3-part catch, 'Quoth Jack on a time,' in Longman's Collection is signed 'Morgan,' but it is doubtful if this is the above.

MORHANGE, CHAS. HENRI VALENTIN, see ALKAN (1).

MORI, (1) NICOLAS (*b.* London, Jan. 24, 1796 or 1797[1]; *d.* June 14, 1839), violinist, was the son of an Italian wigmaker in the New Road, London. He was brought out as a prodigy, and at 8 years of age played in public a concerto of Barthélemon's, from whom he had lessons. Subsequently he studied for six years with Viotti, and not only became an excellent solo violinist, but from his enthusiasm, industry and judgment, occupied a very prominent position in the music of London and England generally from about 1812 till his death. He played in the second concert of the Philharmonic Society in 1814, and from 1816 was for many years one of the leaders of the Philharmonic band and first violin at the Lenten oratorios, the provincial festivals, and the majority of concerts of any importance. He married in 1819 the widow of the music publisher LAVENU, and entered into partnership with her son. Amongst other music they published the second book of Mendelssohn's Songs without Words, and his PF. concerto in G minor. He left a son,[2] (2) FRANK (*b.* Mar. 21, 1820; *d.* Aug. 2, 1873), who was well known in London for many years as a musician. His cantata 'Fridolin' (brought out at the Wor-

[1] 1797 is found on a portrait issued in 1805. (*D.N.B.*)
[2] See E. W. Duffin, *Particulars of the Illness and Death of the late Mr. Mori.* (London, 1839.)

cester Festival of 1851) was performed several times with success; and an operetta, the 'River-sprite,' to words by G. Linley, was produced at Covent Garden, Feb. 9, 1865. A second son, (3) NICHOLAS (*b.* Jan. 14, 1822), having studied with his father and Charles Lucas, as well as in Paris, composed various works, among them a setting of Psalm cxxxvii., and music to Gilbert's 'Wicked World.'

G., with addns.

MORIANI, NAPOLEONE (*b.* Florence, Mar. 10, 1808 ; *d.* Mar. 4, 1878), came of a good family, received a liberal education, and studied the law for some time, intending to embrace it as his profession. Seduced, however, by the applause which his beautiful tenor voice obtained for him in society, he changed his intentions, and attempted the operatic career at Pavia in 1833, with success. After singing in the principal Italian cities, he returned to Florence in 1839, and in the following year was recognised both there and at Milan and Trieste, as the first tenor of Italy. In 1841 he visited Vienna, where he was appointed 'Virtuoso di camera' by the Emperor. In 1844 and 1845 he sang in London, but he pleased little here. He sang with success at Lisbon, Madrid and Barcelona in 1846, and was decorated by the Queen of Spain with the Order of Isabella. He sang at Milan in the autumn of 1847, but his voice was gone, and he soon afterwards retired from the stage. Mendelssohn more than once speaks of him as 'my favourite tenor, Moriani.' 	J. M.

MORIGI, ANGELO (*b.* Rimini, 1752 ; *d.* Parma, 1788), violinist and composer. Tartini was his violin teacher and Valotti instructed him in theory and harmony. In 1758 he was appointed first violin of the Prince of Parma's band, and later, director of the court music, a position which he held for many years. He was a composer of some merit, and excellently spoken of as a teacher of composition. Among his pupils was Bonifazio Asioli, the dramatic composer, who out of deference to his master's memory published his (Morigi's) *Trattato di contrappunto fugato* after his death. Compositions :

Six sonatas for violin alone, op 1. Six trios for two violins and violoncello with a figured bass for the clavecin, op. 2. Six concerti grossi for violin, op. 3. Six others dedicated to the Infanta Donna Philippe.

BIBL.—Fétis ; A. MASON CLARKE, *Fiddlers Ancient and Modern.*

E. H.-A.

MORIN, JEAN BAPTISTE (*b.* Orleans, *c.* 1677; *d.* Paris, 1745), musician to the Duke of Orleans; one of the first composers of French cantatas (3 books 1-3 parts, 1706, 1707, 1712), also 2 books of motets (1704, 1709) ; 'Recueil d'airs à boire à 2 voix'; 'La Chasse du cerf,' 'Divertissement,' 'Le Triomphe de l'amour,' etc.; 'L'Hymen et l'Amour,' 'Épithalame' (*Q.-L.*).

MORISSEAU, a sabot-maker practising at No. 9 Rue des Fontaines du Temple, in Paris, who applied the principles of his art to the manufacture of violins, carving the back and sides and neck all in one piece out of a solid block of practically green wood, the only glue used in their manufacture being that employed to fasten on the tables. This innovation was considered sufficiently serious by the Société d'Encouragement pour l'Industrie Nationale for a *Rapport* to be inserted in their Bulletin [1] drawn up by J. Lissajous, with the assistance of Guérin, professor at the Conservatoire, Deloffre and Ferrand, leaders of the orchestras of the Théâtre Lyrique and the Opéra-Comique respectively.   E. H.-A.

MORITZ (MAURICE) (*b.* May 25, 1572; *d.* Mar. 14, 1632), Landgraf of Hesse-Cassel from 1592–1627, under the musical tuition of George Otto, Kapellmeister at Cassel from about 1588–1619, developed considerable talent [2] for composition and was a patron of musicians (see DOWLAND, John). In 1601 he published a Lutheran Gesangbuch with tunes only, twenty-four of which were his own invention. In 1612 he republished the book, providing all the tunes with his own 4-part harmony. Meantime, in 1605, he had abandoned Lutheran doctrine and embraced Calvinism, even adopting the extreme Calvinistic view that nothing but words of Scripture in the vernacular should be sung in churches. Under the influence of his new convictions he published a musical edition of Lobwasser's German version of the French Calvinistic Psalms, providing the original French tunes with a 4-part harmony, and adding some new tunes of his own. His endeavours to force the Calvinistic form of worship on his Lutheran subjects met with some resistance, and he was obliged to concede the use of the Lutheran hymns. It is all the more strange that so enlightened a prince should have adopted this narrow view of the province of church music, considering that he had himself composed a large number of Latin psalms, motets and Magnificats in the *a cappella* style, *a* 4 to 12, which are still preserved in MS. in the library at Cassel (see *Q.-L.*). It redounds to his credit, however, that he showed himself so munificent a patron to the young Heinrich Schütz who, brought up as a chorister in his chapel at Cassel, was afterwards sent at his expense to Venice to complete his musical education under the tuition of Giovanni Gabrieli. Schütz testified his gratitude to his patron by dedicating to him in 1611 his op. 1, the first-fruits of his Venetian studies, consisting of a book of Italian madrigals *a* 5, concluding with a flattering poem written by the musician himself in praise of his patron, and set for eight voices. Among the MS. works of the Landgraf in the Cassel library there are some Italian madrigals and villanelle *a* 4, also some instrumental pieces, fugues and dances, which all serve to show the

interest taken by him in the various branches of music of his time. He laid down the reins of government of his principality in 1627, having lost the confidence of his Lutheran subjects by his Calvinist policy. A considerable number of his 4-part settings of psalm and hymn tunes have been republished in modern collections, such as those of Erk, Tucher and Winterfeld. A fugal movement for four strings has also been published in score by Hugo Riemann in his first Book of Old Chamber Music (Augener & Co.).

                                              J. R. M.

MORLACCHI, FRANCESCO (*b.* Perugia, June 14, 1784; *d.* Innsbruck, Oct. 28, 1841), composer. He learnt the violin at 7 years old from his father. At 12 he was placed under Caruso, maestro of the cathedral of Perugia, who taught him singing, the clavier and thorough-bass, while he learned the organ from Mazetti, his maternal great-uncle. At 13 he had already composed much, and during his years of boyhood wrote several pieces for the church, among which a short oratorio, 'Gli angeli al sepolcro,' attracted the attention of many amateurs, and among them, of his godfather, Count Pietro Baglioni, who sent him to study counterpoint with Zingarelli at Loreto. But the severe conventional teaching of Zingarelli clashed with the aspirations of his young, impatient mind, and after a year and a half he returned to Perugia. Conscious, however, that he had still a great deal to learn, he went to Bologna to complete his studies under Padre MATTEI (*q.v.*). Here he devoted much attention to ecclesiastical music, besides making a special study of the orchestra, and acquiring a practical knowledge of all the chief instruments. During this time of studentship he was commissioned to write a cantata for the coronation of Napoleon as King of Italy, at Milan, in 1805. In Feb. 1807 a musical farce called 'Il poeta in Campagna' was performed at the Pergoia theatre in Florence, and, later in this year, a Miserere for sixteen voices having won golden opinions, the composer was invited to visit Verona, where he produced his first *buffo* opera, 'Il ritratto.' He achieved his first popular success with the melodrama, 'Il Corradino,' at Parma in 1808. This was followed by 'Enone e Paride,' 'Oreste,' 'Rinaldo d' Asti,' 'La Principessa per ripiego,' 'Il Simoncino' and 'Le avventure d' una giornata.' But all these were surpassed by 'Le Danaïde,' written for the Argentino theatre at Rome in 1810. This work was immensely successful, and once for all established its composer's fame. Through the influence of Count Marcolini, Minister to the court of Saxony, Morlacchi was now appointed musical director of the Italian opera at Dresden, at first for a year, subsequently for life, with a large salary, besides a considerable honorarium for every new opera he might compose, and leave of absence for some months of each year, with liberty to write what he pleased, where he pleased. This appointment he held till his death. The Italian style had long reigned supreme in the Dresden fashionable world, and Morlacchi at once became ' the rage.' His music partook of the styles of Paër and Mayr ; it was melodious and pleasing, but very slight in character. He now acquainted himself to some extent with the works of the German masters, a study which had a happy effect on him, as it led him insensibly to add a little more solidity to his somewhat threadbare harmonies. His earliest compositions at Dresden were a Mass for the Royal Chapel, the operas ' Raoul de Créqui ' (1811) and ' La cappriciosa pentita ' (1813), and an oratorio of the ' Passion ' (1812) (book by Metastasio), extravagantly admired by contemporary enthusiasts.

In 1813 Dresden became the military centre of operations of the allied armies, and the King, Friedrich August, Napoleon's faithful ally, was a prisoner. During this time Morlacchi kept at a wise distance from public affairs, and bewailed the fate of his patron in retirement. He was, however, roughly aroused by a sudden order from Baron Rozen, Russian Minister of Police, to write a cantata for the birthday of the Emperor of Russia. The task was, of course, uncongenial to the composer, and as only two days were available for it, he declined to comply, alleging in excuse that the time allowed was insufficient. By way of answer it was notified to him that his choice lay between obeying and being sent to Siberia. Thus pressed he set to work, and in forty-eight hours the cantata was ready. Not long after this the Russian government having decreed the abolition of the Dresden chapel, Morlacchi obtained an audience of the Czar at Frankfort, when, in consequence of his representations and entreaties, the decree was reversed.

To celebrate the return of the Saxon king to his capital in 1814, Morlacchi wrote another Mass and a sparkling *opera buffa*, ' Il barbiere di Siviglia.' His political principles must have been conveniently elastic, for the year 1814 also saw the production of a Triumphal Cantata for the taking of Paris by the allied armies, and a Mass for voices alone, according to the Greek ritual, for the private chapel of Prince Repuin, who had been the Russian Governor of Dresden.

In June 1816 he was elected member of the Academy of Fine Arts at Florence, and shortly after paid a visit of some months to his native country, where he was received with every kind of honour, gala performances of ' Le Danaïde ' and the oratorio of the ' Passion ' being given at Perugia. For the dedication of this last work, Pope Pius VII. rewarded him with the decoration of the Golden Spur and the title of Count Palatine. An oratorio, ' Il sacrifizio d' Abramo, o l' Isaaco ' (1817), although a feeble work, was remarkable for the employment in

it of a novel kind of rhythmical declamation in place of the ordinary recitative.

In 1817 C. M. von Weber was appointed Kapellmeister of the German opera at Dresden. Morlacchi behaved to him with a studied show of obsequious politeness, while doing his utmost in an underhand way to cripple his activity and bar his progress. Yet he did not disdain to beg for Weber's good word as a critic in the matter of his own compositions, and indeed was too much of an artist not to recognise the genius of his young colleague, to whom, although already overworked, he would frequently delegate the whole of his own duties, while on the plea of ill-health he absented himself in Italy for months together. Between 1817 and 1841 he produced a number of operas and dramatic pieces, among which the principal were ' Laodicea ' (Naples, 1817), ' Gianni di Parigi ' (1818), ' La Morte d' Abel ' (Dresden, 1821), ' Donna Aurora ' (Milan, 1821), ' Tebaldo ed Isolina ' (1822), ' La gioventù di Enrico V ' (1823), ' Ilda d' Avenello ' (1824), ' I Saraceni in Sicilia ' (1827), ' Il Colombo ' (1828), ' Il disperato per eccesso di buon cuore ' (1829) and ' Il rinegato ' (1832), this last opera being a second setting of the book of ' I Saraceni,' ' in a style calculated to suit German taste.' He wrote ten masses for the Dresden chapel, besides a great number of other pieces for the church. The best of these was the Requiem, composed on the occasion of the King of Saxony's death in 1827. He said of himself that, during the composition of the ' Tuba Mirum ' in this Mass he had thought unceasingly of the ' Last Judgment ' in the Sistine Chapel, and his biographer, Count Rossi-Scotti,[1] does not hesitate to affirm that by his harmony he emulates Michel Angelo in the realisation of the tremendous moment. A ' scena ' or ' episode ' for baritone voice with pianoforte accompaniment (the narration of Ugolino, from Canto xxxiii. of the *Inferno*), written in his last years, deserves special mention here, as it became very famous.

In 1841 he once more set off for Italy, but was forced by illness to stop at Innsbruck, where he died. He left an unfinished opera, ' Francesca da Rimini,' for the possession of which Florence, Dresden and Vienna had disputed with each other. Profuse honours were paid to his memory in Dresden and in Perugia.

Weber's good-natured criticism (in one of his letters) on his ' Barbiere di Siviglia ' aptly describes much of Morlacchi's dramatic work :

' There is much that is pretty and praiseworthy in this music ; the fellow has little musical knowledge, but he has talent, a flow of ideas, and especially a fund of good comic stuff in him.'

The best monument he left to his memory was a benevolent institution at Dresden for the widows and orphans of the musicians of the Royal Chapel, which he was instrumental in founding.   F. A. M.

[1] *Della vita e delle opere del Cav. Francesco Morlacchi di Perugia.*

MORLAYE, GUILLEAUME (mid-16th cent.), a French lutenist, pupil of Alberto da Ripa, whose compositions he brought out in a number of books in lute tablature, including also his own compositions and those of other masters (published 1550–58). Fétis mentions also a book of Ghitern tablature by him (published 1550).   E. v. d. s.

MORLEY, THOMAS (b. 1557; [1] d. ? 1603), was pupil of William Byrd, by whose endeavours, says Anthony Wood,

'the said Morley became not only excellent in musick, as well in the theoretical as practical part, but also well seen in the Mathematicks, in which Byrde was excellent.'

In July 1588 he took his degree of Mus.B. at Oxford, and at the close of the same year there is reason to think that he was organist of St. Giles's, Cripplegate, for in the registers of that church is entered the burial of 'Thomas ye sonne of Thomas Morley, Organist,' Feb. 14, 1588/9.[2] His wife had probably been a member of the household of Lady Periam, wife of the Lord Chief Baron of the Exchequer (see the Dedication of the 'First Book of Canzonets to Two Voices,' 1595).

It is most likely that, after leaving St. Giles's, Morley became organist at St. Paul's Cathedral, though from a passage in the *Description of Q. Elizabeth's Entertainment at Elvetham in Sept. 1591*, it might perhaps be inferred that his appointment took place earlier; it is said there that the performance of some musicians so pleased the Queen that 'she gave a newe name unto one of their Pavans, made long since by master Thomas Morley, then organist of Paules church.'[3] However this may be, he was still at St. Paul's in the same year, 1591, for there is an allusion to him as organist there in a letter dated Oct. 3, 1591.[4] From this letter, written from Flanders by one Paget, a Catholic intriguer, it would appear that Morley had been employed there as some kind of political agent.

'Ther is one Morley that playeth on the organies in poules that was with me in my house. He semed here to be a good Catholicke and was reconsiled, but not-with-standing suspecting his behaviour I entercepted letters that Mr. Nowell' [presumably but not-with-standing suspecting his behaviour I entercepted letters that Mr. Nowell' [presumably the Dean of St. Paul's] 'wrote to him, wherby I discovered enoughe to have hanged him. Neverthelis he shewing with teares great repentaunce, and asking on his knees forgivenes, I was content to let him goe. I here since his comming thether he hath played the promotor and apprehendeth Catholickes.'

This is corroborated in the reply.[5]

'It is true that Morley the singing man employeth himselfe in that kind of service . . . and hath browght diverse into danger.'

In 1592 Morley was made gentleman of the Chapel Royal, being 'sworne 24th of July in Mr. Greene's roome'[6]; and in Nov. of the same

year he was appointed to the 'Gospeller's place and waiges,' after having served as Epistler.[7] Between 1596 and 1601 he was living in the parish of St. Helen's, Bishopsgate, his house at the end of this period being in Little St. Helen's. The parish registers (Harleian Soc., 1904) record the baptism of 'Frauncys daughter of Thomas Morley, Musition,' Aug. 19, 1596; and the burial of 'Frauncis d. of Thomas Morley, Gent,' Feb. 9, 1598/9. On June 26, 1599, 'Cristofer, s. of Thomas Morley, gentleman, and Suzan his wyfe,' and on July 28, 1600, 'Anne, d. of Thomas Morley, gentleman, and Suzan his wyfe,' were baptized. There seems no reason to doubt that these entries all refer to the musician. His residence in St. Helen's is further marked by the appearance of his name in two Rolls of Assessments for Subsidies dated 1598 [8] and 1600, in both of which his goods to be taxed were valued at £5, and the assessment was 13s. 4d. An interesting point in connexion with the earlier of these documents is that the name of William Shakespeare occurs in it, his goods being valued at the same amount as were Morley's. It appears that he and Morley both appealed against the assessment, and one may suppose that some amount of personal intercourse existed between the two, especially when it is remembered that of the very little original music for Shakespeare's plays which has survived, Morley composed one if not two songs.

In 1598 Morley was granted a licence for twenty-one years to print song-books of all kinds and music paper, 'with forfeiture of £10 to every person offending against this grant.' The Patent, dated Sept. 28, 1598, is printed in Steele's *Earliest English Music Printing*, 1903. It would seem that it was obtained through the interest of one of the Caesar family (probably Sir Julius), which was connected with the parish of St. Helen's. One book, Carlton's 'Madrigals,' 1601, is said on the title-page to have been 'printed by Thomas Morley dwelling in Little Saint Helen's,' but as a rule East, Barley and others published as Morley's 'assignes' under the Patent. Barley indeed, in 1599 and 1600, seems to have done his printing in Little St. Helen's, and only to have sold his books at his shop in 'Gratious' Street (cf. Farmer's 'Madrigals' and Morley's 'Consort Lessons,' 1599, and Morley's 'First Booke of Ayres,' 1600.[9]) In 1601 the whole question of granting monopolies of this kind was raised in the House of Commons, and Morley's Patent was among those mentioned.[10] The last book which appears to have been printed 'by the

---

[1] According to the Sadler MS. (Bodl. MS. Mus. e. 1-5), in which is entered his *Domine non est exaltatum*, with the inscription 'Thomas Morley ætatis suæ 19, ano domini 1576'
[2] *Mus. T.*, Sept. 1903.   [3] Nichols's *Progresses*.
[4] *State Papers*, Dom. Eliz. vol. ccxl. No. 19.
[5] *Ibid.* No. 53.   [6] Rimbault, *Cheque-book*, p. 5.
[7] *Ibid.* p. 34.
[8] The 1598 Roll is printed in Hunter's *New Illustrations of Shakespeare*, 1845, and is discussed fully in Elton's *William Shakespeare, his Family and Friends*, 1904.
[9] An imperfect copy of this last, at present (1925) in the possession of Mr. Folger of New York, is believed to be unique.
[10] Ames, *Typographical Antiquities*, 1749, p. 569.

assignement of a Patent granted to T. Morley,' was Dowland's 'Third Book of Songs,' 1603. Barley obtained this Patent on Morley's death, and his name appears as owner of it from 1606 onwards.

Morley alludes more than once to his ill-health in his *Plaine and Easie Introduction*, 1597: 'My health since you saw me, hath beene so bad, as if it had beene the pleasure of him who may all things, to have taken me out of the world, I should have beene very well contented; and have wished it more than once'; and he speaks of the 'solitarie life which I lead (being compelled to keepe at home),' as a reason for his undertaking the work. It was perhaps the bad state of his health which caused the severance of his connexion with the Chapel Royal, where he was succeeded by George Woodson, Oct. 7, 1602. His death probably took place in 1603, for the 'commission to administer the goods, etc., of Thomas Morley, late parishioner of St. Botolph's, near Billingsgate,' was granted to his widow 'Margaret Morley' on Oct. 25, 1603.[1] If we may assume that this refers to the musician, we must suppose that he had married a second time. The title-page of the 1606 edition of the 'Canzonets' of 1593, which states that they are 'Now Newly Imprinted with some Songs added by the Author,' may be interpreted in two ways. Weelkes printed in his 'Ayres or Fantastic Spirites,' 1608, a 'Remembrance of my friend M. Thomas Morley,' beginning 'Death hath deprived me of my dearest friend.'

The following is a list of Morley's publications, of some of which he was only the editor:

1. Canzonets. Or Little Short Songs to Three Voyces. 1593. (2nd ed. with four additional Canzonets, 1606. 3rd ed. 1631. German translations, Cassel, 1612: Rostock, 1624.) *Eng. Madr. Sch.* i.
2. Madrigalls to Foure Voyces. 1594. (2nd ed. with two additional Madrigals, 1600.) *Eng. Madr. Sch.* ii.
3. The First Booke of Balletts to fiue voyces. 1595. (2nd ed. 1600. An Italian edition, London, 1595. German edition, Nuremberg, 1609.) *Eng. Madr. Sch.* iii.
4. The First Booke of Canzonets to two voyces. 1595. (2nd ed. 1619.) *Eng. Madr. Sch.* i.
5. Canzonets, Or Little Short Songs to foure voyces. Celected out of the best and approued Italian Authors. 1597. (Contains two by Morley himself.)
6. Canzonets or Little Short Aers to fiue and sixe voices. 1597. *Eng. Madr. Sch.* iv.
7. A Plaine and Easie Introduction to Practicall Musicke, 1597. (2nd ed. 1608. 3rd ed. 1771. Contains eight compositions, chiefly motets, by Morley.)
8. Madrigalls to fiue voyces. Celected out of the best approued Italian Authors. 1598.
9. The First Booke of Consort Lessons, made by diuers exquisite Authors for six Instruments. 1599. (2nd ed. 1611.)
10. The First Booke of Ayres or Little Short Songs; to sing and play to the Lute with the Base Viole. 1600. (Contains 'It was a lover and his lass.')
11. The Triumphes of Oriana to 5 and 6 voices, composed by diuers seuerall aucthors. 1601. (Contains two madrigals by Morley. Reprinted in score by Hawes, 1814.) *Eng. Madr. Sch.* xxxii.

With these should be mentioned, 'The whole Booke of Psalmes. With their woonted Tunes . . . Compiled by sundrie Authors,' etc. 'Printed at London in Little S. Hellens by W. Barley, the assigne of T. Morley, and are to be sold at his shop in Gratious street.' This book, which has no date, contains four settings of tunes by Morley, two of which (with

1 Stated on authority of w. b. s.

another hitherto unprinted setting) appeared later in Ravenscroft's Psalter, 1621. (See PSALTER.) Of his sacred music, Barnard (1641) printed a Morning and Evening Service of four and five parts; an Evening Service of five parts; and a Verse Anthem 'Out of the Deep.' His Burial Service was printed by Boyce. A motet, 'Nolo mortem,' *a* 4, was edited by W. Barclay Squire. See list of Morley's church music below.

The *Fitzwilliam Virginal Book* (ed. Fuller Maitland and Squire) contains music by him; as also does Forster's MS. Virginal Book in the Roy. Lib. B.M. A Fancy *a* 5 is at Christ Church, where are many MS. compositions, chiefly canzonets, by him, some of which may be from the printed collections with altered words.

Morley's contemporaries, such as Meres and Peacham, placed him among the best English musicians of the time, and Ravenscroft speaks of him after his death as 'he who did shine as the Sun in the Firmament of our Art, and did first give light to our understanding with his Præcepts.'[2] At the present day Morley perhaps holds the first place in popular esteem of all the Elizabethan composers, partly because of the cheerfulness and tunefulness of his ballets, a form of composition which he introduced into this country, and in which he is unrivalled in England, unless by his follower Weelkes. Here he owed much to Gastoldi, after whose 'balletti' he modelled his own, sometimes making use of phrases which are plainly suggested by the Italian writer, just as in his canzonets he sometimes adapts phrases from Felice Anerio. But if his material is sometimes borrowed, his treatment of it is original, and the charge of plagiarism, which Oliphant and others brought against him, need not be pressed. If Morley wrote more in the lighter forms of music, his graver compositions are not less masterly, as may be seen by reference to the 'Nolo mortem' or the Burial Service, which is worthy of the praises bestowed on it by Burney. His *Plaine and Easie Introduction* stands by itself. Written in dialogue form, it gives a pleasant impression of Morley's personality, and is of the greatest value for the side-lights which it throws on contemporary musical life; while for the English student of modal music it is indispensable, being still the only important English work on the subject. Here again Morley has been charged with plagiarism, on the ground that some of his examples are the same as some which Tigrini gives in his *Compendio della musica*, 1588. But in these examples, both Tigrini and Morley are simply showing the best ways of making formal Closes; and as the best are not unlimited in number, it is not surprising if, in a crowd of others, the same examples sometimes occur in

2 *Briefe Discourse*, 1614.

different text-books. Morley's notation is not identical with Tigrini's, his arrangement is quite different, and there is no reason to suppose that he ever saw Tigrini's book.

G. E. P. A.

LIST OF CHURCH MUSIC

SERVICES, ETC.

First Service, of 4 and 5 parts, including V.; T.D.; B.; C. M.N. Barnard.
Second Service. B.M. Add. MSS. 30,086/152. Score.
Evening Service, a 4. Harl. 7337/81. Score.
Verse Service, including T.D.; B.; K.; C.; M.N. Durh. E. 4-11.
Preces and Psalms. R.C.M. 1045-51.
Responses. R.C.M. 1045-51.
Burial Anthems. Harl. 7337. Score; B.M. Add. MSS. 5054 and 17,842. Scores.

MOTETS

De profundis clamavi, a 6. B.M. Add. MSS. 29,372-7.
Eheu ! Sustulerunt Dominum, a 4. B.M. Add. MSS. 29,372-5.
Gaude Maria Virgo, a 5.
Virgo prudentissima, 2nd part. } B.M. Roy. Lib. Baldwin's MS.
Heu mihi, Domine, a 5. B.M. Add. MSS. 18,936-9. Incomp.
In manus tuas. Tenb. 389/2. Incomp.
Laboravi in gemitu meo, a 6. B.M. Add. MSS. 29,372-7.
Nolo mortem peccatoris, a 4. B.M. Add. MSS. 29,372-5.
O amica mea, a 5.
Dentes tui sicut greges, 2nd part. } B.M. Add. MSS. 29,372-6.

ANTHEMS

How long. PH.; Durh.
Let my complaint. Tenb. O.B./430.
O Jesu meek. R.C.M. 1051/23. Bassus cantoris part only.
Out of the deepe, a 6. { Durh. C. 4-5.
{ B.M. Add. MSS. 31,405/20. Score.
do. 31,443/141. Score.
Teach me Thy way. PH.

J. Mᴷ.

MORLEY, WILLIAM, Mus.B. (d. Oct. 29, 1731), graduated at Oxford, July 17, 1713. On Aug. 8, 1715, he was admitted a gentleman of the Chapel Royal. He composed some songs published in a collection together with others by John Isham, and a chant in D minor, printed by Boyce, ii. 306, by some believed to be the oldest double chant in existence. (See FLINTOFT.) W. H. H.

MORNINGTON, GARRETT COLLEY WELLESLEY (WESLEY), Earl of, Mus.D. (b. Dangan, Ireland, July 19, 1735; d. May 22, 1781).[1] With little or no assistance from masters he learned to play on the violin and organ and to compose, and when, with the view of improving himself in composition, he consulted Th. Roseingrave and Geminiani, they informed him that he already knew all they could teach him. He graduated B.A. of Dublin in 1754 and proceeded M.A. in 1757. In that year he founded the Academy of Music, an amateur society in which for the first time ladies sang in the chorus. Two years later he married the Hon. Anne Hill Trevor. In 1764 the University of Dublin conferred on him the degree of Mus.D., and elected him professor of that faculty, a post he held till 1774. In 1758 he succeeded his father, who in 1746 had been created Baron Mornington, and in 1760 he was created Viscount Wellesley and Earl of Mornington. His compositions are chiefly vocal; some are for the church, copies of which exist in the choirbooks of St. Patrick's Cathedral, Dublin. His chant in E flat is universally known.[2] But it was as a glee composer that he excelled. He gained prizes from the Catch Club in 1776 and

1777 for two catches, and in 1779 for his popular glee ' Here in cool grot.' He published a collection of ' Six Glees,' and John Sale included three others in a collection with three of his own. Nine glees, three madrigals, an ode and ten catches by him are contained in Warren's collections, and several glees in Horsley's ' Vocal Harmony.' A complete collection of his glees and madrigals, edited by Sir H. R. Bishop, was published in 1846. Three of his sons attained remarkable distinction, viz. Richard, Marquis Wellesley; Arthur, Duke of Wellington; and Henry, Lord Cowley.

W. H. H. ; addns. W. H. G. F.

MORO, JACOPO, of Viadana, Mantua (16th-17th cent.), Servite monk, composed 2 books concerti ecclesiastici, 1-8 v. (1604), 1-4 v. (1613); 1 book psalms, etc. (1595); 1 book Officium et missa defunctorum, 8 v. (1599); 'Sacrarum cantionum cantus vel tenor' (no title-page) (Q.-L.).

MORPHY, GUILLERMO CONDE DE (b. Madrid, Feb. 29, 1836; d. Baden, Switzerland, Aug. 28, 1899), grandson of an exiled Irishman, was tutor and private secretary to King Alfonso XII. from 1869-78. His acquaintance with Gevaert influenced him to take up the study of old Spanish lute tablatures, a study to which he devoted 25 years. His magnum opus was published posthumously, in 1902, namely Les Luthistes espagnols du XVIᵉ siècle, of which there was a German version, edited by Riemann. Morphy was a pioneer in the study of Spanish lute-music. W. H. G. F.

MORRIS, REGINALD OWEN (b. York, Mar. 3, 1886), was educated at Rugby, New College, Oxford, and at the R.C.M., becoming a member of the teaching staff of the last named. In 1926 Morris went to America to take up an appointment at the Curtis Institute in Philadelphia. His Contrapuntal Technique in the 16th Century (1922) is of considerable importance, as an attempt to outline the theory of composition as practised by Palestrina and his contemporaries and to contrast their practice with the theories of scholastic contrapuntists (see under POLYPHONY: Principles of the 16th Century). A later book, Foundations of Practical Harmony and Counterpoint, is a text-book for teaching purposes. Morris's close study of polyphonic methods also appears in his own composition, a ' Fantasy for String Quartet,' published by the Carnegie Trust, remarkable for its strangeness of sound produced by severely diatonic handling of the parts. Some motets for string quartet, songs and particularly arrangements of Elizabethan songs with string quartet accompaniment, have been played with success. c.

MORRIS (MORRICE) DANCE, a sort of pageant, accompanied with dancing, probably derived from the Morisco, a Moorish dance formerly popular in Spain and France. Although

1 Several interesting anecdotes of his early career are related by Daines Barrington, Miscellanies. 1781.
2 It is given in its original form in Mus. T., 1900, p. 173.

the name points to this derivation, there is some doubt whether the Morris Dance does not owe its origin to the MATACINS. In accounts of the Morisco, no mention is made of any sword-dance, which was a distinguishing feature of the Matacins, and survived in the English Morris Dance (in a somewhat different form) so late as the 19th century. Jehan Tabourot, in the *Orchésographie* (Langres, 1588), says that when he was young the Morisco used to be frequently danced by boys who had their faces blacked, and wore bells on their legs. The dance contained much stamping and knocking of heels, and on this account Tabourot says that it was discontinued, as it was found to give the dancers gout. The following is the tune to which it was danced :

The English Morris Dance is said to have been introduced from Spain by John of Gaunt in the reign of Edward III., but this is extremely doubtful, as there are scarcely any traces of it before the time of Henry VII., when it first began to be popular. Its performance was not confined to any particular time of the year, although it generally formed part of the May games. When this was the case, the characters who took part in it consisted of a Lady of the May, a Fool, a Piper and two or more dancers. From its association with the May games, the Morris Dance became incorporated with some pageant commemorating Robin Hood, and characters representing that renowned outlaw, Friar Tuck, Little John and Maid Marian (performed by a boy), are often found taking part in it. A hobby-horse, four whifflers, or marshals, a dragon and other characters were also frequently added to the above. The dresses of the dancers were ornamented round the ankles, knees and wrists with different-sized bells, which were distinguished as the fore bells, second bells, treble, mean, tenor, bass and double bells. In a note to Sir Walter Scott's *Fair Maid of Perth* there is an interesting account of one of these dresses, which was preserved by the Glover Incorporation of Perth. This dress was ornamented with 250 bells, fastened on pieces of leather in twenty-one sets of twelve, and tuned in regular musical intervals. The Morris Dance attained its greatest popularity in the reign of Henry VIII.; thenceforward it degenerated into a disorderly revel, until, together with the May games and other ' enticements unto naughtiness,' it was suppressed by the Puritans. It was revived at the Restoration, but the pageant seems never to have attained its former popularity, although the dance continued to be an

ordinary feature of village entertainments until within the memory of persons now living. In Yorkshire the dancers wore peculiar headdresses made of laths covered with ribbons, and were remarkable for their skill in dancing the sword-dance,[1] over two swords placed crosswise on the ground. A country dance which goes by the name of the Morris Dance is still frequently danced in the north of England. It is danced by an indefinite number of couples, standing opposite to one another, as in ' Sir Roger de Coverley.' Each couple holds a ribbon between them, under which the dancers pass in the course of the dance. In Cheshire the following tune is played to the Morris dance :

Mor-ris Dance is a very pretty tune, I can dance in my new shoon ; My new shoon they are so good, I could dance it if I would. This is it, and that is it, And this is Morris dancing, My poor father broke his leg, and so it fell a chancing.

In Yorkshire the following tune, founded on that of ' The Literary Dustman,' is generally used :

W. B. S.

More or less modernised forms of the Morris dance still linger in certain country places, both in the north, and in the south of England. In Oxfordshire there are Morris dancers who perform to the music of a pipe and tabor. The following tune was noted down by the present

Oxfordshire Morris Dance.

Noted from a pipe and tabor player in 1901.

---

[1] ' Do the sword-dance with any Morris-dancer in Christendom.' (Marston, *Malcontent,* 1604 Act i. Scene 3.)

writer from a pipe and tabor player, as one used for the Morris dance in an Oxfordshire village.

In Yorkshire, and in Northumberland, the sword-dance is a feature of the Morris (see SWORD-DANCE), and in the Whitby and other districts of north Yorkshire the pastime is called ' plew stotting.' ' Plew ' is the local pronunciation of plough, and ' stot ' is a young bull, formerly yoked to the plough. The ' plew stots ' are bands of youths (one dressed as the ' maiden '—no doubt a survival of ' Maid Marian '—and another as the ' old man ') who parade from village to village dancing the sword and other dances, to the accompaniment of a fiddle. In ' Traditional Tunes,' 1891, edited by the present writer, is a Lancashire Morris dance, danced at ' rush bearings ' in that county. It is noticeable that most Morris dances are in either common or 2-4 time, and the ' Helston Furry Dance,' which is a true Morris dance, is a very characteristic example. Of a different type is the following, which we may assume to be a traditional Welsh Morris, printed in a book of country dances issued by John Walsh about 1730–35; it is there entitled ' Welsh Morris dance.'

Welsh Morris Dance.
From *Walsh's Dances, circa* 1730-35.

Many references to the Morris dance are found in 17th-century plays. The monetary accounts of different corporate bodies who have provided the Morris men with their bells and decorations for the dance furnish further details. There are records of the Morris dance lingering in many parts of England, more or less differing from the earlier form. There seem few records of the dancing with make-belief swords in the earlier form, though this seems part of the Morris dance as it survives to-day. In many parts the bells, so characteristic of the Morris, are not present, though the dances appear to have been originally founded on that dance. In the sword-dance the laths representing the swords are finally linked together into a ' rose ' and at the finish of the dance are held up by one man.

There does not appear to have been any steps peculiar to the Morris; the performers had a knack of jerking the leg and stamping so as to make the bells ring clearly and well.

The music of the Morris was played by a pipe and tabor, or in some instances by a bagpipe. The illustration to 'Kemp's Nine Daies Wonder,' 1600, shows an accompanying musician playing on a pipe and tabor. Kemp performed the Morris dance step from London to Norwich in nine days in the year 1599.

In Hone's *Every Day Book* there is a letter from a gentleman who narrates having seen, in June 1826, a Morris dance performed by eight young men, six who were dancers, the seventh playing the pipe and tabor, and the eighth collecting the pence from the spectators.

In 1838 at the Coronation of Queen Victoria there was a Morris danced which is thus described by Mr. Shirley Hibberd, a spectator. Two teams of Morris dancers were performers. They were dressed in clean linen smocks, and the dance took place in Hyde Park. The music was given by a pipe and tabor, and one of the teams had short staves which were struck at certain turns of the dance; the other team had white handkerchiefs which by a trick of the hand were thrown out, when they acquired a momentary rigidity.[1]

The late Cecil J. SHARP (*q.v.*) found a band of Morris dancers at Headington, near Oxford, in 1905, Mr. Kimber being the leader, and later discoveries revealed that Morris dancing was current in many country places in England, more especially in the south. It was also practised at the ' rush bearings ' in Lancashire, and several doggerel verses were chanted by different sets of Morris dancers. It was also popular in Derbyshire. The tunes employed were generally the 18th-century song airs. Those noted by Cecil Sharp include ' Constant Billy,' ' Rigs of Marlow ' (really ' Rakes of Mallow ') and others, all of which will be found in 18th-century song collections.

The following is a very brief bibliography in which the Morris dance is treated :

THOINOT ARBEAU, *Orchésographie.* 1588.
FRANCIS DOUCE, *Illustrations of Shakespeare and Ancient Manners.*
WM. HONE, *Every Day Book, Table-Book, Year-Book.*
JOHN BRAND, *Observations on Popular Antiquities.* 1877.
JOSEPH STRUTT, *The Sports and Pastimes of the People of England.* 1830.
ROBERT CHAMBERS, *The Book of Days.*
WM. CHAPPELL, *Popular Music of the Olden Time.* 1855-59.
C. J. SHARP, *The Morris Book.* 1907.
F. KIDSON and MARY NEAL, *English Folk-song and Dance.* 1915.

COLLECTIONS

C. J. SHARP, *Several Collections giving the Airs and Steps.*
FRANK KIDSON, *Old Country Dances and Morris Tunes.*
JOHN GRAHAM, *Shakespeare Bidford Morris Dances.*
Lancashire and Cheshire Morris Dances.
　　　　　　　　　　　　　　　　　　　　　F. K.

MORTARO, ANTONIO, of Brescia, where he entered the Minorite monastery in 1595. In 1598 he was in the Franciscan monastery, Milan ; in 1602, organist at Novara Cathedral ; from 1606–8 he was again at Brescia. He was a prolific composer of masses, motets, sacred songs, etc. ; also 4 books of 3-part ' Fiamelle amorose,' an Organ Canzon and pieces in collective volumes (*Riemann*; *Q.-L.*).

[1] See *Notes and Queries*, 7th series, vol. 6, p. 105.

MORTELLARI, Michele (b. Palermo, 1750; d. ? London), settled in London c. 1785 where his son was teacher of music. Michele was a pupil of Piccinni, and his first opera was performed 1770 at Rome, followed by others in quick succession; his first opera produced in London was 'Armida,' in 1786, when he composed also a Mass a 4 v. with orchestra; songs, etc. (Q.-L.).

MORTIER DE FONTAINE (b. Warsaw, May 13, 1816; d. London, May 10, 1883), a pianist of celebrity. He was possessed of unusual technical ability, and is said to have been the first person to play the great sonata of Beethoven, op. 106, in public. From 1853–60 he resided in St. Petersburg, and subsequently in Munich, Paris and London.   M.

MORTON (Mourton), Robert, clerk of the chapel of Philipp the Good and Charles the Bold of Burgundy, c. 1464–78. He held a high reputation in his time as a learned musician, greatly honoured as such in a poem of the Dijon MS., quoted by Fétis. His name is undoubtedly English. Davey (Hist. Eng. Mus. p. 38) suggests his identity with Robertus de Anglia, choirmaster at Bologna 1467–72, and with Robertus Anglicus, 1485, singer at St. Peter's, Rome. The former appears unlikely, as it covers the period of Morton's presence at the Burgundian court. Some of his chansons have been preserved in MS. codices mentioned in Q.-L.; others may yet be discovered in the Belgian Archives (Fétis ; Q.-L.).

MOSCAGLIA, Giovanni Battista, a late 16th-century composer, of Rome. He wrote 4 books of madrigals, 5 v., 2 books of madrigals, 4 v., 1 book of 'Napolitane,' 3 v. (published c. 1570–87) ; also single numbers and lute arrangements in collective volumes. (List in Q.-L.)

MOSCHELES, Ignaz (b. Prague, May 30, 1794; d. Leipzig, Mar. 10, 1870), the foremost pianist after Hummel and before Chopin. His precocious aptitude for music aroused the interest of Dionys Weber, the director of the Prague Conservatorium. Weber brought him up on Mozart and Clementi. At 14 years of age he played a concerto of his own in public; and soon after, on the death of his father, was sent to Vienna to shift for himself as a pianoforte teacher and player, and to pursue his studies in counterpoint under Albrechtsberger, and in composition under Salieri.

The first volume of Aus Moscheles Leben, extracts from his diary, edited by Mme. Moscheles (Leipzig, 1872), offers bright glimpses of musical life in Vienna during the first decade of the century, and shows how quickly young Moscheles became a favourite in the best musical circles. In 1814 Artaria & Co., the publishers, honoured him with a commission to make the pianoforte arrangement of Beethoven's

'Fidelio' under the master's supervision. (See Vol. I. pp. 291 and 267.)

Moscheles's career as a virtuoso can be dated from the production of his 'Variationen über den Alexandermarsch,' op. 32, 1815. These brilliant variations met with an unprecedented success, and soon became a popular display piece for professional pianists ; later in life he frequently found himself compelled to play them, though he had outgrown them both as a musician and as a player.

During the ten years following Moscheles led the life of a travelling virtuoso. In the winter of 1821 he was heard and admired in Holland, and wrote his concerto in G minor; in the same year he played in Paris, and subsequently in London, where he first appeared at the Philharmonic on June 11, 1821. Here John Cramer, and the veteran Clementi, hailed him as an equal and friend; his capital duo for two pianofortes, 'Hommage à Händel,' was written for Cramer's concert, and played by the composer and 'glorious John' at the opera concert-room on May 9, 1822. In the season of 1823 he reappeared in London, and in 1824 he gave pianoforte lessons to Felix Mendelssohn, then a youth of 15, at Berlin. In 1826, soon after his marriage, at Hamburg, with Charlotte Embden, he chose London for a permanent residence ; and for a further ten years [1] he led the busy life of a prominent metropolitan musician. He appeared at the concerts of friends and rivals, gave his own concert annually, paid flying visits to Bath, Brighton, Edinburgh, etc., played much in society, did all manner of work to the order of publishers, gave innumerable lessons, and withal composed assiduously. In 1832 he was elected one of the directors of the Philharmonic Society ; and in 1837 and 1838 he conducted Beethoven's Ninth Symphony with signal success at the society's concerts. In 1845, after Sir Henry Bishop's resignation, he acted as regular conductor.

When Mendelssohn, who during his repeated visits to England had become Moscheles's intimate friend, started the Conservatorium of Music at Leipzig, Moscheles was invited to take the post of first professor of the pianoforte. He began his duties in 1846 ; and it is but fair to add that the continued success of the institution, both during the few remaining months of Mendelssohn's life, and for full twenty years after, was in a great manner owing to Moscheles's wide and solid reputation, and to his indefatigable zeal and exemplary conscientiousness as a teacher. Moscheles took quite a paternal interest in his pupils. If the school hours proved insufficient, which was frequently the case, he would invite them to

[1] In 1827 he noted and arranged the traditional airs sung by a troupe of Tyrolese singers who came to London. Two folio volumes of these songs were published by Willis with translation by W. Ball. In this collection first appeared the once favourite song, 'The Merry Swiss Boy.'   F. K.

his private residence, and there continue his
instructions ; and when they left school he
endeavoured to find suitable professional openings for them, and remained their friend, ever
ready with kindly advice and assistance.

As a pianoforte - player Moscheles was distinguished by a crisp and incisive touch, clear
and precise phrasing, and a pronounced preference for minute accentuation. He played
octaves with stiff wrists, and was chary in the
use of the pedals.

Mendelssohn and, with some reservations,
Schumann were the only younger masters
whose pianoforte works were congenial to him.
Those of Chopin and Liszt he regarded with
mingled feelings of aversion and admiration.
Indeed, his method of touch and fingering did
not permit him to play either Chopin's or
Liszt's pieces with ease. He wrote in 1833,
apropos of Chopin's Études, etc. :

'My thoughts, and consequently my fingers, ever
stumble and sprawl at certain crude modulations,
and I find Chopin's productions on the whole too
sugared, too little worthy of a man and an educated
musician, though there is much charm and originality
in the national colour of his motives.'

It is true he somewhat modified this opinion
when he heard Chopin play. Still it remains a
fact that to the end of his days, both the matter
and the manner of Chopin and other modern
pianists appeared to him questionable.

Moscheles was renowned for the variety and
brilliancy of his extempore performances, the
character of which can be guessed at by his
preludes, op. 73. His last improvisation in
public on themes furnished by the audience
formed part of the programme of a concert at
St. James's Hall in 1865, given by Madame
Jenny Lind-Goldschmidt ' in aid of the sufferers
by the war between Austria and Prussia,' where
he improvised for some twenty minutes on ' See
the conquering hero comes,' and on a theme
from the Andante of Beethoven's C minor
symphony, in a highly interesting and
astonishing manner.

The list of his numbered compositions given
in a Thematic Catalogue (Leipzig, Kistner) and
in *Aus Moscheles Leben*, vol. ii., extends to op.
142, and there is besides a long list of ephemera,
written for the market, to please publishers and
fashionable pupils. The latter, and many of
the former, have had their day ; but his best
works, such as the concerto in G minor, op.
60 (1820–21) ; the 'Concerto pathétique,' op.
93; the 'Sonate mélancolique,' op. 49; the duo
for pianoforte, ' Hommage à Händel,' op. 92 ;
the three Allegri di bravura, op. 51 ; and above
all, the twenty-four études, op. 70 (1825 and
1826), and the ' Characteristische Studien,' op.
95, occupy a place in the classical literature of
the instrument from which no subsequent development can oust them. The memoir above
referred to was translated by A. D. Coleridge,
and published in 1873 as *The Life of Moscheles.*

His *Briefe von F. Mendelssohn-Bartholdy an
Ignaz und Charlotte Moscheles* appeared in 1888.
          E. D.

MOSE IN EGITTO, ' oratorio,' libretto by
Tottola, music by Rossini. Produced San
Carlo Theatre, Naples, Mar. 5, 1818 ; Théâtre
Italien, Paris, Oct. 22, 1822 ; in a revised form,
text adapted by Balocchi and De Jouy, Académie, Mar. 26, 1827 ; King's Theatre, Haymarket, as ' Pietro l' Eremita,' Apr. 23, 1822;
at Covent Garden, Feb. 22, 1833, as an oratorio,
' The Israelites in Egypt ; or, The Passage of
the Red Sea,' with scenery and dresses, and
additions from ' Israel in Egypt ' ; at the Royal
Italian Opera, Covent Garden, Apr. 20, 1850,
as ' Zora.' In 1845 it was performed by the
Handel and Haydn Society of Boston, U.S.A.,
in an English version of the original libretto,
and on May 24, 1878, by the Sacred Harmonic
Society, at Exeter Hall, in an English version
by Arthur Matthison.   G.

MOSEL, GIOVANNI FELICE (b. Florence,
1754), a violinist of merit. His father, who had
been a pupil of Tartini, gave him his first instruction in violin-playing, and he also received
lessons from Pietro Nardini. In 1793 he succeeded the latter as director of the music at the
court of the Grand Duke Leopold in Florence,
and in 1812 became first violin in the Theatre
at Pergola. His name is chiefly known in connexion with the history of the ' Tuscan Strad,'
a violin which was one of a quartet made by
Stradivarius for the Grand Duke of Tuscany in
1690. Before 1792 this *chef-d'œuvre* had disappeared from the ducal collection, and was
lost until 1795, when Mosel (whose possession of the instrument is unaccounted for)
sold it to David Ker of Portavoe, Ireland,
for £24.

PUBLISHED COMPOSITIONS.—Six duets for two violins and piano,
published by Pleyel in Paris in 1783. Six quartets for two violins,
alto and bass ; *Ibid.* 1785. Six duets for two violins, op. 3 ; Venice,
1791. Serenade for flute, two violins, and violoncello ; Venice,
1791. MS. sonatas for violin alone ; trios for two violins and
violoncello, and some symphonies.

BIBL.—A. M. CLARKE, *Fiddlers Ancient and Modern* ; Fétis; OLGA
RACSTER, *Chats on Violins* (London, 1905); HILL & SONS, *The
Tuscan Strad* (London, 1889, 1891).   E. H.-A.

MOSEL, IGNAZ FRANZ, EDLER VON (b. Vienna,
Apr. 1, 1772 ; d. there, Apr. 8, 1844), composer and writer on musical subjects, conducted
the first musical festivals of the Gesellschaft der
Musikfreunde in the Imperial Riding-school
(1812–16). He was ennobled, and made a Hofrath. From 1820–29 he was vice-director of
the two court theatres, and from 1829 till his
death principal custos of the Imperial library.
He was one of the three chief mourners at
Beethoven's funeral. In his earlier years he
arranged Haydn's ' Creation ' (Mollo), Cherubini's ' Médée ' and ' Deux journées ' (Cappi),
and ' Così fan tutte' (Steiner) for string-quartet;
and the ' Creation ' and ' Così fan tutte ' for
two pianofortes for the blind pianist Paradies.
For the Gesellschaft der Musikfreunde he put
additional instruments to several of Handel's

oratorios,[1] and translated the text. He also composed three operas (court theatre), one Singspiel, several overtures and entr'actes for plays, a Missa solennis, etc. He published three collections of songs, dedicating one to Vogl, the celebrated singer of Schubert's songs, and another to Rochlitz (Steiner). Among his writings the following are of value : *Versuch einer Ästhetik des dramatischen Tonsatzes* (Vienna, Strauss, 1813) ; *Über das Leben und die Werke des Antonio Salieri* (*ibid.*, Wallishauser, 1827) ; *Über die Originalpartitur des Requiems von W. A. Mozart* (1829) ; *Geschichte der Hofbibliothek* (*ibid.*, Beck, 1835) ; and articles in various periodicals on the history of music, including *Die Tonkunst in Wien während der letzten 5 Dezennien* (1818, revised and republished 1840).   C. F. P.

MOSER, (1) ANDREAS (*b.* Semlin on the Danube, Nov. 29, 1859 ; *d.* Nov. 8, 1925), violinist, was pupil and afterwards colleague and biographer of Joachim. He became teacher at the Hochschule in 1888 and professor there in 1900. His biography of Joachim was first written for the latter's artistic jubilee (1899), and enlarged after Joachim's death to two volumes. Moser also edited the correspondence of Joachim and Brahms and the *Briefe von und an J. Joachim* (3 vols. 1911–12). He collaborated with Joachim in producing the 'Methodik des Violinspiels' (Eng. trans. Moffat), and did much important editing of the classics. (See *Riemann.*)

His son, (2) HANS JOACHIM (*b.* Berlin, May 25, 1889), has written widely on musical subjects (notably in the *Z.M.W.*), and is a professor of musical research at Halle. He has appeared as a bass singer and published a number of compositions.   C.

MOSER, FRANZ (*b.* Vienna, March 20, 1880), first studied music under his father and later at the Conservatorium in Vienna under Schalk, Löwe, Mandyczewski, Grädener and Fuchs. He was Kapellmeister in several provincial towns, and in 1906 was appointed *répétiteur* and assistant to Felix Mottl in Munich. He returned to Vienna in 1919, where he is professor of PF. and theory of music at the State Academy, Chorus-Director at the State Opera, and Lecturer at the University.

WORKS.—Op. 1, Mass ; op. 11, female choir ; op. 12, 'Aus meinem Leben,' PF. work ; op. 18, PF. quartet ; op. 19, str. quartet in G major ; op. 20, 1st symphony in C sharp minor ; op. 23, str. sextet ; op. 28, male choir ; op. 32, str. quartet in F major ; op. 34, 2nd symphony in C minor ; op. 35, serenade for 15 wind instruments ; op. 39, 3rd str. quartet in A minor ; op. 36, 4 fantastic pieces for violin and PF. ; op. 37, suite for 17 wind instruments ; op. 40, chamber symphony for 9 solo instruments ; op. 41, symphony prelude for large orch. ; op. 42, music for play, 'Das Märchen' ; op. 43, scherzo for orch. ; op. 45, 4th str. quartet in C major ; op. 48, 3rd symphony in F sharp. Many songs with orch.

K. D. H.

MOSEWIUS, JOHANN THEODOR (*b.* Königsberg, Prussia, Sept. 25, 1788 ; *d.* Schaffhausen, Sept. 15, 1858), like so many others, forsook the law for music and the theatre. After a

regular musical education he became in 1814 director of the opera in his native town. He married, and in 1816 went to Breslau, and for eight years he and his wife were the pillars of the opera. His wife dying in 1825 he forsook the stage, and founded the Breslau Singakademie. He had before this started the Liedertafel of the town. In 1827 he followed Berner as professor at the University, and in 1832 became director of the music there. In 1831 he succeeded Schnabel as head of the Royal Institution for Church Music, which he appears to have conducted most efficiently, bringing forward a large number of pieces by the greatest of the old Italian masters, as well as the vocal works of Mendelssohn, Löwe, Spohr, Marx, etc. His activity was further shown in the foundation of an elementary class as a preparative for the Singakademie, and a society called the Musikalische Cirkel (1834) for the practice of secular music. He also initiated the musical section of the Vaterländische Gesellschaft of Silesia, and became its secretary. In England he was principally known through two pamphlets—reprints from the *A.M.Z.*—*J. S. Bach in seinen Kirchencantaten und Choralgesängen* (Berlin, 1845), and *J. S. Bach's Matthäus Passion* (Berlin, 1852). In the copious examples which they contain, some Englishmen made their first acquaintance with Bach's finest compositions.   G.

MOSKOWA, JOSEPH NAPOLÉON NEY, PRINCE DE LA (*b.* Paris, May 8, 1803 ; *d.* St. Germain-en-Laye, July 25, 1857), eldest son of Marshal Ney. As a lad he showed great aptitude for music, and composed a Mass, which was performed at Lucca, where he lived after his father's death. In 1831 he was made 'Pair de France,' but sought distinction in a totally different line from that of his brother the Duc d'Elchingen. He contributed to various periodicals, especially some articles in the *Revue des deux mondes* and the *Constitutionnel*, which excited considerable interest. His love of sport was great, and he was one of the founders of the Jockey Club of Paris. In 1828 he married the only daughter of Laffitte, the banker. The services rendered by the Prince to music are considerable. In connexion with Adolphe Adam he founded the Société des Concerts de Musique Religieuse et Classique, an association for the practice of vocal music, and a *Recueil des morceaux de musique ancienne* (11 vols. 8vo), which has now become very scarce,[2] was published for the Society by the Prince. The Prince lived on intimate terms with Delsarte the singer, and with Niedermeyer the composer, whom he materially assisted in the foundation of his École de Musique Religieuse. In 1831 a Mass of his for voices and orchestra was executed by the pupils of Choron, and called forth the strong encomiums of Fétis. Although naturally in-

---

[1] Haslinger published the scores of 'Belshazzar' and 'Jephtha.'

[2] There is a copy in the British Museum.

clined to the madrigal style and sacred music, he also attempted the theatre, producing at the Opéra-Comique, ' Le Cent-Suisse ' (June 7, 1840), a 1-act piece, which had a considerable run, and ' Yvonne ' (Mar. 16, 1855), a 1-act opéra-comique, a clever imitation of the antique style.　　　　　　　　　　　　　　　　G. C.

MOSTO, GIOVANNI BATTISTA (16th cent.), of Udine; pupil of Claudio Merulo; from 1580–89 maestro di cappella at Padua Cathedral; afterwards in the service of the Prince-Cardinal Bathori of Siebenbürgen, where he still was in 1595. He composed 3 books of madrigals, 5 v., and 1 book of madrigals, 6 v. He also published 2 collective volumes of madrigals, 1577 and 1579 (Q.-L.).

MOSZKOWSKI, MORITZ (b. Breslau, Aug. 23, 1854 ; d. Paris, Mar. 8, 1925), pianist and composer, studied first at Dresden and afterwards at Berlin at the academies of Stern and Kullak successively. He was a teacher at the latter for a good many years. After a successful career as a pianist and composer he went in 1897 to live in Paris, and was made a member of the Berlin Academy in 1899. His compositions include two books of Spanish Dances for PF., four hands, a symphony in four movements, ' Jeanne d'Arc,' op. 19, two concertstücke and a scherzo for violin with PF.: 'Aus allen Herren Landen,' for PF. four hands, op. 23 ; three concert studies for PF. op. 24 ; Barcarolle for PF. op. 27 ; three pieces for violoncello and piano, op. 29 ; violin concerto, op. 30 ; two orchestral suites, opp. 39 and 47; PF. concerto in E major; ' Phantastischer Zug ' for orchestra, and many PF. solos and duets, and songs. His opera ' Boabdil ' was produced at Berlin, Apr. 21, 1892, and a 3-act ballet ' Laurin ' in 1896. He appeared at the Philharmonic Concerts in 1886, and frequently in London afterwards as a pianist and conductor. His last appearance in London was in 1908, when he conducted a programme of his own works at Queen's Hall.
　　　　　　　　　　　　　　　　　　M.

MOTET. I. FROM THE EARLIEST TIMES TO THE FIRST FLEMISH SCHOOL, c. 1430.—Giving greater scope for artistic skill and technical ingenuity than did the somewhat more restricted style of the CONDUCTUS (q.v.), the motet was the form of composition most frequently employed by polyphonic composers from the beginning of the 13th century A.D. In all the collections of the more developed (as distinct from the semi-experimental) music of the 13th and 14th centuries the motet form predominates, and by 1450 it has completely ousted the conductus. It was applied to every choral part of divine worship, the Credo of the Mass alone excepted, and is of special interest because, with the occasional exception of FAUX-BOURDON (q.v.), it was the only one of the early forms which was taken over by the group of individual composers in the mid-15th century

associated with the names of Dunstable and Dufay.

The earliest school of any extent was that of Notre Dame at Paris, exhaustively treated by Wooldridge.[1] Other important collections are those of Montpelier, dealt with in the scarce works of C. E. H. de Coussemaker ; Bamberg, edited by Pierre Aubry ; and Worcester.[2] The Spanish manuscripts were described by Aubry in his *Iter Hispanicum* (Paris, Geuthner, 1908), and this writer's many other works are all deserving of study. Two important German monographs are Leichtentritt's *Geschichte der Motette* and (on the literary side) Wilhelm Meyer's *Ursprung der Motette*. The former book is of value for the complete history of the form, and not only for the early period to which this first section relates. The climax of the early mediæval motet is reached in the work of MACHAUT (q.v.), a gifted, prolific and original composer, whose treatment of this form is, however, conservative.

The structure of the motet can be best understood if we approach it in the way in which the mediæval mind would approach it, from the point of view of the text. It was essentially an embroidering of a given (not composed) theme of words-and-music by two or by three other sets of words-and-music. This being so, we are not surprised to find that it is closely connected with that expansion of a liturgical text known as the TROPE (q.v.), and this is especially true of the English motets. And it is for this reason that the motet form is not used for the Credo, the text of which was obviously inviolate.

The title, normally motetus, was spelt in a larger variety of ways than is usual even in mediæval orthography. The different spellings have given rise to various etymological guesses : it is probably either from *mot* (word), or cognate with *motion*. *Motetus* sang the chief text : or it moved, while *tenor* held on, the *triplex* being the third voice (whence is derived our modern treble). In pitch, *triplex* would usually correspond to the modern (male) alto, *motetus* to a high tenor, *tenor* to a baritone. The fourth voice, where found, might be called *quadruplum* or *quartus cantus* ; its range would normally be the same as that of the *triplex*.

The tenor motive, usually but not always a liturgical piece of plainsong, was arranged in one or other of the ORDINES (q.v.), which were arbitrary schemes of rhythm founded on poetic metres, and described at length by the contemporary theorists. The *motetus* and *triplex* (and *quartus cantus* where found) also followed rhythmic schemes, but these were usually simple iambic or trochaic forms (♩ ♪ or ♪ ♩). In France, as time goes on, motets are found in

¹ *Oxf. Hist. Mus.*, vol. i. p. 176 *et seq.*
² See *Proceedings of the Musical Association*, Dec. 1924.

which the triplex, or the two upper voices, or even all three parts, including the stiff and orthodox tenor, are provided with vernacular words borrowed, with their music, from some secular song. This practice is frequently interpreted in a loose and very thoughtless way as indicating the low degree of the singers' sense of propriety and reverence, but a moment's serious reflection will show us that this development was nothing more nor less than the effort made by the monodic troubadour minstrels to adapt for their purposes the more complex technique of the ecclesiastical musicians ; and that the occurrence of these vernacular, or partly vernacular, texts in the performance of divine worship (though it did undoubtedly occur) was not the normal course of the art-development, but an illegitimate side-practice, promptly and fairly effectively dealt with by the church authorities.

The motet, unlike the conductus, was not written in score, but in separate vocal parts. The normal English method was to place the *triplex* on the left-hand page of the opening, the *motetus* on the right, and the *tenor* or *pes* at the foot of one or both pages. Continental practice varied. Occasionally, as in a Florence MS. (probably from Notre Dame at Paris) and once at Worcester, *triplex* and *motetus* are found together in quasi-score, with the tenor following them below.

Mutual Relation of the Individual Voices.— We are forced to admit that the style of harmony in the early mediæval motet, at least as it appears on paper, is still deserving of the title ' crude '—that adjective so freely applied in the last century to all that did not conform to current taste. In the light of the harmonic effects reached by ' Sumer is icumen in ' (1240) and the Agincourt Song (1415), we are disappointed to find that most of the motets of the 13th and 14th centuries consist of a succession of five-three chords, or of open fifths, occasionally relieved by other concords and sometimes by sheer discords. Machaut, whose four-part work is noteworthy for the normal completeness of its chords with third and fifth, and general tendency to harmonic propriety as understood in later times, tends to become ' square,' and to lose the advantages of contrapuntal flow. For the motet must not, of course, be judged along harmonic lines : its beauties lay in its melodic counterpoint ; and by the skilful arrangement of phrases and of pauses (the old masters had a great gift for making a silence speak) considerable effect was undoubtedly attained in performance. The subjoined example shows the measure of skill with which a Worcester composer of about 1325 explored the resources of his limited equipment of one common chord. The pes or tenor phrase, repeated twice in this extract, forms a *basso ostinato* throughout the piece.

Middle section from the motet "Te Domine laudat—Te Dominum clamat."

1.   Worcester Chapter Library, Add. 68.

Ut e-mun-det nos a cri-mi-ni-bus.

Cu-ra qua-rum ti-bi tra-di-tur. O

(*Wordless.*)

O Mi-cha-el, re-gis arch-an-ge-le,

Ra-pha-el, lan-guo-ris me-di-ce, ca-li-gi-

pa-ra-di-si lae-ti prae-po-si-ti,

-nem di-lu-ens To-bi-e, Tu

nos a ma-lis ve-lis e-ru-e-re

lan-gui-dos ve-lis e-ru-e-re a-ba-ra-
  *

* A not F in MS.

ut jun-ga-mur ci-vi-bus glo-ri-ae.

-thri te-tra ca-li-gi-ne. O

O Ga-bri-el, qui sanctae vir-gi-ni nun-ti-

Ga-bri-el, tu re-gis nun-ti-us, per te no-

-as-ti sa-lu-tem po-pu-li, etc.

-bis Ma-ri-ae fi-li-us, etc.

II. FROM c. 1430 TO c. 1500.

—Passing on to the days of the three Flemish or Netherland Schools (see POLYPHONY), we find that the motet now shares with the Mass the greater part of the composers' output until about half-way through the period under review, when the madrigal begins to claim some of their attention. The form of the motet still rests, as a rule, upon a slow-moving tenor, but the words are now frequently identical in all the voices, and the tenor moves faster in proportion to the upper parts than was formerly the case. Sometimes even the upper parts will also move slowly, in longs and breves, slightly reminiscent of the old conductus, as in Ex. 2 below. Or the tenor will abandon for a time, or completely, its steady course, and join in the contrapuntal flow on even terms, as in Ex. 3, while in Ex. 4 the distinctive character of the tenor voice is completely lost.

" Benedicta tu."

4.   MS. Pepysian 1236, Magd. Coll. Camb. c. 1460.

2.
Opening of "Ave regina cœlorum."
LEONEL POWER. c. 1460.

etc.

Ending of the same Motet.

3.
Opening of " Sola Virgo."
Trent MS. 90. c. 1465.

etc.

The great gift of DUNSTABLE, DUFAY, POWER (q.v.) and their followers to music was a certain freedom of thought, and a striving after musical effect, beautiful in itself and unfettered by any excessive adherence to the course of a predetermined plain-song melody. Music henceforward is to be more artistic and less mathematical, and the natural result of such a development in the composers' mental processes is to be seen in this alteration in the form. Contemporaneous with this is found a great advance on the paths of imitation, canon and fugue, as well as on that of harmonic smoothness. With OKEGHEM and OBRECHT (q.v.) we reach a period when the normal three-voice arrangement is expanded to a larger range of voices, though Dufay is usually credited with being the first to regard four as the ideal number. Obrecht, for instance, has left one motet for six voices, six for five voices, seven for four and seven for three, while the large majority of his other extant works, including eighteen of his twenty complete masses, are written in four parts, while Okeghem is the earliest producer of a 36-part experiment.[1]

All through the great settlement and expansion of the art of composition that occurred under the leadership of JOSQUIN DES PRÉS (q.v.) and right up into the time of Palestrina, however, we find the plainsong-motive type predominating, if this be taken to include folk-song, chanson and Lieder motives also; and so much so, that when a group of composers, e.g. those associated with the name of MOUTON (q.v.), breaks away from this type to any extent, historians hail them as a new school. In this period also began the practice so marked in the Palestrina era, of a composer writing a motet and following it with a Mass on the same theme, with similar and varied treatment of the motive. This is the origin of the form known as variations. Rockstro, writing in the first edition of this Dictionary, was of opinion that ' the composer of the motet felt bound to give his whole attention to a careful rendering of the words. . . . Hence

[1] See Ambros, Geschichte, iii. 174.

the character of the text frequently offers a tolerably safe criterion as to the style of work.'

The harmonic and other musical developments in this second period are not dealt with here, being treated in general under the heading of POLYPHONY, and sometimes in particular under the composers' names.

By the year 1500 the motet has reached its final form of a short composition for voices, intended primarily for unaccompanied singing, written in contrapuntal style upon a Latin text which is usually liturgical or quasi-liturgical in character.   A. H.

The above definition marks the point at which the individual history of the motet as an art-form ceases, and to trace it further would be to epitomise the development of style in composition as applied to works included under that name. It must be remarked, however, that it was during the century 1500–1600 that the motet was of paramount importance in practical composition. It blossomed in the works of all the great polyphonic composers of the period, and the volumes of Palestrina's works containing no less than 179 motets are regarded as the purest examples of a great epoch. Among polyphonic composers of all schools and nations the term 'Cantiones Sacrae' became the prevalent description for collections of motets intended for singing in the prescribed place at Mass or elsewhere in the offices of the church. What has been said under MASS (q.v.) about the reaction of secular music on church music applies with equal force to the motet, and to recapitulate names and schools here would be superfluous. But the Mass remained at any rate the musical setting of a given text with an unbroken ritual significance. The motet with its freedom of text, and the latitude allowed to its use in the ecclesiastical offices, so far lost its identity that by the beginning of the 17th century even the broad definition given above ceases to be applicable to all the works called by its name.

For the purposes of classification of English church music we normally take the distinction of language as the dividing line, using Motet for the 'Cantiones sacrae' of Tallis, Byrd and Dering, and indeed of all kindred works set to a Latin text, and ANTHEM (q.v.) for all those written for the English Liturgy. Nevertheless Orlando Gibbons's 'First set of Madrigals and Motets of Five Parts' (published 1612) are all in English, and none are definitely ecclesiastical in text or character. From this time dates the common English habit, which has survived to the 20th century,[1] of using motet to imply merely a choral work of more serious import both in its words and its musical structure than the madrigal or partsong. On the other hand, that part of the definition which confines the term to voices unaccompanied vanished when

[1] Witness Parry's 'Six Motets ; Songs of Farewell.'

all church music became normally accompanied either by organ or orchestra, and the accompanied motet ranges through three centuries of composition.[2] Lutheran Germany, however, maintained the distinction. The motets of J. S. Bach are distinguished from his cantatas primarily in the fact that they are for unaccompanied voices. 'Jesu meine Freude' is in all other respects the strictest form of the choral-cantata, and an examination of the six famous examples shows that, except for their purely vocal character, they exhibit no common principle of structure.

BIBLIOGRAPHY
FRIEDRICH LUDWIG, *Die Quellen der Motetten ältesten Stils.* A.M., July 1923, pp. 185-222.
PIERRE AUBRY, *Cent motets du XIIIe siècle.* 3 vols. 1908.
   Photographic Facsimiles, with commentaries, etc. (The Bamberger Motet Codex. An important work. Publications of the International Musical Society, Paris Section.)
HUGO LEICHTENTRITT, *Geschichte der Motette.* (Leipzig, 1908.)

MOTETT SOCIETY, THE, was established in 1841, its chief promoter being William Dyce, R.A. The object was to print 'A Collection of Ancient Church Music,' adapted to English words, with a compressed score, for the purpose of accompaniment. The subscription was a guinea a year. The musical portion was under the charge of Dr. Rimbault, who acknowledges in his preface that 'the greater part of the Motetts of Palestrina were adapted by William Dyce.'

The works were published in large folio, and in parts, forming three divisions : No. 1, Anthems for Festivals ; No. 2, Services ; No. 3, Miscellaneous Anthems ; in all 192 pages of music, and a few more of introductory matter.   W. C.

MOTIF (Ger. *Motiv*), a word which is in process of naturalisation into English, and which has no less than three distinct meanings, according to which it will be found under separate heads : first, the German word originally means what we call FIGURE, that is, a short group of notes, ' which produces a single, complete, and distinct impression ' ; second, it is used as a synonym for SUBJECT ; third, as equivalent to, and an abbreviation of, LEITMOTIV (q.v.).   M.

MOTION is change of pitch in successive sounds, when they are allotted to a single part or voice, or to groups of parts or voices which sound simultaneously. The motions of a single part are classified according as the successive steps do or do not exceed the limits of a degree of the scale at a time, the former being called ' disjunct,' and the latter ' conjunct ' motion. The following examples illustrate the two forms:

[2] The term has even been used in modern times for purely instrumental music, *e.g.* 'Motet for String Quartet' by R. O. Morris (London, 1925).

The independent motions of different parts sounding together constitute counterpoint, and are classified according to their relations, as ' contrary,' ' similar,' and ' oblique ' motions. In the first the parts either distinctly converge or diverge, one rising when the other falls. In the second the parts either rise or fall together, though not necessarily at equal distances. The third refers to one part only, which moves up or down while another stands still.

Further explanations and examples will be found under the respective headings.

C. H. H. P.

MOTTA, José Vianna da (b. St. Thomas, 1868), Portuguese pianist. After early studies at the Lisbon Conservatoire, he went to Berlin, where he had lessons from Xaver Scharwenka (PF.) and Philipp Scharwenka (composition). He subsequently worked with Liszt at Weimar (1885), Schäfer at Berlin (1886) and von Bülow at Frankfort (1887). Since 1902 he has toured widely in Europe and S. America. He was also Hofpianist in Berlin, and from 1915–17 held the post formerly occupied by Stavenhagen at Geneva. He then returned to Lisbon as Director of the Conservatoire and conductor of the Symphony Orchestra. His compositions include :

Op. 9. Portuguese scenes. (PF.)
Op. 10. 5 Portuguese Rhapsodies. (PF.)
Symphony.
Str. Quartet.
' Lusiads ' (Choir and orch.)
Songs.
Transcriptions for PF. (2 and 4 hands) of Alkan's works for pedal-piano.

He edited the works of Liszt for Breitkopf & Härtel, and has written a number of articles on the technical aspects of his art. J. B. T.

MOTTL, Felix (b. Unter - St. - Veit, near Vienna, Aug. 24, 1856 ; d. Munich, July 2, 1911), a celebrated and highly gifted conductor. As a boy he possessed a fine soprano voice, and obtained admission to the Löwenburgische Convict, the preparatory school of the Imperial Court Chapel. Later on he entered the Vienna Conservatorium, where Josef Hellmesberger soon recognised the eminent gifts of young Mottl, who in due course obtained all the prizes the college could award. The Academical Richard Wagner Verein of Vienna elected him to the post of conductor of the society's concerts, and it was there that his eminent ability as a chef d'orchestre attracted general notice. In 1876 Mottl took part in the Bayreuth Festival performances of Wagner's ' Ring des Nibelungen ' as stage conductor, and he became one of the most active members of the so-called ' Nibelungen-kanzlei.' Upon the recommendation of Dessoff he obtained in 1881 the post of conductor at the Grand Ducal Opera House at Carlsruhe, which post he held until 1903. Mottl's energetic activity raised the performances at this opera-house to a place amongst the finest to be heard in Germany. A sworn enemy of all routine work, he produced at Carlsruhe

many important stage works of modern times, including the complete cycle of operas by Berlioz, and all the musical dramas of Richard Wagner. Mottl also obtained brilliant successes as a conductor of concerts ; he was director of the Philharmonic Society of Carlsruhe until 1892, and was in 1886 appointed by the Bayreuth authorities to conduct the festival performances of ' Tristan und Isolde,' a task which he accomplished to perfection. He conducted a Wagner Concert in the Queen's Hall on Apr. 17, 1894, and appeared often in London subsequently, at many series of similar concerts. In June 1898 he conducted the Nibelungen trilogy at Covent Garden. In 1904 he was made a director of the Berlin Royal Academy of Music. He went to New York to conduct the performance of ' Parsifal ' given there in 1903–04, and in 1907 became director of the opera at Munich. He composed three operas, ' Agnes Bernauer ' (successfully produced at Weimar in 1880), ' Ramin ' and ' Fürst und Sänger,' a ' Festspiel,' ' Eberstein ' (produced at Carlsruhe in 1881), a string quartet, a song-cycle ' Pan im Busch,' besides a considerable number of songs for one voice and pianoforte accompaniment. He edited various works of Berlioz, and the ' Barbier von Bagdad ' of Cornelius ; he orchestrated Liszt's pianoforte solo, ' St. Francis of Assisi preaching to the birds,' Wagner's ' Five Songs,' and edited several of the works of Bach and other classics.

C. A., with addns.

MOULU, Pierre (early 16th cent.), pupil of Josquin des Prés. He wrote masses, motets and other church music. His Mass on a popular song, ' A deux visaiges et plus ' (not villaige, as in Coussemaker and Q.-L.) appears to have been a great favourite. It appeared generally as ' Missa duarum facierum,' or ' Missa sans pause,' as it was without a rest, one of the many tricks of the old contrapuntists. Several of Moulu's works were published by Jacques Moderne (1532, 1540). (See Fétis ; Q.-L.)

MOUNSEY, two sisters, (1) Ann Sheppard (b. London, Apr. 17, 1811 ; d. there, June 24, 1891), organist, composer and teacher, studied under Logier. She is alluded to by Spohr in his account of his visit to Logier's academy in 1820.[1] In 1828 she was elected organist to a church at Clapton ; in 1829 to St. Michael's, Wood Street, E.C., and on Nov. 22, 1837, to St. Vedast's, Foster Lane. In 1834 Miss Mounsey became an associate of the Philharmonic Society. In 1843 she gave the first of six series of Classical Concerts, at Crosby Hall, London, for one of which Mendelssohn[2] composed ' Hear my Prayer' for voices and organ, first performed Jan. 8, 1845. On Apr. 28, 1853 she married W. Bartholomew, and in the same year composed the oratorio of ' The

[1] Autobiography, ii. 99, 100.
[2] See his letter, in Polko's Reminiscences, p. 220. The autograph is now in the South Kensington Museum.

Nativity,' which was performed, Jan. 17, 1855, under the direction of John Hullah at St. Martin's Hall. Mrs. Bartholomew was well known in London as a teacher ; she published upwards of 100 songs, 40 partsongs, and a large number of works for piano and for organ.

(2) ELIZABETH (b. London, Oct. 8, 1819 ; d. there, Oct. 3, 1905), organist and composer, developed considerable musical ability at a very early age. She was appointed organist of St. Peter's, Cornhill, in 1834, when only 14 years old, a post she resigned in 1882. The organ of St. Peter's, a fine instrument by Hill, was one of those on which Mendelssohn frequently played during his visits to London. In 1842 Miss Elizabeth Mounsey was elected an associate of the Philharmonic Society. Besides the organ and piano, she at one time devoted much study to the guitar, and in 1833 and 1834 appeared in public as a performer thereon. She published several works for all three instruments. She lived in the same house, 58 Brunswick Place, City Road, for eighty-three years. See *Mus. T.*, 1905, p. 718.   G.

MOUNTAIN, (1) HENRY (d. Nov. 15, 1794 [1]), a Dublin musician, and violinist of ability, who was also established as a music-seller and publisher in the Irish capital towards the latter end of the 18th century.   In 1751 he was one of the Rotunda band in Dublin, and from 1765–85 was leader of the Dublin City music. From before 1785 he was at 20 Whitefriar Street, but about 1790 removed from thence to 44 Grafton Street.   He published a large number of engraved single songs from the popular operas of the day, and besides, about 1785, issued a small book, ' The Gentleman's Catch Book,' which he edited and dedicated to the Hibernian Catch Club.

(2) JOSEPH, his son, was equally clever on the violin, and came to Liverpool where he was leader at the concert hall, and the theatre. In this town he married (1787) Sarah WILKINSON (q.v.) and came with her to Covent Garden, where he was leader of the orchestra.   In 1820 he was leader at the English Opera House and was still living in 1837.

F. K. ; addns. W. H. G. F.

MOUNTAIN SYLPH, THE, opera in 2 acts; words by J. T. Thackeray, music by Barnett. Produced Lyceum Theatre, Aug. 25, 1834. This was the first ' musicall through ' English opera since Arne's 'Artaxerxes.'

MOUNT - EDGCUMBE, RICHARD EDG-CUMBE, second Earl of (b. Sept. 13, 1764 ; d. Sept. 26, 1839), an amateur musician and composer, whose Italian opera ' Zenobia ' was performed at the King's Theatre in 1800 for the benefit of Banti. He is best known as author of *Musical Reminiscences, containing an Account of the Italian Opera in England from 1773*, London, 1825 ; an amusing, gossiping book,

containing much useful information. Two other editions, with a continuation, appeared, and in 1834 a fourth, including the Musical Festival in Westminster Abbey in that year.

W. H. H.

MOUNTIER, who is called by Burney ' the Chichester boy,' was probably of French origin, and educated musically in the choir of Chichester Cathedral.   He made his first appearance ' in Character on any stage ' as Acis, to the Galatea of Miss Arne (afterwards Mrs. Cibber), May 17, 1732, at the Haymarket Theatre—the performance got up by the elder Arne.   Mountier sang, in the same year, the part of Neptune (though advertised for that of Phœbus, which was given afterwards to Barret) in Lediard's ' Britannia, an English Opera,' with music by Lampe, ' after the Italian manner,' a work not mentioned by the biographers of that composer.   It may be, therefore, interesting to record that the cast included Cecilia Young (Britannia), afterwards Mrs. Arne, Susanna Mason (Publick Virtue), Comano, or Commano (Discord), a basso who had sung the year before on the Italian stage, Waltz (Honour), the well-known singer who, from being 'Handel's cook,' became afterwards the performer of many of that master's principal bass parts in opera and oratorio—and other performers.   In the following year we find Mountier singing the part of Adelberto in Handel's ' Ottone ' (revived), after which his name does not appear again in the bills.   J. M.

MOUNT OF OLIVES, the English name of Beethoven's oratorio, ' Christus am Ölberg.' It was first produced in this country on Feb. 25, 1814, by Sir George Smart, in the Lenten oratorios at Drury Lane ; and the English version was probably made by Arnold, at that time manager of the King's Theatre and a prominent person in all theatrical matters. Another version was made by Thos. Oliphant, and a third by Bartholomew. The strong feeling prevailing in England against the appearance of our Saviour as a personage in the oratorio, which led to the modifications in the versions already mentioned, led to one by Dr. Hudson of Dublin in 1842, in which the story was changed to that of David, and the title to ' Engedi.'   This compromise was adopted as lately as in 1905, at the Bristol Festival.

G. ; addn. M.

MOURET, JEAN JOSEPH (b. Avignon, Apr. 11, 1682 ; d. Charenton, Dec. 20, 1738), was in the service of the Duchess of Maine at Paris from about 1707, and composed his first ballets in 1714 ; his first opera, ' Ariane,' in five acts and a prologue, was produced Apr. 6, 1717 ; ' Les Amours des dieux,' an ' opéra-ballet ' in four scenes and a prologue, came out in 1727, and ' Les Triomphes des sens ' in 1732. The names and dates of other operas and ballets will be found in *Q.-L.* Mouret was appointed

musical director of the Concert Spirituel in
1728, and held the post till the concerts were
taken over by the Académie Royale in 1734.
For this institution he wrote a book of motets,
published in 1742 ; and for the Comédie
Italienne, of which he was for some time the
conductor. His instrumental works, published
before 1739, consist of no less than 47 'divertissements,' 'Fanfares pour des trompettes,
timbales, violons et hautbois . . .'; 'Sim-
phonies pour des violons, des hautbois et des
cors de chasse . . .'; 'Concert de chambre
à deux et à trois parties pour les violons,
flûtes, et hautbois' (2 books).
M. ; addns. M. L. P.

BIBL.—*L'Année musicale* 1911; L. DE LA LAURENCIE and G. DE
SAINT-FOIX, *Contribution à l'histoire de la symphonie française
vers 1750*.

MOUSQUETAIRES DE LA REINE, LES,
opéra-comique in 3 acts ; words by St. Georges,
music by Halévy. Produced Opéra-Comique,
Feb. 3, 1846.   G.

MOUSSORGSKY, MODESTE PETROVICH
(*b.* Karevo, Govt. of Pskov, Mar. 16/28, 1835 ;
d. St. Petersburg, Mar. 16/28, 1881), was born
at his father's country-house and spent his
childhood among rural surroundings. Both
his parents were musical, and his mother taught
him the piano from a very early age. Before
he was 9 he played several of Liszt's compositions and a pianoforte concerto of Field.
While at the ' Ensigns' School ' in St. Petersburg he continued to take lessons from the
pianist Herke (Gerke). On leaving this institution he was gazetted to the famous ' Preo-
brajensky ' regiment, accounted one of the
smartest in the service. Gifted with a pleasant
baritone voice, and a facility for improvising,
his attitude towards music remained purely
that of an amateur until 1857, when he became
acquainted with Dargomijsky, and was thus
brought in contact with all the members of the
New Russian School. He now began to study
the works of Beethoven, Glinka and Schumann,
and generally to enlarge his musical outlook.
Balakirev soon recognised the dramatic tendency in Moussorgsky, and set him to compose
music to ' Œdipus,' of which an excellent translation had just appeared in Russian. He was
also occupied with a project to compose an
opera on the subject of Victor Hugo's ' Han
d'Islande,' but got no further than the libretto.

As he became increasingly absorbed in music,
Moussorgsky found his military duties more
and more irksome. Cui, Rimsky - Korsakov
and Borodin had accepted the necessity of a
dual profession, and Stassov—who entertained
the highest opinion of Moussorgsky's talents—
counselled prudence, and tried to persuade him
that military duties need not prove fatal to their
development. But Moussorgsky had immense
faith in his powers, and even the persuasions of
his mother could not prevent him from sending
in his papers. At 22 he began the long struggle

with poverty which lasted—with scarcely a
bright interval—to the end of his life. Far from
being able to devote himself exclusively to his
art, he was compelled to accept a subordinate
post in a government office in order to live.
This uncongenial work proved a constant hindrance to his artistic projects. Highly strung,
morbidly sensitive and impatient of all checks
to his ambition, Moussorgsky was frequently
tempted to forget his troubles in an excitable
and irregular mode of life which proved injurious to his health. After the death of his mother,
matters grew worse, and in 1866, after a serious
breakdown, he consented to live for a time in
the house of his married brother at Minkino,
and then recovered sufficiently to do some of
his best work. In 1868, having exhausted the
patience of his Department, he returned to St.
Petersburg with the score of his national music-
drama, 'Boris Godounov.' The operatic direction requested Moussorgsky to shorten the work
and give more opportunity to the soloists. In
this revised form the work was first performed
at the Maryinsky Theatre, St. Petersburg, Jan.
24 (Feb. 6), 1874. In spite of much acrimonious criticism it must have interested the public,
since it was given twenty times in the course of
the season. It was performed in Moscow in
1889. In 1896 a new edition was issued, the
instrumentation revised by Rimsky-Korsakov.
It was produced in this form at Drury Lane in
Sir T. Beecham's season, June 24, 1913, and
made a great success in England, and subsequently in America (see CHALIAPIN). After
' Boris Godounov ' Moussorgsky turned his
attention to the dramatic story of the Princes
Khovanstchin, suggested to him by Stassov in
1872.

From 1870–81 Moussorgsky continued to
live and work in St. Petersburg. At first he
shared rooms with Rimsky-Korsakov, but when
the latter married, he found himself once more
upon his own resources. The pinch of poverty
grew intolerable, and his health was more and
more undermined. A tour in South Russia
with the gifted singer Mlle. Leonov gave
promise of comparative prosperity. But it
came too late. During the last years of his life
Moussorgsky frequently had recourse to drugs
and stimulants, in which he sought relief from
constant nervous depression. It is sufficient to
look at Repin's portrait of the composer painted
shortly before his death, and compare it with
Borodin's account of the smart young guards-
man, and we shall need no further biographical
commentary. In this slovenly, broken-down,
but not unlovable personality we may find traces
of the Moussorgsky of earlier days, at once the
most imaginative and realistic of musicians ;
something, too, still lingers of Moussorgsky the
humorist, the composer of such satires upon
his contemporaries as ' The Gallery ' and ' The
Lay of the Classicist '; still more of Mous-

sorgsky the child-lover who had such tender insight into the children's world; but the most haunting impression of the portrait is that of the pitiful, tragic Moussorgsky, dying in the prime of life, his fine genius already dimmed and deteriorated, destined never to know the invigorating joy of recognition and success. He died in the Military Hospital of St. Nicholas, in St. Petersburg, on his forty-second birthday.

Moussorgsky is the closest follower of Dargomijsky. He is not less national in sympathy than the direct disciples of Glinka ; but whereas their tendencies are lyrical and ideal, those of Moussorgsky are emphatically disposed to realism. In this respect, and also because he was pre-eminently a vocal rather than a symphonic composer, his musical temperament accords with that of Dargomijsky. His dominant idea was to bring music into closer relationship with actual life. In a letter to Vladimir Stassov he reveals his artistic intentions :

' To seek assiduously the most delicate and subtle features of human nature—of the human crowd—to follow them into unknown regions, to make them our own: this seems to me the true vocation of the artist . . . to feed upon humanity as a healthy diet which has been neglected—there lies the whole problem of art.'

This view, legitimate in its first expression, led the composer insensibly to an attitude of complete negation. Of all the Russians he is the only one to whom the epithet ' musical Nihilist ' can be applied with any show of justice. Seeing nature in everything and making the exact copying of nature the first duty of the artist, Moussorgsky came to reject the formula of ' art for art's sake ' as meaningless. To attempt in a work of art the union of beauty with the material object seemed to him a puerility belonging to the childhood of art.

In order to understand Moussorgsky's work and his attitude towards art, it is necessary to realise the social conditions under which he lived. He was a true child of the sixties, of that period of moral and intellectual ferment which followed the accession of Alexander II. and the emancipation of the serfs. Of the little group of composers then striving to give musical expression to their newly awakened nationality, none was so entirely carried away by the literary and political movements of the time as Moussorgsky. Every man was asking himself and his comrades the question posed by the most popular novel of the day : ' What shall we do ? ' The answer was : ' Throw aside social and artistic conventions. Make art the handmaiden of humanity. Seek not for beauty but for truth. Go to the people. Hold out the hand of fellowship to the liberated masses and learn from them the true purpose of life.' To this democratic and utilitarian spirit, to this deep compassion for the people, to this contempt for the dandyism and dilettantism of an earlier generation, Moussorgsky strove to give expression in his music, as Perov expressed it in painting, as Tchernichevsky, Dostoievsky and Tolstoi expressed it in fiction. We may disagree with his æsthetic principles, but we must confess that he carried out with logical sequence and conviction a considerable portion of his programme. In his sincere efforts to attain great ends he undoubtedly overlooked the means. He could never submit to the discipline of a thorough musical training as did Tchaikovsky and Rimsky-Korsakov. He preserved his originality intact, but at a heavy cost. The weakness of his technique has been exaggerated by those who put down all his peculiarities to ignorance ; but in some respects —particularly as regards orchestration—his craftsmanship was certainly unequal to the demands of his inspiration, for his aims were very lofty. Had this been otherwise Moussorgsky's name would have been more closely linked with those of Berlioz and Richard Strauss.

His songs are the finest expression of his artistic intentions. The ordinary themes of lyric verse had no attraction for Moussorgsky. Conventional subjects were failures in his hands. His songs are a series of 'human documents' in which the psychology of the Russian people is faithfully reflected. The whole army of the ' humiliated and offended ' supplied him with subjects. He has re-created these types of rural life with extraordinary fidelity to nature. He had also a vein of sardonic humour, and his musical satires upon the critics, priests and minor officials of his day are unique in their clever mimicry and mordant sarcasm. He is the Juvenal of musicians. In the series of songs entitled ' The Nursery ' he has done for the children what he had already done for the peasantry : caught and fixed a whole series of child - types with all their moods, engaging, petulant, capricious and whimsical. The song-cycles, 'No Sunlight' and 'Songs and Dances of Death,' were composed during his last years of suffering, and are indeed the cries of one ' who departeth in darkness.' Had the realistic schools of painting and fiction never come into being, we might still reconstruct from Moussorgsky's songs the whole psychology of Russian life.

The national music-drama, ' Boris Godounov,' was written when Moussorgsky was at the zenith of his power, and is the chief foundation on which rests his reputation as an operatic composer. The libretto is based upon Poushkin's famous historical drama which bears the same title, some scenes being kept intact as regards the original text. It is full of stirring dramatic interest, for it deals with one of the most sensational episodes of Russian history. The heir of Ivan the Terrible was of weak intellect, consequently the real power passed into the hands of the regent, the capable and

L

Photo, H. Leiser, Berlin

RIMSKY-KORSAKOV

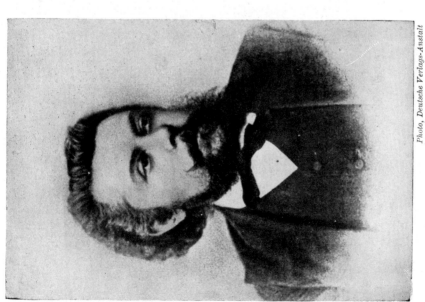

Photo, Deutsche Verlags-Anstalt

MOUSSORGSKY

crafty Boris Godounov. The only obstacle
between the usurper and the crown was the
Tsar's younger brother Dmitri. Boris Godounov did away with him, and ruled wisely and
well for many years. Then Nemesis came in
the person of the False Dmitri, a young monk
who declared himself to be the heir, rescued
at the eleventh hour, and concealed in a
monastery. The remorse, agitation and mad-
ness of Boris are finely depicted by Poushkin,
who obviously had Macbeth in his mind when
creating this character. In ' Boris Godounov '
Moussorgsky discards the conventional divisions and ensemble pieces of Italian opera ;
while the chief interest is centred in the chorus
and dialogue. The period is about 1600, and
the scene is laid partly in the Kremlin, partly
on the borders of Poland.

The action of Moussorgsky's second music
drama ' Khovanstchina ' tàkes place in the
time of Peter the Great, when all Russia was
divided between the Old order and the New.
It would be impossible to point to anything
in Russian music more intensely and touchingly national than the prelude to this work.
The orchestral introduction is built upon
national airs. The scene represents dawn on
the river Moskva. The bells are ringing for
matins, and as the sun rises, the gathering
light reveals the Holy of Holies to all Russian
hearts—the Red Square in Moscow. Tchaikovsky's ' 1812 ' Overture loses its thrill in comparison. The work was given at Drury Lane,
July 1, 1913. The original edition of ' Boris
Godounov ' (1875) was limited, and existing
copies are rare. In 1896 Bessel published
a new edition, edited, somewhat drastically,
by Rimsky-Korsakov, the composer's intimate friend. The corrections which the distinguished theorist made in Moussorgsky's
work became the subject of acrimonious
discussion. In 1906 the firm of Bessel published a further edition, in which the pages
added to the opera at the urgent advice of
friends, were restored to the score. These are
the scenes in the house of the Polish grandee
Mnishek, comprising the love scenes ; the song
of the Hostess of the Inn ; portions of the first
scene of Act I. ; the episodes of the Chiming
Clock and the Parrakeet ; also passages in the
scene between Pimen and Gregory. A fresh
edition, prepared from the original version of
the score, has been issued by J. & W. Chester
(1925), London, edited, with a biographical
and critical essay, by Robert Godet and R.
Aloys Mooser. (The English translation of the
Bessel edition is by Rosa Newmarch ; that of
the Chester edition by M. C. H. Collet.) As in
' Boris Godounov,' so also in ' Khovanstchina,'
religious music is introduced. In the latter
work the ' Rasskolniki ' or ' Old Believers '
play a prominent part, and Moussorgsky has
made their music distinctly archaic in char-

acter, as it should be. Martha, the loyal,
passionate, fanatical Rasskolnik, is one of
Moussorgsky's finest achievements in musical
portraiture. Before his death the composer
entrusted the instrumentation of ' Khovanstchina ' to Rimsky-Korsakov.

Besides these completed operatic works
Moussorgsky in 1868 made an experiment in
what he described as ' opéra dialogué.' He
attempted to set to music, just as it stood, the
prose text of Gogol's comedy ' The Matchmaker.' He abandoned the idea after completing the first act. Another unfinished opera
was based upon Flaubert's ' Salammbô.'
Fragments of this music were afterwards incorporated in other works. A third operatic
subject which he took up for a time was Gogol's
tale ' The Fair at Sorochinsk.'

The following is probably a complete list of
Moussorgsky's compositions : -

VOCAL MUSIC

OPERATIC

' The Matchmaker,' opéra dialogué (one act only) ; ' Boris
Godounov,' national music drama in four acts with a prologue
(completed 1870, first performed at the Maryinsky Theatre,
St. Petersburg, in 1874) ; ' Khovanstchina,' national music drama
in fiv; acts (1872–80) ; fragments of an opera based upon Gogol's
tale ' The Fair at Sorochinsk.'

CHORUS AND ORCHESTRA

' The Destruction of Sennacherib ' (1867) ; ' Joshua Navin ' (1877)
—both these works based on original Hebrew themes ; female
chorus from ' Salammbô ' : mixed chorus from ' Œdipus.'

SONGS

' Saul ' (1863) ; ' Night,' ' Peasant Cradle Song,' ' Savishna ' (The
Idiot's song, 1865) ; ' Gopak,' ' The Wish,' ' The Seminarist ' (1866) ;
' Mushrooming,' ' Hebrew Song,' ' The little Feast,' ' The Goat,' ' The
Magpie ' (?), ' The Swaggerer,' ' The Classicist ' (1867) ; ' The Orphan,'
' The Nurse and Child,' ' The Gallery ' (musical pamphlet, 1870) ;
' The Nursery ' (seven pictures of child-life, 1868–70) , ' Left Behind ' ;
' No Sunlight ' (a cycle of six songs, 1874–75) ; ' Dances of Death '
(four songs, 1875). Published posthumously : ' The quiet Heights ' ;
' O, the Honour ! ' ' Dawn ' ; ' The Vision,' ' Down the Don,' ' The
Dneiper,' ' The Flea,' ' Callistratus,' ' The Traveller.'

ORCHESTRAL

Intermezzo in modo classico (B minor) ; Scherzo in B ; Turkish
March ; fantasia, ' Night in the bare Mountain.'

PIANOFORTE

Pictures from an Exhibition (ten musical sketches, subjects taken
from pictures by the celebrated Russian architect Hartmann) ;
Méditation ; Une Larme ; ' The Sempstress ' ; ' On the Southern
Shores of Crimea ' ; ' In the country ' ; ' A Child's Joke' : Intermezzo.

BIBLIOGRAPHY

Many interesting articles on the composer and his works by
Vladimir Stassov, in his Sobranie Sochinenie (Collected works),
St. Petersburg, 1894 (Russian) ; Mussorgsky, by M. D. Calvocoressi
(Alcan, Paris, 1908 and 1911) ; Eng. trans. 1913 (Kegan Paul) ;
The Russian Opera, by Rosa Newmarch (Herbert Jenkins, 1913) ;
Russkaya Muzyka, by V. V. Berezorsky, 1898 (Russian).
                                                R. N.

MOUTH ORGAN, see ACCORDION.

MOUTHPIECE (Fr. bec, bocal, embouchure ; Ger. Mundstück), that portion of a
wind instrument which, as the name implies,
is inserted into the player's mouth or applied
to his lips.

Of the French words, bec (beak) is applied to
the first variety, and embouchure to the second
or the mouthpieces of brass instruments. As
an Anglicised word the name embouchure is
also applied to the mouth-hole in the head-joint
of the transverse flute, which is never spoken
of as the mouthpiece, although for purposes of
comparison it is convenient to refer to it under
this heading. (For bocal see CROOK.) Including, therefore, the orifice for sound production

ın the transverse flute, mouthpieces may bo classed into four groups, viz.

(1) The open end of a tube, across which a stream of air is blown, as when a note is produced from a Pandean pipe, or from the pipe of a common key. This is the simplest of all forms, and possibly the most ancient ; it is the form adopted in the Nay or Egyptian flute. (See FLUTE.) In the ordinary modern or transverse flute, the open end across which the stream of air is directed is obtained by means of a lateral orifice.

(2) A tubular conduit inserted between the lips by which air is conveyed under pressure to a whistle as in the flageolet ; or to enclosed reeds, either directly as in the cromorne, or indirectly through a wind-bag as in the bagpipe. The beaked mouthpiece of the recorder is merely a modified form of this tubular conduit, but by its name marks the distinction between the Flute-à-bec and the transverse flute.

(3) A beak-shaped chamber forming the upper end of single-reed instruments of the clarinet and saxophone types. One side is flattened to form a bed or table for the reed, and communication is opened with the general tube of the instrument by a slot cut in this table.

This variety of mouthpiece can be applied, although rather ineffectively, to the Bassoon and its diminutives. The Dolcino or small bassoon in the B♭ of the four-foot octave, was actually played in military bands by means of a single reed as late as the early years of the last century, and even since then attempts have been made to revive this means of producing tone on the bassoon.

(4) Cupped mouthpieces, which are applied to the outer surface of the lips, not inserted between them. The lips thus stretched across the calibre of the cup form a kind of double reed, closely resembling the vocal cords of the larynx. Each instrument of this class has a somewhat different form of cup, which is described under their respective headings. In the older examples, however, and in those used by uncivilised tribes, the cup consists of a simple hole, as at the end of a cow's horn for instance, or in the side of an ivory tusk, communicating with the medullary cavity. The transition from this to the shaped cup can be well seen in the Swiss alpenhorn, in which a small globular cavity, like the mouthpiece of the trumpet, is rudely carved out of the wooden strips of which the long tube is built up. In more finished instruments of this class, the mouthpiece is turned out of brass, ivory, aluminium, or silver, with a rounded cushion-shaped edge for the accurate and painless pressure of the lips. Glass has also been used, and of late the cushion has been made of vulcanised indiarubber.

In all the mouthpieces comprised in the third and fourth groups, the exact dimensions and proportions exercise a great effect upon the tone-quality. In those of the clarinet type the ruling factor is the exact degree of opening between the reed and the bed of the mouthpiece ; this is technically called the ' spring' or ' lay.' In the cupped mouthpieces of brass instruments the variations are even greater and of more importance, for in addition to the general size suitable to the range of compass of each class, the exact form of the cup and rim and the diameter of the bore of each mouthpiece have a marked effect.

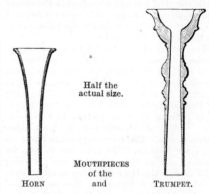

Half the
actual size.

MOUTHPIECES
of the
HORN   and   TRUMPET.

The cups of the mouthpieces of cornets, bugles and saxhorns are intermediate in character between those of the horn and trumpet.

Double-reeds, as used on the oboe and bassoon are mouthpieces only in the literal sense that they are placed in the mouth ; they are described under REED.

W. H. S. ; addns. D. J. B.

MOUTON, a 17th-18th century lutenist, pupil of Gaultier, lived at Turin between 1670–1700. He visited Paris in 1675 and 1678, and lived there entirely from 1700–20. Of his numerous and once popular compositions little is left. One book of ' Pièces de luth sur différents modes' (published Feb. 27, 1699), was or is in private hands at Stockholm. Many MS. pieces are in collective volumes. His portrait has been engraved by Edelinck from a painting by de Troy (Q.-L.).

MOUTON, JEAN (b. dept. of Somme,[1] c. 1475[2]; d. St. Quentin, 1522), French composer. He was a pupil of Josquin, teacher of Willaert, musician to Louis XII. and Francis I. of France, canon of Thérouanne,[3] and afterwards, like Jos-

[1] See Joannis Mouton Sameracensis . . . aliquot moduli ; Paris. Le Roy & Ballard, 1555 (B.M. A. 132)—an edition apparently unknown abroad, or the word ' Sameracensis ' would not have escaped attention. Glarean merely calls Mouton ' Gallus.' Fétis thinks, from the inscription on the tomb, that Hollingue, a little town near Metz, may have been his birthplace. In that case ' Sameracensis ' may refer simply to Mouton's residence at St. Quentin.
[2] Date proposed by Fétis. Mouton's first publication appeared in 1505.
[3] Whence he removed, probably, when the English took the town in 1513.

quin, canon of the Collegiate Church of St. Quentin, in which place he died, and was buried in 1522, the following words being inscribed on his tomb [1]:

'Ce gist maistre Jean de Hollingue dit Mouton, en son vivant chantre du Roy, chanoine de Therouanne et de cet eglise, qui trepassa le penultieme jour d'Octobre MDXXII. Priez Dieu pour son âme.'

When Petrucci began to print music, Mouton was in his prime, and the edition of five masses (a 4), which Fétis assigned to the year 1508, is an early example of a whole book devoted to one composer. This book, which Glarean [2] found 'in manibus omnium,' is now scarce, and Fétis thinks the copy of the second edition [3] in the British Museum the only complete one. Burney carefully examined the fourth Mass, [4] and scored several movements, discovering no variety of measure or subject, no melody, no ingenuity of contrivance, no learning of modulation. Yet the masses were highly valued in their day, reprinted by other publishers [5] and much admired, according to Glarean and Le Roy, [6] by Pope Leo X., Giov. di Medici. [7] As for motets, Mouton saw twenty-one printed in the best collection of his time, Petrucci's Motetti de la Corona. [8] Posthumous publications continued for nearly forty years, and the list of known printed works includes nine masses, [9] about seventy-five motets and psalms, and a few French chansons. (See Q.-L.)

The British Museum has a single voice-part (superius) of Mouton's twenty-two motets printed by Le Roy in 1555, and happily a complete MS. score of the same collection. This gives many interesting pieces: the 'Nesciens Mater' (a 8) with four of the parts derived canonically from the others; the 'Quis dabit oculis' composed in 1514 on the death of Anne of Bretagne, Queen of France; some Easter pieces, 'Alleluia,' and 'In illo tempore,' and one for Christmas, 'Noe, noe, psallite,' on which Arcadelt afterwards wrote a Mass.

Burney has scored, besides the Mass movements, three motets, [10] and in this style of com-

position finds Mouton more smooth and polished than his contemporaries. 'Life in a court' can scarcely account for it. Most great musicians of the time had the same surroundings. Glarean, more reasonably, attributes to zeal and industry the rare facility which separated Mouton from his fellows. The numerous examples drawn from his works for the 'Dodecachordon,' and the evident pride with which Glarean [11] recalls the meeting in Paris, are evidence of the high value set upon the French composer. Had Mouton left no compositions of his own, he would still be remembered as belonging to a remarkable line of great teachers—Okeghem, Josquin, Mouton, Willaert, Zarlino.   J. R. S.-B.

BIBL.—Tribune de Saint Gervais, Dec. 1899; MICHEL BRENET, Jean Mouton, with a full list of his works; E. DROZ and G. THIBAULT, Bibliographie des recueils de chansons du XVe siècle (Paris, 1926).

MOVEMENT, a term most customarily applied to instrumental works of the cyclic order, suite, sonata, symphony, etc. It denotes any portion of such a work sufficiently complete in itself to be regarded as a distinct entity; for example, first *allegro*, *adagio*, *scherzo* or *finale*. In modern music of the kind a movement is rarely so entirely independent as to be detachable from its associated movements, save in the case of the suite.   C.

MOYSES, MIKULÁŠ (b. at Vel'ka Slatina, Zvolen district, Mar. 6, 1872), Slovak composer. His musical gift was precocious, and at 10 he was able to play the organ and accompany the choir in church. His early education was in the gymnasium at Bánská Bystrica and the teachers' normal school at Kláštor. He studied music at the State Academy in Budapest, his chief subjects being the organ and composition, and left it with a teacher's diploma. He then took the post of organist at the cathedra of Jager, and, later on, at Velký Varadín. He held several teaching appointments under the Hungarian Government, and, in 1908, settled down as professor of music in the Training College at Prešov. He remained there after the town had passed from Hungary to Czechoslovakia. His writings include an *Organ School* (1910, Nándor Kalman, Budapest); *Introduction to the Theory of Music* (1912, F. Kalman, Prešov A Slovak edition in preparation). Among his compositions are: Mass in C major; a scherzo for orchestra (Slovak in style); songs, partsongs, compositions for organ and piano, etc.

A. K. and R. N.

MOZART. Of the family to which the great composer belonged six members only call for mention in a musical dictionary: viz. (1) the composer himself; (2) LEOPOLD, his father; (3) MARIANNE, his sister; (4) CONSTANZE, his wife; (5) and (6) KARL and WOLFGANG, his two sons. They are here discussed in the above order.

1 See Études St. Quentinoises (St. Quentin, 1851–62, etc.) tom. i. p. 302. Ch. Gomart, the author took the inscription from a MS. of Quentin Delafons, but does not state where it is to be found. It is the only authority for the date of Mouton's death, and for his two church preferments.
2 'Δωδεκαχορδον' (Basileae, 1548), p. 464.
3 'Missae J. Mouton' (Fossombrone, Petrutius, Aug. 11, 1515), containing 'Missa sine nomine,' 'Alleluia,' 'Alma redemptoris,' another 'Sine nomine,' 'Regina mearum' (B.M. K. 1, d 7).
4 For Burney's examples from Mouton, and critical notes, see Musical Extracts' (vol. ii. pp. 104, 134, 137, 169) in B.M. Add. MSS. 11,582. Most of the notes are incorporated in his History (vol. ii. p. 533).
5 The 'Alma redemptoris' was reprinted, and a new one, 'dittes moy toutes vos pensées.' added in Antiquis's famous 'Liber quindecim missarum' (Rome, 1516).
6 See preface to Joannis Mouton Sameracensis.
7 A passionate lover of music . . . the sounds of which were daily heard floating through the palace, Leo himself humming the airs that were performed' (Ranke's History of the Popes).
8 Eight in book i. (1514); ten in book ii. (1519); three in book iii. (1519).
9 Besides the six mentioned in notes above, the 'Missa d'Allemagne,' 'Tua est potentia' and 'Quem dicunt' were printed. Fétis mentions a MS. 'Missa sans cadence' at Cambrai. Zarlino speaks of a Mass 'Benedicam Dominum,' a 6 (Istitutioni harm. pt. iv. p. 414).
10 'Quis dabit oculis,' 'Non nobis Domine,' composed in 1509 at the birth of Renée, daughter of Louis XII. Also 'Quam pulcra es,' which Burney likes so much that he gives the first movement in his History. This motet had in its own time been ascribed to Josquin.
11 Speaking of it continually in the 'Dodecachordon.' See pp. 296, 320, 464. They conversed by means of an interpreter.

(1) WOLFGANG AMADEUS [1] (*b.* Salzburg, Jan. 27, 1756 ; *d.* Vienna, Dec. 5, 1791).

LIFE

Even as a child of three Mozart showed his love of music in a remarkable manner. He listened eagerly to his sister Marianne's music-lessons, amused himself for hours with picking out thirds, and showed a good memory for the pieces he heard. Encouraged by these indications his father began, almost in play, to teach him little minuets on the harpsichord ; but the boy showed such aptitude that the play soon became real work. Marianne's MS. music-book [2] was called into requisition, the father writing down in it pieces of progressive difficulty. The impulse to compose similar pieces for himself was soon roused in the boy ; these, which already betray his feeling for beauty both of sound and form, he played to his father, who wrote them down in the book. Before long he was able to enter his own compositions. Schachtner the court trumpeter, and a friend of the family, relates many touching instances of his lively and essentially child-like disposition [3] ; of his eagerness in learning anything, especially arithmetic ; of his ear, which was so delicate that he could detect and remember to the next day a difference of half a quarter of a tone, and so susceptible that he fainted away at the sound of a trumpet ; and of his earnestness over his music-lessons. His father wrote to him in 1778 :

'As a child and a boy you were too serious even to be childish : and when sitting at the harpsichord, or doing anything in the shape of music, you would not stand a joke from any one. Indeed, from the precocity of your talent, and the extremely thoughtful expression of your countenance, many people feared you would not live to grow up.'

When a little over five and a half, Mozart took part in a comedy, 'Sigismundus Hungariae Rex,' set to music by Eberlin the court organist, and performed in the hall of the University of Salzburg, Sept. 1 and 3, 1761. There were about 150 performers, including young counts, students and choristers of the chapel.

The father, struck by the rapid progress of his children, determined to travel with them. Their first excursion was in Jan. 1762, to Munich, where the Elector received them kindly, and expressed great admiration ; and encouraged by this success the family next went to Vienna, giving a concert at Linz by the way.

The reputation of the little prodigies had preceded them to Vienna, but the reality far exceeded the expectations formed by the court and nobility. The Emperor was especially taken with the ' kleiner Hexenmeister ' (little magician), and in joke made him play first with one finger only, and then with the keyboard covered. Wolfgang asked expressly for Wagenseil, the court composer, that he might be sure of having a real connoisseur among his hearers. ' I am playing a concerto of yours,' he said, ' you must turn over for me.' He treated the Empress with all the frankness of an unspoilt child, jumping up into her lap, throwing his arms round her neck and kissing her. Of course the upper classes went wild about the children, and ' all the ladies lost their hearts to the little fellow.' But a change soon came, for Wolfgang took the scarlet fever, and even after his recovery people held aloof from fear of infection. After a short excursion to Pressburg the family returned to Salzburg in the beginning of 1763.

The father now considered himself justified in attempting a longer journey, his main objective this time being Paris. They left Salzburg on June 9, and travelled by Munich, Augsburg, Schwetzingen, Mainz, Frankfort, [4] Coblenz, Aix-la-Chapelle and Brussels, giving public concerts, or playing at the various courts. Wolfgang played the violin, and also the organ at the various churches.

They arrived in Paris on Nov. 18, and stayed five months. The children played before the court at Versailles, gave two concerts and excited the greatest enthusiasm. Grimm, the cultivated man of letters, took them up warmly, and was of great use in procuring them introductions and rendering services of various kinds. To show Wolfgang's talent in composition, the father had four sonatas for pianoforte and violin engraved, two (K. 6, 7) [5] being dedicated to the Princess Victoire, the King's second daughter, and two (K. 8, 9) to the witty Comtesse de Tessé. The young musician's portrait was twice painted during his stay in Paris, by Carmontelle in the well-known family group, and by M. B. Ollivier in the picture of a tea-party in the Prince de Conti's salon, which now hangs in the Louvre. [6]

They left Paris, Apr. 10, 1764, and went by Calais to London, where they took lodgings in Cecil Court, St. Martin's Lane. [7] Here also they

---

[1] He was christened in full Joannes Chrysostomus Wolfgangus Theophilus : instead of Theophilus his father wrote Gottlieb—in Latin Amadeus. In his earlier letters Mozart added his confirmation-name Sigismundus. On his first works, and those engraved in Paris in 1764, he signs himself J. G. Wolfgang, afterwards Wolfgang Amade ; in private life he was always Wolfgang.

[2] Now in the Mozarteum at Salzburg. On his seventh name-day (1762) Wolfgang received from his father a music-book of this sort for his own use, now in the possession of Dr. L. Koenig of Kiel. It consisted of a collection of little pieces by various composers written out by Leopold in the form of suites, and designed to serve both as an album of piano music and as a guide to the various forms of composition. It was published in 1922, with an introduction by H. Abert.

[3] Letter to Mozart's sister, dated Salzburg, 1792 ; given entire by Jahn, i. 21. The references throughout are, unless otherwise stated, to the English translation.

[4] Here the father announced in the programme, Aug. 30, that ' he would play with the keyboard covered,' thus turning the Emperor's joke to account. Here also Goethe heard him—' I was about 14, and I still distinctly remember the little man with his frizzled wig, and sword.' Eckermann's *Gespräche mit Goethe* (Leipzig, 1908), ii. 178.

[5] The numbers throughout refer to Köchel's catalogue of Mozart's compositions. For the actual chronology of the works, however, the dates suggested by Wyzewa and Saint-Foix have generally been adopted.

[6] It is possible, however, that this latter picture was painted during the Mozarts' return visit in 1766.

[7] For the details of Mozart's stay, and the condition of music at the time, see Pohl's *Haydn und Mozart in London* (Vienna, 1867). Further particulars may be gleaned from Leopold's own diary published by Dr. A. Schurig in 1920 as *Leopold Mozart : Reiseaufzeichnungen*, and from F. G. Edwards's *Musical Haunts in London* (1895).

met with a gracious reception at court, and the children, especially Wolfgang, made an extraordinary impression. The King put before the 'invincible' Wolfgang pieces by J. C. Bach, Abel, Wagenseil and Handel, which he played at sight, and also made him play on his organ, to the still greater admiration of everybody. He then accompanied the Queen in a song, and a flute-player in his solo, and improvised a charming melody to the bass-part of one of Handel's airs. He became very intimate with the Queen's music-master, J. Christian Bach, and with the singers Tenducci and Manzuoli, the latter of whom gave him singing-lessons of his own accord. He also made the acquaintance of the Hon. Daines Barrington, a man of very versatile attainments, who after putting him to the severest tests, wrote a paper for the Royal Society, in which he detailed the facts and his own admiration and astonishment.[1] After a second performance at court the children gave their first concert on Tuesday, June 5, at the Great Room in Spring Gardens. In the advertisement the father called his children 'prodigies of nature,' and directed special attention to Wolfgang; ' his father had brought him to England, not doubting but that he will meet with success in a kingdom where his countryman Handel, the late famous virtuoso, received during his lifetime such particular protection.' The town was very full for the King's birthday (June 4), and the receipts were as much as 100 guineas ; moreover, many of the professors engaged declined receiving any remuneration for their services. The sensation was immense ; even the father was astonished, and wrote home describing their progress. ' To play the British patriot ' he next allowed Wolfgang to play the harpsichord and organ at a concert at Ranelagh on June 29, ' for the benefit of a useful public charity.' [2] After this the family went to Tunbridge Wells, then at the height of its vogue as a fashionable resort, returning at the end of July ; shortly after the father took cold in returning from a concert at Lord Thanet's, and had a severe illness. During his convalescence they went to Chelsea, then a detached village, and lived at the house of a Dr. Randal in Fivefields (now Lower Ebury Street). Not being able to play any instrument, on his father's account, Wolfgang composed his first symphonies (K. 16, 17, 19),[3] and amused himself with a number of experiments in composition which possess a special interest in that they were never intended for his father's eyes and never underwent correction by him.[4] On their return to town the Mozarts

lodged at a Mr. Williamson's, No. 15 Thrift Street (now Frith Street, Soho) ; and on Oct. 25 were again invited to court. The father had six of Wolfgang's sonatas for harpsichord and violin (K. 10-15) engraved at his own cost, and dedicated to the Queen, who sent him 50 guineas. The last two concerts, in which ' all the overtures were of the little boy's own composition,' took place respectively on Feb. 21, 1765, at the Little Theatre, Haymarket, and May 13, in Hickford's Great Room, Brewer Street, the latter at reduced prices, as the charm of novelty had worn off. Here the children played a piece of Wolfgang's for four hands on the same harpsichord, a thing then quite new.[5] The instrument was one with two manuals and pedals, as well as a Venetian swell, made by Burkhard Shudi for the King of Prussia.[6]

From this time the father put forth repeated invitations to the public to hear and test the youthful prodigies in private, ' every day from 12 to 3, admittance 2/6 each person,' first at their lodgings, and afterwards at the Swan and Hoop Tavern, Cornhill. Playing with the keyboard covered is mentioned as a special attraction. Visitors, however, became constantly fewer, in spite of the increasing urgency with which they were invited (the *Advertiser* of July 11 contains the last advertisement), and some popular disturbances, together with the appearance of the first symptoms of George the Third's malady, made the elder Mozart determine to leave the country. The family, however, first visited the British Museum (opened Jan. 15, 1759), to which the father presented Wolfgang's printed sonatas, and a copy of the engraving from Carmontelle's picture. In memory of his visit Wolfgang composed, by request, a four-part motet,[7] his only vocal piece to English words, and presented the autograph to the Museum, receiving a note of thanks from the secretary, Mr. Maty (July 19, 1765). They left London on July 24, stopped at Canterbury, and at Bourne with Horace Mann, and on Aug. 1 left England for the Hague in consequence of an invitation to the court of Holland.

They were detained a month at Lille by Wolfgang's falling ill, and spent a few days at Ghent and Antwerp. They arrived at the Hague on Sept. 11 and were most graciously received by the Prince of Orange and his sister, Princess Caroline of Nassau Weilburg. On Sept. 30 the children gave a concert at which, according to the announcements, the 'overtures' were again all of Wolfgang's composition. In October, however, the little

---

[1] *Philosophical Transactions*, vol. lx. for the year 1770, p. 54. Reprinted in Barrington's *Miscellanies* (1781).
[2] Probably the Lying-in Hospital (Surrey), the foundation-stone of which was laid in 1765.
[3] K. 18 is merely a copy by Mozart, in score, of an Overture by Abel.
[4] They are preserved in a little music-book now in the Berlin library, and were published by Breitkopf in 1909 under the title ' *Mozart als achtjähriger Componist.*' •The marked difference between them and the work written under Leopold's supervision 's significant.

[5] It is possible that this sonata has been preserved in a unique printed copy in the Bibliothèque Nationale. See G. de Saint-Foix, ' Une Sonate inconnue de Mozart,' *Revue musicale*, May 1921.
[6] See A. J. Hipkins's *History of the Pianoforte* (1897). An account of the concert was given in the *Salzburger Zeitung*, Aug. 6, 1765.
[7] ' God is our Refuge and Strength.' For facsimile of the autograph see Pohl's *Mozart in London* and Wyzewa and Saint-Foix's *W. A. Mozart.* The piece, edited by Dr. W. H. Cummings, was reprinted in *Musical News*, Jan. 27, 1906.

girl fell ill, and then Wolfgang took a violent fever which lasted many weeks. It was not till Jan. 1766 that the family was able to proceed to Amsterdam, where two further concerts were given, at one of which the symphony in B♭ (K. 22) was probably performed. In March they were again at the Hague for the fêtes on the occasion of the installation of the Prince of Orange as Stadtholder, for which Wolfgang composed harpsichord variations on an allegretto, and on the old Volkslied ' Willem van Nassau ' (K. 24, 25), which were immediately printed. He also composed for the Festival a kind of concerto grosso which he called ' Galimathias musicum ' (K. 32) ; it concludes with a fugue on the Volkslied. Six sonatas for PF. and violin (K. 26-31), dedicated to the Princess, were also engraved.

After spending a few days in Amsterdam and Utrecht, in each of which towns a concert was given, the Mozarts started on their return journey. Travelling by Malines, they arrived at Paris towards the end of April. The children played repeatedly at court, and their improvement was appreciated, but here too there was a falling off in interest. On July 9 they left Paris, and passing through Dijon and Lyons to Switzerland, spent many pleasant days at Geneva, Lausanne, Berne, Zurich and Schaffhausen. They were fêted everywhere, but most of all at Zurich by the poet Gesner, from whom they parted with great regret. From Geneva the father took his children over to Ferney, bearing a letter of introduction from Damilaville of Paris. But Voltaire had been in bed for six weeks, and Mme. Denis, Rameau's pupil, was ill too ; ' Comment pourrais-je recevoir votre jeune joueur de clavecin ? Ah ! nous sommes bien loin de donner des fêtes ! ' he wrote to his friend in Paris ; and so this strange encounter between Leopold Mozart the sincere believer and Voltaire the sceptic did not take place.[1] That the former should have desired it is a proof of his readiness to sacrifice even his scruples to the interests of his children. At Donaueschingen they spent twelve pleasant days with the Prince of Fürstenberg, who had music nearly every evening, and after remunerating them very handsomely, took leave of them with tears in his eyes. At Biberach Count Fugger of Babenhausen made Wolfgang compete on the organ with Sixtus Bachmann, a gifted boy two years older than himself ; neither was able to obtain a decided advantage over the other. Passing through Munich, where the Elector was much pleased with Wolfgang's progress, the travellers returned to Salzburg in Nov. 1766.

The father's first care was to carry on Wolfgang's interrupted studies ; and as a solid foundation he took him through Fux's *Gradus*

ad Parnassum. The Archbishop, not believing in the boy's powers, gave him the first part of a sacred cantata, ' Die Schuldigkeit des ersten Gebotes '[2] (K. 35), to compose under strict surveillance. The work was eventually performed on Mar. 12 and Apr. 2, 1767, by the students in the University hall.[3] To this period also belong a Passions-cantate or Grabmusik (K. 42) ; a Latin comedy ' Apollo et Hyacinthus,' performed May 13, at the Aula ; a series of arrangements, in the form of PF. concertos, of movements from sonatas by French composers (K. 37, 39-41) ; and possibly a ' cassation ' (K. 99), a serenade (K. 100) and two symphonies (K. 76, 43). In the beginning of September the family, attracted by the approaching betrothal of the Archduchess Maria Josepha, went to Vienna ; but they came in for a series of misfortunes. The Princess Josepha died of smallpox, the upper classes took flight for fear of infection, and the Mozarts also fled to Olmütz, where, however, both children took the disease, and Wolfgang was blind for nine days. Count Podstatzky generously gave them free quarters, and every care was lavished upon them. After their recovery they made a short stay at Brünn, where they were kindly welcomed by Count Schrattenbach and other nobles.

They arrived in Vienna in Jan. 1768, and were very kindly received at court ; but the Empress was living in retirement after the death of her husband, and the Emperor set an example of parsimony which was scrupulously followed by the aristocracy. Worse than all was the envy and jealousy shown by other musicians. In the midst of these various difficulties and trials, however, the Emperor invited Wolfgang to compose an opera, and conduct it at the harpsichord. Coltellini's ' La finta semplice ' (K. 51) was chosen, but a series of intrigues prevented its being produced. Wolfgang had, however, the satisfaction of producing his little German operetta ' Bastien und Bastienne ' (K. 50)[4] in the private theatre of a Doctor Mesmer, who is probably to be identified with the celebrated discoverer of animal magnetism. He had also an opportunity of appearing in public as a composer, being commissioned to furnish a mass (K. 49), an offertorium (K. 47) and a trumpet-concerto[5] for the consecration of the new church at the Waisenhaus. The ceremony took place Dec. 7, and Wolfgang conducted in presence of the Emperor and the court. During his stay at Vienna Mozart also composed two symphonies (K. 45, 48).[6]

[2] The MS. is at Windsor Castle.
[3] Hammerle (*Mozart und einige Zeitgenossen*, Salzburg, 1877) quotes the notice in the University minutes : ' 1767, 12 Martii, Jovis : Vacatio (Post prandium). Hora media 7 in Aula Oratorium fuit decantatum a D. Wolfgango Mozart adulescentulo 10 annorum in modulos musicos egregie redactum.'
[4] The libretto was a German version, by F. W. Weiskern, of Madame Favart's ' parody ' on Rousseau's ' Devin du village.'
[5] This has not been preserved.
[6] The string quintet, which Köchel assigns to this period (K. 46), is almost certainly an arrangement, possibly by Mozart himself, of the Serenade for Wind Instruments (K. 361) written in 1780. The MS. is not in Mozart's hand, and the superscription ' Salzburg, 25 Jan. 1768,' cannot possibly be correct.

[1] See *Voltaire musicien*, by Edmond van der Straeten (1878).

A great pleasure awaited Wolfgang on his return to Salzburg ; the Archbishop had his rejected opera performed in the palace. He also made him his Konzertmeister, though without salary. Wolfgang again devoted himself to study, composing two masses (K. 65, 66), a Te Deum (K. 141) and a ' Cassation ' (K. 63). His father now determined to carry out a long-cherished plan and to take his son to Italy, the golden land of music, and the one gateway to operatic fame. They left Salzburg in the beginning of Dec. 1769, and travelling by Innsbruck, where Wolfgang was greatly admired at a private concert given by Count Künigl, visited Roveredo, Verona, Mantua, Cremona, Milan, Lodi, where Wolfgang composed his first quartet, Bologna, Rome, Florence, Naples, and on their return, Bologna, Milan and Venice. At Roveredo Wolfgang played at Baron Todeschi's, and the day after played the organ in the parish church to an immense crowd. At Verona one of his symphonies was performed, and his playing at sight, and composing and singing an air to given words, caused great astonishment. His portrait was painted by Cignaroli, and poets celebrated his praises. In Mantua, at a concert of the Società Filarmonica, nine out of fourteen pieces were by Wolfgang. In Milan they were lodged in S. Marco, and Count Firmian, the Governor-General, who was a great connoisseur, introduced them to all the principal families. ' It is the same here as everywhere,' writes the father, 'so there is no need to describe it.' The foremost musician in the city, the aged Giambattista Sammartini (see SAN MARTINI), subjected Wolfgang to severe tests. After a brilliant soirée at Count Firmian's, for which he composed four airs to words by Metastasio (K. 88, 77-79), he was commissioned to write an opera for the next season. At Parma they admired the celebrated singer Agujari.[1] At Bologna they were most hospitably received by Count Pallavicini, who gave a brilliant concert, at which even Padre Martini was present, although he had then given up attending such functions. The father writes[2] that Wolfgang was more admired there than anywhere, and anticipates that from Bologna, the residence of so many artists and scientific musicians, his fame will soon spread over Italy. And he was right ; for the recommendation of Padre Martini, the great church composer, and referee in all musical disputes, at once gave him a position in the eyes of the world. After each visit to the Padre, Wolfgang carried away a fugue to work out at home, and in every case acquitted himself to the satisfaction of the great contrapuntist. His acquaintance, too, with the great singer Farinelli was of service to him from an artistic point of view.

In Florence, where they arrived Mar. 30, the

Mozarts were graciously received by the Archduke Leopold, who had known them in Vienna. Wolfgang played at court, accompanied Nardini the great violinist, and solved, ' as easily as if he were eating a bit of bread,' the hardest problems set him by the Marquis de Ligniville, director of the court music and a thorough contrapuntist. Wolfgang copied for his own use nine pieces from the Marquis's Stabat Mater with thirty canons, and composed in imitation of it a ' Kyrie a cinque con diversi canoni' (K. 89). Here to his great delight he again met Manzuoli, who had taught him to sing in London. He also struck up a great friendship with Thomas Linley, the young composer of 14, who was a pupil of Nardini, and already gave remarkable promise. The two young artists were inseparable for the few days of Mozart's stay, and competed ' not like boys, but like men.' They parted with many tears, but never met again, Linley being drowned in 1778. Long afterwards in Vienna Mozart spoke of him, and lamented his early death.[3] Burney says that the talk throughout Italy was of the two geniuses, little Mozart and ' Tommasino,' from both of whom much was expected.[4]

The travellers reached Rome on Wednesday in Holy Week, and went straight to the Sistine Chapel to hear Allegri's celebrated Miserere, when Wolfgang gave the well-known proof of his ear and memory by writing down the entire work, after one hearing, merely correcting one or two passages during the repetition on Good Friday. (See MISERERE.[5]) This feat made a great sensation. The principal people received him with open arms, and Wolfgang played everywhere. For these concerts he composed a symphony (K. 81) and two soprano airs (K. 82, 83).

On May 8 they went direct to Naples. Wolfgang was not invited to play before the court, but the nobility treated both father and son with great respect ; they also met many previous acquaintances, who were of use to them in various ways, among them the English ambassador Sir William Hamilton. On the 28th Wolfgang gave a concert, which was brilliantly attended, and brought in a good sum. When he played at the ' Conservatorio alla Pietà,' his hearers were superstitious enough to attribute his marvellous execution to the charm of a ring on his finger, and when he laid it aside their astonishment knew no bounds. On June 25 they went back to Rome, and the Pope, in a private audience, bestowed on Wolfgang the order of the ' Golden Spur '— ' the same that Gluck has,' as the father wrote home with pardonable pride. He also told, as a good joke, how the guards let them pass,

---

[1] Wolfgang's letter to his sister of Mar. 24, 1770, affords the chief testimony to the remarkable range of this singer's voice.
[2] Letter to his wife, Mar. 27, 1770.

[3] Kelly's Reminiscences, 1st ed., i. 225.
[4] Present State of Music in France and Italy, 1st ed., p. 247.
[5] The Miserere which Mozart composed, probably in July or Aug. 1770 (K. 85), shows traces of imitation of this model.

taking Wolfgang for a young prince, and himself for his tutor. Now he was Signor Cavaliere
Amadeo, and his father insisted on his thus
signing his compositions. Wolfgang, however,
was less pretentious, and soon let the title
drop.

Leaving Rome on July 10, they arrived on
the 20th in Bologna, where a great distinction
awaited Wolfgang. The Accademia Filarmonica, after testing his powers,[1] admitted him
to their ranks as ' compositore,' although the
statutes, besides other qualifications, required
that members should be at least 20. His
election as ' maestro di cappella '[2] followed on
June 5, 1771. Again they saw much of Padre
Martini, and under his influence Wolfgang
wrote for practice a series of sketches in the
forms of strict counterpoint.[3] Finally Martini
gave him a formal testimonial.[4]

By Oct. 18 they were in Milan, and Wolfgang
set seriously to work on his opera, before the
completion of which the usual battles with the
singers, and in this case with jealous rivals, had
to be gone through. On Dec. 26, however,
' Mitridate Rè di Ponto ' was produced for the
first time, Wolfgang conducting ; and it was
repeated to full houses twenty times, amid cries
of ' Evviva il Maestro ! Evviva il Maestrino ! '
After an excursion to Turin, they again passed
through Milan on their way to Venice, entered
into all the amusements of the Carnival, were
fêted by the nobility, and gave a brilliant concert. On Mar. 12 they went to Padua, where
Wolfgang played the organ in S. Giustina, and
was commissioned to compose an oratorio,
which Jahn conjectures to have been ' Betulia
liberata ' (K. 118), performed in all probability
during Lent, 1772.[5] After some days' deten-
tion in Vicenza and Verona, they arrived at
Salzburg, Mar. 28, 1771. Mozart's success in
Italy procured him two commissions—one from
Milan for an opera for the Carnival of 1773,
and the other from the Empress Maria Theresa
for a dramatic serenata for the marriage of the
Archduke Ferdinand, to take place in Milan
in October. His stay at Salzburg was to
last only five months, but during that brief
period he not only completed his oratorio, but
found time to compose a Regina coeli (K. 108),
a litany (K. 109), an offertory (K. 72), a
psalm (K. 93), three symphonies (K. 75, 73,
110) and three trios with organ continuo (K. 67,
68, 69). Father and son set out again on
Aug. 13, 1771, and arrived in Milan on the
21st ; but the libretto of the serenata was not
ready till the end of the month. Wolfgang
completed the score in a fortnight, a remark-

able instance of rapidity, considering that he
had a violinist overhead, an oboe-player beneath, and a pianoforte - teacher next door,
all hard at work the whole day long—a Babel
of sounds which he, however, pronounced to be
' delightful (*lustig*) for composing, as it gave
him ideas ! ' He was now so firmly established in the favour both of the court and the
public, that he had no intrigues to encounter.
He was on the best terms, too, with Hasse,
who was composing ' Ruggiero,' and who, with
commendable generosity, prophetically remarked, ' This boy will cause us all to be
forgotten ' (Questo ragazzo ci farà dimenticar
tutti). [6] The marriage of the Archduke and
the Princess Beatrice of Modena took place on
Oct. 15 ; Hasse's opera was performed on the
16th, and Wolfgang's serenata ' Ascanio in
Alba ' (K. 111) on the 17th, with a success
which enabled the father to write home, ' I am
sorry to say Wolfgang's Serenata has cut out
Hasse's Opera to an extent I cannot describe.'
Besides his fee, the Empress sent him a gold
watch set with diamonds, with her portrait
at the back. After the opera he composed
another symphony (K. 112), and a divertimento
(K. 113).

They returned home in the middle of Dec.
1771. In the last days of the year Wolfgang
composed another symphony (K. 114), and was
then laid up by serious illness. Meantime the
Archbishop died, and Wolfgang was commissioned to compose an opera for the allegiance
festival of his successor Hieronymus, Count
von Colloredo, whose election caused universal
astonishment and dismay. The work chosen
was Metastasio's ' Il Sogno di Scipione,' an
allegorical piece whose appropriateness to the
occasion is not evident. Mozart does not seem
to have bothered much about it ; at any rate
his setting (K. 126) is one of the dullest things
he ever wrote. It was performed probably in
May 1772. Between Feb. and Oct. of this
year Mozart also composed seven symphonies
(K. 124, 128-130, 132-134), four divertimenti
(K. 131, 136-138), the well-known litany ' de
venerabili ' in B♭ (K. 125), and a Regina coeli
(K. 127).

The travellers again set out for Milan on
Oct. 24, 1772, and arrived on Nov. 4. Here
Wolfgang completed his new opera, ' Lucio
Silla ' (K. 135), produced on Dec. 26, and repeated more than twenty times to crowded and
enthusiastic audiences.[7] Rauzzini was one of
the singers, and Wolfgang composed for him a
motet, ' Exsultate ' (K. 165), which he sang in
the church of the Theatines.

They returned in the beginning of Mar.
1773 to Salzburg, where Wolfgang, still strongly

---

[1] An antiphon was given him to set in four parts (K. 86).
[2] Jahn (2nd Ger. ed.) gives—Minutes, ii. 613 ; Letter from the
Father, i. 126 ; Test-composition, ii. Notenbeilage viii. ; Diploma,
ii. 614.
[3] Jahn (2nd Ger. ed.), ii. Notenbeilage v.
[4] See Jahn (2nd Ger. ed.), ii. 616.
[5] There is, however, no record of this. Anton André is said to
have possessed a copy of the libretto, which bore a note, apparently
in Mozart's hand, to the effect that the work was first performed
in 1786 (Jahn, i. 197).

[6] Mennicke (*Hasse und die Gebrüder Graun als Sinfoniker*, p.
433, etc.) questions the authenticity of this remark, chiefly on the
ground that Leopold Mozart says nothing about it in his letters.
[7] Such is Leopold Mozart's account (letter of Jan. 2, 1773). It
is significant, however, as Dent remarks (*Mozart's Operas*, p. 42),
that Mozart received no further invitation to write for the Italian
stage.

'inder the influence of Italian models, composed four symphonies (K. 184, 181, 162, 182), a divertimento for wind-band (K. 166), a grand concerto for two violins (K. 190), a quartet (K. 160), a violin sonata (K. 56) and a mass (K. 167). In the summer the father and son took the opportunity of the Archbishop's absence in Vienna, to go there themselves. Their immediate object is not known, but probably the father was trying to obtain some court appointment. He had made a similar attempt in Florence, but without success. He wrote to his wife and daughter, 'Things will and must alter ; take comfort, God will help us.' This visit to Vienna, though it failed of its immediate object, had an important bearing on Mozart's artistic career. He was brought once more into contact with German music. We are told that he here made acquaintance with some of Haydn's quartets—probably those numbered as op. 17 and op. 20, the latter being the series known as the 'Sun Quartets' —and that to these we owe the six quartets (K. 168–173) which he wrote in Aug., and to which he specially referred when he spoke of Haydn as his master in this form of composition. The fugal finales of the first and last of these quartets were obviously inspired by similar movements in these works by Haydn. During his stay at the capital he also wrote a serenade for Salzburg (K. 185), and 'was bold enough,' as his father wrote, to play a violin concerto at a festival in the Theatine monastery. His Mass in C major (the Pater Dominicus Missa, K. 66) was performed in Aug. at the Jesuit Church, and made a great impression. Other works of this period were a symphony (K. 199), a divertimento (K. 205) and some piano variations (K. 180).

Wolfgang's return to Salzburg at the beginning of Oct. 1773 was marked by an almost feverish outburst of creative activity. Before the end of the year he had composed a symphony (K. 200), his first PF. concerto (K. 175), refashioned a string quintet (K. 174) which he had written in the previous year, and composed entr'actes and choruses for Gebler's heroic drama 'Thamos, König in Ägypten' (K. 345).[1] In the opening months of 1774 there followed four more symphonies (K. 183, 197, 201, 202) ; the first, in G minor, remarkable for its sustained earnestness of mood, the third, in A, a sparkling composition which marks the beginning of Mozart's conversion to the so-called 'gallant' style—a style in which depth and solidity tended to be sacrificed to brilliance of effect. To this transitional period also belong a sonata for PF. duet (K. 358), a bassoon concerto (K. 191), two masses, in F and D respectively (K. 192, 194), a Dixit and Magnificat [K. 193], a serenade (K. 203), the first of the sonatas for PF. solo (K. 279), and the varia-

tions for PF. on Fischer's minuet (K. 179) that Mozart played so frequently on his tours. The PF. sonatas written during the following autumn (K. 280-283) show Mozart fully converted to the new style.

On Dec. 6 the father and son started for Munich, where Wolfgang was engaged, through the influence of his patron, Count Ferdinand von Zeil, Prince Archbishop of Chiemsee, to compose an opera for the Carnival of 1775. Stimulated, doubtless, by the rich resources at his disposal, Wolfgang exerted himself to the utmost, and 'La finta Giardiniera' (K. 196), produced Jan. 13, 1775, was a great success. Schubart, who had heard it, speaks of the 'wonderful genius' of the composer, and adds, 'unless Mozart should prove to be a mere overgrown product of the forcing - house, he will be the greatest composer that ever lived.' [2] Court and public vied with each other in paying him attentions, and the court chapel performed one of his grand litanies (K. 125), two of his masses,[3] and an offertorium, 'Misericordiae Domini' (K. 222), written in haste at the request of the Elector, and an admirable specimen of strict counterpoint. The PF. sonata in D (K. 284), interesting for its unexpected traces of French influence, appears also to have been written at Munich, at the suggestion of Baron Dürnitz.

Soon after their return to Salzburg in Mar. 1775, a series of fêtes was given at court in honour of the Archduke Maximilian, afterwards Archbishop of Cologne, and Wolfgang's dramatic cantata to Metastasio's much-used ' Il Rè pastore ' (K. 208) was performed on Apr. 23. To the remainder of this year belong two airs for tenor (K. 209, 210) ; an air for soprano (K. 217) ; a divertimento (K. 213) ; a serenade (K. 204) ; a 'sonata' for organ and strings (K. 212) ; and, above all, the five violin concertos (K. 207, 211, 216, 218, 219).[4] All these works are typical examples of Mozart's ' gallant ' style in its extreme development. The concertos show that he was working at the violin, which he did to please his father, as he disliked playing at court, though it was one of his duties. His father writes to him, Oct. 18, 1777, ' You have no idea how well you play the violin ; if you would only do yourself justice, and play with boldness, spirit and fire, you would be the first violinist in Europe.' Again, ' I suspect you have scarcely touched the violin since you were in Munich ; I should be very sorry if that were the case ' ; and later, ' The violin is hanging up on its nail I suppose '—and the conjecture was right. The remark about Munich refers to his Cassation (K. 287), ' Everybody was staring away ; and I

---

[1] Partly rewritten by Mozart in 1779.

[2] *Teutsche Chronik*, 1775, p. 267.
[3] One of these was probably the Missa brevis (K. 220), which seems to date from this time, and bears obvious signs of hurried workmanship.
[4] The authenticity, in the form in which it has been preserved, of the violin concerto in E♭ (K. 268) is open to question. See the article by G. de Saint-Foix in the *Bull. de la Soc. Union Musicologique* année ii. (1922), fasc. i.

playel as if I had been the greatest violinist in Europe.' Later, in Vienna, he preferred taking the viola in quartets.

The whole of 1776, and the greater part of the following year passed quietly in the old routine, numerous compositions testifying to Wolfgang's industry. This period may be divided into three main divisions: in the first, which extends from Jan. to Sept. 1776, Mozart is found refining the cruder features of his 'gallant' style, partly under the influence of a growing acquaintance with some of the more cultured members of Salzburg society such as the Countess Lodron and her daughters; in the second (Oct.-Dec. 1776) we see him, by way of further reaction, devoting himself for a time exclusively to religious music; in the third (Jan.-Sept. 1777) we find him renewing his acquaintance with the works of the older writers and undertaking other preparations for his forthcoming journey to Paris. To the first division belong a grand mass (K. 262); a litany 'de venerabili' (K. 243); an offertorium 'Venite populi' for two choirs (K. 260); four 'organ sonatas' (K. 225, 224, 244, 245); three PF. concertos (K. 238, 242, 246), the second of which, for three pianos, was written for the Countess Lodron and her daughters; three serenades (K. 239, 249 and 250, 101), of which the first is a curious composition for two small orchestras and the second the well-known Haffner [1] serenade; six divertimenti [2] (K. 240, 247 and 248, 251-254), of which the second, written for the Countess Lodron, is one of Mozart's finest works in this kind; and three arias (K. 126, 255, 256) for soprano, alto and tenor respectively. The second division is represented by three masses (K. 257, 259, 258), the last of which marks a definite advance in Mozart's attitude to religious music. To the third division belong a Missa brevis (K. 275); an offertorium (K. 277); the beautiful Sancta Maria (K. 273); two organ sonatas (K. 274, 278); a remarkable PF. concerto written for the French pianist Mlle. Jeunehomme (K. 271); a violin concerto [3] (K. 271a), a 'Nocturne' for four orchestras (K. 286); four divertimenti (K. 270, 287, 289, 188), the second of which was written for the Countess Lodron as a companion piece to the work already mentioned, and is perhaps an even finer composition; a trio for two violins and bass (K. 266); a series of dances (K. 267); and a fine scena written for Mme. Duschek (K. 272).

Mozart was now 21 years of age, a skilled performer on three instruments, and at home in the most varied branches of composition.

His father had given him a conscientious and systematic education, protected him from all injurious influences, and made him concentrate his whole powers on his artistic cultivation. All that teaching could do for him had been done in Salzburg; the time had now come for him to go out into the world, and let the discipline of life complete the work. His existence at Salzburg had long been intolerable to him; beyond a few intimate friends he had no society; he was disgusted at the want of appreciation for art, and his relations with Archbishop Hieronymus became daily more and more strained. On this point both he and his father became anxious. Something must be done. Not daring as yet to send his son alone into the world, the father asked leave to take a professional tour with him. It was refused, the Archbishop's reason being, as he said afterwards, 'that he could not bear people going about begging in that fashion.' The cup was now full, and Wolfgang applied for his discharge.[4] Irritated that any one should dare to leave him so abruptly, and quite aware of what he was losing, the Archbishop granted the request on Aug. 28, adding that, 'after the Gospel [5] both father and son were free to seek their fortune wherever they pleased.' He relented, however, with regard to the father, who came to the painful resolve of sending his son away with his mother. It was true that she had little bodily, and still less intellectual energy; but she was an experienced traveller, and could be useful to her son in many practical ways. The necessary preparations were accordingly made, even to the purchase of a carriage, that they might present a suitable appearance. On Sept. 23, 1777, mother and son left home. The father bore up bravely till they were really off, and then going to his room, sank exhausted on a chair. Suddenly he remembered that in his distress he had forgotten to give his son his blessing. He rushed to the window with outstretched hand, but the carriage was already out of sight. His son, however, breathed freely when once fairly off; the deliverance from a position which he had long groaned under was delightful enough to mitigate even the pain of separation from his father and sister. Fortunately for him he could not foresee the life which lay before him—a life full to its close of crosses and disappointments, and with so few joys!

Their first halting-place was Munich, where Mozart was at once in great demand as a performer, but was not successful in his efforts to obtain a permanent appointment. At Augsburg he visited J. Andreas Stein, the celebrated

---

[1] Composed for the wedding of Elisabeth Haffner, the daughter of the Salzburg burgomaster. The work is so long that it was probably intended to be performed in sections at appropriate intervals in the festivities.
[2] K. 254 is, in form, a PF. trio, but is described by Mozart himself as a divertimento.
[3] This concerto was first published in 1907. The authenticity of the work, which in any case raises many problems, has been questioned by some critics, notably by A. Moser in his *Geschichte des Violinspiels* (1923).

[4] This interesting document was found in the archiepiscopal archives by Pirckmeyer the custodian, and published with other matter under the title of *Zur Lebensgeschichte Mozarts*, Salzburg, 1876; also copied in the Preface to Nohl's *Mozartbriefe*, 2nd ed., 1877.
[5] 'Nach dem Evangelio.' Perhaps this means 'as the Gospel directs,' and is a hit at Mozart's reference, in his petition, to the passage about hiding one's light under a bushel.

maker of organs and pianofortes, and both at his house and in the monastery of St. Ulrich charmed all hearers by his playing. A concert, however, produced but a small sum. On Oct. 30 they reached Mannheim, where they stayed much longer than they anticipated. The good prospects which at first seemed to open before them were not indeed realised; but the visit formed a decisive epoch in Mozart's life. Under the Elector Karl Theodor, Mannheim possessed a good opera, with an orchestra containing virtuosi of the first rank, and at that time considered the first in Europe for instrumental music.[1] Mozart made great friends with Cannabich, an excellent conductor and good teacher, and gave pianoforte lessons to his daughter Rose, who for a time undoubtedly captured his heart. He also made the acquaintance of the poets Wieland[2] and Freiherr von Gemmingen, the composers Holzbauer[3] and Schweitzer, Raaff the great tenor, Wendling, Ramm and Ritter, excellent performers on the flute, oboe and bassoon. Here also his playing, both on the pianoforte and the organ, was much admired, and he had opportunities of measuring himself with Sterkel and Vogler, neither of whom impressed him much. The latter, indeed, he positively disliked. Upon the failure of his attempts to gain admittance to the Elector's Chapel, Wendling, Ramm and Ritter tried to persuade him to accompany them to Paris and give concerts there. He was inclined to the plan, and his father agreed, though with reluctance; but when it came to the point he allowed his friends to start without him. The truth was he had again fallen in love, and this time more seriously. Aloysia, the second daughter of Fridolin Weber, prompter and copyist, was a gifted singer, with a fine voice and considerable beauty, and during an excursion to Kirchheim, where the Princess of Orange kept a private orchestra and had daily concerts, these qualities made a due impression upon Wolfgang. Aloysia returned his attachment, and allowed him to teach her singing; and he, touched by the poverty of the family, conceived the plan of taking her to Italy, and there writing a new opera for her first appearance. So romantic a proposition drove his father nearly out of his senses. In such a case quick action was everything. Urging upon him the doubtful character of the plan, he used all his endeavours to tear him away from these dangerous surroundings. ' Off with you to Paris, and that immediately ! Take up your position among those who are really great—*aut Caesar aut nihil !* From Paris the name and fame of a man of talent spreads throughout the world.' As for his Aloysia, he

advised him to commend her to Raaff, who would not only be able to teach her, but whose good word would have great weight with impresarios. It was a hard struggle for Wolfgang, but his love for his father enabled him to defer to his authority, and the time for departure was fixed. Before leaving, however, he gave some concerts, at which he played, and produced both his compositions and his pupils; and now for the first time Mannheim became aware of what it was losing. Parting with the Webers was hard work; they all wept, and thanked him as their ' greatest benefactor.' In Mannheim he composed : a Kyrie (K. 322); two soprano arias, one for Aloysia Weber (K. 294), the other for Dorothea Wendling (K. 486a); a tenor air for Raaff (K. 295); two Lieder (K. 307, 308); two flute concertos (K. 313, 314); an andante for flute (K. 315); a quartet for flute and strings (K. 285)[4]; seven sonatas for PF. and violin, partly composed in Paris (K. 296, 301-306); three PF. sonatas (K. 309-311), including the beautiful one in A minor. In all these works it is easy to trace the influence of the ' Mannheim school,' especially evident in the sudden alternations of *piano* and *forte*.

Leaving Mannheim on Mar. 14, 1778, the travellers reached Paris on the 23rd. The father's anticipations did not in this instance prove correct; their old friend Grimm was still there, but by no means so devoted to their interests as he had been; the youth was not the same attraction as the marvellous boy had been; and the musical world was absorbed in the Gluck and Piccinni controversy. Nor had they succeeded in obtaining from Vienna a recommendation to Marie Antoinette. They were thus thrown upon their Mannheim friends, and upon Count von Sickingen, to whom von Gemmingen had given them an introduction. Wolfgang renewed his acquaintance with Piccinni, whom he had met in Italy, but they never got beyond the terms of ordinary courtesy; 'I know my business, and he his—that is enough,' writes Wolfgang. Gossec he calls ' my very good friend, and an uncommonly dry man.' There is no trace of any acquaintance with Grétry. Grimm procured him admittance to the Duc de Guisnes, who played the flute superbly, as Mozart says, and whose daughter was a skilful performer on the harp. Accordingly he had to compose a concerto (K. 299) for these two instruments, for which, as solo instruments, he cared less than for any others. To the daughter he gave daily lessons in composition, and he had a few other lady-pupils. But he was not given the opportunity of writing an opera. Noverre, ballet-master at the Opéra, promised to use his influence, which was great, in his favour; but all he did was to employ him to compose twelve

[1] Although Mozart had heard (and had written for) the clarinet before he became acquainted with this orchestra, it was at Mannheim that he first learnt its value as an orchestral instrument.
[2] Mozart draws a very unflattering portrait of the poet in a letter to his father dated Dec. 27, 1777.
[3] Holzbauer's ' Günther von Schwarzburg,' which Mozart heard during his stay, seems to have made a deep impression on him, as even in ' Die Zauberflöte ' there are reminiscences of it.

[4] Wyzewa and Saint-Foix (ii. 404) assign to this period another flute quartet (in G) printed in the Peters' edition but not recorded in Köchel.

pieces for his ballet ' Les petits riens.' [1] He composed a ' sinfonie concertante ' (K. Anh. 9) for oboe, clarinet, bassoon and French horn, at the request of Le Gros, director of the Concert Spirituel, but it was never performed. Some airs in a Miserere by Holzbauer, produced at the Concert Spirituel without Mozart's name, passed unnoticed except by Gossec, who expressed great admiration. Le Gros afterwards ordered another symphony, which pleased greatly—the Paris or French symphony in three movements (K. 297); and at his request Mozart wrote a second Andante in place of the original one.

In the meantime, his mother, who had never been well in Paris, became seriously ill, and died in Wolfgang's arms on July 3. With great thoughtfulness he wrote to their friend Bullinger to prepare his father for the sad news, and then sent a letter direct. He felt he could not remain longer in Paris, and his father even urged his departure, especially as there was now some prospect for him in Salzburg, owing to the deaths of Adlgasser the court organist, and Lolli the old Kapellmeister. Moreover, the Archbishop had promised to allow him to go anywhere to superintend the production of an opera, should he be commissioned to write one. His last few days in Paris were cheered by his old London friend, Christian Bach, who had come over for the performance of his ' Amadis.' ' His joy, and mine too, at meeting again, you can well imagine,' he wrote to his father. With Bach came Tenducci, and the three spent a few pleasant days at the Maréchal de Noailles's château at Saint Germain. Mozart wrote a scena for Tenducci,[2] with accompaniment for pianoforte, oboe, horn and bassoon, and this was played by the Maréchal's servants, who were all Germans. In addition to the works already mentioned, Mozart composed during his stay in Paris : an overture for orchestra (K. Anh. 8) ; a quartet for flute and strings based on favourite airs of the day (K. 298) ; four sets of PF. variations on popular French tunes (K. 264, 265, 353, 354) ; four PF. sonatas (K. 330-333), and, in all probability, the little prelude for PF. (K. 395).

On Sept. 26, 1778, Mozart left Paris, still heavier at heart than he had entered it six months before, but displayed no haste in returning to his native town. He went by Nancy and Strassburg, which he reached in the middle of October. Here he gave three concerts, which produced much applause but little money, and played on Silbermann's two best organs in the Neukirche and St. Thomas. On Nov. 3 he started for Mannheim, although it was, as his father said, a foolish notion to go there when the court, the Webers, and his best friends were all absent at Munich, and there was nothing for him to do. But it did him good to recall the old memories, and, as he said, ' I love Mannheim, and Mannheim loves me.' Besides, he had some prospect of an engagement for an opera. Seyler's troupe was still at the theatre ; they were indeed only an operetta company, but there was some talk of founding a German national opera. Here, too, Mozart saw two of Benda's melodramas, ' Medea ' and ' Ariadne auf Naxos,' and was so delighted with them that he willingly undertook to set von Gemmingen's ' Semiramis ' in the same fashion.[3] Von Dalberg, director of the theatre, also had his eye upon Mozart for his opera ' Cora,' although he was already in negotiation with Gluck and Schweitzer. However, all came to nothing ; and his father, who had run into debt on his account, and had, moreover, great hopes of seeing him well placed in Salzburg, put forth his authority to make him return—' You will start immediately on receipt of this.' The son obeyed, and by Dec. 25 was at Munich ; but his father, anxious lest he should be detained for good, and fearing the proximity of his beloved, did not let him rest there. Cannabich and Raaff were indeed ' working for him hand and foot,' but there was no need for anxiety on Aloysia's account. Her family welcomed him warmly, but she who 'had wept for him ' seemed now scarcely to remember him, and was even displeased that he had altered the fashion of his clothes. Yet he again offered her his musical homage, composing a grand aria (K. 316) suited to her present capabilities, to words taken from Gluck's 'Alceste,' and with an obbligato accompaniment intended for Ramm and Ritter. This air was his farewell to Aloysia Weber, about whom he wrote to his father in May 1781,

' I did love her truly, and feel still that I am not indifferent to her ; but luckily for me her husband is a jealous fool, and never lets her go anywhere, so that I rarely see her.' [4]

In mourning for his mother, disappointed in his first love, and with all his hopes falsified, Mozart returned in the middle of Jan. 1779 to the home of his childhood. In such circumstances the warmth with which he was received was doubly grateful. A good many of his old friends were still there to rally round him, but nothing could overcome his dislike of Salzburg. Even the duties entailed by his position as Konzertmeister and organist to the court and Cathedral [5] were fulfilled as an irksome task.

---

1 Discovered and printed some years ago. See NOVERRE.

2 Tenducci appears to have taken this composition with him to London. Burney (see Barrington's *Miscellanies*, p. 289) speaks of it as a masterpiece of invention and technique (Pohl's *Mozart in London*, p. 121). Unfortunately it has now completely disappeared.

3 He took the libretto home with him to compose ' gratuitously.' ' You see,' he writes to his father, ' how strong my liking for this kind of composition is.' It is uncertain whether Mozart ever completed this work. See Jahn, ii. 78; Abert, i. 752.

4 She was engaged as prima donna in Vienna in 1780, and married Joseph Lange, the court actor. She acknowledged afterwards that as a young girl she had not appreciated Mozart as highly as she ought to have done, but she became a great admirer of his music, and a true friend. She did not live happily with her husband, but their intercourse with Mozart was quite unconstrained. He composed for her in Vienna five more airs, and they gave mutual assistance at each others' concerts. Kelly (*Reminiscences*, i. 253) admired her as a singer of the first rank. Her voice had an exceptionally high range.

5 His father succeeded in getting him appointed successor to Adlgasser, with a salary of 400 florins (about £40).

His desire to write for the stage was rekindled by the presence of the dramatic companies directed by Böhm and Schikaneder. With Schikaneder Mozart was soon on excellent terms, and it was to oblige him that he re-fashioned and supplemented the music to Gebler's 'Thamos' which he had originally composed in 1773. To this period also belongs the uncompleted German opera, on a libretto by Schachtner, to which André afterwards gave the title of 'Zaïde' (K. 344).[1]

During his stay at Salzburg in 1779–80 Mozart produced the following works : two masses (K. 317, the 'Coronation Mass,' and K. 337) ; a Kyrie (K. 323) ; two vespers (K. 321, 339), among his best compositions ; a Regina coeli (K. 276) ; two symphonies (K. 319, 338) ; an 'overture-symphony' [2] (K. 318) ; a 'sinfonie concertante' for violin and viola (K. 364) ; a serenade (K. 320) ; a divertimento for string-quartet and two horns (K. 334) ; a concerto for two PFs. (K. 365) ; and three 'organ sonatas' (K. 328, 329, 336).

His next employment was most congenial. Through the exertions of his friends at Munich the grand opera for the Carnival of 1781 was put into his hands. The libretto was by Abbate Varesco, court chaplain at Salzburg, who con-sulted Mozart at every step, as he began the work at home. He went to Munich in the beginning of November, and at the very first rehearsals the music was highly approved by the Elector and the performers. His father even wrote to him from Salzburg, 'The uni-versal subject of conversation here is your opera.' The Archbishop being in Vienna at the time, his father and sister were able to go to Munich for the first performance on Jan. 29, 1781. 'Idomeneo, Rè di Creta,' opera seria (K. 366; ballet-music, K. 367), was enthusiastic-ally received, and decided once for all Mozart's position as a dramatic composer. During his stay at Munich he also wrote a Kyrie (K. 341) ; two concert airs for soprano (K. 368, 369) ; two Lieder with mandoline accompaniment (K. 349, 351) ; and a quartet for oboe and strings for his friend Ramm (K. 370).

But while he was in the full enjoyment of the pleasures of the Carnival, into which he plunged as soon as his labours were over, he suddenly received a summons from the Archbishop to join him in Vienna.

He started immediately, and on Mar. 16, 1781, after a journey of four days, arrived 'all by himself in a post-chaise'[3] in Vienna, where he was to remain, save for a few brief excursions, for the rest of his life. His first experiences in

the Austrian capital were not encouraging. He was made to live with the Archbishop's house-hold, and dine at the servants' table—treat-ment in striking contrast to that he received from the aristocracy in general. The Countess Thun, 'the most charming and attractive woman I have ever seen in my life,' invited him to dinner, and so did vice-chancellor Count Cobenzl and others. The Archbishop liked the prestige of appearing in society with Mozart, Ceccarelli and Brunetti as his domestic virtuosi, but did not allow Mozart either to play alone in any house but his own, or to give a concert. He was obliged, however, to yield to the entreaties of the nobility and allow him to appear at the concert of the Tonkünstler-Societät. 'I am so happy,' Mozart exclaimed beforehand, and wrote to his father afterwards of his great success. At the Archbishop's private concert, too, he excited the greatest enthusiasm, though he was often addressed in that very house as 'Gassenbube' (low fellow of the streets). It was useless for his father to urge him to forbearance : he was determined not to remain in a position where he had such indignities to endure. The opportunity came only too soon. The Archbishop, detested by the nobility, and above all by the Emperor Joseph, did not receive an invitation to Laxen-burg, the summer residence of the court, and in his disgust determined to leave Vienna. The household was to start first, but Mozart, 'the villain, the low fellow,' was turned out of the house before the others. He took lodgings with the Webers, who were living in the Petersplatz at a house called 'zum Auge Gottes.' At his next audience he was greeted with 'Lump,' 'Lausbube' and 'Fex' (untranslat-able terms of abuse). 'None of his servants treated him so badly,' continued the Arch-bishop. 'Your Grace is dissatisfied with me then ?' said Mozart. 'What ! you dare to use threats ?' (using all the time the contemptuous 'Er'). 'Fex ! there is the door ; I will have nothing more to do with such a vile wretch' ('elenden Buben'). 'Nor I with you,' re-torted Mozart, and turned on his heel. Not having received an answer to his application for his discharge, Mozart drew up a fresh memorial, with which he presented himself in the ante-chamber of this Prince of the Church ; but as a culmination to all the brutal treatment he had already received, Count Arco, the high-steward, addressed him as 'Flegel' (clown), 'Bursch' (fellow), etc., *and kicked him out of the room.* This took place on the 8th of June. Mozart was now free, though he had not received his formal dismissal ; 'I will never have anything more to do with Salzburg,' he wrote to his father, 'I hate the Archbishop almost to fury.' It was summer, the nobility were all going into the country, and there was no demand for either concerts or lessons. The

---

[1] It seems merely to want the overture and the concluding finale. André himself supplied these numbers for his edition. The score contains some of Mozart's most delightful music, and it is a pity that it is not better known.
[2] Generally quoted as overture composed for Bianchi's 'Villanella rapita.' Mozart wrote a trio and a quartet for performance in this opera, but is not known to have written an overture ; nor are there any grounds, apart from tradition, for connecting this symphony with the opera.
[3] Letter of Mar. 17, 1781.

Countess Rumbeck was his only pupil. Composition was of course his resource, and while thus employing his leisure, he fulfilled his long-cherished desire of writing an opera for the National Singspiel (German opera), founded by the Emperor in 1778. The Emperor interested himself in his favour, and he soon received a libretto to his taste. He was hurt, however, at finding himself passed over at the fêtes in honour of the Grand Duke Paul and his wife ; even his ' Idomeneo ' had to give way to two operas of Gluck's. His contest with Clementi, in the presence of the Emperor and the Grand Duchess on Dec. 24,[1] afforded him some slight compensation. He had previously (Nov. 16) played at the house of Archduke Maximilian, who was very fond of him, though under the circumstances unable to do anything for him. It was probably during this winter that he first met Haydn,[2] who visited the Viennese court to superintend the performance of the six quartets (op. 33) dedicated to the Grand Duke Paul. From this meeting dates a ten years' friendship which ceased only at Mozart's death, and which influenced for good the compositions of both masters. It is no coincidence that the greatest works of both were written after 1781. Haydn learned from Mozart a rounder phrase, a richer harmonisation, and a fuller command of the orchestra ; Mozart learned from Haydn a wider range of structure, and a gravity and dignity of expression which are particularly noticeable in his later symphonies. Amongst the works written by Mozart before the production of ' Die Entführung ' may be mentioned : four sonatas and two sets of variations for PF. and violin (K. 376, 377, 379, 380 ; K. 359, 360) ; two serenades for wind instruments (K. 361, 375) ; the sonata for two PFs. (K. 448) ; the prelude and fugue for PF. in C (K. 394) ; and two sets of PF. variations (K. 398, 352). In spite of unremitting intrigues his ' Entführung aus dem Serail ' (K. 384), libretto by Bretzner, was produced by the Emperor's express command, with great success, on July 16, 1782.[3] Mozart was arranging it for wind-band when he received through his father a request for a serenade, to be composed in all haste, for the Haffners of Salzburg. This is the work which was afterwards transformed by Mozart into the well-known Symphony in D (K. 385). He had forgotten all about it, and when he came to rearrange it was quite surprised to find how good it was. At the same time Mozart also composed the fine serenade for wind instru-

ments in C min. (K. 388), better known in his own arrangement of it for string quintet (K. 406).

On the Grand Duke's second visit to Vienna in October, he attended Mozart's opera, which was still attracting ' swarms of people ' ; the composer conducted in person, ' to show himself the father of his own child.' Prague soon produced it with great success ; a foretaste of the many honours Mozart was to receive in that city.

He found his new abode with the Webers very comfortable ; but the world soon began to inquire whether he were not intending to marry one of the daughters. The report reached his father, who admonished him seriously ; but Wolfgang solemnly declared that he was thinking of nothing of the kind, and to prove his statement took another lodging, in the ' Graben.' Here, however, the want of the attentions to which he had been accustomed drove him to a new step, for which we soon find him preparing his father. ' To my mind a bachelor lives only half a life,' he writes, and hesitatingly names the object of his love. ' But surely not a Weber ? ' ' Yes, a Weber, Constanze, the third daughter.' All attempts at dissuasion were vain ; his resolution was fixed, and on Aug. 4, scarcely a month after the production of his opera, he led Constanze to the altar, at St. Stephen's. Bringing home his bride was his ' Entführung aus dem Auge Gottes ' as he told his friends. ' As soon as we were married, my wife and I both began to weep ; all present, even the priest, were touched at seeing us so moved, and wept too.'

His marriage involved Mozart in innumerable troubles. With many good qualities his wife was a thoroughly bad manager, and this was the worst defect possible, since Mozart was naturally careless in money matters, and his life as a busy artist was an unfavourable one for economy. The young couple began house-keeping with next to nothing, and their re-sources were uncertain at the best. No wonder, then, that in six months they were in serious difficulties ; and so it went on to the end. His friends, the worthy Puchberg especially, were always ready to come to his assistance, but they could not prevent his often being put to embarrassing and humiliating straits. Without even a prospect of a fixed appointment he was thrown back upon lessons and concerts. Pupils were scarce, but he was more fortunate as a virtuoso ; and for the next few years he was constantly employed with concerts, his own and those of other artists, and still more in playing at the houses of the nobility. Lent and Advent were the regular concert seasons in Vienna. The Emperor was frequently present, and always had a loud ' bravo ' for Mozart, speaking of him, too, at his own table ' in the highest terms ' as ' un talent décidé.' This makes it

---

[1] The theme of the sonata played by Clementi (Œuvres, vi. 1) on this occasion was utilised by Mozart in the overture to the ' Zauberflöte.'
[2] It is, however, just possible that the Haydn whom the Mozarts met at Augsburg in 1763 was the great Josef. See Schurig, L. Mozart: Reiseaufzeichnungen, pp. 22, 65.
[3] July 12, in Jahn (2nd Germ. ed.), i. 648, is wrong, as is also the alteration to July 13 in the Eng. trans. (ii. 209). The Emperor is reported to have said, ' Too fine for our ears, my dear Mozart, and much too many notes,' meaning that the accompaniments over-powered the voices. Mozart answered frankly, ' Exactly as many notes as are necessary, your Majesty.'

all the more difficult to exonerate His Majesty from the charge of yielding to the efforts of those immediately about him, to prevent his bestowing some suitable post on Mozart. The latter writes on this subject to his father,

'Countess Thun, Count Zichy, Baron van Swieten, even Prince Kaunitz, are all much vexed at the little value that the Emperor puts on men of talent. Kaunitz said lately, when talking to the Archduke Maximilian about me, that men of that stamp only came into the world once in a hundred years, and that they ought not to be driven out of Germany, especially when, as good luck would have it, they were already in the capital.'

After the success of his first concert in Lent 1782, Mozart entered into an engagement with Martin, who had instituted a series of concerts held in the winter at the 'Mehlgrube,' [1] and removed in May to the Augarten,[2] where Mozart played for the first time on May 26. He afterwards joined the pianist Richter, who gave subscription concerts. Among the artists at whose concerts he appeared were the singers Laschi, Teyber and Storace, and his sister-in-law, Mme. Lange.

His own subscription concerts, generally three or four, were held in the theatre, at the Mehlgrube, or in the Trattnerhof, and being attended by the cream of nobility,[3] produced both honour and profit. The programme consisted chiefly, sometimes entirely, of his own compositions—a symphony, two PF. concertos, an orchestral piece with an instrument concertante, three or four airs, and an improvised fantasia. The latter, in which he showed incomparable skill, always roused a perfect storm of applause. For each concert he composed a new PF. concerto, the greatest number and the best belonging to this time. With so much on his hands he might well say, when excusing himself to his sister for writing so seldom, ' Has not a man without a kreutzer of fixed income enough to do and to think of day and night in a place like this ? ' A list he sent to his father of the concerts for 1784 will best show the request he was in. During six weeks (Feb. 26 to Apr. 3) he played five times at Prince Gallitzin's, nine times at Count John Esterhazy's, at three of Richter's concerts, and five of his own.

Tired of waiting for an appointment, which must have been most trying to one of his excitable nature, Mozart seriously thought of going to London and Paris, and began to practise himself in English and French. He had even written to Le Gros in Paris about

engagements for the Concert Spirituel and the Concerts des Amateurs, but his father, horrified at the idea of a newly married man without resources thus wandering about the world, succeeded in putting a stop to the scheme. As a compensation for the postponement of one desire, he was able to fulfil another, that of presenting his young wife to his father. Starting after her recovery from her first confinement (June 17) they reached Salzburg at the end of July 1783.

Before his marriage Mozart had made a vow that if ever Constanze became his wife he would have a new Mass of his own composition performed in Salzburg. The work was nearly ready, and the missing numbers having been supplied from one of his older masses, this fine and broadly designed composition (K. 427) [4] was given at the end of August in the Peterskirche, Constanze herself singing the soprano part. Opera buffa having been reintroduced in Vienna he began a new opera, ' L' oca del Cairo ' (K. 422), but after some progress found the libretto (by Varesco) so wretched that he let it drop.[5] A second opera, ' Lo sposo deluso' (K. 430), only reached the fifth number, partly perhaps because he despaired of being able to produce it, as Sarti and Paisiello were then in Vienna, and the latter in particular was absorbing public attention with the triumph of his ' Il Rè Teodoro ' (1784). In the meantime Mozart rendered a service of love to his friend Michael Haydn, who was incapacitated by illness from completing two duets for violin and viola for the Archbishop. The Archbishop characteristically threatened to stop his Konzertmeister's salary, but Mozart came to the rescue, and undertook to write the two pieces ' with unmistakable pleasure.' His friend retained his salary, and the Archbishop received the duets (K. 423, 424) as Haydn's. Mozart also took an active interest in his father's pupils —Marchand the violinist of 12 (then playing in Vienna), his sister Margarethe, then 14, afterwards Mme. Danzi, the well-known singer, and a child of 9, the daughter of Brochard the celebrated actor. He also became intimate with Marie Thérèse Paradies, the blind pianist, who was then in Salzburg, and for whom he afterwards composed a concerto (K. 456). The main object of his visit, however, was not fulfilled. It was only after long opposition that his father had unwillingly given his consent to his marriage, but Wolfgang hoped that his prejudice against Constanze would disappear on acquaintance ; neither his father nor his sister, however, could ever reconcile themselves to the match.

Leaving Salzburg on Oct. 30, and stopping

---

[1] A very old building, with rooms in which balls and concerts were held. A flour-warehouse in the basement gave its name to the house. It is now the Hotel Munsch.

[2] See AUGARTEN, vol. i.

[3] In the list of his subscribers for 1784 we find, besides his regular patrons, Countess Thun, Baroness Waldstädten, Count Zichy, van Swieten, etc., the Duke of Würtemberg, Princes Lichtenstein, Auersperg, Kaunitz, Lichnowsky, Lobkowitz, Paar, Palm and Schwarzenberg ; the distinguished families of Bathyany, Dietrichstein, Erdödy, Esterhazy, Harrach, Herberstein, Keglewicz, Nostiz, Palfy, Schaffgotsch, Stahrenberg and Waldstein ; the Russian, Spanish, Sardinian, Dutch and Danish ambassadors ; the eminent financiers Fries, Henickstein, Arenfeld, Bienenfeld, Ployer and Wetzlar ; government officials of position, and scientific men, such as Isdenczy, Bedekovich, Nevery, Braun, Greiner, Keess, Puffendorf, Born, Martini, Sonnenfels, etc.

[4] Afterwards converted by Mozart into the cantata ' Davidde penitente ' (K. 469).

[5] It was completed by André, with a Rondeau, quartetto from ' Lo sposo deluso,' finale from ' La villanella rapita,' by Mozart ; was adapted to new words by Victor Wilder, and performed in Paris, Théâtre des Fantaisies-Parisiennes, June 6, 1867 ; at Vienna in the Carltheater, 1868 ; at Drury Lane, May 12, 1870.

at Lambach for Mozart to play the organ in the monastery, they found Count Thun waiting for them at Linz, and stayed with him for some time, being treated with every consideration. For a concert which Mozart gave in the theatre, he composed in haste a new symphony (K. 425).[1]

In 1785 the father returned his son's visit, staying with him in the Grosse Schulerstrasse (now No. 8) from Feb. 11 to Apr. 25. He was rejoiced to find their domestic arrangements and money matters for the time being in good order. He found a grandson too—'little Karl 's very like your brother.' Though not yet on thoroughly good terms with his son or his daughter-in-law, he derived all the old pleasure from his successes as an artist, and listened with delight to his productions. He had come just at the right time, when concerts were succeeding each other as fast as possible, and his son taking part in all; and at the first he attended his eyes filled with tears of happiness at Wolfgang's playing and compositions. The day after his arrival Wolfgang invited his friend Haydn and the two Barons Todi; and his father wrote home [2] a full account of this memorable evening. 'Three new quartets were played,' writes the happy father,

'the three [K. 458, 464, 465] he has added to those we already have [K. 387, 421, 428]; they are perhaps a trifle easier, but excellently composed. Herr Haydn said to me, *I declare to you before God as a man of honour, that your son is the greatest composer that I know, either personally or by reputation; he has taste, and beyond that the most consummate knowledge of the art of composition.*'

In return for this avowal Mozart dedicated to Haydn, with a laudatory preface, these six quartets, 'the fruits of long and arduous toil.' 'It is but his due,' he said, 'for from Haydn I first learnt how to compose a quartet.' The success of his pupil Marchand, and the great progress of Aloysia Lange, both as a singer and actress, also afforded pleasure to Leopold Mozart. It is a significant fact that a man of his way of thinking should have joined the Freemasons, avowedly through his son's influence. This, however, was their last meeting, for soon after his return from Vienna his health began to fail, and on May 28, 1787, he ended a life which had been wholly consecrated to his children.

Mozart the son belonged to the eighth and oldest Freemasons' Lodge (' zur gekrönten Hoffnung ') in Vienna. His interest in the order was great, indeed he at one time thought of founding a society of his own to be called 'Die Grotte,' and had drawn up the rules. A letter to his father, during his illness, in which he enlarges upon the true significance of death to a Mason, is a proof of the serious light in which he considered his obligations. His connexion with the order also inspired many of his compositions. For it he wrote—' Gesellen-

reise' (K. 468); 'Maurerfreude' (K. 471), a short cantata, at the performance of which his father was present shortly before his death; the noble 'Maurerische Trauermusik' (K. 477), for strings and wind; a 'Lied,' with chorus, and a chorus in three parts, both with organ (K. 483, 484), for the ceremony at the opening of the 'Neugekrönte Hoffnung' (by a decree of the Emperor Joseph) in 1785; and a short cantata for tenor, with closing chorus (K. 623), composed Nov. 15, 1791, the last of his recorded works which he conducted himself. A short adagio for two corni di bassetto and bassoon (K. 410), an adagio for two clarinets and three corni di bassetto (K. 411) and an unfinished cantata (K. 429) were also probably intended for Masonic use.

In Mar. 1785 Mozart produced at the concert of the Tonkünstler Societät a cantata, 'Davidde penitente' (K. 469), the materials for which he drew from his last unfinished mass (K. 427), writing the Italian words below the Latin, and adding two new airs.

After a long delay he was again gratified by an opportunity of writing for the stage. An opera-buffa had been organised as far back as Apr. 1783, and the Emperor had secured an excellent company [3]; and after a failure the National-Singspiel had been revived in Oct. 1785. A libretto, 'Rudolf von Habsburg,' sent to Mozart from Mannheim, remained unused, but at length he and Salieri were requested to supply German and Italian 'pièces de circonstance' for some fêtes in honour of distinguished visitors at Schönbrunn. To Mozart's lot fell 'Der Schauspieldirector' (K. 486), a one-act burlesque of operatic life by Stephanie the younger, produced at Schönbrunn, Feb. 7, 1786, and afterwards at the Kärnthnerthor Theatre.[4]

In the next month a gratifying performance of 'Idomeneo' took place at the palace of Prince Auersperg, by a troupe of titled and efficient performers, under Mozart's own supervision.[5] This mark of the favourable disposition of the aristocracy towards him bore fruit, attracting the attention of Lorenzo da Ponte, the well-known dramatist. His proposal to adapt Beaumarchais's 'Mariage de Figaro' for Mozart received the Emperor's consent—reluctantly given on account of the political implications of the original plot—and the first performance of 'Le nozze di Figaro' (K. 492) took place after violent intrigues, on May 1, 1786. The theatre was crowded, and the audience enthusiastic; several numbers were repeated twice, and the little duet three times, and this went on at succeeding representations till the Emperor

---

[1] Dedicated to Count Thun. André imagined K. 444 to have been the one composed for this occasion, but this is a copy by Mozart of a work by Michael Haydn.   [2] Feb. 14, 1785.

[3] Including three English singers, Nancy Storace, her brother Stephen and the tenor Kelly.
[4] See R. Hirsch: *Mozart's Schauspieldirector* (1859). This Singspiel was given several times with a new libretto and several interpolations. A later attempt by Schneider (1861), introducing both Mozart and Schikaneder, was particularly unfortunate.
[5] He composed for it a new duet for soprano and tenor (K. 489) and a rondo for soprano with violin solo (K. 490).

prohibited encores.[1] Kelly, who took the parts of Basilio and Don Curzio, writes with great spirit :

'Never was anything more complete than the triumph of Mozart, and his "Nozze di Figaro," to which numerous overflowing audiences bore witness. Even at the first full band rehearsal, all present were roused to enthusiasm, and when Benucci came to the fine passage, "Cherubino, alla vittoria, alla gloria militar," which he gave with stentorian lungs, the effect was electric, for the whole of the performers on the stage, and those in the orchestra, as if actuated by one feeling of delight, vociferated "Bravo! Bravo, Maestro! Viva, viva, grande Mozart!" Those in the orchestra I thought would never have ceased applauding, by beating the bows of their violins against the music desks.'

And Mozart ?

'I never shall forget his little animated countenance when lighted up with the glowing rays of genius ;— it is as impossible to describe it, as it would be to paint sunbeams.'[2]

And yet, after all this success, nothing was done for him. Earning a living by giving lessons and playing in public was in every respect unsatisfactory. 'You lucky man,' he said to young Gyrowetz as he was starting to Italy, 'and I am still obliged to give lessons to earn a trifle.' Moreover, he soon found himself eclipsed on the stage by two new pieces, which for a time absorbed the public entirely ; these were Dittersdorf's Singspiel, 'Doctor und Apotheker' (July 11), and Martin's 'Cosa rara' (Nov. 17). Again he resolved to go to England, and was again dissuaded by his father. A gleam of light came, however, from Prague, whither he was invited to see for himself the immense success of his 'Figaro,' which, like 'Die Entführung,' had been produced there immediately after its performance at Vienna. Count Johann Jos. Thun, one of the greatest amateurs in Prague, placed his house at Mozart's disposal, and he joyfully accepted the invitation. His first letter[3] gives a vivid picture of what he found at Prague, 'the one subject of conversation here is—Figaro ; nothing is played, sung or whistled but— Figaro ; nobody goes to any opera but—Figaro ; everlastingly Figaro !' He was literally overwhelmed with attentions, and felt himself at the summit of bliss ; at the opera, which was given quite to his satisfaction, he received a perfect ovation. Furthermore, two concerts were brilliantly successful ; at the first, his new symphony (K. 504) having been loudly applauded, he sat down to the piano, and improvised for fully half an hour, rousing the audience to the highest pitch of enthusiasm. Again and yet once again he had to resume, till, obeying the general acclamation, he finished by extemporising variations on 'Non più andrai,' which completed his triumph. The receipts

also were thoroughly satisfactory. He chanced to let fall the remark that he should like to compose an opera for so intelligent and appreciative a public, whereupon the impresario Bondini at once took him at his word, and concluded a contract with him for an opera for the ensuing season, for which he was to receive the usual fee of 100 ducats. The distractions of society in Prague took up all his time, and his only compositions while there were nine contredanses for orchestra (K. 510)[4] written for Count Pachta, who locked him in for an hour before dinner for the purpose, and six German dances for full orchestra (K. 509).

On his return to Vienna after this magnificent reception, he felt his position more galling than ever ; and his desire to visit England was rekindled by the departure of his friends Nancy Storace and her brother, Kelly, and his pupil Attwood, who promised to endeavour to secure him some position there, so that he would be able to go without undue risk.

The libretto of 'Figaro' having proved so satisfactory, Mozart applied again to Da Ponte, and this time their choice fell upon 'Don Giovanni.' In Sept. 1787 Mozart and his wife went to Prague, and took lodgings 'Bei den drei Löwen' No. 420 in the Kohlmarkt. But his favourite resort was the vineyard of his friend Duschek at Koschirz near the city, where are still shown his room and the stone table at which he used to sit working at his score, often in the midst of conversation or skittle-playing.[5] Before the production of his new opera, Mozart conducted a festival performance of 'Figaro' on Oct. 14, in honour of the Archduchess Maria Theresa, bride of Prince Anton of Saxony. He was very anxious about the success of 'Don Giovanni,' although, as he assured Kucharz, the conductor of the orchestra, he had spared neither pains nor labour in order to produce something really good for Prague. On the evening before the representation the overture was still wanting, and he worked at it far into the night, while his wife kept him supplied with punch, and told him fairy stories to keep him awake.[6] Sleep, however, overcame him, and he was obliged to rest for a few hours, but at seven in the morning the copyist received the score, and it was played at sight in the evening. This first performance of 'Don Giovanni' (K. 527) took place on Oct. 29, 1787. On Mozart's appearance in the orchestra he was greeted with enthusiastic applause and a triple flourish of trumpets, and the opera was accompanied from beginning to end with rapturous

---

[1] Kelly relates (*Reminiscences*, i. 262), 'When the singers were one day rehearsing, the Emperor said, "I daresay you are all pleased that I have desired there shall be no more encores." To which they all bowed assent, but Kelly said boldly, "Do not believe them, Sire, they all like to be encored, at least I am sure I always do."'

[2] *Reminiscences*, i. 258, 259.

[3] To his friend Gottfried von Jacquin, Jan. 15, 1787.

[4] There is, however, some doubt whether the dances listed by Köchel as No. 510 are those written for Count Pachta or are even Mozart's work at all. See the note by G. Nottebohm quoted in the 2nd ed. of Köchel.

[5] The villa is now called 'Bertramka.' A bust of Mozart, by Seidan, was placed on a slight eminence in the grounds, and solemnly unveiled on June 3, 1876, by the then possessor, Herr Lambert Popelka.

[6] Unless this is also a fairy story. Various conflicting accounts of the composition of the overture have been preserved. See, *e.g.*, Dent, *Mozart's Operas*, pp. 190, 191.

marks of approval. He had of course no time for other compositions, but his friend Mme. Duschek locked him into her summer-house to ensure his writing an aria he had promised her. He revenged himself by making it difficult, and would only give it her on condition that she should sing it at sight. It is one of his finest airs (K. 528).

About the time of his return to Vienna Gluck died (Nov. 15, 1787), and Mozart had reason to hope that some suitable position would now be open to him.[1] But the Emperor was in no hurry. By way, however, of recognising his recent triumph at Prague, and in order to retain him in Vienna (his hankering after England being well known), he appointed him Kammer-compositor with a salary of 800 gulden [2] (about £80). Mozart looked upon this appointment as a mere beggar's dole, and when, according to custom, he had to send in a sealed letter stating his income, he wrote bitterly, 'Too much for what I produce [3]; too little for what I could produce.' 'Don Giovanni' was not given in Vienna till May 7, 1788, and then did not please.[4] Mozart added a new air for Donna Elvira, a short air for Don Ottavio, and a duet for Zerlina and Leporello.

In spite of the success of his last opera, Mozart's pecuniary condition continued desperate. This is shown convincingly by a letter (June 27) to his friend Puchberg, in which the poor fellow begs piteously for a loan, and speaks of 'gloomy thoughts which he must repel with all his might.' And yet at the very height of his distress he manifests extraordinary power. Besides other compositions, he wrote within six weeks (June 26 to Aug. 10) his three last and finest symphonies, in E♭, G minor and C (Jupiter) (K. 543, 550, 551). But other very congenial work awaited him. From the beginning of his life in Vienna he had been acquainted with van Swieten, director of the Hofbibliothek, who was a great amateur of classical music, and who with a small band of friends devoted every Sunday morning to studying the works of the old masters. He himself sang the treble,[5] Mozart (who sat at the piano) the alto, and Starzer and Teyber tenor and bass. It was for these practices that Mozart sent for his MS. book of pieces by Michael Haydn and Eberlin, and afterwards for the fugues of Bach and Handel.

By 1788, however, van Swieten's practices had assumed larger proportions. At his instigation a number of gentlemen united to provide the necessary funds for performances of oratorios with chorus and orchestra. The fine large hall of the Hofbibliothek served as their concert-room, Mozart conducted and young Weigl took the pianoforte. It was for these performances that Mozart added wind-parts to Handel's 'Acis and Galatea' (Nov. 1788), 'Messiah' (Mar. 1789), 'Ode to St. Cecilia's Day' and 'Alexander's Feast' (July 1790).[6] (See ADDITIONAL ACCOMPANIMENTS.)

The whole-heartedness with which Mozart threw himself into the study of these older masters and strove to assimilate their style is shown not merely by the numerous contrapuntal sketches by him that have been preserved, but also by various compositions in which he has taken them for his model. Of these the most important are a Prelude and Fugue for PF. in C (K. 394); a Fugue in C minor for two PF. (K. 426), afterwards arranged for string quartet and provided with an introductory adagio (K. 546); a Suite for PF. in the Handelian style (K. 399) [7]; and a Fugue for PF. in G minor (K. 401). These were, however, only the more obvious fruits of his new studies, the influence of which can be traced no less certainly in almost everything he wrote from 1782 till his death in 1791.

Such work as this, however, did nothing to improve his pecuniary condition ; and in the hope that the journey might bring to light some means of extricating himself, he gratefully accepted an invitation from his pupil and patron Prince Karl Lichnowsky, to accompany him to Berlin.

Leaving Vienna on Apr. 8, 1789, their first halting-place worth noting was Dresden, where Mozart played at court, exciting great admiration and receiving 100 ducats. He was well received also in private circles, and the general interest was increased by a competition with J. W. Hässler of Erfurt, then distinguished as pianist and organist.[8] Without considering him a formidable opponent, Mozart acknowledged his talent. Here also he made the acquaintance of the poet Körner, and his sister-in-law Dora Stock, who drew a charming portrait of Mozart in silver-point. He produced a still greater effect in Leipzig, where he made the acquaintance of Rochlitz, who has preserved innumerable interesting traits both of the man and the artist.[9] On Apr. 22 he played the organ in the St. Thomas Church, Doles the cantor and Görner the organist pulling out the stops for him. All present were enchanted, especially Doles, who could almost have believed in the

---

[1] Gluck had been ' Kammercompositeur ' to Maria Theresa since Oct. 7, 1774.
[2] His father did not live to see this partial realisation of his hopes ; he had died, as already stated, on May 28.
[3] Viz. the dances for the Imperial Redouten-balls, which it was his duty to supply.
[4] According to Da Ponte the Emperor said, ' The opera is divine, finer perhaps than " Figaro," but it is not the meat for my Viennese.' When the saying was reported to Mozart he replied, ' We must give them time to chew it.'
[5] Diskant.' Mozart's letter, Mar. 12, 1783.

[6] The ' arrangement ' of Judas Maccabæus, sometimes attributed to Mozart, was really the work of Starzer. As to the public adoption of these additional accompaniments in England, see *Mus. T.*, 1899, p. 18. Of the beauty of Mozart's additions, in most instances, there can be no question ; but they are not always faithful to the spirit of Handel's work. In recent years the ' Messiah,' at any rate, has often been performed with Handel's original instrumentation.
[7] The concluding Sarabande of this Suite was not completed.
[8] Hässler played a concerto of Mozart's at his concert in London, May 30, 1792. See Pohl's *Haydn in London*, pt. 2, p. 200.
[9] In a series of articles in the *A.M.Z.* (1797–1802), subsequently reprinted in his *Für Freunde der Tonkunst.* Unfortunately Rochlitz was a born romancer, and must be read with caution.

restoration to life of his teacher, the great Bach himself. In return he made the choir of the Thomas-school sing Bach's 8-part motet ' Singet dem Herrn,' at which Mozart exclaimed with delight, ' Here is something from which one may still learn,' and having secured the parts of the other motets (no score being at hand), spread them out before him, and became absorbed in study.

On their arrival in Berlin the travellers went straight to Potsdam, where Prince Lichnowsky presented Mozart to the King, who had been anxiously expecting him. Frederick William II. was musical, played the violoncello well (he was a pupil of the elder Duport), and had a well-selected orchestra. The opera was conducted by Reichardt, and the concerts by Duport. The King's favourable anticipations were fully realised in Mozart, but Reichardt and Duport were set against him by his candidly replying to the King's question, what he thought of the band, ' It contains great virtuosi, but if the gentlemen would play together, they would make a better effect.'

On May 8 Mozart returned for a while to Leipzig, where, on the 12th, he gave a public concert. The programme consisted entirely of his own unpublished compositions, and at the close he improvised by general request ; but the audience was a scanty one. For Engel, the court-organist, he composed a charming little gigue for pianoforte (K. 574). Returning to Berlin on May 19, he rushed to the theatre, where his ' Entführung ' was being performed, and taking a seat near the orchestra, made observations in a half-audible tone ; the second violins, however, playing D sharp instead of D, he called out, ' Confound it, do take D ! ' and was recognised immediately. He was much pleased to meet his pupil Hummel, who only became aware while playing of his master's presence at his concert. This time Mozart played before the Queen, but gave no public performance. The King sent him 100 Friedrichs d'or, and asked him to compose some quartets for him. As to the pecuniary results of the tour, Mozart wrote laconically to his wife, ' On my return you must be glad to have me, and not think about money.' The story goes that before Mozart left Potsdam the King offered him the post of Kapellmeister at a salary of 3000 thalers (about £600), but that the composer refused the offer, replying with emotion : ' How could I desert my good Emperor.' There is, however, every ground for believing that this story is a pure invention.[1] The musical outcome of the tour was even slighter. Apart from the little gigue already mentioned the only work which Mozart composed during his visit was the PF. variations on a theme by M. Duport (K. 573). He started on his homeward journey on May 28, and passing through Dres-

den and Prague, reached Vienna on June 4, 1789. He set to work immediately on the first quartet (K. 575) for the King of Prussia, and received a kind letter of thanks, with a gold snuff-box and a second 100 Friedrichs d'or. The two others (K. 589, 590) followed in May and June 1790.

His position still continued a most melancholy one, his wife's constant illnesses adding to his expenses. Again he applies to his friend and brother Freemason, Puchberg, ' for immediate assistance. I am still most unfortunate ! Always hovering between hope and anxiety !' On Aug. 29 ' Figaro ' was revived [2] after a long interval, and it was no doubt the success of the revival that induced the Emperor to order a new opera, for which Da Ponte again furnished the libretto (said to have been founded on recent occurrences in Vienna). This was the opera-buffa ' Così fan tutte ' (K. 588), produced Jan. 26, 1790, but soon interrupted by the Emperor's serious illness, terminating in death on Feb. 20. Musicians had little to expect from his successor, Leopold II., and there was no break in the clouds which overshadowed poor Mozart. The rough draft is still preserved of an application for the post of second Kapellmeister, but he did not obtain it. The magistrate did indeed grant (May 9, 1791) his request to be appointed assistant, ' without pay for the present,' to the cathedral Kapellmeister, which gave him the right to succeed to this lucrative post on the death of Hoffmann the Kapellmeister, but Hoffmann outlived him.

The coronation of the Emperor Leopold at Frankfort on Oct. 9 was the occasion of his last artistic tour. Having pawned his plate to procure funds, he started on Sept. 23, and after a journey of six days arrived in the ancient Reichstadt. He gave a concert on Oct. 15, in the Stadttheater, the programme consisting entirely of his own compositions. On the return journey he visited Mainz, Mannheim and Munich. At Munich, at the Elector's request, he played at a court concert given in honour of the King of Naples. He had not been invited to play before the latter in Vienna, and he wrote to his wife with some bitterness, ' It sounds well for the court of Vienna, that members of their own family should hear me for the first time at a foreign court !' Soon after his return to Vienna, Mozart had to take leave of his best friend, for Salomon, the impresario, had come in person to carry Haydn off to London.[3] With a heavy heart he said good-bye to the only artist who understood him thoroughly, and honestly wished to see him prosper. They were never to meet again.

The year 1790 was a critical period in Mozart's life. The previous nine years, with all their hardships, had been for him one prolonged

---

2 Mozart composed a new air (K. 577) for Mlle. Ferrarese del Bene.

3 He made preliminary offers of a similar kind to Mozart.

spell of creative activity, during which he had written nearly 200 compositions of the most varied character. It has not been possible to mention more than a few of these in the course of the preceding narrative ; of the remainder the following are, perhaps, the most important : the great series of PF. concertos (K. 413-415, 449-451, 453, 456, 459, 466, 467, 482, 488, 491, 503, 537) ; two symphonies, in C (K. 425) and in D (K. 504) ; two serenades (K. 361, 375) ; two string quintets, in C (K. 515) and G min. (K. 516) ; the serenade for strings in G (' Eine kleine Nachtmusik,' K. 525) ; a ' musical joke ' for strings and two horns (K. 522) ; the quintet for PF. and wind (K. 452) ; two PF. quartets (K. 478, 493) ; a string quartet in D (K. 499) ; the E♭ divertimento for string trio (K. 563) ; the clarinet trio (K. 498) and quintet (K. 581) ; the PF. trio in E (K. 542) ; the violin sonatas in B♭ (K. 454) and A (K. 526) ; the sonata for two PF. (K. 448) ; of other PF. works the duet in F (K. 497), the sonatas in C minor (K. 457), with the fantasia (K. 475) afterwards associated with it, and in D (K. 576), the allegro and andante in F (K. 533), an adagio (K. 540), a rondo (K. 511), and two sets of variations (K. 455, 460) ; the aria for soprano ' Bella mia fiamma ' (K. 528) ; and, last but not least, the song ' Das Veilchen ' (K. 476). Towards the end of 1789 the strain seems already to have begun to tell, and in 1790 there is a marked falling off in the number of Mozart's compositions, the most important work, apart from ' Così fan tutte,' which was mainly written in 1789, being the quintet in D (K. 593), which was completed in December. In 1791 Mozart's affairs were, if anything, worse than ever, but he seems to have spurred himself to a final effort, with the result that the last year of his life is one of the most prolific periods in his whole career, and musically one of the most interesting. Apart from his last two operas and the Requiem, he wrote the string quintet in E♭ (K. 614) ; adagios for two basset-horns and bassoon (K. 410) and for two clarinets and three bassoons (K. 411) ; an adagio and rondo for harmonika, flute, oboe, violin and violoncello (K. 617) ; an adagio for harmonika solo (K. 356) ; three compositions for a mechanical organ (K. 594, 608, 616) ; his last PF. concerto (K. 595) ; the clarinet concerto (K. 622) ; a set of PF. variations (K. 613) and a minuet for PF. (K. 355) ; three lieder (K. 596-598) ; a bass air with obbligato double-bass and orchestra (K. 612) ; two masonic cantatas (K. 619, 623) ; the beautiful motet ' Ave verum corpus ' (K. 618), and a few compositions of less importance, including the inevitable dance music for the court.

In March, Schikaneder, the Salzburg acquaintance of 1780, now manager of a little theatre in the grounds of Prince Starhemberg's house in the suburb of Wieden, invited Mozart to compose a magic opera to a libretto he had himself written. Mozart, after some hesitation as to his fitness for the task, finally agreed, and set to work on the score, the greater part of which was written in a little pavilion [1] near the theatre, and in a summer-house in the little village of Josefsdorf, on the Kahlenberg, close to Vienna. To keep him in good humour, Schikaneder provided him with wine and amusing society—his enjoyment of which good things, grossly exaggerated, has tended more than anything to throw discredit upon his character.

In July, while hard at work, he received a visit from a stranger, who, enjoining secrecy, commissioned him to write a Requiem for an unknown individual.[2] The price (50, or, according to some, 100 ducats) was fixed, and Mozart set to work with the more ardour in that he had composed no church music since the Mass of 1783. But once more he was interrupted, this time by an urgent invitation from the Estates of Bohemia to compose an opera for the approaching coronation of Leopold II. at Prague. Mozart was on the point of stepping into the travelling carriage when the mysterious messenger suddenly stood before him, and asked what had become of the Requiem. Touched and distressed by the question, Mozart assured the man that he would do his best on his return ; and so saying, departed with his pupil Süssmayer. He worked hard at the opera during the journey, Süssmayer filling in the recitativo secco. The coronation took place on Sept. 6, and ' La clemenza di Tito ' (K. 621) was performed the same evening in the National Theatre, in presence of their Majesties and a select audience, who were too much absorbed by the occurrences of the day to pay great attention to the opera. Indeed, the Empress is said to have made very disparaging remarks on the ' porcheria ' of German music. Mozart, who was not well when he came to Prague, suffered severely from the strain, but he spent a few pleasant hours with his friends, and parted from them with tears.

Disappointed and suffering he reached home in the middle of September, and at once set to work with energy at Schikaneder's opera. The overture and introductory march to the second act were finished Sept. 28, and two days later, on the 30th, the ' Zauberflöte ' (K. 620) was given for the first time. Mozart conducted at the piano, Süssmayer turned over for him, and Henneberg, who had conducted the rehearsals, played the bells. It was coldly received at the outset, and at the end of the first act Mozart, looking pale and agitated, went on the stage to Schikaneder, who endeavoured to comfort him.[3]

[1] Now on the Kapuzinerberg in Salzburg, a gift from Prince Starhemberg.
[2] Proved after his death to have been Count Walsegg, an amateur anxious to be thought a great composer, who really had the Requiem performed under his own name. The messenger was his steward Leutgeb.
[3] Schenk, in his MS. autobiography, tells how he had a place in the orchestra at the first performance, and was so enchanted with the overture that he crept up to the conductor's chair seized Mozart's hand and kissed it. Mozart, putting out his right hand looked kindly at him, and stroked his cheek.

The audience recovered from their coldness so far as to call for Mozart at the close, but he was with difficulty persuaded to appear before the curtain. The interest in the opera increased, however, with each representation, and soon the ' Zauberflöte ' was as great a ' draw ' as Schikaneder could desire.

Mozart now hoped to be able to devote his whole time to the Requiem, but his late exertions and excitement had proved too much for him, sorely tried as he was in other respects. Fainting fits came on, and he fell into a state of deep depression.[1] His wife tried in vain to raise his spirits. During a drive in the Prater, he suddenly began to talk of death, and said with tears in his eyes that he was writing the Requiem for himself. ' I feel certain,' he continued, ' that I shall not be here long ; some one has poisoned me, I am convinced. I cannot shake off the idea.'[2] By the advice of his physicians, his terrified wife took the score away from him, and he rallied sufficiently to compose on Nov. 15 a cantata (K. 623) for his Lodge to words by Schikaneder. He even conducted the performance himself ; but the improvement was of short duration, and he took to his bed. Now, when it was too late, favourable prospects opened before him. He was informed that some of the nobility of Hungary had clubbed together to guarantee him a yearly sum, and at the same time a subscription was got up in Amsterdam, for which he was to furnish compositions to become the property of the subscribers. When the hour for the theatre arrived, he would follow in imagination the performance of the ' Zauberflöte,' and the Requiem continued to occupy his mind. On Dec. 4 he had the score brought to him in bed, and tried a passage, singing the alto himself, while his brother-in-law Hofer took the tenor, and Schack and Gerl from the theatre the soprano and bass. When they got to the first few bars of the Lacrimosa, it suddenly came home to him that he should never finish it, and he burst out crying, and put away the score. In the evening Süssmayer came in, and he gave him some directions about the Requiem, with which his thoughts seemed constantly occupied, for even while dozing he puffed out his cheeks as if trying to imitate the drums. Towards midnight he suddenly sat up with his eyes fixed ; then he turned his head on one side, and appeared to fall asleep. By one o'clock in the morning of Dec. 5, 1791, his spirit had fled. He died of malignant typhus

fever.[3] At three o'clock in the afternoon of the 6th his body was removed to St. Stephen's [4] ; the service was held in the open air, as was the custom with the poorest class of funeral, and van Swieten, Süssmayer, Salieri, Deiner, Roser and Orsler stood round the bier. They followed as far as the city gates, and then turned back, as a violent storm was raging, and the hearse went its way, unaccompanied, to the church-yard of St. Marx. Thus, without a note of music, forsaken by all he held dear, the remains of this prince of harmony were committed to the earth—not even in a grave of his own, but in the common paupers' grave.[5]

C. F. P. ; addns. W. H. H[W].
The whole rev. with further addns. by C. B. O.

PERSONALIA AND PORTRAITS.—Mozart was short, but slim and well-proportioned, with small feet and good hands. As a young man he was thin, and it was then that the prominence of his nose was most noticeable ; later in life he became much stouter. His head was somewhat large in proportion to his body, and he had a profusion of fine hair, of which he was rather vain. His large blue eyes were well-formed, with fine eyebrows and lashes, but as a rule they looked languid, and his gaze was restless and absent. His general appearance was perhaps somewhat insignificant, and it was partly for this reason, no doubt, that he was very particular about his clothes, and wore a good deal of embroidery and jewellery. When playing, however, his appearance was completely different. His countenance changed, his eye settled at once into a steady calm gaze, and every movement of his muscles conveyed the sentiment expressed in his playing.

Of the numerous portraits that tradition has associated with Mozart's name only a few are of indisputable authenticity. These, together with one or two which are probably though not certainly genuine, are set out in the following list [6] :

---

[1] A note (Jahn, iii. 353) to some unknown person (? Da Ponte) strikingly confirms this.
[2] It is notorious that Salieri was very much suspected, but he indignantly repudiated the accusation. His own words (reported by Niemetschek, p. 81) prove that he was not displeased at Mozart's death : ' It is indeed a pity to lose so great a genius, but his death is a good thing for us. If he had lived longer not a soul would have given us a bit of bread for our compositions.' The answer given to the accusation by Salieri's friend, Kapellmeister Schwanenberg, was, to say the least of it, remarkable : ' Pazzi ! non ha fatto niente per meritar un tal onore.' (Geese ! what has he done to deserve so great an honour ?) This legend is the subject of a powerful little sketch by Poushkin which was set to music by Rimsky-Korsakov.

[3] The official certificate gives ' ein hitziges Frieselfieber ' as the cause of death, and Schiedermair (p. 469) quotes a remarkable passage from an unpublished diary by Karl Bursy which seems to support this diagnosis. Dr. J. Barraud, however, in his study De quoi est mort Mozart ? (Chronique médicale, 1905 ; reprinted in his Promenade d'un médecin à travers l'histoire, 1906) unhesitatingly rejects it. His opinion is that Mozart's death was the result of a complete collapse of the system, brought on by prolonged overwork, and culminating in some kind of nephritis. There is no ground for the oft-repeated assertion that Mozart died of consumption.
[4] Rauhensteingasse, on the site of the present Galvan'sche Gebäude, in the vestibule of which the builder has placed a bust of Mozart.
[5] By van Swieten's orders the strictest economy was observed in the funeral arrangements. The site of the actual grave was soon forgotten ; but the city of Vienna erected on the probable spot a handsome monument by Hans Gasser, solemnly unveiled on the anniversary of Mozart's death, Dec. 5, 1859.
[6] For further information see vol. ii. of Dr. Schurig's biography (2nd ed.), pp. 441-52, the same author's Leopold Mozart : Reiseaufzeichnungen, pp. 83-97, and two excellent papers by E. Speyer, one (' Mozart at the National Gallery ') in the Burlington Magazine for Mar. 1916, and the other (' Some Notes on the Iconography of Wolfgang Amadeus Mozart ') in the Musical Quarterly for Apr. 1919. The detailed article by Emil Vogel in the Jahrb der Musikbibl. Peters für 1899 is still of value. With the exception of No. 6, all the portraits here mentioned are reproduced in Schurig's biography, and the majority of them in the 5th vol. of L. Schiedermair's ed. of the Letters.

1. 1762. An oil-painting, by an unknown artist, representing the composer in the Archduke Maximilian's gold-laced suit, given him by the Empress. This now hangs in the Mozart Museum.

2. 1763. A small family picture in water-colour painted by Carmontelle in Paris. Mozart is seated at the harpsichord, presumably accompanying his sister, who is singing. Leopold stands behind his son with his violin, possibly playing an obbligato accompaniment. The picture is preserved in several replicas, one of which is now in the National Gallery.[1] It was engraved by Delafosse,[2] and has been frequently reproduced since.

3. 1763 or 1766. An oil-painting by M. B. Ollivier, now hanging in the Louvre. It represents a tea-party in Prince Conti's salon, with Mozart—a very tiny figure—playing at the harpsichord.

4. 1764–65 ? A portrait of the young Mozart with a bird's nest in his hand, possibly by Zoffany and painted during the Mozarts' visit to London, as Zoffany's name is mentioned in Leopold Mozart's diary among the notabilities whose acquaintance he made there. The portrait, which was formerly in an English collection, was acquired in 1924 by the Salzburg Mozart-Gemeinde.

5. 1770. A portrait painted at Verona, now in the possession of Dr. K. Kupelwieser of Lunz. (See PLATE LI.) Leopold Mozart mentions ' Sgr. Cignaroli, Pittore' in the list of his acquaintance at Verona. The portrait is generally ascribed to one of several painters of that name.

6. 1770. A portrait-group by an unknown artist, painted on the occasion of Mozart's reception into the Accademia Filarmonica of Bologna (Oct. 9, 1770). The composer is shown exhibiting a contrapuntal exercise to a nobleman (Count Baldassare Carrati ?) in the presence of a third person in clerical dress (Petronio Lanzi ?, the Kapellmeister of the Academy). This picture remained unknown until 1925, when it was discovered in the shop of a dealer at Bologna, among a number of canvases purchased from the Municipality, and said to have been formerly in the possession of the Liceo Musicale.[3]

7. 1771 ? A three-quarter length oil-painting, by an unknown artist, representing Wolfgang wearing his diamond ring. This portrait, which has been in the possession of the Salzburg family of Helmreich von Brunfeld ever since Mozart's own day, is said to have been painted in Salzburg in 1771.[4]

8. 1773 ? An ivory miniature, formerly in the possession of Mozart's sister. It was possibly painted by Martin Knoller, who is mentioned by Mozart in a letter dated Feb. 20, 1773, during the composer's stay in Milan.

9. 1777. A portrait in oils representing Mozart as a ' Knight of the Golden Spur.' The original, which was painted at Bologna, has disappeared, but the Liceo Musicale possesses a copy made at Salzburg for the Padre Martini.

10. 1777. An ivory miniature, painted in Mannheim in Nov. 1777 and presented by Mozart to his cousin Marie Anna Thekla Mozart (the ' Bäsle ' of his letters). It is now in the possession of Frau Justizrat Marie Vogel of Regensburg.

11. 1780. A family group painted by J. N. della Croce at Salzburg in the autumn of 1780 and now in the Mozart Museum. The picture shows Wolfgang and Marianne playing a duet upon the harpsichord. The father is seated at the side of the instrument, and the mother's portrait hangs on the wall.

12. 1786. An engraving by G. A. Sasso after a drawing by G. B. Bosio. The original has not been preserved. Mozart is seated at the harpsichord, on the top of which lies a score of 'Figaro.' The portrait, which is certainly not flattering, bears every sign of having been done from the life.

13. 1788. The profile by Leonard Posch, the best-known of all portraits of the composer. This has been preserved in many forms, the relation of

which to one another has only recently been established.[5] There are two main types. In the first the head and neck only are shown ; the hair falls in loose curls, and there is no indication of any clothing. The second shows the complete bust ; the hair is dressed in the typical Mozartian manner and the composer is wearing a cloak. The original of the first type is undoubtedly a wax-relief now in the Mozart Museum at Salzburg. It bears the artist's signature on the back and is dated 1788. In 1820 it was presented by him to the composer's son Franz Xaver Wolfgang, who ultimately presented it to the Museum. Posch seems also to have made a number of plaster copies of it, one of which is now in the possession of Fräulein Hildegard Lehnert of Berlin. The second type represents a later and more realistic treatment of the same portrait, possibly undertaken at the request of Mozart's friends. The original, which was in a mixture of plaster and wax, has now disappeared. It was formerly in the possession of the sculptor C. Waschmann, who took a bronze cast from it in 1904, which is now in the Department of Coins and Medals of the National Museum at Vienna. This version has been preserved in two other forms which may both have been the work of Posch himself : in a box-wood relief, and on a belt-clasp, said to have belonged formerly to the composer's wife. Both are now in the Mozart Museum. The well-known engravings by J. G. Mansfeld (during Mozart's lifetime) and by A. Kohl (1793) were also based on this second type.

14. 1789. A portrait in silver-point by Dora Stock, the sister-in-law of Körner and friend of Schiller, drawn during Mozart's short stay in Dresden in 1789, and now in the Musikbibliothek Peters at Leipzig. Artistically this is the finest of all the portraits.

15. 1791 ? An unfinished portrait by Lange, Mozart's brother-in-law, now in the Mozart Museum. Mozart is shown, seated at the piano, apparently absorbed in improvisation. The date of this picture has been the subject of much discussion.[6] Tradition associates it with the last year of the composer's life, possibly on account of its unfinished character. Some writers, on the other hand, maintain that it was the original of one of a pair of miniatures (now lost, but preserved in the form of lithograph illustrations to Nissen's biography) which Mozart sent to his father in 1783. This, however, is a pure assumption, and in the absence of definite information the later date, which the character of the portrait seems to support, may be accepted.

These are the only portraits of Mozart the credentials of which can be considered satisfactory.[7] Of the doubtful or unauthenticated portraits the best-known are those ascribed to T. Helbling, A. de Saint-Aubin, P. Battoni, Greuze and Tischbein. Full particulars of these and of numerous other portraits will be found in the literature referred to above.

Mozart was fond of active exercise, which was the more necessary as he suffered materially in health from his habit of working far into the night. At one time he took a regular morning ride, but had to give it up, not being able to conquer his nervousness. It was replaced by billiards and skittles, his fondness for which we have already mentioned. He even had a billiard-table in his own house : ' Many and many a game have I played with him,' says Kelly, ' but always came off second best.' When no one else was there he would play with

---

[1] Reproduced in the Burlington Magazine, Mar. 1916. Another is preserved in the Musée Chantilly, and there are at least two versions in private collections in England.

[2] It is curious that Leopold Mozart in a letter dated Apr. 1, 1764, explicitly states that the portrait was being engraved by ' M. de Mechel ' (Christian von Mechel, 1736-1813).

[3] See the articles by H. Prunières (Rev. musicale, Oct. 1925) and by R. Schade (Die Musik, Feb. 1926). Both are accompanied by reproductions of the picture.

[4] Dr. Schurig prefers to date it about 1774, but does not give his reasons. In 1926 it was acquired for the Mozart Museum.

[5] By R. Lewicki, in two papers in the Zeitschrift für Musikwissenschaft, 1919–1920. See also a note in the Mozarteums Mitteilungen for Feb.-May 1921.

[6] See especially the article by E. Speyer in the Musical Quarterly for Apr. 1919, where a good case is made out for the later date.

[7] While Mozart lay on his death-bed Count Deym, for whose mechanical clock he had written one or two pieces, took a death-mask, and with its aid constructed a wax figure which he dressed in the composer's clothes and exhibited in his gallery. The mask, or at least a copy of it, remained in the widow's possession, until she smashed it one day while cleaning. She is said to have remarked that ' she was glad that that was the end of the hateful old thing.' (Schurig, L. Mozart, p. 92, Constanze Mozart, p. 26 ; L. Nohl, Mozart nach der Schilderungen seiner Zeitgenossen, p. 393.)

MOZART

From a painting by an unknown artist, in the collection of the late Dr. Karl Kupelwieser

his wife, or even by himself. His favourite amusement of all, however, was dancing, for which Vienna afforded ample opportunities. This, too, Kelly mentions (i. 226): 'Mme. Mozart told me that, great as his genius was, he was an enthusiast for dancing, and often said that his taste lay in that art, rather than in music.'

In society Mozart found amusement of the highest kind, and inspiration, as well as affection and true sympathy. No house offered him so much of these as that of Countess Thun, whom he described as 'the most charming and attractive lady I have ever seen.' Other associates were the Countess's son-in-law and Mozart's pupil Prince Karl Lichnowsky, Hofrath von Born, Baron Otto von Gemmingen, Hofrath von Spielmann, Prince Kaunitz, Count Cobenzl, Field-Marshal Haddik, Geheimrath von Kees, who had weekly orchestral concerts at his house, the botanist Jacquin and his son and daughter, Count Hatzfeld, an intimate friend who played in his quartets, Kaufmann Bridi, a good tenor who sang in 'Idomeneo,' the families Greiner, Martinez and Ployer, all of whom had constant music, and the Baron van Swieten, who kindled his enthusiasm for the works of Bach and Handel. Another great admirer of his was Barisani the physician, 'that noble man, my best and dearest friend, who saved my life' (when seriously ill in 1784), and whose unexpected death in 1787 was a great shock to him. It is easy to imagine how gratefully the composer enjoyed the refreshment of social intercourse after long hours of solitary creative work. On such occasions he was full of fun, ready at a moment's notice to pour out a stream of doggerel rhymes or irresistibly droll remarks; in short, he was a frank, open-hearted child, whom it was almost impossible to identify with Mozart the great artist. His brother-in-law Lange [1] says that he was never so unlike a 'great man' as when he was occupied with some important work.

It has been reiterated *ad nauseam* that Mozart was a drunkard, whose indulgence in this and cognate vices brought him to an early grave,[2] but that such a charge was totally unfounded no one who has studied his life can doubt for a moment. That, like other people, he enjoyed a good glass of wine nobody can deny, but his laborious life and the prodigious number of his compositions convincingly prove that he was never given to excess. Those who accused him of intemperance also magnified his debts tenfold when he died, and thus inflicted grievous injury on his widow.[3] These 'friends' propagated the worst reports as to his domestic affairs and constant embarrassments. Undoubtedly his

wife was a bad manager, and this was a serious defect in a household which only acquired a regular income (800 fl., about £80!) in 1788, and whose resources before and after that time were most irregular. Her constant illnesses, too, were a great additional burden. Though naturally unfitted for anything of the kind, Mozart made many serious attempts to regulate his expenses, and would every now and then keep strict accounts of income and expenditure, but these good resolutions did not last.[4] In most cases he was led astray by sheer good-nature, as he never could refuse any one in need. His kindness was grievously abused by false friends, whose acquaintance was damaging to his character, but he never learned prudence. The worst offender in this respect was Stadler, the eminent clarinet-player, who often dined at his table, and repeatedly wheedled money out of him under pretext of poverty. After all that had passed, Mozart composed a concerto (K.622) for Stadler's tour, finishing it two days only before the production of the 'Zauberflöte,' when he was, of course, particularly hard pressed.

Mozart was brought up by his father as a pious Catholic, and although subsequently, when he became interested in freemasonry, he found himself drifting further and further away from strict orthodoxy, he never definitely broke with the Church. The peculiar tone— there is more than a trace of mysticism in it —which his religious opinions took on in his later years comes out clearly in a letter which he wrote to his father in Apr. 1787, when Leopold was already lying on his death-bed. 'As death,' he writes, 'is, strictly speaking, the true end and aim of our lives, I have for the last two years made myself so well acquainted with this true, best friend of mankind, that his image no longer terrifies, but calms and consoles me. And I thank God for giving me the opportunity (you know what I mean [5]) of learning to look upon death as the key which unlocks the gate of true bliss. I never lie down to rest without thinking that, young as I am, before the dawn of another day I may be no more; and yet nobody who knows me would call me morose and discontented. For this blessing I thank my Creator every day, and wish from my heart that I could share it with all my fellow-men.' The best commentary on this passage is Mozart's own 'Maurerische Trauermusik,' written some two years before.

A few words on various aspects of Mozart's life as an artist may serve as a suitable transition to a discussion of his music. First, as to his methods of composition. There can be no

1 *Biographie des Joseph Lange k. k. Hofschauspielers* (Vienna, 1808, p. 172).
2 Compare Schlichtegroll's *Nekrolog*: Arnold's language is even worse (*Mozart's Geist*, p. 65).
3 His association with Schikaneder gave some colour to the reports. Hummel protested vehemently against such accusations.

4 In one of these orderly fits he began (1784) a thematic register of all his compositions as they were completed, and continued the practice up to a short time before his death. This invaluable document was first published by André in 1805 (revised ed. 1828).
5 A reference to the doctrine of the Freemasons.

doubt that with Mozart the creative process was to a very large extent completed before he put pen to paper. The work of recording his ideas was in the main a purely mechanical task, and one that he always tried to postpone to the very last moment. But his thoughts were always occupied with music. 'You know,' he wrote to his father, ' that I am, so to speak, swallowed up in music, that I am busy with it all day—speculating, studying, considering.' Many works which seemed to be thrown off on the spur of the moment may thus have been the fruit of long meditation : the rapidity with which he committed them to paper, often in the intervals of playing billiards or skittles, must not be taken to imply a careless and light-hearted attitude towards his art. His handwriting was always, even when he was most hurried, beautifully neat and clear, and he very rarely found it necessary to make any alterations and erasures. Several manuscripts have, however, been preserved which show that he occasionally made preliminary sketches for passages which presented some special difficulty.

As a performer Mozart distinguished himself as a virtuoso on the pianoforte, organ and violin ; the viola, which he preferred to the violin in later life, he played only when he took part in chamber music with his friends. As a pianist he impressed his contemporaries above all by his marvellous gift of extemporisation. ' If I might have the fulfilment of one wish on earth,' said his biographer Niemetschek, ' it would be to hear Mozart improvise once more on the piano ; those who never heard him cannot have the faintest idea what it was.' The qualities in performance on which he laid the greatest stress were a singing tone, a quiet steady hand, a strict sense of time, and a smoothness of execution that made rapid passage-work 'flow like oil.'

As a teacher of music Mozart was never in very great request. Such men as Steffan, Kozeluch and Righini had a far larger number of pupils. Mozart, it is true, hated the work, but poverty often drove him to it, and from 1778 till the end of his life he was scarcely ever free from the necessity of giving lessons, either in clavier-playing or in composition. When he found pupils who could really profit by his instruction he spared no pains, although even with them he was never methodical enough to make an ideal teacher. When Hummel came to him in 1787 he took him into his house in order to be able to supervise his instruction more thoroughly, but, as it turned out, his lessons were extremely irregular, and the less tangible influences of daily intercourse with the master were probably of more value to him than any special tuition that he received. Thomas Attwood, who came to him from Italy in Aug. 1785 to study composition and, accord-

ing to Kelly, became his favourite pupil,[1] used to say that Mozart ' would at any time rather play a game of billiards with him than give him a lesson.' Kelly himself, who had some talent for song-writing, wished to have some instruction from Mozart in composition, but the latter dissuaded him from it, on the ground that it was too late for technical training to do him anything but harm.[2] Mozart also gave lessons in composition to a niece of his friend the Abbé Stadler. The music book in which she worked her exercises is still preserved in the Nationalbibliothek at Vienna, and is interesting as showing how strictly Mozart kept to the orthodox ' theory ' of the day, however much he may have seasoned its exposition with characteristic jokes and playful remarks.[3] His pianoforte pupils were more numerous, and included several ladies, some of them of high rank. Of the majority little is recorded except that they were Mozart's pupils, and perhaps that recognition was all that they sought. Others, however, such as Franziska von Jacquin, Barbara Ployer, Josephine Aurnhammer, and above all Frau von Trattnern, wife of the wealthy bookseller, possessed real talent, and some of the composer's best music was written specially for them.[4]

MUSIC

Köchel's catalogue of Mozart's compositions records roughly some 600 authentic works that have been preserved, and a large number which, when he compiled his list, were considered to be of doubtful genuineness or were known only by name. Very few of these works were printed in Mozart's lifetime, although many were in circulation in manuscript copies. Practically the whole of this vast mass of music has, however, now been published in the standard edition of the master's works issued by Breitkopf & Härtel. The following classified list, based on the catalogue of this edition, and providing a rough index to it, shows at a glance the number and variety of the works included. Wherever possible the year of composition has been added, as established by the latest research. In many cases, however, the dates given are conjectural only.

1 *Reminiscences*, i. 228. ' Attwood is a young man for whom I have a sincere affection and esteem : he conducts himself with great propriety, and I feel much pleasure in telling you that he partakes more of my style than any scholar I ever had, and I predict that he will prove a sound musician.' Mozart's tuition was certainly the making of Attwood. In spite of two years' study under Neapolitan masters he seems to have been amazingly ignorant when he came to Vienna. The exercises which he worked under Mozart have been preserved (they are at present in the possession of the reviser of this article) and show that in spite of the composer's dislike to teaching, he was ready to take great pains even over the most elementary matters once he became interested in his pupil.
2 *Reminiscences*, i. 227.
3 This music book forms the main subject of an excellent monograph by Dr. R. Lach, *W. A. Mozart als Theoretiker* (Vienna, 1918).
4 For Franziska von Jacquin he wrote the Clarinet Trio (K. 498) ; for Barbara Ployer, the Sonata for two pianos (K. 448) and two PF. concertos (K. 449, 453) ; for Josephine Aurnhammer (presumably), the six violin sonatas which he dedicated to 'her (K. 376, 296, 377-380) ; for Frau von Trattnern, the Fantasia and Sonata for PF. in C min. (K. 457, 475), about which he is said to have written her two interesting letters, which have, unfortunately, disappeared.

I. VOCAL

Series 1. 15 Masses: K. 49 in G (1768), K. 65 in D min. (1769), K. 66 in C (1769), K. 139 in C min. (1772), K. 167 in C (1773), K. 192 in F (1774), K. 194 in D (1774), K. 220 in C (1775), K. 257 in C (1776), K. 258 in C (1776), K. 259 in C (1776), K. 262 in C (1776), K. 275 in B♭ (1777), K. 317 in C (1779), K. 337 in C (1780). [See also Ser. 24.]

Series 2. 4 Litanies: K. 109 in B♭ (1771), K. 125 in B♭ (1772), K. 195 in D (1774), K. 243 in E♭ (1776); 2 Vespers: K. 321 in C (1779), K. 339 in C (1780); 1 Dixit and Magnificat: K. 193 (1774).

Series 3. 5 Kyries: K. 33 in F (1766), K. 89 in G (1770), K. 322 in E♭ (1778 ?), K. 323 in C (unfinished, 1779 ?), K. 341 in D min. (1781); 3 'Regina coeli's': K. 108 in C (1771), K. 127 in B♭ (1772), K. 276 in C (1780); 6 Offertories: K. 34 in F (1766), K. 72 in G (1771), K. 117 in C (1770), K. 198 in F (of doubtful authenticity), K. 260 in D (1776), K. 277 in F (1777); and a number of smaller works for the Church, the most important of which is the Motet 'Ave verum corpus' (K. 618, 1791).

Series 4. A Passion Cantata ('Grabmusik,' K. 42, 1767); 'Die Maurerfreude,' cantata (K. 471, 1785); 'Eine kleine Freimaurer-Kantate' (K. 623, 1791); 'La Betulia liberata,' oratorio (K. 118, 1771); 'Davidde penitente,' cantata (K. 469, 1785).

Series 5. 'Die Schuldigkeit des ersten Gebotes' (K. 35, 1766), sacred Singspiel in 3 parts (the first only by Mozart); 'Apollo et Hyacinthus,' Latin comedy (K. 38, 1767); 'Bastien und Bastienne,' German operetta, 1 act (K. 50, 1768); 'La finta semplice,' opera-buffa, 3 acts (K. 51, 1768); 'Mitridate, Rè di Ponto,' opera seria, 3 acts (K. 87, 1770); 'Ascanio in Alba,' theatrical serenade, 2 acts (K. 111, 1771); 'Il sogno di Scipione,' dramatic serenade, 1 act (K. 126, 1772); 'Lucio Silla, dramma per musica,' 3 acts (K. 135, 1772); 'La finta giardiniera (Die Gärtnerin aus Liebe),' opera-buffa, 3 acts (K. 196, 1774); 'Il rè pastore,' dramatic cantata, 2 acts (K. 208, 1775); 'Zaide,' German opera, 2 acts, unfinished (K. 344, 1779 ?); choruses and entr'actes to 'Thamos, König in Ägypten, heroisches Drama' (K. 345, 1773, partly rewritten 1779); 'Idomeneo, Rè di Creta, ossia Ilia ed Idamante,' opera-seria, 3 acts (K. 366, 1780–81); 'Die Entführung aus dem Serail, komisches Singspiel, 3 acts (K. 384, 1782); 'Der Schauspieldirektor,' comedy with music, 1 act (K. 486, 1786); 'Le nozze di Figaro,' opera-buffa, 4 acts (K. 492, 1786); 'Il dissoluto punito, ossia Il Don Giovanni,' opera-buffa, 2 acts (K. 527, 1787); 'Così fan tutte,' opera-buffa, 2 acts (K. 588, 1790); 'La clemenza di Tito,' opera-seria, 2 acts (K. 621, 1791); 'Die Zauberflöte,' German opera, 2 acts (K. 620, 1791). [See also Ser. 24.]

Series 6. 46 airs, duets, terzets and quartets, with orchestral accompaniment, of which the most important are (1) for soprano solo: a scena 'Ah, lo previdi' (K. 272, 1777), a recitative and aria 'Alcandro lo confesso,' 'Non sò donde viene' (K. 294, 1778), a recitative and aria 'Popoli di Tessaglia' (K. 316, 1779), a scena and aria 'Mia speranza,' 'Ah non sai qual pena' (K. 416, 1783), an aria 'Vorrei spiegarvi,' 'Ah Conte, partite' (K. 418, 1783), a scena and rondo 'Ch' io mi scordi,' 'Non temer amato bene,' with PF. obbligato (K. 505, 1786), and a scena 'Bella mia fiamma' (K. 528, 1787); (2) for alto: a recitative and aria 'Ombra felice,' 'Io ti lascio' (K. 255, 1776); (3) for tenor: the arias 'Se al labbro mio' (K. 295, 1778) and 'Per pietà, non ricercate' (K. 420, 1783), and the recitative and aria 'Misero, o sogno!' (K. 431, 1783); and (4) for bass: the recitatives and arias 'Così dunque tradisci' (K. 432, 1783) and 'Non so donde vieni' (K. 512, 1787), and the arias 'Mentre ti lascio, o figlia' (K. 513, 1787) and 'Rivolgete a lui lo sguardo' (K. 584, 1789).

Series 7. 34 Lieder for solo voice with PF. accompaniment, of which the most important are: 'An die Hoffnung' (K. 390, 1780), 'Der Zauberer' (K. 472, 1785), 'Das Veilchen' (K. 476, 1785), 'Als Luise die Briefe ihres ungetreuen Liebhabers verbrannte' (K. 520, 1787), 'Das Lied der Trennung' (K. 519, 1787) and 'Abendempfindung' (K. 523, 1787); a Masonic song 'Zerfliesset heut', geliebte Brüder,' with chorus and organ accompaniment (K. 483, 1785); a Masonic chorus, in three parts, with organ accompaniment (K. 484, 1785); 'eine kleine deutsche Kantate' for solo voice with PF. accompaniment (K. 619, 1791); a comic terzet (Das Bandel) for soprano, tenor and bass (K. 441, 1783); and 21 canons for 2 or more voices.

II. INSTRUMENTAL

(i.) Orchestral Works

Series 8. 39 Symphonies: K. 16 in E♭ (1764), K. 17 in B♭ (1764), K. 19 in D (1765), K. 22 in B♭ (1765), K. 43 in F (1767), K. 45 in D (1768), K. 48 in D (1768), K. 73 in C (1771), K. 74 in G (1771), K. 84 in D (1770), K. 110 in G (1771), K. 112 in F (1771) K. 114 in A (1771), K. 124 in G (1772), K. 128 in C (1772), K. 129 in G (1772), K. 130 in F (1772, K. 132 in E♭ (1772), K. 133 in D (1772), K. 134 in A (1772), K. 162 in C (1773), K. 181 in D (1773), K. 182 in B♭ (1773), K. 183 in G min. (1773–74), K. 184 in E♭ (1773), K. 199 in G (1773), K. 200 in C (1773), K. 201 in A (1774), K. 202 in D (1774), K. 297 in D (the Paris Symphony, 1778), K. 318 in G (1779), K. 319 in B♭ (1779), K. 338 in C (1780), K. 385 in D (the Haffner Symphony, 1782), K. 425 in C (1783), K. 504 in D (1786), K. 543 in E♭ (1788), K. 550 in G min. (1788), K. 551 in C (the Jupiter Symphony, 1788). [See also Ser. 24.]

Series 9. 2 'Cassations,' K. 63 in G (1769), K. 99 in B♭ (1766–1767); 8 Serenades for strings and wind: K. 100 in D (1767 ?), K. 101 in F (1776), K. 185 in D (1773), K. 203 in D (1774), K. 204 in D (1775), K. 250 in D (the Haffner Serenade, 1776), K. 286 in D (Nocturne for 4 orchestras, 1777), K. 320 in D (1779); a Serenade for 2 string orchestras, one with drums (K. 239, 1776); 3 serenades for wind instruments: K. 361 in B♭ (for 13 instruments; 1780, with additions in 1790 ?), K. 375 in E♭ (1781), and K. 388 in C min. (1782); 7 Divertimenti for strings and wind: K. 113 in E♭ (1771), K. 131 in D (1772), K. 205 in D (1773), K. 247 in F (1776), K. 251 in D (1776), K. 287 in B♭ (1777), K. 334 in D (1779); and 10 Divertimenti for wind instruments: K. 166 in E♭ (1773), K. 186 in B♭ (1772–73), K. 187 in C (1773–75), K. 188 in C (1776–77), K. 213 in F (1775), K. 240 in B♭ (1776), K. 252 in E♭ (1776), K. 253 in F (1776), K. 270 in B♭ (1777), and K. 289 in E♭ (1777).

Series 10. 10 sets of Marches for orchestra; 2 symphonic movements; 'Maurerische Trauermusik' for orchestra (K. 477, 1785); 'Ein musikalischer Spass' for 2 vlns., vla., bass, 2 horns (K. 522, 1787); a Sonata for bassoon and violoncello (K. 292, 1774–75); an Adagio for 2 basset horns and bassoon (K. 410, 1789–90); an Adagio for 2 clarinets and 3 basset horns (K. 411, 1789–90); an Adagio for harmonika (K. 356, 1791); an Adagio and Rondo for harmonika, flute, ob., vla. and v'cl. (K. 617, 1791); a Fantasia (K. 608), and an Andante (K. 616) for a mechanical organ, both completed in 1791. [See also Ser. 24.]

Series 11. 23 sets of Dances for orchestra.

Series 12. Concertos other than those for PF., 5 Concertos for vln.: K. 207 in B♭ (1775), K. 211 in D (1775), K. 216 in G (1775), K. 218 in D (1775), K. 219 in A (1775); 2 Rondos for vln.: K. 269 in B♭ (1776), K. 373 in C (1781); a 'Concertone' for 2 solo vlns. (K. 190, 1773); a 'Sinfonie concertante' for vln. and vla. (K. 364, 1779); a bassoon concerto (K. 191, 1774); a concerto for flute and harp (K. 299, 1778); 2 flute concertos: K. 313 in G (1778), K. 314 in D (1778); an Andante for flute (K. 315, 1778); 4 horn concertos: K. 412 in D (1782), K. 417 in E♭ (1783), K. 447 in E♭ (1783 ?), K. 495 in E♭ (1786); and a clarinet concerto (K. 622, 1791). [See also Ser. 24.]

(ii.) Chamber Music Works for PF., etc.

Series 13. 7 Quintets for 2 vlns., 2 vlas. and v'cl.: K. 174 in B♭ (1773), K. 406 in C min. (1782), K. 515 in C (1787), K. 516 in G min. (1787), K. 593 in D (1790); a Quintet for vln., 2 vlas., horn and v'cl. (K. 407, 1782 ?); a Quintet for clarinet 2 vlns., vla. and v'cl. (K. 581, 1789); 'Eine kleine Nachtmusik' for 2 vlns., vla., v'cl. and bass (K. 525, 1787).

Series 14. 23 Quartets for 2 vlns., vla., and v'cl.: K. 80 in G (1770), K. 155 in D (1772), K. 156 in G (1772), K. 157 in C (1772–1773), K. 158 in F (1773 ?), K. 159 in B♭ (1773), K 160 in E♭ (1773), K. 168 in F (1773), K. 169 in A (1773), K. 170 in C (1773), K. 171 in E♭ (1773), K. 172 in B♭ (1773), K. 173 in D min. (1773), K. 387 in G (1782), K. 421 in D min. (1783), K. 428 in E♭ (1783), K. 458 in B♭ (1784), K. 464 in A (1785), K. 465 in C (1785), K. 499 in D (1786), K. 575 in D (1789), K. 589 in B♭ (1790), K. 590 in F (1790); 3 Divertimenti for 2 vlns., vla., and bass (1772): K. 136 in D, K. 137 in B♭, K. 138 in F; an Adagio and Fugue for string quartet (K. 546, 1788); 2 flute quartets: K. 285 in D (1777) and K. 298 in A (1778); 1 oboe quartet: K. 370 (1781).

Series 15. 2 Duos for vln. and vla. (K. 423, 424; completed 1783); a Divertimento for vln., vla. and v'cl. (K. 563, 1788).

Series 16. 25 Concertos for solo, PF. and orchestra, the first 4 adaptations only: K. 37, 39–41 (1767), K. 175 in D (1773), K. 238 in B♭ (1776), K. 246 in C (1776), K. 271 in E♭ (1777), K. 413 in F (1782), K. 414 in A (1782), K. 415 in C (1782), K. 449 in E♭ (1784), K. 450 in B♭ (1784), K. 451 in D (1784), K. 453 in G (1784), K. 456 in B♭ (1784), K. 459 in F (1784), K. 466 in D min. (1785), K. 467 in C (1785), K. 482 in E♭ (1785), K. 488 in A (1786), K. 491 in C min. (1786), K. 503 in C (1786), K. 537 in D (the Coronation Concerto,' 1788), and K. 595 in B♭ (1791); one Rondo for PF. and orchestra (K. 382, 1782); one Concerto for 2 PF. (K. 365, 1779); and one for 3 PF. (K. 242, 1776).

Series 17. A Quintet for PF., ob., clar., horn, and bassoon (K. 452, 1784); 2 Quartets for PF., vln., vla., and v'cl.: K. 478 in G min. (1785), K. 493 in E♭ (1786); 7 Trios for PF., vln., and v'cl.: K. 254 in B♭ (1776), K. 442 in D min. (really 3 unrelated movements), K. 496 in G (1786), K. 502 in B♭ (1786), K. 542 in E (1788), K. 548 in C (1788) and K. 564 in G (1788); a Trio for PF., clar. and vla. (K. 498, 1786).

Series 18. 35 Sonatas for PF. and vln.: K. 6 in C (1763–64), K. 7 in D (1763–64), K. 8 in B♭ (1763), K. 9 in G (1764), K. 10 in B♭ (1764), K. 11 in G (1764), K. 12 in A (1764), K. 13 in F (1764), K. 14 in C (1764), K. 15 in B♭ (1764), K. 26 in E♭ (1766), K. 27 in G (1766), K. 28 in C (1766), K. 29 in D (1766), K. 30 in F (1766), K. 31 in B♭ (1766), K. 296 in C (1778), K. 301 in G (1778), K. 302 in E♭ (1778), K. 303 in C (1778), K. 304 in E min. (1778), K. 305 in A (1778), K. 306 in D (1778), K. 376 in F (1781), K. 377 in F (1781), K. 378 in B♭ (1781), K. 379 in G (1781), K. 380 in E♭ (1781), K. 402 in A (1782), K. 403 in C (1782), K. 454 in B♭ (1784), K. 481 in E♭ (1785), K. 526 in A (1787), K. 547 in F (1788); an Allegro (K. 372, 1781) and an Andante and Allegretto (K. 404, 1782 ?); 2 sets of variations for PF. and vln. (K. 359, K. 360, 1781).

Series 19. 5 Sonatas for PF. duet: K. 357 in G (1786), K. 358 in B♭ (1774), K. 381 in D (1772 ?), K. 497 in F (1786), K. 521 in C (1787); a set of Variations for PF. duet (K. 501, 1786); a Fugue for 2 PF. (K. 426, 1783); a Sonata for 2 PF. (K. 448, 1781).

Series 20. 17 Sonatas for PF. solo: K. 279 in C (1774), K. 280 in F (1774), K. 281 in B♭ (1774), K. 282 in E♭ (1773–74), K. 283 in G (1774), K. 284 in D (1775), K. 309 in C (1777), K. 310 in A min. (1778), K. 311 in D (1777), K. 330 in C (1778), K. 331 in A (1778), K. 332 in F (1778), K. 333 in B♭ (1778), K. 457 in C min. (1784), K. 545 in C (1788), K. 570 in B♭ (1789), K. 576 in D (1789); a Fantasia and Fugue in C (K. 394, 1782); 3 Fantasias: K. 396 in C min. (1782–84), K. 397 in D min. (1782), K. 475 in C min. (1785).

Series 21. 15 sets of variations for PF.: on an Allegretto in G (K. 24, 1766), on 'Willem von Nassau' (K. 25, 1766), on a Minuet by Fischer (K. 179, 1774), on 'Mio caro Adone' (K. 180, 1773), on 'Lison dormait' (K. 264, 1778), on 'Ah, vous dirai-je, Maman' (K. 265, 1778), on a March from Grétry's 'Mariages samnites' (K. 352, 1782), on 'La Belle Françoise' (K. 353, 1778), on 'Je suis Lindor' (K. 354, 1778), on 'Salve tu Domine' (K. 398, 1782 ?), on 'Unser dumme Pöbel' (K. 455, 1784), on 'Come un agnello' (K. 460, 1784), on an Allegretto in B♭ (K. 500, 1786), on a Minuet by Duport (K. 573, 1789), on 'Ein Weib ist das herrlichste Ding' (K. 613, 1791).

Series 22. 18 miscellaneous pieces for PF.: 6 Minuets, including the well-known one in D (K. 355, 1789–90 ?); 3 Rondos: K. 485 in D (1786), K. 494 in F (1786), K. 511 in A min. (1787); an unfinished Suite in the Handelian style (K. 399, 1782–84 ?); a Fugue in G min. (K. 401, 1782); an Allegro in B♭ (K. 3, 1762); an Allegro of a Sonata in G min. (K. 312, 1774 ?); an Allegro and Andante in F and B♭ (K. 533, 1788); an Andantino in E♭ (K. 236, 1790 ?); an Adagio in B min. (K. 540, 1788); a Gigue in G (K. 574, 1789); 36 Cadenzas to 14 of the PF. Concertos (K. 624).

Series 23. 17 Sonatas for Organ with accompaniment (chiefly for 2 vlns. and bass.): K. 67 in E♭ (1771 ?), K. 68 in B♭ (1771 ?), K. 69 in D (1771 ?), K. 144 in D (1772), K. 145 in F (1772),

K. 212 in B♭ (1775), K. 224 in F (1776), K. 225 in A (1775-76), K. 244 in F (1776), K. 245 in D (1776), K. 274 in G (1777), K. 278 in C (1777), K. 328 in C (1779), K. 329 in C (1779), K. 336 in C (1780).

SERIES 24. Supplement containing, in addition to a few doubtful works, some 60 works which are either incomplete or were rediscovered too late for inclusion in their proper classes. The most important are: the Requiem (K. 626, 1791), the unfinished Mass in C min. (K. 427, 1782), the unfinished operas 'L' oca del Cairo' (K. 422) and 'Lo sposo deluso' (K. 430), both completed in 1783, 5 Symphonies (K. 75 in F, 1771; K. 76 in F, 1767; K. 95 in D, 1770; K. 96 in C, 1772; K. 97 in D, 1770), the Ballet Music to the pantomime 'Les Petits Riens' (K. Anh. 10, 1778), a 'Sinfonie concertante' for ob., clar., horn and bassoon, with orchestra accompaniment (K. Anh. 9, 1778), and an Adagio and Allegro for mechanical organ (PF. arrangement; K. 594, 1790). Mozart's adaptations of Handel's 'Acis,' 'Messiah,' 'Alexander's Feast' and 'Ode on St. Cecilia's Day' are also included in this supplement.

It is hardly necessary to say that the compositions contained in this list vary greatly in merit. Some are youthful and immature; others are experiments in which Mozart is endeavouring to assimilate a strange technique; others (and these form a fairly numerous class) are *pièces d'occasion* written without enthusiasm in the fulfilment of his duties as a court composer, or, at the best, to oblige patrons and pupils whose abilities and limitations had carefully to be regarded. But nothing is more remarkable in Mozart's career than the versatility with which he was able to adapt himself to the most varied and hampering conditions, and when everything of merely ephemeral importance has been eliminated, there still remain an astonishingly large number of compositions which, even at the present day, seem to have lost little, if any, of their vitality. We can here do no more than discuss the more important works in each class.[1]

THE PIANO, ETC.—It will be convenient to consider first the compositions for pianoforte solo, as it is through them that the average student gains his first introduction to Mozart's music. On the whole, they do not represent the composer at his best, and they certainly give but an imperfect idea of his pianoforte technique, which is most fully exemplified in the concertos. The majority of them are comparatively early works and exhibit passing mannerisms of style which Mozart soon outgrew. Thus, whilst most sides of his genius—his wit, humour, melancholy and passion—find expression in them, it is only to a limited extent. The customary explanation—that they were written mainly for pupils—will hardly serve. The first six sonatas (K. 279-284), which are on the whole the weakest, were not, so far as is known, written for pupils, and were certainly frequently performed by Mozart himself in the course of his tours. On the other hand, the Sonatas in C min. (K. 457) and in D (K. 576), written respectively for Frau von Trattnern and Princess Frederica of Prussia, are among the composer's best works in this form. The fact that one or two are slight and unpretentious does not preclude the possibility that Mozart wrote them for his own use: he was accustomed to adapt himself to his company. Some of them, moreover, seem

[1] More space has been devoted to the discussion of works which, in the writer's opinion, are unduly neglected or often misinterpreted, than to criticism of the acknowledged masterpieces.

to call for the clavichord for their proper performance, although Mozart soon developed the clavichord style of the earlier works into a technique more suited to the already fashionable pianoforte. The last sonata of the first group (K. 284, written in 1775) already demands the new instrument; in the C min. sonata (K. 457, written in 1784) full use is made of all its resources, including its greatly increased compass. This sonata is undoubtedly the finest of those written for the solo instrument; of the others only the comparatively early work in A min. (K. 310, 1778) displays anything like the same intensity of fire and passion. Next in importance comes the unfinished Sonata in F (K. 533, 1788; afterwards published with the rondo K. 494), the allegro of which is remarkable for the boldness of its counterpoint, and the andante for some interesting harmonic progressions. Ingenuity of contrapuntal treatment also distinguishes the brilliant Sonata in D (K. 576, 1789), sometimes known as the 'Trumpet sonata' from the fanfare-like character of its opening theme. Of the earlier sonatas that in A min. has already been mentioned. In complete contrast with it is the delightful work in A maj. (K. 331, 1778), with a set of variations as opening movement and a spirited 'Rondo alla Turca' as finale. Of other works for PF. solo the Fantasia in C min. (K. 475, 1785) is of special importance: its earnestness of mood and dramatic force make it a worthy prelude to the sonata in the same key with which it was afterwards united. The Fantasias in C (K. 395, 1778), in C min. (K. 396, 1782-84), and in D min. (K. 397, 1782) are in a different style, being indeed strongly reminiscent of Philip Emanuel Bach, particularly the two former works, which are almost of the character of free improvisations. Another Fantasia in C (K. 394, 1782) forms the prelude to a fine fugue in the Handelian manner. Handel also served as model for the unfinished suite (K. 399, 1782-84?), in which Mozart seems to revel in the keen harmonic clashes resulting from an unsparing polyphony. A little masterpiece in the same somewhat impersonal style is the gigue (K. 574) which the composer wrote at Leipzig in 1789 in the album of the court organist Engel. The Rondo in A min. (K. 511, 1787) and the Adagio in B min. (K. 540, 1788) have, on the other hand, all the intimacy of personal confessions, and breathe that spirit of noble resignation which is so characteristic of Mozart's later years. Technically they are of great interest: the rondo for the homogeneity of its form and the adagio for its keen harmonies. In both works the writing is often more quartet-like in style than specifically pianistic. The variations for PF. solo are mostly of the ornamental or 'melismatic' type, in which the melodic outline of the original theme is easily recognisable throughout. Curiously enough the set which is most free in style (the variations on 'Mio caro Adone,' K. 180, 1773) is also one of the earliest. The best of them, such as those on 'Unser dummer Pöbel meint' (K. 455, 1784), on 'Come un' agnello' (K. 460, 1784) and on 'Ein Weib ist das herrlichste Ding' (K. 613, 1791), deserve to be rescued from the neglect into which they have fallen. Of the sonatas for 4 hands that in F (K. 497, 1786) is unquestionably the most important : it is indeed one of the composer's finest works. That in C (K. 521, 1787) is slighter, though extremely effective in performance. Two pieces for a musical clock (K. 594, 608), ordered by Count Deym for his so-called 'Art Gallery,' are only known in the arrangement for PF. duet ; they belong to the close of Mozart's life, and the earnestness of purpose and thoroughness of technique which they exhibit show how conscientiously he executed such works to order. For two PF. there are two important works : the lively Sonata in D (K. 448, 1781), and the vigorous—and, in parts exhilaratingly cacophonous—Fugue in C min. (K. 426, 1783), afterwards arranged by the composer himself for string quartet, with the addition of a moving adagio (K. 546) by way of introduction. It should be added that to do justice to Mozart's pianoforte compositions something more is required than the fastidious and rather finicking elegance with which it was long the custom to perform them. The mature works, at any rate, admit of the employment of the full range of tone at the modern pianist's command, and their rapid alternations of mood and frequent imitation of orchestral effects call for a quick brain and a responsive touch for their proper rendering.

Of the sonatas for PF. and violin the earliest sets (K. 6-9, 10-15, 26-31) are really sonatas for the keyboard instrument with violin obbligato. The sonatas K. 55-60, however, which were long classed with them as juvenile works and consequently omitted from the ordinary editions of Mozart's violin sonatas,[1] are of an entirely different character, and indeed of far greater importance than many of his later works in this form. They really belong, as recent research [2] has shown, to the composer's Italian tour of 1772–73, and betray the influence of the older suite-form of Corelli and Sammartini. Especially interesting is the Sonata in E min. (K. 60), the allegro of which contains a passage strongly reminiscent of a theme in the last movement of Beethoven's Sonata in C♯ min. Even in these works, however, the violin part is mainly of an obbligato character, and Mozart's first sonatas in the modern style, in which both instruments

[1] Both Breitkopf and Peters have now published editions of them.
[2] To the French scholars Wyzewa and Saint-Foix belongs the credit for rehabilitating these delightful works. It should, however, be stated that Dr. Schiedermair (*Mozart, sein Leben und seine Werke*, 1922, p. 452), while reserving his evidence, hints that he expects to be able to prove that these sonatas are not original compositions by Mozart.

are of equal importance, were those written partly at Mannheim and partly at Paris in 1778 (K. 296, 301-6), largely on the model of the 'Duetti' of Josef Schuster (1748–1812), which Mozart took with him on the journey. Of this group the tragic Sonata in E min. (K. 304) is perhaps the finest. But Mozart's most important contributions to this form date from his Viennese period and include the works in E♭ (K. 380, 1781), in B♭ (K. 454) written in 1784 for the brilliant young violinist Mlle. Strinasacchi from Mantua, in E♭ (K. 481, 1785) and in A (K. 526, 1787). In all four the slow movements are of especial beauty. Two sonatas which date from the period of Mozart's absorption in the works of Bach and Handel (K. 402 in A min., K. 403 in C) were unfortunately left unfinished by the composer and were subsequently completed by the Abbé Stadler. The Sonata in F (K. 547), written for beginners, has as its final movement a spirited set of variations that is often printed in editions of the composer's variations for PF. solo.

The PF. trios were mainly written for performance at private music meetings, and two at least (K. 496 and 564) were hastily adapted from works originally written for PF. solo. In all of them the PF. (at which in all probability Mozart himself presided) has the lion's share of the work, but modest as the function of the strings often is (particularly that of the violoncello) they are handled so skilfully that they often produce an effect quite out of proportion to the technical demands made upon them, as, to give but one example, at their entry in the andante of the Trio in E (K. 542). This, which Mozart wrote in 1788 for his friend Puchberg, is the most important of the set, but those in B♭ (K. 502, 1786) and in C (K. 548, 1788) are very little inferior. On a far higher level, however, than any of the trios for PF. and strings is the Clarinet Trio in E♭ (K. 498, 1786), which Mozart wrote for performance with his friends the von Jacquins. The distinctive timbres of the clarinet and viola give the work a peculiarly 'romantic' colouring that at times takes on an almost sombre tinge, particularly in the minuet which, somewhat unexpectedly, is the most serious of the three movements. Of the two quartets for strings and PF., in G min. (K. 478, 1785) and in E♭ (K. 493, 1786), the former is unquestionably the finer. The passionate first movement, the gentle melancholy of the andante, and the exuberant finale, with its long chain of exquisite melodies, make it a veritable epitome of Mozart's art. The Quintet in E♭, for PF., ob., clar., horn and bassoon (K. 452, 1784), is another characteristic work. Nowhere are Mozart's skill in writing for wind instruments and his marvellous sense of tonal balance better exemplified. He himself was particularly proud of it. He played it before Paisiello when the latter was in Vienna in 1784 and described it in a letter to his father as the best work that he had so far written.

STRINGS, ETC.—We now pass to the chamber compositions in which the piano plays no part. The violin duets written for Michael Haydn in 1783 (K. 423 and 424) have already been mentioned. The only string trio, apart from the early work for 2 violins and bass (K. 266), is the great E♭ 'Divertimento' (K. 563) for violin, viola and violoncello, composed in 1788. With the composer's other divertimenti it has little in common beyond the number of its movements (there are six in all) and the 'folk-song' character of some of its themes; its breadth of design and careful workmanship make it more akin to the quartets and quintets. Mozart's first seven string quartets (K. 80, 155-160) were written in Italy, the first in 1770, the remaining six in 1772-73, and the in-fluence of Italian models, of Sammartini in particular, is unmistakable.[1] In 1773, as we have already related, Mozart, during a brief visit to Vienna, fell completely under the spell of Joseph Haydn and wrote six contrapuntal quartets (K. 168-173) in imitation of a similar set by the older master. Henceforward Haydn is the predominant influence in the formation of Mozart's instrumental style, and it is sig-nificant that it was the publication by Haydn of a further series of quartets (op. 33) in 1781 that stimulated Mozart to take up again a form that he had in the meantime neglected. The first of the new group of six was written in Dec. 1782, the last in Jan. 1785, and in Sept. of the latter year Mozart dedicated them to Haydn as 'the fruit of prolonged and laborious toil,' with a generous admission of his indebtedness to him. They are too well known to call for detailed discussion; it is enough that they are now universally recog-nised as amongst the supreme examples of their kind. Such, however, was not the general verdict at the time. A critic of the day found them 'much too highly spiced'; Prince Grassalkowics tore up the parts in a rage on finding that they really contained the 'hideous stuff' that was being played before him; and they were returned from Italy to the pub-lisher Artaria as so full of mistakes that it was impossible to play from them. Even Attwood in sending them to his friend Ferrari at Naples advised him to hear them played through several times before passing an opinion on them. The chief stumbling - block was the much-discussed introduction to the quartet in C.[2] It may have been due to an attempt to meet such criticisms that Mozart's next quartet, that in D (K. 499, 1786), is lighter in style and content,

though technically in no way inferior to its predecessors. The last three (K. 575, 589, 590) were written for the King of Prussia in 1789-90, and, fine as they are (particularly the first, in D) the prominence given to the King's favourite instrument, the violoncello, un-doubtedly disturbs at times the balance of the ensemble. The quartets for flute and strings (K. 285, 1777; K. 298, 1778) and for oboe (K. 370, 1781) are delightful but unpretentious works in Mozart's lightest style.[3]

Of the quintets, in which Mozart invariably doubled the viola instead of the violoncello as Boccherini had done, the earliest (K. 174, 1773) is chiefly of interest on account of the preserva-tion of two versions of the trio of the second minuet and of the finale (the second in each case being probably only some few months later than the earlier), comparison of which affords striking evidence of the rapidity with which the composer's genius developed. The Quintet in C minor (K. 406, 1782) is, again, merely an arrangement by Mozart himself of the fine serenade for wind instruments (K. 388). On the other hand, of the last four quintets (K. 515 in C, K. 516 in G minor, 1787; K. 593 in D, 1790; K. 614 in E♭, 1791), three at least may be reckoned as masterpieces. The greatest is that in G minor, in which a mood of spiritual anguish has by the magic of genius been crystallised into a work of immortal beauty. Very little inferior, however, are the vigorous and highly contrapuntal works in C and D, entirely different as they are in mood. That in E♭ is a sunny and genial composition which does not quite reach the same level. Four other quintets remain to be mentioned. Both the delightful clarinet quintet (K. 581, 1789) written for Anton Stadler, and the less-known horn quintet (K. 407, 1782 ?) written for Leutgeb, are rather solos with string accompaniment than quintets properly so called. In the latter work two violas are employed and only one violin. The quintet for glass harmonica, flute, oboe, viola and violoncello (K. 617), composed in May 1791 for Marianne Kirchgässner, seems doomed to neglect unless the harmonica should one day become fashionable again. Mozart obviously selected his accompanying instruments with a view to its peculiar timbre, and the effect of the whole is spoilt by the use of the pianoforte in its place. Possibly the celesta would be a more satisfactory substitute. Last, but by no means least, comes the delicious 'Nacht-musik' (K. 525, 1787) for 2 violins, viola, violoncello and bass, which was possibly designed not for solo instruments but for a small orchestra, and so occupies a position mid - way between Mozart's chamber - music

---

[1] The 4 quartets K. Anh. 210-213 have recently been discovered in a transcript in the Berlin Library by G. de Saint-Foix, who unhesitatingly accepts them as genuine works by Mozart, and assigns them to the Italian period of 1772-73. (See Bull. de la Soc. Union Musicologique, année 3, fasc. 2, 1923.)

[2] Sarti's objections are admirably summarised and sympathetic-ally discussed in E. Newman's A Musical Critic's Holiday (1925), pp. 131-150.

[3] The poignant little adagio of the oboe quartet is nevertheless a remarkable example of Mozart's genius for saying as much as possible in the smallest possible space.

proper and the group of compositions we shall have next to consider.

THE ORCHESTRA.—The serenades, nocturnes, cassations and divertimenti all conform to the same main type, widely as they differ in detail, particularly as regards their instrumentation. They are essentially what the Germans call ' Unterhaltungsmusik,' and their individual characteristics were determined in the main by the occasion of their performance. The fact that many were intended to be played in the open air accounts, for instance, for the important rôle played by the wind instruments. The staple number of movements was six, but a sort of miniature concerto was often interpolated in which some of the players were given the opportunity of showing their skill as soloists. The main composition was, moreover, frequently introduced and concluded with a march. A good example of the full form is provided by the Cassation in G (K. 63). Mozart's compositions in this kind range from unpretentious works like the cassation just mentioned to others like the serenades for wind in B♭ (K. 361), E♭ (K. 375) and C minor (K. 388), which pass far beyond the sphere of conventional fête-music. Indeed the adagio of the first-named work, written for 13 wind-instruments, is one of the sublimest slow movements that Mozart ever wrote. A divertimento for strings and horns (K. 522, 1787), entitled ' Ein musikalischer Spass ' (a musical joke), deserves special mention as one of the few successful examples of satire in music. Although it does not exempt the performer from ridicule it is essentially a hit at the unskilful composer who can think of nothing but musical clichés, and when he has got an idea doesn't know what to do with it. In these compositions the most unusual combinations of instruments are sometimes employed ; for example, two divertimenti written between 1772 and 1775 (K. 187, 188) are scored for 2 flutes, 5 trumpets and 4 drums, and one of the nocturnes (K. 286, 1777), for four orchestras, each consisting of 2 vlns., vla., bass and 2 horns, by means of which a triple echo is produced.

Quite as remarkable is the orchestration of many of the dances for orchestra which Mozart wrote in such numbers during his Viennese period for performance at the court balls. A striking example is the trio of the last of the three ' Deutsche Tänze ' (K. 605), entitled ' Die Schlittenfahrt,' where post-horns and sleigh-bells are used with piquant effect. Nearly all of them, however, deserve careful study from this point of view.

Mozart's 40 or more symphonies [1] are evenly distributed over practically the whole of his career, and thus afford excellent material for studying the development of his style. We can see him first making sure of his materials and technique, and then observe how the separate parts gradually acquire more freedom and independence, how melody and invention grow, the subjects gain in character and details are better worked out, how the wind instruments, no longer used merely to strengthen the strings, attain an independent existence and materially contribute to the effects of light and shade, until at length the various component parts of the orchestra become one animated whole. We can see him passing from one model to another, Christian Bach and Abel giving place to the Italian masters, and they in turn to the Viennese school represented by Wagenseil, Monn, Starzer, and above all Josef Haydn, whose influence, after a brief period during which the Mannheim composers were paramount, ultimately predominated. More than twenty of the symphonies were written at Salzburg. Of these the first in which Mozart shows something approaching real mastery over the symphonic form are the two works in A (K. 114, 1771 ; K. 134, 1772) and that in F (K. 130, 1772), written on the composer's return from his first Italian tour. Of far higher importance, however, are the symphonies written after the second tour, particularly the impassioned work in G minor (K. 183, 1773–74), a not unworthy precursor of the later work in the same key, and the bright and genial work in A (K. 201, 1774). The brilliant ' Parisian ' Symphony in D (K. 297, 1778) was written with the object of humouring the taste of the French public, but is much more than a mere *pièce d' occasion*, and is specially noteworthy for the large orchestra employed (there are, in addition to the strings, 2 flutes, 2 oboes, 2 clarinets, 2 bassoons, 2 horns, 2 trumpets and drums). Three further symphonies written at Salzburg in 1779 and 1780 include one in G (K. 318) in one movement, performed, according to tradition, as an overture to Bianchi's ' La vilanella rapita,' and a vigorous and broadly designed work in C (K. 338). With the exception of one in C (K. 425) composed at Linz in 1783 and showing visible traces of Haydn's influence, all the rest were written at Vienna. The earliest of these was the bright and energetic symphony in D major (K. 385), composed in 1782 for his friend Haffner of Salzburg ; four years later followed the Prague Symphony (K. 504), also in D major, the orchestration of which reminds us that it had recently been preceded by ' Figaro.' The last three, in E♭, G minor, and C with the fugue (Jupiter) (K. 543, 550, 551), were composed in 1788 between the 26th of June and the 10th August, in a space of just over six weeks ! Like most of Mozart's works which can be treated as a group, these three symphonies are in strong contrast to one

---

[1] Mozart's development as a symphonic composer is admirably treated in D. Schultz's *Mozarts Jugendsinfonien* (1900).

another.　None of the attempts, however, to sum up their respective characteristics in a brief phrase or epithet have been very successful.　Even the title 'Jupiter' is not altogether happy, and still less satisfactory are the descriptions of the E♭ symphony as Mozart's 'swan song' (E. T. A. Hoffmann) or his 'Eroica' (Kretzschmar), or Schumann's phrase about the 'swaying Grecian grace' of the G minor.　It is rather just because each work comprises within it such a wealth and variety of moods that these symphonies represent the very pinnacle of Mozart's achievement as an instrumental composer.

THE CONCERTO FORM.—Equal in historical interest is Mozart's treatment of the concerto, which may justly be regarded as his chief contribution to the growth of the instrumental forms.　Up to the middle of the century the concerto was not distinguished in essential structure from the current types of orchestral or chamber music, and indeed only differed from the overture and the concerted sonata in the opportunity which it afforded for contrasted masses or timbres.　Even in the concertos of Handel and J. S. Bach the solo instruments are only 'primi inter pares'; the distinction of protagonist and chorus is not as yet fully felt. The first to perceive the real æsthetic value of this contrast was C. P. E. Bach, whose clavier-concertos definitely modify the symphonic texture, and his tentative suggestions were developed by Mozart with a richer invention, a wider melodic range, and a far greater command of orchestral effect.　(For a description of the form as he established it see CONCERTO, subsection THE CLASSICAL FORM.)

He composed in all twenty-five concertos for clavier solo, the first four (K. 37-41), which were merely adaptations from works by other composers, at Salzburg in 1767, the next six (K. 175-271) at Salzburg between 1773 and 1777, the last fifteen (K. 413-595) at Vienna between 1782 and 1791.　To these should be added a concerto for three claviers (K. 242), written in 1776, and one for two claviers (K. 365) in 1779.　During the years 1775-77 he wrote six[1] for violin (K. 207, 211, 216, 218, 219, 271 a), mainly, it would appear, as studies for his own practice, and followed them in 1779 with a 'Konzertante Symphonie' (K. 364) for violin and viola.　His other works in this form are a concertone for two violins and a concerto for bassoon (K. 190, 191) written at Salzburg in 1773 and 1774 respectively, a concerto for oboe (K. 293?) written in 1777,[2] one for flute and harp (K. 299) written at Paris in 1778, two for flute solo (K. 313, 314) on his

return to Mannheim, four for horn (K. 412, 417, 447, 495) at Leutgeb's house in Vienna, and the clarinet concerto (K. 622) composed for Stadler in 1791.

These works fall naturally into two groups which respectively precede and follow the beginning of his residence in Vienna.　Those of the earlier group are, comparatively speaking, of less importance, and though they exhibit all his delicacy of touch and daintiness of invention, are mainly interesting as stages in his treatment of the form.　The most noticeable among them are those in D major (K. 175), F major (K. 242), and E♭ major (K. 365) for one clavier or more, together with the six for violin, which make charming use of a medium that has been somewhat neglected by the great masters.　The concerto for flute and harp (K. 298), written apparently with some reluctance on the commission of the Duc de Guisnes, is a brilliant virtuoso-piece[3] with a graceful and tender andante.　The Viennese clavier concertos[4] are all masterly, especially those in D minor (K. 466), C major (K. 467), C minor (K. 491) and C major (K. 503); perfect in style, melody and balance, and often showing a freedom of structural organisation which is not to be found in Mozart's other instrumental works.　It is well known that they were carefully studied by Beethoven, in whose early compositions their influence can clearly be traced.　The horn concertos were evidently intended as a jest; they are written at breakneck speed, and the rondo of the first (K. 412) is scrawled over with extravagant mock-directions.　The concerto for clarinet (K. 622) is, on the other hand, a careful study of one of Mozart's favourite instruments, and may be regarded as the basis of modern clarinet-playing.

VOCAL COMPOSITIONS.—Lieder Mozart wrote only casually; and unfortunately for the most part to very insignificant words.　The greater number are in stanza-form, but some few are continuously composed (*durchcomponirt*), such as 'An Chloe' (K. 524), which is in the style of an Italian canzonet; 'Abendempfindung' (K. 523), fine both in form and expression; 'Unglückliche Liebe' and 'Trennung und Wiedervereinigung' (K. 520, 519), almost passionate in tone; and the sportive 'Zu meiner Zeit' (K. 517).　Of three Kinderlieder (K. 529, 596, 598), the second, 'Komm' lieber Mai,' has passed into a traditional song.　But the finest of Mozart's Lieder is undoubtedly the exquisite setting of Goethe's 'Das Veilchen,' which shows what he might have accomplished if he had devoted himself more seriously to this form.

---

[1] The Concerto in E♭ (K. 268) is, as has already been stated, of doubtful authenticity in its present form.　The Mozartian material which it embodies is probably of a later date than the rest of the concertos.

[2] Mozart appears to have written two concertos for oboe, one of which was not completed.　It seems probable that the work written for Ferlendi in 1777 has disappeared, and that the fragment K. 293 is part of a fresh concerto undertaken later (possibly in 1783).

[3] The finest virtuoso, however, can make little of some of the passages for the harp.　Here, for once, Mozart does not seem to have taken his usual pains to understand the possibilities of an unfamiliar instrument.

[4] Brilliantly analysed by Abert, ii. 202-241.　Cf. F. Blume, *Die formgeschichtliche Stellung der Klavierkonzerte Mozarts* (*Mor. Jahrb.*, 1924).　The question whether the PF. parts as printed were elaborated by Mozart in performance, and should be similarly treated by the present-day soloist, is fully discussed in C. Reinecke's *Zur Wiederbelebung der Mozart'schen Clavier-Concerte* (1891).

The canons require sifting; even our English 'NON NOBIS DOMINE' (*q.v.*) has been set to German words, and ascribed to him. Several are composed to words in the Viennese dialect, and their effect is completely ruined by the modern drawing-room text which is often substituted.

As we have seen already, Mozart was frequently called upon to write airs for concert performance, and for insertion in operas by other composers: many of these are noteworthy examples of Mozart's skill in writing for the voice; for instance, the soprano airs 'Misera dove son' (K. 369), 'Non temer amato bene' with PF. obbligato (K. 505), 'Un moto di gioja' (K. 579), 'Bella mia fiamma' (K. 528), one of his finest airs; the tenor air 'Per pietà' (K. 420), and the bass airs 'Non so d' onde viene' (K. 512), 'Mentre ti lascio' (K. 513), and 'Per questa bella mano' with double-bass obbligato (K. 612).

We will now pass to the consideration of Mozart's religious music, and before discussing his Masses, will deal briefly with his other compositions for the Church. First and foremost come the Litanies and Vespers, each of which consists, like the Mass, of a number of distinct sections. There are two main types of litany: the 'Litania de venerabili (altaris sacramento)' and the 'Litania Lauretana' or 'Marien-litanei' (see LITANY). The chief characteristic of the former is solemnity and of the latter tenderness, and these Mozart has succeeded in preserving in his settings. Of his works in the latter kind, the first, in B♭, composed in 1771 (K. 109), already shows fluency in part-writing, and mastery of form and modulation; but the second, in D (K. 195), composed in 1774, is far more important, the voices being treated contrapuntally against an independent orchestra. There are also two Litanie de venerabili in B♭ and E♭ (K. 125, 243), composed in 1772 and 1776, the lapse of time between the two being clearly marked in the compositions themselves. The fine choruses in Nos. 3 and 5 of the latter point to the Requiem, and, like the fugue 'Pignus futurae,' almost startle by their power, as does also the opening of the 'Panis vivus,' identical with the 'Tuba mirum' in the Requiem. A still stronger sense of the dignity of church music is shown in two vespers in C (K. 321, 339) composed in 1779 and 1780, the greater part of both thoroughly deserving a place among the composer's most important works. The 'Confitebor' in the first, and 'Laudate pueri' and 'Laudate Dominum' in the latter, are real gems. The motet 'Misericordias Domine' (K. 222), which Mozart wrote as an exercise for Padre Martini, who gave him a brilliant testimonial for it in 1775, is in strict counterpoint throughout. In 1776 he composed a 'Venite populi' for double chorus (K. 260); the parts are in imitation, strict or

free, and the whole work is full of force and freshness. A list of innumerable small pieces of church music closes with the beautiful motet 'Ave verum' (K. 618), composed on the 18th of June 1791, at Baden, near Vienna.

Mozart's first Masses (K. 49, 65, 66), written while he was still a mere boy, show how thoroughly he had mastered the forms then in use for that style of music. But there is a tremendous gulf between these early works and the 6th Mass in F [1] (K. 192), written only five years later. This mass, in which the master-hand is clearly discernible, recalls the finest models of the old Neapolitan school; the Credo is based on the subject so well known in the finale to the Jupiter Symphony. It is written in counterpoint throughout with only two violins, bass and organ as accompaniment. The next, in D [2] (K. 194, 1774), is also next in order of merit; it has perhaps more grace, but less earnestness and ideality. These two masses show what Mozart could do when his genius was unfettered; but in the five which followed in 1775 and 1776 [3] (K. 220, 257-259, 262) he was forced to suit his patron's taste by aiming at display, and the result is less fortunate. Unhappily these, being his best-known masses, are generally taken as his standard church works. Hardly more important are the next three [4] (K. 275, 1777; K. 317, 1779; K. 337, 1780), although Mozart himself seems to have had a preference for the first, in B♭, since he chose it to conduct himself in 1791; the second, in C, composed in 1779, is called the 'Coronation-mass'—why, nobody knows; the third, also in C, was composed in 1780; and all three fulfil the conventional requirements, but seldom show a glimpse of the true Mozart, and then only in court uniform. We have already mentioned the last mass, in C minor (K. 427), and the circumstances under which it was written. It is broadly designed, each section being treated as a separate movement, and the whole bears clear traces of his studies at the time (1783) with van Swieten. It is to be regretted that it was never finished; the Kyrie, Gloria, Sanctus and Benedictus alone are complete; of the Credo only half was written.[5] Very remarkable are the varying length of the different movements, the large dimensions of the choruses and fugues, and the bravura style of the solos. The Kyrie, Gloria and Sanctus are excellent; the five-part Gratias and the eight-part Qui tollis, of incomparable beauty.

---

1 Mozart's Masses, arranged by V. Novello, No. 3.
2 Novello, No. 6.
3 The second, in B♭ (K. 257; Novello 2), is called the 'Credo Mass,' from the peculiar treatment of the Credo. Novello printed it in a very mutilated form; even the characteristic subject in the Credo itself being left out whenever possible. The much-used subject from the Jupiter Symphony is introduced again in the Sanctus.
4 Novello, 10, 1, 14.
5 The Credo was completed by the adaptation of other church compositions of the master; for the Agnus Dei, the opening Kyrie was repeated, and the mass, as thus made fit for public performance, was given by the Mozartverein at Dresden Apr. 3, 1901, and at the Bristol Festival of 1905, for the first time in England.

We now come to the Requiem, that work of pain, which the composer was not permitted to finish. The following pieces are in his own handwriting: —(1) Requiem and Kyrie, complete; (2) voice-parts, organ and notes of the accompaniment of Nos. 2 to 9, as follows: Dies irae, 68 bars; Tuba mirum, 62; Rex tremendae, 22; Recordare, 130; Confutatis, 40; Lacrymosa, 8; Domine, 78; Hostias, 54: the last eight bars, containing voice-parts, organ and first violin, go to the words 'Fac eas Domine de morte transire ad vitam,' followed by the direction 'Quam olim Da Capo,' that is to say, repeat the last 35 bars of the Domine. His widow, in her anxiety to have the score completed, and thus satisfy the person who had ordered it, first applied to Eybler, but after a few attempts he threw up the task, and she then entrusted it to Süssmayer, who not only had more courage, but was able to imitate Mozart's hand. He copied what Mozart had sketched in, filled up the gaps, wrote a Sanctus, Benedictus and Agnus Dei, possibly utilising rough sketches left by the master, and, to give unity to the work, wound it up by repeating the fugue of the Kyrie to the words 'Cum sanctis tuis.' The score thus completed was handed to the messenger, who afterwards proved to have been Leutgeb, steward to Count Franz von Walsegg, of Ruppach. The Count, who had lost his wife, Anna Edlen von Flammberg, on Feb. 14, 1791, and wished to perform a Requiem to her memory, copied out the score, inscribed it 'Requiem composto dal Conte Walsegg,' and actually had it performed as his own work on Dec. 14, 1793.[1] After wanderings almost as complicated as those of Ulysses, the various portions, in the original handwriting, at length found their way safely to the Hofbibliothek of Vienna. They consist of — (1) the autograph Requiem[2] and Kyrie, with the remainder complete in Süssmayer's hand, bought by the Hof-bibliothek in 1839 for fifty ducats; (2) Nos. 2 to 9 just as they were left by Mozart; (3) twelve sheets presented by the Abbé Stadler, and (4) thirteen bequeathed by Eybler in 1846.[3] Mozart, it is well known, imagined that he was

writing the Requiem for himself, and traces of the agony of spirit in which he wrote it have passed into his music. For this reason, in spite of all its beauties, it is a work which many lovers of Mozart can never hear without pain.[4]

We have seen Mozart, when a mere boy, turning from childish play to serious occupations: a striking instance of this is his 'Grab-musik' or German cantata (K. 42), written in 1767, which is anything but a boyish composition. About five years later he wrote, apparently in consequence of his visit to Padua, an oratorio by Metastasio called 'Betulia liberata' (K. 118), which in style is not unlike an opera seria of the period. The refrain in the last number but one, alternately sung by solo and chorus, is an ancient canto fermo harmonised in four parts, in fact the same which is introduced in the Requiem to the words 'Te decet hymnus.' This is the only independent work of the kind, the cantata 'Davidde penitente' (K. 469) being made up from the Kyrie and Gloria of the unfinished mass in C min. (K. 427) set to Italian words, with two interpolated airs in concert style, which are not altogether in keeping with the severity of the rest of the piece.

Of smaller cantatas, three written for masonic use (K. 429, 471, 623) are the only specimens. All show much earnestness and depth of feeling. The first was composed in 1783, the second in 1785; the last, consisting of six numbers, written on Nov. 15, 1791, Mozart conducted in person only two days before his last illness.

DRAMATIC COMPOSITIONS.—The long list of Mozart's dramatic compositions[5] is headed by a sacred Singspiel, 'Die Schuldigkeit des ersten Gebotes,' in three parts, the first being composed by him in Salzburg during the winter of 1766–67, and the others added by Michael Haydn and Adlgasser, the court organist. Mozart's work occupies 208 pages, and is in the style of the Italian oratorios of the period, the conventions of which are handled with extraordinary precocity. Mingled with the boy's unsteady writing there are occasional passages, mostly florid, in his father's hand, and the words to the recitatives are by a third person. The third tenor air is interesting, and Mozart himself evidently thought well of it, as he introduced it with slight variations into his first opera. Immediately afterwards followed the music to a Latin comedy 'Apollo et Hyacinthus,' given in the University on May 13, 1767, a dull piece of work on the whole, though it contains a few premonitions of the later Mozart. In Vienna in 1768 he composed a German operetta or pastorale in one act, 'Bastien und Bastienne,' and an opera buffa in three acts, 'La finta semplice.' With the simple

1 This, Mozart's last work, was the first of his vocal works (including his operas) to be performed in England. John Ashley introduced it at Covent Garden Theatre on the first oratorio evening during Lent, Feb. 20, 1801. The piece which preceded it was a Dead March with corni di bassetto, double bassoons, and two pairs of double drums; after it came a PF. concerto played by John Field, and Handel's 'L' Allegro ed il Pensieroso.' Books of the words, with a translation of the Requiem and a biographical sketch of Mozart, were sold at 6d. each. Of the Requiem Parke says, 'It is a composition of infinite science and dulness, from the effects of which the audience was happily relieved by Incledon's song in " L' Allegro," " Haste thee, Nymph." ' The *Morning Post* said, ' The talents which have celebrated the name of Mozart can scarcely be justly appreciated by such a composition as the Requiem ': and wound up with, It is upon the whole a composition which could only have come from the hand of a master. From the performers it received ample justice.' According to the *Porcupine* ' the performance was far from being well managed.' It was repeated on Mar. 4. (Pohl, *Mozart in London*, p. 144.)

2 The whole story of the history of the MSS. and of the long controversy as to the work's authenticity is told with admirable lucidity in W. Pole's *The Story of Mozart's Requiem* (1879). The best analysis of the music is that by Abert (*W. A. Mozart*, ii. 851-87). The heading ' Requiem di me, W. A. Mozart mp 792 ' is touching, as showing how he looked forward to its completion.

3 A facsimile of Mozart's contributions was published at Vienna in 1914, under the editorship of Dr. A. Schnerich.

4 Cf. Dent (*Mozart's Operas*, p. 380), where, however, too much stress is laid upon these traces of morbidity.

5 Special literature: E. J. Dent. *Mozart's Operas* (1913); E. Lert, *Mozart auf dem Theater* (3rd ed., 1921).

emotions of his shepherd and shepherdess Mozart succeeded well enough, and his little piece still makes pleasant hearing, but to the complicated network of emotions—often sordid enough—of the stock Italian opera buffa he was as yet quite unequal. The three works composed and performed in Milan—'Mitridate' (opera seria, 1770), 'Ascanio in Alba' (theatrical serenade, 1771), and 'Lucio Silla' (opera seria, 1772) — are scarcely more important, except as marking stages in the composer's development and as providing him with experience that was to prove invaluable later. The serenade 'Il sogno di Scipione,' written at Salzburg in 1772, was, as has been already described, an uninspired piece written hastily to order. The first version of the incidental music which Mozart wrote to Gebler's masonic drama 'Thamos' dates from the end of 1773, but the two choruses (Nos. 6 and 7b), which are the finest features in the score as we now know it, were written in 1779, when the composer, anxious to come before the public once more as a writer of dramatic music, subjected it to a fairly drastic revision. It is also necessary to distinguish the original score from later accretions in the case of the opera buffa 'La finta giardiniera,' which was first produced in its Italian form at Munich in Jan. 1775, but later, when a German text was substituted, underwent two successive revisions (the first in 1779 or 1780 and the second in 1789). The early score, so far as it can be reconstituted, shows a considerable advance upon Mozart's first attempt at opera buffa. Though largely modelled upon Anfossi's setting of the same text, produced about a year before, and owing much to other masters of opera buffa, such as Piccinni, Traetta and Majo, it is characterised by a gentle poetic charm that is all Mozart's own. As yet, however, there is little attempt at musical characterisation, and it shows only traces of the wit and verve of its Italian models. The treatment of the voice is interesting : it holds no paramount position, but is treated as only one of several strands in the symphonic ensemble. The same general features characterise the serenata 'Il rè pastore,' produced at Salzburg in 1775, now remembered only by the song 'L' amero,' which still finds a place in our concert programmes. Mozart's hopes of writing an opera in Paris in 1778 were disappointed, and he had to console himself with the composition of some of the numbers for Noverre's ballet 'Les Petits Riens.' The most important of these is the spirited overture, containing a theme which afterwards played a part in 'Figaro.' The remaining pieces are graceful and dainty enough but of no special importance. The unfinished opera 'Zaide,' to a wretched text by Schachtner, which busied Mozart for some months at Salzburg in 1779, exhibits that curious mixture of styles which was a feature of the Viennese Singspiel. Italian

arias and German song forms are found side by side, and there are even traces of French influences. To this medley Mozart has added interludes of 'melodrama '—spoken recitative to an orchestral accompaniment—on the model of Benda's experiments. The work contains much fine music, especially in the ensembles, but is chiefly of interest for certain numbers in which Mozart seems to have been striving to evolve a specifically German style.

But Mozart's first great opportunity was to be provided not by a German but by an Italian opera. This was 'Idomeneo,' first performed at Munich in Jan. 1781. The original text to the opera, as written by the Abbé Varesco, the court chaplain of Salzburg, was far from satisfying the composer, and it was only by the exertion of constant pressure that he finally got it altered to suit his wishes. His correspondence with his father about the libretto affords instructive evidence of his remarkable instinct for the dramatically effective. In accordance with the taste of the moment the conventional form of opera seria was, in 'Idomeneo,' modified by the introduction of choruses and ballets after the model of Gluck's French operas, and Mozart's music also pays allegiance to these diverse schools, the influence of Gluck predominating. The whole work is conceived on a grand scale, and its tragic force, the majesty of the choruses, and the brilliance of the orchestration give it a unique place among the composer's works. He himself thought very highly of it, and when he was at Vienna in 1781 hoped to get it performed in a German version, for which he proposed recasting the music 'more in the French style.' He had, however, to wait till 1786, and even then had to be content with a private performance by distinguished amateurs, for which he made several alterations and additions (see e.g. K. 489, 490).

In the year following the production of 'Idomeneo ' Mozart's desire to write a German opera was at length gratified. The text of 'Die Entführung aus dem Serail' was adapted by the younger Stephanie from a libretto by Bretzner, and it is again interesting to observe that Mozart's practical acquaintance with the stage dictated many alterations—much, it may be said, to Bretzner's disgust. Osmin, one of the most original characters in the opera, was entirely the composer's own creation. There remained, however, certain structural weaknesses which even the beauty of Mozart's music could not quite conceal. The general effect is of a series of detached numbers, often developed to a disproportionate length, rather than of a unified whole. What makes the opera so perennially attractive in spite of its defects is that spirit of freshness and youthful exuberance which led Weber to say that 'Of such operas as "Figaro" and "Don Juan" we might have had many more ; but with all the

good will in the world Mozart could never have
written another " Entführung." '

The unfinished scores of ' L' oca del Cairo '
and ' Lo sposo deluso,' which date from 1783,
need not detain us, although Mozart completed
several numbers of each before the poverty of
the libretti compelled him to give them up ; nor
is the amusing skit on theatrical and operatic
life ' Der Schauspieldirektor,' which was performed at Schönbrunn on Feb. 7, 1786, of
sufficient importance to call for discussion here,
in spite of the exquisite finish of the music. We
must pass at once to a brief consideration of the
five works on which, Mozart's operatic fame
chiefly rests : ' Le nozze di Figaro ' (1786),
' Don Giovanni '(1787), ' Così fan tutte '(1790),
' La clemenza di Tito ' (1791) and ' Die Zauberflöte ' (1791).

The unity that was lacking in ' Die Entführung ' is one of the most marked features of
' Figaro,' in some respects the most perfect of
Mozart's operas. In no work is his power of
dramatic characterisation more brilliantly exemplified. In the concerted numbers, which
form so large a proportion of the whole, it is
amazing to see the skill with which the voices,
whilst forming part of a complex musical tissue,
are made to express the personalities of the
various characters. Perhaps they are not the
personages of Beaumarchais' satirical comedy ;
but what does it matter ? Mozart, with the
help of the witty Da Ponte, has created them
afresh, and they are unmistakable flesh and
blood.

If 'Figaro' is not Mozart's finest opera, it is
because it deals after all with a somewhat
narrow range of emotions. In ' Don Giovanni,'
on the other hand, less homogeneous as it is in
style, there is scarcely a feeling known to
humanity that is not expressed in some one of
the situations or characters. It must not be
forgotten, however, that Mozart himself described it as an ' opera buffa,' and even its
most serious moments are tempered with that
spirit of irony which gives such a characteristic
flavour to so much of his music.

This spirit is given full rein in 'Così fan tutte,'
where Da Ponte's amusing comedy of intrigue
gave him full opportunity for its exercise. It
seems incredible that any one should ever have
imagined that this was a work which Mozart
undertook with reluctance, and that he regarded
the libretto as so beneath contempt that he was
satisfied to compose a string of beautiful airs
which had nothing to do with it.

' La clemenza di Tito ' he certainly was
reluctant to undertake, busied as he was already
with ' Die Zauberflöte,' to say nothing of the
Requiem. ' La clemenza ' carries us back to
the old opera seria which Mozart had not
touched since ' Idomeneo.' Metastasio's libretto, written in 1734, required considerable
modifications to adapt it to the altered taste of

the day, the most important being the introduction of ensembles wherever the situations
allowed and the curtailment of the original
three acts to two. Nothing availed, however, to
make the plot or the characters interesting.
Throughout it was evident that the characteristics which had most attracted in Metastasio's
day were now only so many obstacles and
hindrances to the composer. The most important thing in Mozart's score is the finale to
Act, 1, noteworthy as the first instance in which
he employs solo voices in an ensemble, and for
the important dramatic function which the
chorus performs.

In ' Figaro,' ' Don Giovanni ' and ' Così fan
tutte ' Mozart's task had been considerably
lightened by Da Ponte's excellent libretti. At
first sight it would not seem that Schikaneder
deserved much credit for his text to ' Die
Zauberflöte.' On the surface it appears to be
a tissue of improbabilities and absurdities. Its
main characteristics are only explicable in
relation to contemporary theatrical history.
Spectacular operas, of a highly romantic cast,
were the fashion in Vienna at the time, and
numbers of them were produced not only at
Schikaneder's theatre but on other stages also.
For this particular production Schikaneder
drew in the main upon a fairy-tale ' Lulu, oder
die Zauberflöte ' from Wieland's ' Dschinnistan.'
Its peculiar weakness as it is now printed is due
to the fact that at the last moment—when,
indeed, Mozart had already composed a good
deal of the music—it was suddenly decided to
alter the whole character of the story by introducing allusions to Freemasonry and giving
the whole an ideal and symbolical character.
This sudden change has generally been attributed to the influence of a certain Karl
Ludwig Giesecke, who in fact afterwards laid
claim to the authorship of the libretto, but it
may have been largely at the instance of Mozart
himself. Its immediate occasion may have
been the death of the prominent Freemason
Ignaz von Born on July 24, 1791. In any case
there is no evidence that Mozart was at all dissatisfied with the libretto in its final form, and
there is certainly no sign of it in his music. As
a matter of fact, with all its contradictions and
occasional fatuities, it is undoubtedly adapted
to the stage. Goethe, whilst acknowledging its
weaknesses, claimed that ' the author had a
perfect knowledge of the art of contrast and a
wonderful knack of introducing stage effects.'
It is well known that the poet himself began a
continuation of the libretto and entered into
an agreement with Wranizky on the subject in
1796. The deeper signification of the text undoubtedly appealed strongly to Mozart's imagination and called forth some of his sublimest
music. Beethoven declared ' Die Zauberflöte '
to be Mozart's greatest work. Unfortunately
Schindler adds that his reason for estimating

it so highly was that in it were to be found specimens of nearly every species of music from the Lied to the chorale and fugue. It is a composer's explanation : the layman, if he is not content simply to drink in its beauty, will prefer to think of it as the perfect expression of the two complementary—though apparently contradictory—sides of Mozart's character, his ideality and his realism. As Schurig has well remarked, he was himself both Tamino and Papageno.

THE SPURIOUS AND DOUBTFUL WORKS.—No discussion of Mozart's music would be complete without at least a brief mention of some of the spurious works that have been attributed to him. Of these, various Masses are the most important. In the early part of the 19th century Vincent Novello searched the Continent for unpublished masses by Mozart. Unfortunately he does not seem always to have investigated the authenticity of the works that were offered him, with the result that, of the 17 masses ultimately published by him, five (Nos. 7, 8, 9, 12, 18) have since proved to be spurious, and three (Nos. 13, 16 and 17) must be regarded as of doubtful genuineness. The best known of these is the so-called Twelfth Mass (K. Anh. 232), which gained its English title simply from the fact that it formed No. 12 in Novello's collection. This Mass was first published under Mozart's name by Simrock of Bonn in 1821 from a MS. obtained from Carl Zulehner ; but the violinist Leopold Jansa subsequently identified it as a work which he used to sing as a boy in a musical school in his native country of Bohemia, where it was known as ' Müllers Mass.' On purely internal grounds it certainly seems difficult to accept it as a work of Mozart.[1] Of other religious works formerly ascribed to Mozart the Mass K. 140 is by Süssmayer, the Hymn K. 327 by Gasperini, and the Offertory K. 177 probably by Leopold Mozart. Numerous spurious songs were published as Mozart's during the early part of the 19th century ; Köchel (Anh. 245) mentions in particular a collection of 33 published by Rellstab of Berlin, of which only 5 were genuine ! The most important of them is the ' Wiegenlied ' (K. Anh. 284f), which is still frequently sung as a work of Mozart, but has been shown by Dr. Max Friedländer to be by the Berlin composer Bernhard Flies. Almost equally well known is the song ' Vergiss mein nicht ' (K. Anh. 246), which as ' Forget me not ' long enjoyed a considerable vogue in this country. Its real composer was Ludwig Schneider of Coburg. The beautiful bass air ' Io ti lascio, cara, addio ' (K. Anh. 245) was written by Mozart's friend Gottfried von Jacquin. A number of instrumental works have also been erroneously attributed to Mozart. The three symphonies K. 18, K. 444 and K.

[1] For further details of the controversy regarding the authenticity of this Mass, the previous edition of this Dictionary should be consulted.

Anh. 293 are respectively by Abel, Michael Haydn and Leopold Mozart, while the Minuet and Trio for orchestra (K. 25a), preserved in a MS. at the British Museum, is probably a youthful work by Beethoven. Of the large number of spurious piano pieces the best known is the set of variations (really by Förster) on a theme from Sarti's ' I finti eredi ' (K. Anh. 289) that has frequently been printed in editions of Mozart's PF. works. The ' Pastorale variée ' (K. Anh. 209b) is also still published under Mozart's name. The grandiose Sonata in C min. (K. 284a), which was printed by Pleyel as ' Mozart's last Grand Sonata,' was composed by Anton Eberl. Finally, the Rondo for PF. (K. 511a), which is bound with the Minuet and Trio for orchestra mentioned above, is probably, like that, an early work by Beethoven.

BIBLIOGRAPHY

This list is confined to works of a general character. The most important of the books and papers on special subjects have been mentioned in the appropriate place in the body of this article. H. de CURZON's *Essai de bibliographie mozartine* (1906) records some 450 books and articles, and the later literature is fully discussed in the prefaces to the biographies by Jahn, Abert, Schurig and Schiedermair.

1. CHIEF SOURCES.—L. von KÖCHEL : *Chronologisch-thematisches Verzeichnis sämmtlicher Tonwerke W. A. Mozarts*, 1862 ; 2nd ed., 1905. (Not always trustworthy on points of chronology, but indispensable for the identification and description of the works.) —O. JAHN : *Wolfgang Amadeus Mozart*, 4 vols., 1856–59 ; 2nd ed., in 2 vols., 1867 ; 3rd, 1889–91 ; 4th, 1905–7 ; 2nd ed. trans. into English by Miss P. D. Townsend, 3 vols., 1882. (Still the fullest of all the biographies, although as a critical survey of Mozart's music it no longer holds pride of place.)—H. ABERT : *W. A. Mozart*, 2 vols., 1919–21 ; revised ed., 1923–24. (Issued as a revised ed. of Jahn, but practically a new book. The best guide to the music.)—T. de WYZEWA and G. de SAINT-FOIX : *W. A. Mozart. Sa vie musicale et son œuvre de l'enfance à la pleine maturité, 1756–77*, 2 vols., 1912. (An epoch-making book, the first to investigate with any thoroughness the sources and development of Mozart's style. It provides a revised chronology of the whole of the works.)—L. Schiedermair ed. ; *Die Briefe W. A. Mozarts und seiner Familie*, 5 vols., 1914. (The standard ed. of the letters. Vol. 5 is a collection of portraits and other illustrations.)

2. SUPPLEMENTARY LITERATURE. — A. OULIBICHEFF : *Nouvelle Biographie de Mozart*, 3 vols., 1843 ; Germ. trans. by A. Shraishuon, 1847, 2nd ed., 1859. (Still valuable for its musical criticism.)— H. de CURZON : *Mozart*, 1914. (In French. Chiefly critical.)— A. SCHURIG : *Wolfgang Amadeus Mozart*, 2 vols., 1913 ; 2nd ed., 1923. (Useful for biographical details. The illustrations are excellent. The French adaptation by J. G. Prod'homme (1925) omits them, as well as many other distinctive features of the original.)—L. SCHIEDERMAIR : *Mozart, sein Leben und seine Werke*, 1922. (The best critical biography of a handy size. Well illustrated.) Since 1923 an important *Mozart-Jahrbuch* has been published under the editorship of HERMANN ABERT. The reader who only knows English should consult—in addition to the English trans. of Jahn already mentioned—the biographies by E. HOLMES (1845 ; 2nd ed., 1878 ; ' Everyman's Library,' 1912), V. WILDER (trans. by L. LIEBICH, 2 vols., 1906), and E. J. BREAKSPEARE (1902), and the trans. of the letters by Lady WALLACE (2 vols., 1865).

c. b. o. ; incorporating material from c. f. p. and w. h. hw.

(2) JOHANN GEORG LEOPOLD (b. Augsburg, Nov. 14, 1719 ; d. Salzburg, May 28, 1787), father of the great composer, was himself a musician of some note. The son of Johann Georg Mozart, a bookbinder at Augsburg, he determined to push himself beyond the narrow circle of his parental home. He studied for two years (1737–39) at the University of Salzburg with the intention of entering the priesthood, but his love of music proving too strong for him (he was already an excellent violinist), he obtained an appointment in 1740 as musician and chamberlain to Count Thurn and Taxis, Canon of Salzburg. Three years later he was appointed fourth violinist in the private orchestra of the Archbishop of Salzburg, in whose service he ultimately (1763) attained to the post of

vice-Kapellmeister, after having already in 1757 been granted the additional appointment of court composer. On Nov. 21, 1747, he married Anna Maria Pertl, daughter of an official ot St. Gilgen. They were described as the handsomest couple in Salzburg. Of their seven children only two survived—a daughter, Maria Anna, and a son, the illustrious Wolfgang. Both showed great musical gifts at an early age, and Leopold soon found himself compelled to devote almost the whole of his time to their training. The story of his travels with them has been told above. There is perhaps something that smacks a little of the showman in the manner in which he rushed them round Europe and exhibited them as prodigies, and the strain of these years of travel undoubtedly had a very bad effect on Wolfgang's health. On the other hand, the latter owed much to his father's careful training and strict supervision, irksome as this often was to one so different in temperament. The list of Leopold Mozart's compositions is fairly extensive, and includes religious music, symphonies and concertos, divertimenti, and PF. sonatas. A selection, edited by Max Seiffert, was published by Breitkopf & Härtel in 1908.[1] Six divertimenti written about 1760, and included in this collection, possess considerable merit and deserve to be better known. Leopold's great work, however, was his *Versuch einer gründlichen Violinschule* (Augsburg, 1756), which passed through many editions in several languages and was for long the standard method for the violin.

BIBL.—A selection from Leopold Mozart's letters is given in vols. 3 and 4 of L. Schiedermair's *Die Briefe Mozarts und seiner Familie* (1914). In 1920 the diary that he kept during his travels with his children was published by A. Schurig under the title *Leopold Mozart : Reiseaufzeichnungen, 1763–1771* A good study of Leopold's character is to be found in J. Kreitmaier's biography of his son (1919).

(3) MARIA ANNA, Mozart's sister (*b.* Salzburg, July 30, 1751 ; *d.* there, Oct. 29, 1829), was, like her brother, a child prodigy, but, unlike him, never developed into anything more. She shared her brother's successes as a pianist on their joint tours, but later in life was chiefly in request as a teacher. In 1784 she married Baron von Berchthold zu Sonnenberg, Hofrath of Salzburg and Warden of St. Gilgen. On his death in 1801 she returned to Salzburg and again occupied herself with teaching. She became blind in 1820 and ended her days in comparative poverty.

(4) CONSTANZE (*née* Weber), Mozart's wife (*b.* Zell, Lower Austria, Jan. 6, 1763 ; *d.* Salzburg, Mar. 6, 1842), was not herself gifted with any great musical talent, although she had a pleasing, well-trained voice and was possessed of some skill on the piano. She sang the soprano part in her husband's Mass in C minor (K. 427) on its performance in Salzburg in 1783, and after his death appeared in public at one or two of the concerts of his works that she directed. In 1799

[1] *Denkmäler der Tonkunst in Bayern*, ix. 2. There is a valuable Introduction.

she helped to improve her penurious position by selling all her husband's remaining MSS. to André, the composer and music-publisher of Offenbach. In 1809 she married Georg Nikolaus Nissen, an official in the Danish diplomatic service, whose acquaintance she had made at Vienna in 1797. There were no children of this second marriage. On Nissen's retirement from office in 1820, he and Constanze retired to Salzburg, where Nissen collected the materials for his Mozart biography. He died in 1826, however, before its publication, and Constanze had the task of seeing it through the press. The rest of her life was uneventful. Her character is an interesting study. After Mozart's death she seems to have lost all traces of the slovenliness and improvidence that helped to wreck his affairs, and, as her diary and correspondence [2] show, became a capable business woman and a devoted mother to his children.

(5) KARL THOMAS (*b.* Vienna, Sept. 21, 1784 ; *d.* Milan, Oct. 31, 1858), the elder of the two sons who survived the composer, did not become a professional musician, though during his early life in Prague he enjoyed Duschek's instruction and became a gifted pianist. In 1798 he was apprenticed to a merchant at Leghorn. For a long time he still debated the advisability of turning to music as a career, but finally entered the service of the Austrian government and became an official at Milan, where he died unmarried in 1858.

(6) FRANZ XAVER WOLFGANG, later known as WOLFGANG AMADEUS (*b.* Vienna, July 26, 1791 ; *d.* Carlsbad, July 29, 1844), was intended from the first for a musical career. He studied in Vienna under Hummel, Salieri, the Abbé Vogler, and perhaps Albrechtsberger, and gave his first public concert in 1804. From 1808–14 he held posts as music-master to two noble families in Lemberg. In 1819 he set out on a long musical tour, finally settling again in Lemberg in 1822, where he remained for the rest of his life composing, conducting and teaching music. Both as pianist and composer he was held in high esteem, but his name alone was sufficient to preclude his rising to eminence. It is only fair to add, however, that his music has never yet been subjected to a thorough-going examination.

C. B. O.

MOZARTEUM OF SALZBURG, THE. An educational institution for musicians, housed since 1914 in a handsome building which also serves as the headquarters of the Mozart-Gemeinde, an international society which collects funds for the upkeep of Mozart's birthplace and other places associated with the composer, and for the acquisition of Mozart relics. The present director is Dr. Bernhard Paumgartner.

MOZARTSTIFTUNG, see FRANKFORT.

[2] See the collection of *Briefe, Aufzeichnungen, Dokumente*, 1782–1842, published by Dr. A.Schurig in 1922. Her diary was published in full in the *Mozarteums Mitteilungen* for 1920.

MUCH ADO ABOUT NOTHING, opera in 4 acts after Shakespeare, text by Julian Sturgis, music by Stanford. Produced Covent Garden, May 30, 1901. In German (John Bernhoff), Stadttheater, Leipzig, Apr. 25, 1902.

MUCK, KARL (b. Darmstadt, Oct. 22, 1859), a distinguished conductor.

His father was a Bavarian magistrate (Ministerialrat). He studied at Heidelberg and Leipzig, and at the latter place visited both University and Conservatorium, and graduated as Doctor of Philosophy. The same year (1880) he made his début as a pianist in the Gewandhaus. Shortly afterwards he became Kapellmeister at Salzburg, then at Brünn, Graz, and in 1886 first Kapellmeister at Prague. As director of Neumann's Travelling Opera Company he appeared in Berlin, and was appointed in 1892 Kapellmeister at the Royal Opera in that capital, and became General Music Director in 1908. Meantime in 1899 he had conducted Wagner at Covent Garden, and through the winter seasons 1903–06, in conjunction with Mottl, he conducted Philharmonic Concerts in Vienna. His performances of 'Parsifal' at Bayreuth have been famous since 1901. In 1906 he went to America to take charge of the Boston Symphony Orchestra. His second term of office there was abruptly terminated by the war (see BOSTON).

Since the war he has conducted at Munich, Hamburg and Amsterdam.

H. V. H. ; addns. from *Riemann.*

MUDARRA, ALONSO DE (16th cent.), Spanish lutenist, said to have been a canon of Seville, who published a book of lute tablature entitled :

Tres libros de musica en cifras para vihuela . . . 1546. (Bibl. Nac., Madrid ; Escurial.)

It includes sets of variations (*diferencias*) on popular tunes of the day, and settings of Spanish ballads, e.g. on the siege of Antequera (1410) and on the death of Absalom, together with passages from Virgil and Ovid and sonnets by Petrarch and Sannazzaro, and also by the Spanish poets Jorge Manrique, Boscán and Garci-Lasso. There are also pavanes, a galliard and a fantasía, and fragments of psalms and motets by Josquin des Prés (v. Morphy, *Les Luthistes espagnols*, Leipzig, 1902, and P. Villalba, *Canciones españolas de los siglos XV. y XVI.*).

J. B. T.

MUDD (MUDDE, MUDES, MUDS), THOMAS (b. circa 1560), composer of English church music, attended St. Paul's School and went to Cambridge in 1578 with one of the sizarships for the sons of London mercers (Davey, *Hist. Eng. Mus.*). He became a Fellow of Pembroke Hall, and continued to be so until as late as 1590. A fair number of compositions by Mudd are preserved, but as there was also a JOHN MUDD (organist of Peterborough Cathedral from 1583, probably until 1629—West's *Cath. Org.*) living about the same time, it is often difficult to differentiate between them. A service and 4 anthems at Ely Cathedral are by John, but the nine dances for 3 viols (3 Airs, Allemande, Courante, 2 Sarabandes, Courante and 'Eccho') (B.M. Add. MSS. 18,940-1-3-4) are by 'Tho. Mudde.' A 5-part In Nomine, arranged for viols in a MS. of about 1578 (B.M. Add. MSS. 31,390/177), is described simply as by 'Mudd.' The anthem 'God which has prepared' is put down in the MS. (written in 1717) as by 'John or Thomas,' which shows that a certain amount of confusion between them was prevalent even then. An 'In Nomine, De Profundis,' described as by Mudd in Batten's Organ Book at St. Michael's College, Tenbury, is probably by Mundy. The words of an anthem by 'Mudd' are included in Clifford's collection (1663). Below is a list of anthems by Mudd (any designation as to authorship is given as it stands in the MSS.).

God which has prepared ('Thomas or John Mudd'). Durh.; Harl. 7340/436. Score ; B.M. Add. MSS. 30,478-9. Tenor cantoris part only.
I will always give thanks ('Mudd,' 'Mudes'). PH.; B.M. Add. MSS. 30,478-9. Tenor cantoris part only.
Let Thy merciful ears ('Mudd,' 'Muds'). Durh.; B.M. Add. MSS. 30,478-9. Tenor cantoris part only.
Lift up your heads. Durh.; incomp.
Lord hear my voice when I cry ('Tho. Mudde'). Harl. 6347/78. Words only.
O clap your hands. PH.
O God Thou art my God ('Mudd'). B.M. Add. MSS. 30,478. Tenor cantoris part only.

There was also a third Mudd living in the 17th century, organist of Lincoln Cathedral in 1662. As, however, he lived much later than John or Thomas, it is unlikely that he wrote any of the above anthems. Certain extracts from letters written by the precentor to the Dean of Lincoln in 1662, complaining about Mudd's drinking habits, will no doubt confirm this assumption (West's *Cath. Org.*).   J. MK.

MUDIE, THOMAS MOLLESON (b. Chelsea, Nov. 30, 1809 ; d. London, July 24, 1876), one of the ten successful candidates for entry into the R.A.M., in the severe first examination of 1823. Mudie was a pupil of Dr. Crotch for composition, of Cipriani Potter for the pianoforte—who also gave him useful advice as to his writings—and of Willman for the clarinet. His song 'Lungi dal caro bene' was so esteemed that the Committee of Management paid the cost of its publication, an act repeated in the case of Sterndale Bennett's first concerto, but in no other. Several vocal pieces with orchestral accompaniment, a symphony in C and one in B♭ were also works of his student time. Mudie's pupilage terminated in 1832, by his appointment as a professor of the pianoforte in the Academy, which post he held till 1844. The Society of British Musicians, founded in 1834, furnished an arena for the performance of several of the works of Mudie. The symphony in B♭, already mentioned, was played at the concert of Feb. 9, 1835 ; a symphony in F, remarkable for a movement in F minor, Nov. 10, 1835 ; a symphony in D, Mar. 10, 1837 ; a quintet in E♭ for pianoforte and strings, Jan. 5, 1843, and Mar. 7,

1844; a trio in D for pianoforte and strings, Oct. 6, 1843; and several songs and concerted vocal pieces on many occasions. On the death of Alfred Devaux, in 1844, Mudie went to succeed him in his occupation as teacher in Edinburgh. While there he published several pianoforte pieces and songs, and wrote accompaniments to many in Wood's collection of the Songs of Scotland; he also occasionally gave pianoforte recitals. In 1863 he returned permanently to London, but from that time, except with an overture at one of the Crystal Palace concerts, came little before the public. The existing scores of his symphonies and the whole of his printed works are deposited in the library of the R.A.M. He was buried in Highgate Cemetery.   G. A. M.

MÜHLFELD, RICHARD (b. Salzungen, Feb. 28, 1856; d. June 1, 1907), was a member of the Grand Ducal Orchestra of Meiningen from 1873, at first as a violinist, but from 1876 as first clarinet, having taught himself the latter instrument with such success that he rapidly gained an unique position among modern players. He took part in the Bayreuth festival plays from 1884–96, and came to England for the first time in 1892, appearing on Mar. 28 at the Popular Concerts, in Brahms's quintet for clarinet and strings, a work, like the master's trio and the two sonatas in which the same instrument is employed, written with special view to Mühlfeld's great qualities as a player. In all kinds of music his performance was a perfect model of what musical interpretation should be. Many a detail of excellence in the Meiningen orchestra was due to him, for he was accustomed for many years to act as sub-conductor, and to rehearse the players singly and in groups. (*Riemann.*)   M.

MÜLLER, THE BROTHERS, celebrated quartet-players, four sons of the Duke of Brunswick's Hofmusikus, AEGIDIUS CHRISTOPH MÜLLER (b. Nordhausen, July 2, 1766; d. Brunswick, Aug. 14, 1841). All his sons were born in Brunswick.

The brothers were (1) KARL FRIEDRICH (b. Nov. 11, 1797; d. Apr. 4, 1873), first violin and Konzertmeister to the Duke; (2) THEODOR HEINRICH GUSTAV (b. Dec. 3, 1799; d. Sept. 7, 1855), viola player; (3) AUGUST THEODOR (b. Sept.[1] 27, 1802; d. Oct. 20, 1875), violoncellist; (4) FRANZ FERDINAND GEORG (b. July 29, 1808; d. May 22, 1855), second violinist of the quartet and Kapellmeister to the Duke.

Educated by their father expressly with a view to quartet-playing, they brought the art to a perfection then unknown. The Duke of Brunswick's somewhat tyrannical regulation, by which none of his musicians were allowed to take any part in the music of the town, obliged them to prepare in secret for appearing in public, and in 1830 they sent in their resignations. They gave concerts at Hamburg in 1831, and

in 1832 at Berlin, where the public gradually learned to appreciate their wonderful ensemble. In 1833 they left Berlin, and visited in turn all the principal cities of Germany and Paris, extending their tours farther and farther, till 1845, when they went to Russia. Their repertory consisted almost entirely of the works of Haydn, Mozart and Beethoven. Their performance of Haydn's 'Kaiser quartett' especially had a world-wide reputation.

The eldest brother, Karl Friedrich, also had four sons, known as the younger Müller brothers; (5) BERNHARD (b. Feb. 24, 1825; d. Sept. 4, 1895), viola; (6) KARL (b. Apr. 14, 1829; d. Stuttgart, Nov. 11, 1907), first violinist (he married a singer, Elvira Berghaus, and was known as Müller-Berghaus); (7) HUGO (b. Sept. 21, 1832; d. June 26, 1886), second violin; and (8) WILHELM (b. June 1, 1834; d. New York, Sept. 1897), violoncellist, the most important individually, was for ten years a member of the JOACHIM QUARTET (q.v.). They were court quartet-players to the Duke of Meiningen, and also made extended tours, visiting Russia, Denmark and France. In 1866 they settled for a short time in Wiesbaden, and then at Rostock, where Karl became Kapellmeister, his place in the quartet being supplied when travelling by Leopold Auer. It was, however, broken up entirely in 1873, by the appointment of Wilhelm as Kammermusikus, and teacher at the Hochschule für Musik in Berlin. The younger Müllers, though distinguished for their ensemble, did not reach the standard maintained by the elder brothers; the chief reason being that, instead of restricting themselves to genuine quartets, they played music which, though good of its kind, was in reality better suited to a small orchestra.   F. G.

MÜLLER, AUGUST EBERHARDT (b. Nordheim, Hanover, Dec. 13, 1767; d. Dec. 3, 1817). His father, organist at Rinteln, was his first instructor, and he subsequently learnt of J. C. F. Bach of Bückeburg. In 1785 he went to Leipzig to study law, but soon gave it up, and became in 1789 organist of St. Ulrich's Church, Magdeburg. In 1792 he was chosen to direct the concerts, etc., at Berlin, and there became intimate with Marpurg, Fasch, Reichardt and other distinguished men. He was made organist of St. Nicholas' Church, Leipzig, in 1794. He played the organ and harpsichord equally well, and was also a proficient on the flute. In 1800 he was appointed deputy to Hiller at the Thomasschule, and cantor on Hiller's death in 1804. In 1810 he moved to Weimar. The following is a list of his compositions:

(1) Piano: Two concertos; a trio for piano and strings, op. 17; two sonatas for violin and piano; many sonatas for piano solo, besides variations, etc. (2) Organ: Suites, a sonata and Choral, variations. (3) Flute: Eleven concertos; a fantasia with orchestra and twenty-three duets for two flutes. (4) Vocal: Three cantatas for four voices and orchestra; two posthumous operettas (Singspiele); songs with piano accompaniment. (5) Instruction: Method for the piano, and instruction-book for the flute. (See Q.-L.)   M.

---

[1] *Riemann* gives Aug. 27.

MÜLLER, CHRISTIAN, of Amsterdam, between 1720 and 1770 built the finest organs in Holland, and especially the celebrated instrument at Haarlem in 1738.   V. de P.

MÜLLER, HEINRICH (b. Lübeck, Oct. 18, 1631; d. Sept. 17, 1675), pastor and archdeacon of the St. Marienkirche, Rostock, from 1653 till his death. He was also a distinguished professor of theology at the University there.

Among his numerous theological and homiletical works he published in 1659 a book entitled 'Geistliche Seelen-Musik,' containing about 400 hymns, for which 126 tunes are provided with figured bass. As the hymns are characterised by almost an excess of subjective devotional sentiment, some of them by Müller himself, and a large number from Angelus Silesius, so the tunes bear witness to a corresponding change in musical taste, and the gradual suppression of the older rhythmical Choral in favour of the secular aria-form in modern keys. The work is even more of a pioneer in this direction than Crüger's 'Praxis pietatis melica.' Of the tunes fifty new ones are the invention of Nicolaus Hasse, then organist of the Marienkirche.[1] None of these tunes have continued in general use. Müller prefaces his work with a series of ten chapters on the origin and use of spiritual songs, in the course of which he deplores the decay of congregational interest in church music and hymn-singing, and of the devotional sentiment in connexion therewith. Another work of Müller may be mentioned, Geistliche Erquick-stunden (1664–66), the devotions in which were afterwards versified, and provided with tunes in the form of spiritual arias by several Nuremberg poets and musicians, members of the Pegnitz-Blumen-Genossenschaft, and published under the title Poetischer Andacht-Klang (1673–91).

J. R. M.

MÜLLER, IWAN (b. Reval, Dec. 3, 1786; d. Bückeburg, Germany, Feb. 4, 1854), a renowned clarinettist, appeared first in Paris in 1809, where he brought out many of his structural improvements in the instrument, and where, after a residence of some years, and a successful concert tour through all the principal European cities, undertaken 1820–26, he was appointed professor in the Conservatoire. In later life he returned to Germany. His compositions (concertante for two clarinets, three quartets for clarinet, violin, viola and violoncello, etc.) have an educational value for players of his instrument, but beyond that they are of no importance. His best production is a 'Gamme pour la nouvelle clarinette,' published at Berlin in 1825.   M.

MÜLLER, WENZEL (b. Trnava, Moravia, Sept. 26, 1767; d. Baden, near Vienna, Aug. 3,

1835), was for some time a pupil of Dittersdorf, and became conductor in the Brno Theatre in 1783 and three years afterwards, when only nineteen, obtained a similar post at Marinelli's theatre in Vienna, where the rest of his life was spent, with the exception of the years 1808–13. During this period he was director of the opera at Prague, where his daughter Thérèse, afterwards known as Madame Grünbaum, was engaged as a singer. On his return to Vienna, he became conductor at the Leopoldstadt Theatre, and retained the post until within a short time of his death. As a composer of light operas, he enjoyed enormous popularity for many years, and his productions in this kind are said to number over 200. His more ambitious works, as symphonies, masses, etc., were less successful. Among his dramatic works may be mentioned : 'Das Sonnenfest der Braminen' (1790); 'Das neue Sontagskind' (1793); 'Die Schwestern von Prag' (1794); 'Die Teufelsmühle auf dem Wienerberge' (1799). A peculiar interest attaches to his 'Zauberzither' or 'Kaspar der Fagottist,' produced June 8, 1791, since Schikaneder took several suggestions from it for the plot of 'Die Zauberflöte.' In 1818 Müller produced his 'travestierte Zauberflöte' ('The Magic Drum ') (Mendel's Conversations-Lexikon; Riemann's Opernhandbuch).   M.

MÜNTZBERGER (MÜNTZ - BERGER), JOSEPH, called LE JEUNE on some title-pages of his works (b. Brussels, 1769; d. Paris, Jan. 1844), pupil of his father and van Maldere. He chose the violoncello as his principal instrument; went to Paris in 1783, was violoncellist at the Opéra-Comique in 1790, and was later at Favart, retiring with a pension in 1830. He composed 2 concertos, trios, sonatas, solos and studies (E. v. d. Straeten, History of the Violoncello; Q.-L.).

MÜTHEL, JOHANN GOTTFRIED (b. Mölln, Lauenburg, c. 1720), became a pupil of J. P. Kuntzen at Lübeck, and in 1738 received the appointment of chamber-musician and court organist at Schwerin, in which capacity he also gave musical instruction to the members of the ducal family of Mecklenburg-Schwerin. Provided with a letter of introduction from the Duke he went to Leipzig in May 1750 to perfect himself in playing and composition under the tuition of Sebastian Bach. It was the last year of Bach's life, but he received Müthel into his house, and Müthel was with him in his last illness, and at his death. He then went to Naumburg to Bach's son-in-law Altnikol, and afterwards visited Dresden and Potsdam, at which latter place he made the acquaintance of Emanuel Bach, with whom he continued on terms of close friendship. In 1753 he accepted a call to Riga, where he remained for the rest of his life as organist to the Lutheran church, and where he died some time after 1790. Müthel is described as one of the best organ an𝓁

clavier players and composers of his time.   Dr.
Burney speaks of his clavier works in the highest
terms, describing them indeed as more difficult
than those of Handel, Scarlatti, Schobert and
Emanuel Bach ; but as characterised by so
much novelty, taste, grace, and contrivance as
entitle them to be ranked among the best productions of the kind (see his *Present State of
Music in Germany*, 1773, vol. ii. pp. 328-9).
Only a few of his works were published, among
them two concertos, C minor and D minor, for
clavier with accompaniment of strings, published at Riga in 1767 ; three sonatas and two
ariosi with variations published by Haffner at
Nuremberg ; a ' Duetto für 2 Claviere, 2 Flügel,
oder 2 Fortepiano,' Riga, 1771, which appears to
be the earliest work with Fortepiano on the title.
In Madame D'Arblay's *Diary* mention is made
of this duet as played by two members of Dr.
Burney's family at one of his house-concerts.
If Müthel's clavier works have that originality
which Burney and Schubart (*Ideen zur Ästhetik
der Tonkunst*, 1784), ascribe to them, it is
surprising that in these days of revivals none
of them have ever been republished.   J. R. M.

MUETTE DI PORTICI, LA, see MASA-
NIELI O.

MUFFAT, (1) GEORG (*b.* Schlettstadt
c. 1645 ; *d.* Passau, Feb. 23, 1704), highly
esteemed composer, of Scottish extraction,[1]
studied Lully's style for six years in Paris ; was
organist of Strassburg Cathedral till 1675 ; became organist to the Bishop of Salzburg about
1678 ; visited Vienna and Rome ; became in
1690 organist, and in 1695 Kapellmeister and
Master of the Pages to the Bishop of Passau.
He published ' Armonico tributo ' (sonate di
camera, Salzburg, 1682) ; ' Apparatus musico-
organisticus'—twelve toccatas, chaconne, passacaglia, Augsburg, 1690, dedicated to Leopold I.)
—of importance as regards the development
of organ-playing ; ' Svaviores harmoniae. . . .
Florilegium I.' (Augsburg, 1695) ; ' Florilegium
secundum ' (Passau, 1698), both with autobiographical preface in four languages ; ' Auserlesene mit Ernst und Lust gemengte Instru-
mental-Musik ' (1701.)[2]   The 'Apparatus' was
republished in the *Trésor des pianistes*, and the
two works called ' Florilegium ' in *D.T.Ö.*
I. and II., the 'Auserlesene mit Ernst und
Lust gemengte,' etc. in *D.T.Ö.* XI.   His son

(2) GOTTLIEB (Theophil) (*b.* Passau, 1690;
bapt. Apr. 25 ; *d.* Vienna, Dec. 10, 1770), a
pupil of J. J. Fux, became in 1717 court and
chamber-organist to the Emperor Charles VI.,
and to the widowed Empress Amalie Wilhelmine
(*d.* 1742), and music-master to the royal children.   He retired on a pension in 1763.   He
was a distinguished organist and a composer of
taste, and published for organ[3] 72 Versetten

[1] Eitner.
[2] See *Zeitschrift* of the Int. Mus. Ges. vol. v. p. 365.
[3] About seventy years ago Löschenkohl of Vienna republished
from this work ' XII. kleine Fugen sammt II. Toccaten.'

oder Fugen, sammt 12 Toccaten, besonders
zum Kirchendienst bei Choral-Aemtern und
Vespern dienlich ' (Vienna, 1726) ; for harpsichord, ' Componimenti musicali,' containing
overtures, caprices, sarabandes, etc., with a
preface ; and ending with ' Particolari segni
delle maniere ' (see ORNAMENTS) etc., dedicated
to Charles VI., at whose expense it was engraved.   He was one of the many composers
whom Handel laid under contribution for subjects and phrases in his oratorios.   The date of
this work was formerly given as 1727.   Subsequent research by Adler [4] and others fixed it
at or about 1739 ; probably not more than
three or four months, if so many, intervened
before Handel's use of it in the ' Ode on St.
Cecilia's Day ' (Sept. 1739).   The ' Componimenti,' republished in the *Trésor des pianistes*,
were again brought out by Chrysander, as No. 5
of his ' Supplemente.' (See DENKMÄLER, vol. i.
p. 689).   Adler [5] again edited the work for
D.T.Ö. III.

There were two violinists of the same name in
the Imperial Chapel, GOTTFRIED, from 1701–9,
and JOHANN ERNST, appointed in 1730, died in
1746, aged 48.   C. F. P. rev.

BIBL.—HEINRICH JOHANN KNÖLL, *Die Klavier- und Orgelwerke von
Theophil Muffat.* (Vienna Dissertation, 1916.)

MUGNONE, LEOPOLDO (*b.* Naples, Sept. 29,
1858), conductor and composer.   He came of a
musical family and studied at the Conservatoire of S. Pietro a Majella under Cesi and
Serras.   At the age of 12 he wrote a pretty
comic opera, ' Il dott. Bartolo Salsapariglia,'
which was successfully performed at various
academies.   Another, ' Don Bizzarro e le sue
figlie,' was given in 1875 at the Teatro Nuovo,
Naples, together with some of his Neapolitan
songs.   In collaboration with Enrico Goli-
sciani he wrote, when still a youth, several
other comic works, including two, ' Madame
Angot al serraglio ' (3 acts) and ' Il Biric-
chino ' (1 act), which enjoyed lengthy runs,
the latter being given in turn at Venice (1892),
Florence, Rome, Vienna, and Barcelona.   The
opera ' Vita Brettona ' was produced at the
San Carlo, Naples, under his own direction in
1905 and well received.   His career as a conductor began when he was only 16 with a
season of comic opera at the Fenice, in his
native city, after which he had experience
as a chorus-trainer and as accompanist to
Bottesini, the eminent double-bass player.   His
talent was recognised by Sonzogno, the publisher, who engaged him for various operatic
undertakings, including that in Rome (1890)
which gave him the direction of the first performance of ' Cavalleria Rusticana.'   He also
shared with Toscanini the direction of the
special performances at La Scala in honour of
Verdi, whose ' Nabucco ' he conducted with

[4] See *Zeitschrift* of Int. Mus. Ges., Dec. 1907 and Feb. 1908.
[5] See *R.M.I.* iii. 1, where an interesting article by Guido Adler
is to be found.

conspicuous ability. He distinguished himself no less in the handling of symphonic orchestras, particularly in the scores of the modern
Italian school ; a well-known writer, Amintore
Galli, once said of him, 'He is the personifica-
tion of Italian art as well as the manifestation
of a sensitive and essentially musical soul.' His
individuality and sincerity were clearly revealed during the seasons that he conducted
at Covent Garden, where he made his début
('La Bohème') in the autumn of 1905 and
directed the *première* here of Giordano's
'André Chénier.' A year later he brought
out the same composer's 'Fédora' and, in
1919, Mascagni's 'Iris.'   H. K.

MUHAMMEDAN MUSIC. Oriental melodies are almost always handed down orally,
and so we have no direct practical knowledge
of them, and can argue back to their original
condition and subsequent development only
from chronicles and theoretical works.

HISTORY.—We know little of the music of the
pre-Muhammedan Arabs. It was inseparable
from their desert life, and that has remained
unchanged. Perhaps the present Bedouin
music, with its monotonous rhythms, short
compass and faint pipe and string accompaniment, is a fair representative of it.

1. Bedouin Song from Southern Algeria.

Arabic music, as we understand it, is rather
that composite edifice, with a foundation in
Arabic poetry and superstructure of Persian
and Byzantine elements, which has persisted in
Muhammedan centres and dates from the 7th
century. Practised in the first instance by
freedmen and slaves of both sexes and, together
with the wine whose praises it sang, under the
ban of the Church, it became socially indispensable. The zenith of the practice of
music [1] was the period of Haroun al Rashid
(786–809), and its two rival representatives
were the conservative Ishāq-al-Mausilī, a
Persian by blood, and the progressive Ibrāhīm
ibn al-Mahdī, the Caliph's nephew.

The writings on the theory of music which
began about the 8th century culminated in
Al Fārābī (900–950). They were all framed on
Greek theory, but include valuable hints of
Arabic origins. A second climax came three
centuries later in the person of Safī-ud-Dīn, and
with his successors, chief of whom was Abd al
Kadr, 15th century, who wrote in Persian.

Politically, the Muhammedan world divided
itself, after the Arabian expansion, into an
eastern group, running from the Persian Gulf
to the Mediterranean and including Persia, and

[1] See the *Kitab al Aghani* of Ali al Isbahani, 10th century.

a western, comprising N. Africa, Sicily and
Spain. Music naturally followed this division.
In the west, the extension of Muhammedan
sway and the absorption of foreign peoples
introduced new elements. The Syrian 'Umaiy-
yads had carried the court music into Spain,
and the Baghdad tradition obtained a footing
there in the 9th century. Side by side with it
sprang up in Spain a new style of song with
strophic forms. In the course of the 11th and
12th centuries this penetrated N. Africa,

2. Prelude and Song from Morocco.
    (a) *senza misura.*

    (b) *Tempo giusto.*

and remained the prominent type in Andalusia
and Granada, the last stronghold of the Moors.
In the east, the Persian practice had been a
feature from the beginning. The whole area
was gradually overrun by tribes of Central Asia,
who influenced, but did not vitally change, the
character of the music. The kind of influence
exercised by particular tribes of east and west
is to be seen in Examples 1, 2, 3.

3. Dance from Aidin, a Province of Anatolia.

This general grouping of east and west holds
good in the music of to-day. The western
musicians consider themselves to be heirs of
the Andalusian style. The musical centres of
the east are now Cairo and Constantinople. In
both the musical centre of gravity has been
shifted from the courts to the bourgeoisie. The
practitioners are mainly professionals, still as
ever held in disdain, or belong to communities

which originally practised music as an incentive to religious ecstasy. European music has affected principally the military music and the street songs; its effect on the pure style has been chiefly to drive it into corners.

SCALE.—The scale of Al Fārābī's predecessors was, as far as we know it, Pythagorean. This is clear from their description of the fretted string instruments, especially the 'Ud of Persian origin, the classical instrument and the prototype of the European lute. It had either four or five strings tuned in fourths; the little finger stopped a fourth from the open note, the first finger stopped one tone and the third two tones above the open string, and the middle finger a tone below the fourth (all fretted). The middle and third fingers were used only in alternation, and two groups of melodies were distinguished ʰy the practice of Baghdad according as one or other of the frets was used. The particular tonality depended on the combination of this chosen note with the tonic.

The next step was to introduce a fret one tone below the middle finger, giving the Pythagorean *Limma* at the lower as well as the upper end of the tetrachord; thus, in cents (see INTERVAL),

```
Nut. New Fret.        Middle.
 0    90       204    294      408      498
       90   114    90     114      90
```

But there were other methods in actual practice. On the Tanbūr of Baghdad, a long-necked two-stringed lute, the lowest eighth of the string was in pre-Muhammedan times divided into five equal parts. The second string was usually tuned to the lowest note but one of thɔ first. In this there were no Greek intervals, not even the fourth as a terminal. This same system of equal divisions, mechanically arrived at, accounts for the position of certain frets by which the executants of Al Fārābī's time replaced the Pythagorean. Thus the Persian 2nd finger was half-way between the 1st and 3rd, and the 2nd finger of Zalzal, a Baghdad lutenist of the 8th century, was half-way between the 'Persian' and the 3rd. Similarly the 'new' half-way fret, between nut and 1st finger, could also be taken as between the nut and the Persian, or between the nut and Zalzal's.

		String lengths.	Cents.
4th	. . . . .	27	498
3rd	. . . . .	28·44	408
2nd (Middle)	Zalzal . .	29·33	355
	Persian . .	30·22	303
	Pythagorean .	30·38	294
1st	. .	32	204
New	Zalzal . .	32·67	168
	Persian . .	33·11	145
	Pythagorean.	34·17	90
Nut	. . . .	36	0

Besides this division, another common one on the Tanbūr was that of the whole tone into three equal parts (on the string).

Al Fārābī exhibits the Greek *systema teleion* on a five-stringed 'Ud comprising two octaves and one note. The double octave is arrived at by every conceivable arrangement of conjunct and disjunct tetrachords. The principal intervals are 'superparticulars,' that is, fractions[1] of the form $\frac{n+1}{n}$. His tetrachord has two distributions—(i.) the fourth is diminished by a superparticular and its residue is divided in the proportion 1 : 1 or 1 : 2; or (ii.) it is diminished by two equal or unequal superparticulars leaving a residue. Tetrachords of different kinds result from (i.) and (ii.). Safī-ud-Dīn repeats Al Fārābī's tetrachords but rejects a number of them, including those which involve the Greek enharmonic genus 'on account of their defective harmony,' and merges groups which are mathematically distinct, since they are aurally indistinguishable.

The fretting of the 'Ud is from now on exclusively Pythagorean. Zalzal's two frets are shifted to places one tone and two tones above the open string; each semitone is a limma, and each tone two limmas and a Pythagorean comma—

```
Nut          1st              2nd   3rd
 |  90  24  90  |  90  24  90  |  90  |
```

and the octave, being two fourths and a tone, has therefore 17 frets.

The normal type of scale before the Persian period was a Pythagorean G-scale. After that period it was a C-scale in just lutonation, derived possibly from the Tanbūr. With Safī-ud-Dīn the scales can begin either on a common tonic or, as before the 10th century and at the present day, on this or that degree; but the older degrees are more often employed than the later ones in those scales which are in common use.

The theorists of the 19th century construct their scales from 24 degrees of the octave, the increase being due to the need for transposition. They call their divisions 'quarter tones' and usually regard them as equally tempered. The movable frets of the 'Ud have disappeared. The lowest string (of four) is now a tone (not, as before, a fourth) below the 3rd string, and an octave below the first.

The general tendency throughout Arab music is towards finer distinctions of interval.

4. Prelude and (composed) Song from Tunis.

(a) *senza misura.* ♩=140. *Phonogram.*

---

[1] Safī-ud-Dīn held that the consonance of these intervals diminished with their size, and their octave-extensions and their inversions similarly. Aricenna (980–1037) fixed the limit at whic* two pitches could be distinguished as 46/45 (38 cents).

MELODY

GENERAL CHARACTERISTICS.—The old theorists gave rules ; we have to confine ourselves to the practice. The things that strike us in that are the abundance of sequences and grace notes, the preference for descent over ascent and for steps over leaps. Steps are from one to three semitones ; leaps are anything larger. After a third, return is usually made to one of the notes which have been leapt over. Fourths and fifths are mainly used to bring back a sequential ascent or descent to a central position for a new start. Larger intervals than these do not occur within a section, only at a change from one section to another. This helps us to see that their songs are in a framework of tetrachords, either continuous or overlapping, which is more or less what the theory says. In a song a note may often occur in two forms—natural and sharp. At such a place it is common to hear a $\frac{3}{4}$-tone substituted. This points back to the alternative frets of the lute and to the neutral intonation of Zalzal's ' middle finger.'

GROUPING.—Some theorists felt that their system of scales did not do justice to the variety of melody, and they therefore supplemented the system by scales which varied in ascent and descent. The practical musician is not concerned with scales ; he thinks, not in notes, but in melodic figures, and groups the melodies accordingly. These groups are *maqāms*, the exact counterpoint of *Rāgs* (see INDIAN MUSIC). *Maqām* has four distinguishing marks : (1) the selection of constituent notes, (2) compass, (3) position of the important notes, (4) typical phrases. These characteristics of the *maqām* are most fully exhibited in the indispensable prelude to song or piece (see Exs. 2*a*, 4*a*). This prelude is improvised and in free time ; its purpose is to establish the *maqām* in the mind both of performer and listener (cp. the Indian *ālāp*). Melodies in the more elaborate style are not restricted to one *maqām*, but may even run through a series of them. The word *maqām* means ' a recitation from a raised position ' : the term is used in Syria and Turkey ; in Algeria the word is *sana'a* ; in Tunis, *taba'* ; in Egypt, *naghma*. A few individual names of *maqāms* point to a local origin (*e.g. Higāz*, the district of Mecca). The *maqāms* as a whole have sprung from particular folk-songs, or composed songs, or both, and they naturally vary according to the school they come from. The east is distinguished from the west by a preference for leading notes, which entail augmented and diminished intervals, and by a healthy contempt for those who have no such preference.

RHYTHM.—Al Fārābī has a system for time as well as for tune, and later theorists have followed suit. There is, of course, at that period, no notation for either ; he merely describes. He has two systems. (i.) His bar contains anything from one to five units (*chronoi protoi*). It has two to four parts of unequal length, and the last part must be longer than any of the others. (ii.) Instead of piling up from a small duration he splits up a large one into two equal parts. In fact, (i.) provides for any kind of time, and (ii.) only for duple. He finds, as was to be expected, that his system does not cover all the cases, and he falls back on a list and a description of the different times in use in his own day. Theorists have also, at all times, utilised the natural connexion between music and verse to transfer the actual prosodical names to music ; but the connexion does not, and probably never did, amount to identity.

As for the practice, two of our examples will show the difference between the Arab and the European conception. We interpret nine-four as 3×3 ; they can take it as thrice $2 +$ once 3 (as in Ex. 3) or in many other ways. Similarly, in Ex. 4*b*, they divide an eight-four bar into twice $3 +$ once 2.

CROSS-RHYTHM.—All melodies have a rhythmic accompaniment, of drum or string, like a *basso ostinato*. These may coincide in simple pieces like Ex. 3, but the Arabs much prefer cross-rhythm. Here are three usual forms of accentuation in an eight-four bar :

(*a*)	$\underline{1}$	2	$\underline{3}$	4	$\underline{5}$	6	$\underline{7}$	8
(*b*)	$\underline{1}$	2	3	$\underline{4}$	5	6	$\underline{7}$	8
(*c*)	$\underline{1}$	$\underline{2}$	3	$\underline{4}$	5	6	$\underline{7}$	8

The drum may choose any one of these, and stick to it throughout the piece ; and so, independently, may the melody. There will then be cross-rhythm in two out of three of the cases. Besides this, the drum having selected its rhythm, the melody may interchange (*a*) and (*b*), or (*a*) and (*c*), but not (*b*) and (*c*). There is then cross-rhythm in half the possible cases. Of the two regions already mentioned, the east prefers long and metrically intricate rhythms— as many as 88 beats in a bar are known—but employs little cross-rhythm ; the west prefers short bars and elaborate cross-rhythm (see Ex. 4*b*).

FORM.—From a comparison of several hundreds of their songs and pieces the formal structure may be put down in general terms thus. (The letters *a*, *b*, *c* represent melodies of indeterminate length, which may be highly elaborate ; *z* stands for a development section.) These are typical examples only.

Folk music $\begin{cases} a \quad a \quad a, \text{ etc.} \\ a \quad a \quad b \quad a \quad a \quad b, \text{ etc.} \\ a \quad a \quad b \quad a \quad a \quad b \quad c \quad c \quad d \quad c \quad d, \text{ etc.} \end{cases}$

(There is no space for all the varieties.)

Composed music (west) *a a a z a* (voc. and instr.).

,,   ,,   (east) $\begin{cases} a \quad b \quad z \quad b \text{ (voc.).} \\ b \quad a \quad c \quad a \quad d \quad a \quad e \text{ (instr.).} \end{cases}$

Potpourris are a favourite form in folk-music and suites in composed music. In each suite a ' prelude,' representing the *maqām*, is followed by vocal and instrumental pieces gradually increasing in pace. As part of the connexion between music and magic, common to all the East, *maqāms* were, rather than are, appropriate to some one hour of the day.

INSTRUMENTS may be divided into melodic and rhythmic. Melodic are the bowed lute (Kamanja and Rabāb) and the flute held lengthways (Nai). Rhythmic are the tambourine (Duf) and drum (Darbūka, struck by two hands), neither of them tuned. The dulcimer (Qānūn), the short-necked lute ('Ud) and, in the east, the long-necked lute (Tanbūr) may serve both purposes. Choir and orchestra are now unknown. Unison singing and the ensemble of

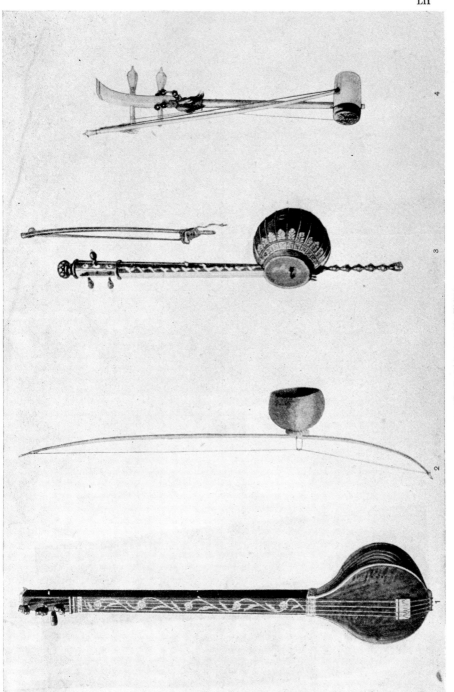

LII

ORIENTAL INSTRUMENTS

1. Indian Lute (*Tamburi*).   2. African Musical Bow (*Gubo*).   3. Persian Fiddle (*Kemantchè*).   4. Chinese Fiddle (*Urheen*).
1 and 3. By permission of Messrs. Novello & Co., Ltd.   2. Galpin Collection.   4. By permission of The Encyclopædia Britannica Co., Ltd.

nomogeneous instruments are hinted at in old books. Unaccompanied solo singing is reserved for the recitation of the Koran and of prayers ; it follows the *maqāms* but is in verbal rhythm. Instrumental solos exhibit virtuosity. Though expression by means of volume or pace is unknown, the performance does not sound meagre; this is due to the various qualities of tone and styles of playing, to the complexity of rhythms, and to the copious *melismata*. The whole forms a heterophony in the Greek sense rather than a monody or polyphony in ours.

BIBLIOGRAPHY

Encyclopédie de la Musique et Dictionnaire du Conservatoire (edited by A. Lavignac) : 1re partie. *Histoire de la musique.* Vol. 5. Paris, 1922. Articles by JULES ROUANET, *La Musique arabe*, and RAOUF YFKTA, *La Musique turque.*
JULIAN RIBERA : *La Musica de las Cantiguas.* Madrid, 1922.
Sammelb. für vergleichetnde Musikwissenschaft (edited by C. Stumpf and E. M. v. Hornbostel). Vol. 1. Munich, 1922.
ROBERT LACHMANN : *Die Musik in den tunisischen Städten* (*Archiv für Musikwissenschaft.* Jhrg. 5. 1923).
CARL BROCKELMANN : *Geschichte der arabischen Litteratur.* 2 vols. Weimar, 1898 ; Berlin, 1902.
The books and essays quoted give references to the whole of the rest of the *l*iterature, including manuscript and printed sources.
R. L. and A. H. F. S.

MUIÑEIRA (MUÑEIRA), see SONG, SPAIN (1).

MUKLE, MAY HENRIETTA (*b.* London, May 14, 1880), violoncellist, was educated at the R.A.M. As her public career began at the age of nine and has been continued since with successful tours at home, in various European countries, and in America, she may be regarded as a pioneer among women violoncellists (see VIOLONCELLO - PLAYING). She is a player of first-rate ability who has constantly set herself to enlarge the repertory of her instrument by the introduction of new works of serious aim.   C.

MULLINGS, FRANK (*b.* Walsall, May 10, 1881), operatic and concert tenor. He received his musical training at the Birmingham and Midland Institute under Prof. Granville Bantock and G. A. Breeden (vocal). In 1904 he won the Maas scholarship at that school, and three years later he made a public appearance in opera at Coventry in the part of Faust. He sang first in London at a Queen's Hall concert in 1911, but his experience as an operatic tenor really dates from a tour which he made with the Denhof company in 1913. Subsequently he came under the notice of Sir Thomas Beecham and extended his growing reputation as a lyric tenor to the metropolis. He made his début at Covent Garden during the Beecham summer season of 1919 as Hadyar in the first English performance of Isidore de Lara's opera ' Naïl.' In the autumn of the same year he did more conspicuous work by appearing as Othello in Verdi's opera and (Nov. 17) as the hero in the first English performance of Wagner's ' Parsifal.' Both these impersonations gained for him warm praise and encouragement, while other rôles in which he appeared to notable advantage were Tristan, Tannhäuser, Siegfried and Radamès After the formation of the B.N.O.C. his work in opera was mainly

associated with that organisation, and among other parts he created that of Apollo in Rutland Boughton's opera ' Alkestis ' on its production at Covent Garden, Jan. 11, 1924. During all this period he was doing important concert work and appearing at most of the principal musical festivals. Both as a singer and an actor he has made consistent improvement, but on the other hand he has never wholly rid himself of certain faults of production and style acquired during his early training. He has a powerful robust organ of genuine tenor quality, and his singing is marked by notable sincerity of expression. He married in 1924 Eleanora Vera Maude Ashbee.   H. K.

MULTIPLE TONALITY, see TONALITY ; HARMONY.

MUNCK, (1) FRANÇOIS DE (*b.* Brussels, 1815 ; *d.* there, 1854), Belgian violoncellist, trained at the Brussels Conservatoire under Platel, in which institution he eventually became that famous teacher's successor as first professor of the violoncello. As a soloist he was well known in Germany. In 1848 he accepted a position in the orchestra of Her Majesty's Theatre, London, but returned to Brussels in 1853. His chroniclers unite in ascribing to him exceptional talents, the development of which was hindered by a somewhat disorderly course of life. His one published composition was a ' Fantaisie et variations sur un thème russe.'

(2) ERNEST (*b.* Brussels, 1840 ; *d.* London, Jan. 19, 1915), son of the above, was a pupil of his father, and of Servais, and was a capable violoncellist at the age of 10. In 1855 he went on tour in Great Britain with Jullien's band, and ultimately settled down in London, where he was engaged as professor at the Guildhall School of Music. His residence in London, however, was not continucus. In 1868 he was in Paris, and in 1870 at Weimar, where he formed part of the court orchestra. He married Carlotta Patti in 1879. In 1893 he was appointed professor at the R.A.M.   W. W. C.

MUNDY (1), WILLIAM (*d. circa* 1591) a vicar-choral of St. Paul's, was sworn a gentleman of the Chapel Royal on Feb. 21, 1563/4. A service and three anthems by him, and also the anthem ' O Lord, the Maker of all thing ' (sometimes assigned to Henry VIII.), are printed in Barnard's ' Selected Church Music.' Another service and two other anthems are contained in Barnard's MS. collections, and eleven Latin motets in a set of MS. parts by him, both in the R.C.M. A number of compositions are in the Christ Church and Music School collections, Oxford. The words of several of his anthems are contained in Clifford's *Divine Services and Anthems*, 1664. He is mentioned by Morley in his *Introduction*, in company with Byrd and others, as never having ' thought it greater sacriledge to spurne against the Image of a Saint then to take two perfect cordes of one kinde together.' The date of his death is not recorded, but it was probably in 1591, as on Oct. 12 in that year Anthony Anderson was sworn gentleman of the Chapel Royal in his room.

(2) JOHN, Mus.D. (d. 1630), son of William (1), gentleman of the Chapel Royal, was educated by his father, became organist of Eton College, and about 1585 succeeded John Marbeck as one of the organists of St. George's Chapel, Windsor. On July 9, 1586, he graduated Mus.B. at Oxford. Both he and his father are mentioned in some verses at the end of a MS. collection of motets and madrigals transcribed in 1591 by John Baldwin, singing man of Windsor, recounting the celebrated musicians of the time. In 1594 he published 'Songs and Psalmes, composed into 3, 4 and 5 parts, for the use and delight of such as either love or learne Musicke,' published in ENGLISH MADRIGAL SCHOOL, vol. xxxv. He contributed a madrigal, 'Lightly she tripped o'er the dales' to 'The Triumphes of Oriana,' 1601. He took his Mus.D. degree in 1624. An anthem by him is contained in Barnard's MS. collections, and three of the pieces in his 'Songs and Psalmes' were scored by Burney (B.M. Add. MSS. 11,588). Burney gives a partsong by him, 'In deep distress,' in his *History*, vol. iii., p. 55. Several of his compositions for the keyboard are contained in the Fitzwilliam Virginal Book, among them a curious fantasia describing 'Faire Wether,' 'Lightning,' 'Thunder,' 'Calme Wether,' and 'A faire Day.' He died in 1630 and was buried in the Cloisters of St. George's Chapel, Windsor.   w. h. h.

MUNICH. Throughout its history until 1918 Munich's musical life has been closely bound up with that of the Bavarian court. To go no farther back, Orlando di Lasso spent the last thirty-four years of his life as Hofkapellmeister, his most prolific if not his best period, to be followed at intervals by his son Ferdinand (1609) and his grandson Ferdinand (1616–29). The first opera recorded at Munich was brought there by the Electress Adelaide from her home in Savoy. This opera seria had given way to the opera buffa by 1745.

The Residenztheater, an interesting example of the theatrical rococo, was begun in 1751 and opened in 1753. Mozart's 'Idomeneo' was produced in Munich in 1781. Side by side with the Italian opera occasional German music-plays were produced. The era of the Italian opera, however, was drawing to a close with the arrival of Gluck. A new opera house had been built in 1818 on the site of the Franciscan convent from plans of Karl von Fischer. In 1818, however, it was burnt down. King Ludwig I. had it rebuilt according to Fischer's plans in 1823, it was re-opened on

Jan. 2, 1825, as the Hof- und Nationaltheater. Shortly afterwards the king disbanded the Italian opera ; it is said that he was finally converted by a performance of 'Fidelio.'

With Johann Aiblinger as chief Kapellmeister came the new period when the German opera at Munich began to rank with the best in the country. The subsequent hundred years of opera in Munich may be said to form an epitome of the development of the opera in Germany. First there came the period of Franz Lachner. With his production of Meyerbeer's 'Les Huguenots' he lifted the Munich opera on to a new plane ; another landmark was his production of 'Tannhäuser' in 1855, in the face of strong opposition and intrigue. After his death in 1860 the second period may be said to have begun. It was signalised by the friendship between the new King, Ludwig II., and Richard Wagner. The composer brought Hans von Bülow to Munich, first as court pianist, but soon to be advanced (in 1867) to general music director. A year later Hans Richter came to Munich as director of the opera chorus, also under the influence of Wagner, and in 1869 Franz Wüllner became chief Kapellmeister. In the year in which Hans von Bülow became general music director, Karl von Perfall was appointed intendant. Under this combination, stimulated by the personality of the composer, the Wagner operas began to be lifted to a world-wide reputation, and to lift the Munich opera with them. 'Tristan' had been produced in 1865 ; it was to be followed by 'Rheingold' (1869), 'Die Walküre' (1870), 'Rienzi' (1871). When 'Siegfried' and the 'Götterdämmerung' were produced in 1878 Hermann Levi had been Kapellmeister for six years, Wüllner had died, and Rheinberger was chief Kapellmeister, assisted by Franz Fischer, who had been a violoncellist in the orchestra.

In the period that followed new influences were at work in Munich. Thuille had begun teaching at the composition school in 1883 (he remained till 1907) and Alexander Ritter came to live in Munich. Ritter had great influence on the younger musicians, and among those who came under him was Richard Strauss, who had a post as Kapellmeister from 1886–89, and again from 1894–98. Ritter died in Munich in 1896. Stavenhagen was Kapellmeister in 1898, Felix Weingartner conducted the Kaim orchestra from 1898–1907, and Max Reger lived in Munich from 1901–07. In 1903 Felix Mottl arrived for his all-too-short career in Munich—he died there in 1911—and set a tradition that was felt through every German school of conducting. He was succeeded by Bruno Walter. At this period Pfitzner, after many vicissitudes, came to Munich as conductor of the Kaim orchestra, and ten years later had his triumph when the Munich opera produced his 'Palestrina' as the climax of a Pfitzner week.

After an interval, due to the revolution of 1918, the Hof- und Nationaltheater was reconstructed and reorganised as the Bayerische Staatstheater, the name covering the Nationaltheater, the Residenztheater and the Prinzregenten-Theater, the last having been built in 1901 as a Wagner memorial theatre for performances after the manner of Bayreuth. Dr. Karl Zeiss then took over the management of the whole, but died in 1923. Baron Frankenstein, the intendant at the time of the revolution, who had then been compelled to retire, now returned, with Hans Knappertsbusch, who had succeeded von Hausegger under Zeiss, as general music director. The Munich festivals were revived in the 2nd and 3rd weeks of Aug. 1924. The centenary of the opera house was celebrated with great ceremony by a gala performance of the 'Meistersinger' on Jan. 1, 1925. Operatic performances are given occasionally at the Theater am Gärtnerplatz (Kapellmeister, Fritz Werther) and at the Münchner Volkstheater (Glinschegg). Light opera is given at the Operettenbuhne (Kurt Pastor).

The principal orchestra is the Orchester des Bayerischen Staatstheaters with 130 members (founded in 1911 as the Hof-Orchester). The Musikalische Akademie gives 10 concerts with this orchestra each season, under the direction of Knappertsbusch. The Münchner Konzertverein Orchestra, with 65 members, gives twelve subscription concerts (director S. von Hausegger), regular weekly popular symphony concerts (Friedrich Munter) and popular Sunday concerts (Friedrich Rammelt). The Philharmonische Konzerte (Julius Rünger) gives symphony and chamber concerts. There are four other orchestral associations.

Among the many chamber-music associations the chief are the Münchner Kammermusik Vereinigung, the Münchner Streichquartett, the Berber Quartett and the Vereinigung für alte Musik (viola da gamba, viola d' amore and cembalo). Chief among the choral associations is the Domchor (Berberich), with state and royal associations and a long history. There are over 100 choirs in Munich, several of which have celebrated their 50 years' jubilee. The Oratorienverein was founded by Karl von Perfall in 1854. The principal halls are the Odeon (1500), Tonhalle (large, 1800; small, 400), Künstlerhaus (600) and Museum (400). The state, city and Konzertverein have planned to build a Musikhaus with a hall to hold 2000–3000 persons.

The leading institution for musical education is the Staatliche Akademie der Tonkunst, founded in 1846 and reconstructed in 1867 under Hans von Bülow. The president is Professor S. von Hausegger. It gives teaching in every branch of music, especially in association with opera, solo and chorus. There are departments devoted to professional classes in composition, conducting, orchestral and church music. The school begins on or about Sept. 16. There are several private music schools, seminaries and singing schools. At the University there is a chair of Musikwissenschaft, held for many years past by Dr. Adolf Sandberger. The Bavarian State Library (librarian Dr. G. Schulz) possesses a fine collection of MSS. of the 15th to 17th centuries and a noteworthy collection of modern literature of music.   H. G. D.

MUNRO, ALEXANDER, a Scottish musician settled in Paris. He published there 'A Collection of the best Scots tunes fitted to the German flute,' folio, license dated 1732. This work is particularly rare—a copy was sold at the Taphouse sale in July 1905. Hawkins criticises the arrangements of the melodies thus : ' The simplicity of the airs is lost in the attempts of the author to accommodate them to the style of the Italian music.'   F. K.

MURCIANA, see FANDANGO ; SONG, subsection SPAIN (4).

MURIS, JOHANNES DE, a celebrated musical theorist of the early part of the 14th century. He has been claimed as an Englishman, but on what grounds it is difficult to say. Gesner, in his Bibliotheca universalis of 1545, p. 441, cites a mathematical treatise of De Muris printed at Mainz in 1538, but gives no indication of his nationality. Bale, who appears to have relied on information received from the learned Oxford mathematician, physician and antiquary Robert Record, included ' Joannes de Muris, quem Anglum fuisse scriptores ferunt,' in the second part of the enlarged edition of his Scriptores illustres Majoris Brittaniae (Basle, 1559, p. 69). Neither Gesner nor Bale makes any reference to his reputation as a musician. At a later date Tanner describes him as ' natione Anglus, philosophus, mathematicus et musicus insignis ' (Bibliotheca Brittanico-Hibernica, 1748, p. 537), and Sir John Hawkins found confirmation of his English origin in the following verses which occur in a treatise ' De origine et effectu Musice ' in MS. Lansdowne 763 of the British Museum, at fol. 17 :

'Pausas. iuncturas. fracturas. atque figuras
Mensuratarum formauit Franco notarum.
Et Jhon de Muris variis floruitque figuris.
Anglia cantorum nomen gignit plurimorum.'

But, in whatever way these lines are punctuated, it is difficult to see how they can be made to attribute an English origin to De Muris. No locality in England is known with an English or Latinised name at all resembling Muri or Muris.

When we look abroad the great Benedictine abbey of Muri in Switzerland at once suggests itself ; but the chronicles of this abbey, which have been published by P. M. Keim (Zürich, 1877), contain no reference to our author. In France there are several communes of the name of Murs or Meurs, and M. l'abbé Normand, who under the pseudonym of Théodore Nisard published a short paper on Jean de Muris in 1886, gives reasons for selecting Murs or Meurs in the cantonne of Sézanne, which lies about half-way between Meaux and Vitry, as the home of the De Muris family. Henri de Muris, bishop of Thérouane (d. 1286), was a benefactor of the abbey of Saint Faron at Meaux. Another Henri de Muris, chevalier, owned land at Saint Fiacre in Brie in 1313. This is in the near neighbourhood.

On the other hand Fétis favours a Norman origin on the ground that De Muris, in a letter written late in life to Pope Clement VI., alludes to the friendship of their youth, and that Clement had in fact been a monk at the Chaise Dieu in Normandy and afterwards Archbishop of Rouen. He cites a Padua manuscript dated 1404, and entitled

'Mag. Joh. de Muris de Normandia alias Parisiensis practica mensurabilis cantus cum expositione Prosdocimi de Beldemandis';

but one may suspect that the title is a later addition. In a mathematical treatise at Oxford dated 1321 (MS. Digby 190, fol. 66) Johannes de Muris is again described as a Norman ; but this is in a colophon which is clearly not part of the original treatise. No place of the name of Murs is known in Normandy.

Whatever doubt there may be about his birthplace, there is abundant evidence that De Muris resided for some part of his life in Paris. He himself speaks of having heard at Paris a triplum composed by Franco (Coussemaker, *Scriptores*, ii. 402a), and at least two of his treatises are dated from the Sorbonne in Paris. One is the *Musica speculativa* printed by Gerbert (*Scriptores*, vol. iii.), the Paris manuscript of which ends with the words : ' Explicit musica speculativa secundum Boetium per magistrum Johannem de Muris abbreviata Parisiis in Sorbona anno Domini 1323.' The other is the *Canones de eclipsi lunae*, the Bodleian manuscript of which (MS. Digby 97, fol. 124b) ends thus : ' Hos autem canones disposuit Johannes de Muris Parisiis in anno Domini 1339 in domo scolarium de Sorbona.' Leopold Delisle (*Le Cabinet des manuscrits de la Bibliothèque Nationale*, 1874, vol. ii. p. 186) has noticed that many of the Sorbonne manuscripts bear the names, and possibly the signatures, of teachers through whose hands they passed. One of them (Latin MS. 16,646) is an Euclid bearing the name of J. de Muris, but this may be the Julianus de Muris who was elected Rector of the Sorbonne in Dec. 1350 (Du Boulay, *Historia Universitatis Parisiensis*, iv. 973). Mersenne (*Harmonicorum libri XII.*, Paris, 1648. i xxv. 8) speaks of De Muris as ' Canonicus et Decanus Ecclesiae Parisiensis ' ; but his

name does not occur in the *Cartulary* of Notre Dame published in four volumes in 1850, nor in the *Gallia Christiana*, nor in *La France pontificale*.

Beyond 1339 the existence of De Muris can be traced down to 1350 or a little later. The authors of the *Gallia Christiana*, writing in 1744 (vol. vii. p. 1636), speak of ' epistolae Johannis Muri famosi theologi anni 1340 ' as attesting Philip de Vitry's skill in music ; but the letters are not now known, unless that mentioned below should prove to be one of them, and it may be doubted whether De Muris the musician is the person referred to. The Paris MS. 7443 of the Bibliothèque Nationale contains a letter of De Muris to Pope Clement the Sixth, who succeeded to the papacy in 1342. MS. Digby 176 of the Bodleian Library contains (at fol. 17b) an astrological treatise by De Muris on the conjunction of Saturn and Jupiter in 1345. Another Paris manuscript of the 15th century (Fonds Latin 14,736) is catalogued as containing: (1) Theorica numerorum auct. Jo. de Muris; (2) Ejusdem epistola metrica ad Philippum de Vitriaco, episcopum Meldensem; (3) De arte mensurandi. If this description be correct, De Muris must have been living at least as late as 1350, the year in which Philip de Vitry was appointed Bishop of Meaux. Weiss in Michaud's *Biographie universelle* (Paris, 1821) asserts that De Muris is known to have been still alive in 1358, but he gives no authority.

The reputation of De Muris, not only as musician, but as mathematician, astronomer and astrologer, is attested by the numerous manuscripts bearing his name to be found in most of the principal libraries of Europe. Mathematical treatises by him were printed at Vienna in 1515 and at Mainz in 1538. A copy of the latter is in the British Museum. The *Musica speculativa*, an abridgment of Boetius attributed to De Muris, was printed at Frankfort in 1508 and is probably the work cited by Panzer, i. 486, as ' Joann. Muris Musica manuscripta et composita. Lipsiae, 1496, fol.' As early as 1404 a commentary on his treatise on mensurable music was written by Prosdocimus de Beldemandis, and his authority is constantly appealed to by the theorists who followed him.

Of the musical works of De Muris by far the most important, and the only one of which the authenticity has never been questioned, is the *Speculum musice*, preserved in two manuscripts of the Bibliothèque Nationale at Paris, Nos. 7207 and 7207A, the former of which is said to date from the end of the 14th century. It is a treatise in seven books, the first five of which deal with the theory and the last two with the practice of music. Owing to its great length it has never been printed in its entirety, but Coussemaker has included the last two books in the second volume of his *Scriptores*, and has also, in the preface to that volume, given us the chapter-headings of the first five books.[1] These treat of intervals and ratios, consonances, proportions, scales, tetrachords and the like, and are professedly based on Boetius. The sixth book is devoted to the church modes, and expounds the doctrines first of Boetius, then (cap. xv.) of Guido and his successors, and finally (cap. lx. to cxiii.) of the moderns. The seventh book deals with mensurable music, and is remarkable for the protest it contains against modern divergence from the theory and practice of Franco and his school, against innovations in notation, exaggerated sentiment in descant, the liberties taken by singers in the matter of embellishment, the excessive use of discords and the abandonment of the old organum and conductus in favour of the motet and cantilena. De Muris never refers to contemporary musicians by name, but the passages he cites from their writings show that Philip de Vitry, the champion of the 'ars nova,' was one of those attacked. This lends point to the sentence at the end of his first chapter, in which De Muris disclaims any personal enmity against those whose doctrines he controverts. It has been thought that the *Speculum musice* is the treatise mentioned with three others at the end of the mathematical treatise of 1321 as having been completed in the same year, and that its publication was the immediate cause of the papal decree of 1322 prohibiting the use of descant in churches (see Ambros, ii. 347). The passage in MS. Digby 190 is as follows :

'Eodemque anno noticia artis musice proferende, figurande, tam mensurabilis quam plane, quantum ad omnem modum possibilem discantandi, non solum per integra sed usque ad minutissimas fracciones ; Cognicioque circuli quadrature perfectissime demonstrata ; Exposicioque tabularum Alphonsi reg's Castelle ; ac Geneologia Astronomie nobis claruit.'

This is not a very apt description of the *Speculum musice*, nor is the expression ' nobis claruit ' such as one would expect an author to use of his own work. On the other hand, it is unlikely that De Muris would have troubled to note down such a list of works unless they were his own, and no other musical treatise of his is known to which the description would at all apply. A further difficulty is caused by the fact that in the *Speculum* De Muris speaks of himself as old and feeble, which is hardly consistent with his having lived another thirty years, and it may be doubted whether the ' ars nova ' could have won by 1321 such general acceptance as is indicated by the language of the seventh book of the *Speculum*.

Several minor treatises attributed to De Muris have been printed by Gerbert and Coussemaker. Some of them do not profess to be more than epitomes of his teaching ; such are

the *Summa Magistri Johannis de Muris* (Gerbert, iii. 190) and the *Ars contrapuncti secundum Johannem de Muris* (Coussemaker, iii. 59). Others contain details of notation which did not come into use till long after his death, and doctrines which are entirely at variance with those of the *Speculum*. Such are the *Libellus practice cantus mensurabilis* (Coussemaker, iii. 46), which authorises the use of white or openheaded notes in *proportio sesquialtera*, and the *Ars discantus*, which is not only inconsistent with the *Speculum* in many respects, but actually cites De Muris as an authority (Coussemaker, iii. 68, 108). Others again contain passages which are quoted verbatim and confuted in the *Speculum*. Such are the *Musica speculativa* and the *Quaestiones super partes musicae* (Gerbert, iii. 256, 301).[2] For these reasons the *Speculum musice* is the only work which, in the present state of our knowledge, can be attributed without hesitation to De Muris. The treatises with the next best claim to authenticity are the *Summa musice*, the *Libellus* and the *Musica speculativa*. The *Summa musice* is not inconsistent with the *Speculum*, and the difference of style may be accounted for by supposing it to be an early work written for the use of students. The *Libellus* is accepted and quoted as the work of De Muris by Prosdocimus de Beldemandis and all the early theorists. The anachronism above referred to may perhaps be explained as a later addition intended to bring the book up to date. On the other hand, in all the manuscripts it is entitled *Libellus secundum* (not *per*) *J. de Muris*, and the mention by name of the contemporary Gulielmus de Mascandio (Guillaume de Machaut) is not in accordance with the practice of the *Speculum*. The *Musica speculativa* follows immediately after the *Speculum* in the Paris MS. 7207, and was printed as the work of De Muris in 1508, but Dr. Hirschfeld's demonstration of the attack made upon it in the *Speculum* seems fatal to its authenticity.

Extravagant claims were formerly made for De Muris as a pioneer and inventor. Nicola Vicentino first made the astonishing statement that musical notes, the long, breve, etc., were the invention of De Muris (*L' antica musica*, Rome, 1555, p. 9). Prior to the publications of Gerbert and Coussemaker this was repeated in many books of reference (as, for instance, in Grassineau's *Musical Dictionary* of 1740), though Mersenne and after him Rousseau (*Dict. de musique*, 1767), both of whom were at pains to consult the Paris manuscripts, had no difficulty in refuting it. If we ask what was the contribution of De Muris to the progress of the art of music, the answer must be that his was purely a restraining influence. Neither on the

---

[1] The text of liber i., cap. i.-xix., is printed in the pamphlet *Die einleitenden Kapitel des Speculum Musicae von Johannes de Muris*, by Walter Grossmann (B. & H., 1924). The pamphlet includes an analysis of the text of this portion of the *Speculum*, together with an attempt to answer the questions raised as to the identity of the author.

[2] See Dr. Robert Hirschfeld's *Johann de Muris*, Leipzig, 1884, pp. 11-26.

theoretical nor on the practical side of the art did he take any step forward. It is to his personality as a teacher, his vast erudition and his lucidity in definition and exposition that his reputation as a musician must be attributed.

J. F. R. S.

MURSCHHAUSER, Franz Xaver Anton (b. Zabern, Alsace, 1663 [1]; d. Munich, Jan. 6, 1738), came early to Munich, and became a pupil of Johann Caspar Kerl, with whom he remained till his death in 1690. From the title-page of his book 'Vespertinus latriae, et hyperduliae cultus' (Ulm, 1700; for four voices, two principal and four ripieno violins), we learn that he was then Kapellmeister to the Frauenkirche at Munich. Besides the work already mentioned, he left : ' Octitonium novum organum' (Augsburg, 1696) ; ' Prototypon longobreve organicum' (Nuremberg, 1700)—preludes and fugues for organ, lately re-edited by Franz Commer. A second part appeared later : ' Fundamentalische . . . Handleitung gewohl zur Figural- als Choral-Musik' (1707) ; ' Opus organicum tripartitum' (1712, 1714). His most important and best-known work is the *Academia musico-poetica bipartita, oder hohe Schule der musikalischen Composition* (Nuremberg, 1721). Towards the close of the first part he incautiously used the words ' to give a little more light to the excellent Herr Mattheson,' for which he was so severely taken to task by that irascible musician in a pamphlet *Melopoetische Lichtscheere in drei verschiedenen Schneutzungen* (*Critica musica*, pp. 1-88), that he relinquished the publication of the *Academia*. An ' Aria pastoralis variata ' of his is given in Pauer's ' Alte Klaviermusik ' ; his organ works have been reprinted in *D.D.T.* (2nd series), xviii.   F. G.

MURSKA, Ilma de (b. 1836; d. Jan. 14, 1889), a native of Croatia, taught singing at Vienna and Paris by Madame Marchesi ; made her début in opera at the Pergola, Florence, in Apr. 1862, sang at Pest, Berlin, Hamburg, Barcelona, etc. ; obtained an engagement in Vienna as a bravura singer in parts such as Constanze (' Seraglio '), Martha, Inez (' L'Africaine '), etc., and appeared in London at Her Majesty's Theatre, as Lucia, May 11, 1865. She played also Linda, Amina and Astrifiammante, and sang at the Philharmonic, May 29, and always with great applause. Between this date and 1873 she acted and sang repeatedly in London, at Her Majesty's, Covent Garden, and Drury Lane, returning to the Continent in the off seasons. One of her most congenial parts and best achievements was Senta in the Italian version of the ' Flying Dutchman,' July 23, 1870. Between 1873 and 1876 she visited America, Australia, New Zealand, etc., returning to this country in 1879. On Dec. 29, 1875, she married for the second

[1] Bapt. July 1, 1663.

time (her first marriage having taken place many years before), Alfred Anderson at Sydney ; and, after his death, she took for her third husband J. T. Hill, at Otago, New Zealand, May 15, 1876. Her voice was a soprano of nearly three octaves compass, with great execution. Her acting was brilliant and original, though sometimes bordering on extravagance. After spending some time from 1879 onwards in London, she went to New York as a teacher of singing, but, finding this work uncongenial, returned to Munich, to live with a married daughter. Interesting and amusing particulars of Murska's career may be read in *Marchesi and Music*, Santley's *Student and Singer*, and *The Mapleson Memoirs*.

A. C.

MUSARD, (1) Philippe (b. Tours, 1793; d. Mar. 31, 1859), took private lessons for some years from Reicha, to whom he dedicated his *Nouvelle Méthode de composition musicale* (1832). This long-forgotten work, of which only eight chapters appeared, contains the announcement of a *Traité complet et raisonné du système musical*, with curious historical notes, implying that Musard was dissatisfied with his position as an obscure violinist and conductor, and proposed to make his mark as a solid and erudite musician. A series of concerts and ' bals masqués,' held in the bazaar in the Rue St. Honoré (afterwards the Salle Valentino), however, gave him the opportunity of distinguishing himself in a different direction. The most salient feature of these promenade concerts (instituted Nov. 1833) was the introduction of the cornet-à-pistons. In fact Dufresne, the cornet-player, owed much of his success to the solos composed for him by the conductor. In 1835 and 1836 Musard conducted the balls at the Opéra, and his band of seventy musicians was rapturously applauded. ' Gustave III.' had set the fashion of the galop, and with Musard's music, and the ' entrain ' of the orchestra, the new dance deserved its nickname of ' Le galop infernal.' Meantime a better room had been built in the Rue Vivienne, and thither Musard removed in 1837. Here he had to sustain a competition with Johann Strauss of Vienna. His first experiment, the introduction of a chorus, having succeeded, he next attempted classical music, and in Holy Week gave a concert, consisting of Handel's music only.

Having secured a reputation in France, he came to England, and made his first appearance at Drury Lane on Monday, Oct. 12, 1840, as conductor of the Promenade Concerts, or Concerts d'hiver, given there under the management of Eliason. The series terminated in Mar. 1841, and on Sept. 30, Musard appeared again as conductor of a set of Promenade Concerts at the Lyceum, under the management of Henri Laurent, which continued up to

Christmas. He was long remembered in London, and his appearance is well described by Hood:

> 'From bottom to top
> There's no bit of the *Fop*,
> No trace of your Macaroni;
> But looking on him,
> So solemn and grim,
You think of the Marshals who served under Boney.'

Up to 1852 Musard was considered the best composer of dance-music and conductor of promenade concerts in France. His quadrilles —'Venise,' 'Les Échos,' etc.—contain many happy and at that time novel effects, and his music is well written and well scored. Having made money he bought a house at Auteuil, where he lived, much respected. Symptoms of paralysis appeared in 1852, and he died in 1859. His son

(2) ALFRED (*b.* Paris, 1828; *d.* Apr. 1881) followed his father's profession. As early as 1847 he conducted the orchestra at a ball given at the Opéra-Comique, and in 1856 Besse-lièvre selected him to conduct the Concerts des Champs-Élysées, but he did not retain the post, and never rose above mediocrity.   G. C.

MUSETTE, (1) a name indiscriminately given to a small keyless oboe or shawm in G, sometimes A flat, and to the Pastoral Oboe or SHEPHERD'S PIPE (*q.v.*), either in its single pipe form or double pipe and drone form. In the latter case the wind is supplied from a leathern reservoir in the manner of the BAG-PIPE (*q.v.*). All are characterised by the use of a double reed, the pipe with its finger holes giving a natural scale similar to that of the OBOE (*q.v.*).

(2) The term is also applied to an air in 2–4, 3–4 or 6–8 time, of a moderate tempo, and smooth and simple character, appropriate to the instrument from which it takes its name. Thus a musette generally has a pedal-bass answering to the drone or *bourdon*, and the upper part abounds in grace-notes and rapid passages. To these airs were arranged pastoral dances, also called musettes, which were in great favour under Louis XIV. and Louis XV., especially the latter, as may be seen by the pictures of Watteau and others of that school.

Among the most celebrated musettes may be mentioned those in 'Callirhoé' and 'Nina,' operas by Destouches and Dalayrac. Musettes are to be found in Bach's English Suites, Nos. 3 and 6, in the sixth of Handel's grand concertos and the overture to 'Alcina.'   G. C.

MUSICA ANTIQUA, a collection of music compiled and edited by John Stafford SMITH (*q.v.*), and published in 1812 in two vols. folio, with a preface and translations of the Provençal songs inserted in the work by John Sidney Hawkins, and some notes by the editor. Its nature and objects will be best described by quoting the very ample title—

'Musica Antiqua. A Selection of Music of this and other countries from the commencement of the twelfth to the beginning of the eighteenth century, comprising some of the earliest & most curious Motetts, Madrigals, Hymns, Anthems, Songs, Lessons & Dance Tunes, some of them now first published from manuscripts and printed works of great rarity & value. The whole calculated to shew the original sources of the melody & harmony of this country, & to exhibit the different styles and degrees of improvement of the several periods.'

The work contains 190 separate pieces. The selections are made with great skill and judgment, but are very ill digested, as instead of being arranged in strict chronological order, they are intermingled in a very confused manner. The composers from whose works the specimens are selected are:

John Ambrose, Hugh Aston, Thibaut de Blason, Dr. John Blow, Gaces Brulez, William Byrd, Dr. Thomas Campion, Peter Certon, Dr. William Child, Clemens non Papa, John Cole, Raoul de Coucy, Perrin Dangecourt, John Dowland, John Earsden, Jehan Erars, Thomas Erars, Francesco Geminiani, Jhan Gero, Orlando Gibbons, Heath, Henry VIII., Pelham Humfrey, Simon Ives, John Jenkins, Robert Johnson, Robert Jones, Nicholas Laniere, Orlando di Lasso, Jehan de Latre, William Lawes, Matthew Locke, George Mason, Tiburtio Massaino, Christofero Morales, Thibaut King of Navarre, Jacob Obrecht, Johannes Okeghem, Parker, monk of Stratford, Francis Pilkington, Jodocus Pratensis, Daniel Purcell, Henry Purcell, Richafort, Dr. Nicholas Staggins, Thomas Tallis, Thierres, Orazio Vecchi, Thomas Weelkes, Giaches Wert, Adrian Willaert and Gioseffo Zarlino, besides others whose names are unknown.

The principal pieces include four ancient chants for the Te Deum as given by Meibomius, Diruta, Lucas Lossius and Merbecke; the canon, 'Sumer is icumen in'; chansons by troubadours of Navarre and Normandy; part of Robert Johnson's music for Middleton's 'Witch'; two or three masques of the time of James I., copious extracts from 'Musick's Handmaid,' two parts, 1678 and 1689; etc., etc.   W. H. H.

MUSICA DIVINA. (1) A collection of 42 madrigals by various composers published in 1583 at Antwerp by PHALÈSE (*q.v.*).

(2) An important collection of church music, edited by Carolus PROSKE, priest and Kapellmeister of the cathedral at Ratisbon, and published there by Pustet. The materials were collected by Proske himself from the libraries of the Papal Chapel, St. Peter's, St. John Lateran, S. Maria Maggiore, S. Maria in Vallicella, the Vatican, the Roman College and other libraries in Rome, and also from the best collections in Naples. The prospectus was issued in Jan. 1853, and the first volume, 'Liber missarum,' was published in the same year. The second volume, 'Liber motettorum,' followed in 1854; the third, 'Liber vesperarum' (Psalms, etc.), in 1859; and the fourth, 'Liber vespertinus' (Passions, Lamentations, etc.), at Easter 1862. All these contained compositions for four voices, and belong to the 'first year.' The publication was continued by a 'Selectus novus missarum' in two vols. (1857–1861), after which Proske died, Dec. 20, 1861. An 'Annus secundus,' four volumes having the same general arrangement as the 'Annus

primus,' was issued subsequently under the editorship of Schremo and Haberl.

MUSICA FICTA, or FALSA, or COLORA-TA (*Cantus Fictus*). Early music presents many insoluble problems to those who set out to reconstruct and interpret it. In few of the problems, however, is it so hazardous to attempt any definite codex of law and practice as in that of *Musica ficta*—*i.e.* the insertion of accidentals into a text. That composers, from the earliest times, intended such occasional modifications to be made by the performers is beyond any possible doubt : indeed the ancient name for an accidental (*signum asininum* or ' asses' mark ') is clear evidence that its insertion by a composer was a reflection on the competence of the singer. But there is little or no agreement amongst the old theorists as to the laws of interpretation ; which seems to imply either that there was no unanimity in practice, or that the theorists themselves suffered from the malady endemic to their tribe. For it is characteristic of all theorists to epitomise and codify the very usages which the creative minds of their contemporaries have decisively abandoned. Nor is there, at the present day, any solid agreement amongst the most thoughtful students of ancient music—no two of whom would, in all probability, produce an identical ' fair-copy ' of any given manuscript from the earliest times down to Orlando Gibbons. The most reasonable course, therefore, is to attempt to state impartially the conditions of the problem and the difficulties inherent in its solution.

' Music is called *Ficta* when we make a tone to be a semitone, or, conversely, a semitone to be a tone.' [1] And the problem for the student consists in this : since the composer did not (or seldom did) tell the performer, by means of accidentals, when these changes were to be made, how could the performer know ?

The most usual cases in which accidentals were assumed to be too obvious for insertion were the following :

Notes to be raised a semitone :

(*a*) The seventh note of the scale, if rising to the tonic, in order to create a major sixth with the supertonic :

(*b*) To avoid a diminished fifth, if rising subsequently :

(*c*) To avoid the tritone :

1 *Ars Contrapuncti*, early 14th century.

(*d*) To avoid the minor third in a full close:

Notes to be lowered a semitone :
(*a*) To avoid the tritone :

(*b*) To avoid the chord of the diminished fifth (*Quinta falsa*).

It is beyond doubt that the singers, in any early period, were capable of a performance comparatively free from error, and it is customary nowadays to marvel at their skill, with an accompanying gibe at the deterioration of their descendants. But such easy wit ignores the fact which lies at the root of the matter : *i.e.* the immense strain on the resources of notation which accompanied, *pari passu*, the transition from the homophonic modal melody to the polyphonic harmonies of the major and minor scales. If an edition of a hymn-book were published to-day with all accidentals omitted any fair musician could play it through with but few catastrophes ; and such accidents as occurred would be due to one of two causes. (1) In equal temperament the music may at any moment modulate anywhere, and therefore cases of ambiguity may arise when the signposts are absent. (2) Certain hymn tunes would be ' modal ' (or pseudo-modal) and the idiom might be unfamiliar to a performer accustomed only to major and minor keys.

But when all music was modal the first of these difficulties was practically non-existent. Given the mode, the excursions from it were circumscribed and definite, and a mistake would betray either culpable ignorance or pure carelessness. The second difficulty, however, was always present from the moment when the simplest two-part harmony existed ; at first involving little more than careful attention, but decade by decade more imperatively demanding concentration of mind. And the appreciation of the ever-growing insistence of this demand gives the key to the whole development of music from the simplicity of a plainsong melody to the complexity of a Bach motet.

A short outline of the functions of the accidental in this evolution may help to make clearer the lines on which it developed. Originally, when melodies were purely modal and structurally simple, no need occurred for the alteration of any note of the mode chosen. Given an appreciation of the relationship of tonic and dominant, the melodies travelled evenly along the path of conjunct motion. But as soon as a more enterprising ambition began to explore the possibilities of disjunct motion, the angularity of the tritone became apparent and was felt to be the bar to progress. And undoubtedly the first use of a note foreign to the mode (i.e. a note chromatically altered) was for the purpose of softening this obtrusion.

Later, when the combination of voices had passed the experimental stage, and normal music had become definitely harmonic, the accidental acquired other functions. For example, the *Clausula vera*, or true CADENCE (q.v.) in two parts, necessitated a penultimate chord which was a major sixth (or its inversion); and the feeling for the ' leading note,' which was destined to revolutionise the whole modal system, was given its first impetus. And when increased harmonic technique had established three-part writing, the laws of acoustics led composers, unconsciously obedient to them, to sharpen the third in the final chord. Once started, the swing away from the severity of diatonic modal melody to the freedom of non-modal chromatic harmony gathered momentum with every experiment. The process is described in a passage from the preface to vol. i. (Taverner) of the Carnegie Edition of *Tudor Church Music*:

' At the present moment the world has so tired of the limitations of the major and minor scales that our composers are deliberately exploring those harmonic fields which are conveniently labelled "modal." But in Taverner's time the musical sense of Europe was moving, in the unconscious fulfilment of an evolution it could not escape, in exactly the reverse direction : *from* the modal system to the system with which we are now surfeited. The modes are for melody, and for melody alone, and the birth of polyphony rang the death-knell of the whole modal system. Consequently, the pioneer of those days was the man who saw his way to cast aside some of the angular conventions that had grown out of the vain attempt to combine modal laws with harmonic exigencies, and to foreshadow the ease and smoothness of texture and progression which later, in the days of equal temperament, were to be the common accomplishment of every student. In the days when the modes were living things such terms as leading-note, dominant, or any sort of cadence, meant something different in kind from what they of necessity meant tc the later polyphonic composer ; for his standpoint was no longer primarily melodic. Horizontal it still was, in the matter of texture and combination of rhythms, but his mind was at last—what it had never been before—chained and tethered to the perpendicular chord as seen from the bass upwards. Smoothness of chord-progression meant manipulation of the notes constituting chords, so that in the passage from austere diatonic modality to the flexibility of the modern tonality, increase of technique and craftsmanship synchronised with increased freedom in the use of accidentals.' (See also HARMONY.)

This inexorable trend towards our modern scales, spread over the centuries, produced in composers a sense of tonality which was never final or stagnant, but continuously developing. Their conception of the material at their disposal, notes, chords, keys and modulations,

was never for any group of years truly static, and in this ceaseless growth of an idea lies the difficulty of the student of to-day in determining the intention of a composer at any given moment. At either end of the period the problem is seldom really baffling : one expert will feel as secure in his transcription of a purely modal melody as another in his reading of one of the Forty-eight : in both cases there may, here and there, be a choice between two possibilities, but not a doubt as to whether any reading at all will ' make sense.' But in the intervening centuries uncertainty dogs every conclusion, and many questions arise. What was the feeling for tonality at this moment ? Was this particular composer a pioneer or a ' die-hard ? ' Is this curious passage a survival of modal influence or an experiment in modernity ? And in such a work as a Tallis motet questions such as these must be answered a dozen times, and no two scholars will coincide in every solution. And when it is added that right up to the end of the period, until the complexities of equal temperament forced composers to say exactly what they meant— there persisted the old tradition that to insert *all* the accidentals was to insult the intelligence of the performer, some conception will be formed of the brambles and briars that bestrew the path of a modern editor.

Scholars who desire first-hand acquaintance with the ancient authorities on *Musica ficta* are referred to

Pietro Aron, 1529.
Zarlino, 1558.
Zacconi, 1596.
Coussemaker : *Scriptorum de musica.*

P. C. B.

MUSICA FIGURATA (Figured music). Used in mediæval music of embellishments to the plain-song itself, but more frequently of descants added by singers in counterpoint with the *canto fermo* or plain-song.

W. S. R.

MUSICAL ANTIQUARIAN SOCIETY, THE (1840–47), ' for the publication of scarce and valuable works by the early English composers,' was established in 1840, and started its publications in November of that year.

Nineteen works were published, in large folio, and to these were added sixteen corresponding folios of compressed scores by Sir G. A. Macfarren. These were undertaken by the publisher on his own responsibility, with a view of increasing the subscription list.

The Society lasted seven years, and in its second year numbered nearly a thousand members. The annual subscription was one pound, and the works were supplied to the members at prime cost.

The nineteen works issued by the Society were :

1. A Mass for five voices, by William Byrd. Edited by E. F. Rimbault.
2. The first set of Madrigals by John Wilbye. Edited by James Turle.

3. Madrigals and Motets for five voices, by Orlando Gibbons. Edited by Sir George Smart.
4. Dido and Æneas, a tragic opera by Henry Purcell. Edited by G. A. Macfarren.
5. The first set of Ballets for five voices by Thomas Morley. Edited by E. F. Rimbault.
6. Book I. of Cantiones Sacrae for five voices, by William Byrd. Edited by W. Horsley.
7. Bonduca, a tragedy by Henry Purcell. Edited by E. F. Rimbault.
8. The first set of Madrigals by Thomas Weelkes. Edited by Edward J. Hopkins.
9. Fantasies in three parts composed for Viols, by Orlando Gibbons. Edited by E. F. Rimbault.
10. King Arthur, an opera, by Henry Purcell. Edited by Professor Edward Taylor.
11. The whole Book of Psalms with their wonted tunes, in four parts, as published by Thomas Este. Edited by E. F. Rimbault.
12. The first set of Songs by John Dowland. Edited by William Chappell.
13. Airs or Fa las by John Hilton. Edited by Joseph Warren.
14. A collection of Anthems by M. Este, T. Ford, Weelkes and Bateson. Edited by E. F. Rimbault.
15. Madrigals by John Bennet. Edited by E. J. Hopkins.
16. The second set of Madrigals by John Wilbye. Edited by George William Budd.
17. The first set of Madrigals by Thomas Bateson. Edited by E. F. Rimbault.
18. Parthenia, or the first music ever printed for the Virginals, by W. Byrd, John Bull and Orlando Gibbons. Edited by E. F. Rimbault.
19. Ode composed for St. Cecilia's Day by Henry Purcell. Edited by E. F. Rimbault.

Dr. Rimbault acted throughout as hon. secretary, and W. Chappell, the projector of the Society, acted for about five years as treasurer and manager of the publications. He was then succeeded by his younger brother, Thomas P. Chappell. The publications of the Society, useful in their day, are now for the most part superseded by later and more authoritative editions, such as those of the PURCELL SOCIETY, the ENGLISH MADRIGAL SCHOOL and TUDOR MUSIC (Carnegie Trust).

w. c., with addns.

MUSICAL ARTISTS' SOCIETY, THE (1873–99). Among the numerous attempts made for the direct encouragement of British music towards the end of the 19th century, those for which this Society was responsible hold no small place. Projected in 1873 by Arthur O'Leary, C. E. Stephens and other musicians, the Society was established in the following year, when a series of semi-private concerts was inaugurated, at which perform-ances were given of chamber music, chiefly by members of the Society—Algernon Ashton, J. F. Barnett, F. Davenport, Dr. F. E. Glad-stone and Sir G. A. Macfarren being some of the composers whose works had a hearing. Among the list of original members may be mentioned J. F. Barnett, H. R. Bird, Alfred Gilbert, A. Randegger and Olaf Svendsen ; while the vice-presidents were Sir G. A. Mac-farren, Sir Arthur Sullivan and others ; the Duke of Beaufort being president. The first concert took place at the premises of Messrs. Stanley Lucas, Weber & Co., others (being three in number a year, though later this number was increased) at such places as the R.A.M., Grosvenor Gallery, and St. Martin's Town Hall, where the last concert was given on June 6, 1898, the Society dissolving itself early in 1899.   N. C. G.

MUSICAL ART SOCIETY OF NEW YORK, see NEW YORK.

MUSICAL ASSOCIATION, THE, initiated by Sir John Stainer and the Rev. Sir F. A. Gore Ouseley, Bart., was established in 1874, after preliminary meetings at the house of W. Spottis-woode, F.R.S., and at South Kensington Museum, at the latter of which, on May 29, John Hullah presided, and several members were enrolled. On Aug. 4, 1874, the first general meeting of the members was held, A. J. Ellis, F.R.S., in the chair ; and it was resolved that the Society's title should be :

'Musical Association for the investigation and dis-cussion of subjects connected with the Science and Art of Music.'

The members, according to the rules,

'consist of practical and theoretical musicians as well as those whose researches have been directed to the science of acoustics, the history of music or other kindred subjects.'

The Association met for many years at the Beethoven Rooms, Harley Street, on the first Monday of every month from Nov. to June, when papers were read and discussed. Later both the place and the day of meeting have varied at convenience. The subscription is one guinea a year, and members are elected by ballot. The first president was the Rev. Sir F. A. G. Ouseley, Bart., whose successor was Sir John Stainer. The vice-presidents were G. Grove ; J. Hullah ; G. A. Macfarren, Mus.D. ; W. Spottiswoode, and J. Tyndall. The original Council included the vice-presi-dents and Messrs. W. Chappell, G. A. Osborne, Dr. W. Pole, Messrs. A. H. D. Prendergast, C. K. Salaman (the first hon. secretary), Dr. Stainer and Dr. W. H. Stone. The Society's Proceedings were published annually by Chap-pell & Co. for the first three years, and then by Stanley Lucas & Weber, until 1887 inclusive ; in 1888 Novello's name appeared on the title-page as publisher. The present publishers (1926) are Whitehead & Miller, Leeds. The early volumes of Proceedings are of extreme rarity. The whole represents an important body of research, and numerous references to the contents will be found in this Dictionary. In 1900 the Association entered into special relations with the INTERNATIONAL MUSICAL SOCIETY (q.v.) with certain privileges in the way of subscription to members of both societies. In 1904 the Association became incorporated. The Secretary of the Musical Association is Mr. J. Percy Baker.   c. m., with addns.

MUSICAL BOW, a primitive type of musical instrument found among savage tribes in such widely distant places as New Mexico, Patagonia, Central and South Africa, India and the Spice Islands (see PLATE LII. No. 2).

The types which have been collected and deposited in our museums are astonishingly similar, the general form being an ordinary bow such as is used for shooting arrows, formed of cane or pliable wood, bent by a tight cord. The size varies from 5 or 6 feet in length to

18 inches or 2 feet. In almost every case a dried gourd or other hollow vessel is fixed to the cane or wood portion, and this acts as a resonator. Generally, the string is also kept taut by a smaller cord passing over it, below the middle, and attached to the wood or cane part. The sound is produced by striking or plucking the tightened string with a piece of wood or bone, and by skilful performance various notes are produced.

It is important to discriminate between the Musical Bow and the Oriental Kite Bows and African Goura, in both of which the string is set in vibration by a current of air ; nor does the Musical Bow appear to have much affinity with the Jew's Harp, another widely distributed sound producer, in which, however, the tones are varied by altering the resonating cavity of the mouth.

BIBL.—H. BALFOUR, (1) *The Natural History of the Musical Bow* (Oxford, 1899) ; (2) *The Goura (Journal of Anthropological Institute*, vol. xxxiii., 1902) ; ANKERMANN, *Die afrikanischen Musikinstrumente* (Berlin. 1901) ; *The American Anthropologist* (vol. ii., 1898).

F. W. G.

MUSICAL BOX, see MECHANICAL APPLIANCES (4).

MUSICAL GLASSES, see HARMONICA.

MUSICAL SNUFFBOX, see MECHANICAL APPLIANCES (4).

MUSICAL SOCIETY OF LONDON, THE (1858–67). This Society was founded in Apr. 1858 by a body of musicians, professional and amateur, who had originally been members of the New Philharmonic Society, and wished to reconstitute it. This being found impracticable, they established a new institution, under the name of the Musical Society of London. Among the names of this body are found those of Charles Salaman, the chief mover of the project, who held the post of honorary secretary until 1865, when G. C. Verrinder succeeded him ; Augustine Sargood (treasurer) ; C. E. Horsley (honorary librarian) ; W. V. Wallace ; G. A. Macfarren ; Henry Smart ; Jules Benedict ; Stephen Elvey ; John Goss ; E. J. Hopkins ; B. Molique ; Sir F. A. Gore Ouseley, Bart. ; and Dr. S. S. Wesley ; besides other prominent musicians. The objects of the Society, as stated in its early prospectuses were :

To promote social intercourse among its members and with musicians of this and other countries ; to form a musical library for the use of members ; to hold conversazioni, at which papers on musical subjects might be read, and subjects of musical interest discussed ; to give orchestral, choral, and chamber concerts, and occasionally lectures ; to afford the opportunity of trying new compositions ; to publish occasional papers calculated to extend the theoretical and historical knowledge of music.

The members consisted of fellows, associates and lady-associates, whose subscription was fixed at one guinea. The following were honorary fellows : Auber, Berlioz, Ernst, Joachim, Meyerbeer, Moscheles, Rossini and Spohr. The conductor of the Society during the whole period of its existence was Alfred Mellon. The

first concert took place on Jan. 26, 1859, when the C minor symphony of Beethoven, the ' Melusina ' overture of Mendelssohn, and a cantata by G. A. Macfarren, ' May-Day,' etc., were given. At the last concert, Mar. 20, 1867, the most interesting feature of the programme was Beethoven's Choral Fantasia, the pianoforte part of which was played by Mme. Schumann.

M.

MUSICAL UNION, THE, see ELLA, JOHN.

MUSICA MENSURATA, or CANTUS MENSURABILIS (Measured Music). The notes of plain-song were originally of indeterminate length ; and were lengthened or shortened indefinitely, in accordance with the rhythm or accent of the words to which they were adapted. But after the invention of figured music it became necessary to design a system of notation capable of expressing the relative duration, as well as the pitch, of every note intended to be sung : and thus arose a new species of song, called *Cantus mensurabilis* or measured music. (See NOTATION, subsection MUSICA MENSURATA, where the system is described ; also RHYTHMIC MODES.)

One of the earliest known writers on this subject was Franco of Cologne (see FRANCO, Magister), author of *Ars cantus mensurabilis*.

Next in point of antiquity to Franco's treatise is one written by our own countryman, Walter ODINGTON (*q.v.*) of Evesham, in the 13th century. Others follow, by Marchettus of Padua, in 1274 ; Johannes de Muris, in 1321 ; Robert de Handlo—another Englishman—in 1326 ; Prosdocimus de Beldemandis, in 1410 ; Franchinus Gafurius, in 1480.

W. S. R., abridged.

BIBLIOGRAPHY

JOHANNES WOLF : *Geschichte der Mensural-Notation von 1250–1460.* 3 Il. (Leipzig, 1904, 1905) ; *Ein Breslauer Mensuraltraktat des 15. Jahrhunderts (A.M. 13. 1919).*
JACQUES HANDSCHIN : ' Die ältesten Denkmäler mensural notierter Musik in der Schweiz ' (*A.M.*, Jan., 1923. Pp. 1–10).

MUSICA TRANSALPINA, the name of the first printed collection of Italian madrigals with English words. It was published in London in 1588 (the dedicatory epistle is dated Oct. 1), soon after Byrd had issued his ' Psalmes, Sonets and Songs,' the first printed collection of English madrigals. The title is :

' Musica Transalpina. Madrigales translated of foure, five and sixe parts, chosen out of diuers excellent Authors, with the first and second part of *La Verginella*, made by Maister *Byrd* vpon two Stanz's of *Ariosto*, and brought to speak English with the rest. *Published by* N. Yonge, *in fauour of such as take pleasure in Musick of voices.* Imprinted at London by Thomas East, the assigné of William Byrd, 1588. *Cum Priuelegio Regiae Maiestatis.*'

Nicholas YONGE (*q.v.*) was the compiler. The collection contains fifty-seven madrigals, viz. sixteen by Ferrabosco, ten by Marenzio, four each by Palestrina and Filippo di Monte, three by Conversi, two each by Byrd, Faignient, Donato, Orlando Lasso, Ferretti and Felis, and one each by di Macque, Pordenoni, de Vert, Verdonck, Palestrina, Rinaldo del Mel, Bertani and Pinello. In the table of contents the original initial Italian words are given, side by side with the English. In 1597 Yonge published a second book under the same name, containing twenty-four madrigals, viz. six by Ferrabosco, three each by Marenzio, Croce and Quintiani, two each by Eremita and Palavicino, and one each by Vecchi, Nanini, Venturi, Feliciani and Bicci. The English words in both books are almost literal translations of the original Italian, and are generally well fitted to the notes, but as verses are singularly crude, and in some instances—notably the well-known 'Cynthia, thy song and chanting' of Giovanni Croce—almost unmeaning.   W. H. H.

MUSICIANS' COMPANY. The Worshipful Company of Musicians of London has a history and associations which carry back the mind to the musical life of the Middle Ages, the days of the troubadours and minstrels. The Charter by which the Company received its corporate existence and legal status dates back no farther, it is true, than 1604, in which year it was granted by James the First. This was not, however, the first instrument by which minstrels in England had been empowered to form themselves into Guilds or Fraternities, for the Patent Roll gives us the Charter granted by King Edward IV. in 1469 to his 'beloved minstrels,' empowering them to constitute themselves into a guild and make rules and regulations for the government of the craft or 'mystery' of musicians, and to adopt measures to remedy grievances and improve the poor estate into which the calling had evidently then fallen from the high esteem in which it had been held in previous centuries. This Charter, preserved by Rymer in his well-known *Foedera*, where the original Latin text is given, possesses great interest, by reason of the light it throws upon the musical practitioners of those days. Though apparently the earliest on record, it cannot have been the first of its kind, for in it we are told that 'the brothers and sisters of the Fraternity of Minstrels' had established and ordained similar brotherhoods or guilds 'in times past.' Of these earlier Charters, unfortunately, no copy is known, but it will be safe to assume that the rules which they contained for the government of the guild differed little from those laid down in the document here referred to.

This earlier Charter was granted in response to the prayer of the King's Minstrels, whose names are given. They were Walter Halliday (Marshall), John Cliff, Robert Marshall, Thomas Grene, Thomas Calthorne, William Cliff, William Christean and William Eynsham. They complain of the wrong done them by 'certain ignorant rustics and craftsmen of various callings, who falsely represent themselves to be minstrels; although they are in that art by no means learned or skilled, they nevertheless move from place to place on festival days and collect all those profits by means of which the King's Minstrels should obtain their living '; and, furthermore, that thus 'much disgrace is brought upon the art or occupation of minstrels.' To remedy the grievances thus complained of, the minstrels named were erected into a corporation with perpetual succession, and were given powers of examination, supervision, control and correction of all minstrels throughout the Kingdom, the County of Chester excepted, for there the minstrels were under other special control (see Sir Peter Leycester's *Historical Antiquities of Cheshire*). What measure of success attended the efforts of the new guild to improve the condition of the members, or what was its eventual fate, is not recorded. Its existence must have been short-lived, however, for at the opening of the 16th century we find mention of a new guild, a 'Fellowship of Minstrels and Freemen of the City of London,' though when and by whom it was instituted there is nothing so far discovered to show. However, in the history of the Pewterers' Company by Welch, under date 1500 and 1501, it is stated that the Pewterers' Hall was frequently let, the Minstrels or Musicians being amongst the principal hirers.

It may be remarked in passing that the term 'Minstrel' is a loose one and has led to some confusion, a notable instance being the Henry Walker, 'citizen and minstrel of London,' from whom Shakespeare held his house in Blackfriars. Walker's connexion with the Musicians' Company is mentioned in his will with codicil proved Aug. 30, 1616, where he describes himself as a 'Musitian of London.'

The association that existed between music and players leads one to suppose that in all probability Shakespeare, too, was a member of the Musicians' Company, but owing to the Roll of the Freemen connected with the Company at that period having been destroyed we are unable to find any proof for this supposition.

In the early days one of the principal duties of these City Musicians or 'waits,' as they were commonly called, was to supply the music for the City Pageants and Festivities.[1]

The Fellowship of the Freemen and Minstrels of the City of London have many complaints to make of precisely the same character as those raised by the minstrels of Edward IV., 'the povertie and decay' to which they are brought by the 'continuell recorse of foreign minstrels daily resorting to the City out of all the Contrays of England.' For the remedy of this, and

---

[1] The livery of the London Waits in 1575 is described in Fairholt's *Lord Mayors' Pageants*, Pt. 1, p. 23, as follows : 'Blue gowns, red sleeves and caps, every one having his silver collar about his neck.' The gowns worn by the Masters and Wardens of the present day are blue, trimmed with fur. In the Diary of Henry Machyn, citizen and merchant-taylor of London, 1550–63, may be seen such entries as the following :
'The furst day of September [1556] was Sant Gylles day, and ther was a goodly processyon abowt the parryche with the whettes (waits) and the canepe borne, and the Sacrement, and ther was a goodly masse songe as bene hard ; and master Thomas Grenelle, waxchandler mad a grett dener for master Garter and my ladye, and master Machylle the shreffe and ys wife, and both the chamburlayns, and mony worshipfull men and women at dener, and the whettes playng and dyvers odur mynsterelles, for ther was a grett dener.'

for the better government of the London Minstrels, the testing of 'their sufficiency in their art,' and the control and regulation of the teaching of music and dancing, we find that rules were continually enacted and re-enacted, but without, as it would seem, any permanent measure of success.[1]

Eventually the Fellowship appears to have been reduced to such a condition that it was deemed necessary to reconstitute it upon a new basis. This was furnished by the Charter of James I., which brought into existence the Worshipful Company of Musicians. It was incorporated at the prayer of the above-mentioned Fellowship of the Minstrels of London (of which it was consequently the direct successor and representative), under the style and title of 'the Master, Wardens and Commonalty of the Musicians of London.' It was to be governed by a master, two wardens and a body of assistants numbering not less than thirteen and not more than twenty, and it was to be invested with full powers for the control and government of all minstrels and musicians in the City of London and within three miles thereof. In accordance with the authority conferred in the Charter, the Company drew up an elaborate series of by-laws for the regulation of the teaching of music within its jurisdiction. These rules, which are too elaborate and extensive to quote here, afford some interesting matter for readers of to-day. It must be admitted, however, that they exhibit a business-like and wise regard for the interests of its members, their proficiency in their art, and also for the training and morals of the apprentices.

The Arms of the Company were granted by Camden, Oct. 15, 1604, and approved by Sir Henry St. George Richmond, 1634, Philip Pikeman being master, Walter Clarke and Philip Janvrin, wardens, and Nicholas Pinny, clerk. We may add that the principal charge of the Arms is the swan, the bird of Apollo and emblem of the musician's or poet's song.

The state of decline into which the art of music as a profession had fallen during the 17th century is no doubt due to the Revolution and Puritan domination. It is therefore not surprising that the Musicians' Company should have sunk into comparative obscurity, as is proved by a MS. dated about 1660, which is preserved in the Bodleian Library, wherein the members of the Company are enumerated as being thirteen in number. Later on, however, it appears to have come once more to the front, for in 1700 the Company was authorised by an Act of Common Council to exercise jurisdiction over dancing-masters. It likewise appears that the Company's jurisdiction was enforced as late as 1763, in which year an action was suc-

cessfully brought by the Musicians' Company before the Recorder of London against Barton Hudson for employing persons not free as musicians at a Lord Mayor's Banquet.

Though the Company is still in active existence, it possesses, unfortunately, no records of its history and acts during the greater part of the last three centuries. These have been lost, and with them, of course, many interesting details of the musical life of London during that period. However, some glimpses of the Company's history may be found in the Records of the City of London.

Times are changed since the Guilds were potent factors in the political and social life of England, when it was necessary for those living in the City to take up the Freedom and Livery of the City Guilds in order to be allowed to carry on their trade or profession in the confines of the City. Nevertheless, many of them still exist, and although they no longer discharge to the full the functions for the exercise of which they were originally founded, most of them have adapted themselves to the new conditions and seek to the best of their power to further the interests of the calling with which they have been so long associated. Such is the case with the Musicians' Company. It is doing all that lies within its limited means, by the institution of scholarships, competitions, the award of medals and in other ways, to stimulate and promote the study and practice of the art which it was established to supervise and control. We may add in passing, however, that the Musicians' Company has never possessed any great wealth.

In addition to the above-mentioned awards, a sum is granted annually for a scholarship in composition to be held at the G.S.M. In 1904 Andrew Carnegie founded in connexion with the Company, of which he was an honorary freeman, two scholarships entitling the holders to three years' free tuition at the G.S.M., and in 1905 Sir S. Ernest Palmer, whose benefactions to the musical world are so well known, presented to the Company, of which he also is an honorary freeman, the sum of £1250. With the interest derived therefrom two other scholarships have been created, tenable, at the same Institution, the one by a boy and the other by a girl. In 1904, in connexion with the tercentenary of the granting of the Company's Charter, prizes were given by Charles T. D. Crews, the Master, and H. T. C. de Lafontaine, liveryman of the Company, for various musical compositions, including a grace for the use of the Company. In addition the Master presented fifty guineas to the G.S.M. to be employed in assisting poor students, a window of St. Cecilia to St. Paul's Cathedral to commemorate the revival in 1904 of the custom of attending a special service on St. Cecilia's Day, and a bust of

[1] Thomas Morley writes as follows in the 'Dedication of First Booke of Consort Lessons,' 1599 ; ' The ancient custome of this honourable and renowned Citie hath been ever to retaine and maintaine excellent and expert Musicians,'

Orlando Gibbons to Westminster Abbey. W. W. Cobbett, a member of the Court of the Company, has also given a prize of £50 for a 'Phantasy' for string quartet, and has instituted the annual presentation of a medal for chamber music. The Company also presents annually silver medals to the R.A.M., R.C.M. and the G.S.M. (in rotation), the Royal Naval and Royal Military Schools of Music, and triennially to the R.C.O. and Trinity College of Music.

Specially worthy of mention is the Exhibition held by the Company in commemoration of its tercentenary at the Fishmongers' Hall, which was opened by the Prince and Princess of Wales on June 28, 1904, under the patronage of the King and Queen, His Majesty heading the list of lenders. Then was brought together a remarkable collection of instruments, books, manuscripts, portraits and other objects bearing upon the history and practice of music, probably more complete, valuable and instructive than anything of the kind that had ever before been got together. A finely illustrated catalogue of the entire collection was published subsequently.

In order that all possible advantage might be derived from the Exhibition, a series of lectures on the exhibits, with musical illustrations, was delivered. (These have since been published in book form.)

At the present time (1926) the Musicians' Company consists of about 140 members. Election to the Company rests with the Court, which consists of the Master, two Wardens and not less than thirteen assistants. Fees, amounting to £52 : 10s., are payable on taking the Livery. The Livery of the Company carries with it the Freedom of the City and the privilege of a vote for Civic elections. The Musicians' Company is the only City Company concerned with the exercise of a profession.

By arrangement the Musicians' Company enjoys the use of the Worshipful Company of Stationers' magnificent old Hall.

The Company, as regards members and influence, is at present in a stronger position than it has been for upwards of a century, and the greater number of the liverymen are connected with and interested in the art of music. The majority are musicians, both professional and amateur. The clerk to the Company is T. C. Fenwick.

The Livery Club of the Musicians' Company, founded in 1902 to promote the interests of the Company and its usefulness to the art of music, has issued for private circulation two handbooks dealing with the history of the Company, reprinting the two Charters and giving the by-laws and other information of interest to the liverymen ; and a third handbook was issued in 1915 by Clifford B. Edgar, a past-master of the Company. During the war of 1914–18 the Company presented a gold watch to each bandsman who won the V.C., such presentation being made at the Mansion House by the Lord Mayor at appropriate functions. In recent years the Company has become possessed of many handsome pieces of plate through the beneficence of its members. King George V. accepted the gold medal of the Company, and the Prince of Wales and the Duke of Connaught were admitted to the Honorary Freedom of the Company in 1921.

A. F. H.

MUSICIANS OF GREAT BRITAIN, Royal Society of, see Royal Society of Musicians.

MUSICIANS' UNION. This Society, a registered Trade Union, was formed in 1921 by the amalgamation of the National Orchestral Association of Professional Musicians and the Amalgamated Musicians' Union, two independent organisations which, under various titles, had been in existence since 1893. Their aims and objects were to improve the status of the professional musician, more especially the orchestral players, amongst whom, for various reasons, chiefly the speculative nature of so many of their engagements, great hardships had frequently arisen in the past. For example, a great deal of time would be expended in rehearsing a musical play which, upon production, would prove to be a complete failure, yet the musicians were expected to rehearse unrestrictedly as though a long run were assured.

The Musicians' Union has proved of the utmost importance in securing adequate payment for rehearsals and fixing their duration, while in other matters its activities extend to controlling the entry into the profession and to ensuring it being sufficiently lucrative to eliminate the necessity of members having to resort to non-professional employment, to the establishment of benefit funds for illness, to the insurance of instruments and to legal assistance when required, etc. The registered offices of the Union are in Manchester, the London offices being in Archer Street, W.1. The general secretary is E. S. Teale.

MUSIC PRINTING, see Printing.

MUSIC SCHOOL, THE, Oxford, is situated on the south side of the Schools quadrangle, under the Bodleian Library. This building was rebuilt in its present form at the beginning of the 17th century, but the interior of the Music School was altered in 1780 by the architect Wyatt under the direction of the then Professor of Music, Dr. Philip Hayes. The expenses of these alterations were defrayed by a grant of £50 from the University and by the proceeds of three choral concerts given at the following Commemoration, at one of which Dr. Hayes's oratorio 'Prophecy' was performed. The Music School was formerly used for the performance of the exercises for the degree of

Mus.B. and Mus.D. The collection of music (see LIBRARIES) which belongs to the Music School is no longer preserved there, having been removed to the Bodleian ; and the famous collection of portraits,[1] of which a list is appended, was moved in 1887 to the New Schools. They were shown at the Music and Inventions Exhibition of 1885, where Salomon's portrait was identified.

C. F. Abel.	Sir JOHN HAWKINS.
Dr. J. BULL.[2]	James Hasletine.
Dr. Burney.	Dr. W. Hayes.
Thomas Blagrave.	Dr. P. Hayes.
Colonel Blaithwait.	John Hingeston.
Dr. Boyce.	R. Hudson.
Lord Crewe, Bishop of	J. Hilton.
Durham.	Nicholas Laniere.
Dr. Child.	HENRY LAWES.
Dr. Croft.	William Lawes.
Corelli.	Orlando di Lasso.
J. P. Eiffert.	Matthew Locke.
Bernard Gates.	Dr. Pepusch.
Christopher Gibbons.	Salomon.
Orlando Gibbons.	Bernard Smith.
W. Gregory.	Christopher Simpson.
Handel.	Dr. Thomas Tudway.
Dr. Heyther.	Dr. Wilson.

Anthony à Wood states that the Music School also possessed busts of King Alfred, Dr. W. Hayes and H. Purcell, as well as portraits of W. Hine, Dr. Parsons and John Weldon.   W. B. S.

MUSIC SOCIETY, THE. This Society was formed in London by André Mangeot in 1920, giving its first concert on Nov. 2. It is run on a subscription basis, and has always paid attention to the production of contemporary chamber-music in addition to the revival of less well-known works in the classical repertory, and to the informality of the performances, which take place at St. John's Hall, Westminster. Among the composers who have been represented in the programme there may be mentioned the names of Bax, Bloch, Goossens, Honegger, de Maleingreau, Turina and Wiener.

MUSIKALISCHES OPFER, *i.e.* Musical Offering ; one of Bach's works, containing various treatments of a subject given him by Frederick the Great to extemporise upon during his visit to Potsdam in May 1747. The work, as published by Breitkopf & Härtel (Nov. 1831) contains two ricercari, one for three voices and one for six voices (the latter in score), one fuga canonica for two voices, five sonatas for flute (the king's own instrument), violin and continuo, and eight canons ; sixteen pieces in all. The work was published by Bach with a dedication dated July 7, 1747—a curious medley of five sheets oblong folio and one sheet upright folio, containing the ricercar a 3 and a canon perpetuus (the third in B. & H.'s edition), five canons, and the fuga canonica. In the dedication copy, now in the Amalienbibliothek at Berlin, Bach has written ' Regis Iussu Cantio Et Reliqua Canonica Arte Resoluta '—' the

theme demanded by the king with other things developed by canonical art.' Four more oblong folio sheets seem to have been afterwards added, containing the ricercar a 6 and two canons, and lastly three sheets containing the sonatas and one canon. (See Spitta's *Bach*, Engl. transl. iii. 191-7, 233, 292, 294.)   G.

MUSIN, OVIDE (b. Nandrin, near Liège, Belgium, Sept. 22, 1854), entered Liège Conservatoire in 1863 ; was a pupil of Hyneberg, and two years later took first prize for violin-playing. In 1870 Henri Léonard was appointed professor at the Liège Conservatoire ; Musin studied with him, and eventually followed him to the Paris Conservatoire, where—at the age of 14—he was awarded the gold medal for solo and quartet playing. A year later he made his début, replacing Léonard at a concert. After touring in France, he visited Holland in 1875, and, meeting the impresario Jarreth, was engaged by him for a prolonged tour. Under Mapleson's direction he came to London in 1877, remaining here for five years. Finally he made a tour round the world, returned to Liège in 1897, and succeeded César Thomson as violin professor at the Conservatoire. His last appearance in London was on May 6, 1888, at the Prince's Hall, where he played Leopold Damrosch's Concertstück for violin and orchestra, under the baton of Walter Damrosch. Subsequently his residence was divided between Brussels and New York. (*Liège Artiste*, Sept. 30, 1905 ; *Baker*.)

                               E. H.-A.

MUSTEL, VICTOR (b. Le Havre, June 13, 1815 ; d. Paris, 1890), a manufacturer of harmoniums, whose several inventions resulted in the instrument known as the ' Mustel Organ.'

Left an orphan at the age of 12, he was apprenticed to a shipbuilder, and in 1838 set up in business for himself in that trade at the little hamlet of Sanvic. Endowed from youth with a peculiarly constructive genius, his first attempts at making musical instruments were devoted to the improvement of an accordion which he had bought in Havre. Elated with his success, he disposed of his workshop in May 1844, and set out for Paris with his wife and two children. For the next nine years he worked in several different workshops, but never obtained high wages. In 1853 he determined to start in business for himself as a harmonium maker, and in 1855 exhibited his harmonium with ' Double Expression,' and a new stop ' Harpe éolienne,' for which he gained a medal of the first class. For the first year after this Mustel (now assisted by his two sons) did fairly well, but business rapidly declined, and he would perhaps have been obliged to succumb but for the sale of a little land which he had inherited from his father. Even in 1866 his receipts did little more than cover the costs, but since that date the firm of ' Victor Mustel et ses Fils ' has gained a reputation that has been as noteworthy in England as in France. The present name of the firm is 'Mustel et Cie.'

The inventions due to the Mustels are—'La Double Expression' (patented 1854), whereby the natural preponderance of the bass tones over those of the treble is, with complete power of increase and decrease in either half, brought under direct control of the player by means of knee pedals (genouillères) that control the energy and pressure of the wind; 'Le Forté expressif,' a divided swell governed by pneumatic agency; and 'La Harpe éolienne,' a tremolo register of two ranks of vibrators, 2 ft. pitch, which offer a gently beating variation to the unison by being slightly less and more than the normal pitch of the instrument, the impression of which remains unimpaired. Mustel subsequently invented 'Le Typophone' and 'Le Métaphone.' The first of these is a keyboard percussion instrument, made of tuning-forks in resonance boxes of the proper acoustic capacity. The principle is very similar to that of the CELESTA (*q.v.*). The Métaphone (patented in 1878) is an invention to soften at pleasure the somewhat strident tones of the harmonium. It is produced by a sliding shutter of leather to each compartment, and is governed by draw-stops, as with other modifications of tone and power. A. J. H.

MUSURGIA UNIVERSALIS, see KIRCHER, ATHANASIUS.

MUTA (Italian), *i.e.* change, a word often seen attached to horn parts—'muta in Es,' 'muta in B,' etc., meaning simply 'change to E♭ or B♭,' etc.; that is, take off the crook in which you are playing and put on that which will make the horn sound in E♭ or B♭. G.

MUTATION (Lat. *mutatio*, from *muto*, 'I change'). (1) When in the Solmisation of a plain-song melody it becomes necessary to pass from one hexachord to another, the process by which the transfer is effected is called a mutation. (See HEXACHORD and SOLMISATION.)

(2) The term is also applied to the change which takes place in a boy's voice, when it passes from treble or alto into tenor or bass. The period of this transformation is uncertain; but it generally declares itself between the ages of 14 and 16, and is very rarely deferred later than the completion of the seventeenth year.

(3) More rarely, the word is used to denote that change in the position of the hand upon the violin, which, by English violinists, is called the SHIFT (*q.v.*). W. S. R.

MUTATION STOPS, in an organ, are those registers which do not produce a sound agreeing with the name of the key pressed down, but either the perfect fifth or the major third to it, as G or E on the C key. The former are called fifth-sounding, or Quint stops; the latter third-sounding, or Tierce stops. The proper relative size of the largest fifth-sounding stop is one-third that of the Foundation stop from which it is deduced; as $10\frac{2}{3}$, $5\frac{1}{3}$ or $2\frac{2}{3}$ from the 32, 16 or 8-foot stops respectively. The largest Tierce-sounding stops are one-fifth the size of the Foundation stops from which they are deduced; as $6\frac{2}{5}$, $3\frac{1}{5}$ and $1\frac{3}{5}$ feet respectively. The third-sounding rank on the manual has been much more sparingly used since the introduction of Equal Temperament, as it does not sound agreeably with that system of tuning; and an additional rank of pipes consequently becomes available for some other purpose.

The only Mutation stop in use in England previously to the arrival of Smith and Harris (1660) was the twelfth ($2\frac{2}{3}$ feet). After that date the Tierce ($1\frac{3}{5}$ foot), Larigot ($1\frac{1}{3}$ foot) and their octaves (among the small Mixture ranks) became not uncommon. (See MIXTURE.) E. J. H.

MUTE,[1] or Damper (Fr. *sourdine*; Ger. *Dämpfer*; Ital. *sordino*). A mechanical device for restricting the tone of instruments.

PIANOFORTE.—In the pianoforte the contrivance is called in English the damper. The first pianofortes, as we find Cristofori's and Silbermann's, were made without stops. In course of time a practice common with the harpsichord was followed in the pianoforte, and led the way to the now indispensable pedals.

The first stops were used to raise the dampers; and by two brass knobs on the player's left hand the dampers could be taken entirely off the strings in two divisions, bass and treble C. P. E. Bach, in his *Versuch*, makes few references to the pianoforte; but in the edition of 1797 he remarks (p. 268) that the undamped register of the Fortepiano is the most agreeable, and that, with due care, it is the most charming of keyed instruments for improvising ('fantasiren'). The higher treble of the piano is not now damped. These short strings vibrate in unison with the overtones of deeper notes, and, as a distinguished pianoforte-maker has said, give life to the whole instrument.[2] The terms 'Senza sordini' and 'Con sordini' applied to the damper stops were used exclusively by Beethoven in his earlier sonatas. He did not use the now familiar 'Ped.' or 'Pedal,' because the pedal was of recent introduction, and was less commonly employed than the stops which the little square pianos then had. The 'Genouillière,' or knee-pedal, replaced the damper stops in the German grands. For the Italian words signifying without and with dampers the signs ⊕ and ✱ were substituted by Steibelt, and eventually became fixed as the constant equivalents. The oldest dated square piano existing, one of Zumpe's of 1766, has the damper stops; as to the Genouillière, Mozart tells us (letter, Oct.

[1] It will be noticed that the metaphors at the root of the Italian and English terms are deafness in one case and dumbness in the other.

[2] Even in Virdung, A.D. 1511, we find the practice of leaving sympathetic strings in the clavichords; as he says to strengthen the resonance.

1777) how Stein had one in his improved grand, and Mahillon's Stein of 1780, or thereabouts, accordingly has one. There is one in Mozart's (Walther) grand at Salzburg, and in each of the two (Huhn, Berlin) grands of 1790, or earlier, preserved at Potsdam. The action of the Genouillière consists of two levers which descend a little below the key-bottom of the piano, and meet opposite the knees of the player, who, pressing the levers together, by an upward thrust moves a bar which takes the whole of the dampers off the strings.[1]

Contemporaneous with the employment of the Genouillière was that of the *piano* stop (Fr. *céleste*, Ger. *Harfenzug*), afterwards transferred, like the dampers, to a pedal. An interesting anonymous Louis Quinze square piano belonging to the painter Gosselin of Brussels had this Céleste as a stop. Its origin is clearly the harp-stop of the harpsichord, the pieces of leather being turned over so as to be interposed between the hammers and the strings.

A note of directions for the use of the pedals prefixed to Steibelt's three sonatas, op. 35, gives an approximate date to the use of the pedals becoming recognised, and put under the composer's direction, instead of being left entirely to the fancy of the player. He says:

'The Author wishing to make more Variety on the Piano Forte finds it necessary to make use of the Pedals, by which alone the tones can be united, but it requires to use them with care, without which, in going from one chord to another, Discord and Confusion would result. Hereafter the Author in all his Compositions will make use of the following signs to denote the Pedals :
⊕ The Pedal which raises the dampers.
✳ The Piano Pedal.
ᐟ To take the foot off the Pedal that was used before.'

Steibelt's op. 35 was published in 1799, by Longman, Clementi & Co.[2]

The leather was applied in one length to mute the strings more effectually, and was then called in French 'sourdine.' John Broadwood was the first to put the 'sordin'—as it is called in his patent of 1783—upon a foot-pedal; he put the dampers upon a pedal at the same time, and for fifty years the pedal-foot was cloven, to divide the dampers into bass and treble sections, as the stops had previously been divided for the same purpose. The use of the pianissimo mute was indicated by the Italian word 'sordino.' This term is used in the sense of a mute as late as Thalberg's op. 41 (Ashdown's edition).

The 'Verschiebung,' or shifting pedal, for shifting the hammer first to two strings and then to one (UNA CORDA (*q.v.*)), ultimately gained the day over the muted pedals or stops. The effect of the 'una corda' was

[1] See Hipkins, *History of the Pianoforte*, pp. 93, 108 and 110: footnote.
[2] Steibelt gives a description of the pedals, with his signs for them, in his *Méthode de piano*, first published by Janet, Paris, 1805. He names Clementi, Dussek and Cramer as having adopted his signs. They differ from and are better than Adam's (*Méthode de piano du Conservatoire*), also published in Paris, 1802. Steibelt calls the 'una corda' *céleste*.

charming and is expressly indicated by Beethoven in his G major concerto, in op. 106, etc. The *pp* and *ppp* soft pedal in course of time shared the fate of the divided damper pedal; such refinements were banished as being of small service in large rooms. In the six-pedal Viennese grand of Nannette Stein at Windsor Castle, the 'Verschiebung' and 'Harfenzug' co-exist.[3] The latter has of late years again come forward, at first in oblique pianos that could not shift, and since more generally; and has, to a certain extent, gained the favour of amateurs. The material used is cloth or felt.[4]   A. J. H.

VIOLIN, etc.—The muting of violin, viola, violoncello and double bass is effected by fixing a three-pronged apparatus on the bridge, the split prongs of which grip firmly and damp the vibrations of the strings. It is also possible to mute by slipping a coin or piece of horn between the strings on the tail-side of the bridge. Mutes are made of metal, wood, ivory or xylonite and vary somewhat in their effect according to the substance employed; but the chief variation in the tone depends upon the firmness with which the prongs grip the bridge. The mute is less satisfactory on the violoncello and double-bass owing to the difficulty in devising one of the requisite weight and gripping power.

WIND INSTRUMENTS.—The horn and trumpet are the most frequently muted wind instruments, the introduction of the hand into the bell of the horn altering the pitch as well as veiling the tone (see HORN). The horn mute is a pear-shaped piece of wood or metal inserted into the bell. A similar device is used for muting the trumpet, cornet, trombone and tuba. There is also what is called the 'echo attachment,' a small double cone of metal which reduces the tone of the cornet to a mere thread.

There are no practical means of muting wood-wind instruments. For the muting of drums see DRUM.   F. C., with addns.

MUWASHSHÄH, see SONG, subsection SPAIN ; VILLANCICO.

MYRIELL, THOMAS (*b.* early 16th cent.), made a most important collection of 16th and early 17th century English (and Italian) compositions, and apparently some of his own. It has an engraved title-page, 'Tristitiae remedium,' and the year 1616. For a detailed description see H. Davey, *Hist. of Eng. Music*, p. 164. Another MS. collection in the Fétis Library, Brussels, bears his autograph signature.   E. V. D. S.

MYSLIWEČEK (MYSLIWECZEK), JOSEF (*b.* Prague, Mar. 9, 1737 ; *d.* Rome, Feb. 4, 1781), a Bohemian composer, son of a miller,

[3] The remaining pedals in Nannette Stein's grand are the 'Fagotzug,' by which a piece of card or stiff paper is brought into partial contact with the strings, and the 'Janissary' drum and triangle. See STEIN.
[4] See also the glossary of terms in Hipkins, *History of the Pianoforte*, p. 123.

had a good education in the common school, and after his father's death devoted himself to music. After many attempts at composition, and much wandering, he went to Venice, studied with Pescetti, and fell upon his feet at Parma, in 1764, with an opera, 'Il Bellerofonte,' the success of which was so great as to make his reputation ; though he returned to the north of Italy he was recalled to Naples no less than nine times. In 1773 his 'Erifile' was given in Munich, and in 1775 his 'Ezio' at Naples. An oratorio 'Abramo ed Isacco' (1777) was for some time ascribed to Haydn. Mozart met him at Bologna in Nov. 1772, and again at Munich in 1777. He was evidently very gifted. Mozart says of his sonatas that 'they are bound to please, not difficult, and very effective,' and urges his sister to learn them by heart.[1] Elsewhere he speaks of him as a prize difficult to replace.[2] He was evidently very fascinating,[3] but as evidently a loose fish,

[1] Letter, Nov. 13, 1777.
[2] Aug. 7, 1778.   [3] Oct. 11, 1777.

unable, with all his engagements, to keep himself respectable.[4]

In 1778 he gave his 'Olimpiade' at Naples, which threw every one into transports of enthusiasm. The famous singer Gabrielli sang his songs everywhere, and was accustomed to say that none were so well suited to her voice. Mysliweček is said to have had a young English friend named Barry, who buried him in San Lorenzo in Lucina, and erected a monument to him there. The Italians called him Venatorini, or, more intimately, Il divino Boëmo, in despair at the pronunciation of his proper name. Four oratorios, thirty operas, many symphonies, concertos, sonatas and arias are mentioned in *Q.-L.*   G. ; rev.

MYSTÈRES D'ISIS, LES, an arrangement of Mozart's 'Zauberflöte,' words by Morel, music adapted by Lachnith ; produced Opéra, Paris, Aug. 20, 1801. (See LACHNITH.)   G.

BIBL.—G. SERVIÈRES. *Épisodes d'histoire musicale* (Paris, 1914).

Feb. 22, 1778 ; Oct. 11, 1777.

N

NAAMAN, oratorio in 2 parts; words by W. Bartholomew, music by Costa; produced Birmingham Festival, Sept. 7, 1864.

NABUCCO, or NABUCODONOSOR, opera in 3 acts; libretto by Solera, music by Verdi. Produced La Scala, Milan, Mar. 9, 1842; Paris, Oct. 16, 1845; at Her Majesty's, as 'Nino,' Mar. 3, 1846.   G.

NACHBAUR, FRANZ (b. Schloss Giessen, near Friedrichshafen, Wurtemberg, Mar. 25, 1835; d. Munich, Mar. 21, 1902), a noted German tenor. He was educated at the Polytechnic School, Stuttgart. As a member of a Gesang-verein, his fine voice attracted the notice of Pischek, who advised him to take regular instruction in singing. He began his career as a chorister at Basle, and afterwards became a member of a German troupe travelling in France. Through the liberality of Passavant, a banker at Lunéville, he found means for the culture of his voice, first through Orth, the bass singer, and afterwards with Lamperti of Milan. He afterwards sang in opera at Mannheim, Prague, Darmstadt, Vienna, and in 1866 at Munich, where he obtained a permanent en-gagement at the opera, enjoying a great repu-tation until his retirement in 1890. He created the part of Walther in 'Die Meistersinger' in 1868, and that of Froh in 'Das Rheingold' in 1869. He also sang in Italy, and appeared as Lohengrin at Rome in 1878. In 1882 he was a member of the German Opera Company at Drury Lane, and on June 3 sang the part of Walther in 'Die Meistersinger.'   A. C.

NACHDRUCK, MIT, 'with pressure,' 'heavily'; corresponding nearly to the Italian pesante.

NACHEZ, TIVADAR (b. Budapest, May 1, 1859), violinist. His first teacher was Saba-thiel, leader of the orchestra at the Royal Hungarian Opera. He remained with him till his 16th year, when he gained one of the travelling scholarships founded by the King of Hungary. With this he went to Berlin, and was for three years a pupil of Joachim. His studies concluded at Paris, where he was a pupil of Léonard for a year, and where he established himself for a time, playing at the Pasdeloup and other concerts. He made several tours on the Continent, and finally settled in London in 1889, where he earned a high reputation as a solo player. He made what was described as a farewell appearance with Thibaut in the autumn of 1926. As a composer he has been mainly successful in writing violin solos based upon Hungarian melodies. In 1923 he published a string quartet and has completed a new violin concerto. He has done much editing of classical works for his instrument.   W. W. C.

NACHSCHLAG, see ORNAMENTS, GERMAN.

NACHSPIEL, 'afterpiece,' a name given by German organists to voluntaries intended to be played at the conclusion of the service, while the congregation is leaving the church. This form of composition is also called Postludium, and has even been Englished as 'Postlude.' The German title corresponds to the word Vorspiel, used as an equivalent to Präludium or Prelude. Examples of the name (Nachspiel) may be found in the works of Joseph André and Rinck, and examples of Postlude in those of Henry Smart and many others.   M.

NACHTGALL, see LUSCINIUS, OTTOMAR.

NACHTLAGER VON GRANADA, DAS, opera in 2 acts; from Fr. Kind's drama, by Frhr. von Braun, music by Conradin Kreutzer. Produced Vienna, 1834.

NADERMANN, FRANCOIS JOSEPH (b. Paris, c. 1773; d. there, Apr. 2, 1835), son of a cele-brated harp-maker, became the second greatest virtuoso of his time on that instrument.[1] He was harpist at the Opéra and in the royal chapel after the Restoration, and professor of harp at the Paris Conservatoire, Jan. 1, 1825. He composed for the harp with and without other instruments: concertos, quartets, trios, duets, sonatas and solos; also (together with Duport) nocturnes for violoncello and harp.[2] Most of his works were published by J. H. Nadermann, probably a relative. With his brother Henri, also a harpist, he engaged in a controversy with Seb. Erard on the subject of the latter's double-action harp which ended in Erard's victory and the gradual disappearance of the once famous Nadermann instruments.   E. V. D. S.

NADESHDA, opera in 4 acts; words by Julian Sturgis, music by A. Goring Thomas. Produced Carl Rosa Co., Drury Lane, Apr. 16, 1885.   M.

NÄGELI, HANS GEORG (b. Zürich, May 26, 1773[3]; d. there, Dec. 26, 1836), composer, teacher, writer on musical subjects and pub-lisher. He received his musical education at Zürich and Berne. In 1792 he started his music publishing business by producing works by Bach, Handel, Frescobaldi and other famous masters in a style surpassing in clear-ness of type and elegance of production most of his predecessors and contemporaries. In 1803 he started the Répertoire des clavecinistes, a periodical in which he published pianoforte com-positions by Clementi, Cramer, Dussek, Steibelt, Beethoven and others, and which in that year contained the first edition of Beethoven's sonatas, op. 30, Nos. 1 and 2 (without opus

[1] De Marin, whom Fétis considered greater, never played in public.
[2] In the library of E. van der Straeten.
[3] Centenary pamphlet by Rudolf Hunziker, *Hans Georg Nägeli* (Winterthur, 1924).

number). In the first of these he committed the error of judgment of adding four bars to the first movement, an error which Beethoven magnanimously forgave, for he wrote to him even on later occasions in affectionate terms and even induced the Archduke Rudolph, in 1824, to subscribe to a volume of his poems. Apart from toccatas and other pianoforte pieces he composed a large amount of vocal compositions for the church, the school and the home, and his 15 books of songs with pianoforte accompaniment contain many numbers which are still popular among students, in elementary schools and among the people, especially his 'Lied vom Rhein' and 'Freut Euch des Lebens' (published in 1794), which became also a favourite in England as 'Life let us cherish.' His merit in the advancement of musical art is very considerable, especially by means of the 'Schweizerbund,' a choral society with branches throughout Switzerland, and the improvement of musical education in elementary schools on the principles of Pestalozzi's system, in which he adopted the method of Michael Traugott Pfeiffer, who had organised the music teaching in Pestalozzi's institute. Nägeli wrote several works on the subject, which became largely textbooks for teachers, and he translated his theory into practice by applying it for a period of 20 years in an elementary school founded by himself. In 1824 he lectured on music particularly for the benefit of musical amateurs in many towns of southern Germany. The lectures, which were published by Cotta (Tübingen, 1826), became the subject of a polemic between Nägeli and Professor Thibaut of Heidelberg, which was also published by the former as *Der Streit zwischen der alten und neuen Musik* (the controversy between old and modern music). To Nägeli belongs the merit of having revived male choir singing (Liedertafel). E. V. D. S.

BIBL.—RUDOLF HUNZIKER, *Hans Georg Nägeli. Gedächtnisrede zur 150. Wiederkehr seines Geburtstages, mit Bildnisse und bibliographischen Anhang*, pp. 40 (Winterthur, 1924).

NÆNIA, cantata for chorus and orchestra on Schiller's words, 'Auch das Schöne muss sterben,' set by Hermann Goetz, op. 10, and by Brahms, op. 82. Nænia or Nenia was a classical term for a funeral dirge. G.

NAGEL, WILIBALD (*b.* Mülheim on the Ruhr, Jan. 12, 1863), the son of a well-known singer, Siegfried Nagel; he studied music at Berlin under Ehrlich, Treibs, Spitta and Bellermann, and after spending some years as a teacher of musical history at Zürich, came to England in order to study the records of our national music. He made many minute and valuable researches which were afterwards embodied in two books, *Geschichte der Musik in England*, 2 vols., 1891 and 1897, and *Annalen der englischen Hofmusik*, 1894–95, published as a supplement to the *Monatshefte*

für Musik. Among his other works are *Über die dramatisch-musikalischen Bearbeitungen der Genovefa-Legende* (1888) and *Beethoven und seine Claviersonaten* (1903), as well as a life of Brahms. In 1896 he went back to Germany and took up his residence at Darmstadt, where in 1898 he became teacher of musical science in the Technische Hochschule, and professor in 1905. In 1913 he gave up this work and returned to Zürich, and later settled in Stuttgart. M.

NAICH, HUBERT, one of the earlier madrigal composers, of whose life nothing is known except that he was a Netherlander living in Italy towards the middle of the 16th century. The only publication which bears his name exclusively is a collection of thirty Italian madrigals *a* 4 and 5, printed at Rome but bearing no date, though probably about 1540. It is dedicated to Bindo Altoviti, the friend of Raphael and patron of Benvenuto Cellini, and at the end Naich himself is described as a member of the Accademia degli Amici at Rome. Other madrigals by Naich appeared in the various collections of Arcadelt and Rore. Among the half-dozen Italian madrigals contained in Ott's *Liederbuch*,[1] 1544, there is one by Naich, 'Rara beltà divina,' a very good specimen of early madrigal composition, and the only means we have at present of judging Naich's work. J. R. M.

NAÏL, opera composed by Isidore de Lara. Produced Théâtre de la Gaieté, Paris, 1911; in English, Covent Garden, July 18, 1919.

NAIL VIOLIN. (In German *Nagelgeige, Nagelharmonika, Eisenvioline*.) This curious musical instrument was invented in the year 1740 by a German violinist named Johann Wilde, at that time living in St. Petersburg. The suggestion for its construction originated in Wilde's accidentally scraping the hair of his bow across the metal peg upon which he was about to hang it, and in so doing producing a musical sound of distinctive quality. The flat wooden sounding-board is in the shape of a half-moon, and the metal nails are firmly fastened perpendicularly around the edge of the curved side. These nails diminish in height as the notes rise in pitch, and the chromatic nails are distinguished by being slightly bent. It was held in the left hand by a hole underneath, and sound was produced by rubbing a strong, well-rosined, black-haired bow across the nails. In 1780 it was improved by the addition of sympathetic strings; and Senal —a Viennese artist—excelled upon it. In 1791 a new arrangement of it, called the 'Nagelclavier,' was produced by Trager of Bamberg, who made it of an oblong shape. It was played upon with a band coated with rosin, instead of a bow, which band was worked by keys. (Carl Engel, *Catalogue of Musical Instruments at South Kensington*.) E. H.-A.

1 Reprinted by Eitner.

NAKERS (O. French, *nacaires*). The mediæval name for the kettledrums, and distinctly showing their Arabian or Saracenic origin; for the old English word is but a corruption of the Arabic *nacareh*, now represented by the *naqqareh* of Turkey, Egypt and Syria—small hand drums with bowl-shaped bodies of wood or metal and covered on their open top with skin. They are generally used in pairs : if small enough the performer holds them with one hand ; if larger, they are placed on the ground, on either side of a camel, or even on the back of an attendant. (See *PLATE XXX*. No. 1.)

They were probably introduced into western Europe at the time of the Crusades, together with the long trumpet known as the buzine. At the close of the 14th century the word appears in English literature, though in 1304 amongst King Edward the First's musicians was one Janino le Nakerer, and in 1349 'nacaires' helped to celebrate the entry of King Edward III. into Calais. Their use in British cavalry regiments was due to King Henry VIII., who sent to Vienna 'for drums that could be played on horseback after the Hungarian manner.' For their later development see DRUM.   F. W. G.

NALDI, GIUSEPPE (*b*. Bologna, Feb. 2, 1770 ; *d*. Paris, Dec. 15, 1820 [1]), baritone singer, was the only son of Giuseppe Naldi, who held a government appointment at Bologna. The son was educated in the universities of Bologna and Pavia, where he made very rapid progress in his studies for the law, the profession of his choice.

He achieved his first success on the stage at Milan. According to Fétis (who, however, is incorrect in some details of his biography), Naldi appeared at Rome in 1789, then at Naples, and next at Venice and Turin. In 1796 and 1797 he reappeared at Milan. In London he made his début Apr. 15, 1806, and he continued to sing here every subsequent season up to 1819 (inclusive). His principal characters were in 'Le cantatrici villane,' 'Così fan tutte' and 'Il fanatico per la musica.' In the latter he showed his skill in playing the violoncello, on which he was no mean performer. Lord Mount-Edgcumbe describes his voice as 'weak and uncertain' ; while another critic [2] calls it 'sonorous and powerful.' All agree, however, that Naldi was extremely clever, could write very fair verses and compose very tolerable music ; had an accurate ear ; could play the piano and violoncello very well ; and read at sight with perfect ease and intonation. As an actor he was excellent, and played with 'irresistible humour, effect, judgment and truth.' A good portrait-sketch of him as Figaro in 'Le nozze,' 'drawn and etched expressly for the British Stage,' appeared in Feb. 1818. In the next year he was engaged at Paris, where he made his début in

[1] *Gentleman's Magazine.*   [2] *Monthly Mirror.*

'Così fan tutte ' ; but his powers were much faded. He returned once more to London in that, his last, season ; and in the following year, at Paris, met an untimely death, in the apartments of his friend Garcia, by the bursting of a newly-invented cooking-kettle, a trial of which he had been invited to witness.

His daughter, Mlle. NALDI, made her début in 1819. She sang at Paris in 1822–23, and is said by Fétis to have shared the public applause with Pasta for some years, particularly in 'Tancredi' and 'Romeo e Giulietta.' She retired in 1824, having married the Conte di Sparre.   J. M.

NALDI, ROMULO, LL.D. (16th-17th cent.), priest, Knight of St. Peter's, Rome ; lived at Rome and Bologna. He composed 1 book of madrigals *a* 5 v. (1589) ; 1 book of motets for double chorus (1600), both published at Venice. Other numbers are in collective volumes (*Q.-L.*).

NALSON, REV. VALENTINE (*d*. 1722), Subchanter of York Cathedral in the early part of the 18th century, composed an Evening Service in G, and also, on the occasion of the Peace of Utrecht in 1713, a Morning Service in the same key, both which are contained in the Tudway Collection, Harl. MSS. 7341 and 7342. Some anthems by him are also extant at Ely.
      W. H. H.

NANGA, a Nubian harp without a fore pillar ; a relic of the harps of ancient Egypt (*PLATE XXXVIII*. No. 1 ; see HARP).
      F. W. G.

NANINI (NANINO), two brothers, important composers of the 16th-century Roman school.

(1) GIOVANNI MARIA (*b*. Tivoli, *c*. 1545 ; *d*. Rome, Mar. 11, 1607) was a chorister at Vallerano, and studied counterpoint at Rome under Gaudio Mell ; and, on the completion of his education, he obtained a place as tenor singer in Sta. Maria Maggiore in Rome, was appointed in 1575 maestro at San Luigi de' Francesi, in 1577 a singer in the Papal Chapel, and in 1579 maestro at Sta. Maria Maggiore.

G. Maria established a public music school— the first ever opened in Rome by an Italian— in the management of which he was assisted by his brother, G. Bernardino (2), as well as by Palestrina himself. The school prospered exceedingly. G. Maria's reputation as a learned contrapuntist and gifted composer was secured. His works were received at the Sistine Chapel with marks of special approbation, and in 1604 he was appointed maestro in that chapel. On his death three years later he was buried in the church of S. Luigi de' Francesi.

Nanini was one of the brightest ornaments of the great Roman school, the highest qualities of which he cultivated in a remarkable degree. His motet for six voices, 'Hodie nobis coelorum rex,' annually sung in the Sistine Chapel on the morning of Christmas Day, is a noble composition; and he has left us many others of equal merit, a large proportion of which still remain in MS. among the archives of the pontifical choir, the Vatican Basilica, the Collegium Romanum, the oratory of S. Maria in Vallicella and other noted collections. P. Martini mentions a MS. collection of Canons, entitled ' Cento cinquanta sette contrappunti e canoni, a 2, 3, 4, 5, 6, 7, 8 e 11 voci, sopra del canto fermo intitolato La Base di Costanzo Festa,' which contains some miracles of ingenuity and learning. Some of these, at least, have already appeared among his published works; but a dissertation on counterpoint, called ' Regole di Giov. Maria e di Bernardo Nanini, per fare contrappunto a mente sopra il canto fermo,' written conjointly by himself and his younger brother in 1619, exists only in a MS. copy— unhappily imperfect—transcribed by Orazio Griffi, and preserved in the library of the Palazzo Corsini alla Lungara. (For other copies see Q.-L.)

The published works of Nanini comprise a volume of ' Motetti, a 3-5 voci ' (Venice, 1586); ' Madrigali,' lib. I. (1579); idem, lib. II. (1581, etc.); id. lib. III. (1586); ' Canzonetti, a 3 voci, per Alessandro Nanini raccolti ' (1593)—all published at Venice, in 4to, by Gardano; some ' Salmi, a 8 voci,' printed in the well-known collection of Fabio Costantini (Naples, 1615); and a number of motets, madrigals and other isolated works included in Costantini's ' Motetti,' Waelrant's ' Symphonia angelica ' and other collections published in Italy, and by P. Phalèse of Antwerp. Some very fine motets—including a masterly ' Hodie Christus natus est,' in which the characteristic Noè! Noè! is introduced with great effect— will be found in Proske's ' Musica divina.' Others are given in the collections of the Prince de la Moskowa, Rochlitz, etc. (See Q.-L.) A bibliography of his works is in the Kirchenmusikalisches Jahrbuch for 1891; see the same publication for 1898, p. 29.　　　w. s. r.

(2) GIOVANNI BERNARDINO (b. Vallerano, c. 1560; d. Rome, 1623) studied counterpoint under his elder brother, Giovanni Maria. Removing at a later period to Rome, he held the appointment of maestro di cappella, first in 1599 at the church of S. Luigi de' Francesi, and afterwards at that of S. Lorenzo in Damaso. Beyond this little is known of his personal history; though it is certain that he took a prominent part in the management of his brother's music school.

As a composer G. B. Nanini takes rank among the best masters of his time; but his works are, for the most part, far less characteristic of the true polyphonic style than those of his brother. He was one of the first who ventured so far to depart from the traditions of the Roman school as to write church music with organ accompaniment. His published

works are: a volume of delightful madrigals entitled ' Madrigali, a 5 voci, lib. I.' (Venice, 1588, 1598); idem, lib. II. (Venice, 1599); id. lib. III. (Rome, 1612); ' Motecta, a i. ii. iii. iv. v. voc. una cum gravi voce ad organi sonitum accommodata, lib. I.' (Rome, 1610); id. lib. II. (Rome, 1611); id. lib. III. (Rome, 1612); id. lib. IV. (Rome, 1618); ' Salmi, a 4 voc. con l' organo ' (Rome, 1620); and ' Venite, exultemus Domino, a 3 voc. coll' organo ' (Assisi, 1620). In addition to these important works, many madrigals and other detached compositions will be found in the collections published by Phalèse and others at the beginning of the 17th century; and many more still remain in MS. (See Q.-L.) Of these last, the most important are some psalms and motets for eight voices and a Salve Regina for twelve, formerly in the collection of the Abbé Santini; and a treatise on counterpoint, written, in conjunction with G. Maria, perhaps for the use of the pupils in the music school. Proske has included four of his Psalms in the ' Musica divina.'　　w. s. r.

NANTIER - DIDIÉE, CONSTANCE BETSY ROSABELLA (b. St. Denis, Île de Bourbon, now Île de la Réunion, Nov. 16, 1831; d. Madrid, Dec. 4, 1867), mezzo-soprano singer, derived her second name from her marriage with a singer. She was at the Paris Conservatoire, under Duprez, from 1847–49, and obtained an accessit in the latter year in his class, and the first prize in the opera class. She made her début on the stage at the Carignan Theatre, Turin, in Mercadante's ' La Vestale.' She played in Paris at the Salle Ventadour in 1851, and afterwards joined an Italian company, of which Giuglini was one, playing at Lyons, Nîmes, Montpelier, etc.

Madame Nantier-Didiée made her first appearance in England at Covent Garden in 1853 as the Chevalier de Gondi in ' Maria di Rohan,' afterwards as Maddalena in ' Rigoletto ' on its production here, and as Ascanio in ' Benvenuto Cellini '; and in all three parts was successful. From 1853–64 inclusive she sang here every year in Italian opera, at Covent Garden and the Lyceum, the usual mezzo-soprano or contralto parts, creating amongst others Nancy in ' Marta,' Rita on the revival of ' Zampa,' L' Amore in ' Orfeo,' Ulrica in Verdi's ' Ballo ' and Siebel in ' Faust.' In this last opera Gounod wrote the popular air ' Quando a te lieta ' expressly for her. During this time Madame Nantier-Didiée sang at court and public concerts, made an operatic provincial tour in 1855, later in that year and the early part of 1856 played in opera in America, and took part at the Bradford Festival of 1859. The rest of each year she was engaged in the Italian Opera of Paris, St. Petersburg, Moscow, Madrid, etc., or sang at concerts in the French provinces.

　　　　　　　　　　　　　　　　　　　　A. C.

NAPIER, WILLIAM (*b. circa* 1740; *d.* London, 1812), a Scottish musician and music-publisher.

For a number of years he played the violin in the private band belonging to George the Third, until gout in his hands prevented this. He was an energetic music-publisher, quick to see latent talent in new composers. His publications include a quantity of instrumental works, and he held the valuable copyright of such ballad operas as ' Rosina,' ' Maid of the Mill,' etc. He disposed of some of these copyrights to Dale for £540. His best-known publication is 'A Selection of Original Scots Songs,' 3 vols. folio, 1790–94, with Bartolozzi frontispieces. His earliest address (before 1773) was 474 Strand, London, at the corner of Lancaster Court. About 1788 he removed from here to 49 Great Queen Street, and finally, about 1800, to 8 Lisle Street. He died in his 72nd year in 1812, at Somers Town (see obituary notice in *The Scots Magazine* for Aug. 1812).   F. K.

In 1792, when his business went through a critical period, Haydn, in order to assist him, arranged for him a book of Scottish songs with accompaniment for pianoforte, violin and violoncello. This proved so successful that Napier paid Haydn afterwards £50 and doubled that sum for a subsequent book.   E. V. D. S.

NAPLES. The first school of music at Naples was founded towards the middle of the 15th century by John Tinctor. His school was short-lived, but it was immediately succeeded by the Neapolitan Conservatorios, which were both the first examples and models of all similar musical institutions, not only in Italy but in the other countries of Europe.

The Conservatorios of Naples, four in number —(1) Santa Maria di Loreto, (2) San Onofrio, (3) De' Poveri di Gesù Cristo, (4) Della Pietà de' Turchini—were originally founded by private benefactors for the purpose of affording shelter and instruction to the homeless orphans of Naples. The children were taken out of the streets and clad in a particular dress, each Conservatorio being distinguished from the others by its peculiar colour. Ecclesiastical music was at first the primary object of these institutions. They were governed after the pattern of a priests' seminary, and each had a church of which the pupils formed the choir. The funds of the institution were increased by the services of the pupils in other city churches and in the Royal Chapel, for which they received a monthly salary ; also by other pious offices, such as prayers over the dead previous to burial. The elder pupils were called ' Paranze ' (*i.e.* a small corps or company) and the younger ones ' Sopranelli ' and ' Contraltini,' according to their voices. Besides these pious services, the pupils were engaged to sing in great musical processions or ' Flottole.' When dramatic music began to revive, they represented the mysteries in the monasteries and convents dur-

ing carnival, and later performed in the theatres. These efforts of the pupils brought in to each Conservatorio an average of 1000 ducats a year, but despite these and private benefactions the endowment of each institution was hardly sufficient to supply the bare necessaries of life to the pupils. Yet from this humble origin sprang the great masters of music whose compositions are inseparably associated with Italy.

(1) SANTA MARIA DI LORETO. This originated in 1535 with a poor artisan of the name of Francesco, who received into his house on the Mercato orphans of both sexes, and caused them to be fed and clothed and instructed in music. The rich citizens of the Mercato assisted his pious design by every means in their power. The fame of the school reached the ears of Giovanni da Tappia, a Spanish priest domiciled in Naples, and he, having the progress of music at heart, volunteered to direct it and extend its powers of usefulness by a permanent endowment. This he obtained by begging alms through the Neapolitan Provinces. At the end of nine years he returned to Naples with a sufficient sum for the purpose. The original humble institution was transferred to a larger building close to the Church of Sta. Maria de Loreto. This building received the title of ' Conservatorio,' and was endowed, in 1566, with the ' Jus del forno ' and ' della beccaria.' Thus established, rich citizens from time to time left their fortunes to this institution, which grew and flourished. The pupils of both sexes reached the number of 800. Among the illustrious musicians whose names are connected with Santa Maria di Loreto are Alessandro Scarlatti, Durante, Porpora, Traëtta, Sacchini, Perez, Guglielmi and many more.

In 1797 the two Conservatorios of San Onofrio and Santa Maria di Loreto were united, the former being absorbed in the latter. In 1806, by order of Joseph Buonaparte, the Conservatorio of Loreto was united to that of the ' Pietà de' Turchini,' and the building of Santa Maria di Loreto then became a hospital.

(2) SAN ONOFRIO A CAPUANA, so called because it was situated in the district of Naples known as Capuana. It was founded in 1576 by private benefactions under the name of the ' confraternity of the Bianchi.' It received 120 orphans, who were instructed in religion and music. The funds of this, as of the other similar institutions, were augmented by the exertions of the pupils as already described. In course of time it was taken out of the hands of the confraternity and established as a Conservatorio by royal warrant, with the title of San Onofrio. The dress of the pupils was black and white—hence the name ' de' Bianchi.' At a later date foreign pupils were admitted on terms of monthly payment, and on the understanding that they should continue to give their services for a few years after the end of their term of

instruction. In 1797 the building of San Onofrio was turned into barracks and the pupils were transferred to Santa Maria di Loreto. A. Scarlatti was a teacher in this Conservatorio *also, likewise Durante, Leo, Feo, Cotumacci ; amongst their pupils were Gizzi, Jommelli, Piccinni, Terradellas and Paisiello. Gizzi, by the advice of Scarlatti, opened in 1720 a school of singing in connexion with this Conservatorio; the famous singer Gioacchino Conti di Arpino was one of his pupils, and out of gratitude to his master took the name of GIZZIELLO (*q.v.*).

(3) DE' POVERI DI GESÙ CRISTO. This was established in 1589 by a Franciscan, Marcello Foscataro di Nicotera, for the foundlings of Naples. By means of alms collected from the Neapolitans, he obtained the necessary funds, and drew up the rules, which were ratified by Alfonso Gesualdo, the then Cardinal Archbishop of Naples. The pupils, 100 in number, varying in age from 7 to 11, and literally taken out of the streets, were clothed at first in the sober dress of the Franciscan order, afterwards in blue and red, fed and instructed in their own language and in music, and were governed by two canons of the cathedral of Naples.

This Conservatorio existed till 1744, when by order of Cardinal Spinelli it was converted into a Diocesan Seminary and the pupils were distributed among the three remaining Conservatorios—San Onofrio, Loreto and the Pietà de' Turchini.

This Conservatorio is by some considered as the oldest of all, and as the cradle of the great Neapolitan school of music. Feo, Greco, Durante, Vinci—all pupils of Scarlatti—Cotumacci, Porpora, Ignazio Gallo and Pergolesi were among the most famous composers which it produced.

(4) DELLA PIETÀ DE' TURCHINI. This originated with the confraternity of Sta. Maria della Incoronatella, who in the year 1583 made their house an asylum both for the homeless orphans of Naples and also for children whose parents were unable to support them. At first the children were only taught to read and write, and were clad in long blue garments (' color turchino '); hence the name of ' Pietà de' Turchini,' which was adopted by the institution instead of that of the ' Incoronatella.' It was not till a century later that musical instruction was given to the pupils. In 1600 it was placed under the protection of Philip III. of Spain, and in 1670 Francesco Provenzale and Gennaro Ursino were appointed to be its professors of music, Provenzale having preceded Scarlatti as maestro of the Palatine Chapel at Naples. It produced many famous composers, such as Fago, Carapella, Leo, Cafaro, Jommelli and Sala. In 1806, on the abolition of the Conservatorio of Sta. Maria di Loreto, the pupils were received into the Pietà

de' Turchini. In 1808 this, the last of the Conservatorios, was also suppressed.

Thus the ' REAL CONSERVATORIO DI MUSICA ' came into existence, first with the title of San Sebastiano and afterwards with that of S. Pietro a Maiella, which it still retains.

Tritta, Paisiello and Fenaroli were the first directors and general administrators of the new Real Conservatorio. They were succeeded in 1813 by Zingarelli. In 1817 ' external ' preparatory schools of music were added ; and the pupils who passed creditable examinations there were admitted into the Real Conservatorio. In the revolution of 1820 half the building of San Sebastiano was seized for the use of the Government, the other half was made over to the Jesuits, and the monastery of San Pietro a Maiella was assigned to the Conservatorio. In 1837 Zingarelli was followed by Donizetti, and he again in 1840 by Mercadante, who made great reforms in the discipline and efficiency of the college. In 1861, on account of his blindness, Carlo Conti was appointed his coadjutor. Conti died in 1868 and was succeeded by Paolo Serrao Mercadante, who retained his post as president till his death in 1870. Since that date the Conservatorio appears to have lost ground. In 1874 the scholarships were reduced from 100 to 50, and 25 of these were thrown open to women, with allowance for lodging ; but in 1879 this allowance was abolished. The Conservatorio is now governed by a Board of professors and amateurs. Bellini, Luigi Ricci, Michael Costa, Martucci, Leoncavallo, Giordano and Cilla are the most distinguished names on the roll of the Real Conservatorio di Napoli. (See LIBRARIES.)

C. M. P.

SAN CARLO, the largest and most beautiful theatre of Naples, has almost the same proportions as La Scala of Milan, with which it contends for the theatrical primacy in Italy. It was built in 1737 by the architect Carasale, on plans by Medrano, a General of the R.E., and was completed in nine months. Some alterations and improvements were made in it by Fuga and Niccolini towards the end of the 18th century. It was completely burnt down in 1816, and rebuilt even more elegantly and quickly than before, in six months, by the said Antonio Niccolini. In 1844 the San Carlo underwent a thorough restoration and considerable improvement. The most notable operas performed for the first time at this theatre are : Rossini's ' Otello ' (1816) and ' Mosé ' (1818) ; Donizetti's ' Lucia ' (1835) ; Verdi's ' Alzira ' (1845) and ' Luisa Miller ' (1849).

F. B.

NAPRAVNIK, EDWARD (*b.* Beišt, near Hradeckrálove, Bohemia, Aug. 12/24, 1839 ; *d.* Nov. 10, 1915), was the son of a teacher. He learnt the rudiments of music from a colleague of his father named Pugonny, and at 13 was able to play for the service in the village church. In 1854 he was left an orphan in very poor circumstances. He determined to become a musician, and succeeded in entering the School of Organists in Prague. He studied instrumentation with Kittel, and also at the pianoforte school established by Maidel, where he soon became an assistant teacher. Several essays in composition, comprising masses, symphonies, overtures on Czech themes, songs, etc., date from this early period. In 1861 Napravnik was called to St. Petersburg to be director of Prince Youssipov's private orchestra. Two years later he was appointed, at Liadov's suggestion, to be his assistant, and the organist of the Imperial Theatres. He rose to be second conductor in 1867, and succeeded Liadov as chief Kapellmeister in 1869; a position which he occupied until his death.

At the time of his appointment Russian opera was in a neglected and languishing condition, and Napravnik carried on the work of restitution begun by his predecessor Liadov with tact and zeal. The existing repertory of the Maryinsky Theatre—where Russian opera was usually performed in St. Petersburg—was largely built up on his recommendation. Mention must be made of the admirable performances of Glinka's ' A Life for the Tsar,' Tchaikovsky's ' Eugene Oniegin,' 'The Oprichnik' and 'Dame de Pique,' and of Rimsky-Korsakov's ' Snow Maiden ' and ' Sadko,' which were distinguishing features of Napravnik's directorship. To his remarkable talent as a conductor Napravnik joined uncommon powers of organisation. Although a strict disciplinarian, he showed great diplomacy in the management of his affairs. Not only did he so greatly improve the orchestra of the Imperial Opera—both as regards numbers and quality—that it came to be regarded as one of the finest in the world, but he did much to raise the social and material position of the players. He was universally respected, and his opinion carried weight in all strata of the musical world of Russia.

At the close of thirty-five years' service, in 1898, Napravnik had conducted over 3000 operas, including sixty-two first productions, of which thirty-six were Russian, and thirty revivals, fifteen of these being by native composers. Besides his onerous work at the Opera, Napravnik distinguished himself as a concert conductor. From 1869–81 he conducted the concerts of the Russian Musical Society, and occasionally those of the Philharmonic Society.

In his compositions Napravnik shows the qualities and defects frequently characteristic of the conductor-composer; a consummate command of technical means and the eclecticism and good taste born of vast experience; but also a certain loss of individuality and distinction, which seems the unavoidable result of perpetually assimilating other men's creations. His

operas have met with marked success, and are certainly not devoid of charm, although the nature of the music is often reminiscent.

Napravnik's early opus numbers, up to thirteen, represent his youthful works composed before leaving Bohemia. The following is a list of his known compositions :

OPERATIC

' The Nije-Novgorodians,' opera in 4 acts, op. 15, first performance St. Petersburg, 1868 (revived in 1888) ; ' Harold,' opera in 5 acts, op. 45, St. Petersburg, 1886 ; ' Doubrovsky,' opera in 4 acts, op. 58, St. Petersburg, 1895 ; ' Francesca da Rimini ' (libretto from Stephen Phillips's play), op. 71, St. Petersburg, 1903.

ORCHESTRAL

Four Symphonies, op. 17 ; ' The Demon,' op. 18, 1879 ; National Dances, opp. 20 and 23 ; Symphonic poem, ' The East,' op. 40 ; Suite, op. 49 ; Solemn Overture, op. 14 ; Marches, opp. 33 and 38.

CHAMBER MUSIC

Three String Quartets, opp. 16, 28, 65 ; two Pianoforte Trios, opp. 24 and 62 ; Pianoforte Quartet, op. 42 ; String Quintet (two violoncellos), op. 19 ; Violin and Pianoforte Sonata, op. 52 ; two Suites for violoncello and pianoforte, opp. 29 and 36.

INSTRUMENTAL AND ORCHESTRAL

Pianoforte Concerto, op. 27 ; Fantasia on Russian themes for pianoforte and orchestra, op. 39 ; Fantasia for violin and orchestra, op. 30 ; Suite for violin and orchestra, op. 60.

VOCAL

Music to A. Tolstoi's ' Don Juan,' for soli, chorus, orchestra and declamation ; ballads, with orchestral accompaniment, ' The Voyevode,' op. 22 (baritone), ' The Cossack ' and ' Tamara,' op. 26. For chorus.—Three male-voice choruses, op. 41 ; five choruses a cappella, op. 50 ; four ditto, op. 55 ; four ditto, op. 63. Songs, op. 21 (4), op. 25 (4), op. 31 (4), op. 35 (4), op. 44 (4), op. 56 (4), op. 59 (6), op. 68 (4), op. 70 (4 duets).

PIANOFORTE

Musical Pictures (5), op. 43 ; Bagatelles (4), op. 46 ; two Valses, op. 48 ; Dance Suite, op. 57 ; six pieces, op. 61 ; three pieces for violin and piano, op. 64 ; three pieces for violoncello and piano, op. 37 ; four ditto, op. 67.   R. N.

NARDINI, PIETRO (b. Fibiana, Tuscany, 1722 ; d. Florence, May 7, 1793), an eminent violinist and composer, received his first musical instruction at Leghorn, and afterwards studied for several years under Tartini at Padua. About the year 1753 he was appointed solo-violinist at the ducal court at Stuttgart, where he remained for fifteen years. In 1767 he returned to Italy, settled at Leghorn, and stayed with his old master Tartini during his last illness. In 1770 he accepted an appointment as director of the music at the court of the Duke of Tuscany.

Nardini was the most eminent of Tartini's disciples. Leopold Mozart, the best possible judge in matters of violin-playing, writes of him:

' The beauty, purity and equality of his tone, and the tastefulness of his cantabile-playing, cannot be surpassed ; but he does not execute great difficulties.'

The well-known poet-musician Schubart relates in his flowery style :

' His playing brings tears into the eyes of stonyhearted courtiers—nay, his own tears run down on his violin ! '

That Nardini was not a mere executant, but a thorough musician, is evident from the character of his compositions for the violin. Vivacity, grace, a sweet sentimentality, are the main characteristics of his style, which is altogether more modern in form and feeling than Tartini's. His allegros are often largely developed, and already display the full sonata form, while his slow movements are not unlike Viotti's. If nevertheless the greater part of his works appear to us old-fashioned and antiquated compared with those of Tartini, the reason is that he has

neither the depth of feeling, the grand pathos nor the concentrated energy of his great master.
His published compositions are :

Six Concertos, op. 1 (Amsterdam) ; six Sonatas for violin and bass, op. 2 (Berlin, 1765 ; a new edition published by Cartier, Paris) ; six Sonatas for two violins (also numbered op. 2), London, Walsh ; six Trios for flute (London) ; six Solos for violin, op. 5 (London, 1770) ; a Solo for violin with thorough-bass (London, 1780) ; six Quartets (Florence, 1782) ; six 'Duos pour deux violons' (Parl.).

Some of his sonatas have latterly been re-edited by Alard in his ' Maîtres classiques,' by F. David in the ' Hohe Schule des Violinspiels,' and by G. Jensen in ' Classische Violinmusik.' Leoni di Pienza published an *Elogio di Pietro Nardini* in Florence, 1793 ; see also J. B. de Rangoni's *Essai sur le goût de musique*, 1790.

P. D. ; addns. E. H.-A.

NARDÒ, Fra Benedetto Serafico di, of the order of the predicatori, was at Naples in 1575, at Leccie in 1581. He composed 3 books of madrigals. (See *Q.-L.*)

NARES, James, Mus.D. (*b.* Stanwell, Middlesex, 1715 [1] ; *d.* Feb. 10, 1783), was a chorister in the Chapel Royal under Bernard Gates and Dr. Croft, and afterwards with Dr. Pepusch. He acted for some time as deputy for Pigott, organist of St. George's Chapel, Windsor, and in 1734 was appointed, on the resignation of Salisbury, organist of York Minster. On Jan. 13, 1756, he was appointed to succeed Dr. Greene as organist and composer to the Chapel Royal, and in the same year graduated as Mus.D. at Cambridge. In Oct. 1757 he was appointed master of the children of the Chapel Royal, *vice* Gates, his old master. In 1770 he gained a prize from the Catch Club for his glee, ' To all Lovers of Harmony.' He resigned the mastership of the Chapel boys July 1, 1780, died in 1783, and was buried in St. Margaret's Westminster.

Nares published ' Eight Sets of Harpsichord Lessons,' 1748 ; ' Five Harpsichord Lessons,' op. 2, 1758; 'Three Easy Harpsichord Lessons'; ' A Treatise on Singing ' ; ' Il Principio, or, A regular Introduction to playing on the Harpsichord or Organ' (1759, the first set of progressive lessons published on a systematic plan) ; ' The Royal Pastoral,' a dramatic ode, 1767 ; ' Collection of Catches, Canons and Glees,' *c.* 1780 ; ' Six Organ Fugues ' ; ' Second Treatise on Singing, with a Set of English Duets ' ; and ' Twenty Anthems,' 1778. ' A Morning and Evening Service and Six Anthems ' were published in 1788, with a portrait of him, *œtat.* 65, engraved by Ward after Engleheart, prefixed. A sketch of his life is also contained in the volume by his son Robert. His Service in F and three anthems are included in Arnold's ' Cathedral Music,' an anthem in Page's ' Harmonia sacra,' and two anthems in Stevens's ' Sacred Music.' Two canons, two glees, two rounds, and a catch by him (the famous ' Wilt thou lend me thy mare ? ') are contained in

1 Baptized Apr. 19.

Warren's collections, and one of his lessons, in three movements, from the set of 1758, was reprinted in the *Oxf. Hist. Mus.* vol. iv., *The Age of Bach and Handel.* W. H. H.

NARVAEZ (Narbais), Luys de (16th cent.), Spanish lutenist (*vihuelista*), said to have been a native of Granada, and of such extraordinary skill that he could give the illusion of playing all the parts in a work for four voices. He published a book of tablature entitled :

Los seys libros del Delphin de musica en cifras para vihuela . . . Valladolid, 1538. (B.M.; Bibl. Nac., Madrid ; Bibl. Provincial, Toledo.)

Narvaez (like Luis Milan) has a definitely instrumental style, well shown in his brilliant setting of the ballad ' Ya se asienta el rey Ramiro,' printed by Morphy (*q.v.*). He introduced into Spanish music the principle of variation, or *diferencias*, usually ascribed to Diego Ortiz. In Spain the variation-form seems to have arisen through the necessity of varying the accompaniment during the singing of a long ballad. Narvaez, however, has another manner of treating *diferencias*, which arose from the first : that is, to treat them as purely instrumental variations. His works for vihuela are in course of publication by E. M. Torner (Madrid : Junta Para Ampliación de Estudios). Two motets were printed between 1539 and 1542.

J. B. T.

NASARRE, Fr. Pablo (*b.* 1664 ; *d.* 1724), a blind organist of Saragossa, author of two theoretical works :

Fragmentos musicos . . . canto llano, canto de organo, contrapunto y composición. Saragossa, 1683 (B.M.) and Madrid, 1700 (Bibl. Nac., Madrid).
Escuela musica segun la practica moderna. Saragossa, Pt. I., 1724 ; Pt. II., 1723. (Paris, Conservatoire ; Madrid, Bibl. Nac.; Barcelona, Orfeó Català.)

Though praised by Fétis, in Spain he has always been considered a pedant. He was described by Eximeno as being ' an organist by birth, and blind by profession.' J. B. T.

NASCIMBENI, (1) Maria Francesca (late 17th cent.) of Ancona, pupil of Scipione Lazarini. She composed canzoni and madrigals (1674), also 2 motets in Lazarini's Motets op. 2 (1674).

(2) Stefano (Nasim-beni) (*b.* Mantua, early 17th cent.), composed 8-part masses (1612) ; vesper-psalms and 8-part psalms (1616) ; concerti ecclesiastici, 12 v. for 3 choirs (1610) ; several songs in collective volumes (1588, 1596) (*Q.-L.*).

NASCO, Giovanni (*d.* before 1560), maestro of a musical academy at Verona, 1548 ; in 1554 and 1557 maestro di cappella at Treviso Cathedral. He composed 3 books of Lamentations (1561, 1564, 1574), and several books of madrigals and canzons, some in several editions (1548-65). (List in *Q.-L.*)

NASOLINI, Sebastiano (*b.* Piacenza, *c.* 1768 ; *d.* Naples, *c.* 1816 ?), at first a pianist, devoted himself afterwards entirely to composition of operas which met with great success all over Europe. He spent some time also in

London. For list of his 38 operas, arias, scenas, etc., see Sonneck's *Catalogue of Opera Librettos.*

NATALI (NATALE), PATER POMPEO, in 1674 described as '.dalla Ripa Transona' (Provincia della Marca), was a singer at S. Maria Maggiore, Rome. He composed between 1656–81, 2 books of madrigals and canzons of 2-3 equal voices, and two books of Solfeggi, 2-3 v. (Q.-L.; *Riemann*).

NATHAN, ISAAC (b. Canterbury, 1791; d. Australia, Jan. 15, 1864), of Hebrew parentage, was intended for the priesthood, and was in 1805 sent to Cambridge to study Hebrew, but his natural bent being for music he was articled to Domenico Corri, and devoted his attention principally to singing and composition. He appeared at Covent Garden as Henry Bertram, in 'Guy Mannering.' After composing several songs, he produced in 1815 – 22 'Hebrew Melodies,' to Lord Byron's poetry, with much success. Byron became very intimate with Nathan, who set many of his poems to music. (See *D.N.B.*) In 1823 he supplied part of the music for the comedy 'Sweethearts and Wives' —one song in which, 'Why are you wandering here, I pray?' became very popular—and published *Musurgia Vocalis, An Essay on the History and Theory of Music and on the qualities, capabilities, and management of the Human Voice.* In 1824 he brought out 'The Alcaid,' comic opera, and in 1827 'The Illustrious Stranger,' operatic farce. In 1836 he published *The Life of Madame Malibran de Bériot.* In 1841 he emigrated to Sydney, where he produced 'Merry Freaks in Troublous Time,' 1851, and ran a periodical, *The Southern Euphrosyne and Australian Miscellany,* from 1846. He was accidentally killed by being run over by a tramway car. He was much esteemed as a singing-master.

w. h. h. ; addns. *D.N.B., B.M. Biog.,* etc.

NATIONAL ANTHEM, see GOD SAVE THE KING.

NATIONAL CONCERTS, a series of concerts given in Her Majesty's Theatre, in Oct., Nov. and Dec. 1850, with Balfe and Charles d'Albert as conductors. The prospectuses promised many new works, most of them by English composers (probably the only origin of the name of the concerts), none of which, however, saw the light. During the season the following works came to a hearing : Spohr's symphony, 'The Seasons'; Mendelssohn's 'Fingal's Cave' and 'Melusina' overtures, one or two symphonies, and a movement or two from a concerto by Beethoven. The following artists appeared : Hallé, Molique, Sainton, Piatti, Arabella Goddard (her first appearance), Stockhausen and Sims Reeves. The concerts were an unequivocal failure, chiefly because of the enormous expectations that were excited but not fulfilled. An attempt was made in Mar.

1852 to start another series with the same title, in Exeter Hall, but the scheme fell to the ground after a few concerts.

NATIONAL TRAINING SCHOOL FOR MUSIC, THE. This institution, which had been projected and discussed since 1854, and the idea of which had emanated from the Prince Consort, was not founded until 1873, when a meeting was held at Clarence House, the Duke of Edinburgh in the chair, at which it was resolved that ' it is desirable to erect a building at a cost not exceeding £20,000 for the purposes of a Training School for Music at Kensington, in connexion with the Society of Arts.' A site on the immediate west side of the Albert Hall was granted by the Commissioners of 1851; the construction of the building,[1] on the design of Captain F. Cole, R.E., was undertaken by Charles J. Freake (afterwards Sir Charles) at his own cost; the first stone was laid on Dec. 18, 1873, and the School was opened at Easter 1876 with 82 free scholarships, of which 4 were founded by the Society of Arts, 2 by members of the Society, 5 by Freake, 10 by the Corporation of London, 14 by City Guilds, 33 by provincial towns, and the remainder by private donors. The scholarships were of the value of £40 a year each, and were founded for five years, by subscription renewable at the end of that term; they carried free instruction for the same period, and were obtainable ' by competitive examination alone.' The Duke of Edinburgh was chairman of the Council, Sullivan was appointed principal, with a staff of teachers; in 1881 he was succeeded by Stainer as principal, and the School continued to flourish till Easter 1882, when it came to an end owing to the determination arrived at to establish the R.C.M. on a wider and more permanent basis. The College, on its formation, took over the building, furniture and fittings, organ and music, and a balance at the banker's of £1100. (See ROYAL COLLEGE OF MUSIC.)   M.

NATURAL, a word formerly applied to the scale of C major, which was called ' the natural scale ' because it has no accidentals. It thus became used for the sign ($\natural$) (Fr. *bécarre*, Ger. *Quadrat*, Ital. *quadro*), which cancels a preceding sharp or flat, whether used as a chromatic accidental or occurring in the signature. In other words, when the use of a sharp or flat has indicated that the note a semitone above or below that in the diatonic series of C major is to be taken, the introduction of a natural indicates that the unaltered note is to be resumed; and hence a naturalised note is always a white key on the pianoforte or organ, unless it be combined with a sharp or flat, as $\natural\sharp$ or $\natural\flat$, to cancel a chromatic double-sharp or double-flat, and indicate the corresponding note of the diatonic series as shown by the existing signature.

Naturals do not occur in the signatures *of*

keys, except when it is necessary to cancel all
or part of a previous signature, at a change of
key in the course of a piece of music ; as at the
change from C minor to C major in the Marcia
Funebre of the Eroica Symphony, or the change
from E♭ to G minor in Chopin's nocturne, op.
37, No. 1. Where a complete change is made
from a sharp key to a flat key, or *vice versa*, the
naturals are often indicated, but with very
little reason, as the mere statement of the new
signature must cancel the former one.

C. H. H. P. ; rev. S. T. W.

NAU, MARIA DOLORES BENEDICTA JOSE-
FINA (b. New York, Mar. 18, 1818 ; d. Levallois,
near Paris, Jan. 1891), singer, of Spanish parentage, entered the Conservatoire at Paris, July
23, 1832, and became a pupil of Mme. Cinti-
Damoreau, soon developing a clear and flexible
voice. This, with a large share of intelligence,
musical feeling and application, enabled her
to take the first prize at the *concours* of 1834.

On Mar. 1, 1836, at the age of 18, Mlle. Nau
made her first appearance at the Opéra, as
the Page in the ' Huguenots,' and achieved a
success, in spite of her inexperience. She remained six years at that establishment, but
playing only secondary parts, which did not
allow her real worth to appear ; and at the end
of that time her engagement was not renewed.
Mlle. Nau determined, therefore, to travel in
the provinces and abroad, where she soon was
appreciated much more highly ; in Brussels,
particularly, her excellent vocalisation and
phrasing produced a marked impression. In
Oct. and Nov. 1844, she sang in London. Her
foreign successes opened the eyes of the Opéra
managers at Paris, where she was re-engaged at
thrice her former salary. She reappeared there
in December, receiving a warm welcome ; and
continued to sing on that stage till the end of
1848, with unabated éclat. Her farewell was
on Oct. 11 of that year, in ' Lucia ' ; after
which she went to London, and thence to the
United States, where she had a triumphal progress. Returning to London, she sang at the
Princess's Theatre for nearly eighteen months,
with great success ; and thence betook herself
once more to the Opéra at Paris, where she
remained during 1851, 1852 and 1853. Mlle.
Nau revisited her native country in 1854, and
received extravagant adoration. She returned
to Paris again in 1856, when she finally quitted
the stage.　　　　　　　　　　　　　J. M.

NAUDIN, EMILIO (b. Parma, Oct. 23, 1823 ;
d. Boulogne, May, 1890), was taught singing by
Giacomo Panizza of Milan, made his début at
Cremona about 1845 in Pacini's ' Saffo,' and
afterwards sang at the principal theatres of
Italy, at Vienna and St. Petersburg. He made
his first appearance in England, June 2, 1858,
at Drury Lane, as the Duke in ' Rigoletto,'
and remained for the season, playing Edgardo,
Ernesto and Arturo, and singing in concerts.

After singing at Madrid and Turin, he reap
peared in England on May 30, 1862, at Mrs.
Anderson's farewell concert at Her Majesty's,
and on the 31st acted Manrico at the same
theatre. In November of that year he appeared
as Ferrando at the Parisian revival of ' Così fan
tutte,' and in Flotow's ' Stradella.' On Apr. 7,
1863, he appeared at Covent Garden as Masaniello, and remained there every season up to
1872 inclusive, except 1865, when he was engaged to create Vasco di Gama, on the production of ' L'Africaine,' Apr. 28 ; he had been
mentioned in Meyerbeer's will as the most
suitable singer for the part. During all these
seasons he undertook several characters in
addition to the above, viz. Don Ottavio, Raoul.
Vasco, Danilowitz, Fra Diavolo, Carlo, etc., as
well as Don Carlos, on the production of Verdi's
opera of that name in England, June 4, 1867 ;
and was always acceptable on account of his
careful singing and acting. In 1873 he sang in
concerts only. In 1874 he sang at Drury Lane
for the season, adding Henrique (' Diamant de
la couronne ') to his already extensive list, and
in 1875 returned to Covent Garden. In the
autumn of that year he played Lohengrin for
the first time in the English provinces. In
Moscow he played Tannhäuser in 1877. In
1879 he sang in Spain and Italy, and added the
part of Eleazar (in ' La Juive ') to his repertory.
He became paralysed and died at Boulogne.

A. C.

NAUDOT, JEAN-JACQUES (Paris, early 18th
cent.), was one of the first of those who distinguished themselves on the traverse flute
in France, and according to Laurent Grillet,
one of the greatest French viellists (hurdy-
gurdy players). He composed between 1726-
1740 trios, duos and sonatas for flutes and bass,
sonatas for vielle and bass, and ' Babioles ' for
2 vielles or musettes (Q.-L.).　　　　E. V. D. S.

NAUMANN, (1) JOHANN GOTTLIEB (GIO-
VANNI AMADEO) (b. Blasewitz, near Dresden,
Apr. 17, 1741 ; d. Dresden, Oct. 23, 1801), a
well-known composer in his day. Though the
child of a peasant he was educated at the
Kreuzschule in Dresden, and intended for a
schoolmaster. He studied music by himself,
until a Swedish musician resident in Dresden named Weestroem, happening to visit his
home, was struck by seeing Bach's (probably
Emanuel's) sonatas on the harpsichord, and
determined to take Naumann on a professional
tour. Starting in May 1757, they first went to
Hamburg, where they were detained ten months
by Weestroem's ill-health, and then to Padua,
where Weestroem took lessons from Tartini, in
which he did not allow Naumann to share. His
treatment was altogether so bad that the young
man left him, but was able to proceed with his
training, as Tartini taught him for nothing, and
an English musician named Hunt gave him
pecuniary assistance. During his stay of three

years in Padua he made the acquaintance of Hasse. He next went to Naples in 1761 with a pupil named Pitscher, to study dramatic music for six months ; and then, armed with a recommendation from Tartini, visited Padre Martini at Bologna, and received from him some instruction in counterpoint. During a lengthened stay at Venice he produced his first opera at San Samuele. In 1763 he returned home, and through the influence of the Electress was appointed court composer of sacred music. In 1765–68 he was again in Italy, composing ' Achille in Sciro ' (1767) for Palermo, and ' Alessandro nelle Indie ' for Venice. In 1769 he produced ' La clemenza di Tito ' (Metastasio's text) in Dresden, and in 1772 ' Solimanno ' and ' Nozze disturbate ' in Venice, ' Armida ' in Padua (1773), and ' Ipermestra ' in Venice (1774). On his return to Dresden in 1774 he declined a flattering invitation from Frederick the Great to Berlin, and in 1776 was rewarded by the Elector with the title of Kapellmeister, and a salary of 1200 thalers. During a temporary residence in Stockholm (1776–78) he produced in Swedish ' Amphion ' (1776) and ' Cora,' his best and most popular work, published for PF. in 1780. He was again in Sweden in 1782–84, producing ' Gustav Vasa ' in 1783. In 1786 he was raised to the dignity of Oberkapellmeister, with a salary of 2000 thalers, for his refusal of a brilliant position at Copenhagen. In 1793 he produced ' Protesilao,' an opera, at Berlin, and an oratorio, ' Davidde in Terebinto,' at Potsdam, for which he received a gold snuff-box with 400 Friedrichs d'or from the King Frederick William II., who also induced Hummel to take lessons from him. His last opera, ' Aci e Galatea,' was produced, Apr. 25, 1801, at Dresden, where he died of apoplexy. For further particulars see Meissner's *Bruchstücke zur Biographie Naumanns* (Prague, 1803–04).

Naumann was also a prolific composer of church music ; 13 oratorios, and 21 masses with Te Deums, and smaller church pieces, being preserved in Dresden.[1] (See *Q.-L.* for list.)

The R.C.M. contains a Mass of his (in G) published in London, with an accompaniment arranged by Edmund Harris; and ' The Pilgrims at the Holy Sepulchre,' an oratorio, edited with a biography by Mainzer. By his marriage with the daughter of Admiral Grotschilling he left three sons, the eldest of whom, Karl Friederich, became a well-known mineralogist, whose son (2) ERNST (*b.* Aug. 15, 1832) studied the organ with Johann Schneider, and composition with Hauptmann, and was from 1860 organist and musikdirector at Jena, and from 1877 professor. He published an excellent treatise, *Über die verschiedenen Bestim-*

[1] He is reported to have composed the beautiful ' Dresden Amen,' immortalised in Wagner's ' Parsifal.'

mungen der Tonverhältnisse (Leipzig, 1858), as well as some music, among which may be named two string quintets, and a serenade for strings and wind.

The elder Naumann's second son, Moritz Ernst Adolf, a well-known physician and professor in Bonn, was father of (3) Dr. EMIL NAUMANN (*b.* Berlin, Sept. 8, 1827; *d.* Dresden, June 23, 1888), pupil of Mendelssohn and Hauptmann, and a composer of merit. An oratorio, ' Christus der Friedensbote,' was given in Dresden in 1848, and an opera, ' Judith,' was given in the same place in 1858. In 1856 his first effort in musical literature, *Die Einführung des Psalmengesangs in die Kirche*, procured him the post of court director of sacred music. Another opera, ' Loreley,' was performed after his death, in 1889. He lived chiefly in Dresden, and published many books, the most notable being *Die moderne musikalische Zopf* (1880), a pamphlet of conservative tendency, and an exhaustive *History of Music* (1880–85), translated into English by F. Praeger, and furnished with very necessary additional chapters on English music by Sir F. A. Gore Ouseley. This appeared in 1886. He succeeded W. Rust as organist of St. Thomas's, Leipzig (Mar. 1880). on the promotion of the latter to be cantor.

BIBLIOGRAPHY

MEISSNER : *Bruchstücke zur Biographie Naumanns.* Prague, 1803–04.)
M. L. NESTLER : *Der kursächsische Kapellmeister Naumann aus Blasewitz.* (1901.)
R. ENGLÄNDER : *J. G. Naumann als Opernkomponist, 1741–1801,* etc. (Leipzig, 1922.)
                                                                F. G.

NAUWACH (NAUWACHEN), JOHANN, in 1627 chamber musician of the Elector of Saxony at Torgau, composed 1 book of German villanelles, 1, 2, and 3 v., for theorbo, lute, harpsichord and other instruments; also ' libro primo di arie ' (1623) (*Riemann*).

NAVA, GAETANO (*b.* Milan, May 16, 1802 ; *d.* Mar. 31, 1875), a distinguished Italian teacher of singing, and writer of vocal exercises. His father, Antonio, taught and composed for the French guitar, then a favourite instrument, but the son received a college education previous to entering the Milan Conservatoire under Federici. Here in 1837 Nava was appointed professor, retaining his connexion with the institution—where he gave instruction both in harmony and in singing—for thirty-eight years, that is, up to the time of his death. His skill as a vocal teacher, enhanced by his cultivated intelligence and uncommon earnestness and honesty of purpose, brought him a large clientele of private pupils. Distinguished among these was Charles SANTLEY (*q.v.*). Nava's works, published at Milan, by the firms Ricordi, Lucca and Conti, comprise numerous books of *solfeggi* and *vocalizzi*, several masses and separate pieces of vocal church music, and a Method of Singing that has appeared also in London and at Leipzig. (See SOLFEGGIO.)   F. T.

NAVARRAISE, LA, 'Lyric Episode' in 2 acts; text by J. Claretie and H. Cain, music by Jules Massenet. Produced Covent Garden Theatre, June 20, 1894; Brussels the same year; Opéra-Comique, Paris, 1895.

NAVARRO, JUAN (b. Seville, c. 1530; d. Mexico, after 1604), Spanish church composer and madrigalist. Like Morales, he was described as *Hispalensis*, a native of Seville; and it has been conjectured that, from his style, he was a pupil of Fernandez de Castilleja, the master of both Morales and Guerrero. Since he was among the unsuccessful candidates for the post of maestro de capilla at Malaga, left vacant through the death of Morales in 1553, he cannot have been born much later than 1530. Espinel, the Spanish novelist, states that Navarro was maestro at Salamanca in the time of SALINAS, professor of music, 1567–87. He may have been in Rome in 1590; at any rate a nephew of his, Fernando Navarro Salazar, who was a jurist at the Papal court, arranged with SOTO DE LANGA for the publication of his uncle's psalms, hymns and Magnificats. The costs of printing were borne by a certain Francisco Reinoso, 'Abbati Fusillensi,' to whom the work was dedicated. Navarro afterwards emigrated to Mexico, where, in 1604, he published a book of Passions and Lamentations (plain-song, not polyphony). His madrigals (Bibl. Medinaceli, Madrid) are good; and if the comic 'Ay Jesus, que mal fraile!' be by him, he had sense of humour not unlike that of Orazio VECCHI.

Navarro's work was approvingly quoted by Padre Martini (*Esemplare*, i. 149, 204); Eslava printed 3 Magnificats and 2 psalms.

PRINTED WORKS

Psalmi, Hymni ac Magnificat totius anni . . . 4, 5 ac 6 v. Rome, 1590. (Rome: St. Cecilia; Bologna; Toledo; Montserrat.)
Liber in quo 4 Passiones Christi Domini continentur. . . . 8 Lamentationes, oratioque Hieremie Prophete. Mexico, 1604 (B.M.), and elsewhere.

MSS.

Malaga: Antifona a San Sebastian.
Seville: Part of Magnificat, 5 tone.
Toledo: 8 pieces.
Valencia, Col. del Patriarca, MS. 6. Partbooks: Madrigal, 5 v., Recuerde el alma dormida (coplas de Jorge Manrique).
Madrid, Bibl. Medinaceli. Madrigals, 7 for 4 v. and 1 for 5 v. Also Bibl. Nac. M. 1262. 'Ay de mi, sin ventura' has been printed by Pedrell (*Canc. Mus. Popular.* iii.).   J. B. T.

NAVOIGILLE (real name GUILLAUME JULIEN) (b. Givet, c. 1745; d. Paris, Nov. 1811) came to Paris, was adopted by an Italian, and patronised by Monsigny. He entered the band of the Duke of Orleans, and opened a free violin school, in which Boucher, the well-known virtuoso, was educated. He composed duets and trios for strings, and two theatrical pieces, the music of which largely consisted of well-known airs. He was a good leader, but his name would have been forgotten but for the mistake of Fétis in attributing to him the authorship of the 'Marseillaise.'   G. C.

NAVRÁTIL, CARL (b. Prague, Apr. 24, 1867), was taught theory by Guido Adler and the violin by Ondriček, and is the composer of many ambitious works of considerable in-

terest and value. The operas 'Hermann' and 'Salammbô' represent his work for the stage; besides a symphony in G minor, five symphonic poems deal respectively with 'John Hus,' 'Ziska,' 'Zalov,' 'Neklan' and 'Der weisse Berg.' Concertos for violin and pianoforte with orchestra, two trios for piano and strings, two quintets for piano and strings, a sonata for violin and piano, one for viola and piano, a string quartet in D minor, two psalms for eight-part chorus, a Mass in D, much pianoforte music and many songs, show great industry, and some of the music is strongly original. Navrátil has written a life of Smetana, and is an honorary member of the Dutch Maatschappij tot Bevordering van Toonkunst.   M.

NAY (NEI), an Egyptian flute consisting of a hollow reed blown across the upper end, and pierced with from 5 to 7 holes for the fingers (*PLATE XXV.* No. 1; see FLUTE). F. W. G.

NAYLOR, (1) JOHN (b. Stanningley, near Leeds, June 8, 1838; d. at sea, May 15, 1897), was organist in succession of St. Mary's and All Saints' Churches, Scarborough, and of York Minster. He composed church music and several cantatas, and died during a voyage to Australia. His son, (2) EDWARD WOODALL (b. Scarborough, Feb. 9, 1867), was musically educated by his father, and gained a choral scholarship at Emmanuel College, Cambridge, in 1884. He took his B.A. degree in 1887, and in 1888 entered the R.C.M., where on July 11, 1892, his scena 'Merlin and the Gleam' was performed. In 1889 he was appointed organist of St. Michael's, Chester Square, and in 1896–97 was organist at St. Mary's, Kilburn. He then returned to Cambridge, as assistant master at the Leys School, and organist of his old college, Emmanuel. He had taken the degrees of Mus.B. and M.A. in 1891, and that of Mus.D. in 1897. He made considerable alterations in the character and quality of the chapel services, and wrote a large number of services and anthems for choirs of tenors and basses. A trio for piano and strings in D is in MS., but many of his church compositions have been published, as well as partsongs, 'The Merry Bells of Yule' (with some nine-part writing at the close) and 'The Charge of the Light Brigade.' A cantata, 'Arthur the King,' was produced at Harrogate, Dec. 24, 1902, in which year he was appointed lecturer on music at Emmanuel College. His lectures are singularly free from 'academicism,' and often present history, etc., in new points of view. Papers were read by him on 'Heinrich Schütz (1905) and 'Jacob Hándl (Gallus)' (1908), before the Musical Association (see the *Proceedings* for those years). A book entitled *Shakespeare and Music* came out in 1896, and an analysis of the 'Fitzwilliam Virginal Book' in 1905. Dr. Naylor's name came before the general musical public most prominently in connexion with his opera 'The Angelus,' which gained the prize offered by Ricordi for an English work. It was performed at Covent Garden, Jan. 27, 1909. It was revived there by the Carl Rosa Company in 1921. For list of compositions see *B.M.S. Ann.*, 1920.   M., with addns.

NEALE, JOHN (*d.* before 1738) and WILLIAM (*d. circa* 1769) (father and son), a firm of Dublin music-sellers and publishers established before the middle of the 18th century in Christ Church Yard. It is very difficult to trace their history, though they played an important part in matters musical in the Dublin of their day, while few of their publications are left to afford clues. The elder, John Neale or 'O'Neil,' was in 1723 connected with a musical club held at a tavern in Christ Church Yard, which club afterwards developed into a very important musical association. He and his son were managers of most of the entertainments in Dublin, and built 'The Musick Hall' in Fishamble Street, opened in Oct. 1741, and wherein Handel in December of the same year conducted the first public performance of 'Messiah.'

William Neale died at an advanced age, his son John, who was a surgeon, becoming the best amateur violinist in Dublin. The above particulars are mainly gathered from Gilbert's *History of Dublin*, 1854. In turning to other references, in Bunting, 1840, p. 4, and in Petrie, 1855, pp. 39, 150-57, some confusion is apparent. They speak of certain publications issued about 1720, and it is difficult to identify these satisfactorily.

John and William Neale published a couple of thin folio works, being the songs and airs in 'The Beggar's Opera,' and in its second part. On these are advertised other of their publications, including three books of 'English Airs'; one each of 'Scotch Tunes,' 'Irish Tunes' and 'Country Dances'; while 'The Songs and Airs in *Merlin*' fixes the date of issue as after 1734 or 1736. The Neales were probably the first Irish music-publishers of any note, though perhaps exception might be made for Robert Thornton, who engraved music in Dublin at the end of the 17th century, and for Samuel Powell, a printer and bookseller, who issued psalmodies and similar works having musical notes, in the early years of the 18th century.   F. K.

NEANDER, ALEXIS, of Kolberg, matriculated, 1580, at Frankfort-on-the-Oder, was music director at the College of St. Kilian, Würzburg, in 1605. He composed 4 books of motets, 4-24 v. (published Frankfort, 1605–06); also motets in various MS. collective volumes and 260 hymns and motets in organ tablature (MS. in Munich Library) (*Q.-L.*; *Fétis*).

NEATE, CHARLES (*b.* London, Mar. 28, 1784; *d.* Brighton, Mar. 30, 1877), received his early musical education from William Sharp, and

afterwards from John Field, with whom he had formed a close intimacy. Besides the pianoforte he performed on the violoncello, he and Field both being instructed on that instrument by Sharp. He first appeared in public as a pianist at Covent Garden at the Lent 'oratorios,' in 1800, and soon established a reputation as an excellent performer of the school of Clementi and Field. He studied composition under Woelfl, and in 1808 published his first work, a sonata in C minor. In 1813 he was one of the original members of the Philharmonic Society, of which he was for many years a director, often a performer, and occasionally conductor, at its concerts. His admiration for Beethoven induced him in 1815 to visit Vienna, where he remained for eight months, enjoying the friendship and profiting by the advice of the great composer. He then went to Munich, where he stayed five months, studying counterpoint under Winter. After an absence of two years he returned to England, and was long esteemed as one of the best performers upon, and teachers of the pianoforte. His compositions were unimportant. He was the first to introduce into England Beethoven's concerto in E♭, Weber's Concertstück, and Hummel's concerto in E and Septuor in D minor. See *Concordia*, Oct. 16, 1875; *Mus. T.*, 1901, pp. 15, 16.   W. H. H.

NEBRA, JOSÉ DE (*d.* Madrid, July 11, 1768), Spanish composer of opera and church music. From the post of organist at the Convent of the Descalzas Reales, Madrid (formerly held by Victoria), Nebra was appointed 2nd organist to the Chapel Royal (1724). After the disastrous fire of 1734 (Dec. 24), when the musical archives of the palace were destroyed, Nebra and LITERES (*q.v.*) were asked to compose church music to replace that which had been lost. The neglect of the master of the Chapel Royal (Corselli), owing to his time being taken up with Italian opera, led to the creation of the post of vice-master for Nebra (1751). The plans for re-organisation were drawn up by him and approved in 1756. The choir was to consist of 4 sopranos (castrati), 4 altos, 4 tenors and 3 basses. There were 3 organists (Nebra, Literes and Rabassa) and an orchestra of 2 flutes, 2 hautboys, 2 *fagotes*, 3 *bajones* (bassoons and tenor bassoons), 2 horns, 2 trumpets, 12 violins, 4 violas. 3 violoncelli and 3 basses. Besides this, a special choir of 18 voices was engaged, with a special organist, for the performance of plain-song. These arrangements were completed by Apr. 1757. The first great occasion for which they were employed was the funeral of Queen Barbara of Braganza, whose music-master had been Domenico Scarlatti, and whose husband had been consoled for twenty years by the same songs sung nightly by FARINELLI (*q.v.*). Queen Barbara died Aug. 27, 1758 (Scarlatti had died the year before, at Naples); the music written by Nebra for the royal funeral included the Requiem for 8 v., flute and strings, publ. by Eslava.

Nebra, however, did not devote all his energies to the Chapel Royal. Between 1744 and 1747 he produced at least three operas ; one of which, ' Ante que celos y amor . . .,' was a version of the story of Briseis and the wrath of Achilles, with two comic characters who sang a seguidilla in the Spanish manner beneath the walls of Troy. Of these, only the libretti have been preserved. Existing MSS. include a Miserere, 8 v. (Paris Conservatoire); 15 psalms, 4 v. (Sistine Chapel); a villancico, 4 v. (Munich), while quantities of his works are to be found in the Escurial and many Spanish cathedrals.

J. B. T.

NEBUŠKA, OTAKAR (b. Mladá Boleslav, 1875), Czech musical writer, one of the leading members of the committee of management of the Hudební Matice, the musical branch of Umělecká Beseda (Society of Arts). He also helped to found the *Hudební Revue*, a periodical chiefly devoted to the interests of national music. He has composed some lyrics and choruses (Fr. Urbánek and Mojmír Urbánek), but his most important services to the art have been effected by his personal integrity and literary gift. He is at present secretary to the Chamber of Deputies. R. N.

NEDBAL, OSKAR (b. Tábor, Bohemia, Mar. 26, 1874), was educated at the Prague Conservatoire, and was the original viola-player of the BOHEMIAN (CZECH) STRING QUARTET (q.v.), as well as conductor of the Prague Philharmonic (1896–1906). Later he pursued his career as conductor chiefly in Vienna, where he directed the Tonkünstler orchestra till 1919 and also conducted at the Volksoper. Nedbal has been a fairly prolific composer, and has had some success with light operas. C.

NEEDLER, HENRY (b. London, 1685 ; d. Aug. 1, 1760), was an amateur violinist, who was instructed on the instrument first by his father and afterwards by the younger Banister, and became a proficient performer. He is said to have been taught harmony by Purcell, which must probably be taken to mean Daniel Purcell. About 1710 he was appointed Accountant-General of the Excise, and in the same year assisted in establishing the Academy of Ancient Music, where he long filled the post of principal violin. He was the first to lead the concertos of Corelli in England. Twenty-eight volumes of music, almost entirely transcribed by him from the libraries at Oxford, were presented by his widow to James Mathias, who, in 1782, bequeathed them to the British Museum, where they form Add. MSS. 5035 to 5062. W. H. H.

NEEFE, CHRISTIAN GOTTLOB (b. Chemnitz, Feb. 5, 1748 ; d. Jan. 26, 1798), a musician of some distinction in his day, whose claim to remembrance is his having been Beethoven's instructor. He was the son of a poor tailor,

and, possessing a lovely voice, sang in the church choir and learnt music in the school. His parents contrived to place him at the University of Leipzig to study law, but all his spare time was spent over the treatises of Marpurg and Emanuel Bach ; and the acquaintance of J. A. Hiller, then cantor of Leipzig, was a great incentive. He broke with law and began his musical career by writing operettas for the theatre. In 1777 he took Hiller's place as conductor of a travelling orchestra known as the Seyler Society, which made him known in the Rhine district. At Frankfort he found a wife, in 1779 settled at Bonn as conductor of another association called the 'Grossmann-Hellmuth Society,' and on Feb. 15, 1781, entered the service of the Elector, Max Friedrich, as aspirant to the post of court organist, *vice* Van den Eeden. With the organ Neefe took over van den Eeden's pupil, Ludwig van Beethoven, then just entered on his eleventh year. Van den Eeden died in June 1782, and on Apr. 26, 1783, Neefe was promoted to the direction of both sacred and secular music at the court. A year after this, Apr. 15, 1784, the Elector died, the theatrical music was put down, and a series of economies begun by the new Elector Max Franz, which resulted in the reduction of Neefe's pay from 400 to 200 florins. In 1788 a new court theatre was organised, with Reicha as director, and Neefe as accompanist and stage manager. Then came the war, and in 1794 the theatre was shut up, the company disbanded, and Neefe lost his place. He led a poor existence as municipal official under the French, his family were dispersed, and at last we hear of him as conductor at the theatre at Dessau. Here his wife fell seriously ill, and ultimately he himself sank under his troubles, and died. Neefe was an industrious musician ; the names of eight pieces are preserved which he wrote for the theatres of Leipzig and Bonn between 1772 and 1782. He wrote also for the church, and a mass of chamber music, besides arranging and adapting many operas. (See Q.-L.) He also published articles on musical subjects in the periodicals of the time, and left an autobiography which was communicated by his wife to the *A.M.Z.* of 1799 (p. 241). (See *Thayer*, i. 81-5, 117, etc. ; *Krehbiel*, i. 67, etc.) G.

BIBL.—New ed. of Neefe's autobiography in Alfred Einstein's series *Lebensläufe deutscher Musiker von ihnen selbst erzählt* (Bd. 2, Leipzig, 1915) ; IRMGARD LEUX, CHR. G. NEEFE, *Biographie und Instrumentalkompositionen* (Munich Dissertation, 1921).

NEFER (NOFRE). It has been conjectured that this was the name of the ancient Egyptian Tamboura or long-necked guitar (see PANDORA), though no direct application of the word to the instrument has been discovered. The hieroglyph which at first sight bears a curious resemblance to the Tamboura, means 'good,' and modern Egyptologists, including Professor

Flinders Petrie, consider that it represents the heart and the throat, conveying the idea that out of the heart the mouth speaks. The marks on the body of the painted hieroglyph are similar to those on that denoting 'the heart,' and although the one cross-bar (as in the earlier form) or the two cross-bars (as in the later) suggest to us tuning pegs, there are no such pegs to be found on pictures of the instrument itself; for, as in many Oriental instruments of to-day, it was the practice to stretch the strings as tightly as possible before winding them round the head of the instrument and then to tune them finely by a slipping loop of cord or leather. The supposed 'pegs' probably represent the mouth or the open lips. Cf. F. L. Griffith, *Hieroglyphs*, 1898, and Biernath, *Die Guitarre*, 1907.   F. W. G.

NEGRI, CESARE, detto il Trombone (*b. circa* 1546), ballet-master at the court of Milan. He published 'Le gratie d' amore' 1602 (modern ed. by Chilesotti; Ricordi, 1883), and 'Nuove inventione di balli' (1604); an historically valuable collection of ancient dance tunes.
                         E. v. d. S.

NEGRO (NEGRI), GIULIO SANTO PIETRO DEL (*b.* Milan, latter half of 16th cent.), an amateur of noble birth. He composed 'Gl' amorosi pensieri. Canzonette, vilanelle et arie napolitane a 3 voci . . .,' 3 books (1607); 'Grazie ed affetti di musica moderna *a* 1, 2 and 3 voci . . .,' 2 books (op. 5, 1613; op. 8, 1614; 'Musica ecclesiastica concertata alla moderna a 2, e 3 voci, op. 9' (1616); 'Canti academici a 2-6 voci, op. 11' (1620) (*Q.-L.*).

NEGRO MUSIC OF THE UNITED STATES. The nearest approach to 'folk-music' in the United States is that played or sung by the negroes in the Southern States. Before the Civil War (1861–65) brought freedom to the slaves, the ability to read was very rare among those held in bondage. Indeed, in many of the States which authorised slavery, education of the slave was a misdemeanour. The tunes to which they danced or to which they sang their songs and hymns were, therefore, traditional. The origin of some of the tunes is held to be African on these grounds: they can be reduced to a pentatonic scale, which is the scale of musical instruments said to be still in use in Abyssinia, Nubia and other countries in Africa; they have the same 'catch' that appears in songs still sung in Africa, according to the observations of several travellers. Both 'catch' and scale are also common in the traditional music of the Scotch, Irish, Welsh and Magyars. There are, however, many tunes in common use among the American negroes which have neither peculiarity. The negroes have the imitative faculties very highly developed, and most of their tunes which do not resemble those of the old races were probably caught from Methodist preachers, whose system

of conducting 'revivals,' with its appeals to the imagination of the hearer, was such as readily to capture these impressionable people. Many of the negro hymns have lines and phrases that show a Wesleyan origin. Traces of Catholic teaching are visible also, but these are infrequent. Resemblances between various sections as to the tunes and the words used are noted by close observers, the differences being such as would naturally be produced in the flight of time or by lapse of memory, as they were handed down from father to son or carried across the country. The tunes are sometimes minor (generally without a sharp seventh) and sometimes major; occasionally a mixed mode is employed, beginning in a major key, and ending in either the relative or tonic minor; or the contrary course may be followed. And there are tunes which end on the subdominant or anywhere but on the tonic or the dominant. The negroes are very sensitive to rhythm. As one dances a jig, his companions gather about him and furnish a percussive accompaniment with bones (played after the manner of castanets) or roughly made tambourines, or, wanting instruments, by alternately slapping their hands together and on their knees, keeping excellent time. They have songs for all occasions where they move in concert, such as loading or unloading ships, or working at the pumps of a fire engine. Their rhythmic sympathies are most strongly active on these occasions. Often one of a gang acts as a precentor, giving a line or two by himself, and the chorus coming in with the refrain. This leader, when his supply of lines gives out or his memory fails, resorts to improvisation (cf. SHANTY).

A similar practice obtains with them at their religious and social gatherings. Sometimes the improvised lines will be given in turn by different ones in the company who have the faculty of inventing them. The women's voices have a peculiarly pathetic timbre within their natural range, which is narrow. When forced they are harsh and strident. As a rule the tenor voices are dry, but the basses are generally rich and sonorous. A quick ear is more common than tunefulness among the race, but the effect produced by the singing of a great number, always in unison, so quickens the hearer's pulse or moves him to tears that defects are forgotten. Their time is sure to be accurate. Of instruments in use among them the variety is small. Bones and tambourines are common, but the banjo is not so generally used by them as has been thought, and fiddlers are very rare. Some of the slave songs, especially those that may be classed as hymns, were made known in the Northern States for the first time by small bands of singers of both sexes who gave concerts in the principal cities in 1871 and subsequently. One troupe (the 'Jubilee singers') came from the Fisk University, Nashville, Tennessee, and in the course of its tours, which included several trips to Europe, raised over 150,000 dollars for the University, which was established especially to educate those who had been born in slavery. Another came from a similar institution at Hampton, Virginia. One effect of their tours was the introduction of some of the songs into the religious services of the Northern negroes. It is observed, however, that the songs are everywhere gradually disappearing from use as the negroes become better educated. Their imitative faculties lead them to prefer music exactly like that which is performed in churches where the worshippers are white. Some of the secular songs of the negroes have acquired peculiar distinction. ' Jim Crow '—said to be the name both of the song and of the negro whose performance of it had a local reputation in Louisville, Kentucky, in 1830—was, indirectly, the origin of the negro minstrel show, the most familiar example of which in England was that long known as Christy's. Many of the plantation songs were introduced into these shows, ' Coal-black Rose,' ' Zip Coon ' and ' Ole Virginny nebber tire ' being the most familiar among them. A plantation song, ' Way down in Raccoon Hollow,' enjoyed a wide popularity set to words beginning ' Near the lake where droops the willow.'

A few examples of the negro melodies and verses are appended. They are taken from the collection ' Slave Songs of the United States.' The reader must understand that all of these are sung much faster than either the tunes or the words would seem to warrant, the rapid pace being a result of the negroes' strong rhythmic instincts. The first example shows a pentatonic scale, and the use of the ' Scotch snap ':

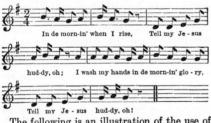

In de morn-in' when I rise, Tell my Je-sus

hud-dy, oh; I wash my hands in de morn-in' glo-ry,

Tell my Je-sus hud-dy, oh!

The following is an illustration of the use of an unconventional ending :

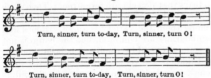

Turn, sinner, turn to-day, Turn, sinner, turn O!

Turn, sinner, turn to-day, Turn, sinner, turn O!

A very popular tune, and full of pathos when sung by a large company, is the following :

No - bo - dy knows de trou-ble I've had,

No - bo - dy knows but Je-sus, No-bo-dy knows de

trou-ble I've had, Glo-ry hal - le - lu! One
[Sing]

morn-in' I was a-walk-in' down, O yes, Lord! I

saw some ber-ries a-hang-in down, O yes, Lord.

Dr. W. Howard Russell describes in chapter xviii. of *My Diary North and South*, a song which made a remarkable impression on him, and which, from his description, appears to be the following :

O graveyard, O graveyard, I'm

walk-in' troo' de graveyard, Lay dis bo - dy down.

The following is a popular song among the Louisiana creoles, and the words give an idea of the dialect :

Belle Layotte.

Chorus.

Mo dé-ja rou-lé tout la côte, Pancor ouar par-eil

Fine. Solo.

belle La-yotte. Mo rou-lé tout la côte, Mo rou-lé tout la

col - o - nie ; Mo pan - cor ouar griff-one la

D.C.

Qua ma gout comme la belle La-yotte. F. H. J.

The peculiarities of negro music have been introduced into works of higher artistic aim. Gottschalk used some of the creole music as subjects for free treatment on the pianoforte ; J. A. Brockhoven, of Cincinnati, wrote a suite for orchestra on creole tunes ; and Dvořák, during his residence in America, adopted some of the musical idioms of the negro music into his ' New World ' symphony and two chamber compositions, opp. 95–97. The cult of the ' negro spiritual,' stimulated by the numerous arrangements of Henry T. BURLEIGH (*q.v.*), has spread among American and English singers, and many American composers, following the lead of Dvořák, have attempted to develop the negro melody as symphonic material. But a still more far-reaching manifestation is all that American product which has gone by the successive names of 'Ragtime,' 'Jazz' and 'Syncopation,' and for which descent from the negro song is claimed. The most useful and comprehensive work on the subject is *Afro-American Folksong* (1914) by H. E. KREHBIEL.

C.

BIBLIOGRAPHY

Dwight's Journal of Music, Nov. 8, 1862. Letter, Miss McKim, Philadelphia ; probably the first occasion when public attention was called to the Slave songs.
Continental Monthly, Philadelphia, Aug. 1863 : article, *Under the Palmettos*, B. G. Spaulding, with specimens of the music.
Atlantic Monthly, June 1867 : article, *Negro Spirituals*, T. W. Higginson, with the words of many of the most popular hymns.
'Slave Songs of the United States,' New York, 1871. Words and tunes, the largest collection published.
The Century, New York, Feb. 1886 : article, *Creole Slave Dance*. Apr. 1886 : article, *Creole Slave Songs*. Both by G. W. Cable. Especially interesting because of the descriptions of negro customs in Louisiana, some of which are of remote African origin, and because of the explanation of the peculiar dialect of the Louisiana negroes—a mixture of French and English, sometimes a little Spanish, but each greatly modified by the negro's own method of speech.
W. F. Allen, article on *Negro Dialect*, New York *Nation*, May 30, 1867 ; John Mason Brown, *Songs of the Slaves*, *Lippincott's Mag.*, Dec. 1868 ; Clarence Deming, *By-ways of Nature and Life*, New York, 1884 ; Marion Alexandra Haskell, *Negro Spirituals*, *Century Mag.*, Aug. 1899 ; Isabella T. Hopkins, *A Description of a Negro Church Service*, *Scribner's Mag.*, 1880, pp. 422-429 ; James M. Trotter, *Music and some highly Musical People*, Boston and New York, 1878 ; Jennie Woodville, *Rambling Talk about the Negro*, *Lippincott's Mag.*, Nov. 1878.—COLLECTIONS : Charles L. Edwards, *Bahama Songs and Stories*, Boston, 1895 ; J. B. T. Marsh, *The Story of the Jubilee Singers*, Boston, 1895 (often reprinted) ; *Cabin and Plantation Songs sung by the Hampton Students*, New York, 1891.

F. H. J. ; with addns. H. E. K.

NEGRO SONG IN ENGLAND

Until about 1835 English people had neither knowledge of, nor interest in, the folk-music of the American negro. Some few examples, though probably not many more than half a dozen, had appeared in print before that time, and one characteristic specimen from Aird's *Selection of Scotch, English, Irish and Foreign Airs*, vol. i. (1782), is appended. It has the incessant repetition of phrase found in so many negro airs. One or two others from Virginia are in the same work.

Pompey ran away.

Negro Jig (Virginia).

The other is taken from *The Gentleman's Amusement*, book 2, c. 1800. The words of these plantation melodies seem to have been merely a string of sentences concocted on the spur of the moment by the singer as he performed the 'Walk Round' (much the same sort of thing as the 'Cake Walk' of to-day), while a steady clapping of hands from the spectators marked the time.

NEGRO DANCE

From *The Gentleman's Amusement*, book 2, c. 1800 (a work containing many airs of American interest).

About 1834–35 one Dan Rice introduced the grotesque song and dance of the negro to the audience of American theatres and concert halls. His first song was 'Jim Crow,' the main burden of which with appropriate actions ran—

Wheel about, and turn about and jump just so,
Every time you wheel about you jump Jim Crow.

Though no doubt this was a plantation lyric, there are signs that the melody has been considerably tampered with. Rice, bringing the song to England about 1835–36, the whole nation became in a perfect ferment over it. 'Coal-black Rose,' 'Sich a getting upstairs,' 'Dandy Jim from Carolina,' and 'Jim along Josey,' whose principal phrase was—

Hey, get along, get along Josey, Hey, get along, Jim, along Joe,

were others of this early period. The singing of negro songs having become general, several bands of 'Ethiopian Serenaders' appeared at the theatres of America and in England during the 'forties. Christy's, the most famous of these, was of a rather later date.

While in the earlier days the entertainments professed to represent the plantation song and dance with banjo, bones and fiddle accompaniment, this soon gave way to the introduction of other songs of better literary merit than the meaningless jumble of words of the original songs. Stephen C. Foster (1826–64) supplied such lyrics as 'Old folks at home,' etc., and an attempt was made to give some picture of the life of the slave in the songs sung.　　F. K.

NEITHARDT, AUGUST HEINRICH (*b.* Schleiz, Aug. 10, 1793; *d.* Berlin, Apr. 18, 1861), founder of the Berlin Domchor (Cathedral choir). His early musical studies were interrupted at twenty years of age by his military service, which lasted through the campaigns of 1813–15. This led to his becoming bandmaster to the Garde-Schützen Battalion (1816–22), for which he composed and arranged a host of pieces. From 1822–40 he was master of the band of the Kaiser Franz Grenadiers, and wrote and did much for the improvement of military music. In 1834 he wrote an opera, 'Julietta,' and in 1839 he was made 'königliche Musikdirector,' and in 1843 was commissioned to found a regular choir for the Berlin Cathedral, which he did by uniting the scholars and seminarists who sang the ordinary Cathedral service with the smaller choir who sang in the court chapel, about eighty strong in all. (See MENDELSSOHN.) In 1846 Neithardt went to St. Petersburg to hear the famous Russian choirs, and in 1850 he and his choir visited London and created much astonishment by their extraordinarily refined and effective performances. He was a remarkably able conductor, indefatigable in drilling his choir and in providing them with masterpieces of all schools, some of which were edited by him in continuation of Commer's 'Musica sacra' (Berlin, Bote & Bock). G.

NEJEDLÝ, ZDENĔK (*b.* Litomyšl, 1878), Czech musical writer and historian ; Ph.D. of Prague University, where he was called to the Chair of Musical Theory and Æsthetics in 1905. His interests are by no means confined to music, for he takes an active part in political journalism, his views tending to socialism. In 1910 he founded a musical periodical, *Smetana,* in which he has carried on some acrimonious campaigns against certain movements and individuals in the world of Czechoslovak music. He would have satisfied Samuel Johnson's predilection for 'a good hater'; but his hostilities, if implacable, are fought out in the light of day. A disciple of HOSTINSKÝ (*q.v.*), he has brought system and consistency into Czech musical criticism. His fine historical sense and the depth of his knowledge are unquestionable. His love of music seems sometimes to come in the rear of his love of politics, literature and dialectics. His devotion to the memory of Smetana, whom he views clearly from the ethical and democratic sides, gives a central idea and distinction to his work. Criticism in Czechoslovakia has not yet shed its elementary tendency to be a question of partisanship. Apart from this disqualification, Nejedlý, because of his general culture, untiring research and admirable literary style, easily takes the highest place in the contemporary musical literature of the Czechs. Nejedlý delivered the public oration upon Smetana at the opening of the centenary celebrations in 1924. Besides constant journalistic activity, he has published the following books :

A History of Pre-Hussite Vocal Music in Bohemia (1904) ; *Beginnings of Hussite Vocal Music* (1907) ; *Hussite Vocal Music during the Hussite Wars* (1913). Books on Smetana: *Smetana's Operas* (1908) ; an exhaustive biography of Smetana in 5 vols., of which vol. i. appeared in 1922 and vol. ii. in 1925 ; a biography on a smaller scale in the series *Zlatoroh* ; a complete edition *de luxe* of Smetana's compositions, of which the first number, 'Youthful Compositions up to 1843,' appeared in 1924 (State Printing Press) ; *Frederick Smetana* (Geoffrey Bles, London). Also : *Zdenko Fibich* (1901) ; *Catechism of Czech Musical History* (1903) ; *Catechism of Æsthetics* (1902) ; *Czech Opera from Smetana onwards* (1911) ; *J. B. Foerster* (1910) ; *Gustav Mahler* ; *Richard Wagner* ; *Vítĕzlav Novák* (1921) ; *A General History of Music* (vol. i.). R. N.

NELSON, SYDNEY (*b.* London, Jan. 1, 1800; *d.* there, Apr. 7, 1862), son of Soloman Nelson, was for some time a pupil of Sir George Smart. About or shortly before 1840 he entered into a partnership with Charles Jefferys (a song-writer for whose lyrics Nelson's music was mainly composed), and as 'Jefferys and Nelson' they began a music-publishing business in Frith Street, removing afterwards into Soho Square. They issued much sheet music, chiefly by Nelson, but in 1843, the concern not proving a success, Nelson left it entirely in Jefferys' hands, who greatly developed it. Nelson now arranged a musical and dramatic entertainment, and with members of his family went on tour to America, Canada and Australia.

His musical works principally consist of drawing-room ballads, which include such once popular melodies as 'The Rose of Allandale,' 'The Pilot,' etc. He also composed a burletta, 'The Grenadier,' produced by Madame Vestris, and 'The Cadi's Daughter,' while a grand opera, 'Ulrica,' was put in rehearsal, though never performed. (Information in part from *D.N.B.*) F. K.

NENNA, POMPONIO (*b.* Bari, old kingdom of Naples, *c.* 1560 ; *d.* before 1618), distinguished himself chiefly as a composer of madrigals in the style of Monteverdi. On the titles of his publications he is described as 'Il cavaliere Cesareo,' having been made a Knight of the Golden Spur. Following further in the path opened up by MONTEVERDI (*q.v.*), he became the teacher and inspirer of GESUALDO, Prince of Venosa, in the direction of free chromatic modulation. He published eight books of madrigals *a* 5, and one *a* 4, appearing in various editions from 1609–24. His death must have occurred before 1618, as appears from the preface to a new edition of his eighth book of madrigals *a* 5. His other works are a set of Responsoria *a* 4 for the Matins of Christmas and Holy Week, published in 1607, and another set of Responsoria *a* 5 for the Matins of Holy Week, published after his death in 1622. The only sacred work of Nenna in modern score is a simple setting of the Veni Creator, printed from a Roman MS. in the continuation of the 'Musica divina' by Haberl. J. R. M.

NEO-MODAL, a term used to describe modern melodic or harmonic idioms derived from scales which have a definite internal organisation other than that associated with the traditional major-minor system. This definition covers (1) inflections and combinations characteristic of the true ecclesiastical modes, when used on a background of classical or later harmonies or tonalities ; (2) idioms derived from such folk-songs or other melodies as are themselves organised on a modal basis, whether derived or local ; (3) any arbitrary scale, such as that of whole tones, which is used with fair consistency as a melodic or harmonic medium. See MODES; SCALES; SONG; HARMONY.

G. D.

NERI, FILIPPO (SAINT) (b. Florence, July 21, 1515; d. Rome, May 26, 1595), of noble family, entered the priesthood in 1551, and joined the order of Hieronymus, where he undertook the teaching of the children. In 1564 he founded the society of the Oratorio for the cultivation of music in the oratory of the monastery of S. Girolamo, supported by Animuccia, who wrote 'Laudi spirituali' specially for this society, and was followed by Palestrina as its conductor and composer. Cavalieri's 'Mysterium Anima e corpo' was first performed here in 1600, and the modern oratorio received its name from that society. A book of 'Canzonette spirituali'—sung at the Oratorio—was published in 1657 (see *Riemann*).

NERI, MASSIMILIANO, first organist at St. Mark's, Venice, 1644, raised to the rank of nobility by the Emperor Ferdinand II. in 1651, court organist of the Elector of Cologne in 1664, composed 1 book of motets *a* 2 and 3 v. (1664), 1 book of 'Sonate e canzone a 4,' op. 1, to be played on sundry instruments in church or chamber (1644); sonatas for 3 to 12 instruments, op. 2 (1651). These sonatas rank among the best early instrumental music (*Q.-L.*; *Riemann*). (See VIOLIN-PLAYING.)

NERITI DA SALÒ (NERITO), Vicenzo, musician and chaplain to the Emperor Rudolph II., 1593; maestro di cappella of the great church at Salò, 1595–99. On a Magnificat published in 1593 he calls himself 'Capellanus et Sacellanus' in the Carmelite monastery at Mantua, and imperial musician. He composed 3 books of canzonets, etc. (1593, 1595, 1599) (*Q.-L.*).

NÉRON, opera in 4 acts; words by Jules Barbier; music by A. Rubinstein. Produced in German, as 'Nero,' Stadt Theater, Hamburg, Nov. 1, 1879, under the direction of the composer.

G.

NERONE, tragedy in 4 acts, written and composed by Boïto. Produced La Scala, Milan, Apr. 30, 1924. The original text included a fifth act which Boïto did not set. The score was edited by Toscanini.

NERUDA, a distinguished family of violinists. According to Dlabacz,[1] the founder was Jakob, who belonged to Rossice, and died Feb. 19, 1732. He left two sons : (1) JOHANN CHRYSOSTOM (b. Rossice, Dec. 1, 1705; d. Dec. 2, 1763) learnt music at Prague, became famous on the violin, and took orders at the Præmonstratensian convent there, a few months after his father's death, becoming choirmaster of the convent.

(2) JOHANN BAPTIST GEORG (b. ? 1707; d. Dresden, 1780) was first at Prague, and then, for thirty years, at the Elector's Chapel at

[1] *Künstler-Lexikon für Böhmen.*

Dresden, where he died, leaving a mass of compositions behind him (see *Q.-L.*). His two sons, LUDWIG and ANTON, were both chamber musicians to the Elector of Dresden.

Another member of the Neruda family was JOSEF (b. 1807; d. Feb. 18, 1875), organist of the Cathedral at Brno, Moravia. He had five children, Victor, Amalie, WILMA, Marie and FRANZ. Amalie adopted the PF., and made no important career.

(3) FRANZ (b. Brno, Dec. 3, 1843; d. Copenhagen, Mar. 19, 1915), became a violoncellist, and joined his father and sister in various concert tours. In 1864–76 he was a member of the royal orchestra at Copenhagen; in 1892 he succeeded to Gade's place as director of the musical society there, and he also directed another society in Stockholm. He wrote many popular and meritorious compositions for orchestra and chamber, a violoncello concerto, string quartet, etc. The best-known of his works is a little berceuse often played by his famous sister.

(4) WILMA (WILHELMINA) (b. Mar. 21, 1839; d. Berlin, Apr. 15, 1911) began to play the violin almost as soon as she could walk, became a pupil of Jansa, and made her first appearance, with her sister, in the winter of 1846 at Vienna, where she excited much astonishment by the extraordinary power of her bow, the deep sentiment of her cantilena, and her great execution, notwithstanding the smallness of her hands.[2] From Vienna the family journeyed northwards, visiting Leipzig, Berlin, Breslau, Hamburg and other cities. In London, Wilma made her first appearance at the Princess's Theatre, Apr. 30, 1849, and appeared eighteen times up to May 24. She played at the Philharmonic Concert of June 11, 1849, in a concerto by De Bériot. The family returned immediately to the Continent, and passed several years in travelling, chiefly in Russia. In 1864 Mlle. Neruda found herself in Paris, where she played at the Pasdeloup Concerts, the Conservatoire, etc., and awakened enthusiasm. At this time she married Ludwig NORMAN (q.v.) a Swedish musician, and was henceforth known as Mme. Norman-Neruda. In 1869 she again visited London, played at the Philharmonic on May 17, and was with some difficulty induced, by the entreaties of Vieuxtemps, to remain till the winter, when she took the first violin at the series of Monday Popular Concerts before Christmas, and at once made her mark. From that time until 1898 she was in England for each winter and spring season, playing at the Popular Concerts, the Philharmonic, the Crystal Palace, Hallé's recitals and Manchester concerts, etc., with ever-increasing power and refinement.

G.; rev. R. N.

Norman died in 1885 and on July 26, 1888, she married Sir Charles HALLÉ (q.v.), and was associated with him on the concert platform

[2] Hanslick.

until 1895, when he died. In 1896 a public subscription was set on foot among her admirers,
under the direction of a committee of which
King Edward VII. (then Prince of Wales) was
president. Associated with him were the King
of Sweden, the King of Denmark, and a vast
number of eminent musicians, statesmen and
others, and the title-deeds of a palazzo at Asolo,
near Venice, were presented to Lady Hallé, on
behalf of the subscribers, by the President of
the Committee at Marlborough House. In
1898, after the death of her eldest son in an
Alpine accident, she made Berlin her headquarters, paying annual visits to England, and
making artistic tours throughout Europe. In
1901 Queen Alexandra conferred upon her the
distinctive title of ' Violinist to the Queen.'
The Stradivarius violin upon which Lady Hallé
played was one of the finest in existence, dating
from 1709, and was presented to her in 1876 as
the joint gift of H.R.H. the Duke of Edinburgh
(afterwards Duke of Saxe-Coburg), Earl Dudley
and the Earl of Hardwicke.

E. H.-A. ; rev. R. N.

NESBET, a 15th-century English composer
who contributed a song to the Pepysian MS.
1236, and figures among the composers of the
lost parts of the Eton College MS. (Hy. Davey,
Hist. Eng. Mus.).

NESSLER, VICTOR E. (b. Baldenheim,
Alsace, Jan. 28, 1841 ; d. Strassburg, May 28,
1890), at first studied theology at Strassburg,
but the success of his essay in operatic composition, a work entitled ' Fleurette,' and produced there in 1864, induced him to devote
himself to music. He then went to Leipzig,
and obtained various posts as conductor of
male choral societies, for the use of which he
wrote a set of partsongs, etc. In 1870 he became choral director at the Stadt Theater, and
in 1879 conductor at the Carolatheater in the
same town. Meanwhile various operas had
been brought out with varying success. The
list is as follows :

' Die Hochzeitsreise ' (1867) ; ' Dornröschens Brautfahrt' (1868) ;
' Nachtwächter und Student' (1868) ; ' Am Alexandertag ' (1869) ;
' Irmingard,' a more ambitious work than the previous productions,
in five acts (1876) ; ' Der Rattenfänger von Hameln ' (1879), an
opera which rapidly spread his fame throughout Germany, and
attained an enormous success ; ' Die wilde Jäger ' (1881) ; ' Der
Trompeter von Säkkingen ' (1884) ; ' Otto der Schütz ' (1886) ;
and ' Die Rose von Strassburg ' (1890).

The success of the ' Trompeter ' was almost as
great as that of the ' Rattenfänger.' Both owe
their popularity to an easy superficiality of
style, which commended itself to the less musical portion of the German public. When the
' Rattenfänger,' under the name of ' The Piper
of Hamelin,' was produced at Covent Garden
Theatre by the English Opera Company on
Jan. 7, 1884, it proved a failure.　　　　M.

NEŠVERA, JOSEF (b. Praskolesíce, Bohemia,
Oct. 24, 1842 ; d. Olomouc, 1914), a Czech
composer some time choirmaster of the Cathedral at Olomouc. He was a prolific composer,
working chiefly in small forms, especially for

the piano (valses, mazurkas, studies) and the
violin (popular Slumber Songs, etc.). His
sacred music includes a Mass in honour of St.
Procopius, the Passion (in Czech), an oratorio,
De Profundis, etc. His best-known operas
are ' Perdita ' (produced Prague, 1897), ' Lesní
vzduch ' (The Forest Breeze), ' Bratránek '
(The Cousin), and ' Radhošt,' produced in Brno
(1906) under the title of ' Černoknĕžnik ' (The
Black Monk), which reflects the folk life of the
Moravians and the charm of their popular
melodies.　　　　　　　　　　　　R. N.

NEUKOMM, SIGISMUND, CHEVALIER VON
(b. Salzburg, July 10, 1778 ; d. Paris, Apr. 3,
1858), was a chorister at the cathedral of Salzburg in 1788–93 and first learned music from
Weissauer and from Michael Haydn, who in
1798 sent him to his brother at Vienna. He
studied music with Joseph Haydn for some
years, and was treated by him more as a son
than a pupil. His first compositions appeared
in 1808, and in 1806 he went via Sweden to St.
Petersburg, where he became Kapellmeister, and
director of the Emperor's German theatre. He
returned to Vienna just before Haydn's death,
and shortly after took up his residence in Paris,
and there lived on terms of intimacy with
Grétry, Cherubini, Cuvier and other eminent
men, and especially with Talleyrand, in whose
establishment he succeeded Dussek as pianist.
Their friendship survived the downfall of the
Empire, and he accompanied Talleyrand to the
Congress of Vienna. There he composed a Requiem for Louis XVI., which was performed at
St. Stephen's before a crowd of notabilities,
and for which in 1815 Louis XVIII. made him
Chevalier of the Legion of Honour, with letters
of nobility. In 1816 he went in the suite of
the Duke of Luxemburg to Rio Janeiro, and
remained there as maître de chapelle to Dom
Pedro till the revolution of 1821 drove that
monarch, and Neukomm with him, back to
Lisbon. Having resigned his pension, he returned to Talleyrand, whom he accompanied on
several of his grand tours. He came to London
in the same year with Mendelssohn (1829), and
they met at the house of Moscheles, with whom
Neukomm remained on terms of great friendship and mutual esteem.[1] The last twenty
years of his life he divided between England and
France.

In England his intelligence and cultivation
gave him a high position. His symphony in
E♭ was played by the Philharmonic, Mar. 21,
1831, and many other pieces at various times.
His oratorio ' Mount Sinai,' was repeatedly performed in London, and at Worcester, Derby,
etc., and he wrote his oratorio ' David ' specially
for the Birmingham Festival of 1834, where so
highly was he prized as to be familiarly called
' the King of Brummagem.'[2] In fact his two

---

[1] See Mendelssohn's letters to Moscheles, pp. 116, 118.
[2] Mendelssohn's *Letters*, ii. 124.

songs 'Napoleon's Midnight Review' and 'The Sea,' the latter to Barry Cornwall's words, may be said to have made him for some months the most popular person in England. But Mendelssohn's arrival at Birmingham in 1837 eclipsed Neukomm's fame, and even caused him to be as unjustly depreciated as he had before been unduly extolled. This reverse he bore with a philosophy which elicited Mendelssohn's warmest expressions.[1]

Neukomm was a man of remarkable diligence and method, which nothing interrupted. The number of his compositions is prodigious. They embrace about 1000 works, including eight oratorios, numerous masses, and music for Schiller's ' Braut von Messina,' in which he endeavoured to resuscitate the ancient Greek chorus. He had a great predilection for Palestrina, and attempted to revive his style. He also wrote for several musical periodicals, especially the *Revue et Gazette musicale de Paris.*　　　　　　　　　　　　　F. G.

NEUMANN, FRANTIŠEK (b. Přerov, Moravia, June 16, 1874), composer and conductor ; at present (1926) chief conductor of the National Theatre in Brno.

His parents removing to Prostějov, he was sent to the Communal School there in 1880, and in 1884 passed on to the Modern School. He entered the Commercial Academy at Chrudím in 1888, and after completing his course, fulfilled his year of military service as a volunteer at Olomouc. At the age of 22 he went to the Conservatorium at Leipzig, and in the following year was appointed chorus-master to the theatre at Carlsruhe. In 1898 he accepted a similar post at the municipal theatre at Hamburg. In 1899 he was first conductor at Regen (Ratisbon), 1900 at Linz, 1901 at Reichenberg, 1902 at Teplice, and 1904 at Frankfort-on-Main, where he remained until 1919. He then returned to his native land and took up the post of conductor-in-chief at the National Theatre in Brno. Here he has accomplished excellent work, thanks to his long and varied experience as an operatic conductor. Among other productions, he has to his credit the admirable first performances of most of Leoš Janáček's operas. Neumann's works include :

OPERAS

'Markýz' (Marquis), Linz, 1901 (unpublished) ; 'Milkováni' (Love-making), Frankfort, 1906 (Schott & Son, Mainz) ; 'Ekvinoce' (Equinox), Berlin, 1919 ('Harmonic,' Berlin) ; 'Beatrice,' Brno, 1922 (Barvič & Novotný, Brno).

MELODRAMA

'Pan' (Barvič & Novotný, Brno).

BALLETS

'V sladké pasti' (In Pleasant Pastures); 'Perý' (The Peri), and 'Pierrot.'

ORCHESTRA

Moravian Rhapsody ; one or two Overtures ; Symphonic Poem, 'Pekelný rej' (Dance of Inferno); Suite, 'Potopeny Zvon' (The Submerged Bell).

CHAMBER MUSIC

An Octet, which won a prize offered by the Czech Academy of Arts (MS.) ; Trio (MS.).
Some songs and choruses, and several masses and motets.
　　　　　　　　　　　　　　　　　　　R. N.

[1] Mendelssohn's *Letters*, ii. 124, 132.

NEUMARK, GEORG (b. Mühlhausen, Thuringia, May 16, 1621 ; d. Weimar, July 8, 1681), poet and musician.

On his way to Königsberg to study law at the University, he was robbed of all his possessions, and was obliged for a time to accept a post as private tutor at Kiel, where, it is said, he indited his best-known hymn, ' Wer nur den lieben Gott lässt walten.' After various wanderings and further misfortunes, he at last in 1651 obtained a settled position as secretary and librarian to the ducal court at Weimar, where his talents were also called into requisition as court poet for festival occasions. He was enrolled in several of the fancifully named literary societies of the time for the cultivation of poetry, such as ' die fruchtbringende Gesellschaft ' and the 'Pegnitz-schäferei.' His chief work is entitled ' Musikalisch-poetischer Lustwald ' (Jena,1657), and consists of a collection of sacred and secular songs, some of which, chiefly the sacred, are provided with melodies by Neumark himself and other musicians. The melodies have a slight instrumental accompaniment of two violins and bass. But the one hymn and tune by which Neumark really lives is the above-mentioned ' Wer nur den lieben Gott,' which, with the rhythm of the tune slightly altered, have been received into most Choralbücher, and form the basis of Bach's Church Cantata of the same name for the Fifth Sunday after Trinity. Spitta, in his comments upon Bach's Cantata, seems to consider Bach's choice of this hymn as not very appropriate to the Sunday ; but it is significant of Bach's thinking otherwise that he chose the same last verse of the hymn to be the concluding Choral to another cantata for this Sunday, ' Siehe ich will viel Fischer aussenden.' Bach must have been fond of the tune, as he has adopted it with other words as the concluding Choral to four other cantatas, and has also employed the tune for organ treatment. (See his Choral-Preludes.) Mendelssohn has also adopted it in ' St. Paul ' to the words (in the English version) ' To Thee, O Lord, I yield my spirit,' with special reference to the death of St. Stephen.　　　　　　　　　　J. R. M.

NEUMES, see NOTATION.

NEUNER, KARL (b. Munich, July 29, 1778 ; d. there, July 1830), studied at Tegernsee and afterwards under Valesi (singing) and Jos. Grätz (violin) at Munich where he entered the court orchestra as violinist. He composed ballets for the court the MSS. of which are in Vienna ; psalms, sacred songs, etc., symphonies, overtures, songs and a book on counterpoint.　　　　　　　　　　E. v. d. s.

NEUSIDLER, the name of a family of German lutenists in the 16th century, of whom two are known by publications of their own. (1) HANS NEUSIDLER (b. Presburg, Hungary ; d. 1563) lived as lutenist and citizen (Bürger) of Nuremberg, where in 1563, 1540 and 1544 he

published various lute-books in German tablature, usually divided into two parts, the first
consisting of instructions and exercises for
beginners, the second (as the titles indicate)
containing fantasias, preludes, motets, secular
songs and dances arranged for the lute. Oscar
Chilesotti's *Lautenspieler des 16. Jhts.* (published
by Breitkopf & Härtel, 1891) contains twelve of
these pieces in modern notation.

(2) MELCHIOR (*d.* 1590), said to be the son of
Hans (though this is not certain), lived chiefly
at Augsburg, partly under the patronage of the
merchant-prince Anton Fugger, but apparently
also employed in the service of the city to provide for what is described as the *Stille Musica*,
that is, the quiet, domestic music for private
festivities.[1] Earlier in his life he must have
been in Italy, since his first publication consists
of two books of lute-pieces in Italian tablature,
issued from the Venetian press of Gardano,
1566. These pieces, besides being received into
Phalèse's 'Theatrum musicum' (Louvain, 1571),
were afterwards republished in German tablature (Frankfort, 1573). In 1574 Neusidler
published at Strassburg his 'Teutsch Lauten-
buch,' which contains motets and secular songs
by the best composers of the time, such as
Josquin, Lassus, Arcadelt, Rore and others,
arranged with little florid variations for the
lute ('artlich und zierlich coloriert' as the title
says), also some dances and fantasias. (See
Q.-L.) In 1626 mention is made of a CONRAD
NEUSIDLER, supposed to be a son of Melchior,
living at Augsburg, and employed as a lutenist
for the *Stille Musica* or private music of the
citizens. No publication of his is known.

J. R. M.

NEVADA, (1) EMMA, *née* WIXOM (*b.* Alpha,
near Nevada City, California, 1862), the
daughter of a doctor, was taught singing by
Mme. Marchesi at Vienna, and on May 17, 1880,
made a successful début on the stage at Her
Majesty's Theatre as Amina, under the name
of Nevada, but did not sing again, owing to
pecuniary difficulties with her manager. She
then sang in all the great cities of Italy, and on
May 17, 1883, made a successful début at the
Opéra-Comique, Paris, as Zora in the revival of
Félicien David's 'Perle du Brésil,' appearing
also as Mignon until Feb. 1884. In the spring
of 1884 she sang as Amina and Lucia in Italian
at the Théâtre des Nations, and in the autumn
at the Norwich Festival in the 'Redemption,'
'Elijah,' etc., and Oct. 16, on the production of
Mackenzie's 'Rose of Sharon,' with great success,
the soprano music having been written expressly
for her. On Nov. 7 she sang in the last work at
the 'Sacred Harmonic,' St. James's Hall. Later
in the year and in 1885 she sang in Italian Opera
on alternate nights with Mme. Patti at New
York, San Francisco, etc., with the greatest
success. On Oct. 1, 1885, she married at

[1] See document printed in *M.f.M.* xxv. 6.

Paris Dr. Raymond Palmer. She returned to
America on an extended concert tour, and reappeared in England for a few nights at Covent
Garden, notably on Apr. 29, 1887, in the revival of ' Mireille.' She then sang in Holland,
Germany, Russia, Italy, Portugal and Spain.
Her medallion as Amina, in company with those
of Pasta and Malibran, was placed on the statue
of Bellini at Naples, on the initiative of her
friend the late Francesco Florimo, the great
personal friend of the composer. A. C.

(2) MIGNON, her daughter, is also a brilliant
soprano, who made her début at the Costanzi
Theatre in Rome, as Rosina in ' Il Barbiere.'
Her first appearance at Covent Garden was in
Thomas's ' Hamlet ' (Beecham season, Oct. 4,
1910), since when she has been frequently engaged in London, and has also sung in most of
the principal opera-houses of Europe. C.

NEVIN, ETHELBERT (*b.* Edgeworth, Penn.,
Nov. 25, 1862 ; *d.* New Haven, Conn., Feb. 17,
1901), an American composer, made famous by
his song ' The Rosary.' He studied in Boston,
the pianoforte under B. J. Lang and composition
under Stephen A. Emery ; he then went to
Berlin, where he spent the years 1884, 1885 and
1886 under the instruction of Karl Klindworth,
and of Von Bülow. He returned to America,
and taught for some years in Boston ; then,
from 1892, in Paris, Berlin, Florence and Venice,
he spent his time in teaching, studying and
composing. He again returned to America in
broken health.

His work as a composer was confined almost
entirely to songs and short pianoforte pieces,
which have a graceful lyric vein, and a feeling
for melody that is sometimes over sentimental,
but often finely expressive of the gentler moods,
amorous, gay and introspective. Among his
best-known publications are a ' Sketch Book '
of songs and pianoforte pieces, op. 2 ; pianoforte
duets, op. 6 ; ' Water Scenes ' for pianoforte,
op. 13, of which one number, ' Narcissus,'
attained a very wide popularity ; ' A Book of
Songs,' op. 20 ; a suite for pianoforte, ' In
Tuscany,' op. 20 ; and a pantomime designed
by Vance Thompson, entitled ' Lady Floriane's
Dream.' R. A.

NEWARK, WILLIAM (*b.* Newark-on-Trent,
c. 1450 ; *d.* Nov. 1509), English choir-trainer
and composer. The following biographical details have been collected by Grattan Flood [2] :

1477. Became a gentleman of the Chapel Royal.
1479. Given a corrody in the Monastery of St. Mary,
Thetford. (Patent Rolls, Nov. 28, 1480.)
1484. Granted a yearly sum of £20 accruing from the
King's Manor at Bletchingley, Surrey.
(Patent Rolls, Apr. 6, 1485.)
1487. Received a corrody from St. Benet's Monastery,
Holme, Norfolk.
1493 (Jan. 1). Received the sum of 20s. for 'making
of a song.' (*Household Book of Hy.,* vii.
B.M. Add. MSS. 7099/7.)
1493 (May 30). Master of the children of the Chapel
Royal.

[2] *Mus. T.,* Nov. 1921.

The corrody at St. Benet's had previously been held by Gilbert Banastir, who was master of the royal children, 1478–83. Newark's name, together with that of Fayrfax and Cornyshe, occurs in a list of the gentlemen who received liveries for the funeral of Queen Elizabeth, wife of Henry VII., Feb. 23, 1503, and later (1509) with Cornyshe, Fayrfax and William Crane (who succeeded Cornyshe in' 1523 as master) for the funeral of Henry VII.[1] Actually, Newark succeeded Lawrence Squire as master of the children. His patent was renewed under Henry VIII., but he died in the first year of that king's reign, and was succeeded by Cornyshe. He was buried in Greenwich Church porch. A 2-part madrigal by him ' O my desyre ' is in the Fayrfax book (B.M. Add. MSS. 5465). Six others by him, in 2 and 3 parts, are also in B.M. Add. MSS. 11,583 ; a duplicate of one of these, ' Thus musing,' is in R.C.M. 808/59.   J. M^K.

NEW ENGLAND CONSERVATORY OF MUSIC, see Boston.

NEWMAN, Ernest (b. Liverpool, Nov. 30, 1868), has succeeded in combining with a busy journalistic career the writing of a number of books which make a solid contribution to criticism.

His first books, Gluck and the Opera (1895) and A Study of Wagner (1899), appeared while he was still engaged in business at Liverpool, and during this time he made a number of contributions to current journalism, some of which were ultimately collected in his volume Musical Studies (1905). From 1903–05 he was on the musical staff of the Midland Institute at Birmingham, which post he left for that of music critic to the Manchester Guardian (1905–1906). The writings of this period showed him to be a keen student of the principles of music drama as formulated by Gluck and pursued by Wagner, as well as a champion of programme music. They proved his possession of a mind capable of combining close analysis with complete independence of outlook and vividness of expression. With them may be classed a second little book on Wagner (Music of the Masters, 1904), Elgar (1906) and Richard Strauss (1908) ; the value of the last two was necessarily limited by their dates. Of greater importance was Hugo Wolf (1907), the first English book to attempt an exhaustive study of Wolf's qualities as a song-writer. It was Newman's method here as elsewhere to state his case at its highest ; his claims for Wolf and his comparisons of him with other German song-writers raised a controversy the echoes of which have hardly died away in close on twenty years, but at least he secured a juster appreciation of Wolf's genius in this country.

From 1906–19 Newman was music critic to the Birmingham Daily Post, and he then settled

in London, first as critic to the Observer (1919–1920), then transferring himself to the Sunday Times. For the winter season of 1924–25 he visited America as ' guest-critic ' to the New York Evening Post. Books of this period are Wagner as Man and Artist (1914), a trenchant criticism of official views of the man as exhibited in Mein Leben, etc., and a sympathetic study of the artist as exhibited in the music-dramas ; a further collection of essays called A Musical Motley (1919), and The Piano-player and its Music (see under Mechanical Appliances). A Musical Critic's Holiday (New York, 1925) is a valuable study in the principles of criticism.

Newman translated the texts of Wagner's music-dramas from ' Der Ring des Nibelungen ' to ' Parsifal ' and also Schweitzer's J. S. Bach. Though his study of Bach deepened the hold of the classics on him the period of his special knowledge has remained the century from Berlioz to Richard Strauss with Wagner at its centre.   c.

NEWMARCH, Rosa Harriet (b. Leamington, Dec. 18, 1857), a writer on music, who has exerted an important influence in England especially through her programme notes (see Analytical Programmes) written for the concerts of the Queen's Hall Orchestra.

The daughter of Samuel Jeaffreson, M.D., and grand-daughter of James Kenney (playwright), she married (1883) Henry Charles Newmarch, and all her writings have appeared under her married name. In 1897 she made the first of a series of visits to Russia, where she worked at the Imperial Public Library of St. Petersburg, under the supervision of Vladimir Stassov (q.v.). The outcome appeared in a number of articles and lectures on Russian music and art in general, which did much to further in England that interest already awakened by Tchaikovsky's music. Her articles on Russian composers, first contributed to the second edition of this Dictionary, were to many English musicians the first source of enlightenment with regard to the aims and accomplishments of the Russian Nationalists. Mrs. Newmarch paid her last visit to Russia in the early summer of 1915, and when political events closed that country to civilisation she directed her interest to Western Slavonic music, particularly that of the Czechs and Slovaks. Here again, in her visits to Czechoslovakia, her lectures and various writings, which include important contributions to the present work, her object has been to effect introductions between the art and artists of her own and other countries. As official programme writer to the Queen's Hall Orchestra (1908–20, since then in conjunction with Eric Blom), Mrs. Newmarch has acted as the advocate before the London public of the new music of all countries, and her qualities of insight and sympathy with

[1] H. C. de Lafontaine, The King's Musick.

every kind of high artistic aim have fitted her ideally for such work.

The following is a list of her chief musical publications:

Johannes Brahms, trans. from the German of Hermann Deiters, with a preface by J. A. Fuller Maitland (1887).
Borodin and Liszt, with an introduction to the study of Russian music (1889).
Tchaikovsky (1900).
The Life and Letters of Peter Ilich Tchaikovsky, edited and translated from the Russian (1906).
César Franck, translated from the French of Vincent D'Indy, with an introduction (1909).
Edits *The Living Masters of Music* series, to which she contributed the volume on *Henry J. Wood*.
The Russian Opera (1914; French ed., 1922).
English translations of Moussorgsky's ' Boris Godounov,' ' Khovantshina,' Tchaikovsky's ' Queen of Spades ' and Rimsky-Korsakov's ' Ivan the Terrible (Pskovityanka).
Edits *The Russian Song Books* and *Russian Folk Songs* (J. & W. Chester).
Non-musical publications include : *Horae Amoris*, songs and sonnets (1903) ; *Songs to a Singer* (1906) ; *Poetry and Progress in Russia* (1907) ; *The Russian Arts* (1916) ; *The Devout Russian* (1918).

NEW PHILHARMONIC SOCIETY, THE (1852–79).

The prospectus, dated from Cramer's, Jan. 1852, states that the Society was founded to give more perfect performances of the great works than had hitherto been attained, and to afford to modern and native composers a favourable opportunity of coming before the public. Classical music was not to be exclusively adhered to ; Exeter Hall was chosen as the locale ; Berlioz was engaged as conductor for the first season ; the band was magnificent (twenty first violins, led by Sibori) ; the chorus was professional ; and the subscription for stalls for six concerts was £2 : 2s., professional subscribers, £1 : 1s. The concerts of the second season were conducted, four by Lindpaintner, and two by Spohr, in combination with Dr. Henry Wylde. The orchestra was enlarged to twenty-four first violins, etc. For the third season the concerts were removed to St. Martin's Hall, and were conducted partly by Lindpaintner, partly by Dr. Wylde. For the fourth season they returned to Exeter Hall. For the fifth and sixth, 1856 and 1857, Hanover Square Rooms were chosen. In 1858 Wylde assumed the entire responsibility of the undertaking, and the concerts were henceforward held in St. James's Hall, season by season, as the 'New Philharmonic Concerts,' until 1879, when Wylde retired in favour of William Ganz. The programmes throughout maintained that preference for novelties which distinguished them at the outset. In 1859 the practice of making the rehearsals public was begun. In 1879 the Society came to an end, the last concert under its name being given on June 21 of that year. The scheme was carried on for three years more as 'Ganz's Orchestral Concerts.'

NEW QUEEN'S HALL ORCHESTRA.

This organisation, originally known as the Queen's Hall Orchestra, was formed in 1895, with Robert Newman (d. 1926) as manager and Henry J. Wood as conductor for a series of PROMENADE CONCERTS (q.v.) given in QUEEN'S HALL (q.v.). The success of these concerts, due to two things, the quickly growing reputation of the conductor as such and the musical policy adopted in the selection of the programmes, led to the establishment of a series of Saturday afternoon concerts given by the orchestra in the same hall. The first concert took place on Jan. 30, 1897, and the series has continued uninterruptedly ever since under the same manager and conductor. In 1904 a dispute arose between the directors and the players over the right to send deputies, which ended in the withdrawal of a large number of the latter, who formed themselves into a separate organisation. (See LONDON SYMPHONY ORCHESTRA.) Wood, however, quickly engaged other players and the orchestra soon acquired the peculiar sensitiveness and perfection of ensemble which are characteristic of his methods of training and, incidentally, of continual performance under a permanent conductor. Orchestra and conductor have, in fact, been inseparable, except through occasional and unavoidable causes. At first the financial responsibilities of the orchestra rested upon Newman ; in 1902 they were undertaken by a syndicate, with Sir Edgar Speyer as head, and in 1915 were transferred to Messrs. Chappell,[1] lessees of Queen's Hall. The title of the orchestra was then changed to that it now bears, personnel, conductor and manager remaining as before. An important feature of the establishment of the orchestra was that Wood insisted upon the introduction of the French pitch. The activities of the orchestra were extended by the Sunday afternoon orchestral concerts started at the Queen's Hall in Oct. 1895, the first two series of which were conducted by Randegger. (See QUEEN'S HALL.) It has taken part in some of the provincial festivals, such as Norwich and Sheffield, and from time to time special series of concerts have been given in London, notably the London Festival of 1911. N. C. G.

NEW SYMPHONY ORCHESTRA, see ROYAL ALBERT HALL ORCHESTRA.

NEW YORK. The history of musical societies in New York City does not extend back further than the middle of the 18th century. Until that period the social customs and tastes of the inhabitants of the town, and the character of their entertainments, were swayed by the original settlers and their descendants. An excerpt from the writer's monograph entitled *The Philharmonic Society of New York* states the case with sufficient comprehensiveness to serve present purposes, and is therefore quoted here :

' The Dutch had brought little or no artistic sensibility with them, and their experiences from the time of their settlement of Manhattan Island till the final occupation of the town by the British were not of a kind calculated to develop a love for music. In social, political and commercial affairs their influence

---

[1] Messrs. Chappell announced the intention of abandoning the orchestra in March 1927.

was much more widespread and enduring; but, having come from a country where music was sadly neglected, to another where life meant a struggle and where of necessity the commercial spirit swayed everything, the Dutch could not fairly be expected to give a very appreciable tinge to the art-tastes of the growing town. After New Amsterdam had become New York, and was firmly settled in the possession of Great Britain, and English merchants and English soldiers had begun to work a change in the social life of the town, the things which embellish civilisation were speedily introduced and, very naturally, in their English types. All the musical impulses of a century ago came from England, though, after the cultivation of the serious forms of music had begun, German musicians were largely instrumental in advancing them in New York as well as Boston and the other large cities of the sea-coast.'

Amateur orchestras came into existence late in the 18th century. One of these, which gave its 48th anniversary concert in 1847, was called the EUTERPEAN. Before the end of the first quarter of the 19th century there were in existence, besides the Euterpean, a PHILHARMONIC SOCIETY and the CONCORDIA, clubs of singers and instrumentalists, the former English in its constitution, the latter predominantly German. There was a professional element in these organisations, and it was in significant degree the creator of the influence which in 1842 crystallised in the present Philharmonic Society, which since then has been the most notable institution in the field of American instrumental music, and with whose foundation the professional record may be said to begin. It is the only concert organisation in New York whose history extends back to the middle of the 19th century.

The history of the choral societies using the vernacular, which preceded the present Oratorio Society, extends back to the last decades of the 18th century, and seems to have begun in its larger phase—there were Glee Unions like those of England at an earlier date—with movements looking to the betterment of church music after the shackles of the old psalmody had been cast off. William Tuckey, who had been a vicar-choral in Bristol, was brought from England in 1752 to be clerk of Trinity parish. He served in that office for four years from Jan. 1, 1753. At first his choir was composed of boys and girls from the Charity School, but he succeeded in eliminating the female element soon after he entered upon his duties. After his departure from Trinity parish he continued to labour in other parishes and outside the church walls. He raised a subscription for which he taught 'ladies and gentlemen' a Te Deum, evidently of his own composition, which he 'guaranteed' to be 'as good a piece of music as any of the common Te Deums sung in any cathedral church in England.' On Jan. 16, 1770, the same musician gave a concert for his own benefit, at which he performed the overture and sixteen numbers of Handel's 'Messiah.' A Handel and Haydn Society, Choral Society and Sacred Music Society all grew out of movements which had their inception in the Episcopal Church, and from 1825 on there was a continuous succession of singing-societies till the field was occupied by the organisations whose histories are told below. The Sacred Music Society, under the direction of Ureli Corelli Hill, one of the founders of the Philharmonic Society, performed Handel's 'Messiah' in 1831 and Mendelssohn's 'St. Paul' in 1838. In 1844 Hill invited Spohr and Mendelssohn to visit New York for the purpose of conducting a festival after the English model. Nothing came of the enterprise at the time, but in Feb. 1847 a Mendelssohn Festival was held in Castle Garden, in which the Philharmonic Society, the German Liederkranz and the Concordia took part.

The musical societies of New York are described below in the chronological order of their foundation.

PHILHARMONIC SOCIETY (1842).—The New York Philharmonic is the oldest orchestral body in continuous service in the United States devoted to the performance of instrumental music. It is also said to be the third oldest in the world, after the like-named societies of London and Vienna, and was formerly a communistic body of professional musicians, the profit-sharing members constituting a little less than two-thirds of the performers at its concerts, who generally numbered from 90–110. Among the honorary members of the Society since its foundation have been Vieuxtemps, the first one, elected in 1843; Spohr, Mendelssohn, Jenny Lind, Sontag, Alboni, William Vincent Wallace, Thalberg, Mme. Parepa-Rosa, Franz Liszt, Richard Wagner, Joachim Raff, Anton Rubinstein and Dvořák.

The history of the Society had its beginning at a meeting of professional musicians called by Ureli Corelli Hill (an American musician, violinist and conductor, pupil of Spohr in Cassel), held on Apr. 2, 1842. The impulse to organise such a Society seems to have come from the artistic success achieved at a 'Musical Solemnity' given in June 1839, in honour of the memory of Daniel Schlesinger, one of the first thoroughly trained musicians to make his home in New York. The most prominent musicians in the city were present at this meeting and the meetings which followed, at which the organisation of the Society was perfected. Among them were Hill; A. P. Heinrich, an eccentric Bohemian composer who presided at the first meeting, but took no further interest in the affair; Charles E. HORN (q. v.); William Vincent Wallace, who was a member during the first two years; Alfred Boucher, a connexion of Alexandre Jean BOUCHER (q.v.); Dr. Edward Hodges, an English Cathedral musician, afterwards organist of Trinity Church; H. C. Timm and William Scharfenberg, pianists of German birth and training; George Loder, a member of the English family of musicians of that name; and D. G. Etienne, a French pianist who could play the horn when required. To Loder, who was connected with the Society throughout the first decade, fell the honour of conducting the first performance in the United States of Beethoven's Choral Symphony at a concert of the Society on May 20, 1846. Three concerts were given in the first season (1842–1843), and the first programme is such excellent testimony to the seriousness of the founders' aims that it deserves publication here.

First Concert, Dec. 7, 1842—Symphony No. 5, in C minor, Beethoven (conducted by U. C. Hill) ; Scena from 'Oberon,' Weber (Madame Otto) ; Quintet in D minor, for pianoforte, violin, viola, violoncello and double-bass, Hummel (Messrs. Scharfenberg, Hill, Derwort, Boucher and Rosier) ; Overture 'Oberon,' Weber (conducted by Mr. Etienne) ; Duet from 'Armida,' Rossini (Madame Otto and Mr. C. E. Horn) ; Scena from 'Fidelio,' Beethoven (Mr. C. E. Horn) ; Aria Bravura from 'The Seraglio,' Mozart (Madame Otto) ; New Overture in D, Kalliwoda (conducted by Mr. Timm). The orchestra during the vocal music was directed by H. C. Timm.

For the next sixteen years four regular concerts were given each season, then for ten years five. In the 27th season the number was increased to six, and this remained the rule until the 56th season, when the number was increased to eight. Out of a custom of admitting amateurs to the rehearsals of the Society, which was inaugurated in the second season, there grew the so-called public rehearsals, which for several decades differed in nothing but name and the time of performance from the regular concerts. In 1906 the title 'public rehearsals' was abandoned for 'Afternoon Concerts.' This explains the statement, heretofore made, that the Society for some years gave sixteen subscription concerts annually. It was the custom during the early years of the Society, when the president was a professional musician and necessarily a member of the Society, to leave the conducting of the concerts in his hands, though for a number of years that official found it expedient to share the duty with the leading members of the Society, especially such as were at the head of singing and other musical societies. Thus in the 1st season, though only three concerts were given, five members officiated at the conductor's desk, viz.: U. C. Hill, H. C. Timm, W. Alpers, Alfred Boucher and George Loder. D. G. Etienne aided Hill, Loder and Alpers in the 2nd season. Two new men, one of whom was destined to play an important rôle in the history of the Society, appeared in the 7th season. They were Theodore Eisfeld, who came from Europe with experience gained in conducting concerts in Paris and elsewhere; and Max Maretzek, whose real activities belonged in the field of opera. In Eisfeld's second season the directors changed their policy and elected Eisfeld sole director for the season. In 1854 Carl BERGMANN was associated with him and H. C. Timm, who was then president, and thereafter for ten years, save the 15th and 16th seasons conducted solely by Eisfeld and the 14th and 17th conducted by Bergmann, these two men conducted alter-

nately. Bergmann was sole conductor from 1865–76. Then came an interregnum of three years with Dr. Leopold DAMROSCH, Theodore THOMAS and Adolph Neuendorff as conductors. Thomas was conductor for the next twelve years, Anton SEIDL for the next seven (holding the position at the time of his death on Mar. 28, 1898), and Emil PAUR for four. Under the artistic administration of Thomas and Seidl the Society grew steadily in prosperity and reached its zenith. A falling off in popular interest during the Paur régime and the one season, the 61st, in which Walter DAMROSCH was conductor, led to the adoption of the custom, which had gained a foothold in some of the European capitals, of engaging a different conductor for each concert, instead of one for the entire season. These 'guests' in the 62nd season were Edouard Colonne of Paris, Gustav F. Kogel of Frankfort, Henry J. Wood of London, Victor Herbert of Pittsburgh, Felix Weingartner of Munich and Richard Strauss of Berlin. In the 63rd season the conductors were Gustav F. Kogel, Edouard Colonne, Wassili Safonov of Moscow, Felix Weingartner and Karl Panzner of Bremen; Theodore Thomas, who had also accepted the invitation of the directors, died before the concert which he was to conduct, and Kogel was called back from Frankfort to take his place. In the 64th season the Society's invitation was accepted by Willem Mengelberg of Amsterdam, Victor Herbert, Max Fiedler of Hamburg, M. Safonov, Dr. Ernest Kunwald of Frankfort and Fritz Steinback of Cologne. At the end of this season an engagement was made with Safonov as sole conductor for three years. To carry out these new policies a number of public-spirited citizens placed a considerable fund at the service of the Society.

Later Philharmonic conductors were; 1909–1911, Gustav Mahler; 1911–23, Josef Stransky; 1921 and half-seasons thereafter, Willem Mengelberg; also occasional conductors, including Artur Bodanzky (1921–22), Henry Hadley (1920–25, for American programmes), Willem Van Hoogstraten (associate, 1923–25), Ernest Schelling (a series of children's concerts, begun 1924–25), Igor Stravinsky (guest, 1925), Arturo Toscanini (guest, 1926), and as Mengelberg's associate for half-seasons, Wilhelm Furtwaengler (1925 and after). The Philharmonic absorbed the National Symphony (active, 1919–1921) and the City Symphony (1921–23). It took over the Stadium Summer Concerts (started by Arnold Volpe, 1917) and the American Orchestral Society (founded 1921 by Mrs. E. H. Harriman and continued under Philharmonic auspices). A bequest of Joseph Pulitzer (1912) provided $500,000 endowment, later said to be doubled; a building fund of $110,000 was subscribed in the 75th jubilee year (1917); and the Society's finances were subsequently guaranteed by a Board of Directors headed by Clarence H. Mackay. Calvin Coolidge, President of the United States, was elected an Honorary Associate, Mar. 16, 1924.

(For a history of the Society see *The Philharmonic Society of New York*, a memorial by Henry Edward Krehbiel published on the occasion of the Fiftieth Anniversary of the founding of the Society, Apr. 1892, London, Novello, Ewer & Co.)

THE DEUTSCHER LIEDERKRANZ (1847) is perhaps the most striking representative in the United States of the musical club developed on the German lines which combine the cultivation of music with good fellowship, social and domestic enjoyments. Naturally the task grows more difficult as the original immigrants die and the younger generation, born and educated in the country, take their places.

When the first steps to organise the Liederkranz were taken in the fall of 1846 the German population in New York was small, but already boasted a singing-society called the Gesangverein der Social-Reformer, a name which betrays its bond of union to have been as much political as artistic. Those who responded to the call numbered 150, but this number was cut down to 25 when it was proposed to assess would-be members twenty-five cents each. Nevertheless an organisation was effected on Jan. 9, 1847, the name Deutscher Liederkranz agreed on and Dr. Hermann E. Ludwig elected president. A musician named Krauskopf was elected conductor. Rehearsals were begun in the Shakespeare Hotel, and the first concert was given in the Apollo Rooms, then the fashionable concert-hall of the city, on May 17, 1847. The chorus numbered about 100. Julius Hecht succeeded as conductor on Aug. 20 of the same year. The Liederkranz participated in the concerts of Jenny Lind, Thalberg, the Mendelssohn Festival of 1848 (which was attended by an audience of 8000), William Vincent Wallace and the Philharmonic Society. In Feb. 1849 Hecht resigned, and was succeeded by Wilhelm Müller, who had been a conductor in Brunswick. He lasted less than a year and one Weisheit, whose tenure of office was no longer, was elected. Then Agriol Paur was elected conductor in May 1850, and remained in active duty till he retired as honorary conductor with salary in 1884. Two years before Theodore THOMAS (*q.v.*) had been elected to perform the duties which were become too onerous for Paur, and at various times during the next two years, Edward Heimendahl and Arthur Mees were frequently called in to assist Thomas, who was unable to devote himself to the work of training the singers. He declining a re-election, in 1884 Reinhold L. Herman was elected and served five years. Heinrich Zoellner was called to the post from Cologne.

and remained in office from 1890–98. From 1898–1903 the conductor was Dr. Paul Klengel, who came from Leipzig, and he was succeeded by Arthur Claassen. The club was active during its early years in manifesting sympathy with the revolutionists in Germany, and the influx of political refugees in 1849 resulted in a strengthening of its membership. Internal dissensions resulted in a defection in the membership and the organisation of the Männergesangverein Arion in 1854.

THE MÄNNERGESANGVEREIN ARION (1854–1918), as compared with the Liederkranz, had a larger devotion to characteristically German things and German methods, and a slightly larger proportion of active members. It also adhered to its original mission as a promoter of songs for men's voices, and never cultivated music for mixed voices, or founded a women's choir. In the summer of 1892 sixty singers were sent by the Society to make a tour of the principal cities of Germany under the direction of Frank van der Stucken, and made a profound impression by the excellence of their performances. In Jan. 1854 fourteen members of the Liederkranz, disagreeing violently with the majority of that Society, seceded and organised a club to which they gave the name Männergesangverein Arion. Within a week they gave a concert in the Apollo Rooms. The first conductor was a musician named Meyerhofer, who was succeeded by Carl BERGMANN (*q.v.*). Bergmann remained in the position, barring a short interregnum in 1862, till 1870. Other conductors for short terms were Carl Anschütz, F. L. Ritter, V. Hartmann and H. Grenier. In 1871 Dr. Leopold DAMROSCH (*q.v.*) was brought from Breslau, and he remained conductor until 1884, when he made way for Frank van der STUCKEN (*q.v.*), who was succeeded in the fall of 1895 by Julius Lorenz, and 1913–18, Carl Hahn. In addition to the customary music for men's voices, the Arion, from the beginning of its career, cultivated operettas. In 1855 a work of this kind, composed by Carl Bergmann and called 'Mordgrundbruck,' was performed, and a year later 'Der Gang zum Eisenhammer' by the same composer. Amusing little works in the same style, which do not call for female voices, were given at long intervals of time, but only for the diversion of the members and their families. The choruses in the first Wagner opera ever performed in America were sung by the active members of the Männergesangverein Arion. This was 'Tannhäuser,' produced under the direction of Carl Bergmann at the Stadt Theatre in the Bowery on Aug. 27, 1859. In 1869 the Society gave a public performance of 'Der Freischütz.' In 1918 the Liederkranz and Arion were reunited, following the vicissitudes of the various German-American societies during the war of 1914–18.

BROOKLYN PHILHARMONIC SOCIETY, incorporated 1857, had for its declared object 'the advancement of music in the city of Brooklyn, by procuring the public performance of the best works in this department of art.' Beginning in the autumn of 1857, five or more concerts were given in each season, that at the close of the 21st season, May 10, 1879, being the 108th—each preceded by three public rehearsals. During the first five seasons the concerts were given at the Brooklyn Athenæum. After 1862 the Brooklyn Academy of Music was made use of. The orchestral conductors have been—Theodore Eisfeld, 1857–62; Theodore Thomas, part of 1862; Eisfeld again, until the election of Carl Bergmann, Sept. 5, 1865; Thomas, re-elected Sept. 4, 1866; Bergmann again, 1870–73; succeeded May 26, 1873, by Thomas, who retained the position until his departure for Chicago, assisted by William G. Dietrich, who had charge of the orchestra at the first two rehearsals of each concert. The concerts were always of a high order; the orchestra large and composed of the best musicians procurable. Important works were produced for the first time in America, including several by native composers. Large choral works occasionally figured on the Society's programmes.

What was formerly the city of Brooklyn, N.Y., is now a borough of the American metropolis. Nevertheless the Philharmonic Society retains the corporate name by which it has been known since 1857. Theodore Thomas, with his orchestra, gave its concerts from 1873–1891. On his departure for Chicago an arrangement was made by which the concerts (five annually, by the Boston Symphony Orchestra, and later by the New York Symphony also) were continued under the joint auspices of the Philharmonic Society and the Institute of Arts and Sciences. After the destruction of the Academy of Music, Nov. 29, 1903, the concerts were transferred to the Baptist Temple until the rebuilding of the Academy on another site.

THE MENDELSSOHN GLEE CLUB (1866), organised on May 21, 1866, and incorporated under the laws of the State of New York on Oct. 21, 1876, cultivates unaccompanied part-songs, and its active membership is composed almost wholly of professional singers. In the formative period of the club's history, meetings having been held in the winter of 1865–66, rehearsals were conducted by a Mr. Schripf and Mr. Albites. In 1867, however, Joseph Mosenthal was elected conductor, and such he remained till his death, which came to him suddenly in one of the club's rooms in 1896. Mosenthal, a native of Cassel, was a violinist, pupil of Spohr, and for many years one of the leading church musicians of New York. The season of 1896 was filled out by Arthur Woodruff, one of the active members, whereupon

Edward A. MACDOWELL (*q.v.*) was elected, serving till May 1898, being succeeded by Arthur Mees, who, in 1904, gave way to Frank DAMROSCH (*q.v.*); 1909, Clarence Dickinson; and 1919, Nelson P. Coffin. Mosenthal wrote a number of songs for the club, among the best known of which are 'The Sailors' Song,' 'Music of the Sea,' 'Blest Pair of Sirens,' 'Thanatopsis.' Reinhold L. Herman wrote for it 'Song of the Seasons,' and W. W. Gilchrist 'Ode to the Sun,' 'Autumn Day' and 'Dreaming Forever.'

ORATORIO SOCIETY (1873).—When Dr. Leopold Damrosch came to New York in 1871 to assume the conductorship of the Männergesangverein Arion he had been for fourteen years conductor of singing-societies as well as the Symphony Orchestra in Breslau. In the spring of 1873 he invited a number of singers to his house, and submitted a proposition to form a singing-society of mixed voices which should consistently cultivate the higher forms of the art. The singers decided to make a beginning. True to its traditions, which show that choral music in New York had its beginnings within its walls, Trinity parish gave the new choir the use of Trinity Chapel as a meeting-place. Fifteen or eighteen persons attended the first rehearsal. Summer interrupted the meetings, and after the customary vacation it was thought wise to change the study room to a ware-room of the Knabe firm of pianoforte manufacturers. There, too, the first concert of the infant Society was held on Dec. 3, 1873. Neither Dr. Damrosch nor the officers, at the head of whom stood Prof. F. A. P. Barnard, president of Columbia College, thought it advisable to ask public support for the concert. The programme embraced a chorale by Bach, Mozart's 'Ave Verum,' the motet 'Adoramus Te,' by Palestrina, a partsong by Mendelssohn, and some of the airs and choruses from Handel's 'Samson.' The choir numbered between fifty and sixty, and the artistic success attained was encouraging. Thus was the Oratorio Society launched, which soon assumed the task of maintaining the oratorio in New York. A public hall was hired for the second concert on Feb. 26, 1874, at which the programme was still of a miscellaneous character, comprising again a chorale by Bach, Orlando Lasso's 'And the Angel,' Michael Haydn's 'Tenebrae factae sunt,' Handel's 'Zadok, the Priest.' At the third concert, on May 12, 1874, the Society entered upon its mission. It, and public interest in it, had grown apace, and it was found possible to perform an entire oratorio with orchestral accompaniment. Naturally the work was 'Samson.' The prospectus issued at the outset stated the purpose of the new Society to be the cultivation 'of the highest style of sacred and secular music,' and though the oratorio was admitted to be the objective point, yet the compositions of masters like Lotti, Anerio, Palestrina, Lasso, Purcell and Bach were admitted to be within the purview of its activities. The third concert was held in Steinway Hall, then the best and most fashionable concert-room in the city. On Christmas night, 1874, the Oratorio Society took from the palsied hands of the Harmonic Society, which went out of existence, the pious duty of an annual performance of the 'Messiah,' a duty which it has performed ever since, and which, indeed, has enabled it to continue its ministrations. The Harmonic Society had performed Handel's sacred oratorio annually in the Christmastide ever since its organisation in 1850. Since its organisation the Oratorio Society, numbering on an average 400 singers, has given three or four concerts annually, first at Steinway Hall, then the Academy of Music, Metropolitan Opera House and Carnegie Hall. Dr. Damrosch was conductor from the beginning down to his death in Feb. 1885. He was succeeded by his son, Walter DAMROSCH (q.v.), who served until the season 1898–99, when he in turn yielded to his brother, Frank DAMROSCH (q.v.). Other conductors were Sir Edward Elgar, 1904, a guest; 1912, Louis Koemmenich; 1917, Walter Damrosch again; and 1921, Albert Stoessel. Following is a list of the less familiar works performed by the Oratorio Society:

L. Damrosch, 'Ruth and Naomi,' 1875 ; Liszt, 'Christus ' (first part), 1876 ; Brahms, ' A German Requiem ' (first time in America), 1877 ; Kiel, 'Christus ' (first time in America), 1879 ; Bach, ' St. Matthew Passion,' 1880 ; Handel, ' L' Allegro, il Pensieroso ed il Moderato,' 1881 ; Rubinstein, ' The Tower of Babel,' 1881 ; L. Damrosch, 'Sulamith ' (first performance), 1882 ; Berlioz, 'Grand Messe des Morts,' 1882 ; Cowen, ' St. Ursula,' 1883 ; Wagner, 'Parsifal ' (as an oratorio), 1886 ; Eduard Grell, Mass *a cappella*, 1889 ; Brahms, 'Commemorative Sentences,' 1890 ; Saint-Saëns, ' Samson and Delilah,' 1892 ; Tinel, ' St. Francis ' (first time in America), 1893 ; Dvořák, ' Psalm cxlix.,' 1895 ; Verdi, ' Manzoni Requiem,' 1896 ; Gounod, ' The Redemption,' 1897 ; Parker, ' St. Christopher,' 1898 ; Goetz, ' 137th Psalm,' 1898 ; Walter Damrosch, 'Manila Te Deum ' (first time), 1898 ; Bach, Mass in B minor, 1900 ; Dvořák, ' Requiem,' 1901 ; Elgar, 'Dream of Gerontius,' 1903 ; Elgar, ' The Apostles ' (first time in America), 1904 ; Richard Strauss, 'Taillefer ' (first time in America), 1905 ; Dvořák, 'Stabat Mater,' 1905 ; Beethoven, Mass in D, 1905. Two popular novelties in later years were Pierné's ' The Children's Crusade,' and Wolf-Ferrari's ' La Vita Nuova,' after Dante.

THE NEW YORK SYMPHONY SOCIETY (1878). —This organisation is a successor, *de jure* if not *de facto*, of a Society of like name, which was founded in 1878 by Dr. Leopold DAMROSCH. During the early years of its existence the New York Symphony Society maintained an exceedingly active competition with the orchestra of Theodore THOMAS, and the rivalry of the organisations had much to do with familiarising the New York public with the works of the German, French and Russian composers as fast as they were published, and even before, since Damrosch and Thomas were both in the habit of securing manuscript copies of their compositions from the leading authors of Europe. After the death of Dr. Damrosch in 1885 his son Walter succeeded to the conductorship of the Society, and has remained its administrative as well as artistic head ever since. The Society has passed through many

vicissitudes, and has several times appeared to be moribund, only to be awakened to renewed life by its energetic and indefatigable conductor. The concerts were permitted to lapse in 1899, when Damrosch devoted a year to composition ; again when he travelled with his own opera company, and still again when he became conductor for a season (1902–03) of the Philharmonic Society of New York. Retiring from that post Damrosch organised what for four years was called the New York Symphony Orchestra, on a co-operative basis, profit and loss being shared by the members of the organisation and a committee of guarantors.

The plan proved to be unsatisfactory, and in the spring of 1907 the guarantors called the old Symphony Society back to life, and resolved to proceed under the old style and in the old manner, paying the players weekly wages throughout the season, and assuming all financial responsibilities. At the same time it was determined to increase the number of concerts in New York City to twenty-eight, half of them to be given on Sunday afternoons. In the season 1905–06 Felix Weingartner alternated with Damrosch in conducting concerts in New York and other cities. This orchestra was among the first to make tours to many cities and towns in the United States. It also remained intact during the summer months, and provided music for large and fashionable resorts near Philadelphia and Chicago.

More recent guest conductors of the Symphony Society, both at Æolian and Carnegie Hall, have been Vincent d'Indy and, since the war, Albert Coates, Vladimir Golschmann, Bruno Walter and Otto Klemperer. The financing of the Society, which like other American orchestras faced an annual deficit of upwards of $100,000, was guaranteed in 1914 and yearly thereafter by Harry Harkness Flagler. In 1920 Mr. Flagler sent the orchestra to Europe at a cost of $250,000. The Sunday concerts were moved in 1925 to the new Mecca Temple, near Carnegie Hall.

APOLLO CLUB (Borough of Brooklyn) (1878). —A glee club devoted chiefly to the performance of partsongs for men's voices. The club is the outgrowth of a meeting of fifteen gentlemen, chiefly church singers, held on Nov. 1, 1877. Membership was later fixed at 80 voices and associates at 250. Three concerts have been given every season since, and have been attended by the élite of Brooklyn society. Dudley BUCK (q.v.) was conductor until 1903 ; he was succeeded by John Hyatt Brewer. Of Buck's many compositions the following were written for the Apollo Club and first brought forward at its concerts: 'The Voyage of Columbus,' 'The Bugle Song,' 'Paul Revere's Ride,' 'The Nun of Nidaros,' 'Twilight,' 'King Olaf's Christmas' and 'Chorus of Spirits and the Hours' from Shelley's 'Prometheus.'

CHURCH CHORAL SOCIETY.—Early in Feb. 1889 a number of gentlemen met in the Rectory of St. Bartholomew's Church for the purpose of discussing a plan formulated by Richard Henry Warren, organist of the church, looking to the production of the larger forms of ecclesiastical music within the walls of metropolitan churches and under conditions calculated to enhance their dignity and solemnity. Gounod's 'Mors et Vita' was presented (for the first time in New York) in St. Bartholomew's Church on Apr. 25, in the presence of a large congregation that had responded to the invitations. The function was treated as strictly religious. At a meeting held in the rooms of St. Bartholomew's Church on Dec. 16, 1889, the Church Choral Society was organised, the officers chosen being J. Pierpont Morgan, president; the Right Rev. H. C. Potter, Bishop of New York, and the Rev. E. Winchester Donald, vice-presidents; Henry W. Hayden, secretary; John Murray Mitchell, treasurer; and Richard Henry Warren, musical director. The Society's services were continued uninterruptedly for seven years, with a tentative resumption in 1903. In its first epoch the Church Choral Society performed, besides other works,

Dvořák's Requiem Mass (first time in America), Mass in D (first time in America); Liszt's Thirteenth Psalm (first time in New York); George W. Chadwick's 'Phoenix expirans' (first time in New York); Mackenzie's 'Veni, Creator Spiritus' (first time in America); Horatio W. Parker's 'Hora Novissima' (first time); Harry Rowe Shelley's 'Vexilla Regis' (first time).

In the second epoch :

Coleridge-Taylor's 'The Atonement' (first time in America); Elgar's 'Light of Life,' 'Te Deum' and 'Benedictus' (first time in America).

THE MANUSCRIPT SOCIETY was founded in Aug. 1889, reorganised in 1899 as the Society of American Musicians and Composers, and again reorganised a year later for the purpose of promoting the interests of American composers. It had an enrolled membership of about 100 in 1906, when, after many futile efforts to enlist the general public in its activities, it was pursuing the policy of holding meetings for its members and invited guests at intervals of a month, for the purpose of hearing compositions by its members in the smaller forms.

Since the war (1914–18) this Society has been followed by many new organisations. Chief among those active in 1925 was the SOCIETY FOR PUBLICATION OF AMERICAN MUSIC.

THE BROOKLYN INSTITUTE's department of music dates from 1891. Brooklyn is the second in importance of the boroughs constituting the city of New York. The Brooklyn Institute of Arts and Sciences is the outgrowth of the Brooklyn Apprentices' Library Association, which was incorporated by the Legislature of the State of New York on Nov. 20, 1824. A charter granted in 1843 widened the scope of the original association, and changed the name to the Brooklyn Institute. There was a still

greater extension of the Institute activities in 1888, and to the other artistic and scientific departments that of music was added in Nov. 1891, the first public function being a lecture on Chinese Music by H. E. Krehbiel. The membership of the department was 54 originally, and Dudley Buck was the first president. Since then the membership has grown steadily. Musical knowledge is promoted by means of lectures and concerts, the largest functions being the concerts of the Brooklyn Philharmonic Society (see above). For the maintenance of these concerts and unspecified concerts of chamber music the department has a fund of $10,000, received as a bequest under the will of Henry K. Sheldon, many years president of the Brooklyn Philharmonic Society. From this latter Society, on the disbandment of its chorus, the department received a large number of vocal scores; it has also received gifts of a collection of exotic instruments and scores from James A. H. Bell and others. In the new Academy of Music provision was made for lecture, class and concert-rooms for the uses of the department.

PEOPLE'S CHORAL UNION AND SINGING-CLASSES were the fruits of a movement begun in the autumn of 1892 by Frank Damrosch to bring choral culture home to the wage-earning classes in the population of New York. It was the outcome of Settlement work and various civic and labour movements. Meetings were held in Settlement homes and Working Girls' Clubs in the section of the city largely occupied by Polish and Russian Jews employed in clothing manufactories. Elementary classes were at first formed to teach singing and sight-reading, Damrosch beginning the work and gradually turning it over to assistants. After the first year the elementary classes, three in number, were consolidated into one class for more advanced study, which met on Sunday afternoons in the hall of Cooper Union, one of the largest rooms in the city. A nominal fee of ten cents for each lesson was exacted, and the classes were self-supporting from the beginning. The study, beginning with the most elementary exercises, led up through simple rounds and partsongs to cantatas and oratorios. For several years, beginning 1897, the Choral Union gave an annual concert, with a chorus sometimes exceeding 1000 voices, at which such works as 'Messiah,' 'Elijah,' 'Samson,' Schubert's 'Miriam's Triumph,' 'Israel in Egypt,' 'The Seasons,' 'St. Paul' and Bruch's 'Cross of Fire' were sung under the direction of Frank Damrosch, later succeeded by Harry Barnhart.

MUSICAL ART SOCIETY, founded in 1894 for the cultivation of the works of Palestrina, Bach and a cappella music generally, consisted of a choir of some seventy professional singers whose performance exhibited the highest standard. After a quarter century, this Society's unique artistic activity ended in 1920. Its conductor, Frank Damrosch, was asked to head the Institute of Musical Art. (See below.)

AMERICAN GUILD OF ORGANISTS.—The work of the Guild, established 1896, has broadened and been reinforced by the NATIONAL ASSOCIATION OF ORGANISTS (1908) and the SOCIETY OF THEATRE ORGANISTS (1919), the last-named formed by professionals in the large moving picture theatres. In certain festivals of organ music, such as the free recitals at Wanamaker's, New York, members of all three organisations take part.

YOUNG PEOPLE'S SYMPHONY CONCERTS OF NEW YORK.—For the purpose of giving children and young people an opportunity not only to hear standard symphonic works, but also to become familiar with their structure and contents, Frank DAMROSCH organised an annual series of concerts under the above title in 1898. Appreciation of the compositions is helped by explanatory remarks made by the conductor, in which the forms are briefly analysed and the poetic contents suggested, themes and phrases being played in illustration by the orchestra. The orchestra has full symphonic dimensions, that of the New York Symphony Society being employed and solo artists are frequently engaged. Expenses were not always covered, though for years all the seats in Carnegie Hall have been subscribed for, and the resulting deficits were first met by private subscription of public-spirited music-lovers.

On Dr. Frank Damrosch's retirement as conductor, the Symphony Society, under Walter Damrosch, took over the Young People's Concerts, adding another series of concerts for children. These last were held on Saturday mornings at Æolian and later at Carnegie Hall, where both series sold out annually in advance of the season and were widely copied by orchestras in other cities and abroad.

PEOPLE'S SYMPHONY CONCERTS OF NEW YORK.—Under this title a series of concerts was annually given by an orchestra of excellent proportions and artistic character, and with programmes of a high class, for which there was little more than a nominal charge for admission, the prices varying from ten cents to fifty. The concerts were given in pairs, first in the large hall of Cooper Union, situated in the densely populated district known as the East Side ; then in Carnegie Hall, the home of all the fashionable concerts, the purpose being to reach all classes of the people whose tastes the concerts were designed to educate. Under the title ' The People's Symphony Concerts ' auxiliary chamber concerts were also given by local combinations of players. All the concerts, which were called into being by Franz Xavier Arens in 1902 and directed by him until his removal to California, were given under the

auspices of an organisation incorporated under the laws of the State of New York, and were maintained largely by the contributions of philanthropic persons interested in musical culture. These contributions ranged from $2500, which sum entitled the donor to be a founder, to a dollar a year. Receipts and expenses were about $12,000 a year, and at the end of 1905 the organisation had a permanently invested fund of the same amount.

Annie Louise Cary, the American opera singer, left a bequest of $50,000 to the People's Symphony Concerts in 1921. With this fund the founder's son, Egbert L. Arens, continued the chamber-music concerts in a municipal hall at Washington Irving High School, in Irving Place, where leading chamber organisations played in turn at a nominal charge to several thousand hearers.

H. E. K. ; rev. with addns. W. B. C. ;
incorp. material from F. H. J.

RUSSIAN SYMPHONY ORCHESTRA (1904-18), organised under Modest Altschuler's direction, and until the war (1914–18) receiving a small annual subsidy from the Russian Ministry of Education. It gave new works by Rachmaninov, Rimsky - Korsakov, Scriabin, Liadov, Ippolitov-Ivanov and others ; assisted at American débuts of Rachmaninov, Scriabin, Lhevinne and Elman, and in festivals on tour.

SCHOLA CANTORUM (founded 1912), originally the women's chorus of the MacDowell Club, recruited to a large mixed choir under the able direction of Kurt Schindler. In addition to Latin and mediæval masters, the Schola's programmes were enriched by folk-songs and modern art-songs of Russia and Finland, old French and English carols, and especially by Schindler's gatherings from Spain.

FRIENDS OF MUSIC (founded 1913) was begun as a private Sunday afternoon assembly, and became influential in producing rare or unknown works with the Metropolitan Opera Orchestra under Artur Bodanzky and the Friends of Music Chorus under Stephen Townsend. It has produced many Bach cantatas. Pfitzner's ' Von deutscher Seele,' Mahler's ' Lied von der Erde ' (1923, 1924), Purcell's ' Dido and Æneas ' and (1925) Honegger's ' Le Roi David.'

NEW YORK CHAMBER MUSIC SOCIETY was founded in 1914 by Carolyn Beebe, pianist, with a dozen men from the string and wind players in local orchestras. In 1925 there were nearly forty groups of chamber musicians, either resident or annual visitors to the concert platforms of New York.

PEOPLE'S CHORUS OF NEW YORK (founded 1916) was organised by Lorenzo Camilieri, and taking part in patriotic occasions during the war, became a permanent enterprise of popular education and participation in music, like its predecessor, the People's Choral Union.

BEETHOVEN ASSOCIATION (founded 1919),

was formed by volunteer artists under the presidency of Harold Bauer, for performance of rarely given chamber music of Beethoven. Its programmes were varied by songs of that master and soon extended to other classic composers. Proceeds were devoted to needy musicians and (1923) to the publication of Krehbiel's translation of Thayer's *Life of Beethoven*.

JUILLIARD FOUNDATION (founded 1919), a bequest nominally of $5,000,000, from Augustus D. Juilliard, which proved double that amount when received (1923) and was estimated later at $20,000,000, the largest sum ever given to music. The fund was incorporated (1920) under Dr. Eugene C. Noble and (1924) awarded its first 100 free scholarships under famous artist teachers.

AMERICAN MUSIC GUILD and INTERNATIONAL COMPOSER'S GUILD (founded 1921), and LEAGUE OF COMPOSERS (founded 1923), three musically 'radical' organisations arising through the spread of interest in modern music generally since the war (1914–18). The International produced (1923–24) Stravinsky's ' Renard,' under Stokowski. The League in recent seasons gave Schönberg's ' Pierrot Lunaire ' and Respighi's ' Sette Canzone.'

STATE SYMPHONY ORCHESTRA (founded 1923), incorporated under the laws of the State of New York by union musicians who elected Josef Stransky as their leader and Carroll Downes, a New York banker, as president. The orchestra gave fourteen concerts in its first season. Stransky, retiring in 1924, was succeeded by Ignaz Waghalter as conductor, and (1925–26) Ernst von Dohnanyi and Alfredo Casella.

AMERICAN NATIONAL ORCHESTRA (founded 1923), established under the leadership of Howard Barlow, gave concerts of serious purpose and merit thrice yearly, bringing forward the more promising works of native composers.   W. B. C.

EDUCATIONAL

THE INSTITUTE OF MUSICAL ART (1904) is the principal Conservatoire of Music in New York. Founded in 1904 with an initial endowment of $500,000 by James Loeb, it was opened in the following year in an already existing building on Fifth Avenue and 12th Street, with Frank Damrosch as director. Subsequent endowments enabled the Institute to remove (1910) up town into a new building, 120 Clarmont Avenue, specially designed and equipped for the purposes of a music school. There its work has been developed under the continued guidance of Frank Damrosch to the dimensions of a full training establishment in every branch of the art on the model of the leading music schools of Europe. There is a theatre for the study of opera, and special emphasis is laid on that branch, on orchestral playing and other ensemble work. Courses for the training of teachers are scientifically planned. The number of students was originally fixed at about 600, but this number has been exceeded. The Institute is staffed by a faculty of over seventy leading musicians. A valuable library, to which students have access, is an important part of the Institute's equipment.

THE COLUMBIA UNIVERSITY of New York provides courses in music under a professor with assistants. The practical side is attended to at Teachers' College, while in the University itself lectures are given in history, form, theory and æsthetics of the art. Edward MacDowell was professor 1896–1904 ; he was succeeded by Cornelius Ryber, 1904–1919, who was followed in turn by Daniel Gregory MASON (*q.v.*).

MUSIC SCHOOL SETTLEMENTS, which had their origin in New York, are a valuable feature of the educational life in many of the greater cities of the United States. The original settlement was that started in New York in 1894 and housed at 51, 53 and 55 East 3rd Street. The object is to provide musical education in the poorer districts for children and young people largely drawn from the foreign immigrants. Many talented artists have been thus discovered, trained and produced. Along with the artistic side of the work goes the social one of producing the sense of American citizenship among the rising generation of these classes. The work has been carried on in a highly efficient manner by several directors, Thomas Tapper (1907–09), David Mannes (1910–15), Arthur Farwell (1915–19) and Melzar Chaffee. The number of pupils is about 1000 annually, and great attention is devoted to orchestral practice in a series of classes graduated according to age and ability. (Information from *The Annual Report* of the Music School Settlement ; *Amer. Supp.*)   C.

NIBELUNGEN, see RING DES NIBELUNGEN.

NICCOLINI (NICOLINI), GIUSEPPE (*b.* Piacenza, Jan. 29, 1763 ; *d.* there, Dec. 18, 1842), studied at the Conservatoire S. Onofrio, Naples, and under Giac. Insanguine. He was a prolific opera composer whose ' Trajano in Dacia ' carried off the palm in 1807 over Cimarosa's ' Horazi e Curiazi,' but he was eventually overshadowed by Rossini and devoted himself chiefly to the composition of church music. In 1819 he became maestro di cappella of Piacenza Cathedral. A list of his operatic works, as also of his masses and other church compositions, appears in *Q.-L.* and *Fétis*.   E. V. D. S.

NICHELMANN, CHRISTOPH (*b.* Treuenbrietzen, in Brandenburg, Aug. 13, 1717 ; *d.* Berlin, July 20, 1762), was pupil and first treble in the choir-school of St. Thomas, Leipzig, and thus enjoyed his first musical instruction from Sebastian Bach. Spitta says it was from Friedemann Bach that he had his lessons on the clavier, although Friedemann can only have been a very young man at the time. Nichelmann betook himself for a time to Hamburg, where he made the acquaintance of Mattheson and Telemann. Coming to Berlin in 1738 he continued his studies in counterpoint under Quanz, and in 1744, probably on the recommendation of Emanuel Bach, was appointed second cembalist or harpsichord player to the Royal Chapel, in which capacity his chief duty was to accompany the flute-playing of King Frederick the Great. In 1756, for some reason or other, he was dismissed from the chapel, but continued to live in Berlin by giving private lessons, though always in straitened circumstances. He was highly esteemed by his Berlin contemporaries as a composer of odes and works for clavier, and many of his works appeared in the various collections of clavier pieces and odes, such as the *Musikalische Allerlei* of 1760, and other similar works edited by F. W. Marpurg. Twelve clavier sonatas, their style resembling that of Emanuel Bach, were published in two parts as op. 1 and op. 2 by Schmid of Nuremberg, and six of them reappeared in London. A large number of clavier concertos and other works, including a serenata, ' Il sogno di Scipione,' performed at Berlin before the King in 1746, exist in MS. Nichelmann is also known as the author of a treatise on the nature of melody (*Die Melodie nach ihrem Wesen*, etc.) published in 1755, which provoked some controversy. The six sonatas forming op. 2, and other pieces, are reprinted in the ' Trésor des pianistes.'   J. R. M.

NICHOLL, HORACE WADHAM (*b.* Tipton, near Birmingham, Mar. 17, 1848 ; *d.* New York, Mar. 10, 1922) (a descendant of the founder of Wadham College, Oxford), was taught music by his father and Samuel Prince, was organist at Dudley, near Birmingham in 1867–70, and at Stoke - on - Trent, 1868–70. While at the latter place he was persuaded to go to Pittsburg, where he became organist of St. Paul's Cathedral, and afterwards at a Presbyterian church. He lived in New York from 1878 onwards, for two years as organist of St. Mark's. As a composer he united great contrapuntal skill with a modern taste ; his organ pieces include twelve symphonic preludes and fugues, a symphonic poem called ' Life,' in six movements, and works in various forms. Among his most important compositions in other forms are a cycle of four oratorios (1880–1890), ' Adam,' ' Abraham,' ' Isaac,' and ' Jacob,' all in MS. ; a setting of ' The Golden Legend,' a ' Cloister Scene ' for choir and orchestra (op. 6) ; and a Mass in E flat, also published. Among his orchestral works are a suite, op. 3, symphonic fantasias, opp. 5 and 7 ; a symphony in G minor, ' The Nation's Mourning,' op. 8 ; another in C, op. 12 ; symphonic poems, ' Tartarus,' op. 11, and ' Hamlet,' op.

14, and a ' scherzo-fugue ' for small orchestra, op. 15. Besides these there are numerous pianoforte pieces, songs, anthems, etc., and some chamber music and text-books. (*Baker.*)
                                                            M.

NICHOLLS, AGNES (*b.* Cheltenham, July 14, 1877), a distinguished soprano singer.
In 1894 she gained a scholarship at the R.C.M., and studied singing there six years under Visetti. During this period she made her débuts on the stage at the Lyceum Theatre, Nov. 20, 1895, as the heroine on the revival of Purcell's ' Dido and Æneas,' and Dec. 11, 1896, as Anne Page, on the production in English of Verdi's ' Falstaff.' In 1897 she sang at the Gloucester Festival. As a student, she sang thrice before Queen Victoria, as Javotte at a private performance at Windsor of Delibes's ' Le Roi l'a dit,' in the ' Hymn of Praise ' on Jubilee Sunday, 1897, with Albani and Lloyd, and in 1899, the principal soprano music in ' Elijah,' on both these latter occasions at St. George's Chapel, under Sir W. Parratt. On leaving the College she had further vocal instruction from John Acton of Manchester. On May 14, 1901, she made her début at Covent Garden as the Dewman in ' Hänsel und Gretel,' and was re-engaged there in 1904–08. She sang the parts of Sieglinde (' The Valkyrie ') and Brunnhilde (' Siegfried ') in the first production under Richter of ' The Ring ' in English (Feb. 1908). Her career in opera has been intermittent but was continued with distinction in Beecham's and Denhof's companies, and in the British National Opera Company, of which she was one of the first directors. But it is as a concert and oratorio singer that she has established her highest reputation ; she has sung at all the principal festivals, the Richter concerts in London and Manchester, the London festivals under Weingartner, the Royal Choral Society, etc. The soprano parts of many of Parry's choral works were written for her and the tenth book of his ' English Lyrics ' (high soprano songs demanding that purity of tone and style for which she is famous) is dedicated to her. She sang the part of the Blessed Virgin in the first production of Elgar's ' The Kingdom,' and it is among her most beautiful performances. She appeared at the Cincinnati Festival and at the Jubilee Concerts at the Crystal Palace in 1904. On July 15 of the same year she married Hamilton HARTY (*q.v.*).
                                     A. C. ; addns. C.

NICHOLSON, CHARLES (*b.* Liverpool, 1795 ; *d.* London, Mar. 26, 1837), son of a flute-player, became the most eminent of English flautists. After performing in the orchestras of Drury Lane and Covent Garden he was engaged, about 1823, as principal flute at the Opera, the Philharmonic Society, the country festivals, etc. His playing was remarkable for purity and brilliance of tone and neatness of execution, and his admirable manner of performing an adagio. He published a flute preceptor and numerous concertos, fantasias, solos and other pieces for his instrument.   w. h. h.

NICHOLSON, Richard (d. 1639), English organist and composer. On Jan. 23, 1595, he became instructor of the choristers and probably organist of Magdalen College, Oxford. He resigned this post in the year of his death. He graduated Mus.B. Feb. 1596, and in 1626 became the first University Professor of Music at Oxford under Dr. William Heyther's foundation. One motet and 3 anthems by him, all for 5 voices, are in B.M. Add. MSS. 17,797. These are :

'Cantate domino'; 'Come, Holy Ghost'; 'O Lord, of whom I do depend'; 'O Lord, turne not away the face.'

Two other anthems, also for 5 voices, 'O pray for the peace' and 'When Jesus sat at meat,' are in Bodl. Mus. Sch. D 212-6. A pavan for 5 viols by him is in R.C.M. 1145. Nicholson contributed a 5-part madrigal, 'Sing, Shepherds all,' to the 'Triumphes of Oriana' (1601). B.M. Add. MSS. 17,797 also contains 13 5-part madrigals, of which 9 are by Nicholson ; the remaining 4 are anonymous, but are probably his also. Nicholson's most interesting composition, however, is a setting of a dialogue 'Joane, quoth John,' apparently for 3 voices, the treble and bassus partbooks of which were once in the library of Carlisle Cathedral, but are now in the possession of J. W. Brown of Carlisle. The poem derived from some of the many 16th-century popular fragments based on the line 'I cannot come every day to woo' treats of the wooing of Joane and John, and is in 11 distinct sections. As, however, they all treat of the same subject and are set consecutively, the series is claimed by J. W. Brown to be the first example of a 'song-cycle' which has come down to us (but see Thomas Ravenscroft). Some portions of this dialogue are in B.M. Add. MSS. 17,786-91; but here it is definitely put down as for 5 voices. For further information about the cycle, and an account of how it came to be composed, see an article by J. W. Brown in the *Cornhill Magazine*, May 1920.   j. mᴋ.

NICHOLSON, Sydney Hugo (b. Feb. 9, 1875), organist of Westminster Abbey in succession to Sir F. Bridge, was educated at Rugby and New College, Oxford. He studied under Parratt and Stanford at the R.C.M., and also at Frankfort-on-Main under Ivan Knorr. He became acting organist of Carlisle Cathedral in 1904 and was organist of Manchester Cathedral (1908–18).

Nicholson came to the Abbey at a critical moment when after the war the traditions of the Abbey services, no less than the fabric, were in need of restoration. He devoted himself to that work, has raised the choral performances to a high level, and has shown remarkable skill in organising the music of special functions held there. In particular he founded and conducts with success the Westminster Abbey Special Choir which gives from time to time performances of oratorios, motets and anthems drawn from all the great periods of church music. As chairman of the Church Music Society (q.v.) he has headed a campaign for the improvement of the general level of church music throughout the country. He has done a considerable amount of composition which, however, has held a comparatively small place in a career devoted to executive and administrative work.
    c.

NICODÉ, Jean Louis (b. Jerczig, near Posen, Aug. 12, 1853; d. Dresden, Oct. 5, 1919). His father, a skilful amateur violinist, pianist, conductor and composer, removed to Berlin in 1856. Here the young Nicodé was taught by his father and the organist Hartkäss, until, in the beginning of 1869, he entered the Neue Akademie der Tonkunst, where he studied the piano under Kullak, harmony under Wüerst, counterpoint and composition under Kiel. When he left the Akademie he was able to succeed well as a teacher in Berlin, and also to establish the Nicodé Concerts, at which he proved himself to be a brilliant and attractive pianist. A concert tour through Galicia and Roumania with Mme. Désirée Artôt increased his reputation so much that in 1878 he was led to remove to Dresden in order to become a professor at the Royal Conservatorium, of which Franz Wüllner was artistic director. Here he remained until Wüllner was ejected from his post as director of the Opera in 1885, when Nicodé left the Conservatorium and became director of the Philharmonic Concerts. He held this post for three years, gaining great success, but in 1888 he gave up his appointment in order to devote himself entirely to composition. However, in 1893 he again appeared as a conductor, and on the establishment of the Dresden 'Neustädt Chorgesangverein' he was appointed director.

As a pianist his style was full of warmth and artistic power ; and as a conductor he showed an artistic insight and a genial warmth of comprehension which led him to give interpretations full of breadth and humanity. Among the larger works for orchestra, 'Marie Stuart,' 'Symphonic Variations,' 'Die Jagd nach dem Glück,' 'Das Meer' and 'Gloria,' Nicodé showed a steady advance in power of invention, construction, development and skill in orchestration. 'Marie Stuart' is a brilliant piece of character-painting. 'Die Jagd nach dem Glück' is a 'Phantasiestück' which, although practically a bravura piece, is not at all commonplace. In the 'Symphonic Variations' a beautiful theme is treated with unusual skill. It was in 1888 that Nicodé produced his more important work 'Das Meer,' a symphony for full orchestra, organ, male chorus and soli, the poem by Karl Wörmann. Nicodé's ' Gloria ' (produced 1904) may be called a symphonic opera without voices, for it occupies a whole evening in performance. Scored for a very large orchestra, organ, harps, male chorus and boys' solo, it is laid out in six movements, in which great use is made of a number of Leit-motive, and ' quotations.' His works are as follows :

Op.
1. Six Songs ⎱ MS.
2. Symphony ⎰
3. Two Waltzes.
4. Marie Stuart.　Symphonic Poem (orchestra).　1881.
5. Characteristic Polonaise.　PF. solo.
6. Andenken an Schumann.　Six ' Phantasiestücke,' PF. solo.
7. Miscellen.　Four pieces (PF. duet).
8. Aphorismen.　(13 Klavierstücke.)
9. Two Characteristic pieces.　(1. E♭ minor, 2. G minor), PF. solo.
10. Waltz Caprices.　PF. duet.
11. Die Jagd nach dem Glück.　Phantasiestück (orchestra.)　1882.
12. Two Studies (1. in C♯ minor, 2. in C minor).
13. Italienische Volkstänze und Lieder (orchestra.)　In two books.
　　Arranged for orchestra from PF. solo.
14. Romanze for violin and orchestra.
15. Three Songs.
16. Scherzo fantastique.　(PF. duet.)　1877.
17. Suite for small orchestra.　(Four movements.)　1892.
18. Variations and Fugue, D♭ major.　1880.　PF. solo.
19. Sonata, F minor.　PF. solo.
20. Jubiläumsmarsch (orchestra) composed for the twenty-fifth
　　anniversary of the Berlin Academy of Music.　1880.
21. Three Studies (1. F♯ minor, 2. F major, 3. D minor).　PF. solo.
22. Ein Liebesleben (Ten Poems).　PF. solo.
23. Sonata for violoncello in B minor.
24. Faschingsbilder.　Four pieces (orchestra).
25. Sonata for violoncello in G major.　1882.
26. Ein Ballscene (Waltzer).　PF. duet.
27. Symphonic Variations.　1883.　(Orchestra.)
28. Waltzes and Burlesques.　PF. solo.
29. Pictures from India.　1886.
30. Dem Andenken an Amarantha.　Song Cycle.
31. Das Meer, Symphonic Ode.　1889.　(Orchestra, organ, male
　　chorus.)
32. Two pieces for string orchestra.　2 oboi, 2 horns.
33. Erbarmen.　Hymn for mezzo-soprano and orchestra.
34. Gloria (1904), in six movements.
　　Works for male choir including ' Morgenwanderung im Gebirge,'
　　' Nach Sonnenuntergang,' ' Requiem.'

　　　　　　　　　　　　　　　　　　　　D. H.

NICOLAI, CARL OTTO EHRENFRIED (b. Königsberg, June 9, 1810 ; d. May 11, 1849), eminent composer and conductor.

His home was unhappy, and his education neglected, except for the piano, which he was well taught. At 16 he ran away, but found a protector in Justizrat Adler of Stargard, who assisted him in his studies, and in 1827 sent him to Berlin, where he took lessons from Zelter and Klein. In 1833 the Chevalier de Bunsen sent for him to Rome as organist to the chapel of the Prussian Embassy, and there, under Baini, he studied the ancient Italian masters, without neglecting those of modern date. Towards the close of 1837 he went to Vienna, and became Kapellmeister and singing-master of the Kärnth-nerthor Theater, returning to Rome in Oct. 1838. He then composed a series of operas in the prevailing taste of the day. ' Enrico secondo ' and ' Rosmonda d' Inghilterra ' (1839) were given at Trieste, and ' Il Templario ' (1840) with great success at Turin ; but ' Odoardo e Gildippe ' (Genoa, 1841) and ' Il proscritto ' (Milan, 1841) were not so well received. In 1841 he accepted the first Kapellmeistership of the court opera at Vienna, and remained till Easter, 1847, highly appreciated as a conductor. Here were produced his ' Templario ' (1841, German, 1845) and ' Die Heimkehr des Ver-

bannten ' (1844), a remodelling of ' Il proscritto,' in which Staudigl was much applauded. With the avowed object of giving first-rate perform-ances of Beethoven's symphonies, he founded the Philharmonic concerts, the first of which took place Mar. 28, 1842. A Mass (composed 1843) dedicated to Frederick William IV., and a Fest-Ouvertüre for the Jubilee of the Uni-versity of Königsberg (1844) led to his appoint-ment as director of the newly founded Domchor, and court Kapellmeister of the opera in Berlin, and he gave a farewell concert in the large Re-doutensaal at Vienna (Apr. 1, 1847), at which Jenny Lind sang, and some of the instrumental music in ' Die lustigen Weiber von Windsor ' was produced for the first time. He completed that opera in Berlin, and the first performance took place on Mar. 9, 1849, with brilliant success, which he did not live to enjoy, as he expired of apoplexy on May 11. The opera was given in Vienna (with recitatives by Proch), Feb. 12, 1852, and in London (as ' Falstaff '), May 3, 1864, and long held its place as one of the most popular of comic operas.

Nicolai had a fine collection of Italian and German scores, which he left to the Imperial library at Berlin. Mendel's *Otto Nicolai* (Berlin, Heimann) contains a catalogue of all his works, printed and in MS., the latter being numerous, and including a symphony, a Requiem and a Te Deum. He was an honorary member of the Società Cecilia of Rome, and of the Filarmonici of Bologna. The Tonkünstler-Verein of Berlin erected in 1851 a monument over his grave in the churchyard of Doro-theenstadt.　　　　　　　　　　　　c. f. p.

NICOLAI, JOHANN MICHAEL, chamber musician at the court of Würtemberg, 1669. He composed ' Erster Theil geistlicher Har-monien ' (sacred songs a 3 v. with 2 violins, 1669) ; 12 sonatas, partly for 2 violins and a viola da gamba, partly for 2 violins and bassoon (Augsburg, 1675), one of the earliest works of sonatas for 2 violins and bass which became so popular in the 18th century.

　　　　　　　　　　　　　　　E. V. D. S.

NICOLAI, DR. PHILIPP (b. Mengeringhausen, Principality of Waldeck, Aug. 10, 1556 ; d. Hamburg, Oct. 26, 1608), served as Lutheran pastor at Dortmund and Cologne, was then for a while court preacher to the Dowager Countess of Waldeck, pastor again at Unna in West-phalia, and finally from 1601 to his death, first pastor of the church of St. Katherine, Ham-burg. It was during a severe visitation of the plague at Unna in Westphalia that he wrote and afterwards published his *Freudenspiegel des ewigen Lebens* (Frankfort, 1599), containing the words and melodies of the two well-known Chorals, ' Wachet auf, ruft uns die Stimme,' and ' Wie schön leuchtet uns der Morgenstern,' on which J. S. Bach based two of his most beautiful church cantatas. Nicolai himself was musician enough to harmonise these and other choral melodies for four voices. Winterfeld erroneously supposed the words of ' Wie schön leuchtet uns der Morgenstern ' to have been a spiritual parody of a secular love-song ' Wie schön leuchten die Äugelein,' to which he concluded that the melody originally belonged, but Wackernagel [1] proved the secular words to be of later origin than the spiritual, so that in this case it is the secular love-song which is the parody of the hymn and not *vice versa*. In the melody Bäumker [2] traces resemblances to the old Christmas carol ' Resonet in laudibus.'

J. R. M.

NICOLAU, ANTONIO (*b.* Barcelona, June 8, 1858), Spanish (Catalan) composer, formerly conductor of the Sociedad de Conciertos at Barcelona and then director of the Music School. He excels as a composer for voices, his choral works being conspicuous in any Spanish programme for his technique in writing for the chorus. He has also done valuable work for musical education.

J. B. T.

NICOLETTI (NICCOLETTI), FILIPPO, of Ferrara, where he was living in 1592. In 1605 he was maestro di cappella at S. Lorenzo in Damasco, Rome. He composed madrigals *a* 5 v. (1578) ; ' I finti amori,' *a* 5 v., op. 2 (1585) ; madrigals, *a* 2 v. (1588 ; 2nd ed. 1605) ; villanelle, *a* 3 v. (1604) ; and various numbers in collective volumes (*Q.-L.*).

NICOLINI (*b.* S. Malo, Feb. 23, 1834 ; *d.* Pau, Jan. 19, 1898), originally ERNEST NICOLAS, son of an hotel-keeper of Dinard, Brittany. He was for a short time a pupil at the Paris Conservatoire, and in 1856 gained a second *accessit* in comic opera. In July 1857 he made his début at the Opéra-Comique in Halévy's ' Mousquetaires de la Reine ' ; he remained there until 1859, without any marked success. In that year he went to Italy, and under the name of Nicolini sang at Milan, Florence, Turin and elsewhere, with fair success. He returned to Paris in 1862, to the Salle Ventadour, with better results than before, and sang there for several seasons till 1870.

His first appearances in England were May 21, 1866, at a concert given by Madame Lucca, at St. James's Hall, and on the 29th of the same month at Covent Garden, as Edgardo, but with such moderate success that he did not return to London until Apr. 25, 1871, when he reappeared at Drury Lane under Mapleson, as Faust, with very fair results, and remained for the season, distinguishing himself especially as Raoul. In 1872 he was engaged at Covent Garden, where he sang every year for some time, took part in the first performance there of 'Lohengrin,' and was associated with Mme. Patti in her various operatic triumphs. They were married on Aug. 10, 1886.

A. C.

NICOLINI (NICOLINO GRIMALDI) (*b.* Naples, *c.* 1673), one of the greatest singers of the 18th century. He received a good education, and could write very fair verses, as appears from the libretti which bear his name as their author. His voice, originally a soprano, soon sank into a fine contralto. The first dramas in which his name has been found are ' Tullo Ostilio ' and ' Serse,' set by Bononcini, at Rome, 1694, in which he sang with the celebrated Pistocchi. During 1697–98 he was the principal singer in the operas at Naples ; and in 1699 and 1700 was again performing at Rome. After this he sang in other Italian cities, including Milan and Venice ; and, being decorated at the latter place with the Order of St. Mark, he was thenceforth always known as the 'Cavaliere Nicolini.'

Late in the autumn of 1708 he came to England, drawn hither by the report of our passion for foreign operas, and ' without any particular invitation or engagement.' [3] Here he made his first appearance, Dec. 14, in the ' Pyrrhus and Demetrius ' of A. Scarlatti, translated into English by Owen Swiney (or MacSwiney), the manager, and arranged by N. Haym, who wrote a new overture and some songs for it. In this, of course, Nicolini sang his part in Italian, while other singers performed theirs in English. Steele describes this opera as ' a noble entertainment,' and declares that he

' was fully satisfied with the sight of an Actor [Nicolini] who, by the Grace and Propriety of his Action and Gesture, does Honour to an Human Figure,' and ' sets off the Character he bears in an Opera by his Action, as much as he does the Words of it by his Voice. Every Limb, and every Finger, contributes to the Part he acts, insomuch that a deaf Man might go along with him in the Sense of it,'—with much more to the same purport. [4]

The opera prices were raised on the arrival of this performer, ' the first truly great singer who had ever sung in our theatre.[5] Some curious papers exist,[6] the collection of Vice-Chamberlain Coke, by which it appears that Nicolini furnished that official with a full account of the system on which the Venetian opera was managed, and that he suggested a similar system for that of London. One chief feature was that a subscription of 1000 gs. should be got from the Queen (Anne) ; and on this Coke founded a calculation which led to the remodelling of the opera subscription and raising of the prices, in order to remedy what Nicolini described as the ' annual and certain loss of money ' which our opera had till then suffered.

Though not attracted to London by an engagement, Nicolini had been immediately secured by Swiney for a year. Tosi, in his *Treatise on Singing*, doubts whether a perfect singer can at the same time be a perfect actor ; but Galliard, the translator of that treatise, says (in a note, 1742)—

1 *Das deutsche Kirchenlied*, i. pp. 617-19.
2 *Das katholische deutsche Kirchenlied*, ii. p. 283.

3 Cibber.   4 *Tatler*, Jan. 3, 1709.
5 Burney.   6 In the writer's possession.

'Nicolini had both qualities, more than any that have come hither since. He acted to perfection, and did not sing much inferior. His variations in the airs were excellent; but in his cadences he had a few antiquated tricks.'

Nicolini next appeared in 'Camilla'; and in May he signed an engagement with Swiney for three years, at a salary of 800 gs.; the singer to receive, in addition, £150 for a new opera ' to be by him fitted for the English stage every season, if such opera shall be approved of.' [1]

On June 4 Nicolini had a concert for his benefit at the Opera House, where he continued to sing as before. In 1710, however, he quarrelled with Swiney, and sought, in a letter dated May 18,[2] to free himself from an 'esclavage inquiet et honteux qu'on ne sçauroit non plus s'immaginer ailleurs hors de l'Angleterre,'—his engagement with Swiney. The principal grievance, as usual, was that he had not been paid his due salary; but the Vice-Chamberlain patched up the quarrel, and Nicolini continued to sing at the theatre in 'Almahide' and 'Hydaspes,' the libretto of the latter being his own, or at least edited by himself. In this piece occurred the famous combat with the lion, about which Addison was so witty, while giving the greatest possible credit to Nicolini for his acting, which gave 'new majesty to kings, resolution to heroes and softness to lovers.'[3] On Feb. 24, 1711, 'Rinaldo' appeared, the chief part being created by Nicolini, who had in it many opportunities for displaying his powers of declamation, execution and acting. He played in 'Antioco,' Dec. 12, and in 'Ambleto' (his own libretto) in the beginning cf 1712. Addison says,[4]

'I am sorry to find, by the Opera bills for this day, that we are likely to lose the greatest performer in dramatic Music that is now living, or that perhaps ever appeared upon a stage. I need not acquaint my readers, that I am speaking of Signor Nicolini. The town is highly obliged to that excellent artist, for having shewn us the Italian Music in its perfection, as well as for that generous approbation he lately gave to an opera of our own country [5] in which the composer endeavoured to do justice to the beauty of the words, by following that noble example which has been set him by the greatest foreign masters in that art.'

Nicolini, who took his benefit, on Mar. 22, in 'the Music performed before the Queen on her birthday, and the famous scene in Thomyris, by Scarlatti,' left England at the end of this season (he sang in Dublin in March-June, 1711), and did not return till 1714, when he appeared, June 14, 'for the last time before his voyage to Italy.'[6] He returned, however, in the following winter, for he sang in 'Rinaldo' (revived), Jan. 4, 1715, and afterwards in 'Amadigi.' According to the idea which tradition gives us of the abilities of Nicolini, his part in this latter opera must have drawn out all his powers, both as singer and actor.[7] He took his benefit in

1 In the writer's possession.   2 *Ibid.*
3 *Spectator*, Mar. 15, 1710-11.
4 *Ibid.*, June 14, 1712.
5 Galliard's 'Calypso and Telemachus,' words by Hughes.
6 *Daily Courant.*   7 Burney.

'Rinaldo.' In the following season (1716) Nicolini appeared in 'Lucio Vero,' 'Amadigi' and 'Clearte'; and in 1717 he sang again in 'Rinaldo' and 'Amadigi'—his last appearances in England. We find him at Venice in a long run of 'Rinaldo' in 1718, again in 1723, singing in Leo's 'Timocrate,' and Quantz met him there in 1726, when his singing was on the decline, though his acting still commanded admiration.   J. M.

NICOLO, the ordinary name in France for Nicolo Isouard (*q.v.*).   G.

NIECKS, FRIEDRICH (FREDERICK), Mus.D., LL.D. (*b.* Düsseldorf, Feb. 3, 1845; *d.* Edinburgh, June 24, 1924), was for twenty-three years Reid Professor of Music at Edinburgh. His father was an orchestral musician, teacher and conductor at Düsseldorf. From him Niecks learnt the elements of music and violin-playing, before studying under a local organist and, subsequently, under Langhans, Julius Grunewald and Leopold Auer, for violin, and under Julius Tausch, for composition and pianoforte-playing. At the age of 13 Niecks made his first public appearance as a violinist at a concert of the Musikverein in Düsseldorf, where he played De Bériot's second concerto; and about the same time he became a regular member of the Theatre and Subscription Concerts Orchestra, a post he retained till after he was 21 years of age, when, owing to ill-health, he had to abandon the idea of a public career as an instrumentalist. Meanwhile his general education had been obtained from private teachers, by self-tuition and at Leipzig University, where he devoted his attention chiefly to philosophy, with a special leaning towards psychology and æsthetics, fine arts and history. In 1868 Niecks was induced by (Sir) A. C. Mackenzie to leave Düsseldorf and settle in Scotland, where later in the year he became viola-player in Mackenzie's Edinburgh quartet, and organist and teacher in Dumfries. In 1875 a letter written to the *Monthly Musical Record*, of which Prout was editor, led to a permanent engagement in connexion with that paper, and in 1879 Niecks became a regular contributor to the *Musical Times*. His *Concise Dictionary of Musical Terms, to which is prefixed an Introduction to the Elements of Music*, appeared in 1884, in which year a second edition, revised and corrected, also was printed; while in 1888 his *Frederick Chopin as Man and Musician* was published, a German edition by W. Langhans appearing in the following year. In 1890 Niecks lectured before the Royal Institution of Great Britain on the early development of the forms of instrumental music, and in November of the next year he was appointed Reid Professor of Music in Edinburgh University. There he lectured on and gave practical teaching in music in all its kinds, and in each winter held a series of not less than four historical concerts, and from 1894–96 he led a string quartet. In 1901 he founded a Musical Education Society, and to it is attached a musical circulating library. Before the Musical Association Niecks read many interesting papers, including one on ' The Flat, the Sharp and the Natural,' and another on ' The Teaching of Musical History.' He wrote *A History of Programme Music from the 16th Century to the Present Time* which was published in 1907, and a volume on *The Nature and Capacity of Modern Music*—the latter a philosophical treatise. In 1898 Dublin University created him Mus.D. *honoris causa*. He married, in 1907, Christina, daughter of Sir John Struthers, M.D. It was under her editorship that his valuable biography, *Robert Schumann*, was published posthumously (1925).   R. H. L.

NIEDERMEYER, ABRAHAM LOUIS (*b.* Nyon, Lake of Geneva, Apr. 27, 1802 ; *d.* Paris, Mar. 14, 1861), composer, studied under Moscheles and Förster in Vienna, Fioravanti in Rome, and Zingarelli in Naples, where he formed a lasting intimacy with Rossini. At Naples he produced his first opera, ' Il reo per amore.' He next settled in Geneva, taught the piano and composed melodies to Lamartine's poetry, one of which, ' Le Lac,' obtained great success, and made his name known in Paris, before his arrival there in 1823. Through Rossini's influence his 1-act opera, ' La casa nel bosco,' was produced at the Théâtre Italien (May 28, 1828), but its reception not satisfying him he left Paris and became music-master at the institute founded in Brussels by Gaggia. Wearied of this drudgery, he returned to Paris, and published melodies distinguished for style and sentiment, and worthy of the poems by Lamartine, Victor Hugo and Emile Deschamps, which they illustrated. The success of these songs made Niedermeyer anxious to return to the theatre, but ' Stradella' (5 acts, at the Opéra, Mar. 3, 1837) failed, though supported by Mlle. Falcon, Nourrit and Levasseur. It was, however, revived in 1843 in 3 acts. ' Marie Stuart,' 5 acts (Dec. 6, 1844), was scarcely more successful, and would be forgotten but for its ' Adieu à la France.' Other numbers, however, deserve attention. The revival of the ' Donna del lago ' having been resolved on at the Opéra, Rossini summoned Niedermeyer to his residence at Bologna, and empowered him to adapt the score to a French libretto entitled ' Robert Bruce,' in 3 acts (Dec. 30, 1846). The opera failed, but the introduction of the saxhorn, the eight trumpets in four different keys in the overture and the skill with which various movements from ' Zelmira ' and ' Armida ' were adapted attracted the attention of musicians. Niedermeyer's last attempt at opera was ' La Fronde ' (5 acts, May 2, 1853) —a failure like its predecessors. His true vocation was sacred music. His Mass with full

orchestra, his ' messes basses,' motets and anthems, pure in style, and abounding with graceful melody, are still sung. We have mentioned elsewhere his connexion with d'Ortigue in the foundation of a periodical for sacred music, intended to maintain the old traditions. (See MAÎTRISE.) Unfortunately he knew but little of either the history or the practice of plain-song, and his *Méthode d'accompagnement du plain chant* (1855), hastily compiled, was severely criticised. The École de Musique still known by his name (a continuation of that founded by Choron) ensured for his sacred works an honourable place in the repertories of the Maîtrises of France. There is little ground for supposing, as Riemann does, that he composed the famous song, ' Pietà, Signore ' attributed to Stradella, of which Rossini was probably the real author.   G. C.

NIEDERRHEINISCHE MUSIKFESTE, *i.e.* LOWER RHENISH MUSICAL FESTIVALS, held in triennial turn at Whitsuntide, at either Düsseldorf, Aix-la-Chapelle or Cologne. The originator is said to have been Dr. Ludwig F. C. BISCHOFF (*q.v.*), who assembled together the musicians in his province, and instituted a ' Thuringian Musical Festival,' held at Erfurt in 1811. In 1817, Johann Schornstein, music director at Elberfeld, following the example of Bischoff, collected the musical forces of Elberfeld and Düsseldorf, and gave a performance on a large scale in the former town. The success of the Elberfeld attempt was decided enough to induce several of the most influential persons in the two towns mentioned to arrange two grand concerts for Whitsuntide, which should take place alternately at Elberfeld and Düsseldorf. The organisation of these concerts exacted so much labour and trouble that it was resolved to propose to a third neighbouring city to take part in them, and an offer of co-operation was made to Cologne, which at first declined the proposal. The first four festivals were therefore held at Elberfeld and Düsseldorf alternately.

From the time of the retirement of Elberfeld in 1827, Aix gave in its definite adhesion, and except during the political disturbances from 1848–50, and also in 1852 and 1859, these festivals have since occurred at Düsseldorf, Aix or Cologne.

The fifteenth meeting, at Düsseldorf, in 1833, marked a new epoch in the history of these renowned festivals. For it was on this occasion that the direction of the music was first entrusted to Mendelssohn.[1] Another distinguishing feature was a third concert improvised by him on the morning of Whit-sun-Tuesday, which was subsequently known as the ' Artists' concert,' in consequence of the introduction at it of detached and solo pieces. In 1835 Mendelssohn conducted at Cologne,

1 See under MENDELSSOHN, p. 392.

and on the following Whitsuntide directed the eighteenth festival at Düsseldorf, on which occasion his oratorio ' St. Paul ' was produced. He reproduced Handel's ' Joshua ' at Cologne in 1838, and on that occasion continued his great work of reviving the choral works of J. S. Bach.

At the twenty-first festival, at Düsseldorf, in 1839, Mendelssohn introduced his 42nd Psalm, ' As the hart pants,' and at the ' Artists' concert ' played his second pianoforte concerto. In 1842 he conducted at Düsseldorf, and made its festival memorable by the introduction of the ' Lobgesang,' which had been already performed at Leipzig and Birmingham ; and in 1846, at Aix, for the seventh and last time, he directed a grand selection, when Jenny Lind sang, and produced extraordinary enthusiasm—the occasion being recorded as the ' Jenny-Lind-Fest.' Her singing of Mendelssohn's ' Auf Flügeln des Gesanges ' and ' Frühlingslied,' at the ' Artists' concert,' is described by chroniclers of this festival as producing an effect wholly unparalleled. In 1852 no festival took place, but in the following year Hiller and Schumann shared the direction at Düsseldorf, respectively contributing a psalm —the 125th, and a symphony—in D minor.

From this time the Rhenish Festivals became in some respects even more than previously interesting. In 1855, at Düsseldorf, Mme. Lind-Goldschmidt sang in Haydn's ' Creation,' Schumann's ' Paradise and Peri,' and at the Artists' concert.

Düsseldorf was fortunate enough in 1863 again to secure her services, and the choral selections were conducted by Otto Goldschmidt. An unusual and interesting feature on this occasion was an organ solo by van Eyken, who played Bach's great prelude and fugue in G minor. The following Whitsuntide, 1866, Madame Lind-Goldschmidt was once more heard at a Düsseldorf festival, in Handel's ' Messiah ' and Schumann's ' Paradise and Peri,' etc., Madame Schumann, Auer and Stockhausen being the other soloists, O. Goldschmidt and Tausch conducting.

The conductors of later festivals have included A. Rubinstein (1872), J. Joachim (1875, 1878), J. Brahms (1883, 1884), Hans Richter (1888, etc.), R. Strauss (1896), Julius Buths (1893, etc.), Fritz Steinbach (1904, etc.). The festival held at Düsseldorf in 1902 was specially interesting to English musicians, for the performance of Elgar's ' Dream of Gerontius ' under Buths. (See ELGAR.) The festivals were discontinued between 1915–19.   H. S. O., rev.

NIEDT, FRIEDRICH ERHARDT (d. Copenhagen, c. 1717), is described on the title-pages of his works as being a native or inhabitant of Jena (Jenensis), and by profession a Notary Public. He afterwards removed to Copenhagen, where he is said to have died in 1717. He is chiefly known as the author of a work on musical composition entitled *Musicalische Handleitung*, which appeared in three parts : the first part, published at Hamburg, 1700 and 1710, treats chiefly of playing from a thorough or figured Bass ; the second part, entitled *Handleitung zur Variation*, published at Hamburg, 1706, treats of the composition of preludes, chaconnes and other dance-forms on one and the same Bass. An improved and enlarged edition of this was issued by Mattheson in 1721, containing, as the title indicates, over sixty different organ-specifications. The third part of Niedt's work appeared posthumously under Mattheson's editorship in 1717, and treats of counterpoint and canon, and the composition of motets and recitative. Another work of Niedt's is entitled *Musicalisches A B C zum Nutzen der Lehr- und Lernenden* (1708), and contains a few practical examples. It would appear from what Spitta says that Bach was familiar with Niedt's *Musicalische Handleitung*, and based his own system of instruction in Thorough-bass upon it.   J. R. M.

NIELSEN, CARL (b. Isle of Fyen, Denmark, 1865), composer, was compelled at an early age to make his own way. In his fourteenth year he joined a military band at Odense remaining there until he was 18, when he was admitted to the Conservatoire in Copenhagen as a pupil of Gade. In 1891 he became a member of the Royal Orchestra, which, in 1908, elected him as its conductor, a post he retained until 1914. Nielsen is now principal of the Conservatoire and conductor of the ' Musical Society,' an appointment formerly held by Gade. He has frequently conducted important symphony concerts (often including his own works) in Scandinavia, Germany, Finland and Holland, and he visited London for a similar purpose in 1923.

Carl Nielsen, who in Denmark is considered as the country's most representative living composer, is known chiefly as a symphonist. He has so far written five symphonies (including one entitled ' The Four Temperaments '), the last of which was produced at Copenhagen in Jan. 1923.   E. B.

NIEMANN, ALBERT (b. Erxleben, Magdeburg, Jan. 15, 1831 ; d. Berlin, Jan. 13, 1917), one of the most famous tenors of Germany. His father kept an hotel in Erxleben. He was placed, when 17 years old, in a machine factory, but want of means prevented his remaining there, and he went on the stage at Dessau in 1849, first as an actor of small parts, and afterwards as a chorus-singer. Here the Hofkapellmeister Friedrich Schneider discovered his musical talent, and gave him some instruction. A baritone singer named Nusch taught him singing, and with such success that Niemann soon obtained engagements at Halle and other small theatres. He thus came under the notice of von Hülsen, who called him to Berlin, and gave him the means of further improvement. He afterwards played at Stuttgart, Königsberg and Stettin, and from 1854–1856 at Hanover. Through the kindness of the King of Hanover he was sent to Paris to study under Duprez. From 1866 until his retirement at the end of 1888 he was engaged at Berlin ; and was created 'Kammersänger' to the Emperor. In Germany he enjoyed a great reputation, especially in 'heroic parts,' for which his handsome person and powerful voice eminently fitted him. He played the parts of the Wagner heroes, also Cortez, Florestan, Joseph, Raoul, John of Leyden, Arnold, George Brown ('La Dame blanche') and Chapelon ('Postillon') ; and was selected by Wagner to play Siegmund in the trilogy at Bayreuth in 1876 ; he appeared at Her Majesty's Theatre in the same part in 1882.

Earlier in his career he played Tannhäuser in Paris, on its production at the Opéra on Mar. 13, 1861, when the opera, received with great disfavour, was only played twice. In 1886–88 he sang in German in New York with great success. He married two eminent actresses, first, in 1859, Marie Seebach, and, second, in 1870, Hedwig Raabe (b. 1831). By his first wife he had a son, Otto, also a tenor singer, who appeared in a selection from 'Parsifal' at one of Henschel's London Symphony Concerts, in Dec. 1887.   A. C.

BIBL.—*R. Wagner und Albert Niemann*, ed. by W. ALTMANN. Berlin, 1924.

NIEMANN, (1) RUDOLPH FRIEDRICH (b. Wesselburen, Holstein, Dec. 4, 1838 ; d. Wiesbaden, May 3, 1898), the son of an organist, made a name for himself as pianist and composer. He studied at Leipzig (1853–56) under Moscheles, at the Paris Conservatoire under Marmontel and Halévy, and in Berlin under von Bülow. He became a teacher at the Conservatoire of Albert Fuchs at Wiesbaden. His compositions for the piano included many character studies.

(2) GUSTAV ADOLF (b. Wesselburen, Dec. 6, 1841 ; d. Helsingfors, Finland, Dec. 5, 1881), brother of the above, was a violinist, pupil of David at Leipzig, who settled at Helsingfors as leader of the orchestra. He had a distinguished career there, especially as a chamber-music player.

(3) WALTER (b. Hamburg, Oct. 10, 1876), son of Rudolph (1), besides being a voluminous composer, has done important research which has resulted in a number of literary works on musical subjects. He studied at the University and Conservatoire of Leipzig under Riemann and Reinecke and graduated with a thesis on Ligatures and Mensural Music before the time of Johannes de Garlandia. His literary works include the following :

Musik und Musiker des 19. Jahrhunderts. (1905.)
Musik Scandinaviens. (1906.)
Das Klavierbuch (shortened from *History of Piano Music*). (1907.)
Grieg (with Schjelderup). (1908.)
Die musikalische Renaissance des 19. Jahrhunderts. (1911.)
Taschenlexikon für Klavierspieler. (1912.)
Die Musik der Gegenwarts (since Wagner). (1913.)
Jean Sibelius. (1917.)
Die nordische Klaviermusik. (1918.)
Die Virginalmusik. (1919.)
Meister des Klaviers. (1919.)
Brahms. (1920.)

For ten years (1907–17) Niemann was music critic to the *Leipzig neuesten Nachrichten*. He has also done much editing of music. (*Riemann.*)

NIGHT DANCERS, THE, opera, in 2 acts, words by G. Soane, music by E. J. Loder. Produced as 'The Wilis, or the Night Dancers,' Princess's Theatre, Oct. 28, 1846. Adam's ballet 'Giselle' and Puccini's 'Le Villi' have the same subject.   G.

NIKISCH, ARTHUR (b. Lébényi Szent Miklos, Hungary, Oct. 12, 1855 ; d. Leipzig, Jan. 23, 1922), famous orchestral conductor, was the third son of the Baron Sina's chief book-keeper, August Nikisch.

At 3 he showed signs of musical aptitude, and at 6 began the study of the pianoforte and theory under Franz Prochazka at Butschowitz, whither the family had withdrawn. Even at 7 years of age Nikisch's musical memory was so remarkable that he was able to write down for pianoforte the 'Tell' and 'Barbiere' overtures, after having heard them played on an orchestrion ; at 8 he made his first public appearance as a pianist, and at 11 became a pupil of Hellmesberger, Schenner and Dessoff at the Vienna Conservatoire. At the entrance examination he so distinguished himself as to be placed in the highest class where his colleagues were ten and more years senior to him. For a time the violin chiefly occupied his thoughts, though at 13 he won the gold medal by the composition of a string sextet, the first prize for violin-playing, and the second for pianoforte-playing. In 1873 Nikisch left the Conservatoire ; at the final concert he conducted part of his own D minor symphony. At this period he had also written a violin sonata, a string quartet, and a cantata, 'Christnacht,' with orchestra. In his student days, Nikisch on one occasion acted as spokesman for a deputation (which included Mottl and Paur) appointed to greet Wagner in 1872 ; and in May of that year Nikisch played among the first violins in the historic performance under Wagner of Beethoven's Choral Symphony at the laying of the foundation-stone of the Bayreuth Festspielhaus. On Jan. 1, 1874, Nikisch became an official member of the Vienna Hofkapelle, which post he occupied during the next three years, playing under such conductors as Herbeck, Dessoff, Rubinstein, Liszt, Brahms and Wagner. But his own ideal, held from childhood, to become a conductor, was ever before him, and at Christmas 1877, Angelo Neumann, the director of the Leipzig Opera, invited him, on Dessoff's recommendation, to become Chorrepetitor there. The invitation was accepted, and on Jan. 15, 1878, Nikisch took up the post in the town with whose musical life he practically became, from that day, indissolubly connected. On Feb. 11 he conducted opera for the first time in the Altes Theater, and with such success that in the following summer he replaced, temporarily, Josef Sucher, and conducted ' Tannhäuser ' and ' Die Walküre.' In 1879, on Sucher's retirement, Nikisch became first conductor of the Opera in Leipzig. For the next ten years he busied himself immensely with the production of the best new operas and the revival of neglected masterpieces. In the concert-room, too, he enjoyed many a triumph, among which were his performances in 1880 of Schumann's D minor symphony, when he was semi-publicly congratulated by Mme. Schumann. In 1881 he conducted the Tonkünstler - Versammlung at Magdeburg, when Borodin's E♭ symphony was introduced, and again at Leipzig in 1883 ; and two years later he startled conservative Leipzig by conducting (from memory, a rare event then) a concert of the Liszt Verein in the Opera House, when the ' Faust ' and ' Dante ' symphonies were played complete.

In July 1889 Nikisch accepted a call to Boston, Mass., to take up the conductorship of the famous Symphony Orchestra ; he took his farewell of Leipzig—for a time only, as events proved—in a memorable performance of ' Fidelio.' In America he remained four years, travelling much ; in 1893, his contract there being at an end, he returned to Europe and became Hofkapellmeister at the Budapest Opera, as well as director. These posts, however, he resigned when, being in London to conduct a series of concerts, he received an invitation to become conductor of the Leipzig Gewandhaus on Reinecke's retirement (1895). He held the post of conductor of the Gewandhaus, together with that of conductor of the Berlin Philharmonic, until his death; with the latter orchestra he visited Paris, St. Petersburg, Moscow, Switzerland, etc. From 1897 he conducted the Philharmonic Concerts in Hamburg in succession to Hans von Bülow. In 1902 he visited London for the second time, when as one of the conductors of the London Musical Festival he directed a memorable performance of Tchaikovsky's fifth symphony, a work he was the first to introduce to England on his first visit. He came to England again in 1904, and frequently conducted the London Symphony Orchestra till 1914, toured in America with that orchestra in 1912, conducted occasional opera performances at Covent Garden (notably the ' Ring,' 1913) and the Leeds Festival, 1913. In

1905–06 he was director of the Leipzig Opera. His retirement was caused partly by his ill-health, and partly, it is said, by the parsimony of the treasury in regard to the mounting of operas. On July 1, 1885, Nikisch married Amelie Heusner, of Brussels, a singer of repute in the operas of Cassel and Leipzig. His son, MITJA, is a fine pianist, and his first appearance in England soon after the death of the father created a considerable impression.

In addition to being one of the finest of orchestral conductors in musical history, Nikisch was a superb pianoforte accompanist, as appeared more particularly in his performance with his pupil Elena GERHARDT (q.v.). At one time he held the theory that all conductors should first be violinists, for as such they are trained to use the wrist and so to avoid the apparently great physical effort of the other class of conductors.

R. H. L., addns.

BIBL.—ARTHUR DETTE, *Nikisch* (Leipzig. 1922. *Meistermusikanten*, Bd. i.) ; *Arthur Nikisch. Leben und Wirken* (a collection of contributions from various authors, edited by Heinrich Chevalley. Berlin, 1922). See also *Mus. T.*, 1905, p. 89, 1522, p. 47; and *M. and L.*, 1922.

NILSSON, CHRISTINE (Kristina) (b. near Wexiö, district of Wederslöf, Sweden, Aug. 20, 1843 ; d. Stockholm, Mar. 22, 1921), famous soprano singer. Her father was a very small farmer on the estate of Count Hamilton, near Wexiö. From an early date she showed great aptitude for music, and her voice proved the means of her introduction to Baroness Leuhusen, née Valerius, herself formerly a singer, from whom the young vocalist received some lessons. She was afterwards instructed by Franz Berwald of Stockholm, and in six months sang at court. She next accompanied the Baroness Leuhusen to Paris, and studied singing under Masset, Wartel and Delle Sedie. She made her début at the Théâtre Lyrique, Oct. 27, 1864, as Violetta in a French version of ' La Traviata '; and afterwards appeared as Lady Henrietta, Astrifiammante, Donna Elvira, etc. She remained at the Lyrique nearly three years, during which time she created the parts of Myrrha in Joncières's ' Sardanapale ' and Estelle in Cohen's ' Bluets,' both in 1867. Between the two she came to England, and made her first appearance, June 8, 1867, at Her Majesty's as Violetta, with great success, subsequently playing in the other characters mentioned above, and as Margaret in ' Faust.' The same season she sang at the Crystal Palace, and also at the Birmingham Festival in oratorio. She was next engaged at the Paris Opéra for the part of Ophélie in Ambroise Thomas's ' Hamlet,' in which she appeared on its production, Mar. 9, 1868, with very great success.

In 1868 Mlle. Nilsson reappeared in Italian opera at Drury Lane, with the same éclat as before, and sang the parts of Lucia and

Cherubino. In that year she sang at the Handel Festival. She sang in the autumn at Baden - Baden, appearing for the first time as Mignon, and in the winter returned to the Opéra, Paris. In 1869 she played Ophélie in the production of 'Hamlet' at Covent Garden, and appeared as Donna Elvira to the Donna Anna of Tietjens and the Zerlina of Patti. In the autumn she made a provincial tour, singing later in London, at Exeter Hall, in the 'Messiah,' 'Creation,' 'Hymn of Praise,' etc., and returning to Paris for the winter. In the summer season of 1870 she sang for the first time in England as Alice, the Countess ('Figaro'), Desdemona and Mignon. On July 17 she sang the scena 'Ah perfido' at the Philharmonic, on the commemoration of the centenary of Beethoven.'s birth. From the autumn of 1870 to the spring of 1872 she sang in America in concerts and Italian opera under Strakosch, when she added to her other parts Mme. Abeille in Flotow's comic opera 'L'Ombre.' She returned to Drury Lane in the summer of 1872, and on July 27 was married at Westminster Abbey to Auguste Rouzeaud of Paris (d. Feb. 22, 1882). From 1872–77 Madame Nilsson sang every season in Italian opera at Drury Lane and Her Majesty's, creating Edith in Balfe's 'Talismano,' June 18, 1874, and Elsa on the production of 'Lohengrin' at Drury Lane in 1875, a part which she had previously played in America. She paid a second visit to America for the winter seasons of 1873–74; in 1876 she made a tour in Scandinavia with remarkable success. In 1877, and in 1879–81, she sang at Her Majesty's Theatre, singing the part of Helen in Boito's 'Mefistofele' in the first performance of that work in England, July 6, 1880. She toured in opera and concerts in Russia, Spain, Vienna, America and Sweden about the same period, and married Count Casa di Miranda in Mar. 1887. On June 20, 1888, she gave the second of her farewell concerts, and definitely retired from the professional career, giving her services once more at what was presumed to be Sims Reeves's final retirement in the same hall, May 11, 1891.

Her voice was of moderate power, great sweetness, brilliancy, and evenness in all the register, the compass being about two and a half octaves, from g to d'''.[1] During her earlier seasons her success was helped by a certain naïveté of look and manner which was very charming.   A. C.

BIBL.—CARLSSON BEYRON, *Kristina Nilsson Grevinna de Casa Miranda. Minnen och upplevelser upptecknade* (464 pp. Stockholm, 1921); G. DE CHARNACÉ, *Les Étoiles du chant* (Paris, 1869); H. DE CURZON, *Croquis d'artistes* (Paris, 1898).

NINETTA, or THE MAID OF PALAISEAU, see GAZZA LADRA.

NINTH. The compound intervals called

[1] It was formerly nearly three octaves, but she spared the higher part on the advice of Rossini, on account of the great strain.

ninths exceed the octave either by a tone or a semitone ; if the former the ninth is called 'major,' if the latter it is called 'minor.' (See INTERVALS ; HARMONY.)

NISARD, THEODORE (real name, Théodule Elzéar Xavier Normand) (b. Quaregnon, Belgium, Jan. 27, 1812; d. Jacqueville, Seine-et-Marne, Feb. 29, 1888), was ordained priest in 1835, and in 1842 became 2nd organist at St. Germain - des - Prés, in Paris, and was employed by a large ecclesiastical bookseller to edit books of plain - song. Being naturally of a controversial turn of mind, he published many pamphlets on questions connected with musical archæology ; but these are of less value than his edition of Dom Jumilhac's treatise on *La Science et la pratique du plain-chant*, from which he extracted his pamphlet *De la notation proportionnelle du moyen âge* (Paris, 1847); his *Études sur les anciennes notations musicales de l'Europe* (no date), directed against Fétis ; and finally his remarkable articles in d'Ortigue's *Dictionnaire liturgique, historique, et pratique du plain-chant*, etc. (1854). Many other titles are given in *Riemann*.

BIBL.—*Tribune de Saint Gervais*, 1899; P. AUBRY, *Les Papiers &c., Th. Nisard*.

NISSEN, ERIKA LIE-, see LIE-NISSEN.

NISSEN, GEORG NICOLAUS VON, Staatsrath of Denmark (b. Hadersleben, Denmark, Jan, 22, 1761 ; d. Salzburg, Mar. 24, 1826). When chargé-d'affaires at Vienna in 1797 he made the acquaintance of Mozart's widow, assisted her in regulating her embarrassed affairs, and in 1809 married her. Retiring from official life in 1820, he settled in Salzburg. His biography of Mozart, compiled from the mass of documents then in existence, and from the recollections of his wife and Mozart's sister, was published after his death by his widow, with preface by Dr. Feuerstein of Pirna, and 'Anhang' (published by Breitkopf & Härtel, with second and cheap edition by G. Senff, Leipzig, 1828).   C. F. P.

NIVERS, GUILLAUME GABRIEL (b. near Melun, c. 1617 ; d. Paris ?, after 1701), pupil of Chambonnières ; organist of St. Sulpice, 1640 ; organist to the King and music-master of the Queen, 1667. His book *La Gamme du si ; nouvelle méthode pour apprendre à chanter sans muances* (4 editions between 1646–96) was mainly responsible for the final abolition of solmisation. Several other theoretical works are in Q.-L. He composed motets and other church music, lute pieces and 3 books of organ pieces, published in modern edition by Vervoitte (*Riemann* ; Fétis ; Q.-L.).

NIXON, (1) HENRY GEORGE (b. Winchester, Feb. 20, 1796 ; d. Southwark, 1849), was successively organist at St. George's Chapel, London Road, 1817–20 ; at Warwick Street Chapel, 1820–36 ; at St. Andrew's Roman

LIII

Photo, C. Reutlinger

NILSSON

LUCCA

From the Title-page of the ' Pauline Waltz'

Photo, H. J. Whitlock

TIETJENS

Photo, C. Reutlinger

PATTI

Catholic Chapel, Glasgow, 1836–39 ; and finally at St. George's (R.C.) Cathedral, Southwark, in 1839, which post he held until his death from cholera. His compositions include five masses, a Te Deum, ' Respice Victimae Paschali,' ' Dominus regnavit'; a cantata written for Malibran ; Vespers for every festival in the year, many of them published after his death in two-folio volumes, besides pianoforte solos and songs. He married in 1818 Caroline Melissa Danby, the daughter of John Danby, the glee composer, who died in 1857, and by whom he had thirteen children ; among them were :

(2) JAMES CASSANA (1823–42), a violinist.

(3) HENRY COTTER, the fourth son (b. London, 1842), who was taught music and the organ by Deval of Hull, Henry Smart, Dr. Steggall and G. A. Macfarren. He was successively organist at churches of various denominations at Hull, Woolwich, Blackheath, Spanish Place and St. Leonard's, where he officiated from 1872–77, being also the local representative of the R.A.M. He received the degree of Mus.B. at Cambridge in 1876. His compositions include a sonata for piano and violin, played by himself and Henry Blagrove in 1871 ; a pianoforte trio, first prize Trinity College, London, in 1880 ; sonata for pianoforte and violoncello ; symphonic poem ' Palamon and Arcite,' overture, ' Titania ' (Cowen's Concerts, Dec. 18, 1880); Concertstück for piano and orchestra ; madrigals, partsongs and songs, etc.   A. C.

NOBLE, THOMAS TERTIUS (b. Bath, May 5, 1867), English organist.

In 1881 an old friend, one of the minor canons of Gloucester Cathedral, who had been appointed rector of All Saints, Colchester, gave Noble his first organ appointment, took him to live in his house, and superintended his general as well as his musical education. He was given further lessons in organ-playing and theory by Edwin Nunn of Ipswich. Early in 1886 he entered the R.C.M., coming to London twice a week for his lessons ; studying with Parratt, Bridge and Stanford. He gained an exhibition soon after entering, and a scholarship in the following year. On the completion of his studies he joined the teaching staff. In 1889 he left Colchester to take the place of organist at St. John's, Wilton Road, S.W., and soon afterwards became assistant organist to Stanford at Trinity College, Cambridge, 1890–92. In 1892 he was appointed organist and choirmaster at Ely Cathedral, and, in 1898, organist of York Minster, a post he filled with great distinction till 1912, when he accepted that of St. Thomas's Church on Fifth Avenue, New York.

Meantime, in 1899 he founded the York Symphony Orchestra, in 1901 he became conductor of the York Musical Society, and in 1906 was appointed conductor of the Hovingham Festival (where his ' Birthday Greeting to Joachim ' had been performed) in succession to Canon T. P. Pemberton, the founder. He was made an honorary fellow of the R.C.O. in 1905, and was Master of the Music and conductor of the York Pageant in 1909.

The post which he went to New York to fill was one of great importance. St. Thomas's had just been rebuilt on a new site. One of the finest Gothic churches in the city, it had been designed to reproduce the conditions of the English cathedral service. It was Noble's task to establish the musical traditions ; a magnificent organ was installed under his supervision, a choir school founded, and under his direction the musical services have been maintained at a high level. His principal compositions have been in the direction of church music ; he has written three full Morning and Evening Services, an Evening Service in G minor, Communion Services in A and F and one for female voices ; one of the Communion Services has accompaniment for organ, wind instruments and brass instruments and drums ; nine unaccompanied anthems and an eight-part motet. Many shorter church compositions, such as offertory sentences, etc., a vigorous choral work, ' The Sound of War,' a cantata for baritone solo, chorus and orchestra, ' Gloria Domini,' a madrigal, ' Come see what pleasure,' and some songs and partsongs. In a lighter vein he won success at Cambridge with his music to an A.D.C. burlesque, ' Jupiter,' and greater renown with his charming music to the Wasps of Aristophanes, 1897. The music for the York Pageant was a work of importance, and Noble has also written a number of orchestral and chamber compositions.   M. ; addns. C.

NOBLEMEN'S AND GENTLEMEN'S CATCH CLUB, see CATCH CLUB.

NOCTURNE, NOTTURNO. The use of the title ' Nocturne ' for a certain kind of quiet, reflective movement for pianoforte, originated with John FIELD (q.v.), and it was adopted by Chopin for his opp. 9, 15, 27, 32, 37, 48, 55, 62 and 72, in which the mood became of a more melancholy nature, as though reflecting the atmosphere of night.

' Notturno ' originally meant a kind of SERENADE (q.v.), and was employed by Mozart in his three-movement work for strings and 2 horns (K. 286). An entr'acte in the ' Midsummer Night's Dream ' music of Mendelssohn bears the same title.

NOCTURNS (Lat. nocturni, nocturnae orationes. The Night Hours), see MATINS.

NODE (Latin nodus, ' a knot '). The vibration of a string may assume many different forms. In Fig. 1 the string is shown vibrating as a whole ; in Fig. 2 it divides into two equal segments ; in Fig. 3 into three equal segments. These segments, where the amplitude of vibration is greatest, are called Loops (l, Figs. 2

and 3), and the points of rest between them are called Nodes (n).

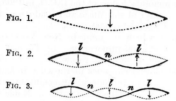

Fig. 1.

Fig. 2.

Fig. 3.

But when a string is plucked, as in the harp and guitar, or bowed as in the violin, it does not vibrate in any one of the simple forms just described, but in several of them at once. The motion of the whole string combined with that of its halves would be represented by Fig. 4.

Fig. 4.

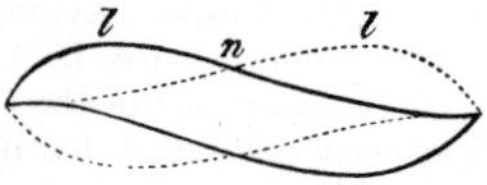

Here the node is no longer a point of complete rest but a point where the amplitude of vibration is least.

If the string while vibrating be touched at $\frac{1}{2}$, $\frac{1}{3}$, $\frac{1}{4}$, etc., of its length, as in playing harmonics on the harp or violin, all forms of vibration which have loops at these points vanish, and all forms which have nodes there become more marked. Thus it is possible to damp the vibrations of the whole string, of its third parts, of its fifth parts, etc., leaving the vibrations of its halves, of its fourth parts, of its sixth parts, etc., unimpeded.

The column of air in an open pipe vibrating as a whole has a node in the centre towards which the particles of air press and from which they again draw back (see Fig. 5, n).

Fig. 5.

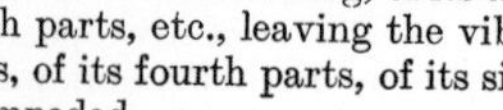

Thus at the node the air does not move but undergoes the greatest changes of density. At the loop (l) there is no change of density but great amplitude of vibration. The open ends of the pipe are always loops, for the density at these points, being the same as that of the outer air, does not change. This remains true whether the pipe have two, three or more nodes, as shown in Figs. 6 and 7.

Fig. 6.

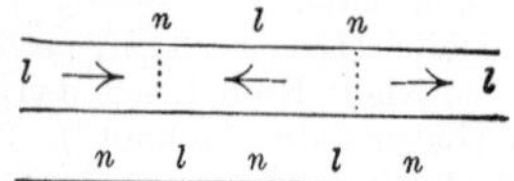

Fig. 7.

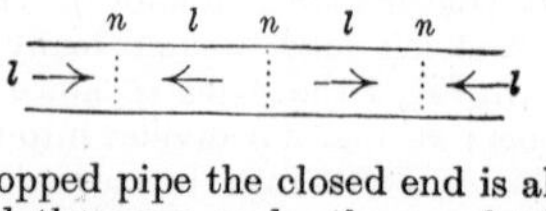

In a stopped pipe the closed end is always a node, and the open end a loop, whether the column of air vibrate as a whole (see Fig. 8)

or divide into segments, as shown in Figs. 9 and 10.

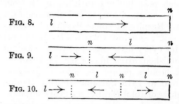

Fig. 8.

Fig. 9.

Fig. 10.

In practice both an open and a stopped pipe vibrate not in any one of the ways just described, but in several of them at once. Here, too, as in the case of strings, the node is not a point of complete rest but of least motion. Chladni showed that sand strewn on vibrating plates or membranes collects along the lines where the motion is least. These are called *nodal lines*, and may assume a variety of symmetric forms (see ACOUSTICS).   J. L.

NODUS SALOMONIS (Solomon's knot), a celebrated canon composed by Pietro VALENTINI (*q.v.*), and described by Fr. Kircher in his 'Musurgia.'

NOËL (Old Fr. *nouel*; Burgundian *noé*; Norman *nuel*; Poitevin *nau*; Ger. *Weihnachtslied*; Eng. *nowell*, *nowell*, Christmas carol), a peculiar kind of hymn or canticle of mediæval origin, composed and sung in honour of the Nativity of Our Lord.

Of the numerous early examples which have fortunately been preserved to us, the most interesting is undoubtedly the famous 'Prose de l'âne.' This curious carol was annually sung at Beauvais and Sens on the Feast of the Circumcision as early as the 12th century, and formed an important part of the ceremonial connected with a certain popular festival called the 'Fête de l'âne,' on which an ass, richly caparisoned and bearing upon its back a young maiden with a child in her arms, was led through the city, in commemoration of the Flight into Egypt, and finally brought in solemn procession to the cathedral, while the crowd chanted a variant of the plain-song melody 'Jesu redemptor omnium'[1]:

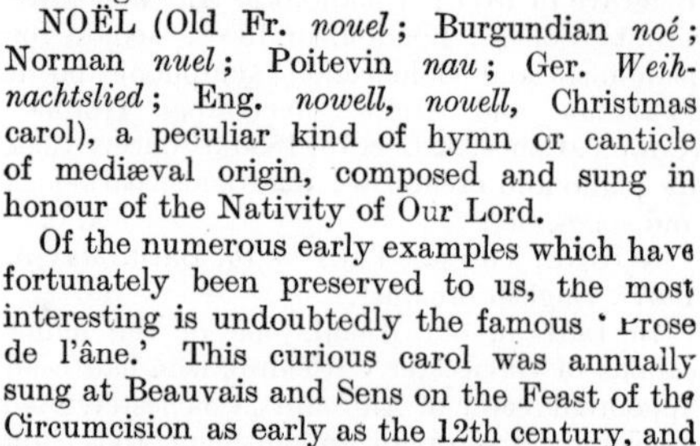

Or - i - en - tis par-ti-bus, Ad-ven-ta-vit as - i - nus,
Hez, sire Asnes, car chantez, Bel-le bouche re-chig-nez,

Pul-cher et for - tis - si-mus, Sar - ci - nis ap - tis - si-mus.
Vous aurez du foin as - sez, Et de l'avoine à plantez.

Hez, sire As - nes, hez!
Hez, sire As - nes, hez!

Scarcely less popular in Germany than the

[1] There is a copy in the British Museum, Egerton MSS., with notes of even length.

'Prose de l'âne' in France were the beautiful carols ' Resonet in laudibus ' (Wir loben all' das Kindelein) and ' Dies est laetitiae ' (Der Tag der ist so freundlich)—the latter equally well known in Holland as ' Tis een dach van vrolichkeit.' Both these examples are believed to be as old as the 13th century, as is also another —' Tempus adest floridum '—of equally tuneful character. ' In dulci jubilo '—a mixture of Latin and patois set to a deliciously simple melody—may possibly be of somewhat later date.

These early forms were succeeded in the 16th and 17th centuries by carols treated, with more or less success, in the polyphonic style. The credit of having first so treated them is generally given to François Eustache du Caurroy, maître de chapelle to Charles IX, Henri III and Henri IV, on the strength of a collection of pieces, entitled ' Mélanges de la musique,' published at Paris in 1610—the year following his decease. But Giovanni Maria Nanini, who died at Rome in 1607, has left us a magnificent example in the form of a motet—' Hodie Christus natus est '—in the course of which he introduces the exclamation, Noé ! Noé ! with striking effect ; and Luca Marenzio published a similar composition adapted to the same words as early as 1588. The same words were set by Sweelinck and many other composers. As Du Caurroy's collection was contained in a posthumous volume, it would perhaps be impossible now to reconcile the claims of the rival composers as to priority of invention ; though the French Noëls bear no comparison with those written in Italy in point of excellence. Still, it is only fair to say that the Italian composers seem to have excited no spirit of emulation among their countrymen ; while for more than a century after the death of Du Caurroy collections of great value appeared from time to time in France, such as Jean François Dandrieu's ' Suite de noëls,' published early in the 18th century ; ' Noei Borguignon de Gui Barôzai,' 1720 ; ' Traduction des noëls bourguignons,' 1735 ; ' Nouveaux Cantiques spirituels provençaux,' Avignon, 1750 ; and many others.

W. S. R.

For a wider treatment of this subject and a full bibliography see CAROL.

NOHL, CARL FRIEDRICH LUDWIG (b. Iserlohn, Westphalia, Dec. 5, 1831 ; d. Heidelberg, Dec. 16, 1885), writer on music and musical subjects. He was educated at the Gymnasium of Duisburg, and in 1850 entered the University of Bonn. From Bonn he proceeded to Heidelberg, in order to pursue his legal studies, which were, however, neglected for musical and literary pursuits. At Heidelberg he determined to make music his profession, but this idea was abandoned in accordance with his father's wishes, and he continued the study of juris-

prudence at Berlin, at the same time receiving instruction in the theory of music from Professor Dehn. In 1853 Nohl entered the Prussian Civil Service as Referendarius, but in 1856 his health broke down, and he had to undertake a journey to France and Italy. He returned to Berlin in 1857, and continued his musical studies under Professor Kiel. In 1858 he finally abandoned the legal profession and settled at Heidelberg, the university of which place conferred upon him the degree of Doctor of Philosophy (1860). In the following year he went to Munich, where in 1865 King Ludwig II. appointed him an honorary professor in the university. In 1872 he returned to Heidelberg, where he resided as teacher of musical history and æsthetics until his death. Many of Nohl's works have been translated into English. His *Mozart's Letters* (1865), *Beethoven's Letters* (1865 and 1867), *Letters of Musicians* (1866), *Gluck and Wagner* (1870), *Die Beethoven Feier* (1871), *Beethoven according to the Representations of his Contemporaries* (1877), *Life of Beethoven* (1864–77), *Mozart according to the Representations of his Contemporaries* (1880), and other works on Mozart and Beethoven, are valuable contributions to the musical literature of the time, and have gone through many editions.

W. B. S.

NOIRE, the French name for a crotchet, or quarter-note.

NOLA, DOMENICO DA (proper name Don Joan Domenico del Giovane) (b. Nola, kingdom of Naples, first quarter of 16th cent.), became maestro di cappella of the Church of the Annunziata, Naples. His publications, appearing between 1541 and 1564, consist of one book of motets *a* 5, some books of villanelle *a* 3, and madrigals *a* 4 and 5. His villanelle were afterwards re-edited by Claudio Merulo in 1567. Several of his madrigals appeared in later collections. Ambros mentions a book of motets *a* 5 and 6 (Venice, 1575), which is not indicated in *Q.-L.* Three of his madrigals, which have melody and good workmanship, have been republished in Torchi's *L'arte musicale in Italia*, vol. i.

J. R. M.

NONE (Lat. *officium* (*vel oratio*) *ad horam nonam, ad nonam*), the last of the ' Lesser Hours ' in the Roman Breviary.

NONET (Ger. *Nonett*; Ital. *nonetto*), a composition for nine instruments. Such works are few in number and are generally designed for a string quartet or quintet (double-bass), with the addition of wind instruments. The varieties of combination are of course manifold. Stanford's op. 95 is scored for quartet, double-bass, flute, clarinet, bassoon and horn. Rheinberger has written for violin, viola, violoncello, double-bass, flute, oboe, clarinet, bassoon and horn. Ravel's ' Poèmes ' are for pianoforte, string quartet, two flutes and two clarinets. (See CHAMBER MUSIC.)

N. C. G.

NONNE SANGLANTE, LA, opera in 5 acts ; words by Scribe and Delavigne, from Lewis's 'Monk'; music by Gounod. Produced Opéra, Oct. 18, 1854.   G.

NON NOBIS DOMINE, a celebrated canon, generally sung in England as a substitute for ' Grace after meat ' at public dinners and on other festive occasions.

English historians are unanimous in describing ' Non nobis Domine ' as the composition of William Byrd ; but it is not to be found in any volume of his published works, though the subject appears in one of the 'Cantiones sacrae' printed by Byrd and Tallis in 1575. Burney tells us that the earliest copy to which Byrd's name is appended is that inserted in Hilton's ' Catch that Catch can.' It is undoubtedly to be found in that curious work, but neither in the edition of 1652 nor that of 1658 is the author's name mentioned ; but on the title-page of Playford's ' Musical Banquet ' (1651) is this canon with Byrd's name. Dr. Pepusch, in his *Treatise on Harmony* (1730–31), distinctly calls it ' the famous Canon by William Byrd.' Mattheson, in the *Vollkom. Capellm.* (1739), refers to it as being Byrd's, and no doubt seems to have been felt on the subject until about the middle of the 18th century, when Carlo Ricciotti published at Amsterdam a concerto, founded on the well-known theme, which he attributed to Palestrina. Palestrina has, indeed, used its opening clause more than once—notably in his madrigal ' When flowery meadows deck the year,' one of the loveliest that ever was written. This, however, proves nothing. He has not treated it as a canon—in which form it bears far less resemblance to his peculiar style than to that of Josquin des Prés. The subject, moreover, is by no means an unusual one, and has even been called, by Morley, ' a most common point.' Handel has used it, in his ' Hallelujah Chorus,' in ' I will sing unto the Lord ' (' Israel ' [1]) and in other places too numerous to mention. Bach has employed it as the subject of an ' Allabreve per organo pleno,' in D (B.-G. xxxviii. p. 121). Mendelssohn has also used the few opening notes in ' Not only unto him '—the last chorus in ' St. Paul ' ; and these notes, phrased exactly as in the canon, will be found among the works of so many composers that it is clear they are looked upon as common property. But the subject is not the canon. It is in the ingenuity of that that the true merit lies. We claim that merit for Byrd. Ricciotti may possibly have been tempted to accord it to Palestrina, on the authority of a very ancient copy, said to be preserved in the Vatican, engraved upon a plate of gold. But it does not appear that Palestrina's name is appended to this copy ; and it is worthy of remark that in the Introduction to Dr. Blow's ' Amphion Anglicus,'

printed in 1700, special mention is made of ' Bird's Anthem in golden notes,' ' Preserv'd intire in the Vatican.'

The canon—a perpetual one, in the Mixolydian Mode—is capable of many solutions, all exhibiting a freedom of treatment not quite consistent with the strict laws of counterpoint. The most noticeable deviations from rule are some hidden octaves, which seem to form an essential element in the construction of the second clause, and a certain changing note in the form of an ascending seventh, which last fault, however, would not appear were the parts made to leave off in the old-fashioned way, one at a time, as they began. The leading part—technically termed the *Guida*—taken at its true pitch is as follows :

Non no - bis Do - mi - ne, non no - bis   sed no-mi-ni

tuo da glo - ri-am,   sed no-mi-ni tuo da glo - ri - am.

The simplest solution of which it seems capable is in two parts, of which the first leads, with the *Guida*, while the second follows, after a breve rest, in the fifth below, singing the B flat in order to preserve the tonality. The chief demerit of this lies in the prominence which it gives to the hidden octaves already mentioned.

In another two-part solution the upper voice, leading with the *Guida*, is followed after a semibreve rest by the lower one in the fourth below, all the F's in the second voice being made sharp.

In a third the *Guida* leads, as before, and the lower voice follows, after three semibreve rests, in the octave below.

The solution usually sung is in three parts. The treble leads. The alto follows after a semibreve rest in the fourth below, singing all the F's sharp. And the tenor enters, three semibreve rests after the *Guida*, in the octave below it.[2]

Another three-part solution may be formed, as follows. The treble leads, with the *Guida*. The alto follows, after a breve rest, in the fifth below, singing the B flat. And the tenor enters, one semibreve later than the alto, in the octave below the *Guida*.

Among the MSS. preserved in the B.M. Roy. Lib. is a solution in four parts. The tenor leads with the *Guida*. The bass follows, after a breve rest, in the fifth below, singing the B flat. The alto enters, a breve after the bass, in the fourth above the *Guida*, singing the B flat. The treble begins a semibreve after the alto, an octave above the *Guida*. In order to work out this solution, the seventh note in the alto must be made a semibreve and the eighth a minim ; and the three last notes in the treble must be F, F, C, instead of B, B, A. No clue can be obtained either as to the authorship or the date of this very interesting MS.

Furthermore, Burney entertains us, on the authority of Hilton, with a solution in which all the parts are inverted ; thus—

Non no-bis Do-mi-ne, non no - bis, sed no-mi-ni

tuo da glo - ri-am, sed no-mi-ni tuo da glo - ri - am.

The *Guida* is here led off by the second voice. The first follows after a semibreve rest, in the fourth above. The third enters, two semibreves after the second, in the twelfth below the *Guida*. We give this solution for what it is worth; but it presents so many crudities that it is impossible to believe it can ever have entered into the composer's original design.   W. S. R.

NOORDEWIER - REDDINGIUS, AALTJE (*b.* Deurne, Holland, Sept. 1, 1868), a soprano singer and a pupil of Messchaert. She was, like her master, a member of the admirable little a cappella choir of Daniel de Lange. Since 1890 she has appeared in almost all European countries as an oratorio singer. She is one of the most distinguished representatives of the new school of Dutch singing, and she is especially a fine interpreter of Bach. Mrs. Noordewier lives at Hilversum, Holland, where she is a well-known teacher.   R. M ^G.

NOORDT (NOORTH), ANTHONY VAN, is only known as being in 1659 organist of the Nieuwe Kerk at Amsterdam. In that year was published his 'Tabulatur-Boeck' for the organ containing a number of the French psalm tunes varied according to the verses, and six fantasias in fugue form. The music appears on a double stave of six lines each with two clef-signatures to each stave, and occasionally there is a part for the left hand given in Old German tablature under the stave. The work has been republished in modern score by the Vereeniging voor Noord-Nederlands Muziekgeschiedenis, vol. xix. One of the fantasias is also given in Ritter, *Geschichte des Orgelspiels*, Bd. ii. No. 35.   J. R. M.

NORCOME (NORCUM), DANIEL (*b.* Windsor, 1576; *d.* before 1626 [1]), son of a lay-clerk of St. George's Chapel, Windsor, was himself a lay-clerk. Having become a Roman Catholic, he was deprived of his lay-clerkship and went to Brussels, where he became one of the instrumentalists in the viceregal chapel. His name occurs in a list of the members of the chapel in 1641. He was at the Danish court (1599), whence he fled with John Meinert (? Maynard), travelling through Germany and Hungary to Venice. He contributed a madrigal, 'With angel's face and brightness,' to 'The Triumphes of Oriana,' 1601. He is mentioned by SYMPSON (*q.v.*) in *The Division Viol*, which contains viol pieces by Norcome. (See copies at Oxford and R.C.M.)   W. H. H., with addns.

NORDICA, LILIAN (LILLIAN), *née* NORTON (*b.* Farmington, Maine, U.S.A., May 12, 1859 ; *d.* Batavia, Java, May 10, 1914), was taught singing by John O'Neill, New England Conservatory, Boston. She first sang in the vocal quartet of Dr. Putnam's church, and afterwards 'in an extended concert tour throughout America, principally with the Handel and Haydn Society and with Theodore Thomas's Orchestra, with unvarying success.' [2] On May 21 and 22, 1878, she came to England and sang at the Crystal Palace with Gilmore's American band. She then studied singing at Milan with Sangiovanni, and on Apr. 30, 1879, made a successful début, under the name of Nordica, at Brescia as Violetta in 'Traviata.' After singing in other cities, Berlin, Dantzig, etc., she was engaged in 1881 at St. Petersburg, and sang as Philine, Amalia in 'Un ballo,' etc. On July 21, 1882, she made her début in 'Faust,' and sang on Dec. 15 in 'Hamlet,' having studied the leading soprano parts under Gounod and Thomas. In the same year she married Frederick A. Gower, and for a time retired into private life. After eighteen months of married life she lost her husband in a balloon accident in an attempt to cross the English Channel. In 1885 she reappeared on the stage at Boston, made a long tour with Mapleson in America and the English provinces, and under him on Mar. 12, 1887, she made her début at Covent Garden as Violetta—appearing later as Gilda and Margaret with instant success, on account of the purity of her style and the richness and roundness of her upper register. On Mar. 24 she sang at the Philharmonic. The same year she was engaged by Harris for his Drury Lane season, where she sang as Lucia, Donna Elvira, Valentine, Aïda, etc. From 1888–93 she sang every season under Harris, at Covent Garden, in a great variety of parts. On July 26, 1893, she sang the part of Zelica in Stanford's 'Veiled Prophet.' She also sang with much success in concerts at the Crystal Palace, in oratorio at Albert Hall and St. James's Hall (Novello concerts), the Handel and provincial festivals, and other concerts. In 1889 she sang in the winter season under Abbey and Grau, and again in 1893. In 1894 she sang Elsa in 'Lohengrin' at Bayreuth. In 1896 she married in America a Hungarian tenor, Zoltan Dome, whom she afterwards divorced. In 1897 she sang again at the Handel Festival. In 1898, 1899 and 1902 she returned to Covent Garden, and added to her repertory Donna Anna, Susanna, Isolde, Brünnhilde, etc. She excelled both in dramatic

<hr>

[1] The registers of St. George's Chapel, Windsor, record the burial of Norcome's widow in this year. (See Fellowes, *English Madrigal Composers*, p. 245.)

[2] Pratt.

and florid singing, though she was a better singer than actress. A. C.

NORDISA, opera in 3 acts, words and music by F. Corder. Produced Carl Rosa Co., Liverpool, Jan. 26, Drury Lane, May 4, 1887. M.

NORDRAAK, RICHARD (b. Christiania, June 12, 1842 ; d. Mar. 20, 1866), a name known mainly to the biographers of Grieg, as he had an important influence on that composer's career. He was a pupil of Kiel and Kullak ; he wrote incidental music to Björnson's ' Mary Stuart ' and ' Sigurd Slembe,' and threw himself with ardour into the cause of Norwegian national music, collecting and editing folksongs, etc. He and Grieg were fellow-workers with this object, and his early death deprived his friend and his country of an enthusiastic supporter. M.

NORLIND, TOBIAS (b. Hvellinge, Sweden, May 6, 1879), studied with Jadassohn at Leipzig and with Thuille at Munich, where he began his studies in musical history and research with Sandberger. He extended them later in Paris, London and Berlin. Returning to his own country he engaged in educational work, and established himself as a teacher of musical science in the University of Lund. He has published many works in Swedish on a variety of musical subjects, including Swedish folklore and history, Allmian Musikhistoria (1920). He has edited the most important Swedish Dictionary of Music, Allmänt Musiklexikon (2 vols., 1916), and is also editor of a musical paper, Svénsk Tidskrift for Musikforskning. (Riemann.) C.

NORMA, opera in 2 acts ; words by Romani, music by Bellini. Produced La Scala, Milan, Dec. 26, 1831 ; Paris, Italiens, Dec. 8, 1835 ; King's Theatre, June 20, 1833 ; in English (Planché), Drury Lane, June 24, 1837 ; New York, Park Theatre, Nov. 13, 1835. G.

NORMAN, BARAK, viol- and violoncellomaker, London, 1688–1740 ; one of the best of the old English school of viol-makers, and one of the first—if not the first—to manufacture violoncellos in England. His earliest work is in imitation of Thomas Urquhart, whose pupil he is thought to have been ; later he copied the Maggini models, especially in the matter of double purfling. His violoncellos and tenors are skilfully modelled ; they are rather high in build, the *f* holes somewhat German in character ; the wood used for the bellies is of good quality ; the varnish is very dark. His name or monogram is found executed in purfling under the finger-board of all his instruments. In 1715 Barak Norman went into partnership with Nathaniel Cross and carried on a joint business with him at the sign of the Bass Viol in St. Paul's Churchyard.

BIBL.—GEORGE HART, *The Violin, its Famous Makers*, etc.; E. HERON-ALLEN, *Violin-Making as it Was and Is*; MORRIS, *British Violin-Makers*; SANDYS and FORSTER, *History of the Violin.*

E. H.-A.

NORMAN, FREDRIK VILHELM LUDVIG (b. Stockholm, Aug. 28, 1831 ; d. there, Mar. 28, 1885), a Swedish composer who has created works of deep and lasting value. He showed an early talent in improvisations on the piano and composition. Already in 1843 a book of 'Songs composed at 11 years of age' was published.

His father's death left Norman poor, but through the kind interest shown him by the Crown Prince Oscar, Jenny Lind and others, he was enabled to continue his musical education in Leipzig, where he remained for four years, studying at the Conservatoire under Hauptmann, Moscheles and Rietz. Through the mediation of Schumann, his first opus, ' Zwei Klavierstücke,' was published in 1851 by Kistner ; this Leipzig firm also later on undertook the publication of his various instrumental compositions.

On his return to Stockholm, Norman, at the age of 30, became conductor of the Royal Orchestra, which post he held till 1879 ; up to the last year of his life he conducted the Symphony Concerts.

But it is as a composer that Norman ranks highest. He was one of the first to show the importance of Franz Berwald's art by following in his footsteps. He wrote three symphonies, four overtures and three sonatas ; also a good deal of chamber music and a number of songs. Many honours were bestowed on the distinguished composer ; he received several orders, and in 1884 the prize medal of the Swedish Academy, for his merits as a musician and author. He edited *The Journal for the Theatre and Music*, and also wrote musical articles and criticisms for various papers. He was a member of the Academy of Music in 1857, and this society in 1910 engraved a medal in commemoration of him. He married in 1864 the celebrated violinist Wilma (Wilhelmina) NERUDA, afterwards Lady Hallé. G. A. S.

NORMAN, JOHN, English organist and church music composer of the late 15th and early 16th centuries. In his MS. *Memoria sacra*, Archdeacon Yardley mentions that in Bishop Vaughan's time (1509–22) ' Mr. John Norman, a Skillful and Learned Musician, was Organist and Master of ye Choristers ' at St. David's Cathedral (West's *Cath. Org.*). Norman was thus a contemporary of Aston, Taverner and Fayrfax, and a Mass, ' Resurrexit,' by him (Bodl. Mus. Sch.) is written out in the same hand as other masses in this collection by these three composers. There is also a motet by him, ' Euge dicta,' in some partbooks at Peterhouse, Cambridge (the tenor book is missing), as well as the score of another 3-part one, in a MS. of Henry VIII.'s time (B.M. Add. MSS. 5665/145). J. MK.

NORRIS, THOMAS, Mus.B. (b. Mere, near Salisbury, Aug. 1741 [1] : d. Himley Hall, near

[1] Baptized Aug. 15, 1741.

Stourbridge, Sept. 3, 1790), was a chorister of Salisbury Cathedral under Dr. Stephens. He appeared as one of the principal soprani at the Worcester Festival, 1761, and Hereford Festival, 1762, and in the latter year at Drury Lane in 'The Spring,' a pasticcio. In 1765 he was appointed organist of Christ Church Cathedral, Oxford; in November of the same year graduated at Oxford as Mus.B., his exercise (two anthems, 'The Lord is king' and 'I will alway give thanks') being performed in the Music School, Nov. 12; and on Dec. 15 was chosen organist of St. John's College. In 1766 he appeared at the Gloucester Festival as a tenor singer, and continued to sing at the meetings of the Three Choirs until 1788. On Nov. 5, 1771, he was admitted a lay-clerk of Magdalen College, Oxford.[1] He sang at the commemoration of Handel in 1784 (where his delivery of the final recitatives in 'Israel in Egypt,' and of 'Thy rebuke' and 'Behold and see' in 'Messiah,' was greatly admired), and at most of the subsequent performances in the Abbey. He sang also at the oratorios in London. In 1790 he was engaged at the Birmingham Festival, but ten days afterwards died at Himley Hall, near Stourbridge, the seat of Lord Dudley and Ward. Norris composed several anthems, only one of which has been printed, six symphonies for strings, with two hautboys and two horns (in the R.C.M.), and some glees and other vocal pieces. A catch by him is in the third volume of Sibbald's Collection of Catches, and he wrote an overture to Purcell's 'Tempest' music, of which a copy is in B.M. Add. MSS. 31,450.

w. H. H.

NORRIS, WILLIAM (d. circa 1710), one of the children of the Chapel Royal at the coronation of James II. in 1685; afterwards a member of the choir, and master of the choristers of Lincoln, his appointment to the latter office being confirmed in 1691. An anthem by him, 'Blessed are those,' was printed in Playford's 'Divine Companion,' and a service and two anthems are in the Tudway collection (Harl. MS. 7340). He composed an ode for St. Cecilia's Day, believed to have been performed in London in 1702; the MS. was in the possession of Benjamin Jacob, and was sold with the rest of his library in 1830, but has not been traced. Norris is supposed to have died about 1710, but his name does not occur in the Chapter Rolls after 1700. w. H. H.

NORTH, (1) FRANCIS, LORD GUILFORD (b. Kirtling, Cambridgeshire, in 1637[2]; d. Sept. 5, 1685), Chief Justice of the Common Pleas, and afterwards Keeper of the Great Seal, one of the best amateur musicians of his time, published anonymously in 1677 A Philosophical Essay on Musick, containing some

curious observations on the phenomena of sounds.

(2) The HON. ROGER, his brother (b. Tostock, Suffolk, Sept. 3, 1653; d. Rougham, Mar. 1, 1733/34), was also bred to the Bar, and became Attorney - General to James II. He wrote several family biographies and other works, but his claim to mention here is as author of Memoires of Musick, a well-written sketch of the progress of the art from the time of the ancient Greeks to 1728. The MS. remained in the family's possession, unpublished, until 1842, when, after being rescued from the shop of a country broker, it came into the hands of George Townshend Smith, then organist of Lynn, Norfolk, through whose exertions it was published in 1846 under the editorship of Dr. Rimbault. The first 185 pages of the MS. contain a treatise, The Musical Grammarian, never printed.

w. H. H.; corr. D.N.B.; addns. F. K.

NORTHBROKE, JAMES (first half of 16th cent.), English church composer. He was a secular chaplain and graduated Mus.B. at Oxford in 1531.[3] There is a motet by him, 'Sum tuam protectionem' (PH.; tenor part-book missing). J. Mᴷ.

NORTH STAFFORDSHIRE FESTIVALS, see HANLEY.

NORWICH FESTIVAL. The establishment of Triennial Festivals at Norwich dates from the year 1824, but previous to this Musical Festivals were held in 1770, 1802, 1809, 1811, 1813, 1814 and 1817. These generally consisted of two or more miscellaneous concerts held either in St. Andrew's Hall or the theatre, and of oratorios and selections of sacred music performed in the church of St. Peter's Mancroft. On these occasions the band was chiefly composed of local musicians, both amateur and professional, led by London principals under different conductors, the most prominent of whom was Dr. Beckwith.

In 1824 the scheme of Triennial Festivals, after having been broached by R. M. Bacon and discussed for some years, was finally adopted on the motion of Philip Martineau, surgeon, of Norwich. A chorus of 150 voices was formed and trained by Edward Taylor, afterwards Gresham Professor, assisted by the Cathedral organist, Zechariah Buck. The band consisted of 110 performers, and the conductor was Sir George Smart. The Festival was attended by 10,087 people, and was a great financial success, the sum of £2411 : 4 : 2 being handed over to the Norfolk and Norwich Hospital after paying all expenses. Thenceforward festivals were held at Norwich triennially until 1911. That proposed for 1914 was postponed by the war, and the Festival was only revived in 1924.

The conductor from 1824–36 was Sir George Smart; from 1839–42, Professor Taylor; from

[1] An amusing extract from the Magdalen Registers is given in West's Cath. Org. p. 66.
[2] Baptized Nov. 2, 1637.
[3] C. F. Abdy Williams, Degrees in Music.

1842–78, Sir Julius Benedict; from 1881–1905, Alberto Randegger; and from 1908–24, Sir Henry Wood.

In 1839 Spohr was present, conducted his 'Calvary,' played his concertino 'Sonst und jetzt,' and with Blagrove a concertante for two violins. A list of all the artists who have sung at these festivals would include the names of all the greatest vocalists of the century, from Mrs. Billington and Braham (in 1802) downwards. Apart from the stock pieces the following may be mentioned: Mozart's 'Davidde Penitente' (1848), Bexfield's 'Israel Restored' (1852), Pierson's 'Jerusalem' (1852) and 'Hezekiah' (1869), Molique's 'Abraham' (1860) and Handel's 'Passion Music' (1866). 'St. Paul' was given for the first time at Norwich in 1881, when the new works were Cowen's 'St. Ursula' and A. Goring Thomas's 'Sun-worshippers,' and, for orchestra alone, Barnett's 'Harvest Festival' and W. Macfarren's 'Henry V.' In 1884 the chief novelties were Mackenzie's 'Rose of Sharon' and Stanford's 'Elegiac Ode.' In 1887 the new works were both Italian oratorios, 'The Garden of Olivet,' by Bottesini, and Mancinelli's 'Isaias.' In 1890 Parry's 'L' Allegro' and Mackenzie's 'Dream of Jubal' were the novelties (the latter had been performed elsewhere previously). In 1893 Paderewski and Sarasate were engaged, the former to play his 'Polish Fantasia' and the latter to introduce Mackenzie's 'Pibroch'; Cowen's 'Water Lily' was the most important new choral work. In 1896 Mancinelli's 'Hero and Leander,' an opera performed as a cantata; Stanford's 'Phaudrig Crohoore,' and a violin concerto by Frederick Cliffe, were the principal new works. In 1899 the three new sacred compositions of Verdi, Dvořák's 'Biblical Songs,' Perosi's 'Passion according to St. Mark,' Parry's 'Song of Darkness and Light' and Elgar's 'Sea Pictures' were given for the first time. From 1902–11 the programmes contain an increasing number of works by native composers, including many new ones in the shorter forms of cantata, choral ballad or orchestral tone-poem. The revival of 1924 was more remarkable for its series of classical masterpieces, including Beethoven's Mass in D, Bach's 'St. John Passion' and Verdi's Requiem. Its English works included Holst's 'Hymn of Jesus' and Vaughan Williams's 'Sea Symphony.'

w. b. s., with addns.

Bibl.—*Annals of the Norfolk and Norwich Triennial Musical Festivals*, by R. H. Legge and W. E. Hansell, 1896.

NOTA CAMBITA (Ital. *nota cambiata*; Ger. *Wechselnote*; Eng. *changing note*). (1) A note of irregular transition; in other words, a passing note, on the strong part of the measure, as opposed to the note of regular transition or true passing note, which occurs upon the weak part of the measure.

In the following example from Cherubini the D is a changing, and the second G a passing note:

(2) Fux applies the term *Nota cambita* [1] to a peculiar licence sometimes known as 'Die Fux'sche Wechselnote' by virtue of which the contrapuntist, instead of resolving a passing discord at once, suffered it to descend a third, and then to rise a second to its resolution. Cherubini condemns this licence as one which should 'neither be admitted nor tolerated in strict Counterpoint.' Fux accounts for it by the omission of an imaginary quaver. The norm of the passage is, he says, as at (*a*) in the following example. By leaving out the first quaver it is made to appear as at (*b*); by leaving out the second, as at (*c*):

Cherubini recommends the form shown at (*b*). The common consent of the great Polyphonic composers justifies the preference of (*c*), and their best defence lies in the exquisitely beautiful effects they produce by means of it. Without multiplying examples we may mention innumerable instances in the 'Missa Papae Marcelli,' and in Orlando Gibbons's full anthem 'Hosanna to the Son of David.' The last-named composition derives a great part of its wonderful beauty from the judicious use of this unjustly condemned licence. (See Changing Note, Counterpoint.)   w. s. r.

NOTARI (Notary, Notario), Angelo (*d*. London, before Nov. 28, 1664), singer and lutenist in the King's private music, London, from 1625. He composed 'Prime musiche nuove, *a* 1, 2 et 3 voci per cantare con la Tiorba, et altri strumenti' (London, 1613).   e. v. d. s.

NOTATION (Lat. *notatio*; Fr. *sémiographie*; Ger. *Notirung, Notenschrift, Tonschrift*; Ital. *annotazione*), the art of expressing musical ideas in writing.

Musical notation is so familiar to us that few are aware of the difficulty of the problems which had to be solved, and the innumerable experiments undertaken for the invention and perfecting of a satisfactory method of recording musical sounds. In early stages the transference of melody from composer to performer is made through the ear only; but as the art develops and increases in complexity the assistance of the eye becomes a necessity, for the memory can no longer retain the growing mass of new compositions. Methods of expressing musical sounds in writing may be conveniently

[1] 'Nota cambita, ab Italis *cambiata* nuncupata.' (*Gradus ad Parnassum*, ed. 1725, p. 65.)

grouped under two heads : (1) the Phonetic, in which words, letters or numerals indicate the degrees of the scale, with the addition of signs to show time values and rhythm ; and (2) the Diastematic, or 'Notation by intervals,' in which the rise and fall of melody is presented to the eye by the relative positions of certain signs called Neumes, or Figures, or Notes (Lat. *figurae, notae, notulae*).

Amongst Phonetic notations are those of (1) the Hindus, one of the oldest in use, consisting of five consonants and two vowels, representing the names of the scale degrees, while the addition of other vowels doubles the value of the notes ; (2) the Chinese, who use characters derived from the names of the scale degrees, with signs for values ; (3) the ancient Greek system of letters and signs ; (4) the Arabs, who divide their octave into thirds of a tone, and write the scale in groups of three Arabic letters or Persian numerals, a survival of the Greek system ; (5) the tablatures, in which letters or figures represented the keys or fingering of instruments rather than the scale degree ; (6) the TONIC SOL-FA (*q.v.*), in which (as in that of the Hindus) letters represent the names of the scale degrees, and other signs show time values ; (7) the Paris - Galin - Chevé (see CHEVÉ), in which numerals are used for the scale degrees.

The Diastematic method embraces the neumes of the Western Church, the notation of the Greek Church (a survival, in a much altered form, of the neumes), the classical notation of Japan, the Mensural music of the Middle Ages, and its descendant, the familiar notation of modern Europe.

The function of a complete notational system is twofold : to indicate relations in pitch and relations in time. There is also a notation to indicate the method of performance, *i.e.* fingering, bowing, etc. ; but this is a separate and accessory development, and except in such cases as TABLATURE (*q.v.*), where the relation in pitch is directly indicated by the notation of performance, the message of notation is directed to the conceptive and not to the executive faculty, or, in other words, it is symbolical and not practical.

For notation to be translated into conception two mental processes must be gone through, recognition and deduction. The brain, presented by the eye with certain symbols, must recognise them, and from their mutual relationship must deduce the corresponding mutual relationship of the musical elements they represent. In the phonetic notations pitch relationships are absolutely represented : the intervals of an unknown melody are as certainly perceived as those of a melody which is already familiar. But in that early form of Diastematic notation which is called neumatic notation, pitch relationship was only approximately conveyed, and the processes of memory or guessing were sub-

stituted for the process of deduction. It was to remedy this deficiency that the Stave, that essential element in our common notation, was evolved ; and it is probable that the continued predominance of staff notation over modern phonetic methods, such as tonic sol-fa, is due to the fact that in the former the exact indication of pitch relationship is reinforced by the pictorial element which it possesses.

THE NEUMES.—All variations and developments of notation are, naturally, determined by the variations and developments of the music which it is its function to convey ; and the neumatic method is the notational equivalent of that style of music known as plain-song. So well fitted was the one to the other that at the present day plain-song retains a specialised neumatic notation, for no other has been found so suitable. The Greek system of notation by alphabetical letters seems gradually to have dropped out of use between A.D. 200 and 500. Boethius and Gaudentius, referring to it, say that the 'ancients made use of little signs, called *notulae*, by which any melody could be noted down.' Boethius knew of no contemporary means of writing music, and the so-called Boethian notation was in reality simply a means of referring to his diagrams of tetrachords by letters of the alphabet, having no connexion with the musical scale. It is probable that up to this time, or even later, the teachers sent out from the singing-schools of Rome and Milan taught the melodies of the church by ear. But with its rapidly advancing development, church music began to feel the pressing need of preserving the purity of its melodies by some means of recording them in writing, and recourse was had to the methods used in rhetoric, in which the rise and fall of the speaking voice was regulated by certain rules, and indicated in writing by signs, called accents, *i.e.* ad cantus, ' belonging to the (rhetorical) song.' A rise of the speaker's voice was indicated by an upward stroke of the pen from left to right, a fall by a downward stroke, and a rise and fall on a single syllable by the junction of the two signs, which thus formed the circumflex accent. The rhetorical accents seem to have originated in Byzantium, and Gevaert supposes that they were first used in connexion with the melodies of the church about A.D. 680.[1] Their adoption was a natural outcome of the singing of the prose words of Scripture, from which metre was absent, and which only differed from rhetoric in that the rise and fall of the voice was regulated by the musical scale. The melodies naturally required additions to the grave, acute and circumflex

[1] A similar system of d_picting upward and downward movements of melody by strokes of the pen is found in the Japanese notation of the 14th century. The reciting note is shown by a stroke like the Punctum of the neumes, while the inflexions are indicated by up-and-down strokes. A new reciting note is indicated by a down or up stroke placed before the first of a series of ' level ' strokes. Signs for ornaments of the nature of the *quilisma, pressus,* etc., together with some other features, make a striking resemblance in the principles of the two notations. This ancient Japanese diastematic notation was in use before there was any known communication between Europe and Japan. (See JAPANESE MUSIC.)

accents : and by the 9th century an organised system of notation had arisen, under the name for the proper accentuation, *crescendo, diminuendo, ritardando*, etc., of the various groups of

1	2	3	4	5	6
Elements	Name of Neume	Elementary Form	St. Gall IX Cent.	North Italy X Cent.	Germany XI Cent.
Grave accent	Punctum	●	●	●	●
Acute accent	Virga	/	/	/	//
Acute and grave accent combined	Clivis or Clinis	∧	⁊	⌒	⋀
Grave and acute accent combined	Podatus or Pes	✓	✓	⌄	♩♩
Two grave and one acute accent	Scandicus	⠂/	⠒⁊	⠒⌒	⠒/
Acute accent and two grave accents	Climacus	/⠂⠂	/⠂⠂	/⠒	/⠒
Grave, acute, and grave accents	Torculus	∿	∿	∿	∿
Acute, grave, and acute accents	Porrectus	⋌	⋀	⋈	⋎
Grave, acute, and one or more grave accents	Podatus subpunctis or sub-bipunctis	✓⠂⠂	✓⠂⠂	✓⠂⠂	✓⠂⠂
Acute, two grave, and one acute accents	Climacus resupinus	/⠂/	/⠂⁊	/⠒/	/⠂/
Two grave, one acute, and one grave accents	Scandicus flexus	⠂⌐	⠂⁊	⠒⌐	⠒⌐
Two grave, one acute, and two grave accents	Scandicus subpunctis or sub-bipunctis	⠂/⠂	⠂/=	⠒/⠂	⠂/⠂
Grave, acute, grave, acute accents	Torculus resupinus	W	ʋ	w	∿
Acute, grave, acute, grave accents	Porrectus flexus	M	ʍ		ʍ
Acute, grave, acute, and two grave accents	Porrectus subpunctis	ʌ⠒	ʋ⠒		ʌ⠒

of neumes, from νεῦμα,[1] a ' nod,' or ' sign.' Each neume was given a name, and there were rules

sounds. No time measurement was required, for the words were sung as they would be pronounced in clear reading, according to the rules of rhetoric.

[1] νεῦμα, a sign, must not be confounded with πνεῦμα, a breathing, hence a long florid passage of plain-song sung without words.

The neumes were originally intended only to refresh the memory of those who had previously important, since they show the proper grouping and accentuation of the sounds.   But

7	8	9	10	11	12	13	14	15
Lombardy XI Cent.	Aquitaine XI Cent. on one line.	Germany XII Cent.	Gothic XIII Cent.	Sarum Gradual XIII Cent. on four lines.	Gothic XIV Cent.	South Italy XV Cent.	Ratisbon 1889	Solesmes 1902

Emery Walker sc.

learned the melodies by ear in the singing-schools; they made no attempt to represent the actual intervals, and hence are in this respect untranslatable; their study is, however, very the numerous photographic reproductions of ancient MSS. published by the Benedictines of Solesmes, and other learned societies, have shown that the church melodies whose structure is known through the square notation on a stave, are the same as those written in the early neumes of the 9th century, whose intervals can thus be known by comparing their notation with that of later times.

The figure shows the elements out of which some of the more important neumes are derived, and the forms they have taken in different countries and at various times. The table (which might be extended indefinitely) shows how carefully the unity of the individual neumes has been preserved in the Gothic and Square notation. A comparison of numbers of photographic facsimiles reveals the fact that the groups of square and lozenge notes found in plain-song MSS. of the 13th century and onwards are not merely haphazard ligatures and arbitrary combinations, but the mediæval forms of the neumes of earlier MSS., and the Benedictines, in their latest editions, have restored to them their proper name of Neumes.

The Punctum appears at first as a dot, and afterwards takes the form of a lozenge, as shown in column 7 ; this shape is due to a short downward stroke of a broad-nibbed pen. When a knowledge of sight-singing became part of the education of all priests and choirmen, a custom arose, which is still continued, for choirs and priests to sing from a single large book, placed on a high reading-desk, the words and music being written so boldly that they could be seen at a distance. The single Punctum then took the form shown in column 13, though it retained its lozenge shape in compound figures. It originally represented a low note.

The Virga, or rod, derived from the acute accent, gradually acquired a head, perhaps at first from the action of the pen in rapid writing ; when the stave came into general use, the head of the Virga was enlarged, and placed on the line or space belonging to the scale degree it indicated. (See columns 11 to 14.) It represented a higher note than the Punctum.

The Clivis and Podatus are compound notes, the component parts of which are rarely found separated. In the square notation the Podatus is represented by two squares placed vertically, and connected by a stem. These two neumes represented respectively a higher followed by a lower, and a lower followed by a higher note.

The Scandicus, an ascending passage, becomes vertical in the Sarum Gradual, but in most MSS. it retains its oblique position.

The Climacus, a descending group, the Torculus (i.e. twisted), a group of low, high, low and its converse, the Porrectus, retain their structural principles throughout : the down stroke of the Porrectus becomes, in the square notation, a thick oblique line, representing two notes, the first higher than the second, while the third note is in the form of a Virga, or Punctum, joined to the lower extremity of the oblique line. The construction of the remaining

neumes can easily be understood by comparing them with those described, and their translation as given in columns 11 to 15.

Space forbids us to give more than a passing reference to the accentuation, on which depend the rhythmical properties of the neumes. It must be understood that neumes, whether in the forms of columns 3 to 10 or 11 to 15, have in themselves no time values ; any variation of time comes, not from the shape of the notes, but from the rules for the verbal and vocal phrasing, etc. The two simple neumes, the Virga and Punctum, take their time and their accent from the words to which they are allied ; the compound neumes are as a rule to have their first note accented, i.e. the first note forms the thesis, and the other notes the arsis; but to this there are many exceptions, which can only be learned from a treatise. The time of the several notes of the compound neumes is that of the syllables of the text; but here again the exceptions are numerous.

Certain ornaments must be mentioned, viz. the Quilisma, written thus in the Solesmes version : ⏗, a kind of mordent, generally occurring on the lower note of an ascending minor third ; the Strophicus (Apostropha, Distropha, Tristropha), representing a sustained sound, sung with a vibrato effect : ⏗ ; the A - men. Pressus, a junction of two neumes by means of a common note, producing an effect of the nature of syncopation ; and the Liquescents, or Seminotes, represented in the Solesmes version by ⏗. They seem to have indicated a kind of mezza voce sound on the liquescent letters L, M, N, R, and became the Plica of the mensuralists.

A complete system of signs of expression is found in many MSS. under the name of Romanian Letters, from its supposed inventor, Romanus, a monk of St. Gall. The most notable example of the system is in an Antiphonary, in the library at Einsiedeln (Codex 121), which is known to have been written before A.D. 996. The signs refer to Intonation, Rhythm, and Intensity ; the following are a few examples :

Intonation : a, ut altius elevetur admonet.
l, levare neumam.
d, ut deprimatur.
Rhythm : c, celeriter.
t, tenere
x, expectare ⎫(ritardando).
m, moderari ⎭
Intensity : f, frangore.
k, clange clamitat.
Any of the signs could be modified by the addition of the letters
b, bene.
v, valde.
m, mediocriter.

It will be seen that non-linear neumatic notation was developed into a system of considerable fullness and expressiveness: and as long as
nothing more was required of it than that it
should suggest to singers the proper execution
of melodies already established in the ecclesiastical repertory it was satisfactory enough; so
satisfactory, indeed, that even when its inherent
deficiencies in regard to establishing exact pitch
and time relationships had brought into being
new systems of notation more satisfactory in
these regards, they were for some time considered as supplementing, not supplanting it.
In this connexion it should be pointed out that
nearly all early notational innovations arose
from a theoretical dissatisfaction with existing
methods; that they were originally products of
the study and not of the scriptorium. The
experiments which we have now to consider
exemplify this in a marked degree. The invention of organum in the 9th century is generally said to have been the spur to these new
developments in notation; it would perhaps
be more correct to suppose that organum on the
one hand, and notational experiments on the
other, were expressions of the fact that music
had reached one point of culmination and was
then entering upon a new stage of its evolution. The first concern was to find some method
of indicating exact intervals. However much
the Greek alphabetical notation had been superseded by the neumes in practical music, some
knowledge of it must have been preserved as a
matter of scholarship; and this was now made
the basis of a series of attempts to evolve a fixed
notation of pitch relationships, either by the
alphabet alone or by combinations of the alphabet and the neumes. An immediate problem
was to fix a convenient nomenclature for the
degrees of the scale, hitherto known by their
unwieldy Greek names. The MONOCHORD (*q.v.*),
the instrument used for teaching the theory
of music, was marked with the letters of the
alphabet, but apparently without system, each
teacher marking it as he liked. Experiments
were made, at first without success, of adapting
the letters of the monochord to the neumes.
Notker Balbulus (*d.* 912) suggests the following nomenclature, showing that the importance
of the modern major mode was already beginning to be recognised, and that the octave had
taken the place of the tetrachord as the basis of
the scale :

A B C D E F G   A B C D E F G etc.

This nomenclature, which is also found in
other treatises, seems to have been applied to
instruments rather than voices.

Two 11th-century treatises—*Musica Enchiriadis* by pseudo-Hucbald, and *Opuscula musica*
by Hermannus Contractus—describe the Dasia

notation, in which the ancient sign for the
aspirate (προσῳδία δασεῖα), with certain additional features attached, is used to indicate the
first, second and fourth notes of each tetrachord, the third being shown by other signs.

The ancient form of the aspirate, ⊢, continued
in use as an alphabetical letter until the 12th
century of our era, and was therefore familiar to
the musicians of the 11th century ; it was also
the ancient instrumental note corresponding to
Lichanos Hypaton, which became the final (D)
of the first mode.

The various additions to the aspirate sign
used in the Dasia notation make it appear
something like the letter **F** in various shapes ;
and it was used in different positions for the
different notes, in accordance with Greek precedent. This notation represented eighteen
notes ; its signs were as follows :

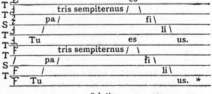

For the sake of beginners it was used in combination with horizontal lines, and the letters
T, S (tone, semitone), the words of the *cantus*,
being written between the lines. This is probably the earliest attempt to invent a Diastematic notation in which the intervals were
indicated with absolute precision:

		es		
T		tris sempiternus / \		
T		pa /	fi \	
S		/		li \
T	Tu	es		us.
T		tris sempiternus / \		
T		pa /	fi \	
S		/		li \
T	Tu			us. ✠

Solution.

Tu pa - tris sem - pi - ter - nus es fi - li - us.

The theorists, however, failed to see what an
immense advance they had accidentally made,
and when the student had become familiar with
the signs of the Dasia notation he was expected
to be able to use them without the lines. They
were then placed over the words, and must have
been even more troublesome to read than Odo's
system described below.

Adelbold, a contemporary writer, being influenced by the Katapyknosis of Greek music,
proposes to use the whole alphabet, to represent
the three genera, with large capitals for ' fixed,'
and small ones for ' movable ' sounds. The
diatonic genus works out by his system as
follows :

A   B   E   G   H   I   M   O   s etc.

An anonymous writer calls Proslambanomenos A, goes up the scale as far as our G in

Latin capitals, uses the round and square *b* for our *b* flat and *b* natural, shows the second and third octaves by small Latin and Greek letters respectively, and the G below Proslambanomenos by a capital Gamma. Odo of Clugny, the inventor of the Guidonian system (*vid. infra*), made an attempt to combine the alphabet with the neumes, after the manner of the Montpellier Antiphonary, where letters from *a* to *k* are placed below the neumes; but this suggestion seems to have been soon given up. In the middle of the 11th century Hermannus Contractus invented a system of indicating intervals thus :

> E = Unison.
> S = Semitone.
> T = Tone.
> TS = Minor Third (Tone & Semitone).
> TT = Major Third.
> D = Diatessaron (Fourth).
> Δ = Diapente (Fifth).
> ΔS = Diapente & Semitone (Minor Sixth).
> ΔT = Diapente & Tone (Major Sixth).
> ΔD = Diapente & Diatessaron (Octave).

A dot above or below the letters indicated, respectively, a rising or falling interval. This notation had the fatal defect that a single mistake in an interval would destroy the whole of the subsequent melody.

Vincenzo Galilei, writing in 1571, says that he found in a MS. of the 10th century, in the monastery of San Salvator at Messina, a notation on lines, the spaces not being utilised, thus :

It cannot be translated with certainty, since the Greek letters belong to no known system of notation. The lines, however, probably represent the degrees of an ascending or descending scale.

The outcome of the experiments was the general adoption of the system known as 'Guidonian,' since it was perfected and utilised by GUIDO D'AREZZO (*q.v.*) (though suggested by Odo of Clugny) in the first decades of the 11th century; and this has remained, with certain modifications, to the present day. Beginning with Gamma for G (whence the French *Gamme* and the English *Gamut*, meaning scale), Latin capitals were given to the note Proslambanomenos[1] and the six notes above it, small Latin letters to the next octave and doubled letters to the third.

thought of, not as a series of octaves, but as a series of Hexachords, or six-note sections. The intervals of each Hexachord were the same, but as they overlapped the B♭ was necessary to the system, not as a chromatic but as an alternative note, thus :

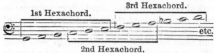

1st Hexachord.   3rd Hexachord.

2nd Hexachord.

Fourth, fifth and sixth Hexachords were the first, second and third repeated an octave higher : thus the fourth Hexachord would introduce a B♮ as against the B♭ of the third ; but the flat and natural B's would be understood as proper to their own Hexachords, and not contradictory, the one being the third note of the Hexachord on G, the other the fourth note of the Hexachord on F. Two different forms of the letter B were used to distinguish these notes in the alphabetical notation : the round or roman b for the flat, the square or Gothic ♮ for the natural. This differentiation has provided notation with the signs ♭ and ♮ ; but it should be remembered that in the Guidonian system they bore none of their later sense of chromatic alteration of pitch.

The Hexachordal system was primarily a teaching system ; and in order to make it easier for singers to learn the different intervals the six syllables *ut, re, mi, fa, sol, la* were associated with the six degrees of the Hexachord.[2] These being invariable, it became possible to note musical intervals with certainty by either alphabetical or phonetic methods.

But the alphabetical notation, however necessary for teaching, was not found satisfactory for recording melodies, since it was inconvenient for sight-singing ; and experiments were now made in another direction. 'Points' were placed at definite distances above the words, and above and below one another. In this system, called by the Solesmes writers *Notation à points superposés*, everything depended on the accuracy with which the points were interspaced ; and the scribes, as a guide to their eye, began to scratch a straight line across the page, to indicate the position of one particular scale degree, from which all the others could be shown by the relative distances of their 'points.' But this was not found sufficiently definite. The scratched line was therefore coloured red, and a second line was added, coloured yellow, indi-

Γ   A   B   C   D   E   F   G   a   b   c   d   e   f   g   or $\begin{cases} \text{aa} & \text{bb} & \text{cc} & \text{dd} \\ \text{a} & \text{b} & \text{c} & \text{d} \\ \text{a} & \text{b} & \text{c} & \text{d} \end{cases}$ etc.

It will be seen that this represents the 'natural' scale, a scale without sharps or flats. Actually the Guidonian scale contained a B♭, and was

cating the interval of a fifth above the first. Neumes placed on these two lines were to repre-

---

[1] The lowest note, and considered as an adjunct to the scale.

[2] For the 'shifting' of the Hexachords, if the interval exceeded the sixth degree, see HEXACHORD and GAMUT.

sent the sounds F and c of the Guidonian alphabet, and the other sounds were shown by the relative position of the neumes between, above or below them. (See GUIDO D' AREZZO.) The pitch of every note within a certain compass was definitely shown by its position on a line or a space, and four lines have continued to form the orthodox stave of plain-song to the present day. Neumes, however, continued to be written without a stave in Germany as late as the 14th century, while staves of one, two and three lines only are of frequent occurrence in 12th- and 13th-century MSS.

When the compass of a melody overlapped that of the stave, it became necessary to alter the names of the lines ; hence arose the practice of placing one or more letters at the beginning of each stave, called *Claves signatae,* our ' Clefs,' since, as explained by several writers, they are ' the *keys,* by which the secrets of the stave are unlocked.'

With the apparatus of the stave, the clefs and the ♭ and ♮ signs the problem of the notation of pitch relationship was practically overcome, and subsequent additions were merely amplifications and adaptations of this existing material. Meanwhile the development of organum and the custom of improvising upon a plain-song (free descant) had been combined into a system of organised descant, the earliest form of true polyphonic composition (cf. CONDUCTUS ; MOTET); and this raised the problem of the exact indication of time relationship. This aspect of notation is distinguished by the terms *Musica mensurabilis, mensurata, figurata,* etc. ; mensural music or ' measured song ' ; or by the phrase ' Franconian notation ' in commemoration of FRANCO OF COLOGNE (*q.v.*), whose treatise upon the subject was the first systematic statement of the new practice.

MUSICA MENSURATA.—The first step was to select from existing material simple and easily recognisable signs for a long and a short note. The square-headed virga (p. 648, col. 6) was chosen to represent the ' Longa ' or long note; the punctum, enlarged into a square or a lozenge, represented the ' Brevis ' or short note. The proportion of the short note to the long was fixed as either two- or threefold. The Brevis was soon subdivided into the ' Semibrevis,' again in the proportion of two or three to one ; and the lozenge-shaped Punctum became the accepted form of the semibrevis, the brevis being represented by a square note. These three signs were further augmented on both the greater and the lesser side, the square head of the virga being extended into an oblong for the ' Maxima,' a note standing to the longa as the longa stood to the brevis, the semibrevis being subdivided into the ' Minima ' or ' Semibrevis Minor,' and graced with a tail, or two tails. Besides these single notes, or ' Figurae,' there were also com-

pound figures of two or more notes, known as Ligatures and derived from the compound neumes, and a sign called the Plica. The Ligatures were brought into conformity with the mensural system by certain fixed rules (see below) ; the Plica did not establish itself in the new notation. It had four figures : ascending long, ⌐⌐ ; ascending short, ⌐⌐ ; descending long, ■ ; descending short, ■ ; equalling :

the ascent or descent of the second note being shown by the position of the tails.

It was with the long, breve and semibreve that the development of measured music was mainly wrought out. It has been mentioned above that the long and the breve were susceptible of a threefold or a twofold division ; moreover, the threefold division could be compounded as two and one, or one and two, *i.e.* ▭ ▭, or ▭ ▭ equalling ▭ · ; and this ambiguity between perfect (threefold) and imperfect (twofold) notes, identical in appearance, was the first problem which the mensural notationers had to overcome.

The first expedient, the system of the rhythmic modes, was not, strictly speaking, a method of mensural notation, but rather a method of mensural structure ; that is to say, it governed the actual music, not the writing of it; but it is properly included in a study of mensural notation, for till it be understood the notational expedients which supplemented and eventually superseded it will scarcely be perceived for what they originally were : a series of experimental safeguards, at first mutually independent, and applied in somewhat haphazard fashion, then overlapping with each other and giving rise to many seeming inconsistencies and redundancies, and only after a long process of shaking down together becoming truly one compound system instead of several single systems in practice at the same time.

The Rhythmic Modes [1] were a quantitative system, based on the poetic metres. As given by Franco, they are as follows [2] :

1. Molossic, all longs : – – –, noted ⌐ ⌐ ⌐
2. Trochaic, long-short : – ◡, noted ⌐ ▭
3. Iambic, short-long : ◡ –, noted ▭ ⌐
4. Dactylic, long-short-short : – ◡ ◡, noted ⌐ ▭ ▭
5. Anapæstic, short-short-long : ◡ ◡ –, noted ▭ ▭ ⌐
6. Tribrachic, all shorts : ◡ ◡ ◡ : noted ▭ ▭ ▭
(Cf. METRE.)

It is clear that if melodies had been constructed in a succession of unaltered poetic feet, the respective values of long and short, long and breve, would have been clear enough ; but this exemplary dullness would be intolerable;

[1] Or moods.
[2] Franco included the molossic and trochaic modes in one, treating the trochee as a dissolved form of the molossic unit, and thereby reducing the number of the modes to five. The above description, however, is the more systematic.

and since the dissolution of a whole into its parts (Molossus into Trochees), or the occasional substitution of one mode for another (Trochee for Iambus), made the value of the long an uncertain quality, the rule was made that the value of a note was determinable by its position.

1. A note was perfect if it was followed by a note or rest of its own denomination.

2. A note was imperfect if it was followed or preceded by a note of the next denomination below it.

Examples given by Franco. Rhythmic translation (values quartered):

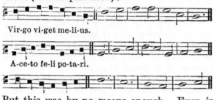

Vir-go vi-get me-li-us.

A-ce-to fe-li po-ta-ri.

But this was by no means enough. Even in the examples given there is room for misunderstanding: for instance, the third, fourth and fifth notes of the third example might be ◠ ⌐ ◠ ·

or ◠ · ⌐ ◠, as the short was either taken to follow the first long or to precede the second. And the Dactylic and Anapæstic modes were even more fruitful in ambiguities; for though appearing to be in duple time they were given a triple significance, the second breve being sung as an imperfect long, to balance with the normal breve the perfect long of the other half of the foot. Here again, if it were understood at the start what value should be given to long and second breve, and if the succession of tripled dactyls or anapæsts was unbroken, the notation of long and breve was adequate representation enough; but the moment another variety of foot was interpolated the notation broke down hopelessly. For example, were the first half of a triple dactyl dissolved into a trochee, the notation ⊒ ◻ ◻ ◻ might be taken for ⊒ · ◻ ◻ ◻ instead of ⊒ ◻ ◻ ⊒; and had other irregularities of dissolved or compounded feet preceded or followed this group, the interpretation of these four notes would be even more conjectural. To remedy this state of things three notational devices were evolved:

(1) The Point of Perfection, or Dot.
(2) The Coloration of Notes.
(3) Time-signatures.

THE POINT OF PERFECTION.—This was a small dot which was placed after the note or group of notes affected, and either on the stave or just above it. In its simplest and best-known form it indicates the perfection or triplicity of a single long, breve or semibreve. Thus used it is most commonly placed on the stave. Its function is to confirm the perfection of the preceding note. Besides confirming perfection, the

dot can be used to confer it. If placed after a note either imperfect by position, i.e. after a long followed by a breve, or imperfect by scheme, i.e. a long in duple measure, the dot added one-half to its value. This was called the dot of addition or of augmentation, and was invariably placed on the stave. These two uses of the dot have persisted to the present day, as, for example, $\frac{3}{4}$ ⊒ · | ♩ · ♪ ♩ |. The first is a dot of perfection, the second of augmentation. These may be called the arithmetical functions of the dot.

The dot could also be used with a mensural purpose, as a sort of bar-line.[1] A dot placed after a long and a breve, or a long and a breve rest, indicated that the long was imperfect and the breve was needed to complete the triple measure. Thus used the dot was a safeguard against a potential redundancy of the mensural material. It could also be used with something like the significance of a tie to show the end of a triple measure when the notes involved were not enough on their face value to make it up. Thus a dot placed after a long and a semibreve showed that the long was to be considered equal to five semibreves, five-sixths of a triple measure.

There was also the dot Divisio modi, used in connexion with the special difficulties of the tripled Dactylic and Anapæstic modes (v.a.). When in deference to the poetic metre the twofold long of the second half of a dactylic foot was noted as a breve, a dot placed before the group of two breves showed that the second breve was a twofold long, i.e. ⊒ · ◻ ◻ = ⊒ · ◻ ◻, or ⊒ ◻ · ◻ ◻ = ⊒ ◻ ◻ ⊒. The position of the dot coming before the two breves, the second of which is to be altered, may seem a little irrational, since in all other cases the dot comes after the note or notes it affects; but the function of the dot divisio modi coming at the hinge of a compound foot (commonly between a trochee and an iamb, hence the name Divisio modi) is that, by showing the triplicity of the note or group of notes preceding it, it also shows that the two apparently equal notes following it need the alteration of the second to convert them into a corresponding triplicity. This conversion of the second breve into a twofold long was known as alteration, or the change from Brevis recta into Brevis altera.

The custom of writing ◻ ⊒ or ◠ ◠ in triple measure as ◻ ◻ or ◠ ◠ persisted long after the rhythmic modes had gone out of use; and if the need for alteration was obscured by what followed (i.e. ◻ ◻ ◠ ◠ ⊒, which might be read as ◻ ◻ ◠ ◠ ⊒ · instead of ◻ ◻ ◠ ◠ ⊒), a dot was sometimes placed after the Brevis altera; but this is, strictly speaking, the dot used in its

[1] It was then placed higher than the notes and generally above the stave.

sense of a point of perfection, *i.e.* to show the perfection of a measure. The true dot of alteration was always placed before the group which was to take alteration.

This completes the mensural functions of the dot, which were to show the perfection of a measure either potentially redundant or seemingly inadequate. One further use of this sign remains to be noted. It could be used extramensurally,[1] and therefore either in perfect or imperfect time, to mark a break or articulation of the melodic flow. Thus used it corresponds to our phrase-marks, either to the end of a slur or to the comma sometimes placed above the stave to show that what follows is the beginning of a new phrase. This use of the dot is of course in direct contradiction to its original nature, which was to assure mensural (*N.B.*—not rhythmical) symmetry. It is, however, common in 16th-century notation, and a simila. change from mensural to extra-mensural significance also marks the later development of the next notational device to be discussed.

COLORATION.—The significant use of colour in notation had already been essayed in the development of the stave, and the same idea was applied to the notes to define their value. At first all notes were filled in with ink, normally black, or red to show change of value. Philip of Vitry (*c.* 1290–1361) says that red notes change what was perfect by position to imperfect and *vice versa*,[2] and a white or empty note is said by Philip of Caserta to bear the same meaning as a red note, if the scribe had no red ink handy. Morley[3] says that the custom of old time was to have four kinds of coloured notes—black full, black void (*i.e.* white or empty), red full, red void. A black void among a dominant notation of black full lost half its value, *i.e.* minim = crotchet ; a red full among black notation, apparently either full or void, lost a fourth part of its value, *i.e.* three red semibreves equalled two black ones. It seems doubtful if red notation ever established itself in a systematised notation ; by Morley's account a red note was on the minus side of value ; on the other hand, if it were considered to be represented equally well by a white note, it is possible that in some usages it may have been on the plus side ; for the custom of indicating an imperfect note by black (black full), as opposed to a perfect note represented by white (black void), was common.

It is reasonable to suppose that the evolution of coloured notation was largely determined by convenience. Scribes availed themselves of the permission to represent a red note by a white one ; the dot was a speedier way of indicating perfection than blackening what was imperfect ;

and the black notation was mainly reserved for the special purposes of indicating (1) changes of note value incident to proportional writing, (2) changes of accentuation.[4] 'There was no real ambiguity in the use of the same notational device for these two different purposes since when the blackening of a series of notes indicated their change of time-value consequent upon the introduction of a PROPORTION (*q.v.*) that indication was reinforced by the appearance of the sign for that Proportion at the place where the changed time-values took effect, and so long as the notes continued to be blackened, they would be understood as being under the influence of the proportional sign. Thus if the Proportion were that of *sesquialtra*, three blackened semibreves, or blackened notes of corresponding value, would be measured against two unaffected white semibreves or their equivalents, either present in another part or, if the *sesquialtra* were universal, mentally acknowledged. The only likelihood of misunderstanding in this class of black notation arises from the fact that, if a minim be blackened, there is nothing to distinguish it from a crotchet. This difficulty was overcome thus : a black minim always represented a minim, so, if crotchets occurred in a blackened passage, they were whitened. Thus treated, there is nothing to distinguish them from minims, but the inconsistency is only to the eye, since the whitening of the crotchet exactly carries out the principle of black proportional notation, which shows the alteration of the time-value of a note by the alteration of its colour.

'Notationers were not so consistent in their treatment of *sesquialtra* breves in black notation. A triple breve in *sesquialtra* is properly noted black with a dot ; but it was sometimes left white, owing to a confusion with non-proportional black notation, where a black breve is imperfect (duple), as against a white one which is perfect (triple). A triple breve in *sesquialtra* is perfect in relation to the rest of the *sesquialtra* passage wherein it occurs, but it is not perfect in relation to the mensural structure of the whole, since it corresponds to an imperfect breve in the normal underlying measure. But though indefensible in theory the white *sesquialtra* breve is perfectly comprehensible in practice.'[5]

A further complication sometimes arises when the scribe in noting a blackened proportional passage wishes to emphasise some specifically triple piece of phrasing : ⌐ ⌐ left white in such a case does not contradict the proportional

[1] Again higher than the notes, and generally above the stave.

[2] And also that in some cases they are used to show that the passage is to be sung an octave higher, a survival of the early stave experiments of connecting colour and pitch.

[3] He gives no authorities for this statement, which is probably his own conflate of the many contradictory earlier rules and exceptions.

[4] The practice of blackening notes was also used in many MSS. to indicate a plain-song canto fermo. No special rules attach to this form of black notation, which may be compared to the practice in modern typography of using a black letter fount to emphasise the antiquity of some rhyme or motto. Another variation of blackened notation came into being with the mid-16th-century movement for a neo-plain-song syllabic style of composition (see MERBECKE). In this also the object was presumably to look old-world : the notation has no points of interest if it be not for the fact that what appears to be a black long ◼▬ is in reality but half the value of the breve figure |◼| .   [5] From *Tudor Church Music*, vol. i. p. xxxviii.

values of these notes, which are still governed by the sign for the proportion ; it merely shows that the notes constitute a triple group, a fact that could be better expressed by the dot.

It has already been said that a blackened note indicates its imperfection or duple value. This principle was extended to the non-proportional blackening of notes to show a duple accentuation. In a passage where the prevailing accentuation is triple, this group of notes ⬜ · ⬚ ⬜ ⬜ by being blackened would be understood as requiring a duple accentuation ⬜ · ⬚ | ⬜ ⬜ | as against the normal ⬜ · ⬚ ⬜ | ⬜ : the time value was unaltered ; the rhythmic significance was reversed.

One other use of non-proportional black notation remains to be noted. If a single triple group of black breve and semibreve, or semibreve and minim, were introduced into prevailing white notation without being preceded by a proportional sign, the effect was equal to a diminution of both note values by half and a dot of augmentation placed after the first ; i.e. ⬛ ⬛ ● ⬜ = ⬜ ⬚ · ⬚ ⬜. This singularly clumsy device is explained by Morley thus :

'The semibreve so blacke is a minime and a dott and the blacke minime a Crochet, as indeede it is.'

As indeed it is : but this will not apply to ⬛ ● = ⬚ · ⬚ ; and if the blackening of the second note is to be theoretically explained, it seems best to suppose that while the first note is blackened for value, the second note (whose lesser value is already determined by the blackening of the first) is blackened for duple accentuation. Morley adds that this method of noting ⬚ · ⬚ frequently led to misunderstanding, the two notes thus blackened being sung as an ordinarily triple proportional group, 3 against 2 ; and there is reason to suppose that in some cases this is the right interpretation, the proportional sign having been omitted by inadvertence. In any case, the interpretation ⬚ · ⬚ only holds good for a single introduction of such blackened triples.

Black notation attained to its most systematic and skilful development in the 16th century, after which it went rapidly out of use. Proportional black notation was the first to be discarded, when the proportions were discovered to be ridiculously old-fashioned and scholastic (cf. Morley's *Plaine and Easie Introduction*, the Third Part); accentual black notation lasted a little longer, though only in certain restricted and conventional forms, and thus used occurs in Barnard's *Church Musick* (1641).

TIME-SIGNATURES.—The essential division of value in measured music has never varied : it was Perfect or Imperfect ; in other words, triple or duple. But the nomenclature and symbolism of the mensural scheme has been complicated by the fact that the relationships of large to long, and long to breve, and breve to semibreve, and of semibreve to minim, have each in turn been endowed with special names and special signs. This is not unnatural, since it must be remembered that the tendency of notation has been for the normal unit of one period to be supplanted by the unit next in value ; in other words, for the fraction of one rhythmic division to become the integer of the next.

The oldest of the mensural divisions was the Moods, major and minor. The major mood expressed the relationship of the theoretically longest note, the Maxima or large, and the long. In major perfect mood the large equalled three longs : in major imperfect mood the large equalled two longs. The minor mood expressed the relationship of the long and the breve. In minor perfect mood the long equalled three breves : in minor imperfect mood the long equalled two breves.

The second mensural division was Time. It expressed the relationship of breve and semibreve.

In perfect time the breve equalled three semibreves.

In imperfect time the breve equalled two semibreves.

The third mensural division was Prolation. It expressed the relationship of semibreve and minim. The division of prolation was also triple and duple ; but instead of being called Perfect and Imperfect, it was called Major and Minor.

In major prolation the semibreve equalled three minims.

In minor prolation the semibreve equalled two minims.

Signs were invented to represent each of these classes of mood, time and prolation. They were placed at the beginning of the stave or in the margin to the left of it. They were as follows [1] :

Mood: Major Perfect.　　　Major Imperfect.

Mood: Minor Perfect.　　　Minor Imperfect.

Time :　Perfect O　　Imperfect C

The signatures for prolation are compounded of the circle and half-circle for time, and a dot expressing triplicity, for the major prolation, the minor (two minims) prolation being shown by the absence of the dot.

Perfect time with the major prolation, ⊙ ; with the minor prolation, ◯.

Imperfect time with the major prolation, ⊙ ; with the minor prolation, C .

[1] The strokes represent the number of breve rests equivalent to the whole note.

This constitutes the basis of the mensural signatures[1]; further additions were (1) the stroke; (2) the retort; (3) numerals. If a stroke were drawn through the circle or semicircle, the notes were understood as having only half their value, i.e. the tempo was twice as fast. An unstroked semicircle ' retorted,' i.e. turned back to front, expressed the same thing.[2] If the circle had two strokes through it, parallel or crossing, the notes were diminished to one-fourth their value. A retorted semicircle with a stroke would express the same thing.

Ex. of diminution   Ⓞ Ⓠ ₵ ℂ Ↄ   1 = ½.
Ex. of double diminution   ⊕ ⊕ ₵ Ↄ   1 = ¼.

It should be realised that these time-signatures expressed no more than an arithmetical scheme of note division. Thus it was possible to employ simultaneously different time-signatures in the different voices (i.e. ◯ in one voice, ☉ in another, ⊙ in a third, the first two equalling each other in the measure, as they contained six minims each, the third equalling a measure and a half of the other two); or in the same voice even, if the composer wanted to show his ingenuity. Bach's signature, ₵ ¹²⁄₈, to the prelude in D ma. (48, bk. ii.) is a later instance of a multiple time-signature.

Numerals were also used; it is necessary that a distinction should be made between the integral figures 3 and 2 sometimes used in conjunction with the signatures for mood and time as an additional emphasis on perfection and imperfection, and the fractional figures which were used to express the Proportions. Properly these were distinct from the normal signatures, but two of them, 3:1 and 3:2, expressing the proportions known as tripla and sesquialtra, came into use in 16th-century notation as subsidiary time-signatures. Tripla expressed the proportion of three to one, sesquialtra of three to two, of the normal unit. (See PROPORTIONS.) As a rule the proportion was only sustained by some of the parts against the normal system of the others; but it could also be expressed by all the voices, when a measure of three semibreves would be sung in the time of one (tripla) or two (sesquialtra). Thus the signs 3:1 and 3:2 came to stand for a brisk triple time. These quasi time-signatures are especially common in the works of the madrigalists (Byrd, further,

employs 6:1, No. 26 of his 1611 Set), either with or without the true time-signatures. Sometimes the fractional 3 alone is given, the integer sign having lost its proportional significance.[3]

Mood, Time, Prolation, Perfection, Imperfection, Major and Minor, led to the construction of enormous time-tables, many examples of which are found in mediæval treatises. Hothby and Prosdoscimus each give no less than twenty-six such tables, the complication of which can be gathered from a remark of Hamboys that, if a larga be perfect, it contains 3 double longs, 27 breves, 81 semibreves, 241 minor semibreves, 721 semiminors and 2187 minims, and each of the notes, perfect and imperfect, is similarly described in detail. In the 16th century we find evidence of a revolt against the complications of the time-tables, which led to the gradual disappearance of the Franconian system and the adoption of simpler and more practical methods of indicating rhythm. The expression ' The Moderns love brevity ' begins to occur in the treatises, and the duple division begins to take on the character of ' the musical time called Natural.' The old rules are collected by Zarlino in his Istitutioni armoniche, 1558, not because they were any longer of practical value to musicians, but ' lest they should be lost.' ' Some musicians might like,' he says, ' to read some ancient cantilena; but if the modern composer should not number his cantilena according to the Moods, he could really say that the matter was of little account, and that he had no knowledge of such things.' Thomas Morley collects the rules in his Plaine and Easie Introduction in 1597, and regrets the loss of the old teaching, saying that ' a more slight and superficial knowledge (is) come in steede thereof; so that it is come nowadays to that, that if they know the Common Moode and some Triples, they seeke no further.'

By the beginning of the 17th century the semibreve was the basis of the time-signatures, as it is with us; the circle still continued to show three semibreves in a measure, but it disappeared in the course of the century, and the only remnant of mediæval signatures now in use is the C, or semicircle, indicating the ' Common,' or ' Natural,' or duple division of the semibreve, and the same figure with a line through it to show diminution.

LESSER NOTE VALUES. — The ' simple '[4] notes other than those already mentioned (large, long, breve, semibreve) were the minim, introduced about the end of the 13th century and mentioned early in the 14th century by Johannes de Muris; the crotchet, mentioned

---

[1] These signatures were not arrived at without many experiments, some of which are referred to by Johannes de Muris the Norman, in his Speculum musicae, written in 1321, where he complains that ' to show Perfect Mood (the moderns) use three lines enclosed in a quadrangle, and for Imperfect Mood two lines in a quadrangle. Some again presume to use M for Perfect Mood, and N for Imperfect, saying that as ◯ and ℂ are used for variations of Time, so M and N may show mood. But others reverse the matter, and use ◯ for Perfect Mood and ℂ for Imperfect Mood. Others use for Perfect Time a circle containing three strokes, and for Imperfect Time a semicircle containing two strokes. Such and many other things do the moderns, which the ancients never did; and thus they have added many burdens to the art, which was formerly free, but has now become like a slave in such matters.'
[2] The doubled semicircle ℂℷ indicates that the note values were doubled. It was, however, a very theoretical signature. It was tentatively revived in Germany as the sign for the four-beat measure called Grosse Allabrevetakt, as opposed to ₵ for the two-beat measure called Kleine Allabrevetakt.

[3] Strozzio, in his Elementorum musicae praxis, 1683, gives a list of proportions in which he makes ³⁄₂ indicate four minims, ⁶⁄₅ six semibreves, ⁸ four semibreves, ³⁄₂ two and a half breves, etc. This shows the proportional signatures in process of emancipation, i.e. ⁶⁄₅ originally meant six falsified semibreves against five normal, not six semibreves absolutely.
[4] As opposed to compound notes, i.e. ligatures.

with disapprobation as a recent introduction, in a treatise (c. 1440) by Thomas de Walsingham (his disapprobation is theoretical: since 'minima' means least note, it is irrational to have new notes of smaller value); the croma or quaver, and the semicroma or semiquaver.

These smaller notes appeared in various forms and under various names. The following table will show something of the development of the 'simple' notes.

N.B.—In the mensural system minim, crotchet, quaver and semiquaver were imperfect notes. They could, of course, be given a triple value by use of the dot; but by system they were capable of a duple division only.

Notes deriving from the Virga

Maxima	
Large	
Long	

These notes could also have their tails going up. The little divisions in the maxima were a way of marking perfection or imperfection. They could also be applied to the large.

Notes deriving from the Punctum

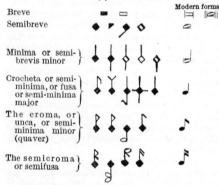

		Modern forms
Breve		
Semibreve		
Minima or semibrevis minor		
Crocheta or semiminima, or fusa or semi-minima major		
The croma, or unca, or semiminima minor (quaver)		
The semicroma or semifusa		

N.B.—Crotchets, quavers and semiquavers were black unless in proportional black notation, when they were white; similarly minims were white except in proportional black notation, when they were black. The tendency with such notes as breve or semibreve was always to write them as empty notes in order to save time.

Lozenge-shaped breves, semibreves, minims, crotchets, etc., slowly gave way to the more rapidly written and more easily read oval and round notes of modern music. In the beginning of the 18th century a new method of saving time and facilitating reading was found by joining the crooks of quavers and semiquavers, etc., instead of writing each crook separately. This had been done in the tablatures some centuries before. Playford, in 1712, describes

notes thus joined as 'the new tyed note,' *e.g.*
 instead of

The corresponding RESTS, called in Latin Pausae or Pausationes, were:

Maxima.	Large.	Long.
Perfect. Imperfect.	Perfect. Imperfect.	Perfect. Imperfect.

	Minim or	Crochet or	Semi-
Breve. Semibreve.	Suspirium.	Semisuspirium. Quaver.	quaver.

A dot was sometimes placed on the stave after the breve rest standing for a perfect breve, and after a triple semibreve rest in the greater prolation. A group of rests, thus,

was a conventional way of indicating that a voice part was to be silent for a prolonged period. These rests need not exactly correspond with the number of silent measures; but the colon corresponded to the close in the other voices which most immediately preceded the entry of the resting voice, and after the colon any rests preceding the entry were exactly given.

Akin to this colon were the REPETITION DOTS placed by the mensuralist on each side of a 'Period' rest, which was double or triple, etc., according to the number of times the passage was to be repeated, thus: :||: :|||: :|||||:. When words were to be repeated a smaller sign was used: :||:. The modern *Segno* 𝄋 was borrowed from the tablatures. The *Presa* ·𝄐· was used in canons, to show where the various voices entered, and the *Fermata*, called in English Pause, ⌒, showed where they closed. The pause was also used both in the tablatures and in mensural music, in its modern sense of showing an indefinite dwelling on a note.

The LIGATURES were survivals of the compound neumes, put into Franconian notation and supplied with rules of mensural value. Any account of the ligatures must be preceded by a general rule, and a general qualification of it. The rule is that one syllable only can be sung to a ligature; the qualification is that ligatures were constantly written in the middle of long melismatic passages, where they can have no significance as regards the words, since several ligatures together with intervening passages of simple notes are all to be sung on a single drawn-out syllable.

Ligatures could be of two or more notes; they were written in two forms—square and oblique:

1. Square.	2. Oblique.

Square and oblique writing could be combined in one ligature. In oblique ligature two notes are expressed — the first where the ligature begins, the second where it ends. Thus in Ex. 2 the notes are C and F.

Ligatures were described as ascending and descending. Ex. 1 is an ascending, Ex. 2 a descending, ligature.

The rules for the mensural values of ligatures are as follows :

(1) If the ligature, either square or oblique, be an ascending one, the first note, being without a tail, is a breve.

(2) If the ligature, either square or oblique, be a descending one, the first note, being without a tail, is a long.

(3) If in a ligature, either square or oblique, either ascending or descending, the first note have a tail downwards on the left side, the first note is a breve.

(4) If in a ligature, either square or oblique, ascending or descending, any note have a tail upwards on the left side, that note and the next are semibreves.

This concludes the rules for initial notes of ligatures

(5) If the last note descends, and is square, it is a long.

(6) If the last note descends, and is oblique, it is a breve.

(7) If the last note ascend, be it square or oblique, it is a breve.

This concludes the rules for the final notes.

(8) The middle note or notes of any ligature is a breve ; unless (a) it be governed by rule 4 ; or (b) has a tail on its right side, when it is a long.

N.B.—Rule 4 takes precedence over rules 5, 6 and 7, i.e. = ▭ ▭ ◿ ◿.

A note having a tail on its right side is a long wherever it occurs, and takes precedence over rule 4, i.e. = ◿ ▭ ▭.

Ligatures can be perfect or imperfect in accordance with the time-signature. They can also be perfected or imperfected by use of the dot or black notation, exactly as though they would be were they written as separate notes.

Franco's definition of ligatures as being *con proprietate, sine proprietate* and *con opposita proprietate* refers them by the position or lack of tails to the corresponding ligature forms in plain-song. A downward tail before a descending ligature is the scribal convention in plain song, hence this corresponding mensural ligature is *con proprietate, i.e.* correct to type.[1]

Towards the end of the 16th century ligatures, except the simple two-semibreve ligature, had almost passed from practical use. How fast they were being forgotten is shown in various MSS. of this period, where the respective value of their constituent notes is added

beneath them in figures. In theoretical works, however, they endured into the 17th century, and an 18th-century example is to be found in Martini's *Essemplare ossia Saggio di contrappunto*, Bologna, 1774.

Measures were called BARS in 1584 by William Bathe, in his *A Brief Introduction to the True Arte of Musicke*, and in 1597 by Morley ; and about this time bar-lines, which had already been used for more than a century in the tablatures, began to take their place on the stave. They were sometimes placed at irregular intervals,[2] and in some instances with such rhythmical fitness that the irregularity would appear to be of musical significance. In other cases, however, notably in some of the early 17th-century MS. organ books, the bar-lines, though irregular, would appear to have no function beyond assuring the eye by a semi-periodic measurement. Bar-lines did not come into general use until about a century after their introduction. Caccini's ' Euridice,' composed in 1600, is barred throughout ; while a book of Solfeggi by Caresana of the year 1693 is unbarred.

Like the other features of our notation, the STAVE passed through many vicissitudes before its general acceptance in the form that we know it. While plain-song has found a stave of four red or black lines sufficient for its needs, measured music, whose whole *raison d'être* was the notation of two or more simultaneous melodies, made use in early times of staves containing lines varying in number from 4 to 15 and even to 25, on which all the voice parts were written. Clefs were given to several lines, and sometimes to all the lines, and even to the spaces. Vertical lines were roughly ' scored ' through the staves at indefinite intervals (hence our word ' Score ') as a guide to the eye and a help to keeping the singers together ; perhaps they were used at rehearsals, in the same way as the capital letters or numerals printed over modern scores, to aid the conductor.

In course of time the inconvenience of so many lines was felt, and they were divided into groups of four for each voice, by the insertion of red lines in the stave, on which no notes were written. The next step was to make a space between the several voice parts by omitting the red lines, and it was found convenient to use five instead of four lines for each voice part, though sometimes, as in the famous rota ' Sumer is icumen in ' (13th century), six lines are used. The stave of five lines first appeared in the 12th century, and its convenience caused its gradual adoption to the exclusion of all others. It must not be imagined, however, that its general acceptance by musicians can be assigned to any particular date, or even any century ; on the contrary, just as we find unstaved neumes continuing to be written for centuries after the

1 See Proc. Mus. Ass., 1900, vol. 26, p. 126.
2 See the Fitzwilliam Virginal Book.

invention of so important an improvement as the stave, so we find, in measured music, staves of eleven to fifteen lines in the 14th century, long after one would have expected composers to have recognised the more practicable and convenient smaller staves. A little two-part composition of the 12th century in the Bodleian Library (Douce MS. 139), 'Fowles in ye frich,'[1] written in square-headed neumes (see p. 649, col. 11), therefore not in measured notes, shows two separate five-lined staves, bearing the soprano and tenor clefs, and, except for the shape of the notes, it might have been written in the 17th century ; while a book of theological treatises and hymns (Brit. Mus., Codex Arundel 248) of the 14th century has staves of varying numbers of lines, from fifteen downwards.

The vocal stave was fixed at five lines by the 15th century ; but this was not the case with instrumental music, which continued to use large staves till well into the 17th century.

The Fitzwilliam and other contemporaneous collections of English harpsichord and organ music make use of staves of six lines ; while the Bolognese, Venetian and Neapolitan organists of the end of the 16th and beginning of the 17th centuries use a stave of six lines for the right hand, and eight for the left hand and feet combined. The so-called ' Great Stave ' of eleven lines has never been used except for the purpose of illustration in modern theoretical works : De Muris and others certainly use staves of eleven lines in their treatises, but not in the sense of the ' Great Stave.'

The invention of Ledger- or Leger-lines in the 16th century enabled composers not only to reduce the instrumental stave to the convenient number of five lines, but also to lessen the number of changes of clef ; though they were slow to perceive the latter advantage, for changes of clef are as frequent in music for keyed instruments in the 18th century as they are in viola and violoncello music to-day. Of the clefs we shall speak later.

EXPRESSION SIGNS,[2] though used by the earliest neume-writers, were entirely absent from mensural music, and seem to have been first reintroduced in connexion with the lute, in whose notation Morley indicates ' Soft and Loud play ' by So : Lo : calling this ' as good a grace as any other.' About 1638 we find in lute music *Piano*, *Forte*, the sign $\vee$ for *Mezzoforte*, $\lessgtr$ for *Crescendo* and *Diminuendo*, besides tempo indications, as *Presto*, *Adagio*, etc. (But see MAZZOCCHI.) Expression words and signs were gradually introduced into vocal music after having found a place in that for instruments, and have always had a tendency to increase in number and refinement. Italian has been the language most used for the purpose, and is generally understood in this connexion,

[1] Published in facsimile by the Plain-song and Med. Mus. Soc. ('Early English Harmony,' Plate 7).
[2] Though not phrasing signs ; for accentual black notation and the extra-mensural use of the dot were early forms of these.

but English, German and French have been employed, latterly with increasing frequency, by composers of those nations. The Staccato sign first appeared in the works of Couperin, J. S. Bach and Rameau, in the form of a dot ; in those of J. C. Bach it is a dot or an upright stroke, according to the degree of staccato required. (See DOT, DASH.) The Legato sign appears early in the 18th century, and is used for the first time in combination with the staccato dots by Mozart.

The CLEFS have varied considerably, both as to form and method of use, in the course of time. Plain-song has practically used only the C and F clefs ; while mensural music, after employing all the letters of the musical alphabet, together with ♮, at different periods, finally reduced its clefs to the three which are now in use, and whose shapes have gradually become conventionalised thus :

F Clefs.

C Clefs.

G Clefs.

The F clef is now always placed on the fourth line, and is called the Bass clef ; in the 17th and 18th centuries it was frequently placed on the middle line, and, when in this position, it was called the Baritone clef. This is the oldest of the clefs, having been the one used when the stave consisted of only a single line. It marked the *mi fa* or semitone of the *Hexachordum naturale*. The C clef was formerly the most used of all for vocal music, but during the last century it has been more and more confined to instruments. It has been used on each of the five lines, though now restricted to three. It is named after the voices it formerly represented, soprano, alto or tenor.

Rockstro gave the following scheme of clefs in use in the time of Palestrina :

Cantus.	Altus.	Tenor.		Bassus.
High Treble. Treble. or Violin.	Sop- Mezzo rano. Sop- rano.	Alto. Tenor.	Con- Bari- tra tone. Tenor.	Bass. Contra Basso.

The G, or treble, clef can hardly be said to have come into general use till the rise of instrumental music into importance during the 16th and 17th centuries ; and even then, on keyed instruments, it had to share a place with the C clefs ; hence it has altered its shape less than the others. Until the 19th century it was hardly looked upon as a vocal clef, and, except in England, it was never used for chorus parts, though it was for solo voices. Its foreign names imply an instrumental rather than a vocal use : Italian, *chiave di violino*; German, *Violonschlüssel*. It was formerly sometimes placed on the lowest line, and called, when in this position, the 'High treble' or 'French violin clef.' C. P. E. Bach in ' Die Israeliten in der Wüste,' 1775, doubles the G clef thus, 𝄞𝄞, to show that two flute parts are written on a single stave. This doubling of the treble clef is now the familiar sign for the tenor clef. It only dates from the middle of the last century, and it is already threatened by the growing use of the sign 𝄞, a combination of the G and C clefs. In either of these clefs it is understood that the music is to be sung an octave lower than it is written.[1] The alto voice part when not written with the C clef on the third line, is written in the G clef at the actual pitch ; but when the G clef first superseded the C clef for the alto voice the music was written an octave higher, as in the tenor G clef.

The clefs are now distributed amongst the instruments and voices in the following way : In full scores the soprano, alto and tenor voices are given either their own proper clefs or three G clefs, and the bass voice always has the F clef. The violins use the G clef, the violas the alto clef, changing to the G to avoid many leger-lines. The violoncellos use the F and tenor clefs, with an occasional passage in the G clef, causing some ambiguity, as in some instances the G clef is used, as in writing for the tenor voice, to indicate sounds an octave below what is written ; all modern writers use this clef only in its real position in writing for the violoncello. The double-basses use the F clef, but sound an octave below the written notes. The flutes, oboes and clarinets use the G clef. The corno di bassetto and the cor anglais play from the G clef. The bassoon uses the F and tenor clefs, and the double bassoon the F clef only, transposing an octave lower. Trumpets and horns use the G clef. The extreme low notes of the horn are, however, written in the F clef in many classical scores. Alto (now almost obsolete), tenor and bass trombones use the corresponding clefs. Drums use the F clef.

The history of the Sharp, Flat and Natural must now be referred to. When the Guidonian alphabet was arranged, the Roman *b*, called B *rotundum*, or B *mollis*, was given to the sound called *Trite synemmenon*, and the Gothic ♮, called B *quadrum*, B *quadratum*, B *durum*, was applied to *Paramese* ; a survival of the two forms of *b* is seen in the modern German nomenclature, in which B flat is called B, and B natural is called H, from the old form of the

square *b*, which was something like the letter *h*. Guido called the hexachord beginning on C, to whose scale the B *quadrum* belonged, *Hexachordum naturale* ; hence arose the English name of ' Natural ' for the sign of the square *b*.

It is obvious that B *rotundum* would be the first to be introduced into stave notation, where all B's, unless qualified by the ♭ sign, would be taken as B natural *per se*. The ♭ was at first applied only to the note immediately below middle C, that being the only B which lay within the strict compass of the ecclesiastical chant, and the common staves of the C clef on the third or fourth line. With the notation of organised descant or prick-song came the need for a ♭ in the octave above, and this was supplied in a doubled form of the letter β, a distinction also employed by some notationers for a ♭ in the octave below. As music became more developed it was necessary for notation to become more systematic, and by the 15th century a ♭ in the signature was accepted as governing all occurrences of a B in that line. Its dominion, however, was restricted to a horizontal significance, and it is common to find in MSS. down to the end of the 16th century either what we should now call a superfluous flat in the signature, 𝄢, or a ♭ implied in the signature appearing as an accidental,

It has been pointed out that in a strict application of the hexachordal system to stave notation there was no logical place for the B *quadratum*. Notation, however, is rightly influenced by the desire to be explicit rather than logical, and the convenient B *rotundum* so soon began to establish itself as the rule and not the exception that the B *quadratum* was introduced to correct or contradict it. In the notation of music in the first modes in which the sixth note, B, is variable, sometimes B, sometimes B♭, according to the inflexions of the plain-chant, the B♭ is strictly an accidental and should alone be indicated ; but notationers introduced the B *quadratum* as a safeguard against the growing tendency of singers to regard the B *rotundum* as the dominant indication. Thus introduced the B *quadratum* is a redundancy, a superfluous natural. In the notation of cadences and *Musica ficta* it assumes the character of a true accidental. In this function, however, it was supplanted by the sign for raising a note by a semitone. This, the origin of our sharp, is said to have been invented by Josquin de Prés (1450–1521). Its form is supposed to be derived from the B *quadratum* ; it was called B *cancellatum*, or *Diesis*, or, from its shape, *Crux* (whence the French *dièse* and German *Kreuz*: the English ' sharp ' and ' flat ' refer to function). A curious little anonymous chapter quoted by de Coussemaker with the heading *de Sinemensis* (evidently a corruption of *synemmenon*) refers to the *crux* as the conjunction between the tones, and gives a complete semitonic scale, explaining, however, that the *crux* between B *rotundum* and C is represented by the sign ♮ ; and according to the vulgar such music is called False Music. (See MUSICA FICTA.)

The new sign, ※, had the great advantage of being easily distinguishable from the B *rotundum*, while the B *quadratum* was not. To us a system in which the same sign is used for sharpening one note and for restoring the pitch of another seems oddly ambiguous. But it is the way of notation to prefer convenience to correctness, to risk an ambiguity in the sense rather than an ambiguity in the presentation. Moreover, it must be borne in mind that key-signatures were extremely simple, one ♭, two at the most, no ♯ signatures ; that the principle that an accidental only affected the note it preceded was still observed,[1] at any rate in the printed partbooks ; and that most of the writing was diatonic. If this be considered it will be seen that B♯ and E♯, to represent the raising of a signatural B♭ and E♭, or even a corrective C♭ introduced as a safeguard to mark that a C just previously sharpened in a cadence is C natural once more, are not such arbitrary absurdities as they seem at first sight.

The use of the ♮ to contradict a ♭ (its function in the innocent days when B *rotundum* and B *quadratum* knew not B *cancellatum*) had been reintroduced by the middle of the 17th century, for Kircher in his *Musurgia* (1650) gives this passage as an example of chromatic notation :

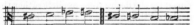

but not until the beginning of the 18th century was the ♮ used to contradict both ♯ and ♭, as in modern notation. A 16th-century expedient of restoring the natural pitch of C, F and G after they had been sharpened, by introducing the capital letter, *i.e.*

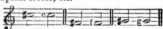

might be attributed to a sensitive notational conscience. It occurs, though not very frequently or at all consistently, in various MSS. ; and four instances of a naturalising capital F are to be found in the printed partbooks of Pilkington's second set of Madrigals, 1624.

---

[1] Except in the case of the common cadence figures such as

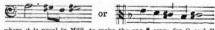

where it is usual in MSS. to make the one ♯ serve for G and F. C and B♭ together. In MSS. the accidental does not always *immediately* precede the note it affects, *i.e.*

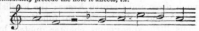

It is a question of scribal convenience, or scribal carelessness.

The flat and natural have never altered their shapes, except that the form ♭ for the higher and lower octave was given up in favour of a uniform ♭. The sharp has undergone many modifications, of which the following are the principal :

※   ×   ♯

The double sharp and double flat became necessary when equal temperament gave composers command of the complete circle of keys. The double sharp was at first represented by the natural of the note above the note affected, but this unscientific and misleading method was successfully combated by Mattheson, who proposed a St. Andrew's cross, and by Leopold Mozart, who proposed an upright cross. Other forms suggested were ✱ and ♯♯♯, but the one proposed by Mattheson has superseded all the others. He also proposed a Greek β for the double flat, but this was given up in favour of the form familiar to us. The conventional way of contradicting a double sharp and flat by ♮♯ and ♮♭ has been objected to by some, and possibly a new method may be invented and find acceptance in the future.

KEY-SIGNATURES were probably suggested by the early use of B *rotundum* as a clef. They are found in the compositions printed by Petrucci at Fossombrone, 1513–23. In the 17th century composers, besides frequently duplicating sharps and flats, frequently omitted the last sharp or flat of the signature. This practice continued to the time of J. S. Bach and Handel. (See ACCIDENTALS.)

The 18th-century composers employed a great number of signs called *Agréments* or Graces, as a kind of shorthand for certain well-recognised ORNAMENTS (*q.v.*). They are now for the most part written out in full by notes of smaller type than the rest, and the only survivals of the old shorthand signs are the shake, the turn and the mordent.

SUMMARY

The successive labours of the neume-writers, the mensuralists, and the tablaturists, and the impetus given to composers by the rise of instrumental and dramatic music during the 17th and 18th centuries, have resulted in a notation that is now accepted by the whole of the civilised world ; that is equally applicable to instruments and voices ; that is easily learned by all who have musical instincts ; that is capable of expansion to meet new requirements ; and whose very inconsistencies (which are a stumbling-block to those who begin to learn it late in life) are, in reality, an assistance to the eye, which would easily become confused by too great a uniformity. Changes will undoubtedly come, as long as music continues to be a living and advancing art ; but they will only come slowly and gradually, as they have done in the past, and it is probable that in its general structural principles our notation will last as long as our present system of music. Its principles may be thus summarised :

1. The relative pitch of sounds is indicated by the position of signs, called notes, on a stave of five lines, which can be extended when required by the addition of ledger- or leger-lines. The clef forms the key of the stave.

2. The relative time values of notes are shown by their shapes.

3. The relative force of accents is shown by the position of the notes with regard to the bar-lines.

4. The key and rhythm of a composition are shown by signatures.

5. The semibreve is the ' mother of the other notes,' [1] the remaining notes taking their values as $\frac{1}{2}$, $\frac{1}{4}$, etc., of the semibreve.[2]

6. The rhythmical scheme is shown by bar-lines.

7. The expressional requirements of the music thus written are shown by easily understood words and signs placed above or below the stave.

Innumerable efforts have been made to supersede this system of notation by the invention of others, which are supposed to be easier to learn or more simple in construction ; but, with one partial exception, TONIC SOL-FA (q.v.), the new notations have not made good. A pinch of practice is worth a peck of theory : whatever its claims on the score of system or facility, no *invented* notation is likely to supplant a notation which has been *evolved*. To suppose, however, that stave notation has attained its final form is to be alike blind to the present outlook of music and singularly unappreciative of the power to adapt itself to new conditions which our notation has shown in the past.

AUTHORITIES.—*Scriptores ecclesiastici de musica sacra potissimum,* edited by GERBERT, 1784 ; *Scriptores de musica medii aevi,* edited by COUSSEMAKER, 1864 – 76 ; ZARLINO, *Istitutioni armoniche,* 1558 ; MORLEY, *A Plaine and Easie Introduction to Practical Music,* 1597. For the history of plain-song notation the chief authority is the *Paléographie musicale,* a periodical published by the Benedictines of Solesmes.

s. t. w., incorporating material
from c. f. a. w.

NOTE, NOTES (Lat. *nota*), the marks or signs by which music is put on paper. (See NOTATION.) Hence the word is used for the sounds represented by the notes. (See SCALE.) Also for the keys of a pianoforte ; and for a tune or song, as the ' note ' of a bird.   G.

NOTKER (b. early 9th cent. ; d. 912), a monk of St. Gall, composer and writer on music, who died at a great age. His chief title to fame rests on his work in the development and popularisation of the SEQUENCES (q.v.), and as his share in that has been overestimated, so the

value of his brief theoretical writings has been much overlooked. There is a letter from him to his colleague, Lambert, on the subject of the so-called ' Romanian letters '—a series of letters found in early MSS. of plain-song giving directions as to the execution of the music. The value of Notker's exposition in all respects may be doubted, but it seems to explain rightly the more important signs and their use by the important but somewhat eccentric school of St. Gall.

Of greater interest are Notker's three short treatises in Old German, on the theory of music and on organs. The first describes a peculiar method of alphabetic notation, and the others have some curious features. His writings are printed in Gerbert, *Scriptores,* i. 95-102. He is generally distinguished from other writers of the same name by the nickname Balbulus—the stammerer.   w. h. f.

NOTOT, JOSEPH (b. Arras, Pas - de - Calais, 1755). From his earliest infancy he manifested a wonderful aptitude for music. His father intended to educate him for the Church or the Bar, and for the purpose of diverting his mind from the pursuit he most loved, sent him to Paris. It happened soon after his arrival in that city that a friend took him to St. Germain - des - Prés, where, having obtained permission of the organist to sit at the organ, he performed extempore in so ingenious a manner that Leclerc would not believe it possible the boy could be playing from his own ideas. Leclerc therefore gave him a subject, upon which the boy instantly formed a fugue, and acquitted himself so admirably that the great composer seized him in his arms and, lifting him up as high as he could, exclaimed, in an ecstasy of delight, ' Tu resteras à Paris.' His father, finding him to have really a genius for music, permitted the boy to adhere to the study of music as his future profession, and he consequently remained in Paris, where he soon acquired a great reputation. On his return to Arras he was appointed organist there. His compositions, which were greatly admired by John Christian Bach, consist of four symphonies, three pianoforte concertos and a number of sonatas for that instrument. And it is said that in his style of accompanying from a full score Joseph Notot was unequalled. At the French Revolution this excellent musician renounced music as a profession and came to reside in England.   c. h. p.

BIBL.—*British Minstrel and Musical Literary Miscellany,* Glasgow No. 58.

NOTTEBOHM, MARTIN GUSTAV (b. Lüdenscheid, near Arnsberg, Westphalia, Nov. 12, 1817 ; d. Gratz, Oct. 29, 1882), composer, teacher and writer on music, son of a manufacturer. In 1838 and 1839, when in Berlin as a volunteer in the Gardeschützenbataillon, he took lessons on the piano and composition

[1] An expression found in 16th-century writers, during the revolt against the Moods.
[2] In Germany and America the notes are named after their values, the old word semibreve, minim, crotchet, etc., being given up in favour of *Ganz-note,* whole-note, *Halb-note,* half-note, *Viertel-note,* quarter-note, etc.

from L. Berger and Dehn. In 1840 he removed to Leipzig, where he became intimate with Mendelssohn and Schumann, particularly the latter. A testimonial from Mendelssohn, stating his qualifications as a musician, procured his discharge from the army, and in Sept. 1846 he settled finally in Vienna. In 1847 he went through a course of counterpoint with Sechter, and was for long esteemed as an *ble and conscientious teacher of the pianoforte *nd composition. But it is as a solid and *cientific writer on music that his name will live; indeed his critical researches on Beethoven's works constitute him an authority of the first rank. His co-operation in the revised editions of the works of Bach, Handel, Beethoven, Mendelssohn and Mozart is of the highest value. If not the first to explore Beethoven's sketch-books, he certainly investigated them more thoroughly and to more purpose than any one else, and his works on this subject deserve the gratitude of every student of the great composer.

Nottebohm wrote:

Musikwissenschaftliche Beiträge in the *Monatsschrift für Theater und Musik* (1855 and 1857, Vienna, Klemm); *Ein Skizzenbuch von Beethoven*, description with extracts (1865, Breitkopf & Härtel); *Thematisches Verzeichniss der im Druck erschienenen Werke von Beethoven*, 2nd ed. enlarged, and with chronological and critical observations (1868, B. & H.); *Beethoveniana* (1872, Rieter-Biedermann); *Beethovens Studien*, vol. i. containing the instruction received by Beethoven from Haydn, Albrechtsberger and Salieri, from the original MSS. (1873, *ibid.*), *Thematisches Verzeichniss der im Druck erschienenen Werke Franz Schuberts* (1874, Vienna, Schreiber); *Neue Beethoveniana*, papers appearing from time to time in the *Musikalisches Wochenblatt*, 1875–79—this last, and the *Beethoveniana*, are founded on the examination of Beethoven's sketch-books to which allusion has been made; *Mozartiana* (1880, B. & H.); *Ein Skizzenbuch von Beethoven aus dem Jahr 1803* (1880, B. & H.)—this contains the sketches for the Eroica.

His compositions include:

Op. 1, piano quartet; op. 4, piano trios (both Peters); solos for PF., opp. 2 and 3 (Peters); opp. 6, 10, 11, 13-15 (Spina); op. 16 (Peters); op. 17, 'Variationen über ein Thema von J. S. Bach,' PF., four hands (B. & H.).

Since then the papers which appeared in the *Mus. Wochenblatt* as *Neue Beethoveniana*, with others of the same nature by him, have been collected by E. Mandyczewski, and published in 1887 by Rieter-Biedermann of Leipzig in a volume of 590 pages, as *Zweite Beethoveniana*. An index to both the Beethoveniana volumes was published in Oct. 1888.   C. F. P.

NOTTURNO, see NOCTURNE.

NOURRIT, (1) LOUIS (*b.* Montpellier, Aug. 4, 1780; *d.* Brunoy, Sept. 23, 1831), tenor singer, educated in the Maîtrise at Montpellier. Through the influence of Méhul he entered the Conservatoire at Paris, became the favourite pupil of Garat, and won prizes. He made his first appearance at the Opéra as Renaud in Gluck's 'Armide.' A good singer, but unambitious and cold, he contented himself with taking Laîné's parts in the old operas, and seldom created new rôles. He retired in 1826, and lived at his country house at Brunoy till his death. During the whole of his operatic career he carried on the business of a diamond merchant, and wished to make a tradesman of his eldest son,

(2) ADOLPHE (*b.* Paris, Mar. 3, 1802; *d.* Naples, Mar. 8, 1839). This gifted youth received a good classical education at the Collège Ste. Barbe, but was then put into an office, the drudgery of which he beguiled by studying music in secret. On the representation of Garcia, however, he was allowed to follow his wishes. His first appearance at the Opéra took place Sept. 10, 1821, as Pylade in Gluck's 'Iphigénie en Tauride,' when he was favourably received, partly because, in voice, manner and appearance, he was strikingly like his father. This resemblance suggested to Méhul an opéra-féerie, 'Les Deux Salem' (July 12, 1824), which, however, failed. On his father's retirement he succeeded him as leading tenor, and for more than ten years created the first tenor rôle in all the operas produced at the Opéra. The following is a list of the parts written for him:

1826, Néoclès in 'Le Siège de Corinthe.' 1827, Aménophis in 'Moïse'; and Douglas in 'Macbeth.' 1828, Masaniello in 'La Muette de Portici'; and 'Le Comte Ory.' 1829, Arnold in 'Guillaume Tell.' 1830, Léonard da Vinci in Ginestet's 'François Ier à Chambord'; and Un Inconnu in 'Le Dieu et la Bayadère.' 1831, Guillaume in 'Le Philtre'; and Robert in 'Robert le Diable.' 1832, Edmond in 'Le Serment.' 1833, Gustave III.; and Nadir in Cherubini's 'Ali Baba.' 1835, Éléazar in 'La Juive.' 1836, Raoul in 'Les Huguenots'; and Phoebus in 'La Esmeralda,' by Louise Bertin. 1837, Stradella in Niedermeyer's opera. In 1831 he sang Adhémar in 'Euryanthe,' and in 1834 Don Juan in a new translation of Mozart's opera.

The writer of this article was a personal friend of Nourrit and heard him in nearly all the rôles which he created, and to which he imparted a distinct stamp of his own. Though rather stout, and short in the neck, he had a fine presence, and could be refined and pleasing in comedy or pathetic and commanding in tragedy, at will. He used his falsetto with great skill, and was energetic without exhausting his powers. He was idolised by the public, and his influence both with them and with his brother artists was great. He was consulted by managers and authors alike; he wrote the words for Eléazar's fine air in 'La Juive,' and suggested the abrupt and pathetic close of the duet in 'Les Huguenots.' His poetic imagination is shown by the libretti for the ballets of 'La Sylphide,' 'La Tempête,' 'L'Île des pirates,' 'Le Diable boiteux,' etc., danced by Taglioni and Fanny Elssler—all of which were written by him. Besides securing large receipts for the Opéra, he popularised Schubert's songs in France, made the fortune of various composers of romances, and was always ready to sing the first act of 'La Dame Blanche' with Mme. Damoreau for any charitable purpose. In conversation he was witty and refined. Duprez's engagement at the Opéra was a severe mortification for so earnest and so popular an artist, and rather than divide honours to which he felt he had an exclusive right, or provoke comparisons which would in all probability have been made in his favour, he resolved to retire. On his last appearance at the Opéra (Apr. 1, 1837) he received the most enthusiastic and flattering ovation ever perhaps accorded to a French artist, but nothing would induce him to remain in Paris. He obtained leave of absence from the Conservatoire in 1837, where he had been professeur de déclamation lyrique from Jan. 1, 1828, started for Brussels, and thence proceeded to Marseilles, Lyons and Toulouse. His idea was to produce during his tour scenas or acts composed expressly for him, and Ambroise Thomas furnished him with a dramatic cantata called ' Silvio Pellico ' (words by Legouvé), which he carried off with expressions of delight at having found something which would display his powers in a new light. Of this piece, however, nothing has ever been heard since. While at Marseilles and Toulouse Nourrit's customary excitement increased to an alarming degree, and was aggravated after his return to Paris by a series of newspaper articles praising Duprez at his expense. These drove him away a second time. He started for Italy in a state of deep depression, but was temporarily restored by Rossini's kindness and by the cordiality of his reception in most of the great towns. Unfortunately ' Polyeucte,' which Donizetti had composed for him, was interdicted in Naples, and he made his first appearance at San Carlo in Mercadante's ' Il giuramento.' He was well received both in this and in ' Norma,' but could not be persuaded of the fact. After singing at a benefit concert in a state of great mental fatigue, he had a sudden access of delirium in the night, and throwing himself out of window, was killed on the spot. His remains were brought to Paris, and interred amid a crowd of sorrowing friends. He was much valued by Mendelssohn, who made his acquaintance in 1831, and who notices his death in terms of great sorrow.[1]

There is a fine marble medallion of Nourrit by Pradier ; and he was often painted in scenes from ' La Muette,' ' Robert,' ' La Juive ' and ' Les Huguenots.' The portrait by F. R. Spencer is very like. M. L. Quicherat, one of his sons-in-law, published *Adolphe Nourrit : sa vie*, etc. (Paris, 1867, 3 vols.), containing ample details. (See also Ferdinand Hiller's *Künstlerleben*, 1880.)

His brother, (3) AUGUSTE (*b.* Paris, 1808 ; *d.* l'Isle-Adam, July 11, 1853), was also a distinguished tenor singer, and for some time directed the chief theatres at The Hague, Amsterdam and Brussels. He visited the United States, and after his return devoted himself to teaching singing.   G. C.

BIBL.—ALPH. DUPRASQUIER, *Adolphe Nourrit* (Lyons, 1839); BOUTET DE MONVEL, *Adolphe Nourrit* (Paris, 1903).

NOVÁČEK, OTTOKAR (*b.* Fehertemplom, Hungary, May 13, 1866 ; *d.* New York, Feb. 3, 1900), violinist and composer, was a pupil first of his father, second, of Dont in Vienna, and lastly of Schradieck and Brodsky at the Leipzig Conservatoire, where he gained the Mendelssohn

[1] Hiller's *Mendelssohn*, p. 137.

prize in 1885. He played at the Gewandhaus, and joined the Brodsky Quartet, first as second violin and later as viola. He was a member of the Boston Symphony Orchestra under Nikisch, and solo viola in the New York Damrosch Orchestra from 1892–93. Weakness of the heart caused him to retire from active work in 1899, and being unable to play he devoted himself to composition. Published compositions :

Three string quartets, No. 1 in E minor, No. 2 in E, No. 3 in C (posthumous) ; concerto for piano (introduced by Busoni) ; two concerto caprices for piano ; eight ditto for violin and piano ; Bulgarian dances for violin and piano ; Perpetuum Mobile for violin and orchestra ; air for violin and pianoforte ; six songs, the words by Tolstoi.

(*Baker*.)   E. H.-A.

NOVÁK, VÍTĚZSLAV (*b.* Kamenice-on-Lipa, Southern Bohemia, Dec. 5, 1870), composer and teacher. Early in the present century he became, in association with his contemporary Josef SUK (*q.v.*), one of the leaders of modern Czech music. He was the son of the local doctor at Kamenice, and, losing his father early in life, he had to maintain his mother and younger brothers and sisters by giving lessons. He attended the Gymnasium at Jindřichův Hradec (Neŭhaus) and afterwards entered the Prague University, where he studied jurisprudence and philosophy. At the same time he worked at the Prague Conservatoire (piano with Josef Jiránek, and composition with Antonin Dvořák). Dvořák took him into special favour, and, acting on the master's advice, Novák decided to devote himself entirely to music. Having passed through the school of composition he began to take private pupils, and soon made a reputation as composer and teacher. During the first decade of the 20th century most of the younger Czech musicians were indebted to him for their training (Štěpan, Vycpálek, Novotný, Vomáčka and others). In 1909 Novák became professor of composition at the Conservatoire. After the political changes in 1918, when the institution was reorganised and passed under State control, Novák was appointed professor in the ' master school,' and was elected director in the years 1919–22.

Novák's early attempts at composition date from his school days. He already inclined towards programme music. Touched by the ' Weltschmerz ' and romanticism of the young generation, he was a devoted admirer of Heine and Byron in poetry, and of Mendelssohn in music ; although afterwards Schumann claimed his special homage, and Grieg enjoyed favour for a time. The violin sonata, the first pianoforte trio (G minor) and the 'Variations on a Theme by Schumann,' reflect the young Novák. At the Conservatoire he also came under the spell of the neo-romantics. We find the influence of Berlioz in the overture ' The Corsair,' and of Liszt in the ballad for piano, ' Manfred.' Dvořák also made some impression upon him. From him Novák learned the strong and logical structure of musical forms, and the need for a thorough study of the classical composers. His ideal now became Brahms, whose influence, together with Dvořák's, prevails in the piano and chamber music. The central point of this period of Novák's activity is found in his music for piano (the Concerto, the Souvenirs, Serenades, Eclogues, Barcarolles, etc.), and his songs (particularly ' A Tale of the Heart '). An erotic feeling, dreamy or passionate, or sometimes linked to a gift of apt irony, distinguishes these little works.

Up to this time the national character is hardly perceptible in Novák's compositions. But the longing for the beauties of nature, which, together with the erotic impulse, has always been one of the chief incitements to his inspiration, attracted him one summer to Moravia, where he suddenly discovered a new horizon. Hitherto he had felt no wish merely to copy Smetana and Dvořák, who specialised in Czech local colour, but now that he had learnt to know the Moravian and Slovak folk, he saw them as his kinsmen, with their peculiar qualities and customs, and, above all, he heard their characteristic songs. He began to compose in this newly recognised spirit. In this respect he approaches the native Moravian musician Leoš JANÁČEK (q.v.), and it is interesting to observe how each works in his own way. Janáček is a realist, an ' expressionist,' who often leaves his raw material intentionally undeveloped ; Novák idealises and polishes the Slovak folk-tunes, and frames them in the logical structure of polyphonic forms. Here we trace the origin of Novák's own music written to Moravian folk-texts, and also of the pianoforte quartet and quintet, the first string quartet, the four choral ballads (with orchestra), the overture to the Moravian folk-drama ' Maryša,' the piano pieces ' My Maytide,' the ' Sonata eroica ' and the Valachian Dances.[1] These works have had a lasting influence upon the successive phases of Novák's art, because, having experienced all the impressions which grew out of intercourse with the folk, he assimilated these national elements with his own individuality. He soon returned to subjective music, inspired from within ; but the Slovak idiom remains a distinguishing feature of all his work.

Novák was next attracted to impressionism. Simultaneously with the renewal of the subjective phase, the element of colour became prominent, and steadily took the ascendant in his orchestral works. The central inspiration of his art was now twofold—love of woman and of nature. His eroticism sometimes rises to an immensity of passion ; while in his description of nature he seeks for the sublime

[1] Moravian Valachia must not be confounded with the Roumanian province Wallachia.

aspects of the mountains and the sea. He often has recourse (like Richard Strauss) to very subtle methods of tone-painting. His modern tendency is first revealed in the song cycle ' Melancholy,' op. 25, followed soon afterwards by the characteristic ballads, and later by the song cycle which marks the climax of his lyrical work, ' In the Valley of a new Kingdom,' op. 31. This valuable series of modern Czech songs ends with the ' Melancholy Songs of Love,' op. 38, and the Eight Nocturnes, op. 39. The pianoforte music belonging to this period includes the ' Winter Night Songs,' a monothematic cycle of pieces. Among the chamber music is the impassioned pianoforte trio ' Quasi una ballata,' op. 27. Novák was the first Czech composer to make use, early in the 20th century, of the single-movement form in which the character of all the sonata movements is preserved. In the same group must be placed the second string quartet (in two movements) in D, which is also monothematic. It contains a fugue in which Novák expresses himself in an unusually calm and clear mood.

Novák's strong, reflective, logical mind progresses continuously from simple to complex forms. He began with pianoforte music and songs, passed on to chamber music, and finally to orchestral composition. His serenade for small orchestra, in which passion is only lightly treated and satirical wit plays an important part, seems to be a kind of episode in his creative work. His programme works for full orchestra are on a large scale : ' In the Tatra ' is a fine picture of nature in the mountain heights ; ' Eternal Longing ' is the outcome of a sublime impression of the Adriatic sea ; ' Toman and the Wood Nymph ' is the most temperamental of all Novák's works, and draws a twofold picture of ideal love and baneful love (sexus necans). Upon these works followed ' Lady Godiva,' the apotheosis of ideal womanly love ; ' The Storm,' a picture of the wild destructive ocean, by the power of which all the emotions and passions of which human nature is capable are brought to naught ; and ' Pan '—originally written for piano—in which is revealed the old god and the joy of the nature-worshipper in the mountains, the sea, the forests and in woman.

' The Spectre's Bride ' already shows the transition to Novák's latest period. Here the resources of tone-painting come to the front. Novák finally turned his attention to opera, the importance of which he had underrated for a time. He first composed a comic opera in one act, ' The Imp of Zvíkov,' in which we find a good deal of that personal irony already familiar in his instrumental works. At this time there is a new departure in the character of his music. It was natural that the passion of his earlier music should calm with advancing years. The works of his maturity are pene-trated by a compensating serenity. Biting irony is softened to kindly humour. He chooses no highly dramatic material for his operas, but rather that which intimately reveals the spirit of the Czechoslovak people and gives sufficient opportunity for nature - painting. 'Karlstein,' which originated during the war, is an expression of profound patriotism. 'The Lantern' is a genre picture depicting the sufferings of the Czechs in the years of their oppression ; but it contains also a good many folk-tale elements which are treated with subtle humour. Whereas in 'The Lantern' Novák gives us a musical picture of the Czechs, in his latest legendary opera [1] he returns to his favourite Slovak environment.

Besides opera, Novák has written in recent years the songs entitled ' Eroticon ' and the piano suite ' Exoticon ' (the outcome of his study of the folk-songs of foreign lands). On the establishment of the Czechoslovak Republic he composed two occasional works — the patriotic choruses for male voice choir, and military marches ; also a number of children's songs and piano pieces, mostly for his little son.

Novák's early works without opus numbers are :

Sonata in D minor (violin and piano) (Hudební Matice, Prague); concert overture, 'The Corsair' (MS.) ; ' Variations on a Theme by Schumann ' (MS.); Serenade in F for small orchestra (with exception of the second number—J. Otto, Prague) ; Piano Concerto (MS.) ; Choruses for female voices (MS.), and some MS. Songs.

The following are published without opus numbers :

Slovak Songs (book 3, with English words by Rosa Newmarch, Hudební Matice, Prague) ; 25 Slovak Songs (Moimir Urbánek, Prague) ; two Festival Choruses to President Masaryk (F. A. Urbánek) ; two marches—' Masaryk March ' and ' Heroes of Czecho-slovakia ' (F. A. Urbánek).

WORKS WITH OPUS NUMBERS
OPERAS

'Zvíkovský rarášek' (The Imp of Zvíkov), op. 47 ; 'A Night at Karlstein,' op. 50 ; 'Lucerna' (The Lantern), op. 56 (all produced at the National Theatre, Prague); 'Dědův odkaz,' op. 87 (Brno, June 1926).

CANTATAS

'Bonře' (The Storm), op. 42, for solo voices, chorus and orchestra; 'Svatební Košile' (The Spectre's Bride), op. 48.

ORCHESTRAL WORKS

Symphonic poems : 'In the Tatra,' op. 26 ; 'Eternal Longing,' op. 23 ; 'Toman and the Wood Nymph,' op. 40. Overtures : 'Maryša,' op. 18; 'Lady Godiva,' op. 41. Serenade in D for small orchestra, op. 36 (Universal Edition, Vienna).

CHORAL WORKS AND SONGS

Ballads for chorus and orchestra : ' Ranořa ' (The Accursed Daughter), 'The Murderer-lover' (Stóji Jano při potoce), 'The Unhappy War' (Nešťastny vojna)—all to Moravian folk-words. Ballads for one voice, with pianoforte or orchestra : 'The Child Ballad ' and 'The Mountain Ballad,' op. 28 (Czech and German words, M. Urbánek, Prague) ; 'The Ballad of the Soul of Jan Neruda,' for bass and orchestra, op. 29 (M. Urbánek). Song cycles : opp. 4, 8, 14 (Gipsy Songs, F. A. Urbánek, Prague), 16, 17, 21, 25 ('Melancholy,' M. Urbánek, Prague), 31 ('In the Valley of a new Kingdom '), 38 ('Melancholy Songs of Love,' Hudební Matice), 39 (Eight Nocturnes, Simrock and Universal Edition); op. 46, 'Eroticon' (Universal Edition, Czech and German) ; op. 52, 'Spring,' children's songs in two books (Universal Edition). Op. 47, Four Poems for mixed chorus ; opp. 37, 44, 51, Songs for male chorus ; op. 53, Three Silesian Songs for chorus and orchestra (Hudební Matice).

FOR PIANO

'Manfred,' ballad, op. 2 ; Ragatelles, op. 5 ; Souvenirs, op. 6 ; Serenades, op. 9 ; Barcarolles, op. 10 ; Eclogues, op. 11 ; ' Twi-light,' op. 13 ; Three Bohemian Dances, op. 15 ; ' My Maytide,' op. 20 (F. A. Urbánek) ; 'Sonata eroica,' op. 24 ; 'Songs of Winter Nights,' op. 30 ; Two Valachian Dances, op. 34 ; 'Pan,' op. 43 (Universal Edition) ; ' Exoticon,' op. 45 ; Six Sonatinas, op. 54 ; ' Youth,' op. 55 (children's pieces, Hudební Matice, Prague).

Three short pieces for violin and piano, op. 3.   R. V.

------
[1] ' The Wood Nymph,' not yet quite finished.

NOVELLO, (1) VINCENT (b. London, Sept. 6, 1781 ; d. Nice, Aug. 9, 1861), son of an Italian father and English mother, was born at 240 Oxford Street. He was a chorister at the Sardinian Chapel, Duke Street, Lincoln's Inn Fields, under Samuel Webbe the organist, and after the breaking of his voice officiated as deputy for Webbe, and also for Danby, organist of the Spanish Chapel, Manchester Square. At 16 years of age he became organist of the Portuguese Chapel in South Street, Grosvenor Square, which office he held until 1822. In 1812 he was pianist to the Italian Opera Com-pany at the Pantheon. He was one of the original members of the Philharmonic Society, and occasionally directed its concerts. Having attained great eminence as an organist, he was selected to take the organ in the ' Creation ' at the Westminster Abbey Festival in 1834. From 1840–43 he was organist of the Roman Catholic Chapel in Moorfields. He was one of the founders of the Classical Harmonists and Choral Harmonists Societies, of both of which he was for some time conductor. In 1849 he quitted England for Nice, where he resided until his death.

Novello's compositions were numerous and varied, and if not remarkable for invention and originality, are marked by grace and solid musicianship. They include 'Rosalba,' a cantata composed for the Philharmonic Society, and first performed in 1834 ; ' Old May Morning,' a ' cheerful glee ' which gained a prize at Man-chester in 1832 ; and ' The Infant's Prayer,' a recitative and air which was long the favourite of every choir-boy who was qualified for concert-singing, and of which nearly 100,000 copies were sold. He also composed many masses, motets and sacred pieces to Latin words. But it was as an editor and arranger that he princi-pally deserves the gratitude of lovers of music. His first work was 'A Collection of Sacred Music' (masses and motets, including many by himself), 2 vols., 1811, 2nd edit. 1825 ; which was fol-lowed by ' Twelve Easy Masses,' 3 vols., 1816 ; ' The Evening Service,' including the Gregorian hymns, 2 vols., 1822 ; ' The Fitzwilliam Music,' a noble selection of sacred pieces by Italian com-posers from MSS. in the Fitzwilliam Museum, Cambridge, 5 vols., 1825 ; ' Purcell's Sacred Music,' 5 vols., 1828–32, containing many an-thems, services and other pieces never before printed, afterwards republished in 4 vols. But for the accident that Novello was allowed, after the York Festival of 1828, to copy the MSS. in the library of the Minster, many of these must have been lost to the world ; 18 masses by Mozart, and 16 by Haydn, of which 10 of the former and 9 of the latter were printed for the first time ; ' Convent Music,' a collection of pieces for treble voices, 2 vols., 1834 ; ' Studies in Madrigalian Scoring,' 1841 ; ' The Psalmist,' a collection of psalm tunes ; 'The Congregational and Chorister's Psalm and Hymn Book'; Croft's Anthems, 2 vols.; Greene's Anthems, 2 vols.; Boyce's Anthems, 4 vols.; Organ part to Boyce's 'Cathedral Music'; the masses of Beethoven, Hummel, etc. He took a number of madrigals by Wilbye and others, originally written for three and four voices, and added two, three and even four additional parts to them with great, if misplaced, ingenuity. For the organ he published, amongst others, 'Select Organ Pieces,' 3 vols.; 'Cathedral Voluntaries,' 2 vols.; and 'Short Melodies,' 1 vol.

Novello possessed well-cultivated literary taste, and numbered among his intimate friends Charles and Mary Lamb, Shelley, Keats, Leigh Hunt, Hazlitt, Edward Holmes and Charles Cowden Clarke, the latter of whom married his eldest daughter, Mary (d. Genoa, Jan. 12, 1898). Lamb mentions him with affection in more than one passage (see 'A Chapter on Ears' in the *Essays of Elia*). His family circle was greatly beloved by those who had access to it, amongst others by Mendelssohn, who was often there during his early visits to this country, and many of whose extraordinary improvisations took place in the Novellos' drawing-room. (See Joseph Bennett's 'A Novello Centenary,' *Mus. T.*, 1881, p. 495; and *D.N.B.*)

The following among Vincent Novello's children followed musical careers :

(2) CECILIA (d. Genoa, June 20, 1890), his second daughter, studied singing under Mrs. Blane Hunt, and appeared upon the stage. She was a good musician, and an excellent and useful singer of secondary parts. She became the wife of Thomas James Serle, actor, dramatist and journalist. Their daughter, EMMA CLARA, a promising soprano singer, died at an early age, Oct. 4, 1877.

(3) CLARA ANASTASIA (b. June 10, 1818; d. Rome, Mar. 12, 1908), his fourth daughter, was at 9 years of age placed under Miss Hill and John Robinson, at York, to learn singing and pianoforte-playing. In 1829 she became a pupil of the Conservatoire at Paris, but returned to England in the following year on account of the Revolution. In 1833 she made her first public appearance at a concert at Windsor, with such success that she was immediately engaged at the Ancient and Philharmonic Concerts and Worcester Festival, and in the next year at the Westminster Abbey Festival. She sang at all the principal concerts and festivals until 1837, when, at the invitation of Mendelssohn, she went to Leipzig, and appeared at the Gewandhaus Concerts, whence she passed on to Berlin, Vienna, St. Petersburg and Düsseldorf. Writing to the secretary of the Philharmonic Society in Jan. 1839, Mendelssohn speaks of her and Mrs. Shaw as 'the best concert-singers we have heard in Germany for a long time,' and Schumann (*Gesamm.*

Schriften, iii. 47) dwells on the extraordinary interest she excited, and the universal surprise at her noble simple style of interpreting Handel. In 1839 she went to Italy to study for the stage, and became a pupil of Micheroux at Milan, with whom she remained for a year. She made her first appearance in opera at Padua, July 6, 1841, in Rossini's 'Semiramide,' with great success. She afterwards sang at Rome, Milan, Bologna, Modena and other places. She returned to England in Mar. 1843, and appeared in opera at Drury Lane, and in oratorio at the Sacred Harmonic Concerts, and the Birmingham Festival. On Nov. 22, 1843, she was married to Count Gigliucci, and withdrew from public life; but circumstances compelled her, a few years later, to return to the exercise of her profession, and in 1850 she sang in opera at Rome and Lisbon. In 1851 she returned to England and appeared in oratorio, in which she achieved her greatest successes, and at concerts. She also made one more appearance here on the stage, namely, in the 'Puritani' at Drury Lane, July 5, 1853. In 1854 she sang in opera at Milan. Her greatest triumphs were at the opening of the Crystal Palace, June 10, 1854, and at the Handel Festivals in 1857 and 1859, where her clear pure notes penetrated the vast space in a manner not to be easily forgotten. In Nov. 1860 she took leave of the public in a performance of 'Messiah' at the Crystal Palace, and at a benefit concert at St. James's Hall, and returned to Italy. Her voice was a high soprano, extending from C below the stave to D *in alt*, retaining till old age its purity of tone, brilliance and power. She excelled in oratorio, particularly in devotional songs, and she enjoyed the distinction of having drawn praise from Charles Lamb, notwithstanding his insensibility to music. Her reminiscences were published in 1910.

(4) MARY SABILLA (d. Genoa, Jan. 8, 1904), the sixth daughter, was also a soprano vocalist, but delicacy of throat and susceptibility to cold compelled her to relinquish singing. She translated several theoretical works into English. From 1849 she resided in Italy.

(5) JOSEPH ALFRED (b. Aug. 12, 1810; d. Genoa, July 16, 1896), the eldest son, was a bass singer, and for many years sang in oratorios and concerts. He was for some time choirmaster at Lincoln's Inn Chapel. He adapted the English text to the 'Lobgesang' and several of the Psalms of Mendelssohn. He was actively engaged in obtaining the repeal of the advertisement duty, the paper duty, the stamp on newspapers, and other imposts generally known as the 'Taxes upon Knowledge.' He was, however, best known as a music publisher. (See NOVELLO & COMPANY.) He retired in 1856 and went to reside at Nice, whence he removed to Genoa.   W. H. H.

NOVELLO & CO. A firm of music pub-lishers founded in 1811 by Vincent Novello. His first issue—' Novello's Sacred Music as per-formed at the Royal Portuguese Chapel '—de-serves mention for two reasons. The work consisted of two folio volumes of music sung at the chapel of the Portuguese Embassy, where Novello was organist. Finding no publisher willing to undertake the risk of production, he issued the works from his private residence, and so laid the foundation of the present house. Apart from the interest that must always attach to the small beginnings of great enterprises, this ' Sacred Music ' is notable for another reason. Hitherto all works of the kind had been issued with figured bass accompaniment only. Novello broke away from custom by writing out the organ part in full—an innovation which was disapproved by organists as a body. It seems certain, however, that the plan, by thus making the music accessible to the less skilled among players, was largely responsible for a success which encouraged Novello to continue and extend his venture. (For a list of the more important of his publications see the article under his name.)

In 1829 his son, JOSEPH ALFRED (q.v.) opened a music - publishing business at 67 Frith Street, Soho, whence he removed, five years later, to 69 Dean Street. Alfred Novello must be credited with the discovery of the possibilities, artistic and commercial, of cheap editions of standard works. A detailed account of the bold and energetic methods by which he carried the idea into practice appears in *A Short History of Cheap Music,* by Joseph Bennett, with a preface by Sir George Grove (Novello, 1887). The present widespread musical activity in this country (especially in choral singing) is due largely to the enterprise of Alfred Novello and his successor, Henry Littleton. A history of the steady growth of the popular interest in classi-cal choral music during the period 1830–70 would be little more than a history of the house of Novello during those years. A few salient points will enable the reader to realise this. Sir George Grove, in the Preface mentioned above (dated 1887), says,

' When the present writer was in his teens [1830–40] the price of music was more than twenty times what it now is. The first guinea that he recollects having given him, in 1837, was expended in a pianoforte score of the ' Messiah ' which is now published at a shilling.'

It is hard to realise to-day that when Alfred Novello began to publish there were few choral societies, and that the members of one of the most important in London—the Cecilian Society—were accustomed to sing the ' Messiah ' from manuscript copies, or from old scores ·ssued by Button and Whitaker, St. Paul's Churchyard, at two guineas each. Not only were cheap copies of Handel's oratorios un-known : so small was the demand for any complete works of large scale, that when in 1836 Alfred Novello announced his purchase of the English copyright of ' St. Paul,' and the issue of the . pianoforte score at thirty-two shillings, the music trade felt that he was court-ing disaster. The step, followed as it was by the publication of other choral works by Mendelssohn—the Psalms, ' Lobgesang,' etc.—proved on the contrary to be a means of con-solidating the position of the firm. The needs of many small bodies that were springing up at this period were met by such issues as ' Novello's Choral Handbook,' issued in separate parts at 3d. a page, and Mainzer's ' Singing for the Million,' a series of choruses published by Novello in penny numbers. Popular choralism was further stimulated by Alfred Novello him-self during his commercial tours, which were

' exalted into the dignity of musical missions. His cheap publications had made the formation of choral societies possible. In the large factories of York-shire and Lancashire many choral unions existed, and the publications of the house were gladly welcomed, because of their modest price and accuracy. The publisher in his progress was always cordially received, and often concerts were given in his honour, the performers making extra exertions to show their advancement since his last issue.' [1]

The year 1844 saw the beginning of *The Musical Times* (see PERIODICALS, MUSICAL). From the first it contained one or more pieces of choral music, and the size adopted for the purpose of the journal led to the idea of the ' Octavo Editions' which have ever since been a prominent feature in the firm's output. In 1846 began the issue of the ' Messiah ' in twelve monthly numbers at 6d. each, the complete work costing 6s. 6d. ' The Creation,' ' Judas Maccabeus,' ' Jeptha,' ' St. Paul,' and other oratorios followed in the same cheap form. Ten years later the ' Messiah ' was issued com-plete for 1s. 4d. These and other steps in the direction of Alfred Novello's goal of cheap music were made possible by the repeal of the various ' Taxes on Knowledge' (a reform in which he played a prominent part), and by his prompt adoption and development of improve-ments in printing.

In 1857 Alfred Novello retired to Italy, leav-ing the rapidly growing business to be managed by Henry Littleton, who had entered his em-ploy as a lad. Four years later Littleton was taken into partnership (the title of the firm becoming Novello & Co.), and soon afterwards he bought the business, having thus risen in about twenty-five years from the humble post of ' collector ' to sole proprietor. In 1867 the business of Ewer & Co. was acquired, and with it all the existing Mendelssohn copyrights. The same year saw the opening of the premises at 1 Berners Street. The present address of the firm is 160 Wardour Street. Henry Littleton's conduct of the business was even more daring [2]

[1] *A Short History of Cheap Music.*
[2] For a detailed account of his operations, which included suc·

than that of his predecessor, and was so successful that on his retirement in 1887 the firm had become one of the largest of its kind in the world.

On Henry Littleton's death (May 11, 1888) he was succeeded by his sons ALFRED (d. Nov. 8, 1914) and AUGUSTUS, the present (1926) chairman, the firm reverting to its former title of Novello & Co.   H. G.

NOVERRE, JEAN GEORGES (b. Paris, Apr. 29, 1727 ; d. St. Germain-en-Laye, Oct.[1] or Nov. 19,[2] 1810 [3]). His father, who had formerly served under Charles XII., intended him for the army, but his love of dancing and the theatre were invincible, and he became the great authority on dancing, and the reformer of the French ballet. A pupil of the celebrated dancer Dupré, he made his début before the court at Fontainebleau in 1743. He was engaged by Frederick the Great in Berlin to organise the opera ballet, and was well received. In 1747 he returned to Paris, and composed several ballets, among them the ' Ballet chinois,' for the Opéra - Comique (where he became ballet-master in 1749), the success of which aroused so much jealousy as to induce him to accept Garrick's invitation to London in 1755 as ballet - master. The ' Chinese Festival,' produced at Drury Lane, Nov. 8, 1755, provoked great opposition owing to political circumstances. There he spent two years, profiting in more ways than one, as may be seen by the more extended knowledge and more elevated imagination of his ballets of that date. He returned to Paris hoping for the appointment of ballet-master to the Académie Royale de Musique, but failing this, he accepted a lucrative engagement at the large theatre of Lyons. Here, in conjunction with Granier, he produced three ballets (1758 and 1759) of which the scenarios were printed. Here also he published his Lettres sur la danse et les ballets (1760, 1 vol. 8vo), which attracted general notice, and greatly increased his reputation. Remaining still without a summons to Paris, he found a patron in the Duke of Wurtemberg, for whom he composed no less than twenty divertissements and ballets-pantomimes. In 1765 he returned to Paris and produced ' Médée.' In 1770 Empress Maria Theresa summoned him to Vienna, as director of the court fêtes, and dancing-master to the Imperial family ; and here again he composed a dozen ballets for the court theatre, the scenarios of

which were printed separately. On the marriage of Archduke Ferdinand, Noverre received the Order of Christ, and permission to take part in the wedding fêtes at Milan, when he produced several new ballets, afterwards given in Vienna. His two letters to Voltaire describing Garrick (printed in the French translation of the Life of Garrick, 1801) probably date from a visit to London which Noverre paid at this time.

On his return to Paris in 1775, Noverre obtained, through his former pupil Marie Antoinette, now Queen of France, the long-coveted post of ' Maître des ballets en chef ' at the Opéra. In addition to revivals of earlier works he composed specially for the Opéra ' Les Caprices de Galathée ' (Sept. 30, 1776) ; ' Annette et Lubin ' (June 9, 1778) ; ' Les Petits Riens ' (June 11, 1778), for which Mozart wrote fourteen pieces ; the music was long supposed to be lost, but was discovered in 1873 in the library of the Opéra in Paris by Nuitter ; it was printed in extenso in C. E. Noverre's Life and Works of the Chevalier Noverre (1882), but is placed by Köchel in his appendix of lost works, where, however, he gives the themes of thirteen out of the fourteen movements ; and ' Médée ' (Jan. 30, 1780). He also arranged the divertissements of several operas by Gluck and Piccinni. In the famous quarrel over these two composers Noverre took the side of Piccinni. He retired with a pension in 1780, and lived at St. Germain-en-Laye. His ' works ' in three volumes were published in an English translation in 1782. On the outbreak of the Revolution he fled to London, and there produced two of his best ballets, ' Les Noces de Thétis ' and ' Iphigénie en Aulide.' After so successful a career he was justified in looking forward to an old age of affluence, but during the Revolution he lost the savings of fifty years and was reduced to poverty, which he bore with dignity and resignation.

Noverre several times remodelled his standard work Lettres sur la danse et les ballets (Lyons ; Stuttgart, 1760 ; Paris, 1760, 1783 ; Vienna, 1767 ; Copenhagen, 1803).[4] An edition published at St. Petersburg (1803–04), Lettres sur la danse, sur les ballets et les arts, 4 vols., scarce, and apparently unknown to Fétis, contains analyses of numerous ballets. The best known is the Paris edition of 1807, Lettres sur les arts imitateurs en général, et sur la danse en particulier, 2 vols., with portrait engraved by Roger after Guérin, and the following lines by Imbert :

' Du feu de son génie il anima la danse :
    Aux beaux jours de la Grèce il sut la rappeler ;
    Et, recourvant par lui leur antique éloquence,
    Les gestes et les pas apprirent à parler ' ;

gigantic concert enterprise as the series of two hundred given at the International Exhibition in 1873–74 ; the nightly concerts launched at the Albert Hall in 1874, which anticipated the present ' Promenades ' by adopting a weekly scheme of ' nights,' ' Classical,' ' Wagner,' ' Oratorio,' ' English,' ' Ballad,' and ' Popular ' ; the formation of the Barnby Choir ; the undertaking of the general direction of the Royal Choral Society when Barnby succeeded Gounod as conductor, the reader is referred to A History of Cheap Music and the biographical sketch which appeared in The Musical Times of Jan. 1923, the centenary of his birth.
1 Choron and Favolle.   2 Fétis
3 Some authorities give 1807, but that is apparently a mistake. The date given in his descendant's biography is Oct. 18, 1809, but no authority is quoted in support.

4 German translation : Briefe über die Tanzkunst (Hamburg and Bremen, 1769), J. H. Cramer ; also in Hamburger Blätter für Unterhaltung, vol. i.

which give a good summary of what Noverre effected. He invented the ballet d'action, reformed the costume of the dancers, abolished routine in favour of taste, compelled composers to conform their music to the situations in the drama and the sentiments of the characters, and succeeded in making the pantomime appeal to the intellect as well as to the eye.

Among Noverre's writings may be specified *Observations sur la construction d'une nouvelle Salle de l'Opéra* (Paris, 1770 [1]; Amsterdam, 1787) ; and *Lettres à un artiste sur les fêtes publiques* (Year IX.). The MS. notes of an eminent bibliophile allude to another, *Théorie et pratique de la danse en général*, which seems not to have been printed, and was doubtless intended for the *Dictionnaire de la danse*, projected by Noverre, but not finished.   G. C.

NOVOTNÝ, JAROSLAV (*b.* Jičín, 1886 ; *d.* 1918), a Czech composer of promise, killed in the Ural district while fighting with the Czech legionaries against the Bolsheviks. He studied under Vít. Novák and was making his mark in the musical world of Prague when he was called upon to serve in the Austrian army. Having been taken prisoner by the Russians, he joined the Czech legion, and, like his compatriot, Rudolf KAREL (*q.v.*) managed to carry on his art amid a strenuous campaign. The choruses written in Russia show a marked tendency to adopt the newest theories of composition. His works include : ' Večna svatba ' (The Eternal Wedding), a cycle of 4 songs, op. 2, and ' Balady duše ' (Ballads of the Soul), four settings of poems by Sova, op. 4 (Hudební Matice) ; children's songs (MS.) ; string quartet; pianoforte sonata; choruses (Hudební Matice).   R. N.

NOWELL, see NOËL.

NOZZE DI FIGARO, LE, opera buffa by Mozart, in 4 acts ; libretto by L. da Ponte after Beaumarchais's ' Mariage de Figaro,' on Mozart's own suggestion. It is dated, in Mozart's Autograph Catalogue, Vienna, Apr. 29, 1786. Produced National Theatre, Vienna, May 1, 1786 ; Opéra, Paris, in 5 acts, with Beaumarchais's spoken dialogue, Mar. 20, 1793; King's Theatre (in Italian), June 18, 1812 ; in English, Covent Garden, Mar. 6, 1819 ; New York in 1823.   G.

NUCIUS (NUX ; NUCIS), JOANNES (*b.* Görlitz, Silesia, *c.* 1556). In the *M.f.M.* xxxvi. 200-209, Reinhold Starke corrects and supplements from documentary evidence the details given in *Q.-L.* as to the life and works of Nucius. From this we learn that Nucius received his musical instruction from a certain Johannes Winckler, whom he describes as a very capable musician. He afterwards took the monastic vows in the Cistercian Abbey of Rauden in Upper Silesia, and in 1591 was elected Abbot of the daughter-house of Him-

melwitz. The Abbey was burnt down in 1617, but Nucius survived the partial rebuilding of it to Mar. 25, 1620. His published works consist of two books of motets for five and six voices (Cantiones Sacrae . . . Prague, 1591, 1595, and Liegnitz, 1609), containing altogether 129 numbers, including second parts. His intention to publish a book of masses does not appear to have been carried out. Two masses with missing parts exist in MS. Nucius also put forth in 1613 a theoretical work entitled *Musices poeticae sive de compositione cantus*. Of this work Starke gives a pretty full account in the *Monatshefte* referred to above. Nucius expresses his great veneration for the works of Josquin des Prés and Orlando Lassus.

BIBL.—BERNHARD WIDMANN, *Johann Nucius, Abt von Himmelwitz. Ein Altmeister der klassischen Polyphonie*, p. 32. (Bregenz, 1922.), Reprinted from the ' Cisterzienser-Chronik,' Jahrg. 32. Cf. Reinhold Starke, *Johannes Nux, M.f.M.* Bd. 36, 1904.

J. R. M.

NUIT DE MAI, opera in 3 acts ; text after Gogol, music by Rimsky-Korsakov. Produced St. Petersburg, 1880 ; Drury Lane, June 26, 1914.

NUITTER,[2] CHARLES LOUIS ÉTIENNE (originally TRUINET) (*b.* Paris, Apr. 24, 1828; *d.* there, Feb. 24, 1899), librettist and French writer on music. In 1849 he was a lawyer, devoting his spare time to the theatre, and from 1855 he collaborated (notably with de Beaume, called Beaumont), in a large number of *vaudevilles* and libretti for opera, operettes, ballets; also translations, amongst others, at the Théâtre Lyrique: Weber's ' Obéron,' ' Preciosa,' ' Abou-Hassan ' (1857–59) ; Bellini's ' Roméo ' (1859) ; Mozart's ' La Flûte enchantée ' (1865) ; Wagner's ' Rienzi ' (1869). At the Opéra: ' Tannhäuser ' (1861), ' Lohengrin ' (1891 ; Brussels, 1870) ; Verdi's ' Aïda ' (1800) ; Delibes' ballets, ' La Source ' and ' Coppélia ' (1866 and 1870) ; Lalo's ballet, ' Namouna ' (1882). At the Bouffes he gave ' La Prise de Trébizonde ' and ' Boule de neige ' with Offenbach (1869 and 1871). At the Nouveautés : ' Le Cœur et la main ' with Lecocq (1880). At the Opéra-Comique: Wagner's ' Le Vaisseau-fantôme ' (1897 ; Brussels, 1872).

In 1865 Nuitter was appointed archivist at the Opéra. With Théodore de Lajarte, keeper of the music, he reorganised the important department which had been put under his care, and he enriched it with numerous works, drawings, autographs, play-bills and documents of all kinds connected with the theatre and music in Paris (notably a very important collection of journals), acquisitions the greater part of which were paid for out of his own pocket.

Nuitter contributed to the *Chronique musicale* (1873 *et seq.*) and published the following : *Le Nouvel Opéra* (1875) ; *Histoire et description du nouvel opéra* (1884) ; with

Thoinan, a fine work, *Les Origines de l'opéra français* (1886); in the *Bayreuther Festspiel-Blätter* (1884), a documented article on the first production of ' Tannhäuser ' in Paris.

BIBL.—WAGNER, *Mein Leben*; G. SERVIÈRES, *Wagner jugé en France* (1887), *Tannhäuser à l'opéra en 1861* (1895), and *Guide musical* (1914).
                                J. G. P.

NUNC DIMITTIS. The first words of the Song of Simeon used as an Evening Canticle from very early days, and especially at Compline, where it was not likely to receive elaborate musical treatment. But in the making of the Anglican Prayer Book it became an integral part of English Evensong; and as such it has been set by a great number of the best English church composers on large lines. (See SERVICE.)   W. H. F.

NURMAHAL, see LALLA ROOKH (2).

NUT. (1) Of the violin (Fr. *sillet*; Ger. *Sattel*). A slip of ebony or ivory (the former chiefly used) glued to the neck of the violin at the upper end of the FINGER-BOARD (*q.v.*), and over which the strings pass. It is slightly raised above the level of the finger-board, and serves to keep the strings from touching it except when pressed down by the finger. It existed in the old instruments which preceded the violin, and in them was ruder and larger.

(2) Of the bow (Fr. *hausse*; Ger. *Frosch*). A piece of ebony or ivory, over which the hairs pass, attached to the end of the bow by a metal shank working in a groove cut in the bow. A screw working in the shank serves to tighten or slacken the hairs. The nut is slightly hollowed in the cheeks, and is accurately fitted to the stick by means of a metallic groove. The nut is as old as the bow itself.

The name in both cases is equivalent to ' knob ' or ' projection.'   E. J. P.

NYASTARANGA (Throat Trumpet), a brass instrument used in the N.W. provinces of India. Though resembling in shape a small trumpet it is not blown by the mouth, but placed on the vibrating chords of the throat. As the performer hums the melody the sound is taken up sympathetically by a delicate membrane (the cocoon or egg-case of a spider, or a piece of very thin rice paper) placed over the hole at the bottom of the shallow cup-mouthpiece, the sound being then reinforced by the resonating tube of the trumpet. In India it is considered a classical instrument and very ancient; it i generally used in pairs, one placed on each side of the throat. The tone is reedy and somewhat uncanny; it is more readily produced if the membrane is slightly moistened.   F. W. G.

O

OAKELEY, Sir Herbert Stanley, Mus.D. (*b.* Ealing, July 22, 1830 ; *d.* Eastbourne, Oct. 26, 1903), second son of Sir Herbert Oakeley, Bart., was educated at Rugby and Christ Church, Oxford. He graduated B.A. in 1853 and M.A. in 1856. He studied harmony under Dr. Stephen Elvey, and the organ under Dr. Johann Schneider at Dresden, and completed his musical studies at Leipzig, with Prof. Breidenstein of Bonn. In 1865 he was elected professor of music in the University of Edinburgh. He received his Mus.D. degree from the Archbishop of Canterbury (Tait) in 1871, and was knighted in 1876. He received in 1879 the degree of Mus.D. from the University of Oxford, and in 1881 that of LL.D. from the University of Aberdeen ; he was created in the same year composer of music to Her Majesty in Scotland. In 1886 the University of Toronto conferred on him the degree of D.C.L., and in 1887 he received the degree of Mus.D. from the University of Dublin. In 1891 he resigned the Edinburgh professorship, and was made Emeritus Professor in the following year. A year after his death a memoir by his brother, E. M. Oakeley, was published in London. Among his own publications are many songs, with pianoforte or orchestral accompaniment, twenty of which were published in a 'Jubilee Album' dedicated to Queen Victoria ; three vocal duets ; twelve partsongs ; students' songs and choral arrangements of eighteen Scottish National melodies, and of various others for male voices. For the church, some dozen anthems, a Jubilee Cantata for 1887, a motet with orchestral accompaniment, a Morning and Evening Service and many hymn-tunes. He also published a few of his compositions for pianoforte and organ, and for orchestra, including a festal and a funeral march.

Sir Herbert Oakeley had a remarkable gift of improvisation, and was an organ-player of exceptional ability. During his tenure of the professorship he gave a great impulse to the public performance of music at the Reid Concert (*q.v.*) ; he inaugurated an annual festival which did a good work for some years. w. h. h.

OBBLIGATO, *i.e.* necessary, a term signifying that the instrument with which it is coupled is indispensable in that place or that piece. It is in this respect the opposite to Ad libitum. (See Accompaniment.) g.

OBERMEYER, Joseph (*b.* Nezabudicz, Bohemia, in 1749), violinist. Kamel was his first master and, owing to the generosity of his patron Count Vincent Waldstein, Tartini was his second. He is said to have closely imitated the broad adagio playing of the great maestro. On his return to Bohemia he resumed his post of valet-de-chambre (which it need hardly be observed was a household position different from that which is nowadays implied by the term) to Count Waldstein. Eventually he relinquished this situation, and becoming a farmer performed but rarely in public. In 1801 he reappeared at Prague with great success, and three years later his playing at some musical fêtes at Strathaw was, according to Fétis, greatly admired. He was then 55. He was still alive in 1816. e. h.-a.

Bibl.—*Fétis* ; Clarke, *Dictionary of Fiddlers* ; Q.-L.

OBERNDÖRFFER, David, an early 17th-century instrumental player at Frankfort-on-M., wrote 'Allegrezza musicale,' an important collection of pavans, galliards, canzonets, etc., for sundry instruments in 4-6 parts, including some by Wm. Brade, Tho. Simpson, J. H. Schein, Val. Haussmann, etc. (*Q.-L.*).

OBERON, opera in 3 acts ; words (English) by J. R. Planché, music by Weber. Produced Covent Garden, Apr. 12, 1826 ; in Italian (Maggione), Her Majesty's (in 4 acts), July 3, 1860, with recitatives by Benedict and six additional numbers from 'Euryanthe' and elsewhere ; in German, Leipzig (Hell's translation), Dec. 23, 1826 ; Théâtre Allemand, Paris, 1830 ; Théâtre Lyrique (transl. by Nuitter, Beaumont Chazot), 1857. g.

OBERTAS. From 'Obracać,' signifying ' to turn round.' ' Obertas ' has a second meaning, ' confusion ' or ' perplexity.' The accent lies on the second syllable. This is described in the *Encyklopedyja Powszechna* (Warsaw, 1884) as the most popular of Polish national dances.

The couples follow their leader, turning from right to left, and describing a circle or oval ring. The woman sometimes dances round her partner, and sometimes *vice versa* ; a song is often sung at the same time. The obertas is evidently regarded by the Poles as their national waltz, though, as will have been seen, it differs from the German waltz in several characteristics of the dance as well as in the style of the music associated with it by modern composers. Wieniawski's 'Mazurka caractéristique' for violin No. 1 bears the sub-title 'Obertas' ; it is deficient in the rough, wild character, without which the dance is scarcely to be distinguished from a mazurka. Boito introduces the obertas into the first scene of Act i. of ' Mefistofele ' ; whether he was guilty of an anachronism in representing his 16th-century Frankfort populace indulging in a national dance of Poland (to say nothing of Polish exclamations) is open to question. The Mazurka found its way into North-Germany only after August III. of Saxony ascended the throne in 1733 (Brockhaus). Had the obertas been adopted at any time by the German people, such writers as Angerstein, Czerwinski, Voss, etc., could not have ignored it in their works on the art and history of the Dance ; though their neglect to include the name of a dance known only in Poland in their enumeration of dances of all nations is at least excusable. However, the charm of these stirring strains, no doubt suggested to Boito by his Polish mother, renders very welcome the composer's possible deviation from historic truth.

Wieniawski and Boito suggest by a drone bass in fifths the rude accompaniment of the bagpipes or other primitive combination of instruments.

> ' Tutto vanno alla rinfusa
> Sulla musica confusa
> Così far la cornamusa—'

writes Boito for his chorus. The wild and romping nature of this dance and music must have proved without attraction for Chopin, who has at any rate not included by name an obertas among his mazurkas. Nevertheless, we may recognise that in C major, op. 56, No. 2 (Vivace), as being in harmony and rhythm the nearest approach to the obertas attempted by this fastidious and undramatic composer.

L. M. M.

OBERTHÜR, Charles (b. Munich, Mar. 4, 1819 ; d. London, Nov. 8, 1895), a distinguished performer on and composer for the harp. His father carried on a manufactory of strings for musical instruments in Munich. His teachers were Elise Brauchle and G. V. Röder, the court Director of Music. In the autumn of 1837 he was engaged by Charlotte Birch-Pfeiffer as harp-player at the Zürich theatre. He stayed there until Sept. 1839, when, after a concert tour through Switzerland, he accepted an engagement at Wiesbaden. In 1842 he went to Mannheim, where he remained until 1844. A difference with V. Lachner, and the representations of English friends then living at Mannheim, induced Oberthür in Oct. 1844 to come to England, where he found a firm protector in Moscheles, and where he took up his residence. He first obtained an engagement at the Italian Opera, but soon gave this up, and devoted himself to private teaching and composition, with occasional appearances as a soloist at the principal concerts in England and abroad.

The list of Oberthür's compositions (more than 200 in number) includes two operas, 'Floris von Namur' and ' Der Berggeist des Harzes,' successfully performed at Wiesbaden ; a Mass, ' St. Philip de Neri ' ; cantatas, ' The Pilgrim Queen,' ' The Red Cross Knight ' and ' Lady Jane Grey'; Overtures (' Macbeth' and ' Rübezahl '); Trios for harp, violin and violoncello ; a Concertino for harp and orchestra ; ' Loreley '—a legend for harp and orchestra ; a Quartet for four harps, etc.   W. B. S.

OBLIQUE PIANO, a cottage pianoforte the

strings of which are disposed diagonally. The greatest angle, however, is at the longest and lowest string, the bias gradually diminishing until the shortest and highest string is vertical or nearly so. The object is to get greater length in the bass strings. The invention of the Oblique Piano is due to Robert Wornum, of London, who, in 1811, took out a patent for an upright piano with the strings set diagonally, and the heads of the hammers in the same rake as the strings. The Oblique Piano was comparatively early adopted in France, especially by Roller & Blanchet, who made very distinguished small instruments in this manner. The principle was then generally adopted by the best French and English makers, and later by the Germans and Americans. (See Pianoforte.)   A. J. H.

OBOE (or Hautboy) (Fr. hautbois; Ger. Oboe, Hoboe, Hochholz; Ital. oboe), a wooden instrument of conical bore played with a double reed. There are several varieties : (1) the Oboe proper, (2) the Cor anglais, (3) the Oboe d' amore, (4) the Baritone Oboe and (5) the obsolete Oboe di caccia. For the Pastoral Oboe see Bagpipe and Shepherd's Pipe.

(1) The orchestral Oboe as now made sounds d' when the six holes controlled by the fingers and others by key-work are closed, and by raising the fingers in succession the scale of D major is obtained as on the flute. Strictly speaking, the instrument is therefore in D, but as the notes sound as written, it is customarily spoken of as being in C. Its tube is conical, enlarging from the reed to the bell, and it therefore overblows to the octave, and is usually built up of three portions, the ' top joint,' ' lower joint ' and ' bell.' In addition to these there is the small metal tube, or ' staple,' to which the blades of cane forming the double reed are secured. To facilitate the fingering of semitones, the third and fourth finger-holes were formerly made double, that is to say, instead of a full-sized hole, two small ones placed side by side were used in each case, one or both of which could be covered by the finger, but although this arrangement was long maintained, the necessity for it has passed away with the modern free use of key-work. By the end of the 17th century two keys giving c' and $e'\flat$ were introduced ; in 1727 Gerard Hofmann of Rastenburg added two keys for $g'\sharp$, $a'\sharp$, and in the 19th century the instrument gradually attained its present delicacy and excellence. The Method by Sellner, published in 1825 at Vienna, describes keys producing c', $c'\sharp$, $d'\sharp$, f', $f'\sharp$, $g'\sharp$, $a'\sharp$, c'', and also an octave key. The present compass of the instrument extends downwards to $b\natural$, and sometimes to $b\flat$, and the fingering of the less complicated models is not dissimilar from that of the flute and the bassoon. (See PLATE V. No. 6.)

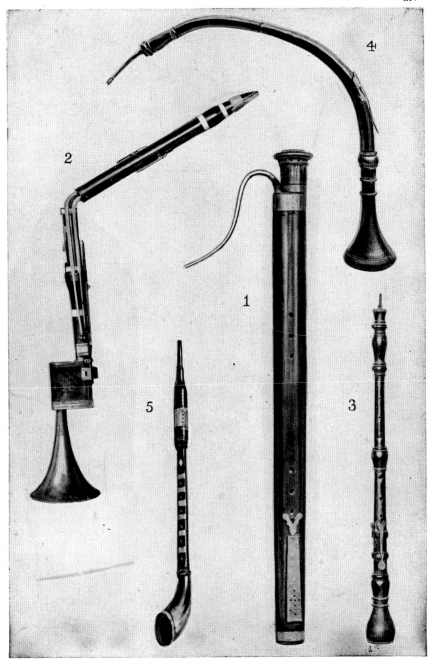

LIV

1. DOLCIAN (Fagotto) (*c.* 1620).   2. BASSET HORN (J. Stengel, *c.* 1820).

2. OBOE D'AMORE (J. Poerschmann, *c.* 1725).   4. OBOE DA CACCIA (C. Strisch, 18th cent.)

5. STOCK HORN (18th cent.).

1, 2. Heyer Museum, formerly Cologne, now Leipzig.   3, 4. Metropolitan Museum, New York.   5. Royal College of Music.

From the lowest note, whether $b\flat$ or $b\natural$ (1) to the $b'\natural$ next above (2), thirteen or twelve consecutive semitones are successively obtained by lifting fingers or depressing keys. For c'' (3) the middle finger of the left hand is kept down and the forefinger lifted, as on the flute, the note being improved by covering the right-hand finger-holes. For $c''\sharp$ all finger-holes are open, or as an alternative the fingering of its lower octave $c'\sharp$ can be used, the emission of the note being aided by a slight opening of the $c'\sharp$ hole, which in this way serves as a vent or speaker. Continuing to repeat the fingering of the lower octave, d' and $d'\sharp$ are obtained by a similar use of the $c''\sharp$ hole. From e'' (4) to a'' (5) the first octave or speaker-key which is worked by the thumb is used, and in all modern instruments there is a second octave key worked by the knuckle of the left forefinger, by means of which the scale can be extended from a'' to a''' (6), though

the f''' below this may be considered as the practical limit of the oboe's compass. In the most recent instruments of all, these two ' vent-holes,' or harmonic keys, which serve only to determine a node in the tube, and which, unlike the corresponding mechanism of the clarinet, do not furnish an independent note of their own, are made automatic, and practically independent of the player's will. For most of the higher notes above a'', the bottom $d'\sharp$ key requires to be raised by the right little finger, just as occurs in the flute.

The above scale, from its close similarity to those of the flute and bassoon, may be looked upon as traditional and fundamental. But hardly any wind-instrument, except the flute, has been so altered and modified of late years in its mechanism as the oboe. The form most in use at the present day is a modification of the older model described above, with many devices borrowed from the Boehm system of fingering. It has thus become by far the most elaborate and complicated of reed instruments, and it is a question whether a return to an older and simpler pattern, by lessening the weight of the machine, and the number of holes breaking the continuity of the bore, and by increasing the vibratory powers of the wooden tube, would not conduce to an improved quality of tone.

The chief improvements due to BARRÉ and TRIEBERT (q.v.) may be briefly named as (1) the introduction of a plate for the left-hand thumb, somewhat similar to that on modern flutes, by which this member, formerly idle, is called into action; (2) the double automatic octave keys, an improvement upon the two separate octave keys, named above; (3) a vast

number of double, triple and even quadruple alternative fingerings for particular notes, which materially reduce the mechanical difficulty of inconvenient passages.[1]

It is not, however, in the mechanism only that the oboe of to-day is entirely different from that used in the early part of the 19th century, but also in the sound-producer or reed, as is shown by the accompanying illustration

 of two examples, half the actual size. The right-hand cut is a reproduction of the modern reed, that on the left is one of several given to the late Dr. W. H. Stone; they belonged to the oboist who accompanied Rossini on his first visit to this country, in 1823, the composer being unwilling to entrust his elaborate oboe parts to any English pretender. It will be at once seen that the latter is a reproduction of the Pifferaro reed, approximating more to that of the bassoon than to that of the modern oboe.

The oboe as above described is the instrument practically in general use both in orchestras and military bands. For the latter, however, the oboe is sometimes, but not often, made in B♭ instead of in C, and a smaller instrument in E♭, or soprano oboe, is also occasionally used; the two instruments thus pitched are in correspondence with the B♭ and E♭ clarinets respectively, and therefore require the same transpositions of the written parts.

A small oboe or shawm was formerly made in G or A flat, without keys, and called Musette.

The development of the modern oboe and its relationship to other double reed instruments can be best traced by reference to some primitive types. The double reed is certainly prehistoric, and the oboe in its rudest form is of the highest antiquity, and has been used in all parts of the globe. It can be traced in the sculptures and paintings of ancient Egypt and Greece; indeed, specimens are preserved in the British and Leyden Museums, which were found with straws beside them, probably to be used in making the reed. Instruments from Arabia, ancient America, China, Hindustan, Italy and Wallachia are deposited in the Victoria and Albert Museum.

HISTORY.—Although some of these ancient instruments were undoubtedly rude, yet others, both in design and workmanship, were of high class, and it is therefore impossible to speak of the modern oboe as an invention of any particular date. It should rather be regarded as the outcome of a gradual differentiation of type, accentuated by the refinement of a particular

1 On these and other points the writer has to thank Mr. Mitcalfe, of Lowestoft, for some valuable suggestions.

member of a family. By the 16th century, two chief families of double reed instruments were well established, and are described by Sebastian Virdung (1511) and by Michael Praetorius (1618). One of these families, in which the double reed is associated with a cylindrical tube, is represented by the KRUMMHORN (q.v.), and lies outside the scope of this article. In the other chief family the double reed is fitted to a conical tube, and the oboe is the aristocratic descendant of one branch of this family. The whole group comprised schalmeys or shawms, and pommers, known also as bombards, from the humming or buzzing tone of the lower-pitched members of the group. The little schalmey with lowest note a' was, according to Praetorius, not much used ; the discant schalmey with lowest note d' has been developed into the modern oboe. These two schalmeys were the treble members of the family, the set or choir of six being completed by the alto, tenor and bass pommers, with the great double-quint pommer descending to the contra F (FF). The typical instrument had six finger-holes, and in the tenor, bass and double-quint instruments these were supplemented by extra holes closed by keys to extend the compass downwards. The differentiation of this primitive type above referred to has resulted in the oboes and bassoons as we now know them, for the distinction between these is not mainly that of pitch as between treble and bass, but one of quality, instruments of the oboe group having a lighter and more delicate quality than bassoons, irrespective of pitch. In the 17th century the little and discant schalmeys, with the alto and tenor pommers, were grouped together and called ' haulx - bois ' or ' haultbois,' to distinguish them from the two larger pommers called ' gros-bois.' We thus obtain the modern French and English names Hautbois and Oboe, and it was early in the 17th century that the discant schalmey assumed the form of the oboe, the addition of key-work since that date being a gradual development, and not the introduction of any distinctively new principle.

The oboe with its congeners was formerly used for town bands and military purposes to an extent not now seen, and long before it was introduced into church and artistic secular music, indeed, military bands were in Germany termed ' Hautboisten,' and a well - known copperplate engraving of the 18th century shows the band of the English Guards passing to St. James's Palace, consisting principally of oboes of different sizes, with bassoons of primitive shape, drums and cymbals.

The tone is peculiarly distinctive, and without being powerful or obtrusive it is very penetrating. A character of sportiveness and light-heartedness seems proper to it in quick movements, and yet in slow passages there is perhaps no instrument which can better give the effect of a ' pleading ' or ' beseeching ' as distinguished from a ' plaintive ' voice.

The oboe appears to have been first introduced into the orchestra in Cambert's opera, ' Pomone,' given in Paris in 1671.

(2) COR ANGLAIS (English Horn) (Ger. englisches Horn; Ital. corno inglese) differs in build from the oboe in that the tube is longer and ends in a globular or pear-shaped bell, and the crook which holds the reed is bent back at an angle. (See PLATE V. No. 5). It is a refined development of the tenor pommer, and in early examples is found with the whole tube bent either into a curve or at an obtuse angle. The derivation of the name is uncertain ; the instrument is neither ' English ' nor is it a ' horn.' ' cor anglé ' (angled horn) has been suggested as being due to the last-named or angled form.

Built in F, it sounds a fifth lower than the oboe and possesses the same compass. The part is written a fifth higher with a key-signature of one flat less or one sharp more than that of the music. In old French scores the part is found written with a mezzo-soprano clef, the player reading it as though from the treble clef. The Italians formerly adopted the plan of writing the part in the bass clef an octave below the sounds required.

The tone-colour possesses a peculiar melancholy or reflective sadness strikingly exemplified by the familiar shepherd's pipe melody in Act iii. of ' Tristan,' or the melody of the slow movement from Dvořák's ' New World ' Symphony. Gluck wrote for the cor anglais in ' Alceste ' and ' Orfeo,' the parts being arranged for clarinet for performance in Paris, as the instrument was not introduced into the opera orchestra until 1808. Although Mozart, Haydn and Beethoven wrote for it occasionally, it did not become a regular member of the German orchestra till Wagner's day.

(3) OBOE D' AMORE (Fr. hautbois d'amour). This instrument is built a minor third lower than the oboe proper, and its part is therefore written in a key with three flats or three sharps less than that of the piece. The compass is

from (there is no key extension

for obtaining the B♭) to the high E sounding

. (See PLATE LIV. No. 3.)

Since the time of Bach, who wrote for it in the ' Christmas Oratorio,' the Passion music and other works, the oboe d' amore appears to have fallen into complete disuse until its revival by Strauss in his ' Sinfonia domestica.'

(4) BARITONE OBOE, BASSET OBOE (Ger. Heckelphon), is a development of the tenor pommer. Various attempts have been made from time to time to establish a bass oboe, an instrument, that is, an octave lower than the

ordinary oboe and with a similar compass. Such an one was exhibited at the Paris Exhibition in 1889. The ' Heckelphon ' is a German instrument of this type made by Heckel, and was used by Strauss in ' Salome.'

(5) OBOE DI CACCIA (hunting oboe), an obsolete type of alto oboe, a development of the alto pommer and possessing the same pitch as the cor anglais, which has now taken its place. Parts for it are to be found in Bach's ' Christmas Oratorio,' the ' St. Matthew ' and ' St. John ' Passions and numerous cantatas. (See *PLATE LIV.* No. 4.)

The late Dr. Stone in earlier editions of this Dictionary seems to have confused the oboe di caccia with the tenor bassoon. (See BASSOON (3).)

OBOE D' AMORE (Fr. *hautbois d'amour*), see OBOE (3).

OBOE DI CACCIA, see OBOE (5).

OBRECHT (HOBRECHT), JACOB (*b.*? Utrecht, *c.* 1430 ; *d.* Ferrara,[1] 1505), one of the great masters of the 15th century. In early life he was maître de chapelle at Utrecht, and Erasmus [2] learnt music from him, as a choir-boy in the cathedral, about the year 1474. Traces of a visit to Italy, where he entered the services of Duke Ercole of Ferrara, in 1474, have been found by Van der Straeten.[3] In 1483–85 he was director of the school of singing at Cambray, and in 1489–1500 held the office of teacher at St. Donat at Bruges. He was also living some time in Florence, where Aaron met him in company with Josquin, Isaac and Agricola at the court of Lorenzo il Magnifico.

In 1491 Obrecht was elected maître de chapelle in Antwerp Cathedral, already a great musical centre, with a fine choir of nearly seventy voices, exclusive of boys. Of the higher honours and emoluments he received there, of the visits paid him by foreign musicians, of his work in the revision of the cathedral music-books, and lastly of his poor health, Léon de Burbure has found ample evidence in the records of that church.[4] Obrecht's Passion Music is a noteworthy and early contribution to the development of that form. It is described under PASSION MUSIC, subsection THE MOTETT PASSION.

Of his works eight masses were printed, the merits of which are fully discussed by Ambros.[5] The finest of these, ' Fortuna desperata,' was first published in modern notation (Amsterdam, 1870) and reprinted as No. IX. of the publications of the Maatschappij tot Bevordering der Toonkunst (1880). Since then a definitive edition of his works edited by Johannes Wolf has appeared under the auspices of the same society (see VEREENIGING).

The first volume of printed music in 1501

contained two secular pieces, and Petrucci included many more in his collection of the next few years. Eitner gives titles of about thirty printed chansons and motets still existing. Burney scored some movements from the Mass ' Si dedero,' in his notebooks, and Forkel gave two examples in his history. (See *Q.-L.*)

J. R. S.-B.

O'BRIEN, VINCENT (*b.* Dublin, May 1870), son of R. V. O'Brien, a Dublin organist, studied at the R.I.A.M. and was organist of Rathmines R.C. church (1885–88), and of the Carmelite church, Dublin (1897–99). He produced an opera, ' Hester,' in 1893, and in 1902 was appointed musical director of the pro-Cathedral Palestrina Choir, a post which he still (1926) fills with distinction. John MacCormack was one of his discoveries in 1902, and he was musical director of MacCormack's first world tour in 1913.　　　　W. H. G. F.

OCA DEL CAIRO, L', opera buffa in 2 acts ; libretto by Varesco, music by Mozart, 1783. Mozart left it unfinished, being dissatisfied with the text. It was completed by André with pieces from other operas of Mozart, adapted to new French words by Victor Wilder, and performed at the Théâtre des Fantaisies Parisiennes, June 6, 1867 ; Vienna, 1868 ; Drury Lane, in Italian, May 12, 1870.　　G.

OCARINA, a family of small terra-cotta instruments, in character somewhat resembling flageolets, made of various sizes, and introduced into this country in the 19th century by a travelling troupe of German or Tyrolese musicians. The fingering is something intermediate between that of the flageolet and that of the ' picco ' pipe. The only point of acoustical importance they illustrate is due to their large internal cavity, and the absence of any bell. They have in consequence a hollow, rather sweet tone, similar to that of a stopped organ pipe. (See ACOUSTICS.)

W. H. S.

O'CAROLAN (CAROLAN), TURLOGH (*b.* Newtown, Co. Meath, 1670 ; *d.* Mar. 25, 1738), one of the last and certainly the most famous of the bards of Ireland. He lost his sight in his 22nd year from smallpox, and, in allusion to this, used to say, ' my eyes are transplanted into my ears.'

He was descended from an ancient and respectable family in Meath, where a district was known as Carolanstown (now Carlanstown). Turlogh began to learn the harp at 12 years of age, but owed nearly all his education to Madam Macdermot Roe of Alderford, a fine dame of the old school, who lived to 80 years of age, and survived her *protégé*. She it was who, when O'Carolan's father settled at Carrick-on-Shannon, perceived the talent of the boy, had him taught the Irish language and music, and provided him with a horse and an attendant, when, at 22, he became an

---

[1] *Riemann.*
[2] Glarean, who was a pupil of Erasmus, mentions this in the *Dodecachordon.*
[3] *Musique aux Pays-Bas.*　　[4] See article ' Obrecht ' in *Fétis.*
[5] *Geschichte der Musik,* iii. 180.

itinerant minstrel. It was said that Geminiani and other foreign artists entertained a very high opinion of his musical talents, but, though some stories are told of his immediately executing from memory long and difficult pieces which the Italian musicians had just played, these tales are musically improbable, and are inconsistent with the generally received accounts of his moderate skill on the harp. It is enough to allow him the decided talent 'or improvising music and words, to which his claim has been undisputed. As early as 1727 several of O'Carolan's airs were printed in Daniel Wright's 'Aria di camera.' His 'Bumpers Squire Jones,' 'One bottle more,' 'Down beside me,' 'Grace Nugent,' and 'O'Rourke's noble feast,' were enormously popular, whilst his 'Princess Royal' was adapted by Shield as 'The Arethusa,' on which account many have considered the melody as of English origin. Lampe introduced two of O'Carolan's airs into a Dublin-printed Wesleyan Hymn-Book (1749). Tom Moore adapted ten of his tunes, including 'Fly not yet,' 'The Young May Moon,' 'Oh! banquet not,' 'Oh! blame not the bard,' 'Oh, the sight entrancing,' and 'The Wandering Bard.' Of his 200 songs all are in Irish, save one, 'O'Carolan's Devotion,' set to English words. His harp became the property of the Right Hon. O'Conor Don, P.C., Clonalis, as also the best-known portrait of the great minstrel. Four editions of his airs were printed between the years 1780 and 1800; and, in 1804, Broderip & Wilkinson published an edition, suppressing the names of the tunes. O'Carolan's skull was presented by George Nugent Reynolds to Sir John Caldwell, for his museum, in 1796.

His son taught the Irish harp in London, and before he quitted Ireland, in 1747, published an imperfect collection of his father's compositions. Turlogh O'Carolan died at Alderford House, where his room is still shown. Of late years the grave of the bard (hardly to be distinguished from those of the Macdermot Roe family amongst whom he lies) has been neatly enclosed, and an inscription placed over the arch of the gateway, by Lady Louisa Tenison. O'Carolan's fecundity as a musician was undoubted; one of the ten harpers assembled at Belfast in 1792 had acquired more than 100 tunes composed by him, and asserted that this was but a small portion of them. In Sept. 1809, a sort of commemoration of him was held in Dublin. Lady Morgan bequeathed £100 for a fine bas-relief of O'Carolan, executed by a son of the Irish sculptor Hogan. It was placed in St. Patrick's Cathedral.

R. P. S.; addns. and corr. W. H. G. F.

OCCASIONAL ORATORIO, THE, a work of Handel, probably intended to celebrate the failure of the Jacobite rising of 1745. It consists of an overture and three parts, among which are 'O liberty,' afterwards transferred to 'Judas Maccabeus,' some of the choruses from 'Israel in Egypt,' and a Coronation Anthem, introduced into Part III. The words of Part I. are in great part taken from Milton's Psalms, and many numbers appear to be written by Dr. Morell. (See pref. to the work in the Händel-Gesellschaft edition.) It was performed at Covent Garden on Feb. 14, 19 and 26, 1746. (Rockstro's *Life of Handel*.)

M.

OCHETTO (Ochetus). See HOCKET.

OCHSENKUHN, SEBASTIAN (*b.* Feb. 6, 1521; *d.* Heidelberg, Aug. 20, 1574), lute-player in the service of the enlightened patron of art and literature, Otho Henry, the Elector Palatine of the Rhine. (Otho Henry was the founder of the famous Palatine Library at Heidelberg, and the builder of the best part of the Castle.) Ochsenkuhn seems to have continued in the service of succeeding Electors till his death at Heidelberg. He is the author of a German Tablature Book for the lute (Heidelberg, 1558), containing transcriptions of motets and French and German secular songs. As his book also contains some of the texts to these songs, it is of some importance in the endeavour to ascertain the original form of the tunes, and is frequently referred to in this connexion by Eitner in his various publications on the German song.

J. R. M.

OCKEGHEM, JOANNES, see OKEGHEM.

OCTAVE. An octave is the interval of eight notes, which is the most perfect consonance in music. The ratio of its sounds is 1 : 2; that is, every note has twice the number of vibrations of its corresponding note an octave lower. For the space-saving device in keyed instruments, known as SHORT OCTAVE, see that article; see also ORGAN and SPINET. For consecutive octaves see CONSECUTIVE.

C. H. H. P.

OCTAVE, or PRINCIPAL, an open metal cylindrical organ-stop, of four feet on the manual and eight feet on the pedal; the scale and strength of tone of which are determined by those of the open diapason on the same department. (See under ORGAN, *Vocabulary of Stops*.)

E. J. H.

OCTAVE FLUTE, see FLUTE.

OCTET (Fr. *octuor, octette*; Ger. *Oktett*; Ital. *ottetto*), a composition for eight solo instruments. Theoretically any number of solo players can be combined in chamber music, but the multiplicity of parts or colour is limited in practice. Octets for strings, four violins, two violas and two violoncellos have been written by Mendelssohn, Gade, Svendsen and Enescu, and for strings and wind by Schubert and Spohr. Beethoven's op. 103, for 2 oboes, 2 clarinets, 2 horns and 2 bassoons is the original form of his string quintet, op. 4. Stravinsky has written an octet for wind instruments. Spohr, realising the limitations of true chamber-music, attempted double string quartets in which antiphonal effects were aimed at. (See CHAMBER MUSIC.)

            N. C. G.

OCTO BASSE, a double bass of gigantic proportions, invented by Vuillaume of Paris in 1849, of which only two specimens are known to exist, the one in the museum of the Paris Conservatoire of Music and the other, made originally for the Moscow Opera House, in Vienna. It is 10 ft. in height with 3 strings tuned to C, G, and C, the lowest note being an octave below that of the violoncello. The neck is 'fretted' like a guitar, and, by a system of lever keys for the left hand placed at the back of the instrument which press the strings upon the frets and seven pedal keys for the same purpose, the performer is able to produce a chromatic scale of 2 octaves and a fifth. Rapid music is not effective, but the tone is said to be full and strong without roughness. Berlioz [1] recommends the employment of at least three of these instruments in an orchestra of over 150 performers.   F. W. G.

ODE (Gr. ᾠδή, from ἀείδω, 'I sing '), a form of poetry which, both in its origin and in its later forms, has been peculiarly adapted for musical expression ; in fact, the words of the earliest odes were probably written to fit music already existing. The form which has been most frequently and successfully set to music in modern times is that of the Greek odes, in which the rhythm and metre are constantly changing, thus giving great scope for variety of treatment. English instances of this kind of odes are Milton's ' L' Allegro ' and ' Il Penseroso,' Dryden's ' Ode on St. Cecilia's Day,' Gray's ' Bard ' and ' Progress of Poesy,' Collins's ' Ode to the Passions,' Wordsworth's ' Ode on Intimations of Immortality ' and Shelley's odes. Another form of ode is one in which the metre of the verses remains the same, as in the Odes of Horace, Milton's ' Ode on the Nativity,' etc. To this class belongs Schiller's ' Ode to Joy,' used by Beethoven in the Ninth Symphony. Among musical settings of odes the following are important, besides those already mentioned : Handel's four odes, a list of which is given in the catalogue of his works (see HÄNDEL-GESELLSCHAFT) ; Purcell's ' Odes and Welcome Songs,' twenty-nine in number (see PURCELL SOCIETY), and others written for the festival of St. CECILIA (q.v.). Sterndale Bennett's setting of Tennyson's ' Ode for the opening of the International Exhibition of 1862 ' ; Parry's setting of Shirley's ode, ' The Glories of our Blood and State ' (1883) ; Stanford's of Whitman's ' Elegiac Ode ' (1884) ; and Parry's of Milton's ' Ode at a Solemn Music ' (1887) were followed by many other odes, and set the fashion in England for short choral works more or less strictly in the ode form.

       [1] Traité de l'instrumentation.

Most of these compositions are for chorus and orchestra, and in many there are solos or semi-choruses interspersed, representing the Strophe and Antistrophe of the classic chorus.   M.

ODINGTON, WALTER DE, or Walter of Evesham (13th cent.), as he appears to have been indifferently called, probably took his name from Oddington, in Gloucestershire. It has been the fashion among musical historians to identify him with the Walter, monk of Canterbury, whose election to the primacy was quashed by the Pope in 1229 ; but unfortunately the true spelling of his name was Einesham or Eynsham.

The subject of this article could not have been born much before the middle of the 13th century, if, as appears beyond doubt, he was the Walter de Evesham who is referred to in a list of mathematicians as living in 1316. Upon this supposition we may accept the date, 1280, at which Leland states that Odington was flourishing. In all probability his musical works were written early in his life, his latter days being given up to astronomy, in which science he is known to have been proficient from several treatises which have come down to us. His only known musical work was the *De speculatione musices*, of which there is a MS. copy in Corpus Christi College, Cambridge. Another copy is supposed to have been contained in one of the Cotton MSS. of which the remains are now at the British Museum. In this treatise Walter shows himself a sound musician as well as a learned writer, supplying in almost all cases examples of his own composition. The principal subjects he handles are musical intervals, notation, rhythm, musical instruments and harmony, which latter term he uses instead of the old ' discantus ' ; he gives interesting definitions of such words as ' rondeau,' ' motet ' (which he calls ' motus brevis cantilenae '), etc. But the treatise is especially important for the study of rhythm in the 13th century. It was printed, by no means accurately, by Coussemaker (*Scriptores*, i.) in 1864, and was discussed at length by Riemann.

All that is known of his life is that he was a Benedictine of the monastery at Evesham, and that he was at Oxford, as stated above, in 1316. He compiled a calendar, beginning with the year 1301 ; and lodged in Merton College about 1330. (*D.N.B.*)   A. H.-H.

ODO (OTTO) (b. 879 ; d. Tours, Nov. 18, 943), Abbot of Cluny from 927–43, is the reputed author of a *Dialogus de musica* [2] printed by Gerbert (*Scriptores*, i. 252). A large amount of biographical material concerning Odo is collected in Mabillon's *Acta Sanctorum Ordinis S. Benedicti* (1685), vol. vii. pp. 124-99. It includes a contemporary memoir by Frater

     [2] Gastoué and M. Brenet ascribe the authorship of the *Dialogus* to Odon de Cluny at the end of the 10th century. See *Tribune de St. Gervais*, 1902, pp. 126-7.

Johannes, an Italian who was brought back from Rome by Odo in 939, and spent two years as a monk at Cluny in immediate attendance on the Abbot.

Odo was brought up at the court of William, Duke of Aquitaine. At the age of 19 he took Holy Orders and joined the establishment of St. Martin's at Tours. He subsequently studied dialectics and music at Paris under Remy d'Auxerre, and on his return to Tours was appointed ' Archicantor,' in which capacity he composed three hymns and twelve antiphons in honour of St. Martin. In 909 he left Tours and entered the Benedictine monastery of Beaume (near Besançon), one of the dependencies of the great monastery of Cluny (near Macon). Here he was entrusted with the care of the choir - school, and here, if anywhere, he probably wrote the *Dialogus*. On the death of Berno in 927 he succeeded to the Abbacy of Cluny itself. Throughout his life he was distinguished for zeal and piety. He was buried in the crypt of St. Julian's at Tours.

On the vexed question of the authorship of the *Dialogus de musica* we learn nothing from the biographers beyond the fact that Odo was a skilled teacher and composer of church music. The dialogue, which is between master and student, treats of the monochord and its use, the ' consonantiae et conjunctiones vocum,' *i.e.* the construction of plain-song melodies, and the eight ecclesiastical modes. In the prologue, addressed to his ' carissimi fratres,' the author states that he was induced to write in consequence of his success in training choirboys, but further on (Gerbert, i. 256 *b*) he speaks of an antiphon ' quae a Domno Oddone curiosissime est emendata,' a statement which has been held to show conclusively that Odo was not the author of the *Dialogus*. The diagram on p. 253 exhibits (1) the ' monochordum Guidonis,' not necessarily Guido of Arezzo, and (2) the gamut divided into tetrachords on Hucbald's system and with Hucbald's letter-signs, with the words ' Enchiriadis Oddonis ' added. In several of the MSS. collated by Gerbert this title ' Enchiridion,' *i.e.* Manual, is given to the *Dialogus*, and it has been generally assumed that this is the book referred to by Guido d' Arezzo in his letter to the monk Michael, where he recommends to students ' librum Enchiridion quem reverendissimus Oddo abbas luculentissime composuit ' (Gerbert, ii. 50). Further, most of the MSS. of the *Dialogus* name Odo as the author, so that the generally received opinion is not lightly to be set aside.

Some writers, however, have claimed the *Dialogus* for Guido of Arezzo, on the ground of the addition of the note *gamma ut* at the bottom of the scale, the insertion of the ' monochordum Guidonis,' and the fact that it is usually found

with Guido's writings and is actually ascribed to him in some of the earliest MSS. But *gamma ut* had certainly been introduced before Guido's time, and no other of the Guidonian ' inventions ' is to be found in the *Dialogus*.

The problem is further complicated by the suggestion that the Enchiridion referred to by Guido is really the *Musica enchiriadis* generally attributed to Hucbald. For this again there is considerable authority, though it is possible that it is all derived from the statement of Guido as quoted above. Hermann Contractus, who died in 1055, speaks hesitatingly of ' quidam enchiriadis musicae auctor,' but William of Hirschau (*d.* 1091) distinctly attributes it to a ' venerable Otto,' and many MSS. name Odo or Otto as the author of both the *Musica enchiriadis* and the *Scholia enchiriadis*. The question is elaborately discussed by Hans Müller in his *Hucbald's echte und unechte Schriften* (Leipzig, 1884). Müller decides that neither Hucbald nor Odo was the author, but it may be questioned whether such a conclusion is justified by his premises.

Of other treatises ascribed to Odo the best authenticated is a Tonarium printed by Coussemaker (*Scriptores*, ii. 117) from a MS. at St. Dié, where it is entitled

' Intonarium a Domino Ottone abbate diligenter examinatum et ordinatum, a Guidone scientissimo monaco, optimo musyco, probatum, legitime approbatum et autenticatum.'

J. F. R. S.

ODOISTIC NOTATION. When the Byzantine Scales were introduced into the Western Church the letter names (in Greek) of the notes were α β γ δ ε ζ η α, but these letters had the meaning of our C D E F G A B C. The Greek letters were replaced by Latin letters A B C D E F G, but these also had the meaning of our C D E F G A B. The Western monks, probably adhering at first to the system which regarded plagal as being a fifth below authentic, were obliged, in order to provide a plagal for the authentic beginning on our D, to introduce the note gamma Γ (*c.* 900). Odo of Cluny appears to have changed the letter pitch meanings so as to cause that which had previously been named *a* to be called *c*, thus altering all these meanings three degrees. The first Western use of the *sign* gamma occurs in Odo, who died 942. However, the Byzantines seem to have used the *note* gamma (see Byzantine Music; Notation).

D. H.

O'DWYER, Robert (*b.* Bristol, 1860), of Irish parentage, was conductor of the Rousbey Opera Company from 1891–96, and settled in Dublin in 1897. He produced the first opera to an Irish libretto, ' Eithne,' in 1909, and has been lecturer in Irish Music at University College, Dublin, since 1914, as well as organist of the Jesuit church in Dublin. W. H. G. F.

OEDIPUS. (1) ' Oedipus Tyrannus ' and ' Oedipus at Colonos,' the second and third parts of a trilogy (of which the first is ' Antigone,' *q.v.*), music by Mendelssohn. ' Oedipus Tyrannus,' though completely sketched, was never performed, and the music appears to be lost. ' Oedipus at Colonos' was produced at Potsdam, Nov. 1, 1845, and was published, before the end of 1851, as op. 93 (22 of the posthumous works). A full analysis by G. A. Macfarren will be found in the earlier numbers of the *Musical World* for 1854.   G.

(2) Incidental music, choruses, etc. were written to the ' Oedipus Tyrannus,' by Stanford, for the performance at Cambridge on Nov. 22-26, 1887.

OEGLIN, ERHART, of Reutlingen, established himself in Augsburg as book and music-printer and publisher at the beginning of the 16th century. He was the first to introduce into Germany Petrucci's invention of music-printing with movable metal types. His practice only differed from that of Petrucci by his printing notes and lines together by one impression. His first known work of the kind is the *Melopoiae sive harmonia* of Tritonius (a musical setting of some odes of Horace), printed in 1507. In 1512 he printed and published without special title a Liederbuch, containing forty-two German secular songs and six Latin motets or hymns, all for four voices. No names of composers are given, but from comparison with other sources five of the secular songs have been ascertained to be by Hofhaimer, two by Heinrich Isaac, and one by Senfl. The whole work has been reprinted in modern score by Eitner in bd. ix. of the *Publikation der Gesellschaft für Musikforschung*, with facsimiles of the original title-pages and some of the music. Oeglin printed another Liederbuch, but of this only the discant part is at present known to exist, preserved in the State Library at Berlin. (See Eitner, *Monatshefte*, xxii. pp. 214-17.)   J. R. M.

OESTEN, THEODOR (*b.* Berlin, Dec. 31, 1813 ; *d.* Mar. 16, 1870), learned various instruments, both wind and string, from Politzki, Stadtmusicus of Fürstenwald, a small town between Berlin and Frankfort-on-the-Oder. At 19 he went to Berlin, and studied composition with Böhmer, Rungenhagen, Schneider and A. W. Bach, but before this he had written a quantity of dance-music, variations, etc. He also learned the clarinet from Tanne, a Kammermusicus. He was soon in great request as a teacher, and in 1843 his PF. rondo called ' Les Premières Violettes,' cleverly written in the sentimental taste of the day, had an enormous success, and was followed by a host of similar pieces, easy to play and with attractive titles, which ruled the market for many years. He had many more or less successful imitators, his own son Max among the number.   F. G.

OESTERREICH, GEORG, of Magdeburg, studied at the school of St. Thomas, Leipzig,

1678–80, when he left on account of the plague. In 1687 he was Kapellmeister at Gottorf, in 1694 at the court of Schleswig-Holstein, and from *c.* 1735 cantor of the ducal chapel, Brunswick. He composed a considerable number of cantatas, the MSS. mostly in the Berlin library (*Q.-L.*).

OFFENBACH, originally LEVY, JACQUES, (*b.* Offenbach-on-Main, June 21, 1819 ; *d.* Paris, Oct. 4, 1880), the most brilliant composer of light opera of his day, was the son of the cantor of the Jewish synagogue at Cologne. He came to Paris as a youth, and in Nov. 1833 entered the violoncello class of Vaslin at the Conservatoire, where he stayed a year. He left in 1837 without having distinguished himself, or shown any taste for serious study. He then entered the orchestra of the Opéra-Comique, where he played by the side of Seligmann, and doubtless picked up much of his knowledge. In early life he wrote several pieces for the violoncello.

He first appears as the composer of some chansonettes to parodies of La Fontaine's poems. He next became conductor of the orchestra at the Théâtre Français, and composed the ' Chanson de Fortunio,' in Alfred de Musset's ' Chandelier ' (1848), a song which is certainly one of the best of his melodies. Henceforward he made use of every expedient to place himself before the public, giving concerts of a kind to excite public curiosity, and in various ways illustrating the saying that ' a grain of wit is better than a bushel of learning ' (le savoir-faire vaut mieux que le savoir). His first piece, ' Pepito,' produced at the Variétés, Oct. 28, 1853, attracted little notice, but he followed it by a host of operettas, and at last found his real field in ' Les Deux Aveugles,' ' Le Violoneux,' and other musical trifles which he gave at the small theatre in the Champs Elysées, of which he became manager in July 1855. In December of that year he took the ' Théâtre Comte ' in the Passage Choiseul, named it the ' Bouffes Parisiens,' and produced a succession of operettas which became immensely popular, and eventually opened to him the doors of the Opéra-Comique, and even of the Opéra, where his ballet-pantomime, ' Le Papillon,' was brought out, Nov. 26, 1860, with considerable success. In 1861 he gave up management on his own account and produced pieces in various other theatres ; but in 1873 he once more became a manager, taking the Théâtre de la Gaîté till 1875, when he went to America, without much success.[1] The following list of his works is arranged for convenience' sake in alphabetical order :

Apothicaire et perruquier, one act ; 1861.	Ba-ta-clan, one act ; 1856.
Arlequin barbier, one act pantomime ; 1855.	Bavards, Les, two acts ; 1863.
	Belle Hélène, La, three acts ; 1865.
Bagatelle, one act ; 1874.	Bergers, Les, three acts ; 1866.
Barbe bleue, three acts ; 1866.	Bergers de Watteau, Les, one act ; 1856.
Barkouf, three acts ; 1861.	

---

[1] See his *Notes d'un musicien en voyage*, 1877.

Boite au lait, La, four acts;
1877.
Bonne d'enfants, La, one act;
1856.
Boulangère, La, a des écus, three
acts; 1875.
Boule de neige, three acts; 1872.
Braconniers, Les, three acts;
1873.
Brigands, Les, three acts; 1869.
Carneval des revues, one act;
1860.
Chanson de Fortunio, La, one
act; 1861.
Château à Toto, Le, three acts;
1867.
Chatte, La, métamorphosée en
femme, one act; 1858.
Corsaire noir, Le, three acts;
Vienna, 1872.
Coscoletto, one act; Ems, 1865.
Créole, La, three acts; 1875.
Croquefer, one act; 1857.
Daphnis et Chloé, one act; 1860.
Deux Aveugles, Les, one act;
1855.
Deux Pêcheurs, Les, one act;
1857.
Diva, La, three acts; 1869.
Docteur Ox, Le, three acts; 1877.
Dragées du baptême, Les, one
act; 1856.
Dragonette, one act; 1857.
Entrez, Messieurs, Mesdames, one
act; 1855.
Fantasio; three acts; 1872.
Fifre enchanté, Le, one act; 1868.
Fille du tambour major, La,
three acts; 1879.
Financier, Le, et le savetier, one
act; 1856.
Foire St. Laurent, La, three acts;
1877.
Geneviève de Brabant, two acts,
Bouffes, 1859 ; five acts,
Gaîté, 1875.
Géorgiennes, Les, three acts;
1864.
Grande duchesse de Gérolstein,
La, three acts; 1867.
Île de Tulipatan, L', one act;
1868.
Jacqueline, one act; 1862.
Jeanne qui pleure et Jean qui
rit, one act; 1865.
Jolie Parfumeuse, La, three acts;
1873.
Leçon des chants, La, one act;
Ems, 1867.
Lischen et Fritzchen, one act;
Ems, 1863.
Madame Favart, three acts; 1878.
Madame l'Archiduc, three acts;
1874.
Mme. Papillon, one act; 1855.

Maître Péronilla, three acts; 1878.
Mariage aux lanternes, Le, one
act ; 1858.
Marocaine, La, three acts ; 1879.
Mesdames de la Halle, one act;
1858.
Monsieur Choufleuri, one act;
1861.
Monsieur et Madame Denis, one
act ; 1862.
Nuit blanche, La, one act; 1857.
Orphée aux Enfers, two acts;
1858 ; 1874, in four acts.
Papillon, Le,ballet, two acts;1860.
Pepito, one act; 1853.
Périchole, La, three acts ; 1868.
Périnette, one act ; 1855.
Permission de dix heures, La, one
act ; 1874.
Petits Prodiges, Les, one act;
1858.
Pierrette et Jacquot, one act;
1876.
Pierrot Clown, one act panto-
mime ; 1855.
Polichinelle dans le monde, one
act ; 1855.
Pomme d'api, one act ; 1873.
Pont des soupirs, Le, two acts ;
1861.
Princesse de Trébizonde, three
acts ; 1869.
Rêve d'une nuit d'été, Le, one
act ; 1855.
Rheinnixen, three acts ; Vienna,
1872.
Robinson Crusoé, three acts ;
1867.
Roi Carotte, Le, four acts ; 1872.
Romance de la rose, La, one
act ; 1870.
Rose de St. Flour, La, one act ;
1856.
Signor Fagotto, one act ; 1864.
Soixante-sixième, Le, one act ;
1856.
Trois Baisers du diable, Les, one
act ; 1857.
Tromb al Cazar, one act ; 1856.
Une Demoiselle en loterie, one
act ; 1857.
Un Mari à la porte, one act; 1859.
Vent du soir, one act; 1857.
Vert-Vert, three acts ; 1869.
Vie parisienne, La, five acts ;
1866.
Violoneux, Le, one act ; 1855.
Vivandières de la grande armée,
Les, one act ; 1859.
Voyage dans la lune, Le, four
acts ; 1875.
Voyage de MM. Dunanan, Le,
three acts ; 1862.
Whittington and his Cat, three
acts; Alhambra, London,1875.

—ninety pieces, written in twenty-five years !
Offenbach visited England at least four
times. In 1844 he played the violoncello in
public and private at the concerts of Ella,
Benedict, Mme. Puzzi, etc. In 1857 he conducted the performances of the Bouffes
Parisiens company at the St. James's Theatre,
and for his benefit played a musette of his own
on the violoncello. In 1866, when his ' Belle
Hélène ' was running at the Adelphi, and in
1870, he made no public appearance.

He died of gout on the heart at his residence
on the Boulevard des Capucines. His posthumous works include ' La Belle Lurette,'
composed within a short time of his death, and
' Les Contes d'Hoffmann,' opéra-comique. The
former was revised by Léo Delibes, and produced at the Renaissance, Oct. 30, 1880, with
Jane Hading, Milly Meyer, Vauthier, Jolly,
etc. (in English at the Avenue Theatre, Mar. 24,
1883). The second opera was the composer's
most cherished work, on which he had been
working for years. For some time Offenbach
had felt his end approaching, and said to
Carvalho, ' Make haste, make haste to mount
my piece ; I am in a hurry, and have only one

wish in the world—that of witnessing the
première of this work.' [1] It was finally revised
and partly orchestrated by Guiraud, and produced at the Opéra-Comique, Feb. 10, 1881,
with Adèle Isaac, Marguérite Ugalde, Talazac,
Taskin, Grivot, etc. It was played no less
than 101 nights in the year of its production.
It was given in Germany, and at the Ring
Theatre, Vienna, at the time of its conflagration. Some of the music was adapted to a
1-act farce by Leterrier and Vanloo, ' Mamzelle
Moucheron,' produced at the Renaissance,
May 10, 1881. Offenbach's widow, to whom
he was married in 1844, died Apr. 19, 1887.
After enjoying extraordinary popularity in
London during the sixties and seventies, Offenbach's music almost completely lost its vogue
in England, though there was a revival of
' La Grande Duchesse ' at the Savoy Theatre
in 1897–98. ' Les Contes d'Hoffmann ' (' Tales
of Hoffmann ') had to wait for popularity in
this country until Beecham gave it at His
Majesty's Theatre in 1910. It is now (1925)
a favourite in the repertory of the British
National Opera Company. In Germany, and
especially in Berlin, the tradition of Offenbach's
light-hearted and witty music has been more
consistently preserved. Revivals take place
fairly often at the Variétés and other Parisian
theatres and ' Contes d'Hoffmann ' remains in
the repertory of the Opéra-Comique.

G. C., with addns.

BIBLIOGRAPHY
E. DE MIRECOURT : *Offenbach*. (1867.)
J. OFFENBACH : *Offenbach in America*, with preface by A. Wolff.
(New York, 1877.)
ANDRÉ MARTINET : *Jacques Offenbach, sa vie et son œuvre* (1892).
P. BEKKER : *Jacques Offenbach*. (1909.)
E. RIEGER : *Offenbach und seine Wiener Schule*. (1920.)
LOUIS SCHNEIDER : *Offenbach*. (Paris, 1923.)

OFFERTORIUM (Eng. *offertory*, Fr. *offer-
toire*), a portion of a Psalm, or verse from
some other part of Holy Scripture, sung by the
choir, at High Mass, immediately after the
Credo, during the time occupied by the priest
in making ready the Oblations and offering
them upon the altar.

In early times there was antiphonal psalm-
singing at this point ; when simple psalmody
gave place to the elaborate performances of
trained singers there arose a form of composition consisting of an elaborate *antiphona ad
offerendum*, with three or four verses to be sung
alternately with the antiphon, and in early
Gregorian music the Offertory takes this form.
The curtailment of the ceremonies in this part
of the service from the 9th century onward led
to a curtailment of the music, the verses were
diminished in number or restricted so much
that after the 12th century it was rare to find
even one left. They survived, however, on
some few occasions right down to the 16th century ; but the modern Roman rite has scarcely
anything left except the Offertory-antiphon
alone.

[1] *Daily Telegraph*, Paris Correspondence, Oct. 7, 1880.

As the plain-song settings have been curtailed until they are not long enough to fill up the interval before the priest is ready to begin the 'Sursum corda,' they are usually supplemented, either by a motet—as in the Pontifical Chapel—or by a grand voluntary on the organ. Palestrina provided for this contingency by setting the special forms for all the Sundays and most of the principal festivals in the year in the motet style, for five voices, and publishing them in the year 1593 in two books, entitled ' Offertoria totius anni.' [1] But when the appointed words have already been sung in plain-song, it is not at all *de rigueur* that they should be repeated in the motet which follows, provided this be an appropriate one for the festival. It is, indeed, in this part of the Mass that the MOTET (*q.v.*), properly so called, finds its strongest *raison d'être*; and a rich store of compositions, well adapted to the end in view, has been bequeathed to us by the great masters of the 15th and 16th centuries.

The Sentences appointed to be used at the Offertory, in the Book of Common Prayer, were printed by John Merbecke in his ' Booke of Common Praier noted ' in 1550, with melodies, evidently adapted from ancient sources.

W. S. R.

OGINSKI, a noble and distinguished Polish family.

(1) Prince MICHAEL CASIMIR (*b.* Warsaw, 1731 ; *d.* there, 1803) resided at Slonin in Lithuania, where he maintained an establishment of orchestra and singers. He is said to have invented the addition of pedals to the harp, and to have proposed the Creation to Haydn as the subject of an oratorio. He formed a canal between two rivers at his own expense—a national work, which connected the Baltic with the Black Sea.

(2) His nephew, MICHAEL CLEOPAS (*b.* Gutzow, near Warsaw, Sept. 25, 1765 ; *d.* Florence, Oct. 31, 1833), was grand treasurer of Lithuania and senator of the Russian Empire. Of his diplomatic and literary achievements we need not speak. In the matter of music he was a pupil of Kozlowski's, and was known for his Polonaises. Of these fourteen are published, one of which became very widely celebrated owing to its merit and to a romantic story attached to its origin. It was printed in the *Musical Library*, with the story referred to. Twelve others were printed in the *Harmonicon* of 1824. He also wrote songs to French words. During his residence in Paris in 1823 Prince Oginski was well known in the best musical circles. He died at Florence and was buried in Santa Maria Novella.

(3) Prince GABRIEL (*b.* 1788 ; *d.* Lithuania, 1843), though a musician and violin-player,

left no compositions. He was driven from home by the revolutions of 1831, but was forced to return by nostalgia.

G.

O'HARA, KANE (*b.* Feb. 1711 ; *d.* Dublin, June 17, 1782), entered T.C.D. 3 March, 1727/8, aged 16 ; B.A. 1732 ; M.A. 1735, was a composer of light operatic pieces (see BURLETTA). Of these ' Midas ' (1762) and ' The Golden Pippin ' (1773) were the most famous. The latter was popularised by the singing of Anne CATLEY (*q.v.*)

OIREACHTAS (pronounced *Urracktus*). In 1896 the executive committee of the Gaelic League in Ireland decided on holding an annual Oireachtas, or Festival, at which competitions were to take place in various subjects, including literary and musical. The first Oireachtas was held in Dublin, in 1897, and was a marked success. Each year has shown that the Irish revival is gaining strength ; and the tenth Oireachtas, in Aug. 1906, was the most representative yet held. In the musical section, prizes are awarded for solo and choral singing, also for harp, fiddle, war pipes, uilleann (union) pipes, and flutes, as well as dancing. For the solo and choral competitions (as well as in the literary section) only Irish words are permitted, and there is a distinction made between ' native ' and ' non-native ' speakers. The Oireachtas, since 1900, lasts five days, but the musical element, which at first predominated, is now (1926) mainly devoted to the language.

W. H. G. F.

OKEGHEM (OCKEGHEM, OCKENHEIM, HOC QUEHAM), JEAN DE (JOANNES) (*b.* probably Termonde,[2] East Flanders, early 15th cent.[3] ; *d. circa* 1495). The form OCKENHEIM was introduced by Glarean, and has been very generally copied, but Okeghem (with such slight variations as Okenghem, Okekem, etc.) appears on his compositions and in all important documents relating to him. There is some reason for supposing Binchois to have been his master, but in any case there was no lack of excellent musicians at the time when he was a boy. He gave up his place as chorister at Antwerp in 1444, from 1446–48 was in the service of the Duke Charles of Bourbon at Moulins, and about 1452 entered that of the King of France. In 1454 he is styled ' Johannes Hoquegan, premier chappellain.' In 1461, the year of Charles VII.'s death, he is mentioned as head of the chapel. With Louis XI. he appears to have been in great favour, and was by him appointed treasurer of the church of St. Martin's at Tours, where he resided the greater part of his life. He made a journey to Spain in 1469, and his post at Tours was filled up in 1496. He is said to have served three kings of France for forty years.

No wonder if by this time he was somewhat out of fashion, and that the invention of music-

---

1 They form the fifth vol. of Alfieri's edition and the ninth of Breitkopf's. Burney has printed one of them—' Exaltabo te Domine,' the Offertory for the eleventh Sunday after Pentecost—in vol. iii. p. 191.

2 Where a family of that name then resided.
3 Fétis suggests about 1430.

printing at the beginning of the 16th century
was more to the advantage of his distinguished
pupils than to his own. In the earliest of
Petrucci's publications five French chansons are
given; but no Mass or motet bearing Okeghem's
name was printed till many years after his
death, and even then the Mass which Petreius
published, ' Missa cujusvis toni,' seems to have
been chosen on account of its special scientific
interest, and no others were printed entire. Extracts from the ' Missa prolationum ' were given
in various theoretical treatises, but both these
Masses exhibit Okeghem as a great teacher
rather than a great church composer. In the
royal collection at Dresden is the MS. Kyrie
from a Mass ' Gaudeamus,' and the court
library at Vienna contains MS. copies of this
whole Mass as well as of the ' Missa cujusvis
toni.' The Brussels library possesses two MS.
Masses, ' Pour quelque peine ' and ' Ecce ancilla
Domini,' and the Papal Chapel one, ' De plus en
plus.' Other masses are in the Sistine Chapel at
Rome and in the cathedral archives at Trient.
A tradition asserts that costly music books
containing many of Okeghem's works were
destroyed when the Imperial troops plundered
the city in 1527, and his compositions at St.
Martin's at Tours were probably lost in the same
way. A motet, ' Alma redemptoris,' and three
songs, ' D'ung aultre amer,' ' Aultre Venus '
and ' Rondo Royal,' in MS., are in the Bibl.
Riccardiana at Florence, and other chansons at
Rome and Dijon. (See Q.-L.)

These compositions are sufficient to separate
him very distinctly from his predecessors, and
show the astonishing progress made during the
forty years of his supremacy (1450–90). He is
regarded as the founder of the second or new
Netherland school, in contradistinction to the
older school of Dufay, Brassart, Eloy, Binchois
and Faugues. Kiesewetter, who first made this
classification, and has given numerous examples
from the works of the earlier period, distinguishes Okeghem and his contemporaries

' by a greater facility in counterpoint and fertility
in invention ; their compositions, moreover, being no
longer mere premeditated submissions to the contrapuntal operation, but for the most part being
indicative of thought and sketched out with manifest
design,[1] being also full of ingenious contrivances of
an obbligato counterpoint, at that time just discovered, such as augmentation, diminution, inversion,
imitation : together with canons and fugues of the
most manifold description.'

One of these canons has gone the round of the
musical histories, but its solution has not always
been successful, and Fétis has had to correct
the editions given by Forkel, Kiesewetter,
Burney and Hawkins. The ' Missa cujusvis
toni,' which Kiesewetter, without sufficient
reason, regards as a comical Mass, is a work
possibly written for the sake of his pupils, but
more probably as an intellectual treat for the

highly educated musicians who formed the
church choirs in those days. It would be
valued by them not only as a test of their
thorough acquaintance with the church modes,
and an exercise in transposition from one mode
to the next, but also for the endless charm of
variety which the special characteristics of the
various modes would impart to it. Another
piece of Okeghem's, famous in its time, was a
motet for thirty-six voices, which was probably
(like Josquin's ' Qui habitat in adjutorio ')
written with six voices, the other parts being
derived from them canonically.[2] Most important among modern reprints are the two
Masses (Trent Codices) in D.T.Ö. Four
chansons are in Ambros's Geschichte, vol. v.

As a teacher Okeghem stands alone in the
whole history of music :

' Through his pupils the art was transplanted into
all countries, and he must be regarded (for it can be
proved by genealogy) as the founder of all schools
from his own to the present age.'[3]

The names of JOSQUIN[4] and DE LA RUE stand
foremost in the list of his pupils. Josquin,
himself a great teacher, carried the new
Netherland art into Italy, and the first important representatives both of German and
French music, Isaac and Mouton, with many
others less famous, learnt through him the
Okeghem traditions.

BIBLIOGRAPHY

E. THOINAN : Déploration de Guillaume Crétin sur le trépas de
   Jean Ockeghem, musicien. (Paris, 1864.)
DE BURBURE : Jean de Ockeghem (Annales du Cercle archéologique
   de Termonde, 2nd series, i. 1868).
MICHEL BRENET : Jean de Ockeghem, maître de la chapelle des rois
   Charles VII et Louis XI. Nagent C. Rotrou, 1893 (extract
   from the Mémoires de la Société de Paris et de l'Ile de France),
   with a bibliography ; republished in Musique et musiciens de
   la vieille France (Paris, Alcan, 1911).
DE MARCY : Jean Ockeghem. (1895.)
E. DROZ and G. THIBAULT : Bibliographie des recueils de chansons
   du XVe siècle. (Paris, 1926.)
DRAGAN PLAMENACZ : Johannes Ockeghem als Motetten- und Chansons-
   Komponist. (1925.) (Thesis for Doctorate at Vienna University).
                    J. R. S.-B. ; with addns. M. L. P.

OKELAND (1st half of 16th cent.), English
composer of church music. A ' Robert Oke-
laund' appears among the ' Gentilmen of the
Chapell ' who received new liveries for the
coronation of Edward VI. in 1547, but his
name is given as ' Hockland ' in a similar list
for the burial of Henry VIII. in that year.[5]
He contributed an anthem, ' Prayse we the
Father,' and a ' prayer,' ' Prayse the Lord, O
our soules,' to Day's ' Certaine Notes ' (1560).
A 4-part Mass by him is in B.M. Add. MSS.
17,802-5.   J. Mᴋ.

OKEOVER (OKER, OKAR), JOHN, organist
in 1619 of Wells Cathedral. His 2 pavans and
7 fancies from early 17th century MSS. in the
British Museum rank with the compositions of
Ward and Peerson. The songs mentioned in
Q.-L. cannot be traced (probably an error on
Eitner's part).   E. v. d. s.

2 Ambros, iii. 174.
3 Kiesewetter's History of Music, English edition. p. 131.
4 The elegy composed by Josquin in memory of his master is
spoken of elsewhere. See JOSQUIN.
5 See H. C. de Lafontaine, The King's Musick.

1 Ambros (iii 175) mentions the motet ' Alma redemptoris ' as
affording a proof of this statement.

OKER (OCKEOVER, OKAR), JOHN (1st half of 17th cent.), organist and English Church music composer. He graduated Mus.B. at Oxford in 1633, was organist of Wells Cathedral, 1619–39, and of Gloucester Cathedral, 1640 (?)–44 (West's *Cath. Org.* p. 108). Some early 17th century MSS. (B.M. Add. MSS. 17,786-89, 17,791) are a collection of 5-part fancies for viols, and include two pavans by 'John Ockeover' or 'Oker'; Add. MSS. 17,792-6 is a similar collection and contains a 5-part fantasia for viols by 'Okar.' Single parts of the following anthems by 'Oker—of Wells Org^t' are in Barnard's MS. collection (now at R.C.M.).

Grant we beseech Thee. R.C.M. 1045/51. Medius decani part only.
God shall send. R.C.M. 1051/57. Bassus Cantoris part only.
The King shall reign. R.C.M. 1051/48. Bassus Cantoris part only.

　　　　　　　　　　　　　　　　　　　J. M^K.

OKTAVGEIGE (OCTAVE FIDDLE), a small violoncello tuned an octave below the violin. (See VIOL FAMILY.)　　　　　　F. W. G.

OLCZEWSKA, MARIA (b. Bavaria, Aug. 12, 1892), operatic contralto, an artist of distinction whose co-operation lent appreciable strength to the revival of German opera which marked the Covent Garden 'grand' season of 1924. She had been singing for the three preceding years at the Vienna Hofoper, and was re-engaged there on a lengthy contract in consequence of her great success. Her first experiences on the stage, after an apprenticeship in 'operette,' were gained at Leipzig through the influence of Nikisch, who heard her at a concert at Hamburg and was much struck by the beauty of her voice and the rare emotional quality of her singing. These were precisely the characteristics that brought her into immediate prominence on her début in London (May 13, 1924) as Fricka, in 'Das Rheingold,' and again even more strongly by her fine delineations of Brangäne, Herodias and Waltraute. She also took part in the German seasons of 1925 and 1926, and added to her reputation by a powerful yet subtle impersonation of Ortrud in the revival of 'Lohengrin,' fifty years after its first production in this country. In fact, in all of these heavy parts she displayed declamatory gifts of the highest order.

BIBL.—NORTHCOTT, *Covent Garden and the Royal Opera.* H. K.

OLD ENGLISH EDITION, THE, a valuable series of musical reprints, edited by G. E. P. Arkwright, was published by Joseph Williams of London, and Parker & Sons of Oxford, from 1889–1902. The list of contents is as follows:

1. Campion, Lupo, and Giles. Masque for Lord Hayes's Marriage, 1607.
2. Arne. Six Songs.
3-5. Kirbye's Madrigals, 1597.
6-9. Byrd's Songs of Sundry Natures, 1589.
10. Tye. Mass, 'Euge bone.'
11-12. Ferrabosco's Madrigals.
13-15. Weelkes's Ballets and Madrigals, 1598.
16-17. Weelkes's Ayres or Phantastick Spirites, 1608.
18-20. Pilkington's Songs or Airs, 1605.
21. White, Kirbye, Wilbye and Daman. Anthems, Motets, etc.
22. Milton. Six Anthems.
23. Blow. Six Songs.
24. Six Songs by Henry Purcell from 'Orpheus Britannicus.'
25. Blow. Masque, 'Venus and Adonis.'

OLDFIELD, THOMAS (16th-17th cent.), known so far only by a prelude in the 'Fitzwilliam Virginal book.'

OLD HUNDREDTH TUNE, THE, is the melody adapted to Beza's version of the 134th Psalm included in the first instalment of psalms, thirty-four in number, added by him to the Genevan Psalter in 1551. No copy of that Psalter containing the tunes to these psalms is known of earlier date than 1554, but there is little doubt that they were added to the psalms either at the time of publication of the latter or in 1552; and this date falls within the time when Bourgeois was musical editor of the Genevan Psalter—that is, from 1542–57. To Bourgeois, therefore, the tune in its present form may be ascribed, but how far it is original is uncertain.

In 1561 Kethe wrote versions of twenty-five psalms for the enlarged edition of Knox's Anglo-Genevan Psalter published in that year. One of these was the long measure version of Psalm C., 'All people that on earth do dwell,' to which the Genevan tune was then for the first time adapted.

The name 'Old Hundredth' is peculiar to England.[1] The psalm was originally known as the 'Hundredth,' but after the appearance of the New Version by Brady and Tate in 1696, the word 'Old' was added to the titles of the tunes continued in use from the preceding Psalter of Sternhold and Hopkins, to which no special names had been given. The name 'Savoy,' sometimes applied to the Old Hundredth in the 18th century, was derived, not as Havergal supposes, from a vague fancy respecting its Savoyard origin, but from its use by the French congregation established in the Savoy, London, in the reign of Charles II. G. A. C.

OLD VIC, THE. The popular name of the Royal Victoria Hall, Waterloo Road, S.E., at which performances of opera in English and of Shakespeare plays are given regularly at popular prices.

This theatre, originally known as the Royal Coburg Theatre, was opened in 1818 for the best kind of theatrical performance; in 1833 it was re-named the Royal Victoria Theatre—it was here that Paganini gave his 'farewell' concert—and after some years of prosperity became the home of melodrama and eventually a place where the entertainment was frequently accompanied by drunkenness and disorder. At this moment the lease was acquired by a small company at the instigation of Emma Cons, an ardent social reformer, and as the Royal Victoria Coffee Hall, the theatre was reopened on Boxing Day, 1880, to provide entertainment of a more refined nature and without drink. In 1884 the lease was taken over by a body of trustees, chiefly owing to the help of Samuel

---

[1] In America the tune is commonly called 'Old Hundred'; probably an English provincialism imported by some of the early colonists.

Morley, and in 1888 the freehold was acquired and a grant obtained from the Charity Commissioners. In 1889 the back of the stage was remodelled to accommodate the Working Men's College instituted as a Morley Memorial. Opera first appeared at the theatre in the form of excerpts which were sung at the ballad concerts which formed so important a part of the entertainment provided by Emma Cons. Having no dramatic licence, it became the practice to give selections from some particular opera in costume, followed by tableaux to illustrate the action. A chorus was employed in 1895, and in the following year whole operas were given under the direction of Alfred Dove; but as a dramatic licence would have prevented smoking in the theatre it was necessary to make a technical break in the continuity of the action, and this was done by drawing the curtain to shut off the scene during the performance of concerted numbers. The regulation about smoking was set aside during the war, and so in 1914, the year when Shakespeare's plays were first given in the theatre, opera was presented in the normal manner. But the alteration that had been made to the stage could not now be accepted by the London County Council, and after the war great efforts were made to raise the money required for the necessary reconstruction, a problem solved in 1923 by the generosity of Sir George Dance.

Meanwhile, upon the retirement of Emma Cons in 1898, her niece, Lilian Baylis, had become manager, and upon her has fallen the difficult rôle of dramatic and operatic manager in one. Naturally an institution which runs both plays and operas at the cheapest possible prices, and with only a small grant, cannot aim at elaboration of production, but the seriousness of purpose and the remarkable receptivity of the audience has gradually built up a standard of performance which in spirit and intelligence sometimes achieves an effect not always obtainable in more favoured circumstances. Operas are given on two nights in the week and on alternate Saturday afternoons. The orchestra is small, but as the policy has been adopted of engaging some first-rate players, the want of volume is balanced by general accuracy, good tone and intonation. A performance of 'Tristan and Isolde' has been given with the score so skilfully reduced by Charles Corri, the musical director, that a remarkable reflection of the original orchestration has been obtained. A valuable interpretative quality was secured in the production of 'Figaro' in 1919 by Clive Carey with E. J. Dent's translation, and this was repeated later in the revivals of 'Don Giovanni' and 'The Magic Flute.' The enterprise of the management has been extended to contemporary British opera in the performances of Ethel Smyth's 'The Boatswain's Mate' and 'Fête galante' and Nicholas Gatty's 'The

Tempest' and 'Prince Ferelon,' the last-named being given for the first time in public. It should be added that the mostly 'part-time' chorus generally includes some young singers who may be called upon to take small parts and thus gain valuable operatic experience. Principal parts have often been taken by singers whose public reputation is in nowise to be measured by the necessarily small fee; but then, to sing at the 'Old Vic' is an experience of a peculiarly happy nature.   N. C. G.

BIBL.—LILIAN BAYLIS and CICELY HAMILTON, *The Old Vic Book* (1925).

OLDYS, VALENTINE, a chemist in the Black Friars, contributed some pieces to Playford's 'Court Ayres,' 1655.

O'LEARY, ARTHUR (b. Tralee, co. Kerry, Ireland, Mar. 15, 1834 ; d. Mar. 13, 1919). He received his early instruction in music at home. When between 7 and 8 years old, his pianoforte-playing attracted the attention of Wyndham Goold, through whose instrumentality he was sent to the Leipzig Conservatorium in Jan. 1847. At a dinner-party given in Goold's honour by Mendelssohn, the boy sat next the composer, who was in many ways most kind to him afterwards. At Leipzig he studied the piano with Moscheles and Plaidy, counterpoint with Hauptmann, and composition with Richter and Julius Rietz. At the house of Preusser he became acquainted with Robert and Clara Schumann, and many other musical celebrities. After a five years' stay at Leipzig, O'Leary returned to London and entered the R.A.M., studying under Cipriani Potter and Sterndale Bennett. In 1856 Lord Westmorland appointed him professor at the Academy, and on the opening of the National Training School for Music, he was appointed to that institution. He retired from the R.A.M. in 1903, but continued to teach privately. O'Leary's compositions include orchestral pieces, songs, dance-music, transcriptions and original pieces for the pianoforte, etc. His toccata in F was played at the Popular Concert of Dec. 14, 1885. He also edited Bach's Christmas Oratorio, Bennett's Pianoforte works, and masses by Hummel, Sechter and Schubert.

His wife, ROSETTA (d. London, June 17, 1909), was the daughter of W. S. Vinning, of Newton Abbot, and was married to O'Leary in Nov. 1860. She was elected King's Scholar at the R.A.M. in 1851, and is known as the composer of several successful songs.

                                        W. B. S.

OLIMPIADE. An opera of Metastasio's, written in 1733 to celebrate the birthday of the Empress Elizabeth, wife of Charles VI., Emperor of Germany. It was set no less than thirty-one times, by the following composers: Caldara (1733), Pergolesi, Leo, Duni, Scolari, Latilla, Perez, Sarti, Hasse, Piccinni

(2), Bernasconi, Gassmann, Bertoni, Jommelli, Cafaro, J. C. Bach, Traetta, Arne, Anfossi, Mysliweczek, Andreozzi, Schwanberg, Gatti, Borghi, Paisiello-Federici, Reichardt, Tarchi, Perrino, Conti (1829), as given in Clement's *Dict. Lyrique.*   **G.**

OLIPHANT (OLIFANT from *olifaunt*, elephant), a short horn or bugle, made from the tusk of an elephant, from which the name comes. These instruments were used for signalling and hunting, and some existing specimens are very richly carved. They have no musical value, but are interesting in connexion with the development of the horn, and of wind instruments generally. (See HORN ; WIND INSTRUMENTS ; *PLATE LXVIII.* No. 3.)   **D. J. B.**

OLIPHANT, THOMAS (*b.* Condie, Perthshire, Dec. 25, 1799 ; *d.* Mar. 9, 1873), was in 1830 admitted a member of the Madrigal Society, and soon afterwards became its honorary secretary. He adapted English words to many Italian madrigals, some of which have become exceedingly popular, notably ' Down in a flow'ry Vale,' adapted to Festa's ' Quando ritrovo.' In 1834 he published *A Brief Account of the Madrigal Society*, and in 1836 *A Short Account of Madrigals*. In 1837 he published an 8vo volume entitled *La musa madrigalesca*, a collection of the words of nearly 400 madrigals, with remarks and annotations. He wrote an English version of Beethoven's ' Fidelio,' and English words to several songs, and edited Tallis's ' Service and Responses.' In his latter years he was president of the Madrigal Society.   **W. H. H.**

OLIVER Y ASTORGA, see ASTORGA, Jean Oliver y.

OLMEDA, P. FEDERICO (*b.* Burgo de Osma, 1865 ; *d.* Madrid, Feb. 11, 1909), Spanish musical historian, organist and composer. After occupying the post of organist at Tudela, Navarre (1887) and Burgos (1888–93), he became maestro de capilla at the Convent of the Descalzas Reales, Madrid, an office once held by Victoria. His importance in Spanish musical research rests mainly on his work on early polyphony ; some of his conclusions are stated in a rare pamphlet, *Viaje musical a Santiago de Galicia* (1895), describing the 12th-century ' Codex Calixti II.' (Santiago Cathedral MS.). He also published a valuable study on the folksongs of the district of Burgos, *Folklore de Castil.a* (1902), and other works concerning the performance of liturgical music. His compositions include 4 symphonies; string quartet; PF. pieces ; Salve Regina for vln. and orch. ; and other church music.   **J. B. T.**

OLSEN, OLE (*b.* Hammerfest, July 4, 1850), distinguished Norwegian musician and composer, who at the early age of 7 was able to take his father's place at the organ and play the services. It was originally intended that he should become an engineer, and he was

sent, in 1865, to study at Drontheim ; but his strong bias in favour of music continued to assert itself, and it was not long before he placed himself under the guidance of Fust Lendermann. This was in 1867 ; and from that date until 1870 Olsen studied regularly during the winter months, while in the summer time he joined various travelling theatrical companies as conductor. In the year 1870, however, he betook himself to Leipzig, where he became the pupil of E. F. Richter, Oscar Paul and Reinecke. After a course of four years at Leipzig Olsen returned to Sweden and settled at Christiania (1874), where he worked as a teacher of the piano, and as a choirmaster. He also made use of his great talent for writing by becoming a musical critic. When Svensden retired from the directorship of the Musical Society the post was offered to Olsen, who accepted it and retained it for many years. In 1884 he became musical director to the 2nd Norwegian Infantry Brigade ; and the experience and skill which he acquired in this leading position led to his being asked to undertake the onerous duties of musical director under the Military Board, when that office was established by the Swedish Government in 1900.

Ole Olsen has produced compositions of all kinds, excepting chamber music. Of his orchestral works the symphony in G major, together with the symphonic poems ' Aasgaardsreien ' and ' Elf-dance ' are accounted very fine examples of their class. In the sphere of operatic music Olsen is well represented by three grand operas, ' Stig Hvide,' ' Lajla,' and ' Stallo,' the libretti of which he wrote himself. He has written one oratorio, ' Nideros,' a fairy comedy, ' Svein Urad,' and four grand cantatas, ' Ludwig Holberg,' ' Griffenfeld,' ' Broderbud,' and the ' Tourist Cantata.'   **D. H.**

OLTHOFF, STATIUS (*b.* Osnabrück, 1555 ; *d.* Rostock, Feb. 28, 1629), was called in 1579 to the post of cantor to the Marien-Kirche at Rostock in Mecklenburg. In 1593 he is described in the account-books of the church as *Magister Statius* and as occupying the higher position of con-rector. At the instigation of Nathan or Nathaniel Chytraeus, the Humanist Professor of Latin and Poetry at the University of Rostock, who also as rector reorganised the chief school of the town, Olthoff composed a series of four-part settings of George Buchanan's famous Latin-verse paraphrases of the Psalms. This work was published at Frankfort 1585 with the title : *Psalmorum Davidis paraphrasis poetica Georgii Buchanan Scoti argumentis ac melodiis explicata atque illustrata*, etc. Eitner enumerates successive editions of this work up to 1656. The musical settings have been republished in the *Vierteljahrsschrift für Musikwissenschaft*, bd. v. Olthoff retired from active work in 1614.   **J. R. M.**

OLYMPIE, tragédie lyrique, in 3 acts, imitated from Voltaire by Dieulafoy, Briffault and Bujac; music by Spontini. Produced Paris Opéra, Dec. 20, 1819; Berlin, in German (E. T. A. Hoffmann), May 14, 1821.

G.; rev. M. L. P.

O'MARA, JOSEPH (b. Limerick, July 16, 1866), son of James O'Mara, J.P., late high sheriff for that city. In 1889 he studied singing in Milan under Perini and Moretti. On Feb. 4, 1891, he made his début as Ivanhoe at the Royal English Opera-House, and was favourably received. He had further teaching from Edwin Holland, and in 1892 he sang at the Popular Concerts. In 1894–95 he sang under Harris, both in English and Italian, at Drury Lane and Covent Garden as Don Cæsar, Hardress Cregan, Faust, Philémon, Don José, Turiddu, etc. On Mar. 2, 1896, he made a great success as Mike Murphy on the production of Stanford's 'Shamus O'Brien' at the Opéra-Comique Theatre. He became a favourite tenor in the Moody-Manners Opera Company in their London and provincial seasons, and added to his repertory many Wagnerian parts, Myles in 'Lily of Killarney,' Raoul, etc. Subsequently he toured the provinces with an opera company bearing his own name. He retired from the operatic stage in 1926.

A. C.

ONDŘIČEK, FRANZ (b. Prague, Apr. 29, 1859; d. Milan, Apr. 13, 1922), violinist, of Czech parentage. His father, a good violinist, was the leader of a small orchestra performing in cafés, ballrooms, etc., and early conveyed a knowledge of his instrument to his son, who, at the age of 7, was able to take a part in the orchestra, and was known in Prague as a prodigy. In 1873 he was sent to the Conservatorium of his native town, where he received free tuition for three years. In 1876 he gave a concert at Prague. Wieniawski, who was present, after hearing Ondříček play a movement from a concerto of Molique, stepped on to the platform and publicly embraced the young artist. The result of this successful appearance was that a rich merchant undertook his further education, and sent him to the Paris Conservatoire, where he entered the class of Massart, gaining a *premier prix* at the end of two years. Had he been eligible he would have won it in his first year. After leaving the Conservatoire he remained in France for two years, played in Paris at Pasdeloup's Concerts, and in other French towns, and then visited London, where he appeared at a concert of the Philharmonic Society, of which he was an honorary member. After returning for a short time to Bohemia, he made a series of tours on the continent, in the course of which he visited Berlin (in 1884) and gave two successful concerts in the opera-house. Later, he played as a soloist in most musical centres

of the world: in Russia, Italy, Holland, America, the East, etc., and was the recipient of many orders and decorations. In 1911 he was appointed professor in the Vienna Conservatoire, remaining there until 1919, when he moved on to the Conservatorium at Prague. He collaborated with Dr. Mittelmann in a *New Method of Learning the Higher Technique of Violin-Playing on Anatomical and Physiological Principles* (1909). His compositions include a rhapsody for orchestra 'Bohème,' a concerto and smaller pieces. He occasionally visited London, playing at the Popular Concerts and elsewhere.

W. W. C.

O'NEILL, NORMAN (b. Kensington, Mar. 14, 1875), composer and musical director of the Haymarket Theatre, London, is son of the painter, G. B. O'Neill. He studied with Dr. A. Somervell in 1890–93 ; in the latter year he entered the Hoch Conservatorium at Frankfort, where he studied until 1897 with Iwan Knorr. In 1899 he married Adine Rückert, a pupil of Mme. Schumann and of Mme. Wilhelmine Clauss-Szarvady ; under her married name she has won much acceptance as a pianist in London. O'Neill's chief work as composer and conductor has been done chiefly in the theatre. He was musical director of the Haymarket (1908–19) and during that time wrote the music for several important plays, including that to Maeterlinck's *The Blue Bird* (1909). Previously he had written music for a production of *Hamlet* (Dublin, 1904, and Lyric Theatre, London, 1905). In 1919 he was transferred to the St. James's Theatre, but returned to the Haymarket in 1920 for the production of *Mary Rose* (J. M. Barrie), for which he wrote music. Since then his connexion with the Haymarket has been maintained, and he wrote again for the revival of *A Kiss for Cinderella* (Barrie) in 1925. In such work O'Neill shows a remarkable aptitude for devising music which will enhance a situation and reflect the stage character, and he brings to the task the accomplishment of thorough musicianship. His connexion with the Royal Philharmonic Society has been a long one, and in 1919 he became its treasurer, a post held by his great-grandfather, Dr. CALLCOTT (q.v.), nearly a hundred years earlier. In September 1924 O'Neill joined the staff of the R.A.M. as a teacher of harmony and composition.

The following is the list of his principal compositions :

Op.
1. Variations for violin, violoncello and piano.
2. Sonata for violoncello and piano.
3. Suite for string orchestra. Played first at Frankfort.
4. Four compositions for piano.
5. Variations and Fugue for piano.
6. Romance and Scherzo for violin and piano.
7. Trio for piano, violin and violoncello.
8. Overture, 'In Autumn.'
10. Quintet for piano and strings.
11. Overture to *Hamlet*. Played at Birmingham, 1903.
12. Ballad for contralto and orchestra.
13. Overture, entr'actes, and incidental music to *Hamlet*. 1904
14. Miniatures for small orchestra.
17. Variations and Fugue on an Irish air for two pianofortes.

Op.
18. Five Rondels.
19. ' Woldemar,' fantasy for solo voices, chorus and orchestra.
21. Overture, ' In Spring Time.' Birmingham, 1906.
22. Overture, entr'actes, and incidental music to J. Comyns Carr's
     play, *A Lonely Queen.* New York.
23. Prelude, intermezzo and musical accompaniment to the play,
     A Tragedy of Truth. Manchester, 1906, and Adelphi Theatre,
     London, 1907.
24. Two pianoforte studies.
25. Miniatures for full orchestra. Birmingham, 1907.
28. Overture, entr'actes, and incidental music to Stephen Phillips's
     The Lost Heir. Glasgow, 1908, and Adelphi Theatre, London,
     1908.
29. Variations for orchestra (orchestral version of op. 17).
30. Scotch Rhapsody for orchestra.
31. ' La Belle Dame sans merci,' ballad for baritone and orchestra,
     London, 1910.
32. Trio for piano, violin and violoncello in one movement. 1908.
34. Eight National Songs for unison chorus and orchestra.
36. Music to *King Lear* (overture, entr'actes and incidental music).
     Haymarket Theatre, Sept. 8, 1909.
37. Music to Maeterlinck's *Blue Bird* (overture, dances and
     incidental music). Haymarket Theatre, Dec. 8, 1909.
     Suite of four dances from the above, for orchestra, published in
     a piano arrangement.

    Music to the following plays :
Julius Cæsar. (St. James's Theatre, 1919.)
Mary Rose. (Haymarket, 1920.)
Macbeth. (Aldwych, 1920.)
The Merchant of Venice. (New York, 1922.)
A Kiss for Cinderella. (Haymarket, 1925.)
Kismet. (New Oxford Theatre, 1925.)

    Ballets :
' The Swinburne Ballet.' (Coliseum, 1917.)
' The Punch and Judy Ballet.' (Duke of York's Theatre, 1924.)
    Publications include many selections from these stage works,
songs, piano pieces, etc.

                      M. ; rev. C.

ONSLOW, George (*b.* Clermont-Ferrand,
Puy-de-Dôme, July 27, 1784 ; *d.* Clermont,
Oct. 3, 1853), was a grandson of the first Lord
Onslow, and descended through his mother,
a de Bourdeilles, from the family of Brantôme.
Although eventually a prolific composer, he
showed as a child no special love for music,
and the lessons he took on the piano from
Hullmandel, Dussek and Cramer, during a
stay of some years in London, developed
nothing beyond manual dexterity. Having
returned to France, and settled in a province
more famous for its scenery than for its opportunities of artistic relaxation, he associated
with some amateurs who played chamber music,
and was thus induced first to study the violoncello, and then after a two-years' visit to
Vienna to compose works modelled after those
which gave so much pleasure to himself and
his friends. Onslow, even after he had composed a considerable amount of chamber-
music, felt the necessity for further instruction
before attempting dramatic composition, and
studied with Reicha. His three opéras-
comiques, ' L'Alcalde de la Vega ' (Aug. 10,
1824), ' Le Colporteur ' (Nov. 22, 1827), and
' Le Duc de Guise ' (Sept. 8, 1837), however,
after securing successive *succès d'estime*, disappeared, leaving the overture to ' The Colporteur,' which for some time was to be heard
in concert rooms, as their only representative.
His three published symphonies, though performed several times by the Société des Concerts du Conservatoire, are also forgotten. He
was elected a member of the Philharmonic
Society in London in 1832, and wrote a symphony for it.

A musician of respectable attainments and
indefatigable industry, an accomplished gentleman, and moreover a man of fortune, he had
no difficulty in finding either publishers or
appreciative friends, as was proved by his
election in 1842 to succeed Cherubini at the
Institut. With the above reservations it must
be admitted that Onslow, by the number of
his works and the elegant style of his best
passages, merited the reputation he enjoyed
during his lifetime.

His works include a scena, ' La Mort d'Abel,'
for bass-solo and orchestra ; four symphonies ;
thirty-four quintets and thirty-six quartets for
strings, six trios for PF., violin and violoncello ;
a sextuor (op. 30) for PF., flute, clarinet, horn,
bassoon and contrabasso, or PF., two violins,
viola, violoncello, and contrabasso ; a nonetto
(op. 77) for violin, viola, violoncello, contrabasso, flute, oboe, clarinet, bassoon and horn,
which he also arranged (op. 77 *bis*) as a sextour
for PF., flute, clarinet, horn, bassoon and
contrabasso, or for PF., two violins, viola,
violoncello and contrabasso ; a septet (op. 79)
for PF., flute, oboe, clarinet, horn, bassoon and
contrabasso ; sonatas and duos for PF. and
violin, or violoncello ; sonatas for PF., four
hands, and many pieces for PF. solo.

His quintets are undoubtedly his best works,
and contain much charming music. No. 15,
called ' Le Quintette de la balle,' describes his
emotions—the pain, the irregular beating of
his pulse, and his gratitude on his recovery—
consequent on an accident that happened to
him in 1829 at a wolf-hunt, where a spent ball
hit him in the face, rendering him somewhat
deaf in one ear for the rest of his life. His
earlier quintets were written for two violoncelli, but at a certain performance in England
the second violoncello failed to arrive, and it
was proposed that Dragonetti should play the
part on his double-bass. Onslow positively
refused, saying the effect would be dreadful.
However, after waiting some time, he was
obliged to consent, and after a few bars was
delighted with the effect. After this he wrote
them for violoncello and double-bass, and the
preceding ones were then rearranged in that
way under his own inspection by Gouffé, the
accomplished double-bass of the Paris Opéra.
Halévy pronounced his eulogium at the Institut, and printed it in his *Souvenirs et portraits*. D'Ortigue collected materials for his
biography, but only published an abstract of
them in the *Ménestrel* (1863–64, p. 113). Fétis
drew his information from these two sources,
to which the reader is referred for further detail.

        G. C. ; addns. *D.N.B.* ; *Riemann.*

OPEN NOTES. On wind instruments those
notes which are proper to the tube employed,
and occur as natural harmonics of the fundamental tone, are known as open notes, and are
thus distinguished from ' stopped ' notes obtained on the horn by the closing of the bell to
a greater or lesser degree by the hand, and from
notes produced by the means of keys or valves.

When keys or valves are used the fundamental length of the tube is changed, and consequently a new series of harmonics is introduced.

D. J. B.

OPEN STRINGS. In instruments of the violin type the term ' Open String ' is employed to indicate the unstopped sound of one of the stretched strings (see STOPPING). Example : On the violin, the note *e″* can be sounded by pressing a finger on the A, D, or G strings, or by vibrating the first string which is tuned to the pitch of that note. There is a difference of quality between stopped and open notes of the same pitch. A small o placed over the note indicates when the ' open string ' is to be played.

O. R.

OPERA (Ital. *opera*, abbrev. of *opera in musica*, a ' musical work,' *dramma per la musica* ; Fr. *opéra* ; Ger. *Oper, Singspiel*), a drama, either tragic or comic, sung throughout, with appropriate scenery and acting, to the accompaniment of an orchestra.

This article outlines the development of operatic style and structure to about the year 1900. References to composers who have attained distinction since that date will be found at the end.

It may seem strange to speak of the Opera as one of the oldest institutions in existence ; yet our search for its origin leads us back to a time long antecedent to the beginning of the Christian era ; and he who would read the story of its infancy aright must collect its details from the history of ancient Greece ; for it is as old as the drama itself. It was nurtured at Athens, in that glorious theatre the acoustic properties of which have never yet been rivalled. Its earliest librettists were Æschylus and Sophocles, and its earliest orchestra a band of lyres and flutes. There is no doubt about this. It is quite certain that not only were the choruses of the ' Agamemnon ' and the ' Antigone ' sung to the grandest music that could be produced at the time they were written, but also that every word of the dialogue was musically declaimed. Musical dialogue has been censured by unmusical critics as contrary to nature. It is, undoubtedly, contrary to the practice of everyday life, but not to the principles of art. It is necessary that the truth of this proposition should be very clearly established, for unless we make it our starting-point we shall never arrive at the true *raison d'être* of the Lyric Drama, nor be prepared with a satisfactory answer to the cavils of those who, like Addison and Steele, condemn it as a monstrous anomaly. It is open to no charge of inconsistency to which the spoken drama is not equally exposed. The poet writes his tragedy in verse, because he thereby gains the power of expressing great thoughts with the greatest amount of dignity that language can command. His verses are sung, in order that they may be invested with a deeper pathos than the most careful form of ordinary declamation can reach. No one objects to the iambics of the ' Seven against Thebes,' or the blank verse of ' King John ' ; yet surely our sense of the fitness of things is not more rudely shocked by the melodious *Ah ! soccorso ! son tradito !* uttered by the Commendatore after Don Giovanni has pierced him through with his sword, than by the touching couplet with which Prince Arthur, at the moment of his death, breaks forth into rhyme—

' O me ! my uncle's spirit is in these stones :—
Heaven take my soul, and England keep my bones ! '

The conventionalities of common life are violated no less signally in the one case than in the other ; yet, in the opera as well as in the play, the result of their violation is an artistic conception, as easily defensible on logical grounds as the proportions of a statue or the colouring of a picture—neither of which are faithful imitations of nature, though founded upon a natural ideal.

These appear to have been the views entertained, towards the close of the 16th century, by a little band of men of letters and musicians —all ardent disciples of the Renaissance—who met in Florence at the house of Giovanni Bardi, Conte di Vernio, with the avowed object of resuscitating the style of musical declamation peculiar to Greek tragedy. This end was unattainable. The antagonism between Greek and modern tonalities would alone have sufficed to make it an impossibility, had there been no other difficulties in the way. But, just as the search for the philosopher's stone resulted in some of the most important discoveries known to chemistry, this vain endeavour to restore a lost art led to the one thing upon which, above all others, the future fate of the Lyric Drama depended—and compassed it, on this wise.

Among the musicians who frequented the Count of Vernio's *réunions* were three whose names afterwards became celebrated. Vincenzo Galilei—the father of the great astronomer— was a pupil of the old school, but burning to strike out something new. Jacopo Peri and Giulio Caccini were young men, with little or no knowledge of counterpoint, but gifted with a wealth of original genius, and sufficient energy of character to enable them to turn it to the best account. All were thoroughly in earnest, thoroughly dissatisfied with the music of the period, and longing for a style of composition better fitted to express the varying shades of human passion than that then generally cultivated. The first result of their tentative efforts to reach this long-cherished ideal was the invention of the cantata—a secular composition for a single voice accompanied by a single instrument. Galilei produced a work of this description entitled ' Il Conte Ugolino,' which has unhappily been lost. Caccini—already celebrated for the beauty of his voice, and the excellence of his performance upon the lute—wrote a number of shorter pieces, which he sang with unbounded applause at Bardi's house, to the accompaniment of a theorbo, played by Bardilla.

Some of these Canzonette were published, in 1602, under the title of ' Le nuove musiche.' They are, indeed, most interesting, as examples of the earliest phase of the style—fitly called Monodic—which exchanged the contrapuntal richness of the polyphonic school for the simplest of melodies, confined to a single part, and accompanied by a bass, which was often not only simple, but of the rudest possible construction. The particular verse to which we have referred—*Diteli voi se di me vi cale*—is exceptionally symmetrical in form. As a general rule, the melodies of this transitional period were so destitute of what we now call ' figure,' as to be all but amorphous ; and it is precisely to this peculiarity that we are indebted for the extraordinary effect they wrought. All that their composers aimed at in constructing them was the exact oratorical rendering of the words with which they had to deal ; and in striving to attain this they unconsciously, and as if by a kind of inspiration, achieved that potent medium of passionate expression which alone was needed to make the Lyric Drama possible—pure, well - accented, declamatory recitative. Not, as they fondly imagined, the exact method of delivery cultivated by the Greek dramatists ; but, we may fairly believe, the nearest approach to it consistent with the modern scale—the true *musica parlante*, or *stilo rappresentativo*, which, by regulating the inflections of the voice in accordance with the principles of sound rhetorical science, invests them, if the experience of three centuries may be trusted, with an amount of dramatic power attainable by no other means.

The necessity for some such provision as this must have been painfully apparent to all thinking men. The polyphonic school, brought to perfection by Palestrina and his great contemporaries, was utterly unfit for dramatic purposes ; yet, in ignorance of a more appropriate form of expression, attempts to turn it to account in that direction had not been wanting.[1] (See INTERMEZZO.) It is certain that great part of Poliziano's ' Orfeo,' written in the latter half of the 15th century, was set to music of some kind ; and Leo Allatius mentions, in his ' Drammaturgia,' the names of eight musical representations produced between the years 1569 and 1582. The bare titles of these works, to one of which the name of Claudio Merulo is attached, are all that now remain to us ; and, unfortunately, we possess no printed copies of three still more important productions—' Il Satiro,' ' La disperazione di Fileno,' and ' Il

giuoco della cieca '—set to music by Emilio del Cavalieri, the two first in 1590, and the last in 1595 : but we may form a tolerably safe estimate of their style from that of Orazio Vecchi's ' L' Amfiparnasso,' performed at Modena in 1594, and printed soon afterwards in Venice.[2] This curious *Commedia armonica*, as the composer himself calls it, is presented in the form of a series of madrigals for five voices, written in the true polyphonic style, and equally remarkable for the beauty of their effect and the learning displayed in their construction. There is no overture ; and no instrumental accompaniment or ritornello of any kind. When the stage is occupied by a single character only, the four superfluous voices are made to sing behind the scenes ; when two persons are needed for the action three are kept out of sight. All doubt on this point is removed by the woodcuts with which the music is illustrated ; but before we condemn the absurdity of the arrangement we must remember that the grand old madrigalist only uses his unseen voices as later composers have used the orchestra. He could not leave his characters to sing without any accompaniment whatever ; and has therefore supported them, and, to the best of his ability, enforced the action of the scene by the only harmonic means within his reach.[3]

It must be confessed that though Vecchi was a skilful contrapuntist and Peri was not, the latter had all the advantage on his side, when, three years after the first performance of ' L' Amfiparnasso,' he produced his music to Rinuccini's ' Dafne.' It was at the Palazzo Corsi that ' Dafne ' was first privately performed in 1597.

1600. PERI'S ' EURIDICE.'—The success of the experiment was so decided that in the year 1600 Peri was invited to provide a still greater work to grace the festivities which followed the marriage of King Henri IV. of France with Maria de' Medici. It was on this occasion that he produced his famous ' Euridice,' the acknowledged prototype of all later developments of the *Dramma per la musica*. The work excited an extraordinary amount of attention. Rinuccini furnished the libretto. Several noblemen took part in the public performance. Behind the scenes, Corsi himself presided at the harpsichord, assisted by three friends, who played upon the chitarrone, the lira grande or viola da gamba, and the theorbo or large lute. These instruments, with the addition of three flutes used in a certain ritornello, seem to have comprised the entire orchestra ; and a considerable amount of freedom must have been accorded to the performers with regard to their manner of employing them ; for in the barred score

[1] See *Some Forerunners of Italian Opera*, by W. J. Henderson (1911).

[2] A modern edition by Eitner is published by Breitkopf & Haertel. [3] On the condition of performance of the earliest operas, see the *Sammelbände* of the Int. Mus. Ges. iv. 175 and 404, by Alfred Heuss ; and the *Monthly Musical Record*, Mar. 1906, article by E. J. Dent.

published at Florence, with a dedication to
Maria de' Medici, in 1600, and reprinted at
Venice in 1608, the accompaniment consists of
little more than an ordinary figured bass.
This score is now exceedingly scarce. Hawkins
did not even know of its existence, and Burney
succeeded in discovering one example only, in
the possession of the Marchese Rinuccini, a
descendant of the poet, at Florence ; but a
copy of the Venice edition is happily preserved
in the library of the British Museum.

Peri himself tells us, in his preface, that a
portion of this interesting work was written by
Caccini, though his own name alone appears
upon the title-page ; but Caccini also set the
entire libretto to music, on his own account,
and published[1] it in Florence in the same year
(1600), with a dedication to Giovanni Bardi.
The style of the two operas is so nearly identical, that whole scenes might easily be transferred
from one to the other without attracting
notice ; though it cannot be denied that there
are situations, such as that in which Orpheus
returns with Euridice from Hades, wherein
Peri has reached a higher level of dramatic
expression than his rival. Caccini's ' Euridice '
seems never to have been honoured with a
public performance ; the young composer
was, however, commissioned to produce for the
wedding festivities another *favola in musica*,
entitled ' Il rapimento di Cefalo,' some
portion of which afterwards appeared among
the ' Nuove musiche.'

The immediate result of these early experiments was the recognition of the opera as a
form of art no longer tentative, but fairly
established upon true æsthetic principles,
embarrassed by no grave practical difficulties,
and perfectly consistent, in all its details, with
the received traditions of classical antiquity
—which last recommendation was no light one,
in the estimation of men whose reverence for
Greek and Roman customs amounted to a
species of insanity.

MONTEVERDI'S ' ORFEO.'—The next development of importance took place in 1607 at
Mantua. At the invitation of Vincenzo Gonzaga, the reigning Duke, Rinuccini prepared
for the festival organised on the occasion
of the marriage of Francesco Gonzaga with
Margherita Infanta of Savoy the libretti of
two operas, entitled ' Dafne ' and ' Arianna,'
the first of which was set to music by Marco di
Zanobi da Gagliano, and the second by Claudio
Monteverdi, the Duke's maestro di cappella
—a man of extraordinary genius, already
famous for the boldness of his innovations in
the style of the Madrigal. Both operas were
written in the *stilo rappresentativo* ; and both
were deservedly successful, though not in an
equal degree. After the first performance of

' Dafne ' we hear of it no more ; but ' Arianna '
produced so extraordinary an effect upon the
audience, more especially in the scene in which
the forsaken Ariadne bewails the departure
of her faithless lover,[2] that Monteverdi was
at once invited to compose another opera, for
the ensuing year. For the subject of this he
chose the story of Orpheus and Eurydice,
dramatised by some poet whose name has
not transpired. The new work — entitled
' Orfeo,' to distinguish it from Peri's setting—
was in many respects immeasurably superior to
any that had preceded it. Dramatic expression
was one of the most prominent characteristics of Monteverdi's genius, and while his
natural love for instrumental music tempted
him to write for a far larger orchestra than any
of his predecessors had ventured to bring
together, his technical skill enabled him to turn
its resources to excellent account.[3] The
instruments used on the occasion of the first
performance were—

2 Gravicembali.	3 Bassi da gamba.
2 Contrabassi de Viola.	4 Tromboni.
10 Viole da brazzo.	1 Regale.
1 Arpa doppia.	2 Cornetti.
2 Violini piccoli alla Fran-	1 Flautino alla vigesima
cese.	seconda.
2 Chitarroni.	1 Clarino, con 3 trombe
2 Organi di legno.	sordine.

Hawkins, strangely misinterpreting the lists
of characters and instruments given at the
beginning of the printed score, imagines every
singer to have been accompanied by an instrument of some particular kind set apart for his
exclusive use. A very slight examination of
the music will suffice to expose the fallacy of
this idea. Nevertheless, the instruments are
really so contrasted and combined as to invest
each character and scene with a marked individuality which added greatly to the interest
of the performance. The recitatives are
accompanied, sometimes by a figured bass only,
and sometimes by two or more instruments, the
names of which are indicated at the beginning.
A complete score of the opera was published
at Venice in 1609, and reprinted in 1615.[4] A
copy of the second edition, now preserved in
the Roy. Lib. B.M., was formerly in the possession of Sir John Hawkins, who quoted from it
largely in vol. iii. of his *History of Music*.

Pietro della Valle, writing in 1640, tells us
that, like Tragedy at Athens under the guidance of Thespis, the Lyric Drama made its first
appearance in Rome upon a cart. During the
Carnival of 1606 this ambulant theatre was

---

[1] Eitner has published a modern edition of Caccini's ' Euridice '
in *Dis Oper* vol. i.

[2] This scene—*Lasciatemi morire*—generally known as the ' Lament
of Ariadne '—is almost the only portion of the opera that has been
preserved to us. It may be found entire in C. von Winterfeld's
Joannes Gabrieli, and has often been reprinted. See *Oxf. Hist. Mus.*
vol. iii. p. 47 *et seq.*
[3] See MONTEVERDI for an account of his organisation of the orchestra in subsequent works.
[4] See *The Life, Work, and Influence of Monteverde*, printed in the
Mus. T. for Apr. 1880. See also Parry's *Music of the 17th Century*
(*Oxf. Hist. Mus.* vol. iii. p. 51), where a close analysis of the whole
work is given. The latest of several modern editions of the ' Orfeo '
is that edited by Francesco Mal'piero, pub. by Chester (1923). An
English text translated by R. L. Stuart was published for the
revival at Oxford, 1925.

driven from street to street, surmounted by a movable stage, whereon five masked performers enacted a little play, set to music for them by Paolo Quagliati. The idea seems to have originated with Della Valle himself. He it was who arranged the performances, and induced Quagliati to write the music ; and so great was the success of the experiment that from four o'clock in the afternoon until after midnight the little band of strollers found themselves surrounded by a never-failing concourse of admiring spectators. Rough indeed must these primitive performances have been when compared with the entertainments presented to the Florentines by Peri and Caccini ; yet it is strange that, notwithstanding their favourable reception, we hear of no attempts either to repeat them or to encourage the introduction of anything better until the year 1632, when a musical drama called ' Il ritorno di Angeiica nell' Indie ' appears to have been privately performed in the palace of one of the Roman nobles. The composition is ascribed in Lady Morgan's *Life and Times of Salvator Rosa*, to a composer named Tignali. This name is considered by S. S. Stratton to be a corruption of Tenaglia, whose ' Clearco ' was produced at Rome in 1661.

VENICE AND CAVALLI, 1637.—The actual transfer of the patronage of opera from the nobles to the people took place in 1637 in Venice, the famous theorbo-player, Benedetto Ferrari, and Francesco Manelli da Tivoli, the composer, opening at their own private risk the first public opera-house, under the name of the Teatro di San Cassiano. For this new theatre Ferrari wrote the words, and Manelli the music, of an opera called ' Andromeda,' which was so well received that in the following year the same two authors brought out a second work, ' La maga fulminata '; while in 1639 the text of Giulio Strozzi's ' La Delia, ossia la sposa del sole ' was set to music, either by Manelli or Paolo Sacrati—it is difficult to say which—and Ferrari produced ' L' Armida ' to poetry of his own. This was an eventful season. Before its close, Monteverdi once more appeared before the public with a new opera called ' L' Adone,' which ran continuously till the Carnival of 1640 ; and his pupil, Pier-Francesco Caletti-Bruni, nicknamed by the Venetians ' il Checco Câ-Cavalli,' [1] made his first appearance as a dramatic composer with ' Le nozze di Peleo e di Tetide.' Cavalli's natural taste suggested the cultivation of a more flowing style of melody than that in which his contemporaries were wont to indulge ; and he was not so bigoted a disciple of the Renaissance as to think it necessary to sacrifice that taste to the insane Hellenic prejudice which would have banished rhythmic melody from the opera for no better reason than that it was unknown in

the time of Pericles. Vincenzo Galilei and his Florentine associates condemned such melody as puerile and degraded to the last degree. But Cavalli—as he is now generally called—not only employed it constantly, for the sake of relieving the monotony of continuous recitative, but even foreshadowed the form of the regular aria, by that return to the first part which was afterwards indicated by the term *da capo*.

Cavalli's predilection for rhythmic melody was fully shared by his talented contemporary, Marc Antonio Cesti — a pupil of Giacomo Carissimi, to whose example, though he himself did not care to write for the stage, the dramatic composers of the day were indebted for a higher ideal than they could possibly have conceived without his assistance. Honest work in one branch of art seldom fails to react favourably upon another ; and it is certain that, by transferring to the opera the methods of phrasing and instrumentation employed by Carissimi in the Cantata di Camera, Cesti not only elevated the former to a more dignified level than it had ever before attained, but at the same time laid the foundation of his own triumphant success. His earliest attempt, ' L' Orontea ' — first performed at Venice in 1649, at the Teatro dei SS. Apostoli, in the teeth of Cavalli's ' Giasone ' at the rival house of S. Cassiano—retained its popularity, throughout the whole of Italy, for more than thirty years.

The honours of the Venetian school were upheld, about this time, by a crowd of popular composers, the most successful of whom were Carlo Pallavicino, D. Giov. Legrenzi, Antonio Sartorio, Pietro and Marc Antonio Ziani, Castrovillari, Strozzi, and some other aspirants for public fame, who found ample employment in the numerous opera houses which before the close of the century sprang up in every quarter of the city. Between 1637 and 1699 eleven theatres came into existence (see VENICE) proving more clearly than any amount of written description the readiness with which the Venetians received the opera as one of their most cherished amusements. They had already learned to look upon it as quite a national institution ; and supported it with a liberality altogether unknown elsewhere. In Rome, for instance, there were at this time three opera-houses only—the Torre di Nona, opened in 1671 with Cavalli's ' Giasone '; the Sala de' Signori Capranica, for the inauguration of which Bernardo Pasquini composed his ' Dov' è amore e pietà ' in 1679 ; and a theatre in the Palazzo Aliberti, which started with Perti's ' Penelope la casta ' in 1696. No public theatre was established in Bologna till 1690.

SCARLATTI.—The next period of our history was a very significant one, and productive of results so important that it may be said to

---

[1] That is, ' Little Frank, of the House of Cavalli.'

mark the boundary between a class of works interesting chiefly from an antiquarian point of view and those grander productions the intrinsic value of which entitles them to be remembered throughout all time.

Alessandro Scarlatti, beyond all comparison the brightest genius of the epoch we are considering, and universally recognised as the most learned musician of his day, took even the best of his contemporaries at an incalculable disadvantage. His knowledge so far aided him in the construction of his basses and the elaboration of his accompaniments that, under his masterly treatment, the timidity which, in the infancy of modern art, so fatally weakened its effect, and rendered it so miserable a substitute for the richer combinations of polyphony, was exchanged for a freedom of style and breadth of design which at once elevated it to the rank of a finished school, capable indeed of future development to an unlimited extent, but no longer either tentative in conception or rudimentary in structure. On the other hand, his splendid natural talents did him good service in quite another way. Tired of the monotony of uninterrupted recitative, he boldly started on a new path, and, rejecting the experience of his immediate predecessors as altogether effete, availed himself of three distinct forms of dramatic expression—the simple form of recitative, called by the Italians *recitativo secco* ; accompanied recitative, or *recitativo stromentato* ; and the regular *aria*. The first of these he employed for the ordinary business of the stage ; the second, for the expression of deep pathos, or violent emotion of any kind ; the third, for impassioned, or at least strongly individualised soliloquy. *Recitativo secco* was supported by a simple ' Thorough-bass,' the chords of which were filled in, in former times, upon the harpsichord, and later, in England, played on the violoncello and double bass. Accompanied recitative has since passed through an infinity of changes, naturally dictated by the gradual enlargement of the orchestra and the increased strength of its resources. But it is still what its inventor intended it to be —a passionate form of declamation, in which the sense of the verbal text is enforced by the continual interposition of orchestral symphonies of more or less elaborate construction. Lastly, the symmetrical form of the aria had only been very imperfectly suggested before Scarlatti stereotyped it by the addition of a ' Second Part,' followed by that repetition of the original strain now known as the DA CAPO (*q.v.*). That this indication of a desire to escape from the dreariness of the interminable monologue which preceded it ultimately led to a formality and a pandering to a singer's vanity, which it was Gluck's task to attempt to sweep away, was not the fault of Scarlatti ; and indeed we owe something to the

composer who first made it a distinctive feature in the dramatic music he did so much to perfect, and whose love of regular design led him to introduce improvements of equal value into the form of the instrumental prelude which was afterwards recognised as the indispensable overture. (See SCARLATTI, Alessandro.)

The most talented of Scarlatti's contemporaries were, among Neapolitans, Alessandro Stradella and Francesco Rossi ; in Venice, Antonio Caldara and Antonio Lotti ; in Bologna, Antonio Perti, Francesco Pistocchi, and Giovanni Maria Buononcini ; and, in Vicenza, Domenico Freschi. But for his untimely death, Stradella's genius would undoubtedly have entitled him to take rank as the founder of an original and highly characteristic school. As it was, he lived but to compose one single opera, ' La forza dell' amor paterno,' the libretto of which was printed at Genoa in 1678. Rossi, though born in Naples, wrote chiefly for Venice, where he met with very great success. Lotti produced eighteen successful operas in that city, between the years 1683 and 1717 ; and one in Dresden. Caldara enriched the Venetian school with five, besides writing many more for Vienna, founded for the most part upon the libretti of Apostolo Zeno and Metastasio. The greater number of Freschi's works were also written for Venice ; but his famous ' Berenice ' was first performed at Padua, in 1680, the year after Scarlatti made his first appearance in Rome, with a *mise en scène* which exceeded in magnificence anything that had ever been previously attempted. Among the attractions mentioned in the printed book of the opera, we find choruses of 100 virgins, 100 soldiers and 100 horsemen in iron armour ; besides 40 cornets, on horseback ; 6 mounted trumpeters ; 6 drummers ; 6 ensigns ; 6 sackbuts ; 6 flutes ; 12 minstrels, playing on Turkish and other instruments ; 6 pages ; 3 sergeants ; 6 cymbaleers ; 12 huntsmen ; 12 grooms ; 12 charioteers ; 2 lions, led by 2 Turks ; 2 led elephants ; Berenice's triumphal car, drawn by 4 horses ; six other cars, drawn by 12 horses ; 6 chariots, for the procession ; a stable containing 100 living horses ; a forest, filled with wild-boar, deer and bears ; and other scenic splendours, too numerous to mention in detail, but highly significant, as indicative of a condition of the drama in which, notwithstanding an honest desire on the part of many a true artist to attain æsthetic perfection, the taste of the general public was as yet unable to soar above the vulgarities of a frivolous peep-show. PISTOCCHI's 'Leandro' (1679) and ' Girello ' (1682) were performed in Venice by puppets, and ZIANA's ' Damira placata ' by mechanical figures, as large as life, while the real singers officiated behind the scenes.

FRENCH OPERA.—The scene now changes to Paris, whither Giovanni Battista Lully was brought from Florence in the year 1646, in the character of page to Mademoiselle de Montpensier, niece of Louis XIV. The earliest suggestion of the opera form in France seems to be the dramas with music of the trouvères of the 13th century; indeed, 'Le Jeu de Robin et de Marion' of Adam de la Hale (*q.v.*), which has been preserved entire, is virtually an 'opéra-comique'—a form to be discussed later—with its dialogue interspersed with musical numbers. But grand opera is to be more definitely connected with the Ballet. As early as the year 1581, a piece, called 'Le Ballet comique de la royne,' arranged by Baltazar de Beaujoyeaulx, with dance tunes, choruses, musical dialogues and ritornelli, composed for the occasion by Beaulieu and Salmon, was acted, at the Château de Moutiers, in presence of Henri III., with extraordinary splendour. The first attempt to introduce Italian music was made by Rinuccini, who visited France in the suite of Maria de' Medici in 1600; but it does not seem to have accorded with the national taste. During the reign of Louis XIII. the Ballet was more warmly patronised at court than any other kind of musical entertainment. Cardinal Mazarin endeavoured to reintroduce the Italian Opera, during the minority of Louis XIV.; but its success was very transient, and far less encouraging than that of the early attempts at French Opera. The first of these was 'Akebar, roi de Mogol,' written and composed by the Abbé Mailly, and performed at Carpentras in 1646, in the presence of the Papal Legate, Cardinal Bichi. In 1659, Perrin wrote a Pastoral, with music by Cambert, which was first privately performed at Issy, and afterwards, in presence of the king, at Vincennes. Louis was delighted with it; and, supported by his approval, its authors produced some other works, of which the most successful was 'Pomone,' played first in 1671 at the Hôtel de Nevers, and in 1677 in the Tennis Court at the Hôtel de Guénégaud. This was the first French opera ever publicly performed in Paris. Meanwhile, Lully was industriously engaged in the composition of ballets, designed to meet the taste of the young king. But in Mar. 1672 he obtained, by Royal Patent, the entire monopoly of the Académie de Musique (*q.v.*), and then it was that he entered upon that portion of his career which exercised the strongest influence upon the subsequent progress of dramatic music in France. Inspired by the verses of Quinault, who wrote twenty pieces for him between the years 1672 and 1686, he substituted for the Italian *recitativo secco* a style of accompanied recitative so well adapted to the spirit of the best French poetry that the declamatory portions of his operas soon became even more attractive than the scenes which depended for their success upon mere spectacular display.

In order to accomplish this purpose, he availed himself of an expedient already well known in the Venetian school—the constant alternation of duple and triple rhythm. Moreover, his bold and highly cultivated taste for instrumental music led him to mould the overture into a form more perfect than any with which it had been previously invested. (See Overture.) For the meagre prelude affected by his Italian contemporaries he substituted a dignified Largo, followed by an Allegro, in the fugato style, with a well-marked subject and points of imitation. Sometimes he added a third movement, in the form of a minuet or other stately dance tune; so successful was the general effect of the whole that before long it was imitated by every composer in Europe.

Of Lully's immediate successors, Colasse, Destouches and Campra, the last-named was the most gifted, and his 'Tancrède,' produced in 1702, held the stage for many years. But at that very date, a decline in the popularity of the Lully style is evidenced by the publication of the Abbé François Raguenet's *Parallèle des Italiens et des Français, en ce qui regarde la musique et les opéras.* Some years before this publication d'Allard and Vanderberg, proprietors of 'marionette' or puppet theatres, had introduced music into their performances at the 'Foire St. Germain' with such success as to excite the jealousy of Lully, who obtained an order forbidding the performance of vocal music in the marionette theatre, and reducing the orchestra to four stringed instruments and an oboe. Moreover the entrepreneurs of the 'Comédie Française,' on whose domain the marionettes would seem considerably to have encroached, obtained another order forbidding even speech in their representations. At the instigation of two ingenious playwrights, Chaillot and Remy, the difficulty created by these orders was in some sort met by furnishing each performer with a placard on which were inscribed the words he would or should have uttered under other circumstances. These placards, of necessity large, being found to impede the action and even sight of the performers, their 'parts' were subsequently appended to the scene. The utterance, musical or other, of the songs of which these were largely made up, though forbidden to the actors, were not unallowable for the audience, who, perfectly familiar with the airs to which (vaudeville-wise) they had been written, took on themselves this portion of the dumb actors' duties—doubtless with sufficient spirit and intensity. The popularity of these performances, which, in spite (or because) of the restrictions upon them, increased day by day, eventually brought about a treaty of peace between the would-be monopolists of speech and song and the 'marionettes.' In 1716 Catherine Vanderberg, then directress, obtained a licence for the presentation of dramatic pieces interspersed with singing and dancing, and accompanied by instruments, to which the name 'opéra-comique' was given, a form in which France was presently to excel.

ENGLISH MASQUES.—The idea of English Opera was suggested neither by the Ballet nor the Tragedy. It was the legitimate offspring of the MASQUE (q.v.); and the Masque, in England at least, was very far from presenting the characteristics of a true Lyric Drama. Its music was, at first, purely incidental—ac much so as that introduced into the plays of Shakespeare. In the masques performed at court, temp. James I. and Charles I., a nearer approach was made to the opera—poetry, music, scenery, machinery and characteristic dresses and decorations being combined in them. Alfonso Ferrabosco junior, Laniere, who in 1617 set an entire masque of Ben Jonson to music in the *stilo recitativo* and may therefore claim the credit of having composed the first English Opera, Coprario, Robert Johnscn, Campian, Simon Ives, and William and Henry Lawes were the principal composers employed. The first approaches towards the revival of dramatic entertainments, which had been suspended by the closing of the theatres during the Civil War, were made during the interregnum through the medium of musical pieces. On Mar. 26, 1653, Shirley's masque, 'Cupid and Death,' with music by Matthew Locke and Christopher Gibbons, was performed before the Portuguese ambassador. Three years later Sir William Davenant gave, in a semi-public manner, 'The First Day's Entertainment at Rutland House by Declamations and Musick,' with music by Colman, Cook, H. Lawes and Hudson. In the prologue it is designated an opera, though it is not one in any respect. In the following year Davenant produced 'The Siege of Rhodes,' the dialogue of which was given in recitative, which Davenant describes as 'unpractised here, though of great reputation amongst other nations.' This piece, to which a second part was subsequently added, maintained its position for some years, but the music has not, so far as is known, been preserved. 'The Siege of Rhodes' was followed by the production by Davenant in 1658 of 'The Cruelty of the Spaniards in Peru, expressed by instrumental and vocal music, and the art of perspective in scenes,' a performance said to have been not only connived at, but secretly encouraged by Cromwell, who was then supposed to be meditating some designs against the Spaniards.

During the four or five years which followed the reopening of the public theatres in 1660, little, beyond occasional repetitions of 'The Siege of Rhodes,' appears to have been done to forward operatic performances on the English stage. The Plague in 1665 and the Great Fire of London in 1666 caused a temporary suspen-

sion of all theatrical performances, but a step onwards was made in 1667 by the production of an adaptation by Davenant and Dryden of Shakespeare's 'Tempest' with large additions to the lyric portions. The vocal music of this version was supplied by Pelham Humfrey and John Banister, and the instrumental by Matthew Locke. Soon after the opening of the theatre in Dorset Gardens (1671), the proprietor resorted to opera as the principal attraction. In 1673 they brought out Shadwell's 'Psyche,' of which the author said 'the great desire was to entertain the town with variety of musick, curious dancing, splendid scenes and machines.' Matthew Locke composed the vocal, and Giovanni Baptista Draghi the instrumental music for 'Psyche,' the dances being arranged by St. André, and the scenery painted by Stephenson. In 1676 Charles Davenant's 'Circe' was produced, with the music of John Banister. The Frenchman Grabu's setting of Dryden's 'Albion and Albanius' appeared in 1685 and failed. About 1688 was 'performed at Mr. Josias Priest's Boarding School at Chelsey by young Gentlewomen' Henry Purcell's opera 'Dido and Aeneas,' the dialogue in recitative. (See PURCELL, subsection THEATRE MUSIC.[1])

BEGINNINGS IN GERMANY.—What Lully did for France, and Purcell began in England, Reinhard Keiser did for Germany. The Opera was first imported into that country from Italy in 1627, when Rinuccini's 'Dafne,' translated into German by Martin Opitz, and set to music by Heinrich Schütz, was performed at Torgau, on the occasion of the marriage of George II., Landgraf of Hesse, with the sister of the Elector of Saxony. At Regensburg, the musical drama made its first appearance with Benedetto Ferrari's 'L'inganno d'Amore,' in 1653. Antonio Draghi's 'Alcindo,' and 'Cloridia,' were produced in 1665 at Vienna; and Giulio Riva's 'Adelaida regia principessa di Susa' at Munich. But all these last-named works were sung in Italian. The true cradle of the German Opera, despite its transient success at Torgau, was Hamburg; in which city Johann Theile produced his 'Adam und Eva'—the first 'Singspiel' ever publicly performed in the German language—in 1678. This was followed, in the same year, by 'Orontes'; and from that time forward the Hamburg Theatre retained the first place among the public opera-houses of Germany for more than half a century. Nikolaus Strungk wrote six operas for it, between the years 1678 and 1685. Between 1679 and 1686 Johann Franck wrote thirteen. Johann

---

[1] Practically the whole of the English Restoration stage music called 'opera,' including Purcell's own works, with the exception of 'Dido and Aeneas,' was an unsatisfactory hybrid. Musical scenes, chiefly concerned with supernatural characters, alternated with spoken scenes, the characters in which had no part in the musical scheme. Such a form was incapable of artistic development. In 'Dido' Purcell merely showed what his operatic style would have been had there been a public stage for its presentation. Failing that he fell back on the opportunity of performance at a girls' school. When he wrote for the public stage he, like his predecessors and contemporaries, accepted the conditions imposed by fashion.   c.

Förtsch wrote twelve, between 1684 and 1690; Johann Conradi eight, between 1691 and 1693; Johann Cousser five, between 1693 and 1697; and Mattheson three, between 1699 and 1704; but between 1694 and 1734 Keiser produced quite certainly not less than 116, and probably many more. Handel also brought out his 'Almira' and 'Nero' there in 1705, and his 'Daphne' and 'Florinda' in 1706; his connexion with Hamburg was, however, of no long duration, and it was to Keiser's exertions alone that the Theatre was indebted for its world-wide fame. Keiser's first attempt, 'Ismene,' was successfully performed at Wolfenbüttel in 1692; and after that his popularity continued undiminished, in spite of variations in his personal fortunes, until in 1734 he took leave of his admiring audience with his last production, 'Circe.' The number of his published works is exceedingly small,[1] but a large collection of the original MSS. are in Berlin. Their style is purely German; less remarkable for its rhetorical perfection than that of Lully, but exhibiting far greater variety of expression, and a more earnest endeavour to attain that spirit of dramatic truth which alone can render such music worthy of its intended purpose.

HANDEL AND 18TH-CENTURY OPERA.— Though Handel, as we have already seen, made his first essay at Hamburg in German opera, his natural taste accorded entirely with the traditions of the Italian school. His first Italian opera, 'Roderigo,' was produced at Florence in 1706, and 'Agrippina,' at Venice in 1709, put the crown on his Italian visit (see HANDEL). Even in these early works his genius asserted itself, but a still more decided triumph awaited him in London, where he brought out his famous 'Rinaldo' at the Queen's Theatre, Haymarket, in 1711, beyond all comparison the finest opera that had as yet been placed upon the stage in any country, and being indebted for its great popularity to the exceeding beauty of its arias.

When Italian operas were first introduced into this country, they were performed by a mixed company of Italians and Englishmen, each of whom sang in his own language. A similar absurdity had long prevailed in Hamburg, where the airs of certain popular operas were sung in Italian, and the recitatives in German; and even in Italy the conventionalities of fashion and the jealousies of favourite singers had already begun to exercise a far more potent influence upon the progress of dramatic art than was consistent with true æsthetic principles. During the greater part of the 18th century the laws which regulated the construction of an opera were so severely formal

that the composer was not permitted to use his own discretion, even with regard to the distribution of the voices he employed. The orthodox number of *personaggi* was six—three women and three men; or, at most, three women assisted by four men. The first woman (*prima donna*) was always a high soprano, and the second or third a contralto. Sometimes a woman was permitted to sing a man's part, especially if her voice, like those of Mrs. Barbier and Mrs. Anastasia Robinson, happened to be a low one; but, in any case, it was *de rigueur* that the first man (*primo uomo*) should be an artificial soprano (see CASTRATO), even though the rôle assigned to him might be that of Theseus or Hercules. The second man was either a soprano, like the first, or an artificial contralto; and the third, a tenor. When a fourth male character (*ultima parte*) was introduced, the part was most frequently allotted to a bass; but operas were by no means uncommon in which, as in Handel's 'Teseo,' the entire staff of male singers consisted of artificial sopranos and contraltos, who monopolised all the principal songs, and upon whose popularity for the time being the success of the work in no small degree depended.

The airs entrusted to these several performers were arranged in five classes, each distinguished by some well-defined peculiarity of style, though not of general design; the same mechanical form, consisting of a first and second part, followed by the indispensable *da capo*, being common to all alike. These were, with variants, the *aria cantabile, aria di portamento, aria di mezzo carattere, aria parlante* and *aria di bravura,* or *d' agilità* (see ARIA).

The sequence and distribution of these varied movements was regulated by laws no less stringent than those which governed their division into separate classes. It was necessary that every scene in every opera should terminate with an air; and every member of the *dramatis personae* was expected to sing one, at least, in each of the three acts into which the piece was almost invariably divided; but no performer was permitted to sing two airs in succession, nor were two airs of the same class allowed to follow each other, even though assigned to two different singers. The most important airs were played at the conclusion of the first and second acts. In the second and third acts, the hero and heroine each claimed a grand scena, consisting of an accompanied recitative followed by an *aria d' agilità* calculated to display the power of the vocalist to the greatest possible advantage; in addition to which the same two characters united their voices in at least one grand duet. The third act terminated with a chorus of lively character, frequently accompanied by a dance; but no trios, quartets or other concerted movements were permitted in any part of the opera, though three or more characters were sometimes suffered—as in

<hr>

[1] See, however, his 'Octavia,' edited by Chrysander as a supplement to the German Handel Societies edition; also *D.D.T.* xxvii. and xxviii., from reprints of 'Krösus' and 'L' inganno felice.'

'Rinaldo'[1]—to join in a harmonised exclamation, at the close of a recitative.

It seems strange that with so many voices at command, so little advantage should have been taken of the opportunity of combining them ; but the law was absolute, and no doubt owed its origin to the desire of popular singers rather to shine alone, at any cost, than to share their triumphs with rival candidates for public favour.

The effect of these formal restrictions, pressing with equal severity on the composer and the author of the libretto, was fatal to the development of a natural and consistent drama. Handel himself but rarely evaded them ; the third act of 'Radamisto,' however, contains an elaborate quartet, and in ' Teseo,' in five acts, two airs in succession are frequently given to the principal characters. Of the numerous poets who wrote for the lyric stage, during the earlier half of the 18th century, two only, Apostolo Zeno and Metastasio, succeeded in producing really good pieces, in spite of the difficulties thrown in their way. Goldoni would probably have been equally successful had he been equally persevering ; but after one or two vexatious failures, he threw up the opera in disgust, and devoted his attention to comedy.

Though Handel's operas so far excelled all others produced, either during his lifetime or for many years after his death, they seem, except in a few isolated cases, to have excited very much less attention on the Continent than in our own country. While they were steadily increasing his fame and ruining his fortune in London, another set of works was progressing successfully on the banks of the Elbe, under the superintendence of one of the greatest of Handel's contemporaries, Johann Adolph Hasse, a native of North Germany, who, after a long course of study in Naples, adopted the Italian style, and eventually settled in Dresden, where, between the years 1731 and 1763, he brought the Italian opera to a higher condition than it enjoyed in any other continental city. He died at Venice in 1783, leaving behind him more than 100 operas, most of which exhibit great merit though little depth of inspiration, while all, probably, owed some part at least of their popularity to the matchless singing of his wife, the celebrated Faustina. To this period belong also the Italian operas produced by Graun, at Brunswick and Berlin, between the years 1726 and 1759, and those written about the same time, by Fux, at Vienna. These compositions, though they never became equally famous, were undoubtedly greater, considered as works of art, than those of Hasse ; as were those, also Italian, given to the world a little later by John Christian Bach. Meanwhile,

[1] More than seventy years afterwards, Mozart used the same expedient, with irresistible effect, in ' Le nozze di Figaro.' The writer well remembers the ' double encore ' which followed the delivery of the words ' E schiatti il Signor Conte al gusto mio ' by Mlle. Jenny Lind, Mme. Grimaldi, Signor Lablache and Herr Staudigl, at Her Majesty's Theatre, in the year 1847.

good service was done in Italy by Vinci.. by his share in the development of the aria form— Domenico Scarlatti, Leonardo Leo, Francesco Feo, Nicolo Porpora and many others, including Bononcini, now chiefly remembered for his unfortunate contest with Handel.

OPERA BUFFA.—We are next transported once more to Naples, where rapid progress was made, about the middle of the 18th century, in a new direction. We have already described, in the article INTERMEZZO, the gradual development of the Opera Buffa from the interludes which were formerly presented between the acts of an Opera Seria, or spoken drama. These light works were, at first, of very simple character ; but a significant change in their construction was introduced when the idea was first entertained of bringing the principal characters on the stage together towards the close of the piece, and combining their voices in a more or less elaborate concerted finale. Originally this consisted of a single movement only, and that, comparatively, a simple one. It was later extended to several movements in succession, often in different keys ; and finally was introduced into the Opera Seria, in which it soon began to play a very important part, naturally leading to the introduction of trios, quartets and the host of richly harmonised *pezzi concertati* upon which the dignity of the Grand Opera was afterwards made so largely to depend.

The distribution of parts in the Opera Buffa differed, in some important particulars, from that which so long prevailed in the Opera Seria ; introducing fewer artificial voices, and giving far greater prominence to the basses. The *personaggi* were grouped in two divisions. The chief, or *buffo* group, consisted of two female performers, called the *prima* and *seconda buffa*, and three men, distinguished as the *primo buffo*, the *buffo caricato* and the *ultima parte,* of whom the first was a tenor, while the second was generally, and the third always, a bass. The subordinate group was limited to the two inevitable lovers, entitled the *donna seria* and *uomo serio*. This arrangement was originally very strictly enforced ; but as time progressed departures from the orthodox formula became by no means uncommon.

Most of the composers of this period excelled equally in Opera Buffa and Opera Seria ; and the style of their melodies was so much more modern than that cultivated either by Handel or Hasse, that we have found it necessary to include among them some whose names, by right of chronology, should rather have been referred to the preceding epoch, with which, however, they can claim but very little æsthetic connexion. First among them stands Pergolesi, whose serious opera ' Sallustia ' produced a furore in Naples in 1731, while his comic Intermezzo, 'La serva padrona,' performed in 1733, was received with acclamations in every capital in Europe. Jommelli's style, though less truly Italian than Pergolesi's, so nearly resembled it, that it would be impossible to class him with any other composer. He wrote an immense number of operas, both serious and comic ; and the melodies he introduced into them obtained for him an amount of public favour which had by no means begun to wane when Burney visited him at Naples in 1770.[1]

Jommelli is also to be credited with an innovation in respect of the *da capo* aria form, thus anticipating one of Gluck's reforms (see JOMMELLI). The work of these men was vigorously supplemented by the efforts of Sacchini, Guglielmi and Perez ; and still more by those of Galappi and Paisiello, both of whom worked on the development of the concerted finale. Piccinni developed the duet form and wrought his finales into long concerted pieces, remarkable for their attempt to make the interest of the piece culminate, as it approaches its conclusion, in the richest harmonies producible by the united voices of the entire *dramatis personae*.

GLUCK'S REFORMS.—The climax, however, of this eventful epoch was created by Christoph Willibold Gluck, whose clear judgment and unerring dramatic instinct was to exercise a powerful influence upon the progress of operatic art. An accomplished rather than a learned musician, Gluck rendered himself remarkable, less by any extraordinary display of technical skill than by his profound critical acumen ; but it was not until he was well advanced in life that this great quality bore the fruit which rendered his name famous.

His first doubt as to the logical consistency of the orthodox Italian Opera seems to have been suggested by the unsatisfactory effect of a pasticcio, called ' Piramo e Tisbe,' which he produced in London in the year 1746. In this piece he contrived to introduce a large collection of airs, chosen from his best and most popular works ; yet it wholly failed to fulfil his expectations, not because the music was in fault, but because it was altogether unsuited to the situations of the drama. The reader will, it is to be hoped, remember the grand principle which we assumed as our *point d'appui* at the opening of the present article— that the Lyric Drama could neither be pronounced inconsistent nor illogical so long as music was employed as a means of intensifying the expression of poetry, and therefore (as a natural consequence) of increasing the dramatic power of the scenes it depicted ; and, theoretically, the position was never disputed. But as the art of composition, assisted by increased orchestral resources and an improved system

of vocalisation, threw off the trammels of its early stiffness and attained, step by step, the perfection of symmetrical form, composers were tempted to sacrifice the interest of the drama to that of the music which should have tended to illustrate it. The real force of the most striking situations was lost in the endeavour to fill them with captivating arias, calculated to gratify, at the same time, the popular taste and the vanity of individual singers. As the number of great singers multiplied, the abuse grew daily more and more antagonistic to the enunciation of æsthetic truth, until the opera was degraded into a mere collection of songs, connected together by recitatives which seemed designed more with the idea of providing breathing-time for the singer than that of developing the plot of the piece or rendering its details intelligible to the audience. Against this state of things, which Benedetto Marcello had already censured in no measured terms, Gluck's hatred of falsehood and incongruity in all that concerned his beloved art could not fail to rebel. He felt that the system was based, from first to last, on a fatal mistake ; yet could not, for the time, suggest a remedy sufficiently potent to remove an evil so deeply rooted. His first operas were written in a style which he himself was rapidly learning to despise, but with which the general public were enchanted. It was not until 1762, sixteen years after his memorable visit to England, that he made any serious attempt to express his new ideas in a tangible form when he produced ' Orfeo ' to the libretto of Calzabigi, written on principles totally opposed to those of Metastasio, with whom he had previously worked in concert. Here Gluck carried out his new theories, as far as he had succeeded in perfecting them ; made his music everywhere subservient to the action of the drama ; finished his airs without the stereotyped *Da capo* ; introduced appropriate choruses and other concerted ɪieces ; and never sacrificed the true rendering of a dramatic situation for the sake of attracting attention to his own powers as a composer, or of affording a popular singer the opportunity of displaying the flexibility of his voice. The result of this conscientious endeavour to carry out a reform which he believed to be not only desirable but absolutely necessary, was a work which, though its success at first seemed doubtful, eventually found a place in the repertory of every theatre in Europe. Even those most violently opposed to innovation felt compelled to applaud it ; for its dramatic force was irresistible, and in flow of melody it was excelled by none of the best operas of the period. Encouraged by the triumph of his first attempt in a new style, he carried out his principles still further, in two other operas, ' Alceste ' (1767), and ' Paride ed Elena ' (1770), which were not

received at Vienna with very great favour.
The critics of the day were not yet fully prepared for the amount of reform indicated in
their construction. Metastasio and Hasse had
reigned too long to be deposed in a moment ;
and Gluck met with so much opposition that
he determined to make his next venture in
Paris, where, in 1774, he brought out his first
French opera, 'Iphigénie en Aulide,' under the
patronage of his old pupil Marie Antoinette.
The result fully justified his reliance upon the
critical discernment of an audience less easily
influenced by the sensuous allurements of
Italian art than by the declamatory powers
of their own old favourites, Lully and his
successor Rameau, who both regarded the perfection of accompanied recitative as a matter
of far greater importance than a continuous
flow of rhythmic melody.

It is necessary at this stage to consider the
position of opera in France which had received
a fresh stimulus by the genius of Rameau.
With his originality of harmony and rhythm
and effective orchestration, Rameau's position
as absolute leader of French music was assured,
but it was not surprising that the arrival of the
Italian troupe of singers, 'Les Bouffons,' as
they were styled, in 1752, performing Italian
intermezzi, should have taken Paris by storm.
There can be no question that Opera Buffa was
at this time a more living thing than Opera
Seria, but even so the fact remains that with
all the faults which had crept into the Italian
style, it was at any rate first and foremost a
lyric art, and it was on the purely vocal side
that the French work showed its chief limitations. It is an interesting fact that Rousseau,
who had just produced his 'Devin du village,'
should have taken the side of the Italians in the
famous 'Guerre des Bouffons,' since it was not
long before the French school was to become
prominent in the domain of Opéra-comique.

'Iphigénie en Aulide' thus came at an
appropriate moment.

To Lully's rhetorical purity Gluck communicated an intensity of passion which,
though it would have scandalised the courtiers
of the Grand Monarque, to whom the voice of
nature was an unknown language, was welcome
enough to those of Louis XVI. He enriched
his scenic effects with an orchestral background
with which the most ambitious attempts of
Rameau would bear no comparison whatever.
In place of Lully's formal fugue, and Rameau's
scarcely less inelastic orchestral prelude, he
introduced an overture, intended—in his own
words—'to prepare the audience for the action
of the piece, and serve as a kind of argument
to it.'

The new opera was received with acclamation, and the only mistake the Parisian critics
made lay in supposing that the principles of its
construction were new. They were not new—

and it is well that we should state this fact
clearly, because we shall have occasion to
refer to it again. The abstract ideal which in
the year 1600 found its highest attainable
expression in Peri's 'Euridice' was not merely
analogous to, but absolutely identical with,
that which, in 1774, Gluck clothed in the outward form of 'Iphigénie en Aulide.'

Gluck's personal triumph was complete, and
his success was accepted as one for French
opera itself as well. A reaction, however,
soon set in. Piccinni had been invited to
Paris in 1776, and with the assistance of
Marmontel as his librettist, produced 'Roland,'
an opera in the Italian style, which excited
general admiration. This, however, was not
enough to satisfy the party spirit of a large
body of malcontents, who, on the arrival of the
Italian composer, divided the art-world of Paris
into two rival factions—the *Gluckiste* and the
Piccinniste—which fought with a bitterness of
prejudice infinitely greater than that displayed
by the followers of Handel and Bononcini in
London. Meanwhile the opera director conceived the idea of inviting Piccinni and Gluck
to write operas on the same subject, 'Iphigénie
en Tauride.' The text supplied to Piccinni
was so poor that it had to be rewritten ; consequently Gluck's version was ready first, and
it was produced with immense success in 1779.
The comparative failure of Piccinni's work two
years later did not put an end to the pretensions
of his party, and the feud was continued with
undiminished violence on either side, until long
after Gluck had retired into private life at
Vienna. Although French composers, with
the exception of Méhul, made no immediate
attempt to carry out the principles laid down
by Gluck as indispensable to the perfection of
dramatic music, they were, after their early
rejection at Vienna, unhesitatingly adopted in
Germany, and have ever since formed one of
the strongest characteristics of German opera.
On the other hand, Piccinni's development of
the finale enriched the Italian school with a
means of effect of which it was not slow to avail
itself, and which its composers did not cease
to cherish with well-directed care. Of the
work wrought by one of the greatest of these
we shall now proceed to speak.

FROM CIMAROSA TO MOZART.—We have already explained that, after formal recognition
of the Opera Buffa as a legitimate branch of art,
it was cultivated with no less assiduity than
serious opera, and that the greatest writers
attained equal excellence in both styles. Of
none can this be more truly said than of Cimarosa, to whose fertility of invention Italian
opera is indebted for the nearest approach to
perfection it had as yet been permitted to
achieve at the hands of a native composer.
The raciness which forms so conspicuous a
feature in 'Il matrimonio segreto' is not more

remarkable than the pathos in ' Gli Orazij e Curiazij.' In neither style do we find a trace of the stiffness which no previous composer was able entirely to shake off. Cimarosa's forms, too, were moulded with equal care in movements of all descriptions. It is, however, in his treatment of the *Pezzo concertato* that he differs most essentially from all his predecessors. Taking full advantage of the improvements introduced by Piccinni, he bestowed upon them an amount of attention which proved the high value he set upon them as elements of general effect and as a powerful means of carrying on the action of the piece, instead of interrupting it, as they had too frequently done in the works of earlier writers.

What Haydn could have done for this period had he devoted his serious attention to dramatic music, at any of the larger theatres, is of course mere matter of conjecture ; though it seems impossible to believe that he would have rested satisfied with the prevailing Italian model. His ' Orfeo ed Euridice,' written for the King's Theatre in the Haymarket in 1791, but not then performed, in consequence of a change in the management, is remarkable rather for its supreme refinement than for dramatic power, a qualification which it would have been unreasonable to expect from a composer whose former operas had been written expressly for Prince Esterhazy's private theatre, and, though well adapted for performances on a small scale (several were written for the marionette theatre), were not, as he himself confessed, calculated to produce a good effect elsewhere. The scores of many of these were destroyed when the little theatre was burned down in 1779 ; but the original autograph of 'Armida,' first performed in 1783, is happily preserved in the R.C.M. (London). ' Orfeo ed Euridice ' was printed at Leipzig in 1806 ; and a beautiful air from it, ' Il pensier sta negli oggetti,' will be found in the collection called ' Gemme d' antichità'(Ashdown & Parry), and will give a fair idea of the general style of the work. Zingarelli, Salieri and their Italian contemporaries, though undoubtedly possessing talents of a very high order, were so far inferior to Cimarosa, in all his greatest qualities, that he will always remain the typical writer of the age ; and to his works alone can we look for the link which connects it with the next period, the most glorious one the lyric drama has ever known, since it witnessed the elevation both of the Italian and German schools to what, in its own way, we must needs regard as absolute perfection.

Though Mozart was born only seven years later than Cimarosa, and died many years before him, the phase of art he represents is infinitely more advanced than that we have just described. His sympathies, like Handel's, were entirely with the Italian school, while his natural feeling for form and his fine technique

enabled him to enlarge a thousandfold upon the ideas of Piccinni and Cimarosa, and produce symmetrical movements the complications of which had never entered into their minds as possible. Thus the sestets ' Sola, sola ' and ' Riconosci in questo amplesso ' surpass in fulness of design the grandest *dénoûments* to be found in any other operas of the period ; while the two concerted finales in ' Le nozze di Figaro ' contain respectively nine and seven, and those in ' Don Giovanni ' no less than eleven distinct movements, are all written with the most masterly skill, and linked together in such natural sequence that each appears as a component part of a single comprehensive idea, as homogeneous as that of a symphony or a concerto. Again, Mozart's command of the orchestra, as a medium of dramatic effect, stands unrivalled. He was accused by some of his contemporaries of overloading the voice with unmeaning accompaniments ; but the charge was made in ignorance of the principle upon which he worked. Grétry, when asked by Napoleon to define the difference between the styles of Mozart and Cimarosa, replied, ' Sire, Cimarosa places his statue on the stage, and its pedestal in the orchestra : Mozart places the statue in the orchestra, and the pedestal on the stage.' The metaphor, though pretty enough, conveyed a palpable untruth. Neither Mozart nor Cimarosa reversed the relative positions of the statue and the pedestal ; but Cimarosa used the latter simply as a means of support, whereas Mozart adorned it with the most exquisite and appropriate *bassirilievi*. His accompaniments are always made to intensify the expression of the voice, and to aid it in explaining its meaning ; and he attains this end by a mode of treatment as varied as it is original. Though his system of instrumentation has served as the basis of every other method, without exception, used by later composers, his own combinations are marked by a freshness which never fails to make known their true authorship at the very first hearing.

THE GERMAN ' SINGSPIEL.'—We must now return to Germany. For long there had been in existence a light form of musical entertainment known as the SINGSPIEL (*q.v.*) and similar to the Intermezzo and Opera Buffa except for the fact that the action was carried on by means of spoken dialogue. It received a great stimulus at Leipzig in 1764 at the hands of J. Adam Hiller. J. F. Reichardt brought forward the ' Liederspiel '—an imitation of the French ' Vaudeville '—while a third form of musical drama was introduced at Gotha in 1774 by George Benda, who, in his ' Ariadne auf Naxos ' and ' Medea,' assisted the effect of a spoken dialogue by means of a highly coloured orchestral accompaniment, carried on uninterruptedly throughout the piece after the manner of what is now called a MELODRAMA (*q.v.*). Mozart heard some of Benda's productions at Mannheim in 1778, and, though he never adopted the method in any of his greater works, was delighted with its effect. Commissioned to write a work for the National opera, founded at Vienna in 1778 by the Emperor Joseph, he threw his best energies into the task, and produced in 1782 a masterpiece—' Die Entführung aus dem Serail '—which at once elevated the Singspiel to the level he had already won for the Italian opera, and secured it a recognised status as the embodiment of a conception peculiar to and truly worthy of the great Teutonic school. It was followed in 1786 by ' Der Schauspiel-direktor,' and in 1791 by ' Die Zauberflöte,' which was described as ' Singspiel ' on the pianoforte score.

' FIDELIO.'—But the history of the next period will teach us that the peculiar phase of German art over which Mozart asserted such absolute supremacy was not the only one in which it was capable of manifesting itself, and that in point of fact the inconsistent form in which singing and speaking alternated could be used impressively for subjects of a serious kind, a matter this of considerable importance. Over Beethoven's early youth the stage seems to have exercised none of that fascination which so frequently monopolises the young composer's interest, and when, in the full maturity of his genius, he turned his attention to it, he does not appear to have been attracted, like Mozart, by the force of uncontrollable instinct, but rather to have arrived at perfection by the assistance of earnest thought and unremitting study. He wrote an opera simply because the manager of the Theater-an-der-Wien found it worth while to offer him an engagement for that purpose ; but having undertaken the work, he threw his whole soul into it, laboured at it, as his sketch-books prove, incessantly, and identified himself so completely with its progress that he seems as much at home in it as he had ever previously been in a sonata or a symphony. The subject selected was Bouilly's ' Léonore, ou l'amour conjugale.' A German translation was made by Sonnleithner ; and that Beethoven was satisfied with it, and was conscious of no inconsistency in the dialogue being spoken, must be inferred from the careful solicitude with which he strove, not only to give due effect to the various situations of the drama, but to bring out the sense of the text, even to its lightest word.

Great, however, as the music is in depth of feeling and dramatic expression, it did nothing towards solving the problem of maintaining musical interest from the rise of the curtain to its fall. The glowing intensity of musical expression was by its very force beginning to make more apparent the gulf between the formal aria and the *recitativo secco* and *stromer-*

tato so far as the latter was developed, or the dialogue, which was spoken. Still ' Fidelio,' with its fine qualities of formal construction and musical beauty, stands alone, and has necessarily become immortal ; while the works of Paër, Süssmayer and other composers who enjoyed a high degree of popularity in the earlier years of the 19th century, have been long since almost forgotten. The only other productions of the period that can for a moment be placed in competition with it are the later operas of Cherubini, who, after writing for many years in the light Neapolitan style, struck out, in ' Lodoiska ' (1791), in a manner of his own strikingly original, and based, like Beethoven's, upon the principles laid down by Gluck, and presenting the curious anomaly of a German method cultivated by an Italian for the amusement of a Parisian audience. Beethoven is known to have spoken of Cherubini as ' the greatest of all living writers for the stage,' and to have admired ' Les Deux Journées ' and ' Faniska ' exceedingly ; and it is worthy of remark that a strong analogy is observable between the libretti of ' Fidelio,' ' Faniska,' ' Les Deux Journées ' and ' Lodoiska,' in each of which the leading incident is the rescue of an unjustly detained prisoner, through the devotion of a faithful friend whose life is risked, though not lost, in the labour of love necessary to effect the desired object.

OPÉRA-COMIQUE, 1800.—The French musicians at this time had been working chiefly in the slighter form of opera styled Opéra-comique.[1] After the retirement of Gluck, Piccinni still enjoyed a certain term of popularity ; but when the excitement of faction had settled down into the calm of sounder judgment, the field was really open to any native composer with talent enough to secure a fair hearing. At this juncture, following on Monsigny, Grétry and Méhul stepped forward to fill the gap. Both were men of more than ordinary talent, and the works of both became extremely popular, and held firm possession of the stage for many years. Grétry's style was light and pleasing, and exactly adapted to the taste of a Parisian audience. Méhul was an even more thorough musician, and aimed at higher things, striving conscientiously to carry out the principles of his instructor, Gluck, for whom he entertained the deepest reverence, and to whose counsels he was indebted for many of the qualities which tended to make his work deservedly famous. It was chiefly by the exertions of these two genial writers and their equally talented countryman and contemporary, Boieldieu, that the Opéra-comique was raised to the position of being one of the most popular branches of French dramatic art. The true Opéra-comique

[1] The lighter form of the *Vaudeville* so much more nearly resembles a play, with incidental songs, than a regular opera, that we do not think it necessary to include a notice of it in the present articles. (See VAUDEVILLE.)

is essentially a French creation. Beginning with the aim of amusement through real wit, piquancy of plot, simplicity and clarity of the music, it gradually developed to a point where not only the spoken dialogue could be dispensed with, but humour too. It ultimately began to differ from ' Grand Opera ' only in the nature of the subject, ' romantic ' rather than ' heroic,' and in the music which, while it could be serious, was at any rate never solemn.

Meanwhile the production of Spontini's ' La Vestale ' (1807) and ' Olympic ' (1819), works oddly enough, like those of Gluck and Cherubini, from an alien composer, marked another stage in the progress of the French type of Grand Opera, a type which preserved the breadth of the classical style, gave the fullest opportunity for scenic display, and demanded subjects of an heroic or historical nature. The music was of course continuous, still, however, leaving unbridged the gulf between the recitative, *secco* or accompanied, and the lyrical moments, the arias, duets, scenas, etc.

WEBER AND THE ROMANTIC OPERA.—The next development of German Opera is that known among musical historians as the Romantic school—a form of art which, at the beginning of the 19th century, exercised a more decided influence upon the progress of dramatic music than any other recognised agent, and of which Weber's ' Der Freischütz ' is the outstanding example. Weber's share in the development of opera lay in his faculty for musical characterisation [1] and in imaginative orchestral colouring, while in his scenas he came near to evolving a successful system of continuous music. It should be remembered, however, in this connexion that German opera at this time was no more than elaborate ' Singspiel ' ; in ' Euryanthe ' only did Weber dispense altogether with spoken dialogue. The success of ' Der Freischütz ' was of great importance in Germany and ultimately elsewhere, since it popularised ' romantic ' subjects, while Weber's distinctly ' national ' style of melody showed that ' classical ' or formal beauty was not indispensable for the lyric stage.

Spohr's imaginative temperament and creative powers enabled him to cultivate romantic opera with success ; while his unlimited command over what were then considered intricacies of the chromatic and enharmonic genera lent a peculiarly luscious and novel colouring to his method of treatment. His ' Faust ' has now been thrust aside to make room for another work of the same name. ' Der Berggeist,' though less generally known, is, in some respects, a finer work. Mention should be made of the once popular ' Zemire und Azor ' and ' Der Alchymist ' and ' Der Kreuzfahrer ' (1845). In ' Jessonda,' produced in 1823, and regarded by

himself as his best opera, Spohr [2] made an attempt, like Weber, to abolish spoken dialogue in favour of accompanied recitative ; but found that popular feeling was too strong to listen to reason on a point concerning which it still held its ground, alike in Germany, France and England. In Italy alone had uninterrupted singing been always regarded as a *sine qua non* at the opera.

Of the romantic operas of Heinrich Marschner, ' Der Vampyr,' ' Der Templer und die Jüdin,' ' Hans Heiling ' and ' Adolph von Nassau ' were among the best works of the kind of their day. Of the eleven operas written by Ernst Theodor Hoffmann, and now preserved in MS. at Berlin, one only, ' Undine,' enthusiastically praised by Weber, seems to have produced any very strong impression.

ENGLISH OPERAS.—Opera in England languished after the death of Purcell, and even when something characteristic did arise there was no trace of any desire for, or appreciation of, the dramatic qualities which Purcell had imparted into his works. During the 18th century Italian opera, and Handel in particular, held the field until the remarkable success of ' The Beggar's Opera ' turned the attention of English composers to a form of entertainment which was cultivated with great assiduity for a number of years. (See BALLAD OPERA.) Arne did, however, try to write an opera on the Italian model with recitatives in place of spoken dialogue and with a classical text (Metastasio's ' Artaserse '). Curiously enough, although the recitative was accepted in the oratorio, the critics condemned it in English opera, and there was no composer of sufficient power and originality to follow Arne's example and convince them of its possibility. It is not necessary to dwell long on this period, the work of men like the Linleys, Shield, Dibdin, Kelly, Storace and many others was no more than melodious ; dramatic qualities are far to seek either in the music or the libretti.[3]

ROSSINI AND HIS CONTEMPORARIES.—Italian opera meanwhile was taking on a new lease of life with the coming of Rossini. He saw how the monotony of the *recitativo secco* could be avoided by a string quartet accompaniment as in ' Elisabetta ' or the addition of wind instruments in ' Otello.' Indeed, his instrumentation showed real mastery and originality. Vocally, however, the operas for the most part ended in once again disturbing the balance between the mere display of effective ornamentation and musical and dramatic expression. While ' Barbiere di Siviglia ' (1816) remains a masterpiece of the Opera Buffa school, the serious operas have lost their hold on the public chiefly through their lack of truth and depth of

---

[1] The use of the *Leitmotiv* throughout ' Der Freischütz ' seems indeed to entitle Weber to the honour of its invention, notwithstanding the suggestive notes sung by the statue in ' Don Giovanni.'

[2] See three articles on Spohr's operas, by F. Corder, in the *Mus. T.* for 1884, pp. 385, 444 and 508.

[3] For a searching analysis of the latter the reader may be referred to Cecil Forsyth's *Music and Nationalism.*

feeling and homogeneity. The chief of Rossini's contemporaries and successors were Bellini and Donizetti. In the work of these men (and of the earlier operas of Verdi as well) the Italian style began to change in that the line of the melodies lost its former elegance and classic formalism, becoming more direct and 'popular' in its appeal. In other respects the music shows no departure from the accepted models of the day, and in fact, during the greater part of the 19th century, Italian opera was structurally at a standstill.

Returning to Paris where, in 1829, Rossini's 'Guillaume Tell' had made a great impression by reason of its breadth of style, wealth of melody and full measure of scenic display, French grand opera was to be still further exploited by yet another alien composer and Rossini's fame to be eclipsed by that of Meyerbeer. Alive to what Weber had achieved in 'Der Freischütz' and fully aware of the claims of the singer—indeed Rossini's example could not be ignored—Meyerbeer succeeded in 'Robert le Diable,' 'Les Huguenots,' 'Le Prophète' and 'L'Africaine' in continuing and carrying further the broad design of the French type. As a musician, however, he had not enough strength to avoid conventionality, and the lack of uniformity of style was bound to end in a reaction after the enormous successes which are said to have made the fortunes of the Paris Opéra. His chief contemporary was Halévy, whose 'La Juive' kept the stage for many years. Berlioz's operas contributed little or nothing to the development of the form. Auber continued the traditions of the opéra-comique which in its still lighter form 'opéra-bouffe' culminated in the work of Jules Offenbach. Meanwhile Gounod created a fresh point of view in grand opera with his 'Faust,' perhaps the most successful opera ever written. Here is crystallised a vein of sentimental expression which was quite novel at the time and which succeeded in giving fresh life to the standardised set forms in which they appear. Structurally, 'Faust' may not be of great importance, but it undoubtedly has exerted considerable influence upon French music in spite of its greatest weakness, the want of a complete unity of style. Thomas's 'Mignon' and the earlier works of Saint-Saëns and Massenet belong to this particular school.

VERDI was a far stronger personality than Donizetti and Bellini. There is a vigour and energy in all that he wrote coupled with a power of self-development which gradually led to remarkable results. He is to be credited also with an advance in the writing of *musica caratteristica* upon which latter-day tendencies so greatly depend. He was to some extent influenced by Meyerbeer, as in his 'Les Vêpres Siciliennes' and again 'Don Carlos,' while in addition to his own natural growth there is a breadth of treatment in 'Aïda,' the culminating point of his earlier style, which is perhaps also to be in part attributed to a like influence. 'Aïda' is marked by the important part the orchestra plays and by the continuity of the musical structure tending towards the gradual elimination of the set aria. For a time it seemed that the Wagnerian movement, shortly to be mentioned, was going to discredit the works of composers trained in the old tradition. But it is now seen that this is by no means the case, and we remain face to face with the *point d'appui* from which this article started, the use of music to intensify the dramatic action. It is only the means whereby this intensification is effected that have gradually changed, and then only, if we go to the root of the matter, from simplicity to varying degrees of complexity. What has not changed is the power of song to enchain the hearer, and thus, in looking back upon what has been so far recorded, there is no difficulty in understanding why 'Figaro,' 'Orfeo,' 'Der Freischütz,' 'Rigoletto,' 'Faust,' etc., can still hold their own alongside of works which structurally are of a vastly different and more complex nature. And here, perhaps, is the place to emphasise the unvarying strength of the Italian school of opera in that, although it has often been extravagant, the instinct to rely on the voice for dramatic expression is unquestionably sound.

WAGNER.—The secret of Wagner's success lay really in his development of a system of musical composition which enabled him to build up long scenes of narration and dialogue and in a far more interesting and compelling way than had been possible with reliance upon *recitativo secco* and *recitativo stromentato* in their stereotyped forms. These passages lead up to the moments of pure lyricism which correspond to the aria and the formal movement. The effect is analogous to that of a symphonic movement where the interest is both continuous and cumulative. Of far less importance, although they have perhaps seemed the most in the public eye, are the *Leitmotiv* and the instrumentation. These and the polyphony are only the means, and the great beauty and power of all three tend to obscure what is really the important fact that the aria, disguised maybe, still remains. The development of a simple ballad into the 'durch-componirt' type of song is akin to Wagner's treatment of the 'lyrical moment.' (See, however, the article WAGNER for fuller details of his aims and methods.) It is sufficient here to state that after the Weber-esque 'Flying Dutchman,' 'Tannhäuser' and 'Lohengrin,' in which there are already many suggestions of what was to come, he acquired the technique whereby a complete unity of style in the writing was possible from the beginning to end of each act and of each opera. No other composer has shown so complete a mastery of variety of expression, and 'Tristan,' 'Parsifal,' 'Der Ring' and 'Die Meistersinger' have their own uniformity and musical character, such as might only have been expected from the pens of four different writers.

Wagner's influence was of course immense, and in a large degree due to his exceptional command over the orchestra. By the end of the 19th century, however, this instrumental glamour fell back into its proper place, while in point of fact the earlier diatribes against the disproportion between voice and orchestra were felt in some measure to be justified by many people. Moreover, the extreme length of the operas was generally recognised. For ordinary purposes the orchestration is out of proportion and the prolixity is such that the operas are generally 'cut.' It is unfortunate that we cannot always hear them under the ideal conditions of the 'festival' as originally intended and with a sunken orchestra.

END OF THE 19TH CENTURY

GERMANY.—Wagner's influence was naturally strongest in Germany, and the immediate result was a quantity of music in which the more obvious characteristics of his style were freely imitated. Only one writer, however, really succeeded in probing deeper into the method and producing something personal, and that only in a single work. Humperdinck's 'Hansel und Gretel' is a singularly successful example of the Wagnerian polyphony and orchestral style, but the use of folk-tune and melody akin to it gives it a character and charm of its own. Strauss's operas are less Wagnerian in texture and in thematic combination ; he has followed up the disproportion between voice and orchestra, but on the other hand has not neglected the 'lyrical moment'; indeed in the latter respect there is something approaching to a keener appreciation of what the Italians have never forgotten, the paramount importance in stage works of the vocal line, than has been shown by many of his contemporaries.

ITALY.—To return to the Italian school, reference must be made to Verdi's friendship and collaboration with Boïto, whose 'Mefistofele' (1866) contributed much towards the advance of Italian opera. There is indeed no comparison musically between the two, but Boïto, who had a share of the reforming element in his mentality, was able to exert some influence upon Verdi, as was shown in 'Otello' and 'Falstaff' of which he wrote the librettos. Verdi remained really unaffected by Wagner except incidentally; he was too original a creator for one thing and, for another, his operatic style was too fixed for his technique to change materially. Indeed, except for the instrumental skill and variety of his immediate successors and the frank adoption of the *Leitmotiv* as a significant part of the musical struc-

ture, the Italian style has developed along lines which are not Wagnerian in the contrapuntal, polyphonic and symphonic sense. The aria in a more or less disguised form holds its place firmly in the operas of the later writers. Mascagni sprang into fame with his 'Cavalleria rusticana' (1890) and Leoncavallo with 'Pagliacci' (1892), both on the same lines of crude, direct melodrama. Puccini's far greater musicianship enabled him to construct scenes of stronger and more musically sustained interest. He relied largely upon the reiteration of significant melodic phrases and generally, as in 'La Bohème' (1896), 'Tosca' (1900) and 'Madama Butterfly' (1904), to name the three universally popular examples of his work, maintained a uniform and homogeneous style. He occasionally leaves the aria and the concerted finale quite clearly defined so that they can be removed as complete wholes from the context. Giordano in 'Andrea Chenier' (1896), 'Fedora' (1898) and 'Siberia' (1904) has shown dramatic power and that feeling for theatrical effect which seem to be the special heritage of Italian musicians. Among other Italian composers who have won some success for a time are Franchetti, Alèa, Tasca and Spinelli. Wolff-Ferrari's representative work belongs chronologically to a later period than that covered by this review.

FRANCE.—French composers were long in seriously responding to Wagner's influence. After 'Faust' and 'Mignon' (A. Thomas), Bizet's 'Carmen,' 1875, was the most original and successful opera ; but here the form is that of opéra-comique with a certain amount of spoken dialogue, and while there are some examples of the use of the *Leitmotiv* the ordinary aria and concerted numbers form the basis of the musical structure. Ernest Reyer's 'Sigurd' (1884), however, bore witness to the growing influence, and Massenet's 'Esclarmonde' (1889) was the most serious attempt that had till then been made to graft the *Leitmotiv* system upon the stock of French opera. Since 'Esclarmonde' Massenet made few attempts to follow up his early excursions upon Wagnerian paths, and his later operas show a growing tendency to fall back upon the slighter form of opéra-comique, though he never altogether relinquished his tendency to trifle with leading motives. Alfred Bruneau in 'Le Rêve' (1891) announced himself as a staunch adherent of the Wagnerian system, and his later works, 'L'Attaque du moulin' (1893), 'Messidor' (1897), 'L'Ouragan' (1901) and 'L'Enfant Roi' (1905), though less uncompromising in style than 'Le Rêve,' are no less saturated with Wagnerian ideals. Vincent d'Indy is another staunch Wagnerian, and his 'Fervaal' (1897) and 'L'Étranger' (1903) are among the most important works produced by French musicians in which Wagner's system is fully accepted.

César Franck's two remarkable operas, 'Hulda' and 'Ghisèle,' both produced after the composer's death in 1890, are Wagnerian in their remarkable command of polyphony rather than in their adherence to the system of leading motives, and in the ' Louise ' (1900) and ' Julien' of Charpentier the Wagnerian methods are only employed in a modified manner. Debussy's ' Pelléas et Mélisande ' (1902) stands rather in a category of its own. Debussy here sought for a closer union between voice, orchestra and action than he considered the symphonic style of Wagner made possible, which was in effect to say that Wagner did not go far enough, that often his symphonic methods delayed the action just as did the formal aria which it superseded. Debussy therefore, while making great use of the *Leitmotiv* and of the orchestra, would not allow the music as music to obtrude. It would seem that the extreme limit has been reached in this imaginative work of a freely moving musical commentary on the action, and to the fact that the opportunities are so few for dramatic expression through the means of pure singing, which, of necessity, brings with it some form of theoretical conflict with reality, must be assigned the reason why it cannot be the foundation of a new school or cannot appeal to the general opera public at large.

ENGLAND.—During the earlier part of the 19th century English opera showed few changes. Sir Henry Bishop was an accomplished musician, but made no attempt to improve upon the form which, in his hands as in those of his predecessors, was still no more than a play diversified by songs, duets and choruses. Such works as ' The Knight of Snowdoun ' (1811), ' The Miller and his Men ' (1813) or ' Guy Mannering ' (1816) could hardly have more than an ephemeral success. There was a grave lack of energy in the right direction at this epoch. Charles Horn, a composer with melodic gifts, could do no more than let the general character of the piece remain as he found it. Balfe, who won his first success with ' The Siege of Rochelle ' in 1835, carried things a little further besides writing in 1843 the most widely known opera in the English language, ' The Bohemian Girl.' Balfe's style is simple, but he had plenty of melody, and by a careful study of the opéra-comique, he certainly raised the standard of the pieces he wrote, so far as their general structure was concerned. Similar work was done by Rooke, J. Barnett, Lavern, Wallace and E. F. Loder. Benedict and Macfarren achieved a higher artistic level, though, with the exception of the former's ' Lily of Killarney,' their operas have not survived. The frequent opportunities afforded for the production of operas during the century were increased by the formation of the Carl Rosa Company in 1875. It is neither possible nor necessary here to give anything approaching a complete list of the various operatic ventures which were embarked on or of the works produced down to the end of the century. It has been often said that the continual performance of alien opera in England has militated against the production of successful native work. There would perhaps be truth in this if production had been denied to the native writer. Such, however, has been far from the case. Failure to produce successful English opera can only be explained by the lack of sufficient musicodramatic talent. Nevertheless the work done by A. Goring Thomas, Mackenzie, Stanford and Ethel Smyth, who by 1901 was only known by her ' Der Wald,' showed an increasing command over the technical requirements of opera and a closer approximation to the advancing tendencies of the day. Moreover, a style of expression less definitely founded upon alien models has been gradually becoming apparent, without which a native school of either opera-writing or opera-performance is an impossibility.

SLAVONIC OPERA.—The history of opera in certain other countries must now be considered. Wherever a really national school of opera has been founded its rise may be dated from the time when the general feeling of society in each country succeeded in resisting the spell of a foreign influence. But it could only do this when something worthy was found to take its place. In the 18th century Italian opera ruled Europe with the sole exception of France. Germany was the first to emancipate herself, and her example was followed by other countries, notably Bohemia (Czechoslovakia) and Russia. The former distinctly national school was founded by Smetana, who became chief conductor of the new National Theatre in Prague in 1866, in which year his most famous opera, 'Prodaná nevěsta ' (The Bartered Bride), was produced. The success of this and of other works naturally opened the way for his immediate successor and disciple Dvořák, whose first opera, ' Kral a Uhlir ' (King and Collier), was produced at Prague in 1874. Karel Kovarovic, chief conductor of the National Opera, Prague, from 1900 till his death, produced his first opera in 1882. The work of these men has achieved popularity, although very few have been performed in other countries.

In Russia national opera was practically founded by Glinka with his ' A Life for the Tsar' (1836) and ' Russlan and Lioudmilla ' (1842), and continued by Dargomijsky, who in ' The Roussalka ' (1856) and ' The Stone Guest ' (performed posthumously 1872) sought to free the style from the Italian influence. Moussorgsky in ' Boris Godounov ' (1874) and ' Khovanstchina ' leaned more to the realistic side than did Borodin in ' Prince Igor ' or Rimsky-Korsakov in his various operas, while Tchaikovský's broad melodic gifts and his greater susceptibility to Western ideals made his work more national in a personal than a general sense. But these composers drew largely upon the musical idiom of their folk-music and upon Russian literature, especially the poems of Poushkin, for their subjects. For fuller details in all cases the reader may be referred to the separate articles on the various composers named.

The above article is a revision of that by w. s. r., incorporating material by r. a. s. and with additions by n. c. g.

OPÉRA BOUFFE, a French comic opera, of exceedingly light character, and constructed on too trivial a scale to entitle it to rank as an opéra-comique. (See BALLAD OPERA ; COMIC OPERA ; INTERMEZZO ; OPERA ; SINGSPIEL.)

w. s. r.

OPERA BUFFA, an Italian opera, of light and playful character, in which the dialogue is carried on in *recitativo secco*, interposed between the airs, duets and choruses, which form the chief attraction of the piece. The subject of the Opera Buffa is always more or less comic, and not unfrequently extravagantly so. Fine examples are : Cimarosa's 'Il matrimonio segreto,' Mozart's 'Così fan tutte,' and Rossini's 'Il barbiere di Siviglia.' (See BALLAD OPERA ; COMIC OPERA ; INTERMEZZO ; OPERA ; SINGSPIEL.)

w. s. r.

OPÉRA-COMIQUE, a designation applied to a form of French opera originally akin to Opera Buffa except that the dialogue was always spoken. (See BALLAD OPERA ; COMIC OPERA ; INTERMEZZO ; OPERA ; SINGSPIEL.)

w. s. r.

OPÉRA-COMIQUE, see PARIS, Vol. IV. p. 46.

OPERETTA, a little opera, generally of a buffo character, too short to furnish an evening's amusement, but useful as an afterpiece or Intermezzo. We can scarcely point out more charming examples of the style than Mozart's 'Schauspieldirektor' and Rossini's 'L' inganno felice.' Both these little masterpieces are in one act, and this condition is really an essential characteristic of the Operetta ; in England the term has been loosely applied to a work better described as COMIC OPERA (*q.v.*), which has no time limitation.

In Italy the dialogue of the Operetta is always carried on in *recitativo secco*. In England, Germany and France it is spoken.   w. s. r.

OPHICLEIDE (Eng. and Ger. ; Fr. *basse d'harmonie*). A barbarous name, compounded of the Greek words for snake and door-key, which was given to an improvement on the serpent and Russian bassoon, or bass-horn.

The invention of this instrument is attributed by Fétis to Frichot, a French musician settled in London about the year 1790. He states, moreover, that Frichot published in London in the year 1800 a description and method of playing it, under the title of *A Complete Scale*

and Gammut of the Bass-horn, a new instrument, invented by M. Frichot, and manufactured by J. Astor. It seems, however, that a musician of the church of St. Peter, at Lille, by name Regibo, had already, in 1780, made improvements on the serpent by adding several keys and modifying the bore, so that Regibo may in fact be considered as the inventor even of the so-called Russian bassoon, 'which returned from the north of Europe about thirty years later.' It seems agreed on all hands that the French were made acquainted with this instrument by the bands of the allied sovereigns when the latter occupied Paris in 1815. In this year its discovery is claimed by Halary of Paris, who patented it in 1821, and whose successor is said to possess the original model, with seven keys and a scale of twenty-seven notes. Labbaye added new keys to it, and the number was raised to eleven or twelve.

The ophicleide, like the serpent and bass-horn which it superseded, has become obsolete. The period of its rise and decline lies within the 19th century, its decline corresponding in time with the improvement of the various bass brass valved instruments ; and as it may be regarded as the final development and latest survival of cup-blown instruments with side-holes (see WIND INSTRUMENTS), a general view of the relationship between the ophicleide and its immediate predecessors may be conveniently given here.

From the family of CORNETT (*zinke*) came the serpent, an instrument of large calibre, descending to the 8-foot C, and originally having six or sometimes seven finger-holes, but no keys. The serpentine form was given to the instrument to bring the finger-holes within convenient reach, but the fundamental defect was that any holes that could be covered by the fingers were necessarily far too small to allow of free ventage and good intonation. The gradual addition of keys improved the instrument, but so long as the finger-holes remained no really good scale was possible. The 'bass-horn,' or 'basson russe,' was essentially a serpent changed in form, so as, by being doubled upon itself, to have some resemblance to the bassoon, but the weakness due to the size and position of the finger-holes remained ; beyond convenience in handling, the improvement upon the serpent was therefore not great. (See *PLATE LXXIV.* No. 8.)

To Halary of Paris appears to be due the credit of dispensing with finger-holes, and of so disposing large side-holes covered with keys as to obtain a chromatic scale with facility, both in the pedal and upper octaves. The 'bass-horn,' or 'basson russe,' thus became the ophicleide, an instrument an octave lower than the 'key' or 'Kent bugle' (and cf the same family), to which similar key-work had already been applied. (See KLAPPENHORN.

There is, however, this distinction between the two instruments, that whereas on the key-bugle the pedal octave *c* to *c'* is not used, and the key-work has therefore only to give the chromatic scale between *c'* and *g'*, on the ophicleide the pedal octave is used, and the key-work had to be schemed to give semitones from C to *c*.

The instrument as finally established had eleven and in some cases twelve keys, and was blown with a large cup mouthpiece of metal or ivory, very similar to those of the bass-trombone and euphonium. Some of the early specimens were made chiefly of wood, like their predecessors the serpents, and were termed serpentcleides, but latterly brass was almost universally used for the whole instrument.

The ophicleide being practically a conical tube possesses the usual harmonic series of all brass instruments, and its open notes are these —C, *c*, *g*, *c'*, *e'*, *g'*, *b♭'*, *c''*; but the last two were usually obtained as harmonics of lower notes produced from side-holes. The C speaks through a side-hole covered by an open-standing key, and the bell of the instrument is prolonged sufficiently to give B♮, when this open-standing key is closed by the thumb of the left hand. The series as above given then becomes B♭, B♮, *f♯*, *b♮*, etc., and in like manner the different effective lengths of the tube, as determined by the successive opening of the other ten keys, yield primes from C♯ to A♯, each of which can give its series of harmonics by changes of lip-pressure.

A compass is thus obtained of thirty-eight semitones, or a little over three octaves—from B♮ to *c''*—but the upper limit is indeterminate, as on nearly all wind instruments. It will be obvious that from the overlapping and coincidence of the various harmonic series many alternative methods of producing the same note with slight enharmonic changes are open to a good player.

The tone of the ophicleide is, from its difference of scale and of material, less tender and veiled than that of its predecessor the serpent, but on the other hand it has greater compass and equality than that rather primitive contrivance.

The ophicleides used in the orchestra were usually made in C, but in military bands they were used in B♭, with A♮ for the lowest note. Alto or tenor instruments in F or E♭ were sometimes made, and also contrabass ophicleides in F or E♭, an octave lower than the tenors. One such was used at the Birmingham Festival of 1834.

The complete falling into desuetude of this instrument, notwithstanding its fairly good intonation and distinctive tone-quality, must be partly attributed to this very distinctiveness, a peculiar ' hollowness ' which did not blend well with other instruments ; and partly to

the improvement in brass valve-instruments, with their much more simple and convenient fingering and richer tone-quality.

The ophicleide was first used in the opera in the production of Spontini's ' Olympie ' in 1819. Ophicleide parts are now played on the tuba, although those in Berlioz's ' Faust ' have been allotted to two trombones.   D. J. B.

OPUS, OPUS-NUMBER, OPERA, ŒUVRE. A method of numbering musical compositions in the order of their publication, using the Latin word *opus* (work), appears first, though rather spasmodically, in the 17th century ; it began to come into general use in the time of Mozart, but was not fully established until Beethoven's time, the numbering not being carried out to all the published works of the former master. No rule is observed as regards the size of an *opus* ; for instance, Beethoven's op. 1 consists of three pianoforte trios, while Schubert's op. 1 is only the song ' Erlkönig.' The opus-number has nothing to do necessarily with the date of composition, but only with that of the publication ; thus some early works, both of Schubert and Mendelssohn, were published (posthumously) with very late opus-numbers. On the other hand, many composers make a practice of assigning opus-numbers to their works on completion and quite irrespective of publication.   M. ; addn. C.

ORACOLO, L', opera in one act ; text adapted by Camillo Zanoni from C. B. Fernald's play, *The Cat and the Cherub* ; music by Franco Leoni. Produced Covent Garden, June 28, 1905 ; New York, Metropolitan Opera House, Feb. 4, 1915.

ORATORIO (Lat. *oratorium* ; Ital. *dramma sacro per musica, oratorio* ; Ger. *Oratorium*). A dramatic poem, usually of a sacred character, sung throughout by solo voices and chorus, to the accompaniment of a full orchestra, but—at least in modern times—without the assistance of scenery, dresses or action.

I. Ancient Oratorio

It is impossible to say when, where or by whom the first dramatic representation of a scene from Holy Writ was attempted. One of the oldest examples of which we have any certain record is the ' Festum asinorum,' celebrated at Beauvais and Sens, in the 12th century, and long remembered in connexion with a famous carol called the ' Prose de l'âne.' But it was not only in France that such representations found favour in the sight of the people. William FitzStephen mentions a Monk of Canterbury who wrote many Miracle-Plays during the reign of King Henry II., and died in 1191 ; and we know, from other sources, that an English audience was always ready to greet entertainments of this description with a hearty welcome. The clergy also took them under their especial protection, and retained their interest in them for so long a period, that, in 1378 the choristers of St. Paul's performed them regularly, under careful ecclesiastical superintendence. In other countries they attained an equal degree of popularity, but at a somewhat later date. In Italy, for instance, we hear of a 'Commedia spirituale' performed for the first time at Padua in 1243, and another at Friuli in 1298; while 'Geistliche Schauspiele' first became common in Germany and Bohemia about the year 1322.

The subjects of these primitive pieces were chosen for the purpose of illustrating certain incidents selected from the history of the Old and New Testaments, the lives of celebrated Saints, or the meaning of allegorical conceits, intended to enforce important lessons in Religion and Morality. For instance, 'Il Conversione di S. Paolo' was sung in Rome in 1440, and 'Abram et Isaac suo figluolo' at Florence in 1449. Traces are also found of 'Abel e Caino' (1554), 'Sansone' (1554), 'Abram et Sara' (1556), 'Il figluolo prodigo' (1565), an allegorical piece, called 'La commedia spirituale dell' anima,' printed at Siena, without date 'and not to be confounded with a very interesting work bearing a somewhat similar title, to be mentioned presently), and many different settings of the history of the Passion of our Lord. This last was always a very favourite subject; and the music adapted to it, combining some of the more prominent characteristics of ecclesiastical plain-song with the freedom of the secular chanson, was certainly not wanting in solemnity. Particular care was always taken with that part of the sacred narrative which described the grief of Our Lady at the crucifixion; and we find frequent instances of the 'Lamentation' of Mary, or of S. Mary Magdalene, or of The Three Maries.

No great improvement seems to have been made in the style of these performances after the 14th century; indeed, so many abuses crept into them that they were frequently prohibited by ecclesiastical authority. But the principle upon which they were founded still remained untouched, and the general opinion seemed to be rather in favour of their reformation than their absolute discontinuance. S. Philip Neri, the founder of the congregation of Oratorians, thought very highly of them as a means of instruction, and warmly encouraged the cultivation of sacred music of all kinds. On certain evenings in the week his sermons were preceded and followed either by a selection of popular hymns (see LAUDI SPIRITUALI), or by the dramatic rendering of a scene from Scripture history, adapted to the comprehension of an audience consisting chiefly of Roman youths of the humbler classes, the discourses being delivered between the acts of the drama. As these observances were first introduced in the Oratory of S. Philip's newly built church of S. Maria in

Vallicella, the performances themselves were commonly spoken of as Oratorios, and no long time elapsed before this term was accepted, not in Rome only, but throughout the whole of Europe, as the distinguishing title of the 'dramma sacro per musica.'

S. Philip died in 1595, but the performances were not discontinued. While Peri and Caccini were feeling their way towards a new style of dramatic music in Florence, Emilio del Cavalieri was endeavouring with equal earnestness to attain the same end in Rome. With this purpose in view he set to music a sacred drama, written for him by Laura Guidiccioni, and entitled 'La rappresentazione dell' anima e del corpo.' The piece was an allegorical one, complicated in structure, and of considerable pretensions; and the music was written throughout in the *stilo rappresentativo* of which Emilio del Cavalieri claimed to be the originator. By a singular coincidence, the year 1600 witnessed the first performance, in Rome, of Emilio's 'Rappresentazione' and, in Florence, of Peri's 'Euridice.' The former was produced at the Oratory of S. Maria in Vallicella in the month of February, ten months before the appearance of 'Euridice' at Florence. Emilio del Cavalieri was then no longer living, but he had left such full directions, in his preface, as to the manner in which the work was to be performed, that no difficulty whatever lay in the way of bringing it out in exact accordance with his original intention, which included scenes, decorations, action and even dancing on a regular stage (*in palco*). The principal characters were Il Tempo (Time), La Vita (Life), Il Mondo (the World), Il Piacere (Pleasure), L' Intelletto (the Intellect), L' Anima (the Soul), Il Corpo (the Body), two youths who recited the Prologue, and the chorus. The orchestra consisted of one lira doppia, one clavicembalo, one chitarrone and two flauti, 'o vero due tibie all' antica.' No part is written for a violin, but a note states that a good effect may be produced by playing one in unison with the soprano voices throughout. The orchestra was entirely hidden from view, but it was recommended that the various characters should carry musical instruments in their hands, and pretend to accompany their voices, and to play the *ritornelli* interposed between the melodies allotted to them. A madrigal, with full instrumental accompaniment, was to take the place of the overture. The curtain then rose, and the two youths delivered the Prologue; after which a long solo [1] was sung by Time. The Body, when singing the words 'Se che hormai alma mia,' was to throw away his golden collar and the feathers from his hat. The World and Life were to be very richly dressed, but when divested of their ornaments, to appear very poor and wretched, and ultimately dead bodies.

[1] Quoted in Burney's *History*, iv. p. 91.

A great number of instruments were to join in the *ritornelli*. And, finally, it was directed that the performance might be finished either with or without a dance. ' If without,' says the stage-direction,

' the vocal and instrumental parts of the last chorus must be doubled. But should a dance be preferred, the verse beginning *Chiostri altissimi e stellati* must be sung, accompanied by stately and reverent steps. To these will succeed other grave steps and figures of a solemn character. During the *ritornelli* the four principal dancers will perform a ballet, embellished with capers (*saltato con capriole*) without singing. And thus, after each verse, the steps of the dance will always be varied, the four chief dancers sometimes using the *Gagliarde*, sometimes the *Canario*, and sometimes the *Corrente*, which will do well in the *Ritornelli*.'

The general character of the music will be readily understood from the following examples [1] of portions of a solo and chorus :

L'Intelletto.

Coro.

The occasion which immediately led to the second period of the oratorio was the Canonisa-

tion of SS. Ignatius Loyola and Francis Xavier. In honour of this event Kapsberger set to music an Allegorical Drama, called ' Apotheosis, seu consecratio SS. Ignatii et Francisci Xaverii,' which was several times performed at the Collegio Romano, with magnificent scenic decorations and full dramatic action, in the year 1622. The music of this piece, which is still extant, is miserably poor and so much inferior, both in originality and dramatic form, to the works of Monteverdi and other popular writers of the period, that it is impossible to believe it could have succeeded, had it not been for the splendour of the *mise en scène* with which it was accompanied. Another piece, on the same subject, entitled ' S. Ignatius Loyola,' was set to music in the same year by Vittorio Loreto. Neither the poetry nor the music of this has been preserved, but Erythraeus [2] assures us that, though the former was poor, the latter was of the highest order of excellence, and that the success of the performance was unprecedented. Vittorio Loreto also set to music ' La pellegrina constante,' in 1647, and ' Il sagrifizio d' Abramo,' in 1648. Besides these, mention is made of ' Il Lamento di S. Maria Vergine,' by Michelagnolo Capellini, in 1627 ; ' S. Alessio,' by Stefano Landi, in 1634 ; ' Erminio sul Giordano,' by Michel Angelo Rossi, in 1637 ; and numerous oratorios by other composers, of which, in most instances, the words only have survived, none appearing to have been held in any great amount of popular estimation. An exception must, however, be made in favour of the works of Domenico MAZZOCCHI (*q.v.*), by far the greatest composer of this particular period, whose ' Querimonia di S. Maria Maddelena ' rivalled in popularity even the celebrated ' Lamento d' Arianna ' of Monteverdi. His oratorio, ' Il martirio di SS. Abbundio ed Abbundanzio,' was produced in Rome in 1631 ; but his fame rests chiefly upon the ' Querimonia,' which when performed at S. Maria in Vallicella, by such singers as Vittorio Loreto, Buonaventura, or Marcantonio, drew tears from all who heard it. The following extract will be sufficient to show the touchingly pathetic character of this famous composition :

S. *Maria Maddelena.*

---

[1] See also *Oxf. Hist. Mus.* vol. iii. pp. 37-40.   [2] *Epistolæ ad diversos,* lib. iv

sa-rà per lei di quel be - a - to sangue senza il doglioso hu-

mor del pian • • • • • • • • • to mi - o
etc.

We now come to Giovanni Carissimi. His first efforts were devoted to the perfection of the sacred cantata, of which he has left us a multitude of beautiful examples ; but he also wrote numerous oratorios, among which the best known are ' Jephte,' ' Ezechias,' ' Baltazar,' ' Abraham et Isaac,' ' Jonas,' ' Judicium Salomonis,' ' L'Histoire de Job,' ' La Plainte des damnés,' ' Le Mauvais Riche,' ànd ' Le Jugement Dernier.' These are all full of beauties, and, in ' Jephte '[1] especially, the composer has reached a depth of pathos which none but the greatest of singers can hope to interpret satisfactorily. The solo ' Plorate colles,' assigned to Jephtha's Daughter, is a model of tender expression ; and the echo, sung by two sopranos at the end of each clause of the melody, adds an inexpressible charm to its melancholy effect.

It was about this time that the spectacular representation began gradually to fall into disuse, though the dramatic character of the poem was still retained, with certain modifications, chief among which was the introduction of a personage called the ' Historicus,' to whom were assigned certain narrative passages interpolated between the clauses of the dialogue for the purpose of carrying on the story intelligibly in the absence of scenic action. This idea was no doubt suggested by the liturgical manner of singing the Passion during Holy Week. (See PASSION MUSIC.) Carissimi used this expedient freely, and his example soon led to its general adoption, both in Italy and Germany.

Carissimi's most illustrious disciple—the only one perhaps whose genius shone more brightly than his own—was Alessandro Scarlatti, a composer gifted with talents so versatile that it is impossible to say whether he excelled most in the cantata, the oratorio or the opera. His sacred music, with which alone we are here concerned, was characterised by a breadth of style and dignity of manner which we cannot but regard as the natural consequence of his great contrapuntal skill. He gave to the aria a definite structure which it retained for more than a century—the well-balanced form, consisting of a first or principal strain, a second part, and a return to the original subject in the shape of the familiar ' Da Capo.' This sym-

[1] Accessible in modern reprints, notably the octavo edition of Novello.

metrical system soon came into general use in every school in Europe. Scarlatti used rhythmic melody of this kind for those highly impassioned scenes which, in a spoken drama, would have been represented by the monologue, reserving accompanied recitative for those which involved more dramatic action combined with less depth of sentiment, and using *recitativo secco* chiefly for the purpose of developing the course of the narrative. Thus carefully planned, his oratorios were full of interest, whether regarded from a musical or a dramatic point of view. The most successful among them were ' I dolori di Maria sempre Vergine ' (Rome, 1693), ' Il sagrifizio d' Abramo,' ' Il martirio di Santa Teodosia,' and ' La Concezzione della beata Vergine ' ; but it is to be feared that many are lost, as very few of the composer's innumerable works were printed. Dr. Burney found a very fine one in MS. in the Library of the Chiesa Nuova at Rome, with 'an admirable overture, in a style totally different from that of Lully,' and a song with trumpet obbligato. He does not mention the title of the work, but the following lovely melody seems intended to be sung by the Blessed Virgin before the finding of our Lord in the Temple :

Il mio fig - lio o - - vè,   che fà,   do-ve

fià   la mia gio - ja,   il mio te-sor, Fig-lio

o - vèche fà, Fig-lio   che fà dove stà? dove

fà   la mia gio - ja   il mio te-sor? etc.

The publication (1905) of E. J. Dent's exhaustive monograph on Alessandro Scarlatti enables us to have a much clearer idea of the composer than was formerly possible. His researches have not unearthed the music of the above - mentioned ' I dolori di Maria sempre

Vergine' and 'Il sagrifizio d' Abramo,' which are ascribed to Alessandro Scarlatti by Fétis, Florimo and others; possibly, however, the manuscripts may still be lying in one of the monastic libraries to which Dent was not able to procure access. Besides these two, three other oratorios are mentioned as having eluded his pursuit: but there remain eighteen ranging in date from a 'St. John Passion,' of about 1680, and 'Agar et Ismaele esiliati,' of 1683, to an unnamed oratorio of 1717 which Gevaert has entitled 'La Vergine addolorata.' Their subjects vary widely: two are Passion oratorios, two others works for performance at Christmas, one a Latin oratorio on the subject of David, and several hagiological—some of a modern character concerning S. Philip Neri or S. Casimir, King of Poland. Many, again, are based on librettos in honour of the Blessed Virgin, 'La Santissima Annuntiata,' 'La Santissima Vergine del Rosario,' and so on; though the general style of the words varies but little throughout the whole group of oratorios. The librettos, indeed, are in many respects very much akin to those of the operas; and even the orchestration is sometimes very unecclesiastical, as in the above-mentioned Rosary oratorio, where 'Penitence' has an air accompanied by a toy-nightingale, played as the performer may please. As Dent remarks:

'except that the operas are in three acts and the oratorios in two, the only difference is in the absence of professedly comic characters, and of the formal statement in which the author protests that the words *Fato, Dio, Deità,* etc., are only *Scherzi poetici* and imply nothing contrary to the Catholic Faith.'

Occasionally, however, as in the 'La Santissima Trinità,' which is simply a string of theological disputations between various allegorical characters, Scarlatti comes very close to the original hortatory standpoint of the oratorio performances of S. Philip Neri, on whose life one of the best of these works is based. They seem to vary much in quality; some are tedious, not through any complexity (there is only one fugal chorus, in the early 'Il martirio di Santa Teodosia,' in the whole group), but through absence of sincerity of touch, yet usually, when human interest is derivable from the words, Scarlatti is able to meet the demand. Dent quotes from the Assumption and Christmas oratorios some singularly delicate and fascinating music which gives rise to strong wishes that the complete works might be readily accessible: the air in which the hymns of the angels and shepherds in the stable at Bethlehem are depicted is particularly interesting as showing a close likeness, which can hardly be altogether accidental, to the 'Pastoral Symphony' in Handel's 'Messiah.'

Among the most popular of Scarlatti's contemporaries were D. Francesco Federici, who wrote two oratorios, 'Santa Cristina' and 'Santa Caterina de Siena,' for the Congregation of Oratorians, in 1676; Carolo Pallavicini, who

dedicated 'Il trionfo della castità' to Cardinal Ottoboni, about the year 1689; Fr. Ant. Pistocchi, whose 'S. Maria Vergine addolorata,' produced in 1698, is full of pathetic beauty; Giulio d' Alessandri, who wrote an interesting oratorio called 'Santa Francesca Romana,' about 1690; and three very much greater writers—Caldara, Colonna and Stradella.[1] Caldara composed—chiefly at Vienna—a large collection of delightful oratorios, most of which were adapted to the poetry of Apostolo Zeno and Metastasio. The most successful of these were 'Tobia,' 'Assalone,' 'Giuseppe,' 'Davidde,' 'La Passione di Gesù Cristo,' 'Daniele,' 'San Pietro a Cesarea,' 'Gesù presentato al Tempio,' 'Gerusalemme convertita,' and most especially 'Sisera,' which, as Zeno himself confesses, owed its reputation entirely to the beauty of the music. Colonna's style—especially that of his choruses—was broader and more dignified than Caldara's, and he did much towards raising the oratorio to the noble level it attained in the 18th century. But in point of natural genius there can be no doubt that Alessandro Stradella excelled all the best writers of this period.

w. s. r.; rev. with addns. by e. w.

II. MODERN ORATORIO

The point that these investigations have now reached is indeed the pivot of the whole history of oratorio. It had its artistic birth in Italy simultaneously with opera; and it at once gravitated in the direction of the sister form, and the two streams flowed side by side, their waters occasionally intermingling till at last they coalesced. Italian oratorio has indeed an exclusive history of its own; it never spoke another language (though in its decay composers of other races handled it), and it never abandoned its intimate connexion with Italian opera. But the spirit that animated the great 16th-century religious liturgical music passed out of Italy with the birth of opera; it met in Germany the spirit of the PASSION MUSIC (q.v.), and the offspring of the two is modern oratorio. All unconsciously, but without any break, Palestrina and Victoria passed on the pure flame to Byrd and Gibbons, and they to Schütz. We may say that all oratorio is religious recreation; but, though the great men rose above the conception, Italian oratorio as a whole, from Cavalieri to Rossini, lays the stress on the recreation, while, though some of its exponents have fallen below their ideal, all other oratorio, from Schütz to Elgar, lays the stress on the religion. Palestrina and Bach would cheerfully have persecuted each other as alien heretics, but they are spiritual brothers in their art; Palestrina and Rossini were of the same blood and professed the same faith, but there is not the slightest real tie between them. It is true that

[1] Leo is sometimes grouped with these; but as practically the whole of his life falls within the limits of the 18th century, he may perhaps be better considered separately.

what we may call modern oratorio was born long before what we may call ancient oratorio had died ; and at times in the 18th century the path of the growing man came very near that of the dying child. But still the line of demarcation is there, and it is the central fact in the history of oratorio.

The actual personal link between the great Italians of the 16th century and Schütz was Giovanni Gabrieli, who received Schütz at Venice as one of his pupils during the last three years of his life (1609–12). Gabrieli was a very remarkable composer of ruggedly sincere aims, who attempted to fuse the religious earnestness of the older generation both of Italians and Netherlanders with the technical methods of the operatic revolution, and produced in the process some most interesting works, though as he wrote nothing that can be called an oratorio, he remains outside the present investigation. Among his own countrymen he left no followers, but Schütz imbibed a large measure of his spirit; and the six works that we may call oratorios (' Historia von der Auferstehung Jesu Christi,' ' Die sieben Worte Jesu Christi am Kreuz,' and four Passions, one according to each Evangelist), which he produced at intervals after his return to Germany, are the real first-fruits of German music. The influence of the old mystery play is no doubt present, as it was present in the earliest Italian oratorio ; but the whole conception is, nevertheless, different. There is no thought of the stage, no attempt at anything like a tune or at anything ' attractive ' ; the solemnity of the subjects is obviously the only thing present to his mind, and his sole aim is to represent them faithfully.

EVOLUTION OF THE GERMAN STYLE.— Schütz was the last composer who was at all strongly influenced by the traditional musical formulæ of the Roman Church ; and in Germany the influence of the plain-song quickly gave way before that of the CHORAL (*q.v.*), which was entirely an indigenous product, and was indeed being treated as the basis of comparatively elaborate artistic work of the motet type even before the time of Schütz, though his own oratorios show no recognisable traces of anything of the kind. In 1672, the year of Schütz's death, Johann Sebastiani produced at Königsberg a Passion oratorio in which all trace of the plain-song had completely disappeared ; and from that time onwards German music knew it no more, apart from passing purely artistic references, as in the ' Credo ' of Bach's Mass in B minor. But though it is certain that the noble choral tunes were more and more used by composers—sometimes in fairly plain, sometimes in highly elaborate settings [1]—yet we are often in the earlier times left

[1] It must be confessed that Bach and all other adapters of chorales were the reverse of purists. Luther and all his contemporaries and followers wrote their melodies in a flexible rhythm that is as innocent of any sort of bar-fetters as plain-song itself ; and a considerable torturing process was often necessary before they

without exact evidence as to the frequency of their introduction as congregational elements into the Passion oratorio, in the manner exemplified later on in Bach and Graun. Thus the two oratorios which are the greatest sacred works by a German composer between Schütz and Bach—Keiser's settings of Brockes's favourite poem *Der für die Sünde der Welt gemartete und sterbende Jesus*, and König's poem *Der zum Tode verurtheilte und gekreuzigte Jesus*, are extant only in selections entitled respectively ' Auserlesene Soliloquiae ' and ' Seelige Erlösungsgedanken,' which contain merely the contemplative numbers and the recitatives of the evangelist-narrator. Keiser, who was born in 1673, the year after Schütz's death, and was consequently twelve years the senior of Bach and Handel, still remains a mere name to most persons : Schütz and Buxtehude, the two greatest of the other great early Germans, have recently come to their own so far as publication is concerned, but Keiser still lacks due recognition. The above-mentioned extracts from his two masterpieces were, however, published by the composer himself, and undoubtedly express a very noble and very mature art. Bach's religious music is steeped through and through with the influence of these works, produced respectively in 1712 and 1715, just indeed at the time when he was passing out of his early rather stiff style into the enjoyment of his full powers ; and though of course it would be out of the question to make any real comparison between the total output of the two men, yet nevertheless there are pages in these works of Keiser which are quite worthy of the younger composer in some of his very finest moods. Indeed, it would need considerable search before we could find six bars more full of supreme pathos than these that open a ' Soliloquium Mariae ' in ' Der gekreuzigte Jesus '—sung, no doubt, ' molto adagio ed espressivo ' :

could be fitted to the more modern conditions which were supposed to be indispensable.

which are followed by a sort of 'accompanied recitative' and an aria 'con affetto,' the whole forming a wonderful piece of the highest expressiveness and beauty. Or again, take from the same work the close of the 'Chor der nach-folgenden Weiber und Verwandten des Herrn Jesu'—an 'aria a tre voci':

or, in a totally different style, the air of the 'Gläubige Seele,' as fresh in its spring-like devotion as anything of the kind in Bach:

or the air of the ' Fromme Schächer,' with its
' violette all' unisono, piano per tutta l' aria,'
playing chiefly reiterated notes with lovely
tranquil effect—or indeed very many other
things. ' Der gekreuzigte Jesus ' is on the
whole considerably the finer of the two works ;
but the earlier ' Der sterbende Jesus ' contains
also some very beautiful numbers, such as the
' Soliloquium ' for the ' Tochter Zion '—' Die
Rosencrönen sonst der ranken Dornen Spitzen '
—consisting of (a) a ' Cavata,' *cantabile*, in A
major, (b) a recitative beginning in C and ending in A major, (c) a ' Larghetta ' in B minor,
(d) a ' Da capo,' presumably the ' Cavata,'
(e) a recitative beginning in F♯ minor and
ending in A major, (f) an aria, *canto cantabile*, in D major, (g) two concluding bars for
the tenor - evangelist. Keiser shows several
examples of this sort of extended solo scena
(which really finds its closest parallel in certain
works of Purcell) ; and though his oratorios
are of course, in general scope and type, much
smaller than those of Bach, yet in maturely
artistic expression of notably fine ideas the
best work of the older man need not be ashamed
of the comparison. One of his most modern
touches is his great fondness for nuances, like
' cantabile,' ' con affetto,' and so on ; in later
years, it is true, German religious music degenerated into a good deal of mere sentimentality, but there is as little of that in Keiser as
in Schütz or Bach.

We have now four oratorios from the pen of
John Sebastian Bach—three Passion oratorios
and a Christmas oratorio [1] : certainly a ' St.
Mark Passion,' and most probably yet another,
have disappeared. Of the Passion oratorios,
that ' according to St. Luke ' was regarded by
Mendelssohn as spurious, but it is now generally accepted as a genuine but very early
work ; it is of but slight importance, and
demands little more than historical mention.
Of the other two great works the ' St. John
Passion ' is the earlier, dating from 1724, five
years before the ' St. Matthew Passion,' and
is the more dramatic and the less reflective of
the two ; in the ' Christmas Oratorio,' written
in 1734, five years after the ' St. Matthew
Passion,' the dramatic element is practically
non-existent, the pastoral music being the only
portion which is not, so to speak, evangelically
mystical in outlook. The title is Bach's own,
but the oratorio is really not a whole singly
conceived work like each of the Passions, but
a collection of six separate cantatas written
for six separate holy-days, beginning with
Christmas and ending with Epiphany.

Telemann, who was Bach's senior by four
years, and survived both him and Handel,
wrote forty-four Passions, and many oratorios on other subjects, among which ' Der

[1] The so-called Easter and Ascension oratorios are merely church
cantatas of the normal pattern.

Tag des Gerichts ' and ' Die Tageszeiten ' seem
to have been the best known ; he was a highly
skilled contrapuntist, and, according to an
anecdote quoted by Schumann, boasted that
' a proper composer should be able to set a
placard to music,' but his bland style lacks any
sort of depth or solidity, and the shallowness
of much of the subsequent ecclesiastical music
in Germany—especially that designed for
definitely liturgical use—is very largely traceable to his widespread influence. Very many
of his works were published, while Bach's
manuscripts were accumulating dust ; and,
anyhow, they were so much more easy and
generally intelligible to the average church-
goer of the period.

HANDEL AND THE 18TH CENTURY.—Handel's
early essays in ecclesiastical music are, however, of different quality ; they lack indeed
the maturity of technical handling that we see
in the great English oratorios, but as regards
at any rate two of them we may perhaps say
that on the whole they show more strictly
religious earnestness of purpose, and that
while we miss the spaciousness of the later
works we miss also their careless conventionalities. In many ways both the ' St. John
Passion ' (1704) and the Passion set to the
often-used poem of Brockes (1715) are distinctly interesting works ; there are many
numbers that are far closer to Keiser's and
Bach's methods than anything else Handel ever
wrote. He had indeed a singular genius for
adaptation to his environment : to German
words he wrote purely German music, while
the English oratorios are totally different, as
indeed again is ' La Resurrezione,' the oratorio
written at Rome in 1708 and built on a purely
Italian model. The Handelian English oratorio is something *sui generis* ; it had no sort
of precursor, and apart from some slight relics
in the works of Beethoven and Spohr and some
rather clearer ones in those of Mendelssohn, it
has left no traces in the work of any great man.
Kinship with the previous religious music of
Handel's own countrymen is practically in-
discoverable ; it is far closer to the models of
the Italians. Apart from ' Messiah,' which
occupies a unique position, the Handelian
oratorio is an ' entertainment,' sometimes consisting, like ' Solomon ' and ' Israel in Egypt,'
chiefly of imposing choruses, sometimes, like
' Joseph ' and ' Jephtha,' of a judicious blend
of Biblical history and decorous ' love-interest,
sometimes again of vivid drama, like ' Saul '
and ' Belshazzar ' ; but compared with Schütz
or Bach it is always ' of the earth, earthy.'
The atmosphere of the theatres in which
they were produced hangs round them all
(some pages indeed, especially in ' Joseph '
and ' Susanna,' seem imperatively to demand gesture and movement) ; and yet they
are sharply differentiated from the Italian

oratorios by the enormous stress which they lay on choral utterance, not by any means exclusively as representing the sentiments of actors in the story, but equally or even more frequently as representing the reflections of the religiously minded listener. But still these reflections are always, so to speak, external; North German pietism found little echo in the breast of the Londoner, whether Christian or Jew,[1] for whom Handel wrote.

As we have seen, Handel's Italian work merely echoed the older type, and had no real influence on his English masterpieces. And, indeed, the whole subsequent history of Italian oratorio is that of the gradual extinction of the ancient type; strictly speaking, it is not modern oratorio, but ancient oratorio *in extremis*. But still, though its last days were brightened by no music worthy to be compared with Carissimi's for really subtle artistic insight, there are yet works that show glimpses of fine music, and several names seem to demand mention, if only as historical landmarks.

The traditions of the best features of the oratorios of musicians like Alessandro Scarlatti and Stradella lingered indeed for some considerable time. Lotti's work in this direction shows much that is of high value, and Marcello's curiously named 'oratorio a quattro voci'—'Il Pianto e il Riso delle quattro Stagioni dell' anno per la Morte, Esaltazione, e Coronazione di Maria sempre Vergine Assunta in Cielo'—contains some fine dignified music, and shows in the alto aria 'Maria, Madre d'Amor' a singularly beautiful Siciliano, which is really equal to all but the very finest of Handel's songs in that measure.[2] Leo's 'Santa Elena al Calvario' has also much of very considerable interest; some of its choruses (particularly 'Di quanta pena è frutta') show fine strong solid workmanship, though on the whole it can perhaps hardly compare with other definitely liturgical sacred music from his pen, nor with certain sacred cantatas for solo voices. Pergolesi produced a Christmas oratorio, and also a sacred drama entitled 'La Conversione di S. Guglielmo,' into which comic intermezzi —after the very curious fashion of those days (1731)—were introduced; and this marks the beginning of the decline. Too much has indeed been made of the mere fact that religious subjects were frequently given stage presentation—from the earliest mystery play down to 'Parsifal,' such things have been done in the spirit of the very purest reverence; but the real cause of the decay was that there was not the least attempt at any elevation of style,

and that these lapses from the true path were not mere occasional accidents (as had happened before), but settled habits that were frankly avowed by the composers, and frankly welcomed by their listeners. Porpora's 'Santa Eugenia,' one of the early works of his Roman period, though not intended for stage presentation, does its best to look like an opera, with its twenty changes of scene in the first act, and seventeen in the second; and in spite of certain relics of sedateness and dignity (as in Eugenia's really pathetic 'Tu lacero esangue con pena infinita'), the work as a whole is thoroughly stilted. Men like Piccinni (whose 'Jonathan' is perhaps his best work) and Sacchini—who had both an inclination towards the serious in art—did, it is true, something to stem the current; and Jommelli's 'La Passione di nostro Signore Giesu Cristo,' which was highly successful, and had the honour of being reprinted in London, tried, with much address, to combine the 'elegance and taste' which the composer's patrons demanded with a certain sort of solidity of technique. But Jommelli's work, though one of the best of its age in this field, is extremely dull on the whole; and almost the only thing that is really noteworthy is the remarkable ending of the last chorus of the first part on the unresolved dominant harmony to the words, 'pensaci, pensaci'—an emotional effect which anticipates by nearly a century Schumann's 'Im wünderschönen Monat Mai.' The 'Assalonne' of Cimarosa, whose main line (for which he had a real genius) was comedy opera, and the oratorios of Zingarelli and Guglielmi are full of bald triviality; and Sarti, Salieri and Paër, who were, especially the first named, men of decidedly more mark, still produced in this field nothing that possesses any sort of vitality. Not indeed that they did not attempt to do things on a somewhat large scale; in the extracts from Paër's 'Il trionfo della Chiesa,' which are preserved in the British Museum, there is a very elaborate movement, 'Dio pietoso, dio clemente,' with a bass aria for an Angel combined with two separate choirs, one of female voices 'coro d'eco celeste da lontano,' and the other an ordinary four-part choir of worshippers—the whole accompanied by a full soft orchestra, with clarinets and harp, but no trumpets and drums, and a great deal of wood-wind *soli*. But experiments of this kind, which were not uncommon, have hardly ever any real sign of vitality about them; Italian oratorio was indeed dying, and it expired in its absolute fusion with opera in Rossini's 'Mosè in Egitto,' which was originally written for the stage (and was so performed, with two different librettos on the subjects of 'Peter the Hermit' and 'Zora' respectively, at London theatres in 1822 and 1850), but was also, under the composer's own direction, entitled 'oratorio,' and very

---

[1] 'Judas Maccabæus' and 'Alexander Balus' were specially written to please the Jews, who had aided Handel in his second bankruptcy in 1745.

[2] The MS. of this work in the British Museum has the word Originale' in large letters at the bottom of the title-page—presumably to show that it is not, like so many works of the period, a pasticcio. The name of the author of the words has been carefully erased, but the words 'della Compagnia di Gesù' can just be traced. Is this perhaps a sign of a performance of the work in some country from which the Jesuit order was excluded?

frequently performed in the concert - room. This curious work marks the final extinction of any trace of the religious spirit, which still lingered very fitfully in Paër. With it Italian oratorio was practically silenced for seventy years ; a very few works were indeed produced by composers of Italian race but cosmopolitan careers, which chiefly saw the light outside their native country, and, anyhow, are of very slight importance. But at the close of the 19th century it was revived, under the direct guidance of the Vatican, by Lorenzo Perosi, whose works were urged upon Europe for several years by the whole driving force of the Roman Church. His numerous oratorios— ' The Resurrection of Lazarus ' is as typical as any—while showing influences ranging from Palestrina to Wagner, remind us, in one way, more of Haydn's works than of any others ; there is the similar attitude of the religiously minded child.

While Italian religious music was waning more and more, German oratorio composers of the generation after J. S. Bach were torn by diverse forces ; on the one hand was the influence of the Passion music, on the other that of Italian opera, the fashionable amusement of all persons of culture and taste. This struggle between the national and the foreign strikes deeply across all the music of the 18th century in all countries north of the Alps ; in Germany we see how Haydn and Mozart looked both ways, and it was indeed only the patriotic uprising at the fall of Napoleon that finally nationalised German music. Some were led more one way than the other, but others tried to keep the balance fairly even ; Graun, for example, wrote both German and Italian operas, and though his style owed far more to Italian influence than to any other, yet his ' Der Tod Jesu,' by which alone his fame has survived, is in design a Passion oratorio on the strict North German model. It starts at once, without any preamble, with the ' O Haupt voll Blut und Wunden ' Choral tune with which Bach's ' Matthäus - Passion ' renders us so familiar ; several more are introduced in the course of the work, and later on the Choral with bass solo is obviously modelled on Bach's structures. Graun was not in truth anything like a great genius, but the best things in ' Der Tod Jesu ' leave a very satisfactory impression behind them ; while the one oratorio of his famous contemporary Hasse that has survived complete, ' I pellegrini aJ Sepolcro,' [1] is (apart from its one and only chorus, which is a vast improvement on the rest of the work) merely the ordinary adequately effective dry machine-made music. And this kind of oratorio lingered on for some time ; Hasse was the great fashionable autocrat of his day, and pleasant

as some of his secular music is, his influence in the oratorio field weighed altogether on the wrong side. His traditions were carried on by men like Naumann, J. C. Bach, Winter, Weigl, Hiller, Dittersdorf, Himmel and many others till they died from sheer inanition about the second decade of the 19th century : and few works are more tedious than theirs, which (save in very rare instances) have neither soul enough to be sacred music nor backbone enough to be secular. Nor indeed have we even the relief that the sight of new librettos might afford, for the same poems were amiably handed over from one oratorio composer to another : Metastasio's ' I pellegrini al Sepolcro' was, for example, set by Naumann as well as by Hasse, his ' Passione di Giesu Cristo ' by Jommelli (as we have just seen), Paisiello, Salieri and Naumann, his ' Santa Elena al Calvario ' by Leo, Hasse and Naumann, and so on ad infinitum. Some of the Italians, like Leo and Jommelli, were, as we have seen, above their school : Leo, indeed, was in some of his religious music a distinctly great man, but, apart from a very few exceptions, the decay of Italian oratorio, whether in its native land or elsewhere, leaves no regret behind it.

But while Hasse and his friends and followers were vainly trying to galvanise a dying art-form, one great composer, whose work has been, till of late years, far too much neglected, produced three oratorios which are of very high interest as well as of special historical importance ; indeed, Carl Philip Emanuel Bach's ' Passions-Cantate,' ' Die Auferstehung und Himmelfahrt Jesu ' and ' Die Israeliten iñ der Wüste ' all, but especially (though it is the earliest) the last named, well repay close study.[2] Like all his contemporaries, he felt the pressure of the conflict of styles, and indeed is the one great man who best exemplifies them. Often he shows extensive traces of his father's influence, most of all perhaps in his recitatives and recitative-like movements in each of the three works, where he combines a large share of J. S. Bach's dignity and pathetic expressiveness with a power of dramatic word-painting that is his own great endowment. And, again, he abolishes altogether the customary overture, which even with Handel (though his workmanship is far more solid than that of the ordinary writer of Italian oratorios) is a more or less perfunctory and, anyhow, entirely irrelevant production ; instead he writes, in both the ' Passions - Cantate ' and ' Die Auferstehung und Himmelfahrt Jesu,' very short movements (one to each part in the latter work) only a few bars long, but obviously aiming, and with considerable success, at the preparation of the right solemn mood. Often, again, he altogether turns his back on his father and looks out in a

<hr/>

[1] The original perished, with many works of Hasse, in the bombardment of Dresden in 1760 ; what we have is a German version published by J. A. Hiller as ' Die Pilgrimme auf Golgotha.'

[2] See especially The Viennese Period (Oxford History of Music, vol. iv.), by W. H. Hadow, for an admirable account of C. P. E Bach.

quite different direction; he introduces a Choral, 'Was der alten Väter Schaar,' into 'Die Israeliten in der Wüste,' but the harmonisation is totally unlike J. S. Bach's style, and in some of the choruses in the same work and in 'Die Auferstehung und Himmelfahrt Jesu,' notably in the very long and elaborate finale of the latter, the whole handling of the voices and the brilliance of the orchestration remind us strongly of Haydn. The one great drawback, however, is that C. P. E. Bach, of all foremost composers, was the most amateurish in technique; his dramatic feeling sometimes outruns his sense of artistic proportion, and we never feel quite certain that his powers will not give out suddenly.

VIENNESE COMPOSERS.—The two great giants of the period, who enriched so many fields of music side by side, took very diverse views of oratorio. Mozart's work in this form is altogether negligible, and consists merely of two compositions. 'La Betulia liberata,' written to a libretto by Metastasio (also set by Jommelli, Naumann and others), at the end of 1771 or beginning of 1772, was the result of a commission given him at Padua when he visited that city in the course of his Italian concert tour; the oratorio is simply an 'opera seria' without action, and, though its composer had then (in his 16th year) written many wonderful things, is of but little interest; one of its numbers contains the ancient 'intonation' introduced at the words 'Te decet hymnus' in the first chorus of the 'Requiem' twenty years later. The only other oratorio, 'Davidde penitente,' of considerably later date, is nothing but a pasticcio from the splendid C minor Mass, arranged to Italian words, and combined with a couple of incongruous and not specially noteworthy arias of a florid character. Mozart also wrote, in the very early 'sacred singspiel,' 'Die Schuldigkeit des ersten Gebotes,'[1] an example of the kind of hybrid production which, as we have seen, was not uncommon at this time; but this again is of no importance, and the composer's genius for sacred music can only be seen in the 'Requiem' and in the many splendid and far too little known liturgical works of smaller dimensions.

Haydn, on the other hand, put much of his greatest music into his oratorios. His earliest, 'Il ritorno di Tobia' (the finest example of 18th-century Italian oratorio that exists), written in 1774 for the Tonkünstler-Societät of Vienna, is laid out on a large scale, and, though it suffers by comparison with its composer's later work, represents, at its date, his largest orchestral as well as Choral manner. In the year 1785 Haydn received a commission from the authorities of the cathedral at Cadiz to write 7 instrumental

adagios for use during Lenten services as interludes between sermons on each of the 'Seven Words on the Cross.' Originally composed for orchestra and afterwards arranged for string quartet, they were yet again published in 1801 with additions and modifications and arranged for solo voices, chorus and orchestra, with an explanatory preface; and in this form, which Haydn obviously considered the best, the work may fairly be ranked as a short oratorio. Next[2] came the masterpiece known in England as the 'Creation,' which was written in 1797–98 on a libretto which Haydn had acquired during his last English visit: it was the culminating success of its composer's life. For his last great work Haydn had again recourse to England, the libretto of the 'Seasons' being an adaptation by van Swieten of Thomson's poem of the same name. The title of 'oratorio' is Haydn's own, but it is what would now be called merely a cantata on a large scale; there is a little 'religious application' in the words of a few numbers in two out of the four sections, but otherwise the subject is throughout purely secular. It is a case of the same mistaken nomenclature that is to be noticed with regard to several works of Handel; but it is almost the last time that we find the word oratorio thus vaguely used, as, with the spread of public music unconnected with either church or stage, other more adequate titles came into use, and the modern definite idea of oratorio as a non-liturgical work of religious character became firmly established. Haydn's work forms a sort of bypath in the history of oratorio; and we can see no reflection of it in sacred music till we come to the 'Stabat Mater' and 'Biblische Lieder' of Dvořák,[3] who, though so much later in date, is the only other composer of such music who was similarly a Slav by blood and a Roman Catholic by faith, and also, like Haydn, steeped through and through in his national folk-tunes.

Though not published till 1811, Beethoven's 'Christus am Ölberge'[4] seems to have been written between the 'Creation' and the 'Seasons'; but the world to which it introduces us is altogether different. Beethoven jokingly compared his own very successful 'Prometheus' ballet music with Haydn's masterpiece[5]; and it is very possible that it was the extraordinary reception of the 'Creation' which suggested to Beethoven the composition of an oratorio. It is Beethoven's only sacred work, apart from the two masses, though late in his life he seems to have contemplated a sort of sequel, to be entitled 'Die Höllenfahrt des Erlösers'; many

---

[1] Only the first of the three parts is by Mozart, the other two being respectively by Michael Haydn and Adlgasser, the court organist of Salzburg, a personage otherwise unknown to fame.

[2] The Mass in B flat, written in 1796, is the main source of an unauthorised pasticcio called the oratorio 'Judah,' which was popular in England in the days when atrocities of this kind were common.

[3] St. Ludmila,' Dvořák's only oratorio, is, as we shall see later, not altogether characteristic of his usual style.

[4] Known in England firstly with a substituted libretto (after the barbarous fashion of older days) on the subject of 'Engedi, or David in the Wilderness,' and now as 'The Mount of Olives.'

[5] The pun on 'Die Schöpfung' and 'Die Geschöpfe des Prometheus' is obvious; but it has been sometimes unwarrantably supposed that the comparison was a piece of mere conceited impertinence.

years subsequently Beethoven expressed to his friend Schindler his dissatisfaction with the work, and especially his regret that the part of Jesus had been treated in too operatic a style.

Schubert's essays in oratorio writing are two: ' Miriams Siegesgesang ' (1828), and ' Lazarus ' (1820)—the latter, for some reason which is unknown, left unfinished. ' Miriam's Song of Victory ' is a short work that might fitly be called an ' oratorietto,' and is designed for soprano solo and chorus, with only a provisional pianoforte accompaniment, after the composer's not infrequent fashion. ' Lazarus ' is, however, merely a fragment of what was designed to be an oratorio on apparently a very large scale ; the libretto is laid out in three acts, but Schubert comes to an abrupt end in the middle of a number in the second of these three. The work is called a ' religious drama,' and is indeed furnished with regular scenic directions ; but it seems in the highest degree unlikely that it can ever have been meant for stage performance, and in all probability the acting indications were (as in many concert-room works by various composers of both earlier and later date) merely designed to give *vraisemblance* to the situations.

GERMAN 19TH-CENTURY WORK.—Neither of Schubert's oratorios was performed during his lifetime, and, as we have seen, one of them was a fragment and the other (as regards the accompaniments) a mere temporary makeshift ; but far different is the case with Spohr's works in this field. Excluding the early and altogether unimportant ' Das jüngste Gericht '—written for the ' Fête Napoléon ' at Erfurt in 1812—he wrote three oratorios, ' Die letzten Dinge ' (' The last Judgment '—a confusing mistranslation) in 1826, ' Des Heilands letzte Stunden ' (' Calvary ') in 1835, and ' Der Fall Babylons ' in 1842 ; on each of them he lavished all the resources of his art, and each met with enormous success, alike in Germany and in England. But with the rise of Mendelssohn worship his star gradually waned. About this time there were signs that Germany, like contemporary England, was passing through a period of oratorio worship for its own sake ; it hardly seems possible on any other supposition to account for the extraordinary popularity of the oratorios of Friedrich Schneider, who between 1810 and 1838 turned out no fewer than 16, all of which were apparently welcomed with enthusiasm. Like Lindpaintner's ' Abraham ' and ' Der Jüngling von Nain,' Schneider's ' Das Weltgericht,' ' Die verlorene Paradies ' and ' Salomonis Tempelbau ' belong to that great company of musical works which, successful as they may be at the time, have no root in themselves and presently wither away. And a similar neglect has overtaken the ' Mount Sinai ' and ' David ' of Neukomm, a cosmopolitan composer who, after studying under Haydn,

spent the rest of his life in Paris and London, with intervals in Russia and Brazil ; especially in England his works were held in very high esteem, and ' David ' was specially written for the Birmingham Festival of 1834.

Very different has been the fate of the oratorios of Mendelssohn. ' St. Paul,' ' Elijah ' and the ' Hymn of Praise ' (which is more fitly grouped with the oratorios than with anything else) long were, and in some quarters still are, household words, and the unfinished ' Christus ' shows enough of the same characteristics to warrant the supposition that, had its composer lived to finish it, it would have equalled the popularity of the others. A comparison of his oratorios with those of Spohr is not without considerable interest. Both men enjoyed unbounded popularity, and we in England welcomed them whole-heartedly as twin kings of religious art. No doubt it has been fitting that Mendelssohn should have had the longer lease of life : his touch is much the firmer, and his command over varied resources much the greater. But yet sometimes, in an uncertain vague sort of way, Spohr seems to have had a glimpse of depths unknown to the serene conservatism of the other ; his visions of ' far-off things ' are dim, and are inextricably mixed up with much that is weak and altogether transient, while Mendelssohn's religious music gives the impression that he lived in untroubled unconsciousness of anything outside mid-19th-century Protestantism. And this would seem to be the real secret of his vitality in this country. He appealed directly and with absolute sincerity to a particular form of religious sentiment which, from early Victorian days, has lain deep in the heart of the average Englishman and Englishwoman ; he is the only great artist, in words or colour or music, who has ever touched this emotional spring, and he has had, and still has, his reward.

In 1843, half-way between the productions of the ' Hymn of Praise ' and ' Elijah,' Wagner's ' Biblical scena ' ' Das Liebesmahl der Apostel ' saw the light ; it is his solitary piece of sacred music, and, as being entirely non-liturgical in character, seems to find a place in this article. It is a comparatively brief work, written for a ' Male-chorus festival ' at Dresden, and consists of two sections of contrasting character ; the first part, comprising some two-thirds of the work, is entirely *a cappella*, but the second part, into which it leads without break, has an independent and elaborate orchestral accompaniment. The work as a whole is one of Wagner's mildest, and would hardly require notice were it not the solitary contribution to the oratorio field of one of the greatest of composers.

The contribution of his great German contemporary to the literature of non-liturgical religious music is, however, of a very different character. Brahms's ' Deutsches Requiem ' is not styled an oratorio, but it is far more that than it is anything else ; it has no sort of connexion with any ecclesiastical service, and its whole being is religious. Indeed, it represents the supreme religious emotions in the language of his own world, as Palestrina represents them in that of mediævalism and Bach in that of the Reformation ; it is alike the permanent and the solitary artistic memorial of the highest aspirations of his generation.

The later German composers have indeed ventured but little into this field ; Schumann never attempted anything that could even approximately be called an oratorio (in the sense in which the term is here used), and his reluctance seems to have spread to nearly all who can in any way be called his followers. Individual works there have no doubt been, but their importance, whether artistic or historical, is very slight ; and on the whole the recent generations of German composers do not seem to have turned their attention much in the direction of religious music in the concert-room, though there is a large output of works intended for liturgical use. Mention might perhaps— among the productions of the older men— be made of Raff's ' Weltende,' one of his last compositions ; but the oratorios of Bruch are deserving of rather more notice. Well known as is much of his violin and violoncello music in this country, Bruch's choral compositions are not at all generally familiar to English concert-goers ; among his religious works the oratorios ' Arminius ' (op. 43) and ' Moses ' (op. 67) are the most important, the latter a ' Biblical oratorio '—so styled probably to differentiate it from the earlier work— designed on a very large scale.

We may now perhaps briefly mention a few oratorios by composers not of German blood, but largely influenced by German methods. Gade, for example, though a pure Dane, is in all but his very earliest works a German composer ; and his short oratorio-cantata ' Zion ' shows many traces of his intercourse with the Mendelssohn school. No really national Scandinavian composer seems to have produced any noteworthy work in the field of oratorio ; and Slavonic composers also have almost always turned their energies in other directions. Rubinstein, though musically he was really a quite denationalised Russian, nevertheless attempted no concert-oratorio, though his sacred opera ' The Tower of Babel ' was once performed at a Crystal Palace concert under its composer's direction, and proved to be a somewhat unsatisfactory attempt at a realistic expression of its title ; and his later strictly national compatriots seem to have done nothing even of this hybrid nature. The two oratorios of Liszt deserve, however, a few words : ' Christus '—a Latin oratorio containing com-

plete settings of the ' Stabat mater dolorosa,' the ' Stabat mater speciosa,' and much more— seems to be very little known in England, but ' St. Elizabeth ' was performed in London several times during the composer's last visit to this country. The former is, as is natural, the more subjective and mystical of the two ; the latter is more dramatic and spectacular, and contains (like most modern oratorios on hagiological subjects) a certain amount of purely ' secular ' music.

Dvořák's ' St. Ludmila ' is also an oratorio on a hagiological theme, and, like ' St. Elizabeth,' includes in one and the same work hunting choruses and solemn cathedral ceremonials. It was written on commission for the Leeds Festival of 1886, but failed to meet with the success that had been won by his ' Stabat Mater ' and ' The Spectre's Bride ' in the years immediately preceding. These works had aroused in England a widespread interest in the Bohemian composer ; and there can be little doubt that ' St. Ludmila ' was written with rather special desire to meet the wishes of the friendly patrons who had been really the first adequately to recognise him. But the result was as unsatisfactory as usually happens when an artist tries to please others rather than himself ; and Dvořák's solitary oratorio does very little to add to his fame.

THE FRENCH SCHOOLS.—French oratorio, always a plant of uncertain growth, shows its earliest fruits in the music of Lully's contemporary, Charpentier, who brought back from his studies in Italy ideas about oratorio-writing which took shape in many works—' David et Jonathan,' ' L'Enfant prodigue,' ' Le Sacrifice d'Abraham,' etc. etc. The fine motets of Lalande and Campra, at the beginning of the 18th century, are as exclusively intended to be portions of an ecclesiastical service as are the contemporary English anthems, to which in many ways some of them, especially by Lalande, bear a close resemblance ; and composers who desired to treat Biblical subjects outside the church resorted frankly to the stage. Rameau wrote an opera on the subject of Samson, and though it does not seem to have come to performance, the contemporary production of another on the subject of Jephtha by Montéclair shows that there was no rooted censorial objection to Biblical drama with costume and scenery. Later on, another example is visible in Méhul's ' Joseph '—the masterpiece of a remarkable composer far too neglected at the present time : also Meyerbeer. who for practical purposes may be counted as a Frenchman, made his first boyish essay in opera with a libretto on the same story as that used by Montéclair. There were, no doubt, concert-oratorios written now and then, chiefly more or less strongly influenced by Italian methods, though not to the extent (as with contemporary Germans) of the abandonment of the native language. Gossec's ' Saul ' seems to have had considerable success, and Lesueur produced a good many works of the kind— a Christmas oratorio, two Passion-oratorios, three Coronation-oratorios, ' Debora,' ' Rachel,' etc. etc.—of which his pupil Berlioz can speak with respect. Cherubini, however, though the list of sacred works produced by him in Paris is a long one, used exclusively liturgical words ; and it was reserved for the wayward pupil of these two pillars of the old regime to produce, in the year 1854, what is really the first French oratorio of lasting artistic importance that exists.

The sub-title of Berlioz's ' L'Enfance du Christ ' is ' trilogie sacrée ' ; and as a matter of fact the work is a mosaic. The second section, ' La Fuite en Égypte,' was written several years before the others, and was published by itself as a ' mystère ' : the oratorio as a whole is of singular beauty, and shows Berlioz in an almost unique light. Though designed for the concert-room, it looks at times towards the stage : and a similar twofold aspect is visible in the (otherwise very different) most recent important French oratorios, d'Indy's ' Légende de St. Christophe ' (1915) and Honegger's ' Le Roi David ' (1921). Of all later French oratorio composers, César Franck is, however, certainly the one who has inherited most of Berlioz's spirit, though his great sacred work ' Les Béatitudes ' is not entitled an oratorio, and is not strictly Biblical in subject : but, as we so often notice, the mere label that a composer may choose to give to his work is of but little importance in broad classification of art-forms. Besides this Franck also produced several ' Scènes bibliques,' or short oratorios ; of these ' Rebecca ' is a typical example. Almost all his vocal writings are much earlier than the instrumental by which he is best known : ' Ruth,' one of his most poetical works, dates in its original form from 1845, and his ' Rédemption ' preceded its better-known namesake by half a generation.

The oratorios of Gounod and Massenet and Saint-Saëns strike other notes. Massenet's ' Ève ' and ' Marie Madeleine ' and Saint-Saëns's ' Le Déluge ' all represent in very clear and definite shape what we may perhaps call the ' salon ' idea of oratorio, though the two composers approach their goal from different sides. Massenet is the more Parisian, Saint-Saëns the more ' dans le style ancien ' : the latter's ' The Promised Land ' (produced at the Gloucester Festival of 1913) is an appeal to what was supposed to be English taste. In the musical career of Gounod operatic composition is a long interlude of some thirty years or more, religious subjects chiefly engrossing his pen both in his early youth and also towards the close of his life. The St. Cecilia

Mass (the first ' Messe solennelle ') was the earliest work to give him fame in England ; and more than thirty years afterwards ' The Redemption ' was produced at Birmingham, in 1882, and was followed at the next festival three years later by ' Mors et Vita.' Gounod's two oratorios are of historical importance to English musicians, inasmuch as they represent one of the latest attempts at foreign domination of English music. While it lasted, it was a serious menace.

A brief paragraph may perhaps be given to the modern Belgian school of oratorio, the chief names in which are Peter Benoît (1834–1901) and, in the younger generation, Edgar Tinel. Franck, whom we have already mentioned, was indeed a Belgian by birth, but he was a Frenchman by long residence ; and his works show no sympathy with the school founded by Benoît, the leading principle of which was the employment of the Flemish language in all vocal music. The list of Benoît's works includes several oratorios, ' Lucifer,' ' De Schelde ' (more properly styled a cantata), a ' Children's Oratorio ' and others ; Tinel's chief work, ' Franciskus,' is laid out on a large scale so as to include musical treatment of all the salient features in the life of St. Francis of Assisi, both before and after his conversion. Neither Benoît nor Tinel can reach the level of their self-denationalised compatriot Franck ; and very possibly their enthusiastic attempts to galvanise an artificial music-school hindered their really natural freedom of utterance, though still Franck would have remained as inherently far the greatest talent.

THE ENGLISH TYPES.—We may now, in conclusion, turn to the English school of oratorio composers since Handel. The great Anglo-German impresario achieved his most brilliant *coup* in his discovery that, although there had not been the very faintest trace of any such thing as English oratorio before he wrote one himself, yet the art-form was, above all others, the one to which the average English person would cling with the most tenacious affection. Directly after the success of ' Esther,' Greene rushed into the field with ' Deborah ' (1732) and ' Jephtha ' (1737) ; but neither these nor Boyce's ' David's Lamentation ' (1736) nor the ' Judith ' (1733) of the much inferior Defesch, a Fleming just then settled in London, seem to have secured more than transient fame. Arne's first oratorio, ' Abel,' dates from 1744, and his second and more important, ' Judith,' from twenty years later ; his technical equipment was never of the most complete kind, but he was saved from complete submission to the Handelian domination by his artistic kinship with his native folk-music. But with Arne's death in 1775 English oratorio music entered on a century of artistic darkness, over which brooded from first to last the elephantine shadow of Handel, to which was added in the final thirty years the almost equally universal though less ostentatiously ponderous shadow of Mendelssohn. The composers of these tons of oratorios were ' all honourable men '; their visions of things outside the organ-loft were usually fitful and reluctant, but they worked hard and conscientiously, and their music is nothing worse than intolerably dull. They set, with apparently absolute indiscrimination, wellnigh every word of the Bible; and when they were not writing oratorios of their own, they were still making them out of the mangled remains of other men's music. Operas of Handel, masses of Haydn, instrumental music of Mozart and Beethoven—all were fish to the net of this insatiable oratorio-demanding public; and most English musicians devoted the greater part of their energies to the task of satisfying it in one way or the other. From the middle of the 18th century down to the renascence more than a hundred years later, English music is a darkness relieved only by the wandering lights of talents that, in happier circumstances, might have been geniuses.

But it is undeniable that these talents did exist; and some of them were very remarkable talents too. All through the century some, with whom we have here no concern, showed their real worth in other fields than oratorio; the greatest of these, Samuel Wesley, the remarkable father of a better-known but hardly on the whole quite so remarkable son, wrote between the ages of 6 and 11 a couple of oratorios, ' Ruth ' and ' The Death of Abel,' which are at least as good as the grown-up work of most of his contemporaries, but he afterwards diverged into liturgical music. Crotch's ' Palestine ' is probably the best specimen of English oratorio during the half-century after Arne's death; and anyhow, the oratorios that were mainly imitations of Handel possess a sort of satisfactory downrightness of attitude which is lacking in most of those of rather later date, where the old influence is weakened by the addition of reminiscences of the inferior moments of Spohr or Mendelssohn. Sterndale Bennett's ' The Woman of Samaria ' is probably the best of the oratorios of this later period; but ' the best in this kind are but shadows.' ' Pierson's Jerusalem ' (1852) represents, however, a side-path; it is a transitional work, owing very little to either Handel or Mendelssohn, and interesting as an early sign of revolt.

The notable revival of English oratorio has been chiefly due to Parry, Stanford, Mackenzie and, in later days, Elgar. Some of these have indeed turned, to a considerable extent, to other fields; Mackenzie's ' Rose of Sharon ' (1883) showed a promise that has hardly been fulfilled, and Stanford produced no strictly non-liturgical religious music except ' The Three

Holy Children ' and ' Eden,' both comparatively early works. But the latter's other religious music also helped on the movement very greatly; and Parry's three oratorios and numerous oratorio-like cantatas are the works that did perhaps most to build up his fame, while Elgar's three chief productions, ' The Dream of Gerontius,' ' The Apostles ' and ' The Kingdom,' approach the problem with equal sincerity from an entirely different side, and, like Walford Davies's ' Everyman,' added yet further impetus to the revival.

CONCLUSION.—As we have seen, the history of oratorio has been that of an art-form with exceedingly ill-defined boundaries. On the one hand, it has in the past often, by insensible degrees, become practically identical with opera or with purely secular cantata; on the other, it still often passes imperceptibly into pure worship-music, or into the recently developed choral art-form that is associated with poetry of a lofty but non-religious character. In these pages the boundary line has been fixed so as to include, along with all works named oratorios by their composers, all those written for chorus and orchestra (on a scale of certain dimensions) to words definitely religious, but at the same time neither by fact nor by implication a mere part of a church service. Consequently, while the more modern Passion-music compositions have been included as complete ' services ' in themselves,[1] the German church cantatas have been ruled out as being nothing more than an incident in regular worship, like the English anthem; and similarly all motets and settings of the ordinary Mass, the Requiem Mass, the Te Deum, the Stabat Mater, or of any Psalms, have been judged outside the field even if designed for self-contained, non-liturgical presentation. The line has been drawn in full and lively consciousness of its very faint character; but a line of some kind is necessary, and all others seemed fainter still. It appears now, however, most probable that certain kinds of oratorio, which in the not so recent past have been much favoured, will attract at any rate the foremost composers no longer. The old type of oratorio libretto, the hack-work of men totally devoid of either religious discrimination or literary instinct, is very justly dead; composers are more and more seeking their inspiration in fine original poetry, whether strictly religious or what may perhaps be called ' ethically religious ' in character, and when preferring to select scriptural words, generally do so with a subtle thoughtfulness very seldom shown in earlier times.

For an art-form undergoing such a process of rejuvenation, there ought normally to be a noteworthy future; but possibly the new birth

---

[1] Keiser's ' Passions,' anyhow, were definitely called oratorios by their composer.

has come too late. All over Europe, and certainly not least in England, the younger musicians are turning their faces elsewhere; but this may be only a passing phase, and the fascination may again make itself felt. But the oratorio of the future will have to recognise that the days of preferential treatment are over, and that the new works must stand or fall as music, and as music alone; the demand to be heard solely in surroundings where non-musical associations are overwhelming and where the voice of criticism is silenced can no longer be tolerated, and the plea that a work can only be fairly judged in a mediæval cathedral must be taken as a confession that it cannot stand on its own merits. The appeal made by a Madonna of Giovanni Bellini loses not one whit of its essential force when addressed to those who are parted by many a long mile from its creator's own ways of thought; similarly the religious music of the future must stand, as the great religious music of the past stands now, in the light of day and in the rush of the world, by its appeal to us as men and as musicians.

E. W.

ORATORIO SOCIETY, see under NEW YORK.

ORAZI ED I CURIAZI, GLI, opera in 3 acts; libretto by Sografi, music by Cimarosa. Produced Venice, 1794; Théâtre Odéon, Paris, June 16, 1813.   G.

ORAZIO DEL VIOLONO (or DE PARMA; real name ORAZIO BASSANI), a 16th-17th century viol-player and composer whose fame spread all over Europe, his compositions becoming very popular. A few of his MS. pieces are in the British Museum library. André Maugars, who speaks of him in his *Réponse faite à un curieux* (1639), knew him personally, at a very advanced age (E. v. d. Straeten, *History of the Violoncello*).

ORCHÉSOGRAPHIE, see ARBEAU.

ORCHESTRA (Gr. ὀρχήστρα — *orchestra*; Fr. *orchestre*; Ger. *Orchester*; Ital. *orchestra*), literally 'a dancing place'; that portion of the Greek theatre between the semicircular seats of the auditorium (in Latin *cavea*; there is no Greek equivalent) and the stage buildings. This space, a few inches below the front row of seats, was about 60 feet in diameter in the theatre of Dionysus at Athens. It was here that the Chorus, numbering from 12 to 15 persons, sang or performed their evolutions round the statue of Dionysus which stood in the centre. They did not obstruct the view of the stage (λογεῖον—*logeion*—or 'speaking place'), which was 12 feet in height. The Greek Orchestra was also known from its shape as σίγμα—*sigma* —from its resembling the curve of the archaic C, the old form of the letter Σ or S. It was also described as κονίστρα — *konistra* — ' the sandy place '—either because at one time it was not paved (as it later was and still is) or in

Roman times because it was used as the arena for gladiatorial contests. With the Romans, copying, as near as need be, the Greek model of the theatre, the 'Orchestra' became absorbed into the auditorium with seats for the audience, while the Chorus performed on the stage. The departure of the word 'Orchestra' from its original meaning and its application to a body of instrumentalists and the position which they occupy in a building have yet to be explained. It may have been chosen under the mistaken idea that instrumental music was prominent in Greek choruses, whereas it was subordinate to the words and simple in character. It crept into the currency of language like other musical terms. In the comedies of Molière, in which music plays so important a part, the musicians at first were concealed behind a trellis, but in 1671 they appeared on the stage in appropriate costume. Their position varied; sometimes they were behind the audience, sometimes at the back of the stage, sometimes before the footlights as with us, or in the wings — the position adopted (1871) in the Théâtre Français when a play of Molière is being performed. When the Orchestra was not on the stage or before the footlights, the leader had to remember his cues to obviate the prompter's shouting to him 'Jouez!'

The practice initiated by Wagner at Bayreuth of placing the orchestral players out of sight of the audience has been generally adopted, but the idea was foreshadowed by Grétry.

W. W.

ORCHESTRATION (or INSTRUMENTATION). The art of combining in a musical work instruments of different timbres, so as to obtain contrast of colour, individuality and balance of tone. Composition and orchestration have gone hand in hand. At times one has been a little in advance of the other, the composer calling to his aid the maker of instruments when desiring a special effect; the maker inventing models to improve or replace instruments already in existence; the instrumentalist in his turn studying and practising the new or enlarged technique demanded by these innovations.

There are plentiful references to musical instruments from the year 1300 onwards, but we do not know what music was played in the earlier days. Voice parts at first supplied the material, and could have been followed only when the music was simple, for the instruments, with their primitive construction, could not have kept up with the complicated meanderings of mediæval counterpoint. The accounts and inventories of the Lord Chamberlain from the reign of Edward III. contain long lists of musicians attached to and paid by the English court. Edward IV. in the 14th century had trumpets, lutes, rebec, trombone, viol, cornemuse, flute, virginals and drums In France at the beginning of the 16th century, in the reign of Francis I., orchestras were common, and performed on all occasions. These bands were attached to a court establishment, known as the *écurie*, which had two divisions, the *grande* and the *petite*. It was from the first of these that Lully obtained his extra instruments. Stringed instruments, such as the viol family and lute, supplied the music at court, but for the dances of the people there were added oboes, flutes, trumpets, trombones and drums. In England there was much viol-playing, and in an inventory of Henry VIII., made in 1547, there were 64 stringed instruments, 215 wind instruments, not to speak of innumerable keyboard instruments In the National Portrait Gallery there is a painting, dated 1596, in which musicians are represented playing from music on a viol, flute, cittern, pandore, lute and viola da gamba.[1] In Italy the nobility had their own private bands. The best known was that of the Duke of Ferrara, Alfonzo II., whose maestro di cappella was Fiorino, born in 1540. In connexion with this band we come across one of the earliest references to the use of a baton, and also to a woman conductor. But while the strictest discipline was enforced among the musicians of Ferrara, there is a description, published in 1554, of a concert in Italy in which those taking part amused themselves by singing or playing out of time and tune. In the 16th century a curious practice crept in. It was called counterpoint *alla mente*. A theme was given out, usually one from the church ritual, which each singer embroidered according to his fancy, the instrumentalists following suit (cf. DISCANT). It came to an end about 1625, but some fifty years later a composer, Graziani, went the length of suggesting that the instrumentalist might improvise on the accompaniments of his hymns.

In Tudor days in England music was well established in royal favour. Queen Elizabeth had an orchestra of about 40, and her own prowess as a virtuoso is beyond all challenge. While the English school of players on stringed instruments reigned supreme (see FANCY; IN NOMINE), there was not yet a clear understanding as to the most fitting types of instruments. Consistency was not to be expected when everything depended on the means at hand.

In the three-score years between Queen Elizabeth's orchestra and that of Landi it is evident that composers had to make the most of their musical environment. The strings were approaching some consistency, but the instrumental body showed wide divergencies in each case. There was no recognised standard, and a score which had served its purpose in Italy could not be performed elsewhere unless local talent and conditions could be guaranteed. Technique was not within the reach of every-

[1] Cf. Morley's *Consort Lessons*.

body, and those who had attained it were not always disposed to impart their secrets to others. It is difficult to give a comparative table of the orchestras of this period owing to confusion as to what instruments were included under the generic names of VIOL and LUTE (*q.v.*). Later on a similar problem was to arise in the case of instruments which, though bearing the same name, could not have sounded alike owing to mechanical improvements, apart from the question of technique.

The foregoing survey of a large and important period may be summed up in a few words. The voice at first dominated the situation and the instrumentalists followed. But gradually composers, who were instrumentalists as well, rebelled against this subservience, even though they had acquired from the quartet of voices that just balance which little by little influenced their string parts. In falling back upon such instruments of the wind-type as were available, they discovered a means of escape from the tyranny of that which was meant to be sung. They contrived devices of their own; agreeable combinations of sounds of different timbres, doubtless harsh enough to modern ears, but the discovery was far-reaching. Like all innovations which aim at levelling up a groove, the response was not encouraging. Even in the section of bowed instruments the crescendo mark provoked a mutiny: the tremolo and pizzicato were regarded by viol and violin players as vulgar and degrading. But the art of music was coming into its kingdom, and whatever was new proved its worth. (See VIOLIN-PLAYING.)

There is no need to dwell upon the absurdities found in some scores of the 16th and 17th centuries—giant double basses, windmills strung with ropes, cannons and bombs. It is, however, interesting to find Wagner's use of the harp in the Fire Music of 'Die Walküre' anticipated by over 150 years by Brossard in a cantata on a subject taken from the Book of Daniel. To the eye, at least, the account of the score has a modern look, with flutes, oboes, bassoons, trumpets and drums, in addition to violins.

Composers appear to have been occupied more with the construction of their theme than with the manner of presenting it. Lully was content to write the melody and the bass, leaving the middle parts and such scoring as was requisite to his copyists Lalouette and Colasse. Grétry was equally indifferent, and it was said of his scores that you could drive a coach-and-four between the treble and bass. With the advanced technique of modern times it comes as a surprise to learn that some of Lully's violin passages were declared impossible and often raised storms among his instrumentalists. It is even more strange that in the first quarter of the 18th century there were scarcely any violinists at the court of France who could read at sight. (See VIOLIN-PLAYING.)

THE CLASSICAL STYLE.—The point was reached when there were three elements to be considered, the music of the day, the person to play it, and the instrument itself. The last opens up a very large question. With the exception of the trombone and drums every instrument in the orchestra has been altered or modified structurally, and mechanical improvements have had their effect upon their tone or timbre. There was no organised system of laying out an orchestral score till the middle of the 18th century, when Gossec, followed by Haydn, in spite of obstacles and limitations, laid the foundations of the modern orchestra (see SCORE). This, however, needs qualification. It is by no means certain that orchestral works written before the first quarter of the 19th century, when played by a modern orchestra, would convey to modern ears what their several composers heard. At best it is only a paper estimate that can be formed : the resemblance is only in name. The flute as we know it is not the instrument that a flautist of the 18th or early 19th century had in his hands. If some of Bach's flute passages are unplayable even on the modern model with Boehm's principle, they would have been the more impossible on the contemporary instrument. The mechanism of keys and levers now enables the fingers to control holes scientifically cut at points which otherwise would have been awkward to reach. This mechanism was in use on a very primitive but unscientific scale in Haydn's day, and tentatively in Bach's. The modern flute is different in tone as well. The diameter of the holes and their position have been altered to the extent that the flute-tone in its lower compass approaches that of the clarinet. The lever system was not invented by Boehm : it was in use throughout the wood-wind group ; obviously some appliance of the kind was necessary for big instruments like the obsolete ophicleide and serpent. The task for all the wood-wind group was to play the notes and to keep in tune ; expression and delicacy of phrasing were an afterthought. Even the violin was not to escape reconstruction, imperative in many cases owing to worm-holes. It is safe to say that there is scarcely an instrument of the string family in use in our orchestras, from the violin to the double bass, which has not been rebuilt. The neck of the violin was lengthened and the tilt of the finger-board increased so as to conform with the height of the modern bridge. Its architecture was revised in the light of the higher pitch, and even the bow was reformed. (See BOW and VIOLIN FAMILY.) It is clear that these modifications, introduced almost imperceptibly, affected the tone of the instruments, the technique of those who handled them, and, above all, the scope of the composer.

But beyond these a further mechanical device was to open up a fresh field, namely, the application of valves to horn and trumpet. To grasp the full significance of these revolutions a backward glance is necessary. A score of Bach, for example, corresponds with a modern score only in name. His instrumental technique was greatly determined by the limitations of the keyboard instrument of the period. The harpsichord had not sustaining power, consequently it was necessary to keep the parts moving. Hence much of his orchestration appears at first sight as if transcribed from a score for some keyboard instrument which allowed for rapidity of execution. We are left in doubt how some parts were played. It has just been pointed out that there are flute passages outside the capacity of the average player, and the same may be said of the much-debated trumpet passages, the problem of which remains unsolved. Trumpet-players there are who declare that the high and rapid passages were never played ; others have suggested that these and similar florid parts were performed on appropriate organ stops. A further theory is that they demanded a technique which is now lost. This is the less credible ; for the lip-pressure or embouchure of a trumpet-player cannot have changed in less than two hundred years.

Brandenburg Concerto, No. 2.
Ex. 1. Tromba in F, sounding a fourth higher.

It has been generally assumed that these so-called trumpet passages were actually played on the trumpet, but were they ? Again, a theory, hitherto not put forward, may clear the air. It is on record that instrumentalists jealous of their proficiency deliberately concealed their technique from others. Might there not have been among Bach's friends some executant who, by means of a secret invention of his own, was able to play the critical phrases and to soften what to modern ears are almost invariably harsh and piercing tones ? The ' Bach trumpet ' in use to-day cannot be accepted as an agreeable substitute. Bach's resources were by no means limited. On paper he had as wide a field as the most exacting and unreasonable modern composer. He did not, however, employ all his instruments in every score, but selected those which he considered appropriate for each work ; possibly, too, he was limited as to use by local conditions. We find flutes, oboes, oboe d' amore, oboe da caccia, bassoons ; horns, trumpets, trombones, drums, bells. There are violins, viol, piccolo, viola d' amore, viola pomposa (midway between viola and violoncello), viola da gamba, violoncello and double bass : organ and harpsichord or clavichord. The variety of type of single instruments is striking. The difficulty of obtaining competent players for out-of-the-way instruments may partly explain why Bach's music did not travel far beyond his own frontier. Neither to him nor to Handel was the art of the orchestra indebted for signs of development. To them the function of the orchestra was accompaniment for the most part, and the persistent figured bass left the empty bars to be filled in by an improvisation which may not have been discreet in hands other than the composer's. (See ADDITIONAL ACCOMPANIMENTS ; THOROUGH-BASS.)

No greater contrast could there have been between the orchestration of Bach and Handel and the school of instrumental and operatic music that was arising. In accomplishment it was a protest against the shallowness of the French and Italian music in vogue in the first half of the 18th century. Bach founded his style upon structure, colour taking a secondary, almost an accidental place. Nevertheless he had a free hand in his little preludes leading up to the entrance of his voices, and, within his limited means, with the economy of timbres which tied him to the resources of his day, he embroidered his themes in his own distinctive fashion. It was not for him to erect an orchestral tradition ; his instruments for the most part were destined to silence in the glass cases of museums ; but he still speaks in his own tongue.

The first steps towards obtaining some consistency in the orchestral organism were taken by Rameau. Apart from his conception of the overture as a formal movement, he was a colourist as well. To colour, then, he gave his mind, and opera, not altogether formless with its slavish adherence to patterns, became the canvas for his brush. In his scores the instruments are the same in name as in Beethoven's, with the exception of the clarinet, which did not make its début in the orchestra till later. If he did nothing more than follow convention by doubling wood-wind with strings and give them holding notes, at least he gave composers an opportunity for hearing strings and wind in combination, along with timid adventurings towards thematic development. The static quality of the orchestra, however, had not yet been established, for in certain of his MSS. there were additions by another hand. Thus this composer, like Lully, and Grétry, whose *aide d'orchestre* was Panseron, seems to have been the victim of tradition in this respect.

The art of music had advanced to a point when fashion intruded. The taste of the period required of a composition that it should illustrate a thunder-storm, a tempest, the murmur of a stream, the song of a nightingale, and Rameau conceded. Was Beethoven aware of this ? Rameau went further : he invented character in his orchestration, and did not hesitate to combine two opposing forms of dramatic thought. The incongruity of two antagonistic personages singing the same air with different feelings struck him as capable of interpretation only by orchestral means.

To Gossec belongs the credit of having established the symphonic orchestra, just a shade in advance of Haydn. By adding two clarinets he completed the small symphonic orchestra as we know it.[1] But the progress of the clarinet was slow, for the reason that it was still in an embryonic state, and composers who used it were limited to two keys only. Whatever its timbre at this stage of its life, it was recognised as a valuable addition to the wood-wind section, and the instrument-makers had to keep pace with the composers. Gossec was an innovator in another direction with his two orchestras in his 'Messe des Morts.' The second of these consisted of clarinets, horns or trumpets and three trombones which alternated with the first.

We now arrive at the composer who was to reform not only the orchestra but the opera as well. Gluck, born in Bavaria, greatly influenced by Handel, greatly influencing Berlioz, departed from the empty librettos which were used as stopgaps for vacuous operas and went to poets for his material. His great discovery was the emotional side of the orchestra. Not content to allow it to play a passive rôle in accompanying, he used it as the interpreter of character, as colouring, adding to the force of the words that were being sung, and heightening the dramatic situation and action. This was a marked change from the practice of earlier composers, who were content with a single line or phrase upon which to hang an entire aria. One of Gluck's greatest innovations was his emphasising the importance and function of the overture. Up to his day, in opera, at least, it served merely to play the audience in, and often it had no connexion with the work that followed, or had done duty elsewhere. In two of his operas, 'Naïs' and 'Acanto et Céphise,' Rameau had attempted to crystallise a résumé of the whole, but it was left to Gluck, and after him Mozart, to make the overture an integral part of the work. Like the preludes to 'Tristan,' 'Die Meistersinger' and 'Parsifal,' Gluck's overtures were continuous with the opening scene, and it was Wagner himself who provided a formal ending[2] for 'Iphigenia in Aulis' for concert

[1] See also the symphonies of Stamitz and others of the Mannheim school. *D.D.T.* 2nd series, viii. 2.
[2] He did a good deal more. He practically rewrote the entire work and introduced a new character.

oerformance. As for the orchestra, Gluck banished the harpsichord, which hitherto had its
place among the other instruments, and with it
the last trace of the basso continuo. (The purpose of the keyboard instrument had been to
supply from the figured bass the accompaniments to recitative, and also, it may be assumed, to give confidence to and prompt the
singers in opera. The conductor presided at it,
and constant were the differences between him
and the leader of the first violins as to which
was the more important personage.) Although
the trombone—the oldest instrument in the
orchestra—had appeared in many an earlier
score, it was left to Gluck to discover its secrets,
which he revealed with imposing effect in the
famous ' Divinités du Styx.' [1] Other regular
constituents of his orchestra were the harp,
cymbals, triangle and bass drum. While his
works were being performed in Italy he employed two English horns (cor anglais), which
were obtainable there, but in Paris the parts
were transposed for the clarinets then coming
into use. While opera in France about the
middle of the 18th century was said to be a
fracas, and, as Molière had earlier remarked,
the most expensive of all noises, in Italy the
orchestra was said to be treated like a huge
guitar. So much attention was given to the
voice that the orchestra was subordinated, and
there was less freedom for purely instrumental
music. Hence it was that Italian composers
contributed little to the development of the
orchestra, although it was mainly to them that
we are indebted—whether in a good or bad
sense — for the rise and spread of virtuoso
violin-playing. Opera everywhere monopolised
the attention, as much because there was a
popular demand as because it was profitable. [2]

We are now at the point when the ear began
to decide which instruments were to survive as
fittest. It is difficult to understand how the
survival came about, for, as has already been
pointed out, the wood-wind up to Beethoven's
day could not have sounded exactly as we hear
these instruments to-day. The lack of good
players on the clarinet, even in Mozart's time,
probably delayed the adoption of this instrument until after the flute, oboe and bassoon
had become regular members. There is not a
clarinet in Mozart's ' Jupiter' symphony,
written in 1788, but in his E flat symphony
he employs two, omitting the oboe. There
is no need to draw far-fetched conclusions from
these happenings ; it is just as likely that some
very commonplace explanation was at the root.
We know that Mozart often had to work
against time—witness the overture to ' Don

Giovanni,' written in a night, parts copied next
day and played at sight in the evening, probably very badly. (See Mozart, ante, p. 551.)
It may be pointed out that owing to the conditions under which they lived Haydn and
Mozart frequently had to write at high pressure
in order to satisfy their patrons.

It is not unlikely that the wood-wind group
was selected because the instruments composing it were the least disagreeable at the time,
and had the more efficient players. The
Haydn and Mozart orchestra consisted of
about 35 players, the wind and percussion
accounting for from 11 to 13 instruments—
flutes, oboes, clarinets (occasionally), bassoons, horns, trumpets, trombones (occasionally, though not in symphonies), percussion and
strings. The same force was used by Beethoven, with double bassoon and cymbals
added. The Dresden Opera Orchestra of 1754
consisted of 8 first and 7 second violins, 4
violas, 3 violoncellos, 3 basses, 2 flutes, 5
oboes, 5 bassoons, 2 horns, 3 trumpets and
3 timpani. This balance on paper looks too
reedy in tone and probably harsh. In contrast the numbers of the performers in the
Handel Commemoration Festival in Westminster Abbey in 1784 may be given. The
chorus of 274 was made up of 59 sopranos, 48
altos, 83 tenors and 84 basses. With them
were 48 first and 47 second violins, 26 violas,
21 violoncellos, 15 double basses. The wind
section comprised 6 flutes, 6 oboes, 26
bassoons, 1 double bassoon, 12 trumpets, 12
horns, 6 trombones and 4 pairs of drums. [3]
Burney mentions that twelve oboes played
a solo as one man, and that a bassoon solo was
' performed by twenty-four bassoons, of which
the unity of effect was truly marvellous.' He
rejoiced that there was no ' Manuductor' [4] or
conductor, and that there was only one full
rehearsal ! An examination of these forces
indicates a predominance of tenors and basses
over the female voices. As for the orchestra,
it may be asked if the proportion of 6 flutes to
26 oboes and 26 bassoons throws any light
upon the relative penetrating power of these
instruments in the period in which they were
used.

It is interesting to note how much Mozart
made of certain sections of the wood-wind
when he discovered their capabilities. A
Divertissement of 1771 is written for 2 clarinets
and 2 English horns. [5] But on one occasion
when clarinets were not at hand, he transposed
their parts for English horns, forming a quartet
of these instruments. Another Divertissement of 1773 has 2 oboes, 2 clarinets, 2
English horns, 2 horns and 2 bassoons (K. 186).

1 See Berlioz's *Instrumentation* (English edition, Novello), p. 157.
2 If we read contemporary accounts in diaries and records of
travel, it appears that opera, as far as public support was concerned,
was no more than a social affair in which music was the excuse for
intrigue and rendezvous. At this period the opera-house and the
composers of operas had lowered themselves to the prevailing
unworthiness of taste and morals.

3 A pair of the last were known as the Tower drums, lent by the
Ordnance from the Tower stores. They were captured by Marlborough at Malplaquet in 1709.
4 *Commemoration of Handel*, p. 15.
5 See Köchel, *Verzeichnis*, note to 113

Mozart was fond of the basset horn (see CLARINET), an instrument which should be used more frequently. He wrote an adagio for three, combined with two clarinets, and from this it is to be inferred that players on these instruments were available (K. 411). We do not know if all his performances passed off without a hitch, but it is likely that he had trustworthy wind players, for he wrote 10 concertos for wind and only 6 for violin amid his immense output.

Important as were the mechanical improvements in the wood - wind, reforms of greater moment were approaching. The scope of horns and trumpets up to the time of Beethoven and for some little time after was restricted. They could not play a complete chromatic scale, but only the notes of the harmonic chord. Beethoven, with rare exceptions, used about a bare dozen of these notes. In the last movement of Mozart's 'Jupiter' symphony there are only eight, of which only one complete triad, that of C, can be constituted, while the dominant chord of G has the bare fifth owing to the difficulty of producing the B. (See HORN; TRUMPET; VALVE.)

Some further instances will illustrate the restrictions. The overture to 'Fidelio' is in E, but Beethoven prescribed trumpets in C, in whose harmonic series the only note common to the key is E, the major third of C. Whenever, therefore, the tonic chord of E occurs in the movement, the trumpet can play, and play it does, its single note of E, and that one hundred times, no less. In the andante of the C minor symphony, which is in the key of A flat, the horns are crooked in C, providing only one note, C, the third of A flat, but playing tonic and dominant in the key of C when the movement modulates to that key. Again, in the 'Eroica' (movement and horns in E flat), after the well-known passage with the horn playing the tonic chord against the dominant seventh of the violins, the first horn changes to his F crook when the theme appears in that key. In Schubert's 'Unfinished' symphony, in the second movement the second trumpet in the midst of a *tutti* is given rests in bars in which the then impracticable F sharp is the note required. In 'Fidelio,' in the aria 'Komm, Hoffnung,' the three horns have passages which must have sounded doubtful on the natural horn, and there is the famous passage for the fourth horn in the ninth symphony, which has given rise to various explanations.[1] It is singular that composers employed horns and trumpets at all with their obvious limitations. At the present day, even with the parts played on instruments furnished with valves, the persistence of tonic and dominant can be particularly monotonous and irritating to a mind that has grown accustomed to a wider province of

harmony. Their sudden entry and equally sudden silence suggest to those unaware of the technical defects of the instruments mistakes on the part of the musician or carelessness on the part of the conductor.

In a long work, such as an opera, the horn-player had to provide himself with a number of crooks, and be constantly putting them in or taking them out according to the directions in his part. Forsyth[2] mentions 35 of these changes in 'Don Giovanni.' For the four horns in 'Fidelio' there are over 25, comprising 9 different crooks. With valves the horn-player now uses one crook only, that in F, which gives him a complete chromatic scale of four octaves. With this he transposes at sight, no matter what crook other than the F is indicated, but occasionally he has to substitute the crook required in the score when the notes to be played are outside his compass.

When composers were agreed upon the constitution of the orchestra, or when it appeared to become stereotyped, the instrument-makers set to work to improve the types in vogue, with sundry excursions in search of new timbres. But even with the accepted material it was possible to carry orchestration further. It may be of antiquarian interest here to consider to whom innovations were due. It is claimed for Philidor that he introduced the tam-tam; Méhul employed four horns; Cherubini divided his violoncelli into four parts; Lesueur, in an opera based upon Ossian, had 6 first and 6 second harps. Méhul went to the same source, and in his opera 'Uthal' dispensed with violins; he also wrote a part in 'Joseph' for the tuba, probably to represent the shofar. (See HEBREW MUSIC.) In the year 1795 there was a professor of the 'tuba curva' at the Paris Conservatoire. In another direction Boieldieu, who was praised as heartily by Weber as 'La favorita' was condemned at a later date by Schumann for its 'marionette music,' outlined a definite programme in 'Le Petit Chaperon rouge,' in which the story is illustrated by music in minute detail.

In the evolution of the orchestra there are many *petits-maîtres* now forgotten whose happy ideas were captured by greater men and afterwards accredited to them. The fact, however, remains that music was reaching out and bringing into the fold such diversities of thought and of invention that he would be rash who would assign to any composer the honour of having been the first to suggest a proceeding which in time became the common currency. Therefore while claims have been made on the part of this or that composer, surely enough in some corner of the world there will be produced evidence to demolish that claim.

Although orchestral music towards the close of the 18th century strikes us as simple in char-

---

[1] See the *Mus. T.* for Feb. and Mar. 1925.

[2] Cecil Forsyth, *Orchestration*, p. 82, note.

acter, it is strange to read the protest made by Grétry, Lemoine, Cherubini, Méhul and Lesueur against the contemporary school of music. They said :

> ' Harmony to-day is complicated to the last degree. Singers and instruments have exceeded their natural compass. The rapidity of execution makes our music inappreciable by the ear, and one step more will plunge us into chaos.'

This was Grétry's opinion, and it may be compared with another manifesto of a later date. The protest was made during the lifetime of Mozart, but from the progress of music it would be difficult to understand or to justify it nowadays. Whatever contemporaries felt as to style, with the exception of Beethoven there appears a sameness, if not a monotony, in the compositions that date from the beginning of the 19th century. It is not easy to differentiate between one composer and another. Their names, if not their music, may be familiar, but there are no very marked grounds for putting each into a self-contained compartment and considering him apart from his contemporaries. We have to resort to chronology for our bearings, rather than to schools, for there was a great deal of overlapping, and many composers were so entangled in the snares of opera that, with all that we know and have heard, we might not find arresting qualities in style between two works of the same period. There may be points in construction and development which are of interest, but orchestration was proceeding upon lines which had become conventional. But there were exceptions, and they are still with us.

We have independence of thought in Schubert, as shown in his ' Unfinished ' and C major symphonies. It is inconceivable that a young composer, living in the same city with Beethoven, should not have acquired a tinge of his idiom. Almost the only music that he could have heard must have been that of his great predecessors, Haydn and Mozart, and of his contemporary, yet of their styles there is no trace in these symphonies. Like Weber in opera, Schubert went in search of character and melody in instruments that hitherto had often been humble but necessary servants. It was a great discovery that the horn was a melodic instrument, that the clarinet's independence commanded respect, that it was grateful to hear violas and violoncellos and even double basses emancipated from routine.

While the orchestra was growing in strength, its development was to have a profound effect upon composition. The art was being rent within itself by discord. Five years after the first performance of Beethoven's Choral Symphony there came the ' Symphonie fantastique ' of Berlioz. The one was incomprehensible to many ; the other, devastating. Whatever views that were held it is clear that a rift had appeared, and that tradition on its complacent side had received a shock. Composers still held to the style of Mozart or the earlier Beethoven, to the Italian or the French school of opera ; some felt that the frontier of music had been extended.

The greater certainty of accurate performances assured composers and enlarged their opportunities. The fiascos in Beethoven's day —Meyerbeer's blunder with the big drum in ' The Battle of Vittoria,' when Beethoven was conducting ; the extraordinary performance of the Choral Symphony, when the conductor, Polenz, was ordered to sit down—these fiascos were to be repeated up to the year 1876, when the scenic gear at Bayreuth went awry. But what at one time had been called ' the infallible test ' by the pianoforte of music primarily written for the orchestra no longer could be applied. The orchestral horizon was reaching far beyond the compass of a pair of hands ; themes arose suggested by the timbres of the various instruments and became intimately associated with them. At the same time composers grew conscious of a definite quality in orchestration, which, though they heard it, they were unable to analyse. Beethoven in his deafness could only fall back upon his earlier recollection of timbres ; for him it was the greater glory that he was able to summon at will the tones that in less afflicted days he had treasured. He knew well what effect he wished to produce, witness his direction, *sul ponticello*, in his op. 131, 18 bars of it, corrected to *da capo per l' ordinario*.

It is difficult to account for Berlioz and Wagner, for neither was in a position to learn the amplitude of orchestration from predecessor or contemporary, with the exception of Meyerbeer In some respects Meyerbeer was not unlike a well-to-do chemist, with the orchestra as his laboratory, and however much his results may be derided in an artistic sense, they were appreciated by those who were gifted with, and reacted to, a richer musical thought. So it was that Berlioz stampeded into darkness even those whom he had held up before all. It cannot be said of him or of Wagner at any period of their lives that they were fully aware of the bitter - sweetness produced on the ear by a studied combination of the upper partials of the wood-wind. (See ACOUSTICS.) Yet the ear, shackled to one pitch of a series, hears a good deal more, although it cannot define it in terms other than the sounds resulting from the written notes.

MODERN ORCHESTRATION may be said to date from the ' Symphonie fantastique ' of Berlioz. In the 63 bars of the opening Largo there are more expression marks and indicated nuances than in a Mozart symphony. This shows that he attached the utmost importance to tone and phrasing, and left nothing to the caprice of the individual player. With him it was not so much the material of the music as the method of handling it. In the strings he followed the conventions, for even the *col legno* effect was by no means new, it having dated from the technical studies of Michel Waldemar (1750–1816). It was copied by Meyerbeer in 'L'Africaine' some years later. In 'Also sprach Zarathustra' (p. 38, miniature score) Richard Strauss indicates a *tremolo col ligno* (*sic*) not quite to the advantage of the polish on the bow.

Berlioz raised the status of the wood-wind, adding importance to the English horn and E flat clarinet. The possibilities of the horn were ever in his mind, but he was handicapped by the system of crooks and had to devise complicated means whereby he could use the instrument more freely. It was not till a later day that he could avail himself of the valve mechanism. Melodically his horn passages were rare, and probably the instrumentalists upon whom he could depend preferred the valveless form. While using for the most part the orchestra required for Beethoven's ninth symphony, he added to the scope of each instrument, not always to the improvement of the balance of tone, and in many instances apparently to display his technical knowledge. Anticipated by Boieldieu in writing harmonics for the harp, he employed them effectively in the 'fairy' music in 'Faust' and 'Romeo.' Muted horns and trumpets make their way, but while he did not exceed their conventional number he had a singular leaning towards doubling instruments of which composers in modern times are content with one. He had triangles and tambourines in pairs in 'Romeo'; 2 ophicleides in the old edition of 'Faust' in the 'Amen' fugue (now 3 trombones and tuba); 2 tubas in 'Pandaemonium' in the same work; 4 bassoons with work for two; 4 harps (two first and two second, *al meno*, he stipulated); and 6 pianofortes in the 'Ronde du Sabbat' to sustain the two bell notes, foreshadowing the device that was adopted in 'Parsifal' for the same end.

It has never been explained why composers were reluctant to avail themselves of the advantages and facilities conferred by the use of instruments with valves. It may be that the difficulty lay with the horn-players and others, who were unwilling to accustom themselves to a new technique and were content to blare out tonic and dominant with abundance of rests. Berlioz, who had the flair for the capabilities of instruments more than any of his predecessors or contemporaries, devised an unnecessary complication of crooks for trumpets and cornets in addition to horns, in order to avail himself of their colour. Yet, though unable to play any instrument beyond the flute and guitar — if indeed he carried his experience of them beyond the elementary stage—he had mastered the mysteries of the brass instruments, of which those who used them constantly had not even dreamed. So we

find intricate problems of crooks which scarcely justified the pains. Wagner in 'Rienzi' was not timid; he asked for French horns in D, the key of the overture, pistons (? cornets) in G, valve trumpets in D, ordinary trumpets in D, three trombones, serpent and euphonium. A pretty affair this, and having got the length of 'The Dutchman' he required horns in F and D, trumpets in F, three trombones and an ophicleide.

To return to Berlioz; it is not certain where composition with him ended and orchestration began. He was so deeply read in all that concerned instruments that it is likely that he had them in mind more than any finely conceived theme. It was not always the noisy and macabre that appealed to him. The Queen Mab movement in 'Romeo' and the dance of Will-of-the-Wisps in 'Faust' belie this. The harmonics of harps and strings in the one, combined with the wood-wind, give an ethereal effect which, if not so delicate in the other, shows the importance that Berlioz attached to the wood-wind while subordinating the strings. Again in 'Faust' there are extensive passages for wood-wind, in which the strings are silent or have little to do. Striking effects are those in which what may be called the 'column' of brass is clearly balanced, but, as has been suggested, he gave himself needless trouble in crooking his horns, trumpets and cornets. In at least one movement he has six separate crooks for these instruments. It will ever be a mystery that with his analytical ear, surely the most sensitive to sound, he did not listen more to what his instruments could give forth. There are few of his bars that do not enshrine a secret; other composers, if they did not capture it wholly, at least learned from it, profited by it and then ungratefully scorned it. In the history of music there is no figure more pathetic than that of Berlioz, who, in despite, lacked the crowning gift. (See BERLIOZ; subsection THE ART OF BERLIOZ.)

These reinforcements of his outline to some extent reveal the drift of his thought as well as his profound knowledge of the orchestra. At the same time it may not be wide of the mark to assume that they indicated the general standard of ability of those who were to interpret his scores. Whatever may have been fortuitous or haphazard as regards innovations, whether conventional or standardised by custom in orchestration, it cannot be gainsaid that, apart from the unexpectedness of many of his effects, his *Traité de l'instrumentation*, published in 1844, came as an awakening and a message which no one in the world of music could afford to disregard. It is a sign of the progress of music in minds of vastly different calibre that strict chronological sequence cannot now be observed. The claims of one composer to a new orchestral device are always subject to challenge. In the opening bars of 'Die Walküre' Wagner gave the violins a double D, on the open string third and the stopped fourth string. Berlioz, in the 'Carnaval romain' had done the same on the first E string.[1] The 'many inventions' were being gathered into the common stock. To these Meyerbeer was no small contributor. Born six years before Schubert, twelve years before Berlioz, twenty-two before Wagner, he swiftly appreciated the tendencies of popular taste, and after following them at first, ultimately dictated them. A man of many styles and an incorrigible borrower, in his orchestration he indicated, more than any of his predecessors, the way to the employment of solo instruments. He would start with a Handelian phrase and then slip into Bellini. He certainly gave the public what the public wanted, writing his music round his audiences, trying effects at rehearsal, writing and rewriting till he hit upon what he thought would be effective, and this accounts for the five months that were spent in rehearsing 'The Huguenots' for the first performance in Berlin. He worked on a huge canvas, sometimes with miniature brushes, sometimes with a whitewash weapon, but whatever may be thought of his music now, in his orchestration he suggested combinations and effects by which every composer since has profited, none more than Wagner. Meyerbeer extended the use of the wood-wind, especially in the lower octaves. The emotional character of each in the various sections of its register was being developed. Thanks to him the bass clarinet, two of which were employed in 'L'Africaine,' became a regular member of the orchestra, and he added an alto clarinet as well. In the same opera he had two English horns. The 'Shadow Song' in 'Dinorah' was accompanied by flutes, harmonics of the harp, and violoncellos. There was also a fifth horn. In 'Le Prophète' he introduced saxhorns, and could not resist having a good quantity of brass on the stage in 'L'Étoile du nord.'

While Meyerbeer's influence was far-reaching in the domain of orchestration, there were those who viewed with misgivings the immense popularity of his operas in France. It was not the music that gave them anxiety, but the political and historical ideas in the librettos. Particularly in the provinces, where the opera was the only distraction, people who never opened a book but accepted the stories of the operas as veracious, derived false impressions of the Middle Ages, the French Monarchy, the Wars of Religion and the Inquisition. This was curious in the light of the complacency with which the French people tolerated the misplaced accents and ungrammatical lines in the texts.

It is not necessary to refer to all the great names inscribed on the orchestral roll. Mendelssohn with his marvel of the 'Midsummer Night's Dream' overture, perhaps retouched in the light of maturer experience, took things as they came. Schumann was acquiescent, plodding along with more thought for the idea of the theme and its development than for the heightening of its colour.[2] Reference, however, must be made to a composer, as exotic as Meyerbeer was, but more lasting in influence. Liszt, envied for his popularity and facility, generous and not over-critical, was destined to be associated with the greatest musical movement of the 19th century. The reign of the orchestra, mild and suave as it was in those days, compared with its later tyranny, demanded fresh forms, uncomprehended or mistrusted by the formalists. It was a phase of evolution to be spread far and wide while those of the more conservative school were content to remain primly in a comfortable groove. Liszt, with greater musical acumen than Berlioz, but influenced by him, brought to light his SYMPHONIC POEMS (q.v.). What directed his steps to the orchestra was very likely his arrangement for pianoforte of the 'Symphonie fantastique,' the details of which he had to analyse and master. It was an invaluable lesson, and answers the question which has been asked, how he learned orchestration. The friendship between him and Wagner was more one-sided than is generally known. Wagner was independent of him in his earlier days, from 'Rienzi' to 'Lohengrin,' and it was only when the last-named was accepted by Liszt for production at Weimar that the intimacy ripened. In the composition or form of these works he owed nothing to Liszt. But eventually Liszt's plan of development and metamorphosis of theme, suggested by the *idée fixe* of Berlioz, must have indicated to Wagner a wider sphere in which *Leitmotive* were to predominate. It was clear that the reiteration of a theme employed as a LEITMOTIV (q.v.) could become commonplace if set forth always in the same orchestral colour, hence the composer's palette had to provide contrast of tone. Wagner's earlier experience as a conductor of opera at Magdeburg, Königsberg and Riga had introduced him to the conventions of orchestration. But occasions must have arisen when he had to devise makeshifts and rescore parts which were beyond the resources of his bands. Five or six years of this work were not wasted when the result was the four operas just mentioned. Before a note of 'The Ring' was written Liszt had composed eight of his symphonic poems, and although the *idée fixe*, theme-metamorphosis and *Leitmotiv* were not identical in their ultimate content, they stood for the aim of each composer towards securing a unity

---

[1] Mozart, however, was before either. In his symphony in D (K. 385) the first note, D, is written as two semibreves touching one another.

[2] See under SCHUMANN the account of the modification which had to be made in the theme of the first symphony.

of design opposed to the older kinds of structure. Wagner was at pains to disclaim his indebtedness to Liszt in this respect, or was evasive when challenged to state his position, but whatever the divergencies due to the use of the orchestra alone and the compliance with textual exigencies, their common ancestry cannot be doubted.

Like Mendelssohn and Schumann, Brahms, too, intent upon musical form, orchestrated in such a way as to leave to conductors of his works the problem of bringing his ideas into the broad light of day. To these conductors he owes his position as a writer of orchestral music. Impervious to contemporary movements in the art he went on in his own sturdy fashion, tethered to the past, and hammering out imperishable themes. He had a sense of orchestral colour which was quite as personal as Wagner's was, but at first sight it was not clear, and the reading of one of his symphonies was in his day a test of a conductor's insight more severe than that of any contemporary work. His influence lay rather in the direction of musical form and thought than in orchestral effects, and he was content to leave his symphonies in the hands of his interpreters to discover the means of solving the many *cruces* that lay therein.

WAGNER'S CONTRIBUTION.—To those whose receptive faculties have been educated by listening to music written up to the end of the 19th century it is difficult to comprehend the ferocity with which Wagner's music was attacked in some quarters. May not the explanation lie partly in the bearing of the man himself? However that may be, every page of his orchestral work bears witness to restraint, even to reticence. These qualities perhaps, have not been without their effect on some French works that followed his day ; the economy of means, the simplicity carried even to emptiness in the scoring were scarcely noticed in the pregnancy of the theme. The opening bars of 'Tristan,' for instance, on paper seem bare and inadequate. At first sight they appear wavering and indecisive, without the manliness of many another opening phrase. But the dramatic instinct was there, and the gradual working up to that tremendous climax and catastrophe justified the slenderness and tenderness of the opening bars. There are pages in Wagner's later works in which there would appear almost nothing in the orchestra ; a touch of colour, a shudder of divided violoncellos and violas, a single drum-roll ; a broken line, as it were, of dry-point left for the mind to complete the design ; a broad expanse of colour when the situation demanded polychromatic treatment. The mystery is how Wagner, with none too many opportunities of hearing his own works, and tied as he was in Dresden and elsewhere to conducting the works of others, discovered the genius of one instru-

ment after another, held it captive and made it his servant.

As suggested above, the 'prentice hand may have had to turn to in order to make good deficiencies in the scramble of operatic performances up to the Riga period. These must have borne their lesson. But after he had recovered from the infection of opera that was grand, with the usual sequelae, in his convalescence, he found himself, as in many such cases, renewed in vigour and in experience. To conduct operas composed by others, not to speak of recomposing Gluck, with now and then performances of his own, was a schooling more direct, more practical, than a wilderness of textbooks. It is significant that for the well-being of his music the circumstances that embroiled him in, and banished him from Dresden and Munich were just those that ruptured the link with the State observances of opera that passed as music. Henceforth, out of the depths of his experience, out of the darkness of his travail, he was to bring forth a new light. Influenced by Beethoven, of whom a trace is to be found in the 'Faust' overture, passing through his mind Mozart, Weber and Meyerbeer, he discovered himself in 'Tristan.' Henceforward he was on his own ground and in his full estate. The appeal, howsoever it might be interpreted as conforming with musical design in an extended fashion, was not so much to the austerity of musical architecture, as to that curiosity which is not far removed from emotion. What he said in words—the least component in his music dramas—he magnified and exalted in sound.

THE RUSSIAN SCHOOL.—Contemporary with, if not in advance of, Wagner was the Russian School, evolved more by innate musical instinct than by systematic training. In this respect it is notable that the leading exponents were men who had begun life in careers in which music was as it were an afterthought, and not a dominating prepossession. The forerunner was Glinka who created an idiom as much as he founded a style. His case was not very different from those who came after him and spread the spirit of his example, for his early musical training was desultory and he had reached his thirtieth year before he addressed himself to serious technical study. Following him, of the Group of Five, Balakirev was alone in having pursued a musical vocation from youth. Of the others, Cui at an early age had reached a high rank in the military hierarchy, Moussorgsky was a commissioned officer, Borodin to the day of his death was a lecturer on chemistry, and Rimsky-Korsakov, a naval cadet, had put in some service at sea. Self-taught and self-trained, but charged with their earlier experiences in matters unrelated to music, they brought into the fold fresh strains in more senses than one. It was

Berlioz with his work on the orchestra who aroused curiosity. It was his teaching that drove one Russian composer after another to intervene and pontificate. As in life in Russia, so also was it in Russian music. There was docility on the one side in a composer who allowed another to take in hand and reconstruct his work : autocracy on the other, till it became a problem to trace the work of the original composer. There was a pretty state of chaos when Rimsky-Korsakov was set the task of putting in order what would have been called in the 18th century the ' Respectable Remains ' of Moussorgsky and Borodin.

While it may be said of the group of Five that their tendency was ethnological, Tchaikovsky, aloof from them, went further afield than they. Not concentrated as they were upon a purely national art which geographically led nowhither eastwardly, while westwardly there were forbidden frontiers, Tchaikovsky followed the course of the sun and grafted his native song upon the stripling that had been reared in more congenial climes. Sentiment did the rest ; his last symphony, and then the rumours about his death. But orchestration on the great lines owes as much to him as to the others of his nationality in consistency. In his case it was a matter of assimilation and adaptation rather than self-assertiveness and dogmatism. Music must ever remain a mystery : to the present generation at least it is incomprehensible why stylists so divergent as Tchaikovsky and Gounod should have pinned their faith to Mozart, a composer who on the face of it had little affinity with either. Again, it may be asked how it was that what came to be characteristic of the French School, to mention Debussy alone of many, should have been foreshadowed some score or two years earlier by a Russian soldier on active service.

Orchestral technique in western Europe assumed a new guise as Russian music became known. While Rimsky - Korsakov and his associates were burrowing deep into the *Traité* of Berlioz, involving themselves in perplexing horn passages as Wagner did in the sterile pre-valve era, they discovered much virtue in the spacing and combining of timbres so that the breadth of sound was not cramped. The fascination lay in technique, not in the obsolete quotations that Berlioz supplied. Many another has spoken and written : among them Gevaert, for the most part faithful to tradition ; but in the end it was, and is, the instinct of the individual that moulds the orchestra.

Apart from the question of composition attention was paid to the ' laying out,' especially of the wind section, as if the ear had become sensitive to those combinations which coalesced, without the prominence of some particular timbre. A test that was severe was the rehearsing of strings alone and wind

alone. But as orchestration advanced at the expense of co-ordinated theme, there grew up an independence on the part of every instrument, in derision, as it were, of its neighbours.

STRAUSS.—The departure from classic forms and the aim at poetic and literal or concrete effects brought a new element into orchestration, the most striking example being found in the second variation of ' Don Quixote ' (1896–1897) by Richard Strauss, a unique instance of minute sound-analysis solved by instruments. But before this piece of realism, in his ' Till Eulenspiegel ' (1895) Strauss had taxed the orchestra to the uttermost, and called for a revision and extension of technique in every department. What appeared impossible at that period became child's play as he proceeded from one Rabelaisian work to another, almost every page of which shows some daring feat of orchestration. There may be views as to the value of his thematic material, but on the orchestral side there can be no question of his having indicated advances in directions hitherto looked on as insurmountable and impassable.

Encouraged by the *réclame* of these works Strauss ventured a composition on a still larger scale—his 'Symphonia (*sic*) domestica.' It is dated December 31, 1903. As music nothing need be said here, but as orchestration in this period it reached the extreme point in the use of instruments. Not content with the orchestral force of his earlier works he asked for piccolo, three flutes, 2 oboes and oboe d' amore, an English horn, a clarinet in D, one in A, two in B flat, a bass clarinet, 4 saxophones (' *ad libitum* only in extreme necessity '—when ?), 4 bassoons, a double bassoon, 8 horns, 4 trumpets, 3 trombones, a bass tuba, 4 timpani, 1 triangle, a tambourine, glockenspiel, cymbals, bass drum and 2 harps. Against these forty-nine the string formula was 16, 16, 12, 10, 8. What with uncles and aunts, a child having a bath at 7 P.M., wakened at 7 A.M., and doubtless other intimate details considerately withheld, one misses two instruments in the orchestra which would have added colour to this charming picture of homeliness, namely, a sewing-machine, and a vacuum cleaner in B flat *alt*.

It is too soon to say whether the presently regarded ' extra' instruments which he employs will in time become regular members of the orchestra. The question often has been asked if the composer is the ideal interpreter of his own scores. It might not be quite a bad thing to let him loose and invite him to interpret himself. The impression cannot be dispelled that a large amount of modern music is being written, like the dogmatic music of the mid or late 19th century, by what the eye sees and not by what the ear hears. A glaring instance of this occurred when a composer, conducting one of his own works and reading his score by eye alone, turned by mistake two pages at once and indicated a ' lead ' some bars before its entrance.

The later French school, basing its style, like its great writers, upon the *mot juste*, punctilious (the word is here in its full sense) as to orchestral colour, resorts to the utmost economy of means, but at the same time to so exact a valuation of timbre that the very simplicity of the score would be barren if it were not fully observed and respected. Thought in the orchestra is then expressed in a welding of timbres, almost a breath, but ample for the purpose.

GENERAL CONSIDERATIONS.—Almost every bar of orchestral music should enshrine a secret, but it is not found in all. The obvious and commonplace often enough ' lag superfluous ' when the orchestra is ' busy ' : an apparent idleness may be part of the design in order to prepare an effective entry. Towards the end of his days Haydn was warned against being pushed by eccentricity to caricature. Will many to-day endorse that opinion? The lucidity and limpidity of Mozart, as we with perfected instruments find him, may not have struck his contemporaries. Beethoven's performances did not escape collapse on many an occasion. Routine and an enlarged comprehension have intervened. Some names, notable in their time, have become shadows, but in the progress of music the heavenly maid still keeps her eternal youth. The fracas that Molière called the music of his day is now as words of one syllable. The clamourings of a past age become mere lispings, but there is wisdom still to be learnt out of the mouths of babes and sucklings.

Orchestration for the sake of orchestration because ' the instruments are there ' tends to thrust aside the pure expression of ideas. A complicated texture that seeks out many inventions exalts colour at the expense of design. The older reign of the fingers on the keyboard imposed a surrender of the ear of the mind, and fettered the analysis of sound and the fitness of the instrument appropriate to produce it. As the ear of the mind awoke to fuller consciousness the labour at the pianoforte ceased to be worthy of transmission. Man had to hear with his ears rather than with his eyes and his fingers.

Recent excursions have scorned the preachings of the elders and it would seem as if the goodly fellowship among instruments were to be sacrificed to an antagonistic and jealous clamour for supremacy. Whither the present mood is tending, or for how long it will persist, nothing can be said. The perception of the human ear may have been strained either to welcome new sounds or to return to earlier delights. From that which is new can be learnt the simple beauties of music that was in its childhood. Again, it may yet be that a great art may be built up on the debris of failures.

But it is not well for music that the orchestra should be employed for the rags and tatters of scraps of themes which ill accord with the eloquence and noble purpose of the art.

To invent new devices, such as uncertain harmonics on the double bass, to discover that a section of a plucked harp-string has its own colour—these in themselves, while technically interesting and novel, are not exactly on the same plane with the just combination of timbres so as to obtain their full value. There is no royal road to the orchestra, however paved it may be with good intentions. A *tutti* passage may be ' indicated ' *fff*, but the horse-power, if a simile may be allowed, will be far below the pressure demanded if the judicious balance of tone is disregarded. The vast column of sound, thick where it should be thin, thin where it should be compact, close-knit where it should be open, muddy where it should be filigree— these are ' faults ' in musical architecture which even the greatest masters have left to conductors to make good by tempering some member and enforcing some other unit of the orchestra. The surest hand is that of the composer who has spent hours, if not days, in analysing in silence and then placing for good his orchestral thought on paper. The weakest hand is his who gropes hesitatingly, rewrites, bespatters his score with alterations in red ink : who has not heard with his ears but only with his eyes. Such demolitions and reconstructions point to an uncertainty of thought, a wavering, to which no one sure of his building and his inner orchestral ear would confess for a moment. The deeper questionings, the capturings in solitude, are not for some rough and ready ' filling in,' but for a certainty of expression which is proof against later revision.

In spite of much that has been written of orchestration at the present day, the last word lies with the theme itself. The grim anatomy of music, like that of man, is changeless.

W. W.

BIBLIOGRAPHY

BERLIOZ : *Traité de l'instrumentation.* For modern editions and translations see under BERLIOZ.
GEVAERT : *Traité général d'instrumentation. Cours méthodique d'orchestration.* For translations, etc., see under GEVAERT.
LAVOIX : *Histoire de l'instrumentation.* (1878.)
RIMSKY-KORSAKOV : *The Foundations of Instrumentation.* (Eng. trans.)
C. FORSYTH : *Orchestration.* (London, 1914.) (The most exhaustive original English work on the subject.)
J. LYON : *A Practical Guide to the Modern Orchestra.* (A concise and useful handbook.)
ADAM CARSE : *The History of Orchestration.* (Kegan Paul, 1925.)
F. VOLBACH : *Das moderne Orchester in seiner Entwickelung,* p. 118. (Leipzig, 1910.)

ORCHESTRELLE, see MECHANICAL APPLIANCES (5).

ORCHESTRINA DI CAMERA, the title of a series of little instruments of the harmonium tribe. They were invented and made by W. E. Evans, of London, and represent the orchestral clarinet, oboe, flute, French horn and bassoon. They imitate the timbre of the instruments after which they are called, and have the same compass of notes. The clarinet and French

LV

MUSICAL INSTRUMENTS — SPAIN, c. 1270

(Library of the Escorial. Cantigas de S. Maria)

1. Portative Organ (*Organo de coll*).   2. Organistrum (*Cinfonie*).   3. Chimebells (*Cimbalos*).
4. Cymbals (*Platillos*).   5. Clackers (*Tabillos*).   6. Drum (*Atambor*).

horn are furnished with shifting keyboards, in order to arrange for the mechanical transposition of the parts when these are not written in the key of C. The different qualities of tone are obtained by making the vibrating reeds of varying dimensions, and by the peculiar shape of the channels conveying the wind to them. The orchestrinas are chiefly intended to be employed as convenient substitutes for the real instruments at performances where players of the orchestral instruments cannot be obtained. Hullah, in his *Music in the House*, recommended them as valuable for the practice of concerted music as well as for the purpose of supplying obbligato accompaniments.   T. L. S.

ORDINES. A conventional grouping of a number of feet of one of the first five of the RHYTHMIC MODES (*q.v.*), ending always with a rest of the duration necessary to complete the last foot. The scheme is as follows :

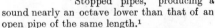

Ordo.	Mode.	Number of Feet.
I.	1–4	2
I.	5	1⅓ (*i.e.* ○.○.○. ▬▪–▪)
II.	1–4	3
II.	5	2
III.	1–4	4
III.	5	2⅔

A. H.

ORDOÑEZ, PEDRO (*b.* Palencia, *c.* 1500 ; *d.* Rome, 1550), Spanish church composer. He went to Rome and entered the Capella Pontificia (Apr. 29, 1539) some four years after Morales, being described as of the diocese of Palencia. In 1545 (Jan. 11) he was created *Abbas*, and was among the singers who took part in the opening ceremony of the Council of Trent (Dec. 13, 1545). He also accompanied the council when it removed to Bologna in 1547. (The question of church music did not come up until 1562.) In 1549 Ordoñez was still a member of the Capella Pontificia, and is mentioned as having leave of absence to visit some baths near Bologna. MSS. of his works exist in certain Spanish cathedrals.   J. B. T.

ORDRE, another name for SUITE (*q.v.*), used by Couperin and some of his contemporaries. There is no difference of arrangement or structure which would account for the employment of the two names.   M.

OREFICE, GIACOMO (*b.* Vicenza, 1865 ; *d.* Milan, Dec. 22, 1922), composer, studied at the Liceo of Bologna under Busi and Mancinelli. Unlike many Italian composers of his time, Orefice was not exclusively devoted to the stage. His most important operas are :

' Consuelo ' (Bologna, Teatro Comunale, 1895), ' Chopin ' (Milan, Teatro Lirico, 1901), ' Cecilia ' (Vicenza, Teatro Comunale, 1902), ' Mosè ' (Genoa, Teatro Carlo Felice, 1905), ' Pane altrui ' (Venice, Teatro Fenice, 1907), ' Radda ' (Milan, Teatro Lirico, 1913) and ' Il Castello del Sogno.'

The symphonic works include :

' Sinfonia del Bosco,' symphony in D minor, suite for violoncello and orchestra and ' Anacreontiche,' a work in four movements (Ad Artemide, A Fauna, Ad Eros, A Dionisio).

Among his chamber music may be mentioned:

Two sonatas for violin and piano and one for violoncello and piano, a trio and ' Rifles ioni ed ombre ' for quintet.

There are also a number of songs and piano

pieces (Preludi del mare, Quadri di Boecklin, Crespuscoli, Miraggi, etc.). Orefice was professor of composition at the Conservatorio of Milan.   E. B.

ORFEO, see ORPHEUS (1).

ORGAN (Fr. *orgue* ; Ital. *organo* ; Ger. *Orgel*). A wind instrument, the basic principle of which is that its tones are produced by means of a number of pipes, each pipe producing only one note. The instrument is here discussed under three heads : 1, History ; 2, Description of Mechanism ; 3, The Modern Organ.

1. HISTORY

There can be little doubt that the principle of the three great classes of organ-pipe— Stopped, Open and Reed—was known at a very early period, as we shall have occasion to show. (See PIPES, EVOLUTION AND DISTRIBUTION OF MUSICAL.)

The first idea of such an instrument was doubtless suggested to man by the passing breezes as they struck against the open ends of broken reeds. A few such reeds or tubes, of varied growths or diameters, and of graduated lengths, bound together in a row, with their open tops arranged in a horizontal line, would form an instrument possessing sufficient capacity for the performance of primitive melodies.

The myth that Pan was the originator of the syrinx led to its being called ' Pan's-pipe,' under which name, or that of ' Mouth-organ,' it is known to the present day. (PANDEAN PIPE.)

The pipes of the syrinx being composed of  reeds cut off just below the knot —which knot did not permit the wind to escape, but caused it to return to the same place where it entered, thus traversing the length of the tube twice—were in principle so many examples of the first class of pipes mentioned

FIG. 1.   above. They were practically ' Stopped pipes,' producing a sound nearly an octave lower than that of an open pipe of the same length.[1]

The mode of playing upon this earliest organ must have been troublesome and tiring, as either the mouth had to be in constant motion to and fro over the tubes, or they had incessantly to be shifted to the right or left under the mouth. Some other method of directing wind into them must in course of time have been felt to be desirable ; and the idea would at length occur of conducting wind into the tube from below instead of above. This result—an enormous step forward—could be obtained by selecting a reed, as before, but with a short additional portion left below the knot to serve as a mouthpiece or wind-receiver (the modern ' foot ') ; by making a straight narrow slit through the knot, close to the front, to serve as a passage-way for the breath ; and by cutting a small horizontal opening immediately above that slit, with a sloping notch, bevelling upwards and outwards over that again. The breath blown in at the lower end, in passing through the slit would strike against the edge of the notch above, and there produce rapid flutterings, which would be communicated to the air in the tube, and would cause a sound to be emitted. In this manner a specimen of the second class of pipe mentioned above—that of the open species —would be brought into existence.

When the first ' squeaker ' was made, such as country lads still delight to construct of osiers in spring-time, a primitive model of a pipe of the third kind mentioned above, a ' Reed-pipe,' was produced. It consisted of a ' vibrator' and a tube ; the former sounded by being agitated by compressed wind from an air-cavity —the breath from the human mouth. Reed-pipes, although freely used as separate wind instruments in ancient times — the bagpipe among the number—were not introduced into organs until the 15th century, so far as can be ascertained, and need not therefore be further considered in this place.

A series of pipes of the second class (receiving air from below) would be less conveniently under the immediate control of the mouth than their predecessors; hence a wooden box was devised (now the wind-chest), containing a row of holes along the top into which were placed the lower ends of the pipes ; and the wind was sometimes provided by two attendants, who blew with their mouths alternately into pliable tubes, the one while the other took breath.

An antique organ supplied in this manner is sculptured under a monument in the Museum at Arles, bearing the date of XX.M.VIII.[1]

FIG. 2.

The pipes are held in position by a crossband, just as were those of the earlier syrinx. The carving represents the *back* of the instrument, as is indicated not only by the ' blowers '

[1] From Dom Bedos, *L'Ar du facteur d'orgues* (Paris, 1766)

being there, but also by the order of the pipes from large to small, appearing to run the wrong way, namely, from right to left instead of the reverse. The pipes of the early organs are said to have sounded at first all together, and those which were not required to be heard had to be silenced by means of the fingers or hands. An arrangement so defective would soon call for a remedy ; and the important addition was made of a slide, rule or tongue of wood, placed beneath the hole leading to each pipe, and so perforated as either to admit or exclude the wind as it was drawn in or out. Kircher [2] gives a

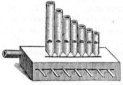

drawing, here reproduced, to show this improvement. (He conceives it to be the Mashokithra or Magraketha of the Chaldees.)

FIG. 3.

The wind was conveyed to the chest through the tube projecting from the right-hand side, either from the lips or from some kind of hand-bellows. In either case the stream would be only intermittent.

Another drawing given by Kircher (said to be that of the Hebrew instrument called *Magrephah*) exhibits the important addition of two small bellows, which would afford a continuous wind-supply, the one furnishing wind while the other was replenishing.

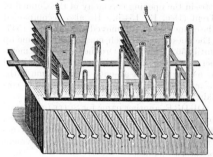

FIG. 4.

It is very doubtful, however, whether this is an authentic representation.

Although nothing very precise can be deduced from the ancient writers as to the time, place or manner in which some of the progressive steps in the invention of the organ already detailed were made, yet it is certain that the germ of many of the most important parts of the instrument had been discovered before the Christian era.[3]

[2] *Musurgia*, Bk. ii. ch. iv. § 3, p. 3.
[3] A paper by Miss Kathleen Schlesinger, *Researches into the Origin of the Organs of the Ancients*, in the *Sammelbände* of the Int. Mus. Ges. vol. ii. p. 167 ff., may be referred to. *The Organ of the Ancients from Eastern Sources (Hebrew, Syriac and Arabic)*, by Dr. Henry Farmer (in the press, 1926), is looked forward to as an authoritative treatment of the subject.

THE CHRISTIAN ERA TO A.D. 1000.—During the first ten centuries but little appears to have been done to develop the organ in size, compass or mechanism ; in fact, no advances are known to have been made in the practice of music itself of a kind to call such improvements into existence. Yet a number of isolated records exist as to the materials used in the construction of the instrument ; the great personages who exerted themselves about it ; and its gradual introduction from Greece, where it is said to have taken its origin, into other countries, and into the church ; and these have only to be brought together and placed in something approaching to chronological order, with a few connecting words here and there, to form an interesting and continuous narrative.

In the organ of Ctesibius, described by Hero,[1] it appears that the lower extremity of each pipe was enclosed in a small shallow box, something like a domino box inverted, the sliding lid being downwards. Each lid had an orifice which, on the lid being pushed home, placed the hole in correspondence with the orifice of the pipe, and the pipe then sounded. When the sliding lid was drawn forward, it closed the orifice, and so silenced the pipe. With certain improvements as to detail, this action is in principle substantially the same as that shown in Figs. 3 and 4 and it continued in use up to the 11th century. But the most interesting part of this description is the reference to the existence of a simple kind of key-action which pushed in the lid on the key being pressed down, the lid being pulled back by a spring of elastic horn and a cord on the key being released. Claudian the poet, who flourished about A.D. 400, has in his poem De consulatu F. Manlii Theodori (316-19) left a passage describing an organist's performance upon an instrument of this kind, and also its effect, of which the following is a literal version:

'Let there be also one who by his light touch forcing out deep murmurs, and managing the un-numbered tongues of the field of brazen tubes, can with nimble finger cause a mighty sound ; and can rouse to song the waters stirred to their depths by the massive lever.'

(For a technical description of the instrument see HYDRAULUS, also PLATE XXXVI.)

A Greek [2] epigram, attributed to the Emperor Julian the Apostate (d. A.D. 363), conveys some particulars concerning another kind of 4th-century organ, of which the following is a literal translation :

'I see a strange species (lit. " nature ") of reeds : surely they have rather sprung up from a foreign (lit. another) brazen field (lit. furrow) : wild—ncr are they swayed by our winds ; but a blast, rushing forth from a cavern of bull's hide, forces its way from beneath, under the root of the well-bored reeds. And a skilful man having nimble fingers stands feeling the yielding rods of pipes, and they, gently dancing, press out song.'

This account describes a wind organ, and one which had no keyboard. Both accounts

particularise the material of which the pipes were made, and it is not improbable that pipes of metal were at that time a novelty.

Theodoret (b. about 393, d. 457) also refers to musical organs as being furnished with pipes of copper or of bronze.

On an obelisk at Constantinople, erected by Theodosius (d. 393), is a representation of an organ, which is here copied.

FIG. 5.

The pipes are eight in number, and appear to be formed of large reeds or canes. They are not sufficiently varied in length to indicate the production of a proper musical scale, which is possibly an error of the sculptor. They are supported like those shown in Fig. 2. This example is very interesting as affording the earliest illustration known of a method of compressing the organ wind which some centuries afterwards became common—namely, by the weight of human beings. From the drawing it seems as if the two youths were standing on the same bellows, whereas they were more probably mounted on separate ones placed side by side. St. Jerome (d. 420) is said [3] to mention an organ at Jerusalem, with twelve brazen pipes, two elephants' skins and fifteen smiths' bellows, which could be heard at the Mount of Olives,— it is nearly a mile from the centre of the city to the top of the mount,—and therefore must have been an instrument of great power. Cassiodorus, who was consul of Rome under King Vitigas the Goth in 514, described the organ of his day as an instrument composed of divers pipes, formed into a kind of tower, which, by means of bellows, is made to produce a loud sound ; and in order to express agreeable melodies, it is constructed with certain tongues [4] of wood from the interior, which the finger of the master duly pressing or forcing back, elicits the most pleasing and brilliant tones.

The exact period at which the organ was first used for religious purposes is not positively known ; but according to Julianus, a Spanish bishop who flourished A.D. 450, it was in common use in the churches of Spain at that time. One is mentioned as existing ' in the most ancient city of Grado,' in a church of the nuns before the year 580. It is described as

---

[1] See W. Chappell's account, History of Music, i. 343, etc.
[2] Palatine Anthology, Bk. ix. No. 365.

[3] Kitto, Cyc. Bib. Lit., 3rd ed., ii. 255b. Kitto's reference (A1 Dardanum), however, does not appear to be correct
[4] The term ' tongues ' (linguae) remained in use for the sliders up to the time when the slide-box was superseded by the spring-box about the end of the 11th century.

being about two feet long, six inches broad, and furnished with fifteen playing-slides and thirty pipes, two pipes to each note. Hawkins[1] has given a drawing of the slide-box of this organ, the ' tongues ' of which are singularly ornate. The number of notes on the slide-box (fifteen in a length of two feet) would show that the pipes were of small diameter, and therefore that the notes were treble ones.

The advantage of using the organ in the services of the church was so obvious that it would soon be perceived ; and accordingly in the 7th century Pope Vitalian, at Rome (about the year 666), introduced it to improve the singing of the congregations. Subsequently, however, he abolished the singing of the congregations, and substituted in its place that of canonical singers.

At the beginning of the 8th century the use of the organ was appreciated, and the art of making it was known in England. The native artificers had even introduced the custom of pipe decoration, for, according to Aldhelm (d. 709), the Anglo-Saxons ornamented the front pipes of their organs with gilding. Organ-making was introduced into France about the middle of the same century. Pepin (714–68), the father of Charlemagne, perceived that an organ would be an important aid to devotion ; and as the instrument was at that time unknown either in France or Germany, he applied (about the year 757) to the Byzantine Emperor Constantine Copronymus the Sixth, requesting him to send one to France. Constantine not only complied with this solicitation by presenting him with a large organ, but forwarded it by a special deputation, headed by the Roman bishop Stephanus. The organ was deposited in the church of St. Cornelius at Compiègne. It was a wind organ, with pipes of lead : and is said to have been made and played by an Italian priest, who had learnt the method of doing both at Constantinople.

The first organ introduced into Germany was one which the Emperor Charles the Great, in 811 or 812, caused to be made at Aix-la-Chapelle after the model of that at Compiègne. The copy was successful, and several writers expressed themselves in terms of high praise at its powerful yet pleasing tone.

Shortly after the year 800 an organ was sent to Charlemagne by the Caliph Haroun Alraschid, constructed by an Arabian maker of the name of Giafar, which was placed in a church at Aix-la-Chapelle. It was a wind organ of extraordinarily soft tone.

Venice was favourably known for its organ-makers about this time ; a monk of that city, of the name of Georgius, a native of Benevento, having in the year 822 constructed an instrument for Louis le Debonnaire, which was an hydraulic organ, and was erected in the palace

1 History of Music, i. 401.

of the king at Aix-la-Chapelle. Its pipes were of lead.

The progress of Germany in making and using organs in the latter half of the 9th century, particularly in East Franconia, was so great, that Pope John VIII. (880), in a letter to Anno, Bishop of Friesingen, requests that a good organ may be sent to him, and a skilful player to instruct the Roman artists.

By this time organ-building had apparently made its way into Bavaria ; and a large instrument, with boxwood pipes, is said to have been erected in the Cathedral of Munich at a very early date.

In the 9th century organs had become common in this country, the English artificers furnishing them with pipes of copper, which were fixed in gilt frames. In the 10th century the English prelate St. Dunstan (925–88), famous for his skill in metal work, erected or fabricated an organ in Malmesbury Abbey, the pipes of which were of brass. He also gave an organ to Abingdon Abbey, and is said to have furnished many other English churches and convents with similar instruments. In this same century Count Elwin presented an organ to the convent at Ramsey, on which he is said to have expended the then large sum of thirty pounds in copper pipes, which are described as emitting a sweet melody and a far-resounding peal.

A curious representation of an organ of about this date is given [2] in a MS. Psalter of Edwin preserved in the library of Trinity College, Cambridge.[3] The pipes are placed within a frame, apparently after the manner referred to above. The surface of the organ is represented as being perforated to receive a second set of pipes, though the draughtsman appears to have sketched one hole too many. The two organists, whose duties seem for the moment to have been brought to an end by the inattention of the blowers, are intent on admonishing their assistants, who are striving to get up the wind-supply, which their neglect has apparently allowed to

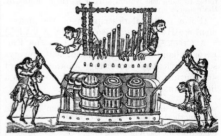

FIG. 6.

run out. The four bellows are blown in a manner which we here meet with for the first time—namely, through the intervention of

2 It is a bad copy of a picture in the Utrecht Psalter.
3 Part of the representation is here engraved from a photograph, by the kind permission of the authorities.

handles instead of directly by the hands ; and as in so small an organ there could not have been room for four persons to compress the wind by standing upon the bellows, it is possible that they were loaded with weights in the manner that has generally been supposed not to have been introduced until some centuries later.

At the end of the 10th century several organs existed in Germany (St. Paul's, Erfurt ; St. James's, Magdeburg ; and Halberstadt Cathedral), which, although small and unpretending instruments, were objects of much astonishment and attraction at the time.

In the 11th century we find a treatise [1] on the construction of organs, included in a larger work on *Divers Arts*, by a monk and priest of the name of Theophilus, which is of considerable interest as showing the exact state of the art of organ-making at that period. It is too long to quote *in extenso*, and is also rather obscure in parts ; but the following particulars may be gathered from it : that the slide-box was made two and a half feet in length, and rather more than one foot in breadth ; that the pipes were placed upon its surface ; that the compass consisted of seven or eight notes ; that the length of the slide-box was measured out equally for the different notes or slides, and not on a gradually decreasing scale as the pipes became smaller, since the playing-slides would not in that case have been of one width or at one distance apart ; that the organ was played by these movable slides ; that each slide worked in little side-slits, like the lid of a box of dominoes ; that there were two or perhaps even more pipes to each note ; that the projecting ' tongue ' of each slide was marked with a letter to indicate to which note it belonged— a custom that continued in use for centuries afterwards (as, for instance, in the Halberstadt organ finished in 1361 ; and in the old organ in the church of St. Ægidius, in Brunswick, built in the latter part of the 15th century, and illustrated on p. 744) ; that a hole was cut through the slide under each pipe about an inch and a half across, for the passage of the wind ; that all the pipes of a note sounded together ; that a note was sounded by the slide being pushed in, and silenced by its being drawn forward ; and that in the front of each slide, immediately behind the handle or tongue, a narrow hole about two inches long was cut, in which was fixed a copper-headed nail, which regulated the motion of the slide and prevented its being drawn out too far.

The following illustration, deduced from Theophilus's description, shows the slide, and three passages for wind to as many pipes above. The slide intercepts the wind, but will allow it

[1] *Theophili, qui et Rugerus, Presbyteri et Monachi libri III., de diversis artibus.* Opera et studio Roberti Hendrie. Londini, Johannes Murray, MDCCCXLVII. 8vo.

to pass on being moved so that its openings, shown by the unshaded parts, correspond with those below and above.

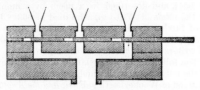

FIG. 7.

Gori's *Thesaurus diptychorum*, 1759, vol. ii., contains a most interesting engraving, copied from an ancient MS., said to be as old as the time of Charlemagne, which shows a person playing upon an instrument of the Theophilus type. (See Fig. 8.)

But of all the information given by Theophilus, the most important, because previously unknown and unsuspected, is that which relates to the finishing of the pipes so as to produce different qualities of tone. They were

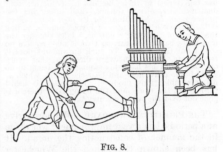

FIG. 8.

made of the finest copper ; and the formation of a pipe being completed, Theophilus thus proceeds :

' He (the maker) can bring it (the pipe) to his mouth and blow at first slightly, then more, and then strongly ; and, according to what he discerns by hearing, he can arrange the sound, so that if he wish it strong the opening is made wider ; but if slighter, it is made narrower. In this order all the pipes are made.'

Here we see that the means for producing a fuller tone by a wide or high mouth, and a more delicate sound by a narrower or lower one, were well known in the 11th century ; and that the manner of testing the ' speech ' by blowing the pipe with the mouth in various ways is precisely that often employed by the ' voicer ' of the present day when ' regulating ' or ' finishing ' a stop. It is worthy of observation that although Theophilus incidentally recognises an addition to the number of pipes to a note as one means of increasing the utility of the organ, he as distinctly indicates its range or compass as simply seven or eight notes.

We have intentionally introduced the account of Theophilus somewhat before its due chronological place, as it materially assists in elucidating the description of the remarkable organ erected in Winchester Cathedral in the 10th century by order of Bishop Elphege (*d.* 951), and described in a poem by a monk of the name of Wulstan, who died in 963. It is of further use in this place, since Wulstan's description had formerly been a great puzzle to writers on the history of the organ.

The following is a translation of the portion of the Latin poem with which we are concerned, as given in Wackerbarth's *Music and the Anglo-Saxons*, pp. 12-15 :

'Such organs as you have built are seen nowhere, fabricated on a double ground. Twice six bellows above are ranged in a row, and fourteen lie below. These, by alternate blasts, supply an immense quantity of wind, and are worked by seventy strong men, labouring with their arms, covered with perspiration, each inciting his companions to drive the wind up with all his strength, that the full-bosomed box may speak with its four hundred pipes which the hand of the organist governs. Some when closed he opens, others when open he closes, as the individual nature of the varied sound requires. Two brethren (religious) of concordant spirit sit at the instrument, and each manages his own alphabet. There are, moreover, hidden holes in the forty tongues, and each has ten (pipes) in their due order. Some are conducted hither, others thither, each preserving the proper point (or situation) for its own note. They strike the seven differences of joyous sounds, adding the music of the lyric semitone. Like thunder the iron tones batter the ear, so that it may receive no sound but that alone. To such an amount does it reverberate, echoing in every direction, that every one stops with his hand his gaping ears, being in no wise able to draw near and bear the sound, which so many combinations produce. The music is heard throughout the town, and the flying fame thereof is gone out over the whole country.'

THE PRIMITIVE KEYBOARD.—We now arrive at a period when a vast improvement was made in the manner of constructing the organ. It has been shown that when the Winchester organ was made, and onwards to the date of the treatise by Theophilus, the method of admitting wind to, or of excluding it from, the pipes of a note was by a slide, which alternately covered and exposed the underside of the holes leading up to its pipes. The frictional resistance of the slides, at all times trying, would inevitably be increased by their swelling in damp weather and becoming tight; they would certainly have to be lengthened for every pipe added, which would make them heavier and harder to move with the hand; and they involved the twofold task, already mentioned, of simultaneously thrusting one slide back while another was being drawn out. These circumstances, added to the fact that a given resistance can be overcome with less difficulty by a blow than by a pull with the fingers and thumb, must have directed attention to the possibility of substituting pressure for traction in the manipulation of the organ. Thus it is recorded that towards the end of the 11th century huge keys, or rather levers, began to be used as the means for playing the instrument; and however unwieldy these may have been, they were nevertheless the first rude steps towards providing the organ with a keyboard. A spring-box, too, of some kind was almost of necessity also an improvement of the same period; for without some restoring power, a key, on being knocked down, would have remained there until picked up; and that restoring power would be the most readily supplied by a spring or springs. In some of the early spring-boxes a separate valve seems to have been placed against the hole leading up to every pipe of each note, where it was held in position by an elastic appliance of the nature just named. The valves were brought under outward control by strings or cords, which passed through the bottom of the spring-box, and were attached to the key lying in a direct line beneath. As the keys must have been hung at their inner end, and have had their greatest fall in front, the smallest pipes of a note were no doubt from the first placed quite inside, and the largest in front, with those of graduating scale occupying an intermediate position in proportion to their size; and thus the small valves, opening a lesser distance, were strung where the key had the least fall, and the larger pallets where they had the greatest motion.

Edmund Schulze, of Paulinzelle, about the middle of the 19th century made for the present writer a rough sketch of the spring-box of an organ about 400 years old which he assisted in taking to pieces when he was quite a youth; from which sketch the drawing for the following illustration was prepared.

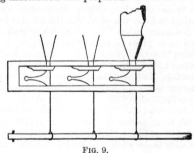

FIG. 9.

The early keys are described as being from three to five inches wide, or even more; an inch and a half thick; from a foot and a half to a yard or more in length, with a fall sometimes of as much as a foot in depth. They must at times, therefore, have been as large as the treadle of a knife-grinder's machine. Their size and amount of resistance would on first thought appear to have been most unnecessarily great and clumsy; but this is soon accounted for. We have seen that the gauge of the keys was influenced by the size of pipe necessary for the lowest note. Their width would be increased when the compass was extended downwards with larger pipes; and their length would be increased with the number of valves that had to be strung to them ; while the combined resistance of the many strong springs of the larger specimens would render the touch insensible to anything short of a thump.

It was in the cathedral at Magdeburg, towards the end of the century of which we have been speaking (the 11th), that the earliest organ with a keyboard of which we have any authentic record was erected. It is said to have had a compass of sixteen notes, but no mention is made as to what the notes were.

In the 12th century the number of keys was sometimes increased ; and every key further received the addition of two or three pipes, sounding the fifth and octave to the unison. According to Seidel [1] a third and tenth were added. All sounded together, and there was no escaping from the strong incessant 'Full Organ' effect.

There is a curious account written by Lootens [2] —an author but little known—of a Dutch organ said to have been erected in the church of St. Nicholas at Utrecht in the year 1120. The organ had two manuals and pedals. The compass of the former was from F, represented by a pipe of 6 feet standard length, up to $b'b$, namely two octaves and a half. The chief manual had twelve pipes to each key, including one set of which the largest pipe would be 12 feet in length,[3] and which therefore was identical with the Double Open Diapason of subsequent times. The sound-board was without grooves or draw-stops, consequently there were probably nearly as many springs for the organ-beater to overcome as there were pipes to sound. The second manual was described as having a few movable draw-stops ; and the pedals one independent stop—oddly enough a Trumpet—details and peculiarities which strongly point to the last two departments having been additions made at a much later period ; for a 'double organ' is not known to have existed for two centuries after the date at which this one is said to have been completed ; still less a triple one.

One of the greatest improvements effected in the organ in the 14th century was the gradual introduction of the four remaining chromatic semitones. F♯ was added in the early part of the century ; then followed C♯ and E♭ ; and next G♯. The B♭ already existed in the Winchester and other mediæval instruments. By Dom Bedos the introduction of these four notes is assigned to the 13th century ; while others place the first appearance of three of them as late as the 15th. Praetorius gives them an

intermediate date—the middle of the 14th century ; and he is undoubtedly correct, as they were certainly in the Halberstadt organ, finished in the year 1361.

Dom Bedos refers to a curious MS. of the 14th century in the Bibliothèque Nationale, as affording much further information respecting the organ of that period. This MS. records that the clavier of that epoch sometimes comprised as many as thirty-one keys, namely, from B up to f'', two octaves and a fifth ; that wooden rollers, resembling those used in English organs as late as the 19th century, were employed to transmit the movement of the keys to the valves ; that the bass pipes were distributed, right and left, in the form of wings ; and that those of the top notes were placed in the centre of the instrument, as they now are.

To appreciate the importance of the improvements just mentioned, and others that are necessarily implied, it is necessary to remember that so long as it was a custom in organ making to have the pipes above and the keys below placed parallel one to the other, every little expansion of the organ involved an aggravation of the unwieldy size of the keys, at the same time that the convenient reach of the player set most rigid bounds to the legitimate expansion of the organ, and fixed the extent of its limits. The ingenious contrivance of the roller-board at once left the dimensions of the organ free to be extended laterally, irrespective of the measure of the keyboard.

This emancipation was necessary before the additional semitones could be conveniently accommodated ; for as they would materially increase the number of pipes in each rank, so they would require wider space to stand in, a larger spring-box, such as was then made, to stand upon, and rollers equal in length to the sum of the distance to which the pipes were removed from a parallel with each key.

With regard to the distribution of the pipes, they had generally been placed in a single row, as shown in mediæval drawings, but as the invention of the chromatic notes nearly doubled the number in the septave—increasing them from seven to twelve—half the series would now form nearly as long a row as the entire diatonic range previously did. The two smallest pipes were, therefore, placed in the centre of the organ, and the remainder alternately on each side ; and their general outline—spreading outwards and upwards—gave them the appearance of a pair of outstretched wings. The 'zigzag' plantation of pipes was doubtless a subsequent arrangement.

In 1350 Poland appears in connexion with our subject. In that year an organ was made by a monk at Thorn in that kingdom, which had twenty-two keys. As this is the exact number possessed by the Halberstadt organ, completed eleven years later, it is possible that

[1] Johann Julius Seidel, *Die Orgel und ihr Bau* (Breslau, 1842).
[2] *Nouveau Manuel complet de l'organiste* (Paris).
[3] No record is known to exist as to the pitch to which the very early organs were tuned, or whether they were tuned to any uniform pitch whatever, which is extremely doubtful. In referring to the lowest pipe as being 12 feet in speaking length, a system of pipe measurement is made use of which is not known to have been adopted until centuries after the date at which this organ is stated to have been made.

the Thorn organ may have been an anticipation of that at Halberstadt, as far as the chromatic keyboard is concerned.

The Halberstadt Cathedral organ, although, strictly speaking, a ' *single* organ,' only, with a compass of scarcely three octaves, had three claviers, and pipes nearly equal in size to any that have ever been subsequently made. It was built by Nicholas Faber, a priest, and was finished on Feb. 23, 1361. Our information regarding it is obtained from the description of Michael Praetorius in his *Syntagma musicum*. It had twenty-two keys, fourteen diatonic and eight chromatic, extending from B♮ up to a′, and twenty bellows blown by ten men. Its largest pipe, B, stood in front, and was 31 Brunswick feet in length, and 3½ ft. in circumference, or about 14 inches in diameter. This note would now be marked as the semitone below the C of 32 feet, and the pipe would naturally be expected to exceed the pipe of that note in length ; but the pitch of the Halberstadt organ is known to have been more than a tone sharper than the highest pitch in use in England at the present day, which accounts for the want of length in its B♮ pipe.[1]

In the Halberstadt instrument a successful endeavour was made for the first time to obtain some relief from the constant 'full organ' effect, which was all that had previously been commonly produced. For this purpose a means was devised for enabling the pipes standing in front (afterwards the Principal, Praestant, or Open Diapason), and the larger pipes in the side towers (subsequently part of the Great Bass Principal, or 32-foot Diapason), to be used separately and independently of the other tiers of pipes, which were located behind, and hence called the *Hintersatz*, or ' hinderposition.' This result was obtained by introducing three claviers instead of one only ; the upper one for the full organ, consisting of all the tiers of pipes combined ; the middle one, of the same compass as the upper, and called ' Discant,' for the Open Diapason alone ; and the lower one, with a compass of an octave, from ♮ (B♮) to H (b♮), for the lower portion of the Bass Diapason. Praetorius mentions incidentally that the large bass pipes, which sounded the *third* octave below the unison, would have been scarcely definable, but being accompanied by the numerous pipes of other pitches in the general mixture organ, they became effective.

The claviers of the Halberstadt organ presented several interesting features ; and being

1 As the history of musical PITCH is treated of under its proper head, it is only necessary here to refer briefly to the remarkable fact that the pitch of old organs sometimes varied to no less an extent than half an octave, and that too at one and the same date, as shown by Arnold Schlick in 1511. One reason given for this great shifting of the pitch was, that the organ should be tuned to suit higher or lower voices, without the organist having to ' play the chromatics, which was not convenient to every one ' ; a difficulty that must have arisen as much from the construction of the keyboards, and the tuning in unequal temperament, as from lack of skill ᵥ the performer to use them.

the earliest examples of chromatic keyboards known, are here engraved from Praetorius.

The keys of the Halberstadt organ were made at a time when the five chromatic notes were placed in a separate row from the ' naturals,' almost as distinctly so as a second manual of the present day. The keys of the upper (*Hintersatz*) and middle (*Discant*) claviers (Fig. 10) measured four inches from centre to centre and the diatonic notes were ornamentally shaped and *lettered*, thus preserving the ' alphabetic ' custom observed in the 16th-century organ at Winchester, and described by Theophilus in the 11th. The chromatic notes were square-shaped, and had their surface about two and a half

FIG. 10.

FIG. 11.

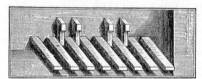

FIG. 12.

inches above that of the diatonic, were two inches in width, and one inch in thickness, and had a fall of about an inch and a quarter. The chromatic keys were no doubt pressed down by the three inner fingers, and the diatonic by the wrist end of the hand. The diatonic notes of the lower clavier (Fig. 11), eight in number, namely ♮ (B♮), C, D, E, F, G, A, H (B♮), were quite differently formed, being square-fronted, two inches in breadth, and with a space of about the same width on each side. These keys were evidently thrust down by the left hand, by pressure from the shoulder, like handles, the space on each side being left for the fingers and thumb to pass through. This clavier had four chromatic notes, C♯, E♭, F♯, and G♯, but curiously enough, not B♭, although that was the ' lyric semitone ' of which so much is heard long before.

The contrast between the *forte* and *piano* effect on the Halberstadt organ—from the full organ to a single set of pipes—must have been very violent ; but the experiment had the good effect of directing attention to the fact that a change, if less marked, would be grateful and useful ; for Seidel (p. 9) records that from this time instruments were frequently made comprising *two* manual organs, the upper one, interestingly enough, being named ' discant ' ; and he further gives it as his opinion that this kind of construction probably led to the invention of Couplers.

He likewise mentions that large churches were often provided with a second and smaller organ ; and Praetorius speaks of primitive little organs which were hung up against a column in the church ' like swallows' nests,' and contained twelve or thirteen notes almost or entirely diatonic, thus,

B, C, D, E, F, G, A, B,   C, D, E, F ; or
   C, D, E, F, G, A, B♭, C, D, E, F, G, A.

Dom Bedos relates that in the 14th century an organ was erected in the church of St. Cyprian, at Dijon, which not only had two manuals, but had the choir organ in front. The front pipes were made of tin, those inside of lead ; there were said to be sound-board grooves, covered underneath with white leather ; three bellows 4 feet 7 inches long, and 2 feet 1 inch wide ; and an arrangement by which a continuous wind could be provided from one bellows only. This, however, is manifestly the account of an organ which had received improvements long after its construction, such additions afterwards coming to be described as part of the original work.

MECHANICAL ADVANCE IN THE 15TH CENTURY.—We now come to the 15th century, which was prolific in its improvements of the spring-box, keys, pedals, wind-supply, etc. And first of the spring-box.

The first endeavour was to obtain more than one strength of tone from the same manual. It appears that to establish the power of preventing some of the sets of pipes (doubtless those that afterwards constituted the mixture and other bright-sounding ranks) from speaking when required to be silent, a sliding board was placed over the valves that opened and closed the entrance for the wind at the feet of those pipes. The remaining tiers of pipes, doubtless those sounding the unison (8), octave (4), and sub-octave (16), could thus be left in readiness to sound alone when desired. The effect of this contrivance must have greatly resembled that of the ' shifting movement ' of subsequent times.

Two distinct effects were thus obtained from one organ and one set of keys ; and the question would soon arise, ' If two, why not more ? ' A further division of the organ-sound soon followed ; and according to Praetorius the credit of first dividing and converting the *Hintersatz* into an instrument of several single sets of pipes (afterwards called registers or stops) is due to a German artificer of the appropriate

name of Timotheus, who constructed a sound-board possessing this power for an organ which he rebuilt for the monastery of the Bishop's palace at Würzburg.

The ' Spring sound-board ' was formed in the following manner. The valves of each note were closed in on each side by two diminutive walls (sound-board bars) extending from the back to the front of the wind-box, and, together with the top and bottom, forming and enclosing each valve within a separate canal (sound-board) groove of its own. The entire area of the former wind-box was partitioned off in this manner, and occupied by the ' bars ' and ' grooves ' of the newly devised sound-board. A playing-valve (sound-board pallet) was necessary below each groove to admit or exclude wind. These were collectively enclosed within a box (wind-chest) now added to fulfil the duty of the transformed wind-box. The valves immediately under the several pipes of a note were no longer drawn down from below by cords, but were pressed down from above, as shown in the following cut, which is a transverse section of a small spring sound-board for three stops.

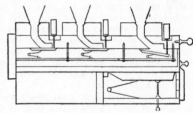

FIG. 13.

A metal pin passed down through the surface of the sound-board and rested on the front end of the ' register-valve ' as it was called. A movement or draw-stop was provided, on drawing which the longitudinal row of metal pins was pressed down, and the valves lowered. The combined resistance of the set of springs beneath the valves was very considerable, hence great force was necessary in drawing a stop, which had to be hitched on to an iron bar to keep it ' drawn.' When released it sprang back of its own accord. The set of pipes of which the register-valves were open would then be ready for use ; and in the woodcut the front set is shown as being thus prepared. The wind would be admitted into the groove by drawing down the sound-board pallet, which is seen immediately below.

By this means the power was created of using each separate set of pipes, except the small ones, singly or in any desired combination, so that the organ could be played loudly or softly, or at any intermediate strength between the two extremes ; and they now for the first time received distinctive names, as Principal (Open

Diapason, 8 feet) ; Octave (Principal, 4 feet) ; Quint (Twelfth, 2⅔ feet) ; Super-octave (Fifteenth, 2 feet) ; etc. ; and each separate series was then called a Register (Stop). The smaller sets of pipes were left to be used in a group, and were called 'Mixture '[1] (Sesquialtera, etc.). The stops sounding a note in accordance with the key struck, as C on the C key, were afterwards called Foundation-stops ; those which produced a different sound, as G or E on the C key, were named Mutation - stops ; while those that combined the two classes of sounds were distinguished as Compound or Mixture Stops.

The spring sound-board was much admired by some Hollanders ; and some organ-builders from the Low Countries, as well as from Brabant, went to see it, and constructed sound-boards on the same system for some time afterwards.

The pipe-work, however, was all of one class, —open, metal, cylindrical, and of full proportionate scale—similar in general model to the second great class of pipe referred to at the beginning of this article as Open. Great therefore as was the gain resulting from the invention of the registers, the tone still remained of one general character or quality. It then occurred to some of the thinking men of the time that other qualities of tone would probably ensue if modifications were made either in the shape, proportion, outline, or material of the pipes, etc. ; and the experiments justified the hypothesis.

Stopped pipes (our first great class) were made either of wood closed with a plug, or of metal covered with a sliding cap ; and so a soft pleasing mild tone was obtained. Thus originated the Gedact (Stopped Diapason), Bordun (Bourdon), Klein-gedact (Flute), etc. Some Reed-stops (our third class) were also invented about this time, as the Posaune (Trombone), Trumpet, Vox humana, etc. Stops composed of cylindrical pipes of small diameter were likewise constructed, and made to produce the string-tone, which stops were hence called Violone (Double Bass), Viol di gamba, etc. ; and further modifications of tone were secured by either making the pipes taper upwards, as in the Spitz-flote, Gemshorn, etc., or spread out, as in the Dolcan. Thus was brought about as great a contrast in the organ ' tone-tints ' as there is between the graduated but similar tones of a photograph and the varied tints of a coloured drawing.

In the course of the 15th century the keys were reduced in size several times, as fresh contrivances for manipulating the instrument

[1] Dr. Burney, Dr. Crotch, Kiesewetter and other writers, took considerable pains to ventilate and enforce their various theories as to the origin of the Mixture-stop in an organ ; but they all omitted to remember that for centuries the whole organ was nothing but one huge stop of the kind ; and that when the larger sets of pipes were separated off for use, the Mixture was self-formed out of the residue, consisting of rows of little pipes that were thought scarcely worth the trouble of ' drawing on' separately.

were from time to time thought of, or new requirements arose.

An early improvement consisted in combining the ' long and short keys ' on one manual, and so far reducing their size that they could be played by perhaps a couple of fingers and the thumb alternately. The manuals of the old organ in the church of St. Ægidius, in Brunswick, presented this advance ; and as they are early examples, perhaps the very first to foreshadow the modern keyboard, a representation of a few notes of one of them is here given from Praetorius.

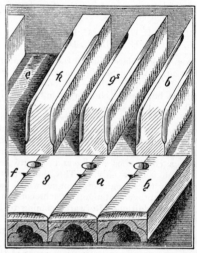

FIG. 14.

The naturals of the Great manual were about an inch and three-quarters in width, two inches and three-eighths in length in front of the short keys, while the short keys, three inches long and an inch wide, stood an inch and a half above the naturals. The keys of the second manual (Rück-positif), curiously enough, appear to have been made to a somewhat smaller gauge, the naturals being an inch and a half in width. On this organ the intervals of a third, fourth and fifth lay within the span of the hand.

It will be observed that the plan of lettering the keys was still followed ; but the formation of the clavier was quickly becoming so compact, well defined and susceptible of being learnt without such assistance, that the ' alphabet ' probably fell into disuse as superfluous soon after this time.

The name given to the second manual,— Rück-positif, Back-choir organ, or, as it is called in England, ' Choir organ in front,'—is interesting as showing that at this time the double organ (to the eye) was certainly in existence.

Franchinus Gaffurius, in his Theorica musica, printed at Milan in 1492, gives a curious engraving of an organist playing upon an early clavier of this period, with broad keys, of which a copy is given (Fig. 15).

The keys of the organs in the Barefooted Friars' church at Nuremberg (Rosenberger, 1475), the cathedral at Erfurt (Castendorfer, 1483), and the collegiate church of St. Blasius at Brunswick (Kranz, 1499), were less again in size than the foregoing, so that an octave was brought within about a note of its present width. The next reduction must, therefore, have introduced the scale of key still in use. Seidel (p. 10) mentions that in 1493 Rosen-

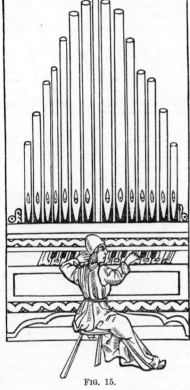

FIG. 15.

berger built for the cathedral at Bamberg a still larger organ than his former work at Nuremberg. and with more keys. He further observes that the manual of the organ in the Barefooted Friars' church had the upper keys of ivory and the under keys of ebony. Here, then, we reach a period when the keys were certainly capped with light and dark-hued materials, in the manner which continued to be followed up to the end of the 18th century, when the naturals were usually black, and the sharps and flats white. Seidel states also that all the above-named organs were provided with pedals.

The invention of the pedals ranks among the most important improvements that were effected in the 15th century. For a long time they did not exceed an octave in compass, and consisted of the diatonic notes only—♮ (B♮), C, D, E, F, G, A, H (B♮)—and their use was for some time confined, as might have been expected, to the holding of long sustained sounds only. The manual clavier was attached to them by cords. This kind of 'pedal action' could only be applied conveniently when the pedals were made to a similar gauge to the manual clavier as the clavier keys had previously been made to accord in position with the valves in the early spring-box. This correspondence of gauges was actually observed by Georgius Kleng in the pedals which he added to the organ at Halberstadt in 1495 ; and as those pedals were at the same time the earliest of which a representation is to be traced, an engraving has already been given of them below the Halberstadt claviers (Fig. 12). It will be observed that in addition to the diatonic keys already mentioned, they had the four chromatic notes corresponding with those on the lower manual with which they communicated. The naturals were made of the kind that were afterwards called 'toe pedals.'

In the early part of the 15th century—in the year 1418—the pedals received the important accession of a stop of independent pedal-pipes, and thus were initiated the 'Pedal Basses' which were destined to impart so much dignity and majesty to the general organ tone.

The manner in which the date of the construction of the first pedal stop was discovered is thus related in the Leipzig *Allgem. mus. Zeitung* for 1836 (p. 128) :

'In the year 1818 a new organ was erected in the church of Beeskow, five miles from Frankfort on the Oder, on which occasion the organ-builder, Marx, senior, took some pains to ascertain the age of the old organ which he had to remove. On a careful investigation it appeared that the old organ had been built just four hundred years, the date MCCCCXVIII being engraved on the upper side of the partition (*kern*) of the two principal pedal-pipes, for that these two pipes did belong to the pedal was clear from their admeasurement.'

This may, however, have indicated some kind of arrangement similar to that of SHORT OCTAVE (see below).

In 1468–69 Traxdorff, of Mainz, made an organ for the church of St. Sebald at Nuremberg, with an octave of pedals, which adjuncts led to his being afterwards at times quoted as the originator of them. Their invention has more usually been attributed to Bernhard in 1470 or 1471, organist to the Doge of Venice ; but there can be little doubt that they were known before his time.

Several improvements connected with the pedals seem not to have been traced to their originators ; such as the introduction of the semitones, the formation of the frame pedal-board as now made, the substitution of rollers for the rope-action when the breadth of the manual keys was made less than that of the pedals ; the separation of the 32-foot stop from the manual, and its appropriation, together with that of other registers, exclusively to the use of the pedals, etc. Bernhard may perhaps have been the first to originate some of these alterations, and Traxdorff others.

Dom Bedos mentions that in the course of the 15th century, 16- and even 32-foot pipes began to be heard of, and that they necessitated a general enlargement of the several parts of the organ, particularly of the bellows. Pipes of 16 and *nearly* 32 feet were, as we have seen, in existence a century earlier than the period to which Dom Bedos assigns them. His observation, therefore, may be taken as applying more probably to the fact that means, which he specifies, had been taken to rectify the feebleness existing in the tones of large pipes, such, for instance, as those at Halberstadt. Hand-bellows were no longer adequate to the supply of wind, either in quantity or strength, and hence more capacious ones were substituted. Praetorius, in 1620, illustrates this improvement by giving a representation of the twenty bellows which he found existing in the old organ in the church of St. Ægidius in Brunswick, and which we have copied (Fig. 16).[1]

Fig. 16.

Upon each bellows was fixed a wooden shoe ; the blowers held on to a transverse bar, and each man, placing his feet in the shoes of two bellows, raised one as he lowered the other. Great ingenuity and constructive labour were bestowed on such bellows ; but a supply of wind of uni-

[1] The reader will remember that this method of compressing the organ-wind had been thought of upwards of a thousand years earlier at Constantinople.

form strength could never have been obtained from them, and consequently the organ could never have sounded strictly in tune.

About the beginning of the 16th century the very ingenious but complicated spring sound-board was discontinued as being subject to frequent and very difficult repairs, and for it was substituted the sound-board with sliding registers.

In this sound-board were ingeniously combined the chief features of the two kinds of wind-controlling apparatus that had been in use in previous centuries. Between the holes in the top of the grooves, and those now made parallel therewith in the pipe-stocks, into which the feet of the pipes fitted, were now introduced the *slides*, shown in section in the following cut ;

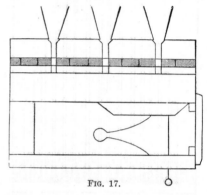

Fig. 17.

which were now laid the length-way of the sound-board, instead of the cross-way as in the old spring-box ; and as they were placed in the opposite direction they likewise operated in the reverse way ; that is, each slide opened or closed one pipe or rank of the several notes, whereas before it acted on the several pipes of one note, as shown in Fig. 7. The pallets and springs in the wind-chest were of course retained; but the forest of valves, etc., which had been imbedded in the grooves was done away with, and the sound-board simplified and perfected in the form in which it still continues to be made. (Fig. 17.)

In the early part of the 16th century (1516–18) a large and handsome organ was erected in St. Mary's Church, Lübeck, which had two manuals from DD to *a'''* and a separate pedal down to C. The latter had a great Principal of 32 feet, and a second one of 16 feet, made of the finest English tin, and both 'in front.' This organ, however, was tuned to a very sharp pitch—a whole tone above the highest now in use. Its largest pipe, therefore, although named C, really sounded D, and was therefore scarcely so long as the biggest pipe at Halberstadt, made a century and a half earlier. This organ received the addition of a 'hird Manual (then called 'Positiv im Stuhl') in 1560 and 1561, and subsequently underwent many other enlargements and improvements; so that by the beginning of the 18th century, when the celebrated Buxtehude was organist, its disposition stood nearly as follows; though the list may possibly include a few subsequent additions of minor importance.

HAUPTWERK. 13 stops.

	Feet.		Feet.
Principal	16	Rausch-pfeife (12 & 15).	
Quintatön	16	Mixture, 7 ranks.	
Octav	8	Scharff, 4 ranks.	
Spitz-flöte	8	Trompete	16
Octav	4	Trompete	8
Rohr-flöte	4	Zink	8
Nassat	2⅔		

UNTER-WERK. 14 stops.

Bordun	16	Sesquialtera (12 & 17).	
Principal	8	Mixture, 4 ranks.	
Rohr-flöte	8	Scharff, 5 ranks.	
Viola di Gamba	8	Fagott	16
Quintatön	8	Bar-pfeife	8
Octave	4	Trichter-Regal	8
Spitz-flöte	2	Vox humana	8

BRUST-WERK. 15 stops.

Principal	8	Oboe	8
Gedact	8	Cormorn	8
Rohr-flöte	8	Regal	8
Octave	4	(In a swell)	
Nassat	2⅔	Flöte	8
Sesquialtera (12 & 17)	2	Trompete	8
Mixture, 8 ranks.		Trompete	8
Cimbal, 3 ranks.		Vox humana	8

PEDAL. 15 stops.

Principal	32	Mixture, 6 ranks.	
Principal	16	Posaune	32
Sub-bass	16	Posaune	16
Octave	8	Basson	16
Gedact	8	Trompete	8
Octav	4	Cormorne	8
Nacht-horn	4	Trompete	4
Octav	2		

Having traced the history and growth of the organ in various kingdoms, attention may now be devoted to its special progress in England.

ELY CATHEDRAL ACCOUNTS.—The earliest record known to exist that gives any particulars as to the cost of making an organ in England is that preserved in the Precentor's accounts of Ely Cathedral, under the date 1407. The items, translated from the Latin, read as follows:

	s.	d.
20 stones of lead	16	9
4 white horses' hides for 4 pair of bellows	7	8
Ashen hoops for the bellows	0	4
10 pairs of hinges	1	10
The carpenter, 8 days, making the bellows	2	8
12 springs	0	3
1 pound of glue	0	1
1 pound of tin	0	3
6 calf skins	2	6
12 sheep skins	2	4
2 pounds of quicksilver	2	0
Wire, nails, cloth, hoops and staples	1	0
Fetching the organ-builder, and his board, 13 weeks	40	0
Total	3 17	8

These particulars, although scanty, contain entries that help us to trace a few of the features of this early instrument. The 'ashen hoops' indicate that the bellows were of the forge kind. The '12 springs' were presumably the 'playing springs,' and if so, denote that the organ had a compass of 12 notes, C to F, with the B♭ added. The metal for the pipes, compounded of '1 pound of tin' only to '20 stones of lead,' must

have been rather poor in quality and texture. The circumstance of the organ-builder being fetched, and his board paid for, indicates that the useful class of artificers to which he belonged sometimes led rather an itinerant life, as we shall presently see they continued to do two centuries later.

About the year 1450, Whethamstede, Abbot of St. Albans, presented to his church an organ on which he expended, including its erection, fifty pounds—an enormous sum in those days. This instrument, we are told, was superior to everything of the kind then in England for size, tone and workmanship; but no record is left as to where or by whom it was made, nor as to what its contents or compass were.

A PAIR OF ORGANS.—The term 'pair of organs,' so much used in the 16th and the greater part of the 17th centuries, has been a source of as much difficulty to the commentators as the spelling of the words themselves became to the scribes of the period. (See note below.) It grew gradually into use; and the most interesting fact connected with it, namely that there were various *kinds* of 'pairs' in use, has passed without hitherto receiving sufficient notice. At York in 1419, 1457, 1469 and 1485, the instrument is spoken of in the singular number, as 'The organ,' or 'The great organ.' In 1475 it is referred to as 'An organ.' In 1463 we meet with 'yᵉ players at yᵉ orgenys,' and in 1482 a payment is made for 'mending of organys.' In 1501 the complete expression is met with, 'one peyre of orgynys'; and it continued in use up to the time of Pepys, who wrote his 'Diary' in the second half of the 17th century.

One commentator considered the term 'pair' to refer to the '*double* bellows'; but besides the fact that a *single* bellows is sometimes itself called a 'pair,' a 'pair of virginals,' containing wires, required no wind whatever. Another annotator thought that a 'pair' signified two organs conjoined, with two sets of keys, one above the other—'one called the choir organ, and the other the great organ'; but this explanation is answered by an entry of the expense incurred for 'a pair of new organs' for the Church of St. Mary at Hill, in the year 1521, which, including the cost 'for bringing them home,' amounted altogether to 'xs. viijd.' only. If this were not sufficient, there would be the fact that many churches contained 'two payre of orgyns'[1]; and if they were of the bulk supposed, there would be the question how much room, if any, could have remained in the church for the accommodation of the congregation. A third writer suggested that a 'pair' meant an organ with two pipes to each note; but 'a pair of regals' sometimes had but a

[1] Ashford.   'Item ij payer of great organes.'
Canterbury (Westgate).   'Item, two paire of organs.'
Guildford (Holy Trinity).   'Item, ij paire of orgaynes.'
Norwich (St. Andrew).   'Item, ij peir of orgonnes.'
Singfield.   'Item, ij peyr of orgens,'

single pipe to each key. The term in all probability meant simply an instrument with at least one complete set of pipes.[1] It might have more, as in Duddington's organ noticed farther on.

The most interesting question here, however, is not simply the fact that a church had frequently two pairs of organs, but, when so, why one was generally ' the grete orgones ' and the other ' the small orgones.' It is quite possible that the custom mentioned by Praetorius, and already quoted, may have prevailed in England, of regulating the pitch of the organ according to the prevailing pitch of the voices (whether high or low), and that when there were two organs, one was made to suit each class of voice ; and as an alteration of pitch, made for this purpose, of say half an octave, would have caused one organ to be nearly half as large again as the other, their difference of size may have led to the distinction of name as a natural sequence. This opinion seems to receive support from the fact that at Bethersden they had not a ' great ' but ' a *base* peare of organes.'

AN EARLY SPECIFICATION.—Under the date 1519 we meet with the earliest specification of an English organ that is known to exist. It is found embodied in an ' endenture ' or ' bargayn ' entered into by ' Antony Duddyngton, citezen of London,' to make a ' payer of organs ' for the ' P'isshe of Alhalowe, Barkyng, next yᵉ Tower of London.' It was to have three stops, namely, a ' Diapason, containing length of x foot or more,' and ' dowble principalls throweout, to contain the length of v foote.' The compass was to be ' dowble *Ce-fa-ut*,' and comprise ' xxvij playne keyes,' which would doubtless be the old four-octave short octave range, in which the *apparent* EE key sounded CC, up to *c″*. It was further specified that ' the pyppes wᵗ inforth shall be as fyne metall and stuff as the utter parts, that is to say of pure Tyn, wᵗ as fewe stoppes as may be convenient ' ; and the cost was to be ' fyfty poundes sterlinge.' It was also a condition ' that the aforesaid Antony shall convey the belowes in the loft abowf, wʰ a pype to the sond boarde.' It is interesting to note that although made so few years after the invention of ' stops ' and the ' sound-board ' abroad, the English builder had made himself acquainted with these improvements, and here inserted them.

Many entries follow closely on the date given above ; but none that supply any additional matter of sufficient interest to be quoted here, until nearly the end of the century, when the list of payments made to John Chappington for an organ he built in 1597 for Magdalen College, Oxford, shows that the practice of painting the

front pipes was sometimes observed at that period. It is short, and runs thus :

	£	s.	d.
Paid Mr. Chappington for the organ	35	13	8
For colour to decorate the same .	2	2	0
For wainscot for the same . .	3	14	0
	41	9	8

SHORT OCTAVES.—By the end of the 15th century the manuals had in continental organs been extended to four octaves in compass, and those of this country had most likely also reached the same range, the lowest octave, however, being either a ' short octave ' or a ' broken octave.' In the short octave two of the natural keys were omitted, and the succession stood thus : CC (on the EE key), FF, G, A, B, C.[2] A short octave manual, CC to C in alt, therefore, had only twenty-seven natural keys instead of twenty-nine. The three short keys in the lower octave were not all chromatic notes, but sounded DD on the FF♯ key, EE on the G♯ key, and B♭. The object of this device no doubt was to obtain a deep sound for the tonic of as many of the scales and chords in use at the time as was practicable. When the lowest octave was made complete, the EE♭ note was present ; DD occupied its correct position ; and the CC♯ key sounded AA. Father Smith's organs at the University Church, Oxford, the Danish Chapel, Wellclose Square, and St. Nicholas, Deptford, were originally made to this compass. A key was sometimes added beyond CC, sounding GG, which converted the compass into ' GG short octaves.' There is a painting in the picture gallery at Holyrood, of about the date of the end of the 15th century, representing St. Cecilia playing upon a Positive Organ, which shows quite clearly the lower keys and pipes of a GG short octave manual. Both Smith and Harris sometimes constructed organs to this compass, and subsequent builders also did so throughout the 18th and early part of the 19th centuries. The FFF short octave manual, which would seem to have existed, although we have at present no record of it, might have had the note acting on the AA long key, or on a supplementary short key between the BB and CC keys.

RECORD OF INSTRUMENTS BY THE DALLAM FAMILY.—A great progressive step was made when Thomas DALLAM (*q.v.*), in 1605-06, built for King's College Chapel, Cambridge, the handsome ' double organ,' the case of which remains to this day. It was a complete two-manual organ, the earliest English specimen of which we have a clear trace ; and to construct it Dallam and his assistants closed their workshop in London and took up their residence in Cambridge. As this instrument is the first of importance out of several that were made before the time of the Civil War, but of which the accounts are more or less vague or incom-

---

[1] It is possible that the word ' pair ' was used in a sense equivalent to the German ' Paar,' of several things, not exclusively two. Traces of this use in England remain in the vulgar phrase ' a pair of stairs.' If this be so, the expression might refer to an instrument with a number of pipes.

[2] In the system of nomenclature now used apart from the special method employed by organists, these notes are C F, G, A, B, c.

plete, it will be worth while to follow out some of their leading particulars.

No record is known to exist of the contents or compass of this instrument. The only stop mentioned is the ' shaking stoppe ' or tremulant. The compass, however, can be deduced with some approach to certainty. Mr. Thomas Hill, who with his father rebuilt this organ in the 19th century, stated that the ' fayre great pypes ' mentioned by Dallam still occupied their original positions in the eastern front of the case, where they are utilised as part of the Double Diapason. As the largest pipe sounds the GG of the present lower pitch (nearly a whole tone below what is known to have been the high ecclesiastical pitch of the first half of the 17th century), there can be little doubt that the King's College Chapel organ was originally of FFF compass, as Father Smith's subsequent instruments were at the Temple, St. Paul's (choir organ) and Durham. Smith in that case must simply have followed an old tradition. More is said on this subject farther on. The east front pipes, as well as those in the ' Chayre Organ,' were handsomely embossed, gilded and coloured.

On Mar. 20, 1632, Robert Dallam, ' citizen and blacksmith of London,' entered into an agreement with ' the right worshippfull John Scott, deane of the cathedrall and metropoliticall church of St. Peter of Yorke, touchinge the makinge of a great organ for the said church.' Most of the particulars respecting this instrument have fortunately been preserved, from which we learn that ' the names and number of the stoppes or setts of pipes for the said great organ, to be new made ; every stopp containeinge fiftie-one pipes ; the said great organ containeing eight stoppes,' were as follows :

GREAT ORGAN. 9 stops.

1 and 2. Imprimis two open diapasons of tynn, to stand in sight, many of them to be chased.
3. Item one diapason stopp of wood.
4 and 5. Item two principals of tynn.
6. Item one twelft to the diapason.
7. Item one small principall of tynn. (15.)
8. Item one recorder, unison to the said principall. (15.)
9. Item one two and twentieth.

' The names and number of stoppes of pipes for the chaire organ, every stopp containeinge fiftie-one pipes, the said chaire organ containeinge five stoppes,' were as follows :

CHAIRE ORGAN. 5 stops.

10. Imprimis one diapason of wood.
11. Item one recorder of tynn, unison to the voice.
12. Item one principal of tynn, to stand in sight, many of them to be chased.
13. Item one flute of wood.
14. Item one small principall of tynn. (15.)
    Three bellows.

It will be noticed that this organ contained neither reeds nor mixtures, and but one mutation-stop, namely the ' twelfth.'

No mention is made as to what was the compass of the old York Minster organ. All that is stated is that each ' stoppe ' had a series of ' fiftie-one pipes '—an unusual number. The old case of the organ remained until the in-cendiary fire of 1829, and contained the two original Diapasons ; and as the largest pipes of these stops sounded the GG of the lowered pitch of the 18th century, it is quite possible that the compass was originally FFF, short octave (that note sounding on the AA key), up to C in alt (F, to c′′′), which range would have required exactly the number of notes specified in the agreement. Robert Dallam built organs similar to that at York for St. Paul's and Durham Cathedrals, the latter costing £1000. If they were of FFF compass, that circumstance would perhaps account for the schemes for Smith's new organs for both those churches having been prepared for that exceptional range.

In Aug. and Sept. 1634 three musical enthu-siasts, ' a Captaine, a Lieutenant, and an Ancient (Ensign), of the Military Company in Norwich,' went on ' a Seaven Weekes' Journey' through a great part of England, in the course of which they occasionally took particular notice of the organs. At York they ' saw and heard a faire, large, *high* organ, newly built '—the one just noticed ; at Durham they ' were wrapt with the sweet sound and richness of a fayre organ ' ; at Lichfield ' the organs were deep and sweet ' ; at Hereford was ' heard a most sweet organ ' ; at Bristol they found a ' neat, rich, melodious organ ' ; while at Exeter the organ was ' rich, delicate, and lofty, with more additions than any other ; and large pipes of an extraordinary length.' Some of these in-struments were destined in a few years to fall a prey to ' axes and hammers.' The organ at Carlisle, however, was described as being ' like a shrill bagpipe.'

MAGDALEN COLLEGE, OXFORD.—Three years afterwards (in 1637) a maker of the name of HARRIS (*q.v.*)—the first of four generations of organ-builders of that name—built a ' double organ ' (Great Organ, with Choir Organ in front) for Magdalen College, Oxford. Its Manuals ranged from ' Do Sol Re ' (double C) without the CC♯ up to D in alt (C to d′′′) fifty notes ; and the Great Organ had eight stops, while the Choir had five. The following was its specification :

GREAT ORGAN. 8 stops.

	Feet.			Feet.
1 & 2. Two open Diapasons	8		5 & 6. Two Fifteenths .	. 2
3 & 4. Two Principals	. 4		7 & 8. Two Two-and-twentieths	1

CHOIR ORGAN. 5 stops.

	Feet tone.			Feet tone.
9. One Stopped Diapason	8		12. One Recorder	. 4
10 & 11. Two Principals	4		13. One Fifteenth	. 2

This was the organ which Cromwell had taken down and conveyed to Hampton Court, where it was placed in the great gallery. It was restored to the college in 1660, and remained there until 1737, when it was removed to Tewkesbury Abbey. The Diapasons and Principal of the Great Organ, and the Principal in the Choir still remain, and are made of tin alloyed with about eight pounds of lead to the hundredweight.

This organ was tuned to a high pitch, as is shown by one of the items in Renatus Harris's agreement for improving it (1690), which specifies that he ' shall and will alter the pitch of the said organs half a note lower than they are now.'

This is the last organ of which we have any authentic particulars as being made previously to the outburst that checked the art of organ-building in this country for several years.

On Aug. 23, 1643, an ordinance was passed by the Lords and Commons assembled in Parliament for abolishing superstitious monuments. On May 9, 1644, a second ordinance was passed ' for the further demolishing of monuments of Idolatry and Superstition,' in which the destruction of organs was enjoined.[1]

In consequence of this ordinance collegiate and parochial churches were stripped of their organs and ornaments ; some of the instruments were sold to private persons, who preserved them ; some were totally and others partially demolished ; some were taken away by the clergy to prevent their being destroyed, and some few escaped injury altogether.

Among the organs that escaped destruction or removal were those of St. Paul's, York, Durham and Lincoln Cathedrals ; St. John's College, Oxford ; Christ's College, Cambridge, etc.

During the sixteen years that elapsed between the date of the ordinance already quoted and that of the Restoration, most of the English organ-builders had been dispersed, and compelled to work as ordinary joiners, carpenters, etc. ; so that at the expiration of the period just mentioned, there was, according to Sir John Hawkins, ' scarce an organ-maker that could be called a workman in the kingdom,' excepting the Dallams (three brothers) ; Thamar of Peterborough, concerning whom, however, nothing is known ; Preston of York, who repaired the organ in Magdalen College, Oxford, in 1680—and who, among other doings, according to Renatus Harris (1686), spoiled one stop and several pipes of another ; and Henry Loosemore of Exeter, who built the organ in the cathedral of that city. Inducements were, therefore, held out to encourage artists from the Continent to settle in this country ; and among those who responded to this invitation were a German, Bernhard Schmidt, known as ' Father Smith,'[2] with his two nephews, Bernard (Christian) and Gerard ; and Thomas Harris, an Englishman, who had taken refuge in France during the troublous

[1] For the proposal to abolish organ-playing in churches as early as 1550 see MERBECKE.
[2] No particulars of Smith's first organ at Whitehall exist. That which Hopkins originally described here was the organ of the Banqueting Hall Chapel built in 1699, i.e after his Temple and St. Paul's organs (see *Father Smith*, by the Rev. A. Freeman). This diminishes the historical importance of the instrument and disposes of Hopkins's suggestion that it was a model for the Restoration

times, together with his son Renatus, a young man of great ingenuity and spirit.

Smith and the Dallams had for some years the chief business of the kingdom, the Harrises not receiving an equal amount of encouragement ; but on the death of Robert and Ralph Dallam, in 1665 and 1672 respectively, and of the elder Harris shortly after, Renatus Harris became a formidable rival to Smith.

Smith seems to have settled at once in London, was appointed ' organ-maker in ordinary ' to King Charles II. and put into possession of apartments in Whitehall, called in an old plan of the palace ' The Organ-builder's Workhouse.' The Harrises appear to have taken up their abode at Old Sarum, but on the death of the father, Renatus removed to the metropolis.

To illustrate the gradual progress from this starting-ground, a description will now be given of a series of representative organs, the accounts of which are derived from sources not now generally accessible, including notices of many historical instruments which, since the time of their original construction, have either been much altered or removed altogether.

THE RESTORATION ORGANS

Soon after the Restoration, Ralph Dallam built an organ for St. George's Chapel, Windsor, containing the recently imported novelties of Compound and Trumpet Stops (Nos. 6 and 7, below). It was a single-manual organ only ; and its specification, given below, is very interesting, as showing that means were taken even at that early time to compensate, as far as might be, for the lack of a second manual, by the adoption of mechanical arrangements for obtaining variety of effect from a limited number of registers governed by a single set of keys. Thus there were two ' shifting movements,' or pedals, one of which reduced the ' Full Organ ' to the Diapasons and Principal, and the other to the Diapasons alone. Thus two reductions of tone, in imitation of choir organ strength, could quickly be obtained ; which, in a place like St. George's Chapel, where choral service was celebrated, was very necessary. Besides this, the Compound and the

organ builders. Its specification is retained here for comparison with others.
C.

GREAT ORGAN. 10 stops.

	Pipes.			Pipes.
1. Open Diapason .	. 53	7. Block Flute, metal to		
2. Holflute .	. 53		middle C♯ .	. 24
3. Principal .	. 53	8. Sesquialtera, 3 ranks .		159
4. Nason .	. 53	9. Cornet, to middle C, do.		72
5. Twelfth .	. 53	10. Trumpet .	.	. 53
6. Fifteenth .	. 53			
				626

CHOIR ORGAN. 5 stops.

11. Stopped Diapason	. 53	14. Cremona, through	.	53
12. Principal .	. 53	15. Vaux Humane .	.	53
13. Flute, wood, to middle C	25			
				237

ECCHO ORGAN. 4 stops.

16. Open Diapason .	. 29	19. Trumpet .	.	. 29
17. Principal .	. 29			145
18. Cornet, 2 ranks (12 & 17)	58	Total		1008

Compass, Great and Choir, GG, without GG♯ to C in alt, 53 notes.
Eccho, Fiddle G to C in alt, 29 notes.

Trumpet stops were both made to draw in halves at middle C, that is to say, the Treble portion could be used without the Bass, so that a solo could be played prominently with the right hand and a soft accompaniment with the left ; and the solo stop could also be suddenly shut off by the foot at pleasure.[1]

GREAT ORGAN. 9 draw-stops.

	Pipes.			Pipes.
1. Open Diapason to CC, then Stopped and Octave pipes	54	5. Fifteenth		52
		6. Cornet Treble, 3 ranks		78
		Sesquialtera Bass, 3 ranks		78
2. Stopped Diapason	52			
3. Principal	52	7. Trumpet Treble		26
4. Twelfth	52	Trumpet Bass		26

Compass, GG, short octaves, to D in alt, 52 notes.

EXETER. DOUBLE DIAPASON, ETC. — The organ in Exeter Cathedral, constructed by John Loosemore, possessed a remarkable feature in its Double Open Diapason, which contained the largest pipes ever made in this country. The fourteen pipes of which this stop consisted were grouped in two separate sets of seven each, against the columns at the south entrance of the choir,[1] and therefore at some distance from the main body of the organ ; and were acted upon by an additional set of pallets. The dimensions of the largest pipe (GGG) were as follows :

Speaking part, long	20 ft. 6 in.	Contents of the speaking part,
Nose	4 „ 0 „	3 hogs. 8 gal.
Circumference	3 „ 11 „	Weight, 360 lbs.
Diameter	1 „ 3 „	

The large Exeter pipes, like those at Halberstadt, did not produce much effect when tried by themselves, for an old writer, the Hon. Roger North, says of them, ' I could not be so happy to perceive that in the musick they signified anything at all ' ; but (like those at Halberstadt) they manifested their influence when used in combination ; for another writer, at the beginning of the 19th century, observes respecting them, ' no effect alone, but very fine with the Diapasons and Principal.'

The following was the scheme of the Exeter Cathedral organ, in which we find the Open Diapasons duplicated :

GREAT ORGAN. 10 stops.

	Pipes.			Pipes.
1. Double Diapason	14	7. Fifteenth		55
2. Open Diapason	55	8. Sesquialtera 5 ranks		275
3. Open Diapason	55	9. Cornet to middle C, do.		135
4. Stopped Diapason	55	10. Trumpet		55
5. Principal	55			
6. Twelfth	55			809

CHOIR ORGAN. In front 5 stops.

	Pipes.			Pipes.
11. Stopped Diapason	55	15. Bassoon		55
12. Principal	55			275
13. Flute	55			
14. Fifteenth	55	Total		1084

Compass, Great and Choir, GG, long octaves, no GG♯, to D in alt, 55 notes.

THE TEMPLE. TWO QUARTER NOTES.—In Sept. 1682 the treasurers of the two Hon. Societies of the Inner and Middle Temple had some conversation with Smith respecting the construction of an organ for their church. Renatus Harris, who was then residing in ' Wyne Office Court, Fleet Street,' and was therefore close upon the spot, made interest

___
[1] The ' Cornet ' quickly became a favourite ' solo ' stop and continued to be so for nearly 150 years,

with the Societies, who were induced to arrange that if each of these excellent artists would set up an organ, the Societies would retain that which, in the greatest number of excellences, deserved the preference. This proposal was agreed to, and by May 1684, the two organs were erected in the church. Smith's stood in the west-end gallery, and Harris's on the south (Inner Temple) side of the Communion Table. They were at first exhibited separately on appointed days, and then tried on the same day : and it was not until the end of 1687, or beginning of 1688, that the decision was given in favour of Smith's instrument ; Harris's organ being rejected without reflecting any loss of reputation on its ingenious builder.[2]

Smith's organ reached in the bass to FFF ; and from FF upwards it had two additional keys or ' quarter notes ' in each octave, ' which rarityes,' according to an old book preserved in the library of the Inner Temple, ' no other organ in England hath ; and can play any tune, as for instance yᵉ tune of yᵉ 119th Psalm (in E minor), and severall other services set by excellent musicians ; which no other organ will do.' The order of the keys ran thus : FFF, GG, AA, BB♭, BB♮, then semitones to gamut G, after which the two special quarter tones in each octave ; the compass ending on C in alt, and the number of keys on each manual being sixty-one.[3]

The keys for the two extra notes (A♭ and D♯) were provided by those for G♯ and E♭ being cut across midway ; the back halves, which acted on the additional pipes, rising as much above the front halves as the latter did above the long keys.[4]

Smith's organ had three complete manuals, which was also a novelty. Two complete stops were allotted to the upper set of keys, forming a kind of Solo organ, with which the ' Ecchos ' acted in combination.

___
[2] The interesting details of this musical contest are not given here, as they have been printed separately by one of the Benchers of the Middle Temple, the late Edmund Macrory, under the title A Few Notes on the Temple Organ. (See also PURCELL, Henry.)

[3] Dr. Armes, the organist of Durham Cathedral, brought under the notice of the present writer a very curious discovery—namely, that the organ in that Church was originally prepared for, and afterwards received, quarter notes exactly similar to those at the Temple. The original order for the organ, dated Aug., 18, 1683, does not provide for them, the number of pipes to each single stop being specifically given, ' fifty-four,' which would indicate the same compass as the Temple organ, viz. FFF to C in alt without the quarter tones ; but the sound-boards, roller-boards, etc., were unquestionably made from the first with two extra grooves, movements, etc., for each octave from FF upwards, and the large extra diapason pipes, as being required for the east and west fronts, were also inserted. The original contract was completed by May 1, 1685 ; and Dr. Armes is of opinion that the £50, paid in 1691 to Smith by ' the Worshl, the Dean and Chapter of Durham for work done at ye Organ ' was for the insertion of the quarter-tone pipes. Smith made use of several different pitches. His highest, arising from placing a pipe of one English foot in speaking length on the A key, he used at Durham Cathedral. His next, resulting from placing a similar pipe on the B♭ key, he used for Hampton Court Chapel. The pitch a semitone lower than the last, produced by placing the 1-ft. pipe on B♮, was used by Renatus Harris towards the latter part of the 17th century. It was Handel's pitch, and that of the organ-builders generally of the 18th and early part of the 19th centuries, as well as of the Philharmonic Society at the time of its establishment (1813). The lowest pitch of all, arising from placing the 1-ft. pipe on the C key, was used by Smith at Trinity College, Cambridge. These variations were first clearly pointed out by Mr. Alexander Ellis in his History of Musical Pitch, 1880. (See PITCH.)

[4] The organ built by Parker for the foundling chapel in 1769 had four quarter notes, D♭, D♯, A♭ and A♯. These were not furnished with extra keys but were controlled by a substituting mechanism.

The following is a copy of the Schedule of Father Smith's organ as delivered to the two Societies, signed, and dated June 21, 1688.

GREAT ORGAN. 10 stops.

	Pipes.	Foote Tone.			Pipes.	Foote Tone.
1. Prestand of Mettle	61	12	6. Super Octavo	.	61	03
2. Holflute of Wood			7. Sesquialtera of			
and Mettle	. 61	12	Mettle	. 183	03
3. Principall of Mettle	61	06	8. Mixture of Mettle	226	03
4. Gedackt of Wains-			9. Cornette of Mettle	112	02
cott	. . . 61	06	10. Trumpet of Mettle	61	12
5. Quinta of Mettle	. 61	04			948

CHOIR ORGAN. 6 stops.

	Pipes.	Foote Tone.			Pipes.	Foote Tone.
11. Gedackt of Wains-			15. A Violl and Violin			
cott	. . . 61	12	of Mettle	. . 61	12
12. A Sadt of Mettle	. 61	06	16. Voice humane of			
13. Holflute of Mettle	61	06	Mettle	. . 61	12
14. Spittsflute of Met-					
tle	. . . 61	03			366

ECCHOS. 7 stops.

	Pipes.	Foote Tone.			Pipes.	Foote Tone.
17. Gedackt of Wood	. 61	06	21. Sesquialtera of			
18. Super Octaveo of			Mettle	. . 105	
Mettle	. . 61	03	22. Cornett of Mettle	87	
19. Gedackt of Wood	. 29		23. Trumpett	. . 29	
20. Flute of Mettle	. 29				401

Total 1715

With 3 full setts of Keys and quarter notes to C in alt, 61 notes.

ST. PAUL'S CATHEDRAL. — Father Smith's success at the Temple doubtless had much to do with his being invited to erect an organ in St. Paul's Cathedral ; the contract for which was dated and signed Dec. 19, 1694.[1] The instrument was to consist of Great and Chayre Organs, and Echoes, it was to be completed by Lady Day, 1696, and the price to be £2000. The compass was to be the same as that at the Temple, namely ' Double F fa ut to C sol fa in Alt inclusive,' 54 notes. Smith's contract was for the inside of the organ only ; the case being provided by Sir Christopher Wren. The list of stops originally agreed upon was as follows :

GREAT ORGAN. 12 stops.

1. Open Diapason.	7. Fifteenth.
2. Open Diapason.	8. Small Twelfth.
3. Stop Diapason.	9. Sesquialtera.
4. Principal.	10. Mixture.
5. Holfleut.	11. Cornet.
6. Great Twelfth.	12. Trumpet.

CHAYRE ORGAN. 9 stops.

13. Stop Diapason.	18. Fifteenth.
14. Quinta dena Diapason.	19. Cymball.
15. Principal.	20. Voice Humane.
16. Holfleut.	21. Crumhorne.
17. Great Twelfth.	

ECHOES or halfe stops ; 6.

22. Diapason.	25. Fifteenth.
23. Principal.	26. Cornet.
24. Nason.	27. Trumpet.

After the contract was signed, Smith extended his design, and made the Great Manual to the compass of 16 ft., instead of 12 ft. only ; and he added the six large extra notes—CCC, DDD, EEE♭, EEE♮, FFF♯, and GG♯—at his own expense. He had previously given Sir Christopher Wren the dimensions of the case he would require for his 12-ft. organ ; and he now desired these to be increased, but this Sir Christopher refused, declaring that the building was already spoiled by the ' confounded box of whistles.' Smith took his revenge on Wren

1 It is given in *Mus. T.*, 1880, p. 21 ; an illustration of the organ is in the same periodical, 1900, p. 794 ; see also 1901. p. 230.

by letting the larger open Diapason pipes in the two side towers project through the top of the case nearly a foot, which vexed Sir Christopher exceedingly, and compelled him to add ornaments several feet in height to hide the disfigurement. The Choir Organ case, too, was made so small that it had no room for the Quinta-dena, which therefore, though made, had to be left out.

EARLY 18TH CENTURY.—An organ at St. Saviour's, Southwark (now Southwark Cathedral), is said to have been built by ' one Jordan, a distiller, who,' as Sir John Hawkins tells us in his *History of Music*, ' had never been instructed in the business, but had a mechanical turn, and was an ingenious man, and who, about the year 1700, betook himself to the making of organs, and succeeded beyond expectation.' He certainly built several excellent and substantial instruments. The one under notice had a 16-ft. octave of metal pipes acting on the Great Organ keys from tenor C down to CC. These large pipes originally stood in the front of the case, where they made a very imposing appearance, as their full length was presented to view, without nearly a yard of the upper part being hidden behind the case, as at St. Paul's. This organ possibly had an Echo ; but no account of it has been preserved.

GREAT ORGAN. 13 stops.

	Pipes.		Pipes.
1. Double Open Diapason,		8. Fifteenth . . 54
CCC to CC, no CCC♯ . 12		9. Sesquialtera, 4 ranks. 216
2. Open Diapason . . 54		10. Furniture, 3 ranks . 162
3. Open Diapason . . 54		11. Cornet, 5 ranks . 145
4. Stopped Diapason . . 54		12. Trumpet . . . 54
5. Principal . . . 54		13. Clarion . . . 54
6. Flute . . . 54		
7. Twelfth . . . 54		1021

CHOIR ORGAN. 7 stops.

14. Open Diapason, wood 54		19. Mixture, 3 ranks . 162
15. Stopped Diapason . 54		20. Vox Humana . . 54
16. Principal . . . 54		486
17. Flute . . . 54		
18. Fifteenth . . . 54		Total 1507

Compass, GG, short octaves, up to E in alt, 54 notes.

In the year 1710 Renatus Harris erected in Salisbury Cathedral, in place of the instrument put up by his father, an organ possessing four manuals (for the first time in England) and fifty stops, including ' eleven stops of Echos,' and on which ' may be more varietys express'd, than by all ye organs in England, were their several excellencies united.' Such was the glowing account given of the capabilities of this new organ, on the engraving of its ' East Front.' The extra department consisted of a complete borrowed organ of thirteen stops derived from the Great Organ. The Choir organ had its own real stops ; and the ' eleven Stops of Echos ' were to a great extent made up of the single ranks of the ordinary Cornet. There was a ' Drum Pedal, CC,' the ' roll ' of which was caused by the addition of a second pipe sounding a semitone below the first pipe, with which it caused a rapid beat. Smith had previously put ' a Trimeloe ' into his organ at St. Mary-at

Hill, and ' a Drum,' sounding D, into that at St. Nicholas, Deptford.

FIRST GREAT ORGAN. 15 real stops.

	Pipes.		Pipes.
1. Open Diapason .	50	10. Sesqualtera, 4 ranks .	200
2. Open Diapason .	50	11. Cornet, 5 ranks .	125
3. Stopped Diapason	50	12. Trumpet .	50
4. Principal .	50	13. Clarion .	50
5. Flute .	50	14. Cromhorn	50
6. Twelfth .	50	15. Vox Humana .	50
7. Fifteenth .	50		
8. Tierce .	50		975
9. Larigot .	50		

SECOND GREAT ORGAN. 13 borrowed stops.

	Pipes.		Pipes.
a. Open Diapason .	00	h. Larigot .	00
b. Stopped Diapason	00	i. Sesqualtera .	00
c. Principal .	00	j. Trumpet .	00
d. Flute .	00	k. Clarion .	00
e. Twelfth .	00	l. Cromhorn .	00
f. Fifteenth .	00	m. Vox Humana .	00
g. Tierce .	00		

CHOIR ORGAN. 7 stops.

	Pipes.		Pipes.
16. Open Diapason, to Gamut	42	21. Fifteenth .	50
17. Stopped Diapason .	50	22. Bassoon .	50
18. Principal .	50		
19. Flute .	50		342
20. Twelfth .	50		

ECHO. 11 stops.

	Pipes.		Pipes.
23. Open Diapason .	25	30. Larigot .	25
24. Stopped Diapason	25	31. Trumpet .	25
25. Principal .	25	32. Vox Humana .	25
26. Flute .	25	33. Cromhorn .	25
27. Twelfth .	25		275
28. Fifteenth .	25		
29. Tierce .	25	Total	1592

Compass Gt. and Chr. GG, short 8ves, to C in alt, 50 notes. Echo, middle C to C in alt, 25 notes.

THE FIRST SWELL.—In 1712 the Jordans (Abraham, sen. and jun.) built an organ for the church at the opposite end of London Bridge to St. Saviour's, namely St. Magnus, which deserves special notice as being the first instrument that contained a Swell. This organ also had four sets of keys, the fourth no doubt being a counterpart of the third (Echo) but ' adapted to the act of emitting sounds by swelling the notes,' so that passages played with expression could be contrasted with those played without. A list of the stops in the Swell has not been preserved ; but we know from those subsequently made, that its compass and capacity must have been very limited, though sufficient to illustrate the importance of the improvement.

FIRST OCTAVE COUPLER.—In 1726 John Harris and John Byfield, sen., erected a fine and imposing-looking organ for the church of St. Mary Redcliff, Bristol, which had a ' 16 ft. speaking front.' The compass of this instrument was in some respects unusually complete, the Great Organ descending to CCC, including CCC♯, and the Choir Organ going down to GG with GG♯ ; the Swell consisted of the unusual number of nine stops. Four of the Stops in the Great Organ descended to GG only ; and one of the open Diapasons had stopped-pipes to the last four notes. There was ' a spring of communication ' attached to the Great Organ, by which CC was made to act on the CCC key, and so on throughout the compass. The Redcliff organ, therefore, contained the first 'octave coupler ' that was ever made in England ; in fact, the first coupler of any kind with which any organ in this country was provided. Some old printed accounts of this organ state that

the Swell originally went to tenor C, with the lower notes of the reeds very fine ; and that it was afterwards shortened to the fiddle G compass ; but Vowles, organ-builder of Bristol, who reconstructed the organ, and had all its original mechanism under his eye, assured the present writer that the statement was erroneous, and probably took its rise from the circumstance that the key-maker, doubtless by mistake, made the Swell Manual down to tenor C, and that the seven extra keys were, therefore, allowed to remain as ' dummies.'

GREAT ORGAN. 11 stops.

	Pipes.		Pipes.
1. Open Diapason .	63	7. Tierce, to GG .	56
2. Open Diapason, metal to EEE; stopped pipes below	63	8. Sesqualtera, 5 ranks, to GG	250
3. Stopped Diapason .	63	9. Cornet, to mid. C, 5 rks.	135
4. Principal .	63	10. Trumpet .	63
5. Twelfth, to GG .	56	11. Clarion .	63
6. Fifteenth, to GG	56		961

CHOIR ORGAN. 6 stops.

	Pipes.		Pipes.
12. Stopped Diapason .	56	16. Sesqualtera, 3 ranks	168
13. Principal .	56	17. Bassoon .	56
14. Flute .	56		
15. Block flute	56		448

SWELL ORGAN. 9 stops.

	Pipes.		Pipes.
18. Open Diapason .	32	24. Trumpet .	32
19. Stopped Diapason .	32	25. Cremona .	32
20. Principal .	32	26. Vox Humana .	32
21. Flute .	32		352
22. Cornet, 3 ranks .	96		
23. Hautboy .	32	Total	1761

Compass, Great Organ, CCC with CCC♯ to D in alt, 63 notes.
Choir do. GG with GG♯ to D in alt, 56 notes.
Swell do. Fiddle G to D in alt, . 32 notes.
Four Bellows.

1790. INTRODUCTION OF PEDALS.—Although as we have seen, pedals were known in Germany upwards of four hundred years ago, yet they were not introduced into England until nearly the close of the 18th century. Who first made them, or which was the first organ to have them, are matters of some doubt. The organs in Westminster Abbey, the German Lutheran Church in the Savoy, and St. Matthew's, Friday Street, each claim the priority. The first organ that is known for certain to have had them, was that made in 1790 by G. P. England, and erected by him at St. James's, Clerkenwell, which instrument, according to the words of the original specification, was ' to have pedals to play by the feet.' These, like the early German specimens, were an octave only in compass, GG to Gamut G ; and also, as at Halberstadt, etc., had no pipes of their own, but only drew down the manual keys. Before 1793 Avery put pedals to the Westminster Abbey organ, together with an octave of unison wood GG pedal-pipes ; and from that date he frequently introduced both into his own instruments. In 1811 G. P. England built an organ for Lancaster with 1½ octave of Pedals, GG to tenor C ; and two couplers, Great and Choir to Pedal. He also, like Avery, became a strong advocate for separate pipes for the pedals, introducing them in 1803 into his organ at Newark, which had the FFF (12 ft.) pipe.

After a time pipes of double size, speaking down to GGG (21⅓ feet length) were made, as by Elliott & Hill at Westminster Abbey, etc.

Besides the unison and double pedal-pipe ranges, a mongrel scale crept into use, which, though most defective, was for a few years the most frequently followed. This consisted of an octave of double pipes from CC down to CCC, and then five unison pipes from BB down to GG. The five pedal keys, B to G, at each extremity of the pedal-board, were thus without any difference in the pitch of their five sounds.

In 1809 J. C. Bishop effected the improvement on the old Shifting movement which afterwards became so generally known as the COMPOSITION PEDALS (q.v.).

The most complete GG Pedal Organ that was ever made, both as to compass and stops, was the one erected by J. C. Bishop in St. James's Church, Bermondsey, in 1829. It had three stops of a range of two octaves each.

There was a keyboard on the left-hand side of the manuals, acting on the Pedal Organ; and the writer remembers seeing in print a copy of Handel's chorus, ' But the waters overwhelmed their enemies,' arranged for *three* performers,— a duet for the manuals, with the rolling bass part for a third player at the side keyboard,— prepared expressly for and played at the opening of this organ.

1832. THE PNEUMATIC LEVER.—In a large organ with several pallets to a key, and perhaps some stops on a heavy pressure of wind, the touch becomes heavier than the most muscular finger (or foot) can control without experiencing great exhaustion.[1] The number of springs in the several sound-boards to some extent bring back the resistance existing in the old 16th-century spring-boxes, which resistance, however, can now no longer be overcome by brute force, but must be controlled by the elastic action from the knuckles or ankle. The power to do this is supplied by the pneumatic lever.

Joseph Booth, of Wakefield, was the first organ-builder to whom the idea seems to have occurred of establishing pneumatic agency, and of thus ingeniously turning the wind-power, one of the organist's antagonists, into his assistant. It was to some of the bass pipes of the organ he built for the church of Attercliffe, near Sheffield, in the year 1827, that Booth first applied his little invention. The lower notes of the wood open Diapason of the GG manual were placed on a small separate sound-board, and to the pull-down of each pallet he attached a small circular bellows below. From the great organ sound-board groove a conveyance conducts wind into this bellows, which, opening downwards, draws the pallet with it. These small bellows Booth used to call *puff-valves.*

It was in 1832 that Charles Spackman Barker first thought of the invention that has since been called the pneumatic lever. On the com-

[1] The organist at Haarlem was accustomed to strip like a blacksmith preparatory to giving his usual hour's performance, and at the end of it retired, covered with perspiration.

pletion of the organ in York Minster, the touch of which, in consequence of the great size of the instrument, was of course very heavy, he wrote to Dr. Camidge, then the organist of the Cathedral, begging to be allowed to attach one of his levers in a temporary way to one of the heaviest notes of his organ. Dr. Camidge admitted that the touch of his instrument was ' sufficient to paralyse the efforts of most men'; but financial difficulties stood in the way of the remedy being applied; and in 1837 Barker went to France to superintend its introduction into the organ then being built by the eminent builder Cavaillé-Coll for the royal Church of St. Denis, near Paris. Cavaillé had, among his other experiments, made Flue and Reed pipes to produce harmonic tones by means of wind of heavy pressure, but these discoveries he had looked upon as practically useless on account of their leading to the production of a touch which no human muscles could overcome. Barker's apparatus, which simply overpowered the resistance that could not be removed, was therefore an opportune presentation; and Cavaillé immediately introduced it, together with several Harmonic stops, into the large organ he was then (1841) building for the Abbey Church of St. Denis.

In 1835 David Hamilton, of Edinburgh, made a pneumatic movement, which he applied to the organ in St. John's Episcopal Church in that city; and in 1839 a paper was read at a meeting of the British Association at Birmingham explanatory of a pneumatic lever which he then exhibited.

The pneumatic lever consists of a bellows shaped very like a small concussion bellows, two or three inches in width, and about ten inches in length. The key of the clavier opens a small circular valve beneath this, and compressed air being thus admitted, the bellows rises, drawing with it a tracker that communicates the motion to the pallets and to such of the coupling movements, etc., as may be ' drawn '; all of which immediately answer to the putting down of the key. When the key is released the valve that admitted the air is closed and another opened, the bellows consequently closing. The key is thus relieved from the combined resistance of the main pallets, coupling movements, and the heavy wind-pressure; and the touch can consequently be adjusted to any degree of elastic resistance pleasant to the performer.

1834. IMPROVEMENTS AT YORK MINSTER. RADIATING PEDAL-BOARD.—The organ in York Minster, which had been twice enlarged—about 1754, and again in 1813—was a third time altered and considerably increased in size in 1823, by Ward of York; who among other things added a Pedal Organ of thirteen stops to FFF, containing two Double Diapasons down to FFFF, 24 feet length, etc. The fire of

1829 cleared all this away ; and Messrs. Elliott & Hill were then engaged to erect an entirely new organ, under the superintendence of Dr. Camidge.

It had been found from experience that the vast area of York Minster required an immense amount of organ tone to fill it adequately, and with the view of supplying this, Dr. Camidge seems to have selected as the foundation of his plan, the type of a large ordinary Great Organ of the period, of twelve stops, which he followed almost literally, and then had that disposition inserted twice over. The compass of the Great and Choir Manuals he extended downwards to CCC, 16 feet and upwards to *c in altissimo* ; and the Pedal Organ he designed to include four ' Double ' Stops of 32 feet, and four ' Unisons ' of 16 feet. The great fault in the scheme lay in the entire omission from the Manuals of all sub-octave Foundation-stops— *i.e.* stops sounding the 16-foot tone on the 8-foot key—and consequently also of all the Mutation-stops due to that sound. In spite of the great aggregation of pipes, therefore, the numerous manual stops produced no massiveness of effect, while as the Pedal had no less than four ponderous sub-octave registers,[1] and, with the manuals coupled, a total of over forty stops, the only possible result from such an arrangement was a ' top-and-bottom ' effect.

The original scheme of the organ—which underwent thorough revision and improvement in 1859—is given below. This organ had a radiating pedal-board. The organ erected in Mitcham church in 1834, and originally made by Bruce of Edinburgh, also had a radiating pedal-board, of peculiar construction.

GREAT ORGAN. 24 stops.

(East sound-boards.)	Feet.	(West sound-boards.)	Feet.
1. Open Diapason .	16	13. Open Diapason .	16
2. Open Diapason .	16	14. Open Diapason .	16
3. Stopped Diapason .	16	15. Stopped Diapason .	16
4. Principal .	8	16. Principal .	8
5. Principal .	8	17. Principal .	8
6. Principal, wood (Flute)	8	18. Principal, wood (Flute)	8
7. Twelfth .	5⅓	19. Twelfth .	5⅓
8. Fifteenth .	4	20. Fifteenth .	4
9. Sesquialtera, 7 ranks .		21. Sesquialtera, 7 ranks .	
10. Mixture .		22. Mixture .	
11. Trumpet .	16	23. Trumpet .	16
12. Trumpet .	16	24. Trumpet .	16

CHOIR ORGAN. 9 stops.

	Feet.		Feet.
25. Open Diapason .	16	30. Principal .	8
26. Open Diapason .	16	31. Flute .	8
27. Dulciana .	16	32. Fifteenth .	4
28. Stopped Diapason .	16	33. Bassoon .	16
29. Horn Diapason .	16		

SWELL ORGAN. 12 stops.

	Feet.		Feet.
34. Open Diapason .	8	40. Fifteenth .	2
35. Stopped Diapason .	8	41. Sesquialtera, 4 ranks	
36. Dulciana .	8	42. Horn .	8
37. Harmonica .	8	43. Trumpet .	8
38. Principal .	4	44. Oboe .	8
39. Principal, wood .	4	45. Cremona .	8

PEDAL ORGAN. 9 stops.

	Feet.		Feet.
46. Double open, wood .	32	51. Open Diapason, metal	16
47. Double open, metal .	32	52. Sacbut (reed), wood .	32
48. Double stopped, wood .	32	53. Trumpet, wood .	16
49. Open Diapason, wood .	16	54. Trumpet, metal .	8
50. Open Diapason, wood .	16		

Compass, Gt. and Chr. CCC to C in alt[mo] (6 octaves) ; 73 notes. Swl. CC to C in alt[mo] (5 octaves) ; 61 notes. Pedal Organ, CCC to Tenor C ; 25 notes.

Manual and Pedal couplers. Radiating Pedal-board.

[1] It was stated at the time this organ was made that the largest pedal-pipe would hold a glass of ale for every man, woman and child then residing within the walls of the city of York.

Not long after the completion of the York organ H. J. GAUNTLETT (*q.v.*) made a praiseworthy effort to introduce some of the leading features of the continental principle of organ-building into England ; and being heartily seconded by William Hill, his endeavours were attended with a considerable amount of success. The 8-feet compass was gradually accepted as the proper range for the Manuals, although at times greatly opposed ; the sub-octave (16 feet) manual stops, which had been essayed successively by Parker, Snetzler and Lincoln, at last obtained favourable recognition, together with the Twelfth thereto, viz. the Quint of 5⅓ feet. Double manual[2] reeds were incorporated ; and the importance of and necessity for the independent Pedal Organ was also demonstrated. The weak points were the number of half and incomplete stops, which retarded the process of quick registering ; and the short range of the Pedal Organ, which, instead of being, like the pedals themselves, upwards of two octaves in compass, from CCC, consisted of a single octave only, which then repeated. This defect—a continuation of the old ' return pedal-pipe ' system—had to be remedied before a clear and intelligible reading of Bach's Fugues, or any other essentially organ music, could be given.

1851. EXHIBITION ORGANS.—Of four organs shown at the great Industrial Exhibition of 1851, three were by foreign builders (Ducroquet, Schulze, Ducci[3]), the other by Henry Willis. This instrument had three manuals and pedal, seventy sounding stops and seven couplers. There were four different pressures of wind. The Swell had its own separate bellows placed within the swell-box, as in Green's organ at St. George's, Windsor. It also presented several novelties, the principal of which was the introduction of studs or pistons projecting through the key-slips, acting on the draw-stops, operated by the thumbs, and designed as a substitute for the ordinary Composition Pedals. This was effected by the aid of a pneumatic apparatus on the same principle as that applied to the keys. A stud, on being pressed, admitted compressed air into a bellows, which immediately ascended with sufficient power to act, by means of rods and levers, on the machinery of the stops, drawing those which the given combination required, and pushing in those that were superfluous. In most cases there was a duplicate stud for each combination, so that it could be obtained by using either the right or the left thumb.

[2] A double reed-stop (double bassoon, down to the DDD pipe) formed a portion of the Great Organ of the instrument erected by John Byfield, jun., in Christ Church Cathedral, Dublin, in 1751.
[3] These were fully described and many specifications of contemporary organs were given in previous editions of this Dictionary. As organs in public buildings, and particularly in the English cathedrals, are continually being rebuilt according to modern requirements, no attempt has been made to reproduce this feature of Hopkins's article in the present edition.   C.

2. DESCRIPTION OF MECHANISM

It has been shown in the preceding history traced to the middle of the 19th century how the organ became virtually the instrument of to-day, and sometimes consists really of as many as five separate and distinct organs—Great, Swell, Choir, Solo, and Pedal, with the occasional addition of an Echo, Celestial or Altar Organ. To describe such an organ completely and in detail would require a volume, which is impossible here, and is besides unnecessary, as the smallest specimen equally with the largest comprises a certain number of necessary parts ; namely, (1) the apparatus for collecting and distributing the wind, viz. the bellows, wind-trunk, the wind-chest, and the sound-board-grooves ; (2) the mechanism for playing the organ, viz. the clavier and the key movement ; (3) the mechanism for controlling the use of the tiers of pipes, viz. the draw-stop action. To these have to be added (4) the couplers, composition pedals, pistons, etc.

(1) THE BELLOWS that collect and compress the wind are shown in the accompanying wood-cut occupying their usual position in the lower part of the organ ; the reservoir being marked *r,r,r,r*, and the feeder *t,t,t.* From the reservoir of the bellows the wind is conducted through a large service-pipe or ' wind-trunk ' to the wind-cisterns or wind-chests *z,z*, where it remains for further use in smaller quantities. The wind-trunk, which could not be conveniently shown in the woodcut, is made either of wood or metal, and traverses the distance between the reservoir and wind-chest by the shortest convenient route. The wind-chest is a substantial box of wood extending the whole length of the sound-board ; about equal to it in depth ; and about two-thirds its width. In this chest are located the sound-board pallets (*d* and *k*), which prevent the wind proceeding any farther, unless one or more of them are drawn down (or opened) by the means next to be noticed.

(2) THE KEY ACTION is the system of mechanism by which the performer is able to open the pallets, which are otherwise far beyond his reach. In an action of simple construction this consists of a key (*a*), sticker (*b*), roller and tracker (*c*), communicating with a pull-down (*d*) attached to the pallet. On pressing down the front end of the key (*a*)—which key works on a metal pin or centre—the further end rises, lifting with it the vertical sticker (*b*). This sticker, lifting the first arm of the horizontal roller, causes the roller partly to revolve. At the opposite end of this roller is a second arm projecting from the back, which consequently descends (*c*). To this is attached a tracker made to any length necessary to reach from the second roller-arm to the pull-down (*d*). The course of the motion transmitted by these **parts is as follows** : The key-tail carries the

motion inwards, the sticker carries it upwards ; the roller conveys it to the necessary distance laterally, while the tracker again carries it upwards to the pallet. Small discs of crimson cloth, placed at each end of the sticker, prevent any rattling between the contiguous parts of the mechanism. A pin passes down from the sticker, through the key-tail, to prevent the former from slipping off the latter. A second one is placed on the top, and passes through an eye in the roller-arm to secure the certain action of the roller. The two studs into which the roller-pins pass to sustain the roller are lined with cloth, or ' bushed,' as it is termed, also to secure silence in action ; and the rollers themselves are made of iron tubing, which is more firm and rigid than the old wooden rollers, and has the additional advantage of taking much less space.

It is a matter of much importance to lessen the strain on the key-movement just noticed by reducing the resistance at the pallet as much as possible, and thus also relieving the finger of the player from all unnecessary labour and fatigue. For this purpose builders make use of what are called *relief* pallets. When wind, in however small quantity, gains admission above a pallet, the wind-pressure ceases by becoming equal all round, and there remains only the elastic resistance of the spring to be overcome. To effect this relief numerous devices have been thought of, as the ' jointed pallet,' in which two or three inches of the fore part move first, and then the remainder, perhaps for nearly a foot in length. There is also the ' double pallet,' in which a small valve is placed on the back of the large one, and opens first, etc. etc. In large organs some builders use relief pallets to obviate the necessity for ' pneumatics,' though the two are sometimes used at the same time.

(3) THE DRAW-STOP ACTION is a second system of mechanism, by means of which the performer is enabled to draw out or push in any slider that lies beneath a separate set of pipes or ' stop.' In the accompanying drawing each separate pipe depicted represents a single member of a different stop, and the slider-ends are the little shaded portions that are shown immediately over the ' sound-board groove ' (*e,e,e* and *o,o,o,o*). The unshaded intermediate parts are the ' bearers,' which sustain the weight of the ' upper-boards ' on which the pipes are seen standing, as well as of the pipes themselves ; the sliders being thus left unfettered to move freely to and fro. In the small movable (Portative) organs of the Middle Ages, when the surface of the sound-board, or ' table ' on which the pipes stood, was scarcely any higher above the keys than the top of a modern square pianoforte above its clavier, and when the sound-board measured only about a couple of feet in length, the slider-ends could

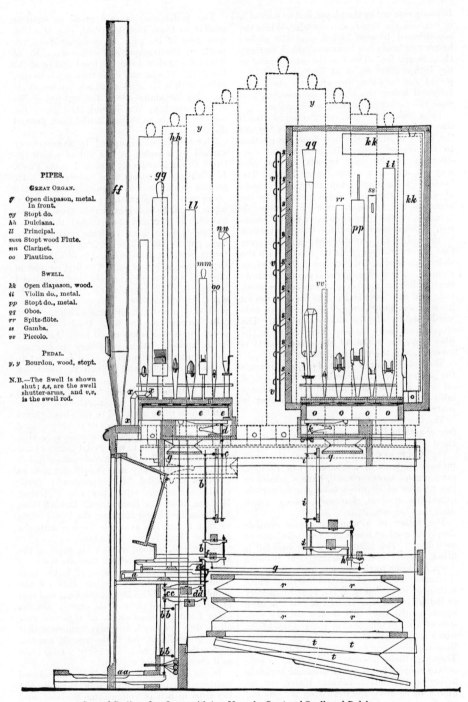

PIPES.

GREAT ORGAN.

ff Open diapason, metal.
    In front.
gg Stopt do.
hh Dulciana.
ll Principal.
mm Stopt wood Flute.
nn Clarinet.
oo Flautino.

SWELL.

kk Open diapason, wood.
ii Violin do., metal.
pp Stopt do., metal.
qq Oboe.
rr Spitz-flöte.
ss Gamba.
vv Piccolo.

PEDAL.

y, y Bourdon, wood, stopt.

N.B.—The Swell is shown
    shut; *s,s*, are the swell
    shutter-arms, and *v,v*,
    is the swell rod.

General Section of an Organ with two Manuals, Great and Swell, and Pedals.

be easily reached by the player, and be moved in or out with the fingers and thumb. When the sound-board became longer, and the sliders longer and heavier, a lever was added, to move them to and fro. This was the arrangement in the 16th-century organ at Radnor. At that period, and for a long time after, the stops were arranged before the playing commenced, and were not varied during the performance.

In a modern organ, even one of small dimensions, the slider-ends are always beyond the reach of the performer, being, in relation to the claviers, generally farther in, considerably to the right or left, as the case may be, and at a much higher level. The 'action' to a single stop therefore consists of a 'draw-stop rod,' which passes into the organ to the necessary extent; a movable 'trundle,' which turns the corner; a 'trace-rod,' which spans the distance from the trundle to the end of the sound-board; and the lever that is in connexion at its upper end with the slider. These attached parts act in the following manner. The draw-stop rod is drawn forward; the trundle partly revolves and moves the trace-rod; and the lower end of the lever is drawn inwards, causing the upper end to move outwards, and to take the slider-end with it. The stop is now ready for use. On pushing in the draw-stop, the action of the several parts is reversed, and the stop is silenced.

The end of the draw-stop rod projects through the jamb at the side of the keys, and is finished off with a knob ornamented with an ivory label bearing the name of the stop that it controls.

The Concussion-bellows is shown in position (see q) attached to the under-side of the wind-chest.

(4) COUPLERS, ETC. — Besides the two primary systems of mechanism just noticed, most organs, however small, have a greater or less number of members belonging to certain subsidiary systems, foremost among which rank the Couplers.

The action of a manual-coupler consists simply of a set of levers or 'backfalls,' one to each key. The front end of the backfall is lifted, the far end descending, and pressing down a sticker resting on the back end of the T-shaped backfall of the swell-action, which is then set in motion (g, h, i, i, k) as completely as though it had been started at f by the swell upper-manual key. An octave coupler consists of a set of diagonal or splayed backfalls, which extend sufficiently to the right to reach from any given key to the tracker of its octave. The upper backfall above h shows this. A sub-octave coupler has a set of diagonal backfalls acting on the octave below. When not required to be used, the draw-stop is 'put in,' which raises the frame and backfalls from the stickers at the front end.

The pedal-couplers are made in manner similar to those just described, one of which may here be traced. On pressing down the pedal aa the trackers and roller-arms, bb, bb, descend, drawing down the front end cc of the backfall. The far end dd is thus made to rise, lifting with it the sticker, which, communicating with the under-side of the tail (ee) of the great-organ key, lifts it and thus plays the note as exactly as though it had been pressed down by a finger.

The 'Sforzando coupler' is a movement worked by a pedal, by the aid of which the Great Organ is suddenly attached to the Swell. It reinforces the strength of the Swell to a far greater extent, and more quickly than by the 'crescendo' pedal; and is therefore useful when a quick and remarkable accent is required. It is formed of a backfall, the far end of which presses down a sticker resting on the back part of the square backfall of the Great Organ, which it depresses, and so sets the Great Organ tracker in motion. The first coupler of the kind was made by Lincoln, and introduced by him into his organ at St. Olave's, Southwark, erected in 1844. This coupler is always worked by a pedal, on pressing which the backfalls descend into position. On releasing the pedal the backfalls are raised from their work by a spring. Other subsidiary pedals are now frequently introduced, such as ' Great to Pedal, on or off,' and ' Swell to Great, on or off.'

The Composition Pedals have already been noticed. Their use is so generally felt that in addition to those attached to the Great Organ stops, there are usually two or three provided for the Swell of organs of even average size. In instruments that have a Pedal Organ of fair dimensions, the Great Organ composition pedals usually do, or at any rate should, act also on those of the Pedal, ' in proportion '; particularly where the latter has any Mutation, Mixture, or 16-foot Reed stops. In such cases a ' Piano Pedal ' for reducing the Pedal organ so that it may be available for use with the Swell or Choir, is very desirable.

Sometimes, instead of silencing some of the stops by composition pedals, they are rendered mute by means of a trap or ventil in the local wind-trunk, which, by closing, cuts off the supply of wind. This lessens the wear and tear of the mechanical parts of the organ. On the other hand the draw-stops, or registers, may all be duly prepared, and may announce that all is in readiness, yet if the ventils are forgotten there may be as distinctly a false start as if there were ' no wind in.'

In his large organs Henry Willis introduced combination pistons projecting through the key-slips in lieu of composition pedals; and devoted the width over the pedal-board to pedals acting on the various couplers, etc.

ELECTRIC AND TUBULAR PNEUMATIC ACTIONS.—Notice may now be taken of two substitutes which modern thought has devised for the first of the primary systems of organ mechanism already described under the title of ' Key-movement.'

1. Seeing what had been accomplished by telegraphy, by which the most delicate movements could be transmitted with rapidity and precision, and to indefinite distances, the thought occurred as to whether it might be possible to apply the principle of electricity to the organ, in which case the key-board would represent the manipulator and the pallets of the organ the receptors. To Dr. Gauntlett belongs the credit of having been the first to start this theoretical idea. His first proposal, made at the time of the Great Exhibition of 1851, was to play all the organs in the place at one and the same time ; but the suggestion met with no response. When the intention of the Crystal Palace Company to build an immense organ was announced in 1852, he met the Provisional Committee and proposed the erection of facsimiles of the eight most celebrated continental organs in various parts of the Palace, and of playing them, either all together or separately, in the centre of the building ; but this suggestion also remained unembodied. Dr. Gauntlett patented his invention in 1852, and in 1863 another plan was patented by Goundry ; but no organs appear to have been built to illustrate the practicability of either of them.

In 1867 Barker erected an electric organ in the church of St. Augustin in Paris, which attracted the attention of Bryceson, who was then paying a visit to the Paris Exhibition, and who made arrangements with Barker for introducing the electric system into England. Barker's English patent was taken out in Jan. 1868. It protected his special applications for playing the manual and pedal organs ; for coupling the various manuals as well as the pedals, either in the unison, or in the octave or sub-octave, and for commanding the large traps in the wind-trunks known in England as ventils, to which was afterwards added an arrangement for drawing the stops. Bryceson added in Apr. 1868 a perfectly new form of pallet which offered no resistance in opening ; and he subsequently introduced several other improvements, including an arrangement for using attenuated air instead of pressure ; and Henry Willis took out a patent almost simultaneously with Bryceson for using exhaust and power alternately for actuating a ' floating valve,' in connexion with a novel arrangement of draw-stop action ; neither builder manifestly being aware of the conclusion arrived at by the other.

Among the electric organs erected or reconstructed by Bryceson were included St. Michael's, Cornhill ; St. George's, Tufnell Park ; St. Augustine's, Highbury ; Milney Manor.

2. A second substitute for the long tracker movements, etc., in large or separated organs, is the ' tubular pneumatic system.' The germ of this application existed of course in Booth's contrivance (already noticed), which consisted of a tube receiving compressed wind at one end, and having a motor at the other ; but there is as much difference between the primitive device of 1827 and the more perfected ' system,' as between the early trials of Papin and the steam engines of Watt and Stephenson. It was not till 1867 that the principle was turned to practical account, when it was applied to an organ that was publicly shown at the Paris Exhibition of that year. Its importance was recognised by Henry Willis, who introduced it with improvements into his organ in St. Paul's Cathedral in 1874 ; and employed it extensively in that at the Alexandra Palace ; and it was used by Bryceson in the organ removed from St. Paul's to the Victoria Rooms, Bristol ; by T. Hill in his organ at Manchester Cathedral ; by Bishop in the Yarmouth organ ; by Foster & Andrews at the City Temple ; and by Lewis & Co., for the Pedal Organ of their new instrument at Ripon.

The invention of some mechanical means for blowing the bellows, and for increasing or decreasing the speed of the supply, according as much or little might be required, became a matter of some concern and much importance.

The first piece of mechanism devised for this purpose was the Hydraulic Engine of Joy and Holt — afterwards David Joy, of Middlesborough. This consisted of a cylinder similar to that of an ordinary steam-engine, but deriving its motion from the pressure of a column of water, admitted alternately to the top and bottom of the piston. Engines of this kind were attached to the organs at the Town Hall, Leeds ; the Parish Church, Leeds ; Rochester Cathedral ; the Temple Church, etc. etc.

The Liverpool Water Meter, as patented by Thomas Duncan, and made by Forrester & Co., of Liverpool, consisted of two cylinders, with pistons and slotted piston-rods working a short crank-shaft. Gas engines also came into use for blowing organs.   E. J. H. ; rev. T. E.

The following English works (from Rev. J. H. Burn's Bibliography) deal with the History of the organ.

G. C. BEDWELL : *The Evolution of the Organ.*
Rev. ANDREW FREEMAN, in the second edition of the *Dictionary of Organs and Organists.*
Rev. F. W. GALPIN : *Notes on a Roman Hydraulus.*
ARTHUR G. HILL : *The Organ Cases, etc., of the Middle Ages.*
HOPKINS and RIMBAULT : *The Organ, its History and Construction.*
EDWARD JOHN HOPKINS : *The English Mediæval Church Organ.*
Dr. CHARLES W. PEARCE : *Notes on English Organs of the Period 1800 1810.*
Old London City Churches, their Organs, etc.
EDWARD F. RIMBAULT : *The Early English Organ Builders.*
SIR JOHN SUTTON : *A Short Account of Organs, etc.*
JOHN W. WARMAN : *The Hydraulic Organ of the Ancients.*
C. F. ABDY WILLIAMS : *The Story of the Organ.*

NOTE.—Technical works of every description may be consulted at the Library of the Patent Office, Chancery Lane, London.

3. The Modern Organ

Since the preceding article was written enormous strides have been taken in the organ world. Not only in the actual construction of the instrument has this been the case, but in every department or branch of science or art connected with the organ there is progress to report.

Organ - building, organ - playing, balance, quality, and power of tone, marvellous actions and systems of control, development of flue, string and reed tone, acoustics, compass, pitch, tuning, wind pressures and blowing machinery stand prominently out from amongst the multitude of minor subjects and their attendant problems that have called for earnest study, and have received the unremitting attention of some of the foremost men of our time, whose combined labours and achievements in these directions have resulted in an almost perfect instrument, the fruits of which are so well displayed in the organ recital as we hear it to-day. (Cf. ORGAN-PLAYING and REGISTRATION.)

It is scarcely within the scope of this article to deal minutely with the innumerable factors or influences to which this happy state of affairs is due, but mention must be made of the continual improvement in organ action, stop control, tonal development and kindred matters accruing from the indefatigable investigations of a host of labourers in the field.

BELLOWS. — The wind - consumption of the large modern tubular - pneumatic organ is enormous.

It is not only a question of the quantity of wind required to sound the multitudinous pipes —many of which are very large and greedy of wind—but its quality also must be taken into consideration. It must fulfil several conditions. The supply must be ample for the Full Organ. Several different pressures must be provided, some of which are heavy. There must be no unsteadiness when a sudden demand (or cessation of demand) on the wind is created by the player.

Not only is wind required for filling the several reservoirs and sounding the pipes, but sufficient must be raised for operating the pneumatics and for satisfying the demands of numerous couplers and extensions of pipes, especially in the Pedal department.

It is indeed a far cry from the small and primitive diagonal (blacksmith's) bellows to the latest elaborate power-blowing installation, of which there are now several varieties.

In course of time the weighted reservoir (or upper portion of the bellows) was made to rise horizontally instead of diagonally. Later on the large *single* feeder (or lower portion of the bellows) was superseded by double (or triple) feeders, which, by being smaller and acting alternately, supply the wind much more steadily

and regularly than the full-sized single feeder acting intermittently. Upon the introduction of blowing by power, the feeders, as well as the reservoir, were made to rise horizontally instead of diagonally, thereby doubling the supply of wind per stroke. With power-blown bellows the wind is automatically fed off to the lower pressures. When all the reservoirs are full the blowing-power likewise is automatically cut off. Rotary fan-blowers are now largely used. The wind may be generated at the lowest pressure and raised step by step to the higher pressures.

The problem of securing steady wind has claimed the attention of all who have had the best interests of the organ at heart. A great step forward was made when (in 1825) the ' Concussion Bellows ' was introduced by J. C. Bishop.

This consists of a feeder attached to the wind-trunk or to the wind-chest, and open to the wind inside. Normally—with the wind ' on '—springs connected with the feeder are so adjusted as to allow it to stand half-way open. Consequently, when fluctuation arises the feeder gives or takes pressure as occasion requires.

In the year 1894 the attention of John Turnell Austin was drawn to the unequal pressure arising from the conveyance of wind to the pipes through trunks and grooves of a comparatively small fixed capacity. This resulted in the construction of the ' Universal Air Chest,' in which a large portion of the lower part of the instrument is normally under wind. Springs, instead of weights, are used to give pressure, constituting practically a huge ' Concussion.'

The organ at Rushden Chapel, Northampton, is an early example, since when a very large number of instruments have been built on this system in the United States.

English organ-builders plant their wind-devouring manual basses over an independent supply, and provide each chief department or sound-board with its own separate reservoir.

ACTIONS.—Organ action may be divided into two classes—mechanical and supplementary.

Tracker or ' mechanical ' action (as organ-builders term it) consists of stickers, backfalls, (or squares), rollers and trackers, by means of which the movement is conveyed from the key to the pallet ; and is operated entirely by the energy of the performer.

The term ' mechanical ' in organ-builders' phraseology may therefore be taken to imply that the whole of the energy required to open the pallet (or operate other mechanism) must be supplied by the performer.

Actions of this description have the advantage of cheapness, durability and promptness of response.

But when the instrument contains more than about twenty speaking stops or the couplers are numerous, the touch becomes too heavy for the finger to overcome, and rapid playing (on anything like the full organ) becomes an impossibility.

To remedy this, class number two is employed, in which a secondary agent, such as pneumatic work, or a combination of electric and pneumatic work intervenes between the key and the pallet, and provides the power for overcoming the resistance. In this class of action the personal control of the pallet is almost entirely lost, constituting one of the most serious penalties which have to be paid for its use.

Supplementary actions are of several kinds. In the Barker pneumatic lever action depression of the key admits heavy pressure wind to a small external motor (something like a feeder), causing it to distend or inflate, and operate an ordinary tracker action leading to the pallet. Upon releasing the key a small valve is opened, emptying or exhausting the motor, which deflates and collapses, allowing the pallet spring to close the pallet.

Tubular-pneumatic action is of two kinds :

1. The supply, charge, or pressure system.
2. The exhaust system.

In supply pneumatics, depression of the key admits wind to a tube conveying it to further pneumatic work, which in turn exhausts an inflated motor subject to wind pressure within and without, causing it to collapse or deflate and pull down the pallet attached to it.

In the exhaust system depression of the key exhausts the tube and motors from the key end of the tube, opening the pallet as before.

Electro-pneumatic action is a combination of electric and pneumatic work. Depression of the key makes an electrical contact, which in turn causes the exhaustion of the inflated motor opening the pallet.

This action has the advantages of rapidity and of occupying very little room, allowing of a wide distribution of parts if desired. The wires necessary for the control of a large instrument may be formed into a cable and be led to a movable console.

No description of this action (which is largely used in America) would be complete without reference to the work of the late Robert Hope-Jones.

The latest development is an all-electric action, of which Compton, of Nottingham, is an exponent.

The following are useful works on actions :

Thomas Casson : *Modern Pneumatic Organ Mechanism.*
W. E. Dickson : *Practical Organ Building.*
Dr. J. W. Hinton : *Story of the Electric Organ.*
F. E. Robertson : *A Practical Treatise on Organ Building.*
Mark Wicks : *Organ Building for Amateurs.*

Double Touch.—Hope-Jones's electro-pneumatic organs were usually provided with double touch. In such case the depth of touch was divided into two dips or touches, the first touch resting upon the second, which resisted further depression until extra pressure is brought to bear upon it. When only the first depth of touch was made use of, a combination of stops suitable for accompaniment was heard, but upon overcoming the resistance of the spring belonging to the second touch, and depressing the key to its full depth, an additional solo stop or more powerful combination came into operation, enabling the performer to pick out any part as a solo, or obtain contrasting powers on the same manual, by skilful manipulation of the two touches. The invention, however, did not win general approval.

Stop Keys and Stop Control.—The introduction of supplementary action has led to its employment as an agent for the entire control. Pivoted stop keys or rocking tablets, adjustable pistons and composition pedals (sometimes having double touch), reversing movements, and every other imaginable device for controlling the resources of the instrument, combine to the production of the elaborate and efficient console as it is seen to-day, especially in America.[1]

In England draw-stops with splayed drawstop jambs still find favour.

Compass and Extension.—The compass of the manuals now extends from CC to c'''', five octaves (61 notes), and that of the pedal board from CCC to g (32 notes), the concave and radiating modified Wesley-Willis pattern for the latter being generally adopted.

In connexion with the compass of both manual and pedal organs it has been the custom of late to make considerable use of what is known as the ' Extension ' system of organ-building, in which the compass of the *pipes* is extended beyond that of the keyboard or clavier, thereby rendering them available for completing the compass of an octave (or sub-octave) coupler, or for use, by suitable means or mechanism, as a separate (borrowed) stop of octave or sub-octave pitch.

Also a stop may be ' borrowed ' in its entirety from one manual to another, or from a manual organ to the pedal organ. Both extension and borrowing are open to abuse.

Extension,[2] if adopted and used indiscriminately, upsets the balance of tone.

Borrowing is open to objection when it depletes the proper tonal balance.

But it is now generally conceded that such methods have a perfectly legitimate value when properly applied and used.

By means of the judicious employment of the numerous couplers or stops suggested by the principle of manual and pedal extension (to say nothing of stops borrowed bodily from one manual to another), ' effects ' can be

[1] See *The Evolution of the Modern Organ and its Control*, by J. M. B. (Boustead).
[2] *Reform of the Church Organ* by Kenneth G. Burns, deals with the principle of extension as exemplified in the organ at the Church of St. Matthias, Richmond Hill (Extension, Transfer and Multiple Swell-box System).

obtained (with or without the use of the Unison Off) which are otherwise impossible.

SWELL PEDAL.—In all new instruments the Swell pedal is balanced.

American organ - builders frequently put several departments (including the Great organ) into separate swell-boxes. In England separate boxes for Choir and Solo organs are becoming general. The new organ at Liverpool Cathedral (1926) contains a large portion of the Pedal Organ in a swell-box of its own.

PIPES AND WIND PRESSURE.—Although the pipes of the chief foundation and chorus stops remain much about the same as formerly, great advances have been made in the 'voicing' of the pipes and in the power obtained by the use of wind varying in pressure from about three or four inches to fifty.

The power of the large modern organ ranges from the merest whisper of the Echo Dulciana to the Tuba, or the mighty Diaphone, of which it is said that it may be set over a variable pressure of wind without materially affecting its pitch.[1]

PEDAL ORGAN.—The earlier development of the Pedal Organ was strongly championed by the late Dr. E. J. Hopkins and by Mr. Thomas Casson, whose organ at the London Music School exemplifies also his system of Octave Duplication, Stop Control and other inventions.

The Pedal Organ is now augmented by extension and borrowing to a condition of efficiency. Free use is made of the resultant Acoustic Bass produced by the sounding of two notes a fifth apart.[2]

PITCH AND TUNING.—The Diapason Normal, C = 517·3 vibrations per second, is now generally adopted for new instruments.[3]

Shortening a pipe sharpens it ; lengthening a pipe flattens it. Large open metal pipes are tuned by means of a tongue or tongues of metal near the top of the pipe. By pulling the tongue outward the pitch is sharpened, and by pressing closer it is flattened.

Large open wood pipes are tuned by shifting a wooden slide so as to cover partially or uncover a slot or aperture cut in the top end of the pipe, or, more clumsily, by nailing a piece of wood over a portion of the top of the pipe to flatten it, or by making the opening larger to sharpen it.

Small open metal pipes are tuned by pressing the pointed end of a tuning-horn or cone into the tops of the pipes to sharpen them, and by pressing the hollow end of the cone over the tops to flatten them. A better and more recent plan is to provide the pipes with lapped tuning-slides, which clasp the top of the pipe. These

can be raised to flatten, or lowered to sharpen, by tapping them with a thin square-edged tuning knife, thus avoiding injury to the tops of the pipes.

Small open wood pipes are provided with metal shades at the top, for partially shading or covering and uncovering the top of the pipe. Shading the top of the pipe flattens it, and uncovering sharpens it.

Stopped pipes are tuned by shifting the stoppers or tompions upward to flatten, and downward to sharpen.

Reed pipes are provided with a hooked wire (near the boot of the pipe), which can be tapped upward to flatten and downward to sharpen, by which means the speaking portion of the tongue is lengthened or shortened.

The tuning of the organ should not be proceeded with until every other part of the instrument has been thoroughly overhauled, and all irregularities with regard to touch, actions, draw-stops or the speech of the pipes have received attention and been remedied. Tuning should always be done under normal conditions. This is especially necessary as regards the temperature of the building, which should be the same for tuning as when the instrument is in use.

The following are the chief particulars relating to the process of tuning.

In keyed instruments required to be playable in every key, but having only twelve notes to the septave, every interval except the octave must deviate slightly from just or true intonation, i.e. be slightly out of tune. (See EQUAL TEMPERAMENT, TEMPERAMENT, and TUNING.)

When two notes of a unison or of a consonant interval are perfectly in tune, they coalesce, but as soon as any departure from purity occurs waves or beats arise. The greater the departure or error the faster the beats, and the nearer the approach to purity the slower they become.

It is by means of these beating-rates that the instrument is tuned, the intervals employed being fifths, fourths and octaves.

All beats (following the law of vibrations) double their rate at the octave above.

It is important to bear this in mind, as the same degree of interval, say a fifth, beats quicker as the pitch rises.

Each fifth must be slightly *narrower* than a perfect fifth, and each fourth must be *wider* than a perfect fourth, the fourths being rather more imperfect (pitch for pitch) than the fifths. The major thirds accruing will be still more imperfectly *wide*.

Now hold middle C of the Principal 4 ft. on the Great organ with the G above, and tune the G slightly flat, or narrower than a perfect fifth.

Hold the same G with the D below, and tune

---

[1] See *Organ Voicing and Tuning*, Anon. ; *Studies in Organ Tone* by the Rev. Noel A. Bonavia-Hunt, M.A.
[2] See Thomas Casson, *The Pedal Organ.*
[3] As the pitch of an organ depends upon the length of its pipes, it cannot be materially altered except at considerable trouble and expense, especially when it requires to be flattened, which is generally the case with instruments of Victorian build.

the D slightly flat, or wider than a perfect fourth.

Hold the same D with the A above, and tune the A slightly flat.

Hold the same A with the E below, and tune the E slightly flat.

Hold the same E with the B above, and tune the B slightly flat.

Hold the same B with the F♯ below, and tune the F♯ slightly flat.

Hold the same F♯ with the C♯ *below*, and tune the C♯ slightly flat.

Hold the same C♯ with the G♯ above, and tune the G♯ slightly flat.

Now hold the middle C with the F above, and tune the F slightly sharp.

Hold the same F with the A♯ (B♭) above, and tune the A♯ slightly sharp.

Hold the same A♯ with the D♯ below, and tune the D♯ slightly sharp.

When this is done correctly, this D♯ should prove to be a slightly wide fourth with the G♯ above, which can be tested by holding the tuning-cone over the top of the G♯ pipe and shading it slightly to flatten it, when such slight temporary flattening should cause it to sound a perfect fourth.

By this method each note within the compass of the septave is tuned, and it remains only to tune the octaves above and below to complete the compass.

As each octave note is tuned it should be tested for accuracy by holding it with its fifth and fourth already tuned. Ultimately the tuning is tested by the degree of smoothness or roughness of the resulting major thirds and tenths.

See THOMAS ELLISTON, *Organs and Tuning*; A. HEMSTOCK, *On Tuning the Organ*; HERMANN SMITH, *Modern Organ Tuning*.

GENERAL REMARKS. — In reviewing the course of recent events attention may be drawn to (1) the great size, power, variety of tone, completeness and the general efficiency of the modern organ.

(2) The fuller appreciation of the complete Pedal organ and of the Foundation, String and Orchestral tone ; also of softer mutation work.

(3) The increased refinement and variety of qualities in modern flue and reed work.

(4) The discrimination displayed in regard to the legitimacy of extension and borrowing, the free use of couplers, accessories, etc., and of the means taken to give control and expression.

(5) The great strides made in the United States of America, especially regarding the Unit System, in which widely extended ranks of pipes are made to serve as family stops, separately available.

(6) The use of the organ in kinematographic work.

(7) The great increase in the number of high-class organ recitals, and of text-books on the organ and organ-playing.

VOCABULARY OF STOPS [1]

The following are the chief of the many names under which organ stops are classified. Brief definitions are given.

Acoustic Bass. 32 ft. Resultant tone yielded by pure fifths.

Acute Mixture. See Sharp Mixture.

Bass Flute. 8 ft. A pedal stop (frequently borrowed from the Bourdon—extended).

Bassoon. 16 ft. The Bass of the Oboe or Clarinet. A light pedal reed.

Bell Gamba. 8 ft. A Gamba surmounted by a bell or inverted cone.

Bombarde. Similar to Bombardon but more powerful.

Bombardon. 16 ft. A reed stop.

Bourdon. 16 ft. *tone.* A Stopped Diapason.

Carillons. Metal bars, gongs or bells.

'Cello. Contraction of Violoncello.

Clarabella. ⎫ 8 ft. An open wood flue stop
Claribel. ⎬ usually from mid C upward.
Claribel Flute. ⎭

Clarinet (Clarionet). 8 ft. A reed stop resembling the tone of that instrument.

Clarion. 4 ft. A manual reed stop.

Clarionet Flute. 8 ft. *tone.* A reedy-toned Stopped Diapason having a hole through the stopper.

Clarion Mixture. A flue-work Mixture of Clarion tone.

Closed Horn. 8 ft. A reed stop.

Contra. A prefix denoting the octave below.

Cor Anglais. 8 ft. A reed stop of thin tone.

Cor-de-Nuit. 8 ft. A closed flue stop of tin or metal.

Cornet. A compound stop of the Mixture tribe.

Corno-di-Bassetto. 8 ft. A Clarinet with its Bass.

Corno Dolce. 8 ft. A metal stop of soft tone.

Cornopean. 8 ft. A reed stop resembling the tone of that instrument.

Cor-Oboe. 8 ft. A flue substitute for the reed of that name.

Couplers. Explain themselves.—Ex. Swell (organ) to Great (organ).

Cremona. See Clarinet.

Cymbal. A Mixture.

Diapason. See Open Diapason and Stopped Diapason.

Diaphone. 32 ft., 16 ft. and 8 ft. A Tremulant stop of enormous power.

Dolcan, Dolce. 8ft. A metal stop of soft tone.

Double. A prefix denoting the octave below.

Dulciana. 16 ft., 8 ft. and 4 ft. An Open Diapason of small scale and delicate tone.

Dulciana Mixture. A Mixture consisting of Dulciana pipes.

Echo. A prefix signifying distant effect.

Fagotto. 16 ft. A reed stop of moderate power.

Fifteenth. 2 ft. A Diapason fifteen diatonic notes above pitch.

Flageolet. 2 ft. A soft flue stop.

Flautina. 2 ft. Virtually a soft Fifteenth. The octave of the Gemshorn.

Flauto Traverso. 4 ft. Resembles the orchestral flute.

Flute. 8 ft., 4 ft. An open or stopped pipe of flute-like tone.

Flûte à Cheminée. 8 ft. *tone.* A stopped metal pipe having a tube or chimney in the stopper.

Flute Bass. See Bass Flute.

Flute d'Amour. 8 ft., 4 ft. A soft flue stop.

Flute Harmonic. 8 ft., 4 ft. An open metal pipe of double speaking-length.

Furniture (Fourniture). A Mixture.

Gamba. 16 ft., 8 ft. and 4 ft. An open metal stop of small scale and stringy tone.

Gedact, Gedackt, Gedeckt. 8 ft. *tone.* A soft Stopped Diapason.

Geigen Principal. 8 ft. A small Open Diapason.

Gemshorn. 4 ft. An open (conical) stop of soft tone.

Grave Mixture. A Mixture consisting of pipes sounding the lower members of partial tones. Cf. Sharp Mixture.

Great Quint. 5⅓ ft. A rank of pipes speaking the fifth above pitch.

[1] Many of the more representative stops also receive short notice under their own names throughout the Dictionary The pitches indicated here in feet are the most usual, but others are built. No list can be exhaustive.

Harmonic. A prefix signifying that the pipes being of double, triple or quadruple speaking-length, the pitch yielded is harmonic.

Harmonic Bass. 32 ft. See Acoustic Bass.

Harmonic Flute. See Flute Harmonic.

Hautboy, Oboe. 8 ft. A reed stop resembling the instrument of that name.

Hohl Flute. 8 ft. Similar to the Clarabella but having the mouth on the wide side of the pipe.

Horn. 8 ft. A powerful reed stop.

Horn Diapason. 8 ft. A slotted Open Diapason of stringy tone.

Keraulophon. 8 ft. A slotted Gamba of small scale and delicate tone.

Lieblich. A prefix meaning sweet of tone.

Lieblich Flute. 4 ft. The octave of Lieblich Gedact.

Lieblich Gedact. 8 ft. See Gedact.

Major Bass. 32 ft. An open pedal stop.

Mixture. A compound stop consisting of ranks of pipes representative of partial tones.

Oboe. See Hautboy.

Octave. See Principal.

Open. A prefix signifying that the pipes are open at the top, i.e. of full speaking-length.

Open Diapason. 32 ft., 16 ft. and 8 ft. Open wood or metal pipes. The foundation of organ tone.

Ophicleide. 16 ft. A powerful pedal reed.

Orchestral. A prefix signifying that the stop resembles the orchestral instrument.

Piccolo. 2 ft. A stop of piccolo tone.

Posaune. 16 ft., 8 ft. A powerful reed stop.

Principal. 4 ft. An Open Diapason of octave pitch. Of 8 ft. pitch in the pedal organ and in German instruments.

Quint. See Great Quint.

Quintaton. A stop in which the twelfth is a feature in the tone of the pipes.

Rohr Flute. 8 ft. tone. A metal Stopped Diapason.

Salicional, Salicet. 8 ft. An open metal stop of small scale and unobtrusive power.

Sesquialtera. Virtually a Mixture.

Sharp Mixture. A Mixture consisting of pipes sounding the higher partial tones.

Stopped. A prefix denoting that the top of the pipe is closed, i.e. a pipe of half true speaking length.

Stopped Diapason. 32 ft., 16 ft., 8 ft. and 4 ft. tone. Of wood or metal.

Suabe Flute. 4 ft. Similar to Clarabella, but of smaller scale and having the lip of the pipe inverted.

Sub. A prefix. See Contra or Double.

Sub Bass. 16 ft. tone. Another name for Bourdon.

Sub Bourdon. 32 ft. tone. A Contra Bourdon.

Super. A prefix signifying the octave above.

Super Octave. On a coupler means the octave above, but in pipe-work two octaves above, i.e. a fifteenth.

Tremulant. A draw-stop (or pedal) bringing on the action of the Tremulant.

Tromba. See Trumpet.

Trombone. 16 ft. A pedal reed of the Trumpet tribe.

Trumpet. 8 ft. A powerful reed stop.

Tuba. 8 ft. A very powerful reed stop.

Twelfth. 2⅔ ft. A stop sounding twelve diatonic notes above pitch.

Unda Maris. Similar in principle to the Voix Céleste.

Unison Off. A draw-stop silencing the unison note when the octaves only are required to sound in using the octave couplers.

Viol. 8 ft. Short for Viol d'Orchestre.

Viola. 8 ft. A Violin Diapason.

Viol d'Amour. 8 ft. Similar to Violin Diapason.

Viol di Gamba. 8 ft. A string-toned Gamba.

Viol d'Orchestre. 8 ft. A very keen string-toned Gamba of small scale.

Violin Diapason. 8 ft. A string-toned Open Diapason of small scale.

Violoncello. 8 ft. The octave of the Violone.

Violone. 16 ft. A string-toned stop of small scale.

Voix Céleste. 8 ft. A stop of two ranks of soft pipes which produce a waving effect in consequence of one of the ranks being tuned sharp.

Vox Angelica. 8 ft. A very delicate-toned open metal stop. Also applied to the Céleste when one rank is tuned flat.

Vox Humana. 8 ft. A reed stop intended to represent the voice.

Wald Flute. 8 ft., 4 ft. Similar to Clarabella with inverted mouth.

BIBLIOGRAPHY OF STOPS

Dr. G. A. Audsley : Organ-Stops and their Artistic Registration.
Rev. Noel A. Bonavia-Hunt : Modern Organ Stops (with a Glossary of Technical Terms).
Carl Locher : An Explanation of the Organ Stops. (English translation.)
G. B. Nevin : A Primer of Organ Registration (with a Dictionary of Organ Stops).
Everett E. Truette : Organ Registration.
James Ingall Wedgwood : Dictionary of Organ Stops.

GENERAL BIBLIOGRAPHY
(Compare sectional Bibliographies given above)

Dr. G. A. Audsley : The Art of Organ Building.
   The Organ of the Twentieth Century.
Charles K. K. Bishop : Notes on Church Organs.
Rev. Noel A. Bonavia-Hunt : The Church Organ.
Thomas Casson : Reform in Organ Building.
   The Modern Organ.
C. A. Edwards : Organs and Organ Building.
Rev. Andrew Freeman : English Organ Cases.
John Wallace Goodrich : The Organ in France.
John Hiles : Catechism of the Organ.
Arthur G. Hill : The Organ Cases and Organs of the Middle Ages and Renaissance.
Dr. J. W. Hinton : Organ Construction.
Walter and Thomas Lewis : Modern Organ Building.
John Matthews : The Organ Described.
   The Restoration of Organs.
J. Norbury : The Box of Whistles.
W. Shepherdson : The Organ : Hints, etc.
John W. Warman : The Organ : its Compass, Tablature, etc.
   The Organ : Writings and Other Utterances, etc.
James Ingall Wedgwood : Tonal Design in Modern Organ Building.

American Works

William Horatio Clarke : Standard Organ Building.
Oliver C. Faust : A Treatise on the Construction, Repairing and Tuning of the Organ.
George Laing Miller : The Recent Revolution in Organ Building.
Ernest M. Skinner : The Modern Organ.
Dr. G. A. Audsley : The Temple of Tone. (1926.)   T. E.

French Works

Dom Bédos de Celles : L'Art du facteur d'orgues (Paris, 1766–1778).
Cavaillé-Coll : Études expérimentales sur les tuyaux d'orgues (Paris) ; and De l'orgue et de son architecture (Paris, 1872).
Comte P. de Fleury : Dictionnaire des facteurs d'orgues français (Paris, 1926).
Jean Huré : L'Esthétique de l'orgue (Paris, 1921).
A. Gastoué : L'Orgue en France de l'antiquité au début de la période classique (Paris, 1921).
Henri Mulet : Les Tendances néfastes et antireligieuses de l'orgue moderne (Paris, 1922).
A. Peschard : Les Premiers Applications de l'électricité aux grandes orgues (Paris, 1890).
F. Raugel : Les Orgues de l'abbaye de Saint-Mihiel (Paris, 1919) ; Les Organistes (Paris) ; Recherches sur les maîtres de l'ancienne facture d'orgues françaises (Paris) ; Les Anciens Buffets d'orgues du département de Seine-et-Oise (Paris) ; Les Grandes Orgues des églises de Paris (Paris, 1926).
G. Servières : La Décoration des buffets d'orgues aux XVe et XVIe siècles (Gazette des Beaux Arts, Dec. 1916 and Mar. 1917).
                                                                F. R.

A bibliography of the organ appeared in Notes and Queries at various dates between Apr. 12 and Dec. 6, 1890.

Robertson's Organ Building contains a bibliography of 225 works on the organ, most of which are in the British Museum.

But the most complete is that of 756 works compiled by the Rev. John Henry Burn, B.D., for the second edition of the Dictionary of Organs and Organists, 1921, supplemented in Sept. 1923 by an article written by him, entitled The Literature of the Organ, which not only brings the bibliography up to that date, but contains much sound advice concerning the best course to pursue in following up the subject.

Barrel organs and instruments played by means of suitably perforated interchangeable paper tune-rolls are dealt with under the heading of Mechanical Appliances.   T. E.

ORGANISTRUM, see Hurdy Gurdy.

ORGANISTS, Royal College of, see Royal College of Organists.

ORGANO denotes the organ part in a score. Organo pieno means Full organ—that is, the entire power of the instrument.   E. J. H.

ORGANOPHONE, a variety of the Harmonium invented by A. Debain of Paris, wherein the reeds or vibrators are raised within instead of being beneath the channels. The result of this disposition is the production of a tone-quality assimilating to that of the American organ.   A. J. H.

ORGANO PLENO, see REGISTRATION.

ORGAN-PLAYING. In England, from the earliest until comparatively recent times, the organ has been the most important of all musical instruments. Our Cathedral choirs and choir-schools were for centuries the only training-grounds for composers and theoreticians, and until the foundation (in 1823) of the Royal Academy of Music there can have been few serious musicians whose early education had not centred round an organ-loft. Furthermore, it may be said, with scarcely any qualification, that in every town and village in the land the organist has been for centuries, for good or for bad, the focus and origin of all musical activities.

For various reasons this predominance of the organist is now gradually disappearing. But to its existence we undoubtedly owe the fact that for a long time no country has approached England (and no country approaches her now) either in the high standard of playing at which organists aim, or in the very large number of executants who reach that standard. Of late years we have been visited by many foreign organists of eminence whose press-agents have persuaded the public, even before their arrival, that England has lost her pride of place ; but, welcome as our visitors are, and skilful as some of them have proved to be, those capable of judging agree that they are in no way superior, and in some ways definitely inferior, to many less-advertised Englishmen.

It is proposed to discuss briefly three aspects of organ-playing : (a) Technique and interpretation ; (b) The special characteristics of organ-music ; (c) The future of the organ itself ; and the consideration of these must be preceded by an epitome of the idiosyncrasies of the instrument.

The organ is the chief of those wind-instruments on which chords can be played. It possesses several keyboards (called manuals), and also pedals. Each manual is provided with its own set of ' stops ' (i.e. collections of pipes of varying strengths and qualities) which can be used either separately or together, and the different manuals can also be ' coupled.' The stops vary in pitch, and are said to be of 32-, 16-, 8-, 4-, or 2-ft. pitch according to the approximate length of the lowest (i.e. longest) pipe ; and these various pitches are an octave apart—8 ft. stops being at ' piano-pitch.' Thus by depressing a single note such as middle C, when 5 stops of the above varieties have been drawn, we can obtain 5 different C's,

two above and two below the actual note held down. Consequently the compass of the organ, though apparently two octaves less than that of the piano, is in reality greater than that of any other keyed instrument.

(a) THE TECHNIQUE of organ-playing is sui generis. Leaving aside the use of the feet, which has a special technique of its own, and the peculiar mental and muscular difficulties in combining hand and foot movements, the actual finger-technique of the manuals differs from that of the only instrument with which it can be compared—the pianoforte. In the old days of the tracker-action there was scarcely any similarity between the two in the use of hands and fingers ; and although the invention of pneumatic action (c. 1832) and electric action (c. 1851) has approximated methods by lightening the touch, there is still considerable divergence. In elementary respects—e.g. the fingering of scales and chords—the basis of technique is now identical ; but there are other cardinal aspects of technique in which, owing to the fundamental differences of the instruments, divergence of method must always exist. On the pianoforte tone is, and always must be, dependent on touch, since it is governed by a hammer hitting a string ; whereas on the organ the pipe alone provides the tone, and every note, be it pianissimo or fortissimo, is struck in the same way, since impact makes no difference to tone. Again, the existence of a sustaining pedal gives pianists facilities in legato passages which an organist must secure solely by ingenuity of fingering, and the existence of stops to be manipulated adds at all times tasks for his hands from which the pianist is exempt. In addition to the above considerations, the weight of touch still differs markedly in the two instruments. Messrs. Broadwood give their standard as ' 3 oz. in the bass, 2½ oz. in the centre, 2 oz. in the treble,' whereas Messrs. Walker & Sons, a leading firm of organ-builders, state that in their organs the touch-weight throughout is ' about 4½ oz. on end of key.'

INTERPRETATION, on the organ, is also governed to a considerable extent by the nature and limitations of the instrument. Apart from the ' Swell-pedal '—a device for opening the shutters of the box in which are contained the pipes of one manual—no accent is obtainable. The difficulty of playing rhythmically becomes, in consequence, so great that the crucial test of the musicianship of an organist is his ability to produce the illusion of rhythm. A further difficulty of interpretation lies in the curious fact that, whereas no inner part can be ' brought out ' by means of touch, it is universally agreed that the music most germane to the organ is that in contrapuntal style, where the inner parts are of equal importance with the outer. To these two difficulties is probably due the tendency of organists to shift the bearing of the word 'interpretation' on to the less musical aspects of organ-playing, such as registration. With all the resources of a modern organ at command it is so much easier to give a striking performance of, let us say, the 'Meistersinger' prelude than, confining oneself to single stops, to give an interpretation of a Bach sonata, wherein the necessity for phrasing and rhythm is supreme. It may be that the inability of audiences to appreciate the subtler qualities of good playing has bred a tendency in organists to discard music that will not prove 'popular,' but it is certain that nowadays the term 'Organ recital' has become suspect amongst musicians, and that few recital programmes—even of the best players—consist entirely of music which, to a non-organist, appears to be of a high calibre.

(b) To the composer the organ has always been a problem. Some, like Brahms, without any intimate understanding of the instrument, have introduced it into their orchestral scores, attracted by its obvious power of contributing volume and building up climax, or by the sonorous depth of its larger pipes. Others, like Mendelssohn, being themselves performers, have used it to the same ends with greater effect. There have also been experiments in the way of concertos for organ and orchestra in which, broadly speaking, contrast supersedes the attempt to blend. But organ and orchestra do not really 'mix,' and none of the numerous concertos that exist—even those of Handel and Mozart—have ever secured a firm foothold amongst musicians, in spite of many attractive movements.

Organ-music proper is something of a hybrid. Bach alone seems to have been able to work with ease at his highest level, but a complete programme, even of Bach, is apt to become wearisome to the ear, though never to the mind. The truth would seem to be that the organ, in spite of its variety of tone-colour, is a monotonous instrument, and composers for it, confronted *ab initio* with this fact, have never succeeded in solving the problem. The German school of the last generation, headed by Rheinberger and Merkel, accepted the fact, and in consequence their music, in the lump, is incontrovertibly dull. Their contemporaries in France, led by Guilmant and Widor, aimed at lightness and fancy, but the results, though often strikingly original, were too often fantastic or undignified. The best work, both in originality of treatment and in musical value, was probably that of César Franck; but even this, highly valued as it is by organists, is not completely successful. Nor was the solution of the problem much advanced by the immediate successors of those mentioned—men such as Max Reger and Vierne. But in more recent works there does seem to be a clear recognition

that the problem is worth attacking, and that by a combination of the contrapuntal style with the modern spirit the organ may prove to possess a dignity and charm which will once again bring it into the realm of serious music. It would be easy to name composers of standing who are contributing to this renaissance, and not least amongst them would be those who are gradually but firmly laying the foundations of a definite English School.

(c) But if the organ is to be rehabilitated, it is necessary, above all things, that it should be improved as a musical instrument. People who buy organs are in the hands—one might almost say at the mercy—of organ-builders; and English organ-builders—at their best still immeasurably the finest in the world—are in the main characterised by an adamantine conservatism. Lovers of the organ seem blissfully unaware that by musicians at large their instrument is looked on as a noisy and inartistic abomination. There is more than a little justification for this attitude in the way that the organ is frequently played; and also more than a little justification for the style of playing in the nature of the instruments with which organ-builders supply us. A few possible improvements may be mentioned which, it is safe to prophesy, will be part and parcel of every organ in a hundred years' time, and all of them could be embodied in any organ this year if the abandonment of stern conservatism were aided by talent for mechanical invention.

(1) The whole of an organ should obviously be enclosed in a swell-box. A dead equality of tone is the negation of all expression, and is not tolerated on any other instrument. Any one who has ever played (as the writer has) on Great Diapasons so enclosed, and realised the overwhelming gain in effect, must for ever be dissatisfied with a Great in which variation of intensity is only possible by the addition or subtraction of stops—*i.e.* by variation of quality.

(2) In very few organs is the number of 8-ft. stops, in comparison with the total number, anything approaching adequate.

(3) The shibboleth of an organ-builder is 'building up tone.' This means that stops are so voiced and graded that we get a series of volumes, from *pp.* to *ff.*, all satisfactorily balanced. The result is that, on practically all but the very largest organs, there is only one way of 'playing loud,' whereas there might quite easily be six or eight. To have to listen to a 'jubilant' piece of music on the organ is, to a non-organist, an almost intolerable experience.

(4) In most instruments the presence of overtones is recognised and definite steps are taken (*e.g.* in the pianoforte) to reduce them and keep them within bounds. The organ is

an instrument where, owing to its sustaining power, overtones are specially numerous and offensive ; but so far from trying to suppress them we add mixture stops (tuned, too, to *unequal* whilst the rest of the organ is tuned to *equal* temperament) to emphasise and exaggerate them. It is a curious example of perverse ingenuity that man invents such an apparatus for the one instrument that needs it least, and the result, labelled ' cacophony ' by Sir Walter Parratt in the first edition of this Dictionary, is distressing in the extreme to all but hardened organists. Berlioz and Helmholtz both expressed astonishment at their being tolerated, yet it is with great difficulty that any organ-builder can be persuaded to omit them.

(5) If an orchestral writer desired to brighten an effect, he would add to his score a few notes in the higher ranges : the last thing he would do would be to ' thicken ' the lower parts. But when an organist desires brightness he cannot do the one without the other. If, for instance, the chord at (*a*) were played on an 8-ft.

flute, and then a 4-ft. flute were drawn, the result is the chord at (*b*)—an entirely haphazard chord in which three of the middle notes are being sounded at double strength. If, however, a 4-ft. flute were merely an extension of an 8 ft. by one octave, then the chord at (*c*) would result and the player would realise his desire in a completely musical way. Any 8-ft. stop, by having an octave added at each end of its compass, can provide three stops of 16-, 8-, and 4-foot tone of homogeneous quality, and there can be little doubt that this principle of ' extension ' will one day be universal. It is economical both of money and space, it is what all musicians desire, and it helps enormously to eliminate that ' thickness ' in the sound of the organ which now destroys the texture of the music. Yet organ-builders with one accord seem to have set their faces against it.

It was Spitta who spoke of ' the mechanical soulless material of the organ ' (*Life of Bach*, i. 284), and there have been too many converts to his view for lovers of so noble an instrument to view the situation with complacent equanimity (cf. REGISTRATION).

P. C. B.

BIBLIOGRAPHY

WALTER G. ALCOCK : *The Organ.*
FREDERICK ARCHER : *The Organ.*
W. T. BEST : *The Art of Organ-Playing.*
   The Modern School for the Organ.
Dr. PERCY C. BUCK : *The Organ.*
HERBERT F. ELLINGFORD : *The Organ.*
HARVEY GRACE : *The Complete Organist.*
Dr. A. EAGLEFIELD HULL : *Organ Playing.*
   Organ Tutor.
A. PAGE : *On Organ Playing.*
Dr. H. W. RICHARDS : *The Organ Accompaniment of the Church Service.*
A. M. RICHARDSON : *Modern Organ Accompaniment.*
SIR JOHN STAINER : *The Organ.*
HAWKES & SON : *The Orchestral and Cinema Organist.*

AMERICAN WORKS
EDITH LANG and GEORGE WEST : *Musical Accompaniment of Moving Pictures.*
M. M. MILLS : *The Art of Organ Playing for Motion Pictures.*

ORGANUM. (1) A general term for measurable music as opposed to unmeasured plain-song. Johannes de Garlandia opens his treatise *De musica mensurabili* with these words:

' Habito de ipsa plana musica quae immensurabilis dicitur, nunc est presens intentio de ipsa mensurabili, quae organum dicitur quantum ad nos prout organum generale dicitur ad omnem mensurabilem musicam ' —' Having dealt with plain music which is called unmeasurable, we now propose to treat of measurable music, which is called organum.' [1]

(2) Organum *per se* or organum *communiter sumptum* is ' quilibet cantus ecclesiasticus tempore mensuratus ' (Franco), or ' quidquid profertur secundum aliquem modum ' (J. de Garlandia), *i.e.* any ecclesiastical melody composed in one of the six RHYTHMIC MODES (*q.v.*) of measurement, as opposed to the unmeasured plain-song chant (C. i. 114*a*, 118*b*).

(3) An early synonym for diaphony or descant in the sense of polyphony.

' Diaphonia vocum disjunctio sonat *quam nos organum vocamus*, cum dis unctae ab invicem voces et concorditer dissonant et dissonanter concordant ' — ' Diaphony means the division of notes which we call organum, in which notes of different pitch are sounded together in concord or discord.' [2]
' Multiplex armonica est plurium vocum dissimilium, ut gravis cum acuta, concussio, quam diaphoniam dico, *quae communiter organum appellatur* ' — ' Multiple harmony is the sounding together of several different notes of varying pitch. This I term diaphony, which is commonly called organum.' [3]

(4) The name given by Hucbald and Guido to the added part in diaphony, taken by the vox organalis or subsecutor. (See DIAPHONIA.)

(5) Organum *purum* or *duplum* or *proprie sumptum*, an ancient form of descant, properly speaking in two parts only, consisting of a measured counterpoint above an unmeasured canto fermo. It is variously defined.

' Pure organum est, quando cuilibet notae de plano cantu ultra mensuram existenti correspondent de discantu duae notae, longa scilicet et brevis, vel his aliquid equipollens ' — ' Organum proper is when each unmeasured note of the plain-song has answering to it in descant notes of two values, namely long and breve, or their equivalents.' [4]
' Cantus non in omni parte sua mensuratus ' — ' Vocal music which is not measured in all its parts.' [5]
' Genus cantus organici in quo tantum attenditur coherentia vocum immensurabilium, et Organum Purum appellatur : et hoc genus antiquissimum est, et duorum tantum ' — ' There is one species of part-singing in which the due adjustment of unmeasured notes is alone regarded. This is called Organum Purum. It is the most ancient species, and consists of two parts only.' [6]
' Discantus igitur, cum magis proprie duos cantus respiciat quam plures, antiquitus de Organo Duplo dicebatur, in quo non sunt nisi duo cantus ' — ' Descant, therefore, since it properly has reference to two melodies only, was originally derived from Organum Duplum, in which there are no more than two parts.' [7]

1 Coussemaker, *Scriptores*, i. 175*a.*
2 Guido ap. Gerbert, *Scriptores*, ii. 21*a.*
3 Walter of Odington ap. Coussemaker, *Scriptores*, i. 212*b*, 235*a.*
4 *Discantus positio vulgaris* ap. C. i. 96*a.*
5 Franco ap. C. i. 134*b.*
6 Walter of Odington, *ib.* i. 245*b.*
7 Johannes de Muris, *ib.* ii. 386*a.*

There is some ambiguity about the expression 'ultra mensuram' in the first of the above extracts. The author of the *Discantus positio vulgaris* seems to apply 'mensura' only to the subdivision of the perfect long of three beats, which he takes as his unit. The plain-song, therefore, consisting entirely of perfect longs, is 'ultra mensuram' in the sense of not having any notes of less value that require to be measured. Later writers, however, understood 'ultra mensuram' as meaning unrhythmical. This is plain from the directions given by Franco and Odington for the conduct of the tenor, who has to watch closely the movement of the descant and wait for an opportunity of bringing in each note of his plain-song on a concord.[1]

Odington gives an example of organum purum, in which the descant appears to be written in the third or dactylic mode of rhythm. The following transcription is given with some hesitation, because the example presents an arrangement of ligatures which does not exactly correspond to the rules laid down by Odington himself for the notation of this mode.

Wooldridge, following up the researches of Meyer of Göttingen, has been able to present us, in the first volume of the *Oxford History of Music*, with facsimiles and transcriptions of several specimens of this kind of composition, taken from a manuscript in the Laurentian Library at Florence. He observes that in none of these is the organum purum carried through from beginning to end; and it was in fact often introduced for a few bars only as a special feature, like *copula* or *ochetus*. Walter of Odington, for instance, says that one, two, or three notes of plain-song only should be taken for the canto fermo.[2] An episode of this sort was usually placed either at the beginning or end of a composition, and was called a 'punctus organicus' or 'floratura.'[3] Good examples may be seen at pp. 195 and 206 of Wooldridge's book.

Of the mode of performance we are told :

1 Coussemaker, i. 135 a, 245 b.   2 *Ibid.* i. 246 b.
3 *Ibid.* i. 193 a, 361 a, ii. 385 b.

'Cantandum est leniter et subtiliter; descensus vero equaliter. Tenor autem tremule teneatur, et cum discordia offendit'—' It must be sung smoothly and finely, and in descending passages evenly. The tenor should be sustained in a tremulous tone, even when a discord is sounded.'[4]

MUSICA FICTA (*q.v.*) was doubtless employed in this, as in other forms of descant, and we are expressly told that the tenor might on occasion 'fingere in concordantiam,' *i.e.* sharpen or flatten the written note.[5]

The specimens of organum purum printed by Wooldridge confirm the impression given by Odington's example,[6] that the descant in this form of composition was extremely free; but the difficulties of performance must have been considerable, and these led to its gradual abandonment in favour of methods less free in some respects, but simpler in execution. By the middle of the 14th century it had fallen into disuse, and Johannes de Muris[7] writes regretfully of the 'organum purum de quo forsan pauci sciunt modernorum'—'Organum purum, of which probably few living musicians have any knowledge.' (See DESCANT.)

J. F. R.

BIBL.—ERICH STEINHARD, *Zur Frühgeschichte der Mehrstimmigkeit. A.M.*, Apr. 1921, pp. 220–231. Gives a list of the chief treatises on the question of diaphony and discusses Riemann's theory of the reversion of polyphonic music in the 11th and 12th century to the principles of the 9th century. Also quotes from two unpublished MSS.

ORGENI, ANNA MARIA AGLAJA (real surname GÖRGER ST. JORGEN) (*b.* Rima Szombat, Hungary, Dec. 17, 1841; *d.* Vienna, Mar. 1926), was a pupil of Mme. Viardot-Garcia, and made her first appearance on the stage Sept. 28, 1865, as Amina, at the Royal Opera-House, Berlin, and was highly successful, both on account of her excellent singing and acting, and of the natural charm of her person and manner. She first appeared in England, Apr. 7, 1866, at the Royal Italian Opera, Covent Garden, as Violetta, and was very well received, subsequently playing Lucia and Marta. She also sang in concerts, and gained great praise for her singing of Agatha's scena from 'Der Freischütz' (of which a contemporary remarked, 'we have not heard anything better than the opening of the great scene . . . her measure and expression in delivery of the Largo bespoke a real artist'[8]); and also of Bach's 'Mein gläubiges Herze' to the violoncello obbligato of Piatti, of which the same writer remarks that 'the elegance and distinction of her manner and her real musical acquirements have secured her a public.'[9] In spite of the large measure of favour given her, she never played on the stage again in England, but in 1870 sang in concerts for a short period, being well received at the Philharmonic in the above scena of Weber, and that from 'Lucia.' After her first season in London she went to Vienna in September of that year, and played

4 *Ibid.* i. 246 b.   5 *Ibid.* i. 135 a
6 *Ibid.* i. 246 b.   7 *Ibid.* ii. 429 a.
8 *Athenæum*, May 19, 1866.   9 *Ibid.* June 7, 1866.

there with success, and afterwards was heard in opera, festivals and concerts, at Leipzig, Hanover and Dresden. She sang for a few nights at the Lyrique, Paris, in 1869, as Violetta. In 1881 she reappeared in England, and sang with success at the Crystal Palace, Philharmonic and other concerts. She subsequently became a teacher of singing at the Dresden Conservatorium, and was the first woman to receive there (1908) the title of Professor. A. C.

At about the beginning of the war (1914) she went to Vienna, where she had a great number of singing pupils.

ORGUE EXPRESSIF, a French name for the reed organ or HARMONIUM. A. J. H.

ORIANA, TRIUMPHES OF, see TRIUMPHES OF ORIANA.

ORIANA MADRIGAL SOCIETY, see SCOTT, Charles Kennedy.

ORIENTAL MUSIC, see MUHAMMEDAN.

ORLANDINI, GIUSEPPE MARIA (b. Bologna, Feb. 4, 1688; d. Florence, c. 1750), opera composer, for some time maestro di cappella to the Duke of Tuscany. He wrote 44 operas between 1708-45, which enjoyed great popularity; also oratorios, cantatas, etc.; on the subject of his comic opera ' Il giocatore,' see O. G. Sonneck, *Mus. Ant.*, Apr. 1913 (*Q.-L.*; *Riemann*).

ORNAMENTS (Fr. *agréments*, properly *agréments du chant* or *de musique*; Ger. *Manieren*; Ital. *abbellimenti*; Eng. *graces*), are commonly described by the French word *agréments* (*agrémens*), owing to the fact that they were standardised by the French. In the following articles the subject is treated under FRENCH, GERMAN and ENGLISH, and to these are added an explanation of the purely vocal ornamentation developed in the earlier Italian schools of music. Certain ornaments introduced into vocal or instrumental melody, indicated either by signs, or by small notes, are performed according to certain rules.

FRENCH.—The custom of ornamenting the melody is as ancient as music; perfect examples of *agréments* are to be found in Gregorian chant and in the measured music (Musica mensurata or Cantus mensurabilis) of the mediæval ages. At the time of the Renaissance the principal part was frequently enriched with vocalisations, of which many specimens have been retained by the theorists.

It is difficult to ascertain at what period the French style (*goût français*) took birth; it is inaccurate to impute the invention of *agréments* to Chambonnières (1670), as already in 1636 the famous Père Mersenne mentions them in his *Harmonie universelle*.

Lully greatly contributed to codify their use. Between 1690 and 1800 the French *agréments* perfectly defined have remained unchanged; their performance is absolutely necessary, for,

(says Blanchet in his *Art du chant*, 1756), ' they are greatly befitted to move powerfully the soul; to deprive music of such ornaments would be depriving it of the most beautiful part of its essence.' A similar doctrine is to be found in Ph. E. Bach, in his *Versuch über die wahre Art das Clavier zu spielen*, in 1753. (See below.) The principal *agréments* of the French School are the following :

To these must be added the Passages, Diminutions, Coulades, Fusées, Traits, which are arbitrary features left to the discretion of the performers.

BIBL.—E. BORREL, *Contribution à l'interprétation de la musique française au XVIIIe siècle*, Paris, 1916; J. ARGER, *Les Agréments et le rythme*, Paris, 1917; E. BRUNOLD, *Les Agréments chez les clavecinistes*. E. B^L.

GERMAN.—C. P. E. Bach, in his *Versuch über die wahre Art das Clavier zu spielen,* in 1753, speaks of the great value of the *agréments* :

They serve to connect the notes, they enliven them, and when necessary give them a special emphasis, . . . they help to elucidate the character of the music ; whether it be sad, cheerful, or otherwise, they always contribute their share to the effect, . . . an indifferent composition may be improved by their aid, while without them even the best melody may appear empty and meaningless.

At the same time he warns against their too frequent use, and says they should be as the ornament with which the finest building may be overladen, or the spices with which the best dish may be spoilt.

The *agréments*, according to C. P. E. Bach, are the Bebung,[1] Vorschlag, Triller, Doppelschlag, Mordent, Anschlag, Schleifer, Schneller, and Brechung.

The PRALL-TRILLER (*q.v.*) is included as a species of triller. In addition to these, Marpurg treats of the Nachschlag or 'Aspiration,' which Emanuel Bach does not recognise, or at least calls 'ugly, although extraordinarily in fashion,' but which is largely employed by modern composers.

ENGLISH.—The graces peculiar to English music differed considerably from the above. The 'Fitzwilliam Virginal Book,' which may be taken as typical of Elizabethan practice, that is, before the exertion of any French influence on English music, includes only two. These

---

[1] The Bebung (Fr. *balancement*, Ital. *tremolo*) cannot be executed on the modern pianoforte. It consisted in giving to the key of the clavichord a certain trembling pressure, which produced a kind of pulsation of the sound, without any intervals of silence. On stringed instruments a similar effect is obtained by a rocking movement of the finger without raising it from the string.

are : (1) The slide of a third upwards or double appoggiatura,  probably occasionally treated as a mordent.

(2) The shake, short or long.

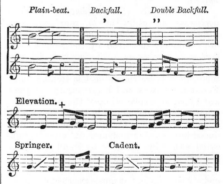

A complete table, though of a later date and devised primarily for stringed instruments, is given by Christopher SIMPSON (*q.v.*) in *The Division Violist* (1659). In giving it, Simpson admits his indebtedness to COLEMAN (*q.v.*) in the words, 'for these I am obliged to the ever-famous Dr. Coleman.' The graces of this table are divided into two classes, the 'smooth and shaked graces.' The smooth graces are only adapted to stringed instruments, as they are to be executed by sliding the finger along the string ; they include the Plain-beat or Rise, the Backfall, the Double Backfall, the Elevation, the Cadent, and the Springer which ' con-

cludes the Sound of a Note more acute, by clapping down another Finger just at the expiring of it.' The effect of this other finger upon the violin would be to raise the pitch of the last note but one (the upper of the two written notes) so that the Springer would resemble the French *accent*. The ' shaked graces ' are the Shaked Backfall Close Shake, a slight undulation of pitch by oscillation of the finger (note Simpson's curiosity of notation), Shaked Beat, Elevation and Cadent, which are similar to the plain graces with the addition of a shake, and lastly the Double Relish, of which no explanation in words is attempted, but an example in notes given as below. It will be worth while to compare with the above the simpler list given in Henry Purcell's ' Choice

Collection of Lessons for the Harpsichord or Spinnet,' published by his widow (1696), the more so since the comparison emphasises the influence exerted by the French school between the times of Coleman and of Purcell. The following is condensed from the instructions given in the 'Choice Collection' (edition 3, 1669).

The Ornaments used in later music of the classical period, ACCIACCATURA, APPOGGIATURA, ARPEGGIO, MORDENT, PRALL-TRILLER, SHAKE (TRILL) and TURN, are further described under their own names. (See also the masterly treatise on *Musical Ornamentation* by E. Dann-reuther in two volumes of Novello's *Music Primers*.)   **F. T.**

BIBL.—E. DANNREUTHER, *Musical Ornamentation* (2 vols.); R. LACH. *Studien zur Entwicklungsgeschichte der ornamentalen Melopöie* (Leipzig, 1913).

VOCAL ORNAMENTS OF THE ITALIAN SCHOOL

VOCAL.—The origins of the various crna-ments employed in vocal music are lost in the mists of antiquity. Between the time of Charlemagne and the close of the 16th century the Latin writers, beginning with the Romanian letters, which were marks of expression, used a set of terms which clearly described orna-ments. The most important were *crispatio*, a shake; *trepidatio*, also meaning a shake, *reverberatio* (mediæval Latin) ' beats '—perhaps the beginning of our vibrato—*vinnulae* ('sweet'), probably, though not certainly, *mezza voce*, *voces tremulae*, tremulous voices, *copula*, a pass-age sung by a tenor over a hold in the bass, and *hocheti*, meaning staccati (see HOCKET). Appoggiaturas single and double, ascending and descending, were known in the 11th century. Grupetti were common from the earliest days, when they appeared in simple forms in the Kyrie. They were the roots of the ' passages ' so much discussed toward the close of the 16th century.

These passages disclosed themselves first in the simple variation form called diminutions, from which ultimately developed the elaborate floridity of 16th- and 17th-century music. A clear illustration of the construction of a pass-age in diminution form on a plain chant is furnished by Giovanni Battista Bovicelli, a famous teacher, in his *Regole di musica* (1594).

Al - le - - - - - - lu - ia

The trill existed at least as far back as the 3rd century, for it is defined by Pomponius Festus, the grammarian, who wrote at that time. The name was subsequently applied to other orna-ments. At the time of Giulio Caccini, the end of the 16th century, the name *trillo* was applied to an ornament long since discarded. The example is from Herbst.

Ve - ni ve   ni

The trill of contemporaneous music was called *gruppo* by Caccini and his contemporaries, and written thus:

Johann Crüger, in his *Precepta musicae practicae figuralis* (1625), and Johann Andreas Herbst in *Musica practica sive Instructio pro symphoniacis* (1642), call this ornament *tremolo*. In the employment of florid passages much latitude was allowed to the singer, and Bovicelli lays stress on the importance of avoiding monotony by making rhythmic changes. A favourite device for this purpose was called the ' Lombard figure ' and was merely a syncopation in this form.

The swell tone, later known as the *messa di voce*, was assiduously cultivated in the late years of the 16th century, if not earlier, and was then practised in several forms under the general title of *esclamazio*. The *esclamazio languida* consisted of a crescendo, a diminuendo and a crescendo. The *esclamazio viva* was a diminuendo followed by a crescendo. The latter was not usually employed in dramatic recitative, but was regarded as more suitable to canzone. The crescendi in these ornaments (which were also means of expression) did not go beyond a mezzo forte in Caccini's time. The 18th-century *messa di voce* was more vigorous and at one period was used on every long tone. An example from Caccini's ' Nuove musiche ' will throw light on the *esclamazio*.

The development of ornamentation in vocal art began after the Council of Laodicea in 367 placed the music of the service entirely in the hands of trained choirs. The solo chanters quickly seized the opportunity for vocal display, and cultivated an ornate style. The Schola Cantorum, founded by Gregory the Great in 590, trained singers for the Papal Choir and the choirs of other churches of the Holy See. The most accomplished of its singers were made solo chanters. The vanity of these solo singers led to abuse of the ornaments of the

chant. In the 9th century we find the appoggiatura, syncopation, the mordent, portamento and other graces used indiscriminately. In the late years of the 16th century the church singers freely introduced passages in the polyphonic music. When Peri and Caccini, who complained vigorously of the inartistic employment of passages, introduced the new *stile parlante*, the ecclesiastical singers appeared to be more anxious than ever to preserve floridity in the church service. Pope John XXII., in the 14th century, had commanded the abolition of all ornaments from sacred chant, which shows us that abuses must have reached a lamentable state. But it is probable that Pope John's decree was not generally obeyed. It was after the public opera house came into existence and audiences encouraged opera singers and composers to the cultivation of a brilliantly florid style that the stage furnished what the Church gradually abandoned. Before the close of the 17th century all the ornaments had assumed the forms in which we now use them, and the extraordinary cadenzas of Handel's day had been already equalled.   W. J. H.

ORNITHOPARCUS (ORNITOPARCHUS), ANDREAS, the author of a rare Latin treatise, entitled ' Musicae activae micrologus,' which was published at Leipzig in 1516. (See MICROLOGUS.) His real name was Vogelsang or Vogelgesang, and he seems to have adopted the Greek pseudonym of Ornithoparcus on account of the many countries which he had visited, and of which he gives a list at the end of the third book of his work. Little further is known about him, except that he was a native of Meiningen, that he was M.A. of Tübingen, and was connected in Oct. 1516 with the University of Wittenberg. (*Monatshefte*, 1878, p. 54.) His book was translated into English by JOHN DOWLAND (London, 1609).   W. B. S.

ORNSTEIN, LEO (*b.* Kremenchug, Russia, Dec. 11, 1895), Russian-American pianist and composer. As a child he studied at the Conservatoire in St. Petersburg, where he was a pianistic prodigy; after 1906 he was a pianoforte pupil of Mrs. Thomas Tapper at the Institute of Musical Art in New York. His début as pianist was made in New York in 1911 ; since then he has played in concerts in numerous cities of Europe and America. A radical and anarchistic composer, he is reported to have declared himself ' not concerned with form or with standards of any nature.' His compositions include 2 piano concertos ; 2 symphonic poems, ' The Life of Man ' and ' The Fog,' and other orchestral pieces ; chamber music and sonatas ; choral pieces ; piano pieces and songs.
W. S. S.

OROLOGIO, ALESSANDRO. According to Eitner (*Monatshefte*, xxx. 36, and *Q.-L.*) there were two musicians of this name, living at the same time, and employed in very much the same capacity at two different German courts, whose published works, too, it is almost impossible to separate. One is described as in 1580 violinist and in 1603 vice-Kapellmeister to the court chapel of the Emperor Rudolf at Prague. The other appears as in 1590 instrumentalist (Zinkenist) in the Electoral Chapel at Dresden, and also in 1603 promoted to the position of vice-Kapellmeister. DOWLAND (*q.v.*) made the acquaintance of this latter in 1584 at the court of the Landgrave of Hesse-Cassel. The works of both Orologios consist of Books of Madrigals and Canzonets *a* 3-6, but to the Dresden musician of this name is ascribed a Book of Instrumental Intradas *a* 5-6 dedicated to King Christian IV. of Denmark and published at Helmstädt, 1597. Morley has a Madrigal of Orologio with English words in his Book of 1598.   J. R. M.

ORPHÉE AUX ENFERS, opéra bouffe, in 2 acts and 4 tableaux; words by Hector Crémieux, music by Offenbach. Produced Bouffes-Parisiens, Oct. 21, 1858; in London in French (Hortense Schneider) St. James's Theatre, July 12, 1869.   G.

ORPHÉON. This word was used about 1830 by Bocquillon-Wilhem to designate men's choral societies. In 1815 it had been one of Choron's aims to introduce the practice of music in the elementary instruction of French schools. In 1819 Wilhem opened special courses, taught at the École Polytechnique, and at the City of Paris schools. Introduced into nine schools in 1830, singing became obligatory in 1835; in 1865 it was inaugurated at the schools of the Paris suburbs, and a wide popular movement of Orphéonistes resulted, for which many popular composers have written suitable music. The directors of the Orphéon societies (Paris) have been: Wilhem until 1842; Hubert, Gounod, Hubert, 1852; Bazin, Pasdeloup, 1863; Bazin, 1873-78; Dannhauser, 1879; Chapuis, 1894, who reorganised the municipal 'Orphéon.' An annual concert is given at the Trocadero with 1500 performers. The Orphéon - concourses date from 1849. In the provinces (Lyons), a military Orphéon was performed in 1843, and 700 provincial societies were existing in 1859; 3000 'Orphéonists' were heard in London in 1860.

From 1862, 300 societies have been steadily growing, attaining 2200 in about 1900. The movement is comparable with that of the British COMPETITION FESTIVALS (*q.v.*).

BIBLIOGRAPHY

See also the article ORPHÉON, ORPHÉONISTE in former editions of this Dictionary.
J. COMBARIEU : *Histoire de la musique*, iii. pp. 313-15.
J. WEBER: *La Situation musicale et l'instruction publique en France.* (1889.)
H. MARECHAL et G. PARÈS : *Monographie universelle de l'Orphéon, Sociétés Chorales, fanfares.* (1910.)   M. L. P.

ORPHEOREON (ORPHEORON, ORPHARION); an instrument of the cither kind, with flat back, but with the ribs shaped in more than one incurvation. The varieties of the orpheoreon also differed from the usual cither in the bridge being oblique, rising towards the treble side. According to Praetorius (*Organographia*, Wolfenbüttel, 1619, p. 54) the orpheoreon was tuned like a LUTE (*q.v.*) in ' Kammerton ' (*a*). The strings were of brass or iron, in six or seven pairs, and were played with a plectrum. A larger orpheoreon was called Penorcon, and a still larger one Pandore—Praetorius spells this Pandorra or Bandore. According to his authority it was invented in England ; to which another adds the name of John Rose, citizen of London, living in Bridewell, and the date of about 1560. It must, however, have been a rather different orpheoreon. Following Praetorius, the pandore, and we presume its congeners, had no chanterelle or melody string, and could therefore have been used only for accompaniment, like the common cither, *sutoribus et sartoribus usitatum instrumentum.* He gives cither tunings for seven strings, including the common ' four-course ' (*b*) and ' Italian ' (*c*) ; old tunings (*d*), (*e*), often used an octave lower on the lute in France, and the old Italian six-course (*f*), but no other than the lute tuning above mentioned for the orpheoreon family. The player probably tuned as he chose. The forms ' Orpharion ' and ' Pandora ' occur in a book on the Lute and other instruments, entitled *The Schoole of Musicke*, by Thomas Robinson, London, 1603. A copy is in the British Museum. There is another instrument which Praetorius describes as being like a pandore in the back ; this was the Quinterna, or Chiterna. It differed, however, in other respects, as the ribs, belly, etc., were of simple outline, and the bridge was straight. He says it was tuned like the very earliest lutes (*g*), and depicts it in his illustrations as not unlike a guitar.

An orpheoreon was sold at Christie's in 1898 ; another is in the possession of Lord Tollemache, at Helmingham.   A. J. H.

ORPHEUS (1), a collection of partsongs or vocal quartets by German composers, with English words, published in parts and compressed score. It was started by Ewer in 1836, and continued by their successors, Novello.

A similar work—but for equal voices only—appeared in Germany, entitled ' Orpheus : Sammlung auserlesene mehrstimmige Gesänge für Männerstimmen,' in many volumes, published at Leipzig, by Friedlein, and by Zöllner   G.

ORPHEUS (2). The story of Orpheus and Eurydice was the subject of the first actual operas in the history of music, (1) the ' Euridice' of Caccini and Peri to Rinuccini's words, 1600 ; this was shortly afterwards followed by (2) Monteverdi's ' Orfeo ' in Mantua, 1607. Later in the 17th century there were many operas on the same subject, as, for example, by Sartorio (1672), Draghi (1683), the sons of Lully (1690), Reinhard Keiser (1699), Fux (1715), Pergolese (1734), Wagenseil (1740), and Graun (1752). The most important is (3) the ' Orfeo ed Euridice,' words by Calzabigi, music by Gluck ; produced Vienna, Oct. 5, 1762 ; Paris, 1764 ; in a slightly altered form as ' Orphée,' Opéra, Aug. 2, 1774 ; revived Théâtre Lyrique, Nov. 19, 1859 ; Covent Garden, June 27, 1860 ; New York, Metropolitan Opera House (in German), 1885. For later operas on the same story, see Riemann's *Opern Handbuch*.

M.

ORPHEUS BRITANNICUS, the first attempt towards a collection of Henry Purcell's vocal music. It was issued by Henry Playford, in folio, shortly after the composer's death, and the first volume, which is dedicated to Lady Elizabeth Howard, is dated 1698. The second bears the date 1702, and both have the portrait engraved by White after Closterman.

The second edition has the dates 1706 and 1711 (also in two volumes), and the third edition 1721. Of this last named few copies appear to have been printed, for Handel's music had begun to be more in favour than Purcell's.

About 1735 John Walsh published a volume of Purcell's songs under the title ' Orpheus Britannicus,' pp. 120, these being printed from engraved plates, which had been used for single songs.

The title-page of the original issue of 1698 runs :

' Orpheus Britannicus, a collection of all the choicest songs for One, Two, and Three voices, composed by Mr. Henry Purcell ; together with such symphonies for violins or flutes as were by him designed for any of them, and a Thorough-bass to each song figured for the Organ, Harpsichord, or Theorbo lute. London : printed by J. Heptinstall for Henry Playford in the Temple Change in Fleet St. MDCXCVIII.' fol.

F. K.

ORPHEUS CALEDONIUS, the first published collection of Scottish songs united to their melodies, for though a prior collection of Scottish airs had been issued, in 1700 (second edition 1701) by Henry Playford, yet these were merely noted for the violin, and did not include the most popular ones. The ' Orpheus Caledonius ' was edited, with the bass added to the tunes, by William Thomson, who entered the work at Stationers' Hall on Jan. 5, 1725. The words are chiefly taken from the first volume of Allan Ramsay's *Tea-Table Miscellany*, 1724. It was dedicated to the Princess of Wales (afterwards Queen Caroline), who appears to have patronised Thomson. There is, no doubt in consequence of this patronage,

a very lengthy list of distinguished subscribers names. There are fifty songs and airs printed, and to several of them is affixed a mark attributing them to David Rizzio, the first appearance of this oft-repeated myth.

In 1733 Thomson again issued the ' Orpheus Caledonius,' but in two volumes octavo. The first contained the same fifty songs and airs as in the 1725 edition, with some slight changes in the melodies. The second volume had fifty more Scottish songs.

As the first edition is rare and of great interest, the following copy of the title-page and index may be of service.

Except the dedication and the list of subscribers, etc., the whole work is engraved.

' Orpheus Caledonius, or a Collection of the best Scotch Songs set to Musick by W. Thomson. London : Engraved and Printed for the Author at his house in Leicester Fields Enter'd at Stationers' Hall according to Act of Parliament.' 1725, Jan. 5. ' Index (the songs mark'd thus * were composed by David Rizzio.) '

*The Lass of Patie's Mill.	Love is the cause of my mourning.
*Bessie Bell.	Bonny Jean.
*The Bush aboon Traquair.	Mary Scott.
Thro' the Wood, Laddie.	The Mill, Mill-O.
Bless'd as the Immortal Gods.	I'll never leave thee.
The Last time I came o'er the moor.	Katherine Ogie.
The Yellow-hair'd Laddie.	*Ann thou were my ain thing.
*The Bonny Boatman.	Polwart on the Green.
Woe's my heart that we should sunder.	A Health to Betty.
The Broom of Cowdenknowes.	Fy let us a' to the bridal.
A Cock Laird fu' cadgie.	Saw ye na my Maggy.
Fy gar rub her o'er wi' Strae.	My Nannio.
Muirland Willy.	Maggie's Tocher.
Peggy, I must love thee.	Were na my heart light I wad die.
*Auld Rob Morris.	Sow'r plumbs of Gallow Shiels.
Auld Lang Sine.	There's my thumb, I'll ne'er beguile ye.
My Apron Dearie.	The Gaberlunzie Man.
My Daddy's a Delver of Dikes.	The Collier's Bonny Lassie.
Wale, wale up yon Bank.	The Bob of Dunblain.
John Hay's Bonny Lassie.	The Carle he came o'er the croft.
Hap me with thy Petticoat.	O'er Bogie.
Bonny Christy.	The Lass of Livingston.
Nancy's to the Greenwood gane.	William and Margaret.
The Highland Laddie.	*Down the burn, Davie.
Blinko'er the burn, Sweet Betty.	
Tweed Side.	F. K.

ORPHEUS CHORAL SOCIETY, see under DUBLIN.

ORTIGUE, JOSEPH LOUIS D' (*b.* Cavaillon, May 22, 1802 ; *d.* Paris, Nov. 20, 1866), musical *littérateur*.

He studied at first merely as an amateur, under the Castil Blazes, father and son. He went to Aix in Provence to study law, but music proved more powerful, and he finally resolved to abandon the law for musical literature. With this view he came to Paris in 1829, and began by writing musical critiques in the *Mémorial Catholique* ; then, becoming intimate with Lamennais, he wrote for *L'Avenir*, and, after its failure, for *La Quotidienne*, besides the *Gazette musicale* and *La France musicale*. After his marriage in 1835 he redoubled his exertions and contributed to half a score of periodicals, including the *Temps*, *Revue des deux Mondes*, *National*, *L'Univers*, *L'Université Catholique*, *L'Opinion Catholique*, and above all the *Journal des Débats*, on which paper he succeeded Berlioz as musical critic. To this last paper he mainly owed his reputation, and his place in several commissions, historical and scientific, to which he was appointed by government. In 1863 he became chief editor of *Le Ménestrel*,

His important works are *De la guerre des dilettanti* (1829) ; his large *Dictionnaire liturgique, historique, et théorique de plain-chant et de musique religieuse* (Paris, 1854 and 1860, small 4to), and *La Musique à l'Église* (*ibid.*, 1861, 12mo). To the former of these the Abbé Normand contributed a number of articles under the *nom de guerre* of Théodore Nisard. D'Ortigue was associated with Niedermeyer in founding *La Maîtrise* (1857), a periodical for sacred music, and in the *Traité théorique et pratique de l'accompagnement du plain-chant* (Paris, 1856, large 8vo). In 1862 he started, with Félix Clément, the *Journal des Maîtrises*, a periodical of reactionary principles in sacred music, which soon collapsed. He was an honest and laborious writer ; his name will live through his *Dictionnaire*, which contains some excellent articles on church music, but his other books are mere musical miscellanies, thoughtfully written, but not endowed with any of those qualities of style or matter which ensure any lasting influence. He died suddenly.

G. C.

BIBL.—M. BARBER, *Joseph d'Ortigue* (with list of works), 1919.

ORTIZ, DIEGO (*b.* Toledo ; fl. 1547–65), Spanish composer, famous as being one of the first to employ the principle of variation. He is first heard of in 1547 as a composer of motets, printed in lute tablature in the ' Silva de Sirenas ' of Enriquez de Valderrabano. In 1553 and 1558 he was maestro de capilla to the Duke of Alba, Viceroy of Naples. His singers and players were almost all Spaniards and included the blind organist Francisco de SALINAS (*q.v.*).

His famous book of variations for bass-viol and *cymbalo* appeared in Rome in 1553, in Spanish and Italian versions. If not the first to use variation-form, he certainly realised something of its artistic possibilities. Priority in this seems to belong to Hugh Aston and the composer of ' My Lady Carey's Dompe ' (B.M. Royal MSS. App. 58), whose work dates from the beginning of the 16th century. In Italy the beginnings of variation are seen in the works of Silvestro Ganassi for flute (1535) and bass-viol (1542–43) ; while in Spain definite variations are found in the lute book of Luis de NARVAEZ (1538).

The published works of Diego Ortiz are as follows :

Tratado de glosas sobre clausulas . . . en la musica de violones. Rome, 1553. (Berlin.) Reprinted by Max Schneider, Berlin, 1913.
Il primo libro di Diego Ortiz Tolletano, nel qual si tratta delle glose sopra le cadenze. . . . Rome, 1553. (Bibl. Nac., Madrid.) An Italian version of the above.
Musicæ Liber I. Hymnos, Magnificat, Salves, Motecta, Psalmos. . . . Venice, 1565 ; Gardano. (Augsburg ; Berlin ; Bologna ; Rome, St. Cecilia ; Vienna.) Of these, 8 were reprinted by Proske, one by Eslava and others by Pedrell.

J. B. T.

ORTO, MARBRIANO DE, a Flemish musician of the end of the 15th and beginning of the 16th centuries, to whom Fétis wrongly gives the Christian name Jean, and conjectures the surname to have been originally Dujardin, was a singer in the Papal chapel at Rome from 1484–

1494, contemporary therefore with Josquin des Prés.

From 1505 he was first chaplain and singer at the court of Philip the Fair of Burgundy, and his name appears in the chapel lists up to 1516. In 1505 Petrucci printed a book of five Masses *a* 4 by De Orto, bearing the titles *Dominicalis, l'ay pris amours* (containing two settings of the Creed), *L'omme armé, La belle se sied, Petite camusette.* The miscellaneous collections of Petrucci also contain a few motets, chansons and a lamentation lesson by De Orto. Two masses and parts of masses, including another ' L'omme armé ' *a* 5, are contained in the choir-books of the Sistine chapel at Rome. The Imperial Library at Vienna has also two important unprinted masses of De Orto, one entitled ' Mi-mi,' indicating the main theme, in accordance with the hexachord solmisation system, as consisting of the constant succession of the two notes E–A, the other entitled ' Le Serviteur,' both *a* 4. The very remarkable Agnus of the Mass ' Mi-mi,' with the tenor based on the canon ' descende gradatim ' is reproduced in modern score in the Beilagen to Ambros's *Geschichte der Musik,* also the motet Ave Maria, from Petrucci, 1501.   J. R. M.

BIBL.—E. DROZ and G. THIBAULT, *Bibliographie des recueils de chansons du XVe siècle* (1926).

O SALUTARIS HOSTIA, probably part of the hymn of Aquinas, beginning *Verbum supernum prodiens,* for the office of Corpus Christi, but better known through its being sung at the service of Benediction, or more rarely from its being sung after the Benedictus at Mass.

Its plain-song melody is borrowed from the Ascensiontide hymn, ' Eterne Rex altissime.' [1]

O sa - lu - ta - ris hos-ti - a, Quæ cæ - li pandis os - ti-um,

Bella premunt hos-ti - li - a, Da ro-bur, fer aux - i - li-um.

It is one of the more elaborate hymn melodies, and in the eighth mode ; the melody has become current in a debased and simplified form, thus :

O sa - lu - ta - ris hos - ti - a,   Quæ cæ-li pan-dis os - ti - um,

Bel-la premunt hos-ti - li - a,   Da ro-bur, fer aux-i - li-um.

(See RUE, Pierre de la.)   W. S. R.

OSBORNE, GEORGE ALEXANDER (*b.* Limerick, Sept. 24, 1806 ; *d.* London, Nov. 16, 1893). His father was organist and lay-vicar at Limerick.

Osborne was a self-instructed pianist until

1 *Hymns Ancient and Modern,* No. 167.

he reached the age of 18, when he determined on making music his profession and seeking instruction on the Continent. In 1825 he repaired to Belgium, and found a home in the house of the Prince de Chimay, Cherubini's friend, the well-known musical amateur, who made him acquainted with the works of the best German composers. During his residence in Brussels he taught the eldest son of the Prince of Orange, afterwards King of the Netherlands, by whom he was subsequently decorated. In 1826 he went to Paris, and studied the pianoforte under Pixis, and harmony under Fétis. He afterwards placed himself under Kalkbrenner, and soon obtained a good position among the pianists of the day, took his full share in the musical life at that time so abundant in Paris, and amongst other advantages enjoyed the privilege of an intimate acquaintance with Chopin and Berlioz.[1] In 1843 Osborne settled in London, where he was for many years one of the most esteemed and genial teachers. He died there, and was buried in Highgate Cemetery. He wrote three trios for piano and strings, and a sextet for piano, flute, oboe, horn, violoncello and double-bass. Of the many duets for piano and violin, thirty-three were written with De Bériot, the greater part of which are original, one was written in conjunction with Lafont, one with Artôt, and two with Ernst. His pianoforte solo, 'La Pluie des perles,' enjoyed extraordinary popularity in its day.   W. H. H.

OSIANDER, Lucas (b. Nuremberg, Dec. 16, 1534; d. Stuttgart, Sept. 7, 1604), son of the Protestant controversialist, Andreas Osiander. Besides being himself a theologian of some eminence, pastor at Esslingen and elsewhere in Würtemberg, he had received a thorough musical training, both theoretical and practical, which qualified him to bring out what is sometimes described as the first real German Chorale-Book, the first, that is, in which the melody is definitely placed in the descant or soprano part, and provided with a simple note-for-note counterpoint a 4. Though not absolutely the first to put the chorale melody in the descant (it had been occasionally done by Le Maistre and others), he was the first to do it systematically, and for the express purpose of enabling the whole congregation to join in the singing of it. The full title of his work is ' Fünfzig geistliche Lieder und Psalmen mit 4 Stimmen auf contrapunctsweise also gesetzt, dass eine ganze christliche Gemein durchaus mitsingen kann,' Stuttgart, 1586. In the preface he says :

' I know, indeed, that composers otherwise usually put the Choral in the Tenor, but when that is done, the Choral is not sufficiently recognisable among the other voices, and the congregation (der gemeine Mann) cannot follow or join in the singing. I have, therefore, put the Choral always in the Descant.'

This preface also shows the original meaning of the word ' choral ' as applied to the melody only, in contradistinction to the word ' figural ' as applied to every polyphonic setting, however simple. ' Pastors and schoolmasters,' he says, ' should see that the Choral and the Figured Music go well together, so as to form an agreeable concord.' A few of his settings were received into Schöberlein's Schatz, and Friedrich Zelle of Berlin republished the whole book (' Das erste evangelische Choralbuch ') as his Easter programme, by way of appendix to his school report of 1903.   J. R. M.

OSSIA (Oppure, Ovvero) (Ital. ' or else '); these words are used indifferently to mark a passage, generally printed above the treble or below the bass, which may be substituted for that written in the body or text of the work, being in most cases an easier version of the same kind of effect. These words were also used when the compass of the piano was in process of alteration ; thus Moscheles sometimes adapts passages, originally written for a full-sized piano, to the smaller compass, writing the passage for the smaller piano above that of the full-sized one.

The same object is attained by the words plus facile or leichter.   M.

OSTINATO, i.e. obstinate. ' Basso ostinato ' is the Italian term for a GROUND BASS (q.v.), which recurs obstinately throughout the composition. ' I shall seem to you,' says Mendelssohn,[2] ' like a Basso ostinato, always grumbling over again, and at last becoming quite tiresome.'   G.

OSTRČIL, Otakar (b. Smichov, Prague, Feb. 25, 1879), Czechoslovak, composer and conductor. His father was a medical man. Both parents feared the uncertain career of a musician for their son, and he therefore entered the philosophical faculty of the Prague University, and, in 1901, became professor of modern languages at the Commercial Academy, Prague. While pursuing his philological studies, he worked hard at music, taking private piano lessons from Prof. Ad. Mikeš of the Conservatoire, and from 1895 studying piano and composition with Zdenko Fibich (q.v.). He remained with this master until his death in 1900, and in his last years became his assistant, correcting his proofs, helping him in the scoring of his works and with their pianoforte editions. From 1909–22 Ostrčil was conductor of the amateur orchestra, Orchestralni Idruženi (The Orchestral Association), and brought it into prominence. From 1914–19 he was operatic conductor at the Vinohrady theatre, in Prague, and in the same year was appointed dramaturge at the National Theatre. On the death of Karel Kovařovic, in 1920, Ostrčil was chosen as his successor after he had resigned his professorship. In this new post

---

[1] See Proc. Mus. Assn. Apr. 1883.

[2] Letter, Jan. 8, 1838.

he has shown himself a zealous and convinced propagandist of modern tendencies in dramatic music.

As a composer Ostrčil attracted attention early by the maturity of his technique. The symphonic poem, 'The Legend of Šemik,' is linked to the patriotic-mythical material of Smetana's and Fibich's works, and resembles the latter in the working of the motives and the formal structure. The same may be said of the music drama, 'The Death of Vlasta,' the libretto of which by K. Pippich was originally written for Fibich and, at his recommendation, set to music by his pupil. The suite in G major and the string quartet in B major are also allied to Fibich's style.

It was natural that at this period Ostrčil should pay some attention to melodrama, also his teacher's favourite form. He only composed, however, two concert-melodramas for orchestra, opp. 6 and 8 (see List below). The symphony in A major is still in an old-fashioned style and of minor importance. On the other hand, opus 9, 'Osiřelo Dítě (The orphaned child) introduces a fresh point of view. Here Ostrčil moves in modern paths with the spirit of the time ; he sets folk poetry in the manner of V. NOVÁK (q.v.). Henceforth there came a gradual inward change in his development.

There is something novel in the opera 'Kunálovy Oči' (Kunala's Eyes). This Indian legend, steeped in the mysticism of the Buddhist spirit, written by the Czech poet Julius Zeyer—who possessed a richly-coloured imagination and specially chose exotic material for his poems—gave Ostrčil a good opportunity to display his musical art in its fulness. He accentuates to the utmost the dramatic treatment and also the mystical and passionate elements, while avoiding the musical exoticism to which the Indian atmosphere might lead him. In harmony the work reflects much that is bold and rugged. The same applies in a still greater degree to his next opera, 'Poupě' (The Bud), which is therefore the more interesting, because here the composer is dealing with a comedy from modern life, in one act, in which he hits off brilliantly the colloquial style ; and the scoring for small orchestra (without trombones) is quite lightly and transparently treated. In his succeeding works Ostrčil makes considerable advances, more particularly in polyphony, whereby the independent melodic movement of all the parts results in greater harmonic boldness. The work, however, which stands as a landmark in this respect is his impromptu for full orchestra, op. 13. It is an important step in his technical progress, but, artistically speaking, the suite in C minor (op. 14) stands higher. It is an intimately poetic and almost grotesquely humorous work. Entirely modern in polyphony are the compositions which follow the above : 'Cizí Host' (The Strange Guest),

'Legende o Svaté Zitě' (The Legend of St. Zita) and the 'Sinfonietta'; the last named employs a male voice *a cappella* chorus in the same style. For his latest opera, 'Legenda z Erinu' (A Legend of Erin) Ostrčil has again had recourse to one of Zeyer's dramas. The exceedingly tragic work contains many stirring dramatic situations.

LIST OF WORKS

Operas.—'Vlasty Skon,' op. 6 (The Death of Vlasta), music drama in 3 acts ; libretto by K. Pippich, produced at National Theatre, Prague, Dec. 14, 1904, under Kovařovic, MS. ; 'Kunálovy Oči,' op. 12 (Kunala's Eyes), opera in 3 acts, based on Zeyer's novel, National Theatre, Prague, Nov. 25, 1908, conducted by Kovařovic, (piano score, Hudebni Matice, Prague) ; 'Poupě' (The Bud), comic opera in 1 act, op. 13, National Theatre, Prague, Jan. 25, 1911, under the composer (piano score, Hudebni Matice) ; 'Legenda z Erinu' (Legend of Erin), op. 19, opera in 4 acts, on Zeyer's drama, National Theatre, Prague, 1923 (piano score, Foerster Society, Prague).

Orchestral.—'Selska Slavnost' (Rustic Festival), orchestral sketch, op. 1, MS. ; suite in G, for full orch., op. 2, MS. ; 'Pohádka o Šemíku' (The tale of Šemik), symphonic poem, op. 3, MS. ; two melodramas for orch., 'Ballada o mrtvém ševci, a mladé tanečnice' (Ballad of the Dead Cobbler and the young Dancing-girl), op. 6, and 'Ballada Česká' (Czech ballad), op. 8 ; symphony in A maj., op. 7, MS. ; impromptu for orch., op. 13, MS. ; suite in C min., op. 14, MS. ; 'Sirotek' (The Orphan), music to a drama by Kvapil, op. 11, MS. ; 'Sinfonietta,' for orch., op. 20 (score pub. by the Foerster Soc.).

Choral and Vocal.— Osiřelo Dítě' (A child became an orphan), ballad for mezzo-soprano and orch., op. 9 (piano score, Mojmír Urbánek, Prague ; 'Česká Legenda Vanočni' (Czech Christmas legend) for male voice choir *a capella*, op. 15 (Hudebni Matice) ; 'Cizi Host' (The stranger guest), ballad for tenor and orch., op. 16 (piano score with Czech and German texts, Hudebni Matice) ; 'Legende o Svaté Zitě' (Legend of St. Zita), for mixed chorus, tenor solo, orch. and organ, op. 17 (piano score and parts, Hudebni Matice) ; 'Homely Motives,' four male voice part-songs, op. 21 (score and parts, Hudebni Matice). Also three songs, op. 18, with piano accompaniment (Hudebni Matice).

Chamber Music.—String quartet in B maj., op. 4, MS. ; sonatina for violin, viola and piano, op. 22, MS.   R. V.

O'SULLIVAN, DENIS (*b.* San Francisco, Apr. 25, 1868 ; *d.* Columbus, Ohio, Feb. 1, 1908), son of Cornelius O'Sullivan of Skibbereen, Co. Cork, Ireland, first studied singing at San Francisco, as an amateur, under Ugo Talbo (Hugh Talbot Brennan) and Karl Formes. He was afterwards taught, for some time by Vannuccini at Florence, by Santley and Shakespeare in London, and later by Sbriglia in Paris. On Mar. 6, 1895, he made his début at Miss Ethel Bauer's concert, Prince's Hall, and sang six of Schumann's 'Dichterliebe' with the greatest success, on account of his excellent phrasing and enunciation. On Aug. 25 of the same year he made his début with the Carl Rosa Company at Dublin as Ferrando in 'Trovatore,' and also sang on tour as Prince John in 'Ivanhoe,' the Mayor in 'Son and Stranger,' Lothario in 'Mignon,' Vanderdecken in 'Flying Dutchman,' a part he sang at five hours' notice without rehearsal, etc. On Jan. 20, 1896, he sang at Daly's Theatre with the above company as Biterolf in 'Tannhäuser,' and in Feb. as Alfio in 'Cavalleria.' On Mar. 2 he made a great success as the hero on the production of Stanford's 'Shamus O'Brien' at the Opéra-Comique Theatre (London), and sang throughout the run of that opera. Between 1897 and 1899 he divided his time between England and America, singing in the latter country on tours with 'Shamus O'Brien,' and for two seasons in his native San Francisco ; also Sept. 19, 1898, at New York as the Marquis de Saint André in

Englander's 'Little Corporal.' On Jan. 27, 1902, he sang as Shaun the Smith on production of Esposito's operetta ' The Post Bag,' at a performance given by the Irish Literary Society at St. George's Hall, and in the same year sang at the Westmorland and Northampton Festivals. On Oct. 17, 1903, he sang as Lefebvre in Caryll's ' Duchess of Dantzig ' at the Lyric Theatre. On Nov. 7, 1904, he sang as Barry Trevor in the musical play ' Peggy Machree,' written by Patrick Bidwell (i.e. Mrs. O'Sullivan), with music by Esposito, produced at the Grimsby Theatre. He also acted in Boucicault's plays in America. A book of poems (dedicated to his memory) was published in 1911 by his widow. It contains a fine drawing of O'Sullivan by John Sargent.

A. C.

OSWALD, JAMES (d. Jan. 1769), a popular composer of the middle of the 18th century. He was originally a dancing-master at Dunfermline, and is first heard of in Aug. 1734, when he advertises in the *Caledonian Mercury* that he is publishing a collection of minuets. In 1736 he had taken up his residence in Edinburgh, and appears to have made a position quickly as a performer on the violin, as organist, composer and as teacher of dancing. From here he issued several collections of 'Scots Tunes ' and chamber music. He advertised in 1740 that he was leaving for Italy, but it is doubtful whether he ever made the journey, though it is certain that in 1741 he left Edinburgh for London. His departure from Scotland is made the subject of a poetical ' Epistle ' in the *Scots Magazine* for October 1741, which gives many interesting details of his compositions, his arrangements and his playing. Especially significant are the lines—

> ' Or when some tender tune compose again
> And cheat the town wi' David Rizo's name.'

Arrived in London, probably with influence from the Earl of Bute, he seems to have obtained patronage from the Prince and Princess of Wales, to whom he dedicated some of his works, and it is not unlikely he had some share in the early musical education of their son, afterwards George III., to whom he was appointed chamber composer in 1761. As court patronage would certainly not supply all necessities, there are indications that he obtained employment with JOHN SIMPSON (q.v.), who published all Oswald's early London work. It must be confessed that Oswald's life in London is much of a mystery, but it is pretty well ascertained that though his name had some degree of value, he worked both anonymously and under assumed names. It is likely that Oswald was a sort of musical editor to the several miscellaneous collections which Simpson published. Simpson having died in 1747, Oswald about this date set up a music-shop on the north side of St. Martin's Church, at the

corner of St. Martin's Lane. From this address were published many works of antiquarian musical interest, including the well-known collection of Scots tunes, twelve parts, entitled ' The Caledonian Pocket Companion,' the two first having been issued by John Simpson ; ' Airs for the Spring,' ' Summer,' ' Autumn ' and ' Winter ' ; his several collections of ' Scots Tunes,' etc. etc. ' The Comic Tunes in Queen Mab . . . by the Society of the Temple of Apollo ' and ' Six Solos . . . by I. R. Esq.' (General Reid) were afterwards republished with a mysterious note that they were really by the ' late Mr. Oswald, who for certain reasons could not openly claim them during his life.' ' The Music in the Masque of Alfred . . . by the Society of the Temple of Apollo ' (not Dr. Arne's) was doubtless one of these anonymous compositions.

The mysterious ' Society of the Temple of Apollo ' was apparently a small society of musicians gathered round Oswald[1] which included Charles Burney, and probably John REID (then Captain, afterwards General, q.v.) and the Earl of Kelly. The several works which bear this society's name were all published by Oswald.

Meanwhile Oswald's name as composer of music for the popular fashionable song is very frequent in collections of the period, and one set of songs, ' Colin's Kisses,' attained some degree of fame. He died, so far as can be ascertained, in Jan. 1769, and was buried on the 9th of that month at Knebworth.

The writer broached the theory in *The Minstrelsy of England*, first series (Bayley Ferguson), that to Oswald we are indebted for either the composition of GOD SAVE THE KING (q.v.), or for its modern revival.   F. K.

OTELLO. (1) Opera ; libretto based on Shakespeare's play, music by Rossini. Produced Fondo, Naples, Dec. 4, 1816 ; in French, Académie, as ' Othello,' Sept. 2, 1844 ; King's Theatre, May 16, 1822.

(2) Opera in 4 acts ; libretto, founded on Shakespeare, by Arrigo Boito, music by Verdi. Produced La Scala, Milan, Feb. 5, 1887 ; New York, Academy of Music, Apr. 16, 1888 ; Lyceum Theatre, July 5, 1889 ; in English, Carl Rosa Co., Royal Court Theatre, Liverpool, 1895.   G.

OTGER, an early writer on musical theory, whose life is obscure, and whose very existence has been hitherto almost ignored. To him, probably, are due the treatises called *Musica enchiriadis* and *Scolica enchiriadis*, which on the authority of a few MSS. or notes in MSS. have been ascribed to Hucbald. The best of the MSS., however, give Abbot Otger (also called Hoger or Noger) as their author, and among them is a MS. (now at Valenciennes)

[1] See *Mus. Ant.* ii. 34, *James Oswald and the Temple of Apoll* by F. Kidson.

from the Monastery of St. Amand, which was the home of Hucbald ; it is therefore good evidence against the ascription of these treatises to him. They, with the *Commemoratio brevis*, form a little group of treatises distinguished by a special method of notation (see HUCBALD) which, as well as the general tenor of the teaching, distinguishes the group sharply from the one unquestioned work of Hucbald (*De harmonica institutione*), or the writings of Odo of Cluny, to whom also the group is sometimes ascribed. No particulars of the life of Otger are known, but his treatises are among the most valuable of the sort. They are printed in Gerbert, *Scriptores*, vol. i. See further on the matter H. Müller, *Hucbalds echte und unechte Schriften* (Leipzig, 1884).   W. H. F.

OTHMAYR, KASPAR (*b*. Amberg, Upper Palatinate, Mar. 12, 1515 ; *d*. Nuremberg, Feb. 7, 1553), was a fellow-student with Georg Forster, the song-book editor, at the University of Heidelberg, and fellow-pupil with him in music under Lorenz Lem'in, the Heidelberg Kapellmeister. In 1545 he was rector of the Convent School at Heilsbronn. In 1547 he obtained a canonry at the church of St. Gumbert in Ansbach which had become Lutheran, and in 1548 was chosen to be provost ; but the elections being contested, probably in consequence of the religious disputes of the time, he retired to Nuremberg. Forster speaks of him as a widely celebrated musician, and received twenty-six of his settings of secular songs [1] into his great collection. Othmayr's own publications are sacred works chiefly, and the titles of some of them bear witness to the religious confusion of the time, as, for instance, ' Cantilenae aliquot . . . quibus his turbulentis temporibus ecclesia Christi utitur' (Nuremberg, 1546). Epitaphium D. Martin Lutheri *a* 4. Other works are ' Bicinia sacra ' (1547), German hymns *a* 2 and ' Tricinia ' (1549), Latin motets *a* 3.   J. R. M.

OTT, JEAN, a Nuremberg lute-maker who worked during the first half of the 15th century, and, according to Fétis, was alive in 1463. Together with Hans Frey, the father-in-law of Albert Dürer the painter, he was the earliest maker of viols in Germany, and they are generally named together with Joan Kerlino (1449), who was the first to manufacture viols in Italy.   E. H.-A.

OTT (OTTO), JOHANNES, a bookseller and music-publisher at Nuremberg in the first half of the 16th century, who edited, in union with the typographer Hieronymus Formschneider or Graphæus, several very valuable collections of the older music. In his prefaces to these collections Ott shows himself to have been an excellent connoisseur of the older music, possessing good knowledge and refined taste. The

composers whom he chiefly loves to exalt are, first, Josquin, whom he describes as the hero of his art, having in him something truly divine and inimitable, and next to Josquin, Heinrich Isaac and Ludwig Senfl. His collections are as follows : 1533, ' Der erst Theil : 121 neue Lieder, von berümbten diser Kunst gesetzt, lustig zu singen und auf allerley Instrument dienstlich, vormals dergleichen im Truck nie ausgangen.' This work is dedicated to the composer Arnold von Bruck, and contains twenty German songs by him, eighty-two by Senfl, the rest by other composers, all *a* 4 to 6. 1537, ' Novum et insigne opus musicum,' etc. This work is dedicated to the Emperor Ferdinand, and contains fifty-seven motets, *a* 4 to 6, chiefly by German composers, but fourteen of them by Josquin, among them the celebrated Miserere, *a* 5, to the beauties of which Ott himself calls special attention. 1538, ' Secundus tomus novi operis musici,' etc., contains forty-three motets, *a* 4 to 6, among them eleven by Josquin including his famous Stabat Mater. 1539, ' Missae tredecim 4 voc.,' dedicated to the Senate of Nuremberg, contains masses by Josquin, Isaac and others. 1544, ' 115 guter neuer Liedlein.' This last work has been completely reprinted in modern score by the Gesellschaft für Musikforschung. In one of his prefaces Ott had expressed his intention of bringing out a complete edition of the ' Coralis Constantinus ' of Heinrich Isaac, but death would appear to have overtaken him before its publication by his associate Formschneider in 1550. Although his name is not mentioned in connexion with them, he is also supposed to have had some share in the publication by Formschneider of Senfl's Magnificats in 1532, and Heinrich Fink's Lieder in 1536.   J. R. M.

OTTANI, ABBATE BERNARDINO (*b*. Bologna, Sept. 8, 1736 ; *d*. Turin, Oct. 26, 1827), pupil of Padre Martini ; maestro di cappella at Bologna, 1758, and at Turin Cathedral, 1779. He composed 12 operas and a large amount of church music (46 masses), also instrumental music (*Q.-L.* ; *Riemann*).

OTTAVINO, an octave flute.   (See FLUTE.)

OTTER, FRANZ JOSEPH (*b*. Nandlstadt, Bavaria, 1760 [2] or 1764 [3] ; *d*. Sept. 1, 1836), violinist.

Bishop von Freising sent him to Florence, where he became a pupil of Pietro Nardini. After the death of his patron Franz Otter was forced to return to Germany and seek employment. Together with his brother Ludwig, he received an appointment as violinist at the Salzburg Cathedral, with an annual stipend of 200 gulden. He occupied this position from 1803–07, and, upon retiring with a pension, settled in Vienna as a teacher and violinist at the Hofkapelle. Reichard's *Gothaer Kalendar* for 1798 states that Otter, in that year, was

[1] For a description of these see Eitner, *Monatshefte*, xxvi. pp. 115-17.

[2] According to *Q.-L.*   [3] According to *Fétis*.

Konzertmeister at the Vienna Hoftheater, and Musikdirector in 1800. Michael Haydn taught him composition. He wrote several concertos and sonatas for violin, but has left (so far as is known) only one published work, viz. Nineteen variations on the German air 'Ich bin liederlich,' with accompaniment for a second violin (Haslinger, Vienna). Amongst Michael Haydn's unpublished songs in the Berlin Museum there is a canon for nine voices by Otter, and in Prince Esterhazy's Library at Eisenstadt there is a canon for seven voices, composed by Otter, to celebrate Joseph Haydn's birthday. This is in manuscript. (*Fétis*; *Q.-L.*)　　　　　　　　E. H.-A.

OTTEY, MRS. SARAH, (*b. circa* 1695), one of the earliest female professional performers on the violin in London. Dr. Burney, mentioning her in his *History*, says : 'This and the preceding year (1721–22) Mrs. Sarah Ottey frequently performed solos at concerts on three several instruments—Harpsichord, bass-viol and violin.'

BIBL.—DUBOURG, *The Violin*; LAHEE, *Famous Violinists.*
　　　　　　　　　　　　　　　　E. H.-A.

OTTO, (1) ERNST JULIUS (*b.* Königstein, Sept. 1, 1804 ; *d.* Dresden, Mar. 5, 1877), composer, more especially of works for men's voices, passed his 'maturity examination' at Dresden in 1822 with honour, and studied theology for three years at Leipzig. While doing this he worked at music with Schicht and Weinlig. His compositions are of a solid character— oratorios ; masses ; an opera (' Schloss am Rhein ') performed at Dresden, 1838, and another at Augsburg ; sonatas ; cycles of songs for men's voices, etc. In 1830 he was appointed cantor at Dresden, a post which he held with honour to himself up till his death.

His brother, (2) FRANZ (*b.* June 3, 1809 ; *d.* Apr. 30, 1842), a bass singer, and also composer of popular works for men's choir, came with another brother, a tenor, to England in 1833 as directors of a part-singing society.
　　　　　　　　　　　　　　　　　　G.

OTTO, GEORG (*b.* Torgau, Electoral Saxony, *c.* 1544), spent the best part of his life from before 1588 to 1619 at Cassel as Kapellmeister to the Landgrave of Hesse-Cassel. He was the instructor in composition of the Landgraf Moritz. Otto's published works are : ' Geistliche deutsche Gesenge,' *a* 5 and 6 (Erfurt, 1588) ; ' Opus musicum divinum ' (Cassel, 1604), in three books, containing motets *a* 5 to 8 on Latin texts from the Gospel for every Sunday and Festival and other occasions in the Church's year. Among unpublished works in the Library at Cassel are a series of introits for the Church's year *a* 5, and various Latin psalms and Magnificats *a* 5 to 12.　　J. R. M.

OTTO, JACOB AUGUSTUS (*b.* Gotha, 1762 ; *d.* Jena, 1830), the author of a valuable treatise upon the construction of the violin, in which

the mathematical ' rules ' of Bagatella are simplified and explained. An excellent maker and repairer of stringed instruments, he was at one time attached to the court of the Grand Duke of Weimar in that capacity. From time to time his profession required him to visit Halle, Leipzig, Magdeburg and Berlin, journeys which assisted him in enlarging his remarkable knowledge and judgment of ancient instruments of the violin class. In 1817 his *Über den Bau und die Erhaltung der Geige und aller Bogeninstrumente* is said to have been published by Reinecke in Halle, and an enlarged edition of the same, with the title *Über den Bau der Bogeninstrumente und über die Arbeiten der vorzüglichsten Instrumentenmacher*—published by Bran in Jena—appeared in 1828. Of this the second edition appeared in 1873 and the third in 1886. In 1833 Longmans brought out T. Fardeley's English translation, and John Bishop's English version entitled *Treatise on the Structure and Preservation of the Violin*, etc., was published by Robert Cocks in London in 1848 (second edition, 1850 ; third edition, 1875). The first edition, though often quoted, does not exist, as far as can be ascertained, in any public or private library, but an article by Otto bearing the original title is to be found at p. 3 of vol. i. (1809) of the *Neues Magazin aller neuer Erfindungen, Entdeckungen und Verbesserungen* (Leipzig). It is mainly an eulogy of Jacobus Stainer. Otto left five sons, all of whom became violin-makers.

BIBL.—FÉTIS, *Biog. des Mus.*; DAVIDSON, *The Violin*; DUBOURG, *The Violin*; HART, *The Violin*; BROWN, *Dictionary of Musicians*; Q.-L.
　　　　　　　　　　　　　　　　E. H.-A.

OTTO, MELITTA, *née* ALVSLEBEN (*b.* Dresden, Dec. 16, 1842 ; *d.* there, Jan. 13, 1893), was taught singing there by Thiele at the Conservatorium, and sang in opera as a light soprano from 1860–73 ; in 1866 she married Max Otto, commissioner of customs. Her parts comprised Anna in ' Hans Heiling,' Rowena in ' Templer und Jüdin,' Queen of Night, Alice, Martha, Eva, etc. She acquired a great reputation as a concert singer, and was the solo soprano at the Beethoven Centenary at Bonn in 1871. She first appeared in England at Mme. Schumann's concert, St. James's Hall, Mar. 20, 1873 ; at the Crystal Palace, Mar. 22 ; at Manchester, in Bach's Passion music ; at the Albert Hall, Apr. 2 and 7. She made a great success, and remained in England until 1875, appearing most frequently at the Crystal Palace and Albert Hall, notably in the revivals of ' Theodora,' Oct. 30, 1873, and the ' Christmas Oratorio,' Dec. 15, 1873. She sang at the Philharmonic, Mar. 25, 1874 ; at the Leeds Festival in ' St. John the Baptist ' and Schumann's ' Paradise and the Peri,' etc., in 1874 ; at the Sacred Harmonic, the Wagner, Bache's, the Ballad and principal provincial concerts. She returned to Germany in 1875, and sang in opera at Hamburg, and from 1877–1883 at Dresden. In 1879 she sang at the Cincinnati Festival.   A. C.

OTTO, Stephan (b. Freiberg, Saxony, c. 1594), received his musical instruction from the Freiberg cantor, Christoph Demantius. After holding some subordinate appointment at Augsburg, he became succentor or assistant cantor at Freiberg from 1632–33, during which time he also had Andreas Hammerschmidt for his pupil. Becoming cantor at Schandau, he afterwards, in 1643, made an unsuccessful application for the post of cantor at Freiberg in succession to Demantius. He was still living at Schandau in 1648. His chief published work bears the peculiar title :

'Kronen-Krönlein oder Musicalischer Vorlauffer auff geistliche Concert-Madrigal-Dialog-Melod-Symphon-Motetische Manier mit 3, 4, 5, 6, 7, 8 Stim. . . .' (Freiberg, 1648).

The title would indicate the compositions as being in the sacred concerto and dialogue style of Schütz and Hammerschmidt. It may be a question whether Otto did not precede Hammerschmidt in the adoption of the dialogue style of composition for church music, although this work is published later than similar works of Hammerschmidt. Another work of Otto, existing only in MS., consists of a setting of the hymn ' Ein' feste Burg,' for nineteen voices divided into four choirs, intended for a special occasion. The full title of this work [1] would lend some degree of sanction to the tradition that Luther wrote the hymn on the occasion of his citation before the Diet of Worms, 1521.   J. R. M.

OTTO, Valerius (b. Leipzig), organist in 1607 of the Lutheran church, Prague ; musician in 1611 at the court of Prince Lichtenberg. He composed psalms, a Magnificat and a book of 5-part pavans, galliards, etc. (Q.-L. ; Riemann).

OUDIN, Eugène Espérance (b. New York, Feb. 24, 1858 ; d. Nov. 4, 1894), singer, of French parentage, was a graduate of Yale University, and for a time practised at the American bar. In 1886, while on a holiday in London, he adopted a musical career on the advice of friends, and received instruction from Moderati in America. On Aug. 30 of the same year he made his début on the stage at Wallack's Theatre, New York, with the M'Caul Opéra-Comique Company, as Montosol in an English version of Victor Roger's ' Joséphine vendue par ses sœurs,' his future wife, Miss Louise Parker, also making her début as Joséphine. Both artists were successful during the two months' run of the opera at New York and on tour. On Dec. 4, 1886, they were married at Detroit. In 1889 Oudin sang again in private concerts in London. On Jan. 31, 1891, he first appeared on the English stage, with the greatest success, both as a singer and actor, as the

[1] See Monatshefte, xx., Die älteren Musikalien der Stadt Freiberg, pp. 22, 23.

Templar, on the production of Sullivan's ' Ivanhoe ' at the Royal English Opera House (Palace Theatre), having been engaged at the instance of the composer, and sang throughout the run of the opera. On Oct. 17, 1892, he made a distinct success as the hero on the production of Tchaikovsky's ' Eugen Onegin ' at the Olympic, and on Nov. 17 he sang as Henri Quatre on the production of Lacome's ' Ma mie Rosette ' at the Globe, and later at the Prince of Wales's Theatre. Oudin then devoted himself in England exclusively to concerts, gaining great applause for his delivery of songs, ancient and modern, at the Popular and other concerts. He was the translator of many modern songs, also of the lyrics of Messager's ' Basoche,' for which he was greatly commended by the composer, and also of Saint-Saëns's ' Samson et Dalila,' wherein on Sept. 25, 1893, he sang on its production in a concert version under Cowen at the Promenade Concerts, Covent Garden. He composed a set of four songs, words and music ; but his best composition is an ' O Salutaris ' for two voices. In 1893 and 1894 he sang again in opera with great success at St. Petersburg as Wolfram, Telramund, the High Priest in ' Samson et Dalila,' Albert in ' Werther ' ; also in concerts throughout Russia. In 1894 he sang at the Birmingham Festival, where his rendering of Doctor Marianus's music in the third part of Schumann's ' Faust ' made the greatest impression on all who heard him. On Oct. 20, after a Richter concert, he was struck down with apoplexy in the artists' room at the Queen's Hall. He never recovered from the stroke. Mrs. Oudin left the stage soon after her marriage, occasionally sang in concerts with her husband, and became a successful teacher of singing.   A. C.

OULIBICHEFF, Alexander von (b. Dresden, 1795 ; d. near Nijni-Novgorod, Jan. 24, 1858), Russian nobleman and enthusiastic amateur, whose father was Russian ambassador in Dresden. From his earliest years he was devoted to music, and studied the violin sufficiently to become a good quartet-player. He served first in the army, and then as a diplomatist, but retired on the accession of the Emperor Nicholas, and lived on his estates near Nijni-Novgorod till his death. Mozart was his idol, and he reawakened attention to his works at a time when Germany at least was entirely preoccupied with Meyerbeer and Spontini. Oulibicheff's great work, Nouvelle Biographie de Mozart, 3 vols. (Moscow, 1844), contains much valuable matter, biographical and æsthetical, and has been largely used by Otto Jahn. His admiration for Mozart, however, led him to depreciate Beethoven, and for this he was attacked by Lenz. In his reply, Beethoven, ses critiques et ses glossateurs (Leipzig and Paris, 1857), he expressed with even greater vehemence his opinion on the extravagance of Beethoven's later works, and drew down a storm of abuse and controversy with which he was little fitted to cope, and which is said to have hastened his end. It is but just to admit that his views, less caustically expressed, were held by many eminent musicians, including Ries and Spohr.   F. G.

OURAGAN, L', lyric drama in 4 acts; text by Émile Zola, music by Alfred Bruneau. Produced Opéra-Comique, Paris, Apr. 29, 1901.

OURY, (1) ANTONIO JAMES (b. probably London, 1800; d. Norwich, July 25, 1883 [1]), violinist.

His father was an Italian of noble descent, who served as an officer in Napoleon's army. Taken prisoner by the English, he settled in this country, married a Miss Hughes, and became a professor of dancing and music. Antonio began playing the violin at the age of 3, and showed considerable promise. His first master was Christopher Gottfried Kiesewetter, a German violinist, who travelled about the continent, was appointed the leader of the Hanoverian court band, and finally settled in London. In 1820 Oury went to Paris, and studied under Kreutzer, Baillot and Lafont, and in 1828 returned to London and made his début (on Feb. 20), at a concert given for the benefit of Kiesewetter's widow and children. His performance provoked enthusiastic applause, and was considered to be ' as fine a specimen of finished violin-playing as was ever heard in this country.' [2] On the 25th of the same month he played with equal success at the first Philharmonic Concert of the season, held at the Argyll Rooms. On Mar. 28 he again played at the Philharmonic, and on May 21 led a quartet by Meyseder—with Lindley for violoncello—at another Philharmonic Concert. He held the post of ' leader of the ballet ' at the King's Theatre, a position which admitted of many opportunities for displaying his graceful solo-playing. In 1831 he married Mlle. Belleville, and shortly after accompanied his wife on a nine years' concert tour, visiting Russia, Germany, Austria and France. (See below.)

BIBL.—DUBOURG, The Violin; PARKE, Musical Memoirs, p. 257; Athenæum, Feb. 1828 ; Times, 1828 ; LAHEE, Famous Violinists ; The Violinists' Kalendar for 1902 ; published by W. E. Hill & Sons.   E. H.-A.

(2) ANNA CAROLINE DE BELLEVILLE (b. Landshut, Bavaria, Jan. 24, 1808 ; d. Munich, July 22, 1880), his wife, a pianist of note, was the daughter of a French nobleman, director of the opera in Munich. She spent the first ten years of her life at Augsburg with her parents, studying with the cathedral organist, on whose recommendation she was taken to Vienna in 1816, and placed under the direction of Czerny for four years, during which time she was introduced to Beethoven, and heard him

improvise on the piano. She appeared on two occasions in Vienna, on one of which (Madame Catalini's farewell concert) she played a Hummel concerto with orchestra. In 1820 she returned to her parents at Munich, and played there with great success. The next year was spent in Paris, where she was well received. She resumed her studies with Andreas Streicher in Vienna in 1829, after which she made a professional tour to Warsaw, Berlin, etc. In 1831 she came to London, and made her début at Her Majesty's Theatre at Paganini's concert in July. Her own concert took place in August, and in October she married Oury, with whom she then proceeded to make a long tour to Russia, where they remained two years, to the principal cities of Germany, Austria and Holland, settling at length in Paris for two years and a half. In Apr. 1839 they returned to England, which from that time became their home. Until 1846 Madame Oury divided her time between London and Brighton, being particularly successful at the latter place. From that time she devoted herself entirely to composition, and during the 20 years that followed published no less than 180 pieces, principally of the class known as ' drawing-room ' music. In 1866 she retired from all artistic pursuits, and continued to live near London. Schumann made an elaborate comparison between her playing and that of Clara Wieck (Music and Musicians, p. 68).   M.

OUSELEY, the REV. SIR FREDERICK ARTHUR GORE, Bart. (b. London, Aug. 12, 1825 ; d. Hereford, Apr. 6, 1889), son of the Rt. Hon. Sir Gore Ouseley, Bart., Ambassador at the courts of Persia and St. Petersburg, from early childhood evinced great talent for music, and an extraordinarily accurate ear.[3] His skill in playing and extemporising was very unusual, and at the age of 8 he composed an opera, ' L' isola disabitata.' In 1844 Sir Frederick succeeded his father, having entered, the year before, as a gentleman commoner at Christ Church, Oxford, at which University he graduated B.A. in 1846, and M.A. in 1849. In that year he was ordained, and until the close of 1850 held a curacy at St. Paul's, Knightsbridge. In 1850 he took the degree of Mus.B. at Oxford, his ' exercise ' being a cantata, ' The Lord is the true God,' and in 1854 took the higher grade of Mus.D. for which his oratorio ' The Martyrdom of St. Polycarp ' was composed and performed. In that year the foundation-stone was laid of St. Michael's College, Tenbury, with which he was so intimately connected for the rest of his life. Upon the death of Sir Henry R. Bishop in 1855, Sir Frederick was elected to the professorship of music at Oxford, an office which he held till his death. The same year he was ordained priest and appointed precentor of Hereford Cathedral. In 1856 he was ad-

1 Date of death furnished by Arthur Hill.   2 The Times.   3 See the Harmonicon, 1833, pp. 102, 103.

mitted to the *ad eundem* degrees of Mus.B. and Mus.D. at Durham, and became vicar of St. Michael's, Tenbury, as well as warden of St. Michael's College[1] there for the education of boys in music and general knowledge, of which establishment he was the principal munificent founder and maintainer (see LIBRARIES). The daily choral service in the beautiful church of St. Michael's, which Sir Frederick erected adjoining his college, is served by the masters and boys. He received the honorary degrees of Mus.D. Cantab. in 1862, LL.D. Cantab. 1883, and LL.D. Edinburgh, 1885. He died suddenly of heart disease, and was buried on Apr. 11 at Tenbury.

Ouseley was skilled both as pianist and organist. He excelled in extemporaneous performance on the organ, especially in fugue-playing and in contrapuntal treatment of a given theme. He published treatises on *Harmony, Counterpoint and Fugue, Form and General Composition.*

As composer Sir Frederick is known chiefly by his works for the church. In these he adhered closely to the traditions of the Anglican school. He composed 11 services, one in 8 parts, another with orchestral accompaniment. He also published upwards of 70 anthems, and edited the sacred works of Orlando Gibbons. His compositions for organ include a set of 6, one of 7, and one of 18 preludes and fugues, also 6 preludes, 3 andantes, and 2 sonatas. He also wrote some dozen glees and partsongs, several solo songs with PF. accompaniment, and 2 string-quartets. His oratorio, 'Hagar,' was produced at the Hereford Festival of 1873, and performed in the following year at the Crystal Palace.

As Oxford professor he effected considerable improvements and reforms. The office of Choragus, which had fallen into disuse, was re-established, and was held at first by Corfe, who was succeeded in 1884 by C. H. H. Parry, Sir F. A. Gore Ouseley's successor in the professorship; the standard of qualifications for degrees was raised, and the professor also induced his University to grant honorary degrees in music, which had never been given by Oxford previous to 1879.[2]

In addition to the works already named, Ouseley edited a collection of Cathedral Services (1853), and with Dr. E. G. Monk, 'Anglican Psalter Chants' (1872). (See *Memorials of Sir F. A. Gore Ouseley, Bart.,* by F. T. Havergal, 1889; a more extensive memoir by the Rev. F. W. Joyce was published in 1896.)   H. S. O.

OVER-BLOWING is the production of a higher note than the natural note of a pipe, by forcing the wind. In the flute the upper

octaves are legitimately so produced. In the organ it is apt to arise when the feeders of a bellows pump wind into the reservoir in greater quantities or at greater speed than its consumption, and when the reservoir is full this is liable to cause undue strain. If more wind were then to be supplied it might become more compressed,—stronger,—causing the pipes to produce a momentary scream rather than a musical sound. To prevent this natural consequence of 'over-blowing,' a safety-valve or *waste-pallet* is provided, which allows the super-added wind to pass from the reservoir.

          E. J. H.

OVEREND, MARMADUKE (*d.* June 1790), organist of Isleworth in 1760 and scholar of Dr. Boyce, whose MSS. on the theory of music he acquired, enjoyed much repute as a theorist. He composed an 'Epithalamium' for the marriage of George III. in 1761, 'Twelve Sonatas for two Violins and a Violoncello,' published in 1763.[3] In 1783 he published *A Brief Account of, and Introduction to Eight Lectures on the Science of Music.* (It does not appear that the lectures were ever delivered.) A canon for eight voices by him, 'Glory be to the Father,' is printed in Warren's collection. In his will, dated 1781, he described himself as 'Student in Music.' He was buried on June 25, 1790. His library was sold in 1791, and his MSS. (including those of Dr. Boyce), passed into the hands of Callcott.   W. H. H.

OVERSPUN, equivalent to the German *übersponnen,* applied to the large strings in a pianoforte, or the G string in a violin, etc., which are wound or spun round with fine wire to increase their weight and also the depth and richness of their tone.   A. J. H.

OVERSTRINGING, a method adopted by some pianoforte-makers of raising the lower bass strings and leading them diagonally over the others, to obtain length and a different arrangement of the scale. (See PIANOFORTE.)

          A. J. H.

OVERTONES. A word formed in imitation of the German *Obertöne* which Helmholtz uses as a contraction for *Oberpartialtöne,* meaning Upper PARTIAL TONES (*q.v.*). (See ACOUSTICS, subsection HARMONIC SERIES.)   J. L.

OVERTURE (Fr. *ouverture*; Ger. *Ouvertüre, Vorspiel, Einleitung*; Ital. *overtura*), *i.e.* opening. This term was originally applied to the instrumental prelude to an opera and later to orchestral works of an independent, self-existing type. The first important development is due to Lully, as exemplified in his series of French operas and ballets, dating from 1672–1686. The earlier Italian operas were generally preceded by a brief introduction for instruments, usually called 'Sinfonia,' sometimes 'Toccata.' Monteverdi's opera 'Orfeo' (1607) begins with a short prelude of nine bars, termed

[1] See *Mus. T.*, 1900, p. 713.
[2] The degree offered to Handel was refused because it was not Honorary.' Haydn presented an 'exercise' for his, and presumably paid his fees.
[3] Advertisement in *Lloyd's Evening News.*

'Toccata,' to be played three times through—being, in fact, little more than a mere preliminary flourish of instruments. Such small beginnings became afterwards somewhat amplified, both by Italian and French composers; but only very slight indications of the overture, as a composition properly so called, are apparent before the time of Lully, who justly ranks as an inventor in this respect. He fixed the form of the dramatic prelude; the overtures to his operas having not only served as models to composers for nearly a century, but having also been themselves extensively used in Italy and Germany as preludes to operas by other composers.

The form of the overture of Lully's time consisted of a slow Introduction, generally repeated, and followed by an allegro in the fugued style; and occasionally included a movement in one of the many dance-forms of the period, sometimes two pieces of this description. The distinction between the French and Italian styles, on which so much trouble was expended by the musical writers of the 18th century, seems to amount to little more than this; that the French type of overture began with a slow introductory movement, the Italian type with a quick movement.[1] The development of the ballet and of the opera having been concurrent, and dance-pieces having formed important constituents of the opera itself, it was natural that the dramatic prelude should include similar features, and no incongruity was thereby involved, either in the overture or the serious opera which it heralded, since the dance music of the period was generally of a stately, even solemn, kind.

Up to the time of Gluck the dramatic overture had no special relevance to the character and sentiment of the work which it preceded. In the dedication of his 'Alceste' Gluck refers to this among his other reforms in stage composition. (See GLUCK; OPERA, ante, p. 699.) He did not, however, always identify the overture with the opera to which it belonged so thoroughly as was afterwards done by including a theme or themes in anticipation of the music which followed, but he certainly made the orchestral prelude what, as a writer has well said, a literary preface should be—'something analogous to the work itself, so that we may feel its want as a desire not elsewhere to be gratified.' His overtures to 'Alceste' and 'Iphigénie en Tauride' run continuously into the first scene of the opera—and the latter is perhaps the most remarkable instance up to that time of special identification with the stage music which it heralds; inasmuch as it is a distinct foreshadowing of the opening storm scene of the opera into which the prelude is merged. Perhaps the finest specimen of the dramatic overture of the

period, viewed as a distinct orchestral composition, is that of Gluck to his opera 'Iphigénie en Aulide.'

The influence of Gluck on Mozart is clearly to be traced in Mozart's first important opera, 'Idomeneo' (1781), the overture to which, both in beauty and power, is far in advance of any previous work of the kind; but, beyond a general nobility of style, it has no special dramatic character that inevitably associates it with the opera itself, though it is incorporated therewith by its continuance into the opening scene. However, in the overture to his 'Don Giovanni' (1787) we have a distinct identification with the opera by the use, in the introductory 'Andante,' of some of the music introducing the entry of the statue in the last scene, while the solemn initial chords for trombones of the overture to 'Die Zauberflöte' may be supposed to be suggestive of the religious element of the libretto. Since Mozart's time the overture adopted the same general principles of form which govern the first movement of a symphony or sonata, without the repetition of the first section.

Reverting to the French school, we find a characteristic overture of Méhul's to his opera 'La Chasse du Jeune Henri' (1797), the prelude to which alone has survived. Cherubini, all of whose great works were produced at Paris, must be specially mentioned as having been one of the first to depart from the pattern of the overture as fixed by Mozart. Cherubini indeed marks the transition point between the regular symmetry of the style of Mozart, and the developments effected by Beethoven. In the dramatic effect gained by the gradual and prolonged *crescendo*, both he and Méhul seem to have anticipated one of Rossini's favourite resources, as is observable in the overture to his opera 'Anacréon' (1803).

The next step in the development of the overture was taken by Beethoven. In the 'Leonore' overtures, Nos. 1, 2 and 3, we find references to music in the opera itself.[2] Other overtures of Beethoven, such as 'Coriolan' and 'Egmont,' written as preludes to the plays, really belong to the class of independent overtures referred to later.

The overtures of Weber are impressed with the character and tone of the opera to which they belong, anticipating themes from the following stage music, while the Mozart model is adhered to in the regular recurrence of the principal subject and the episode.

Berlioz left two overtures to his opera of 'Benvenuto Cellini,' one bearing the name of the drama, the other called the 'Carnaval romain,' and usually played as an entr'acte. The themes of both are derived more or less from the opera itself.

---

[1] See *Oxf. Hist. Mus.* vol. iv. p. 286 ff.

[2] There is a curious anticipation of the famous trumpet-call in the overture to Méhul's 'Hélène.'

Since Weber there have been no such fine examples of the operatic overture—suggestive of and identified with the subsequent dramatic action—as those of Wagner. That to 'Tannhäuser' is of especial importance in the history of the overture, as Wagner remodelled it so as to make it a prelude to the drama, rather than an overture in the usual sense. In the later works his practice varies, for sometimes he is content with a mere prelude suggestive of what is to follow; compare the 'Ring' introductions with 'Die Meistersinger' or 'Tristan und Isolde.'

The later tendency seems to be to dispense with overtures of an elaborate nature, sometimes indeed a few bars of introductory matter are considered sufficient, just enough to put the hearer into the right frame of mind before the curtain rises.

Reference has already been made to the title 'Overture' as applied to orchestral pieces intended merely for concert use, sometimes with no special purpose, in other instances bearing a specific title indicating the composer's intention to illustrate some poetical or legendary subject. Formerly a symphony, or one movement therefrom, was entitled 'Grand Overture,' or 'Overture,' in the concert programmes, according to whether the whole work or only a portion thereof was used. Thus in the announcements of Salomon's London concerts (1791-94), Haydn's symphonies, composed expressly for them, are generally so described. Like the opera overture such self-existing works have generally been written in the 'first movement' form; they are often called 'Concert-overtures' and form a valued part of the orchestral repertory. (See ENTRÉE; INTRADA; INTRODUCTION; PRELUDE; SYMPHONY.)　　　H. F. L.; rev. N. C. G.

OXFORD. The ancestry of all Oxford Musical Societies may be traced to the 'weekly music meetings' which are described in detail by Anthony Wood. In 1656 they were taking place at the house of 'William Ellis, late organist of St. John's College,' and were attended by an enthusiastic company of amateurs. Wood says that if he missed a meeting 'he could not well enjoy himself the week after.' During the early part of the 18th century the practice seems to have fallen into abeyance; but in 1733 it received new impetus from the visit of Handel, who gave five concerts in the theatre; and by 1750 the author of the *Academic* could write that 'a Taste for Musick, modern Languages, and other polite Entertainments of the Gentlemen have succeeded to Clubs and Bacchanalian Routs.'[1] When Haydn received his degree in 1791 the concerts given at Oxford were probably better than those of any provincial town in England, and they maintained for some years a high

[1] Godley, *Oxford in the Eighteenth Century*, p. 136,

standard of excellence. But about the middle of the 19th century there succeeded another period of apathy and indifference. Crotch, who held the professorship for fifty years, and in 1819 founded the Oxford Choral Society, was non-resident during the latter part of his life; Bishop who succeeded him in 1848 was not a man of much strength or energy; and matters were going from bad to worse when in 1855 a new chapter of Oxford history was opened by Ouseley's appointment to the chair. The difficulties which he encountered and overcame were those which commonly beset the path of the reformer. To his ability, his patience and his power of organisation the subsequent activity of Oxford music is largely due.

In 1865 Sir John Stainer founded the Philharmonic Society, and after its first concert handed over the conductorship to Dr. James Taylor, organist of New College. In 1869 the Choral Society was remodelled by Allchin, organist of St. John's, and for some quarter of a century these two societies divided the larger choral music of Oxford between them. Allchin was succeeded by Sir Walter Parratt (1881), C. H. Lloyd (1882) and J. V. Roberts (1886); soon after this Taylor resigned the conductorship of the Philharmonic and was succeeded by Lloyd. Meanwhile a third society, for the performance of madrigals, had been founded in 1885, under the conductorship of J. V. Roberts. Among the works performed during this period by the Choral Society may be mentioned Handel's 'Israel in Egypt,' Schumann's 'Pilgrimage of the Rose,' Macfarren's 'Joseph' and 'John the Baptist,' Stainer's 'Daughter of Jairus,' Barnett's 'Ancient Mariner,' Sullivan's 'Martyr of Antioch,' and Parry's 'Prometheus Unbound': by the Philharmonic, Beethoven's 'Choral Fantasia,' Cherubini's 'Requiem in C minor,' Schubert's 'Song of Miriam,' Spohr's 'Fall of Babylon,' Bennett's 'Woman of Samaria' and Schumann's 'Paradise and the Peri.'

In 1890, shortly after Sir John Stainer's appointment as professor, the societies were all amalgamated under the title of 'Choral and Philharmonic,' conducted successively by J. V. Roberts (1890), F. Cunningham Woods (1893), and G. H. Betjemann (1895). The enlarged resources enabled a wider range of work to be chosen, and during the first few years of its existence the combined Society gave Mozart's Requiem, Sullivan's 'Golden Legend,' Dvořák's 'Stabat Mater' and 'Spectre's Bride,' and Parry's 'Judith' and 'Blest Pair of Sirens.'

In 1896 the OXFORD BACH CHOIR was founded under the conductorship of Harwood, and soon indicated its distinctive character by performances of the Christmas Oratorio, the St. John Passion, and the cantata 'My Spirit was in heaviness.' In 1901 H. P. Allen came to

Oxford as organist of New College, and was at once appointed conductor both of the Bach Choir and of the Choral and Philharmonic Society. For a time the two institutions worked together in entire accord, retaining their separate committees and their separate organisation, but uniting their forces in the concert-room. Among the works given in these conditions may be mentioned Bach's St. Matthew Passion and B minor Mass, Beethoven's Choral Fantasia, Choral Symphony and Mass in D, Brahms's 'Song of Destiny,' 'Nänie,' 'Begräbnissgesang,' and Requiem, Verdi's Stabat Mater, Parry's 'Blest Pair of Sirens,' 'The Glories of our Blood and State,' and 'Job,' Walker's 'Hymn to Dionysus,' and Harwood's 'As by the streams of Babylon.' Later the two societies were completely amalgamated with the title of the Oxford Bach Choir, which under the inspiring energy of Allen has given a wide range of choral music annually to the present time (1926). Outstanding events under Allen's direction have been a Festival of Bach (May 13-15, 1914), a whole week's festival of miscellaneous music (May 8-13, 1922) and a week's festival to commemorate the 300th anniversary of the Heyther foundation (see HEYTHER and PROFESSOR) May 3-8, 1926.

The membership of all these societies has been open alike to the University and the town, and the same is true of the Oxford Orchestral Society, which was brought to a high pitch of efficiency by Lloyd, and, after his departure from Oxford, maintained by Harwood. Allen reconstituted the orchestra, which was first called by his name and then became the Oxford Orchestra. Besides taking part with the choral societies in all their activities, the orchestra, an admirable amateur organisation, has given periodic concerts of the larger kinds of orchestral music. Since 1919 it has been conducted by Maurice BESLY (*q.v.*).

Among several operatic productions by members of the University and town the first performance on the modern stage of Monteverdi's 'Orfeo' (Dec. 7, 1925), under the musical direction of W. H. Harris, was an event of more than local importance.

Two chamber-music societies are, except under special conditions, restricted to members of the University. The first inception of the OXFORD MUSICAL CLUB may be traced to the informal music meetings held in the rooms of Hubert Parry when he was an undergraduate at Exeter College; its actual foundation is due to C. H. Lloyd (then scholar of Hertford College) who became its first president in 1872. For some time the concerts were given mainly by members of the Club—often with a professional violinist to lead the quartet; then the professional element was gradually increased until it took a preponderating share in the performance.

As an offset to this the OXFORD MUSICAL UNION was founded in 1884 by J. H. Mee, with the object of providing for its members a larger opportunity of ensemble-playing in practice and performance : and the continued prosperity for many years of the two societies provided clear indication that the University had ample room for both. In 1916, however, the two were brought together, provision being made for both the professional and amateur performances under one organisation.

The LADIES' MUSICAL SOCIETY, founded on the lines of the Musical Club, also provides chamber-music performances for its members fortnightly during term. In addition to its own weekly meetings the Musical Club established in 1891 a series of public classical concerts, partly of chamber-music, partly of orchestral, which were continued until 1913.

A special place in the history of Oxford Music must be assigned to the Sunday evening concerts which have been given since 1885 in the Hall of Balliol College. They were founded by John Farmer, on his appointment as organist of Balliol, and soon attained a popularity which they well merited by their excellent programmes and their high standard of performance. In 1892 the direction of these concerts was shared by Ernest Walker, who from 1900 till 1925 took the entire control of them. On his retirement these concerts were successfully maintained on generally similar lines under W. H. Harris, organist of New College.

During the latter half of the 19th century many Oxford colleges formed separate musical societies, meeting for weekly practice, and giving at least one concert a year, usually in the summer term. Some of these societies have been intermittent, others have preserved an unbroken continuity, all alike have contributed in their measure to the progress of University Music. (See also DEGREES IN MUSIC, LIBRARIES.)

w. h. h^w.; rev. c. (with information from E. W.).

OXFORD HOUSE CHORAL SOCIETY, THE. This Society was first formed in 1898 by two residents of the Oxford House (the University Settlement in Bethnal Green), Hugh A. Burry, who became conductor, and A. P. Charles, hon. secretary. Burry was succeeded at the beginning of 1901 by Cuthbert Kelly, who has been conductor of the Society ever since that date.

The object of the Society was to provide the people of Bethnal Green and its neighbourhood with an opportunity for practising and performing the best choral music. The members have always been recruited entirely in East London, and concerts have been given during every winter since the Society's formation, at Excelsior Hall, Bethnal Green.

In 1903 the Society made its first appearance

in West London at the old St. James's Hall in Piccadilly. From 1904–21 a concert was given annually at Queen's Hall. Since 1921 the annual West End appearances have been made at the church of St. Martin-in-the-Fields, Trafalgar Square.

Among the works which have been performed both in Bethnal Green and in West London are Elgar's ' The Dream of Gerontius ' (in 1912, 1914 and 1922); ' The Music Makers ' (in 1913—the work's second performance); ' For the Fallen'; Brahms ' 'Requiem' (in 1915 and 1923) and ' A Song of Destiny '; Parry's ' Blest Pair of Sirens ' and ' The Pied Piper'; Vaughan Williams's ' Toward the Unknown Region.'   C. K.

END OF VOL. III